Roger Ebert's
Movie Yearbook
2004

Roger Ebert's Movie Yearbook 2004

**Andrews McMeel
Publishing**

Kansas City

This book is dedicated
to Robert Zonka, 1928–1985.
God love ya.

Contents

Introduction

One hot summer evening in August I watched a movie with ten thousand other people in the Piazza Grande in Locarno, Switzerland. There were people as far as you could see—some in the countless rows of chairs supplied by the Locarno Film Festival, others in cafés ringing the square, some in windows overlooking all of us. Included in the crowd were the presidents of Switzerland and Germany. It was a British film, a comedy named *Calendar Girls*, about a group of middle-aged committee women who posed for a mildly daring cheesecake calendar to raise money for the leukemia unit of their local hospital. It was in English with Italian subtitles. I had the sense that many audience members spoke neither language, yet the movie communicated in its own way to everyone in the square. It "worked," which is to say, it summoned an alternative experience out of the imaginations of all of us, so that for a time, in a way, we were in that little British village, sharing the hope and the scandal as the calendar girls became famous beyond their wildest dreams.

That night I thought a little about our delight in going to the movies. I've seen films in the Piazza San Marco in Venice, in a vast Bollywood palace in India, in smoky little dens on the Left Bank in Paris, under the stars in Telluride, Colorado, and in Grant Park in Chicago. The crowds arrive, they sit, they watch the movie, they form an audience. François Truffaut observed that the most beautiful sight in any movie theater is to walk down to the front and look at all the faces turned up to the screen. If the movie is accessible at all, if it is not fiercely insistent on turning each of us into an island, it is creating a shared experience by calling on what is universal in all of us.

The compleat moviegoer understands that experience. He or she is not a snob but a student and does not reject films because they are too vulgar, too broad, or too shameless in their desire to be liked, but only because they are bad—which is to say, because they do not succeed in interesting their intended audiences. That is a belief I have come to slowly during a career of moviegoing. As a young man, fresh from graduate school, I was more of a snob, or pretended to be. You couldn't sneak a Doris Day movie past me, because I knew it was corny. That despite the fact that, growing up, I loved Doris Day with an affection that was unforced and genuine. I had to unlearn my natural feelings in order to teach myself to think as a "critic." It was only gradually that I grew out of that phase and could look at *Young at Heart* or *Pillow Talk* and enjoy them as the skillful and joyous movies that they were.

In the summer of 2003 I approved of a few films that scandalized some of my readers. I liked *Lara Croft Tomb Raider: The Cradle of Life*, for example. And *American Wedding*. Although I disapproved of *Gigli*, I did not hate it with sufficient passion to please some of my readers. I received unkind e-mails asking me how large a bribe I had received—since, if I disagreed with them, obviously they could not be mistaken and so equally obviously I must be corrupt. I once had that sort of cocky confidence and cynicism myself, but I have outgrown it.

American Wedding is a vulgar comedy. It occupies a genre of vulgarity, inspired in one way or another by the original *American Pie* and *There's Something About Mary.* I disapprove of most vulgar comedies, yet these titles made me laugh. One of the crimes a critic must not commit is to laugh and then pretend he did not. Laughter, like sexual arousal, is a genuine emotion, impossible to fake, and it must be respected. I disapprove of vulgarity except when it works, and then I embrace it, because the filmmaker has taken a chance and succeeded.

As for the *Lara Croft* film, one of its qualities was old-fashioned craftsmanship. At a time when well-made adventure films are a rarity, when nonstop wall-to-wall mindless violence has replaced them (see *Bad Boys 2*), here was a movie in the tradition of *The Guns of Navarone* and the Indiana Jones pictures, a film with a plot, characters, stylish dialogue, exotic locations, and stunts—yes, real stunts, not computer fabrications. When the two heroes jump off the top of a skyscraper and fly to earth using wings built into the fabric of their suits, those are actual stunt doubles, and the stunt is real, and you can see it is real.

Earlier in the summer I was at an event honoring the directors Andrew Davis and Harold Ramis and a clip was shown from Davis's *Code of Silence*, a Chuck Norris thriller that is a good deal better than you might expect. In the movie, two men are fighting on top of an elevated train as it crosses the Chicago River. One jumps in, and the other follows—and those were real stunt men, really jumping off a real train into a real river. There was an unfakeable quality about the stunt. Spiderman swings from skyscrapers and all we're seeing is an animated cartoon stunt.

It's not that I like a movie merely because of its stunts or locations or plot. It's that when I see craftsmanship expended on making a film as good as it can be, when I sense love and respect for the audience, I respond well. That was how I felt during *Gigli*. This is not a successful film, true. But as its reading on the Tomatometer crept down toward a historic low, I asked myself if it was one of the worst films of all time, and of course it was not.

Gigli had the misfortune to ride the crest of public gossip about the romance of its stars, Jennifer Lopez and Ben Affleck. Its advance buzz was negative. It was known as a troubled picture, and so critics went after it as predators will single out the weakest member of a herd. What I and a few other critics (Owen Gleiberman, Joe Baltake, *Variety*) saw was a real attempt to do something unusual and good. The writer-director, Martin Brest, is a man whose work is distinguished by a quirky pushing of the envelope. Compare his *Midnight Run* with the average action comedy. Here, he was trying a revisionist romantic comedy. By making the Lopez character a lesbian, he was employing one of the oldest devices in comedy—the unavailable character who becomes more desirable because of being unavailable. Some of the dialogue in the movie was unconventional and daring, edgy, including the characters' speeches in praise of their competing forms of genitalia. It is not much of a stretch to imagine George Bernard Shaw writing such speeches for his characters. Then there's that moment when Lopez instructs Affleck to "gobble," and although many critics threw up their hands in horror, I responded with delight—because, yes, in the privacy of sexual play, people really do talk like that, and we know it.

I have come to the conclusion that a critic grows, not by elevating his tastes, but by broadening them. It is in the nature of my upbringing and education that I came equipped to admire what Dwight Macdonald called "high cult," or high culture. Through eight years of undergraduate and graduate school, I learned to admire Shakespeare (whom I love above all others) and the classics. I needed no prompting to understand the greatness of Bergman, Welles, Ozu, Truffaut. Even at the beginning, however, I responded directly to something in Fellini even as others were bemoaning his descent from neorealism into mere autobiographical entertainments. So help me, I liked *La Dolce Vita* more than *La Strada,* and I could not help myself. And although I knew that Laurence Olivier was a great actor, I knew that Robert Mitchum was better in the movies.

The critic can learn from the audience, which is rarely wrong. Even on opening night of a movie destined to "do" a $60 million weekend, you can sense which movies delight the audience *(Titanic, Star Wars)* and which are merely marketing ploys, soon to be forgotten *(Godzilla, Star Wars: Episode II—Attack of the Clones).* If you listen, you can hear audiences discussing *The Matrix* months or years later, and you can ask yourself why absolutely no one ever brings up *Pearl Harbor.*

Dwight Macdonald had three categories: high cult, mid cult, low cult. His point was that excellence could reside in all three. The gift of the French New Wave was to educate us on the excellence of *film noir,* musicals, Westerns, and other American genres residing at the intersection of mid and low. What is essential above all is taste—the taste, for example, to know the difference between Vulgar Sublime and Vulgar Contemptuous. A movie that loves its audience will be loved by its audience, and about that the audience always seems to be right.

* * *

Where should you start in compiling a movie library? *For Keeps,* by Pauline Kael, brings together a generous selection from her many previous books of reviews, providing an overview of the career of the most influential of film critics. The newly revised and expanded edition of David Thomson's *New Biographical Dictionary of Film* is an opinionated, informed, concise summary of hundreds of key careers. The late Ephraim Katz's *Film Encyclopedia* is an invaluable one-volume survey of the world of film. And *Distinguishing Features,* by Stanley Kauffmann, is the latest collection of reviews by the critic whose superb writing and scholarship have distinguished the *New Republic* for decades. Jonathan Rosenbaum's recent book *Movies as Politics* showcases the work of one of the best contemporary critics. David Bordwell's *On the History of Film Style* tells you more about how to look at a movie than any other book I have ever found. The best place to start, if you want to learn more about movies and moviegoing, is Louis D. Giannetti's *Understanding Movies,* now in a new edition and the best introduction to the art, craft, and medium.

For decades Donald Richie has been an unfailingly literate and perceptive guide to

Japanese films. His new *Donald Richie Reader: 50 Years of Writing on Japan* (compiled by Arturo Silva) brings together his film and Japanese writings in a book of remarkably original organization and design. It is not for sale everywhere, so use the Internet; the book is like a window into the mind of a wise, perceptive, and amusing man.

For the critics who shaped today's film criticism, I recommend the collected works of Kael, Kauffmann, Manny Farber, Andrew Sarris, Dwight Macdonald, James Agee, and Graham Greene. If you can find used copies of Macdonald's *On Movies*, Farber's *Negative Space*, or Sarris's *The American Cinema*, buy them and treasure them.

On the Web, Rotten Tomatoes (www.rottentomatoes.com) has the famous Tomatometer, which supplies links to many differing reviews. For a quick search, I use the Movie Review Query Engine (www.mrqe.com). For parents who require *detailed* factual information about the contents of movies, supplied without a political or religious agenda, there is no better site than Screen It! (www.screenit.com); make a sample visit to Jim Judy's site and you will be amazed at the completeness and usefulness of his concrete details about every movie. The most valuable one-stop movie resource on the Web is the Internet Movie Database (www.imdb.com). And the new Movie City News (www.moviecitynews.com) is a daily stop for me, a clearinghouse of commentary, information, and links.

* * *

My muse is my wife, Chaz. People ask her if she goes to "all those movies Roger goes to," and the answer is, yes, she does—and more, too. Amidst the madness of festivals she is an oasis of sanity, and in times of trouble an unfailing support. To her, my love and gratitude.

ROGER EBERT

Acknowledgments

My editor is Dorothy O'Brien, tireless,
cheerful, all-noticing. She is assisted by the
equally invaluable Julie Roberts. My friend
and longtime editor Donna Martin
suggested this new approach to the annual
volume. The design is by Cameron Poulter,
the typographical genius of Hyde Park.
My thanks to production editor Christi
Clemons-Hoffman, who renders
Cameron's design into reality. I have been
blessed with the expert and discriminating
editing of John Barron, Laura Emerick,
Miriam DiNunzio, Jeff Wisser, Darel Jevins,
Avis Weathersbee, Jeff Johnson, and Teresa
Budasi at the *Chicago Sun-Times;* Sue
Roush at Universal Press Syndicate; and
Michelle Daniel at Andrews McMeel
Publishing. Many thanks are also due to
the production staff at *Ebert & Roeper,*
and to Marsha Jordan at WLS-TV. My
gratitude goes to Carol Iwata, my expert
personal assistant, and to Marlene Gelfond,
at the *Sun-Times.* And special thanks and
love to my wife, Chaz, for whom I can only
say: If more film critics had a spouse just
like her, the level of cheer in the field would
rise dramatically.

ROGER EBERT

Key to Symbols

★★★★ A great film
★★★   A good film
★★   Fair
★   Poor

G, PG, PG-13, R, NC-17:
Ratings of the Motion Picture
Association of America

G   Indicates that the movie is suit-
        able for general audiences

PG   Suitable for general audiences
        but parental guidance is sug-
        gested

PG-13   Recommended for viewers 13
        years or above; may contain ma-
        terial inappropriate for younger
        children

R   Recommended for viewers 17 or
        older

NC-17   Intended for adults only

141 m. Running time

2003   Year of theatrical release

☞   Refers to "Questions for the
        Movie Answer Man"

Reviews

A

Abandon ★ ★ ½
PG-13, 93 m., 2002

Katie Holmes (Catherine Burke), Benjamin Bratt (Detective Wade Handler), Charlie Hunnam (Embry Larkin), Melanie Lynskey (Mousy Julie), Zooey Deschanel (Samantha), Gabrielle Union (Friend), Joseph Scarimbolo (Sean), John Fallon (Mime). Directed by Stephen Gaghan and produced by Gary Barber, Roger Birnbaum, Lynda Obst, and Edward Zwick. Screenplay by Gaghan.

Abandon is a moody, effective thriller for about 80 percent of the way, and then our hands close on air. If you walk out before the ending, you'll think it's better than it is. Or maybe I'm being unfair: Maybe a rational ending with a reasonable explanation would have seemed boring. Maybe this is the ending the movie needed, but it seems so arbitrary as it materializes out of thin air.

Or maybe I'm still being unfair. Maybe it doesn't come from thin air. Students of *Ebert's Bigger Little Movie Glossary* will be familiar with the Law of Economy of Characters, which states that no movie introduces a character unnecessarily, so that the apparently superfluous character is the one to keep an eye on. That rule doesn't precisely apply here, but it's relevant in a reverse sort of way. Think of "The Purloined Letter."

Enough of this. The movie finally did not satisfy me, and so I cannot recommend it, but there is a lot to praise, beginning with Katie Holmes's performance as Catherine Burke, a smart and articulate student who is on the fast track to a corporate boardroom. She's a student at an unnamed university (McGill in Montreal provided the locations), has just aced an interview with a big firm, studies hard, doesn't date. Her ex-boyfriend Embry Larkin (Charlie Hunnam) vanished mysteriously two years ago, but then he was the kind of weirdo genius who was always pulling stunts like that.

The key question: Did Embry disappear himself, or was he disappeared? Detective Wade Handler (Benjamin Bratt) is on the case, and

although Catherine at first cuts him off, she starts to like the guy. Meanwhile, in what is not as much of a spoiler as it might appear, Embry Larkin reappears on campus, and starts stalking Catherine.

That's all of the plot you'll get from me. I want to talk about casting, dialogue, and the film's general intelligence. This is a movie that convincingly portrays the way students talk, think, get wasted, philosophize, and hang around on a college campus. I emphasize that because when *The Rules of Attraction* opened, I questioned its scenes in which topless lesbians were ignored by male students at campus parties. I have here a letter from Joseph Gallo of Auburn, Alabama, who says such a sight is not uncommon on his campus. Uh-huh.

The students in *Abandon* talk smart. Especially Catherine. Watch the way Katie Holmes handles that interview with the high-powered corporate recruiters. It could be used as a training film. Watch her body language and word choices when she rejects an advance from her counselor. Notice the scene where a friend invites her to attend an "antiglobalization rally." In an ordinary movie, a line like that would be boilerplate, designed to move the plot to its next event. In this movie, Catherine responds. She has an opinion about antiglobalization. Astonishing.

The movie was written and directed by Stephen Gaghan, who won an Oscar for the *Traffic* screenplay and is making his directorial debut. Gaghan has written such convincing characters, including the snotty know-it-all played by Melanie Lynskey and the best friends played by Zooey Deschanel and Gabrielle Union, that it's kind of a shame this is a thriller. A real campus movie, about fears and ambitions, could have been made from this material. Deschanel's drunk scene with the cop is an example of material that is spot-on.

But the movie is a thriller, and so we must watch as the human elements and the intelligence, which have absorbed and entertained us, are ground up in the requirements of the Shocking Climax. Too bad. Here is a movie that never steps wrong until the final scenes, and then, having answered all of our questions up until then, closes with questions even it, I suspect, cannot answer.

About a Boy ★ ★ ★ ½
PG-13, 100 m., 2002

Hugh Grant (Will), Nicholas Hoult (Marcus), Rachel Weisz (Rachel), Toni Collette (Fiona), Victoria Smurfit (Suzie), Sharon Small (Christine). Directed by Paul Weitz and Chris Weitz and produced by Jane Rosenthal, Robert De Niro, Brad Epstein, Tim Bevan, and Eric Fellner. Screenplay by Peter Hedges, Chris Weitz, and Paul Weitz, based on the book by Nick Hornby.

Hugh Grant, who has a good line in charm, has never been more charming than in *About a Boy.* Or perhaps that's not quite what he is. "Charming" in the Grant stylebook refers to something he does as a conscious act, and what is remarkable here is that Grant is—well, likable. Yes, the cad has developed a heart. There are times, toward the end of the film, where he speaks sincerely and we can actually believe him.

In *About a Boy,* he plays Will, a thirty-eight-year-old bachelor who has never had a job, or a relationship that has lasted longer than two months. He is content with this lifestyle. "I was the star of the Will Show," he explains. "It was not an ensemble drama." His purpose in life is to date pretty girls. When they ask him what he does, he smiles that self-deprecating Hugh Grant smile and confesses that, well, he does—nothing. Not a single blessed thing. In 1958, his late father wrote a hit song named "Santa's Super Sleigh," and he lives rather handsomely off the royalties. His London flat looks like a showroom for Toys for Big Boys.

Will is the creation of Nick Hornby, who wrote the original novel. This is the same Hornby who wrote *High Fidelity,* which was made into the wonderful John Cusack movie. He depicts a certain kind of immature but latently sincere man who loves Women as a less-demanding alternative to loving a woman. Will's error, or perhaps it is his salvation, is that he starts dating single mothers, thinking they will be less demanding and easier to dump than single girls.

The strategy is flawed: Single mothers invariably have children, and what Will discovers is that while he would make a lousy husband he might make a wonderful father. Of course, it takes a child to teach an adult how to be a parent, and that is how Marcus (Nicholas Hoult) comes into Will's life. Will is dating a single mom named Suzie, whom he meets at a support group named Single Parents Alone Together (SPAT). He shamelessly claims that his wife abandoned him and their two-year-old son, "Ned."

Suzie has a friend named Fiona (Toni Collette), whose son Marcus comes along one day to the park. We've already met Marcus, who is round-faced and sad-eyed and has the kind of bangs that get him teased in the school playground. His mother suffers from depression, and this has made Marcus mature and solemn beyond his years; when Fiona tries to overdose one day, Will finds himself involved in a trip to the emergency room and other events during which Marcus decides that Will belongs in his life whether Will realizes it or not.

The heart of the movie involves the relationship between Will and Marcus—who begins by shadowing Will, finds out there is no "Ned," and ends by coming over on a regular basis to watch TV. Will has had nothing but trouble with his fictional child, and now finds that a real child is an unwieldy addition to the bachelor life. Nor is Fiona a dating possibility. Marcus tried fixing them up, but they're obviously not intended for each other—not Will with his cool bachelor aura and Fiona with her Goodwill hippie look and her "health bread," which is so inedible that little Marcus barely has the strength to tear a bite from the loaf. (There is an unfortunate incident in the park when Marcus attempts to throw the loaf into a pond to feed the ducks, and kills one.)

Will finds to his horror that authentic emotions are forming. He likes Marcus. He doesn't admit this for a long time, but he's a good enough bloke to buy Marcus a pair of trendy sneakers, and to advise Fiona that since Marcus is already mocked at school, it is a bad idea, by definition, for him to sing "Killing Me Softly" at a school assembly. Meanwhile, Will starts dating Rachel (Rachel Weisz), who turns out to be a much nicer woman than he deserves (she also has a son much nastier than she deserves).

This plot outline, as it stands, could supply

the materials for a film of complacent stupidity—a formula sitcom with one of the Culkin offspring blinking cutely. It is much more than that; it's one of the year's most entertaining films, not only because Grant is so good but because young Nicholas Hoult has a kind of appeal that cannot be faked. He isn't a conventionally cute movie child, seems old beyond his years, can never be caught in an inauthentic moment, and helps us understand why Will likes Marcus—he likes Marcus because Marcus is so clearly in need of being liked, and so deserving of it.

The movie has been directed by the Weitz brothers, Paul and Chris, who directed *American Pie,* which was better than its countless imitators, and now give us a comedy of confidence and grace. They deserve some of the credit for this flowering of Hugh Grant's star appeal. There is a scene where Grant does a double take when he learns that *he* has been dumped (usually it is the other way around). The way he handles it—the way he handles the role in general—shows how hard it is to do light romantic comedy, and how easily it comes to him. We have all the action heroes and Method script-chewers we need right now, but the Cary Grant department is understaffed, and Hugh Grant shows here that he is more than a star, he is a resource.

About Schmidt ★ ★ ★ ½
R, 124 m., 2002

Jack Nicholson (Warren Schmidt), Kathy Bates (Roberta Hertzel), Hope Davis (Jeannie), Dermot Mulroney (Randall Hertzel), Howard Hesseman (Larry), Len Cariou (Ray), June Squibb (Helen Schmidt). Directed by Alexander Payne and produced by Michael Besman and Harry Gittes. Screenplay by Payne and Jim Taylor, based on a novel by Louis Begley.

Warren Schmidt is a man without resources. He has no intellectual curiosity. May never have read a book for pleasure. Lives in a home "decorated" with sets of collector's items accumulated by his wife, each in the display case that came with the items. On his retirement day, he is left with nothing but time on his empty hands. He has spent his entire life working at a job that could have been done by any-

body or, apparently, nobody. He goes to the office to see if he can answer any questions that the new guy might have, but the new guy doesn't. In a lifetime of work, Warren Schmidt has not accumulated even one piece of information that is needed by his replacement.

"The mass of men," Thoreau famously observed, "lead lives of quiet desperation." Schmidt is such a man. Jack Nicholson is not such a man, and is famous for the zest he brings to living. It is an act of self-effacement that Nicholson is able to inhabit Schmidt and give him life and sadness. It is not true to say that Nicholson disappears into the character, because he is always in plain view, the most watchable of actors. His approach is to renounce all of his mannerisms, even the readiness with which he holds himself on-screen, and withdraw into the desperation of Schmidt. Usually we watch Nicholson because of his wicked energy and style; here we are fascinated by their absence.

About Schmidt, directed by Alexander Payne, written by Payne and Jim Taylor, is not about a man who goes on a journey to find himself, because there is no one to find. When Schmidt gets into his thirty-five-foot Winnebago Adventurer, which he and his wife, Helen, thought to use in his retirement, it is not an act of curiosity but of desperation: He has no place else to turn.

The film's opening scenes show him suffering through a meaningless retirement dinner and returning home to ask himself, after forty-two years of marriage, "Who is this old woman who is in my house?" His wife might ask the same question about her old man. They have lived dutiful and obedient lives, he as an actuary for the Woodman of the World Insurance Co. in Omaha, Nebraska, she as a housewife and mother, and now that the corporate world has discarded them they have no other role to assume.

Helen (June Squibb) makes an effort to be cheerful, and surprises him with breakfast in the Adventurer the morning after his retirement dinner, but breakfast is a cheerless meal when it does not begin a day with a purpose. Then Helen drops dead. Warren is astonished and bereft, not at the enormity of his loss, but that he had so little to lose. Here is a man who did not "plan for retirement."

About Schmidt has backed itself into a corner

with its hero, who is so limited it would be torture to watch him for two hours, even played by Nicholson. The film puts Schmidt on the road, in a reversal of Nicholson's youthful journey in *Easy Rider*. He and the film are in search of life, and find it in his daughter's plans to marry a man he (correctly) perceives as a buffoon and a fraud.

The humor in the film comes mostly from the daughter (Hope Davis, fed up with him) and the family she is marrying into. Schmidt's new in-laws include Randall Hertzel (Dermot Mulroney), a waterbed salesman and promoter of pyramid schemes, and his mother, Roberta (Kathy Bates), who embraces the life force with a bone-crushing squeeze. Schmidt, who has hardly had a surprise in forty years, now finds himself wrestling with a water bed, and joined in a hot tub by the topless and terrifyingly available Roberta.

Roberta is intended as a figure of fun, but at least she approaches life hungrily and with good cheer. This is one of Bates's best performances, as a woman of outsize charm and personality, who can turn on a dime to reveal impatience and anger. Her selfishness helps us observe that Schmidt is not a selfish man, mostly because there is nothing he has that he wants and nothing he lacks that he cares about.

Schmidt has one relationship in his life that gives him a place to spill out his fears and discontent. After watching a TV ad for a world children's charity, he "adopts" a six-year-old Tanzanian named Ndugu. Encouraged to write to the boy, he spills out his thoughts in long confessional letters. It is impossible to be sure if he thinks Ndugu can read the letters or understand them, or if he has such a painful need to find a listener that Ndugu will do. Certainly there is no one in America who Schmidt would be able to talk to with such frankness.

About Schmidt is essentially a portrait of a man without qualities, baffled by the emotions and needs of others. That Jack Nicholson makes this man so watchable is a tribute not only to his craft, but to his legend: Jack is so unlike Schmidt that his performance generates a certain awe. Another actor might have made the character too tragic or passive or empty, but Nicholson somehow finds within Schmidt a slowly developing hunger, a desire to start living now that the time is almost gone.

About Schmidt is billed as a comedy. It is funny to the degree that Nicholson is funny playing Schmidt, and funny in terms of some of his adventures, but at bottom it is tragic. In an RV camp, Schmidt is told by a woman who hardly knows him, "I see inside of you a sad man." Most teenagers will probably not be drawn to this movie, but they should attend. Let it be a lesson to them. If they define their lives only in terms of a good job, a good paycheck, and a comfortable suburban existence, they could end up like Schmidt, dead in the water. They should start paying attention to that crazy English teacher.

Adam Sandler's Eight Crazy Nights ★ ★
PG-13, 71 m., 2002

With the voices of: Adam Sandler (Davey/Whitey/Eleanor), Jackie Titone (Jennifer), Austin Stout (Benjamin). Other voices by Kevin Nealon, Rob Schneider, Norm Crosby, Jon Lovitz, and Tyra Banks. Directed by Seth Kearsley and produced by Adam Sandler, Allen Covert, and Jack Giarraputo. Screenplay by Brooks Arthur, Covert, Brad Isaacs, and Sandler.

Heaven help the unsuspecting families that wander into *Adam Sandler's Eight Crazy Nights* expecting a jolly, animated holiday funfest. The holidays aren't very cheerful in Sandlerville, which is why the PG-13 rating mentions "frequent and crude sexual humor." The MPAA doesn't mention it, but there's also a lot of scatological humor in the film, in keeping with Sandler's inexplicable fascination with defecation, flatulence, and bodily fluids.

If this is not a family film, what is it? Well, the audiences for *Jackass* may enjoy a scene where Davey, the hero, slams a sweet little old man into a Porta-Potty and shoves it down a hill. When the geezer emerges at the bottom, he is still alive, but covered from head to toe with excrement. Then Davey sprays him with a garden hose, and he freezes solid. Ho, ho.

Davey (who looks like and is voiced by Sandler) is "a thirty-three-year-old crazy Jewish guy," the film informs us, who is up before the judge on the latest in a long series of brushes with the law, this time for drunkenness. The judge is prepared to send him away for a long time, but kindly little Whitey (voice also by

Sandler) pipes up. Whitey explains that he is the referee of the local youth basketball league, and he could use an assistant. The judge releases Davey to Whitey's custody, not explaining why he thinks this drunk and vandal would be a good role model.

Whitey and his twin sister, Eleanor (also voiced by Sandler), take the lad into their home, but he remains stubbornly ill-mannered, not to mention pathologically violent, until the movie's eventual collapse into obligatory peace and goodwill, etc. If there was ever a movie where the upbeat ending feels like a cop-out, this is the one.

I can understand why Sandler might want to venture into *South Park* territory with a raunchy animated cartoon, but not why he links it to Christmas and Hanukkah. The advertising will inevitably use holiday images, and in the minds of most people those images will not suggest a film this angry and vulgar. There is also an odd disconnect between Sandler's pride in his Jewishness, which is admirable, and his willingness to display the obnoxious behavior of this particular Jewish character to an audience that may not get the point.

That point is, I think, that Davey has lost his way through alcoholism and antisocial neurosis, and is finally redeemed by the elfish saints Whitey and Eleanore, plus the beneficial side effects of working with the basketball team. All well and good, but the movie lingers on the scatological stuff and adds the happy ending as if paying its dues. Did it occur to Sandler that he could touch his bases and make his points in a film that was not quite so offensive? That was, in fact, sweet and cheerful and family-friendly? Considering that his popularity and the movie's holiday packaging will attract large numbers of teenage Middle Americans not necessarily familiar with Jews, does he think this is a good way to get them started?

Yes, I've argued against the requirement that ethnic groups must present "positive" images of themselves in the movies. I've defended Justin Lin's *Better Luck Tomorrow,* with its criminal Chinese-American teenagers, and Chris Eyre's *Skins,* with its portrait of alcoholics and vigilantes on an Indian reservation, and Tim Story's *Barbershop,* with its free-for-all African-American dialogue. But those films are positioned to reach audiences that will understand them—decode them as the directors hoped they would.

Won't *Adam Sandler's Eight Crazy Nights* attract an audience for reasons (holiday images, Sandler's popularity) that have nothing to do with the material? What are people who want to see an Adam Sandler movie going to take home from this one? Sandler's most recent film, the inspired and wonderful *Punch Drunk Love,* was not well received by Sandler fans; I heard from readers appalled by the way his audience responded to the film—before, in some cases, walking out. (How can someone in the dark of a movie theater tell "his audience" from themselves? Easily: The giveaway is inappropriate laughter, especially during serious moments.)

Sandler has painted himself into a corner. His comedies have included generous amounts of antisocial hostility, sudden violence, dodgy material about urination, defecation, and flatulence, and a general air of defiance. A lot of people like that. But they are not the people likely to understand the Hanukkah message in *Eight Crazy Nights.* And those who appreciate the message are likely to be horrified by a lot of the other material in the film. What Sandler has made here is a movie for neither audience.

Adaptation ★ ★ ★ ★
R, 114 m., 2002

Nicolas Cage (Charlie/Donald Kaufman), Meryl Streep (Susan Orlean), Chris Cooper (John Laroche), Tilda Swinton (Valerie), Brian Cox (Robert McKee), Cara Seymour (Amelia), Judy Greer (Alice), Maggie Gyllenhaal (Caroline), John Cusack (Himself), Catherine Keener (Herself). Directed by Spike Jonze and produced by Jonathan Demme, Vincent Landay, and Edward Saxon. Screenplay by Charlie Kaufman and Donald Kaufman, based on the book *The Orchid Thief* by Susan Orlean.

What a bewilderingly brilliant and entertaining movie this is—a confounding story about orchid thieves and screenwriters, elegant New Yorkers and scruffy swamp rats, truth and fiction. *Adaptation* is a movie that leaves you breathless with curiosity, as it teases itself with the directions it might take. To watch the film is to be actively involved in the challenge of its creation.

It begins with a book named *The Orchid Thief,* based on a *New Yorker* article by Susan Orlean (Meryl Streep). She writes about a Florida orchid fancier named John Laroche (Chris Cooper), who is the latest in a long history of men so obsessed by orchids that they would steal and kill for them. Laroche is a con man, and believes he has found a foolproof way to poach orchids from the protected Florida Everglades: Since they were ancestral Indian lands, he will hire Indians, who can pick the orchids with impunity.

Now that story might make a movie, but it's not the story of *Adaptation.* As the film opens, a screenwriter named Charlie Kaufman (Nicolas Cage) has been hired to adapt the book, and is stuck. There is so *much* about orchids in the book, and no obvious dramatic story line. Having penetrated halfway into the book myself, I understood his problem: It's a great story, but is it a movie?

Charlie is distraught. His producer, Valerie (Tilda Swinton), is on his case. Where is the first draft? He hardly has a first page. He relates his agony in voice-over, and anyone who has ever tried to write will understand his system of rewards and punishments: Should he wait until he has written a page to eat the muffin, or . . .

Charlie has a brother named Donald (also played by Cage). Donald lacks Charlie's ethics, his taste, his intelligence. He cheerfully admits that all he wants to do is write a potboiler and get rich. He attends the screenwriting seminars of Robert McKee (Brian Cox), who breaks down movie classics, sucks the marrow from their bones, and urges students to copy the formula. At a moment when Charlie is suicidal with frustration, Donald triumphantly announces he has sold a screenplay for a million dollars.

What is Charlie to do? To complicate matters, he has developed a fixation, even a crush, on Susan Orlean. He journeys to New York, shadows her, is too shy to meet her. She in turn goes to Florida to interview Laroche, who smells and smokes and has missing front teeth, but whose passion makes him . . . interesting.

And now my plot description will end, as I assure you I have not even hinted at the diabolical developments still to come. *Adaptation* is some kind of a filmmaking miracle, a film

that is at one and the same time (a) the story of a movie being made, (b) the story of orchid thievery and criminal conspiracies, and (c) a deceptive combination of fiction and real life. The movie has been directed by Spike Jonze, who with Charlie Kaufman as writer made *Being John Malkovich* the best film of 1999. If you saw that film, you will (a) know what to expect this time, and (b) be wrong in countless ways.

There are real people in this film who are really real, like Malkovich, Jonze, John Cusack, and Catherine Keener, playing themselves. People who are real but are played by actors, like Susan Orlean, Robert McKee, John Laroche, and Charlie Kaufman. People who are apparently not real, like Donald Kaufman, despite the fact that he shares the screenplay credit. There are times when we are watching more or less exactly what must (or could) have happened, and then a time when the film seems to jump the rails and head straight for the swamps of McKee's theories.

During all of its dazzling twists and turns, the movie remains consistently fascinating not just because of the direction and writing, but because of the lighthearted darkness of the performances. Chris Cooper plays a con man of extraordinary intelligence, who is attractive to a sophisticated New Yorker because he is so intensely *himself* in a world where few people are anybody. Nicolas Cage, as the twins, gets so deeply inside their opposite characters that we can always tell them apart even though he uses no tricks of makeup or hair. His narration creates the desperate agony of a man so smart he understands his problems intimately, yet so neurotic he is captive to them.

Now as for Meryl Streep, well, it helps to know (since she plays in so many serious films) that in her private life she is one of the merriest of women, because here she is able to begin as a studious New Yorker author and end as, more or less, Katharine Hepburn in *The African Queen.*

I sat up during this movie. I leaned forward. I was completely engaged. It toyed with me, tricked me, played straight with me, then tricked me about that. Its characters are colorful because they care so intensely; they are more interested in their obsessions than they are in the movie, if you see what I mean. And all the time, uncoiling beneath the surface of the film, is the audacious surprise of the last twenty minutes, in which—well, to say the movie's ending works on more than one level is not to imply it works on only two. ☞

The Affair of the Necklace ★ ★
R, 120 m., 2001

Hilary Swank (Jeanne de la Motte Valois), Simon Baker (Retaux de Vilette), Adrien Brody (Nicolas de la Motte), Joely Richardson (Marie Antoinette), Jonathan Pryce (Cardinal da Rohan), Christopher Walken (Cagliostro), Brian Cox (Minister Breteuil). Directed by Charles Shyer and produced by Broderick Johnson, Andrew A. Kosove, Redmond Morris, and Shyer. Screenplay by John Sweet.

Fed up with historical dramas, Jack Warner is said to have snarled at his producers: "Don't give me any more pictures where they write with feathers." He could have had *The Affair of the Necklace* in mind. This is the kind of movie that used to be called a bodice-ripper, and still could, if only more bodices were ripped. It tells the story of a scandal that prepares the way for the French Revolution, and involves a silly girl who thinks she can outsmart the cardinal, the royal jeweler, Marie Antoinette—and Cagliostro, the leader of the Illuminati, played by Christopher Walken. One look at Cagliostro and she should know she's in over her head.

The movie stars Hilary Swank as Jeanne St. Remy de Valois, who after her marriage of convenience becomes Jeanne de la Motte Valois. The operative name is "Valois." It is her family name, and she was orphaned as a child after her parents were involved in schemes against the crown. She dreams of restoring the glory of her family name and returning to the family house where she spent her childhood, and to do this she unfolds a scheme of audacious daring.

She knows that Cardinal Louis de Rohan (played by Jonathan Pryce in a congenial state of sin) wishes to be prime minister. She convinces him that Marie Antoinette will be more favorably disposed toward his cause if he presents the queen with a fabulous necklace containing 647 diamonds. She gets the money from the cardinal, obtains the necklace from the royal jeweler, keeps it for herself, uses it to repurchase her family home, and forges letters from the queen to the cardinal to cover the deception. What was she thinking? That the queen had so many necklaces she would never be able to account for one more or less? And that the cardinal would never dare refer directly to the transaction?

This kind of skullduggery (a word actually used in the film) would be more appropriate in the hands of an actress who includes devious scheming among her specialties—a Helena Bonham Carter, say, or Catherine Zeta-Jones. Hilary Swank, who was so wonderful in her Oscar-winning work in *Boys Don't Cry* (1999), exudes truthworthiness, which is the wrong quality for this assignment. She also embodies a certain plucky vulnerability, when what is wanted for Jeanne Valois is the Monica Lewinsky gene, the ability to imagine herself in the embrace of the great. Above all, she needs a kind of Bette Davis imperiousness. Hilary Swank, I fear, believes we should feel sorry for Jeanne. So does Charles Shyer, who directed this movie and sends Swank on the wrong assignment. *The Affair of the Necklace* only works if it understands Jeanne is one villain among many, not a misguided heroine.

The supporting cast offers incidental pleasures. Joely Richardson is an imperious, silly Marie Antoinette, able to deceive herself but not often deceived by anyone else. Jonathan Pryce makes the cardinal into a venal and greedy schemer, and Christopher Walken, as always, inspires hope when he walks into a scheme. Adrien Brody plays Jeanne's first, ineffectual, husband, and Simon Baker plays the ladies' man who plays Jeanne the way she is trying to play the crown.

But the storytelling is hopelessly compromised by the movie's decision to sympathize with Jeanne. We can admire someone for daring to do the audacious, or pity someone for recklessly doing something stupid, but when a character commits an act of stupid audacity, the admiration and pity cancel each other, and we are left only with the possibility of farce.

7

Agent Cody Banks ★ ★ ½
PG, 110 m., 2003

Frankie Muniz (Cody Banks), Hilary Duff (Natalie Connors), Angie Harmon (Ronica Miles), Keith David (CIA Director), Cynthia Stevenson (Mrs. Banks), Daniel Roebuck (Mr. Banks), Arnold Vosloo (Molay), Ian McShane (Brinkman), Martin Donovan (Dr. Connors). Directed by Harald Zwart and produced by David Glasser, Andreas Klein, David Nicksay, Guy Oseary, and Dylan Sellers. Screenplay by Zack Stentz, Ashley Miller, Scott Alexander, and Larry Karaszewski.

Imagine James Bond as a suburban American fifteen-year-old, and you have *Agent Cody Banks*, a high-speed, high-tech kiddie thriller that's kinda cute but sorta relentless. Frankie Muniz stars as Cody, whose martial arts skills, skateboarding, ceiling-walking, and extreme snowboarding are all the more remarkable when you consider that he goes into action before the CIA has time to give him much more than what in the Bond pictures is the Q routine with the neat gizmos.

Frankie lives with his parents (Cynthia Stevenson and Daniel Roebuck), who mean well but are so inattentive they don't notice their son has become a spy with international missions. His CIA handler (Angie Harmon, low-cut and sexy) wants him to become friends with a classmate named Natalie Connors (Hilary Duff, from *Lizzie McGuire*). Frankie is, alas, so tongue-tied around girls that his grade-school brother boasts, "Cody's almost sixteen and I've had twice as many dates as he has." Cody fights back ("Sitting in a treehouse doesn't count"), but the kid is serene ("It does when you're playing Doctor").

Natalie attends the ultraexclusive William Donovan Prep School, no doubt named for the famous World War II spy "Wild Bill" Donovan, and Frankie transfers there, uses his karate skills to silence hecklers, and ends up on a mission to liberate Natalie's father, Dr. Connors (Martin Donovan), from the clutches of the evil masterminds Brinkman and Molay (Ian McShane and Arnold Vosloo), who want to (we know this part by heart) attain world domination by using the doctor's inventions—microscopic nanorobots that can eat through anything.

The movie imitates its Bond origins with a lot of neat toys. Cody is given a BMW skateboard that has unsuspected versatility, and a jet-powered snowboard, and a sports car, and X-ray glasses (Hello, Angie Harmon!), and a watch that will send electricity through your enemies, although I think (I'm not sure about this) you should not be wearing it yourself at the time.

The set design includes the scientist's laboratory in underground World Domination Headquarters—which includes, as students of *Ebert's Bigger Little Movie Glossary* will not be surprised to learn, commodious and well-lighted overhead air ducts so that Cody can position himself in comfort directly above all important conversations. There also is CIA regional headquarters, with a conference table that looks like it was designed by Captain Nemo in a nightmare. We learn that the CIA runs summer camps to train kids to become junior spies, although why Angie Harmon, who seems to be playing Young Mrs. Robinson, is their handler is hard to explain—maybe she's there for the dads, in the movie and in the audience.

The movie will be compared with the two *Spy Kids* pictures, and it looks more expensive and high-tech, but isn't as much fun. It has a lot of skill and energy, but its wit is more predictable and less delightful. It's a well-made movie, to be sure, and will probably entertain its target audience, but its target audience is probably not reading this review, and you (for whatever reason) are. The difference is, I could look you in the eye and recommend you go see the *Spy Kids* movies, but this one, if you're not a kid, I don't think so.

A.I. Artificial Intelligence ★ ★ ★
PG-13, 145 m., 2001

Haley Joel Osment (David), Jude Law (Gigolo Joe), Frances O'Connor (Monica Swinton), Brendan Gleeson (Lord Johnson-Johnson), Sam Robards (Henry Swinton), William Hurt (Professor Hobby), Jake Thomas (Martin Swinton). Directed by Steven Spielberg and produced by Kathleen Kennedy, Spielberg, and Bonnie Curtis. Screenplay by Spielberg and Ian Watson, based on the short story "Supertoys Last All Summer Long" by Brian Aldiss.

Greatness and miscalculation fight for screen space in Steven Spielberg's *A.I. Artificial Intelligence,* a movie both wonderful and maddening. Here is one of the most ambitious films of recent years, filled with wondrous sights and provocative ideas, but it miscalculates in asking us to invest our emotions in a character that is, after all, a machine.

"What responsibility does a human have to a robot that genuinely loves?" the film asks, and the answer is: None. Because the robot does not genuinely love. It only genuinely seems to love. We are expert at projecting human emotions into nonhuman subjects, from animals to clouds to computer games, but the emotions reside only in our minds. *A.I.* evades its responsibility to deal rigorously with this trait, and goes for an ending that wants us to cry but had me asking questions just when I should have been finding answers.

At the center of the movie is an idea from Brian Aldiss's 1969 short story, "Supertoys Last All Summer Long," about an advanced cybernetic pet that is abandoned in the woods. When real household animals are abandoned, there is the sense that humans have broken their compact with them. But when a manufactured pet is thrown away, is that really any different from junking a computer? (I hope Buzz Lightyear is not reading these words.) From a coldly logical point of view, should we think of David, the cute young hero of *A.I.*, as more than a very advanced gigapet? Do our human feelings for him make him human?

Stanley Kubrick worked on this material for fifteen years, before passing it on to Spielberg, who has not solved it either. It involves man's relationship to those tools that so closely mirror our own desires that we confuse them with flesh and blood; consider that Charles Lindbergh's autobiography, *We,* is about himself and an airplane. When we lose a toy, the pain is ours, not the toy's, and by following an abandoned robot boy rather than the parents who threw him away, Spielberg misses the real story.

The film opens with cerebral creepiness, as Professor Hobby (William Hurt) presides at a meeting of a company that makes humanoid robots (or "mechas"). We are in the future; global warming has drowned the world's coastlines, but the American economy has survived thanks to its exploitation of mechas. "I propose that we build a robot that can love," Hobby says. Twenty months later, we meet Monica and Henry (Frances O'Connor and Sam Robards), a married couple whose own child has been frozen until a cure can be devised for his disease. The husband brings home David (Haley Joel Osment), a mecha who looks as lifelike and lovable as—well, Haley Joel Osment.

"There's no substitute for your own child!" sobs Monica, and Henry tries to placate her: "I'll take him back." Cold, but realistic; David is only a product. Yet he has an advanced chip that allows him to learn, adapt, and "love," when Monica permanently "imprints" him. In some of the most intriguing passages in the film, Spielberg explores the paradoxes that result, as David wins their love and yet is never—quite—a real boy. He doesn't sleep, but he observes bedtime. He doesn't eat, but so fervent is his desire to belong that he damages his wiring by ingesting spinach (wouldn't a mecha be programmed not to put things into its mouth?). David is treated with cruelty by other kids; humans are frequently violent and resentful against mechas. Why? Maybe for the same reason we swear at computers.

Events take place that cause David's "mother" to abandon him in the woods, opening the second and most extraordinary section of the movie, as the little mecha, and Teddy, his mecha pet bear, wander lost through the world, and he dreams of becoming a real boy and earning Monica's love. He knows *Pinocchio* from his bedtime reading, and believes that the Blue Fairy might be able to make him real. David and Teddy are befriended by Gigolo Joe (Jude Law), a love mecha living the life of a hustler. There is a sequence at a Flesh Fair, not unlike a WWF event, at which humans cheer as damaged mechas are destroyed grotesquely. Eventually, after a harrowing escape, they arrive at Rouge City, where a wizard tells David where to look for the Blue Fairy.

It's here that *A.I.* moves into its most visionary and problematical material, in spectacular scenes set in a drowned New York. There are secrets I won't reveal, but at one point David settles down to wait a very long time for the Blue Fairy, and the movie intends his wait to be poignant, but for me it was a case of a looping computer program—not a cause for tears, but a cause for rebooting. In the final scenes, David

9

is studied in a way I will not reveal; it is up to us to determine who, or what, his examiners are.

The movie is enormously provocative, but the story seems to skew against its natural grain. It bets its emotional capital on David and his desire to be a real boy, but it's the old wood-carver Geppetto, not the blockhead puppet, who is the poignant figure in *Pinocchio*. The movie toys with David's nature in the edgy party scenes, but then buys into his lovability instead of balancing on the divide between man and machine. Both of the closing sequences—the long wait and an investigation—are unsuccessful. The first goes over the top. The second raises questions it isn't prepared to answer. There are a couple of possible earlier endings that would have resulted in a tougher movie.

Haley Joel Osment and Jude Law take the acting honors (and, of course, Hurt is perfect at evoking the professor). Osment, who is on-screen in almost every scene, is one of the best actors now working. His David is not a cute little boy but a cute little boy *mecha;* we get not the lovable kid from *The Sixth Sense* but something subtly different. The movie's special effects are awesome. The photography by Janusz Kaminski reflects Spielberg's interest in backlighting, bright whites, and the curiously evocative visible beams of flashlights. The effects seamlessly marry the real with the imaginary.

A.I. is audacious, technically masterful, challenging, sometimes moving, ceaselessly watchable. What holds it back from greatness is a failure to really engage the ideas it introduces. The movie's conclusion is too facile and sentimental, given what has gone before. It has mastered the artificial, but not the intelligence.

Alex & Emma ★ ½

PG-13, 96 m., 2003

Kate Hudson (Emma, Eulva, Elsa, Eldora, and Anna), Luke Wilson (Alex, Adam), Sophie Marceau (Polina), David Paymer (John Shaw), Alexander Wauthier (Andre), Leili Kramer (Michele), Rip Taylor (The General), Gigi Birmingham (Madame Blanche), Jordan Lund (Claude). Directed by Rob Reiner and produced by Todd Black, Alan Greisman, Jeremy Leven, Reiner, and Elie Samaha. Screenplay by Reiner, Leven, Adam Scheinman, and Andrew Scheinman.

Alex & Emma is a movie about a guy who has to write a novel in thirty days in order to collect the money from his publisher to pay two gamblers who will otherwise kill him. So he hires a stenographer to take dictation, and they fall in love. But the thing is, it's a bad novel. Very bad. Every time the author started dictating, I was struck anew by how bad it was—so bad it's not even good romance fiction.

I guess I didn't expect him to write *The Gambler* by Dostoyevsky—although, come to think of it, Dostoyevsky dictated *The Gambler* in thirty days to pay off a gambling debt, and fell in love with his stenographer. I just expected him to write something presentable. You might reasonably ask why we even need to know what he's writing in the first place, since the movie involves the writer and the girl. But, alas, it involves much more: There are cutaways to the story he's writing, and its characters are played by Kate Hudson and Luke Wilson, the same two actors who star in the present-day story.

This other story takes place in 1924 and involves people who dress and act like the characters in *The Great Gatsby*. Not the central characters, but the characters who at*tend* Gatsby's parties and are in those long lists of funny names. It might have been a funny idea for the novelist to actually steal *The Great Gatsby*, confident that neither the gamblers nor his publisher would recognize it, but funny ideas are not easy to come by in *Alex & Emma*.

Alex is played by Luke Wilson. Emma is played by Kate Hudson. He also plays Adam, the young hero of the story within the story, and she plays four different nannies (Swedish, German, Latino, and American) who are employed by a rich French divorcée (Sophie Marceau) who plans to marry a rich guy (David Paymer) for his money, but is tempted by the handsome young Adam, who is a tutor to her children, who remain thoroughly untutored.

So the story is a bore. The act of writing the story is also a bore, because it consists mostly of trying out variations on the 1924 plot and then seeing how they look in the parallel story. Of course chemistry develops between Alex and Emma, who fall in love, and just as well: There is a Hollywood law requiring fictional characters in such a situation to fall in love, and the penalty for violating it is death at the box office. A lot of people don't know that.

Curious, the ease with which Alex is able to dictate his novel. Words flow in an uninterrupted stream, all perfectly punctuated. No false starts, wrong word choices, or despair. Emma writes everything down and then offers helpful suggestions, although she fails to supply the most useful observation of all, which would be to observe that the entire novel is complete crap.

Despite the deadly deadline, which looms ever closer, the young couple find time to get out of the apartment and enjoy a Semi-Obligatory Lyrical Interlude, that old standby where they walk through the park, eat hot dogs, etc., in a montage about a great day together. I do not remember if they literally walk through the park or eat hot dogs, but if they don't, then they engage in parklike and hot dog–like activities.

Now about his apartment. It's at the top of a classic brownstone, with balconies and tall windows, and should cost thousands of dollars a month, but he's flat broke, see, and just to prove it, there's a place where the plaster has fallen off the wall and you can see the bare slats underneath. He has art hanging all over his apartment, except in front of those slats. All Alex has to do is sublet, and his financial worries are over.

The movie has been directed by Rob Reiner and is not as bad as *The Story of Us* (1999), but this is a movie they'll want to hurry past during the AFI tribute. Reiner has made wonderful movies in the past (*Misery, The Princess Bride, Stand by Me*) and even wonderful romantic comedies (*The Sure Thing, When Harry Met Sally*). He will make wonderful movies in the future. He has not, however, made a wonderful movie in the present.　　☞

Ali ★ ★

R, 157 m., 2001

Will Smith (Muhammad Ali), Jamie Foxx (Drew "Bundini" Brown), Jon Voight (Howard Cosell), Mario Van Peebles (Malcolm X), Ron Silver (Angelo Dundee), Jeffrey Wright (Howard Bingham), Michael Bentt (Sonny Liston), Candy Ann Brown (Odessa Clay), Giancarlo Esposito (Ali's Dad). Directed by Michael Mann and produced by Paul Ardaji, A. Kitman Ho, James Lassiter, Mann, and Jon Peters. Screenplay by Eric Roth and Mann, based on the story by Gregory Allen Howard, Stephen J. Rivele, and Christoper Wilkinson.

Ali is a long, flat, curiously muted film about the heavyweight champion. It needs more of the flash, fire, and humor of Muhammad Ali and is shot more in the tone of a eulogy than a celebration. There is little joy here. The film is long and plays longer because it permits itself sequences that are drawn out to inexplicable lengths, while hurrying past others that should have been dramatic high points. It feels like an unfinished rough cut that might play better after editing.

Consider, for example, a training sequence set in Zaire, after Ali travels there for the Rumble in the Jungle. He begins his morning run, which takes him past a panorama of daily life. All very well, but he runs and runs and runs, long after any possible point has been made—and runs some more. This is the kind of extended scene you see in an early assembly of a film, before the heavy lifting has started in the editing room.

The film considers ten years in the life of Ali, from 1964, when he won the heavyweight championship as Cassius Clay, to 1974, when as Muhammad Ali he fought in the Rumble. This is the key decade in Ali's life, interrupted for three years when he was barred from boxing because of his refusal to be drafted.

Although many mistakenly believe he refused to serve because of guidance from the Nation of Islam, the film makes it clear that he took his stand on principle, and it cost him both his title and his religion; the Nation disapproved of his decision and suspended him. By the time the U.S. Supreme Court ruled 8–0 in his favor, he had lost what should have been his prime years as a young fighter. When he went into the ring against George Foreman in Zaire, he was thirty-two, the champion twenty-four.

Michael Mann's story of these ten years is told in the style of events overheard—this isn't a documentary, but it seems to lack a fiction's privileged access to its hero. Key scenes play out in enigmatic snippets of dialogue. We work to make connections. We see Ali's wives, but don't feel we know them; they fade in and out of focus like ghosts. The screenplay by Eric Roth and Mann seems reluctant to commit to a point of view, and leaves us to draw our own conclusions. During some scenes you can almost sense it shrugging. Ali remains an enigma.

This is despite what is actually a good job of acting by Will Smith in the title role. He has bulked up and looks convincing in the ring, but the key element of his performance is in capturing Ali's enigmatic, improvisational personality. He gets the soft-spoken, kidding quality just right, and we sense Ali as a man who plays a colorful public role while keeping a private reserve. There are times when he grows distant from even those close to him, and they look at him as if into a mystery.

The real problem with Smith's performance is the movie it finds itself in. Smith is the right actor for Ali, but this is the wrong movie. Smith is sharp, fast, funny, like the Ali of trash-talking fame, but the movie doesn't unleash that side of him or his character. Ali was not only the most famous man of his time, but had fun with his fame. I can't claim any special insights, but I did once spend a day with him, and I saw a man enormously entertained by life, twinkling with bemusement, lowering the tinted glass window of his Rolls limousine so that pedestrians could do a double take when they saw it was the Champ. Smith could play that man, but *Ali* doesn't know or see him; it sees Ali as more meditative and subdued—as sad, sometimes, when sadness is the last thing you feel when you risk everything on principle. The film feels under a cloud.

Among the many key players in his life—his wives, his trainer Angelo Dundee, his right-hand man Bundini Brown, his mentor Malcolm X, his father, his leader Elijah Muhammad—Ali's most authentic relationship in the film seems to be with the sportscaster Howard Cosell. Played by Jon Voight in a performance that captures his theatrical weirdness and forthright honesty, Cosell comes across as a man who slipped into TV before the cookie cutting began. His voice, his toupee, his sublime self-assurance are all here, along with a tender, almost paternal regard for Ali, a man he clearly loves and worries about. Ali responds in kind, and Smith is able to suggest that in a world that surrounded him with toadies, bootlickers, and yes-men, Ali turned to Cosell almost in relief at being able to hear the truth, plainly spoken. Jamie Foxx is also engaging and appealing as Bundini, the self-destructive mascot who sold the Champ's belt "and put it into my arm."

The fight scenes are convincing and well staged. Smith looks at home in the ring. But the unique thing about the life of Muhammad Ali is precisely that it was not just about the fighting. More than any other heavyweight champion and few athletes in any sport, Ali changed the subject: His life was not about boxing, but about a black man who dared to triumph in American society without compromise, apology, or caution.

Those who called him a coward for refusing to fight in the war will learn here that he'd been offered a sweetheart deal by the army; all he had to do was go along, be inducted, not play the angry black rebel, and he'd be entertaining the troops and defending his title and getting nowhere close to combat. To turn down that deal and the heavyweight title, and to lose the blessing of the Nation of Islam in the process, was to show himself as a brave man entirely governed by ethics.

"No Viet Cong ever called me nigger," Ali famously said, and the movie makes it clear that the American establishment was terrified of a black uprising in the tumultuous Vietnam era, and that J. Edgar Hoover, whose G-men tracked and tricked Martin Luther King and Ali, was one of the great villains of his time.

The movie includes scenes involving King and Malcolm X, but doesn't really deal with them (you find out more in Spike Lee's *Malcolm X*). After King is shot, Ali watches a city burn, but curiously has no dialogue. We wait for issues to be clarified, for points to be made, for the movie to punch up what is important, but the dramatic high points slowly slip back down into a miasma of unfocused and undisciplined footage. The visual look of the picture mirrors its lack of energy; the colors are subdued, the focus often a little soft. *Ali* looks like a movie that was never properly prepared and mounted, that got away from its makers in the filming, that has been released without being completed.

All About Lily Chou-Chou ★ ★
NO MPAA RATING, 146 m., 2001

Hayato Ichihara (Yûichi Hasumi), Shûgo Oshinari (Shusuke Hoshino), Yû Aoi (Shiori Tsuda), Ayumi Ito (Yôko Kuno), Takao Osawa (Tabito Takao), Miwako Ichikawa (Shimabukuro), Izumi Inamori (Izumi Hoshino). Directed by Shunji Iwai and produced by Koko Maeda. Screenplay by Iwai.

All About Lily Chou-Chou is like an ancient text that requires modern commentary. It's not an old film (it's cutting-edge Japanese techno-angst), but it's so enigmatic, oblique, and meandering that it's like coded religious texts that require monks to decipher. In this case, the monks are the critics. They won't tell you anything you haven't figured out for yourself, but they will confirm that there's no more to the movie than you thought there was. This movie is maddening. It conveys a simple message in a visual style that is willfully overwrought.

The story: Lily Chou-Chou is a Japanese pop idol who must be real, since she appears in concert, but whom we never see. Ironically, then, one of her songs consists of repetitions of "I see you and you see me." She is idolized by Yûichi (Hayato Ichihara), a student in high school. He has a crush on the real-life Yôko (Ayumi Ito), a gifted pianist. Both Yûichi and Yôko are the targets of cliques of school bullies.

For a while, Yûichi has a friend, Shusuke Hoshino (Shûgo Oshinari), a fellow student who turns into a sadist and forces Yûichi to steal money and give it to him. Shusuke has another sideline: He pimps Shiori (Yû Aoi) to businessmen, and makes her give him most of the money. Shiori has a secret crush on Yûichi, but is under Shusuke's control and pathetically confides on the telephone, "Lately, when I think of men I think of customers."

The elements are in place for a powerful story of alienated Japanese teenagers, but the writer-director, Shunji Iwai, cannot bring himself to make the story accessible to ordinary audiences. He and his cinematographer, Noboru Shinoda, are in love with their lightweight digital camera and give us jerky, handheld, out-of-focus shots. Some sequences are so incomprehensible they play as complete abstractions. I know, it's a style. It's a style that was interesting for a brief season and is now tiresome and pretentious.

Either you make an experimental film that cuts loose from narrative, characters, and comprehensible cinematography, or you do not. Iwai seems to want to tell the story of his characters, and it could be a compelling one (some of the scenes are poignant or wounding), but he cannot allow himself to make the film in a way that can communicate. That would be, I guess, a compromise. He has made a film that few reasonable ticket-buyers will have the patience to endure. It will be appreciated by a handful of highly evolved film watchers who can generate a simultaneous analysis in their minds, but what is the point, really, in making a film that closes out most moviegoers?

The world that swims murkily to the surface of *All About Lily Chou-Chou* is certainly a frightening one, eclipsing even the anomie of the Columbine killers. These students drift without values or interests, devoting all the passion of their young lives to creatures who may exist only on the Internet. Shiori has sex with strangers for pay, but is too shy to tell Yûichi she likes him. Yûichi's life has been turned into hell by Shusuke, who seems to act not so much out of hatred as boredom. The film's teachers and adults care, but are hopelessly misinformed about what is really going on.

There is a movie here somewhere. Shunji Iwai has gone to a great deal of trouble to obscure it. *Lily Chou-Chou* has been compared by some to Truffaut's *The 400 Blows,* which was also stylistically groundbreaking in its time, but Truffaut broke with traditional styles in order to communicate better, not to avoid communicating at all.

All or Nothing ★ ★ ★ ★
R, 128 m., 2002

Timothy Spall (Phil Bassett), Lesley Manville (Penny Bassett), Alison Garland (Rachel Bassett), James Corden (Rory Bassett), Ruth Sheen (Maureen), Marion Bailey (Carol), Helen Coker (Donna). Directed by Mike Leigh and produced by Simon Channing-Williams. Screenplay by Leigh.

Mike Leigh's *All or Nothing* looks behind three doors in a South London public housing estate and finds loneliness, desperation, and a stubborn streak of spunky humor. His characters try to remember a time when they were light-hearted and had hope. But there is little to cheer them now, except for food and sleep, the telly, the pub on Saturday night, and, for the young, thoughtless sex to hurry them along into raising thankless kids of their own.

Phil Bassett, played by the sad-faced and wounded Timothy Spall, is a minicab driver who stares straight ahead as dramas unfold in his backseat. His common-law wife, Penny (Lesley Manville), is a checkout clerk at the Safeway. They have two fat, unattractive children: Rachel (Alison Garland), who is a cleaner at an old-folks' home and buries herself in romance novels, and Rory (James Corden), who lurches from the table to the sofa, his eyes hypnotically fixed on the television, his voice wavering between anger and martyrdom.

Their flat is on an outside corridor of an anonymous housing project, but it has a wooden door with a knocker—a reminder of when they had hopes for it as a home. Now it's a place where they barely meet. Phil sleeps late, his wife goes to work early, Rachel is in a world of her own, and Rory vibrates with hostility. For Penny, there is at least the companionship of neighbors along the corridor; she hangs out with Carol (Marion Bailey) and Maureen (Ruth Sheen), and they go to karaoke night at the pub. Maureen is a single mom whose daughter Donna (Helen Coker) is abused by a boyfriend. Carol, whose husband, Ron, also drives a minicab, is a drunk sliding off into walking hallucinations.

This sounds grim and is grim, but it is not depressing, because Leigh, who in his earlier films might have found a few laughs at the expense of his characters, clearly loves these people and cares for them. They are, we realize, utterly without resources; they lack the skills to enjoy life and are trapped on an economic treadmill. Phil has the makings of a philosopher, and observes sadly that you work all day and sleep all night and then you die. When a fellow driver complains of a car crash, Phil looks on the bright side: "You might have driven around the corner and killed a little girl."

The film pays attention to the neighbors, but its main attention is on the Bassetts, and one day something unforeseen happens—I will not reveal what it is—and it acts as a catalyst to jolt them out of their depression and lethargy. It is the kind of bad thing that good things come from. Watch carefully how it happens, and who reacts to it and how, and you will see that Leigh has made all of the neighbors into characters whose troubles help to define their response.

There are moments in *All or Nothing* of such acute observation that we nod in understanding. Consider the way Maureen learns that Donna is pregnant and how she deals with the news (at first, and then later), and how she treats the boyfriend. Watch joy and beauty flash briefly in the pub when the women are singing. And observe how Timothy Spall goes through an entire life crisis while scarcely saying a word, and tells us all we need to know with his eyes.

There is a scene that establishes the Bassett family as well as any scene possibly could. Phil needs to put together a sum of money, and he visits his wife and children separately. He searches for a coin under Rory's sofa cushion, but Rory finds it and piggishly snatches it. Rachel lends him money as if money is the least of her worries. Penny tries to find out what he is thinking. He keeps repeating that he will pay her back tomorrow. This is his companion of twenty years, and he treats her loan like one he would get in a pub.

Mike Leigh is now the leading British director— ironic, since after his brilliant *Bleak Moments* (1972) he spent long years making TV films because no one would finance his features. He and his actors improvise their scripts during long periods of living as the characters. His subject is usually working- and middle-class life in Britain, although his jolly *Topsy-Turvy* (2000) entered the backstage world of Gilbert and Sullivan. In *All or Nothing* he returns to more familiar material, in one of his very best films.

The closing scenes of the movie are just about perfect. Rory is the center of attention, and notice when, and how, he suddenly speaks in the middle of a conversation about him. When a director gets a laugh of recognition from the audience, showing that it knows his characters and recognizes typical behavior, he has done his job. These people are real as few movie characters ever are. At the end, it looks as if they will be able to admit a little sunshine into their lives, and talk to each other a little more. We are relieved.

All the Queen's Men ★
NO MPAA RATING, 105 m., 2002

Matt LeBlanc (Steven O'Rourke), Eddie Izzard (Tony Parker), James Cosmo (Archie), Nicolette Krebitz (Romy), Udo Kier (General Lansdorf), David Birkin (Johnno), Oliver Korittke (Franz), Karl Markovics (Liebl), Edward Fox (Colonel Aiken). Directed by Stefan Ruzowitzky and produced by Zachary Feuer, Gabrielle Kelly, and Marco Weber. Screenplay by David Schneider.

All the Queen's Men is a perfectly good idea for a comedy, but it just plain doesn't work. It's dead in the water. I can imagine it working well in a different time, with a different cast, in black and white instead of color—but I can't imagine it working like this.

The movie tells the World War II story of the "Poof Platoon," a group of four Allied soldiers parachuted into Berlin in drag, to infiltrate the all-woman factory where the Enigma machine is being manufactured. This story is said to be based on fact. If it is, I am amazed that such promising material would yield such pitiful results. To impersonate a woman and a German at the same time would have been so difficult and dangerous that it's amazing how the movie turns it into a goofy lark.

The film stars Matt LeBlanc, from *Friends,* who is criminally miscast as Steven O'Rourke, a U.S. officer famous for never quite completing heroic missions. He is teamed with a drag artist named Tony (Eddie Izzard), an ancient major named Archie (James Cosmo), and a scholar named Johnno (David Birkin). After brief lessons in hair, makeup, undergarments, and espionage, they're dropped into Berlin during an air raid, and try to make contact with a resistance leader.

This underground hero turns out to be the lovely and fragrant Romy (Nicolette Krebitz), a librarian who, for the convenience of the plot, lives in a loft under the roof of the library, so that (during one of many unbelievable scenes) the spies are able to lift a skylight window in order to eavesdrop on an interrogation.

The plot requires them to infiltrate the factory, steal an Enigma machine, and return to

England with it. Anyone who has seen *Enigma, U-571,* or the various TV documentaries about the Enigma machine will be aware that by the time of this movie, the British already had possession of an Enigma machine, but to follow that line of inquiry too far in this movie is not wise. The movie has an answer to it, but it comes so late in the film that although it makes sense technically, the damage has already been done.

The four misfit transvestites totter about Berlin looking like (very bad) Andrews Sisters imitators, and O'Rourke falls in love with the librarian Romy. How it becomes clear that he is not a woman is not nearly as interesting as how anyone could possibly have thought he was a woman in the first place. He plays a woman as if determined, in every scene, to signal to the audience that he's absolutely straight and only kidding. His voice, with its uncanny similarity to Sylvester Stallone's, doesn't help.

The action in the movie would be ludicrous anyway, but is even more peculiar in a cross-dressing comedy. There's a long sequence in which Tony, the Izzard character, does a marked down Marlene Dietrich before a wildly enthusiastic audience of Nazis. Surely they know he is, if not a spy, at least a drag queen? I'm not so sure. I fear the movie makes it appear the Nazis think he is a sexy woman, something that will come as a surprise to anyone who is familiar with Eddie Izzard, including Eddie Izzard.

Watching the movie, it occurred to me that Tony Curtis and Jack Lemmon were not any more convincing as women in *Some Like It Hot.* And yet we bought them in that comedy, and it remains a classic. Why did they work, while the Queen's Men manifestly do not? Apart from the inescapable difference in actual talent, could it have anything to do with the use of color?

B&w is better suited to many kinds of comedy because it underlines the dialogue and movement while diminishing the importance of fashions and eliminating the emotional content of various colors. Billy Wilder fought for b&w on *Some Like It Hot* because he thought his drag queens would never be accepted by the audience in color, and he was right.

The casting is also a problem. Matt LeBlanc

15

does not belong in this movie in any role other than, possibly, that of a Nazi who believes Eddie Izzard is a woman. He is all wrong for the lead, with no lightness, no humor, no sympathy for his fellow spies, and no comic timing. I can imagine this movie as a black-and-white British comedy, circa 1960, with Peter Sellers, Kenneth Williams, et al., but at this time, with this cast, this movie is hopeless.

All the Real Girls ★ ★ ★ ★
R., 108 m., 2003

Paul Schneider (Paul), Zooey Deschanel (Noel), Shea Whigham (Tip), Danny McBride (Bust-Ass), Maurice Compte (Bo), Heather McComb (Mary-Margaret), Benjamin Mouton (Leland), Patricia Clarkson (Elvira). Directed by David Gordon Green and produced by Jean Doumanian and Lisa Muskat. Screenplay by Green.

We like to be in love because it allows us to feel idealistic about ourselves. The other person ennobles, inspires, redeems. Our lover deserves the most wonderful person alive, and that person is ourselves. Paul (Paul Schneider), the hero of *All the Real Girls,* has spent his young manhood having sex with any girl who would have sex with him and some who were still making up their minds, but when he meets Noel he doesn't want to rush things. He wants to wait, because this time is special.

Noel (Zooey Deschanel), who has spent the last several years in a girls' boarding school, is crazy in love with him and is a virgin. She is eighteen, an age when all the hormones in our bodies form ranks and hurl themselves against the ramparts of our inhibitions. That they can discuss these matters with romantic idealism does not entirely work as a substitute.

All the Real Girls, David Gordon Green's second film, is too subtle and perceptive, and knows too much about human nature, to treat their lack of sexual synchronicity as if it supplies a plot. Another kind of movie would be entirely about whether they have sex. But Green, who feels tenderly for his vulnerable characters, cares less about sex than about feelings and wild, youthful idealism. He comes from North Carolina, the state where young Thomas Wolfe once prowled the midnight campus, so in love with life that he uttered wild goat cries at the moon.

Most movies about young love trivialize and cheapen it. Their cynical makers have not felt true love in many years, and mock it, perhaps out of jealousy. They find something funny in a twenty-year-old who still doesn't realize he is doomed to grow up to be as jaded as they are. Green is twenty-seven, old enough to be jaded, but he has the soul of a romantic poet. Wordsworth, after all, was thirty-six when he published:

The rainbow comes and goes,
And lovely is the rose;

How many guys that age would have that kind of nerve today? Green knows there are nights when lovers want simply to wrap their arms around each other and celebrate their glorious destinies.

He centers these feelings on characters who live in the same kind of rusty, overgrown southern mill town he used for his great first film, *George Washington* (2000). His characters grew up together. They look today on the faces of their first contemporaries. Paul's best friend, Tip (Shea Whigham), has been his best friend almost from birth. That he is Noel's brother is a complication, since Tip knows all about Paul's other girls. And more than a complication, because your best friend's sister embodies a history that includes your entire puberty, and may be the first person you noticed had turned into a girl.

Green likes to listen to his characters talk. They don't have much to do. Some of them work at the few remaining mill jobs, and we learn some details about their lives (an hourly sprinkler system washes the fibers out of the air). They stand around and sit around and idly discuss the mysteries of life, which often come down to whether someone did something, or what they were thinking of when they did it, or if they are ever going to do it. I had relatives who lived in towns like these, and I know that when you go to the salad bar it includes butterscotch pudding.

Paul's single mom, Elvira (Patricia Clarkson), works as a clown at parties and in the children's wards of hospitals. Some critics have mocked this occupation, but let me tell you something: A small-town woman with a family to feed can make better money with a Bozo wig and a putty nose than she can working unpaid overtime at Wal-Mart. People will pay you nothing to clean their houses, but they pay the going rate when their kids have birthdays. The fact that Green knows this and a lot of people don't is an indicator of his comfort with his characters.

Green's dialogue has a kind of unaffected, flat naturalism. ("You feel like waffles or French toast?" "No, the places I go are usually not that fancy.") That doesn't mean their speech is not poetic. His characters don't use big words, but they express big ideas. Their words show a familiarity with hard times, disappointment, wistfulness; they are familiar with all the concepts on television, but do not lead lives where they apply.

Two emotional upheavals strike at the narrative. One is inevitable; Tip is enraged to learn that Paul and Noel are dating. The other is not inevitable, and I will not even hint about it. There is a scene where it is discussed in a bowling alley, using only body language, in long shot.

The thing about real love is, if you lose it, you can also lose your ability to believe in it, and that hurts even more. Especially in a town where real love may be the only world-class thing that ever happens.

Almost Salinas ★ ½
PG, 92 m., 2003

John Mahoney (Max Harris), Linda Emond (Nina Ellington), Lindsay Crouse (Allie), Virginia Madsen (Clare), Ian Gomez (Manny), Nathan Davis (Zelder Hill), Tom Groenwald (Leo Quinlan), Ray Wise (Jack Tynan). Directed by Terry Green and produced by Wade W. Danielson. Screenplay by Green.

Almost Salinas is a sweet and good-hearted portrait of an isolated crossroads and the people who live there, or are drawn into their lives. Shame about the plot. The people are real, but the story devices are clunkers from Fiction 101; the movie generates goodwill in its setup, but in the last act it goes haywire with revelations and secrets and dramatic gestures. The movie takes place in Cholame, the California town where

James Dean died in 1955, and maybe the only way to save it would have been to leave out everything involving James Dean.

John Mahoney stars as Max Harris, the proprietor of a diner in a sparsely populated backwater. He's thinking of reopening the old gas station. Virginia Madsen is Clare, his waitress, and other locals include Nathan Davis, as an old-timer who peddles James Dean souvenirs from a roadside table, and Ian Gomez, as the salt-of-the-earth cook.

The town experiences an unusual flurry of activity. A film crew arrives to shoot a movie about the death of James Dean. Max's ex-wife, Allie (Lindsay Crouse), turns up. And a magazine writer named Nina Ellington (Linda Emond) arrives to do a feature about the reopening of the gas station. If this seems like an unlikely subject for a story, reflect that she stays so long she could do the reporting on the reopening of a refinery. She gradually falls in love with Max, while one of the young members of the film crew falls for Clare's young assistant behind the counter.

The place and the people are sound. Mahoney has the gift of bringing quiet believability to a character; his Max seems dependable, kind, and loyal. Virginia Madsen is the spark of the place, not a stereotyped, gum-chewing hash-slinger, but a woman who takes an interest in the people who come her way. If Emond is not very convincing as the visiting reporter, perhaps it's because her job is so unlikely. Better, perhaps, to make her a woman with no reason at all to be in Cholame. Let her stay because she has no place better to go, and then let her fall in love.

From the movie's opening moments, there are quick black-and-white shots of Dean's 1955 Porsche Spyder, racing along a rural highway toward its rendezvous with death. The arrival of the film crew, with its own model of the same car, introduces a series of parallels between past and present that it would be unfair to reveal.

Spoiler warning! Without spelling everything out, let us observe, however, that it is unlikely that a character who was locally famous in 1955 could stay in the same area and become anonymous just by changing his name. It is also unlikely that he would be moved, so many years later, to the actions he takes in the film. And cosmically unlikely that they would have the results that they do. Not to mention how pissed off the film company would be.

As the movie's great revelations started to slide into view, I slipped down in my seat, fearful that the simple and engaging story of these nice people would be upstaged by the grinding mechanics of plot contrivance. My fears were well grounded. *Almost Salinas* generates enormous goodwill and then loses it by betraying its characters to the needs of a plot that wants to inspire pathos and sympathy, but inspires instead, alas, groans and the rolling of eyes.

Along Came a Spider ★ ★
R, 105 m., 2001

Morgan Freeman (Detective Alex Cross), Monica Potter (Agent Jezzie Flannigan), Michael Wincott (Gary Soneji), Jay O. Sanders (Detective Kyle Craig), Dylan Baker (Mayor Carl Monroe), Raoul Ganeev (Agent Charles Chakley), Billy Burke (Agent Michael Devine), Penelope Ann Miller (Katherine Rose Dunne). Directed by Lee Tamahori and produced by David Brown and Joe Wizan. Screenplay by Marc Moss, based on a novel by James Patterson.

A few loopholes I can forgive. But when a plot is riddled with them, crippled by them, made implausible by them, as in *Along Came a Spider*, I get distracted. I'm wondering, since Dr. Alex Cross is so brilliant, how come he doesn't notice yawning logical holes in the very fabric of the story he's occupying?

Dr. Cross (Morgan Freeman) is a District of Columbia police detective, a famous forensic psychologist whose textbook is quoted by other cops. As the movie opens, he loses his partner in one of those scenes where you're thinking, gee, I didn't know the police had *that* kind of technology. A woman cop has a small camera concealed on her being, which takes a TV signal of the killer, who is driving a car, and relays it to Cross in a helicopter, causing us to wonder if there is a way to arrest this guy at less taxpayer expense.

After this chase, Cross goes into a depression and passes the time building model boats— until his phone rings and it's another diabolical killer, who once again has devised an elaborate cat-and-mouse game for the detective to play. No killers in Washington ever just want to murder somebody; they're all motivated by the desire to construct elaborate puzzles for Cross.

No one is better than Morgan Freeman at being calm and serious and saying things like, "He's really after somebody else." Freeman was brilliant at unraveling the diabolical pattern in *Seven* (1995), and the success of that movie inspired the splendid *Kiss the Girls* (1997), where he first played Cross, the hero of six novels by James Patterson. In *Girls*, he intuited that the madman wasn't killing his victims but collecting them. Now comes another criminal who has read way too many James Patterson novels.

I will tread carefully to avoid revealing surprises, since the movie socks us with one every five minutes, counting on our astonishment to distract us from implausibilities. The film opens with a strangling and a kidnapping at an exclusive private school. The kids have parents so important that the Secret Service has agents permanently assigned. Because the hostage is the daughter of a senator, Cross finds himself working with Agent Jezzie Flannigan (Monica Potter), who found time for a career despite a lifetime of explaining to people how her name is spelled.

The school's students have computer monitors at every desk, and are challenged by their teacher to see who can find Charles Lindbergh's home page in the fewest possible clicks. (Answer: Go to Google, type in "Lindbergh," get 103,000 results, discover he doesn't have a home page.) Most kids their age are already busy creating viruses to bring the economy to its knees. Why such a lamebrained exercise? Dr. Cross figures it out.

The correct Lindbergh page, which he finds immediately out of 103,000 possibilities, has been put up by the kidnapper (or come to think of it, has it?), and includes a live cam shot with resolution so high Cross can read the name on a bottle of pills. This clue, plus the kidnapper's insistence on communicating through Cross, gets him on the case, partnered with Agent Flannigan.

Kiss the Girls, directed by Gary Fleder, had a palpable sense of time and place; deep, moist, shadowy, ominous woodlands figured heavily.

Along Came a Spider, directed by Lee Tamahori (of the great *Once Were Warriors*), is also thick with atmosphere, and evokes the damp, wet gloom of a chilly season. As Cross and Flannigan follow leads, we also see the kidnapper and his victim, and are filled with admiration for her imagination; she is able to escape, set fires, swim toward shore, and perform other feats far more difficult than a Google search.

But then . . . well, there's not much more I can say without giving away astonishing surprises. The film contains two kinds of loopholes: (1) those that emerge when you think back on the plot, and (2) those that seem like loopholes at the time, and then are explained by later developments which may contain loopholes of their own.

Of Morgan Freeman as a movie actor, no praise is too high. Maybe actors should be given Oscars not for the good films they triumph in, but for the weak films they survive. The focus of his gaze, the quiet authority of his voice, make Dr. Cross an interesting character even in scenes where all common sense has fled. And the look and texture of the film are fine; Tamahori and cinematographer Matthew F. Leonetti have created a convincing sense of place (to be sure, they shot their Virginia exteriors in British Columbia, but, hey, that's a place too). Michael Wincott makes a satisfactory bad guy, especially when his mastermind schemes start blowing up in his face.

But, man, are you gonna be talking when you come out of this movie! Saying things like "but why . . ." and "if she . . ." and "wouldn't he . . ." and "how come . . ." as you try to trace your way back through the twisted logic of the plot. Here's a sample question: Dr. Cross mentions a $12 million ransom and later explains that the person he was talking to should have known it was $10 million but never said anything. And I'm thinking, should that person have even known about the ransom at all? Well, maybe, if . . . but I dunno. There are places in this movie you just can't get to from other places in this movie.

Amandla! ★ ★ ★
PG-13, 105 m., 2003

Featuring Hugh Masekela, Abdullah Ibrahim, Miriam Makeba, and Vusi Mahlasela. A documentary directed by Lee Hirsch and produced by Hirsch and Sherry Simpson.

"We'll catch the early staff boat and get there before the tourists arrive," A. M. Kathrada told my wife and me, in Cape Town in November 2001. We were going the next morning to visit Robben Island, where for twenty-seven years Nelson Mandela and others accused of treason, including Kathrada, were held by the South African apartheid government. We were having dinner with Kathrada, who is of Indian descent, and his friend Barbara Hogan, who won a place in history as the first South African white woman convicted as a traitor.

In those days it was easy to become a traitor. *Amandla!,* a new documentary about the role of music in the overthrow of apartheid, begins with the exhumation of the bones of Vuyisile Mini, who wrote a song named "Beware, Verwoerd! (The Black Man Is Coming!)," aimed at the chief architect of South Africa's racist politics of separation. Mini was executed in 1964 and buried in a pauper's grave.

Robben Island lies some twenty miles offshore from Cape Town, and the view back toward the slopes of Table Mountain is breathtaking. When I was a student at the University of Cape Town in 1965, friends pointed it out, a speck across the sea, and whispered that Mandela was imprisoned there. It would be almost twenty-five years until he was released and asked by F. W. DeKlerk, Verwoerd's last white successor, to run for president. No one in 1965 or for many years later believed there would be a regime change in South Africa without a bloody civil war, but there was, and Cranford's, my favorite used book shop, can now legally be owned by black South Africans; it still has a coffee pot and crooked stairs to the crowded upstairs room.

Kathrada, now in his early seventies, is known by everyone on the staff boat. At the Robben Island Store, where we buy our tickets, he introduces us to the manager—a white man who used to be one of his guards, and who smuggled forbidden letters ("and even the occasional visitor") on and off the island. On the island, we walk under a crude arch that welcomes us in Afrikaans and English, and enter the prison building, which is squat and unlovely, thick with glossy lime paint. The office is not yet open and Kathrada cannot find a key.

"First I am locked in, now I am locked out," he observes cheerfully. Eventually the key is discovered and we arrive at the object of our visit, the cell where Mandela lived. It is about long enough to lie down in. "For the first seven years," Kathrada said, "we didn't have cots. You got used to sleeping on the floor."

White political prisoners like Barbara Hogan were kept in a Pretoria prison. There were not a lot of Indian prisoners, and Kathrada was jailed with Mandela's African group.

"They issued us different uniforms," he observed dryly. "I was an Indian, and was issued with long pants. Mandela and the other Africans were given short pants. They called them 'boys,' and gave them boys' pants."

A crude nutritional chart hung on the wall, indicating that Indians were given a few hundred calories more to eat every day, because South African scientists had somehow determined their minimal caloric requirements were a little greater than those of blacks.

Weekdays, all of the men worked in a quarry, hammering rocks into gravel. No work was permitted on Sunday in the devoutly religious Afrikaans society. The prisoners were fed mostly whole grains, a few vegetables, a little fruit, very little animal protein. "As a result of this diet and exercise, plus all of the sunlight in the quarry," Kathrada smiled, "we were in good health and most of us still are. The sun on the white rocks and the quarry dust were bad for our eyes, however."

During the 1970s the apartheid government clamped such a tight lid on opposition that it seemed able to hold on forever. The uplifting film *Amandla!* argues that South Africa's music of protest played a crucial role in apartheid's eventual overthrow. Mandela's African National Congress was nonviolent from its birth until the final years of apartheid, when after an internal struggle one branch began to commit acts of bombing and sabotage (murder and torture had always been weapons of the whites). Music was the ANC's most dangerous weapon, and we see footage of streets lined with tens of thousands of marchers, singing and dancing, expressing an unquenchable spirit.

"We lost the country in the first place, to an extent, because before we fight, we sing," Hugh

Masekela, the great South African jazzman, tells the filmmakers. "The Zulus would sing before they went into battle, so the British and Boers knew where they were and when they were coming."

There was a song about Nelson Mandela that was sung at every rally, even though mention of his name was banned, and toward the end of the film there is a rally to welcome him after his release from prison, and he sings along. It is one of those moments where words cannot do justice to the joy.

Amandla! (the Xhosa word means "power") was nine years in the making, directed by Lee Hirsch, produced with Sherry Simpson. It combines archival footage, news footage, reports from political exiles like Masekela and his former wife, Miriam Makeba, visits with famous local singers, an appearance by Archbishop Desmond Tutu, and a lot of music. The sound track CD could become popular like "The Buena Vista Social Club."

After the relatives of Vuyisile Mini disinter his bones, he is reburied in blessed ground under a proper memorial, and then his family holds a party. Among the songs they sing is "Beware, Verwoerd!" It is not a nostalgia piece, not dusty, not yet. They sing it not so much in celebration as in triumph and relief.

The Amati Girls ★
PG, 91 m., 2001

Cloris Leachman (Dolly), Mercedes Ruehl (Grace), Dinah Manoff (Denise), Sean Young (Christine), Lily Knight (Dolores), Paul Sorvino (Joe), Lee Grant (Aunt Spendora), Edith Field (Aunt Loretta), Cassie Cole (Carla), Marissa Leigh (Laura), Doug Spinuzza (Armand), Mark Harmon (Lawrence). Directed by Anne De Salvo and produced by James Alex, Melanie Backer, Steven Johnson, Michael I. Levy, and Henry M. Shea Jr. Screenplay by De Salvo.

A lot of saints are mentioned in *The Amati Girls*, including Christopher, Lucy, Cecelia, Theresa (the Little Flower), and the BVM herself, but the movie should be praying to St. Jude, patron saint of lost causes. Maybe he could perform a miracle and turn this into a cable offering, so no one has to pay to see it.

The movie's a tour of timeworn clichés

about family life, performed with desperation by a talented cast. Alone among them, Mercedes Ruehl somehow salvages her dignity while all about her are losing theirs. She even manages to avoid appearing in the shameless last shot, where the ladies dance around the kitchen singing *Doo-wah-diddy, diddy-dum, diddy-dum.*

The movie is about a large Italian-American family in Philadelphia. Too large, considering that every character has a crisis, and the story races from one to another like the guy on TV who kept all the plates spinning on top of the poles. This family not only has a matriarch (Cloris Leachman) but her superfluous sister (Lee Grant) and their even more superfluous sister (Edith Field). There are also four grown daughters, two husbands, two hopeful fiancées, at least three kids, and probably some dogs, although we never see them because they are no doubt hiding under the table to avoid being stepped on.

The adult sisters are Grace (Ruehl), who is married to macho-man Paul Sorvino ("No Padrone male will ever step foot on a ballet stage except as a teamster"); Denise (Dinah Manoff), who is engaged to Lawrence (Mark Harmon) but dreams of show biz (she sings "Kiss of Fire" to demonstrate her own need for St. Jude); Christine (Sean Young), whose husband, Paul (Jamey Sheridan), is a workaholic; and poor Dolores (Lily Knight), who is retarded. Denise and Christine think Grace is ruining her life with guilt because when she was a little girl she ran away and her mother chased her and fell, which of course caused Dolores to be retarded.

Sample subplot. Dolores decides she wants a boyfriend. At the church bingo night, she sits opposite Armand (Doug Spinuzza), who, we are told "has a head full of steel" after the Gulf War. This has not resulted in Armand being a once-normal person with brain damage, but, miraculously, in his being exactly like Dolores. At the movies, after they kiss, he shyly puts his hand on her breast, and she shyly puts her hand on his.

You know the obligatory scene where the reluctant parent turns up at the last moment for the child's big moment onstage? No less than two fathers do it in this movie. Both Joe (Sorvino) and Paul have daughters in a ballet recital, and not only does Joe overcome his loathing for ballet and even attend rehearsals, but Paul overcomes his workaholism and arrives backstage in time to appear with his daughter.

The movie has one unexpected death, of course. That inspires a crisis of faith, and Dolores breaks loose from the funeral home, enters the church, and uses a candlestick to demolish several saints, although she is stopped before she gets to the BVM. There are also many meals in which everyone sits around long tables and talks at once. There is the obligatory debate, recycled from *Return to Me*, about who is better, Frank Sinatra or Tony Bennett. And an irritating editing twitch: We are shown the outside of every location before we cut inside. There is also one priceless conversation, in which Lee Grant explains to Cloris Leachman that her hair is tinted "copper bamboo bronze." For Cloris, she suggests "toasted desert sunrise." The Little Flower had the right idea. She cut off her hair and became a Carmelite.

Amelie ★ ★ ★ ½
R, 115 m., 2001

Audrey Tautou (Amelie Poulain), Mathieu Kassovitz (Nino Quicampoix), Rufus (Raphael Poulain), Yolande Moreau (Madeleine Wallace), Arthus De Penguern (Hipolito [The Writer]), Urbain Cancellier (Collignon [The Grocer]), Dominique Pinon (Joseph), Maurice Benichou (Bretodeau [The Box Man]), Claude Perron (Eva [The Stripteaser]). Directed by Jean-Pierre Jeunet and produced by Claudie Ossard. Screenplay by Guillaume Laurant and Jeunet. In French with English subtitles.

Jean-Pierre Jeunet's *Amelie* is a delicious pastry of a movie, a lighthearted fantasy in which a winsome heroine overcomes a sad childhood and grows up to bring cheer to the needful and joy to herself. You see it, and later when you think about it, you smile.

Audrey Tautou, a fresh-faced waif who looks like she knows a secret and can't keep it, plays the title role, as a little girl who grows up starving for affection. Her father, a doctor, gives her no hugs or kisses, and touches her only during checkups—which makes her heart beat so fast he thinks she is sickly. Her mother dies as the result of a successful suicide leap off the towers of Notre Dame, a statement that reveals less of the plot than you think it does.

Amelie grows up lonely and alone, a waitress in a corner bistro, until one day the death of Princess Diana changes everything. Yes, the shock of the news causes Amelie to drop a bottle cap, which jars loose a stone in the wall of her flat, which leads her to discover a rusty old box in which a long-ago boy hoarded his treasures. And in tracking down the man who was that boy and returning his box, Amelie finds her life's work: She will make people happy. But not in any old way. So, she will amuse herself (and us) by devising the most extraordinary stratagems for bringing about their happiness.

I first began hearing about *Amelie* last May at the Cannes Film Festival, where there was a *scandale* when *Amelie* was not chosen for the official selection. "Not serious," sniffed the very serious authorities who decide these matters. The movie played in the commercial theaters of the back streets, where audiences vibrated with pleasure. It went on to win the audience awards at the Edinburgh, Toronto, and Chicago festivals, and I note on the Internet Movie Database that it is currently voted the twelfth best film of all time.

I am not sure *Amelie* is better than *Fargo* (No. 64) or *The General* (No. 85), but I know what the vote reflects: immediate satisfaction with a film that is all goodness and cheer—sassy, bright, and whimsical, filmed with dazzling virtuosity, and set in Paris, the city we love when it sizzles and when it drizzles. Of course this is not a realistic modern Paris, and some critics have sniffed about that, too: It is clean, orderly, safe, colorful, has no social problems, and is peopled entirely by citizens who look like extras from *An American in Paris*. This is the same Paris that produced Gigi and Inspector Clouseau. It never existed, but that's okay.

After discovering the box and bringing happiness to its owner, Amelie improvises other acts of kindness: painting word-pictures of a busy street for a blind man, for example, and pretending to find long-lost love letters to her concierge from the woman's dead husband, who probably never mailed her so much as a lottery ticket. Then she meets Nino (the director Mathieu Kassovitz), who works indifferently in a porn shop and cares only for his hobby, which is to collect the photos people don't want from those automated photo booths and turn them into collages of failed facial expressions.

Amelie likes Nino so much that one day when she sees him in her café, she dissolves. Literally. Into a puddle of water. She wants Nino, but some pixie quirk prevents her from going about anything in a straightforward manner, and success holds no bliss for her unless it comes about through serendipity. There must be times when Nino wonders if he is being blessed or stalked.

Jean-Pierre Jeunet has specialized in films of astonishing visual invention but, alas, impenetrable narratives *(Delicatessen, The City of Lost Children)*. He worked for Hollywood as the director of *Alien Resurrection* (1997), placing it, I wrote, "in what looks like a large, empty hangar filled with prefabricated steel warehouse parts." With *Amelie* he has shaken loose from his obsession with rust and clutter, and made a film so filled with light and air it's like he took the cure.

The film is filled with great individual shots and ideas. One of the best comes when Amelie stands high on the terrace of Montmartre and wonders how many people in Paris are having orgasms at that exact instant, and we see them, fifteen in all, in a quick montage of hilarious happiness. It is this innocent sequence, plus an equally harmless childbirth scene, that has caused the MPAA to give the movie an undeserved R rating (in Norway it was approved for everyone over eleven).

It is so hard to make a nimble, charming comedy. So hard to get the tone right, and find actors who embody charm instead of impersonating it. It takes so much confidence to dance on the tightrope of whimsy. *Amelie* takes those chances, and gets away with them.

American Outlaws ★

PG-13, 94 m., 2001

Colin Farrell (Jesse James), Scott Caan (Cole Younger), Ali Larter (Zee Mimms), Gabriel Macht (Frank James), Gregory Smith (Jim Younger), Harris Yulin (Thaddeus Rains), Will McCormack (Bob Younger), Kathy Bates (Ma James), Timothy Dalton (Allan Pinkerton). Directed by Les Mayfield and produced by

James G. Robinson and Bill Gerber. Screenplay by Roderick Taylor and John Rogers.

For years there have been reports of the death of the Western. Now comes *American Outlaws,* proof that even the B Western is dead. It only wants to be a bad movie, and fails. Imagine the cast of *American Pie* given a camera, lots of money, costumes and horses, and told to act serious and pretend to be cowboys, and this is what you might get.

The movie tells the story of the gang formed by Jesse James and Cole Younger after the Civil War—a gang which, in this movie, curiously embodies the politics of the antiglobalization demonstrators in Seattle, Sweden, and Genoa. A railroad is a-comin' through, and they don't want it. When the railroad hires Pinkertons to blow up farms, and Jesse and Frank's mother is blowed up real good, the boys vow revenge. They will steal the railroad's payroll from banks, and blow up tracks.

It is curious that they are against the railroad. In much better movies like *The Claim,* the coming of the railroad is seen by everybody as an economic windfall, and it creates fortunes by where it decides to lay its tracks. For farmers, it was a lifeblood—a fast and cheap way to get livestock and crops to market. But the James farm is one of those movie farms where nothing much is done. There are no visible herds or crops, just some chickens scratching in the dirt, and Ma James (Kathy Bates) apparently works it by herself while the boys are off to war. Her hardest labor during the whole movie is her death scene.

Jesse James is played by Colin Farrell, who turned on instant star quality in the Vietnam War picture *Tigerland* (2001) and turns it off here. That this movie got a theatrical push and *Tigerland* didn't is proof that American distribution resembles a crap shoot. Scott Caan plays Jesse's partner, Cole Younger, Gabriel Macht is Frank James, and Jim and Bob Younger are played by Gregory Smith and Will McCormack. Farrell here seems less like the leader of a gang than the lead singer in a boy band, and indeed he and the boys spend time arguing about their billing. Should it be the James Gang? The James-Younger Gang? The Younger-James Gang? (Naw, that sounds like there's an Older James Gang.) There was a great American film about the James-Younger Gang, Philip Kaufman's *The Great Northfield, Minnesota, Raid* (1972), and this movie crouches in its shadow like the Nickelodeon version.

According to *American Outlaws,* Jesse James was motivated not by money but by righteous anger (and publicity—all the boys liked being famous). After getting his revenge and knocking over countless banks, what he basically wants to do is retire from the gang and get himself a farm and settle down with pretty Zee Mimms (Ali Larter). His delusion that the most famous bank robber in America—the perpetrator, indeed, of "the first daylight bank robbery in American history"—could peacefully return to the farm is an indication of his grasp of reality, which is limited.

While we are musing about how many nighttime robberies there had been in American history, we meet the villains. The railroad is owned by Thaddeus Raines (Harris Yulin), who lectures about "the righteousness of progress," and the hired goons are led by Allan Pinkerton (Timothy Dalton), who spends most of the movie looking as if he knows a great deal more than he is saying, some of it about Jesse James, the rest about this screenplay.

There is some truth to the story; the James home really was bombed by the Pinkertons, although Ma didn't die, she only lost an arm. But there's little truth in the movie, which makes the James-Younger Gang seem less like desperadoes than ornery cutups. The shootouts follow the timeless movie rule that the villains can't aim and the heroes can't miss. Dozens of extras are killed, countless stuntmen topple forward off buildings, but the stars are treated with the greatest economy, their deaths doled out parsimoniously according to the needs of the formula screenplay.

Should cruel mischance lead you to see this movie, do me a favor and rent Kaufman's *The Great Northfield, Minnesota, Raid* and then meditate on the fact that giants once walked the land in Hollywood. The style, class, and intelligence of a Western like that (in an era which also gave us *The Wild Bunch*) is like a rebuke to *American Outlaws.* What happened to the rough-hewn American intelligence that gave us the Westerns of Ford, Hawks, and Peckinpah? When did cowboys become teen pop idols?

American Pie 2 ★ ★ ★
R, 100 m., 2001

Jason Biggs (Jim), Shannon Elizabeth (Nadia), Alyson Hannigan (Michelle), Chris Klein (Oz), Natasha Lyonne (Jessica), Thomas Ian Nicholas (Kevin), Tara Reid (Vicky), Seann William Scott (Stifler), Mena Suvari (Heather), Eugene Levy (Jim's Dad). Directed by J. B. Rogers and produced by Warren Zide, Craig Perry, and Chris Moore. Screenplay by Adam Herz, based on a story by David H. Steinberg and Herz.

This may seem crushingly obvious, but here goes: The problem with a sequel like *American Pie 2* is that it's about the same characters and the elements of surprise and discovery are gone. In the first movie, Stifler's mom appeared unexpectedly like a gift from above. In this movie, she has become a standing joke (except to Stifler). In the first movie, Jim didn't know that he and Nadia were making love in streaming video on the Internet. In this one, there's a sequence where strangers pick up a sex scene on their CB radios, and we're thinking: this year's version of Internet broadcast.

That said, I had a good time at *American Pie 2*, maybe because the characters are broad comic types, well played; because the movie feels some sympathy for their dilemmas; and because it's obsessed with sex. Also because it has Jim's dad (Eugene Levy), the world's most understanding and supportive parent, meet his son in the emergency room during the most embarrassing and humiliating evening of the kid's life (and remember, this is the kid who made love on the Internet), and tell him, "I'm proud of you, son."

I will not tell you why Jim is in the emergency room. There's a lot I can't tell you about the movie because it's filled with turnabouts, sight gags, and horrifying sexual adventures. Also a lot of sex lore, as that three is the magic number in sexual histories: When a woman tells you how many men she has slept with, you should multiply by three, and when a man tells you, you should divide by three.

The cast of *American Pie* is back for this sequel, no doubt because their original contracts provided for it, and just as well: The first film cost $11 million and grossed more than $150 million worldwide. Now they've graduated from high school, just finished their first year of college, and decided to spend the summer by renting a place on the lake at Grand Haven, Michigan. And the party's on.

Jim (Jason Biggs) is first among equals in the cast. His experience on the Internet, his first sexual encounter, left him badly shaken, and a prom night experience was a fiasco. His current girlfriend invites him to have "friendly good-bye sex" before the school term ends, but he observes gloomily that they've never had "friendly hello sex." When he learns that Nadia (Shannon Elizabeth), the Internet girl, is heading back for the summer, in desperation he enlists Michelle (Alyson Hannigan) to give him lessons. She's the strange but lovable girl he took to the prom, and is a good sport, even strapping her brassiere around a pillow so he can practice unfastening it with one hand.

The movie's longest comic sequence is not exactly its best. It involves three of the guys being trapped inside the house they're painting by its two residents, who they think are lesbians. The girls agree to put on a show, if the guys will do everything to each other that they want to see the girls doing to each other. Some of this works, some loses the right note, and it goes on too long. A subtler and funnier way could have been found to indicate the guys' homophobic feelings. A scene in which Jim is mistaken for a retarded trombone player doesn't play well, either.

One nice thing about the movie is that the girls are portrayed as equal opportunity predators, and not simply as objectified sex objects. Heather (Mena Suvari), for example, suggests phone sex to her boyfriend, and we consider for the first time the detumescent effect of call-waiting.

I laughed at *American Pie 2*, yes, but this is either going to be the last *Pie* movie or they're going to have to get a new angle. I'd hate to see the freshness of the series grind down into the repetition of the same formula to wring a few more dollars out of the brand name. One hopeful sign that the filmmakers can learn and grow is that the sequel does not contain a single pie, if you know what I mean.

Note: I am informed it does indeed contain one pie, although not to the same purpose.

An American Rhapsody ★ ★ ★
PG-13, 102 m., 2001

Nastassja Kinski (Margit), Scarlett Johansson (Suzanne [at fifteen]), Tony Goldwyn (Peter), Agi Banfalvy (Helen), Zoltan Seress (George), Zsuzsa Czinkoczi (Teri), Balazs Galko (Jeno). Directed by Eva Gardos and produced by Colleen Camp and Bonnie Timmermann. Screenplay by Gardo.

An American Rhapsody is told from the point of view of a fifteen-year-old American girl, but in a way it's more her mother's story. The girl is named Suzanne, and until the age of six she was raised in her native Hungary by two foster parents she loved dearly. Then, the way she understands it at the time, she's stolen away from them and put on an airplane to join her "real" family in America.

As she grows older, she understands more: Her parents, Margit and Peter, escaped Hungary with her older sister at the height of the Stalin horror. Babies were not allowed to be brought along, so they left the infant Suzanne with her grandmother—who, after being arrested, passed her on to the older childless couple. Stalin dies, the grandmother is released from jail, she reclaims Suzanne for a "day's visit," and puts her on the plane to America.

These are two versions of the same events, and they have much different emotional loads. Little Suzanne is happy to have her own room in a Los Angeles bedroom suburb, but she misses the only people she has ever known as her parents. The wound remains. As she grows older, she coexists with her father (Tony Goldwyn), but has an uneasy truce with her mother (Nastassja Kinski). We meet her at fifteen, in the full flood of adolescent rebellion.

Suzanne (Scarlett Johansson) is a budding Valley Girl, with a best friend, a boyfriend, and a habit of smoking cigarettes when she's out of sight of her parents. Her mother is protective of her to a degree approaching panic. When she sees the girl kissing her boyfriend, she yanks her away, puts bars on her bedroom window, and a dead bolt on the door. The way Suzanne responds to imprisonment is direct and extreme, and has the advantage of getting everyone's attention.

Suzanne is allowed to return to Hungary to meet again with her grandmother, Helen (Agi Banfalvy), and her foster parents, Teri (Zsuzsa Czinkoczi) and Jeno (Balazs Galko). She learns things about her mother's childhood that help her understand, if not fully accept, her mother's extreme protectiveness.

Along the way what we get is a view of the way unhealthy states create unhealthy citizens, and the way evil at the top can poison even the trust between a mother and a daughter. *An American Rhapsody* was written and directed by Eva Gardos, who is the model for Suzanne. It is her story. Her mother's story is told obliquely, but it is her mother who really suffered, who is the victim more than the daughter.

Nastassja Kinski, in one of her most affecting performances, does much to convey the turmoil going on in her soul, but has the handicap of being offscreen much of the time, or seen through her daughter's eyes. She wears fresh American dresses and keeps her home spotless and enjoys prosperity, but it must at times all seem like a mirage to her—to this survivor of World War II, this victim of sudden violence, this refugee from Stalinism and worse. There is good reason to be protective of a child, but at some point childhood is over and life will collect its dues one way or another, and parents who deny that are practicing a form of insanity.

Scarlett Johansson, so good in *Ghost World,* plays Suzanne in a sort of a glower; immersed in the culture celebrated by the Beach Boys, she wants to be a California Girl and have fun, fun, fun, and her mother treats her like a bomb about to explode. I appreciated the way Johansson created this character not as a colorful victim, but as an ordinary teenage girl who retreats into secrecy and passive hostility. She wisely sees that Suzanne is not meant to be a rebel with or without a cause, but more like the bystander at a sad historical accident.

We can understand why Eva Gardos wants to tell her own story (we all do), but at the end of the day she had it easy compared to her mother. I suppose the film, in a way, is about how she comes to realize that. The American children of immigrants from anywhere will probably find moments they recognize in this movie.

America's Sweethearts ★ ★
PG-13, 100 m., 2001

Julia Roberts (Kiki Harrison), Billy Crystal (Lee Phillips), Catherine Zeta-Jones (Gwen Harrison), John Cusack (Eddie Thomas), Hank Azaria (Hector), Stanley Tucci (Dave Kingman), Christopher Walken (Hal Weidmann), Seth Green (Danny Wax), Alan Arkin (Wellness Guide). Directed by Joe Roth and produced by Susan Arnold, Billy Crystal, and Donna Roth. Screenplay by Crystal and Peter Tolan.

America's Sweethearts recycles *Singin' in the Rain* but lacks the sassy genius of that 1952 musical, which is still the best comedy ever made about Hollywood. Both movies open with profiles of famous couples whose on-screen chemistry masks an offscreen split. Both have canny studio heads and eager-beaver assistants. Both have plain little wall-flowers who suddenly blossom. Both climax with sneak previews that are fraught with disaster. One difference is that a Hedda Hopper-style gossip columnist, in the earlier picture, is replaced by a whole junket-load of freeloading journalists in this one.

Here's a quick casting key. The movie stars Julia Roberts in the Debbie Reynolds role, Catherine Zeta-Jones as Jean Hagen, John Cusack as Gene Kelly, Billy Crystal as Donald O'Connor, and Stanley Tucci as Millard Mitchell (the studio head). Added to the mix are two grotesque caricatures—one funny (Christopher Walken's auteur director), one overdone (Hank Azaria's Spanish lover). Both movies are about a troubled megamillions production that could save, or sink, the studio.

In principle, there's nothing wrong with returning to a classic for inspiration. But *Singin' in the Rain* unreeled with effortless grace, and *America's Sweethearts* lacks inner confidence that it knows what it is and where it's going. The opportunities are here for a classic comedy, but the fangs never sink in and the focus isn't sharp enough.

I was especially disappointed by the junket scene; in this season of fake critics and phony quotes, the time was ripe for savage satire, but this movie goes way too easy on the junket blurbsters. They've been invited to a remote desert location for the premiere of a movie that may not even exist; the studio P.R. ace (Crystal) claims he can distract them from the missing movie by convincing them the stars are in love again. While it's true that most junketeers care more about celeb gossip than the movies themselves, the movie goes too easy on them. One can imagine a scene, modeled on real life, where Crystal writes quotes praising the unseen movie and asks the freebie hounds to sign up for them, and they eagerly line up to claim their blurbs so they can get to the open bar and the complimentary buffet.

Julia Roberts and Catherine Zeta-Jones play sisters, Kiki and Gwen. Gwen is the sleek and famous beauty. Kiki has always been sixty pounds overweight, her sister's lapdog and gofer. John Cusack is Eddie, Gwen's costar, as they say, on-screen and off. But Gwen has been lured away by the oily charms of Hector (Azaria), a Latin lover with a lisp and too much jewelry, and Eddie has gone ballistic, attacking them with his motorcycle before being bundled off to a rehab center run by "wellness guide" Alan Arkin.

Meanwhile, Hal Weidmann (Christopher Walken) is the mad-dog auteur who has directed Eddie and Gwen in their latest epic (for solitude while editing his film, he has purchased the Unibomber's cabin and erected it in his backyard). The studio head gnashes his teeth with frustration: Hal has spent $86 million and shown him only twenty seconds of titles, along with a note: "We could also do these in blue."

These early scenes are promising. But then . . . well, I think the problem is that years of read-my-lips filmmaking have drained Hollywood of the quick intelligence of the screwball comedy. It's obvious that Kiki the wallflower has slimmed down into a beauty, that Gwen is a tiresome egomaniac, that Hector's days are numbered, that Eddie must realize that Kiki, not Gwen, is the sister he has always loved. But in the romantic scenes, there's too much earnestness and not enough rapid-fire cynicism. The movie forgets it's a comedy at times, and goes for conviction and insight when it should be running in the opposite direction.

The movie moves from a bright beginning and a passable middle to a disastrous closing act, when Hal Weidmann helicopters in with the long-awaited print of his masterpiece. The scenes showing the premiere of this movie don't work for a number of reasons, including their lack of a proper comeuppance for Gwen. Remember the unmasking and humiliation of the Jean Hagen character in *Singin' in the Rain* and compare it with the unfocused, dull-edged result of this screening.

Part of the problem is with the movie-within-a-movie itself—the masterpiece Hal unveils. We get the idea behind what he's trying to do, but *America's Sweethearts* never lets him do it. There are no scenes in Hal's movie that pay off on their own and really skewer the stars sitting in the audience. We want revenge and payoff time, and we get a muddled sequence that eventually degenerates into a routine series of shots tying up the loose ends.

You can't blame the actors (although you might blame the casting for Azaria, who doesn't seem plausible as a movie star or a lover). Julia Roberts is sweet and lovable, Catherine Zeta-Jones is chilly and manipulative, John Cusack is desperately heartsick, and Billy Crystal is, as we'd expect, convincing as the wise-guy publicist. But the screenplay, by Crystal and Peter Tolan, is all over the map, and director Joe Roth should have ordered rewrites and a new ending. Isolated scenes work but don't add up. Godard said the way to criticize a movie is to make another movie. Even while you're watching *America's Sweethearts,* it gets shouldered aside by *Singin' in the Rain.*

Amores Perros ★ ★ ★ ½
R, 153 m., 2001

Emilio Echevarria (El Chivo), Gael Garcia Bernal (Octavio), Goya Toledo (Valeria), Alvaro Guerrero (Daniel), Vanessa Bauche (Susana), Jorge Salinas (Luis), Laura Almela (Julieta), Marco Perez (Ramiro). Directed and produced by Alejandro González Iñárritu. Screenplay by Guillermo Arriaga.

Amores Perros arrives from Mexico trailing clouds of glory—it was one of this year's Oscar nominees—and generating excitement on the Internet, where the fanboys don't usually flip for foreign films. It tells three interlinked stories that span the social classes in Mexico City, from rich TV people to the work-ing class to the homeless, and it circles through those stories with a nod to Quentin Tarantino, whose *Pulp Fiction* had a magnetic influence on young filmmakers. Many are influenced but few are chosen: Alejandro Gonzalez Inarritu, making his feature debut, borrows what he can use but is an original, dynamic director.

His title translates as *Love's a Bitch,* and all three of his stories involve dogs who become as important as the human characters. The film opens with a disclaimer promising that no animals were harmed in the making of the film. That notice usually appears at the ends of films, but putting it first in *Amores Perros* is wise, since the first sequence involves dog fights and all three will be painful for soft-hearted animal lovers to sit through. Be warned.

"Octavio and Susana," the first segment, begins with cars hurtling through city streets in a chase and gunfight. The images are so quick and confused, at first we don't realize the bleeding body in the backseat belongs to a dog. This is Cofi, the beloved fighting animal of Octavio (Gael Garcia Bernal), a poor young man who is helplessly in love with Susana (Vanessa Bauche), the teenage bride of his ominous brother, Ramiro (Marco Perez). Flashbacks show how Cofi was shot after killing a champion dog; now the chase ends in a spectacular crash in an intersection—a crash that will involve all three of the movie's stories.

In the second segment, "Daniel and Valeria," we meet a television producer (Alvaro Guerrero) who has abandoned his family to live with a beautiful young model and actress (Goya Toledo). He's rented a big new apartment for her; Valeria's image smiles in through a window from a billboard. But then their happiness is marred when Valeria's little dog chases a ball into a hole in the floor, disappears under the floorboards, and won't return. Is it lost, trapped, or frightened? "There are thousands of rats down there," they warn each other.

Then Valeria is involved in the same crash; we see it this time from a different angle, and indeed it comes as a shock every time it occurs. Her leg is severely injured, and one complication leads to another—while the dog still snuffles under the floor, sometimes whining piteously, sometimes ominously silent. This sequence surely owes something to the great

Spanish director Luis Buñuel, who made some of his best films in Mexico, and whose *Tristana* starred Catherine Deneuve as a beauty who loses her leg. The segment is sort of dark slapstick—morbid and ironic, as the romance is tested by the beauty's mutilation and by the frustration (known to every pet owner) of a dog that *will not* come when it is called.

From time to time during the first two segments, we've seen a street person, bearded and weathered, accompanied by his own pack of dogs. The third segment, "El Chivo and Maru," stars the famous Mexican actor Emilio Echevarria, who, we learn, is a revolutionary turned squatter, and supports himself by killing for hire. He is approached by a man who wants to get rid of his partner, and is inspired to add his own brutal twist to this murder scheme. The three stories have many links, the most interesting perhaps that El Chivo has rescued the wounded dog Cofi and now cares for it.

Amores Perros at 153 minutes is heavy on story—too heavy, some will say—and rich with character and atmosphere. It is the work of a born filmmaker, and you can sense Inarritu's passion as he plunges into melodrama, coincidence, sensation, and violence. His characters are not the bland, amoral totems of so much modern Hollywood violence, but people with feelings and motives. They want love, money, and revenge. They not only love their dogs but also desperately depend on them. And it is clear that the lower classes are better at survival than the wealthy, whose confidence comes from their possessions, not their mettle.

The movie reminded me not only of Buñuel but also of two other filmmakers identified with Mexico: Arturo Ripstein and Alejandro Jodorowsky. Their works are also comfortable with the scruffy underbelly of society, and involve the dangers when jealousy is not given room to breathe. Consider Jodorowsky's great *Santa Sangre*, in which a cult of women cut off their own arms to honor a martyr. *Amores Perros* will be too much for some filmgoers, just as *Pulp Fiction* was and *Santa Sangre* certainly was, but it contains the spark of inspiration.

Analyze That ★ ★
R, 95 m., 2002

Robert De Niro (Paul Vitti), Billy Crystal (Dr. Ben Sobel), Lisa Kudrow (Laura Sobel), Joe Viterelli (Jelly), Cathy Moriarty (Patti LoPresti), Joe D'Onofrio (Gunman), Joseph Bono (Wiseguy), John Finn (Richard Chapin). Directed by Harold Ramis and produced by Jane Rosenthal and Paula Weinstein. Screenplay by Peter Tolan, Peter Steinfeld, and Ramis.

The success of *Analyze This* (1999) made *Analyze That* inevitable, but was it necessary? What seemed like a clever idea the first time feels like a retread the second, as mob boss Paul Vitti (Robert De Niro) goes back into therapy with Dr. Ben Sobel (Billy Crystal). The first film more or less exhausted the possibilities of this idea, as the second one illustrates.

Analyze This was never more than a sitcom, but the casting gave it an aura. De Niro as a neurotic mobster was a funny idea, and Crystal as a shrink was good casting because of his ability to seem smart even during panic attacks. Lisa Kudrow, then the shrink's girlfriend, now his wife, has a nice off-balance disbelieving way with dialogue that plays against Crystal instead of merely outshouting him, and there was also the mammoth presence of Joe Viterelli as Jelly, the boss's loyal chauffeur and sidekick.

All of that worked the first time, and it kind of works, sometimes, in the second film. But the story has the ring of contrivance. If the first film seemed to flow naturally from the premise, this one seems to slink uneasily onto the screen, aware that it feels exactly like a facile, superficial recycling job.

As the film opens, Sobel is attending his father's funeral, but takes a cell call from Sing Sing, right there in the front row at temple. Turns out Vitti has turned goofy and does nothing all day but sing songs from *West Side Story*. Is he crazy, or faking it? Whether he's faking it or not, he knows all the words. He gets no less goofy after he's released into the custody of Sobel and his wife, Laura (Kudrow), and placed under their supervision—in their home. Laura *hates* this idea, but the FBI insists on it: Vitti's good behavior is Sobel's responsibility.

The film then descends into an unconvincing, contrived heist subplot, with Sobel linked with the robbers. And Cathy Moriarty (De Niro's wife in *Raging Bull*) turns up as the head of a rival gang, in a rivalry that never seems anything more than the excuse for some routine mob-war threat routines. Harold Ramis, who directed and cowrote (as he did with the first film), is a gifted filmmaker, the author of many great laughs in the movies, but he should reflect that there is a reason most sequels are not directed by the same men who made the originals: A movie that inspires a sequel, if it is any good, incorporates qualities that cannot be duplicated.

What we get in *Analyze That* are several talented actors delivering their familiar screen personas in the service of an idiotic plot. There is undeniable pleasure to be had in hearing De Niro say, yet once again, "You're good. No! You're good!" to Crystal, and watching De Niro use that beatific smile as if his character is saintly to bestow such praise (a compliment from De Niro is somewhat like being knighted). And Crystal, in this character as in life, is able to suggest that his mind runs so rapidly it spits out the truth before his better judgment can advise him. Lisa Kudrow, sadly underused here, plays not the wife who doesn't understand, but the wife who understands all too well.

There is also the question of Joe Viterelli as Jelly. Writing about his work in the first movie, I saw him playing not just a mobster, but "an older man who is weary after many years in service, but loyal and patient with his weirdo boss." The sad thing about *Analyze That* is that Viterelli is invited back but not made to feel welcome at the party. We miss the sense that De Niro counts on him, that he comes as part of the package. Now De Niro's focus is on Crystal. And if Vitti and Sobel are a double act, the point of the movie is missing.

Angel Eyes ★ ★ ★
R, 104 m., 2001

Jennifer Lopez (Sharon), Jim Caviezel (Catch), Terrence Howard (Robby), Sonia Braga (Mrs. Pogue), Jeremy Sisto (Larry), Victor Argo (Mr. Pogue), Shirley Knight (Elanora Davis). Directed by Luis Mandoki and produced by Mark Canton and Elie Samaha. Screenplay by Gerald DiPego.

Jennifer Lopez is the real thing, one of those rare actresses who can win our instinctive sympathy. She demonstrates that in *Angel Eyes*, playing a tough cop who does everything she can to wall out the world, and yet always seems worthy of trust and care. The film's story involves the cop's skittish, arm's-length relationship with a man named Catch (Jim Caviezel), whose walls are higher than her own.

Who is this Catch, anyway? He walks the streets in a long overcoat, head down, lonely, depressed, looking like one of the angels in *Wings of Desire*. Once a week he brings groceries to a shut-in named Nora (Shirley Knight). The first time he sees Sharon, the Lopez character, he stops and stares at her through a restaurant window—not with lust or curiosity, but as if he's trying to repair some lost connection.

Lopez constructs Sharon, not out of spare parts from old cop movies, but in specific terms. She is a good cop from a technical point of view—firm, confident, brave. She wants to do well and punish evil, and only gradually do we learn that her orientation toward this career may have been formed early, when she called the cops on her abusive father (Victor Argo) as he beat up her mother (Sonia Braga). Her father has disowned her for that, her brother is still mad about it, and even her mother defends the man. He never did it again, after all, she argues, to which Sharon replies that perhaps he would have if she hadn't acted. Fighting other lawbreakers may be her way of proving she was right in the first place.

The movie, directed by Luis Mandoki, has intriguing opening scenes. Is this a thriller? A supernatural movie? Who do the angel eyes belong to? An angel? Or does Catch only come on like a guardian angel, while reserving secrets of his own? We are still asking these questions during a stretch of the film where Sharon is staring at a gun in her face, and her life is saved by . . . Catch.

They talk. It is like a verbal chess game. Catch doesn't simply answer questions, he parries them; his responses redefine the conversation, as an unexpected move changes the logic on the board. She invites him home. He pokes through drawers. She likes him. She begins to kiss him. He doesn't want to be kissed. They settle into a cat-and-mouse rhythm in which one and then the other flees, and one and then the other pursues. She follows him to his apartment. It is empty except for a futon. "This is it," he says. "I live here. I walk around town. That's it, except for how I feel about you."

But how does he feel about her? *Angel Eyes* is a complex, evasive romance, involving two people who both want to be inaccessible. It's intriguing to see their dance of attraction and retreat. Meanwhile, secrets about both their family situations emerge; credit the screenwriter, Gerald DiPego, for not resolving the standoff with the father with an easy payoff.

There are lots of movies about cops because their lives lend themselves to excitement in a movie plot. They get involved with bad guys. They see action. They spend a lot of time drinking coffee in diners because a booth in a diner provides an ideal rationale for a face-to-face two-shot that doesn't look awkward or violate body language. For these and other reasons *Angel Eyes* is a cop movie, but its real story doesn't involve the police; it involves damaged lives and the possibility that love can heal.

Jim Caviezel, who has been in movies for ten years, emerged in *The Thin Red Line* (1998) and then played Dennis Quaid's son in *Frequency*—the one who contacts his father with a radio signal that travels back in time. Here he has an elusive, dreamy quality, using passivity as a mask for sharp, deep emotions. Since he apparently has no desire to meet anyone, why is he so attracted to Sharon? The answer has been waiting for us since the opening scene.

Lopez has a hard assignment here, remaining plausible in action scenes and touchy, slippery dialogue scenes. She and Caviezel play tricky notes, and so do the other actors, especially Victor Argo as a stubborn, hard man and Sonia Braga as his conflicted wife. The screenplay doesn't let them off the hook. And notice what simplicity and conviction the veteran Shirley Knight brings to her role, never straining for an effect, never punching up false emotions, embodying acceptance. This is a surprisingly effective film.

Note: Because Angel Eyes *steps so surely for so long, I suspect the movie's very last seconds* *were dictated over the director's dead body. The movie arrives at exactly the right note at the end, and then the sound track bursts prematurely into David Gray singing "Sail Away With Me Honey" and shatters the mood. I know Hollywood believes every audience must be patronized with an upbeat ending, but this movie has earned its final silence, and deserves it. Couldn't the screen have at least decently faded to black before the jarring music crashes in?*

Anger Management ★ ★
PG-13, 101 m., 2003

Jack Nicholson (Dr. Buddy Rydell), Adam Sandler (Dave Buznik), Marisa Tomei (Linda), Luis Guzman (Lou), Allen Covert (Andrew), Lynne Thigpen (Judge Daniels), Woody Harrelson (Galaxia), John Turturro (Chuck). Directed by Peter Segal and produced by Barry Bernardi, Derek Dauchy, Todd Garner, Jack Giarraputo, John Jacobs, and Joe Roth. Screenplay by David Dorfman.

The concept is inspired. The execution is lame. *Anger Management,* a film that might have been one of Adam Sandler's best, becomes one of Jack Nicholson's worst. Because Nicholson has a superb track record and a sure nose for trash, it's obvious the movie was a Sandler project with Nicholson as hired talent, not the other way around. The fact that four of the producers were involved in *The Master of Disguise* and *The Animal* indicates that quality control was not an issue.

Everything about the way the movie goes wrong—the dumbing down of plot developments, the fascination with Sandler's whiny one-note character, the celebrity cameos, the cringing sentimentality—indicates a product from the Sandler assembly line. No doubt Sandler's regular fans will love this movie, which is a return to form after the brilliant *Punch-Drunk Love.* Nicholson's fans will be appalled.

And yet there might really have been something here. When I heard the premise, I began to smile. Sandler plays a mild-mannered guy named Dave Buznik, who just got a promotion at work and is in love with his fiancée, Linda (Marisa Tomei). Through a series of bizarre misunderstandings on an airplane trip, he is misdiagnosed as a person filled with rage, and is assigned to therapy with the famed anger specialist Dr. Buddy Rydell (Jack Nicholson).

Nicholson's early scenes are his best because he brings an intrinsic interest to every character he plays, and we don't yet know how bad the movie is. He wears a beard making him look like a cross between Stanley Kubrick and Lenin, and works his eyebrows and sardonic grin with the zeal of a man who was denied them during the making of *About Schmidt*. He introduces Dave to a therapy group including the first of many guest stars in the movie, Luis Guzman and John Turturro. Both are clearly nuts—and so is Dr. Rydell, as Dave finds himself trapped in an escalating spiral of trouble, climaxing in a bar fight and a court appearance where he explains, "I was being attacked by someone while stealing a blind man's cane."

The blind man is played by Harry Dean Stanton. Also on display in the movie are Woody Harrelson (as a drag queen), John C. Reilly (as a Buddhist monk who gets a wedgie), Heather Graham, Mayor Rudolph Giuliani, and (ho, ho) the angry Bobby Knight. The use of celebrity walk-ons in a movie is often the sign of desperation, but rarely does one take over the movie and drive it to utter ruin, as Giuliani's role does. The closing scenes in Yankee Stadium, with the hero proposing to his girl over a loudspeaker, passed into the realm of exhausted cliché before Sandler was born.

Most good comedy has an undercurrent of truth. The genius of *Punch-Drunk Love* was that it identified and dealt with the buried rage that does indeed seem to exist in most of Sandler's characters. The falsity of *Anger Management* is based on the premise that Dave Buznik is not angry enough—that he needs to act out more and assert himself. That provides the explanation for the plot's "surprise," which will come as old news to most audiences.

I said that Nicholson brings an intrinsic interest to his characters. Sandler does not. His character is usually a blank slate waiting to be written on by the movie. While Nicholson has infinite variations and notes, Sandler is usually much the same. It's said the difference between character actors and stars is that the star is expected to deliver the same elements in every movie, while the character actor is supposed to change and surprise.

Nicholson, who has been a star character actor since he grinned triumphantly on the back of the motorcycle in *Easy Rider,* was part of a revolution that swept away old-model stars and replaced them with such character-stars as Dustin Hoffman, Robert De Niro, and, recently, Nicolas Cage, William H. Macy, or Steve Buscemi.

Sandler was wonderful in *Punch-Drunk Love* because, for once, he was in a smart movie that understood his screen persona. Paul Thomas Anderson, who wrote and directed that film, studied Sandler, appreciated his quality, and wrote a story for it. Most of Sandler's other movies have been controlled by Sandler himself (he is executive producer this time), and repeat the persona but do not seem willing to see it very clearly. This is particularly true in the cloying romantic endings, in which we see what a very good fellow he is after all.

That there is a market for this I do not deny. But imagine, just imagine, a movie in which Dave Buznik truly was exploding with rage, and Dr. Buddy Rydell really was an anger therapist. This movie should be remade immediately, this time with Jack Nicholson as executive producer, and Adam Sandler as hired gun.

The Anniversary Party ★ ★ ★
R, 115 m., 2001

Alan Cumming (Joe Therrian), Jennifer Jason Leigh (Sally Therrian), Gwyneth Paltrow (Skye Davidson), John Benjamin Hickey (Jerry Adams), Parker Posey (Judy Adams), Kevin Kline (Cal Gold), Jennifer Beals (Gina Taylor), Phoebe Cates (Sophia Gold), Jane Adams (Clair Forsyth), John C. Reilly (Mac Forsyth), Mina Badie (Monica Rose), Denis O'Hare (Ryan Rose), Michael Panes (Levi Panes). Directed by Alan Cumming and Jennifer Jason Leigh and produced by Cumming, Leigh, and Joanne Sellar. Screenplay by Cumming and Leigh.

The Anniversary Party is a long night's journey into day with a group of Hollywood types—actors, directors, photographers, agents—and a couple of neighbors who are invited over. The occasion is a get-back-together party for Joe and Sally Therrian (Alan Cumming and Jennifer Jason Leigh), he a writer-director, she an actress who hears time's winged chariot

31

drawing near. It's their sixth anniversary, although they've lived apart for most of the past year; the issues between them involve his infidelity, sometime bisexuality and drug use, and his decision not to cast his wife in a role obviously inspired by her. He believes that, in her late thirties, she's too old to play herself. (I am reminded of Margaret Cho's documentary *I'm the One That I Want*, where she describes the CBS sitcom producer who told her she was too fat to play herself, and should be a little less Chinese-y.)

This is not an original idea for a movie. I can think of a dozen movies about all-night parties at which painful truths are revealed. What makes *The Anniversary Party* intriguing is how close it cuts to the bone of reality—how we're teased to draw parallels between some of the characters and the actors who play them. Cumming is not a stranger to sexual ambiguity, Leigh is indeed in her thirties (although, unlike her character, at the top of her form), and look at some of the others.

Kevin Kline plays an actor who is no longer the first choice to play romantic leading men. Phoebe Cates, his real-life wife, plays an actress who has retired from acting to be a mother and wife. Gwyneth Paltrow plays the rising young star who gets multimillion-dollar paychecks, and has been cast in Joe's new movie. Other stars play recognizable types. Jennifer Beals is a savvy photographer who once slept with Joe. John Benjamin Hickey is the couple's business manager, and Parker Posey is his motormouth wife. Michael Panes plays Levi Panes (no coincidence, I assume), Sally's best pal and court jester. John C. Reilly is the director who desperately needs a hit, and is troubled because Sally is sleepwalking through her role in his new movie. Jane Adams is his neurotic, anorexic wife, in the throes of postpartum depression; she looks typecast, until you see her as a robust country schoolteacher in *Songcatcher*, and realize it's just acting. The next-door neighbors, happy to be invited to a party with so many stars, are played by Denis O'Hare and Mina Badie.

In the earlier days of this genre, the characters got drunk in order to blurt out what they were really thinking (see such examples as *Long Day's Journey Into Night* and *The Boys in the Band*). The truth serum this time is the drug ecstasy, brought along by the Paltrow character and inspiring an orgy of truth-telling, sexual cheating, and other reasons they're going to hate themselves in the morning. The movie doesn't use the drug simply as a story element, but knows it is dangerous and weaves it into a subtle thread of material about addiction and recovery; unless you watch carefully, you may miss the alcoholic who chooses this night to have a relapse.

The appeal of the film is largely voyeuristic. We learn nothing we don't already more or less know, but the material is covered with such authenticity and unforced, natural conviction that it plays like a privileged glimpse into the sad lives of the rich and famous. We're like the neighbors who are invited. Jennifer Jason Leigh and Alan Cumming cowrote and codirected, and are confident professionals who don't indulge their material or themselves. This isn't a confessional home movie, but a cool and intelligent look at a lifestyle where smart people are required to lead their lives according to dumb rules.

The movie was shot with a digital camera. Yes, you can tell. (Critics who say it looks as good as film are like friends who claim you don't look a day older.) It doesn't have the richness and saturation of film, but on the other hand, it does capture a spontaneity that might have been lost during long setups for lighting and camera (the shooting schedule was only four weeks). There are perfect uses for digital, and a movie like this is one of them. Leigh and Cumming and their cinematographer, the veteran John Bailey, wisely prefer the discipline of classic cinematography to the dizziness of handheld, and treat their little camera as if it were a big one. (Every digital camera should come with a warning label: "Just because you can move this around a lot doesn't mean you have to.")

I mentioned that some of the actors seem to be playing themselves. It might be more correct to say they are playing characters who we think of as being like themselves. Paltrow, for example, is not a mock-humble diva, but a smart pro who grew up in the industry and probably eavesdropped on parties like this from the top of the stairs. The tone we get from the whole movie reflects that knowingness: Being invited to a party like this (and leading these lives) is not the gold at the end of the rainbow, but what you get instead of the rainbow.

AntiTrust ★ ★
PG-13, 108 m., 2001

Ryan Phillippe (Milo Hoffman), Tim Robbins (Gary Winston), Rachael Leigh Cook (Lisa Calighan), Claire Forlani (Alice Poulson), Yee Jee Tso (Teddy Chin), Tygh Runyan (Larry Banks), Ned Bellamy (Phil Grimes), Douglas McFerran (Bob Shrot), Zahf Hajee (Desi). Directed by Peter Howitt and produced by Keith Addis, David Nicksay, and Nick Wechsler. Screenplay by Howard Franklin.

They might have been able to make a nice little thriller out of *AntiTrust*, if they'd kept one eye on the Goofy Meter. Just when the movie is cooking, the needle tilts over into Too Goofy and breaks the spell. What are we to make of a brainy nerd hero who fears his girlfriend is trying to kill him by adding sesame seeds to the Chinese food, and administers himself a quick allergy test at a romantic dinner by scratching himself with a fork and rubbing on some of the brown sauce? Too goofy.

The movie uses a thinly disguised fictional version of Bill Gates as its hero—so thinly, I'm surprised they didn't protect against libel by having the villain wear a name tag saying, "Hi! I'm not Bill!" This billionaire software mogul, named Gary Winston, is played by Tim Robbins as a man of charm, power, and paranoia. "Anybody working in a garage can put us out of business," he frets, and he's right. Cut to a garage occupied by Milo Hoffman (Ryan Phillippe) and his best buddy, Teddy Chin (Yee Jee Tso), who are on the edge of a revolutionary communications breakthrough.

Winston's company, which seems a *whole* lot like Microsoft, is working toward the same goal. In fact, Winston claims his new Synapse global communications system will, and I quote, "link every communications device on the planet." Too goofy. In order to discourage his competitors, Winston has announced a release date for his new software while it is still being written (details like this are why the company seems a whole lot like Microsoft).

He needs a software breakthrough, and he thinks Milo and Teddy can provide it. He in-

vites them up for a tour of his company's campus in the Pacific Northwest. Teddy declines: He hates the megacorp and believes code should be freely distributed. Milo accepts, and before he goes is visited by an agent from the (pre-Bush) Department of Justice (Richard Roundtree), who is preparing an antitrust case against Winston. "If you see something up there that hits you the wrong way, do the right thing," the agent says, offering Milo, who stands on the brink of untold millions, a salary much higher than you can earn at McDonald's.

Milo takes the junket to the software campus, and is shown around by cool young software dudes and a sexy software babe named Lisa (Rachel Leigh Cook), whose vibes suggest she likes him. Then he gets a tour of Winston's palatial high-tech lakeside home, which even includes computers that sense when you're in a room and play your favorite music while displaying your favorite art on the digital wall screens. "Bill Gates has a system like this," says Milo, just as we were thinking the exact same words. "Bill who?" says Winston. "His is primitive."

Milo decides to go to work for the megacorp, and is flattered by all the personal attention he gets from Winston, a friendly charmer who has a habit of dropping around even in the middle of the night. At one point when Milo is stuck, Winston hands him a disk with some code on it that "might help," just as a TV set in the background is reporting a news story about the death of a gifted software programmer. Hmmm.

Milo's girlfriend from his garage days was the loyal and steadfast Alice Poulson (Claire Forlani), who comes to visit and smells a rat in Lisa. And sure enough the little software vixen gets her talons in Milo and begins to seduce him away from Alice, although if Milo were not such a nerd and had seen a few thrillers in between programming worldwide communications, he would be able to predict her secret agenda as easily as we can.

There's a moment in the movie you should savor, if you see it. Teddy continues to work back in the garage, and has a breakthrough he summarizes as, "It's not in the box. It's in the band." Soon after, Teddy is beaten senseless in what is disguised as a racist attack. Soon after that, Winston tells Milo: "It's not in the box. It's in the band." Milo's delusions collapse as he realizes Winston will kill for code, and to eliminate the competition. This is a realization we have long since arrived at, but for Winston it is earth-shattering, as we can see because the movie's editing goes into hyperdrive. There's a berserk montage of remembered dialogue, jagged images, tiling cameras, echo chamber effects, everything but a woo-woo-woo alarm horn. Too goofy. In Ingmar Bergman's *Persona*, when one character realizes the other one isn't nice, the film itself seems to break. In *AntiTrust* it's like the projector explodes.

The movie then degenerates into fairly conventional thriller material, like chases, deadly stalkings through dark interior spaces, desperate sesame-seed allergy tests, and so on. At the end we are left with an argument that software code should not be copyrighted because "human knowledge belongs to the world." Stirring sentiments, although it is unlikely that a free digital version of this movie will be posted on the Net anytime soon.

Antwone Fisher ★ ★ ★ ½
PG-13, 113 m., 2002

Derek Luke (Antwone Fisher), Joy Bryant (Cheryl Smolley), Denzel Washington (Jerome Davenport), Salli Richardson (Berta Davenport), Earl Billings (Uncle James), Kevin Connolly (Slim), Viola Davis (Eva), Vernee Watson-Johnson (Antwone's Aunt). Directed by Denzel Washington and produced by Todd Black, Randa Haines, and Washington. Screenplay by Antwone Fisher.

Antwone Fisher is a good sailor, but he has a hair-trigger temper, and it lands him in the office of the base psychiatrist, Dr. Jerome Davenport. He refuses to talk. Davenport says he can wait. Naval regulations require them to have three sessions of therapy, and the first session doesn't start until Antwone talks. So week after week Antwone sits there while the doctor does paperwork, until finally they have a conversation:

"I understand you like to fight."
"That's the only way some people learn."
"But you pay the price for teaching them."

This conversation will continue, in one form or another, until Fisher (Derek Luke) has returned to the origin of his troubles, and Davenport (Denzel Washington) has made some discoveries as well. *Antwone Fisher,* based on the true story of the man who wrote the screenplay, is a film that begins with the everyday lives of naval personnel in San Diego, and ends with scenes so true and heartbreaking that tears welled up in my eyes both times I saw the film.

I do not cry easily at the movies; years can go past without tears. I have noticed that when I am deeply affected emotionally, it is not by sadness so much as by goodness. Antwone Fisher has a confrontation with his past, and a speech to the mother who abandoned him, and a reunion with his family, that create great, heartbreaking, joyous moments.

The story behind the film is extraordinary. Fisher was a security guard at the Sony studio in Hollywood when his screenplay came to the attention of the producers. Denzel Washington was so impressed he chose it for his directorial debut. The newcomer Derek Luke, cast in the crucial central role after dozens of more-experienced actors had been auditioned, turned out to be a friend of Antwone's; he didn't tell that to the filmmakers because he thought it would hurt his chances. The film is based on truth but some characters and events have been dramatized, we are told at the end. That is the case with every "true story."

The film opens with a dream image that will resonate through the film: Antwone, as a child, is welcomed to a dinner table by all the members of his family, past and present. He awakens from his dream to the different reality of life onboard an aircraft carrier. He will eventually tell Davenport that his father was murdered two months before he was born, that his mother was in prison at the time and abandoned him, and that he was raised in a cruel foster home. Another blow came when his closest childhood friend was killed in a robbery. Antwone, who is constitutionally incapable of crime, considers that an abandonment, too.

As Antwone's weekly sessions continue, he meets another young sailor, Cheryl Smolley (Joy Bryant). He is shy around her, asks Davenport for tips on dating, keeps it a secret that he is still a virgin. In a time when movie romances end in bed within a scene or two, their relationship is sweet and innocent. He is troubled, he even gets in another fight, but she sees that he has a good heart and she believes in him.

Davenport argues with the young man that all of his troubles come down to a need to deal with his past. He needs to return to Ohio and see if he can find family members. He needs closure. At first Fisher resists these doctor's orders, but finally, with Cheryl's help, he flies back. And that is where the preparation of the early scenes pays off in confrontations of extraordinary power.

Without detailing what happens, I will mention three striking performances from this part of the movie, by Vernee Watson-Johnson as Antwone's aunt, by Earl Billings as his uncle, and by Viola Davis as his mother. Earlier this year Davis appeared as the maid in *Far from Heaven* and as the space station psychiatrist in *Solaris*. Now this performance. It is hard to believe it is the same actress. She hardly says a word, as Antwone spills out his heart in an emotionally shattering speech.

Antwone's story is counterpointed with the story of Dr. Davenport and his wife, Berta (Salli Richardson). There are issues in their past, too, and in a sense Davenport and Fisher are in therapy together. There is a sense of anticlimax when Davenport has his last heartfelt talk with Antwone, because the film has reached its emotional climax in Ohio and there is nowhere else we want it to take us. But the relationship between the two men is handled by Washington, as the director, with close and caring attention. Hard to believe Derek Luke is a newcomer; easy to believe why Washington decided he was the right actor to play Antwone Fisher. ☞

Apocalypse Now Redux ★ ★ ★ ★
R, 197 m., 2001

Marlon Brando (Kurtz), Robert Duvall (Kilgore), Martin Sheen (Willard), Frederic Forrest (Chef), Dennis Hopper (Photographer), Aurore Clement (Roxanne), Laurence Fishburne (Clean), Albert Hall (Chief), Harrison Ford (Colonel Lucas). Directed by Francis Ford Coppola and produced by Coppola and Kim Aubry. Screenplay by John Milius and Coppola.

More than ever it is clear that Francis Ford Coppola's *Apocalypse Now* is one of the great films of all time. It shames modern Hollywood's timidity. To watch it is to feel yourself lifted up to the heights where the cinema can take you, but so rarely does. The film is a mirror reflecting our feelings about the war in Vietnam, in all their complexity and sadness. To those who wrote me defending the banality of *Pearl Harbor,* I wrote back: "See *Apocalypse Now* and reflect on the difference."

The movie comes to us now in a new version, forty-nine minutes longer than the original. The most unexpected thing about *Apocalypse Now Redux* may not be the restored footage, however, but the new Technicolor dye-transfer prints. An expert on prints, Jeff Joseph, tells me: "This is essentially a reworking of the old three-strip Technicolor process. Instead of the chemical development of colors, color dyes are transferred to the film directly, resulting in the stunning 'Technicolor' look of the '40s and '50s: lush, gorgeous, bright, sharp, and vivid, with deep, rich, true blacks."

The physical look of the film is therefore voluptuous and saturated. This is what would be at risk with digital projection. Coppola also pushes the envelope with the remastered sound track, and I was reminded of the film's world premiere at Cannes in 1979, when the old Palais was so filled with light and sound that I felt enveloped; the helicopters in the famous village assault could first be heard behind me, and then passed overhead, and yes, there were people who involuntarily ducked. To be able to come home from the hellish production conditions on the Philippines locations with a film of such technical mastery is miraculous.

The story concerns a journey upriver by Captain Willard (Martin Sheen), who commands a patrol boat to penetrate behind enemy lines and discover the secret redoubt of the almost mythical Colonel Kurtz (Marlon Brando)—one of the army's most decorated soldiers, now leading his own band of tribesmen. The story is based on Joseph Conrad's *Heart of Darkness,* but replaces the implacable mystery of the upper reaches of the Congo with the equally unfathomable mystery of the American venture in Vietnam. When you get to the bottom of who Kurtz has become and what he is thinking, you can see how the war transformed the original American idealism.

The movie consists of a series of set pieces.

35

The most famous is the assault on the village, opening with the helicopter loudspeakers blasting Wagner at the terrified students and teachers, and continuing with Lieutenant Kilgore (Robert Duvall) and his swashbuckling bravado on the beach ("I love the smell of napalm in the morning"). Other sequences are also in the permanent memory of moviegoers: the drugged monotony of the river journey, the sudden gunfire that kills everyone on the sampan, the Playboy Playmates entertaining the troops, the dreamlike final approach to Kurtz's compound, the shadowed Kurtz and his bleak aphorisms, and the giggling assent of the stoned photographer (Dennis Hopper), who is the Fool to his Lear.

To the majesty of these scenes in their progression to Kurtz's words "the Horror," Coppola has now added forty-nine minutes, most of them devoted to a visit by the crew to a French plantation, a colonial leftover that somehow survives. At dinner the Americans and French discuss the colonial history of Vietnam, and Willard's eyes meet those of Roxanne (Aurore Clement), a widow who will spend the night in his arms. Other new footage includes dialogue and byplay on the boat, a second encounter with the Playmates, and additional dialogue by Kurtz.

In a note released with the film, Coppola emphasizes that this new material was not simply shoehorned into the original version of the film, but that *Redux* is "a new rendition of the movie from scratch." He and his longtime editor Walter Murch "re-edited the film from the original unedited raw footage—the dailies," he says, and so possibly even some of the shots that look familiar to us are different takes than the ones we saw before. The 1979 version "terrified" him, he says, because it was "too long, too strange and didn't resolve itself in a kind of classic big battle at the end." Facing financial disaster, he shaped it for the "mainstream audience of its day," and twenty years later, seeing it again, he found it "relatively tame."

To consider *Apocalypse Now* mainstream or tame in either form is a bizarre judgment for Coppola to pass on his picture, but then he has a history of incautious and inexplicable remarks about it, going back to the infamous Cannes press conference where he confessed he had "problems with the ending," and many critics thought he was talking about the Kurtz episode, and not (as he was) the closing titles.

My own feeling is that the original cut was neither mainstream nor tame, but epic filmmaking on a scale within the reach of only a few directors—Tarkovsky, Lean, Eisenstein, Kurosawa. The new version therefore triggered my suspicion. I was happy to see the additional footage, and indeed had seen it before, in outtake form. Did the movie require it?

Some of the footage enters seamlessly into the work and disappears, enriching it. That would include the river footage and some moments with the photographer. The new Brando footage, including some more pointed analysis of the war, is a valuable addition. The Playmate footage simply doesn't work; it was left out of the original because a typhoon prevented him from completing its filming, Coppola says, but "Walter found a way to get in and out of the sequence." Perhaps, but no reason to be there.

It is the French plantation sequence that gives me the most pause. It is long enough, I think, that it distracts from the overall arc of the movie. The river journey sets the rhythm of the film, and too much time on the banks interrupts it (there is the same problem with the feuding families in *Huckleberry Finn*). Yet the sequence is effective and provoking (despite the inappropriate music during the love scene). It helps me to understand it when Coppola explains that he sees the French like ghosts; I questioned how they had survived in their little enclave, and accept his feeling that their spirits survive as a cautionary specter for the Americans.

Longer or shorter, *Redux* or not, *Apocalypse Now* is one of the central events of my life as a filmgoer. To have it in this beautiful print is a luxury. This new version will make its way to DVD and be welcome there, but the place to see it is in a movie theater, sitting not too far back, your eyes and ears filled with its haunting vision. Now this is a movie.

Ararat ★ ★ ½
R, 116 m., 2002

David Alpay (Raffi), Charles Aznavour (Edward Saroyan), Eric Bogosian (Rouben), Brent Carver (Philip), Marie-Josée Croze (Celia), Bruce

Greenwood (Martin/Clarence Ussher), Arsinée Khanjian (Ani), Elias Koteas (Ali/Jevdet Bey), Christopher Plummer (David). Directed by Atom Egoyan and produced by Egoyan and Robert Lantos. Screenplay by Egoyan.

Atom Egoyan has something he wants us to know. In 1915, he tells us in his new film *Ararat*, Turkey committed genocide against its Armenian population, massacring two-thirds of its 1.5 million citizens of Armenian descent. This crime, denied to this day by Turkey, has largely been wiped from the pages of history.

Egoyan is one of Canada's best and most respected directors. He and his wife, the actress Arsinée Khanjian, are Canadians of Armenian descent. When he told his children of the massacre, he has said in interviews, they wanted to know if Turkey had ever apologized. His answer is contained in *Ararat*. Unfortunately, it is couched in such a needlessly confusing film that most people will leave the theater impressed, not by the crime, but by the film's difficulty. Egoyan's work often elegantly considers various levels of reality and uses shifting points of view, but here he has constructed a film so labyrinthine that it defeats his larger purpose.

The story has three central strands: (1) A film is being made about the atrocity; (2) some of the scenes of this film-within-the-film recreate historical incidents for our information; (3) there is a web of connections between the people working on the film and other characters in the story.

We meet an art historian named Ani (Arsinée Khanjian) who lectures on the Armenian artist Arshile Gorky, whose mother was one of the Turkish victims. Ani's husband died in an attempt to assassinate a Turkish official some fifteen years earlier. She has a son named Raffi (David Alpay) from her first marriage, and a stepdaughter named Celia (Marie-Josée Croze) from a second marriage with a man who, Celia believes, was driven to suicide by Ani. When Ani lectures on Gorky, Celia often attends in order to heckle her with questions about her dead father. Further complicating this emotional tangle, Raffi and Celia are sleeping with each other.

There is another sexual-political connection. When Raffi attempts to pass through Canadian customs with several film cans from Europe, he is questioned at length by a customs inspector named David (Christopher Plummer), who is on his last day on the job. Raffi says the cans contain unexposed documentary footage needed for the movie. We know, because of a scene at breakfast that day, that David's son Philip (Brent Carver) is the lover of an actor named Ali (Elias Koteas), who plays the barbaric Turkish general Jevdet Bey in the film. Thus David is in a position to know the film being brought in by Raffi may not be needed for the project.

We meet the director of the film, named Edward (Charles Aznavour), and see him on the set, filming scenes that are often presented as reality before the camera pulls back to reveal another camera. And we meet the screenwriter, Rouben (Eric Bogosian). Both Aznavour and Bogosian, who are of Armenian ancestry, are used to provide more information about the atrocities, as is the character of Clarence Ussher (Bruce Greenwood), a character in Aznavour's film. He was an American physician who was an eyewitness to the massacres and wrote a book about them.

The questioning at the customs station goes on, apparently, for hours, because David, on his last day on the job, is trying to determine through sheer skill whether the cans contain film or heroin. He could open them (in a dark room to avoid spoiling the film), but that would be too simple, and perhaps he thinks that by understanding the young man before him, he can gain a better insight into his own son.

The scenes in the movie-within-a-movie document horrendous acts by the Turks against the Armenians, including one sequence in which women are burned alive. The film also shows Gorky as a young boy, shouldering arms against the Turks. There are flashbacks to show the adult Gorky painting in exile in New York. And discussion of the relative truth of two portraits: one a photo of Gorky with his mother, the other the painting he has based on this portrait. It is the same painting we have heard Ani lecturing about.

You may be feeling some impatience at the complexity of this plot. It is too much, too heavily layered, too needlessly difficult, too opaque. Individual scenes leap out and have a life of their own: Khanjian makes the difficulties of her own character very affecting, the Plummer episode is like a small, perfect character study, and I remember the re-created atrocities as if from another film, which is indeed how they are presented.

Ararat clearly comes from Egoyan's heart, and it conveys a message he urgently wants to be heard: that the world should acknowledge and be shamed that a great crime was committed against his people. The message I receive from the movie, however, is a different one: that it is difficult to know the truth of historical events, and that all reports depend on the point of view of the witness and the state of mind of those who listen to the witness. That second message is conveyed by the film, but I am not sure it presents Eyogan's intention. Perhaps this movie was so close to the director's heart that he was never able to stand back and get a good perspective on it—that he is as conflicted as his characters, and as confused in the face of shifting points of view.

Note: In the film, Hitler is quoted discussing his plans for genocide and asking, "Who remembers the extermination of the Armenians?" The film presents this as fact, although there is enormous controversy over whether Hitler actually ever said it.

Assassination Tango ★ ★ ★

R, 114 m., 2003

Robert Duvall (John J. Anderson), Ruben Blades (Miguel), Kathy Baker (Maggie), Luciana Pedraza (Manuela), Julio Oscar Mechoso (Orlando), James Keane (Whitey), Frank Gio (Frankie), Katherine Micheaux Miller (Jenny). Directed by Robert Duvall and produced by Rob Carliner and Duvall. Screenplay by Duvall.

Robert Duvall's *Assassination Tango* is not entirely about crime or dance, and that will be a problem for some audiences. "More assassination, less tango!" demands the on-line critic Jon Popick. But I have seen countless movies about assassination and not a few about the tango, and while Duvall's movie doesn't entirely succeed, what it attempts is intriguing. It wants to lock itself inside the mind of a man whose obsessions distract him from the wider world.

John J. Anderson (Duvall) talks to himself a lot, carrying on a bemused commentary that

may eventually descend into dementia, but not yet. No longer young, he is a professional hit man who plans to retire and devote his life to his woman, Maggie (Kathy Baker), and especially to her ten-year-old daughter, Jenny (Katherine Micheaux Miller). He likes Maggie but loves Jenny with a rather alarming intensity: "She is my soul, my life, my eyes, my everything."

Is he a suppressed child molester? Later in the film a hooker reports, "He wanted me to call him 'daddy.'" But no, I don't believe he represents a threat. He is not an actor-out but a holder-in, a brooder whose emotional weather is stormy but unseen. Most of the people he deals with, including Frankie (Frank Gio), the mobster who employs him, have no idea who he really is or what he really needs.

Sent to Buenos Aires on his final job, assassinating a wealthy general, Anderson meets with local contacts but keeps his own counsel. We realize this is not a conventional crime story; he rejects most of the advice of the local bad guys, drifts off by himself, seems preoccupied or distracted, and happens by chance into a dance club where he is entranced by one of the performers, Manuela (Luciana Pedraza). He returns. He asks her to dance. She has no idea what to make of him. He requests tango lessons. They begin a relationship impossible to define, and it seems for a time that the movie will deny us both of the usual payoffs: no murder, no romance.

Whether or not it delivers on those fronts I will leave for you to discover. Duvall, who wrote as well as directed, never makes them the point. His movie is not about a killer or a lover, but about a man who has been damaged in some unspecified way, and wanders through the world in an unorganized search for something to make him whole again. This could be love for a young girl, mastery of the tango, idealization of a dancer's skill, or exercise of his assassin's craft.

Audiences impatient for plot may miss Duvall's movie altogether. Yes, he spends a lot of time in cafés doing nothing. Yes, his conversation is limited. Yes, not even Manuela knows what he wants. Yes, he meanders toward assassination in maddening digressions. Yes, there are dance scenes that slow the progress—but if, and only if, the progress is the point.

The tango is a dance in which partners join

in meticulously rehearsed passion, with such exact timing that no improvisation or error is possible. (You can tell a bad tango dancer by the bruises on the shins.) Why is Anderson so attracted to this dance? Obviously, because it provides a framework for his emotional turmoil—laces it in, gives it structure, allows him to show the world he is disciplined when he is not. For him it is about control, and it supplies rigid rules for how to interact with his partner.

What *Assassination Tango* is about, I think, is John J. Anderson's quiet and inward attempt to slow his descent toward incompetence. He has Maggie but cannot visualize their future. He meets Manuela but does not know whether to offer a future. He has a job but suspects it is a trap. People threaten him but his biggest threat is interior: He is falling to pieces, falling into confusion, losing his sense of himself. The tango is a fragment to shore up against his ruin.

The movie is not quite successful. It is too secretive about its heart. It seems unfocused unless we are quick to get the clues, to look at Anderson in a certain way, to realize it will not be about murder or love but about coping strategies. John J. Anderson has so many secrets from the world that even this movie preserves some of them. Duvall has created it from the inside out, seeing it not through the eyes of the audience but through the mind of Anderson. *Assassination Tango* is all the same a fascinating effort, and I am happy to have seen it. It taught me something about filmmaking strategy.

Atlantis: The Lost Empire ★ ★ ★ ½
PG, 95 m., 2001

With the voices of: Michael J. Fox (Milo), James Garner (Rourke), Cree Summer (Princess Kida), Don Novello (Vinny), Phil Morris (Dr. Sweet), Claudia Christian (Helga), Jacqueline Obradors (Audrey), John Mahoney (Preston Whitmore), Corey Burton (Moliere), Jim Varney (Cookie), Florence Stanley (Mrs. Packard), Leonard Nimoy (King of Atlantis). Directed by Gary Trousdale and Kirk Wise and produced by Don Hahn. Screenplay by Tab Murphy, based on a story by Wise, Trousdale, Joss Whedon, Bryce Zabel, Jackie Zabel, and Murphy.

Disney's *Atlantis: The Lost Empire* is an animated adventure movie with a lot of gusto

and a wowser of a climax. It's an experiment for the studio. Leaving behind the song-and-dance numbers and the cute sidekicks, Disney seems to be testing the visual and story style of anime—those action-jammed animated Japanese movies that occupy shelves in every video store, meaning someone must be renting them.

The movie is set in 1914, a favorite period for stories like this, because technology was fairly advanced while people could still believe that a sunken continent or lost world or two might have gone overlooked. Just as the *Jurassic Park* movies owe something (actually, a lot) to Arthur Conan Doyle's *The Lost World,* so does *Atlantis* spring from the old Edgar Rice Burroughs novels about a world in the center of Earth. (There is also discussion on the Web about how it springs even more directly from a 1989 Japanese anime named *Nadia: The Secret of Blue Water.*)

All stories like this require a rich, reclusive billionaire to finance an expedition to the lost corners of Earth, and *Atlantis* has Preston Whitmore (voice by John Mahoney), who lives Citizen Kane–style behind vast iron gates in a mysterious citadel, and puts together a team to go to the bottom of the sea.

Whitmore summons the linguist Milo Thatch (voice by Michael J. Fox) to join the expedition; he knew Milo's grandfather, and trusts an ancient notebook in which the old man perhaps recorded the secret of Atlantis. Milo himself has spent much time trying to convince Smithsonian scientists of the possibility of a sunken continent; he works at the institute—as a janitor.

The diving team, which uses a sub Captain Nemo would have envied, is led by the rough-and-ready Rourke (James Garner) and includes a mixed bag of adventurers, including Vinny the explosives man (Don Novello), who has voluptuous ambitions for blowing up stuff real good; Moliere the Mole (Corey Burton), the digging expert; Rourke's first mate Helga (Claudia Christian), a scheming vamp; Audrey the mechanic (Jacqueline Obradors); Doctor Sweet (Phil Morris); Cookie the cook (the late Jim Varney); and Mrs. Packard (Florence Stanley), who chain-smokes while handling communications.

You will note among this crew no dancing

teacups, even though the movie was directed by Gary Trousdale and Kirk Wise, who made the wonderful *Beauty and the Beast* for Disney. Perhaps that's because of the influence of a comic-book artist named Mike Mignola, previously unknown to me but described by my colleague Elvis Mitchell as the creator of an underground comic character named Hellboy; his drawing style may have something to do with the movie's clean, bright, visual look, which doesn't yearn for the 3-D roundness of *Toy Story* or *Shrek*, but embraces the classic energy of the comic-book style. You especially see that in the movie's spectacular closing sequence—but I'm getting ahead of the story.

Atlantis is protected by fearsome robotic sea leviathans, which all but destroy the expedition before Rourke, Milo, and the crew succeed in penetrating a volcano and reaching the ocean floor in their sub, where Milo is befriended by Princess Kida (Cree Summer). The submerged land is ruled by her father the king (Leonard Nimoy), who wants to banish the outsiders, but Kida has eyes for Milo in a subplot owing more than a little to *The Little Mermaid*.

Atlantis itself seems desperately in need of fresh blood—not for population (since the residents are 1,000 years old and going strong) but for new ideas, since the land has fallen into apathy and disrepair. Princess Kida is kind of a reformist, nudging her father to get off his throne and organize some public works projects.

Now about that closing sequence. If you recall the ballroom scene in *Beauty and the Beast*, you will remember the exhilarating way directors Trousdale and Wise liberated their characters not only from gravity but from the usual rules of animation, so that they careered thrillingly through the air. Multiply that several times, and you get the excitement of a final battle that brings to animated life the kind of explosive energy we sense imprisoned in the printed KA-BOOM!s, KERRR-ASSHHHH!es, and THUNK!s of those full-page drawings in action comic books, where superheroes battle for control of the universe.

The story of *Atlantis* is rousing in an old pulp science fiction sort of way, but the climactic scene transcends the rest, and stands by itself as one of the great animated action sequences. Will the movie signal a new direction for Disney animation? I doubt it. The synergy of animated musical comedies is too attractive, not only for entertainment value but also for the way they spin off hit songs and stage shows. What *Atlantis* does show is a willingness to experiment with the anime tradition—maybe to appeal to teenage action fans who might otherwise avoid an animated film. It's like *20,000 Leagues Under the Sea* set free by animation to look the way it dreamed of looking.

Austin Powers in Goldmember ★ ★
PG-13, 94 m., 2002

Mike Myers (Austin Powers/Dr. Evil/Fat Bastard/Goldmember), Beyoncé Knowles (Foxxy Cleopatra), Michael York (Basil Exposition), Michael Caine (Nigel Powers), Verne Troyer (Mini Me), Heather Graham (Ms. Felicity Shagwell), Seth Green (Scott Evil), Robert Wagner (Number Two). Directed by Jay Roach and produced by John S. Lyons, Eric McLeod, Demi Moore, Mike Myers, Jennifer Todd, and Suzanne Todd. Screenplay by Myers and Michael McCullers.

Like the James Bond series that provided it with comic inspiration, the Austin Powers series benefits from a certain familiarity. Not every Bond movie is good, but once you get started going to them you would never think of missing one. Same with Austin Powers. The third movie about the shagadelic one, *Austin Powers in Goldmember,* is a step or two down from the first and second, but it has some very funny moments, and maybe that is all we hope for.

The familiar characters are back, including Austin, Dr. Evil, and Fat Bastard (all played by Mike Myers), and Mini Me (Verne Troyer). Is this a good thing? The first time we saw them, they had the impact of novelty, but Dr. Evil is growing a little repetitious, and Fat Bastard, in his attempt to keep our attention, has escalated his adventures with bodily functions into a kind of manic bathroom zeal. There are some things we do not want to know about his bowels, and he informs us of all of them.

Myers adds a new character this time, Goldmember, whose name more or less explains his name. This is a Dutchman with flaking skin, which he likes to peel off and eat. He doesn't really grab the imagination the way Evil and Bastard did, although he provides the inspiration for a large number of Dutch jokes, all of which are supposed to be funny because they're not funny.

One new character I did like was Foxxy Cleopatra (Beyoncé Knowles, from Destiny's Child). With an Afro out to here, she's a 1970s blaxploitation heroine, inspired by the characters played by Pam Grier and Tamara Dobson. Alas, the movie doesn't do much with her except assign her to look extremely good while standing next to Austin. Having journeyed back to her period of 1975 in a time-traveling pimpmobile, it's too bad Austin doesn't do more with the opportunity.

He makes the journey because Dr. Evil has kidnapped Austin's father, Nigel (Michael Caine), and hidden him in 1975. Once found, Nigel has a heart-to-heart with his neglected son, and Caine's comic timing brings a certain zip to the movie. Meanwhile, we learn that Dr. Evil plans to flood Earth with a beam projected from an orbiting satellite that looks like a gigantic brassiere. (He likes things that look like other things; we first saw him in a satellite modeled on Bob's Big Boy, and in this film he cruises in a submarine modeled on himself.)

The funniest parts are self-contained inspirations that pop up from time to time out of the routine. One involves Austin's desperate attempt to stand in for a tinkling statue that has lost its water pressure. Another involves a shadow show when Austin disappears behind a screen to give a urine sample; he's trying to hide Mini Me, but in silhouette the effect suggests he has an extraordinarily versatile anatomy. There is also a lot of fun with subtitles in a Japanese sequence, where white backgrounds obscure some of the words, so that what's left looks obscene. Consider what can be done with "Please eat some shiitake mushrooms."

Those scenes are funny, and so is the title sequence, which introduces the first of a great many cameos involving very big stars, whose names I will not reveal. I also like the whole tone of the Powers enterprise—its wicked joy in Austin's cheerful hedonism. The movie is a little tired; maybe the original inspiration has run its course. It's a small disappointment, but I'm glad I saw it. Sorta.   ☞

Auto Focus ★ ★ ★
R, 107 m., 2002

Greg Kinnear (Bob Crane), Willem Dafoe (John Carpenter), Maria Bello (Patricia Crane), Rita Wilson (Anne Crane), Ron Leibman (Lenny). Directed by Paul Schrader and produced by Scott Alexander, Larry Karaszewski, Todd Rosken, Pat Dollard, and Alicia Allain. Screenplay by Michael Gerbosi, based on the book by Robert Graysmith.

Eddie Cantor once told Bob Crane, "Likability is 90 percent of the battle." It seems to be 100 percent of Bob Crane's battle; there is nothing there except likability—no values, no self-awareness, no judgment, no perspective, not even an instinct for survival. Just likability and the need to be liked in a sexual way every single day. Paul Schrader's Auto Focus, based on Crane's life, is a deep portrait of a shallow man, lonely and empty, going through the motions of having a good time.

The broad outlines of Crane's rise and fall are well known. How he was a Los Angeles DJ who became a TV star after being cast in the lead of Hogan's Heroes, a comedy set in a Nazi prison camp. How his career tanked after the show left the air. How he toured on the dinner theater circuit, destroyed two marriages, and was so addicted to sex that his life was scandalous even by Hollywood standards. How he was found bludgeoned to death in 1978 in a Scottsdale, Arizona, motel room.

Crane is survived by four children, including sons from his first and second marriages who differ in an almost biblical way, the older appearing in this movie, the younger threatening a lawsuit against it, yet running a Website retailing his father's sex life. So strange was Crane's view of his behavior, so disconnected from reality, that I almost imagine he would have seen nothing wrong with his second son's sales of photos and videotapes of his father having sex. "It's healthy," Crane argues in defense of his promiscuity, although we're not sure if he really thinks that, or really thinks anything.

The movie is a hypnotic portrait of this sad, compulsive life. The director, Paul Schrader, is no stranger to stories about men trapped in sexual miscalculation; he wrote Taxi Driver and wrote and directed *American Gigolo*. He sees Crane as an empty vessel, filled first with fame and then with desire. Because he was on TV, he finds that women want to sleep with him, and seems to oblige them almost out of good manners. There is no lust or passion in this film, only mechanical courtship followed by desultory sex. You can catch the women looking at him and asking themselves if there is anybody at home. Even his wives are puzzled.

Greg Kinnear gives a creepy, brilliant performance as a man lacking in all insight. He has the likability part down pat. There is a scene in a nightclub where Crane asks the bartender to turn the TV to a rerun of *Hogan's Heroes*. When a woman realizes that Hogan himself is in the room, notice how impeccable Kinnear's timing and manner are, as he fakes false modesty and pretends to be flattered by her attention. Crane was not a complex man, but that should not blind us to the subtlety and complexity of Kinnear's performance.

Willem Dafoe is the costar, as John Carpenter, a tech-head in the days when Hollywood was just learning that television could be taped and replayed by devices in the consumer price range. Carpenter hangs around sets, flattering the stars, lending them the newest Sony gadgets, wiring their cars for stereo and their dressing rooms for instant replays. He is the very embodiment of Mephistopheles, offering Crane exactly what he wants to be offered.

The turning point in Crane's life comes on a night when Carpenter invites him to a strip club. Crane is proud of his drumming, and Carpenter suggests that the star could "sit in" with the house band. Soon Crane is sitting in at strip clubs every night of the week, returning late or not at all to his first wife, Anne (Rita Wilson). Sensing something is wrong, he meets a priest one morning for breakfast, but is somehow not interested when the priest suggests he could "sit in" with a parish musical group.

Dafoe plays Carpenter as ingratiating, complimentary, sly, seductive, and enigmatically needy. Despite their denials, is there something homosexual in their relationship? The two men become constant companions, apart from a little tiff when Crane examines a video and notices Carpenter's hand in the wrong place. "It's an orgy!" Carpenter explains, and soon the men are on the prowl again. The video equip-

ment has a curious relevance to their sexual activities; do they have sex for its own sake, or to record it for later editing and viewing? From its earliest days, home video has had an intimate buried relationship with sex. If Tommy Lee and Pamela Anderson ever think to ask themselves why they taped their wedding night, this movie might suggest some answers.

The film is wall-to-wall with sex, but contains no eroticism. The women are never really in focus. They drift in and out of range, as the two men hunt through swinger's magazines, attend swapping parties, haunt strip clubs, and troll themselves like bait through bars. If there is a shadow on their idyll, it is that Crane condescends to Carpenter, and does not understand the other man's desperate need for recognition.

The film is pitch-perfect in its decor, music, clothes, cars, language, and values. It takes place during those heady years between the introduction of the pill and the specter of AIDS, when men shaped as adolescents by *Playboy* in the 1950s now found some of their fantasies within reach. The movie understands how celebrity can make women available—and how, for some men, it is impossible to say no to an available woman. They are hardwired, and judgment has nothing to do with it. We can feel sorry for Bob Crane, but in a strange way, because he is so clueless, it is hard to blame him; we are reminded of the old joke in which God tells Adam he has a brain and a penis, but only enough blood to operate one of them at a time.

The movie's moral counterpoint is provided by Ron Leibman, as Lenny, Crane's manager. He gets him the job on *Hogan's Heroes* and even, improbably, the lead in a Disney film named *Superdad*. But Crane is reckless in the way he allows photographs and tapes of his sexual performances to float out of his control. On the Disney set one day, Lenny visits to warn Crane about his notorious behavior, but Crane can't hear him, can't listen. He drifts toward his doom, unconscious, lost in a sexual fog.

* * *

Postscript: Bob Crane's two sons are on opposite sides in a legal dispute about the biopic *Auto Focus*. Robert David Crane, the son by the first marriage, supports the movie and appears in it as "Bob Crane Jr." Robert Scott Crane, from the second marriage, says it is filled with inaccuracies, and has started a Website to oppose it. The site somewhat undermines its own position by offering for sale photographs and videos taken by Crane of his sexual indiscretions.

"There is no such person as Bob Crane Jr.," says Lee Blackman, the Los Angeles attorney representing the second wife, Patricia, and her son. "Both sons had Robert as a first name, and different middle names. Bob Crane's own middle name was Edward." In life, he told me, the older son is called Bobby, and the younger, his client, is Scotty.

By taking money for his participation in the movie and billing himself Bob Crane Jr., Blackman said, Bobby has compromised himself. (In the movie, the older son has a small role as a Christian TV interviewer.)

But what about his client Scotty's Website, with the Crane sex tapes for sale?

"He is trying to set the record straight. The Website only came into existence because of the film. For example, on Scotty's site you will find the Scottsdale coroner's autopsy on Bob Crane, clearly indicating he never had a penile implant, although the movie claims he did. You will see that his movies were really just homemade comedies: He would edit the sex stuff with cutaways to Jack Benny or Johnny Carson, and a musical sound track."

Other complaints by Blackman and his clients:

"He was reconciled with Patricia, his second wife, at the time of his death. The movie shows her drinking in the middle of the day, but she has an allergic reaction to hard liquor."

"DNA tests have proven Scotty is Bob Crane's son, despite implications in the movie that he is not."

"Bob Crane was not a dark monster. The night he was killed, he was editing *Star Wars* for Scotty, to take out the violence."

"He didn't meet John Carpenter (the Willem Dafoe character) until 1975. The movie has him meeting him in 1965. It implies Bob needed Carpenter to teach him all that technical stuff, but in fact Bob Crane was very knowledgeable about home electronics, and was making home movies even in the 1950s."

"Legally," said Blackman, "you can defame the dead. This movie has massive quantities of defamation. We're trying to work with the distributor, Sony, to tweak the film in a couple of little places to make it more accurate. When it's released, if it still contains actionable material, we'll determine what to do." ☞

B

Baby Boy ★ ★ ★ ½
R, 129 m., 2001

Tyrese Gibson (Jody), Omar Gooding (Sweetpea),
A. J. Johnson (Juanita), Taraji P. Henson (Yvette),
Snoop Dogg (Rodney), Tamara LaSeon Bass
(Peanut), Ving Rhames (Melvin). Directed
and produced by John Singleton. Screenplay
by Singleton.

John Singleton's *Baby Boy* is a bold criticism of young black men who carelessly father babies, live off their mothers, and don't even think of looking for work. It is also a criticism of the society that pushes them into that niche. There has never been a movie with this angle on the African-American experience. The movie's message to men like its hero is: Yes, racism has contributed to your situation—but do you have to give it so much help with your own attitude?

In the opening sequence, we meet Jody (Tyrese Gibson), a twenty-year-old who has children by two women and still lives in his room in his mother's house. He drives his girlfriend Yvette (Taraji P. Henson) home from a clinic where she has just had an abortion. She is understandably sad and in pain, a little dopey from pills. She doesn't want to talk. In that case, says Jody, she won't mind if he borrows her car. He does, and uses it to visit his other girlfriend.

That scene will not come as a shock to Mary A. Mitchell, the *Chicago Sun-Times* columnist who has written a series of sad, angry articles about absentee fathers and "man-sharing" in the black community, where drugs, crime, and prison have created a shortage of eligible men. Her columns are courageous; the African-American community prefers to present a positive front and keep its self-criticism behind closed doors. She takes heat for what she writes. Now Singleton, too, dares to take a hard look at his community. Ten years ago, in *Boyz N the Hood*, he told a brilliant story about young men in a movie made by a young man. Now he returns to the same neighborhood, South Central in Los Angeles. His characters are a little older, and he is older, too, and less forgiving.

Baby Boy doesn't fall back on easy liberal finger-pointing. There are no white people in this movie, no simplistic blaming of others; the adults in Jody's life blame him for his own troubles, and they should. At some point, as Jody's mother, Juanita (A. J. Johnson), tells him again and again, he has to grow up, move out, get a job, and take care of his family.

Jody doesn't even bother to answer, except to accuse her of not loving him. He likes the life he leads, and doesn't consider employment as an option. He sponges off of two women: his mother, and Yvette, who has a job. Also in the picture is Peanut (Tamara Laseon Bass), the mother of his other child. But it's Yvette he loves. Still, he plays around, and she knows it and in a certain way accepts it, although she gets mad when she can never drive her own car, which she's making payments on. She screams that he lies to her, and his answer is a logical masterpiece: "I'm out in these streets telling these ho's the truth. I lie to you because I care about you."

All would be well if Jody could keep on sleeping in his childhood bedroom (where he still builds model cars), eat his mother's cooking, drive Yvette's car, sleep with his women, and hang with his boys—especially his best friend, Sweetpea (Omar Gooding). But Yvette is fed up. Sweetpea is getting involved with dangerous gang types. Yvette's old boyfriend (Snoop Dogg) is out of prison and hanging around. And at home, most disturbingly, his mother has a new boyfriend named Melvin (Ving Rhames), who has no patience with him. Melvin has spent ten years in the slammer, is determined to go straight, has a landscaping business, and moves in and marks his territory. Jody knows things are different when he finds Melvin stark naked in the kitchen, scrambling eggs for Juanita. "I was like you, Jody," he says. "Young, dumb, and out of control."

Juanita herself is a piece of work, a still-youthful woman who loves her backyard garden and tries patiently, over and over, to cut through Jody's martyrdom and evasion. When he complains to her that Yvette has locked him out, she levels: "What would *you* do if Yvette f——— around on you, took your car, and left you in a hot house all day with a baby?" An excellent question. Yvette answers it, in a way, by stealing back her own car, so the "baby boy" is reduced to riding his childhood bicycle around the neighborhood.

When John Singleton burst on the scene with *Boyz N the Hood*, he brought the freshness of direct, everyday experience to movies about black Americans. He was still in his mid-twenties, fresh out of South Central, already a legend for the way, at sixteen, he started hanging around the USC film school—volunteering as a gofer until the dean concluded, "We might as well make him a student, since he acts like he is one anyway." Singleton comes from the same background as his characters, knows them, sees aspects of himself and his friends in them. Like many self-made men, he is impatient with those, like Jody, who do not even try.

He has a gift for finding good actors. *Boyz* was Cuba Gooding Jr.'s first movie. Here we meet Cuba's brother Omar, also gifted. Tyrese Gibson, already known as a singer, model, and music video DJ, is a natural, unaffected actor who adds a spin of spoiled self-pity to Jody. Taraji P. Henson has some of the most difficult scenes as Yvette, who does love her man, but despairs of him, and is tired to the bone of working, child care, and caring, too, for Jody, the twenty-year-old "baby boy." And there is a wonderful rapport between A. J. Johnson and Ving Rhames as the mother and her ex-con boyfriend; they have an exuberant sex life, feel they deserve a second chance at happiness, and have lived long enough and paid enough dues to be impatient with Jody's knack for living off the land.

Baby Boy has a trailer that makes it look like a lot of fun—like a celebration of the lifestyle it attacks. I was reminded of the trailer for *Boyz N the Hood*, which seemed to glorify guns and violence, although the movie deplored them. I asked Singleton about it at the time, and he said, "Maybe some kids will see the trailer and come to see the movie, and leave with a lot of ideas they didn't have before." Maybe so. I have a notion the Yvettes of the world are going to love this movie, and march their Jodys in to see it.

Bad Company ★ ★
PG-13, 111 m., 2002

Anthony Hopkins (Gaylord Oakes), Chris Rock (Jake Hayes), Garcelle Beauvais-Nilon (Nicole), Gabriel Macht (Seale), Peter Stormare (Adrik Vas), Kerry Washington (Julie), John Stattery (Roland Yates). Directed by Joel Schumacher and produced by Jerry Bruckheimer and Mike Stenson. Screenplay by Jason Richman, Michael Browning, Gary Goodman, and David Himmelstein.

Hard on the heels of *The Sum of All Fears*, here's Jerry Bruckheimer's *Bad Company*, another movie about an American city threatened by the explosion of a stolen nuclear device. This one is an action comedy. There may come a day when the smiles fade. To be sure, the movie was made before 9/11 (and its original autumn 2001 release was delayed for obvious reasons), but even before 9/11 it was clear that nuclear terrorism was a real possibility. While *The Sum of All Fears* deals in a quasi-serious way with the subject (up until the astonishingly inappropriate ending), *Bad Company* is more lighthearted. Ho, ho.

The nuclear device is really only the Maguffin. It could be anything, as long as bad guys want it and good guys fight to keep them from it. The movie's a collision among three durable genres: Misfit Partners, Fish Out of Water, and Mistaken Identity. After an opening scene in which the Chris Rock character is killed, we learn that he had a twin brother named Jake Hayes; the babies were separated at birth and never knew about each other. The first was adopted by a rich family, went to Ivy League schools, and joined the CIA. Jake is a ticket scalper and chess hustler who's in love with a nursing student (Kerry Washington).

One problem with the movie, directed by Joel Schumacher, is that it jams too many prefabricated story elements into the running time. Consider the training sequence, in which Rock has nine days to perfect the mannerisms and absorb the knowledge of his dead brother. Odd that most of the coaching sessions have him learning to recognize fine vintages of wine and evaluate ancient cognacs; is he going to be dining with the terrorists? Meanwhile, he's apparently expected to learn to speak Czech from a dictionary tossed onto his bunk.

His minder at the CIA is Gaylord Oakes (Anthony Hopkins), a spookily calm veteran operative whose plan is to substitute this twin for the other in a sting operation designed to buy a stolen nuclear device. When another would-be buyer enters the picture, the film descends into a series of chase scenes, which are well enough done, but too many and too long.

Hopkins plays his character right down the middle, hard-edged and serious. Rock has some effective scenes played straight, but at other times he goes into a nonstop comic monologue that is funny, yes, but unlikely; when he's being shot at, how can he think of all those one-liners? The movie's strategy is to make every sequence stand on its own, with no thought to the overall tone of the film, so that we go from the deadly serious to something approaching parody.

Of the plot I can say nothing except that it exists entirely at the whim of the stunts, special effects, chases, and action. The two competing teams of would-be evil bomb buyers function entirely to supply an endless number of guys who fire machine guns a lot but hardly ever hit anything. The motive for blowing up New York is scarcely discussed. And could I believe my eyes? Here in 2002—another Red Digital Readout counting down to zero, just when I thought that was one cliché that had finally outlived its viability.

As for the girls, well, Kerry Washington is sweet and believable as Rock's girlfriend, but a Bruckheimer movie is not the place to look for meaningful female performances. No doubt there was a nice payday, but meanwhile, Washington's fine performance in *Lift*, the shoplifting film from Sundance 2001, goes unheralded. Even more thankless is the role by Garcelle Beauvais-Nilon as a CNN correspondent who was the girlfriend of the first twin, and spots this one because he kisses differently. She disappears entirely from the film after an ironically appropriate slide down a laundry chute. (By the way: During the shoot-out in that hotel, how come not a single guest or employee is ever seen?)

I won't tell you I didn't enjoy parts of *Bad Company*, because I did. But the enjoyment came at moments well separated by autopilot action scenes and stunt sequences that outlived their interest. As for the theme of a nuclear device that might destroy New York, I have a feeling that after this generation of pre-9/11 movies plays out, we won't be seeing it much anymore.

Baise-Moi ★
NO MPAA RATING, 77 m., 2001

Raffaela Anderson (Manu), Karen Bach (Nadine), Delphine MacCarty (La Colocataire), Lisa Marshall (Karla), Estelle Isaac (Alice), Herve P. Gustave (Martin), Marc Rioufol (L'architecte), Ouassini Embarek (Radouan). Directed by Virginie Despentes and Coralie Trinh Thi and produced by Philippe Godeau. Screenplay by Despentes and Trinh Thi, based on the novel by Despentes.

Baise-Moi is (a) a violent and pornographic film from France about two women, one a rape victim, the other a prostitute, who prowl the countryside murdering men. Or, *Baise-Moi* is (b) an attempt to subvert sexism in the movies by turning the tables and allowing the women to do more or less what men have been doing for years—while making a direct connection between sex and guns, rather than the sublimated connection in most violent movies.

I pose this choice because I do not know the answer. Certainly most ordinary moviegoers will despise this movie—or would, if they went to see it, which is unlikely. It alternates between graphic, explicit sex scenes, and murder scenes of brutal cruelty. You recoil from what's on the screen. Later, you ask what the filmmakers had in mind. They are French, and so we know some kind of ideology and rationalization must lurk beneath the blood and semen.

The film has been written and directed by Virginie Despentes, based on her novel; she enlisted Coralie Trinh Thi, a porno actress, as her codirector (whether to help with the visual strategy or because of her understanding of the mechanical requirements of on-screen sex, it is hard to say). The movie's central characters, Manu and Nadine, are played by Raffaela Anderson and Karen Bach, who act in hardcore films, and some of the men are also from the porno industry. This is, in fact, the kind of film the director in *Boogie Nights* wanted to make—"porn, but artistic"—although he would have questioned the box-office appeal of the praying mantis approach to sex, in which the male is killed immediately after copulation.

As it happens, I saw a Japanese-American

coproduction named *Brother* not long after seeing *Baise-Moi*. It was written and directed by Takeshi Kitano, who starred under his acting name, Beat Takeshi. Kitano under any name is the Japanese master of lean, violent, heartless action pictures, and in this one the plot is punctuated every five minutes or so by a blood-bath in which enemies are shot dead. Many, many enemies. We're talking dozens. The killings are separated in *Brother* by about the same length of time as those in *Baise-Moi*, or the sex acts in a porno film. Obviously all three kinds of film are providing payoffs by the clock. Would *Brother* be as depressing as *Baise-Moi* if all the victims had sex before they were gunned down? I don't know, but I'm sure *Baise-Moi* would be perfectly acceptable if the women simply killed men, and no sex was involved. At some level it seems so . . . cruel . . . to shoot a man at his moment of success.

A case can be made that *Baise-Moi* wants to attack sexism in the movies at the same time it raises the stakes. I'm not interested in making that argument. Manu and Nadine are man-haters, and clinically insane, and not every man is to blame for their unhappiness—no, not even if he sleeps with them. An equally controversial new American movie named *Bully* is also about stupid, senseless murder, but it has the wit to know what it thinks about its characters. *Baise-Moi* is more of a bluff. The directors know their film is so extreme that most will be repelled, but some will devise intellectual defenses and interpretations for it, saving them the trouble of making it clear what they want to say. I can't buy it. Ernest Hemingway, who was no doubt a sexist pig, said it is moral if you feel good after it, and immoral if you feel bad after it. Manu and Nadine do not feel bad, and that is immoral.

Ballistic: Ecks vs. Sever ½★
R, 91 m., 2002

Antonio Banderas (Jeremiah Ecks), Lucy Liu (Sever), Gregg Henry (Robert Gant), Talisa Soto (Vinn Gant/Rayne), Ray Park (A. J. Ross), Miguel Sandoval (Julio Martin). Directed by Wych Kaosayananda and produced by Chris Lee, Elie Samaha, and Kaosayananda. Screenplay by Alan B. McElroy.

There is nothing wrong with the title *Ballistic: Ecks vs. Sever* that renaming it *Ballistic* would not have solved. Strange that they would choose such an ungainly title when, in fact, the movie is not about Ecks *versus* Sever but about Ecks *and* Sever working together against a common enemy—although Ecks, Sever, and the audience take a long time to figure that out.

The movie is a chaotic mess, overloaded with special effects and explosions, light on continuity, sanity, and coherence. So short is its memory span that although Sever kills, I dunno, maybe forty Vancouver police officers in an opening battle, by the end, when someone says, "She's a killer," Ecks replies, "She's a mother."

The movie stars Lucy Liu as Sever, a former agent for the Defense Intelligence Agency, which according to www.dia.mil is a branch of the U.S. government. Antonio Banderas is Ecks, a former ace FBI agent who is coaxed back into service. Sever has lost her child in an attack and Ecks believes he has lost his wife, so they have something in common, you see, even though . . .

But I'll not reveal that plot secret, and will discuss the curious fact that both of these U.S. agencies wage what amounts to warfare in Vancouver, which is actually in a nation named Canada that has agencies and bureaus of its own and takes a dim view of machine guns, rocket launchers, plastic explosives, and the other weapons the American agents and their enemies use to litter the streets of the city with the dead.

Both Sever and Ecks, once they discover this, have the same enemy in common: Gant (Gregg Henry), a DIA agent who is married to Talisa Soto and raising her child, although Sever kidnaps the child, who is in fact . . . but never mind, I want to discuss Gant's secret weapon. He has obtained a miniaturized robot so small it can float in the bloodstream and cause strokes and heart attacks.

At one point in the movie a man who will remain nameless is injected with one of these devices by a dart gun, and it kills him. All very well, but consider for a moment the problem of cost overruns in these times of economic uncertainty. A miniaturized assassination robot small enough to slip through the bloodstream would cost how much? Millions? And it is delivered by dart? How's this for an idea: Use a poison dart and spend the surplus on school lunches.

Ballistic: Ecks vs. Sever is an ungainly mess, submerged in mayhem, occasionally surfacing for clichés. When the FBI goes looking for Ecks, for example, they find him sitting morosely on a bar stool, drinking and smoking. That is, of course, where sad former agents always are found, but the strange thing is, after years of drinking he is still in great shape, has all his karate moves, and goes directly into violent action without even a tiny tremor of DTs.

The movie ends in a stock movie location I thought had been retired: a steam and flame factory where the combatants stalk each other on catwalks and from behind steel pillars, while the otherwise deserted factory supplies vast quantities of flame and steam. Vancouver itself, for that matter, is mostly deserted, and no wonder, if word has gotten around that two U.S. agencies and a freelance killer are holding war games. *Ballistic: Ecks vs. Sever* was directed by Wych Kaosayananda of Thailand, whose pseudonym, you may not be surprised to learn, is Kaos.

Bandits ★ ★

PG-13, 123 m., 2001

Bruce Willis (Joe), Cate Blanchett (Kate), Billy Bob Thornton (Terry), Troy Garity (Harvey), Rocky La Rochelle (Tomales Bank Manager), Jaye K. Danford (Alamo Bank Manager), Anthony Burch (Phil), Norman Fessler (Alamo Bank Hostage). Directed by Barry Levinson and produced by Michael Birnbaum, Michele Berk, Levinson, Paula Weinstein, Ashok Amritraj, David Hoberman, and Arnold Rifkin. Screenplay by Harley Peyton.

Bandits is a movie so determined to be clever and whimsical that it neglects to be anything else. That decision wouldn't be fatal if the movie had caved in and admitted it was a comedy, but no, it also wants to contain moments of pathos, suspense, and insight, and it's too flimsy to support them. It's an anthology of unrelated tones; individual scenes may play well, but seem unaware of the movie they're in. And the love triangle never decides if it's

romance or romantic comedy. If the movie won't commit, why should we?

It's rare for a movie to have three such likable characters and be so unlikable itself. Bruce Willis and Billy Bob Thornton star as "America's most famous bank robbers," and Cate Blanchett is Kate, the executive's wife who starts as their hostage and becomes their lover. Yes, both of them (or neither of them; the PG-13 movie is cagey about what happens in between those knocks on the motel room doors). She can't choose. She likes Joe (Willis) because he's brave, strong, and handsome, and Terry (Thornton) because he's sensitive and cute.

Thornton's character is the jewel—a neurotic, fearful hypochrondiac who is lactose intolerant, hears a ringing in his ears, suffers from psychosomatic paralysis, and has a phobia about antique furniture. (You never know what's real and what they're making up in the movies; Billy Bob Thornton has a real-life phobia about antique furniture, in fact, and almost had a meltdown once during a visit to Johnny Cash's antique-filled home.)

The plot: The partners break out of prison after Joe steals a cement truck, and there's a nice shot of it plowing its way through suburban backyards. Terry comes up with the idea of taking bank managers hostage in their homes the night before a job, so they can get into the bank before business hours in the morning. They steal a lot of loot, become celebrities, and stay on the loose for an amazing length of time, considering their driver, lookout, and "outside man" is Joe's moronic cousin Harvey (Troy Garity), who dreams of being a stuntman.

The movie, directed by Barry Levinson and written by Harley Peyton (*Twin Peaks*), is told in a flashback and actually begins with the news that the two men have been shot dead after a failed hostage situation. Cut to a tabloid TV show whose host got an exclusive interview shortly before the final shoot-out; Joe and Terry narrate their career, try to justify themselves, and say Kate was an innocent hostage and not a fellow criminal. Eventually the film works its way back to the fatal robbery it began with and to the classic line, "The suspects are in a shoot-out with themselves."

The film has laughs sprinkled here and there.

I liked the way the confused Terry asks Joe, "What's on our mind?" And the way Kate's preoccupied husband, a self-involved hotshot, goes on TV to tell the kidnapped woman: "I'm going to Spain next week. If the kidnappers want to reach me, they can get in touch with my people." And I liked the jolly little fireplug of a bank manager who is delighted to meet the "Sleepover Bandits" in person, but cannot take them seriously.

Problem is, the movie doesn't commit to any of the several directions where it meanders. Is the romantic triangle poignant, or a gimmick? Do the guys joke and make small talk during robberies because this is a comedy, or because they are pathological narcissists? The flashback structure is an annoyance, and by the time it is justified, it's too late: We've already been annoyed. One of the joys of Barry Levinson's *Wag the Dog* (1997) was the way he juggled tones, moving from satire to suspense to politics. This time it's the audience that feels juggled.

The Banger Sisters ★ ★ ★
R, 97 m., 2002

Susan Sarandon (Lavinia), Goldie Hawn (Suzette), Geoffrey Rush (Harry), Robin Thomas (Raymond), Erika Christensen (Hannah), Eva Amurri (Ginger). Directed by Bob Dolman and produced by Elizabeth Cantillon and Mark Johnson. Screenplay by Dolman.

When you get right down to it, *The Banger Sisters* is pretty thin, but you grin while you're watching it. Later you reflect that it has an obvious story arc and sketchy minor characters, and awkwardly tries to get down and provide uplift at the same time. The screenplay could have used an overhaul before production, but I'm glad I saw it.

I'm glad primarily because of Goldie Hawn. She's infectious and likable in this movie, but not in that ditzy way we remember. Although she plays a legendary groupie who, in her day, "rattled" most of the rock stars ("and roadies") in the business, she plays a woman who has taken her youthful sense of freedom and combined it with a certain amount of common sense.

Hawn is Suzette. Her costar, Susan Saran-don, is Lavinia. Together, some (cough) years ago, they were such legendary groupies that Frank Zappa named them the Banger Sisters. Hawn has stayed true to her school, and as we meet her she's bartending in a West Hollywood club where she is more beloved by the customers than by the owner, who fires her. (She thinks that's not fair: "See that toilet? Jim Morrison passed out in there one night with me underneath him.") Broke and without plans, she points her pickup to Phoenix for a reunion with Lavinia, whom she hasn't seen in years.

Along the way, in need of gas money, she picks up a lost soul named Harry (Geoffrey Rush), a screenwriter whose dreams have not come true, and who is traveling to Phoenix with one bullet in his gun, to shoot his father. Harry is one of those finicky weirdos who doesn't want anyone upsetting his routine. The very sight of Suzette, with her silicone treasures, is disturbing in more ways than he can bear to think of.

In Phoenix, Lavinia lives with her lawyer husband, Raymond (Robin Thomas), and her two spoiled teenagers, Hannah (Erika Christensen) and Ginger (Eva Amurri). She is so respectable she doesn't even want to think about her former life, which her husband knows nothing about. Are you counting the formulas? And so here we have not one but two fish out of water (Harry and Suzette), plus two examples (Lavinia and Harry) of that other reliable element, the repressed sad sack who needs a taste of freedom.

Give the movie a moment's thought and you see the screenplay's gears turning. This is a movie that could have been a term paper. But Hawn and Sarandon hit the ground running, and are so funny and goofy that they distract and delight us. Lavinia at first resists Suzette's appeal, but then she realizes, "I'm the same color as the Department of Motor Vehicles—and you're like a flower." The girls go out for a wild night on the town, and Suzette brings much-needed reality into the cocooned existence of the two daughters.

The most underwritten character is Lavinia's husband, Raymond. The movie doesn't know what to do with him. They let him be a little surprised, a little shocked, a little too straight, but mostly he just stands there waiting for dialogue that is never supplied. Comic opportunities were lost here. And the Geoffrey Rush character, while more filled in, also seems oddly unnecessary. I can easily imagine the movie without him and with more about the family in Phoenix. He is not and never will be a workable life partner for Suzette, no matter how the movie tries to sentimentalize him.

What Goldie Hawn does is to play Suzette sincerely—as if she really were a groupie who still holds true to her partying past. Her daughter Kate Hudson, of course, played the groupie Penny Lane in *Almost Famous,* and Suzette could be the same character further down the road. The movie's buried joke is that Suzette, the wild girl from West Hollywood, has more commonsense knowledge about life than the movie's conventional types. Listen to how she talks to Harry on the phone. I guess you learn something about human nature after (cough) years as a bartender.

Baran ★ ★ ★ ½
PG, 94 m., 2002

Hossein Abedini (Latif), Zahra Bahrami (Baran), Mohammad Amir Naji (Memar), Hossein Rahimi (Soltan), Gholam Ali Bakhshi (Najaf). Directed by Majid Majidi and produced by Majidi and Fouad Nahas. Screenplay by Majidi.

What are they like, over there in Iran? Are they all glowering fanatics, stewing in resentment of America? What's your mental image? When a land is distant, unknown, and labeled as an enemy, it's easy to think in simple terms. No doubt Iranians are as quick to think evil about us as we are to think evil about them. The intriguing thing about an Iranian movie like *Baran* is that it gives human faces to these strangers. It could be a useful learning tool for those who have not traveled widely, who never see foreign films, who reduce whole nations to labels.

The movie is a romantic fable about a construction worker. His name is Latif, and he labors on a building site not far from the border with Afghanistan. All of the labor here is manual, including hauling fifty-pound bags of cement up a series of ramps. Latif doesn't actually work very hard, since he is Iranian and most of the labor is being done by under-paid refugees from Afghanistan. Latif is the tea boy, bringing hot cups to the workers and drinking more than his own share.

We learn at the beginning of the movie that millions of Afghans have poured into Iran as refugees. Since it is illegal to hire them, they work secretly for low wages, like undocumented Mexicans in America. Many are fleeing the Taliban for the comparatively greater freedom and prosperity of Iran, a distinction that may seem small to us, but not to them. (The title cards carrying this information were already in place when the film debuted at the 2001 Montreal and Toronto festivals, and were not added post-9/11.)

One day there is an accident on the site. A man named Najaf injures his leg, and that is a catastrophe because he has five children to feed in the squatters' camp where his family lives. Najaf sends his son Rahmat to take his place, but the son is small, slight, and young, and staggers under the burden of the concrete sacks. So Memar, the construction boss, who pays low wages but is not unkind, gives Rahmat the job of tea boy and reassigns Latif to real work.

Latif is lazy, immature, resentful. He trashes the kitchen in revenge, and makes things hard for Rahmat. Yet at the same time he finds something intriguing about the new tea boy, and eventually Latif discovers the secret: The boy is a girl. So desperate for money was Rahmat's family that in a society where women are strictly forbidden from mixing with men on a job like this, a deception was planned. In keeping the secret, Latif begins his journey to manhood and tolerance.

The outlines of *Baran,* as they emerge, seem as much like an ancient fable as a modern story. Middle Eastern society, so insistent on the division between men and women, has a literature filled with stories about men and women in disguise, passing through each other's worlds. The vast gulf between Latif and Rahmat is dramatized by the way they essentially fall in love without exchanging a single word. Meanwhile, watching conditions on the work site and seeing raids by government agents looking for illegal workers, we get an idea of Iran's ground-level economy.

My description perhaps makes the film sound grim and gray, covered with a silt of concrete dust. Not at all. It is the latest work by Majid Majidi, whose *Children of Heaven* (1997) was a heartwarming fable about a brother and sister who lose a pair of sneakers and try to hide this calamity from their parents. The director uses natural colors and painterly compositions to make even the most spartan locations look beautiful, and as Stephanie Zacharek of Salon.com observes: "Majidi uses sunlight, a completely free resource if you can time your filmmaking around it, as a dazzling special effect."

What happens between Rahmat and Latif I will leave you to discover. There are many surprises along the way, one of the best involving a man Latif meets during a long journey—an itinerant shoemaker, who has thoughtful observations about life. *Baran* is the latest in a flowering of good films from Iran, and gives voice to the moderates there. It shows people existing and growing in the cracks of their society's inflexible walls.

Barbershop ★ ★ ★
PG-13, 102 m., 2002

Ice Cube (Calvin), Cedric the Entertainer (Eddie), Leonard Earl Howze (Dinka), Troy Garity (Isaac), Eve (Terri), Sean Patrick Thomas (Jimmy), Michael Ealy (Ricky), Anthony Anderson (J. D.), Lahmard Tate (Billy), Keith David (Lester). Directed by Tim Story and produced by Mark Brown, Robert Teitel, and George Tillman Jr. Screenplay by Brown, Don D. Scott, and Marshall Todd.

I've become embroiled in a controversy recently about whether women engage in audible and detailed discussions of their sexual activities while sitting in beauty salons. Doesn't happen, say some of my correspondents, while a woman from Texas says it happens there all the time—although, being from Michigan, she naturally doesn't join in. I got started on this subject while reviewing a movie named *Never Again,* where there's a scene of sex talk in a salon that's enough to make your hair curl.

My hunch is that most women don't talk that way in most salons. Do I know? No, because I've never been in a beauty salon. But now comes *Barbershop* to argue the question from the male side. The movie takes place during one long day in a barbershop on Chicago's South Side, where seven barbers (six men, one woman; six blacks, one white) man the chairs. Judging by this film, the conversation ranges far beyond sex, but is not above spirited discussions of booty: Who has it, who needs it, who wants it. But sex as a general topic would be far too limiting for this crowd, and the movie plays like a talk show where everyone is the host.

The barbershop is owned by Calvin (Ice Cube), who inherited it from his father. It scrapes by, but doesn't feed his hungers for bigger things—like a recording studio, for example (he dreams of platinum records issuing from his basement). One day, heedlessly, he sells the shop for $20,000 to Lester the loan shark (Keith David), who promises the word "barbershop" will be permanently on the store, but privately has in mind a gentleman's club by the same name.

The barbers and regular customers are devastated by this news. The shop provides more than employment or service for them; it is community, forum, friendship, camaraderie, continuity. Realizing his error, Calvin tries to buy back the shop, but finds the price is now $40,000. So it appears this will be the last day that the little shop acts as a stage for all the regulars.

The barbers are perhaps too many to be supported by such a shop, but they provide a nice cross section: In addition to Calvin, there's old Eddie (Cedric the Entertainer), who never seems to have a customer but is installed as chief pontificator; Jimmy (Sean Patrick Thomas), a college student who tries to impress everyone with his knowledge (are scallops a mollusk?); Terri (Eve), who knows somebody has been drinking her apple juice from the refrigerator in the back room; Ricky (Michael Ealy), who has two strikes against him and will get life for a third; Dinka (Leonard Earl Howze), from Nigeria, who likes Terri but is too rotund for her tastes; and Isaac (Troy Garity), the token white barber, who explains that, inside, he's blacker than some of the others.

A parallel plot involves J. D. (Anthony Anderson) and Billy (Lahmard Tate), who stage a spectacularly incompetent theft of an ATM machine that has been recently installed in the Indian grocery on the corner. Since they "borrowed" Ricky's van for this job, if they get

51

caught he goes up for life. The unending conversation in the shop is intercut with J. D. and Billy wrestling with the ATM machine, which at one point they even attempt to check in with at a motel.

If nothing significant gets settled in the rambling barbershop conversations, at least many issues are aired, and by the end, in classic sitcom fashion, all problems have been solved. The talk is lively, but goes into overdrive when Eddie is onstage; Cedric the Entertainer has the confidence, the style, and the volume to turn any group into an audience, and he has a rap about Rosa Parks, Rodney King, and O. J. Simpson that brought down the house at the screening I attended.

The film is ungainly in construction but graceful in delivery. I could have done without both of the subplots—the loan shark and the ATM thieves—and simply sat there in Calvin's barbershop for the entire running time, listening to these guys talk. There is a kind of music to their conversations, now a lullaby, now a march, now a requiem, now hip-hop, and they play with each other like members of an orchestra. The movie's so good to listen to, it would even work as an audio book. ☞

Bartleby ★ ★ ½
PG-13, 82 m., 2002

David Paymer (The Boss), Crispin Glover (Bartleby), Glenne Headly (Vivian), Joe Piscopo (Rocky), Maury Chaykin (Ernie), Seymour Cassel (Frank Waxman), Carrie Snodgress (Book Publisher), Dick Martin (Mayor). Directed and produced by Jonathan Parker. Screenplay by Parker and Catherine DiNapoli, based on the story "Bartleby the Scrivener" by Herman Melville.

The mass of men lead lives of quiet desperation.
—Thoreau

The life work of the employees in the Public Record Office can be easily described: They take enormous quantities of printed documents they have no interest in, and they file them. They are surrounded by the monument to their labor: lots of file cabinets. No wonder they go mad. Vivian distracts herself by flirting. Rocky pretends he has the inside line on everything. For Ernie, changing the toner cartridge in a Xerox machine is an invitation to disaster. Their boss patiently oversees their cheerless existence trying not to contemplate the devastating meaningless of the office.

One day a new employee is hired. His name is Bartleby. The boss asks him to do something. "I would prefer not to," Bartleby says. That becomes his reply to every request. He would prefer not to. He would prefer not to work, not to file, not to obey, not to respond, *not* to. What he prefers to do is stand in the center of the office with his neck cocked at an odd angle, staring at the ceiling.

The boss is checkmated. Bartleby is not doing bad work; he isn't working at all. His refusal to work subverts the entire work ethic of the organization. Everyone in the office— Vivian, Rocky, Ernie, and the boss himself— would prefer not to work. But that way madness lies. Our civilization is founded on its ability to get people to do things they would prefer not to do.

Bartleby is set in the present day in a vast, monolithic office building that crouches atop a hill like an Acropolis dedicated to bureaucracy. It is based on "Bartleby the Scrivener," a famous story published in 1856 by Herman Melville, who not only wrote *Moby-Dick*, but also labored for many empty years as a clerk in a customs house. Although the story is nearly 150 years old, it is correct to observe, as A. O. Scott does in the *New York Times*, that Melville anticipated Kafka—and Dilbert. This kind of office work exists outside time.

David Paymer plays the boss, a sad-eyed man who has a private office of his own, its prestige undermined by the fact that his window directly overlooks a Dumpster. Glenne Headly is Vivian, who flirts because if a man shows interest in her, that may be evidence that she exists. Joe Piscopo is Rocky, who dresses flamboyantly to imply he is not as colorless as his job. Maury Chaykin is the hopeless nebbish Ernie, who elevates strategic incompetence to an art form.

And Crispin Glover is Bartleby. The teen star of the eighties appears here like a ghost, pale and immobile, arrested by some private grief or fear. When he says, "I would prefer not to," it doesn't sound like insubordination, rebellion, or resistance, but like a flat statement of fact—a fact so overwhelming it brings all possible alternatives to a dead halt.

The film has been directed by Jonathan Parker; he adapted the Melville story with Catherine DiNapoli. It's his first work, and a promising one. I admire it and yet cannot recommend it, because it overstays its natural running time. The Melville short story was short because it needed to be short—to make its point and then stop dead without compromise or consideration. *Bartleby* is short for a feature film, at eighty-two minutes, but might have been more successful at fifty or sixty minutes. Too bad there seems to be an unbreakable rule against features that short, or short subjects that long. In a perfect world, *Bartleby* would establish the office and its workers, introduce Bartleby, develop response to the work, and stop. Side stories, such as Vivian's attraction to the city manager (Seymour Cassel), would not be necessary.

And yet there is a kind of uncompromising, implacable simplicity to *Bartleby* that inspires admiration. In a world where most movies are about exciting people doing thrilling things, here is a film about a job that is living death, and a man who prefers not to do it. My friend McHugh worked his way through college at Acme Pest Control of Bloomington, Indiana. One day while he was crawling under a house with a spray gun, a housewife invited him into the kitchen for a lemonade. As he drank it, while covered in cobwebs and mud, she told her son, "Study your lessons hard, Jimmy, or you'll end up like him." Or like Bartleby.

Basic ★
R, 98 m., 2003

John Travolta (Agent Tom Hardy), Connie Nielsen (Lieutenant Julia Osborne), Samuel L. Jackson (Sergeant Nathan West), Giovanni Ribisi (Levi Kendall), Brian Van Holt (Raymond Dunbar), Taye Diggs (Pike), Timothy Daly (Colonel Bill Styles), Roselyn Sanchez (Nunez), Harry Connick Jr. (Pete Vilmer). Directed by John McTiernan and produced by Mike Medavoy, James Vanderbilt, Arnie Messer, and Michael Tadross. Screenplay by Vanderbilt.

I embarked on *Basic* with optimism and goodwill, confident that a military thriller starring John Travolta and Samuel L. Jackson, and directed by John McTiernan *(Die Hard),* might be entertaining action and maybe more. As the plot unfolded, and unfolded, and unfolded, and unfolded, I leaned forward earnestly in my seat, trying to remember where we had been and what we had learned.

Reader, I gave it my best shot. But with a sinking heart I realized that my efforts were not going to be enough, because this was not a film that *could* be understood. With style and energy from the actors, with every sign of self-confidence from the director, with pictures that were in focus and dialogue that you could hear, the movie descended into a morass of narrative quicksand. By the end, I wanted to do cruel and vicious things to the screenplay.

There's a genre that we could call the Jerk-Around Movie, because what it does is jerk you around. It sets up a situation and then does a bait and switch. You never know which walnut the truth is under. You invest your trust and are betrayed.

I don't mind being jerked around if it's done well, as in *Memento.* I felt *The Usual Suspects* was a long ride for a short day at the beach, but at least as I traced back through it, I could see how it held together. But as nearly as I can tell, *Basic* exists with no respect for objective reality. It is all smoke and no mirrors. If I were to see it again and again, I might be able to extract an underlying logic from it, but the problem is, when a movie's not worth seeing twice, it had better get the job done the first time through.

The film is set in a rainy jungle in Panama. I suspect it rains so much as an irritant, to make everything harder to see and hear. Maybe it's intended as atmosphere. Or maybe the sky gods are angry at the film.

We are introduced to the hard-assed Sergeant Nathan West (Jackson), a sadistic perfectionist who is roundly hated by his unit. When various characters are killed during the confusion of the storm, there is the feeling the deaths may not have been accidental, may indeed have involved drug dealing. A former DEA agent named Tom Hardy (Travolta) is hauled back from alcoholism to join the investigation, teaming with Lieutenant Julia Osborne (Connie Nielsen).

The murders and the investigation are both told in untrustworthy flashbacks. We get versions of events from such differing points of view, indeed, that we yearn for a good old-fashioned omnipotent POV to come in and slap everybody around. There are so many different views of the same happenings that, hell, why not throw in a musical version?

Of course, there are moments that are engaging in themselves. With such actors (Giovanni Ribisi, Taye Diggs, Brian Van Holt, Roselyn Sanchez, and even Harry Connick Jr.), how could there not be? We listen and follow and take notes, and think we're getting somewhere, and then the next scene knocks down our theories and makes us start again. Finally we arrive at an ending that gives a final jerk to our chain and we realize we never had a chance.

What is the point of a movie like *Basic*? To make us feel cleverly deceived? To do that, the film would have to convince us of one reality and then give us another, equally valid (classics like *Laura* did that). This movie gives no indication even at the end that we have finally gotten to the bottom of things. There is a feeling that *Basic II* could carry right on, undoing the final shots, bringing a few characters back to life and sending the whole crowd off on another tango of gratuitous deception.

Beautiful Creatures ★ ½
R, 88 m., 2001

Rachel Weisz (Petula), Susan Lynch (Dorothy), Iain Glen (Tony), Maurice Roeves (Ronnie McMinn), Alex Norton (Hepburn), Pauline Lynch (Sheena), Tom Mannion (Brian McMinn). Directed by Bill Eagles and produced by Simon Donald and Alan Wands. Screenplay by Donald.

I spent last week at the Conference on World Affairs at the University of Colorado, Boulder, where one of my fellow panelists created a stir by standing up and shouting that the women on his panel were "man-haters," and he was fed up and wasn't going to take it anymore.

He would have had apoplexy if he'd seen *Beautiful Creatures,* from Scotland. Here is a movie about two of the most loathsome women in recent cinema, and the movie thinks the male characters are the villains. It gets away with this only because we have been taught that women are to be presumed good and

men are to be presumed evil. Flip the genders in this screenplay, and there would not be the slightest doubt that the characters named Petula and Dorothy are monsters.

Consider, for example, the setup. Dorothy (Susan Lynch) has been unwise enough to shack up with a boyfriend who is not only a junkie but also a golfer. This makes her a two-time loser. She pawns his golf clubs. He gets revenge by throwing her brassiere in boiling water, dyeing her dog pink, and stealing her money, which is from the pawned golf clubs. Any golfer (or junkie) will tell you that at this point, they are approximately morally even.

Dorothy leaves the house and comes upon a disturbance in the street. Petula (Rachel Weisz) is being beaten by Brian (Tom Mannion). Why is he doing this? Because the movie requires this demonstration of typical male behavior. Dorothy is already mad, and now she loses it. She slams Brian with a pipe to the back of the head, and the two women, instantly bonding, carry his unconscious body to Dorothy's flat, where they share a joint while Brian dies in the bathtub. "You just get sick listening to all that gonna (bleeping) kill you stuff," Dorothy explains.

Imagine a scene where a man slams a woman with a pipe, and then joins her boyfriend in dragging the body into the bathtub and sharing a joint while she dies. Difficult. Even more difficult in a comedy, which, I neglected to mention, *Beautiful Creatures* intends to be. But I don't want to get mired in male outrage. Men are more violent than women, yes, and guilty of abuse, yes, although the percentage of male monsters is incalculably higher in the movies than in life. Like Thelma and Louise, Dorothy and Petula commit crimes that are morally justifiable because of their gender. We even like them for it. They have to conceal the death, for example, because "no one would believe" they had not committed murder. My own theory is that any jury in Scotland would believe their story that the man was violent and Dorothy had come to the defense of a sister.

The movie, set in Glasgow and one of the many offspring of *Trainspotting,* uses local color for a lot of its gags. Instead of picketing *The Sopranos,* Italian-Americans should protest the new wave of films from Scotland, which indicate Scots make funnier, more violent, more eccentric, and more verbal gangsters than they do. Films and TV shows that portray ethnic groups as interesting and colorful are generally a plus, since those viewers dumb enough to think every story is an "accurate portrait" are beyond our help anyway.

The plot. The dead man has a brother who is a rich bad guy. The women cut off the corpse's finger and send it with a ransom demand. A detective (Alex Norton) comes to investigate, gets in on the scheme, and alters it with designs of his own. Meanwhile, the junkie boyfriend turns up again, and one thing leads to another. You know how it is.

There is some dark humor in the movie, of the kind where you laugh that you may not gag. And the kind of convoluted plotting that seems obligatory in crime films from Scotland (consider *Shallow Grave*). I am not really offended by the movie's gender politics, since I am accustomed to the universal assumption in pop (and academic) culture that women are in possession of truth and goodness and men can only benefit from learning from them. In fact, if the movie had been able to make me laugh, I might have forgiven it almost anything.

A Beautiful Mind ★ ★ ★ ★
PG-13, 129 m., 2001

Russell Crowe (John Forbes Nash Jr.), Ed Harris (William Parcher), Jennifer Connelly (Alicia Nash), Paul Bettany (Charles), Adam Goldberg (Sol), Austin Pendleton (Thomas King), Vivien Cardone (Marcee), Judd Hirsch (Helinger), Christopher Plummer (Dr. Rosen). Directed by Ron Howard and produced by Brian Grazer and Howard. Screenplay by Akiva Goldsman, based on the book by Sylvia Nasar.

The Nobel Prize winner John Forbes Nash Jr. still teaches at Princeton and walks to campus every day. That these commonplace statements nearly brought tears to my eyes suggests the power of *A Beautiful Mind,* the story of a man who is one of the greatest mathematicians, and a victim of schizophrenia. Nash's discoveries in game theory have an impact on our lives every day. He also believed for a time that the Russians were sending him coded messages on the front page of the *New York Times.*

A Beautiful Mind stars Russell Crowe as Nash, and Jennifer Connelly as his wife, Alicia, who is pregnant with their child when the first symptoms of his disease become apparent. It tells the story of a man whose mind was of enormous service to humanity while at the same time betraying him with frightening delusions. Crowe brings the character to life by sidestepping sensationalism and building with small behavioral details. He shows a man who descends into madness and then, unexpectedly, regains the ability to function in the academic world. Nash has been compared to Newton, Mendel, and Darwin, but was also for many years just a man muttering to himself in the corner.

Director Ron Howard is able to suggest a core of goodness in Nash that inspired his wife and others to stand by him, to keep hope, and, in her words in his darkest hour, "to believe that something extraordinary is possible." The movie's Nash begins as a quiet but cocky young man with a West Virginia accent, who gradually turns into a tortured, secretive paranoid who believes he is a spy being trailed by government agents. Crowe, who has an uncanny ability to modify his look to fit a role, always seems convincing as a man who ages forth-seven years during the film.

The early Nash, seen at Princeton in the late 1940s, calmly tells a scholarship winner, "There is not a single seminal idea on either of your papers." When he loses at a game of Go, he explains: "I had the first move. My play was perfect. The game is flawed." He is aware of his impact on others ("I don't much like people, and they don't much like me") and recalls that his first-grade teacher said he was "born with two helpings of brain and a half-helping of heart."

It is Alicia who helps him find the heart. She is a graduate student when they meet, is attracted to his genius, is touched by his loneliness, is able to accept his idea of courtship when he informs her, "Ritual requires we proceed with a number of platonic activities before we have sex." To the degree that he can be touched, she touches him, although often he seems trapped inside himself; Sylvia Nasar, who wrote the 1998 biography that informs Akiva Goldsman's screenplay, begins her book by quoting Wordsworth about "a mind forever voyaging through strange seas of thought alone."

Nash's schizophrenia takes a literal, visual form. He believes he is being pursued by a federal agent (Ed Harris), and finds himself in chase scenes that seem inspired by 1940s crime movies. He begins to find patterns where no patterns exist. One night he and Alicia stand under the sky and he asks her to name any object, and then connects stars to draw it. Romantic, but it's not so romantic when she discovers his office thickly papered with countless bits torn from newspapers and magazines and connected by frantic lines into imaginary patterns.

The movie traces his treatment by an understanding psychiatrist (Christopher Plummer), and his agonizing courses of insulin shock therapy. Medication helps him improve somewhat—but only, of course, when he takes the medication. Eventually newer drugs are more effective, and he begins a tentative re-entry into the academic world at Princeton.

The movie fascinated me about the life of this man, and I sought more information, finding that for many years he was a recluse, wandering the campus, talking to no one, drinking coffee, smoking cigarettes, paging through piles of newspapers and magazines. And then one day he paid a quite ordinary compliment to a colleague about his daughter, and it was noticed that Nash seemed better.

There is a remarkable scene in the movie when a representative for the Nobel committee (Austin Pendleton) comes visiting, and hints that Nash is being "considered" for the prize. Nash observes that people are usually informed they have won, not that they are being considered: "You came here to find out if I am crazy and would screw everything up if I won." He did win, and did not screw everything up.

The movies have a way of pushing mental illness into corners. It is grotesque, sensational, cute, funny, willful, tragic, or perverse. Here it is simply a disease, which renders life almost but not quite impossible for Nash and his wife, before he becomes one of the lucky ones to pull out of the downward spiral.

When he won the Nobel, Nash was asked to write about his life, and he was honest enough to say his recovery is "not entirely a matter of joy." He observes: "Without his 'madness,' Zarathustra would necessarily have been only another of the millions or billions of human individuals who have lived and then been forgotten." Without *his* madness, would Nash have also lived and then been forgotten? Did his ability to penetrate the most difficult reaches of mathematical thought somehow come with a price attached? The movie does not know and cannot say.

Beauty and the Beast ★ ★ ★ ★
G, 94 m., revised 2002

With the voices of: Paige O'Hara (Belle), Robby Benson (Beast), Richard White (Gaston), Jerry Orbach (Lumiere), David Ogden Stiers (Cogsworth), Angela Lansbury (Mrs. Potts), Jesse Corti (LeFou). Directed by Gary Trousdale and Kirk Wise and produced by Don Hahn. Art direction by Brian McEntee. Animation screenplay by Linda Woolverton.

With *The Little Mermaid* (1989) and *Beauty and the Beast* (1991), Disney in two strokes reinvented the animated feature and the movie musical. Both genres were languishing in the 1980s—musicals seemed like a lost art—and these two films brought them to a new kind of life. All the big animated hits since (*The Lion King, Aladdin, Toy Story, Monsters, Inc., Shrek*) descend from that original breakthrough, which blasted animated films out of the kiddie-film category and saw them, as Walt Disney originally saw them, as popular entertainments for all ages.

The Little Mermaid was the film that reminded audiences how entertaining animation could be, and *Beauty and the Beast* was the breakthrough—the first animated film to win an Oscar nomination in the Best Picture category. Disney itself groups the film with *Snow White* and *Pinocchio* as one of its three best. Now *Beauty* is back, in a new version so vibrant it's like experiencing the film anew. For its engagements on giant IMAX screens around the country, the movie has received a frame-by-frame restoration (since even the tiniest blemish isn't tiny on an IMAX screen). The sound track has been prepped for IMAX's seventy-four-speaker surround sound. And there's even new footage.

"Human Again," the added footage, is not a "deleted scene" that has been added to this rerelease in the spirit of countless recent "director's cuts." Although a scene is occasionally dropped from an animated film, the preplanning that goes into them, and the labor-intensive nature of the work, make it rare for scenes to be fully animated and then cut. What Disney started with was an original song by Howard Ashman and Alan Menken, written for the *Beauty and the Beast* score but then dropped from the screenplay. The song was put back in for the Broadway stage version of *Beauty*, was a hit, and belatedly won a place in the movie. It has now been animated for the first time.

The new scene stars three of the Beast's household servants, who fell under the same curse as their master, and were transformed into (hardly inanimate) objects. Lumiere (voice by Jerry Orbach) is a candelabra, Cogsworth (David Ogden Stiers) is the clock, and Mrs. Potts (Angela Lansbury) is the teapot (Chip, of course, is her son, the teacup). Joined by a chorus line of other household utensils, products, and tools, they sing in anticipation of being restored to human form if the Beast makes his deadline and falls in love with Belle before the last petal falls from the enchanted rose.

Sitting in front of the IMAX screen, I was reminded again that the giant format is a major part of the experience. There is a theory that quick cuts in such a large format tend to disorient the audience, and many IMAX films move in a stately manner from one static composition to another, but the quick pace of *Beauty* presented no problems. To be sure, the picture was not originally filmed with IMAX cameras, but this restoration is not a blowup of an existing 35mm print; it's a digital re-creation of it for the bigger screen.

Disney pioneered this form of giant-screen rerelease with its *Fantasia 2000* (1999). Seeing *Beauty and the Beast* again this way, I began to daydream about other classics that could be showcased on IMAX. The year 2001 came and went without a proper national rerelease of *2001: A Space Odyssey*, and although Francis Ford Coppola's *Apocalypse Now Redux* got somewhat more exposure, imagine it on the giant screen. As the average American movie screen grows smaller and smaller, as palaces are phased out for multiplexes, why isn't IMAX the natural home for the great Hollywood epics?

Before Night Falls ★ ★ ★ ½

R, 143 m., 2001

Javier Bardem (Reinaldo Arenas), Olivier Martinez (Lazaro Gomez Carilles), Andrea Di Stefano (Pepe Malas), Johnny Depp ("Bon Bon"/Lieutenant Victor), Sean Penn (Cuco Sanchez), Michael Wincott (Herberto Zorilla Ochoa), Najwa Nimri (Fina Correa), Vito Maria Schnabel (Teenage Reinaldo). Directed by Julian Schnabel and produced by Jon Kilik. Screenplay by Cunningham O'Keefe, Lazaro Gomez Carilles, and Schnabel, based on the memoirs of Reinaldo Arenas.

Born into crushing poverty in pre-Castro Cuba, young Reinaldo Arenas was told by a teacher than he had a gift for poetry. When his father heard this news, he slammed his fist down on the table and beat the boy. That more or less sets the pattern for Arenas's life: He tries to exercise his gifts as a poet and a novelist, and society slaps him down. It doesn't help that he's a homosexual.

Arenas believed the great betrayal in his life was by Fidel Castro. As a teenager, Reinaldo hitchhiked to the hills and joined the revolution, but once Castro came to power he showed little sympathy for artists and none for homosexuals. Arenas was an outcast and for seven years a prisoner in Cuba—until 1980, when he took advantage of the boat exodus for criminals, gays, the mentally ill, and others considered unfit to be Cubans. Ten years later, in Manhattan, dying of AIDS, he committed suicide, using pills and (just to be sure) a plastic "I Love NY" bag over his head.

Before Night Falls tells the story of Arenas's life through the words of his work and the images of Julian Schnabel's imagination. Schnabel, the painter, makes his screen a rich canvas of dream sequences, fragmented childhood memories, and the wild Cuban demimonde inhabited by Arenas and others who do not conform. There is no sequence more startling than one where Arenas stumbles onto a ragtag commune of refuseniks and finds that in the roofless ruin of an old cathedral they are building a hot-air balloon with which they hope to float to Florida. The balloon actually makes one brief flight. Did this episode actually happen? I would like to think that it did.

This is Schnabel's second film, and his second about an artist who is also a moody, difficult outcast. The first film was *Basquiat* (1996), about Jean Michel Basquiat, the Manhattan graffiti artist who rose briefly from homelessness to fame before sinking into madness. Arenas describes a similar trajectory. For both men, joy seems to come primarily at those moments when they are actually creating. Sex (for Arenas) and drugs (for Basquiat) are a way to avoid work, loneliness, and pain, but they lead to trouble, not release. Arenas claimed to have slept with 5,000 men by the age of twenty-five. That is not the record of a man who finds sex satisfying, but of one who does not.

Arenas is played by Javier Bardem, a Spanish actor with a specialty in macho heterosexuality (if you doubt me, see *Jamon, Jamon*). He doesn't play Arenas as a gay man so much as a man whose body fits like the wrong suit of clothes. We accept Arenas as gay in the movie because the story says he is, and because there are after all no rules about how a homosexual should look or behave—but there is somehow the feeling that the movie's Arenas is not gay from the inside out, but has chosen the lifestyle as part of a compulsion to defy Castro in every way possible. The film contains two more-convincing homosexual characters, both played by Johnny Depp: Lieutenant Victor, a sleek, tight-trousered military officer, and "Bon Bon," a flamboyant transvestite who struts through Castro's prisons and proves incredibly useful by smuggling out one of Arenas's manuscripts, concealing it in that place where most of us would be most inconvenienced by a novel, however brilliant.

What is most heroic about Arenas is his stubbornness. He could make his life easier with a little discretion, a little cunning, a little tact, and even a small ability to tell the authorities what they want to hear. There must have been a lot of gay men in Cuba who didn't make their lives as impossible as Arenas did. Consider the character of Diego, in *Strawberry and Chocolate,* the 1993 movie by the great Cuban director Tomas Gutierrez Alea. The movie is set in 1979, Diego is clearly gay,

and yet he lives more or less as he wants to, because he is clever and discreet.

There is a little something of the spoiled masochist about Arenas. One would not say he seeks misery, but he wears it like a badge of honor, and we can see his mistakes approaching before he does. This is not a weakness in the film but one of its intriguing strengths: Arenas is not presented as a cliché, as the heroic gay artist crushed by totalitarian straightness, but as a man who might have been approximately as unhappy no matter where he was born. That angle between Arenas and his society is perhaps what inspired his work. Trapped on the margin, he wrote in spite of everything, and the anguish of creation was a source of energy. One is reminded a little of the Marquis de Sade, as portrayed in *Quills*. It was never simply what they wrote, but that, standing outside convention, taunting the authorities, inhabiting impossible lives, they wrote at all.

Behind Enemy Lines ★ ½
PG-13, 93 m., 2001

Owen Wilson (Burnett), Gene Hackman (Reigart), Joaquim de Almeida (Piquet), Vladimir Mashkov (Tracker), David Keith (O'Malley), Olek Krupa (Lokar), Eyal Podell (Kennedy), Gabriel Macht (Stackhouse). Directed by John Moore and produced by John Davis. Screenplay by David Veloz and Zak Penn, based on a story by Jim Thomas and John Thomas.

The premiere of *Behind Enemy Lines* was held aboard the aircraft carrier USS *Carl Vinson*. I wonder if it played as a comedy. Its hero is so reckless and its villains so incompetent that it's a showdown between a man begging to be shot, and an enemy that can't hit the side of a Bosnian barn. This is not the story of a fugitive trying to sneak through enemy terrain and be rescued, but of a movie character magically transported from one photo opportunity to another.

Owen Wilson stars as Burnett, a hotshot navy flier who "signed up to be a fighter pilot—not a cop on a beat no one cares about." On a recon mission over Bosnia, he and his partner, Stackhouse (Gabriel Macht), venture off mission and get digital photos of a mass grave and illegal troop movements. It's a Serbian operation in violation of a fresh peace treaty, and the Serbs fire two missiles to bring the plane down. The plane's attempts to elude the missiles supply the movie's high point.

The pilots eject. Stackhouse is found by Tracker (Vladimir Mashkov), who tells his commander, Lokar (Olek Krupa), to forget about a big pursuit and simply allow him to track Burnett. That sets up the cat-and-mouse game in which Burnett wanders through open fields, stands on the tops of ridges, and stupidly makes himself a target, while Tracker is caught in one of those nightmares where he runs and runs but just can't seem to catch up.

Back on the USS *Vinson*, Admiral Reigart (Gene Hackman) is biting his lower lip. He wants to fly in and rescue Burnett, but is blocked by his NATO superior, Admiral Piquet (Joaquim de Almeida)—who is so devious he substitutes NATO troops for Americans in a phony rescue mission, and calls them off just when Burnett is desperately waving from a pickup area. Admiral Piquet, who sounds French, is played by a Portuguese actor.

The first-time director is John Moore, who has made lots of TV commercials, something we intuit in a scene where Reigart orders Burnett to proceed to another pickup area, and Burnett visualizes fast-motion whooshing tracking shots up and down mountains and through valleys before deciding, uh-uh, he ain't gonna do that.

What Burnett does do is stroll through Bosnia like a bird-watcher, exposing himself in open areas and making himself a silhouette against the skyline. He's only spotted in the first place because when his buddy is cornered, he's hiding safely but utters a loud involuntary yell and then starts to run up an exposed hillside. First rule of not getting caught: No loud involuntary yells within the hearing of the enemy.

This guy is a piece of work. Consider the scene where Burnett substitutes uniforms with a Serbian fighter. He even wears a black ski mask covering his entire face. He walks past a truck of enemy troops, and then what does he do? Why, he *removes the ski mask*, revealing his distinctive blond hair, and then he *turns back toward the truck* so we can see his face, in case we didn't know who he was. How did this guy get through combat training? Must have been

a social promotion to keep him with his age group.

At times Burnett is pursued by the entire Serbian army, which fires at him with machine guns, rifles, and tanks, of course never hitting him. The movie recycles the old howler where hundreds of rounds of ammo miss the hero, but all he has to do is aim and fire, and—pow! another bad guy jerks back, dead. I smiled during the scene where Admiral Reigart is able to use heat-sensitive satellite imagery to look at high-res silhouettes of Burnett stretched out within feet of the enemy. Maybe this is possible. What I do not believe is that the enemies in this scene could not spot the American uniform in a pile of enemy corpses.

Do I need to tell you that the ending involves a montage of rueful grins, broad smiles, and meaningful little victorious nods, scored with upbeat rock music? No, probably not. And of course we get shots of the characters and are told what happened to them after the story was over—as if this is based on real events. It may have been inspired by the adventures of air force pilot Scott O'Grady, who was rescued after being shot down over Bosnia in 1995, but based on real life, it's not.

Behind the Sun ★ ★
PG-13, 94 m., 2002

Jose Dumont (Father), Rodrigo Santoro (Tonio), Rita Assemany (Mother), Ravi Ramos Lacerda (Pacu), Luis Carlos Vasconcelos (Salustiano), Flavia Marco Antonio (Clara), Everaldo De Souza Pontes (Old Blind Man). Directed by Walter Salles and produced by Arthur Cohn. Screenplay by Karim Ainouz and Sergio Machado.

Behind the Sun describes a blood feud elevated to the dignity of tragedy. It takes place in a rural area of Brazil, but it could be set instead in the Middle East, in Bosnia, in India, in Africa, in any of those places where people kill each other because of who their parents were.

Religion, which is often cited as a justification for these killings, is just a smoke screen for tribalism. The killings spring out of a universal human tendency to dislike anyone who is not like we are.

The movie takes place in 1910. Two families live on either side of a cane field. The Ferreiras are richer, live in a sprawling villa, have an extended family. The Breves are poorer, humble, hardworking. Since time immemorial there has been a feud between these two families, springing from some long-forgotten disagreement over land. Over time a set of ground rules has grown up: First a Ferreira man (or a Breves man) kills a Breves (or a Ferreira) man, and then the tables are turned.

If it amounted only to that, all the Breves and Ferreiras would be dead, or one side would have won. Certain customs somewhat slow the pace of the killing. When someone has been killed, his bloodstained shirt is left out in the sun to dry, and there is a truce until the red has turned yellow. Despite the predictable timetable that would seem to operate, the next victim is somehow always unprepared, as we see when a young Breves stalks his quarry one night after a shirt has turned yellow.

We meet the Kid (Ravi Ramos Lacerda), youngest son of the Breves family, who knows that since his adored older brother Tonio (Rodrigo Santoro) has killed a Ferreira, it is only a matter of time until the blood fades and Tonio is killed. While the ominous waiting period continues, a troupe of itinerant circus performers passes through, and the Kid meets the ringmaster and his sultry fire-eating star. They give him a picture book about the sea, which, wouldn't you know, encourages him to dream about a world different from the one he knows.

The circus itself offers an alternative vision, not that the cheerless sugar cane feud doesn't make anything look preferable. Tonio meets the fire-breather and is thunderstruck by love, and there is the possibility that, yes, he might run away with the circus. More than this I dare not reveal, except to hint that the age-old fate of the two families must play out under the implacable sun.

Behind the Sun is a good-looking movie, directed by Walter Salles, who was much praised for his 1998 Oscar nominee *Central Station,* also about a young boy whose life is scarred by the cruelty of his elders. It has some of the simplicity and starkness of classical tragedy, but what made me impatient was its fascination with the macho blood lust of the two families. Since neither family has evolved to the point where it can see the futility of killing and the pointlessness of their deadly ritual, it

was hard for me to keep from feeling they were getting what they deserved. Sure, I hoped Tonio would get the girl and the Kid would see the ocean, but these are limited people and we can care about them only if we buy into their endless cycle of revenge and reprisal. After a certain point no one is right and no one is wrong, both sides have boundless grievances, and it's the audience that wants to run away with the circus.

The Believer ★ ★ ★
R, 98 m., 2002

Ryan Gosling (Danny Balint), Summer Phoenix (Carla Moebius), Theresa Russell (Lina Moebius), Billy Zane (Curtis Zampf), A. D. Miles (Guy Danielson), Joshua Harto (Kyle), Glenn Fitzgerald (Drake), Garret Dillahunt (Billings). Directed by Henry Bean and produced by Susan Hoffman and Christopher Roberts. Screenplay by Bean.

Censors feel *they* are safe with objectionable material, but must protect others who are not as smart or moral. The same impulse tempts the reviewer of *The Believer.* Here is a fiercely controversial film about a Jew who becomes an anti-Semite. When I saw it at Sundance 2000, where it won the Grand Jury Prize, I wrote, "Some feared the film could do more harm than good." I shared those fears. The film's hero is so articulate in his retailing of anti-Semitic beliefs that his words, I thought, might find the wrong ears. I understand the film, I was saying—but are you to be trusted with it?

Certainly the movie has been a hot potato. After a screening at the Simon Weisenthal Center inspired audience members to protest it, no major distributor would pick it up. Showtime scheduled it for a cable showing, which was canceled in the aftermath of 9/11. Then it was finally shown in the spring, and now has theatrical distribution from small Fireworks Pictures. In the meantime, to its Sundance awards it has added Independent Spirit Awards for best screenplay and best first feature (both to director Henry Bean), best actor (Ryan Gosling), and best supporting actress (Summer Phoenix). Few doubt it is a good film. But do we really need a movie, right now, about a Jewish neo-Nazi?

I am not the person to answer that question

for you. You have to answer it for yourself. The film's anti-Semitism is articulate but evil, and the conflict between what the hero says and what he believes (or does not want to believe) is at the very center of the story.

Gosling's character, named Danny Balint, is based on a real person. The *Jerusalem Report* writes: "The film has its roots in a true story. Daniel Burros was a nice Jewish boy from Queens who somehow went from being his rabbi's star pupil to a hotheaded proponent of the long-defunct Third Reich. After a stint in the army, he became involved with the American Nazi Party and the Ku Klux Klan. In 1965, following Burros's arrest at a KKK event in New York City, the *New York Times* disclosed that he was Jewish. Hours after the paper hit the stands, Burros took his own life."

In the film, Danny is seen as a bright young yeshiva student who gets into impassioned arguments with his teachers. Why must Abraham sacrifice his son Isaac? What kind of a God would require such an act? "A conceited bully," Danny decides. As a young man, Danny rejects his Orthodox upbringing, confronts Jews on the street and in subway cars, beats and kicks one, and expresses contempt for a race which, as he sees it, did not fight back during the Holocaust. Eventually he falls into the orbit of a neo-Nazi organization run by Theresa Russell and Billy Zane, who are impressed by his rhetoric but want him to dial down on the subject of Judaism: "It doesn't play anymore."

For Danny, anti-Semitism and the self-hate it implies is the whole point; he is uninterested in the politics of fascism. For Danny, the weakness of Jews is what he sees as their willingness to be victims, and after a court assigns him to an encounter group with Holocaust survivors, he bluntly asks one why he didn't fight back. Israelis, he believes, are not Jews because they own their own land and defend it, and therefore have transcended their Jewishness. You can see this reasoning twisting back into his own unhappy soul; he objects to Abraham taking instructions from God, and he objects to taking instructions from his church. His values involve his muscles, his fighting ability (both physical and rhetorical), his willingness to confront. In some kind of sick way, he attacks Jews, hoping to inspire one to beat him up.

Ryan Gosling (who, incredibly, was a Mouse-keteer contemporary of Britney Spears), is at twenty-two a powerful young actor. He recently starred in *Murder by Numbers* as one of two young killers resembling Leopold and Loeb in their desire to demonstrate their superiority by committing a perfect crime. In *The Believer,* he reminds us of Edward Norton in *American History X,* another movie about a bright, twisted kid who is attracted to the transgressive sickness of racism. The movie is not very convincing in its portrayal of the fascist group (Zane and Russell seem less like zealots than hobbyists), but his personal quest is real enough.

When he involves himself in a raid on a temple, there is a revealing paradox: He resents the skinheads who come along with him because they don't understand the traditions they are attacking. What good is it to desecrate the Torah if you don't know what it is? He knows, and we begin to understand that he cares, that he accepts Judaism in the very core of his soul, and that his fight is against himself.

The ending of *The Believer,* if not exactly open, is inconclusive, and this is the kind of movie where you need to budget in time afterward for a cup of coffee and some conversation. The movie is better at portraying Danny's daily reality than at making sense of his rebellion (if sense can be made), but perhaps the movie plus the discussion can add up to a useful experience. Although his film needs more clarity and focus, Henry Bean has obviously taken a big chance because of his own sincere concerns. And if the wrong people get the wrong message—well, there has never been any shortage of wrong messages. Or wrong people.

Below ★ ★ ½
R, 103 m., 2002

Matt Davis (O'Dell), Bruce Greenwood (Brice), Olivia Williams (Claire), Holt McCallany (Loomis), Scott Foley (Coors), Zach Galifianakis (Weird Wally), Jason Flemyng (Stumbo), Dexter Fletcher (Kingsley). Directed by David N. Twohy and produced by Sue Baden-Powell and Michael Zoumas. Screenplay by Twohy, Lucas Sussman, and Darren Aronofsky.

Even before the woman is taken on board, the USS *Tiger Shark* is a submarine in trouble. The captain has been lost overboard, or at least that's the story, and tempers run high in the confined space. Then the sub rescues three drifters in a life raft, one of them a woman, whose presence on board is agreed by everyone to be bad luck on a sub, although her arrival does result in the crew wearing cleaner underwear.

Now dangers increase. The sub is tracked by Germans, who drop depth bombs and later come back to troll for it with giant grappling hooks. There is fearful damage to the periscope and the control tower. An oil leak threatens to betray the sub's position. Oxygen is running low, and hydrogen in the air is a danger to the crew's safety and sanity. And perhaps there is a ghost on board. The creepy sounds from outside the hull—of seaweed, whale songs, and bouncing depth bombs—increase apprehension.

Yes, a ghost. How else to explain why a record of Benny Goodman's "Sing, Sing, Sing" seems to play itself at inopportune times—as when the Germans are listening for the slightest sound from below? And when the late skipper was a Goodman fan? Of course, there could be a saboteur on board, in addition to, or perhaps instead of, the ghost.

Below is a movie where the story, like the sub, sometimes seems to be running blind. In its best moments it can evoke fear, and it does a good job of evoking the claustrophobic terror of a little World War II boat, but the story line is so eager to supply frightening possibilities that sometimes we feel jerked around. Isn't it possible for a submarine to be haunted without turning it into a museum of horror film devices?

Of those devices, the most tiresome is the convention that surprises make sounds. In most horror movies, including many less clever than *Below*, there is a visual strategy in which a character is shown in relative close-up (limiting our ability to see around him) and then startled by the unexpected appearance of another character or other visual surprise. This moment is invariably signaled on the sound track with a loud, alarming musical chord, or perhaps by the sound of a knife being sharpened. But surprises don't make sounds, and the cliché has become so tiresome that I submit a director might be able to create a *more* frightening sequence by playing the unexpected appearance in total silence.

There are a lot of surprise apparitions in *Below*, and many times we expect them even when they don't arrive. Consider the effective sequence in which four divers have to penetrate the ballast space between the inner and outer hulls to search for the oil leak. Will they find a ghostly body, or what?

The acting skipper of the ship is Brice (Bruce Greenwood). The absence of the former skipper is a secret at first, and the explanations for his disappearance are contradictory; even by the end of the movie, we are not sure we have the correct story. Has he returned to haunt the boat? Oxygen deprivation can encourage hallucinations.

The bad-luck woman on board, Claire (Olivia Williams), turns out to be a nurse from a sunken hospital ship. Who sunk that ship with its big red cross, and why? And what about the two survivors in the boat with her? What are their stories? Although the arrival of a woman on board inspires some heavy-handed scenes in which some men seem to be warming up for an assault, that plot thread is quickly abandoned, and Claire begins to take a surprisingly active role in the onboard discussions. Siding with her is O'Dell (Matt Davis), maybe because he agrees, maybe because he likes her. Brice's command of the ship may include decisions made with a hidden agenda.

The movie is skillfully made by David N. Twohy, whose *The Arrival* (1996) was an uncommonly intelligent science fiction thriller about a hidden alien plot against Earth. But his overpraised *Pitch Black* (2000), which launched Vin Diesel, was weakened by the same faults as *Below*. It had too many obligatory startles, too many unclear possibilities, and not enough definition of the crucial players. But Twohy showed with *The Arrival* that he is a gifted director. *Below* has ambitions to be better than average, but doesn't pull itself together and insist on realizing them.

Bend It Like Beckham ★ ★ ★ ½
PG-13, 112 m., 2003

Parminder K. Nagra (Jesminder ["Jess"] Bhamra), Keira Knightley (Juliette ["Jules"]), Jonathan Rhys-Meyers (Joe), Anupam Kher (Mr. Bhamra), Shaheen Khan (Mrs. Bhamra), Archie Panjabi (Pinky Bhamra), Juliet Stevenson

(Paula). Directed by Gurinder Chadha and produced by Chadha and Deepak Nayar. Screenplay by Chadha, Paul Mayeda Berges, and Guljit Bindra.

I saw more important films at Sundance 2003, but none more purely enjoyable than *Bend It Like Beckham*, which is just about perfect as a teenage coming-of-age comedy. It stars a young actress of luminous appeal, it involves sports, romance, and, of course, her older sister's wedding, and it has two misinformed soccer moms—one who doesn't know a thing about the game and another who doesn't even know her daughter plays it.

The movie, set in London, tells the story of Jesminder Bhamra, known as "Jess," who comes from a traditional Indian family. Her parents are Sikhs who fled from Uganda to England, where her dad works at Heathrow airport. They live in the middle-class suburb of Hounslow, under the flight path of arriving jets, where her mother believes that Jess has two great duties in life: to learn to prepare a complete Indian meal, and to marry a nice Indian boy, in exactly that order.

Jess plays soccer with boys in the park. In her family's living room is a large portrait of a Sikh spiritual leader, but above Jess's bed is her own inspiration—the British soccer superstar David Beckham, better known to some as Posh Spice's husband. To Beckham's portrait she confides her innermost dream, which is to play for England. Of course, a girl cannot hope to be a soccer star, and an Indian girl should not play soccer at all, since in her mother's mind the game consists of "displaying your bare legs to complete strangers."

Jess is seen in the park one day by Juliette (Keira Knightley), who plays for the Hounslow Harriers, a woman's team, and is recruited to join them. The coach is a young Irishman named Joe (Jonathan Rhys-Meyers), and it is love at second or third sight—complicated because Joe cannot date his players, and Juliette has a crush on him, too.

But all of these elements make the film sound routine, and what makes it special is the bubbling energy of the cast and the warm joy with which Gurinder Chadha, the director and cowriter, tells her story. I am the first to admit that Gurinder Chadha is not a name on every-

body's lips, but this is her third film and I can promise you she has an unfailing instinct for human comedy that makes you feel good and laugh out loud.

Her previous film was the wonderful *What's Cooking,* about four American ethnic families (African-American, Latino, Jewish, and Vietnamese) all preparing a traditional Thanksgiving dinner, while their younger generations are connected in unsuspected ways. There is an emerging genre of comedies about second- and third-generation young people breaking loose from traditional parents (*My Big Fat Greek Wedding* is the most spectacular example), and I've seen these rite-of-entry comedies by directors with Filipino, Indian, Chinese, Mexican, Iranian, and Korean backgrounds, and even one, *Mississippi Masala,* where Denzel Washington and Sarita Choudhury played two such characters whose stories meet.

Bend It Like Beckham, which adds a British flavor to its London metroland masala, is good not because it is blindingly original but because it is flawless in executing what is, after all, a dependable formula. The parents must be strict and traditional, but also loving and funny, and Mr. and Mrs. Bhamra (Anupam Kher and Shaheen Khan) are classic examples of the type. So is Juliette's mother, Paula (the wry, funny British star Juliet Stevenson), who tries to talk her tomboy daughter into Wonderbras, and spends most of the movie fearing that a girl who doesn't want to wear one must be a lesbian ("There's a reason why Sporty Spice is the only one without a boyfriend"). The editing by Justin Krish gets laughs all on its own with the precision that it uses to cut to reaction shots as the parents absorb one surprise after another.

Jess, played by Parminder K. Nagra, is a physically exuberant girl whose love of soccer crosses over into a love of life. She runs onto the field as if simply at play, she does cartwheels after scoring goals, and although she deceives her parents about her soccer dreams, she loves them and understands their point of view. Her father, who played cricket in Uganda but was discriminated against by the local London club, still bears deep wounds, but "things are different now," Jess tells him, and there is the obligatory scene where he sneaks into the crowd at a match to see for himself.

Can there be an Indian comedy without a

wedding? *Monsoon Wedding* is the great example, and here too we get the loving preparation of food, the exuberant explosion of music, and the backstage drama. All ethnic comedies feature scenes that make you want to leave the theater and immediately start eating, and *Bend It Like Beckham* may inspire some of its fans to make Indian friends simply so they can be invited over for dinner.

The movie's values run deep. It understands that for Jess's generation soccer is not about displaying bare legs (Jess has another reason to be shy about that), but it also understands the hopes and ambitions of parents—and, crucially, so does Jess, who handles the tentative romance with her coach in a way that combines tenderness with common sense. A closing scene at the airport, which in a lesser movie would have simply hammered out a happy ending, shows her tact and love.

Like all good movies, *Bend It Like Beckham* crosses over to wide audiences. It's being promoted in the magazines and on the cable channels that teenage girls follow, but recently we showed it on our Ebert & Roeper Film Festival at Sea to an audience that ranged in age from seven to eighty-one, with a fiftyish median, and it was a huge success. For that matter, the hip Sundance audience, dressed in black and clutching cell phones and cappuccinos, loved it, too. And why not, since its characters and sensibility are so abundantly lovable. ☞

Better Luck Tomorrow ★ ★ ★ ★

R, 98 m., 2003

Parry Shen (Ben), Jason Tobin (Virgil), Sung Kang (Han), Roger Fan (Daric), John Cho (Steve), Karin Anna Cheung (Stephanie). Directed by Justin Lin and produced by Lin, Ernesto M. Foronda, and Julie Asato. Screenplay by Lin, Foronda and Fabian Marquez.

Justin Lin's *Better Luck Tomorrow* has a hero named Benjamin, but depicts a chilling hidden side of suburban affluence that was unseen in *The Graduate*. Its heroes need no career advice; they're on the fast track to Ivy League schools and well-paying jobs, and their straight-A grades are joined on their résumés by an improbable array of extracurricular credits: Ben

lists the basketball team, the academic decathlon team, and the food drive.

What he doesn't mention is the thriving business he and his friends have in selling cheat sheets. Or their drug sideline. Or the box hidden in his bedroom and filled with cash. Ben belongs to a group of overachieving Asian-American students in a wealthy Orange County suburb; they conform to the popular image of smart, well-behaved Asian kids, but although they have ambition they lack values, and step by step they move more deeply into crime. How deep is suggested by the film's opening scene, where Ben (Parry Shen) and his best friend, Virgil (Jason Tobin), are interrupted while sunbathing by the sound of a cell phone ringing on a body they have buried in Virgil's backyard.

Better Luck Tomorrow is a disturbing and skillfully told parable about growing up in today's America. These kids use money as a marker of success, are profoundly amoral, and project a wholesome, civic-minded attitude. They're on the right path to take jobs with the Enrons of tomorrow, in the dominant culture of corporate greed. Lin focuses on an ethnic group that is routinely praised for its industriousness, which deepens the irony, and also perhaps reveals a certain anger at the way white America patronizingly smiles on its successful Asian-American citizens.

Ben, Virgil, and their friends know how to use their ethnic identity to play both sides of the street in high school. "Our straight A's were our passports to freedom," Ben says in his narration. No parents are ever seen in the movie (there are very few adults, mostly played by white actors in roles reserved in most movies for minority groups). The kids get good grades, and their parents assume they are studying while they stay out late and get into very serious trouble.

Better Luck Tomorrow has all the obligatory elements of the conventional high school picture. Ben has a crush on the pretty cheerleader Stephanie Vandergosh (Karin Anna Cheung), but she dates Steve (John Cho), who plays the inevitable older teenager with a motorcycle and an attitude. Virgil is unlucky with girls, but thinks he once spotted Stephanie in a porno film (unlikely, but gee, it kinda looks like her). Han (Sung Kang) comes up with the scheme to sell homework for cash, and Daric (Roger Fan) is the overachiever who has, no doubt, the longest entry under his photo in the school yearbook.

These students never refer to, or are identified by, specific ethnic origin; they're known as the "Chinese Mafia" at school because of their low-key criminal activities, but that's not a name they give themselves. They may be Chinese, Japanese, Korean, Filipino, but their generation no longer obsesses with the nation before the hyphen; they are Orange County Americans, through and through, and although Stephanie's last name and Caucasian little brother indicate she was adopted, she brushes aside Ben's tentative question about her "real parents" by saying, "These are my real parents."

Better Luck Tomorrow is a coming-of-age film for Asian-Americans in American cinema. Like African-American films that take race for granted and get on with the characters and the story, Lin is making a movie where race is not the point but simply the given. After Ben joins the basketball team, a writer for the high school paper suggests he is the "token Asian" benchwarmer, and when students form a cheering section for him, he quits the team in disgust. He is not a token anything (and privately knows he has beaten the NBA record for free throws).

The story is insidious in the way it moves stealthily into darker waters, while maintaining the surface of a high school comedy. There are jokes and the usual romantic breakthroughs and reversals, and the progress of their criminal career seems unplanned and offhand, until it turns dangerous. I will not reveal the names of the key characters in the climactic scene, but note carefully what happens in terms of the story; perhaps the film is revealing that a bland exterior can hide seething resentment.

Justin Lin, who directed, cowrote, and co-produced, here reveals himself as a skilled and sure director, a rising star. His film looks as glossy and expensive as a mega-million studio production, and the fact that its budget was limited means that his cinematographer Patrice Lucien Cochet, his art director Yoo Jung Han, and the other members of his crew were very able and resourceful. It's one thing to get an expensive look with money, and another thing to get it with talent.

Lin keeps a sure hand on tricky material; he has obvious confidence about where he wants to go and how he wants to get there. His film is uncompromising, and doesn't chicken out with a U-turn ending. His actors expand and breathe as if they're captives just released from lesser roles (the audition reel of one actor, Lin recalls, showed him delivering pizzas in one movie after another). Parry Shen gives a watchful and wary undertone to his all-American boy, and Karin Anna Cheung finds the right note to deal with a boy she likes but finds a little too goody-goody. *Better Luck Tomorrow* is not just a thriller, not just a social commentary, not just a comedy or a romance, but all of those in a clearly seen, brilliantly made film. 🖙

Big Bad Love ★ ★

R, 111 m., 2002

Arliss Howard (Leon Barlow), Debra Winger (Marilyn), Paul Le Mat (Monroe), Rosanna Arquette (Velma), Angie Dickinson (Mrs. Barlow), Michael Parks (Mr. Aaron). Directed by Arliss Howard and produced by Debra Winger. Screenplay by James Howard and Arliss Howard, based on stories by Larry Brown.

It all comes down to whether you can tolerate Leon Barlow. I can't. *Big Bad Love* can, and is filled with characters who love and accept him even though he is a full-time, gold-plated pain in the can. Leon is a college graduate (no doubt of creative writing classes) who has adopted a Good Old Drunk persona that wavers between the tiresome and the obnoxious. The movie has patience with his narcissistic self-pity. My diagnosis: Send Barlow to rehab, haul him to some AA meetings, and find out in a year if he has anything worth saying.

I know there are people in real life who smoke as much as Barlow (Arliss Howard) does, but at today's cigarette prices he is spending $400 a month on cigarettes and almost as much on the manuscripts he ships out to literary magazines. His bar bill is beyond all imagining. The first thing you learn as a poor writer is to cut back on the overhead. Here at H & R Ebert ("Budget Control for Unpublished Drunks"), we could pare $25,000 a year from his costs just by cutting out his bad habits.

Barlow smokes more or less all the time. He becomes a character whose task every morning is to get through sixty to eighty cigarettes that day. Everything else is a parallel activity. He lives in a colorfully rundown house in rural Mississippi—the sort that passes for genteel poverty in the movies and is priced at $300,000 and up, with land, in the real-estate ads. He pounds away on his Royal typewriter as if engaged in a mano-a-mano with Robert E. *(Conan the Barbarian)* Howard in *The Whole Wide World*. Since he is a man without a glimmer of awareness of his own boorishness, one wonders what he writes. Epic fantasy, perhaps?

Like many drunks, he is enabled by his loved ones (or, as is often the case, his former loved ones). His ex-wife, Marilyn, well played by Debra Winger (Arliss Howard's real-life wife), has divorced him but still has a soft spot for the crazy lug. His buddy Monroe (Paul Le Mat) loves him, maybe because you protect your drinking buddy just like you protect your drinking money. Monroe's old lady, Velma (Rosanna Arquette), has a fate that was preordained when she was christened Velma, a name that summons up Raymond Chandler novels and long-suffering girlfriends. Velma sees more than she lets on, but is stuck in her sexpot act.

The movie's basic problem is that it has no distance on Barlow—no way to criticize him. The screenplay, written by Arliss Howard and James Howard, based on stories by the Mississippi writer Larry Brown, lets Barlow get away with murder. We all have a tendency to go easy on ourselves, and *Big Bad Love* is unaware that its hero is a tiresome jerk. Larry Brown writes about "hard-bitten, hard-drinking, hard-living male characters," according to a Website about his work, and is a "bad-boy novelist." One suspects that the movie lacks perspective on Barlow because Brown is, in some respects, Barlow.

Because a movie must be about something more than smoking, drinking, and talking as if you are the best-read drunk in town, *Big Bad Love* delivers two tragedies, both foreshadowed, right on time. It also involves some visual touches, such as an indoor rainstorm, that may perplex audiences not familiar with the work of Tarkovsky.

Arliss Howard is not a bad actor or a bad director, but in this film he shows himself an unreliable judge of character. Leon Barlow could

be saved by an emergency transfusion of irony, or even a film that is cheerfully jaundiced about him. But the martyr act doesn't work. Here is a man who wants us to like him because of his marriage that did not work, his stories that do not sell, and his children that he is not doing a very good job of parenting. Then we are asked to pity him because of all the cigarettes he must smoke and all the booze he has to drink, and because they make him feel so awful in the morning. He's a familiar type, imprisoned by self-monitoring: How am I doing? How do I feel? How long can I continue to abuse myself and those around me? In the movie, he's blessed by people who can see through the facade to the really great guy inside. All I could see was a cry for help.

Big Eden ★ ★
PG-13, 118 m., 2001

Arye Gross (Henry Hart), Eric Schweig (Pike Dexter), Tim DeKay (Dean Stewart), George Coe (Sam Hart), Louise Fletcher (Grace Cornwell), Nan Martin (Widow Thayer), Veanne Cox (Mary Margaret). Directed by Thomas Bezucha and produced by Jennifer Chaiken. Screenplay by Bezucha.

Big Eden tells a story of gay love in a small Montana town whose citizens are so accepting of homosexuality that the old coots around the cracker barrel at the general store rush to the window to monitor the progress of a triangle involving the local hunk, the artist feller from New York, and a tall, silent Indian. Earlier, the Widow Thayer, who failed to fix up the New Yorker with the local girls, discovers her error and throws a party so he can meet the local boys.

This is the same Montana that's next door to Wyoming, where a gay man named Matthew Shepard was murdered not long ago. Or rather, it is not the same Montana, but some kind of movie fantasy world in which all the local folk know and approve of the fact that Henry Hart (Arye Gross) is gay; by the end of the film, they're ready to use crowbars on the door to Henry's closet. This is the kind of movie small town with no ordinary citizens; everyone has a speaking role, and they all live in each other's pockets, know each other's business, and have jobs that allow them to drop into the general store and each other's kitchens with the frequency of neighbors on a sitcom.

That's not to say the movie doesn't have a lot of sweetness and warmth. Until the plot becomes intolerably cornball, there's charm in the story of how the withdrawn Henry returns to Big Eden after his granddad (George Coe) has a stroke. He's welcomed by Grace (Louise Fletcher), the local teacher, and learns immediately that "Dean is back in town." That would be Dean Stewart (Tim DeKay), Henry's hunky best friend in high school, and the object of an unrequited crush that spans the decades. Now Dean is divorced, and smiling at Henry during Sunday church services.

Grandpa starts to mend, Henry helps Grace in the local school, and the Widow Thayer is hired to cook meals for the two men. But Widow Thayer is a fearsomely bad cook, and soon the wonderfully named Pike Dexter (Eric Schweig) is secretly preparing gourmet meals from recipes on the Internet, and feeding the widow's swill to his dog. Pike is an Indian who runs the general store, despite painful shyness and a deep reluctance to say more than three words at a time.

We think the plot may involve local homophobia. But no: Everybody in this town is pro-gay. Then we think perhaps Henry and Dean will fall in love. They seem headed in that direction until a scene so awkwardly written and acted that it seems to have been pounded into the plot with sledgehammers (you'll know the scene I mean; ask yourself exactly how and why it justifies Henry's later anger, in another awkward scene). Finally it turns out that Henry's future lies in the arms of Pike, whose life changes the day he checks *The Joy of Cooking* out of his own lending library. (The movie misses a golden opportunity; Pike should have selected *The Settlement Cook Book*, with its cover motto, "The way to a man's heart is through his stomach.")

There are things in the movie that are very good. I admired George Coe's work in a difficult role (listen to his reading of the line, "God has done a good job here"). I liked Louise Fletcher's unforced intelligence and goodwill. Ayre Gross plays a character who at times is willfully obtuse, but it would be fatal to be more open—since the moment he acknowl-edges his gayness, the plot, which depends on him being the least liberated person in town, would collapse.

I had real troubles, I must admit, with the coots who gather at the general store. I doubt that in the real world all six of these bewhiskered, pipe-puffing, jeans-wearing, cowboy-hatted old cowboys would be cheerleaders for a gay romance. I also found Pike's character a puzzle. In the opening scenes he seems either retarded or mentally ill, but by the end love has conquered all and repaired it. The last scene is painfully overdone; a shy "like to dance?" and a fade-out would have worked a lot better than the current ending. When you lay it on too thick, the audience is distracted by implausibility rather than identifying with the characters.

Whether Henry will find happiness in Big Eden we can only wonder. Some may think him courageous to abandon his art career in Manhattan to join the circle of Pike's admirers around the cracker barrel. I think it is a prudent decision. Based on the one example of Henry's painting that we see, his artistic talents are best suited to designing gift-wrap paper.

Big Fat Liar ★ ★ ★
PG, 87 m., 2002

Frankie Muniz (Jason Shepherd), Paul Giamatti (Marty Wolf), Amanda Bynes (Kaylee), Amanda Detmer (Monty), Donald Faison (Frank). Directed by Shawn Levy and produced by Brian Robbins and Michael Tollin. Screenplay by Dan Schneider and Robbins.

Big Fat Liar takes the smartest fourteen-year-old fibber in Michigan and pairs him up against the dumbest thirty-something fibber in Hollywood. Jason Shepherd is an eighth-grader who lies about almost everything, so when a movie producer steals his homework and turns it into a movie, naturally Jason's parents and teacher don't believe him. So he enlists his girlfriend Kaylee, and goes to Hollywood to confront the creep and prove he was telling the truth. (Naturally, he lies to cover up his absence from home.)

This premise, which sounds like something a fourteen-year-old might have dreamed up, becomes a surprisingly entertaining movie—

one of those good-hearted comedies like *Spy Kids* where reality is put on hold while bright teenagers outsmart the best and worst the adult world has to offer. It's ideal for younger teens, and not painful for their parents.

Jason is played by Frankie Muniz (who was wonderful in *My Dog Skip*), Kaylee is Amanda Bynes, a TV actress making her film debut, and the reprehensible Marty Wolf, Hollywood sleazo supremo, is played by Paul Giamatti with the kind of teeth-gnashing venom the Beagle Boys used against Uncle Scrooge.

Marty, the "Wolfman," has indeed stolen Jason's eighth-grade story, which fell from his backpack into Wolf's limousine, for reasons too complicated to explain. The story, which is autobiographical, involves, of course, an eighth-grader who tells so many lies that no one believes him when he tells the truth. Marty is astonished when confronted in his studio office by the kid, who doesn't want money or even a share of ownership, but just for the guy to call his dad and admit, yes, it's true, I stole your kid's story. Marty laughs incredulously: That'll be the day.

The story is an excuse to take the kids on a tour of Hollywood, starting with the Universal back lot, which, like all back lots in movies, is jammed with countless extras dressed as Romans, aliens, cowboys, biblical figures, and can-can dancers. Jason and Kaylee get onto the lot via the Universal tour, and hide out in the wardrobe and props department, which has everything they need for their skulduggery.

Marty Wolf is such a seven-letter word that Jason quickly wins the sympathy of two key allies: his limo driver, Frank (Donald Faison), and his secretary, Monty (Amanda Detmer). Frank has reason for revenge. He was a hopeful actor until Marty wrote "loser" on his composite and sent it to every casting director in town. Monty does, too: She gets blamed for the Wolfman's every mistake.

A lot of the funniest scenes involve Giamatti, who is the target of so many practical jokes by the two kids that his life becomes miserable. The best: They fill his swimming pool with blue dye, so that on the day of his big meeting with the studio chief, he looks like an understudy for the Blue Man Group. His broad humor here is dramatically different from his

needy, imploding documentary producer in Todd Solondz's *Storytelling*.

The movie's charm is that it has confidence in this goofy story, and doesn't push it too hard. Muniz and Bynes have an easy prepubertal relationship (she's a lot taller, of course). It's based on wisecracks and immunity from the problems of the real world, where Hollywood might be a lot more dangerous for fourteen-year-olds. Giamatti's slow burn alternates with his fast burn and his explosive rages, and his comeuppance at the end is entirely appropriate in movie terms. And certain lines have a charm of their own, as when the kids send the Wolfman (now bright blue) not to the studio head's house as he expects, but to a birthday party, where the little guests joyfully cry, "Hey, it's the clown! Let's hurt him!"

Biggie & Tupac ★ ★ ★ ½
R, 107 m., 2002

A documentary directed by Nick Broomfield and produced by Michele D'Acosta. Featuring Tupac Shakur, Christopher ("Biggie Smalls," "Notorious B.I.G.") Wallace, and Suge Knight.

Nick Broomfield is the Geraldo Rivera of celebrity documentarians, plunging fearlessly into combat zones, protected only by his pluck, his boom mike, and his apparent cluelessness. Looking something like the guy who sidles up to you in Best Buy and offers advice on bug zappers, Broomfield persuades his subjects to say astonishing things on camera. His *Kurt and Courtney* (1998) more or less blamed Courtney Love for her husband's death; his *Heidi Fleiss: Hollywood Madam* (1996) argued that a Hollywood sleazehead named Ivan Nagy was the real villain and Heidi was the fall girl.

And now here is *Biggie & Tupac*, which claims to solve the murders of rap artists Tupac Shakur and Christopher Wallace (a.k.a Biggie Smalls, a.k.a. the Notorious B.I.G.). According to Broomfield, both killings were ordered and paid for by recording tycoon Suge Knight, and the hit men were off-duty Los Angeles police officers. He produces an eyewitness who names one of Tupac's killers, and a bag man willing to say, on camera, that he delivered the money for the Notorious B.I.G. hit. And in an astonishing sequence, he marches into a California prison and confronts the surprised Suge Knight on camera.

Before moving on to Broomfield's argument, it's worth lingering for a moment or two over that interview with Suge Knight. Knight is the millionaire boss of Death Row Records, has been known to post death threats on his Website, and is a big, intimidating man—so fearsome that Broomfield's photographer, the fellow documentarian Joan Churchill, refused to go into the prison with him, and he had to hire a freelancer for the day. A freelancer so nervous that at one crucial moment the camera was pointed at the clouds overhead.

Broomfield describes all of this in his voice-over track. His movies are, in a sense, about his experiences in making them. Appearing unannounced at the prison, his two-man band is unprepossessing: The sloppy Broomfield with a recorder slung over his shoulder and a boom mike in his hand, and the cameraman trailing nervously behind. A network crew would have required clearances, but maybe Broomfield looks harmless. He says he has an interview scheduled with Suge Knight, and the warden, who takes this at face value, nervously observes that "Mr. Knight" is on the phone.

Broomfield walks fearlessly up to Knight, who carries a mean-looking walking stick and has a couple of apparent bodyguards, and announces he is "here for the interview." What interview? "Your message to the kids," Broomfield brilliantly improvises. Knight, a media creature on autopilot, doesn't miss a beat in delivering his message ("Don't get in trouble because you can't afford high-powered lawyers like artists can"). Then Broomfield segues to Tupac and Biggie, predictably without success.

Tupac Shakur was said to be the leading rap artist of his time, and his work in *Gridlock'd* (1997) showed him as a talented actor. He was shot in Las Vegas in September 1996, while his car was in a motorcade following one containing Suge Knight. In March 1997, his rival Biggie Smalls was shot down outside a Los Angeles party.

Broomfield assembles a case charging that Shakur was ordered killed by Knight because the executive owed the singer unpaid royalties and had heard Shakur planned to jump to another record label. Then he ordered B.I.G.'s death in order to make the two murders seem like part of a fictitious East–West rap rivalry. The film observes that Suge Knight had thirty to forty LAPD officers on his payroll for off-duty bodyguard and other duties. And he produces an LAPD detective whose own investigation into the Shakur murder was stonewalled, leading to his resignation from the force. If nothing else, Broomfield proves that the LAPD bent over backward to avoid questioning the most obvious suspects.

There is another theory about the two murders, developed in a long *Los Angeles Times* investigation by Chuck Phillips, published September 6, 2002. His findings in a nutshell: Shakur was killed by the Crips street gang to avenge Shakur's beating of one of their members, and the gun used was supplied by Notorious B.I.G., who agreed to pay the Crips $1 million. As for B.I.G.'s death: It remains unresolved.

Whether either of these theories is correct is not my purpose to decide. What can be said is that *Biggie & Tupac* is compulsively watchable and endlessly inventive as it transforms Broomfield's limited materials into a compelling argument.

Broomfield himself is the star of the film, complaining about his gas mileage, forcing himself to listen to one of Tupac's tapes, complaining about his incompetent employees, confessing to fear as he walks into dangerous situations. There is something so disarming about the man as he persuades people to say things on camera that, presumably, could land them in trouble. That no trouble has resulted from those things being said seems to support his argument—that the killings were covered up within the LAPD and there is no interest, these days, in being inconvenienced by any additional facts. It goes without saying that the killings only enhanced the aura around rap music, encouraging other artists to adopt the popular gangsta image.

Big Trouble ★ ★ ½
PG-13, 84 m., 2002

Tim Allen (Eliot Arnold), Rene Russo (Anna Herk), Stanley Tucci (Arthur Herk), Tom Sizemore

(Snake), Patrick Warburton (Walter), Zooey Deschanel (Jenny Herk), Dennis Farina (Henry Algott), Omar Epps (Seitz), Heavy D (Greer), Jason Lee (Puggy), Janeane Garofalo (Monica Romero), Ben Foster (Matt Arnold). Directed by Barry Sonnenfeld and produced by Tom Jacobson, Barry Josephson, and Sonnenfeld. Screenplay by Robert Ramsey and Matthew Stone, based on the novel by Dave Barry.

Big Trouble is based on a novel by Dave Barry, and I have no trouble believing that. The genius of Dave Barry is that he applies a logical and helpful analysis to a situation that can only be worsened by such intervention. It is impossible, for example, to explain to a policeman why he is wasting his time on your illegal left turn while real criminals go free. Or to the IRS agent that Enron is robbing billions from widows and orphans while he ponders your business-related need to buy lots of CDs. Or to your wife why it is pointless to do the dishes on a daily basis when you can save hot water by letting them accumulate for a week in the dishwasher—which, being airtight, will not stink up the kitchen if you slam it right after adding more dishes.

All of these positions, which make perfect sense, only infuriate the cop, tax man, spouse, etc., by applying logic to a situation they have invested with irrational passion. As a sane voice in a world gone mad, Barry alone sees clearly. The Dave Barry figure in *Big Trouble,* I think, is Puggy (Jason Lee), a man who when he first addresses the camera seems to be Jesus, until he starts munching Fritos between his words of wisdom, observing, "You really can't beat these when they're fresh." Puggy is a homeless man who was living in the rainy north inside a cardboard box, when an article in *Martha Stewart's Living* inspired him to move to sunny southern Florida.

He is the film's omniscient narrator, not because he knows everything in a godlike way, but because he lives outdoors and happens to be ideally positioned during an evening when most of the film's other characters meet at the luxury home of Arthur Herk (Stanley Tucci), who is "one of the few Floridians who actually did vote for Pat Buchanan." (Saddened by the inability of many Republicans to express even

token pity about the Jewish senior citizens whose mistaken votes for the Great Foamer tilted the election, I am always happy to have this event recalled.)

Arthur Herk is . . . ah, but if I begin a plot synopsis, we will be here all day, and I have already squandered three paragraphs with fancy writing. There is a plot in *Big Trouble,* quite a logical one actually, with all the threads tied into neat knots at the end, but to explain it would leave you banging your forehead against the newspaper and crying, "Why must I know this?" It might be simpler to describe the characters and let you discover their interactions for yourself.

Herk is a rich man who owes money to the wrong people and wants to buy a bomb. Rene Russo is his wife, Anna, who no longer remembers why she married this jerk. Zooey Deschanel is their daughter Jenny, who is the target of Matt Arnold (Ben Foster), a school classmate who needs to squirt her with a one-gallon water gun. Tim Allen is Eliot Arnold, Matt's father, who was the two-time Pulitzer Prize–winning columnist of the *Miami Herald* until he kicked in the computer screen of an editor who gave him idiotic assignments while refusing to meet his eyes. (It would seem to the casual moviegoer that Eliot Arnold is the Dave Barry figure in the movie, since he closely resembles the author, but no, it's Puggy.)

Then there are Dennis Farina and Jack Kehler as two hit men assigned to kill Arthur Herk. And Janeane Garofalo and Patrick Warburton as two cops who answer a call to the Herk home. And Lars Arenta-Hansen and Daniel London, who have a nuclear bomb they can sell to Arthur Herk. And Omar Epps and Heavy D as FBI agents on the trail of the bomb sellers. And Sofia Vergara as Nina, the Herks's maid, whom Arthur wants to have sex with. She despises Herk, but instantly lusts for Puggy—another clue he is the Dave Barry character. And Tom Sizemore and Johnny Knoxville as Snake and Eddie, who try to stick up the bar where the bomb dealers meet Arthur Herk while the FBI stakes it out. (Sample dialogue: "Snake, let's get the hell out of here. I think I hear one of them silent alarms.") There is also a toad whose spit is hallucinogenic.

The film has been directed by Barry Sonnenfeld, who made *Get Shorty*. It's not in that class—indeed, it seems so crowded that it sometimes feels like the casting call for an eventual picture not yet made—but it has its charms. It's the kind of movie you can't quite recommend because it is all windup and not much of a pitch, yet you can't bring yourself to dislike it. A video or airplane or cable movie. Originally scheduled for an autumn opening, it was pulled from the release schedule after 9/11 because it involves terrorists and a nuclear bomb. But these are terrorists and bombs from a simpler and more innocent time. The movie is a reminder of an age when such plots were obviously not to be taken seriously. It is nice to be reminded of that time.

Biker Boyz ★ ★
PG-13, 111 m., 2003

Laurence Fishburne (Smoke), Derek Luke (Kid), Orlando Jones (Soul Train), Djimon Hounsou (Motherland), Lisa Bonet (Queenie), Brendan Fehr (Stuntman), Larenz Tate (Wood), Kid Rock (Dogg), Vanessa Bell Calloway (Anita), Eriq La Salle (Slick Will). Directed by Reggie Rock Bythewood and produced by Stephanie Allain, Gina Prince-Bythewood, and Erwin Stoff. Screenplay by Bythewood.

Biker Boyz has an idea, but not an approach. The idea comes from an article in the *Los Angeles New Times* about motorcycle clubs that meet for scheduled but illegal road races. The members are affluent enough to maintain expensive bikes (even mechanics are on the payroll) and polite enough that the movie's language slipped in under the ropes at PG-13.

Many but not all of the boys are African American; some are still literally boys but others are men in their forties, and the (unexplored) subtext is that these are successful men who enjoy the excitement of street racing. Not much mention is made of jobs, but you can't buy and maintain these machines without a good one.

We meet Smoke (Laurence Fishburne), longtime undefeated champion of street racing, and his mechanic Slick Will (Eriq La Salle). Slick's son is Kid (Derek Luke). Smoke's longtime fierce competitor is Dogg (Kid Rock).

Races involve money (bets to $5,000) and, even more significant, racing helmets: If you lose, you hand over your helmet to the guy who beat you.

All of this is intriguing material, but the movie doesn't do much with it. There are several races in the film, but they don't generate the kind of pulse-quickening suspense that the races did in *The Fast and the Furious,* a four-wheel street-racing picture. As a general rule the right people win for the right reasons, and during some of the races the spectators inexplicably cluster at the starting line, so there's time for soul-to-soul conversations at the finish line.

Some of those involve a secret revealed halfway through the film; stop reading now unless you want to learn that Kid's mother, Anita (Vanessa Bell Calloway), tells him, after the death of the man he thinks is his father, that Smoke is his real father. This leads to less trauma and more niceness than you might think, in a movie that is gentler and tamer than the ads might suggest. Even insults, when they are traded, seem more written than felt.

This is the third film I've seen Derek Luke in, after *Antwone Fisher* and the Sundance 2003 hit *Pieces of April.* It's his least significant role, and yet confirms his presence: He's a rising star, all right, with a particular way of holding back, as if sizing up a situation to find the best entry point. Like Denzel Washington, who cast him as Antwone, he'll spend most of his career playing nice guys. (Does he have a *Training Day* in him? I can't tell from here.)

Laurence Fishburne is a strong presence in the central role, but the character isn't very interesting; he's good at racing, he's not a bad man, he has few complexities. Vanessa Bell Calloway, a crucial woman in both men's lives, has a kind of sultry power that suggests if she ever got on a bike, she'd have all the helmets.

I think what happened here is that the filmmakers were fascinated by the original article, did some research that hooked them on this world, and then trusted the world would be enough to power the movie. It isn't. We need a stronger conflict, as we had in *The Fast and the Furious,* and better and more special effects (the crashes all seem to happen at a distance). The father–son scenes have an earnestness and sincerity that would be right in another kind of movie, but seem like sidebars to the main story.

Birthday Girl ★ ★
R, 93 m., 2002

Nicole Kidman (Nadia/Sofia), Ben Chaplin (John Buckingham), Vincent Cassel (Yuri), Mathieu Kassovitz (Alexei), Stephen Mangan (Bank Manager). Directed by Jez Butterworth and produced by Eric Abraham, Steve Butterworth, and Diana Phillips. Screenplay by Jez Butterworth and Tom Butterworth.

Anyone who orders a mail-order bride over the Internet deserves more or less who he gets. The bride may or may not be looking forward to a lifetime as a loving and devoted spouse, but she is certainly looking forward to an air ticket, a visa, and citizenship in a Western democracy. Would-be husbands who do not understand this probably believe that beautiful women gladly offer themselves sight unseen to men merely because they have mastered such skills as logging on, typing, and possessing a credit card.

Yet hope springs eternal. John Buckingham (Ben Chaplin), a bank teller in a small British town, is a lonely guy who clicks forlornly on the photos of Russian mail-order brides and finally orders Nadia, who says she is tall, blonde, speaks English, and is a nonsmoker. When, at the airport, Nadia turns out to look exactly like Nicole Kidman, you would think John might be satisfied. But no: She is tall, all right, but she is a chain-smoker, speaks no English, and throws up out the car window. He tests her language skills in a brief conversation: "Are you a giraffe?" "Yes."

John calls the marriage agency to complain. He wants to return Nadia and get himself a nonsmoking English speaker. Nadia keeps smiling, discovers his secret horde of porn magazines and videos, and cheerfully reenacts some of the scenarios she finds there. Soon John is beginning to reevaluate his consumer complaint.

So goes the setup for *Birthday Girl*, a comedy that starts out lightheartedly and makes some unexpected turns, especially after Nadia's two alleged cousins arrive from Russia. Yuri and Alexei, played by those two hard-edged French actors Vincent Cassel and Mathieu Kassovitz, reminded me of Emil and Oleg, the two Russians who turn up in *15 Minutes*, with the difference that they are not quite as ambitious and sinister; it appears at first they are basically after a free lunch.

There is a curious problem with *Birthday Girl*, hard to put your finger on: The movie is kind of sour. It wants to be funny and a little nasty, it wants to surprise us and then console us, but what it mostly does is make us restless. Strange, how the personalities of characters can refuse to match the work laid out for them by the script. I did not much like anyone in the movie, not even poor John Buckingham, and as for Nadia, she has to go through so many twists and turns that finally we don't know what to believe, nor do we much care.

The movie's downfall is to substitute plot for personality. It doesn't really know or care about the characters, and uses them as markers for a series of preordained events. Since these events take us into darker places than we expect, and then pull us back out again with still more arbitrary plotting, we lose interest; these people do not seem plausible, and we feel toyed with. Even the funny moments feel like nothing more than—well, the filmmakers inventing funny moments.

Black Hawk Down ★ ★ ★ ★
R, 143 m., 2002

Josh Hartnett (Eversmann), Ewan McGregor (Grimes), Tom Sizemore (McKnight), Eric Bana (Hoot), William Fichtner (Sanderson), Ewen Bremner (Nelson), Sam Shepard (Garrison), Gabriel Casseus (Kurth), Kim Coates (Wex). Directed by Ridley Scott and produced by Jerry Bruckheimer and Scott. Screenplay by Ken Nolan and Steve Zaillian, based on the book by Mark Bowden.

Ridley Scott's *Black Hawk Down* tells the story of a U.S. military raid that went disastrously wrong when optimistic plans ran into unexpected resistance. In Mogadishu, Somalia, in October 1993, eighteen Americans lost their lives, seventy more were wounded, and within days President Bill Clinton pulled out troops that were on a humanitarian mission. By then some 300,000 Somalians had died of starvation, and the U.S. purpose was to help deliver UN food shipments. Somalian warlords were more interested in protecting their turf than feeding their people—an early warning of the kind of zeal that led to September 11.

The movie is single-minded in its purpose. It wants to record as accurately as possible what it was like to be one of the soldiers under fire on that mission. Hour by hour, step by step, it reconstructs the chain of events. The plan was to stage a surprise raid by helicopter-borne troops, joined by ground forces, on a meeting of a warlord's top lieutenants. This was thought to be such a straightforward task that some soldiers left behind their canteens and night vision gear, expecting to be back at the base in a few hours. It didn't work out that way.

What happened is that enemy rockets brought down two of the helicopters. The warlord's troops gathered quickly and surrounded the U.S. positions. Roadblocks and poor communications prevented a support convoy from approaching. And a grim firefight became a war of attrition. The Americans gave better than they got, but from any point of view the U.S. raid was a catastrophe. The movie's implied message was that America on that day lost its resolve to risk American lives in distant and obscure struggles, and that mind-set weakened our stance against terrorism.

The engagement itself seems to have degenerated into bloody chaos. Ridley Scott's achievement is to render it comprehensible to the audience. We understand, more or less, where the Americans are, and why, and what their situation is. We follow several leading characters, but this is not a star-driven project and doesn't depend on dialogue or personalities. It is about the logistics of that day in October, and how training did help those expert fighters (Army Rangers and Delta Force) to defend themselves as well as possible when all the plans went wrong and they were left hanging out to dry.

His longest day begins with a briefing by Major General William F. Garrison (Sam Shepard), who explains how intelligence has discovered the time and location of a meeting by lieutenants of the warlord Mohamed Farah

Aidid. A taxi with a white cross on its roof will park next to the building to guide the airborne troops, who will drop down on ropes, be joined by ground forces, secure the building, and take prisoners. The problem with this plan, as Garrison discovers in steadily more discouraging feedback, is that the opposition is better armed, better positioned, and able to call on quick reinforcements.

We follow several stories. A man falls from a helicopter and is injured when he misses his descent rope. A pilot is taken prisoner. Desperate skirmishes unfold in streets and rubble as darkness falls. The Americans are short on ammo and water, facing enemies not particularly shy about exposing themselves to danger.

Black Hawk Down doesn't have heroic foreground figures like most war movies. The leading characters are played by stars who will be familiar to frequent moviegoers, but may be hard to tell apart for others. They include Josh Hartnett, much more convincing here than in *Pearl Harbor*, as a staff sergeant in command of one of the raiding teams; Ewan McGregor as a Ranger specialist whose specialties are paperwork and coffee making until he is pressed into service; Tom Sizemore as a veteran who provides steady counsel for younger troops; and William Fichtner as a fighter who seems to have internalized every shred of training, and embodies it instinctively.

The cinematography by Slawomir Idziak avoids the bright colors of upbeat combat movies, and its drab, dusty tones gradually drain of light as night falls. The later scenes of the movie feel chilly and forlorn; the surrounded troops are alone and endangered in the night. The screenplay by Ken Nolan and Steve Zaillian, working from a book by Mark Bowden, understands the material and tells it so clearly and efficiently that we are involved not only in the experience of the day but also in its strategies and unfolding realities.

Films like this are more useful than gung ho capers like *Behind Enemy Lines*. They help audiences understand and sympathize with the actual experiences of combat troops, instead of trivializing them into entertainments. Although the American mission in Somalia was humanitarian, the movie avoids speechmaking and sloganeering, and at one point, discussing why soldiers risk their lives in situations like this, a veteran says, "It's about the men next to you. That's all it is."

Blade II ★ ★ ★ ½
R, 110 m., 2002

Wesley Snipes (Blade), Kris Kristofferson (Whistler), Ron Perlman (Reinhardt), Luke Goss (Nomak), Leonor Varela (Nyssa), Matt Schulze (Chupa), Norman Reedus (Scud). Directed by Guillermo del Toro and produced by Peter Frankfurt and Patrick Palmer. Screenplay by David S. Goyer.

Blade II is a really rather brilliant vomitorium of viscera, a comic book with dreams of becoming a textbook for mad surgeons. There are shots here of the insides of vampires that make your average autopsy look like a slow afternoon at Supercuts. The movie has been directed by Guillermo del Toro, whose work is dominated by two obsessions: war between implacable ancient enemies, and sickening things that bite you and aren't even designed to let go.

The movie is an improvement on *Blade* (1998), which was pretty good. Once again it stars Wesley Snipes as the Marvel Comics hero who is half-man, half-vampire. He was raised from childhood by Whistler (Kris Kristofferson), a vampire hunter who kept Blade's vampirism in check, and trained him to fight the nosferatus. Time has passed, Whistler has been captured by vampires and floats unconscious in a storage tank while his blood is harvested, and Blade prowls the streets in his lonely war.

One night, acrobatic creatures with glowing red eyes invade Blade's space and engage in a violent battle that turns out to be entirely gratuitous, because after they remove their masks to reveal themselves as vampires—a ferocious warrior and a foxy babe—they only want to deliver a message: "You have been our worst enemy. But now there is something else on the streets worse than you!" This reminded me of the night in O'Rourke's when McHugh asked this guy why he carried a gun and the guy said he lived in a dangerous neighborhood and McHugh said it would be safer if he moved.

The Vampire Nation is under attack by a new breed of vampires named Reapers, who drink the blood of both humans and vampires, and are insatiable. Blade, who is both human and vampire, is like a balanced meal. If the Reapers are not destroyed, both races will die. This news is conveyed by a vampire leader whose brain can be dimly seen through a light blue, translucent plastic shell, more evidence of the design influence of the original iMac.

Blade and Whistler (now rescued from the tank and revived with a "retro-virus injection") join the vampires in this war, which is not without risk, because of course if the Reapers are destroyed, the vampires will turn on them. There is a story line, however quickly sketched, to support the passages of pure action, including computer-aided fight scenes of astonishing pacing and agility. Snipes once again plays Blade not as a confident superhero, but as a once-confused kid who has been raised to be good at his work and uncertain about his identity. He is attracted to the vampire Nyssa (Leonor Varela), but we sense a relationship between a creature of the night and Blade, known as the Daywalker, is sooner or later going to result in arguments over their work schedules.

The Reapers are the masterpieces of this movie. They all have what looks like a scar down the center of their chins. The first time we see one, it belongs to a donor who has turned up at a blood bank in Prague. This is not the kind of blood bank you want to get your next transfusion from. It has a bug zapper hanging from the wall, and an old drunk who says you can even bring in cups of blood from outside and they'll buy them.

The chin scar, it turns out, is not a scar but a cleft. These Reapers are nasty. They have mouths that unfold into tripartite jaws. Remember the claws on the steam shovels in those prize games at the carnival, where you manipulated the wheels and tried to pick up valuable prizes? Now put them on a vampire and make them big and bloody, with fangs and mucous and viscous black saliva. And then imagine a tongue coiled inside with an eating and sucking mechanism on the end of it that looks like the organ evolution forgot— the sort of thing diseased livers have nightmares about. Later they slice open a Reaper's chest cavity and Blade and Whistler look inside.

Blade: The heart is surrounded in bone! Whistler: Good luck getting a stake through it!

Del Toro's early film *Cronos* (1993) was about an ancient golden beetle that sank its claws into the flesh of its victims and injected an immortality serum. His *Mimic* (1997) was about a designer insect, half-mantis, half-termite, that escapes into the subway system and mutates into a very big bug. Characters would stick their hands into dark places and I would slide down in my seat. His *The Devil's Backbone* (2001), set in an orphanage at the time of the Spanish civil war, is a ghost story, not a horror picture, but does have a body floating in a tank.

Still in his thirties, the Mexican-born director doesn't depend on computers to get him through a movie and impress the kids with fancy fight scenes. He brings his creepy phobias along with him. You can sense the difference between a movie that's a technical exercise *(Resident Evil)* and one steamed in the dread cauldrons of the filmmaker's imagination.

Blood Work ★ ★ ★ ½

R, 111 m., 2002

Clint Eastwood (Terry McCaleb), Wanda De Jesus (Graciella Rivers), Jeff Daniels (Buddy Noone), Anjelica Huston (Dr. Bonnie Fox), Tina Lifford (Detective Jaye Winston), Paul Rodriguez (Detective Arrango), Dylan Walsh (Waller). Directed and produced by Clint Eastwood. Screenplay by Brian Helgeland, based on the novel by Michael Connelly.

Clint Eastwood's *Blood Work* opens with an FBI agent of retirement age chasing a killer and collapsing of a heart attack. Two years later, we meet him living on a boat in a marina, with another person's heart in his chest. A woman asks him to investigate the murder of her sister. He says he is finished with police work. Then she shows him her sister's photograph, and softly adds a personal reason why he might want to help.

Unlike some action stars who want to remain supermen forever, Eastwood has paid attention to his years and found stories to exploit them. *Space Cowboys* (2000) was about proud

old astronauts called out of retirement. In *Absolute Power* (1997), accused of climbing a rope to an upper window, he says he'll have to tell that one at his next AARP meeting. In *Blood Work*, he plays Terry McCaleb, a man conscious of his mortality at every moment; all during the movie, other characters tell him how bad he looks.

McCaleb shouldn't be doing police work. His doctor (Anjelica Huston) threatens to stop seeing him if he doesn't slow down. But from the moment he sees the photograph, and meets the dead woman's little boy, and looks in the eyes of her sister, he has no choice.

The movie is not simply a sentimental revenge picture, however, but a police procedural that leads us into an intriguing investigation. Based on a novel by Michael Connelly, the movie is like one of those Ed McBain stories in which the facts add up but make no sense until the key is supplied in a sudden observation.

Before his retirement, McCaleb was on the trail of a man named the Code Killer. Now there seems to be a similar serial killer operating in Los Angeles, one with a particular interest in McCaleb. "Catch me, McCaleb," he writes on a mirror (a nice echo of *Call Northside 777*). The investigation takes McCaleb to distant corners of Los Angeles County, and involves a friendly L.A. cop (Tina Lifford) and her hostile partner (Paul Rodriguez). Because he doesn't want to drive so soon after heart transplant surgery, Eastwood hires a neighbor at the marina (Jeff Daniels) as an assistant. And gradually he grows closer to Graciella (Wanda De Jesus), the dead woman's sister, and to the little boy.

The film establishes a muted, elegiac tone in its early scenes, and sticks to it. There is no false bravado. Terry McCaleb is not a well man, he sometimes touches his chest wonderingly, he develops a fever. But the logic of the chase is a relentless goad, and he pushes on. His health adds an additional dimension to the movie, inspiring a concern in Graciella that eventually, but very slowly, leads to love.

The strength of the picture, directed by Eastwood, is that it has three intersecting story arcs: the investigation, the health issues, and the relationship that builds, step by step. Almost every scene involves one of these concerns, and the screenplay by Brian Helgeland (*L.A. Confidential*) moves smoothly between them, so that we develop an unusual degree of personal interest in McCaleb; he isn't just the hero of a thriller, but a man with human qualities we grow concerned about.

There is action and violence in *Blood Work*, but not the pumped-up, computer-aided pyrotechnics of so many summer thrillers. Here the action involves people, and the things that people can do. A final confrontation aboard two boats is handled in a way that makes the action seem difficult—but like hard physical labor, not martial arts gymnastics.

And when the movie was all over, what I cared about most was the love between Terry and Graciella. Wanda De Jesus is an actress who has done a lot of television work, but her film work has usually been limited to secondary supporting roles. Here she is crucial to the success of the picture. She avoids all temptations to leap into romance, she plays her scenes not as the hero's sidekick but as a dead woman's sister, and there is such a tenderness in the way she eventually starts to regard Terry that when finally they acknowledge how they feel, it isn't a plot point but an actual emotional transition that feels right and warm.

Clint Eastwood has directed himself in twenty movies, and that may represent the most consistent director-actor relationship in modern movies. He knows himself, he knows his craft; his pride as a director is dominant over his ego as an actor, and the results are films that use a star aura with an uncommon degree of intimacy. Terry McCaleb is one of Eastwood's best characters because, in a way, he's not a new character at all but just the same guy further down the road.

Bloody Sunday ★ ★ ★ ½
R, 107 m., 2002

James Nesbitt (Ivan Cooper), Tim Pigott-Smith (Major General Ford), Nicholas Farrell (Brigadier Maclellan), Gerard McSorley (Chief Superintendant Lagan), Kathy Keira Clarke (Frances), Allan Gildea (Kevin McCorry), Gerard Crossan (Eamonn McCann), Bernadette Devlin (Mary Moulds). Directed by Paul Greengrass and produced by Arthur Lappin and Mark

Redhead. Screenplay by Greengrass, based on the book by Don Mullan.

Both sides agree that on January 30, 1972, a civil rights march in Derry, Northern Ireland, ended with a confrontation between some of the marchers and British Army paratroopers. At the end of the day, thirteen marchers were dead and thirteen in hospital, one of whom later died. No British soldiers were killed. An official inquiry declared that the soldiers had returned the fire of armed marchers. Some of the soldiers involved were later decorated by the Crown.

Beyond this agreement, there is a disagreement so deep and bitter that thirty years later, Bloody Sunday is still an open wound in the long, contested history of the British in Northern Ireland. A new inquiry into the events of the day was opened in 1998, and continued at the time of the film.

Paul Greengrass's film *Bloody Sunday,* which shared the Golden Bear at the Berlin Film Festival this year, is made in the form of a documentary. It covers about twenty-four hours, starting on Saturday evening, and its central character is Ivan Cooper (James Nesbitt), a civil rights leader in Derry. He was a Protestant MP from the nationalist Social Democratic Labour Party. Most of the 10,000 marchers on that Sunday would be Catholic; that a Protestant led them, and stood beside such firebrands as Bernadette Devlin, indicates the division in the north between those who stood in solidarity with their coreligionists, and those of all faiths who simply wanted the British out of Northern Ireland.

Cooper is played by Nesbitt as a thoroughly admirable man, optimistic, tireless, who walks fearlessly through dangerous streets and has a good word for everyone. He knows the day's march has been banned by the British government, but expects no trouble because it will be peaceful and nonviolent. As Cooper hands out leaflets in the streets, Greengrass intercuts preparations by the British Army, which from the top down is determined to make a strong stand against "hooliganism." More than two dozen British soldiers have been killed by the Provisional IRA in recent months, and this is a chance to crack down.

Greengrass also establishes a few other characters, including a young man who kisses his girlfriend good-bye and promises his mother no harm will come to him—always ominous signs in a movie. And we meet the Derry police chief (Gerard McSorley), who is alarmed by the fierce resolve of the soldiers and asks, not unreasonably, if it wouldn't be wiser to simply permit the march, since it is obviously going to proceed anyway.

Greengrass re-creates events with stunning reality. (When he shows a movie marquee advertising *Sunday Bloody Sunday* it's a small glitch, because it seems like a calculated shot in a movie that feels like cinema verité). He is aided by the presence of thousands of extras, who volunteered to be in the movie (some of them marched on Bloody Sunday and are in a way playing themselves). Northern Ireland is still a tinderbox where this film could not possibly be made; streets in a poor area of Dublin were used.

Cooper and the other leaders are on the bed of a truck that leads the column of marchers, and from their vantage point we can see that when the march turns right, away from the army's position, some hot-headed marchers turn left and begin to throw rocks at the soldiers. In the army's HQ, where Major General Ford (Tim Pigott-Smith) is in charge, an order is given to respond firmly. Communications are confused, orders are distorted as they pass down the chain of command, and soon rubber bullets and gas grenades are replaced by the snap of real bullets.

Greengrass shows marchers trying to restrain a few of their fellows who are armed. His film is clear, however, in its belief that the British fired first and in cold blood, and he shows one wounded marcher being executed with a bullet in the back. One of the marchers is apparently inspired by Gerald Donaghey, whose case became famous. After being wounded, he was searched twice, once by doctors, and then taken to an army area where he died. Soldiers then found nail bombs in his pockets that had been "overlooked" in two previous searches. For Greengrass, this is part of a desperate attempt by the army to plant evidence and justify a massacre.

Of course there are two sides to the story of Bloody Sunday, although the score (Army 14,

Marchers 0) is significant. The Greengrass view reflects both the theories and the anger of the anti-British factions, and the army's smugness after being cleared in the original investigation was only inflammatory. *Bloody Sunday* is one view of what happened that day, a very effective one. And as an act of filmmaking, it is superb: A sense of immediate and present reality permeates every scene.

Note: The official Website of the inquiry into Bloody Sunday is at www.bloody-sunday-inquiry.org.uk. Thomas Kinsella's famous poem about the day, "Butcher's Dozen," is at www.usm.maine.edu/~mcgrath/poems/butchrs.htm.

Blow ★ ★ ½
R, 119 m., 2001

Johnny Depp (George Jung), Penelope Cruz (Mirtha), Franka Potente (Barbara), Paul Reubens (Derek Foreal), Ray Liotta (Fred Jung), Jacque Lawson (Biker), Cliff Curtis (Pablo Escobar), Ethan Suplee (Tuna), Rachel Griffiths (Ermine Jung). Directed by Ted Demme and produced by Demme, Denis Leary, and Joel Stillerman. Screenplay by David McKenna and Nick Cassavetes, based on the book by Bruce Porter.

Blow stars Johnny Depp in a biopic about George Jung, a man who claims that in the late 1970s he imported about 85 percent of all the cocaine in America. That made him the greatest success story in drugs, an industry that has inspired more movies than any other. So why is he such a sad sack? Why is his life so monotonous and disappointing? That's what he'd like to know. The last shot in the film shows the real George Jung staring out at us from the screen like a man buried alive in his own regrets.

The story begins in a haze of California dreamin' for George, who escapes West from an uninspiring Massachusetts childhood, a relentless mother (Rachel Griffiths), and a father (Ray Liotta) who doesn't want to deal with bad news about his son. In the Los Angeles environs of Manhattan Beach, George smokes pot, throws Frisbees, meets stewardesses, and engages in boozy plans with his friend Tuna (Ethan Suplee), who asks him, "You know how we were wondering how we were gonna get money being that we don't want to get jobs?"

The brainstorm: Import marijuana from Mexico in the customs-free luggage of their stewardess pals and sell it to eager students at eastern colleges. This is a business plan waiting to be born, and soon George is wealthy, although not beyond his wildest imaginings. His first love is a stewardess named Barbara (Franka Potente, from *Run, Lola, Run*) and it's fun, fun, fun, and her daddy never takes her T-Bird away.

These opening chapters in the life of George Jung tell a story of small risk and great joy, especially if your idea of a good time is having all the money you can possibly spend and hopelessly conventional ideas about how to spend it. How big a house can you live in? How many drugs can you consume? George never actually planned to become a drug dealer and is a little bemused at his good luck. Even a 1972 bust in Chicago seems like a minor bump in the road (speaking in his own defense, he tells the judge, "It ain't me, babe").

Back on the streets, George finds clouds obscuring the California sun. Barbara dies unexpectedly (i.e., not because of drugs), and his success attracts the interest of a better class of narcotics cop. He becomes a fugitive, and it is his own mother who rats on him with the cops, even while his father is beaming at what might seem to be his success.

In Danbury Prison, he tells us, "I went in with a bachelor's of marijuana and came out with a doctorate in cocaine." As the 1970s roll on, the innocence of pot has been replaced by the urgency of cocaine. Soon George is making real money as a key distributor for his new friend Pablo Escobar (Cliff Curtis) and the Medellin drug cartel of Colombia. It's with their cocaine that he racks up his record market share. And there is a new woman, Mirtha (Penelope Cruz), sexy as hell, but a real piece of work in the deportment department. At one point she gets him arrested by throwing a tantrum in their car.

The Colombians, of course, are heavy-hitters, and George tries to protect his position by concealing the identity of his key California middleman, a onetime hairdresser named Derek Foreal (Paul Reubens). But the Colombians want to know that name really bad, and

meanwhile George might be asking, is a rich man under the shadow of sudden death measurably happier than a man with a more mundane but serene existence?

This is not, alas, a question that occurs to George Jung. Indeed, not many questions occur to him that are not directly related to getting, spending, and sleeping with. The later chapters of his life grow increasingly depressing. He was never an interesting person, never had thoughts worth sharing or words worth remembering, but at least he represented a colorful type in his early years: the kid who smokes a little weed, finds a source, starts to sell, and finds himself with a brand-new pair of roller skates. By his middle years, George is essentially just the guy the Colombians want to replace and the feds want to arrest. No fun.

The dreary story of his final defeats is a record of backstabbing and broken trusts, and although there is a certain poignancy in his final destiny, it is tempered by our knowledge that millions of lives had to be destroyed by addiction so that George and his onetime friends could arrive at their crossroads.

That's the thing about George. He thinks it's all about him. His life, his story, his success, his fortune, his lost fortune, his good luck, his bad luck. Actually, all he did was operate a tollgate between suppliers and addicts. You wonder, but you never find out, if the reality of those destroyed lives ever occurred to him.

The movie, directed by Ted Demme and written by David McKenna and Nick Cassavetes (from an as-told-to book by Bruce Porter), is well made and well acted. As a story of the rise and fall of this man, it serves. Johnny Depp is a versatile and reliable actor who almost always chooses interesting projects. The failure is George Jung's. For all the glory of his success and the pathos of his failure, he never became a person interesting enough to make a movie about. The appearance of Ray Liotta here reminds us of Scorsese's *GoodFellas*, which took a much less important criminal and made him an immeasurably more interesting character. And of course Al Pacino's *Scarface* has so much style he makes George Jung look like a dry-goods clerk. Which essentially he was. Take away the drugs, and this is the story of a boring life in wholesale.

The Blue Angel ★ ★ ★ ½

NO MPAA RATING, 106 m., 1929 (rereleased 2001)

Emil Jannings (Professor Immanuel Rath), Marlene Dietrich (Lola Lola), Kurt Gerron (Kiepert, the Magician), Rosa Valetti (Guste, His Wife), Hans Albers (Mazeppa, the Strong Man), Reinhold Bernt (The Clown), Eduard von Winterstein (The Headmaster), Hans Roth (The Caretaker), Rolf Muller (Angst [Rath's Pupil]). Directed by Josef von Sternberg and produced by Erich Pommer. Screenplay by Robert Liebmann, Karl Vollmoeller, and Carl Zuckmayer, based on the novel *Professor Unrat* by Heinrich Mann.

The Blue Angel will always have a place in film history as the movie that brought Marlene Dietrich to international stardom. At the time it was made, at the birth of the sound era in 1929, it was seen as a vehicle for Emil Jannings, the German actor who had just won the first Academy Award for Best Actor (for both *The Last Command* and *The Way of All Flesh*) after starring in such silent landmarks as *The Last Laugh* and *Faust*. Dietrich's overnight stardom inspired distributors to recut the film, ending it with one of her songs instead of his pathetic closing moments, and this restored version shows the entire film for the first time in years.

Even then there is a choice to be made. Jannings and his director, Josef von Sternberg, had established themselves in the silent era, when films knew no language barriers, and they shot the film in both English and German. This is the English version, with Dietrich and Jannings fluent (the Swiss Jannings claimed, falsely, that he had been born in Brooklyn), but many prefer the German version because the actors feel more at home with the dialogue.

Whatever its language, *The Blue Angel* looks and feels more like a silent film, with its broad performances that underline emotions. Von Sternberg, who was raised in Europe and America and began his career in Hollywood, was much influenced by German expressionism, as we see in early street scenes where the buildings tilt toward each other at crazy angles reminiscent of *The Cabinet of Dr. Caligari.* He was a bold visual artist who liked shots where the actors shared space with foreground props and dramatic shadows, and he makes the dressing room beneath the stage of the Blue Angel nightclub into a haunting psychic dungeon.

Lotte Eisner observes in *The Haunted Screen,* her study of German expressionism, that Sternberg was more at ease with sound than many of his contemporaries (this was his second talkie), and was perhaps the first director to deal with how offstage sounds alter as doors are opened and closed. Sound itself was seen as self-sufficient in the earlier days, but von Sternberg was already modulating it, tilting it toward realism.

His story involves the fall and humiliation of Professor Immanuel Rath (Jannings), a respected high school professor who one day confiscates a postcard showing Lola Lola (Dietrich), the dancer at a local nightclub. Visiting the club to reprimand any students he might find there, the professor falls under the spell of Dietrich, who looks fleshier and more carnal than she later appeared. Soon he is lost. He marries her (in a showbiz wedding of grotesque toasts and whispered gossip), goes on the road, and returns to his hometown some years later as a bit player in her stage show—the stooge of a magician who produces eggs from the professor's nose and cracks them on the old man's head.

Jannings specialized in roles where he was humiliated; *The Last Laugh,* where he plays a proud hotel doorman who loses his position, is the most famous. His performance in *The Blue Angel* is odd; he plays a high school teacher and is presumably intelligent, yet his thoughts and actions seem slowed-down and laborious, as if he's puzzling things out as he goes along. Dietrich had made seven silent films before this one, but seems to adapt easily to the quickened pace of talkies, and of course her stardom depended on sound; her singing of "Falling in Love Again" in this film established it as her trademark. (Three years later, in von Sternberg's *Shanghai Express,* she would utter that masterpiece of understatement, "It took more than one man to change my name to Shanghai Lily.")

The puzzle throughout *The Blue Angel* is why Lola Lola marries the sad, besotted professor. It appears they have a sex life, at least for one night, although it is not appealing to imagine its nature. There are times when she seems fond of him, times when she is indifferent, times when she is unfaithful, and yet she has a certain stubborn affection for this pathetic figure. Perhaps he acts as a front for her shadow life of discreet prostitution; perhaps, in a world that regards her as a tramp, she values the one man who idealizes her.

Dietrich, in any event, never seemed to embody romance; the sexual identity she offered, in film after film, was that of a predator, disillusioned by men, satisfying her physical needs but indifferent to their providers. She seems to have all of the equipment of a woman except for the instruction manual, and it's interesting that Dietrich is a favorite role for female impersonators, in movies like *The Damned* and in life; if you are a man who wants to play a woman, Dietrich meets you halfway.

The Blue Angel lumbers a little on its way to a preordained conclusion, but is intriguing for its glimpses of backstage life in shabby German prewar vaudeville, and for Dietrich's performance, which seems to float above the action as if she's stepping fastidiously across gutters. The final humiliation of the professor is agonizing and protracted, and Siegfried Kracauer, in his study *From Caligari to Hitler,* found it one more example of the way German movies mirrored their society in humiliating intellectuals and glorifying the physical. You can glimpse the sadomasochism of the Nazi pose in the strange relationship of Professor Rath and Lola Lola.

Blue Car ★ ★ ★ ½
R, 96 m., 2003

David Strathairn (Auster), Agnes Bruckner (Meg), Margaret Colin (Diane), Regan Arnold (Lily), Frances Fisher (Delia). Directed by Karen Moncrieff and produced by Peer J. Oppenheimer, Amy Sommer, and David Waters. Screenplay by Moncrieff.

Blue Car watches with horror as a vulnerable teenage girl falls into the emotional trap set by her high school English teacher. The teacher watches with horror, too: He knows what he is doing is wrong, but he is weak, and pities himself more than the sad girl he is exploiting. Step by step, they move in a direction only he understands.

The girl is named Meg (Agnes Bruckner). She is beautiful, and her teacher knows that with a desperate urgency. He is Auster (David Strathairn), who poses in the classroom as a stern but inspiring romantic. Meg reads a poem one day about how her father left her family. Auster asks her to stay after class, tells her she can reach deeper, asks her to find more truth. "We need a map of your nerve centers," he says. He thinks maybe the poem is good enough to get her into a poetry competition in Florida.

Meg's home life is in turmoil. Her mother, Diane (Margaret Colin), is distant and overworked, attending night school, complaining that her ex-husband is behind on his payments. Meg is baby-sitter and substitute mother for her kid sister, Lily (Regan Arnold), who is seriously disturbed and sometimes cuts herself.

Auster's approach to Meg is subtle and guarded. He flatters her with his attention. He maintains his authority and seems to keep his distance, but somehow she is sharing his sandwich at the noon hour and getting a ride home in his car. And then, when a family tragedy occurs, Auster comforts her a degree too eagerly.

This teacher is a piece of work. He knows that an open appeal to Meg would be rejected, that she would be creeped out by his lust. But by maintaining a position of power and then overpraising her work, he gets inside her defenses. Her poem is a good poem, but not that good. Sometimes he reads to her from his novel in progress, which sounds like subpar Thomas Wolfe but is as much a fraud as the rest of him. Notice the cruelty in the scene where he gives her a little speech about how we can't all be winners all of the time, and then, after she thinks she has lost the poetry competition, tells her she is a winner.

We see a bright, sad, lonely girl with absent parents, drifting into danger. She thinks she may be able to get a ride to Florida with a friend's family. That falls through. She takes the bus, sleeps on the beach, turns up for the competition, and even finds Auster on the beach, sunning with his wife (Frances Fisher) and son. Fisher has a brief scene, but it is played with acute observation. Watch the way she sizes up Meg and immediately reads her husband's intentions.

Blue Car, written and directed by Karen

Moncrieff, is wise in the way it follows the progress of the story. Auster wants to have sex with Meg, but it must be within the twisted terms of his own compromised morality. She must in some sense seem to agree to it. I will leave it to you to witness how this scenario plays out, and to observe the sadness with which he pursues his pathetic goal.

The ending of the film is as calculated and cruel as a verbal assault by a Neil LaBute character. In a few merciless words and an unmistakable implication, Meg fights back. The story has its basis in everyday realism. The teacher is made not a stereotyped monster but a pathetic and weak one. The girl is not a sexpot nor childishly naive, but distracted and deceived. Moncrieff doesn't exploit the situation, but deplores it.

Bruckner, an eighteen-year-old veteran of soap opera and four smaller feature roles, negotiates this difficult script with complete conviction. Strathairn's role is even trickier, because Moncrieff doesn't want to make him into a stereotyped molester, but wants to show how he is about to manipulate himself into a situation where it seems, because he wants it to seem, that the girl accepts him. He is rotten in an everyday way, not in a horror movie way—and that makes him much more frightening.

Because the movie is an honest and forthright drama about a teenager in danger, of course the MPAA has rated it R. That despite the fact that it contains no nudity, no explicit sex, and only ordinary adolescent language. The theory of the ratings board, apparently, is that all manner of vulgarity and pop violence is suitable for those under seventeen, but any movie that addresses the actual conditions of teenage life must be off-limits. What the MPAA standards amount to is: Let students learn about sexual predators in their lives, not in the movies. *Blue Car* is a valuable cautionary tale.

Blue Collar Comedy Tour: The Movie
★ ★ ★
PG-13, 105 m., 2003

Featuring Jeff Foxworthy, Bill Engvall, Ron White, Larry the Cable Guy, Heidi Klum, and David Allen Grier. A documentary directed by C. B. Harding and produced by Alan C. Blomquist, Casey LaScala, Joseph Williams, Hunt Lowry, and J. P. Williams.

Jeff Foxworthy, the "you know you're a redneck" guy, was ice-fishing in Minnesota once and started thinking of the experience from the point of view of the fish.

"Suppose you get caught and you're thrown back in. What do you tell your buddies? 'Man, I had an out-of-the-body experience. I was just minding my own business, living my life, when suddenly I felt myself under the control of a powerful force. I was drawn up toward the light. I went through a hole in the sky and found myself surrounded by all my dead relatives. And God was wearing a flannel shirt and a Budweiser hat.'"

The humor in that story is typical of all four performers in *Blue Collar Comedy Tour: The Movie,* a concert film starring Foxworthy, Bill Engvall, Ron White, and Larry the Cable Guy. I am informed that their national tour, just closing after four years, is the most successful in history, although whose history is not specified, and all tours say that. Certainly they're popular, and this film, which is kind of a redneck version of *The Original Kings of Comedy,* is the way to see them without having to find your car in the middle of all the pickups in the parking lot.

White and Cable Guy are the warm-ups, Foxworthy and Engvall are the stars, and then all four come on stage to share stories and listen to Foxworthy's redneck litany. ("If the wedding rehearsal dinner is at Hooter's—you know you're a redneck.") His uncle is such a NASCAR fan, he always gets into his car through the window.

But there I go, stealing his material. How do you review a movie like this without reprinting the jokes? The film consists of four concert segments, larded with "documentary" footage of the four buddies fishing, visiting Victoria's Secret, etc. The concert stuff is consistently funny, good-humored, and surprisingly clean; there's a lot more bathroom humor than sex or profanity, and the PG-13 rating is probably about right.

I do have some doubts about the other stuff. When they go shopping for underwear at Victoria's Secret, the sales clerk is played by supermodel Heidi Klum, which clues us that it's a setup and probably halfway scripted. What's the point? Why not let the boys walk into a real Victoria's Secret and start filming and see what happens? I was also a little puzzled by the role played by David Allen Grier, as the chauffeur and valet. Why have a recognizable star and not make any use of him?

These are minor quibbles. The underlying secret of the four comedians is the way they find humor in daily life, and in their families. In this they're a lot like the Kings of Comedy, and Engvall (the "here's your sign" guy) gets as much mileage out of his family as K of C's Bernie Mac.

Okay, I got a couple more. I liked the whole riff about leaf blowers being banned from airplanes. And I suppose it is thought-provoking that nobody ever has to stop to pee while tubing down a river.

Blue Crush ★ ★ ★
PG-13, 103 m., 2002

Kate Bosworth (Anne Marie), Michelle Rodriguez (Eden), Matthew Davis (Matt Tollman), Sanoe Lake (Lena), Mika Boorem (Penny), Kala Alexander (Kala), Chris Taloa (Drew). Directed by John Stockwell and produced by Brian Grazer and Karen Kehela. Screenplay by Lizzy Weiss and Stockwell.

Blue Crush knows something most surfing movies don't acknowledge—that many nonpro surfers endure blue-collar jobs as a way to support their surfing, which is the only time they feel really alive. Surfers in the movies have traditionally been golden boys and girls who ride the waves to Beach Boys songs—and live, apparently, on air. In *Blue Crush,* we meet three Hawaiian surfers who work as hotel maids, live in a grotty rental, and are raising the kid sister of one of them. Despite this near-poverty, they look great; there is nothing like a tan and a bikini to overcome class distinctions.

The women are Anne Marie (Kate Bosworth), Eden (Michelle Rodriguez), and Lena (Sanoe Lake). Anne Marie was a contender three years earlier in a major surfing competition on Oahu, but nearly drowned. Now she's edging back into competition, encouraged by the others, who seem to take Anne Marie's career more seriously than she does. Life for the women includes surfing at dawn, working hard as a three-maid team at a local luxury resort, and surfing at dusk. Since her mother bailed out, Anne Marie has been raising Penny (Mika Boorem), who attends a local school but is not always delivered quite on time.

The movie, based on Susan Orlean's magazine article named "Surf Girls of Maui," resembles the Nik Cohn journalism that inspired *Saturday Night Fever.* Both stories are about working-class kids escaping into the freedom and glamour of their obsessions. We hear fascination in their voices when they stop at a gas station and see, at another pump, famous professional women surfers who are in Hawaii for a big tournament. While it is true that Anne Marie might be able to make money as a member of a pro surfing team, it is also true, as it was of Tony Manero in *Saturday Night Fever,* that other things distract her, especially romance. She is not single-mindedly focused on her career.

The movie's surfing scenes are well photographed, and yet we've seen versions of them in many other movies, going all the way back to the lodestone, Bruce Brown's *Endless Summer* (1967). What we haven't seen, what has the delight of life, are the scenes in the hotel, where the three maids deal with the aftermath of a messy party held by pro football players and try on expensive bathing suits in the room of a rich woman.

Anne Marie has a fierce working woman's pride, and at one point gets herself fired by daring to march out onto the beach and demonstrate to a huge football lineman the correct procedure for wrapping a used condom in a Kleenex. She also has a working woman's realism, as when she advises the others not to resign in sympathy because they have rent payments to meet.

The date for the big competition is approaching, and Anne Marie is focused on it when the run-in with the football players (who are not bad guys) changes everything. The quarterback, Matt Tollman (Matthew Davis), asks her out, and although she talks about nonfraternization policies, she accepts, and finds herself falling for him. Here is the crucial question: Is this a vacation romance, or does it really mean something? Matt seems nice, attentive, and genuine, but is it an act? The movie is realistic here too: Anne Marie would not *mind* a vacation romance, but she wants to know if that's what it is—she doesn't want to risk her heart needlessly.

Eden is tougher and more cynical than her friend, and we remember Michelle Rodriguez's performance as an amateur boxer in *Girlfight* (2000). She's alarmed when her friend starts spending too much time with the quarterback and not enough time preparing for the impending competition ("Some guy thinks you look good in a bikini and you forget all about the contest"). And then of course the movie ends with the big showdown, with waves of awesome strength and feats of great surfing, with all the necessary dangers and setbacks. Even here, it doesn't settle for what we thought was the predictable outcome.

Blue Crush was directed by John Stockwell, who made *Crazy/Beautiful* (2001), the movie where Kirsten Dunst plays the wild daughter of a congressman, and her boyfriend is a responsible young Mexican-American. Here again we get the footloose Anglo and the Latino looking out for her, but in an unexpected context. Looking at the posters for *Blue Crush*, which show Bosworth, Rodriguez, and Lake posing with bikinis and surfboards, I expected another mindless surfing movie. *Blue Crush* is anything but.

Boat Trip ½ ★

R, 93 m., 2003

Cuba Gooding Jr. (Jerry), Horatio Sanz (Nick), Vivica A. Fox (Felicia), Roselyn Sanchez (Gabriela), Maurice Godin (Hector), Richard Roundtree (Malcolm), Roger Moore (Lloyd). Directed by Mort Nathan and produced by Frank Hübner, Brad Krevoy, Gerhard Schmidt, and Andrew Sugerman. Screenplay by Nathan and William Bigelow.

Boat Trip arrives preceded by publicity saying many homosexuals have been outraged by the film. Now that it's in theaters, everybody else has a chance to join them. Not that the film is outrageous. That would be asking too much. It is dim-witted, unfunny, too shallow to be offensive, and way too conventional to use all of those people standing around in the background wearing leather and chains and waiting hopefully for their cues. This is a movie made for nobody, about nothing.

The premise: Jerry (Cuba Gooding Jr.) is depressed after being dumped by his girl (Vivica A. Fox). His best buddy Nick (Horatio Sanz) cheers him up: They'll take a cruise together. Nick has heard that the ships are jammed with lonely women. But they offend a travel agent, who books them on a cruise of gay men, ho, ho.

Well, it could be funny. Different characters in a different story with more wit and insight might have done the trick. But *Boat Trip* requires its heroes to be so unobservant that it takes them hours to even figure out it's a gay cruise. And then they go into heterosexual panic mode, until the profoundly conventional screenplay supplies the only possible outcome: The sidekick discovers that he's gay, and the hero discovers a sexy woman on board and falls in love with her.

Her name is Gabriela (Roselyn Sanchez), and despite the fact that she's the choreographer on a gay cruise, she knows so little about gay men that she falls for Jerry's strategy: He will pretend to be gay, so that he can get close to her and then dramatically unveil his identity, or something. Uh-huh. Even Hector, the crossdressing queen in the next stateroom, knows a straight when he sees one: "You want to convince people you are gay, and you don't know the words to 'I Will Survive'?"

The gays protesting the movie say it deals in stereotypes. So it does, but then again, so does the annual gay parade, and so do many gay nightclubs, where role-playing is part of the scene. Yes, there are transvestites and leather guys and muscle boys on the cruise, but there are also more conventional types, like Nick's poker-playing buddies. The one ray of wit in the entire film is provided by Roger Moore, as a homosexual man who calmly wanders through the plot dispensing sanity, as when, at the bar, he listens to the music and sighs, "Why do they always play Liza?"

One of the movie's problems is a disconnect between various levels of reality. Some of the scenes play as if they are intended to be realistic. Then Jerry or Nick goes into hysterics of overacting. Then Jerry attempts to signal a helicopter to rescue him, and shoots it down with a flare gun. Then it turns out to be carrying the Swedish suntanning team on its way to the Hawaiian Tropic finals. Then Jerry asks Gabriela to describe her oral sex technique, which she does with the accuracy and detail of a porn film, and then Jerry—but that pathetic moment you will have to witness for yourself. Or maybe you will not.

Note: The credit cookies weren't very funny, either, but at least they kept me in the theater long enough to notice the credits for the film's Greek support team.

Borstal Boy ★ ★
NO MPAA RATING, 93 m., 2002

Shawn Hatosy (Brendan Behan), Danny Dyer (Charlie), Eva Birthistle (Liz), Michael York (Warden), Robin Laing (Jock), Mark Huberman (Mac). Directed by Peter Sheridan and produced by Arthur Lappin and Pat Moylan. Screenplay by Nye Heron and Sheridan, based on the book by Brendan Behan.

For a dozen years of my life, I gazed into the face of Brendan Behan almost nightly. There was an enormous photograph of him on the wall of O'Rourke's Pub on North Avenue, and it didn't take a lip-reader to guess which word began with his upper teeth posed on his lower lip. Drunk and disheveled, he must have been in a late stage of his brief and noisy progress through life. He wrote that to be drunk in Ireland in his youth was not a disgrace but a sign of status, because it showed you had enough money to pay for the drink. By that measurement, Behan was a millionaire.

Still beloved and read by those who remember him, the boy-o has long since faded from his time of great celebrity, when he enlightened talk shows with his boisterous proletarian philosophy. The recent equivalent of his risky performances as a late-night chat star would be Farrah Fawcett crossed with Andrew Dice Clay. He also wrote some good plays and the classic memoir *Borstal Boy*, and died at forty-one—which was old age, considering how he lived.

That is the Behan I remember. The Behan of *Borstal Boy* (Shawn Hatosy) is another person altogether, an idealistic young lad who naively goes to England on a mission for the IRA, is

arrested, sent to juvenile prison ("borstal") and there learns to love those he thinks he hates, including the English (through the warden's daughter) and "queers" (through his prison pal Charlie). After being discharged as a presumably pacified bisexual, he returns to Ireland and the movie ends quickly, before having to deal with the facts that he once again took up arms for the IRA, shot a cop, was sent back to prison, and (despite marriage to the saintly Beatrice) found love most reliably in the arms of the bottle.

Is the Brendan Behan of *Borstal Boy* simply the young man before alcoholism rewrote his script? I haven't read the book in years, but my strongest memory is of Behan's defiance—of his unshakable belief that carrying bombs to Liverpool and shooting cops was not criminal because he was a soldier at war. That has been the policy of the IRA from the beginning, that they are not terrorists but soldiers or prisoners of war. It is the same today with terrorists, with the difference that things were ever so much more innocent in the 1950s, so that the borstal warden (Michael York) could see Brendan as a lad with a good heart who just needed a chance to settle down and think things through.

The story hinges on parallel love affairs, both depending on a permissiveness one is a little startled to find in an English juvenile prison in the 1950s. Young Brendan makes best friends with his fellow prisoner Charlie (Danny Dyer), a young sailor who is "openly gay" (says Stephen Holden of the *New York Times*), although I believe being openly gay in those days, when it was against the law, was more a matter of sending signals to those who knew them and staying prudently in the closet otherwise. Certainly Brendan is slow to catch on, both to Charlie's homosexuality and to the promptings of his own heart. He is more obviously attracted to Liz (Eva Birthistle), the warden's daughter.

My guess is that the likelihood of a borstal boy being allowed to spend quality time with the warden's daughter is approximately the same as his chances of making friends with an "openly gay" prisoner, which is to say less likely than being invited to tea with the queen.

Of course, Liz and Charlie may come directly from the pages of the book and I have simply forgotten them. But my problem with *Borstal*

Boy isn't so much with the facts as with the tone. If this is an accurate portrait of Brendan Behan at sixteen, then *Borstal Boy* makes the same mistake *Iris* does—gives us these writers before (and in the case of *Iris,* after) the years in which they were the people they became famous for being. True, Behan's book is *about* that period in his life, but written with a gusto and rudeness that's lacking in Peter Sheridan's well-mannered film.

Yes, I know I've defended *A Beautiful Mind* against charges that it left out seamy details from the earlier years of John Forbes Nash, but the difference is, *A Beautiful Mind* focused intently on the central story, which is that he was a schizophrenic whose work won the Nobel Prize. Does anyone much think the central story of Brendan Behan is that he was a bisexual sweetheart before he took to drink? The photo on the wall at O'Rourke's shows him forming the first letter of the first word of his response to that theory.

The Bourne Identity ★ ★ ★
PG-13, 118 m., 2002

Matt Damon (Jason Bourne), Franka Potente (Marie Kreutz), Chris Cooper (Ted Conklin), Clive Owen (The Professor), Brian Cox (Ward Abbott), Adewale Akinnuoye-Agbaje (Wombosi). Directed by Doug Liman and produced by Patrick Crowley, Richard N. Gladstein, and Liman. Screenplay by Tone Gilroy and William Blade Herron, based on the novel by Robert Ludlum.

The Bourne Identity is a skillful action movie about a plot that exists only to support a skillful action movie. The entire story is a setup for the martial arts and chases. Because they are done well, because the movie is well crafted and acted, we give it a pass. Too bad it's not about something.

Well, perhaps it is. Perhaps it is about the amoral climate in spy agencies like the CIA. There are no good guys in the movie—certainly not the hero, played by Matt Damon, who is a trained assassin—and no bad guys, either. Even the people who want to kill Damon are only doing their jobs. Just as the guardians of the Navaho windtalkers in another movie are told to kill their charges rather than let them fall

into enemy hands, so is Bourne, or whatever his name is, targeted for death after he fails to assassinate an African leader. (There's a good possibility he would also be targeted if he had succeeded.)

As the movie opens, a fisherman on a boat out of Marseilles spots a body floating in what is obviously a studio back-lot tank. Hauled aboard, the body turns out to be alive, to have two bullet wounds, and to have a capsule embedded under the skin that contains the code to a Swiss bank account. The friendly fisherman gives the rescued man (who doesn't remember who he is) money to take the train to Switzerland, and he is welcomed in that nation and withdraws a fortune from a bank despite lacking a name or any form of personal identification.

Indeed, he finds out who he may be by looking inside the red bag from the bank, where he finds several passports, one saying his name is Bourne. Determined to find out his real name and why he was floating in the Mediterranean, Bourne pays $10,000 to a gypsy named Marie (Franka Potente from *Run, Lola, Run*) to drive him to Paris. Meanwhile, the movie cuts to CIA headquarters in Virginia, where we meet Bourne's handler, Conklin (Chris Cooper), and his boss, Abbott (Brian Cox). Bourne was thought to be dead. Now that he is alive, he must be killed, and the assignment goes to several assassins, including the Professor (Clive Owen), who is as highly trained as Bourne.

I forgot to say that Bourne is trained. Is he ever. He speaks several languages, is a formidable martial artist, has highly trained powers of observation and memory, knows all the spy tricks, and is a formidable driver. We see that during a sensational chase scene through the streets of Paris, much of it through narrow alleys, down flights of steps, and against traffic.

There comes a point at which we realize there will be no higher level to the screenplay, no greater purpose than to expend this kinetic energy. The movie's brutally cynical happy ending reveals that it doesn't take itself seriously. And we catch on (sooner than Marie) that the girl stays in the picture only because—well, there has to be a girl to provide false suspense and give the loner hero someone to talk to.

I kind of enjoyed *The Bourne Identity.* I had to put my mind on hold, but I was able to. I am less disturbed by action movies like this, which are frankly about nothing, than by action movies like *Windtalkers,* which pretend to be about something and then cop out. Doug Limon, the director of *Bourne,* directs the traffic well, gets a nice wintry look from his locations, absorbs us with the movie's spycraft, and uses Damon's ability to be focused and sincere. The movie is unnecessary, but not unskilled.

Bowling for Columbine ★ ★ ★ ½
R, 120 m., 2002

Featuring Michael Moore, George W. Bush, Dick Clark, Charlton Heston, Marilyn Manson, John Nichols, and Matt Stone. A documentary directed by Michael Moore and produced by Charles Bishop, Jim Czarnecki, Michael Donovan, Kathleen Glynn, and Moore. Screenplay by Moore.

McHugh and I were sitting in O'Rourke's one day when a guy we knew came in for a drink. The guy pulled back his coat and we could see he had a handgun in his belt. "Why are you carrying a gun?" McHugh asked. "Because I live in a dangerous neighborhood," the guy said. "It would be safer if you moved," said McHugh.

Michael Moore's *Bowling for Columbine,* a documentary that is both hilarious and sorrowful, is like a two-hour version of that anecdote. We live in a nation with millions of handguns, but that isn't really what bothers Moore. What bothers him is that we so frequently shoot them at each other. Canada has a similar ratio of guns to citizens, but a tenth of the shooting deaths. What makes us kill so many times more fellow citizens than is the case in other developed nations?

Moore, the jolly populist rabble-rouser, explains that he's a former sharpshooting instructor and a lifelong member of the National Rifle Association. No doubt this is true, but Moore has moved on from his early fondness for guns. In *Bowling for Columbine,* however, he is not so sure of the answers as in the popular *Roger & Me,* a film in which he knew who the bad guys were, and why. Here he asks questions he can't answer, such as why we as a nation seem so afraid, so in need of the reassurance of guns. Noting that we treasure urban legends designed to make us fearful of strangers, Moore

notices how TV news focuses on local violence ("If it bleeds, it leads") and says that while the murder rate is down 20 percent in America, TV coverage of violent crime is up 600 percent. Despite paranoia that has all but sidetracked the childhood custom of trick-or-treat, Moore points out that in fact no razor blades have ever been found in Halloween apples.

Moore's thoughtfulness doesn't inhibit the sensational set pieces he devises to illustrate his concern. He returns several times to Columbine, at one point showing horrifying security-camera footage of the massacre. And Columbine inspires one of the great confrontations in a career devoted to radical grandstanding. Moore introduces us to two of the students wounded at Columbine, both still with bullets in their bodies. He explains that all of the Columbine bullets were freely sold to the teenage killers by K-Mart, at seventeen cents apiece. And then he takes the two victims to K-Mart headquarters to return the bullets for a refund.

This is brilliant theater, and would seem to be unanswerable for the hapless K-Mart public relations spokespeople, who fidget and evade in front of Moore's merciless camera. But then, on Moore's third visit to headquarters, he is told that K-Mart will agree to completely phase out the sale of ammunition. "We've won," says Moore, not believing it. "This has never happened before." For once, he's at a loss for words.

The movie is a mosaic of Moore confrontations and supplementary footage. One moment that cuts to the core is from a stand-up routine by Chris Rock, who suggests that our problem could be solved by simply increasing the price of bullets — taxing them like cigarettes. Instead of seventeen cents apiece, why not $5,000? "At that price," he speculates, "you'd have a lot fewer innocent bystanders being shot."

Moore buys a map to the stars' homes to find where Charlton Heston lives, rings the bell on his gate, and is invited back for an interview. But Heston clearly knows nothing of Moore's track record, and his answers to Moore's questions are borderline pathetic. Heston recently announced he has symptoms associated with Alzheimer's disease, but there is no indication in this footage that he is senile;

it's simply that he cannot explain why he, as a man living behind a gate in a protected neighborhood, with security patrols, who has never felt himself threatened, needs a loaded gun in the house. Heston is equally unhelpful when asked if he thinks it was a good idea for him to speak at an NRA rally in Denver ten days after Columbine. He seems to think it was all a matter of scheduling.

Bowling for Columbine thinks we have way too many guns, don't need them, and are shooting each other at an unreasonable rate. Moore cannot single out a villain to blame for this fact, because it seems to emerge from a national desire to be armed. ("If you're not armed, you're not responsible," a member of the Michigan militia tells him.) At one point he visits a bank that is giving away guns to people who open new accounts. He asks a banker if it isn't a little dangerous to have all these guns in a bank. Not at all. The bank, Moore learns, is a licensed gun dealership.

Note: The movie is rated R, so that the Columbine killers would have been protected from the "violent images," mostly of themselves. The MPAA continues its policy of banning teenagers from those films they most need to see. What utopian world do the flywheels of the ratings board think they are protecting? ☞

The Bread, My Sweet ★ ★ ★
NO MPAA RATING, 105 m., 2002

Scott Baio (Dominic), Kristin Minter (Lucca), Rosemary Prinz (Bella), John Seitz (Massimo), Zachary Mott (Eddie), Shuler Hensley (Pino). Directed by Melissa Martin and produced by Adrienne Wehr and William C. Halley. Screenplay by Martin.

The Bread, My Sweet tells an improbable love story in such a heartfelt way that it's impossible to be cynical in the face of its innocence. Filmed in Pittsburgh, where it has been playing to full houses since January, it now gets a national release thanks to the success of *My Big Fat Greek Wedding*, another unlikely hit about ethnic romance. It's likely to appeal to the same kinds of audiences.

The movie stars Scott Baio as Dominic, who has two careers. He works downtown as a corporate raider whose job is to fire people at the companies he acquires. And he also owns a little pastry shop in an old Italian neighborhood, which provides jobs for his two brothers: Pino (Shuler Hensley), who is retarded, and Eddie (Zachary Mott), who floats through life without direction.

Upstairs over the shop live their landlords, Bella (Rosemary Prinz) and Massimo (John Seitz), who are salt-of-the-earth types, loud, demonstrative, extravagant with affection, always fighting but forever in love. They have a daughter named Lucca (Kristin Minter) who, instead of marrying and providing them with grandchildren, has joined the Peace Corps and disappeared from their lives. Now the boys downstairs are a surrogate family: "Three years ago, I don't know your name," Bella tells Dominic. "Now you are my son."

Like many stories that are too good to be true, this one has some truth in it. I learn from a review by Ron Weiskind of the *Pittsburgh Post-Gazette* that the movie, written and directed by Melissa Martin, "was inspired by a beloved Italian couple who lived above the Strip District bakery Enrico Biscotti, which is run by Martin's husband, Larry Lagatutta." The bakery in the movie is his actual bakery.

The first act establishes these people, their personalities and needs, and shows that Dominic is increasingly unhappy with his corporate job. Having opened the bakery out of love for his brothers, he finds he loves it too—and the old couple who live upstairs. I must explain what happens next to deal with the movie at all, so you might want to file this if you don't want to know that . . .

Bella falls ill. And now her heart is breaking. She doesn't mind dying, but she is filled with grief that she will die with her only child still single and wandering somewhere in the Peace Corps wilderness. Dominic tracks down the daughter and advises her to come home quickly. Lucca materializes, turning out to be a good and loving daughter (perhaps the Peace Corps was a hint), and she and Dominic discuss what is to be done. It quickly becomes obvious to Dominic that only one thing will make a difference: He and Lucca must be married so that the old woman can die in peace.

This development is straight out of romantic comedy, and *The Bread, My Sweet* is rather daring to take it seriously. There is a crucial scene where Dominic explains his thinking to Lucca, and this scene somehow, against all odds, works. Scott Baio and Kristin Minter, who could so easily bog down in soppy truisms, discuss his plan objectively. She is of course astonished by his suggestion, but he keeps talking. "I do deals," he says, and this will be his biggest deal. "We have a very small window of opportunity."

Of course they can get divorced after Bella dies, etc., and need not have sex, etc., but all of these footnotes are brushed aside by the enormity of the deception they are planning, and then—well, two nice young people like that, don't they deserve each other?

The film misses scarcely a chance to tug at our heartstrings. As Bella grows more ill and loses her appetite, Pino bakes smaller and smaller pies for her to eat, until finally in tears he admits that he cannot make a pie any smaller. Martin even adds a touch of magic realism, with a mysterious gypsy woman who dances with a tambourine on the street outside.

What makes the movie special is its utter sincerity. For all of the contrivances in the plot, there is the feeling that the actors love their characters and are trying to play them honestly. Yes, the movie is corny, but no, it's not dumb. It's clever and insightful in the way it gets away with this story, which is almost a fable. The turning point is the key conversation between Dominic and Lucca. Once that works, we can believe almost anything. Now if only Bella will.

Bread and Roses ★ ★ ★ ½
R, 106 m., 2001

Pilar Padilla (Maya), Adrien Brody (Sam), Elpidia Carrillo (Rosa), Jack McGee (Bert), George Lopez (Perez), Alonso Chavez (Ruben), Monica Rivas (Simona). Directed by Ken Loach and produced by Rebecca O'Brien. Screenplay by Paul Laverty.

If you work in a building with janitors, how much do they get paid? Is it enough to decently support a family? Have you given any thought to the question? I haven't. Ken Loach's *Bread and Roses*, a drama about a janitorial strike in Los Angeles, made me think. It suggests that the people who manage your building pay the

janitors as little as they possibly can, and pass the savings on to your employers. Here is a statistic: In 1982, union janitors in Los Angeles were paid $8.50 an hour. In 1999, nonunion janitors were paid $5.75. Do they have a health plan? Don't make me laugh.

Under the trickle-down theory, if the boss makes millions and the janitor makes $5.75, in the long run we all benefit. How does this work in practice? A simple illustration will suffice. When both parents have to moonlight in underpaid jobs, that gives their children an opportunity to get in trouble on the streets, leading to arrests, convictions, and millions of dollars pumped into the economy through the construction of new prisons and salaries for their guards. Right now America has a larger percentage of its population in prison than any other Western nation, but that is not good enough.

Bread and Roses tells its story through the eyes of Maya (Pilar Padilla), an illegal immigrant newly arrived in Los Angeles. Her sister Rosa (Elpidia Carrillo) gets her a job in a sleazy bar, but Rosa is a good girl and doesn't like it: "I want to work with you cleaning the offices." Rosa gets Maya hired in a high-rise, where she has to kick back her first month's salary. Maya meets Sam (Adrien Brody), an organizer for the janitor's union, who is trying to sign up the workers in the building.

For some of my readers, the key words in the previous paragraph were "illegal immigrant." Why, they are thinking, should such a person have a job in America at all, let alone complain about the low wages? This attitude is admirable in its idealism, but overlooks the fact that the economy depends on workers who will accept substandard wages. The man who hires Maya certainly knows she is illegal. That man's boss, as they say, "knows but doesn't know." The man above him doesn't know and doesn't care—he's only interested in delivering janitorial services to the building management at the lowest possible price.

If the janitors were paid a decent wage plus health benefits, there would be no shortage of American citizens to take the jobs, so it is better this way, especially since the illegal workers have no rights and are easily intimidated. If the Mexican border were sealed, Los Angeles would be a city without janitors, gardeners, car washes, and maids. And in Michigan, who would pick the fruit?

Sam the organizer encourages Maya and her friends to organize for the union within the building—secretly, of course. Rosa, the sister, is not so enthusiastic: "We could all lose our jobs, and then who would pay the bills?" There is a juicy scene where the striking janitors invade a housewarming by a big Hollywood agency which has just taken offices in the building. Do the star clients know their agents are exploiting the workers? (Credit here to Ron Perlman and other actors who play recognizable extras.)

Sam is played by Brody as a complex character, filled with anger but also with a streak of zany street comedian. He's trapped in the middle, since the union's bosses, like all bosses, are basically establishment. When his boss argues that a strike might cost the union too much money, Sam snaps back: "No more $40 million to give the Democrats." Sam and Maya are drawn to one another, and there is a shy little love scene, but Ken Loach is not the kind of director to confuse his real story with the love story; he knows that no matter what happens between Sam and Maya, the janitors are still underpaid and the strike is still dangerous. That same stubborn integrity prevents him from giving the movie a conventional happy ending. Just think. If he had directed *Pearl Harbor*, it would have ended sadly.

Loach is left-wing but realistic. The best scene in *Bread and Roses* argues against Sam, Maya, and the union. It is a searing speech by Rosa, delivered by Elpidia Carrillo with such force and shaming truth that it could not have been denied the Oscar—if the Academy voters in their well-cleaned buildings ever saw movies like this. Rosa slices through Maya's idealism with hard truths, telling her sister that she worked as a prostitute to pay for Maya's education, and indeed slept with the supervisor to get Rosa her job. "I've been whoring all my life, and I'm tired," she says. Now she has a sick husband and kids to feed and they take priority over the union and the college-boy organizer.

The more you think about it, the more this movie's ending has a kind of nobility to it. Loach, who has always made films about the working class *(Riff-Raff, My Name Is Joe, Ladybird, Ladybird)*, is too honest to believe in easy solutions. Will the union get its contract? Will Maya and Sam live happily ever after? Will the national minimum wage ever be a living wage? Will this movie change anything, or this review make you want to see it? No, probably not. But when you come in tomorrow morning someone will have emptied your wastebasket.

Bread and Tulips ★ ★ ★ ½
PG-13, 115 m., 2001

Licia Maglietta (Rosalba), Bruno Ganz (Fernando), Giuseppe Battiston (Costantino), Marina Massironi (Grazia), Antonio Catania (Mimmo), Felice Andreasi (Fermo), Vitalba Andrea (Ketty), Tatiana Lepore (Adele), Ludovico Paladin (Eliseo). Directed by Silvio Soldini and produced by Daniele Maggioni. Screenplay by Doriana Leondeff and Soldini.

It's all in the casting. Silvio Soldini's *Bread and Tulips* tells a story that seems born to be remade in Hollywood with Sandra Bullock or Julia Roberts, but look at Licia Maglietta and tell me what you see. Not a classic beauty, not a "movie star," but a fortyish dreamer who's just a little overweight, with the kind of sexiness that makes you think of bread baking, clean sheets, and that everything is going to be all right. Maglietta is the secret of this film's romantic charm because we like her so much.

We like her, and we like the dignified and sad waiter Fernando (Bruno Ganz), and we like her friend Grazia (Marina Massironi), who is a "holistic beautician and masseuse," and we like the sweet old florist Fermo (Felice Andreasi), and we like the plump, perspiring Costantino (Giuseppe Battiston) who is the plumber and amateur detective hired to track her down.

We like them to begin with, and we like them more because they occupy an obscure corner of Venice, that city above all others that encourages us to yield to our romantic impulses. We like them, and so did the David Di Donatello Awards, the Italian version of the Oscars, which showered *Bread and Tulips* with Davids for Best Picture, Actor, Actress, Supporting Actor, Supporting Actress, Director, and three more besides. The Italians say this is their favorite movie in years, and they are not without reason.

Licia Maglietta plays Rosalba, a housewife who is taken utterly for granted by her family. When she loses an earring down the drain at a highway rest stop, her husband and teenage children board their tourist bus and it pulls away without anyone even missing her. Rosalba's husband calls on his cell phone; he's mad at her—because, of course, it was her fault that they didn't miss her. Rosalba impulsively hitches a ride with a friendly woman, and later, more impulsively, hitches another ride—to Venice, where she has never been. Suddenly this has turned into *her* vacation.

In the serene city she meets characters who are not likely to exist in real life—but here is the point, they're *played* as if they were. With a few lira in her handbag, she visits a lonely little restaurant near the train station, and meets Fernando, a waiter played by Bruno Ganz with a sad countenance and dignified charm. The cook is sick, but Fernando prepares a cold dish for her and serves it as if she were a queen. One thing leads to another, not in an obvious way, and soon she has a job with the florist, is living in an extra room of Fernando's flat, and has made friends with Grazia, whose profession may extend beyond massage, or at least liberally define it.

Bruno Ganz is the actor who will be forever remembered as the angel in *Wings of Desire*—the angel whose love and sympathy for mankind caused him to turn in his wings and take his chances in the physical universe. Here he's something of an angel, too—a melancholy one. When Rosalba unexpectedly knocks on his door on the second day, he has to take down the noose from his ceiling before he can let her in. He has no carnal designs on his houseguest, and she is too abashed at her rebellion to even think in those terms, but they are both confronted with the inescapable fact that their souls match.

The movie intercuts events in Venice with a human comedy involving Mimmo (Antonio Catania), Rosalba's husband, who has long enjoyed the favors of a mistress but is now dismayed to find that she refuses to perform Rosalba's domestic tasks in her absence. Rosalba has sent him postcards that announce she is safe in Venice, but they are vague about the possibility of her return. Mimmo enlists the services of Costantino, the plumber, who fancies himself a detective and goes off to Venice to track her down; his mission provides first a guided tour of Venice and then experiences of his own in applied holism.

I am aware that stories like this have been told before. Venice has been put on earth as an opportunity for underappreciated women of a certain age to make one more roll of the romantic dice. The film is haunted by Katharine Hepburn's adventures in *Summertime,* and by films as unlike as *Blume in Love, Wings of the Dove, Only You,* and *Everyone Says I Love You.* But I don't require the story to be original. I am not at the movies for lonely-hearts tips. I require the characters to be strange and wonderful, romantic and quirky, and above all lovable. It may be that a relationship like the one here between Rosalba and Fernando is impossible in real life. All the more reason for this movie.

Bride of the Wind ½★
R, 99 m., 2001

Sarah Wynter (Alma Mahler), Jonathan Pryce (Gustav Mahler), Vincent Perez (Oskar Kokoschka), Simon Verhoeven (Walter Gropius), Gregor Seberg (Franz Werfel), Dagmar Schwarz (Anna Moll), Wolfgang Hubsch (Karl Moll), August Schmolzer (Gustav Klimt), Francesca Becker (Maria). Directed by Bruce Beresford and produced by Lawrence Levy and Evzen Kolar. Screenplay by Marilyn Levy.

"I'm not just any widow! I'm Mahler's widow!"
—Alma Mahler

She must have been a monster. The Alma Mahler depicted in *Bride of the Wind* is a woman who prowls restlessly through the beds of the famous, making them miserable while displaying no charm of her own. Whether this was the case with the real woman I do not know. But if she was anything like the woman in this movie, then Gustav Mahler, Gustav Klimt, Oskar Kokoschka, Walter Gropius, and Frank Werfel should have fled from her on sight.

Bride of the Wind, which tells her story, is one of the worst biopics I have ever seen, a leaden march through a chronology of Alma's affairs, clicking them off with the passion of an encyclopedia entry. The movie has three tones: overwrought, boring, laughable. Sarah Wynter, who plays Alma, does not perform the dialogue but recites it. She lacks any conviction as a seductress, seems stiff and awkward, and should have been told that great women in turn-of-the-century Vienna didn't slouch.

We first meet her going to a ball her father has forbidden her to attend. He is stern with her when she returns. So much for her adolescence. We move on to a dinner party where she flirts with the artist Klimt (August Schmolzer), who labors over one-liners like, "Mahler's music is much better than it sounds." She insults Mahler (Jonathan Pryce) at dinner, offending and fascinating him, and soon the older man marries her.

She has affairs throughout their marriage. She cheats with the architect Gropius (Simon Verhoeven), who unwisely writes a love letter to Alma but absentmindedly addresses it to Gustav—or so he says. "You drove me to him," she pouts to her husband. Mahler is always going on about his music, you see, and thinks himself a genius. Well, so does Gropius. The screenplay shows the egos of the men by putting big, clanging chunks of information in the dialogue. Sample:

"You've been very kind, Herr Gropius."
"Dancing is one of the two things I do well."
"And what is the other?"
"I am an architect."

Since Alma already knows this, the movie misses a bet by not having her ask, winsomely, "Is there a ... third ... thing you at least do not do badly?"

There is. Another affair is with the sculptor and painter Oskar Kokoschka (Vincent Perez), who goes off to fight the war, is shot through the head, and bayoneted after falling wounded. In what the movie presents as a dying vision, he imagines Alma walking toward him. Since his head is flat on the ground, she walks toward him sideways, rotated ninety degrees from upright. But, of course, a vision stands upright no matter what position one's head is in, or dreams would take place on the ceiling.

Oskar's mother posts herself outside Alma's house with a pistol, seeking revenge for her son's death. "I was never popular with mothers," Alma sighs. She becomes involved with the writer Werfel. Just when we are wondering if Oskar's mother is still lying in ambush outside the gates, Kokoschka himself returns a year later—alive!—and surprises her in her drawing room. "It's not every man who is shot in the head, bayoneted, and lives to tell about it," he observes. Then he sees she is pregnant and rejoices that she decided to have his baby after all, instead of an abortion. "But it has been a year," Alma tells him. "Think, Oskar! A year."

The penny falls. He stalks away, disgusted either at the fact that she is bearing another man's child, or that he cannot count. I meanwhile am thinking that when one is reported dead in action, it is only common good manners to wire ahead before turning up unexpectedly at a lover's house. Ben Affleck makes the same mistake in *Pearl Harbor*.

Bride of the Wind was directed by Bruce Beresford, who has made wonderful films *(Tender Mercies, Crimes of the Heart, The Fringe Dwellers, Driving Miss Daisy)*. At a loss to explain this lapse, I can only observe that another of his filmed biographies, *King David* (1985), was also very bad. Maybe there is something about a real-life subject that paralyzes him.

If Sarah Wynter is not good as Alma Mahler, the other actors seem equally uneasy—even the usually assured Pryce and Perez. Something must have been going wrong on this production. Even that doesn't explain the lack of Bad Laugh Control. Filmmakers need a sixth sense for lines that might play the wrong way. For example: After Alma has slept with as many Viennese artists as she can manage without actually double-booking, she quarrels with the latest. Her winsome little daughter, Maria (Francesca Becker), whines, "Is he going to leave us? Are you going to send him away?" Alma replies, "What made you think that?" Wrong answer. At the end of the movie there are titles telling us what happened to everyone; Gropius moved to America and went on to become a famous architect, etc. We are not surprised to learn that little Maria went on to be married five times.

Bridget Jones's Diary ★ ★ ★ ½
R, 95 m., 2001

Renée Zellweger (Bridget Jones), Colin Firth (Mark Darcy), Hugh Grant (Daniel Cleaver), Honor Blackman (Penny), Crispin Bonham-Carter (Greg), Gemma Jones (Bridget's Mum), Jim Broadbent (Bridget's Dad), James Callis (Tom), Embeth Davidtz (Natasha). Directed by Sharon Maguire and produced by Tim Bevan, Jonathan Cavendish, and Eric Fellner. Screenplay by Richard Curtis, Andrew Davies, and Helen Fielding, based on the novel by Fielding.

Glory be, they didn't muck it up. *Bridget Jones's Diary,* a beloved book about a heroine both lovable and human, has been made against all odds into a funny and charming movie that understands the charm of the original, and preserves it. The book, a fictional diary by a plump, thirty-something London office worker, was about a specific person in a specific place. When the role was cast with Renée Zellweger, who is not plump and is from Texas, there was gnashing and wailing. Obviously the Miramax boys would turn London's pride into a Manhattanite, or worse.

Nothing doing. Zellweger put on twenty-something pounds and developed the cutest little would-be double chin, as well as a British accent that sounds reasonable enough to me. (*Sight & Sound,* the British film magazine, has an ear for nuances and says the accent is "just a little too studiedly posh," which from them is praise.)

As in the book, Bridget arrives at her thirty-second birthday determined to take control of her life, which until now has consisted of smoking too much, drinking too much, eating too much, and not finding the right man, or indeed much of any man. In her nightmares, she dies fat, drunk, and lonely, and is eaten by Alsatian dogs. She determines to monitor her daily intake of tobacco and alcohol units, and her weight, which she measures in stones. (A stone is fourteen pounds; the British not only have pounds instead of kilos but stones on top of pounds, although the other day a London street vendor was arrested for selling bananas by the pound in defiance of the new European marching orders; the next step is obviously for Brussels to impound Bridget's diary.)

Bridget's campaign proceeds unhappily when her mother (who "comes from the time when pickles on toothpicks were still the height of sophistication") introduces her to handsome Mark Darcy (Colin Firth), who is at a holiday party against his will and in a bad mood and is overheard (by Bridget) describing her as a "verbally incontinent spinster." Things go better at work, where she exchanges saucy e-mails with her boss, Daniel Cleaver (Hugh Grant). His opener: "You appear to have forgotten your skirt." They begin an affair, while Darcy circles the outskirts of her consciousness, still looking luscious but acting emotionally constipated.

Zellweger's Bridget is a reminder of the first time we became really aware of her in a movie, in *Jerry Maguire* (1996), where she was so cute and vulnerable we wanted to tickle and console her at the same time. Her work in *Nurse Betty* (2000) was widely but not sufficiently praised, and now here she is, fully herself and fully Bridget Jones, both at once. A story like this can't work unless we feel unconditional affection for the heroine, and casting Zellweger achieves that; the only alternate I can think of is Kate Winslet, who comes close but lacks the self-destructive puppy aspects.

The movie has otherwise been cast with dependable (perhaps infallible) British comic actors. The first time Hugh Grant appeared on-screen, I chuckled for no good reason at all, just as I always do when I see Christopher Walken, Steve Buscemi, Tim Roth, or Jack Nicholson—because I know that whatever the role, they will infuse it with more than the doctor ordered. Grant can play a male Bridget Jones (as he did in *Notting Hill*), but he's better as a cad, and here he surpasses himself by lying to Bridget about Darcy and then cheating on her with a girl from the New York office. (An "American stick insect," is what Bridget tells her diary.)

Colin Firth on the other hand must unbend to become lovable, and when we do finally love him, it's largely because we know what an effort it took on his part. *Bridget Jones's Diary* is famously, if vaguely, patterned after Jane Austen's *Pride and Prejudice*; Firth played Mr. Darcy in the BBC's 1995 adaptation of the novel, and now plays another Darcy here. I didn't see the TV version but learn from the critic James Berardinelli that Firth "plays this part exactly as he played the earlier role, making it evident that the two Darcys are essentially the same."

It is a universal rule of romantic fiction that all great love stories must be mirrored by their low-comedy counterpoints. Just as Hal woos Katharine, Falstaff trifles with Doll Tearsheet. If Bridget must choose between Mark and Daniel, then her mother (Gemma Jones) must choose between her kindly but easy-chair-loving husband (Jim Broadbent) and a dashing huckster for a TV shopping channel.

The movie strings together one funny set-piece after another, as when Bridget goes in costume to a party where she *thought* the theme was "Tarts & Vicars." Or when she stumbles into a job on a TV news show and makes her famous premature entrance down the fire pole. Or when she has to decide at the beginning of an evening whether sexy underwear or tummy-crunching underwear will do her more good in the long run. Bridget charts her own progress along the way, from "tragic spinster" to "wanton sex goddess," and the movie gives almost unreasonable pleasure as it celebrates her bumpy transition.

Bringing Down the House ★ ★
PG-13, 105 m., 2003

Steve Martin (Peter Sanderson), Queen Latifah (Charlene Morton), Eugene Levy (Howie Rosenthal), Jean Smart (Kate Sanderson), Michael Rosenbaum (Todd Gendler), Betty White (Mrs. Klein), Joan Plowright (Mrs. Arness). Directed by Adam Shankman and produced by Ashok Amritraj and David Hoberman. Screenplay by Jason Filardi.

I confess I expected Steve Martin and Queen Latifah to fall in love in *Bringing Down the House*. That they avoid it violates all the laws of economical screenplay construction, since they are constantly thrown together, they go from hate to affection, and they get drunk together one night and tear up the living room together, which in movies of this kind is usually the closer.

But, no, all they fall into is Newfound Respect, which, in a world of high-performance star vehicles, is the minivan. Eugene Levy is

brought off the bench to console the Queen, and Martin ends up back with his divorced wife (Jean Smart), who exists only so that he can go back to her. These two couples had better never double-date, because under the table Queen and Steve are going to have their socks up each other's pants.

Why, I asked myself, is their mutual sexual attraction disguised as roughhousing when they are the stars, and movie convention demands that they get it on? There isn't a shred of chemistry between Latifah and Levy (who likes the Queen's wildness and is infatuated with her cleavage, which is understandable but shallow—his infatuation, not her cleavage). I think it's because the movie, coproduced by Latifah, was making a point, which is that the rich white lawyer had better learn to accept this bitch on her own terms instead of merely caving in to her sex appeal. This may be a point worth making, but not in a comedy.

I use the word "bitch" after some hesitation, to make a point: The movie is all about different ethnic styles of speech. It uses the B-word constantly (along, of course, with lots of "hos"), and I argue that since the MPAA rates the language PG-13, I can use it in a review. You kids under thirteen who are reading this better be getting parental guidance from a POS.

(Emergency definition: POS [n., slang]. Abbreviation used in teenage chat rooms, warning person at other end: "Parent over shoulder!")

Martin plays Peter Sanderson, a high-powered lawyer with a trophy ex-wife who lives in a posh Los Angeles neighborhood and speaks with meticulous precision he elevates to a kind of verbal constipation. Queen Latifah plays Charlene Morton, whom he meets in an Internet chat room, where she is LawyerGirl.

They both misrepresent their appearance—well, all right, she's guiltier than he is—and when they meet he's appalled to find, not a blond legal bimbo, but a trash-talking black ex-con who wants him to handle her case. Charlene *can* talk like a perfect middle-class lady, as she demonstrates, but the movie's point of pride is that she shouldn't have to. Peter can also talk like a black street dude, sort of. Maybe he learned it from his kids' rap records.

The movie's conceit is that Peter keeps throwing Charlene out and she keeps coming back because she's determined to prove her legal innocence. She breaks into his house, throws wild parties, embarrasses him at his club, and so on, until a magic night when she gets him drinking and dancing, plants his hands squarely on what Russ Meyer used to rhapsodically refer to as garbanzos, and breaks down his inhibitions. At this point—what? Wild nuzzling, rapturous caresses, shredded knickers, wild goat cries in the night? Peter takes her case, that's what, while Eugene Levy crawls out of his eyebrows and joins the tag team.

This is all wrong. It violates the immortal Stewart/Reagan principle: Steve Martin for Latifah, Eugene Levy for best friend. A comedy is not allowed to end with the couples incorrectly paired. It goes against the deeply traditional requirements of the audience. Here is a movie that ignores the Model Airplane Rule: First, make sure you have taken all of the pieces out of the box, then line them up in the order in which they will be needed. *Bringing Down the House* is glued together with one of the wings treated like a piece of tail. ☞

Brother ★ ★

R, 114 m., 2001

Beat Takeshi (Yamamoto), Omar Epps (Denny), Claude Maki (Ken), Masaya Kato (Shirase), Susumu Terajima (Kato), Royale Watkins (Jay), Lombardo Boyar (Mo), Ren Osugi (Harada). Directed by Takeshi Kitano and produced by Masayuki Mori and Jeremy Thomas. Screenplay by Kitano.

The actor Beat Takeshi is a Japanese original, but if you made a list of the American stars he resembles, it would start with Clint Eastwood. The director Takeshi Kitano is also a Japanese original, but if you made a list of the Western filmmakers he resembles, it would reach from Sergio Leone to Jim Jarmusch, with Eastwood somewhere in the middle. But there is no one in Hollywood quite like the two of them put together, and, of course, they are the same man, using two names to separate his many jobs on the set.

Kitano, for so we will call him, is revered in Japan as an auteur of hard-boiled, minimalist action. His films consist of periods of quiet in which you can feel violence coiling out of sight, and then sudden explosions of mayhem. He is a weathered, deadpan, wary-looking man, a yakuza Jack Webb. He usually wears dark glasses, rarely has much to say, and occasionally barks out an amazed little laugh at what life has to offer him. When part of his face was paralyzed in a motorcycle accident, it became part of his lore that you couldn't tell which side, because he never moved his facial muscles anyway.

Brother is Kitano's deliberate attempt to enter the American market, in a movie set in Los Angeles and essentially in English, although Kitano, unlike Jackie Chan, doesn't pretend fluency. Many of the movie's key situations depend on who speaks English or Japanese, and why—although one enemy dies right after Kitano tells him, in perfect English, "I understand 'dirty Jap.'"

As the movie opens, Yamamoto, Kitano's character, has had to leave Japan suddenly after a gang war has gone against him. In Los Angeles, he teams up with a half-brother (Claude Maki), his African-American partner Denny (Omar Epps), and others in a drug ring. Yamamoto is the catalyst in many situations, simplifying them with the sudden elimination of those he disagrees with. Soon the gang is riding high, and has its own headquarters with a private basketball court (a tattooed yakuza complains when the blacks won't pass the ball to him).

Kitano is as much an existentialist as a action hero, however, and his crime movies (like *Sonatine*) rarely end with victory for himself and his friends. He is more in love with doom-laden irony, with grand gestures in defeat. His final scene in *Brother* owes more to the defiant last gestures of 1930s Warner Bros. gangsters than to simpleminded modern action pictures that end after all the enemies have been eliminated.

What's fascinating about Kitano is the way he pounces. He specializes in moments of action almost too fast to see (here he resembles Eastwood as The Man With No Name—and Eastwood, of course, was ripping off Mifune in *Yojimbo*). An opponent will say the same thing, there will be a flash of action, and he'll have chopsticks stuck halfway up his nose. A pause for the realization to sink in, and then the sudden blow to push them the rest of the way in. All over in a moment.

Brother is a typical Kitano film in many ways, but not one of his best ones. Too many of the killing scenes have a casual, perfunctory tone: lots of gunfire, a row of enemies lies dead, the plot moves on. Finally so many people are dead that the movie looks more like a shooting gallery or a video game than a stylized crime parable. Kitano, both Beat and Takeshi, is a name that belongs on the list of anyone who wants to be familiar with the key players in modern world cinema, but don't start with *Brother*. Rent *Sonatine* or *Fireworks*, and then double back.

Brotherhood of the Wolf ★ ★ ★
R, 146 m., 2002

Samuel Le Bihan (Fronsac), Vincent Cassel (Jean-Francois), Mark Dacascos (Mani), Monica Bellucci (Sylvia), Emilie Dequenne (Marianne), Jeremie Renier (Thomas de'Apcher), Jacques Parrin (Old Thomas). Directed by Christophe Gans and produced by Samuel Hadida and Richard Grandpierre. Screenplay by Stephane Cabel. In French with English subtitles.

Brotherhood of the Wolf plays like an explosion at the genre factory. When the smoke clears, a rough beast lurches forth, its parts cobbled together from a dozen movies. The film involves quasi-werewolves, French aristocrats, secret societies, Iroquois Indians, martial arts, occult ceremonies, sacred mushrooms, swashbuckling, incestuous longings, political subversion, animal spirits, slasher scenes, and bordellos, and although it does not end with the words "based on a true story," it is.

The story involves the Beast of Gevaudan that, in 1764, terrorized a remote district of France, killing more than sixty women and children, and tearing out their hearts and vitals. I borrow these facts from Patrick Meyers of TheUnexplainedSite.com, who reveals that the Beast was finally found to be a wolf. Believe me, this information does not even come close to giving away the ending of the movie.

Directed by Christophe Gans, *Brotherhood of the Wolf* is couched in historical terms. It begins in 1794, at the time of the Revolution, when its narrator (Jacques Parrin), about to be carried away to the guillotine, puts the finishing touches on a journal revealing at last the true story of the Beast. Although a wolf was killed and presented to the court of the king, that was only a cover-up, he says, as we flash back to . . .

Well, actually, the Beast attacks under the opening credits, even before the narrator appears. For the first hour or so we do not see it, but we hear fearsome growls, moans, and roars, and see an unkempt but buxom peasant girl dragged to her doom. Enter Gregoire de Fronsac (Samuel Le Bihan), an intellectual and naturalist, recently returned from exploring the St. Lawrence Seaway. He is accompanied by Mani, an Iroquois who speaks perfect French and perfect tree (he talks to them). Mani is played by Mark Dacascos, a martial arts expert from Hawaii whose skills might seem out of place in eighteenth-century France, but no: Everyone in this movie fights in a style that would make Jackie Chan proud.

Fronsac doubts the existence of a Beast. Science tells us to distrust fables, he explains. At dinner, he passes around a trout with fur, from Canada, which causes one of the guests to observe it must really be cold for the fish there, before Fronsac reveals it is a hoax. The Beast, alas, soon makes him a believer, but he sees a pattern: "The Beast is a weapon used by a man." But what man? Why? How? Charting the Beast's attacks on a map, he cleverly notices that all of the lines connecting them intersect at one point in rural Gevaudan. Fronsac and Mani go looking.

The local gentry include Jean-Francois (Vincent Cassel), who has one arm, but has fashioned a rifle he can brace in the crook of his shoulder. It fires silver bullets (this is also a historical fact). His sister Marianne (Emilie Dequenne) fancies Fronsac, which causes Jean-Francois to hate him, significantly. Also lurking about, usually with leaves in her hair, is the sultry Sylvia (Monica Bellucci), who travels with men who might as well have "Lout" displayed on a sign around their necks, and likes to dance on tabletops while they throw knives that barely miss her.

I would be lying if I did not admit that this is all, in its absurd and overheated way, entertaining. Once you realize that this is basically a high-gloss werewolf movie (but without a werewolf), crossed with a historical romance, a swashbuckler, and a martial arts extravaganza, you can relax. There is, of course, a deeper political message (this movie is nothing if not inclusive), and vague foreshadowings of fascism and survivalist cults, but the movie uses its politics only as a plot convenience.

Brotherhood of the Wolf looks just great. The photography by Dan Laustsen is gloriously atmospheric and creepy; he likes fogs, blasted heaths, boggy marshes, moss, vines, creepers, and the excesses of eighteenth-century interior decorating. He has fun with a completely superfluous scene set in a bordello just because it was time for a little skin. The Beast, when it finally appears, is a most satisfactory Beast indeed, created by Jim Henson's Creature Shop. There are times when its movements resemble the stop-motion animation of a Ray Harryhausen picture, but I like the oddness of that kind of motion; it makes the Beast weirder than if it glided along smoothly.

The one thing you don't want to do is take this movie seriously. Because it's so good-looking, there may be a temptation to think it wants to be high-toned, but no: Its heart is in the horror-monster-sex-fantasy-special-effects tradition. "The Beast has a master," Fronsac says. "I want him." That's the spirit.

The Brothers ★ ★ ★

R, 103 m., 2001

Morris Chestnut (Jackson Smith), D. L. Hughley (Derrick West), Bill Bellamy (Brian Palmer), Shemar Moore (Terry White), Tamala Jones (Sheila West), Gabrielle Union (Denise Johnson), Julie Benz (Jesse Caldwell), Jenifer Lewis (Louise Smith), Clifton Powell (Fred Smith). Directed by Gary Hardwick and produced by Darin Scott and Paddy Cullen. Screenplay by Hardwick.

The Brothers is another movie about black guys who have been friends since childhood and how wedding bells are breaking up that old gang of theirs. This is getting to be a genre; I was reminded of *The Wood* (1999). What makes this one interesting is the way one couple actually deals with the crisis that threatens to keep them apart, instead of saying all the wrong things at the wrong times in traditional Idiot Plot fashion.

An early scene, of course, shows the friends playing basketball together. This is obligatory, showing how they cling to the innocence of those earlier days before romance and responsibility cluttered their lives. We meet Jackson the pediatrician (Morris Chestnut), Brian the lawyer (Bill Bellamy), Terry the executive (Shemar Moore), and Derrick the teacher (D. L. Hughley), who married young and regrets it. Now there's a crisis: Terry announces that he's going to get married.

The others, of course, oppose this decision, especially the married Derrick, whose marriage is approaching a crisis stage because of his wife's refusal to engage in oral sex. Derrick takes this as a personal affront—as proof she doesn't love him—and the arguments they have on this subject are among the movie's more tedious.

Jackson is a fervent opponent of premature marriage; they are, after all, young urban professionals, the cream of the crop, and deserve to play the field for a few more years. Then he meets a freelance photographer named Denise (Gabrielle Union), and is thunderstruck by love. Their relationship redeems the movie, because it involves real issues, and not simply plot points that are manipulated to keep them apart until it's time to push them together.

At first, Jackson and Denise seem too good to be true. They were made for each other. They're happy not simply in romantic montages, but even in dialogue sequences where we sense a meeting of the minds. Then Jackson finds out something from Denise's past, which I will not reveal, except to say that Denise is blameless, and that Jackson has all the information he needs to realize this. (In an Idiot Plot, she would be blameless, but Jackson would be kept in the dark by contortions of the screenplay.)

No, it's not information Jackson needs, but a better understanding of himself, and of his troubled relationship with his divorced parents. And as he works on that, there is a strong scene where Denise tries to reason with him. She is persuasive and logical and emotional; she's arguing for her own happiness as well as his. This is precisely the kind of scene I yearn for in Idiot Plots, where the characters should say something but never do. She gives it her best shot, and so when Jackson stubbornly sticks to his wrongheaded position, it's about the characters, not the screenplay mechanics.

Gabrielle Union you may recall from *Bring It On* (2000), the dueling cheerleader comedy. This movie demonstrates how teenager comedies can obscure real talent. The cast is generally good, but writer-director Gary Hardwick doesn't give them the scenes that Chestnut and Union get. There is, for example, an awkward scene in a restaurant; the lawyer (Bellamy) brings in a white date (Julie Benz) who is a karate expert, and they run into a black woman judge who is one of his former girlfriends. There is a fight, which is stagy, artificial, and leads to race-based dialogue from the lawyer that seems out of character.

Even the divorced parents of the Morris Chestnut character get good scenes (his whole family seems to be in a better movie than the others). His mother, Louise (Jenifer Lewis), and his father, Fred (Clifton Powell), have had their good and bad times; their son resents the father and sides with the mother, and doesn't see their marriage with an adult's sense of complexity. It's interesting how he has to deal with his parents in order to learn how to deal with the woman he loves, and both parents have well-written scenes.

As for the others, well, the less said about the marriage in crisis over oral sex, the better. There might be useful or entertaining things to say about such a dilemma, but this movie doesn't find them. The subplot about Terry's approaching marriage is pretty standard sitcom stuff. And so on. The movie's a mixed bag, but worth seeing for the good stuff, which is a lesson in how productive it can be to allow characters to say what they might actually say.

Brown Sugar ★ ★ ★
PG-13, 108 m., 2002

Taye Diggs (Dre), Sanaa Lathan (Sidney), Nicole Ari Parker (Reese), Boris Kodjoe (Kelby Dawson), Mos Def (Chris V.), Queen Latifah (Francine). Directed by Rick Famuyiwa and produced by Peter Heller. Screenplay by Michael Elliot and Famuyiwa.

She is the editor of an important music magazine. He produces hip-hop for a major label. They've been best friends since childhood, but never more than that, although they came close a few times. Now, as both approach thirty, Dre (Taye Diggs) feels his career has lost its way. And Sidney (Sanaa Lathan) is working so hard she doesn't have time for romance: "You're turning into a Terry McMillan character," her girlfriend Francine warns her.

Brown Sugar, which charts romantic passages in these lives, is a romantic comedy, yes, but one with characters who think and talk about their goals, and are working on hard decisions. For both Sidney and Dre, hip-hop music symbolizes a kind of perfect adolescent innocence, a purity they're trying to return to as more cynical adults.

The first question Sidney asks an interview subject is always, "How did you fall in love with hip-hop?" For her, it was July 18, 1984, when she discovered for the first time a form that combined music, rhythm, performance, and poetry. Dre, her best buddy even then, grew up to become an important hip-hop producer, working for a label that compromised its standards as it became more successful. Now he's faced with the prospect of producing "Rin and Tin," one white, one black, who bill themselves as "The Hip-Hop Dalmatians."

Dre gets engaged to the beautiful Reese (Nicole Ari Parker). Sidney can't believe he'll marry her, but can't admit she loves him—although she comes close on the night before their wedding. Francine (Queen Latifah) lectures her to declare her love: "You'll get the buddy and the booty!" When Dre quits his job rather than work with the Dalmatians, he turns instinctively to Sidney for advice, and Reese begins to understand she's sharing his heart.

Sidney, meanwhile, interviews the hunky athlete Kelby Dawson (Boris Kodjoe), and soon they're engaged. Is this the real thing or a rebound? Dre still needs her for encouragement, as he pursues a hip-hop taxi driver named Chris V. (Mos Def), who he believes has potential to return the form to its roots. And Chris, articulate in his music but lacking confidence in his life, doesn't have the nerve to ask out Francine.

Brown Sugar, advertised as a hip-hop comedy, is more like a slice of black professional life (there's not even an entire hip-hop song in the whole movie). Directed and cowritten by Rick Famuyiwa, the movie returns to a world similar to his *The Wood* (1999). But the characters are deeper and more complex.

Consider Reese, the Nicole Ari Parker character. In a less thoughtful movie, she'd be the shallow, bitchy life-wrecker. Here she is blameless and basically reasonable: Mad at Dre for quitting his job without talking it over with her, jealous of Sidney because she (correctly) suspects Sidney and Dre have always been in love, but lied to themselves about it. That feeling comes to a head at the gym where both women work out, during a sparring match that gets a little too sincere.

There's a scene in *Brown Sugar* I never thought I'd see in a movie, where after Reese and Dre have a "final" fight, and in a more conventional film she would disappear forever from the screenplay, she returns to suggest counseling and says they need to work harder at their marriage. How many movie romances are that thoughtful about their characters?

Brown Sugar may be pitching itself to the wrong audience. The ads promise: "The Rhythm . . . the Beat . . . the Love . . . and You Don't Stop!" But it's not a musical, and although it's sometimes a comedy, it's observant about its people. Francine is onto something. They're all Terry McMillan characters.

Bruce Almighty ★ ★ ★
PG-13, 95 m., 2003

Jim Carrey (Bruce Nolan), Jennifer Aniston (Grace), Morgan Freeman (God), Lisa Ann Walter (Debbie), Philip Baker Hall (Jack Keller), Catherine Bell (Susan Ortega), Steven Carell (Evan Baxter), Nora Dunn (Ally Loman), Sally Kirkland (Waitress). Directed by Tom Shadyac and produced by Michael Bostick, James Brubaker, and Shadyac. Screenplay by Steve Oedekerk, Steve Koren, and Mark O'Keefe.

There is about Jim Carrey a desperate urgency that can be very funny, as he plunges with manic intensity after his needs and desires. In *Bruce Almighty,* he plays a man for whom the most important thing on Earth is to become an anchor on the Buffalo TV station. When he fails to achieve this pinnacle, he vents his anger at the very heavens themselves, challenging God to show and explain himself.

One could argue that Bruce Nolan, Carrey's character, is not necessarily qualified to be anchor, on the basis of two remote reports we see him delivering, one from the scene of a choco-

late chip cookie of record-breaking size, the other from onboard an anniversary cruise of the *Maid of the Mist,* the famous Niagara Falls tour boat. During the cruise he learns, while on the air live, that he will not be getting the coveted anchor job, and he goes ballistic, even uttering the dread f-word in his dismay.

Now that may argue that he is a loose cannon and not fit to anchor anyway (although he would be replacing a man whose primary skill seems to be smiling). Nevertheless, in anger and grief, and facing the loss of the love of his faithful girlfriend, Grace (Jennifer Aniston), he calls upon God, and God answers.

God is, in this case, a man in a white suit, played by Morgan Freeman with what can only be described as godlike patience with Bruce. Since Bruce is so dissatisfied with the job God is doing, God turns the controls of the universe over to him—or at least, the controls over his immediate neighborhood in Buffalo, although at one point this limited power seems to extend directly above Buffalo to such an extent that Bruce is able to change the distance of the moon, causing tidal waves in Japan.

Bruce Almighty, directed by Tom Shadyac and written by Steve Oedekerk, Steve Koren, and Mark O'Keefe, is a charmer, the kind of movie where Bruce learns that while he may not ever make a very good God, the experience may indeed make him a better television newsman.

The problem with playing God, the movie demonstrates, is that when such powers are entrusted to a human, short-term notions tend to be valued higher than long-term improvement plans. Consider, for example, the way Bruce deals with a dog that pees in the house (the payoff shot, showing the dog learning a new way to use the newspaper, had me laughing so loudly people were looking at me). And consider Bruce's methods for dealing with traffic jams, which work fine for Bruce but not so well for everyone else; when you're God, you can't think only of yourself.

Morgan Freeman plays God with a quality of warm detachment that is just about right, I think. You get the feeling that even while he's giving Bruce the free ride, he has a hand on the wheel, like a driver's training instructor. Jennifer Aniston, as a sweet kindergarten teacher and fiancée, shows again (after *The Good Girl*) that she really will have a movie career, despite the small-minded cavils of those who think she should have stayed on television. She can play comedy, which is not easy, and she can keep up with Carrey while not simply mirroring his zaniness; that's one of those gifts like being able to sing one song while typing the words to another.

Whether *Bruce Almighty* is theologically sound, I will leave to the better qualified. My own suspicion is that if you have God's power, even in a small area like Buffalo, it's likely to set things spinning weirdly everywhere. If a butterfly can flap its wings in Samoa and begin a chain of events leading to a tropical storm in the Caribbean, think what could happen when Bruce goes to work.

Bulletproof Monk ★ ★
PG-13, 103 m., 2003

Chow Yun-Fat (Monk with No Name), Seann William Scott (Kar), Jamie King (Jade/Bad Girl), Karel Roden (Struker), Victoria Smurfit (Nina), Patrick Hagarty (Mr. Funktastic). Directed by Paul Hunter and produced by Terence Chang, Charles Roven, John Woo, and Douglas Segal. Screenplay by Ethan Reiff and Cyrus Voris, based on the comic book by Brett Lewis and RA Jones.

Let us first consider the Scroll of the Ultimate. "Whoever reads it aloud in its entirety," an ancient monk explains to his young acolyte, "will gain the power to control the world." It is Tibet in 1943. The Nazis are there to capture the Scroll of the Ultimate. We recall from *Raiders of the Lost Ark* that the Third Reich was also trying to capture the Ark of the Covenant, perhaps so that Leni Riefenstahl, Hitler's favorite filmmaker, could direct *The Scroll of the Ultimate vs. the Ark of the Covenant*, a title I have just registered with the Writers Guild.

The young acolyte accepts responsibility for the Scroll and renounces his name, becoming the Monk with No Name, a name Clint Eastwood should have registered with the Writers Guild. No sooner does the Monk (Chow Yun-Fat) take possession than the sky churns with sensational visual effects, high winds blow, and the Nazis attack the temple. The Monk escapes by jumping off a high cliff, after first taking a Nazi bullet, which hits him right in the Scroll. He survives the jump, as he later explains, because gravity exists only if you think it does.

Since he walks around on the ground a lot, apparently he thinks it does, most of the time. The knack is to learn how to turn your belief on and off. Sixty years later, which is how long any one monk can guard the Scroll, the Monk is in New York City when he happens upon a pickpocket named Kar (Seann William Scott). Kar is working the subway, and has indeed just picked the Scroll from the Monk's briefcase, when he is forced into the subterranean lair of a gang of young toughs who look as dangerous as the crowd in a leather bar on date night. This gang is led by Mr. Funktastic (Patrick Hagarty), who has his name tattooed across his chest, and also includes the beautiful Bad Girl (Jamie King), who turns out to be a good girl. Kar engages in a violent martial arts struggle with the gang for a long time, after which they stop, because the scene is over, and Mr. Funktastic issues a dire warning should Kar ever stray their way again. Like he wants to hang out down there in the subterranean lair.

The Monk with No Name has secretly observed the fight, perhaps because Mr. Funktastic's men failed to notice the arrival of an unexpected monk, and he becomes friends with Kar, who seems to fit the Three Prophecies made about the one who will be chosen to guard the Scroll for the next sixty years. Of course, Kar is a reckless youth and must learn much about life, and meanwhile the Nazis turn up again and at one point have the Monk with No Name strapped to a torture machine crucifix-style, and are about to screw things into his brain.

Bulletproof Monk is a cross between a traditional Hong Kong martial arts movie and various American genres, incorporating the dubious notion that the wisest and most skilled practitioners of the ancient Asian arts have nothing better to do than tutor young Americans. To be sure, Kar has been studying on his own. "Where do you study fighting?" the Monk asks him. "The Golden Palace," he says. This is the broken-down movie palace where he is the projectionist, and he copies the moves from old karate movies.

The fight scenes in *Bulletproof Monk* are not

99

as inventive as some I've seen (although the opening fight on a rope bridge is so well done that it raises expectations it cannot fulfill). The film demonstrates, *Matrix*-style, that a well-trained fighter can leap into the air and levitate while spinning dozens of times, although why anyone would want to do this is never explained. Chow Yun-Fat and Seann William Scott do as much with the material as they can, although it's always a little awkward trying to shoehorn a romance into a movie like this, especially when you have to clear time for Bad Girl and Nina (Victoria Smurfit), who is a third-generation Nazi and the real bad girl, to have their obligatory hand-to-hand combat.

Bulletproof Monk was written by Ethan Reiff and Cyrus Voris, based on the comic book by Brett Lewis and RA Jones, and will appeal to more or less the same audience as the comic book. The ads and trailer hope we confuse it with *Crouching Tiger, Hidden Dragon,* but this is more like the Young Readers' version.

Bully ★ ★ ★ ★
NO MPAA RATING, 112 m., 2001

Brad Renfro (Marty Puccio), Rachel Miner (Lisa Connelly), Nick Stahl (Bobby Kent), Bijou Phillips (Ali Willis), Michael Pitt (Donny Semenec), Kelli Garner (Heather Swaller), Daniel Franzese (Derek Dzvirko), Leo Fitzpatrick (Hit Man). Directed by Larry Clark and produced by Chris Hanley, Don Murphy, and Fernando Sulichin. Screenplay by Zachary Long and Roger Pullis, based on the book *Bully: A True Story of High School Revenge* by Jim Schutze.

Larry Clark's *Bully* calls the bluff of movies that pretend to be about murder but are really about entertainment. His film has all the sadness and shabbiness, all the mess and cruelty and thoughtless stupidity of the real thing. Based on a real incident from 1993, it tells the story of a twisted high school bully and a circle of friends who decide to kill him. But this is not about the evil sadist and the release of revenge; it's about how a group of kids will do something no single member is capable of. And about the moral void these kids inhabit.

Clark moved to the Hollywood, Florida, suburb where the actual murder took place, and sees it as a sterile expanse of identikit homes, strip malls, and boredom, where the kids drift from video arcades to fast-food hangouts, and a car means freedom. There is no doubt a parallel universe in this same suburb, filled with happy, creative, intelligent people and endless opportunities—there always is—but these kids are off that map. They are stupid by choice, not necessity; they have fallen into a slacker subculture that involves leading their lives in a void that can be filled only by booze, drugs, sex, and the endless, aimless analysis of their pathetic emptiness.

The movie is brilliantly and courageously well acted by its young cast; it's one of those movies so perceptive and wounding that there's no place for the actors to hide, no cop-out they can exercise. Their characters bleed with banality and stupid, doped reasoning. Their parents are not bad and, for the most part, not blamed; their children live in a world they do not understand or, in some cases, even see.

We meet Marty Puccio (Brad Renfro) and Bobby Kent (Nick Stahl). For as long as Marty can remember, Bobby has picked on him, and we see it as a daily ordeal: the ear twisting, the hard punches, the peremptory orders ("Get back in the car now!"), the demands that he go where he doesn't want to go and do what he doesn't want to do. In a key scene, Bobby takes him to a gay strip club and makes him dance on the stage while patrons stuff bills into his shorts. Marty is not gay. Bobby may be; certainly his relationship with Marty is sublimated S&M.

Marty and Bobby meet Lisa and Ali (Rachel Miner and Bijou Phillips). Bobby eventually rapes both girls. He also likes to watch Marty and Lisa in the backseat. He is, we sense, evil to the core; something has gone very wrong in his life, and maybe it was engendered by the authoritarian style of his father, who likes to dominate people under the guise of only doing what's right for them.

The movie establishes these kids in a larger circle of friends, including the tall, strong, and essentially nice Donny (Michael Pitt), the anything-goes Heather (Kelli Garner), and Derek (Daniel Franzese), along for the ride. It watches as they drift from coffee shops to malls to each other's cars and bedrooms, engaged in an endless loop of speculation about the only subject available to them, their lives. The leadership in this circle shifts according to who has a strongly held opinion; the others drift into line. A consensus begins to form that Bobby deserves to be killed. At one point, Lisa simply says, "I want him dead."

It's chilling, the way the murder is planned so heedlessly. The kids decide they don't know enough to do it themselves and need to hire a "hit man." This turns out to be Leo Fitzpatrick (from Clark's powerful first film, *Kids*), who is essentially a kid himself. The conspirators vaguely think his family is "Mafia," although his qualifications come into question when he worries that car horns will bother the neighbors; eventually we get the priceless line, "The hit man needs a ride."

The details of the murder are observed unblinkingly in a scene of harrowing, gruesome sadness. It is hard, messy work to kill someone. Once the body is disposed of, the arguments begin almost immediately: Everybody had a hand in the assault, but nobody actually can be said to have delivered the fatal blow, and we watch incredulously as these kids cave in to guilt, remorse, grief, blaming each other, and the irresistible impulse to tell an outsider what happened.

Clark's purpose in the film is twofold. He wants to depict a youth culture without resources, and to show how a crowd is capable of actions its members would never commit on their own. In *Kids* (1995) and in this film, the adult society has abandoned these characters—done little to educate or challenge them, or to create a world in which they have purpose. One of Bobby's sins, which I neglected to mention, is that he is still in high school and plans to go to college; the others live with fast-food jobs and handouts from parents, and Ali has a revealing line: "I was married once, for about three weeks. I have a little boy, but it's no big deal—my parents take care of him." *Kids* takes place in Manhattan and *Bully* in south Florida, but these kids occupy essentially the same lives, have the same parents, share the same futures.

It may be that *Bully* helps to explain the high school shootings. We sense the chilling disconnect between an action and its consequences, the availability of firearms, the buildup of teenage resentments and hatreds, the moral vacuum, the way they can talk themselves into doing unthinkable things, and above all, the need to talk about it. (So many high school shooters leave diaries and Web pages, and tell their friends what they plan to do.) Yes, Bobby Kent is a bully (and one of the most loathsome characters I've seen in a movie). But he dies not for his sins, but because his killers are so bored and adrift, and have such uncertain ideas of themselves.

Larry Clark is obviously obsessed by the culture of floating, unplugged teenagers. Sometimes his camera seems too willing to watch during the scenes of nudity and sex, and there is one particular shot that seems shameless in its voyeurism (you'll know the one). But it's this very drive that fuels his films. If the director doesn't have a strong personal feeling about material like this, he shouldn't be making movies about it. Clark is not some objectified outside adult observer, making an after-school special, but an artist who has made a leap into this teenage mindscape. Some critics have attacked him as a dirty old man with a suspect relationship to his material; if this film had been directed by a twenty-five-year-old, some of these same critics might be hailing it. I believe *Bully* is a masterpiece on its own terms, a frightening indictment of a society that offers absolutely nothing to some of its children—and an indictment of the children, who lack the imagination and courage to try to escape. Bobby and his killers deserve one another.

The Business of Strangers ★ ★ ★
R, 83 m., 2001

Stockard Channing (Julie Styron), Julia Stiles (Paula Murphy), Frederick Weller (Nick Harris). Directed by Patrick Stettner and produced by Susan A. Stover and Robert H. Nathan. Screenplay by Stettner.

The Business of Strangers starts as a merciless dissection of a high-powered business executive, turns into a confrontation between two styles of being a tough woman, and ends as an upmarket version of a Pam Grier revenge melodrama. It keeps you watching.

The movie centers on two performances that are closely observed in their details and nuances. Stockard Channing plays Julie Styron, a road warrior for a software company, who is divorced, childless, curt, dismissive, and paranoid.

When she hears that the boss is flying in to have dinner with her, she immediately assumes she's being fired and instructs her secretary to copy all her files and messenger them to her house.

She's having a bad day. Her tech person turned up forty-five minutes late and blew an important presentation. That would be Paula Murphy (Julia Stiles), a Dartmouth grad who considers this "only a money job," is "really" a writer, and has a lot of tattoos, including a spider on the back of her neck and what looks like the Chrysler logo centered on her chest. (Why do some women believe tattoos enhance their breasts? Aren't they bringing coals to Newcastle?)

"As far as I'm concerned, she's fired," Julie says into her cell phone, ignoring Paula, who is standing next to her. As the older woman gets into her limo, the younger one calls her "uberfrau," but by that night in the hotel bar they find that they get along just fine as drinkers.

The third character in Patrick Stettner's original screenplay is Nick Harris (Frederick Weller), an executive headhunter, who flies in on a false alarm when Julie thinks she's being fired, and stays overnight after all of their flights are canceled. He's tall, slick, saturnine, and uses a lot of hair products.

The movie for at least its first hour is simply a very close study of how road warriors live. Their briefcases, their cell calls, their flight schedules, their hotel rooms, their use of the hotel bar and restaurant, their alienation and loneliness. Yet there is something uncoiling beneath this surface, based on the fact that Paula is a woman who doesn't like to be messed with, and Julie messed with her more than she realizes.

At first this manifests itself in daring one-upmanship, as when Julie offers to buy Paula a drink, Paula specifies a brand of cognac, the waiter says, "That's $20 a shot," Paula says,

"Make it a double," and Julie says she'll have the same thing. Later, after three or four more stiff drinks, Paula uses an elevator full of men to play a mind game—whispering to Julie about unusual sexual practices. Only gradually do we understand that Paula is challenging Julie, as when they're in the sauna and she asks, "Is this what a hot flash is like?" Julie responds with a description of her first hot flash, but that isn't why Paula asked.

What happens later in the film would not be fair to reveal. But I can express my ambivalence about it. Although the climactic scenes in the film have a certain weird fascination, I am not sure they're in character—maybe not for Paula, and certainly not for Julie, unless she's more drunk than she seems. The movie, having started with acute psychological observation, moves beyond realism into melodrama, and although some audiences will be fascinated (I was, to a degree), I think we lose something in the transfer.

Here's the paradox: If the first half of the film hadn't been so good, I might not question the second half so much. Channing and Stiles are so accurate in the way they create their two recognizable types that, well, the types are enough. We're fascinated by the dynamic between the two women, both smart and hard-edged, both obscurely wounded, both seeing themselves in the other. We like the way the younger woman goes after the older one ("Your best friend is your secretary. That's pathetic"). We want *this* to be the story, and when *The Business of Strangers* veers off into a series of manufactured plot developments, we're not sure we like it as much. Either way, it's a good movie, and Stockard Channing and Julia Stiles are the right choices for these roles. They zero in on each other like heat-seeking missiles.

C

Captain Corelli's Mandolin ★ ★
R, 127 m., 2001

Nicolas Cage (Captain Antonio Corelli), Penelope Cruz (Pelagia), John Hurt (Dr. Iannis), Christian Bale (Mandras), David Morrissey (Captain Gunther Weber), Irene Papas (Drosoula), Patrick Malahide (Colonel Barge), Aspasia Kralli (Mrs. Stamatis), Gerasimos Skiadaressis (Stamatis). Directed by John Madden and produced by Tim Bevan, Eric Fellner, Mark Huffam, and Kevin Loader. Screenplay by Shawn Slovo, based on the novel by Louis de Bernieres.

Perhaps *Captain Corelli's Mandolin* would have worked with subtitles. That way we would have had Greek, Italian, and German actors flavoring the story with the sound of their languages, and perhaps more local quirkiness too. In this film there is a scene where something is said in English pronounced with one accent, and a character asks, "What did he say?" and he is told—in English pronounced with another accent.

The story takes place on a small Greek island that serves as a microcosm for the Second World War, and as the backdrop for scenes of battle and romance. Its love story coexists with the war much more intelligently than the romance in *Pearl Harbor,* but it has a similar lack of passion: The lovers seem to be acting on assignment, rather than being compelled by passion.

I am increasingly suspicious of love at first, or even second, sight, because it inevitably means the two lovers stare fixedly at each other as if something Extremely Important has just happened, and the music tells us they have fallen in love—and the screenplay takes it as a given, and doesn't do the heavy lifting and tell us how, and why, and with what words, and for what reasons. To be required to love by the needs of a genre formula is no kind of fun.

The lovers in *Captain Corelli's Mandolin* are a Greek girl named Pelagia (Penelope Cruz) and the Italian Captain Corelli (Nicolas Cage). She is the daughter of the village physician, Dr. Iannis (John Hurt). Raised by her father and educated by him in literature and medi-

cine, she is smarter than the other village women, and when, earlier, she falls in love with the muscular, handsome Mandras (Christian Bale), her father warns her: "I would expect you to marry a foreigner." Greek men, he explains, expect to be dominant in a marriage, and "he is not your equal."

Mandras enlists in the Greek army to fight for freedom, ships out, and in the best-selling novel by Louis de Bernieres, has detailed and harrowing adventures that the movie avoids through a general downgrading of his role. Corelli arrives at the head of an invading "force"—a handful of Italian soldiers who sing opera and spend a lot of time at the beach with friendly prostitutes. When the mayor of the town is asked to surrender, he stands on his dignity, requiring a German officer to accept his surrender, as he doesn't take the Italians seriously. (He would rather surrender to the German officer's dog than to an Italian, he explains helpfully.)

The most delicate and fetching passages in the novel involve the stages by which Pelagia falls in love with Corelli, despite her engagement to Mandras, her dislike of foreigners, and her father's watchful eye. Then there are some effective scenes in which the Italians try to follow Mussolini's lead in surrendering, and the Germans respond. The novel's touching passages about Corelli's long secret stay in the Iannis house are, alas, compressed so painfully they lose all their meaning.

What we get is kind of a condensed version of some of the sights and sounds of the novel, without the heart, the spirit, and the juicy detail. The movie seems to exist on some sort of movie stage, and not in the real world. Curious, because it looks right. Dr. Iannis's house and its surrounding hillside looked uncannily like the scene I imagined while reading the novel, and the locations have a color the characters lack.

All except for one of them. Mandras's mother is played by the fierce Irene Papas, great spirit of the Greek cinema, now seventy-two. Her presence, and even some of her brief scenes, are a reminder that the Greeks are a little stormier and more unforgiving than some Mediterranean peoples. Penelope Cruz is Spanish, and with all the best intentions plays a Greek girl more motivated by sentiment than passion. Cage is American, and plays an Italian man for whom what is really important about love is that he is adored and forgiven by this enemy woman. A Greek and an Italian might have played these characters like romantic kickboxers.

There is a moment when the Irene Papas character sees Pelagia and Corelli dancing in the town square, and realizes Pelagia has betrayed her son Mandras (who is away fighting for freedom) with this foreign enemy. In the movie, the Papas character looks sorrowful and turns away. In life, I have a feeling, she would have come after the doctor's daughter with her teeth bared.

Capturing the Friedmans ★ ★ ★ ½
NO MPAA RATING, 107 m., 2003

Featuring Arnold Friedman, David Friedman, Elaine Friedman, and Jesse Friedman.
A documentary directed by Andrew Jarecki and produced by Jarecki and Marc Smerling.

After the Sundance screenings of *Capturing the Friedmans,* its director, Andrew Jarecki, was asked point-blank if he thought Arnold Friedman was guilty of child molestation. He said he didn't know. Neither does the viewer of this film. It seems clear that Friedman is guilty in some ways and innocent in others, but the truth may never be known—may not, indeed, be known to Friedman himself, who lives within such a bizarre personality that truth seems to change for him from moment to moment.

The film, which won the Grand Jury Prize at Sundance 2003, is disturbing and haunting, a documentary about a middle-class family in Great Neck, Long Island, that was torn apart on Thanksgiving 1987 when police raided their home and found child pornography belonging to the father. Arnold was a popular high school science teacher who gave computer classes in his basement den, which is where the porn was found—and also where, police alleged, he and his eighteen-year-old son, Jesse, molested dozens of young boys.

Of the porn possession there is no doubt, and in the film Arnold admits to having molested the son of a family friend. But about the

multiple molestation charges there is some doubt, and it seems unlikely that Jesse was involved in any crimes.

As Jarecki's film shows the Friedmans and the law authorities who investigated their case, a strange parallel develops: We can't believe either side. Arnold seems incapable of leveling with his family, his lawyers, or the law. And the law seems mesmerized by the specter of child abuse to such an extent that witnesses and victims are coached, led, and cajoled into their testimony; some victims tell us nothing happened, others provide confused and contradictory testimony, and the parents seem sometimes almost too eager to believe their children were abused. By the end of the film there is little we can hang onto, except for our conviction that the Friedmans are a deeply wounded family, that Arnold seems capable of the crimes he is charged with, and that the police seem capable of framing him.

Our confusion about the facts is increased, not relieved, by another extraordinary fact: All during the history of the Friedmans, and even during the period of legal investigations, charges, and court trials, the family was videotaped by another son, David. A third son, Seth, is visible in some of this footage, but does not otherwise participate in the film. At the very time when Arnold is charged with possession of child porn, when the abuse charges make national headlines, when his legal strategy is being mapped and his and Jesse's trials are under way, David is there, filming with the privileged position of a family insider. We even witness the last family council on the night before Arnold goes to prison.

This access should answer most of our questions, but does not. It particularly clouds the issue of Jesse's defense. It would appear—but we cannot be sure—that he was innocent but pled guilty under pressure from the police and his own lawyer, who threaten him with dire consequences and urge him to make a deal. Given the hysteria of the community at the time, it seems possible he was an innocent bystander caught up in the moment.

The dynamics within the family are there to see. The mother, Elaine, who later divorced and remarried, seems in shock at times within a family where perception and reality have only a nodding acquaintance. She withdraws, is passive-aggressive; it's hard to know what she's thinking.

Arnold is so vague about his sexual conduct that sometimes we can't figure out exactly what he's saying. He neither confirms nor denies. Jesse is too young and shell-shocked to be reliable. The witnesses contradict themselves. The lawyers seem incompetent. The police seem more interested in a conviction than in finding the truth. By the end of *Capturing the Friedmans,* we have more information, from both inside and outside the family, than we dreamed would be possible. We have many people telling us exactly what happened. And we have no idea of the truth. None.

The film is an instructive lesson about the elusiveness of facts, especially in a legal context. Sometimes guilt and innocence are discovered in court, but sometimes, we gather, only truths about the law are demonstrated. I am reminded of the documentaries *Paradise Lost* and *Paradise Lost 2: Revelations,* which involve the trials of three teenage boys charged with the murders of three children. Because the boys were outsiders, dressed in black, listened to heavy metal, they were perfect suspects—and were convicted amid hysterical allegations of "satanic rituals," even while the obvious prime suspect appears in both films doing his best to give himself away. Those boys are still behind bars. Their case was much easier to read than the Friedman proceedings, but viewers of the films are forced to the conclusion that the law and the courts failed them.

Catch Me If You Can ★ ★ ★
PG-13, 140 m., 2002

Leonardo DiCaprio (Frank Abagnale Jr.), Tom Hanks (Carl Hanratty), Christopher Walken (Frank Abagnale Sr.), Martin Sheen (Roger Strong), Nathalie Baye (Paula Abagnale), Amy Adams (Brenda Strong), Jennifer Garner (Cheryl Ann). Directed by Steven Spielberg and produced by Walter F. Parkes and Spielberg. Screenplay by Jeff Nathanson, based on the book by Frank Abagnale Jr. and Stan Redding.

The trailer for *Catch Me If You Can* is so obvious it could have written itself. It informs us that Frank Abagnale Jr. practiced medicine without attending medical school, practiced law without a law degree, and passed as a pilot without attending flight school—all for the excellent reason that he did all of these things before he was nineteen, and had not even graduated from high school.

That this is a true story probably goes without saying, since it is too preposterous to have been invented by a screenwriter. Abagnale also passed millions of dollars in bogus checks, dazzled women with his wealth and accomplishments, and was, a lot of the time, basically a sad and lonely teenager. At the time the only honest relationships in his life were with his father and with the FBI agent who was chasing him.

In Steven Spielberg's new film, Abagnale is played by Leonardo DiCaprio as a young man who succeeds at his incredible impersonations by the simple device of never seeming to try very hard. While an airline employee might be suspicious of a very young-looking man who insists he is a pilot, what could be more disarming than a man offered a trip in the jump seat who confesses, "It's been a while. Which one is the jump seat?"

DiCaprio, who in recent films like *The Beach* and *Gangs of New York* has played dark and troubled characters, is breezy and charming here, playing a boy who discovers what he is good at, and does it. There is a kind of genius flowing in the scene where he turns up for classes at a new school, walks into the classroom to discover that a substitute teacher is expected and, without missing a beat, writes his name on the blackboard and tells the students to shut up and sit down and tell him what chapter they're on.

It is probably true that most people will take you at face value until they have reason to do otherwise. I had a friend who had risen to a high level in her organization and was terrified her secret would be discovered: She never attended college. My guess, and it proved accurate, was that nobody would ever think to ask her. It is probably an even better guess that no patient in a hospital would ask to see a doctor's medical school diploma.

The movie makes some attempt to explain Abagnale's behavior through adolescent trauma. He is raised by loving parents; his father, Frank Sr. (Christopher Walken), brought his French mother, Paula (Nathalie Baye), back from Europe after military service, and Frank

Jr.'s childhood is a happy one until Paula cheats on her husband and walks out. Is that why her son was driven to impersonation and fraud? Maybe. Or maybe he would have anyway. Once he discovers how much he can get away with, there is a certain heady exhilaration in how easily he finds status, respect, and babes.

The movie costars Tom Hanks as Carl Hanratty, an FBI agent whose mission in life evolves into capturing Abagnale. As the only person who really has a comprehensive overview of the scope and versatility of Abagnale's activities, Hanratty develops—well, not an admiration, but a respect for a natural criminal talent. There is a scene where he actually has Abagnale at gunpoint in a motel room, and the kid, a cool customer and quick thinker, tries impersonating a Secret Service agent who is also on the suspect's tail.

Much of the pleasure of the movie comes from its enjoyment of Abagnale's strategies. He doesn't seem to plan his cons very well, but to take advantage of opportunities that fall his way. At one point, in New Orleans, he finds himself engaged to the daughter (Amy Adams) of the local district attorney (Martin Sheen). At a dinner party with his prospective in-laws, he seems to contradict himself by claiming to be both a doctor and a lawyer, when he doesn't look old enough to be either. When the D.A. presses him for an explanation, there is a kind of genius in his guileless reply: "I passed the bar in California and practiced for a year, before saying, 'Why not try out pediatrics?'"

Uh-huh. And then he makes the mistake of saying he graduated from law school at Berkeley. Turns out the Sheen character did, too, and quizzes him about a legendary professor before adding, "Does he still go everywhere with that little dog?" Here is where Abagnale's quickness saves him. Considering the thirty-year age difference between himself and the girl's father, he simply observes, "The dog died." Yes, although the professor may well have died, too, and when the D.A. calls his bluff, he responds by being honest (although that is sort of a lie, too).

This is not a major Spielberg film, although it is an effortlessly watchable one. Spielberg and his writer, Jeff Nathanson, working from the memoir by the real Frank Abagnale Jr. and

Stan Redding, don't force matters or plumb for deep significance. The story is a good story, directly told, and such meaning as it has comes from the irony that the only person who completely appreciates Abagnale's accomplishments is the man trying to arrest him. At one point, when the young man calls the FBI agent, Hanratty cuts straight to the point by observing, "You didn't have anyone else to call."

Cats and Dogs ★ ★ ★
PG, 87 m., 2001

Jeff Goldblum (Professor Brody), Elizabeth Perkins (Carolyn Brody), Alexander Pollock (Scott Brody). With the voices of: Tobey Maguire (Lou), Alec Baldwin (Butch), Sean Hayes (Mr. Tinkles), Susan Sarandon (Ivy), Joe Pantoliano (Peek), John Lovitz (Calico), Michael Clarke Duncan (Sam), Charlton Heston (The Mastiff). Directed by Lawrence Guterman and produced by Andrew Lazar, Chris Defaria, Warren Zide, and Craig Perry. Screenplay by John Requa and Glenn Ficarra.

Dogs are man's best friend, and that makes cats insanely resentful, in *Cats and Dogs,* a family comedy that uses every trick in the book to turn its dogs and cats into talking, scheming warriors. This movie probably has more special effects in it than *Lara Croft Tomb Raider,* although you don't notice them so much because you think you're looking at real animals even when you're not.

The movie reveals that cats and dogs have been at war since time immemorial, and in recent decades have escalated into high-tech battle technology, just like humans. Early in the film, a shepherd named Butch (voice by Alec Baldwin) trots into a doghouse, pushes a button, and is transported to a secret underground canine war room worthy of Dr. Strangelove. Later in the film, in a scene that is inexplicably even funnier than it should be, Ninja cats parachute to Earth wearing night-vision goggles.

The current battle in the long-running pet war involves the Brody family, and especially Professor Brody (Jeff Goldblum), whose research may eradicate man's allergies to dogs. The cats think that would be a very bad idea, and have mobilized on two fronts: (1) They want to sabotage Brody's research, and (2) in a lab of their own, they are developing a plan to make all humans allergic to all dogs.

Assigned to guard the Brody family is the inexperienced little beagle puppy Lou (voice of Tobey Maguire). He gets the job through a mix-up, and is briefed by Butch and introduced to the secrets of the canine war machine. Leading the opposition is the waspish cat Mr. Tinkles (voice of Sean Hayes) and his assistant Calico (voice of Jon Lovitz).

Warner Bros. says dozens of cats and dogs were used in the filming of the movie, but that doesn't even begin to suggest the result, which combines real animals with realistic puppets and computer-generated effects. The dogs and cats talk a lot, with perfect lip-synch, and they do things we somehow doubt any animals, however well trained, could really do. So advanced are the special-effects techniques that the filmmakers even combine animated faces with real animal bodies with such uncanny skill that after a while you give up trying to find the seams.

One of the movie's most enjoyable in-jokes is the way some of the animals actually look a little like the humans doing their voices. Not a lot—that would spoil the illusion—but subtly. Baldwin and Maguire are fairly easy to identify behind the ears and whiskers, and look for Susan Sarandon, Michael Clarke Duncan, Joe Pantoliano, and (as the general, of course) Charlton Heston.

This has been a year for inventive family movies. In addition to the animated features like *Atlantis* and *Shrek,* there have been three live-action films: *Spy Kids, Dr. Dolittle 2,* and now *Cats and Dogs.* I'd make *Cats and Dogs* a strong second on that list, for the remarkably convincing animals, the wild action and, not least, the parachuting Ninja cats. You really have to see them. Know how something will get you started giggling?

The Cat's Meow ★ ★ ★
PG-13, 110 m., 2002

Kirsten Dunst (Marion Davies), Cary Elwes (Thomas Ince), Edward Herrmann (William Randolph Hearst), Eddie Izzard (Charlie Chaplin), Joanna Lumley (Elinor Glyn), Jennifer Tilly (Louella Parsons). Directed by Peter Bogdanovich and produced by Kim Bieber and Carol Lewis. Screenplay by Steven Peros.

William Randolph Hearst did, or did not, get away with murder on board his private yacht *Oneida* on November 15, 1924. If he did, there is no question he was powerful enough to cover it up. Hearst was the carnivorous media tycoon of the age, proprietor of newspapers, magazines, radio stations, wire services, movie production companies, a private castle, and his mistress Marion Davies, an actress of great but perhaps not exclusive charms. He was above the law not so much because of clout or bribery but because of awe; the law enforcement officials of the day were so keenly aware of their inferior social status that they lacked the nerve to approach him. The silent movies of the time are filled with scenes in which cops arrest a millionaire, discover who he is, respectfully tip their hats to him, and apologize.

On that day in 1924, the Hollywood producer Thomas Ince possibly died, or was murdered, on board the *Oneida.* Or perhaps not. According to one story, he was shot dead by Hearst through an unfortunate misunderstanding; Hearst mistook him for Charlie Chaplin, and thought Chaplin was having an affair with Davies. Other theories say Hearst accidentally stuck Ince with a hat pin, precipitating a heart attack. Or that Ince drank some bad rotgut. There is even the possibility that Ince died at home. There was no autopsy, so the official cause of death was never determined. No guests on the yacht were ever questioned; indeed, no one can agree about who was on the yacht during its cruise.

In Hollywood at the time, whispers about Ince's death and Hearst's involvement were easily heard, and the story told in Peter Bogdanovich's *The Cat's Meow* is, the film tells us, "the whisper heard most often." Bogdanovich is not much interested in the scandal as a scandal. He uses it more as a prism through which to view Hollywood in the 1920s, when the new medium had generated such wealth and power that its giants, like Chaplin, were gods in a way no later stars could ever be. Hearst (Edward Herrmann) liked to act the beneficent host, and on the *Oneida* for that cruise were the studio head Ince (Cary Elwes), the stars Davies (Kirsten Dunst) and Chaplin (Eddie Izzard), the British wit Elinor Glyn (Joanna Lumley), and an ambitious young gossip columnist named Louella Parsons (Jennifer Tilly). There were also various stuffed shirts and their wives, and a tame society doctor.

In this company Hearst is an insecure loner, an innocent barely the equal of the life of sin he has chosen for himself. He has the *Oneida* bugged with hidden microphones, and scarcely has time to join his guests because he needs to hurry away and eavesdrop on what they say about him in his absence. Davies knows about the microphones and knows all about Willie; she was a loyal mistress who loved her man and stood by him to the end. Whether she did have an affair with Chaplin is often speculated. According to this scenario, she may have, and Willie finds one of her brooches in Chaplin's stateroom (after tearing it apart in a scene mirroring Kane's famous destruction of Susan's bedroom in the Welles picture).

Bogdanovich has an exact way of conveying the forced and metronomic gaiety on the yacht, where guests are theoretically limited to one drink before dinner, Marion Davies has to order the band to play the Charleston to cover awkward silences, every guest has a personal agenda, and at night, as guests creep from one stateroom to another and deck planks creak, they seem to be living in an English country house mystery—*Gosford Yacht.*

Apart from its theory about the mistaken death of Ince and its cover-up, the movie's most intriguing theory is that Louella Parsons witnessed it, which might explain her lifetime contract with the Hearst papers. In the exquisite wording of a veiled blackmail threat, she tells the tycoon: "We're at the point in our careers where we both need real security." Since she was making peanuts and he was one of the richest men in the world, one can only admire the nuance of "our careers."

The film is darkly atmospheric, with Edward Herrmann quietly suggesting the sadness and obsession beneath Hearst's forced avuncular chortles. Dunst is as good, in her way, as Dorothy Comingore in *Citizen Kane* in showing a woman who is more loyal and affectionate than her lover deserves. Lumley's zingers

as Glyn cut right through the hypocritical grease. Tilly, we suspect, has the right angle on Parsons's chutzpah.

There is a detail easy to miss toward the end of the film that suggests as well as anything what power Hearst had. After the society doctor ascertains that Ince, still alive, has a bullet in his brain, Hearst orders the yacht to moor at San Diego, and then dispatches the dying producer by private ambulance—not to a local hospital, but to his home in Los Angeles! Hearst is on the phone to the future widow, suggesting a cover story, long before the pathetic victim arrives home. ☞

The Caveman's Valentine ★ ★ ★
R, 105 m., 2001

Samuel L. Jackson (Romulus), Colm Feore (Leppenraub), Ann Magnuson (Moira), Damir Andrei (Arnold), Aunjanue Ellis (Lulu), Tamara Tunie (Sheila), Peter MacNeill (Cork), Jay Rodan (Joey/No Face). Directed by Kasi Lemmons and produced by Danny DeVito, Michael Shamberg, Stacey Sher, Elie Samaha, and Andrew Stevens. Screenplay by George Dawes Green, based on his novel.

The detective in *The Caveman's Valentine* is a raving lunatic on his bad days, and a homeless man on a harmless errand on his good ones. Once he was a brilliant pianist, a student at Julliard. Now he lives in a cave in a park. His dreadlocks reach down to his waist, and his eyes peer out at a fearsome world. You'd be fearful, too, if your enemy lived at the top of the Chrysler Building and attacked you with deadly rays.

Romulus Ledbetter is one of Samuel L. Jackson's most intriguing creations, a schizophrenic with sudden sharp stabs of lucid thought and logical behavior, whose life is changed one day when the frozen body of a young man is found outside his cave in a city park. The police believe the man, a transient, froze to death. Romulus thinks he knows better. And his desire to unmask the real killer draws him out of his cave and into a daring foray into the New York art world.

Romulus is not without connections. His daughter, Lulu (Aunjanue Ellis), is a policewoman. But she is hardly convinced by his first suspect: his enemy in the Chrysler Building. By the time he discards that hypothesis and zeroes in on a fashionable photographer named Leppenraub (Colm Feore), it's too late for anyone to take him seriously—if they ever could have in the first place.

The challenge for Jackson and his director, Kasi Lemmons, is to make Romulus believable both as the caveman and as a man capable of solving a murder. Too much ranting and raving, and Romulus would repel the audience. Too much logic, and we don't buy him as mentally ill. Even the clothes and the remarkable hair have to be considered; this is not a man you would want to sit next to during a three-day bus trip, but, on the other hand, he doesn't tilt over into repellent grunge (like the aliens in *Battlefield Earth*). It's remarkable the way Jackson begins with the kind of character we'd avert our eyes from, and makes him fascinating and even likable.

This is Lemmons's second film; after her remarkable debut *Eve's Bayou* (1997), she repeats her accomplishment in fleshing out a story with intriguing supporting characters. Chief among these is Leppenraub, a gay photographer who savors S and M imagery, and his employee/lover Joey (Jay Rodan), who makes digital videos. If Leppenraub killed the dead young man, did Joey film it? Romulus is able to enter the photographer's world through an unlikely route, involving a bankruptcy lawyer who befriends him, cleans him up, and enlists him as a pianist at a party. At one of Leppenraub's openings, the dreadlocked caveman looks at the photographs with the clear eye of the mad but logical, and says exactly what he thinks.

Is this a reach, suggesting that the caveman and the photographer could find themselves in the same circles? Not in the art world, where unlikely alliances are forged every day; the movie *Basquiat* is about an artist who made the round trip from the streets to the galleries. It's also plausible, if unlikely, that the cleaned-up Romulus, an exciting man with an electric presence, could attract the sexual attention of Leppenraub's sister, Moira (Ann Magnuson), who seduces him because she likes to shock, she likes to try new things, and she likes the guy (of course, she doesn't know his whole story).

The actual solution to the murder mystery was, for me, the least interesting part of the movie. *The Caveman's Valentine* is based on a crime novel by George Dawes Green, who also wrote the screenplay, and like many procedurals it has great respect for clues, sudden insights, logical reasoning, holes in stories, and all the beloved devices of the detection genre. Although the detective in this case may be completely original, his method (under the madness) is traditional. At the end all is settled and solved, but I agree with Edmund Wilson in his famous essay on detective novels when he concluded, essentially, "so what?"

The solution simply allows the story to end. The engine that makes the story live is in the life of Romulus: in how he survives, how he thinks, how people see in him what they are looking for. To watch Samuel L. Jackson in the role is to realize again what a gifted actor he is, how skilled at finding the right way to play a character who, in other hands, might be unplayable. I think the key to the whole performance is in his walk. It's busy and bustling, as if he's late for an appointment that he's rather looking forward to. He seems absorbed in his thoughts and plans, a busy man, with the jam-packed calendar of the mad.

The Center of the World ★ ★ ★ ½
NO MPAA RATING, 86 m., 2001

Peter Sarsgaard (Richard Longman), Molly Parker (Florence), Carla Gugino (Jerri), Balthazar Getty (Brian Pivano). Directed by Wayne Wang and produced by Peter Newman and Wang. Screenplay by Ellen Benjamin Wong (pseudonym for Wang, Paul Auster, and Siri Hustvedt).

Sex isn't the subject of *The Center of the World*. It's the arena. The subject is making money, and the movie is about two people who hate their jobs. Richard (Peter Sarsgaard) is a computer whiz whose company is about to go public and make him a millionaire. Florence (Molly Parker) is a lap dancer in a strip club, but technically not a prostitute. You can be aroused by her, but you can't touch her. Richard is the same way. He skips a meeting with investors, and disappears as his company floats its IPO. You can profit from his skills, but you can't have him.

Here are two people who want to succeed only on their own terms. The big difference between them, as she points out, is "money. You have it and I don't." As a sex worker, her strategy is to get the client's money without giving herself. She meets Richard in a coffee shop. He finds out where she works, turns up, and buys a lap dance. He's fascinated. He asks her to go to Las Vegas for a weekend. She says she's not that kind of person. "I can compensate you," he says. "Compensate" is a revealing word in this context. He offers her $10,000. She says he'll have to observe her rules. He agrees.

He may actually be happy to agree. She's spared him from performance anxiety. He gets the intrigue, the excitement, the mystique, and her full attention, and avoids physical and psychological risk. Nice deal. Good for her, too, because she needs money but doesn't think of herself as a prostitute (she's "really" a drummer in a rock band). Wayne Wang says his film was inspired by the strip clubs of the Silicon Valley. They bring together men who have too much money and no interest in relationships with women who have too little money and no interest in relationships.

Sex supplies the stakes. It's the currency of the microeconomy created for a weekend by Richard and Flo. She manufactures sex, he consumes it, and cash flow is generated. When she goes a little further than her guidelines permit, that's like Alan Greenspan lowering interest rates. The casual observer may think the weekend is all about sex; more evolved viewers will notice that the sex is not very fulfilling, very original, or very good; what is fascinating are the mind games. They're like negotiations. Flo is the better negotiator, but then of course she's the market-maker.

In theory, a prostitute and her client form a closed system, in which everything in their private lives, even their real names, may be kept secret. Because Richard and Flo met socially before entering into their agreement, information leaked out. She knows he's about to make millions of dollars, although all she wants is $10,000. The commitment involved in getting the millions would interfere with her idea of herself. We in the audience get more information because we eavesdrop during their private moments; he deals by e-mail with part-

ners who are enraged that he stiffed the investors and (they hear) is in Vegas with a hooker on the company's biggest day. She calls a Vegas friend named Jerri (Carla Gugino), who gives her technical advice; she tells Jerri she "kinda likes" the guy.

Now look at their sex. Her rules permit action only between 10 P.M. and 2 A.M. The rest of the time, they sightsee, visit restaurants, play video games. The sex in theory will not involve intercourse. They have connecting rooms. At 10 P.M. she throws open the doors, dressed dramatically in "erotic" clothes that are pretty routine. She does advanced versions of a lap dance. He wants to go further. "You want real?" she asks. "I'll show you real." What she shows him is real, all right, but scant consolation for an onlooker.

At one point they practice something called "fire and ice," which involves ice cubes and hot sauce, and has been compared by credulous reviewers with the most famous scene in *Last Tango in Paris*. The difference is, in *Last Tango* something was really happening between two unpaid and involved participants; in *The Center of the World,* it's erotic showbiz. (Show me a sexual practice that involves ice cubes and hot sauce, and I will show you a sexual practice that would be improved without them.) The movie has also been compared to *Leaving Las Vegas,* but couldn't be more different. That was about agony and redemption, and the hooker was a healing angel. This movie is about two entrepreneurs.

The suspense in *The Center of the World* is not about whether Flo and Richard will have real sex. The suspense involves whether they'll start to like each other. He tells her he's in love, but guys always say that. She kinda likes him, but having started off in this way, can she ever have sex with him that will not seem, in some way, like a subtle extension of prostitution? To this intrigue is added another level when Jerri, the friend, visits their suite with a story of being beaten up. Is Richard being scammed by the two women?

In a scenario like this, it's impossible to figure out what's real. Does Richard love Flo, or the erotic illusion she creates, or the freedom from responsibility she makes possible? Does Flo like Richard, or his money, or the gamesmanship of dancing closer to the flame? When they spontaneously find themselves turned on outside the four-hour time zone, is that real, or does it feed off the excitement of breaking the rules? The situation is complicated because all of their interruptus brinksmanship has been a turn-on. They're only human.

If you understand who the characters are and what they're supposed to represent, the performances are right on the money. Flo is not supposed to be a sexy tart, and Richard is not supposed to be a lustful client. They're sides of the same coin, and very much alike. You want real? This movie shows you real. For Richard and Flo, real is a weekend in Vegas trying to figure out what they really want, and how much they're willing to sell off in order to buy it.

Changing Lanes ★ ★ ★ ★
R, 100 m., 2002

Ben Affleck (Gavin Banek), Samuel L. Jackson (Doyle Gipson), Toni Collette (Michelle), Sydney Pollack (Delano), William Hurt (Doyle's Sponsor), Amanda Peet (Cynthia), Kim Staunton (Valerie Gipson), Dylan Baker (Fixer). Directed by Roger Michell and produced by Scott Rudin. Screenplay by Chap Taylor and Michael Tolkin.

"One wrong turn deserves another," say the ads for *Changing Lanes*. Yes, both of the movie's dueling hotheads are in the wrong—but they are also both in the right. The story involves two flawed men, both prey to anger, who get involved in a fender bender that brings out all of their worst qualities. And their best. This is not a dumb formula film about revenge. It doesn't use rubber-stamp lines like, "It's payback time." It is about adults who have minds as well as emotions, and can express themselves with uncommon clarity. And it's not just about the quarrel between these two men, but about the ways they have been living their lives.

The story begins with two men who need to be in court on time. Gavin Banek (Ben Affleck) needs to file a signed form proving that an elderly millionaire turned over control of his foundation to Banek's law firm. Doyle Gipson (Samuel L. Jackson) needs to show that he has loan approval to buy a house for his family; he hopes that will persuade his fed-up wife to stay in New York and not move with the kids to Oregon. Banek and Gipson get into a fender bender. It's not really anybody's fault.

Of course they are polite when it happens: "You hurt?" Nobody is. Banek, who is rich and has been taught that money is a solution to human needs, doesn't want to take time to exchange insurance cards and file a report. He hands Gipson a signed blank check. Gipson, who wants to handle this the right way, doesn't want a check. Banek gets in his car and drives away, shouting, "Better luck next time!" over his shoulder, and leaving Gipson stranded in the middle of the expressway with a flat tire.

Gipson gets to court twenty minutes late. The case has already been settled. In his absence, he has lost. The judge isn't interested in his story. Banek gets to court in time, but discovers that he is missing the crucial file folder with the old man's signature. Who has it? Gipson.

At this point, in a film less intelligent and ambitious, the vile Banek would pull strings to make life miserable for the blameless Gipson. But *Changing Lanes* doesn't settle for the formula. Gipson responds to Banek's rudeness by faxing a page from the crucial file to Banek with "Better luck next time!" scrawled on it. Banek turns to his sometime mistress (Toni Collette), who knows a guy who "fixes" things. The guy (Dylan Baker) screws with Gipson's credit rating so his home mortgage falls through. Gipson finds an ingenious way to counterattack. And so begins a daylong struggle between two angry men.

Ah, but that's far from all. *Changing Lanes* is a thoughtful film that by its very existence shames studio movies that have been dumbed down into cat-and-mouse cartoons. The screenplay is by Chap Taylor, who has previously worked as a production assistant for Woody Allen, and by Michael Tolkin, who wrote the novel and screenplay *The Player* and wrote and directed two extraordinary films, *The Rapture* and *The New Age*. The writers, rookie and veteran, want to know who these men are, how they got to this day in their lives, what their values are, what kinds of worlds they live in. A dumb film would be about settling scores after the fender bender. This film, which breathes, which challenges, which is ex-

111

citingly alive, wants to see these men hit their emotional bottoms. Will they learn anything?

Doyle Gipson is a recovering alcoholic. His AA meetings and his AA sponsor (William Hurt) are depicted in realistic, not stereotyped terms. He's sober, but still at the mercy of his emotions. As he stands in the wreckage of his plans to save his marriage, his wife (Kim Staunton) tells him, "This is the sort of thing that always happens to you—and never happens to me unless I am in your field of gravity." And his sponsor tells him, "Booze isn't really your drug of choice. You're addicted to chaos." At one point, seething with rage, Gipson walks into a bar and orders a shot of bourbon. Then he stares at it. Then he gets into a fight that he deliberately provokes, and we realize that at some level he walked into the bar not for the drink but for the fight.

Gavin Banek leads a rich and privileged life. His boss (Sydney Pollack) has just made him a partner in their Wall Street law firm. It doesn't hurt that Banek married the boss's daughter. It also doesn't hurt that he was willing to obtain the signature of a confused old man who might not have known what he was signing, and that the firm will make millions as a result. His wife (Amanda Peet) sees her husband with blinding clarity. After Banek has second thoughts about the tainted document, Pollack asks his daughter to get him into line, and at lunch she has an extraordinary speech.

"Did you know my father has been cheating on my mother for twenty years?" she asks him. He says no, and then sheepishly adds, "Well, I didn't know it was for twenty years." Her mother knew all along, his wife says, "but she thought it would be unethical to leave a man for cheating on his marriage, after she has enjoyed an expensive lifestyle that depends on a man who makes his money by cheating at work." She looks across the table at her husband. "I could have married an honest man," she tells him. She did not, choosing instead a man who would go right to the edge to make money. You don't work on Wall Street if you're not prepared to do that, she says.

And what, for that matter, about the poor old millionaire whose foundation is being plundered? "How do you think he got his money?" Pollack asks Affleck. "You think those factories in Malaysia have day-care centers?"

He helpfully points out that the foundation was set up in the first place as a tax dodge.

Such speeches are thunderbolts in *Changing Lanes*. They show the movie digging right down into the depths of the souls, of the values of these two men. The director, Roger Michell, has made good movies, including *Persuasion* and *Notting Hill*, but this one seems more like Neil LaBute's *In the Company of Men*, or Tolkin's work. It lays these guys out and X-rays them, and by the end of the day, each man's own anger scares him more than the other guy's. This is one of the best movies of the year.

Charlie's Angels: Full Throttle ★ ★ ½
PG-13, 105 m., 2003

Cameron Diaz (Natalie Cook), Drew Barrymore (Dylan Sanders), Lucy Liu (Alex Munday), Demi Moore (Madison Lee), Bernie Mac (Jimmy Bosley). Directed by McG and produced by Drew Barrymore, Leonard Goldberg, and Nancy Juvonen. Screenplay by John August, Cormac Wibberley, and Marianne Wibberley, based on the television series by Ivan Goff and Ben Roberts.

Sometimes it has more to do with mood than with what's on the screen. *Charlie's Angels: Full Throttle* is more or less the same movie as the original *Charlie's Angels* (2000), and yet I feel more forgiving this time. Wow, did I hate the first one: "a movie without a brain in its three pretty little heads." I awarded it one-half of a star.

But what, really, was so reprehensible about that high-tech bimbo eruption? Imagine a swimsuit issue crossed with an explosion at the special-effects lab, and you've got it. Maybe I was indignant because people were going to spend their money on this instead of going to better movies that were undoubtedly more edifying for them. But if people wanted to be edified every time they went to the movies, Hollywood would be out of business.

Charlie's Angels: Full Throttle is not a funny movie, despite a few good one-liners, as when Bernie Mac explains that the Black Irish invented the McRib. It is not an exciting movie, because there is no way to genuinely care about what's happening, and it doesn't make much sense, anyway. It is not a sexy movie, even though it stars four sexy women, because you just can't get aroused by the sight of three babes running toward you in slow motion with an explosion in the background. I've tried it.

So what is it? Harmless, brainless, good-natured fun. Leaving *Full Throttle*, I realized I did not hate or despise the movie, and so during a long and thoughtful walk along the Chicago River, I decided that I sort of liked it because of the high spirits of the women involved.

Say what you will, Drew Barrymore, Cameron Diaz, Lucy Liu, and Demi Moore were manifestly having fun while they made this movie. They're given outrageous characters to play, an astonishing wardrobe (especially considering the fact that they go everywhere without suitcases), remarkable superpowers, and lots of close-ups in which they are just gorgeous when they smile.

It's a form of play for them, to be female James Bonds, just as male actors all like to be in Westerns because you get to ride a horse and shoot up saloons. There is a scene where the three angels discuss what Dylan Sanders (Drew Barrymore) was named before she went into the witness protection program. It turns out she was named Helen Zas. Now there's a name to go in the books with Norma Stitz. Natalie (Cameron Diaz) and Alex (Lucy Liu) kid her mercilessly about her name, and as Lucy Liu comes up with wicked puns, you almost get the impression she's thinking them up herself.

The plot . . . but why should I describe the plot? It is an arbitrary and senseless fiction designed to provide a weak excuse for a series of scenes in which the angels almost get killed, in Mongolia and elsewhere, mostly elsewhere, while blowing up stuff, shooting people, being shot at, almost getting killed, and modeling their PG-13-rated outfits.

Two new faces this time: Demi Moore, as Madison Lee, a fallen angel, and Bernie Mac, taking over for Bill Murray in the Bosley role, as Bosley's brother, who I think is also called Bosley. The Angels confront Madison high atop Los Angeles at the Griffith Observatory, which for mysterious reasons is completely deserted during their showdown and shoot-out.

So. I give the movie 2½ stars, partially in expiation for the half-star I gave the first one. But if you want to see a movie where big stars trade witty one-liners with one another in the midst of high-tech chase scenes and all sorts of explosive special effects, the movie for you is *Hollywood Homicide.*

Charlotte Gray ★ ★

PG-13, 123 m., 2002

Cate Blanchett (Charlotte Gray), Billy Crudup (Julien Lavade), Rupert Perry-Jones (Peter), Michael Gambon (Levarde), Anton Lesser (Benech), Ron Cook (Mirabel). Directed by Gillian Armstrong and produced by Sarah Curtis and Douglas Rae. Screenplay by Jeremy Brock, based on the novel by Sebastian Faulks.

Consider now Cate Blanchett, a wondrous actress. Born in Melbourne in 1969, honored for her stage work in Australia, a survivor of U.S. TV-like *Police Rescue*, she made her first film in 1997 (*Paradise Road*, about female prisoners of war in the Pacific) and then arrived immediately at stardom in the title role of *Elizabeth* (1998), winning an Oscar nomination.

In the four years since then she has played in an astonishing range of roles: as a calculating Londoner in *An Ideal Husband*, as a strong-willed nineteenth-century gambler from the Outback in the wonderful *Oscar and Lucinda*, as an Italian-American housewife from New Jersey in *Pushing Tin*, as a rich society girl in *The Talented Mr. Ripley*, as a gold-digging Parisian showgirl in *The Man Who Cried*, as an Appalachian redneck with psychic powers in *The Gift*, as the woman who convinces both Billy Bob Thornton and Bruce Willis they love her in *Bandits*, as Galadriel in *Lord of the Rings*, as a lanky-haired Poughkeepsie slattern in *The Shipping News*, and now as a British woman who parachutes into France and fights with the Resistance in *Charlotte Gray*. Oh, and also in 2001 she had a baby.

Name me an actress who has played a greater variety of roles in four years, and I'll show you Meryl Streep. Were you counting Blanchett's accents? British, Elizabethan English, Edwardian English, Scots, Australian, French, American southern, midwestern, New England, New Joisey. And she has the kind of perfect profile they used in the "Can You Draw This Girl?" ads. She can bring as much class to a character as Katharine Hepburn, and has a better line in sluts.

While I was watching *Charlotte Gray,* I spent a lot of time thinking about Blanchett's virtues, because she, Billy Crudup, and Michael Gambon were performing life support on a hopeless screenplay. This is a movie that looks great, is well acted, and tells a story that you can't believe for a moment. I have no doubt that brave British women parachuted into France to join the Resistance; indeed, I have seen a much better movie about just such a woman—*Plenty* (1985), starring, wouldn't you know, Meryl Streep. It's just that I don't think such women were motivated primarily by romance. After *Pearl Harbor,* here is another movie where World War II is the backdrop for a love triangle.

Blanchett plays the title character, a Scottish woman in London who speaks perfect French and meets a young airman named Peter (Rupert Perry-Jones) at a publisher's party. They fall instantly in love, they have a one-night stand, he's shot down over France, and (she hears and believes) finds shelter with the Resistance. Charlotte allows herself to be recruited into British Special Operations, goes through training, and is dropped into France—near where Peter is thought to be. She is going to—what? Rescue him? Comfort him in her arms? Get him back to Britain? The movie doesn't spell this out very well.

In France, she comes into contact with a Resistance group led by Julien (Billy Crudup), a Communist, whose father, Levarde (Michael Gambon), disapproves of his son's politics, but keeps quiet because he hates the Nazis. Soon Charlotte is taken along on a raid that underlines the screenplay's basic problem, which is her utterly superfluous presence.

Crudup and his men hide in a ditch, blow up a Nazi train, are chased and nearly killed by Nazi soldiers. The next morning, Charlotte is told: "You did a good job last night." Why? How? What did she accomplish but tag along on a mission she had nothing to do with, watch the men blow up the train, and run for her life? A stranger, not needed, why was she taken along in the first place? This is the Resistance version of the practice of taking a girl along with you on a hunting trip so she can admire you shooting the big bad birds.

Soon Charlotte and Julien are drifting into unacknowledged love, while a subplot involves the fate of two local Jewish children whose parents have been shipped to the camps. Charlotte touches base with a dyspeptic local contact who seems to exist primarily to raise doubts about himself, and . . . but see for yourself, as the plot thickens. One question you might ask: How wise is it for Julien, an important Resistance fighter who wants to remain unnoticed, to shout curses at arriving Nazi troops? Another is: How important is that final letter Charlotte risks her life to type?

Blanchett, Crudup, and Gambon stand above and somehow apart from the absurdities of the screenplay. Their presence in their characters is convincing enough that we care about them and hope they survive—if not the war, at least the screenplay. The movie was directed by Gillian Armstrong, usually so good (*My Brilliant Career,* the overlooked and inspired *Oscar and Lucinda*). This time she excels in everything but her choice of material.

It is Cate Blanchett's fate to be born into a time when intelligence is fleeing from mainstream movies. The script for *Plenty* was based on a great play by David Hare. *Charlotte Gray* is based on a best-selling novel by Sebastian Faulks, unread by me, and on the basis of this movie, not on my reading list. Next Blanchett appears in *Heaven,* based on a screenplay by the late Krzysztof Kieslowski and directed by Tom Tykwer (*Run Lola Run, The Princess and the Warrior*). Good career move.

Charlotte Sometimes ★ ★ ★ ½
NO MPAA RATING, 85 m., 2003

Michael Idemoto (Michael), Jacqueline Kim (Darcy), Eugenia Yuan (Lori), Matt Westmore (Justin), Shizuko Hoshi (Auntie Margie), Kimberly Rose (Annie). Directed by Eric Byler and produced by Marc Ambrose and Byler. Screenplay by Byler.

The man lives alone in his apartment, sometimes reading, sometimes standing quietly in the dark. Through the walls he can hear passionate lovemaking. After a time there is a knock on his door. It is, we know, the young woman who lives next door. She can't sleep, she says. The man and his neighbor sit on his couch to watch television, and in the morning she is still asleep in his arms.

This simply, Eric Byler's *Charlotte Sometimes* draws us into its mysterious, erotic story. The man is named Michael (Michael Idemoto). His neighbor—actually his tenant in a two-unit building—is Lori (Eugenia Yuan). Her lover is Justin (Matt Westmore), and while their sex life is apparently spectacular she seems to have a deep, if platonic, love for Michael. What is their relationship, exactly? Michael is so quiet, so reserved, we cannot know for sure, although it seems clear in his eyes that he does not enjoy what he hears through the wall.

Lori asks Michael if he would like to meet a girl—she knows someone she could introduce him to. Before that can happen, one night in a neighborhood bar, he sees a young woman sitting alone across the room. He looks at her; she looks at him. He leaves, but comes back just as she is leaving—clearly to find her, although he claims he forgot something.

This is Darcy (Jacqueline Kim). She is tall and grave, the opposite of the pretty, cuddly Lori. "Men don't want me," she says. "They only think they want me." She reveals little about herself. As they talk into the night, they develop that kind of strange intimacy two people can have when they know nothing about each other but feel a deep connection. Eventually she offers to have sex with him, but Michael doesn't want that. It's too soon. Sex may be a shortcut to intimacy, but he values something more: perhaps his privacy, perhaps his growing attraction for her, which he doesn't want to reduce to the physical just yet.

Byler's screenplay never says too much, never asks the actors to explain or reveal in words what we sense in their presence and guarded, even coded, conversations. Jacqueline Kim, an experienced classical stage actress (from the Goodman in Chicago and the Guthrie in Minneapolis), brings a quality to Darcy that is intriguing and unsettling at the same time. She leaves and returns unpredictably. There is something she is not saying. Michael feels attracted, and yet warned.

This story, which is almost Gothic in its undertones, is filmed in an ordinary Los Angeles neighborhood. The house is on a winding road on a hillside. Michael owns a garage. "You're a mechanic—and you read," Darcy muses. He took over the family garage, but lives inside his ideas and his loneliness. How does he feel that

Lori has sex with Justin but prefers to spend her nights with him? That Darcy is willing to have sex with him but then disappears, and withholds herself and her secrets?

The film has been photographed by Rob Humphreys in dark colors and shadows, sometimes with backlighting that will catch part of a face or an expression and leave the rest hidden. Then there are ordinary daytime scenes, such as a double date when the two couples have lunch. There is subtle verbal fencing; Michael, Darcy, and Lori are Asian, Justin is half-Asian, and when Darcy asks which of his parents taught him to use chopsticks, there is an undercurrent they all feel, and when he says he cannot remember the time when he could not use chopsticks, he is answering more than her question.

The movie has revelations I must not reveal, but let it be said that Byler conceals nothing from us except what is concealed from the characters, and what they learn, we learn. It becomes clear that Darcy came into Michael's life in the wrong way and cannot undo that, and that Lori is deeply disturbed that her platonic friend may become this other woman's lover. Little is actually said about any of this; it is all there in the air between these guarded and wounded characters.

Charlotte Sometimes drew me in from the opening shots. Byler reveals his characters in a way that intrigues and even fascinates us, and he never reduces the situation to simple melodrama, which would release the tension. This is like a psychological thriller, in which the climax has to do with feelings, not actions.

Idemoto brings such a loneliness to his role, such a feeling of the character's long hours of solitary thought, that we care for him right from the start, and feel his pain about this woman who might be the right one for him, but remains elusive and hidden. Kim has a way of being detached and observant in her scenes, as if Darcy is seeing it all happen within a context only she understands. At the end, when we know everything, the movie has not cheated; we sense the deep life currents that have brought these people to this place. There is sadness and tenderness here, and the knowledge that to find true love is not always to possess it.

Chasing Papi ★ ★ ½
PG, 92 m., 2003

Roselyn Sanchez (Lorena), Sofia Vergara (Cici), Jaci Velasquez (Patricia), Eduardo Verastegui (Papi), Lisa Vidal (Carmen), D. L. Hughley (Rodrigo), Freddy Rodriguez (Victor), Maria Conchita Alonso (Maria), Paul Rodriguez (Costas Delgado). Directed by Linda Mendoza and produced by Tracey Trench and Forest Whitaker. Screenplay by Laura Angelica Simon, Steven Antin, Alison Balian, and Liz Sarnoff.

Chasing Papi is a feature-length jiggle show with Charlie's Angels transformed into Latina bimbos. Well, not entirely bimbos: The movie's three heroines are smart and capable, except when they're in pursuit of the man they love, an occupation that requires them to run through a lot of scenes wearing high heels and squealing with passion or fear or delight, while a stupendous amount of jiggling goes on.

These are great-looking women. Forgive me if I sound like a lecher, but, hey, the entire purpose and rationale of this film is to display Roselyn Sanchez, Sofia Vergara, and Jaci Velasquez in a way that would make your average *Maxim* reader feel right at home. So high are the movie's standards of beauty that even two supporting roles feature the ravishing Lisa Vidal and the immortal Maria Conchita Alonso.

The three stars are veterans of Spanish-language TV soap operas, a genre that celebrates cleavage with single-minded dedication. In the story, they are the three girlfriends of Thomas Fuentes (Eduardo Verastegui), aka Papi, an advertising executive whose travels require him to visit Lorena (Sanchez) in Chicago, Cici (Vergara) in Miami, and Patricia (Velasquez) in New York. He does not intend to be a three-timer and sincerely loves them all, but asks: "How can you choose between the colors of nature's beautiful flowers?"

All three women happen to be watching the same astrologer on TV, and take the seer's advice to drop everything and race to the side of their man. This leads to an improbable scene when all three burst through doors leading into Papi's bedroom while wearing his gift of identical red lingerie. Papi is not home at the time, supplying an opportunity for the women to discover his betrayal and decide to gang up and have what is described as revenge but looks more like a fashion show by Victoria's Secret.

Meanwhile, let's see, there's a plot about a bag of money, and an FBI agent (Vidal) trails the women to Los Angeles while some tough guys, led by Paul Rodriguez, also are on the trail of the money, and this all leads inevitably to the girls making their onstage dancing debut at a festival headlining Sheila E.

Chasing Papi is as light as a feather, as fresh as spring, and as lubricious as a centerfold. Its three heroines are seen in one way or another as liberated women, especially Lorena, who is said to be a lawyer, but their hearts go a-flutter in the presence of Papi. The movie's purpose is to photograph them as attractively as possible, while covering up the slightness of the plot with wall-to-wall Latin music, infectiously upbeat scenes, and animated sequences that introduce New York, Miami, Chicago, and Los Angeles. (The use of these cartoon intervals is an inspired solution to the problem that the movie was shot entirely in Canada.)

I cannot recommend *Chasing Papi*, but I cannot dislike it. It commits no offense except the puppylike desire to please. It celebrates a vibrant and lively Latino world in which everyone speaks English with a charming accent, switching to Spanish only in moments of intense drama. There is something extroverted and refreshing in the way these women enjoy their beauty and their sexiness. They've got it, and they flaunt it.

The movie could have been smarter and wittier. The plot could have made a slight attempt to be original. There are better ways to pass your time. But it will make you smile, and that is a virtue not to be ignored.

Chelsea Walls ★ ★ ★
R, 109 m., 2002

Rosario Dawson (Audrey), Vincent D'Onofrio (Frank), Kris Kristofferson (Bud), Robert Sean Leonard (Terry), Natasha Richardson (Mary), Uma Thurman (Grace), Steve Zahn (Ross), Tuesday Weld (Geta), Mark Webber (Val), Jimmy Scott (Skinny Bones). Directed by Ethan Hawke and produced by Alexis Alexanian, Pamela Koffler, Christine Vachon, and Gary

Winick. Screenplay by Nicole Burdette, based on her play.

A rest stop for rare individuals.
—Motto of the Chelsea Hotel

Chelsea Walls is the movie for you if you have a beaten-up copy of the Compass paperback edition of Kerouac's *On the Road* and on page 124 you underlined the words, "The one thing that we yearn for in our living days, that makes us sigh and groan and undergo sweet nauseas of all kinds, is the remembrance of some lost bliss that was probably experienced only in the womb and can only be reproduced (though we hate to admit it) in death." If you underlined the next five words ("But who wants to die?"), you are too realistic for this movie.

Lacking the paperback, you qualify for the movie if you have ever made a pilgrimage to the Chelsea Hotel on West 23rd Street in New York, and given a thought to Dylan Thomas, Thomas Wolfe, Arthur C. Clarke, R. Crumb, Brendan Behan, Gregory Corso, Bob Dylan, or Sid and Nancy, who lived (and in some cases died) there. You also qualify if you have ever visited the Beat Bookshop in Boulder, Colorado, if you have ever yearned to point the wheel west and keep driving until you reach the Pacific Coast Highway, or if you have never written the words "somebody named Lawrence Ferlinghetti."

If you are by now thoroughly bewildered by this review, you will be equally bewildered by *Chelsea Walls,* and had better stay away from it. Ethan Hawke's movie evokes the innocent spirit of the Beat Generation fifty years after the fact, and celebrates characters who think it is noble to live in extravagant poverty while creating Art and leading untidy sex lives. These people smoke a lot, drink a lot, abuse many substances, and spend either no time at all or way too much time managing their wardrobes. They live in the Chelsea Hotel because it is cheap, and provides a stage for their psychodramas.

Countless stories have been set in the Chelsea. Andy Warhol's *Chelsea Girls* (1967) was filmed there. Plays have between written about it, including one by Nicole Burdette that inspired this screenplay. Photographers and painters have recorded its seasons. It is our American Left Bank, located at one convenient address. That Ethan Hawke would have wanted to direct a movie about it is not surprising; he and his wife, Uma Thurman, who could relax with easy-money stardom, have a way of sneaking off for dodgy avant-garde projects. They starred in Richard Linklater's *Tape* (2001), about three people in a motel room, and now here is the epic version of the same idea, portraying colorful denizens of the Chelsea in full bloom.

We meet Bud (Kris Kristofferson), a boozy author who uses a typewriter instead of a computer, perhaps because you can't short it out by spilling a bottle on it. He has a wife named Greta (Tuesday Weld) and a mistress named Mary (Natasha Richardson), and is perhaps able to find room for both of them in his life because neither one can stand to be around him all that long. He tells them both they are his inspiration. When he's not with the Muse he loves, he loves the Muse he's with.

Val (Mark Webber) is so young he looks embryonic. He buys lock, stock, and barrel into the mythology of bohemia, and lives with Audrey (Rosario Dawson). They are both poets. I do not know how good Audrey's poems are because Dawson reads them in close-up—just her face filling the screen—and I could not focus on the words. I have seen a lot of close-ups in my life but never one so simply, guilelessly erotic. Have more beautiful lips ever been photographed?

Frank (Vincent D'Onofrio) is a painter who thinks he can talk Grace (Uma Thurman) into being his lover. She is not sure. She prefers a vague, absent lover, never seen, and seems to know she has made the wrong choice but takes a perverse pride in sticking with it. Ross (Steve Zahn) is a singer whose brain seems alarmingly fried. Little Jimmy Scott is Skinny Bones, a down-and-out jazzman. Robert Sean Leonard is Terry, who wants to be a folk singer. The corridors are also occupied by the lame and the brain-damaged; every elevator trip includes a harangue by the house philosopher.

Has time passed these people by? Very likely. Greatness resides in ability, not geography, and it is futile to believe that if Thomas Wolfe wrote *Look Homeward, Angel* in Room 831, anyone occupying that room is sure to be equally inspired. What the movie's characters are seeking is not inspiration anyway, but an audience. They stay in the Chelsea because they are surrounded by others who understand the statements they are making with their lives. In a society where the average college freshman has already targeted his entry-level position in the economy, it's a little lonely to embrace unemployment and the aura of genius. To actors with a romantic edge, however, it's very attractive: No wonder Matt Dillon sounds so effortlessly convincing on the audiobook of *On the Road*.

Hawke shot the film for $100,000 on digital video, in the tradition of Warhol's fuzzy 16mm photography. Warhol used a split screen, so that while one of his superstars was doing nothing on the left screen, we could watch another of his superstars doing nothing on the right screen. Hawke, working with Burdette's material, has made a movie that by contrast is action-packed. The characters enjoy playing hooky from life and posing as the inheritors of bohemia. Hawke's cinematographers, Tom Richmond and Richard Rutkowski, and his editor, Adriana Pacheco, weave a mosaic out of the images, avoiding the temptation of a simple realistic look: The film is patterned with color, superimposition, strange exposures, poetic transitions, grainy color palettes.

Movies like this do not grab you by the throat. You have to be receptive. The first time I saw *Chelsea Walls*, in a stuffy room late at night at Cannes 2001, I found it slow and pointless. This time I saw it earlier in the day, fueled by coffee, and I understood that the movie is not about what the characters do, but about what they are. It may be a waste of time to spend your life drinking, fornicating, posing as a genius, and living off your friends, but if you've got the money, honey, take off the time.

Cherish ★ ★ ★
R, 99 m., 2002

Robin Tunney (Zoe), Tim Blake Nelson (Deputy Bill), Brad Hunt (D.J.), Liz Phair (Brynn), Jason Priestley (Andrew), Nora Dunn (Bell), Lindsay Crouse (Therapist), Ricardo Gil (Max). Directed by Finn Taylor and produced by Mark Burton and Johnny Wow. Screenplay by Taylor.

In most locked-room mysteries, the death takes place inside the room and the hero tries to figure out how it was done. *Cherish* is a variation on the theme: The death takes place outside the room, and then the heroine is locked into it, and has to find the killer without leaving. Throw in a love story, a touch of *Run, Lola, Run*, and a lot of Top 40 songs, and you have *Cherish*, a lightweight charmer with a winning performance by Robin Tunney.

She plays Zoe, the kind of clueless office worker that her coworkers subtly try to avoid (I was reminded of the Shelley Duvall character in Altman's *Three Women*). She has a hopeless crush on coworker Andrew (Jason Priestley), and that leads her one night to a nightclub and to a fateful encounter with a masked man who enters her car, steps on the accelerator, mows down a cop, and then flees on foot.

Zoe is arrested for drunken vehicular homicide and several other things, and given little hope by her attorney, who gets the case continued in hopes that the heat will die down. The court orders her confined to a walk-up San Francisco apartment, with a bracelet on her ankle that will sound alarms if she tries to leave. In charge of the bracelet program: a nerdy technician named Daly (Tim Blake Nelson, from *O Brother, Where Art Thou?*), who tries his best to keep everything on a businesslike footing.

By limiting Zoe to her apartment, the movie creates the opportunity to show her fighting boredom, testing the limits of the bracelet, and making friends with Max (Ricardo Gil), the gay dwarf who lives downstairs. It also allows her, through quite a coincidence to be sure, to get a lead on that masked man who is the real cop-killer. But since absolutely no one believes her story about the masked man in the first place (and since her Breathalyzer test was alarming), it's up to her to gather evidence and nail the perp—all, apparently, without straying from her apartment.

How the movie manages to exploit and sidestep her limitations is a lot of the fun. It's good, too, to see Zoe growing and becoming more real, shedding the persona of office loser. And although as a general rule I deplore movies that depend on chase scenes for a cheap third act, I concede that in a locked-room plot, a chase scene of any description is a tour de force.

Robin Tunney has a plucky charm that works nicely here; it's quite a shift from her best movie, the overlooked *Niagara, Niagara* (1997), where she played a runaway with Tourette's; and she needed considerable pluck, to be sure, to play the mother of the Antichrist in *End of Days* (1999). Here she brings a quiet goofiness to the role, which is a much better choice than grim heroism or calm competence or some of the other speeds she could have chosen. Tim Blake Nelson is a case study as the kind of man who looks at a woman as if desperately hoping to be handed an instruction manual. And I liked the fire and ingenuity of Ricardo Gil, as the little man downstairs.

Chicago ★ ★ ★ ½
PG-13, 113 m., 2002

Catherine Zeta-Jones (Velma Kelly), Renée Zellweger (Roxie Hart), Richard Gere (Billy Flynn), John C. Reilly (Amos Hart), Queen Latifah (Matron "Mama"), Christine Baranski (Mary Sunshine), Taye Diggs (The Bandleader), Lucy Liu (Go-to-Hell Kitty), Dominic West (Fred Casely). Directed by Rob Marshall and produced by Marty Richards and Harvey Weinstein. Screenplay by Bill Condon, based on the musical by Fred Ebb and Bob Fosse.

Chicago continues the reinvention of the musical that started with *Moulin Rouge*. Although modern audiences don't like to see stories interrupted by songs, apparently they like songs interrupted by stories. The movie is a dazzling song-and-dance extravaganza, with just enough words to support the music and allow everyone to catch their breath between songs. You can watch it like you listen to an album, over and over; the same phenomenon explains why *Moulin Rouge* was a bigger hit on DVD than in theaters.

The movie stars sweet-faced Renée Zellweger as Roxie Hart, who kills her lover and convinces her husband to pay for her defense; and Catherine Zeta-Jones as Velma Kelly, who broke up her vaudeville sister act by murdering her husband and her sister while they were en-gaged in a sport not licensed for in-laws. Richard Gere is Billy Flynn, the slick, high-priced attorney who boasts he can beat any rap, for a $5,000 fee. "If Jesus Christ had lived in Chicago," he explains, "and if he'd had $5,000, and had come to me—things would have turned out differently."

This story, lightweight but cheerfully lurid, fueled Bob Fosse and Fred Ebb's original stage production of *Chicago*, which opened in 1975 and has been playing somewhere or other ever after—since 1997 again on Broadway. Fosse, who grew up in Chicago in the 1930s and 1940s, lived in a city where the daily papers roared with the kinds of headlines the movie loves. Killers were romanticized or vilified, cops and lawyers and reporters lived in each other's pockets, and newspapers read like pulp fiction. There's an inspired scene of ventriloquism and puppetry at a press conference, with all of the characters dangling from strings. For Fosse, the Chicago of Roxie Hart supplied the perfect peg to hang his famous hat.

The movie doesn't update the musical so much as bring it to a high electric streamlined gloss. The director, Rob Marshall, a stage veteran making his big-screen debut, paces the film with gusto. It's not all breakneck production numbers, but it's never far from one. And the choreography doesn't copy Fosse's inimitable style, but it's not far from it, either; the movie sideswipes imitation on its way to homage.

The decision to use nonsingers and non-dancers is always controversial in musicals, especially in these days when big stars are needed to headline expensive productions. Of Zellweger and Gere, it can be said that they are persuasive in their musical roles and well cast as their characters. Zeta-Jones was, in fact, a professional dancer in London before she decided to leave the chorus line and take her chances with acting, and her dancing in the movie is a reminder of the golden days; the film opens with her "All That Jazz" number, which plays like a promise *Chicago* will have to deliver on. And what a good idea to cast Queen Latifah in the role of Mama, the prison matron; she belts out "When You're Good to Mama" with the superb assurance of a performer who knows what good is and what Mama likes.

The story is inspired by the screaming headlines of the "Front Page" era and the decade after. We meet Roxie Hart, married early and unwisely to Amos Hart (John C. Reilly), a credulous lunkhead. She has a lover named Fred Casely (Dominic West), who sweet-talks her with promises of stardom. When she finds out he's a two-timing liar, she guns him down, and gets a one-way ticket to Death Row, already inhabited by Velma and overseen by Mama.

Can she get off? Only Billy Flynn (Gere) can pull off a trick like that, although his price is high and he sings a song in praise of his strategy ("Give 'em the old razzle-dazzle"). Velma has already captured the attention of newspaper readers, but after the poor sap Amos pays Billy his fee, a process begins to transform Roxie into a misunderstood heroine. She herself shows a certain genius in the process, as when she dramatically reveals she is pregnant with Amos's child, a claim that works only if nobody in the courtroom can count to nine.

Instead of interrupting the drama with songs, Marshall and screenwriter Bill Condon stage the songs more or less within Roxie's imagination, where everything is a little more supercharged than life, and even lawyers can tap-dance. (To be sure, Gere's own tap dancing is on the level of performers in the Chicago Bar Association's annual revue.) There are a few moments of straight pathos, including Amos Hart's pathetic disbelief that his Roxie could have cheated on him; he sings "Mr. Cellophane" about how people see right through him. But for the most part the film runs on solid-gold cynicism.

Reilly brings a kind of pathetic, sincere naïveté to the role—the same tone, indeed, he brings to a similar husband in *The Hours*, where it is also needed. It's surprising to see the confidence in his singing and dancing, until you find out he was in musicals all through school. Zellweger is not a born hoofer, but then again Roxie Hart isn't supposed to be a star; the whole point is that she isn't, and what Zellweger invaluably contributes to the role is Roxie's dreamy infatuation with herself, and her quickly growing mastery of publicity. Velma *is* supposed to be a singing and dancing star, and Zeta-Jones delivers with glamour, high style, and the delicious confidence the world forces on you when you are one of its most beautiful inhabitants. As for Queen Latifah, she's too young to remember Sophie Tucker, but not to channel her.

Chicago is a musical that might have seemed unfilmable, but that was because it was assumed it had to be transformed into more conventional terms. By filming it in its own spirit, by making it frankly a stagy song-and-dance revue, by kidding the stories instead of lingering over them, the movie is big, brassy fun.

Chopper ★ ★ ★
NO MPAA RATING, 90 m., 2001

Eric Bana (Chopper), Simon Lyndon (Jimmy Loughnan), Kenny Graham (Keith Read), Dan Wyllie (Bluey), David Field (Keithy George), Vince Colosimo (Neville Bartos), Kate Beahan (Tanya). Directed by Andrew Dominik and produced by Michele Bennett. Screenplay by Dominik, based on books by Mark Brandon Read.

It is not agreed how "Chopper" Read got his nickname. Some say it was because he chopped off the toes of his enemies. Others believe it was because he had his own ears chopped off, or because he had his teeth capped in metal. He is Australia's most infamous prisoner, a best-selling author, a vicious killer, a seething mass of contradictions. *Chopper* tells his story with a kind of fascinated horror.

Is everyone in Australia a few degrees off from true north? You can search in vain through the national cinema for characters who are ordinary or even boring; everyone is more colorful than life. If England is a nation of eccentrics, Australia leaves it at the starting line. Chopper Read is the latest in a distinguished line that includes Ned Kelly, Mad Max, and Russell Crowe's Hando in *Romper Stomper*. The fact that Chopper is real only underlines the point.

Since the real Chopper is again behind bars, the film depends entirely on its casting, and in a comedian named Eric Bana the filmmakers have found, I think, a future star. He creates a character so fearsome and yet so clueless and wounded that we can't tell if the movie comes to praise or bury him. There is a scene in the movie where Chopper is stabbed by his best friend, and keeps right on talking as if nothing has happened; his nonchalance is terrifying.

And another where he shoots a drug dealer and then thoughtfully drives him to the emergency room. Bana's performance makes the character believable—in fact, unforgettable. We feel we're looking at a hard man, not at an actor playing one.

As the film opens, Chopper is in prison watching himself on television. He seems curiously conflicted about what he sees—as if the Chopper on TV has been somehow constructed by others and then installed inside his skin. The writer-director Andrew Dominik and producer Michele Bennett, who met Chopper Read while preparing the film, sensed the same thing. "After we'd passed some time with him," says Bennett, "we could see that he was waiting to gauge our reaction before he proceeded. We did offer to show him the script, but he declined, remarking, 'Anything I say would be fiddling. I want to know what you think of me,' so we didn't pursue it. He pretends that he doesn't care how he's perceived by others, but I suspect he really does."

That's how he comes across as a film—as a man who seems to stand outside himself and watch what Chopper does. He's as fascinated by himself as we are, and isolated from his actions. Even pain doesn't seem to penetrate. He looks down at blood pouring from his body as if someone else has been wounded, and then up at his attacker as if expressing regret that it should have come to this.

The movie wisely declines to offer a psychological explanation for Chopper's violent amorality. But it provides a clue in the way he stands outside criminal gangs and has no associates; he is not a "criminal," if that word implies a profession, but a violent psychopath who is seized by sudden rages. There is a startling moment in the film, during a brief stretch on the streets between prison sentences, when he revisits old haunts and old friends and seems genial and conciliatory—until his mad-dog side leaps out in uncontrolled fury. The earlier niceness was not an act to throw people off their guard, we sense; he really was feeling friendly, and did not necessarily anticipate the sudden rush of rage.

Eric Bana's performance suggests he will soon be leaving the comedy clubs of Australia and turning up as a Bond villain or a madman in a special-effects picture. He has a quality no

acting school can teach and few actors can match: You cannot look away from him. The performance is so . . . strange. The parts you remember best are the times when he seems disappointed in others, or in himself, as if filled with sadness that the world must contain so much pain caused to or by him. Of course in creating this Chopper, he may simply be going along with the original Chopper's act, and the real Chopper Read with his TV interviews and best-sellers may be a performance too. Whatever the reality, Chopper is a real piece of work, and so is Bana.

Note: Chopper Read speaks in an unalloyed Australian accent that may be difficult for some North American audiences; he's no toned-down mid-Pacific Crocodile Dundee. I understood most of what he was saying. And when you don't catch the words, you get the drift.

Cinema Paradiso: The New Version
★ ★ ★ ½
R, 170 m., 2002

Salvatore Cascio (Salvatore [Young]), Marco Leonardi (Salvatore [Teenager]), Agnese Nano (Elena [Teenager]), Jacques Perrin (Salvatore [Adult]), Brigitte Fossey (Elena [Adult]), Philippe Noiret (Alfredo), Leopoldo Trieste (Father Adelfio). Directed by Guiseppe Tournatore and produced by Mino Barbera, Franco Cristaldi, and Giovanna Romagnoli. Screenplay by Tournatore.

When *Cinema Paradiso* won the Academy Award as Best Foreign Film in 1990, it was an open secret that the movie the voters loved was not quite the same as the one director Guiseppe Tournatore made. Reports had it that Harvey Weinstein, the boss at Miramax, had trimmed not just a shot here or there, but a full fifty-one minutes from the film. Audiences loved the result, however, and the movie is consistently voted among the 100 best movies of all time at the Internet Movie Database.

Now comes a theatrical release of *Cinema Paradiso: The New Version*, with an ad campaign that promises, "Discover what really happened to the love of a lifetime." Considering that it was Miramax that made it impossible for us to discover this in the 1990 version, the ad is sublime chutzpah. And the movie is now so much longer and covers so much more detail that it almost plays as its own sequel.

Most of the first two hours will be familiar to lovers of the film. Little Salvatore (Salvatore Cascio), known to one and all as Toto, is fascinated by the movies and befriended by the projectionist Alfredo (Philippe Noiret). After a fire blinds Alfredo, Toto becomes the projectionist, and the Cinema Paradiso continues as the center of village life, despite the depredations of Father Adelfio (Leopoldo Trieste), who censors all of the films, ringing a bell at every kissing scene.

The new material of the longer version includes much more about the teenage romance between Salvatore (Marco Leonardi) and Elena (Agnese Nano)—a forbidden love, since her bourgeoisie parents have a better match in mind. And then there is a long passage involving the return of the middle-aged Salvatore (Jacques Perrin) to the village for the first time since he left to go to Rome and make his name as a movie director. He contacts the adult Elena (Brigitte Fossey), and finds out for the first time what really happened to a crucial rendezvous, and how easily his life might have turned out differently. (His discoveries promote the film to an MPAA rating of R, from its original PG.)

Seeing the longer version is a curious experience. It is an item of faith that the director of a film is always right, and that studios who cut films are butchers. Yet I must confess that the shorter version of *Cinema Paradiso* is a better film than the longer. Harvey was right. The 170-minute cut overstays its welcome, and continues after its natural climax.

Still, I'm happy to have seen it—not as an alternate version, but as the ultimate exercise in viewing deleted scenes. Anyone who loves the film will indeed be curious about "what really happened to the love of a lifetime," and it is good to know. I hope, however, that this new version doesn't replace the old one on the video shelves; the ideal solution would be a DVD with the 1990 version on one side and the 2002 version on the other.

The Circle ★ ★ ★ ½

NO MPAA RATING, 91 m., 2001

Mariam Palvin Almani (Arezou), Nargess Mamizadeh (Nargess), Fereshteh Sadr Orfani (Pari), Monir Arab (Ticket Seller), Elham Saboktakin (Nurse), Fatemeh Naghavi (Mother), Mojhan Faramarzi (Prostitute). Directed and produced by Jafar Panahi. Screenplay by Kambozia Partovi.

Few things reveal a nation better than what it censors. In America, the MPAA has essentially eliminated adult sexuality from our movies, but smiles on violence and films tailored for the teenage toilet-humor market. Now consider *The Circle*, a film banned in Iran. There is not a single shot here that would seem offensive to a mainstream American audience— not even to the smut-hunting preacher Donald Wildmon. Why is it considered dangerous in Iran? Because it argues that under current Iranian law, unattached women are made to feel like hunted animals.

There is no nudity here. No violence. No drugs or alcohol, for sure. No profanity. There is a running joke that the heroines can't even have a cigarette (women cannot smoke in public). Yet the film is profoundly dangerous to the status quo in Iran because it asks us to identify with the plight of women who have done nothing wrong except to be female. *The Circle* is all the more depressing when we consider that Iran is relatively liberal compared to, say, Afghanistan under the Taliban.

Jafar Panahi's film begins and ends with the same image, of a woman talking to someone in authority through a sliding panel in a closed door. In the opening shot, a woman learns that her daughter has given birth to a girl when the ultrasound promised a boy; she fears angry reprisals from the in-laws. In the closing shot, a woman is in prison, talking to a guard. In closing the circle, the second shot suggests that women in strict Muslim societies are always in prison in one way or another.

The film follows a series of women through the streets of a city. We follow first one and then another. We begin with two who have just been released from prison—for what crime, we are not told. They want to take a bus to a city where one of them hopes to find a safe harbor. But they have no money and lack the correct identification. They run through the streets and down back alleys at the sight of policemen, they crouch behind parked cars, they ask a ticket-seller to give them a break and sell them a ticket though they have no ID. At one point it's fairly clear that one of the women prostitutes herself (offscreen) to raise money to help the other. Men all over the world are open-minded about exempting themselves from the laws prohibiting other men from frequenting prostitutes.

If you have no ID, you cannot leave town. If you have no ID, you cannot live in a town. Your crime, obviously, is to be a woman living outside the system of male control of women; with a husband or a brother to vouch for you, you can go anywhere, sort of like baggage. The argument is that this system shows respect for women, just as Bantustans in South Africa gave Africans their own land, and American blacks in Jim Crow days did not have to stand in line to use white rest rooms. There is a universal double-speak in which subjugation is described as freedom.

We meet another woman, who has left her little daughter to be found by strangers. She hides behind a car, her eyes filled with tears; as a single mother she cannot care for the girl, and so dresses her up to look nice, and abandons her. We meet another woman, a prostitute, who is found in the car of a man and cannot prove she is related to him. She is arrested; the man seems to go free. Has there ever been a society where the man in this situation is arrested and the woman goes free? The prostitute at least gets to smoke on the prison bus (not when she wants to, but after the men light up, so the smoke will not be noticed).

The movie is not structured tautly like an American street thriller. There are handheld shots that meander for a minute or two, just following women as they walk here or there. The women seem aimless. They are. In this society, under their circumstances, there is nowhere they can go and nothing they can do, and almost all of the time they have to stay out of doors. They track down rumors: A news vendor, for example, is said to be "friendly" and might help them. From time to time, a passing man will say something oblique, like "Can I help you?" but that is either casual harassment or a test of availability.

The Iranian censors may ban films like *The Circle*, but it got made, and so did the recent *The Day I Became a Woman*, about the three ages of women in such a society. One suspects that videotapes give these films wide private circulation; one even suspects the censors know that. I know a director from a communist country where the censor had been his film school classmate. He submitted a script. The censor read it and told his old friend, "You know what you're really saying, and I know what you're really saying. Now rewrite it so only the audience knows what you're really saying."

City by the Sea ★ ★ ★
R, 108 m., 2002

Robert De Niro (Detective Vincent La Marca), Frances McDormand (Michelle), James Franco (Joey La Marca), Eliza Dushku (Gina), Patti LuPone (Maggie), George Dzundza (Reg Duffy), William Forsythe (Spyder). Directed by Michael Caton-Jones and produced by Matthew Baer, Caton-Jones, Brad Grey, and Elie Samaha. Screenplay by Ken Hixon and Mike McAlary.

City by the Sea tells the sad, fatalistic story of a cop whose father was a baby-killer, and whose son now seems to be a murderer too. Robert De Niro stars as Detective Vincent La Marca, a pro whose years of hard experience have made him into a cop who dismisses sociology and psychology and believes simply that if you did it, you have to pay for it. This code extends to his father and he will apply it if necessary to his son.

La Marca works homicide in a shabby beachfront area; Asbury Park, New Jersey, supplied the locations. He knows so much about police work his autopilot is better than most cops' bright ideas. His partner, Reg (George Dzundza), who has eaten too many doughnuts over the years, soldiers along with him. La Marca walked out on his wife (Patti LuPone) and son fourteen years ago, and now tentatively dates his upstairs neighbor, Michelle (Frances McDormand).

The cop's story is intercut with the life of his son, Joey (James Franco), a strung-out addict who has worked himself into a fearful situation involving debt and need. In a confusing struggle, he knifes a drug dealer and eventually, inevitably, La Marca is working the case and discovers that the killer may have been Joey.

If this story sounds a little too symmetrical and neat, and in a way it does, real life supplies a rebuttal: *City by the Sea* is based on a true story, as described by writer Mike McAlary in a 1997 *Esquire* article. I learn from *Variety*, however, that in fact the murder the son committed was vicious and premeditated, and not, as it is here, more or less an accident.

The plot takes us places we have been before, right down to the scene where La Marca resigns from the force and places his gun and badge on the captain's desk. There is also the possibility in La Marca's mind that his son is innocent—he claims he is—and there is the enormous psychic burden caused by the fact that La Marca's own father was convicted of a heartless murder. The last act of the movie is the sort of cat-and-mouse chase we have seen before, staged with expertise by director Michael Caton-Jones, but the movie's heart isn't in the action but in the character of Vince La Marca.

De Niro has worked so long and so frequently that there is sometimes the tendency to take him for granted. He is familiar. He has a range dictated by his face, voice, and inescapable mannerisms, but he rarely goes on autopilot and he makes an effort to newly invent his characters. Here he is a man with a wounded boy inside. Most of the time the cop routine provides him with a template for behavior: He keeps his head low, he does his job well. But inside is the kid who found out his dad was a killer. That provides the twist when he finds himself on his own son's case. There is hurt here, and De Niro is too good an actor to reduce it to a plot gimmick. He feels it.

Details of the plot I will not reveal, except to observe that the context of the murder and the condition of the son leave enough room for the La Marca character to believe, or want to believe, that his son may be innocent. That leads to the scene where he turns in his badge and gun, accusing his boss of having already made up his mind. And it leaves La Marca freefloating, because without the protection of the job he is now nakedly facing a situation that churns up his own past.

Frances McDormand takes a routine, even obligatory, character and makes her into an important part of the movie. The female confidante is usually dispensable in cop movies, except for a few scenes where she provides an ear for necessary exposition. Not here. McDormand's Michelle likes La Marca, but more important, she worries about him, sees the inner wounds, provides a balm, and knows about tough love.

City by the Sea is not an extraordinary movie. In its workmanship it aspires not to be remarkable but to be well made, dependable, moving us because of the hurt in the hero's eyes. A better movie might have abandoned the crime paraphernalia and focused on the pain between the generations, but then this director, Michael Caton-Jones, has already made that movie with De Niro. *This Boy's Life* (1993) had De Niro as a harsh adoptive father and Leonardo DiCaprio as his resentful son. A better movie, but *City by the Sea* is a good one.

City of Ghosts ★ ★ ★
R, 116 m., 2003

Matt Dillon (Jimmy Cremming), James Caan (Marvin), Natascha McElhone (Sophie), Gérard Depardieu (Emile), Kem Sereyvuth (Sok), Stellan Skarsgard (Casper), Rose Byrne (Sabrina). Directed by Matt Dillon and produced by Willi Bar, Michael Cerenzie, and Deepak Nayar. Screenplay by Dillon and Barry Gifford.

When a hurricane wipes out large parts of the East Coast, many homeowners are understandably alarmed to learn that their insurer, the Capable Trust Co., is incapable of paying their claims because it has no money in the bank. Jimmy Cremming is also upset, or so he tells the cops. Played by Matt Dillon, he runs the U.S. office of the company, which is owned by a shady figure named Marvin, who when last heard from was in Cambodia. When federal agents start asking difficult questions, Jimmy leaves for Phnom Penh to find Marvin.

This is, you will agree, a preposterous setup for a movie. And the rest of the plot of *City of Ghosts* is no more believable. But believability is not everything, as I have to keep reminding myself in these days of *The Matrix Reloaded*. Character and mood also count for something—and so does location, since Matt Dillon shot his movie mostly on location in Cambodia; it's the first picture primarily filmed there since *Lord Jim* in 1965.

Dillon and his cinematographer, Jim Denault, find locations that don't look like locations; they have the untidiness and random details of real places, as indeed they are, and I particularly liked the hotel and bar run by Gérard Depardieu, who shambles around with a big shirt hanging over his belly and breaks up fights while casually holding a baby in his arms. Although such bars, and such exiles as proprietors, are standard in all *film noir* set in exotic locations, this one had a funky reality that made me muse about a sequel in which we'd find out more about Depardieu, the baby, and a monkey he seems to have trained as a pickpocket.

In such movies, all visitors to Asia from the West quickly find a local helper who is instantly ready to risk his life to help the foreigner. Mel Gibson's character found Billy Kwan in *The Year of Living Dangerously*, and Dillon's character finds Sok (Kem Sereyvuth), a pedicab driver who serves as chauffeur, spy, and adviser to the outsider. Also hanging around the bar is Casper (Stellan Skarsgard), who says he works with the mysterious Marvin and conveys enigmatic messages. The one character who seems unlikely, although obligatory, is the beautiful woman Sophie (Natascha McElhone), who is an art historian but finds time to get tender with Jimmy. (I wonder if movie Americans who land in Asia are supplied with a list, so they can check off Friendly Bartender, Local Helper, Sinister Insider, Beautiful Girl, Monkey . . .)

Marvin is kept offscreen so long that he begins to take on the psychic heft of Harry Lime in *The Third Man*. Such a concealed character needs to have presence when he is revealed, and James Caan rises to the occasion, as a financial hustler who not only stiffed the policyholders of Capable Trust but now seems to be in bed with the Russian Mafia in a scheme to build a luxury hotel and casino.

When and how Jimmy finds Marvin, and what happens then, are surprises for the plot to reveal. What can be said is that the details of Marvin's scheme, and the plans of his enemies, seem more than a little muddled, and yet Dillon, as director, handles them in a way that makes the moments convincing, even if they don't add up.

City of Ghosts reminded me of *The Quiet American*, which likewise has visiting Westerners, beautiful women, sinister local figures, etc. It lacks a monkey, but has a more sharply told story, one with a message. *The Quiet American* was based on Graham Greene's novel about America's illegal activities, circa 1960, in Vietnam. The screenplay for *City of Ghosts*, by Dillon and sometime David Lynch collaborator Barry Gifford, avoids a rich vein of true Cambodian stories and recycles the kind of generic financial crimes that Hollywood perfected in the 1940s.

Still, sometimes the very texture of the film, and the information that surrounds the characters on the screen, make it worth seeing. I didn't believe in James Caan's cons, but I believed him, and at times like that it's helpful to stop keeping score and live in the moment. Between the Caan and Dillon characters there are atmosphere, desperation, and romance, and, at the end, something approaching true pathos. Enough.

City of God ★ ★ ★ ★
R, 135 m., 2003

Matheus Nachtergaele (Sandro Cenoura), Seu Jorge (Knockout Ned), Alexandre Rodrigues (Rocket), Leandro Firmino da Hora (L'il Ze), Philippe Haagensen (Bene [Benny]), Johnathan Haagensen (Cabeleira [Shaggy]), Douglas Silva (Dadinho), Roberta Rodriguez Silvia (Berenice), Graziela Moretto (Marina), Renato de Souza (Goose). Directed by Fernando Meirelles and produced by Andrea Barata Ribeiro and Mauricio Andrade Ramos. Screenplay by Bráulio Mantovani, based on the novel by Paulo Lins. In Portuguese with English subtitles.

City of God churns with furious energy as it plunges into the story of the slum gangs of Rio de Janeiro. Breathtaking and terrifying, urgently involved with its characters, it announces a new director of great gifts and passions. Fernando Meirelles. Remember the name. The film has been compared with Martin Scorsese's *GoodFellas*, and it deserves the comparison. Scorsese's film began with a narrator who said that for as long as he could remember he wanted to be a gangster. The narrator of this film seems to have had no other choice.

The movie takes place in slums constructed by Rio to isolate the poor people from the city center. They have grown into places teeming with life, color, music, and excitement—and also with danger, for the law is absent and violent gangs rule the streets. In the virtuoso sequence opening the picture, a gang is holding a picnic for its members when a chicken escapes. Among those chasing it is Rocket (Alexandre Rodrigues), the narrator. He suddenly finds himself between two armed lines: the gang on one side, the cops on the other.

As the camera whirls around him, the background changes and Rocket shrinks from a teenager into a small boy, playing soccer in a housing development outside Rio. To understand his story, he says, we have to go back to the beginning, when he and his friends formed the Tender Trio and began their lives of what some would call crime and others would call survival.

The technique of that shot—the whirling camera, the flashback, the change in colors from the dark brightness of the slum to the dusty, sunny browns of the soccer field—alert us to a movie that is visually alive and inventive as few films are. Meirelles began as a director of TV commercials, which gave him a command of technique—and, he says, trained him to work quickly, to size up a shot and get it and move on. Working with the cinematographer Cesar Charlone, he uses quick cutting and a mobile, handheld camera to tell his story with the haste and detail it deserves. Sometimes those devices can create a film that is merely busy, but *City of God* feels like sight itself, as we look here and then there, with danger or opportunity everywhere.

The gangs have money and guns because they sell drugs and commit robberies. But they are not very rich because their activities are limited to the City of God, where no one has much money. In an early crime, we see the stickup of a truck carrying cans of propane gas, which the crooks sell to homeowners. Later there is a raid on a bordello, where the customers are deprived of their wallets. (In a flashback, we see that raid a second time, and understand in a chilling moment why there were dead bodies at a site where there was not supposed to be any killing.)

As Rocket narrates the lore of the district he knows so well, we understand that poverty has undermined all social structures in the City of God, including the family. The gangs provide structure and status. Because the gang death rate is so high, even the leaders tend to be surprisingly young, and life has no value except when you are taking it. There is an astonishing sequence when a victorious gang leader is killed in a way he least expects, by the last person he would have expected, and we see that essentially he has been killed not by a person but by the culture of crime.

Yet the film is not all grim and violent. Rocket also captures some of the Dickensian flavor of the City of God, where a riot of life provides ready-made characters with nicknames, personas, and trademarks. Some, like Benny (Philippe Haagensen), are so charismatic they almost seem to transcend the usual rules. Others, like Knockout Ned and L'il Ze, grow from kids into fearsome leaders, their words enforced by death.

The movie is based on a novel by Paulo Lins, who grew up in the City of God, somehow escaped it, and spent eight years writing his book. A note at the end says it is partly based on the life of Wilson Rodriguez, a Brazilian photographer. We watch as Rocket obtains a (stolen) camera that he treasures, and takes pictures from his privileged position as a kid on the streets. He gets a job as an assistant on a newspaper delivery truck, asks a photographer to develop his film, and is startled to see his portrait of an armed gang leader on the front page of the paper.

"This is my death sentence," he thinks, but no: The gangs are delighted by the publicity, and pose for him with their guns and girls. And during a vicious gang war, he is able to photograph the cops killing a gangster—a murder they plan to pass off as gang-related. That these events throb with immediate truth is indicated by the fact that Luiz Inacio Lula da Silva, the newly elected president of Brazil, actually reviewed and praised *City of God* as a needful call for change.

In its actual level of violence, *City of God* is less extreme than Scorsese's *Gangs of New York*, but the two films have certain parallels. In both films, there are really two cities: the city of the employed and secure, who are served by law and municipal services, and the city of the castaways, whose alliances are born of opportunity and desperation. Those who live beneath rarely have their stories told. *City of God* does not exploit or condescend, does not pump up its stories for contrived effect, does not contain silly and reassuring romantic sidebars, but simply looks, with a passionately knowing eye, at what it knows. ☞

The Claim ★ ★ ★ ½
R, 120 m., 2001

Peter Mullan (Daniel Dillon), Sarah Polley (Hope Dillon), Wes Bentley (Donald Dalglish), Milla Jovovich (Lucia), Nastassja Kinski (Elena Dillon), Julian Richings (Bellanger), David Lereaney (Saloon Actor), Sean McGinley (Sweetley). Directed by Michael Winterbottom and produced by Andrew Eaton. Screenplay by Frank Cottrell Boyce, based on the novel *The Mayor of Casterbridge* by Thomas Hardy.

In the town of Kingdom Come, winter is more of a punishment than a season. High in a pass of the Sierra Nevada, its buildings of raw lumber stand like scars on the snow. The promise of gold has drawn men here, but in the winter there is little to do but wait, drink, and visit the brothel. The town is owned and run by Mr. Dillon, a trim Scotsman in his forties who is judge, jury, and (if necessary) executioner.

I dwell on the town because the physical setting of Michael Winterbottom's *The Claim* is central to its effect. Summer is a season for work, but winter is a time for memory and regret. Mr. Dillon (Peter Mullan) did something years ago that was wrong in a way a man cannot forgive himself for. He lives in an ornate Victorian house, submits to the caresses of his mistress, settles the affairs of his subjects, and is haunted by his memories.

Two women arrive in Kingdom Come. One is a fading beauty named Elena (Nastassja Kinski), dying of tuberculosis. The other is her daughter, about twenty, named Hope (Sarah Polley). They have not journeyed to Kingdom Come to forgive Mr. Dillon his trespasses. It becomes clear who they are, but the movie is not about that secret. It is about what happened twenty years ago, and what, as a result, will happen now.

To the town that winter also comes Donald Dalglish (Wes Bentley), a surveyor for the railroad. Where the tracks run, wealth follows. What they bypass will die. Dalglish is young, ambitious, and good at business. He attracts the attention of Lucia (Milla Jovovich), who is not only Mr. Dillon's comfort but the owner of the brothel. She kisses him boldly on the lips in full view of a saloon-full of witnesses, sending a message to Mr. Dillon: If he doesn't want to keep her, others will. Dalglish is not indifferent, but he is more intrigued by the strange young blonde woman, Hope, who stands out in this grimness like the first bud of spring.

The past comes crashing down around them all—and then the future arrives to finish them off. Mr. Dillon's fate, which he fashions for himself, is all the more complex because he has done great evil but is in some ways a good man. Nor is Dalglish morally uncomplicated. In the hard world they inhabit, no one can afford to act only on a theoretical basis.

The Claim is parsimonious with its plot, which is revealed on a need-to-know basis. At first, we're not even sure who is who; dialogue is half-heard, references are unclear, the townspeople know things we discover only gradually. The method is like Robert Altman's in *McCabe and Mrs. Miller,* and Antonia Bird's in the underrated 1999 Western *Ravenous* (a movie that takes place in about the same place and time as this one). Like strangers in town, we put the pieces together for ourselves.

The movie is so rooted in the mountains of the American West that it's a little startling to learn *The Claim* is based on Thomas Hardy's 1886 British novel *The Mayor of Casterbridge.* Winterbottom filmed *Jude,* a version of Hardy's *Jude the Obscure,* in 1996. By transmuting Hardy into a Western here, he has not made a commercial decision (Westerns are not as successful these days as British period pictures), but an artistic one, perhaps involving his vision of Kingdom Come, a town which is like a stage waiting for this play.

Winterbottom is a director of great gifts and glooms. His *Butterfly Kiss* (also 1996) starred Amanda Plummer in a great performance as a kind of homeless flagellant saint. Here he tells the story of another kind of self-punishing character, and Peter Mullan's performance is private and painful, as a man whose first mistake is to give away all he has, and whose second mistake is to try to redeem himself by giving it all away again. Mullan *(My Name Is*

Joe) is like a harder, leaner, younger (but not young) Paul Newman, coiled up inside, handsome but not depending on it, willing to go to any lengths to do what he must. Intriguing, how he makes a villain sympathetic, in a movie where the relatively blameless Dalglish seems corrupt.

A movie like this rides on its cinematography, and Alwin H. Kuchler evokes the cold darkness so convincingly that Kingdom Come seems built on an abyss. Like the town of Presbyterian Church in *McCabe and Mrs. Miller,* it is a folly built by greed where common sense would have steered clear. There are two great visual scenes, the arrival of the railroad and the moving of a house, one exercising public will, the other private will. And an ending uncannily like *McCabe and Mrs. Miller*'s, although for an entirely different reason.

Winterbottom is a director comfortable with ambiguity. In movies like *Wonderland* (1999), *Welcome to Saravejo* (1997), and others, he's reluctant to corner his characters into heroism or villainy. In the original Hardy novel, the Dillon character, named Henchard, is a drunk who pays so well for his sins that he seems more like Job than a sinner being punished. Dillon, who was also a drunk, tells the woman he has wronged, "I don't drink anymore. I want you to know that." For his time and place, he has grown into a hard but not bad man, and when he has a citizen horsewhipped, the man explains that the town would have lynched him—the whipping saved his life. The strength of *The Claim* is that Dillon and Dalglish are on intersecting paths; Dillon is getting better, while Dalglish started out good and is headed down.

Clockstoppers ★ ★ ½

PG, 90 m., 2002

Jesse Bradford (Zak Gibbs), French Stewart (Dr. Earl Dopler), Paula Garces (Francesca De La Cruz), Michael Biehn (Henry Gates), Robin Thomas (Dr. George Gibbs), Gariyaki Mutambirwa (Danny Meeker). Directed by Jonathan Frakes and produced by Gale Anne Hurd and Julia Pistor. Screenplay by Rob Hedden, J. David Stem, and David N. Weiss.

In an early scene of *Clockstoppers,* a student in a college physics class is unable to complete the phrase, "Einstein's Theory of . . ." And just as well, too, since any time-manipulation movie has to exist in blissful ignorance of Einstein's theory. Not that it can't be done, at least in the movies. *Clockstoppers* has a new twist: The traveler doesn't travel through time but stays right where he is and lives faster. This is closer to Einstein's Theory of Amphetamines.

Dr. George Gibbs (Robin Thomas) has invented a way for a subject to live much faster than those around him, so that they seem to stand in place while he whizzes around. He is like the mayfly, which lives a lifetime in a day—and that is precisely the trouble. The system works well, but experimenters age so quickly that they return looking worn and wrinkled, like Keir Dullea in *2001,* who checks into that alien bedroom, doesn't check out. Gibbs needs to iron out a few kinks.

Before he can perfect his discovery, intrigue strikes. His teenage son, Zak (Jesse Bradford), is informed by the friendly Dr. Earl Dopler (French Stewart) that Gibbs has been kidnapped into hyperspace by the evil and scheming millionaire Henry Gates (Michael Biehn). Dopler is named after the Effect. I have no idea how they came up with the name of Gates.

Zak has just met the beautiful Francesca De La Cruz (Paula Garces), a pretty student from Venezuela, at his high school, and they find themselves teamed on a mission to venture into hyperspace, rescue his father, outsmart Gates, and return without becoming senior citizens. (That's if hyperspace is the same place as speeded-up-time-space, and frankly the movie lost me there.) To assist in their mission they use a gun that fires marbles filled with liquid nitrogen, which burst on impact and instantly freeze their targets. That this gun is not fatal is a fact the movie wisely makes no attempt to explain.

Clockstoppers has high energy, bright colors, neat sets, and intriguing effects as the speeded-up characters zip around. There is a time when Zak outsmarts characters who are merely speeded-up by speeding up while *in* speed-space, or whatever it's called, so that he whizzes around the whizzers while emitting a kind of pulsing glow.

The movie has been produced by Nickelodeon, and will no doubt satisfy its intended audience enormously. It does not cross over into the post-Nickelodeon universe. Unlike *Spy Kids* or *Big Fat Liar,* it offers few consolations for parents and older brothers and sisters. It is what it is, efficiently and skillfully, and I salute it for hitting a double or maybe a triple. I also like the dialogue of Dr. ("Don't blow your RAM") Dopler. No one can be altogether uninteresting who makes a verb out of "ginzu."

Note: At one point the characters pass a high-security checkpoint and have to submit to a retinal scan. In a subtle bow to the Americans with Disabilities Act, the retinal scan device is at waist level.

The Closet ★ ★ ½

R, 85 m., 2001

Daniel Auteuil (Francois Pignon), Gerard Depardieu (Felix Santini), Thierry Lhermitte (Guillaume), Michele Laroque (Mlle. Bertrand), Michel Aumont (Belone), Jean Rochefort (Kopel), Alexandra Vandernoot (Christine). Directed by Francis Veber and produced by Alain Poire. Screenplay by Veber.

Francois Pignon is the most boring employee at the condom factory, a meek accountant who seems so unnecessary that he's told he'll be fired after twenty years of loyal service. That figures. His wife divorced him two years earlier, his son despises him as a nobody, and at work they snicker about what a nerd he is.

Pignon returns to his depressing bachelor apartment, finds a kitten on the balcony, gives it a saucer of milk, and hears a knock at the door. It is his new neighbor, an older man who is looking for the kitten—and sees immediately that Francois is miserable. "Give me a drink," he says. "I'm lonelier than you are."

Pignon is played by Daniel Auteuil, the sad-eyed, crooked-nose star of some of the best French films of recent years *(The Widow of St. Pierre, The Girl on the Bridge).* His neighbor is Belone (Michel Aumont), large, expansive, sympathetic. Soon Pignon is pouring out his story. Belone listens and comes up with a way for Francois to keep his job: He must pretend to be gay. That way, the condom company will be terrified of bad publicity if it fires him. *The Closet* is a new French comedy that turns

the tables on *La Cage aux Folles.* That was about a gay man trying to appear straight; this is about a straight, conservative, timid man who is transformed in the eyes of the world when he seems to be gay. Belone, who is gay himself, uses his computer to fabricate photographs that seem to show Pignon being very friendly with a leather-clad gay man, and mails it to coworkers at the factory. The news spreads instantly, and Pignon's office mates now interpret his inhibited behavior as just a cover-up.

The movie is a box-office hit in France, not least because it has four top actors in unusual roles. Gérard Depardieu, the most macho of French actors, plays Santini, a homophobe who stops gay-bashing and tries to befriend Pignon. Jean Rochefort, is the magisterial boss of the company. And Thierry Lhermitte is the troublemaker who inflames Depardieu's fears by telling him he'll be fired for his political incorrectness. To understand this casting in Hollywood terms, think of Auteuil, Depardieu, Rochefort, and Lhermitte as Tom Hanks, Brendan Fraser, Michael Douglas, and Kevin Pollack. (Given the success of the Hollywood remake of *La Cage aux Folles,* we may actually be seeing casting like this before long.)

At least two of Pignon's coworkers are intrigued by the revelations about his sexuality. Ms. Bertrand (Michele Laroque), his superior, found him boring when he was straight but sexy now that he's gay, and wants to seduce him. And the rugby-playing Santini, who picked on Pignon when he thought he was a sissy, tries to save his own job by taking the accountant out to lunch and being nice to him—suspiciously nice, some might think.

The movie passes the time pleasantly and has a few good laughs (the loudest is when Pignon rides in a gay pride parade wearing a crown that looks like a jolly giant condom). But the screenplay relies too much on the first level of its premise and doesn't push into unexpected places. Once we get the setup, we can more or less anticipate the sitcom payoff, and there aren't the kinds of surprises, reversals, and explosions of slapstick that made *La Cage aux Folles* so funny. In the rating system of the Michelin guide, it's worth a look, but not a detour or a journey.

Collateral Damage ★ ★ ★

R, 115 m., 2002

Arnold Schwarzenegger (Gordon Brewer), Elias Koteas (CIA Agent Peter Brandt), Francesca Neri (Selena Perrini), Cliff Curtis (Claudio "The Wolf" Perrini), John Leguizamo (Felix Ramirez), John Turturro (Sean Armstrong). Directed by Andrew Davis and produced by David Foster, Peter MacGregor-Scott, and Steven Reuther. Screenplay by David Griffiths and Peter Griffiths.

Collateral Damage is a relic from an earlier (if not kinder and gentler) time, a movie about terrorism made before terrorists became the subject of our national discourse. "You Americans are so naive," says the movie's terrorist villain. "You see a peasant with a gun, you change the channel. But you never ask why a peasant needs a gun." Well, we still don't wonder why the peasant needs the gun (we think we should have the gun), but we're not so naive anymore.

The movie stars Arnold Schwarzenegger as Brewer, a Los Angeles fireman who sees his wife and son killed by a terrorist bomb. Vowing revenge, he flies to Colombia, escapes several murder attempts, survives an improbable trip down a waterfall, penetrates guerrilla territory, kills a lot of people, and blows up a lot of stuff. He is your typical Los Angeles fireman if the fire department sent all of its men through Delta Force training.

To review this movie in the light of 9/11 is not really fair. It was made months earlier, and indeed its release date was postponed in the aftermath of the attack. That has escaped the attention of the Rev. Brian Jordan, a priest who, according to the Associated Press, ministers to workers at Ground Zero. "Making the main character a firefighter who becomes a vigilante is an insult to the firefighters who became heroes after the terrorist attacks," he says. He adds that the film discriminates against Colombians; his fellow protesters said the movie will "cement stereotypes that Colombians are drug traffickers and guerrillas, rather than hardworking, educated people."

Jordan added that he has not seen the film. His criticism is therefore theoretical. He believes making a firefighter a vigilante in a movie made before the attacks is an insult now that the attacks have taken place. Would it have been an insult even if the attacks had not taken place? Why is it an insult? Should a firefighter not feel like avenging the murder of his family? As to the film's view of Colombia, since the guerrillas are shown as drug traffickers and enemies of the government, it seems clear they are not considered the majority of Colombians. The AP, which would not run the review of a critic who had not seen the film, felt Jordan was sufficiently qualified to attack it sight unseen. We await his further insights once he has seen it.

My guess is that the average firefighter, like the average American moviegoer, might sort of enjoy the movie, which is a skillfully made example of your typical Schwarzenegger action film. The Arnold character is uncomplicated, loyal, brave, and resourceful, and does only six or seven things that are impossible in the physical universe. The villains, it is true, give a bad name to Colombian guerrillas and drug traffickers. The only ambiguity comes in the person of a government agent played by Elias Koteas, who first refuses to share information with the FBI, and then appears to be an FBI agent himself. It's the kind of movie where you don't give that a passing thought.

I kept expecting a subtext in which the CIA or other American agencies were involved in skulduggery in Colombia, but no: The plot leads us to believe there may be a double agent on our side, but that's a blind alley. Instead, all leads up to a climax involving the planned destruction of a Washington skyscraper, which is creepy and disturbing given our feelings about 9/11, but traditional in movies made earlier—when terrorism plots were standard in the movies. You may not want to attend *Collateral Damage* because of 9/11, but it hardly seems fair to attack it for not knowing then what we all know now.

That leaves me with a couple of tactical questions. There is an air attack on a guerrilla base where the fireman is being held captive. How can they be sure their rockets won't kill him? Or do they want to kill him? And there is a neatly timed rendezvous involving a terrorist and a man on a motorcycle that leads us to wonder, thinking back through the plot, how this plan could have been made. There are also some coincidences that are a little too neat, like how a fire ax saves lives in the first scene and then, at the end, becomes the fireman's handy and symbolic tool for creating one of those booby traps where you wonder how in the hell he could have figured that one out.

There will not be any more action stories like this for a long time. We're at the end of the tunnel, the light is out, the genre is closed. *Collateral Damage* may stir unwanted associations for some viewers. Others may attend it with a certain nostalgia, remembering a time when such scenarios fell under the heading of entertainment.

Comedian ★ ★

R, 100 m., 2002

As themselves: Jerry Seinfeld, Orny Adams, Bill Cosby, Robert Klein, Jay Leno, Chris Rock, and Garry Shandling. A documentary directed by Christian Charles and produced by Gary Streiner.

If it takes this much agony to be a stand-up comic, I don't think I could survive a movie about a brain surgeon. *Comedian* follows Jerry Seinfeld and other stand-ups as they appear on stage and then endlessly analyze, discuss, rerun, regret, denounce, forgive, and rewrite their material. To say they sweat blood is to trivialize their suffering.

It looks to the audience as if stand-up comics walk out on a stage, are funny, walk off, and spend the rest of the time hanging around the bar being envied by wannabes. In fact, we discover, they agonize over "a minute," "five minutes," "ten minutes," on their way to nirvana: "I have an hour." When Chris Rock tells Seinfeld that Bill Cosby does two hours and twenty minutes *without an intermission,* and he does it *twice in the same day,* he becomes very sad and thoughtful, like a karaoke star when Tony Bennett walks in.

Seinfeld can't believe his good fortune. He reached the top with one of the biggest hit TV shows of all time. And yet: "Here I am in Cleveland." After retiring his old nightclub act with an HBO special, he starts from scratch to devise a new act and take it on the road to comedy clubs, half of which are called the Improv. He stands in front of the same brick walls, drinks the same bottled water, handles the same microphones as kids on the way up. Of course,

he flies into town on a private jet that costs more than the comedy club, but the movie doesn't rub this in.

Seinfeld is a great star, yet cannot coast. One night he gets stuck in the middle of his act—he loses his train of thought—and stares baffled into space. Blowing a single word can depress him. If it's still a battle for Seinfeld, consider the case of Orny Adams, a rising comedian whom the film uses as counterpoint. Adams shows Seinfeld a room full of boxes, drawers, cabinets, file folders stuffed with jokes. There are piles of material, and yet he confides: "I feel like I sacrificed so much of my life. I'm twenty-nine, and I have no job, no wife, no children." Seinfeld regards him as if wife, children, home will all come in good time, but stand-up, now—stand-up is life.

Orny Adams gets a gig on the David Letterman program, and we see him backstage, vibrating with nervousness. The network guys have been over his material and suggested some changes. Now he practices saying the word "psoriasis." After the show, he makes a phone call to a friend to explain, "I opened my first great network show with a joke I had never used before." Well, not a *completely* new joke. He had to substitute the word "psoriasis" for the word "lupus." But to a comedian who fine-tunes every syllable, that made it a new joke and a fearsome challenge.

Seinfeld pays tribute to Robert Klein ("he was the guy we all looked up to"). We listen to Klein remember when, after several appearances on *The Tonight Show,* he received the ultimate recognition: He was "called over" by Johnny. Seinfeld recalls that when he was ten he memorized the comedy albums of Bill Cosby. Now he visits Cosby backstage and expresses wonderment that "a human life could last so long that I would be included in your life." Big hug. Cosby is sixty-five, and Seinfeld is forty-eight, a seventeen-year difference that is therefore less amazing than that Shoshanna Lonstein's life could last so long that she could meet Jerry when she was eighteen and he was thirty-nine, but there you go.

Comedian was filmed over the course of a year by director Christian Charles and producer Gary Streiner, who used two "store-bought" video cameras and followed Seinfeld around. If that is all they did for a year, then this was a waste of their time, since the footage, however interesting, is the backstage variety that could easily be obtained in a week. There are no deep revelations, no shocking moments of truth, and many, many conversations in which Seinfeld and other comics discuss their acts with discouragement and despair. The movie was produced by Seinfeld, and protects him. The visuals tend toward the dim, the gray, and the washed-out, and you wish instead of spending a year with their store-boughts, they'd spent a month and used the leftover to hire a cinematographer.

Why, you might wonder, would a man with untold millions in the bank go on a tour of comedy clubs? What's in it for him, if the people in Cleveland laugh? Why, for that matter, does Jay Leno go to comedy clubs every single week, even after having been called over by Johnny for the ultimate reward? Is it because to walk out on the stage, to risk all, to depend on your nerve and skill, and to possibly "die," is an addiction? Gamblers, they say, don't want to win so much as they want to play. They like the action. They tend to keep gambling until they have lost all their money. There may be a connection between the two obsessions, although gamblers at least say they are having fun, and stand-up comics, judging by this film, are miserable, self-tortured beings to whom success only represents a higher place to fall from.

Company Man ½★
PG-13, 81 m., 2001

Douglas McGrath (Allen Quimp), Sigourney Weaver (Daisy Quimp), John Turturro (Crocker Johnson), Anthony LaPaglia (Fidel Castro), Ryan Phillippe (Rudolph Petrov), Denis Leary (Fry), Woody Allen (Lowther), Alan Cumming (General Batista). Directed by Peter Askin and Douglas McGrath and produced by Guy East, Rick Leed, John Penotti, and James W. Skotchdopole. Screenplay by Askin and McGrath.

Company Man is the kind of movie that seems to be wearing a strained smile, as if it's not sure we're getting the jokes. If it could, it would laugh for us. It's an arch, awkward, ill-timed, forced political comedy set in 1959 and seemingly stranded there.

Astonishing, that a movie could be this bad and star Sigourney Weaver, John Turturro, Anthony LaPaglia, Denis Leary, Woody Allen, Alan Cumming, and Ryan Phillippe. I am reminded of Gene Siskel's classic question, "Is this movie better than a documentary of the same actors having lunch?" In this case, it is not even better than a documentary of the same actors ordering room service while fighting the stomach flu.

In addition to the cast members listed above, the movie stars Douglas McGrath, its author and codirector, who is a low-rent cross between Jack Lemmon and Wally Cox and comes across without any apparent comic effect. He plays Allen Quimp, rhymes with wimp, a grammar teacher from Connecticut whose wife (Weaver) frets that he needs a better job. To get her and his own family off his back, he claims to be a CIA agent, and that leads, through a series of events as improbable as they are uninteresting, to his involvement in the defection of a Russia ballet star (Phillippe) and his assignment to Cuba on the eve of Castro's revolution.

His contact agent there is Fry, played by Denis Leary, who looks appalled at some of the scenes he's in. Example: As Fry denies that a revolutionary fever is sweeping the island, a man with a bottle full of gasoline approaches them and borrows a light from Quimp. Soon after, the man runs past in the opposite direction and they pass (without noticing—ho, ho) a burning auto. And not any burning auto, but an ancient, rusty, abandoned hulk filled with phony gas flames obviously rigged and turned on for the movie. How does it help the revolution to restage ancient auto fires?

But never mind. Fry introduces Quimp to Lowther (Woody Allen), the CIA's man in charge, who also denies a revolution is under way, while turning aside to light his cigarette from a burning effigy of Batista (ho, ho). The mystery of what Woody Allen is doing in this movie is solved in a two-name search on the Internet Movie Database, which reveals that McGrath cowrote the screenplay for Allen's *Bullets Over Broadway.* Now Allen is returning the favor, I guess.

Well, that was a funny movie, and the same search identifies McGrath as the writer-director of *Emma* (1996), a nice little comedy with Gwyneth Paltrow. So he is obviously not without talent—except in this movie. Maybe the mistake was to star himself. He doesn't have the presence to anchor a comedy; all those jokes about Quimp the nonentity ring true, instead of funny.

As bad movies go, *Company Man* falls less in the category of Affront to the Audience and more in the category of Nonevent. It didn't work me up into a frenzy of dislike, but dialed me down into sullen indifference. It was screened twice for the Chicago press, and I sat through the first thirty minutes of the second screening, thinking to check it against a different crowd. I heard no laughter. Just an occasional cough, or the shuffling of feet, or a yawn, or a sigh, like in a waiting room.

Confessions of a Dangerous Mind
★ ★ ★ ½
R, 113 m., 2002

Sam Rockwell (Chuck Barris), Drew Barrymore (Penny), George Clooney (Jim Byrd), Julia Roberts (Patricia Watson), Rutger Hauer (Keeler), Kristen Wilson (Loretta). Directed by George Clooney and produced by Andrew Lazar. Screenplay by Charlie Kaufman, based on the book by Chuck Barris.

I had not read the autobiography of Chuck Barris when I went to see *Confessions of a Dangerous Mind*. Well, how many people have? So I made an understandable error. When the movie claimed that the game show creator had moonlighted as a CIA hit man, I thought I was detecting a nudge from the screenwriter, Charlie Kaufman. He is the man who created the portal into John Malkovich's mind in *Being John Malkovich,* and gave himself a twin brother in *Adaptation.* Now, I thought, the little trickster had juiced up the Barris biopic by making the creator of *The Gong Show* into an assassin. What a card.

I am now better informed. Barris himself claims to have killed thirty-three times for the CIA. It's in his book. He had the perfect cover: The creator of *The Dating Game* and *The Gong*

Show would accompany his lucky winners on trips to romantic spots such as Helsinki in midwinter, and kill for the CIA while the winners regaled each other with reindeer steaks. Who, after all, would ever suspect him?

When I met Barris I asked him, as everyone does, if this story is true. He declined to answer. The book and the movie speak for themselves—or don't speak for themselves, depending on your frame of mind. As for myself, I think he made it all up and never killed anybody. Having been involved in a weekly television show myself, I know for a melancholy fact that there is just not enough time between tapings to fly off to Helsinki and kill for my government.

It matters not whether the story is true or false, because all autobiographies are fictional, made up out of that continuous subconscious rewriting process by which we make ourselves blameless and heroic. Barris has a particular need to be heroic, because he blamed himself for so much. As the movie opens in 1981, he is holed up in a New York hotel (the Chelsea, I think), mired in self-contempt and watching TV as his penance. It is here, he tells us in a confiding voice-over, that he began to record "my wasted life."

That this would be the first project to attract George Clooney as a director is not so surprising if you know that his father directed game shows, and he was often a backstage observer. That Clooney would direct it so well is a little surprising, and is part of that reeducation by which we stop thinking of Clooney as a TV hunk and realize he is smart and curious. His first movie is not only intriguing as a story but great to look at, a marriage of bright pop images from the 1960s and 1970s and dark, cold spyscapes that seem to have wandered in from John le Carré.

Sam Rockwell plays Barris as a man who was given gifts but not the ability to enjoy them. He is depressed not so much because he thinks he could have done better in his life, but because he fears he could not. From his start as an NBC page in 1955, through his backstage work on Dick Clark's *American Bandstand,* to the crushing blow of having ABC choose *Hootenanny* over his *Dating Game* pilot, Barris comes across as a man who wants to succeed in order to

133

confirm his low opinion of himself. When his shows finally make the air, the TV critics blame him for the destruction of Western civilization, and he doesn't think they're so far off.

The movie has fun with the TV shows. We are reminded once again of the Unknown Comic and Gene-Gene the Dancing Machine, and on an episode of *The Dating Game* we see a contestant choose Bachelor No. 3 when we can see that Bachelors 1 and 2 are Brad Pitt and Matt Damon. Early in his career, Barris is recruited by a CIA man named Jim Byrd (George Clooney), and agrees to become a secret agent, maybe as a way of justifying his existence. "Think of it as a hobby," Clooney says soothingly. "You're an assassination enthusiast."

Two women figure strongly in his life. Patricia Watson (Julia Roberts) is the CIA's Marlene Dietrich, her face sexily shadowed at a rendezvous. She gives him a quote from Nietzsche that could serve as his motto: "The man who despises himself still respects himself as he who despises." And then there's Penny (Drew Barrymore), the hippie chick who comes along at first for the ride, and remains to be his loyal friend, trying to talk him out of that hotel room.

Confessions of a Dangerous Mind makes a companion to Paul Schrader's *Auto-Focus*, the story of the rise and fall of *Hogan's Heroes* star Bob Crane. Both films show men whose secret lives are more exciting than the public lives that win them fame. Barris seems to want to redeem himself for the crimes he committed on television, while Crane uses his fame as a ticket to sex addiction. Both films lift up the cheerful rock of television to find wormy things crawling for cover. The difference is that Crane comes across as shallow and pathetic, while Barris—well, any man who would claim thirty-three killings as a way to rehabilitate his reputation deserves our sympathy and maybe our forgiveness. ☞

Confidence ★ ★
R, 98 m., 2003

Edward Burns (Jake Vig), Rachel Weisz (Lily), Andy Garcia (Gunther Butan), Dustin Hoffman (King), Paul Giamatti (Gordo), Donal Logue (Whitworth), Luis Guzman (Manzano), Frankie G. (Lupus), Brian Van Holt (Miles). Directed by James Foley and produced by Michael Burns, Marc Butan, Michael Ohoven, and Michael Paseornek. Screenplay by Doug Jung.

Confidence is a flawless exercise about con games, and that is precisely its failing: It is an exercise. It fails to make us care, even a little, about the characters and what happens to them. There is nothing at stake. The screenplay gives away the game by having the entire story narrated in flashback by the hero, who treats it not as an adventure but as a series of devious deceptions that he can patiently explain to the man holding a gun on him—and to us. At the end, we can see how smart he is and how everybody was fooled, but we don't care.

The obvious contrast is with David Mamet's *House of Games*, which also told a story of cons within cons, but which had stakes so high that at the end the victim called the con man's bluff by—well, by shooting him dead, after which he didn't have any twists left. We cared about those characters. *Confidence* lacks that passion and urgency; there are times when the narration sounds like the filmmakers at a pitch meeting, explaining how tricky their plot is and unable to keep the enthusiasm out of their voices.

That's not to say the movie, directed by James Foley, is badly made. It's great-looking, with its *film noir* reds and greens and blues, its neon Bud Ice signs, its shadows and mean streets, its sleazy strip clubs, and its use of wipes and swish-pans (sideways, up, down, sometimes two at a time). You know this is a crime movie, which is nice to be reminded of, except that every reminder also tells us it's only a movie, so that there is no possibility that we can commit to the characters, worry about them, want them to succeed or fail.

The movie stars Edward Burns as Jake Vig, a confidence mastermind, who has a crew of regulars and uses them to stage fake murders in order to scare marks into running away without their money. One day he makes the mistake of stealing $150,000 from the bagman for a nasty crimelord, the King (Dustin Hoffman). He confronts the King in his strip club and tells him he'll get the money back, but first he wants the King to supply an additional $200,000 as seed money for a $5 million scam Jake has in mind.

Jake's last name, Vig, is possibly short for "vigorish," the word gamblers use to describe the money the house takes off the top. If I were looking for someone to play with $200,000 of my money, I don't think I would choose a con man named Vig. But the King is confident that no one would even dream of cheating him, because he has such a fearsome reputation. And to keep an eye on Jake, he sends along his henchman Lupus (Frankie G.) to watch Jake's every move.

Dustin Hoffman's performance as the King is the best thing in the movie—indeed, the only element that comes to life on the screen. The King runs a strip club as a front, launders money for the mob, and suffers from attention deficit disorder—or, as he meticulously specifies, "attention deficit hyperactivity disorder." To control his condition, he takes pills that slow him way down. "Feel my heart," he says to one of the strippers in his club, to prove that it is hardly beating. Hoffman, chewing gum, wearing a beard and glasses, looks like the gnome from hell, and fast-talks his way into a brilliant supporting performance.

So brilliant, I couldn't help wondering how much energy the film would have gained if Hoffman, say, had played the lead instead of Burns. With Hoffman, you look at him and try to figure out what he's thinking. With Burns, you look at him and either you already know, or he doesn't make you care. Burns is the right actor for a lot of roles, especially young men tortured by the pangs of romance, but as a con man he lacks the shadings and edges. Once again, the comparison is with Joe Mantegna in *House of Games*.

Jake Vig's crew includes fellow hoods Gordo (Paul Giamatti) and Miles (Brian Van Holt). He has recently enlisted Lily (Rachel Weisz), who is very pretty and whom he likes—two ominous signs for a con man. And when he needs two guys to turn up and pretend to be L.A. cops, he has two real cops (Donal Logue and Luis Guzman) to play the roles. There is also the enigmatic federal agent Gunther Butan (Andy Garcia), whose name means "butane" in German, and who spends a great deal of time relighting his cigar. Garcia has been on Jake's tail for years, we learn, although he may simply represent a higher level in the game.

Confidence is a jerk-around movie, a film that works by jerking us around. I don't mind being misled and fooled in a clever way, especially when the movie makes me care about the characters before pulling the rug out from under them, or me. But there is no sense of risk here. No real stakes. It's all an entertainment, even for the characters, and at the end of the movie, as one surprise after another is revealed, there is no sense that these amazing revelations are really happening; no, they're simply the screenplay going through its final paces so the audience will appreciate the full extent to which it has been duped. What a shame that such a well-made movie is never able to convince us it is anything more than merely well made.

The Core ★ ★ ½
PG-13, 135 m., 2003

Aaron Eckhart (Josh Keyes), Hilary Swank (Major Rebecca Childs), Delroy Lindo (Dr. Edward Brazzleton), Stanley Tucci (Dr. Conrad Zimsky), Tchéky Karyo (Serge Leveque), Bruce Greenwood (Colonel Robert Iverson), DJ Qualls (Taz "Rat" Finch), Richard Jenkins (General Thomas Purcell), Alfre Woodard (Talma Stickley). Directed by Jon Amiel and produced by Sean Bailey, David Foster, and Cooper Layne. Screenplay by Layne and John Rogers.

Hot on the heels of *Far from Heaven*, which looked exactly like a 1957 melodrama, here is *The Core*, which wants to be a 1957 science fiction movie. Its special effects are a little too good for that (not a lot), but the plot is out of something by Roger Corman, and you can't improve on dialogue like this:

"The Earth's core has stopped spinning!"

"How could that happen?"

Yes, the Earth's core has stopped spinning, and in less than a year the Earth will lose its electromagnetic shield and we'll all be toast—fried by solar microwaves. To make that concept clear to a panel of U.S. military men, professor Josh Keyes of the University of Chicago (Aaron Eckhart) borrows a can of room freshener, sets the propellant alight with his Bic, and incinerates a peach.

To watch Josh Keyes and the generals contemplate that burnt peach is to witness a scene that cries out from its very vitals to be cut from the movie and made into ukulele picks. Such goofiness amuses me.

I have such an unreasonable affection for

this movie, indeed, that it is only by slapping myself alongside the head and drinking black coffee that I can restrain myself from recommending it. It is only a notch down from *Congo, Anaconda, Lara Croft, Tomb Raider,* and other films that those with too little taste think they have too much taste to enjoy.

To be sure, *The Core* starts out in an unsettling manner, with the crash landing of the space shuttle. Considering that *Phone Booth,* scheduled for release in October 2002, was shelved for six months because it echoed the Beltway Sniper, to put a shuttle crash in a March 2003 movie is pushing the limits of decorum, wouldn't you say?

And yet the scene is a humdinger. Earth's disturbed magnetic field has confused the shuttle's guidance system, causing it to aim for downtown Los Angeles. Pilot Richard Jenkins insists, "It's Mission Control's call," but copilot Hilary Swank has an idea, which she explains *after* the shuttle passes over Dodger Stadium at an altitude of about 800 feet.

If the shuttle glided over Wrigley Field at that altitude, I'm thinking, it would have crashed into the 23d Precinct Police Station by now, or at the very least a Vienna Red Hot stand. But no, there's time for a conversation with Mission Control, and then for the shuttle to change course and make one of those emergency landings where wings get sheared off and everybody holds on real tight.

Other portents show something is wrong with Gaia. Birds go crazy in Trafalgar Square, people with pacemakers drop dead, and then Josh Keyes and fellow scientist Conrad Zimsky (Stanley Tucci) decide that Earth's core has stopped spinning. To bring such an unimaginable mass shuddering to a halt would result, one assumes, in more than confused pigeons, but science is not this film's strong point. Besides, do pigeons need their innate magnetic direction-sensing navigational instincts for such everyday jobs as flying from the top of Nelson's column to the bottom?

Dr. Zimsky leads the emergency team to the Utah salt flats, where eccentric scientist Edward Brazzleton (Delroy Lindo) has devised a laser device that can cut through solid rock. He has also invented a new metal named, I am not making this up, Unobtainium. (So rare is this substance that a Google search reveals only 8,060 sites selling Unobtainium ski gear, jackets, etc.) Combining the metal and the laser device into a snaky craft that looks like a BMW Roto-Rooter, the United States launches a $50 billion probe to Earth's core, in scenes that will have colonoscopy survivors shifting uneasily in their seats.

Their mission: Set off a couple of nuclear explosions that (they hope) will set the core a-spinnin' again. Earth's innards are depicted in special effects resembling a 1960s underground movie seen on acid, and it is marvelous that the crew have a video monitor so they can see out as they drill through dense matter in total darkness. Eventually they reach a depth where the pressure is 800,000 pounds per square inch—and then they put on suits to walk around outside. Their suits are obviously made of something stronger and more flexible than Unobtainium. Probably corduroy.

The music is perfect for this enterprise: ominous horns and soaring strings. The cast includes some beloved oddballs, most notably DJ Qualls *(The New Guy),* who plays Rat, a computer hacker who can talk to the animals, or at least sing to the dolphins. The only wasted cast member is Alfre Woodard, relegated to one of those Mission Control roles where she has to look worried and then relieved.

The Core is not exactly good, but it knows what a movie is. It has energy and daring and isn't afraid to make fun of itself, and it thinks big, as when the Golden Gate Bridge collapses and a scientist tersely reports, "The West Coast is out." If you are at the video store late on Saturday night and they don't have *Anaconda,* this will do. ☞

Corky Romano ½★
PG-13, 86 m., 2001

Chris Kattan (Corky Romano), Peter Falk (Pops Romano), Vinessa Shaw (Kate Russo), Peter Berg (Paulie), Fred Ward (Leo Corrigan), Chris Penn (Peter), Richard Roundtree (Howard Shuster). Directed by Rob Pritts and produced by Robert Simonds. Screenplay by David Garrett and Jason Ward.

Corky Romano continues the *Saturday Night Live* Jinx, which in recent years has frustrated the talented members of the TV program in their efforts to make watchable movies. It's a desperately unfunny gangster spoof, starring Chris Kattan as the kid brother in a Mafia family, so trusting and naive he really does believe his father is in the landscaping business.

This is the third time the jinx has claimed Kattan as a victim, after *A Night at the Roxbury* (1998) and this year's *Monkey Bone*, two films that will be among the first to go when Blockbuster destroys 25 percent of its VHS tape inventory, and will not be leading the chain's list of DVD replacement titles.

Now when I use the words "desperately unfunny," what do I mean? Consider one of Corky's earlier scenes, where we see him as an assistant veterinarian. Clumsy beyond belief, he knocks over everything in a room full of ailing animals, and a snake crawls up his pants and eventually, inevitably, emerges from his fly.

I submit as a general principle that it is not funny when a clumsy person knocks over *everything* in a room. The choreography makes it obvious that the character, in one way or another, is deliberately careening from one collision to another. It always looks deliberate. Indeed, it looks like a deliberate attempt to force laughs instead of building them. One movie where it does work is *The Mummy*, where Rachel Weisz knocks over a bookcase and a whole library tumbles over domino-style. But there an original accident builds and builds beyond her control; Corky Romano's approach would be to reel around the room knocking over every bookcase individually.

In the movie, Corky's father is played by Peter Falk. True, Falk is one of the first guys you'd think of for the role, but they should have kept thinking. He has played similar roles so many times that he can sleepwalk through his dialogue; a completely unexpected casting choice might have been funnier. Corky has two very tough brothers (Peter Berg and Chris Penn) who doubt their father's plan, which is that the youngest son should infiltrate the FBI in order to destroy the evidence against the old man.

That brings Corky into contact with Howard Schuster (Richard Roundtree), the local FBI chief, who is given the thankless comic task of never knowing more than he needs to know in order to make the wrong decision. There's also Vinessa Shaw as an FBI agent who goes under-cover as a sexy nurse. Or maybe she's a sexy agent who goes undercover as a nurse. Such a thin line separates the two concepts.

Corky Romano is like a dead zone of comedy. The concept is exhausted, the ideas are tired, the physical gags are routine, the story is labored, the actors look like they can barely contain their doubts about the project.

The Count of Monte Cristo ★ ★ ★
PG-13, 118 m., 2002

Guy Pearce (Fernand Mondego), James Caviezel (Edmond Dantes), Richard Harris (Faria), Dagmara Dominczyk (Mercedes), Luis Guzman (Jacobo), Henry Cavill (Albert Mondego), James Frain (Villefort), Albie Woodington (Danglars). Directed by Kevin Reynolds and produced by Gary Barber, Roger Birnbaum, and Jonathan Glickman. Screenplay by Jay Wolpert, based on the novel by Alexandre Dumas.

The Count of Monte Cristo is a movie that incorporates piracy, Napoleon in exile, betrayal, solitary confinement, secret messages, escape tunnels, swashbuckling, comic relief, a treasure map, Parisian high society, and sweet revenge, and brings it in at under two hours, with performances by good actors who are clearly having fun. This is the kind of adventure picture the studios churned out in the Golden Age—so traditional it almost feels new.

James Caviezel stars, as Edmond Dantes, a low-born adventurer betrayed by his friend Fernand Mondego (Guy Pearce). Condemned to solitary confinement on the remote prison island of Chateau d'If, he spends years slowly growing mad and growing his hair, until one day a remarkable thing happens. A stone in his cell floor moves and lifts, and Faria (Richard Harris) appears. Faria has even more hair than Dantes, but is much more cheerful because he has kept up his hope over the years by digging an escape tunnel. Alas, by digging in the wrong direction, he came up in Dantes's cell instead of outside the walls, but c'est la vie.

"There are 5,119 stones in my walls," Dantes tells Faria. "I have counted them." Faria can think of better ways to pass the time. Enlisting Dantes in a renewed tunneling effort, Faria also tutors him in the physical and mental arts; he's the Mr. Miyagi of swashbuckling.

137

Together, the men study the philosophies of Adam Smith and Machiavelli, and the old man tutors the younger one in what looks uncannily like martial arts, including the ability to move with blinding speed.

This middle section of the movie lasts long enough to suggest it may also provide the end, but no: The third act takes place back in society, after Faria supplies Dantes with a treasure map, and the resulting treasure finances his masquerade as the fictitious Count of Monte Cristo. Rich, enigmatic, mysterious, he fascinates the aristocracy and throws lavish parties, all as a snare for Mondego, while renewing his love for the beautiful Mercedes (Dagmara Dominczyk).

The story, of course, is based on the novel by Alexandre Dumas, unread by me, although I was a close student of the *Classics Illustrated* version. Director Kevin Reynolds redeems himself after *Waterworld* by moving the action along at a crisp pace; we can imagine Errol Flynn in this material, although Caviezel and Pearce bring more conviction to it, and Luis Guzman is droll as the count's loyal sidekick, doing what sounds vaguely like eighteenth-century stand-up ("I swear on my dead relatives—and even the ones that are not feeling so good...").

The various cliffs, fortresses, prisons, treasure isles, and chateaus all look suitably atmospheric, the fight scenes are well choreographed, and the moment of Mondego's comeuppance is nicely milked for every ounce of sweet revenge. This is the kind of movie that used to be right at home at the Saturday matinee, and it still is.

The Country Bears ★ ★
G, 87 m., 2002

Christopher Walken (Reed Thimple), Stephen Tobolowsky (Mr. Barrington), Meagen Fay (Mrs. Barrington), M. C. Gainey (Roadie), Diedrich Bader (Officer Cheets). And the voices of: Haley Joel Osment (Beary Barrington), Diedrich Bader (Ted Bedderhead), Candy Ford (Trixie St. Claire), James Gammon (Big Al), Brad Garrett (Fred Bedderhead). Directed by Peter Hastings and produced by Jeffrey Chernov and Andrew Gunn. Screenplay by Mark Perez.

The formidable technical skills in *The Country*

Bears must not be allowed to distract from the film's terminal inanity. Here is a story about a young music fan who convinces his favorite band to reunite after ten years for a concert—and the fan and the band members are all bears. Why they are bears, I do not know. Do they know they are bears? Not necessarily. Do any of the humans mention that they are bears? Only in passing. Are there real bears in the woods who would maul and eat their victims, or are all bears benign in this world?

These are not questions one is expected to pose about a movie based on a stage show at Disneyland. We simply have to accept that some of the characters in the movie are people and others are bears, and get on with it. If Stuart Little's family can have a two-inch mouse as a son, then why not musical bears? We must celebrate diversity.

The movie stars Beary Barrington (voice by Haley Joel Osment), whose human parents treat him as one of the family. Then his brother breaks the news that he was adopted after being found by a park ranger, and little Beary runs away from home. His goal: Visit legendary Country Bear Hall, the Grand Ole Opry of singing bears, and pay tribute to the band he idolizes.

Alas, the band has broken up, its members have scattered, and now even Country Bear Hall itself faces the wrecker's ball, thanks to the evil banker Reed Thimple (Christopher Walken). Since the hall is an elegant wooden structure, it is a little hard to understand why Thimple wants to replace it with a vacant lot, but there you have it. Little Beary then begins to meet the members of the Country Bears, and to persuade them, in a series of adventures, to reunite and stage a benefit concert to save the hall.

One of the movie's running gags is that recording stars appear as themselves, talking about the Bears. We see Willie Nelson, Bonnie Raitt, Elton John, Queen Latifah, and others, all talking about the band's influence on them, none mentioning that they are bears. Is the music good enough to influence Willie and the Queen? Don't make me laugh.

It's hard to figure who the movie is intended for. In shape and purpose it's like a G-rated version of *This Is Spinal Tap*, but will its wee target audience understand the joke? Anyone old enough to be interested in the music is unlikely to be interested in the bears—at least, interested in the movie's routine and wheezy plot. True, the movie does a good job of integrating the bears into the action, with animatronics by Jim Henson's Creature Shop and no doubt various CGI effects, not to mention the strong possibility that in some shots we are basically watching actors in bear suits. It's done well, yes, but why?

Cradle 2 the Grave ★ ★
R, 100 m., 2003

Jet Li (Su), DMX (Fait), Anthony Anderson (Tommy), Kelly Hu (Sona), Tom Arnold (Archie), Mark Dacascos (Ling), Gabrielle Union (Daria). Directed by Andrzej Bartkowiak and produced by Joel Silver. Screenplay by John O'Brien and Channing Gibson.

The funniest scene in *Cradle 2 the Grave* comes over the end credits, as supporting actors Tom Arnold and Anthony Anderson debate how the story should be filmed. This scene, which feels ad-libbed, is smart and self-aware in a way the movie never is. The film itself is on autopilot and overdrive at the same time: It does nothing original, but does it very rapidly.

Jet Li and DMX are the stars, both ready for better scripts, playing enemies who become buddies when it turns out they have a common antagonist. DMX plays a character pronounced "fate" but spelled "Fait," which would give you a neat pun you could use in French class, if the spelling of his name were ever seen. Jet Li plays a boy named Su. After Fait and his accomplices break into a Los Angeles diamond vault, their caper is interrupted by Su, who is working for the Taiwanese police.

Bad guys end up with the diamonds and kidnap Fait's beloved little daughter, in a plot that started out as a remake of Fritz Lang's *M* (1931). The journey from *M* to *2* was downhill all the way. The result is a Joel Silver nonstop action thriller, well produced, slickly directed, sure to please slackjaws who are not tired to death of this kind of material recycled again and again and again.

It makes at least a sincere attempt to one-up previous cop-crook-buddy-sex-chase-caper-martial-arts thrillers. Jet Li doesn't merely take on a lot of opponents at the same time, he gets in a fight with all of the competitors in an illegal extreme fighting club. He doesn't merely do stunts, but drops in free-fall from one high-rise balcony to the next. Tom Arnold doesn't merely play a black market arms dealer, he supplies a tank. The black diamonds are not merely black diamonds, but are actually a superweapon that would bring down the cost of weapons of mass destruction into the price range of a nice private jet. There is not merely a hood who has special privileges in jail, but one with a private cell where the prison guards melt butter for his fresh lobster while he waits impatiently. There is not merely a chase, but one involving an all-terrain vehicle, which is driven up the stairs of a store and then jumps from one rooftop to another more or less for the hell of it. And the girl is not merely sexy but Gabrielle Union.

I can see that this movie fills a need. I have stopped feeling the need. The problem with action movies is how quickly state of the art becomes off-the-shelf. We yearn for wit and intelligence, and a movie like *Shanghai Knights* looks sophisticated by comparison.

Cradle 2 the Grave will, however, be a box-office hit, I imagine, and that will be demographically interesting because it demonstrates that a savvy producer like Silver now believes a white star is completely unnecessary in a mega-budget action picture. At one point, there were only white stars. Then they got to have black buddies. Then they got to have Asian buddies. Then *Rush Hour* proved that black and Asian buddies could haul in the mass audience. Long ago a movie like this used a black character for comic relief. Then an Asian character. Now the white character is the comic relief. May the circle be unbroken.

Not only is Gabrielle Union the female lead, but Kelly Hu is the second female lead, slapping the kid around and engaging in a catfight with Union. Lots of mild sex in the movie, although an opening scene assumes a security guard is a very slow study. First Gabrielle Union goes in to flirt with him so he won't look at the TV security monitors. When he turns out to be gay, she sends in the second team, Anthony Anderson, to flirt with him. When two people try to pick you up in ten minutes and you're a security guard on duty, do you suspect anything?

139

It's a common complaint that the cops are never around during sensational movie chase scenes and shoot-outs. Dozens of squad cars turn up twice in *Cradle 2 the Grave*, however—once when they're told a robbery is in progress, and again at the end, when a battle involving guns, rockets, explosives, and a tank blowing a helicopter out of the sky inspires an alert response after only twenty minutes.

Crazy/Beautiful ★ ★ ★

PG-13, 95 m., 2001

Kirsten Dunst (Nicole Oakley), Jay Hernandez (Carlos Nunez), Joshua Feinman (Football Player), Bruce Davison (Tom Oakley), Lucinda Jenney (Courtney Oakley), Taryn Manning (Maddy), Keram Malicki-Sanchez (Foster). Directed by John Stockwell and produced by Rachel Pfeffer, Harry J. Ufland, and Mary Jane Ufland. Screenplay by Phil Hay and Matt Manfredi.

She's a wild child, a drinker, a truant, sexually bold, deliberately reckless. He's a model student, serious, responsible, who wants to attend Annapolis. She's the daughter of a liberal white congressman. He's the son of a hardworking Mexican-American woman. She goes after him because he's a hunk. He likes her but is frightened by her wildness, which is against his nature. Will she lead him into trouble, or will he help her grow up and quiet her demons? *Crazy/Beautiful,* which is about these questions, is an unusually observant film about adolescence.

The movie stars Kirsten Dunst and Jay Hernandez as Nicole and Carlos. Both actors are natural and unaffected—they level with their characters, instead of trying to impress us. They're students at a magnet high school in Pacific Palisades; she lives in Malibu, he lives in the barrio, and when she gets him into trouble and he's assigned to detention, he's angry: "I'm bussed two hours both ways. If I wanted to screw up, I'd do it in my own school, and get a lot more sleep." Nicole is self-destructive and parties with the wrong crowd; perhaps because Carlos uses his intelligence and has goals, he represents not just a cute guy but a self that she lost along the way.

Of course they are in love. Hormones take over when you're seventeen. But even during sex he's worried by her behavior. She brings him home, they get into bed, he insists on a condom, and then he sees her father wandering by the pool outside her window. He's alarmed, but she laughs: "That's my dad. He doesn't care. I can do anything. We're using a condom—he'd be so proud. And a person of color in his daughter's bed!"

Actually, it isn't quite that simple, and her father, Tom (Bruce Davison), is a good man who is written without resorting to the usual stereotypes about well-meaning but clueless adults. At one point he forbids Carlos to see his daughter—for the boy's own good, since he considers his daughter irredeemable, a lost cause. There are times when we agree.

Both characters find elements in the other they envy. "You don't care about what people think, and when I'm with you I don't care about what people think," says Carlos, who actually cares a great deal. Nicole works hard on her reputation for trouble, but there's a part of her that mourns, "I wish I wasn't the child that everybody learned what not to do from."

One of Nicole's problems is that her mother is dead, and her father's second wife has given him a perfect little child that they both dote on. The mother is obsessed by the tiniest rash on her child, but indifferent to the entire scope of Nicole's life. Carlos has problems at home, too, but of a different nature: His father is absent, and he carries the burden of his family's hopes. His mother and older brother are fiercely protective of him and hostile to Nicole, partly because she is white, even more because she is obviously trouble.

Crazy/Beautiful, directed by John Stockwell, written by Phil Hay and Matt Manfredi, is like a tougher, less-sentimental mirror version of *Save the Last Dance.* In that one, a white girl attends a black boy's inner-city high school, but in both films there are cultural differences, resentment because of color, a feeling of star-crossed loves, and the sense that each can help the other.

Crazy/Beautiful is tougher, and would have been tougher still, I understand, if the studio hadn't toned it down to get the PG-13 rating. It was originally intended to include drug use and irresponsible sex, and play as a cautionary message—but the R rating would have limited it to those over seventeen, and these days, alas, the warnings need to come a little sooner. As it stands, the movie sets up real tension between Nicole's self-destructive behavior and Carlos's responsible nature. And because of the real conviction that Dunst and Hernandez bring to the roles, we care about them as people, not case studies.

The Crime of Father Amaro ★ ★ ★
R, 120 m., 2002

Gael García Bernal (Padre Amaro), Ana Claudia Talancón (Amelia), Sancho Gracia (Padre Benito), Angélica Aragón (Sanjuanera), Luisa Huertas (Dionisia), Damián Alcázar (Padre Natalio), Ernesto Gómez Cruz (Bishop), Andrés Montiel (Rubén). Directed by Carlos Carrera and produced by Daniel Birman Ripstein and Alfredo Ripstein. Screenplay by Vicente Leñero, based on the novel by Eça de Queirós.

The Crime of Father Amaro arrives surrounded by controversy. One of the most successful Mexican films in history, it has been denounced by William Donohue of the Catholic League for its "vicious" portrait of priests; on the other hand, Father Rafael Gonzalez, speaking for the Council of Mexican Bishops, calls it an "honest movie" and describes it as "a wake-up call for the church to review its procedure for selecting and training priests and being closer to the people."

Both sides treat the film as a statement about the church, when in fact it's more of a melodrama, a film that doesn't say priests are bad but observes that priests are human and some humans are bad. What may really offend its critics is that young Father Amaro's crime is not having sex with a local girl and helping her find an abortion. His crime is that he covers up this episode and denies his responsibility because of his professional ambitions within the Church. Young Father Amaro thinks he has a rosy future ahead of him.

The movie is based on an 1875 Portuguese novel by Eça de Queirós, transplanted to modern Mexico. It gives us Padre Amaro (Gael García Bernal) as a rising star in the Church, a protégé of the bishop (Ernesto Gómez Cruz), who ships him to the provincial capital of Los Reyes to season a little under an old clerical

hand, Padre Benito (Sancho Gracia). Benito has been having a long-running affair with the restaurant owner Sanjuanera (Angélica Aragón), whose attractive daughter Amelia (Ana Claudia Talancón) may possibly be theirs.

There is the implication that the bishop knows about Benito's sex life but doesn't much care, and sends Amaro to Los Reyes for exposure to the Church's realpolitik; that the bishop knows Benito's ambitious program of hospital construction is financed through money he launders for local drug lords. It is likely the bishop approves more of priests like Benito, who raise money and get results, than of another local priest, Padre Natalio (Damián Alcázar), who supports the guerrillas waging war against the drug lords.

Once established in the local basilica, Amaro cannot help but notice the fragrant Amelia. And she develops an instant infatuation with the handsome young priest, whose unavailability makes him irresistible. Amelia has been dating a local newspaperman named Rubén (Andrés Montiel), but drops him the moment Amaro expresses veiled interest. Soon Amaro and Amelia are violating the Church's laws of priestly celibacy, and eventually she is pregnant, and this fate leads them to an illegal abortion clinic on a back road in the jungle.

The film has been attacked for the sacrilege of showing a priest paying for an abortion, but since he related to Amelia as a man, not a priest, there is a certain consistency in his behavior. It is also consistent that he would attempt to hide his crime because, like Benito, he finds it easy to make himself a personal exception to general rules. There is still a little seminary idealism in Amaro, enough to be shocked that Benito is taking drug money to build the hospital, but part of Amaro is already warming to Benito's logic: "We are taking bad money and making it good." This theology is not unique to that time or place, or even to that church; we are reminded of the CIA using drug money to finance its friends.

The film is directed in a straightforward way by Carlos Carrera, who makes it direct and heartfelt, like a soap opera. The presence of Gael García Bernal in the cast is a reminder of his work as one of the two young men in *Y Tu Mamá También* (2002), a film where the ethical issues were more complex and deeply buried.

141

There are no complexities here, unless they involve Amaro's gradual corruption in the real world of Church politics and money.

Is the film harmful to the Church? I tend to agree with Father Gonzalez, who finds that fresh air is a help, not a harm. Donohue and his league predictably denounce every movie that is unfavorable to the Church, undeterred by the fact that their opposition helps publicize the films and sell tickets (no movie has ever been harmed by being called "controversial").

Predictably, the film's critics are most upset by Amaro's sexual behavior, when in fact the film's real questions run deeper and are political: Has the Church sometimes kept company with unsavory sources of financing? Is the policy of celibacy more observed in the breach than in the observance? Are laws against abortion made by men in the daylight and violated by them in the darkness? Is the Church more comfortable allied with an amoral establishment than with a moral opposition? These questions are lost in the excitement about sex, which is often the way it works: Carnal guilt clouds our minds, distracting us from more important issues.

The Crimson Rivers ★ ★ ★ ½
R, 105 m., 2001

Jean Reno (Pierre Niemans), Vincent Cassel (Max Kerkerian), Nadia Fares (Fanny Ferreira), Laurent Avare (Remy Caillois), Jean-Pierre Cassel (Dr. Bernard Cherneze), Karim Belkhadra (Captaine Dahmane), Dominique Sanda (Sister Andree). Directed by Mathieu Kassovitz and produced by Alain Goldman. Screenplay by Kassovitz and Jean-Christophe Grange, based on the novel by Grange.

If the makers of the next Hannibal Lecter picture don't hire Mathieu Kassovitz to direct it, they're mad. His new thriller *The Crimson Rivers* is a breathtaking exercise in the macabre, a gruesome thriller with quirky cops and a killer of Lecterian complexity, and even when the movie is perfect nonsense it's so voluptuous that you're grateful to be watching it anyway. This is the work of a natural filmmaker.

The film begins with parallel stories involving two cops, who eventually meet. One is Niemans (Jean Reno), a famed investigator from Paris, such a lone wolf that when he's asked about his unit, he says, "I'm the unit." The other is Kerkerian (Vincent Cassel), a provincial policeman. Niemans is investigating the murder of a man who is found hanging 150 feet in the air in the fetal position, blinded, his hands amputated. Kerkerian is investigating the desecration of a tomb containing a child whose mother said she was killed by the devil.

The investigations are in a spectacularly forlorn valley in the French Alps, where a famous university clings to the slopes. The children of its teachers go to school here, and eventually become professors themselves; there are hints of problems with inbreeding. The university dean is the "mayor of the valley," and he haughtily tells Niemans: "We all live in perfect harmony. To accuse one of us is to accuse all of us, including me."

Niemans has nobody he wants to accuse. The murder is baffling. "The hands and eyes are the body parts that belong to us alone," the surgeon tells him after the autopsy, adding that in his opinion the victim was tortured for hours. Plodding through his investigation, morose, inward, afraid of dogs, Niemans meets Kerkerian and then meets him again. Why do their two cases seem to lead to the same places?

The movie is as good-looking as any film this year. It is cold, wet, and gray, like *The Silence of the Lambs*, and its mountain fastness doesn't look like a place for a ski holiday, but like a place where you could be lost and never found. Kassovitz's camera gives us the sensation of these peaks and altitudes by moving with uncanny grace through high, empty spaces: There was one shot that had me frankly baffled about where the camera could possibly be positioned.

Notice, too, the way an innocuous visit to a university library somehow becomes a venture into the research room of hell. The room is architecturally beautiful (so is the university—Guernon, in Modane-Avrieux), but Kassovitz and his cinematographer, Thierry Arbogast, somehow light it and move through it so that every innocent student seems to glance up from satanic studies. The entire university—the grounds, the labs, the dean's office—has this unwholesome quality, and if you could figure out how Kassovitz does it you'd learn something about the craft of filmmaking, because he starts with a picture postcard.

The two cops establish a grumpy, monosyllabic relationship, based on the isolationist Niemans's gradual realization that Kerkerian is not a complete fool. There is a moment when they visit a grubby little rental apartment where somehow Kassovitz conjures suspense out of thin air. And a scene where Niemans and a local woman mountaineer lower themselves down a sheer ice face to find a ten-year-old sample of acid rain needed as a clue. They find another clue: a second victim.

All of this, alas, eventually yields a solution to the mystery. Along the way we have been much too interested in current developments to bother formulating our own hypothesis. When the answer comes, it comes all in a package, like one of Sherlock Holmes's wrap-ups for the admiring Watson. The dialogue is such a rush, indeed, that I was reminded of Russ Meyer's analysis of *Vixen*: "I put all the socially redeeming stuff in one speech at the end, so the audience knows when that comes on, it's safe to leave."

What Kassovitz may be doing here, consciously or not, is demonstrating that we go to a mystery thriller for the windup, not the delivery. All the fun is in the atmosphere, the setup, the surprises, and murky sense of danger. The whodunit part is usually either (a) too predictable, or (b) so unpredictable it's a cheat. Joseph Conrad said he didn't like popular adventure stories because they were all based on accidents—random adventures, not generated by the nature of the characters. For almost all of its length, *The Crimson Rivers* is anchored by the natures of Niemans and Kerkerian, as tested by criminal events. Kassovitz holds off telling us whodunit as long as possible, and then grits his teeth like a runner who finds a puddle at the finish line. Look at this movie and tell me this director shouldn't have a date with Hannibal Lecter.

Crocodile Dundee in Los Angeles ★ ★
PG, 95 m., 2001

Paul Hogan (Mick Dundee), Linda Kozlowski (Sue Charlton), Jere Burns (Arnan Rothman), Jonathan Banks (Milos Drubnik), Aida Turturro (Jean Ferraro), Paul Rodriguez (Diego), Alec Wilson (Jacko), Serge Cockburn (Mikey Dundee). Directed by Simon Wincer and produced by Paul Hogan and Lance Hool. Screenplay by Matthew Berry and Eric Abrams.

I don't want to see a movie about Crocodile Dundee; I just want to hang out with him. Anyone who can rassle crocodiles and be that nice must know the secret of life. If he knew the secret of making movies, there'd be no stopping the bloke.

Crocodile Dundee in Los Angeles is a movie about a genial man and his sweet wife and nice son, and how they leave the Outback and fly to L.A. and foil an international smuggling ring. I've seen audits that were more thrilling.

The movie recycles the formula of the original *Crocodile Dundee* movie from 1986, and the 1988 sequel. Together those two titles rang up a worldwide gross in the neighborhood of $610 million for Paul Hogan. Good on ya, mate! The only mystery about the third movie, more intriguing than anything in its plot, is why there was a thirteen-year delay before the next title in such a lucrative series.

Paul Hogan is just plain a nice guy. He's low-key and folksy, and hardly ever gets mad, and has such a studied naïveté regarding life in the big city that he not only comes from the Outback but must live in a soundproof hole out there. Like the hero of *Memento* he seems to suffer from short-term memory loss, which is why in movie after movie he can expose himself to would-be muggers, or walk into gay bars without realizing it.

In *Crocodile Dundee in Los Angeles*, he lives in a town with a population of twenty with his partner, Sue (Linda Kozlowski), who met him in the first movie when she was a New York TV reporter. He runs Outback safaris, traps crocodiles, and picks his son, Mikey, up after school. Sue, whose father is an international press baron, is happy to live so far from town, as indeed she might be, considering that Croc does the dishes and only occasionally puts an animal trap in to soak with the china. Now her father asks her to fill in for a deceased reporter in his Los Angeles bureau, and that leads Sue and Croc to stumble over a scheme in which money-losing movies are made in order to cover up a scam.

The movie is pokey and the jokes amble on-screen, squat down on their haunches, and draw diagrams of themselves in the dust. But enough Croc-bashing. Truth in journalism compels me to report that *Crocodile Dundee* is at least genial family entertainment, quite possibly of interest to younger audiences, and entirely lacking in the vomitous content of such other current films as *See Spot Run, Joe Dirt,* and *Freddy Got Fingered.*

Since the studios are advertising those excremental exercises in places where kids develop a desire to see them, it is good, after they see *Spy Kids,* to have an innocent and harmless entertainment like *Crocodile Dundee in Los Angeles* as another choice. It may not be brilliant, but who would you rather your kids took as role models: Crocodile Dundee, David Spade, or Tom Green? It is a melancholy milestone in our society when parents pray, "Please, God, let my child grow up to admire a crocodile rassler," but there you have it.

The Crocodile Hunter: Collision Course
★ ★ ★
PG, 90 m., 2002

Steve Irwin (Steve Irwin), Terri Irwin (Terri Irwin), Magda Szubanski (Brozzie), Kenneth Ransom (Vaughan Archer), Lachy Hulme (Robert Wheeler), David Wenham (Sam Flynn), Aden Young (Ron Buckwhiler), Kate Beahan (Jo Buckley). Directed by John Stainton and produced by Judy Bailey, Arnold Rifkin, and Stainton. Screenplay by Holly Goldberg Sloan and Stainton.

There are scenes in *The Crocodile Hunter: Collision Course* where Steve Irwin jumps into rivers at night and wrestles crocodiles bare-handed, while his wife, Terri, helps him tie their jaws shut and haul them onto the boat. In another movie you would question the possibility of such scenes.

But there is something about this one that argues they are true: a certain straightforward, matter-of-fact approach that suggests Steve has been wrestling crocodiles all his life. And he has; according to his bio, Steve's dad, Bob, who ran the Queensland Reptile and Fauna Park in Australia, "taught the young Steve everything there was to know about reptiles—even teaching his nine-year-old how to jump in and catch

crocodiles in the rivers of North Queensland at night!"

How, I am wondering, *do* you teach a nine-year-old to jump in and catch crocodiles in the rivers of North Queensland at night? Is rehearsal possible, or do you just get a lot of theory and then jump in? Is it child abuse to tell your nine-year-old to wrestle crocodiles, or only tough love? I urgently await a film titled *Young Steve: The Education of a Croc Hunter.*

Studying the bio more closely, I realize that many of its sentences end with an exclamation point. In the movie, nearly every sentence uttered by Irwin does, although supporting players are allowed periods and question marks. Half of his sentences have only one word: "Crikey!" He says this frequently while handling the dangerous creatures of the outback, which he likes to get real close to, so they can snap at him during his lectures.

There is a plot to this movie, which I hardly need to mention, since it's irrelevant to the experience. A secret communications satellite falls to Earth and its black box is gobbled up by a croc, and two rival U.S. intelligence agencies send teams to the outback to retrieve it. Meanwhile, Steve and Terri don't realize it's in the stomach of the croc they plan to move to another river system.

Forget the plot. The movie is really about Steve and Terri taking us on a guided tour of the crocs, snakes, deadly insects, and other stars of the outback fauna. Steve's act is simplicity itself. He holds a deadly cobra, say, by its tail and looks straight at the camera and explains that the cobra has enough venom to kill him one hundred times over. The cobra twists and tries to strike at Steve's bare leg. He jerks it away. Crikey! Steve's monologues about the incredible danger he's in do sometimes run a bit long, but he has the grace to interrupt them to slap at flies that are biting him.

Later we meet a "bird-eating" spider whose fangs contain venom that would kill Steve, I dunno, a thousand times over, and he pokes it with a stick to make it display its fangs, and it almost bites Steve's thumb. Crikey! Then he shows us the spider's nest, and sticks his finger down it and yanks it back as if he's been bitten. Crikey! But he was only fooling, mate.

The movie is entertaining exactly on the level I have described it. You see a couple of likable people journeying though the outback, encountering dangerous critters and getting too close for comfort, while lecturing us on their habits and dangers and almost being killed by them. The stunts are not faked, and so there is a certain fascination. Steve and Terri are not exactly developed as deeply realized characters, and only on their Website did I discover they were married in 1992 and in 1998 gave birth to little Bindi Sue Irwin, who is now four, and started in as a baby by wrestling tiny gecko lizards. Crikey.

Crossroads ★ ½

PG-13, 90 m., 2002

Britney Spears (Lucy), Zoe Saldana (Kit), Anson Mount (Ben), Taryn Manning (Mimi), Justin Long (Henry), Dan Aykroyd (Lucy's Dad), Kim Cattrall (Lucy's Mom). Directed by Tamra Davis and produced by Ann Carli. Screenplay by Shonda Rhimes.

I went to *Crossroads* expecting a glitzy bimbo fest and got the bimbos but not the fest. Britney Spears's feature debut is curiously low-key and even sad. Yes, it pulls itself together occasionally for a musical number, but even those are so locked into the "reality" of the story that they don't break loose into fun.

The movie opens with three eighth-graders burying a box filled with symbols of their dreams of the future. Four years later, on high school graduation day, the girls are hardly on speaking terms, but they meet to dig up the box, tentatively renew their friendship, and find themselves driving to California in a convertible piloted by a hunk.

Lucy (Spears) hopes to find her long-indifferent mother in Arizona. Kit (Zoe Saldana) wants to find her fiancé in Los Angeles; he has become ominously vague about wedding plans. Mimi (Taryn Manning) is pregnant, but wants to compete in a record company's open audition. Spoiler warning! Stop reading now unless you want to learn the dismal outcome of their trip, as Lucy's mom informs her she was a "mistake," Kit's fiancé turns out to have another woman *and* to be guilty of date rape, and Mimi, who was the rape victim, has a miscarriage.

I'm not kidding. *Crossroads*, which is being promoted with ads showing Britney bouncing on the bed while lip-synching a song, is a downer that would be even more depressing if the plot wasn't such a lame soap opera.

This is the kind of movie where the travelers stop by the roadside to yell "Hello!" and keep on yelling, unaware that there is no echo. Where Britney is a virgin at eighteen and enlists her lab partner to deflower her. Where when that doesn't work out she finds herself attracted to Ben (Anson Mount), the guy who's giving them the ride, even though he is alleged to have killed a man. Where the apparent age difference between Spears and Mount makes it look like he's robbing the cradle. (In real life, he's twenty-nine and she's twenty, but he's an experienced twenty-nine and she's playing a naive eighteen-year-old.)

Of the three girls, Mimi has the most to do. She teaches Kit how to land a punch, tells the others why she doesn't drink, and deals almost casually with her miscarriage. Kit is a slow study who takes forever to figure out her fiancé has dumped her. And Spears, as Lucy, seems to think maybe she's in a serious Winona Ryder role, but with songs.

"What are you writing in that book?" Ben asks her. "Poems," she says. He wants her to read one for him. She does. "Promise not to laugh," she says. He doesn't, but the audience does. It's the lyrics for her song "I'm Not a Girl, Not Yet a Woman." Didn't anyone warn her you can't introduce famous material as if it's new without risking a bad laugh? Later, Ben composes music for the words, and he plays the piano while she riffs endlessly to prove she has never once thought about singing those words before.

The movie cuts away from the payoffs of the big scenes. We get the foreplay for both of Britney's sex scenes, but never see what happens. Her big meeting with her mother lacks the showdown. We can be grateful, I suppose, that after Mimi falls down some stairs after learning that Kit's fiancé is the man who raped her, we are spared the details of her miscarriage and cut to her later in the hospital. Perhaps study of the live childbirth scene in the Spice Girls movie warned the filmmakers away from obstetric adventures in this one.

Like *Coyote Ugly*, a movie it resembles in the wardrobe department, *Crossroads* is rated

145

PG-13 but is going on 17. Caution, kids: It can be more dangerous to get a ride in a convertible with a cute but ominous guy than you might think (see *Kalifornia*).

And you can't always support yourself by tips on Karaoke Night. When the girls sing in a karaoke contest, a three-gallon jug is filled with bills which, after they're piled in stacks on the bar, are enough to pay for car repairs and the rest of the trip. Uh-huh. Curious thing about that karaoke bar: It has a position on the stage with an underlight and one of those poles that strippers twine around. You don't see those much in karaoke clubs.

Crush ★ ★ ★
R, 115 m., 2002

Andie MacDowell (Kate), Imelda Staunton (Janine), Anna Chancellor (Molly), Kenny Doughty (Jed), Bill Paterson (Rev. Gerald Farquar-Marsden). Directed by John McKay and produced by Lee Thomas. Screenplay by McKay.

If I were reviewing *Crush* in England, I would work the name of Joanna Trollope into the first sentence, and my readers would immediately be able to identify the terrain. Trollope, a best-seller who is often quite perceptive and touching, writes at the upper range of the category just below serious fiction. She is a good read for those, like myself, who fantasize about living prosperously in the Cotswolds in an old but comfortably remodeled cottage not far from the village green, the churchyard, the tea shop, the bookstore, and the rail line to London, while growing involved in a web of imprudent adulterous sex. (As a happily married man, you understand, I do not want to *perform* adulterous imprudent sex, only to be involved in a web with such entertaining neighbors.)

This is not England. Few North Americans read Joanna Trollope, and fewer still respond to key words in her vocabulary such as "Aga." An Aga cookstove is so expensive and versatile it does everything but peel the potatoes, and its presence in a kitchen tells you so much about the occupants that in the Brit book review pages, the phrase "Aga romance" perfectly categorizes a novel.

Crush is an Aga romance crossed with modern retro-feminist soft porn, in which liberated women discuss lust as if it were a topic and not a fact. We begin by meeting the three heroines, who are forty-something professionals who meet once a week to (1) drink gin, (2) smoke cigarettes, (3) eat caramels, and (4) discuss their lousy love lives. My advice to these women: stop after (3).

The characters: Kate (Andie MacDowell) is the American headmistress of the local upscale school, Janine (Imelda Staunton) is a physician, and Molly (Anna Chancellor) is the police chief. That these three professional women at their age would all still be smoking can be explained only by a movie that does not give them enough to do with their hands. One day Kate goes to a funeral, is immeasurably moved by the music, and meets the organist. His name is Jed (Kenny Doughty), and he was once a student of hers. She is between fifteen and eighteen years older, but their conversation drifts out of the church and into the churchyard, and soon they are performing the old rumpy-pumpy behind a tombstone while the mourners are still stifling their sobs.

This is, you will agree, an example of lust. In a rabbit, it would be simple lust. In a headmistress, it is reckless lust. (In a twenty-five-year-old organist, it is what comes from pumping the foot pedals for thirty minutes while observing Andie MacDowell.) The movie cannot leave it at lust, however, because then it would be a different movie. So it elevates it into a Love That Was Meant to Be, in which the two lovers overcome differences of age, class, and grooming, and determine to spend their lives together. Because they are attractive people and we like them, of course we identify with their foolishness and feel good when romance triumphs.

A sixth sense tells us, however, that romance has triumphed a little too early in the movie. The only way for *Crush* to get from its romantic triumph to the end of the film is to supply setbacks, and does it ever. I will not reveal what episodes of bad judgment, bad karma, and plain bad luck lead to the ultimate bittersweet denouement, and will distract myself from the temptation by telling you that the pastor of the local church is named the Rev.

Gerald Farquar-Marsden, a name to rival Cats-meat Potter-Pirbright.

The movie does its best to work us over, with second helpings of love, romance, tragedy, false dawns, real dawns, comic relief, two separate crises during marriage ceremonies, and the lush scenery of the Cotswolds (or, as the Website refers to the district, "Cotswold"). It's the kind of world where romance begins in tombs among the headstones, or vice versa, and almost immediately requires engraved invitations. Jed is described as being twenty-five years old and Kate is described as being forty "cough," but Andie MacDowell is the definition of a dish, and Jed, just by being a church organist, is mature for his age. Besides, what is an age difference of fifteen or even eighteen years when my old friend Betty Dodson, at seventy-two, is in the third year of a steamy romance with a twenty-five-year-old? You can look it up at Salon.com, under "sex."

The Curse of the Jade Scorpion ★ ★ ½
PG-13, 103 m., 2001

Woody Allen (C. W. Briggs), Dan Aykroyd (Chris Magruder), Elizabeth Berkley (Jill), Helen Hunt (Betty Ann Fitzgerald), Brian Markinson (Al), Wallace Shawn (George Bond), David Ogden Stiers (Voltan), Charlize Theron (Laura Kensington). Directed by Woody Allen and produced by Letty Aronson. Screenplay by Allen.

Woody Allen's *The Curse of the Jade Scorpion* takes place in an insurance office not unlike the one in *Double Indemnity*, where the very woodwork and the reassuring bulk of the filing cabinets seem to guarantee the company's solidity. But after the company's fraud investigator and its efficiency expert are hypnotized by a nightclub charlatan, none of the company's clients are safe.

In *Double Indemnity*, Billy Wilder's classic *noir*, Fred MacMurray was an investigator who betrayed his company after a slinky seductress (Barbara Stanwyck) lured him into a scheme to murder her husband for profit. The comic angle in Allen's approach is that C. W. Briggs, the investigator (Allen himself), is an obsessive-compulsive perfectionist, and the slinky sex bomb, Betty Ann Fitzgerald (Helen Hunt), is

his archenemy (although that doesn't discourage him from asking her out). When "Fitz" has her wits about her, she describes C.W. with an impressive array of insults ("mealymouthed little creep," "inchworm," "snoopy little termite," "squirming little trapped rat"). They hate each other. "I love where you live," she tells him. "A grimy little rat hole. I find it strangely exciting standing here in a grungy hovel with a myopic insurance investigator." Then the hypnotic trigger is pulled, and they think they're in love.

To this inspiration Allen adds another; they have separate cue words, so that one can be under the hypnotic spell while the other isn't. And then he surrounds them with dependable comic types. Dan Aykroyd is Magruder, the cost-cutting boss who has brought in Fitz. Elizabeth Berkley is Jill, the curvy secretary he's having an affair with. And Charlize Theron is Laura Kensington, a rich kid who is attracted to C.W. when she catches him in midtheft, but is helpless in the face of the hypnotic depth bomb.

David Ogden Stiers plays Voltan the hypnotist, a great convenience to the story, because all he has to do is telephone C.W., utter a magic word into the telephone, and order him to do whatever he wishes—in this case, to break into houses C.W. himself has burglar-proofed, and steal precious diamonds.

All of this sounds like the setup for a wicked screwball comedy, but somehow *Curse of the Jade Scorpion* never quite lifts off. The elements are here, but not the magic. There are lines that you can see are intended to be funny, but they lack the usual Allen zing. Allen is as always a master of the labyrinthine plot (his characters turn up in the wrong place at the right time, and vice versa, with inexhaustible ingenuity), but we never much care how things turn out.

That said, there are pleasures in the film that have little to do with the story. Its look and feel are uncanny; it's a tribute to a black-and-white era, filmed in color, and yet the colors seem burnished and aged. No *noir* films were shot in color in the 1940s, but if one had been, it would have looked like this. And great attention is given to the women played by Hunt, Berkley, and Theron; they look not so much like the women in classic *film noir* as like the women on *film noir* posters—their costumes and styles elevate them into archetypes. Hunt in particular has fun with a wisecracking dame role that owes something, perhaps, to Rosalind Russell in *His Girl Friday*.

Woody Allen's characters depend on self-deprecating, double-reverse ironic wit for their appeal, and C.W. doesn't seem to have an infallible ear for it. (Example: He says that she went to Harvard but he went to driving school; that's first-level and Allen usually gets to second or third.) He should be invulnerable in a verbal exchange, but here sometimes he seems brought to a halt by Fitz. He's funny in the nightclub hypnosis scene, when he slumps like a puppet with loose strings, but later he seems wide of the target. The movie is a pleasure to watch, the craft is voluptuous to regard, but *The Curse of the Jade Scorpion* lacks the elusive zing of inspiration.

Note: The two hypnotic triggers are "Madagascar" and "Constantinople." Did Allen miss comic opportunity by not making them "Istanbul" and "Constantinople"? Like all of his films, Jade Scorpion is scored with jazz and pop classics of the period, and I imagine a scene where C.W. and Fitz both hear the famous song "Istanbul (not Constantinople)," and are inadvertently launched into loveland without the participation of Voltan.

D

Daddy Day Care ★
PG, 93 m., 2003

Eddie Murphy (Charlie Hinton), Jeff Garlin (Phil), Anjelica Huston (Miss Harridan), Steve Zahn (Marvin), Khamani Griffin (Ben Hinton), Regina King (Kim Hinton). Directed by Steve Carr and produced by John Davis, Matt Berenson, and Wyck Godfrey. Screenplay by Geoff Rodkey.

Daddy Day Care is a woeful miscalculation, a film so wrongheaded audiences will be more appalled than amused. It imagines Eddie Murphy and sidekick Jeff Garlin in charge of a day-care center that could only terrify parents in the audience, although it may look like fun for their children. The center's philosophy apparently consists of letting kids do whatever they feel like, while the amateur staff delivers one-liners.

I realize that the movie is not intended as a serious work about day-care centers. It is a comedy (in genre, not in effect). But at some point we might expect it to benefit from real life, real experiences, real kids. Not a chance. It's all simply a prop for the Eddie Murphy character. Aggressively simpleminded, it's fueled by the delusion that it has a brilliant premise: Eddie Murphy plus cute kids equals success. But a premise should be the starting point for a screenplay, not its finish line.

In the film, Murphy plays Charlie Hinton, an advertising executive assigned to the account of a breakfast cereal based on vegetables. This leads eventually to desperate scenes involving Murphy dressed in a broccoli suit, maybe on the grounds that once, long ago, he was funny in a Gumby suit. The cereal fails, and he's fired along with his best pal, Phil (Garlin). Charlie's wife, Kim (Regina King), goes to work as a lawyer, leaving her husband at home to take care of their son, Ben (Khamani Griffin). Next thing you know, Charlie has the idea of opening a day-care center.

Enter the villainess, Miss Harridan (Anjelica Huston), whose own day-care center is so expensive that Charlie can no longer afford to send Ben there. Huston plays the role as your standard dominatrix, ruling her school with an iron hand, but you know what? It looks to me like a pretty good school, with the kids speaking foreign languages and discussing advanced science projects. Obviously, in the terms of this movie, any school where the kids have to study is bad, just as a school where the kids can run around and raise hell is good. This bias is disguised as Charlie's insight into child psychology.

The new school is successful almost from the outset, and empty seats begin to turn up in Miss Harridan's school as parents switch their kids to the cheaper alternative. No sane parent would trust a child to Charlie and Phil's chaotic operation, but never mind. Soon the partners hire an assistant, Marvin, played by Steve Zahn as a case of arrested development. Miss Harridan, facing the failure of her school, mounts a counterattack and of course is vanquished. She appears in the movie's final shot in a pathetically unfunny attempt to force humor long after the cause has been lost.

What the movie lacks is any attempt to place Murphy and his costars in a world of real kids and real day care. This entire world looks like it exists only on a studio lot. A few kids are given identifiable attributes (one won't take off his superhero costume), but basically they're just a crowd of rug rats in the background of the desperately forced comedy. Even the movie's poop joke fails, and if you can't make a poop joke work in a movie about kids, you're in trouble.

The movie's miscalculation, I suspect, is the same one that has misled Murphy in such other recent bombs as *I Spy* and *The Adventures of Pluto Nash* (which was unseen by me and most of the rest of the world). That's the delusion that Murphy's presence will somehow lend magic to an undistinguished screenplay. A film should begin with a story and characters, not with a concept and a star package. ☞

The Dancer Upstairs ★ ★ ★
R, 128 m., 2003

Javier Bardem (Augustin Rejas), Laura Morante (Yolanda), Juan Diego Botto (Sucre), Elvira Minguez (Llosa), Alexandra Lencastre (Sylvina), Oliver Cotton (General Merino), Luis Miguel Cintra (Calderon), Abel Folk (Ezequiel/Duran). Directed by John Malkovich and produced by

Malkovich and Andrés Vicente Gómez. Screenplay by Nicholas Shakespeare, based on his novel.

John Malkovich's *The Dancer Upstairs* was filmed before 9/11 and is based on a novel published in 1997, but has an eerie timeliness in its treatment of a terrorist movement that works as much through fear as through violence.

Filmed in Ecuador, it stars Javier Bardem as Augustin, an inward, troubled man who left the practice of law to join the police force because he wanted to be one step closer to justice. Now he has been assigned to track down a shadowy terrorist named Ezequiel, who is everywhere and nowhere, and strikes at random to sow fear in the population. His trademark is to leave dead dogs hanging in public view. In China, a dead dog is symbolic of a tyrant executed by the people, we learn.

The movie's story, based on a novel by Nicholas Shakespeare, is inspired by the Shining Path, a terrorist group in Peru. But this is not a docudrama; it is more concerned with noticing the ways in which terrorism takes its real toll in a nation's self-confidence. Ezequiel commits bold and shocking but small-scale public executions, many of helpless civilians in remote districts, but the central government is paralyzed by fear, martial law is declared, and the army steps into Augustin's investigation. The cure may be more damaging than the crime.

Augustin is a very private man. He seems to be happily married and to dote on his daughter, but he is happy to spend long periods away from home, and doesn't really seem to focus on his wife's obsession with getting herself an improved nose. He never gives a convincing explanation of why he left the law. His approach to the Ezequiel crimes is largely intuitive; faced with an enemy who works through rumor and legend, he looks more for vibes than clues, and at one point revisits the rural district where his family owned a coffee farm, since confiscated. There he will find—well, whatever he will find.

The movie is contemplative for a police procedural; more like Georges Simenon or Nicolas Freeling than like Ed McBain. Bardem, who was so demonstrative as the flamboyant writer in *Before Night Falls,* now turns as subtle and guarded as—well, as John Malkovich. It is typical that when he falls in love with Yolanda (Laura Morante), his daughter's ballet teacher, both he and she are slow to realize what has happened, and reluctant to act on it.

When Ezequiel is finally discovered, it is through a coincidence that I will not reveal here, although his location is made clear to the audience long before Augustin discovers it. I cannot resist, however, quoting one of the film's most cutting lines. We have heard that Ezequiel represents what Marx called "the fourth stage of communism," and when the terrorist is finally dragged into the light of day, Augustin says, "The fourth stage of communism is just a big fat man in a cardigan."

Malkovich has not set out to make a thriller here, so much as a meditation about a man caught in a muddle of his own thinking. By rights, Augustin says at one point, he should be a coffee farmer. The government's confiscation of his family's farm paradoxically did him a favor, by pushing him off the land and into law school, and he is caught between a yearning for the land and a confused desire to make a difference in his society.

As a cop he is trusted by his superiors with great responsibility, but we see him more as a dreamy idealist who doesn't have a firm program for his life and is pushed along by events. He hates the cruelty of Ezequiel, but is baffled, as the whole nation is, by Ezequiel's lack of a program, focus, or identity. His violent acts function as classic anarchism, seeking the downfall of the state with the hope that a new society will somehow arise from the wreckage.

The Dancer Upstairs is elegantly, even languorously, photographed by Jose Luis Alcaine, who doesn't punch into things but regards them, so that we are invited to think about them. That doesn't mean the movie is slow; it moves with a compelling intensity toward its conclusion, which is not a "climax" or a "solution" in the usual police-movie mode, but a small moral victory that Augustin rescues from his general confusion.

When he finally gets to the end of his five-year search for the figure who has distracted and terrorized the country all of that time, his quarry turns out to be a little like the Wizard of Oz. And having pulled aside the curtain, Augustin now has to return to Kansas, or in this case to his wife, who will soon be talking once again about plastic surgery.

Note: The movie, cast with Spanish and South American actors, is entirely in English.

The Dangerous Lives of Altar Boys ★ ★ ½

R, 105 m., 2002

Kieran Culkin (Tim Sullivan), Jena Malone (Margie Flynn), Emile Hirsch (Francis Doyle), Vincent D'Onofrio (Father Casey), Jodie Foster (Sister Assumpta), Jake Richardson (Wade), Tyler Long (Joey Scalisi). Directed by Peter Care and produced by Meg LeFauve, Jay Shapiro, and Jodie Foster. Screenplay by Jeff Stockwell, based on the book by Chris Furhman.

There were times when *The Dangerous Lives of Altar Boys* evoked memories of my own Catholic school days—not to confirm the film, but to question it. There is a way in which the movie accurately paints its young heroes, obsessed with sex, rebellion, and adolescence, and too many other times when it pushes too far, making us aware of a screenplay reaching for effect. The climax is so reckless and absurd that we can't feel any of the emotions that are intended.

Yet this is an honorable film with good intentions. Set in a small town in the 1970s, it tells the story of good friends at St. Agatha's School, who squirm under the thumb of the strict Sister Assumpta (Jodie Foster) and devise elaborate plots as a rebellion against her. At the same time, the kids are growing up, experimenting with smoking and drinking, and learning more about sex than they really want to know.

The heroes are Tim Sullivan (Kieran Culkin) and Francis Doyle (Emile Hirsch). We look mostly through Francis's eyes, as the boys and two friends weave a fantasy world out of a comic book they collaborate on called *The Atomic Trinity*, with characters like Captain Asskicker and easily recognized caricatures of Sister Assumpta and Father Casey (Vincent D'Onofrio), the distracted, chain-smoking pastor and soccer coach who seems too moony to be a priest.

The movie has a daring strategy for representing the adventures of the Trinity: It cuts to animated sequences (directed by Todd McFarlane) that cross the everyday complaints and resentments of the authors with the sort of glorified myth-making and superhero manu-facture typical of Marvel comics of the period. (These sequences are so well animated, with such visual flair and energy, that the jerk back to the reality sequences can be a little disconcerting.) The villainess in the book is Sister Nunzilla, based on Sister Assumpta right down to her artificial leg.

Does the poor sister deserve this treatment? The film argues that she does not, but is unconvincing. Sister Assumpta is very strict, but we are meant to understand that she really likes and cares for her students. This is conveyed in some of Jodie Foster's acting choices, but has no payoff, because the kids apparently don't see the same benevolent expressions we sometimes glimpse. If they are not going to learn anything about Sister Assumpta's gentler side, then why must we?

The kids are supposed to be typical young adolescents, but they're so rebellious, reckless, and creative that we sense the screenplay nudging them. Francis feels the stirrings of lust and (more dangerous) idealistic love inspired by his classmate Margie Flynn (Jena Malone), and they have one of those first kisses that makes you smile. Then she shares a family secret that is, I think, a little too heavy for this film to support, and creates a dark cloud over all that follows.

If the secret is too weighty, so is the ending. The boys have been engaged in an escalating series of pranks, and their final one, involving plans to kidnap a cougar from the zoo and transport it to Sister Assumpta's living quarters, is too dumb and dangerous for anyone, including these kids, to contemplate. Their previous stunt was to steal a huge statue of St. Agatha from a niche high on the facade of the school building, and this seems about as far as they should go. The cougar business is trying too hard, and leads to an ending that doesn't earn its emotional payoff.

Another hint of the overachieving screenplay is the running theme of the boys' fascination with William Blake's books *Songs of Innocence* and *Songs of Experience*. I can believe that boys of this age could admire Blake, but not these boys. And I cannot believe that Sister Assumpta would consider Blake a danger. What we sense here is the writer, Jeff Stockwell, sneaking in material he likes even though it doesn't pay its way. (There's one other cultural reference in the movie, unless I'm seeing it where none was intended: Early in the film, the boys blow up a telephone pole in order to calculate when it will fall, and they stand just inches into the safe zone. I was reminded of Buster Keaton, standing so that when a wall fell on him, he was in the exact outline of an open window.)

The movie has qualities that cannot be denied. Jena Malone *(Donnie Darko, Life as a House)* has a solemnity and self-knowledge that seems almost to stand outside the film. She represents the gathering weather of adulthood. The boys are fresh and enthusiastic, and we remember how kids can share passionate enthusiasms; the animated sequences perfectly capture the energy of their imaginary comic book. Vincent D'Onofrio muses through the film on his own wavelength, making of Father Casey a man who means well but has little idea what meaning well would consist of. If the film had been less extreme in the adventures of its heroes, more willing to settle for plausible forms of rebellion, that might have worked. It tries too hard, and overreaches the logic of its own world.

Note: The movie is rated R, consistent with the policy of the flywheels at the MPAA that any movie involving the intelligent treatment of teenagers must be declared off-limits for them.

Daredevil ★ ★ ★
PG-13, 97 m., 2003

Ben Affleck (Matt Murdock/Daredevil), Jennifer Garner (Elektra Natchios), Michael Clarke Duncan (Kingpin), Colin Farrell (Bullseye), Jon Favreau (Franklin "Foggy" Nelson), Joe Pantoliano (Ben Urich), David Keith (Jack Murdock), Scott Terra (Young Matt Murdock). Directed by Mark Steven Johnson and produced by Avi Arad, Gary Foster, and Arnon Milchan. Screenplay by Johnson, based on the comic by Stan Lee, Bill Everett, and Frank Miller.

The origin is usually similar: A traumatic event in childhood, often involving the loss of parents, leaves the future superhero scarred in some ways but with preternatural powers in others. Daredevil came out of the Marvel Comics stable in the same period as Spider-Man, and both were altered by accidents, which gave Peter Parker his spidey-sense, and blinded Matt Murdock but made his other four senses

hypersensitive. They grew up together in Marvel Comics, sometimes sharing the same adventures, but you won't see them fraternizing in the movies because their rights are owned by different studios.

Daredevil stars Ben Affleck as the superhero, wearing one of those molded body suits that defines his six-packs but, unlike Batman's, doesn't give him dime-size nipples. His mask extends over his eyes, which are not needed, since his other senses fan out in a kind of radar, allowing him to visualize his surroundings and "see" things even in darkness.

By day (I love that "by day") he is a lawyer in the Hell's Kitchen area of Manhattan. By night, he tells us, he prowls the alleys and rooftops, seeking out evildoers. Of these there is no shortage, although most of the city's more lucrative crime is controlled by the Kingpin (Michael Clarke Duncan) and his chief minister, Bullseye (Colin Farrell).

There must be a woman, and in *Daredevil* there is one (only one, among all those major male characters), although the fragrant Ellen Pompeo has a slink-on. She is Elektra Natchios (Jennifer Garner), who, like her classical namesake, wants to avenge the death of her father. By day she is, well, pretty much as she is by night. She and Daredevil are powerfully attracted and even share some PG-13 sex, which is a relief, because when superheroes have sex at the R level I am always afraid someone will get hurt. There is a rather beautiful scene where he asks her to stand in the rain because his ears are so sensitive they can create an image of her face from the sound of the raindrops.

Matt Murdock's law partner is Franklin "Foggy" Nelson (Jon Favreau). He has little suspicion of whom he is sharing an office with, although he is a quick study. Another key character is Ben Urich (Joe Pantoliano), who works for the *New York Post*, the newspaper of choice for superheroes.

Daredevil has the ability to dive off tall buildings, swoop thorough the air, bounce off stuff, land lightly, and so forth. There is an explanation for this ability, but I tend to tune out such explanations because, after all, what do they really explain? I don't care what you say, it's Superman's cape that makes him fly. Comic fans, however, study the mythology and methodology with the intensity of academics. It is reassuring, in this world of inexplicabilities, to master a limited subject within a self-contained universe. Understand, truly understand, why Daredevil defies gravity, and the location of the missing matter making up 90 percent of the universe can wait for another day.

But these are just the kinds of idle thoughts I entertain during a movie like *Daredevil*, which may have been what the Vatican had in mind when it issued that statement giving its limited approval of Harry Potter, as long as you don't start believing in him. Daredevil describes himself as a "guardian devil," and that means there are guardian angels, and that means God exists and, by a process of logical deduction, that Matt Murdock is a Catholic. Please address your correspondence to Rome.

The movie is actually pretty good. Affleck and Garner probe for the believable corners of their characters, do not overact, are given semi-particular dialogue, and are in a very good-looking movie. Most of the tension takes place between the characters, not the props. There is, of course, a fancy formal ball to which everyone is invited (Commissioner Gordon must have been at the rival affair across town).

Affleck is at home in plots of this size, having just recently tried to save Baltimore from nuclear annihilation and the world from *Armageddon,* but Garner, Farrell, and Duncan are relatively newer to action epics, although Garner did see Affleck off at the station when he took the train from Pearl Harbor to New York, and Duncan was Balthazar in *The Scorpion King.* They play their roles more or less as if they were real, which is a novelty in a movie like this, and Duncan in particular has a presence that makes the camera want to take a step back and protect its groin.

The movie is, in short, your money's worth, better than we expect, more fun than we deserve. I am getting a little worn-out describing the origin stories and powers of superheroes, and their relationships to archvillains, gnashing henchmen, and brave, muscular female pals. They weep, they grow, they astonish, they overcome, they remain vulnerable, and their enemies spend inordinate time on wardrobe, grooming, and props, and behaving as if their milk of human kindness has turned to cottage cheese. Some of their movies, like this one, are better than others.

Dark Blue ★ ★ ★
R, 116 m., 2003

Kurt Russell (Eldon Perry Jr.), Scott Speedman (Bobby Keough), Ving Rhames (Arthur Holland), Brendan Gleeson (Jack Van Meter), Michael Michele (Beth Williamson), Lolita Davidovich (Sally Perry). Directed by Ron Shelton and produced by David Blocker, Caldecot Chubb, Sean Daniel, and James Jacks. Screenplay by David Ayer, based on a story by James Ellroy.

Two cops. One a veteran, one a rookie. One corrupt, the other still learning. Two sets of bad guys. One pair guilty of a heartless crime, the other pair guilty, but not of this crime. Two women, one a disillusioned wife, the other a disillusioned girlfriend. Two superior officers, one rotten, the other determined to bring him down. All the action takes place in the final days before the Rodney King verdict was announced in April 1992, and in the immediate aftermath, when the LAPD abandoned some neighborhoods to looters and arsonists.

Dark Blue is a formula picture in its broad outlines, but a very particular film in its characters and details. It doesn't redeem the formula or even tinker with it very much, but in a performance by Kurt Russell and in some location work on the angry streets, it has something to say and an urgent way of saying it.

The movie is based on a story by James Ellroy, a novelist who knows Los Angeles like the back of his hand, just after it has been stepped on. The screenplay for *L.A. Confidential* came from him, and a lot of hard-boiled fiction, punched out in short paragraphs, as if he has to keep ducking. He's been trying to get this story made into a movie for so long it was originally set during the Watts riots. The update works better, because the King verdict fits more neatly with his police department ripe for reform.

Kurt Russell and Scott Speedman star as Perry and Keough, two detectives who prowl the streets like freelance buccaneers; we know this type and even the veteran–rookie relationship from *Training Day, Narc,* and many other movies. The older cop explains you have to play tough to get things done, and the younger one tries to go along, even though he keeps failing the Hemingway test (it's immoral if you feel bad after you do it). They're the street agents, in a sense, of top cop Jack Van Meter (Brendan Gleeson). He has a couple of snitches he's protecting, and after they murder four people in a convenience store robbery, he orders Perry and Keough to frame and kill a couple of sex criminals for the crimes. Now young Keough, having balked at his first chance to execute a perp in the streets, gets a second chance.

The movie surrounds this situation with a lot of other material—too much, so that it sometimes feels hurried. Perry is married to one of those cop wives (Lolita Davidovich) who is stuck with the thankless task of telling him he just doesn't see her anymore ("You care more about the people you hate"). Keough is dating a young black woman (Michael Michele) who insists they not tell each other their last names. A man who sleeps with a woman who will not reveal her last name is marginally to be preferred, I suppose, to a man who will sleep with a woman who tells him her name but he forgets it in the morning.

The good cop, Deputy Chief Arthur Holland, played by Ving Rhames, knows Van Meter is crooked and has to decide whether to stay and prove it, or take an offer to become police chief of Cleveland. Meanwhile, the clock ticks toward an "innocent" verdict for the cops who were videotaped while beating Rodney King. (This does not stop the police academy from scheduling a promotion ceremony at the very same time, so that everyone will be in the same room when they are required for the big scene.)

I'm making the film sound too obvious. It follows well-worn pathways, but it has a literate, colloquial screenplay by David Ayer (*Training Day, The Fast and the Furious*), whose dialogue sounds as if someone might actually say it, and the direction is by Ron Shelton (*White Men Can't Jump, Bull Durham*), who marches us right up to clichés and then pulls them out from under us.

Above all, the movie has the Kurt Russell performance going for it. Every time I see Russell or Val Kilmer in a role, I'm reminded of their *Tombstone* (1993), which got lost in the year-end holiday shuffle and never got the recognition it deserved. Russell has reserves he can draw on when he needs them, and he needs them here, as Perry descends into self-disgust

and then, finally, understands the world and the role he has chosen. There is a late shot in which we look over his character's shoulder as Los Angeles burns all the way to the horizon. It takes a lot of setup to get away with a payoff like that, but Shelton and Russell earn it.

Dark Blue is not a great movie, but it has moments that go off the meter and find visceral impact. The characters driving through the riot-torn streets of Los Angeles provide some of them, and the savage, self-hating irony of Russell's late dialogue provides the rest. It is a clanging coincidence that the LAPD would be indicted just at the moment it was being exonerated, but then that's what the movies are for sometimes: to provide the outcomes that history overlooked.

Dark Blue World ★ ★
R, 114 m., 2002

Ondrej Vetchy (Franktisek Slama), Krystof Hadek (Karel Vojtisek), Tara Fitzgerald (Susan), Charles Dance (Colonel Bentley), Oldrich Kaiser (Machaty), Linda Rybova (Hanicka), Lukas Kantor (Tamtam), Hans-Jorg Assmann (Dr. Blaschke). Directed by Jan Sverak and produced by Eric Abraham and Jan Sverak. Screenplay by Zdenek Sverak.

Dark Blue World recycles some of the aerial combat footage shot for *Battle of Britain* (1969), and indeed, some of the same old-fashioned war movie clichés, like the faithful dog pining for its master. Told mostly in English, it's the story of two Czech pilots who escape their Nazi-occupied homeland, go to England, and enlist in the RAF to fight the Germans. Returning to Czechoslovakia after the war, one is rewarded for his pains by being jailed (exposure to British values might cause him to question communism). He finds that former S.S. men are his guards.

The Czech scenes are bookends for the heart of the story, which intercuts aerial dogfights with a love triangle in which both pilots have romances with the same English woman. Susan (Tara Fitzgerald) is minding a houseful of orphans in the countryside, and befriends Karel (Krystof Hadek). They fall in the wartime equivalent of love (her husband is missing in action), and Karel proudly introduces her to his friend Franktisek (Ondrej Vetch). Alas, not long after, he feels embittered and betrayed.

With *Pearl Harbor* fresh in my mind, here is yet another movie in which World War II supplies a backdrop for a love triangle. And not even a convincing, psychologically complex love triangle, but one imposed upon us by the requirements of the screenplay: The participants are attractive and sweet and we like them, but they get shuffled around for pragmatic reasons.

The aerial footage is good. It should be; in many cases, those are real planes, really in the air. Some of the shots come from the 1969 Harry Saltzman production, and well do I remember visiting a British airfield near Newmarket to see the actual Spitfires and other real planes purchased or rented for *Battle of Britain.* I even met Battle of Britain aces Douglas Bader, Ginger Lacey, and Group Captain Peter Townsend, although I inform you at this late date primarily because that old memory is more interesting than this movie.

The director, Jan Sverak, works from a screenplay by his father, Zdenek Sverak. They also made the splendid *Kolya* (1997), in which Zdenek starred as an ideologically untrustworthy cellist who is bounced from the philharmonic, marries a woman to save her from being returned to Russia, and (when she skips town) ends up in an uneasy but eventually heartwarming relationship with her five-year-old son. *Kolya* was as emotionally authentic and original as *Dark Blue World* is derivative and not compelling.

The movie's open and close will be significant in Czechoslovakia, where communism turned out to be preferable only to Nazism, which isn't saying much. As the German doctor observes in the prison hospital: "I'll bet back in England you never thought they'd welcome you back with such a sad song."

Das Experiment ★ ★ ★

NO MPAA RATING, 113 m., 2002

Moritz Bleibtreu (Tarek Fahd, No. 77), Justus von Dohnanyi (Berus), Christian Berkel (Steinhoff, No. 38), Oliver Stokowski (Schutte, No. 82), Wotan Wilke Mohring (Joe, No. 69), Stephan Szasz (No. 53), Polat Dal (No. 40), Danny Richter (No. 21), Ralf Müller (No. 15), Maren Eggert (Dora). Directed by Oliver Hirschbiegel and produced by Marc Conrad, Norbert Preuss, and Friedrich Wildfeuer. Screenplay by Don Bohlinger, Christoph Darnstädt, Mario Giordano, Hirschbiegel, and Wildfeuer, based on the novel *Black Box* by Giordano.

Human behavior is determined to some degree by the uniforms we wear. An army might march more easily in sweatpants, but it wouldn't have the same sense of purpose. School uniforms enlist kids in the "student body." Catholic nuns saw recruitment fall off when they modernized their habits. If you want to figure out what someone thinks of himself, examine the uniform he is wearing. Gene Siskel amused himself by looking at people on the street and thinking: When they left home this morning, they thought they looked good in that.

Das Experiment, a new film from Germany, suggests that uniforms and the roles they assign amplify underlying psychological tendencies. In the experiment, twenty men are recruited to spend two weeks in a prison environment. Eight are made into guards and given quasi-military uniforms. Twelve become prisoners and wear nightshirts with numbers sewn on them. All twenty know they are merely volunteers working for a $1,700 paycheck.

The movie is based on a novel, *Black Box,* by Mario Giordano. The novel was probably inspired by the famous Stanford Prison Experiment of 1971, a classic of role-playing. On that experiment's Website, its director, Philip G. Zimbardo, writes:

How we went about testing these questions and what we found may astound you. Our planned two-week investigation into the psychology of prison life had to be ended prematurely after only six days because of what the situation was doing to the college students who participated. In only a few days, our guards became sadistic and our prisoners became depressed and showed signs of extreme stress.

So there, I've given away the plot. Some critics of *Das Experiment* question the fact that the guards become cruel so quickly, but the real-life experiment bears that out. What is fascinating is how most of the members of both groups tend to follow charismatic leaders. None of the other guards is as sadistic as Berus (Justus von Dohnanyi) and none of the other prisoners is as rebellious as Tarek Fahd (Moritz Bleibtreu), who remembers, "My father would say 'don't do this,' and I'd do it."

Perhaps uniforms turn us into packs, led by the top dog. There are a few strays. One prisoner seems custom-made to be a victim, but another, a man with military experience, holds back and tries to analyze the situation and provide cool guidance. But he's more or less powerless because—well, the guards are in charge. One of the guards has misgivings about what is happening, but it takes a lot of nerve to defy the pack.

It would make perfect sense for the guards to say, "Look, we're all in this together and we all want the $1,700 at the end of the two weeks. So let's make it easy on ourselves." But at Stanford as in this movie (and in life), that is not human nature. The outcome of the experiment is clear from the setup. We would be astonished if the guards became humane.

What impressed me is how effective the movie was, even though the outcome is a foregone conclusion. That's a tribute to the director, Oliver Hirschbiegel, and the actors, who have been chosen with the same kind of typecasting that perhaps occurs in life. The sadist *looks* mean. The rebel *looks* like a troublemaker. The military guy *looks* competent. The victim *looks* submissive. We see them and read them. Is it the same in life?

By halfway through, I was surprised how involved I was, and I see that I stopped taking notes at about that point—stopped thinking objectively and began to identify. Of course, I identified with the troublemaker. But give me a uniform and who knows what I would have done. The fact that the movie is German inspires thoughts about the Holocaust: The Nazi command structure needed only strong leaders at the top for Hitler to find, as one book called them, willing executioners in the ranks. But is the syndrome limited to Nazi Germany? This movie argues not.

Thinking of World War II, we're reminded not only of the Nazi uniforms, which were fetishistic, but of the genial sloppiness of the average American GI, as unforgettably portrayed by the great Bill Mauldin. His Willie and Joe, unshaven, their helmets askew, cigarettes dangling from their lips, resented authority, but they won the war.

Note: The Stanford Prison Experiment is at www.prisonexp.org.

The Day I Became a Woman ★ ★ ★ ½
NO MPAA RATING, 78 m., 2001

Fatemeh Cheragh Akhtar (Hava [Young Girl]), Hassan Nabehan (Boy [Her Friend]), Shahrbanou Sisizadeh (Mother), Ameneh Pasand (Grandmother), Shabnam Toloui (Ahoo [Bicyclist]), Cyrus Kahouri Nejad (Ahoo's Husband), Mahram Zeinal Zadeh (Osman), Nourieh Mahiguirian (Rival Cyclist), Azizeh Seddighi (Hourfa [Old Woman]), Badr Irouni Nejad (Young Boy). Directed by Marziyeh Meshkini and produced by Makhmalbaf Film House. Screenplay by Mohsen Makhmalbaf. In Farsi with English subtitles.

The Day I Became a Woman links together three stories from Iran—the three ages of women— involving a girl on the edge of adolescence, a wife determined not to be ruled by her husband, and a wealthy widow who declares "whatever I never had, I will buy for myself now."

All three of the stories are told in direct and simple terms. They're so lacking in the psychological clutter of Western movies that at first we think they must be fables or allegories. And so they may be, but they are also perfectly plausible. Few things on the screen could not occur in everyday life. It is just that we're not used to seeing so much of the *rest* of everyday life left out.

The first story is about Hava, a girl on her ninth birthday. As a child she has played freely with her best friend, a boy. But on this day she must begin to wear the chador, the garment which protects her head and body from the sight of men. And she can no longer play with boys. Her transition to womanhood is scheduled for dawn, but her mother and grandmother give her a reprieve, until noon. They put an upright stick in the ground, and tell her that when its shadow disappears, her girlhood is over. She measures the shadow with her fingers, and shares a lollypop with her playmate.

The second episode begins with an image

that first seems surrealistic, but has a pragmatic explanation. A group of women, all cloaked from head to toe in black, furiously pedal their bicycles down a road next to the sea. A ferocious man on horseback pursues one of the women, Ahoo, who is in the lead. This is a women's bicycle race, and Ahoo's husband does not want her to participate. He shouts at her, at first with solicitude (she should not pedal with her bad leg) and then with threats (a bike is "the devil's mount," and he will divorce her). She pedals on as the husband is joined by other family members, who finally stop her forcibly.

The third story begins like an episode from a silent comedy, as a young boy pushes a wheelchair containing an old woman, who is alert as a bird. She directs him into stores where she buys things—a refrigerator, a TV, tables and chairs—and soon she is at the head of a parade of boys pushing carts filled with consumer goods. We learn she inherited a lot of money and plans to spend it while she can, on all the things she couldn't buy while she was married. The scene concludes with a Felliniesque image I will not spoil for you; it is the film's one excursion out of the plausible and into the fantastic, but the story earns it.

The Day I Became a Woman is still more evidence of how healthy and alive the Iranian cinema is, even in a society we think of as closed. It was directed by Marziyeh Meshkini, and written by her husband, Mohsen Makhmalbaf (whose own *Gabbeh*, from 1996, found a story in the tapestry of a rug). It is a filmmaking family. Their daughter, Samira, directed *The Apple* in 1998, and last year her *Blackboards* was an official selection at Cannes (not bad for a twenty-year-old). Unlike the heroines of this film, the women of the Makhmalbaf family can think about the day they became directors. In fact, Iranian women have a good deal more personal freedom than the women of many other Islamic countries; the most dramatic contrast is with Afghanistan.

One of the strengths of this film is that it never pauses to explain, and the characters never have speeches to defend or justify themselves (the wife in the middle story just pedals harder). The little girl will miss her playmate, but trusts her mother and grandmother that she must, as they have, modestly shield herself from men who are not family members. Only

the old grandmother, triumphantly heading her procession, seems free of the system—although she, too, has a habit of pulling her shawl forward over her head, long after any man could be seduced by her beauty; the gesture is like a reminder to herself that she is a woman and must play by the rules.

Death to Smoochy ½★
R, 105 m., 2002

Robin Williams (Rainbow Randolph), Edward Norton (Sheldon Mopes [Smoochy]), Danny DeVito (Burke), Jon Stewart (Stokes), Catherine Keener (Nora), Harvey Fierstein (Merv Green), Vincent Schiavelli (Buggy Ding Dong). Directed by Danny DeVito and produced by Andrew Lazar and Peter MacGregor-Scott. Screenplay by Adam Resnick.

Only enormously talented people could have made *Death to Smoochy*. Those with lesser gifts would have lacked the nerve to make a film so bad, so miscalculated, so lacking any connection with any possible audience. To make a film this awful, you have to have enormous ambition and confidence, and dream big dreams.

The movie, directed by Danny DeVito (!), is about two clowns. That violates a cardinal rule of modern mass entertainment, which is that everyone hates clowns almost as much as they hate mimes. (*Big Fat Liar*, a much better recent showbiz comedy, got this right. When the clown arrived at a birthday party, the kids joyfully shouted, "Hey, it's the clown! Let's hurt him!") Most clowns are simply tiresome (I exempt Bozo). There are, however, two dread categories of clowns: clowns who are secretly vile and evil, and clowns who are guileless and good. *Death to Smoochy* takes no half-measures, and provides us with one of each.

We begin with Rainbow Randolph, played by Robin Williams, an actor who should never, ever play a clown of any description, because the role writes a license for him to indulge in those very mannerisms he should be striving to purge from his repertoire. Rainbow is a corrupt drunk who takes bribes to put kids on his show. The show itself is what kiddie TV would look like if kids wanted to see an Ann Miller musical starring midgets.

The good clown is Smoochy (Edward Norton), a soul so cheerful, earnest, honest, and uncomplicated you want to slap him and bring him back to his senses. Sample helpful Smoochy song for kids: "My Stepdad's Not Bad, He's Just Adjusting." Both of these clowns wear the kinds of costumes seen at the openings of used-car lots in states that doubt the possibility of evolution. Rainbow is convoluted, but Smoochy is so boring that the film explains why, on a long bus ride, you should always choose to sit next to Mrs. Robinson, for example, rather than Benjamin.

Enter the film's most engaging character, a TV producer named Nora (Catherine Keener), who, like Rachel Griffiths, cannot play dumb and is smart enough never to try. She's taking instructions from the network boss (Jon Stewart, who might have been interesting as one of the clowns). They're trapped in an inane subplot involving two bad guys, Burke (DeVito) and Merv Green (played by the gravel-voiced Harvey Fierstein, who, as he puts on weight, is becoming boulder-voiced). There is also Vincent Schiavelli as a former child star, now a crackhead.

The drama of the two clowns and their battle for the time slot is complicated by Rainbow Randolph's attempts to smear Smoochy by tricking him into appearing at a neo-Nazi rally. One wonders idly: Are there enough neo-Nazis to fill a thundering convention center? Do they usually book clowns? The answer to the second question may be yes.

The movie ends by crossing an ice show with elements of The Manchurian Candidate. It involves an odd sexual predilection: Nora has a fetish for kiddie show hosts. It has a lesbian hit-squad leader with a thick Irish brogue. It uses four-letter language as if being paid by the word. In all the annals of the movies, few films have been this odd, inexplicable, and unpleasant.

The Debut ★ ★ ★
NO MPAA RATING, 89 m., 2002

Dante Basco (Ben Mercado), Bernadette Balagtas (Rose Mercado), Tirso Cruz III (Roland Mercado), Gina Alajar (Gina Mercado), Eddie Garcia (Lolo Carlos), Joy Bisco (Annabelle), Darion Basco (Augusto), Dion Basco (Rommel), Fe de Los Reyes (Alice). Directed by Gene Cajayon and produced by Lisa Onodera. Screenplay by Cajayon and John Manal Castro.

There is a moment in The Debut where a white man, who has married into a Filipino-American family, solemnly informs a dinner party of Filipinos that they are "not considered Asians, but Malays." He doesn't realize how offensive and condescending it is for an outsider to tell people about themselves, but there is another reason to put the dialogue in this first-ever Filipino-American film: Most Americans don't know that. And now, knowing it, they don't know what a Malay is. And unless they've been in the Philippines, they don't have much idea of the heritage of the islands, where the cultures of the Pacific and Spain intersect with America. And they don't know that Tagalog is the national language, coexisting with English. And that the Philippine film industry is one of the few outside the United States and India to possess more than 50 percent of its own market.

Given the health of the film industry and the availability of English, it's surprising that it took so long for this first Filipino-American feature to be born. It joins a group of films about second-generation immigrants, standing between the traditions of their parents and their own headlong dive into American culture. Maryam is about an Iranian-American teenage girl in conflict with strict Iranian parents. ABCD and American Desi are about Indian-Americans. Real Women Have Curves is about a Mexican-American teenager whose mother opposes her college plans. Bread and Roses is about a Mexican-American strike leader whose sister opposes her. Mi Familia is a multigenerational story about Mexican-Americans, and The Joy Luck Club is a Chinese-American version. For that matter, Stolen Summer has an Irish-American dad who wants his son to follow him into the fire department instead of going to college.

The films have elements in common: A bright young person who dreams of personal fulfillment. Parents who worked hard to support their families in a new land, and now want to dictate the choices of their children. A father who is stern, a mother who is a mediator. And with surprising frequency, a stiff, unyielding older man, a grandfather or "sponsor," who is like the ghost at the family feast. The message of all of the movies: The older generation must bend and let the kids follow their dreams. That's not surprising, since the kids make the films, and all of these filmmakers must have had parents who thought they were crazy to dream of becoming movie directors.

The Debut is familiar in its story arc, but fresh in its energy and lucky in its choice of actors. Filmed on a low budget, it looks and plays like an assured professional film, and its young leads are potential stars. The story involves a high school student named Ben Mercado (Dante Basco), who works in a comic-book store and in the opening scene is selling his comics collection to help pay his way into Cal Arts.

He wants to be a graphic artist. His father, Roland (Tirso Cruz III), a postman, has other plans for Ben, who has won a pre-med scholarship to UCLA. The boy will be a doctor, period. Everything comes to a head at the eighteenth birthday party of Ben's sister Rose (Bernadette Balagtas), the "debut" of the title.

Ben has assimilated by always keeping a certain distance between his friends and his family. His best buddies are an Anglo and a Mexican-American, who are curious about Ben's home life, but keep getting shuffled aside. When they mention the inviting cooking aromas, Ben takes that as a criticism of the way his home smells. On the night of Rose's party, Ben has made plans to meet a pretty Anglo girl at a high school party, and is torn between the two events (unlike his friends, who have more fun at Rose's party).

The movie involves some melodrama when Ben meets Rose's pretty Filipino-American friend Annabel (Joy Bisco) and it's love at first sight; Annabel is breaking up with a tough boyfriend who, in the modern equivalent of male possessiveness, wants her to wear a pager. In a scene at a burger joint, there's casual racism in jibes that Filipinos eat dogs, and Ben is called a "Chink." "I'm not Chinese," he murmurs, and we realize one reason for the white man's gauche line about Malays is to get information into the screenplay that Filipinos would hardly tell one another.

The outcome of all of this is not hard to anticipate, but the setting is new, and the birthday party provides an excuse for traditional songs and dances (as well as for a virtuoso performance of hip-hop turntabling, an art where Filipino-Americans often win U.S. contests). In Dante Basco, Bernadette Balagtas, and Joy Bisco the movie has likable, convincing young actors with marquee potential, and all of the major roles are filled with capable pros. There is one surprise. In most movies about artists, the artwork never looks as good as the movie thinks it does. But when Ben shows his father his portfolio, we see he does have the talent to realize his dream of writing graphic novels. Or maybe even go into animation and make some real dough.

The Deep End ★ ★ ★ ½
R, 99 m., 2001

Tilda Swinton (Margaret Hall), Goran Visnjic (Alek Spera), Jonathan Tucker (Beau Hall), Peter Donat (Jack Hall), Josh Lucas (Darby Reese), Raymond J. Barry (Carlie Nagle), Tamara Hope (Paige Hall), Jordon Dorrance (Dylan Hall), Margo Krindel (Jackie). Directed and produced by Scott McGehee and David Siegel. Screenplay by McGehee and Siegel, based on the book *The Blank Wall* by Elisabeth Sanxay Holding.

The Deep End uses relentless ingenuity to dig its heroine into deeper and deeper holes—until finally, when she seems defeated by the weight of her problems, it's equally ingenious in digging her out again. This is one of those plots like *Blood Simple* where one damn thing leads to another—although it has an entirely different tone, because the heroine is a completely ordinary woman we begin to care about.

Tilda Swinton stars as Margaret, a mother of three who lives in a handsome home on the shores of Lake Tahoe. Her husband is an admiral, away at sea. She lives with her kids and her querulous, distant father-in-law. She's worried about the oldest son, Beau (Jonathan Tucker), who is seventeen and has started to run with dangerous company.

The movie's opening shot shows her visiting a gay club in Reno to ask a thirty-year-old man named Darby (Josh Lucas) to stay away from her son; while they were both drunk, Beau crashed the car they were driving. Darby is handsome, but in a way that makes us mistrust him because he uses his looks so obviously. He's got a gambling problem, apparently, and offers to stay away—for $5,000.

The movie shows a quiet delicacy in dealing with Margaret's feelings about her son's recently revealed homosexuality. It wisely doesn't make his sexuality the subject of the story; she gently tries to approach the subject once, he roughly avoids it, and that's all they really say. What she sees is a good child, a talented musician with a scholarship on the way, who has been temporarily dazzled by Darby.

We also see a household filled with silences. Margaret is lonely and isolated, maintains a distance from her father-in-law, performs motherly duties for her children, but seems vaguely worried most of the time. One reason the movie works is because she's so practiced at keeping secrets. That reserve, linked to a strong will, sets up the *noir* plot. If she weren't so capable and secretive . . . but she is.

When Darby visits Beau late one night, the two men fight in a boathouse, and after Beau stalks away, the drunken Darby stumbles, falls, and kills himself. The next morning, Margaret finds the body, assumes her son killed Darby, and sets about trying to conceal the corpse. Scott McGehee and David Siegel, the writer-directors, are merciless in creating one difficulty after another—the problem of the car keys, for example—and there is a long, sustained sequence in which we follow Margaret as she does her best.

Then a man comes knocking on the door. This is Alek Spera (Goran Visnjic). He thinks he has incriminating information and wants $50,000 to keep quiet and destroy some evidence. What is intriguing here, and elsewhere, is that we know more about the actual death than anyone in the movie, and *The Deep End* creates that kind of suspense Hitchcock likes, in which an innocent person is wrongly accused, looks guilty, tries to cope, and lacks essential information.

The movie is based on a 1947 crime novel named *The Blank Wall*, by Elisabeth Sanxay Holding (it was filmed in 1949 by Max Ophuls as *The Reckless Moment*, with James Mason and Joan Bennett). This version changes the gender of the child and adds homosexuality, but relishes the freedom of 1940s melodrama to pile on complications and dark coincidences.

When the film played at Sundance and Cannes, some critics complained that the later developments were simply too implausible. But there are times at the movies when we have to cut loose from plausibility and enjoy the ride; this movie would not be better if the ending were more believable, because there is a part of us that enjoys melodrama stretched to the limit.

What's skillful, too, is the way McGehee and Siegel go for broke in the plot but keep the performances reined in. Tilda Swinton is the key. She is always believable as this harassed, desperate, loving mother. She projects a kind of absorption in her task; she juggles blackmail, murder, bank loans, picking up the kids after school—it's as if the ordinary tasks keep her sane enough to deal with the dangers that surround her. Swinton's career has included one extraordinary movie after another. In *Orlando*, she was a man who became a woman and lived for four centuries. In *Love Is the Devil*, the Francis Bacon story, she presided over London's most notorious drinking club. In Tim Roth's *The War Zone* she was a pregnant wife in a family harboring dark secrets. And you may remember her in *The Beach* as the imperious leader of the tropical commune Leonardo DiCaprio stumbles across. Her American housewife here is, in a way, a bigger stretch than most of those; she is believable and touching.

The Deep End is the kind of crime movie where the everyday surroundings make the violence seem all the more shocking and gruesome. Nobody much wants to really hurt anybody, and in a nice twist even one of the villains doesn't have much heart for the task, but once the machinery of death and deception has been set into motion, it carries everyone along with it. It's intense and involving, and it doesn't let us go.

Deliver Us from Eva ★ ★
R, 105 m., 2003

Gabrielle Union (Eva), LL Cool J (Ray), Essence Atkins (Kareenah), Mel Jackson (Tim), Meagan Good (Jacqui), Dartanyan Edmonds (Darrell), Robinne Lee (Bethany), Duane Martin (Mike). Directed by Gary Hardwick and produced by Len Amato and Paddy Cullen. Screenplay by Hardwick, James Iver Mattson, and B. E. Brauner.

Deliver Us from Eva is the second movie of the same weekend based on a romantic bet. See my review of *How to Lose a Guy in 10 Days* for my general comments on this unhappy genre. *Eva* has the advantage of being about one bet, not two, preserving at least one of the protagonists as a person we can safely like. But it proceeds so deliberately from one plot point to the next that we want to stand next to the camera, holding up cards upon which we have lettered clues and suggestions.

The movie stars two tall and striking actors, Gabrielle Union and LL Cool J, who have every reason to like each other anyway, even if Union's brothers-in-law were not paying him $5,000 to take her out, make her fall in love, and move with her to a town far, far away. They can't stand the woman. Well, hardly can we.

Union plays Eva, oldest of the four Dandridge sisters. After the untimely death of their parents, Eva took on the task of raising the girls, and has never been able to stop giving the orders—no, not even now that they're grown up. The sisters are Kareenah (Essence Atkins), who won't get pregnant, on Eva's orders; Bethany (Robinne Lee), whom Eva won't let live with her cop boyfriend; and Jacqui (Meagan Good), who is married to a mailman who always feels like there's postage due.

The Dandridge sisters like their local fame and kind of enjoy being under Eva's motherly thumb. The director, Gary Hardwick, often films them cresting a hill, four abreast, hair and skirts flying, arms linked, while straggling after them are their luckless men, left in the rear. Much of the action centers on a beauty parlor, serving, like the title location in *Barbershop*, as the stage upon which daily soap operas are played out to loud acclaim or criticism.

The Dandridge family logjam is broken, as we can easily foresee, when Eva actually begins to fall for that big lug Ray (played by LL Cool J, who says after this movie he is changing his name back to James Todd Smith, a victory for punctuationists everywhere). He wins her over by admiring her spicy beans, which are too hot for the wimps she usually dates. If the way to a man's heart is through his stomach, the way to

a woman's heart is through adoring a recipe that only she thinks is edible.

But let's back up. The problem with their love affair, of course, is that although Eva loves Ray and Ray loves Eva, Eva is certain to find out about the bet, causing a scene of heartbreak and betrayal that would be moving if I hadn't also seen it in *How to Lose a Guy in 10 Days* and every other movie in history where lovers begin with secret deception and arrive at the truth.

Any two lovers with the slightest instinct for each other, with the most perfunctory ability to see true romance glowing in the eyes of the beloved, would not have the fight because they would not need the fight. They would know their love was true. I live to see the following scene:

> She: You mean . . . you only went out
> with me on a bet!?!
> He: That's right, baby.
> She: Well, you won, you dumb lug. Now
> haul your lying ass over here and
> make me forget it.

The Devil's Backbone ★ ★ ★
R, 106 m., 2001

Marisa Paredes (Carmen), Eduardo Noriega (Jacinto), Federico Luppi (Casares), Fernando Tielve (Carlos), Irene Visedo (Conchita), Inigo Garces (Jaime). Directed by Guillermo del Toro and produced by Agustin Almodovar and Bertha Navarro. Screenplay by del Toro, Antonio Trashorras, and David Munoz.

Ghosts are more interesting when they have their reasons. They should have unfinished affairs of the heart or soul. Too many movies use them simply for shock value, as if they exist to take cues from the screenplay. *The Devil's Backbone,* a mournful and beautiful new ghost story by Guillermo del Toro, understands that most ghosts are sad, and are attempting not to frighten us but to urgently communicate something that must be known so that they can rest.

The film takes place in Spain in the final days of the civil war. Franco's fascists have the upper hand, and in a remote orphanage the children of left-wing families await the end. An enormous crucifix has been put on display to disguise the institution as a Catholic school, and the staff is uneasily prepared to flee. In the courtyard, a huge unexploded bomb rests, nose down, like a sculpture. "They say it's switched off," says one of the kids, "but I don't believe it. Put your head against it. You can hear it ticking."

A young boy named Carlos (Fernando Tielve) has been brought to the school in a car riding across one of those spaghetti Western landscapes. He is assigned Bed No. 12—"Santi's bed," the children whisper. Santi is a boy who died and whose ghost is sometimes seen, sometimes heard sighing. Carlos learns the ways of the school, its rules, the boys who will be his friends and his enemies.

The most ominous presence is Jacinto (Eduardo Noriega), a former student who is now the janitor. The orphanage is run by Dr. Casares (Federico Luppi), elderly and self-absorbed, and by Carmen (Marisa Paredes), who has a wooden leg. There is also Conchita (Irene Visedo), the sexy maid; Jacinto sleeps with her, but also goes through the motions of courting Carmen because he suspects she has gold hidden somewhere on the grounds and he wants it.

This information unfolds gradually, as Carlos discovers it. He also begins to see the ghost, a sad, gray, indistinct figure who seems associated with a deep water tank in the basement. There's a creepy sequence in which the other boys dare Carlos to make a forbidden nighttime expedition to the kitchen to bring back water; he is venturing into the world of the orphanage's dread secrets.

What happens, and why, must remain a secret. The Mexican director, del Toro, is a master of dark atmosphere, and the places in his films seem as frightening as the plots. He is only thirty-seven; he began with *Cronos* (1994), the story of an antique dealer who invents a small, elegant golden beetle that sinks its claws into the flesh and imparts immortality. In 1997, he made a Hollywood film, *Mimic*, starring Mira Sorvino and Jeremy Northam, which trapped them in a subway system with a fearsome bug that mutates out of control. That makes it sound dumb, but it was uncanny in its ability to transcend the creature genre, to create complex characters and an incredible interior space (an abandoned subway station).

Now this film. Del Toro is attracted by the horror genre, but not in thrall to it. He uses the golden beetle, the mimic insects, the school ghost, not as his subjects but as the devices that test the souls of his characters. Here he uses buried symbolism that will slip past American audiences not familiar with the Spanish civil war, but the impotent school administrators and the unexploded fascist bomb do not need footnotes, nor does the grown child of the Left (Jacinto), who seduces the younger generation while flattering the older for its gold. Carlos, I suppose, is the Spanish future, who has a long wait ahead. Such symbols are worthless if they function only as symbols; you might as well hand out name tags. Del Toro's symbols work first as themselves, then as what they may stand for, so it doesn't matter if the audience has never heard of Franco, as long as it has heard of ghosts.

Any director of a ghost film is faced with the difficult question of portraying the ghost. A wrong step, and he gets bad laughs. The ghost in *The Devil's Backbone* is glimpsed briefly, is heard sighing, is finally seen a little better as a dead boy. What happens at the end is not the usual action scene with which lesser ghost films dissipate their tension, but a chain of events that have a logic and a poetic justice. *The Devil's Backbone* has been compared to *The Others*, and has the same ambition and intelligence, but is more compelling and even convincing.

Diamond Men ★ ★ ★ ½
NO MPAA RATING, 100 m., 2002

Robert Forster (Eddie Miller), Donnie Wahlberg (Bobby Walker), Bess Armstrong (Katie Harnish), Jasmine Guy (Tina), George Coe (Tip Rountree), Jeff Gendelman (Brad), Douglas Allen Johnson (John Ludwig), Kristin Minter (Cherry). Directed and produced by Daniel M. Cohen. Screenplay by Cohen.

Robert Forster has a note of gentle sadness in some of his roles, revealing a man who has lived according to a code, not always successfully. Whether that is true of his acting career, I cannot say, but it is often true of his characters. Here is an actor who has been bringing special qualities to his work as long as I have been a critic, in early movies like John Huston's *Reflections in a Golden Eye* (1967) and Haskell Wexler's *Medium Cool* (1969), and recent ones like Quentin Tarantino's *Jackie Brown* (1997) and Joe Mantegna's *Lakeboat* (2000). But for the most part he has been relegated to exploitation movies like *Maniac Cop 3* and *Original Gangstas.*

Now here he is in his best performance, in *Diamond Men,* as a man in his fifties who is about to lose the job he loves. Forster plays Eddie Miller, a diamond salesman who has long traveled the mid-sized cities of Pennsylvania, selling to the owners of jewelry stores. He has a heart attack, recovers, and is told that he is no longer "insurable" to drive around with $1 million in stock in his car. His boss introduces him to Bobby Walker (Donnie Wahlberg), a brash kid whose sales experience is limited mostly to pretzels. Eddie is to train Bobby to take over his route.

He takes on the kid because he has no choice. There is a generation gap. Eddie likes jazz; Bobby likes heavy metal. Eddie keeps a low profile: "I stay at out-of-the-way motels, I eat in quiet restaurants, I don't talk about what I do." Bobby is a party animal who has a girl in every town, or hopes to. Eddie winces as Bobby tries to sell diamonds, and fails. "How do you do it?" Bobby asks the older man. "What's the magic word? I never ever saw a diamond until a week ago. I'm afraid of them." Eddie, who has nurtured his clients for years and plays them skillfully, tries to explain: "When they say 'no,' they're looking for a way to say 'yes.'"

Bobby is not a bad kid. He's in over his head, but he wants to learn. And he wants Eddie to have more fun. Eddie's wife, we learn, died of cancer; Forster's reading as he remembers her is an exercise in perfect pitch: "She didn't want to go into a facility because . . . well, you know. And I don't blame her." Bobby takes it as his personal assignment to get Eddie laid, and after various schemes fail because Eddie is too old to attract the barflies Bobby recruits, Bobby takes Eddie to the Altoona Riding Club, which is a discreet rural brothel run by Tina (Jasmine Guy).

Here, too, Eddie strikes out: He doesn't *want* to get laid. He wants to check into that obscure motel and find that quiet restaurant. Finally Tina suggests Katie (Bess Armstrong), who is, she explains, a secretary who lost her job and needs money but doesn't want to go all the way. That's fine with Eddie. Katie treats him politely, calls him "Edward," and administers a gentle massage, and so moved is Eddie that he invites her to dinner. Really, to dinner. A quiet restaurant.

The story, written and directed by Daniel M. Cohen (himself a former diamond salesman), seems to be shaping up as a buddy movie with a good woman at the end of the road. But Cohen has laid the preparations for a series of unexpected developments, which I will not reveal. The movie keeps surprising us. First it's about salesmen, and then it's about lonely men, and then it's about sex, and then it's about romance, and then it's about crime. It reinvents itself with every act.

Among its gifts is a quick perception of human nature. Eddie is a thoroughly good man, honest and hardworking. Bobby sees work as an unpleasant necessity. Katie is a character study, a woman who has so surrounded her occupation (hooker) with her beliefs (yoga, inner truth, meditation, transcendence) that sex is like a by-product of redemption. As in *Jackie Brown,* where he had a lovely, subtle, almost unstated courtship with the Pam Grier character, Forster plays a man for whom romance sometimes seems like more trouble than it's worth. There is truth in the wary way he regards the women Bobby finds for him.

Diamond Men is the kind of movie the American distribution system is not set up to handle. It does not appeal to teenagers. It doesn't fit into an easy category, but moves from one to another. It has actors who, by playing many different kinds of characters, have never hardened into brand names. It has fun with a crime plot and a twist at the end, but stays true to its underlying direction. It looks and listens to its characters, curious about the unfolding mysteries of the personality. It is a treasure.

The Diaries of Vaslav Nijensky
★ ★ ★ ½
NO MPAA RATING, 95 m., 2002

Derek Jacobi (Voice of Nijinsky), Delia Silvan

(Romola), Chris Haywood (Oscar), Hans Sonneveld (Doctor), Oliver Streeton (Psychiatrist), Jillian Smith (Emilia), Kevin Lucas (Diaghilev). Directed by Paul Cox and produced by Cox and Aanya Whitehead. Screenplay by Cox, from the diaries of Vaslav Nijinsky.

I attended the world premiere of Paul Cox's *The Diaries of Vaslav Nijinsky* in September 2001 at the Toronto Film Festival. It was not a serene event. The film started very late, some audience members found it difficult, and there were walkouts and even audible complaints. Cox took the microphone afterward to castigate those who had left (and could therefore not hear him) and to explain passionately why he had made the film.

His comments came down to: Art defends the final battlements against ignorance and violence. When he read the diaries, he said, "it was the first time I had read something somebody had written not out of his head but out of his heart." And to those who had stayed, in an oblique reference to mainstream commercial cinema: "At least when you walk out of the door you have not become a more disgusting human being."

The screening was held a few days after 9/11, there was borderline hysteria in the air, and the film's own examination of insanity was no doubt more disturbing than it might have been. Nor is it an easy film. I recall a conversation at the Sundance Film Festival with Ken Turan of the *Los Angeles Times*. He asked me about another difficult film.

"Well," I said, "it's the kind of movie it takes an experienced observer to appreciate. Someone who has seen a lot of movies and thought deeply about them."

"Someone like us," Turan said.

"Exactly. The average viewer is going to be incapable of accepting it as only what it is."

Pure snobbery, with our tongues in cheek, and yet not without merit. *The Diaries of Vaslav Nijinsky* is not a biography of the great dancer, or a dramatic reenactment of events in his life, but pure cinema in an experimental form, anchored by the voice of Derek Jacobi reading from the diaries. The images sometimes represent episodes in Nijinsky's life, sometimes symbolize them obliquely, sometimes represent images in his mind, sometimes simply

want to evoke his state of mind. The music by Paul Grabowsky, Cox's longtime collaborator, is similarly motivated.

"I made this film in the editing room," Cox said. Out of his heart, not his head, I believe. It took him many months. Although he is a director capable of making films that communicate with anyone (such as his wonderful *Innocence* from 2000), this film will baffle those moviegoers who expect to have everything laid out for them like a buffet supper. If you have never heard of Nijinsky, this film is not going to function like a lecture. It is sensuous, not informational. Those who have seen what we once called underground films will respond, and those familiar with experimental films going back to the silent era. The structure of the film is musical, not dramatic, and attempts a sweep through Nijinsky's psyche during a period in 1919 when he danced for the last time and then was institutionalized. His diaries commenced at just this time.

Any reaction to this film must be intensely personal; it is not a mass-market entertainment but an uncompromising attempt by one artist to think about another. My own subjective feelings are all I can convey. I do not have much knowledge of Nijinsky (I know him mostly through the 1980 Herbert Ross film and countless secondhand references), or much curiosity. I do, however, have a lot of knowledge about the work of Paul Cox, a heroic filmmaker of great gifts and curiosity about everything he does. I was watching not a film about Nijinsky, but a film evoking Cox's need to make it.

What I got then is likely to be different than what a Nijinsky person would understand. I sensed at once in Jacobi's reading and Cox's images the fact of Nijinsky's madness, his identification with God, the oneness between his art and his ego. I sensed his feeling that great currents in the world mirrored and even flowed from his own spirit. I saw how, for him, madness (or whatever it should be called) was the wellspring of creativity. Art can lead (but rarely does) to such ecstasy that it resembles derangement. I think that Cox saw Nijinsky not as a madman but as a man too inspired to be sane.

I sat in the theater in much the same state I might attend a concert of serious music. I do not ask music to have a plot, a story, or characters. It does not make sense in any literal way. It is a collection of feelings, pushed forward through time, expressed by artists who want to flow through the inspiration of the composer. If the technique is good enough not to call attention to itself, it is all emotion.

The Diaries of Vaslav Nijinsky is a film with that musical kind of effect. I have tried to describe it accurately. You will either be in sympathy with it, or not. Much depends on what you bring into the theater. It is possible that those who know the most about Nijinsky will be the most baffled, because this is not a film about knowing, but about feeling.

Die Another Day ★ ★ ★
PG-13, 123 m., 2002

Pierce Brosnan (James Bond), Halle Berry (Jinx), Toby Stephens (Gustav Graves), Rosamund Pike (Miranda Frost), Rick Yune (Zao), John Cleese (Q), Judi Dench (M), Michael Madsen (Damian Falco), Samantha Bond (Miss Moneypenny). Directed by Lee Tamahori and produced by Barbara Broccoli and Michael G. Wilson. Screenplay by Neal Purvis and Robert Wade.

I realized with a smile, fifteen minutes into the new James Bond movie, that I had unconsciously accepted Pierce Brosnan as Bond without thinking about Sean Connery, Roger Moore, or anyone else. He has become the landlord, not the tenant. Handsome if a little weary, the edges of an Irish accent curling around the edges of the Queen's English, he plays a preposterous character but does not seem preposterous playing him.

Die Another Day is the twentieth Bond film in forty years, not counting *Casino Royale*. Midway through it, Bond's boss, M, tells him, "While you were away, the world changed." She refers to the months he spent imprisoned at the hands of North Korean torturers, but she might also be referring to the world of Bondian thrillers. This movie has the usual impossible stunts, as when Bond surfs down the face of a glacier being melted by a laser beam from space. But it has just as many scenes that are lean and tough enough to fit in any modern action movie.

It also has a heroine who benefits from forty years of progress in the way we view women.

When Halle Berry, as Jinx, first appears in the movie there is a deliberate and loving tribute to the first Bond girl, Ursula Andress, in *Dr. No* (1962). In both movies, the woman emerges from the surf wearing a bikini which, in slow motion, seems to be playing catch-up. Even the wide belt is the same. But Jinx is a new kind of Bond girl. She still likes naughty double entendres (Bond says he's an ornithologist, and she replies, "Well, that's a mouthful"). But in *Die Another Day* her character is not simply decoration or reward, but a competent and deadly agent who turns the movie at times into almost a buddy picture.

The film opens with an unusual touch: The villains are not fantastical fictions, but real. The North Koreans have, for the time being, joined the Nazis as reliable villains, and Bond infiltrates in order to—I dunno, deal with some "African Conflict Diamonds," if I heard correctly, but I wasn't listening carefully because the diamonds are only the maguffin. They do, however, decorate the memorable cheekbones of one of the villains, Zao (Rick Yune), who seems to have skidded facedown through a field of them at high impact.

A chase scene involving hover tanks in a minefield is somewhat clumsy, the hover tank not being the most graceful of vehicles, and then Bond is captured and tortured for months. He's freed in a prisoner exchange, only to find that M (Judi Dench) suspects him of having been brainwashed. Is he another "Manchurian candidate"? Eventually he proves himself, and after a visit to Q (John Cleese) for a new supply of gadgets, including an invisible car, he's back into action in the usual series of sensational stunt sequences. For the first time in the Bond series, a computer-generated sequence joins the traditional use of stunt men and trick photography; a disintegrating plane in a closing scene is pretty clearly all made of ones and zeroes, but by then we've seen too many amazing sights to quibble.

The North Koreans are allied with Gustav Graves (Toby Stephens), a standard-issue world-dominating Bond villain, whose orbiting space mirror is not exactly original. What is original is Gustav's decision to house his operation in a vast ice building in Iceland; since his mirror operates to focus heat on Earth, this seems like asking for trouble, and indeed, before long the ice palace is melting down, and Jinx is trapped in a locked room with the water level rising toward the ceiling. (Exactly why the room itself doesn't melt is a question countless readers will no doubt answer for me.)

Other characters include the deadly Miranda Frost (Rosamund Pike), whose name is a hint which side she is on, and Damian Falco (Michael Madsen), whose name unites two villainous movie dynasties and leaves me looking forward to Freddy Lecter. Oh, and Miss Moneypenny (Samantha Bond), who seems to have been overlooked, makes a last-minute appearance and virtually seduces Bond.

The film has been directed by Lee Tamahori (*Once Were Warriors, Mulholland Falls*), from New Zealand, who has tilted the balance away from humor and toward pure action. With *Austin Powers* breathing down the neck of the franchise, he told *Sight & Sound* magazine, it seemed like looking for trouble to broaden the traditional farcical elements. *Die Another Day* is still utterly absurd from one end to the other, of course, but in a slightly more understated way.

And so it goes, Bond after Bond, as the most durable series in movie history heads for the half-century. There is no reason to believe this franchise will ever die. I suppose that is a blessing.

Dinner Rush ★ ★ ★
R, 98 m., 2002

Danny Aiello (Louis Cropa), Edoardo Ballerini (Udo Cropa), Sandra Bernhard (Jennifer), Vivian Wu (Nicole), Mark Margolis (Fitzgerald), Mike McGlone (Carmen), Kirk Acevedo (Duncan), Summer Phoenix (Marti), John Corbett (Ken). Directed by Bob Giraldi and produced by Louis DiGiaimo and Patti Greaney. Screenplay by Rick Shaughnessy and Bryan Kalata.

"Unbelievable. Only in New York can a double murder triple your business."

So it is observed in *Dinner Rush*, a movie set in one of those Italian restaurants that the customers are tickled to believe is mob-connected even though it isn't, because it makes it more thrilling that way. (Rosebud, the Chicago eatery, had billboards saying, "We serve the whole mob.") The story unfolds during one long night at an Italian place in Tribeca that is un-dergoing an identity crisis. The owner, Louis (Danny Aiello), likes traditional Italian fare. His son Udo (Edoardo Ballerini) is into nouvelle, or nuovo, cuisine, and boasts: "Sausage and peppers is not on my menu."

Louis is in despair. He wants to turn the place over to his son, but not if it means abandoning dishes that make you think of bread sticks and red-and-white checkerboard tablecloths. There are other problems. A man has been murdered, and the identity of his killers may be known to Louis. And two men have come into the restaurant, taken a table, called Louis over, and informed him, "We're not leaving here until we're partners in the business." Louis says they can have the book he runs, but not the restaurant. Never the restaurant. They don't leave.

It's a busy night. The party at one long table is presided over by Fitzgerald (Mark Margolis), a gravel-voiced snob who talks slooow-ly so the cretins of the world can understand him. He runs an art gallery and is treating a visiting Greek artist. The entertainment consists of insulting his waitress (Summer Phoenix) and the maitresse d' (Vivian Wu). At another table, Sandra Bernhard plays a food critic as if she considers the performance personal revenge on every theater and movie critic who has ever said a word against her.

So there's a crisis in management and a crisis in the dining room. A third crisis is unfolding in the kitchen, where Duncan (Kirk Acevedo), the only cook who will still make Louis "salsiccia e peperoni," is deep in debt to a bookmaker. Louis, who takes bets but is a reasonable man, tells Duncan's bookmaker: "Stop taking his action. The kid's a pathological gambler. He needs help, not another bookmaker."

There are enough plots here to challenge a Robert Altman, specialist in interlocking stories, but the director, Bob Giraldi, masters the complexities as if he knows the territory. He does. He owns the restaurant, which in real life is named Giraldi's. His center of gravity is supplied by Danny Aiello, who plays his cards close to his vest—closer than we suspect—and like a man who has been dealing with drunks for a very, very long time, doesn't get worked up over every little thing. He talks to his accountant and the visiting gangsters as if they're in the same business.

Like *Big Night*, a film it resembles, *Dinner Rush* has a keen appreciation for the intricacies of a restaurant. In front, everybody is supposed to have a good time. In the kitchen, the chef is a dictator and the workers are galley slaves. Udo has a scene right at the start where he makes one thing clear: Do it his way or get out. The scenes in the kitchen show the bewildering speed with which hard and exact work is accomplished, and Giraldi is able to break these scenes down into details that edit together into quick little sequences; not surprising, since he has directed hundreds of commercials.

In a plot like this, there isn't a lot of time to establish characters, so the actors have to bring their characters into the film with them. They do. The gangsters walk in menacing. Mark Margolis has a manner that makes Fitzgerald hateful on sight. Bernhard and her long-suffering companion play out nightly private dramas over the work of the city's chefs. And Aiello suggests enormous depths of pride, sympathy, worry, and buried anger.

The last scenes are fully packed, with developments that come one after another, tempting critics to complain it's all a little too neat. Maybe, but then you wouldn't want those story strands left dangling, and to spend any more time on them would be laboring the point: Like a good meal, this movie is about the progression of the main courses and not about the mints at the door.

The Dish ★ ★ ★ ½
PG-13, 101 m., 2001

Sam Neill (Cliff Buxton), Kevin Harrington (Ross "Mitch" Mitchell), Tom Long (Glenn Latham), Patrick Warburton (Al Burnett), Genevieve Mooy (May McIntyre), Tayler Kane (Rudi Kellerman), Bille Brown (Prime Minister), Roy Billing (Mayor Bob McIntyre), Eliza Szonert (Janine Kellerman), Lenka Kripac (Marie McIntyre). Directed by Rob Sitch and produced by Michael Hirsh, Santo Cilauro, Tom Gleisner, Jane Kennedy, and Sitch. Screenplay by Cilauro, Gleisner, Kennedy, and Sitch.

In a sheep pasture outside the little town of Parkes in New South Wales stands the pride and joy of Australian astronomy, a radio telescope the size of a football field. Most days it eavesdrops on the stars. In 1969, it gets a momentous assignment: Relaying the television signals from the Moon that will show Neil Armstrong's one small step for man, one giant leap for mankind.

Parkes is agog. This is the town's shining hour. *The Dish*, a smiling human comedy, treats the Moon walk not as an event 240,000 miles away, but as a small step taken by every single member of mankind, particularly those in Parkes. Resigned to thinking of themselves as provincials in a backwater, they're thrilled and a little humbled by their role on the world stage. True, NASA is relying on its primary telescope in Goldstone, California, and Parkes is only the backup—but still!

Mayor Bob McIntyre and his wife, Maisie (Roy Billing and Genevieve Mooy), nervously prepare for visits from the prime minister and the U.S. ambassador. Out at the telescope, Cliff Buxton (Sam Neill), the imperturbable, pipe-smoking scientist in charge of the telescope, steadies his team. There's Glenn (Tom Long), the soft-spoken mathematician, Mitch (Kevin Harrington), in charge of keeping the equipment humming, and Al (Patrick Warburton), the American observer from NASA, whose black horn-rims and foursquare demeanor make him seem like Clark Kent. Patrolling the parameters of the site, prepared to repel foreign invaders and curious sheep, is Rudi the security guard (Tayler Kane), whose sister, Janine (Eliza Szonert), is in love with Mitch and effortlessly penetrates Rudi's defenses.

Since we all know Neil Armstrong and his shipmates returned safely from the Moon, *The Dish* can't develop suspense over the outcome of the mission. But it's a cliffhanger anyway, through the ingenious device of making the movie more about Parkes than about the Moon. The movie is "inspired by fact" (very loosely, I suspect), but who can remember if the historic TV signals were relayed by Parkes or Goldstone? Since we've met the locals in Parkes, we're as eager as they are to have it be them.

But it won't be simple. Director and cowriter Rob Sitch (whose *The Castle* is one of the funniest comedies of recent years) intercuts the drama of the approaching Moon walk with the drama of the momentous visit to Parkes by the prime minister and the ambassador. At the observatory, embarrassing technical problems pop up when the town blows a fuse. And at a crucial moment, high gusts of wind threaten to topple the telescope right over onto the sheep.

Sitch laces the Moon walk and the local plots together so effortlessly that it would be unfair to describe his plot developments. I will be vague, then, in mentioning the visit by the U.S. ambassador, who arrives at the telescope at a particularly delicate moment, but leaves satisfied that he has at least heard Neil Armstrong speaking from the Moon. There is also the inspired solution to another crisis, when Parkes "loses" the spacecraft after a power outage, and Glenn tries to find it with frantic mathematical calculations before the team hits upon a solution of stunning simplicity.

The Dish is rich in its supporting characters. I like the mayor's daughter Marie (Lenka Kripac), who has moved on from the sunny, idealistic 1960s and already embodies the sullen, resentful 1970s. I like the way Mayor Bob and his wife so cheerfully and totally dote on each other—and the way she tries to get him to use the upscale name "May" for her, when he's been calling her "Maisie" as long as he can remember. And the way Rudi the security guard is in fact the town's greatest security threat.

With *The Dish* and *The Castle*, Sitch and his producing partner Michael Hirsh have made enormously entertaining movies. Perhaps just as important, they've made good-hearted movies. Recent Hollywood comedy has tilted toward vulgarity, humiliation, and bathroom humor. Sometimes I laugh at them, even a lot; but I don't feel this good afterward. *The Dish* has affection for every one of its characters, forgives them their trespasses, understands their ambitions, doesn't mock them, and is very funny. It placed second for the People's Choice Award at the 2000 Toronto Film Festival—after *Crouching Tiger, Hidden Dragon*. That's about right.

Divine Intervention ★ ★ ★

NO MPAA RATING, 89 m., 2003

Elia Suleiman (E. S.), Manal Khader (The Woman), Nayef Fahoum Daher (The Father), Amer Daher (Auni), Jamel Daher (Jamel). Directed by Elia Suleiman and produced by Humbert Balsan. Screenplay by Suleiman.

Divine Intervention is a mordant and bleak comedy, almost without dialogue, about Palestinians under Israeli occupation. Its characters live their daily lives in ways that are fundamentally defined by the divisions between them, and the scene with the most tension simply involves two drivers, one Israeli, one Palestinian, who lock eyes at a traffic light. Neither will look away. In their paralysis, while the light turns green and motorists behind them start to honk, the film sums up the situation in a nutshell.

The movie stars Elia Suleiman, who also wrote and directed it, and who has probably included more political references than an outsider is likely to understand. Most of his ideas are conveyed in scenes that would be right at home in a silent comedy, and on the few occasions when the characters talk, they say nothing more than what could be handled in a title card.

One running gag, for example, involves a household that throws its daily bag of garbage into the neighbor's yard. When the neighbor one day angrily throws it back, the original litterer complains. The neighbor responds: "The garbage we threw in your yard is the same garbage you threw in our garden." Nevertheless, the offender says, it is bad manners to throw it back.

This is the sort of parable that can cut both ways, and I get the sense that, for Suleiman, it doesn't matter at this point which neighbor represents an Israeli and which a Palestinian. The same simmering hostility is reflected in other scenes, as in one where a man takes a sledgehammer to a driveway so that his neighbor's car will get stuck in a hole.

There is a romance in the movie, involving the Suleiman character and a woman played by Manal Khader. Because they live in different districts and cannot easily pass from one to another, they meet in the parking lot of a checkpoint and sit in his car, holding hands and staring with hostility at the Israeli guards. In one stunning shot, she boldly walks across the border and right past the guards, who level their rifles at her but are unwilling to act.

Later, marksmen do shoot at her, in a weird scene involving special effects. After taking target practice at cardboard dummies that resemble her, the riflemen are amazed to see the woman herself materialize before them. She whirls and levitates. They shoot at her, but the bullets pause in midair and form themselves in a crown around her head, an image not impossible to decipher.

The film has been compared to the comedies of Jacques Tati, in which everyday actions build up to an unexpected comic revelation. I was reminded also of the Swedish film *Songs from the Second Floor*, set in a city where all seems normal but the inhabitants are seized with a strange apocalyptic madness. Suleiman's argument seems to be that the situation between Palestinians and Israelis has settled into a hopeless stalemate, in which everyday life incorporates elements of paranoia, resentment, and craziness.

The film was so well received around the world that it seemed likely to get an Oscar nomination but was rejected by the Motion Picture Academy because entries must be nominated by their nation of origin, and Palestine is not a nation. That's the sort of catch-22 that Suleiman might appreciate.

Divine Secrets of the Ya-Ya Sisterhood ★ ½
PG-13, 116 m., 2002

Sandra Bullock (Sidda), Ellen Burstyn (Vivi), Fionnula Flanagan (Teensy), James Garner (Shep Walker), Ashley Judd (Younger Vivi), Shirley Knight (Necie), Maggie Smith (Caro), Angus MacFadyen (Connor). Directed by Callie Khouri and produced by Bonnie Bruckheimer and Hunt Lowry. Screenplay by Khouri and Mark Andrus, based on the novels by Rebecca Walls.

Divine Secrets of the Ya-Ya Sisterhood has a title suggesting that the movie will be cute and about colorful, irrepressible, eccentric originals. Heavens deliver us. The Ya-Ya Sisterhood is rubber-stamped from the same mold that has produced an inexhaustible supply of fictional southern belles who drink too much, talk too much, think about themselves too much, try too hard to be the most unforgettable character you've ever met, and are, in general, insufferable. There must be a reason these stories are never set in Minnesota. Maybe it's because if you have to deal with the winter it makes you too realistic to become such a silly goose.

There is not a character in the movie with a shred of plausibility, not an event that is believ-able, not a confrontation that is not staged, not a moment that is not false. For their sins the sisterhood should be forced to spend the rest of their lives locked in a Winnebago camper. The only character in the movie who is bearable is the heroine as a young woman, played by Ashley Judd, who suggests that there was a time before the story's main events when this creature was palatable.

The heroine is Vivi, played by Ellen Burstyn in her sixties, Judd in her thirties and, as a child, by a moppet whose name I knoweth not. Yes, this is one of those movies that whisks around in time, as childhood vows echo down through the years before we whiplash back to the revelations of ancient secrets. If life were as simple as this movie, we would all have time to get in shape and learn Chinese.

As the film opens, four little girls gather around a campfire in the woods and create the Ya-Ya Sisterhood, exchanging drops of their blood, no doubt while sheriff's deputies and hounds are searching for them. Flash forward to the present. Vivi's daughter Sidda (Sandra Bullock) is a famous New York playwright, who tells an interviewer from *Time* magazine that she had a difficult childhood, mostly because of her mother. Whisk down to Louisiana, where Vivi reads the article and writes the daughter forever out of her life—less of a banishment than you might think, since they have not seen each other for years and Vivi doesn't even know of the existence of Sidda's Scottish fiancé, Connor (Angus MacFadyen).

Connor seems cut from the same mold as Shep Walker (James Garner), Vivi's husband. Both men stand around sheepishly while portraying superfluous males. No doubt their women notice them occasionally and are reminded that they exist and are a handy supply of sperm. Shep's role for decades has apparently been to beam approvingly as his wife gets drunk, pops pills, and stars in her own mind. Both men are illustrations of the impatience this genre has for men as a gender; they have the presence of souvenirs left on the mantel after a forgotten vacation.

Anyway. We meet the other adult survivors of the Ya-Ya Sisterhood: Teensy (Fionnula Flanagan), Necie (Shirley Knight), and Caro (Maggie Smith). Why do they all have names like pet animals? Perhaps because real names, like Martha,

Florence, or Esther would be an unseemly burden for such featherweights. Summoned by Vivi so that she can complain about Sidda, Teensy, Necie, and Caro fly north and kidnap Sidda, bringing her back to Louisiana so that they can show her that if she really knew the secrets of her mother's past, she would forgive her all shortcomings, real and imagined. Since the central great mystery of Vivi's past is how she has evaded rehab for so long, this quest is as pointless as the rest of the film.

Why do gifted actresses appear in such slop? Possibly because good roles for women are rare, for those over sixty precious. Possibly, too, because for all the other shortcomings of the film, no expense has been spared by the hair, makeup, and wardrobe departments, so that all of the women look just terrific all of the time, and when Vivi is distraught and emotional, she looks even more terrific. It's the kind of movie where the actresses must love watching the dailies as long as they don't listen to the dialogue.

The movie is a first-time directing job by Callie Khouri, author of *Thelma and Louise*. She seems uncertain what the film is about, where it is going, and what it hopes to prove apart from the most crashingly obvious clichés of light women's fiction. So inattentive is the screenplay that it goes to the trouble of providing Vivi with two other children in addition to Sidda, only to never mention them again. A fellow critic, Victoria Alexander, speculates that the secret in Vivi's past may have been that she drowned the kids, but that's too much to hope for.

Dogtown and Z-Boys ★ ★ ★
PG-13, 89 m., 2002

Themselves: Jay Adams, Tony Alva, Bob Biniak, Paul Constantineau, Shogo Kubo, Jim Muir, Peggy Oki, Stacy Peralta, Nathan Pratt, Wentzle Ruml, and Allen Sarlo. Directed by Stacy Peralta and produced by Agi Orsi. Screenplay by Peralta and Craig Stecyk.

Dogtown and Z-Boys, a documentary about how the humble skateboard became the launch pad for aerial gymnastics, answers a question I have long been curious about: How and why was the first skateboarder inspired to go aerial, to break contact with any surface and do acrobatics in midair? Consider that the pioneer was doing this for the very first time over a vertical drop of perhaps fifteen feet to a concrete surface. It's not the sort of thing you try out of idle curiosity.

The movie answers this and other questions in its history of a sport that grew out of idle time and boundless energy in the oceanfront neighborhood between Santa Monica and Venice. Today the area contains expensive condos and trendy restaurants, but circa 1975 it was the last remaining "beachfront slum" in the Los Angeles area. Druggies and hippies lived in cheap rentals and supported themselves by working in hot-dog stands, tattoo parlors, head shops, and saloons.

Surfing was the definitive lifestyle, the Beach Boys supplied the sound track, and tough surfer gangs staked out waves as their turf. In the afternoon, after the waves died down, they turned to skateboards, which at first were used as a variation of roller skates. But the members of the Zephyr Team, we learn, devised a new style of skateboarding, defying gravity, adding acrobatics, devising stunts. When a drought struck the area and thousands of swimming pools were drained, they invented vertical skateboarding on the walls of the empty pools. Sometimes they'd glide so close to the edge that only one of the board's four wheels still had a purchase on the lip. One day a Z-boy went airborne, and a new style was born—a style reflected today in Olympic ski acrobatics.

I am not sure whether the members of the Zephyr Team were solely responsible for all significant advances in the sport, or whether they only think they were. *Dogtown and Z-Boys* is directed by Stacy Peralta, an original and gifted team member, still a legend in the sport. Like many of the other Z-boys (and one Z-girl), he marketed himself, his name, his image, his products, and became a successful businessman and filmmaker while still surfing concrete. His film describes the evolution of skateboarding almost entirely in terms of the experience of himself and his friends. It's like the vet who thinks World War II centered around his platoon.

The Southern California lifestyle in general, and surfing and skateboarding in particular, are insular and narcissistic. People who live indoors have ideas. People who live outdoors have style. Here is an entire movie about looking cool while not wiping out. Call it a metaphor for life. There comes a point when sensible viewers will tire of being told how astonishing and unique each and every Z-boy was, while looking at repetitive still photos and home footage of skateboarders, but the film has an infectious enthusiasm, and we're touched by the film's conviction that all life centered on that place, that time, and that sport.

One question goes unanswered. Was anyone ever killed? Maimed? Crippled? There is a brief shot of someone on crutches, and a few shots showing skateboarders falling off their boards, but since aerial gymnastics high over hard surfaces are clearly dangerous and the Z-boys wear little or no protective gear, what's the story?

That most of them survived is made clear by info over the end credits, revealing that although one Zephyr Team member is in prison and another was "last seen in Mexico," the others all seem to have married, produced an average of two children, and found success in business. To the amazement, no doubt, of their parents.

Domestic Disturbance ★ ½
PG-13, 88 m., 2001

John Travolta (Frank Morrison), Vince Vaughn (Rick Barnes), Teri Polo (Susan Morrison Barnes), Matthew O'Leary (Danny Morrison), Steve Buscemi (Ray Coleman), Chris Ellis (Detective Warren), Nick Loren (Officer Foxx), Charles E. Bailey (Streetwalker). Directed by Harold Becker and produced by Becker, Donald De Line, and Jonathan D. Krane. Screenplay by Lewis Colick, William S. Comanor, and Gary Drucker.

John Travolta plays a nice guy better than just about anybody else, which is why it's hard to figure out why his seemingly intelligent wife would divorce him, in *Domestic Disturbance,* to marry Vince Vaughn, who plays a creep better than just about anybody else. Maybe that's because it's not until the wedding day that her new husband's best friend turns up, and it's Steve Buscemi, who plays the creep's best friend absolutely better than anybody else.

All of this is a setup for a child-in-terror movie, in which a child is the eyewitness to a brutal murder and the incineration of the body. Then the kid sees his father hammered to within an inch of his life, his mother beaten until she has a miscarriage, and himself as the unwitting cause of an electrocution. I mention these details as a way of explaining why the flywheels at the MPAA Ratings Board gave the movie a PG-13 rating. Certainly it doesn't deserve an R, like *Amelie* or *Waking Life.*

The movie is a paid holiday for its director, Harold Becker. I say this because I know what Becker is capable of. This is the same director who made *The Onion Field, The Boost,* and *Sea of Love.* If this is the best screenplay he could find to work on, and it probably was, all I can do is quote Norman Jewison at this year's Toronto Film Festival: "You wouldn't believe the shit the studios want you to make these days."

Sad, because there are scenes here showing what the film could have been, if it hadn't abandoned ambition and taken the low road. Travolta plays Frank Morrison, a boatbuilder and all-around nice guy—so nice he's even optimistic about the approaching marriage of his ex-wife, Susan (Teri Polo). Frank's son, Danny (Matthew O'Leary), is a little dubious about this new guy, so Frank even takes the three of them on a fishing trip together. But Danny is still upset, and has a habit of lying, running away, and not turning up for basketball games. He's Trying To Tell Them Something.

The fiancé is Rick Barnes (Vaughn), new in town, who has made a lot of money and is about to be honored by the chamber of commerce. But when his old buddy Ray (Buscemi) turns up uninvited at the wedding, Rick's eyes narrow and his pulse quickens and it is only a matter of time until the domestic drama turns into a domestic monster movie. You know it's a bad sign when you're Frank, the understanding ex-husband, standing around at the reception, and Ray tells you your ex-wife "must know some pretty good tricks to make old Rick settle down."

Suspense builds, not exactly slowly, in scenes involving an ominous game of catch. Then there's a scene that flies in the face of all logic, in the way the child is made to be an eyewitness to murder. The physical details are so unlikely they seem contrived even in a thriller. All leads up to a final confrontation so badly choreographed that I was not the least bit

171

surprised when the studio called to say the Chicago critics had seen "the wrong last reel," and would we like to see the correct reel on Monday? I agreed eagerly, expecting revised footage—but, no, the only problem was the earlier reel was lacking the final music mix.

Music is the last thing wrong with that reel. Apparently the filmmakers saw no problem with the way a key character enters on cue, at a dead run, without any way of knowing (from outside) where to run to, or why. No problem with a fight scene so incomprehensibly choreographed it seems to consist mostly of a chair. And no problem with a spectacularly inappropriate speech at a crucial moment (it's the one beginning, "Too bad..."). This speech provides additional information that is desperately unwanted, in a way that inspires only bad laughs from the audience, just when you want to end the movie without any more stumbles.

Donnie Darko ★ ★ ½
R, 122 m., 2001

Jake Gyllenhaal (Donnie Darko), Mary McDonnell (Rose Darko), Holmes Osborne (Eddie Darko), Jena Malone (Gretchen Ross), Drew Barrymore (Ms. Pomeroy), Daveigh Chase (Samantha Darko), Patrick Swayze (Jim Cunningham), Katharine Ross (Dr. Thurman), Noah Wyle (Dr. Monnitoff). Directed by Richard Kelly and produced by Adam Fields and Sean McKittrick. Screenplay by Kelly.

There is a kind of movie that calls out not merely to be experienced but to be solved. The plot coils back on itself in intriguing mind-puzzles, and moviegoers send bewildering e-mails to one another explaining it. First came *Mulholland Dr.*, which has inspired countless explanations, all convincing, none in agreement, and now here is *Donnie Darko*, the story of a teenage boy who receives bulletins about the future from a large and demonic rabbit.

The film stars Jake Gyllenhaal, from *October Sky*, as Donnie Darko, a high school student whose test scores are "intimidating," whose pose is to be likable and sardonic at once, and who occasionally forgets to take his medication, for unspecified but possibly alarming reasons. He is seeing a psychiatrist (Katharine Ross),

who uses hypnosis to discover that he has a nocturnal visitor who leads him on sleepwalking expeditions. One of these trips is fortunate, because while he's out of the house a 747 jet engine falls directly through his bedroom.

The movie is grounded solidly in a leafy suburban setting, where the neighbors gather behind police lines while a big flatbed truck hauls the engine away and the FBI questions the Darko family. There is much unexplained. For example, no airline is reporting that an engine is missing from one of its jets. Where did the engine come from? Donnie has no more idea than anyone else, and we follow him through high school days with an English teacher (Drew Barrymore) who is sympathetic, and a gym teacher who requires the class to locate imaginary experiences on a "lifeline" between Fear and Love. When Donnie suggests what the gym teacher can do with her lifeline, he and his parents are called in for a conference with the principal—and one of the movie's charms is that they are not shocked but amused.

Donnie comes from a happy enough home. His mother (Mary McDonnell) is sensible and cheerful, and his father (Holmes Osborne) is imperturbable. An older sister announces at dinner that she will vote for Dukakis (it is autumn 1988), and a younger sister is a sly instigator, but *Donnie Darko* doesn't go the well-traveled route of making its hero the tortured victim of an unhappy home. Donnie even gets a girlfriend (Jena Malone) during the course of the movie.

Yet disturbing undercurrents are gathering. Donnie's nocturnal rabbit-wizard informs him the end of the world is near. Donnie becomes able to see time lines in front of his family—semitransparent liquid arrows that seem to lead them into the future. He becomes fascinated by the theory of wormholes, and discovers that a key book, *The Philosophy of Time Travel*, was written by a neighbor, Roberta Sparrow—known to the neighborhood as Grandma Death, and now, at 100, reduced to endless round trips to her mailbox for a letter that never comes.

This setup and development is fascinating, the payoff less so. I could tell you what I think happens at the end, and what the movie is about, but I would not be sure I was right. The movie builds twists on top of turns until the plot wheel revolves one time too many and we're left scratching our heads. We don't demand answers at the end, but we want some kind of closure; Keyser Soze may not explain everything in *The Usual Suspects,* but it *feels* like he does.

Richard Kelly, the first-time writer-director, is obviously talented—not least at creating a disturbing atmosphere out of the materials of real life. His mysterious jet engine is a masterstroke. He sees his characters freshly and clearly, and never reduces them to formulas. In Jake Gyllenhaal he finds an actor able to suggest an intriguing kind of disturbance; the character is more curious than frightened, more quixotic than eccentric, and he sets a nice tone for the movie. But somehow the control fades in the closing scenes, and our hands, which have been so full, close on emptiness. *Donnie Darko* is the one that got away. But it was fun trying to land it.

Don't Say a Word ★ ★ ½
R, 110 m., 2001

Michael Douglas (Dr. Nathan Conrad), Sean Bean (Patrick B. Koster), Brittany Murphy (Elisabeth Burrows), Sky McCole Bartusiak (Jessie Conrad), Guy Torrey (Martin J. Dolen), Jennifer Esposito (Detective Sandra Cassidy), Oliver Platt (Dr. Sachs). Directed by Gary Fleder and produced by Arnon Milchan, Arnold Kopelson, and Anne Kopelson. Screenplay by Anthony Peckham and Patrick Smith Kelly, based on the book by Andrew Klavan.

Don't Say a Word is one of those movies where a happy professional couple suddenly find their lives threatened by depraved outsiders. Like airline owner Mel Gibson in *Ransom* and Dr. Harrison Ford in *Frantic,* psychiatrist Michael Douglas has to discover if he possesses the basic instincts to fight to the death for the ones he loves.

The movie turns this into a race against the clock when kidnappers take his eight-year-old daughter and give him a five P.M. deadline. To do what? To pry a six-digit number from the memory of a mental patient. And that's not all. For the second half of the movie, there are four parallel plots, involving Douglas working

over the patient, his wife struggling to defend herself with her leg in a cast, his daughter trying to outsmart the kidnappers, and a woman detective stumbling over the crime during a related investigation.

Plotting this dense is its own reward. We cast loose from the shores of plausibility and are tossed by the waves of contrivance. I like thrillers better when they put believable characters in possible situations (*The Deep End,* with Tilda Swinton, was accused of implausibility but is *cinema verité* compared to this). But I also have a sneaky affection for Douglas thrillers where he starts out as a sleek, rich businessman and ends up with an ax in his hand. Who else can start out so well groomed and end up as such a mad dog?

The movie was directed by Gary Fleder, whose *Kiss the Girls* (1997) was taut and stylish. Here again he shows a poetic visual touch, cutting between cozy domestic interiors and action scenes shot in gritty grays and blues. The look of his pictures shows the touch of an artist, and he has a fondness for character quirks that flavors the material. Consider Douglas's fellow psychiatrist, played by Oliver Platt, who has his own reasons for immediate results.

The bank robbery opening the movie is recycled from countless similar scenes, but then the movie makes a twist and the plot keeps piling it on. What's remarkable is how certain performances, especially Brittany Murphy's as the mental patient and Sky McCole Bartusiak's as the kidnapped girl, find their own rhythm and truth in the middle of all that urgency.

Some might wonder (actually, I might wonder) why the villain can wait ten years and then give Douglas only eight hours to work with his patient. Or at the way Murphy's character is sane and insane to suit the conveniences of the plot (a glib explanation doesn't account for what should be the lingering effects of drugs). And the police detective (Jennifer Esposito) is pushing it when she arrives in the nick of time. Sean Bean, as the villain who wants his "property," is as malevolent as he can be without suffering serious dental damage.

Douglas has made roles like this his own, and redeems them by skirting just barely this side of overacting—which is about where a character in this plot should be positioned.

Shame that his subtler and more human work in movies like *Wonder Boys* is seen by smaller audiences than his fatal/basic/instinct/attraction/disclosure movies.

The end of *Don't Say a Word* does descend, as so many thrillers do, to a species of a chase. But the final locations are darkly effective, and I liked the way the villain arrives at a spectacular end. But the movie as a whole looks and occasionally plays better than it is. There is a point, when the wife is struggling with her leg cast and crutches and the daughter is cleverly signaling her whereabouts and Douglas is trying to perform instant psychiatry at an emergency room tempo, and flashbacks accompany the time-honored Visit to the Scene of the Previous Trauma, when it just all seemed laid on too thick. There is a difference between racing through a thriller and wallowing in it.

Double Take ★
PG-13, 88 m., 2001

Orlando Jones (Daryl Chase), Eddie Griffin (Freddy Tiffany), Gary Grubbs (T. J. McCready), Daniel Roebuck (Agent Norville), Sterling Macer Jr. (Agent Gradney), Benny Nieves (Martinez), Garcelle Beauvais (Chloe Kent), Vivica A. Fox (Shari). Directed by George Gallo and produced by David Permut and Brett Ratner. Screenplay by Gallo, based on *Across the Bridge* by Graham Greene.

Double Take is the kind of double-triple-reverse movie that can drive you nuts because you can't count on *anything* in the plot. Characters, motivations, and true identities change from scene to scene at the whim of the screenplay. Finally, you weary of trying to follow the story. You can get the rug jerked out from under you only so many times before you realize the movie has the attention span of a gnat, and thinks you do too.

Orlando Jones stars as Daryl Chase, a businessman who becomes the dupe of a street hustler named Freddy Tiffany (Eddie Griffin). The movie opens with Daryl as the victim of a complicated briefcase-theft scam, which turns out not to be what it seems, and to involve more people than it appears to involve. Freddy is at the center of it, and Daryl soon learns that Freddy will be at the center of everything in his life for the rest of the movie.

Who is this guy? He seems to have an almost supernatural ability to materialize anywhere, to know Daryl's secret plans, to pop up like a genie, and to embarrass him with a jive-talking routine that seems recycled out of the black exploitation pictures of the 1970s. The movie's attitudes seem so dated, indeed, that when I saw a computer screen, it came as a shock: The movie's period feels as much pre-desktop as it does pretaste.

Freddy embarrasses Daryl a few more times, including during a fashion show, where he appears on the runway and shoulders aside the models. Meanwhile, Daryl discovers he is under attack by mysterious forces, for reasons he cannot understand, and to his surprise Freddy turns out to be an ally. The obnoxious little sprite even helps him out of a dangerous spot in a train station by changing clothes with him, after which the two men find themselves in the dining car of a train headed for Mexico. The switch in wardrobe of course inspires a switch in personalities: Freddy orders from the menu in a gourmet-snob accent, while Daryl is magically transformed into a ghetto caricature who embarrasses the waiter by demanding Schlitz Malt Liquor.

And so on. Wardrobes, identities, motivations, and rationales are exchanged in a dizzying series of laboriously devised "surprises," until we find out that nothing is as it seems, and that isn't as it seems, either. It's not that we expect a movie like this to be consistent or make sense. It's that when the double-reverse plotting kicks in, we want it to be funny, or entertaining, or anything but dreary and arbitrary and frustrating.

The movie was directed by George Gallo, who wrote the much better *Midnight Run* and here again has latched onto the idea of a nice guy and an obnoxious one involved in a road trip together. One of his problems is with Eddie Griffin. Here is a fast-thinking, fast-talking, nimble actor who no doubt has good performances in him, but his Freddy Tiffany is unbearable—so obnoxious he approaches the fingernails-on-a-blackboard category. You know you're in trouble when your heart sinks every time a movie's live wire appears on the screen. I realized there was no hope for the movie, because the plot and characters had alienated me beyond repair. If an audience is going to be entertained by a film, first they have to be able to stand it.

Down to Earth ★
PG-13, 87 m., 2001

Chris Rock (Lance Barton), Regina King (Suntee), Mark Addy (Cisco), Eugene Levy (Keyes), Frankie Faison (Whitney), Jennifer Coolidge (Mrs. Wellington), Greg Germann (Sklar), Chazz Palminteri (Mr. King). Directed by Chris Weitz and Paul Weitz and produced by Sean Daniel, James Jacks, and Michael Rotenberg. Screenplay by Elaine May, Warren Beatty, Chris Rock, Lance Crouther, Ali LeRoi, and Louis C.K.

Down to Earth is an astonishingly bad movie, and the most astonishing thing about it comes in the credits: "Written by Elaine May, Warren Beatty, Chris Rock, Lance Crouther, Ali LeRoi, and Louis C.K." These are credits that deserve a place in the Writer's Hall of Fame, right next to the 1929 version of *The Taming of the Shrew* ("screenplay by William Shakespeare, with additional dialogue by Sam Taylor").

Yes, Chris Rock and his writing partners have adapted Elaine May's Oscar-nominated 1978 screenplay for *Heaven Can Wait* (Warren Beatty falls more in the Sam Taylor category). It wasn't broke, but boy, do they fix it.

The premise: Lance Barton (Rock) is a lousy stand-up comic, booed off the stage during an amateur night at the Apollo Theater. Even his faithful manager, Whitney (Frankie Faison), despairs for him. Disaster strikes. Lance is flattened by a truck, goes to heaven, and discovers from his attending angel (Eugene Levy) that an error has been made. He was taken before his time. There is a meeting with God, a.k.a. "Mr. King" (Chazz Palminteri), who agrees to send him back to Earth for the unexpired portion of his stay.

The catch is, only one body is available: Mr. Wellington, an old white millionaire. Lance takes what he can get and returns to Earth, where he finds a sticky situation: His sexpot wife (Jennifer Coolidge) is having an affair with his assistant, who is stealing his money. Meanwhile, Lance, from his vantage point inside Mr. Wellington, falls in love with a young African-American beauty named Suntee (Regina King).

Let's draw to a halt and consider the situation as it now stands. The world sees an old white millionaire. So does Suntee, who has disliked him up until the point where Lance occupies the body. But we in the audience see Chris Rock. Of course, Rock and Regina King make an agreeable couple, but we have to keep reminding ourselves he's a geezer, and so does she, I guess, since soon they are holding hands and other parts.

The essential comic element here, I think, is the disparity between the two lovers, and the underlying truth that they are actually a good match. Wouldn't that be funnier if Mr. Wellington looked like . . . Mr. Wellington? He could be played by Martin Landau, although, come to think of it, Martin Landau played an old white millionaire who got involved with Halle Berry and Troy Beyer in *B.A.P.S.* (1997), and don't run out to Blockbuster for *that* one.

The real problem with Mr. Wellington being played by an old white guy, even though he is an old white guy, is that the movie stars Chris Rock, who is getting the big bucks, and Chris Rock fans do not want to watch Martin Landau oscillating with Regina King no matter *who* is inside him. That means that in the world of the movie everyone sees an old white guy, but we have, like, these magic glasses, I guess, that allow us to see Chris Rock. Well, once or twice we sort of catch a glimpse of the millionaire, in reflections and things, but nothing is done with this promising possibility.

The story then involves plots against and by Mr. Wellington, plus Lance's scheming to get a better replacement body, plus Suntee being required to fly in the face of emotional logic and then fly back again, having been issued an emotional round-trip ticket. If I were an actor, I would make a resolution to turn down all parts in which I fall in and out of love at a moment's notice, without logical reason, purely for the convenience of the plot.

Chris Rock is funny and talented, and so I have said several times. I even proposed him as emcee for the Academy Awards (they went for an old white millionaire). This project must have looked promising, since the directors are the Weitz brothers, Chris and Paul Weitz, fresh from *American Pie*. But the movie is dead in the water.

Down with Love ★ ★ ★
PG-13, 94 m., 2003

Renée Zellweger (Barbara Novak), Ewan McGregor (Catcher Block), David Hyde Pierce (Peter MacMannus), Sarah Paulson (Vikki Hiller), Tony Randall (Theodore Banner). Directed by Peyton Reed and produced by Bruce Cohen and Dan Jinks. Screenplay by Eve Ahlert and Dennis Drake.

Down with Love opens with the big Cinema-Scope logo that once announced 20th Century Fox mass-market entertainments. The titles show animated letters bouncing each other off the screen, and the music is chirpy. The movie's opening scenes confirm these clues: This is a movie set in 1962, and filmed in the style of those Doris Day–Rock Hudson classics about the battle of the sexes. That it adds an unexpected twist is part of the fun.

Maybe the filmmakers believe that movies lost something when they added irony. *Far from Heaven* was in the style of a 1957 Universal melodrama, and now this wide-screen comedy, with bright colors and enormous sets filled with postwar modern furniture, wants to remember a time before the sexual revolution.

Well, just barely before. Its heroine is determined to usher it in. She is Barbara Novak (Renée Zellweger), a New Englander whose new best-seller, *Down with Love,* has just pushed John F. Kennedy's *Profiles in Courage* off the charts (and about time, too, since JFK's book was published in 1956). Novak's book announces a new woman who will not be subservient to men in the workplace, and will call her own shots in the bedroom.

This attracts the attention of Catcher Block (Ewan McGregor), a womanizing male chauvinist pig who works as a magazine writer, specializing in exposés. He bets his boss Peter MacMannus (David Hyde Pierce) that he can seduce Barbara, prove she's an old-fashioned woman at heart, and write a sensational article

about it. Meanwhile, Barbara's publisher, Vikki Hiller (Sarah Paulson), announces a publicity coup: She's arranged an interview with . . . well, Catcher Block, of course.

Any movie fan can figure out the 1962 casting of these characters. Barbara and Catcher are Doris Day and Rock Hudson, Vikki is Lauren Bacall, and Peter is Tony Randall; Randall himself, in fact, is in this movie, as chairman of the board. And the plot resembles Doris Day's movies in the sex department: Barbara Novak talks a lot about sex and gets in precarious positions, but never quite compromises her principles.

The movie has a lot of fun with the split-screen techniques of the 1960s, which exploited the extra-wide screen. If you remember the split-screen phone calls in *Pillow Talk,* you'll enjoy the same technique here, in a series of calls where Catcher stands up Barbara on a series of dinner dates. *Down with Love* borrows a technique from the Austin Powers series (itself a throwback to the 1960s) with scenes in which the split screen is used to suggest strenuous sexual activity that is, in fact, quite innocently nonsexual.

I don't believe anyone will equal whatever it was that Doris Day had; she was one of a kind. But Renée Zellweger comes closest, with her wide eyes, naive innocence, and almost aggressive sincerity. She has a speech toward the end of the movie where the camera simply remains still and regards her, as a torrent of words pours out from her character's innermost soul.

Down with Love is no better or worse than the movies that inspired it, but that is a compliment, I think. It recalls a time when society had more rigid rules for the genders, and thus more adventure in transcending them. And it relishes the big scene where a hypocrite gets his comeuppance. The very concept of "comeuppance" is obsolete in these permissive modern times, when few movie characters have a sense of shame and behavior is justified in terms of pure selfishness. Barbara Novak's outrage at sneaky behavior is one of the movie's most refreshing elements from the 1960s—not to say she isn't above a few neat tricks herself.

Dracula: Pages from a Virgin's Diary
★ ★ ★ ½
NO MPAA RATING, 75 m., 2003

Zhang Wei-Qiang (Dracula), Tara Birtwhistle (Lucy Westernra), David Moroni (Dr. Van Helsing), CindyMarie Small (Mina Murray), Johnny Wright (Jonathon Harker), Stephane Leonard (Arthur Holmwood), Matthew Johnson (Jack Seward), Keir Knight (Quincy Morris). Directed by Guy Maddin and produced by Vonnie Von Helmolt. Screenplay by Mark Godden.

The ballet as a silent movie with an orchestra. I'd never thought of it that way before. The dancers embody the characters, express emotion with their bodies and faces, try to translate feeling and speech into physical movement. They are borne up on the wings of the music. *Dracula: Pages from a Virgin's Diary* uses (and improvises on and kids and abuses) the style of silent films to record a production of *Dracula* by the Royal Winnipeg Ballet. The film is poetic and erotic, creepy and melodramatic, overwrought and sometimes mocking, as if F. W. Murnau's *Nosferatu* (1922) had a long-lost musical version.

The director is Guy Maddin, who lives in Winnipeg and is Canada's poet laureate of cinematic weirdness. His films often look as if the silent era had continued right on into today's ironic stylistic drolleries; he made a 2000 short named *The Heart of the World* that got more applause than most of the films it preceded at the Toronto film festival. Imagine *Metropolis* in hyderdrive.

In *Dracula: Pages from a Virgin's Diary* he begins with the Royal Winnipeg Ballet's stage production of *Dracula,* choreographed and produced by Mark Godden, and takes it through a series of transformations into something that looks a lot like a silent film but feels like avant-garde theater. The music is by Mahler (the first and second symphonies), the visuals include all the favorite devices of the silent period (wipes, iris shots, soft framing, intertitles, tinting), and the effect is—well, surprisingly effective. The emphasis is on the erotic mystery surrounding Dracula, and the film underlines the curious impression we sometimes have in vampire films that the victims experience orgasm as the fangs sink in.

The Dracula story is so easily mocked and satirized that it is good to be reminded of the unsettling erotic horror that it possesses in the hands of a Murnau or Werner Herzog (1979) or now Maddin. Not that Maddin is above poking it in the ribs (sample titles: "Why can't a woman marry two men? Or as many as want her?" and "She's filled with polluted blood!").

It deals primarily with Count Dracula's seduction, if that is the word, of Lucy Westernra (Tara Birtwhistle), whose name in Bram Stoker's novel was Westenra. The "westernization" is no doubt to underline Dracula's own relocation from Transylvania to the mysterious East; he is played here by the ballet's Zhang Wei-Qiang, whose stock melodramatic Asian characteristics are made not much more subtle than D. W. Griffith's Cheng Haun in *Broken Blossoms* (1919).

Jonathon Harker (Johnny Wright), the hapless estate agent, and his fiancée, Mina (Cindy-Marie Small), who both played major roles in the Stoker novel and most of the resulting films, have been somewhat downgraded in importance here, but Van Helsing (David Moroni), the vampire expert and hater, is well employed, and there are the usual crowds of townspeople to exhume coffins and perform other useful tasks. The story is less a narrative than an evocation of the vampire's world. Maddin shoots on sets and locations that resemble silent films in their overwrought and bold imagery, and he combines a number of low-tech filming formats, including 16 mm and Super 8; among the evocative stills on the movie's Website (www.zeitgeistfilms.com) is one in which Maddin is seen photographing with a tiny camera.

For the purposes of this film, the original images are only a starting point. Madden manipulates them with filters, adds grain, softens focus, moves through them with wipes, and takes the silent technique of tinting to a jolly extreme with blood and capes that suddenly flood the screen with red.

Dracula: Pages from a Virgin's Diary is not concerned with the story mechanics of moving from A to B. At times it feels almost like one of those old silent films where scenes have gone missing and there are jumps in the chronology.

This is not a problem but an enhancement, creating for us the sensation of glimpsing snatches of a dream. So many films are more or less alike that it's jolting to see a film that deals with a familiar story but looks like no other.

Dr. Dolittle 2 ★ ★ ★
PG, 88 m., 2001

Eddie Murphy (Dr. John Dolittle), Jeffrey Jones (Joseph Potter), Kevin Pollak (Jack Riley), Steve Irwin (Himself), Kyla Pratt (Maya Dolittle), Raven-Symone (Charisse Dolittle), Kristen Wilson (Lisa Dolittle). With the voices of: Norm Macdonald (Lucky), Lisa Kudrow (Ava), Steve Zahn (Archie), and Molly Shannon. Directed by Steve Carr and produced by John Davis and Joseph Singer. Screenplay by Larry Levin, based on the stories of Hugh Lofting.

Dr. Dolittle 2 is a cute, crude, and good-hearted movie about a doctor who can talk to the animals—and listen, too, often to them loudly passing gas. It combines the charm of the 1998 movie with the current Hollywood obsession with intestinal tracts, resulting in a movie that kids, with their intense interest in digestive details, may find fascinating.

Eddie Murphy stars as a famous veterinarian who now runs his own animal clinic (complete with twelve-step therapy groups for ownerless dogs). His home life is almost more demanding than his work: His daughter Charisse (Raven-Symone) is sixteen and starting to date, and his wife (Kristen Wilson) is remarkably patient with a house full of pets and a yard full of animals, including a raccoon who comes to summon the doctor to an emergency.

The crisis: A forest is about to be leveled by a plump, sneering enemy of the ecology (Jeffrey Jones), and the animals, led by a Godfather-style beaver, hope Dolittle can help. The forester is represented by a slick attorney (Kevin Pollack), and Dolittle recruits his lawyer wife to defend his case in court.

Much depends on the fact that the land is the habitat of a female bear, member of a protected species. But since she can't reproduce all by herself, the villain's lawyer argues, what's the use of preserving her habitat? Dolittle, thinking fast, recruits a male performing bear from a circus. Can the bear be persuaded to perform those functions that a male bear in the wild does naturally? When the bear proves shy, Dolittle turns into an animal sex counselor.

All of this is helped immeasurably by the doctor's ability to speak to the animals (who all speak the same language—English, curiously enough). There are no nasty animals in the movie, except for a crocodile who does his dirty work just offscreen, and the bear is so accommodating he actually visits Dolittle in a rustic restaurant, enters the toilet, and seems familiar with the function, if not the limitations, of a toilet seat. The bear, in fact, is one of the funniest elements in the movie; it is about as happy to be in the forest as Woody Allen would be.

There's also a sequence, perhaps inspired by a scene in *The Edge*, where the bear creeps out onto a precariously balanced log to try to grab some honey and prove himself a man, or bear. Will the bear master the intricacies of the reproductive process? Will Dr. and Mrs. Dolittle accept a measly compromise offer of ten acres? The story takes an unexpected twist when the animals of the world go on strike and shut down Sea World.

Dr. Dolittle 2 is not the kind of movie that rewards deep study, and it's an easy assignment for Murphy, whose work in the *Nutty Professor* movies is much more versatile (and funnier). As the PG rating suggests, this is a movie aimed at younger audiences, who are likely to enjoy the cute animals, the simple plot, the broad humor, and Dolittle's amazingly detailed explanation (to the bear) of how a bear's elimination system shuts itself down during hibernation.

Dreamcatcher ★ ½
R, 134 m., 2003

Morgan Freeman (Colonel Abraham Curtis), Thomas Jane (Dr. Henry Devlin), Jason Lee (Joe "Beaver" Clarendon), Damian Lewis (Gary "Jonesy" Jones), Timothy Olyphant (Pete Moore), Donnie Wahlberg (Douglas "Duddits" Cavell), Tom Sizemore (Captain Owen Underhill). Directed by Lawrence Kasdan and produced by Kasdan and Charles Okun. Screenplay by William Goldman and Kasdan, based on the novel by Stephen King.

Dreamcatcher begins as the intriguing story of

friends who share a telepathic gift, and ends as a monster movie of stunning awfulness. What went wrong? How could director Lawrence Kasdan and writer William Goldman be responsible for a film that goes so awesomely cuckoo? How could even Morgan Freeman, an actor all but impervious to bad material, be brought down by the awfulness? Goldman, who has written insightfully about the screenwriter's trade, may get a long, sad book out of this one.

The movie is based on a novel by Stephen King, unread by me, apparently much altered for the screen version, especially in the appalling closing sequences. I have just finished the audiobook of King's *From a Buick 8*, was a fan of his *Hearts in Atlantis*, and like the way his heart tugs him away from horror ingredients and into the human element in his stories.

Here the story begins so promisingly that I hoped, or assumed, it would continue on the same track: Childhood friends, united in a form of telepathy by a mentally retarded kid they protect, grow up to share psychic gifts and to deal with the consequences. The problem of *really* being telepathic is a favorite science-fiction theme. If you could read minds, would you be undone by the despair and anguish being broadcast all around you? This is unfortunately not the problem explored by *Dreamcatcher*.

The movie does have a visualization of the memory process that is brilliant filmmaking; after the character Gary "Jonesy" Jones (Damian Lewis) has his mind occupied by an alien intelligence, he is able to survive hidden within it by concealing his presence inside a vast memory warehouse, visualized by Kasdan as an infinitely unfolding series of rooms containing Jonesy's memories. This idea is like a smaller, personal version of Jorge Luis Borges's *The Library of Babel*, the imaginary library that contains all possible editions of all possible books. I can imagine many scenes set in the warehouse—it's such a good idea it could support an entire movie—but the film proceeds relentlessly to abandon this earlier inspiration in its quest for the barfable.

But let me back up. We meet at the outset childhood friends Henry Devlin, Joe "Beaver" Clarendon, Jonesy Jones, and Pete Moore. They happen upon Douglas "Duddits" Cavell, a retarded boy being bullied by older kids, and they defend him with wit and imagination. He's

grateful, and in some way he serves as a nexus for all of them to form a precognitive, psychic network. It isn't high-level or controllable, but it's there.

Then we meet them as adults, played by (in order) Thomas Jane, Jason Lee, Lewis, and Timothy Olyphant (Duddits is now Donnie Wahlberg). When Jonesy has an accident of startling suddenness, that serves as the catalyst for a trip to the woods, where the hunters turn into the hunted as alien beings attack.

It would be well not to linger on plot details, since if you are going to see the movie, you will want them to be surprises. Let me just say that the aliens, who look like a cross between the creature in *Alien* and the things that crawled out of the drains in that David Cronenberg movie, exhibit the same problem I often have with such beings: How can an alien that consists primarily of teeth and an appetite, that apparently has no limbs, tools, or language, travel to Earth in the first place? Are they little clone creatures for a superior race? Perhaps; an alien nicknamed Mr. Gray turns up, who looks and behaves quite differently, for a while.

For these aliens, space travel is a prologue for trips taking them where few have gone before; they explode from the business end of the intestinal tract, through that orifice we would be least willing to lend them for their activities. The movie, perhaps as a result, has as many farts as the worst teenage comedy—which is to say, too many farts for a movie that keeps insisting, with mounting implausibility, that it is intended to be good. These creatures are given a name by the characters that translates in a family newspaper as Crap Weasels.

When Morgan Freeman turns up belatedly in a movie, that is usually a good sign, because no matter what has gone before, he is likely to import more wit and interest. Not this time. He plays Colonel Abraham Curtis, a hard-line military man dedicated to doing what the military always does in alien movies, which is to blast the aliens to pieces and ask questions later. This is infinitely less interesting than a scene in King's *Buick 8* where a curious state trooper dissects a batlike thing that seems to have popped through a portal from another world. King's description of the autopsy of weird alien organs is scarier than all the gnashings and disembowelments in *Dreamcatcher*.

When the filmmakers are capable of the first half of *Dreamcatcher*, what came over them in the second half? What inspired their descent into the absurd? On the evidence here, we can say what we already knew: Lawrence Kasdan is a wonderful director of personal dramas *(Grand Canyon, The Accidental Tourist, Mumford)*. When it comes to Crap Weasels, his heart just doesn't seem to be in it.

Driven ★ ★ ½
PG-13, 109 m., 2001

Sylvester Stallone (Joe Tanto), Til Schweiger (Beau Brandenburg), Kip Pardue (Jimmy Bly), Burt Reynolds (Carl Henry), Estella Warren (Sophia Simone), Cristian de la Fuente (Memo Moreno), Gina Gershon (Cathy Moreno), Robert Sean Leonard (DeMille Bly), Stacy Edwards (Lucretia "Luc" Jones). Directed by Renny Harlin and produced by Elie Samaha, Sylvester Stallone, and Harlin. Screenplay by Stallone, based on a story by Stallone and Harlin.

Whether they admit it or not, many fans go to auto races to see crashes, and they'll see a lot of them in *Driven*. Cars slam into walls, tumble upside down, come apart in midair, land in water, explode in flames, fall on top of other cars and disintegrate. So serious are these crashes that one of the movie's heroes injures his ankle. No one is killed, I guess. There is a horrible multicar pileup in the final race, but it serves only to clear the field for the movie's stars and is never referred to again.

Most of the crashes are apparently done with special effects, and there are subtle moments when you can tell that: A car in midair will jerk into split-second freeze-frames, or pieces of sheet metal will fly toward us more slowly than in real life. But we get our money's worth; the races consist of quick cutting between long shots of real races, close-ups of narrowed eyes behind face masks, close-ups of feet pushing the pedal to the metal, POV shots of the track (sometimes in a blur or haze), the crashes, and the finish lines.

Director Renny Harlin, an expert at action, has made better pictures *(Die Hard 2, Cutthroat Island)*, but delivers the goods here and adds a wall-to-wall music track that pumps up the volume. He cuts almost as quickly in the dialogue scenes; his camera, often handheld, circles the actors and sometimes he cuts after every line of dialogue. The music continues. *Driven* is a movie by, for, and about the attention deficit disordered.

Sylvester Stallone stars and wrote the screenplay, which was originally inspired by his desire to make a biopic about the Brazilian racing great Ayrtan Senna, who was killed in 1994. The first drafts may have contained bio, but the final draft is all pic, and the characters are off the shelf. Stallone plays a hotshot retired driver whose comeback problems are quickly dealt with ("What about the fear?" "The fear is gone"). Burt Reynolds is the wheelchair-bound owner of a racing team. Til Schweiger plays the defending champion from Germany. Kip Pardue plays a rookie phenom, in a role once penciled in for Leonardo DiCaprio. And Robert Sean Leonard is the phenom's brother, required to utter the thankless dialogue: "I saw this eight-year-old goofy-looking kid on a go-kart come from three laps behind to beat kids twice his age." Think about that. Three laps on a go-kart track. At Captain Mike's Go-Kart Track in Sawyer, Michigan, where I practice the sport, you don't even get enough time to *fall* that far behind.

The movie is rated PG-13, and so the women, like the drivers, have to act with their eyes, lips, and shoulders. The gorgeous Canadian supermodel Estella Warren plays Sophia, who is dumped by the champ, dates the rookie, and is taken back by the champ. She has lips that could cushion a nasty fall and swimmer's shoulders that look great except in that off-the-shoulder dress that makes them look wider than Stallone's. Gina Gershon plays the mean girl who used to date Stallone and dumped him for another driver ("He's a younger, better you," she explains). Gershon has sexy lips too, but goes for sneers, pouts, and curls—she's doing a self-satire. Then there's a journalist played by Stacy Edwards who will follow the team for the season. "She's doing an exposé on male dominance in sports," explains Reynolds, only smiling a little, as if to himself, at this line.

It's tough to fit all these relationships in

between the races, but Harlin uses an interesting device. Not only does Reynolds communicate with his team members by headset, but so do the girls; there are times when three people are shouting advice at a guy doing 195 miles per hour. The Edwards character nevertheless disappears so inexplicably from the story (apart from reaction shots) that when she's there at the end, Stallone (who has been holding hands with her) says, "Glad you stuck around."

The movie is so filled with action that dramatic conflict would be more than we could handle, so all of the characters are nice. There are no villains. There is a shoving match over the girl, but no real fights, and afterward a character actually apologizes.

One of the action sequences is noteworthy. The phenom, mad at the girl, steals a race car from an auto show in Chicago and hits 195 miles per hour through the Chicago Loop with Stallone chasing him in another race car. Although this high-speed chase is tracked by helicopters, so inefficient are the Chicago police that after the kid pulls over, Stallone has time to give him the first trophy he ever won *and* deliver a lecture about faith and will—and *still* we don't even hear any sirens in the background from the Chicago police—perhaps because, as students of geography will observe, the two characters are now in Toronto.

I mentioned that all of the characters are nice (except for Gershon, who sticks to bitchiness in a stubborn show of integrity). The feel-good ending is a masterpiece even in a season where no audience can be allowed to exit without reassurance. There's an endless happy-happy closing montage at a victory celebration, with hugs and champagne, and all the characters smile at all the other characters, and outstanding disagreements are resolved with significant little nods.

Drumline ★ ★ ★
PG-13, 134 m., 2002

Nick Cannon (Devon), Zoë Saldana (Laila), Orlando Jones (Dr. James Lee), Leonard Roberts (Sean), GQ (Jayson), Jason Weaver (Ernest), Earl Poitier (Charles), J. Anthony Brown (Mr. Wade). Directed by Charles Stone and produced by Timothy M. Bourne, Wendy Finerman, and Jody Gerson. Screenplay by Tina Gordon Chism and Shawn Schepps.

When the first half is over, the show begins. So *Drumline* advises us, in a story centered on the marching band of a predominantly black university in Atlanta. Devon (Nick Cannon), a drummer so good he was personally recruited by the bandmaster, journeys from Harlem to the middle-class world of Atlanta A&T, where he is the best drummer in the band, and the most troublesome.

He's a cocky hotshot, a showboat who adds a solo to the end of his audition piece and upstages his section leader in front of thousands of fans during a half-time show. The movie shows him gradually drumming himself out of the band, and out of favor with Laila (Zoë Saldana), the dance major he's dating. It also shows him growing up, learning some lessons, and making a friend out of a former enemy.

The film sets Devon's story against the background of the BET Big Southern Classic, a (fictional) annual competition among marching bands that's held in Atlanta. His school's traditional rival is crosstown Morris Brown College, a real school whose band is famed for its half-time shows. MBC's band is flashy and high-stepping, doing anything to please the crowd, while Atlanta A&T's bandmaster, Dr. James Lee (Orlando Jones), has more serious musical tastes and believes the primary job of a band member is to learn.

Drumline, directed by Charles Stone and written by Tina Gordon Chism and Shawn Schepps, is entertaining for what it does, and admirable for what it doesn't do. It gets us involved in band politics and strategy, gives us a lot of entertaining half-time music, and provides a portrait of a gifted young man who slowly learns to discipline himself and think of others. That's what it does.

What it doesn't do is recycle all the tired old clichés in which the Harlem kid is somehow badder and blacker than the others, provoking confrontations. Devon makes the nature of his character clear in a heartbreaking early scene when, after high school graduation, he talks to his father, who abandoned the family, and tells him he doesn't do drugs, doesn't have a lot of little kids running around, and has a full scholarship to a university. This is a movie that celebrates black success instead of romanticizing gangsta defeatism. Nick Cannon plays Devon as a fine balance between a showoff and a kid who wants to earn admiration

The key rivalry in the film is between Devon and Sean (Leonard Roberts), head of the drum section and the band's best drummer—until Devon arrives. They develop a personal animosity that hurts the band, Dr. Lee believes. He disciplines Devon for violations of the band rule book, for provoking a fight with another band member and, most painful, for keeping a secret that Sean makes sure is revealed.

Dr. Lee has a problem, too, with the school president, who likes Devon's showboating and thinks the band needs more pizzazz to please the alums. Orlando Jones makes his character a thoughtful teacher, a little old-fashioned, who believes in values. In creating this character, the writers must have been thinking about real teachers they admired, since they avoid the usual *Mr. Chips/Dead Poets* clichés.

The love story between Devon and Laila is sweet and remarkably innocent, for a contemporary movie. They share one tender kiss, although the eagle-eyed MPAA rates the film PG-13 for "innuendo." Oh, I forgot: The MPAA also singles out "language," although this is one of the cleanest-talking urban movies in history. If this isn't a PG film in today's world, what is?

It is also, in a very sincere way, touching. It pays attention to its characters, gives them weight and reality, doesn't underline the morals but certainly has them. *Drumline* joins titles like *love jones, Soul Food, Barbershop,* and *Antwone Fisher* in the slowly growing list of movies about everyday African-American lives. What a good-hearted film.

Note: The filmmakers filled the Georgia Dome with 50,000 extras for the rousing marching band showdown, which features the actual bands of Morris Brown College and Clark Atlanta University, Bethune-Cookman College in Daytona Beach, and Louisiana's Grambling State. Morris Brown was a good sport to allow its bandmaster to be portrayed as the villain.

DysFunKtional Family ★ ★ ★
R, 83 m., 2003

A concert documentary by Eddie Griffin. Directed by George Gallo and produced by Griffin, David Permut, and Paul Brooks.

Eddie Griffin uses the N-word 382 times in his new concert film, *DysFunKtional Family*. I know this because David Plummer of the Ebert & Roeper staff counted them. It isn't uncommon for speakers to use placeholders, such as "you know" or "uh" or "like," but in Griffin's case the N-word functions more as a lubricant. It speeds his sentences ahead, provides timing, delays punch words until the right moment. The N-word in his act is so omnipresent that it becomes invisible, like air to a bird or water to a fish. It's his rhythm section.

Much has been written about how African-American musicians, comedians, and writers began to use the N-word in order, they said, to rob it of its poison. When Dick Gregory titled his 1963 autobiography *Nigger,* it was shocking and controversial, but he was making a bold gesture to strip the word of its hurtful power. ("Also," he told his mother, "whenever you hear it, they're advertising my book.")

The N-word is now spoken mostly by those who mean it as a sign of affection and bonding. The rules are: Blacks can say it, but whites should be very sure how, where, when, and why they are using it. (Not all agree. The black scholar Randall Kennedy's new book, *Nigger: The Strange Career of a Troublesome Word,* argues that the word is always wrong.)

I mention this because on a single day recently I received a curiously large number of e-mails criticizing my use of the word "redneck." I've used the word in several reviews over the years, but the occasion this time was a review of *Blue Collar Comedy Tour,* another new comedy concert film. It stars Jeff Foxworthy, who is famous for his litany ending ". . . you may be a redneck." (Example: If the wedding rehearsal dinner is at Hooter's, you may be a redneck.)

Whether these e-mails were all inspired by the same source, I cannot say. Odd that they came in a cluster. They made the same point: "Redneck" is as offensive to white Americans as the N-word is to African Americans. I doubt that this is the case, and suspect some of my correspondents may have even laughed at a Jeff Foxworthy concert.

One correspondent writes: "I notice that as a liberal you are highly sensitive to the rights of minority groups and would never apply a derogatory adjective to an African-American, a Hispanic-American or a Jew. However, when it comes to White Americans, it seems that you apply a different standard."

The implication is that a conservative would not be so "highly sensitive," I guess, although every true conservative would be. The reasoning behind this message derives from David Duke's European-American Unity and Rights Organization, and it's pretty obvious what they're getting at.

Is "redneck" an offensive term? Yes and no. It does not refer to all white people (as the N-word refers to all blacks, or certain terms refer to all Jews or all Mexicans). It is a term for a specific character type. The dictionary says it is "disparaging," but it is often used affectionately, as Foxworthy does. It is in wide usage. A Google search turns up 524,000 sites using "redneck"— amazingly, two and a half times as many as those using the N-word. Among "redneck" sites, Foxworthy's places second and Redneck World is sixth. I doubt that my correspondents have complained to Redneck World.

Of course, "redneck" would be an insult if used against a given person in a particular situation. Most of the time, it is not used in that way. Everything depends on who you are, how you use a word, who you use it to, and in what

spirit. Words are not neutral. My use of "redneck" was not intended to offend, but by taking offense at it, my correspondents have made a not very subtle equation of civil rights in general and their own specialized version of white civil rights, which in Duke's case slides smoothly into white supremacy.

Foxworthy's act is genial, not hurtful, and his definitions of "redneck" include so much basic human nature that we often laugh in recognition. Griffin is also not hurtful (the word "genial" does not occur in connection with his sharp-edged material), but his N-word usage creates uncertainty among whites, who are unsure how to respond. It may limit his crossover appeal to general audiences. As he grows and deepens he may find he can live without it, as Bill Cosby, the greatest of all standup comedians, has always been able to.

I haven't said much about Eddie Griffin's film itself, perhaps because it made me think more about the N-word than about his comedy. Griffin is quick, smart, and funny, and presents the critics with the usual challenge in reviewing a comedy concert: What do you write about, apart from quoting his funniest lines? I have a few quibbles about the way he ropes in his actual family members, especially two uncles, one a pimp, the other addicted to porn; although they seem cheerful enough about going along with the joke, is the joke on them? Still, Griffin made me laugh.

As for "redneck," well, as someone who comes from a part of Illinois where the salad bar includes butterscotch pudding, I can use it, but don't you call me that.

E

Eight Legged Freaks ★ ★ ★
PG-13, 99 m., 2002

David Arquette (Chris McCormack), Kari Wuhrer (Sheriff Sam Parker), Scott Terra (Mike Parker), Scarlett Johansson (Ashley Parker), Doug E. Doug (Harlan), Eileen Ryan (Gladys). Directed by Ellory Elkayem and produced by Dean Devlin and Roland Emmerich. Screenplay by Jesse Alexander, Elkayem, and Randy Kornfield.

Eight Legged Freaks may be the movie that people were hoping for when they went to see *Men in Black II.* They no doubt walked into the theater hoping for laughs, thrills, wit, and scary monsters, and they backed their hopes with something like $133 million over twelve days. It is depressing to contemplate that many people spending that much money on a limp retread that runs out of gas long before it's over. Now here is *Eight Legged Freaks,* which has laughs, thrills, wit, and scary monsters, and is one of those goofy movies like *Critters* that kids itself and gets away with it.

The movie is about spiders, but it doesn't make the mistake of *Arachnophobia* (1990), which was about little spiders. Research shows that small insects don't play on the big screen. See also *The Swarm* from 1978, which, despite its Oscar for the beekeeper's uniforms, failed to excite audiences with its clouds of little buzzing dots. No, these spiders are built along the lines of the one Woody Allen encountered in *Annie Hall;* the females are as big as a Buick, and even the jumpers are as big as a dirt bike. I am reminded of the bird-eating spider in *Crocodile Hunter.*

The movie takes place in bankrupt Prosperity, Arizona, which the mayor wants to sell lock, stock, and barrel to a company that will fill its abandoned mines with toxic wastes. Outside of town, an eccentric spider lover (an unbilled Tom Noonan) lives surrounded by glass tanks containing hundreds of exotic species. An ever-reliable fifty-five-gallon drum, that standby of all toxic waste movies, spills into a nearby river and makes the grasshoppers grow so big they're like "spider steroids." Soon a spider escapes and bites the collector, who of course thrashes around in such methodical agony that he overturns every single glass case, releasing all of his spiders, who soon start dining on dirt bikers, etc.

The movie stars David Arquette as a local boy who has returned after ten years and still has a crush on cute Sheriff Sam Parker (Kari Wuhrer). Her son, Mike (Scott Terra), is the owl-eyed little friend of the spider man; her daughter, Ashley (Scarlett Johansson), seems superfluous at first but becomes indispensable in scenes involving a stun gun and, of course, lots of spiders. Little Mike has learned a lot about spiders from his dead friend, and becomes the local expert.

The town is populated mostly by kooks, whose paranoia is led and fed by Harlan (Doug E. Doug); he runs a radio station from his mobile home and warns of alien attacks. The townsfolk are fed up with the mayor, whose get-rich-quick schemes have included a mall and an ostrich farm, but the mall provides a convenient locale for a last-ditch stand (like in *Dawn of the Dead*), and the ostriches disappear gratifyingly when hauled under by giant trap-door spiders.

The movie's director, Ellory Elkayem, has a sure comic touch; he first handled this material in a short subject that played at the Telluride Film Festival and then was hired by Dean Devlin and Roland Emmerich, of *Godzilla* fame, to direct the feature. I like the way he keeps the characters likable and daffy and positions the spiders just this side of satire. The arachnids make strange nonspidery gurgles and chirps, are capable of double takes, and are skilled at wrapping their victims in cocoons to be devoured later.

The movie contains creepy but reliable clichés (sticking your hand into dark places), funny dialogue ("Please! Not the mall!"), and bizarre special effects, as when a spider slams a cat so hard against plasterboarding that its face can be seen on the other side in bas-relief. The chase scene with jumping spiders and dirt bikes adds a much-needed dimension to the boring sport of dirt bike racing. And I liked the way the cute sheriff dismisses her daughter's spider ravings as "media-induced paranoid delusional fantasies." Meanwhile, a love story blossoms, sort of.

I am not quite sure why the basement of the widow Gladys (Eileen Ryan) would lead directly into a mine shaft, or how the exoskeleton of a spider is strong enough to pound through a steel wall, or how, once again, the hero is able to outrun a fireball. But I am not much bothered. *Eight Legged Freaks* is clever and funny, is amused by its special effects, and leaves you feeling like you've seen a movie instead of an endless trailer.   ☞

8 Mile ★ ★ ★
R, 118 m., 2002

Eminem (Jimmy Smith Jr.), Kim Basinger (Stephanie Smith), Brittany Murphy (Alex), Mekhi Phifer (David Porter/Future). Directed by Curtis Hanson and produced by Brian Grazer, Hanson, and Jimmy Iovine. Screenplay by Scott Silver.

Pale, depressed, Jimmy Smith Jr. (Eminem), skulks through a life that has been so terribly unkind to him. His girlfriend has gotten pregnant and broken up with him, and although he did the right thing by her—he gave her his old car—he now faces the prospect of moving back into his mother's trailer home with her boyfriend who hates him. Jimmy carries his clothes around in a garbage bag. He has a job as a punch press operator.

We see him, early in *8 Mile*, about to do the only thing he does well and takes joy in doing. He is about to go onstage at the Shelter, a rap club that looks uncannily like a deserted building, and engage in the hip-hop version of a poetry slam. In this world he is known as "Rabbit."

He rehearses in a mirror in the men's room, fiercely scowling at his own reflection and practicing those hand gestures all the rappers use, their outboard fingers pointed down from jerking arms as they jab spastically like Joe Cocker. Then Rabbit throws up. Then he goes onstage, where he has forty-five seconds to outrap his competitor in a showdown. And then he freezes. The seconds creep by in total silence, until Rabbit flees the stage and the Shelter.

We are hardly started in *8 Mile*, and already we see that this movie stands aside from routine debut films by pop stars. It stands aside from Britney Spears and the Spice Girls and the other hit machines who have unwisely tried to transfer musical ability into acting careers. Like Prince's *Purple Rain*, it is the real thing.

Eminem insists on Rabbit's proletarian roots, on his slattern mother, on his lonely progress as a white boy in a black world.

Whether *8 Mile* is close to Eminem's own autobiographical truths, I do not know. It is a faithful reflection of his myth, however, beginning with the title, which refers to the road that separates Detroit from its white suburbs. He lives on the black side of the road, where he has found acceptance and friendship from a posse of homies, and especially from Future (Mekhi Phifer), who emcees the contests at the Shelter. When Rabbit gets into fights with black rivals, and he does, they are motivated not by racism but by more wholesome feelings, like sexual jealousy and professional envy.

The genius of Rabbit is to admit his own weaknesses. This is also the approach of Eminem, who acknowledges in his lyrics that he's a white man playing in a black man's field. In the climactic performance scene in *8 Mile*, he not only skewers his opponent, but preempts any comeback by trashing himself first, before the other guy can. At one point, devastatingly, he even calls another rapper "too generic." They must read rock critics in the inner city.

The movie, directed by Curtis Hanson *(Wonder Boys)* and written by Scott Silver, is a grungy version of a familiar formula, in which the would-be performer first fails at his art, then succeeds, is unhappy in romance but lucky in his friends, and comes from an unfortunate background. He even finds love, sort of, with Alex (Brittany Murphy), who is loyal if not faithful. What the movie is missing, however, is the third act in which the hero becomes a star. We know that Eminem is awesomely successful, but *8 Mile* avoids the rags-to-riches route and shows Rabbit moving from rags to slightly better rags.

There has been criticism of Kim Basinger, who is said to be too attractive and even glamorous to play Rabbit's mother, but this strikes me as economic discrimination: Cannot poor people as well as rich people look like Kim Basinger? Given the numbers of ugly people who live in big houses, why can't there be beautiful people living in trailers? Her performance finds the right note somewhere between love and exasperation; it cannot be easy to live with this sullen malcontent, whose face lights up only when he sees his baby sister, Lily.

As an actor, Eminem is convincing without being electric. Perhaps the Rabbit character doesn't allow for joy; he seems to go through life forever remembering why he shouldn't be happy. As it happens, on the same day that *8 Mile* was screened in Chicago, I also saw *Standing in the Shadows of Motown,* a documentary about the studio musicians who created the Motown sound. The contrast was instructive. On the one hand, a Detroit white boy embracing the emblems of poverty and performing in a musical genre that involves complaint, anger, and alienation. On the other hand, black Detroit musicians making good money, performing joyously, having a good time, and remembering those times with tears in their eyes. What has happened to our hopes, that young audiences now embrace such cheerless material, avoiding melody like the plague? At least in their puritanism they still permit rhymes.

Eminem survives the X-ray truth-telling of the movie camera, which is so good at spotting phonies. He is on the level. Here he plays, if not himself, a version of himself, and we understand why he has been accepted as a star in a genre mostly owned by blacks. Whether he has a future as a movie actor is open to question: At this point in his career, there is no reason for him to play anyone other than himself, and it might even be professionally dangerous for him to try. He can, of course, play versions of Rabbit in other movies, and would probably play them well, but Rabbit, let it be said, is a downer. I would love to see a sequel (maybe *8½ Mile*) in which Rabbit makes millions and becomes world-famous, and we learn at last if it is possible for him to be happy. ☞

8 Women ★ ★ ★
R, 113 m., 2002

Danielle Darrieux (Mamy), Catherine Deneuve (Gaby), Isabelle Huppert (Augustine), Virginie Ledoyen (Suzon), Ludivine Sagnier (Catherine), Fanny Ardant (Pierrette), Emmanuelle Béart (Louise), Firmine Richard (Madame Chanel). Directed by François Ozon and produced by Olivier Delbosc and Marc Missonnier. Screenplay by Ozon and Marina de Van, adapted from the play by Robert Thomas.

Here it is at last, the first Agatha Christie musical. Eight women are isolated in a snowbound cottage, there is a corpse with a knife in his back, and all of the women are potential suspects, plus six song-and-dance numbers. The cast is a roll call of French legends. In alphabetical order: Fanny Ardant, Emmanuelle Béart, Danielle Darrieux, Catherine Deneuve, Isabelle Huppert, Virginie Ledoyen, Firmine Richard, and Ludivine Sagnier.

From the opening shot, the film cheerfully lets us know it's a spoof of overproduced Hollywood musicals. We pan past tree branches impossibly laden with picturesque snow, and find a charming cottage where guests are just arriving. Eight women have gathered to celebrate Christmas with Marcel, who is the husband of Gaby (Deneuve), the son-in-law of Mamy (Darrieux), the brother-in-law of Aunt Augustine (Huppert), the father of Catherine (Sagnier) and Suzon (Ledoyen), the employer of the domestic servants Madame Chanel (Richard) and Louise (Béart), and the brother of the late-arriving Pierrette (Ardant).

"Monsieur died in his bed with a knife in his back," the assembled company is informed. And (significant detail required in all isolated rural murders) "the dogs didn't bark all night." The women absorb this news while dressed in stunning designer fashions (even the maids look chic) and deployed around a large, sunny room that looks like nothing so much as a stage set—even to the detail that all the furniture is behind the actresses most of the time. Only a couple of brief excursions upstairs prevent the movie from taking place entirely on this one bright set, where nothing looks used or lived with.

The artificiality is so jolly that we're not surprised when the first song begins, because *8 Women* is in no sense serious about murder, its plot, or anything else. It's an elaborate excuse to have fun with its cast, and we realize we've been waiting a long time for Catherine Deneuve to come right out and say of Isabelle Huppert: "I'm beautiful and rich. She's ugly and poor." I had also just about given up hope of ever seeing Deneuve and Fanny Ardant rolling around on the floor pulling each other's hair.

In a cast where everybody has fun, Huppert has the most, as Augustine. She and her mother

(Darrieux) have been living rent-free in Marcel's cottage with her sister (Deneuve), but that has not inspired Augustine to compromise in her fierce resentment and spinsterish isolation. She stalks around the set like Whistler's mother, frowning from behind her horn-rims and making disapproval into a lifestyle.

The other characters quickly fall into approved Agatha Christie patterns. Young Suzon appoints herself Sherlock Holmes, or perhaps in this case Hercule Poirot, and begins sniffing for clues. The sexy Louise is established as the late Marcel's mistress. Madame Chanel, from French Africa, has been with the family for years and lives out back in the guest cottage, where, as it develops, she often plays cards with Pierrette. And Pierrette herself, who arrives late with the kind of entrance that only the tall, dark, and forcible Ardant could pull off, has secrets that are as amazing as they are inevitable.

I dare not reveal a shred of the plot. And the movie is all plot—that, and stylish behavior, and barbed wit, and those musical numbers. Watching 8 Women, you have a silly grin half of the time. Astonishing that François Ozon, who directed this, also made *Under the Sand* (2001), that melancholy record of a wife (Charlotte Rampling) whose husband disappears, apparently drowned, and who refuses to deal with the fact that he is dead.

Movies like 8 Women are essentially made for movie lovers. You have to have seen overdecorated studio musicals, and you have to know who Darrieux and Deneuve and Béart and Huppert and Ardant are, to get the full flavor. It also helps if you have seen Agatha Christie's *The Mousetrap*, now more than fifty years into its London run, with its cast still trapped with the corpse in the isolated cottage. "Do not give away the secret!" the program notes exort. And here too. Not that the secret is anything more than one more twist of the plot's peppermill.

Elling ★ ★ ★

R, 89 m., 2002

Per Christian Ellefsen (Elling), Sven Nordin (Kjell Bjarne), Marit Pia Jacobsen (Reidun Nordsletten), Jorgen Langhelle (Frank Asli), Per Christensen (Alfons Jorgensen), Hilde Olausson (Gunn), Ola Otnes (Hauger), Eli Anne Linnestad (Johanne), Cecilie A. Mosli (Cecilie Kornes).

Directed by Petter Naess and produced by Dag Alveberg. Screenplay by Axel Hellstenius, based on a novel by Ingvar Ambjornsen.

Here are two men, both around forty, with no desire to cope with the world: Elling, who lived all of his life as a mama's boy and had to be hauled by the police out of a cupboard, where he was crouched and trembling, after his mother's death. And Kjell Bjarne, who has been institutionalized so long it is the only world he knows—although he fantasizes endlessly about nubile women in other worlds. Elling is assigned as Kjell's roommate in a care home, and two years later they are moved into an apartment in Oslo and given a shot at independent living.

Elling, the deadpan Norwegian comedy that tells their stories, was nominated for an Oscar in 2002 in the Best Foreign Film category. It's the kind of story that in the wrong hands would be cloying and cornball, but director Petter Naess has the right hands. He gives the movie edge and darkness, is unsentimental about mental illness, makes his heroes into men instead of pets, and still manages to find a happy ending.

Elling (Per Christian Ellefsen) is slight, fastidious, fussy, and extremely reluctant to go outdoors. Kjell Bjarne (Sven Nordin) is burly, unkempt, goes for days without a bath, and knows a certain amount about the world, mostly by hearsay. When their social worker Frank (Jorgen Langhelle) tells them they must leave the apartment to buy food and eat in restaurants, Elling is incredulous: What's the use of putting the Norwegian welfare state to all the expense of renting them a nice flat if they are expected to leave it?

The movie is narrated by Elling, who depends on Kjell Bjarne (always referred to by both names) and is threatened when Reidun, an upstairs neighbor, pregnant and drunk, gets Kjell's attention. Yet Elling is a fiercely honest man who tells both Kjell and Reidun (Marit Pia Jacobsen) that the other is in love. Then he ventures out into the night to poetry readings, having written down some words about Reidun's fall on the stairs and realized, as he puts it, "My God, Elling, all your life you have walked the Earth not knowing you were a poet!"

At a reading he befriends an old man who turns out to be a famous poet and to own a wonderful car, a 1958 Buick Century hardtop.

Kjell Bjarne can fix the car, and soon the four of them are heading for the poet's country cottage for a weekend at which matters of love and identity will be settled, not without difficulties, not least when Kjell Bjarne discovers that Reidun is prepared to sleep with him but does not suspect he has been wearing the same underwear for more than a week.

In a subtle, half-visible way, *Elling* follows the movie formula of other movies about mentally impaired characters (the picnic outing is an obligatory scene). But *Elling* has no lessons to teach, no insights into mental illness, no labels, no morals. It is refreshingly undogmatic about its characters, and indeed Elling and Kjell may not be mentally ill at all—simply unused to living in the real world. The humor comes from the contrast between Elling's prim value system, obviously reflecting his mother's, and Kjell Bjarne's shambling, disorganized, good-natured assault on life. If Felix and Oscar had been Norwegian, they might have looked something like this.

The Emperor's Club ★ ★ ★
PG-13, 109 m., 2002

Kevin Kline (William Hundert), Emile Hirsch (Sedgewick Bell), Embeth Davidtz (Elizabeth), Rob Morrow (James Ellerby), Edward Herrmann (Headmaster Woodbridge), Harris Yulin (Senator Bell), Paul Dano (Martin Blythe). Directed by Michael Hoffman and produced by Andrew Karsch and Marc Abraham. Screenplay by Neil Tolkin, based on the short story "The Palace Thief" by Ethan Canin.

The Emperor's Club tells the story of a teacher who fixes the results of an academic competition and twice allows a well-connected student to get away with cheating. Because he privately tells the cheater he is a heel, the film presents him as a great educator, but he is correct when he tells that student: "I failed you." The chief curiosity of the film is how it seems to present one view of the teacher, but cannot prevent itself from revealing another.

The film will not be generally interpreted in this way, and will be hailed in the latest of a series of sentimental portraits of great teachers, which include *Goodbye, Mr. Chips, The Prime of Miss Jean Brodie, The Dead Poets' Society,* and

Mr. Holland's Opus. All of those are enjoyable films, except for *Dead Poets,* which is more of a showbiz biopic with students as the audience. None of them have the nerve to venture into the tricky ethical quicksand of *The Emperor's Club.* The movie is too methodical, but it doesn't avoid the hard questions.

Kevin Kline plays William Hundert. who as the film opens has retired after teaching the classics for thirty-four years at St. Benedictus School for Boys, a private East Coast institution that has an invisible conveyor belt leading directly from its door to the Ivy League and the boardrooms of the Establishment. The students are the children of rich men. The purpose of the school is theoretically to mold them into leaders. Hundert tells them, "A man's character is his fate," and asks them, "How will history remember you?" But more truth is contained in the words of a U.S. senator whose son is in trouble at the school: "You, sir, will not mold my son! I will mold him."

The troubled student is Sedgewick Bell (Emile Hirsch), a smart aleck who interrupts in class, disrespects the teacher, and has a valise under his bed that is jammed with men's magazines, booze, condoms, and a pack of Luckies. Despite all of the molding and shaping St. Benedictus has performed on its students, the other boys of course idolize Sedgewick. Strange how, among the young, there is nothing sillier than a man who wants you to think hard and do well, and nothing more attractive than a contemporary who celebrates irony and ignorance.

Mr. Hundert is a bachelor, ferociously dedicated to being a good teacher, and silently in love with the fragrant Elizabeth (Embeth Davidtz), wife of another faculty member. She also loves him, but marriage and rectitude stand between them, and there is an effective scene when she says good-bye—forever, she thinks. Hundert redoubles his teaching efforts, which climax, every school year, with the Mr. Julius Caesar contest, in which the three best students compete in a sort of quiz show.

[Spoilers follow.] After a rocky start, Sedgewick begins to apply himself to his work—not so much because of Hundert as because of dire threats from his father, the no doubt thoroughly corrupt U.S. senator (Harris Yulin). When final exams are written, Sedgewick has so improved that he finishes fourth. But because Hundert wants to reward that improvement, and because even for him a rebel is more attractive than a bookworm, the professor takes another long look as Sedgewick's paper and, after much brow-furrowing, improves his grade and makes him a finalist.

The movie wisely never says if Sedgewick deserves to be upgraded, although we suspect that if he had placed third in the first place, Hundert would not have taken another long look at the fourth-place paper. In any event, Sedgewick competes in the big contest, and cheats, and is seen by Hundert, who finds a silent and tactful way to force him to lose.

Now many years pass. Sedgewick is himself a rich man and wants to run for senator, and will give an enormous endowment to St. Benedictus on the condition that there be a rerun of the original Mr. Julius Caesar contest. Does he at last redeem himself? You will have to see for yourself.

What is interesting about the movie is that Mr. Hundert is fully aware of his ethical shortcomings in the matter of young Sedgewick. He does not let him win, but does not expose him. And the movie does not provide the kind of ending we fear the material is building up to, but finds its own subtle way to see that justice is done. The mechanics of the eventual confrontation between Sedgewick and his own son are ingenious, devastating, and unanswerable.

We are so accustomed to noble teachers that *The Emperor's Club* surprises us by providing one who is dedicated, caring, and skillful, but flawed. As a portrait of the escalator that speeds the sons of the rich upward toward power, it is unusually realistic. Kevin Kline's performance shows a deep understanding of the character, who is, after all, better than most teachers, and most men. We care for him, not because he is perfect, but because he regrets so sincerely that he is not.

The Emperor's New Clothes ★ ★ ★
PG, 105 m., 2002

Ian Holm (Napleon/Eugene Lenormand), Iben Hjejle (Pumpkin), Tim McInnerny (Dr. Lambert), Tom Watson (Gerard), Nigel Terry (Montholon), Hugh Bonneville (Bertrand), Murray Melvin (Antommarchi), Eddie Marsan (Marchand), Clive Russell (Bommel). Directed by Alan Taylor and produced by Uberto Pasolini. Screenplay by Kevin Molony, Taylor, and Herbie Wave, based on the novel *The Death of Napoleon* by Simon Leys.

Napoleon did not die on the island of St. Helena in 1821. That was Eugene Lenormand, who looked a lot like him. *The Emperor's New Clothes,* a surprisingly sweet and gentle comedy, tells how it happened. Lenormand is smuggled onto St. Helena to act as a double for the emperor, who is smuggled off as a cargo hand on a commercial ship ("A position above decks would have been more appropriate"). The theory is, he will arrive in Paris, the impostor will reveal his true identity, and France will rise up to embrace the emperor.

"So many have betrayed me," Napoleon announces grandly at the outset of this adventure. "I place my trust in only two things now: my will, and the love of the people of France." He forgets that he has also placed his trust in Eugene Lenormand—a poor man who grows to enjoy the role of Napoleon, is treated well by his British captors, dines regularly, and refuses to reveal his real identity: "I have no idea what you're talking about."

Both Napoleon and Lenormand are played by Ian Holm (Bilbo Baggins from *The Lord of the Rings*), that invaluable British actor who actually looks so much like Napoleon he has played him twice before, in *Time Bandits* (1981) and on a 1974 TV miniseries. Another actor might have strutted and postured, but Holm finds something melancholy in Bonaparte's fall from grace.

To begin with, the escape ship goes astray, lands at Antwerp instead of a French port, and Napoleon has to use his limited funds for a coach journey with an unscheduled stop at the battlefield of Waterloo—where he can, if he wants, buy souvenirs of himself. Finally in Paris, he goes to see a loyalist named Truchaut, who will engineer the unveiling. Truchaut, alas, has died, and so confidentially has he treated his secret that not even his widow, Pumpkin (Iben Hjejle, from *High Fidelity*), knows the story.

She has no sympathy with this madman who claims to be Napoleon. There is no shortage of those in Paris. But after he injures himself she calls a doctor and grows tender toward this little man, and insightful: "I think you've been in prison." During his convalescence, Napoleon comes to treasure the pleasant young widow, and learns of a guild of melon-sellers who are barely making a living. Planning their retail sales like a military campaign, he dispatches melon carts to the key retail battlefields of Paris, greatly increasing sales.

The story, inspired by Simon Leys's 1992 novel *The Death of Napoleon,* could have gone in several directions; it's not hard to imagine the Monty Python version. But Holm, an immensely likable actor, seems intrigued by the idea of an old autocrat finally discovering the joys of simple life. The director, Alan Taylor, avoids obvious gag lines and nudges Bonaparte gradually into the realization that the best of all worlds may involve selling melons and embracing Pumpkin.

Of course, there must have been countless people in Paris at that time who could have identified Napoleon—but how could he have gotten close enough to them? The government was hostile to him. The British insisted they had the emperor locked up on St. Helena. And at home, Pumpkin wants no more of his foolish talk: "You're not Napoleon! I hate Napoleon! He has filled France with widows and orphans! He took my husband. I won't let him take you."

For Napoleon, this last adventure is a puzzling one: "I have become a stranger to myself." But who knows who we are, anyway? We affix names and identities to ourselves to provide labels for the outside world. When the labels slip, how can we prove they belong to us? Like a modern victim of identity theft, Napoleon has had his name taken away and is left as nothing. Well, not nothing. Pumpkin loves him. And the melon merchants are grateful.

Empire ★ ★ ½
R, 100 m., 2002

John Leguizamo (Victor Rosa), Peter Sarsgaard (Jack), Delilah Cotto (Carmen), Denise Richards (Trish), Vincent Laresca (Jimmy), Isabella Rossellini (La Colombiana), Sonia Braga (Iris), Nestor Serrano (Rafael Menendez), Treach (Chedda), Fat Joe (Tito). Directed by Franc Reyes and produced by Daniel Bigel and Michael Mailer. Screenplay by Reyes.

Empire comes so close to working that you can see there from here. It has the right approach and the right opening premise, but it lacks the zest and goes for a plot twist instead of trusting the material. I recently saw *GoodFellas* again, and this film is similar; they're both about the rise and fall of a gangster, narrated by himself, and complicated by a wife who walks out when she catches him with another woman. And *Empire* has a story hook that could have transformed this story into another classic.

The story is told by Victor Rosa (John Leguizamo), a successful drug distributor of Puerto Rican background who controls a territory in the Bronx. He describes his world in a rich, fact-packed voice-over. He works for La Colombiana (Isabella Rossellini), a rich, ruthless suburban woman with a vicious enforcer. He understands the business inside out; turf wars are not meaningless when "twenty feet of sidewalk means thirty grand a week, easy." He is in love with Carmen (Delilah Cotto), a college student.

Victor is upwardly mobile. He deals with hard street people and is hard himself, a killer, yet we sense an inner goodness trying to be born, a desire to better himself. One day his girlfriend, Carmen, meets Trish (Denise Richards) at school, and they're invited to a party being given by Trish's boyfriend, Jack (Peter Sarsgaard). He's a hotshot young Wall Street wizard who is attracted to Victor's criminal glamour: "We're the same . . ." He offers Victor a chance to invest in a sure thing, an offshore deal that will double his money, and explains to Trish: "He's a businessman. If he were born in the suburbs he'd be running a *Fortune* 500 company."

Investing with Jack fits in with Victor's plans. Carmen is pregnant, and he wants to launder his drug money, leave the business to his top lieutenant, and move to Manhattan with her. When Jack offers him the use of a luxury loft, he grabs at it; he sees himself going legit and becoming an investment wizard like Jack. Carmen isn't so sure. She misses the old neighborhood: "This loft will never be home for me." Especially not after Victor is depressed one day, Jack sends the compliant Trish over to cheer him up, and Carmen walks in on them. Victor is telling the truth when he says, "It's not what it looks like," but tell that to Carmen.

So now we have the setup. I will not reveal the payoff or the twist. For that, you will need to visit the movie's trailer at www.apple.com/trailers, which gives away the surprise with a heedlessness that is astonishing even in these days of trailers that tell too much.

I will couch my objection to the movie cautiously, to preserve its secrets. What disappointed me is that the movie didn't follow through with its original premise and show us a bright, resourceful drug dealer trying to start all over on Wall Street. Is it possible? Is the high-finance club open to outsiders? Does Wall Street play even dirtier than drug dealers, and have more vicious criminal types? The possibility exists in a time when CEOs have led their accountants in the theft of billions from American shareholders.

But no. The movie lacks the ambition or nerve to make the moral critique of American finance that it seems to be heading for. It settles instead for a series of developments that will be familiar to students of similar films. There is poignancy in the situation Victor finds himself in, yes, and real drama in his relationship with Carmen (both Leguizamo and Cotto give full-hearted, convincing performances). And his relationship with the Isabella Rossellini character unfolds with implacable logic, although its final result could have been handled with more imagination.

But *Empire* fails because it lacked the nerve to really be about its people and went for the fancy plot gimmick, which no doubt played better at the pitch meeting. It takes imagination to visualize a movie that sees clearly how finance and morality have diverged (as Oliver Stone's *Wall Street* did), but very little imagination to green-light a mechanical plot device that the audience can see coming long before the characters do. Leaving the theater, still impressed by the reality of Victor, Carmen, and many of the others, I felt a sense of loss. What would La Colombiana have done if Victor really had taken over a *Fortune* 500 company? Now there's a story for you.

The Endurance ★ ★ ★ ½
G, 93 m., 2002

A documentary of Sir Ernest Shackleton's 1914–1916 expedition to Antarctica. Directed by George Butler and produced by Butler, Caroline Alexander, and Louise Rosen. Screenplay by Alexander and Joseph Dorman, based on the book by Alexander.

Footage from a remarkable silent documentary has been combined with new photography, music, and a narration to produce an even more remarkable sound documentary, *The Endurance*, the story of Ernest Shackleton's doomed 1914 expedition to the South Pole. The expedition failed when its ship, the *Endurance*, became trapped in ice and eventually broke up and sank. It was then that the heroism of Shackleton and his twenty-eight-man crew proved itself, as they survived a long polar winter and a hurricane while eventually finding rescue through an 800-mile journey in a lifeboat.

Shackleton's expedition was not necessarily noble, but its failure created the opportunity for legend. The South Pole had already been reached by the Norwegian Roald Amundsen, who outraced Robert Falcon Scott in 1911–12, in a competition that ended in Scott's death. Shackleton's plan was to cross Antarctica via the pole, and claim it for England; explorers of his generation were inflamed by visions of daring conquests.

What made Shackleton's adventure so immediate to later generations was that he took along a photographer, Frank Hurley, who shot motion picture film and stills (and entered the sinking *Endurance* to rescue it). That film was the basis of *South* (1916), a silent documentary that was restored and rereleased in 2000. It was not a sophisticated film; Hurley employed the point-and-shoot approach to cinematography, but his simple shots spoke for themselves: men with frost on their beards, dogs plowing through snow, the destruction of the *Endurance* in the ice. Above all they underlined the might of nature and the impudence of men; we are surprised by how small the *Endurance* is, and how the crew members seem like dots of life in a frozen world.

That footage has now been used by the documentarian George Butler (*Pumping Iron*) as the basis for *The Endurance*, a new documentary based on Caroline Alexander's book about the expedition. The narration is by Liam Neeson. The old black-and-white footage, retaining all of its power, is intercut with new color footage of the original locations, including Elephant Island, where the *Endurance* crew wintered in the endless night, crouching inside shelters for six months.

Determining that his expedition would have to rescue itself, Shackleton set forth in the lifeboat with six men to try to cross 800 miles of open sea and reach a whaling port at South Georgia Island. That they survived this journey of seventeen days is extraordinary. Then they had to find the courage to face what they found on the island: "A chaos of peaks and glaciers that had never been crossed." Exhausted, without adequate food or water, they trekked for three more days through this landscape to find the village and bring rescue back to the men who were left behind.

Amazingly, not a single life was lost. When the *Endurance* crew returned to England, it was at the height of World War I; instead of being greeted as heroes, they were suspected of malingering. Some volunteered for the army, and died in the trenches.

The physical toll of polar exploration has taken a psychic price as well from many of its survivors. The best book about Polar ordeals is *The Worst Journey in the World* by Apsley Cherry-Garrard, a member of Scott's expedition, who walked by himself over hundreds of miles of ice to study penguin behavior. In later life he was a broken shell of the confident young man who set out with Scott. *The Endurance* interviews surviving descendants of Shackleton's expedition, including Peter Wordie, the son of James Wordie, who says of his father: "He would never let us read his diaries."

Enemy at the Gates ★ ★ ★
R, 131 m., 2001

Jude Law (Vassili), Joseph Fiennes (Danilov), Ed Harris (Konig), Rachel Weisz (Tania), Bob Hoskins (Khrushchev), Ron Perlman (Koulikov), Gabriel Marshall-Thomson (Sacha), Eva Mattes (Mother Filipov), Matthias Habich (General von Paulus). Directed by Jean-Jacques Annaud and produced by Annaud and John D. Schofield. Screenplay by Annaud and Alain Godard.

Enemy at the Gates opens with a battle sequence that deserves comparison with *Saving Private Ryan,* and then narrows its focus until it is about two men playing a cat-and-mouse game in the ruins of Stalingrad. The Nazi is sure he is the cat. The Russian fears he may be the mouse.

The movie is inspired by true events, we're told, although I doubt real life involved a love triangle; the film might have been better and leaner if it had told the story of the two soldiers and left out the soppy stuff. Even so, it's remarkable, a war story told as a chess game where the loser not only dies, but goes by necessity to an unmarked grave.

This is a rare World War II movie that does not involve Americans. It takes place in the autumn of 1942 in Stalingrad, during Hitler's insane attack on the Soviet Union. At first it appeared the Germans would roll over the ragged Russian resistance, but eventually the stubbornness of the Soviets combined with the brutal weather and problems with supply lines deliver Hitler a crushing defeat and, many believe, turn the tide of the war.

We see the early hopelessness of the Soviet cause in shots showing terrified Russian soldiers trying to cross a river and make a landing in the face of withering fire. They are ordered to charge the Germans across an exposed no-man's-land, and when half are killed and the others turned back, they are fired on by their own officers, as cowards. This is a sustained sequence as harrowing, in its way, as Spielberg's work.

One of the Russians stands out. His name is Vassili (Jude Law), and we know from the title sequence that he is a shepherd from the Urals, whose marksmanship was learned by killing wolves that preyed on his flock. In the heat of battle, he kills five Germans, and is noticed by Danilov (Joseph Fiennes), the political officer assigned to his unit. As Russian morale sinks lower, Danilov prints a leaflet praising the heroic shepherd boy.

We learn that Vassili is indeed a good shot, but has little confidence in his own abilities (in the opening sequence, he has one bullet to use against a wolf, and misses). Danilov encourages him, and as the battle lines solidify and both sides dig into their positions, Vassili continues to pick off Germans and star in Danilov's propaganda. Even Nikita Khrushchev (Bob Hoskins, looking uncannily like the real thing), the leader of the Soviet defense of Stalingrad, praises the boy and the publicity strategy.

As German resolve falters, they bring in their own best sniper, a sharpshooter named Konig (Ed Harris), a Bavarian aristocrat who in peacetime shoots deer. He is older, hawk-faced, clear-eyed, a professional. His assignment is to kill Vassili and end the propaganda. "How will you find him?" he's asked. "I'll have him find me."

The heart of the movie is the duel between the two men, played out in a blasted cityscape of bombed factories and rubble. The war recedes into the background as the two men, who have never had a clear glimpse of each other, tacitly agree on their ground of battle. The director, Jean-Jacques Annaud, makes the geography clear—the open spaces, the shadows, the hollow pipes that are a way to creep from one point to another.

The duel is made more complicated when Vassili meets Sacha (Gabriel Marshall-Thomson), a boy of seven or eight who moves like a wraith between the opposing lines and is known to both snipers. Through Sacha, Vassili meets his neighbor Tania (Rachel Weisz), a Jewish woman whose parents were killed by the Nazis. Vassili falls in love with Tania—and so does Danilov, and this triangle seems like a plot device to separate the scenes that really interest us.

Sacha is a useful character, however. As a child of war he is old beyond his years, but not old enough to know how truly ruthless and deadly a game he is involved in. His final appearance in the film brings a gasp from the audience, but fits into the implacable logic of the situation.

Annaud (*Quest for Fire, In the Name of the Rose, Seven Years in Tibet*) makes big-scale films where men test themselves against their ideas. Here he shows the Nazi sniper as a cool professional, almost without emotion, taking a cerebral approach to the challenge. The Russian is quite different; his confidence falters when he learns who he's up against, and he says, simply, "He's better than me." The strategy of the final confrontation between the two men has a kind of poetry to it, and I like the physical choices that Harris makes in the closing scene.

Is the film also about a duel between two opposing ideologies, Marxism and Nazism? Danilov, the propagandist, paints it that way, but actually it is about two men placed in a situation where they have to try to use their intelligence and skills to kill each other. When Annaud focuses on that, the movie works with rare concentration. The additional plot stuff and the romance are kind of a shame.

Enigma ★ ★ ★
R, 117 m., 2002

Dougray Scott (Tom Jericho), Kate Winslet (Hester Wallace), Jeremy Northam (Wigram), Saffron Burrows (Claire Romilly), Nikolaj Coster-Waldau ("Puck" Pukowski), Tom Hollander (Logie), Corin Redgrave (Admiral Trowbridge), Matthew MacFadyen (Cave). Directed by Michael Apted and produced by Mick Jagger and Lorne Michaels. Screenplay by Tom Stoppard, based on a book by Robert Harris.

World War II may have been won by our side because of what British code-breakers accomplished at a countryside retreat named Bletchley Park. There they broke, and broke again, the German code named Enigma, which was thought to be unbreakable, and was used by the Nazis to direct their submarine convoys in the North Atlantic. Enigma was decoded with the help of a machine, and the British had captured one, but the machine alone was not enough. My notes, scribbled in the dark, indicate the machine had 4,000 million trillion different positions—a whole lot, anyway—and the mathematicians and cryptologists at Bletchley used educated guesses and primitive early computers to try to penetrate a message to the point where it could be tested on Enigma.

For those who get their history from the movies, *Enigma* will be puzzling, since *U-571* (2000) indicates Americans captured an Enigma machine from a German submarine in 1944. That sub is on display at the Museum of Science and Industry in Chicago, but no Enigma machine was involved. An Enigma machine *was* obtained, not by Americans but by the British ship HMS *Bulldog*, when it captured U-110 on May 9, 1941.

Purists about historical accuracy in films will nevertheless notice that *Enigma* is not blameless; it makes no mention of Alan Turing, the genius of British code-breaking and a key theoretician of computers, who was as responsible as anyone for breaking the Enigma code. Turing was a homosexual, eventually hounded into suicide by British laws, and is replaced here by a fictional and resolutely heterosexual hero named Tom Jericho (Dougray Scott). And just as well, since the hounds of full disclosure who dogged *A Beautiful Mind* would no doubt be asking why *Enigma* contained no details about Turing's sex life.

The movie, directed by the superb Michael Apted, is based on a literate, absorbing thriller by Robert Harris, who portrays Bletchley as a hothouse of intrigue in which Britain's most brilliant mathematicians worked against the clock to break German codes and warn North Atlantic convoys. As the film opens, the Germans have changed their code again, making it even more fiendishly difficult to break (from my notes: "150 million million million ways of doing it," but alas I did not note what "it" was). Tom Jericho, sent home from Bletchley after a nervous breakdown, has been summoned back to the enclave because even if he is a wreck, maybe his brilliance can be of help.

Why did Jericho have a breakdown? Not because of a mathematical stalemate, but because he was overthrown by Claire Romilly (Saffron Burrows), the beautiful Bletchley colleague he loved, who disappeared mysteriously without saying good-bye. Back on the job, he grows chummy with Claire's former roommate, Hester Wallace (Kate Winslet), who may have clues about Claire even though she doesn't realize it. Then, in a subtle, oblique way, Tom and Hester begin to get more than chummy. All the time Wigram (Jeremy Northam), an intelligence operative, is keeping an eye on Tom and Hester, because he thinks they may know more than they admit about Claire—and because Claire may have been passing secrets to the Germans.

Whether any of these speculations are fruitful, I will allow you to discover. What I like about the movie is its combination of suspense and intelligence. If it does not quite explain exactly how decryption works (how could it?), it at least gives us a good idea of how decrypters work, and we understand how crucial Bletchley was—so crucial its existence was kept a secret for thirty years. When the fact that the British had broken Enigma finally

became known, histories of the war had to be rewritten; a recent biography of Churchill suggests, for example, that when he strode boldly on the rooftop of the Admiralty in London, it was because secret Enigma messages assured him there would be no air raids that night.

The British have a way of not wanting to seem to care very much. It seasons their thrillers. American heroes are stalwart, forthright, and focused; Brits like understatement and sly digs. The tension between Tom Jericho and Wigram is all the more interesting because both characters seem to be acting in their own little play some of the time, and are as interested in the verbal fencing as in the underlying disagreement. It is a battle of style. You can see similar fencing personalities in the world of Graham Greene, and, of course, it is the key to James Bond.

Kate Winslet is very good here, plucky, wearing sensible shoes, with the wrong haircut— and then, seen in the right light, as a little proletarian sex bomb. She moves between dowdy and sexy so easily it must mystify even her. Claire, when she is seen, is portrayed by Saffron Burrows as the kind of woman any sensible man *knows* cannot be kept in his net—which is why she attracts a masochistic romantic like Tom Jericho, who sets himself up for his own betrayal. If it is true (and it is) that *Pearl Harbor* is the story of how the Japanese staged a sneak attack on an American love triangle, at least *Enigma* is not about how the Nazis devised their code to undermine a British love triangle. That is true not least because the British place puzzle solving at least on a par with sex, and like to conduct their affairs while on (not as a substitute for) duty.

Enough ★ ½
PG-13, 115 m., 2002

Jennifer Lopez (Slim), Billy Campbell (Mitch), Juliette Lewis (Ginny), Russell Milton (Alex), Tessa Allen (Gracie), Dan Futterman (Joe), Chris Maher (Phil), Noah Wyle (Robbie), Fred Ward (Jupiter). Directed by Michael Apted and produced by Rob Cowan and Irwin Winkler. Screenplay by Nicholas Kazan.

Enough is a nasty item masquerading as a feminist revenge picture. It's a step or two above

I Spit on Your Grave, but uses the same structure, in which a man victimizes a woman for the first half of the film, and then the woman turns the tables in an extended sequence of graphic violence. It's surprising to see a director like Michael Apted and an actress like Jennifer Lopez associated with such tacky material.

It is possible to imagine this story being told in a good film, but that would involve a different screenplay. Nicholas Kazan's script makes the evil husband (Billy Campbell) such an unlikely caricature of hard-breathing, sadistic testosterone that he cannot possibly be a real human being. Of course there are men who beat their wives and torture them with cruel mind games, but do they satirize themselves as the heavy in a B movie? The husband's swings of personality and mood are so sudden, and his motivation makes so little sense, that he has no existence beyond the stereotyped Evil Rich White Male. The fact that he preys on a poor Latino waitress is just one more cynical cliché.

The story: Jennifer Lopez plays Slim, a waitress in a diner where she shares obligatory sisterhood and bonding with Ginny (Juliette Lewis), another waitress. A male customer tries to get her to go on a date, and almost succeeds before another customer named Mitch (Billy Campbell) blows the whistle and reveals the first man was only trying to win a bet. In the movie's headlong rush of events, Slim and Mitch are soon married, buy a big house, have a cute child, and then Slim discovers Mitch is having affairs, and he growls at her: "I am, and always will be, a person who gets what he wants." He starts slapping her around.

Although their child is now three or four, this is a Mitch she has not seen before in their marriage. Where did this Mitch come from? How did he restrain himself from pounding and strangling her during all of the early years? Why did she think herself happy until now? The answer, of course, is that Mitch turns on a dime when the screenplay requires him to. He even starts talking differently.

The plot (spoiler warning) now involves Slim's attempts to hide herself and the child from Mitch. She flees to Michigan and hooks up with a battered-wife group, but Mitch, like the hero of a mad slasher movie, is always able to track her down. Along the way Slim appeals for help to the father (Fred Ward) who has never acknowledged her, and the father's dialogue is so hilariously over the top in its cruelty that the scene abandons all hope of working seriously and simply functions as haywire dramaturgy.

Slim gets discouraging advice from a lawyer ("There is nothing you can do. He will win."). And then she gets training in self-defense from a martial arts instructor. Both of these characters are African-American, following the movie's simplistic moral color-coding. The day when the evil husband is black and the self-defense instructor is white will not arrive in our lifetimes.

The last act of the movie consists of Slim outsmarting her husband with a series of clever ploys in which she stage-manages an escape route, sets a booby trap for his vehicle, and then lures him into a confrontation where she beats the shinola out of him, at length, with much blood, lots of stunt work, breakaway furniture, etc. The movie, in time-honored horror movie tradition, doesn't allow Mitch to really be dead the first time. There is a plot twist showing that Slim can't really kill him—she's the heroine, after all—and then he lurches back into action like the slasher in many an exploitation movie, and is destroyed more or less by accident. During this action scene Slim finds time for plenty of dialogue explaining that any court will find she was acting in self-defense.

All of this would be bad enough without the performance of Tessa Allen as Gracie, the young daughter. She has one of those squeaky, itsy-bitsy piped-up voices that combines with babyish dialogue to make her more or less insufferable; after the ninth or tenth scream of "Mommy! Mommy!" we hope that she will be shipped off to an excellent day-care center for the rest of the story.

Jennifer Lopez is one of my favorite actresses, but not here, where the dialogue requires her to be passionate and overwrought in a way that is simply not believable, maybe because no one could take this cartoon of a story seriously. No doubt she saw *Enough* as an opportunity to play a heavy, dramatic role, but there is nothing more dangerous than a heavy role in a lightweight screenplay, and this material is such a melodramatic soap opera that the slick production values seem like a waste of effort.

Equilibrium ★ ★ ★
R, 106 m., 2002

Christian Bale (Clerick John Preston), Emily Watson (Mary O'Brian), Taye Diggs (Clerick Brandt), Angus MacFadyen (Master Clerick/Father), Sean Bean (Partridge), Oliver Brandl (The Technician), Francesco Cabras (Leader of the Rebels), Daniel Lee Clark (Lead Sweeper), Christian Kahrmann (Special Squad Officer). Directed by Kurt Wimmer and produced by Jan de Bont and Lucas Foster. Screenplay by Wimmer.

Equilibrium would be a mindless action picture, except that it has a mind. It doesn't do a lot of deep thinking, but unlike many futuristic combos of SF and f/x, it does make a statement: Freedom of opinion is a threat to totalitarian systems. Dictatorships of both the left and right are frightened by the idea of their citizens thinking too much, or having too much fun.

The movie deals with this notion in the most effective way, by burying it in the story and almost drowning it with entertainment. In a free society many, maybe most, audience members will hardly notice the message. But there are nations and religions that would find this movie dangerous. You know who you are.

The movie is set in the twenty-first century—hey! that's our century!—at a time after the Third World War. That war was caused, it is believed, because citizens felt too much and too deeply. They got all worked up and started bombing each other. To assure world peace and the survival of the human race, everyone has been put on obligatory doses of Prozium, a drug that dampens the emotions and shuts down our sensual side. (Hint: The working title of this movie was *Librium*.)

In the movie, enforcers known as Clericks have the mandate to murder those who are considered Sense Offenders. This is a rich irony, since True Believers, not Free Thinkers, are the ones eager to go to war over their beliefs. If you believe you have the right to kill someone because of your theology, you are going about God's work in your way, not His.

Christian Bale stars as Clerick John Preston,

partnered with Partridge (Sean Bean) as a top-level enforcer. Nobody can look dispassionate in the face of outrageous provocation better than Christian Bale, and he proves it here after his own wife is incinerated for Sense Offenses. "What did you feel?" he is asked. "I didn't feel anything," he replies, and we believe him, although perhaps this provides a clue about his wife's need to Offend.

Preston is a top operative, but is hiding something. We see him pocketing a book that turns out to be the collected poetry of W. B. Yeats, a notorious Sense Offender. He has kept it, he explains, to better understand the enemy (the same reason censors have historically needed to study pornography). His duties bring him into contact with Mary O'Brian (Emily Watson), and he feels — well, it doesn't matter what he feels. To feel at all is the offense. Knowing that, but remembering Mary, he deliberately stops taking his Prozium: He loves being a Clerick, but, oh, you id.

If *Equilibrium* has a plot borrowed from *1984, Brave New World,* and other dystopian novels, it has gunfights and martial arts borrowed from the latest advances in special effects. More rounds of ammunition are expended in this film than in any film I can remember, and I remember *The Transporter.*

I learn from Nick Nunziata at www.CHUD. com that the form of battle used in the movie is "Gun-Kata," which is "a martial art completely based around guns." I credit Nunziata because I think he may have invented this term. The fighters transcribe the usual arcs in midair and do impossible acrobatics, but mostly use guns instead of fists and feet. That would seem to be cheating, and involves a lot of extra work (it is much easier to shoot someone without doing a backflip), but since the result is loud and violent it is no doubt worth it.

There is an opening sequence in which Preston and Partridge approach an apartment where Offenders are holed up, and Preston orders the lights to be turned out in the apartment. Then he enters in the dark. As nearly as I could tell, he is in the middle of the floor, surrounded by Offenders with guns. A violent gun battle breaks out, jerkily illuminated by flashes of the guns, and everyone is killed but Preston. There is nothing about this scene that even *attempts* to be plausible, confirming a suspicion

I have long held, that the heroes of action movies are protected by secret hexes and *cannot* be killed by bullets.

There are a lot more similar battles, which are pure kinetic energy, made of light, noise, and quick cutting. They seem to have been assembled for viewers with Attention Deficit Disorder, who are a large voting block at the box office these days. The dispassionate observer such as myself, refusing to Sense Offense my way through such scenes, can nevertheless admire them as a technical exercise.

What I like is the sneaky way Kurt Wimmer's movie advances its philosophy in between gun battles. It argues, if I am correct, that it is good to feel passion and lust, to love people and desire them, and to experience voluptuous pleasure through great works of music and art. In an early scene Clerick Preston blowtorches the *Mona Lisa*, the one painting you can be pretty sure most moviegoers will recognize. But in no time he is feeling joy and love, and because he is the hero, this must be good, even though his replacement partner, Clerick Brandt (Taye Diggs), suspects him, and wants to expose him.

The rebel group in *Equilibrium* preserves art and music (there is a touching scene where Preston listens to a jazz record), and we are reminded of Bradbury and Truffaut's *Fahrenheit 451*, where book lovers committed banned volumes to memory. One is tempted to look benevolently upon *Equilibrium* and assume thought control can't happen here, but of course it can, which is why it is useful to have an action picture in which the Sense Offenders are the good guys.

Evelyn ★ ★ ★

PG, 94 m., 2002

Pierce Brosnan (Desmond Doyle), Sophie Vavasseur (Evelyn Doyle), Julianna Margulies (Bernadette Beattie), Aidan Quinn (Nick Barron), Stephen Rea (Michael Beattie), Alan Bates (Thomas Connolly), John Lynch (Mr. Wolfe), Andrea Irvine (Sister Brigid), Karen Ardiff (Sister Felicity). Directed by Bruce Beresford and produced by Pierce Brosnan, Michael Ohoven, and Beau St. Clair. Screenplay by Paul Pender.

Evelyn is set in 1953, and could have been filmed then. Told with the frank simplicity of a classic, well-made picture, it tells its story, nothing more, nothing less, with no fancy stuff. We relax as if we've found a good movie on cable. Story is everything here. Even though Pierce Brosnan is a movie star, he comes across here as an ordinary bloke, working-class Irish, charming but not all that charming. We hardly need to be told the movie is "based on a true story."

Brosnan plays Desmond Doyle, a drunk and a carpenter, more or less in that order. He has two sons and a daughter. When his wife runs away from the family, the government social workers come around, size up the situation, and advise, "send in the nuns." The children are sent to orphanages on the grounds, then sanctified in Irish law, that a father cannot raise children by himself.

Desmond is devastated. At first that translates into drinking, but eventually he meets an understanding woman (a barmaid, of course, since where else would he meet a woman?). She is Bernadette Beattie (Julianna Margulies), who advises Desmond to get his act together if he ever hopes to have his children back again. With her encouragement, he meets her brother, an attorney named Michael Beattie (Stephen Rea), who holds out little hope of a successful court case. For one thing, Desmond will need the consent of his wife, who is conspicuously unavailable.

Before settling into the rhythms of a courtroom drama, the movie takes a look at the conditions in the orphanage where Evelyn (the fetching Sophie Vavasseur) is being cared for. It apparently contains only two staff members: the fearsome, strict, and cruel Sister Brigid (Andrea Irvine), and the sweet, gentle Sister Felicity (Karen Ardiff). The orphanage itself is one step up from the conditions shown in *The Magdalene Sisters*, another current film, which shows how many Irish women were incarcerated for life for sexual misdeeds, stripped of their identities, and used as cheap labor in church-owned laundries.

In 1953 there was no daylight between the Catholic Church and the Irish government, and Doyle's chances in court are poor. He is trying not merely to regain custody of his children, but to overturn Irish law. The case has great symbolic value, and soon Beattie finds himself joined by an Irish-American lawyer

197

named Nick Barron (Aidan Quinn), and finally by a retired Irish legal legend named Thomas Connolly (Alan Bates).

Courtroom scenes in movies are often somewhat similar, and yet almost always gripping. The format fascinates us. There is great suspense here as Evelyn herself takes the stand to denounce Sister Brigid, and Sophie Vavasseur is a good actress, able to convincingly make us fear she won't choose the right words, before she does.

Evelyn depicts Irish society of fifty years ago with a low-key cheerfulness that shows how humor cut the fog of poverty. The Irish in those days got much of their entertainment in pubs, which often had a lounge bar with a piano and an array of ready singers, and it is a true touch that Desmond Doyle takes a turn with a song (Brosnan does his own singing, no better but no worse than a competent pub singer). The movie also enjoys the Irish humor based on paradox and logic, as when one of Desmond's sons, told Joseph was a carpenter, asks, "Did Joseph ever do a bit of painting and decoration like my dad?"

Evelyn is directed by Bruce Beresford *(Driving Miss Daisy, Crimes of the Heart)*, who may have chosen the straightforward, classic style as a deliberate decision: It signals us that the movie will not be tarted up with modern touches, spring any illogical surprises, or ask for other than genuine emotions. Brosnan, at the center, is convincing as a man who sobers up and becomes, not a saint, but at least the dependable person he was meant to be. And Irish law is changed forever.

Everybody's Famous ★ ½
R, 92 m., 2001

Josse De Pauw (Jean Vereecken), Werner De Smedt (Willy van Outreve), Eva van der Gucht (Marva Vereecken), Thekla Reuten (Debbie), Victor Low (Michael Jansen), Gert Portael (Chantal Vereecken). Directed by Dominique Deruddere and produced by Loret Meus and Deruddere. Screenplay by Deruddere.

Everybody's Famous opens at a dreary talent contest at which the plump, desperate Marva demonstrates that she cannot sing, and could not deliver a song if she could. The judges, including the local mayor, hold up Olympic-style paddles scoring her with twos and threes, and we feel they're generous. But Jean, Marva's father, remains fanatically convinced that his daughter is talented and has a future—this despite the thankless girl's rudeness toward her old man.

Poor Jean (Josse De Pauw) is a good man, endured by his patient wife, Chantal (Gert Portael), treasured by his best friend, Willy (Werner De Smedt), and chained to the night shift at a factory where he has to inspect endless lines of bottles for hours at a time. At home, he joins his family in admiring the concerts of a pop singer named only Debbie (Thekla Reuten), who wears an incandescent blue polyester wig.

One day a bolt of coincidence joins Debbie and Jean. He finds an opportunity to kidnap her, and does, enlisting Willy to help him. His ransom demand: Debbie's manager (Victor Low) must record and release a song that Jean has written and that Marva (Eva van der Gucht) must sing.

This sets into motion a plot that begins with the same basic situation as *The King of Comedy,* where the Robert De Niro character kidnapped a TV host played by Jerry Lewis, but the difference here is that *Everybody's Famous* is cheerful and optimistic, and if by the end everybody is not famous at least everybody has gotten what they want in life.

Three of the characters—the mother, the best friend, and the pop star—are so bland they're essentially place-holders. Josse De Pauw does what he can with the lead role, as a simple, good-hearted man who can't even get a good-night kiss from the daughter he has sacrificed everything for. Victor Low seems like a very low-rent pop impresario, especially considering he can get a song scored, recorded, and on the charts in about twenty-four hours. But Eva van der Gucht brings some pouting humor to the role of the untalented daughter, whose costumes look like somebody's idea of a cruel joke, and who is bluntly told that she sings with a complete absence of emotion.

The big scene at the end involves one of those TV news situations that never happen in real life, where a reporter and camera materialize at a crucial point and are seemingly at the pleasure of the plot. And there's a surprise during a televised talent show, which will not come as that much of a surprise, however, to any sentient being.

The movie, from the Flemish community of Belgium, was one of this year's Oscar nominees for Best Foreign Film, leading one to wonder what films were passed over to make room for it. It is as pleasant as all get-out, sunny and serendipitous, and never even bothers to create much of a possibility that it will be otherwise. By the time the police spontaneously applaud a man they have every reason to believe is holding a hostage, the movie has given up any shred of plausibility and is simply trying to be a nice comedy. It's nice, but it's not much of a comedy.

Evolution ★ ★ ½
PG-13, 103 m., 2001

David Duchovny (Ira Kane), Orlando Jones (Harry Block), Ted Levine (Dr. Woodman), Julianne Moore (Allison Reed), Seann William Scott (Wayne Green), Dan Aykroyd (Governor Lewis), Wayne Duvall (Dr. Paulson), Michael Bower (Danny Donald), Wendy Braun (Nurse Tate). Directed by Ivan Reitman and produced by Daniel Goldberg, Joe Medjuck, and Reitman. Screenplay by David Diamond, David Weissman, and Don Jakoby.

I can't quite recommend *Evolution,* but I have a sneaky affection for it. It's not good, but it's nowhere near as bad as most recent comedies; it has real laughs, but it misses real opportunities. For example, by giving us aliens who are sort of harmless, it sets up a situation where the heroes should be trying to protect them. But no. Everybody wants to kill them, apparently because the national psyche has reverted to the 1950s, when all flying saucers were automatically fired on by the army.

Ivan Reitman, who directed the film, also made *Ghostbusters,* and there are times when you can see that he remembers his earlier success all too well. Both movies have vast gaseous monsters, although only this one, keenly alert to the bodily orifice du jour, gives us "Help! I'm Trapped Up the Alien's Sphincter!" jokes. I have days on the movie beat when I don't know if I'm a critic or a proctologist.

As the film opens, a would-be fireman (Seann

William Scott) is practicing by rescuing an inflatable doll from a burning shack, when a flaming meteor crashes nearby. Harry Block (Orlando Jones), a scientist from nearby Glen Canyon Community College, is called to investigate and brings along his friend, science instructor Ira Kane (David Duchovny). They discover the meteor has "punched through" to an underground cavern, where it is oozing strange sluglike little creatures.

Kane and Bloch have a nice double-act together; like the characters in *Ghostbusters* they talk intelligently and possess wit and irony, and are not locked into one-liners. Jones even gets a laugh out of a significant nod, which is not easy in a movie with this decibel level. I also liked the way they came up with a popular drugstore item as a weapon against the invaders.

The alien creatures have the amazing ability to evolve in brief generations into whatever the screenplay requires: flying dinosaurs, creepy-crawlies, savage reptiles, even a sad-eyed ET clone that has an *Alien* tooth-monster hiding down its throat. The army is called in, led by Dr. Woodman (Ted Levine), a soldier-scientist who worked with Ira Kane once before ("he's a dangerous disgrace"). Turns out Ira inoculated platoons of soldiers with a substance with such side effects as diarrhea, blindness, facial paralysis, and hair loss. The army named this tragic syndrome after Kane; I found myself thinking of funnier names for it, starting with the Bald Runs.

Dr. Woodman's assistant is Allison Reed (Julianne Moore), whose character trait is that she falls over everything. She is, however, funny in other ways, and sides with the two community college guys when her boss tries to freeze them out of the investigation. Meanwhile, the evolving creatures take on weird manifestations while the Mother of All Creatures is expanding down there in that cavern, generating all manner of strange offspring, while preparing to make an appearance in the grand finale.

The aliens are clever and bizarre movie creatures, designed by special-effects wizard Phil Tippett, who applied "the basic theory of panspermia," according to the press notes, which I always study after movies like this. It will come as news to panspermists that pansperm can evolve into amphibians, reptiles, birds, and mammals within a week; *Evolution* parts company with the basic theory almost before the publicist can get it into the notes, but never mind: One does not attend this movie for scientific facts. That is what the *Star Trek* movies are for.

Would it surprise you if I said that after ninety minutes of preparation, we discover that the entire movie has been leading up to a moment when the Orlando Jones character finds himself occupying the business end of a giant alien's digestive tract? Not if you have a sense of fair play. Earlier in the movie, a little alien crawls under Jones's skin and lodges in *his* intestines, inspiring emergency measures by a doctor who cries, "There's no time for lubricant!"—inspiring Jones to utter the best line in the movie, "There's *always* time for lubricant!"

The Eye ★ ★ ½
NO MPAA RATING, 99 m., 2003

Lee Sin-Je (Mun), Lawrence Chou (Dr. Wah), Chutcha Rujinanon (Ling), Yut Lai So (Yingying), Candy Lo (Yee), Yin Ping Ko (Mun's Grandmother), Pierre Png (Dr. Eak), Edmund Chen (Dr. Lo). Directed by Oxide Pang Chun and Danny Pang and produced by Lawrence Cheng. Screenplay by Jo Jo Yuet-chun Hui, Pang Chun, and Pang.

The Eye is a thriller about a blind young violinist from Hong Kong whose sight is restored through surgery, but who can then see a little too well, so that she observes the grim reaper leading the doomed in solemn procession to the other side, and shares the anguish of the donor of her eyes. What's more, she's thrown out of the blind orchestra now that she can see.

All I know about restored sight I learned in the books of Oliver Sacks, who writes about a patient whose sight was miraculously restored. The problem turns out to be knowing what you're looking at. Babies do all the hard work in the first months after birth, learning to interpret shapes and colors, dimension and distance. For an adult who relates to the world through the other four senses, the addition of sight is not always a blessing.

The movie touches on that, in a scene where the blind girl, named Mun (Lee Sin-Je) is shown a stapler and asked what it is. She can tell by feeling it. But she's a quick study, and in no time is moving independently through the world and falling in love with Dr. Wah, her handsome young therapist (Lawrence Chou).

Lee has an expressive face, which is crucial to the success of the film, because she has an extraordinary number of reaction shots, and no wonder: The movie is about what Mun sees and how she reacts to it. Unlike the overwrought heroines of most women-in-danger films, Mun is quiet, introspective, reasonable, and persuasive.

Perhaps that's why Dr. Wah believes her. She becomes convinced that she can see the dead leaving this Earth and anticipate tragedies before they happen. She thinks this may be connected in some way with the donor of her new eyes, and Dr. Wah begins to believe her, not least because he falls in love with her. His uncle, Dr. Lo (Edmund Chen), takes a jaundiced view of this development, which violates medical ethics and perhaps common sense, and refuses to divulge the name of the donor.

But Wah and Mun eventually do figure out that the corneas came from a girl in Thailand, and journey there for a conclusion that includes a startling scene of carnage that's all the more unexpected because it comes at the end of a relatively quiet and inward movie.

The Eye is better than it might have been, especially in moments of terror involving Mun's ability to see what no one else can see, and in her relationship with a little girl at the hospital who seems to be dying, and becomes her special friend. But the notion that body parts retain the memories of their owners is an outworn horror cliché, as in *The Beast with Five Fingers* and Oliver Stone's early screenplay, *The Hand*. This is the kind of movie you happen across on TV, and linger to watch out of curiosity, but its inspired moments serve only to point out how routine, and occasionally how slow and wordy, the rest of it is.

F

Faithless ★ ★ ★ ½
R, 142 m., 2001

Lena Endre (Marianne), Erland Josephson (Bergman), Krister Henriksson (David), Thomas Hanzon (Markus), Michelle Gylemo (Isabelle), Juni Dahr (Margareta), Philip Zanden (Martin Goldman), Therese Brunnander (Petra Holst). Directed by Liv Ullmann and produced by Kaj Larsen. Screenplay by Ingmar Bergman.

The island is Faro, where Ingmar Bergman lives, and the house is Bergman's house, and the beach is where he walks, and the office is where he works, and we can see a shadowy 16mm film projector in the background, and remember hearing that the Swedish Film Institute sends him weekly shipments of films to watch. And the old man in the film is named "Bergman," although we don't learn that essential piece of the jigsaw until the final credits.

Or perhaps the house and its office are a set. And perhaps "Bergman" is partly Ingmar Bergman and partly the director's fictional creation. And surely, we think, he has a DVD player by now. *Faithless,* a film made from his screenplay and directed by Liv Ullmann, is intriguing in the way it dances in and out of the shadow of Bergman's autobiography. We learn in his book *The Magic Lantern,* for example, that in 1949 he was involved in an affair something like the one in this film—but we sense immediately that *Faithless* is not a memoir of that affair, but a meditation on the guilt it inspired.

Bergman, the son of a Lutheran bishop, has in his eighties forsaken the consolations of religion but not the psychic payments that it exacts. His film feels like an examination of conscience, and he's hard on himself. It's with a start we realize that Ullmann is also one of his former lovers, that they have a child together, and that in her vision he has clearly been forgiven his trespasses.

The movie is about a messy affair from "Bergman's" past, and it is about the creative process. As it begins, the old man (Erland Josephson) has writing paper on the desk before him, and is talking with an actress (Lena Endre). It becomes clear that this actress is not physically present. The dialogue suggests the director has enlisted this woman, or her memory, to help him think through a story he is writing. But she is also the woman the story is about. And she sometimes seems to be reading her story from his notes—as if he created her and she exists only in his words.

The woman is named Marianne. She is married to Markus (Thomas Hanzon), a symphony conductor, often away on tours. They have a daughter of eight or nine, Isabelle (Michelle Gylemo). David (Krister Henriksson) is Markus's best friend. One night while Markus is away David asks Marianne if he may sleep with her. She laughs him off, but then agrees they can share the same bed as brother and sister. Soon they have hurtled into a passionate affair, unforeseen and heedless.

It is clear that David is "Bergman" at an earlier age. He is a film director with vague projects in mind, he has long been attracted to Marianne, and he is, let us say, a louse. What becomes clear during the course of the film is that Markus is no saint either, and that he uses his daughter as a hostage in the unpleasantness that results.

Ullmann has a sure sense for the ways people behave in emotional extremity. *Faithless* is not made of soap opera sincerity, but from the messiness of people who might later wish they had behaved differently. When Markus surprises the naked David in bed with Marianne, he projects not jealous anger, but a kind of smarmy "gotcha!" triumph (for their part, they giggle nervously).

It is David who feels sexual jealousy; when Marianne returns from Markus with the news she has regained custody of her child, David thinks "something doesn't sound right," and cross-examines her until he forces out a description of how Markus raped her as the cost of custody. (This rape, described but not seen, has the same kind of reality in the mind's eye as the monologue about the boys on the beach in *Persona.*)

At one point in the film, "Bergman" reaches out and tenderly touches the cheek of David, and Ullmann has said this is the old man forgiving the young man, even though the old man can never forgive himself.

Ingmar Bergman has had his name on films for nearly sixty years. Some are among the best ever made. In old age he has grown more inward and personal, writing versions of his autobiography, usually to be directed by close friends. The films shot on Faro are in a category by themselves: chamber films, spare, chilly, with grateful interiors warmed by fires or candles. In *Faithless,* scenes in Stockholm and Paris show cozy interiors, boudoirs, restaurants, theaters, cafés. And then all is reduced to the spare, stark office—almost a monk's cell—where "Bergman" sits and remembers, summons his muses, and writes.

Far from Heaven ★ ★ ★ ★
PG-13, 107 m., 2002

Julianne Moore (Cathy Whitaker), Dennis Quaid (Frank Whitaker), Dennis Haysbert (Raymond Deagan), Patricia Clarkson (Eleonor Fine), Viola Davis (Sybil), James Rebhorn (Dr. Bowman), Celia Weston (Mona Lauder). Directed by Todd Haynes and produced by Jody Patton and Christine Vachon. Screenplay by Haynes.

Todd Haynes's *Far from Heaven* is like the best and bravest movie of 1957. Its themes, values, and style faithfully reflect the social melodramas of the 1950s, but it's bolder and says out loud what those films only hinted at. It begins with an ideal suburban Connecticut family, a husband and wife "team" so thoroughly absorbed into corporate culture they're known as "Mr. and Mrs. Magnatech." Then it develops that Mr. Magnatech is gay, and Mrs. Magnatech believes that the black gardener is the most beautiful man she has ever seen.

They are the Whitakers, Cathy and Frank (Julianne Moore and Dennis Quaid). They live in a perfect split-level house on a perfect street, where the autumn leaves are turning to gold. Their little son is reprimanded for rude language like "Aw, shucks." Of course she drives a station wagon. Mona Lauder (Celia Weston), the local society editor, is writing a profile about their perfection.

One slight shadow clouds the sun. While being interviewed by Celia, Cathy sees a strange black man in the yard and walks outside to ask, ever so politely, if she can "help" him. He introduces himself: Raymond Deagan (Dennis

Haysbert), son of their usual gardener, who has died. Cathy, who has a good heart, instinctively reaches out to touch Raymond on the shoulder in sympathy, and inside the house the gesture is noted by Celia, who adds to her profile that Cathy is a "friend to Negroes."

Frank Whitaker is one of those big, good-looking guys who look like a college athlete gone slightly to seed, or drink. One night Cathy has to pick him up at the police station after an incident involving "one lousy cocktail." In another scene we see him enter a gay bar, where in these days long before Stonewall, the men exchange furtive, embarrassed glances as if surprised to find themselves there. One night Cathy makes the mistake of taking Frank his dinner when he works late, and opens his office door to find him kissing a man.

The movie accurately reflects the values of the 1950s, and you can see that in a scene where Frank says his homosexuality makes him feel "despicable," but he's "going to lick this problem." The key to the power of *Far from Heaven* is that it's never ironic; there is never a wink or a hint that the filmmakers have more enlightened ideas than their characters. This is not a movie that knows more than was known in 1957, but a movie that knows exactly what mainstream values were in 1957—and traps us in them, along with its characters.

Frank and Cathy have no sex life. Cathy is not attracted to Raymond so much sexually, however, as she's in awe of his kindness and beauty, which is so adamantly outside her segregated world. She hardly knows how to talk with him. At one point she says that "Mr. Whitaker and I support equal rights for the Negro." Raymond looks at her level-eyed and says, "I'm happy to hear that." He has a business degree, but has inherited the same gardening business that supported his father; a widower, he dotes on his eleven-year-old daughter.

The plot advances on a public and a private front. Publicly, word starts to get around that Cathy has been "seen" with the black gardener. Only that—"seen." Once when they take a ride in his truck, they enter a black diner, where their reception is as frosty as it would have been in a white place. Neither race approves of mixed couples. Soon people start to "talk," and Frank, the hypocrite, screams at her about all he's done to build up the reputation of the family, only to hear these stories.

Frank's homosexuality, of course, remains deeply buried. A psychiatrist (James Rebhorn) muses about "aversion therapy" but warns that the "majority of cases cannot be cured." Frank drinks heavily and turns ugly, and Cathy's feelings for Raymond grow, but she has no idea how to act on them. Mr. and Mrs. Magnatech need a repairman.

Far from Heaven uses superb craftsmanship to make this film look and feel like a film from the 1950s. Todd Haynes says he had three specific inspirations: Douglas Sirk's *All That Heaven Allows* (1955), which starred Jane Wyman and Rock Hudson in the story of a middle-aged widow and her handsome young gardener; Sirk's *Imitation of Life* (1959), with Lana Turner as a rich woman whose maid's daughter (Susan Kohner) passes for white; and Max Ophuls's *The Reckless Moment* (1949), about blackmail. In Sirk's films you often have the feeling that part of the plot is in code, that one kind of forbidden love stands for another.

The movie benefits enormously from its cinematography by Ed Lachman, who faithfully reproduces the lush 1950s studio style; the opening downward crane shot of autumn leaves is matched by the closing upward crane shot of spring blossoms, and every shot has the studied artifice of 1950s "set decoration," which was not so different, after all, from 1950s "interior decoration." The musical score, by Elmer Bernstein, is true to the time, with its underlining of points and its punching-up of emotions. Haynes said in an interview that "every element" of his film has been "drawn from and filtered through film grammar."

One detail is particularly true to the time: Interracial love and homosexual love are treated as being on different moral planes. The civil rights revolution predated gay liberation by about ten years, and you can see that here: The movie doesn't believe Raymond and Cathy have a plausible future together, but there is bittersweet regret that they do not. When Frank meets a young man and falls in love, however, the affair is not ennobled but treated as a matter of motel rooms and furtive meetings. Haynes is pitch-perfect here in noting that homosexuality, in the 1950s, still dared not speak its name.

Because the film deliberately lacks irony, it has a genuine dramatic impact; it plays like a powerful 1957 drama we've somehow never seen before. The effect is oddly jolting: Contemporary movies take so many subjects for granted that they never really look at them. Haynes, by moving back in time, is able to bring his issues into focus. We care about the characters in the way its period expected us to. (There is one time rupture; Frank uses the f-word to his wife and the fabric of the film breaks, only to be repaired when he apologizes.)

Julianne Moore, Dennis Quaid, and Dennis Haysbert are called on to play characters whose instincts are wholly different from their own. By succeeding, they make their characters real, instead of stereotypes. The tenderness of Cathy and Raymond's unrealized love is filled with regret that is all the more touching because they acknowledge that their society will not accept them as a couple. When Raymond and his daughter leave town, Cathy suggests maybe she could visit them sometime in Baltimore, but Raymond gently replies, "I'm not sure that would be a good idea." ☞

The Fast and the Furious ★ ★ ★
PG-13, 101 m., 2001

Vin Diesel (Dominic Toretto), Paul Walker (Brian), Jordana Brewster (Mia Toretto), Michelle Rodriguez (Letty), Rick Yune (Johnny Tran), Beau Holden (Ted Gessner). Directed by Rob Cohen and produced by Neal H. Moritz. Screenplay by Ken Li, Gary Scott Thompson, Erik Bergquist, and David Ayer.

The Fast and the Furious remembers summer movies from the days when they were produced by American-International and played in drive-ins on double features. It's slicker than films like *Grand Theft Auto,* but it has the same kind of pirate spirit—it wants to raid its betters and carry off the loot. It doesn't have a brain in its head, but it has some great chase scenes, and includes the most incompetent cop who ever went undercover.

According to the "In a World" Guy, who narrates the trailer, the movie takes place "In a world . . . beyond the law." It stars Vin Diesel, the bald-headed, mug-faced action actor who looks like a muscular Otto Preminger. He plays

Toretto, a star of the forbidden sport of street racing who rockets his custom machine through Los Angeles at more than 100 mph before pushing a button on the dashboard and *really* accelerating, thanks to a nitrous oxide booster. He also runs a bar where his sister Mia (Jordana Brewster) serves "tuna salad on white bread, no crusts" every day to Brian (Paul Walker), who looks a little like white bread, no crusts himself.

Brian hangs out there because he wants to break into street racing, and because he likes Mia. Toretto's gang is hostile to him, beats him up, disses him, and he comes back for more. He ends up winning Toretto's friendship by saving him from the cops. The races involve cars four abreast at speedway speeds down city streets. This would be difficult in Chicago, but is easy in Los Angeles, because, as everybody knows, L.A. has no traffic and no cops.

Actually, Brian is a cop, assigned to investigate a string of multimillion-dollar truck hijackings. The hijackers surround an eighteen-wheeler with three Honda Civics, shoot out the window on the passenger side, fire a cable into the cab, and climb into the truck at high speeds. This makes for thrilling action sequences when it works, and an even more thrilling action sequence when it doesn't, in a chase scene that approaches but does not surpass the climax of *The Road Warrior*.

During the chases, we observe that there is *no* other traffic on the highway—just the trucks and the Hondas. Anyone who has ever driven a Honda next to an eighteen-wheeler will know that a Humvee is the wiser choice, but never mind. And only a hopeless realist would observe that leaping through the windshield of a speeding truck is a dangerous and inefficient way of stealing VCRs. In Chicago, the crooks are more prudent, and steal from parked trucks, warehouses, and other unmoving targets. Toretto should try it.

Anyway, Brian at first seems just like a guy who wants to race, but is revealed as a cop in an early scene, although not so early the audience has not guessed it. He works for a unit that has its undercover headquarters in a Hollywood house, and as he enters it his boss says, "Eddie Fisher built this house for Elizabeth Taylor in the 1950s." I am thinking: (1) This is almost certainly true or it would not be said in

a movie so stingy with dialogue, and (2) Is this the first time Brian has seen his unit's office?

One of the nice things about the movie is the way it tells a story and explains its characters. It's a refreshing change from such no-plot, all-action movies as *Gone in 60 Seconds*. We learn a little about Toretto's father and his childhood, and we see Brian and Mia falling in love—although I think in theory you are not supposed to date the sister of a guy you are undercover to investigate. Michelle Rodriguez, the star of the underappreciated boxing movie *Girlfight*, costars as a member of the hijack gang, and gets to land one solid right on a guy's jaw, just to keep her credentials.

The Fast and the Furious is not a great movie, but it delivers what it promises to deliver, and knows that a chase scene is supposed to be about something more than special effects. It has some of that grandiose, self-pitying dialogue we've treasured in movies like this ever since *Rebel Without a Cause*. "I live my life a quarter-mile at a time," Toretto tells Brian. "For those ten seconds, I'm free." And, hey, even for the next thirty seconds, he's decelerating.

Fast Food, Fast Women ★ ½
R, 95 m., 2001

Anna Thomson (Bella), Jamie Harris (Bruno), Louise Lasser (Emily), Robert Modica (Paul), Lonette McKee (Sherry-Lynn), Victor Argo (Seymour), Angelica Torn (Vitka), Austin Pendleton (George). Directed by Amos Kollek and produced by Hengameh Panahi. Screenplay by Kollek.

There's nothing wrong with *Fast Food, Fast Women* that a casting director and a rewrite couldn't have fixed. The rewrite would have realized that the movie's real story involves a sweet, touching romance between two supporting characters. The casting director would have questioned the sanity of using Anna Thomson in the lead role.

The sweet love story stars Louise Lasser in her best performance, as Emily, a widow who finds Paul (Robert Modica) through a personals ad. Their courtship is complicated by pride and misunderstanding, and by way too many plot contrivances. The lead role involves Thomson as Bella, a waitress who is said to be thirty-five.

A gentleman does not question a lady about her age, but Thomson was playing adult roles twenty years ago, has obviously had plastic surgery, and always dresses to emphasize her extreme thinness and prominent chest, so that we can't help thinking she's had a boob job.

Faithful readers will know I rarely criticize the physical appearance of actors. I would have given Thomson a pass, but the movie seems to be inviting my thoughts about her character, since Lasser's character has one big scene where she confesses she's not really as young as she claims, and another where she wonders if she should have her breasts enlarged—and then Thomson's character asks the taxi driver, "Aren't I voluptuous enough?" It's unwise to have one character being honest about issues when we're supposed to overlook the same questions raised by another character.

The movie takes place in one of those movie diners where everybody hangs out all day long and gets involved in each other's business. Bella rules the roost, pouring coffee for Paul and his pal Seymour (Victor Argo). The diner has so many regulars, it even has a regular hooker, Vitka (Angelica Torn), who stutters, so that guys can't tell she's asking them if they feel like having a good time. We learn that for years Bella has been having an affair with the married George (Austin Pendleton), who claims to be a Broadway producer, but whose shows sound like hallucinations. He spends most of their time together looking away from her and grinning at a private joke.

Bella meets a cab driver named Bruno (Jamie Harris), who has become the custodian of two children, leading to more misunderstandings that threaten to derail their future together. And then Bruno meets Emily, Seymour falls for Wanda, a stripper in a peep show, and there comes a point when you want to ask Amos Kollek, the writer-director, why the zany plot overkill when your real story is staring you in the face? (You want to ask him that even before the zebras and the camels turn up, and long before the unforgivable "happy ending.")

Lasser and Modica, as Emily and Paul, are two nice, good, lovable people who deserve each other, and whenever the movie involves their story, we care (even despite some desperate plot contrivances). Lasser's vulnerability, her courage, and the light in her eyes all bring

those scenes to life, as does Paul's instinctive courtesy and the way he responds to her warmth. There's the movie. If it has to pretend to be about Bella, Kollek as the director should at least have been able to see the character more clearly—clearly enough to know the audience cannot believe she is thirty-five, and thinks of her whenever anyone else mentions plastic surgery.

The Fast Runner ★ ★ ★ ★
NO MPAA RATING, 172 m., 2002

Natar Ungalaaq (Atanarjuat), Sylvia Ivalu (Atuat), Peter-Henry Arnatsiaq (Oki), Lucy Tulugarjuk (Puja), Madeline Ivalu (Panikpak), Paul Qulitalik (Qulitalik), Eugene Ipkarnak (Sauri, the Chief), Pakkak Innushuk (Amaqjuaq). Directed by Zacharias Kunuk and produced by Paul Apak Angilirq, Norman Cohn, and Zacharias Kunuk. Screenplay by Paul Apak Angilirq.

We could begin with the facts about The Fast Runner. It is the first film shot in Inuktitut, the language of the Inuit peoples who live within the Arctic Circle. It was made with an Inuit cast, and a 90 percent Inuit crew. It is based on a story that is at least 1,000 years old. It records a way of life that still existed within living memory.

Or we could begin with the feelings. The film is about romantic tensions that lead to tragedy within a small, closely knit community of people who depend on one another for survival, surrounded by a landscape of ice and snow. It shows how people either learn to get along under those circumstances, or pay a terrible price.

Or we could begin with the lore. Here you will see humans making a living in a world that looks, to us, like a barren wasteland. We see them fishing, hunting, preparing their kill, scraping skins to make them into clothing, tending the lamps of oil that illuminate their igloos, harvesting the wild crops that grow in the brief summertime, living with the dogs that pull their sleds.

Or we could begin with the story of the film's production. It was shot with a high-definition digital video camera, sidestepping the problems that cinematographers have long experienced while using film in temperatures well below zero. Its script was compiled from versions of an Inuit legend told by eight elders. The film won the Camera d'Or, for best first film, at Cannes, and was introduced at Telluride by the British stage director Peter Sellars; telling the story of its origin, he observed, "In most cultures, a human being is a library."

We could begin in all of those ways, or we could plunge into the film itself, an experience so engrossing it is like being buried in a new environment. Some find the opening scene claustrophobic. It takes place entirely inside an igloo, the low lighting provided only by oil lamps, most of the shots in close-up, and we do not yet know who all the characters are. I thought it was an interesting way to begin: to plunge us into this community and share its warmth as it shelters against the cold, and then to open up and tell its story.

We meet two brothers, Amaqjuaq (Pakkak Innushuk), known as the Strong One, and Atanarjuat (Natar Ungalaaq), known as the Fast Runner. They are part of a small group of Inuit including the unpleasant Oki (Peter-Henry Arnatsiaq), whose father is the leader of the group. There is a romantic problem. Oki has been promised Atuat (Sylvia Ivalu), but she and Atanarjuat are in love. Just like in Shakespeare. In the most astonishing fight scene I can recall, Atanarjuat challenges Oki, and they fight in the way of their people: They stand face to face while one solemnly hits the other, there is a pause, and the hit is returned, one blow after another, until one or the other falls.

Atanarjuat wins, but it is not so simple. He is happy with Atuat, but eventually takes another wife, Puja (Lucy Tulugarjuk), who is pouty and spoiled and put on Earth to cause trouble. During one long night of the midnight sun, she is caught secretly making love to Amaqjuaq, and banished from the family. It is, we gather, difficult to get away with adultery when everybody lives in the same tent.

Later there is a shocking murder. Fleeing for his life, Atanarjuat breaks free, and runs across the tundra—runs and runs, naked. It is one of those movie sequences you know you will never forget.

At the end of the film, over the closing titles, there are credit cookies showing the production of the film, and we realize with a little shock that the film was made now, by living people,

with new technology. There is a way in which the intimacy of the production and the 172-minute running time lull us into accepting the film as a documentary of real life. The actors, many of them professional Inuit performers, are without affect or guile: They seem sincere, honest, revealing, as real people might, and although the story involves elements of melodrama and even soap opera, the production seems as real as a frozen fish.

I am not surprised that *The Fast Runner* has been a box-office hit in its opening engagements. It is unlike anything most audiences will ever have seen, and yet it tells a universal story. What's unique is the patience it has with its characters: The willingness to watch and listen as they reveal themselves, instead of pushing them to the front like little puppets and having them dance through the story. *The Fast Runner* is passion, filtered through ritual and memory.

Fat Girl ★ ★ ★ ½
NO MPAA RATING, 83 m., 2001

Anais Reboux (Anais), Roxane Mesquida (Elena), Libero De Rienzo (Fernando), Arsinee Khanjian (Mother), Romain Goupil (Father), Laura Betti (Fernando's Mother), Albert Goldberg (The Killer), Claude Sese (Police Officer), Marc Samuel (Inspector). Directed by Catherine Breillat and produced by Fredy Lagrost and Jean-Francois Lepetit. Screenplay by Breillat.

Young love is idealized as sweet romance, but early sexual experiences are often painful and clumsy and based on lies. It is not merely that a boy will tell a girl almost anything to get her into bed, but that a girl will pretend to believe almost anything because she is curious too. *Fat Girl* is the brutally truthful story of the first sexual experiences of a fifteen-year-old sexpot and her pudgy twelve-year-old sister.

The movie was written and directed by Catherine Breillat, a French woman who is fascinated by the physical and psychological details of sex. Her characters may talk of love, but rarely feel it, and are not necessarily looking for it: Her women, as well as men, have a frank curiosity about what they can do, and what can be done, with their bodies. Her previous film, the notorious *Romance*, was about a sexually unsatisfied woman who goes on a deliberate quest for better sex—and if that sounds like a porn film, *Romance* is not about ecstasy but about plumbing, sweating, hurting, lying and loathing.

Fat Girl, seemingly more innocent, at times almost like one of those sophisticated French movies about an early summer of love, turns out to be more painful and shocking than we anticipate. It is like life, which has a way of interrupting our plans with its tragic priorities. True, Anais (Anais Reboux) achieves a personal milestone, but at what a cost.

The movie takes place in a summer resort area. Anais and her sexy fifteen-year-old sister, Elena (Roxane Mesquida), are vacationing with their mother (Arsinee Khanjian). Their father (Romain Goupil) is a workaholic for whom the family is just one more item on his to-do list. Elena attracts the attention of the local boys, and her overweight kid sister looks on with smoldering jealousy: Anais at twelve is smarter and in certain ways more grown-up. She is eager for a sexual experience, although she has little idea what that would entail (in one sad-sweet scene in a swimming pool, she imagines a romantic rivalry for her affections between . . . a pier and a ladder). In another scene, she eats a banana split in the backseat while watching Elena necking in the front.

Fernando (Libero De Rienzo) comes sniffing around. He is older, a law student, also on vacation. Elena finds his attention flattering. He speaks of love, is vague about the future, insistent about his demands. What Breillat sees clearly is that Elena is not an innocent who is deceived by his lies, but a curious girl with high spirits who wants to believe. Yes, she says she wants to keep her virginity (Anais wants to lose hers). But virginity and purity for Elena are two very different things. Like a lover in a Latin farce, Fernando climbs in through the bedroom window one night, and the "sleeping" Anais watches as Elena and Fernando have sex. What do they do? There is no doubt a French phrase for the words "everything but."

Breillat has no false sentimentality about women, no feeling that men are pigs. Sentiment and piggishness are pretty equally distributed between the sexes in her movies. Consider a sequence in which Fernando steals one of his mother's rings and gives it to Elena, not quite saying what he promises by it. And then how

Fernando's mother calls on Elena's mother to get the ring back. We discover that the ring is part of a little collection Fernando's mother has, of jewelry given to her by lying men; if she had a sense of humor, she would see the irony in how it has been passed on.

The private scenes between Anais and Elena are closely observed. The girls say hateful and insulting things to each other, as young adolescents are likely to do, but they also share trust and affection, and talk with absolute frankness about what concerns them. Elena's dalliance with Fernando ends unhappily, but then of course, in a way she knew it would. Anais is left raging with jealousy that she is still a virgin, and she is at least more realistic about life than Elena: When she loses her virginity, she says, it will be without love, to a man she hardly knows, because she just wants to get it out of the way and move on.

The film has a shocking ending, which Breillat builds to with shots that are photographed and edited to create a sense of menace. This ending leaves the audience stunned, and some will be angered by it. But consider how it works in step with what went before, and with the drift of Breillat's work. This is not a film softened and made innocuous by timid studio executives after "test screenings." There is a jolting surprise in discovering that this film has free will, and can end as it wants, and that its director can make her point, however brutally. And perhaps only with this ending could Anais's cold, hard, sad logic be so unforgivingly demonstrated.

FearDotCom ★ ★

R, 90 m., 2002

Stephen Dorff (Mike Reilly), Natascha McElhone (Terry Huston), Stephen Rea (Alistair Pratt), Udo Kier (Polidori), Amelia Curtis (Denise), Jeffrey Combs (Styles), Nigel Terry (Turnbull), Gesine Cukrowski (Jeannine), Elizabeth McKechnie (Alice Turnbull). Directed by William Malone and produced by Limor Diamant and Moshe Diamant. Screenplay by Josephine Coyle, based on a story by Moshe Diamant.

Strange, how good *FearDotCom* is, and how bad. The screenplay is a mess, and yet the visuals are so creative this is one of the rare bad films you might actually want to see. The plot is a bewildering jumble of half-baked ideas, from which we gather just enough of a glimmer about the story to understand how it is shot through with contradictions and paradoxes. And yet I watched in admiration as a self-contained nightmare formed with the visuals. Not many movies know how to do that.

I'll get to the plot later, or maybe never. Let me talk about what I liked. The film takes place in a city where it always rains and is nearly always night, where even people with good jobs live in apartments that look hammered together after an air raid. Computers and the Internet exist here, and indeed telephones, televisions, and all the other props of the present day, but windows are broken, walls are punctured, lights flicker, streets are deserted, and from time to time a dramatic thunderstorm threatens to sweep everything away. This is like *Dark City* after a hurricane.

It is the kind of city where a man can walk down into a subway and be the only person there, except for a little girl bouncing her ball against the third rail. Or . . . is the man really alone? Is that his fantasy? Whether it is or not, he gets slammed by the next train, and the cops are startled by the expression on his face. It looks, they agree, as if he had just seen something terrifying. Apparently something even worse than the train. And he is bleeding from the eyes.

The film's premise is that a Website exists that channels negative energy into the mind of the beholder, who self-destructs within forty-eight hours, a victim of his or her deepest fear. Our first glimpse of this Website suggests nothing more than a reasonably well-designed horror site, with Shockwave images of dark doorways, screaming lips, rows of knives, and so forth. The movie wisely doesn't attempt to develop the site much more than that, relying on the reactions of the victims to imply what other terrors it contains. And it does something else, fairly subtly: It expands the site to encompass the entire movie, so that by the end all of the characters are essentially inside the fatal Web experience, and we are, too.

The last twenty minutes are, I might as well say it, brilliant. Not in terms of what happens, but in terms of how it happens, and how it

looks as it happens. The movie has tended toward the monochromatic all along, but now it abandons all pretense of admitting the color spectrum, and slides into the kind of tinting used in silent films: browns alternate with blues, mostly. The images play like homage to the best Grand Guignol traditions, to *Nosferatu* and some of the James Whale and Jacques Tourneur pictures, and the best moments of the Hammer horror films. Squirming victims are displayed on the Internet by the sadistic killer, who prepares to autopsy them while still alive; subscribers to the site, whose crime is that they want to watch, are addressed by name and are soon paying dearly for their voyeurism.

The movie is extremely violent; it avoided the NC-17 rating and earned an R, I understand, after multiple trims and appeals, and even now it is one of the most graphic horror films I've seen. (The classification is for "violence including grisly images of torture, nudity and language," the MPAA explains, but you'll be disappointed if you hope to see grisly images of language).

Stephen Dorff and Natascha McElhone star, as a cop and a public health inspector, and Stephen Rea, who was so unexpectedly deceived in *The Crying Game,* plays the host of the Website and the torturer. The movie keeps trying to make some kind of connection between Rea and the ghostly little girl, who was his first victim, but if the site is her revenge, why is he running it? And how can what happens to him in the end not have happened before?

Never mind. Disregard the logic of the plot. Don't even go there. Don't think to ask how the Internet can channel thoughts and commands into the minds of its users. Disregard the dialogue (sample: "We will provide a lesson that reducing relationships to an anonymous electronic impulse is a perversion"). This is a movie that cannot be taken seriously on the narrative level. But look at it. Just look at it. Wear some of those Bose sound-defeating earphones into the theater, or turn off the sound when you watch the DVD. If the final twenty minutes had been produced by a German impressionist in the 1920s, we'd be calling it a masterpiece. All credit to director William Malone, cinematographer Christian Sebaldt, production designer Jerome Latour, and art directors Regine Freise and Markus Wollersheim.

Now. Do I recommend the film? Not for the majority of filmgoers, who *will* listen to the dialogue, and *will* expect a plot, and *will* be angered by the film's sins against logic (I do not even mention credibility). But if you have read this far because you are intrigued, because you can understand the kind of paradox I am describing, then you might very well enjoy *FearDotCom*. I give the total movie two stars, but there are some four-star elements that deserve a better movie. You have to know how to look for them, but they're there.

Fellini: I'm a Born Liar ★ ★ ½
NO MPAA RATING, 105 m., 2003

With Roberto Benigni, Italo Calvino, Federico Fellini, Donald Sutherland, Terence Stamp, and Giuseppe Rotunno. A documentary directed by Damian Pettigrew and produced by Olivier Gal. Screenplay by Pettigrew and Gal.

Federico Fellini created a world that was gloriously his own, and there is scarcely a shot— certainly not a scene—in his work that doesn't announce its maker. That's also true of Hitchcock, Ozu, Tati, and a few other filmmakers; their work gives us the impression, somehow, of being in their presence.

Fellini: I'm a Born Liar is a documentary centering on a lengthy interview Fellini gave to the filmmakers in 1993, shortly before his death. As a source of information about his life and work, this interview is almost worthless, but as an insight into his style, it is priceless. Having interviewed the master twice, once on the location of his *Fellini Satyricon,* I was reminded of his gift for spinning fables that pretend to be about his work but are actually fabricated from thin air.

Consider, for example, the way he confides to the camera that he gets on very well with actors, because he loves them and understands them. Then listen to two of the actors he worked with, Donald Sutherland and Terence Stamp, who recall the experience as if their skins are still crawling.

Fellini, we learn, sometimes gave no direction at all, expecting his actors to intuit his desires. At other times (seen in footage of the director at work) he stood next to the camera and verbally instructed his actors on every move

and nuance. This was possible because he often didn't record sound, preferring to dub the dialogue later, and some of his actors simply counted, "one, two, three," knowing the words would be supplied. It is clear that Stamp and Sutherland did not enjoy the experience, and so much did Fellini treat them like his puppets that at one point Sutherland says "Fellini" when he means his own character.

The actor he worked with most often and successfully, Marcello Mastroianni, was the most cooperative: "He would turn up tired in the morning, sleep between takes, and do whatever Fellini told him to do without complaining." That this approach created the two best male performances in Fellini's work (in *La Dolce Vita* and *8½*) argues that Mastroianni may have been onto something.

The documentary includes many clips from Fellini's work, none of them identified, although his admirers will recognize them immediately. And we revisit some of the original locations, including a vast field with strange concrete walls (or are they crypts?) where Fellini's hero helped his father climb down into a grave in *8½*.

The movie does not do justice to Fellini's love of sensuous excess, both in his films and in his life, although when he says he "married the right woman . . . for a man like me" he may be telling us something. The film assumes such familiarity with Fellini that although that woman, the actress Giulietta Masina, is seen more than once, she is never identified.

No doubt the existence of the extended Fellini interview is the movie's reason for existing, and yet it is less than helpful. Fellini is maddeningly nonspecific, weaves abstractions into clouds of fancy, rarely talks about specific films, actors, or locations. When he mentions his childhood home of Rimini, it is to observe that the Rimini in his films is more real to him. And so it should be, but why not even a word about his youthful days as a cartoonist, hustling on the Via Veneto for assignments? Why no mention of his apprenticeship in neorealism? Why not a word about the collapse and death of the Rome studio system?

I love Fellini, and so I was happy to see this film, and able to add it to my idea of his charming but elusive personality. But if you know little about Fellini, this is not the place to start. Begin with the films. They are filled with joy, abundance, and creativity. You cannot call yourself a serious filmgoer and not know them.

Fellini Satyricon ★ ★ ★ ★
R, 129 m., 1970 (rereleased 2001)

Martin Potter (Encolpio), Hiram Keller (Ascilto), Max Born (Gitone), Salvo Randone (Eumolpo), Mario Romagnoli (Trimalcione), Magali Noel (Fortunata), Capucine (Trifena), Alain Cuny (Lica), Fanfulla (Vernacchio). Directed by Federico Fellini and produced by Alberto Grimaldi. Screenplay by Fellini and Bernardino Zapponi, based on the book by Petronius.

"I am examining ancient Rome as if this were a documentary about the customs and habits of the Martians."
—Fellini in an interview, 1969

Fellini Satyricon was released in 1970, and I was ready for it: "Some will say it is a bloody, depraved, disgusting film," I wrote in a fever. "Indeed, people by the dozens were escaping from the sneak preview I attended. But *Fellini Satyricon* is a masterpiece all the same, and films that dare everything cannot please everybody." Today I'm not so sure it's a masterpiece, except as an expression of the let-it-all-hang-out spirit of the 1970 world that we both then occupied. But it is so much more ambitious and audacious than most of what we see today that simply as a reckless gesture, it shames these timid times. Films like this are a reminder of how machine-made and limited recent product has become.

The movie is based on a book that retold degenerate versions of Roman and Greek myth. Petronius's *Satyricon,* written at the time of Nero, was lost for centuries and found in a fragmented form, which Fellini uses to explain his own fragmented movie; both book and film end in midsentence. Petronius was a sensualist who celebrated and mocked sexual decadence at the same time. So does Fellini, who observes that although the wages of sin may be death, it's nice work if you can get it.

The movie was made two years after the Summer of Love—it came out at about the same time as the documentary *Woodstock*—and it preserves the postpill, pre-AIDS sexual frenzy

of that time, when penalty-free sex briefly seemed to be a possibility (key word: seemed). The characters in the Fellini film may be burned alive, vivisected, skewered, or crushed, but they have no concerns about viruses, guilt, or psychological collapse. Like most of the characters in ancient myth, indeed, they have no psychology; they act according to their natures, without introspection or the possibility of change. They are hard-wired by the myths that contain them.

The film loosely follows the travels and adventures of several characters, notably the students Encolpio (Martin Potter) and Ascilto (Hiram Keller), as they fight over the favors of the comely slave boy Gitone (Max Born). Gitone is won by Ascilto, who sells him to the repulsive actor Vernacchio (Fanfulla), whose performances include mutilation of prisoners. True to the nature of the film, Gitone doesn't mind such treatment and indeed rather enjoys the attention, but the story moves on, presenting a series of masters and slaves in moments of grotesque drama and lurid fantasy. It is all phantasmagoria, said Pauline Kael, who hated the film, and wrote, "Though from time to time one may register a face or a set or an episode, for most of the time one has the feeling of a camera following people walking along walls."

Well, yes and no. There are scenes that are complete playlets, as when a patrician couple free their slaves and then commit suicide, or when a dead rich man's followers gather on the seashore to consider his final request that his body be eaten. These moments pop out from the fresco as they must have popped out of Petronius, but Fellini is unconcerned with beginnings, middles, and ends, and wants us to walk through the film as through a gallery in which an artist tries variations on a theme. This would increasingly be his approach in the films that followed; set against this ancient Rome is the fragmented modern city in *Fellini Roma,* which is a series of episodes in search of a destination, and lacks the structure of his great Roman film, *La Dolce Vita* (1959).

Does *Satyricon* work? Depends. Certainly the visuals are rich (Kael's wall-image doesn't do justice to their grungy, spermy, tactile fertility). Is there anyone we care about as we watch the film? We share the joy during a couple of sexual romps, and are touched by the suicides of the patricians, but—no, we don't care about them, because they seem defined not by their personalities but by their mythical programming. Like the figures in Keats's "Ode on a Grecian Urn," they are forever caught in the act of demonstrating their natures, without prologue or outcome.

In no other Fellini film do we see a more abundant demonstration of his affection for human grotesques (although *Fellini Casanova* comes close). I visited the set of this film one day, on the coast near Rome, when he was shooting the funeral of the man who wanted to be cannibalized. We were surrounded by dwarfs and giants, fat people and beanpoles, hermaphrodites and transvestites, some grotesquely painted or costumed, some deformed by nature or choice. "People ask, where did you find these faces?" Fellini said. "None of them are professional actors; these faces come from my private dreams. I opened a little office in Rome and asked funny-looking people to come in. Did you know Nero had a hang-up on freaks? He surrounded himself with them." And so does Fellini, perhaps because ordinary-looking extras would bring too much normality into his canvas.

What is the sum of all this effort? A film that deals in visual excess like no other, showing a world of amorality, cruelty, self-loathing, and passion. Did Fellini see his *Satyricon* as a warning to modern viewers, an object lesson? Not at all, in my opinion. He found an instinctive connection between Petronius and himself—two artists fascinated by deviance and excess—and in the heady days of the late 1960s saw no reason to compromise. *Fellini Satyricon* is always described as a film about ancient Rome, but it may be one of the best films about the Summer of Love—not celebrating it, but displaying the process of its collapse. What is fun for a summer can be hard work for a lifetime.

Femme Fatale ★ ★ ★ ★
R, 110 m., 2002

Rebecca Romijn-Stamos (Laure Ash), Antonio Banderas (Nicolas Bardo), Peter Coyote (Bruce Hewitt Watts), Eriq Ebouaney (Black Tie), Edouard Montoute (Racine), Rie Rasmussen (Veronica), Thierry Frémont (Serra). Directed by Brian De Palma and produced by Tarak Ben Ammar and Marina Gefter. Screenplay by De Palma.

Sly as a snake, Brian De Palma's *Femme Fatale* is a sexy thriller that coils back on itself in seductive deception. This is pure filmmaking, elegant and slippery. I haven't had as much fun second-guessing a movie since *Mulholland Drive*. Consider such clues as the overflowing aquarium, the shirt still stained with blood after many days, the subtitles for dialogue that is not spoken, the story that begins in 2001 and then boldly announces: "Seven years later."

The movie opens with a $10 million diamond theft, with a difference: The diamonds adorn the body of a supermodel attending a premiere at the Cannes Film Festival, and they are stolen with erotic audacity as the model is seduced in a rest room of the Palais du Cinema by the tall, brazen Laure Ash (Rebecca Romijn-Stamos). Her team includes the usual crew of heist-movie types, and we get the usual details, like the guy in the wet suit, the laser cutter, and the TV spycam that attracts the attention of an inquisitive cat. But the movie announces its originality when none of these characters perform as they expect to, and Laure Ash steals the diamonds not only from the model but also from her fellow criminals.

No, I have not given away too much. The fact is, I have given away less than nothing, as you will fully appreciate after seeing the film. The long opening sequence, about forty minutes by my clock, is done almost entirely without dialogue, and as De Palma's camera regards these characters in their devious movements, we begin to get the idea: This is a movie about watching and being watched, about seeing and not knowing what you see.

Romijn-Stamos plays Laure Ash as a supremely self-confident woman with a well-developed sense of life's ironies. Chance plays a huge role in her fate. Consider that not long after the theft, while trying to avoid being spotted in Paris, she is mistaken for a grieving widow, taken home from a funeral, and finds herself in possession of an airplane ticket to

New York and a passport with a photo that looks exactly like her. And then . . .

But no. I cannot tell any more. I will, however, describe her relationship with Nicolas Bardo (Antonio Banderas), a paparazzo who photographs her in 2001 on that day she is mistaken for the widow, and photographs her again seven years later (!) when she returns to Paris as the wife of the American ambassador (Peter Coyote). She wants that film: "I have a past here." And then . . .

Well, the movie's story, written by De Palma, is a series of incidents that would not be out of place in an ordinary thriller, but here achieve a kind of transcendence since they are what they seem, and more than they seem, and less than they seem. The movie tricks us, but not unfairly, and for the attentive viewer there are markers along the way to suggest what De Palma is up to.

Above all he is up to an exercise in superb style and craftsmanship. The movie is very light on dialogue, and many of the words that are spoken come across as if the characters are imitating movie actors (the film opens with Laure watching *Double Indemnity*—for pointers in how to be a vixen, no doubt). I've seen the movie twice; it's one of those films like *Memento* that plays differently the second time. Only on the second viewing did I spot the sly moment when the subtitles supply standard thriller dialogue—but the lips of the actors are not moving. This is a movie joke worthy of Buñuel.

Rebecca Romijn-Stamos may or may not be a great actress, but in *Femme Fatale* she is a great Hitchcock heroine—blond, icy, desirable, duplicitous—with a knack for contemptuously manipulating the hero. She is also very sexy, and let it be said that De Palma, at least, has not followed other directors into a sheepish retreat from nudity, seduction, desire, and erotic wordplay. The man who made *Body Double* is still prepared to make a movie about a desirable woman, even in these days of buddy movies for teenage boys. When it comes to sex, the characters in *Femme Fatale* have all been around the block a few times, but it takes this scenario to make them wonder what side of the street they're on.

De Palma deserves more honor as a director. Consider also these titles: *Sisters, Blow Out,*

The Fury, Dressed to Kill, Carrie, Scarface, Wise Guys, Casualties of War, Carlito's Way, Mission: Impossible. Yes, there are a few failures along the way *(Snake Eyes, Mission to Mars, The Bonfire of the Vanities)*, but look at the range here, and reflect that these movies contain treasure for those who admire the craft as well as the story, who sense the glee with which De Palma manipulates images and characters for the simple joy of being good at it. It's not just that he sometimes works in the style of Hitchcock, but that he has the nerve to. ☞

15 Minutes ★ ★ ★
R, 120 m., 2001

Robert De Niro (Eddie Flemming), Edward Burns (Jordy Warsaw), Kelsey Grammer (Robert Hawkins), Karel Roden (Emil Slovak), Oleg Taktarov (Oleg Razgul), Melina Kanakaredes (Nicolette Karas), Vera Farmiga (Daphne Handlova). Directed by John Herzfeld and produced by Keith Addis, David Blocker, Herzfeld, and Nick Wechsler. Screenplay by Herzfeld.

I want to know if you think this is possible. Two creeps videotape themselves committing murder, and then attempt to sell the video to a reality news show for $1 million. They plan to beat the murder charges with an insanity plea, adding that they were abused as children.

I think it is possible. I heard about a documentary at Sundance this year where a fraternity boy videotaped his friend in a sex act that the woman claimed was rape. The video, later sold to the press by law enforcement officials, is included in the documentary, so you can decide for yourself.

What kind of person would do something like that? (I refer both to the fictional murder plot and to the rape footage.) The kind of person, I imagine, who appears on the Jerry Springer show, a program I study for signposts on our society's descent into barbarism. When you say these people have no shame, you have to realize that "shame" is a concept and perhaps even a word with which they are not familiar. They will eagerly degrade themselves for the fifteen minutes of fame so famously promised them by Andy Warhol.

15 Minutes is a cynical, savage satire about

violence, the media, and depravity. It doesn't have the polish of *Natural Born Killers* or the wit of *Wag the Dog*, but it's a real movie, rough edges and all, and not another link from the sausage factory. A couple of the early reviews have called it implausible. They doubt that real killers would sell their footage to TV and then watch it in a Planet Hollywood, hoping to be spotted and arrested. See, that's the funny thing. I think there are people who would.

The movie stars Robert De Niro as a Manhattan detective who has become a celebrity, Edward Burns as a fire inspector, and Kelsey Grammer as a cross between Springer and Geraldo Rivera. Working the other side of the street are Karel Roden and Oleg Taktarov as Emil and Oleg, one Czech, one Russian, who fly into Kennedy airport and are robbing an electronics store within hours of getting off the plane. Emil dreams of becoming rich and famous through violence, and Oleg videotapes his efforts—at first just for fun, later as part of a scheme. Emil loves America because "no one is responsible for what they do!" and Oleg idolizes Frank Capra, the poet of the little man who shoves it to the system.

The movie, written and directed by John Herzfeld, is the work of a man intoxicated by characters and locations. His previous film, *2 Days in the Valley* (1997), was the same way, filled with characters who spinned into each other and bounced apart like pinballs. His movie may overachieve, may weary sometimes as it hurries between plotlines, but I prefer this kind of energy and ambition to a plodding exercise in action clichés. Herzfeld has something he wants to say.

His premise depends on Emil and Oleg being perfectly amoral idiots, shaped in their homelands by overdoses of American TV and movies. Since their countries are saturated with U.S. entertainment, and since the most popular exports are low-dialogue action shows, this is not a stretch. Is their view of America hopelessly brutal and unrealistic? Yes, but it is the view we export for study abroad.

They shoot, slash, burn, and pillage their way through Manhattan, attacking former friends, call girls, and bystanders. Meanwhile, Burns, as the fire inspector, finds evidence that a fire was set to conceal a murder, and De Niro

engages in a little jockeying for position in the media spotlight because he wants credit for the investigation. His publicity efforts are helped by his friendship with Grammer, a star of reality TV, and by his affair with a TV reporter (Melina Kanakaredes).

Emil and Oleg are really the center of the movie. They reminded me of Dick Smith and Perry Hickock from *In Cold Blood*, except the vicious amorality of the 1968 movie no longer seems so totally alien to the society surrounding it; programs like Grammer's *Top Story* are based on, feed on, depend on there being people like these.

The movie is far from unflawed. I have a private theory that half the time you see a character tied to a chair, the screenwriter ran out of ideas. Some of the getaways are unlikely. The ending is on autopilot. But there's an absolutely sensational scene where Burns tries to help a woman escape from a burning apartment; it's the best work along these lines since *Backdraft*. And poignant personal moments for De Niro that keep his character from simply being a publicity hound. And performances by Karel Roden and Oleg Taktarov that project the kind of flat, empty-headed, blank-faced evil that is so much scarier than evil by people who think about what they're doing.

Some movies, however good, seem to be simply technical exercises. Others, even if flawed, contain the seed of inspiration. John Herzfeld has not made a great movie yet, but on the basis of his first two, he might. He cares, he strives, he's not content. While you're watching the movie, you question details and excesses. Afterward, you admire it for the passion of its attack, and the worthiness of its targets.

The Fighter ★ ★ ★
NO MPAA RATING, 91 m., 2002

With Arnost Lustig and Jan Wiener. A documentary directed by Amir Bar-Lev and produced by Bar-Lev, Jonathan Crosby, and Alex Mamet.

The Fighter is named after one of its two subjects, Jan Wiener, seventy-seven years old, who describes himself as a "professor, wilderness guide, and old fart," and adds: "But I still can connect." We see him pounding a punching bag to prove it. His friend is Arnost Lustig, seventy-two. Both of them were born in Czechoslovakia and now live in America. The story of Wiener's escape from the Nazis, how he flew for the RAF against Germany, how he returned to his homeland and was imprisoned by the Communists as a spy, has inspired more than one movie. Lustig has long planned to write a book about it, and the two old men set off on a trip to the places of their youth and their war.

Following them is Amir Bar-Lev, an American documentary filmmaker, born in Israel, who could hardly have anticipated what would happen. *The Fighter* could have been just a travelogue about two old-timers reliving their wartime memories. Even a heroic story can slow in the retelling. But *The Fighter* picks up surprising energy, as old wounds are reopened and the two men express strong opinions that may be unforgivable. What unfolds on-screen is remarkable: The passions and arguments of the past are resurrected in the present.

At first the trip goes smoothly. Both men are fit and quick, not slowed by the ravages of age. Both teach at universities. They retrace Wiener's steps as he recalls the collapse of Czechoslovakia (he and other pilots never dreamed the Nazis would roll in so decisively). In a scene of stunning power, he visits the house where his parents committed suicide rather than be captured by the Nazis. He recalls his father saying: "Tonight I am going to kill myself. That is the only freedom we have left." He remembers how it happened, his father telling him, "I have taken the pills. Hold my hand." And then, says Wiener, sitting in the same chair he sat in all those years ago, "he was asleep."

They visit Terezienstadt, a model concentration camp set up by the Nazis to fool a Swiss Red Cross inspection team (the notorious Nazi documentary *The Fuhrer Gives a City to the Jews* was filmed there). Lustig was a prisoner there, and remembers how the prisoners were terrified to speak to the inspectors, and how food and comforts disappeared along with the Swiss. Together, the two men retrace the route of Wiener's escape, ending in Italy, where a compassionate Italian cop did not betray him to the Nazis. He later became a POW in Italy, later still a pilot for the British.

After the war their lives diverged. Wiener returned home to Czechoslovakia only to be suspected of spying and sentenced to prison. Lustig became a Communist official until he became disillusioned and left for America. The old friends met again in the United States.

And so the story might end, gripping, fascinating, happily—but then they have a fight. There is a disagreement over why the Italian cop spared Wiener. Another one over why Lustig could have survived Nazism only to become a Communist. Filming shuts down for three days during this impasse, and when it begins again it is clear that the old men are friends no longer. We understand that for them the war is a wound that has not healed, and that it led to decisions that cannot be explained. We stand a little outside: No one who was not there knows for sure what he would have done. Suddenly, we are not in the past but in the present, seeing real emotions, not remembered ones. In this movie the war is not quite over. For those who survived it, maybe it will never be.

Note: The 2002 feature Dark Blue World *also tells a story about a Czech pilot who flies for the British.*

Final ★ ★
R, 111 m., 2002

Denis Leary (Bill), Hope Davis (Ann), J. C. MacKenzie (Todd), Jim Gaffigan (Dayton), Jim Hornyak (Orderly), Maureen Anderman (Supervisor), Marin Hinkle (Sherry), Madison Arnold (Bill's Father), Caroline Kava (Bill's Mother). Directed by Campbell Scott and produced by Gary Winik, Alexis Alexanian, Mary Frances Budig, Steve Dunn, and Campbell Scott. Screenplay by Bruce McIntosh.

In a mental hospital in Connecticut, a patient defends his paranoid fantasies against a psychiatrist who gently tries to bring him back to reality. He says it is the year 2399, that he has been cyrogenically frozen for 400 years, and that he has been thawed and awakened so that his organs can be harvested. She says he was in a serious truck accident, was in a coma, and is now being treated to remove his delusions. While they discuss this rather basic disagreement, it becomes clear they are gradually falling in love.

Campbell Scott's *Final* is a movie told mostly through dialogue. It lacks the life and humor of his wonderful *Big Night*, codirected with Stanley Tucci, and burrows into its enigmatic situation with cheerless intensity. Only the innate energy of its actors, Denis Leary and Hope Davis, keep it on its feet. Both are very good—Leary at trying to talk his way out of what looks like a trap he has set for himself, and Davis at remaining professionally responsible even while getting emotionally involved, if that is possible. She cares for him.

Then the plot takes a turn that I will not even begin to reveal, and we have to reevaluate the meaning of their relationship, their characters, their situation. By even mentioning the turn, I know I will get protests from readers who complain that they would have never known there was going to be a turn if I hadn't revealed it, etc., but really, what is a critic to do? Stop writing after the first two paragraphs and completely misrepresent the film? *Final* is "difficult to discuss without giving away the surprise that pops up halfway through," A. O. Scott observes in the first sentence of his *New York Times* review, thereby giving away the surprise that there *is* a surprise. You see what I mean.

So, yes, there is a surprise. I will have nothing to say about it. You will have to deal with it on your own. But if you should see *Final* and start to analyze it, ask yourself these questions: Why is the therapy necessary in the first place? Why are this patient and this psychiatrist even talking? What do they have to accomplish? Unless my logic is flawed (and if it is, other audience members are going to make the same mistake), the entire movie is a red herring.

That doesn't mean it lacks certain virtues. The movie, shot on video by Dan Gillham, creates a convincing space around the characters; the institution seems real enough, if underpopulated, and the claustrophobia it brings on helps define the relationship. Although the screenplay by Bruce McIntosh suffers from that plausibility gap, the characters of course don't know this and establish a rapport so nuanced and subtle it deserves a better story. Maybe one without a surprise.

Final Desination 2 ★ ½

R, 100 m., 2003

Ali Larter (Clear Rivers), A. J. Cook (Kimberly Corman), Michael Landes (Thomas Burke), David Paetkau (Evan Lewis), James Kirk (Tim Carpenter), Lynda Boyd (Nora Carpenter), Keegan Connor Tracy (Kat), Jonathan Cherry (Rory). Directed by David Ellis and produced by Warren Zide and Craig Perry. Screenplay by J. Mackye Gruber and Eric Bress.

"Look, we drove a long way to get here, so if you know how to beat death, we'd like to know."

So say pending victims to a morgue attendant in *Final Destination 2*, which takes a good idea from the first film and pounds it into the ground, not to mention decapitating, electrocuting, skewering, blowing up, incinerating, drowning, and gassing it. Perhaps movies are like history, and repeat themselves, first as tragedy, then as farce.

The earlier film involved a group of friends who got off an airplane after one of them had a vivid precognition of disaster. The plane crashed on takeoff. But then, one by one, most of the survivors died, as if fate had to balance its books.

That movie depends on all the horror clichés of the Dead Teenager Movie (formula: Teenagers are alive at beginning, dead at end). But it is well made and thoughtful. As I wrote in my review: "The film in its own way is biblical in its dilemma, although the students use the code word 'fate' when what they are really talking about is God. In their own terms, in their own way, using teenage vernacular, the students have existential discussions."

That was then; this is now. Faithful to its genre, *Final Destination 2* allows one of its original characters, Clear Rivers (Ali Larter), to survive, so she can be a link to the earlier film. In the new film, Clear is called upon by Kimberly Corman (A. J. Cook), a twenty-something, who is driving three friends in her SUV when she suddenly has a vision of a horrendous traffic accident. Kimberly blocks the on-ramp, saving the drivers behind her when logs roll off a timber truck, gas tanks explode, etc.

But is it the same old scenario? Are the people she saved all doomed to die? "There is a sort of force—an unseen malevolent presence

215

around us every day," a character muses. "I prefer to call it death."

The malevolent presence doesn't remain unseen for long. Soon bad things are happening to good people, in a series of accidents that Rube Goldberg would have considered implausible. In one ingenious sequence, we see a character who almost trips over a lot of toys while carrying a big Macintosh iMac box. In his house, he starts the microwave and lights a fire under a frying pan, then drops his ring down the garbage disposal, then gets his hand trapped in the disposal while the microwave explodes and the frying pan starts a fire, then gets his hand loose, breaks a window that mysteriously slams shut, climbs down a fire escape, falls to the ground, and finally, when it seems he is safe . . . well, everything that could possibly go wrong does, except that he didn't get a Windows machine.

Other characters die in equally improbable ways. One is ironically killed by an air bag, another almost chokes in a dentist's chair, a third is severed from his respirator, and so on, although strange things do happen in real life. I came home from seeing this movie to read the story about the teenager who was thrown twenty-five feet in the air after a car crash, only to save himself by grabbing some telephone lines. If that had happened in *Final Destination 2*, his car would have exploded, blowing him off the lines with a flying cow.

There is a kind of dumb level on which a movie like this works, once we understand the premise. People will insist on dying oddly. Remember the story of the woman whose husband left her, so she jumped out the window and landed on him as he was leaving the building?

The thing about *FD2* is that the characters make the mistake of trying to figure things out. Their reasoning? If you were meant to die, then you owe death a life. But a new life can cancel out an old one. So if the woman in the white van can safely deliver her baby, then that means that someone else will be saved, or will have to die, I forget which. This is the kind of bookkeeping that makes you wish Arthur Andersen were still around.

Note: The first Final Destination *(2000) had characters named after famous horror-film figures, including Browning, Horton, Lewton,*

Weine, Schreck, Hitchcock, and Chaney. The sequel has just two that I can identify: Corman and Carpenter.

Final Fantasy: The Spirits Within
★ ★ ★ ½
PG-13, 105 m., 2001

Voices of: Ming-Na (Dr. Aki Ross), Alec Baldwin (Gray Edwards), Steve Buscemi (Neil), Peri Gilpin (Jane Proudfoot), Ving Rhames (Ryan), Donald Sutherland (Dr. Sid), James Woods (General Hein). Directed by Hironobu Sakaguchi and produced by Jun Aida, Chris Lee, and Akio Sakai. Screenplay by Al Reinert, Sakaguchi, and Jeff Vintar.

Other movies have been made entirely on computers, but *Final Fantasy: The Spirits Within* is the first to attempt realistic human characters. Not Shrek with his trumpet ears, but the space soldier Gray Edwards, who looks so much like Ben Affleck that I wonder if royalties were involved. The movie, named after a famous series of video games, creates Planet Earth, circa 2065, where humans huddle beneath energy shields and wraithlike aliens prowl the globe.

The film tells a story that would have seemed traditional in the golden age of Asimov, van Vogt, and Heinlein. But science-fiction fans of that era would have wept with joy at the visuals, and they grabbed me too. I have a love of astonishing sights, of films that show me landscapes and cityscapes that exist only in the imagination, and *Final Fantasy* creates a world that is neither live-action nor animation, but some parallel cyber universe.

The characters live in that cyberspace too. Not for an instant do we believe that Dr. Aki Ross, the heroine, is a real human. But we concede she is *lifelike*, which is the whole point. She has an eerie presence that is at once subtly unreal and yet convincing; her movements (which mirror the actions of real actors) feel about right, her hair blows convincingly in the wind, and the first close-up of her face and eyes is startling because the filmmakers are not afraid to give us a good, long look—they dare us not to admire their craft. If Aki is not as real as a human actress, she is about as real as a Playmate who has been retouched to a glossy perfection.

The story involves a struggle by Aki and a band of Deep Eyes (futuristic human warriors) to defend the survivors of an alien invasion of Earth. Humans live inside energy shields that protect some of the largest cities, and they venture out cautiously, armored and armed, to do battle with the aliens, who look like free-form transparent monster nightmares; I was reminded of the water creature in *The Abyss*. The aliens can infect humans with their virus, or essence, and Aki (Ming-Na) thinks she can defeat them by channeling the eight "spirit waves" of Earth—or Gaia, the planetary soul.

Her allies include Gray (Alec Baldwin), the leader of the Deep Eyes troop, and Dr. Sid (Donald Sutherland), her wise old teacher. Her other teammates include the pilot Neil (Steve Buscemi) and the fighters Ryan (Ving Rhames) and Jane Proudfoot (Peri Gilpin). Leading the forces of evil is General Hein (James Woods), who wants to blast the aliens with his high-tech orbiting space cannon.

Those who find a parallel between Hein's cannon and George W. Bush's missile shield will find it easy to assign Aki and her friends to the environmentalists; they believe Earth's mantle sits above a Gaia-sphere containing the planet's life force, and that if the cannon destroys it, not only the aliens but all human life will die. One of Aki's early expeditions is to find, rescue, and tend a tiny green growing thing that has survived in the wasteland caused (I think) when a giant meteorite crashed into Earth and released the aliens it contained.

The aliens are strange creatures, made stranger still by the film's inconsistency in handling them. Without revealing one major secret about their essence, I can ask how they seem to be physical and conceptual both at once. They defeat a human not by physically attacking him, but by absorbing his life essence. Yet they can be blasted to smithereens by the weapons of the Deep Eyes. Maybe the human weapons are not conventional, but operate on the aliens' wavelength; either I got confused on that point, or the movie did.

Enough about the plot, which is merely the carrier for the movie's vision. The reason to see this movie is simply, gloriously, to look at it. Aki has dream scenes on another planet, where a vast, celestial sphere half fills the sky. We see New York City in 2065, ruined, ghost-like, except for the portions under the protective dome. There are action sequences that only vaguely obey the laws of gravity, and yet seem convincing because we have become familiar with the characters who occupy them: shots like the one where we look straight up at Aki standing on the surface of a shimmering lake. The corridors and machines composing the infrastructure of the protective dome surpass any possible real-world sets.

Final Fantasy took four years to create. A computer animation team, half-Japanese, half-American, worked in Hawaii with director Hironobu Sakaguchi; they shot many of the physical movements and then rotoscoped them, and artists were assigned to specialize in particular characters. The most realistic are probably Dr. Sid and Ryan. It all comes together into a kind of amazing experience; it's as if you're witnessing a heavy-metal story come to life.

Is there a future for this kind of expensive filmmaking ($140 million, I've heard)? I hope so, because I want to see more movies like this, and see how much further they can push the technology. Maybe someday I'll actually be fooled by a computer-generated actor (but I doubt it). The point anyway is not to replace actors and the real world, but to transcend them—to penetrate into a new creative space based primarily on images and ideas. I wouldn't be surprised if the Star Wars series mutated in this direction; George Lucas's actors, who complain that they spend all of their time standing in front of blue screens that will later be filled with locations and effects, would be replaced by computerized avatars scarcely less realistic.

In reviewing a movie like this, I am torn between its craft elements and its story. The story is nuts-and-bolts space opera, without the intelligence and daring of, say, Spielberg's *A.I.* But the look of the film is revolutionary. *Final Fantasy* is a technical milestone, like the first talkies or 3-D movies. You want to see it whether or not you care about aliens or space cannons. It exists in a category of its own, the first citizen of the new world of cyberfilm.

Finding Nemo ★ ★ ★ ★
G, 101 m., 2003

With the voices of: Albert Brooks (Marlin), Ellen DeGeneres (Dory), Alexander Gould

(Nemo), Willem Dafoe (Gill), Geoffrey Rush (Nigel), Brad Garrett (Bloat), Barry Humphries (Bruce), Allison Janney (Peach). Directed by Andrew Stanton and produced by Graham Walters. Screenplay by Stanton.

Finding Nemo has all of the usual pleasures of the Pixar animation style—the comedy and wackiness of *Toy Story* or *Monsters Inc.* or *A Bug's Life*. And it adds an unexpected beauty, a use of color and form that makes it one of those rare movies where I wanted to sit in the front row and let the images wash out to the edges of my field of vision. The movie takes place almost entirely under the sea, in the world of colorful tropical fish—the flora and fauna of a shallow warm-water shelf not far from Australia. The use of color, form, and movement make the film a delight even apart from its story.

There is a story, though, one of those Pixar inventions that involves kids on the action level while adults are amused because of the satire and human (or fishy) comedy. The movie involves the adventures of little Nemo, a clownfish born with an undersized fin and an oversized curiosity. His father, Marlin, worries obsessively over him because Nemo is all he has left: Nemo's mother and all of her other eggs were lost to barracudas. When Nemo goes off on his first day of school, Marlin warns him to stay with the class and avoid the dangers of the drop-off to deep water, but Nemo forgets and ends up as a captive in the saltwater aquarium of a dentist in Sydney. Marlin swims off bravely to find his missing boy, aided by Dory, a bright blue Regal Tang fish with enormous eyes whom he meets along the way.

These characters are voiced by actors whose own personal mannerisms are well known to us; I recognized most of the voices, but even the unidentified ones carried buried associations from movie roles, and so somehow the fish take on qualities of human personalities. Marlin, for example, is played by Albert Brooks as an overprotective, neurotic worrywart, and Dory is played by Ellen DeGeneres as helpful, cheerful, and scatterbrained (she has a problem with short-term memory).

The Pixar computer animators, led by writer-director Andrew Stanton, create an undersea world that is just a shade murky, as it should be; we can't see as far or as sharply in sea water, and so threats materialize more quickly, and everything has a softness of focus. There is something dreamlike about *Finding Nemo's* visuals, something that evokes the reverie of scuba diving.

The picture's great inspiration is to leave the sea by transporting Nemo to that big tank in the dentist's office. In it we meet other captives, including the Moorish Idol fish Gill (voice by Willem Dafoe), who are planning an escape. Now it might seem to us that there is no possible way a fish can escape from an aquarium in an office and get out of the window and across the highway and into the sea, but there is no accounting for the ingenuity of these creatures, especially since they have help from a conspirator on the outside—a pelican with the voice of Geoffrey Rush.

It may occur to you that many pelicans make a living by eating fish, not rescuing them, but some of the characters in this movie have evolved admirably into vegetarians. As Marlin and Dory conduct their odyssey, for example, they encounter three carnivores who have formed a chapter of Fish-Eaters Anonymous and chant slogans to remind themselves that they abstain from fin-based meals.

The first scenes in *Finding Nemo* are a little unsettling, as we realize the movie is going to be about fish, not people (or people-based characters like toys and monsters). But of course animation has long since learned to enlist all other species in the human race, and to care about fish quickly becomes as easy as caring about mice or ducks or Bambi.

When I review a movie like *Finding Nemo*, I am aware that most members of its primary audience do not read reviews. Their parents do, and to them and adults who do not have children as an excuse, I can say that *Finding Nemo* is a pleasure for grown-ups. There are jokes we get that the kids don't, and the complexity of Albert Brooks's neuroses, and that enormous canvas filled with creatures that have some of the same hypnotic beauty as—well, fish in an aquarium. They may appreciate another novelty: This time the dad is the hero of the story, although in most animation it is almost always the mother. ☞

Focus ★ ★ ★
PG-13, 106 m., 2001

William H. Macy (Lawrence Newman), Laura Dern (Gertrude Newman), David Paymer (Mr. Finkelstein), Meat Loaf Aday (Fred). Directed by Neal Slavin and produced by Robert A. Miller and Slavin. Screenplay by Kendrew Lascelles and Arthur Miller, based on the novel by Miller.

Focus is a parable about Lawrence Newman, a meek office manager who hasn't had a day of trouble in his life until he gets a new pair of glasses and everyone, even his own mother, decides he "looks Jewish." In Brooklyn in 1944, even during a war against Nazism, anti-Semitism runs deep and help-wanted ads specify "Christians only." Newman's neighbor, the bully Fred (Meat Loaf Aday), scowls at Finkelstein's convenience store on the corner and tells Newman, "That Yid is moving in all of his relatives." Newman is supposed to nod in agreement, and you can see that Fred is watching closely for his reaction.

Newman is not Jewish, or particularly Christian (he is played by William H. Macy, who is often cast as a gentile everyman). He's a secular nerd, a little man who is precise in his habits and exact in his work, and has never married. His job is to oversee a room full of women typists and hire replacements. He hires a woman named Kipinski, and his boss complains, "We can't have her kind here." Soon he is being shifted to a new job in a remote office, apparently because with his new glasses he makes the wrong impression.

Focus doesn't reach for reality; it's a deliberate attempt to look and feel like a 1940s social problems picture, right down to the texture of the color photography. The movie is based on a novel by Arthur Miller, which he says was written during a period of disillusionment with the stage; angered by American anti-Semitism even during the war against Hitler, he wrote it in a white heat. It's a didactic warning that it *can* happen here.

Well, of course it can. Tribalism is deeply ingrained in the American culture, and even though we are all outsiders we look with fear on *other* outsiders. The truest words in the movie are spoken by Finkelstein (David Paymer), at a time when a native Nazi group is trying to intimidate everyone on the block: "For God's sake, don't you see what they're doing?! There's hundreds of millions of people in this country, and a couple of million Jews. It's you they want, not me! They are a gang of devils, and they want this country." This is an insight into the methods of the far right, which uses scapegoats and prejudice to lure people out of the middle and into their corner. They need the Jews, because without them how can they create anti-Semitism? Hatred of another group is what binds their group together. That process feeds nicely on the sick impulses of xenophobics.

Frightened for his job, Newman turns down a job applicant named Gertrude Hart (Laura Dern) because her name "sounds Jewish." She's more world-wise than he is, and knows exactly what he's doing. Later, after being shifted away from his position of twenty years, Newman resigns in anger, and can't get hired elsewhere because he looks "too Jewish"—until he is hired at a Jewish firm by . . . Miss Hart. He apologizes to her, they begin to talk, and soon are married, with Fred next door eyeing the new bride suspiciously.

Fred puts Newman to an acid test, pressuring him to attend a meeting of the Union Crusaders, a neo-Nazi group that feeds off the rantings of a right-wing radio broadcaster. (Father Charles Coughlin, the anti-Semitic priest who had a national following, is the model.) "Either you go to the meeting or we get out now," Gertrude tells him. He goes, but is thrown out for displaying insufficient enthusiasm. ("I never applaud," he lamely explains as he's being hustled to the door.)

The purpose of the movie is to take a man who might be willing to go along with anti-Semitic values, and show him what it's like to be discriminated against as a Jew. The climax of this experience comes late one night in Finkelstein's store, when the merchant asks him, "What do you see when you look at me?" The problem in all societies throughout history, the opening for all prejudice, is that we don't look at all. We look away, or at our prejudices, or we allow the worst among us to look on our behalf, and accept their reports.

219

Formula 51 ★
R, 92 m, 2002

Samuel L. Jackson (Elmo McElroy), Robert Carlyle (Felix DeSouza), Emily Mortimer (Dakota Phillips), Meat Loaf (The Lizard), Sean Pertwee (Detective Virgil Kane), Ricky Tomlinson (Leopold Durant), Rhys Ifans (Iki). Directed by Ronny Yu and produced by Andras Hamori, Seaton McLean, Malcolm Kohll, David Pupkewitz, and Jonathan Debin. Screenplay by Stel Pavlou.

Pulp Fiction and *Trainspotting* were two of the most influential movies of the past ten years, but unfortunately their greatest influence has been on rip-offs of each other—movies like *Formula 51*, which is like a fourth-rate *Pulp Fiction* with accents you can't understand. Here, instead of the descent into the filthiest toilet in Scotland, we get a trip through the most bilious intestinal tract in Liverpool; instead of a debate about Cheese Royales, we get a debate about the semantics of the word "bollocks"; the F-word occupies 50 percent of all sentences, and in the opening scenes Samuel L. Jackson wears another one of those Afro wigs.

Jackson plays Elmo McElroy, a reminder that only eight of the seventy-four movies with characters named Elmo have been any good. In the prologue, he graduates from college with a pharmaceutical degree, is busted for pot, loses his license, and thirty years later is the world's most brilliant inventor of illegal drugs.

Now he has a product named "P.O.S. Formula 51," which he says is fifty-one times stronger than crack, heroin, you name it. Instead of selling it to a drug lord named The Lizard (Meat Loaf), he stages a spectacular surprise for Mr. Lizard and his friends, and flies to Liverpool, trailed by Dakota Phillips (Emily Mortimer), a skilled hit woman hired by The Lizard to kill him, or maybe keep him alive, depending on The Lizard's latest information.

In Liverpool, we meet Felix DeSouza (Robert Carlyle), a reminder that only 6 of the 200 movies with a character named Felix have been any good. (The stats for "Dakota" are also discouraging, but this is a line of inquiry with limited dividends.) Felix has been dispatched by the Liverpudlian drug king Leopold Durant (Ricky Tomlinson), whose hemorrhoids require that a flunky follow him around with an inner tube that makes whoopee-type whistles whenever the screenplay requires.

The movie is not a comedy so much as a farce, grabbing desperately for funny details wherever possible. The Jackson character, for example, wears a kilt for most of the movie. My on-line correspondent Ian Waldron-Mantgani, a critic who lives in Liverpool but doesn't give the home team a break, points out that the movie closes with the words "No one ever found out why he wore a kilt," and then explains why he wore the kilt. "You get the idea how much thought went into this movie," Waldron-Mantgani writes, with admirable restraint.

Many of the jokes involve Felix's fanatic support of the Liverpool football club, and a final confrontation takes place in an executive box of the stadium. Devices like this almost always play as a desperate attempt to inject local color, especially when the movie shows almost nothing of the game, so that Americans will not be baffled by what Brits call football. There are lots of violent shoot-outs and explosions, a kinduva love affair between Felix and Dakota, and an ending that crosses a red herring, a maguffin, and a shaggy dog.

40 Days and 40 Nights ★ ★ ★
R, 93 m., 2002

Josh Hartnett (Matt Sullivan), Shannyn Sossamon (Erica), Maggie Gyllenhaal (Samantha), Emmanuelle Vaugier (Susie), Keegan Connor Tracy (Mandy), Vinessa Shaw (Nicole), Paulo Costanzo (Ryan), Adam Trese (John), Monet Mazur (Candy). Directed by Michael Lehmann and produced by Tim Bevan, Eric Fellner, and Michael London. Screenplay by Rob Perez.

Matt is weary of sex. Weary of himself as a sex partner. Weary of the way he behaves around women, weary of the way women make him behave, and weary of his treacherous ex-girl. So weary that he swears off sex for Lent in *40 Days and 40 Nights*. On the scale of single guy sacrifice, this is harder than not drinking but easier than asking for directions.

Matt (Josh Hartnett) is a nice guy who is disgusted by his predatory sexual nature—at the way his libido goes on autopilot when he sees an attractive woman. The breakup with Nicole (Vinessa Shaw) is the final straw. She loved him, dumped him, still excites him, and no wonder; as Bagel Man, who makes morning deliveries to the office, observes, "She's so hot you need one of those cardboard eclipse things just to look at her." Matt gets some support from his brother John (Adam Trese), who is studying to be a priest and offers advice that is more practical than theologically sound, but nobody else in Matt's life believes he can go forty days without sex. Certainly not a co-worker (Monet Mazur), who gives him her phone number on a photocopy of her butt.

Then Matt meets Laundromat Girl. She is sweet, pretty, smart, and something clicks. He tries to keep his distance and end the conversation before his dreaded instincts click in, but a week later he's back in the Laundromat and so is she. Her name is Erica (Shannyn Sossamon), and soon they are engaged in a courtship that proceeds, from her point of view, rather strangely. On their first real date, when the moment comes for their first kiss, they grow closer and quieter and then he gives her a high-five. What's up with this guy?

40 Days and 40 Nights was directed by Michael Lehmann, who has a sympathy for his characters that elevates the story above the level of a sexual sitcom. He uses humor as an instrument to examine human nature, just as he did in the wonderful, underrated *The Truth About Cats and Dogs*. Amazing, what a gulf there is between movies about characters governed by their genitals, and this movie about a character trying to govern his genitals.

The world seems to conspire against him. The movie's single funniest scene involves dinner with his parents, where his father, who has just had a hip replacement, is delighted to show him a checklist of sexual positions still workable even while he is wearing the cast. The second funniest scene involves a roommate who bursts into Matt's flat with an ultraviolet lamp to check for telltale secretions on the sheets.

Then Matt discovers to his horror that his coworkers have not only got up an office pool on how long he can go without sex, but also have put the pool on a Website. Matt looks at the site in disbelief: "You're selling banner ads?" When Erica sees the site, there's hell to pay.

Josh Hartnett shows here a breezy command of his charming, likable character. It is a reminder of his talent and versatility. After an actor stars in a movie that's widely disparaged, as Hartnett did with *Pearl Harbor,* there is an unfair tendency to blame the film on him. The same thing happened to Kevin Costner after *The Postman.* Actors we liked fall out of favor, as if they didn't work just as hard, and hope as much, for their flops as for their hits. Walking into this movie, I heard *Pearl Harbor* jokes ("40 days that will live in infamy"), but during the film the screenplay kicked in and the next stage of Hartnett's career was officially declared open.

40 Days and 40 Nights does observe the plot conventions of a standard comedy, requiring Erica to persist in unreasonably obtuse behavior far beyond its logical time span, but the details are fresh and writer Rob Perez's dialogue about sex has more complexity and nuance than we expect. And a romantic scene involving flower blossoms is unreasonably erotic. The ending, alas, goes astray, for reasons I cannot reveal, except to suggest that Nicole's entire participation is offensive and unnecessary, and that there was a sweeter and funnier way to resolve everything.

Note: Not even under the end titles does the movie use the Muddy Waters classic 40 Days and 40 Nights. In an age when every song title seems to be recycled into a movie, what were they thinking of?

The Four Feathers ★ ★
PG-13, 128 m., 2002

Heath Ledger (Harry Faversham), Wes Bentley (Lieutenant Jack Durrance), Kate Hudson (Ethne Eustace), Djimon Hounsou (Abou Fatma), Michael Sheen (Trench). Directed by Shekhar Kapur and produced by Paul Feldsher, Robert Jaffe, Stanley R. Jaffe, and Marty Katz. Screenplay by Michael Schiffer and Hossein Amini, based on the novel by A.E.W. Mason.

Looking ahead to the Toronto Film Festival, I

foolishly wrote that I was looking forward to Shekhar Kapur's *The Four Feathers* because I was "intrigued by the notion that a story of British colonialism has now been retold by an Indian director. We await the revisionist *Gunga Din*." That was foolish because the film is not revisionist at all, but a skilled update of the same imperialist swashbuckler that's been made into six earlier films and a TV movie (the classic is the 1939 version with Ralph Richardson and C. Aubrey Smith). I do not require Kapur to be a revisionist anti-imperialist; it's just that I don't expect a director born in India to be quite so fond of the British Empire. To be sure, his previous film was the wonderful *Elizabeth* (1998), about Elizabeth I, so perhaps he's an Anglophile. So am I. It's permitted.

The Four Feathers tells the story of Harry Faversham (Heath Ledger), a young British soldier, circa 1875, whose father is a general and who finds himself in the army without having much say in the matter. He is engaged to the comely Ethne Eustace (Kate Hudson), and when his regiment is ordered to the Sudan he cannot bear to part from her, and resigns his commission. He acts primarily out of love, but of course his comrades consider the timing, conclude he is a coward, and send him three white feathers—the sign of cowardice. A fourth is added by the patriotic Ethne.

Disowned by his father, renounced by his fiancée, disgraced in society, Harry must regain his good name. He ships out to the Sudan on his own, disguises himself as an Arab, and lives anyhow in the desert, shadowing his former regiment and doing undercover work on their behalf. He is much helped by the noble Abou Fatma (Djimon Hounsou, from *Amistad*), a desert prince who selflessly devotes himself to helping and protecting the Englishman, for reasons I could never quite understand.

The picture is handsomely mounted (the cinematographer is the Oscar winner Robert Richardson). Red British uniforms contrast with the sand of the desert, and Oriental details make many frames look like a painting by David Roberts. Epic battle scenes, including one where the British form a square and gun down waves of horsemen, are well staged and thrilling. And Harry is a dashing hero, if we can distract ourselves from the complete impossibility of his actions; any man naive enough to think he could resign his commission on the eve of battle and not be considered a coward is certainly foolish enough to become a freelance desert commando—a dry run for T. E. Lawrence.

A newly restored print of *Lawrence of Arabia*, as it happens, is opening on the same day as *The Four Feathers* in many cities, and this is bad luck for the new picture. If you want to see drama in the desert, you're best off with the real thing. The problem with *The Four Feathers* is that the characters are so feckless, the coincidences so blatant, and the movie so innocent of any doubts about the White Man's Burden that Kipling could have written it—although if he had, there would have been deeper psychology and better roles for the locals.

Wes Bentley, from *American Beauty*, costars as Harry's best friend, Lieutenant Jack Durrance. He and Hudson are Americans; Ledger is Australian; obviously no British actors existed who could fill these roles. Non-British actors are often skilled at British accents, but the younger ones usually don't have the right moves or body language. There is an American/Australian manner of informality, casual demeanor, even slouching, that a certain kind of British actor can never be caught committing; British society, it is said, is a stage on which everyone is always playing a role, but Ledger, Hudson, and Bentley seem to be playing dress-up.

I also have problems with the faithful Abou Fatma. Why do the dark-skinned natives always get to be the best buddy, never the hero? Why would a callow, badly trained, unequipped English boy be able to walk into the desert and command the services of a skilled desert warrior as his sidekick? What's in it for Abou? Movies like this are big on those solemn exchanges of significant looks during which deep truths remain unspoken, primarily because there is no way on earth they *can* be spoken without the cast and audience joining in uncontrolled laughter.

But I must not dismiss the qualities of the movie. It looks good, it moves quickly, and it is often a jolly good time. As mindless swashbuckling in a well-designed production, it can't be faulted. The less you know about the British Empire and human nature, the more you will like it, but then that can be said of so many movies.

Frailty ★ ★ ★ ★
R, 100 m., 2002

Bill Paxton (Dad), Matthew McConaughey (Fenton Meiks), Powers Boothe (Agent Wesley Doyle), Matthew O'Leary (Young Fenton Meiks), Jeremy Sumpter (Young Adam Meiks), Luke Askew (Sheriff Smalls), Derk Cheetwood (Agent Griffin Hull), Blake King (Eric). Directed by Bill Paxton and produced by David Blocker, David Kirschner, and Corey Sienega. Screenplay by Brent Hanley.

Heaven protect us from people who believe they can impose their will on us in this world, because of what they think they know about the next. *Frailty* is about such a man, a kind and gentle father who is visited by an angel who assigns him to murder demons in human form. We are reminded that Andrea Yates believed she was possessed by Satan and could save her children by drowning them. *Frailty* is as chilling: The father enlists his two sons, who are about seven and ten, to join him in the murders of victims he brings home.

This is not, you understand, an abusive father. He loves his children. He is only following God's instructions: "This is our job now, son. We've got to do this." When the older son, terrified and convinced his father has gone mad, says he'll report him to the police, his father explains, "If you do that, son, someone will die. The angel was clear on this." The pressure that the children are under is unbearable and tragic, and warps their entire lives.

Frailty is an extraordinary work, concealing in its depths not only unexpected story turns but also implications, hidden at first, that make it even deeper and more sad. It is the first film directed by the actor Bill Paxton, who also plays the father, and succeeds in making "Dad" not a villain but a sincere man lost within his delusions. Matthew McConaughey plays one of his sons as a grown man, and Powers Boothe is the FBI agent who is investigating the "God's Hand" serial murders in Texas when the son comes to him one night, with the body of his brother parked outside in a stolen ambulance.

The movie works in so many different ways that it continues to surprise us right until the end. It begins as a police procedural, seems for a time to be a puzzle like *Usual Suspects*, re-veals itself as a domestic terror film, evokes pity as well as horror, and reminded me of *The Rapture*, another film about a parent who is willing to sacrifice a child in order to follow the literal instructions of her faith.

As the film opens, Matthew McConaughey appears in the office of FBI agent Wesley Doyle (Powers Boothe), introduces himself as Fenton Meiks, and says he knows who committed the serial killings that have haunted the area for years. His story becomes the narration of two long flashbacks in which we see Paxton as the elder Meiks, and Matthew O'Leary and Jeremy Sumpter as young Fenton and Adam. Their mother is dead; they live in a frame house near the community rose garden, happy and serene, until the night their father wakes them with the news that he has been visited by an angel.

The film neither shies away from its horrifying events nor dwells on them. There is a series of ax murders, but they occur offscreen; this is not a movie about blood, but about obsession. The truly disturbing material involves the two boys, who are played by O'Leary and Sumpter as ordinary, happy kids whose lives turn into nightmares. Young Adam simply believes everything his father tells him. Fenton is old enough to know it's wrong: "Dad's brainwashed you," he tells Adam. "It's all a big lie. He murders people and you help him."

The construction of the story circles around the angel's "instructions" in several ways. The sons and father are trapped in a household seemingly ruled by fanaticism. There is, however, the intriguing fact that when Dad touches his victims, he has graphic visions of their sins—he can see vividly why they need to be killed. Are these visions accurate? We see them, too, but it's unclear whether through Dad's eyes or the movie's narrator—if that makes a difference. Whether they are objectively true is something I, at least, believe no man can know for sure about another. Not just by touching him, anyway. But the movie contains one shot, sure to be debated, that suggests God's hand really is directing Dad's murders.

Perhaps only a first-time director, an actor who does not depend on directing for his next job, would have had the nerve to make this movie. It is uncompromised. It follows its logic right down into hell. We love movies that play and toy with the supernatural, but are we prepared for one that is an unblinking look at where the logic of the true believer can lead? There was just a glimpse of this mentality on the day after 9/11, when certain TV preachers described it as God's punishment for our sins, before backpedaling when they found such frankness eroded their popularity base.

On the basis of this film, Bill Paxton is a gifted director; he and his collaborators, writer Brent Hanley, cinematographer Bill Butler, and editor Arnold Glassman, have made a complex film that grips us with the intensity of a simple one. We're with it every step of the way, and discover we hardly suspect where it is going.

Note: Watching the film, I was reminded again of the West Memphis Three (www.wm3.org), those three Arkansas teenagers convicted of the brutal murder of three children. One faces death and the other two long sentences. The documentaries Paradise Lost *(1992) and* Paradise Lost 2: Revelations *(2000) make it clear they are probably innocent (a prime suspect all but confesses on-screen), but the three are still in jail because they wore black, listened to heavy metal music, and were railroaded by courts and a community convinced they were Satanists—which must have been evidence enough, since there wasn't much else, and the boys could prove they were elsewhere.*

Freddy Got Fingered no stars
R, 93 m., 2001

Tom Green (Gord Brody), Rip Torn (Jim Brody), Harland Williams (Darren), Julie Hagerty (Julie Brody), Marisa Coughlan (Betty), Eddie Kaye Thomas (Freddy). Directed by Tom Green and produced by Larry Brezner, Lauren Lloyd, and Howard Lapides. Screenplay by Green and Derek Harvie.

It's been leading up to this all spring. When David Spade got buried in crap in *Joe Dirt,* and when three supermodels got buried in crap in *Head Over Heels,* and when human organs fell from a hot-air balloon in *Monkey Bone* and were eaten by dogs, and when David Arquette rolled around in dog crap and a gangster had his testicles bitten off in *See Spot Run,* and when a testicle was eaten in *Tomcats,* well, somehow the handwriting was on the wall. There had to be a movie like *Freddy Got Fingered* coming along.

This movie doesn't scrape the bottom of the barrel. This movie isn't the bottom of the barrel. This movie isn't below the bottom of the barrel. This movie doesn't deserve to be mentioned in the same sentence with barrels.

Many years ago, when surrealism was new, Luis Buñuel and Salvador Dali made a film so shocking that Buñuel filled his pockets with stones to throw at the audience if it attacked him. Green, whose film is in the surrealist tradition, may want to consider the same tactic. The day may come when *Freddy Got Fingered* is seen as a milestone of neosurrealism. The day may never come when it is seen as funny.

The film is a vomitorium consisting of ninety-three minutes of Tom Green doing things that a geek in a carnival sideshow would turn down. Six minutes into the film, his character leaps from his car to wag a horse penis. This is, we discover, a framing device— to be matched by a scene late in the film where he sprays his father with elephant semen, straight from the source.

Green plays Gord Brody, a twenty-eight-year-old who lives at home with his father (Rip Torn), who despises him, and his mother (Julie Hagerty), who wrings her hands a lot. He lives in a basement room still stocked with his high school stuff, draws cartoons, and dreams of becoming an animator. Gord would exhaust a psychiatrist's list of diagnoses. He is unsocialized, hostile, manic, and apparently retarded. Retarded? How else to explain a sequence where a Hollywood animator tells him to "get inside his animals," and he skins a stag and prances around dressed in the coat, covered with blood?

His romantic interest in the movie is Betty (Marisa Coughlan), who is disabled, and dreams of rocket-powered wheelchairs and oral sex. A different kind of sexual behavior enters the life of his brother, Freddy, who gets the movie named after him just because, I suppose, Tom Green thought the title was funny. His character also thinks it is funny to falsely accuse his father of molesting Freddy.

Tom Green's sense of humor may not resemble yours. Consider, for example, a scene where Gord's best friend busts his knee open while skateboarding. Gord licks the open wound. Then he visits his friend in the hospital. A woman in the next bed goes into labor. Gord rips the baby from her womb and, when it appears to be dead, brings it to life by swinging it around his head by its umbilical cord, spraying the walls with blood. If you wanted that to be a surprise, then I'm sorry I spoiled it for you.

Frida ★ ★ ★ ½
R, 120 m., 2002

Salma Hayek (Frida Kahlo), Alfred Molina (Diego Rivera), Antonio Banderas (David Alfaro Siqueiros), Valeria Golino (Lupe Marín), Ashley Judd (Tina Modotti), Mía Maestro (Cristina Kahlo), Edward Norton (Nelson Rockefeller), Geoffrey Rush (Leon Trotsky). Directed by Julie Taymor and produced by Lindsay Flickinger, Sarah Green, Nancy Hardin, Salma Hayek, Jay Polstein, Roberto Sneider, and Lizz Speed. Screenplay by Diane Lake, Clancy Sigal, Gregory Nava, and Anna Thomas, based on the book *Frida: A Biography of Frida Kahlo* by Hayden Herrera.

Early in their marriage, Frida Kahlo tells Diego Rivera she expects him to be "not faithful, but loyal." She holds herself to the same standard. Sexual faithfulness is a bourgeois ideal that they reject as Marxist bohemians who disdain the conventional. But passionate jealousy is not unknown to them, and both have a double standard, permitting themselves freedoms they would deny to the other. During the course of *Frida*, Kahlo has affairs with Leon Trotsky and Josephine Baker (not a shabby dance card), and yet rages at Diego for his infidelities.

Julie Taymor's biopic tells the story of an extraordinary life. Frida Kahlo (Salma Hayek), born of a German-Jewish father and a Mexican mother, grew up in Mexico City at a time when it was a hotbed of exile and intrigue. As a student she goes to see the great muralist Diego Rivera at work, boldly calls him "fat," and knows that he is the man for her.

Then she is almost mortally injured in a trolley crash that shatters her back and pierces her body with a steel rod. She was never to be free of pain again in her life, and for long periods had to wear a body cast. Taymor shows a bluebird flying from Frida's hand at the moment of the crash, and later a gold leaf falls on the cast: She uses the materials of magic realism to suggest how Frida was able to overcome pain with art and imagination.

Diego was already a legend when she met him. Played by Alfred Molina in a great bearlike performance of male entitlement, he was equally gifted at art, carnal excess, and self-promotion. The first time Frida sleeps with him, they are discovered by his wife, Lupe (Valeria Golino), who is enraged, of course, but such is Diego's power over women that after Frida and Diego are wed, Lupe brings them breakfast in bed ("This is his favorite. If you are here to *stay*, you'd better learn how to make it").

Frida's paintings often show herself, alone or with Diego, and reflect her pain and her ecstasy. They are on a smaller scale than his famous murals, and her art is overshadowed by his. His fame leads to an infamous incident, when he is hired by Nelson Rockefeller (Edward Norton) to create a mural for Rockefeller Center, and boldly includes Lenin among the figures he paints. Rockefeller commands the mural to be hammered down from the wall, thus making himself the goat in this episode forevermore.

The director, Taymor, became famous for her production of *The Lion King* on Broadway, with its extraordinary merging of actors and the animals they portrayed. Her *Titus* (2000) was a brilliant reimaging of the Shakespeare tragedy, showing a gift for great, daring visual inventions. Here, too, she breaks out of realism to suggest the fanciful colors of Frida's imagination. But real life itself is bizarre in this marriage, where the partners build houses side by side and connect them by a bridge between the top floors.

Artists talk about the "zone," that mental state when the mind, the eye, the hand, and the imagination are all in the same place, and they are able to lose track of time and linear thought. Frida Kahlo seems to have painted in order to seek the zone and escape pain: When she was at work, she didn't so much put the pain onto the canvas as channel it away from conscious thought and into the passion of her work. She *needs* to paint not simply to "express herself," but to live at all, and this is her closest bond with Rivera.

Biopics of artists are always difficult because the connections between life and art always seem too easy and facile. The best ones lead us back to the work itself, and inspire us to sympathize with its maker. *Frida* is jammed with incident and anecdote—this was a life that ended at forty-six and yet made longer lives seem underfurnished. Taymor obviously struggled with the material, as did her many writers; the screenwriters listed range from the veteran Clancy Sigal to the team of Gregory Nava and Anna Thomas, and much of the final draft was reportedly written by the actor Edward Norton. Sometimes we feel as if the film careens from one colorful event to another without respite, but sometimes it must have seemed to Frida Kahlo as if her life did, too.

The film opens in 1953, on the date of Frida's only one-woman show in Mexico. Her doctor tells her she is too sick to attend it, but she has her bed lifted onto a flatbed truck and carried to the gallery. This opening gesture provides Taymor with the setup for the movie's extraordinary closing scenes, in which death itself is seen as another work of art.

Friday After Next ★ ★
R, 85 m., 2002

Ice Cube (Craig Jones), Mike Epps (Day-Day), John Witherspoon (Mr. Jones), Don "D. C." Curry (Uncle Elroy), Anna Maria Horsford (Mrs. Jones), Bebe Drake (Miss Pearly), Terry Crews (Damon), Katt Micah Williams (Money Mike). Directed by Marcus Raboy and produced by Matt Alvarez and Ice Cube. Screenplay by Ice Cube.

Craig and Day-Day are back in the ghetto as *Friday After Next* opens, after a relative's lottery win allowed them to spend the previous film, *Next Friday*, in the lap of luxury. They're behind on the rent, unemployed, and as the picture opens their Christmas presents are being stolen by Santa Claus. That's the ghetto for you—a point the movie makes again and again, with humor that will cause some to laugh and others to cringe. There's already a controversy about the movie's TV spots, which "coincidentally" superimpose Santa's "Ho, ho, ho" over shots of black women.

As it happens, I saw the movie at about the same time as *Adam Sandler's 8 Crazy Nights*, another holiday picture with an ethnic angle. That probably helped me get in a better spirit. Sandler's film is so mean-spirited that *Friday After Next*, for all of its vulgarity (and scatology and obscenity), seems almost benevolent by contrast. At least its characters just wanna have fun and don't seem mad at the world.

The plot involves cousins Craig (Ice Cube) and Day-Day (Mike Epps) as roommates who have made one promise too many to their landlady (Bebe Drake), especially now that her man-mountain son Damon (Terry Crews) is out on parole. Desperate to raise cash, they get jobs as security guards in the neighborhood mall where their fathers, Mr. Jones (John Witherspoon) and Uncle Elroy (Don "D. C." Curry) run Bros. Bar-B-Que. Other stores include Pimp and Ho Fashions and Toys N the Hood, which is a nod to Ice Cube's debut picture *Boys N the Hood* but leaves an opening for *We Be Toys*.

The action mostly centers around attempts to raise the rent money and apprehend the thieving Santa, and there's a rent party that fills the screen with a lot of music and dancing and an improbable number of great-looking women. The landlady complains about the noise until she is rewarded with favors both mind-altering and sexual from upstairs, leading to the usual broad humor when Mrs. Jones (Anna Maria Horsford) finds her husband cheating.

A team of cops, one white, one black, both with ribald names, drift in and out. At one point they find a thriving marijuana bush in the cousins' apartment, and Craig desperately explains that it's for "municipal use." It turns out, once the cops confiscate the plant, that he's right.

Some of the better laughs come from Money Mike (Katt Micah Williams), who is short but, because of his wardrobe, not easy to miss. He plays the neighborhood pimp. Which leads me to wonder: Why, really, does this movie need a pimp? And "hos" that are not part of Santa's dialogue? And as much pot smoking as in a Cheech and Chong movie?

I guess there's an audience for it, and Ice Cube has paid dues in better and more positive movies (*Barbershop* among them). But surely laughs can be found in something other than this worked-over material. The original *Friday* movie, back in 1995, benefited not only from the presence of Chris Tucker but from a sweeter approach more based on human nature. The third picture has reduced the *Friday* series to loud, broad vulgarity, including Mr. Jones's obligatory battle with world-class flatulence. There's an audience for it, but it could have been funnier and more innocent. It's rated R, but when it hits the video stores you somehow know it will be viewed at home as a family movie, and that's kind of sad.

From Hell ★ ★ ★
R, 137 m., 2001

Johnny Depp (Frederick Abberline), Heather Graham (Mary Kelly), Ian Holm (Sir William Gull), Katrin Cartlidge (Dark Annie), Robbie Coltrane (Peter Godley), Bryon Frear (Robert Best). Directed by Albert Hughes and Allen Hughes and produced by Don Murphy and Jane Hamsher. Screenplay by Terry Hayes and Rafael Yglesias, based on the graphic novel by Alan Moore and Eddie Campbell.

"One day men will say I gave birth to the twentieth century."
—dialogue by Jack the Ripper

I'd like to think Darwin has a better case, but I see what he means. The century was indeed a stage for the dark impulses of the soul, and recently I've begun to wonder if Jack didn't give birth to the twenty-first century, too. Twins.

During ten weeks in autumn 1888, a serial killer murdered five prostitutes in the White-chapel area of London. The murders were linked because the Ripper left a trademark, surgically assaulting the corpses in a particularly gruesome way. "I look for someone with a thorough knowledge of human anatomy," says Inspector Abberline of Scotland Yard. An elementary knowledge would have been sufficient.

The story of Jack the Ripper has been fodder for countless movies and books, and even periodic reports that the mystery has been "solved" have failed to end our curiosity. Now comes *From Hell*, a rich, atmospheric film by the Hughes brothers *(Menace II Society)*, who

call it a "ghetto film," although knowledge of film, not the ghetto, is what qualifies them.

Johnny Depp stars as Inspector Frederick Abberline, an opium addict whose smoke-fueled dreams produce psychic insights into crime. The echo of Sherlock Holmes, another devotee of the pipe, is unmistakable, and *From Hell* supplies its hero with a Watsonoid sidekick in Peter Godley (Robbie Coltrane), a policeman assigned to haul Abberline out of the dens, gently remind him of his duty, protect him from harm, and marvel at his insights. Depp plays his role as very, very subtle comedy—so droll he hopes we think he's serious.

The movie feels dark, clammy, and exhilarating—it's like belonging to a secret club where you can have a lot of fun but might get into trouble. There's one extraordinary shot that begins with the London skyline, pans down past towers and steam trains, and plunges into a subterranean crypt where a Masonic lodge is sitting in judgment on one of its members. You get the notion of the robust physical progress of Victoria's metropolis, and the secret workings of the Establishment. At a time when public morality was strict and unbending, private misbehavior was a boom industry. Many, perhaps most, rich and pious men engaged in private debauchery.

The Hughes brothers plunge into this world, so far from their native Detroit, with the joy of tourists who have been reading up for years. Their source is a 500-page graphic novel (that is, transcendent comic book) by Alan Moore and Eddie Campbell, and some of their compositions look influenced by comic art, with its sharp obliques and exaggerated perspectives. The movie was shot on location with the medieval streets of Prague doubling for London, and production designer Martin Childs goes for lurid settings, saturated colors, deep shadows, a city of secret places protected by power and corruption.

We meet some of the prostitutes, particularly Mary Kelly (Heather Graham), who is trying to help her sisters escape from the dominance of the pimps. We see Abberline and Kelly begin a romance that probably would have been a lot more direct and uncomplicated at that time than it is in this movie. We see members of Victoria's immediate family implicated in whoring and venereal mishaps, and we meet the queen's surgeon, a precise and, by his own admission, brilliant man named Sir William Gull (Ian Holm).

The investigation is interrupted from time to time by more murders, graphically indicated, and by forms of official murder, like lobotomy. Sir William is an especially enthusiastic advocate of that procedure, reinforcing my notion that every surgeon of any intelligence who practiced lobotomy did so with certain doubts about its wisdom, and certain stirrings of curious satisfaction.

Watching the film, I was surprised how consistently it surprised me. It's a movie "catering to no clear demographic," *Variety* reports in its review, as if catering to a demographic would be a good thing for a movie to do. Despite its Gothic look, *From Hell* is not in the Hammer horror genre. Despite its Sherlockian hero, it's not a Holmes and Watson story. Despite its murders, it's not a slasher film. What it is, I think, is a Guignol about a cross section of a thoroughly rotten society, corrupted from the top down. The Ripper murders cut through layers of social class designed to insulate the sinners from the results of their sins.

Full Frontal ★ ½
R, 101 m., 2002

Blair Underwood (Nicholas/Calvin), Julia Roberts (Catherine/Francesca), David Hyde Pierce (Carl), Catherine Keener (Lee), Mary McCormack (Linda), Erika Alexander (Lucy), Rainn Wilson (Brian), David Duchovny (Bill/Gus). Directed by Steven Soderbergh and produced by Gregory Jacobs and Scott Kramer. Screenplay by Coleman Hough.

Every once in a while, perhaps as an exercise in humility, Steven Soderbergh makes a truly inexplicable film. There was the Cannes "secret screening" of his *Schizopolis* in 1996, which had audiences filing out with sad, thoughtful faces, and now here is *Full Frontal,* a film so amateurish that only the professionalism of some of the actors makes it watchable.

This is the sort of work we expect from a film school student with his first digital camera, not from the gifted director of *Traffic* and *Out of Sight.* Soderbergh directs at far below his usual level, and his cinematography is also

wretched; known as one of the few directors who shoots some of his own films, he is usually a skilled craftsman, but here, using a digital camera and available light, he produces only a demonstration of his inability to handle the style. Many shots consist of indistinct dark blobs in front of blinding backlighting.

The plot involves a film within a film, on top of a documentary about some of the people in the outside film. The idea apparently is to provide a view of a day in the life of the Los Angeles entertainment industry and its satellites. The movie within the movie stars Julia Roberts as a journalist interviewing Blair Underwood; shots that are supposed to be this movie are filmed in lush 35mm, and only serve to make us yearn for the format as we see the other scenes in digital.

The doc is not quite, or entirely, a doc; there are voice-overs describing and analyzing some of the characters, but other scenes play as dramatic fiction, and there's no use trying to unsort it all, because Soderbergh hasn't made it sortable. If this movie is a satire of the sorts of incomprehensible, earnest "personal" films that would-be directors hand out on cassettes at film festivals, then I understand it. It's the kind of film where you need the director telling you what he meant to do and what went wrong and how the actors screwed up and how there was no money for retakes, etc.

The other characters include Catherine Keener and David Hyde Pierce, as an unhappily married couple. She leaves him a good-bye note in the morning, then goes off to work as a personnel director, spending the day in a series of bizarre humiliations of employees (forcing them, for example, to stand on a chair while she throws an inflated world globe at them). In these scenes she is clearly deranged, and yet there is a "serious" lunch with her sister Linda (Mary McCormack), a masseuse who has never met Mr. Right.

Linda does, however, meet Gus (David Duchovny), a producer who is having a birthday party in a big hotel, hires her for a massage, and then offers her $500 to "release his tension." She needs the money because she is flying off the next day to see a guy she met on the Internet. She thinks he's twenty-two, but in fact he's about forty, and is not an artist as he says, but a director whose new play features Hitler as a guy who, he tells Eva Braun, has "so many responsibilities I can't think of a relationship right now."

Meanwhile, Pierce is fired at work ("He said I have confused my personality quirks with standards") and returns home to find his beloved dog has overdosed on hash brownies, after which he has a heart-to-heart with the veterinarian's assistant. All of these scenes feel like improvs that have been imperfectly joined, with no through-line. The scenes that work (notably McCormack's) are perhaps a tribute to the professionalism of the actor, not the director. Among the false alarms are little details like this: A love note that Underwood's character thinks came from Roberts's character is written on the same kind of red stationery as Keener's note to her husband. Is there a connection? Short answer: No.

Just yesterday I saw *Sex and Lucía,* also shot on digital, also involving a story within a story, with double roles for some of the characters. With it, too, I was annoyed by the digital photography (both films have more contrast between shadow and bright sunlight than their equipment seems able to handle). *Sex and Lucía* was even more confusing when it came to who was who (*Full Frontal* is fairly easy to figure out). But at least *Sex and Lucía,* was made by a director who had a good idea of what he wanted to accomplish, and established a tone that gave the material weight and emotional resonance. There is a scene in *Full Frontal* where a character comes to a tragic end while masturbating. That could symbolize the method and fate of this film.

G

Gangs of New York ★ ★ ★ ½
R, 168 m., 2002

Leonardo DiCaprio (Amsterdam Vallon), Daniel Day-Lewis (Bill the Butcher), Cameron Diaz (Jenny Everdeane), Jim Broadbent (Boss Tweed), John C. Reilly (Happy Jack), Henry Thomas (Johnny Sirocco), Brendan Gleeson (Monk McGinn), Gary Lewis (McGloin), Liam Neeson (Priest Vallon). Directed by Martin Scorsese and produced by Alberto Grimaldi, Scorsese, and Harvey Weinstein. Screenplay by Jay Cocks, Steven Zaillian, and Kenneth Lonergan.

Martin Scorsese's *Gangs of New York* rips up the postcards of American history and reassembles them into a violent, blood-soaked story of our bare-knuckled past. The New York it portrays in the years between 1830 and the Civil War is, as a character observes, "the forge of hell," in which groups clear space by killing their rivals. Competing fire brigades and police forces fight in the streets, audiences throw rotten fruit at an actor portraying Abraham Lincoln, blacks and Irish are chased by mobs, and the navy fires on the city as the poor riot against the draft.

The film opens with an extraordinary scene set beneath tenements in catacombs carved out of the Manhattan rock. An Irish-American leader named Priest Vallon (Liam Neeson) prepares for battle almost as if preparing for the Mass—indeed, as he puts in a collar to protect his neck, we think for a moment he might be a priest. With his young son Amsterdam trailing behind, he walks through the labyrinth of this torchlit Hades, gathering his forces, the Dead Rabbits, before stalking out into daylight to fight the forces of a rival American-born gang, the Nativists.

Men use knives, swords, bayonets, cleavers, cudgels. The ferocity of their battle is animalistic. At the end, the field is littered with bodies—including that of Vallon, slain by his enemy William Cutting, a.k.a. Bill the Butcher (Daniel Day-Lewis). This was the famous gang fight of Five Points on the Lower East Side of Manhattan, recorded in American history but not underlined. When it is over, Amsterdam disappears into an orphanage, the ominously named Hellgate House of Reform. He emerges in his early twenties (now played by Leonardo DiCaprio) and returns to Five Points, still ruled by Bill, and begins a scheme to revenge his father.

The vivid achievement of Scorsese's film is to visualize this history and people it with characters of Dickensian grotesquerie. Bill the Butcher is one of the great characters in modern movies, with his strangely elaborate diction, his choked accent, his odd way of combining ruthlessness with philosophy. The canvas is filled with many other colorful characters, including a pickpocket named Jenny Everdeane (Cameron Diaz), a hired club named Monk (Brendan Gleeson), the shopkeeper Happy Jack (John C. Reilly), and historical figures such as Boss Tweed (Jim Broadbent), ruler of corrupt Tammany Hall, and P. T. Barnum (Roger Ashton-Griffiths), whose museum of curiosities scarcely rivals the daily displays on the streets.

Scorsese's hero, Amsterdam, plays much the same role as a Dickens hero like David Copperfield or Oliver Twist: He is the eyes through which we see the others, but is not the most colorful person on the canvas. Amsterdam is not as wild, as vicious, or as eccentric as the people around him, and may not be any tougher than his eventual girlfriend Jenny, who, like Nancy Sykes in *Oliver Twist*, is a hellcat with a fierce loyalty to her man. DiCaprio's character, more focused and centered, is a useful contrast to the wild men around him.

Certainly Daniel Day-Lewis is inspired by an intense ferocity, laced with humor and a certain analytical detachment, as Bill the Butcher. He is a fearsome man, fond of using his knife to tap his glass eye, and he uses a pig carcass to show Amsterdam the various ways to kill a man with a knife. Bill is a skilled knife artist, and terrifies Jenny, his target for a knife-throwing act, not only by coming close to killing her but also by his ornate and ominous word choices.

Cameron Diaz plays Jenny as a woman who at first insists on her own independence; as a pickpocket, she ranks high in the criminal hierarchy, and even dresses up to prey on the rich people uptown. But when she finally caves in to Amsterdam's love, she proves tender and loyal in one love scene where they compare their scars, and another where she nurses him back to health.

The movie is straightforward in its cynicism about democracy at that time. Tammany Hall buys and sells votes, ethnic groups are delivered by their leaders, and when the wrong man is elected sheriff he does not serve for long. That American democracy emerged from this cauldron is miraculous. We put the Founding Fathers on our money, but these Founding Crooks for a long time held sway.

Martin Scorsese is probably our greatest active American director (Robert Altman is another candidate), and he has given us so many masterpieces that this film, which from another director would be a triumph, arrives as a more measured accomplishment. It was a difficult film to make, as we know from the reports that drifted back from the vast and expensive sets constructed at Cinecitta in Rome. The budget was enormous, the running time was problematical.

The result is a considerable achievement, a revisionist history linking the birth of American democracy and American crime. It brings us astonishing sights, as in a scene that shows us the inside of a tenement, with families stacked on top of one another in rooms like shelves. Or in the ferocity of the draft riots, which all but destroyed the city. It is instructive to be reminded that modern America was forged not in quiet rooms by great men in wigs, but in the streets, in the clash of immigrant groups, in a bloody Darwinian struggle.

All of this is a triumph for Scorsese, and yet I do not think this film is in the first rank of his masterpieces. It is very good but not great. I wrote recently of *GoodFellas* that "the film has the headlong momentum of a storyteller who knows he has a good one to share." I didn't feel that here. Scorsese's films usually leap joyfully onto the screen, the work of a master in command of his craft. Here there seems more struggle, more weight to overcome, more darkness. It is a story that Scorsese has filmed without entirely internalizing. The gangsters in his earlier films are motivated by greed, ego, and power; they like nice cars, shoes, suits, dinners, women. They murder as a cost of doing business. The characters in *Gangs of New York* kill

because they like to and want to. They are bloodthirsty and motivated by hate. I think Scorsese liked the heroes of *GoodFellas, Casino*, and *Mean Streets*, but I'm not sure he likes this crowd.

Gangster No. 1 ★ ★ ★
R, 105 m., 2002

Malcolm McDowell (Gangster 55), David Thewlis (Freddie Mays), Paul Bettany (Young Gangster), Saffron Burrows (Karen), Kenneth Cranham (Tommy), Jamie Foreman (Lennie Taylor), Eddie Marsan (Eddie Miller), Andrew Lincoln (Maxie King). Directed by Paul McGuigan and produced by Norma Heyman and Jonathan Cavendish. Screenplay by Johnny Ferguson.

If Alex DeLarge of *A Clockwork Orange* had become a London gangster, he might have turned out like the hero of *Gangster No. 1*. The movie encourages that connection by casting Malcolm McDowell, the original Alex, as the character grown old. Paul Bettany, who plays Young Gangster, is often photographed with his eyes glaring up from beneath lowered brows, which was the signature look Stanley Kubrick gave Alex. Another connection: The movie contains a beating of startling brutality, scored by a pop song played at top volume.

The movie is inspired, as all modern London gangster movies are inspired, by the notorious Kray brothers. It isn't based on their lives or deeds, but on the aura of evil they so successfully projected; they often got their way without violence, because they seemed so capable of it. In *Gangster No. 1*, the crime family is led by Freddie Mays (David Thewlis), who in 1968 is a young, sleek, expensively groomed hood who runs a nightclub and surrounds himself with hard men; he's known as the Butcher of Mayfair. One day he summons Young Gangster (Paul Bettany), tosses him a roll of bills, hires him, and seals his own fate.

The movie, directed by Paul McGuigan, begins in 1999, with Young Gangster grown middle-aged and cold-eyed. McDowell plays the character as a man who has lost all joy, retaining only venom. We see him with cronies at a private boxing club; they're laughing uglies, drinking champagne, smoking cigars, recalling the violent days of their youth (significantly, their memories are starting to be unreliable). Then he learns that Freddie is getting out of prison, his eyes narrow, and we go into the flashback.

The 1968 events have been called Shakespearean, which is fair enough, since just about everything is Shakespearean. They also have a touch of Freud. Everything has a touch of Freud. Young Gangster admires Freddie enormously, wants to be like him, and is probably half in love with him. When Freddie falls in love with the nightclub singer Karen (Saffron Burrows), Young Gangster is consumed with jealousy. In one of the movie's strongest scenes, he confronts Karen, who not too subtly offers to help him find a girl, and then spits in his face.

Paul Bettany's reaction shot is a piece of work. His face screws into a rictus of hate, he seems about to hit her, and then, by an act of will, he starts smiling—which is even more frightening. There has been a gangland feud between Freddie and a rival named Lennie Taylor (Jamie Foreman), and when Young Gangster learns of a planned hit on Freddie and Karen, he goes to the location, stays in his car, and watches it like a drama. Then he kills Lennie to frame Freddie for the murder.

The sequence involving this murder is one of the most brutal and, it must be said, successfully filmed acts of violence I have seen. Chilling, how Young Gangster breaks down the door of Lennie's flat, shoots him in the knee, then carefully takes off his coat, shirt, tie, and pants, because he doesn't want them bloodied in the events ahead. Then he unpacks a tool kit, including a hatchet, a hammer, and a chisel. The attack is seen through Lennie's point of view, as he fades in and out of consciousness. Another piece of work.

The movie is exact in its characters and staging, using Freddie's sunken living room conversation pit as a kind of stage; the man in power towers over the others. But I am not sure the ending really concludes anything. We see Freddie and Young (now Old) Gangster in a final exchange of information, revelation, and emotional brinksmanship, but then there's a coda with the older gangster on a rooftop, shouting for all the world like the bitter loser in a 1930s Warner Bros. crime movie.

This conclusion is too pat to be satisfying, but the film has a kind of hard, cold effect.

George Washington ★ ★ ★
NO MPAA RATING, 89 m., 2001

Candace Evanofski (Nasia), Donald Holden (George), Curtis Cotton III (Buddy), Eddie Rouse (Damascus), Paul Schneider (Rico Rice), Damian Jewan Lee (Vernon), Rachael Handy (Sonya), Jonathan Davidson (Euless), Janet Taylor (Ruth). Directed by David Gordon Green and produced by Green, Sacha W. Mueller, and Lisa Muskat. Screenplay by Green.

There is a summer in your life that is the last time boys and girls can be friends until they grow up. The summer when adolescence has arrived, but has not insisted on itself. When the stir of arriving sexuality still makes you feel hopeful instead of restless and troubled. When you feel powerful instead of unsure. That is the summer *George Washington* is about, and all it is about. Everything else in the film is just what happened to happen that summer.

This is such a lovely film. You give yourself to its voluptuous languor. You hang around with these kids from the poor side of town, while they kill time and share their pipe dreams. A tragedy happens, but the movie is not about the tragedy. It is about the discovery that tragedies can happen. In the corresponding summer of my life, a kid tried to be a daredevil by riding his bicycle up a ramp, and fell off and broke his leg, and everybody blamed that when he got polio. I tell you my memory instead of what happens in this film, because the tragedy in the film comes so swiftly, in the midst of a casual afternoon, that it should be as surprising to you as to the kids.

The movie takes place in a rusting industrial landscape, which the weeds are already returning to nature. It is in North Carolina. We meet some black kids, between ten and thirteen, and a few white kids. They're friends. They are transparent to one another. They are facts of life. You wake up every morning and here they are, the other kids in your life. They are waiting to grow up. There are some adults around, but they're not insisted upon. Some of them are so stranded by life they kill time with the kids. Nothing better to do.

Buddy (Curtis Cotton III) has a crush on Nasia (Candace Evanofski). She leaves him for George (Donald Holden). This is all momentous because it is the first crush and the first leaving of their lives. Buddy asks for one last kiss. "Do you love me?" asks Nasia. Buddy won't say. He wants the kiss voluntarily. No luck. George has his own problems: The plates in his skull didn't meet right, and he wears a football helmet to protect his skull. "When I look at my friends," Nasia muses, "I know there's goodness. I can look at their feet, or when I hold their hands, I pretend I can see the bones inside."

George fears for his dog because his Uncle Damascus (Eddie Rouse) doesn't like animals. "He just don't like to get bothered," says Aunt Ruth (Janet Taylor). "Do you remember the first time we made love to this song?" Damascus asks Ruth. "We were out in that field. You buried me in that grass." "Why is it," Ruth asks him, "every time you start talkin', you sound like you gonna cry?"

The heat is still, the days are slow, there is not much to do. A kid with freckles gets in trouble in the swimming pool and George jumps in to save him, even though he's not supposed to get his head wet. Then George starts wearing a cape, like a superhero. Buddy wears a Halloween dinosaur mask while he stands in a rest room, which is one of their hangouts, and delivers a soliloquy that would be worthy of Hamlet, if instead of being the prince of Denmark, Hamlet had been Buddy. Buddy disappears. Nasia thinks he ran away "because he still has his crush on me." Others know why Buddy disappeared but simply do not know what to do with their knowledge. Vernon (Damian Jewan Lee) has a soliloquy beginning with the words "I wish," that would be worthy of Buddy, or Hamlet.

The film has been written and directed by David Gordon Green. The cinematography, by Tim Orr, is the best of the year. The mood and feel of the film has been compared to the work of Terence Malick, and Green is said to have watched The Thin Red Line over and over while preparing to shoot. But this is not a copy of Malick; it is simply in the same key. Like Malick's Days of Heaven, it is not about plot, but about memory and regret. It remembers a summer that was not a happy summer, but there will never again be a summer so intensely felt, so alive, so valuable.

Gerry ★ ★ ★
R, 103 m., 2003

Casey Affleck (Gerry), Matt Damon (Gerry). Directed by Gus Van Sant and produced by Dany Wolf. Screenplay by Casey Affleck, Matt Damon, and Van Sant.

Not long after Gus Van Sant got the bright idea of doing a shot-by-shot remake of Hitchcock's Psycho in color, I ran into him at the Calcutta Film Festival, and asked him why in the hell he'd come up with that bright idea. "So that no one else would have to," he replied serenely. With his new film, Gerry, he has removed another project from the future of the cinema and stored it prudently in the past. He is like an adult removing dangerous toys from the reach of reckless kids.

Gerry stars Casey Affleck and Matt Damon as two friends named Gerry who go for a walk in the desert and get lost. There, I've gone and given away the plot. They walk and walk and walk. For a while they talk, and then they walk in silence, and then they stagger, and then they look like those New Yorker cartoons of guys lost in the desert who reach out a desperate hand toward a distant mirage of Jiffy-Lube. It would have been too cruel for Van Sant to add Walter Brennan on the sound track, listenin' to the age-old story of the shiftin', whisperin' sands.

A movie like this doesn't come along every day. I am glad I saw it. I saw it at the 2002 Sundance Film Festival, where a fair number of people walked out. I would say half. I was reminded of advice once given me by the veteran Chicago movie exhibitor Oscar Brotman: "Roger, if nothing has happened by the end of the first reel, nothing is going to happen." If I were to advise you to see Gerry, you might have a good case on your hands for a class-action suit.

And yet, and yet—the movie is so gloriously bloody-minded, so perverse in its obstinacy, that it rises to a kind of mad purity. The longer the movie ran, the less I liked it and the more I admired it. The Gerrys are stuck out there, and it looks like no plot device is going to come along and save them. The horizon is

233

barren for 360 degrees of flat wasteland. We have lost most of the original eight hours of *Greed* (1925), Erich von Stroheim's film that also ends with its heroes lost in Death Valley, but after seeing *Gerry* I think we can call off the search for the missing footage.

The screenplay for *Gerry*, by Affleck, Damon, and Van Sant, is not without humor. Before they realize the enormity of their predicament, the two Gerrys discuss this dumb contestant they saw on *Jeopardy*, and Affleck expresses frustration about a video game he has been playing (he conquered Thebes, only to discover he needed twelve horses and had but eleven).

One morning one of the characters finds himself standing on top of a tall rock, and is not sure how he got there, or whether he should risk breaking an ankle by jumping down. If I ever get lost in Death Valley, it will be more or less exactly like this.

After seeing the film at Sundance, as I reported at the time, I got in a conversation with three women who said they thought it was "existential."

"Existential?" I asked.

"Like, we have to choose whether to live or die."

"They do not have a choice to make," I said. "They're lost and they can't find their car. They have no water and no food."

"What I think," said one of the women, "is that it's like Samuel Beckett's *Waiting for Godot*, except without the dialogue."

"It has dialogue," her friend said.

"But not serious dialogue."

"The dialogue in *Godot* is not serious," I said. "At least, it is not intended by the speakers to be serious."

"In *Godot*," the woman said, "they wait and wait and Godot never comes. In *Gerry*, they walk and walk and they never get anywhere."

"There you have it," I said.

I arrive at the end of this review having done my duty as a critic. I have described the movie accurately, and you have a good idea what you are in for, if you go to see it. Most of you will not. I cannot argue with you. Some of you will—the brave and the curious. You embody the spirit of the man who first wondered what it would taste like to eat an oyster.

Ghost Ship ★ ★

R, 88 m., 2002

Gabriel Byrne (Murphy), Julianna Margulies (Epps), Ron Eldard (Dodge), Desmond Harrington (Ferriman), Isaiah Washington (Greer), Alex Dimitriades (Santos), Karl Urban (Munder), Emily Browning (Katie). Directed by Steve Beck and produced by Joel Silver, Robert Zemeckis, and Gilbert Adler. Screenplay by Mark Hanlon and John Pogue, based on the story by Hanlon.

Ghost Ship recycles all the usual haunted house material, but because it's about a haunted ocean liner, it very nearly redeems itself. Yes, doors open by themselves to reveal hanging corpses. Yes, there's a glimpse of a character who shouldn't be there. Yes, there's a cigarette burning in an ashtray that hasn't been used in forty years. And yes, there's a struggle between greed and prudence as the dangers pile up.

These are all usual elements in haunted house movies, but here they take place aboard the deserted—or seemingly deserted—hulk of the *Antonia Graza*, an Italian luxury liner that disappeared without a trace during a 1962 cruise to America, and has how been discovered forty years later, floating in the Bering Straits. A salvage crew led by Murphy the skipper (Gabriel Byrne) and Epps the co-owner (Julianna Margulies) sets out to capture this trophy, which could be worth a fortune.

Echoes from long-ago geography classes haunted me as I watched the film, because the Bering Sea, of course, is in the North Pacific, and if the *Antonia Graza* disappeared from the North Atlantic, it must have succeeded in sailing unattended and unnoticed through the Panama Canal. Or perhaps it rounded Cape Horn, or the Cape of Good Hope. Maybe its unlikely position is like a warning that this ship no longer plays by the rules of the physical universe.

The salvage crew is told about the ship by Ferriman (Desmond Harrington), a weather spotter for the Royal Canadian Air Force. He got some photos of it, and tips them off in return for a finder's fee. Onboard the salvage tug are Murphy, Epps, and crew members Greer (Isaiah Washington), Dodge (Ron Eldard), Munder (Karl Urban), and Santos (Alex Dimitriades). Under the time-honored code of horror movies, they will disappear in horrible ways in inverse order to their billing—although of course there's also the possibility they'll turn up again.

The most absorbing passages in the film involve their exploration of the deserted liner. The quality of the art direction and photography actually evoke some of the same creepy, haunting majesty of those documentaries about descents to the grave of the *Titanic*. There's more scariness because we know how the original passengers and crew members died (that opening scene has a grisly humor), and because the ship still seems haunted—not only by that sad-eyed little girl, but perhaps by others.

The mystery eventually yields an explanation, if not a solution, and there is the obligatory twist in the last shot, which encourages us to reinterpret everything in diabolical terms, and to think hard about the meanings of certain names. But the appeal of *Ghost Ship* is all in the process, not in the climax. I liked the vast old empty ballroom, the deserted corridors, and the sense of a party that ended long ago (the effect is of a nautical version of Miss Havisham's sealed room). I knew that there would be unexpected shocks, sudden noises, and cadaverous materializations, but I have long grown immune to such mechanical thrills (unless they are done well, of course). I just dug the atmosphere.

Is the film worth seeing? Depends. It breaks no new ground as horror movies go, but it does introduce an intriguing location, and it's well-made technically. It's better than you expect, but not as good as you hope.

Ghosts of Mars ★ ★ ★
R, 98 m., 2001

Ice Cube (Desolation Williams), Natasha Henstridge (Melanie Ballard), Jason Statham (Jericho Butler), Clea DuVall (Bashira Kincaid), Pam Grier (Helena), Joanna Cassidy (Whitlock), Richard Cetrone (Big Daddy Mars), Duane Davis (Uno). Directed by John Carpenter and produced by Sandy King. Screenplay by Larry Sulkis and Carpenter.

John Carpenter's *Ghosts of Mars* is a brawny space opera, transplanting the conventions of Western, cop, and martial arts films to the Red Planet. As waves of zombified killers attack the heroes, action scenes become shooting galleries, and darned if in the year 2176 they aren't still hurling sticks of dynamite from moving trains. All basic stuff, and yet Carpenter brings pacing and style to it, and Natasha Henstridge provides a coolheaded center.

As the film opens, a ghost train pulls into Chryse City, so named for a flat plain north of the Martian equator. No driver is at the helm, and only one passenger is on board. She is Melanie Ballard (Henstridge), a cop who headed a detail to an outlying mining town named Shining Canyon to bring back a killer named Desolation Williams (Ice Cube). Called up before a tribunal in the matriarchal Martian society, she tells her story, and most of the action is in flashback.

The mining camp seems empty when the cops arrive. Henstridge is joined by Helena (Pam Grier), Bashira (Clea DuVall), Jericho (Jason Statham), and Uno (Duane Davis). They start finding bodies. Desolation is still in jail, proving he could not be the killer, and eventually a survivor named Whitlock (Joanna Cassidy) tells the story of how the miners found the entrance to a long-buried tunnel. It led to a door that, when merely touched, crumbled into dust and released, yes, the ghosts of Mars. They possessed humans and turned them into killing machines, to take, she says, "vengeance on anyone who tries to lay claim to their planet."

That's the setup. The payoff is a series of well-staged action sequences, made atmospheric by the rusty red atmosphere that colors everything. At one point the cops barricade themselves inside the mining camp's police station, which will remind Carpenter fans of his early feature, *Assault on Precinct 13*. There is also something about the ghoulish way the possessed miners lurch into action that has a touch of the *Living Dead* movies.

These ghouls or zombies or ghost-creatures are not, however, slow. They're pretty fast in the martial arts scenes, especially their leader, Big Daddy Mars (Richard Cetrone). But like all similar movie creatures, they're just a little slower than the heroes. They keep coming but never quite catch up.

Natasha Henstridge has come full circle. Her

movie career began in *Species* (1995), where she played Sil, an alien who looked like Natasha Henstridge part of the time, and like gloppy puke-monsters the rest of the time. Now she's fighting the aliens, and for most of the movie is partnered with Desolation, the Ice Cube character, played by Mr. Cube with solid authority.

Ghosts of Mars delivers on its chosen level and I enjoyed it, but I wonder why so many science-fiction films turn into extended exercises in Blast the Aliens. *Starship Troopers* was another. Why must aliens automatically be violent, angry, aggressive, ugly, mindless, and hostile? How could they develop the technology to preserve their spirits for aeons, and exhibit no civilized attributes? And, for that matter, if Earth creatures came along after, oh, say, 300 million years of captivity and set you free, would you be mad at them?

These are all questions for another movie. This one does have one original touch. After Melanie is possessed by a ghost, Desolation administers a fix from her stash, and the drug, whatever it is, inspires the alien to get out of her body fast. It is encouraging to learn that the ancient races of our solar system learned to just say no to drugs.

Ghosts of the Abyss ★ ★ ★
G, 59 m., 2003

Narrated by Bill Paxton, and featuring Lewis Abernathy, Dr. Lori Johnston, Don Lynch, Ken Marschall, Dr. Charles Pellegrino, and Tava Smiley. A documentary directed and written by James Cameron. Produced by Cameron, Chuck Comisky, and Andrew Wight.

The wreck of *Titanic*, which for decades seemed forever out of reach, has in recent years been visited by documentaries that bring back ghostly images of a party that ended in midsong. These films have an undeniable fascination, and none has penetrated more completely and evocatively than James Cameron's *Ghosts of the Abyss.*

The earliest films about *Titanic* were marvelous just because they existed at all. Cameron mounts a much more ambitious expedition to the bottom of the sea, involving a powerful light "chandelier" that hangs above the wreck and illuminates it, and two remote-controlled cameras named Jake and Elwood that propel themselves into tight corners and explore the inside of the ship.

Guiding them are expedition members in deep-diving exploration subs, including Bill Paxton, who starred in Cameron's *Titanic* and now narrates this documentary and shoots some of it himself. The result is often spellbinding, and to mention some of the sights we see is to praise the film's ambition.

The agile little camera-bots are able, for example, to snake their way into the ship's grand ballroom, and to discover that the Tiffany cutglass windows are, astonishingly, still intact. Later, Cameron is able to position one of the minisubs outside the ship to shine its light through the windows for the camera inside, and we see the colors brought alive by light for the first time since the ship hit the fatal iceberg.

Other scenes actually discover the brass bed in the suite occupied by the "unsinkable" Molly Brown, who was such a famous survivor she had a Broadway musical named after her, and who always insisted her bed was brass, not wood. We also see a bowler hat, still waiting atop a dresser, and glasses and a carafe, left where they were put down after a final drink.

Cameron, who achieved so much with digital effects in *Titanic,* here uses similar technology to animate his haunted undersea scenes. He shoots the *Titanic* today—its empty corridors, its deserted grand staircase, its abandoned decks—and then populates the ship with a ghostly overlay showing the restored ship with its elegant passengers on their cruise to doom.

The movie is an impressive achievement, but that is not because of its trumpeted sellingpoint, the fact that it was shot in 3-D. I saw the first 3-D movie *(Bwana Devil)* and I have seen most of them since, as the technology has been improved and perfected, and I have arrived at the conclusion that 3-D will never be ready for prime time: It is an unnecessary and distracting redundancy. It can be done very well (as with the custom-made $200 glasses supplied with some IMAX features) and we can admire its quality and yet doubt its usefulness. Oldfashioned 2-D provides an illusion of reality that has convinced moviegoers for one hundred years. We accept it and do not think about it. The 3-D process is a mistake because it distracts attention away from the content and toward the process.

Ghosts of the Abyss is being shown around the country in 3-D on IMAX screens and also in some regular theaters. Do not feel deprived if your theater does not have 3-D. You won't be missing a thing.

Note: I learn that Cameron's next fiction film, his first since Titanic, *will be a feature shot in 3-D. "People are looking for a new way to be stimulated," industry analyst Paul Dergarabedian said in the announcement story.*

He is correct about people, but wrong that 3-D is a new way to be stimulated. It is an old way that has never lived up to its promise. If Cameron wants to be a pioneer instead of a retro hobbyist, he should obviously use Maxivision 48, which provides a picture of such startling clarity that it appears to be 3-D in the sense that the screen seems to open a transparent window on reality. Ghosts of the Abyss would have been incomparably more powerful in the process.

Maxivision 48 would be cheaper than 3-D, would look dramatically better, would not require those silly glasses, would be backward-compatible for standard theaters, and would allow Cameron to introduce the next step forward in movie projection, rather than returning to the obsolete past. Cameron has the clout and the imagination to make this leap forward, not just for his next film but for an industry that needs something dramatic and new and realizes it isn't going to be digital projection. This is his chance to explore the future of cinema as bravely as he ventured to the ocean floor.

Ghost World ★ ★ ★ ★
R, 111 m., 2001

Thora Birch (Enid), Scarlett Johansson (Rebecca), Steve Buscemi (Seymour), Brad Renfro (Josh), Illeana Douglas (Roberta), Bob Balaban (Enid's Dad), Teri Garr (Maxine). Directed by Terry Zwigoff and produced by Lianne Halfon, John Malkovich, and Russell Smith. Screenplay by Daniel Clowes and Zwigoff, based on the comic book by Clowes.

There's a small tomb in Southwark Cathedral that I like to visit when I am in London. It contains the bones of a teenage girl who died three centuries ago. I know the inscription by heart:

This world to her
Was but a tragic play.
She came, saw, dislik'd,
And passed away.

I thought of those words while I was watching *Ghost World*, the story of an eighteen-year-old girl from Los Angeles who drifts forlorn through her loneliness, cheering herself up with an ironic running commentary. The girl is named Enid, she has just graduated from high school, and she has no plans for college, marriage, a career, or even next week. She's stuck in a world of stupid, shallow phonies, and she makes her personal style into a rebuke.

Unfortunately, Enid is so smart, so advanced, and so ironically doubled back upon herself that most of the people she meets don't get the message. She is second-level satire in a one-level world, and so instead of realizing, for example, that she is mocking the 1970s punk look, stupid video store clerks merely think she's twenty-five years out of style.

Enid is played by Thora Birch, from *American Beauty,* and in a sense this character is a continuation of that one—she certainly looks at her father the same way, with disbelief and muted horror. Her running mate is Rebecca (Scarlett Johansson). There's a couple like this in every high school: the smart outsider girls who are best friends for the purpose of standing back-to-back and fighting off the world. At high school graduation, they listen to a speech from a classmate in a wheelchair, and Enid whispers: "I liked her so much better when she was an alcoholic and drug addict. She gets in one stupid car crash and suddenly she's Little Miss Perfect."

But now Rebecca is showing alarming signs of wanting to get on with her life, and Enid is abandoned to her world of thrift shops, strip malls, video stores, and 1950s retro diners. One day, in idle mischief, she answers a personal ad in a local paper, and draws into her net a pathetic loner named Seymour (Steve Buscemi). At first she strings him along. Then, unexpected, she starts to like him—this collector who lives hermetically sealed in a world of precious 78 rpm records and old advertising art.

By day, Seymour is an insignificant fried chicken executive. By night, he catalogs his records and wonders how to meet a woman. Why does Enid like him? "He's the exact opposite of all the things I hate." Why does he like her? Don't get ahead of the story. *Ghost World* isn't a formula romance where opposites attract and march toward the happy ending. Seymour and Enid are too similar to fall in love; they both specialize in complex personal lifestyles that send messages no one is receiving. Enid even offers to try to fix up Seymour, but he sees himself as a bad candidate for a woman: "I don't want to meet someone who shares my interests. I hate my interests."

Seymour resembles someone I know, and that person is Terry Zwigoff, who directed this movie. It's his first fiction film. Zwigoff earlier made two docs, the masterpiece *Crumb* (1995), about the comic artist R. Crumb, and *Louie Bluie*, about the old-timey Chicago string band Martin, Bogan, and the Armstrongs. He looks a little like Buscemi, and acts like a Buscemi character: worn down, dubious, ironic, resigned. Zwigoff was plagued by agonizing back pain all during the period when he was making *Crumb*, and slept with a gun under his pillow, he told me, in case he had to end his misery in the middle of the night. When Crumb didn't want to cooperate with the documentary, Zwigoff threatened to shoot himself. Crumb does not often meet his match, but did with Zwigoff.

Both Zwigoff and his character Seymour collect old records that are far from the mainstream. Both are morose and yet have a bracing black humor that sees them through. Seymour and Enid connect because they are kindred spirits, and it's hard to find someone like that when you've cut yourself off from mankind.

The movie is based on a graphic novel by Daniel Clowes, who cowrote the screenplay with Zwigoff. It listens carefully to how people talk. Illeana Douglas, for example, has a perfectly observed role as the art teacher in Enid's summer makeup class, who has fallen for political correctness hook, line, and sinker, and praises art not for what it looks like but for what it "represents." There are also some nice moments from Teri Garr, who plays the take-charge girlfriend of Enid's father (Bob Balaban).

One scene I especially like involves a party of Seymour's fellow record collectors. They meet to exchange arcane information, and their conversations are like encryptions of the way most people talk. This event must seem strange to Enid, but see how she handles it. It's Seymour's oddness, his tactless honesty, his unapologetic aloneness, that Enid responds to. He works like the homeopathic remedy for angst: His loneliness drives out her own.

I wanted to hug this movie. It took such a risky journey, and never stepped wrong. It created specific, original, believable, lovable characters, and meandered with them through their inconsolable days, never losing its sense of humor. The Buscemi role is one he's been pointing toward during his entire career; it's like the flip side of his alcoholic barfly in *Trees Lounge*, who also becomes entangled with a younger girl, not so fortunately.

The movie sidesteps the happy ending Hollywood executives think lobotomized audiences need as an all-clear to leave the theater. Clowes and Zwigoff find an ending that is more poetic, more true to the tradition of the classic short story, in which a minor character finds closure that symbolizes the next step for everyone. *Ghost World* is smart enough to know that Enid and Seymour can't solve their lives in a week or two. But their meeting has blasted them out of lethargy, and now movement is possible. Who says that isn't a happy ending?

The Gift ★ ★ ★
R, 110 m., 2001

Cate Blanchett (Annie Wilson), Giovanni Ribisi (Buddy Cole), Keanu Reeves (Donnie Barksdale), Greg Kinnear (Wayne Collins), Hilary Swank (Valerie Barksdale), J. K. Simmons (Sheriff Pearl Johnson), Michael Jeter (Defense Attorney), Gary Cole (David Duncan). Directed by Sam Raimi and produced by James Jacks, Tom Rosenberg, and Robert G. Tapert. Screenplay by Billy Bob Thornton and Tom Epperson.

Psychics and hairdressers have three things in common: They can appoint themselves, they can work out of their homes, and they don't have a lot of overhead—a Tarot deck, shampoo, candles, scissors, incense, mousse. It helps if they have a reassuring manner, because many of their clients want to tell their troubles and receive advice.

Poor neighborhoods have a lot of women working as beauticians or soothsayers. If you're a woman with few options, no husband, and a bunch of kids, you can hang out the shingle and support yourself. The advice dispensed by these professionals is often as good as or better than the kind that costs $200 an hour, because it comes from people who spent their formative years living and learning. The problems of their clients are not theoretical to them.

Consider Annie Wilson (Cate Blanchett), the heroine of *The Gift*. Her husband was killed in an accident a year ago. She has three kids. She gets a government check, and supplements it by reading cards and advising clients. She doesn't go in for mumbo jumbo. She takes her gift as a fact of life; her grandmother had it, and so does she. She looks at the cards, she listens to her clients, she feels their pain, she tries to dispense common sense. She is sensible, courageous, and good.

She lives in a swamp of melodrama; that's really the only way to describe her hometown of Brixton, Georgia, which has been issued with one example of every standard Southern Gothic type. There's the battered wife and her redneck husband; the country club sexpot; the handsome school principal; the weepy mama's boy who is afeared he might do something real bad; the cheatin' attorney; the salt-of-the-earth sheriff; and various weeping willows, pickup trucks, rail fences, country clubs, shotguns, voodoo dolls, courtrooms, etc. When you see a pond in a movie like this, you know that sooner or later it is going to be dragged.

With all of these elements, *The Gift* could have been a bad movie, and yet it is a good one, because it redeems the genre with the characters Cate Blanchett's sanity and balance as Annie Wilson provide a strong center, and the other actors in a first-rate cast go for the realism in their characters, instead of being tempted by the absurd. The movie was directed by Sam Raimi and written by Billy Bob Thornton and Tom Epperson. They know the territory. Raimi directed Thornton in *A Simple Plan* (1998), that great movie about three bud-

dies who find a fortune and try to hide it; and Thornton and Epperson wrote *One False Move* (1991), about criminals on the run and old secrets of love.

The Gift begins by plunging us into the daily lives of the characters, and then develops into a thriller. One of Annie's kitchen-table clients is Valerie Barksdale (Oscar winner Hilary Swank), whose husband, Donnie (Keanu Reeves), beats her. Another is Buddy Cole (Giovanni Ribisi), who is haunted by nightmares and is a seething basket case filled with resentment against his father. Annie advises Valerie to leave her husband before he does more harm, and then Keanu Reeves has two terrifying scenes—one threatening her children, the other a midnight visit where he uses the voodoo doll as a prop.

Social interlude: Annie attends a country club dance, where she has a flirty conversation with the school principal (Greg Kinnear). He's engaged to Jessica King (Katie Holmes), a sultry temptress (i.e., country club slut) who Annie accidentally sees having a quickie with another local man. Not long after, Jessica disappears, and Sheriff Pearl Johnson (J. K. Simmons), frustrated by an absence of clues, appeals to Annie for some of her "hocus-pocus."

Annie has a dream that leads the law to Donnie Barksdale's pond, where the dead body is found, and Donnie looks like the obvious killer, but Annie's visions don't stop, and we are left (1) with the possibility that the murder may have been committed by several other excellent candidates, and (2) with suspicion falling on the psychic herself.

The movie is ingenious in its plotting, colorful in its characters, taut in its direction, and fortunate in possessing Cate Blanchett. If this were not a crime picture (if it were sopped in social uplift instead of thrills), it would be easier to see the quality of her work. By the end, as all hell is breaking loose, it's easy to forget how much everything depended on the sympathy and gravity she provided in the first two acts. This role seems miles away from her Oscar-nominated *Elizabeth* (1998), but after all isn't she once again an independent woman surrounded by men who want to belittle her power, seduce her, frame her, or kill her? A woman who has to rely on herself and her gifts, and does, and is sufficient.

Girls Can't Swim ★ ★

NO MPAA RATING, 101 m., 2002

Isild Le Besco (Gwen), Karen Alyx (Lise), Pascale Bussières (Céline), Pascal Elso (Alain), Marie Rivière (Anne-Marie), Yelda Reynaud (Solange), Sandrine Blancke (Vivianne), Julien Cottereau (Frédo), Dominique Lacarrière (Rose). Directed by Anne-Sophie Birot and produced by Philippe Jacquier. Screenplay by Birot and Christophe Honoré.

Gwen is a tall, toothy fifteen-year-old who lives with her parents in a French beachfront village. Her father is a drunk, given to spurts of rage, but otherwise, hey, a nice guy. Her mother seems like a sweet, decent person, which makes us wonder if she knows what movie she's in, since her reactions to the events around her seem inexplicably passive. Gwen waits impatiently for her friend Lise to join them for a summer holiday at the beach, and meantime engages in what the movie thinks of as adolescent sex and I think drifts over into wanton promiscuity.

During the course of just a few days, she makes love twice with her boyfriend, and then picks up two boys on the beach and has sex with both of them. Her father slaps her, once, for staying out all night. Later, finding her and the boyfriend having sex on his boat, he stands by as the boy flees and then takes no particular action. Still later, when both parents find Gwen, the boyfriend, and Lise in bed together, the boyfriend flees again (he seems to be constantly pulling on his pants and hopping out of the frame) and the mother says she'll take care of things and then essentially does nothing. Those French.

The story follows Gwen for the first act, then cuts to Lise for a story that parallels the same time frame, then joins the two stories at the beach. As we meet Lise, news comes that her father has been killed in an accident. She barely remembers him (he abandoned the family), and her mother says: "We slept alone for ten years. Your father's death doesn't mean anything." Lise says, "Well, I'm sad," but the depth

of her sadness can be estimated by another line: "But the beach is still on?"

The two girls were apparently very close the summer before, in a sort of quasi-Sapphic teenage friendship, but now Lise is disturbed to learn from two boys on the beach that they shared Gwen. Lise is a little behind Gwen on the maturation and hormone curve, which may explain the awkward scene where she tries to join Gwen and the boyfriend, just before the parents break in.

There are all sorts of issues about fathers in the movie. Lise's father is absent and then dead. Gwen's father is unpredictable in his behavior, and his marriage seems to lurch between truce and rage. Life at home is a thrill a minute; Gwen's father rents their front yard to some campers, only to throw them out while tearing down their tent and tossing their things around.

Gwen (Isild Le Besco) is obviously headed for some kind of crisis, and signals this by her emotional swings. Most of the time she's smiling or laughing inappropriately, and the rest of the time she's in rebellion and acting self-destructively. Poor Lise (Karen Alyx), who is more balanced, can't keep up, although in a misplaced attempt at revenge she more or less agrees to be almost seduced by Gwen's father, in a scene that ends in an event that I will not divulge, except to say that Lise's line to Gwen ("Now we're the same!") sounds like one of those brainstorms from writing school that force authors to work backward in order to set them up.

The phrase "coming of age," when applied to movies, almost always implies sex, but *Girls Can't Swim* has nothing useful to say about sex (certainly not compared to Catherine Breillat's brilliant *Fat Girl* from last year), and is too jerky in structure to inspire much empathy from us. I felt sad for Lise not so much because of what happens, as because she was captured by this movie when she obviously belongs in something lighter and sunnier, by Rohmer, for example. As for Gwen, she is unpleasant and reckless, and the movie is too easy on her. The parents remain inconsistent enigmas. Even the title is a puzzle, since, as nearly as I can tell, both girls can swim.

The Glass House ★ ★
PG-13, 101 m., 2001

Diane Lane (Erin Glass), Leelee Sobieski (Ruby Baker), Stellan Skarsgard (Terry Glass), Rita Wilson (Grace Baker), Bruce Dern (Lawyer), Michael O'Keefe (Dave Baker), Trevor Morgan (Rhett Baker). Directed by Daniel Sackheim and produced by Heather Zeegen. Screenplay by Wesley Strick.

The Glass House brings skilled technique to a plot that's a foregone conclusion. Since it's clear from early in the film what must have happened and why, it's a film about waiting for the characters to catch up to us. The movie's trailer doesn't help, with its comprehensive betrayal of the movie's key secrets. It should even be a secret that this is a thriller—we should walk in thinking it's about kids surviving the loss of their parents. No chance of that.

The film opens with one of those irrelevant shock buttons that have become annoying in recent years—five or ten minutes that have nothing to do with the rest of the story, but fool us with misleading footage. In this case, there's a horror scene, and then we see it's a film, and then we see the heroine and her friends watching it—and, yes, they're cute as they giggle at their own reactions, but openings like this are empty stylistic exercises. Once was a time when the well-made film used its opening scenes to dig in, not just spin its wheels.

The movie was directed by the TV veteran Daniel Sackheim, who worked on *ER, X Files, Law and Order,* and other series that are smarter than this. It stars Leelee Sobieski, one of the best young actresses, as Ruby Baker, who with her little brother Rhett (Trevor Morgan) is orphaned when their parents die in a car crash. The family lawyer (Bruce Dern) explains that the parents had arranged for their close friends Erin and Terry Glass to be their guardians in the case of tragedy, and soon the kids are moving into the Glasses' big glass house (uh-huh), which is luxurious, although Ruby and Rhett are a little too old to be sharing the same bedroom.

It's a detail like that we find annoying. Why would the Glasses, who have acres of living space on their Malibu hilltop, put the kids into one room? Given the Glasses' long-term plans, why not make the kids as happy as possible? There's a kind of thriller in which the events unfold as they might in real life, and we have to decide which way to take them—and another kind of thriller, this kind, where the events unfold as a series of ominous portents, real and false alarms, and music stingers on the sound track. The first kind of thriller is a film; the second is a technical exercise.

What makes *The Glass House* sad is that resources have been wasted. Diane Lane and Stellan Skarsgard, as the Glasses, are so good in the dialed-down "realistic scenes" that we cringe when they have to go over the top and make everything so very absolutely clear for the slow learners in the audience. Sobieski is fine, too—as good an upscale Los Angeles high school student as Kirsten Dunst in the recent *crazy/ beautiful,* but in a genre exercise that strands her instead of going someplace interesting and taking her along.

It was good to see Bruce Dern again. He's one of those actors, like Christopher Walken, who you assume on first glance has a secret evil agenda. Here he's the family lawyer the kids can or can't trust, and is wise enough to play the character absolutely straight, with no tics or twitches, so that he keeps us wondering—or would, if Wesley Strick's screenplay wasn't one of those infuriating constructions where the key outside characters turn up at the wrong times, believe the wrong people, and misinterpret everything.

Speaking of turning up, Sobieski's character turns up at too many right times. How fortunate that she drops in on Mr. Glass's office just at the right moment to eavesdrop, unobserved, on crucial dialogue. And how unfortunate that she seems to be proving the Glasses right and herself wrong when a social worker walks in on a crucial moment and, of course, misinterprets it.

If you want to see a great movie about a couple of kids endangered by a sinister guardian, rent *Night of the Hunter.* Watching *The Glass House* has all the elements for a better film, but doesn't trust the audience to keep up with them. Having criticized the Strick screenplay, I should in fairness observe that the way it usually works is, the writer puts in the smart stuff and then it comes out in the story conferences with executives who figure if they don't understand it, nobody will.

The Gleaners and I ★ ★ ★ ★
NO MPAA RATING, 82 m., 2001

A documentary by Agnes Varda.

In our alley we see men searching through the garbage for treasure. *The Gleaners and I* places them in an ancient tradition. Since 1554, when King Henry IV affirmed the right of gleaning, it has been a practice protected by the French constitution, and today the men and women who sift through the Dumpsters and markets of Paris are the descendants of gleaners who were painted by Millet and van Gogh.

Gleaners traditionally follow the harvest, scavenging what was missed the first time around. In Agnes Varda's meditative new film we see them in potato fields and apple orchards, where the farmers actually welcome them (tons of apples are missed by the first pickers, because the professionals work fast and are not patient in seeking the hidden fruit). Then we meet urban gleaners, including an artist who finds objects he can make into sculpture, and a man who has not paid for his food for more than ten years.

Everybody seems to know this practice is protected by law, but no one seems to know quite what the law says. Varda films jurists standing in the fields with their robes and law books, who say gleaning must take place between sunup and sundown, and she shows oyster-pickers in rubber hip boots, who say they must come no closer than ten, or twenty, or twelve, or fifteen yards of the oyster beds, and cannot take more than eight, or twenty, or ten pounds of oysters—not that anybody is weighing them.

In a provincial city, Varda considers the case of young unemployed people who overturned the Dumpsters of a supermarket after the owner drenched the contents with bleach to discourage them. Perhaps both parties were violating the law; the young people had the right to glean, but not to vandalize. But as she talks to the young layabouts in the town square, we realize they don't have the spirit of the other gleaners, and in their own minds see themselves as getting away with something instead

of exercising a right. They have made themselves into criminals, although the French law considers gleaning a useful profession.

The true gleaner, in Varda's eyes, is a little noble, a little idealistic, a little stubborn, and deeply thrifty. We meet a man who gleans for his meals and to find objects he can sell, and follow him back to a suburban homeless shelter where for years he has taught literature classes every night. We look over the shoulders of him and his comrades as they find perfectly fresh tomatoes left after a farmer's market. Varda and her cinematographer find a clock without hands—worthless, until she places it between two stone angels in her house, and it reveals a startling simplicity of form.

Agnes Varda, of course, is a gleaner herself. She is gleaning the gleaners. And in what appears to be a documentary, she conceals a tender meditation about her own life, and life itself. Who is this woman? I have met her, with her bangs cut low over her sparkling eyes in a round and merry face, and once had lunch in the house she shared with her late husband, the director Jacques Demy *(The Umbrellas of Cherbourg)*. The house itself was in the spirit of gleaning: not a luxury flat for two famous filmmakers, but a former garage, with the bays and rooms around a central courtyard parceled out, one as a kitchen, one as Jacques's office, one a room for their son, Mathieu, one Agnes's workroom, etc.

Varda is seventy-two and made her first film when she was twenty-six. She was the only woman director involved in the French New Wave, and has remained truer to its spirit than many of the others. Her features include such masterpieces as *One Sings, the Other Doesn't*, *Vagabond*, and *Kung Fu Master* (which is not about kung fu but about love). Along the way she has made many documentaries, including *Uncle Yanco* (1968), about her uncle who lived on a houseboat in California and was a gleaner of sorts, and *Daguerreotypes* (1975), about the other people who live on her street. Her *A Hundred and One Nights* (1995) gleaned her favorite moments from a century of cinema.

In *The Gleaners and I*, she has a new tool—a modern digital camera. We sense her delight. She can hold it in her hand and take it anywhere. She is liberated from cumbersome equipment. "To film with one hand my other hand," she says, as she does so with delight. She shows how the new cameras make a personal essay possible for a filmmaker—how she can walk out into the world and, without the risk of a huge budget, simply start picking up images as a gleaner finds apples and potatoes.

"My hair and my hands keep telling me that the end is near," she confides at one point, speaking confidentially to us as the narrator. She told her friend Howie Movshovitz, the critic from Boulder, Colorado, how she had to film and narrate some scenes while she was entirely alone, because they were so personal. In 1993, she directed *Jacquot de Nantes,* the story of her late husband, and now this is her story of herself, a woman whose life has consisted of moving through the world with the tools of her trade, finding what is worth treasuring.

Glitter ★ ★
PG-13, 103 m., 2001

Mariah Carey (Billie Frank), Max Beesley (Julian Dice), Da Brat (Louise), Tia Texada (Roxanne), Valarie Pettiford (Lillian Frank), Isabel Gomes (Young Billie), Padma Lakshmi (Sylk), Terrence Howard (Timothy Walker), Ann Magnuson (P.R. Woman). Directed by Vondie Curtis-Hall, produced by Laurence Mark. Screenplay by Kate Lanier, based on a story by Cheryl L. West.

Glitter is not *The Mariah Carey Story,* but it's tempting to try to read it that way. The movie is based not on Carey's life but on a kind of mirror image, in which she has a black mother and a white father instead of the other way around, and is taken under the wing of a club DJ instead of a record executive. Her character, named Billie Frank (after the two great vocalists?), makes all the usual stops on the rags-to-riches trail, but the movie rushes past them. We're in the strange position of knowing everything that's going to happen and wishing it would take longer.

Young Billie (Isabel Gomes) is first seen in a smoky dive, invited up onstage to join her mother, Lillian (Valarie Pettiford), in a duet. Soon after, Lillian falls asleep while smoking and burns the house down, and we are left to conclude she is a junkie, although the movie is so reticent it only confirms this years later,

with a report that Lillian is now clean and sober. Billie is shipped off to an orphanage, where she makes instant friends (a black, a white, and a Puerto Rican), identifies herself as "mixed" and—well, that's it for the orphanage.

Fast-forward to grown-up Billie, now played by Carey, who is a backup singer behind the untalented protégé of a would-be record producer (Terrence Howard). She ghosts the other singer's voice and is spotted by a DJ named Dice (Max Beesley), who buys her contract from the would-be producer for $100,000, but unwisely neglects to make the payment.

Dice guides her into a record contract, a hit single, and so on, before undergoing a sudden, unexplained personality change; he seems to become Mr. Hyde purely as a plot device. The closing several scenes of the movie are a blinding whirl of developments, jammed so close together that there's barely time for Billie to get tragic news before she rushes onto the stage of Madison Square Garden and then into the arms of her long-lost mother.

You can see, here and there, what the movie was aiming at. It makes some sly digs at self-important music video directors, has an affectionate cameo by Ann Magnuson as a hyper publicist, and does a good job of showing how a young talent attracts friends, enemies, leeches, and hangers-on. Always steadfast are Billie's two backup singers, Louise (Da Brat) and Roxanne (Tia Texada), who seem to spend twenty-four hours a day in their apartment so they are always available to take her calls, see her on TV, listen to her song on the radio, and take her in when she needs a home. Those girls should get out more.

Carey sings a lot, well, in footage that would be at home in a concert video. Her acting ranges from dutiful flirtatiousness to intense sincerity; she never really lets go. The title *Glitter* is perhaps intended to evoke *Sparkle* (1976), which was grittier, livelier, and more convincing. The name "Billie" evokes *Lady Sings the Blues* (1972), which was miles better. And for a biopic of a singer's hard road to the top, the touchstone is *What's Love Got to Do With It* (1993), where Angela Basset took the seemingly impossible assignment of playing Tina Turner and triumphed.

One problem with *Glitter* is that it doesn't step up and offer itself as Mariah Carey's real story, and yet is so afraid of being taken that way that it goes easy on the details anyway. Was being a mixed-race child as much of a nonissue in Carey's childhood as it is in this movie? Billie searches for her birth mother, and yet there's a scene so confusingly handled that we're not sure if she sees her on the street one night or not. We're given a triumphant concert in Madison Square Garden, but it's unlikely she could even sing under the circumstances shown. And the film is lacking above all in joy. It never seems like it's fun to be Billie Frank.

Gloomy Sunday ★ ★ ★
NO MPAA RATING, 114 m., 2003

Erika Marozsán (Ilona Varnai), Joachim Król (László Szabo), Ben Becker (Hans Wieck), Stefano Dionisi (András Aradi). Directed by Rolf Schübel and produced by Michael André and Richard Schöps. Screenplay by Schübel and Ruth Toma, based on the novel by Nick Barkow.

Odd, how affecting this imperfect film becomes. It's a broad romantic melodrama set in Budapest before and during the Holocaust, and that is not, you will agree, an ideal time to set a love story. And if it is true that the title song drove hundreds to commit suicide, some of them may have merely been very tired of hearing it.

And yet *Gloomy Sunday* held my attention, and there were times when I was surprisingly involved. It's an old-fashioned romantic triangle, told with schmaltzy music on the sound track and a heroine with a smoky singing voice, and then the Nazis turn up and it gets very complicated and heartbreaking.

The movie opened Friday in Chicago. So far as I can tell, this is its first American theatrical booking. But listen to this: In New Zealand, it ran for more than a year and became a local phenomenon.

The story begins in Budapest in the 1930s, where László Szabo (Joachim Król) runs a restaurant celebrated for its beef rolls. His hostess is the young and fetching Ilona (Erika Marozsán), and he is in love with her. Together they hire a piano player named András (Stefano Dionisi), and András falls in love with Ilona, and she with him, but she still loves László, and

since they all like one another, they arrive at a cozy accommodation.

A regular customer in the 1930s is a German named Hans Wieck (Ben Becker), who also falls in love with Ilona, and says if she will marry him, he will build Germany's largest import-export business, just for her. But as she already has her hands full, she turns him down.

András meanwhile composes a song named "Gloomy Sunday" that sweeps the world and which he has to play every night at the restaurant. Soon a legend grows up around the song, that people who hear it commit suicide. Strangely enough, this detail is based on fact; it was written in 1933 by Rezsó Seress, became an international hit, was recorded by such as Artie Shaw and Billie Holiday (and later Bjork and Elvis Costello), and was banned by the BBC because of its allegedly depressing effect. On the night that Ilona rejects Hans, indeed, he casts himself into the Danube and is hauled out by László. You see what I mean about melodrama.

The war comes. It is well known what the Nazis are doing to the Jews, but László, who is Jewish, has never given much thought to religion and believes such things will never happen in Hungary. He has more than one chance to escape, but remains, and his restaurant becomes even more popular in wartime. A regular customer is none other than Hans Wieck, now in charge of the Hungarian final solution, and he gives László an exemption; his beef rolls are a contribution to the war effort. Wieck, too, is said to be based on a historical figure, a Nazi named Kurt Becher who held a similar job in Budapest.

The movie, which has been fanciful and romantic, now descends into tragedy and betrayal. The carefree days of romance and denial are over, and the closing scenes of the film have an urgency that blindsides us, given the movie's earlier innocence. Then there is an epilogue, which is gratuitous and overlong; we could have done without it.

But the main story has the strength of its characters, who feel deeply and are brave and foolish in equal measure. András is a basket case who wears his emotions on his sleeve, but Ilona loves him for his vulnerability, and László is one of those good souls who find the calm in every situation, think the best of people, are generous and not jealous, and trusting—too trusting. The actors give the characters a touching presence and reality.

The movie will play for a week or two and disappear from Chicago and, for all I know, from North America. Maybe not. Maybe it will play for eighty weeks, like in Auckland.

Note: My information about the legend of Gloomy Sunday was obtained at www.phespirit. info/gloomysunday, which includes several sets of lyrics.

Gods and Generals ★ ½
PG-13, 216 m., 2003

Jeff Daniels (Lieutenant Colonel Joshua Chamberlain), Stephen Lang (General "Stonewall" Jackson), Robert Duvall (General Robert E. Lee), Chris Conner (John Wilkes Booth), C. Thomas Howell (Tom Chamberlain), Kevin Conway (Sergeant "Buster" Kilrain), Patrick Gorman (Brigadier General John Bell Hood), Brian Mallon (Brigadier General Winfield Scott Hancock). Directed and produced by Ronald F. Maxwell. Screenplay by Maxwell, based on the book by Jeff M. Shaara.

Here is a Civil War movie that Trent Lott might enjoy. Less enlightened than *Gone with the Wind*, obsessed with military strategy, impartial between South and North, religiously devout, it waits seventy minutes before introducing the first of its two speaking roles for African-Americans; Stonewall Jackson assures his black cook that the South will free him, and the cook looks cautiously optimistic. If World War II were handled this way, there'd be hell to pay.

The movie is essentially about brave men on both sides who fought and died so that . . . well, so that they could fight and die. They are led by generals of blinding brilliance and nobility, although one Northern general makes a stupid error and the movie shows hundreds of his men being slaughtered at great length as the result of it.

The Northerners, one Southerner explains, are mostly Republican profiteers who can go home to their businesses and families if they're voted out of office after the conflict, while the Southerners are fighting for their homes. Slavery is not the issue, in this view, because it would have withered away anyway, although a liberal professor from Maine (Jeff Daniels)

makes a speech explaining it is wrong. So we get that cleared up right there, or for sure at Strom Thurmond's birthday party.

The conflict is handled with solemnity worthy of a memorial service. The music, when it is not funeral, sounds like the band playing during the commencement exercises at a sad university. Countless extras line up, march forward, and shoot at each other. They die like flies. That part is accurate, although the stench, the blood, and the cries of pain are tastefully held to the PG-13 standard. What we know about the war from the photographs of Mathew Brady, the poems of Walt Whitman, and the documentaries of Ken Burns is not duplicated here.

Oh, it is a competently made film. Civil War buffs may love it. Every group of fighting men is identified by subtitles, to such a degree that I wondered, fleetingly, if they were being played by Civil War reenactment hobbyists who would want to nudge their friends when their group appeared on the screen. Much is made of the film's total and obsessive historical accuracy; the costumes, flags, battle plans, and ordnance are all doubtless flawless, although there could have been no Sergeant "Buster" Kilrain in the 20th Maine, for the unavoidable reason that "Buster" was never used as a name until Buster Keaton used it.

The actors do what they can, although you can sense them winding up to deliver pithy quotations. Robert Duvall, playing General Robert E. Lee, learns of Stonewall Jackson's battlefield amputation and reflects sadly, "He has lost his left arm, and I have lost my right." His eyes almost twinkle as he envisions that one ending up in *Bartlett's*. Stephen Lang, playing Jackson, has a deathbed scene so wordy, as he issues commands to imaginary subordinates and then prepares himself to cross over the river, that he seems to be stalling. Except for Lee, a nonbeliever, both sides trust in God, just like at the Super Bowl.

Donzaleigh Abernathy plays the other African-American speaking role, that of a maid named Martha who attempts to jump the gun on Reconstruction by staying behind when her white employers evacuate, and telling the arriving Union troops it is her own house. Later, when they commandeer it as a hospital, she looks a little resentful. This episode, like many others, is kept so resolutely at the cameo level that we realize material of such scope and breadth can be shoehorned into three and a half hours only by sacrificing depth.

Gods and Generals is the kind of movie beloved by people who never go to the movies, because they are primarily interested in something else—the Civil War, for example—and think historical accuracy is a virtue instead of an attribute. The film plays like a special issue of *American Heritage*. Ted Turner is one of its prime movers, and gives himself an instantly recognizable cameo appearance. Since sneak previews must already have informed him that his sudden appearance draws a laugh, apparently he can live with that.

Note: The same director, Ron Maxwell, made the much superior Gettysburg *(1993) and at the end informs us that the third title in the trilogy will be* The Last Full Measure. *Another line from the same source may serve as a warning: "The world will little note, nor long remember, what we say here."*

The Golden Bowl ★ ★ ★
R, 130 m., 2001

Nick Nolte (Adam Verver), Kate Beckinsale (Maggie Verver), Uma Thurman (Charlotte Stant), Jeremy Northam (Prince Amerigo), Anjelica Huston (Fanny Assingham), James Fox (Bob Assingham). Directed by James Ivory and produced by Ismail Merchant. Screenplay by Ruth Prawer Jhabvala, based on the novel by Henry James.

There are four good people in *The Golden Bowl* and four bad people, making, in all, four characters. The genius of Henry James's greatest novel is that these four people have placed themselves in a moral situation that alters as you rotate them in your view. If you come to the movie without reading the book, you may find yourself adrift; it's not easy to know who to like when everyone is a sinner, and all have their reasons.

The story involves two marriages, with the same dreadful secret hidden at the heart of both of them. Adam Verver (Nick Nolte), an American billionaire, has been traveling in Europe with his daughter, Maggie (Kate Beckinsale), buying things. Having grown rich on the backs of his workers (he frets about their long

hours), he now vows to brighten their lives by filling a museum with his treasures, which they can admire while he no doubt feels virtuous. Having purchased innumerable statues, houses, and paintings, he finds it time to buy Maggie a husband. Prince Amerigo (Jeremy Northam) seems a good investment: He is handsome and refined, and his old Italian family occupies the Pallazzo Ugolini in Florence. The prince needs Verver's money, and will provide a title for his grandson; Maggie is swayed by his charm.

There is a complication, which is revealed in the very first scene of the movie. The prince was long involved in an affair with Charlotte Stant (Uma Thurman), Maggie's best friend. Since the story takes place in 1902, when such affairs could ruin reputations, it has been a secret—even from Maggie. The prince is prepared to marry Maggie for her father's money, and also because she is lithe and fragrant. But where does that leave poor Charlotte?

In her drawing room in London, Fanny Assingham (Anjelica Huston) thinks she knows the answer. She's one of those middle-aged American exiles, much beloved by James, who lurks at the center of a web of social connections, waiting for twitches. She boldly suggests that the widower billionaire Verver is the perfect match for Charlotte. That will mean that the father and daughter will be married to former lovers, a fact known to Mrs. Assingham, who can live with it.

Now, does that make Charlotte and the prince dishonest? Yes, they share a secret. But both the prince and Charlotte must, because they are poor, marry money. They are marrying people who want them. Perhaps they are making a sacrifice—especially if they behave themselves, which they are determined to do. Or are Maggie and her father dishonest, since she is marrying to please her father and he is marrying her best friend to please his daughter? No one at the altar is blameless. But no one is marrying for love, except Maggie, whose definition of love is too specialized to be entirely idealistic.

Soon the two couples settle into a routine that satisfies Maggie and Mr. Verver, who dote on each other and spend all of their time together, to the dissatisfaction of their mates. Charlotte complains that her husband and his daughter are always together. "What becomes of me when they're so happy?" she asks the prince. "And what becomes of you?" Soon enough the two former lovers find themselves at a house party in the country without their spouses, and one thing apparently leads to another (it is difficult to be sure with James, since no novelist ever used the word "intercourse" more frequently without quite making it clear what he meant by it).

It is not sexual infidelity that causes trouble, however, but the slight shade of suspicion— and then a darker shade, when a golden bowl in an antique shop provides Maggie with absolute proof that the prince and Charlotte knew each other before they had, presumably, met. Now comes the diabolical unfolding of James's plan, since at no time do the four people ever openly discuss what each one of them privately knows. Instead, wheels of unspoken priorities grind mercilessly, and Charlotte, in my opinion, becomes the character we have most reason to pity.

The Golden Bowl would seem to be an ideal project for director James Ivory, producer Ismail Merchant, and screenwriter Ruth Prawer Jhabvala; they specialize in literary adaptations, and previously collaborated on James's *The Europeans* and *The Bostonians*. But here they've taken on the most difficult of James's novels—a story told largely through what remains unsaid. James has not made it easy for the modern moviegoer who expects good and evil to be clearly labeled and lead to a happy ending. His villain is a system based on wealth and class, which forces the poor to deal on the terms of the rich and then sometimes spits them out anyway—or, in Charlotte's case, buries her alive. That James spent his career chronicling people like these characters does not mean he loved them, and in a novel like *The Ambassadors* you can hear him cheering as a female version of Verver is frustrated in her desire to control her son.

I admired this movie. It kept me at arm's length, but that is where I am supposed to be; the characters are, after all, at arm's length from one another, and the tragedy of the story is implied but never spoken aloud. It will help, I think, to be familiar with the novel, or to make a leap of sympathy with the characters; they aren't dancing through a clockwork plot,

but living their lives according to rules which, once they accept them, cannot ever be broken.

The Good Girl ★ ★ ★ ½
R, 93 m., 2002

Jennifer Aniston (Justine Last), Jake Gyllenhaal (Holden Worther), John C. Reilly (Phil Last), Tim Blake Nelson (Bubba), Zooey Deschanel (Cheryl), Mike White (Corny). Directed by Miguel Arteta and produced by Matthew Greenfield. Screenplay by Mike White.

After languishing in a series of overlooked movies that ranged from the entertaining (*Office Space*) to the disposable (*Picture Perfect*), Jennifer Aniston has at last decisively broken with her *Friends* image in an independent film of satiric fire and emotional turmoil. It will no longer be possible to consider her in the same way. In *The Good Girl*, she plays Justine, a desperately bored clerk at Retail Rodeo, a sub-K-Mart where the customers are such sleepwalkers they don't even notice when the "Attention, Shoppers!" announcements are larded with insults and nonsense.

Recent headlines tell of a lawsuit against Wal-Mart for forcing its employees to work unpaid overtime. Retail Rodeo is by contrast relatively benign. Management is particularly flexible with Justine's coworker Cheryl (Zooey Deschanel), who, after getting carried away once too often on the PA system, is reassigned to Women's Makeovers, where she improvises dubious advice. A new makeup style is called "Cirque du Face," she tells one customer. "It's all the rage with the Frenchies."

Justine, who is thirtyish, is married to a house painter named Phil (John C. Reilly), who is attached vertically to the living room sofa and horizontally to his best friend, Bubba (Tim Blake Nelson). Phil and Bubba paint houses during the day and are couch potatoes at night, smoking weed and peering at the television. After a day of drudgery, Justine comes home to stoned indifference. No wonder she's intrigued by Holden (Jake Gyllenhaal), the new checkout kid, who's reading *The Catcher in the Rye* and tells her its hero is a victim of the world's hypocrisy.

Quite a coincidence, that a kid named Holden would be reading a book about a character named Holden. When they become better friends, Holden invites Justine to his house, where his mother calls him "Tom." In the safety of his room, he explains: "Tom is my slave name." Soon Justine and Tom, who is a college dropout with a drinking problem, are having sex everywhere they can: in the car, in his room, in the stockroom at Retail Rodeo, and in a fleabag motel, where, unluckily, Bubba sees them.

For Bubba, this is an ideal opening for emotional blackmail. He has long explained that he is single because he despairs of ever finding a wife as "perfect" as Justine. Now he demands sex with her so his life will be complete. Otherwise, he will tell Phil about her affair. In a decision that Jennifer Aniston would never make but Justine might (this is a crucial distinction), she deals with this demand and with another crisis, when she discovers she is pregnant. She also finds out what she should have suspected, that Bubba would never tell Phil about her secrets, because he adores Phil too much, and, as Phil's wife, she is protected by his immunity.

The Good Girl has been directed by Miguel Arteta and written by Mike White, who plays the Retail Rodeo's security guard. They also collaborated on *Chuck and Buck,* and on the basis of these two strange movies with their skewed perspectives, they are talents with huge promise. They know how much satire and exaggeration is enough but not too much, so that in a subterranean way their movies work on serious levels while seeming to be comedies.

Certainly the last big scene between Aniston and Reilly is an unexpected payoff, delivering an emotional punch while at the same time we can only admire Justine's strategy involving the father of her child. She says it's Phil, and cannot be disproven on the basis of Phil's information; having confessed to cheating, she allows him to suspect someone who could not have a black-haired child; therefore, the father is the dark-haired Phil. Right? Right.

Good Housekeeping ★ ★ ★
R, 90 m., 2002

Bob Jay Mills (Don), Petra Westen (Donatella), Tacey Adams (Marion), Al Schuermann (Joe), Zia (Chuck), Andrew Eichner (Don Jr.), Maeve Kerrigan (Tiffany). Directed by Frank Novak and produced by Mark G. Mathis. Screenplay by Novak.

I watch the guests on *Jerry Springer* with the fascination of an ambulance driver at a demo derby. Where do these people come from? Their dialogue may be "suggested," but their lives are all too evidently real, and they have tumbled right through the safety net of taste and self-respect and gone spiraling down, down into the pit of amoral vulgarity. Now comes *Good Housekeeping,* a film about how the people on *Springer* live when they're not on camera.

No, it's not a documentary. It was written and directed by Frank Novak, otherwise a trendy Los Angeles furniture manufacturer, who regards his white trash characters with deadpan neutrality. How is the audience expected to react? Consider this dialogue:

Don: "Maybe if we cut her in half we could get her in there."

Chuck: "We can't cut her in half!"

Don: "So what are you? Mr. Politically Correct?"

Don and Chuck are brothers. Don (Bob Jay Mills) uneasily shares his house with his wife, Donatella (Petra Westen), while Chuck (credited only as Zia) sleeps with his girlfriend Tiffany (Maeve Kerrigan) in Don's car. Things are not good between Don and Donatella, and he uses two-by-fours and plasterboard to build a wall that cuts the house in two ("She got way more square feet than I got," he tells the cops during one of their frequent visits). Realizing he has forgotten something, Don cuts a crawl hole in the wall so that Don Jr. (Andrew Eichner) can commute between parents. Soon Donatella's new lesbian lover Marion (Tacey Adams) is poking her head through the hole to discuss the "parameters" Don is setting for his son.

Donatella is a forklift operator. Don is self-employed as a trader of action figures, with a specialty in Pinhead and other Hellraiser characters. When Chuck tries to sell him a Sad-Eye Doll, he responds like a pro: "Couldn't you Swap-Meet it? I'm not gonna put that on my table and drag down my other merch." Don Jr. has less respect for action figures, and occasionally saws off their heads.

Terrible things happen to the many cars in this extended family, both by accident and on purpose. One of the funniest sequences shows a big blond family friend, desperately hungover, methodically crunching into every other car in the driveway before she runs over the mailbox. Don lives in fear of Donatella running him down, and at one point discusses his defense with a gun-show trader (Al Schuermann) who scoffs, "You would use a .38 to defend yourself?" He comes back with real protection against vehicular manslaughter: a shoulder-mounted rocket launcher.

Marion, the well-mannered lesbian lover, is the source of many of the film's biggest laughs because of the incongruity of her crush on Donatella. She watches Donatella smoke, eat, talk, and blow her nose all at the same time, and her only reaction is to eat all the more politely, in the hope of setting an example. Marion is an accountant at the factory where Donatella works; she dresses in chic business suits, has smart horn-rimmed glasses and a stylish haircut, and plunges into Springerland with an arsenal of liberal clichés. At one point, after a nasty domestic disturbance, she tries to make peace by inviting Don out to brunch. "There's no way the cops can make you go to brunch," Don's beer-bellied buddies reassure him.

It is perhaps a warning signal of incipient alcoholism when the family car has a Breathalyzer permanently attached to the dashboard. Yet Don is not without standards, and warns his brother against making love in the car because "I drive Mom to church in it." Family life follows a familiar pattern. Most evenings end with a fight in the yard, and Novak and his cinematographer, Alex Vandler, are skilled at getting convincing, spontaneous performances out of their unknown actors; many scenes, including the free-for-alls, play with the authenticity of a documentary.

Just as mainstream filmmakers are fascinated by the rich and famous, so independent filmmakers are drawn to society's hairy underbelly. *Good Housekeeping* plunges far beneath Todd Solondz's territory and enters the suburbs of John Waters's universe in its fascination for people who live without benefit of education, taste, standards, hygiene, and shame. Indeed, all they have enough of are cigarettes, used cars, controlled substances, and four-letter words. The movie is, however, very funny, as you peek at it through the fingers in front of your eyes.

Note: Good Housekeeping *has had its ups and downs. It won the grand jury prize at Slamdance 2000, was the only U.S. film chosen for Critic's Week at Cannes that year, and was picked up for distribution by the Shooting Gallery—which alas went out of business, leaving the film orphaned.*

The Good Thief ★ ★ ★ ½
R, 109 m., 2003

Nick Nolte (Bob), Tchéky Karyo (Roger), Nutsa Kukhianidze (Anne), Saïd Taghmaoui (Paulo), Gérard Darmon (Raoul), Ralph Fiennes (Tony), Marc Lavoine (Remi). Directed by Neil Jordan and produced by Steven Woolley, John Wells, and Seaton McLean. Screenplay by Jordan, based on the film by Jean-Pierre Melville.

Nick Nolte plays a great shambling wreck of a wounded Hemingway hero in *The Good Thief*, a film that's like a descent into the funkiest dive on the wrong side of the wrong town. He's Bob, the child of an American father and a French mother, so he claims—but he seems to change his story every time he tells it. He lives in Nice, on the French Riviera, moving easily through the lower depths of crime and drugs, and—this is the tricky part—liked by everyone. When it's rumored he is up to a new heist, the policeman Roger (Tchéky Karyo) tells his partner, "Find out before he does it!" He doesn't want to arrest Bob; he wants to save him from himself.

Bob is a thief and a heroin addict. "Heroin is his lady," his friend Raoul observes. "I thought luck was his lady," says another friend. "When one runs out he turns to the other," says Raoul. Bob is intimately familiar with the language of AA, talking about the Twelve Steps and "one day at a time" and even at one point citing the Serenity Prayer. But his only visit to a Narcotics Anonymous meeting involves walking in one door and out the other to elude pursuit ("I'm Bob, and I'm an addict," he says on the way through).

Bob is a good man, a good thief, to the bottom of his soul, a gentleman who rescues a teenage Bosnian hooker (Nutsa Kukhianidze) from a vicious pimp and then becomes her protector, although to be sure he introduces her to bad company. He is headed toward some kind of showdown with his fate. Down to his last 70,000 francs, he goes to the races. "What if you lose?" asks his friend. "I'll have hit rock bottom. I'll have to change my ways."

He hits rock bottom. He changes his ways. "I feel a confinement coming on," he says in that deep gravel voice. He chains himself to a bed, eats ice cream, goes through an agonizing detox, and is ready to consider an ingenious plan to steal the treasures of a Monte Carlo casino. No, not the money. The paintings.

The Good Thief, directed by Neil Jordan *(Mona Lisa, The Crying Game),* is a remake of a famous 1955 French film named *Bob le Flambeur* by Jean-Pierre Melville. *The Good Thief* is drawn to the affectionate study of a character who is admirable in every way except that he cannot bring himself to stop breaking the law. But it is juicier, jazzier, with a more charismatic hero.

Bob le Flambeur was filmed in elegant black and white, with Roger Duchesne playing Bob as a trim, self-contained, sleek operator. Nolte, on the other hand, has such a bulldog look that even his clothes have jowls. He told a press conference at the Toronto Film Festival that he used "a little heroin" every day while making the movie, just to get in the mood. Not long ago, it is well known, he was arrested while driving under the influence, and his mug shot, widely circulated, showed a man who had made dissipation his life's work. Nolte recently said he was on his way to an AA meeting when something made him turn away and led eventually to his arrest. Maybe he wanted to be arrested, he speculated, so he could get help. *The Good Thief* looks like the direction he took when he turned away.

Whether or not Nolte topped up every day on the set, it is clear that he was born to play Bob. It is one of those performances that flows unhindered from an actor's deepest instincts. Jordan and his cinematographer, Chris Menges, place him in a world of smoke, shadows, and midnight blues, where cops and robbers supply work for each other. Into this world drift occasional outsiders like the kinky art dealer (Ralph Fiennes), who talks like a Batman villain: "If I don't get my money back by Monday, what I do to your faces will definitely be Cubist."

The plot I will not breathe a word about, since it is so elegantly ironic in the way Bob outflanks the cops, his partners, the casino, and ourselves. It leads up to a deeply satisfying conclusion, but along the way what we enjoy is the portrait of this man who is engaged in some kind of lifelong showdown between his goodness and his weakness. This is a struggle Nolte seems to know a great deal about.

Gosford Park ★ ★ ★ ★
R, 137 m., 2002

Eileen Atkins (Mrs. Croft), Bob Balaban (Morris Weissman), Alan Bates (Jennings), Charles Dance (Lord Stockbridge), Stephen Fry (Inspector Thompson), Michael Gambon (Sir William McCordle), Richard E. Grant (George), Derek Jacobi (Probert), Kelly Macdonald (Mary Maceachran), Helen Mirren (Mrs. Wilson), Jeremy Northam (Ivor Novello), Clive Owen (Robert Parks), Ryan Phillippe (Henry Denton), Maggie Smith (Constance, Countess of Trentham), Kristin Scott Thomas (Lady Sylvia McCordle), Emily Watson (Elsie). Directed by Robert Altman and produced by Altman, Bob Balaban, and David Levy. Screenplay by Julian Fellowes, based on an idea by Altman and Balaban.

Robert Altman's *Gosford Park* is above all a celebration of styles—the distinct behavior produced by the British class system, the personal styles of a rich gallery of actors, and his own style of introducing a lot of characters and letting them weave their way through a labyrinthine plot. At a time when too many movies focus every scene on a $20 million star, an Altman film is like a party with no boring guests. *Gosford Park* is such a joyous and audacious achievement it deserves comparison with his very best movies, such as *M*A*S*H, McCabe and Mrs. Miller, Nashville, The Player, Short Cuts,* and *Cookie's Fortune.*

It employs the genre of the classic British murder mystery, as defined by Agatha Christie: Guests and servants crowd a great country house, and one of them is murdered. But *Gosford Park* is a Dame Agatha story in the same sense that *M*A*S*H* is a war movie, *McCabe* is a Western, and *Nashville* is a musical: Altman uses the setting, but surpasses the limitations and redefines the goal. This is no less than a comedy about selfishness, greed, snobbery, eccentricity, and class exploitation, and Altman is right when he hopes people will see it more than once; after you know the destination, the journey is transformed.

The time is November 1932. Sir William McCordle (Michael Gambon) and Lady Sylvia McCordle (Kristin Scott Thomas) have invited a houseful of guests for a shooting party. They include Sir William's sister Constance, the Countess of Trentham (Maggie Smith), who depends on an allowance he is constantly threatening to withdraw. And Lady Sylvia's sister Louisa (Geraldine Somerville), who like Sylvia had to marry for money (they cut cards to decide who would bag Sir William). And Louisa's husband, Commander Anthony Meredith (Tom Hollander). And their sister Lavinia (Natasha Wightman), married to Raymond, Lord Stockbridge (Charles Dance). And the Hollywood star Ivor Novello (Jeremy Northam). And Morris Weissman (Bob Balaban), a gay Hollywood producer who has brought along his "valet," Henry Denton (Ryan Phillippe).

Below stairs we meet the butler Jennings (Alan Bates), the housekeeper Mrs. Wilson (Helen Mirren), the cook Mrs. Croft (Eileen Atkins), the footman George (Richard E. Grant), and assorted other valets, maids, grooms, and servers. When the American Henry comes to take his place at the servants' table and says his name is Denton, Jennings sternly informs him that servants are addressed below stairs by the names of their masters, and he will be "Mr. Weissman" at their table—where, by the way, servants are seated according to the ranks of their employers.

It has been said that the most enjoyable lifestyle in history was British country house life in the years between the wars. That is true for some of the people upstairs in this movie, less true of most of those downstairs. Altman observes exceptions: Some of the aristocrats, like Lady Constance, are threatened with financial ruin, and others, like Novello, have to sing for their supper; while below stairs, a man like Jennings is obviously supremely happy to head the staff of a great house.

The classic country house murder story begins with perfect order, in which everyone up and down the class ladder fits securely into his or her place—until murder disrupts that order and discloses unexpected connections between the classes. That's what happens here, when one of the characters is poisoned and then stabbed, suggesting there are two murderers to be apprehended by Inspector Thompson (Stephen Fry).

Half of those in the house have a motive for the murder, but the investigation isn't the point, and Altman has fun by letting Thompson and his assistant Constable Dexter (Ron Webster) mirror the relative competence of the upper and lower classes in the house. Thompson, like the aristocrats, sets great store by his title and dress (he puffs a pipe that will be recognized by anyone who knows the name Monsieur Hulot). Dexter, like the servants, just gets on with it, doggedly pointing out clues (footprints, fingerprints on a tea cup, a secret door) that Thompson ignores.

The cast of *Gosford Park* is like a reunion of fine and familiar actors (I have not yet even mentioned Derek Jacobi, Kelly Macdonald, Clive Owen, Emily Watson, and James Wilby). This is like an invitation for scene-stealing, and Maggie Smith effortlessly places first, with brittle comments that cut straight to the quick. When Novello entertains after dinner with one song, and then another, and then another, and shows no sign of stopping, Smith crisply asks, "Do you think he'll be as long as he usually is?" and then stage-whispers, "Don't encourage him."

Altman has a keen eye and ear for snobbery. Note the way that when Mr. Weissman introduces himself, Lady Sylvia asks him to repeat his name, and then she repeats it herself. Just that, but she is subtly underlining his ethnicity. And the way Constance puts Novello in his place by mentioning his most recent film and observing, ostensibly with sympathy, "It must be rather disappointing when something flops like that."

The screenplay by Julian Fellowes, based on an idea by Altman and Balaban, is masterful in introducing all of the characters and gradually making it clear who they are, what they've done, and what it means. Like guests at a big party, we are confused when we first arrive: Who are all these people? By the end, we know. No director has ever been better than Altman at providing the audience with bearings to find its way through a large cast. The sense of place is also palpable in this film; the downstairs and attics were entirely constructed on sound stages by production designer Steven Altman, Altman's son, who also supervised the real country house used for the main floors. Andrew Dunn's photography is sumptuous upstairs, while making the downstairs look creamy and institutional. The editor, Tim Squyres, must have been crucial in keeping the characters in play.

Gosford Park is the kind of generous, sardonic, deeply layered movie that Altman has made his own. As a director he has never been willing to settle for plot; he is much more interested in character and situation, and likes to assemble unusual people in peculiar situations and stir the pot. Here he is, like Prospero, serenely the master of his art.

Go Tigers! ★ ★ ★
R, 103 m., 2001

Featuring Dave Irwin, Danny Studer, Ellery Moore, and the rest of the team. A documentary directed by Ken Carlson and produced by Sidney Sherman and Carlson. Screenplay by Carlson.

I don't know if Massillon, Ohio, has the best high school football team in the country, but since the annual Massillon-McKinley rivalry is the only prep game that carries Vegas odds, doesn't that tell you something? *Go Tigers!* is a documentary about a town of 33,000 so consumed by football it makes South Bend and Green Bay look distracted.

The film was directed by Ken Carlson, a Massillon native and, it must be said, a Tiger booster. He raises an eyebrow at the widespread local practice of holding boys back to repeat the eighth grade, whether they need to or not, because they'll be older and bigger as high school seniors. He listens to a couple of kids observe that if you aren't into football you're an automatic outsider ("I can't wait to get out of this dump"). But the movie argues that Massillon lives for football, that it creates identity and pride, and on the evidence I would have to agree.

Consider a town where a live tiger cub is the team mascot (and cringe as it plants a friendly paw on a small child). Where the "Tiger Lady" fills her house so full of tiger paraphernalia that there is scant room for her husband, jammed into his chair in a corner. Where the high school band has mayoral permission to march and play anywhere within the city limits on the day of the McKinley game (it marches through department stores, cafeterias, and the library). Where more fans attend the games than at many (maybe most) colleges. Where there are so many assistant coaches one specializes in strength and fitness.

Massillon is a steel town, working class and moderately prosperous, and one of the things we notice (the movie doesn't make a point of it) is that there seems to be racial harmony. Possibly the team is such a strong binding and unifying force that it rolls over the divisive feelings that might exist in another town. The Tigers are a secular religion. And mainstream religion gets in the act, too, with a Jewish speaker at the breakfast on the day of the big game, followed by a Catholic mass, the Lord's Prayer in the locker room, and other evocations to the Almighty (Massillon has lost to McKinley the last four years, inspiring a certain urgency).

We meet two of the team's cocaptains, Dave Irwin and Ellery Moore. Like other Massillon players going back four generations, they see football as their ticket to college scholarships. Irwin, the quarterback, is a gifted passer, and during the 1999 season (shown in the film) throws seventeen touchdown passes in nine games before the McKinley game, whose outcome I will leave for you to discover. He works part-time as a drill press operator, and shortly before the big game injures the index finger of his passing hand. So much is at stake: If he loses that finger, he can look forward to the drill press instead of college.

It looks like Massillon would be fun to live in if you're a football fan (one good player from nearby Petty transfers just to get in on the action). To *not* be a football fan in Massillon would be a lonely and unrewarding enterprise. Underlying tension is created because the local schools face severe budget cuts unless a tax levy passes. Opponents argue that the football program is so expensive it drives up the budget— but it seems more likely that the better the team does, the more likely the voters are to approve the levy. "I've seen more good come from that pigskin than from a lot of schoolbooks," observes one local sage. If it gets the kids into college, he may have a point.

Note: The movie has an R rating because its high school kids talk and drink beer exactly like high school kids.

Greenfingers ★ ★
R, 90 m., 2001

Clive Owen (Colin Briggs), Helen Mirren (Georgina Woodhouse), David Kelly (Fergus Wilks), Warren Clarke (Governor Hodge), Danny Dyer (Tony), Adam Fogerty (Raw), Paterson Joseph (Jimmy), Natasha Little (Primrose Woodhouse). Directed by Joel Hershman and produced by Travis Swords, Daniel J. Victor, and Trudie Styler. Screenplay by Hershman.

Greenfingers is a twee little British comedy in which hardened prisoners became gifted gardeners and are allowed to enter their prize flowers in the Hampton Court Garden Show. Their entry, a garden that seems to bloom in a junkyard, is no more bizarre than entries I've seen in the Chelsea Flower Show.

The movie populates this story with standard types: the salvageable murderer, the elderly lifer with a secret, the ferocious bouncer, the punk kid, the Caribbean guy. There is a warden who glows and beams and nods as approvingly as a Wodehousian vicar, and a formidable gardening expert (Helen Mirren). Would it amaze you to learn that the expert comes supplied with a comely daughter who catches the eye of the salvageable murderer?

If you follow little British TV comedies on PBS, many of the cast members will be familiar to you—especially the priceless David Kelly, who took the immortal nude motorcycle ride in *Waking Ned Devine*. The lead is Clive Owen, who made an impression in the breakthrough thriller *Croupier*. Mirren's Georgina Woodhouse, the garden lady, wears big hats and is a TV star and is based, we assume, on British media types not familiar over here; she has some fun with the distance between vast wealth and celebrity on the one hand and domestic and gardening skills on the other, and we wonder if the name Martha Stewart might not sometimes pass through her mind.

The film is set in an "open prison" in the Cotswolds, where long-term convicts with good behavior records are trusted to work on a farm or in craft shops. When the Owen character accidentally raises a patch of double violets, the warden decides he has a green thumb—or fingers, in this case—and assigns him to cultivate a garden, with the mixed lot of other prisoners as his assistants. Soon they're studying horticulture books and creating a prize garden that inspires Miss Woodhouse to suggest an entry in the big garden show.

It's not that I disliked the movie. It has nothing in it to dislike—or to like very much. It's relentlessly pleasant and good-tempered, positive and eager to amuse, as it goes through the various obligatory stages of such stories. We know, for example, that the prisoners will succeed at gardening, but that there'll be some kind of setback to their hopes. That the officials at the Hampton Court show will include snobs who do not want to admit prisoners. That a young man and a young woman are written into movies like this for the express purpose of falling in love. And that the story will not end on the gallows.

It's as if this current round of small British (and Irish and Welsh and Scots) comedies started strong, with titles like *The Full Monty, The Commitments, The Snapper,* and *Ned Devine* and then started to lose energy about the time of *Saving Grace* (2000) and is now, for the time being, out of gas. The wellsprings of the genre are the Ealing comedies of the 1950s, with Peter Sellers, Terry Thomas, and others as dotty eccentrics; *Local Hero, Gregory's Girl,* and *Comfort and Joy* are interim high points. *Greenfingers* is amusing enough to watch and passes the time, but it's the kind of movie you're content to wait for on your friendly indie cable channel.

The Grey Zone ★ ★ ★ ★
R, 108 m., 2002

David Arquette (Hoffman), Daniel Benzali (Schlermer), Steve Buscemi (Abramowics), David Chandler (Rosenthal), Allan Corduner (Dr. Nyiszli), Harvey Keitel (Muhsfeldt), Natasha Lyonne (Rosa), Mira Sorvino (Dina), Kamelia Grigorova (Girl). Directed by Tim Blake Nelson and produced by Pamela Koffler,

Nelson, and Christine Vachon. Screenplay by Nelson, based on the play by Nelson and the book *Auschwitz: A Doctor's Eyewitness Account* by Miklos Nyiszli.

"How can you know what you'd really do to stay alive, until you're asked? I know now that the answer for most of us is—anything."

So says a member of the Sonderkommandos, a group of Jews at the Auschwitz II–Birkenau death camp, who sent their fellow Jews to die in the gas chambers and then disposed of the ashes afterward. For this duty they were given clean sheets, extra food, cigarettes, and an extra four months of life. With the end of the war obviously drawing closer, four months might mean survival. Would you refuse this opportunity? Would I?

Tim Blake Nelson's *The Grey Zone* considers moral choices within a closed system that is wholly evil. If everyone in the death camp is destined to die, is it the good man's duty to die on schedule, or is it his duty to himself to grasp any straw? Since both choices seem certain to end in death, is it more noble to refuse or cooperate? Is hope itself a form of resistance?

These are questions no truthful person can answer without having been there. The film is inspired by the uprising of October 7, 1944, when members of the 12th Sonderkommando succeeded in blowing up two of the four crematoria at the death camp; because the ovens were never replaced, lives were saved. But other lives were lost as the Nazis used physical and mental torture to try to find out how the prisoners got their hands on gunpowder and weapons.

I have seen a lot of films about the Holocaust, but I have never seen one so immediate, unblinking, and painful in its materials. *The Grey Zone* deals with the daily details of the work gangs—who lied to prisoners, led them into gas chambers, killed them, incinerated their bodies, and disposed of the remains. All of the steps in this process are made perfectly clear in a sequence that begins with one victim accusing his Jewish guard of lying to them all, and ends with the desperate sound of hands banging against the inside of the steel doors. "Cargo," the workers called the bodies they dealt with. "We have a lot of cargo today."

The film has been adapted by Nelson from his play, and is based in part on the book *Auschwitz: A Doctor's Eyewitness Account,* by Miklos Nyiszli, a Jewish doctor who cooperated on experiments with the notorious Dr. Josef Mengele, and is portrayed in the film by Allan Corduner.

Is it a fact of human nature that we are hardwired to act for our own survival? That those able to sacrifice themselves for an ethical ideal are extraordinary exceptions to the rule? Consider a scene late in the film when Rosa and Dina (Natasha Lyonne and Mira Sorvino), two women prisoners who worked in a nearby munitions factory, are tortured to reveal the secret of the gunpowder. When ordinary methods fail, they are lined up in front of their fellow prisoners. The interrogator repeats his questions, and every time they do not answer, his arm comes down and another prisoner is shot through the head. What is the right thing to do? Betray the secrets and those who collaborated? Or allow still more prisoners to be murdered? And if all will die eventually anyway, how does that affect the choice? Is it better to die now, with a bullet to the brain, than after more weeks of dread? Or is any life at all worth having?

The film stars David Arquette, Daniel Benzali, Steve Buscemi, and David Chandler as the leaders of the Sonderkommandos, and Harvey Keitel as Muhsfeldt, an alcoholic Nazi officer in command of their unit. Although these faces are familiar, the actors disappear into their roles. The Jewish workforce continues its grim task of exterminating fellow Jews, while working on its secret plans for a revolt.

Then an extraordinary thing happens. In a gas chamber, a young girl (Kamelia Grigorova) is found still alive. Arquette rescues her from a truck before she can be taken to be burned, and now the Jews are faced with a subset of their larger dilemma: Is this one life worth saving if the girl jeopardizes the entire revolt? Perhaps not, but in a world where there seem to be no choices, she presents one, and even Dr. Nyiszli, so beloved by Mengele, helps to save the girl's life. It is as if this single life symbolizes all the others.

In a sense, the murders committed by the Nazis were not as evil as the twisted thought that went into them and the mental anguish they caused for the victims. Death occurs thoughtlessly in nature every day. But death with sadistic forethought, death with a scenario forcing the victims into impossible choices, and into the knowledge that those choices are inescapable, is mercilessly evil. The Arquette character talks of one victim: "I knew him. We were neighbors. In twenty minutes his whole family and all of its future was gone from this Earth." That victim's knowledge of his loss was worse than death.

The Grey Zone is pitiless, bleak, and despairing. There cannot be a happy ending, except that the war eventually ended. That is no consolation for its victims. It is a film about making choices that seem to make no difference, about attempting to act with honor in a closed system where honor lies dead. One can think: If nobody else knows, at least I will know. Yes, but then you will be dead, and then who will know? And what did it get you? On the other hand, to live with the knowledge that you behaved shamefully is another kind of death—the death of the human need to regard ourselves with favor. The Grey Zone refers to a world where everyone is covered with the grey ash of the dead, and it has been like that for so long they do not even notice anymore.

H

Half Past Dead ½ ★
PG-13, 99 m., 2002

Steven Seagal (Sascha Petrosevitch), Morris
Chestnut (Donny/49er One), Ja Rule (Nick
Frazier), Matt Battaglia (49er Three), Richard
Bremmer (Sonny Ekvall), Art Camacho (49er
Eleven), Steven J. Cannell (Hubbard), Claudia
Christian (E. Z. Williams). Directed by Don
Michael Paul and produced by Elie Samaha,
Steven Seagal, and Andrew Stevens. Screenplay
by Paul.

Half Past Dead is like an alarm that goes off
while nobody is in the room. It does its job and
stops, and nobody cares. It goes through the
motions of an action thriller, but there is a
deadness at its center, a feeling that no one
connected with it loved what they were doing.
There are moments, to be sure, when Ja Rule
and Morris Chestnut seem to hear the music,
but they're dancing by themselves.

The plot is preposterous, but that's acceptable with a thriller. The action is preposterous,
too: Various characters leap from high places
while firing guns, and the movie doesn't think
to show us how, or if, they land. A room is filled
with tear gas, but what exactly happens then?
The movie takes the form of a buddy movie,
but is stopped in its tracks because its hero,
played by Steven Seagal, doesn't have a buddy
gene in his body. (I know, he takes seven bullets for his partner Nick, but I don't think he
planned it: "I'll take seven bullets for Nick!")

Seagal's great contribution to the movie is to
look very serious, even menacing, in close-ups
carefully framed to hide his double chin. I do
not object to the fact that he's put on weight.
Look who's talking. I object to the fact that he
thinks he can conceal it from us with knee-
length coats and tricky camera angles. I would
rather see a movie about a pudgy karate fighter
than a movie about a guy you never get a good
look at.

The film has little dialogue and much action. It places its trust so firmly in action that it
opens with a scene where the characters have
one of those urban chase scenes where the car
barely misses trailer trucks, squeals through
180-degree turns, etc., *and they're not even being
chased.* It's kind of a warm-up, like a musician
practicing the scales.

Do not read further if you think the plot
may have the slightest importance to the movie.
Seagal plays an undercover FBI guy who has
teamed up with the crook Nick Frazier (Ja
Rule), who vouched for him with the master
criminal Sonny Ekvall (Richard Bremmer),
who runs, if I have this correct, "the biggest
crime syndicate between Eastern Europe and
the Pacific Rim." He doesn't say whether the
syndicate extends easterly or westerly between
those demarcations, which would affect the
rim he has in mind. Maybe easterly, since Seagal's character is named Sascha Petrosevitch.
"You're Russian, right?" he asks Seagal, who
agrees. Seagal's answer to this question is the
only time in the entire movie he has a Russian
accent.

Nick gets thrown into New Alcatraz. Sascha
Petrosevitch gets thrown in, too. Later, after his
cover is blown, he explains to Nick that the FBI
thought if he did time with Nick, it would help
him get inside the criminal organization. The
sentence is five years. What a guy.

Then, let's see, the prison contains an old
man who is about to go to the chair with the
secret of $200 million in gold bars. Bad guys
want his secret and cooperate with an insider
(Morris Chestnut) to break into the prison,
taking hostage a female U.S. Supreme Court
justice who is on a tour of death row (she's one
of those liberals). They want to escape with the
old guy and get the gold. Among their demands: a fully fueled jet plane to an "undisclosed location." My advice: At least disclose
the location to the pilot.

Nick and Sascha Petrosevitch team up to risk
their lives in a nonstop series of shoot-outs, explosions, martial arts fights, and shoulder-
launched rocket battles in order to save the
Supreme Court justice. We know why Sascha
Petrosevitch is doing this. But why is Nick? Apparently he is another example of that mysterious subset of the law of gravitation that
attracts the black actor with second billing in
an action movie to the side of the hero.

At the end of *Half Past Dead* there is a scene
where Nick looks significantly at Sascha Petrosevitch and nods and smiles a little, as if to say,

you some kinda white guy. Of course, Sascha Petrosevitch has just promised to spring him from New Alcatraz, which can easily inspire a nod and a little smile.

Meanwhile, I started wondering about that $200 million in gold. At the end of the movie, we see a chest being winched to the surface and some gold bars spilling out. If gold sells at, say, $321 per troy ounce, then $20 million in gold bars would represent 623,052 troy ounces, or 42,720 pounds, and would not fit in that chest. You would expect the FBI guys would know this. Maybe not these FBI guys.

Note: I imagine the flywheels at the MPAA congratulating each other on a good day's work as they rated Half Past Dead *PG-13, after giving the antigun movie* Bowling for Columbine *an R.*

Hannibal ★ ★ ½
R, 131 m., 2001

Anthony Hopkins (Hannibal Lecter), Julianne Moore (Clarice Starling), Ray Liotta (Paul Krendler), Frankie R. Faison (Barney), Giancarlo Giannini (Pazzi), Francesca Neri (Signora Pazzi), Zeljko Ivanek (Dr. Cordell Doemling), Hazelle Goodman (Evelda Drumgo). Directed by Ridley Scott and produced by Dino De Laurentiis and Martha De Laurentiis. Screenplay by David Mamet and Steven Zaillian, based on the novel by Thomas Harris.

Ridley Scott's *Hannibal* is a carnival geek show elevated in the direction of art. It never quite gets there, but it tries with every fiber of its craft to redeem its pulp origins, and we must give it credit for the courage of its depravity; if it proves nothing else, it proves that if a man cutting off his face and feeding it to his dogs doesn't get the NC-17 rating for violence, nothing ever will.

The film lacks the focus and brilliance of *The Silence of the Lambs* for a number of reasons, but most clearly because it misplaces the reason why we liked Hannibal Lecter so much. He was, in the 1991 classic, a good man to the degree that his nature allowed him to be. He was hard-wired as a cannibal and mass murderer, true, but that was his nature, not his fault, and in his relationship with the heroine, FBI Agent Clarice Starling, he was civil and even kind. He did the best he could. I remember sitting in a restaurant with Anthony Hopkins as a waitress said, "You're Hannibal Lecter, aren't you? I wish my husband was more like you."

Hopkins returns here as Lecter, although Jodie Foster has been replaced by Julianne Moore as Clarice. We do not miss Foster so much as we miss her character; this Clarice is drier, more cynical, more closed-off than the young idealist we met ten years ago. A decade of law enforcement has taken the bloom off her rose. She is credited, indeed, by the *Guinness Book* as having killed more people than any other female FBI agent, although like all cops in movies, she still doesn't know what to say when her boss demands her badge and her gun. (Suggestion: "I ordered the D.C. police to stand down, and they opened fire anyway.")

Exiled to a desk job, she soon finds herself invited back to the chase by Lecter himself, who writes her from Florence, where he is now a wealthy art curator. On his trail is another millionaire, Mason Verger, who wants revenge. Verger was a child molester assigned to Dr. Lecter for therapy, which Lecter supplied by drugging him and suggesting he cut off his face and feed it, as mentioned, to the dogs. Now horribly disfigured, with no eyelids or lips, he remembers: "It seemed like a good idea at the time." (Verger is played with repellent ooze by an uncredited and unrecognizable star; search the end credits.)

A Florence policeman named Pazzi (Giancarlo Giannini) suspects that the curator is actually Hannibal Lecter, and decides to shop him to Verger for a $3 million reward. This turns out to be a spectacularly bad idea, he realizes, as he ends up spilling his guts for Lecter. Giannini has always had sad eyes, never sadder than in his big scene here.

But do we like Lecter on the loose? It was the whole point of *Silence* that he could never hope to escape. Clarice descended seven flights of stairs and passed through seven locked doors before arriving at the Plexiglas wall that contained his shackled body. Only his mind was free to roam and scheme; the only way he could escape was to think himself out. In *Hannibal,* Lecter can move freely, and that removes part of the charm. By setting him free to roam, the movie diminishes his status from a locus of evil to a mere predator. He can escape from traps seemingly at will, but that misses the point. He is never more sympathetic here than when he's strapped to a cruciform brace and about to be fed, a little at a time, to wild boars. His voice at that point sounds a note of pity for his tormentors, and we remember the earlier Lecter.

Having read the Harris novel, I agreed with earlier reviewers who doubted it could be filmed in its original form. What is amazing is that Ridley Scott, with screenwriters David Mamet and Steven Zaillian, has kept most of the parts I thought would have to go. Verger's muscle-bound lesbian dominatrix sister is missing, along with her electric eel, and the very ending of the novel is gone, perhaps to spare Clarice irreversible humiliation in case there is a sequel. But the face-eating and voracious boars are still here, along with the man whose skull is popped open so that nonessential parts of his brain can be sliced off and sautéed for his dinner.

Many still alive will recall when a movie like this could not be contemplated, let alone filmed and released. So great is our sophistication that we giggle when earlier generations would have retched. The brain-eating scene is "special effects," the face-eating is shot in deep shadow and so quickly cut that you barely see the dogs having their dinner, and Julianne Moore explains in interviews that the story is a fable of good and evil (although she cautions that she "actually talked to my shrink about it").

I cannot approve of the movie, not because of its violence, which belongs to the Grand Guignol tradition, but because the underlying story lacks the fascination of *The Silence of the Lambs*. Lecter on the loose loses power, Clarice is harder and less likable, the story unsuccessfully joins its depravity with its police procedural details, and the movie is too bold in its desire to shock (*Silence* somehow persuaded us the shocks were forced upon it).

Still, I'm left with admiration for Scott's craft in pulling this off at all, and making it watchable and (for some, I'm sure) entertaining. The Mason Verger character is a superb joining of skill and diabolical imagination, Julianne Moore's agent is probably an accurate portrait of how Clarice would have changed in ten years, and Anthony Hopkins makes Lecter fascinating every second he is on the screen. The old cannibal still has his standards. "He said that whenever possible," his former jailer Barney recalls, "he preferred to eat the rude—the free-range rude."

Happy Accidents ★ ★ ★
R, 110 m., 2001

Marisa Tomei (Ruby Weaver), Vincent D'Onofrio (Sam Deed), Nadia Dajani (Gretchen), Tovah Feldshuh (Lillian), Holland Taylor (Therapist), Richard Portnow (Trip), Sean Gullette (Mark), Cara Buono (Bette), Anthony Michael Hall (Famous Actor). Directed by Brad Anderson and produced by Susan A. Stover. Screenplay by Anderson.

Sam tells Ruby he has back-traveled in time from May 8, 2439—starting in Dubuque, Iowa, "on the Atlantic Coast." Guys have used weirder pickup lines. Ruby has heard them. She's a "fixer," an emotional codependent who seems to attract the losers, the needy, and the fetishists. In some ways, Sam is the most normal guy she's dated. *Happy Accidents* is their love story.

Ruby (Marisa Tomei) is deep in analysis. She repeats after her therapist, "I am willing to find a balance between my own needs and my concern for others." Sam (Vincent D'Onofrio) is not who she needs to meet at this stage in her recovery. He explains that mankind has survived two ice ages, that most humans are clones created by corporations, and that his parents are "anachronists" who live in a reservation and practice the officially discouraged practice of reproducing through sex. He found a photo of Ruby, he says, and felt compelled to travel through time to find her, love her, and save her from certain death.

Uh-huh. And yet there is something strangely convincing about Sam. D'Onofrio has played some odd characters in his time (notably Robert E. Howard, the creator of Conan the Barbarian, in *Whole Wide World*). This time, given an astonishing background, he plays the character persuasively and realistically; if a man came back from 2439, he might act something like this. Indeed, if an otherwise absolutely normal man of the present time *thought* he came back from 2439, he might act like this in all details other than the time-travel business.

It is Ruby who seems from another time. The first time we meet her, she's working as a directory assistance operator and is fired for inappropriate verbal interactions with the customers. Her shrink thinks maybe she has some kind of a need to look for trouble, and thinks Sam is trouble with a capital T. Yet Sam and Ruby fall in love. And although it would seem in the nature of things that there is no way for Sam to prove that his story is on the level, things do sometimes oddly turn out as if he might possibly be telling the truth. (The camera allows us to see, as he sees, coffee running backward out of his cup and up into the pot, in what is possibly an example of Residual Temporal Drag Syndrome.)

Whether or not he is really from 2439, I will not say. *Happy Accidents* isn't really about that anyway. It's about the collision of these two personalities, and the catalyst of love. Brad Anderson, the writer-director, chose wisely in casting Tomei and D'Onofrio because they can both look normal one moment and then have a strange light in their eyes a second later. Watch the way Tomei screws up her mouth in unhappiness at an art gallery opening. See how D'Onofrio seems absolutely, convincingly, bottom-line credible—and then pushes just a smidgen further.

Happy Accidents is essentially silliness crossed with science fiction. The actors make it fun to watch. And Anderson is good with the supporting roles, including Tovah Feldshuh as Ruby's mother, Lillian, who advises her to seize the moment (Lillian's husband was an alcoholic, and she learned too late that she liked him better when he was drinking). There is also a cameo for Anthony Michael Hall that is the best thing in its line since Marshall McLuhan stepped out from behind the movie poster in *Annie Hall.*

Happy Times ★ ★
PG, 106 m., 2002

Dong Jie (Wu Ying), Zhao Benshan (Zhao), Dong Lihua (Stepmother). Directed by Zhang Yimou and produced by Zhang Weiping , Zhou Ping, and Zhao Yu. Screenplay by Gui Zi.

One of the challenges of foreign movies is to determine how they would play on their native soil. Here, for example, is *Happy Times,* from the sometimes great Chinese director Zhang Yimou. It is about a group of unemployed men who build a fake room in an abandoned factory, move a blind girl into it, tell her it is in a hotel, and become her clients for daily massages, paying her with blank pieces of paper they hope she will mistake for money.

On the basis of that description, you will assume that this movie is cruel and depraved. But turn now to the keywords under "Tones" in the movie's listing at allmovie.com, and you will find: "sweet, reflective, light, humorous, easygoing, compassionate, affectionate." *Happy Times* is a comedy, and has been compared to Chaplin's *City Lights,* which was also about a jobless man trying to help a blind girl.

Consider first how this movie would play if it were a Hollywood production. Imagine a good-hearted everyman (Steve Martin, let's say) with a group of cronies (we'll cast Harvey Keitel, Jeff Daniels, Bill Paxton, Steve Buscemi, and Danny DeVito). They build a fake room and install a young, naive, blind girl (Christina Ricci), and go for daily massages, etc. Is there any way your imagination can stretch widely enough for this scenario to become a compassionate and affectionate comedy?

I say not. There must be something cultural at work here. When American critics praise the movie (and most of them have), they are making some kind of concession to its Chinese origins. A story that would be unfilmable by Hollywood becomes, in Chinese hands, "often uproariously funny" (*New York* magazine), "subtle and even humorous" *(Film Journal International),* and "wise, gentle and sad" *(New York Times).* The movie's message, according to *FJI,* is that "the underpinning of paternalistic values which once protected the old and ensured a future for the young is now a pretense."

Uh-huh. I can even halfway understand those reviews, because the movie sets up like a comedy, plays like a comedy, and barks like a comedy, so it must be a comedy. It opens with a retired man named Zhao (Zhao Benshan) proposing marriage to a jolly divorcée (Dong Lihua), who meets his high standards for chubbiness. He needs money to bring about the match, however, and so teams up with a buddy to turn an abandoned bus into a "love hotel," which lonely couples can rent by the hour.

He tells his intended he is a hotel owner, but then the bus is hauled away. He meets Wu Ying (Dong Jie), his fiancée's stepdaughter, who is blind and has been abandoned by her father, the divorcée's most recent husband. Acting the big shot, Zhao tells them he will give the girl work in his hotel, and then enlists his buddies in building the fake room, paying the fake money for the massages, etc.

This is all done good-heartedly, you see. The cronies are warm and caring men, who, when they are not receiving massages, sit on the rafters to look down into the roofless room; they nod approvingly at "Little Wu's" happiness, and the movie argues that they practice their deception to make her happy.

That assumes their definition of happiness for a blind young teenage girl is to let her sit in a "hotel room" waiting for one of her newfound friends to come in for a massage. This would not be my definition of happiness, or perhaps yours, although it might fit for the hero of John Fowles's novel *The Collector*. To me it sounds like a cruel deception carried out by men of marginal intelligence, reactionary ideas about women, and a total lack of empathy.

There is a poignant ending that I found particularly inexplicable. Please do not read further unless you are prepared for spoilers. It turns out that Little Wu was aware of the deception all along (we see her using a stick to prove to herself that the room has no ceiling). With the acute hearing and memory of the blind, she also no doubt noticed that the "street noises" outside her "room" were a tape recording, played over and over. She went along with the deception, she tells Zhao, because she was so incredibly touched and moved by the care of her new friends, and the lengths they went to, trying to make her happy. This is all revealed in a tape recording she leaves behind, and then we see her, all by herself, setting out alone on the road of life, while sentimental music plays.

The movie seems to come from a simpler, more innocent culture. There is never a hint of sex in it, for one thing. The massages are completely chaste, the men like them that way, and it never occurs to the girl that it is creepy that she is giving massages to a bunch of anonymous men in a fake hotel room. Apparently the men never, ever, look down into the room while Little Wu undresses. No, the movie is sweet, reflective, light, humorous, easygoing, compassionate, affectionate.

If I did not find it that way, if I found it creepy beyond all reason, that is no doubt because I have been hopelessly corrupted by the decadent society I inhabit. Or, are there moviegoers in China who also find *Happy Times* odd in the extreme? I searched the Chinese Movie Database and the sites of the *People's Daily,* the *South China Morning Post,* and English-language papers from Shanghai and Beijing, without finding any mention of the film at all. The Web is worldwide and perhaps I will hear from a Chinese reader or two. Please slug your message *Happy Times* so it will stand out from all the offers I get for discount Viagra.

Hardball ★ ★ ½
R, 106 m., 2001

Keanu Reeves (Conor O'Neill), Diane Lane (Elizabeth Wilkes), DeWayne Warren (G-Baby), John Hawkes (Ticky), Bryan Hearne (Andre), Julian Griffith (Jefferson), Michael B. Jordan (Jamal), Alan Ellis Jr. (Miles), Kristopher Lofton (Clarence). Directed by Brian Robbins and produced by Tina Nides, Robbins, and Michael Tollin. Screenplay by John Gatins, based on the book *Hardball: A Season in the Projects* by Daniel Coyle.

Hardball tells the story of a compulsive gambler whose life is turned around by a season of coaching an inner-city baseball team. That sounds like a winning formula for a movie, and it might be, if the story told us more about gambling, more about the inner city, and more about coaching baseball. But it drifts above the surface of its natural subjects, content to be a genre picture. We're always aware of the formula—and in a picture based on real life, we shouldn't be.

Keanu Reeves stars as Conor O'Neill, whose life revolves around sports bars and the point spread on the post-Jordan Bulls. True, betting on the Bulls is just about the only way to develop interest in the team these days, but compared to movies like *The Gambler* and *California Split*, *Hardball* uses gambling just for motivation and atmosphere; we never feel the urgency and desperation of a man deeply in debt to bad people. Oh, we see a man *acting* urgent and desperate, but the juice isn't there. Consider the scene where O'Neill negotiates a weekly payment plan with a collector; they could be working out the installments on a car.

O'Neill turns to a friend in the investment business for a loan, and the friend makes him an offer: 500 bucks a week to coach a kids' baseball team in the Chicago Housing Authority league. This is not something O'Neill wants to do, but he needs the money. We meet the kids (one too small, one with birth certificate problems, one with asthma, etc.) and of course they're a bunch of unmotivated losers, and of course by the end of the movie they will be champions, because the formula demands it. (It would take more imagination than this movie has to show the kids and the coach redeemed by a losing season.)

There's little detail about who these kids really are and what kinds of homes they come from. A few dialogue scenes with worried parents, and that's it. Toward the end, in a truly heartbreaking scene where an older kid cradles the body of a younger one who has been shot in a drive-by, there's genuine emotion that makes us realize how much was missing earlier.

As the coach, O'Neill mostly addresses the kids as a group, not individually. His dialogue consists of the announcement of plot points (he likes them, he doesn't, he's quitting, he's staying, he's taking them to a Cubs game, they have to believe in themselves). There is not, as nearly as I can remember, a single one-on-one scene in which he tells a kid anything specific about baseball strategy. For that matter, does he know anything about baseball? In many scenes he just lines them up and hectors them, and they look like kids patiently watching some crazy white guy work out his issues.

There's a low-key love story involving Diane Lane as Elizabeth, who teaches some of the kids and keeps an eye on O'Neill because she would like him if (can you see this coming?) he could learn to like himself. I liked the freshness of a moment when O'Neill breaks into a conversation to say, "You like me! You just looked at me a certain way and I could see you liked me." The rhythm of the formula was broken for a moment, and it felt nice.

The movie is based on the book *Hardball: A Season in the Projects* by Daniel Coyle, based on life. I doubt the book, unread by me, is as inauthentic as the movie; the screenplay shows signs of having been tilted in the direction of the basic Hollywood workshop story structure in which we get a crisis because it's time for one. And Keanu Reeves seems subdued in the role—so glum and distant we wonder why we should care if he doesn't. He retails some of his dialogue with excessive hand movements, as if trying to guide his sentences in for a landing.

There was controversy when the movie was made because the dialogue included various words that would be used by most kids on any baseball team. I think I spotted a couple of times when an eight-letter word was dubbed in for its seven-letter synonym. Why bother? Kids talk this way. We might as well face it.

The Hard Word ★ ★ ½

R, 102 m., 2003

Guy Pearce (Dale), Rachel Griffiths (Carol), Robert Taylor (Frank), Joel Edgerton (Shane), Damien Richardson (Mal), Rhondda Findleton (Jane), Kate Atkinson (Pamela). Directed by Scott Roberts and produced by Al Clark. Screenplay by Roberts.

The Twentyman brothers—Dale, Shane, and Mal—are stickup men with the motto "Nobody gets hurt." Despite their benevolence, they end up in prison, where Mal practices the butcher's trade and Dale works as a librarian. Then their lawyer, Frank, springs them for one last brilliant job. The job is much complicated by the fact that Dale's wife has become Frank's mistress.

The wife-slash-mistress is Carol, played by Rachel Griffiths with her intriguing ability to combine the qualities of a tomboy and a sex kitten. She's married to Dale Twentyman (Guy Pearce), insists she loves him, yet is having an affair with the crooked lawyer Frank (Robert Taylor). Which one does she really love? Sometimes she seems to be smiling to herself with the evil contentment of a woman whose bread is buttered on both sides.

It is good to hear Pearce (*L.A. Confidential, Memento*) and Griffiths (a star of HBO's *Six Feet Under*) speaking in their native Australian accents in *The Hard Word,* a movie that exists halfway between Tarantinoland and those old black-and-white British crime comedies. The characters seem to have devised themselves as living works of art, as if personal style and being "colorful" is the real point of being a criminal, and the money is only a bothersome technicality.

Consider Shane Twentyman (Joel Edgerton), the brother with a big-time problem with anger. A big guy who looks a little like young Albert Finney, he's assigned a prison counselor named Jane (Rhondda Findleton), and they fall in love with startling speed. Mal Twentyman (Damien Richardson) also has a magnetic attraction for women, which comes as a surprise to him, since he is usually much abashed around them. After the gang steals a getaway car, its owner and driver, Pamela (Kate Atkinson), comes down with a critical case of Stockholm Syndrome and falls in love with Mal.

These scenes have a charm that works all the better considering that they are surrounded by a good deal of startling violence. Frank's big plan involves the brothers stealing the bookies' money after the running of the Melbourne Cup, but an outsider, brought in to keep an eye on them, opens fire and there is blood and carnage as the brothers flee on foot.

The foot chase has a quality missing in a lot of modern action movies, and that is the sensation of physical effort. William Friedken achieved it, too, in the underrated *The Hunted.* The robbers run through malls and down stairs and across pedestrian overpasses and are hauling the money and panting and sweating, and we realize belatedly that one of the things wrong with Spiderman was that he never seemed to go to any effort.

Griffiths is at the center of both of the movie's key relationships, with her husband the crook and her lover the lawyer. Robert Taylor's lawyer is one of those devious creatures from 1940s movies who seem more interested in taking the woman away from a man than in actually having her. If he were a fisherman he would throw her back in. Does Griffiths's character know this? There is the suggestion that she does and is in love with Dale the whole time, but she is so good at looking a guy straight in the eye and telling him she loves him that her actions are

eventually going to have to speak louder than her words.

The movie has room for quirky little side trips, as when the loot is hidden in a peculiar place, and for classic *film noir* moments, as when several key characters gather for a showdown that is not quite what some of them had in mind, but they get to engage in a lot of high-style crime dialogue before they find that out.

And then there's more. Too much more. *The Hard Word* feels like it should be more or less over after the Melbourne Cup heist, but it's barely getting started, as writer-director Scott Roberts supplies twists and double crosses and startling developments and surprise revelations and unexpected appearances and disappearances, until finally we give up. This movie could obviously go on fooling us forever, but we are good sports only up to a point, and then our attention drifts. Shame, since there's so much good stuff in it, like how effortlessly Rachel Griffiths keeps two tough guys completely at her mercy.

Harrison's Flowers ★ ★ ½
R, 122 m., 2002

Andie MacDowell (Sarah Lloyd), David Strathairn (Harrison Lloyd), Elias Koteas (Yeager Pollack), Adrien Brody (Kyle Morris), Brendan Gleeson (Marc Stevenson), Alun Armstrong (Samuel Bruceck). Directed by Elie Chouraqui and produced by Chouraqui and Albert J. Cohen. Screenplay by Chouraqui, Michael Katims, Isabel Ellsen, and Didier LePecheur.

I am pleased we have women in our fighting forces, since they are so much better at war than men. *Harrison's Flowers* is about an American wife who journeys to the Balkans to rescue her husband from a hotbed of genocide. In *Charlotte Gray,* a British woman parachuted behind German lines in France to rescue her boyfriend. I can just about believe that Charlotte Gray could deceive the Germans with her perfect French, but that Sarah Lloyd could emerge alive from the Balkans hell is unlikely; much of the movie's fascination is with the way Croatians allow this woman and her new friends to wander through the killing zones intact.

I doubt, for that matter, that a Los Angeles fireman could fly to Colombia in *Collateral Damage* and single-handedly outfight guerrillas and drug empires, but that is an Arnold Schwarzenegger picture and not supposed to be realistic. *Harrison's Flowers* is not based on fact but plays like one of those movies that is, and the scenes of carnage are so well staged and convincing that they make the movie's story even harder to believe. Strong performances also work to win us over, wear us down, and persuade us to accept this movie as plausible. Who we gonna believe, the screenplay or our lyin' eyes?

Andie MacDowell stars, in another reminder of her range and skill, in what is essentially an action role. She plays Sarah Lloyd, mother of two, wife of the celebrated war photographer Harrison (David Strathairn). In an obligatory scene that triggers an uh-oh reflex among experienced filmgoers, he tells his boss he wants to retire and is persuaded to take One Last Job. Off he flies to the early days of the war in the Balkans to investigate "ethnic cleansing," which was I think a term not then quite yet in use. He is reported dead, but Sarah knows he's still alive: "Something would have happened inside if he were dead."

She watches TV obsessively, hoping for a glimpse of Harrison among POWs, and takes up chain-smoking, which is the movie symbol for grief-stricken obsession and is dropped as soon as it's no longer needed. Because of a hang-up call in the middle of the night and other signs, she decides to fly to the Balkans to find Harrison. A more reasonable spouse might reason that since (a) her husband is reliably reported dead, and (b) she has no combat zone skills, (c) she should stay home with her kids so they will not become orphans, but no.

The war scenes have undeniable power. Violence springs from nowhere during routine moments and kills supporting characters without warning. Ordinary streets are transformed instantly into warscapes. Sarah joins up with three of Harrison's photographer friends who accompany her quest: pill-popping, wisecracking Morris (Adrien Brody), shambling, likable Stevenson (Brendan Gleeson), and bitter, existentialist Yeager Pollack (Elias Koteas). (If any of them are killed, can you predict from the character descriptions which order it will happen in?) They commandeer cars and jeeps, and essentially make a tour of the war zone, while bullets whiz past their ears and unspeakable horrors take place on every side.

They are protected, allegedly, by white flags and large letters proclaiming "TV" on the sides of their cars. But there is a scene where troops are methodically carrying out an ethnic massacre, and the photographers wander in full view at the other end of the street: Does their status as journalists render them invisible? At one point, Sarah wears fatigues, which (I learn from an article by a war correspondent) is the last thing she should do. Civilian clothes mark her as a noncombatant; camouflage marks her as a target even before her gender is determined.

Whether Sarah finds her husband I will leave you to discover. Whether, when she is in a burning building, the flames shoot up everywhere except precisely where she needs to be, you already know. There is a way in which a movie like this works no matter what. Andie MacDowell is a sympathetic actress who finds plausible ways to occupy this implausible role. Brendan Gleeson is a comforting force of nature, and Adrien Brody's work is a tour de force, reminding me of James Woods in *Salvador* in the way he depends on attitude and cockiness to talk his way through touchy situations. Watch the way he walks them all through a roadblock. I don't believe it can be done, but I believe he did it.

As for the war itself, the movie exhibits the usual indifference to the issues involved. Although it was written and directed by Elie Chouraqui, a Frenchman, it is comfortably xenophobic. Most Americans have never understood the differences among Croats, Serbs, and Bosnians, and this film is no help. (I am among the guilty, actually mislabeling the bad guys in my review of *Behind Enemy Lines*, another film set in the region.) All we need to know is: The Americans are tourists in a foreign war involving ruthless partisans with fierce mustaches. Why are those people killing one another? Why is the war being fought? With those crazy foreigners, who knows? The New Jersey housewife wants to return her man to the arms of his family and the peace of his greenhouse. The movie's buried message is that domestic order must be restored. Just like in Shakespeare.

Harry Potter and the Chamber of Secrets ★ ★ ★ ★
PG, 161 m., 2002

Daniel Radcliffe (Harry Potter), (Rupert Grint (Ron Weasley), Emma Watson (Hermione Granger), Jason Isaacs (Lucius Malfoy), Alan Rickman (Professor Snape), Maggie Smith (Professor McGonagall), Robbie Coltrane (Hagrid the Giant), David Bradley (Mr. Argus Filch), Kenneth Branagh (Gilderoy Lockhart), Miriam Margolyes (Professor Sprout), John Cleese (Nearly Headless Nick), Richard Harris (Professor Dumbledore), Tom Felton (Draco Malfoy), Bonnie Wright (Ginny Weasley), Harry Melling (Dudley Dursley). Directed by Chris Columbus and produced by David Heyman. Screenplay by Steve Kloves, based on the novel by J. K. Rowling.

The first movie was the setup, and this one is the payoff. *Harry Potter and the Chamber of Secrets* leaves all of the explanations of wizardry behind and plunges quickly into an adventure that's darker and scarier than anything in the first Harry Potter movie. It's also richer: The second in a planned series of seven Potter films is brimming with invention and new ideas, and its Hogwarts School seems to expand and deepen before our very eyes into a world large enough to conceal unguessable secrets.

What's developing here, it's clear, is one of the most important franchises in movie history, a series of films that consolidate all of the advances in computer-aided animation, linked to the extraordinary creative work of J. K. Rowling, who has created a mythological world as grand as *Star Wars,* but filled with more wit and humanity. Although the young wizard Harry Potter is nominally the hero, the film remembers the golden age of moviemaking, when vivid supporting characters crowded the canvas. The story is about personalities, personal histories, and eccentricity, not about a superstar superman crushing the narrative with his egotistical weight.

In the new movie, Harry (Daniel Radcliffe, a little taller and deeper-voiced) returns with his friends Ron Weasley (Rupert Grint) and Hermione Granger (Emma Watson, in the early stages of babehood). They sometimes seem to stand alone amid the alarming mysteries of Hogwarts, where even the teachers, even the august headmaster Albus Dumbledore (Richard Harris), even the learned professors Snape (Alan Rickman) and McGonagall (Maggie Smith), even the stalwart Hagrid the Giant (Robbie Coltrane) seem mystified and a little frightened by the school's dread secrets.

Is there indeed a Chamber of Secrets hidden somewhere in the vast pile of Hogwarts? Can it only be opened by a descendent of Salazar Slytherin, the more sinister of the school's co-founders? Does it contain a monster? Has the monster already escaped, and is it responsible for paralyzing some of the students, whose petrified bodies are found in the corridors, and whose bodies are carried to the infirmary still frozen in a moment of time? Do the answers to these questions originate in events many years ago, when even the ancient Dumbledore was (marginally) younger? And does a diary by a former student named Tom Marvolo Riddle—a book with nothing written in it, but whose pages answer questions in a ghostly handwriting—provide the clues that Harry and his friends need? (Answer to all of the above: probably.)

This puzzle could be solved in a drab and routine movie with characters wandering down old stone corridors, but one of the pleasures of Chris Columbus's direction of *Harry Potter and the Chamber of Secrets* is how visually alive it is. This is a movie that answers any objection to computer animation with glorious or creepy sights that blend convincingly with the action. Hogwarts itself seems to have grown since the first movie, from a largish sort of country house into a thing of spires and turrets, vast rooms and endlessly convoluted passageways, lecture halls and science labs, with as much hidden below the ground as is visible above it. Even the Quidditch game is held in a larger stadium (maybe rich alumni were generous?). There are times, indeed, when the scope of Hogwarts seems to approach that of Gormenghast, the limitless edifice in the trilogy by Mervyn Peake that was perhaps one of Rawling's inspirations.

The production designer is Stuart Craig, returning from *Harry Potter and the Chamber of Secrets*. He has created (there is no other way to put it) a world here, a fully realized world with all the details crowded in, so that even the corners of the screen are intriguing. This is one of the rare recent movies you could happily watch with the sound turned off, just for the joy of his sets, the costumes by Judianna Makovsky and Lindy Hemming, and the visual effects (the Quidditch match seems even more three-dimensional, the characters swooping across the vast field, as Harry finds himself seriously threatened by the odious Malfoy).

There are three new characters this time, one delightful, one conceited, one malevolent. Professor Sprout (Miriam Margolyes) is on the biology faculty and teaches a class on the peculiar properties of the mandrake plant, made all the more amusing by students of John Donne who are familiar with the additional symbolism of the mandrake only hinted at in class. The more you know about mandrakes, the funnier Sprout's class is.

She is the delightful addition. The conceited new faculty member, deliciously cast, is Gilderoy Lockhart (Kenneth Branagh), author of the autobiography *Magical Me*, who thinks of himself as a consummate magician but whose spell to heal Harry's broken arm has unfortunate results. And then there is Lucius Malfoy (Jason Isaacs), father of the supercilious Draco, who skulks about as if he should be hated just on general principles.

These characters and plot elements draw together in late action sequences of genuine power, which may be too intense for younger viewers. There is a most alarming confrontation with spiders and a scary late duel with a dragon, and these are handled not as jolly family movie episodes, but with the excitement of a mainstream thriller. While I am usually in despair when a movie abandons its plot for a third act given over entirely to action, I have no problem with the way *Harry Potter and the Chamber of Secrets* ends, because it has been pointing toward this ending, hinting about it, preparing us for it, all the way through. What a glorious movie.

Harry Potter and the Sorcerer's Stone
★ ★ ★ ★
PG, 152 m., 2001

Daniel Radcliffe (Harry Potter), Rupert Grint (Ronald Weasley), Emma Watson (Hermione Granger), Tom Felton (Draco Malfoy), Richard Harris (Albus Dumbledore), Maggie Smith (Professor Minerva McGonagall), Alan Rickman (Professor Severus Snape), Ian Hart (Professor Quirrell), Robbie Coltrane (Gamekeeper Rubeus Hagrid), Julie Walters (Mrs. Weasley), Harry Melling (Dudley Dursley), Warwick Davis (Professor Flitwick), Zoe Wanamaker (Madame Hooch). Directed by Chris Columbus and produced by David Heyman. Screenplay by J. K. Rowling and Steven Kloves, based on the novel by Rowling.

Harry Potter and the Sorcerer's Stone is a red-blooded adventure movie, dripping with atmosphere, filled with the gruesome and the sublime, and surprisingly faithful to the novel. A lot of things could have gone wrong, and none of them have: Chris Columbus's movie is an enchanting classic that does full justice to a story that was a daunting challenge.

The novel by J. K. Rowling was muscular and vivid, and the danger was that the movie would make things too cute and cuddly. It doesn't. Like an *Indiana Jones* for younger viewers, it tells a rip-roaring tale of supernatural adventure, where colorful and eccentric characters alternate with scary stuff like a three-headed dog, a pit of tendrils known as the Devil's Snare, and a two-faced immortal who drinks unicorn blood. Scary, yes, but not too scary—just scary enough.

Three high-spirited, clear-eyed kids populate the center of the movie. Daniel Radcliffe plays Harry Potter, he with the round glasses, and like all of the young characters, he looks much as I imagined him, but a little older. He once played David Copperfield on the BBC, and whether Harry will be the hero of his own life in this story is much in doubt at the beginning. Deposited as a foundling on a suburban doorstep, he is raised by his aunt and uncle as a poor relation, then summoned by a blizzard of letters to become a student at Hogwarts School, an Oxbridge for magicians.

265

Our first glimpse of Hogwarts sets the tone for the movie's special effects. Although computers can make anything look realistic, too much realism would be the wrong choice for *Harry Potter*, which is a story in which everything, including the sets and locations, should look a little made-up. The school, rising on ominous Gothic battlements from a moonlit lake, looks about as real as Xanadu in *Citizen Kane*, and its corridors, cellars, and Great Hall, although in some cases making use of real buildings, continue the feeling of an atmospheric book illustration.

At Hogwarts, Harry makes two friends and an enemy. The friends are Hermione Granger (Emma Watson), whose merry face and tangled curls give Harry nudges in the direction of lightening up a little, and Ronald Weasley (Rupert Grint), all pluck, luck, and untamed talents. The enemy is Draco Malfoy (Tom Felton), who will do anything, and plenty besides, to be sure his house places first at the end of the year.

The story you either already know or do not want to know. What is good to know is that the adult cast, a who's who of British actors, play their roles more or less as if they believed them. There is a broad style of British acting, developed in Christmas pantomimes, that would have been fatal to this material; these actors know that, and dial down to just this side of too much. Watch Alan Rickman drawing out his words until they seem ready to snap, yet somehow staying in character.

Maggie Smith, still in the prime of Miss Jean Brodie, is Professor Minerva McGonagall, who assigns newcomers like Harry to one of the school's four houses. Richard Harris is Headmaster Dumbledore, his beard so long that in an Edward Lear poem birds would nest in it. Robbie Coltrane is the gamekeeper, Hagrid, who has a record of misbehavior and a way of saying very important things and then not believing that he said them.

Computers *are* used, exuberantly, to create a plausible look in the gravity-defying action scenes. Readers of the book will wonder how the movie visualizes the crucial game of Quidditch. The game, like so much else in the movie, is more or less as I visualized it, and I was reminded of Stephen King's theory that writers practice a form of telepathy, placing ideas and images in the heads of their readers. (The reason some movies don't look like their books may be that some producers don't read them.)

If Quidditch is a virtuoso sequence, there are other set pieces of almost equal wizardry. A chess game with life-size, deadly pieces. A room filled with flying keys. The pit of tendrils, already mentioned, and a dark forest where a loathsome creature threatens Harry but is scared away by a centaur. And the dark shadows of Hogwarts's library, cellars, hidden passages, and dungeons, where an invisibility cloak can keep you out of sight but not out of trouble.

During *Harry Potter and the Sorcerer's Stone*, I was pretty sure I was watching a classic, one that will be around for a long time, and make many generations of fans. It takes the time to be good. It doesn't hammer the audience with easy thrills, but cares to tell a story and to create its characters carefully. Like *The Wizard of Oz, Willy Wonka and the Chocolate Factory, Star Wars*, and *E.T.*, it isn't just a movie but a world with its own magical rules. And some excellent Quidditch players.

Hart's War ★ ★ ★
R, 125 m., 2002

Bruce Willis (Colonel William McNamara), Colin Farrell (Lieutenant Tommy Hart), Terrence Howard (Lieutenant Lincoln Scott), Vicellous Shannon (Lieutenant Lamar Archer), Cole Hauser (Staff Sergeant Bedford), Marcel Iures (Commandant Visser), Linus Roache (Captain Peter Ross). Directed by Gregory Hoblit and produced by David Foster, Hoblit, David Ladd, and Arnold Rifkin. Screenplay by Billy Ray and Terry George, based on the novel by John Katzenbach.

"Your colonel is throwing you to the wolves," the Nazi commandant of a POW camp tells the young American lieutenant. It looks that way. A white racist American has been murdered, a black officer is charged with the crime, and Lieutenant Tommy Hart (Colin Farrell) has been assigned to defend him in a court-martial. The Nazi has permitted the trial as a gesture (he is a Yale man, not uncivilized, likes jazz). But Colonel William McNamara (Bruce

Willis), the senior officer among the American prisoners, doesn't seem much interested in justice.

Because the movie is told mostly from Hart's point of view, we lack crucial pieces of information available to McNamara, and as these are parceled out toward the end of the film, the meaning of the events shifts. But one underlying truth does not change: Racism during World War II in America and in the army was a reality that undercut duty, patriotism, and truth.

As the movie opens, Hart has been captured, interrogated, and sent to Stalag VI in Belgium. He is a senator's son, destined for a desk job. At the POW camp he is cross-examined by Willis, who senses he's lying about the interrogation, and assigns him to a barracks otherwise filled with enlisted men. It's a problem of space, Willis explains, and a few days later the officers' barracks is again too crowded to accommodate two black air corps pilots who have been shot down: Lieutenant Lincoln Scott (Terrence Howard) and Lieutenant Lamar Archer (Vicellous Shannon).

Bunking with black men does not sit well with Vic Bedford (Cole Hauser), a staff sergeant who calls the pilots "flying bellhops." Soon a tent spike, which could be used as a weapon, is found under Archer's mattress, and he's summarily shot by the Nazis without a trial. Since it is pretty clear that Bedford planted the spike, no one is very surprised not long after when the man is found dead with Scott standing over his body.

A clean-cut case of murder, right? Not according to Hart, who believes this is another setup and demands that a trial be held. Colonel McNamara is not enthusiastic about the idea, but the Nazi commandant is, and soon a court-martial is under way with Hart (who has no legal experience) as the defense attorney.

All of this is absorbing, if of course manipulative, but what makes it more intriguing is the sense that something else is going on underneath the action—that McNamara's motives may be more complicated than we know. One hitch is that both the dead man and his alleged killer left the barracks by a secret route at night, a route that cannot be revealed without jeopardizing the other American prisoners. So Hart agrees to a cover story about how his man left the barracks, and then, in a scene built on devastating logic, has to stand mute while the phony cover story is used against his client.

Colin Farrell, the young star of Joel Schumacher's powerful but hardly released *Tigerland* (2000), is a twenty-five-year-old Dublin native obviously destined for stardom. He does a good job with the conflicted, anguished Lieutenant Hart, and Bruce Willis brings instinctive authority to the colonel. Marcel Iures, a Romanian actor, is sharp-edged and intriguing as the Nazi commandant; when he gets condolences on the death of his son in battle, he muses, "I killed my share of English and French soldiers in the first war. They had fathers too." There is a shade of the Erich von Stroheim character in *Grand Illusion* here, the suggestion of a German whose military ideas do not depend on that little twerp Hitler.

But for all the interest in these performances, *Hart's War* would be just another military courtroom drama if it were not for the work by Terrence Howard as Lincoln Scott, the man on trial. He expects no justice from an American court-martial. He enlisted in the air corps, trained at Tuskegee, wanted to serve his nation, and has seen racism and contempt from whites in uniform. He makes one statement that is chilling because we know it was true: German POWs held in the Deep South were allowed to attend movies and eat in restaurants that were off limits to blacks, even those in uniform. "If I wanted to kill a cracker," Scott says, "I could have stayed at home in Macon."

The movie worked for me right up to the final scene, and then it caved in. Bowing to ancient and outdated convention, director Gregory Hoblit and writers Billy Ray and Terry George put the plot through an awkward U-turn so that Willis can end up as a hero. How and why he does so is ingenious, yes, but the ending gives the impression it is a solution when it is only a remedy. And I would have liked it better if the far-off bugle had been playing under a black character at the end and not a white one. It's as if the movie forgot its own anger.

Harvard Man ★ ★ ★
R, 100 m., 2002

Adrian Grenier (Alan Jensen), Sarah Michelle Gellar (Cindy Bandolini), Joey Lauren Adams (Chesney Cort), Eric Stoltz (Teddy Carter), Rebecca Gayheart (Kelly Morgan), Gianni Russo (Andrew Bandolini), Ray Allen (Marcus Blake), Michael Aparo (Russell). Directed by James Toback and produced by Daniel Bigel and Mike Mailer. Screenplay by Toback.

James Toback is a gambler and an intellectual—a Harvard graduate who at times in his life has been deeply involved in betting. His first screenplay, for Karel Reisz's masterpiece *The Gambler* (1974), was about a university literature teacher with a compulsion not merely to gamble, but to place himself at risk. "I play in order to lose," his character says. There is a point at which he contemplates the excellent possibility of having his kneecaps shattered. The only reason Toback himself has never been kneecapped, I suspect, is because he likes to talk even more than he likes to gamble.

Harvard Man stars Adrian Grenier as Alan Jensen, a member of the Harvard basketball squad. He is having an affair with his philosophy professor (Joey Lauren Adams), but also has a more conventional girlfriend, Cindy Bandolini (Sarah Michelle Gellar). Her father is widely believed to be a Mafia boss, although Alan brushes aside all such suggestions with the information that he is a "businessman and investor."

Toback is not above using melodrama as a shortcut, and does so here: Alan's parents lose their house in a Kansas tornado, and he needs to raise $100,000, fast, to help them. He turns to Cindy and suggests that perhaps, ah, if the stories about her father are true, he might be in a position to throw the Dartmouth game and make a lot of money for everybody, including his homeless parents. And now it gets interesting, because Cindy, as played by Gellar, is not your standard-issue Mafia princess, but a sharp and shrewd operator who is no pushover and doesn't like unpleasant surprises. What makes the movie work is that the premise, which sounds like a comedy, is treated with the seriousness of life and death. You do not disappoint a Mafia bookmaker and laugh it off.

Some of my favorite scenes involve Joey Lauren Adams, as the professor. You may remember her as the third wheel in *Chasing Amy*. She has a face like your sister's best friend and a voice like Lauren Bacall crossed with an all-night waitress. She would not be your first idea for an actress to play a philosophy professor; you might go with Meryl Streep, say, or someone smart and nervous, like Jennifer Jason Leigh. She seems more like the philosophy professor's secretary. But that's before she starts to talk. She and Alan have several heart-to-hearts about love, gambling, and drugs, and she deals not only in practical advice but in the meaning of it all.

And that's how the whole movie proceeds. "The unexamined life is not worth living," Socrates reminds us, and in a Toback film the characters examine their lives almost more assiduously than they live them. Alan realizes he's in very deep, with possible criminal characters on the one hand and possible Mafia reprisals on the other. It all grows even more complicated when two of the Mafia's gambling advisers (Eric Stoltz and Rebecca Gayheart) turn out to be more, or less, than they seem.

Alan does what any Toback hero might do when boxed into such a corner, and drops acid. This is not a good idea, and the movie's visuals, distorting faces and summoning up scenes that may or may not be happening, create a nightmare for him. How can one man juggle two women, possible expulsion, Mafia baseball bats, and the meaning of life while on acid? This is the kind of question only a Toback film thinks to ask, let alone answer.

Head of State ★ ★ ★
PG-13, 95 m., 2003

Chris Rock (Mays Gilliam), Bernie Mac (Mitch Gilliam), Dylan Baker (Martin Geller), Nick Searcy (Brian Lewis), Lynn Whitfield (Debra Lassiter), Robin Givens (Kim), Tamala Jones (Lisa Clark), James Rebhorn (Senator Bill Arnot), Stephanie March (Nikki). Directed by Chris Rock and produced by Ali LeRoi, Rock, and Michael Rotenberg. Screenplay by Rock and LeRoi.

Head of State is an imperfect movie, but not a boring one, and not lacking in intelligence. What it does wrong is hard to miss, but what it does right is hard to find: It makes an angry and fairly timely comic attack on an electoral system where candidates don't say what they really think, but simply repeat safe centrist banalities.

In *Head of State,* the presidential and vice presidential candidates of an unnamed party, obviously the Democrats, are killed when their campaign planes crash into each other less than two months before the election. Seeking a replacement candidate, the party settles on Mays Gilliam, an obscure Washington, D.C., alderman (Chris Rock), who has saved a woman and her cat from a burning building. He seems to have no chance of victory, but of course party boss Senator Bill Arnot (James Rebhorn) doesn't want him to win—he wants to exploit him as a token black candidate who will lose, but win painless points for the party.

If Mays can't win, then he has nothing to lose, and his strategy is obvious: Instead of trying to please everyone, he should say the unsayable. We've seen this strategy before from movie candidates, notably Kevin Kline in *Dave,* Warren Beatty in *Bulworth,* and Eddie Murphy in *Distinguished Gentleman,* and the notion runs back to Frank Capra. What Chris Rock brings to it is brashness—zingers that hurt. "What kind of a drug policy," he wants to know, "makes crack cheaper than asthma medicine?"

The movie, directed and cowritten by Rock, is wickedly cynical about the American electoral system. It shows Mays being supplied with a prostitute named Nikki (Stephanie March) because, campaign manager Martin Geller (Dylan Baker) explains, "We got tired of getting caught up in sex scandals, so we commissioned our own team of superwhores." And it gives him an opponent, the incumbent vice president (Nick Searcy), whose claim to fame is he's Sharon Stone's cousin, and whose motto has a certain resonance: "God bless America—and no place else."

Mays bumbles through the first weeks of his campaign, following the instructions of his profoundly conventional campaign advisers, Geller and Debra Lassiter (Lynn Whitfield), until his brother, a Chicago bail bondsman named Mitch (Bernie Mac), asks him when he's going to start speaking his mind. When he does, the first thing he says is that he wants Mitch as his running mate.

This is one of the areas that doesn't work.

Bernie Mac could be a funny veep candidate, but not as a bondsman whose peculiar personal quirk is to hit people as hard as he can as a sign of friendship. The character should have been redefined, and a scene where Mays and Mitch batter each other should have been edited out; it works only as an awkward puzzlement for the audience.

Another element that doesn't work is the character of Kim (Robin Givens), who begins the movie as Mays's fiancée, is dumped, and then turns into a crazy stalker who follows him everywhere, overacting on a distressingly shrill note until she exits in a particularly nasty way. This character could have been dumped, especially since Mays meets a cute caterer named Lisa (Tamala Jones), who looks like first lady material.

Chris Rock is a smart, fast-talking comedian with an edge; I keep wondering when the Academy will figure out he could host the Oscars. Here he plays his usual persona, more or less, in a movie where some of the edges are rough and others are serrated. We keep getting these movie fantasies where political candidates say what they think, are not afraid to offend, cut through the crap, and take stands. Must be wish fulfillment.

Head Over Heels ★ ½
PG-13, 91 m., 2001

Monica Potter (Amanda Pierce), Freddie Prinze Jr. (Jim Winston), Shalom Harlow (Jade), Ivana Milicevic (Roxana), Sarah O'Hare (Candi), Tomiko Fraser (Holly), Raoul Ganeev (Harold). Directed by Mark S. Waters and produced by Julia Dray and Robert Simonds. Screenplay by Ron Burch and David Kidd.

Head Over Heels opens with fifteen funny minutes and then goes dead in the water. It's like they sent home the first team of screenwriters and brought in Beavis and Butt-Head. The movie starts out with sharp wit and edgy zingers, switches them off, and turns to bathroom humor. And not funny bathroom humor, but painfully phony gas-passing noises, followed by a plumbing emergency that buries three supermodels in a putrid delivery from where the sun don't shine. It's as if the production was a fight to the death between bright people with a sense of humor and cretins who think the audience is as stupid as they are.

Monica Potter and Freddie Prinze Jr. star, in another one of those stories where it's love at first sight and then she gets the notion that he's clubbed someone to death. The two characters were doing perfectly well being funny as *themselves,* and then the movie muzzles them and brings in this pea-brained autopilot plot involving mistaken identities, dead bodies, and the Russian mafia.

Why? I wanted to ask the filmmakers. Why? You have a terrific cast and the wit to start out well. Why surrender and sell out? Isn't it a better bet, and even better for your careers, to make a whole movie that's smart and funny, instead of showing off for fifteen minutes and then descending into cynicism and stupidity? Why not make a movie you can show to the friends you admire, instead of to a test audience scraped from the bottom of the IQ barrel?

Monica Potter is radiant as Amanda, an art restorer at the Museum of Modern Art. She has been betrayed by a boyfriend, and vows to focus on her job. "I love art better than real life," she says, because the people in paintings "stay in love forever." True of the Grecian urn, perhaps, if not of Bosch, but never mind; her latest challenge is to restore a priceless Titian, which the curator hauls into the room with his fingers all over the paint, banging it against the doorway.

Moving out from her faithless boyfriend, she finds a $500-a-month room (i.e., closet) in a vast luxury apartment occupied by "the last four nonsmoking models in Manhattan" (Shalom Harlow, Ivana Milicevic, Sarah O'Hare, and Tomiko Fraser). And then she falls head over heels in love with a neighbor, Jim (Prinze), who walks a big dog that knocks her over and sets up a conversation in which she says all of the wrong things. That's the dialogue I thought was so funny.

In a film with more confidence, the comedy would continue to be based on their relationship. This one prefers to recycle aged clichés. She thinks she sees him club someone to death. We know he didn't, because—well, because (a) it happens in silhouette, so the movie is hiding something, and (b) Freddie Prinze is not going to play a *real* club-murderer, not in a movie with a cute dog. Idiot Plot devices prevent either one of them from saying the two or three words that would clear up the misunderstanding. Meanwhile, the exhausted screenwriters haul in the Russian mafia and other sinister characters in order to make this movie as similar as possible to countless other brain-dead productions.

As my smile faded and I realized the first fifteen minutes were bait-and-switch, my restless mind sought elsewhere for employment. I focused on Amanda's job, art restoration. Her challenge: An entire face is missing from a grouping by Titian. She "restores" it by filling the gap with, yes, Freddie Prinze's face and head, complete with a haircut that doesn't exactly match the Renaissance period.

But never mind. Give the movie the benefit of the doubt. Maybe one of those Renaissance geniuses like Michelangelo invented Supercuts clippers at the same time he invented bicycles and submarines. What's really odd is that the face is not in the style of Titian, but in the style of Norman Rockwell. Obviously it was only with the greatest restraint that Amanda was able to prevent herself from adding a soda fountain to the background.

Now what about that eruption of unspeakable brown stuff that coats the supermodels as they hide behind a shower curtain in a bathroom? Why was that supposed to be funny? The scene betrays a basic ignorance of a fundamental principle of humor: It isn't funny when innocent bystanders are humiliated. It's funny when they humiliate themselves. For example, *Head Over Heels* would be funny if it were about the people making this movie.

Heartbreakers ★ ★ ★
PG-13, 123 m., 2001

Sigourney Weaver (Max), Jennifer Love Hewitt (Page), Ray Liotta (Dean Cumanno), Jason Lee (Jack), Gene Hackman (William B. Tensy), Anne Bancroft (Gloria Vogal/Barbara), Nora Dunn (Miss Madress). Directed by David Mirkin and produced by John Davis and Irving Ong. Screenplay by Robert Dunn, Paul Guay, and Stephen Mazur.

Heartbreakers is *Dirty Rotten Scoundrels* plus Gene Hackman as W. C. Fields, plus Jennifer

Love Hewitt and Sigourney Weaver walking into rooms wearing dresses that enter about a quarter of an inch after they do. I guess that's enough to recommend it. It's not a great comedy, but it's a raucous one, hardworking and ribald, and I like its spirit.

Weaver and Hewitt play Max and Page, a mother-and-daughter con team. Their scam: Max (Weaver) marries a rich guy and then surprises him in a compromising position with Page (Hewitt), after which there's a big divorce settlement. This has worked thirteen times, according to Max, whose latest victim is Dean (Ray Liotta), a chop-shop owner who falls for what my old buddy Russ Meyer would describe as Hewitt's capacious bodice.

Hewitt spends the entire film with her treasures on display, maybe as product placement for the Wonder Bra, and for that matter, Heather Graham is identically costumed in *Say It Isn't So*. The moviegoers of America owe something, possibly gratitude, to Erin Brockovich, the most influential movie style-setter since Annie Hall.

Weaver and Hewitt attack their roles with zeal, but the movie doesn't really start humming until Hackman enters. He plays William B. Tensy, a chain-smoking tobacco zillionaire who lives on the water in Palm Beach with a draconian housekeeper (Nora Dunn) and lots of ashtrays. He believes everyone, especially children, should take up smoking, and has a cigarette in his mouth at all times except when violently choking with bronchial spasms, which is frequently.

My guess is that Hackman decided to take the role when he hit on the approach of playing Tensy as W. C. Fields. There is nothing in the role as written that suggests Fields, but everything in the role as played, including Hackman's recycling of Fields's wardrobe from the famous short *The Golf Specialist* (1930).

Weaver seems tickled by the sheer awfulness of Tensy, a man most women would cross not only the room but perhaps the state to avoid. With the Liotta character she was within the guidelines of traditional farce, but with Hackman she's working without a net: What strategy *can* a woman adopt in dealing with such an astonishing combination of the gauche and the obnoxious? Their relationship concludes with a sight gag involving, of course,

cigarette smoke; I wouldn't dream of revealing one more thing about it.

Weaver's approach to Tensy is a devious one; she pretends to be Russian, which leads into a precarious situation when she's called up on the stage in a Russian nightclub and expected to sing; her response to this emergency is inspired. Not so brilliant is another strategy she and her daughter use. In restaurants, they sneak broken glass onto their salads and then complain loudly, refusing to pay. Nice, but wiser if they'd eat some of the salad course before complaining; by dropping the glass immediately, they defeat the purpose.

Anyway. While Max courts the disgusting Tensy, Hewitt, as Page, is developing a relationship with Jack (Jason Lee), the owner of a Palm Beach bar. She's torn between falling in love with him and fleecing him, especially after she learns he's been offered 3 million bucks for his bar and its waterfront property. This is the moment that will get the biggest laughs in Palm Beach, where the last time this much ocean frontage went for $3 million was when Roxanne Pulitzer was taking trumpet lessons. That both Jack and Page are dumb enough to be dazzled by the offer is a hint that they may be made for each other.

The movie has been directed by David Mirkin, who made the sly and charming *Romy and Michele's High School Reunion* (1997). *Heartbreakers* is not as sly and has no ambition to be charming, but in a season of dreary failed comedies it does what a comedy must: It makes us laugh.

The Heart of Me ★ ★ ★
R, 96 m., 2003

Helena Bonham Carter (Dinah), Olivia Williams (Madeleine), Paul Bettany (Rickie), Eleanor Bron (Mrs. Burkett), Luke Newberry (Anthony), Alison Reid (Bridie), Tom Ward (Jack), Gillian Hanna (Betty), Andrew Havill (Charles). Directed by Thaddeus O'Sullivan and produced by Martin Pope. Screenplay by Lucinda Coxon, based on the novel *The Echoing Grove* by Rosamond Lehmann.

The lovers in *The Heart of Me* have a line of poetry by William Blake as their touchstone: "And throughout all eternity, I forgive you and you forgive me." This implies much to forgive, and the movie involves a decade of suffering, punctuated by occasional bliss, and inspired by their misfortune in falling in love with one another. For theirs is not an ordinary adultery, but one complicated by the inconvenience that he is married to her sister.

The film is a soapy melodrama set from about 1936 to 1946 and done with style—Jerry Springer crossed with *Masterpiece Theater.* Helena Bonham Carter stars as Dinah, a raffish bohemian who is the despair of her sister, Madeleine (Olivia Williams), and their mother (Eleanor Bron). Madeleine at last contrives to get Dinah engaged to a presentable man, but when the intended nuptials are announced at a family dinner, we notice that Madeleine's husband, Rickie, winces. We notice, and so does Dinah, who sends him a barely perceptible shrug. Later that night Rickie (Paul Bettany) opens her bedroom door and announces, "You are not going through with this. Break it off."

She agrees. His statement clarifies what has been vibrating in the air between them, a romantic love of the abandoned, hopeless variety that is most irresistible when surrounded by the codes of a society that places great value on appearances. The family maintains "the smartest house in London," Rickie has one of those jobs in the city that provides a large income for tasks hard to define, and while there is no love between him and his wife, it is simply not done to cheat with your sister-in-law.

The movie is based on a 1953 novel by Rosamond Lehmann, and while it is hard to say it was inspired by her affair with C. Day Lewis, they had an affair, and she wrote a novel about an affair, and there you are. No doubt the facts are different, but the feelings are similar. Helena Bonham Carter does suggest a woman with something of Lehmann's flair for romantic drama; her Dinah is the kind of person it is easy to criticize until you look into her heart and see with what fierce integrity she opposes the strictures of society. It is really Dinah, and not Rickie, who is taking the big chances, because no matter what sins Rickie commits he will always be required to remain on display as Madeleine's husband, while the punishment for Dinah must be exile. "I love you!" Madeleine cries at a crucial moment, and Rickie's reply is dry and exact: "Madeleine, I

think if that were true, you would have said it sooner."

Madeleine is not a bad person either, really; she is the aggrieved party, after all, and has good reason to be cross with her sister and her husband. But it never occurs to her to cut loose from Ricky; this man who has betrayed her remains necessary for her to keep up appearances, and she and her mother tell appalling lies to both Dinah and Rickie in trying to force the relationship to an end. The great sadness in the movie is the waste of love, which is a rare commodity and must be consumed in season.

An intriguing supporting character in the movie is Bridie (Alison Reid), who serves as Dinah's confidante and companion in exile, and who, like many privileged insiders, cannot resist sharing what she knows with just those people who least should know it. As Dinah waits sadly in lovers' nests and French hideaways, it is Bridie who harbors resentments.

There are major developments in the story that I will not reveal, but, oh! how sad these people are by the end. And how pathetic. There is a certain nobility in the way Rickie, a wrecked man, displays what is left of himself to Madeleine and bitterly tells her, "This is what you fought so hard to hold onto." If they only had attended to the entire poem by Blake ("My spectre around me night and day") they would not have taken such comfort from its promise of forgiveness.

The movie has won only a mixed reception. Many of the complaints have to do with the fact that the characters are wealthy and upper-class and speak English elegantly. The names of Merchant and Ivory are used like clubs to beat the film. This is the same kind of thinking that led Jack Warner to tell his producers, "Don't give me any more pictures where they write with feathers." The movie is *about* the punishment of being trapped in a system where appearances are more important than reality. After she breaks her engagement at the beginning of the movie, Dinah has lunch with Madeleine, who says, "You've put us all in a very awkward position." Dinah said, "I thought that preferable to marrying a man I didn't love." Madeleine, on the other hand, believes it is better to marry a man you do not love than be put in an awkward position. And just as well, as that turns out to be the story of her marriage.

Hearts in Atlantis ★ ★ ★ ½
PG-13, 101 m., 2001

Anthony Hopkins (Ted Brautigan), Anton Yelchin (Bobby Garfield), Hope Davis (Liz Garfield), Mika Boorem (Carol Gerber), Will Rothhaar (Sully), David Morse (Adult Bobby Garfield), Alan Tudyk (Monte Man), Tom Bower (Len Files), Celia Weston (Alana Files). Directed by Scott Hicks and produced by Kerry Heysen. Screenplay by William Goldman, based on the book by Stephen King.

Hearts in Atlantis weaves a strange spell made of nostalgia and fear. Rarely does a movie make you feel so warm and so uneasy at the same time, as Stephen King's story evokes the mystery of adolescence, when everything seems to be happening for the very first time.

Set in 1960, the movie tells the story of an eleven-year-old named Bobby (Anton Yelchin) whose father left when he was five, whose mother (Hope Davis) seems too distracted to love him, whose life centers on his best friend, Sully (Will Rothhaar), and Carol Gerber (Mika Boorem), with whom he will share a first kiss by which he will judge all the others. As is often the case in King stories, the period is re-created through an intense memory of cars, radio shows, clothes, baseball mitts— material treasures in an uncertain world.

Then a man comes as a boarder in the upstairs apartment at Bobby's house. This is Ted Brautigan (Anthony Hopkins). "I never trust a man who carries his possessions in grocery bags," says Bobby's mother, as Ted stands on the curb without much in the way of possessions. Bobby is often home alone (his mother is much distracted by her office job), and Ted offers root beer, conversation, and even a dollar a day to read him the paper. Then he reveals a more shadowy assignment for Bobby: keeping a lookout for Low Men, who are seeking Ted because they want to use his gift. By now Bobby does not have to be told that Ted can sometimes foresee the future; Bobby has the same ability, but muted.

"One feels them first at the back of one's eyes," Ted tells Bobby, and we note how Anthony Hopkins takes this line, which could come from a cheap horror film, and invests it with nuance. The Low Men themselves are as sym-bolic as real. In the King story it's hinted they may come from another world or time, and in the movie they may be FBI agents who want to use Ted's powers for the government, but it hardly matters; in either version, they are the hard realities of an adult world that takes the gifted and the unconforming and either uses them or destroys them.

Scott Hicks and Piotr Sobocinski, who directed and photographed the movie, have wisely seen that atmosphere is everything in *Hearts of Atlantis*. They evoke a shady lower-middle-class neighborhood in a town of hills and trees, and the sleepy Sunday 1950s feel of the newspaper, root beer, Chesterfields, and a game on the radio. In this world Bobby grows up. He is threatened by an older neighborhood bully, he is in love with Carol Gerber, he is in awe of Ted. When Bobby's mother gives him an adult library card for his birthday, it is Ted who advises him which authors bear reading.

There are wonderful set pieces in the film. One of the best is the way Ted tells Bobby the story of the great Chicago Bears running back Bronco Nagurski, who came out of retirement, old and hurt, and seemed to carry the whole Chicago team on his back as he marched down the field in a last hurrah. Another is a visit to a pool hall in a neighboring town, where Ted wants to place a bet, and Bobby meets a woman who knew his father.

The movie ends as childhood ends, in disillusionment at the real world that lies ahead. Bobby's mother is cruelly divested of her illusions, and later lashes out at the innocent Ted, and then the Low Men come, as they always do. But Bobby's summer had to end, and at least he experienced the best of all possible kisses.

A movie like this is kind of a conjuring act. Like a lot of Stephen King's recent work, it is not a horror story so much as an everyday story with horror lurking in the margins. It's not a genre movie, in other words, but the story of characters we believe in and care about. Anton Yelchin is not just a cute kid but a smart and wary one, and Mika Boorem is not just the girl down the street but the kind of soul who inspires the best in others. And Anthony Hopkins finds just the tired, truthful note for Ted Brautigan—who knows the worst about men and fears for his future, but still has enough faith to believe it will do a kid good to read the right books.

Note: So should you therefore read the book after seeing the movie? I would recommend the audiobook; William Hurt's reading is one of the best audio performances I have ever heard.

Heaven ★ ★ ★
R, 96 m., 2002

Cate Blanchett (Philippa), Giovanni Ribisi (Filippo), Remo Girone (The Father), Stefania Rocca (Regina), Alessandro Sperduti (Ariel), Mattia Sbragia (Major Pini), Stefano Santospago (Mr. Vendice). Directed by Tom Tykwer and produced by Stefan Arndt, Frédérique Dumas-Zajdela, William Horberg, and Maria Köpf. Screenplay by Krzysztof Kieslowski and Krzysztof Piesiewicz.

There is a moment early in *Heaven* when the character played by Cate Blanchett is told something she did not expect to hear. This news piles grief upon unbearable grief, and she cries out in pain. She is a good woman who is prepared to sacrifice her life against evil, but through a great misfortune she has done evil herself.

She plays Philippa, a teacher of English in Turin, Italy. She has seen drugs kill her husband and some of her students. Her complaints to the police have been ignored. She knows the man behind the Turin drug traffic, and one day she plants a bomb in his office. A cleaning lady removes it with the trash, and it explodes in an elevator, killing the cleaner, a man, and his two children. Four innocent dead.

Philippa has lost her husband and her students, and stands ready to lose her freedom. But the deaths of these four crush her. We are reminded of *Running on Empty*, the 1988 Sidney Lumet film about antiwar radicals in America who did not know there would be someone in the building they chose to blow up. As Philippa sits in police headquarters, undergoing a cross-examination, unaware that one of the men in the room is himself connected to the drug trade, she makes a conquest.

His name is Filippo (Giovanni Ribisi). He is a rookie cop, the son of a veteran officer. When Philippa insists on testifying in her native tongue, Filippo offers to act as her translator.

This is after she heard the horrifying news, and passed out, and grasped his hand as she came to, and he fell in love with her.

After the ten films of *The Decalogue* and the great trilogy *Blue, White,* and *Red,* the Polish director Krzysztof Kieslowski and his writing partner Krzysztof Piesiewicz began writing a new trilogy: *Heaven, Purgatory,* and *Hell.* Kieslowski died in 1996 before the project could be filmed. Many good screenplays have died with their authors, but occasionally a director will step forward to rescue a colleague's work, as Steven Spielberg did with Kubrick's *A.I.* and now as Tom Tykwer has done with *Heaven.*

This is, and isn't, the sort of project Twyker is identified with. It is more thoughtful, proceeds more deliberately, than the mercurial haste of *Run Lola Run* and *The Princess and the Warrior.* At the same time, it has a belief in fateful meetings that occur as a side effect of violence or chance, as both of those films do. And it contains the same sort of defiant romanticism, in which a courageous woman tries to alter her fate by sheer willpower.

Philippa and Filippo have almost identical names for a reason, and later when they shave their heads and dress alike, it is because they share a common lifeline. It is not a case of merger so much as of Filippo being assumed into Philippa. She is older, stronger, braver, and he invests the capital of his life in her account. He betrays his uniform to do whatever he can to help her escape.

After she agrees to his brilliant plan, she tells him: "Do you know why I said I agree? I don't want to escape punishment. I want to kill him." Him—the man behind the drugs. Whether she gets her wish is not the point. What she focuses on is her original plan; if she can finally carry it out, she will have made amends, however inadequately, for the innocents who died.

Kieslowski was fascinated by moral paradoxes, by good leading to evil and back again. In *The Decalogue,* a child's brilliance at the computer leads to a drowning. A woman wants to know if her husband will die, because if he will not, she will have her lover's baby aborted. A wife breaks it off with her lover—but her husband tarnishes her decision by spying on them. To do good is sometimes to cause evil. We can make plans, but we can't count on the consequences.

The ending of *Heaven* is disappointing. It becomes just what it should not be, the story of an escape. I wonder if Kieslowski and Piesiewicz ended their version this way, in a fable of innocence regained. The tough ending would have had Philippa and Filippo paying for their crimes. It would not have been an unhappy ending for them; they are fully prepared to take the consequences, and that is what's most admirable about them.

Still, many lesser films—almost all commercial films these days, in fact—contrive happy endings. This one is poetic in its sadness, and the Cate Blanchett performance confirms her power once again. She never goes for an effect here, never protects herself, just plays the character straight ahead as a woman forced by grief and rage into a rash action, and then living with the consequences. We require theology to get to the bottom of the story: It is wrong to commit an immoral act in order to bring about a good outcome. No matter how beneficial the result, it is still a sin. This is a good movie that could have been great if it had ended in a form of penance.

Hedwig and the Angry Inch ★ ★ ★
R, 95 m., 2001

John Cameron Mitchell (Hansel/Hedwig), Miriam Shor (Yitzhak), Michael Pitt (Tommy Gnosis), Andrea Martin (Phyllis Stein), Alberta Watson (Hedwig's Mother), Ben Mayer-Goodman (Hansel [six years old]), Stephen Trask (Skszp), Theodore Liscinski (Jacek). Directed by John Cameron Mitchell and produced by Pamela Koffler, Katie Roumel, and Christine Vachon. Screenplay by Mitchell, based on the musical by Mitchell and Stephen Trask.

Hedwig and the Angry Inch occupies an almost extinct movie category: It's an original rock musical—indeed, according to its maker, a "postpunk neo–glam-rock musical," a category almost as specialized as the not dissimilar *Beyond the Valley of the Dolls*, which was a "camp-rock horror musical." Filmed with ferocious energy and with enough sexual variety to match late Fellini, it may be passing through standard bookings on its way to a long run as the midnight successor to *The Rocky Horror Picture Show.*

Hedwig began life in 1997 as an off-Broadway musical, and now arrives as a movie with its cult status already established. It tells the story of an East German boy named Hansel who grows up gay, falls in love with a U.S. master sergeant, and wants to go to America with him. The master sergeant explains that, as Hansel, that will be impossible, but if the lad undergoes a sex-change operation, they can get married and then the passport will be no problem ("To walk away, you gotta leave something behind").

Hansel becomes Hedwig (John Cameron Mitchell) in a botched operation that leaves a little too much behind (thus the title), and she soon finds herself abandoned in a Kansas trailer park. She turns tricks at a nearby military base, becomes a baby-sitter for the general, and meets the general's son, Tommy Gnosis (Michael Pitt). They're lovers, until Tommy discovers the secret of Hedwig's transsexualism and abandons her—quickly becoming a rock star on the basis of songs stolen from Hedwig.

All of this we discover in flashback. The movie opens with Hedwig on a national tour with her own band ("The Angry Inch"). Her itinerary makes her into a virtual stalker of Tommy Gnosis, with the difference that while Tommy plays stadiums, Hedwig plays behind the salad bar of a fast-food chain called Bilgewater's. The customers look on in disbelief, and would be even more disbelieving if they could study the lyrics and discover that the songs (by Stephen Trask and Mitchell) add up to an Aristotelian argument about gender and wholeness.

John Cameron Mitchell electrifies the movie with a performance that isn't a satire of glam-rock performers so much as an authentic glam-rock performance. The movie may have had a limited budget, but the screen is usually filled with something sensational, including a trailer home that transforms itself in an instant into a stage. Michael Pitt's performance as Tommy is all the more astonishing if you've recently seen him, as I did, playing Donny, the overgrown tough kid, in *Bully.*

This material could have been glib and smug, but it isn't. There's some kind of pulse of sincerity beating below the glittering surface, and it may come from Mitchell's own life story. He was raised in Berlin as the son of the general in charge of the U.S. military garrison there.

275

(The defense secretary at the time was Dick Cheney; did they discuss their gay children?) The fall of the Berlin Wall must have made an impression on young John Cameron Mitchell, as did also the wild nightlife scene in Berlin, and in a way the movie is about a collision between those two inspirations.

The filmmaking is as free-form as such movies as *Pink Floyd the Wall*. There's an animated sequence to illustrate one of the songs, and a bouncing ball for a sing-along; the musical numbers spill out from behind the salad bar to become as exuberant as something from MGM. Hedwig stands astride the material, sometimes literally, and it's interesting that the character is presented as someone whose sex change was not eagerly sought, but seemed to be a necessary by-product of love. Does Hedwig really want to be a boy or a girl? And what about Yitzhak (Miriam Shor), who may be her boyfriend, although the movie doesn't say for sure. Strange, how the movie seems to be loud, flashy, and superficial, and yet gives a deeper dimension to its characters.

Heist ★ ★ ★ ½
R, 107 m., 2001

Gene Hackman (Joe Moore), Danny DeVito (Mickey Bergman), Delroy Lindo (Bobby Blane), Sam Rockwell (Jimmy Silk), Rebecca Pidgeon (Fran), Ricky Jay (Pinky Pincus), Patti LuPone (Betty Croft), Jim Frangione (D. A. Freccia). Directed by David Mamet and produced by Art Linson, Elie Samaha, and Andrew Stevens. Screenplay by Mamet.

David Mamet's *Heist* is about a caper and a con, involving professional criminals who want to retire but can't. It's not that they actually require more money. It's more that it would be a sin to leave it in civilian hands. Gene Hackman plays a jewel thief who dreams of taking his last haul and sailing into the sunset with his young wife (Rebecca Pidgeon). Danny DeVito is the low-rent mastermind who forces him into pulling one last job. Hackman complains he doesn't need any more money. DeVito's wounded reply is one of the funniest lines Mamet has ever written: "Everybody needs money! That's why they call it money!"

Hackman plays Joe Moore, a thief whose real love is building and sailing boats. His crew includes Bobby Blane (Delroy Lindo) and Pinky Pincus (Ricky Jay); his wife, Fran (Pidgeon), is a groupie who has confused danger with foreplay. They pull off a big job, with one hitch: Moore is caught on a security camera. Time to haul anchor and head for Caribbean ports—but not according to Mickey Bergman (DeVito), who pressures Joe into pulling one last job and insists he take along his feckless nephew Jimmy Silk (Sam Rockwell). Jimmy is the kind of hothead who carries a gun because he lives in a dangerous neighborhood, which would be safer if he moved.

The plot moves through labyrinthine levels of double cross. Mamet loves magic, especially sleight of hand (his favorite supporting actor, Ricky Jay, is a great card artist), and the plot of *Heist*, like those of *The Spanish Prisoner* and *House of Games*, is a prism that reflects different realities depending on where you're standing. It also incorporates a lot of criminal craft, as in the details of the diamond robbery that opens the movie, and the strategy for stealing gold bars from a cargo plane at the end.

When the movie played at the Venice, Toronto, and Chicago festivals, some critics disliked the details I enjoyed the most. We learn from *Variety* that "some late-reel gunplay could have benefited enormously from more stylish handling." This is astonishingly wrongheaded. Does *Variety* mean it would have preferred one of those by-the-numbers high-tech gunfights we're weary of after countless retreads? "Stylish handling" in a gunfight is for me another way of saying the movie's on autopilot.

What I like about the "late-reel" gunplay in *Heist* is the way some of the shooters are awkward and self-conscious; this is arguably the first gunfight of their lives. And the way DeVito dances into the path of the bullets hysterically trying to get everybody to stop shooting ("Let's talk this over!"). The precision with which Hackman says, "He isn't gonna shoot me? Then he hadn't oughta point a gun at me. It's insincere." And the classical perfection of this exchange:

"Don't you want to hear my last words?"
"I just did."

I am also at a loss to understand why critics pick on Rebecca Pidgeon. Yes, she has a distinctive style of speech that is well suited to Mametian dialogue: crisp, clipped, colloquial. Mamet loves to fashion anachronisms for her ("You're the law west of the Pecos"). She is not intended as a slinky *film noir* seductress, but as a plucky kid-sister type who can't quite be trusted. Mamet goes to the trouble of supplying us with style and originality, and is criticized because his films don't come from the cookie cutter.

Hackman, of course, is a dab hand at tough, grizzled veterans. ("Dab hand"—that could be a Pidgeon line.) He and Lindo inhabit their characters so easily they distract from the plot twists by the simple sincerity with which they confront them. Their world-wise dialogue is like a magician's patter, directing our attention away from the artifice. And DeVito is one of the most consistently entertaining actors in the movies, with an energy that makes his dialogue vibrate. "I've just financialized the numbers," he explains. He is not a bad man in this movie. Just an unprincipled greedy-guts with dangerous associates.

Close attention may reveal a couple of loopholes in the plot. One wonders why the Pidgeon character would do what she does after the truck crashes. Whether we can be sure that her last revelation is, indeed, her last revelation. And the film ends with a character who gives us a little smile that seems wrong, because he is smiling at the audience and not at what has happened. Unless, of course, he knows the last revelation is not the last revelation.

Heist is the kind of caper movie that was made before special effects replaced wit, construction, and intelligence. This movie is made out of fresh ingredients, not cake mix. Despite the twists of its plot, it is about its characters. Consider the exchanges between Lindo and Hackman: They have a shorthand that convinces us they've worked together for a very long time and are in agreement on everything that matters. Most modern caper movies convince us the characters met this morning on the set.

Herod's Law ★ ★
R, 120 m., 2003

Damián Alcázar (Juan Vargas), Leticia Huijara (Gloria), Pedro Armendáriz Jr. (López), Delia Casanova (Rosa), Juan Carlos Colombo (Ramírez), Alex Cox (Gringo), Guillermo Gil (Padre), Eduardo López Rojas (Doctor), Salvador Sánchez (Pek), Isele Vega (Doña Lupe). Directed and produced by Luis Estrada. Screenplay by Estrada, Jaime Sampietro, Fernando León, and Vicente Leñero.

Juan Vargas is a simple man with unswerving loyalty to the party, and that is why he is chosen to be the mayor of San Pedro. There is an election coming up, three mayors have been killed in the last five years, and López, the regional party leader, hopes Vargas can keep the lid on and not cause much trouble. As Juan (Damián Alcázar) and his wife, Gloria (Leticia Huijara), drive to San Pedro in the dusty Packard supplied by the party, they dream of his assignment to bring "Modernity, Peace, and Progress" to the little town, little suspecting how little it is.

"Where is San Pedro?" Juan asks a man. "This is it," the man replies. "I am Pek, your secretary." Vargas and his wife look around in dismay at the pathetic hamlet he is to lead. Pek (Salvador Sánchez) will be invaluable, because he speaks the Indian language, and few of the residents speak Spanish. Vargas quickly meets other important local figures, including the doctor (Eduardo López Rojas), the priest (Guillermo Gil), and Doña Lupe (Isele Vega), the madam of the local brothel.

All of the trouble in San Pedro comes from the brothel, the doctor bitterly tells Vargas. It is responsible for disease, corruption, murder. The padre is more forgiving: "San Pedro lacks many things, and Doña Lupe performs an important social function." The priest advises Vargas to accept Doña Lupe's bribes so that village life will continue as before. This is a mercenary padre: In the confessional, he charges one peso per sin and pointedly informs Vargas he would like a car: "A Ford . . . or perhaps a Packard, like yours."

Herod's Law uses Vargas and his backwater town to form a parable about political corruption in Mexico in 1949—and before and since, we have no doubt. It is a savage attack on the Institutional Revolutionary Party (PRI), which ruled Mexico from the days of revolution until the recent rise of President Vicente Fox and his National Action Party. In the figure of Juan Vargas, it sees a humble working-class man with

277

high ideals, who caves in to the temptations of high office, even in so low a town, and is soon demanding bribes, making himself mayor for life, and paying free visits to Doña Lupe's girls. He justifies his actions with a motto learned from his party leader, who quotes Herod's Law, which is (somewhat reworded), "Either you screw them or you get screwed."

His wife, who is not blind to Juan's visits to the brothel, finds consolation from a visiting American (Alex Cox). The gringo's function in the parable is not difficult to decipher: He repairs Juan's car, demands an exorbitant payment, moves into Juan's house, and has sex with his wife. I think (I am pretty sure, actually) this is intended to suggest the helpful role of American advisers in Mexico.

The film is bold and passionate, but not subtle, and that is its downfall. Luis Estrada, the writer and director, uses his characters so clearly as symbols that he neglects to give them the complexity of human beings. Juan Vargas begins as a simple and honest idealist and then converts to corruption so instantly at the sight of money that we have little idea of who he really was before or after. His escalation into a madman and murderer is laying it on a little thick; the recent Mexican film *The Crime of Father Amaro* made a similar critique of Mexican society and the church without such heavy-handed, almost comic, melodrama.

There are a couple of scenes that suggest a more moderate approach Estrada might have taken. One involves a dinner in the midst of all the chaos, at which the principal characters sit down to discuss their nation. The American is asked his opinion, and refers to Mexico as a "dictatorship," which makes the others, except the doctor, laugh. The doctor observes, "In Mexico if there were true democracy, the president would be a priest."

Note: Isele Vega, who plays Doña Lupe, starred as a prostitute in Sam Peckinpah's Bring Me the Head of Alfredo Garcia. *It must be a nod to that movie that this one has a character named Alfredo Garcia.*

High Crimes ★ ★ ★
PG-13, 115 m., 2002

Ashley Judd (Claire Kubik), Morgan Freeman

(Charles Grimes), James Caviezel (Tom Kubik), Adam Scott (Lieutenant Terrence Embry), Amanda Peet (Jackie Grimaldi), Michael Gaston (Major Waldron), Tom Bower (FBI Agent Mullins), Jesse Beaton (Ramona Phillips). Directed by Carl Franklin and produced by Arnon Milchan, Janet Yang, and Jesse B'Franklin. Screenplay by Yuri Zeltser and Cary Bickley, based on the novel by Joseph Finder.

Although I believe Ashley Judd could thrive in more challenging roles, and offer *Normal Life* (1996) as an example, her career seems to tilt toward thrillers, with the occasional comedy. She often plays a strong, smart woman who is in more danger than she realizes. Although her characters are eventually screaming as they flee brutal killers in the long tradition of Women in Danger movies, the setups show her as competent, resourceful, independent.

High Crimes is a movie like that. Judd plays Claire Kubik, a high-profile defense attorney for a big firm. When her ex-soldier husband (Jim Caviezel) is arrested by the FBI, charged with murder, and arraigned before a military tribunal, she defiantly says she will defend him herself. And because she doesn't know her way around military justice, she enlists a lawyer named Grimes (Morgan Freeman) as co-counsel. Grimes is that dependable character, a drunk who is on the wagon but may (i.e., will) fall off under stress.

This is the second movie Judd and Freeman have made together (after *Kiss the Girls* in 1997). They're both good at projecting a kind of southern intelligence that knows its way around the frailties of human nature. Although Freeman refers to himself as the "wild card" in the movie, actually that role belongs to Caviezel, whose very identity is called into question by the military charges. "Is your name Tom Kubik?" Claire asks her husband at one point. She no longer knows the answer.

The plot involves a massacre in a Latin American village and a subsequent cover-up. Did Claire's husband gun down innocent civilians, or was he framed by a scary marine vet and his straight-arrow superior? Does the military want justice or a cover-up? We are not given much reason to trust military tribunals—evidence the screenplay was written before 9/11—and the Freeman character intones the familiar refrain, "Military justice is to justice as military music is to music."

And yet . . . well, maybe there's more to the story. I wouldn't dream of revealing crucial details. I do like the way director Carl Franklin and writers Yuri Zeltser and Cary Bickley, working from Joseph Finder's novel, play both ends against the middle, so that the audience has abundant evidence to believe two completely conflicting theories of what actually happened. In the very season of the DVD release of *Rashomon,* which is the template for stories with more than one convincing explanation, here's another example of how Kurosawa's masterpiece continues to inspire movie plots.

High Crimes works to keep us involved and make us care. Although Freeman's character may indeed start drinking again, it won't be for reasons we can anticipate (of course, like all heroic movie drunks, he retains the exquisite timing to sober up on demand). The unfolding of various versions of the long-ago massacre is handled by Franklin in flashbacks that show how one camera angle can refute what another angle seems to prove. And if we feel, toward the end, a little whiplashed by the plot manipulations, well, that's what the movie promises and that's what the movie delivers.

As for Miss Judd. From the first time I saw her, in *Ruby in Paradise* (1993), I thought she had a unique sympathy with the camera, an ability that cannot be learned but only exercised. In the years since then, she has often been better than her material—or do her advisers choose mainstream commercial roles for her as the safest course? When she strays out of genre, as she did in *Smoke, Heat, Normal Life,* and *Simon Birch,* she shows how good she is. Of course, she's good in *High Crimes,* too, and involves us more than the material really deserves. But this is the kind of movie any studio executive would green light without a moment's hesitation—always an ominous sign.

Himalaya ★ ★ ★

NO MPAA RATING, 104 m., 2001

Thinlin Lhondup (Tinle), Gurgon Kyap (Karma), Karma Wangiel (Passang/Tsering), Lhakpa Tsamchoe (Pema), Karma Tenzing Nyima Lama (Norbou). Directed by Eric Valli and produced by Jacques Perrin and Christophe Barratier. Screenplay by Olivier Dazat and Valli.

Himalaya tells the story of a village that since time immemorial has engaged in a winter trek to bring salt to its people and send out goods to be traded. The journeys are conducted by yak caravans. For many years the old chief, Tinle, led the treks, but he retired in favor of his son. Now his son is dead, his body brought back to the village by Karma, who wants to take his place at the head of the caravans.

Tinle (Thinlin Lhondup) is not so sure. He is half-convinced Karma (Gurgon Kyap) has something to do with the death of the son. And he believes the position of honor should remain within his own family. He goes to visit another son, who is a monk in a Buddhist monastery. This son wants to stay where he is. So Tinle defiantly says he will come out of retirement and lead the next caravan. And Karma says, no, he will lead it instead.

So begins *Himalaya,* a film of unusual visual beauty and enormous intrinsic interest. Set in the Dolpo area of Nepal, it has been directed by Eric Valli, a photographer who has lived in Nepal for years, filmed it for *National Geographic,* and made documentaries about it. Now in this fiction film he uses conflict to build his story, but it's clear the narrative is mostly an excuse; this movie is not so much about what its characters do, as about who they are.

It is astonishing to think that lives like this are still possible in the twenty-first century. We are less surprised when we see such treks reflecting modern realities—as in *A Time for Drunken Horses* (2000), about the Kurdish people of Iran, who use mule caravans to transport contraband truck tires into Iraq. We suspect that the story of *Himalaya* re-creates a time that has now ended, but no: Such caravans still exist, and were the subject of *The Saltmen of Tibet,* a 1997 documentary by Ulrike Koch.

Much of the film is simply pictorial, as Karma and Tinle make rival journeys, and Tinle ominously squints at the clear sky and foresees snow. There is one passage of pure suspense, as part of a narrow mountain path slips away, and the yaks and their masters have to traverse a dangerous stretch; we are reminded of similar situations involving trucks in *The Wages of Fear* and *Sorcerer.*

The actors are not experienced and sometimes simply seem to be playing men very much like themselves, but we are not much concerned with subtle drama here. The real movie takes place in our minds, as we think about these people who share the planet with us right now, and yet lead unimaginably different lives. Would it be a trial or a blessing to be a member of a community like this? That would depend, I imagine, on whether your view of the world has expanded to encompass more than villages and salt journeys. There must be something deeply satisfying about knowing your place in an ancient social structure, and fitting into it seamlessly. So I thought as I watched this film, although it did not make me want to lead a yak caravan.

Holes ★ ★ ★ ½
PG, 111 m., 2003

Sigourney Weaver (The Warden), Jon Voight (Mr. Sir), Patricia Arquette (Kissin' Kate), Tim Blake Nelson (Mr. Pendanski), Dule Hill (Sam), Shia LaBeouf (Stanley IV), Henry Winkler (Stanley III),Nathan Davis (Stanley II), Khleo Thomas (Hector Zero), Eartha Kitt (Madame Zeroni). Directed by Andrew Davis and produced by Davis, Lowell D. Blank, Mike Medavoy, and Teresa Tucker-Davies. Screenplay by Louis Sachar, based on his novel.

"You take a bad boy, make him dig holes all day long in the hot sun, it makes him a good boy. That's our philosophy here at Camp Green Lake."

So says Mr. Sir, the overseer of a bizarre juvenile correction center that sits in the middle of the desert, surrounded by countless holes, each one five feet deep and five feet wide. It is the fate of the boys sentenced there to dig one hole a day, day after day; like Sisyphus, who was condemned to forever roll a rock to the top of a hill so that it could roll back down again, they are caught in a tragic loop.

Holes, which tells their story, is a movie so strange that it escapes entirely from the family genre and moves into fantasy. Like *Willy Wonka and the Chocolate Factory,* it has fearsome depths and secrets. Based on the much-honored young adult's novel by Louis Sachar, it has been given the top-shelf treatment: The director is Andrew Davis *(The Fugitive)* and the cast includes not only talented young stars but also weirdness from such adults as Jon Voight, Sigourney Weaver, Tim Blake Nelson, and Patricia Arquette.

In a time when mainstream action is rigidly contained within formulas, maybe there's more freedom to be found in a young people's adventure. *Holes* jumps the rails, leaves all expectations behind, and tells a story that's not funny ha-ha but funny peculiar. I found it original and intriguing. It'll be a change after dumbed-down, one-level family stories, but a lot of kids in the upper grades will have read the book, and no doubt their younger brothers and sisters have had it explained to them. (If you doubt the novel's Harry Potter–like penetration into the youth culture, ask a seventh-grader who Armpit is.)

The story involves Stanley Yelnats IV (Shia LaBeouf), a good kid who gets charged with a crime through no fault of his own, and is shipped off to Camp Green Lake, which is little more than a desert bunkhouse surrounded by holes. There he meets his fellow prisoners and the ominous supervisory staff: Mr. Sir (Jon Voight) and Mr. Pendanski (Tim Blake Nelson) report to the Warden (Sigourney Weaver), and both men are thoroughly intimidated by her. All three adult actors take their work seriously; they don't relax because this is a family movie, but create characters of dark comic menace. Voight's work is especially detailed; watch him spit in his hand to slick back his hair.

Holes involves no less than two flashback stories. We learn that young Stanley comes from a long line of Yelnatses (all named Stanley, because it is the last name spelled backward). From his father (Henry Winkler) and grandfather (Nathan Davis) he learns of an ancient family curse, traced back many generations to an angry fortune-teller (Eartha Kitt; yes, Eartha Kitt). The other flashback explains the real reason the Warden wants the boys to dig holes; it involves the buried treasure of a legendary bandit queen named Kissin' Kate Barlow (Arquette).

There is a link between these two back stories, supplied by Zero (Khleo Thomas), who becomes Stanley's best friend and shares a harrowing adventure with him. Zero runs away despite Mr. Sir's warning that there is no water for miles around, and when Stanley joins him they stumble upon ancient clues and modern astonishments.

Shia LaBeouf and Khleo Thomas are both new to me, although LaBoeuf is the star of a cable series, *Even Stevens*. They carry the movie with an unforced conviction, and successfully avoid playing cute. As they wander in the desert and discover the keys to their past and present destinies, they develop a partnership which, despite the fantastical material, seems like the real thing.

The whole movie generates a surprising conviction. No wonder young viewers have embraced it so eagerly: It doesn't condescend, and it founds its story on recognizable human nature. There are all sorts of undercurrents, such as the edgy tension between the Warden and Mr. Sir that add depth and intrigue; Voight and Weaver don't simply play caricatures.

Davis has always been a director with a strong visual sense, and the look of *Holes* has a noble, dusty loneliness. We feel we are actually in a limitless desert. The cinematographer, Stephen St. John, thinks big, and frames his shots for an epic feel that adds weight to the story. I walked in expecting a movie for thirteen-somethings, and walked out feeling challenged and satisfied. Curious, how much more grown-up and sophisticated *Holes* is than *Anger Management.*

Hollywood Ending ★ ★ ½
PG-13, 114 m., 2002

Woody Allen (Val Waxman), Tea Leoni (Ellie), George Hamilton (Ed), Debra Messing (Lori), Mark Rydell (Al Hack), Tiffani Thiessen (Sharon Bates), Treat Williams (Hal), Barney Cheng (Translator). Directed by Woody Allen and produced by Letty Aronson. Screenplay by Allen.

Val Waxman is a movie director going through a slow period in his career. Maybe it's more like a slow decade. He left his last movie project, explaining, "I quit over a big thing." What was that? "They fired me." Then he gets a big break:

Galaxie Studios has just green-lighted *While the City Sleeps,* and his ex-wife has convinced the studio head that Val, despite his laundry list of psychosomatic anxieties and neurotic tics, is the right guy to direct it.

Woody Allen's new comedy, *Hollywood Ending,* quickly adds a complication to this setup: Waxman goes blind. It may all be in his mind, but he can't see a thing. For his ever-smiling agent, Al Hack (Mark Rydell), this is insufficient cause to leave the project. Al says he will glide through the picture at Waxman's elbow, and no one will ever notice. When the studio demurs at the agent being on the set, Al and Val recruit another seeing-eye man: the business student (Barney Cheng) who has been hired as the translator for the Chinese cinematographer. The translator says he'll blend right in: "I will practice casual banter."

Further complications: Waxman's ex-wife, Ellie (Tea Leoni), is now engaged to Hal (Treat Williams), the head of Galaxie Studios. Waxman casts his current squeeze, Lori (Debra Messing), to star in the movie, but while Lori is away at a spa getting in shape, costar Sharon (Tiffani Thiessen) moves on Waxman. In his dressing room, she removes her robe while explaining that she is eager to perform sexual favors for all of her directors (Waxman, who cannot see her abundant cleavage, helpfully suggests she advertise this willingness in the *Directors Guild* magazine).

What is Val Waxman's movie about? We have no idea. Neither does Waxman, who agrees with every suggestion so he won't have to make any decisions. He's not only blind but apparently has ears that don't work in stereo, since he can't tell where people are standing by the sound of their voices, and spends much of his time gazing into space. No one notices this, maybe because directors are such gods on movies that they can get away with anything.

The situation is funny, and Allen of course populates it with zingy one-liners, orchestrated with much waving of the hands (he's a virtuoso of body language). But somehow the movie doesn't get over the top. It uses the blindness gimmick in fairly obvious ways, and doesn't bring it to another level—to build on the blindness instead of just depending on it. When Waxman confesses his handicap to the wrong woman—a celebrity journalist—because he thinks he's sitting next to someone he can trust, that's very funny. But too often he's just seen with a vacant stare, trying to bluff his way through conversations.

Why not use the realities of a movie set to suggest predicaments for the secretly blind? Would Val always need to take his translator into the honey wagon with him? Could there be tragic misunderstandings in the catering line? Would he wander unknowingly into a shot? How about the cinematographer offering him a choice of lenses, and he chooses the lens cap? David Mamet's *State and Main* does a better job of twisting the realities of a movie into the materials of comedy.

Because Allen is a great verbal wit and because he's effortlessly ingratiating, I had a good time at the movie even while not really buying it. I enjoyed Tea Leoni's sunny disposition, although she spends too much time being the peacemaker between the two men in her life and not enough time playing a character who is funny in herself. George Hamilton, as a tanned studio flunky, suggests a familiar Hollywood type, the guy who is drawing a big salary for being on the set without anybody being quite sure what he's there for (he carries a golf club to give himself an identity—the guy who carries the golf club). And Mark Rydell smiles and smiles and smiles, as an agent who reasons that anything he has 10 percent of must be an unqualified good thing. As Waxman's seeing eyes, Barney Cheng adds a nice element: Not only is Waxman blind, but he is being given an inexact description of the world through the translator's English, which is always slightly off-track.

I liked the movie without loving it. It's not great Woody Allen, like *Sweet and Lowdown* or *Bullets Over Broadway*, but it's smart and sly, and the blindness is an audacious idea. It also has moments when you can hear Allen editorializing in the dialogue. My favorite is this exchange:

"He has made some very financially successful American films."

"That should tell you everything you need to know about him."

Hollywood Homicide ★ ★ ★
PG-13, 111 m., 2003

Harrison Ford (Joe Gavilan), Josh Hartnett (K. C. Calden), Lena Olin (Ruby), Lolita Davidovich (Cleo), Bruce Greenwood (Bennie Macko), Keith David (Lieutenant Fuqua). Directed by Ron Shelton and produced by Lou Pitt and Shelton. Screenplay by Robert Souza and Shelton.

The most popular occupations in movies about Hollywood are cops, crooks, hookers, psychics, and actors, and to this list we must add the people they are all terrified of, real estate brokers.

Hollywood Homicide covers these bases with a murderer, a cop who is a realtor, a cop who wants to be an actor, and a psychic who can visualize that the murderer will be in an SUV on Rodeo Drive in half an hour. There are also two hookers, although one scarcely counts, being an undercover cop in drag. Still, in Hollywood, maybe that does count.

The movie stars Harrison Ford and Josh Hartnett as the two cops, named Joe Gavilan and K. C. Calden, who are detectives assigned to Hollywood. Gavilan is so preoccupied with his real estate business that he tries to sell a house to the owner of a club where four rappers have just been killed, and later negotiates the purchase price during a police chase. Calden has decided he wants to be an actor, and makes Gavilan run lines for him from *A Streetcar Named Desire*. Gavilan is not impressed: "Who wrote this stuff?"

The movie was directed by Ron Shelton, who cowrote with Robert Souza. Shelton also made *Bull Durham* and *White Men Can't Jump* and specializes in funny dialogue for guy characters who would rather talk than do just about anything else. One of the pleasures of *Hollywood Homicide* is that it's more interested in its two goofy cops than in the murder plot; their dialogue redeems otherwise standard scenes. It's kind of a double act, between a man who has seen everything and a man who's seen too much.

Consider a scene where K. C. commandeers a vehicle containing a mother and her two small children. He needs it to chase a bad guy. "We're gonna die!" whines one of the kids. "Yes," agrees

K. C., who moonlights as a yoga instructor, "we *are* all going to die someday, but . . ." His philosophical observations are cut short by a crash.

The movie opens with a hit on a rap group in a music club. Four people are dead when Joe and K.C. turn up to investigate. Joe immediately sends out for food. K.C. tells the club owner he is an actor. Their investigation is hampered by an inconvenient development: They are under investigation by Bennie Macko (Bruce Greenwood), the Internal Affairs guy who hates Joe, and who reminds us once again that movie villains usually have a hard C or K in their names.

Joe is suspected of "mingling funds," which is to say, he confuses his personal debts and the debts of his real estate business. He has been seen with Cleo (Lolita Davidovich), who is a known hooker. No wonder; you do not get to be an unknown hooker by being chauffeured around town in your own stretch limousine. Internal Affairs thinks he is fooling around with Cleo, but he isn't; he's fooling around with Ruby the psychic (Lena Olin). She's yet another in the baffling legion of Los Angeles women who believe it is fun to make love on a blanket on the hardwood floor of an empty house while surrounded by a lot of candles.

At Harrison Ford's age, this qualifies as a dangerous stunt. But Ford just gets better, more distilled, more laconic, and more gruffly likable year after year. It is hard to catch him doing anything at all while he's acting, and yet whatever it is he isn't doing, it works. You don't feel he's going for laughs when he tries to sell the club owner a house while the two of them are standing in fresh pools of blood, metaphorically speaking; you feel he desperately needs to unload the house.

Hartnett makes an able partner for Ford, trading deadpan dialogue and telling everyone he's really an actor. He's given one of Shelton's nicest little scenes, when he goes to the morgue and looks at the dead bodies of the murder victims (he hates looking at dead bodies), and then notices some other dead bodies that have just arrived at the morgue, checks their shoe sizes, and says, "Hey . . . those guys shot these guys."

There is a chase and a half near the end of the movie, a lot of it near the Kodak Theatre at Hollywood and Highland. That gives the movie a chance to interrupt Robert Wagner as he's leaving his handprints in front of Graumann's Chinese Theater, and indeed the movie is filled with cameos and walk-bys, including Frank Sinatra Jr. as a showbiz lawyer, Martin Landau very funny as a fading producer who needs to unload his mansion, Lou Diamond Phillips as Wanda the cop in drag, Gladys Knight, Dwight Yoakam, Isaiah Washington, Master P, Kurupt, Eric Idle, Dr. Dre, and just plain Dre.

Much of the closing excitement depends on the Fallacy of the Climbing Killer, that dependable chase cliché in which the killer climbs to a high place, from which he cannot escape unless he can fly. *Hollywood Homicide* uses this as an excuse to show police helicopters and TV news helicopters crowding each other out of the skies. It's a skillful chase, well done, but the dialogue is the reason to see the movie. This may be the most exciting film ever made about real estate.

Home Movie ★ ★ ★
NO MPAA RATING, 65 m., 2002

As themselves: Linda Beech, Francis Mooney, Diana Peden, Ed Peden, Darlene Satrinano, Ben Skora, Bill Tregle, Bob Walker. A documentary film directed by Chris Smith and produced by Barbara Laffey and Susane Preissler.

The five homes in Chris Smith's *Home Movie* are no doubt strange and eccentric. Not everyone would choose to live on a houseboat in alligator country, or in a missile silo, or in a tree house, or in a house modified for the comfort of dozens of cats, or in a house that looks like Rube Goldberg running berserk.

But what is a normal house, anyway? In *The Fast Runner*, we see a civilization that lives in igloos. In *Taiga*, we visit the yurt dwellers of Outer Mongolia. Their homes are at least functional, economical, and organic to the surrounding landscape. It's possible that the most bizarre homestyles on Earth are those proposed by Martha Stewart, which cater to the neuroses of women with paralyzing insecurity. What woman with a healthy self-image could possibly dream of making those table decorations?

The five subjects of *Home Movie* at least know exactly why they live where they do and as they do, and they do not require our permission or approval. There is Bill Tregle, whose Louisiana houseboat is handy for his occupation of trapping, selling, and exhibiting alligators. He catches his dinner from a line tossed from the deck, has electric lights, a microwave and a TV powered by generator, pays no taxes, moves on when he feels like it, and has decorated his interior with the treasures of a lifetime.

Or consider the Pedens, Ed and Diana, who live in a converted missile silo. The concrete walls are so thick that they can have "tornado parties," and there's an easy commute down a buried tunnel from the living space to the work space. True, they had to build a greenhouse on the surface to get some sun or watch the rain, because otherwise, Diana observes, it's too easy to stay underground for days or weeks at a time. Their living room is the silo's former launch center: interesting karma.

Linda Beech speaks little Japanese, yet once starred on a Japanese soap opera. Now she lives in the Hawaiian rain forest, in a tree house equipped with all the comforts of home. To be sure, family photos tend to mildew, but think of the compensations, such as her own waterfall, which provides hydroelectric power for electricity, and also provides her favorite meditation spot, on a carefully positioned "water-watching rock." She can't imagine anyone trying to live without their own waterfall.

Bob Walker and Francis Mooney have dozens of cats. They've renovated the inside of their house with perches, walkways, and tunnels, some of them linking rooms, others ending in hidey-holes. They speculate about how much less their house is worth today than when they purchased it, but they're serene: They seem to live in a mutual daze of cat-loving. The cats seem happy too.

Ben Skora lives in a suburb of Chicago. His house is an inventor's hallucination. Everything is automatic: the doors, which open like pinwheels, the toilets, the lights, the furniture. The hardest task, living in his house, must be to remember where all the switches are and what they govern. He also has a remote-controlled robot that is a hit at shopping malls. The robot will bring him a can of pop, which is nice, although the viewer may reflect that it is easier to get a can out of the refrigerator than build a robot to do it for you. Skora's great masterwork is a ski jump that swoops down from his roof.

Are these people nuts? Who are we to say? I know people whose lives are lived in basement rec rooms. Upstairs they have a living room with the lamps and sofas still protected with plastic covers from the furniture store. What is the purpose of this room? To be a Living Room Museum? What event will be earth-shaking enough to require the removal of the covers? Do they hope their furniture will appreciate in value?

There is no philosophy, so far as I can tell, behind Chris Smith's film. He simply celebrates the universal desire to fashion our homes for our needs and desires. Smith's previous doc was the great *American Movie*, about the Wisconsin man who wanted to make horror movies, and did, despite all obstacles. Perhaps the message is the same: If it makes you happy and allows you to express your yearnings and dreams, who are we to enforce the rules of middle-class conformity?

The Hot Chick ★ ½

PG-13, 101 m., 2002

Rob Schneider (Clive), Anna Faris (April), Matthew Lawrence (Billy), Rachel McAdams (Jessica Spencer). Directed by Tom Brady and produced by Carr D'Angelo and John Schneider. Screenplay by Tom Brady and Rob Schneider.

The Hot Chick is about a woman who is magically transported into a man's body, and takes several days to learn how to urinate correctly with her new equipment. This despite getting a how-to lecture from a helpful washroom attendant. Luckily, she finds that passing gas is a skill that ports easily between the genders. Meanwhile, the former occupant of her male body has been magically transported into her former female body, and immediately becomes a hooker and a stripper.

How is this switch possible? It happens because of a pair of magic earrings. Their history is shown in an introductory scene helpfully subtitled, "Abyssinia, 50 B.C." The scene is clearly inspired by *The Arabian Nights;* the screenplay is by the director, Tom Brady, and the star, Rob Schneider, who have confused Africa with the Middle East, but the prologue is over before we can grow depressed by its geographical and ethnographic ignorance.

In modern times, we are introduced to a cadre of hot chicks who all go to the same high school. The Rob Schneider character, named Clive, no doubt after Clive of India, who would have been a much more interesting character, mugs one of the hot chicks and gets one of her earrings. When Clive and the chick put on the earrings, they are wondrously transported into each other's bodies. Jessica (Rachel McAdams) occupies Clive.

Clive also occupies Jessica, but only gets a couple of scenes, in which he quickly masters feminine skills, starting with buying tampons and progressing quickly to stripping. The movie's conviction that we would rather see the outside of Rob Schneider's body than the outside of Rachel McAdams's body is not the least of its miscalculations. Rob Schneider's outside has most of its scenes with Jessica's best friend, played by Anna Faris, whose resemblance to Britney Spears in the hair and makeup departments is a complete coincidence.

The way the movie handles the switch is that Rob Schneider, visually appearing as himself, has Jessica trapped inside. He/she convinces his/her best girlfriends of this transformation. This is one of the most astonishing events in the history of mankind, incredible and miraculous, and so what inflames the curiosity of the three girlfriends? His penis.

That they are stupid goes without saying. That the filmmakers could think of nothing more creative to do with their premise is a cause for despair. Body-switch movies had a brief vogue in the 1980s, when there were some cute ones *(Big, Vice Versa)*, but Hollywood has so downgraded its respect for the audience that *The Hot Chick* is now considered acceptable.

The movie resolutely avoids all the comic possibilities of its situation, and becomes one more dumb high school comedy about sex gags and prom dates. Jessica, as Clive, becomes the best boy/girl friend a girl could want, during a week in which the female Jessica's parents absentmindedly observe that she has been missing for days. (That a girl looking exactly like the most popular girl in high school is stripping and hooking escapes the attention of the local slackwits.)

Lessons are learned, Jessica sees things from a different point of view, sweetness triumphs, and the movie ends with one of those "deleted" scenes over the final credits. This particular credit cookie is notable for being even more boring and pointless than the movie. Through superhuman effort of the will, I did not walk out of *The Hot Chick*, but reader, I confess I could not sit through the credits.

Note: The MPAA rates this PG-13. It is too vulgar for anyone under thirteen, and too dumb for anyone over thirteen.

The Hours ★ ★ ★ ½
PG-13, 114 m., 2002

Meryl Streep (Clarissa Vaughn), Julianne Moore (Laura Brown), Nicole Kidman (Virginia Woolf), Stephen Dillane (Leonard Woolf), Ed Harris (Richard), John C. Reilly (Dan Brown), Claire Danes (Julia), Allison Janney (Sally). Directed by Stephen Daldry and produced by Robert Fox and Scott Rudin. Screenplay by David Hare, based on the novel by Michael Cunningham.

Three women, three times, three places. Three suicide attempts, two successful. All linked in a way by a novel. In Sussex in 1941, the novelist Virginia Woolf fills the pockets of her coat with rocks and walks into a river to drown. In Los Angeles in 1951, Laura Brown fills her purse with pills and checks into a hotel to kill herself. In New York in 2001, Clarissa Vaughn watches as a friend she loves decides whether to let himself fall out of a window, or not.

The novel is *Mrs. Dalloway*, written by Woolf in 1925. It takes place in a day during which a woman has breakfast, buys flowers, and prepares to throw a party. The first story in *The Hours* shows Virginia writing about the woman, the second shows Laura reading the book, the third shows Clarissa buying flowers after having said one of the famous lines of the book. All three stories in *The Hours* begin with breakfast, involve preparations for parties, end in sadness. Two of the characters in the second story appear again in the third, but the stories do not flow one from another. Instead, they all revolve around the fictional character of Mrs. Dalloway, who presents a brave face to the world but is alone, utterly alone within herself, and locked away from the romance she desires.

The Hours, directed by Stephen Daldry and based on the Pulitzer Prize–winning novel by Michael Cunningham, doesn't try to force these

285

three stories to parallel one another. It's more like a meditation on separate episodes linked by a certain sensibility—Woolf's, a great novelist who wrote a little book named *A Room of One's Own*, which in some ways initiated modern feminism. Her observation was that throughout history women did not have a room of their own, but were on call throughout a house occupied by their husbands and families. Jane Austen wrote her novels, Woolf observed, in a corner of a room where all the other family activities were also taking place.

In *The Hours*, Woolf (Nicole Kidman) has a room of her own, and the understanding of her husband, Leonard (Stephen Dillane), a publisher. Laura (Julianne Moore), whom we meet in the 1950s, is a typical suburban housewife with a loving and dependable husband (John C. Reilly) she does not love, and a son who might as well be from outer space. A surprising kiss midway through her story suggests she might have been happier living as a lesbian. Clarissa (Meryl Streep), whom we meet in the present, is living as a lesbian; she and her partner (Allison Janney) are raising a daughter (Claire Danes) and caring for their friend (Ed Harris), now dying of AIDS. (We may know, although the movie doesn't make a point of it, that Virginia Woolf was bisexual.)

If this progression of the three stories shows anything, it demonstrates that personal freedom expanded greatly during the decades involved, but human responsibilities and guilts remained the governing facts of life. It also shows that suicides come in different ways for different reasons. Woolf's suicide comes during a time of clarity and sanity in her struggle with mental illness; she leaves a note for Leonard saying that she feels the madness coming on again, and wants to spare him that, out of her love for him. Laura attempts suicide out of despair; she cannot abide her life and sees no way out of it, and the love and gratitude of her husband is simply a goad. Richard, the Ed Harris character, is in the last painful stages of dying, and so his suicide takes on still another coloration.

And yet—well, the movie isn't about three approaches to sexuality, or three approaches to suicide. It may be about three versions of Mrs. Dalloway, who in the Woolf novel is outwardly a perfect hostess, the wife of a politician, but

who contains other selves within, and earlier may have had lovers of both sexes. It would be possible to find parallels between *Mrs. Dalloway* and *The Hours*—the Ed Harris character might be a victim in the same sense as the shell-shocked veteran in the novel—but that kind of list-making belongs in term papers. For a movie audience, *The Hours* doesn't connect in a neat way, but introduces characters who illuminate mysteries of sex, duty, and love.

I mentioned that two of the characters in the second story appear again in the third. I will not reveal how that happens, but the fact that it happens creates an emotional vortex at the end of the film, in which we see that lives without love are devastated. Virginia and Leonard Woolf loved each other, and Clarissa treasures both of her lovers. But for the two in the movie who do not or cannot love, the price is devastating. ☞

House of Fools ★ ★ ★
R, 104 m., 2003

Julia Vysotsky (Janna), Sultan Islamov (Akhmed), Bryan Adams (Himself), Vladas Bagdonas (Doctor), Stanislav Varkki (Ali). Directed by Andrei Konchalovsky and produced by Konchalovsky and Felix Kleiman. Screenplay by Sergei Kozlov.

Why are madhouses seen as such useful microcosms of human society? Why are their inhabitants invariably seen, in the movies anyway, as saner than the rest of us? The inmates are invariably choreographed as a group, acting like a Greek chorus. These groups I like to describe as the Baked Potato People, a name suggested by my old friend Billy ("Silver Dollar") Baxter, who once found a flag stuck into his baked potato, which read: "I've been tubbed, I've been rubbed, I've been scrubbed! I'm lovable, hugable, and eatable!"

Andrei Konchalovsky's *House of Fools* begins with ominous signs that it will be yet another recycling of simple fools, angelic heroines, and Baked Potatoes, with the familiar moral that it's the outside world that's crazy. It doesn't help that the movie is "based on a true story." But Konchalovsky was not born yesterday, has no doubt seen *King of Hearts, One Flew Over the Cuckoo's Nest,* and all the others, and shows courage in pressing ahead into this fraught territory. To my amazement, he salvages a good film from the genre—a film that succeeds not by arguing that the world is crazier than the asylum, but by arriving at the melancholy possibility that both are equally insane.

His true story: In 1996, during the Chechen war, the staff of a mental institution abandoned their posts as Russian and Chechen troops approached, and the inmates ran the place by themselves. Konchalovsky, a Russian who has worked for Hollywood (and made two admirable pictures there, *Shy People* and *Runaway Train*), not only shot in a real mental asylum, but used its actual inmates, who are blended with actors in the leads. This lends an authenticity and a certain unpredictability to the story.

We meet Janna (Julia Vysotsky), blonde and cheerful, in her twenties, an inmate who cheers the others with her accordion; so effective is her music that the image, usually a gray-green-blue, brightens up and admits yellow tones when she plays. In charge is the doctor (Vladas Bagdonas), who goes in search of a bus to evacuate his charges, and Ali (Stanislav Varkki), a poet who never goes anywhere without his knapsack, and even sleeps with it.

For the inmates, the daily high point comes right before bedtime, when they cluster around a window to watch a train roll past. Improbably bedecked with glittering lights like a Christmas tree, it still more improbably has an engineer who not only looks like the Canadian singer Bryan Adams but *is* the Canadian singer Bryan Adams, who sings "Have You Ever Really Loved a Woman?" while he guides the train.

A later shot of a passing train shows that it carries Russian tanks, and there is a good possibility, I think, that so does the Bryan Adams train. But Janna believes Adams is her fiancé and will come to marry her, and has a giant poster of him over her bed, like the poster of David Beckham in *Bend It Like Beckham*. She is all primed for love, and so when Chechen troops arrive it is only a matter of time until she transfers her affections to an Adamesque blond soldier named Akhmed (Sultan Islamov), who goes along with the joke and agrees to be engaged to her.

The early scenes in the asylum are conventionally in Baked Potato land, but the arrival of the troops nudges the film into new and riskier territory, and there are frightening moments when the inmates wander oblivious in the face of danger. One shot shows Janna completely unaware that a helicopter has crashed and exploded behind her. Intriguingly, the soldiers are shown, not as violent outsiders, but as essentially confused and alarmed creatures who are as surprised to find themselves in this situation as the inmates are. One adroit bit of plotting even allows a soldier to enlist in the ranks of the mad.

House of Fools doesn't take sides in the Chechen conflict but offers us two groups of soldiers equally uncomfortable with the situation. The masterstroke is the use of Bryan Adams, who seems like a joke when he first appears (the movie knows this), but is used by Konchalovsky in such a way that eventually he becomes the embodiment of the ability to imagine and dream—an ability, the movie implies, that's the only thing keeping these crazy people sane.

How I Killed My Father ★ ★ ★ ½
NO MPAA RATING, 100 m., 2002

Michel Bouquet (Maurice), Charles Berling (Jean-Luc), Natacha Régnier (Isa), Stéphane Guillon (Patrick), Amira Casar (Myriem), Hubert Koundé (Jean-Toussaint), Karole Rocher (Laetitia). Directed by Anne Fontaine and produced by Philippe Carcassonne. Screenplay by Jacques Fieschi and Fontaine. In French with English subtitles.

One day a letter comes from Africa, regretting to inform him that his father has died and was not able to return to France "as he had planned." That night, during a party in his honor, Jean-Luc sees his father standing among the other guests in the garden, beaming, nodding, his eyes twinkling: *Yes, it's really me.* Is this the father returned from the dead, or was the letter mistaken? The end of the film presents a third possibility.

How I Killed My Father is not about murder in the literal sense, although that seems a possibility. It is about a man who would like to kill his father, and who may have been killed spiritually by his father. Because his father abandoned him and embraced freedom on a continent far away, the son has turned in the opposite direction and jammed himself into a corner, denying himself love, freedom, even children. This is a harrowing movie about how parents know where all the buttons are, and how to push them. Unlike most such stories, however, it doesn't blame the father for pushing the buttons, but the son for having them. We choose to be unhappy.

The background is easily told. Thirty years ago, when Jean-Luc (Charles Berling) was about ten, his father, Maurice (Michel Bouquet), walked out and never returned. Jean-Luc's younger brother Patrick (Stéphane Guillon) doesn't remember the old man, isn't as wounded, but is a feckless failure whom Jean-Luc has hired as a driver and assistant. It's almost as if this relationship forces Jean-Luc to take over the father's responsibility for Patrick.

Jean-Luc is a wealthy doctor in Versailles, running a clinic that promises to combat the process of aging. A woman client asks about botox. A man complains he will be elderly when his two-year-old is grown. At home, Jean-Luc lives with his wife, Isa (Natacha Régnier), a "perfect" wife, hostess, and adornment. He has determined it would be dangerous for her to have children.

And then old Maurice materializes in the garden. Michel Bouquet, whose thin lips and twinkling eyes have added a knowing mystery to so many films by Chabrol and others, has returned unexplained. He would like money to reopen his clinic in Africa, but that doesn't seem to be his real motive. Perhaps he has returned simply because he is curious. He and Jean-Luc have that sort of infuriating relationship where the father does not have to say anything at all in order to be critical. His very silences are a reproach. His pleasantries carry an edge of irony. Like many parents, he is more beloved by strangers than by his children. Isa, for example, is drawn to him. And Patrick, who has no history with him, likes him. Only hard, cold Jean-Luc, who has founded his life on resentment, who takes no chances so he can never be hurt, hates him.

The film, cowritten and directed by Anne Fontaine, plays like a thriller that is toying with us by delaying its explosion of violence. But the violence in the film doesn't involve guns or blood. It involves quiet little statements, some

of them pleasantries, by which the father literally devastates his son's system of defenses. By the end, hardly having raised his voice, Maurice has returned to the son he hurt so much and finished the job.

Fontaine tells the story with many scenes of unexpected insight. Curious, how Jean-Luc wants to buy an expensive apartment for his mistress (Amira Casar), who doesn't want one. Odd how he dotes on her child. One night a hooker takes him home, and Fontaine shows him looking through a door that is ajar, so he can see the hooker's parents at their evening meal. What are these scenes for? To show him always yearningly on the outside of a family? Who put him there? Is his wife really not capable of child-bearing?

How I Killed My Father is about cold people and their victims. It is the misfortune of the brother and the wife to have Jean-Luc to deal with. He treats them both with financial generosity, but they can never heal his wound, and he lets them know that. So imagine Jean-Luc's pain when a young African appears in Versailles to visit old Maurice. This visitor is a doctor, too: "Your father was my mentor." One night Jean-Luc glimpses them laughing together in a way he has never laughed with his father.

Sometimes in life we trade parents. Others are closer to our parents than we are. We are closer to the parents of others than they are. Maybe it is so hard to be successful as a parent and a child that this is what we're forced to do. Jean-Luc's tragedy is not that he lost a father, but that he never found another. He refused to look for one. And the father he never found is the one he killed.

How to Lose a Guy in 10 Days ★ ½
PG-13, 116 m., 2003

Kate Hudson (Andie), Matthew McConaughey (Ben), Adam Goldberg (Tony), Michael Michele (Spears), Shalom Harlow (Green), Bebe Neuwirth (Lana), Robert Klein (Phillip). Directed by Donald Petrie and produced by Christine Forsyth-Peters, Lynda Obst, and Robert Evans. Screenplay by Kristen Buckley, Brian Regan, and Burr Steers, based on the book by Michele Alexander and Jeannie Long.

I am just about ready to write off movies in

which people make bets about whether they will, or will not, fall in love. The premise is fundamentally unsound, since it subverts every love scene with a lying subtext. Characters are nice when they want to be mean, or mean when they want to be nice. The easiest thing at the movies is to sympathize with two people who are falling in love. The hardest thing is to sympathize with two people who are denying their feelings, misleading each other, and causing pain to a trusting heart. This is comedy only by dictionary definition. In life, it is unpleasant and makes the audience sad.

Unless, of course, the characters are thoroughgoing rotters in the first place, as in *Dirty Rotten Scoundrels* (1988), in which Steve Martin and Michael Caine make a $50,000 bet on who will be the first to con the rich American Glenne Headly. They deserve their comeuppance, and we enjoy it. *How to Lose a Guy in 10 Days* is not, alas, pitched at that modest level of sophistication, and provides us with two young people who are like pawns in a sex game for the developmentally shortchanged.

He works at an ad agency. She works for a magazine that is *Cosmopolitan,* spelled a different way. She pitches her editor on an article about how to seduce a guy and then drive him away in ten days. He pitches his boss on an idea that involves him being able to get a woman to fall in love with him in ten days. They don't even Meet Cute, but are shuffled together by a treacherous conspirator.

Now, of course, they will fall in love. That goes without saying. They will fall in love even though she deliberately creates scenes no man could abide, such as nicknaming his penis Princess Sophia. She allows her disgusting miniature dog to pee on his pool table. She even puts a plate of sandwiches down on top of the pot in their poker game, something Nancy would be too sophisticated to do to Sluggo.

He puts up with this mistreatment because he has his own bet to win, and also because, doggone it, he has fallen in love with this vaporous fluffball of narcissistic cluelessness. That leaves only one big scene for us to anticipate, or dread: the inevitable moment when they both find out the other made a bet. At a moment like that, a reasonably intelligent couple would take a beat, start laughing, and head for the nearest hot-sheets haven. But no. These

characters descend from the moribund fictional ideas of earlier decades and must react in horror, run away in grief, prepare to leave town, etc., while we in the audience make our own bets about their IQs.

Matthew McConaughey and Kate Hudson star. I neglected to mention that, maybe because I was trying to place them in this review's version of the Witness Protection Program. If I were taken off the movie beat and assigned to cover the interior design of bowling alleys, I would have some idea of how they must have felt as they made this film.

Hulk ★ ★ ★
PG-13, 138 m., 2003

Eric Bana (Bruce Banner), Jennifer Connelly (Betty Ross), Sam Elliott (Ross), Josh Lucas (Talbot), Nick Nolte (Father), Paul Kersey (Young David Banner), Cara Buono (Edith Banner), Todd Tesen (Young Ross). Directed by Ang Lee and produced by Avi Arad, Larry J. Franco, Gale Anne Hurd, and James Schamus. Screenplay by John Turman, Michael France, Schamus, Jack Kirby, and Stan Lee, based on the story by Schamus.

The Hulk is rare among Marvel superheroes in that his powers are a curse, not an advantage. When rage overcomes Dr. Bruce Banner and he turns into a green monster many times his original size, it is not to fight evil or defend the American way, but simply to lash out at his tormentors. Like the Frankenstein stories that are its predecessors, *Hulk* is a warning about the folly of those who would toy with the secrets of life. It is about the anguish of having powers you did not seek and do not desire. "What scares me the most," Banner tells his only friend, Betty Ross, "is that when it happens, when it comes over me, when I totally lose control, I like it."

Ang Lee's *Hulk* (the movie's title drops "the") is the most talkative and thoughtful recent comic book adaptation. It is not so much about a green monster as about two wounded adult children of egomaniacs. Banner (Eric Bana) was fathered by a scientist (Nick Nolte) who has experimented on his own DNA code and passed along genes that are transformed by a lab accident into his son's hulkhood. Betty Ross

(Jennifer Connelly) is his research partner; they were almost lovers, but it didn't work out, and she speaks wryly of "my inexplicable fascination with emotionally distant men." Her cold father is General Ross (Sam Elliott), filled with military bluster and determined to destroy the Hulk.

These two dueling Oedipal conflicts are at the heart of Hulk, and it's touching how in many scenes we are essentially looking at damaged children. When the Hulk's amazing powers become known, the military of course tries to kill him (that's the routine solution in most movies about aliens and monsters), but there's another villain who has a more devious scheme. That's Talbot (Josh Lucas), a venal entrepreneur who wants to use Banner's secret to manufacture a race of self-repairing soldiers. Lots of money there.

The movie brings up issues about genetic experimentation, the misuse of scientific research, and our instinctive dislike of misfits, and actually talks about them. Remember that Ang Lee is the director of such films as The Ice Storm and Sense and Sensibility, as well as Crouching Tiger, Hidden Dragon; he is trying here to actually deal with the issues in the story of the Hulk, instead of simply cutting to brainless special effects.

Just as well, too, because the Hulk himself is the least successful element in the film. He's convincing in close-up but sort of jerky in long shot—oddly, just like his spiritual cousin, King Kong. There are times when his movements subtly resemble the stop-frame animation used to create Kong, and I wonder if that's deliberate; there was a kind of eerie oddness about Kong's movement that was creepier than the slick smoothness of modern computer-generated creatures.

King Kong is of course one of Lee's inspirations, in a movie with an unusual number of references to film classics. Bride of Frankenstein is another, as in a scene where Hulk sees his reflection in a pond. No prizes for identifying Dr. Jekyll and Mr. Hyde as the source of the original comics. Other references include Citizen Kane (the Hulk tears apart a laboratory) and The Right Stuff (a jet airplane flies so high the stars are visible). There is also a shade of General Jack D. Ripper in General Ross, who is played by Sam Elliott in a masterful demonstration of controlled and focused almost-overacting.

The film has its share of large-scale action sequences, as rockets are fired at the Hulk and he responds by bringing down helicopters. And there are the obligatory famous landmarks, real and unreal, we expect in a superhero movie: the Golden Gate Bridge, Monument Valley, and of course an elaborate secret laboratory where Hulk can be trapped in an immersion chamber while his DNA is extracted.

But these scenes are secondary in interest to the movie's central dramas, which involve the two sets of fathers and children. Banner has a repressed memory of a traumatic childhood event, and it is finally jarred loose after he meets his father again after many years. Nolte, looking like a man in desperate need of a barber and flea powder, plays Banner's dad as a man who works in the same laboratory, as a janitor. He uses DNA testing to be sure this is indeed his son, and in one clandestine conversation tells him, "You're going to have to watch that temper of yours."

Connelly's character also has big issues with her father—she trusts him when she shouldn't—and it's amusing how much the dilemma of this character resembles the situation of the woman she played in A Beautiful Mind. Both times she's in love with a brilliant scientist who's a sweetheart until he goes haywire, and who thinks he's being pursued by the government.

The movie has an elegant visual strategy; after countless directors have failed, Ang Lee figures out how split-screen techniques can be made to work. Usually they're an annoying gimmick, but here he uses moving frame-lines and pictures within pictures to suggest the dynamic storytelling techniques of comic books. Some shots are astonishing, as foreground and background interact and reveal one another. There is another technique, more subtle, that reminds me of comics: He often cuts between different angles in the same close-up—not cutting away, but cutting from one view of a face to another, as graphic artists do when they need another frame to deal with extended dialogue.

Whether Hulk will appeal to its primary audience—teenage science fiction fans—is hard to say. No doubt it will set the usual box office records over the weekend, but will it reach audiences who will respond to its dramatic ambition? Ang Lee has boldly taken the broad outlines of a comic book story and transformed them to his own purposes; this is a comic book movie for people who wouldn't be caught dead at a comic book movie.　　　☞

Human Nature ★ ★ ★
R, 96 m., 2002

Tim Robbins (Nathan Bronfman), Patricia Arquette (Lila Jute), Rhys Ifans (Puff), Miranda Otto (Gabrielle), Robert Forster (Nathan's Father), Mary Kay Place (Nathan's Mother), Rosie Perez (Louise). Directed by Michel Gondry and produced by Anthony Bregman, Ted Hope, Spike Jonze, and Charlie Kaufman. Screenplay by Kaufman.

Is human life entirely based on sex, or is that only what it seems like on cable television? *Human Nature*, a comedy written and produced by the writer and director who made us the great gift of *Being John Malkovich*, is a study of three characters at war against their sexual natures.

Lila (Patricia Arquette) fled to the woods at the age of twenty, after hair entirely covered her body. She becomes a famous reclusive nature writer, a very hairy Annie Dillard, but finally returns to civilization because she's so horny. Puff (Rhys Ifans) is a man who was raised as an ape, thinks he's an ape, and is cheerfully eager on all occasions to act out an ape's sexual desires. And Nathan (Tim Robbins) was a boy raised by parents so strict that his entire sexual drive was sublimated into the desire to train others as mercilessly as he was trained.

With these three characters as subjects for investigation, *Human Nature* asks if there is a happy medium between natural impulses and the inhibitions of civilization—or if it is true, as Nathan instructs Puff, "When in doubt, don't ever do what you really want to do." The movie involves these three in a ménage à trois that is (as you can imagine) very complicated, and just in order to be comprehensive in its study of human sexual behavior, throws in a cute French lab assistant (Miranda Otto).

None of which gives you the slightest idea of the movie's screwball charm. The writer, Charlie Kaufman, must be one madcap kinda guy. I imagine him seeming to wear a funny hat even when he's not. His inventions here lead us down strange comic byways, including Disneyesque song-and-dance numbers in which the hairy Arquette dances nude with the cute little animals of the forest. (Her hair, like Salome's veil, prevents us from seeing quite what we think we're seeing, but the MPAA's eyeballs must have been popping out with the strain.)

Early scenes show poor Nathan as a boy, at the dinner table with his parents (Robert Forster and Mary Kay Place), where every meal involves as much cutlery as a diplomatic feast, and using the wrong fork gets the child sent to his room without eating. As an adult, Nathan dedicates his life to training white mice to eat with the right silver, after the male mouse politely pulls out the female mouse's chair for her.

Then he gets a really big challenge, when the ape-man (Ifans) comes into his clutches. Nicknaming him Puff, Nathan keeps him in a Plexiglas cage in his lab, and fits Puff with an electrified collar that jolts him with enough juice to send him leaping spasmodically into the air every time he engages in sexual behavior, which is constantly. Lila, the hairy girl, meanwhile has turned herself over to a sympathetic electrologist (Rosie Perez), who fixes her up with Nathan—who does not know she is covered with hair and, if he did, would be sure it was bad manners.

The movie has nowhere much to go and nothing much to prove, except that Stephen King is correct and if you can devise the right characters and the right situation, the plot will take care of itself—or not, as the case may be. Ifans is so dogged in the determination of his sex drive, despite the electrical shocks, that when the professor sets his final examination at a Hooters-type place, we're grinning before he gets inside the door.

The movie is the feature debut of Michel Gondry, who directed a lot of Bjork's videos and therefore in a sense has worked with characters like these before. His movie is slight without being negligible. If it tried to do anything more, it would fail and perhaps explode, but at this level of manic whimsy, it is just about right. You had better go alone, because in any crowd of four there will be three who find it over their heads, or under their radar. They would really be better off attending

National Lampoon's Van Wilder, unless you want to go to the trouble of having them fitted with electric collars.

The Hunted ★ ★ ★ ½
R, 94 m., 2003

Tommy Lee Jones (L. T. Bonham), Benicio Del Toro (Aaron Hallam), Connie Nielsen (Abby Durrell), Jenna Boyd (Loretta Kravitz), Leslie Stefanson (Irene Kravitz), Robert Blanche (Crumley), Aaron Brounstein (Stokes), Ron Canada (Van Zandt). Directed by William Friedkin and produced by James Jacks and Ricardo Mestres. Screenplay by David Griffiths, Peter Griffiths, and Art Monterastelli.

The Hunted is a pure and rather inspired example of the one-on-one chase movie. Like *The Fugitive,* which also starred Tommy Lee Jones, it's about one man pursuing another more or less nonstop for the entire film. Walking in, I thought I knew what to expect, but I didn't anticipate how William Friedkin would jolt me with the immediate urgency of the action. This is not an arm's-length chase picture, but a close, physical duel between its two main characters.

Jones plays L.T. Bonham, a civilian employee of the U.S. Army who trains elite forces to stalk, track, hunt, and kill. His men learn how to make weapons out of shards of rock, and forge knives from scrap metal. In a sequence proving we haven't seen everything yet, they learn how to kill an enemy by the numbers—leg artery, heart, neck, lung. That Jones can make this training seem real goes without saying; he has an understated, minimalist acting style that implies he's been teaching the class for a long time.

One of his students is Aaron Hallam (Benicio Del Toro), who fought in Kosovo in 1999 and had experiences there that warped him ("his battle stress has gone so deep it is part of his personality"). Back home in Oregon, offended by hunters using telescopic sights, he claims four victims—"those hunters were filleted like deer." Bonham recognizes the style and goes into the woods after him ("If I'm not back in two days that will mean I'm dead").

Hallam's stress syndrome has made him into a radical defender of animal rights; he talks about chickens on assembly lines, and asks one

cop how he'd feel if a higher life form were harvesting mankind. Of course, in killing the hunters, he has promoted himself to that superior life form, but this is not a movie about debate points. It is a chase.

No modern director is more identified with chases than Friedkin, whose *The French Connection* and *To Live and Die in L.A.* set the standard. Here the whole movie is a chase, sometimes at a crawl, as when Hallam drives a stolen car directly into a traffic jam. What makes the movie fresh is that it doesn't stand back and regard its pursuit as an exercise, but stays very close to the characters and focuses on the actual physical reality of their experience.

Consider an early hand-to-hand combat between Bonham and Hallam. We've seen so many fancy, high-tech, computer-assisted fight scenes in recent movies that we assume the fighters can fly. They live in a world of gravity-free speedup. Not Friedkin's characters. Their fight is gravity-based. Their arms and legs are heavy. Their blows land solidly, with pain on both sides. They gasp and grunt with effort. They can be awkward and desperate. They both know the techniques of hand-to-hand combat, but in real life it isn't scripted, and you know what? It isn't so easy. We are involved in the immediate, exhausting, draining physical work of fighting.

The chase sequences—through Oregon forests and city streets, on highways and bridges—are also reality-oriented. The cinematography, by the great Caleb Deschanel *(The Right Stuff),* buries itself in the reality of the locations. The forests are wet and green, muddy and detailed. The leaves are not scenery but right in front of our faces, to be brushed aside. Running, hiding, stalking, the two men get dirty and tired and gasp for breath. We feel their physical effort; this isn't one of those movies where shirts are dry again in the next scene and the hero has the breath for long speeches.

The Hunted requires its skilled actors. Ordinary action stars would not do. The screenplay, by David Griffiths, Peter Griffiths, and Art Monterastelli, has a kind of minimalist clarity, in which nobody talks too much and everything depends on tone. Notice scenes where Del Toro is interrogated by other law officials. He doesn't give us the usual hostile, aggressive clichés, but seems to be trying to explain himself from a place so deep he can't make it real to outsiders. This man doesn't kill out of rage but out of sorrow.

There are moments when Friedkin lays it on a little thick. The early how-to sequence, where Bonham's trainees learn how to make weapons from scratch, implies there will be a later sequence where they need to. Fair enough. But would Hallam, in the heat of a chase, have the time to build a fire from shavings, heat an iron rod and hammer it into a knife? Even if Bonham cooperates by meanwhile pausing to chip his own flint weapon? Maybe not, or maybe the two hunters are ritualistically agreeing to face each other using only these tools of their trade. The resulting knife fight, which benefits from the earlier knife training sequence, is physical action of a high order.

There are other characters in the movie, other relationships. A woman with a child, whom Hallam visits (she likes him but is a little afraid). A woman who is an FBI field officer. Various cops. They add background and atmosphere, but *The Hunted* is about two hardworking men who are good at their jobs, although only one can be the best.

I

I Am Sam ★ ★
PG-13, 133 m., 2002

Sean Penn (Sam Dawson), Michelle Pfeiffer (Rita), Dakota Fanning (Lucy Dawson), Dianne Wiest (Annie), Doug Hutchison (Ifty), Stanley DeSantis (Robert), Brad Silverman (Brad), Joseph Rosenberg (Joe), Richard Schiff (Turner), Laura Dern (Randy). Directed by Jessie Nelson and produced by Marshall Herskovitz, Nelson, Richard Solomon, and Edward Zwick. Screenplay by Kristine Johnson and Nelson.

"Daddy, did God mean for you to be like this, or was it an accident?"

That's little Lucy Dawson, asking her father why he isn't quite like other people. She's a bright kid and figures out the answer herself, and when a classmate at grade school asks, "Why does your father act like a retard?" she explains, "He is."

I Am Sam stars Sean Penn as Lucy's dad, Sam, who has the IQ of a seven-year-old but is trying to raise the daughter he fathered with a homeless woman. The mother disappeared right after giving birth (her farewell words: "All I wanted was a place to sleep"), and now Sam is doing his best to cope, although sometimes Lucy has to help him with her homework. Eventually Lucy decides to stop learning so she won't get ahead of her dad. "I don't want to read if you can't," she tells him.

Sam loves the Beatles (his favorite is George). He named his daughter after "Lucy in the Sky With Diamonds," and has learned most of life's lessons from Beatles songs. The lesson *I Am Sam* wants to teach us is, "All you need is love." This is not quite strictly true. Sam loves his daughter more than anyone else, and she loves him, but it will take more than love for him to see her through grade school and adolescence and out into the world. Since the movie does not believe this, it has a serious disagreement with most of the audience.

Sean Penn does as well as can be expected with Sam, but it is painful to see an actor of his fire and reach locked into a narrow range of emotional and intellectual responses. Not long ago a veteran moviegoer told me that when he sees an actor playing a mentally retarded person, he is reminded of a performer playing "Lady of Spain" on an accordion: The fingers fly, but are the song or the instrument worthy of the effort? The kind of performance Sean Penn delivers in *I Am Sam,* which may look hard, is easy compared, say, to his amazing work in Woody Allen's *Sweet and Lowdown.* As Robert Kohner observes in his *Variety* review: "In a way, Edward Norton's turn in *The Score,* in which his thief used a mental handicap as a disguise, gave the trade secret away when it comes to this sort of performance."

The movie sets up the Department of Children and Family Services and its attorney as the villains when they take Lucy away from Sam and try to place her with a foster family. The heroine is a high-velocity Beverly Hills lawyer named Rita (Michelle Pfeiffer), who takes Sam's case on a pro bono basis to prove to the other people in her office that she's not a selfish bitch. This character and performance would be perfect in an edgy comedy, but they exist in a parallel universe to the world of this film.

Sam has the kinds of problems that come up in story conferences more than in life. For example, he's sitting in a diner when an attractive young woman smiles at him. He smiles back. She comes over and asks him if he would like to have a good time. He says he sure would. Then a cop pounces and arrests him for frequenting a prostitute. Back at the station, the cop admits, "This is the first time in nineteen years I actually believe a guy who says he didn't know she was a hooker." Hey, it's the first time in history that a man has been arrested on sex charges for talking to a woman in a diner before any clothes have come off, money has changed hands, or services have been discussed.

The movie climaxes in a series of courtroom scenes, which follow the time-honored formulas for such scenes, with the intriguing difference that this time the evil prosecutor (Richard Schiff) seems to be making good sense. At one point he turns scornfully to the Pfeiffer character and says, "This is an anecdote for you at some luncheon, but I'm here every day. You're out the door, but you know who I see come back? The child." Well, he's right, isn't he?

The would-be adoptive mother, played by Laura Dern, further complicates the issue by not being a cruel child-beater who wants the monthly state payments, but a loving, sensitive mother who would probably be great for Lucy. Sam more or less understands this, but does the adoptive mother? As the film ends, the issue is in doubt.

I Am Sam is aimed at audiences who will relate to the heart-tugging relationship between Sam and Lucy (and young Dakota Fanning does a convincing job as the bright daughter). Every device of the movie's art is designed to convince us Lucy must stay with Sam, but common sense makes it impossible to go the distance with the premise. You can't have heroes and villains when the wrong side is making the best sense.

Ice Age ★ ★ ★
PG, 88 m., 2002

Denis Leary (Diego the Saber-Toothed Tiger), John Leguizamo (Sid the Sloth), Ray Romano (Manfred the Mammoth), Goran Visnjic (Soto the Saber-Toothed Tiger), Jack Black (Zeke), Tara Strong (Roshan), Cedric the Entertainer (Rhino). Directed by Chris Wedge and produced by Lori Forte. Screenplay by Peter Ackerman, Michael Berg, and Michael Wilson.

Ice Age is a pleasure to look at and scarcely less fun as a story. I came to scoff and stayed to smile. I confess the premise did not inspire me: A woolly mammoth, a saber-toothed tiger, and a sloth team up to rescue a human baby and return it to its parents. Uh-huh. But the screenplay is sly and literate, and director Chris Wedge's visual style so distinctive and appealing that the movie seduced me.

The film takes place during a southward migration of species during a great ice age. Such migrations took place over millennia and were not the pre-Cambrian equivalent of going to Florida for the winter months, but no matter: As the ice packs advance, the animals retreat. There is no time to lose. Baby mammoths, playing in a tar pit, are told by their parents to hurry up: "You can play Extinction later."

We meet Manfred the Mammoth (voice by Ray Romano) and Sid the Sloth (John Legui-

zamo). Of course they can speak. (It is the humans, they believe, who have not yet mastered language.) When Sid and Manfred come upon a small, helpless human child, they decide to protect it and return it to its parents— even though those same parents, they know, have developed weapons for killing them. Along the trail they are joined by Diego the Saber-Toothed Tiger (Denis Leary), who has a hidden agenda. They are potentially each other's dinners, and yet through Sid's insouciance and Manfred's bravery in saving Diego from certain death, they bond and become friends.

It is true that altruism is a positive evolutionary trait; a species with individuals willing to die for the survival of the race is a species that will get somewhere in the Darwinian sweepstakes. But listen closely. When Diego the Saber-Toothed Tiger asks Manfred the Mammoth why he saved him, Manfred replies, "That's what you do as a herd." Yes, absolutely. But herds are by definition made up of members of the same species (and tigers are not herd animals anyway). If Manfred's philosophy were to get around in the animal kingdom, evolution would break down, overpopulation would result, there would be starvation among the nonvegetarians, and it would be an ugly picture. Much of the serenity and order of nature depends on eating the neighbors.

Ice Age does not preach Darwinian orthodoxy, however, but a kinder, gentler worldview: Ice Age meets New Age. And the philosophy scarcely matters anyway, since this is an animated comedy. Enormous advances have been made in animation technology in recent years, as computers have taken over the detail work and freed artists to realize their visions. But few movies have been as painterly as *Ice Age*, which begins with good choices of faces for the characters (note the tiger's underslung jaw and the sloth's outrigger eyes). The landscape is convincing without being realistic, the color palate is harmonious, the character movements include little twists, jiggles, hesitations, and hops that create personality. And the animals blossom as personalities.

That's because of the artwork, the dialogue, and the voice-over work by the actors; the filmmakers have all worked together to really see and love these characters, who are not "cartoon animals" but as quirky and individual as human actors, and more engaging than most.

I would suggest the story sneaks up and eventually wins us over, except it starts the winning process in its very first shots, showing a twitchy squirrel desperately trying to bury an acorn in an icy wilderness. We follow the progress of this squirrel all through the picture, as a counterpoint to the main action, and he is such a distinctive, amusing personality I predict he'll emerge as the hero of a film of his own.

Identity ★ ★ ★
R, 90 m., 2003

John Cusack (Ed), Ray Liotta (Rhodes), Amanda Peet (Paris), Alfred Molina (Doctor), Clea DuVall (Ginny), Rebecca De Mornay (Caroline), John C. McGinley (George York), John Hawkes (Larry), William Lee Scott (Lou), Jake Busey (Robert Maine), Pruitt Taylor Vince (Man), Leila Kenzle (Alice York), Bret Loehr (Timothy York). Directed by James Mangold and produced by Cathy Konrad. Screenplay by Michael Cooney.

It is a dark and stormy night. A violent thunderstorm howls down on a lonely Nevada road. A family of three is stopped by a blowout. While the father tries to change the tire, his wife is struck by a passing limousine. Despite the protests of the limo's passenger, a spoiled movie star, the driver takes them all to a nearby motel. The roads are washed out in both directions. The phone lines are down. Others seek shelter in the motel, which is run by a weirdo clerk.

Altogether, there are ten guests. One by one, they die. Agatha Christie fans will assume that one of them is the murderer—or maybe it's the clerk. Meanwhile, the story intercuts an eleventh-hour hearing for a man (Pruitt Taylor Vince) convicted of several savage murders. A grumpy judge has been awakened for this appeal, and unless he overturns his own ruling, the man will die. His psychiatrist (Alfred Molina) comes to his defense.

We don't know yet how these two stories will intersect, although they eventually must, but meanwhile events at the motel take our attention. We know the formula is familiar, and yet the treatment owes more to horror movies than to the classic whodunit. The group gathered at the motel includes the limousine driver

(John Cusack), who says he is a former cop and seems kind of competent. There's another cop (Ray Liotta), who is transporting a killer (Jake Busey) in leg irons. The driver with the blowout (John C. McGinley) tenderly cares for his gravely injured wife (Leila Kenzle) while his solemn little son (Bret Loehr) looks on.

Also at the rain-swept rendezvous are the movie star (Rebecca De Mornay) that Cusack was driving, a hooker (Amanda Peet) on her way out of Nevada, and a young couple (William Lee Scott and Clea DuVall) who recently got married, for reasons still in dispute. The motel manager (John Hawkes) finds them all rooms—numbered from 1 to 10, of course.

While lightning rips through the sky and the electricity flickers, gruesome events start to occur. I will not describe them in detail, of course, since you will want to be horrified on your own. Although many in the group fear a mad killer is in their midst, and the Busey character is a prime suspect, some of the deaths are so peculiar it is hard to explain them—or to know whether they are murders, or a case of being in the wrong place at the wrong time.

That there is an explanation goes without saying. That I must not hint at it also goes without saying. I think it is possible that some audience members, employing the Law of Economy of Characters, so usefully described in my *Bigger Little Movie Glossary*, might be able to arrive at the solution slightly before the movie does, but this isn't the kind of movie where all is revealed in a sensational final moment. The director, James Mangold, and the writer, Michael Cooney, play fair, sort of, and once you understand their thinking you can trace back through the movie and see that they never cheated, exactly, although they were happy enough to point to the wrong conclusions.

A movie like this is an acid test for actors. Can they keep their self-respect while jammed in a room while grisly murders take place, everybody is screaming and blaming one another, heads turn up without bodies, bodies disappear—and, of course, it is a dark and stormy night?

John Cusack does the best job of surviving. His character is a competent and responsible person, while all about him are losing their heads (sometimes literally) and blaming it on him. I also liked Amanda Peet's hooker, who suggests she's seen so much trouble that all of this is simply more of the same. And there is something to be said for the performance of John Hawkes as the motel manager, although I can't say what it is without revealing a secret (no, it's not the secret you think).

I've seen a lot of movies that are intriguing for the first two acts and then go on autopilot with a formula ending. *Identity* is a rarity, a movie that seems to be on autopilot for the first two acts and then reveals that it was not, with a third act that causes us to rethink everything that has gone before. Ingenious, how simple and yet how devious the solution is.

Igby Goes Down ★ ★ ★ ½
R, 97 m., 2002

Kieran Culkin (Jason "Igby" Slocumb Jr.), Susan Sarandon (Mimi Slocumb), Jeff Goldblum (D. H. Baines), Claire Danes (Sookie Sapperstein), Ryan Phillippe (Oliver Slocumb), Bill Pullman (Jason Slocumb), Amanda Peet (Rachel). Directed by Burr Steers and produced by Lisa Tornell and Marco Weber. Screenplay by Steers.

Holden Caulfield formed the mold, and Jason "Igby" Slocumb Jr. fits it perfectly in *Igby Goes Down*, an inspired example of the story in which the adolescent hero discovers that the world sucks, people are phonies, and sex is a consolation. Because the genre is well established, what makes the movie fresh is smart writing, skewed characters, and the title performance by Kieran Culkin, who captures just the right note as an advantaged rich boy who has been raised in discontent.

Igby is the child of a malevolently malfunctioning family. His mother, Mimi (Susan Sarandon), is a tart, critical, perfectionist mandarin ("I call her Mimi because Heinous One is a bit cumbersome"). His father, Jason (Bill Pullman), went through meltdown and is in a mental hospital, staring into space. His godfather, D. H. (Jeff Goldblum), is a slick operator, who converts both lofts and the young girls he installs in them. His brother, Oliver (Ryan Phillippe), is a supercilious Columbia student who regards Igby as a species of bug. Igby, like Citizen Kane before him, has been thrown out of all the best schools, and early in the movie

he escapes from a military school and hides out in New York City.

Of course a boy with his advantages is fortunate even in hideouts. He has an understanding meeting with his godfather, finds shelter in one of his lofts, and soon is on very good terms with Rachel (Amanda Peet), his godfather's mistress, who is an artist in every respect except producing anything that can be considered art. Through Rachel he meets Sookie Sapperstein (Claire Danes), a Bennington student who likes him because he makes her laugh. Among the lessons every young man should learn is this one: All women who like you because you make them laugh sooner or later stop laughing, and then why do they like you?

The movie has a fairly convoluted plot, involving who is sleeping with whom, and why, and who finds out about it, and what happens then. There is also the problem of the older brother, who does not make women laugh, which may be his strong point. The Goldblum character is especially intriguing, as a charmer with unlimited personal style and a hidden vicious streak.

Movies like this depend above all on the texture of the performances, and it is easy to imagine *Igby Goes Down* as a sitcom in which the characters don't quite seem to understand the witty things they're saying. All of the actors here have flair and presence, and get the joke, and because they all affect a kind of neo-Wildean irony toward everything, they belong in the same world. It is refreshing to hear Igby refer to his "Razor's Edge" experience without the movie feeling it is necessary to have him explain what he is talking about.

The Culkins are approaching brand-name status, but the thing is, the kids can act. Kieran emerges here as an accomplished, secure comic actor with poise and timing, and there is still another younger brother, Rory, who appears as a younger Igby. Kieran's role is not an easy one. He is not simply a rebellious, misfit teenager with a con man's verbal skills, but also a wounded survivor of a family that has left him emotionally scarred. One of the movie's touching scenes has him visiting his father in the mental hospital, where his father's total incomprehension suggests a scary message: I don't understand my family or anything else, and I've given up thinking about it.

297

Sarandon, as Mimi the Heinous One, treats her boys as if they're straight men in the ongoing sitcom of her life. That there are tragic secrets involved, which I will not reveal, makes her all the more frightening: Is nothing entirely sincere with this woman? Goldblum's sense of possession is the scariest thing about him, since Igby finds out it's bad to be considered his property and worse not to be. And Ryan Phillipe is pitch-perfect as the affected college student, whose elevated style and mannered speech seem designed to hide the same wounds that Igby bears.

There is a lot of sex in the movie, but it is sane sex, which is to say, sex performed by people who seem to have heard of sex and even experienced it before the present moment. Sex is seen here as part of the process of life, rather than as cinematic mountain-climbing. Everyone except Igby is fairly casual about it, which is kind of sad, and among the things Igby has been deprived of in life, one is an early romance with a sincere girl of about the same age who takes him seriously. Perhaps the sad inherited family trait among the Slocumbs is premature sophistication.

The movie was written and directed by Burr Steers (who acted in *Pulp Fiction* and *The Last Days of Disco,* among others). It is an astonishing filmmaking debut, balancing so many different notes and story elements. What Steers has not lost sight of, in all the emotional chaos, is heart. The film opens and closes on different kinds of pain, and by the end Igby has discovered truths that Holden Caulfield, we feel, could not have handled.

I'm Going Home ★ ★ ★
NO MPAA RATING, 90 m., 2002

Michel Piccoli (Gilbert Valence), Antoine Chappey (George), Leonor Baldaque (Sylvia), Catherine Deneuve (Marguerite), John Malkovich (John Crawford). Directed by Manoel de Oliveira and produced by Paulo Branco. Screenplay by de Oliveira.

There are a few movies where you can palpably sense the presence of the director behind the camera, and *I'm Going Home* is one of them. The movie is about an old actor who has lost many of those he loves, but continues to work. The actor is played by France's great Michel Piccoli, who at seventy-seven has appeared in 200 movies since 1945. And the director, whose breathing we can almost hear in our ear, is Manoel de Oliveira of Portugal, who is ninety-four and directed his first film in 1931.

When we first see the actor, named Gilbert Valence, he is onstage in a production of Ionesco's *Exit the King,* and the film lingers on speeches in which the old man rails against his mortality and defines the unending memorials that he fancies will keep his name alive. After the play, he learns of a tragic accident that has robbed him of his wife, daughter, and son-in-law. "Some time later," we see him living with his young grandson and the nanny.

Gilbert's offstage life is one of routine, and it is here, in a touch both subtle and glancing, that de Oliveira makes his most poignant observation about how we die but life heedlessly goes on without us. Gilbert takes his coffee every morning in the same Paris café, sitting in the same chair at the same table and always reading the same morning paper, *Liberation.* As he gets up to go, another man enters, sits at the same table, and unfolds his copy of *Le Figaro.* This happens day after day.

One morning, the other man arrives early and takes another table. But when Gilbert frees his regular table, the man gets up with alacrity to claim it—only to be headed off by a stranger who sits down first. These little scenes had a surprising impact on me. I often think of myself as a ghost at places I have visited: There is "my" café, and "my" table, and when I return to a city there is a satisfaction in occupying them again, because it proves my own continuity. Of course those cafés also "belong" to others I will never know, and someday I will never return to them, and someday neither will the others, and someday the café will not be there. Yet daily ritual encourages us to believe that because things have been the same for a long time, they will always be the same.

The old actor sees a handsome pair of shoes in a store window, and buys them. For a man past a certain age, to buy new shoes is an act of faith. (One is reminded of the Irish story about the shoe clerk who assured an old man, "These will see you out.") We see the shoes in close-up as Gilbert talks with his agent, a venal man who hints that a young actress might like to meet him. After all, the agent says, when Pablo Casals was in his eighties, he married a teenage student. "But I am nowhere near my eighties," Gilbert snaps. "And I am not Casals."

What eventually happens to these shoes is a reminder that we can make plans, but we cannot count on them. There are tender little scenes in which the old man and his grandson play with battery-powered trucks and enjoy each other's company, and fraught scenes in which the agent tries to get the actor to take a tawdry TV show. And a scene from a production of *The Tempest*, in which Gilbert gives Prospero's speech beginning, "Our revels now are ended . . ."

How the film plays out you will have to see for yourself. Few films seem so wise and knowing about the fact of age and the approach of the end. And at his great age, de Oliveira dispenses with the silliness of plot mechanics and tells his story in a simple, unadorned fashion, as episodes and observations, trusting us to understand.

In the very final scene, as Gilbert leaves a café without drinking the wine he has ordered, the camera lingers to watch another man walk in and order a beer. Life goes on. You might think that *I'm Going Home*, about an artist at the end of his career, is de Oliveria's own farewell, but no: He made a new film in 2002, named *The Uncertainty Principle*, and it played at Cannes in May. Some directors burn out early, others flower late. Luis Buñuel began a remarkable series of twelve great films when he was sixty-one. De Oliveira has made thirteen films since 1990. There is a time when going to the café is a habit, but if you go long enough it becomes a triumph.

The Importance of Being Ernest
★ ★ ★
PG, 100 m., 2002

Rupert Everett (Algernon Moncrieff), Colin Firth (Jack Worthing), Reese Witherspoon (Cecily Cardew), Judi Dench (Lady Bracknell), Frances O'Connor (Gwendolen Fairfax), Tom Wilkinson (Dr. Chasuble), Anna Massey (Miss Prism), Edward Fox (Lane). Directed by Oliver Parker and produced by Uri Fruchtmann and Barnaby Thompson. Screenplay by Parker, based on the play by Oscar Wilde.

Be careful what you ask for; you might get it. Recently I deplored the lack of wit in *Star Wars: Episode II—Attack of the Clones*, which has not one line of quotable dialogue. Now here is *The Importance of Being Earnest*, so thick with wit it plays like a reading from *Bartlett's Familiar Quotations*. I will demonstrate. I have here the complete text of the Oscar Wilde play, which I have downloaded from the Web. I will hit "page down" twenty times and quote the first complete line from the top of the screen:

"All women become like their mothers. That is their tragedy. No man does. That's his."

Now the question is, does this sort of thing appeal to you? Try these:

"Really, if the lower orders don't set us a good example, what on earth is the use of them?"

"To lose one parent, Mr. Worthing, may be regarded as a misfortune. To lose both looks like carelessness."

It appeals to me. I yearn for a world in which every drawing room is a stage, and we but players on it. But does anyone these days know what a drawing room is? The Universal Studios theme park has decided to abolish its characters dressed like the Marx Brothers and Laurel and Hardy because "a majority of people no longer recognize them." I despair. How can people recognize wit who begin with only a half-measure of it?

Oscar Wilde's *The Importance of Being Earnest* is a comedy constructed out of thin air. It is not really about anything. There are two romances at the center, but no one much cares whether the lovers find happiness together. Their purpose is to make elegant farce out of mistaken identities, the class system, mannerisms, egos, rivalries, sexual warfare, and verbal playfulness.

Oliver Parker's film begins with music that is a little too modern for the period, circa 1895, following the current fashion in anachronistic movie scores. It waltzes us into the story of two men who are neither one named Ernest and who both at various times claim to be.

299

Jack Worthing (Colin Firth) calls himself Jack in the country and Ernest in town. In the country, he is the guardian of the charming Miss Cecily Cardew (Reese Witherspoon), who is the granddaughter of the elderly millionaire who adopted Jack after finding him as an infant in a handbag he was handed in error at the cloakroom in Victoria Station. When Jack grows bored with the country, he cites an imaginary younger brother named Ernest who lives in London and must be rescued from scrapes with the law.

This imaginary person makes perfect sense to Jack's friend Algernon Moncrieff (Rupert Everett), who lives in town but has a fictitious friend named Bunbury who lives in the country and whose ill health provides Algernon an excuse to get out of town. I have gone into such detail about these names and alternate identities because the entire play is constructed out of such silliness, and to explain all of it would require—well, the play.

In town Jack is much besotted by Gwendolen Fairfax (Frances O'Connor), daughter of the formidable Lady Bracknell (Judi Dench), Algernon's aunt, who is willing to consider Jack as a suitor for the girl but nonplussed to learn that he has no people—none at all—and was indeed left in a bag at the station. Thus her remark about his carelessness in losing both parents.

Algernon in the meantime insinuates himself into the country estate where young Cecily is being educated under the watchful eye of Miss Prism (Anna Massey), the governess; eventually all of the characters gather at the manor house, Woolton, where there's some confusion since Algernon has taken the name Ernest for his visit and proposed to Cecily, so that when Cecily meets Gwendolen, they both believe they are engaged to Ernest, although Cecily, of course, doesn't know that in town Gwendolen knows Jack as Ernest.

But now I have been lured into the plot again. The important thing about *The Importance* is that all depends on the style of the actors, and Oliver Parker's film is well cast. Reese Witherspoon, using an English accent that sounds convincing to me, is charming as Jack's tender ward, who of course falls for Algernon. She is a silly, flighty girl, just right for Alger-

non, for whom romance seems valuable primarily as a topic of conversation. Frances O'-Connor is older and more sensuous as Gwendolen, and gently encourages the shy Jack to argue his case ("Mr. Worthing, what have you got to say to me?"). Judi Dench keeps a stern eye on the would-be lovers and a strong hand on the tiller.

The Importance of Being Earnest is above all an exercise in wit. There is nothing to be learned from it, no moral, no message. It adopts what one suspects was Wilde's approach to sex—more fun to talk about than to do. As Algernon observes, romance dies when a proposal is accepted: "The very essence of romance is uncertainty." Wilde takes this as his guide. When the play's uncertainties have all been exhausted, the play ends. The last line ("I've now realized for the first time in my life the vital importance of being earnest") takes on an interesting spin if we know that "earnest" was a vernacular term for "gay" in 1895. Thus the closing line may subvert the entire play, although not to the surprise of anyone who has been paying attention.

The In-Laws ★ ★
PG-13, 98 m., 2003

Michael Douglas (Steve Tobias), Albert Brooks (Jerry Peyser), Robin Tunney (Angela Harris), Ryan Reynolds (Mark Tobias), Candice Bergen (Judy), David Suchet (Jean-Pierre Thibodoux), Lindsay Sloane (Melissa Peyser), Maria Ricossa (Katherine Peyser). Directed by Andrew Fleming and produced by Bill Gerber, Elie Samaha, Joel Simon, and Bill Todman Jr. Screenplay by Nat Mauldin and Ed Solomon, based on a screenplay by Andrew Bergman.

The In-Laws is an accomplished but not inspired remake of a 1979 comedy that was inspired and so did not need to be accomplished. The earlier movie was slapdash and at times seemed to be making itself up as it went along, but it had big laughs and a kind of lunacy. The remake knows the moves but lacks the recklessness.

Both movies begin with the preparations for a wedding. The father of the bride is a dentist in 1979, a podiatrist this time. The father of the groom is a secret agent, deeply involved in dubious international schemes. The spy takes the doctor along on a dangerous mission, and they encounter a loony foreign leader who cheerfully proposes to kill them.

Now consider the casting: Peter Falk and Alan Arkin in the earlier film, versus Michael Douglas and Albert Brooks this time. Splendid choices, you would agree, and yet the chemistry is better in the earlier film. Falk goes into his deadpan lecturer mode, slowly and patiently explaining things that sound like utter nonsense. Arkin develops good reasons for suspecting he is in the hands of a madman.

Michael Douglas makes his character more reassuring and insouciant, as if he's inviting his new in-law along on a lark, and that's not as funny because he seems to be trying to make it fun, instead of trying to conceal the truth of a deadly situation. Albert Brooks is portrayed as neurotic and fearful by nature, and so his reactions are not so much inspired by the pickle he's in as by the way he always reacts to everything.

These are small adjustments in the natures of the two characters, but crucial to the success of the films. Comedy works better when the characters seem utterly unaware that they are being funny. And something else is missing, too: the unexpected craziness of the foreign leader, who in the 1979 film brought the movie almost to a halt (I wrote that I laughed so hard, I laughed at myself laughing). The new film plows much more familiar comic terrain.

Richard Libertini was the South American dictator in the earlier film, a sublime nutcase who had an intimate relationship with a sock puppet he addresses as Señor Wences. His two North American visitors desperately try to play along with the gag, without being sure whether the guy really believes the sock puppet is alive or is only testing them.

In the new version, the foreign madman is an international arms dealer named Thibodoux. He's played by David Suchet with sublime comic timing, and is very funny in a scene where he explains that he was once ruthless, but after studying under Depak Chopra has become more gentle, and now allows his victims a running start before shooting at them. All very well, but where is the sock puppet? Why remake a movie and leave out its funniest element—a sequence so funny, it's all a lot of people can remember about the movie? My guess is that

David Suchet could have risen to the occasion with a masterful sock puppet performance.

There are moments when the movie seems perverse in the way it avoids laughs. Consider a scene where Douglas is at the controls of a private jet and Brooks is terrified not simply because he hates flying, but also because they are flying so low—"to come in under the radar," Douglas explains. Why, oh why, isn't there an exterior shot showing the jet ten feet above the ground?

Another missed opportunity: Since the arms dealer develops a crush on the podiatrist, why no sex scenes involving toes? Or not toes necessarily, but anything involving the bad guy discovering a new kind of bliss while the podiatrist improvises desperately with nail clippers and corn removal techniques? True, the podiatrist defends himself by pressing on the dealer's painful foot nerve. But that's level one. The sock puppet was level three.

I'm suggesting such notions not because I want to rewrite the screenplay, but because I miss a certain kind of zany invention. *The In-Laws* seems conventional in its ideas about where it can go and what it can accomplish. You don't get the idea anyone laughed out loud while writing the screenplay. It lacks a strange light in its eyes. It is too easily satisfied. The one moment when it suggests the lunacy of the earlier film is when the Brooks character refuses to get into the water because, he explains, he was born with an unusual condition; his skin is not waterproof.

Now consider the character of Douglas's ex-wife, played by Candice Bergen, who has a lot of fun with it. She hates the guy, but confides that at least the sex was great. "Great, great, great." This is the setup for a scene of potential comic genius, but the movie uses it only for a weak curtain line. The notion of Michael Douglas and Candice Bergen having great sex while she continues to hate him is, I submit, a scene this movie should not be lacking. Think how mad you'd be at someone who could arouse you as no one else before or since, but who is such a complete jerk you can't stand to have him around. Bergen could have an orgasm while screaming passionate vituperations. Now that's a scene I'd like to see.

Innocence ★ ★ ★ ★
NO MPAA RATING, 94 m., 2001

Julia Blake (Claire), Charles "Bud" Tingwell (Andreas), Terry Norris (John), Kristien Van Pellicom (Young Claire), Kenny Aernouts (Young Andreas). Directed and produced by Paul Cox. Screenplay by Cox.

Here is the most passionate and tender love story in many years, so touching because it is not about a story, not about stars, not about a plot, not about sex, not about nudity, but about *love itself.* True, timeless, undefeated love. *Innocence* tells the story of two people who were lovers in Belgium as teenagers and discover each other, incredibly, both living in Adelaide, Australia, in their late sixties. They meet for tea and there is a little awkward small talk and then suddenly they realize that all the old feelings are still there. They are still in love. And not in some sentimental version of love for the twilight years, but in mad, passionate, demanding, forgiving, accepting love.

Paul Cox's *Innocence* is like a great lifting up of the heart. It is all the more affirming because it is not told in grand, phony gestures, but in the details of the daily lives of these two people. Life accumulates routines, obligations, habits, and inhibitions over the years, and if they are going to face their feelings then they're going to have to break out of long, safe custom and risk everything.

Their names are Claire (Julia Blake) and Andreas (Charles "Bud" Tingwell). Both actors are respected in Australia, both unknown in North America, which is all the better, because the purity of this story would be diffused by the presence of familiar faces (perhaps, for example, *The Bridges of Madison County* would have seemed riskier without the familiarity of Clint Eastwood and Meryl Streep). Andreas is a retired music teacher. His wife died thirty years ago. Claire has long been married to John (Terry Norris), in a marriage she thinks, in that bittersweet phrase, will see her out. Both Claire and Andreas have children, friends, people who count on their predictability. How, for example, does Andreas's housekeeper of many years feel when she discovers (as a housekeeper must) that he is sleeping with someone?

Not that sleeping with someone is that easy. In the movies, characters fall into bed with the casual ease of youth or experience, and no film ever stops to consider that questions of modesty, fear, or shyness might be involved. Paul Cox is a director who never loses sight of the humor even in the most fraught situations, and there is a moment in the film that is just about perfect, when Claire and Andreas find themselves at last unmistakably alone in a bedroom, and she says: "If we're going to do this—let's do it like grown-ups. First, close the curtains. Then, close your eyes."

Innocence has no villains. The treatment of John, Claire's husband, is instructive. He is not made into a monster who deserves to be dumped. He is simply a creature of long habit, a man who is waiting it out, who wears the blinders of routine, who expects his life will continue more or less in the same way until accident or illness brings it to a close. When Claire decides to tell him about Andreas ("I'm too old to lie"), his reaction is a study in complexities, and Paul Cox knows human nature deeply enough to observe that in addition to feeling betrayed, disappointed, and hurt, John also feels—well, although he doesn't acknowledge it, somehow grateful for the excitement. At last something unexpected has happened in the long slow march of his life.

The casting of Blake and Tingwell must have been a delicate matter. It is necessary for them to look their age (unlike aging Hollywood stars who seem stuck at forty-five until they die). But they must not seem dry and brittle, as if left on the shelf too long. Both of them seem touchable, warm, healthy, alive to tenderness and humor. And there is a sweet macho stubbornness in Tingwell's Andreas, who refuses to accept the world's verdict that he must be over "that sort of thing" at "his age." He is not over it, because, as he writes her in the letter that brings them together, he always imagined them on a journey together, and if she is still alive then the possibility of that journey is alive. If sixty-nine is a little late to continue what was started at nineteen—what is the alternative?

Many things happen in the movie that I have not hinted at. You must share their discoveries as they happen. By the end, if you are like me, you will feel that something transcendent has taken place. This is the kind of film that makes critics want to reach out and shake their readers. Andrew Sarris, for example, who usually maintains a certain practiced objectivity, writes: "The climax of the film is accompanied by a thrilling musical score that lifts the characters to a sublime metaphysical level such as is seldom attained in the cinema." Then he goes on to call *Innocence* a "film for the ages." You see what I mean.

For myself, *Innocence* is a song of joy and hope, and like its characters it is grown up. Here is a movie that believes love leads to sex, made at a time when movies believe that sex leads to love. But sex is only mechanical unless each holds the other like priceless treasure, to be defended against all of the hazards of the world. This movie is so wise about love it makes us wonder what other love stories think they are about.

In Praise of Love ★

NO MPAA RATING, 98 m., 2002

Bruno Putzulu (Edgar), Cecile Camp (Elle), Jean Davy (Grandfather), Françoise Verny (Grandmother), Audrey Klebaner (Eglantine), Jérémy Lippmann (Perceval), Claude Baignères (Mr. Rosenthal). Directed by Jean-Luc Godard and produced by Alain Sarde and Ruth Waldburger. Screenplay by Godard.

What strange confusion besets Jean-Luc Godard? He stumbles through the wreckage of this film like a baffled Lear, seeking to exercise power that is no longer his. *In Praise of Love* plays like an attempt to reconstruct an ideal film that might once have existed in his mind, but is there no more.

Yes, I praised the film in an article from the 2001 Cannes Film Festival, but have now seen it again, and no longer agree with those words. Seeing Godard's usual trademarks and preoccupations, I called it "a bittersweet summation of one of the key careers in modern cinema," and so it is, but I no longer think it is a successful one.

Godard was the colossus of the French New Wave. His films helped invent modern cinema. They were bold, unconventional, convincing. To see *Breathless, My Life to Live,* or *Weekend* is to be struck by a powerful and original mind. In the late 1960s he entered his Maoist period,

making a group of films *(Wind from the East, Vladimir and Rosa, Pravda)* that were ideologically silly but still stylistically intriguing; those films (I learn from Milos Stehlik of Facets, who has tried to find them) have apparently been suppressed by their maker.

Then, after a near-fatal traffic accident, came the Godard who turned away from the theatrical cinema and made impenetrable videos. In recent years have come films both successful *(Hail Mary)* and not, and now a film like *In Praise of Love,* which in style and tone looks like he is trying to return to his early films but has lost the way.

Perhaps at Cannes I was responding to memories of Godard's greatness. He has always been fascinated with typography, with naming the sections of his films and treating words like objects (he once had his Maoist heroes barricade themselves behind a wall of Little Red Books). Here he repeatedly uses intertitles, and while as a device it is good to see again, the actual words, reflected on, have little connection to the scenes they separate.

He wants to remind us that *In Praise of Love* is self-consciously a movie: He uses not only the section titles, but offscreen interrogators, polemical statements, narrative confusion, a split between the b&w of the first half and the saturated video color of the second. What he lacks is a port of entry for the viewer. Defenses of the film are tortured rhetorical exercises in which critics assemble Godard's materials and try to paraphrase them to make sense. Few ordinary audience members, however experienced, can hope to emerge from this film with a coherent view of what Godard was attempting.

If you agree with Noam Chomsky, you will have the feeling that you would agree with this film if only you could understand it. Godard's anti-Americanism is familiar by now, but has spun off into flywheel territory. What are we to make of the long dialogue attempting to prove that the United States of America is a country without a name? Yes, he is right that there are both North and South Americas. Yes, Brazil has united states. Yes, Mexico has states and is in North America. Therefore, we have no name. This is the kind of tiresome language game schoolchildren play.

It is also painful to see him attack Hollywood as worthless and without history, when (as Charles Taylor points out on Salon.com), Godard was one of those who taught us about our film history; with his fellow New Wavers, he resurrected film noir, named it, celebrated it, even gave its directors bit parts in his films. Now that history (his as well as ours) has disappeared from his mind.

His attacks on Spielberg are painful and unfair. Some of the fragments of his film involve a Spielberg company trying to buy the memories of Holocaust survivors for a Hollywood film (it will star, we learn, Juliette Binoche, who appeared in *Hail Mary* but has now apparently gone over to the dark side). Elsewhere in the film he accuses Spielberg of having made millions from *Schindler's List* while Mrs. Schindler lives in Argentina in poverty. One muses: (1) Has Godard, having also used her, sent her any money? (2) Has Godard or any other director living or dead done more than Spielberg, with his Holocaust Project, to honor and preserve the memories of the survivors? (3) Has Godard so lost the ability to go to the movies that, having once loved the works of Samuel Fuller and Nicholas Ray, he cannot view a Spielberg film except through a prism of anger?

Critics are often asked if they ever change their minds about a movie. I hope we can grow and learn. I do not "review" films seen at festivals, but "report" on them—because in the hothouse atmosphere of three to five films a day, most of them important, one cannot always step back and catch a breath. At Cannes I saw the surface of *In Praise of Love*, remembered Godard's early work, and was cheered by the film. After a second viewing, looking beneath the surface, I see so little there: It is all rote work, used to conceal old tricks, facile name-calling, the loss of hope, and emptiness.

Insomnia ★ ★ ★ ½
R, 118 m., 2002

Al Pacino (Will Dormer), Robin Williams (Walter Finch), Hilary Swank (Ellie Burr), Martin Donovan (Hap Eckhart), Maura Tierney (Rachel), Jonathan Jackson (Randy Stetz). Directed by Christopher Nolan and produced by Broderick Johnson, Paul Junger Witt, Andrew A. Kosove, and Edward McDonnell.

Screenplay by Hillary Seitz, Nikolaj Frobenius, and Erik Skjoldbjaerg.

He looks exhausted when he gets off the plane. Troubles are preying on him. An investigation by Internal Affairs in Los Angeles may end his police career. And now here he is in—where the hell is this?—Nightmute, Alaska, land of the midnight sun, investigating a brutal murder. The fuels driving Detective Will Dormer are fear and exhaustion. They get worse.

Al Pacino plays the veteran cop, looking like a man who has lost all hope. His partner, Hap Eckhart (Martin Donovan), is younger, more resilient, and may be prepared to tell the Internal Affairs investigators what they want to know—information that would bring the older man down. They have been sent up north to help with a local investigation, flying into Nightmute in a two-engine prop plane that skims low over jagged ice ridges. They'll be assisting a local cop named Ellie Burr (Hilary Swank), who is still fresh with the newness of her job.

Insomnia, the first film directed by Christopher Nolan since his famous *Memento* (2001), is a remake of a Norwegian film of the same name, made in 1998 by Erik Skjoldbjaerg. That was a strong, atmospheric, dread-heavy film, and so is this one. Unlike most remakes, the Nolan *Insomnia* is not a pale retread, but a reexamination of the material, like a new production of a good play. Stellan Skarsgard, who starred in the earlier film, took an existential approach to the character; he seemed weighed down by the moral morass he was trapped in. Pacino takes a more physical approach: How much longer can he carry this burden?

The story involves an unexpected development a third of the way through, and then the introduction of a character we do not really expect to meet, not like this. The development is the same in both movies; the character is much more important in this new version, adding a dimension I found fascinating. Spoilers will occur in the next paragraph, so be warned.

The pivotal event in both films, filmed much alike, is a shoot-out in a thick fog during a stakeout. The Pacino character sets a trap for the killer, but the suspect slips away in the fog, and then Pacino, seeing an indistinct figure loom before him, shoots and kills Hap—his partner from L.A. It is easy enough to pin the murder on the escaping killer, except that one person knows for sure who did it: the escaping killer himself.

In the Norwegian film, the local female detective begins to develop a circumstantial case against the veteran cop. In a nice development in the rewrite (credited to original authors Nikolaj Frobenius and Erik Skjoldbjaerg, working with Hillary Seitz), the killer introduces himself into the case as sort of Pacino's self-appointed silent partner.

The face of the killer, the first time we see it, comes as a shock, because by now we may have forgotten Robin Williams was even in the film. He plays Walter Finch, who does not really consider himself a murderer, although his killing was cruel and brutal. These things happen. Everyone should be forgiven one lapse. Right, detective? Pacino, sleepless in a land where the sun mercilessly never sets, is trapped: If he arrests Finch, he exposes himself and his own cover-up. And the local detective seems to suspect something.

Unusual for a thriller to hinge on issues of morality and guilt, and Nolan's remake does not avoid the obligatory Hollywood requirement that all thrillers must end in a shoot-out. There is also a scene involving a chase across floating logs, and a scene where a character is trapped underwater. These are thrown in as—what? Sops for the cinematically impaired, I suppose. Only a studio executive could explain why we need perfunctory action, just for action's sake, in a film where the psychological suspense is so high.

Pacino and Williams are very good together. Their scenes work because Pacino's character, in regarding Williams, is forced to look at a mirror of his own self-deception. The two faces are a study in contrasts. Pacino's is lined, weary, dark circles under his eyes, his jaw slack with fatigue. Williams has the smooth, open face of a true believer, a man convinced of his own case. In this film and *One Hour Photo*, which played at Sundance 2002, Williams reminds us that he is a considerable dramatic talent—and that, while over the years he has chosen to appear in some comedic turkeys (*Death to Smoochy* leaps to mind), his serious films are almost always good ones.

Why Christopher Nolan took on this remake is easy to understand. *Memento* was one of a kind; the thought of another film based on a similar enigma is exhausting. *Insomnia* is a film with a lot of room for the director, who establishes a distinctive far-north location, a world where the complexities of the big city are smoothed out into clear choices. The fact that it is always daylight is important: The dilemma of this cop is that he feels people are always looking at him, and he has nowhere to hide, not even in his nightmares.

Intacto ★ ★ ½
R, 108 m., 2003

Leonardo Sbaraglia (Tomás), Eusebio Poncela (Federico), Max von Sydow (Sam), Mónica López (Sara), Antonio Dechent (Alejandro). Directed by Juan Carlos Fresnadillo and produced by Sebastián Álvarez. Screenplay by Fresnadillo and Andrés M. Koppel.

The Spanish film *Intacto*, like the recent Sundance entry *The Cooler*, believes that luck is a commodity that can be given and received, won or lost, or traded away. Most people have ordinary luck, some have unusually good or bad luck, and then there is a character like Tomás, who is the only survivor of an airplane crash, beating the odds of 237 million to 1. (I am not the statistician here, only the reporter.)

The movie involves a man named Sam (Max von Sydow), who survived the Holocaust and now operates a remote casino at which rich people bet against his luck, usually unsuccessfully. So unshakable is his confidence that he will remove one bullet from a gun holding six and then bet that he will not die. That he is alive to be a character in the movie speaks for itself.

Von Sydow, who in *The Seventh Seal* played a game of chess with Death, believes that he will lose his luck if the wrong person looks on his face at the wrong time, or takes his photograph. To guard himself, he must often sit in a closed room with a hood over his face. We wonder, but he does not tell us, if he thinks this is a high price to pay for good fortune. He has a young man named Federico (Eusebio Poncela) as his confederate; Federico also has good luck, and searches for others who have his gift. When Sam steals his luck from him, he goes searching for a protégé of his own, and finds Tomás.

The single-mindedness of these men assumes that winning at gambling is the most important thing in the world. Certainly there are gamblers who think so. Another of the Sundance entries, *Owning Mahowny,* starred Philip Seymour Hoffman as a Toronto bank clerk who steals millions in order to fund his weekend getaways to Atlantic City and Las Vegas. He has a winning streak at roulette that in its intensity of focus has a kind of awesome power. In *The Cooler,* William H. Macy plays a man whose luck is so bad that he is employed by a casino to merely rub up against someone in a winning streak; then his luck changes.

The two North American films are pretty straightforward in telling their stories. *The Cooler* involves an element of fantasy, but it involves the story, not the visual approach. *Intacto,* directed by the talented young Juan Carlos Fresnadillo, is wilder visually, using the fractured narrative and attention-deficit camera style that can be effective or not, but often betrays a lack of confidence on the simple story level.

The story involves another more human element, centered on Sara (Mónica López), a cop who is chasing Tomás while grieving a tragic loss of her own. Will his luck protect him? What happens when it's luck versus luck?

I admired *Intacto* more than I liked it, for its ingenious construction and the way it keeps a certain chilly distance between its story and the dangers of popular entertainment. It's a Hollywood premise, rotated into the world of the art film through mannerism and oblique storytelling. The same ideas could be remade into a straightforward entertainment, and perhaps they already have been.

There's a fashion right now among new writers and directors to create stories of labyrinthine complexity, so that watching them is like solving a puzzle. I still haven't seen Alejandro Amenabar's *Open Your Eyes,* which a lot of people admire, but when I saw Cameron Crowe's American remake, *Vanilla Sky,* I knew as I walked out of the theater that I would need to see it again. I did, and got a different kind of overview, and liked the film. I liked it the first time, too, but through instinct, not understanding.

When you solve a film like this, have you learned anything you wouldn't have learned in a straight narrative, or have you simply had to pay some dues to arrive at the same place? Depends. *Pulp Fiction,* which jump-started the trend, depends crucially on its structure for its effect. *Intacto,* which is not as complex as the other films I've mentioned, may be adding the layer of style just for fun. That is permitted, but somewhere within that style there may be a hell of a thriller winking at us.

In the Bedroom ★ ★ ★ ★
R, 130 m., 2001

Tom Wilkinson (Matt Fowler), Sissy Spacek (Ruth Fowler), Nick Stahl (Frank Fowler), William Mapother (Richard Strout), Marisa Tomei (Natalie Strout), William Wise (Willis Grinnel), Celia Weston (Katie Grinnel), Karen Allen (Marla Keyes). Directed by Todd Field and produced by Field, Ross Katz, and Graham Leader. Screenplay by Robert Festinger and Field, based on a short story by Andre Dubus.

Todd Field's *In the Bedroom* only slowly reveals its real subject, in a story that has a shocking reversal at the end of the first act, and then looks more deeply than we could have guessed into the lives of its characters. At first it seems to be about a summer romance. At the end, it's about revenge—not just to atone for a wound, but to prove a point. The film involves love and violence, and even some thriller elements, but it is not about those things. It is about two people so trapped in opposition that one of them must break.

The story opens in sunshine and romance. Frank Fowler (Nick Stahl) is in love with Natalie Strout (Marisa Tomei). He'll be a new graduate student in the autumn. She is in her thirties, has two children, is estranged from Richard (William Mapother), who is a rich kid and an abusive husband. Frank's parents are worried.

"This is not some sweetie from Vassar you can visit on holidays," his mother tells him. "You're not in this alone."

"We're not serious, Mom," Frank says. "It's a summer thing."

"I see," says his mother. She sees clearly that Frank really does love Natalie—and she also sees that Frank's father may be vicariously enjoying the relationship, proud that his teenage son has conquered an attractive woman.

Ruth Fowler (Sissy Spacek) is a choral director at the local high school. Her husband, Matt (Tom Wilkinson), is the local doctor in their Maine village. On the local social scale, they are a step above the separated Natalie and her husband, whose money comes from the local fish business. Is she a snob? She wouldn't think so. The Fowlers pride themselves on being intelligent, open-minded, able to talk about things with their son (who does not want to talk about anything with them). We sense that their household accommodates enormous silences; that the parents and their son have each retreated to a personal corner to nurse wounds.

Then something happens. A review should not tell you what it is. It changes our expectations for the story, which turns out to be about matters more deeply embedded in the heart than we could have imagined. The film unfolds its true story, which is about the marriage of Matt and Ruth—about how hurt and sadness turns to anger and blame. There are scenes as true as movies can make them, and even when the story develops thriller elements, they are redeemed, because the movie isn't about what happens, but about why.

In the Bedroom is the first film directed by Todd Field, an actor *(Eyes Wide Shut, The Haunting)*, and one of the best-directed films this year. It's based on a story by the late Andre Dubus, the Massachusetts-based writer who died in 1999, and who worked with Field on the adaptation before his death. It works with indirection; the events on the screen are markers for secret events in the hearts of the characters, and the deepest insight is revealed, in a way, only in the last shot.

Every performance has perfect tone: Nick Stahl as the man who is half in love with a woman and half in love with being in love; Marisa Tomei, who is wiser than her young lover, and protective toward him, because she understands better than he does the problems they face; William Mapother as the abusive husband, never more frightening than when he tries to be conciliatory and apologetic; William Wise and Celia Weston as the Grinnels, the Fowlers' best friends.

And Sissy Spacek and Tom Wilkinson. They know exactly what they're doing, they understand their characters down to the ground, they are masters of the hidden struggle beneath the surface. Spacek plays a reasonable and civil wife and mother who has painful issues of her own; there is a scene where she slaps someone, and it is the most violent and shocking moment in a violent film. Wilkinson lives through his son more than he admits, and there is a scene where he surprises Frank and Natalie alone together, and finds a kind of quiet relish in their embarrassment. When Matt and Ruth lash out at each other, when the harsh accusations are said aloud, we are shocked but not surprised; these hard notes were undertones in their civilized behavior toward each other. Not all marriages can survive hard times.

Most movies are about plot, and chug from one stop to the next. Stephen King, whose book *On Writing* contains a lot of good sense, argues for situation over plot, suggests that if you do a good job of visualizing your characters, it is best to put them into a situation and see what happens, instead of chaining them to a plot structure. Todd Field and Andre Dubus use the elements of plot, but only on the surface, and the movie's title refers not to sex but to the secrets, spoken, unspoken, and dreamed, that are shared at night when two people close the door after themselves.

In the Mood for Love ★ ★ ★
PG, 97 m., 2001

Tony Leung (Chow Mo-wan), Maggie Cheung (Su Li-zhen), Rebecca Pan (Mrs. Suen), Lai Chin (Mr. Ho), Siu Ping-lam (Ah Ping), Cin Tsi-ang (The Amah). Directed and produced by Wong Kar-wai. Screenplay by Wong.

They are in the mood for love, but not in the time and place for it. They look at each other with big damp eyes of yearning and sweetness, and go home to sleep by themselves. Adultery has sullied their lives: His wife and her husband are having an affair. "For us to do the same thing," they agree, "would mean we are no better than they are."

The key word there is "agree." The fact is, they do not agree. It is simply that neither one has the courage to disagree, and time is passing. He wants to sleep with her and she wants to sleep with him, but they are both bound by the moral stand that each believes the other has taken.

You may disagree with my analysis. You may think one is more reluctant than the other. There is room for speculation, because whole continents of emotions go unexplored in Wong Kar-wai's *In the Mood for Love,* a lush story of unrequited love that looks the way its songs sound. Many of them are by Nat King Cole, but the instrumental "Green Eyes," suggesting jealousy, is playing when they figure out why her husband and his wife always seem to be away at the same times.

His name is Mr. Chow (Tony Leung). Hers is Su Li-zhen (Maggie Cheung). In the crowded Hong Kong of 1962, they have rented rooms in apartments next to each another. They are not poor; he's a newspaper reporter, she's an executive assistant, but there is no space in the crowded city and little room for secrets.

Cheung and Leung are two of the biggest stars in Asia. Their pairing here as unrequited lovers is ironic because of their images as the usual winners in such affairs. This is the kind of story that could be remade by Tom Hanks and Meg Ryan, although in the Hollywood version there'd be a happy ending. That would kind of miss the point and release the tension, I think; the thrust of Wong's film is that paths cross but intentions rarely do. In his other films, like *Chungking Express,* his characters sometimes just barely miss connecting, and here again key things are said in the wrong way at the wrong time. Instead of asking us to identify with this couple, as an American film would, Wong asks us to empathize with them; that is a higher and more complex assignment, with greater rewards.

The movie is physically lush. The deep colors of *film noir* saturate the scenes: reds, yellows, browns, deep shadows. One scene opens with only a coil of cigarette smoke, and then reveals its characters. In the hallway outside the two apartments, the camera slides back and forth, emphasizing not their nearness but that there are two apartments, not one.

The most ingenious device in the story is the way Chow and Su play-act imaginary scenes between their cheating spouses. "Do you have

a mistress?" she asks, and we think she is asking Chow, but actually she is asking her husband, as played by Chow. There is a slap, not as hard as it would be with a real spouse. They wound themselves with imaginary dialogue in which their cheating partners laugh about them. "I didn't expect it to hurt so much," Su says, after one of their imaginary scenarios.

Wong Kar-wai leaves the cheating couple offscreen. Movies about adultery are almost always about the adulterers, but the critic Elvis Mitchell observes that the heroes here are "the characters who are usually the victims in a James M. Cain story." Their spouses may sin in Singapore, Tokyo, or a downtown love hotel, but they will never sin on the screen of this movie, because their adultery is boring and commonplace, while the reticence of Chow and Su elevates *their* love to a kind of noble perfection.

Their lives are as walled in as their cramped living quarters. They have more money than places to spend it. Still dressed for the office, she dashes out to a crowded alley to buy noodles. Sometimes they meet on the grotty staircase. Often it is raining. Sometimes they simply talk on the sidewalk. Lovers do not notice where they are, do not notice that they repeat themselves. It isn't repetition, anyway—it's reassurance. And when you're holding back and speaking in code, no conversation is boring, because the empty spaces are filled by your desires.

Intimacy ★ ★ ★
NO MPAA RATING, 119 m., 2001

Mark Rylance (Jay), Kerry Fox (Claire), Timothy Spall (Andy), Alastair Galbraith (Victor), Philippe Calvario (Ian), Marianne Faithfull (Betty), Susannah Harker (Susan), Rebecca Palmer (Pam), Fraser Ayres (Dave). Directed by Patrice Chereau and produced by Jacques Hinstin and Patrick Cassavetti. Screenplay by Chereau and Anne-Louise Trividic, based on the stories "Intimacy" and "Night Light" by Hanif Kureishi.

Intimacy is a movie in which a man and a woman meet for short, brutal, anonymous sex every Wednesday afternoon. They want to keep it to that: no names, no small talk.

After the screening at Sundance 2001, I ran

into Kristina Nordstrom, who runs the Women Filmmakers Symposium in Los Angeles.

"Of course no woman would be attracted to sex like that," she said.

"Why not?"

"The sex in the movie all involves the bottom of the ninth inning. A woman would be turned off by a man who doesn't spend time being tender and sweet, and showing that he cares for her. There's no foreplay. She walks in, they rip off each other's clothes, and a few seconds later they're in a frenzy. Any woman would know that this movie was directed by a man."

A man might know that too. The film, which is brave but not perceptive, stars Mark Rylance as Jay, a former musician, a divorced husband and father, who now works as a barman and lives in a barely furnished London hovel. In an early scene, he is angry about an assistant hired to work with him behind the bar, because the new man is not a professional bartender but is an actor between jobs. The rage wells up because Jay fit that description himself until he left behind music six years ago and masochistically buried himself behind the bar.

The woman is named Claire (Kerry Fox). How they met we do not learn. At first she's simply a woman who turns up at his door every Wednesday afternoon to relieve an urgent physical need. They tear off each other's clothes and have passionate sex on the floor of a messy room. Then they part. She is so single-minded she courageously avoids the line we know every other woman on Earth would have eventually said: "I could help you fix up this place."

Their arrangement of raw sex begins to go wrong when he follows her one day. He discovers her real life, as a housewife, mother, and actress who is playing Laura in a London fringe theater production of *The Glass Menagerie* (a door in a pub is helpfully labeled "Toilets and Theater"). At one performance, he sits next to her husband, Andy (Timothy Spall), and son. Andy is a taxi driver, jovial with strangers. One day Jay asks Andy, "What would you think of a mother who has it off on the sly and then goes back home in the evenings as if nothing has happened?"

He *wants* Andy to know. He all but tells him about the affair. He reveals that he meets a woman every Wednesday afternoon. His eyes burn with intensity: Is Andy getting the message? Andy gets it, but keeps his thoughts to himself.

Apparently Jay needs more than anonymous sex. The film at first suggests that he wants contact, that he is dying of loneliness. But the material, based on stories by the London writer Hanif Kureishi and directed by Patrice Chereau, tilts in a different direction. We see, I think, that what Jay really wants is revenge—revenge against women and against a happy marriage.

Much depends on what went on in Jay's failed marriage. We see him bathing his two small sons, looking like a doting father, and then his wife asks him if he loves them, and he is unable to answer. This may be the most important moment in the movie. If he did love them, would he enter Claire's personal life so violently? Would he attack their marriage, having met her own son? His anger toward women is terrifying.

Andy, the taxi driver, has a surprising scene, too, finally telling Claire what he really thinks of her. We find his issues revolve not around sex but around honesty. And there are scenes at an amateur acting workshop Claire teaches where the line between acting and reality is the real subject; it has not occurred to her, in the workshop or in life, that the point of acting is not to reproduce reality but to improve upon it.

Intimacy is a raw, wounding, powerfully acted film, and you cannot look away from it. Its flaws are honestly come by, in the service of a failed search for truth. Its failure, I think, is an inability to look hard enough at what really drives Jay. His long, antagonistic relationship with a gay colleague might provide an answer, particularly since his taste for quick, anonymous sex seems to reflect a cruising sensibility.

Does he hate women because his inability to accept his homosexuality forces him to use them as substitutes for the partners he would prefer? Only a theory, suggested but not proven by the film. But *Intimacy* stays shy of any theory. It lets Jay off the hook, lets him retreat into the safe haven of loneliness and alienation. It should demand more of Jay, should insist on knowing him better. We leave the film with the conviction that the story is not over—that Jay is finished with Claire, but not with himself.

Invincible ★ ★ ★ ★
PG-13, 133 m., 2002

Tim Roth (Erik-Jan Hanussen), Jouko Ahola (Zishe Breitbart), Anna Gourari (Marta Farra), Max Raabe (Master of Ceremonies), Jacob Wein (Benjamin), Gustav-Peter Wöhler (Landwehr). Directed by Werner Herzog and produced by Gary Bart and Herzog. Screenplay by E. Max Frye and Herzog.

Werner Herzog's *Invincible* tells the astonishing story of a Jewish strongman in Nazi Germany, a man who in his simple goodness believes he can be the "new Samson" and protect his people. He is a blacksmith in Poland in 1932 when discovered by a talent scout, and soon becomes the headliner in the Palace of the Occult in Berlin, which is run by the sinister Hanussen (Tim Roth), a man who dreams of becoming minister of the occult in a Nazi government.

The strongman, named Zishe Breitbart, is played by a Finnish athlete named Jouko Ahola, twice winner of the title World's Strongest Man. Much of the movie's uncanny appeal comes from the contrast between Ahola's performance, which is entirely without guile, and Roth's performance, which drips with mannered malevolence. Standing between them is the young woman Marta (Anna Gourari), who is under Hanussen's psychological power, and whom the strongman loves.

Invincible is based, Herzog says, on the true story of Breitbart, whose great strength contradicted the Nazi myth of Aryan superiority. I can imagine a dozen ways in which this story could be told badly, but Herzog has fashioned it into a film of uncommon fascination, in which we often have no idea at all what could possibly happen next. There are countless movies about preludes to the Holocaust, but I can't think of one this innocent, direct, and unblinking. In the face of gathering evil, Zishe trusts in human nature, is proud of his heritage, and believes strength and goodness (which he confuses) will triumph.

The movie has the power of a great silent film, unafraid of grand gestures and moral absolutes. Its casting of the major characters is crucial, and instinctively correct. Tim Roth is a sinister charlatan, posing as a man with real psychic powers, using trickery and showmanship as he jockeys for position within the emerging Nazi majority. There is a scene where he hypnotizes Marta, and as he stares boldly into the camera I wondered, for a moment, if it was possible to hypnotize a movie audience that way. Late in the film there is a scene where his secrets are revealed, and he makes a speech of chilling, absolute cynicism. Another actor in another movie might have simply gnashed his teeth, but Roth and Herzog take the revelations as an opportunity to show us the self-hatred beneath the deception.

As for Jouko Ahola, this untrained actor, who seems by nature to be good-hearted and uncomplicated, may never act again, but he has found the one perfect role, as Maria Falconetti did in *The Passion of Joan of Arc.* He embodies the simple strongman. The camera can look as closely as it wants and never find anything false. As a naive man from a backward town, not especially devout, he gets into a fight when Polish customers in a restaurant insult him and his little brother as Jews. A little later, entering a circus contest, he watches as the strongman lifts a boulder—and then puts an end to the contest by lifting the strongman *and* the boulder.

The talent scout takes him to see his first movie. Soon he is in Berlin, where Hanussen sizes him up and says, "We will Aryanize you. A Jew should never be as strong as you." Zishe is outfitted with a blond wig and a Nordic helmet, and presented as "Siegfried." He becomes a great favorite of Nazi brownshirts in the audience, as Hanussen prattles about "the strength of the body against the dark powers of the occult." But Zishe's mind works away at the situation until finally he has his solution, tears off the helmet and wig, and identifies himself as a Jew.

Here as throughout the film Herzog avoids the obvious next scene. Is Hanussen outraged? To a degree. But then he reports: "There's a line three blocks long outside! It's the Jews. They all want to see the new Samson." And then, at a time when Hitler was on the rise but the full measure of Jewish persecution was not yet in view, the Palace of the Occult turns into a dangerous pit where audience members are potentially at one another's throats.

This is the first feature in ten years from Werner Herzog, one of the great visionaries among directors. He strains to break the bonds of film structure in order to surprise us in unexpected ways. His best films unashamedly yearn to lift us into the mythical and the mystical. "Our civilization is starving for new images," he once told me, and in *Invincible* there is an image of a bleak, rocky seashore where the sharp stones are littered with thousands or millions of bright red crabs, all mindlessly scrabbling away on their crabby missions. I think this scene may represent the emerging Nazi hordes, but of course there can be no literal translation: Perhaps Herzog wants to illustrate the implacable Darwinian struggle from which man can rise with good heart and purpose.

The strongman in *Invincible* is lovable and so deeply moving precisely because he is not a cog in a plot, has no plan, is involved in no machinations, but is simply proud of his parents, proud to be a Jew, in love with the girl, and convinced that God has made him strong for a reason. He may be wrong in his optimism, but his greatest strength is that he will never understand that. The Roth character is equally single-minded, but without hope or purpose—a conniver and manipulator.

Watching *Invincible* was a singular experience for me, because it reminded me of the fundamental power that the cinema had for us when we were children. The film exercises the power that fable has for the believing. Herzog has gotten outside the constraints and conventions of ordinary narrative, and addresses us where our credulity keeps its secrets.

Invisible Circus ★ ½
R, 98 m., 2001

Jordana Brewster (Phoebe), Christopher Eccleston (Wolf), Cameron Diaz (Faith), Blythe Danner (Gail), Patrick Bergin (Gene), Camilla Belle (Young Phoebe), Isabelle Pasco (Claire), Moritz Bleibtreu (Eric). Directed by Adam Brooks and produced by Julia Chasman and Nick Wechsler. Screenplay by Brooks, based on the book by Jennifer Egan.

Adam Brooks's *Invisible Circus* finds the solution to searing personal questions through a tricky flashback structure. There are two stories here, involving an older sister's disappearance and a younger sister's quest, and either one would be better told as a straightforward narrative. When flashbacks tease us with bits of information, it has to be done well, or we feel toyed with. Here the mystery is solved by stomping in thick-soled narrative boots through the squishy marsh of contrivance.

Jordana Brewster stars as Phoebe, eighteen years old in 1976. In the summer of 1969, she tells us in her narration, her sister Faith went to Europe and never came back. The story was that Faith (Cameron Diaz) killed herself in Portugal. Phoebe doesn't buy it. After a heart-to-heart with her mother (Blythe Danner), Phoebe sets off on a quest to solve the mystery, message, meaning, method, etc., of Faith's disappearance.

The search begins with Wolf (Christopher Eccleston), Faith's old boyfriend, now engaged and living in Paris. Since Wolf knows all the answers, and that's pretty clear to us (if not to Phoebe), he is required to be oblique to a tiresome degree. And there is another problem. In any movie where a lithesome eighteen-year-old confronts her older sister's lover, there is the inescapable possibility that she will sleep with him. This danger, which increases alarmingly when the character is named Wolf, is to be avoided, since the resulting sex scene will usually play as gratuitous, introducing problems the screenplay is not really interested in exploring. I cringe when a man and a woman pretend to be on a disinterested quest, and their unspoken sexual agenda makes everything they say sound coy.

Wolf and Faith, we learn, were involved in radical 1960s politics. Faith was driven by the death of her father, who died of leukemia caused by giant corporations (the science is a little murky here). Phoebe feels her dad always liked Faith more than herself. What was Dad's reason? My theory: Filial tension is required to motivate the younger sister's quest, so he was just helping out.

The movie follows Faith, sometimes with Wolf, sometimes without, as she joins the radical Red Army, becomes an anarchist, is allowed to help out on protest raids, fails one test, passes another, and grows guilt-ridden when one demonstration has an unexpected result. Phoebe traces Faith's activities during an odyssey/travelogue through Paris, Berlin, and Portugal, until we arrive at the very parapet Faith jumped or fell from, and all is revealed.

I can understand the purpose of the film, and even sense the depth of feeling in the underlying story, based on a novel by Jennifer Egan. But the clunky flashback structure grinds along, doling out bits of information, and it doesn't help that Wolf, as played by Eccleston, is less interested in truth than in Phoebe. He is a rat, which would be all right if he were a charming one.

There is a better movie about a young woman who drops out of sight of those who love her and commits to radical politics. That movie is *Waking the Dead* (2000). It has its problems, too, but at least it is unclouded by extraneous sex, and doesn't have a character who withholds information simply for the convenience of the screenplay. And its Jennifer Connelly is much more persuasive than Cameron Diaz as a young woman who becomes a radical; she enters a kind of solemn holy trance, unlike Diaz, who seems more like a political tourist.

I Remember Me ★ ★ ★
NO MPAA RATING, 74 m., 2001

Featuring Kim A. Snyder, Michelle Akers, Blake Edwards, Stephen Paganetti. A documentary directed, produced, and written by Kim A. Snyder.

I now believe in Chronic Fatigue Syndrome. I was one of many who somehow absorbed the notion that it was an imaginary illness. I am ashamed of myself. At the Hamptons Film Festival, I met Kim A. Snyder, who was working as an assistant producer on a Jodie Foster film when she contracted CFS in 1995. For the last five years, while still battling the disease herself, she directed *I Remember Me*, a documentary that does what the Centers for Disease Control in Atlanta shamefully failed to do: connects the dots.

Snyder begins in Lake Tahoe, where the disease struck hundreds of people. She talks to Dr. Daniel L. Peterson, who first started treating CFS patients there in 1984, has had seven who committed suicide because of the disease, and has no doubt it is real. She also talks to a spokesperson for the nearby Incline Village Visitors' Bureau, who says CFS is promoted by "quack doctors and mostly overweight women."

This person succeeds in becoming the living embodiment of the mayor in *Jaws*, who doesn't want anyone to believe there's a shark.

Yes, Dr. Peterson sighs, investigators from the CDC in Atlanta looked into the Lake Tahoe outbreak: "They came out here and skied and looked at a few charts." The conclusion was that Chronic Fatigue Syndrome was psychosomatic or hysterical or misdiagnosed. We are reminded that until the 1950s multiple sclerosis was also considered a hysterical condition.

Kim Snyder is an investigative journalist who does her own detective work. She identifies many earlier outbreaks with the same symptoms as CFS, and goes to Punta Gorda, Florida, to visit five women who had the disease forty years ago. Investigators visiting their community at the time concluded it was a real disease and not an imaginary condition, and said so in a report—which the women never saw. Snyder shows one woman the report on camera. She expresses her anger; this report would have informed her she was not, as many assured her, going crazy.

Snyder interviews two famous CFS sufferers: the film director Blake Edwards, who has continued to work during remissions in a fifteen-year struggle with the disease, and the Olympic gold medalist soccer player Michelle Akers, who walked off a field one day and collapsed.

But her most touching is the depressing visit to the bedside of Stephen Paganetti, a high school senior in Connecticut. He has been on his back in bed for years. The slightest exercise exhausts him. He is fed through tubes. Determined to attend his high school graduation, he's taken there by ambulance and wheeled in on a gurney. Few of his classmates had come to see him imprisoned in his bedroom; one says, "You get better—and we'll talk!" They give him a quilt they have all contributed patches to. Just what a high school kid wants for his graduation. By the end of filming, Stephen is still suffering, and indeed fewer than 20 percent of CFS sufferers get better, Snyder says.

The movie claims the disease strikes as many women as HIV. There has been recent progress. Robert J. Suhadolnik, a biochemist at Temple University, has identified a blood enzyme that acts as a marker of CFS, after many doctors claimed it had no physical symptoms. A whistle blower at the Centers for Disease Control has revealed to government accountants that $13 million was illegally diverted from CFS study to other diseases. Yet TV comics still joke about the disease as a form of laziness. Ironic, isn't it, that Kim Snyder wasn't too lazy to make this film—while the CDC and the medical establishment are only now stirring into action.

Iris ★ ★
R, 90 m., 2002

Judi Dench (Iris Murdoch), Jim Broadbent (John Bayley), Kate Winslet (Young Iris Murdoch), Hugh Bonneville (Young John Bayley). Directed by Richard Eyre and produced by Robert Fox and Scott Rudin. Screenplay by Eyre and Charles Wood.

I must look into myself and ask why I disliked *Iris* so intensely. Was it entirely a complaint against the film, or was it also a protest against the fate that befell the great novelist? There is no modern writer whose work I admire more than Iris Murdoch's, and for that mind to disappear in Alzheimer's is so sad that perhaps I simply refused to accept a film about it. Perhaps. Or perhaps it is true that the movie fails to do her justice—simplifies the life of one whose work was open to such human complexities.

Iris Murdoch (1919–1999) was one of the most important and prolific British novelists of her century, and wrote and taught philosophy as well. She wrote twenty-eight novels (between books, she said, she "took off for about half an hour"). Her novels involved "the unique strangeness of human beings," played against philosophical ideas. There were also touchstones that her readers looked forward to: a lonely child, a magus, an architectural oddity, an old friendship sorely tested, adulteries and unexpected couplings, intimations of the supernatural, theoretical conversations, ancient feuds. Her novel *The Sea, The Sea* won the Booker Prize and is a good place to start.

For years I looked forward to the annual Murdoch. Then her final novel arrived, shorter than usual, and at about the same time the dread news that she had Alzheimer's. "I feel as if I'm sailing into darkness," she said, a line

used in the movie. After her death, her husband, John Bayley, wrote two books about her, dealing frankly and compassionately with her disease.

The film *Iris*, directed by the London stage director Richard Eyre and written by Eyre and the playwright Charles Wood, is literate, fair, and well acted, but is this particular film necessary? It moves between the young and old Iris, painting her enduring relationship with Bayley while at the same time suggesting her openness to affairs and sexual adventures. As a young woman she is played by Kate Winslet, as an older woman by Judi Dench (Bayley is played by Hugh Bonneville and Jim Broadbent). We see her high spirits and fierce intelligence at the beginning, and the sadness at the end. What is missing is the middle.

What Iris Murdoch basically did is to write books. It is notoriously difficult to portray a writer, because what can you show? The writer writing? It isn't the writing that makes a writer interesting—it's the having written. In Murdoch's case, that would suggest that instead of making a film of her life, it might be a good idea to make a film of one of her books. Only one Murdoch novel has ever been made into a film (the undistinguished *A Severed Head*, 1971). Her stories are rich in characters, conflict, and sexual intrigue, and I'm surprised more haven't been filmed.

Instead of honoring the work, *Iris* mourns the life. It's like a biopic of Shakespeare that cuts back and forth between his apprentice days and his retirement in Stratford. Alzheimer's is especially tragic because it takes away the person while the presence remains. The character of Bayley, meanwhile, is presented as a befuddled and ineffectual man who contends with the baffling Murdoch, young and old, accepting her infidelity at the beginning and giving her love and support at the end. Yes, but there is much more to Bayley. He is one of the most brilliant of literary critics, whose essays grace the *New York Review of Books* and the *Times Literary Supplement,* but on the basis of this film you would think of him, frankly, as a fond old fool.

Because the film is well acted and written with intelligence, it might be worth seeing despite my objections. I suspect my own feelings. Perhaps this is so clearly the film I did not want to see about Iris Murdoch that I cannot see the film others might want to see. Stanley Kauffmann's case in praise of the film in *The New Republic* is persuasive, but no: I cannot accept this Iris. The one in my mind is too alive, too vital, too inspiring.

The Iron Ladies ★ ★

NO MPAA RATING, 104 m., 2001

Chaichan Nimpoonsawas (Jung), Sahaparp Virakamin (Mon), Giorgio Maiocchi (Nong), Gokgorn Benjathikul (Pia), Jessdaporn Pholdee (Chai), Ekachai Buranapanit (Wit), Siridhana Hongsophon (Coach Bee). Directed by Yongyoot Thongkongtoon and produced by Visute Poolvoralaks. Screenplay by Visuthichai Boonyakarinjana, Jira Maligool, and Thongkongtoon.

The Iron Ladies would have been a fearless statement for gay pride if it had been released in, oh, say, 1960. Its attitudes are so dated it plays like a float in a Gay and Lesbian Pride Parade, featuring drag stereotypes of the past. That the movie is fun is undeniable. That it is bad is inarguable.

The film is about a Thai volleyball team made up of gays, transvestites, a transsexual, and one allegedly straight member (ho, ho). Locked out of volleyball courts, scorned by the league, the victims of cheating and pig-headed officials, they fight their way to the national finals. Think of *The Mighty Ducks*, with a slight adjustment in spelling.

That gays can excel at volleyball is beyond question. That they can play their best game only when wearing a lot of makeup is questionable. That they must win by shocking their homophobic opponents with flouncing, flaunting, flamboyant behavior and limp-wristed serves is offensive—especially in Thailand, where transsexuality and transvestism are minor tourist industries.

The story arc of the movie is familiar to anyone who has ever seen a formula sports film about an underdog team. Every act seems recycled from the archives. We see the early setbacks. The recruitment of a team of misfits, losers, and reluctant heroes. The key player who needs a lot of convincing. The coach with personal issues of her own (she may be a lesbian,

but the movie refuses to commit). The sports authorities who want to ban the team. The early victories. The setbacks. Capturing the popular imagination. The big game. The crisis. The realization that the team can win only by returning to its True Nature (that is, gobs of foundation, lots of lipstick).

It's a good thing *The Iron Ladies* is about a gay team, because if this team were straight, the film would be an exercise in formula. The characters redeem the material by giving us somewhere else to look. It is, alas, too shy to look very hard. Judging by this movie, gay volleyball players have no sex lives at all, and don't even smooch a little in public. The Iron Ladies make admirable role models for celibacy in drag.

I found myself intrigued, however, by the matter-of-fact Coach Bee (Siridhana Hongsophon). Her performance is so utterly without spin, style, or affect that it could be lifted intact from a documentary. She is utterly convincing as—a volleyball coach. It's as if a real coach is being filmed with a hidden camera. There is no attempt to "perform," no awareness of punch lines, no artificial drama. Just a flat, straight-ahead, no-nonsense coaching job. It is either one of the most convincing performances I have ever seen, or no performance at all.

At the end of the film, we see newsreel footage of the real Iron Ladies, who are indeed a gay Thai volleyball team, and did indeed become national favorites. I understand that the story of the film is adjusted only slightly from real life (although greatly adjusted, I suspect, from real sex lives). This is the kind of movie you kind of enjoy, in a dumb way, with half your mind on hold, wishing they'd tell you more about some of the characters—especially Pia (Gokgorn Benjathikul), the glamorous transsexual. There's something sexy about the way she says, "Your serve."

Iron Monkey ★ ★ ★

PG-13, 85 m., 2001

Donnie Yen (Wong Kei-Ying), Rongguang Yu (Dr. Yang/Iron Monkey), Jean Wang (Orchid Ho), Yee Kwan Yan (Hiu Hing), James Wong (Governor Cheng), Hou Hsiao (Disfigured Swordsman), Sze-Man Tsang (Young Wong Fei-Hung), Sai-kun Yam (Hin Hung), Shun-Yee

Yuen (Master Fox), Fai Li (Witch). Directed by Woo-ping Yuen and produced by Hark Tsui. Screenplay by Tai-Muk Lau, Cheung Tan, Pik-yin Tang, and Hark.

The enormous popularity of *Crouching Tiger, Hidden Dragon* has inspired Miramax to test the market for other upmarket martial arts movies, and its resident kung-fu fan, Quentin Tarantino, has gone plunging back into the stacks of classics to "present" a beautifully restored version of *Iron Monkey.* This 1993 film, produced by the action master Hark Tsui, is seen in all its 35mm glory.

The film includes a young version of Wong Fei-Hung, whose adult exploits were chronicled in *The Legend of Drunken Master,* a 1994 Jackie Chan film released in 2000 by Miramax's Dimension division. Wong was a nineteenth-century folk hero who ranged the Chinese countryside doing, one suspects, very few of the things he is seen doing in this film. (For that matter, in *Iron Monkey* he is played by Sze-Man Tsang, a girl.) One of his specialties was "drunken fighting," in which, by pretending to be drunk, he could loosen himself up enough to be a better fighter.

Here we see twelve-year-old Wong Fei-Hung traveling with his father, Wong Kei-Ying (Donnie Yen), when they are caught in a dragnet set to snare the Iron Monkey, a mysterious Robin Hood figure. Hauled before the provincial governor, Wong Kei-Ying is charged with being the Iron Monkey, but then the real Monkey materializes in the court. The governor tells Wong Kei-Ying his son will be held captive until he captures the Iron Monkey.

Since such a standoff would have the movie's two heroes fighting each other, obviously unacceptable, we see young Wong Fei-Hung escaping, which frees his father to partner with the Iron Monkey, who is actually Dr. Yang (Rongguang Yu), a freelance idealist who fights for the poor against the rich. They find a common enemy in an evil monk.

The story is essentially a clothesline for a series of spectacular action scenes, culminating, as *Drunken Master* did, with one involving fire. This one is pretty spectacular, as the fighters balance on tall wooden poles over an inferno, battering each other with blazing battering rams while leaping from one precarious perch

to another. At one point the two allies are balanced one on top of the other on one shaky pole, and at another point they're balanced on either end of a shaky horizontal pole (this scene may have inspired a similar predicament involving ladders in the recent *The Musketeer;* Western movies are stealing martial arts stunts with shameless abandon).

Iron Monkey is a superior example of its genre without transcending it. The Jackie Chan movie benefited from our knowledge that Chan does most of his own stunts, and *Crouching Tiger* was not simply action scenes but also a poetic story, told with great visual beauty. This movie is great-looking, slick and highly professional, but stops at that. Donnie Yen has great moves, but how many of them are real?

What you can see, watching *Iron Monkey,* is what martial arts fans have been telling me via e-mail ever since *Crouching Tiger* came out: Its scenes of characters running across rooftops and floating in air were far from original, and had been well established in movies like this one. The technique of using invisible wires to "fly" the characters is not new (on the Web, in fact, it has a name: "wire-fu"). The reason *Crouching Tiger, Hidden Dragon* is a better movie is not in the technology but in the art; it incorporates the stunt and action techniques but is not satisfied with them, and aims higher, while a film like *Iron Monkey* is basically aimed at audiences who want elaborate fight sequences and fidget at the dialogue in between. It's for the fans, not the crossover audience.

Irreversible ★ ★ ★
NO MPAA RATING, 99 m., 2003

Monica Bellucci (Alex), Vincent Cassel (Marcus), Albert Dupontel (Pierre), Philippe Nahon (Philippe), Jo Prestia (Le Tenia), Stéphane Drouot (Stéphane), Mourad Khima (Mourad). Directed by Gaspar Noé and produced by Christophe Rossignon and Richard Grandpierre. Screenplay by Noé.

Irreversible is a movie so violent and cruel that most people will find it unwatchable. The camera looks on unflinchingly as a woman is raped and beaten for several long, unrelenting minutes, and as a man has his face pounded in with a fire extinguisher, in an attack that continues until after he is apparently dead. That the movie has a serious purpose is to its credit, but makes it no more bearable. Some of the critics at the screening walked out, but I stayed, sometimes closing my eyes, and now I will try to tell you why I think the writer and director, Gaspar Noé, made the film in this way.

First, above all, and crucially, the story is told backward. Two other films have famously used that chronology: Harold Pinter's *Betrayal* (1983), the story of a love affair that ends (begins) in treachery, and Christopher Nolan's *Memento* (2001), which begins with the solution to a murder and tracks backward to its origin. Of *Betrayal*, I wrote that a sad love story would be even more tragic if you could see into the future, so that even this joyous moment, this kiss, was in the shadow of eventual despair.

Now consider *Irreversible.* If it were told in chronological order, we would meet a couple very much in love: Alex (Monica Bellucci) and Marcus (Vincent Cassel). In a movie that is frank and free about nudity and sex, we see them relaxed and playful in bed, having sex and sharing time. Bellucci and Cassel were lovers at the time the film was made, and are at ease with each other.

Then we would see them at a party, Alex wearing a dress that makes little mystery of her perfect breasts. We would see a man hitting on her. We would hear it asked how a man could let his lover go out in public dressed like that: Does he like to watch as men grow interested? We would meet Marcus's best friend, Pierre (Albert Dupontel), who himself was once a lover of Alex.

Then we would follow Alex as she walks alone into a subway tunnel, on a quick errand that turns tragic when she is accosted by Le Tenia (Jo Prestia), a pimp who brutally and mercilessly rapes and beats her for what seems like an eternity, in a stationary-camera shot that goes on and on and never cuts away.

And then we would follow Marcus and Pierre in a search for Le Tenia, which leads to an S&M club named the Rectum, where a man mistaken for Le Tenia is finally discovered and beaten brutally, again in a shot that continues mercilessly, this time with a handheld camera that seems to participate in the beating.

As I said, for most people, unwatchable. Now consider what happens if you reverse the chronology, so that the film begins with shots of the body being removed from the nightclub and tracks back through time to the warm and playful romance of the bedroom scenes. There are several ways in which this technique produces a fundamentally different film:

1. The film doesn't build up to violence and sex as its payoff, as pornography would. It begins with its two violent scenes, showing us the very worst immediately, and then tracking back into lives that are about to be forever altered.

2. It creates a different kind of interest in those earlier scenes, which are foreshadowed for us but not for the characters. When Alex and Marcus caress and talk, we realize what a slender thread all happiness depends from. To know the future would not be a blessing but a curse. Life would be unlivable without the innocence of our ignorance.

3. Revenge precedes violation. The rapist is savagely punished before he commits his crime. At the same time, and this is significant, Marcus is the violent monster of the opening scenes, and Le Tenia is a victim whose crime has not yet been seen (although we already know Alex has been assaulted).

4. The party scenes, and the revealing dress, are seen in hindsight as a risk that should not have been taken. Instead of making Alex look sexy and attractive, they make her look vulnerable and in danger. While it is true that a woman should be able to dress as she pleases, it is not always wise.

5. We know by the time we see Alex at the party, and earlier in bed, that she is not simply a sex object or a romantic partner, but a fierce woman who fights the rapist for every second of the rape. Who uses every tactic at her command to stop him. Who loses, but does not surrender. It makes her sweetness and warmth much richer when we realize what darker weathers she harbors. This woman is not simply a sensuous being, as women so often simply are in the movies, but a fighter with a fierce survival instinct.

The fact is, the reverse chronology makes *Irreversible* a film that structurally argues against rape and violence, while ordinary chronology would lead us down a seductive narrative path toward a shocking, exploitative payoff. By placing the ugliness at the beginning, Gaspar Noé forces us to think seriously about the sexual violence involved. The movie does not end with rape as its climax and send us out of the theater as if something had been communicated. It starts with it, and asks us to sit there for another hour and process our thoughts. It is therefore moral at a structural level.

As I said twice and will repeat again, most people will not want to see the film at all. It is so violent, it shows such cruelty, that it is a test most people will not want to endure. But it is unflinchingly honest about the crime of rape. It does not exploit. It does not pander. It has been said that no matter what it pretends, pornography argues for what it shows. *Irreversible* is not pornography.   ☞

The Isle ★ ★ ★

NO MPAA RATING, 89 m., 2003

Suh Jung (Hee-Jin), Yoosuk Kim (Hyun-Shik), Sung-hee Park (Eun-A), Jae-Hyun Cho (Mang-Chee), Hang-Seon Jang (Middle-aged Man). Directed by Ki-duk Kim, and produced by Eun Lee. Screenplay by Kim.

The audiences at Sundance are hardened and sophisticated, but when the South Korean film *The Isle* played there in 2001, there were gasps and walkouts. People covered their eyes, peeked out, and slammed their palms back again. I report that because I want you to know: This is the most gruesome and queasiness-inducing film you are likely to have seen. You may not even want to read the descriptions in this review. Yet it is also beautiful, angry, and sad, with a curious sick poetry, as if the Marquis de Sade had gone in for pastel landscapes.

The film involves a lake where fishermen rent tiny cottages, each on its own raft, and bob with the waves as they catch and cook their dinners. It is the ultimate getaway. Once they have been delivered to their rafts by Hee-Jin, a woman who lives in a shack on the bank and operates a motorboat, they depend on her for all of their supplies and for the return to shore. She also sometimes brings them prostitutes, or services them herself.

Hee-Jin (Suh Jung) does not speak throughout the film, and is thought to be a mute, until she utters one piercing scream. She is like the heroine of *Woman of the Dunes*, ruling a domain in which men, once lured, can be kept captive. Most of the time she simply operates her business, ferrying the fishermen back and forth to their floating retreats. The men treat Hee-Jin and the prostitutes with brutality and contempt, even making them dive into the water to get their payments; that these women are willing to work in this way is a measure of their desperation.

Hee-Jin is indifferent to most of the men, but becomes interested in Hyun-Shik (Yoosuk Kim). Because we share his nightmares, we know that he was a policeman, killed his girlfriend, and has come to the floating hut to hide and perhaps to die. Watching him one day, she sees that he is about to commit suicide and interrupts his chain of thought with sudden violence, swimming under his raft and stabbing him through the slats of the floor. They develop what on this lake passes for a relationship, but then he tries suicide again (you might want to stop reading now) by swallowing a line knotted with fishhooks and pulling it up again. This leads to a sex scene I will not describe here, and later to an equally painful sequence involving Hee-Jin's use of fishhooks.

It is not uncommon for South Korean films to involve sadomasochism, as indeed do many films from Japan, where bondage is a common subject of popular adult comic books. The material doesn't reflect common behavior in those countries, but is intended to evoke extremes of violent emotion. It also dramatizes hostility toward women, although in *The Isle* the tables are turned. Between these two people who have nothing in common, one of them mute, sex is a form of communication—and pain, this movie argues, is even more sincere and complete.

Why would you want to see this film? Most people would not. I was recently at a health resort where a movie was shown every night, and one of the selections was Pedro Almodóvar's *All About My Mother*, which involves transgendered characters. "Why," a woman asked me, "would they show a movie with things I do not want to see?" She is not unusual. Most people choose movies that provide exactly what they expect, and tell them things they already know. Others are more curious. We are put on this planet only once, and to limit ourselves to the familiar is a crime against our minds.

The way I read *The Isle*, it is not about

fishhooks and sex at all. It is a cry of pain. The man on the raft, as we have seen in flashbacks, is violent and cruel, and he killed his girlfriend because he was jealous. Of course, jealousy is the face of low self-esteem. The woman sells her body and dives into the water for her payment. Her power is that she can leave these hateful men stranded on their rafts. I believe that Hee-Jin comes to "like" Hyun-Shik, although that is the wrong word. Maybe she feels possessive because she saved his life. His second attempt, with the fishhooks, reveals the depth of his sad self-loathing. When she employs the fishhooks on herself, what is she saying? That she understands? That she feels the same way too? That even in agony we need someone to witness and share?

The film, as I said, is beautiful to look at. The little huts are each a different color. The mist over the water diffuses the light. What a lovely postcard this scene would make, if we did not know the economy it reflects, and the suffering it conceals. Now there's a subject for meditation.

I Spy ★ ★

PG-13, 96 m., 2002

Eddie Murphy (Kelly Robinson), Owen Wilson (Alexander Scott), Famke Janssen (Rachel), Malcolm McDowell (Gundars), Gary Cole (Carlos). Directed by Betty Thomas and produced by Mario Kassar, Thomas, Jenno Topping, and Andrew G. Vajna. Screenplay by Marianne Wibberley, Cormac Wibberley, David Ronn, and Jay Scherick.

The thing about old TV shows is they have established brand names. People have heard of them and maybe enjoyed them once. So when Hollywood recycles them into movies, they have instant name recognition, and if the casting is plausible, audiences are intrigued. Some shows, like *Mission: Impossible*, get the A-list treatment, but *I Spy* is more of a throwaway, an attempt, as *Variety* might put it, to rake in quick coin during a hasty playoff.

Having written that, I turned to the *Variety* review to see if my hunch was correct. I was close. *Variety* writes: "Snoops should sneak out of the B.O. with a nifty opening sum, but expect steep dropoffs in the ensuing weeks. . . ."

Yes. But it's a shame that Eddie Murphy and Owen Wilson should be wasted on a ho-hum project like this. Why not either (1) save them for something worth doing, or (2) have the nerve to remake *I Spy* into an offbeat, contemporary project that slices and dices the old clichés?

Not a chance. This is a remake by the numbers, linking a half-witted plot to a series of stand-up routines in which Wilson and Murphy show how funny they could have been in a more ambitious movie. When they riff with each other, there's an energy that makes us smile. When they slog through the plot, we despair. Does *anyone* other than a Hollywood producer believe that in an Eddie Murphy movie the audience cares about special effects, action sequences, and desperate struggles to save the world? That kind of material is played out; it can be brought briefly back to life in a James Bond movie or an all-out thriller, but in a comedy, what we want to do is, we want to laugh.

Murphy and Wilson play Kelly Robinson and Alexander Scott. Students of the 1960s TV series will note that the roles have switched their races; Murphy is playing the Robert Culp character, and Wilson is in the Bill Cosby role. This makes not the slightest difference, since nothing in this movie refers to the TV series in a way that matters. There is a little color-coding going on, I think, in the decision to change the Culp occupation (tennis player) into a prizefighter for Eddie Murphy to play, the filmmakers apparently not having heard that there are black tennis stars.

The plot: Kelly Robinson (who always refers to himself as "Kelly Robinson") is recruited by spy Alexander Scott. Robinson is about to fight a title bout in Budapest, and an evildoer named Gundars (Malcolm McDowell) will be there. Robinson will provide entrée for Scott, who is trying to get back an invisible spy plane named the *Switchblade*, which Gundars has stolen and plans to use for, I dunno, world domination or something.

Murphy and Wilson are very funny men, and occasionally one of their lines swims up from out of the murk of the screenplay and winks at us. I like Wilson looking at his new spy gear and observing, "My stuff looks like you could get it from Radio Shack in 1972." And later, in a briefing, they learn that the

Switchblade is, "in the hands of the evildoers, a delivery system for weapons of mass destruction." One of the signs that the White House announced its anti-Saddam policy prematurely is when key catchphrases are recycled in movie comedies and the invasion is still in the talking stage. That's too much lead time.

The spy plane shimmers in and out of sight thanks to special effects, while the loyalties of a beautiful spy named Rachel (Famke Janssen) also shimmer in and out of sight, as does the Hispanic accent of the enigmatic spy Carlos (Gary Cole). The movie comes to life when Murphy and Wilson are trading one-liners, and then puts itself on hold for spy and action sequences of stunning banality. Don't moviemakers know that action scenes without context have got to be really, really good or our eyes glaze over? We've seen it all. We don't need one more boring fight on a rooftop with the future of the world hanging in the balance. If the characters are interesting, the story is involving, or the effects are really special, that's another story. *I Spy*, alas, is the same old story.

Italian for Beginners ★ ★ ★
R, 112 m., 2002

Anders W. Berthelsen (Andreas), Ann Eleonora Jorgensen (Karen), Anette Stovelbaek (Olympia), Peter Gantzler (Jorgen Mortensen), Lars Kaalund (Hal-Finn), Sara Indrio Jensen (Giulia), Elsebeth Steentoft (Kirketjener), Rikke Wolck (Sygeplejerske). Directed by Lone Scherfig and produced by Ib Tardini. Screenplay by Scherfig.

What a masterstroke it was for Lars von Trier to invent the Dogma movement! Every review of a Dogma film must begin with the announcement that it is a Dogma film, and then put it to the Dogma test to see if it conforms. Von Trier's name is often mentioned more prominently than the name of the film's actual director. He exacts a tax on our attention to the film. Since most people reading reviews don't know what Dogma is and don't care, this discussion puts them off the movie. Wise Dogma directors should no more trumpet their affiliation than should a movie begin with an announcement of the film stock it was shot on.

I say this because *Italian for Beginners* is a charming Danish comedy, and the fact that it's a Dogma film has little to do with its appeal. Yes, like all Dogma films, it's shot on video, on location, with only music found at the source—but so what? You see how Dogma changes the subject. What is appealing about it, the freshness and quirkiness of its characters and their interlinked stories, has nothing to do with Dogma—although, of course, lower costs may have helped it get made.

The movie takes place near Copenhagen, mostly in a small complex that includes a sports facility, a restaurant, a hair salon, and a nearby church. New to the church is Pastor Andreas (Anders W. Berthelsen), taking the place of a former pastor who took his ideas about services a little too seriously (he pushed the organist off the balcony). Short tempers seem to run in this little community; we meet Hal-Finn (Lars Kaalund), manager of the restaurant, who treats his job like a military command and is hilariously rude to customers who have bad manners.

Ordered to get a haircut, he meets the hairdresser Karen (Ann Eleonora Jorgensen). Everyone seems to cross paths in Karen's salon, including Pastor Andreas, who stops in for a haircut and has to dispense emergency spiritual advice to Olympia (Anette Stovelbaek), a bakery employee who gets a crush on Andreas.

Giulia (Sara Indrio Jensen) is an Italian waitress in the restaurant. It is not beside the point that she is Italian. Jorgen (Peter Gantzler), the manager of the complex, likes her so much he signs up for Italian classes. The Italian teacher suddenly drops dead, and Hal-Finn, who finds himself with some free time, decides to take over the class, which he teaches as if he is instructing Cub Scouts on fire-building techniques.

The movie gradually reveals certain unsuspected connections between some of the characters, and allows romances to bloom or fade among others, and all comes to a head during a class trip to Venice, which they all take more or less in desperation. The film has been written and directed by Lone Scherfig, who has a real affection for her characters, and likes to watch them discovering if happiness can be found in the absence of crucial social skills.

Because it comes attached to the Dogma label, I suppose we assume going into it that *Italian for Beginners* will test our taste or our

319

patience. The film only wants to amuse. It's a reminder that Dogma films need not involve pathetic characters tormented by the misuse of their genitalia, but can simply want to have a little fun. This is the sort of story American independent filmmakers also like to tell, right down to the setting in a restaurant—which, like a bar or an apartment in a sitcom, is convenient because all the characters can drop in without explanation. I was surprised how much I enjoyed *Italian for Beginners,* and made a mental note not to get all hung up on the Dogma movement in my review.

The Italian Job ★ ★ ★
PG-13, 105 m., 2003

Mark Wahlberg (Charlie Croker), Charlize Theron (Stella Bridger), Edward Norton (Steve Frezelli), Seth Green (Lyle), Jason Statham (Handsome Rob), Mos Def (Left-Ear), Donald Sutherland (John Bridger). Directed by F. Gary Gray and produced by Donald De Line. Screenplay by Donna Powers and Wayne Powers.

I saw *The Italian Job* in a Chicago screening room, in the midst of a rush of new summer releases. I recollect it now from the Cannes Film Festival, which has assembled one unendurable film after another for its worst year in memory. That doesn't make *The Italian Job* a better film, but it provides a reminder that we do, after all, sometimes go to the movies just to have a good time, and not to be mired in a slough of existential despond. Don't get me wrong. I like a good mire in despond now and again; it's just that the despond at Cannes has been so unadmirable.

F. Gary Gray's *The Italian Job,* on the other hand, is nothing more, or less, than a slick caper movie with stupendous chase scenes and a truly ingenious way to steal $35 million in gold bars from a safe in a Venetian palazzo.

The safe is stolen by a gang led by Donald Sutherland, who must be relieved to note that Venice has no dwarfs in red raincoats this season. His confederates include Charlie (Mark Wahlberg), a strategic mastermind; second-in-command Steve (Edward Norton); the computer whiz Lyle (Seth Green); the getaway driver Handsome Rob (Jason Statham); and Left-Ear (Mos Def), who can blow up stuff real good.

After a chase through the canals of Venice, which in real life would have led to the loss of six tourist gondolas and the drowning of an accordion player, the confederates go to an extraordinary amount of trouble to meet, with the gold, in a high Alpine pass apparently undisturbed since Hannibal. I have no idea how hard it is to move $35 million in gold from Venice to the Alps with Interpol looking for you, or for that matter how hard it would be to move it back down again, but golly, it's a pretty location.

After betrayal and murder, the action shifts to Los Angeles. Think of the overweight baggage charges. Wahlberg and company, who have lost the gold, are determined to get it back again, and enlist Sutherland's daughter, Stella (Charlize Theron), who is a safecracker. A legal one, until they enlist her.

Stella drives a bright red Mini Cooper, which is terrifically important to the plot. Eventually there is a fleet of three. That the crooks in the original *Italian Job* (1968) also drove Mini Coopers is one of the few points of similarity between the two movies. Good job that the Mini Cooper was reintroduced in time for product placement in this movie.

Actually, that's unfair; they need Mini Coopers because their size allows them to drive through very narrow spaces, although they have no idea how handy the little cars will become when they drive down the stairs and onto the tracks of the Los Angeles subway system. They're also handy in traffic jams, and there are nice sequences in which traffic lights are manipulated by the Seth Green character, who hilariously insists he is the real inventor of Napster, which was stolen by his roommate while he was taking a nap, thus the name.

There are a couple of nice dialogue touches; Edward Norton is not the first actor to say, "I liked him right up until the moment I shot him," but he is certainly the latest. The ending is suitably ironic. This is just the movie for two hours of mindless escapism on a relatively skilled, professional level. If I had seen it instead of the Cannes entry *The Brown Bunny,* I would have wept with gratitude.

It All Starts Today ★ ★ ★
NO MPAA RATING, 117 m., 2001

Philippe Torreton (Daniel), Maria Pitarresi

(Valeria), Nadia Kaci (Samia), Veronique Ataly (Mrs. Lienard), Nathalie Becue (Cathy), Emmanuelle Bercot (Mrs. Tievaux), Francoise Bette (Mrs. Delacourt), Lambert Marchal (Remi). Directed by Bertrand Tavernier and produced by Alain Sarde and Frederic Bourboulon. Screenplay (in French, with English subtitles) by Dominique Sampiero, Tiffany Tavernier, and Bertrand Tavernier.

Daniel, the kindergarten teacher in *It All Starts Today,* finds himself doing a lot more than teaching. He is also expected to be a social worker, child abuse investigator, hot lunch provider, political activist, fund-raiser, administrator, son, and lover, and now his girlfriend wants him to become a father as well. Philippe Torreton plays the role with a kind of desperate energy, relaxing only with the kids in the schoolroom and one night when he dances at a birthday party.

There is not much good cheer in the town where he teaches, a depressed mining village in the very area of France that inspired Zola's great exposé of mine conditions, *Germinal.* Today the typical miner is more like Daniel's dad, a broken figure who shuffles through the living room with his oxygen tank strapped to his back. Unemployment is widespread, government funds are lacking, and the mayor complains that schools and social services eat up his budget.

Not that the services are that good. Early in the film, Daniel locks out a social worker (Nadia Kaci) after she hangs up on him. Later they get to be friends and bend a few rules to make things happen. But what can they do about the pathetic mother who pushes her baby carriage into the schoolyard to pick up her preschooler, collapses on the asphalt, and then runs away, leaving behind both her baby and her little girl?

"She reeked of red wine," another teacher tells Daniel (the French would note the color). He visits her home, to find that the power has been turned off. It is winter, and cold. It's against the law to turn off a customer's power in the winter, but the power company gets around that by turning it off in the autumn. This woman, her kids, and her dispirited husband have no money, no hope, no plans.

The movie is a tender and passionate protest, not without laughter, by Bertrand Tavernier—a director who is not only gifted but honorable, and who since his debut with the wonderful *The Clockmaker* in 1973 has never put his hand to an unworthy film. He works all over the map, from the fantasy of *Death Watch* to the politics of *The Judge and the Assassin* to the character study *A Week's Vacation* to the jazz biopic *'Round Midnight* to the heartbreaking *Daddy Nostalgia* and the angry *L.627,* about the impossibility of being an effective drug cop.

It All Starts Today has most in common with *L.627.* Both films are about talented professionals who are hamstrung by the French bureaucracy and driven to despair by the untidy lives of their citizen clients. The screenplay, written by Tavernier with his daughter Tiffany and a schoolteacher named Dominique Sampiero, works by looking at everyday challenges. What is Daniel to say, for example, when the schoolyard woman and her husband explain that their son has stopped coming to school because it is just too much effort for them to set the alarm and get him out of bed? Irresponsible? Or would you also be defeated by months without heat and light?

The movie sketches Daniel's run-ins with a world that seems determined to make it impossible for him to be a good kindergarten teacher. He is considered a troublemaker, but what can he do? Consider the insufferable school inspector who advises him not to "move among groups" while teaching. "What should I do about the other three groups?" Daniel asks. "Make them self-reliant," advises the inspector, who obviously knows little about the self-reliance skills of two- to five-year-olds.

Maria Pitarresi plays Daniel's girlfriend, a sculptor with a young son who resents him. Her character seems a little unlikely, especially when she dreams up the school fete that ends the film, with classrooms filled with sand and Berber tents made from sheets, and a schoolyard filled with a maze of brightly colored bottles. As the town band plays and the children dance, we're aware that the upbeat ending changes absolutely nothing about the grim prospects for these kids when they someday look for work in this dying region. They'll end up paralyzed in front of the TV, like their parents. No wonder two of the students are named Starsky and Hutch.

It Runs in the Family ★ ★ ½
PG-13, 101 m., 2003

Michael Douglas (Alex Gromberg), Kirk Douglas (Mitchell Gromberg), Cameron Douglas (Asher Gromberg), Diana Douglas (Evelyn Gromberg), Bernadette Peters (Rebecca Gromberg), Rory Culkin (Eli Gromberg), Sarita Choudhury (Peg Maloney), Irene Gorovaia (Abigail Staley). Directed by Fred Schepisi and produced by Michael Douglas. Screenplay by Jesse Wigutow.

I have no idea how accurately the story of *It Runs in the Family* parallels the actual story of the Douglas family, whose members play four of the characters. My guess is that most of the facts are different and a lot of the emotions are the same. Like *On Golden Pond*, which dealt obliquely with the real-life tensions between Jane Fonda and her father Henry, this new film seems like a way for the Douglases to test and resolve assorted family issues—to reach closure, that most elusive of psychobabble goals.

The film is certainly courageous in the way it deals with Kirk Douglas's stroke, Michael Douglas's infidelity, and the drug problems of a son played by Cameron Douglas. Even if the movie doesn't reflect real life, any attentive reader of the supermarket sleaze sheets will guess that it comes close. In a way, just by making the film, the Douglases have opened themselves up to that.

My wish is that they'd opened up a little more. The movie deals with these touchy subjects, and others, but in a plot so jammed with events, disputes, tragedies, and revelations that the most serious matters don't seem to receive enough attention. The film seems too much in a hurry.

It introduces us to the Grombergs. Alex (Michael Douglas) is a prosperous attorney whose father, Mitchell (Kirk Douglas), was a founder of the firm. Not a bad man, Alex volunteers in a soup kitchen, where a sexy fellow volunteer (Sarita Choudhury) finds him so attractive that she all but forces them to have sex, which they do—almost. Their scenes are stun-

ningly unconvincing, except as a convenience to the plot.

At home, Alex is married to Rebecca (Bernadette Peters) and his father is married to Evelyn (Diana Douglas, who was, in an intriguing casting choice, Kirk's real-life first wife). Alex and Rebecca have two sons, the college student Asher (Cameron Douglas, Michael's son by his first marriage) and the eleven-year-old Eli (Rory Culkin, whose family could also inspire a movie). Mitchell also has a brother who is senile and lives in a care facility.

During the course of the movie, there will be two deaths, Alex's marriage will almost break up because of suspected infidelity, Asher will get in trouble with the law, Eli will go on a walk on the wild side with a nose-ringed eleven-year-old girlfriend, and Alex and Mitchell will seem incapable of having a conversation that doesn't descend into criticism and resentment. Only the old folks, Mitchell and Evelyn, seem to have found happiness, perhaps out of sheer exhaustion with the alternatives.

The film, directed by Fred Schepisi, has moments I fear are intended to be more serious than they play. One involves a midnight mission by Alex and Mitchell to set a rowboat adrift with an illegal cargo. I did not for a moment believe this scene, at least not in an ostensibly serious movie. Would two high-powered lawyers collaborate on such an act? When it is clear they can be traced? Really?

The scenes between Michael and Kirk Douglas, which are intended as the heart of the movie, seem inadequately realized in Jesse Wigutow's screenplay. They fret, fence, and feud, but without the sense of risk and hurt we felt between the two Fondas. Even less satisfying are the marital arguments between Alex and Rebecca, who has found a pair of panties in her husband's pocket. How they got there and what they mean, or don't mean, could be easily explained by the defensive husband—but he can never quite get the words out, and his dialogue remains infuriatingly inconclusive. As a result, all of the tension between them feels like a plot contrivance.

There are some good moments. I liked Kirk Douglas's fierce force of personality, and I liked moments, almost asides, in which Michael Douglas finds simple humanity amid the emotional chaos. There is a lovely scene involving Rory Culkin and his first date (Irene Gorovaia), in which their dialogue feels just about right for those two in that time and place. Their first kiss is a reminder that few first kisses are exactly wonderful. And a scene where Kirk and Diana Douglas dance has a simple warmth and truth.

But the movie is simply not clear about where it wants to go and what it wants to do. It is heavy on episode and light on insight, and although it takes courage to bring up touchy topics it would have taken more to treat them frankly.

What about a movie in which a great actor, now somewhat slowed by a stroke, collaborates with his successful son in a movie that will involve other family members and even the great actor's first wife? What does the great actor's second wife (who has been married to him for almost fifty years) think of that? What about a movie in which the son divorces his first wife to marry a famous beauty, who then wins an Oscar? These musings may seem unfair, but *It Runs in the Family* makes them inevitable. The Douglas family would have to make one hell of a movie to do justice to their real lives.

Ivans xtc. ★ ★ ★ ★
NO MPAA RATING, 94 m., 2002

Danny Huston (Ivan Beckman), Peter Weller (Don West), Lisa Enos (Charlotte White), Adam Krentzman (Barry Oaks), Alex Butler (Brad East), Morgan Vukovic (Lucy Lawrence), Tiffani-Amber Thiessen (Marie Stein), James Merendino (Danny McTeague), Caroleen Feeney (Rosemary). Directed by Bernard Rose and produced by Lisa Enos. Screenplay by Rose and Enos, based on *The Death of Ivan Ilyich* by Leo Tolstoy.

There is much sadness but little mourning at the funeral of Ivan Beckman. All agree he brought about his own death. He had few close friends. It is said he died from cancer. Insiders whisper, "The cancer is a cover story." You know you have lived your life carelessly when cancer is your cover story.

Ivans xtc., a remarkable film by Bernard Rose, stars Danny Huston, the rich-voiced, genial, tall son of John Huston, as a powerful Hollywood agent whose untidy personal life becomes a legend. Cocaine was the solution to his problems, which were caused by cocaine. He is headed for a shipwreck anyway when the diagnosis of lung cancer comes, but instead of looking for medical help he bulldozes ahead with cocaine, denial, and call girls.

The film opens with his funeral. There is a fight between a writer fired from a new movie and the star (Peter Weller) who fired him. Their disagreement cannot wait upon death. In voiceover, we hear the voice of the dead agent, who says that at the end, "the pain was so bad I took every pill in the house." And he tried, he says, "to find one simple image to get me through it."

Then we flash back through his life, as Ivan appears on-screen, one of those charming but unknowable men who have perfect courtesy, who lean forward with the appearance of great attention, and whose minds seem to be otherwise involved. As it happens, that is precisely the impression I had of John Huston on the three or four occasions when I met him: He was a shade too courteous, too agreeable, too accommodating, leaning forward too attentively from his great height, and I felt that he was playing a nice man while thinking about other things.

Danny Huston plays Ivan Beckman as the sort of man who believes he cannot be touched. Who has been given a pass. To whom all things come because they must, and for whom addictions like cocaine do not bring the usual ravages. I am told that if you have enough money for enough cocaine you can hold out like that for quite a while, which is not good, because you are building up a deficit in your mind and body that eventually cannot be repaid.

When Ivan doesn't return phone calls, when he doesn't appear at the office, when clients can't find him, he doesn't get in the same kind of trouble that a less legendary agent might experience, because—well, that's Ivan. When his girlfriend Charlotte (Lisa Enos) can't find him, and then discovers he was partying with hookers—well, who did she think he was when she started going out with him? Surely she heard the stories? Surely this doesn't come as news? When his bosses grow restless at his irresponsibility—hey, he has the big client list. If the clients like him, then the agency must.

The diagnosis of cancer comes like a telegram

that should have been delivered next door. It is the final, irrefutable reply to his feeling of immunity. There are two painful scenes where he tries, in one way or another, to deal with this news. One comes in a meeting with his father, whose ideas have made him a stranger. One comes during a party with two call girls, who are happy with the money, happy with the cocaine, happy to be with Ivan Beckman, and then increasingly unhappy and confused as their services are needed, not to pretend, but to be real. You cannot hire someone to really care about you.

The movie is allegedly inspired by *The Death of Ivan Ilyich* by Leo Tolstoy. I say "allegedly," because Bernard Rose has charged that the powerful Creative Artists Agency tried to prevent the film, seeing it as a transparent version of the life of Jay Moloney, an agent who at one time (I learn from a news story) represented Leonardo DiCaprio, Steven Spielberg, Bill Murray, Uma Thurman, Tim Burton—and Rose himself. Fired from CAA in 1996 because of cocaine, the story says, he moved to the Caribbean and killed himself in 1999.

Well, the story could be based on a lot of lives. The parabola of serious addiction often looks a lot the same. If the victim has more money, the settings are prettier. The tragedy of Ivan Beckman is that he doesn't know how to call for help, and has no one to call if he did. It is important to recognize that he is not a bad man. He can be charming, does not wish to cause harm, is grateful for company, and, as such people like to say, "If I'm hurting anybody, I'm only hurting myself." It is not until too late that he discovers how much it hurts.

Note: The story of the making of Ivans xtc. *is*

the story of how a lot of movies can now be made, according to Bernard Rose, its director.

Because of its controversial subject matter and because the Hollywood establishment has no wish to fund the thinly veiled story of the death of one of its own, the movie could not find conventional financing.

"So we went ahead and filmed it anyway," Rose told me after the film's screening at Cannes 2001. *"We got a 24-fps digital video camera, and we shot it in our own homes, and the crew was the cast and the cast was the crew and we took care of catering by calling for carryout."*

Rose, forty-two, is the British-born director of a number of commercial hits, notably Candyman *(1992) and* Immortal Beloved *(1995), and he is known for the power of his visual imagery. In* Paperhouse *(1988), he created a real landscape based on a child's imaginary drawings. In* Immortal Beloved, *a boy runs through the woods at night and plunges into a lake, floating on his back as the camera pulls back to show him surrounded by the reflections of countless stars.*

Ivans xtc., *made on a $500,000 budget, did not support or require such images. Produced by Lisa Enos, who also stars in it, it was directed by Rose on high-def video, which looks—appropriate, I think, is the word. Some shots are beautiful, others are functional, and there are no shots that do not work.*

"We finished the movie, we took it to Artisan Entertainment, and we made a deal," he said. "A 50-50 split of all the proceeds from dollar one. It was made so cheaply that we'll make out and so will they."

Does he wish he'd had film? "It's no use saying you'd rather have film, because this project on film could not have existed."

J

Jackpot ★ ★
R, 100 m., 2001

Jon Gries (Sunny Holiday), Garrett Morris (Lester Irving), Daryl Hannah (Bobbi), Peggy Lipton (Janice), Ricky Trammell (Candy Singer), Allen Fawcett (KJ Number One), Patrick Bauchau (Sevon Voice/Santa Claus), Adam Baldwin (Mel James), Rosie O'Grady (Sweet Dreams Singer), Rick Overton (Roland), Anthony Edwards (Tracy). Directed by Michael Polish and produced by Mark Polish and Michael Polish. Screenplay by Mark Polish and Michael Polish.

Sailing in a big pink Chrysler boat from one sad saloon to another, Sunny Holiday and Lester Irving travel the highways of the West, seeking fame. Sunny (Jon Gries) is the singer, Lester (Garrett Morris) is his manager. Their plan: By gradually building a constituency among karaoke fans, Sunny will position himself for his big breakthrough into the world of pop music. "Our winnings total ... thousands," Sunny assures an interviewer. One of his prizes looks more like a Waring blender (Lester, as manager, gets 15 percent, and keeps the lid).

Jackpot is the new movie by the Polish brothers, directed by Michael, coproduced and co-written by Mark. Their first film, *Twin Falls Idaho* (1999), was a virtuoso dark melodrama about conjoined twins approaching an inescapable separation. This one feels more like when the pianist noodles on the keyboard before breaking into the melody. All the pieces are in place—the characters, the seedy milieu, the look and tone—but we never get to the nod inviting the drums and bass to come in. It's all warm-up, no pitch.

Yet you can tell these guys have a feel for film. This is a sophomore lapse on the way to a real career. There are moments that zing. One comes when Sunny seduces Janice (Peggy Lipton), who lives in a trailer near his motel. First they sleep together. Then he spills his coffee. Then he goes out to his car to get a gallon jug of industrial soap. "None of those big chain stores carry this kind of power," he assures her. Then he tries to sell her the soap. Lesser filmmakers would have stopped there. Not the Polish brothers. "You screwed me once. Why are you trying to screw me again?" asks Janice, in words to that effect.

Sunny and Lester have a relationship like George and Lennie in *Of Mice and Men,* except that both of them are more like Lennie. They travel through life side by side, the fortyish white man and sixtyish black man, toward success that always remains out there on the horizon. Sunny dresses like a caller at a Saturday night square dance, Lester like an unsuccessful undertaker. Lester prays before every competition, and gives advice (no matter how bad things are going, never, ever just walk off the stage).

Sunny has abandoned a wife and child for this quest. Bobbi (Daryl Hannah) waits at home during what she calls his "fantasy tour," raising their baby and waiting for child support. It's her pink Chrysler. She reports it stolen. Sunny does religiously send her a $1 lottery ticket every week, which if it was a winner (he points out) would more than make up for the missing support payments, but somehow for Bobbi this is not enough.

The film has a nice way of getting into scenes. I like the way Sunny and Lester are discovered sitting at the counter of a diner, an empty seat between them, caught in midflow of a conversation they have been having for months. And the way Sunny's brother Tracy (Anthony Edwards) turns up to defend and support him. And the way the fans in the karaoke bars have to think the contestants are stars—because if they're not, what does that make the fans?

In its mastery of its moments, *Jackpot* has charm, humor, and poignancy. What it lacks is necessity. There's a sense in which we're always waiting for it to kick in. If we saw *Duets*, the 2000 Gwyneth Paltrow and Huey Lewis movie, we know this world of competitive karaoke. *Jackpot* is not so much about the karaoke as about the relationship between Sunny and Lester. But do they have a relationship, or it is a double act, so long in rehearsal that all the lines are set? Somebody has to break out if anything is to happen. *Jackpot* was made by twins, and both of their films are about two men joined at the hip, either literally or figuratively. Maybe it's time for them to go in for the operation.

Note: I learn on the Web that the film was photographed with Sony's new Cine Alta digital video camera, the same one George Lucas is using for the next Star Wars *movie. I don't know whether the movie's look (described by Elvis Mitchell as "left on the dashboard faded") is the result of the camera, or of cinematographer M. David Mullen—more Mullen's choice, I assume, or* Star Wars *fans are going to be plenty displeased. It's right for this film, but it's not ready for prime time.*

Jason X ½★
R, 93 m., 2002

Kane Hodder (Jason Voorhees), Lexa Doig (Rowan), Lisa Ryder (Kay-Em 14), Chuck Campbell (Tsunaron), Jonathan Potts (Professor Lowe), Peter Mensah (Sergeant Brodski), Melyssa Ade (Janessa), Todd Farmer (Dallas), Melody Johnson (Kinsa). Directed by James Isaac and produced by Noel Cunningham and Isaac. Screenplay by Victor Miller and Todd Farmer.

"This sucks on so many levels."
—Dialogue from *Jason X*

Rare for a movie to so frankly describe itself. *Jason X* sucks on the levels of storytelling, character development, suspense, special effects, originality, punctuation, neatness, and aptness of thought. Only its title works. And I wouldn't be surprised to discover that the name *Jason X* is copyrighted © 2002, World Wrestling Federation, and that Jason's real name is Dwayne Johnson. No, wait, that was last week's movie.

Jason X is technically *Friday the 13th, Part 10*. It takes place centuries in the future, when Earth is a wasteland and a spaceship from Earth II has returned to the Camp Crystal Lake Research Facility and discovered two cryogenically frozen bodies, one of them holding a machete and wearing a hockey mask.

The other body belongs to Rowan (Lexa Doig), a researcher who is thawed out and told it is now the year 2455: "That's 455 years in the future!" Assuming that the opening scenes take place now, you've done the math and come up with 453 years in the future. The missing two years are easily explained: I learn from the Classic Horror Website that the

movie was originally scheduled to be released on Halloween 2000, and was then bumped to March 2001, summer 2001, and Halloween 2001 before finally opening on the sixteenth anniversary of Chernobyl, another famous meltdown.

The movie is a low-rent retread of the *Alien* pictures, with a monster attacking a spaceship crew; one of the characters, Dallas, is even named in homage to the earlier series. The movie's premise: Jason, who has a "unique ability to regenerate lost and damaged tissue," comes back to life and goes on a rampage, killing the ship's plentiful supply of sex-crazed students and staff members. Once you know that the ship contains many dark corners and that the crew members wander off alone as stupidly as the campers at Camp Crystal Lake did summer after summer, you know as much about the plot as the writers do.

With *Star Wars Episode II: Attack of the Clones* opening, there's been a lot of talk lately about how good computer-generated special effects have become. On the basis of the effects in *Jason X* and the (much more entertaining) *Scorpion King*, we could also chat about how bad they are getting. Perhaps audiences do not require realistic illusions, but simply the illusion of realistic illusions. Shabby special effects can have their own charm.

Consider a scene where the spaceship is about to dock with *Solaris*, a gigantic mother ship, or a city in space, or whatever. Various controls go haywire because Jason has thrown people through them, and the ship fails to find its landing slot and instead crashes into *Solaris*, slicing off the top of a geodesic dome and crunching the sides of skyscrapers (why *Solaris* has a city-style skyline in outer space I do not presume to ask).

This sequence is hilariously unconvincing. But never mind. Consider this optimistic dialogue by Professor Lowe (Jonathan Potts), the greedy top scientist who wants to cash in on Jason: "Everyone OK? We just overshot it. We'll turn around." Uh-huh. We're waiting for the reaction from *Solaris* Air Traffic Control when a dull thud echoes through the ship and the characters realize *Solaris* has just exploded. Fine, but how could they hear it? Students of *Alien* will know that in space, no one can hear you blow up.

The characters follow the usual rules from Camp Crystal Lake, which require the crew members to split up, go down dark corridors by themselves, and call out each other's names with the sickening certainty that they will get no reply. Characters are skewered on giant screws, cut in half, punctured by swords, get their heads torn off, and worse. A veteran pilot remains calm: "You weren't alive during the Microsoft conflict. We were beating each other with our own severed limbs."

There is one good effects shot, in which a scientist's face is held in supercooled liquid until it freezes, and then smashed into smithereens against a wall. There is also an interesting transformation, as the onboard regenerator restores Jason and even supplies him with superhero armor and a new face to replace his hockey mask and ratty army surplus duds. I left the movie knowing one thing for sure: There will be a *Jason XI*—or, given the IQ level of the series, *Jason X, Part 2*.

Jay and Silent Bob Strike Back ★ ★ ★
R, 95 m., 2001

Kevin Smith (Silent Bob), Jason Mewes (Jay Phat Buds), Shannen Doherty (Rene Mosier), Renee Humphrey (Tricia "The Dish" Jones), Ben Affleck (Holden McNeil/Himself), James Van Der Beek (Himself/Bluntman), Jason Biggs (Himself/Chronic), Matt Damon (Himself/Will Hunting), Jason Lee (Banky Edwards). Directed by Kevin Smith and produced by Laura Greenlee and Scott Mosier. Screenplay by Smith.

The Movie Answer Man got a question earlier this year about whether movie characters know about other movie characters and movies. *Jay and Silent Bob Strike Back* is like an answer to that question. It is becoming clear that the film universe of Kevin Smith is interconnected, that characters from one movie can expect to run into characters from another—like Faulkner's Yoknapatawpha County, Smithland has a permanent population, even though we may not meet all of them in every movie.

The connecting threads, apparently, are Jay and Silent Bob, who we met in Smith's first movie, *Clerks*, where they were permanently stationed outside a convenience store, ostensibly pot dealers, more accurately waiting for

something to happen. They moved inside in *Mallrats*, had their lives ripped off to make a comic book in *Chasing Amy*, and risked salvation in *Dogma*. Having visited all of Smith's other movies, they are now given their own, in which characters and stars from the earlier pictures return the favor.

Consider the metaphysics. Ben Affleck and Matt Damon appear as themselves in this movie, making a sequel to their movie *Good Will Hunting*, and then we go into the fourth dimension and begin to suspect wormholes in the plot, because they also starred in *Dogma*, in which Chris Rock played an angel—and now he turns up in *Jay and Silent Bob* as the director of *Bluntman and Chronic*, which is the movie based on the lives of Jay and Silent Bob, which is an adaptation of the comic book created in *Chasing Amy*. And before he appears as himself, Affleck appears as Holden, his *Chasing Amy* character, and introduces Jay and Silent Bob to the Internet.

And look—isn't that Joey Lauren Adams, from *Chasing Amy*? And hey—wasn't Ben Affleck one of the comic artists in *Chasing Amy*? And while Affleck does not play his *Chasing Amy* character in *Jay and Silent Bob*, Jason Lee, the cocreator of the Bluntman comic, does, turning up in this one to warn Jay and Silent Bob that the comic is being made into a movie by Miramax. And Miramax is the studio releasing this movie, which . . .

Jay and Silent Bob will be seen as a self-indulgence by Kevin Smith to those outside the circle of his films—and by those within it as Kevin Smith's indulgence to them. And don't get me started on whether it's plenary or temporal. This is one of those movies where the inmates take over the asylum, by which I mean that the director was obviously unrestrained by any timid notions of "reaching the biggest possible audience," and allowed to make an in-joke of epic proportions. Like the Monty Python movies, it depends for full enjoyment on your encyclopedia knowledge of the world that generated it.

The story begins more or less at birth, as we discover that Jay (Jason Mewes) and Silent Bob (Kevin Smith) were deposited as infants in front of the convenience store in *Clerks* and have more or less been there ever since. Now a restraining order has encouraged them to budge, and in a comic-book store they run into Banky Edwards (Jason Lee), who based his *Bluntman and Chronic* comic on them, and now informs them it's been sold to Miramax.

Jay: Miramax? I thought they only made classy pictures like *The Piano* or *The Crying Game.*

Banky: After they made *She's All That,* everything went to hell.

Jay and Silent Bob decide to hitchhike to the coast, and encounter George Carlin as a hitchhiker who tells them of the one thing guaranteed to get you a ride, and Carrie Fisher as a nun who represents an exception to Carlin's advice. Then they get a ride from four animal activist babes (Shannon Elizabeth, Eliza Dushku, Ali Larter, and Jennifer Smith), who pose as friends but want to exploit them in the theft of a monkey.

Once in Los Angeles, we and they go through the looking-glass into a world where director Gus Van Sant, Affleck, and Damon appear as themselves on the set of *Good Will Hunting,* and Chris Rock is the race-card-playing director of the *Bluntman* movie, which stars James Van Der Beek and Jason Biggs as Jay and Silent Bob. And Silent Bob finally arrives at the monologue we patiently await in every picture, and reveals himself to be as least as articulate as Chris Matthews.

The charm of a Kevin Smith movie is that it assumes you do not enter the theater as a blank slate. *Chasing Amy* assumes a little knowledge of the world of serious comic books and collectors, *Dogma* required you to know something about Catholic theology, and *Jay and Silent Bob* has moments like the one where the Affleck character defines the Internet for Jay: "It's a place used the world over where people can come together to bitch about movies and share pornography together." This is a much more sophisticated idea of the Net than we find in high-tech cyberthrillers, where the Net is a place that makes your computer beep a lot.

Whether you will like *Jay and Silent Bob* depends on who you are. Most movies are made for everybody. Kevin Smith's movies are either made specifically for you, or specifically not made for you. If you read this review without a smile or a nod of recognition, I would recom-

mend *Rush Hour II,* which is for everybody or nobody, you tell me.

Note: The Gay and Lesbian Alliance Against Discrimination has chosen the wrong target in attacking Jay and Silent Bob *for alleged antigay material. GLAAD should give audiences credit for enough intelligence to know the difference between satire and bigotry. Smith agreed to add a disclaimer to the end of the movie saying "the use of antigay slurs in real life is not acceptable," as if this will (a) come as news, or (b) act as a wake-up call for those who use them. But he refused to apologize for his film, which describes Jay and Silent Bob as "hetero life-partners," and said in a statement: "I'm not sorry, because I didn't make the jokes at the expense of the gay community. I made jokes at the expense of two characters who neither I nor the audience have ever held up to be paragons of intellect. They're idiots."*

Jet Lag ★ ★
R, 85 m., 2003

Jean Reno (Felix), Juliette Binoche (Rose), Sergi Lopez (Sergio), Scali Delpeyrat (Doctor), Karine Belly (Air France Hostess), Raoul Billerey (Felix's father). Directed by Daniele Thompson and produced by Alain Sarde. Screenplay by Christopher Thompson and Daniele Thompson.

Jet Lag is sort of a grown-up version of *Before Sunrise.* In both films two travelers Meet Cute by chance and spend a long night in a strange city, talking and eating and flirting and concealing and revealing. The difference between the two films is sort of depressing.

In *Before Sunrise* (1995), Ethan Hawke and Julie Delpy were young students, and they wandered all over Vienna, encountering fortune-tellers, street poets, and friendly bartenders. In *Jet Lag,* Jean Reno and Juliette Binoche are meant to be twenty years older, and although they are in Paris they do not wander the streets or meet fascinating people, but huddle in airport lounges, hotel rooms, and tourist restaurants. The younger people talk about reincarnation, dreams, death, etc. The older people talk about abusive boyfriends, parental alienation, and cuisine.

That's the whole story, right there: The young people have their lives ahead of them and are filled with hope. The older ones are stuck with responsibilities, relationships, careers, and fears. Although *Jet Lag* has a certain morose appeal, we cannot help thinking that this night they've spent together is the most interesting time either character has had in years, and if they get married, they will look back on it as if they were out of their minds.

There are, however, moments of intrigue. Some of them involve Juliette Binoche's makeup. If you know her from her many movies (she won the Oscar for *The English Patient*), you know she has a fresh, natural complexion. As we first see her in *Jet Lag*, she is wearing too much makeup of the wrong kind, and it doesn't flatter her. Makeup is her business, in a vague way. At one point she wipes it all off, and looks younger and more beautiful. Because the director, Daniele Thompson, devotes a lot of the movie to the close-up scrutiny of her actors, this transformation has a fascination entirely apart from the character Binoche plays.

Jean Reno is a rough-hewn French star, always with what looks like a two-week-old beard, often seen in action movies (*La Femme Nikita*). Here he shows gentleness and humor, and we believe him as a celebrity chef who was once great but is now merely rich. When the Binoche character mixes a vinaigrette for him and he likes it, their fate seems possibly sealed.

The plot is based on contrivance. They meet because she needs to borrow his cell phone. When their flights are canceled, he offers to let her stay in his hotel room, the last one available at the airport. We meet her current, former, and perhaps future boyfriend, a jealous creep. We hear about how the Reno character walked out of the life of his father, also a famous chef. They keep getting calls on the wrong phone.

But somehow none of this really matters. The movie is set up as if it should matter—as if much depends on whether they fall in love. The beauty of *Before Sunrise* was that nothing was supposed to matter. They talked, they walked, and the movie (directed by Richard Linklater) was content to let them do that, without forcing false obstacles and goals upon them.

I don't know if the distance between the two films is because of the difference in filmmakers or the difference in ages. It may be that we have a heedlessness around twenty that we have lost,

perhaps prudently, around forty. One thing I know for sure: When you're twenty you know that one night could change your life forever, and when you're forty, not only do you doubt that, but you're sort of relieved.

Jimmy Neutron: Boy Genius ★ ★ ★
G, 90 m., 2001

Debi Derryberry (Jimmy Neutron), Candi Milo (Cindy Vortex), Rob Paulsen (Carl Wheezer), Martin Short (Ooblar), Patrick Stewart (King Goobot). Directed by John A. Davis and produced by Davis, Albie Hecht, and Steve Oedekerk. Screenplay by Davis, David N. Weiss, J. David Stem, and Oedekerk.

The animated comedy *Jimmy Neutron: Boy Genius* takes place in those carefree years right before puberty strikes kids down with zits and self-consciousness. "We don't like girls yet, do we, Jimmy?" asks fearful Carl Wheezer, the hero's best friend. "No, no, not yet," Jimmy reassures him. But he broods about what is on the horizon: "Hormones over which we have no control will overpower our better judgment."

Jimmy Neutron, sometimes called "Nerdtron" by his jeering classmates on the school bus, is a boy inventor who pilots his own rocket plane and is seen, as the movie opens, trying to launch a satellite before breakfast. He makes Tom Swift look slow. His dog, for example, is not a mammal but a robot named Goddard (after the father of rocketry). When Goddard makes a mess, it consists of nuts and bolts.

At home, Jimmy has inventions to brush his teeth and comb his hair. During show-and-tell at school, he unveils a device that will shrink people, and inadvertently shrinks his teacher, who is attacked by the worm in her apple. Jimmy also has a communicator capable of picking up signals from space, and becomes convinced he has been contacted by an advanced civilization. "I don't care how advanced they are," his mother says. "If your father and I haven't met them, they're strangers."

A crisis strikes. Alien spaceships suck up all of the adults in town. At first the kids celebrate, but after eating too much popcorn and candy and drinking forbidden coffee, they're as green in the morning as the lads on the

Island of Lost Boys in *Pinocchio*. Jimmy enlists the other kids in an expedition to find the alien planet and rescue the parents.

Their space travel is conceived by the filmmakers in a way that is not only charming but kind of lovely. Jimmy converts some of the rides in an amusement park into spaceships, and we see a Ferris wheel, an octopus ride, and a merry-go-round journeying across the field of stars. In another inspired conceit, they stop for the night on an asteroid, build a campfire, and frighten each other with campfire ghost stories.

Jimmy Neutron: Boy Genius is a Nickelodeon production, frankly aimed at grade-schoolers. It doesn't have the little in-jokes that make *Shrek* and *Monsters, Inc.* fun for grown-ups. But adults who appreciate the art of animation may enjoy the look of the picture, which is a kind downsized *Toy Story* with a lot of originality in the visual ideas. All movies for kids currently pay intense attention to bodily functions, and it is progress of a sort, I suppose, that Jimmy Neutron's rude noise of choice is merely the belch.

Joe Dirt ★ ½
PG-13, 93 m., 2001

David Spade (Joe Dirt), Brittany Daniel (Brandy), Dennis Miller (Zander Kelly), Adam Beach (Kicking Wing), Christopher Walken (Clem), Jaimie Pressly (Jill), Kid Rock (Robby), Erik Per Sullivan (Little Joe Dirt), Carson Daly (Himself). Directed by Dennie Gordon and produced by Robert Simonds. Screenplay by David Spade and Fred Wolf.

I wrote the words *Joe Dirt* at the top of my notepad and settled back to watch the new David Spade movie. Here is the first note I took: "Approx. 6 min. until first cow fart set afire." *Joe Dirt* doesn't waste any time letting you know where it stands.

This is the kind of movie where the hero finds two things that have fallen from the skies—a meteor and an atomic bomb—and both turn out to be a case of mistaken identity. Yes, the meteor is actually a large chunk of frozen treasure from an airplane lavatory, and the bomb is actually a large human waste storage unit.

We professional movie critics count it a banner week when only one movie involves eating, falling into, or being covered by excrement (or a cameo appearance by Carson Daly). We are not prudes. We are prepared to laugh. But what these movies, including *Joe Dirt*, often do not understand is that the act of being buried in crap is not in and of *itself* funny.

Third-graders might think so (they're big on fart jokes, too), but trust me: When Joe Dirt thinks he has an atom bomb until the cap gets knocked off and a geyser of brown crud pours out, and he *just stands there* while it covers him—that's not funny. Especially since we know he's only standing there to be sure we get the joke. Otherwise, he would move to avoid being entirely covered. Wouldn't you? (Direct quote from the press release, in connection with a scene where Spade is nearly eaten by an alligator: "David Spade performed his own stunts with the animatronic reptile. Trapped in a tangle of cable while lodged in the beast's mouth, he joked to the crew that he hoped he'd never have to get a job at a zoo." To which I can only add, "What? And leave show business?!")

Spade plays Joe Dirt, who is white trash. The movie uses that expression constantly, even observing at one point that his facial hair has grown in "white trash style" without the need for trimming. Joe's haircut is one of those 1970s mullet jobs; we learn it's not real hair but a wig supplied by his parents to cover a crack in his infant head that exposed his brain (Note: This is also supposed to be funny). The wig is a rare gift from his parents, who apparently abandoned him at the Grand Canyon when he was eight and happily playing in a garbage can.

Joe's origins and adventures are related many years later, when he happens into the studio of a talk jock played by Dennis Miller, whose own facial hair makes him look uncannily like the BBC's recent computer reconstruction of historical Jesus. Little Joe has been on his own ever since he was eight, he says, wandering the country as kind of a low-rent Forrest Gump, stumbling into interesting people and strange experiences. Where Forrest might meet a president, however, Joe is more likely to accidentally find himself in the gondola of a hot-air balloon in the shape of a tooth.

The movie's production notes further inform us: "Spade says this is the first time he has ever played a character that is likable. 'It's a big switch for me,' he says." I think he may still have his first likable character ahead of him. Joe Dirt is so obviously a construction that it is impossible to find anything human about him; he is a concept, not a person, and although Spade arguably looks better in the mullet wig than he does with his trademark mop-top, he still has the same underlying personality. Here is a man born to play the Peter Lorre role.

The movie has a very funny moment. (Spoiler alert!) It involves Christopher Walken, an actor with so much identity and charisma that his mere appearance on a screen generates interest in any audience (and gratitude and relief from this one). He plays a character named Clem, who has good reasons for not wanting to appear on television. Eventually he reveals that he has gone underground with a new identity and is now Gert B. Frobe.

Note: The movie's PG-13 rating is one more plaque on the Jack Valenti Wall of Shame. The press kit quotes Spade on the movie: "Honestly, I think it's kind of good for kids. I mean, here's a guy that's just trying to be a good guy. He's not mean to people, and he's not sarcastic, and he's not a jerk." That could be an apology for the mean, sarcastic jerks he's played up until now, but probably not.

Joe Somebody ★ ½
PG, 98 m., 2001

Tim Allen (Joe Scheffer), James Belushi (Chuck Scarett), Julie Bowen (Meg Harper), Patrick Warburton (Mark McKinney), Greg Germann (Jeremy Callahan), Kelly Lynch (Callie Scheffer), Hayden Panettiere (Natalie Scheffer). Directed by John Pasquin and produced by Kenneth Atchity, Matthew Gross, Anne Kopelson, Arnold Kopelson, and Brian Reilly. Screenplay by John Scott Shepherd.

Joe Somebody plays like an after-school special with grown-ups cast in the kids' roles. It's a simple, wholesome parable, crashingly obvious, and we sit patiently while the characters and the screenplay slowly arrive at the inevitable conclusion. It needs to take some chances and

surprise us. Everybody in the movie is kinda nice (except for the bully), and the principal—I mean, the boss—is patient while they learn their lessons and Joe finds out he really is somebody when the smart girl smiles at him.

Tim Allen is likable as the hero named Joe, but is likable enough? He's a Milquetoast video guy at a marketing agency, divorced, lonely, with nothing much to talk about, who makes up stuff to say to the cute Meg (Julie Bowen) when he runs into her in the office, because his real life is too boring to contemplate. The most exciting point in the day is when he staples his sleeve to the wall.

He dotes on his daughter, Natalie (Hayden Panettiere), and takes her along on Bring Your Daughter to Work Day. But in the company parking lot for employees with ten years or more of service, he is cut off by a big SUV driven by the bully (Patrick Warburton), who is not only rude and reckless but also doesn't even have ten years of service. When Joe protests, he is slapped and knocked down in front of his daughter, and decides, thinking it over, that he won't take her to work that day after all.

We feel really bad for him. He seems on the edge of tears. His spirit is crushed, he enters into a depression, and then he decides to get even. Enter Chuck Scarett (James Belushi), a martial arts instructor who is, I think, intended to remind us of Steven Seagal (and who looks rather more sleek and fit than Seagal himself has recently). Chuck has an ancient and obligatory role as the coach who will take the underdog and turn him into a contender. And Joe demands a rematch with the bully.

This pays the unexpected dividend of making his stock rise at the office, although his boss's reasons for promoting him are suitably devious. He even has more to talk about with Meg now, although she looks at his changes with concern, and we are reminded of the schoolmarm in a Western who gets worried when the farmer takes to carrying a rifle.

What happens, and how and why, will be perfectly clear to any sentient moviegoer as soon as the plot lays down its tracks. There are few experiences more disheartening (at the movies, anyway) than a film that suffers from preordination. By the end of *Joe Somebody*, we are faced with the dismal prospect of being denied a climax which, if it occurred, would be just as predictable as its substitute.

Joe Somebody is Tim Allen's third film directed by John Pasquin; they worked together on TV's *Home Improvement.* Their previous movies were *The Santa Clause* (1994) and *Jungle2Jungle* (1997). The first was mediocre, the second was aggressively awful, and now we get this movie, well-meaning but pretty thin soup.

I agree with all the sentiments in *Joe Somebody*, and indeed I can see them being cobbled into a parable of considerable power, especially if Joe were played by somebody who really seemed to have a capacity for violence. But Tim Allen plays Joe as a guy who never really changes, while the screenplay desperately tells us he does. And when the girl seems to turn away—isn't that what the girl always does in these plots, so that later she can turn back again?

John Q. ★ ½
PG-13, 118 m., 2002

Denzel Washington (John Q.), Robert Duvall (Grimes), James Woods (Dr. Turner), Anne Heche (Rebecca Payne), Ray Liotta (Monroe), Shawn Hatosy (Mitch), Kimberly Elise (Denise), Keram Malicki-Sanchez (Freddy), Daniel E. Smith (Mike). Directed by Nick Cassavetes and produced by Mark Burg and Oren Koules. Screenplay by James Kearns.

John Q. is the kind of movie *Mad* magazine prays for. It is so earnest, so overwrought, and so wildly implausible that it begs to be parodied. I agree with its message—that the richest nation in history should be able to afford national health insurance—but the message is pounded in with such fevered melodrama, it's as slanted and manipulative as your average political commercial.

The film stars Denzel Washington as John Q. Archibald, a Chicago factory worker whose apparently healthy son collapses during a Little League game. John Q. and his wife, Denise (Kimberly Elise), race the kid to an emergency room, where his signs are stabilized, and then a cardiologist (James Woods) explains that young Mike's heart is three times normal size.

There are two options: a heart transplant, or optimizing Mike's "quality of life" during

the "months . . . weeks . . . days" left to him. Joining the doctor is appropriately named hospital administrator Rebecca Payne (Anne Heche), who already knows the Archibalds have no money and argues for the "quality of life" choice.

John Q. thinks he's covered by insurance, but no: His company switched to a new HMO that has a $20,000 ceiling, and since John has been downsized to twenty hours a week, he's lucky to have that much coverage. Payne demands a $75,000 down payment on the $250,000 operation, and explains the harsh realities of life for "cash patients." John Q. considers taking the kid to County Hospital, but is urged by a friendly hospital employee to stay right there at the ominously named Crisis of Hope Memorial Hospital.

The TV ads helpfully reveal that John Q. exhausts all his options and eventually pulls a gun and takes hostages, demanding that his son be put at the top of the list of eligible recipients. (He wouldn't be jumping the queue because the Heche character explains Mike is so sick he would automatically be the first recipient—if the money were available.)

The hostages are your usual cross section of supporting roles: a gunshot victim, a battered woman and her violent boyfriend, a pregnant mother who has "started to dilate!" and so on. Plus Dr. Turner. The cops surround the building, and veteran negotiator Grimes (Robert Duvall) tries to build a relationship with John Q., while hotshot police chief Monroe (Ray Liotta) grandstands for the TV cameras—displaying sixteen stars on his uniform, four each on both collars and both lapels. Any more and he'd be Tinker Bell.

The underlying situation here is exactly the same as in *Dog Day Afternoon* (1975), an infinitely smarter hostage picture. What *John Q.* lacks is the confidence to allow its characters to act intelligently. Chief Monroe is almost hilariously stupid. Consider this. A local TV station somehow manages to tap the police feed from the hospital's security cameras, and broadcasts live video and sound of John Q. inside the hospital. Monroe smuggles a sniper into the hospital who has John Q. in his sights. John Q. is in the act of having an emotional and heartbreaking telephone conversation with his little boy when Monroe, who is (a) unaware of the TV feed, or (b) too dumb to live, orders the marksman to fire.

Does John Q. die? That's a question you find yourself asking a lot during this film. To avoid spoilers, I won't go into detail, but there is a moment when the movie just plain cheats on the question of John Q.'s status, and I felt conned.

There are passages where the actors transcend the material. John Q.'s farewell to his son is one. Kimberly Elise's relationship with her husband is well handled. But in a sense special honors should go to James Woods and Robert Duvall for achieving what they can with roles so awkwardly written that their behavior whipsaws between good, evil, and hilarious. Anne Heche is deep sixed by her role, which makes her a penny-pinching shrew and then gives her a cigarette to smoke just in case we missed that she's the villain. The Grim Reaper would flee from this woman.

Josie and the Pussycats ½★
PG-13, 95 m., 2001

Rachael Leigh Cook (Josie McCoy), Tara Reid (Melody Valentine), Rosario Dawson (Valerie Brown), Parker Posey (Fiona), Alan Cumming (Wyatt Frame), Gabriel Mann (Alan M. Mayberry), Paulo Costanzo (Alexander Cabot), Missi Pyle (Alexandra Cabot). Directed by Harry Elfont and Deborah Kaplan and produced by Tony DeRosa-Grund, Tracey E. Edmonds, Chuck Grimes, and Marc E. Platt. Screenplay by Elfont and Kaplan.

The heroines of *Josie and the Pussycats* are not dumber than the Spice Girls, but they're as dumb as the Spice Girls, which is dumb enough. They're a girl band recruited as they're crossing the street by a promoter who wants to use their songs as a carrier for subliminal messages. The movie is a would-be comedy about prefab bands and commercial sponsorship, which may mean that the movie's own plugs for Coke, Target, Starbucks, Motorola, and Evian are part of the joke.

The product placement for Krispy Kreme doughnuts is, however, an ominous development, since it may trigger a war with Dunkin' Donuts, currently the most visible product placer in the movies. With Krispy and Dunkin' dukin' it out, there may soon be no doughnut-free movies not actually featuring gladiators.

The movie, based on a comic book from the Archie stable, stars Rachel Leigh Cook as Josie McCoy, its lead singer; Tara Reid as Melody Valentine, the bubble-brained blonde; and Rosario Dawson as Valerie Brown. None of these women have families, friends, or employers, apparently, and are free to move randomly through the plot as a unit without ever calling home. After a prologue in which a previous prefab boy band disappears in a plane crash, a nefarious record producer named Wyatt Frame (Alan Cumming, the gay villain du jour) hires them on first sight, without hearing them sing a note, to be his newest promotion.

The prologue has some vaguely *Spinal Tap* overtones (I liked the detail that its members wear headsets at all times, not just onstage). But *Josie* ignores bountiful opportunities to be a satire of the Spice Girls and other manufactured groups, and gets dragged down by a lame plot involving the scheme to control teen spending with the implanted messages. (The movie calls them "subliminal." Since they're sound waves, they're actually "subaural," but never mind; the Pussycats would probably think subaural was a kind of foreplay.)

One curiosity about the movie is its stiff and sometimes awkward dialogue; the words don't seem to flow, but sound as if the actors are standing there and reciting them. The movie's market on verbal wit is cornered by Cumming, in the Richard E. Grant role, who has one (1) funny moment in which he demonstrates how very well trained the boy band is. The rest of the time, he has the thankless task of acting as if he is funny in a plot that is not funny.

The music is pretty bad. That's surprising, since Kenneth (Babyface) Edmunds is one of the producers, and knows his way around music. Maybe it's *supposed* to sound like brainless preteen fodder, but it's not good enough at being bad to be funny, and stops merely at the bad stage.

Parker Posey has one of those supporting roles from hell, where she has to make her entrance as a cliché and then never even gets to play with the conventions of her role. She's Cummings's boss, one of the masterminds of the nefarious subaural marketing scheme, and since she is, in fact, a funny and talented actress with wicked timing, her failure to make anything of this role is proof there's nothing for her to work with. Also drifting aimlessly through the plot is a character named Alexandra Cabot (Missi Pyle), who at least has the best explanation for why she's in the movie, as well as the movie's second (2nd) funny line of dialogue. "Why are you here?" she's asked, and replies with serene logic, "I'm here because I was in the comic book."

Joy Ride ★ ★ ★ ½
R, 96 m., 2001

Steve Zahn (Fuller), Paul Walker (Lewis), Leelee Sobieski (Venna), Jessica Bowman (Charlotte), Stuart Stone (Danny), Basil Wallace (Car Salesman), Brian Leckner (Officer Keeney). Directed by John Dahl and produced by J. J. Abrams and Chris Moore. Screenplay by Clay Tarver and Abrams.

There is a kind of horror movie that plays so convincingly we don't realize it's an exercise in pure style. *Halloween* is an example, and John Dahl's *Joy Ride* is another. Both films have an evil, marauding predator who just keeps on coming, no matter what, and always seems to know what the victims will do next. *Joy Ride* adds the detail that we never see the villain. We only hear his voice and see his truck.

The film is anchored by convincing characters in a halfway plausible setup. Paul Walker *(The Fast and the Furious)* plays Lewis, a college student who has pretended for years to be the best friend of Venna (Leelee Sobieski) when actually he wants to be her boyfriend. He's at school in California, she's in Boulder, Colorado, and after a sudden inspiration he offers to drive them both back East for the holidays.

True to the *Ebert's Little Glossary* entry that explains that all movie heroes on cross-country journeys drive gas-guzzling classics, Lewis buys a 1971 Chrysler Newport (most of the cars since 1980 look nerdy). Ordinarily the Newport would be a convertible; it needs to be a hardtop this time, so they can be trapped inside.

Lewis makes a detour along the way—to Salt Lake City, where his feckless brother Fuller (Steve Zahn, with a "What? Me worry?" expression) needs to be bailed out on drunk charges. Then it's on to Boulder, while we have lots of time to wonder why the movie spends so much time repeating that Venna goes to Boulder, Boulder, Boulder—only to show us an absolutely flat, neocolonial campus with no mountains in the background. This evens the score, I guess, for the mountains that *were* in the background in *Rumble in the Bronx*.

No matter. The plot has already tightened its screws. Fuller, who has a gift for attracting trouble, and another gift for seeking it out when it doesn't come to him, talks Lewis into buying a $40 citizen's band radio ("kind of a prehistoric Internet"), and then eggs him into imitating a woman's voice on the air. As Candy Cane, Lewis makes a date with a trucker named Rusty Nail. "She" says she'll be in Room 17 of a roadside motel—which, Lewis and Fuller know, will be occupied by a customer who's a particularly obnoxious racist. The practical jokers are next door in Room 18.

The device of the never-seen enemy is particularly effective here, as Rusty Nail pounds on the door of the neighbor, there are some indistinct voices, and then a long silence. Later, when the guy in Room 17 is found in the middle of the road in a coma and Fuller is talking to the police, he says he heard a noise like—well, you have to hear Zahn performing it. He somehow finds a note of realistic goofiness; he's funny, but you believe he's like this all the time.

The movie then settles into a series of high-tension action scenes as Rusty Nail, driving an enormous semi, tracks the Chrysler down the back roads of the Plains states. It is a convention in road movies that the heroes never take the interstate and always find ramshackle gas stations that in real life have been bankrupt for years; the atmosphere of menace is further underlined by the obligatory redneck bar with the menacing drunks who threaten the girl (Zahn's character defuses this situation with a brilliant improvisation).

It will be impossible for critics to review this movie without mentioning Steven Spielberg's TV debut film, *Duel* (1971), and it does admittedly feature an implacable foe in a big truck, but the details are all different and original, and John Dahl *(Red Rock West, The Last Seduction)* is a master of menace in everyday life. His writers, Clay Tarver and J. J. Abrams, find the details and pacing to make the unlikely into the inevitable.

It's puzzling at first how Rusty Nail, whose truck would seem to be hard to hide, is apparently able to follow them everywhere and know what they're doing; my guess is, when he tells them to "look in the trunk" and they find their CB radio there, he's rigged it so he can eavesdrop on them. That would also explain some (but not all) of his info about Venna's roommate Charlotte (Jessica Bowman). Also, other truckers could be spotting for him, and every semi in the background looks ominous.

One sequence was both effective and distracting at the same time. The truck pursues the three characters through a cornfield at night, its powerful searchlight looking for suspiciously waving stalks, and there is a great shot of the heroes running toward the camera with the truck right on top of them. At moments like this, I always wonder why they don't jump out of the way and run in the opposite direction, since it's a big operation to turn a rig like that around in a cornfield.

Quibbles. *Joy Ride* is a first-rate pure thriller, an exercise that depends on believable characters and the director's skill in putting the pieces together. The final motel sequence, in which everything breathlessly and bloodily comes together, is relentlessly well crafted. You want to be scared and have a few laughs and not have your intelligence insulted? Here you go.

Jump Tomorrow ★ ★ ★
PG, 96 m., 2001

Tunde Adebimpe (George), Hippolyte Girardot (Gerard), Natalia Verbeke (Alicia), James Wilby (Nathan), Patricia Mauceri (Consuelo), Isiah Whitlock Jr. (George's Uncle), Kaili Vernoff (Heather Leather), Gene Ruffini (Old Man), Abiola Wendy Abrams (Sophie). Directed by Joel Hopkins and produced by Nicola Usborne. Screenplay by Hopkins.

People are always asking George to smile, and he obliges, with a self-conscious twitch of the lips that reveals less happiness than wariness. What is he afraid of? Of smiling, I think. George (Tunde Adebimpe) is a serious, dutiful Nigerian who always wears glasses and usually wears a suit and needs to learn to listen to his heart.

We meet him at the airport in Buffalo, where he plans to meet his bride-to-be; it is an arranged marriage with a Nigerian woman his family has known for years. Alas, she arrived on yesterday's plane, and finding no one to meet her, has already gone on to Niagara, where the wedding is to take place. George's uncle (Isiah Whitlock Jr.) is apoplectic: The marriage makes good "sense," and George is blowing it.

That's the setup for the low-key screwball comedy *Jump Tomorrow*, which takes a 1930s Hollywood formula and recasts it with unexpected types. At the airport, George meets Alicia (Natalia Verbeke), a Latina who flirts with him and tells him about a party that night. And he meets Gerard (Hippolyte Girardot), a disconsolate Frenchman who has just proposed marriage and been slammed down.

George is not a demonstrative man, but for some reason he inspires others to enlist in his cause. He ends up at Alicia's party with Gerard, and by the end of the evening it is clear to Gerard, if not to George, that George is in love with Alicia. Gerard sees George as an assignment from heaven: If Gerard cannot find happiness in love, perhaps he can help George find it. He offers to drive George to Niagara. Along the way they encounter Alicia and her unpromising British boyfriend Nathan (James Wilby). Everyone ends up in Gerard's car (license plate: AMOUR), their romantic futures in doubt.

The title of *Jump Tomorrow* refers to helpful advice for potential suicides. It may also refer to taking a big romantic leap. The movie has been written and directed by Joel Hopkins, a recent graduate of the NYU film school, whose short subject *Jorge* starred the same character and was a hit on the festival and on-line circuits. The movie doesn't have an unkind thought in its head. It's all sweetness and understated charm, and after a while even George begins to grow on us.

That is a slow process, because Tunde Adebimpe plays the character as a man who values probity above all else, and has an instinctive loathing for instinctive gestures. If he were happy-go-lucky, the movie would lose much of its charm; the buried question is whether this sober, severe young man is capable of a grand romantic gesture. The movie plays with ethnic stereotypes by having the Gallic Gerard and the Latin Alicia as his emotional prods; the Englishman Nathan is as uptight as George, but while George's personality is a challenge, Nathan's is a trial.

Is there a market for a movie like this? It doesn't punch out its comic points but lets the story gradually reveal them. It takes us time to like George. The plot unfolds with the gradual richness of something by Eric Rohmer, who has the whole canvas in view from the beginning but uncovers it a square inch at a time. By the end of *Jump Tomorrow* I was awfully fond of the picture. Is that enough for a first-run admission, or should you wait until it turns up on one of the indie cable channels? You tell me.

The Jungle Book 2 ★ ½
G, 72 m., 2003

With the voices of: Haley Joel Osment (Mowgli), John Goodman (Baloo), Mae Whitman (Shanti), Connor Funk (Ranjan), Tony Jay (Shere Khan), Bob Joles (Bagheera), Jim Cummings (Kaa/Colonel Hathi), Phil Collins (Lucky). An animated film directed by Steve Trenbirth and produced by Christopher Chase and Mary Thorne. Screenplay by Karl Geurs.

The Jungle Book 2 is so thin and unsatisfying it seems like a made-for-DVD version, not a theatrical release. Clocking in at seventy-two minutes and repeating the recycled song "The Bare Necessities" three if not four times, it offers a bare-bones plot in which Mowgli wanders off into the jungle, is threatened by a tiger and a snake, is protected by a bear, takes care of his little girlfriend, and sings and dances with Baloo.

There's none of the complexity here, in story or style, we expect in this new golden age of animation. It's a throwback in which cute animals of no depth or nuance play with the hero or threaten him in not very scary ways.

As the film opens, Mowgli (who once, long ago and at another level of literacy, was the hero of stories by Rudyard Kipling) lives in a village and is forbidden to cross the river. But "you can take boy out of the jungle, but you can't take the jungle out of boy," we learn. Whoever wrote that dialogue must have gone home weary after a hard day's work.

Mowgli (voice by Haley Joel Osment) and his little village playmate Shanti (voice by Mae Whitman) do, however, venture into the forest, where Mowgli's old friend Baloo the Bear (John Goodman) is delighted to see him, although a little jealous of all the attention he is paying to Shanti. Maybe Baloo should discuss this problem with a counselor. They dance and sing and peel mangos, and then Mowgli and/or Shanti wander off alone to be threatened by the tiger and the snake (whose coils are cleverly animated), and to be rescued by Baloo, with a reprise or two of "The Bare Necessities."

In a time that has given us Miyazaki's great animated film *Spirited Away* (also a Disney release), parents have some kind of duty to take a close look at the films offered. I got in an argument at Sundance with a Salt Lake City man who sells software that automatically censors DVDs in order to remove offending scenes and language. (Theoretically, there could be a version of *Fight Club* suitable for grade-schoolers, although it would be very short.) By this yardstick, *The Jungle Book 2* is inoffensive and harmless.

But it is not nutritious. A new book argues that the average American child spends twice as much time watching television than interacting with his parents, and movies like *The Jungle Book 2* are dim-witted baby-sitters, not growth experiences. If kids grow up on the movie equivalent of fast food, they will form an addiction to that instant action high and will never develop the attention span they need to love worthwhile fiction.

Disney can do better, will do better, usually does better. To release this film theatrically is a compromise of its traditions and standards. If you have children in the target age range, keep them at home, rent an animated classic or Miyazaki's great *My Neighbor Totoro*, and do them a favor.

Jurassic Park III ★ ★ ★
PG-13, 91 m., 2001

Sam Neill (Dr. Alan Grant), William H. Macy (Paul Kirby), Tea Leoni (Amanda Kirby), Alessandro Nivola (Billy Brennan), Trevor Morgan (Eric Kirby), Michael Jeter (Udesky), John Diehl (Cooper), Bruce A. Young (Nash), Laura Dern (Ellie). Directed by Joe Johnston and produced by Kathleen Kennedy and

Larry Franco. Screenplay by Peter Buchman, Alexander Payne, and Jim Taylor, based on characters created by Michael Crichton.

This movie does a good job of doing exactly what it wants to do. *Jurassic Park III* is not as awe-inspiring as the first film or as elaborate as the second, but in its own B-movie way it's a nice little thrill machine. One of its charms is its length—less than 90 minutes, if you don't count the end credits. Like the second half of a double bill in the 1940s, it doesn't overstay its welcome.

One of the ways it saves time is by stunningly perfunctory character development. There's hardly a line of dialogue that doesn't directly serve the plot in one way or another. Even Sam Neill's pontifications about those who would trifle with the mystery of life are in the movie only as punctuation, to separate the action scenes. In a summer when B-movie ideas like this have been blown up to gargantuan size and length with A-movie budgets, here is an action picture we actually wish was a little longer.

Part of its brevity is explained by the abrupt ending, which comes with little preparation and will have you racing to the dictionary to look up "deus ex machina." Trained by the interior tides and rhythms of most action movies, we get the ending when we expect the false crisis, followed by the false dawn, and then the real crisis and the real dawn. We can't believe the movie is really over, and when some flying pteranodons appear, we expect another action scene, but no—they're just flapping their way overseas to set up the next sequel.

The movie begins with a fourteen-year-old named Eric (Trevor Morgan) parasailing with his mother's boyfriend over the forbidden island of Isla Sorna, off the coast of Costa Rica. You will recall that this is the location of the doomed theme park in *The Lost World: Jurassic Park II.* The towboat disappears into a mist of fog and emerges sans crew, and the parasailers crash on the island. Cut to America, where two people (William H. Macy and Tea Leoni) offer a big bucks donation to the research of famous paleontologist Alan Grant (Sam Neill) if he will be their guide for a flight over the island.

They are in fact not just tourists; their secret is that they are Eric's parents, and they plan to land the plane on the island and rescue him.

Along for the ride are Neill's gung ho assistant (Alessandro Nivola) and three other crew members, some of whom are quickly eaten by dinosaurs, although for a change the black character doesn't die first. The search for Eric consists mostly of the survivors walking through the forest shouting "Eric!" but the movie is ingenious in devising ways for prehistoric beasts to attack. There are some truly effective action sequences—one involving flying lizards and a suspension bridge, another involving an emergency rescue with the recycled parasail—that are as good as these things get.

I also liked the humor that's jimmied into the crevices of the plot. There are two nice gags involving the ringer on a cell phone, and a priceless exchange of dialogue between the fourteen-year-old and the expert paleontologist:

Dr. Grant: This is T-Rex pee? How'd you get it?
Eric: You don't want to know.

I am aware that *Jurassic Park III* is shorter, cheaper, and with fewer pretensions than its predecessors, and yet there was nothing I disliked about it, and a lot to admire in its lean, efficient storytelling. I can't praise it for its art, but I must not neglect its craft, and on that basis I recommend it.

Note: That last shot obviously means that the giant flying pteranodons are headed to civilization for Jurassic Park IV. *I am reminded of the 1982 movie* Q, *in which a flying reptile monster builds its nest atop the Chrysler Building and flies down to snack on stockbrokers. The movie was screened at Cannes, after which its proud producer, Samuel Z. Arkoff, hosted a gathering for film critics, at which I overheard the following conversation:*

Rex Reed: Sam! I just saw your picture! What a surprise! All that dreck—and right in the middle of it, a great Method performance by Michael Moriarity!
Arkoff: The dreck was my idea.

Just a Kiss ★
R, 89 m., 2002

Ron Eldard (Dag), Kyra Sedgwick (Halley), Patrick Breen (Peter), Marisa Tomei (Paula), Marley Shelton (Rebecca), Taye Diggs (Andre), Sarita Choudhury (Colleen), Bruno Amato (Joe),

Zoe Caldwell (Jessica). Directed by Fisher Stevens and produced by Matthew H. Rowland. Screenplay by Patrick Breen.

If only it were clever, *Just a Kiss* would be too clever by half. Here is a movie that was apparently made by working its way through a list of styles, so that we have poignancy jostling against farce, thoughtful dialogue elbowed aside by one-liners, and a visual style that incorporates rotoscope animation for no apparent reason except, maybe, that it looks neat.

Just a Kiss, directed by the actor Fisher Stevens, begins with a kiss between two people who should not be kissing, and ends after those people, and their significant others and assorted insignificant others, undergo sexual and emotional misunderstandings, survive plane crashes, end up in hospital or comatose, etc., while occasionally appearing to be animated like the characters in *Waking Life.*

Now *Waking Life* was an accomplished movie, in which Richard Linklater took live-action footage of his characters and passed it through a software program that kept their basic appearances and movements while allowing artists to overlay an animated layer. It worked. It does not work in *Just a Kiss,* and I'm about to explain why.

In *Waking Life,* all of the characters are animated. That is what they are and how we accept them, and whatever reality they have is conveyed visually through the animation. But in *Just a Kiss,* the characters are photographed realistically, so that when they suddenly undergo "rotomation," their reality is violently displaced and our attention is jerked up to the surface of the movie. They exist now, not as characters, but as animated displays who used to be characters and may be characters again.

I can imagine a way in which this could work, in a *Roger Rabbit*–type movie that moves in and out of the cartoon dimension. But it doesn't work here, because it is manifestly and distractingly only a stunt. And the whole movie, in various ways, has the same problem: It's all surface, without an entry point into whatever lurks beneath. The characters, dialogue, personal styles, and adventures are all mannerisms. The actors are merely carriers of the director's contrivances.

Consider, for example, a sequence in which one character on an airplane uses his cell phone to tell another that he loves her. His phone emits lethal transmissions that cause the plane to crash. Everyone in first class lives; everyone in tourist class dies. I smile as I write the words. This would be a good scene in *Airplane!* What is it doing here, in a movie where we are possibly expected to care about the characters' romances and infidelities? To admit farce into a drama is to admit that the drama is farce.

But is it a drama? I haven't a clue. The movie seems to reinvent itself from moment to moment, darting between styles like a squirrel with too many nuts. There is one performance that works, sort of, and it is by Marisa Tomei, as a bartender whose psychic gifts allow her to find meaning in the rings left by cold beers. She is a crazy, homicidal maniac, but, hey, at least that means that nothing she does is out of character.

As for the other actors, they know Stevens from the indie films they've made together and were good sports to volunteer for this project. Ron Eldard, Kyra Sedgwick, Patrick Breen (who wrote the screenplay), Marley Shelton, Taye Diggs, Sarita Choudhury, and Bruno Amato do what they can with characters who are reinvented from minute to minute. And Zoe Caldwell, as a choreographer who is the mother of the Shelton character, has moments of stunningly effective acting that are so isolated from the rest of the movie that they appear like the result of channel-surfing.

Just Married ★ ½
PG-13, 94 m., 2003

Ashton Kutcher (Tom Leezak), Brittany Murphy (Sarah McNerney), Christian Kane (Peter Prentis), Monet Mazur (Lauren McNerney), David Moscow (Kyle), Valeria (Wendy), David Rasche (Mr. McNerney), Veronica Cartwright (Mrs. McNerney), Raymond Barry (Mr. Leezak). Directed by Shawn Levy and produced by Robert Simonds. Screenplay by Sam Harper.

Just Married is an ungainly and witless comedy, made more poignant because its star, Brittany Murphy, made such a strong impression as Eminem's sometime girlfriend in *8 Mile.* With her fraught eyes and husky voice, she has a rare and particular quality (I think of Jennifer Jason Leigh), and yet here she's stuck in a dumb sitcom.

She and Ashton Kutcher play newlyweds in a plot that proves that opposites repel. She's a rich kid named Sarah, expensively raised and educated. He's Tom, an example of the emerging subspecies Sports Bar Man. They have a perfect relationship, spoiled by marriage (I think that may even be one of the lines in the movie). They're too tired for sex on their wedding night, but make up for it on their honeymoon flight to Europe with a quickie in the toilet of the airplane. There is perhaps the potential for a glimmer of comedy there, but not in Sam Harper's overwritten and Shawn Levy's overdirected movie, which underlines and emphasizes like a Power Point presentation for half-wits.

Consider. It may be possible to find humor in a scene involving sex in an airplane rest room, but not by pushing the situation so far that Tom's foot gets caught in the toilet and the bitchy flight attendant suffers a broken nose. Later, in their honeymoon hotel in Venice, it may be possible that energetic sex could break a bed frame—but can it actually destroy the wall to the adjoining room? And it may be possible for an improper electrical device to cause a short in a hotel's electrical system, but need the offending device be a vibrator? And for that matter, isn't it an alarming sign of incipient pessimism to take a vibrator along on your honeymoon?

Europe was not the right choice for this honeymoon. He should have gone to Vegas, and she should have stayed single. Sarah wants to visit every church and museum, but Tom abandons her in the middle of Venice when he finds a bar that's showing an American baseball game. This is as likely as a sports bar in Brooklyn televising *boules* in French.

Sarah and Tom have nothing to talk about. They are a pathetic, stupid couple and deserve each other. What they do not deserve, perhaps, is a screenplay that alternates between motivation and slapstick. Either it's character-driven or it isn't. If it is, then you can't take your plausible characters and dump them into Laurel and Hardy. Their rental car, for example, gets a cheap laugh, but makes them seem silly in the wrong way. And earlier in the film, Tom is responsible for the death of Sarah's dog in a sce-

nario recycled directly from an urban legend everyone has heard.

Would it have been that much more difficult to make a movie in which Tom and Sarah were plausible, reasonably articulate newlyweds with the humor on their honeymoon growing out of situations we could believe? Apparently.

Just Visiting ★ ★ ★
PG-13, 88 m., 2001

Jean Reno (Thibault), Christina Applegate (Rosalind/Julia), Christian Clavier (André), Matthew Ross (Hunter), Tara Reid (Angelique), Bridgette Wilson-Sampras (Amber), John Aylward (Byron), George Plimpton (Dr. Brady), Malcolm McDowell (Wizard). Directed by Jean-Marie Poire and produced by Patrice Ledoux and Ricardo Mestres. Screenplay by Poire, Christian Clavier, and John Hughes.

A medieval sorcerer accidentally sends a French knight and his serf on a trip into the future—landing them in today's Chicago, where the elevated trains terrify them. But they grow to like the city, and when the sorcerer prepares to return them to the Middle Ages, the serf is against it: "I want to stay here, where I can eat doughnuts, and wear exciting men's fashions at rock-bottom prices."

Just Visiting, which tells their story, is one of those rare American remakes of a French film that preserves the flavor of the original and even improves upon it. The movie is a remake of *The Visitors*, or *Les Visiteurs* (1993), which was the top-grossing comedy in French history, but did only moderate business in America. Like the original, it's broad and swaggering, but somehow it plays better in English— maybe because the fish-out-of-water concept works better with French and American accents, instead of everybody speaking in subtitles.

The movie, directed by Jean-Marie Poire, wisely centers on its two original French stars, Jean Reno (of *Mission: Impossible* and *Godzilla*) and Christian Clavier. They look and sound the part; I can imagine the roles being assigned to Adam Sandler and David Spade, but I don't want to. Reno is Sir Thibault, a French knight who goes to Sussex to marry the beautiful Rosalind (Christina Applegate). His vassal André (Clavier) follows along, trotting obediently behind the cart and being whacked occasionally just to honor the class divide.

After a setup heavy on special effects and overacting, involving witches, cauldrons, and royal schemers, Thibault convinces a sorcerer (Malcolm McDowell) to jump them back a little in time, so they can get things right on a second try. The wizard, alas, miscalculates and sends them to modern Chicago, where the knight and serf are terrified by semis, awestruck by skyscrapers, and soon involved in the life of Thibault's great-great-great-great-great (I think) granddaughter Julia (Applegate again).

She's the heir to the family's old European fortune, founded all those years ago by Thibault, and the spitting image of his beloved Rosalind. But her boyfriend, the sneering Hunter (Matthew Ross) wants her to sell the family's European estate, so he can get his claws on the money. Thibault and André understandably have difficulty convincing Chicagoans they are really from the twelfth century, but their behavior certainly seems authentic enough (in a restaurant, Thibault expects André, as his servant, to eat off the floor).

Thibault cannot actually fall in love with Julia, since she is his great, etc., granddaughter, but since she looks exactly like the woman he loved, he cares for her deeply, and tries to protect her from Hunter's schemes while schooling her in the ways of medieval gallantry. This involves a sword-fighting lesson in which they slice up refrigerators and Dumpsters, and a horsemanship adventure in which they actually ride their horses up the stairs, across an L platform, and onto the train.

André meanwhile falls in love with Angelique (Tara Reid), providing a counterpoint to the courtly idealism of his master. And every day is an adventure. Their first ride in a car, for example, is a terrifying experience. "Slower! Slower!" cries Thibault, as the car creeps at twenty miles per hour and both visitors hurl out the windows.

Is it only because the movie is in English that I like it more than the original? I hope I'm not that provincial. It strikes me that *Just Visiting* is brighter and sprightlier than *Les Visiteurs*, and the contrasts are funnier. Modern Europe is filled with Gothic and medieval piles, but in

Chicago, when the visitors go looking for castles and turrets, they find them in the architecture of bars—where the regulars are always ready to drink with a man in armor, as long as he pays for his round.

There's something else too. *Just Visiting* isn't low and dumb like so many recent American comedies. It depends on the comedy of personality and situation, instead of treading meekly in the footsteps of the current gross-out manure-joke movies. Jean Reno, who usually plays a tough guy (remember him in *The Professional?*), plays Thibault more or less straight, taking his chivalric code seriously. Both he and Clavier try to appear truly baffled by what they see, instead of going straight for the gags.

Note: It must be said, all chauvinism aside, that the city of Chicago itself makes an important contribution. John Hughes, who sets almost all of his movies here, is one of the movie's producers and cowriters, and he knows the town better than any other director (maybe it's a tie with Andrew Davis). Chicago locations have not been better used in any movie since Davis's Code of Silence *and* The Fugitive *and Hughes's* Ferris Bueller's Day Off, *and they work not simply as backdrops but as dramatic settings. Given a knight on a horse in a city with elevated trains, it may seem inevitable that sooner or later he'd ride the horse onto the train, but it certainly looked like an inspired idea to me.*

Juwanna Mann ★ ★
PG-13, 91 m., 2002

Miguel A. Nunez Jr. (Jamal/Juwanna Mann), Vivica A. Fox (Michelle Langford), Tommy Davidson (Puff Smokey Smoke), Kevin Pollak (Lorne Daniels), Ginuwine (Romeo), Kim Wayans (Latisha Jansen), Kimberly "Lil' Kim" Jones (Tina Parker). Directed by Jesse Vaughan and produced by Bill Gerber, James G. Robinson, and Steve Oedekerk. Screenplay by Bradley Allenstein.

Let us now consider predictability. Most of the time, I consider it an insult to the audience. We can sense when a movie is on autopilot, and we wonder, not unreasonably, why the filmmakers couldn't be bothered to try a little harder. Then a movie like *Juwanna Mann* comes along and is predictable to its very core, and in a funny way the predictability is part of the fun. The movie is in on the joke of its own recycling.

How predictable is it? It begins with a pro basketball star who is thrown out of the league (he gets so angry at a referee's call that he takes off all of his clothes and flashes the audience). He's faced with foreclosure, bankruptcy, and the loss of all his commercial endorsements, is fired by his manager, and has no skills except the ability to play basketball. In desperation, he dresses in drag and passes himself off as Juwanna Mann, a female player, and is soon a star of the women's pro basketball league.

With that information in mind, there are scenes we can all predict: (1) A date with an obnoxious man who doesn't know Juwanna is male. (2) Weird times in the shower. (3) A crush on a beautiful teammate who likes Juwanna as a friend but, of course, doesn't realize she's a man. (4) Unruly erections. (5) Ill-disciplined falsies. We can also predict that Juwanna will lead her team into the finals, become a big star, learn useful lessons about human nature, be faced with a crisis and exposure, and emerge as a better person, all of her problems solved, while the team wins the big game.

These predictable scenes are, I submit, inevitable. There is no way to make this movie without them—not as a comedy, anyway. So the pleasure, if any, must come from the performances, not the material. Up to a point, it does. Although *Juwanna Mann* is not a good movie, it isn't a painful experience, and Miguel A. Nunez Jr. is plausible as Juwanna, not because he is able to look like a woman, but because he is able to play a character who thinks he can look like a woman.

Vivica A. Fox plays Michelle, the teammate Juwanna falls in love with, and it is a challenging assignment, because almost all her dialogue needs to be taken two ways. Screenplay gimmicks like this are hard for actors, because if they are too sincere they look like chumps, and if they seem to be grinning sideways at the audience, they spoil the illusion. Fox finds the right tone and sticks to it; there is skilled professionalism at work, even in a rent-a-plot like this.

Since the entire movie is, of course, completely implausible, it seems unkind to single out specific examples of implausibility. But there's a difference between the implausibility of the basic gimmick (man passing as a woman) and the implausibility of plot details *within* the gimmick. The most obvious comes at the end, when Juwanna is exposed as a man. The movie deals with that exposure, but ignores another fact that almost every audience member will pick up on: If Juwanna's team played the season with an ineligible player, doesn't it have to forfeit all of its games?

We aren't supposed to ask questions like that, I suppose, but there's another glitch that stands out because the movie insists on it. Early in the film, Juwanna is informed that dunking is illegal in the women's league. Late in the film, she wins a game with a last-second dunk. Say what? Has everyone in the league forgotten the rules?

Such glitches would matter more, I suppose, if the movie were serious. In a comedy, they're distractions, suggesting the filmmakers either weren't paying attention or didn't care. I can't recommend *Juwanna Mann,* and yet I admire the pluck of the actors, especially Nunez, Fox, and Tommy Davidson, as a spectacularly ineligible lothario, and I liked the way Kevin Pollak soldiers away as the manager who must be perpetually offended, astonished, or frustrated. *Juwanna Mann* is unnecessary, but not painful.

K

Kandahar ★ ★ ★ ½
NO MPAA RATING, 85 m., 2002

Nelofer Pazira (Nafas), Hassan Tantai (Tabib Sahid), Sadou Teymouri (Khak). Directed and produced by Mohsen Makhmalbaf. Screenplay by Makhmalbaf.

When she was a child, Nafas was taken to Canada, while her sister stayed behind in Afghanistan. Now Nafas has received a letter from her sister, who lost both legs after stepping on a land mine, and plans to kill herself during the final eclipse of the twentieth century. Nafas sets off on a desperate journey to smuggle herself from Iran into Afghanistan, to convince her sister to live. *Kandahar* follows that journey in a way that sheds an unforgiving light on the last days of the Taliban.

I saw the movie, by Iran's Mohsen Makhmalbaf, at Cannes 2001, where it was admired but seemed to have slim chances of a North American release. Of course, 9/11 changed that, and Kandahar became a familiar place name. The movie is especially accessible because most of it is in English—the language of the heroine, who keeps a record of her journey on a tape recorder, and also the language of one of the other major characters.

Nafas (Nelofer Pazira) is unable to get into Afghanistan by conventional means, perhaps because her family fled for political reasons. In Iran, she pays an itinerant trader, who travels between the two countries, to bring her in as one of his wives; she wears a burka, which covers her from head to toe, making the deception more possible. And as she sets out, we begin to realize that the journey, not the sister's fate, is the point of the film: Nafas is traveling back into the world where she was born.

Makhmalbaf and his cinematographer, Ebraham Ghafouri, show this desert land as beautiful but remote and forbidding. Roads are tracks from one flat horizon to another. Nafas bounces along in the back of a truck with other women, the burka amputating her personality. There are roadblocks, close calls, confusions, and eventually the merchant turns back, leaving her in the company of a boy of ten or twelve named Khak (Sadou Teymouri). With that terrible wisdom that children gain in times of trouble, he knows his way around the dangers and takes $50 to lead her to Kandahar. At one point they trek through a wilderness of sand dunes, and when he finds a ring on the finger of a skeleton he wants to sell it to her.

Nafas grows ill, and Khak takes her to a doctor. She stands on one side of a blanket, the doctor on the other, and he talks to her through a hole in the fabric. The Taliban forbids any more intimate contact between unmarried men and women; he can ask her to say "ah," and that's about it. But this doctor (Hassan Tantai) has a secret—a secret he reveals when he hears her English with its North American accent. Khak hangs around, hungry for any information he can sell, until the doctor bribes him with peanuts and sends him away.

Kandahar does not provide deeply drawn characters, memorable dialogue, or an exciting climax. Its traffic is in images. Who will ever forget the scene of a Red Cross helicopter flying over a refugee camp and dropping artificial legs by parachute, as one-legged men hobble on their crutches to try to catch them? The movie makes us wonder how any belief system could convince itself it was right to make so many people miserable, to deny the simple human pleasures of life. And yet the last century has been the record of such denial.

Khak, the boy, has been expelled from school. We see one of the Taliban schools. All of the students are boys, of course—women are not permitted to study. That may be no great loss. The boys rock back and forth while chanting the Koran. Not studying or discussing it, simply repeating it. Then they are drilled on the parts of a rifle. "Weapons are the only modern thing in Afghanistan," the doctor tells Nafas.

Kate & Leopold ★ ★ ★
PG-13, 118 m., 2001

Meg Ryan (Kate), Liev Schreiber (Stuart), Hugh Jackman (Leopold), Josh Stamberg (Bob), Bradley Whitford (J.J.), Philip Bosco (Otis), Bill Corsair (Morty). Directed by James

Mangold and produced by Cathy Konrad. Screenplay by Mangold and Steven Rogers.

Kate & Leopold is a preposterous time-travel romance in which the third Duke of Albany leaves the New York of 1876 and arrives in the New York of Meg Ryan. Well, of course it's preposterous: Time travel involves so many paradoxes that it is wise, in a romantic comedy like this, to simply ignore them. The movie is not really about time travel anyway, but about elegant British manners versus American slobbiness. Like the heroine of one of those romance novels her best friend reads, our gal Meg is swept off her feet by a wealthy and titled English lord.

Ryan plays Kate, who works in market research and is responsible for promoting products of dubious value. She's been dating Stuart (Liev Schreiber), a half-loony inventor who discovers an opening in the matrix of time, jumps off the Brooklyn Bridge, finds himself in 1876—and returns with his own great-great-grandfather, Leopold, Duke of Albany (Hugh Jackman).

It is inevitable that Kate will overcome her lukewarm affection for Stuart and fall in love with the dashing Englishman (even though the first time she sees him in military costume, she thinks he's dressed as Sergeant Pepper). Meg Ryan does this sort of thing about as well as it can possibly be done, and after *Sleepless in Seattle* and *You've Got Mail,* here is another ingenious plot that teases us with the possibility that true love will fail, while winking that of course it will prevail.

Kate & Leopold wisely does not depend on the mechanics of the developing romance for its humor. Instead, it uses its fish-out-of-water plot to show Leopold as a proper, well-behaved English aristocrat, astonished by what he finds in modern Manhattan. He's struck not so much by the traffic and the skyscrapers as by the manners. Walking a dog, he's asked by a cop if he plans to scoop the poop, and draws himself to his full height to intone: "Are you suggesting, madam, there exists a law compelling gentlemen to lay hold of canine bowel movements?"

Both Leopold and his descendant Stuart are inventor types. Leopold, we learn, designed the Brooklyn Bridge and invented the elevator.

Stuart not only discovered the portal in time, but had enough confidence in his calculations to jump off the bridge and trust that it would open for him. Why he lands on his feet instead of falling to his death in the 1876 river is a question the movie prudently ignores.

The movie, directed by James Mangold *(Heavy; Girl, Interrupted)* and written by Mangold and Steven Rogers, has some droll scenes after Kate enlists Leopold to appear in a TV commercial for Farmer's Bounty, a low-calorie spread. Leopold's accent and his sincere conviction are perfect, and the spot goes well until he actually tastes the product, and compares it to saddle soap or raw suet: "It's revolting!" Kate tries to calm him: "It's diet. It's *supposed* to taste awful."

One of the reasons the movie works is because we like the goodness of the characters; it's wise, I think, to let Schreiber get over his romantic disappointment as quickly as possible and become a coconspirator for love. (Apart from any other reason, Stuart knows that unless Albany returns to 1876 and starts a family, Stuart will never exist.) We know there will be scenes where Kate the practical and cynical girl is swept off her feet by old-fashioned romance, and there are: a candlelit rooftop dinner, and a moment when Leopold tucks her in, she asks him to stay, and he does, in full uniform.

I have here a precautionary message from Will Shank of Toronto, Ontario, who writes that before I review *Kate & Leopold* there are a couple of things I should know: "Prince Leopold, the Duke of Albany, was a hemophiliac and although he has been described as daring and high-spirited, would not have been foolish enough to participate in the dangerous stunts seen in the trailer. He was sickly all his life and his mother, Queen Victoria, expressed surprise that he lived long enough to be married and have a child. Also, Victoria and her children spoke German among themselves, not English. People who knew them related that when they did speak English, it was with a strong German accent."

Thanks, Will. The next time I meet James Mangold, I'll ask him why he didn't make *Kate & Leopold* the story of a hemophiliac with a German accent who was afraid to jump off bridges. Sounds like a movie we are all waiting to see.

Keep the River on Your Right ★ ★ ★
R, 110 m., 2001

A documentary directed and produced by David Shapiro and Laurie Gwen Shapiro.

In the mid-1950s, a New York artist and anthropologist named Tobias Schneebaum walked into the rain forests of Peru, planning to paint some pictures there. His geographical knowledge was limited to the advice: Keep the river on your right. A year later, he walked out of the jungle naked, covered with body paint, having found and lived with an Indian tribe.

At some point during that year, the tribe went on a raid, killed enemies, and ate them. Schneebaum joined them in consuming human flesh. "Didn't you try to stop them?" someone asks him in this documentary. It is the kind of question asked by a person who has never had to live with cannibals, on their terms.

Schneebaum is not the kind of man you would immediately think of in connection with this adventure. Seventy-eight when the film was made, he is a homosexual aesthete who lectures on art and works as a tour guide on cruise ships. Yet his adventures were not limited to Peru, and in the extraordinary documentary *Keep the River on Your Right: A Modern Cannibal Tale,* he also revisits the jungles of New Guinea, where he lived with a tribe, took a male lover, and has a reunion with his old friend. Many years have passed, but the friend accepts him as warmly as if he'd been away for a week or two.

The visits to his old homes in New Guinea and Peru are not without hazards. Schneebaum isn't worried about jungle animals or diseases, but has more practical concerns on his mind, like breaking a hip: "If I slip on the mud, I've had it."

The movie is the work of a brother and sister, David Shapiro and Laurie Gwen Shapiro, who learned about Schneebaum and became determined to make a movie about him. It is a story he has been telling for years; he wrote a memoir about his adventures, and we see clips of him chatting about the book with Mike Douglas and Charlie Rose. He also, I imagine,

gets good mileage out of his stories on those cruise ships, although he is not particularly eager to discuss cannibalism, and we sense pain that his dry, laconic style tries to mask. Asked how people taste, he answers shortly, "I don't remember." At another point, in another context, he observes: "I kind of died. Something I had that was made of me, and then it was gone after the Peruvian experience."

Can we speculate that he penetrated so close to the fault line of human existence that he lost the unspoken security we walk around with every day? Things may get bad for us, even hopeless, but we will not be naked in the jungle, face-to-face with life's oldest and most implacable code, eat or be eaten. Schneebaum doesn't strike us as the Indiana Jones sort. He didn't go into the jungle as a lark. Whatever happened there he prefers to describe in terms of its edges, its outside.

The sexuality he encountered in New Guinea is another matter, and there he cheers up. The men of the tribe he lived with have sex with both men and women and consider it natural. We sense this is not the kind of sex people go looking for in big Western cities, but more of a pastime and consolation among friends. There is a certain shy warmth in the reunion with his former lover, but subtly different on Schneebaum's side than on the other man's, because sex between men means something different to each of them.

Tobias Schneebaum could probably develop a stand-up act based on his adventures, but he is more of a muser and a wonderer. "You're there to study them, not to play with them," he says sharply at one point. I met him at the 2000 Toronto Film Festival, where in interview and question sessions he answered as if he were a teacher or a witness, not a celebrity. We get glimpses of his earlier life in Greenwich Village (former neighbor Norman Mailer remembers him as "our house homosexual—terrified of a dead mouse"), and learn something of his painting and his books.

But mostly we are struck by the man. *Keep the River on Your Right* could have been quite a different kind of film, but the Shapiros wisely focus on the mystery of this man, who was spectacularly ill-prepared for both of his jungle journeys, and apparently walked away from civilization prepared to rely on the kindness of strangers. Perhaps it was his very naïveté that shielded him. The cannibals obviously had nothing to fear from him. Today, we learn, they no longer practice cannibalism, and indeed are well on their way down the capitalist assembly line, shedding their culture and learning to eat fast food. Tobias Schneebaum was not only their first visitor from "civilization," but their most benign.

Note: The flywheels at the MPAA Ratings Board have given this sweet and innocent movie an R rating, explaining "mature thematic material." Yes, but the cannibalism is not seen, only discussed. How can this film and Freddy Got Fingered, *with Tom Green biting a newborn baby's umbilical cord in two, deserve the same rating?*

The Kid Stays in the Picture ★ ★ ★ ½
R, 93 m., 2002

A documentary film about Robert Evans, directed by Brett Morgen and Nanette Burstein and produced by Graydon Carter, Morgen, and Burstein. Screenplay by Morgen, based on the book *The Kid Stays in the Picture* by Robert Evans.

"If you could change one thing about your life," someone in the audience asked Robert Evans, "what would it be?"

"The second half," he said.

Everyone in the Sundance Film Festival audience knew what he meant. We had just seen *The Kid Stays in the Picture,* a new documentary about the life of this producer who put together one of the most remarkable winning streaks in Hollywood history, and followed it with a losing streak that almost destroyed him. It's one of the most honest films ever made about Hollywood; maybe a documentary was needed, since fiction somehow always simplifies things.

Evans made the kinds of movies that would never have played at Sundance; it's poetic justice that he finally got into the festival with a documentary. As the boy-wonder head of production at Paramount, he took the studio from last to first in annual ticket sales, dominating the late 1960s and 1970s with *The Godfather, Chinatown, Love Story, Rosemary's Baby, The Odd Couple, Black Sunday, Popeye,* and *Urban*

Cowboy. And he married Ali MacGraw, his star in *Love Story.*

Then everything that had gone right started to go wrong. MacGraw left him for Steve McQueen. He had exited the studio job with a lucrative personal production deal when disaster struck. He was involved in a cocaine-purchasing sting set up by the DEA, rehabilitated himself with a series of public-service broadcasts, tried a comeback by producing a high-visibility flop *(The Cotton Club),* and then was linked by innuendo and gossip with the murder of a man obscurely involved in the film's financing.

Evans was never charged with anything. But to this day people vaguely remember the drug and murder stories, and at one point in the 1980s he was so depressed he committed himself to a mental hospital, afraid he would kill himself.

The Kid Stays in the Picture is narrated by Evans himself, in a gravely, seen-it-all, told-it-all tone of voice. The film edits out some details, such as his other marriages, but only for purposes of time, we feel. Certainly nothing is papered over; Evans sounds like a man describing an accident he barely survived. Based on his autobiography, the doc is a collage of film and TV clips, countless photographs, news headlines, and magazine covers assembled by Brett Morgen and Nanette Burstein, whose documentary *On the Ropes* was an Oscar nominee two years ago. Remarkable, how they animate the photos with graphics, animation, and juxtapositioning so that instead of looking like a collection of stills it feels like, well, moving pictures.

In the beginning, Evans was a man who seemed blessed with luck. A child actor, he had joined his brother in manufacturing women's clothes when he was spotted poolside at the Beverly Hills Hotel by Norma Shearer, and asked to play her husband, the producer Irving Thalberg, in the Jimmy Cagney picture *The Man With 1,000 Faces.* Then came the prize role of a bullfighter in *The Sun Also Rises.* Author Ernest Hemingway and actors Tyrone Power, Ava Gardner, and Eddie Albert sent studio head Darryl F. Zanuck a telegram saying the film would be a disaster with Evans. Zanuck flew to the Mexican location, took a look, and said, "The kid stays in the picture."

Evans's next film, *The Fiend Who Walked the*

345

West, ended his acting career. But after being tapped to run Paramount by Charles Bludhorn, whose conglomerate Gulf and Western had inhaled the studio, he had more than a decade of success, and then a decade of disaster. Early on, he purchased the legendary home of Shearer and Thalberg. He sold it in the 1980s, then realized he could not live without it. His loyal pal Jack Nicholson flew to Monte Carlo and "got down on his knees" (perhaps Evans exaggerates slightly) to convince its new owner, a French millionaire, to sell it back.

Evans stood on the stage at Sundance, still trim and handsome at seventy-two, and answered the questions of filmmakers half or a third his age. Here was a room full of young people who dream of the kind of success he had. Did they find his life an object lesson? Probably not. At Sundance, they're still trying to change the first halves of their lives.

Kingdom Come ★ ★
PG, 95 m., 2001

LL Cool J (Ray Bud Jr.), Jada Pinkett Smith (Charisse), Vivica A. Fox (Lucille), Loretta Devine (Marguerite), Anthony Anderson (Junior), Toni Braxton (Juanita), Cedric the Entertainer (Reverend Hooker), Whoopi Goldberg (Raynelle Slocumb), Darius McCrary (Royce). Directed by Doug McHenry and produced by Edward Bates and John Morrissey. Screenplay by David Dean Bottrell and Jessie Jones, based on their play *Dearly Departed*.

In an opening scene of *Kingdom Come*, Whoopi Goldberg's husband drops dead at the breakfast table. This triggers a funeral, and Raynelle Slocumb (Goldberg) welcomes her children, in-laws, and descendants to a disorganized family reunion in which three or four subplots jostle for attention.

The movie is based on the play *Dearly Departed*, much performed by local theater groups, and has been adapted by the playwrights, David Dean Bottrell and Jessie Jones. The director, Doug McHenry, also has a long list of credits; as a producer or director he's been involved with *New Jack City, House Party II, Jason's Lyric,* and *The Brothers*. Together, they've made a movie that has generated a terrific trailer, making the film look like a warm-

hearted comedy. But the movie doesn't match the trailer.

Somewhere along the line a curious disconnect has taken place between the Whoopi Goldberg character and the others. She doesn't seem like their mother, their relative, or even an inhabitant of the same social milieu as the other members of her family. She's more like a wise, detached oracle, and when she's given comedy lines, they just don't fit. Early on, for example, she declares that her late husband was "mean as a snake, and surly." Later she insists that "Mean and Surly" be engraved on his tombstone. But she doesn't seem to hear them or feel them; they're words for another character in another movie, and have no connection to how she, or her children, feel about the dearly departed. With those and certain other lines, it's as if she's quoting a stranger.

We meet the family members, played by an all-star cast that never seems to mesh. Raynelle's son Ray Bud Jr. (LL Cool J) is married to Lucille (Vivica A. Fox). She's a scold; he's a good guy trying to handle a drinking problem. Her daughter Charisse (Jada Pinkett Smith) is married to another Junior (Anthony Anderson), who cheats on her. She's over the top in most of her scenes, which aren't played to the scale of the other performances. Another daughter, Marguerite (Loretta Devine), has her hands full with her son Royce (Darius McCrary), who apparently plans to nap through life, and taunts his mother with his shiftlessness. Then there's rich Cousin Juanita (Toni Braxton), and the pious Reverend Hooker (Cedric the Entertainer), who must officiate at the funeral and keep the peace.

Reverend Hooker makes some unwise dietary choices shortly before the funeral begins and farts all the way through it, causing the congregation to break up at this solemn moment. This material is an example of the movie's approach, which is all over the map. Fart jokes have their place, I concede, when the Klump family is at the dinner table. They may even have their place at a funeral—but not one where Raynelle has so recently had a heart-to-heart with Ray Bud Jr. The film changes tone so quickly we get whiplash.

There are times when the movie plays like a pilot for a TV comedy. Each family unit is given a costume, speaking style, and lifestyle that seems self-contained, so that when they assemble it's like a collision involving separate sitcoms. Some of the humor is broad and bawdy, some is observational, some is whimsical, and sometimes the humor collapses into sentiment. The central problem is that the movie seems unsure whether the late Bud Slocumb was indeed mean and surly—and if he was, how it feels about it. Is his death a loss or a liberation?

The pieces are here for a better movie. The cast is capable. A rewrite or two might have helped. *Kingdom Come* has passably funny moments, but they don't connect; it might work on video for viewers who glance up at the screen from time to time. The more attention you pay to it, the less it's there.

The King Is Alive ★ ★ ★
R, 105 m., 2001

Jennifer Jason Leigh (Gina), Miles Anderson (Jack), Romane Bohringer (Catherine), David Bradley (Henry), David Calder (Charles), Bruce Davison (Ray), Brion James (Ashley), Peter Khubeke (Kanana), Vusi Kunene (Moses), Janet McTeer (Liz). Directed by Kristian Levring and produced by Patricia Kruijer and Vibeke Windelov. Screenplay by Anders Thomas Jensen and Levring, based on *King Lear* by William Shakespeare.

In the Namibian desert in southwest Africa, a tourist bus strays far off course and runs out of petrol. The passengers stumble into the blinding sun and find themselves at an abandoned German mining station, its only occupant an old African who surveys them impassively. Jack (Miles Anderson) is the only passenger with any desert experience. He lectures them: There are five things you need to survive in the desert, and in descending order of importance they are water, food, shelter, making yourself visible, and keeping up your spirits.

Well, there is food here (rusted cans of carrots), water (they can collect the morning dew), and old buildings. They tend a signal fire at night. Jack walks off in search of help. Those left behind consider a suggestion by Henry (David Bradley) that they rehearse a production of *King Lear* to keep their spirits up. *Lear* is not the first play one thinks of when spirits

sink, but perhaps in this desolate landscape it is a better choice than *The Producers*.

We meet the tourists, without ever discovering what they were seeking in Namibia (they took the bus after their flight was canceled). Many seem more appropriate for a play by Beckett, and Ray and Liz (Bruce Davison and Janet McTeer) are a squabbling couple out of Albee (when Ray asks her what *King Lear* is about, she replies: "You don't have to worry, you know. Nobody has to fall in love and everybody gets to die in the end").

Hardly anybody dies in the end of the movie, but a lot of them have sex, which seems inspired less by pleasure than by the desire to annoy. There are moments of truth and despair, marital crises, denunciations, renunciations, false hopes, and raving madness. Henry writes out the roles for the play (chosen, we suspect, simply because he happened to know it by heart), there are rehearsals, and finally a performance of sorts. But although the movie's credits say "Based on *King Lear* by William Shakespeare," I was unable to sift through the cast finding specific characters who represented Cordelia, Regan, Kent, the Fool, etc. I think perhaps the play acts more as a mirror; like Lear, they are lost in the wilderness and no longer have faith in goodness.

The King Is Alive is the fourth of the Dogma 95 movies, so called because of a "vow of chastity" signed by the four Danish directors Kristian Levring (who directed this one), Thomas Vinterberg *(Celebration)*, Søren Kragh-Jacobsen *(Mifune)*, and Lars von Trier *(The Idiots)*. Dogma wanna-bes have been produced by Harmony Korine *(julien donkey-boy)*, and von Trier made a half-Dogma, half-musical *(Dancer in the Dark)*. What they have in common is a rough, immediate feel: The drama isn't too formed, the dialogue isn't tamed, the lighting and music are found on the set, the performances seem raw and improvisational.

In *The King Is Alive*, the Dogma approach helps the film look like what might have resulted if one of the characters had used a digital camera. It has the same relationship to a commercial film that their production of *King Lear* has to a conventional staging. It's built from raw materials, needs, and memories, instead of off-the-shelf parts from the movie store.

On one level, of course, we're aware of the

artifice. It's an old dramatic formula to strand a group of characters somewhere and have them try to survive while conditions edge toward the primitive. Cross *Lord of the Flies* with *Flight of the Phoenix* and add *Lifeboat* and you have this film's second cousin. On another level, this kind of story gives great opportunities to actors, who can test their emotional range. But what does the audience get out of it?

I imagine many people would be actively hostile to *The King Is Alive*. It doesn't make the slightest effort to cater to conventional appetites. But the more you appreciate what they're trying to do, the more you like it. I saw it for the first time at Cannes in May 2000, and it stuck with me. It didn't fade in the memory. Ungainly, ill-formed, howling, and desperate, it was there and endured—while, of the more forgettable films, I could observe with Lear that nothing will come of nothing.

Kissing Jessica Stein ★ ★ ★
R, 94 m., 2002

Jennifer Westfeldt (Jessica Stein), Heather Juergensen (Helen Cooper), Scott Cohen (Josh Meyers), Tovah Feldshuh (Judy Stein), Jackie Hoffman (Joan), Michael Mastro (Martin), Carson Elrod (Sebastian), David Aaron Baker (Dan Stein). Directed by Charles Herman-Wurmfeld and produced by Eden Wurmfeld and Brad Zions. Screenplay by Heather Juergensen and Jennifer Westfeldt.

Same-sex romance, a controversial topic in movies millions now alive can still remember, is a lifestyle choice in *Kissing Jessica Stein*. Yes, a "choice"—although that word is non-PC in gay circles—since one of the two women in the movie is nominally straight, and the other so bisexual she pops into her art gallery office during an opening for a quickie with her boy toy. Helen (Heather Juergensen), the gallery manager, is a lesbian in about the same way she would be a vegetarian who has steak once in a while. Jessica (Jennifer Westfeldt), disillusioned after a series of blind dates with hopeless men, answers Helen's personals ad not because she is a woman but because she quotes the poet Rilke.

Jessica is above all a hopeless perfectionist. This places her in contrast with her mother

(Tovah Feldshuh), whose idea of an eligible mate for her daughter is any single Jewish male between the ages of twenty and forty-five in good enough shape to accept a dinner invitation. Like many perfectionists, Jessica works as a copy editor and fact checker, finding writers' mistakes with the same zeal she applies to the imperfections of would-be husbands. In a funny montage, she goes through a series of disastrous dates, including one with a man whose word choices would make him a copy editor's nightmare (he uses the phrase "self-defecating").

Helen is more flexible, knowing, and wise. She seeks not perfection in a partner, but the mysteries of an intriguing personality. She finds it challenging that Jessica has never had a lesbian experience, and indeed approaches sex with the enthusiasm of a homeowner considering the intricacies of a grease trap. Jessica arrives at their first real date with an armload of how-to manuals, and makes such slow progress that Helen is driven all but mad by weeks of interrupted foreplay.

The movie makes of this situation not a sex comedy but more of an upscale sitcom in which the romantic partners happen both to be women. Jessica is fluttery and flighty, breathy and skittish; Helen is cool, grounded, and amused. Adding spice is Jessica's panic that anyone will find out about her new dating partner. Anyone like Josh (Scott Cohen), her boss at work and former boyfriend. Or Joan (Jackie Hoffman), her pregnant coworker. Or especially her mother, who brings single IBM executives to dinner as if they are the Missing Link.

There are a couple of serious episodes to give the story weight. One involves Jessica's reluctance to invite Helen to her brother's wedding, thus revealing to the family the sex of the mysterious "person" she has been dating. The other is a heart-to-heart talk between Jessica and her mother, during which Feldshuh takes an ordinary scene and makes it extraordinary by the way she delivers the simple, heartfelt dialogue.

What makes the movie a comedy is the way it avoids the more serious emotions involved. I reviewed a movie about a man who gives up sex for Lent, and received a reader's letter asking, hey, aren't Catholics supposed to give up extramarital sex all of the time? A theologically excellent question; I am reminded of the priest in *You Can Count on Me*, asked about adultery and reluctantly intoning "That . . . would . . . be . . . wrong."

The would-be lovers in *Kissing Jessica Stein* are not having sex, exactly, because of Jessica's skittish approach to the subject, but if they did, it would be a leisure activity like going to the movies. If it really meant anything to either one of them—if it meant as much as it does to the mother—the comedy would be more difficult, or in a different key. We can laugh because nothing really counts for anything. That's all right. But if Jessica Stein ever really gets kissed, it'll be another story. Right now she's like the grade-school girl at the spin-the-bottle party who changes the rules when the bottle points at her.

Kiss of the Dragon ★ ★ ★
R, 98 m., 2001

Jet Li (Liu Jian), Bridget Fonda (Jessica), Tcheky Karyo (Jean-Pierre Richard), Max Ryan (Lupo). Directed by Chris Nahon and produced by Luc Besson, Steve Chasman, Jet Li, and Happy Walters. Screenplay by Besson and Robert Mark Kamen.

There is a point early in *Kiss of the Dragon* when the Chinese cop played by Jet Li is being searched for weapons. Around his wrist they find a band with a lot of little needles stuck into it. This doesn't indicate that he does tailoring in his spare time. These are acupuncture needles, and he can cure or kill with one deftly inserted point.

The title of the movie refers to the ultimate use of a needle, which he describes as "highly illegal," as indeed it must be, altering the body's flow of blood so that it all rises to the head and bursts from every available orifice. I hate it when that happens. The Jet Li character is also master of the full array of the martial arts, and in this movie he needs them, since he is opposed by more or less every villain in Paris.

The plot has been described as hard to follow. It is simplicity itself, if all you want is a scorecard of the heroes and villains. It admittedly gets murky when it comes to motivation and logic, but never mind: In a movie where the physical actions border on the impossible, why expect the story to be reasonable?

Jet Li's character is apparently the most skilled law enforcement officer in China, brought to Paris to assist a high-level official in dealings that may involve some off-the-record drug traffic. The official is entertained by two hookers in a way that leaves him with his lust unslaked, and dead. Jet Li quickly determines that the mastermind behind the murder, the drug traffic, and much of the crime in modern France is Inspector Jean-Pierre Richard (Tcheky Karyo), a crooked cop with a limitless supply of henchmen.

That's all you're really told about the plot, and all you need to be told, since all else is action, except for some heartfelt scenes between Jet Li and Bridget Fonda, as Jessica, a farm girl from North Dakota whom the evil inspector has hooked on drugs and enslaved as a prostitute by separating her from the young daughter she loves.

Jet Li is one of the best-known martial arts stars, although you might pass him without noticing. He's compact, quiet, good-looking, not a show-off; the Alan Ladd of the genre. His action scenes involve a lot of physical skill (on his part, and also on the part of the editor) and the ingenious use of actual props that come to hand—a flying billiard ball, for example. There's a nice sequence involving a laundry chute and a hand grenade that's so effective only a churl would wonder why a place as expensive as the Hotel Bristol in Paris has an alarm system that doesn't notice a fiery explosion.

Fonda's scenes are mostly played out in evil-looking dens on grotty streets lined with hookers who look as if they were costumed for *Sweet Charity*. Their costumes look so good one wonders how her character gets work; she's grimy and beat-up most of the time, making it easier for us to believe she's an addict than a hooker. She is, however, effective as a desperate woman who finds unlikely friendship with this Chinese cop.

The movie looks great. The producer and coauthor of the screenplay is Luc Besson (*The Fifth Element, La Femme Nikita*), who loans his ace cameraman Thierry Arbogast to the director, Chris Nahon. They get a kind of gray-green, saturated *noir* feeling that's a perfect match for Tcheky Karyo's face—the face of a man whose next visit to the confessional, should he ever make it, will take days or weeks.

I like the movie on a simple physical level. There is no deeper meaning and no higher skill involved; just professional action, well staged and filmed with a certain stylistic elegance. Jet Li is the right star for the material, not too cocksure, not too flashy. His character isn't given a lot of motivation, but one key element is that he's never been in Paris before. He's a stranger in a strange land; that helps him bond with the Bridget Fonda character in a way that gives the movie what emotional center it needs.

A Knight's Tale ★ ★ ★
PG-13, 132 m., 2001

Heath Ledger (William), Rufus Sewell (Count Adhemar), Shannyn Sossamon (Jocelyn), Paul Bettany (Chaucer), Laura Fraser (Kate), Mark Addy (Roland), Alan Tudyk (Wat), Berenice Bejo (Christiana). Directed and produced by Brian Helgeland. Screenplay by Helgeland.

It is possible, I suppose, to object when the audience at a fifteenth-century jousting match begins to sing Queen's "We Will Rock You" and follows it with the Wave. I laughed. I smiled, in fact, all through Brian Helgeland's *A Knight's Tale*, which tells the story of a low-born serf who impersonates a knight, becomes a jousting champion, and dares to court the daughter of a nobleman.

Some will say the movie breaks tradition by telling a medieval story with a sound track of classic rock. They might as well argue it breaks the rules by setting a 1970s rock opera in the Middle Ages. To them I advise: Who cares? A few days after seeing this movie, I saw Baz Luhrmann's *Moulin Rouge*, which was selected to open the Cannes Film Festival despite being set in 1900 and beginning with the hero singing "The Sound of Music." In the case of *A Knight's Tale*, Helgeland has pointed out that an orchestral score would be equally anachronistic, since orchestras hadn't been invented in the 1400s. For that matter, neither had movies.

The film stars Heath Ledger, said to be the next big thing on the Australian sex symbol front, as William, a servant to a knight. The knight is killed, and his servants will be eating parboiled hedgehogs unless someone comes up with an idea. Along happens a desperate and naked man who makes them an offer: "Clothe, feed, and shoe me, and I'll give you your patents!" *Brewer's Dictionary* teaches us that "letters patent" are documents signed by a sovereign, conferring such rights as a title of nobility. The man offering to forge them introduces himself as Chaucer (Paul Bettany), and indeed, *A Knight's Tale* is a very, very, *very* free adaptation of one of his *Canterbury Tales*.

With the forged patents and the dead knight's suit of armor to disguise him, William and his sidekicks Roland and Wat (Mark Addy and Alan Tudyk) put themselves through one of those standard movie training montages and are soon ready to enter a joust, which is the medieval version of golf, with your opponent as the ball. There are many fearsome jousting matches in the movie, all of them playing with perspective and camera angles so that the horses and their riders seem to thunder at high speed for thirty seconds down a course that would take about five, until one knight or the other unseats his opponent three times and takes the victory.

This is not handled with great seriousness but in the spirit of high fun, and there is the evil Count Adhemar (Rufus Sewell) as an opponent. Since the knights wear armor guarding their faces, it might seem hard to distinguish them, but since time immemorial the movies have solved this dilemma by giving good knights attractive facial armor, and bad knights ugly little asymmetrical slits to peer through. I imagine a bad knight going into the armor store and saying, "I want the ugliest facial mask in the place!" Darth Vader is the only villain in the movies with a cool face plate.

Anyway, there are lots of babes in jousting land, especially the lady Jocelyn (Shannyn Sossamon), whose father is the ruler (at a banquet after the first tournament, she dances with William as David Bowie sings "Golden Years"). There is also a cute blacksmithess named Kate (Laura Fraser), who must be good, as she has obviously not been kicked in the head much.

The movie is centered around a series of jousting matches, alternating with threats to unveil the secret of William's identity. Finally we arrive at the World Championships in

London, alas without the movie supplying a definition of what in these pre-Columbian times is considered the "world." My guess is that the World Championship of Jousting is to England as the World Series is to North America. Another thing they have in common: Both events feature "The Boys Are Back in Town."

The movie has an innocence and charm that grows on you. It's a reminder of the days before films got so cynical and unrelentingly violent. *A Knight's Tale* is whimsical, silly, and romantic, and seeing it after *The Mummy Returns* is like taking Tums after eating the Mummy.

K-19: The Widowmaker ★ ★ ★
PG-13, 138 m., 2002

Harrison Ford (Captain Alexi Vostrikov), Liam Neeson (Captain Mikhail Polenin), Peter Sarsgaard (Vadim Radtchenko), Christian Camargo (Pavel Loktev), George Anton (Konstantin Poliansky), Shaun Benson (Leonid Pashinski), Dmitry Chepovetsky (Sergei Maximov). Directed by Kathryn Bigelow and produced by Bigelow, Edward S. Feldman, Chris Whitaker, and Joni Sighvatsson. Screenplay by Christopher Kyle.

Movies involving submarines have the logic of chess: The longer the game goes, the fewer the possible remaining moves. *K-19: The Widowmaker* joins a tradition that includes *Das Boot* and *The Hunt for Red October* and goes all the way back to *Run Silent, Run Deep.* The variables are always oxygen, water pressure, and the enemy. Can the men breathe, will the sub implode, will depth charges destroy it? The submarine *K-19* is not technically at war, so there are no depth charges, but the story involves a deadlier threat: Will the onboard reactor melt down, causing a nuclear explosion and possibly triggering a world war?

The movie is set in 1961, at the height of the cold war, and is loosely based on a real incident. A new Soviet nuclear sub is commissioned before it is shipshape, and sails on its first mission as a bucketful of problems waiting to happen. Many of the problems are known to its original captain, Mikhail Polenin (Liam Neeson). But when he insists after a test run that the submarine is not capable, he is joined on board by Captain Alexi Vostrikov (Harrison Ford), who outranks him and is married to the niece of a member of the Politboro.

Both men are competent naval officers, and Polenin does his best to work with Vostrikov; his men consider Polenin their captain but are persuaded to go along with the senior man, even after Vostrikov orders a dive that tests the ultimate limits of the sub's capabilities. (Such scenes, with rivets popping and the hull creaking, are obligatory in submarine movies.) Most of the big scenes take place in close quarters on the command desk, where dramatic lighting illuminates the faces and eyes of men who are waiting for the sub's shell to crack. By casting the two leading roles with authoritative actors, *K-19* adds another level of tension; if one were dominant and the other uncertain, there would be a clear dramatic path ahead, but since both Vostrikov and Polenin are inflexible, self-confident, and determined, their rivalry approaches a standoff.

The sub's mission is to demonstrate the Soviet Union's new nuclear submarine power to the spy planes of the Kennedy administration. The sub's voyage is shadowed by a U.S. destroyer, which is not unwelcome, since the purpose of this mission is to be seen. When there is an accident involving one of the onboard nuclear reactors, however, the game changes: If the reactor explodes and destroys the U.S. ship, will that event be read, in the resulting confusion, as an act of war? *K-19* could surface and put its men in lifeboats, but for Vostrikov the thought of the United States capturing the new technology is unthinkable. Therefore, the options are to repair the reactor or dive the boat to its destruction.

More problems. The *K-19*'s original reactor officer, an experienced man, has been fired for alcoholism and replaced with a recent naval academy graduate. This man, Vadim (Peter Sarsgaard), is not only inexperienced but scared to death, and he freezes when the accident occurs. As the reactor core overheats, the crew comes up with a jury-rigged quick fix—diverting the onboard water supply—but that involves men entering the sealed reactor compartment to weld pipes and make repairs. They should wear protective radiation suits, but alas, the captains are told, "the warehouse was out. They sent us chemical suits instead." Neeson: "We might as well wear raincoats."

351

The scenes involving the repair of the reactor are excruciating, and director Kathryn Bigelow creates a taut counterpoint between the men who take ten-minute shifts in the high-radiation zone, and the growing tension between the two captains. Footage involving radiation sickness is harrowing. A mutiny is not unthinkable. And meanwhile, in Moscow, *K-19*'s sudden radio silence inspires dark suspicions that the sub has been captured or given away by traitors.

The physical limitations of a submarine create technical difficulties for filmmakers—who can, after all, only move their cameras back and forth within the narrow tube. That claustrophobia also heightens the tension, and we get a sense of a small group of men working desperately together under the pressure of death. *K-19* draws out the suspense about as far as possible, and Bigelow, whose credits include *Point Break* and *Strange Days*, is an expert technician who never steps wrong and is skilled at exploiting the personal qualities of Ford and Neeson to add another level of uncertainty.

It is rare for a big-budget Hollywood production to be seen entirely through the eyes of foreigners, and rarer still for actors like Neeson and Ford to spend an entire role with Russian accents. There isn't even a token role for an American character, and the movie treats the Soviets not as enemies but as characters we are expected to identify with; the same approach allowed us to care about the German U-boat crew in *Das Boot*.

Are Harrison Ford and Liam Neeson, both so recognizable, convincing as Russians? Convincing enough; we accept the accents after a few minutes, and get on with the story. The fact that both men seem unyielding is crucial, and the fact that Vostrikov may be putting political considerations above the lives of his men adds an additional dimension. There is one surprise in the movie, a decision having nothing to do with the reactor, that depends entirely on the ability of the characters to act convincingly under enormous pressure; casting stars of roughly equal weight helps it to work.

Knockaround Guys ★ ★ ★

R, 93 m., 2002

Barry Pepper (Matty Demaret), Vin Diesel (Taylor Reese), Seth Green (Johnny Marbles), Andrew Davoli (Chris Scarpa), Dennis Hopper (Benny Chains), John Malkovich (Teddy Deserve), Tom Noonan (Sheriff). Directed by Brian Koppelman and David Levien and produced by Lawrence Bender, Koppelman, and Levien. Screenplay by Koppelman and Levien.

When Matty Demaret is twelve, he fails a test. His uncle gives him a gun and asks him to shoot a squealer. Matty just can't do it. "That's all right," his uncle says. "You're just not cut out for it." Matt grows into a young man determined to make a place for himself in the mob, and hangs around with other young heirs to a shrinking empire. Their fathers sat around counting money, but they're expected to work the noon and evening shifts at the family restaurant.

Matty (Barry Pepper) wants a chance to prove himself. He begs his dad, Benny Chains (Dennis Hopper) for a job, and finally gets one—picking up some money in Spokane. His friend Johnny Marbles (Seth Green) owns a private plane, and Matty asks him to fly the money back east. In the small town of Wibaux, Montana, Johnny Marbles gets rattled by cops in the airport, drops the bag in a luggage zone, and loses it. This is not good.

Knockaround Guys is inspired by the same impulse as *The Sopranos*. It considers gangsters in the modern age, beset by progress, unsure of their roles, undermined by psychobabble. "Used to be there was a way to do things and things got done," Matty's Uncle Teddy (John Malkovich) complains. "Now everybody's *feelings* are involved."

The heart of the movie takes place in Wibaux, a town ruled by a tall, taciturn, ominous sheriff, played by that unmistakable actor Tom Noonan. Matty flies out to Montana with backup: his friends Taylor (Vin Diesel) and Chris (Andrew Davoli). They stick out like sore thumbs in the little town. "Looks like they're multiplying," the sheriff observes to his deputy. He assumes they're involved with drugs, doesn't much care "as long as they move on through," but is very interested in the possibility of money.

The movie crosses two formulas, Fish Out of Water and Coming of Age, fairly effectively. Because it isn't wall-to-wall action but actually bothers to develop its characters and take an interest in them, it was not at first considered commercial by its distributor, New Line, and languished on the shelf for two years until the growing stardom of Vin Diesel *(XXX)* and Barry Pepper *(We Were Soldiers)* made it marketable. It's more than that—it's interesting in the way it shows these guys stuck between generations. And it makes good use of Diesel, who as he develops into an action superstar may not get roles this juicy for a while. He's a tough guy, yes, a street fighter, but conflicted and with a kind of wise sadness about human nature.

The movie's basic question, I suppose, is whether the rising generation of mobsters is so self-conscious it will never gain the confidence of its ancestors. If it's true that the mob in the 1930s learned how to talk by studying Warner Bros. crime pictures, it's equally true that *The Sopranos* and all the other post-Scorsese *GoodFellas* stories bring in an element of psychological complexity that only confuses an occupation that used to have a brutal simplicity. *Knockaround Guys* opens with Matty being turned down for a job because of his infamous last name. It ends with him not living up to it. "To the regular people we're nothing but goombas," Matty complains. "But to our fathers, we're nothing but errand boys."

K-PAX ★ ★ ★
PG-13, 120 m., 2001

Kevin Spacey (Prot), Jeff Bridges (Dr. Mark Powell), Mary McCormack (Rachel Powell), Alfre Woodard (Claudia Villars), David Patrick Kelly (Howie), Melanee Murray (Bess), Saul Williams (Ernie), Peter Gerety (Sal), Celia Weston (Mrs. Archer), Ajay Naidu (Dr. Chakraborty). Directed by Iain Softley and produced by Lawrence Gordon, Lloyd Levin, and Robert F. Colesberry. Screenplay by Charles Leavitt, based on the novel by Gene Brewer.

If a visitor from another planet appeared among us in human form and told the truth about his origins, no doubt he would be treated like Prot, the hero of *K-PAX*, who finds himself locked in a closed ward of the Psychiatric Institute of Manhattan. He might not, however, be as lucky as Prot in his psychiatrist. "This is the most convincing delusional I've ever come across," says Dr. Mark Powell, and his voice toys with the notion that Prot might not be delusional.

Certainly the patient tells a good story. Played by Kevin Spacey, who has made a career out of being the smartest character in the movie, Prot describes his intergalactic travels, dismisses Einstein's theories about the speed of light, and amazes a group of astronomers in a scene that suggests, as it is intended to, Christ addressing the elders in the temple.

Jeff Bridges plays the shrink, and brings to the role exactly what is required, a weary workaholic who thinks he has seen everything, and is relieved to discover that he hasn't. His sessions with Prot turn into two-way experiences, with Prot offering advice and insights, and seeming intelligent and normal—all except for his impression that his home is 1,000 light-years away. There is also the matter of how he eats a banana. "K-PAX is a planet," he explains to his doctor, "but don't worry—I'm not going to leap out of your chest."

The movie doesn't force its parallel with Christ (who said he was the son of God at a time when, luckily for him, the Psychiatric Institute of Manhattan was not yet admitting patients). But the analogy is there, not least in Prot's relationships with his fellow mental patients; he quietly goes about trying to cure them. The movie populates its ward with the usual job lot of colorful eccentrics, who behave as if they have intensely studied *One Flew Over the Cuckoo's Nest*. The most intriguing, because she never speaks, is Bess (Melanee Murray).

The movie intercuts the psychiatric sessions with Prot and domestic scenes at home, where the doctor's wife, Rachel (Mary McCormack), frets that his mind is always on his work. Why must all men involved in great enterprises have wives who are obsessed with whether they come home for dinner on time? Is it forbidden that the wife also become fascinated with the case and get involved?

No matter. The heart of the movie is in the Spacey performance, and knowing that less is more, he plays Prot absolutely matter-of-factly. *K-PAX* avoids an ending that invites tears, and supplies one that encourages speculation. Is Prot really from another planet? What happens to him at the end is not quite the answer it seems to be. And consider his range of vision, his versatile blood pressure, his tolerance for Thorazine, and the fact that he describes the intricate orbit of his planet to astronomers who have just discovered it. Against this we must balance the investigative road trip that Powell makes to New Mexico, which offers a persuasive answer and then snatches it away (perhaps Prot simply borrowed a human form).

A final answer is unprovable on the basis of what we're told, and I like it that way. I admired how the movie tantalized us with possibilities and allowed the doctor and patient to talk sensibly, if strangely, about the difference between the delusional and that which is simply very unlikely. Whether Prot is right or wrong about where he comes from is not as important as what he does with his conviction.

Kwik Stop ★ ★ ★ ½
NO MPAA RATING, 110 m., 2002

Michael Gilio (Mike), Lara Phillips (Didi), Rich Komenich (Emil), Karin Anglin (Ruthie). Directed by Michael Gilio and produced by Rachel Tenner. Screenplay by Gilio.

Kwik Stop starts out with a shoplifter and a teenager who sees him stealing. She threatens to turn him over to the cops, but actually all she wants is to escape from her life in a Chicago suburb. He explains he's going to Los Angeles to become a movie actor. "Take me with you," she says. "Can I kiss you?" he says.

At this point, maybe ten minutes into the story, we think we know more or less where the movie is going: It'll be a road picture. We are dead wrong. *Kwik Stop*, which never quite gets out of town, blindsides us with unexpected humor and sadness, and is one of the unsung treasures of recent independent filmmaking.

The movie is the work of Michael Gilio, who wrote it, directed it, and stars in it as Mike, the guy who thinks he could be a movie star. Gilio, in fact, is already an established actor; he played opposite Sidney Poitier in the TV movie *To Sir with Love 2*, and has appeared in four other films, but this movie proves he's not only an actor but has a genuine filmmaking talent. In the way it is developed, and seen, and especially in the way it ends, *Kwik Stop* shows an imagination that flies far beyond the conventions it seems to begin with.

Mike is a complicated guy. He dreams of going to Los Angeles and breaking into the movies, yes—but perhaps the dream is more important than actually doing it. He's like a lot of people who are stuck in the planning stage and like it there. Didi (Lara Phillips) has no plans but she has urgent desires and is prepared to act on them. We learn all we need to know about her home life in a shot taken from the curb that watches her go inside to get some stuff and come back out again, unconcerned that she is leaving town, she thinks, forever.

Neither one is dumb. They talk about Henry Miller and Harvey Keitel, two names that suggest you have advanced beyond life's training wheels. Gilio finds a motel room for them with its own disco ball hanging from the ceiling, and as its twinkle disguises the shabbiness, they make and pledge love, and then the next morning Mike is gone. If this couple is going to make it through the entire film, we realize, they are going to have to do it without using the usual clichés.

They meet again. Never mind how. Mike takes Didi to a diner for a meal, where a waitress named Ruthie (Karin Anglin) greets them with a strangely skewed attitude. Watch the way Gilio introduces mystery into the scene and then resolves it, getting humor out of both the mystery and the solution. The diner scene suggests strangeness deep in Mike's character: He doesn't need to go to Los Angeles since he stars in his own drama, and doubles back to be sure he hasn't lost his audience.

Mike and Didi try to burgle a house. Didi is whammed by a homeowner's baseball bat, and ends up imprisoned in the Midwest School for Girls. Mike has a plan to spring her, which involves Ruthie making what is, under the circumstances, a truly selfless gesture (she explains she doesn't want to "waste the time I put into you").

Just as Mike never gets out of town, just as the plot doubles back to pick up first Didi and then Ruthie, so Emil (Rich Komenich), the homeowner with the baseball bat, is also not abandoned. *Kwik Stop* is the opposite of the picaresque journey in which colorful characters are encountered and then left behind. It gathers them all up and takes them along.

The movie contains genuine surprises, some delightful (like the plan to spring Didi from the home) and others involving loneliness, loss, and desperation. I cannot say much more without revealing developments that are unexpected and yet deeply satisfying. Poignancy comes into the movie from an unexpected source. Depths are revealed where we did not think to find them. The ending is like the last paragraph of a short story, redefining everything that went before.

Kwik Stop, made on a low budget, has all the money it needs to accomplish everything it wants to do. It has the freedom of serious fiction, which is not chained to a story arc but follows its characters where they insist on going. Gilio, Phillips, Komenich, and Anglin create that kind of bemused realism we discover in films that are not about plot but about what these dreamy people are going to do next.

L

La Cienaga ★ ★ ★
NO MPAA RATING, 103 m., 2001

Martin Adjemian (Gregorio), Diego Baenas (Joaquin), Leonora Balcarce (Veronica), Silvia Bayle (Mercedes), Sofia Bertolotto (Momi), Juan Cruz Bordeu (Jose), Graciela Borges (Mecha), Noelia Bravo Herrera (Agustina), Mercedes Moran (Tali), Daniel Valenzuela (Rafael), Andrea Lopez (Isabel). Directed by Lucrecia Martel and produced by Lita Stantic. Screenplay by Martel.

La Cienaga is a dank, humid meditation on rotting families. By its end we are glad to see the last of most of its characters, but we will not quickly forget them. The film opens in a crumbling vacation home on a rainy plateau in northern Argentina, and I suspect, although I am not sure, that it expresses the director's feelings about the current downturn in the country's fortunes. These are people who once were rich, and now squat in the ruins of their own lives.

The title translates as "the swamp." Not too hard to spot the symbolism. Thunder rumbles unceasingly on the sound track. It rains and rains. In every room circulating fans look back and forth for relief from the heat. The children find something they are good for: When you put your mouth right in front of the whirling blades and talk, your words get chopped up. Neat. I had forgotten that.

The opening shots show the mottled, exhausted bodies of the slack characters. They've flung themselves on deck chairs next to a stagnant pool. They drink. A woman stands up to carry some wine glasses, slips on the mossy surface, falls, and badly cuts herself. The others do not even look up. She lies in her own blood until her children raise the alarm and take her to a hospital. An alcoholic, she does not seem much interested in what has happened.

The name of the vacation home is La Mandragora ("the mandrake")—"a poisonous plant," the *Concise Oxford* explains, "with emetic and narcotic properties." It is said to shriek when it is plucked. Charming. The mother is named Mecha (Graciela Borges) and her husband is Gregorio (Martin Adjemian). They have four teenage children. In the nearby town of La Cienaga live her cousin Tali (Mercedes Moran), her husband, Rafael (Daniel Valenzuela), and their four younger children.

The older children go hunting in the swamp and kill cattle mired in the mud. One son is missing an eye. Of the younger children in town, one needs to be taken to the dentist because he has a tooth growing out of the roof of his mouth. Later, he cuts his leg. These are potentially cute kids, but not here, where every time they look at their parents they see what's in store for them.

Graciela Borges's performance as Mecha is the centerpiece of the movie. She hints darkly that the "native servants" are stealing the towels. Indeed, when the beautiful servant Isabel (Andrea Lopez) brings towels to stop the flow of blood after she falls, Mecha's first words are, "So that's where the towels went." She stays in bed all day, watching television, sipping wine, complaining, her cuts healing into scars.

Various adulteries have taken place, are taking place, will take place. Mecha's oldest daughter Momi (Sofia Bertolotto) thanks God in her nightly prayers for Isabel, and perhaps is in love with her. Whatever. There is talk by both Mecha and Tali about driving to nearby Bolivia to buy back-to-school supplies, since they are cheaper there. The implication is that Argentineans have fallen from the heights when they consider Bolivia a shopping destination.

This is the first film by writer-director Lucrecia Martel, who doesn't want to tell a story so much as re-create the experience of living in the same houses with these people. Her film is like everyday life in the way events do not always fit together, characters don't know what happens while they're offscreen, and crucial events, even a death, can go unobserved. It's better to know going in that you're not expected to be able to fit everything together, that you may lose track of some members of the large cast, that it's like attending a family reunion when it's not your family and your hosts are too drunk to introduce you around.

The Lady and the Duke ★ ★ ★
PG-13, 129 m., 2002

Lucy Russell (The Lady, Grace Elliott), Jean-Claude Dreyfus (Duke of Orleans), Francois Marthouret (Dumouriez), Leonard Cobiant (Champcenetz), Caroline Morin (Nanon), Alain Libolt (Duc de Biron), Helena Dubiel (Madame Meyler). Directed by Eric Rohmer and produced by Francoise Etchegaray. Screenplay by Eric Rohmer, based on the memoir *Journal of My Life During the French Revolution* by Grace Elliott.

In the Paris of the mob, during the French Revolution, a patrician British lady supports the monarchy and defies the citizens' committees that rule the streets. She does this not in the kind of lamebrained action story we might fear, but with her intelligence and personality—outwitting the louts who come to search her bedroom, even as a wanted man cowers between her mattresses.

Eric Rohmer's *The Lady and the Duke* is an elegant story about an elegant woman, told in an elegant visual style. It moves too slowly for those with impaired attention spans, but is fascinating in its style and mannerisms. Like all of the films in the long career of Rohmer, it centers on men and women talking about differences of moral opinion.

At eighty-one, Rohmer has lost none of his zest and enthusiasm. The director, who runs up five flights of stairs to his office every morning, has devised a daring visual style in which the actors and foreground action are seen against artificial tableaux of Paris circa 1792. These are not "painted backdrops," but meticulously constructed perspective drawings that are digitally combined with the action in a way that is both artificial and intriguing.

His story is about a real woman, Grace Elliott (Lucy Russell), who told her story in a forgotten autobiography Rohmer found ten years ago. She was a woman uninhibited in her behavior and conservative in her politics, at one time the lover of the prince of Wales (later King George IV), then of Phillipe, the duke of Orleans (father of the future king Louis Phillipe). Leaving England for France and living in a Paris town house paid for by the duke (who remains her close friend even after their ardor has cooled),

she refuses to leave France as the storm clouds of revolution gather, and survives those dangerous days even while making little secret of her monarchist loyalties.

She is stubbornly a woman of principle. She dislikes the man she hides between her mattresses, but faces down an unruly citizens' search committee after every single member crowds into her bedroom to gawk at a fine lady in her nightgown. After she gets away with it, her exhilaration is clear: She likes living on the edge, and later falsely obtains a pass allowing her to take another endangered aristocrat out of the city to her country house.

Her conversations with the duke of Orleans (attentive, courtly Jean-Claude Dreyfus) suggest why he and other men found her fascinating. She defends his cousin the king even while the duke is mealymouthed in explaining why it might benefit the nation for a few aristocrats to die; by siding with the mob, he hopes to save himself, and she is devastated when he breaks his promise to her and votes in favor of the king's execution.

Now consider the scene where Grace Elliott and a maid stand on a hillside outside Paris and use a spyglass to observe the execution of the king and his family, while distant cheering floats toward them on the wind. Everything they survey is a painted perspective drawing—the roads, streams, hills, trees, and the distant city. It doesn't look real, but it has a kind of heightened presence, and Rohmer's method allows the shot to exist at all. Other kinds of special effects could not compress so much information into seeable form.

Rohmer's movies are always about moral choices. His characters debate them, try to bargain with them, look for loopholes. But there is always clearly a correct way. Rohmer, one of the fathers of the New Wave, is Catholic in religion and conservative in politics, and here his heroine believes strongly in the divine right of kings and the need to risk your life, if necessary, for what you believe in. Lucy Russell, a British actress speaking proper French we imagine her character learned as a child, plays Grace Elliott as a woman of great confidence and verve. As a woman she must sit at home and wait for news; events are decided by men and reported to women. We sense her imagination placing her in the middle of the action, and we are struck by how much more clearly she sees the real issues than does the muddled duke.

The Lady and the Duke is the kind of movie one imagines could have been made in 1792. It centers its action in personal, everyday experience—an observant woman watches from the center of the maelstrom—and has time and attention for the conversational styles of an age when evenings were not spent stultified in front of the television. Watching it, we wonder if people did not live more keenly then. Certainly Grace Elliott was seldom bored.

Lagaan: Once Upon a Time in India
★ ★ ★ ½
PG, 225 m., 2002

Aamir Khan (Bhuvan), Gracy Singh (Gauri), Rachel Shelley (Elizabeth Russell), Paul Blackthorne (Captain Andrew Russell), Suhasini Mulay (Yashodamai), Kulbhushan Kharbanda (Rajah Puran Singh), Raghuvir Yadav (Bhura), Rajendra Gupta (Mukhiya), Yashpal Sharma (Lakha), Rajesh Vivek (Guran), Pradeep Rawat (Deva). Directed by Ashutosh Gowariker and produced by Aamir Khan. Screenplay by Kumar Dave, Sanjay Dayma, Gowariker, and K. P. Saxena.

Lagaan is an enormously entertaining movie, like nothing we've ever seen before, and yet completely familiar. Set in India in 1893, it combines sports with political intrigue, romance with evil scheming, musical numbers with low comedy and high drama, and is therefore soundly in the tradition of the entertainments produced by the Bombay film industry, "Bollywood," which is the world's largest.

I have seen only five or six Bollywood movies, one of them in Hyderabad, India, in 1999, where I climbed to the highest balcony and shivered in arctic air conditioning while watching a movie that was well over three hours long and included something for everyone. The most charming aspect of most Bollywood movies is their cheerful willingness to break into song and dance at the slightest pretext; the film I saw was about a romance between a rich boy and a poor girl, whose poverty did not prevent her from producing backup dancers whenever she needed them.

Lagaan is said to be the most ambitious, expensive, and successful Bollywood film ever

made, and has been a box-office hit all over the world. Starring Aamir Khan, who is one of the top Indian heartthrobs, it was made with an eye to overseas audiences: If *Crouching Tiger, Hidden Dragon* could break out of the martial arts ghetto and gross $150 million, then why not a Bollywood movie for non-Indians? It has succeeded in jumping its genre; it won an Academy Award nomination in 2002 as Best Foreign Film, and has been rolling up amazing per-screen averages in North American theaters.

All of which evades the possibility that most readers of this review have never seen a Bollywood movie and don't want to start now. That will be their loss. This film is like nothing they've seen before, with its startling landscapes, architecture, and locations, its exuberant colors, its sudden and joyous musical numbers right in the middle of dramatic scenes, and its melodramatic acting (teeth gnash, tears well, lips tremble, bosoms heave, fists clench). At the same time, it's a memory of the films we all grew up on, with clearly defined villains and heroes, a romantic triangle, and even a comic character who saves the day. *Lagaan* is a well-crafted, hugely entertaining epic that has the spice of a foreign culture.

The story takes place at the height of the Raj, England's government of occupation in India. In a remote province, the local British commander is Captain Russell (Paul Blackthorne), a lip-curling rotter with a racist streak, who insults the local maharajah to his face and thinks nothing of whipping a Hindu upstart. Even his fellow officers think he's over the top. He administers "lagaan," which is the annual tax the farmers must pay to their maharajah, and he to the British. It is a time of drought and hunger, and the farmers cannot pay.

Enter Bhuvan (Aamir Khan), a leader among his people, who confronts Russell and finds his weak point: The captain is obsessed by cricket, and believes it's a game that can never be mastered by Indians. Bhuvan says it is much like an ancient Indian game, and that Indians could excel at it. Russell makes Bhuvan a bet: The Brits and a village team will play a cricket match. If the Indians win, there will be no lagaan for three years. If the Brits win, lagaan will be tripled. The villagers think Bhuvan is insane, since a triple tax would destroy them, but he points out that since they cannot pay the current tax, they have nothing to lose.

Bhuvan assembles and starts to coach a local team. Elizabeth Russell (Rachel Shelley), the evil captain's sister, believes her brother's deal is unfair, and secretly sneaks out to the village to provide pointers on cricket. Her closeness to Bhuvan disturbs Gauri (Gracy Singh), a local woman who has believed since childhood that she and Bhuvan are fated to marry. There's another coil of the plot with the two-faced Lakha (Yashpal Sharma), who wants Gauri for himself, and acts as a spy for Russell because he feels that if Bhuvan loses face, he'll have a better chance with her.

We meet the members of the village team, an oddly assorted group that includes a low-caste fortune-teller named Guran (Rajesh Vivek), whose crippled arm allows him to throw a wicked curve ball. There is also Deva (Pradeep Rawat), whose service in the British army has fueled his contempt for his former masters. As training proceeds in the village and the British sneer from their regimental headquarters, the action is punctuated by much music.

The British hold dances, at which single young women who have come out from home hope to find an eligible young officer. (Elizabeth, dreaming about Bhuvan, is not much interested in the candidate selected for her.) And in the village music wells up spontaneously, most memorably when storm clouds promise an end to the long drought. In keeping with Bollywood tradition, the singing voices in these sequences are always dubbed (the voice-over artists are stars in their own right), as the camera plunges into joyous choreography with dancers, singers, and swirls of beautifully colored saris. Such dance sequences would be too contrived and illogical for sensible modern Hollywood, but we feel like we're getting away with something as we enjoy them.

Lagaan somehow succeeds in being suspenseful at the same time it's frivolous and obvious. The final cricket match (which we can follow even if we don't understand the game) is in the time-honored tradition of all sports movies, and yet the underlying issues are serious. And there is the intriguing question of whether the hero will end up with his childhood sweetheart, or cross color lines with the Victorian woman (this is hard to predict, since

both women are seen in entirely positive terms).

As a backdrop to the action, there is India itself. It is a long time since I praised a movie for its landscapes; I recall *Dr. Zhivago* or *Lawrence of Arabia,* and indeed, like David Lean, director Ashutosh Gowariker is not shy about lingering on ancient forts and palaces, vast plains, and the birthday-cake architecture of the British Raj, so out of place and yet so serenely confident. Watching the film, we feel familiarity with the characters and the showdown, but the setting and the production style are fresh and exciting. Bollywood has always struck a bargain with its audience members, many of them poor: You get your money's worth. Leaving the film, I did not feel unsatisfied or vaguely shortchanged, as after many Hollywood films, but satisfied: I had seen a *movie.*

Lakeboat ★ ★ ★
R, 98 m., 2001

Charles Durning (Skippy), Peter Falk (The Pierman), Denis Leary (The Fireman), Robert Forster (Joe Pitko), J. J. Johnston (Stan), Tony Mamet (Dale Katzman), Jack Wallace (Fred), George Wendt (First Mate Collins), Andy Garcia (Guigliani). Directed by Joe Mantegna and produced by Tony Mamet, Mantegna, and Morris Ruskin. Screenplay by David Mamet.

Lakeboat was the tenth play by David Mamet to be produced, but it feels like the wellspring. Here in the rough, awkward, poetic words of the crew members of a Lake Michigan ore boat, he finds the cadences that would sound through his work. The play was first produced in 1981, and three years later came *Glengarry Glen Ross.* Both draw from his early jobs, when as a college student he supported himself working on a lake steamer and as a real-estate salesman. Both are unusual because their young protagonists are not heroes, but witnesses. These plays are not about a young man coming of age, but about older men who have come of age. In *Lakeboat,* a veteran crew member, a thoughtful loner who spends all of his free time reading books, tells the young cook, "You got it made."

We sense that men like these taught the young Mamet how his characters would think and talk. They're not narrow proletarians but men confident of themselves and their jobs, and yet needful of the isolation and loneliness of long lake voyages. No one quotes Melville, who said a ship was his Yale and his Harvard, but his words must have been in Mamet's mind as he created Dale Katzman, a second-year graduate student from "a school outside Boston," who signs on as a cook and sails with the *Seaway Queen*.

Dale is played by Tony Mamet, David's brother. The music is by Bob Mamet, another brother. The screenplay adaptation is by David and the direction is by Joe Mantegna, who has appeared in countless Mamet plays. The key actors include two who have been with him from the beginning, Jack Wallace and J. J. Johnston, and others who show how the poignancy and rhythm of the material allows them living space inside the words: Robert Forster, Charles Durning, Peter Falk, George Wendt, Denis Leary, Andy Garcia. I once taught a class on Mamet's films. I wish I could have opened it with this one, because for Mamet it all starts here.

It is important to note that nothing "happens" in the film in conventional movie-plot terms. It is not about a storm, a mutiny, a personal conflict, an old grudge. There is some mystery about why the regular cook, Guigliani (Garcia), is missing on the voyage, but he makes a space for Dale to be hired, and when the ship sails there is nothing much to be done but get the ore to the other end. Denis Leary plays the fireman, who tells Dale: "I keep my eye on the gauges. I watch them constantly." Yes, and studies porno magazines, although why a man would sign on for a world without women and then yearn for them is a question Mamet asks just by creating the character.

Another crew member with theories about women is Fred, played by Jack Wallace in a performance of such crude sweetness you can hear echoes of those very first Mamet plays, when Wallace was onstage in church basements and rented storefronts. Like most limited men, Fred knows a few things very well, and repeats them often to give himself the air of an expert. He thinks he knows all about women (they like to be smacked around a little, so they can see that the guy really cares). Fred delivers a meditation on the use of the f-word that could be printed as an introduction to Mamet's plays.

If Fred's obsession is with women, Stan (J. J. Johnston) is fascinated and baffled by drink. Booze too is a companion, always there to underline the good times and drown the bad ones, and Stan lectures Dale on drink the way Fred does on women. Both of them give extraordinarily bad advice, but not without having given their subjects a good deal of misguided thought.

The captain (Charles Durning) and first mate (George Wendt) are heavy-set men whose weight makes their movements into commitments. They have worked together a long time, long enough so that the skipper can ask the mate to make him a sandwich without giving offense. Without being sexual, their relationship seems domestic. They fiercely love their jobs.

It is the crew member Joe Pitko (Robert Forster) who is young Dale's mentor, the one he will remember with the most affection many years later. This is a working man who hungers for the life of the mind, and who leads two parallel lives, one in his work, the other in his books. There was perhaps a turning point in his life when he might have gone to school or tested some secret dream, but he took the safe bet of a regular paycheck and now finds himself working with men he cannot have nourishing conversations with. The college boy is a godsend. Pitko, in an unspoken way, gives his blessing to the fact that the boy may someday turn this summer of work into a story or a play. Pitko is not so narrow that he sees himself only as the subject for something the kid might write: He also sees himself as audience and critic.

The lakeboat sails on. Mantegna gives us just enough detail, enough exterior shots, so that we feel we're on a ship. All the rest is conversation and idleness. What do men think about on a long uneventful voyage? The routine of their work, the personalities of their crewmates, the certainty of their paychecks, the elusiveness of their dreams, the rhythms of their anecdotes, and sex. The lakeboat is a lot like life.

Lantana ★ ★ ★ ½
R, 121 m., 2002

Anthony LaPaglia (Leon Zat), Geoffrey Rush (John Sommers), Barbara Hershey (Dr. Valerie

Sommers), Kerry Armstrong (Sonja Zat), Rachael Blake (Jane), Vince Colosimo (Nik), Daniella Farinacci (Paula), Peter Phelps (Patrick). Directed by Ray Lawrence and produced by Jan Chapman. Screenplay by Andrew Bovell, based on the play *Speaking in Tongues*.

Lantana opens with a camera tracking through dense Australian shrubbery to discover the limbs of a dead woman. We are reminded of the opening of *Blue Velvet*, which pushed into lawn grass to suggest dark places hidden just out of view. Much of the movie will concern the identity of the dead woman, and how she died, but when the mystery is solved it turns out to be less an answer than a catalyst—the event that caused several lives to interlock.

Ray Lawrence's film is like Robert Altman's *Short Cuts* or Paul Thomas Anderson's *Magnolia* in the way it shows the lives of strangers joined by unsuspected connections. It discovers a web of emotional hope and betrayal. At its center is a cop named Leon Zat (Anthony LaPaglia) in the process of meltdown; he is cheating on his wife, he has chest pains, he beats a suspect beyond any need or reason, he is ferocious with his son, he collides with a man while jogging and explodes in anger.

Zat's wife, Sonja (Kerry Armstrong), worried about him, is seeing a psychiatrist named Valerie Sommers (Barbara Hershey). Valerie is married to John (Geoffrey Rush). A few years ago their daughter was killed. Valerie wrote a book as a way of dealing with the experience. John hides behind a stolid front. One of her clients (Peter Phelps) is a gay man who wants to talk about his married lover, and Valerie comes to suspect that the lover is, in fact, her own husband.

Other characters. Jane (Rachel Blake) is the separated housewife who is cheating with Leon. Her neighbors are the happily married Nik and Paula (Vince Colosimo and Daniella Farinacci). When Valerie's car is found abandoned and she is missing, murder is feared, and Leon is assigned to the case. He suspects her husband, John, and there is another suspect—Nik, the father of three, seen throwing a woman's shoe into the underbrush by Jane. When Leon arrives to question Jane it is significant, of course, that they were lovers.

This description no doubt makes the film seem like some kind of gimmicky puzzle. What's surprising is how easy it is to follow the plot, and how the coincidences don't get in the way. Lawrence's film, based on a play by Andrew Bovell, only seems to be a murder mystery. As it plays out, we're drawn into the everyday lives of these characters—their worries, their sorrows, the way they're locked into solitary sadness. Nik and Paula are the only happy couple, blessed with kids, happiness, and uncomplicated lives. When the evidence seems overwhelming against Nik, we can hardly believe it. Certainly Valerie's husband, or even an ominous dance instructor, might make better suspects.

Anthony LaPaglia makes his cop into a focus of pain: He cheats, takes no joy in cheating, is violent, takes no joy in violence, is shut inside himself. LaPaglia is so identified with American roles that *Lantana* comes as a little surprise, reminding us that he has an Australian background. The other actors, especially Hershey, Rush, and the two unhappy women in the cop's life (played by Armstrong and Blake) are so attentive to the nuances of their characters, so tender with their hurts, that maybe we shouldn't be surprised when the crime plot turns out to be a form of misdirection.

One particularly effective scene involves a conversation between LaPaglia and Rush. It comes at a point when LaPaglia clearly thinks the other man has murdered his wife, and the Rush character almost willfully says things that will not help his case. In another kind of movie, his dialogue could be cheating—deliberately misleading the audience. Here we sense it grows out of a disgust he feels that he is not a better man.

Lawrence and Bovell ground their stories in a lot of domestic details, involving children: the daughter Valerie and John lost; the sons Leon is alienated from; Nik and Paula's kids, who need baby-sitting and get earaches. After Jane reports her suspicions about the neighbors, she ends up minding the kids, and there is a wonderfully observed moment when the little one gets sick and the slightly older one knows just what medication is necessary.

Lantana is, we learn, the name of a South American plant that, transplanted to Sydney, prospered and became a nuisance. What is its connection to the film? Perhaps suspicion can also grow out of control, when people get out of the habit of assuming that others are good and mean well.

Lara Croft Tomb Raider ★ ★ ★
PG-13, 96 m., 2001

Angelina Jolie (Lara Croft), Daniel Craig (Alex Marrs), Leslie Phillips (Wilson), Mark Collie (Larson), Rachel Appleton (Young Lara), Chris Barrie (Hilary the Butler), Iain Glen (Manfred Powell), Julian Rhind-Tutt (Pimms), Jon Voight (Lord Croft). Directed by Simon West and produced by Colin Wilson, Lawrence Gordon, and Lloyd Levin. Screenplay by Patrick Massett, West, and John Zinman.

Lara Croft Tomb Raider elevates goofiness to an art form. Here is a movie so monumentally silly, yet so wondrous to look at, that only a churl could find fault. And please don't tell me it makes no sense. The last thing I want to see is a sensible movie about how the Illuminati will reunite the halves of the severed triangle in order to control time in the ruins of the ancient city that once rose in the meteor crater—if, and it's a big "if," the clue of the all-seeing eye inside the hidden clock can be used at the moment of planetary alignment that comes every 5,000 years, and if the tomb raiders are not destroyed by the many-armed Vishnu figure and the stone monkeys. The logic is exhausting enough even when it doesn't make sense.

This is, at last, a real popcorn movie. I have been hearing for weeks from fans of *The Mummy Returns* and *Pearl Harbor,* offended that I did not like those movies—no, not even as "popcorn movies." I responded that *The Mummy* was a good popcorn movie, but *The Mummy Returns* was a bad popcorn movie. It is my job to know these things. That *Pearl Harbor* is even discussed in those terms is depressing.

The plot of *Lara Croft Tomb Raider* exists as a support system for four special-effects sequences. Right away you can see that the movie is relatively advanced; *The Mummy Returns* had no plot and one special-effects sequence, which was 121 minutes long.

The film opens with Lara Croft doing desperate battle with a deadly robot, in what turns out to be an homage to the openings of the *Pink Panther* movies where Clouseau took on Kato. When the dust settles, we learn that she is Lady Lara Croft (Angelina Jolie), daughter of the tomb raider Lord Croft (Jon Voight), whose memorial stone sadly informs us, "Lost in the Field, 1985." Lady Lara lives in a vast country estate with a faithful butler and a private hacker and weapons system designer. Elaborate research-and-development and manufacturing facilities must be tucked away somewhere, but we don't see them.

Lara Croft is a major babe with a great set of ears. She hears a faint ticking under the stairs, demolishes the ancient paneling (with her bare hands, as I recall), and finds an old clock that conceals the all-seeing eye. This is the key to whatever it is the Illuminati plan to do with the lost city, etc., in their plan to control time, etc. Why they want to do this is never explained. A letter from her father is discovered sewn into the binding of an old edition of William Blake; "I knew you would figure out my clues," it says. And a good thing, too, since fate hangs in the balance while she plays his parlor games.

We now visit "Venice, Italy," where the Illuminati gather, and then there is an expedition to the frozen northern land where the ancient city awaits in a dead zone inside the crater created by the meteor that brought the key to time here to Earth—I think. Machines do not work in the dead zone, so Lara and the others have to use dogsleds. It is cold on the tundra, and everyone wears fur-lined parkas. Everyone but Lara, whose light gray designer cape sweeps behind her so that we can admire the tight matching sweater she is wearing, which clings tightly to those parts of her body which can be found a foot below and a little to the front of her great ears.

The inside of the city is an inspired accomplishment in art direction, set design, and special effects. A giant clockwork model of the universe revolves slowly above a pool of water, and is protected by great stone figures that no doubt have official names, although I think of them as the "crumbly creatures," because whenever you hit them with anything, they crumble. They're like the desert army in *The Mummy Returns* and the insect alien soldiers in *Starship Troopers*—they look fearsome, but they explode on contact, just like (come to think of it) targets in a video game.

Angelina Jolie makes a splendid Lara Croft, although to say she does a good job of playing the heroine of a video game is perhaps not the highest compliment. She looks great, is supple and athletic, doesn't overplay, and takes with great seriousness a plot that would have reduced a lesser woman to giggles. In real life she is a good actress. Lara Croft does not emerge as a person with a personality, and the other actors are also ciphers, but the movie wisely confuses us with a plot so impenetrable that we never think about their personalities at all.

Did I enjoy the movie? Yes. Is it up there with the *Indiana Jones* pictures? No, although its art direction and set design are (especially in the tomb with all the dead roots hanging down like tendrils). Was I filled with suspense? No. Since I had no idea what was going to happen, should happen, shouldn't happen, or what it meant if it did happen, I could hardly be expected to care. But did I grin with delight at the absurdity of it all? You betcha.

The Last Castle ★ ★ ★
R, 91 m., 2001

Robert Redford (General Irwin), James Gandolfini (Colonel Winter), Mark Ruffalo (Yates), Steve Burton (Captain Peretz), Delroy Lindo (General Wheeler), Paul Calderon (Dellwo), Samuel Ball (Duffy), Jeremy Childs (Cutbush), Clifton Collins Jr (Aguilar), George W. Scott (Thumper), Robin Wright (Daughter). Directed by Rod Lurie and produced by Robert Lawrence. Screenplay by David Scarpa and Graham Yost.

The Last Castle tells the story of a war hero who becomes the prisoner of a tin soldier. Robert Redford stars as General Irwin, much-decorated former Hanoi POW, hero of the Gulf and Bosnian campaigns, now sentenced to a military prison under the command of Colonel Winter (James Gandolfini), a sadistic sentimentalist who obsessively dotes on his collection of military memorabilia.

"They should have given him a medal instead of sending him to prison," Winter tells an underling, as he watches Irwin in the prison yard through the plate-glass window of his office. He admires Irwin, who was found guilty of disobeying a direct command (for heroic rea-

sons, of course). Winter's infatuation is short-lived; he overhears the general telling the orderly, "Any man who has a collection like this has never set foot on a battlefield."

That does it. Winter's true nature emerges: He is a sadist who hides behind military law to run a reign of terror. The Redford character wants only to do his time and go home. But inevitably he finds himself in conflict with Winter, tells him he's "a disgrace to the uniform," and finds himself leading a clandestine uprising. "He's building a structure of loyalty," Winter frets. *The Last Castle*, directed by Rod Lurie *(The Contender)*, builds this bitter personal rivalry into a struggle for power that involves psychological strategy and armed conflict.

There are similarities to *Cool Hand Luke* and its battle of wills. The film does such a good job of creating its oppressive, claustrophobic prison atmosphere and peopling it with sharply defined characters that it grips us, and we shake away logical questions. Lurie shows again, as he did in *The Contender*, that he can tell a dramatic, involving story, even if later we're wondering about loopholes and lapses.

Redford and Gandolfini are two reasons the movie plays so well. Redford, because he does what's expected, as a calm, strong, unbreakable leader. Gandolfini, because he does what is not expected, and creates not simply a villain, but a portrait of a type that is so nuanced, so compelling, so instinctively right that we are looking at the performance of a career. This actor, who can be so disarmingly genial (see his scene-stealing in *The Mexican*), who can play bad guys we enjoy (see *The Sopranos*), here transforms his face and posture to make himself into a middle-aged boy, a hulking schoolyard bully. He does a lot with his mouth, making the lips thin and hurt, as if he is getting back for a lifetime of wounds and disappointments. Colonel Winter's childhood must have been hell.

The immediate experience of watching *The Last Castle* is strongly involving, and the action at the end is exciting. It's the kind of movie people tell you they saw last night and really liked. I really liked it last night too. It's only this morning that I'm having trouble with.

Standing back from the excitement of the engagement, it occurs to me that the Irwin character, in his way, is no less a monster than

Winter. Both men delight in manipulating those they can control; Irwin is simply better at masking his puppet-mastery in nobility. If Winter has been responsible for the injury and death of some of the men under his command, Irwin is responsible for more. If Winter is a disgrace to the uniform, so in a way is Irwin, who could achieve his objectives with less carnage than he does. Much of the plot hinges on a convenient character named General Wheeler (Delroy Lindo), who is wheeled on and off like a Shakespearean chorus. He trusts Irwin, despises Winter, yet makes his decisions entirely for the convenience of the plot. In the real world, he could have easily brought about a peaceful solution.

I was also surprised at the equipment unveiled in the later stages of the film. One of the delights of prison movies like *Stalag 17* and *The Great Escape* is the way the prisoners manufacture props or dig tunnels under the eyes of the guards. All of that ingenuity takes place offscreen in *The Last Castle*, and when we see what Irwin has secretly prepared, we're surprised that Winter could miss such large-scale activities.

There's also a plot thread left hanging. Irwin gets a bitter prison visit from his daughter (Robin Wright), who tells him, "You weren't a father at all." He wants to make peace, but she says it's too late. Fair enough—but this relationship is then dropped. So what was the purpose of the visit? To set up a quest for personal closure in later scenes that have been cut from the film? Or simply because the filmmakers felt that they should supply some family angst from the past because that's what all prison movies do?

Because of these lapses in story logic and character development, *The Last Castle* falls short of the film it could have been. It relies too much on a conflict between colorful characters and a thrilling finish. On those levels it works— I enjoyed watching this movie. It could have been more, could have been a triumph and a classic, instead of simply an effective entertainment. The performances by Redford and Gandolfini are there, ready to be used in the service of something better.

The Last Kiss ★ ★
R, 114 m., 2002

Stefano Accorsi (Carlo), Giovanna Mezzogiorno (Giulia), Stefania Sandrelli (Anna), Giorgio Pasotti (Adriano), Claudio Santamaria (Paolo), Marco Cocci (Alberto), Martina Stella (Francesca), Pierfrancesco Favino (Marco). Directed by Gabriele Muccino and produced by Domenico Procacci. Screenplay by Muccino.

The Last Kiss is a comedy, I guess, about male panic at the specter of adult responsibility. If you're a guy and want to figure out what side of the question you're on, take this test. You're a young, single man. Your girlfriend announces at a family dinner that she is pregnant. You (a) accept the joys and responsibilities of fatherhood; (b) climb up into a treehouse at a wedding to begin a passionate affair with an eighteen-year-old; (c) join three buddies in discussing their plan to buy a van and trek across Africa.

Carlo (Stefano Accorsi), the hero of the film, is torn between (b) and (c). Marriage looms like a trap to him, and he complains to Francesca (Martina Stella), the eighteen-year-old, that he fears "the passion is going" from his life. When his girlfriend, Giulia (Giovanna Mezzogiorno), takes him along to look at a house they could buy, he complains that buying a house seems so "final." Not encouraging words for a pregnant fiancée to hear. "If I catch him cheating, I'll kill him," she says, in the ancient tradition of Italian movie comedy.

But the movie isn't all comedy, and has fugitive ambitions, I fear, to say something significant about romance and even life. Consider some of Carlo's friends. Paolo (Claudio Santamaria) is expected to take over his father's clothing store, has no interest in retail, but is wracked with guilt because his father is dying and this is his last wish. Marco (Pierfrancesco Favino) is a serial lover. Adriano (Giorgio Pasotti) is depressed because his girlfriend has lost all interest in sex after giving birth. Their thirties and indeed their forties are breathing hot on the necks of these friends, who cling to golden memories of adolescence.

There is also the case of Anna (Stefania Sandrelli), Carlo's mother, who is married to a detached and indifferent psychiatrist, and seeks out a former lover with hopes of, who knows, maybe now taking the path not chosen. The lover is delighted to see her for a chat over lunch, but reveals that he has recently married and is the proud father of a one-year-old. How cruelly age discriminates against women (at least those prepared to consider it discrimination and not freedom).

The Last Kiss specializes in dramatic exits and entrances. Anna bursts into her husband's office when he is deep in consultation with a patient, who seems alarmed that his own house is so clearly not in order. Carlo awakens with dread after a night spent imprudently, and flees. Giulia makes a dramatic appearance at a deathbed after discovering Carlo lied to her. And so on.

The problem is that the movie has no idea whether it is serious or not. It combines heartfelt self-analysis with scenes like the one where Carlo is taken by his teenage squeeze to her friend's birthday, and tries to party with the kids. This is either funny or sad, not both, but the movie doesn't know which.

The message behind all of this is difficult to nail down. Mars and Venus? Adults who haven't grown up? The last-fling syndrome? Doing what you want instead of doing what you must? I have just finished *Without Stopping*, the autobiography of the novelist and composer Paul Bowles, who as nearly as I can tell always did exactly what he wanted, and was married to Jane Bowles, who did the same. The answer, obviously, is not to choose between marriage and the van trip through Africa, but to dump the buddies and find a wife who wants to come along.

Last Orders ★ ★ ★ ½
R, 109 m., 2002

Michael Caine (Jack), Tom Courtenay (Vic), David Hemmings (Lenny), Bob Hoskins (Ray), Helen Mirren (Amy), Ray Winstone (Vince), Laura Morelli (June). Directed by Fred Schepisi and produced by Elisabeth Robinson, Schepisi, and Gary Smith. Screenplay by Schepisi, based on the novel by Graham Swift.

Too many films about the dead involve mourning, and too few involve laughter. Yet at lucky funerals there is a desire to remember the good times. The most charismatic man I ever knew was Bob Zonka, an editor at the *Chicago Sun-Times*, and even five years after his death his friends gathered just to tell stories and laugh about them. Yes, he was infuriating in the way he treasured his bad habits, but it was all part of the package. There is the impulse to try to analyze the departed, figure out their motives, ask the questions they never answered, wonder what they were really thinking.

Last Orders, Fred Schepisi's new film, based on the Booker Prize–winning novel by Graham Swift, knows all about those stages in the process of grieving and celebration. It is about four old friends in London who, at one level, simply drank together for years at a pub called the Coach and Horses, and at another level came as close as people can to sharing each others' lives. Now one has died—the most enigmatic and problematical of the four— and the three survivors and the dead man's son gather in the pub with his ashes and set off on a journey to Margate, where he thought to retire. His wife does not make the journey but chooses to spend the day with their retarded daughter.

The three friends and the widow all have faces that evoke decades of memories for moviegoers. In a certain way, we have lived our lives with them, so it feels right to find them on this mission at the end.

Tom Courtenay electrified me in *Loneliness of the Long Distance Runner* when I was still in college. I had lunch with him in 1967 in London, and in a sense have just gotten up from that meal. David Hemmings was the photographer in *Blow-Up*, the movie everybody was talking about when I became a film critic. Michael Caine was one of the first stars I ever interviewed (about *Hurry, Sundown*, a film he had a hard time keeping a straight face about). Bob Hoskins joined the crowd later, with *The Long Good Friday*, walking onto the screen with the authority of a lifelong leaseholder. Helen Mirren I became aware of when I saw *Cal* at the 1984 Cannes festival. Ever since, she has been brave in her film choices, going her own way, so that her character's behavior here mirrors her career.

Because I share history and memories with these actors, it is easy to stand at the bar with their characters as they regard the urn of ashes. "So that's Jack, is it?" they say, looking at the

365

container as if it might explode. Have you noticed that although people feel odd around a corpse, they sometimes have a little smile when looking at ashes, because the ashes so clearly are *not* the departed—who has left for other pastures, leaving behind this souvenir. Having scattered a few ashes myself, I find it more cheerful than putting someone into the ground. It's a way the dead have of telling the living to go outdoors to some nice place and remember them.

The fact that Jack wants his ashes to be scattered into the sea at Margate has a lot to do with his widow Amy's decision not to go along. It was there they met, as kids from London, gathering hops as a summer job. It was there that their daughter was conceived. And when June (Laura Morelli) was born retarded, Jack refused to deal with her—refused even to acknowledge her existence. All these years Amy (Mirren) has visited the daughter in an asylum once a week. The girl has never given the slightest sign of recognizing her mother, and so Amy is trapped between two great gulfs of disregard. That Jack would think Amy would want to retire to a place associated with these memories is—well, typical of the deep misunderstandings a marriage can engender and somehow accommodate.

Jack, we might as well say, is the character played by Michael Caine. It is no secret after the first scene of the film. We get to know him well, because Schepisi's flashback structure shows Jack as a young man at war, as a second-generation butcher, as a young man courting Amy, and as a jolly regular in the pub. The other friends include benign Vic (Courtenay), an undertaker; Ray (Hoskins), who likes to play the ponies; and Lenny (Hemmings), once a boxer, now a portly greengrocer. The actors have logged time in pubs and know the form. Notice how Caine captures the look of a drinker late at night, with the saggy lower eyelids and the slight loosening of tension in the lips.

They all live and work in the same south London neighborhood, and are joined at the pub by Vince (Ray Winstone), who is Jack and Amy's son. It was Jack's wish that Vince join him in the family butcher business, but Vince instead became a car dealer, and turns up in a Mercedes to drive the pals and the ashes to Margate. Many old secrets are revealed in the

course of the journey, but they are not really what the movie is about. The details are not as important as the act of memory itself.

A death in the family is a sudden interruption of the unconscious assumption that things will go on forever. There can be a certain exhilaration at this close contact with eternal truths; we were not aware at our births, so death is the only conscious contact we have with this mysterious journey. The final shot of Schepisi's movie finds a visual way to suggest the great silence that surrounds us. Another scene near the end puts it in human terms. On the day the friends go to scatter Jack's ashes, Amy pays her usual visit to June—to the daughter who was denied the gift of awareness; as Amy tells Ray, "Not once in fifty years did she ever give me a sign—not even a flicker—that she knew me." As we consider June's uncomprehending eyes and fixed smile, we think, death is not so bad. Not knowing we live, not knowing we die, that would be bad. Ashes are scattered in more ways than one in the film's closing scenes.

Note: Some reviews have complained about the Cockney accents. All of these actors can speak the Queen's English if they choose to. The Cockney is their gift to us in creating the world of their characters. You may miss a word or two, but you hear the music.

Last Resort ★ ★ ★
NO MPAA RATING, 76 m., 2001

Paddy Considine (Alfie), Dina Korzun (Tanya), Artiom Strelnikov (Artiom), Lindsay Honey (Les). Directed by Pawel Pawlikowski and produced by Ruth Caleb. Screenplay by Pawlikowski and Rowan Joffe.

Tanya's fiancé was going to meet them in England, but he is not at the airport, the rat. The Russian woman with the small boy and the uncertain English tries to deal with British immigration officials, who are not unkind but have seen this scenario countless times before. She talks about her fiancé, she cites vague employment plans, and finally, in desperation, she requests political asylum.

Asylum is not really what she wants, but it's what she gets: asylum inside the British bureaucracy, which ships Tanya (Dina Korzun) and her son, Artiom (Artiom Strelnikov), to a bleak and crumbling seaside resort named Dreamland, where she's given some food coupons and a barren apartment, and told to wait for a decision that may take months, or years.

Tanya learns over the telephone that the fiancé is never going to show. But in making the call she has also made a crucial connection; using an unfamiliar phone card at a rundown seaside arcade, she meets its owner, Alfie (Paddy Considine). He is an enigma, a seemingly nice man who perhaps has a subtle romantic agenda, or perhaps simply feels sorry for her and wants to help. Having been betrayed by her fiancé, Tanya is not much interested in a new man. But Alfie doesn't push it.

The movie was directed for the BBC films division by Pawel Pawlikowski, who has a background in documentaries and does a good job of sketching in everyday life in the area, where the cold concrete and joblessness of a housing project has bred a generation of young outlaws. It's not clear whether the barbed wire is to keep people out, keep them in, or simply supply a concentration camp decor.

Young Artiom is an enterprising lad who makes friends with Alfie more quickly than his mother will, and is soon hanging out in the arcade, finding his niche in the Dreamland ecology. ("Mom, why can't we stay here with him?") His mother, desperately poor, fields a job offer from a pornographer named Les (Lindsay Honey) who wants to pay her to writhe on a bed for his Internet customers (he demonstrates with a teddy bear, in a scene balancing humor and the grotesque). Les is a sleazeball but a realist, the heir to generations of Cockney enterprisers. He points out that Tanya at least will not have to see, or be touched by, any of her "clients," and that the money's not bad. Such employment would be a change; in Russia, Tanya was an illustrator of children's books.

It's intriguing the way Pawlikowski keeps his hand hidden for most of the movie. We can't guess where things are headed. The movie is not on a standard Hollywood romantic arc in which the happy ending would be Alfie and Tanya in each other's arms. That's only one of several possibilities, and economic factors affect everything. Dina Korzun's performance holds our interest because she bases every scene on the fact that her character is a stranger in a strange land with no money and a son to protect. *Last Resort* avoids all temptations to reduce that to merely the setup for a romantic comedy; it's the permanent condition of her life.

Some movies abandon their soul by solving everything with their endings. Life doesn't have endings, only stages. To pretend a character's problems can be solved is a cheat—in a realistic film, anyway (comedies, fantasies, and formulas are another matter). I like the way *Last Resort* ends, how it concludes its emotional journey without pretending the underlying story is over. You walk out of the theater curiously touched.

The Last Waltz ★ ★ ★
PG, 117 m., 2002

Featuring The Band, Eric Clapton, Neil Diamond, Bob Dylan, Emmylou Harris, Joni Mitchell, Van Morrison, Robbie Robertson, The Staples, Muddy Waters, Ronnie Wood, Neil Young, and Martin Scorsese. A concert documentary directed by Martin Scorcese and produced by Robbie Robertson.

I wonder if the sadness comes across on the CD. The music probably sounds happy. But the performers, seen on-screen, seem curiously morose, exhausted, played out. Recently I was at a memorial concert for the late tenor sax man Spike Robinson, and the musicians—jazz and big-band veterans—were cheerful, filled with joy, happy to be there. Most of the musicians in *The Last Waltz* are, on average, twenty-five years younger than Spike's friends, but they drag themselves onstage like exhausted veterans of wrong wars.

The rock documentary was filmed by Martin Scorsese at a farewell concert given on Thanksgiving Day 1976 by The Band, which had been performing since 1960, in recent years as the backup band for Bob Dylan. "Sixteen years on the road is long enough," says Robbie Robertson, the group's leader. "Twenty years is unthinkable." There is a weight and gravity in his words that suggests he seriously doubts if he could survive four more years.

Drugs are possibly involved. Memoirs recalling the filming report that cocaine was everywhere backstage. The overall tenor of the documentary suggests survivors at the ends of their ropes. They dress in dark, cheerless clothes, hide behind beards, hats, and shades, pound out rote performances of old hits, don't seem to smile much at their music or each other. There is the whole pointless road warrior mystique, of hard-living men whose daily duty it is to play music and get wasted. They look tired of it.

Not all of them. The women (Joni Mitchell, Emmylou Harris) seem immune, although what Mitchell's song is about I have no clue, and Harris is filmed in another time and place. Visitors like the Staples Singers are open-faced and happy. Eric Clapton is in the right place and time. Muddy Waters is on sublime autopilot. Lawrence Ferlinghetti reads a bad poem, badly, but seems pleased to be reading it. Neil Diamond seems puzzled to find himself in this company, grateful to be invited.

But then look at the faces of Neil Young or Van Morrison. Study Robertson, whose face is kind and whose smile comes easily, but who does not project a feeling of celebration for the past or anticipation of the future. These are not musicians at the top of their art, but laborers on the last day of the job. Look in their eyes. Read their body language.

The Last Waltz has inexplicably been called the greatest rock documentary of all time. Certainly that would be *Woodstock,* which heralds the beginning of the era that The Band gathered to bury. Among 1970s contemporaries of The Band, one senses joy in the various Rolling Stones documentaries, in Chuck Berry's *Hail! Hail! Rock and Roll,* and in concert films by the Temptations or Rod Stewart. Not here.

In *The Last Waltz,* we have musicians who seem to have bad memories. Who are hanging on. Scorsese's direction is mostly limited to close-ups and medium shots of performances; he ignores the audience. The movie was made at the end of a difficult period in his own life, and at a particularly hard time (the filming coincided with his work on *New York, New York*). This is not a record of serene men, filled with nostalgia, happy to be among friends.

At the end, Bob Dylan himself comes on. One senses little connection between Dylan and The Band. One also wonders what he was thinking as he chose that oversize white pimp hat, a hat so absurd that during his entire performance I could scarcely think of anything else. It is the haberdashery equivalent of an uplifted middle finger.

The music probably sounds fine on a CD. Certainly it is well rehearsed. But the overall sense of the film is of good riddance to a bad time. Even references to groupies inspire creases of pain on the faces of the rememberers: The sex must have been as bad as anything else. Watching this film, the viewer with mercy will be content to allow the musicians to embrace closure, and will not demand an encore. Yet I give it three stars? Yes, because the film is such a revealing document of a time.

Late Marriage ★ ★ ★
NO MPAA RATING, 100 m., 2002

Lior Louie Ashkenazi (Zaza), Ronit Elkabetz (Judith), Moni Moshonov (Yasha [Father]), Lili Kosashvili (Lily [Mother]), Sapir Kugman (Madona), Aya Steinovits Laor (Ilana). Directed by Dover Kosashvili and produced by Marek Rozenbaum and Edgard Tenembaum. Screenplay by Kosashvili.

When children are grown they must be set free to lead their own lives. Otherwise it's no longer a parent guiding a child, but one adult insisting on authority over another. Wise parents step back before they cross this line. Wise children rebel against parents who do not. *Late Marriage* is about parents who insist on running the life of their thirty-two-year-old son, and a son who lets them. The characters deserve their misery.

The film is set in Israel, within a community of Jewish immigrants from the former Soviet republic of Georgia. Zaza at thirty-one has still not filled his obligation to marry and produce children. His parents have marched a parade of potential wives past him, without success. His secret is that he's in love with Judith, a divorcée from Morocco, four years older, with a daughter. His parents would never approve of Zaza marrying such a woman.

As the movie opens, Zaza and his family descend on the home of Ilana, a sulky seventeen-year-old who has been proposed as a prospective bride. There may be a difference in age and education, but at least she is single, childless, and arguably a virgin. In a scene of excruciating social comedy, the two families arrange themselves in the living room and discuss Zaza and Ilana as if they were this week's Tupperware specials. Then Ilana is produced and the would-be couple dispatched to her bedroom "to get to know one another."

"Is that a dress or a nightgown?" Zaza (Lior Louie Ashkenazi) asks her when they are alone. "What do you think?" asks Ilana (Aya Steinovits Laor). She shows him her portfolio and confides her desire to be a dress designer. She seems to be designing for the hostesses in an Havana hooker bar, circa 1959. "I want a rich man," she tells him. Obviously he will not do, but they fall on her bed and neck for a while until summoned back to the family council.

Zaza's parents find out about Judith (Ronit Elkabetz), the divorcée. They stake out her house and eventually break in upon the romantic couple, calling Judith a whore and demanding that the relationship end. Does Zaza stand up to his mother, Lily (Lili Kosashvili—the director's own mother)? No, he doesn't, and Judith sees this, and wisely drops him because there is no future for her.

The contest between arranged marriages and romantic love is being waged in novels and movies all over those parts of the world where parents select the spouses of their children. Art is on the side of romance, tradition on the side of the parents. Sometimes, as in Mira Nair's wonderful *Monsoon Wedding,* set in Delhi, there is a happy medium when the arranged couple falls in love. But look at Rohinton Mistry's new novel, *Family Matters,* about a man who spends a lifetime of misery after having a widow foisted on him by a family that disapproves of the Christian woman from Goa he truly loves.

The most important sequence in *Late Marriage* is a refreshingly frank sex scene involving Zaza and Judith. We don't often see sex like this on the screen. The scene is not about passion, performance, or technique, but about (listen carefully) familiarity and affection. They know each other's bodies. They have a long history of lovemaking, and you can see how little movements and gestures are part of a shared physical history. Watching this scene,

we realize that most sex scenes in the movies play like auditions.

Late Marriage is not a one-level film, and one of its most revealing moments shows the strong-minded mother expressing respect for the equally iron-willed Judith. These women understand each other, and the mother even realistically discusses the chances that her Zaza will defy her and choose the divorcée. The mother would, if forced to, actually accept that—but Zaza is too frightened of her to intuit that there is a crack in his mother's heart of stone.

I know couples whose marriage were arranged, and who are blissful. I know couples who married for love, and are miserable. I am not saying one way is right and another wrong. The message of *Late Marriage,* I think, is that when a marriage is decided by the parents crushing the will of the child, it is wrong for the child and unfair to the new spouse. I have more thoughts on this subject, but have just remembered this is not the advice column, so I will close with the best all-purpose advice I have heard on this subject: Never marry anyone you could not sit next to during a three-day bus trip.

L'Auberge Espagnole ★ ★ ★
R, 122 m., 2003

Romain Duris (Xavier), Cécile De France (Isabelle), Judith Godrèche (Anne-Sophie), Audrey Tautou (Martine), Kelly Reilly (Wendy), Kevin Bishop (William), Federico D'Anna (Alessandro), Christian Pagh (Lars), Cristina Brondo (Soledad), Barnaby Metschurat (Tobias). Directed by Cédric Klapisch and produced by Bruno Levy. Screenplay by Klapisch.

Xavier, a French student worried about his career choices, is advised by a family friend that learning Spanish will be his ticket to success. He signs up for the Erasmus program of the European Community, which arranges student exchanges as a way for the young people of the New Europe to get to know one another by living and studying together for a year.

L'Auberge Espagnole is the story of Xavier's adventures during a year in Barcelona with, if I have this straight, fellow students from Spain,

England, Belgium, Germany, Italy, and Denmark. An American wanders through, but makes no impression. Although all of their languages make cameo appearances, English is the common language of choice.

That makes the title all the more puzzling. I saw this movie for the first time at the 2002 Karlovy Vary Film Festival in the Czech Republic, where it won the audience award under the title *Europudding*. It opened in England as *Pot Luck,* in Spain as *Una Casa de Locos,* was announced for North America as *The Spanish Hotel,* and now arrives with the Spanish version of that title. This is not a good omen for the movie's message about the harmony of national cultures.

The movie has Xavier (Romain Duris) say good-bye for a year to his French girlfriend (Audrey Tautou, of *Amelie*) and fly to Spain on an odyssey which he narrates, not very helpfully (much dialogue along the lines of, "My story starts here . . . no, not here, but . . . "). In Barcelona he shares an apartment with six other students plus a revolving roster of lovers, most straight, one gay. Imagine the American students in *The Real Cancun* as if they were literate, cosmopolitan, and not substance abusers, and you've got it.

The subplots edge up to screwball comedy without ever quite reaching it, except in a sequence where a girl is in bed with the wrong boy and her current boyfriend arrives unexpectedly at the apartment. Writer-director Cédric Klapisch uses a three-way split screen to show the roommates racing to head off the boyfriend and provide an alibi, and what they come up with provides the movie's biggest laugh.

The romantic adventures of all of the students provide, not surprisingly, most of the movie's plot. I don't remember a whole lot of discussion about the euro as a currency. Unlike *The Real Cancun,* which was dripping with sex but was subtly homophobic, *L'Auberge Espagnole* is refreshingly frank about its lesbian, the Belgian girl named Isabelle (Cécile De France, who won the César Award as most promising newcomer). Although Xavier fancied himself an adequate lover when he arrived in Spain, he benefits greatly from Isabelle's expert lecture-demonstration about what really turns a woman on.

The movie is as light and frothy as a French comedy, which is what it is, a reminder that Cédric Klapisch also directed *When the Cat's Away* (1996), the lighthearted story of a woman who involves an entire neighborhood in the search for her cat. Klapisch likes a casual tone in which human eccentricity is folded into the story and taken for granted.

For Xavier, the year in the Erasmus program leads to a fundamental change in his career goals; he can't face a lifetime of French bureaucracy after the anarchy of his year of Europudding. Travel broadens the mind, they say, and certainly living for a year or so outside your native land helps you view it as part of the larger world. Depressing to contrast these young people with the cast of *The Real Cancun,* who hardly realize they're in Mexico.

Laurel Canyon ★ ★
R, 103 m., 2003

Frances McDormand (Jane), Christian Bale (Sam), Kate Beckinsale (Alex), Natascha McElhone (Sara), Alessandro Nivola (Ian). Directed by Lisa Cholodenko and produced by Susan A. Stover and Jeffrey Levy-Hinte. Screenplay by Cholodenko.

Frances McDormand's first film was *Blood Simple* (1984), but I really noticed her for the first time in *Mississippi Burning* (1988), standing in that doorway, talking to Gene Hackman, playing a battered redneck wife who had the courage to do the right thing. From that day to this I have been fascinated by whatever it is she does on the screen to create such sympathy with the audience.

Her Marge Gunderson in *Fargo* is one of the most likable characters in movie history. In almost all of her roles, McDormand embodies an immediate, present, physical, functioning, living, breathing person as well as any actor ever has, and she plays radically different roles as easily as she walks.

Laurel Canyon is not a successful movie—it's too stilted and preprogrammed to come alive—but in the center of it McDormand occupies a place for her character and makes that place into a brilliant movie of its own. There is nothing wrong with who she is and what she does, although all around her actors are cracking up in strangely written roles.

She plays Jane, a woman in her forties who has been a successful record producer for a long time—long enough to make enough money to own one house in the hills of Laurel Canyon and another one at the beach, which in terms of Los Angeles real estate prices means that when she goes to the Grammys a lot of people talk to her. A sexual free spirit from her early days, she is currently producing an album with a British rock singer named Ian (Alessandro Nivola), who is twenty years younger and her lover.

Jane has a son about Ian's age named Sam (Christian Bale), who is the product of an early and fleeting liaison. Sam is the opposite of his mother, fleeing hedonism for the rigors of Harvard Medical School, where he has found a fiancée named Alex (Kate Beckinsale). He studies psychiatry, she studies fruit flies, and true to their professions he will grow neurotic while she will buzz around seeing who lands on her.

Sam and Alex drive west; he'll do his residency, she'll continue her studies, and they'll live in the Laurel Canyon house while Jane moves to the beach. Alas, Laurel Canyon is occupied by Jane—and Ian and various members of the band—when they arrive because Jane has given the beach place to an ex-husband who needed a place to live.

Significant close-ups and furtive once-overs within the first few scenes make the rest of the movie fairly inevitable. Ian and Jane, whose relationship is so open you could drive a relationship through it, telepathically agree to include Alex in their embraces. Alex is intrigued by a freedom that she never experienced, shall we say, at Harvard Medical School, while Sam meanwhile meets the sensuous Sara (Natascha McElhone), a colleague at the psychiatric hospital, and soon they are in one of those situations where he gives her a ride home and they get to talking so much that he has to turn the engine off. (That act—turning the key in the ignition—is the often-overlooked first step in most adulteries.)

Sam and Alex are therefore on separate trajectories, and *Laurel Canyon* makes that so clear with intercutting that we uneasily begin to sense the presence of the screenplay. The movie doesn't have the headlong inevitability of *High Art* (1998), by the same writer-director, Lisa Cholodenko. The earlier movie starred Radha Mitchell in a role similar to Alex, as a woman

lured away from a safe relationship by the dark temptations of new friends. But *High Art* seemed to *happen,* and *Laurel Canyon* seems to unfold from an obligatory scenario.

Still, there is Frances McDormand, whose character happens and does not unfold, and who is effortlessly convincing as a sexually alluring woman of a certain age. In fact, she's a babe. Of the three principal female characters in the movie—played by McDormand, Beckinsale, and McElhone—it's McDormand whom many wise males (and females) would choose. She promises playful carnal amusement while the others threaten long, sad conversations about their needs.

How McDormand creates her characters I do not understand. This one is the opposite of the mother who worries about her rock-writer son in *Almost Famous.* She begins with a given—her physical presence—but even that seems to transmute through some actor's sorcery. In this movie she's a babe, a seductive, experienced woman who trained in the 1970s and is still a hippie at heart. Now go to the Internet Movie Database and look at the photo that goes with her entry. Who does she look like? A high school teacher chaperoning at the prom. How she does it is a mystery, but she does, reinventing herself, role after role. *Laurel Canyon* is not a success, but McDormand is ascendant.

Lawless Heart ★ ★ ★
R, 102 m., 2003

Bill Nighy (Dan), Tom Hollander (Nick), Douglas Henshall (Tim), Clementine Celarie (Corrine), Stuart Laing (David), Josephine Butler (Leah), Ellie Haddington (Judy), Sukie Smith (Charlie), Dominic Hall (Darren), David Coffey (Stuart). Directed by Tom Hunsinger and Neil Hunter and produced by Martin Pope. Screenplay by Hunsinger and Hunter.

Lawless Heart begins with a funeral, which, like all funerals, assembles people who may not often see one another but have personal connections—old, new, hidden, and potential. The dead man, named Stuart, ran a restaurant on the Isle of Man, off the British coast. To his funeral come Nick, who was his lover; Dan, who was his brother-in-law; and Tim, a childhood friend who has been long absent from the village.

The film opens with the reception after the funeral. We meet the characters and get to know them a little, we think, and we hear the kinds of profundities and resolutions that people utter when reminded of the possibility of their own deaths. The conversation is bright and quick, the people are likable, and at the end of the afternoon they go their various ways.

It's then that the film, written and directed by Tom Hunsinger and Neil Hunter, reveals its own hidden connections. It follows the three men, one after another, in sequences that take place at the same time but change their meaning depending on the point of view, so that the sight of a man crouching out of sight behind a car makes perfect sense, or no sense at all, depending on what you know about why he is doing it.

Nick (Tom Hollander) helped Stuart run the restaurant, and if Stuart had left a will, we learn, he would have left the business to his lover. But he left no will. Stuart's sister Judy therefore inherits the business, but discusses with her husband, Dan (Bill Nighy), the possibility of giving it to Nick anyway.

Nick, meanwhile, discovers that the long-lost friend Tim (Douglas Henshall) is broke and homeless, and lets him stay in the house he shared with Stuart. Tim moves in, drinks too much, and throws a party. The next morning Nick finds a girl named Charlie (Sukie Smith) in his bed, and she wants to know if they had sex. She had sex, all right, but not with the gay Nick—who throws out Tim but begins a friendship with Charlie that leads, to his own amazement, to them having sex after all. Judy discovers this heterosexual excursion by her brother's lover, and takes it as a reason (or an excuse) to keep the restaurant for herself.

Meanwhile, her husband, Dan, follows up on an intriguing conversation he had at the funeral with Corrine (Clementine Celarie), a Frenchwoman who lives in the town, thinks he is single, and boldly invites him to dinner. Will he accept? The way that he handles himself on the crucial night is true, funny, and ultimately ironic.

These intrigues and others are all interconnected, as we gradually understand. *Lawless Heart* is an exercise in interlocking narratives,

in which the same scene means first one thing and then another, the more we know about it. But it isn't simply an exercise; the characters are full-bodied and authentic, capable of surprising themselves, and their dialogue is written with a good ear for how smart people try to be truthful and secretive at the same time.

We discover, for example, that the reason Tim threw his apparently senseless party at Nick's was to create a place to which he could invite Leah (Josephine Butler), whom he met at the funeral. What Tim doesn't know is that his brother David had an unhappy affair with Leah. Tim is in love with Leah himself, or thinks he is, and the outcome of this liaison is one that none of the three could have anticipated.

My description of the plot no doubt makes it sound like a jigsaw puzzle, and yet it's surprising how clear all these relationships become when we're actually seeing and hearing the characters. They're so well drawn, so clear in their needs and fears, that we get drawn into the plot just as we might get drawn into the intrigues of a real village; the movie watches its characters like a nosy neighbor, changing its view as more information surfaces.

The purpose of the movie is perhaps to show us, in a quietly amusing way, that while we travel down our own lifelines, seeing everything from our own points of view, we hardly suspect the secrets of the lives we intersect with. We tend to think people exist when we are with them, but stay on hold the rest of the time. Our lives go forward—but so, *Lawless Heart* reminds us, do theirs.

The League of Extraordinary Gentlemen ★
PG-13, 110 m., 2003

Sean Connery (Allan Quatermain), Shane West (Tom Sawyer), Stuart Townsend (Dorian Gray), Peta Wilson (Mina Harker), Jason Flemyng (Jekyll and Hyde), Naseeruddin Shah (Captain Nemo), Tony Curran (Rodney Skinner), Richard Roxburgh (M). Directed by Stephen Norrington and produced by Trevor Albert and Don Murphy. Screenplay by James Robinson, based on comic books by Alan Moore and Kevin O'Neill.

The League of Extraordinary Gentlemen assembles a splendid team of heroes to battle a plan for world domination, and then, just when it seems about to become a real corker of an adventure movie, plunges into incomprehensible action, idiotic dialogue, inexplicable motivations, causes without effects, effects without causes, and general lunacy. What a mess.

And yet it all starts so swimmingly. An emissary from Britain arrives at a private club in Kenya, circa 1899, to invite the legendary adventurer Allan Quatermain (Sean Connery) to assist Her Majesty's Government in averting a world war. Villains have used a tank to break into the Bank of England and have caused great destruction in Germany, and each country is blaming the other. Quatermain at first refuses to help, but becomes annoyed when armored men with automatic rifles invade the club and try to kill everybody. Quatermain and friends are able to dispatch them with some head butting, a few rights to the jaw, and a skewering on an animal horn, and then he goes to London to attend a meeting called by a spy master named—well, he's named M, of course.

Also assembled by M are such fabled figures as Captain Nemo (Naseeruddin Shah), who has retired from piracy; Mina Harker (Peta Wilson), who was involved in that messy Dracula business; Rodney Skinner (Tony Curran), who is the Invisible Man; Dorian Gray (Stuart Townsend), who, Quatermain observes, seems to be missing a picture; Tom Sawyer (Shane West), who works as an agent for the U.S. government; and Dr. Henry Jekyll (Jason Flemyng), whose alter ego is Mr. Hyde.

These team members have skills undreamed of by the authors who created them. We are not too surprised to discover that Mina Harker is an immortal vampire, since she had those puncture wounds in her throat the last time we saw her, but I wonder if Oscar Wilde knew that Dorian Gray was also immortal and cannot die (or be killed!) as long as he doesn't see his portrait; at one point, an enemy operative perforates him with bullets, and he comes up smiling. Robert Louis Stevenson's Mr. Hyde was about the same size as Dr. Jekyll, but here Hyde expands into a creature scarcely smaller than the Hulk and gets his pants from the same tailor, since they expand right along with him while his shirt is torn to shreds. Hyde looks uncannily like the WWF version of Fat Bastard.

Now listen carefully. M informs them that the leaders of Europe are going to meet in Venice, and that the mysterious villains will blow up the city to start a world war. The league must stop them. When is the meeting? In three days, M says. Impossible to get there in time, Quatermain says, apparently in ignorance of railroads. Nemo volunteers his submarine, the *Nautilus,* which is about ten stories high and as long as an aircraft carrier, and which we soon see cruising the canals of Venice.

It's hard enough for gondolas to negotiate the inner canals of Venice, let alone a sub the size of an ocean liner, but no problem; *The League of Extraordinary Gentlemen* either knows absolutely nothing about Venice, or (more likely) trusts that its audience does not. At one point, the towering *Nautilus* sails under the tiny Bridge of Sighs and only scrapes it a little. In no time at all there is an action scene involving Nemo's newfangled automobile, which races meaninglessly down streets that do not exist, because there are no streets in Venice and you can't go much more than a block before running into a bridge or a canal. Maybe the filmmakers did their research at the Venetian Hotel in Las Vegas, where Sean Connery arrived by gondola for the movie's premiere.

Bombs begin to explode Venice. It is Carnival time, and Piazza San Marco is jammed with merrymakers as the basilica explodes and topples into ruin. Later there is a scene of this same crowd engaged in lighthearted chatter, as if they have not noticed that half of Venice is missing. Dozens of other buildings sink into the lagoon, which does not prevent Quatermain from exalting, "Venice still stands!"

Now back to that speeding car. Its driver, Tom Sawyer, has been sent off on an urgent mission. When he finds something—an underwater bomb, I think, although that would be hard to spot from a speeding car—he's supposed to fire off a flare, after which I don't know what's supposed to happen. As the car hurtles down the nonexistent streets of Venice, enemy operatives stand shoulder-to-shoulder on the rooftops and fire at it with machine guns, leading us to hypothesize an enemy meeting at which the leader says, "Just in case they should arrive by submarine with a fast car, which hasn't been invented yet, I want thousands of men to line the rooftops and fire at it, without hitting anything, of course."

But never mind. The action now moves to the frozen lakes of Mongolia, where the enemy leader (whose identity I would not dream of revealing) has constructed a gigantic factory palace to manufacture robot soldiers, apparently an early model of the clones they were manufacturing in *Attack* of the same. This palace was presumably constructed recently at great expense (it's a bitch getting construction materials through those frozen lakes). And yet it includes vast, neglected, and forgotten rooms.

I don't really mind the movie's lack of believability. Well, I mind a little; to assume audiences will believe cars racing through Venice is as insulting as giving them a gondola chase down the White House lawn. What I do mind is that the movie plays like a big wind came along and blew away the script and they ran down the street after it and grabbed a few pages and shot those. Since Oscar Wilde contributed Dorian Gray to the movie, it may be appropriate to end with his dying words: "Either that wallpaper goes, or I do." ☞

Le Cercle Rouge ★ ★ ★ ★
NO MPAA RATING, 140 m., 2003

Alain Delon (Corey), Gian Maria Volonté (Vogel), Yves Montand (Jansen), André Bourvil (Captain Mattei), François Périer (Santi), Paul Crauchet (The Fence), Pierre Collet (Prison Guard), André Ekyan (Rico). Directed by Jean-Pierre Melville and produced by Robert Dorfmann. Screenplay by Melville.

Gliding almost without speech down the dawn streets of a wet Paris winter, these men in trench coats and fedoras perform a ballet of crime, hoping to win and fearing to die. Some are cops and some are robbers. To smoke for them is as natural as breathing. They use guns, lies, clout, greed, and nerve with the skill of a magician who no longer even thinks about the cards. They share a code of honor that is not about what side of the law they are on, but about how a man must behave to win the respect of those few others who understand the code.

Jean-Pierre Melville watches them with the eye of a concerned god in his 1970 film *Le Cercle Rouge*. His movie involves an escaped pris-

oner, a diamond heist, a police manhunt, and mob vengeance, but it treats these elements as the magician treats his cards; the cards are insignificant, except as the medium through which he demonstrates his skills.

Melville is a director whose films are little known in America; he began before the French New Wave, died in 1973, worked in genres but had a stylistic elegance that kept his films from being marketed to the traditional genre audiences. His *Bob le Flambeur*, now available on a Criterion DVD, has been remade as *The Good Thief* and inspired elements of the two *Ocean's Eleven* films, but all they borrowed was the plot, and that was the least essential thing about it.

Melville grew up living and breathing movies, and his films show more experience of the screen than of life. No real crooks or cops are this attentive to the details of their style and behavior. Little wonder that his great 1967 film about a professional hit man is named *Le Samourai;* his characters, like the samurai, place greater importance on correct behavior than upon success. (Jim Jarmusch's *Ghost Dog* owes something to this value system.)

Le Cercle Rouge, or *The Red Circle* (restored for 2003 release by his admirer John Woo), refers to a saying of the Buddha that men who are destined to meet will eventually meet, no matter what. Melville made up this saying, but no matter; his characters operate according to theories of behavior, so that a government minister believes all men, without exception, are bad; and a crooked nightclub owner refuses to be a police informer because it is simply not in his nature to inform.

The movie stars two of the top French stars of the time, Alain Delon and Yves Montand, as well as Gian Maria Volonté, looking younger here than in the spaghetti Westerns, and with hair. But it is not a star vehicle—or, wait, it is a star vehicle, but the stars ride in it instead of the movie riding on them. All of the actors seem directed to be cool and dispassionate, to guard their feelings, to keep their words to themselves, to realize that among men of experience almost everything can go without saying.

As the film opens, we meet Corey (Delon) as he is released from prison. He has learned of a way to hold up one of the jewelry stores of Place Vendôme. Then we meet Vogel (Volonté), who is a handcuffed prisoner on a train, but he picks the locks of the cuffs, breaks a window, leaps from the moving train, and escapes from the veteran cop Mattei (André Bourvil).

Fate brings Vogel and Corey together. On the run in the countryside, Vogel hides in the trunk of Corey's car. Corey sees him do this, but we don't know he does. He drives into a muddy field, gets out of his car, stands away from it, and tells the man in the trunk he can get out. The man does, holding a gun that Corey must have known he would find in the trunk. They regard each other, face to face in the muddy field. Vogel wants a smoke. Corey throws him a pack and a lighter.

Notice how little they actually say before Corey says, "Paris is your best chance," and Vogel gets back in the trunk. And then notice the precision and economy of what happens next. Corey's car is being tailed by gunmen for a mob boss he relieved of a lot of money. It was probably due him, but still, that is no way to treat a mob boss. Corey pulls over. The gunsels tell him to walk toward the woods. He does. Then we hear Vogel tell them to drop their guns and raise their hands. Vogel picks up each man's gun with a handkerchief and uses it to shoot the other man—so the fingerprints will indicate they shot each other. Corey risked his life on the expectation that Vogel would know what to do and do it, and Corey was right.

There is one cool, understated scene after another. Note the way the police commissioner talks to the nightclub owner after he knows that the owner's son, picked up in an attempt to pressure the owner, has killed himself. Note what he says and what he doesn't say, and how he looks. And note, too, how Jansen, the Yves Montand character, comes into the plot, and think for a moment about why he doesn't want his share of the loot.

The heist itself is performed with the exactness we expect of a movie heist. We are a little startled to realize it is not the point of the film. In most heist movies, the screenplay cannot think beyond the heist, and is satisfied merely to deliver it. Le Cercle Rouge assumes that the crooks will be skillful at the heist because they are good workmen. The movie is not about their jobs but about their natures.

Melville fought for the French Resistance during the war. Manohla Dargis of the Los Angeles Times, in a review of uncanny and poetic perception, writes: "It may sound far-fetched, but I wonder if his obsessive return to the same themes didn't have something to do with a desire to restore France's own lost honor." The heroes of his films may win or lose, may be crooks or cops, but they are not rats.

Left Luggage ★ ★

NO MPAA RATING, 100 m., 2001

Laura Fraser (Chaja), Isabella Rossellini (Mrs. Kalman), Maximilian Schell (Chaja's Father), Marianne Sagebrecht (Chaja's Mother), Jeroen Krabbe (Mr. Kalman), Adam Monty (Simcha), Chaim Topol (Mr. Apfelschnitt). Directed by Jeroen Krabbe and produced by Ate de Jong, Hans Pos, and Dave Schram. Screenplay by Edwin de Vries.

Left Luggage is one of those movies where the audience knows the message before the film begins and the characters are still learning it when the film ends. No matter how noble a film's sentiments, it's wearying to wait while elementary truths dawn gradually on slow learners. Add to this yet one more tiresome story in which the women possess all the wisdom and humanity and the men are cruel, stubborn, and crazed, and you have a long slog through a parched landscape.

The movie takes place in 1972 in Antwerp, where a young woman named Chaja (Laura Fraser) gets a job as a nanny for the Kalmans, a family of Hasidic Jews. Chaja is a Jew herself, but so indifferent to her identity that one of her best friends doesn't even realize she's Jewish. She finds the Hasidim, with their traditional black garments, strict observances, and unyielding patriarchy, absurd throwbacks. But she needs the money and takes the job, and soon bonds with Mrs. Kalman (Isabella Rossellini) and her children, especially a four-year-old named Simcha (Adam Monty).

Simcha has not started to speak. One reason for this may be the fierce tyranny with which Mr. Kalman (Jeroen Krabbe, the film's director) rules his family. He is strict, forbidding, and unforgiving, in accordance with the convention in which most movie fathers are deeply flawed repositories of character defects, while their wives are bubbling reservoirs of life, wit, and humanity. Gene Siskel called this the Bad Dad Syndrome, noting that we could go months at a time between films where a father was smart, gentle, and caring.

At home, Chaja's parents are stuck in their own pasts. Both her father and mother (Maximilian Schell and Marianne Sägebrecht) are Holocaust survivors whose lives are still governed by the experience. The mother compulsively bakes cakes and endlessly tries to feed them to everyone within sight. The father prowls Antwerp with a map and a shovel, trying to find the spot where he buried two precious suitcases before being shipped off by the Nazis. "They're probably all moldy by now," his wife warns—and so is the labored plot device. Surely there is a more creative way to suggest a search for lost roots than to have poor Maximilian Schell up to his armpits in holes he is frantically digging in Antwerp's gardens and backyards.

Chaja becomes close with little Simcha, who eventually reveals that he can indeed speak. His first word is "quack." It is inspired by a toy duck he pushes along so that it quacks too. It goes without saying that the toy duck arouses the ire of Mr. Kalman, who wants to banish it from the house ("My son is saying 'quack, quack' when he should be asking the four questions for the Seder"). Later, when Chaja teaches little Simcha the four questions (remember, this is a child who was thought to be mute), the beast of a father criticizes a mistake and the kid pees in his pants. My notion is that a great many Hasidic fathers succeed in combining their religion with love and kindness for their children, and that this particular father is an example of melodramatic overkill crossed with gender bias.

Ah, but there's more. The Kalmans have succeeded in being the only family still resident in a building where the concierge is a vicious anti-Semite. This is no doubt a great convenience for the plot, since by stationing him at the door to hiss and swear at the Jews every time they enter or leave, the screenplay doesn't have to waste valuable screen time importing anti-Semites from elsewhere. And then there is a development at the end which, as tear-jerking goes, is shameless.

In the midst of this contrivance, both Isabella Rossellini and Laura Fraser give solid and affecting performances, and Schell makes his character less of a caricature than he might have been. But the very last shot of the film, intended as uplifting, seems to solve nothing and to condemn the characters to continue to let the past destroy their present and future. With limitless possibilities for stories involving essentially these same characters, Krabbe and his writer, Edwin de Vries, are trapped by sentimentality and awkward contrivance.

Legally Blonde ★ ★ ★
PG-13, 96 m., 2001

Reese Witherspoon (Elle Woods), Luke Wilson (Emmett), Selma Blair (Vivian), Matthew Davis (Warner Huntington III), Victor Garber (Professor Callahan), Ali Larter (Brooke), Jennifer Coolidge (Paulette), Holland Taylor (Professor Stromwell). Directed by Robert Luketic and produced by Ric Kidney and Marc E. Platt. Screenplay by Kirsten Smith and Karen McCullah Lutz, based on the novel by Amanda Brown.

Legally Blonde is a featherweight comedy balanced between silliness and charm. It is impossible to dislike, although how much you like it may depend on your affection for Reese Witherspoon. She is so much the star of the movie that the other actors seem less like costars than like partners in an acting workshop, feeding her lines. They percolate; she bubbles.

Witherspoon plays Elle Woods, named perhaps for the magazine, perhaps because the word means "she" in French. Work on that pun a little more and you could name the movie *The Vengeance of Elle,* since Elle gets her revenge on the stuck-up snob who dumps her, and thus inspires a brilliant legal career.

We meet Elle as she basks in general approval as president of the Delta Nu house on a Los Angeles campus. She moves in a cloud of pink, dispensing advice on grooming, hair care, and accessorizing; she has a perfect grade point average in her major, which is fashion. She thinks Warner Huntington III (Matthew Davis) plans to propose to her, but actually he wants to break up. He plans to be a senator by the time he's thirty, he explains, and for that career path, "I need to marry a Jackie, not a Marilyn."

Outraged, Elle determines to follow Warner to Harvard Law School and shame him with her brilliance. And so she does, more or less, after being taken on as an intern by the famous Professor Callahan (Victor Garber) and assigned to help him in the case of a famous weight-loss consultant (Ali Larter) accused of murdering her much older husband. The defense hinges on such matters as whether a Delta Nu would sleep with a man who wears a thong, and the chemistry of perms.

Reese Witherspoon effortlessly animates this material with sunshine and quick wit. Despite the title and the implications in the ads, this is a movie about smart blondes, not dumb ones, and she is (I think) using her encyclopedic knowledge of fashion and grooming to disguise her penetrating intelligence. On the other hand, maybe not; maybe it's just second nature for her to win a client's confidence by visiting her in prison with Calvin Klein sheets, Clinique skin care products, and the latest issue of *Cosmo*.

I smiled a lot during the movie, laughed a few times, was amused by the logic of the court case. *Legally Blonde* is not a great movie (not comparable with *Clueless*, which it obviously wants to remind us of, or Witherspoon's own wonderful *Election*). But Witherspoon is a star, and the movie doesn't overstay its welcome. It also contains at least one line I predict will enter the repertory: Elle Woods is asked, "A spa? Isn't that kind of like your mother ship?"

Legally Blonde 2: Red, White and Blonde ★ ★
PG-13, 105 m., 2003

Reese Witherspoon (Elle Woods), Sally Field (Representative Victoria Rudd), Bob Newhart (Sidney Post), Luke Wilson (Emmett Richmond), Jennifer Coolidge (Paulette Bonafonte), Regina King (Grace Stoteraux), Jessica Cauffiel (Margot), Alanna Ubach (Serena McGuire), Bruce McGill (Stanford Marks). Directed by Charles Herman-Wurmfeld and produced by David Nicksay and Marc Platt. Screenplay by Kate Kondell.

Legally Blonde 2: Red, White and Blonde evokes a fairy-tale America in which a congresswoman's ditzy blonde junior staff member, pretty in pink, is asked to address a joint session of Congress and sways them with her appeal for animal rights. Not in this world. It might happen, though, in the world of the movie— but even then, her big speech is so truly idiotic she'd be laughed out of town. That the movie considers this speech a triumph shows how little it cares about its "ideas." The model for the movie is obviously *Mr. Smith Goes to Washington*, but in that one James Stewart's big speech was actually sort of about something.

The movie chronicles the continuing adventures of Elle Woods, the Reese Witherspoon character introduced in the winning *Legally Blonde* (2001). Elle, for whom pink is not a favorite color but a lifestyle choice, is like a walking, talking beauty and cosmetics magazine, whose obsession with superficial girly things causes people, understandably, to dismiss her at first sight. Ah, but beneath the Jackie Kennedy pillbox hat there lurks a first-class brain; Elle is a Harvard Law graduate who, as the sequel opens, has a job in a top legal firm.

It's impossible to determine if Elle knows what she's doing—if it's all a strategy—or whether she truly is *über*-ditzy. Always smiling, never discouraged, deaf to insults, blind to sneers, dressed in outfits that come from a fashion universe of their own, she sails through life like the good ship *Undefeatable*. How she stumbles upon the cause of animal rights is instructive. It begins with her search for the biological birth parent of Bruiser, her beloved Chihuahua. When she finds the mother captive in an animal testing laboratory ("We test makeup on animals so you don't have to"), she becomes an animal rights advocate, is fired from her law firm, and finds herself on the staff of Representative Victoria Rudd (Sally Field), who is sponsoring an animal-rights bill.

The movie's vision of Congress is hopelessly simplistic and idealistic. Characters have the same kinds of instant conversions that are standard on sitcoms, where the unenlightened oppose something, have a sudden epiphany, and then see the light. Consider the character of Stan, a self-described Southern conservative who discovers, along with Elle, that both their dogs are gay and have fallen in love with each other. This softens him up on the pending legislation because he loves his gay dog, you see.

The movie has its share of funny lines ("This is just like C-SPAN except it's not boring") and moments (congressional interns form a pom-

pom squad), but the plot developments in Congresswoman Rudd's office are heavy-handed. Rudd's top aide (Regina King) is cold and antagonistic to Elle when the plot needs her to be and then turns on a dime. Rudd herself admits to dropping her bill in return for big campaign contributions. And Elle's top adviser is a hotel doorman (Bob Newhart) who knows how Washington works because of what he overhears. Uh-huh. Meanwhile, back home in Boston, Elle's fiancé (Luke Wilson) is incredibly understanding when his marriage is put on hold during Elle's legislative campaign. There could be a whole comedy just about being engaged or married to the creature in pink.

Ramping up for this review, I came across a curious column by Arianna Huffington, who attended a preview screening and wrote, "Sitting between my teenage daughters while watching Elle take on the U.S. Congress, I was struck by the palpable effect it had on them: They left the theater inspired, empowered, and talking about the things they wanted to change and the ways they might be able to change them." She quotes approvingly from Elle's big speech: "So speak up, America. Speak up for the home of the brave. Speak up for the land of the free gift with purchase. Speak up, America!"

Amazing, that the usually tough-minded Huffington fell for the movie. Amazing, too, that two teenage girls who have their own mother as a role model were inspired and empowered by the insipid Elle. I have a movie for them to see together: *Whale Rider*. Now there's a great movie about female empowerment, and the heroine doesn't even wear makeup.

America will no doubt speak up, alas, by spending millions of dollars on *Legally Blonde 2* in obedience to the movie's advertising blitz (buses in several cities have been painted entirely pink). And so the myth of a populist Congress will live on, entirely apart from the real world of lobbyists, logrolling, punishment to the disloyal, and favors for friends. In the real world, Elle Woods would be chewed up faster than one of little Bruiser's Milk-Bones.

The Legend of Rita ★ ★ ★ ½
NO MPAA RATING, 101 m., 2001

Bibiana Beglau (Rita), Martin Wuttke (Hull), Nadja Uhl (Tatjana), Harald Schrott (Andi), Alexander Beyer (Jochen), Jenny Schily (Friederike), Mario Irrek (Klatte), Thomas Arnold (Gerngross). Directed by Volker Schlondorff and produced by Arthur Hofer and Emmo Lempert. Screenplay by Wolfgang Kohlhasse and Schlondorff.

It's said that European films are about adults, Hollywood films about adolescents. For evidence, compare two recent films: *The Legend of Rita* and *Invisible Circus*. Both are about young women who become involved with German terrorist gangs. The German film is told through the eyes of a woman who tries to remain true to her principles while her world crumbles around her. The American film is told through the eyes of a kid sister, who seeks the truth of her older sister's death, and ends up sleeping with her boyfriend, etc. The German woman is motivated by political beliefs. The American woman is motivated by family sentiment, lust, and misguided idealism, in keeping with Hollywood's belief that women are driven more by sex than ideas, and that radicalism is a character flaw.

The Legend of Rita, directed by the gifted German Volker Schlondorff *(The Tin Drum)*, won two acting prizes and the award as best European film at the 2000 Berlin Film Festival. It stars Bibiana Beglau as Rita, a West German who belongs to a left-wing terrorist group in the 1970s. The group robs banks, kills people, and inspires a dragnet after a jailbreak. The movie doesn't make it easy for us: Rita is not an innocent bystander, and kills a policeman herself. But this isn't a simplistic parable about her guilt or motivation; it's about the collapse of belief during the last decade of the Cold War. Schlondorff believes his audience may be grown-up enough to accept a story about a woman who is not a heroine. Imagine that.

The setup comes as Rita, who has been in Lebanon, attempts to enter East Germany with a revolver in her luggage. She is questioned by Hull (Martin Wuttke), an agent for Stasi, the East German secret police, and allowed to enter the country with the weapon but without her bullets. Later, because Hull (and Stasi, it is implied) sympathizes with her group's opposition to capitalism, she is offered a new identity.

Cutting her ties to her name, her past and everyone she knows, Rita becomes a cog of the working class. This is all right with her: She isn't a naive hobbyist but seriously believes in socialism. With a new name and identity, she goes to work in a textile factory and becomes friendly with a fellow worker named Tatjana (Nadja Uhl); their affection nudges toward a love affair, but when her identity is discovered, Hull yanks her into another life, this time running a summer camp for the children of factory workers. Here she falls in love with a man. But can she marry a man who doesn't know who she really is?

The movie isn't about love, unrequited or not. It's about believing in a cause after the cause abandons you. Here the intriguing figure is Hull, who is not the evil East German spy of countless other movies, but a bureaucrat with ideals who likes Rita and believes he is doing the right thing by protecting her. When the Berlin Wall collapses, there is an astonishing exchange between Hull and the general who is his superior. The general says West Germany demands the extradition of Rita and other terrorists.

"How did they know they were here?" asks Hull.

"They always knew," says the general.

"How did they find out?"

"From us, perhaps."

The Legend of Rita shows a lot of everyday East Germans, workers and bureaucrats, who seem unanimously disenchanted by the people's paradise. Rita's original cover story was that she moved to the East from Paris because of her ideals; not a single East German can believe that anyone from the West would voluntarily move to their country. In the last days of the East, as the wall is coming down, Rita makes a touching little speech in the factory cafeteria, saying the ideals of socialism were good, even if they were corrupted in practice. The East German workers look at her as if she's crazy.

The Legend of Rita doesn't adopt a simplistic political view. It's not propaganda for either side, but the story of how the division and reunification of Germany swept individual lives away indifferently in its tide. In 1976, Schlondorff and his wife, Margarethe von Trotta, made another strong film, *The Lost Honor of Katharina Blum,* set in West Germany. It was about an innocent bystander caught in the aftermath of raids by the Baader-Meinhof

Gang, the same group Rita presumably belongs to. From West or East, from right or left, his stories have the same message: When the state's interests are at stake, individual rights and beliefs are irrelevant.

Les Destinées ★ ★ ★ ½
NO MPAA RATING, 180 m., 2002

Emmanuelle Béart (Pauline), Charles Berling (Jean Barnery), Isabelle Huppert (Nathalie), Mathieu Genet (Max Barnery), Rémi Martin (Dahlias). Directed by Oliver Assayas and produced by Bruno Pésery. Screenplay by Jacques Fieschi and Assayas, based on the novel by Jacques Chardonne. In French with English subtitles.

Les Destinées is a long, attentive epic about the span of a life and the seasons of a love. It will not appeal to the impatient, but those who like long books and movies will admire the way it accumulates power and depth. It is about youthful idealism, headstrong love, and fierce ambition, and is pessimistic about all of them. At the end, its hero, who has accomplished a great deal and always tried to do his duty, can only say, "Everything I've done is worthless. I was always wrong."

He's wrong about that, too. The film follows Jean Barnery (Charles Berling), born into a porcelain-manufacturing family in the Limoges region of France. The ruling families here make china and cognac, laying down their stocks, treasuring their vintages, transferring power in an orderly way from one generation to the next.

Jean steps outside the mold. He leaves the family business and becomes a Protestant minister, filled with conviction. When he learns that his wife, Nathalie (Isabelle Huppert), may have had affection for another, he divorces her. She is probably innocent (certainly of any physical adultery), but he has read a compromising letter and there is no room in his heart for forgiveness. So concerned is he to appear just in the eyes of the world, however, that he signs over the bulk of his fortune to Nathalie and their daughter, Aline.

In the congregation one day is Pauline (Emmanuelle Béart), just returned from study in England. She loves this stiff and proper man with an inexplicable passion, and soon they have married. He leaves the church. He grows ill, and they move to a chalet in Switzerland for his health, and there they are happy, living a simple life, alone with each other.

Then Jean's father dies, and he is summoned home to take over the firm from his brother, who is incapable of running it. Jean gets the necessary takeover votes from—Nathalie, who continues to think of herself as his wife. Pauline is against the move back to the factory: "This is the end of our love." Not really, but the end of the sweet and uncomplicated part of it, because now their love must survive in the real world.

The film by Oliver Assayas, written by Jacques Fieschi from a novel by Jacques Chardonne, assumes a French audience as familiar with the traditions and politics of fine porcelain and cognac as we are with the Detroit auto dynasties. At three hours, the film is long enough to show us how the factory works, and how the laborers, underpaid, are skilled craftsmen alert to the slightest nuance of tone and texture. Jean becomes an artist, driven by his search for colors he likens to the face of the moon, or to seawater, and he is unable to compromise quality even as he pushes for a modern factory.

The film covers more than thirty years, enough to show us how people change and marriages must change to accommodate them. One of the most startling scenes comes when Jean volunteers for the First World War, and Pauline, visiting him near the front, finds him a crude, rough man, shoveling food into his mouth, made gross by the hard life of the trenches. Later he returns, slowly, to civilization, and even to tenderness, symbolized by a sunny afternoon in their orchard that both remember as a blessed moment.

Social currents thrust into the complacency of the Barnery family. It faces strikes, Marxist organizers, competition from cheap German goods. The film is remarkable in the way it gains epic sweep without ever descending into the merely picturesque. These are always people living in a real world—except for one scene, toward the beginning, where Pauline stars at a formal dance, her head turning left and then right as she sweeps through the room. Emmanuelle Béart, always beautiful,

has never looked more radiant, and Jean Barnery agrees.

As long as the film is, there are loose ends. In the dance scene, for example, Pauline is approached by Dahlias (Rémi Martin), an ugly-handsome man who inspires much gossip. He is attracted to her, stands too close, speaks with too much familiarity, violates her space, creates a threat, excites our interest. And then disappears from the movie. There is also the sense of something missing in the transition of the daughter, Aline, from an adolescent who is scandalously "seen everywhere" to a young woman who takes the vows of a deaconess and walls herself from the world.

But nothing is missing in the central relationship. Jean lives according to his driven inner codes, and Pauline, who loves him, cannot make him happier. But she is able to bring him a perfect example of his new design of china and spread it on the counterpane of his deathbed. Their marriage is not perfect, but it endures and stands for something. This is not a movie about episodes but about the remorseless bookkeeping of life, which sends such large payments so early, and collects so much interest at the end.

Levity ★ ½
R, 100 m., 2003

Billy Bob Thornton (Manuel Jordan), Morgan Freeman (Miles Evans), Holly Hunter (Adele Easley), Kirsten Dunst (Sofia Mellinger), Manuel Aranguiz (Señor Aguilar), Geoffrey Wigdor (Abner Easley), Luke Robertson (Young Abner Easley), Dorian Harewood (Mackie Whittaker). Directed by Ed Solomon and produced by Richard N. Gladstein, Adam Merims, and Solomon. Screenplay by Solomon.

Levity is an earnest but hopeless attempt to tell a parable about a man's search for redemption. By the end of his journey, we don't care if he finds redemption, if only he finds wakefulness. He's a whiny slug who talks like a victim of overmedication. I was reminded of the Bob and Ray routine about the Slow Talkers of America.

That this unfortunate creature is played by Billy Bob Thornton is evidence, I think, that we have to look beyond the actors in placing blame. His costars are Morgan Freeman, Holly Hunter, and Kirsten Dunst. For a director to assemble such a cast and then maroon them in such a witless enterprise gives him more to redeem than his hero. The hero has merely killed a fictional character. Ed Solomon, who wrote and directed, has stolen two hours from the lives of everyone who sees the film, and weeks from the careers of these valuable actors.

The movie stars Thornton as Manuel Jordan, a man recently released from custody after serving twenty-two years of a sentence for murder. That his first name reminds us of Emmanuel and his surname echoes the Jordan River is not, I fear, an accident; he is a Christ figure, and Thornton has gotten into the spirit with long hair that looks copied from a bad holy card. The only twist is that instead of dying for our sins, the hero shot a young convenience store clerk—who died, I guess, for Manuel's sins.

Now Manuel returns to the same district where the killing took place. This is one of those movie neighborhoods where all the characters live close to one another and meet whenever necessary. Manual soon encounters Adele Easley (Holly Hunter), the sister of the boy he killed. They become friendly and the possibility of romance looms, although he hesitates to confess his crime. She has a teenage son (Geoffrey Wigdor), named Abner after her late brother.

In this district a preacher named Miles Evans (Freeman) runs a storefront youth center, portrayed so unconvincingly that we suspect Solomon has never seen a store, a front, a youth, or a center. In this room, which looks ever so much like a stage set, an ill-assorted assembly of disadvantaged youths are arrayed about the room in such studied "casual" attitudes that we are reminded of extras told to keep their places. Preacher Evans intermittently harangues them with apocalyptic rantings, which they attend patiently. Into the center walks Sofia Mellinger (Dunst), a lost girl who is tempted by drugs and late-night raves, who wanders this neighborhood with curious impunity.

We know that sooner or later Manuel will have to inform Adele that he murdered her brother. But meanwhile the current Abner has fallen in with bad companions, and a silly grudge threatens to escalate into murder. This generates a scene of amazing coincidence, during which in a lonely alley late at night, all of the necessary characters coincidentally appear as they are needed, right on cue, for fraught action and dialogue that the actors must have studied for sad, painful hours, while keeping their thoughts to themselves.

Whether Manuel finds forgiveness, whether Sofia finds herself, whether Abner is saved, whether the preacher has a secret, whether Adele can forgive, whether Manuel finds a new mission in life, and whether the youths ever tire of sermons, I will leave to your speculation. All I can observe is that there is not a moment of authentic observation in the film; the director has assembled his characters out of stock melodrama. A bad Victorian novelist would find nothing to surprise him here, and a good one nothing to interest him. When this film premiered to thunderous silence at Sundance 2003, Solomon said he had been working on the screenplay for twenty years. Not long enough.

Liam ★ ★ ★ ½
R, 90 m., 2001

Ian Hart (Dad), Claire Hackett (Mam), Anthony Borrows (Liam), Megan Burns (Teresa), David Hart (Con). Directed by Stephen Frears and produced by Colin McKeown and Martin Tempia. Screenplay by Jimmy McGovern.

Set among the Irish working people of Liverpool in the 1930s, Stephen Frears's *Liam* shows us a family where the children are terrified of sin and their parents of poverty. The first is more easily combated than the second; in two crucial personal transformations, the eight-year-old boy makes his first confession and communion, and his father joins the fascist brownshirts of Oswald Mosley. Both are obsessed with blame; the father blames the Jews for his unemployment and poverty, and his son blames—himself.

This is, says Charles Taylor of *Salon*, the movie that *Angela's Ashes* might have been, and he is correct: It is harder-edged, more unsparing, and when the father tells his wife, "We're skint," he is not making an announcement but accepting a doom. Broke and unemployed, he is expected to outfit little Liam (Anthony Borrows) in a nice new suit from the tailor shop for his first communion.

The way he sees it, to pay the Jewish tailor, he has to get funds from the Jewish pawnbroker, and when, on First Communion Sunday, the priest in his pulpit compliments the children on how well they are dressed, Dad (Ian Hart) stands up furious in his pew to cry out in the church: "Do you know how much it costs to dress the children, Father?" He then goes on to blame the Jews, although he might better blame the church itself for not welcoming the children of the poor in whatever clothes they have.

Times change. I was reminded of Ken Loach's *Raining Stones* (1994), in which it is the unemployed father who is determined that his girl have a nice communion dress, and the priest who tries to talk him out of it. That priest even goes on to make a tricky moral judgment that seems to owe more to situational ethics than to church doctrine; he is that rarity in the movies, a clergyman who is good, flexible, and sympathetic. The priest in *Liam* seems straight from the pages of James Joyce, terrifying the children with visions of hell and informing them that their sins drive the nails deeper into the hands of Christ, which may be more than you can handle when you are eight years old.

The film is built on strong performances, but two stand out. Little Anthony Borrows, short, stout, and always in earnest as Liam, has a stutter that makes it almost impossible for him to get the words out. Sometimes this works to his advantage: He takes a suit to the pawnshop instructed to get "seven and a tanner" but seizes up and gets nine and a tanner when another customer appeals to the good heart of the pawnbroker. During Liam's first confession, he literally cannot say a word until he hits upon a sudden inspiration that releases the flow.

What he wants to confess is that his sins have caused his mother to grow hair upon her body. This he knows from having accidentally seen her in her bath, and comparing her body with the hairless perfection of the art reproductions so thrillingly studied in secret by the boys at school. The priest, who is not a bad man but simply clueless about children, is able to relieve him of this great burden.

The other performance is by Ian Hart, a British actor you may not even recognize, although he has given a series of brilliant, self-effacing performances. He plays the kind of man who cannot bear the pain of seeming insufficient, and must blame somebody. We see him lining up with the other unemployed men outside a factory, hoping to be chosen by the foreman. We see him buying a pint of Guinness for the foreman as a bribe—and *still* being passed over, and spitting in the man's face. And we see how for him the attraction of fascism and anti-Semitism is that it removes the guilt from his shoulders; it is his form of absolution, and when he puts on his fascist shirt and marches out to join a rally, you get a vision of hate groups as clusters of the weak, clinging together to seek in the mob qualities they lack in themselves.

Two children have work: Con (David Hart), the older brother, brings home a paycheck but is at war with his father, and Teresa (Megan Burns) is a housemaid for a wealthy Jewish family, and gets bribes from the wife for keeping quiet about an affair she is having. There is a Jewish daughter, about Teresa's age, who wants to be friendly across the class divide. When Teresa is given some of her dresses, it's no problem that they're hand-me-downs; what breaks Teresa's heart is when she is asked by her mother to select one so the others can be pawned.

Some will find Dad's last big act in the movie too melodramatic. I think it follows from a certain logic, and leads to the very last shot, which is heartbreaking in its tenderness. The film as a whole suggests that Catholicism (in those days, in that society) came down more heavily upon children than some of them could bear, and that children thus diminished in self-esteem might grow up to seek it in unsavory places. It suggests a connection, in some cases, between extreme guilt and low self-esteem in childhood and an adult attraction to the buck-passing solutions of racism, fascism, and even, as Dad's final big scene makes perfectly clear, terrorism.

L.I.E. ★ ★ ★
NC-17, 97 m., 2001

Brian Cox (Big John Harrigan), Paul Franklin Dano (Howie Blitzer), Billy Kay (Gary Terrio), Bruce Altman (Marty Blitzer), James Costa

(Kevin Cole), Tony Donnelly (Brian), Walter Masterson (Scott). Directed by Michael Cuesta and produced by Rene Bastian, Linda Moran, and Michael Cuesta. Screenplay by Stephen M. Ryder, Michael Cuesta, and Gerald Cuesta.

Some pederasts are besotted by sentimentality, seeing their transgression through a misty-eyed desire to be understood. The popular arts usually paint them as monsters, and even a great novel like Michel Tournier's *The Ogre* goes straight for a link between the pederast's idealization of young men and the psychosexual impulses of Nazism. The most remarkable thing about *L.I.E.*, a drama about a fifteen-year-old boy and a middle-aged ex-marine, is that it sees both of its characters without turning them into caricatures. The man is helpless in the face of his compulsion, but he seeks only where he is possibly welcome.

The title is an abbreviation for the Long Island Expressway, and in the opening shot we see Howie (Paul Franklin Dano) hazardously balanced on one foot on a guard rail above the speeding traffic. In narration, he tells us the expressway "has taken a lot of people and I hope it doesn't get me." He lists some of the victims: "Harry Chapin, the director Alan Pakula, and my mother."

Howie lives with his father, who has taken a bimbo girlfriend with unseemly haste. He skips school, hangs out with the kinds of boys his mother would have warned him against, breaks into houses, deals uncertainly with the erotic feelings he has for his best friend, Gary (Billy Kay). Gary is actively gay, we learn, and hustles older guys for money, but he keeps that side of his life secret from his friends.

One of the houses they break into belongs to Big John Harrigan (Brian Cox, who played Hannibal Lecter in *Manhunter*). Big John, a client of Gary's, tracks Howie down, confronts him with proof of his crime, and offers him a choice between arrest and friendship. He does not quite require sex as part of the bargain, and perhaps Howie does not quite understand the nature of the older man; some of his naïveté is real, and some is deliberately chosen.

When Howie's father is arrested on fraud charges connected to his business, Howie ends up at Big John's home, and uncertainly begins to offer what he thinks is expected. Big John turns him away: "It's not about sex, Howie." Isn't it? We have a feeling that for Big John sex is an activity that takes place at the local parks where male hustlers do business, and Howie represents something more complex and, in a twisted way, idealistic.

Make no mistake: *L.I.E.* is not an apologia for pederasty. It does not argue in defense of Big John. But its director, Michael Cuesta, has the stubborn curiosity of an artist who won't settle for formulas but is intrigued by the secrets and mysteries of his characters. My guess is that for every actual sexual liaison of this sort, there are dozens or hundreds of ambiguous, unfulfilled, tentative "friendships." Many men can remember that when they were boys there were sometimes older men around who used friendship or mentoring as a metaphor for a vague, unexpressed yearning. This movie is balanced along that murky divide just as Howie is balanced above the expressway.

Brian Cox has been a superb actor in more than fifty movies, from *Braveheart* to *Rob Roy* to *Rushmore* to Shakespeare. His character here is macho to an extreme (his doorbell plays a patriotic march). He is a man's man in both meanings of the phrase. His achievement in *L.I.E.* is to remain just outside our comprehension: We do not approve of what he does, but he is just subtle enough so that we are sometimes not sure exactly what he's doing. The courts would judge this case in black and white, but the movie occupies the darker shades of gray.

The ending is a cheap shot. An inconclusive ending would have been better, and perhaps more honest. The movie and the ending have so little in common that it's as if the last scene is spliced in from a different film. Although *L.I.E.* is rated NC-17 as it is, one almost suspects that this ending replaces another one that was removed for one reason or another. That is the only plausible explanation.

Life and Debt ★ ★ ★
NO MPAA RATING, 86 m., 2001

A documentary directed and produced by Stephanie Black. Narration written by Jamaica Kincaid.

Most Americans have been bewildered by the

antiglobalization protesters at recent meetings of the International Monetary Fund and the World Bank. Isn't free trade a good thing? Isn't a global economy great for everyone? What could the protesters possibly be objecting to?

Life and Debt, a documentary by Stephanie Black with a commentary written by Jamaica Kincaid, looks at the effect of the International Monetary Fund on the economy of Jamaica. The result, she argues, has been the destruction of Jamaican industry and agriculture, the end of Jamaica as a self-sufficient economic entity, and its conversion into a market for North American goods and a source of underpaid labor.

A harsh indictment, but the film is persuasive, showing how powdered milk from America (purchased from subsidized American dairy farmers and dumped at a loss), has destroyed the Jamaican fresh milk industry, and how even the one remaining market for Jamaican bananas—England—is threatened by the Chiquita–Dole–Del Monte forces, who think one Jamaican banana not sold by them is too many. Latin American banana workers earn $1 a day; Jamaicans can't live on that. Other markets reflect the same policies: Subsidized Idaho potatoes have bankrupted Jamaican potato farmers, McDonald's refuses to buy local meat, sweet Jamaican onions are underpriced by American onions sold at a loss, and so on.

One scheme to help the Jamaican economy, the film says, has been the establishment of "free zones," fenced-in manufacturing areas where workers are paid $30 a week to assemble goods that arrive and leave by container ship without legally being on Jamaican soil. Labor unions are banned, working conditions are subhuman, strikers are forced back to work at gunpoint, and paychecks are taxed for health and retirement schemes that don't seem to exist. The Hanes clothing division of Chicago's Sara Lee company was one of the beneficiaries, until, the movie says, it pulled out to find even cheaper workers elsewhere.

The IMF ideally loans money that can be used to help local businesses, but as former Jamaican prime minister Michael Manley observes, it charges twice the world rate for interest and forbids the country from charging its own lenders less. An IMF-backed small business loan in Jamaica might carry 25 percent interest.

"You ask, whose interest is the IMF serving?" Manley says. "Ask—who set it up?" IMF policies can be changed only by an 80 percent vote. The United States, Japan, Germany, England, Canada, and Italy control more than 80 percent of the votes. The bottom line: Developing economies of the Third World are deliberately destroyed and turned into captive markets for the rich nations, while their once self-sufficient inhabitants become cheap labor, and local competition is penalized.

Are these charges true? I do not have the expertise to say. I only bring you the news that this documentary, which has played twice on PBS and is now in theaters, exists. If you're curious about why the demonstrators are so angry, this is why they're so angry.

Life as a House ★ ★ ½
R, 128 m., 2001

Kevin Kline (George), Kristin Scott Thomas (Robin), Hayden Christensen (Sam), Jena Malone (Alyssa), Mary Steenburgen (Coleen), Mike Weinberg (Adam), Scotty Leavenworth (Ryan), Ian Somerhalder (Josh), Jamey Sheridan (Peter), Sam Robards (David). Directed by Irwin Winkler and produced by Winkler and Rob Cowan. Screenplay by Mark Andrus.

Life as a House has much heart and not enough brain, and to the degree that you can put your centers of higher intelligence on hold, it works as a tragicomic weeper. Because it is slick and classy and good to look at, and the actors are well within their range of competence, you can enjoy the movie on a made-for-TV level, but you wish it had been smarter and tougher. It is a little deadening to realize, at about the twenty-five-minute mark, that the problems of every single major character will be resolved by the end.

Those characters include George (Kevin Kline), a model maker who has just been fired from his job at an architect's firm. Robin (Kristin Scott Thomas), his ex-wife, now trapped in a loveless marriage with the absentminded Peter (Jamey Sheridan). Sam (Hayden Christensen), George and Robin's angst-ridden, pierced, drug-using, and self-loathing son. Coleen (Mary Steenburgen), the next-door neighbor, and her daughter, Alyssa (Jena Malone). And Josh (Ian Somerhalder), Sam's friend and Alyssa's boyfriend, and a part-time pimp.

I cannot proceed further without informing you that very early in the movie (spoiler warning), George discovers he has about four months to live. For a time we assume he has Ali MacGraw's Disease (the sicker you get the better you look), but a specific diagnosis is revealed toward the end. George got a severance package when he was fired, and he determines to tear down the shack he lives in, build a new house, and win the love and respect of his son, all in one summer.

George's shack sits in a cul-de-sac high on a cliff overlooking the Pacific in Orange County, California. Owners of ocean frontage in that area will be interested to learn that with twenty-six weeks of severance pay as a model maker, George can afford to tear down his house and build another one. Some will be surprised he could even pay the taxes.

Any sentient being will be able to predict, after sizing up the characters and their establishing dialogue, that Sam will remove the hardware from his face and learn through hard work to become clean and sober and love his father. That Robin will want to share the experience with Sam (and her two young children by the second marriage), and will recall her early love for George. That Sam and Alyssa will become friends, and a little more. And that two unassigned characters of opposite genders are required by the laws of screenwriting to get together, even if one is a teenage pimp and the other a yuppie housewife.

But I am getting way too cynical. You have to approach Life as a House knowing that it has no interest in life as it is really lived or people as they really are, and offers lovable characters whose personality traits dictate their behavior, just like on TV. What is remarkable is how Kline and Thomas, in particular, are able to enrich their characters by sheer skill and depth of technique, so that we like them and care what happens to them. (Whether it is George and Robin we like or Kline and Thomas is beside the point—the characters and actors amount to the same thing.)

Some episodes in the movie seem especially contrived. One involves a character who discovers something astonishing and falls off the roof. In my experience, people on roofs tend to hold on while digesting astonishing discoveries. Another involves the comeuppance of a nasty neighbor (Sam Robards). The nature of his comeuppance is dictated by the Law of Character Economy, which decrees, I believe, that the purpose of concealing his identity in an earlier scene is to reveal it in a later one. There is also a scene involving Christmas lights that strains geography, plausibility, visibility, and special effects to the breaking point. It gets distracting when some scenes in a movie exist on a different plane of possibility than the others.

Hollywood has fallen on dark days, dumbing down many of its films to the point where the actors seem measurably brighter than their dialogue and decisions. The current *My First Mister* has surprisingly similar situations, more effectively handled. *Life as a House* is aimed at the audience that admired a movie like *Terms of Endearment* (1983), but exists, alas, on the level of its pale sequel, *The Evening Star* (1996). The scenes that play best are not the ones of high drama and tear-jerking intensity, but the moments of simple affection between Kline and Thomas. Those moments have truth, and they humble some of the other material.

The Life of David Gale no stars
R, 130 m., 2003

Kevin Spacey (Dr. David Gale), Kate Winslet (Elizabeth [Bitsey] Bloom), Laura Linney (Constance Harraway), Gabriel Mann (Zack), Matt Craven (Dusty), Rhona Mitra (Berlin), Leon Rippy (Braxton Belyeu). Directed by Alan Parker and produced by Nicolas Cage and Parker. Screenplay by Charles Randolph.

The Life of David Gale tells the story of a famous opponent of capital punishment, who, in what he must find an absurdly ironic development, finds himself on Death Row in Texas, charged with the murder of a woman who was also opposed to capital punishment. This is a plot, if ever there was one, to illustrate King Lear's complaint, "As flies to wanton boys, are we to the gods; They kill us for their sport." I am aware this is the second time in two weeks

I have been compelled to quote Lear, but there are times when Eminem simply will not do.

David Gale is an understandably bitter man, played by Kevin Spacey, who protests his innocence to a reporter named Bitsey Bloom (Kate Winslet), whom he has summoned to Texas for that purpose. He claims to have been framed by right-wing supporters of capital punishment, because his death would provide such poetic irony in support of the noose, the gas, or the chair. Far from killing Constance Harraway (Laura Linney), he says, he had every reason not to, and he explains that to Bitsey in flashbacks that make up about half of the story.

Bitsey becomes convinced of David's innocence. She is joined in her investigation by the eager and sexy intern Zack (Gabriel Mann), and they become aware that they are being followed everywhere in a pickup truck by a gaunt-faced fellow in a cowboy hat, who is either a right-wing death penalty supporter who really killed the dead woman, or somebody else. If he is somebody else, then he is obviously following them around with the maguffin, in this case a videotape suggesting disturbing aspects of the death of Constance.

The man in the cowboy hat illustrates my recently renamed Principle of the Unassigned Character, formerly known less elegantly as the Law of Economy of Character Development. This principle teaches us that any prominent character who seems to be extraneous to the action will probably hold the key to it. The cowboy lives in one of those tumbledown shacks filled with flies and peanut butter, with old calendars on the walls. The yard has more bedsprings than the house has beds.

The acting in The Life of David Gale is splendidly done, but serves a meretricious cause. The direction is by the British director Alan Parker, who at one point had never made a movie I wholly disapproved of. Now has he ever. The secrets of the plot must remain unrevealed by me, so that you can be offended by them yourself, but let it be said this movie is about as corrupt, intellectually bankrupt, and morally dishonest as it could possibly be without David Gale actually hiring himself out as a joker at the court of Saddam Hussein.

I am sure the filmmakers believe their film is against the death penalty. I believe it supports it and hopes to discredit the opponents of the penalty as unprincipled fraudsters. What I do not understand is the final revelation on the videotape. Surely David Gale knows that Bitsey Bloom cannot keep it private without violating the ethics of journalism and sacrificing the biggest story of her career. So it serves no functional purpose except to give a cheap thrill to the audience slackjaws. It is shameful.

One of the things that annoys me is that the story is set in Texas and not just in any old state—a state like Arkansas, for example, where the 1996 documentary Paradise Lost: The Child Murders at Robin Hood Hills convincingly explains why three innocent kids are in prison because they wore black and listened to heavy metal, while the likely killer keeps pushing himself on-screen and wildly signaling his guilt. Nor is it set in my own state of Illinois, where Death Row was run so shabbily that Governor George Ryan finally threw up his hands and declared the whole system rotten.

No, the movie is set in Texas, which in a good year all by itself carries out half the executions in America. Death Row in Texas is like the Roach Motel: Roach checks in, doesn't check out. When George W. Bush was Texas governor, he claimed to carefully consider each and every execution, although a study of his office calendar shows he budgeted fifteen minutes per condemned man (we cannot guess how many of these minutes were devoted to pouring himself a cup of coffee before settling down to the job). Still, when you're killing someone every other week and there's an average of 400 more waiting their turn, you have to move right along.

Spacey and Parker are honorable men. Why did they go to Texas and make this silly movie? The last shot made me want to throw something at the screen—maybe Spacey and Parker.

You can make movies that support capital punishment (The Executioner's Song) or oppose it (Dead Man Walking) or are conflicted (In Cold Blood). But while Texas continues to warehouse condemned men with a system involving lawyers who are drunk, asleep, or absent; confessions that are beaten out of the helpless; and juries who overwhelmingly prefer to execute black defendants instead of white ones, you can't make this movie. Not in Texas. ☞

Life or Something Like It ★

PG-13, 104 m., 2002

Angelina Jolie (Lanie Kerigan), Stockard Channing (Deborah Connors), Edward Burns (Pete), Melissa Errico (Andrea), Tony Shalhoub (Prophet Jack), Christian Kane (Cal Cooper), Gregory Itzin (Dennis), Lisa Thornhill (Gwen). Directed by Stephen Herek and produced by Kenneth Atchity, John Davis, Toby Jaffe, Arnon Milchan, and Chi-Li Wong. Screenplay by John Scott Shepherd and Dana Stevens.

Someone once said, live every day as if it will be your last.

Not just someone once said that. Everyone once said it, over and over again, although *Life or Something Like It* thinks it's a fresh insight. This is an ungainly movie, ill-fitting, with its elbows sticking out where the knees should be. To quote another ancient proverb, "A camel is a horse designed by a committee." *Life or Something Like It* is the movie designed by the camel.

The movie stars Angelina Jolie as Lanie Kerigan, a bubbly blond Seattle TV reporter whose ignorance of TV is equaled only by the movie's. I don't know how the filmmakers got their start, but they obviously didn't come up through television. Even a *viewer* knows more than this.

Example. Sexy Pete the cameraman (Edward Burns) wants to play a trick on Lanie, so he fiddles with her microphone during a stand-up report from the street, and her voice comes out like Mickey Mouse's squeak—like when you talk with helium in your mouth. Everybody laughs at her. Except, see, your voice comes out of your *body*, and when it goes through the air it sounds like your voice to the people standing around. When it goes into the microphone, it kind of *stays* inside there, and is recorded on videotape, which is not simultaneously played back live to a street crowd.

Lanie dreams of going to New York to work on *AM USA*, the network show. She gets her big invitation after attracting "national attention" by covering a strike and leading the workers in singing "Can't Get No Satisfaction" while she dances in front of them, during a tiny lapse in journalistic objectivity. Meanwhile, she is afraid she will die, because a mad street person named Prophet Jack has pre-

dicted the Seattle Mariners will win, there will be a hailstorm tomorrow morning, and Lanie will die next Thursday. They win, it hails, Lanie believes she will die.

This leads to a romantic crisis. She is engaged to Cal Cooper (Christian Kane), a pitcher with the Mariners. He's on the mound, he looks lovingly at her, she smiles encouragingly, he throws a pitch, the batter hits a home run, and she jumps up and applauds. If he sees that, she may not last until Thursday. Meanwhile, she apparently hates Pete the sexy cameraman, although when Cal is out of town and she thinks she's going to die, they make love, and *then* we find out, belatedly, they've made love before. The screenplay keeps doubling back to add overlooked info.

Cal comes back to town and she wants a heart-to-heart, but instead he takes her to the ballpark, where the friendly groundskeeper (who hangs around all night in every baseball movie for just such an opportunity) turns on the lights so Cal can throw her a few pitches. Is she moved by this loving gesture? Nope: "Your cure for my emotional crisis is batting practice?" This is the only turning-on-the-lights-in-the-empty-ballpark scene in history that ends unhappily.

Lanie and Pete the sexy cameraman become lovers, until Pete whipsaws overnight into an insulted, wounded man who is hurt because she wants to go to New York instead of stay in Seattle with him and his young son. This about-face exists *only* so they can break up so they can get back together again later. It also inspires a scene in the station's equipment room, where Jolie tests the theoretical limits of hysterical overacting.

Lanie's *AM USA* debut involves interviewing the network's biggest star, a Barbara Walters type (Stockard Channing), on the star's twenty-fifth anniversary. So earthshaking is this interview, the *AM USA* anchor breathlessly announces, "We welcome our viewers on the West Coast for this special live edition!" It's 7 A.M. in New York. That makes it 4 A.M. on the West Coast. If you lived in Seattle, would you set your alarm to 4 A.M. to see Barbara Walters plugging her network special?

Lanie begins the interview, pauses, and is silent for thirty seconds while deeply thinking. She finally asks, "Was it worth everything?"

What? "Giving up marriage and children for a career?" Tears roll down Channing's cheeks. Pandemonium. Great interview. Network president wants to hire Lanie on the spot. Has never before heard anyone ask, "Was it worth it?" The question of whether a woman can have both a career and a family is controversial in *Life or Something Like It*—even when posed by Ms. Jolie, who successfully combines tomb-raiding with Billy Bob Thornton.

I want to close with the mystery of Lanie's father, who is always found stationed in an easy chair in his living room, where he receives visits from his daughters, who feel guilty because since Mom died they have not been able to communicate with Dad, who, apparently as a result, just sits there waiting for his daughters to come back and feel guilty some more. Eventually there's an uptick in his mood, and he admits he has always been proud of Lanie and will "call in sick" so he can watch Lanie on *AM USA*. Until then I thought he *was* sick. Maybe he's just tired because he's on the night shift, which is why he would be at work at 4 A.M.

Like Mike ★ ★ ★
PG, 100 m., 2002

Lil' Bow Wow (Calvin Cambridge), Morris Chestnut (Tracey Reynolds), Jonathan Lipnicki (Murph), Jesse Plemons (Ox), Robert Forster (Coach Wagner), Crispin Glover (Stan Bittleman), Anne Meara (Sister Theresa), Eugene Levy (Frank Bernard). Directed by John Schultz and produced by Peter Heller and Barry Josephson. Screenplay by Michael Elliot and Jordan Moffet.

Kids can't be Michael Jordan, but they can wear his basketball shoes, and in their fantasies the shoes give them the power to be like Mike. Sports shoes are one of the most powerful totems in kid society, in part because of M. J.'s TV ads, and *Like Mike* is not merely a good idea for a movie, but an inevitable one.

Lil' Bow Wow (whose name should properly be spelled Li'l' Bow Wow, but never mind) stars as Calvin Cambridge, an orphan who comes into possession of a pair of faded Nikes with the initials "MJ" written inside the tongue. We might doubt that Michael Jordan writes his initials in his shoes (and if he does, he probably has someone to do it for him), but

Calvin has no doubts, not even when the shoes are a perfect fit, which seems unlikely.

He lives in an orphanage that seems to be running as a profitable scam. His best buddy is Murph (Jonathan Lipnicki) and his worst enemy is Ox (Jesse Plemons). Ox throws the shoes so they hang by their laces from a power line, Calvin climbs up a tree in a storm to retrieve them, lightning strikes, and somehow the shoes and the lightning magically combine to make him like Mike.

Really like Mike. The kind coach of the local NBA team (Robert Forster) gives him some tickets to a game, he ends up in a half-time shooting contest with an NBA star, and, wearing the shoes, outshoots the star so dramatically that the team owner signs him up—as a gimmick, of course, although Calvin is soon in the starting lineup and leading his team to the finals. Wearing the magic shoes, he makes Air Jordan look like a puddle-jumper.

Lil' Bow Wow is responsible for a lot of the movie's success. He is confident and relaxed on the screen, engaging, and has good moves on the basketball court. In a role that could have been deadly with the wrong kind of kid actor, he's the right kind, a no-nonsense professional who wisely plays the fantasy as if it were real.

A lot of the surrounding plot is recycled from other movies, of course, including the playground bully, the tried-and-true orphanage situations (the kids are like puppies hoping for new owners), and the last-minute cliffhanging plays of the big games. But the movie overcomes its lack of originality in the setup by making good use of its central idea, that a pair of shoes could make a kid into an NBA star. This is a message a lot of kids have been waiting to hear.

Lilo & Stitch ★ ★ ★ ½
PG, 85 m., 2002

With the voices of: Daveigh Chase (Lilo), Chris Sanders (Stitch) Jason Scott Lee (David Kawena), Tia Carrere (Nani), Kevin McDonald (Pleakley), Ving Rhames (Cobra Bubbles), David Ogden Stiers (Jumba). Directed by Chris Sanders and Dean Deblois and produced by Clark Spencer. Screenplay by Sanders and Deblois.

Only a week ago I deplored the wretched

Scooby-Doo as a blight on the nation's theaters. My fellow critics agreed. Checking the Websites that monitor reviews, I find that at Rotten-Tomatoes.com the movie scored a 26, at Metacritic.com a 27. Passing grade is 60. The American public effortlessly shrugged off this warning cry and raced to the box office to throw away $57 million.

Now here comes a truly inspired animated feature named *Lilo & Stitch*. How will it do? It's one of the most charming feature-length cartoons of recent years, funny, sassy, startling, original, and with six songs by Elvis. It doesn't get sickeningly sweet at the end, it has as much stuff in it for grown-ups as for kids, and it has a bright offbeat look to it.

If *Scooby-Doo* grossed $57 million in its first weekend, then if there is justice in the world, *Lilo & Stitch* will gross $200 million. But there is not justice. There is a herd instinct. On Monday a man on an elevator asked me what I thought about *Scooby-Doo*. I said it was a very bad movie. "My kids want to see it," he said. Yes, I said, because they've heard of nothing else all week. But, I said, there is a *much better* animated family film opening this weekend, named *Lilo & Stitch*, that your kids are sure to like much more than *Scooby-Doo*, and you will enjoy it too. Take my word, I said; I do this for a living. Take the kids to *Lilo & Stitch*.

I could see from the man's eyes that he was rejecting my advice. How could I possibly be right when $57 million said I was wrong? How could human taste be a better barometer of movie quality than the success of a marketing campaign? Prediction: This weekend, more parents and their children will dutifully file into the idiotic wasteland of *Scooby-Doo* than will see the inspired delights of *Lilo & Stitch*.

That will be a shame. *Lilo & Stitch*, produced by the same Disney team that made *Mulan*, is a toothy fantasy about an alien monster that accidentally finds itself adopted as the pet of a little girl in Hawaii. The creature, named Stitch (voice by Chris Sanders), was produced by an illegal genetic mutation, and is so horrifyingly hostile that it's been locked up by its inventors. It escapes to Earth, is mistaken for a very strange dog, and adopted by Lilo (voice by Daveigh Chase), who essentially uses her innocence and the aloha spirit to confuse and even civilize the creature.

This all takes place against a cheerful background of pop-culture references, including scenes spoofing *Men in Black*, *Jaws*, and *Godzilla* (with Stitch first building a model of San Francisco, then destroying it). And the film firmly positions itself in Hawaii—both the Hawaii of tourist kitsch, and the Hawaii of the aloha spirit. The plot revolves around concepts of "ohana," or family, since Lilo is being raised by her big sister Nani (voice by Tia Carrere), who is disorganized and not always a perfect substitute mom, and is up against a disapproving social worker named Cobra Bubbles (voice by Ving Rhames).

Nani works as a waitress in one of those "traditional" Hawaiian musical revues, where her boyfriend, David Kawena (Jason Scott Lee), is a fire dancer. Lilo takes Stitch to the show, and Stitch is much confused, especially after David sets the stage on fire, but even more confusing episodes are ahead, as the little girl teaches her alien pal how to be an Elvis imitator.

Lilo and Stitch, of course, have trouble communicating, since Lilo is very young and Stitch speaks no English, but the alien, who is a quick study, picks up some words and, more important, some concepts that challenge its existence as a destructive being. Lilo and Nani are learning, too, how to be a family and take care of each other, but the movie doesn't get all soppy at the end and is surprisingly unsentimental for a Disney animated feature. It keeps its edge and its comic zest all the way through, and although it arrives relatively unheralded, it's a jewel.

Note: I was far off in my prediction; Lilo & Stitch opened like gangbusters and was a huge box-office success.

Lilya 4-Ever ★ ★ ★
R, 109 m., 2003

Oksana Akinshina (Lilya), Artyom Bogucharsky (Volodya), Lyubov Agapova (Lilya's mother), Liliya Shinkaryova (Aunt Anna), Elina Benenson (Natasha), Pavel Ponomaryov (Andrei), Tomas Neumann (Witek). Directed by Lukas Moodysson and produced by Lars Jonsson. Screenplay by Moodysson.

Lilya 4-Ever provides a human face for a story that has become familiar in the newspapers. It follows a sixteen-year-old girl from the former

Soviet Union as she is abandoned by her mother, places her faith in the wrong stranger, and is sold into prostitution. She is naive and innocent, and what looks like danger to us looks like deliverance to her. That there are countless such stories makes this one even more heartbreaking.

Lilya (Oksana Akinshina) lives in a barren urban wasteland of shabby high-rises and wind-swept vacant lots. Her best friend Volodya (Artyom Bogucharsky) plays basketball by throwing a tin can through a rusty hoop. Her mother announces that she is engaged to marry a Russian who now lives in the United States. Lilya is joyous, and brags to Volodya that she is going to America. But her mother has other plans, and explains Lilya must stay behind, to be "sent for" later.

The mother is heartless, but then this is a society crushed by poverty and despair. There must be better neighborhoods somewhere, but we do not see them and Lilya does not find them. Within a day of her mother's departure, she is ordered by an embittered aunt to clear out of her mother's apartment and move into the squalor of a tenement room. Here she hosts glue-sniffing parties for her friends, and Volodya comes to live after his father throws him out. Volodya is young—perhaps eleven or twelve—and although he talks hopefully about sex, he is a child and she treats him like a little brother.

Lilya's descent into prostitution does not surprise us. There is no money for food, no one cares for her, she is pretty, she is desperate, and when she finds her first client in a disco, the movie focuses closely on her blank, indifferent face, turned away from the panting man above her. Later there is a montage of clients, seen from her point of view (although she is not seen), and it says all that can be said about her disgust with them.

The money at least allows her to buy junk food and cigarettes, and give a basketball to Volodya, whose father is enraged by the gift. Then friendship seems to come in the form of a young man named Andrei (Pavel Ponomaryov), who does not want sex, offers her a ride home, takes her on a date (bumper cars, that reliable movie cliché), and says he works in Sweden and can get her a job there. We see through him, and

even Volodya does, but she is blinded by the prospect he describes: "You'll make more money there in a week than a doctor here makes in a month." Perhaps, but not for herself.

The movie, written and directed by Lukas Moodysson, has the directness and clarity of a documentary, but allows itself touches of tenderness and grief. It is so sad to see this girl, even after weeks of prostitution, saying the Lord's Prayer in front of a framed drawing of a guardian angel. And there are two fantasy sequences toward the end that provide her with an escape, however illusory.

The movie should inspire outrage, but I read of thousands of women from Eastern Europe who are lured into virtual slavery. I hope some of their clients will attend this movie, even if for the wrong reasons, and see what they are responsible for.

Little Secrets ★ ★ ★
PG, 107 m., 2002

Evan Rachel Wood (Emily), Michael Angarano (Philip), David Gallagher (David), Vivica A. Fox (Pauline). Directed by Blair Treu and produced by Don Schain, Treu, and Jessica Barondes. Screenplay by Barondes.

The biggest surprise in *Little Secrets* is that Ozzie and Harriet don't live next door. The movie takes place in an improbably perfect suburban neighborhood where all the kids wear cute sportswear and have the kinds of harmless problems that seem to exist only so that they can be harmless problems. Then, of course, there are some Big Problems, which are rendered harmless, too. This is a very reassuring film.

The heroine of the movie, Emily (Evan Rachel Wood), is a budding young violinist who as a sideline runs a Little Secrets stand in her backyard, where kids can tell her their secrets at fifty cents apiece. The secrets are then written on scraps of paper and locked in a chest.

The theological and psychological origins of her practice would be fascinating to research. The neighborhood kids sure take it seriously. When she's a few minutes late in opening her stand, there's an impatient line of kids clamoring to unburden themselves. The fifty-cent price tag doesn't discourage them; these are not kids who remember the days when a quarter used to buy something.

But what kinds of kids are they, exactly? Consider Philip and David. Philip tells David: "Her name is Emily. Like Emily . . ." " . . . Dickinson?" says David. "And Emily Brontë," says Philip. Heartened as I am to know that the grade-school kids in this movie are on first-name terms with these authors, I am nevertheless doubtful that Dickinson and Brontë will ring many bells in the audience.

Vivica A. Fox is the only widely known star in the film, playing a violin teacher who is wise and philosophical. Much suspense centers around Emily's audition for the local symphony orchestra (every suburb should have one). The problems of the kids range from a girl who hides kittens in her room to a boy who is digging a hole to China. Larger issues, including adoption, are eventually introduced.

I am rating this movie at three stars because it contains absolutely nothing to object to. That in itself may be objectionable, but you will have to decide for yourself. The film is upbeat, wholesome, chirpy, positive, sunny, cheerful, optimistic, and squeaky-clean. It bears so little resemblance to the more complicated worlds of many members of its target audience (girls four to eleven) that it may work as pure escapism. That it has been rated not G but PG (for "thematic elements") is another of the arcane mysteries created by the flywheels of the MPAA. There is not a parent on Earth who would believe this film requires "parental guidance."

Live Nude Girls Unite! ★ ★ ★
NO MPAA RATING, 70 m., 2001

A documentary directed by Julia Query and Vicky Funari and produced by Query and John Montoya. Screenplay by Query and Funari.

This Union Maid was wise,
To the tricks of company spies.
She couldn't be fooled by company stools—
She'd always organize the guys.
　　　　　　　　　　　—Old labor song

And not only the guys. When the strippers at the Lusty Lady, a San Francisco peep empo-

rium, decided to organize themselves into a labor union, there were jolly news stories all over the country. People thought it was hilarious. This may be because in the popular mind strippers do not really work.

Opposing the strike, the management of the Lusty Lady argued that taking off your clothes in a peep show is not real labor so much as an enjoyable part-time job. The women putting in ten-hour shifts didn't see it that way—but their customers did. "What's your job?" one of the clients asks one of the girls. "I'm a stripper," she says. "I mean," he says, "how do you earn a living?"

There is the curious notion that strippers and prostitutes do what they do because they enjoy it. This is a fiction that is good for business. I am sure that some strippers and hookers do sometimes enjoy what they do, but not that they do it over and over, all day long, week after week, for a living. By way of illustration, it is possible to take pleasure in making a ham sandwich, but you might not want to work behind the counter at Mr. Submarine, especially when the customers always leave with the sandwiches.

When you think of strippers, you think of a stage, but the strippers at the Lusty Lady work in a small mirrored room. The clients enter little booths surrounding the room and put a quarter in a slot; a panel slides up and they can see the girls for fifteen seconds. Another quarter, another fifteen seconds. It's enough to bring back the silver dollar. The veteran girls make $20 an hour, and there are always two to four on duty, which makes you realize that the hardest job at the Lusty Lady belongs to the guy who collects the quarters.

Live Nude Girls Unite! is a documentary made by Julia Query, a stripper at the club, and Vicky Funari. It is an advertisement for the possibilities of the consumer digital video camera. It's not slick, it has some lapses, it sometimes looks like a home movie, but it's never boring. It follows some eighty strippers as they hire a lawyer, demand a contract, and threaten to strike. Query, Funari, and two other filmmakers simply took the camera along with them and shot whatever happened.

Miss Query is not your average stripper—but then no stripper ever is. She dropped out of graduate school, has worked as a domina-trix, and has a mother who is a famous public health advocate. The mother pilots a van around Manhattan handing out free condoms to hook-ers, and tells Barbara Walters in a *20/20* segment that her group facilitates 500,000 safe sex acts a year. "Peppermint?" Miss Walters asks, hold-ing up one of the condoms.

When Julia turns up as a speaker and stand-up comic at the same conference where her mother is delivering a paper, the result is one of the more unusual mother-daughter argu-ments in movie history. Julia was raised to "do the right thing" and expects her mother to be proud of her as a union organizer, but the mother somehow cannot get around the strip-ping. This although Query tries to stir indig-nation about the club's discrimination against strippers who are not white (or, for that mat-ter, white but not blond).

Julia is a disarmingly honest narrator. When she decided to earn money by stripping, she says, she was terrified by the thought of going on the stage, because "I can't dance." The mir-rored room at the Lusty Lady, which reminded her of an aquarium, seemed less of a challenge, especially since it has silver poles in it. The other girls use these for posing, but we gather Julia may need to grab one to keep from falling down. Still, she's a spirited Union Maid, and she and her sister organizers make labor his-tory. She's the kind of woman Studs Terkel was born to interview.

The Lord of the Rings: The Fellowship of the Ring ★ ★ ★
PG-13, 178 m., 2001

Elijah Wood (Frodo Baggins), Ian McKellen (Gandalf the Grey), Viggo Mortensen (Aragorn, aka Strider), Sean Astin (Samwise "Sam" Gamgee), Liv Tyler (Arwen), Cate Blanchett (Galadriel), John Rhys-Davies (Gimli), Billy Boyd (Peregrin "Pippin" Took), Ian Holm (Bilbo Baggins), Christopher Lee (Saruman), Hugo Weaving (Elrond). Directed by Peter Jackson and produced by Jackson, Barrie M. Osborne, and Tim Sanders. Screenplay by Frances Walsh, Philippa Boyens, and Jackson, based on the novel *The Fellowship of the Ring* by J. R. R. Tolkien.

We invest hobbits with qualities that cannot be visualized. In my mind, they are good-hearted, bustling, chatty little creatures who live in twee houses or burrows, and dress like the merry men of Robin Hood—in smaller sizes, of course. They eat seven or eight times a day, like to take naps, have never been far from home, and have eyes that grow wide at the sounds of the night. They are like children grown up or grown old, and when they rise to an occasion it takes true heroism, for they are timid by nature and would rather avoid a fight.

Such notions about hobbits can be found in *The Lord of the Rings: The Fellowship of the Ring,* but the hobbits themselves have been pushed off center stage. If the books are about brave little creatures who enlist powerful men and wizards to help them in a dangerous cru-sade, the movie is about powerful men and wizards who embark on a dangerous crusade and take along the hobbits. That is not true of every scene or episode, but by the end *Fellowship* adds up to more of a sword-and-sorcery epic than a realization of the more naive and guile-less vision of J. R. R. Tolkien.

The Ring Trilogy embodies the kind of in-nocence that belongs to an earlier, gentler time. The Hollywood that made *The Wizard of Oz* might have been equal to it. But *Fellowship* is a film that comes after *Gladiator* and *Matrix,* and it instinctively ramps up to the genre of the overwrought special-effects action picture. That it transcends this genre—that it is a well-crafted and sometimes stirring adventure—is to its credit. But a true visualization of Tolkien's Middle-Earth it is not.

Wondering if the trilogy could possibly be as action-packed as this film, I searched my memory for sustained action scenes and finally turned to the books themselves, which I had not read since the 1970s. The chapter "The Bridge of Khazad-Dum" provides the basis for perhaps the most sensational action scene in the film, in which Gandalf the wizard stands on an unstable rock bridge over a chasm, and must engage in a deadly swordfight with the monstrous Balrog. This is an exciting scene, done with state-of-the-art special effects and sound that shakes the theater. In the book, I was not surprised to discover, the entire scene requires less than 500 words.

Settling down with my book, the one-volume 1969 India paper edition, I read or skimmed for an hour or so. It was as I remembered it. The trilogy is mostly about leaving places, going places, being places, and going on to other places, all amid fearful portents and speculations. There are a great many mountains, valleys, streams, villages, caves, residences, grottos, bowers, fields, high roads, and low roads, and along them the hobbits and their larger companions travel while paying great attention to mealtimes. Landscapes are described with the faithful detail of a Victorian travel writer. The travelers meet strange and fascinating characters along the way, some of them friendly, some of them not, some of them of an order far above hobbits or even men. Sometimes they must fight to defend themselves or to keep possession of the ring, but mostly the trilogy is an unfolding, a quest, a journey, told in an elevated, archaic, romantic prose style that tests our capacity for the declarative voice.

Reading it, I remembered why I liked it in the first place. It was reassuring. You could tell by holding the book in your hands that there were many pages to go, many sights to see, many adventures to share. I cherished the way it paused for songs and poems, which the movie has no time for. Like *The Tale of Genji*, which some say is the first novel, *The Lord of the Rings* is not about a narrative arc or the growth of the characters, but about a long series of episodes in which the essential nature of the characters is demonstrated again and again (and again). The ring, which provides the purpose for the journey, serves Tolkien as the ideal MacGuffin, motivating an epic quest while mostly staying right there on a chain around Frodo Baggins's neck.

Peter Jackson, the New Zealand director who masterminded this film (and two more to follow, in a $300 million undertaking), has made a work for, and of, our times. It will be embraced, I suspect, by many *Rings* fans and take on aspects of a cult. It is a candidate for many Oscars. It is an awesome production in its daring and breadth, and there are small touches that are just right; the hobbits may not look like my idea of hobbits (may, indeed, look like full-sized humans made to seem smaller through visual trickery), but they have the right combination of twinkle and pluck in

their gaze—especially Elijah Wood as Frodo and Ian Holm as the worried Bilbo.

Yet the taller characters seem to stand astride the little hobbit world and steal the story away. Galdalf the good wizard (Ian McKellen) and Saruman the treacherous wizard (Christopher Lee) and Aragorn (Viggo Mortensen), who is the warrior known as Strider, are so well seen and acted, so fearsome in battle, that we can't imagine the hobbits getting anywhere without them. The elf Arwen (Liv Tyler), the elf queen Galadriel (Cate Blanchett), and Arwen's father Elrond (Hugo Weaving) are not small like literary elves ("very tall they were," the book tells us), and here they tower like Norse gods and goddesses, accompanied by so much dramatic sound and lighting that it's a wonder they can think to speak, with all the distractions.

Jackson has used modern special effects to great purpose in several shots, especially one where a massive wall of water forms and re-forms into wraiths of charging stallions. I like the way he handles crowds of Orcs in the big battle scenes, wisely knowing that in a film of this kind realism has to be tempered with a certain fanciful fudging. The film is remarkably well made. But it does go on, and on, and on—more vistas, more forests, more sounds in the night, more fearsome creatures, more prophecies, more visions, more dire warnings, more close calls, until we realize this sort of thing can continue indefinitely. "This tale grew in the telling," Tolkien tells us in the famous first words of his Foreword; it's as if Tolkien, and now Jackson, grew so fond of the journey they dreaded the destination.

That *The Fellowship of the Ring* doesn't match my imaginary vision of Middle-Earth is my problem, not yours. Perhaps it will look exactly as you think it should. But some may regret that the hobbits have been pushed out of the foreground and reduced to supporting characters. And the movie depends on action scenes much more than Tolkien did. In a statement last week, Tolkien's son Christopher, who is the "literary protector" of his father's works, said: "My own position is that *The Lord of the Rings* is peculiarly unsuitable for transformation into visual dramatic form." That is probably true, and Jackson, instead of transforming it, has transmuted it into a sword-and-sorcery epic in the modern style, containing many of the same characters and incidents.

Lord of the Rings: The Two Towers
★ ★ ★
PG-13, 179 m., 2002

Elijah Wood (Frodo Baggins), Ian McKellen (Gandalf the White), Viggo Mortensen (Aragorn), Sean Astin ("Sam" Gamgee), Billy Boyd ("Pippin" Took), Liv Tyler (Arwen Undomiel), John Rhys-Davies (Gimli/voice of Treebeard), Dominic Monaghan ("Merry" Brandybuck), Christopher Lee (Saruman), Miranda Otto (Éowyn), Brad Dourif (Grima Wormtongue), Orlando Bloom (Legolas), Cate Blanchett (Galadriel), Karl Urban (Éomér), Bernard Hill (Théoden). Directed by Peter Jackson and produced by Barrie M. Osborne, Frances Walsh, and Jackson. Screenplay by Walsh, Philippa Boyens, Stephen Sinclair, and Jackson, based on the novel by J. R. R. Tolkien.

With *Lord of the Rings: The Two Towers* it's clear that director Peter Jackson has tilted the balance decisively against the hobbits and in favor of the traditional action heroes of the Tolkien trilogy. The star is now clearly Aragorn (Viggo Mortensen), and the hobbits spend much of the movie away from the action. The last third of the movie is dominated by an epic battle scene that would no doubt startle the gentle medievalist Tolkien.

The task of the critic is to decide whether this shift damages the movie. It does not. *The Two Towers* is one of the most spectacular swashbucklers ever made, and, given current audience tastes in violence, may well be more popular than the first installment, *The Fellowship of the Ring*. It is not faithful to the spirit of Tolkien and misplaces much of the charm and whimsy of the books, but it stands on its own as a visionary thriller. I complained in my review of the first film that the hobbits had been shortchanged, but with this second film I must accept that as a given, and go on from there.

This is a rousing adventure, a skillful marriage of special effects and computer animation, and it contains sequences of breathtaking beauty. It also gives us, in a character named Gollum, one of the most engaging and convincing computer-generated creatures I've

seen. Gollum was long in possession of the Ring, now entrusted to Frodo, and misses it ("my precious") most painfully; but he has a split personality and (in between spells when his dark side takes over) serves as a guide and companion for Frodo (Elijah Wood) and Sam (Sean Astin). His body language is a choreography of ingratiation and distortion,

Another CGI character this time is Treebeard, a member of the most ancient race in Middle Earth, a tree that walks and talks and takes a very long time to make up its mind, explaining to Merry and Pippin that slowness is a virtue. I would have guessed that a walking, talking tree would look silly and break the spell of the movie, but no, there is a certain majesty in this mossy old creature.

The film opens with a brief reprise of the great battle between Gandalf the Gray (Ian McKellen) and Balrog, the monster made of fire and smoke, and is faithful to the ancient tradition of movie serials by showing us that victory is snatched from certain death, as Gandalf extinguishes the creature and becomes in the process Gandalf the White.

To compress the labyrinthine story into a sentence or two, the enemy is Saruman (Christopher Lee), who commands a vast army of Uruk-Hai warriors in the battle of Helm's Deep, assaulting the fortress of Théoden (Bernard Hill). Aragorn, with Legolas (Orlando Bloom) and Gimli the Dwarf (John Rhys-Davies), joins bravely in the fray, but the real heroes are the computer effects, which create the castle, landscape, armies, and most of the action.

There are long stretches of *The Two Towers* in which we are looking at mostly animation on the screen. When Aragorn and his comrades launch an attack down a narrow fortress bridge, we know that the figures toppling to their doom are computer-generated, along with everything else on the screen, and yet the impact of the action is undeniable. Peter Jackson, like some of the great silent directors, is unafraid to use his entire screen, to present images of wide scope and great complexity. He paints in the corners.

What one misses in the thrills of these epic splendors is much depth in the characters. All of the major figures are sketched with an attribute or two, and then defined by their actions. Frodo, the nominal hero, spends much of his time peering over and around things, watching others decide his fate, and occasionally gazing significantly upon the Ring. Sam is his loyal sidekick on the sidelines. Merry and Pippin spend a climactic stretch of the movie riding in Treebeard's branches and looking goggle-eyed at everything, like children carried on their father's shoulders. The Fellowship of the first movie has been divided into three during this one, and most of the action centers on Aragorn, who operates within the tradition of Viking swordsmen and medieval knights.

The details of the story—who is who, and why, and what their histories and attributes are—still remain somewhat murky to me. I know the general outlines and I boned up by rewatching the first film on DVD the night before seeing the second, and yet I am in awe of the true students of the Ring. For the amateur viewer, which is to say for most of us, the appeal of the movies is in the visuals. Here there be vast caverns and mighty towers, dwarves and elves and Orcs and the aforementioned Uruk-Hai (who look like distant cousins of the aliens in *Battlefield Earth*). And all are set within Jackson's ambitious canvas, and backdropped by spectacular New Zealand scenery.

The Two Towers will possibly be more popular than the first film, more of an audience-pleaser, but hasn't Jackson lost the original purpose of the story somewhere along the way? He has taken an enchanting and unique work of literature and retold it in the terms of the modern action picture. If Tolkien had wanted to write about a race of supermen, he would have written a Middle Earth version of *Conan the Barbarian*. But no. He told a tale in which modest little hobbits were the heroes. And now Jackson has steered the story into the action mainstream. To do what he has done in this film must have been awesomely difficult, and he deserves applause, but to remain true to Tolkien would have been more difficult, and braver.

Lost and Delirious ★ ★ ★ ½
NO MPAA RATING, 102 m., 2001

Piper Perabo (Paulie Oster), Jessica Pare (Victoria Moller), Mischa Barton (Mary Bradford ["Mouse"]), Jackie Burroughs (Fay Vaughn), Mimi Kuzyk (Eleanor Bannet), Graham Greene (Joe Menzies), Luke Kirby (Jake). Directed by Lea Pool and produced by Greg Dummett, Lorraine Richard, Louis-Philippe Rochon, and Richard Rochon. Screenplay by Judith Thompson, based on the novel *The Wives of Bath* by Susan Swan.

Lost and Delirious is a hymn to teenage idealism and hormones. It has been reviewed as a movie about steamy lesbian sex in a girls' boarding school, which is like reviewing Secretariat on the basis of what he does in the stable. The truest words in the movie are spoken by Paulie, the school rebel, when she says she is not a lesbian because her love rises above mere categories and exists as a transcendent ideal.

Indulge me while I tell you that as a teenager I was consumed by the novels of Thomas Wolfe. His autobiographical heroes were filled with a passion to devour life, to experience everything, to make love to every woman, read every book in the library. At night he could not sleep, but wandered the campus, "uttering wild goat cries to the moon."

I read every word Wolfe ever published. Today I find him unreadable—yes, even *Look Homeward, Angel* and *You Can't Go Home Again*. I have outlived that moment when all life seemed spread before me, all possibilities open to me, all achievements within my reach. Outlived it, but not forgotten it. *Lost and Delirious* stirred within me memories of that season in adolescence when the heart leaps up in passionate idealism—and inevitably mingles it with sexual desire.

Yes, there is nudity in *Lost and Delirious*, and some intimate moments in the dorm room when the movie recalls the freedoms of the 1970s, before soft-core sex had been replaced by hard-core violence. The movie would be dishonest if it didn't provide us with visuals to match the libidos of its two young lovers—the heedless rebel girl Paulie (Piper Perabo) and the cautious rich kid Victoria (Jessica Pare), who is excited by her schoolgirl affair, but not brave enough to risk discovery; after all, her parents may not take her to Europe if they find out.

Paulie and Victoria represent two types familiar from everyone's high school—the type who acts out, and the type who wants to get all the right entries under her photo on the yearbook. At reunions years from now, Paulie will be the one they tell the stories about. Piper Perabo plays her with wonderful abandon and conviction, and Jessica Pare's "Tori" is sweet in her timidity. Perabo has scenes that would merely seem silly if she weren't able to invest them with such sincerity. The scene where she stalks into the library in her fencing gear, for example, and leaps onto a table to declare her love for Victoria. The scene where she challenges Victoria's new boyfriend to a duel. The scenes where she identifies with the wounded eagle she tends in the forest. The way she quotes great love poetry, promising, "I will make me a willow cabin at thy gate."

Their school is a vast, beautiful brick pile (actually Bishop's University in Lennoxville, Quebec). It seems to have only two faculty members: the headmistress and English teacher Fay Vaughn (Jackie Burroughs), who teaches Shakespeare's *Antony and Cleopatra* as if she sees herself as Cleopatra—or Antony. And the math teacher, Eleanor Bannet (Mimi Kuzyk). Paulie spots Bannet as a woman not quite brave enough to follow "to thine own self be true," and insolently calls her "Eleanor" in a classroom. Fay Vaughn, on the other hand, feeds into Paulie's hungers by being as romantic as she is—although Paulie doesn't always see that. Also on the staff is Joe Menzies (Graham Greene), a wise old gardener who acts as a Greek chorus, uttering wry epigrams.

The story is told through the eyes of a new girl named "Mouse" (Mischa Barton), who is a little slow to catch on that her roommates are sapphic (the first time she sees them kissing, "I thought they were just practicing for boys"). In the immortal words of every high school movie—for Mouse, after this year, things will never be the same again. Of course, after every year, nothing is ever the same again for anyone, but when you're sixteen it seems to be all about you.

When I saw *Lost and Delirious* at Sundance, I wrote that it was one of the best crafted, most professional films at the festival. The director, Lea Pool, creates a lush, thoughtfully framed and composed film; her classical visual style lends gravitas to this romantic story. It seems important partly because the movie

makes it look important, regarding it with respect instead of cutting it up into little emotional punch lines.

There is a temptation, I suppose, to try to stand above this material, to condescend to its eagerness and uncompromising idealism. To do that is to cave in to the cynicism that infects most modern films. This is a movie for those who sometimes, in the stillness of the sleepless night, are so filled with hope and longing that they feel like—well, like uttering wild goat cries to the moon. You know who you are. And if you know someone who says, "Let's go to *Scary Movie 2* instead," that person is not worthy to be your friend.

Note: The movie is being released "unrated," *which means it is too poetic, idealistic, and health-* *fully erotic to fit into the sick categories of the* *flywheels at the MPAA. Mature teens are likely* *to find it inspirational and moving.*

Lost in La Mancha ★ ★ ★
R, 93 m., 2003

Featuring Terry Gilliam, Phil Patterson, Toni Grisoni, Nicola Pecorini, René Cleitman, Bernard Bouix, Johnny Depp, and Jean Rochefort. Narrated by Jeff Bridges. A documentary directed by Keith Fulton and Louis Pepe and produced by Lucy Darwin. Screenplay by Fulton and Pepe.

Blow, winds, and crack your cheeks! rage! blow! *You cataracts and hurricanoes, spout* *Till you have drench'd our steeples . . .*

History does not record whether these words of King Lear passed through Terry Gilliam's mind as his beloved film about Don Quixote turned to ashes. It is hard to believe they did not. *Lost in La Mancha,* which started life as one of those documentaries you get free on the DVD, ended as the record of swift and devastating disaster.

Gilliam, the director of such films as *Brazil,* *12 Monkeys,* and *The Fisher King,* arrived in Spain in August 2000 to begin filming a project he had been preparing for ten years. *The Man Who Killed Don Quixote* would star Johnny Depp as a modern-day hero who is transported back in time, and finds himself acting as Sancho Panza to old Don Quixote, who tilts at windmills and remains the most bravely romantic figure in Western literature.

The film was budgeted at $32 million, making it the most expensive production ever financed only with European money, although, as Gilliam observes, that's "far below what a film like this would usually cost."

In the title role he had cast Jean Rochefort, the tall, angular French star of more than 100 films, including *The Tall Blond Man with One Black Shoe* and *The Hairdresser's Husband*. Rochefort arrives on the set looking suitably gaunt and romantic, and showing off the English he has learned during seven months of lessons.

The first day of the shoot begins ominously. Someone has forgotten to rehearse the extras who are yoked to Depp in a chain gang. F-16 fighter planes roar overhead, spoiling shot after shot. Gilliam's optimism remains unchecked, and we get a notion of the film from his sketches and storyboards and his conferences with members of the production team. There's an amusing episode when he casts three men as giants.

Day two involves a change of location and an adjustment in the shooting schedule. The actors have arrived late in Spain, but are on hand, and as Gilliam and his first assistant director, Philip Patterson, juggle the schedule, the location becomes too windy and dusty. And then all hell breaks loose.

Thunderheads form overhead and rain begins to fall. Then hail. Winds blow over sets, tents, props. A flash flood crashes down the mountain and turns the area into a muddy quagmire. The damned jets continue to fly. Gilliam and his team regroup and are able to cobble together a shot involving Don Quixote on his horse. But: "Did you see Jean Rochefort's face as he was riding on the horse? He was in pain."

So much pain, as it develops, that although the actor is an experienced horseman, he cannot mount the horse alone, and needs two men and an hour of struggle to get himself down from it. Rochefort flies off to Paris to see his doctors, and the company shuts down, except for a day when they go through some motions to impress a busload of doomed visiting investors.

Rochefort will be gone three days, a week, ten days, indefinitely. His problem is described as two herniated discs. Or perhaps prostate trouble. Like vultures, the insurance agents begin to gather, followed by the completion bond guarantors, who step in when a film goes over budget. There are discussions, not with the optimism of Don Quixote, about what constitutes an act of God.

Midway through the second week of the shooting schedule, with brutal swiftness, *The Man Who Killed Don Quixote* is shut down. Some films end with a whimper; this one banged into a stone wall. The camera often rests on Gilliam's face, as the enormity of the disaster sinks in. "The movie already exists in here," he says, tapping his head. "I have visualized it so many times." But that is the only place it will ever exist.

Many films play dice with nature. I once stood in a barren field outside Durango, Colorado, as workers placed thousands of melons on the ground because the melon crop had failed, and the movie was about a melon farmer. I watched on the Amazon as an expensive light and all of its rigging slowly leaned over and fell forever beneath the waters. Once in the Ukraine, I waited for days with 20,000 extras, all members of the Red Army, who were dressed as Napoleon's Old Guard—and who could not be filmed without a lens that was being held up in customs.

There are many sad sights in *Lost in La Mancha*. One comes when the producers try to evoke the oldest rule in the book: "Fire the first assistant director." Gilliam stands firm behind his longtime assistant Patterson. It is not his fault. Day by day, it becomes increasingly clear that the film will never be made. Finally comes the shot of props being loaded into cardboard shipping boxes and sealed with tape. Maybe they are destined for eBay.

Other men have tilted at Quixote's windmill. Orson Welles famously spent years trying to piece together a film of the material, even after some of his actors had died. Peter O'Toole starred in *Man of La Mancha* (1972), not a good movie. Of that production I wrote: "I've always thought there was a flaw in the logic of *Man of La Mancha*. What good does it do to dream the impossible dream when all you're doing anyway is killing time until the Inquisition chops your block off?"

Love Liza ★ ★ ★
R, 90 m., 2003

Philip Seymour Hoffman (Wilson Joel), Kathy Bates (Mary Ann Bankhead), Jack Kehler (Denny), Sarah Koskoff (Maura Haas), Stephen Tobolowsky (Tom Bailey), Erika Alexander (Brenda). Directed by Todd Louiso and produced by Ruth Charny, Corky O'Hara, Chris Hanley, Jeffrey Roda, and Fernando Sulichin. Screenplay by Gordy Hoffman.

Diane Lane, who worked on Philip Seymour Hoffman's second movie, remembers that the cast almost tiptoed around him, he seemed so fragile. He's a bulky man, substantial, and yet in many of his roles he seems ready to deflate with a last exhausted sigh. It is a little startling to meet him in person and discover he is outgoing, confident, humorous. On the other hand, who knows him better than his brother Gordy, whose screenplay for Love Liza creates a Hoffman role teetering on the brink of implosion.

Hoffman plays Wilson Joel, a tech-head whose wife has recently committed suicide, although it takes us a while to figure that out. He presents a facade of conviviality in the office, sometimes punctuated by outbursts of laughter that go on too long, like choked grief. His home seems frozen in a state of mid-unpacking, and he sleeps on the floor. Eventually he stops going in to work altogether.

What he feels for his late wife is never usefully articulated. She left a letter for him, but he has not opened it; her mother, played by Kathy Bates, would like to know what it says, but what can she do to influence this man whose psyche is in meltdown? Wilson gives the sense of never having really grown up. One day he begins sniffing gasoline, a dangerous way to surround himself with a blurred world. He doesn't even have grown-up vices like drinks or drugs, but reverts to something he may have tried as a teenager.

The movie proceeds with a hypnotic relentlessness that hesitates between horror and black comedy. Searching to explain all the gas he's buying, he blurts out that he needs it for his model airplanes (this would have been a teenager's alibi). A friendly coworker thinks maybe this is an opening to lure him back into life, and sends over a relative who is an enthusiast of remote-controlled planes and boats. This sends Wilson careening into a series of cover-ups; he has to buy a model airplane, he finds himself attending remote control gatherings in which he has not the slightest interest, and finally, after a series of events that Jim Carrey could have performed in another kind of movie, he finds himself inexplicably swimming in a lake while angry little remote-controlled boats buzz like hornets around him.

Love Liza, directed by Todd Louiso, is not about a plot but about a condition. The condition is familiar to students of some of Hoffman's other characters, and comes to full flower in Happiness (1998), where he plays a man who lives in solitary confinement with his desperate and antisocial sexual fantasies. Sex hardly seems the issue with Wilson Joel, but he seems incapable of any kind of normal socializing, other than a kind of fake office camaraderie he might have copied from others. The mystery is not why Liza killed herself, but why she married him.

The purpose of a movie like this is to inspire thoughts about human nature. Most movies do not contain real people; they contain puppets who conform to popular stereotypes and do entertaining things. In the recent and relatively respectable thriller The Recruit, for example, Colin Farrell doesn't play a three-dimensional human, nor is he required to. He is a place-holder for a role that has been played before and will be endlessly played again—the kid who chooses a mentor in a dangerous spy game. He is pleasant, sexy, wary, angry, baffled, ambitious, and relieved, all on cue, but these emotions do not proceed from his personality. They are generated by the requirements of the plot. Leaving the movie, we may have learned something about CIA spycraft (and a lot more about the manufacture of thrillers), but there is not one single thing we will have learned about being alive.

Al Pacino is the costar of that movie, defined and motivated as narrowly as Farrell is. In a new movie named People I Know, he plays a breathing, thinking human being, a New York press agent driven by drugs, drink, duty, and a persistent loyalty to his own political idealism.

We learn something about life from that performance. Pacino teaches us, as he is always capable of doing in the right role.

Philip Seymour Hoffman is a teacher, too. You should see *Love Liza* in anticipation of his new movie, *Owning Mahowny*, which I saw at Sundance this year (*Love Liza* was at the 2002 festival, where it won the prize for best screenplay). The Mahowny character is at right angles to Wilson, but seems similarly blocked at an early stage of development. Observing how Mahowny, an addicted gambler, relates to his long-suffering fiancée (Minnie Driver), we can guess at the ordeal Wilson put Liza through. He's not cruel or angry or mean; he's simply not ... there. His eyes seek other horizons.

In an age when depression and Prozac are not unknown, when the popularity of New Age goofiness reflects an urgent need for reassurance, Hoffman may be playing characters much closer to the American norm than an action hero like Colin Farrell. We cannot all outsmart the CIA and win the girl, but many of us know what it feels like to be stuck in doubt and confusion, and cornered by our own evasions.

There is a kind of attentive concern that Hoffman brings to his characters, as if he has been giving them private lessons, and now it is time for their first public recital. Whether or not they are ready, it can be put off no longer, and so here they are, trembling and blinking, wondering why everyone else seems to know the music.

Lovely and Amazing ★ ★ ★ ★
R, 89 m., 2002

Catherine Keener (Michelle Marks), Brenda Blethyn (Jane Marks), Emily Mortimer (Elizabeth Marks), Raven Goodwin (Annie Marks), Aunjanue Ellis (Lorraine), Clark Gregg (Bill), Jake Gyllenhaal (Jordan), James LeGros (Paul), Dermot Mulroney (Kevin McCabe), Michael Nouri (Dr. Crane). Directed by Nicole Holofcener and produced by Anthony Bregman, Eric d'Arbeloff, and Ted Hope. Screenplay by Holofcener.

The four women in *Lovely and Amazing* have been described as a dysfunctional family, but they function better than some, and at least they're out there looking. Here is a movie that knows its women, listens to them, doesn't give them a pass, allows them to be real: It's a rebuke to the shallow *Ya-Ya Sisterhood*.

Jane Marks (Brenda Blethyn), the mother, fiftyish, had two daughters at the usual season of her life, and now has adopted a third, eight-year-old Annie (Raven Goodwin), who is African-American. Her grown daughters are Michelle (Catherine Keener), who tries to escape from a pointless marriage through her pointless art, and Elizabeth (Emily Mortimer), who is an actress who cares more about dogs than acting.

All of these women are smart, which is important in a story like this. The mistakes they make come through trying too hard and feeling too insecure. They're not based on dumb plot points. They're the kinds of things real people do. And thank God they have a sense of humor about their lives, and a certain zest: They aren't victims but participants. They're even mean sometimes.

Men are a problem. Michelle's husband, Bill (Clark Gregg), is tired of paying all the bills while she sits at home making twee little chairs out of twigs. She accuses him of stepping on one of the chairs deliberately. He informs her that her "art" is worthless. Indeed her chairs are the sorts of collectibles made by the clueless for the clueless. But there is a deeper impulse at work: Her art allows her a zone free of her husband, a zone that insists she is creative and important.

Elizabeth, the actress, is like most actresses, filled with paralyzing doubt about her looks, her body, her talent. Annie, the adopted child, understandably wonders why she is black when everyone else in the family is white, and asks blunt questions about skin and hair. She also eats too much, and is already learning denial: "I'm not gonna eat *all* this," she tells Michelle, who finds her at McDonald's after she has disappeared from home. "I just couldn't make up my mind."

Where did she learn that reasoning? Perhaps from her mother. As the film opens, Jane has gone into the hospital to have liposuction, and there is a complicated dynamic going on because in some sense she dreams that her handsome surgeon (Michael Nouri) will first improve her, then seduce her.

All of these women are obsessed by body

image. There is a scene of uncomfortable truth when Elizabeth sleeps with Kevin, a fellow actor (an indifferent, narcissistic hunk played by Dermot Mulroney), and then stands before him naked, demanding that he subject her body to a minute commentary and critique. When he misses her flabby underarms, she points them out.

When I saw the movie for the first time at Telluride, I noticed a curious thing about the audience. During most nude scenes involving women, men are silent and intent. During this scene, which was not focused on sexuality but on an actual female body, attractive but imperfect, it was the women who leaned forward in rapt attention. Nicole Holofcener, who wrote and directed *Lovely and Amazing,* is onto something: Her movie knows how these women relate to men, to each other, to their bodies, and to their prospects of happiness.

Consider Elizabeth again. She picks up stray dogs—even dogs not much hoping to be adopted. One of them bites her. We have already seen how obsessed she is with her body, and yet she never even mentions the scarring that will result; it's as if the dog bite releases her from a duty to be perfect. Little Annie is certainly obsessed by being plump—she got that from Jane, probably along with the overeating—but she finds another unexpected image problem. An adult black woman, who volunteers to be her big sister, is disappointed: "When I signed up, I thought I was going to get somebody who was poor."

Michelle's husband is manifestly no longer interested in her. When he insists she get a job, she goes to work at a one-hour photo stand, where a fellow employee, a teenage boy (Jake Gyllenhaal), gets a crazy crush on her. She is not impervious to being adored. She likes this kid. She even winds up in his bedroom. And here Holofcener does something almost no other movie ever does: holds an adult woman to the same standard as an adult man. Michelle knows the age difference makes them wrong as a couple. The kid's mother calls the cops and accuses Michelle of statutory rape. There is some doubt about what exactly has taken place, but at least *Lovely and Amazing* doesn't repeat the hypocrisy that it's all right for adult women to seduce boys, but wrong for adult men to seduce girls.

Scene after scene in this movie has the fascination of lives lived by those willing to break loose, to try something new. *Lovely and Amazing* is not about the plight of its women but about their opportunities, and how in their disorganized, slightly goofy way they persist in seeking the good and the true. I hope I haven't made the film sound like a docudrama or a message picture: It has no message, other than to celebrate the lives of these imperfect women, and the joy of their imperfections.

Love the Hard Way ★ ★ ★
NO MPAA RATING, 104 m., 2003

Adrien Brody (Jack), Charlotte Ayanna (Claire), Jon Seda (Charlie), August Diehl (Jeff), Pam Grier (Linda Fox). Directed by Peter Sehr and produced by Wolfram Tichy. Screenplay by Marie Noelle and Sehr.

The Pianist was not only a fine movie but also served the purpose of bringing Adrien Brody into focus for moviegoers who might otherwise have missed this lean, smart, tricky actor. Odd, that his Oscar-winning role displayed him as passive and quiet, when Brody fits more comfortably into roles like Jack in *Love the Hard Way*—a street hustler and con artist, playing the angles, getting into danger "to feel the juice." He teams up with his partner, Charlie (Jon Seda), and a couple of young actresses to play a risky game of street theater: The actresses pretend to be hookers, and then Jack and Charlie, dressed as cops, bust them in hotel rooms—and can be bribed by the johns, of course, to drop the charges.

There is another side to Jack, in this movie made in 2001 but released now on the strength of *The Pianist.* He drops certain names in conversation—Pound, Kerouac, Melville—that lead us to suspect he is not your average street guy, and in the opening scene of the movie we glimpse his secret life. He rents a cubicle in a storage facility, and inside he jams a cramped office where he keeps a journal and works on a novel. He's not exactly a con artist only to get material, however; it's more like one of his personalities is criminal and the other personality is a shy intellectual watching to see what the first guy will do next.

One day he goes to the movies at a Lower

Manhattan art theater (I guess this is the shy guy) and meets Claire (Charlotte Ayanna), a Columbia student. He uses the usual pickup lines, which should turn off your average college woman, but Claire is intrigued, and agrees to meet him again, and the better half of him falls in love with all of her.

This story, written by director Peter Sehr and Marie Noelle, is a little like David Mamet's *House of Games,* in which an academic woman falls for the dangerous appeal of a con man. The difference is Mamet's heroine took revenge on the guy who deceived her, and Claire, in a way, wants to be deceived and degraded. When she takes revenge, it is against herself.

One day a con goes wrong. Jack and Charlie are not arrested, but to stay in business they're going to need new bait. "Maybe we should give Claire a try," Charlie muses. "She's not built for it," Jack says, and indeed he tries his best to break up with her, maybe because he senses how dangerous he is to a woman like her.

But Claire will not be rejected, keeps coming back, wants to know the secret of Jack's other life, and eventually turns a trick—after which, in a pitiful and lonely scene, she sits alone with her sadness in a photo booth. Jack did not intend this, tries again to alienate her, and then is repaid in full for his deceptions when Claire drops out of school to become a hooker full-time, as if proving something.

This is the kind of psychological self-punishment we might expect in a French film, not in an American film where plot is usually more important than insight. But *Love the Hard Way* is curious about the twisted characters it has set into motion and follows them through several more twists and turns—perhaps a few more than necessary. The film approaches several possible endings as if flirting with them.

Charlotte Ayanna is very good as Claire—we realize, as the film goes on and the character deepens, how challenging the role really is. Brody brings a kind of slick complexity to his role; he's so conflicted about what he's doing and why that he may be the real target of all his own cons.

It is not unknown for authors to embrace the experiences they want to write about (of Jack's heroes, Melville went to sea, Kerouac went on the road, and Pound journeyed into madness), but we sense that Jack is on the edge of schizophrenia; his criminal persona scares him, despite all his bravado, and he wants to push Claire away to save her. The secret Jack, huddled in the container, writing in his journal, is an attempt to diagnose and understand himself.

Love the Hard Way is not perfect; a vice cop played by Pam Grier is oddly conceived and unlikely in action, and the movie doesn't seem to know how to end. But as character studies of Jack and Claire, it is daring and inventive and worthy of comparison with the films of a French master of criminal psychology like Jean-Pierre Melville. The success of *The Pianist* made Adrien Brody visible, probably won this film a theatrical release, and promises him many more intriguing roles. Surely Brody was born to play Bobby Fischer.

The Low Down ★ ★ ★
NO MPAA RATING, 96 m., 2001

Aidan Gillen (Frank), Kate Ashfield (Ruby), Dean Lennox Kelly (Mike), Tobias Menzies (John), Rupert Proctor (Terry), Samantha Power (Lisa), Dena Smiles (Susan), Maggie Lloyd Williams (Jean). Directed by Jamie Thraves and produced by John Stewart and Sally Llewellyn. Screenplay by Thraves.

You probably went through a time in your life like the one Frank is going through in *The Low Down.* I know I did. You may be going through it now. It passes. At the time, you hardly notice it. Later, you look back and wonder how you could have been so clueless. Frank is stuck. He should have quit his job, changed his apartment, and found a steady girl a long time ago, but he drifts in vagueness, unable to act. There are times when he may be terrified in social situations, but we can't be sure—and maybe he can't, either.

Frank (Aidan Gillen) works with Mike (Dean Lennox Kelly) and John (Tobias Menzies) in a London shop where they manufacture jokey props for TV shows and magic acts. He lives in a grotty walk-up above a hairdresser's and next door to a crack house. All night long junkies stand on the sidewalk beneath his window, shouting "Paul! Paul!" to their dealer. Frank knows he should move, but jokes about buying Paul a doorbell.

Thinking it is time to buy his own flat, he

goes to a real-estate office and meets Ruby (Kate Ashfield). As they look at apartments together, they begin to like each other. The writer-director, Jamie Thraves, uses freeze-frames to show how they're struck with each other. A stylistic device like that leaps out because the movie is so low-key. It has no plot, no objective, no purpose other than to show a few days in the lives of a group of friends. They work, they gossip, they hang out, they go to parties, they sit on each other's beds and talk, and Frank and Ruby draw as close to each other as Frank can stand before he has to retreat. There is a subtle subplot about how he has stopped drinking, and starts again.

The British critics said the movie was about nothing. Depends on how you see it. I think it's about Frank's paralyzing inability to move, socially or any other way. The more you look at this guy, the more you realize he's trembling inside. Aidan Gillen is handsome in a Richard Gere–Timothy Hutton sort of way, and can be charming at first, but soon Ruby is looking at him strangely because he seems distant and tentative. He has a way of breaking dates, or turning up late; once he hides and watches her waiting for him.

The movie provides key scenes which are like tests. In one of them, he plays handball with a stranger he meets at the court, and then they have a drink together and it is possible that the other man wants to know if Frank is gay, and interested. I say "possible" because Frank is not receiving on that frequency. In another scene, he's in a pub with a friend at closing time, and an ugly drunk gets in Frank's face and Frank avoids a fight by meekly saying what the drunk wants to hear. A little later, when one of Frank's coworkers screws up by spilling paint on a prop, Frank attacks him violently for no real reason; the poor sap gets to stand in for the drunk, I guess.

Two other scenes intrigued me. Both involve encounters with a street woman who wants money. Frank gives the money both times. The second time, the woman offers her body in payment. Frank turns her down. But watch his body language. He takes her up to his flat, and when he goes into the bedroom to get the money, he straightens the cover on the bed, and runs his hand through his hair. Why? Because he doesn't really know if he will have

sex with her or not. And, despite the fact that she's a junkie offering her body, she activates old habits and "manners" involving his uncertainty about women.

A movie like *The Low Down* gets better the more attention you pay. To say "nothing happens" is to be blind to everyday life, during which we wage titanic struggles with our programming. Someday a woman (or a man) will come along who can blast Frank out of his bunker. Someday he will give up the after-college job and find his real work. At the end of the film he at least moves to a different apartment. From time to time, he will remember Ruby, and wonder what went wrong—wonder, for a fleeting moment, if he had anything to do with it.

Lucky Break ★ ★ ★
PG-13, 107 m., 2002

James Nesbitt (Jimmy), Olivia Williams (Annabel), Timothy Spall (Cliff), Bill Nighy (Roger), Lennie James (Rudy), Christopher Plummer (Graham Mortimer). Directed by Peter Cattaneo and produced by Barnaby Thompson. Screenplay by Ronan Bennett.

Lucky Break is the new film by Peter Cattaneo, whose *The Full Monty* is the little British comedy that added a useful expression to the language. This movie is set in prison but uses much the same formula: A group of guys without much hope decide to band together and put on a show. This time they stage a musical comedy written by the prison warden, which means that instead of stripping they perform in costume. I am not sure if this is the half-monty, or no monty at all.

British prisons are no doubt depressing and violent places in real life, but in *Lucky Break,* the recent *Borstal Boy,* and the summer 2001 movie *Greenfingers,* they are not only benign places with benevolent governors, but also provide remarkable access to attractive young women. Jimmy (James Nesbitt), the hero of *Lucky Break,* finds abundant time to fall in love with Annabel, the prison anger-management counselor (Olivia Williams). Brendan Behan, the hero of the biopic *Borstal Boy,* has a youthful romance with Liz, the warden's daughter. And in *Greenfingers,* which is about a prize-winning team of prison gardeners, one of the green-thumbsmen falls in love with the daughter of a famous TV garden lady. Only in these movies is prison a great place for a wayward lad to go in order to meet the right girl.

Lucky Break stars James Nesbitt and Lennie James as Jimmy and Rudy, partners in an ill-conceived bank robbery that lands them both in prison. The prison governor (Christopher Plummer) is an amateur playwright who has written a musical based on the life of Admiral Nelson, whose statue provides a congenial resting place for pigeons in Trafalgar Square. The lads agree to join in a prison production of the musical after learning that the play will be staged in the old prison chapel—which they consider the ideal place from which to launch a prison break.

Much of the humor of the film comes from the production of *Nelson, the Musical,* with book and lyrics by the invaluable actor and comic writer Stephen Fry; we hear a lot of the songs, see enough of the scenes to get an idea of the awfulness, and hardly notice as the prison break segues into a movie about opening night and backstage romance.

I am not sure that the average prisoner has unlimited opportunities to spend time alone with beautiful young anger-management counselors, wardens' daughters, or assistant TV gardeners, but in *Lucky Break,* so generous is the private time that Jimmy and Annabel even share a candlelight dinner. To be sure, a can of sardines is all that's served, but it's the thought that counts.

The key supporting role is by Timothy Spall, sort of a plump British Steve Buscemi—a sad sack with a mournful face and the air of always trying to cheer himself up. What keeps him going is his love for his young son; this whole subplot is more serious and touching than the rest of the film, although it leads to a scene perhaps more depressing than a comedy should be asked to sustain.

The climax of the film, as in *The Full Monty,* is the long-awaited stage performance, which goes on as various subplots solve themselves, or not, backstage. There is not much here that comes as a blinding plot revelation, but the movie has a raffish charm and good-hearted characters, and like *The Full Monty* it makes good use of the desperation beneath the comedy.

Lumumba ★ ★ ★
NO MPAA RATING, 115 m., 2001

Eriq Ebouaney (Patrice Lumumba), Alex Descas (Joseph Mobutu), Theophile Moussa Sowie (Maurice Mpolo), Maka Kotto (Joseph Kasa Vubu), Dieudonne Kabongo (Godefroid Munungo), Pascal Nzonzi (Moise Tshombe), Andre Debaar (Walter J. Ganshof Van der Meersch), Cheik Doukoure (Joseph Okito). Directed by Raoul Peck and produced by Jacques Bidou. Screenplay by Peck and Pascal Bonitzer.

Why does the United States so often back the reactionary side in international disputes? Why do we fight against liberation movements and in favor of puppets who make things comfy for multinational corporations? Having built a great democracy, why are we fearful of democracy elsewhere? Such thoughts occurred as I watched *Lumumba,* the story of how the United States conspired to bring about the death of the Congo's democratically elected Patrice Lumumba—and to sponsor in his place Joseph Mobutu, a dictator, murderer, and thief who continued for nearly four decades to enjoy American sponsorship.

Pondering the histories of the Congo and other troubled lands of recent decades, we're tempted to wonder if the world might not better reflect our ideals if we had not intervened in those countries. American foreign policy has consistently reflected not American ideals but American investment interests, and you can see that today in the rush toward Bush's insane missile shield. There is little evidence it will work, it will be obsolete even if it does, and yet as the largest peacetime public works project in American history it is a gold mine for the defense industries and their friends and investors.

Patrice Lumumba is a footnote to this larger story. Raoul Peck's film (a feature, not a documentary) begins with his assassinated body being dug up by Belgian soldiers so it can be hacked into smaller pieces and burned in oil drums. Lumumba's disfigured corpse begins the narration that runs through the film. He recalls his early days as a beer salesman, a trade that helps him develop a talent for speaking and leadership. As it happens, the beer he promotes has a rival owned by Joseph Kasa

403

Vubu—who later becomes president while Lumumba is named prime minister and defense minister. It is Kasa Vubu who eventually orders the arrest that leads to Lumumba's murder.

In the 1950s, Lumumba becomes a leader of the Congolese National Movement. His abilities are spotted early by the Belgians, who after a century of inhuman despoliation of a once-prosperous land are fearful of powerful Africans. Lumumba is jailed, beaten, and then released to fly to Brussels for the conference granting the Congo its freedom. He takes office to find the armed forces still commanded by the white officers who tortured him, and when he tries to replace one of the most evil, he is targeted by the CIA, the Belgians, and the resident whites as a dangerous man, and his fate is sealed.

Most of the natural riches in the Congo are concentrated in Katanga Province, which declared independence from the mother country in a coup masterminded by the West. Lumumba's attempts to put down this rebellion got him tagged as a Communist, particularly when he considered asking the Russians to support the central government. Well, of course the opportunistic Russians would have been glad to oblige—but why did a democratic leader need help from the Russians to protect himself from the Western democracies?

The movie re-creates scenes that will be familiar, from another angle, to readers of Barbara Kingsolver's great novel, *The Poisonwood Bible*, which tells the story of an American missionary family that finds itself in the Congo at about the same time. Jailed by Kasa Vubu, Lumumba escapes and tries to flee with his family to a safe haven, but is captured and shot by a firing squad, without a trial.

We do not learn much about Lumumba the man. Eriq Ebouaney, a French actor whose family is from the Cameroons, plays Lumumba as a stubborn, fiery leader, good at speeches, but unskilled at strategy and diplomacy. Time and again, we see him making decisions that may be right but are dangerous to him personally. Although the narration is addressed to his wife, we learn little about her, his family, or his personal life; he is used primarily as a guide through the milestones of the Congo's brief two-month experiment with democracy.

Writer-director Raoul Peck has a long-standing interest in Lumumba, and made a documentary about him in 1991. He is a Haitian by birth, a onetime cultural minister there, and so knows firsthand how despotic regimes find sponsorship from Western capitals. His film is strong, bloody, and sad. He does not editorialize about Mobutu, except in one montage of shattering power. On his throne, guarded by soldiers with machine guns, Mobutu gives a speech on his country's second Independence Day. Mobutu asks for a moment of silence in Lumumba's memory, and as the moment begins, Peck cuts away to show the execution, burial, disinterment, dismemberment, and burning of Lumumba—and then back again to Mobutu's throne as the moment of silence ends.

The Luzhin Defence ★ ★ ½
PG-13, 108 m., 2001

John Turturro (Alexander Luzhin), Emily Watson (Natalia), Geraldine James (Vera), Stuart Wilson (Valentinov), Christopher Thompson (Jean de Stassard), Fabio Sartor (Turati), Peter Blythe (Ilya), Orla Brady (Anna). Directed by Marleen Gorris and produced by Stephen Evans, Philippe Gulz, and Caroline Wood. Screenplay by Petter Berry, based on the novel by Vladimir Nabokov.

"There is a pattern emerging!" cries the eccentric chess genius Alexander Luzhin. "I must keep track—every second!" To which the woman he loves can only reply, "It sounds like such a lonely battle." It is the 1920s in Italy, and they've met at a chess tournament, where Luzhin has the ability to become world champion, if his demons do not drive him mad. As anyone who has played chess knows, the game is utterly absorbing, driving out thoughts of anything else. The better you play, the deeper it becomes, until finally, among the very strongest players, it becomes an abyss. Some fall in. Where is Bobby Fischer?

The Luzhin Defence, based on a novella by Vladimir Nabokov, is about love, genius, and madness, but it is also about life among the wealthy emigrés of Europe in the years after World War I. They dress and move with elegance, their wealth preserving around them an illusion of the social order that was destroyed by the guns of August. They move from spa to spa, and although I am not sure where the movie is set, its villa looks as if it could be on the shore of Lake Como.

Here chess masters arrive from all over the world, as well as the debutante Natalia (Emily Watson) and her socially ambitious mother, Vera (Geraldine James). Alexander Luzhin (John Turturro) wanders in like a dreamer from another planet, absentminded, careless of his dress, in a world of his own. "That man is a genius," an onlooker whispers to Natalia. "He can accomplish anything he sets his mind to."

Well, perhaps. He sets his mind on Natalia. After having had no real conversation with her, he approaches her and announces, "I want you to be my wife. I implore you to agree." She doesn't turn him down as a madman, but asks for time to consider, and then agrees. She is won by his absolute simplicity and honesty. She is repelled by the corrupt marriage candidates sponsored by her mother. And something in her needs to protect Alexander.

The film follows a match between Luzhin and a grandmaster whose patience for chess is equaled only by his patience for Luzhin. But there is an evil presence on the premises: Valentinov (Stuart Wilson), who was the boy's chess teacher. The older man has never forgiven young Alexander for crushing him time and again at the board—emasculating him, ignoring him—and has tried for years on end to sabotage the dreamer's chess career. Now he turns up at the villa with more schemes. At one point, totally absorbed by a chess problem, Luzhin is driven away from the tournament by a chauffeur paid by Valentinov. Luzhin solves the problem and gets out of the car, belatedly noticing that he is stranded in the countryside.

The film is elegiac and sad, beautifully mounted, but not as compelling as it should be. It was directed by Marleen Gorris, whose *Antonia's Line* is what *Chocolat* wanted to be in its celebration of a female life-spirit. Here she captures Nabokov's elegance but not his passion. Perhaps we are never convinced by the bond between Alexander and Natalia. She pities him, she cares for him, she tries to protect him—but their relationship is so new we cannot understand the depth of her devotion, unless it involves madness too. And his love for her, after its first dramatic flourish in the marriage proposal, seems to recede into the clutter of his mind and its systems and patterns.

Turturro does something in his performance that demands more of an anchor than the film provides. He is floating in Luzhin's own interior monologue, entranced by the infinity of chess, and to the outer world seems childlike, innocent, incapable of protecting himself. At one point a doctor says he must stop playing to save his life. But it is never the Luzhins who are burnt out by chess. It is their opponents. The mad geniuses play on obsessively, while their opponents play at a level only high enough to understand how much higher there is to go. Turturro looks uncannily like Bobby Fischer, and I irreverently wish Gorris had abandoned Nabokov and his world and used Turturro in a movie about the match between Fischer and Spassky in Iceland in 1972. I see Bjork as Natalia.

M

Made ★ ★ ★
R, 95 m., 2001

Jon Favreau (Bobby), Vince Vaughn (Ricky), Peter Falk (Max), Famke Janssen (Jess), Sean "Puffy" Combs (Ruiz), Vincent Pastore (Jimmy), Dustin Diamond (Himself), Jennifer Bransford (Flight Attendant), Jenteal (Wendy), Faizon Love (Horrace). Directed and produced by Jon Favreau. Screenplay by Favreau.

There's a theory that American gangsters of the 1930s learned how to talk by studying Hollywood movies. Now comes *Made,* about two low-level modern gangsters who have possibly learned most of what they know about life by viewing *The Sopranos.* Bobby and Ricky (Jon Favreau and Vince Vaughn) have been best buddies since childhood, and played football at Hollywood High. Now they dream of success as professional boxers, while Bobby scrapes together a living as a personal manager—that is, he drives his girlfriend to her job as a stripper at bachelor parties.

They were made for each other: Bobby, the earnest, plodding, analytical seeker after success, and Ricky, the clueless instigator who can't involve himself in a situation without making it worse. There are some people with a gift for saying the wrong thing at the wrong time, and Ricky is one of them, talking when he should shut up, helpfully revealing secrets, blurting out the truth when a lie is desperately called for.

Made, a peculiarly entertaining comedy, revisits the rapport that Favreau and Vaughn had in *Swingers* (1996), and rotates it into a deadpan crime comedy. The movie was written, directed, and produced by Favreau, who plays Vaughn's straight man and loyal friend; think of Martin and Lewis. Vaughn gets many of the best moments, and knows just what to do with them; his performance is a tricky balancing act since it depends entirely on tone—Ricky always has to be a little off-key.

The story. Bobby makes a lousy driver for his girlfriend, Jess (Famke Janssen, from *X-Men*). He's consumed by jealousy, and ends up getting in a fight with one of her clients. The wrong client. This lands him in trouble with

his boss Max (Peter Falk), who books the strippers and has to pay eight grand in damages. Falk's character owes a little to some of the Cassavetes roles he's played; he operates out of an office that is meant to be impressive (and probably is, to the Rickys and Bobbys of the world). He has his thumbs in a lot of criminal pies, none of them very lucrative. He likes the sound of his own voice, and the way it coils through irrelevant details on its way to a triumphant, if murky, conclusion.

Max makes Ricky and Bobby an offer they can't, as they know from the movies, refuse. Actually, he makes Bobby the offer: Fly to New York and deliver a package. Bobby insists that Ricky come along because, well, Ricky always comes along. Ricky is like a faithful sidekick who would be lost without Bobby, since screwing up Bobby's plans is the only thing he does well.

They fly to New York. Jennifer Bransford is the flight attendant who deals severely with Ricky's belief that to sit in first class is to be king of the world. They meet a big, wide, tall, ominous driver (Vincent Pastore), who connects them, after many phone calls and mysterious trips to unlikely parts of town, with crime boss Ruiz (Sean Combs). With Ruiz they have at last elevated themselves to a meaningful level in the crime hierarchy, and Ruiz does not look kindly on these two goofballs from the West Coast. We gather he considers Max essentially an elder version of the same species.

The movie is difficult to describe because it's not what happens that matters, it's how it happens and why. Mostly, it happens because Ricky exercises his genius for creating trouble where none need exist. He and Bobby are no more gangsters than they are boxers, and Combs (in an understated, convincing performance) has priceless reaction shots as he listens to their idea of how they should talk.

Comedies like *Made* are hard to make. It's easier when the payoffs are big, obvious laughs or intentional punch lines. Here we have a comedy of manners. The humor comes from the displacement between what any reasonable person would do, and what Ricky would do. Vaughn's work, in its own way, is masterful. Also thankless, because although to do what he does here is as hard as an acting assignment can be, it doesn't work unless it seems almost accidental. The proof of its quality is that it *does* work; another actor might take his dialogue and turn it to lead. And another director might not have the faith that Favreau has in his material. Maybe they made this movie together because no one else could understand how it could work. But they could, and it does.

Maid in Manhattan ★ ★ ★

PG-13, 105 m., 2002

Jennifer Lopez (Marisa Ventura), Ralph Fiennes (Christopher Marshall), Tyler Garcia Posey (Ty Ventura), Natasha Richardson (Caroline), Marissa Matrone (Stephanie Kehoe), Bob Hoskins (Lionel Bloch), Stanley Tucci (Jerry Siegel). Directed by Wayne Wang and produced by Elaine Goldsmith-Thomas, Paul Schiff, and Deborah Schindler. Screenplay by Kevin Wade.

Maid in Manhattan is a skillful, glossy formula picture, given life by the appeal of its stars. It has a Meet Cute of stunning audacity, it has a classic Fish Out of Water, it works the Idiot Plot Syndrome overtime to avoid solving a simple misunderstanding, and there won't be a person in the audience who can't guess exactly how it will turn out. Yet it goes through its paces with such skill and charm that, yes, I enjoyed it.

We go to the movies for many reasons, and one of them is to see attractive people fall in love. This is not shameful. It is all right to go to a romantic comedy and not demand it be a searing portrait of the way we live now. What we ask is that it not be dumb, or at least no dumber than necessary, and that it involve people who embody star quality.

Maid in Manhattan is not dumb; the Kevin Wade screenplay deals with several story lines and makes them all interesting. And Jennifer Lopez and Ralph Fiennes make an intriguing couple because their characters have ways of passing the time *other* than falling in love. (I grow impatient when movie characters are so limited they can think of nothing better to do than follow the plot.)

Lopez plays Marisa Ventura, a maid in a posh Manhattan hotel. She has a bright grade-schooler named Ty (Tyler Garcia Posey) who for reasons of his own has become an expert on Richard M. Nixon. Marisa hopes to be promoted to management one day, but despite the nudging of fellow maid and best friend Stephanie (Marissa Matrone) is hesitant about applying.

Fiennes plays Christopher Marshall, a Republican candidate for U.S. senator. Camera crews and herds of paparazzi follow him everywhere, perhaps under the impression that he is Rudolph Giuliani. He has a personal assistant named Jerry (Stanley Tucci) whose job is to advise him not to do almost everything that he thinks of doing.

The movie uses the device of a hotel staff briefing to fill us in on various VIP guests, including an exhibitionist, two sticky-fingered French ladies, and especially Caroline (Natasha Richardson), a flighty airhead from Sotheby's who has checked into an expensive suite. Future senator Marshall has checked into another one.

And then, in a dazzling display of time-honored movie developments, writer Wade and director Wayne Wang arrange for Marisa to be trying on one of Caroline's expensive dresses just as her son meets Marshall and talks them all into walking the senatorial dog in Central Park. Marshall understandably thinks this impostor is the inhabitant of the other suite. Prince Charming, of course, falls instantly in love with Cinderella, who must race back to the hotel and resume her life of scrubbing and bed-making. Marshall meanwhile invites the inhabitant of the expensive suite to lunch, only to find that it is the real Caroline, not the mistaken one.

And so on. One word by Marisa at any moment could have cleared up the confusion, but perhaps she fears a Republican candidate would not want to date a Puerto Rican maid, except under false pretenses. It is the duty of the screenplay to keep them separated through various misunderstandings and devices, but the movie makes this process surprisingly interesting by dealing with Marisa's application to become an assistant manager. A kind veteran butler (Bob Hoskins, self-effacing but lovable) teaches her the ropes, even when the two of them are called upon to serve Marshall and the real Caroline at the luncheon from hell.

Other issues arise. Marisa's mother, of course, does not think she deserves to be anything more than a maid (hasn't she learned from the mother in *Real Women Have Curves*?). Young Ty, of course, sees clearly that his mom belongs in the arms of this Republican. And the press turns a series of meetings into a front-page romance.

There's a little spunk in the movie. Marisa tells Marshall what's wrong with his ideas about housing and poverty. He's teachable. Marisa attends a charity benefit, looking gorgeous in a dress borrowed from the hotel boutique and wearing Harry Winston diamonds supplied, no doubt, in return for the plug. And when she runs away from the ball and he follows her, well, it worked in *Cinderella* and it works here, too.

The Majestic ★ ★ ★ ½
PG, 143 m., 2001

Jim Carrey (Peter Appleton/Luke Trimble), Martin Landau (Harry Trimble), Laurie Holden (Adele Stanton), Allen Garfield (Leo Kubelsky), David Ogden Steirs (Dr. Stanton), Bruce Campbell (Brett Armstrong/Roland), Amanda Detmer (Sandra Sinclair), Daniel von Bargen (FBI Agent Ellerby), Bob Balaban (Elvin Clyde), Brent Briscoe (Sheriff Coleman), Hal Holbrook (Johnston T. Doyle), Matt Wiens (Spencer Wyatt), James Whitmore (Stan Keller). Directed and produced by Frank Darabont. Screenplay by Darabont.

The Majestic is a proud, patriotic hymn to America, sung in a key that may make some viewers uncomfortable. At a time when our leaders are prepared to hold trials that bypass the American justice system, here is a film that unapologetically supports the Constitution and the Bill of Rights. It is set in the early 1950s, but the parallels with today are unmistakable and frightening.

Yet this is not a sober political picture. It's a sweet romantic comedy starring Jim Carrey, and it involves a case of mistaken identity and an attack of amnesia, those handy plot devices from time immemorial. It flies the flag in honor of our World War II heroes, and evokes nostalgia for small-town movie palaces and the people who run them. It makes us feel about as good as any movie made this year.

I imagine every single review of *The Majestic* will compare it to the works of Frank Capra, and that's as it should be. Frank Darabont has deliberately tried to make the kind of movie Capra made, about decent small-town folks standing up for traditional American values. In an age of Rambo patriotism, it is good to be reminded of Capra patriotism—to remember that America is not just about fighting and winning, but about defending our freedoms. If we defeat the enemy at the cost of our own principles, who has won?

Darabont, the director of *The Shawshank Redemption* and *The Green Mile*, works on big canvases with lots of characters we can sympathize with. Carrey (who has never been better or more likable) plays Peter Appleton, a shallow, ambitious Hollywood scriptwriter who once, in college, attended a left-wing political meeting because he wanted to pick up a girl there. That wins him a place on the blacklist of the House Un-American Activities Committee, and he's subpoenaed to testify. No one believes he was a Communist (which was not against the law in any case), but to keep his job he is required to kowtow to the committee and "name names"—read a list of other Communists. Since he doesn't know any, the committee will helpfully supply it.

Depressed and confused (his current starlet girlfriend has dropped him like a hot potato), Peter drives north along the coast. His car plunges off a bridge, and he's discovered the next morning with no memory of who he is or how he got there. A kindly dog-walker (James Whitmore) takes him into the nearby town, where he looks kind of familiar to everyone. Finally old Harry Trimble (Martin Landau), who ran the local movie theater, blurts it out: This is his son Luke, lost in the war, now returned from the dead after nine years.

The town embraces Luke, and so does Adele Stanton (Laurie Holden), his onetime girlfriend. The town lost more than sixty of its young men in the war and has fallen into a depression. Somehow Luke's miraculous return inspires them to pick up the pieces and make a new start. Why, old Mr. Trimble even decides to reopen the Majestic Theater again.

The second act of the film involves Peter's gradual absorption in the identity of Luke. Darabont paints the town with a Capra palette: Everyone hangs out at the diner, there's a big-band dance down at the Point, Luke and Adele walk home down shady streets just like Jimmy Stewart and Donna Reed. Some, including Adele, have their doubts that this could really be Luke, but keep them to themselves.

Without getting into plot details, let me point out one moment when the screenplay by Michael Sloane does something exactly right. We know, because such stories require it, that sooner or later Peter's true identity will be discovered. In a routine formula picture, there would be a scene where Adele feels betrayed because she was deceived, and a giant misunderstanding would open up, based on the ancient Idiot Plot device in which no one says what they should obviously say.

Not here. In one of the movie's crucial turning points, Peter tells Adele the truth before he has to. Her reaction is based on true feelings, not misunderstandings. The movie plays fair with its plot, and with us. It even has townspeople raise the obvious questions about where Luke spent the past decade, and whether he's built another life. So we're on solid ground for the third act, in which Peter goes back to Los Angeles and testifies before the House committee.

The scenes of his testimony evoke memories of Gary Cooper, Jimmy Stewart, Spencer Tracy, and other Capra heroes standing up for traditional American beliefs ("That's the First Amendment, Mr. Chairman. It's what we're all about—if only we live up to it"). These scenes are also surprisingly funny (Peter defends himself against charges of subversion with the defense that he was feeling horny). Hal Holbrook is the committee chairman, Bob Balaban is the mean little inquisitor, and the committee evokes fears of communism as an excuse to shelve the Bill of Rights.

Darabont makes films long enough to sink into and move around in. *The Majestic* is not as long as *The Green Mile* (182 minutes), but at 143 minutes it's about the same length as *Shawshank*. It needs the time and uses it. It tells a full story with three acts, it introduces characters we get to know and care about, and

it has something it passionately wants to say. When *The Majestic* went into production there could have been no hint of the tragedy of September 11, but the movie is uncannily appropriate right now. It expresses a faith that our traditional freedoms and systems are strong enough to withstand any threat, and that to doubt it is—well, un-American.

Malibu's Most Wanted ★ ★ ½
PG-13, 86 m., 2003

Jamie Kennedy (Brad Gluckman), Taye Diggs (Sean), Anthony Anderson (P. J.), Blair Underwood (Tom Gibbons), Damien Dante Wayans (Tec), Regina Hall (Shondra), Ryan O'Neal (Bill Gluckman), Snoop Dogg (Ronnie Rizat), Bo Derek (Bess Gluckman). Directed by John Whitesell and produced by Fax Bahr, Mike Karz, and Adam Small. Screenplay by Bahr, Nick Swardson, Small, and Jamie Kennedy.

"This is my ghetto—the mall," Brad Gluckman explains at the beginning of *Malibu's Most Wanted*. He's the son of a millionaire who is running for governor of California under the slogan "California is my family," but the candidate has had little time for his own son, who has morphed into a gangsta rapper. Since he's rich and white and lives in Malibu, he's warned against "posing," but explains, "I ams who I say I ams."

Brad is played by Jamie Kennedy, star of the Fox show *JKX: The Jamie Kennedy Experiment*. The movie has a good satirical idea and does some nice things with it, but not enough. Flashes of inspiration illuminate stretches of routine sitcom material; it's the kind of movie where the audience laughs loudly and then falls silent for the next five minutes.

Brad's parents (Ryan O'Neal and Bo Derek) have not been around much to raise him; in a flashback to his childhood, they're seen communicating with him via satellite video from Tokyo and Paris. Although Brad has "never been east of Beverly Hills," he identifies with "his" homies in the inner city and talks about the hardships of his youth, for example when "the public be up on your private beach." He and his mall-rat friends like to pose as gangstas, but one ferocious and intimidating visit to a

409

convenience store turns out to be about getting parking validation, and picking up some aromatherapy candles.

Brad's image is awkward for his father, especially when the kid unfurls a new political slogan on live TV: "Bill Gluckman is down with the bitches and hos." Gluckman's black campaign manager (Blair Underwood) advises a desperation move: Have the boy kidnapped by actors posing as gangstas and let them take him on a tour of the hood, so that he'll understand his own act is a fake.

Taye Diggs and Anthony Anderson play Sean and P. J., the two actors hired for the roles. They know exactly nothing about the hood. "I studied at Julliard," Sean explains. "I was at the Pasadena Playhouse," says P. J. Still, the campaign manager's money talks, and they enlist the help of the only hood dweller they know, P. J.'s cousin Shondra (Regina Hall). Before long the kidnappers and their victim are kidnapped by real gangstas, led by Tec (Damien Dante Wayans), and there's a gun battle that's supposed to be funny because Brad thinks it's all an act and the bullets aren't real.

The movie has one comic insight: The gangsta lifestyle is not authentic to any place or race, but is a media-driven behavioral fantasy. Why should it be surprising that Eminem is the most successful rapper in America when most rap music is purchased by white suburban teenagers? Many of those who actually live in the ghetto have seen too much violence firsthand to be amused by gangsta rap.

Jamie Kennedy is a success on TV, where this same character, nicknamed B-Rad, originated. He's fresh and aggressive, a natural clown, and has a lot of funny lines, as when he's asked where he learned to handle an automatic rifle and he replies, "Grand Theft Auto 3." This inspires a detailed conversation with a real gangster about competing game platforms.

The elements here might have added up to a movie with real bite, but *Malibu's Most Wanted* plays it safe. It doesn't help that Eminem's *8 Mile* provided a recent and convincing treatment of what it might be like for a white rapper in the inner city. The subject is touchy, of course—race often is—but the solution might have been to push harder, not to fall back on reliable formulas.

A Man Apart ★ ★
R, 114 m., 2003

Vin Diesel (Sean Vetter), Larenz Tate (Demetrius Hicks), Timothy Olyphant (Hollywood Jack Slayton), Geno Silva ("Memo" Lucero), George Sharperson (Big Sexy), Jacqueline Obradors (Stacy Vetter), Mateo Santos (Juan Fernandez). Directed by F. Gary Gray and produced by Robert John Degus, Vincent Newman, Joey Nittolo, and Tucker Tooley. Screenplay by Christian Gudegast and Paul Scheuring.

A Man Apart sets chunks of nonsense floating down a river of action. The elements are all here—the growling macho dialogue, the gunplay, the drugs, the cops, the revenge—but what do they add up to? Some sequences make no sense at all, except as kinetic energy.

The movie stars Vin Diesel and Larenz Tate as drug cops named Vetter and Hicks. They're partners in the DEA, attempting to slam shut the Colombia-Mexico-California cocaine corridor. When they capture a cartel kingpin named Memo Lucero (Geno Silva), the cartel has its revenge by attacking Vetter's home and killing his beloved wife, Stacy (Jacqueline Obradors).

I have not given anything away by revealing her death; the movie's trailer shows her dying. Besides, she has to die. That's why she's in the movie. My colleague Richard Roeper has a new book named *Ten Sure Signs a Movie Character Is Doomed.* One of the surest signs is when a wife or girlfriend appears in a cop-buddy action picture, in gentle scenes showing them dining by candlelight, backlit by the sunset on the beach, dancing in the dawn, etc. Action movies are not about dialogue or relationships, and women characters are a major dialogue and relationship hazard. The function of the woman is therefore inevitably to die, inspiring revenge. This time, as they say, it's personal.

Vin Diesel inhabits *A Man Apart* easily, and continues to establish himself as a big action star. Tate gets good mileage from the thankless sidekick role. Geno Silva, as the drug kingpin, gives us glimpses of a character who was probably more fully developed in the earlier drafts: There is very little of Memo, but what there is suggests much more.

The plot is routine. Cops capture kingpin. Kingpin is replaced by shadowy successor named El Diablo. Successor sends hit men to shoot at Vetter and wife. Vetter loses his cool during a drug bust when a guy disses dead wife. As a result, three cops are killed. The chief takes away Vetter's badge. Then the rogue ex-cop goes on a personal mission of revenge against El Diablo, with ex-partner obligingly helping. We have seen this plot before. But Vin Diesel has an undeniable screen charisma. And the movie is good-looking, thanks to cinematographer Jack N. Green, who gives scenes a texture the writing lacks. So everything is in place, and then we find ourselves confused about the basic purpose of whole sequences.

Example. Early in the movie, the DEA raids a club where Memo is partying. "You expect us to go into a building full of drunken cartel gunmen unarmed?" asks Vetter, who conceals a gun. So does everyone else, I guess, since the subsequent gun battle is loud and long and includes automatic weapons. While I was trying to find the logic of the "unarmed" comment, Memo flees from the club through an underground tunnel and emerges on the street to grab a getaway cab.

Okay. Later in the film, Vetter and Hicks return to the same club, enter through the getaway hatch, wade through waist-high water in the tunnels, emerge in the original room, and find a man sitting all by himself, who they think is El Diablo. "You think . . . I am El Diablo?" the man asks, all but cackling. As an action sequence unfolds and the guys retrace their steps through the flooded tunnel, etc., I'm asking what the purpose of this scene was. To provide mindless action, obviously. But was it also a strategy to use the same set twice, as an economy move?

The closing scene is even more illogical. I will give away no details except to say that, from the moment you see Vetter in the funny sun hat, smoking the cigarette and walking in the dusty village street, the entire scene depends on backward choreography: The omnipotent filmmakers know what is going to happen at the end of the scene and rewind it to the beginning. (Even so, the specific logistics of the payoff shot are muddled.)

Faithful readers will know I am often willing to forgive enormous gaps of logic in a movie that otherwise amuses me. But here the Vin Diesel character often seems involved in actions that are entirely without logical purpose. The movie's director is F. Gary Gray, whose *Set It Off* (1996) and *The Negotiator* (1998) were notable for strong characters and stories. This time the screenplay tries to paper over too many story elements that needed a lot more thought. This movie has been filmed and released, but it has not been finished.

The Man from Elysian Fields ★ ★ ★ ★
R, 106 m., 2002

Andy Garcia (Byron Tiller), Mick Jagger (Luther Fox), Julianna Margulies (Dena Tiller), Olivia Williams (Andrea Allcott), James Coburn (Tobias Allcott), Anjelica Huston (Jennifer Adler), Michael Des Barres (Greg). Directed by George Hickenlooper and produced by Andy Garcia, David Kronemeyer, Andrew Pfeffer, and Donald Zuckerman. Screenplay by Phillip Jayson Lasker.

"Elysian Fields is an escort service. We tend to the wounds of lonely women in need of emotional as well as spiritual solace."
"Only women?"
"Call me old-fashioned."

It's not just the reply, it's the way Mick Jagger delivers it. The way only Mick Jagger could deliver it. There is a brave insouciance to it, and George Hickenlooper's *The Man from Elysian Fields* finds that tone and holds it. This is a rare comedy of manners, witty, wicked, and worldly, and one of the best movies of the year. It has seven principal characters, and every one of them is seen sharply as an individual with faults, quirks, and feelings.

With the craftsmanship of a sophisticated film from Hollywood's golden age, with the care for dialogue and the attention to supporting characters that have been misplaced by the star system, the movie is about what people want and need, which are not always the same thing. It contains moments of tender romance, but is not deceived that love can solve anything.

Byron Tiller (Andy Garcia), the hero, is the author of a good first novel and now has written a bad second one. He is afraid to tell his wife, Dena (Julianna Margulies), that his new novel has been rejected, and that they desperately need money. In a bar, he meets a man with the obscurely satanic name Luther Fox (Mick Jagger). Fox runs Elysian Fields, an escort service for wealthy women. Byron agrees to take an assignment, and finds himself with the lovely Andrea Allcott (Olivia Williams). Why would she need to pay for companionship? It is a form of loyalty to her husband, who is old and diabetic, and whom she loves. It would be cheating to go out with an available man.

Her husband is Tobias Allcott (James Coburn), who has won Pulitzer prizes for his novels. He knows about his wife's arrangement, treats Byron in a dry, civilized manner, and enlists the younger writer's help with his current novel. Soon Byron is providing solace, of different kinds to be sure, to both of the Allcotts. He's a little dazzled by their qualities. And then there are two other characters, who add depth to the peculiar emotional complexity of the escort business: Jennifer Adler (Anjelica Huston), who pays for Luther Fox's services but doesn't want them for free; and Greg (rock star Michael Des Barres), a successful escort who gives Byron helpful tips on the clients.

The literate, sophisticated screenplay by Phillip Jayson Lasker understands that what happens to one character affects how another one feels; there's an emotional domino effect. By working for Elysian Fields, Byron supports his family, but it loses his attention. By risking everything in telling Jennifer that he loves her, Luther discovers his own self-deception. By accepting Byron's help with his novel, Tobias loses stature in his own eyes. Andrea fiercely tells Byron of the old man: "The only thing he has left is his reputation, and when he dies I want him holding onto it." Yes, but she saves it in public by destroying it in private. She isn't very sensitive that way.

This is a grown-up movie, in its humor and in its wisdom about life. You need to have lived a little to understand the complexities of Tobias Allcott, who is played by James Coburn with a pitch-perfect balance between sadness and sardonic wit. Listen to his timing and his word choices in the scene where he opens his wife's bedroom door and finds Byron, not without his permission, in his wife's bed. You can believe he is a great novelist. The scene is an example of the dialogue's grace and irony. Another example: "This business you're in," Byron asks Luther. "Does it ever make you ashamed?" Luther replies: "No. Poverty does that."

Julianna Margulies, as Byron's wife, has what could have been the standard role of the wronged woman, but the screenplay doesn't dismiss her with pathos and sympathy. Dena stands up and fights, holds her ground, is correctly unforgiving. Olivia Williams, as Andrea, has a hint of selfishness: Her concern for Tobias's reputation is connected to the way it reflects on her. There is a scene between Luther and Byron on the beach, where the older man shares a lesson he has just learned; it makes exactly the point it needs to make, and stops. The movie is confident enough it doesn't need to underline everything. It makes its point about the Michael Des Barres character even more economically; for him, the song "Just a Gigolo" is sad or jolly, depending on his mood.

Andy Garcia's performance took some courage because his Byron is not a very strong man. Not strong enough to tell his wife the novel didn't sell. Not strong enough to resist the temptations of Elysian Fields, or the flattery of Tobias's attention. By the time the ending comes around, we observe that it is happy, but we also observe that the movie has earned it: Most movies are too eager to wrap things up by providing forgiveness before it has been deserved. Not this one.

Manic ★ ★
R, 100 m., 2003

Don Cheadle (David), Joseph Gordon-Levitt (Lyle), Michael Bacall (Chad), Zooey Deschanel (Tracey), Cody Lightning (Kenny), Elden Henson (Michael), Sara Rivas (Sara). Directed by Jordan Melamed and produced by Trudi Callon and Kirk Hassig. Screenplay by Michael Bacall and Blayne Weaver.

I haven't seen *Manic* before, but it feels like I have. The opening scenes place us in a familiar setting and more or less reveal what we can expect. In an institution for troubled teenagers, an encounter group is overseen by a therapist who tries his best to steer his clients toward healing. But the unruly young egos have wills of their own, and there will be crisis and tragedy before the eventual closure.

The plot is a serviceable device to introduce characters who need have no relationship to one another, and to guarantee conflict and drama. We are all indoctrinated in the wisdom of psychobabble, and know that by the end of the film some of the characters will have learned to deal with the anger, others will have stopped playing old tapes, and with any luck at all there will even be a romance.

The screenplay by Michael Bacall and Blayne Weaver finds no new approaches to the material, but it does a skillful job of assembling the characters and watching them struggle for position within the group dynamic. Don Cheadle, who plays the counselor, has a thankless task, since the heroes and heroines will all eventually heal themselves, but Cheadle is a fine actor and finds calm and power in the way he tries to reason with them: "You don't think you chose the actions that caused you to be in this room with me?"

Joseph Gordon-Levitt, from *Third Rock from the Sun*, shows the dark side of his funny TV personality, as Lyle, a newcomer to the group, who was institutionalized for outbursts of angry violence in school, one leading to the serious injury of a classmate. His challenge now is to somehow learn to control his rage despite the provocations of the aggressive fellow inmate Michael (Elden Henson), who learns how to push his buttons. He shows promise as a serious actor.

With admirable economy, the screenplay provides Lyle not only with an antagonist, but also with a close friend, his Native American roommate, Kenny (Cody Lightning), and a romance (with Tracey, played by Zooey Deschanel). In stories of this sort, a minority group member who is the best friend of the hero has a disquieting way of dying when the movie requires a setback. Just as the romance must seem to have ended just before it finds a new beginning.

If the movie is not original, at least it's a showcase for the actors and writers. It does not speak as well, alas, for director Jordan Melamed and his cinematographer, Nick Hay. The movie was shot on video, which is an appropriate choice, giving the story an immediate, pseudo-documentary quality, but Melamed and Hay made an unfortunate decision to use the handheld style that specializes in gratuitous camera

movement, just to remind us it's all happening right now. There are swish-pans from one character to another, an aggressive POV style, and so much camera movement that we're forced to the conclusion that it's a deliberate choice. A little subtle handheld movement creates a feeling of actuality; too much is an affectation.

There are moments of truth and close observation in *Manic*, and a scene where the Cheadle character does what we're always waiting for a long-suffering group leader to do, and completely loses it. Deschanel and Gordon-Levitt succeed in keeping their problems in the foreground of their romance, so those scenes don't simply descend into courtship. But at the end of *Manic* I'd seen nothing really new, and the camera style made me work hard to see it at all.

Manito ★ ★ ★ ½
NO MPAA RATING, 77 m., 2003

Franky G. (Junior Moreno), Leo Minaya (Manny Moreno), Manuel Cabral (Oscar Moreno), Julissa Lopez (Miriam), Jessica Morales (Marisol), Héctor González (Abuelo). Directed by Eric Eason and produced by Allen Bain and Jesse Scolaro. Screenplay by Eason.

Manito sees an everyday tragedy with sadness and tenderness, and doesn't force it into the shape of a plot. At the end, the screen goes dark in the same way a short story might end; there isn't one of those final acts where we learn the meaning of it all. Sometimes in life, bad things happen, and they just happen. There's nothing you could have done, and no way to fix them, and you are never going to get over the pain.

The movie, a heartfelt debut by writer-director Eric Eason, takes place in Washington Heights, a Latino neighborhood of New York City, where we meet the Moreno family. Junior (Franky G.) runs a plastering and painting crew, and his kid brother, Manny (Leo Minaya), is an honor student who is graduating today from high school, and headed to Syracuse on a scholarship.

In an unforced, natural way, we meet the characters. Junior spent time in prison, and is determined to stay straight. Manny, known as Manito, is not tough like his brother. Junior is a ladies' man; there's a well-observed scene with his wife, Miriam (Julissa Lopez), who won't even listen to his excuses when he sends her home without him. Manito is more shy, but gets up the nerve to ask Marisol (Jessica Morales), his classmate, to the graduation party in his honor.

This party is a big deal. The family is proud of Manito and his scholarship, and has rented a hall and hired a band—paid for by Junior, and also by Abuelo (Héctor González), who in a scene of sly comedy visits a local bordello and brings out his line of trashy lingerie. Humor pops up unexpectedly, as when Junior needs to hire day laborers and discovers that all of the prospects are wearing white shirts and ties. Why? A restaurant closed, and they lost their jobs.

There is a man on the fringes of the story, seen drinking alone, and that is Oscar (Manuel Cabral), the father. We learn later that he was responsible for Junior going to jail; he let his son take the rap for him. Now he wants to send one of those six-foot sub sandwiches to the party, but Junior furiously takes it right back.

Will this man, drinking heavily, do something violent to spoil the big day? It's a possibility. But the movie isn't about overplotted angst between family members. It's about how the city is a dangerous place to live, and has people in it who are not nice, and how it can break your heart and change your destiny in the blink of an eye. One thing leads to another and the result is tragedy. But *Manito* pushes further, to what happens then, and can never be fixed, and helps nothing, and leads to a place where all you can do is sob helplessly.

The film has been compared to *Mean Streets*, and has the same driving energy as the 1973 picture. But some of Scorsese's characters wanted to be criminals—you could see that again in *GoodFellas*. The Morales family has had all the crime it wants, thanks to the father, and wants only to pay the bills, have a party, and see Manito succeed.

Where do the actors come from, who can walk into their first picture and act with such effortless effect? Franky G. has had three roles since he finished *Manito*, in big pictures like *The Italian Job*, and we'll hear more of him. Leo Minaya and Jessica Morales have not worked before or since, but what freshness and truth they bring to their performances.

The film's flaw, not a crucial one, is in the handheld camera style. There are times when the camera is too close for comfort, too jerky, too involved. Just because you can hold a digital camera in your hand doesn't mean you have to; the danger is that a shot will not be about what is seen, but about the act of seeing it. *Manito* settles down a little after the opening scenes, too absorbed in its story to insist on its style.

The Man on the Train ★ ★ ★ ★
R, 90 m., 2003

Jean Rochefort (Manesquier), Johnny Hallyday (Milan), Charlie Nelson (Max), Pascal Parmentier (Sadko), Jean-François Stévenin (Luigi), Isabelle Petit-Jacques (Viviane). Directed by Patrice Leconte and produced by Philippe Carcassonne. Screenplay by Claude Klotz.

Two men meet late in life. One is a retired literature teacher. The other is a bank robber. Both are approaching a rendezvous with destiny. By chance, they spend some time together. Each begins to wish he could have lived the other's life.

From this simple premise, Patrice Leconte has made one of his most elegant films. It proceeds as if completely by accident and yet foreordained, and the two men—who come from such different worlds—get along well because both have the instinctive reticence and tact of born gentlemen. When the robber asks the teacher if he can borrow a pair of slippers, we get a glimpse of the gulf that separates them: He wants them, not because he needs them, but because, well, he has never worn a pair of slippers.

The teacher is played by Jean Rochefort, seventy-three, tall, slender, courtly. It tells you all you need to know that he was once cast to play Don Quixote. The robber is played by Johnny Hallyday, fifty-nine, a French rock legend, who wears a fringed black leather jacket and travels with three handguns in his valise. This casting would have a divine incongruity for a French audience. In American terms, think of James Stewart and Johnny Cash.

Leconte is a director who makes very specific films, usually with an undertone of comedy, about characters who are one of a kind. His *The Hairdresser's Husband*, which also starred Rochefort, was about a man who loved to watch women cut hair. His *The Girl on the Bridge* was about a sideshow knife-thrower. His *The Widow of Saint Pierre* was about a nineteenth-century community on a French-Canadian fishing island that comes to love a man condemned to death. His *Ridicule* was about an eighteenth-century provincial who has an ecological scheme, and is told that the king favors those who can make him laugh. His *Monsieur Hire* was about a meek little man who spies on a woman, who sees him spying, and boldly challenges him to make his move.

These films have nothing in common except the humor of paradox, and Leconte's love for his characters. He allows them to talk with wit and irony. "Were you a good teacher?" the robber asks the teacher, who replies: "Not one pupil molested in thirty years on the job." "Not bad," the robber says dryly.

I have seen *The Man on the Train* twice, will see it again, cannot find a flaw. The man gets off the train in a drear November in a French provincial town, and falls into conversation with the teacher, who is quietly receptive. The teacher's elegant old house is unlocked ("I lost the key"). The village hotel is closed for the winter. "I know," the teacher says when the man returns. "I'll show you to your room."

Over a period of a few days, they talk, eat together, drink, smoke, gaze at the stars. There is no reason for them to be together, and so they simply accept that they are. There is a coincidence: At 10:00 A.M. on Saturday, the teacher is scheduled for a triple heart bypass, and the man from the train is scheduled to stick up a bank. The teacher offers the man money if he will abandon the plan, but the man cannot, because he has given his word to his confederates.

Early in the film, the teacher goes into the man's room, tries on his leather jacket, and imitates Wyatt Earp in the mirror. A little later, he gets a new haircut, telling the barber he wants a style "halfway between fresh out of jail, and world-class soccer player." One day when the teacher is away, one of his young tutorial pupils appears, and the robber says, "I'll be your teacher today," and leads him through a lesson on Balzac while successfully concealing that he has never read the novel, or perhaps much of anything else.

It is so rare to find a film that is about male friendship, uncomplicated by sex, romance, or any of the other engines that drive a plot. These men become friends, I think, because each recognizes the character of the other. Yes, the bank robber is a criminal, but not a bad man; the teacher tells him, quite sincerely, that he wishes he could help with the holdup. They talk about sex (the teacher points out the 200-year-old oil painting he masturbated before when he was young). They agree "women are not what they once were." The robber observes that, after a point, they're simply not worth the trouble. When the teacher's longtime friend Viviane (Isabelle Petit-Jacques) chatters away during dinner, the robber snaps, "He wants tenderness and sex, not news of your brat."

At the end of the film, the two men do exchange places, in a beautiful and mysterious way. Leconte brings his film to transcendent closure without relying on stale plot devices or the clanking of the plot. He resorts to a kind of poetry. After the film is over, you want to sigh with joy, that in this rude world such civilization is still possible.

The Man Who Cried ★ ★ ★
R, 97 m., 2001

Christina Ricci (Suzie), Cate Blanchett (Lola), John Turturro (Dante), Johnny Depp (Cesar), Harry Dean Stanton (Felix), Claudia Lander-Duke (Young Suzie), Oleg Yankovsky (Father), Danny Scheinman (Man in Suit). Directed by Sally Potter and produced by Christopher Sheppard. Screenplay by Potter.

Sally Potter makes movies about women who use art and artifice to escape from the roles society has assigned them. *Orlando* (1993) is about a character who lives for four centuries, first as a man, then as a woman. *The Tango Lesson* (1997) is about a British film director (Potter herself) who becomes a tango dancer. Now here is *The Man Who Cried,* about a little Jewish girl from Russia who becomes a little British girl and then a Parisian dancing girl and then a wartime refugee, and finally, once again, her father's daughter.

This is an amazingly ambitious movie, not so much because of the time and space it covers (a lot), but because Potter trusts us to follow her heroine through one damn thing after another. There is a moment when Suzie is on a bicycle, chasing Gypsy horsemen through the streets of Paris, and I thought: Yes, of course, realism at last—a woman in that situation *would* use a bicycle to chase a man on a horse. By the time a ship is torpedoed near the end of the film, we're reflecting that most movies are too timid to offend the gods of plausibility.

Potter puts her money where her mouth is. If she personally, in her forties, can go to Argentina and become a tango dancer, then we can't complain about anything that happens to Suzie. Not that we'd want to. The story begins in Russia in 1927, when the girl's father determines to move the family to America. The girl and her father are separated, the girl is mislabeled by adults, and ends up being adopted by a well-meaning but grim British couple. When she sees Gypsies in the lanes of Britain, she is reminded of her own Jewish community in Russia.

Britain cannot hold a spirit like this. In Paris, Suzie is taken under the arm of a gold-digging showgirl named Lola (Cate Blanchett), who wants to marry well, and has her eyes on a famous opera singer named Dante (John Turturro). Suzie meanwhile falls for Cesar (Johnny Depp), the Gypsy on the white horse, and finds that he is a ride-on extra in Dante's current production. As the clouds of World War II gather, Dante reveals himself as a supporter of Mussolini and a hater of Gypsies and Jews, and Lola's appetite begins to fade.

Potter drenches her movies in bold, romantic music, and in wildly involved visuals. Her camera (here choreographed by the great European veteran Sacha Vierny) does not observe but joins. She loves rich images, unexpected whirls, camera movements that join unexpected elements. The music this time is mostly opera, evoking grand emotions that the action mirrors. *The Man Who Cried* is like an arthouse companion for *Moulin Rouge*.

Some of the actors are indulged, others reined in. Turturro's Dante is a character basking in his own glory, an ego with a voice, less an artist than a man who knows which way the wind is blowing. Blanchett uses a thick accent as a tart with a heart of pawned gold (consider the reach between this role and her Appalachian fortune-teller in *The Gift*). Depp more or less imports his soulful Gypsy from *Chocolat,* sensitive and moody. Christina Ricci's Suzie is at the still center, and very still herself; can a heroine ever have had less dialogue in a talking picture?

And here is Harry Dean Stanton as the Parisian opera impresario. Yes, Harry Dean Stanton. Well, why not?—and with a scene where he takes a stand no matter what it costs him.

The Man Who Cried himself does not turn up until very late in the movie. He might once have cried for other reasons, but by then he is crying mostly for himself. He has paid a price for his decisions. As for Suzie, she ends up in Hollywood—and no, that is not giving away the ending. No doubt she grew old and became one of those strange women I would sometimes meet up in the Hollywood Hills, when David Bradley threw his dinner parties for the survivors of the silent era, or at Telluride, where they were the widows of legendary emigrés. Old women who told their stories and said, "But you'll never believe this."

The Man Who Wasn't There ★ ★ ★
R, 116 m., 2001

Billy Bob Thornton (Ed), Frances McDormand (Doris), Michael Badalucco (Frank), James Gandolfini (Big Dave), Katherine Borowitz (Ann Nirdlinger), Jon Polito (Creighton Tolliver), Scarlett Johansson (Birdy Abundas), Richard Jenkins (Walter Abundas), Tony Shalhoub (Freddy Riedenschneider), Adam Alexi-Malle (Carcanogues). Directed by Joel Coen and produced by Ethan Coen. Screenplay by Joel Coen and Ethan Coen.

The Coen brothers' *The Man Who Wasn't There* is shot in black and white, so elegant it reminds us of a 1940s station wagon—chrome, wood, leather, and steel all burnished to a contented glow. Its star performance by Billy Bob Thornton is a study in sad-eyed, mournful chain-smoking, the portrait of a man so trapped by life he wants to scream. The plot is one of those *film noir* twisters made of gin and adultery, where the right man is convicted of the wrong crime.

The look, feel, and ingenuity of this film are so lovingly modulated you wonder if anyone else could have done it better than the Coens. Probably not. And yet, and yet—for a movie about crime, it proceeds at such a leisurely pace. The first time I saw it, at Cannes, I emerged into the sunlight to find Michel Ciment, the influential French critic, who observed sadly, "A ninety-minute film that plays for two hours."

Now I have seen it again, and I admire its virtues so much I am about ready to forgive its flow. Yes, it has a deliberate step—but is that entirely a fault of the film, or is it forced by the personality of Ed Crane (Thornton), the small-town barber who narrates it? He is not a swift man, and we get the impression that the crucial decisions in his life—his job, his marriage—were made by default. He has the second chair in a two-barber shop, next to his talkative brother-in-law Frank (Michael Badalucco). He spends most of his waking hours cutting hair and smoking, the cigarette dangling from his lips as he leans over his clients. (This is exactly right; the movie remembers a time in America when everyone seemed to smoke all the time, and I cannot think of Darrel Martin, the barber on Main Street in Urbana, Illinois, without remembering the smoke that coiled from his Camel into my eyes during every haircut.)

Ed Crane has the expression of a man stunned speechless by something somebody else has just said. He is married to Doris (Frances Mc-Dormand), who is the bookkeeper down at Nirdlinger's Department Store. She works for Big Dave (James Gandolfini), and when Dave and his wife come over to dinner, Doris and Dave laugh at all the same things while Ed and Dave's wife stare into thin air. Ed thinks his wife may be having an affair. He handles this situation, as he handles most social situations, by smoking.

The story then involves developments I will not reveal—double and triple reverses in which two people die in unanticipated ways, at unanticipated hands, and Doris ends up in jail. Ed mortgages the house to pay for the best lawyer in California, Freddy Riedenschneider (Tony Shalhoub), who is the defense attorney at two trials in the movie. Ed, who narrates the entire movie with deadpan objectivity, reports his summation for the jury: "He told them to look not at the facts, but at the meaning of the facts. Then he said the facts had no meaning."

The Coens have always had a way with dialogue. I like the way Ed's narration tells us everything we need to know about Ed while Ed seems to be sticking strictly to the facts. I like the way Freddy Riedenschneider tells Ed: "I'm an attorney. You're a barber. You don't know anything." And a conversation in Ed's car between Ed and Birdy Abundas (Scarlett Johansson), a teenage pianist he has taken an interest in. "You know what you are?" she asks him, after he insists she has talent. "You're an enthusiast!" Yes, and he is mostly enthusiastic not about Birdy's music but about Birdy, but too fearful to make the slightest admission of his feelings. She lacks all such inhibition, and when she attempts to demonstrate her gratitude in an extremely direct way, all he can think of to say is, "Heavens to Betsy!"

Classic *film noir* specialized in bad luck and ironic turns of fate. A crime would be committed flawlessly, and then the perp would be trapped by an inconsequential, unrelated detail. That's what happens here, but with the details moved laterally one position, so that you are obviously guilty—not of the crime you committed, but of the crime you didn't commit. *Film noir* is rarely about heroes, but about men of small stature, who are lured out of their timid routines by dreams of wealth or romance. Their sin is one of hubris: These little worms dare to dream of themselves as rich or happy. As the title hints, *The Man Who Wasn't There* pushes this one step further, into the realm of a man who scarcely exists apart from his transgressions. I kill, therefore I am. And he doesn't even kill who, or how, or when the world thinks he does (although there is a certain justice when he receives his last shave).

Joel and Ethan Coen are, above all, stylists. The look and feel of their films is more important to them than the plots—which, in a way, is as it should be. Here Michel Ciment is right, and they have devised an efficient ninety-minute story and stretched it out with style. Style didn't used to take extra time in Hollywood; it came with the territory. But *The Man Who Wasn't There* is so assured and perceptive in its style, so loving, so intensely right, that if you can receive on that frequency, the film is like a voluptuous feast. Yes, it might easily have been shorter. But then it would not have been this film, or necessarily a better one. If the Coens have taken two hours to do what hardly anyone else could do at all, isn't it churlish to ask why they didn't take less time to do what everyone can do?

The Man Without a Past ★ ★ ★ ½
PG-13, 97 m., 2003

Markku Peltola (Man), Kati Outinen (Irma), Juhani Niemela (Nieminen), Kaija Pakarinen (Kaisa Nieminen), Sakari Kuosmanen (Anttila), Annikki Tahti (Flea Market Manageress), Anneli Sauli (Bar Owner), Elina Salo (Shipyard Clerk). Directed and produced by Aki Kaurismäki. Screenplay by Kaurismäki.

We sense that the parcel the man clutches contains everything he owns, or has managed to hang onto. He gets off the train as if it doesn't much matter what city it is. He settles down on a park bench, falls asleep, and is beaten by muggers to within an inch of his life. He flatlines in the hospital, then suddenly awakens and walks out onto the street with no idea who he is. He finds a community of people who live in shipping containers. There is a kind of landlord, who agrees to rent him one.

"If you don't pay up," the landlord says, "I'll send my savage dog to bite your nose off."

"It only gets in the way," the man says.

"You wouldn't be able to smoke in the shower," the landlord points out.

The dog regards all of this, curious and friendly. He never barks once during the entire film.

Aki Kaurismäki's *The Man Without a Past*, from Finland, was a 2003 Oscar nominee for best foreign film. It follows the adventures of its nameless hero in a series of episodes that are dry, deadpan, and either funny or sad, maybe both. The man has no job, no name, no memory, and yet his face reflects such a hard and sorrowful past that we suspect he has never been happier.

The man (Markku Peltola) gets to know his neighbors. A security guard and his wife help him settle in; their generosity is casual, not dramatic. He goes to the Salvation Army for help, work, anything, and meets an Army officer named Irma (Kati Outinen). I remember her from Kaurismäki's *Drifting Clouds* (1996), where she and her husband both lost their jobs and faced destitution with quiet resolve. She has a face, too; one of those faces that tells us there are sometimes small joys in the midst of the general devastation.

To describe the plot is sort of pointless, because it doesn't unfold so much as just plain happen. Without a name, a plan, or (despite the evidence of his callused hands) even an occupation, the man depends on luck and the kindness of strangers—and the love of the Salvation Army woman, who sees him as a soul only marginally more bereft than herself. The only thing keeping her going is rock 'n' roll.

Eventually, through a happy or perhaps unhappy chance, he is identified and journeys to meet the woman who says she was his wife. "You were my first love," she tells him. "That was beautifully said," he says. "Yes," she says. She tells him a little about the past he has forgotten: "You gambled. You lost all your LPs playing blackjack." The former wife is living with a man now, and the two men step outside because they think they probably ought to fight, but that turns out to be unnecessary.

Kaurismäki is an acquired taste—hard to acquire, because most of his films have never played here. You may have come across *Leningrad Cowboys Go America* (1989), about a group of Finnish rock 'n' rollers who hope to make the big time in this country. His characters tend to plant their feet and deliver their dialogue as if eternal truths are being spoken, and the camera tends to plant itself and regard them without a lot of fancy work. His characters don't smile much; they nod sadly a lot, they smoke and think and expect the worst.

And yet there is a joy in them, a deep humor that's all the richer because it springs from human nature and the absurdity of existence, instead of depending on one-liners and gags. If there is something funny about a container having a landlord with a savage watchdog, we have to figure that out for ourselves, because the movie is not going to nudge us in the ribs and laugh for us.

At the end of *The Man Without a Past*, I felt a deep but indefinable contentment. I'd seen a comedy that found its humor in the paradoxes of existence, in the way that things may work out strangely, but they do work out. I felt a real affection for the man, and for the Salvation Army officer, and for the former wife who is not too happy to see her onetime husband again, and even for the poor sap who thinks he has to fight to preserve appearances.

Martin Lawrence Live: Runteldat
★ ★ ★
R, 100 m., 2002

A live performance by Martin Lawrence,
directed by David Raynr and produced by
Michael Hubbard, David Gale, Beth Hubbard,
Loretha C. Jones, Lawrence, and Van Toffler.
Screenplay by Lawrence.

There is no bodily fluid, secretion, emission,
odor, ejaculate, orifice, protuberance, function,
or malfunction that Martin Lawrence overlooks in *Martin Lawrence Live: Runteldat.* The
word "runteldat" is short for "run and tell that,"
but Lawrence doesn't abbreviate much else,
spelling out his insights into the human phys-
iognomy in detail that would impress a gyne-
cologist. If it proves nothing else, this movie
establishes that it is impossible for a film to get
the NC-17 rating from the MPAA for language
alone. This takes the trophy for dirty talk, and
I've seen the docs by Richard Pryor, Eddie
Murphy, and Andrew Dice Clay.

Pryor and Murphy are genteel humanists in
comparison to Lawrence. Clay is a contender.
He doesn't rise to quite the same standard of
medical detail, but he has the same rage, and
the same tendency to reduce the female gender
to its orifices and functions. When Lawrence
reveals that he was married but is now divorced
because "it didn't work out," we think, "No
kidding!" His attitude toward women is that of
a man who has purchased a cooperative household device that works perfectly until the day it
astonishes him by giving birth.

The film is nevertheless funny, if you can get
beyond the language or somehow learn to relate to it as the rhythm and not the lyrics. (If
you can't, don't go. This movie is as verbally
offensive as Lawrence can make it, and he gives
it his best shot.) It is funny because Lawrence is
a gifted performer with superb timing and an
ability to mimic many characters and suggest
attitudes and postures with lightning-quick
invention. There's something almost musical
in the way his riffs build, turn back on themselves, improvise detours, find the way again,
and deliver.

Curious, but the humor is almost *all* generated by the style. Buddy Hackett once demonstrated to me how you can do Catskills-style

humor with irrelevant words and it's still funny
because the timing and delivery instruct the
audience to laugh. Lawrence elevates that technique to an art form. If you read the script of
this concert film, I doubt if you'd laugh much,
because the content itself is not intrinsically
funny. There are no jokes here that you can
take home and use on your friends. You have
to be there. It's all in the energy and timing of
the delivery, in the way Lawrence projects astonishment, resentment, anger, relief, incredulity, and delight.

The film opens with a montage devoted to
his well-publicized troubles, including an arrest for disturbing the peace and a collapse
from heat exhaustion that put him into a coma.
There are segments from news programs reporting on these difficulties—not real programs, curiously, but footage shot for this
movie. Then he launches into a tired attack on
"the media," as if somehow it created his problems by reporting them. He also discusses those
problems, not in the confessional style of
Richard Pryor, but almost as if he was a bystander. He moves on to berate critics, which is
unwise, because the average audience correctly
decodes attacks on critics as meaning the performer got bad reviews. (No performer has
ever attacked a critic for a good review.)

This opening segment is shaky, as Lawrence
finds his footing and gets a feel for the audience. Then he's off and running, for nearly
ninety minutes, in what can only be described
as a triumph of performance over the intrinsic
nature of the material. His description of childbirth, for example, makes it sound simultaneously like a wonderful miracle, and like a
depraved secret that women hide from men.
His descriptions of sexual activities, in all
imaginable variations, depend heavily on what
can go wrong in terms of timing, cleanliness,
technique, equipment, and unforeseen developments. Sex for Lawrence seems like the kind
of adventure for which you should wear protective gear.

You wonder how long Lawrence can keep
this up, and at the end you conclude he could
keep it up forever. I would summarize more of
it, except that a lot of his riffs are about events
and activities that cannot tactfully be described
in print. I urge you to stay for the closing credits, not because there are hilarious outtakes,

but because there is one of the most astonishing credits I can imagine: a thanks to the Daughters of the American Revolution for the use of their Constitution Hall in Washington, D.C. This is the same hall once denied because of racism to Marian Anderson, who then sang instead, at the invitation of Eleanor Roosevelt, from the steps of the Lincoln Memorial. Now Martin Lawrence records a concert film there. RuntelDAT!

Maryam ★ ★ ★ ½
NO MPAA RATING, 90 m., 2002

Mariam Parris (Mary/Maryam Armin), David Ackert (Ali Armin), Shaun Toub (Darius Armin), Shohreh Aghdashloo (Homa Armin), Maziyar Jobrani (Reza), Sabine Singh (Jill), Victor Jory (Jamie), Michael Blieden (Pete). Directed by Ramin Serry and produced by Shauna Lyon. Screenplay by Serry.

Girls just want to have fun, says Cyndi Lauper, and Maryam, a high school senior, is one of them. Yes, she's an honor student and anchors the news on the in-school TV program, but she also likes to hang out at the roller rink with her slacker boyfriend, and pot and booze are not unknown to her. In New Jersey in 1979, she is a typical teenage girl—until the Iran hostage crisis slaps her with an ethnic label that makes her an outsider at school and a rebel in her own home.

Maryam (Mariam Parris) is Iranian-American—or Persian, her father would say. Her parents immigrated from Iran before the fall of the shah, and settled comfortably into suburbia; her father is a doctor, her mother a warm, chatty neighbor, and Maryam (or "Mary," as she calls herself at school) doesn't think much about her Iranian or Muslim heritage. Then two things happen to force her to confront her history. The hostage crisis inspires knee-jerk hostility from her classmates (whose families also come from somewhere else), and her radical cousin Ali arrives from Tehran.

Ramin Serry's *Maryam*, a film that cares too deeply for its characters to simplify them, doesn't indulge in tired clichés about the generation gap. Maryam's home life is strict but not unreasonable. Her father doesn't want her

to date, places great emphasis on her grades, doesn't know about her boyfriend. He is not a cruel or domineering man, and Maryam, to her credit, knows her parents love her. She's caught between trying to be a good daughter and a typical teenager, and has found a workable middle ground before Ali arrives.

With Ali comes a history of family tension she knows nothing about. Ali is an orphan, the son of Mary's uncle, and so he must be taken in. It is more complicated than that. Her father, we learn, turned his brother in to the shah's secret police; he felt he had no choice, but is consumed by guilt. The bloodstained backgammon board Ali brings as a "gift" is an ominous reminder of times past.

Ali is such an observant Muslim that he cannot touch his cousin Maryam, even to shake her hand. Pressed into service as a chaperone, he finds himself plunged into teenage culture that offends and attracts him. He calls Maryam a "whore" to her mother, but subtly flirts with her. More disturbing is his alliance with a campus radical, and his obsession with the deposed shah, who has just entered a New York hospital for cancer treatment. (Maryam's take on this: "He calls the U.S. the Great Satan. I mean, the guy could lighten up a little.")

Maryam was made before 9/11, and indeed I first saw it at the 2000 Hawaii Film Festival and invited it to my own Overlooked Film Festival in April 2001. It is, I learned, the somewhat autobiographical story of writer-director Ramin Serry, who grew up in Chicago and was made sharply aware of his Iranian heritage during the 1979 hostage crisis.

In the film, Maryam's neighbors put a yellow ribbon around the tree in their front yard, and discontinue their friendly chats and visits. Maryam's boyfriend drops her like a hot potato. She is deposed from her TV show (she suggests her newly arrived cousin might make a good interview; the other students prefer to cover a homecoming controversy). A brick comes through the front window. A public demonstration turns into shouts of "Iranians go home." Through all of this, the gifted actress Mariam Parris (British, but seamlessly playing American) finds the right notes: wounded, sad, angry, but more balanced than distraught.

Whatever hostility Serry felt in 1979 is no doubt much worse today for Arab-Americans, who have, like most immigrants since the Pilgrims, left a native land to seek the American dream. Strange how many Americans, themselves members of groups that were hated a few generations ago, now turn against newcomers. (I could hear the pain in my German-American father's voice as he recalled being yanked out of Lutheran school during World War I and forbidden by his immigrant parents ever to speak German again.) *Maryam* is more timely now than ever.

The Master of Disguise ★
PG, 80 m., 2002

Dana Carvey (Pistachio), Jennifer Esposito (Jennifer), Harold Gould (Grandfather), James Brolin (Fabbrizio), Brent Spiner (Bowman), Edie McClurg (Mama), Maria Canals (Sophia), Austin Wolff (Barney). Directed by Perry Andelin Blake and produced by Sid Ganis, Alex Siskin, Todd Garner, and Barry Bernardi. Screenplay by Dana Carvey and Harris Goldberg.

The Master of Disguise pants and wheezes and hurls itself exhausted across the finish line after barely sixty-five minutes of movie, and then follows it with fifteen minutes of end credits in an attempt to clock in as a feature film. We get outtakes, deleted scenes, flubbed lines, and all the other versions of the "credit cookie," which was once a cute idea but is getting to be a bore.

The credits go on and on and on. The movie is like a party guest who thinks he is funny and is wrong. The end credits are like the same guest taking too long to leave. At one point they at last mercifully seemed to be over, and the projectionist even closed the curtains, but no: There was Dana Carvey, still visible against the red velvet, asking us what we were still doing in the theater. That is a dangerous question to ask after a movie like *The Master of Disguise*.

The movie is a desperate miscalculation. It gives poor Dana Carvey nothing to do that is really funny, and then expects us to laugh because he acts so goofy all the time. But *acting* funny is not funny. Acting in a situation that's funny—that's funny.

The plot: Carvey plays an Italian waiter named Pistachio Disguisey, who is unfamiliar with the First Law of Funny Names, which is that funny names in movies are rarely funny.

Pistachio comes from a long line of masters of disguise. His father Fabbrizio (James Brolin), having capped his career by successfully impersonating Bo Derek, retires and opens a New York restaurant. He doesn't tell his son about the family trade, but then, when he's kidnapped by his old enemy Bowman (Brent Spiner), Pistachio is told the family secret by his grandfather (Harold Gould).

Grandfather also gives him a crash course in disguise craft, after locating Fabbrizio's hidden workshop in the attic (a Disguisey's workshop, we learn, is known as a nest). There is now a scene representative of much of the movie, in which Pistachio puts on an inflatable suit, and it suddenly balloons so that he flies around the room and knocks over granddad. That scene may seem funny to kids. Real, real little, little kids.

Carvey, of course, is himself a skilled impersonator, and during the film we see him as a human turtle, Al Pacino from *Scarface*, Robert Shaw from *Jaws*, a man in a cherry suit, a man with a cow pie for a face, George W. Bush, and many other guises. In some cases the disguises are handled by using a double and then employing digital technology to make it appear as if the double's face is a latex mask that can be removed. In other cases, such as Bush, Carvey simply impersonates him.

The plot helpfully supplies Pistachio with a girl named Jennifer (Jennifer Esposito) who becomes his sidekick in the search for Fabbrizio, and they visit a great many colorful locations. One of them is a secret headquarters where Bowman keeps his priceless trove of treasures, including the lunar landing module, which is used for one of those fight scenes where the hero dangles by one hand. The movie's director, Perry Andelin Blake, has been a production designer on fourteen movies, including most of Adam Sandler's, and, to be sure, *The Master of Disguise* has an excellent production design. It is less successful at disguising itself as a comedy. ☞

The Matrix Reloaded ★ ★ ★ ½
R, 138 m., 2003

Keanu Reeves (Neo), Laurence Fishburne (Morpheus), Carrie-Anne Moss (Trinity), Hugo Weaving (Agent Smith), Jada Pinkett

Smith (Niobe), Gloria Foster (Oracle), Monica Bellucci (Persephone), Collin Chou (Seraph), Nona Gaye (Zee), Randall Duk Kim (Keymaker), Harry Lennix (Commander Lock), Harold Perrineau (Link), Neil and Adrian Rayment (Twins), Lambert Wilson (Merovingian), Helmut Bakaltis (Architect). Directed by Andy Wachowski and Larry Wachowski and produced by Joel Silver. Screenplay by Wachowski and Wachowski.

Commander Lock: *"Not everyone believes what you believe."*

Morpheus: *"My beliefs do not require that they do."*

Characters are always talking like this in *The Matrix Reloaded,* which plays like a collaboration involving a geek, a comic book, and the smartest kid in Philosophy 101. Morpheus in particular unreels extended speeches that remind me of Laurence Olivier's remarks when he won his honorary Oscar—the speech that had Jon Voight going "God!" on TV, but in print turned out to be quasi-Shakespearean doublespeak. The speeches provide, not meaning, but the effect of meaning: It sure sounds like those guys are saying some profound things.

That will not prevent fanboys from analyzing the philosophy of *The Matrix Reloaded* in endless Web postings. Part of the fun is becoming an expert in the deep meaning of shallow pop mythology; there is something refreshingly ironic about becoming an authority on the transient extrusions of mass culture, and Morpheus (Laurence Fishburne) now joins Obi Wan Kenobi as the Plato of our age.

I say this not in disapproval, but in amusement. *The Matrix* (1999), written and directed by the brothers Andy and Larry Wachowski, inspired so much inflamed pseudophilosophy that it's all *The Matrix Reloaded* can do to stay ahead of its followers. It is an immensely skillful sci-fi adventure, combining the usual elements: heroes and villains, special effects and stunts, chases and explosions, romance and oratory. It develops its world with more detail than the first movie was able to afford, gives us our first glimpse of the underground human city of Zion, burrows closer to the heart of the secret of the Matrix, and promotes its hero,

Neo, from confused draftee to a Christ figure in training.

As this film opens, we learn that the Machines need human bodies, millions and millions of them, for their ability to generate electricity. In an astonishing sequence, we see countless bodies locked in pods around central cores that extend out of sight above and below. The Matrix is the virtual reality that provides the minds of these sleepers with the illusion that they are active and productive. Questions arise, such as, is there no more efficient way to generate power? And, why give the humans dreams when they would generate just as much energy if comatose? And, why create such a complex virtual world for each and every one of them when they could all be given the same illusion and be none the wiser? Why is each dreamer himself or herself occupying the same body in virtual reality as the one asleep in the pod?

But never mind. We are grateful that 250,000 humans have escaped from the grid of the Matrix and gathered to build Zion, which is "near the Earth's core—where there is more heat." And as the movie opens we are alarmed to learn that the Machines are drilling toward Zion so quickly that they will arrive in thirty-six hours. We may also wonder if Zion and its free citizens really exist, or if the humans only think so, but that leads to a logical loop ending in madness.

Neo (Keanu Reeves) has been required to fly, to master martial arts, and to learn that his faith and belief can make things happen. His fights all take place within virtual reality spaces, while he reclines in a chair and is linked to the cyberworld, but he can really be killed, because if the mind thinks it is dead, "the body is controlled by the mind." All of the fight sequences, therefore, are logically contests not between physical bodies, but between videogame players, and the Neo in the big fight scenes is actually his avatar.

The visionary Morpheus, inspired by the prophecies of the Oracle, instructs Neo—who gained the confidence to leap great distances, to fly, and in *Reloaded* destroys dozens of clones of Agent Smith (Hugo Weaving) in martial combat. That fight scene is made with the wonders of digital effects and the choreography of the Hong Kong action director Yuen Wo Ping, who also did the fights in *Crouching Tiger, Hid-*

den Dragon. It provides one of the three great set pieces in the movie.

The second comes when Morpheus returns to Zion and addresses the assembled multitude—an audience that looks like a mosh pit crossed with the underground slaves in *Metropolis.* After his speech, the citizens dance in a percussion-driven frenzy, which is intercut with Neo and Trinity (Carrie-Anne Moss) having sex. I think their real bodies are having the sex, although you can never be sure.

The third sensational sequence is a chase involving cars, motorcycles, and trailer trucks, with gloriously choreographed moves including leaps into the air as a truck continues to move underneath. That this scene logically takes place in cyberspace does not diminish its thrilling fourteen-minute fun ride, although we might wonder—when deadly enemies meet in one of these virtual spaces, who programmed it? (I am sure I will get untold thousands of e-mails explaining it all to me.)

I became aware, during the film, that a majority of the major characters were played by African Americans. Neo and Trinity are white, and so is Agent Smith, but consider Morpheus; his superior, Commander Lock (Harry Lennix); the beautiful and deadly Niobe (Jada Pinkett Smith), who once loved Morpheus and now is with Lock, although she explains enigmatically that some things never change; the programmer Link (Harold Perrineau); Link's wife, Zee (Nona Gaye), who has the obligatory scene where she complains he's away from home too much; and the Oracle (the late Gloria Foster, very portentous). From what we can see of the extras, the population of Zion is largely black.

It has become commonplace for science fiction epics to feature one or two African-American stars, but we've come a long way since Billy Dee Williams in *Return of the Jedi.* The Wachowski brothers use so many African Americans, I suspect, not for their box-office appeal, because the Matrix is the star of the movie, and not because they are good actors (which they are), but because to the white teenagers who are the primary audience for this movie, African Americans embody a cool, a cachet, an authenticity. Morpheus is the power center of the movie, and Neo's role is essentially to study under him and absorb his mojo.

The film ends with "To Be Concluded," a reminder that the third film in the trilogy arrives on November 5, 2003. Toward the end there are scenes involving characters who seem pregnant with possibilities for part three. One is the Architect (Helmut Bakaltis), who says he designed the Matrix, and revises everything Neo thinks he knows about it. Is the Architect a human, or an avatar of the Machines? The thing is, you can never know for sure. He seems to hint that when you strip away one level of false virtual reality, you find another level beneath. Maybe everything so far is several levels up?

Stephen Hawking's *A Brief History of Time* tells the story of a cosmologist whose speech is interrupted by a little old lady who informs him that the universe rests on the back of a turtle. "Ah, yes, madame," the scientist replies, "but what does the turtle rest on?" The old lady shoots back: "You can't trick me, young man. It's nothing but turtles, turtles, turtles, all the way down." ☞

Max ★ ★ ★ ½
R, 106 m., 2002

John Cusack (Max Rothman), Noah Taylor (Adolf Hitler), Leelee Sobieski (Liselore Von Peltz), Molly Parker (Nina Rothman), Ulrich Thomsen (Captain Mayr). Directed by Menno Meyjes and produced by Andras Hamori. Screenplay by Meyjes.

Und . . . der Fuhrer vas a better artist than Churchill!
                                                    —The Producers

The central mystery of Hitler, William Boyd writes in a recent *Times Literary Supplement,* is: "How on earth could a dysfunctional, deranged, down-and-out homeless person in pre–First World War Vienna become, twenty years later, chancellor of Germany?" A peculiar and intriguing film named *Max* argues that he succeeded because he had such a burning need to be recognized—and also, of course, because of luck, good for him, bad for us. If Hitler had won fame as an artist, the century's history might have been different. Pity about his art.

Max imagines a fictional scenario in which the young Adolf Hitler (Noah Taylor) is befriended by a one-armed Jewish art dealer named Max Rothman (John Cusack) in Munich in the years following World War I. Both served in the German army and fought in the same battle, where Rothman lost his arm. The dealer opens an avant-garde art gallery in a vast abandoned factory, showcasing artists like George Grosz and attracting important collectors—and Hitler, clutching his portfolio of kitsch. Rothman takes pity on this man and is friendly to him, moved by the pathos beneath his bluster.

The film, written and directed by Menno Meyjes, who scripted *The Color Purple*, has been attacked because it attempts to "humanize" a monster. But of course, Hitler was human, and we must understand that before we can understand anything else about him. To dehumanize him is to fall under the spell that elevated him into the führer, a mythical being who transfixed Germans and obscured the silly little man with the mustache. To ponder Hitler's early years with the knowledge of his later ones is to understand how life can play cosmic tricks with tragic results.

Max suggests that Hitler's real work of art was himself and the Nazi state he first envisioned in fantasy terms; even as a young man we see him doodling with swastikas and designing comic-book uniforms. Clothes make the man, and to some extent Hitler's skill as a fashion designer made men into Nazis. "I am the new avant-garde and politics is the new art," he tells Rothman, not inaccurately.

If Hitler is a mystery, what are we to make of Max Rothman? John Cusack plays him as a man of empathy, who endures the tantrums of his artists, and feels pity for this bedraggled Hitler whom he first meets as a liquor deliveryman. Rothman himself wanted to be an artist but has put that on hold after losing his arm. He has returned to a comfortable bourgeois life in Munich, with his doctor father-in-law, his secure wife, Nina (Molly Parker), and his stimulating mistress, Liselore (Leelee Sobieski). When he's quizzed about his friendship with the pathetic Hitler, his answers are simple: "He came back from the war to nothing. He doesn't have any friends."

Yes, Hitler is anti-Semitic and makes no secret of it. But in Germany in those days anti-Semitism was like the weather; you couldn't do anything about it, and you had to go out in it.

Rothman takes Hitler's rantings with weariness and sadness, and at one point tells Liselore, "I told him his insane f------ ideas are holding him back as an artist."

There is never, even for a moment, a glimmer of evidence to suggest that Hitler could have been a successful artist. His drawings look like the kind of cartoon caricatures that bored boys create in their notebooks in the back row of geometry class, playing with their protractors and dreaming of supermen. Hitler instinctively fails to see the point of abstract act; at one point he suggests that Rothman frame his diarrhea. We are reminded that, in power, both the Nazis and the Soviets banned and burned abstract art. Curious, that art which claimed to represent nothing nevertheless represented so much to them. Perhaps art is a threat to totalitarianism when it does not have a clear, censurable subject, and is left to the musings of the citizen.

As the title suggests, *Max* centers more on Rothman than on Hitler. Max is a kind, dreamy, hopeful man, who we presume saw his share of the horrors of that particularly nasty war, and trusts that art is taking him in the right direction. He is also smooth and sophisticated, a master of one-armed cigarette technique, who moves seamlessly between his bourgeois home and the cafés and dives of bohemian Munich. He is worldly in a way that Hitler is not, and their differences are suggested when he says in exasperation to the fierce failed artist, "Listen—do you want to meet some girls?"

Hitler's other patron is an army propagandist named Mayr (Ulrich Thomsen), like Hitler an outcast in the German economic ruin. He is attached to a small splinter party and thinks Hitler might make a good spokesman. What Mayr sees in this hapless nonentity is hard to say, but he is quite right, and soon Hitler is fascinating crowds in beer halls with his emerging Nazi vision. (Mayr, I learn, is an actual historical figure, who later, for his pains, was beheaded by Hitler.)

But what, we may ask, parroting Soviet realism, is the *purpose* of this movie? What is its *message?* It is not abstract but presents us with two central characters whose races have a rendezvous with destiny. I think the key is in Max, who is a kind, liberal humanist, who cares for the unfortunate, who lives a life of the mind that blinds him to the ominous rising tide of Nazism. Can a man like this, with values like this, survive against a man like Hitler, who has no value except the will for power? It is the duty of the enlightened state to assure that he can. Dissent protects the body politic from the virus of totalitarianism.

Max Keeble's Big Move ★ ★
PG, 101 m., 2001

Zena Grey (Woodwind Girl), Alex D. Linz (Max Keeble), Larry Miller (Principal Jindraike), Justin Berfield (Caption Writer), Noel Fisher (Troy McGinty), Orlando Brown (Dobbs), P. J. Byrne (D. J./Young Executive), Robert Carradine (Don Keeble), Clifton Davis (Superintendent Knebworth). Directed by Tim Hill and produced by Mike Karz. Screenplay by Jonathan Bernstein, Mark Blackwell, and James Greer.

I sat down to write a review of *Max Keeble's Big Move* and found myself consumed by a certain indifference. It is the kind of movie one enjoys more at eight, or even twelve, than at sixteen and up. I am up. I stalled. I checked the Movie Answer Man's e-mail. I found a message from Brendan Staunton of London, who writes: "Don't you think that kids are a little, or perhaps even a lot, too wise in American movies—yes, even in serious ones? It's an understandable fault, I suppose, but I've never in my life come across the kind of kids you see in movies or TV dramas."

Brendan, I couldn't agree more. We have a touching faith in childhood wisdom in this country, matched only by our cynicism about adults. I am reminded of our poet e.e. cummings, who wrote "down they forgot as up they grew." The wise children in *The Sixth Sense* and *The Kid* know occult secrets hidden even from Bruce Willis. I imagine that K–6 teachers must go to these movies as a form of escapism, to see children totally unlike the real kids they teach every day.

Kids in comedies are especially clever. They see through adults in a wink, outsmart their opponents, plot to get what they want, and are cute, articulate, and never have pimples. Take Max Keeble (Alex D. Linz), for example. It is his first day of junior high school, and his hormones have recently started to send him messages which, when he sees Woodwind Girl (Zena Grey), he finds himself finally able to decode.

He likes junior high school, all except for those two obligatory characters in all junior high school movies, the bully and the obnoxious principal. The bully, named Troy McGinty (Noel Fisher), is taller, blond, and looks (as bullies always seem to look in these movies) like a twelve-year-old Gary Busey. The principal is named Principal Jindraike (Larry Miller) and looks (as principals always seem to look in these movies) like Larry Miller.

Max is beginning to make headway with Woodwind Girl, in his struggle against Troy, and in his campaign to prevent the principal's insane zeal to tear down an animal shelter and build a stadium. But then disaster strikes when his father (Robert Carradine) tells his mother (Nora Dunn) that they are moving in a week so he can take a new job. And just when she finally had the house decorated perfectly!

You will imagine that this is not the kind of movie that holds me spellbound. It explains why I am so grateful for a film like *Spy Kids*, that the entire family (including adults) can enjoy. This is more like an after-school Nickelodeon romp, with bright colors, broad jokes, lots of sight gags, characters landing in deep, wet puddles, and a plot assembled from off-the-shelf parts.

There's a tendency with these movies to spend money to conceal the lack of creativity. There is, for example, an ice-cream truck that at one point is hoisted aloft by a crane so that it can spill hundreds of gallons of melted ice cream over the villains, and we wonder if a funnier and more economical solution was not available.

Some moments are funny. I liked Larry Miller, who seemed to regard the movie's characters with about as much affection as I did, and makes schoolwide telecasts from his office with a U.S. Capitol photographic backdrop behind him, just like our lawmakers. And Alex D. Linz (*Home Alone 3*) is a talented young actor; I suspect this is a film about which he had private thoughts too, since anyone as smart as he is would not be much entertained by what he is made to do.

So, yes, Brendan Staunton, I agree that kids are a little, or perhaps even a lot, too wise in

American movies. But you have to remember that when the movie is good enough, we forgive them. Look at *E.T.*, for example. And over here in America we are all enthralled by your Harry Potter, who is a lot, or even a whole lot, too wise.

May ★ ★ ★ ★
R, 95 m., 2003

Angela Bettis (May Canady), Jeremy Sisto (Adam Stubbs), Anna Faris (Polly), James Duval (Blank), Nichole Hiltz (Ambrosia), Kevin Gage (Papa), Merle Kennedy (Mama), Chandler Hect (Young May). Directed by Lucky McKee and produced by Marius Balchunas and Scott Sturgeon. Screenplay by McKee.

May is a horror film and something more and deeper, something disturbing and oddly moving. It begins as the story of a strange young woman, it goes for laughs and gets them, it functions as a black comedy, but then it glides past the comedy and slides slowly down into a portrait of madness and sadness. The title performance by Angela Bettis is crucial to the film's success. She plays a twisted character who might easily go over the top into parody, and makes her believable, sympathetic, and terrifying.

The movie will inevitably be compared with *Carrie*, not least because Bettis starred in the 2002 TV version of that story. Like *Carrie*, it is about a woman who has been wounded by society and finds a deadly revenge. But *May* is not a supernatural film. It follows the traditional outlines of a horror or slasher film, up to a point—and then it fearlessly follows its character into full madness. We expect some kind of a U-turn or cop-out, but no; the writer and director, Lucky McKee, never turns back from his story's implacable logic. This is his solo directing debut, and it's kind of amazing. You get the feeling he's the real thing.

Bettis plays May Canady, who as a girl had a "lazy eye" that made her an outcast at school. After a brief prologue, we meet her in her twenties, as an assistant in a veterinary clinic. She is shy, quirky, askew, but in a curiously sexy way, so that when she meets the good-looking Adam Stubbs (Jeremy Sisto), he is intrigued. "I'm weird," she tells him. "I like weird," he says. "I like weird a lot."

Uh-huh. His idea of weird is attending the revival of a Dario Argento horror film. He shows May his own student film, which begins with a young couple kissing and caressing and then moves on inexorably into mutual cannibalism. May likes it. She snuggles closer to him on the sofa. Afterward, she gives him her review: "I don't think that she could have gotten his whole finger in one bite, though. That part was kind of far-fetched."

Bettis makes May peculiar but fully human. There are scenes here of such close observation, of such control of body language, voice, and behavior, evoking such ferocity and obsession, that we are reminded of Lady Macbeth. It is as hard to be excellent in a horror film as in Shakespeare. Harder, maybe, because the audience isn't expecting it. Sisto's performance as Adam is carefully calibrated to show an intelligent guy who is intrigued, up to a point, and then smart enough to prudently back away. He's not one of those horror movie dumbos who makes stupid mistakes. Notice the look in his eye after he asks her to describe some of the weird stuff that goes on at the animal hospital, and she does, more graphically than he requires.

May's colleague at the clinic is Polly (Anna Faris), a lesbian, always open to new experiences. One day when May cuts herself with a scalpel, Polly is fascinated. Then May unexpectedly cuts her. Polly recoils, screams, considers, and says, "I kind of liked it. Do me again." Like Adam, she is erotically stirred by May's oddness—up to a point. There is an erotic sequence involving May and Polly, not explicit but very evocative, and it's not just a "sex scene," but a way to show that for Polly sex is entertainment and for May it is of fundamental importance.

McKee uses various fetishes in an understated way. May is not a smoker, but she treasures a pack of cigarettes that Adam gave her, and the precious cigarettes are measured out one by one as accomplices to her actions. She has a doll from childhood that gazes from its glass cabinet; in a lesser movie, it would come alive, but in this one it does all the necessary living within May's mind. When May volunteers to work with blind kids, we fear some kind of exploitation, but the scenes are handled to engender suspense, not disrespect.

The movie subtly darkens its tone until,

when the horrifying ending arrives, we can see how we got there. There is a final shot that would get laughs in another kind of film, but *May* earns the right to it, and it works, and we understand it.

There are so many bad horror movies. A good one is incredibly hard to make. It has to feel a fundamental sympathy for its monster, as movies as different as *Frankenstein, Carrie,* and *The Silence of the Lambs* did. It has to see that they suffer, too. The crimes of too many horror monsters seem to be for their own entertainment, or ours. In the best horror movies, the crimes are inescapable, and the monsters are driven toward them by the merciless urgency of their natures.

Maze ★ ★ ★
R, 97 m., 2001

Rob Morrow (Lyle Maze), Laura Linney (Callie), Craig Sheffer (Mike), Rose Gregorio (Lyle's Mother), Robert Hogan (Lyle's Father), Gia Carides (Julianne). Directed by Rob Morrow and produced by Paul Colichman, Mark R. Harris, Stephen P. Jarchow, and Morrow. Screenplay by Morrow and Bradley White.

Lyle Maze is a painter who has Tourette's syndrome and obsessive-compulsive disorder. His work should look like Jackson Pollock attacked a Mark Rothko, but no, his inner peace emerges when he's painting. He falls into a sort of reverie then, and "the house could burn down and I wouldn't notice." The rest of the time, there are problems; when he suddenly hurls paint into a model's eye, we sense it's happened before by his instant response: "Don't worry. It's nontoxic. Just wash it with water."

Maze (Rob Morrow) lives alone because, in his words, he's a "freak" and a normal relationship is impossible. His best friends are a doctor named Mike (Craig Sheffer) and Mike's girlfriend, Callie (Laura Linney). Mike is a do-gooder who does not believe humanitarianism begins at home, and leaves Callie for seven months to work as a volunteer doctor in Burundi. Callie is pregnant when he leaves, but Mike doesn't know, care, or notice, and that leaves best friend Maze to be her partner in the natural childbirth classes.

Maze and Callie are drawn toward each other, but Maze doesn't want to be disloyal to his best (only) friend. Callie, who knows Mike better, is more open. Maze experiments with a date: Julianne (Gia Carides) admires his work, but is less entranced when he throws wine at her during dinner.

Maze's OCD is a mild case, involving an obsession with the tongues of shoes and other harmless manifestations. His Tourette's doesn't involve the sudden shouting of obscenities, which is the widespread but limited view of the condition. He sometimes has sudden muscular spasms, or emits strange noises and pops (when that happens, we see a jerky worldview through a handheld video camera). He sees the humor in the situation; when Callie offers him a TV set, he asks her, "Have you ever seen an obsessive-compulsive with a remote control?"

The heart of the story is hard to resist, not least because Linney (the Oscar nominee from *You Can Count on Me*) is sweet and understanding, and Morrow has a shaggy appeal. It is a rite of passage required of all actors that they participate in at least one live childbirth scene, with somebody shouting "Push! Push!" but you have to hand it to the scene in *Maze.* It's original—a duet for screams and Tourette's.

There are small but telling scenes involving Maze's parents (Rose Gregorio and Robert Hogan). When the father needs a blood transfusion, he doesn't want his son's blood, even though his wife tells him what he should have long since known, that you can't "catch" nonorganic disorders. The father has always believed Maze could control his twitches if he wanted to. Morrow and Gregorio have a quiet scene together, son and mother sitting side by side on a bed, where one of her speeches unforgettably sums up her marriage.

The movie is Morrow's directorial debut, and he wrote the screenplay with Bradley White. The story arc is straight out of screenplay workshops, including setbacks that arrive right on time (an ultrasound test, a tantrum). The departure and return of Dr. Mike are so timely he must have had a copy of the script. There are several Idiot Plot moments when a simple line of dialogue ("He has Tourette's syndrome") would work wonders but is never said. And yet the movie has a sweetness and care that is touching.

Mean Machine ★ ★ ★
R, 98 m., 2002

Vinnie Jones (Danny Meehan), Jason Statham (Monk), David Kelly (Doc), David Hemmings (Prison Governor), Vas Blackwood (Massive), Jason Flemyng (Bob), Danny Dyer (Billy the Limpet), Robbie Gee (Trojan). Directed by Barry Skolnick and produced by Guy Ritchie. Screenplay by Tracy Keenan Wynn, Charlie Fletcher, Chris Baker, and Andrew Day.

The formula is familiar but enjoyable. A group of British tough guys are assembled for an enterprise that combines violence with humor, while cherishing their peculiar personalities and even finding goodness where none should grow. We've had prisoners winning a gardening competition, pot dealers helping little old ladies, and crooks leaving crime for life as real-estate agents. Now here is *Mean Machine*, about a corrupt British soccer champion, jailed for rigging an important match and ordered by the prison governor to coach the inmates' team. The big match will be against the guards' team.

If this premise rings a faint, far-off bell, you may be remembering Robert Aldrich's *The Longest Yard* (1974), with one of Burt Reynolds's best performances, that told the same story, more or less, in terms of American football. Barry Skolnick's *Mean Machine* is more than inspired by *The Longest Yard*; it's based on the same Tracy Keenan Wynn screenplay, and indeed *The Mean Machine* was even the original title of *The Longest Yard*.

The movie stars Vinnie Jones, a real-life footballer so tough he didn't even play for England; he played for Wales. According to the BBC Website, he was known for dirty football, just like Danny Meehan, his character in the film. You may recognize Jones's Fearless Fosdick features from *Lock, Stock and Two Smoking Barrels*, directed by Guy Ritchie, who produced this film. And he has appeared as a fearsome background presence in *Snatch, Gone in 60 Seconds*, and *Swordfish*. In his first lead role, he handles the dialogue like meat and potatoes, one line at a time, chewed carefully.

The deal: The prison governor (David Hemmings) has a gambling problem and is crazy about football. He orders his new celebrity prisoner to coach the team. This does not sit well with the head guard, who coaches the guards' team, but what can he say? Danny doesn't much want to enter the coaching profession, but the governor makes him a threat he can't ignore.

The most enjoyable passages are some of the most predictable, recycled out of countless other movies where a leader has to pick his men. Danny finds himself with the prison contraband retailer, Massive (Vas Blackwood), as his right-hand man, and a violent, feared con named Monk (Jason Statham) as his star player. He gets a lot of valuable prison lore and advice from the ancient convict Doc (David Kelly, whom you will remember from his naked scooter ride in *Waking Ned Devine*). Kelly has had a whole late flowering playing twinkly geezers, clouded only by the distressing tendency of his characters to end up in sentimental death scenes.

All leads up to the big match, which of course involves hard play and dirty tricks, and dovetails neatly with the governor's gambling problem. *Mean Machine* lacks the social satire of *The Longest Yard*, which was a true early 1970s film and therefore antiestablishment. It's interested only in the characters and the game. Guy Ritchie, who started out as such an innovator in *Lock, Stock, etc.*, seems to have headed directly for reliable generic conventions as a producer. But they *are* reliable, and have become conventions for a reason: They work. *Mean Machine* is what it is, and very nicely too.

Memento ★ ★ ★
R, 113 m., 2001

Guy Pearce (Leonard), Carrie-Anne Moss (Natalie), Joe Pantoliano (Teddy), Mark Boone Junior (Burt), Stephen Tobolowsky (Sammy), Jorja Fox (Leonard's Wife), Harriet Harris (Mrs. Jankis). Directed by Christopher Nolan and produced by Jennifer Todd and Suzanne Todd. Screenplay by Christopher Nolan, based on the short story by Jonathan Nolan.

I have here a message from Vasudha Gandhi of Queens Village, New York, about the movie *Memento*:

"Although I loved the film, I don't understand one key plot point. If the last thing the main character remembers is his wife dying, then how does he remember that he has short-term memory loss?"

Michael Cusumano of Philadelphia writes with the same query. They may have identified a hole big enough to drive the entire plot through. Perhaps a neurologist can provide a medical answer, but I prefer to believe that Leonard, the hero of the film, has a condition similar to Tom Hanks's "brain cloud" in *Joe vs. the Volcano*—Leonard suffers from a condition brought on by a screenplay that finds it necessary, and it's unkind of us to inquire too deeply.

Leonard is played by Guy Pearce, in a performance that is curiously moving, considering that by definition it has no emotional arc. He has witnessed the violent death of his wife, and is determined to avenge it. But he has had short-term memory loss ever since the death, and has to make copious notes—he even has memos tattooed to his body in order.

If Leonard keeps forgetting what has already happened, we in the audience suffer from the opposite condition. We begin at the end, and work our way back toward the beginning, because the story is told backward. Well, not exactly; it begins with a brilliant idea, a Polaroid photograph that fades instead of developing, but every individual scene plays with time running forward, and there are some lateral moves and flashbacks that illuminate, or confuse, the issue. Essentially, Leonard is adrift in time and experience, and therefore so are we.

The idea of a narrative told backward was famously used by Harold Pinter in the 1983 film *Betrayal*, based on his play. He told a story of adultery and betrayed friendship, beginning with the sad end and then working his way back through disenchantment to complications to happiness to speculation to innocence. His purpose was the opposite of the strategy used by writer-director Christopher Nolan in *Memento*. Pinter's subject was memory and regret, and the way adulteries often begin playfully and end miserably. There was irony in the way the characters grew happier in each scene, while the audience's knowledge of what was ahead for them deepened.

Nolan's device of telling his story backward, or sort of backward, is simply that—a device. It does not reflect the way Leonard thinks. He

still operates in chronological time, and does not know he is in a time-reversed movie. The film's deep backward and abysm of time is for our entertainment and has nothing to do with his condition. It may actually make the movie too clever for its own good. I've seen it twice. The first time, I thought I'd need a second viewing to understand everything. The second time, I found that greater understanding helped on the plot level, but didn't enrich the viewing experience. Once is right for this movie. Confusion is the state we are intended to be in.

That said, *Memento* is a diabolical and absorbing experience, in which Pearce doggedly plays a low-rent Fugitive who patiently makes maps, jots notes, and explains over and over that he has to talk fast, because in a few minutes he'll start forgetting the conversation. A motel clerk takes advantage of his condition to charge him for two rooms at the same time, and cheerfully admits his fraud, pointing out Leonard will forget it. "Even if you get revenge, you're not going to remember it," he's told at one point, but his reply has a certain logic: "My wife deserves revenge whether or not I remember it."

One striking element of the film is a series of flashbacks to a case Leonard investigated when he worked for an insurance company. This involves a man named Sammy, who appears to have memory loss, although he seems otherwise just like good old Sammy. His wife, a diabetic, can't be sure he isn't faking his condition, and arranges a test I will not reveal. This story has relevance to Leonard's own plight, in an indirect way.

The other major characters are Natalie (Carrie-Anne Moss) and Teddy (Joe Pantoliano). Of Natalie, he has a Polaroid inscribed: "She has also lost someone. She will help you out of pity." Their relationship keeps starting over from the beginning. As for Teddy, his identity and role shifts mysteriously.

The purpose of the movie is not for us to solve the murder of the wife. ("I can't remember to forget you," he says of her.) If we leave the theater not sure exactly what happened, that's fair enough. The movie is more like a poignant exercise in which Leonard's residual code of honor pushes him through a fog of amnesia toward what he feels is his moral duty. The movie doesn't supply the usual payoff of a thriller (how can it?), but it's uncanny in evoking a state of mind. Maybe telling it backward is Nolan's way of forcing us to identify with the hero. Hey, we all just got here.

Men in Black II ★ ½
PG-13, 88 m., 2002

Tommy Lee Jones (Kay), Will Smith (Jay), Rip Torn (Zed), Lara Flynn Boyle (Serleena), Johnny Knoxville (Scrad/Charlie), Rosario Dawson (Laura Vasquez), Tony Shalhoub (Jeebs), Patrick Warburton (Tee), (voice of) Tim Blaney (Frank). Directed by Barry Sonnenfeld and produced by Walter F. Parkes and Laurie MacDonald. Screenplay by Robert Gordon and Barry Fanaro, based on the Malibu Comic by Lowell Cunningham.

Some sequels continue a story. Others repeat it. *Men in Black II* creates a new threat for the MIB, but recycles the same premise, which is that mankind can defeat an alien invasion by assigning agents in Ray-Bans to shoot them into goo. This is a movie that fans of the original might enjoy in a diluted sort of way, but there is no need for it—except, of course, to take another haul at the box office, where the 1997 movie grossed nearly $600 million worldwide.

The astonishing success of the original *MIB* was partly because it was fun, partly because it was unexpected. We'd never seen anything like it, while with *MIB II* we've seen something exactly like it. In the original, Tommy Lee Jones played a no-nonsense veteran agent, Will Smith was his trainee, Rip Torn was their gruff boss, and makeup artist Rick Baker and a team of f/x wizards created a series of fanciful, grotesque aliens. Although the aliens had the technology for interplanetary travel, they were no match for the big guns of the *MIB*.

In *MIB II*, the guns are even bigger and the aliens are even slimier, although they do take sexy human form when one of them, Serleena, morphs into Lara Flynn Boyle. Another one, named Scrad (Johnny Knoxville), turns into a human who has a second neck with a smaller version of the same head, although that is not as amusing as you might hope.

The plot: The aliens are here to capture something, I'm not sure what, that will allow them to destroy Earth. The top MIB agent is now Jay (Smith), who needs the help of Kay (Jones), but Kay's memory has been erased by a "deneuralizer" and must be restored so that he can protect whatever it is the aliens want. Kay is currently working at the post office, which might have inspired more jokes than it does.

Smith and Jones fit comfortably in their roles and do what they can, but the movie doesn't give them much to work with. The biggest contribution is a dog named Frank (voice by Tim Blaney), whose role is much expanded from the first movie. Frank is human in everything but form, a tough-talking streetwise canine who keeps up a running commentary as the reunited MIB chase aliens through New York. One of the eyewitnesses they question is a pizza waitress named Laura, played by the beautiful Rosario Dawson, who Jay likes so much he forgets to deneuralize.

The special effects are good, but often pointless. As the movie throws strange aliens at us, we aren't much moved—more like mildly interested. There's a subway worm at the outset that eats most of a train without being anything more than an obvious special effect (we're looking at the technique, not the worm), and later there are other aliens who look more like doodles at a concept session than anything we can get much worked up about. There is, however, a very odd scene set in a train-station locker, which is occupied by a chanting mob of little creatures who worship the keyholder, and I would have liked to see more of them: What possible worldview do they have? If *Men in Black III* opens with the occupants of the locker, I will at least have hope for it.

Merci Pour le Chocolat ★ ★ ★
NO MPAA RATING, 99 m., 2002

Isabelle Huppert (Mika Muller-Polonski), Jacques Dutronc (André Polonski), Anna Mouglalis (Jeanne Pollet), Rodolphe Pauly (Guillaume Polonski), Brigitte Catillon (Louise Pollet), Michel Robin (Dufreigne), Mathieu Simonet (Axel). Directed by Claude Chabrol and produced by Marin Karmitz. Screenplay by Caroline Eliacheff and Chabrol, based on the

Charlotte Armstrong novel, *The Chocolate Cobweb*.

Isabelle Huppert has the best poker face since Buster Keaton. She faces the camera with detached regard, inviting us to imagine what she is thinking. Since so often the thoughts of her characters run toward crime, revenge, betrayal, lust, and sadism, it is just as well she can seem so passive; an actress who tried to *portray* these inner emotions would inevitably go hurtling over the top and into the next movie.

Consider *Merci Pour le Chocolate,* her new film, directed by her longtime admirer Claude Chabrol. There is hardly any suspense about what she's up to. The title, and the fact that it is a thriller, inspire us to regard the movie's frequent cups of hot chocolate with as much suspicion as the arsenic-laced coffee in Hitchcock's *Notorious.* Even if an early scene hadn't warned us that the chocolate contains a date-rape drug, we'd be wary just because of the dispassionate way Huppert serves it. She doesn't seem like a hostess so much as a clinician.

Huppert plays Mika Muller-Polonski, the first and third wife of the famous pianist André Polonski (tired-eyed Jacques Dutronc). They were married "for a few minutes" many years ago. After their divorce, he remarried, had a son named Guillaume, and then lost his wife in a car crash. She apparently dozed off while they were all visiting . . . Mika.

The movie opens with the remarriage of Mika and André, eighteen years after their first ceremony. The spectators look less than ecstatic. The new family moves into Mika's vast, gloomy Gothic mansion in Lausanne, paid for with the profits from her family's chocolate company. One of the rituals is hot chocolate at bedtime, personally prepared by Mika ("In this house, I serve the chocolate").

An unexpected development. An attractive young piano student, Jeanne Pollet (Anna Mouglalis), finds a clipping in her mother's papers reporting that on the day of her birth, she was briefly switched with Guillaume. Using this as a pretext, she calls on the Polonski family, not because she thinks she is André's daughter, but because she wants, she says, piano lessons. Her arrival causes Guillaume to recede into more of a funk than usual, Mika to greet her with the outward show of friendliness, and André to devote himself with unseemly enthusiasm to her piano lessons.

Curious, isn't it, that Jeanne is a piano virtuoso, and Guillaume has a tin ear? Thought-provoking, too, that Guillaume is not Mika's son, but the son of her husband's second wife, who died so tragically during that visit to . . . Mika's. And interesting that André has taken such an interest in Jeanne. And Mika keeps serving the hot chocolate.

There is no mystery about what Mika is doing with the hot chocolate. The mysteries are: to whom, and why. The motives may differ. She may, indeed, simply be amusing herself. Huppert's bland expression masks her motives to such a degree that even when she *does* smile or frown, we suspect the honesty of the expression: What is she really thinking?

Claude Chabrol is a master of domestic suspense, and he has used Huppert before as a cold-blooded killer, notably in *Violette Nozière* (1978). What is fascinating is how little Huppert has seemed to change in the intervening years. She has worked ceaselessly, usually in good pictures, often with good directors. Filmmakers seem drawn to her because of her mysterious detachment; while many actors seek out the secrets of their characters, Huppert keeps such secrets as she may have discovered, and invites us to figure them out for ourselves.

The appeal of *Merci Pour le Chocolate* is not in the somewhat creaky old poisoning plot, not in the hints of suppressed family secrets, not in the suspense about what will happen next—but in the enigma within which Huppert conceals her character. While all those around her plot, scheme, hope, and fear, she simply looks on and pours the chocolate. What is she thinking? What does she want? Who is she? Her appeal in film after film is maddening, perverse, and seductive.

Metropolis ★ ★ ★

PG-13, 107 m., 2002

With the voices of: Jamieson Price (Duke Red), Yuka Imoto (Tima), Kei Kobayashi (Kenichi), Kouki Okada (Rock), Toshio Furukawa (General), Dave Mallow (Pero), Scott Weinger (Atlas). Directed by Taro Rin and produced by

Yutaka Maseba and Haruyo Kanesaku. Screenplay by Osamu Tezuka and Katsuhiro Otomo, based on Tezuka's comic book. Dubbed into English.

There's something about vast futuristic cities that stirs me. Perhaps they awaken memories of my twelfth year, when I sat in the basement on hot summer days and read through the lower reaches of science-fiction magazines: *Imagination, Other Worlds, Amazing.* On the covers, towering cities were linked by sky-bridges, and buses were cigar-shaped rockets. In the foreground a bug-eyed monster was attacking a screaming heroine in an aluminum brassiere. Even now, the image of a dirigible tethered to the top of the Empire State Building is more thrilling to me than the space shuttle, which is merely real.

Those visions are goofy and yet at the same time exhilarating. What I like about Tokyo is that it looks like a 1940s notion of a future city. I placed *Dark City* first on my list of the best films of 1998, loved *Blade Runner*'s visuals more than its story, liked the taxicabs in the sky in *The Fifth Element.* Now here is *Metropolis,* one of the best animated films I have ever seen, and the city in this movie is not simply a backdrop or a location, but one of those movie places that colonize our memory.

The Japanese anime is named after the 1926 Fritz Lang silent classic, and is based on a 1949 *manga* (comic book) by the late Osamu Tezuka, which incorporated Lang's images. The movie was directed by Taro Rin and written by the anime legend Katsuhiro Otomo, who directed *Akira* and wrote *Roujin Z.* It uses the Lang film as a springboard into a surprisingly thoughtful, ceaselessly exciting sci-fi story about a plot to use humanoids to take over the city. In the romance between Tima, the half-human heroine, and Kenichi, the detective's nephew who falls in love with her, the movie asks whether a machine can love. The answer is an interesting spin on *A.I.* and *Blade Runner,* because the debate goes on within Tima herself, between her human and robotic natures.

The film opens with astonishing visuals of the great city, which, like Lang's Metropolis, exists on several levels above- and below-ground. We see the skyscraping Ziggurat, a complex of towers linked by bridges and braces.

The building seems to be a symbol of progress, but actually masks a scheme by the evil Duke Red to wrest control of the city from elected officials. Deep inside Ziggurat is a throne suspended in a hall filled with giant computer chips; it is intended for Tima, a humanoid in the image of Duke Red's dead daughter, built for him by the insane Dr. Lawton. Tima's role will be to merge the power of computers and the imagination of the human brain into a force that will possess the city.

Rock, the adopted son of Duke Red, hates this plan and wants to destroy Tima. He is jealous that his father prefers this artificial girl to his son, and believes Duke Red himself should sit on the throne. Other characters include an elderly detective who arrives in the city to explore the mystery of Ziggurat; his nephew Kenichi becomes the hero.

The story is told with enormous energy; animation is more versatile than live action in making cataclysmic events comprehensible. Mob scenes at the beginning and explosions and destruction throughout have a clarity and force that live action would necessarily dissipate. The animation owes less to mainstream American animation than to the comic book or *manga* tradition of Japan, where both comics and animation are considered art forms worthy of adult attention.

In the figures of Tima and Kenichi, the movie follows the anime tradition of heroes who are childlike, have enormous eyes, seem innocent and threatened. The other characters have more realistic faces and proportions, and indeed resemble Marvel superheroes (the contrast between these characters' looks is unusual: Imagine Nancy visiting Spider-Man). The backgrounds and action sequences look like the anime version of big-budget Hollywood f/x thrillers.

The music, too, is Western. The introduction to the city is scored with Dixieland, Joe Primrose sings "St. James Infirmary" at one point, and the climactic scene is accompanied by Ray Charles singing "I Can't Stop Loving You" (the effect is a little like "We'll Meet Again" at the end of *Dr. Strangelove*).

The movie is so visually rich I want to see it again to look in the corners and appreciate the details. Like all the best Japanese anime, it pays attention to little things. There is a scene where an old man consults a book of occult lore. He opens it and starts to read. A page flips over. He flips it back in place. Considering that every action in an animated film requires thousands of drawings, a moment like the page flip might seem unnecessary, but all through the movie we get little touches like that. The filmmakers are not content with ordinary locations. Consider the Hotel Coconut, which seems to be a lobby with a desk clerk who checks guests into ancient luxury railway carriages.

Metropolis is not a simpleminded animated cartoon, but a surprisingly thoughtful and challenging adventure that looks into the nature of life and love, the role of workers, the rights (if any) of machines, the pain of a father's rejection, and the fascist zeal that lies behind Ziggurat. This is not a remake of the 1926 classic, but a wild elaboration. If you have never seen a Japanese anime, start here. If you love them, *Metropolis* proves you are right.

Me Without You ★ ★ ★ ½
R, 107 m., 2002

Anna Friel (Marina), Michelle Williams (Holly), Oliver Milburn (Nat), Kyle MacLachlan (Daniel), Trudie Styler (Linda). Directed by Sandra Goldbacher and produced by Finola Dwyer. Screenplay by Goldbacher and Laurence Coriat.

Marina and Holly's childhood friendship evolves into a toxic relationship when they grow up, but they still remain close because even when they're hurting each other, there's no one else they'd rather hurt. Ever had a friend like that? Although Marina is more neurotic and Holly is more the victim, maybe it's because they like it that way. If Holly knew the whole story of how Marina betrays her, she'd be devastated — but then, of course, she doesn't.

Me Without You has a bracing truth that's refreshing after the phoniness of female-bonding pictures like *Divine Secrets of the Ya-Ya Sisterhood*. It doesn't mindlessly celebrate female friendship, but looks at it with a level gaze. If Holly and Marina remain friends despite everything—well, maybe it would be a shame to throw away all that history.

Sandra Goldbacher's film begins in London in 1974 and continues for another twenty years,

paying close attention to changing fashions in clothing, music, and makeup, while not making too big a point of it. We meet Holly (Michelle Williams, from *Dawson's Creek*) and Marina (Anna Friel) as adolescents who seal their friendship by placing treasures in a box and hiding it (there is a law requiring all female friends to perform this ritual in the movies). We meet their parents. Marina has a mother who fancies herself a sexpot and is a little drunk all day long, and a father who is, understandably, distant. Holly comes from a Jewish family that is warm but not especially supportive; she learns from her mother that she is more clever than pretty, and is not clever enough to figure out that she's pretty too.

Marina has a brother named Nat (Oliver Milburn) whom Holly has always been in love with. He is a decent sort, and likes her too, and one night during their hippie party phase he makes love to her, but this is not on Marina's agenda, and she destroys a crucial letter that could have changed everything.

Another rivalry over a male takes place at college, when both women fall for a handsome dweeb American lecturer named Daniel (Kyle MacLachlan). And here the movie does something that few female bonding pictures have the nerve to do, and introduces a fully formed, fascinating male. In a superbly modulated performance by MacLachlan, Daniel comes across as a man who can easily be tempted but not easily secured. He's willing to be seduced but frightened of commitment; his posture is always that of the male prepared to back away and apologize at the slightest offense. He has a highly developed line in chitchat, quoting all the best poets, and Holly is deceived by him while the more cynical Marina strip-mines him and moves on.

What's fascinating about the Daniel character is that he illustrates how men are not always the villains in unfaithful relationships, but sometimes simply the pawns of female agendas. Daniel gives both women what they want, and they want it more than he wants to give it. So although he appears to be a two-timer, he's more of a two-time loser. Rare, to see a character portrayed in this depth instead of simply being used as a plot ploy.

Michelle Williams is the surprise. I am not a student of *Dawson's Creek,* but I know she uses an American accent on it, and here, like Renée Zellweger in *Bridget Jones's Diary*, she crosses the Atlantic, produces a perfectly convincing British accent, and is cuddly and smart both at once. Anna Friel, as Marina, has a tricky role because she is only ostensibly the sexy, world-wise woman, and in fact is closer to her insecure mother. What eats at her is that in the long run Holly is more appealing to men, and it has nothing to do with hair or necklines.

The movie isn't entirely free of clichés (the secret treasure box, dredged up from a pond after decades, of course is still intact). But the screenplay, by Sandra Goldbacher and Laurence Coriat, plays as if the authors have based it on their observations of life, not of movies. There is ultimately a species of happy ending, although you realize it represents maturity and weariness more than victory. The struggles of the teens and twenties are so fraught, so passionate, so seemingly desperate, that when you grow older and learn balance and perspective, there's a bittersweet sense of loss. In years to come Marina and Holly may reflect that they were never happier than when they were making each other miserable.

The Mexican ★ ★ ★
R, 123 m., 2001

Brad Pitt (Jerry Welbach), Julia Roberts (Samantha Barzel), James Gandolfini (Leroy), Bob Balaban (Nayman), J. K. Simmons (Ted), David Krumholtz (Beck), Richard Coca (Car Thief), Michael Cerveris (Frank), Gene Hackman (Margolese). Directed by Gore Verbinski and produced by Lawrence Bender and John Baldecchi. Screenplay by J. H. Wyman.

The Mexican stars Brad Pitt and Julia Roberts, and involves a quirky, offbeat relationship—but it's not between Brad and Julia, it's between Julia and James Gandolfini. I like it that way. Considering how badly Jerry and Samantha, the Brad and Julia characters, get along when they're together, a whole movie involving them would be a long, shrill slog. Gandolfini comes in from left field and provides a character with dimension and surprises, bringing out the best in Roberts. Their dialogue scenes are the best reason to see the movie.

The setup: The Mexican of the title is a priceless handgun that a Mafioso named Margolese (Gene Hackman) desires above all else. Margolese is in prison for complicated reasons, and Jerry, who was sort of responsible, has been trying to work off his debt (and stay alive) by running errands for Margolese's lieutenant, Nayman (Bob Balaban). But Jerry is unreliable because he's under the thumb of the demanding Samantha. His excuse for blowing an important assignment: "When you told me to pick up the thing at the thing, well, Samantha, she wanted the car to pick up some things."

Jerry gets one more chance: Go to Mexico, meet a man in a bar, pick up the handgun, and bring it back to America. Samantha blows her top: Jerry promised to take her to Vegas. Jerry explains that if he does not do the errand, he will be killed. Samantha is unmoved and throws his clothes out the window. Jerry leaves for Mexico. Samantha says she will never speak to him again. She leaves for Vegas, and is kidnapped by Leroy, the Gandolfini character.

That means Jerry and Samantha spend most of the movie apart, and that has drawn complaints from critics who would have preferred these two megastars to share lots of screen time. But Roberts, curiously, hardly ever makes love stories involving people her age. Maybe she has so much wattage all by herself that pairing her with an equivalent dude would blow the fuses. Most of her movies involve older men (Richard Gere in *Pretty Woman*), or unavailable men (Dr. Jekyll and Mr. Hyde in *Mary Reilly*), or unacceptable men *(Runaway Bride)*, or make her the heroine of stories with less significant men *(Erin Brockovich, Notting Hill)*. She hardly ever goes knee-to-knee with a guy she's in love with.

Here Gandolfini (from *The Sopranos*) comes in as Leroy, a big bruiser who kidnaps her for reasons that start out simple and grow increasingly complicated as the plot unfolds. They're both talkers, and soon they're bathing each other in confessions and insights. She talks a lot about Jerry, who is guilty of "blame-shifting," etc., and he nods in sympathy and offers advice at least as sound as she could find in a women's magazine. Then, while they're sitting in a diner, he exchanges a look with a guy sitting at the counter, and she says, "You had a moment there. What was that about?"

And then their psychobabble moves into sublime territory.

These scenes make the movie special. The screenplay, by J. H. Wyman, could have easily been one of those dreary road stories where the guy and the girl head south together on a rendezvous with steamy love scenes and lots of bloody chases. Instead, this movie is *about* something. Not something terrifically profound, to be sure, but at least it prefers style and wit to tired, old ideas.

Wyman and the director, Gore Verbinski, intercut the story with various versions of the legend of the Mexican. The movie goes to sepiatone as we learn why the handgun is so valued and legendary. None of these legends agree, which is part of the fun, and meanwhile the real Mexican in the movie runs rings about Jerry, a character so brain-swoggled by Samantha that he can think of little else.

There are lots of things I like in *The Mexican*. Jerry's idiotic attempts to change English into Spanish by adding an "o" to the end of every word. And the way a supporting character keeps explaining, "I'm just trying to do my portion." And the way Samantha zeroes in on Leroy and sees right through his defenses. And the way the movie is amused by its plot, and keeps a wry distance from it, instead of breathlessly chasing it around the screen.

Pitt and Roberts are good, too—maybe better like this than if they were together. I don't see what purpose it serves to complain they don't have every scene together. Usually when $20 million stars are put into movies, we have to look at them every second so the producers can be sure they're getting their money's worth. *The Mexican* is more like a 1940s Warner Bros. picture where the stars get a breather while the supporting actors entertain us. If it had been a Pitt/Roberts two-hander, there wouldn't have been room for Gandolfini's wonderful character, and that would have been a shame.

Me You Them ★ ★ ★
PG-13, 107 m., 2001

Regina Case (Darlene), Lima Duarte (Osias), Stenio Garcia (Zezinho), Luiz Carlos Vasconcelos (Ciro), Nilda Spencer (Raquel). Directed by Andrucha Waddington and produced by Flavio R. Tambellini, Leonardo M. de Barros, Pedro B. de Hollanda, and Waddington. Screenplay by Elena Soarez.

Me You Them tells the story of a peasant woman who creates a happy home with three men—one a provider, one genial, one lustful—while producing children who hardly resemble their reputed father. The film has inspired the usual analysis in feminist terms, with some critics finding the woman strong and others finding her victimized. I don't think ideology has as much to do with it as poverty. In a poor and dusty backwater of Brazil, this woman and all three men find a pragmatic solution to their problems.

The movie could have been a dumb sex comedy, but cares too much for its characters, and is too intrigued by how this unlikely household came into being. It stars Regina Case, "the Oprah of Brazil," as Darlene, a strong country girl who isn't beautiful, but has an earth-mother energy that men are drawn helplessly toward. She has big teeth, she wipes her hands on her dress, she can work in the fields all day, and if she takes you to her bed, you'll have your work cut out for you.

The film opens with Darlene leaving her provincial town. Three years later she's back from the city, with a baby but no husband. She wants her grandmother to bless the child. But her grandmother is dead, and now she is bereft until Osias (Lima Duarte) offers her a deal: Marry him, and she can move into his house. "Tomorrow I'll give you an answer," she says, and her answer is yes.

Osias is not a prize. He raises goats. As a married man, he assigns Darlene to care for the goats while he swings in his hammock, listening to his portable radio. Soon another child arrives, curiously a good deal darker in hue than Osias. A local colonel may know something about this. And eventually another man drifts into Darlene's life. This is Zezinho (Stenio Garcia), Osias's cousin, who is easygoing, gets along with everybody, helps Darlene with the goats, and seems to sort of move in. Osias rationalizes this as providing a home for his cousin rather than thinking about the sexual implications, even though in due time another baby arrives, this one with blue eyes that Osias didn't supply.

Life continues peacefully, Osias listening to his radio and content to play the husband and father rather than to perform such duties in the flesh. Then down by the river Darlene encounters a sexy young man named Ciro (Luiz Carlos Vasconcelos), and feels passionate lust for the first time. When Ciro turns up at the compound, he doesn't like the arrangements, and wants Darlene to leave with him. Osias is possessive and angry, and it's up to Zezinho to explain the facts of life to him: Either they build another room for Ciro, or Darlene will leave, and then they will be lonely and sad.

Me You Them is "based on a true story," we are told, although movies should follow those words with the disclaimer, "as fictionalized according to our needs." It takes place in a remote Brazilian state of stark landscapes and scarce water, where it is usually autumn and the trees stand sad without their leaves. The director, Andrucha Waddington, has worked with cinematographer Breno Silveira to make this a place of dusty beauty, the reds, browns, and ochres fading into deep shadows. The key to the story is that these people so clearly seem to live here, to depend on this land, to have no place else to go. In a society with more movement and choice, the *Me You Them* household would lack what it has here: necessity.

It has been observed that Darlene essentially needs three men to give her one complete husband. One provides shelter, one provides companionship, one provides sex. This doesn't mean she exploits them; the movie also demonstrates that each man is given the opportunity to provide what is in his nature. That is why the household works. None of these men really wants the role of the other two. Even the jealousy of Osias is based more on pride of possession than pride of paternity; if the children are technically considered his, he is content not to have to rouse himself from his hammock to actually father them.

Me You Them, written by Elena Soarez, works because the story is sympathetic to the feelings of the characters, observes them as individuals, is not concerned with the sensational aspects of their household but in the gradual way practical matters work themselves out. In the end this is not a story about sex but about economics. The characters have probably never heard of Marx, but they find his formula useful: From each, according to his abilities; to each, according to his needs.

A Mighty Wind ★ ★ ½
PG-13, 92 m., 2003

Christopher Guest (Alan Barrows), Michael McKean (Jerry Palter), Fred Willard (Mike LaFontaine), Catherine O'Hara (Mickey), Eugene Levy (Mitch), Bob Balaban (Jonathan Steinbloom), Parker Posey (Sissy Knox), Ed Begley Jr. (Lars), Harry Shearer (Mark Shubb), David Blasucci (Tony Pollono), Laura Harris (Miss Klapper), Michael Hitchcock (Lawrence Turpin), Jane Lynch (Laurie Bohner). Directed by Christopher Guest and produced by Karen Murphy. Screenplay by Guest and Eugene Levy.

If your idea of the ultimate circle of hell is singing along with Burl Ives on "I Know an Old Lady Who Swallowed a Fly"—if even as a child you refused to go "hee haw, hee haw"—then *A Mighty Wind* will awaken old memories. Christopher Guest's new mockumentary is about a reunion of three groups from the 1960s folk boom, and in the film's final concert the audience is indeed required to imitate chickens and horses.

The premise: The beloved folk promoter Irving Steinbloom has passed away, and his son Jonathan (Bob Balaban) wants to stage a concert in his honor at Town Hall, legendary site of so many folk performances. He assembles the relentlessly upbeat New Main Street Singers, the Folksmen (Christopher Guest, Harry Shearer, Michael McKean) and—the stars of the show—the long-estranged Mitch and Mickey (Eugene Levy and Catherine O'Hara).

These acts are all uncannily close to types we vaguely remember from *Hootenanny* and other shows, if we are over forty, and *A Mighty Wind* does for aging folkies what Rob Reiner's *This Is Spinal Tap* did for aging heavy-metal fans. If you ever actually spent money on an album by the Brothers Four, you may feel you vaguely remember some of the songs.

Guest follows the general outlines of the real (and wonderful) documentary *The Weavers: Wasn't That a Time!*, joining his characters in their current lives and then leading them through apprehensions and rehearsals to their big concert. The Folksmen are the most analytical about their comeback ("It wasn't retro then, but it's retro now"), the New Main Street Singers the most inanely cheerful (most of the members weren't born when the original group was formed), and Mitch and Mickey the most fraught with painful old memories and (in Mitch's case) new emotional traumas.

Mitch and Mickey dominate the film, providing a dramatic story that takes on a life of its own. Mitch is played by Levy as a deeply neurotic man who doubts he can still sing or even remember lyrics, and who still has a broken heart because a famous onstage kiss with Mickey did not lead to lasting offstage romance. When he disappears from backstage shortly before show time, we may be reminded of Ringo's solo walk in *A Hard Day's Night.*

Guest surrounds his talent with the usual clueless types he likes to skewer in his films. Fred Willard, hilarious as the color commentator in *Best in Show,* is back playing a promoter and onetime TV star who was famous for five minutes for the catchphrase "Wha' happened?" He laughs at his own jokes to demonstrate to his silent listeners that they are funny. Ed Begley Jr. plays an obtuse public television executive named Lars, whose speech is punctuated by an impenetrable thicket of Yiddish. Bob Balaban, as the dutiful son and impresario, frets over every detail of the performance, and is the singularly ill-at-ease emcee.

A lot of the movie consists of music, much of it written by Guest and other collaborators in the cast, and that is an enjoyment and a problem. The songs actually do capture the quality of the lesser groups of the time. They are performed in uncanny imitations of early TV musical staging. The movie demolishes any number of novelty songs with the Folksmen's version of "Eat at Joe's," based on a faulty neon sign that reads, "E ... A ... O."

But there comes a point when the movie becomes ... well, performances and not comedy. The final act of the movie mostly takes place during the televised concert, and almost against its will takes on the dynamic of a real concert and not a satirical one.

There is another difficulty: Christopher Guest is rather fond of his characters. He didn't hate his targets in *Best in Show* or *Spinal Tap,* but he skewered them mercilessly, while the key characters in *A Mighty Wind,* especially Levy and

O'Hara, take on a certain weight of complexity and realism that edges away from comedy and toward sincere soap opera.

There were many times when I laughed during *A Mighty Wind* (not least at lines like, "the kind of infectious that it's good to spread around"). But the edge is missing from Guest's usual style. Maybe it's because his targets are, after all, so harmless. The deluded *Spinal Tap* and the ferocious dog owners in *Best in Show* want to succeed and prevail. The singers in *A Mighty Wind* are grateful to be remembered, and as we watch them, we cut them the kind of slack we often do for aging comeback acts. Hey, the Beach Boys may be old, fat, and neurotic, but we don't want to spoil the fun by taking their T-Bird away.

Minority Report ★ ★ ★ ★
PG-13, 145 m., 2002

Tom Cruise (John Anderton), Samantha Morton (Agatha [Precog]), Max von Sydow (Lamarr Burgess), Colin Farrell (Danny Witwer), Tim Blake Nelson (Gideon), Steve Harris (Jad), Neal McDonough (Officer Fletcher). Directed by Steven Spielberg and produced by Jan de Bont, Bonnie Curtis, Gerald R. Molen, and Walter F. Parkes. Screenplay by Scott Frank and Jon Cohen, based on a short story by Philip K. Dick.

At a time when movies think they have to choose between action and ideas, Steven Spielberg's *Minority Report* is a triumph—a film that works on our minds and our emotions. It is a thriller and a human story, a movie of ideas that's also a whodunit. Here is a master filmmaker at the top of his form, working with a star, Tom Cruise, who generates complex human feelings even while playing an action hero.

I complained earlier this summer of awkward joins between live action and CGI; I felt the action sequences in *Spider-Man* looked too cartoonish, and that *Star Wars: Episode II,* by using computer effects to separate the human actors from the sets and CGI characters, felt disconnected and sterile. Now here is Spielberg using every trick in the book and matching them without seams, so that no matter how he's achieving his effects, the focus is always on the story and the characters.

The movie turns out to be eerily prescient, using the term "precrime" to describe stopping crimes before they happen; how could Spielberg have known the government would be using the same term in the summer of 2002? In his film, inspired by, but much expanded from, a short story by Philip K. Dick, Tom Cruise is John Anderton, chief of the Department of Precrime in the District of Columbia, where there has not been a murder in six years. Soon, it appears, there will be a murder—committed by Anderton himself.

The year is 2054. Futuristic skyscrapers coexist with the famous Washington monuments and houses from the nineteenth century. Anderton presides over an operation controlling three "precogs," precognitive humans who drift in a flotation tank, their brain waves tapped by computers. They're able to pick up thoughts of premeditated murders and warn the cops, who swoop down and arrest the would-be perpetrators before the killings can take place.

Because this is Washington, any government operation that is high-profile and successful inspires jealousy. Anderton's superior, bureau director Burgess (Max von Sydow), takes pride in him, and shields him from bureaucrats like Danny Witwer (Colin Farrell) from the Justice Department. As the precrime strategy prepares to go national, Witwer seems to have doubts about its wisdom—or he is only jealous of its success?

Spielberg establishes these characters in a dazzling future world, created by art director Alex McDowell, that is so filled with details large and small that we stop trying to figure out everything and surrender with a sigh. Some of the details: a computer interface that floats in midair, manipulated by Cruise with the gestures of a symphony conductor; advertisements that crawl up the sides of walls and address you personally; cars that whisk around town on magnetic cushions; robotic "spiders" that can search a building in minutes by performing a retinal scan on everyone in it. *Blade Runner,* also inspired by a Dick story, shows a future world in decay; *Minority Report* offers a more optimistic preview.

The plot centers on a rare glitch in the visions of the precogs. Although "the precogs are never wrong," we're told, "sometimes . . . they disagree." The dissenting precog is said to have filed a minority report, and in the case of Anderton the report is crucial, because otherwise he seems a certain candidate for arrest as a precriminal. Of course, if you could outsmart the precog system, you would have committed the perfect crime.

Finding himself the hunted instead of the hunter, Anderton teams up with Agatha (Samantha Morton), one of the precogs, who seemed to be trying to warn him of his danger. Because she floats in a fluid tank, Agatha's muscles are weakened (have precogs any rights of their own?), and Anderton has to half-drag her as they flee from the precrime police. One virtuoso sequence shows her foreseeing the immediate future and advising Anderton about what to do to elude what the cops are going to do next. The choreography, timing, and wit of this sequence make it, all by itself, worth the price of admission.

But there are other stunning sequences. Consider a scene where the "spiders" search a rooming house, and Anderton tries to elude capture by immersing himself in a tub of ice water. This sequence begins with an overhead cross section of the apartment building and several of its inhabitants, and you would swear it has to be done with a computer, but no: This is an actual, physical set, and the elegant camera moves were elaborately choreographed. It's typical of Spielberg that, having devised this astonishing sequence, he propels it for dramatic purposes and doesn't simply exploit it to show off his cleverness. And watch the exquisite timing as one of the spiders, on its way out, senses something and pauses in midstep.

Tom Cruise's Anderton is an example of how a star's power can be used to add more dimension to a character than the screenplay might supply. He compels us to worry about him, and even in implausible action sequences (like falls from dizzying heights) he distracts us by making us care about the logic of the chase, not the possibility of the stunt.

Samantha Morton's character ("Agatha" is a nod to Miss Christie) has few words and seems exhausted and frightened most of the time, providing an eerie counterpoint for Anderton's man of action. There is poignance in her helplessness, and Spielberg shows it in a virtuoso two-shot, as she hangs over Anderton's shoulder while their eyes search desperately in opposite directions. This shot has genuine mystery. It has to do with the composition and lighting and timing and breathing, and like the entire movie, it furthers the cold, frightening hostility of the world Anderton finds himself in. The cinematographer, Janusz Kaminski, who has worked with Spielberg before (not least on *Schindler's List*), is able to get an effect that's powerful and yet bafflingly simple.

The plot I will avoid discussing in detail. It is as ingenious as any *film noir* screenplay, and plays far better than some. It's told with such clarity that we're always sure what Spielberg wants us to think, suspect, and know. And although there is a surprise at the end, there is no cheating: The crime story holds water.

American movies are in the midst of a transition period. Some directors place their trust in technology. Spielberg, who is a master of technology, trusts only story and character, and then uses everything else as a workman uses his tools. He makes *Minority Report with* the new technology; other directors seem to be trying to make their movies *from* it. This film is such a virtuoso high-wire act, daring so much, achieving it with such grace and skill. *Minority Report* reminds us why we go to the movies in the first place.   ☞

Monkeybone ★ ½
PG-13, 87 m., 2001

Brendan Fraser (Stu Miley), Bridget Fonda (Julie McElroy), Whoopi Goldberg (Death), Chris Kattan (Organ Donor), David Foley (Herb), Giancarlo Esposito (Hypnos), John Turturro (Monkeybone's Voice), Rose McGowan (Kitty). Directed by Henry Selick and produced by Mark Radcliffe and Michael Barnathan. Screenplay by Sam Hamm.

A character played by Brendan Fraser spends half of *Monkeybone* on life support, and so does the movie. Both try to stay alive with injections of nightmare juice. The movie labors hard, the special effects are admirable, no expense has been spared, and yet the movie never takes off; it's a bright idea the filmmakers were unable to breathe into life.

Fraser plays a cartoonist named Stu Miley ("S. Miley"—ho, ho). He's created a character named Monkeybone, which has become enor-mously popular and might soon star on its own TV show—except that Stu is one of those unsullied artists who shies away from success. He flees a fancy reception with his girlfriend Julie (Bridget Fonda), but as they're driving away a giant plastic Monkeybone toy in the backseat suddenly inflates, causing a crash. Julie is unharmed, but Stu goes into a coma, with his sister negotiating with the hospital about how soon they can pull the plug.

The coma is, in fact, action-packed. In his mind, Stu has taken an escalator to Downtown, a nightmare dreamland nightclub ruled by Hypnos (Giancarlo Esposito); it's not far from Thanatopolis, ruled by Death (Whoopi Goldberg). Here Monkeybone is the emcee, and exit passes are hard to come by. That leads to a scheme by Monkeybone ("I'm tired of being a figment!") to occupy Stu's body and escape from Downtown.

Meanwhile, on Earth, Stu's time is drawing short and his sister has her hand on the plug. Julie scans a brain chart and intuits that Stu is trapped in a "nightmare loop." She thinks maybe an emergency injection of Nightmare Juice might scare him awake. Through a coincidental miracle of timing, Monkeybone leaves Downtown and possesses Stu's body just as the juice hits, so when he comes out of the coma and starts acting strangely, she blames it on the juice.

And so on. The plot is not exactly the issue here. *Monkeybone* was directed by Henry Selick, who also made *The Nightmare Before Christmas* and *James and the Giant Peach.* His ability to blend live action with makeup, special effects, and computer effects is about as good as it gets—and he leans away from computers and in the direction of bizarre sets and makeup and stop-action animation, which gives his work an eerie third-dimensionality unmatched by slicker computer effects.

Here he achieves technical marvels, but the movie just doesn't deliver. The Monkeybone character doesn't earn its screen time; it's just a noxious pest. Brendan Fraser has been at home before in cartoon roles *(George of the Jungle, Dudley Do-Right),* but here he seems more like the victim of the joke than the perpetrator, and Bridget Fonda's girlfriend is earnest and plucky, but not funny (she has to look concerned about Stu all the time).

One sequence made me smile. It involves Chris Kattan, from *Saturday Night Live*, as an organ transplant donor snatched from the hospital in midoperation and lofted over the city by a hot air balloon, while spare parts fall from his incision and are greeted below by grateful dogs.

Downtown itself looks like the amusement park from (or in) hell, and there's a lot of *Beetlejuice* in the inspiration for the strange creatures, one-eyed and otherwise, who live there. But strangeness is not enough. There must also be humor, and characters who exist for some reason other than to look bizarre. That rule would include Whoopi Goldberg's Death, who is sadly underwritten, and played by Whoopi as if we're supposed to keep repeating: "Wow! Look! Death is being played by Whoopi Goldberg!" It is a truth too often forgotten that casting a famous actor in a weird cameo is the setup of the joke, not the punch line.

Monsoon Wedding ★ ★ ★ ½
R, 114 m., 2002

Naseeruddin Shah (Lalit Verma), Lillete Dubey (Pimmi Verma), Shefali Shetty (Ria Verma), Vasundhara Das (Aditi Verma), Parvin Dabas (Hemant Rai), Vijay Raaz (P. K. Dubey), Tilotama Shome (Alice), Rajat Kapoor (Tej Puri), Neha Dubey (Ayesha), Randeep Hooda (Rahul). Directed by Mira Nair and produced by Caroline Baron and Nair. Screenplay by Sabrina Dhawan.

Mira Nair's *Monsoon Wedding* is one of those joyous films that leaps over national boundaries and celebrates universal human nature. It could be the first Indian film to win big at the North American box office; like *Tampopo*, the Japanese noodle-shop romance, or *Crouching Tiger, Hidden Dragon*, which escaped the subtitled martial arts ghetto, it's the kind of film people tell their friends they ought to see.

The movie follows the events in the large Verma family of New Delhi, as their daughter Aditi prepares to marry Hemant, a computer programmer from Houston. He is an "NRI" (nonresident Indian), who has returned to meet the bride selected by his parents for an arranged marriage. Such marriages are an ancient tradition, but these are modern young people, and in the opening scene we see Aditi

in a hurried exchange with her married lover, a TV host. She has agreed to the arranged marriage partly out of impatience with her lover's vague talk about someday divorcing his wife.

As in an Altman film, we plunge into the middle of an event and gradually figure out who everyone is—just as the members of the two families must. The key players are the parents of the bride, Lalit (Naseeruddin Shah) and Pimmi (Lillete Dubey). He worries about the weather, the happiness of his family, his duties as a host, and especially about the cost of everything. In charge of the festivities and apparently overcharging him is the wedding planner, P. K. Dubey (Vijay Raaz), who does not reassure Lalit with his use of such invaluable Indian English expressions as "exactly and approximately."

All of the characters speak English. Also Hindi and, in some cases, Punjabi, sometimes in the same sentence. The effect is delightful. We have the pleasure of seeing a foreign film and the convenience of understanding almost everything that's said. The spontaneous movement between languages, typical of modern middle-class Indians, reflects the mixture of characters: Some are returning from America or Australia and work with computers or on television, while others occupy ancient life patterns. One young family member wants to study creative writing in America, and a relative, no doubt aware of the current boom in English-language best-sellers about India, tells her, "Lots of money in writing."

The wedding creates a certain suspense: What if the bride and groom do not like each other? They sneak off for quiet talks and find that they do like each other—at least, each other's looks and as much as they can learn in a few hours. Meanwhile, subterranean romances surround them. Aditi's pretty cousin Ayesha (Neha Dubey) makes no mystery of her attraction to Rahul (Randeep Hooda), the visitor from Australia; P. K. Dubey is thunderstruck by the beauty of the Verma's family maid, Alice (Tilotama Shome). And there is intrigue of a darker sort as Aditi's cousin observes a family friend who once assaulted her and now may have his eye on a young relative.

I have not even started on the groom's family. You will meet them at the wedding. What strikes you immediately about *Monsoon Wedding* is the quickness of the comedy, the deft way Nair moves between story lines, the brilliant colors of Declan Quinn's cinematography, and the way music is easily woven into the narrative. Nair, whose films include *Salaam Bombay!* and *Mississippi Masala,* says she wanted to make a Bollywood movie in her own way, and she has. "Bollywood" is the term for the Bombay film industry, the world's largest, which produces broad popular entertainments in which the characters are likely to start singing and dancing at any moment, in any context. There is a lot of singing and dancing in *Monsoon Wedding,* but all of it emerges in a logical way from the action, as it might in a Hollywood musical.

There are moments of truth in the romance between Aditi and Hemant, especially when they level with each other about their pasts. But the real heart-tugging moment, the moment audiences will love, is when P. K. Dubey falls to his knees before a heart made of marigolds, in a hopeless gesture of adoration before Alice. A harsher moment of truth comes when Aditi's father, who places loyalty to family above everything, breaks with tradition to do the right thing in a painful situation, no matter what.

The hope for *Monsoon Wedding* is that those who like it will drag their friends into the theater. There's such an unreasonable prejudice in this country against any film that is not exactly like every other film. People cheerfully attend assembly-line junk but are wary of movies that might give them new experiences or take them new places. *Monsoon Wedding,* which won the Golden Lion as the best film at Venice 2001, is the kind of film where you meet characters you have never been within 10,000 miles of, and feel like you know them at once.

Monsters, Inc. ★ ★ ★
G, 86 m., 2001

With the voices of: Billy Crystal (Mike Wazowski), John Goodman ("Sulley" Sullivan), James Coburn (Henry J. Waternoose), Jennifer Tully (Celia), Bonnie Hunt (Flint), Mary Gibbs (Boo), Steve Buscemi (Randall Boggs), Sam "Penguin" Black (George Sanderson). Directed by Peter Docter and produced by Darla K. Anderson.

Screenplay by Dan Gerson and Andrew Stanton. Art direction by Tia W. Kratter and Dominique Louis.

Kids and movie monsters have a lot in common. They feel conspicuous. They stand out in a crowd. They can't make small-talk with grown-ups. They are always stepping on stuff and breaking it. Anything that goes wrong is blamed on them. Now it turns out they share something else. Not only are kids scared of monsters, but according to *Monsters, Inc.,* monsters are scared of kids.

The new animated feature from Pixar reveals that it is true (as every child knows) that there are monsters in the bedroom closet, especially after the lights have been put out. What we did not realize is that the monsters are on assignment. A closet door, which by day leads to a closet, at night leads directly to Monstropolis, the world of monsters, which is powered by Scream Heat. The only reason monsters jump out of closets and scare kids is to collect their screams, which are to Monstropolis as power plants are to the rest of us.

As the movie opens, Monstropolis faces a crisis: Kids are getting too hard to scare, and there's a scream shortage. "Rolling blackouts" are predicted. A complete energy shutdown is a possibility. Responsibility falls on the broad shoulders of a big blue monster named Sulley (voice by John Goodman), who is the leading scream-producer. Sulley looks like a cross between a gorilla and a bear. His best pal, Mike Wazowski (voice by Billy Crystal), is a green eyeball with arms and legs. Sulley is brave and dedicated. Wazowski is phobic, frightened, and malingering. Together they cover the spectrum of work traits. The sexy Celia (voice by Jennifer Tilly) has a crush on Wazowski. What she sees in him is beyond me, although if there is anyone who can figure out how to have sex with a green eyeball, that would be Jennifer Tilly. I can imagine her brassy voice: "Blink! Blink!"

There must be villains, and this time they are Henry J. Waternoose (voice by James Coburn), who looks like a crab crossed with a cartoon of Boss Tweed, and Randall Boggs (voice by Steve Buscemi), a snaky schemer who wants to dethrone Sulley as the champion scream collector. Their competition grows more urgent when a human child named Boo (voice by Mary Gibbs) goes where no human ups has gone before, through the closet door and into the monster world.

Monsters, Inc. follows the two *Toy Story* movies and *A Bug's Life* from Pixar, and once again shows off the studio's remarkable computer-aided animation, which creates an uncanny sense of dimension and movement. Monsters, like toys and bugs, come in every conceivable shape, size, and color, which must have been one of their attractions, and the movie is jolly to look at. And since the monsters are terrified of Boo, whose very name is a rebuke to their lifelong missions, there are screams and chases on both sides of the closet doors. ("There's nothing more toxic or deadly than a human child," Waternoose warns. "A single touch could kill you!")

Speaking of those doors—turns out they're manufactured in Monstropolis, to such exacting specifications that no one ever figures out they didn't come with the house. The most entertaining sequence in the movie is a roller-coaster chase scene involving hundreds of doors on an endless conveyor line that loops the loop at a breakneck speed.

Voice-over dubbing used to be what actors did instead of dinner theater. Now, with the multimillion-dollar grosses of the top animated films, it's a lucrative job that is finally getting the credit it deserves for the artistic skills necessary. Not everyone is a good looper, and stars like Goodman, Crystal, Coburn, Buscemi, and Bonnie Hunt bring a dimension to the film that both borrows from their screen personas and kids them. As for the invaluable Tilly, she has the only voice that has ever made me think simultaneously of Mae West and Slim Pickens.

The animation of Wazowski is interesting because the animators apparently had so little to work with. Instead of an expressive face and a lot of body language, they're given, as one of the leads of the picture—an eyeball. Luckily, the eyeball has an eyelid, or maybe it's a brow, and with this to work with the artists are able to supply him with all the facial expressions a monster would ever need—especially one without a face. It's a tour de force.

Monsters, Inc. is cheerful, high-energy fun, and like the other Pixar movies has a running supply of gags and references aimed at grown-ups (I liked the restaurant named Harryhausen's, after the animation pioneer). I also enjoyed the sly way that the monster world mirrors our own, right down to production quotas and sales slogans. "We Scare," they assure us, "Because We Care."

Monster's Ball ★ ★ ★ ★
R, 111 m., 2002

Billy Bob Thornton (Hank Grotowski), Halle Berry (Leticia Musgrove), Heath Ledger (Sonny Grotowski), Peter Boyle (Buck Grotowski), Sean "Puffy" Combs (Lawrence Musgrove), Coronji Calhoun (Tyrell Musgrove). Directed by Marc Forster and produced by Lee Daniels. Screenplay by Milo Addica and Will Rokos.

Monster's Ball is about a black woman and a white man who find, for a time anyway, solace in each other for their pain. But their pain remains separate and so do they; this is not a message movie about interracial relationships, but the specific story of two desperate people whose lives are shaken by violent deaths, and how in the days right after that they turn to each other because there is no place else to turn. The movie has the complexity of great fiction, and requires our empathy as we interpret the decisions that are made—especially at the end, when the movie avoids an obligatory scene that would have been conventional and forces us to cut straight to the point.

Billy Bob Thornton and Halle Berry star as Hank and Leticia, in two performances that are so powerful because they observe the specific natures of these two characters and avoid the pitfalls of racial clichés. What a shock to find these two characters freed from the conventions of political correctness and allowed to be who they are: weak, flawed, needful, with good hearts tested by lifetimes of compromise. They live in a small Georgia town, circa 1990. She works the night shift in a diner, has a fat little son, and an ex-husband on Death Row. He works as a guard on Death Row, has a mean, racist father and a browbeaten son, and will be involved in her husband's execution. ("Monster's Ball" is an old English term for a condemned man's last night on Earth.)

At first Hank and Leticia do not realize the connection they have through the condemned man. For another movie that would be enough plot. We can imagine the scenes of discovery and revelation. How this movie handles that disclosure is one of its great strengths: how both characters deal with it (or don't deal with it) internally, so that the movie blessedly proceeds according to exactly who they are, what they need, what they must do, and the choices open to them.

The screenplay by Milo Addica and Will Rokos is subtle and observant; one is reminded of short fiction by Andre Dubus, William Trevor, Eudora Welty, Raymond Carver. It specifically does not tell "their" story, but focuses on two separate lives. The characters are given equal weight and have individual story arcs, which do not intersect but simply, inevitably, meet. There is an overlay of racism in the story; Hank's father, Buck (Peter Boyle), is a hateful racist, and Hank mirrors his attitudes. But the movie is not about redemption, not about how Hank overcomes his attitudes, but about how they fall away from him like a dead skin because his other feelings are so much more urgent. The movie, then, is not about overcoming prejudice, but sidestepping it because it comes to seem monstrously irrelevant.

Hank is an abused son and an abusive father. His old man, Buck, confined to a wheelchair and a stroller, still exercises an iron will over the family. All three generations live under his roof, and when Hank's son, Sonny (Heath Ledger), opts out of the family sickness, Buck's judgment is cruel: "He was weak." We do not learn much about Leticia's parents, but she is a bad mother, alternately smothering her son, Tyrell (Coronji Calhoun), with love, and screaming at him that he's a "fat little piggy." She drinks too much, has been served with an eviction notice, sees herself as a loser. She has no affection at all for Tyrell's father, Lawrence (Puffy Combs), on Death Row, and makes it clear during a visitation that she is there strictly for her son. There is no side story to paint Lawrence as a victim; "I'm a bad man," he tells Tyrell. "You're the best of me."

Leticia is all messed up. She sustains a loss that derails her, and it happens by coincidence that Hank is there when he can perform a service. This makes them visible to each other. It is safe to say that no one else in the community is visible, in terms of human need, to either one. Hank's shy, slow courtship is so tentative it's like he's sleepwalking toward her. Her response is dictated by the fact that she has nowhere else to turn. They have a key conversation in which the bodies of both characters are tilted away from each other, as if fearful of being any closer. And notice another conversation, when she's been drinking, and she waves her hands and one hand keeps falling on Hank's lap; she doesn't seem to notice and, here is the point, he doesn't seem willing to.

Their intimate scenes are ordinary and simple, a contrast to Hank's cold, mercenary arrangement with a local hooker. The film's only flaw is the way Marc Forster allows his camera to linger on Halle Berry's half-clothed beauty; this story is not about sex appeal, and if the camera sees her that way we are pretty sure that Hank doesn't. What he sees, what she sees, is defined not by desire but by need.

Students of screenwriting should study the way the film handles the crucial passages at the end, when she discovers some drawings and understands their meaning. Here is where a lesser movie would have supplied an obligatory confrontation. Leticia never mentions the drawings to Hank. Why not? Because it is time to move on? Because she understands why he withheld information? Because she has no alternative? Because she senses that the drawings would not exist if the artist hated his subject? Because she is too tired and this is just one more nail on the cross? Because she forgives? What?

The movie cannot say. The characters have disappeared into the mysteries of the heart. *Monster's Ball* demonstrates that to explain all its mysteries, a movie would have to limit itself to mysteries that can be explained. As for myself, as Leticia rejoined Hank in the last shot of the movie, I was thinking about her as deeply and urgently as about any movie character I can remember.

Moonlight Mile ★ ★ ★
PG-13, 112 m., 2002

Jake Gyllenhaal (Joe Nast), Dustin Hoffman (Ben Floss), Susan Sarandon (JoJo Floss), Holly Hunter (Mona Camp), Ellen Pompeo (Bertie Knox), Dabney Coleman (Mike Mulcahey). Directed by Brad Silberling and produced by

Mark Johnson and Silberling. Screenplay by
Silberling.

After the funeral is over, and the mourners have
come back to the house for coffee and cake and
have all gone home, the parents and the
boyfriend of Diana, the dead girl, sit by themselves. Her mother criticizes how one friend expressed her sympathy. And the father asks, what
could she say? "Put yourself in their shoes."

That little scene provides a key to Brad Silberling's *Moonlight Mile.* What do you say when
someone dies—someone you cared for? What
are the right words? And what's the right thing
to do? Death is the ultimate rebuke to good
manners. The movie, which makes an unusually intense effort to deal with the process of
grief and renewal, is inspired by a loss in Silberling's own life. The TV actress Rebecca
Schaeffer, his girlfriend at the time, was killed in
1989 by a fan. Silberling has grown very close to
her parents in the years since then, he told me,
and more than a decade later he has tried to use
the experience as the starting point for a film.

Moonlight Mile, which takes place in 1973,
opens in an elliptical way. At first only quiet
clues in the dialogue allow us to understand
that someone has died. We meet Joe Nast (Jake
Gyllenhaal), the fiancé of the dead girl, and her
parents, Ben and JoJo Floss (Dustin Hoffman
and Susan Sarandon). They talk not in a sentimental way, but in that strange, detached tone
we use when grief is too painful to express and
yet something must be said.

After the funeral and the home visitation,
the film follows what in a lesser film would be
called the "healing process." *Moonlight Mile* is
too quirky and observant to be described in
psychobabble. Joe stays stuck in the Floss house,
living in an upstairs bedroom, his plans on
hold. Ben, who has lost a daughter, now in a
confused way hopes to gain a son, and encourages Joe to join him in his business as a real estate developer. JoJo, protected by intelligence
and wit, looks closely and suspects a secret Joe
is keeping, which leaves him stranded between
the past and future.

Gyllenhaal, who in person is a jokester, in the
movies almost always plays characters who are
withdrawn and morose. Remember him in
Donnie Darko, The Good Girl, and *Lovely and
Amazing.* Here, too, he is a young man with

troubled thoughts. At the post office, and again
at a bar where she has a night job, he meets
Bertie Knox (Ellen Pompeo), who sees inside
when others only look at the surface. They
begin to talk. She has a loss too: Her boyfriend
has been missing in action in Vietnam for three
years. While it is possible that they will mend
each other's hearts by falling in love, the movie
doesn't simplemindedly pursue that plot path,
but meanders among the thoughts of the living.

Silberling's screenplay pays full attention to
all of the characters. Ben and JoJo are not simply a backdrop to a romance involving Joe and
Bertie. The movie provides key scenes for all of
the characters, in conversation and in monologue, so that it is not only about Joe's grieving
process but about all four, who have lost
different things in different ways.

Anyone regarding the Hoffman character
will note that his name is Benjamin and remember Hoffman's most famous character, in
The Graduate. But Joe is the Benjamin of this
film, and Hoffman's older man has more in
common with another of his famous roles:
Willy Loman, the hero of *Death of a Salesman.*
Ben occupies a low-rent storefront office on
Main Street in Cape Anne, Massachusetts, but
dreams of putting together a group of properties and bringing in a superstore like K-Mart.
This will be his big killing, the deal that caps
his career, even though we can see in the eyes
of the local rich man (Dabney Coleman) that
Ben is too small to land this fish. Ben's desire
to share his dream with his surrogate son Joe
also has echoes from the Arthur Miller
tragedy.

Sarandon's JoJo is tart, with a verbal wit to
protect her and a jaundiced view of her husband's prospects. The deepest conversation JoJo
has with Joe ("Isn't it funny, that we have the
same name?") is about as well done as such a
scene can be. She intuits that Joe is dealing not
only with the loss of Diana's life, but with the
loss of something else.

Ellen Pompeo, a newcomer, plays Bertie with
a kind of scary charisma that cannot be written, only felt. She knows she is attractive to Joe.
She knows she likes him. She knows she is faithful to her old boyfriend. She is frightened by
her own power to attract, especially since she
wants to attract even while she tells herself she
doesn't. She is so vulnerable in this movie, so

sweet, as she senses Joe's pain and wants to help him.

Holly Hunter is the fifth major player, as the lawyer who is handling the case against Diana's killer. She embodies the wisdom of the law, which knows, as laymen do not, that it moves with its own logic regardless of the feelings of those in the courtroom. She offers practical advice, and then you can see in her eyes that she wishes she could offer emotional advice instead.

Moonlight Mile gives itself the freedom to feel contradictory things. It is sentimental but feels free to offend, is analytical and then surrenders to the illogic of its characters, is about grief and yet permits laughter. Everyone who has grieved for a loved one will recognize the moment, some days after the death, when an irreverent remark will release the surprise of laughter. Sometimes we laugh that we may not cry. Not many movies know that truth. *Moonlight Mile* is based on it.

Morvern Callar ★ ★ ★ ½
NO MPAA RATING, 97 m., 2002

Samantha Morton (Morvern Callar), Kathleen McDermott (Lanna), Raife Patrick Burchell (Boy in Room 1022), Dan Cadan (Dazzer), Carolyn Calder (Sheila Tequila), Jim Wilson (Tom Boddington), Dolly Wells (Susan), Ruby Milton (Couris Jean). Directed by Lynne Ramsay and produced by George Faber, Charles Pattinson, and Robyn Slovo. Screenplay by Liana Dognini and Ramsay, based on the novel by Alan Warner.

In the opening scene of *Morvern Callar*, a young woman awakens next to the body of her boyfriend, who has committed suicide during the night. Lights blink on their Christmas tree. His blood is all over the floor. His presents for her are still wrapped and under the tree. On his computer he has left a suicide note ("It just seemed like the right thing to do"), instructions on how to withdraw money from his account, and the manuscript of a novel that he wants her to submit to a list of publishers.

Morvern reads the note, opens the presents (she likes the leather jacket), and walks out into the winter gloom of Glasgow. She stands for a long time on a train platform until a pay phone rings. She listens to the stranger on the other end of the line and finally says, "I'm sure he'll be all right." That night, she dresses sexy and meets her best friend, Lanna, for a night at the pub that ends with drunken, confused sex with strangers. The boyfriend's body remains on the floor.

Morvern is played by Samantha Morton, who, like Isabelle Huppert, has a face that can convey enormous emotions without visibly changing. Because she reveals so little, we are drawn into her, fascinated, trying to read her thoughts. You may remember Morton as the musician's deaf-mute girlfriend in Woody Allen's *Sweet and Lowdown*, or as the pale, limp "pre-cog" in Spielberg's *Minority Report*. Here she is a working-class girl, prisoner of a thankless job in a supermarket, whose boyfriend is better educated and more successful.

One of the mysteries of the early stages of *Morvern Callar* is Morvern's behavior after finding the body. She cries, inwardly and privately, but such is her aura that we don't know if she's crying for him or for herself. He left money for a funeral, but after several days, when she can ignore the body no longer, she cuts it up and throws it away. There is a close-up of the computer screen as she deletes his name on the title page of the novel and types in her own. Is she heartless, crazy, or what?

I think the answer is right there in the film, but less visible to American viewers because we are less class-conscious than the filmmakers (the director, Lynne Ramsay, is the daughter of a bartender; Samantha Morton is a survivor of foster homes).

Consider. Morvern lives in her boyfriend's fairly expensive and comfortable Glasgow flat, but still works at the supermarket. If they were truly a couple with a future and had been together for some time, isn't it reasonable to expect that she would no longer be holding onto that job? My guess is that their relationship began fairly recently, based on sex between incompatibles and fueled by a lot of drinking, and that by killing himself he has, from her point of view, shown how unimportant she was to him and how lightly he took their relationship and his life. (When a young person who is not dying or in unbearable crisis commits suicide, it is often an act of selfish, unforgivable egotism.)

By signing her name to his novel, Morvern is sending a message beyond the grave: "I will not clean up this mess and finish your life for you." She will begin to live her own. Unfortunately, she has few resources. She lacks even her friend Lanna's gift for silly, aimless hedonism. After she actually sells the novel, she uses the publisher's check to buy them both a package holiday in Spain, where Lanna is skilled at drinking, partying, and getting laid, but Morvern is a ghost at the feast, a silent, inward person who looks not so much sad as disengaged.

Her style is passive-aggressive. She withholds herself, is not quite present. She sits at times alone and silent, and we feel she is not alone with her thoughts, but only with her feelings. There is the sense that she broods about hurt. We have little idea what her early life was like, but when we learn that Samantha Morton never talks about her own foster childhood, we are bold enough to wonder if the sense-memories she draws upon for the performance have converted her early years into Morvern's.

The movie doesn't have a plot in the conventional sense, and could not support one. People like Morvern Callar do not lead lives that lend themselves to beginnings, middles, and ends. She is on hold. Somehow, in some way, she's stuck in neutral. The gray-brown tones of her life in Glasgow reflect her emotional habitat, and the bright colors of Spain cause her to wince in pain. She can only handle so much incoming experience at a time. "Sorry, Morvern," her boyfriend wrote in that note. "Don't try to understand." What a bloody condescending jerk. Yet she is not drifting because of his death. She drifts anyway, and always has. What great wrong has made her so damaged? We watch Samantha Morton so closely, with such fascination, because she is able to embody a universe of wounded privacy.

This is Lynne Ramsay's second film, after *Ratcatcher* (1999). That one was about a small boy living with the guilt of a terrible act. Her short films include one in which two small girls, half-sisters, try to understand the wreckage of the marriages that created them. She has been signed to direct the film of Alice Sebold's best-seller *The Lovely Bones*, narrated by the ghostly voice of a young girl who has been raped and murdered. These stories all seem to explore similar dread lifescapes. Why she knows it so well we cannot guess, but she does.

The Mothman Prophecies ★ ★
PG-13, 119 m., 2002

Richard Gere (John Klein), Laura Linney (Sergeant Connie Parker), Will Patton (Gordon), Debra Messing (Mary Klein), Shane Callahan (Nat Griffin), Alan Bates (Alexander Leek), Nesbitt Blaisdell (Chief Josh Jarrett). Directed by Mark Pellington and produced by Gary W. Goldstein, Gary Lucchesi, and Tom Rosenberg. Screenplay by Richard Hatem, based on the novel by John A. Keel.

The Mothman Prophecies claims to be based on a true story, which sent me racing to the Web for a little research. And, yes, there is a belief among the folks in Point Pleasant, West Virginia, that a mothlike creature with red eyes can occasionally be glimpsed in the area. Some say he is a spirit evoked by a long-dead Indian chief. Others blame him for a deadly bridge collapse.

John A. Keel has written a book about Mothman, and now here is this movie. The "true story" part involves the possible existence of Mothman; the human characters are, I believe, based not on facts but on an ancient tradition in horror movies, in which attractive people have unspeakable experiences.

Richard Gere stars as a *Washington Post* reporter named John Klein, who is so happily married (to Debra Messing) that when they agree to buy a new house, they decide to test the floor of a closet for lovemaking purposes, to the surprise of the real-estate agent who walks in on them. If there's one thing you demand in a real-estate agent, it's the good judgment to leave a closet door closed when he hears the unmistakable sounds of coitus coming from behind it. Furthermore: Richard Gere is fifty-three. He's in great shape, but to make love at fifty-three on the floor of a closet with a real-estate agent lurking about is, I submit, not based on a true story.

Then Klein and his wife are in a crash. "You didn't see it, did you?" she asks, and before she dies she draws a picture of a mothlike creature she saw flattened against the windshield. Unlike most windshield bugs, this creature has many forms and lives, as Klein discovers when his life takes a turn into the twilight zone. Driving, as he thinks, to Virginia, he ends up hundreds of miles away in West Virginia, and when he knocks on a door for help the frightened householder accuses Klein of having harassed him for three nights in a row.

Laura Linney plays Connie Parker, a local cop. She trusts Klein, and together they get involved in a strange series of events that culminate in a bridge collapse and a dramatic rescue of the sort that is always particularly annoying to me, because it displaces the focus of the movie. Is this a movie about the Mothman, or about a daring rescue after a bridge collapse? And since the Mothman presumably still exists, how does the happy end after the bridge collapse really settle the story? It's lazy for a movie to avoid solving one problem by trying to distract us with the solution to another.

The director is Mark Pellington (*Arlington Road*), whose command of camera, pacing, and the overall effect is so good it deserves a better screenplay. The Mothman is singularly ineffective as a threat because it is only vaguely glimpsed, has no nature we can understand, doesn't operate under rules that the story can focus on, and seems to be involved in space-time shifts far beyond its presumed focus. There is also the problem that insects make unsatisfactory villains unless they are very big.

Richard Gere and Laura Linney have some nice scenes together. I like the way he takes a beat of indecision before propelling himself into an action. This is Linney's first movie since *You Can Count on Me,* which won her an Oscar nomination. I saw it again recently and was astonished by her performance. The melancholy lesson seems to be, if you make a small independent movie for very little money and are wonderful in it, you can look forward to being paid a lot of money to appear in a big-budget production in which the talent that got you there is scarcely required.

Moulin Rouge ★ ★ ★ ½
PG-13, 126 m., 2001

Nicole Kidman (Satine), Ewan McGregor (Christian), John Leguizamo (Toulouse-Lautrec), Jim Broadbent (Zidler), Richard Roxburgh (Duke of Monroth), Kylie Minogue (The Green Fairy), Christine Anu (Arabia), Natalie Jackson Mendoza (China Doll). Directed by Baz Luhrmann and produced by Fred Baron, Martin Brown, and Luhrmann. Screenplay by Luhrmann and Craig Pearce.

Like almost every American college boy who ever took a cut-rate flight to Paris, I went to the Moulin Rouge on my first night in town. I had a cheap standing-room ticket way in the back, and over the heads of the crowd, through a haze of smoke, I could vaguely see the dancing girls. The tragedy of the Moulin Rouge is that by the time you can afford a better seat, you've outgrown the show.

Moulin Rouge the movie is more like the Moulin Rouge of my adolescent fantasies than the real Moulin Rouge ever could be. It isn't about tired, decadent people, but about glorious romantics who believe in the glitz and the tinsel—who see the nightclub not as a shabby tourist trap but as a stage for their dreams. Even its villain is a love-struck duke who gnashes his way into the fantasy, content to play a starring role, however venal.

The film is constructed like the fevered snapshots created by your imagination before an anticipated erotic encounter. It doesn't depend on dialogue or situation but on the way you imagine a fantasy object first from one angle and then another. Satine, the heroine, is seen not so much in dramatic situations as in poses—in postcards for the yearning mind. The movie is about how we imagine its world. It is perfectly appropriate that it was filmed on sound stages in Australia; Paris has always existed best in the minds of its admirers.

The film stars Nicole Kidman as Satine, a star dancer who has a deadly secret; she is dying of tuberculosis. This is not a secret from the audience, which learns it early on, but from Christian (Ewan McGregor), the would-be writer who loves her. Toulouse-Lautrec (John Leguizamo), the dwarf artist, lives above Christian, and one day comes crashing through the ceiling of their flimsy tenement, sparking a friendship and collaboration: They will write a show to spotlight Satine's brilliance, as well as "truth, beauty, freedom, and love." (I was reminded of Gene Kelly and Donald O'Connor's motto in *Singin' in the Rain*: "Dignity. Always dignity.") The show must be financed; enter the venal Duke of Monroth (Richard Rox-burgh), who wants to pay for the show and for Satine's favors. The ringmaster is Zidler (Jim Broadbent), impresario of the Moulin Rouge.

All of these characters are seen in terms of their own fantasies about themselves. Toulouse-Lautrec, for example, is flamboyant and roman-tic; Christian is lonely and lovelorn; Satine has a good heart and only seems to be a bad girl; Zidler pretends to be all business but is a softy; and the duke can be so easily duped because being duped is the essence of his role in life. Those who think they can buy affection are suckers; a wise man is content to rent it.

The movie has been directed by Baz Luhr-mann, an Australian with a background in opera, whose two previous films were also ex-periments in exuberant excess. *Strictly Ball-room* made a ballroom competition into a flamboyant theatrical exercise, and his *William Shakespeare's Romeo + Juliet* updated the play into a contempo teenage rumble. He con-structs *Moulin Rouge* with the melodrama of a nineteenth-century opera, the Technicolor brashness of a 1950s Hollywood musical, and the quick-cutting frenzy of a music video. Nothing is really "period" about the movie—it's like a costume revue taking place right now, with hit songs from the 1970s and 1980s (you will get the idea if I mention that Jim Broadbent sings "Like a Virgin").

I am often impatient with directors who use so many cuts that their films seem to have been fed through electric fans. For Luhrmann and this material, it is the right approach. He uses so many different setups and camera angles that some of the songs seem to be cut not on every word of the lyrics, but on every syllable. There's no breathing room. The whole movie is on the same manic pitch as O'Con-nor's "Make 'Em Laugh" number in *Singin' in the Rain*. Everything is screwed to a breakneck pitch, as if the characters have died and their lives are flashing before our eyes.

This means the actors do not create their characters but embody them. Who is Satine? A leggy redhead who can look like a million in a nightclub costume, and then melt into a guy's arms. Who is Christian? A man who embodies longing with his eyes and sighs—whose very essence, whose entire being, is composed of need for Satine. With the duke, one is reminded

of silent films in which the titles said "The Duke," and then he sneered at you.

The movie is all color and music, sound and motion, kinetic energy, broad strokes, op-eratic excess. While it might be most conve-nient to see it from the beginning, it hardly makes any difference; walk in at any moment and you'll quickly know who is good and bad, who is in love and why—and then all the rest is song, dance, spectacular production num-bers, protestations of love, exhalations of regret, vows of revenge, and grand destructive ges-tures. It's like being trapped on an elevator with the circus.

Mr. Deeds ★ ½
PG-13, 96 m., 2002

Adam Sandler (Longfellow Deeds), Winona Ryder (Babe Bennett), John Turturro (Emilio), Steve Buscemi (Crazy Eyes), Jared Harris (Mac), Peter Gallagher (Chuck Cedar), Allen Covert (Marty), Conchata Ferrell (Jan), Roark Critchlow (William). Directed by Steven Brill and produced by Sidney Ganis and Jack Giarraputo. Screenplay by Tim Herlihy.

At one point during the long ordeal of *Mr. Deeds*, it is said of the Adam Sandler character, "He doesn't share our sense of ironic detach-ment." Is this a private joke by the writer? If there's one thing Sandler's Mr. Deeds has, it's ironic detachment. Like so many Sandler characters, he seems fundamentally insincere, to be aiming for the laugh even at serious mo-ments. Since the 1936 Frank Capra film *Mr. Deeds Goes to Town* was above all sincere, we wonder how this project was chosen; did Adam Sandler look at Gary Cooper and see a role for himself?

He plays Longfellow Deeds, pizzeria owner in the hamlet of Mandrake Falls, New Hamp-shire. The pizzeria is one of those establish-ments required in all comedies about small towns, where every single character in town gathers every single day to provide an audience for the hero, crossed with a Greek chorus. No-body does anything in Mandrake Falls except sit in the pizzeria and talk about Deeds. When he leaves town, they watch him on the TV.

Turns out Deeds is the distant relative of an elderly zillionaire who freezes to death in the very act of conquering Everest. Control of his media empire and a $40 billion fortune goes to Deeds, who is obviously too good-hearted and simpleminded to deserve it, so a corporate executive named Cedar (Peter Gallagher) conspires to push him aside. Meanwhile, when Deeds hits New York, a trash TV show makes him its favorite target, and producer Babe Bennett (Winona Ryder) goes undercover, convinces Deeds she loves him, and sets him up for humiliation. Then she discovers she loves him, too late.

Frank Capra played this story straight. But the 2002 film doesn't really believe in it, and breaks the mood with absurdly inappropriate "comedy" scenes. Consider a scene where Deeds meets his new butler Emilio (John Turturro). Emilio has a foot fetish. Deeds doubts Emilio will like his right foot, which is pitch black after a childhood bout of frostbite. The foot has no feeling, Deeds says, inviting Emilio to pound it with a fireplace poker. When Deeds doesn't flinch, Turturro actually punctures the foot with the point of the poker, at which point I listened attentively for sounds of laughter in the theater and heard none.

There's no chemistry between Deeds and Babe, but then how could there be, considering that their characters have no existence except as the puppets in scenes of plot manipulation. After Deeds grows disillusioned with her, there is a reconciliation inspired after she falls through the ice on a pond and he breaks through to save her using the black foot. In story conferences, do they discuss scenes like this and nod approvingly? Tell me, for I want to know.

The moral center of the story is curious. The media empire, we learn, controls enormous resources and employs 50,000 people. The evil Cedar wants to break it up. The good-hearted Deeds fights to keep it together so those 50,000 people won't be out of work. This is essentially a movie that wants to win our hearts with a populist hero who risks his entire fortune in order to ensure the survival of Time-AOL-Warner-Disney-Murdoch. What would Frank Capra have thought about the little guy bravely standing up for the monolith?

Of the many notes I took during the film, one deserves to be shared with you. There is a scene in the movie where Deeds, the fire chief in Mandrake Falls, becomes a hero during a

Manhattan fire. He scales the side of a building and rescues a woman's cats, since she refuses to be rescued before them. One after another, the cats are thrown onto a fireman's net. Finally there is a cat that is on fire. The blazing feline is tossed from the window and bounces into a bucket of water, emerging wet but intact, ho, ho, and then Deeds and the heavy-set cat lady jump together and crash through the net, but Deeds's fall is cushioned by the fat lady, who is also not harmed, ho, ho, giving us a heartrending happy ending.

That is not what I wrote in my notes. It is only the setup. What I noted was that in the woman's kitchen, nothing is seen to be on fire except for a box of Special K cereal. This is a species of product placement previously unthinkable. In product placement conferences, do they discuss scenes like this and nod approvingly? Tell me, for oh, how I want to know.

Mulholland Dr. ★ ★ ★ ★
R, 146 m., 2001

Justin Theroux (Adam Kesher), Naomi Watts (Betty Elms), Laura Elena Harring (Rita), Ann Miller (Coco Lenoix), Dan Hedaya (Vincenzo Castigliani), Mark Pellegrino (Joe), Brian Beacock (Studio Singer), Robert Forster (Detective Harry McKnight), Michael J. Anderson (Mr. Roque). Directed by David Lynch and produced by Neal Edelstein, Joyce Eliason, Tony Krantz, Michael Polaire, Alain Sarde, and Mary Sweeney. Screenplay by Lynch.

David Lynch has been working toward *Mulholland Dr.* all of his career, and now that he's arrived there I forgive him *Wild at Heart* and even *Lost Highway*. At last his experiment doesn't shatter the test tubes. The movie is a surrealist dreamscape in the form of a Hollywood *film noir*, and the less sense it makes, the more we can't stop watching it.

It tells the story of . . . well, there's no way to finish that sentence. There are two characters named Betty and Rita whom the movie follows through mysterious plot loops, but by the end of the film we aren't even sure they're different characters, and Rita (an amnesiac who lifted the name from a *Gilda* poster) wonders if she's really Diane Selwyn, a name from a waitress's name tag.

Betty (Naomi Watts) is a perky blonde, Sandra Dee crossed with a Hitchcock heroine, who has arrived in town to stay in her absent Aunt Ruth's apartment and audition for the movies. Rita (Laura Elena Harring) is a voluptuous brunette who is about to be murdered when her limousine is front-ended by drag racers. She crawls out of the wreckage on Mulholland Drive, stumbles down the hill, and is taking a shower in the aunt's apartment when Betty arrives.

She doesn't remember anything, even her name. Betty decides to help her. As they try to piece her life back together, the movie introduces other characters. A movie director (Justin Theroux) is told to cast an actress in his movie or be murdered; a dwarf in a wheelchair (Michael J. Anderson) gives instructions by cell phone; two detectives turn up, speak standard TV cop show dialogue, and disappear; a landlady (Ann Miller—yes, Ann Miller) wonders who the other girl is in Aunt Ruth's apartment; Betty auditions; the two girls climb in through a bedroom window, Nancy Drew style; a rotting corpse materializes; and Betty and Rita have two lesbian love scenes so sexy you'd swear this was a 1970s movie, made when movie audiences liked sex. One of the scenes also contains the funniest example of pure logic in the history of sex scenes.

Having told you all of that, I've basically explained nothing. The movie is hypnotic; we're drawn along as if one thing leads to another—but nothing leads anywhere, and that's even before the characters start to fracture and recombine like flesh caught in a kaleidoscope. *Mulholland Dr.* isn't like *Memento,* where if you watch it closely enough you can hope to explain the mystery. There is no explanation. There may not even be a mystery.

There have been countless dream sequences in the movies, almost all of them conceived with Freudian literalism to show the characters having nightmares about the plot. *Mulholland Dr.* is all dream. There is nothing that is intended to be a waking moment. Like real dreams, it does not explain, does not complete its sequences, lingers over what it finds fascinating, dismisses unpromising plotlines. If you want an explanation for the last half-hour of the film, think of it as the dreamer rising slowly to consciousness as threads from the dream fight for space with recent memories from real life, and with fragments of other dreams—old ones and those still in development.

This works because Lynch is absolutely uncompromising. He takes what was frustrating in some of his earlier films, and instead of backing away from it, he charges right through. *Mulholland Dr.* is said to have been assembled from scenes he shot for a 1999 ABC television pilot, but no network would air (or understand) this material, and Lynch knew it. He takes his financing where he can find it, and directs as fancy dictates. This movie doesn't feel incomplete because it could never be complete—closure is not a goal.

Laura Elena Harring and Naomi Watts take the risk of embodying Hollywood archetypes, and get away with it because they *are* archetypes. Not many actresses would be bold enough to name themselves after Rita Hayworth, but Harring does, because she can. Slinky and voluptuous in clinging gowns, all she has to do is stand there and she's the first good argument in fifty-five years for a *Gilda* remake. Naomi Watts is bright-eyed and bushy-tailed, a plucky girl detective. Like a dream, the movie shifts easily between tones; there's an audition where a girl singer performs "Sixteen Reasons" and "I Told Every Little Star," and the movie isn't satirizing *American Bandstand,* it's channeling it.

This is a movie to surrender yourself to. If you require logic, see something else. *Mulholland Dr.* works directly on the emotions, like music. Individual scenes play well by themselves, as they do in dreams, but they don't connect in a way that makes sense—again, like dreams. The way you know the movie is over is that it ends. And then you tell a friend, "I saw the weirdest movie last night." Just like you tell him you had the weirdest dream.

Note: See also my essay about a shot-by-shot analysis of Mulholland Dr. *in Boulder, Colorado.*

The Mummy Returns ★ ★
PG-13, 121 m., 2001

Brendan Fraser (Rick O'Connell), Rachel Weisz (Evelyn), John Hannah (Jonathan Carnahan), Arnold Vosloo (Imhotep), Adewale Akinnuoye-Agbaje (Lock-Nah), Freddie Boath (Alex

O'Connell), Oded Fehr (Ardeth Bay), Patricia Velasquez (Anck-Su-Namun), The Rock (Scorpion King). Directed by Stephen Sommer and produced by Sean Daniel and James Jacks. Screenplay by Sommer.

It is a curiosity of movie action that too much of it can be boring. Imagine yourself on a roller coaster for two hours. After the first ten minutes, the thrills subside. The mistake of *The Mummy Returns* is to abandon the characters, and to use the plot only as a clothesline for special effects and action sequences. If it were not for references to *The Mummy* (1999), this sequel would hardly have a plot at all.

Nine years have passed. Brendan Fraser is back again as Egyptologist Rick O'Connell, and Rachel Weisz, the librarian he met in the first film, is now his wife; they have an eight-year-old son named Alex (Freddie Boath). Also back are John Hannah as the twitty brother-in-law Jonathan, and Arnold Vosloo as the mummy Imhotep, whose name sounds more than ever like an ancient Egyptian chain of pancake houses. Oded Fehr is the worried sage Ardeth Bay, who begins sentences ominously with, "It is written that . . ." until Rick finally snaps, "Where is all this written?"

A good question, since much of the story involves a magical pyramid of which it is written, "No one who has seen it has ever returned alive." That logically leads us to wonder who told them about it. But logic applied to this movie will drive you mad. So will any attempt to summarize the plot, so I will be content with various observations:

1. The ads give The Rock, the WWF star, equal billing with Fraser. This is bait-and-switch. To call his appearance a "cameo" would be stretching it. He appears briefly at the beginning of the movie, is transmuted into a kind of transparent skeletal wraith, and disappears until the end of the film, when he comes back as the dreaded Scorpion King. I am not sure, at the end, if we see the real Rock, or merely his face, connected to computer-generated effects (his scorpion is blown up to giant size, which has the unfortunate effect of making him look more like a lobster tail than a scorpion). I continue to believe The Rock has an acting career ahead of him, and after seeing this movie I believe it is still ahead of him.

2. Alex, the kid, adds a lot to the movie by acting just like a kid. I particularly enjoyed it when he was kidnapped by a fearsome adversary of his parents, chained, and taken on a long journey, during which he drove his captor crazy by incessantly asking, "Are we there yet?"

3. The dialogue, "You have started a chain reaction that could bring about the next Apocalypse" is fascinating. Apparently we missed the first Apocalypse, which does not speak well for it.

4. I have written before of the ability of movie characters to outrun fireballs. In *The Mummy Returns*, there is a more amazing feat. If the rising sun touches little Alex while he is wearing the magical bracelet, he will die (it is written). But Rick, carrying Alex in his arms, is able to outrace the sunrise; we see the line of sunlight moving on the ground right behind them. It is written by Eratosthenes that Earth is about 25,000 miles around, and since there are twenty-four hours in a day, Rick was running approximately 1,041 miles an hour.

5. One of the big action sequences involves a battle between two vast armies, which stretch as far as computer-generated effects can see. One army is human. The other army is made of countless creatures named Anubis that look like giant savage dogs that stand upright and run on their hind legs (it is not done well, but one is surprised to find it done at all). These armies clash in bloody swordplay. Each dog-creature, as it is killed, reverts to the desert sand from whence it sprang. Finally all the creatures are destroyed, and we see the victors standing around feeling victorious and wishing that high-fives had been invented. And we notice that *not one single member* of the victorious army is dead or even wounded. Pathetic, that thousands of years of ancient curses and spells could engender such an incompetent army of dog-sand-creatures.

6. Several readers have argued with the rule in *Ebert's Little Movie Glossary* that teaches us: "No good movie has ever featured a hot-air balloon." To be sure, there are exceptions, but *The Mummy Returns* is not one of them. Its hot-air balloon looks like the ship that sailed to Winken, Blinken, and Nod.

7. At one point the action returns to London, and we see Tower Bridge, the dome of St. Paul's, and Big Ben clustered closely together in one

shot. This is no doubt to make it easy for the geographically challenged. Perhaps adding a few snapshots from Madonna's wedding would not have been too much.

Murder by Numbers ★ ★ ★

R, 119 m., 2002

Sandra Bullock (Cassie Mayweather), Ryan Gosling (Richard Haywood), Michael Pitt (Justin Pendleton), Ben Chaplin (Sam Kennedy), Agnes Bruckner (Lisa), Chris Penn (Ray), R. D. Call (Rod), Tom Verica (Al Swanson). Directed by Barbet Schroeder and produced by Richard Crystal and Susan Hoffman. Screenplay by Tony Gayton.

Richard and Justin, the high school killers in *Murder by Numbers,* may not have heard of Leopold and Loeb, or seen Hitchcock's *Rope,* or studied any of the other fictional versions *(Compulsion, Swoon)* of the infamous murder pact between two brainy and amoral young men. But they're channeling it. *Murder by Numbers* crosses Leopold/Loeb with a police procedural, and adds an interesting touch: Instead of toying with the audience, it toys with the characters. We have information they desperately desire, and we watch them dueling in misdirection.

The movie stars Sandra Bullock as Cassie Mayweather, a veteran detective, experienced enough to trust her hunches and resist the obvious answers. Ben Chaplin is Sam Kennedy, her by-the-books partner, the kind of cop who gets an A for every step of his investigation, but ends up with the wrong conclusion. Paired against them are Richard Haywood and Justin Pendleton (Ryan Gosling, from *The Believer,* and Michael Pitt, from *Hedwig and the Angry Inch*). These are two brainy high school kids, fascinated, as Leopold and Loeb were, by the possibility of proving their superiority by committing the perfect murder.

Their plan: Pick a victim completely at random, so that there is no link between corpse and killers, and leave behind no clues. The film opens with the suggestion of a suicide pact between the two teenagers, who face each other, holding revolvers to their heads, in a crumbling Gothic building so improbably close to the edge of a seaside cliff that we intuit someone is going to be dangling over it by the end of the film.

Bullock's Cassie is the central character, a good cop but a damaged human being, whose past holds some kind of fearsome grip on her present. Cassie and Sam are assigned to a creepy case; the body of a middle-aged female has been found in a wooded area, and close analysis of clues (hair, strands from a rug) seem to lead back to a suspect. Sam is happy to follow the clues to their logical conclusion. Cassie isn't so sure, and a chance meeting with one of the young sociopaths leads to a suspicion: "Something's not right with that kid."

We learn a lot about police work in *Murder by Numbers,* and there's a kind of fascination in seeing the jigsaw puzzle fall into place, especially since the audience holds some (not all) of the key pieces. Many of the best scenes involve an intellectual and emotional duel between the two young men, who seem to have paused on the brink of becoming lovers and decided to sublimate that passion into an arrogant crime. Richard and Justin are smart—Justin smarter in an intellectual way, Richard better at manipulating others. The movie wisely reserves details of who did what in the killing, and why.

These are affluent kids with absent parents, who are their own worst enemies because their arrogance leads them to play games with the cops to show how smart they are. They'd be better off posing as vacant-headed slackers. It is Cassie's intuition that the boys are inviting her attention, are turned on by the nearness of capture. Meanwhile, of course, her partner and the brass at the station are eager for a quick solution. A janitor is the obvious suspect? Arrest the janitor.

The movie has been directed by the versatile Barbet Schroeder, who alternates between powerful personal films *(Our Lady of the Assassins)* and skillful thrillers *(Single White Female).* When the two strands cross you get one-of-a-kind films like *Reversal of Fortune* and *Barfly.* After the semidocumentary freedom and scary Colombian locations of *Our Lady of the Assassins,* here's a movie that he directs as an exercise in craft—only occasionally letting his mordant humor peer through, as in an inexplicable scene where Cassie is bitten by a monkey.

Sandra Bullock does a good job here of working against her natural likeability, creating a character you'd like to like, and could like, if she weren't so sad, strange, and turned in upon herself. She throws herself into police work not so much because she's dedicated as because she needs the distraction, needs to keep busy and be good to assure herself of her worth. As she draws the net closer, and runs into more danger and more official opposition, the movie more or less helplessly starts thinking to itself about that cliff above the sea, but at least the climax shows us that Bullock can stay in character no matter what.

The Musketeer ★ ★ ½
PG-13, 105 m., 2001

Justin Chambers (D'Artagnan), Tim Roth (Febre), Mena Suvari (Francesca), Catherine Deneuve (Queen of France), Stephen Rea (Cardinal Richelieu), Joachim Paul Assbock (Hessian), Jean-Pierre Castaldi (Planchet), Jeremy Clyde (Lord Buckingham), Patrick Dean (Febre's Man), Stefan Jurgens (Darcy), Jan Gregor Kremp (Athos). Directed by Peter Hyams and produced by Rudy Cohen and Moshe Diamant. Screenplay by Gene Quintano, based on the novel by Alexandre Dumas.

Peter Hyams's *The Musketeer* combines traditional swashbuckling with martial arts in a movie where the men wear plumes in their hats but pounce like crouching tigers and scheme like hidden dragons. No wonder; the choreography of the fight scenes is by Xin Xin Xiong—not a name on every tongue, I grant you, but he is one of the top action designers in Hong Kong.

The big-budget extravaganza, with sensational sets and battle scenes, is set in seventeenth-century France, where a Spanish invasion is feared and Cardinal Richelieu (Stephen Rea) has raised a private army while King Louis XIII's loyal musketeers are in disgrace. Then young D'Artagnan (Justin Chambers), who saw his parents murdered by the evil Febre (Tim Roth), rides to the rescue, jump-starts the musketeers, saves the queen, falls in love with the queen's comely dresser, and so on.

The history is not the point, and neither is the story. Both exist only to supply excuses for a series of action sequences, which steal the show to such an extent that if you like martial arts scenes you'll admire this movie, and if you don't, you won't.

Like Hong Kong fight movies, *The Musketeer* makes great use of handy props, folding them into the action scenes. Nowhere is this more dramatic (or ludicrous, depending on your point of view) than in a final duel between D'Artagnan and Febre, which takes place in a warehouse stacked to the ceiling with shelves of big wine barrels. Of course to reach the barrels, you need ladders—*lots* of ladders, with the two fighters leaping from one to another, walking them across the floor, swinging through space clinging to them, and finally, incredibly, balancing one on a center beam and using it as a teeter-totter for their final showdown. This is harder than it looks.

Oh, and I forgot to mention what led up to that. D'Artagnan has freed all the imprisoned musketeers, who form an army to attack the castle where the queen (Catherine Deneuve) and the comely dresser (Mena Suvari, from *American Beauty* and *American Pie*) are being held prisoner by the vile Febre. After the queen drops a marble bust at his feet to attract his attention (lucky she didn't hit him on the head), D'Artagnan fires a rope to the top of the tower and climbs up, hand over hand, to rescue them—but then defenders lower their own ropes, and soon four or five fighters are swaying in big arcs back and forth high above the ground, holding on with one hand while swordfighting, which is harder than it looks.

An earlier chase sequence involves an attempt by Febre to capture the coach containing the queen and the comely dresser, where D'Artagnan single-handedly holds off the entire force, at one point leaping from the saddle of his galloping horse to the saddle of the horse in front (harder than it looks). And there is an early scene where D'Artagnan is able to support himself between two ceiling beams with pressure from his legs and one arm, while the free arm wields a sword. So much harder than it looks that it borders, I would hazard, on the impossible.

There are barrels in this movie. So many barrels they supply the leitmotiv, as they roll, thunder, spill, explode, and impede. At one point D'Artagnan actually balances on top of a barrel and rolls it beneath his feet while swordfighting. Harder than it looks.

Occasionally the action is interrupted by dialogue scenes, which are easier than they look. None of the drama in this movie would stretch Errol Flynn—or Errol Morris, for that matter. Tim Roth already holds the crown for the single best swashbuckling scene in modern film history (in *Rob Roy*). This time, where most of the action is special effects, stunts, rope-flies, and animation, he focuses on being hateful. I love it when the queen tells him, "You have no mercy in your heart" and he replies: "No mercy. No heart."

I cannot in strict accuracy recommend this film. It's such a jumble of action and motivation, ill-defined characters and action howlers. I am not even quite sure if Richelieu and Febre are on the same side, or if there are three or even four sides in the story. But the banquet scene is a marvel of art design. The action scenes are wonders to behold. And when Tim Roth vows vengeance on the man who blinded him, I, for one, believe him.

My Big Fat Greek Wedding ★ ★ ★
PG, 95 m., 2002

Nia Vardalos (Toula Portokalos), John Corbett (Ian Miller), Lainie Kazan (Maria), Michael Constantine (Gus), Gia Carides (Nikki), Louis Mandylor (Nick), Joey Fatone (Angelo), Bruce Gray (Rodney Miller). Directed by Joel Zwick and produced by Gary Goetzman, Tom Hanks, and Rita Wilson. Screenplay by Nia Vardalos.

All the people in this movie look like they could be real people. The romance involves not impossibly attractive people, but a thirty-year-old woman who looks okay when she pulls herself out of her Frump Phase, and a vegetarian high school teacher who urgently needs the services of SuperCuts. Five minutes into the film, I relaxed, knowing it was set in the real world, and not in the Hollywood alternative universe where Julia Roberts can't get a date.

My Big Fat Greek Wedding is narrated by Toula Portokalos (Nia Vardalos), who, like all Greek women, she says, was put upon this Earth for three purposes: to marry a Greek man, to have Greek children, and to feed everyone until the day she dies. Toula is still single and works in the family restaurant (Dancing Zorbas), where, as she explains, she is *not* a waitress, but a "seating hostess." One day a guy with the spectacularly non-Greek name of Ian Miller (John Corbett) walks in, and she knows instinctively that marriage is thinkable.

The movie is warmhearted in the way a movie can be when it knows its people inside out. Watching it, I was reminded of Mira Nair's *Monsoon Wedding*, about an Indian wedding. Both cultures place great emphasis on enormous extended families, enormous extended weddings, and enormous extended wedding feasts. Nia Vardalos, who not only stars but based the screenplay on her own one-woman play, obviously has great affection for her big Greek family, and a little exasperation, too—as who wouldn't, with a father who walks around with a spray jar of Windex because he is convinced it will cure anything? Or a mother who explains, "When I was your age, we didn't *have* food."

Vardalos was an actress at Chicago's Second City when she wrote the play. The way the story goes, it was seen by Rita Wilson, a Greek-American herself, and she convinced her husband, Tom Hanks, that they had to produce it. So they did, making a small treasure of human comedy. The movie is set in Chicago but was filmed in Toronto—too bad, because the dating couple therefore doesn't have a chizbooger at Billy Goat's.

As the film opens, Toula the heroine is single at thirty and therefore a failure. Ian Miller causes her heart to leap up in love and desire, and Ian likes her too. Really likes her. This isn't one of those formula pictures where it looks like he's going to dump her. There's enough to worry about when the families meet. "No one in our family has ever gone out with a non-Greek," Toula warns him uneasily, and indeed her parents (Lainie Kazan and Michael Constantine) regard Ian like a lesser life form.

The movie is pretty straightforward: Ian and Toula meet, they date, they bashfully discover they like each other, the families uneasily coexist, the wedding becomes inevitable, and it takes place (when Ian's mother brings a bundt cake to the wedding, no one has the slightest idea what it is). One key shot shows the church with the bride's side jammed, and the groom's handful of WASP relatives making a pathetic show in their first four rows. Toula explains to Ian that she has twenty-seven first cousins, and at a prenuptial party, her dad even introduces some of them: "Nick, Nick, Nick, Nick, Nick, Nick, Nicky—and Gus."

The underlying story of *My Big Fat Greek Wedding* has been played out countless times as America's immigrants have intermarried. If the lovers have understanding (or at least reluctantly flexible) parents, love wins the day and the melting pot bubbles. This is nicely illustrated by Toula's father, Gus. He specializes in finding the Greek root for *any* word (even "kimono"), and delivers a toast in which he explains that "Miller" goes back to the Greek word for apple, and "Portokalos" is based on the Greek word for oranges, and so, he concludes triumphantly, "in the end, we're all fruits." ☞

My First Mister ★ ★ ★

R, 109 m., 2001

Leelee Sobieski (Jennifer), Albert Brooks (Randall), Carol Kane (Mrs. Benson), Michael McKean (Bob), Desmond Harrington (Randy), Mary Kay Place (Patty [Nurse]). Directed by Christine Lahti and produced by Mitchell Solomon, Sukee Chew, Anne Kurtzman, Carol Baum, and Jane Goldenring. Screenplay by Jill Franklyn.

Consider now Leelee Sobieski, who is nineteen years old and has been acting since she was twelve. *My First Mister* is the latest in a series of wonderful performances in a career so busy that earlier in 2001 she appeared in *The Glass House* and *Joy Ride*. I did not much notice her in *Deep Impact* (1998) and wanted to avert my eyes from the entire movie during *Jungle2-Jungle* (1997). But in 1998, she came into her own as the heroine of *A Soldier's Daughter Never Cries*, based on the autobiographical story by Kaylie Jones, the daughter of the novelist James Jones. And in 1999, she found time to be Joan of Arc on TV, costar with Drew Barrymore in *Never Been Kissed*, and play a small role in Kubrick's *Eyes Wide Shut*.

A new star doesn't always explode. Sometimes she just . . . occurs to you. I was so involved in the story of *A Soldier's Daughter Never Cries* that my review said nothing specific about her performance, although in a sense the whole review was in praise of it. Only with *The Glass House* and *Joy Ride*, seen so close to each other, with the memory of *My First Mister* still warm from Sundance 2001, did it become inescapable that she is an important new talent, an actress who has arrived at the top without having to make a single teenage horror film or *American Pie* rip-off.

She usually plays intelligent, well-scrubbed characters, convincingly. Here she's Jennifer, smart but alienated—a pierced, tattooed Goth. Stomping around in zip-up boots, her chains clanking, she is the despair of a ditzy mother (Carol Kane) who thinks the answer to everything is getting dinner on the table on time. She has refused to go to college, has no job or boyfriend, is a loner wandering through the mall—and one day sees a man adjusting the window display at a men's clothing store. Something about his personal style, his manner of carrying himself, strikes her, and she drifts in to ask about a job.

This is Randall (Albert Brooks). "Hire you?" he says. "For every suit you sell, you're gonna send thirty customers fleeing out of the store." "Dress me," she says. He does. "I look like a Republican," she says. He's forty-nine; she's seventeen. It's odd how they become friends while tacitly sidestepping the idea of sex, although she does raise the subject once, so bluntly that he sprays his Sanka at a hip coffee shop.

The movie is not about sex, not about a Lolita, but about a friendship between two loners. He has her number. "Do you have a copy of *The Bell Jar* next to your bed?" he asks. It's a good guess. "Who do you talk to? Who are your friends?" he asks. "You," she says.

These two characters are so particular and sympathetic that the whole movie could simply observe them. In a way, I wish it had. The film, directed by Christine Lahti from a screenplay by Jill Franklyn, is best in the first hour or more, when things seem to be happening spontaneously. I was a little disappointed when it narrowed down into more conventional channels, involving a crisis and a long-lost son. And a closing dinner scene, assembling the characters, seemed like a convenient plot device.

Still, Sobieski and Brooks stay true to their characters even as the movie gives them less room for spontaneity. Brooks is always able to enrich a role with specific, precise touches. Watch him straightening the stacks of magazines in his house, and listen to him tell a tattoo artist: "I want the smallest tattoo you have. Can you give me a dot, or a period?" Sobieski is wise to make Jennifer practical in the way she abandons her lifestyle: Instead of making it seem like a corny transformation, she makes it a pragmatic choice. It works for her, and when it stops working, she ditches it.

The bravest thing about the movie is the way it doesn't cave in to teenage multiplex demographics with another story about dumb adults and cool kids. *My First Mister* is about reaching out, about seeing the other person, about having something to say and being able to listen. So what if the ending is on autopilot? At least it's a flight worth taking.

Note: There is no earthly reason this movie is rated R. The flywheels at the MPAA have taken flight from the values of the world we inhabit.

The Mystic Masseur ★ ★ ★
PG, 117 m., 2002

Aasif Mandvi (Ganesh), Om Puri (Ramlogan), James Fox (Mr. Stewart), Sanjeev Bhaskar (Beharry), Ayesha Dharker (Leela), Jimi Mistry (Partap), Zohra Segal (Auntie), Sakina Jaffrey (Suruj Mooma). Directed by Ismail Merchant and produced by Nayeem Hafizka and Richard Hawley. Screenplay by Caryl Phillips, based on the novel by V. S. Naipaul.

The West Indies were a footnote to the British Empire, and the Indian community of Trinidad was a footnote to the footnote. After slavery was abolished and the Caribbean still needed cheap labor, thousands of Indians were brought from one corner of the empire to another to supply it. They formed an insular community, treasuring traditional Hindu customs, importing their dress styles and recipes, re-creating India far from home on an island where it seemed irrelevant to white colonial rulers and the black majority.

The great man produced by these exiles was

V. S. Naipaul, the 2001 Nobel laureate for literature, whose father was a newspaperman with a great respect for books and ideas. *A House for Mr. Biswas* (1961) is Naipaul's novel about his father and his own childhood, and one of the best books of the century. But Naipaul's career began in 1957 with *The Mystic Masseur*, a novel casting a fond but dubious light on the Indian community of Trinidad. It is now the first of Naipaul's novels to be filmed, directed by Ismail Merchant, himself an Indian, usually the producing partner for director James Ivory.

The Mystic Masseur is a wry, affectionate delight, a human comedy about a man who thinks he has had greatness thrust upon him when in fact he has merely thrust himself in the general direction of greatness. It tells the story of Ganesh, a schoolteacher with an exaggerated awe for books, who is inspired by a dotty Englishman to write some of his own. Abandoning the city for a rural backwater, he begins to compose short philosophical tomes which, published by the local printer on a foot-powered flatbed press, give him a not-quite-deserved reputation for profundity.

If Ganesh allowed his success to go to his head, he would be insufferable. Instead, he is played by Aasif Mandvi as a man so sincere he really does believe in his mission. Does he have the power to cure with his touch and advise troubled people on their lives? Many think he does, and soon he has become married to the pretty daughter of a canny businessman, who runs taxis from the city to bring believers to Ganesh's rural retreat.

There is rich humor in the love-hate relationship many Indians have with their customs, which they leaven with a decided streak of practicality. In no area is this more true than marriage, as you can see in Mira Nair's wonderful comedy *Monsoon Wedding*. The events leading up to Ganesh's marriage to the beautiful Leela (Ayesha Dharker) are hilarious, as the ambitious businessman Ramlogan positions his daughter to capture the rising young star.

Played by the great Indian actor Om Puri with lip-smacking satisfaction, Ramlogan makes sure Ganesh appreciates Leela's dark-eyed charm, and then demonstrates her learning by producing a large wooden sign she has lettered, with a bright red punctuation mark after every word. "Leela know a lot of punctuation marks," he boasts proudly, and soon she has Ganesh within her parentheses. The wedding brings a showdown between the two men; custom dictates that the father-in-law must toss bills onto a plate as long as the new husband is still eating his kedgeree, and Ganesh, angered that Ramlogan has stiffed him with the wedding bill, dines slowly.

The humor in *The Mystic Masseur* is generated by Ganesh's good-hearted willingness to believe in his ideas and destiny, both of which are slight. Like a thrift shop Gandhi, he sits on his veranda writing pamphlets and advising supplicants on health, wealth, and marriage. Leela meanwhile quietly takes charge, managing the family business, as Ganesh becomes the best-known Indian on Trinidad. Eventually he forms the Hindu Association, collects some political power, and is elected to Parliament, which is the beginning of his end. Transplanted from his rural base to the capital, he finds his party outnumbered by Afro-Caribbeans and condescended to by the British governors; he has traded his stature for a meaningless title, and is correctly seen by other Indians as a stooge.

The masseur's public career has lasted only from 1943 to 1954. The mistake would be to assign too much significance to Ganesh. His lack of significance is the whole point. He rises to visibility as a homegrown guru, is co-opted by the British colonial government, and by the end of the film is a nonentity shipped safely out of sight to Oxford on a cultural exchange. Critics of the film have slighted Ganesh for being a pointless man leading a marginal life; they don't sense the anger and hurt seething just below the genial surface of the novel. The young Trinidadian Indian studying at Oxford, who meets Ganesh at the train station in the opening scene, surely represents Naipaul, observing the wreck of a man who loomed large in his childhood.

Movies are rarely about inconsequential characters. They favor characters who are sensational winners or losers. But Ganesh, one senses, is precisely the character Naipaul needed to express his feelings about being an Indian in Trinidad. He has written elsewhere about the peculiarity of being raised in an In-

dian community thousands of miles from "home," attempting to reflect a land none of its members had ever seen. The empire created generations of such displaced communities, not least the British exiles in India, sipping Earl Grey, reading the *Times,* and saluting "God Save the Queen" in blissful oblivion to the world around them.

Ganesh gets about as far as he could get, given the world he was born into, and he is such an innocent that many of his illusions persist. Shown around the Bodleian Library in Oxford by his young guide, the retired statesman looks at the walls of books, and says, "Boy, this the center of the world! Everything begin here, everything lead back to this place." Naipaul's whole career would be about his struggle with that theory.

My Wife Is an Actress ★ ★ ½
R, 95 m., 2002

Charlotte Gainsbourg (Charlotte), Yvan Attal (Yvan), Terence Stamp (John), Noémie Lvovsky (Nathalie), Laurent Bateau (Vincent), Keith Allen (David), Jo McInnes (David's assistant), Ludivine Sagnier (Géraldine). Directed by Yvan Attal and produced by Claude Berri. Screenplay by Attal.

The thing about movie love scenes is that they are acting and they are not acting, both at the same time. Two actors play "characters" who kiss or caress or thrash about. They are only "acting." When the director shouts, "Cut!" they disengage and wander off to their trailers to finish the crossword puzzle. That at least is the idea they give in interviews.

But consider. Most movie actors are attractive. They come wrapped in a mystique. Everyone is curious about them, including their costars. When the director says, "Action!" and they find themselves in bed, there is the presence and warmth of the other person, the press of bosom or thigh, the pressure of a hand, the softness of lips. Does something happen that is not precisely covered by the definition of acting?

If it does not, then the actors are not humans and should not be playing them. If we in the audience sometimes feel a stirring of more than artistic interest in some of the people we see on the screen, should actors, whose experience is so much more immediate, be any different? The fact that they are not different provides the subtext for half the articles in the supermarket tabloids.

Consider all that, and I will tell you a story. I interviewed Robert Mitchum many times. He costarred with Marilyn Monroe. I never asked him anything as banal as "what was it like to kiss Marilyn Monroe?" but of course there is no woman in the history of the movies who would inspire a greater desire to ask that question. Once, though, as I was Q&Aing Mitchum at the Virginia Film Festival, somebody in the audience asked him about Marilyn.

"I loved her," he said. "I had known her since she was about fifteen or sixteen years old. My partner on the line at the Lockheed plant in Long Beach was her first husband. That's when I first met her. And I knew her all the way through. And she was a lovely girl; very, very shy. She had what is now recognized as agoraphobia. She was terrified of going out among people. At that time they just thought she was being difficult. But she had that psychological, psychic fear of appearing among people. That's why when she appeared in public, she always burlesqued herself. She appeared as you would hope that she would appear. She was a very sweet, loving, and loyal—unfortunately loyal— girl. Loyal to people who used her, and a lot who misused her."

So there you have it. Not what it was like to kiss her, but what it was like to know her. In one paragraph, probably as much truth as can be said about Monroe.

An answer like that is beyond the new movie

My Wife Is an Actress. This is a French serio-comedy written, directed by, and starring Yvan Attal, who plays a Paris sportswriter whose wife is a famous actress. She is played by Charlotte Gainsbourg, who in real life is Attal's wife. No doubt if he were to write a serious novel about his marriage, Attal would have some truths to share, but his film feels like an arm's-length job, a comedy that deliberately avoids deep waters.

Yvan is a jealous man. He is driven to it by an unrelenting barrage of questions from members of the public, some of whom assume as a matter of course that Charlotte really does sleep with her costars. He smashes one guy in the nose, but that doesn't help, and when Charlotte goes to London to work with a big star (Terence Stamp), Yvan all but pushes her into his arms to prove his point.

Stamp, who is very good in a thankless role, plays a man so wearied by life and wear and tear that he sleeps with women more or less as a convenience. He seduces to be obliging. There is a funny moment when he propositions a woman and soberly accepts her refusal as one more interesting development, nodding thoughtfully to himself.

If the movie were all comedy, it might work better. It has an ambition to say something about its subjects, but not a willingness. It circles the possibility of mental and spiritual infidelity like a cat wondering if a mouse might still be alive. Watching it, I felt it would be fascinating to see a movie that was really, truthfully, fearlessly about this subject. ☞

N

Naqoyqatsi ★ ★ ★
PG, 89 m., 2002

A documentary directed by Godfrey Reggio and produced by Joe Beirne, Reggio, and Lawrence Taub. Screenplay by Philip Glass and Reggio.

Naqoyqatsi is the final film in Godfrey Reggio's "qatsi" trilogy, a series of impressionistic documentaries contrasting the nobility of nature with the despoliation of mankind. The titles come from the Hopi Indian language. *Koyaanisqatsi* (1983) translated as "life out of balance." *Powaqqatsi* (1988) means "life in transition." And now comes *Naqoyqatsi,* or "war as a way of life."

Like the others, *Naqoyqatsi* consists of images (450 of them, Reggio said at the Telluride premiere). We see quick streams of briefly glimpsed symbols, abstractions, digital code, trademarks, newsreels, found images, abandoned buildings, and cityscapes, and snippets of TV and photography. An early image shows the Tower of Babel; the implication is that the confusion of spoken tongues has been made worse by the addition of visual and digital languages.

Koyaanisqatsi, with its dramatic fast-forward style of hurtling images, made a considerable impact at the time. Clouds raced up mountainsides, traffic flowed like streams of light through city streets. The technique was immediately ripped off by TV commercials, so that the film's novelty is no longer obvious. Now that he has arrived at the third part of his trilogy, indeed, Reggio's method looks familiar, and that is partly the fault of his own success. Here he uses speed-up less, and relies more on quickly cut montages. It's a version of the technique used in Chuck Workman's films on the Oscarcast, the ones that marry countless shots from the movies; Reggio doctors his images with distortion, overlays, tints, and other kinds of digital alteration.

The thinking behind these films is deep but not profound. They're ritualistic grief at what man has done to the planet. "The logical flaw," as I pointed out in my review of *Powaqqatsi,* is that "Reggio's images of beauty are always found in a world entirely without man—

without even the Hopi Indians. Reggio seems to think that man himself is some kind of virus infecting the planet—that we would enjoy the Earth more, in other words, if we weren't here."

Although *Naqoyqatsi* has been some ten years in the making, it takes on an especially somber coloration after 9/11. Images of marching troops, missiles, bomb explosions, and human misery are intercut with trademarks (the Enron trademark flashes past), politicians, and huddled masses, and we understand that war is now our way of life. But hasn't war always been a fact of life for mankind? We are led to the uncomfortable conclusion that to bring peace to the planet, we should leave it.

This line of reasoning may, however, be missing the point. In reviewing all three Reggio films, I have assumed he was telling us something with his images, and that I could understand it and analyze it. That overlooks what may be the key element of the films, the sound tracks by composer Philip Glass (this time joined by Yo-Yo Ma, who also contributes a solo). Can it be that these films are, in the very best sense of the word, music videos? The movie is not simply "scored" by Glass; his music is a vital component of every frame, fully equal with the visuals, and you can watch these films again and again, just as you can listen to a favorite album.

Perhaps the solution is to stop analyzing the images altogether and set ourselves free from them. Just as it is a heresy to paraphrase classical music by discovering "stories" or "messages," perhaps *Naqoyqatsi* and its brothers need to be experienced as background to our own streams of consciousness—nudges to set us thinking about the same concerns that Reggio has. I have problems with *Naqoyqatsi* as a film, but as a music video, it's rather remarkable.

Narc ★ ★ ★
R, 105 m., 2003

Ray Liotta (Lieutenant Henry Oak), Jason Patric (Sergeant Nick Tellis), Chi McBride (Captain Cheevers), Busta Rhymes (Beery), Anne Openshaw (Kathryn Calvess), Richard Chevolleau (Steeds), John Ortiz (Ruiz), Thomas Patrice (Marcotte), Alan Van Sprang (Michael

459

Calvess). Directed by Joe Carnahan and produced by Diane Nabatoff, Julius Nasso, Ray Liotta, and Michelle Grace. Screenplay by Carnahan.

Joe Carnahan's *Narc* is a cold, hard film about Detroit narcotics detectives. Ray Liotta and Jason Patric star, as a veteran whose partner has been killed, and a younger cop assigned to join him in the investigation. If many cop-partner movies have an undertone of humor, even a splash of *The Odd Couple*, this one is hard-bitten and grim: The team consists of Bad Cop and Bad Cop. The twist is that both of them are good at their work; their problem is taking the job too personally.

The film opens with a virtuoso handheld chase scene, as Nick Tellis (Patric) pursues a suspect through backyards and over fences until the chase ends in a shooting—and it's not the perp who is hit, but a pregnant woman. Tellis is put on suspension and cools off at home with his wife and a baby he loves. It's clear this is a man with big problems involving anger and overcompensation; is there such a thing as being too dedicated as a cop?

More than a year later, his captain (Chi McBride) calls in Tellis and makes him an offer: He can be reinstated on the force if he becomes the partner of Henry Oak (Liotta). Oak's former partner, a cop named Calvess, has been murdered. The captain thinks Tellis's contacts with drug dealers and other lowlifes, plus his unique brand of dedication, are needed to track down the cop killer. He warns Tellis that Oak is a good cop but sometimes unstable, and there are quick subjective cuts to the older man beating a prisoner.

Tellis and Oak do not fit the usual pattern of cop partners in the movies. Either of them could be the lead. Neither one is supporting. As cops, they think independently and are self-starters, and cooperation doesn't come easily. Tellis is startled, too, at Oak's methods, which are quick and practical and amoral, and produce results, but are not always legal.

The movie's writer and director, Joe Carnahan, brings a rough, aggressive energy to the picture. His first film, *Blood, Guts, Bullets & Octane* (1998), was all style, but here he creates believable characters. His screenplay stays within the broad outlines of the cop-buddy formula, but brings fresh energy to the obligatory elements. It is no surprise, for example, that Tellis's wife doesn't want him back out on the streets, and that there's tension between his home life and his job. This is an ancient action cliché: A man's gotta do what a man's gotta do. But the details of the domestic scenes ring true.

In terms of its urban wasteland, the movie descends to a new level of grittiness. These streets aren't mean, they're cruel, and to work them is like being the garbageman in hell. Liotta's character stalks them as a man on a mission, driven by private agendas we only begin to suspect. The Patric character is stunned to see the other man not only violating protocol, but apparently trying to shut him out of the investigation, as if this business can only be settled privately between him and his demons.

Both Liotta and Patric have played similar roles. Patric starred in *Rush* (1992), in a brilliant performance as an undercover narcotics cop who, along with his rookie partner (Jennifer Jason Leigh), gets hooked on drugs himself. Liotta has appeared in countless crime pictures, both as a cop and most memorably in *GoodFellas* (1990) as a cocaine-addled criminal. Here they bring a kind of rawness to the table. Liotta, heavier, wearing a beard, leaves behind his days as a handsome leading man and begins edging into interesting Brian Cox territory. Patric, ten years after *Rush*, looks less like he's playing a cop and more like he might be one.

The investigation itself must remain undescribed here. But its ending is a neat and ironic exercise in poetic justice. Pay attention during one of the very last shots, and tell me if you think the tape recorder was on or off. In a way, it makes a difference. In another way, it doesn't.

National Lampoon's Van Wilder ★
R, 95 m., 2002

Ryan Reynolds (Van Wilder), Tara Reid (Gwen), Kal Penn (Taj), Tim Matheson (Vance Wilder Sr.), Kim Smith (Casey), Daniel Cosgrove (Richard Bagg), Tom Everett Scott (Elliot Grebb), Chris Owen (Timmy [the Jumper]). Directed by Walt Becker and produced by Peter Abrams, Robert L. Levy, Jonathon Komack Martin, and Andrew Panay. Screenplay by Brent Goldberg and David Wagner.

Watching *National Lampoon's Van Wilder*, I grew nostalgic for the lost innocence of a movie like *American Pie*, in which human semen found itself in a pie. In *NatLampVW*, dog semen is baked in a pastry. Is it only a matter of time until the heroes of teenage gross-out comedies are injecting turtle semen directly through their stomach walls?

National Lampoon's Van Wilder, a pale shadow of *National Lampoon's Animal House*, tells the story of Van Wilder (Ryan Reynolds), who has been the Biggest Man on Campus for seven glorious undergraduate years. He doesn't want to graduate, and why should he, since he has clout, fame, babes, and the adulation of the entire campus (except, of course, for the professor whose parking space he swipes, and the vile fraternity boy who is his sworn enemy).

Van Wilder is essentially a nice guy, which is a big risk for a movie like this to take; he raises funds for the swimming team, tries to restrain suicidal students, and throws legendary keg parties. Ryan Reynolds is, I suppose, the correct casting choice for Van Wilder, since the character is not a devious slacker but merely a permanent student. That makes him, alas, a little boring, and Reynolds (from ABC's *Two Guys and a Girl*) brings along no zing: He's a standard leading man when the movie cries out for a manic character actor. Jack Black in this role would have been a home run.

Is Van Wilder too good to be true? That's what Gwen (Tara Reid) wonders. She's a journalism student who wants to do an in-depth piece about Van for the campus paper. Of course she's the girlfriend of the vile frat boy, and of course her investigation inspires her to admire the real Van Wilder while deploring his public image. Tara Reid is remarkably attractive, as you may remember from *Josie and the Pussycats* and *American Pie 2*, but much of the time she simply seems to be imitating still photos of Renee Zellweger smiling.

That leaves, let's see, Kal Penn as Taj, the Indian-American student who lands the job as Van Wilder's assistant, and spends much of his time using a stereotyped accent while reciting lists of synonyms for oral sex. I cannot complain, since the hero's buddy in every movie in this genre is always a sex-crazed zealot, and at least this film uses nontraditional casting. (Casting directors face a catch-22: They cast a white guy, and everybody wants to know why he had to be white. So they cast an ethnic guy, and everybody complains about the negative stereotype. Maybe the way out is to cast the ethnic guy as the hero and the white guy as the horny doofus.)

The movie is a barfathon that takes full advantage of the apparent MPAA guidelines in which you can do pretty much anything with bodily functions except involve them in healthy sex. The movie contains semen, bare breasts and butts, epic flatulence, bizarre forms of masturbation, public nudity, projectile vomiting, and an extended scene of explosive defecation with sound effects that resemble the daily duties of the Port-a-Loo serviceman, in reverse. There are also graphic shots of enormous testicles, which are allowed under the *National Geographic* loophole since they belong to Van Wilder's pet bulldog. Presumably the MPAA would not permit this if it had reason to believe there were dogs in the audience.

"On a scale of 1 to 10 shots of bourbon needed to make a pledge ralph," writes Bob Patterson of the Website Delusions of Adequacy, "this film will get a very strong five from most college-age film fans who are not offended by vulgar humor. Older filmgoers who might be offended by such offerings are encouraged to do something that is physically impossible (i.e., lift yourself up by your bootstraps)."

Although this is obviously the review the movie deserves, I confess the rating scale baffles me. Is it better or worse if a film makes you ralph? Patterson implies that older filmgoers might be offended by vulgar humor. There is a flaw in this reasoning: It is not age but humor that is the variable. Laughter for me was such a physical impossibility during *National Lampoon's Van Wilder* that had I not been pledged to sit through the film, I would have lifted myself up by my bootstraps and fled.

Never Again ★ ★
R, 97 m., 2002

Jeffrey Tambor (Christopher), Jill Clayburgh (Grace), Bill Duke (Earl), Caroline Aaron (Elaine), Eric Axen (College Girl-Boy), Michael McKean (Alex), Sandy Duncan (Natasha). Directed by Eric Schaeffer and produced by

Robert Kravitz, Terence Michael, and Dawn Wolfrom. Screenplay by Schaeffer.

Here's a case of two actors who do everything humanly possible to create characters who are sweet and believable, and are defeated by a screenplay that forces them into bizarre, implausible behavior. It is not even the behavior I object to; in a raucous sex farce, it would be understandable. It is the film's refusal to come down on one side of the fence or the other: to find a tone and believe in it. It wants to be heartfelt and sincere *and* vulgar, dirty, and shocking. And it is willfully blind to human nature.

Never Again stars Jeffrey Tambor and Jill Clayburgh as Christopher and Grace, two lonely people in their fifties. She is divorced; he has never married. They both believe another romance is probably impossible. During the course of this film they will Meet Cute and have a relationship that no two people have ever or will ever have, outside the overheated imagination of Eric Schaeffer, the film's writer and director.

Christopher runs an exterminating service by day and in the evenings plays jazz piano in a Greenwich Village nightclub; the combination of those two jobs says more about an overwrought screenplay than about employment possibilities in the real world. You might assume a jazz pianist in the Village would have seen something of life and even gathered some knowledge of homosexuality, but Christopher is as naive as a thirteen-year-old, and wonders if perhaps his failure to form relationships with women is because he is gay. To test this theory, he makes a date with the least convincing transsexual in cinematic history (Michael McKean), and then, fleeing the scene but still in an investigative mood, he enters a gay bar and meets the most unconvincing male hustler in cinematic history—before eventually trying to pick up Grace, who he thinks might be a more convincing transsexual.

She is a woman, she informs him, and has simply fled to the nearest bar after an unhappy experience in her own dating career. They decide to go out for a meal, and show in a few brief scenes that a sane and plausible version of this relationship might have made a wonderful movie. But no. Schaeffer wants it both ways, and has written a screenplay that periodically runs off the rails.

The most unlikely scenes involve Clayburgh's eagerness to make up for lost time in the department of sexual experimentation. She walks into a sex shop to buy an enormous dildo, and also walks out with whips, chains, and what I guess is supposed to be an S&M uniform, although why a complete set of medieval armor would be necessary is beyond me; how about something simple, in leather or rubber? The appurtenance later pays off, so to speak, in a scene where she straps it on and can't get it off when Christopher unexpectedly comes calling with his mother. I do not pretend to know if it could possibly be true that she could not remove the offending device, but there is one thing as certain as the sun in the morning, and that is that no fifty-four-year-old woman would open the door to her fiancé and his mother while wearing such an appliance, however well concealed by a bathrobe.

There is another scene in *Never Again* that strikes a false note. Grace walks into a beauty parlor and describes an impressive array of sexual practices in a voice clearly audible to other women in the shop, whom she does not know. I am prepared to believe that a woman will tell her hairdresser anything, but that same instinct informs me that such women speak in hushed tones, because they don't want everyone in the shop to spread gossip about events usually found in the pages of *Penthouse Forum,* if indeed that publication still exists. ("An interesting thing happened the other night between me and my boyfriend, a piano-playing exterminator. . . .")

All of this is discouraging because in scene after scene Clayburgh and Tambor show themselves ready and able to create Grace and Christopher as realistic characters. There is a remarkable scene where it appears that he's about to break up with her, and she lets him have it, in a merciless verbal dissection; it's a reminder of Clayburgh's gifts as an actress. And other scenes where his loneliness is a fact instead of a setup for gimmicks. But *Never Again* plays like a head-on collision between two ideas in conflict. Is it a movie about people, or about gags? What purpose is there in creating believable people, only to put them into situations that clash and jar? Who's in charge here? ☞

The New Guy ★ ★
PG-13, 100 m., 2002

D. J. Qualls (Dizzy/Gil), Lyle Lovett (Bear Harrison), Eddie Griffin (Luther), Eliza Dushku (Danielle), Zooey Deschanel (Nora), Parry Shen (Glen), Laura Clifton (Emily). Directed by Ed Decter and produced by Mark Ciardi, Todd Garner, and Gordon Gray. Screenplay by David Kendall.

D. J. Qualls stars in *The New Guy* as a high school misfit who switches schools and gets a fresh start. At Rocky Creek, he was the target of cruel jokes almost daily (sample: being tied to a chair while wearing false breasts), but now, at Eastland High and with a new haircut, he is seen as a cool hero. "The point is," he explains with relief, "today nobody stuffed me in my locker or singed off my ass hairs."

The movie made from this material is quirkier than I would have expected, considering that the building blocks have been scavenged from the trash heap of earlier teenage comedies. Much of the credit goes to Qualls (from *Road Trip*), who not only plays the son of Lyle Lovett in this movie but looks biologically descended from him, no mean feat. He has a goofy grin and an offhand way with dialogue that make him much more likable than your usual teenage comedy hero.

Known at one school by his nickname Dizzy and at the other by his first name Gil, Dizzy/Gil does not approach the dating game with high expectations. Here's how he asks a popular girl out on a date: "Maybe sometime if you would like to drink coffee near me, I would pay." There is a school scandal at Rocky Creek when a librarian does something painful and embarrassing I cannot describe here to that part of his anatomy I cannot name, and he ends up in prison. (His condition or crime—I am not sure—is described as Tourette's syndrome, which is either a misdiagnosis, a mispronunciation, or an example of Tourette's in action.)

Yes, prison. The movie begins with a direct-to-camera narration by Luther (Eddie Griffin), who is in prison for undisclosed reasons and is the narrator of this film for reasons even more deeply concealed. Perhaps my attention strayed, but I was unable to discern any connection between Luther and the other characters, and was baffled by how Dizzy/Gil was in prison whenever he needed to get advice from Luther, and then out again whenever it was necessary for him to rejoin the story in progress. Perhaps a subplot, or even a whole movie, is missing from the middle.

In any event, Dizzy/Gil is seen as a neat guy at the new school, especially after he unfurls a giant American flag at football practice and stands in front of it dressed as George C. Scott in *Patton* and delivers a speech so rousing that the team wins for the first time in five years. He also steals a horse and rides around on it more than is necessary.

The movie has all the shots you would expect in a movie of this sort: cheerleaders, football heroics, pratfalls. Some of them are cruel, as when a bully stuffs a midget in a trash can and rolls it downhill. Others are predictably vulgar, as when Dizzy snatches a surveillance camera from the wall and (aided by its extension cord of infinite length) uses it to send a live broadcast into every classroom of a hated teacher struggling with a particularly difficult bowel movement. Sometimes even verbal humor is attempted, as when a high school counselor (Illeana Douglas) tells our hero he is in denial, and helpfully explains, "Denial is not just a river in Egypt."

I don't know why this movie was made or who it was made for. It is, however, not assembly-line fodder, and seems occasionally to be the work of inmates who have escaped from the Hollywood High School Movie Asylum. It makes little sense, fails as often as it succeeds, and yet is not hateful and is sometimes quite cheerfully original. And D. J. Qualls is a kid you can't help but like—a statement I do not believe I have ever before made about the hero of a teenage vulgarian movie.

Nicholas Nickleby ★ ★ ★ ½
PG, 132 m., 2003

Charlie Hunnam (Nicholas Nickleby), Hugh Mitchell (Young Nicholas), Jamie Bell (Smike),

Nathan Lane (Vincent Crummles), Barry Humphries (Mrs. Crummles), Christopher Plummer (Ralph Nickleby), Tom Courtenay (Newman Noggs), Jim Broadbent (Wackford Squeers), Edward Fox (Sir Mulberry Hawk), Timothy Spall (Charles Cheeryble), Gerald Horan (Ned Cheeryble), Juliet Stevenson (Mrs. Squeers), Romola Garai (Kate Nickleby), Anne Hathaway (Madeline Bray), Stella Gonet (Mrs. Nickleby), Alan Cumming (Mr. Folair). Directed by Douglas McGrath and produced by Simon Channing-Williams, John Hart, and Jeff Sharp. Screenplay by McGrath, based on the novel by Charles Dickens.

Nicholas Nickleby was the third novel by Charles Dickens, following *The Pickwick Papers* and *Oliver Twist* and sharing with them a riot of colorful characters. One of them, the sadistic boarding school proprietor Wackford Squeers, was a portrait taken so much from life that it resulted in laws being passed to reform the private education industry. The novel followed a familiar Dickens pattern—a young man sets out in the world to win fortune and love despite a rogue's gallery of villains. It contained characters improbably good or despicable, and with admirable economy tied together several of the key characters in a web of melodramatic coincidences. It is not placed in the first rank of Dickens's art, but I would place it near the top for sheer readability.

The new film version by Douglas McGrath, who made *Emma* (1996), is much more reasonable than the 1980 nine-hour stage version of the Royal Shakespeare Company, which I have on laser disk and really mean to get to one of these days. The movie is jolly and exciting and brimming with life, and wonderfully well acted. McGrath has done some serious pruning, but the result does not seem too diluted; there is room for expansive consideration of such essential characters as Nicholas's vindictive Uncle Ralph (Christopher Plummer), secretly undermined by his dipsomaniac and disloyal servant Newman Noggs (Tom Courtenay). The movie gives full screen time to Wackford Squeers (Jim Broadbent, looking curiously Churchillian) and his wife (Juliet Stevenson)—and hints that psychosexual pathology inspired their mistreatment of students. Their most pathetic target, Smike (Jamie

Bell, who played *Billy Elliott*), is seen as less of a caricature and more of a real victim.

To balance the scales are two of the happiest comic couples Dickens ever created: the touring theatricals Vincent and Mrs. Crummles (Nathan Lane and Barry Humphries), and the brothers Cheeryble (Timothy Spall and Gerald Horan). The Crummles rescue Nicholas (Charlie Hunnam) after his escape from the Squeers's school, turn him into an actor, and even find talent in the hapless Smike. Their touring company is a loving exaggeration of companies Dickens must have worked with, and is rich with such inspirations as their aging and expanding daughter the Child Phenomenon. Barry Humphries uses his alter ego, Dame Edna Everage, to play Mrs. Crummles, and if you look closely you will notice Humphries as a man, playing opposite the formidable Dame.

The Cheerybles are the lawyer brothers who agree on everything, especially that Nicholas must be hired in their firm, all of his problems solved, and his romantic future secured through a liaison with Madeline Bray (Anne Hathaway), whose tyrannical father has long ruled her life. It is particularly good to see Timothy Spall nodding and smiling as brother Charles, after seeing him so depressed in role after role.

Nicholas himself is more of a placeholder than a full-blooded character: the handsome, feckless, and earnest young man who leads us through the story as he encounters one unforgettable character after another. The most striking member of the Nickleby family is, of course, Uncle Ralph, played by Plummer in a performance so cold-blooded it actually reminded me of his stage Iago. Ralph lives only for the accumulation of money. His opinion of the poor is that poverty is their own fault, and they deserve as a result to be put to work to enrich him (in this he reflects some of the latest tax reforms). Nicholas he more or less sells to Squeers, and he lodges Mrs. Nickleby (Stella Gonet) and her daughter Kate (Romola Garai) in a hovel while Kate is put to work doing piecework. Kate is a beauty, however, and so Ralph's larger scheme is to marry her off to the vile Sir Mulberry Hawk (Edward Fox), in return for various considerations involving their business interests.

The actors assembled for *Nicholas Nickleby*

are not only well cast, but well typecast. Each one by physical appearance alone replaces a page or more of Dickens's descriptions, allowing McGrath to move smoothly and swiftly through the story without laborious introductions: They are obviously who they are. The result is a movie that feels like a complete account of Dickens's novel, even though the Royal Shakespeare found an additional seven hours of inspiration.

The physical production is convincing without being too charming or too realistic. The clothes of some of the characters remind us that in those days their wardrobes would have consisted only of what they wore. The countryside is picturesque but falls short of greeting cards (except for the Nicklebys' cottage at the end). The story takes place at about the same time as Scorsese's *Gangs of New York,* but London is heavier on alehouses, lighter on blood in the gutters. The movie makes Dickens's world look more pleasant to inhabit than it probably was, but then so did his novels.

What animates the story is Dickens's outrage, and his good heart. *The Pickwick Papers* was essentially a series of sketches of comic characters, but in *Oliver Twist* and *Nicholas Nickleby* we find him using fiction like journalism, to denounce those who would feed on the poor and exploit the helpless. One senses that in Dickens's time there were more Uncle Ralphs than Cheerybles, but that perhaps he helped to improve the ratio.

Nico and Dani ★ ★ ★

NO MPAA RATING, 90 m., 2001

Fernando Ramallo (Dani), Jordi Vilches (Nico), Marieta Orozco (Elena), Esther Nubiola (Berta), Chisco Amado (Julian), Ana Gracia (Sonia), Myriam Mezieres (Marianne). Directed by Cesc Gay and produced by Marta Esteban and Gerardo Herrero. Screenplay by Gay and Tomas Aragay, based on the play *Krampack* by Jordi Sanchez.

Nico and Dani considers ten days in the lives of two teenage Spanish boys, during which one finds that he is gay and the other finds that he is not. Oh, but it's a lot more complicated than that. Adolescence always is. The movie takes place at a Spanish beach resort; Dani's parents have gone on vacation, leaving him with a tutor and a cook in the daytime, but on his own at night. His best friend, Nico, comes from Barcelona to spend the week.

The boys are both seventeen, both virgins, both frank about their sexual aspirations but murky about the details. They meet two girls their own age—girls they met the previous summer, but a lot can change in a year when you're a teenager. Elena (Marieta Orozco) likes Nico (Jordi Vilches), and that leaves Berta (Esther Nubiola) and Dani (Fernando Ramallo) to pair off, until Dani realizes he'd rather pair off with Nico.

If this were an American teenage sex comedy . . . but don't get me started. Thanks to the MPAA's determination to steer American teenagers toward material that is immature and vulgar, this movie would never get made except with an R or NC-17 rating. Too bad, since an observant film like *Nico and Dani* could be useful to a confused teenager, suggesting that we all have to choose our own paths in life. Teenagers masturbate and worry about it, and this movie considers the subject in a healthy and helpful way, while the MPAA prefers jokes about despoiled apple pies.

Summer at the shore is casual and aimless. The two couples meet for drinks, go to parties and dances, and visit the beach, where Nico can show off his back flips. It gradually becomes clear that all four of them have concluded that these ten days of freedom are an opportunity to lose their virginity at last. Not all of them do, but the possibility is there.

Nico and Dani return to Dani's house after an evening with the girls, feeling the universal horniness of the teenage boy. They experiment. For Nico, it's a casual, meaningless experience, but for Dani it's more than that, and Nico becomes a little alarmed at Dani's urgency. They just don't share the same feelings.

Elena, meanwhile, has an agenda of her own, which Nico doesn't discover until a night when they meet to "do it," and she reveals—well, that Nico is expected to play a role but not make any long-range plans. That's okay with Nico, who like many teenage boys will agree to almost anything if his goal is in view.

The movie is more concerned with Dani. His English teacher, Sonia (Ana Gracia), has observed subtle signs of Dani's sexuality, and tries in a quiet way to let him know his feelings are not unique in all the world. She has a gay friend, Julian (Chisco Amado), and one night they all end up at Julian's for dinner, and Dani has too much to drink. Dani knows Julian is gay, and the next morning he makes a bold, if uncertain, pass; Julian knows Dani is underage, and so does Sonia—who warns Julian to keep his hands off. This episode ends inconclusively, like so much in life.

The movie, directed by Cesc Gay, reminds me of one of Eric Rohmer's movies about teenagers on summer vacation; it has the same lightness of feeling and delicacy of touch, although it's more directly concerned with sex than Rohmer would be. It has a plot—who will lose his or her virginity, and how?—but it's not *about* the plot. It isn't so stupid as to think the answer to Who and How is the whole point, since eventually all will lose their virginity, one way or another. American teenage movies tidy things up by pairing off the right couples at the end. In Europe they know that summers end and life goes on.

Nico and Dani is more concerned with values: with what is right and wrong, ethical or not. There's the night, for example, when the boys put Valium in the sangria they serve to the girls. Wrong, and dangerous. When Berta is half-unconscious, Dani begins to take advantage of her; the technical word is rape, although here it's more of a muddle, since Dani finds he's just not that interested in a girl. Spiking the drinks is immoral. So is the way Julian casually but unmistakably makes his life available to Dani. The movie trusts us to arrive at these conclusions, and doesn't add a lot of laborious plotting to pound home the message. We've all done things that we regret; with any luck we learned something from them. Next summer, Dani and Nico will know who they are, Elena will have moved on to another boy, and Berta—well, she's already told Nico, "Elena is Elena and I'm not. I'm me." It's the way she smiles when she says it that lets Nico know what that means.

Nine Queens ★ ★ ★

R, 114 m., 2002

Ricardo Darin (Marcos), Gaston Pauls (Juan), Leticia Bredice (Valeria), Tomas Fonzi (Federico), Ignasi Abadal (Gandolfo). Directed by Fabian Bielinsky and produced by Cecilia Bossi and Pablo Bossi. Screenplay by Bielinsky.

Fabian Bielinsky's *Nine Queens* is a con within a con within a con. There comes a time when we think we've gotten to the bottom, and then the floor gets pulled out again, and we fall for another level. Since nothing is as it seems (it doesn't even seem as it seems), watching the film is like observing a chess game in which all of the pieces are in plain view but one player has figured out a way to cheat. "David Mamet might kill for a script as good," Todd McCarthy writes in *Variety.* True, although Mamet might also reasonably claim to have inspired it; the setup owes something to his *House of Games,* although familiarity with that film will not help you figure out this one.

The film starts with *a seemingly* chance meeting. Indeed, almost everything in the film is "seemingly." A young would-be con man named Juan (Gaston Pauls) is doing the $20 bill switch with a naive cashier—the switch I have never been able to figure out, where you end up with $39 while seemingly doing the cashier a favor. Juan succeeds. The cashier goes off duty. Juan is greedy, and tries the same trick on her replacement. The first cashier comes back with the manager, screaming that she was robbed. At this point Marcos (Ricardo Darin), a stranger in the store, flashes his gun, identifies himself as a cop, arrests the thief, and hauls him off.

Of course, Marcos is only seemingly a cop. He lectures Juan on the dangers of excessive greed and buys him breakfast, and then the two of them seemingly happen upon an opportunity to pull a big swindle involving the "nine queens," a rare sheet of stamps. This happens when Valeria (Leticia Bredice), seemingly Marcos's sister, berates him because one of his old criminal associates tried to con a client in the hotel where she seemingly works. The old con seemingly had a heart attack, and now the field is seemingly open for Marcos and Juan to bilk the seemingly rich and drunk Gandolfo (Ignasi Abadal).

Now before you think I've given away the game with all those "seeminglys," let me point out that they may only seemingly be seeminglys. They may in fact be as they seem. Or seemingly otherwise. As Juan and Marcos try to work out their scheme, which involves counterfeit stamps, we wonder if in fact the whole game may be a pigeon drop with Juan as the pigeon. But, no, the fake stamps are stolen, seemingly by complete strangers, requiring Marcos and Juan to try to con the owner of the *real* nine queens out of stamps they can sell Gandolfo. (Since they have no plans to really pay for these stamps, their profit would be the same in either case.)

And on and on, around and around, in an elegant and sly deadpan comedy set in modern Buenos Aires. A plot, however clever, is only the clockwork; what matters is what kind of time a movie tells. *Nine Queens* is blessed with a gallery of well-drawn character roles, including the alcoholic mark and his two bodyguards; the avaricious widow who owns the nine queens and her much younger bleached-blond boyfriend; and Valeria the sister, who opposes Marcos's seamy friends and life of crime, but might be willing to sleep with Gandolfo if she can share in the spoils.

Juan meanwhile falls for Valeria himself, and then there are perfectly timed hiccups in the plot where the characters (and we) apparently see through a deception, only to find that deeper reality explains everything—maybe. The story plays out in modern-day Buenos Aires, a city that looks sometimes Latin, sometimes American, sometimes Spanish, sometimes German, sometimes modern, sometimes ancient. Is it possible the city itself is pulling a con on its inhabitants, and that some underlying reality will deceive everyone? The ultimate joke of course would be if the Argentinean economy collapsed, so that everyone's gains, ill-gotten or not, would evaporate. But that is surely too much to hope for.

Note: Nine Queens is like a South American version of Stolen Summer, *the movie that won the contest sponsored by HBO, Miramax, and Matt Damon and Ben Affleck. According to* Variety, *some 350 screenplays were submitted in an Argentinean competition, Bielinsky's won, and he was given funds to film. It's illuminating that in both cases such competitions yielded more literate and interesting screenplays than the studios are usually able to find through their own best efforts.*

No Man's Land ★ ★ ★ ½
R, 98 m., 2001

Branko Djuric (Chiki), Rene Bitorajac (Nino), Filip Sovagovic (Cera), Simon Callow (Soft), Katrin Cartlidge (Jane). Directed by Danis Tanovic and produced by Marc Baschet, Frederique Dumas-Zajdela, and Cedomir Kolar. Screenplay by Tanovic.

Set in the same place and about the same war, *No Man's Land* is like the grown-up version of *Behind Enemy Lines*. It's a bleakly funny parable that could be titled *Between Enemy Lines*. In Bosnia in 1993, Serbs and Bosnians find themselves trapped in the same trench. Anyone who sticks his head up gets shot. And when will that land mine explode?

The setup seems artificial until you reflect that things like this probably do happen in the confusion of war. As the film opens, a few Bosnian fighters are lost in a battlefield fog, and decide to wait until dawn to go farther. When the sun burns away the mist, they find themselves staring directly at Serbian troops. Some are killed. Chiki (Branko Djuric) falls into a trench and is spared.

Serbs come to inspect the trench. Chiki hides, and watches as they place one of his dead comrades onto a land mine as a booby trap. About to be discovered, he kills one Serb and wounds Nino (Rene Bitorajac). A stalemate is developing when the apparently dead man comes back to life. If he moves, the mine explodes and they're all dead.

And no, I haven't revealed too much of the plot because these are just the opening moves in a war game that eventually involves a UN observer (Simon Callow) and a cable news reporter (Katrin Cartlidge)—who assures, as the saying goes, that the whole world is watching. Untold thousands can die unremarked in a war, but when a situation like this develops, people are intrigued. Will the mine explode? How long can the poor guy lie on top of it? Will the two enemies kill each other?

The movie has been written and directed by Danis Tanovic, and it's a first feature that plays like a natural because the situation is so intriguing. Although the Serb and Bosnian debate who is right and wrong in their war, Tanovic's position is that the conflict has escalated into the arena of the absurd: There are so many grievances on both sides that revenge and redress are impossible, and the land mine symbolizes the unhappy situation Bosnia finds itself in. A movie like this helps illustrate the brilliance of the Truth and Reconciliation Commission in South Africa, which argued that it is wise to put the past at rest and start again in the morning.

No Man's Land has been compared to *Catch-22*, *M*A*S*H*, and *Waiting for Godot*—which means, I suppose, that it contains equal parts of irony and futility. There is something funny about characters stuck in the middle of a process; movement would solve everything (they'd all either live or die), but waiting is intolerable. Into this standoff comes Simon Callow's officious UN observer, appropriately named Soft, who must recite platitudes as if he believed them when the situation itself has underlined the absurdity of the whole "peace process."

The film is curiously beautiful. Knowing something about its story, I didn't expect that. I was visualizing characters and dialogue, and I got them, but Tanovic is also intrigued by the way this situation, by bringing the war to a halt, has allowed everyone to notice that it is being fought in—why, nature! A field. With growing things and a sky above. Dr. Johnson observed that the knowledge that one is about to be hanged concentrates the mind wonderfully. The knowledge that you are lying on your back on a land mine likewise, I imagine, inspires a fresh appreciation of clouds and birds and the deep blue sky.

Northfork ★ ★ ★ ★
PG-13, 103 m., 2003

Peter Coyote (Eddie), Anthony Edwards (Happy), Duel Farnes (Irwin), Daryl Hannah (Flower Hercules), Nick Nolte (Father Harlan), Mark Polish (Willis O'Brien), James Woods (Walter O'Brien), Claire Forlani (Mrs. Hadfield), Robin Sachs (Cup of Tea), Ben Foster (Cod), Clark Gregg (Mr. Hadfield). Directed by Michael Polish and produced and written by Mark Polish and Michael Polish.

There has never been a movie quite like *North-fork*, but if you wanted to put it on a list, you would also include *Days of Heaven* and *Wings of Desire*. It has the desolate open spaces of the first, the angels of the second, and the feeling in both of deep sadness and pity. The movie is visionary and elegiac, more a fable than a story, and frame by frame it looks like a portfolio of spaces so wide, so open, that men must wonder if they have a role beneath such indifferent skies.

The film is set in Montana in 1955, as the town of Northfork prepares to be submerged forever beneath the waters of a dam. Three two-man evacuation teams travel the countryside in their fat black sedans, persuading the lingering residents to leave. The team members have a motivation: They've all been promised waterfront property on the lake to come. Most of the residents have already pulled out, but one stubborn citizen opens fire on the evacuators, and another plans to ride out the flood waters in his ark, which does not have two of everything but does have two wives, a detail Noah overlooked.

Other lingerers include Irwin (Duel Farnes), a pale young orphan who has been turned back in by his adoptive parents (Claire Forlani and Clark Gregg) on the grounds that he is defective. "You gave us a sick child, Father," they tell Father Harlan, the parish priest (Nick Nolte). "He can't stand the journey." The priest cares for the child himself, although the lonely little kid is able to conjure up company by imagining four angels who come to console him. Or are they imaginary? They are real for little Irwin, and that should be real enough for us.

The town evokes the empty, lonely feeling you get when you make a last tour of a home you have just moved out of. There is a scene where the six evacuators line up at the counter in a diner to order soup. "Bowl or cup?" asks the waitress, and as they consider this choice with grave poker faces, we get the feeling that only by thinking very hard about soup can they avoid exploding in a frenzy of madness. One of Father Harlan's final church services is conducted after the back wall has already been removed from his church, and the landscape behind him looks desolate.

This is the third film by the Polish twins. Michael directs, Mark acts, and Mark and Michael coproduce and cowrite. Their first was the eerie, disquieting *Twin Falls Idaho*, about

Siamese twins who deal with the fact that one of them is dying. The next was *Jackpot*, about a man who tours karaoke contests, looking for his big break. Now *Northfork*, which in its visual strategy presents Montana not as a scenic tourist wonderland, but as a burial ground of foolish human dreams. Indeed, one of the subplots involves the need to dig up the bodies in the local cemetery, lest the coffins bob to the surface of the new lake; Walter O'Brien (James Woods), one of the evacuators, tells his son Willis O'Brien (Mark Polish) that if they don't move the coffin of the late Mrs. O'Brien, "When this small town becomes the biggest lake this side of the Mississippi, your mother will be the catch of the day."

Funny? Yes, and so is the soup scene in the diner, but you don't laugh out loud a lot in this film because you fear the noise might echo under its limitless leaden sky. This is like a black-and-white film made in color. In some shots, only the pale skin tones contain any color at all. In talking with the Polish brothers after the film premiered at Sundance 2003, I learned that they limited all the costumes, props, and sets to shades of gray, and the cinematographer, M. David Mullen, has drained color from his film so that there is a bleakness here that gets into your bones.

Against this cold is the pale warmth of the angels, who are evoked by Irwin. To console himself for being abandoned by his adoptive parents, he believes that he is a lost angel, fallen to Earth and abducted by humans who amputated his wings. Indeed, he has scars on his shoulder blades. The angels include Flower Hercules (Daryl Hannah), who seems neither man nor woman; Cod (Ben Foster), a cowboy who never speaks; Happy (Anthony Edwards), who is almost blind, but perhaps can see something through the bizarre glasses he wears, with their multiple lenses; and Cup of Tea (Robin Sachs), who talks enough to make up for Happy.

Of these the most moving is Flower Hercules, who seems to feel Irwin's loneliness and pain as her/his own. Daryl Hannah evokes a quality of care for the helpless that makes her a tender guardian angel. Since the evacuators have a stock of angel's wings, which they sometimes offer as inducements to reluctant home-

owners, the thought persists that angels are meant to be real in the film, just as they are in *Wings of Desire*, and only those who cannot believe think Irwin has dreamed them up.

Northfork is not an entertaining film so much as an entrancing one. There were people at Sundance, racing from one indie hipness to another, who found it too slow. But the pace is well chosen for the tone, and the tone evokes the fable, and the fable is about the death of a town and of mankind's brief purchase on this barren plat of land, and it is unseemly to hurry a requiem. The film suggests that of the thousands who obeyed the call, "Go West, young man!" some simply disappeared into the wilderness and were buried, as Northfork is about to be buried, beneath the emptiness of it all.

No Such Thing ★

R, 111 m., 2002

Sarah Polley (Beatrice), Robert John Burke (Monster), Helen Mirren (TV Producer), Julie Christie (Doctor), Baltasar Kormakur (Dr. Artaud). Directed by Hal Hartley and produced by Fridrik Thor Fridriksson, Hartley, and Cecilia Kate Roque. Screenplay by Hartley.

Hal Hartley has always marched in the avant-garde, but this time he marches alone. Followers will have to be drafted. *No Such Thing* is inexplicable, shapeless, dull. It doesn't even rise to entertaining badness. Coming four years after his intriguing if unsuccessful *Henry Fool*, and filmed mostly on location in Iceland with Icelandic money, it suggests a film that was made primarily because he couldn't get anything else off the ground.

The film's original title was *Monster*. That this is a better title than *No Such Thing* is beyond debate. The story involves a monstrous beast who lives on an island off the Icelandic coast, and is immortal, short-tempered, and alcoholic. As the film opens the monster (Robert John Burke) has killed a TV news crew, which inspires a cynical New York network executive (Helen Mirren) to dispatch a young reporter (Sarah Polley) to interview him. Polley's fiancé was among the monster's victims.

Her plane crashes in the ocean, she is the

sole survivor and therefore makes good news herself, and is nursed back to life by Julie Christie, in a role no more thankless than the others in this film. Since the filming, Julie Christie had a face-lift and Helen Mirren won an Oscar nomination. Life moves on.

We seek in vain for shreds of recognizable human motivation. By the time she meets the monster, Polley seems to have forgotten he killed her fiancé. By the time she returns with the monster to New York, the world seems to have forgotten. The monster wants to go to New York to enlist the services of Dr. Artaud (Baltasar Kormakur), a scientist who can destroy matter and therefore perhaps can bring an end to the misery of the immortal beast. We are praying that in the case of this movie, matter includes celluloid.

Elements of the movie seem not merely half-baked, but never to have seen the inside of an oven. Helen Mirren's TV news program and its cynical values are treated with the satirical insights of callow undergraduates who will be happy with a C-plus in film class. Characterizations are so shallow they consist only of mannerisms; Mirren chain-smokes cigarettes, Dr. Artaud chain-smokes cigars, the monster swigs from a bottle. At a social reception late in the film, Sarah Polley turns up in a leather bondage dress with a push-up bra. Why, oh why?

Hal Hartley, still only forty-two, has proudly marched to his own drummer since I first met him at Sundance 1990 with *The Unbelievable Truth*, a good film that introduced two of his favorite actors, Adrienne Shelly and Robert Burke (now Robert John Burke, as the monster). Since then his titles have included *Trust* (1991), *Simple Men* (1992), *Amateur* (1994), *Flirt* (1995), and *Henry Fool*. My star ratings have wavered around 2 or 2½, and my reviews have mostly expressed interest and hope—hope that he will define what he's looking for and share it with us.

Now I'm beginning to wonder how long the wait will be. A Hartley film can be analyzed and justified, and a review can try to mold the intractable material into a more comprehensible form. But why does Hartley make us do all the heavy lifting? Can he consider a film that is self-evident and forthcoming? One that doesn't require us to plunder the quarterly film magazines for deconstruction? I don't mind heavy lifting when a film is challenging or fun, like *Mulholland Drive*. But not when all the weight is in the packing materials.

In *No Such Thing* we have promising elements. The relationship between the monster and the TV reporter suggests *Beauty and the Beast* (more the Cocteau than the Disney version), but that vein is not mined, and the TV news satire is too callow to connect in any way with real targets. Many of the characters, like Dr. Artaud, seem like houseguests given a costume and appearing in the host's play just to be good sports. That gifted actors appear here show how desperate they are for challenging parts, and how willing to take chances. Hartley has let them down.

Not Another Teen Movie ★ ★
R, 82 m., 2001

Chyler Leigh (Janey Briggs), Chris Evans (Jake Wyler), Jaime Pressly (Priscilla), Mia Kirshner (Catherine Wyler), Eric Christian Olsen (Austin), Deon Richmond (Malik), Eric Jungmann (Ricky), Ron Lester (Reggie Ray). Directed by Joel Gallen and produced by Neal H. Moritz. Screenplay by Michael G. Bender, Adam Jay Epstein, Andrew Jacobson, Phil Beauman, and Buddy Johnson.

I suppose I should be grateful. After years of ridiculing teen movies, here's one that does it for me. It's like that soup that heats itself. *Not Another Teen Movie* assembles the clichés, obligatory scenes, and standard characters from three recent subgenres of the teen movie (prom, cheerleader, and tasteless sex) and cross-fertilizes them, if that is the word, with the John Hughes teenager movies of the 1980s. Of course, Hughes was a lot better than his recent imitators, but people who know that are likely to be in their thirties now and won't be going to *Not Another Teen Movie* anyway.

Who does that leave in the theater? The current audience for teen movies, I suppose. But if they're dumb enough to like them, why would they be smart enough to appreciate a satire? Maybe this will simply play for them like—just another teen movie.

Did I laugh during the movie? Yes, I did, a few times, although not as much as I did at the better teen movies like *American Pie* or *Scary Movie*. I liked the way the characters pointed out the clichés they were inhabiting (although that was done first in *Scary Movie*). And the way that when the hero bets he can turn the plain girl into the prom queen, the black guy tells him, "You'll lose the bet, but learn valuable lessons." And the way the subtitles left spaces for the naughty bits in the scene with the nude foreign exchange student. And the awareness of the Slow Clap, a cliché that is rapidly getting to be a public nuisance.

It was good to see familiar faces from old movies, like Molly Ringwald, who offers some hard-learned advice, and John Vernon, who engages in some almost hallucinatory dialogue with a student in detention class. But it was not good to see yet still more wretched excess in the jokes about characters being sprayed with vast quantities of excrement. The movie does not understand that all fart jokes depend on context to be funny. And the opening sequence involving a vibrator is just plain embarrassing.

I have here a heartfelt message from a reader who urges me not to be so hard on stupid films, because they are "plenty smart enough for the average moviegoer." Yes, but one hopes being an average moviegoer is not the end of the road—that one starts as a below-average filmgoer, passes through average, and, guided by the labors of America's hardworking film critics, arrives in triumph at above average.

You will know you have reached that personal goal for yourself when it takes but a moment of thought to calculate that in the month of December, when the studios traditionally showcase Oscar candidates, when movies like *Harry Potter, Vanilla Sky,* and *Ocean's Eleven* are in theaters, when *Lord of the Rings, In the Bedroom,* and twenty-one other ambitious movies are circling for landings, to spend eighty-two minutes watching *Not Another Teen Movie* would be a reckless waste of your time, no matter how many decades you may have to burn.

Novocaine ★ ★ ★
R, 95 m., 2001

Steve Martin (Frank Sangster), Helena Bonham Carter (Susan Ivey), Laura Dern (Jean Noble), Elias Koteas (Harlan Sangster), Scott Caan (Duane Ivey), Keith David (Lunt), Lynne Thigpen (Pat), Kevin Bacon (Actor). Directed by David Atkins and produced by Paul Mones and Daniel M. Rosenberg. Screenplay by Atkins.

In the flat, too-calm tone of a man who still cannot understand why he was singled out for such bad luck, Steve Martin narrates *Novocaine.* It is the story of Dr. Frank Sangster, a dentist who wants only to do a good day's work at the side of his oral-retentive hygienist and fiancée, Jean Noble (Laura Dern). He is dutiful, stable, contented, and boring, until his chair is occupied one day by the pleading eyes and yearning body of Susan Ivey (Helena Bonham Carter). Soon he finds himself implicated in charges involving drugs, perjury, and murder. He got the wrong end of the lollipop.

His name, with its suggestions of blood and gangsters, is a harbinger of his fate. Frank is, in fact, not contented and boring at all, but a volcano of seething passion. Although he cannot admit it even to himself, he is driven to distraction by the blameless perfection of his fiancée, Jean, since if he could blame her for something, anything, he might like her a lot more.

Susan Ivey, on the other hand, is trouble right from the moment she asks for a prescription for Demerol. "Demerol?" he says knowingly. "I'm not that kind of dentist." He grudgingly fills out a prescription for five (5) pills, which after she has improved it on her way to the pharmacy becomes a prescription for fifty (50) pills. "She's just walked out the door," the druggist tells Frank; he waited too late to check on a prescription that seemed suspiciously large, even for a root canal.

If only Susan had taken the pills and kept going, life might still have been uneventful for Frank, with nothing more exciting to look forward to than the inevitable marriage to and divorce from Jean Noble. But Susan appears again in his office, her mind no doubt on the other controlled substances under his command, and soon they are discovering that modern dental chairs recline almost to the horizontal.

Novocaine is a screwball *film noir* with a lot of medium laughs and a few great big ones, written and directed by David Atkins. All I

471

know about him for sure is that he wrote the screenplay for *Arizona Dream*, the only American film of the Yugoslavian mad genius Emir Kusturica. It was a comedy involving Johnny Depp as a fish warden in New York harbor, Jerry Lewis as an Arizona car dealer, and Faye Dunaway as a widow with an accordion-playing daughter and an eye for Depp. Most of these elements I think we can safely assign to Atkins, not Kusturica. Now in the director's chair, Atkins shows the same offbeat taste for crime, sex, comedy, and labyrinthine plotting.

What complicates *Novocaine* is not the triangle involving the dentist, his patient, and his oral hygienist, but the addition of two brothers, who form the movie's little herd of black sheep. Frank's brother Harlan (Elias Koteas) is a ne'er-do-well freeloader with an unpleasant habit of seeming willing to hang around forever until he sees cash. Susan's brother Duane (Scott Caan) is a violent psychopath who shares her appetite for drugs and far exceeds her capacity. By making the crucial mistake of lying to DEA agents at a time when the simple truth would have done just fine, Frank finds himself drawn into a web with these people that leads to a nightmare of murder, guilt, remorse, and confusion. He becomes a textbook illustration for Hitchcock's favorite character, The Innocent Man Wrongly Accused.

I have been vague about the details because the movie needs its surprises. You will gather that Frank and Susan are not among the dead. They find themselves, indeed, rather sweet on each other—to his surprise, because he thought he was happily engaged, and to hers, because she thought all she wanted was the drugs.

At just about that point when every comedy needs a little laughing gas, *Novocaine* gets a charge from a surprise appearance by Kevin Bacon, playing an actor who is following the police around to get insights for his starring role in a reality TV show. Bacon is playing not "himself," although that is what the reviews will say, but an actor he builds from the ground up as a type he must often have seen: an actor extremely, even obsessively, concerned that you understand he is not "just an actor," but in fact a person of rare intelligence and penetrating insight.

Novocaine is funny all the way through, and ingenious all the way through. I am not sure it

plugs all its loopholes, but in a comedy, that's not such a problem. The key to the film is Helena Bonham Carter, whose passionate character is the engine that pulls the train. Martin is very funny by somehow being simultaneously terrified that he will be framed for murder and that his hair will get mussed. The movie opens with X rays of the teeth of its stars, closes with bite marks as a clue, and uses root canals as its organizing symbol in more ways than one.

Nowhere in Africa ★ ★ ★ ★
NO MPAA RATING, 140 m., 2003

Juliane Köhler (Jettel Redlich), Merab Ninidze (Walter Redlich), Lea Kurka (Younger Regina), Karoline Eckertz (Teenage Regina), Sidede Onyulo (Owuor [Cook]), Matthias Habich (Süsskind). Directed by Caroline Link and produced by Peter Herrmann. Screenplay by Link, based on the novel by Stefanie Zweig.

It is so rare to find a film where you become quickly, simply absorbed in the story. You want to know what happens next. Caroline Link's *Nowhere in Africa* is a film like that, telling the story of a German Jewish family that escapes from the Nazis by going to live and work on a farm in rural Kenya. It's a hardscrabble farm in a dry region, and the father, who used to be a lawyer, is paid a pittance to be the manager. At first his wife hates it. Their daughter, who is five when she arrives, takes to Africa with an immediate and instinctive love.

We see the mother and daughter, Jettel and Regina Redlich (Juliane Köhler and Lea Kurka), in their comfortable world in Frankfurt. The mother likes clothes, luxury, elegance. Her husband, Walter (Merab Ninidze), reading the ominous signs of the rise of Nazism, has gone ahead to East Africa, and now writes asking them to join him—"and please bring a refrigerator, which we will really need, and not our china or anything like that." What Jettel brings is a ballroom gown, which will be spectacularly unnecessary.

The marriage is a troubled one. Jettel thinks herself in a godforsaken place, and Walter, who works hard but is not a natural farmer, has little sympathy with her. Their sex life fades: "You only let me under your shirt when I'm a lawyer," he tells her once when his advance is turned away. But little Regina loves every moment of every day. She makes friends with the African children her age, with that uncomplicated acceptance that children have, and seems to learn their language overnight. She picks up their lore and stories, and is at home in the bush.

Jettel, meanwhile, has a rocky start with Owuor (Sidede Onyulo), the farm cook. He is a tall, proud, competent man from the regional tribe, the Masai, who soon loves Regina like his own daughter. Jettel makes the mistake of treating him like a servant when he sees himself as a professional. He never compromises local custom regarding cooks. Asked to help dig a well, he explains, "I'm a cook. Cooks don't dig in the ground." And for that matter, "Men don't carry water."

They are outsiders here in three ways: as white people, as Germans, and as Jews. The first presents the least difficulty, because the tribal people on the land are friendly and helpful. Their status as Germans creates an ironic situation when war is declared and they are rounded up by the British colonial authorities as enemy aliens; this is absurd, since they are refugees from the enemy, but before the mistake can be corrected they are transported to Nairobi and interred—ironically, in a luxury hotel that has been pressed into service. As high tea is served to them, a British officer asks the hotel manager if the prisoners need to be treated so well. "These are our standards, and we are not willing to compromise," the manager replies proudly.

To the Africans, they are not Jews, Germans, or aliens, but simply white farmers; the rise of anticolonialism is still in the future in this district. Regina, so young when she left Europe, therefore hasn't tasted anti-Semitism until her parents send her into town to a boarding school. Now a pretty teenager (played by Karoline Eckertz), she is surprised to hear the head-master say, "The Jews will stand outside the classroom as we recite the Lord's Prayer."

As time passes and the beauty and complexity of the land become clear to Jettel, she begins slowly to feel more at home. Her husband is vindicated in moving his family to Africa; letters arrive with sad news of family members deported to death camps. But he always considers Africa a temporary haven, and his attention is focused on a return to Europe. Each member of the Redlich family has a separate arc: The mother grows to like Africa as the father likes it less, and their daughter loves it always.

The story is told through the eyes of the daughter (Eckertz is the narrator); Caroline Link's screenplay is based on a best-selling German novel by Stefanie Zweig, who treats such matters as Jettel's brief affair with a British officer as they might have been perceived, and interpreted, by the daughter. Link's style permits the narrative to flow as it might in memory, and although there are dramatic high points (such as a fire and a plague of locusts), they are not interruptions but part of the rhythm of African life, and are joined by the sacrifice of a lamb (for rain) and an all-night ritual ceremony that the young girl will never forget.

Link's film, which won five German Oscars, including best film, won the 2003 Academy Award as best foreign film, and comes after another extraordinary film, her 1997 *Beyond Silence*, which was an Oscar nominee. That one was also about the daughter of a troubled marriage; the heroine was the hearing child of a deaf couple. I respond strongly to her interest in good stories and vivid, well-defined characters; this film is less message than memory, depending on the strength of the material to make all of the points. We feel as if we have lived it.

O

O ★ ★ ★
R, 95 m., 2001

Mekhi Phifer (Odin James), Josh Hartnett
(Hugo Goulding), Julia Stiles (Desi Brable),
Elden Henson (Roger Rodriguez), Andrew
Keegan (Michael Casio), Rain Phoenix (Emily),
John Heard (Dean Brable), Anthony Johnson
(Dell), Martin Sheen (Coach Goulding).
Directed by Tim Blake Nelson and produced by
Daniel Fried, Eric Gitter, and Anthony Rhulen.
Screenplay by Brad Kaaya, based on the play
Othello by William Shakespeare.

Odin, the star basketball player at a private
school in the South, is the only African-
American student there. He dates the daughter of the dean, who may disapprove but keeps
his thoughts to himself because Odin (Mekhi
Phifer) is so useful to the school. Some reviews
of *O* have questioned the plausibility of these
details, but they are perfectly faithful to Shakespeare's *Othello*, the source of the movie: Othello
was the only Moor in Venice, Desdemona was
a senator's daughter, Othello's skill as a general
protected Venice against its enemies.

Odin James (whose initials, "O.J.," are surely
not a coincidence) is also, like Othello, too
easily made jealous—it is his fatal flaw. Desi
(Julia Stiles) loves him and is faithful to him,
but he cannot bring himself to trust her, and
that is his downfall. His supposed friend Hugo
(Josh Hartnett) plants the seeds of doubt, suggesting Desi is secretly sleeping with another
student, Michael (Andrew Keegan). And there
is an antique scarf that Odin gives to Desi and
that seems to become evidence of the cheating.

Again, all from Shakespeare, although the
movie creates Hugo's (Iago's) motivation. Hugo's
father is the basketball coach (Martin Sheen),
but dinnertime at their house is a grim and
silent affair, and when the coach says of Odin,
"I love him like my own son," look for Hugo's
reaction shot. It is sometimes forgotten that
Iago doesn't want Desdemona for himself. He
simply uses her as a way to bring about
Othello's downfall, correctly observing that
jealousy triggers his enemy's weakness. It is
Roderigo who was Desdemona's former lover
(here presented as Roger Rodriguez, and played

by Elden Henson as Hugo's gullible accomplice in treachery).

There have been and will be many modern
retreads of Shakespeare. *O* is close in spirit to
Baz Luhrmann's teen-gang version of *Romeo
and Juliet*. It isn't a line-by-line update of *Othello*,
but an attempt to reproduce the passion of the
original play, and for younger viewers new to
Shakespeare it would only enhance a reading
of the real thing. The film's misfortune, however, is that it was being made at the time of the
Columbine tragedy, and was immediately
deemed unreleasable by Miramax, which shelved
it for three years; Lions Gate is now the distribution company.

We have a peculiar inability in our country
to understand the contexts of things; when it
comes to art, we interpret troublesome works
in the most literal and simple-minded way. In
the aftermath of Columbine, Washington leg-
islators called on Hollywood to police itself,
and rumbled about possible national censorship. Miramax caved in by suppressing this
film. To suggest that *O* was part of the solution
and not part of the problem would have required a sophistication that our public officials
either lack, or are afraid to reveal for fear of
offending the bottom-feeders among their
constituents.

So now here is *O*, a good film for most of
the way, and then a powerful film at the end,
when, in the traditional Shakespearean manner,
all of the plot threads come together, the victims
are killed, the survivors mourn, and life goes
on. It is clearly established that Hugo is a psychopath, and that his allies are victims of that
high school disease that encourages the unpop-
ular to do anything in order to be accepted.
Those who think this film will inspire events
like Columbine should ask themselves how
often audiences want to be like the despised
villain.

Mekhi Phifer makes a strong, tortured Odin,
and delivers a final speech that in its heartbreaking anguish inspires our pity much as
Othello's does. Josh Hartnett showed here,
three years before *Pearl Harbor*, that he is capable of subtleties and complexities that epic
did not dream of. Julia Stiles, who is developing
into one of the best young actresses, adds this

modern Desdemona to her modern Ophelia in *Hamlet* (2000), and reminds us, too, of her interracial romance in *Save the Last Dance.*

True, some of the plot threads seem unlikely. Is it that easy to overhear and completely misunderstand crucial conversations? How much more use can a scarf be put to? But those are problems in Shakespeare, too—or perhaps simply plot mechanisms that allow the characters to arrive at their tragic destinations. And then there's the unexpected additional level, the suggestion that high school sports have become like a kind of warfare. What is insane in most American high schools is that sports are considered more important than study, generating heroism and resentment too powerful for most kids to cope with, and inspiring in their bitter backwash the kind of alienation we saw at Columbine.

Ocean's Eleven ★ ★ ★
PG-13, 116 m., 2001

George Clooney (Danny Ocean), Brad Pitt (Rusty Ryan), Andy Garcia (Terry Benedict), Julia Roberts (Tess Ocean), Casey Affleck (Virgil Malloy), Scott Caan (Turk Malloy), Don Cheadle (Basher Tarr), Matt Damon (Linus Caldwell). Directed by Steven Soderbergh and produced by Jerry Weintraub. Screenplay by Ted Griffin.

Serious pianists sometimes pound out a little honky-tonk just for fun. That's like what Steven Soderbergh is doing in *Ocean's Eleven.* This is a standard genre picture, a remake of the 1960 Frank Sinatra caper, and Soderbergh, who usually aims higher, does it as a sort of lark. It's slick, all right: Directors this good don't usually handle material this routine. It has yearnings above its natural level, as if hoping to redeem itself and metamorphose into a really good movie.

The movie stars George Clooney, who can be powerfully impassive better than almost anybody, as Danny Ocean, fresh out of prison and eager for a new job. He's a smooth operator who, his parole board notes, figured in a dozen investigations where he was never charged. He contacts his old sidekick Rusty Ryan (Brad Pitt) with a scheme to steal millions from not one but three Las Vegas casinos. Amazingly, the movie specifies and shoots in real casinos (the Mirage, the MGM Grand, and the Bellagio) and incorporates the destruction of the Desert Inn.

Casing the job, Rusty sees the casino owner (Andy Garcia) with a woman he recognizes: Tess Ocean (Julia Roberts), Danny's ex-wife. "Tell me it isn't about her," Rusty begs Danny. Of course it is. Ocean wants to steal from his ex-wife's current lover *and* get her back again. They assemble a team, including Matt Damon, Don Cheadle, and Casey Affleck. I suppose there are eleven in all, although even during a long tracking shot I forgot to count.

The outlines of a caper movie are long and well established: The scary external shot of the impenetrable targets, the inside information, and voice-over as we see guards going about their work, the plan with the split-second timing. *Ocean's Eleven* even includes an elaborate full-scale mock-up of the strong room used by the three casinos, leading to such practical questions as (1) why does it need to be this elaborate? (2) how much did it cost? and (3) who contracted it for them, or did they knock it together themselves overnight?

The movie excels in its delivery of dialogue. The screenplay by Ted Griffin is elegantly epigrammatic, with dialogue that sounds like a cross between Noel Coward and a 1940s *noir* thriller.

Roberts: You're a thief and a liar.
Clooney: I only lied about being a thief.
R: You don't do that anymore?
C: Steal?
R: Lie.

They do this so well I was reminded of the classic exchanges between Bogart and Bacall. And notice, too, the conversation involving Clooney, Roberts, and Garcia, when the casino boss finds the ex-husband at Tess's table in the dining room. The two men, of course, despise each other, but are so smooth and cool we note it only in the precision of their timing and word choices, leading up to a final exchange in which Danny, leaving the table, says "Terry" in a way that uses the first name with inappropriate familiarity, and Terry responds, "Danny," on precisely the same note.

Brad Pitt has a nice dialogue passage too, when he's briefing the Matt Damon character. The jargon is all about strategy and entirely in modern terms, but listen to the music instead of the words and you realize it's a riff on Hamlet's instructions to the players.

As movie capers go, the specifics in *Ocean's Eleven* are not necessarily state of the art. I can think of more ingeniously executed plans, most recently in *The Score*, but then this is not a movie about suspense but about suavity. George Clooney and Julia Roberts deliberately evoke the elegance of stars like Cary Grant and Ingrid Bergman, Andy Garcia is as smooth, groomed, polished, and tailored as George Raft, and the movie blessedly ends not with a shoot-out but with a complicated plot finesse. I enjoyed it. It didn't shake me up and I wasn't much involved, but I liked it as a five-finger exercise. Now it's time for Soderbergh to get back to work.

Note: The 1960 Rat Pack version of Ocean's Eleven *was itself a remake. The original is* Bob le Flambeur, *a 1956 French film by Jean-Pierre Melville, now available on DVD in the Criterion Collection.*

Old School ★
R, 90 m., 2003

Luke Wilson (Mitch), Will Ferrell (Frank), Vince Vaughn (Beanie), Ellen Pompeo (Nicole), Juliette Lewis (Heidi), Jeremy Piven (Gordon), Craig Kilborn (Mark), Leah Remini (Lara). Directed by Todd Phillips and produced by Daniel Goldberg, Joe Medjuck, and Phillips. Screenplay by Phillips and Scot Armstrong.

Luke Wilson, Will Ferrell, and Vince Vaughn clock in at an average age of thirty-four, which is a little old to be a frat boy. It is not their age but their longevity, however, that I question. In *Old School*, where they occupy a series of off-campus party houses, they follow lifestyles more appropriate for the college students in *Flatliners*. Anyone stuck in the jugular by an animal-disabling tranquilizer dart who then rolls into a swimming pool is not likely to have to face the kinds of questions about retirement confronting the hero of *About Schmidt*.

There is a type of older student who never seems to leave the campus. Some are actually graduate students, some are "finishing their thesis," others are gaining job experience (i.e., are bartenders or drug dealers). I graduated

from Illinois, returned ten years later, and found my old friend Mike still at his usual table in the Illini Union, drinking the bottomless cup of coffee and working the crossword puzzle.

Wilson, Ferrell, and Vaughn do not play this type of student. They are not really students at all, in fact. Wilson plays a businessman who returns home early to discover that his fiancée (Juliette Lewis) is hosting an orgy. Ferrell is engaged to be married, and Vaughn is married. They stumble into founding their own fraternity after discovering by accident that you can get a lot of action if you throw nude wrestling matches in K-Y jelly.

Old School wants to be *National Lampoon's Animal House,* but then, don't they all. It assumes that the modern college campus is a hotbed, or is it a sinkhole, of moral squalor, exhibitionism, promiscuity, kinky sex, and rampant rampantness. Perhaps it is.

I have also heard, on the other hand, that the politically correct modern male undergraduate, terrified of sexual harassment charges, must have a notarized statement in hand giving him permission to even think about getting to first base, and a judge's order authorizing him to advance to second. (All women in movies set on such campuses are issued at birth a blanket license to kick groins.)

Unsure of myself, I avoid altogether the question of *Old School*'s veracity, and move on to its humor, which is easier to master because there is so little of it. This is not a funny movie, although it has a few good scenes and some nice work by Will Ferrell as an apparently compulsive nudist.

It follows the same old story about a bunch of fun-loving guys who only want to throw orgies and meet chicks, and a young fogey dean (Jeremy Piven) who wants to spoil their fun. One of the cute co-eds is played by Ellen Pompeo, who was so absolutely wonderful in *Moonlight Mile*. She should not be discouraged by this sophomore effort. Even Meryl Streep had to make a second movie after *Julia*. Oh, and I just found the title right here: *The Deer Hunter*.

The movie has been slapped together by director Todd Phillips, who careens from scene to scene without it occurring to him that humor benefits from characterization, context, and continuity. Otherwise, all you have is a lot of people acting goofy. The movie was screened before an "invited audience" in a Chicago theater, where two small groups of audience members laughed loudly at almost everything, and just about everybody else waited politely until it was over and they could leave. Critics are sometimes required to see comedies at such screenings because we can appreciate them better when we see them with a general audience, and to be sure, I learn a lot that way.

The One ★ ½
PG-13, 87 m., 2001

Jet Li (Gabe, Yulaw, Lawless), Carla Gugino (T. K., Massie Walsh), Delroy Lindo (Roedecker), Jason Statham (Funsch), James Morrison (Aldrich), Dylan Bruno (Yates), Richard Steinmetz (D'Antoni). Directed by James Wong and produced by Glen Morgan and Steven Chasman. Screenplay by Morgan and Wong.

There is a vast question lurking at the center of The One, and the question is: Why? Assuming there are 124 universes and that you existed in all of them and could travel among them, why would you want to kill off the other 123 versions of you? This is, I submit, a good question, but not one discussed in any depth by Yulaw (Jet Li), the villain of the film. Jet Li also plays the film's hero and one of its victims, but neither of them understandably knows the answer.

The film opens with a narration informing us that there are parallel universes, and that "a force exists who seeks to destroy the balance so that he can become—The One!" Apparently every time one of your other selves dies, his power is distributed among the survivors. If Yulaw kills 123 selves, he has the power of 124. Follow this logic far enough, and retirement homes would be filled with elderly geezers who have outlived their others and now have the strength of 124, meaning they can bend canes with their bare hands and produce mighty bowel movements with scornful ease.

What does Yulaw hope to accomplish with his power? He might, the narrator suggests, become God—and thus, if killed, might bring all of creation to an end. A guy like this, you don't want him getting in fights and taking chances. But the God theory is theologically unsound, because God works from the top

down and didn't get where he is by knocking off the competition. Maybe Yulaw is just a megalomaniac who gets off on being able to beat up everyone in the room. Maybe one of the differences between a good martial arts movie and one that is merely technically competent is that in the good ones, the characters have a motivation, and in the others life is just a competitive sport.

Yulaw defeats Lawless, one of his other selves, fairly early in the film, and then zeroes in on Gabe, who is a Los Angeles County sheriff's deputy. Gabe knows nothing of the multiverses, but is, under the rules, as strong as half of the dead men, and so a good match for Yulaw. Meanwhile, Yulaw is pursued from his home universe by Roedecker (Delroy Lindo) and Funsch (Jason Statham), agents of the Multiverse Bureau of Investigations. His wife, woman, girlfriend, or sidekick in all of these worlds is played by Carla Gugino.

The possibilities with this plot are endless. Alas, the movie is interested only in fight scenes, and uses the latest in computer-generated effects to show the various Jet Li characters as they throw enemies into the air, dodge bullets, hold a motorcycle in each hand and slam them together against an opponent, etc. The final epic confrontation features Jet Li fighting himself. Both are wearing black jumpsuits at the start of the fight, but the evil Jet Li shows consideration for the audience by stripping down to a blue top, so we can tell him apart from the good Jet Li.

This titanic closing fight, by the way, may use cutting-edge effects, but has been written with slavish respect for ancient clichés. It begins with the venerable It's Only a Cat Scene, in which a cat startles a character (but not the audience) by leaping at the lens. Then the characters retire to a Steam and Flame Factory, one of those Identikit movie sets filled with machines that produce copious quantities of steam, flames, and sparks. Where do they have their fight? On a catwalk, of course. Does anyone end up clinging by his fingertips? Don't make me laugh.

The movie offers brainless high-tech action without interesting dialogue, characters, motivation, or texture. In other words, it's sure to be popular. Seeing a movie like this makes me feel bad that I applied such high standards to Don-

nie Darko, which also deals with logical paradoxes, and by comparison is a masterpiece.

One Day in September ★ ★ ★
R, 92 m., 2001

A documentary featuring Ankie Spitzer, widow
of Israeli fencing coach Andre Spitzer; terrorist
Jamal Al Gashey; ITN News reporter Gerald
Seymour; Alex Springer, son of Jacov Springer,
Israeli and judge; and Gad Zabari, Israeli
wrestler who escaped from the terrorists.
Directed by Kevin Macdonald and produced
by John Battsek and Arthur Cohn.

In September 1972, Palestinian terrorists in-
vaded the athletes' quarters of the Munich
Olympiad and took Israeli athletes hostage.
By the following evening, eleven Israelis and
five of the eight terrorists were dead. Kevin
Macdonald's documentary *One Day in September* retells these events in the style of a
thriller, which is a little unsettling. It's one
thing to see a fictional re-creation of facts,
such as the re-creation of the Cuban missile
crisis in *Thirteen Days,* and another to see
facts tarted up like fiction. Oh, it's exciting,
all right, but do we feel ennobled to be thus
entertained?

Macdonald brings remarkable research to
the film. He has managed to obtain interviews
with most of the key figures who are still alive,
including the one surviving terrorist, Jamal Al
Gashey, now in hiding "in Africa" (the two
other survivors were killed by Israeli assassination squads). He talks to an Israeli athlete
who escaped, the son of another, and the widow
of a third, to Israeli coaches and security experts, to German generals and policemen, to
journalists who covered the event. His reporting is extraordinary, as he relentlessly builds
up a case against the way the Germans and the
International Olympic Committee handled
the crisis.

Much is made of "German efficiency," Macdonald observes, but the Germans were so
inefficient that they had no trained antiterror-
ist squad, no security around the compound,
no contingency plans, not even effective communication (a police sniper and a helicopter
pilot were shot by German police who had not

been told where they were). In a development
that would be funny if it were not so sad, the
Germans stationed a 747 on an airport runway
as a getaway plane for the terrorists, and staffed
it with cops dressed as the plane's crew, but
minutes before the plane was to be used, the
cops took a vote, decided they were not competent to handle the assignment, and walked
off the plane.

In a film filled with startling charges, the
most shocking is that the three captured terrorists escaped from custody as part of a secret
deal with the German government, which essentially wanted the whole matter to be over
with. A German aircraft was hijacked by Palestinians, who demanded that the three prisoners be handed over, which they were, with
"indecent haste." The film says the plane suspiciously contained only twelve passengers,
none of them women or children; now Jamal
Al Gashey confirms it was a setup.

As for the Olympic committee, at first it intended to continue the Games during the
hostage crisis, and we see athletes of other nations training and relaxing within sight of the
dorms where the Israelis were being held. After
the Games were suspended, thousands watched
the standoff as if it were a show, while the Germans continued to bungle (officers crept onto
the roof of the building, but the scene was
broadcast live on TV, and the terrorists, of
course, were watching the news).

The death of the innocent athletes was an
avoidable tragedy, we conclude. If the Israeli secret service had been able to stage a raid as they
wanted, it's likely many lives would have been
saved. The final bloodbath resulted more from
German bumbling than from anything else.

Still, one wonders why newsreel shots of
Hitler and reminders of the Nazi past are necessary in a film that has almost no time at all
to explain who the Palestinians were or why
they made such a desperate raid. The raid had
nothing to do with the Nazi past, and the current Germans seemed like comic-opera buf-
foons from a Groucho Marx comedy. If the
purpose of a documentary is to inform, it
could be argued that audiences already know
a great deal about Hitler but are not likely to
learn much from a couple of perfunctory shots
of Palestinian refugee camps.

One Day in September grips the attention and is exciting and involving. I recommend it on that basis—and also because of the new information it contains. I was disturbed, however, by Macdonald's pumped-up style, and by a tasteless conclusion in which images of action, bloodshed, and corpses are cut together into a montage and backed with rock music. What was he thinking of?

Note: When One Day in September *won the Academy Award in 2000, its producer, Arthur Cohn, held up the Oscar and boasted, "and I won this without showing it in a single theater!" The documentary community is still angry about that remark. Cohn exhibits his Oscar entries at screenings peopled largely by those on his invitation list, and to as few other people as possible. Under the Academy bylaws, only those who have seen all five docs can vote, and by limiting those who have seen his, Cohn shrinks the voting pool and improves his odds. Documentary groups and many individual filmmakers have protested this Oscar to the Academy.*

One Hour Photo ★ ★ ★ ½
R, 98 m., 2002

Robin Williams (Seymour "Sy" Parrish), Connie Nielsen (Nina Yorkin), Michael Vartan (Will Yorkin), Dylan Smith (Jake Yorkin), Gary Cole (Bill Owens), Eriq La Salle (Detective Van Der Zee), Erin Daniels (Maya Burson). Directed by Mark Romanek and produced by Pamela Koffler, Christine Vachon, and Stan Wlodkowski. Screenplay by Romanek.

One Hour Photo tells the story of Seymour "Sy" Parrish, who works behind the photo counter of one of those vast suburban retail barns. He has a bland, anonymous face and a cheerful voice that almost conceals his desperation and loneliness. He takes your film, develops it, and has your photos ready in an hour. Sometimes he even gives you five-by-sevens when all you ordered were four-by-sixes. His favorite customers are the Yorkins—Nina, Will, and cute young Jake. They've been steady customers for six years. When they bring in their film, he makes an extra set of prints—for himself.

Sy follows an unvarying routine. There is a diner where he eats, alone, methodically. He is

an "ideal employee." He has no friends, a coworker observes. But the Yorkins serve him as a surrogate family, and he is their self-appointed Uncle Sy. Only occasionally does the world get a glimpse of the volcanic side of his personality, as when he gets into an argument with Larry, the photo machine repairman.

The Yorkins know him by name and are a little amused by his devotion. There is an edge of need to his moments with them. If they were to decide to abandon film and get one of those new digital cameras, a prudent instinct might lead them to keep this news from Sy.

Robin Williams plays Sy, another of his open-faced, smiling madmen, like the killer in *Insomnia*. He does this so well you don't have the slightest difficulty accepting him in the role. The first time we see Sy behind his counter, neat, smiling, with a few extra pounds from the diner routine, we buy him. He belongs there. He's native to retail.

The Yorkin family is at first depicted as ideal: models for an ad for their suburban lifestyle. Nina Yorkin (Connie Nielsen), pretty and fresh-scrubbed, has a cheery public persona. Will (Michael Vartan) is your regular clean-cut guy. Young Jake (Dylan Smith) is cute as a picture. Mark Romanek, who wrote and directed the film, is sneaky in the way he so subtly introduces discordant elements into his perfect picture. A tone of voice, a half-glimpsed book cover, a mistaken order, a casual aside . . . they don't mean much by themselves, but they add up to an ominous cloud gathering over the photo counter.

Much of the film's atmosphere forms through the cinematography by Jeff Cronenweth. His interiors at "Savmart" are white and bright, almost aggressive. You can hear the fluorescent lights humming. Through choices involving set design and lens selection, the one-hour photo counter somehow seems an unnatural distance from the other areas of the store, as if the store shuns it, or it has withdrawn into itself. Customers approach it across an exposed expanse of emptiness, with Sy smiling at the end of the trail.

A man who works in a one-hour photo operation might seem to be relatively powerless. Certainly Sy's boss thinks so. But in an era when naked baby pictures can be interpreted as child abuse, the man with access to your photos can cause you a lot of trouble. What would happen, for example, if Will Yorkin is having an affair, and his mistress brings in photos to be developed, and Uncle Sy "mistakenly" hands them to Nina Yorkin?

The movie at first seems soundly grounded in everyday reality, in the routine of a predictable job. When Romanek departs from reality, he does it subtly, sneakily, so that we believe what we see until he pulls the plug. There is one moment I will not describe (in order not to ruin it) when Sy commits a kind of social trespass that has the audience stirring with quiet surprise: surprise, because until they see the scene they don't realize that his innocent, everyday act can be a shocking transgression in the wrong context.

Watching the film, I thought of Michael Powell's great 1960 British thriller *Peeping Tom*, which was about a photographer who killed his victims with a stiletto concealed in his camera. Sy uses a psychological stiletto, but he's the same kind of character, the sort of man you don't much notice, who blends in, accepted, overlooked, left alone so that his rich secret life can flower. There is a moment in *Peeping Tom* when a shot suddenly reveals the full depth of the character's depravity. In *One Hour Photo* a shot with a similar purpose requires only a lot of innocent family snapshots, displayed in a way that is profoundly creepy.

The movie has also been compared to *American Beauty*, another film where resentment, loneliness, and lust fester beneath the surface of suburban affluence. The difference, I think, is that the needs of the Kevin Spacey character in *American Beauty*, while frowned upon and even illegal, fall generally within the range of emotions we understand. Sy Parrish is outside that range. He was born with parts missing, and has assembled the remainder into a person who has borrowed from the inside to make the outside look okay.

One Night at McCool's ★ ★ ½

R, 93 m., 2001

Liv Tyler (Jewel Valentine), Matt Dillon (Randy), John Goodman (Detective Dehling), Paul Reiser (Lawyer Carl), Michael Douglas (Mr. Burmeister), Andrew Dice Clay (Utah/Mormon Brother),

Reba McEntire (Carl's Psychiatrist), Richard Jenkins (Priest). Directed by Harald Zwart and produced by Michael Douglas and Allison Lyon Segan. Screenplay by Stan Seidel.

When a man tells a woman she's the one he's been searching for, this is not a comment about the woman but about the man. The male mind, drenched in testosterone, sees what it needs to see. *One Night at McCool's*, a comedy about three men who fall for the same woman, shows how the wise woman can take advantage of this biological insight.

The movie stars Liv Tyler as Jewel Valentine, a woman who walks into a bar one night and walks out, so to speak, with the hearts of three men. Each one sees a different woman. For Randy the bartender (Matt Dillon), she's the sweet homemaker he has yearned for ever since his mother died and left him a house. For Carl the lawyer (Paul Reiser), she's a sexpot with great boobs and legs that go all the way up to here. When Dehling the detective (John Goodman) sees her a few days later, she's like an angel, backlit in soft focus, as if heaven has reincarnated his beloved dead wife.

Much of the humor of the case comes because when Jewel looks at Randy, Carl, and Dehling, she sees three patsys—men who can feed her almost insatiable desire for consumer goods. She may sorta like them. She isn't an evil woman; she's just the victim of her nature. She's like the Parker Posey character in *Best in Show* who considers herself "lucky to have been raised among catalogs."

Like movie sex bombs of the past, Tyler plays Jewel not as a scheming gold digger, but as an innocent, almost childlike creature who is delighted by baubles (and by DVD machines, which she has a thing for). At least, I think that's what she does. Like the audience, I have to reconstruct her from a composite picture made out of three sets of unreliable testimony. Perhaps there is a clue in the fact that the first time we see her, she's with a big, loud, obnoxious, leather-wearing, middle-aged hood named Utah (Andrew Dice Clay). On the other hand, perhaps Utah is a nicer guy, since we see him only through the eyes of his rivals.

We see everything in the movie through secondhand testimony. Like Kurosawa's *Rashomon*, the film has no objective reality; we depend on what people tell us. Jewel Valentine waltzes into each man's life and gets him to do more or less what she desires, and what she desires is highly specific and has to do with her relationship to the consumer lifestyle (to reveal more would be unfair). Each guy, of course, filters her behavior through the delusion that she really likes him. And each guy creates a negative, hostile mental portrait of the other two guys.

Each witness has someone to listen to him. Randy the bartender confides in Mr. Burmeister (Michael Douglas, buck-toothed and in urgent need of a barber). He's a hit man Randy wants to pay to set things straight. Carl the lawyer talks to his psychiatrist (Reba McEntire), who thinks the whole problem may be related to his relationship with his mother, and may be right. And Dehling the detective talks to his brother the priest (Richard Jenkins).

Jewel is not the only character who is seen in three different ways. Consider how Randy the bartender comes across as a hardworking, easygoing, nice guy in his own version, but appears to others as a slow-witted drunk and a letch.

The movie isn't only about three sets of testimony. Far from it. Jewel has a scam she's had a lot of luck with, and enlists Randy in helping her out—against his will, since he sees her as a sweet housewife. He can't imagine her as a criminal, and neither can the cop, who tortuously rewrites the evidence of his own eyes in order to make her into an innocent bystander who needs to be rescued by—well, Detective Dehling, of course.

One Night at McCool's doesn't quite work, but it has a lot of fun being a near miss. It misses, I think, because it is so busy with its crosscut structure and its interlocking stories that it never really gives us anyone to identify with—and in a comedy, we have to know where everybody stands in order to figure out what's funny, and how, and to whom. The same flaw has always bothered me about *Rashomon*—a masterpiece, yes, but one of conception rather than emotion.

We enjoy the puzzle in *McCool's*, and Tyler and her costars do a good job of seeming like different things to different people, but it's finally an exercise without an emotional engine to pull it, and we just don't care enough.

Does it matter if we don't care about a comedy? Yes, I think, it does: Comedy needs victims, and when everybody is innocent in their own eyes, you don't know where to look while you're laughing.

On_Line ★ ★
R, 97 m., 2003

Josh Hamilton (John Roth), Harold Perrineau (Moe Curley), Isabel Gillies (Moira Ingalls), John Fleck (Al Fleming), Vanessa Ferlito (Jordan Nash), Eric Millegan (Ed Simone), Liz Owens (Angel). Directed by Jed Weintrob and produced by Tanya Selvaratnam and Adam Brightman. Screenplay by Andrew Osborne and Weintrob.

I refuse to sign up for instant messaging for the same reason I won't carry a cell phone: Don't call me, I'll call you. The characters in Jed Weintrob's *On_Line* are on call more or less all the time, living their barren lives in cyberspace, where the members of a suicide Webcam chat are bored, waiting around for someone to overdose. The film's redeeming feature is that it knows how sad these people are and finds the correct solution to their problems: They meet in the flesh.

The movie stars Josh Hamilton and Harold Perrineau as John and Moe, roommates who run an on-line sex site named InterconX. It's a little like the real-life iFriends.com; on screens that display simultaneous cybercams, its members flirt, chat, engage in virtual sex, and charge for interaction. So mesmerized is John by this process that he follows, on another screen, a twenty-four-hour live cam where Angel (Liz Owens) lives her life in public view.

This can get to be a way of life. I have a friend who became so obsessed with one woman's Webcam that he kept its window constantly open on his desktop, no doubt getting up in the night to check that she was sleeping well. This is the geek equivalent of looking in on the kids. And at Sundance 1999 I saw *Home Page*, a documentary about a pioneering on-line blogger (as they were not called then) named Justin Hall, whose life seemed to be lived just so he could report on it.

That would also describe John, who keeps his own on-line journal in which he sighs about the emptiness of his existence and the futility of it all, and whose sex life at one point is reduced to masturbating not into his own sock, which would be pathetic enough, but into his roommate's.

The movie charts its lives through a split-screen technique that resembles the Web pages where the characters hang out. Digital video is combined with screen shots in a way that is intriguing and sometimes beautiful; the way the movie chops up the screen to follow simultaneous events is a little like Ang Lee's technique in *Hulk,* and the visuals use filters, textures, and colored lighting to create an effect not unlike some of the weirder pages of the early *Wired* magazine. Even when my interest in the characters flagged, I liked looking at the movie; credit to cinematographer Toshiaki Ozawa and visual effects supervisor Christian D. Bruun.

The film's relationships suggest that although you might find a soul mate on-line, you might be better off sticking with your roommate's sock. John, for example, falls for Jordan (Vanessa Ferlito), one of the women who pays him to rent space on InterconX. When he dates her in real life, he discovers she is frighteningly real and maybe more than he can handle; we hear his thoughts while he watches her dance at a nightclub, and suspect he would be happier going home and experiencing the date on-line.

Another couple consists of an older gay man in New York (John Fleck) who develops a friendship with a teenager (Eric Millegan) who fears he is the only adolescent homosexual in Ohio. When the kid gets off the bus in New York City, I was not ready to cheer this as a victory over the loneliness of cyberspace, because I believe that teenage boys in Ohio, whatever their sexual identity, cannot solve their problems by meeting strange older men in New York. The movie is more optimistic here than I am.

The movie's weakness is in its strength. It does a good job of portraying the day-to-day life of these on-line obsessives, but we realize eventually that they are more interesting *because* they are on-line. Their problems and personalities would not necessarily be movie material if it weren't for the cyberspace overlay. When it comes to those who try to live in cyberspace, I am reminded of Dr. Johnson's comment about a

dog standing on its hind legs: "It is not done well, but you are surprised to find it done at all."

On the Line ★
PG, 85 m., 2001

Lance Bass (Kevin Gibbons), Emmanuelle Chriqui (Abbey), Joey Fatone (Rod), GQ [Gregory Qaiyum] (Eric), James Bulliard (Randy), Richie Sambora (Mick Silver), Jerry Stiller (Nathan), Kristin Booth (Sam), Al Green (Himself). Directed by Eric Bross and produced by Wendy Thorlakson, Rich Hull, Peter Abrams, and Robert Levy. Screenplay by Eric Aronson and Paul Stanton.

Just when you think a dating movie can't conceivably involve more impossible coincidences and Idiot Plot situations, along comes another movie to prove you wrong. After *Serendipity,* here is *On the Line,* starring Lance Bass of 'N Sync in an agonizingly creaky movie that laboriously plods through a plot so contrived that the only thing real about it is its length. In both movies, a boy and a girl Meet Cute and instantly realize they are destined for each other, and then they plunge into a series of absurd contrivances designed to keep them apart.

Just once, could they meet and fall in love, and then the movie would be about their young lives together? I'm weary of romances about lovers who devote years to living far apart and barely missing chances to meet again. If this genre ever inspires a satire, it will end with the boy and girl sitting next to each other on an airplane—*still* not realizing they are together again, because by then they will be eighty, having spent sixty years missing each other by seconds.

Lance Bass plays Kevin Gibbons, a low-level Chicago ad executive who has no trouble with girls unless he really likes them. Then he freezes up and can't close the deal. One day on the el he meets Abbey (Emmanuelle Chriqui), who has a sunny smile and a warm personality, and can recite all of the American presidents, in order! So can Lance! Somewhere between Buchanan and Bush they realize they are meant for each other. But Kevin just *can't* ask for her phone number. And despite decades of feminist advances, all Abbey can do is smile helplessly and leave their future in his hands. They part with rueful smiles. No, make that Rueful Smiles.

Later, Kevin kicks himself and moans to his roommates about the perfect girl who got away. These roommates include fellow 'N Sync-er Joey Fatone, as Rod, who sings in an open-mike saloon and specializes in kicking the amp; Eric (the comedian GQ), a devoted mope; and Randy (James Bulliard), the brains of the outfit. The four guys spend countless precious screen minutes hanging around their flat engaging in redundant dialogue while we desperately want the movie to *lose the roommates* and *bring back the girl!*

But no. Films for the teenage demographic are terrified of romance and intimacy between the sexes, and shyly specialize in boys plotting about girls and girls plotting about boys, with as few actual scenes between boys and girls as possible. So after Kevin papers the town with posters seeking the girl he met on the train, and dozens of calls flood in, the roommates divide up the calls and date the girls (not telling Kevin, of course).

Well, obviously, only the right girl would know she was not going out with Kevin. So when Eric dates Abbey and she knows he's not Kevin—*that's the girl!* Right? But no. Eric is dense to the point of perversity, and spends their date not saying the few obvious words that need to be said, while acting like a pig and giving Abbey the impression that Kevin planned this humiliation. This is the Idiot Plot gone berserk. One sentence—*one word!*—and all would be solved, but Eric and the screenplay contort themselves into grotesque evasions to avoid stating the crashingly obvious.

So of course Abbey is crushed, and so are we, because we realize we are in the grip of a power greater than ourselves—Hollywood's determination to make films at the level of remedial reading. No one involved in the making of this film is as stupid as the characters, so why do they think the audience is? Why not for once allow young lovers to be smart, curious, articulate, and quick?

It must be said that Lance Bass and Emmanuelle Chriqui have sweet chemistry together, in the few moments they are able to snatch away from the forces designed to separate them. Bass is likable (but then likability is the

primary talent of 'N Sync), and Chriqui, from Montreal via *Snow Day* and *A.I.,* is warm and charming and has a great smile. I can imagine a lovely love story involving these two actors. Too bad *On the Line* goes to such lengths to avoid making it.

Open Hearts ★ ★ ★
R, 114 m., 2003

Sonja Richter (Cecilie), Mads Mikkelsen (Niels), Paprika Steen (Marie), Nikolaj Lie Kaas (Joachim), Stine Bjerregaard (Stine), Birthe Neumann (Hanne), Niels Olsen (Finn), Ulf Pilgaard (Thomsen), Ronnie Hiort (Gustav). Directed by Susanne Bier and produced by Jonas Frederiksen and Vibeke Windelov. Screenplay by Anders Thomas Jensen.

A life can be forever changed in an instant. Joachim proposes marriage to Cecilie, they are in love, they kiss, he steps heedlessly out of the car, he is struck by another car, and is paralyzed from the neck down. All of that happens at the outset in *Open Hearts,* which is about how this instant echoes in the lives of others.

Most movies about such injuries are sentimental, like *The Other Side of the Mountain.* What I have learned from disabled friends who have had such devastating events in their lives is that sentimentality is for greeting cards. They face a new reality, and they have to be hard and brave, and sometimes they use dark humor as a relief or shield. I will never forget the puckish humor of Heather Rose, the star and author of *Dance Me to My Song,* who could control only one finger of one hand, and used it to tap out a computer message to a college audience that had just seen her film: "Let's go get pissed."

What is unusual about *Open Hearts* is how forthright it is about the reaction of Joachim (Nikolaj Lie Kaas) to his injury. We have seen him as an athlete, a rock climber, an extrovert, a man in love. But when Cecilie (Sonja Richter) is at his bedside, after he hears that he will never walk again, he turns away from her pledges of love and tells her to get lost. He is angry and doesn't even want to look at her.

This is not unreasonable. He is furious at the instant of fate that has taken his youth and his movement from him. Furious that he cannot do the things he loves. And he recoils from her love because . . . because . . . well, because it hurts him too much, and because he wants to release her from their engagement, spare her a lifetime with him on these new terms.

His anger is a stage that he has to go through. Eventually will come the other stages we hear about, involving negotiation, acceptance, and so on. Kübler-Ross's five stages for the dying get reversed for the gravely handicapped: They awaken feeling they are dead, and have to track back into accepting and embracing life.

Open Hearts is not simply about Joachim and Cecilie, however. It is about a matrix of lives affected by the accident. We meet Marie (Paprika Steen), who was driving the car that struck Joachim. While the accident was not precisely her fault, she was distracted at the time and believes she might have been able to avoid it. Her husband, Niels (Mads Mikkelsen) is by coincidence the doctor on duty in the emergency ward where Joachim is taken. He's the one who has to break the news to Cecilie.

In the weeks and months that follow, Joachim continues to be hostile to Cecilie. He issues orders that she is not to be allowed in his room. He is also startlingly hostile to a nurse, who can take it, and does, creating an intriguing dynamic. Cecilie, who has no one to confide in, begins to share her feelings with Niels, the doctor. His wife knows and approves, but does not know that Niels is falling helplessly, obsessively, in love with the younger woman.

The movie is fascinated by the nature of his love. This is not a romance, not adultery, not an affair, not any of the things that can be explained with a word. It is helpless intoxicating infatuation, so powerful he is ready to consider leaving his long and happy marriage with Marie, which has given him three children he loves.

Now it is up to us. What do we think? Two men have decided to abandon women who love them. Cecilie is in the middle—pushed away by one, loved by another. Joachim and Marie are the outsiders—he by choice, she by—well, you could call this an accident, too, a blow of fate when she does not expect it. Marie's way of dealing with Neils's new love is seen with clarity and intelligence by Susanne Bier, the director. She doesn't respond on cue

with screaming and accusations, like soap opera wives, but tries to size up the new reality and see what can be saved or salvaged.

As for Joachim—well, I feel he's a rat. He should not leave his wife and children to move in with the sort-of fiancée of his patient. As Pascal once said (and Woody Allen once quoted), "The heart has its reasons of which reason knows nothing." At the end, it's all a mess. Love causes such pain and regret. Can Neils be strong and reject his love for Cecilie? Can he be as strong as Joachim? Why do we want Neils to abandon his love and Joachim to reassert his? And what is so amazingly unique about Cecilie, anyway? She is sweet and pretty but not in any way extraordinary, yet has taken possession of both these men.

It must be noted that *Open Hearts* is a Dogma film, subscribing to the Danish manifesto calling for a simpler, more direct, and less artful approach to filmmaking. This was the twenty-eighth film to receive the Dogma certificate, but I am weary of sifting each Dogma production through the same dogmatic sieve, and will simply note that it is filmed directly, intimately, without heightened effects or facile emotion-boosters. It is intensely curious about these people, sees them clearly, has no answers. I wish there were a manifesto that forgot about the stylistic stuff and simply required that.

Orange County ★ ★ ★
PG-13, 90 m., 2002

Colin Hanks (Shawn Brumder), Schuyler Fisk (Ashley), Catherine O'Hara (Cindy Beugler), Jack Black (Lance Brumder), John Lithgow (Bud Brumder), Kevin Kline (Marcus Skinner), Lily Tomlin (Guidance Counselor), Harold Ramis (Don Durkett). Directed by Jake Kasdan and produced by David Gale and Scott Rudin. Screenplay by Mike White.

Orange County has the form of a teenage movie, the spirit of an independent comedy, and the subversive zeal of Jack Black, whose grin is the least reassuring since Jack Nicholson. It's one of those movies like *Ghost World* and *Legally Blonde* where the description can't do justice to the experience. It will sound like the kind of movie that, if you are over seventeen, you don't usually go to see. But it isn't.

The movie is a launching pad for three members of Hollywood's next generation. The stars are Colin Hanks (son of Tom Hanks) and Schuyler Fisk (daughter of Sissy Spacek and Jack Fisk). The director is Jake Kasdan (son of Lawrence and Meg Kasdan). All have worked before, but this is one of those happy projects where everything seems to fall naturally into place.

Hanks plays Shawn Brumder, heedless and carefree teenage Orange County surfer—until one day he finds a novel half-buried in the sand. It's by Marcus Skinner, one of those authors who can strike a kid of the right age as a conduit to truth and beauty. Shawn casts aside his old surfer lifestyle (to the grief of his pot-brained buddy) and determines to get into Stanford and study at the feet of the great Skinner (Kevin Kline).

This should be a cinch, since his test scores are very high. But he's rejected by Stanford because the daffy high school counselor (Lily Tomlin) has sent in the wrong scores under his name. This disappointment is crushing to Shawn, less disturbing to the other members of his definitively dysfunctional family. His father, Bud (John Lithgow), is workaholic and distant, his mother, Cindy (Catherine O'Hara), is—well, Catherine O'Hara, and his brother, Lance (Jack Black), is a couch potato, although potatoes may be the one substance he doesn't abuse. There is also Ashley (Schuyler Fisk), his loyal girlfriend, who believes in him, supports him, and is, in a stunning breakthrough for the teenage comedy genre, a blonde who is as intelligent as he is, maybe more.

The movie was written by Mike White, who you may remember as the author and star of *Chuck and Buck* (2000). He has one of those sideways, sardonic, nerd-savant approaches, getting a lot of his laughs by the application of logic to situations where it is not usually encountered. His characters tend to take things literally; in this case, Lance, the Jack Black character, is usually so stoned that his tunnel vision gives him an extraordinary, if misguided, clarity. Lance loves Shawn, even though he doesn't see the point of ambition or achievement, and so he offers to drive him to Palo Alto so that he can personally confront the Stanford admissions counselor.

It's around this point that we see the strategy of *Orange County*. It wants to appear to be a formula teenage screenplay (sex and dope jokes, girlfriend who is almost alienated and then reunited, personal redemption at last possible moment after maximum contrived suspense). At the same time, it goes under and over this mark: under with gags that would distinguish a Farrelly brothers picture, and over with surprisingly touching attention to Shawn's personality changes, his hopes and dreams, and especially his support from the stalwart Ashley.

The movie's cast looks like a roll call from the comedy hall of fame. If you have Harold Ramis, Jane Adams, Garry Marshall, Chevy Chase, Ben Stiller, and Mike White himself in supporting roles, and Kevin Kline (unbilled) finding just the right balance between charming nobility and weary pomposity, you have a movie that can be undone only in the making. Jake Kasdan is still in his mid-twenties, but is sure-footed and has a nice skewed sense of comic timing; this movie is a world apart from his fine first feature, *Zero Effect* (1998), a Sherlockian web that could go on the puzzler shelf with *Memento* and *Mulholland Drive*. He has also directed a lot of episodic comedy on TV (*Freaks and Geeks, Grosse Pointe*).

I was in New York when the movie was previewed for the press, and heard some idle talk about how this movie was proof that if you had the right parents you could get hired in Hollywood. True, and not true. Certainly Kasdan, Hanks, and Fisk have connections. On the other hand, studios invest real money. If your father is a famous actor, you may be able to get hired as an intern or an assistant still photographer, or get an acting job in a TV series. If you're making a feature on your own, it's because somebody with money thought you were right for the job. In this case, somebody was right.

Original Sin ★ ★ ★
R, 112 m., 2001

Antonio Banderas (Luis Durand), Angelina Jolie (Julia Russell), Thomas Jane (Walter Downs),

Joan Pringle (Sarah), Allison Mackie (Augusta). Directed by Michael Cristofer and produced by Denise Di Novi, Kate Guinzburg, and Carol Lees. Screenplay by Cristofer, based on the novel *Waltz Into Darkness* by Cornell Woolrich.

The first shot on the screen is a close-up of Angelina Jolie's lips. And what lips they are, plump and pouting and almost bruised. Eventually we tear ourselves away from the sight and realize she's talking. She's telling the story of why she happens to be in a jail cell; these flashbacks will eventually reveal that she has been condemned to death by garroting—a nasty way to go, as the executioner turns a screw to tighten an iron collar around your neck.

This prologue undermines any romantic illusions as the story itself begins, circa 1900, introducing us to a wealthy Cuban coffee planter named Luis Durand (Antonio Banderas), who anticipates the arrival of a mail-order bride named Julia Russell (Jolie). Handsome and rich, he has never married ("Love is not for me. Love is for those people who believe in it"). His expectations for the bride are realistic: "She is not meant to be beautiful. She is meant to be kind, true, and young enough to bear children."

"You don't recognize me, do you?" Julia murmurs in a thrilling low register, as he finds her standing before him at the dock. He does not. This sultry vision is not the plain woman in the photograph he holds. She confesses she sent the wrong photo because she did not want a man who was attracted only to her beauty. He confesses too: He owns his plantation and is not simply a worker there. He didn't want to attract a gold digger. "Then we have something in common," she says. "Neither one of us can be trusted." Actually, he can.

Original Sin is based on the novel *Waltz Into Darkness*, by the famous *noir* writer Cornell Woolrich. Another of his books inspired Hitchcock's *Rear Window*—and indeed this one was earlier filmed as *Mississippi Mermaid* by François Truffaut in 1969 (Jean-Paul Belmondo and Catherine Deneuve played the roles). Like many good thrillers, it only really gets rolling after we think we've already seen through the plot. There are surprises on top of surprises, and I will tread carefully to preserve them.

The purpose of the movie is not really to tell its story, anyway, but to use it as an engine to pull Banderas and Jolie through scenes of lurid melodrama, dramatic ultimatums, and stunning revelations. Another purpose is to show off these two splendid human beings, and I am happy to report that there is even a certain amount of nudity—which you would expect with this passionate story, but then again you never know, now that studios are scurrying into the shelter of the PG-13 to hide from pruny congressmen.

Jolie continues to stalk through pictures entirely on her own terms. Her presence is like a dare-ya for a man. There's dialogue in this movie so overwrought it's almost literally unspeakable, and she survives it by biting it off contemptuously and spitting it out. She makes no effort to pretend to be a nice woman—not even at the first, when Luis believes her story. She's the kind of woman who looks a man in the eye and tells him what she wants and how soon she expects to get it. Banderas skillfully plays up to this quality, spaniel-eyed, lovestruck, so overwhelmed he will follow her literally anywhere.

The movie is not intended to be subtle. It is sweaty, candlelit melodrama, joyously trashy, and its photography wallows in sumptuous decadence. The ending is hilariously contrived and sensationally unlikely, as the movie audaciously shows an irrevocable action and then revokes it. I don't know whether to recommend *Original Sin* or not. It's an exuberant example of what it is—a bodice-ripping murder melodrama—and as that it gets a passing grade. Maybe if it had tried to be more it would have simply been watering the soup.

Osmosis Jones ★ ★ ★
PG-13, 98 m., 2001

Bill Murray (Frank), Elena Franklin (Shane), Molly Shannon (Mrs. Boyd), Chris Elliott (Bob), With the voices of: Chris Rock (Osmosis), Laurence Fishburne (Thrax), David Hyde Pierce (Drix), Brandy Norwood (Leah), William Shatner (The Mayor), Ron Howard (Tom Colonic). Directed by Peter Farrelly and Bobby Farrelly and produced by Bradley Thomas, Peter Farrelly, Bobby Farrelly, Zak Penn, and Dennis Edwards. Animation directed by Piet Kroon and Tom Sito. Screenplay by Marc Hyman.

Osmosis Jones is like the dark side of those animated educational films depicting the goings-on in the bowels. It takes us inside the human body for a tour of such uncharted neighborhoods as the Lower East Backside, and such useful organs as the Puke Button. These sights are depicted in colorful, gloppy, drippy animation, and then we switch to live action for the outside of the body in question, which belongs to a man named Frank (Bill Murray).

Frank follows the Ten-Second Rule, which teaches us that if food is dropped and stays on the ground less than ten seconds, it's still safe to eat. In the case of the hard-boiled egg in question, he might also have reflected that before the egg dropped, he had to pry it from the mouth of a monkey. The egg is crawling with germs, sending the inside of his body into emergency mode.

At the cellular level, we meet Osmosis Jones (voice by Chris Rock), a maverick cop, always being called into the chief's office for a lecture. In the first animated microbiological version of a buddy movie, he teams up with Drix (David Hyde Pierce), a timed-release cold capsule, to fight the viral invasion, which threatens to kill Frank after Thrax (Laurence Fishburne) introduces a new and deadly infection.

The live-action scenes, directed by Peter and Bobby Farrelly *(There's Something About Mary)*, use Bill Murray's seedy insouciance as a horrible object lesson in what can happen to you if you don't think all the time about germs. His second, potentially lethal, infection comes as he visits a science fair where his daughter, Shane (Elena Franklin), has an entry. Chatting with another entrant, he learns that the lad's experiment involves the cleansing of polluted oysters; assured that the oysters are cleansed, he eats one.

The inner, animated sequences, which occupy about two-thirds of the movie, were directed by Piet Kroon and Tom Sito. Imagine the journey through the human body undertaken by Dennis Quaid in *Innerspace* (1987) as if it were drawn by Matt Groening *(Life in Hell)* on acid, and you will have an approximation. I especially liked the way various parts of the body represented neighborhoods in the City of Frank (the stomach is the airport, with regular departures to the colon; the Mafia hangs out in the armpit; lawyers can be found in a hemorrhoid).

Inside Frank City, the mayor (William Shatner) tries to maintain the status quo in the face of campaigning by his opponent, Tom Colonic (Ron Howard), a "regular guy." Outside, the unshaven Frank embarrasses his spic-and-span daughter with his uncouth behavior, and mortally offends the science teacher (Molly Shannon) by throwing up on her after eating the wrong oyster. (I am reminded of Dr. Johnson observing to Mr. Boswell: "Sir, he was a brave man who ate the first oyster.") Back inside Frank, Osmosis Jones frets that he acted too quickly in pushing the Puke Button.

Who is the movie for? Despite my descriptions, it is nowhere near as gross as the usual effort, and steers clear of adventures in the genital areas. It was originally classified PG-13, but was upgraded to PG after some trims, and is likely to entertain kids, who seem to like jokes about anatomical plumbing. For adults, there is the exuberance of the animation and the energy of the whole movie, which is just plain clever.

The Others ★ ★ ½
PG-13, 104 m., 2001

Nicole Kidman (Grace), Christopher Eccleston (Charles), Fionnula Flanagan (Mrs. Mills), Elaine Cassidy (Lydia), Eric Sykes (Mr. Tuttle), Alakina Mann (Anne), James Bentley (Nicholas). Directed by Alejandro Amenabar and produced by Fernando Bovaira, Jose Luis Cuerda, and Park Sunmin. Screenplay by Amenabar.

The Others is a haunted house mystery—from which you assume, trained by recent movies, that it is filled with flashy special effects, violent shocks, bloodcurdling apparitions, undulating staircases, telescoping corridors, graves opening in the basement, doors that will not lock or will not open, and dialogue like, "There's something in this house! Something . . . diabolic!"

You would be right about the dialogue. This is a haunted house movie, dark and atmospheric, but it's quiet and brooding. It has less in common with, say, *The House on Haunted Hill* than with *The Sixth Sense* or a story by Oliver Onions. It's not a freak show but a waiting game, in which an atmosphere of dread slowly envelops the characters—too slowly. Comparing this movie with *The Sixth Sense,* we feel a renewed admiration for the way M. Night Shyamalan was able to maintain tension through little things that were happening, instead of (this film's strategy) big things that seem about to happen.

The film takes place in an isolated mansion on the island of Jersey off the French coast. In this house lives Grace (Nicole Kidman) and her two children, the tremulous Nicholas (James Bentley), and the cheeky Anne (Alakina Mann). To the house one day come three servants, who are responding, or say they are responding, to Grace's advertisement for domestic help. There are vacancies because the previous servants decamped in the middle of the night without a word of notice. The three new applicants have the advantage of being familiar with the house.

It is a sound tradition of British fiction that servants do not leave a house only to later return and be rehired (the sole exception is George Wellbeloved, Lord Emsworth's pig-keeper at Blandings Castle). But these are the days immediately after World War II, which claimed, or seems to have claimed, Grace's husband, and so perhaps help is hard to find. She hires them: Mrs. Mills (Fionnula Flanagan), the middle-aged Irish woman with the know-it-all nods, the young mute girl Lydia (Elaine Cassidy), and the gardener Mr. Tuttle (Eric Sykes), who is so ancient that for him planting a seed is an act of wild optimism.

There are odd rules in the house. Each of the fifty doors must be locked before another can be opened. The curtains must always be drawn. These measures are necessary because Anne and Nicholas are so allergic to the sunlight that they might die if exposed to it.

The events in the film are such that I must not describe them. Even a hint might give away the game. Of course they are elusive and mysterious, reported by some, not seen by others, explained first one way and then another. By the time we arrive at the line, "There's something in this house!" we are not only prepared to agree, but to suspect that in supernatural terms it's as crowded as the Smithsonian's attic.

The director, Alejandro Amenabar, has the patience to create a languorous, dreamy atmosphere, and Nicole Kidman succeeds in convincing us that she is a normal person in a disturbing situation and not just a standard-issue horror movie hysteric. But in drawing out his effects, Amenabar is a little too confident that style can substitute for substance. As our suspense was supposed to be building, our impatience was outstripping it. As Houdini said, or should have if he didn't, you can only listen to so much spectral knocking before you want to look under the table.

Otomo ★ ★ ★
NO MPAA RATING, 85 m., 2001

Isaach De Bankole (Otomo), Eva Mattes (Gisela), Hanno Friedrich (Heinz), Barnaby Metschurat (Rolf), Lara Kugler (Simone). Directed by Frieder Schlaich and produced by Thomas Lechner, Claudia Tronnier, and Irene van Alberti. Screenplay by Schlaich and Klaus Pohl.

On August 9, 1989, as a black man was stopped on a bridge in Stuttgart, Germany, for questioning, he knifed two officers to death and wounded three others before being shot dead himself. This man's name was Frederic Otomo. At about 6:15 that morning, he had been confronted on a subway train by a ticket inspector, who told him he had to get off at the next stop. The inspector got aggressive with Otomo, who head-butted him and fled from the train, setting up the manhunt that ended on the bridge.

Those facts are known. What happened between the two incidents is unknown, and inspires this film by Frieder Schlaich, who tries to imagine what went through Otomo's mind between the two confrontations. Along the way, Schlaich portrays a society in which some are racists who act cruelly toward the black man, and others, even strangers, go out of their way to help him.

Otomo, we learn, came from Liberia by way of the Cameroons, where his father fought for the Germans in World War II and was endangered as a German sympathizer. Technically, as one of the police officers observes, he may have had the right to German citizenship. But his only official papers are a temporary passport, not good enough to qualify him for a minimum-wage job he's turned away from at dawn. Before he's turned down, men make fun of his shoes—slippers they call "jungle creepers." Why is it assumed that the poor want to dress the way they must?

There is a moment on the subway line that the film interestingly leaves unclear. The inspector tells Otomo his ticket is only good for one zone, and he must get off. "You know it's a good ticket!" Otomo cries. Later, as the inspector and his woman partner sit in a police station to file a report, she looks at Otomo's ticket and holds it up to show it to the inspector. Why does she do this? I think it is because she notices the ticket is valid, although of course she doesn't mention that as her partner files his complaint.

Otomo (Isaach De Bankole) wanders through Stuttgart, avoiding police cars and helicopters (the scale of the manhunt seems a little large for the severity of his crime). In a restaurant, a waitress gives him food although he can only pay for coffee, and later when the police ask her if she has seen him, she says, "A nigger? Not in here." Using the word puts her on their side; lying for a man she doesn't know reveals, perhaps, an instinctive sympathy for the underdog.

On a river bank, Otomo is offered a flower by a little girl. This is a direct quote from *Frankenstein*, but the episode ends differently, with the girl's grandmother (Eva Mattes) taking him in and agreeing to lend him money to pay for a ride out of town. Why does she do this? Otomo is not talkative, says little to explain himself, yet somehow seems able to inspire sympathy. (Like Frankenstein's monster, he inspires fear on first sight from some, and is inarticulate in explaining himself.)

The movie's case for him is made, not by Otomo himself, but by the manager of the flophouse where he lives, who describes the lives of undocumented "guest workers" in simple terms: They are useful for undesirable jobs, but have no security and live constantly on the edge of destitution. "Is he violent?" a cop asks the manager. "Rather gentle," the manager says. "He'll talk to you for hours about the Bible."

The movie is about a man who reaches his snapping point. The ceremonial funerals for his police victims are contrasted with the three or four people who gather at his pauper's grave. The film doesn't believe the police deserved to die (or that the ticket inspector should have

been assaulted), but then again it doesn't believe a society should so treat a man that this is what he comes to do.

Isaach De Bankole was seen most memorably in Jim Jarmusch's *Ghost Dog*, as the French-speaking African who carried on a long conversation with Forest Whitaker, the two speaking different languages. He also starred in *Chocolat*, Clair Denis's evocative 1988 film set in French West Africa. Eva Mattes was in many Fassbinder movies, including *Jailbait* (1972), made when she was seventeen. Now she plays a grandmother. "You old hippie!" her daughter calls her—needing to find a reason why her mother would befriend a desperate man.

Our Lady of the Assassins ★ ★ ★ ½
R, 98 m., 2001

German Jaramillo (Vallejo), Anderson Ballesteros (Alexis), Juan David Restrepo (Wilmar), Manuel Busquets (Alfonso), Wilmar Agudelo (Child Sniffing Glue), Juan Carlos Alvarez (4X4 Thief), Cenobia Cano (Alexis's Mother), Zulma Arango (Waitress). Directed by Barbet Schroeder and produced by Margaret Menegoz, Jaime Osorio Gomez, and Schroeder. Screenplay by Fernando Vallejo, based on his novel.

Vallejo is a writer who returns home to Colombia to die. By the end of Barbet Schroeder's *Our Lady of the Assassins*, he is almost the only person he knows who is still alive. His hometown is Medellín, company town of the cocaine industry, seen here as a cursed city of casual death, where machine gunners on motorcycles roam the streets settling gang feuds.

The writer knew this town thirty years ago, when it must have been a beautiful place. Now killings are common, bystanders look the other way, and in the movie (at least) the police seem absent. Vallejo (German Jaramillo) has arrived at a time in his life when he hardly seems to care: Did he come home half-expecting to find death before it found him?

A homosexual, he goes to a male brothel and meets Alexis (Anderson Ballesteros), a teenage boy. They spend the night. Not long after, Alexis moves into Vallejo's barren high-rise apartment. "There is no furniture," the boy observes. "There is a table, two chairs, a mattress," said Vallejo. "What else does one need?" A television and a boom box, Alexis explains. But soon the boom box goes over the edge of the balcony; Vallejo is maddened by the music, as he is also annoyed by the ceaseless drumming of a neighbor, and by the musical tastes of a taxi driver who will not turn down the radio. Alexis, a gang member who is always armed, helpfully kills both the neighbor and the taxi driver. Vallejo is appalled and yet detached; the events in this city do not fully register—he is preoccupied by an inner agenda.

Our Lady of the Assassins, based on an autobiographical novel by the Colombian writer Fernando Vallejo, resonates also with Barbet Schroeder's own life; he was raised in Colombia, has worked mostly in the United States and France, at sixty is an extraordinary figure. "No other person in the film world can match his record of diversity," notes Stanley Kauffmann in his *New Republic* review. Schroeder's interests are astonishingly wide. He produces all the films of Eric Rohmer, whose work could not be more different than his own, and he has made movies about Charles Bukowski *(Barfly)*, the accused wife-killer Claus von Bulow *(Reversal of Fortune)*, and *Idi Amin Dada,* a doc about the dictator.

He made this Spanish-language film on the independent fringe, shooting on high-def video without permits, using guerrilla snatch-and-run video techniques, protected by bodyguards. Despite the danger involved in its production, the violence that weaves through all of its moments, and the documentary feel of the location photography in Medellín ("a city entirely without tourists," Schroeder notes), *Our Lady of the Assassins* is not a grim exercise in social realism. Vallejo's detachment sets the tone. He cannot easily be shocked or dismayed, because he's on the way out of life. He is saddened by the death of Alexis (the two grow genuinely close to each other), but that does not prevent him from finding another teenage lover, Wilmar (Juan David Restrepo). And when he discovers that Wilmar was Alexis's killer—well, Alexis killed Wilmar's brother, and what goes around comes around.

Can a man of sixty have a romantic relationship with a boy of sixteen? In a sane world, no. They would drive each other crazy. In a world

where both expect to die in the immediate future, where plans are meaningless, where poverty of body and soul has left them starving in different ways, there is something to be said for sex, wine, music, and killing time in safety. And there is an agelessness in Vallejo, who has no family, no plans, no bourgeois preoccupations, and has simplified his life to a zen emptiness—he and these boys share the same cool disinterest in tomorrow. The morality of their arrangement, of course, is irrelevant in a city with no morality. (Every time a shipment of cocaine reaches the United States, the drug lords treat the people to a fireworks display.)

The film's title is appropriate. A desperate Catholicism flavors the doomed city. "He's happy it's Our Lady's day or I would have killed him," Alexis serenely observes after one violent episode. Drug deals take place in the cathedrals, and beggars fall on their knees to receive bakery handouts as if they are the Eucharist. Cocaine has brought billions to Colombia but little of it has trickled down; unlike a boomtown during the Gold Rush, Medellín does not share in the prosperity of its rich, but inherits only their depravity. A sign on a waste ground warns: NO DUMPING OF CORPSES.

Our Song ★ ★ ★
R, 96 m., 2001

Kerry Washington (Lanisha), Anna Simpson (Joycelyn), Melissa Martinez (Maria), D'Monroe (Terell), Kim Howard (Eleanor), The Jackie Robinson Steppers Marching Band (Themselves). Directed by Jim McKay and produced by McKay, Paul Mezey, and Diana E. Williams. Screenplay by McKay.

Three teenage girls, three possible futures. During a hot August in the Crown Heights section of Brooklyn, they hang out together, talk about boys and clothes, and attend band practice. One will get pregnant. One may drift away from these friends and find a new crowd. One may go back to school, even though the close local school has been closed (asbestos problems) and that means three hours on the bus every day. The theory is, their marching band may be sponsored for a trip to Alaska, a prospect that more or less brings conversation to a halt, since they are at a loss for opinions about Alaska one way or the other.

Our Song is the new movie by Jim McKay, whose *Girls' Town* (1996) was also about adolescent girls making their plans. I admired that film, and like this one more, perhaps because the actors are closer to the ages of the characters and seem to inhabit their lives more easily. *Girls' Town* felt the need to have a plot. *Our Song,* like *George Washington,* has the courage to work without a net, aware that when you're a teenager your life is not a story so much as a million possible stories.

The movie stars Kerry Washington, Anna Simpson, and Melissa Martinez, all in their first roles, and it's impossible not to think a little of *Mystic Pizza,* which introduced Lili Taylor, Annabeth Gish, and Julia Roberts. I have a feeling we'll be seeing these newcomers again; indeed, Washington, who has a face the camera loves, has already made *Save the Last Dance* (as the white girl's new best friend) and *Lift* (a Sundance hit, where she plays a shoplifter).

In *Our Song,* Washington is Lanisha, with a divorced black father and Hispanic mother. She's a good student, has plans, lives in a neighborhood where dying young is a fact of life; she says she "sometimes thinks about being shot, like it would be okay." But then she snaps out of it and decides, "Today's a good day."

Anna Simpson plays Joycelyn, who has a job in retail and is beginning to bond with the other clerks at work. They begin to seem cooler to her than her old friends, and having a paycheck and money to spend seems cooler than going to school; she doesn't see yet that employment at that level is a life sentence.

Melissa Martinez plays Maria, whose boyfriend, Terell (D'Monroe), says he wants to break up. Her friends' theory: He's just trying to get out of buying her a birthday present. She discovers she is pregnant and tells her boyfriend. "I'll be around," Terell says, although he clearly prefers spending time on the streets with "my boys." Maria is realistic: "You barely act like you like me now." The sad truth is, she will probably have this baby and set the course of her life out of misplaced love for an indifferent boy who is already on his way to the exit door.

There is a counterpoint to her decision. Eleanor (Kim Howard), a young local girl with a baby, takes her child in her arms and jumps out of her project window. Friends and neighbors gather at a makeshift shrine of flowers and Polaroids, giving Eleanor the attention now that she needed yesterday.

The thread connecting the girls' lives is their marching band, the Jackie Robinson Steppers. It is a real band, something we don't have to be told after we see them. I learn that McKay got the idea for his film when he saw the Steppers in a parade, and began to wonder about the lives of some of its members. The band provides a focus, discipline, pride. It is very good. And the bandmaster provides a friendly but firm male presence for young people who often come from fatherless homes.

Interesting, the differences between this film and *Crazy/Beautiful,* another new film about young people about the same age. Both are good movies. *Crazy/Beautiful* has an established star (Kirsten Dunst), more plot, a more showy and entertaining sort of angst. It seems more sure of exactly what it wants to tell us. *Our Song* is not on the same fast track; it ambles, observes, meditates, has patience. Most audiences will connect more with *Crazy/Beautiful,* which does the lifting for them. *Our Song* requires us to look and listen to these girls, and make our own connections.

Example. Lanisha, the Kerry Washington character, has asthma. One day she starts to have an attack, and her friend takes her to the emergency room, where the receptionist of course exhibits the usual blindness toward a health crisis while demanding insurance forms, identification, and so on. In a different kind of film, this scene would have built up into a dramatic climax—*E.R.* lite. *Our Song* knows that things like this happen every day, that Lanisha will be frightened but will survive, that life goes on, that emergency rooms are more familiar to teenage girls from this neighborhood than to Kirsten Dunst's friends in Malibu.

Our Song is content with the rhythms of life, and so performs one of the noble functions of the movies, which is to give us the opportunity to empathize with characters not like ourselves.

Note: Because Our Song *deals with the daily reality of many girls under seventeen, it has been rated R by the MPAA, so that they can be prevented from learning from the movie's insights.*

Owning Mahowny ★ ★ ★ ★
R, 107 m, 2003

Philip Seymour Hoffman (Dan Mahowny),
Minnie Driver (Belinda), John Hurt (Victor Foss),
Maury Chaykin (Frank Perlin), Sonja Smits
(Dana Selkirk), Ian Tracey (Ben Lock), Roger
Dunn (Bill Gooden). Directed by Richard
Kwietniowski and produced by Andras Hamori
and Seaton McLean. Screenplay by Maurice
Chauvet, based on a book by Gary Ross.

Owning Mahowny is about a man seized helplessly with tunnel vision, in the kind of tunnel
that has no light at either end. He is a gambler.
Cut off temporarily by his bookie, he asks incredulously, "What am I supposed to do? Go
out to the track and *watch?*" Given the means
to gamble, he gambles—thoughtless of the consequences, heedless of the risks, caught in the
vise of a power greater than himself. Like all addictive gamblers he seeks the sensation of losing more money than he can afford. To win a
great deal before losing it all back again creates
a kind of fascination: Such gamblers need to
confirm over and over that they cannot win.

The film is based on the true story of a
Toronto bank vice president who began by stealing exactly as much as he needed to clear his
debts at the track ($10,300) and ended by taking
his bank for $10.2 million. So intent is he on
this process that he rarely raises his voice, or his
eyes, from the task at hand. Philip Seymour
Hoffman, that fearless poet of implosion, plays
the role with a fierce integrity, never sending
out signals for our sympathy because he knows
that Mahowny is oblivious to our presence.
Like an artist, an athlete, or a mystic, Mahowny
is alone within the practice of his discipline.

There have been many good movies about
gambling, but never one that so single-mindedly
shows the gambler at his task. Mahowny has
just been rewarded at work with a promotion
and a raise. He drives a clunker even the parking lot attendants kid him about. His suits
amuse his clients. He is engaged to Belinda
(Minnie Driver), a teller who is the very embodiment of a woman who might be really
pretty if she took off those glasses and did
something about her hair.

He is so absorbed in gambling that even his
bookie (Maury Chaykin) tries to cut him off, to
save himself the trouble of making threats to
collect on the money Mahowny owes him. "I
can't do business like this," the bookie complains, and at another point, when Mahowny is
so rushed he only has time to bet $1,000 on all
the home teams in the National League and all
the away teams in the American, the bookie
finds this a breach of ethics: He is in business to
separate the gambler from his money, yes, but
his self-respect requires the gambler to make
reasonable bets.

When Mahowny moves up a step by stealing
larger sums and flying to Atlantic City to lose
them, he encounters a more ruthless and amusing professional. John Hurt plays the manager
of the casino like a snake fascinated by the way
a mouse hurries forward to be eaten. Hurt has
seen obsessive gamblers come and go and is familiar with all the manifestations of their sickness, but this Mahowny brings a kind of
grandeur to his losing.

The newcomer is quickly singled out as a
high roller, comped with a luxury suite, offered
French cuisine and tickets to the Pointer Sisters, but all he wants to do is gamble ("and
maybe . . . some ribs, no sauce, and a Coke?").
Hurt sends a hooker to Mahowny's room, and
a flunky reports back: "The only woman he's
interested in is Lady Luck." Certainly Mahowny
forgets his fiancée on a regular basis, standing
her up, disappearing for weekends, even taking
her to Vegas and then forgetting that she is upstairs waiting in their suite. (The fiancée is a
classic enabler, excusing his lapses, but Vegas is
too much for her; she tries to explain to him
that when she saw the size of the suite she assumed they had come to Vegas to get married:
"That's what normal people do in Vegas.")

It is impossible to like Mahowny, but easy to
identify with him, if we have ever had obsessions of our own. Like all addicts of anything,
he does what he does because he does it. "He
needs to win in order to get more money to
lose," one of the casino professionals observes.

Of course he will eventually be caught. He
knows it, we know it, but being caught is beside the point. The point is to gamble as long
as he can before he is caught. Mahowny refers
at one point to having had a lot of luck, and he
is referring not to winning, but to being able to
finance a great deal of gambling at a level so
high that, asked by a psychiatrist to rate the ex-

citement on a scale of zero to one hundred, he unhesitatingly answers, "One hundred." And his greatest excitement in life outside of gambling? "Twenty."

Philip Seymour Hoffman's performance is a masterpiece of discipline and precision. He spends a lot of time adjusting his glasses or resting his fingers on his temples, as if to enhance his tunnel vision. He never meets the eye of the camera, or anyone else. Even when a casino security guard is firmly leading his fiancée away from his table, he hardly looks up to notice that she is there, or to say a word in her defense. He is . . . gambling. The movie has none of the false manipulation of most gambling movies, in which the actors signal their highs and lows. Hoffman understands that for this gambler, it is not winning or losing, but all process.

The movie, written by Maurice Chauvet, has been directed by Richard Kwietniowski, whose only other feature was *Love and Death on Long Island* (1998). That one also starred John Hurt, playing a reclusive British literary intellectual who becomes as obsessed as Mahowny, but with an erotic fixation. So unworldly he does not own a television and never goes to the movies, the Hurt character takes refuge from the rain in a cinema, finds himself watching a teenage comedy starring Jason Priestley, and becomes so fascinated by this young man that he keeps a scrapbook like a starstruck teenager and eventually travels to Long Island just in the hopes of meeting him. We get the impression that the Hurt character has been unaware of his homosexuality and indeed even his sexuality before being thunderstruck by this sudden fixation. In both films, Kwietniowski understands that conscious choice has little to do with his characters, that risk and humiliation are immaterial, that once they are locked in on the subjects of their obsessions, they have no choice but to hurry ahead to their dooms. ☞

P

Paid in Full ★ ★ ½
R, 93 m., 2002

Wood Harris (Ace), Mekhi Phifer (Mitch), Kevin Carroll (Calvin), Esai Morales (Lulu), Chi McBride (Pip), Cam'ron (Rico), Remo Green (Sonny), Cynthia Martells (Dora), Elise Neal (Aunt Jane), Regina Hall (Kiesha). Directed by Charles Stone III and produced by Damon Dash, Jay-Z, and Brett Ratner. Screenplay by Azie Faison Jr. and Austin Phillips.

Paid in Full tells the story of the rise and fall of a gifted young businessman. His career might have taken place at Enron, as a talented manager, staging a fake energy crisis to steal from California consumers. But opportunity finds us where we live, and Ace lives in Harlem and lacks an MBA, so he becomes a drug dealer. The skills involved are much the same as at Enron: Lie to the customers, hide or fake the income, shuffle the books, and pay off powerful friends. It is useful, in viewing a movie like *Paid in Full,* to understand that it is about business, not drugs. Breaking the law is simply an unfortunate side effect of wanting to make more money than can be done legally.

Because many drug dealers and consumers are poor and powerless, laws come down on them more ferociously than on the white-collar criminals whose misdeeds are on a larger scale. Three strikes and you're out, while three lucrative bankruptcies and you're barely up and running. *Paid in Full* might have been fascinating if it had intercut between Ace's career and the adventures of an Enron executive of about the same age. I guess in a way that's what *Traffic* did.

Paid in Full takes place in the 1980s and is based on the true stories of famous drug lords (Alpo, A. Z., Richard Porter) during that era of expanding crack addiction. Names are changed. Ace, based on A. Z. and played by Wood Harris, is a deliveryman for a dry cleaner named Pip (Chi McBride). Moving on the streets all day, it is impossible for him to miss seeing the good fortune of drug dealers, and he learns of the fortunes to be made by delivering something other than pressed pants.

He tells his story himself, in a narration like the ones in *GoodFellas* or *Casino,* and in an early scene we see money that has become so meaningless that small fortunes are bet on tossing crumpled paper at wastebaskets. When another dealer (Kevin Carroll) goes off to the pen, Ace moves quickly to grab his territory, and soon has so much money that his life demonstrates one of the drawbacks of growing up in poverty: You lack the skills to spend it fast enough. He prospers, learning from the more experienced Lulu (Esai Morales). Then another young hotshot, Rico (Cam'ron), comes along, and Ace becomes the veteran who's a target.

The movie is ambitious, has good energy, and is well acted, but tells a familiar story in a familiar way. The parallels to Brian De Palma's *Scarface* are underlined by scenes from that movie that are watched by the characters in this. The trajectory is well known: poverty, success, riches, and then death or jail. This plot describes countless lives, and is so common because the laws against drugs do such a good job of supporting the price and making the business so lucrative. The difference between drugs and corporate swindles, obviously, is that with drugs the profits are real.

Panic ★ ★ ★ ★
R, 88 m., 2001

William H. Macy (Alex), John Ritter (Josh Parks), Neve Campbell (Sarah), Donald Sutherland (Michael), Tracey Ullman (Martha), Barbara Bain (Deidre), David Dorfman (Sammy). Directed by Henry Bromell and produced by Andrew Lazar, Lori Miller, and Matt Cooper. Screenplay by Bromell.

"I've got two jobs. I run a small mail-order business out of the house. Lawn ornaments, kitchen geegaws, sexual aids—things like that."
"And the rest of the time?"
"I work for my father. I kill people."

The sad-eyed patient speaks calmly. His psychiatrist says, "You're kidding, right?" No, he is not kidding. He was raised in the family business. His father was a hit man, and he's a hit man too. Not even his wife knows; she believes the mail-order story. But now he's in his forties, has a young son he loves, and wants to stop murdering for a living.

It tells you something—it may even tell you enough—that the man, named Alex, is played by William H. Macy. This wonderful actor has a gift for edgy unhappiness, repressed resentment, and in *Panic* he speaks too calmly and moves too smoothly, as if afraid of trip wires and booby traps. He spent his childhood afraid to stand up to his father, and in a sense his childhood has never ended.

Henry Bromell's *Panic* seeps with melancholy, old wounds, repressed anger, lust. That it is also caustically funny and heartwarming is miraculous: How does it hit so many different notes and never strain? It has a relationship between Alex and his son, Sammy, that reminds us of *The Sixth Sense,* and one between Alex and the sexy young Sarah (Neve Campbell) that evokes *American Beauty.* And Alex himself, trying to keep everyone happy, trying to keep secrets, trying to separate the compartments of his life, has the desperation of the character Macy played in *Fargo.*

But this is not a movie assembled from spare parts. Bromell began as a writer *(Northern Exposure, Chicago Hope),* and this is a first film made with joy and with a writer's gift for character and dialogue. It involves a situation rich with irony and comic possibilities but isn't cynical about it; it's the kind of story that is funny when you hear about it from someone else, but not funny if it happens to you.

Alex was raised by his father, Michael (Donald Sutherland), to be a hit man. They started with squirrels and worked up from there. Alex didn't like killing squirrels, and in all of his killings since, it has been his father's finger pulling the trigger of Alex's tortured psyche. Alex is good at his job. But it makes him sick.

In the waiting room of his psychiatrist (John Ritter), he meets the patient of another doctor. This is Sarah, played by Neve Campbell as bright, cheeky, and with a gift for sharp observation. She has a complicated love life, is aware of her appeal, asks Alex if he's a guy in midlife crisis who thinks a sexy young girl might be just the ticket. In *American Beauty,* Kevin Spacey did indeed think that about the pom-pom girl, but Alex is looking not for sex but for approval, forgiveness, redemption; sex with Sarah would be less lust than rehab.

There are other important women in the picture. Tracey Ullman is Martha, Alex's wife, and Barbara Bain is Deidre, his mother. Martha has no idea how Alex really earns his living. Deidre knows all about everything, and when Alex confides that he wants out, she delivers a merciless lecture about how his father spent his whole life building up the family business, and Alex is an ungrateful child to destroy that dream. Yes, this is ironic, discussing murder in business terms, but it is so easy to separate success from morality. This could be any business in which the father insists that the son surrender his own dreams for the old man's.

Alex doesn't confide much in his wife; his secrets have built a wall. He loves her, but hopelessly, and he loves his son (David Dorfman, the little boy in *Bounce*). Their talks at bedtime are long and rich, and Sammy sees that something is deeply troubling his father: "Dad, are you all right?"

The movie takes these strands and weaves them into an emotional and logistical trap for Alex. His relationship with Sarah, a complicated girl, creates more issues than it solves. His father assigns him to perform an execution that demonstrates the old man's inexorable power over his son. Flashbacks show Alex's anguish as a child, and there is also a flashback showing how he met his wife, and how he was attracted to her goofiness.

The elements of the movie stand on their own. The Neve Campbell character is not simply the younger woman in Alex's life, but creates plot space of her own, where Alex is a visitor. The parents, Michael and Deidre, have a relationship that depends on their son but excludes him. Alex and Sammy have a private bond. We come to see Alex as a desperate man running from one secret compartment to another, seeking a place where he can hide.

Macy is as easy to identify with as any actor working. He doesn't push it. As Alex, he approaches his problems doggedly, sometimes bravely, hoping for a reprieve. Sutherland makes the old hit man into a particularly unlikable person: There's something about the way he gobbles an outdoor meal, his hat askew, that sets our teeth on edge. Bain's mother in her cold confidence is even more hateful. Ullmann, that gifted character actress, creates a woman who knows her life is coming apart but doesn't know what her life is. Neve Campbell takes a tricky role and enriches it, brings it human dimension instead of being content with the "sexpot" assignment. And the little boy is heartbreaking, particularly in a conversation late in the movie. This is one of the year's best films.

Note: Panic *was a success at Sundance 2000, but didn't get a major release after a test audience disliked it. I don't blame the test audience; this is not a look-alike movie. But the executives who believed the audience instead of their own eyes should be ashamed of themselves. Now the film has won a national release and, like* Croupier, *could be discovered by filmgoers who make up their own minds.*

Panic Room ★ ★ ★
R, 112 m., 2002

Jodie Foster (Meg Altman), Kristen Stewart (Sarah Altman), Forest Whitaker (Burnham), Jared Leto (Junior), Dwight Yoakam (Raoul), Patrick Bauchau (Stephen), Ian Buchanan (Evan), Ann Magnuson (Lydia Lynch). Directed by David Fincher and produced by Cean Chaffin, Judy Hofflund, David Koepp, and Gavin Polone. Screenplay by Koepp.

As a critic I indulge myself by scoffing at loopholes in thrillers that could not exist without them. I guess I'm seeking the ideal of a thriller existing entirely in a world of physical and psychological plausibility. *Panic Room* is about as close as I'm likely to get. Yes, there are moments when I want to shout advice at the screen, but just as often the characters are ahead of me. They also ask the same questions I'm asking, of which the most heartfelt, in a thriller, is, "Why didn't *we* do that?"

The movie, directed by David Fincher and written by David Koepp, embraces realism almost as a challenge. The movie resembles a chess game: The board and all of the pieces are in full view, both sides know the rules, and the winner will simply be the better strategist. Once we sense *Panic Room* isn't going to cheat, it gathers in tension, because the characters are operating out of their own resources, and that makes them the players, not the pawns.

Jodie Foster and Forest Whitaker star, as the chessmasters. She's Meg, a rich woman, recently divorced, who is spending her first night in a big Manhattan brownstone with her teenage daughter, Sarah (Kristen Stewart). He's Burnham, a home invader lured by tales of millions hidden in the house by its former owner. The house includes a "panic room" on the third of four stories—a reinforced retreat with independent supplies of air, electricity, and water, which can be locked indefinitely to keep the occupants safe. Burnham's day job: "I spent the last twelve years of my life building rooms like this specifically to keep out people like us."

He's talking to his partners, Junior (Jared Leto) and Raoul (Dwight Yoakam). Junior brought Burnham and Raoul onto the job, and Burnham hates it that Raoul brought along a gun. Their plan is to get in, find the money, and get out. According to Junior's information, the house is empty. It is not, and soon Meg and Sarah are locked in the safe room, the three men are outside, and it looks like a stalemate except that neither side can afford to concede.

We already know the layout of the house. We got the tour when the real-estate agent showed the women through the rooms, and again in a vertiginous shot that begins in the upstairs bedroom, swoops down two floors, zooms into the keyhole, pulls back, and careens upstairs again. The shot combines physical and virtual camera moves, a reminder that Fincher *(Seven, The Game, Fight Club)* is a visual virtuoso. He's also a master of psychological gamesmanship, and most of the movie will bypass fancy camerawork for classical intercutting between the cats and the mice (who sometimes trade sides of the board).

I have deliberately not described much of the strategy itself. That would be cheating. Once you know what everyone wants and how the safe room works, the plot should be allowed to simply unfold. There is a neat twist in the fund of knowledge about the room; Burnham, who builds them, knows a lot more about how they work, their strengths and limitations, than Meg and Sarah, who start out basically knowing only how to run inside and lock the door.

The role of Meg was originally filled by Nicole Kidman. I learn from *Variety* that she had to drop out after a knee injury and was replaced by Foster. I have no idea if Foster is better or worse than Kidman would have been. I only know she is spellbinding. She has the gutsy, brainy resilience of a stubborn scrapper, and when all other resources fail her she can still think fast—and obliquely, like a chessmaster hiding one line of attack inside another.

The intruders are ill matched, which is the idea. Burnham has the knowledge, Junior has the plan, and Raoul has the gun. Once they are all inside the house and know the plan, therefore, Junior is not entirely necessary, unless the others are positively determined to split the loot three ways. On the other hand, Burnham hates violence, and Raoul is such a wild card he may shoot himself in the foot.

The end game in chess, for the student of the sport, is its most intriguing aspect. The loss of pieces has destroyed the initial symmetry and created a skewed board—unfamiliar terrain in which specialized pieces are required to do jobs for which they were not designed. There is less clutter; strategy must run deeper because there are fewer alternative lines. Sacrifices may be brilliant, or they may be blunders, or only apparent blunders. Every additional move limits the options, and the prospect of defeat, swift and unforeseen, hangs over the board. That is exactly the way *Panic Room* unfolds, right down to the detail that even at the end the same rules apply, and all the choices that were made earlier limit the choices that can be made now.

Pearl Harbor ★ ½
PG-13, 183 m., 2001

Ben Affleck (Rafe McCawley), Josh Hartnett (Danny Walker), Kate Beckinsale (Evelyn Johnson), Cuba Gooding Jr. (Dorie Miller), William Lee Scott (Billy), Greg Zola (Anthony), Ewen Bremner (Red), Alec Baldwin (Doolittle), James King (Betty), Mako (Admiral Yamamoto). Directed by Michael Bay and produced by Bay and Jerry Bruckheimer. Screenplay by Randall Wallace.

Pearl Harbor is a two-hour movie squeezed into three hours, about how on December 7, 1941, the Japanese staged a surprise attack on an American love triangle. Its centerpiece is forty minutes of redundant special effects, surrounded by a love story of stunning banality. The film has been directed without grace, vision, or originality, and although you may walk out quoting lines of dialogue, it will not be because you admire them.

The filmmakers seem to have aimed the film at an audience that may not have heard of Pearl Harbor, or perhaps even of World War II. This is the *Our Weekly Reader* version. If you have the slightest knowledge of the events in the film, you will know more than it can tell you. There is no sense of history, strategy, or context; according to this movie, Japan attacked Pearl Harbor because America cut off its oil supply and they were down to an eighteen-month reserve. Would going to war restore the fuel sources? Did they perhaps also have imperialist designs? Movie doesn't say.

So shaky is the film's history that at the end, when Jimmy Doolittle's Tokyo raiders crash-land in China, they're shot at by Japanese patrols with only a murky throwaway explanation about the Sino-Japanese war already under way. I predict some viewers will leave the theater sincerely confused about why there were Japanese in China.

As for the movie's portrait of the Japanese themselves, it is so oblique that Japanese audiences will find little to complain about apart from the fact that they play such a small role in their own raid. There are several scenes where the Japanese high command debates military tactics, but all of their dialogue is strictly expository; they state facts but do not emerge with personalities or passions. Only Admiral Yamamoto (Mako) is seen as an individual, and his dialogue seems to have been singled out with the hindsight of history. Congratulated on a brilliant raid, he demurs, "A brilliant man would find a way not to fight a war." And later, "I fear all we have done is to awaken a sleeping giant."

Do you imagine at any point the Japanese high command engaged in the 1941 Japanese equivalent of exchanging high-fives and shouting "Yes!" while pumping their fists in the air? Not in this movie, where the Japanese seem to have been melancholy even at the time about the regrettable need to play such a negative role in such a positive Hollywood film.

The American side of the story centers on

two childhood friends from Tennessee with the standard-issue screenplay names Rafe McCawley (Ben Affleck) and Danny Walker (Josh Hartnett). They enter the Army Air Corps and both fall in love with the same nurse, Evelyn Johnson (Kate Beckinsale)—first Rafe falls for her, and then, after he is reported dead, Danny. Their first date is subtitled "Three Months Later" and ends with Danny, having apparently read the subtitle, telling Evelyn, "Don't let it be three months before I see you again, OK?" That gets almost as big a laugh as her line to Rafe, "I'm gonna give Danny my whole heart, but I don't think I'll ever look at another sunset without thinking of you."

That kind of bad laugh would have been sidestepped in a more literate screenplay, but our hopes are not high after an early newsreel report that the Germans are bombing "downtown London"—a difficult target, since although there is such a place as "central London," at no time in 2,000 years has London ever had anything described by anybody as a "downtown."

There is not a shred of conviction or chemistry in the love triangle, which results after Rafe returns alive to Hawaii shortly before the raid on Pearl Harbor and is angry at Evelyn for falling in love with Danny, inspiring her timeless line, "I didn't even know until the day you turned up alive—and then all this happened."

Evelyn is a hero in the aftermath of the raid, performing triage by using her lipstick to separate the wounded who should be treated from those left to die. In a pointless stylistic choice, director Michael Bay and cinematographer John Schwartzman shoot some of the hospital scenes in soft focus, some in sharp focus, some blurred. Why? I understand it's to obscure details deemed too gory for the PG-13 rating. (Why should the carnage at Pearl Harbor be toned down to PG-13 in the first place?) In the newsreel sequences, the movies fades in and out of black-and-white with almost amusing haste, while the newsreel announcer sounds not like a period voice but like a Top-40 DJ in an echo chamber.

The most involving material in the film comes at the end, when Jimmy Doolittle (Alec Baldwin) leads his famous raid on Tokyo, flying army bombers off the decks of navy carriers and hoping to crash-land in China. He and his men were heroes, and their story would make a good movie (and indeed has: *Thirty Seconds*

Over Tokyo). Another hero in the movie is the African-American cook Dorie Miller (Cuba Gooding Jr.), who because of his race was not allowed to touch a gun in the racist prewar navy, but opens fire during the raid, shoots down two planes, and saves the life of his captain. Nice to see an African-American in the movie, but the almost total absence of Asians in 1941 Hawaii is inexplicable.

As for the raid itself, a little goes a long way. What is the point, really, of more than half an hour of planes bombing ships, of explosions and fireballs, of roars on the sound track and bodies flying through the air and people running away from fighters that are strafing them? How can it be entertaining or moving when it's simply about the most appalling slaughter? Why do the filmmakers think we want to see this, unrelieved by intelligence, viewpoint, or insight? It was a terrible, terrible day. Three thousand died in all. This is not a movie about them. It is an unremarkable action movie; Pearl Harbor supplies the subject, but not the inspiration.

Personal Velocity ★ ★ ★ ½
R, 86 m., 2002

Kyra Sedgwick (Delia), Parker Posey (Greta), Fairuza Balk (Paula), Nicole Murphy (May Wurtzle), Tim Guinee (Lee), Ron Leibman (Avram), Seth Gilliam (Vincent), David Warshofsky (Kurt Wurtzle), Brian Tarantina (Pete Shunt), Mara Hobel (Fay), Leo Fitzpatrick (Mylert), Wallace Shawn (Mr. Gelb), John Ventimiglia (Narrator [voice]). Directed by Rebecca Miller and produced by Alexis Alexanian, Lemore Syvan, and Gary Winick. Screenplay by Miller.

Wandering through a bookstore a few weeks ago, I picked up *The Best American Short Stories 2002*, and it launched me into a marathon of short story reading: "The O. Henry Prize Awards 2002," the collected stories of Alice Munro, Ha Jin, Michael Chabon, and William Trevor, and even one evening the works of Mr. Henry himself, long waiting on a distant shelf.

I mention this because it was a well-timed preparation for Rebecca Miller's *Personal Velocity*, which films three of her own short stories in segments of about half an hour each. This was the Grand Jury prize winner at Sundance 2002. I was in the mood for these focused, economic stories, in which we plunge into the middle of a life, witness crucial developments, and end with a moment of bittersweet insight into the character. If novels and feature films are about the arc of a life or at least a significant portion of one, short stories and films are about unexpected moments of truth: "epiphanies," James Joyce called them.

Miller's characters are Delia (Kyra Sedgwick), Greta (Parker Posey), and Paula (Fairuza Balk). These three actresses almost always appear in interesting work, often from the indie segment, and their casting is a clue about the movie: It is likely to be about specific, not generic, women, and in one way or another they will be defiantly out of step. They also share big problems about men: fathers, husbands, lovers, dates.

Delia is a battered wife, once famed as a high school slut. Greta edits cookbooks, until a famous novelist asks her to handle his next novel. Paula is running away from her life when she picks up a hitchhiker who is running away from a worse one. All three women have problems with men, and none of them find the solution in this film—which is, I think, a recommendation.

Paula's segment touched me the most. Balk's Paula is a resilient woman with much to be resilient about. She's pregnant. She has just narrowly escaped one of those senseless accidents that can forever change your life. Shaken, she gets in her car and starts driving and finds herself at her mother's home. Her mother's new husband is a jerk, and her mother won't defend her daughter against him. Paula picks up a sullen, sad, withdrawn young hitchhiker and gets a sudden insight both into what has happened to him—and how it has wounded and hardened him. What she learns is that she still has feelings, can care, is not as crippled as she thinks.

Parker Posey is a natural comedienne, and that is a gift she draws on in the not very funny story of Greta, a cookbook editor who is engaged to a fact-checker at *The New Yorker*. When the famous novelist comes along, he is looking for both an editor and a lover. Will she be loyal to her boyfriend, who her father thinks is a loser? Is the question complicated by this opportunity with a winner? Because she has

never felt very deeply about anything in life, this decision looks easier to her than it should.

The first story, about Delia, stars Kyra Sedgwick as a woman who is at first intrigued when her sex life turns a little rough, until she discovers that once her husband gets the taste for hurting her, he likes it. She flees with her children, lives for a time in a friend's garage, gets a job at a diner, and then is propositioned in an oily, callow way by the owner's son (Leo Fitzpatrick). He is amazed when she calls his bluff and says yes. He is more amazed by the contemptuous, dismissive way she deals with his lust. The segment ends with her regarding him thoughtfully, as if considering her future, or her past.

These stories are commented on by a narrator (John Ventimiglia), who uses Miller's prose to draw larger lessons and look for deeper currents. Miller (the daughter of the playwright Arthur) refuses to draw morals for her characters. They are not yet through learning, and life has more lessons for them. We see them so sharply, however, in the few days we glimpse each one. The actors are gifted at establishing character with just a few well-chosen strokes (as a short story writer must also be able to do). We learn as much about each of these women in half an hour as we learn about most movie characters in two hours. More, really, because the movie doesn't pretend to solve their situations, only to dramatize them.

Much has been made of the Sundance Award–winning cinematography by Ellen Kuras, because it is digital, and cheerfully makes that obvious. No doubt the quickness and economy of digital made the film possible. But I didn't much think about the cinematography while watching the film—or if I did, I had the same thoughts I would have had while watching 35mm. My thoughts were focused on the characters. That is a compliment to Kuras and Miller. If I had been thinking about the visual medium, they would have been doing something wrong.

Phone Booth ★ ★ ★
R, 81 m., 2003

Colin Farrell (Stu Shepard), Forest Whitaker (Captain Ramey), Katie Holmes (Pamela McFadden), Radha Mitchell (Kelly Shepard), Kiefer Sutherland (The Caller [voice]). Directed by Joel Schumacher and produced by Gil Netter and David Zucker. Screenplay by Larry Cohen.

Phone Booth is a religious fable, a showbiz fable, or both. It involves a fast-talking, two-timing Broadway press agent who is using the last phone booth in Manhattan (at 53d and Eighth) when he's pinned down by a sniper. The shooter seems to represent either God, demanding a confession of sins, or the filmmakers, having their revenge on publicists.

The man in the crosshairs is Stu Shepard (Colin Farrell), who we've already seen striding the streets, lying into his cell phone, berating his hapless gofer. Why does he now use a pay phone instead of his cellular? Because he's calling his mistress Pamela (Katie Holmes) and doesn't want the call to turn up on the monthly bill scrutinized by his wife, Kelly (Radha Mitchell).

The phone in the booth rings, and Stu follows the universal human practice of answering it. The voice is harsh, sardonic, sounds like it belongs to a man intelligent and twisted, and with a sense of humor. For the next hour or so, in a movie that is only eighty-one minutes long, Stu will be trying to keep the man on the other end from pulling the trigger. The Voice (for so we may call him) seems to know a lot about Stu—personal secrets, but also things anyone could see, like the way he rudely treated a pizza delivery man. He seems to think Stu is a reprehensible man who deserves to die—and may, unless Stu can talk or think his way out of this situation.

The movie is essentially a morality play, and it's not a surprise to learn that Larry Cohen, the writer, came up with the idea twenty years ago—when there were still phone booths and morality plays. If the movie had been conceived more recently, Stu would have been the hero for the way he lies and cheats. The movie is an instructive contrast to *People I Know*, which played at Sundance 2003 and stars Al Pacino as a press agent who doggedly tries to do the right thing despite all of his (many) sins.

The director, Joel Schumacher, discovered Colin Farrell in the tense, quirky basic training drama *Tigerland* (2000). Farrell played a recruit who was too smart and too verbal to be a good trainee, and stirred up trouble in a fraught situation. Now comes a similar character, further twisted by civilian life. The movie is Farrell's to

win or lose, since he's on-screen most of the time, and he shows energy and intensity.

As the crisis builds in tension, he forms a rapport with Captain Ramey (Forest Whitaker), a cop experienced at hostage situations, who at first believes Stu might be the perp and not the victim. The two actors have to communicate nonverbally to keep the sniper from realizing what's happening, and the movie shows them figuring that out.

The movie was premiered at Toronto 2002, scheduled for immediate release, and then yanked when the Beltway Sniper went into action. Then it opened during the Iraqi war. Hard to pick a safe opening date these days. Schumacher is the director of many blockbuster titles, like two of the *Batman* movies, but he sometimes leaves the big budgets behind (he shot *Phone Booth* on one set in ten days).

For the voice of his sniper, he calls on Kiefer Sutherland, who also starred in Schumacher's *The Lost Boys* (1987), *Flatliners* (1990), and *A Time to Kill* (1996) and here takes the mostly (but not quite entirely) invisible role as a very useful favor to Schumacher—because if the voice doesn't work, neither does the movie. It does. I especially like the way the caller taunts Stu: "Do you see the tourists with their video cameras, hoping the cops will shoot so they can sell the tape?" ☞

The Pianist ★ ★ ★ ½
R, 148 m., 2002

Adrien Brody (Wladyslaw Szpilman), Daniel Caltagirone (Majorek), Thomas Kretschmann (Captain Wilm Hosenfeld), Frank Finlay (Father), Maureen Lipman (Mother), Emilia Fox (Dorota), Ed Stoppard (Henryk), Julia Rayner (Regina). Directed by Roman Polanski and produced by Robert Benmussa, Polanski, and Alain Sarde. Screenplay by Ronald Harwood, based on the book by Wladyslaw Szpilman.

The title is an understatement, and so is the film. Roman Polanski's *The Pianist* tells the story of a Polish Jew, a classical musician, who survived the Holocaust through stoicism and good luck. This is not a thriller, and avoids any temptation to crank up suspense or sentiment; it is the pianist's witness to what he saw and what happened to him. That he survived was not a victory when all whom he loved died; Polanski, in talking about his own experiences, has said that the death of his mother in the gas chambers remains so hurtful that only his own death will bring closure.

The film is based on the autobiography of Wladyslaw Szpilman, who was playing Chopin on a Warsaw radio station when the first German bombs fell. Szpilman's family was prosperous and seemingly secure, and his immediate reaction was, "I'm not going anywhere." We watch as the Nazi noose tightens. His family takes heart from reports that England and France have declared war; surely the Nazis will soon be defeated, and life will return to normal.

It does not. The city's Jews are forced to give up their possessions and move to the Warsaw Ghetto, and there is a somber shot of a brick wall being built to enclose it. A Jewish police force is formed to enforce Nazi regulations, and Szpilman is offered a place on it; he refuses, but a good friend, who joins, later saves his life by taking him off a train bound for the death camps. Then the movie tells the long and incredible story of how Szpilman survived the war by hiding in Warsaw, with help from the Polish resistance.

Szpilman is played in the film by Adrien Brody, who is more gaunt and resourceless than in Ken Loach's *Bread and Roses* (2000), where he played a cocky Los Angeles union organizer. We sense that his Szpilman is a man who came early and seriously to music, knows he is good, and has a certain aloofness to life around him. More than once we hear him reassuring others that everything will turn out all right; this faith is based not on information or even optimism, but essentially on his belief that, for anyone who plays the piano as well as he does, it must.

Polanski himself is a Holocaust survivor, saved at one point when his father pushed him through the barbed wire of a camp. He wandered Krakow and Warsaw, a frightened child, cared for by the kindness of strangers. His own survival (and that of his father) are in a sense as random as Szpilman's, which is perhaps why he was attracted to this story. Spielberg tried to enlist Polanski to direct *Schindler's List,* but he refused, perhaps because Schindler's story involved a man who deliberately set out to frustrate the Holocaust, while from personal experience he knew that fate and chance played an inexplicable role in most survivals.

The film was shot in Poland (where he had not worked since his film *Knife in the Water,* in 1962), and also in Prague and in a German studio. On giant sets he re-creates a street overlooked by the apartment where Szpilman is hidden by sympathizers; from his high window the pianist can see the walls of the ghetto and make inferences about the war, based on the comings and goings at the hospital across the street. Szpilman is safe enough here for a time, but hungry, lonely, sick, and afraid, and then a bomb falls and he discovers with terror that the running water no longer works. By now it is near the end of the war and the city lies in ruins; he finds some rooms standing in the rubble, ironically containing a piano that he dare not play.

The closing scenes of the movie involve Szpilman's confrontation with a German captain named Wilm Hosenfeld (Thomas Kretschmann), who finds his hiding place by accident. I will not describe what happens, but will observe that Polanski's direction of this scene, his use of pause and nuance, is masterful.

Some reviews of *The Pianist* have found it too detached, lacking urgency. Perhaps that impassive quality reflects what Polanski wants to say. Almost all of the Jews involved in the Holocaust were killed, so all of the survivor stories misrepresent the actual event by supplying an atypical ending. Often their buried message is that by courage and daring, these heroes saved themselves. Well, yes, some did, but most did not and—here is the crucial point—most could not. In this respect Tim Blake Nelson's *The Grey Zone* (2002) is tougher and more honest, by showing Jews trapped within a Nazi system that removed the possibility of moral choice.

By showing Szpilman as a survivor but not a fighter or a hero—as a man who does all he can to save himself, but would have died without enormous good luck and the kindness of a few non-Jews—Polanski is reflecting, I believe, his own deepest feelings: that he survived, but need not have, and that his mother died, and left a wound that has never healed.

After the war, we learn, Szpilman remained in Warsaw and worked all of his life as a pianist. His autobiography was published soon after the war, but was suppressed by Communist authorities because it did not hew to the party line (some Jews were flawed and a German was kind). Republished in the 1990s, it caught Polanski's attention and resulted in this film, which refuses to turn Szpilman's survival into a triumph and records it primarily as the story of a witness who was there, saw, and remembers. ☞

The Piano Teacher ★ ★ ★ ½
NO MPAA RATING, 130 m., 2002

Isabelle Huppert (Erika Kohut), Benoit Magimel (Walter Klemmer), Annie Girardot (The Mother), Susanne Lothar (Mrs. Schober), Udo Samel (Dr. Blonskij), Anna Sigalevitch (Anna Schober), Cornelia Kondgen (Mme. Blonskij), Thomas Weinhappel (Baritone). Directed by Michael Haneke and produced by Viet Heiduschka. Screenplay by Haneke, based on the novel by Elfriede Jelinek.

There is a self-assurance in Isabelle Huppert that defies all explanation. I interviewed her in 1977, asking her how she got her start in the movies. She knocked on the door of a Paris studio, she said, and announced, "I am here." Was she kidding? I peered at her. I thought not.

In Michael Haneke's *The Piano Teacher*, which won three awards at Cannes 2001 (best actress, actor, and film), she plays a bold woman with a secret wound. She is Erika Kohut, fortyish, a respected instructor at a conservatory of music in Vienna. Demanding, severe, distant, unsmiling, she leads a secret life of self-mutilation. That she sleeps in the same bed with her domineering mother is no doubt a clue—but to what?

Erika is fascinated with the sexual weaknesses and tastes of men. There is a scene where she visits a porn shop in Vienna, creating an uncomfortable tension by her very presence. The male clients are presumably there to indulge their fantasies about women, but faced with a real one, they look away, disturbed or ashamed. If she were obviously a prostitute they could handle that, but she's apparently there to indulge her own tastes, and that takes all the fun out of it, for them. She returns their furtive glances with a shriveling gaze.

She has a handsome young student named Walter (Benoit Magimel). She notices him in a

particular way. They have a clash of wills. He makes it clear he is interested in her. Not long after, in one of the school's rest rooms, they have a sexual encounter—all the more electrifying because while she shocks him with her brazen behavior, she refuses to actually have sex with him. She wants the upper hand.

What games does she want to play? A detailed and subtle plan of revenge against her mother is involved, and Walter, who is not really into sadomasochism, allows himself to be enlisted out of curiosity, or perhaps because he hopes she will yield to him at the end of the scenario. Does it work out that way? Some audience members will dislike the ending, but with a film like this any conventional ending would be a cop-out.

Most sexual relationships in the movies have a limited number of possible outcomes, but this one is a mystery. Another mystery is, what's wrong with Erika? She is not simply an adventuress, a sexual experimenter, a risk taker. Some buried pathology is at work. Walter's idle thoughts about an experienced older woman have turned into nightmares about experiences he doesn't even want to know about.

Huppert often plays repressed, closed-off, sexually alert women. At forty-seven, she looks curiously as she did at twenty-two; she is thin, with fine, freckled skin that does not seem to weather, and seems destined to be one of those women who was never really young and then never really ages. Many of her roles involve women it is not safe to scorn. Magimel won his best actor award for standing up to her force. He doesn't play the standard movie character we'd expect in this role (the immature twentysomething boy who flowers under the tutelage of an older woman). Instead, he's a capable, confident young man who thinks he has met hidden wildness and then finds it is madness.

The movie seems even more highly charged because it is wrapped in an elegant package. These are smart people. They talk about music as if they understand it, they duel with their minds as well as their bodies, and Haneke photographs them in two kinds of spaces: Sometimes they're in elegant, formal conservatory settings, and at other times in frankly vulgar places where quick release can be snatched from strangers. There is an old saying: Be careful what you ask for, because you might get it. *The Piano Teacher* has a more ominous lesson: Be especially careful with someone who has asked for you.

Pirates of the Caribbean:
The Curse of the Black Pearl ★ ★ ★
PG-13, 134 m., 2003

Johnny Depp (Captain Jack Sparrow), Geoffrey Rush (Captain Barbossa), Orlando Bloom (Will Turner), Keira Knightley (Elizabeth Swann), Jack Davenport (Commodore Norrington), Jonathan Pryce (Governor Weatherby Swann). Directed by Gore Verbinski and produced by Jerry Bruckheimer. Screenplay by Ted Elliott and Terry Rossio.

There's a nice little 90-minute B movie trapped inside the 134 minutes of *Pirates of the Caribbean: The Curse of the Black Pearl,* a movie that charms the audience and then outstays its welcome. Although the ending leaves open the possibility of a sequel, the movie feels like it already includes the sequel; maybe that explains the double-barreled title. It's a good thing that Geoffrey Rush and Johnny Depp are on hand to jack up the acting department. Their characters, two world-class goofballs, keep us interested even during entirely pointless swordfights.

Pointless? See if you can follow me here. Captain Jack Sparrow (Depp) has a deep hatred for Captain Barbossa (Rush), who led a mutiny aboard Sparrow's pirate ship, the *Black Pearl,* and left Captain Jack stranded on a deserted island. Barbossa and his crew then ran afoul of an ancient curse that turned them into the Undead. By day they look like normal if dissolute humans, but by the light of the moon they're revealed as skeletal cadavers.

Now here's the important part: Because they're already dead, they cannot be killed. Excuse me for supplying logic where it is manifestly not wanted, but doesn't that mean there's no point in fighting them? There's a violent battle at one point between the *Black Pearl* crew and sailors of the Royal Navy, and unless I am mistaken the sailors would all eventually have to be dead, because the skeletons could just keep on fighting forever until they won. Yes?

The only reason I bring this up is that the battle scenes actually feel as if they go on forever. It's fun at first to see a pirate swordfight,

but eventually it gets to the point where the sword clashing, yardarm swinging, and timber shivering get repetitious. I also lost count of how many times Jack Sparrow is the helpless captive of both the British and the pirates, and escapes from the chains/brig/noose/island.

And yet the movie made me grin at times and savor the daffy plot and enjoy the way Depp and Rush fearlessly provide performances that seem nourished by deep wells of nuttiness. Depp in particular seems to be channeling a drunken drag queen, with his eyeliner and the way he minces ashore and slurs his dialogue ever so insouciantly. Don't mistake me: This is not a criticism, but admiration for his work. It can be said that his performance is original in its every atom. There has never been a pirate, or for that matter a human being, like this in any other movie. There's some talk about how he got too much sun while he was stranded on that island, but his behavior shows a lifetime of rehearsal. He is a peacock in full display.

Consider how boring it would have been if Depp had played the role straight, as an Errol Flynn or Douglas Fairbanks (Sr. or Jr.) might have. To take this material seriously would make it unbearable. Captain Sparrow's behavior is so rococo that other members of the cast actually comment on it. And yet because it is consistent and because you can never catch Depp making fun of the character, it rises to a kind of cockamamy sincerity.

Geoffrey Rush is relatively subdued—but only by contrast. His Barbossa, whose teeth alone would intimidate a congregation of dentists, brings gnashing to an art form. Only the film's PG-13 rating prevents him from doing unthinkable things to the heroine, Elizabeth Swann (Keira Knightley), whose blood, it is thought, can free the captain and his crew from the curse of the *Black Pearl.* Elizabeth is the daughter of the governor (Jonathan Pryce) of Port Royal, a British base in the Caribbean, and seems destined to marry Commodore Norrington (Jack Davenport), a fate that we intuit would lead to a lifetime of conversations about his constipation.

She truly loves the handsome young swordsmith Will Turner (Orlando Bloom), whom she met when they were both children, after spotting him adrift on a raft with a golden pirate medallion around his neck, which turns out to hold the key to the curse. Jack Sparrow takes a fatherly interest in young Turner, especially when he discovers who his father was . . . and that is quite enough of the plot.

Orlando Bloom is well cast in a severely limited role, as the heroic straight arrow. He has the classic profile of a silent film star. Keira Knightley you will recall as the best friend of the heroine in *Bend It Like Beckham,* where she had a sparkle altogether lacking here. Truth be told, she doesn't generate enough fire to explain why these swashbucklers would risk their lives for her, and in close-up seems composed when she should smolder. Parminder K. Nagra, the star of *Beckham,* might have been a more spirited choice here.

The movie is based on the theme park ride at Disney World, which I have taken many times. It is also inspired (as the ride no doubt was) by the rich tradition of pirate movies and excels in such departments as buried treasure, pirates' caves, pet parrots, and walking the plank, although there is a shortage of eye patches and hooks. The author Dave Eggers has opened a pirates' store, complete with planks measured and made to order, and the movie plays like his daydreams. 👉

Planet of the Apes ★ ★ ½
PG-13, 110 m., 2001

Mark Wahlberg (Leo), Tim Roth (General Thade), Helena Bonham Carter (Ari), Kris Kristofferson (Karubi), Estella Warren (Daena), Paul Giamatti (Limbo), Michael Clarke Duncan (Attar), David Warner (Senator Sandar), Charlton Heston (Thade's Father). Directed by Tim Burton and produced by Richard D. Zanuck. Screenplay by William Broyles Jr., Lawrence Konner, and Mark D. Rosenthal, based on the novel by Pierre Boulle.

Tim Burton's *Planet of the Apes* wants to be all things to all men, and all apes. It's an action picture and a satire of an action picture. It's a comedy and then it gets serious. It's a social satire and then backs away from pushing that angle too far. It even has a weird interspecies romantic triangle in it. And it has a surprise ending that I loved.

The movie could have been more. It could have been a parable of men and animals, as daring as *Animal Farm.* It could have dealt in social commentary with a sting, and satire that hurt. It could have supported, or attacked, the animal rights movement. It could have dealt with the intriguing question of whether a man and a gorilla having sex is open-mindedness or bestiality (and, if bestiality, in both directions?). It could have, but it doesn't. It's a cautious movie, earning every letter and numeral of its PG-13 rating. Intellectually, it's science fiction for junior high school boys.

I expected more. I thought Burton would swing for the fence. He plays it too safe, defusing his momentum with little nudges to tell you he knows it's only a movie. The 1968 *Planet of the Apes* was made before irony became an insurance policy. It made jokes, but it took itself seriously. Burton's *Planet* has scenes that defy us to believe them (his hero survives two bumpy crash landings that look about as realistic as the effects in his *Mars Attacks!*). And it backs away from any kind of risky complexity in its relationships.

The key couple consists of Leo (Mark Wahlberg), who is the human hero, and Ari (Helena Bonham Carter), who is the Eleanor Roosevelt of the apes. They're attracted to each other but don't know what to do about it, and the screenplay gives them little help. Leo is also supposed to be linked romantically, I guess, with a curvy blond human named Daena (Estella Warren), but her role has been so abbreviated that basically all she does is follow along looking at Leo either significantly or winsomely, as circumstances warrant. At the end, he doesn't even bid her a proper farewell.

Leo, to be sure, is not one for effusive emotional outbursts. He's played by Wahlberg as a limited and narrow person with little imagination, who never seems very surprised by anything that happens to him—like, oh, to take a random example, crash-landing on a planet where the apes rule the humans. He's a space jockey type, trained in macho self-abnegation, who is great in a crisis but doesn't offer much in the way of conversation. His basic motivation seems to be to get himself off the planet, and to hell with the friends he leaves behind; he's almost surly sometimes as he leads his little band through the wilderness.

The most "human" character in the movie is, in fact, the chimpanzee Ari, who believes all species were created equal, casts her lot with the outcast humans, and tells Leo, "You're sensitive—a welcome quality in a man." Helena Bonham Carter invests this character with warmth, personality, and distinctive body language; she has a way of moving that kids itself. There's also juice in a character named Limbo (Paul Giamatti), a scam artist who has a deal for everyone, and a lot of funny one-liners. That he sounds like a carnival pitchman should not be held against him.

The major ape characters include the fearsome General Thade (Tim Roth), his strong but occasionally thoughtful gorilla lieutenant Attar (Michael Clarke Duncan), and Senator Sandar (David Warner), who is a parliamentary leader and Ari's father. There's also a cameo for Charlton Heston, as a wise old ape who inevitably introduces a gun into the plot, and has a curmudgeonly exit line. Watching the apes is fun all during the movie, while watching the humans usually isn't; the movie works hard to bring the apes to life, but unwisely thinks the humans can take care of themselves.

It's interesting that several different simian species coexist in the planet's ape society. It may be a little hard to account for that, given the logic of the movie, although I will say no more. One major change between this film and the earlier one is that everyone—apes and humans—speak English. The movie explains why the apes speak English, but fudges on how they learned to speak at all.

The movie is great looking. Rick Baker's makeup is convincing even in the extreme close-ups, and his apes sparkle with personality and presence. The sets and locations give us a proper sense of alien awe, and there's one neat long shot of the ape city-mountain that looks, when you squint a little, like Xanadu from *Citizen Kane*. There are lines inviting laughs ("Extremism in the defense of apes is no vice") and others unwisely inviting groans ("If you show me the way out of here—I promise I'll show you something that will change your life forever"). And a priceless moment when Leo wants to stop the squabbling among his fugitive group of men and apes and barks: "Shut up! That goes for all species!"

Planet of the Apes is the kind of movie that you enjoy at times, admire at times, even really like at times, but is it necessary? Given how famous and familiar Franklin J. Schaffner's 1968

film is, Tim Burton had some kind of an obligation to either top it, or sidestep it. Instead, he pays homage. He calls this version a "reimaging," and so it is, but a reinvention might have been better. Burton's work can show a wild and crazed imagination, but here he seems reined in. He's made a film that's respectful to the original, and respectable in itself, but that's not enough. Ten years from now, it will be the 1968 version that people are still renting.

The Pledge ★ ★ ★ ½
R, 124 m., 2001

Jack Nicholson (Detective Jerry Black), Sam Shepard (Eric Pollack), Mickey Rourke (Jim Olstand), Benicio Del Toro (Toby Jay Wadenah), Helen Mirren (Doctor), Robin Wright Penn (Lori), Vanessa Redgrave (Annalise Hansen), Aaron Eckhart (Stan Krolak). Directed by Sean Penn and produced by Michael Fitzgerald, Penn, and Elie Samaha. Screenplay by Jerzy Kromolowski and Mary Olson-Kromolowski, based on the book by Friedrich Durrenmatt.

Sean Penn's *The Pledge* begins as a police story and spirals down into madness. It provides Jack Nicholson with one of his best roles in recent years, as a retired cop who makes a promise and tries to keep it. Like their previous film together as director and actor, *The Crossing Guard* (1995), it isn't a simple revenge story but shows the desire for justice running out of control and becoming dangerous. The story has the elements of a crime thriller (cops, suspects, victims, clues) but finally it's a character study, and in Detective Jerry Black, Nicholson creates a character we follow into the darkness of his compulsion.

As the film opens, Jerry is retiring as a cop—a good cop—in Reno. He's from an earlier generation; you can see that by the way he looks for ashtrays in the offices of colleagues who don't smoke. News comes that the mutilated body of a young girl has been found. Jerry goes on the call (he wants to work out his last day), and eventually finds himself delivering the tragic news to the parents of the little girl.

This scene, staged by Penn on the turkey farm the parents operate, is amazing in its setting (Nicholson wading through thousands of turkey chicks) and its impact (holding a crucifix made by the murdered Ginny, he swears "by his soul's salvation" that he will find the killer). This is the pledge of the movie's title, and eventually it obsesses him.

It appears at first that the killer has been found. Benicio Del Toro plays an Indian, obviously retarded, who was seen running away from the murder scene. Clues seem to link his pickup with the crime. A knife-edged detective (Aaron Eckhart) gets a confession out of him, with Jerry squirming behind the one-way glass and saying the Indian "doesn't understand the question." Then the Indian grabs a gun and shoots himself. Guilty, and dead. Case closed.

Jerry doesn't think so. His years as a cop tell him something is not right. In retirement, he continues to investigate the case, eventually finding that the dead Ginny had made friends with a "giant" she called "the Wizard." Who was this man? Was he the killer? Was he linked with other unsolved killings of young children?

Until this point, The Pledge has been a fairly standard, if well-done, police procedural. Now Penn, working from a novel by Friedrich Durrenmatt and screenplay by Jerzy Kromolowski and Mary Olson-Kromolowski, begins the film's descent into Jerry's obsession. He does a strange thing. He buys a gas station and convenience store halfway between two towns where he thinks the "wizard" might have committed crimes. Studying drawings by the dead Ginny, he thinks he knows what kind of vehicle the killer might have used. The store is a trap.

An unexpected thing happens. He meets a mother (Robin Wright Penn) and her young daughter, and they feel an instinctive sympathy which blossoms to his surprise into love. After a couple of divorces, Jerry discovers at last what a happy domestic life can be. We immediately realize that the daughter is a potential victim of the killer, if he is indeed still at large. We assume Jerry realizes this too. But surely he would not use this beautiful little girl as bait?

One problem with Jerry's quest is that he is the only person who believes in it. His former police colleagues think he's gone around the bend; even the chief (Sam Shepard), an old friend, looks sadly at Jerry's unhinged zeal. His gas station trap may be a long shot, or an inspiration, or simply proof he's losing touch with reality. The last third of the movie is

where most police stories go on autopilot, with obligatory chases, stalkings, and confrontations. That's when The Pledge grows most compelling. Penn and Nicholson take risks with the material and the character, and elevate the movie to another, unanticipated, haunting level.

Sean Penn has been saying for years that he wants to quit acting and be a director. That would be a loss, because he is one of the finest actors alive (consider Dead Man Walking). What is clear from the three films he has directed (also including The Indian Runner in 1991) is that he has no interest in making ordinary films. He is fascinated by characters under stress. He is bored by the working out of obvious psychological processes.

The character of Jerry here is not merely a good cop, but a retired man, an older man, a man possessed by a fixed idea. He is able at one level to exude charm and stability (one reason the younger woman likes him is that he offers calm and strength after her violent marriage). But we sense deeper, darker currents, and issues he isn't fully aware of himself. By the end of The Pledge, the suspense hinges mostly on Jerry, and the solution of the crime is a sideshow. It is here that Nicholson's skill is most needed, and most appreciated: He has to show us a man who has embarked on a terrifying and lonely quest into the unknown places of his mind.

Pollock ★ ★ ★ ★
R, 122 m., 2001

Ed Harris (Jackson Pollock), Marcia Gay Harden (Lee Krasner), Amy Madigan (Peggy Guggenheim), Jennifer Connelly (Ruth Klingman), Jeffrey Tambor (Clement Greenberg), Bud Cort (Howard Putzel), John Heard (Tony Smith), Val Kilmer (Willem de Kooning). Directed by Ed Harris and produced by Fred Berner, Harris, and John Kilik. Screenplay by Barbara Turner and Susan Emshwiller, based on the book Jackson Pollock: An American Saga by Steven Naifeh and Gregory White Smith.

Reporter from Life magazine: "How do you know when you're finished with a painting?"

Jackson Pollock: "How do you know when you're finished making love?"

Jackson Pollock was a great painter. He was

also a miserable man who made everyone around him miserable a lot of the time. He was an alcoholic and manic-depressive, and he died in a drunken car crash that killed an innocent woman. What Ed Harris is able to show in *Pollock* is that when he was painting, he got a reprieve. He was also reasonably happy during those periods when he stopped drinking. Then the black cloud would descend again.

Pollock avoids the pitfall of making simplistic one-to-one connections between the artist's life and his paintings. This is not a movie about art but about work. It is about the physical labor of making paintings, and about the additional labor of everyday life, which is a burden for Pollock because of his tortured mind and hungover body. It is said that it takes more will for an alcoholic to get out of bed in the morning than for other people to go through the day, and there are times when Pollock simply stops, stuck, and stares into space. He didn't have de Kooning's luck and find sobriety.

Pollock is often depressed, but *Pollock* is not depressing. It contains all the hum and buzz of the postwar New York art world, the vibrant courage of Pollock's wife, Lee Krasner, the measured presence of the art critic Clement Greenberg (who more or less validated abstract expressionism), and the fun-loving energy of the millionaire art patron Peggy Guggenheim, who collected paintings and painters. It was a time when Pollack traded a painting to pay a $56 bill at a store, and found himself in *Life* magazine not long after. Things were on the move.

This is Ed Harris's movie. He started thinking about it fifteen years ago, after reading a book about Pollock. He commissioned the screenplay. He raised the money. He stars in it, and he directed it. He knew he looked a lot like Pollock (his father saw the book and thought the cover photo resembled his son). But his similarity to Pollock is not just superficial; he looks a little like Picasso, too, but is unlikely to find the same affinity. He seems to have made a deeper connection, to have felt an instinctive sympathy for this great, unhappy man.

The movie wears its period lightly. It gets rolling in postwar Greenwich Village. Everybody smokes all the time. Rents are cheap, but the first time Peggy Guggenheim visits Pollock's studio is almost the last: "I do not climb up five flights of stairs to nobody home!" Why did Pollock almost miss his first meeting with the famous patron? Some damn fool reason. He had a knack for screwing up, and it's arguable that his career would never have happened if Lee Krasner hadn't poked her head around his door one day.

Krasner (played by Marcia Gay Harden, evoking enormous sympathy and patience) comes calling because she wants to see his paintings. She passes her hand over them as if testing their temperature. She knows they are good. She senses that Pollock takes little initiative in personal matters, and takes charge of their relationship, undressing while Pollock is still looking for his cigarettes. She goes in with her eyes open. She knows she's marrying a troubled man, but stands by him, and is repaid with a couple of happy years when they get a place in the country, and he doesn't drink. Then the troubles all start again—a bottle of beer, a fight, an upset table at Thanksgiving, and affairs with hero-worshipping girls like Ruth Klingman (Jennifer Connelly).

I don't know if Ed Harris knows how to paint, but I know he knows how to look like he's painting. There's a virtuoso scene where he paints a mural for Peggy's townhouse, utterly confident, fast and sure, in the flow. And others where we see the famous drip technique (and see that "anyone" could not do it). His judge and jury is the critic Clement Greenberg, played with judicious, plummy certainty by Jeffrey Tambor. He says what he thinks, praising early work and bringing Guggenheim around, then attacking later work even as the world embraces it ("pretentious muddiness").

Pollock is confident, insightful work—one of the best films of the year. Ed Harris is always a good actor but here seems possessed, as if he had a leap of empathy for Pollock. His direction is assured, economical, knows where it's going, and what it wants to do. No fancy visual gimmicks, just the look and feel of this world.

I first saw the movie at the Toronto Film Festival and a day later ran into the painter Julian Schnabel. I mentioned Pollock's suffering. "What happened to Jackson Pollock when he was painting," Schnabel said, "is, he was free." That's what Ed Harris communicates in the film. A man is miserable but he is given a gift. The gift lifts his misery while he employs it. It brings joy to himself and others. It creates space he can hide in, space he can breathe in, space he can escape to. He needs that space, and given his demons, painting is the only way he can find it.

Poolhall Junkies ★ ★ ★

R, 94 m., 2003

Gregory "Mars" Callahan (Johnny Doyle), Chazz Palminteri (Joe), Rick Schroder (Brad), Rod Steiger (Nick), Michael Rosenbaum (Danny Doyle), Alison Eastwood (Tara), Christopher Walken (Mike). Directed by Gregory "Mars" Callahan and produced by Karen Beninati, Vincent Newman, and Tucker Tooley. Screenplay by Chris Corso and Callahan.

One of the things I like best about *Poolhall Junkies* is its lack of grim desperation. Its characters know that pool is a game, and do not lead lives in which every moment is a headbutt with fate. Yes, there are fights, weapons are drawn, and old scores are settled, but the hero's most important bet is made to help his girl get a job she wants, the two archrivals are clearly destined to become friends, and Christopher Walken gets to deliver one of his famous monologues. He starts out, "Have you ever watched one of those animal channels?" and we are grinning already.

This is a young man's film, humming with the fun of making it. It was directed and cowritten by Gregory "Mars" Callahan, who also plays the leading role, Johnny Doyle, who was so good when he was a kid that "the cue was part of his arm and the balls had eyes." He never wanted to grow up to be a pool hustler. He wanted to join the pro tour. He's a good player, but he's not one of those nuts whose eyeballs spin like pinwheels when he's lining up a shot.

Johnny was more or less abandoned by his parents, and adopted by Joe (Chazz Palminteri), a manager of young pool talent. Joe likes taking his cut from the kid's earnings, and Johnny grows up before he discovers that Joe destroyed his invitation to join the pros. That leads to a scene in which Joe breaks the kid's hand, but not his thumb, and then seeks more revenge by taking a new protégé named Brad (Rick Schroder) under his management. Joe also involves

Johnny's kid brother Danny (Michael Rosenbaum) in big trouble.

Johnny has a girlfriend named Tara (Alison Eastwood), who's in law school and doesn't approve of pool hustling, so Johnny gets a job as a construction carpenter, but the nails do not have eyes. Johnny and Tara are invited to a party at the home of a rich lawyer, where they meet her uncle Mike (Walken), one of the few actors in movie history who always draws a quiet rustle of pleasure from the audience the first time he appears on the screen.

And so on. The plot you are already generally familiar with. There will be high-stakes games of pool with lives and fortunes, etc., hanging in the balance. That goes with the territory. *Poolhall Junkies* is a pleasure not because it rivets us with unbearable poolhall suspense, but because it finds a voluptuous enjoyment in the act of moviemaking. You get the sense that "Mars" Callahan, whom I have never met, woke during the night to hug himself that he was getting to make this movie.

Poolhall Junkies has big moments of inspiration, like the Walken speech and a couple of other monologues. It has movie-fan moments, as when Rod Steiger, as the manager of a poolhall, gets to stick out his lower jaw and lay it on the line (this was Steiger's final role). It has Callahan as a serious kid with chiseled dark Irish features, who is cool like McQueen was cool—no big thing, just born that way.

And then it has, well, this corny stuff that Callahan kept in the screenplay because he's no doubt the kind of guy who doesn't like to walk into a bar without a joke to tell. There's a lawyer joke ("What do you call it when you have 10,000 lawyers buried up to their necks in the sand?"). And the oldest trick bet in the book ("I'll bet you I can tell you where you got your shoes"). And a barroom hustle recycled directly out of Steve Buscemi's *Trees Lounge* ("I'll bet I can drink both of these pints faster than you can drink both of those shots"). I mean, come on.

These little hustles set up bigger ones that are also the oldest gags in the book, but the movie delivers on them and has fun while it's doing it. Callahan plays the character of Johnny Doyle not to convince you he's the meanest mother in the city, but simply to demonstrate that it would not be wise to bet large sums of money against him in the game of pool. There is an innocence at work here that reminds me of young Sylvester Stallone, who gave Rocky Balboa pet turtles named Cuff and Link.

Is this a great movie? Not at all. Is it more or less consistently entertaining? Yes. Do Walken and Palminteri do things casually that most actors could not do at all? Yes. Did I feel afterward as if I had been dragged through the blood and grime of the mean streets? No, but I felt like I had a good time at the movies.

Pootie Tang ½★
PG-13, 79 m., 2001

Lance Crouther (Pootie Tang), JB Smoove (Trucky), Jennifer Coolidge (Ireenie), Reg E. Cathey (Dirty Dee), Robert Vaughn (Dick Lecter), Wanda Sykes (Biggie Shorty), Chris Rock (Pootie's Father/JB), Cathy Trien (Stacy), David Attel (Frank). Directed by Louis C.K. and produced by Cotty Chubb, David M. Gale, Ali LeRoi, Michael Rotenberg, Dave Becky, and Chris Rock. Screenplay by C.K.

Pootie Tang is not bad so much as inexplicable. You watch in puzzlement: How did this train wreck happen? How was this movie assembled out of such ill-fitting pieces? Who thought it was funny? Who thought it was finished? For that matter, was it finished? Take away the endless opening titles and end credits, and it's about seventy minutes long. The press notes say it comes "from the comedy laboratory of HBO's Emmy Award–winning *Chris Rock Show*." It's like one of those lab experiments where the room smells like swamp gas and all the mice are dead.

Lance Crouther stars as Pootie Tang, a folk hero who has gained enormous popularity even though nobody can understand a word he says. He crusades against the evil Lecter Corp., which sells cigarettes, booze, drugs, and fast food to kids. Pootie is a regular character on *The Chris Rock Show*, and has a following, but he's more suited to skits than to a feature film—or at least to this feature film, which is disorganized, senseless, and chaotic.

Characters appear and disappear without pattern. Pootie has funny scenes, as when he dodges bullets, and other scenes, as when a woman eats a pie off his face, that seem left in the movie by accident. His secret weapon is

his daddy's belt, which he uses against criminals. His daddy (Chris Rock) gave it to him on his deathbed, after being mauled by a gorilla at the steel mill. When the belt is stolen by an evil woman named Ireenie (Jennifer Coolidge), he loses his powers, but is helped by a good woman named Biggie Shorty (Wanda Sykes, who provides more personality than the movie deserves).

Biggie Shorty is a hooker but spends most of her time boogying on street corners and encouraging Pootie Tang. She has a farm in Mississippi she loans Pootie, who, during his recuperation there, is encouraged by the white sheriff to date his daughter. This leads in the direction of a shotgun marriage, until the story thread evaporates and Pootie ends up in bed with Biggie. There is another villain named Dirty Dee (Reg E. Cathey), who is very dirty, and a villain, Dick Lecter, played by Robert Vaughn as if he may have a touch of lockjaw. Bob Costas plays an interviewer on one of those dreadful assignments where the writers thought it was funny simply *that* he was in the movie, instead of giving him anything funny to do.

Material this silly might at least be mindless entertainment for children, but *Pootie Tang* for no good reason includes a lot of language it has no need for. The studios put enormous pressure on the MPAA to award PG-13 ratings to what once would have been R-rated material, and the MPAA obliges. Here is dialogue your MPAA rates PG-13: "You can't hurt a ho with a belt. They like it." Women are routinely described as bitches and slapped around a lot (so are men). I have no problem with street language in movies with a use for the language. But why use it gratuitously in a movie that has no need for it, with a lead character whose TV exposure will attract younger viewers? What's the point?

Anyway, I'm not so much indignant as confused. Audiences will come out scratching their heads. The movie is half-baked, a shabby job of work. There are flashes of good stuff: a music video in the closing titles, some good songs on the sound track, Lance Crouther heroically making Pootie Tang an intriguing character even though the movie gives him no help. This movie is not in a releasable condition.

Possession ★ ★ ★ ½
PG-13, 102 m., 2002

Gwyneth Paltrow (Maud Bailey), Aaron Eckhart (Roland Michell), Jeremy Northam (Randolph Henry Ash), Jennifer Ehle (Christabel LaMotte), Lena Headey (Blanche Glover), Trevor Eve (Professor Morton Cropper), Toby Stephens (Fergus Wolfe), Anna Massey (Lady Bailey), Holly Aird (Ellen), Felicity Brangan (Lucy). Directed by Neil LaBute and produced by Barry Levinson and Paula Weinstein. Screenplay by David Henry Hwang, Laura Jones, and LaBute, based on the novel by A. S. Byatt.

A visiting American scholar is paging through an old volume at the British Museum when he comes upon a letter stuffed between the pages—a love letter, it would appear, from Queen Victoria's poet laureate, addressed to a woman not his wife. The poet has been held up for more than a century as a model of marital fidelity. The letter is dynamite. The scholar slips the letter out of the book and into his portfolio, and is soon displaying it, with all the pride and uncertainty of a new father, to a British woman who knows (or thought she knew) everything about the poet.

The American, named Roland Michell (Aaron Eckhart), is professionally ambitious but has a block against personal intimacy. The British expert, named Maud Bailey (Gwyneth Paltrow), is suspicious of love, suspicious of men, suspicious of theories that overturn a century of knowledge about her specialty. Together, warily, edgily, they begin to track down the possibility that the happily married Randolph Henry Ash did indeed have an affair with the nineteenth-century feminist and lesbian Christabel LaMotte. Two modern people with high walls of privacy are therefore investigating two Victorians who in theory never even met.

This setup from A. S. Byatt's 1990 Booker Award–winning novel would seem like the last premise in the world to attract the director Neil LaBute, whose *In the Company of Men* and *Your Friends and Neighbors* were about hard-edged modern sexual warfare. But look again at the romantic fantasies in his overlooked *Nurse Betty* (2000) about a housewife in love with a

soap opera character and a killer in love with a photograph of the housewife, and you will see the same premise: Love, fueled by imagination, tries to leap impossible divides.

The film, written by David Henry Hwang, Laura Jones, and LaBute, uses a flashback structure to move between the current investigation and the long-ago relationship. Jeremy Northam plays Ash, an upright public figure, and Jennifer Ehle is Christabel, a pre-Raphaelite beauty who lives with the darkly sensuous Blanche Glover (Lena Headey). The nature of their relationship is one of the incidental fascinations of the movie: At a time before lesbianism was widely acknowledged, female couples were commonly accepted and the possibility of a sexual connection didn't necessarily occur. Blanche is the dominant and possessive one, and Christabel is perhaps not even essentially lesbian, but simply besotted with friendship. When she and Ash make contact, it is Blanche, not Ash's unbending wife, who is the angered spouse.

In the way it moves between two couples in two periods, *Possession* is like Karel Reisz's *The French Lieutenant's Woman* (1981). That film, with a screenplay by Harold Pinter, added a modern couple that didn't exist in the John Fowles novel, and had both couples played by Meryl Streep and Jeremy Irons. The notion of two romances on parallel trajectories is common to both films, and intriguing because there seem to be insurmountable barriers in both periods.

Ash and Christabel are separated by Victorian morality, his marriage, and her relationship. The moderns, Maud and Roland, seem opposed to any idea of romance; she has her own agenda, and he is reticent to a fault. "You have nothing to fear from me," he tells her early on, because he avoids relationships. Later, when they find themselves tentatively in each other's arms, he pulls back: "We shouldn't be doing this; it's dangerous."

This might be convincing if Roland and Maud looked like our conventional idea of literary scholars: Mike White, perhaps, paired with Lili Taylor. That they are both so exceptionally attractive is distracting; Paltrow is able to project a certain ethereal bookishness, but a contemporary man with Eckhart's pumped-up physique and adamant indifference to Paltrow would be read by many observers as gay. That he is not—

that his reticence is a quirk rather than a choice—is a screenplay glitch we have to forgive.

We do, because the movie is not a serious examination of scholarship or poetry, but a brainy romance. In a world where most movie romances consist of hormonal triggers and plumbing procedures, it's sexy to observe two couples who think and debate their connections, who quote poetry to one another, who consciously try to enhance their relationships by seeking metaphors and symbols they can attach to. Romance defined by the body will decay with the flesh, but romance conceived as a grand idea—ah, now that can still fascinate people a century later.

LaBute is a director who loves the spoken word. No surprise that between movies he writes and directs plays. I suspect he would be incapable of making a movie about people who had nothing interesting to say to one another. What he finds sexy is not the simple physical fact of two people, but the scenario they write around themselves; look at the way the deaf woman in *In the Company of Men* so completely defeats both men by discovering their ideas of themselves and turning those ideas against them. By the end of the movie, with the egos of both men in shards at her feet, the woman seems more desirable than we could have imagined possible.

What happens in *Possession* is not the same, but it is similar enough to explain LaBute's interest in the story. He likes people who think themselves into and out of love, and finds the truly passionate (like Blanche) to be the most dangerous. He likes romances that exist out of sight, denied, speculated about, suspected, fought against. Any two people can fall into each other's arms and find that they enjoy the feeling. But to fall into someone else's mind — now that can be dangerous.

The Price of Milk ★ ★
PG-13, 89 m., 2001

Danielle Cormack (Lucinda), Karl Urban (Rob), Willa O'Neill (Drosophilia), Rangi Motu (Auntie), Michael Lawrence (Bernie). Directed by Harry Sinclair and produced by Fiona Copland. Screenplay by Sinclair.

Somewhere in New Zealand, a nation apparently inhabited by less than a dozen people, Lucinda and Rob run a dairy farm. So lonely is Rob that he knows all 175 of his cows by their names—or numbers ("Good morning, 47!"). So carnal is Lucinda that she surprises Rob at strange times and places with sudden, bold invitations to make love. So besotted is Rob that he produces a wedding ring and proposes. So fearful is Lucinda that she seeks advice to be sure that Rob really loves her. So realistic am I that I'm thinking—he'd better, since there is, so far, no other man in the movie.

Lucinda turns to her friend Drosophilia, who advises her to be absolutely sure of Rob's love by setting up a series of tests. In the first Lucinda goes bathing in a vat containing $1,500 worth of milk, spoiling it. Rob is angered, but so fetching is Lucinda's smile and so real her dismay that he plunges in with her, and so fervent are their ecstasies that the milk all but churns into butter right before our eyes.

We are thinking, meanwhile, that whatever else you can say for them, Lucinda, Rob, and Drosophilia are healthy-looking specimens, and look right at place on a farm. No wonder; they are played by Danielle Cormack, Karl Urban, and Willa O'Neill, who have all appeared on TV's *Xena* or *Hercules* (Cormack is the Amazon Ephiny). They were cast in *The Price of Milk* by its writer-director, Harry Sinclair—who, I learn from *Film Journal International*, "started out his project not with a story line, or a face in mind, but a bit of a Russian symphony by early-20th-century composer Anatol Liadov, accidentally heard over the radio while location-scouting. Sinclair was inspired by the music and the place, and themes appeared and fell into line for him."

If true, this would indicate Sinclair was scouting for locations before he knew what his story was about, which may explain the rather awkward tension between the cow farm and what is basically a fairy tale. He adds supernatural elements involving a Maori woman named Auntie (Rangi Motu). One day Lucinda runs straight into Auntie with her car, but Auntie is miraculously untouched, and disappears into the woods.

A few nights later, mysterious hands steal the quilt from Lucinda and Rob's bed, and Lucinda sees it soon after in Auntie's hands. Tracking her down to a cottage in the woods, she sees Auntie sleeping under a pile of dozens of quilts—all stolen for her, we learn, by her nephews (who are golfers, and practice putts between quilt raids). Lucinda demands her quilt back, and is given a series of demands by Auntie that *really* test Rob's love.

There is a place for whimsy and magic realism, and that place may not be on a cow farm in New Zealand. Or perhaps it is, but not with this story. I was never much convinced by the romantic chemistry between Rob and Lucinda, never believed in Drosophilia's jealous scheming, found Auntie tiresome, and was most intrigued by her golfing nephews, small though their roles may be. Imagine a golf movie involving six or seven Maoris on the pro Tour with a magic Auntie. Now there's a movie.

The Princess and the Warrior ★ ★ ★ ½
R, 130 m., 2001

Franka Potente (Sissi), Benno Furmann (Bodo), Joachim Krol (Walter), Marita Breuer (Sissi's Mother), Jurgen Tarrach (Schmatt), Lars Rudolph (Steini), Melchior Beslon (Otto). Directed by Tom Tykwer and produced by Stefan Arndt and Maria Kopf. Screenplay by Tykwer.

The positive but puzzled reviews for *A.I.* all agreed on one thing: The film was the work of an artist. I feel more positive and less puzzled about *The Princess and the Warrior,* which is also the work of an artist. Both titles are reminders that it is better to see an imperfect movie that lives and breathes than a perfect one that is merely a genre exercise.

The Princess and the Warrior is one astonishment after another. It uses coincidence with reckless abandon to argue that deep patterns in life connect some people. It uses thriller elements—not to thrill us, but to set up moral challenges for its characters. It is about a woman convinced she has met the one great love of her life, and a man convinced he is not that person. It is about a traffic accident, a bank robbery, an insane asylum, and it does not use any of those elements as they have been used before. Above all, it loves its characters too much to entrap them in a mediocre plot.

The movie was written and directed by Tom Tykwer, from Germany, who had international success with *Run, Lola, Run,* and now has

made a deeper and more ambitious film. It stars Franka Potente, who played Lola (she was also the stewardess married to Johnny Depp in *Blow*). It uses the same kind of crazy looping energy as *Lola,* and is just as open to intersecting fates, but *Lola* was essentially about kinetic energy, and this is a film about the thin membranes that separate life and death, good and evil, success and failure, love and fear.

Potente plays Sissi, a nurse in the psychiatric hospital where she was born. She is much loved by her strange patients, and so shut off from the outside world that when she shares a secret erotic moment with one of them we sense they're performing a mutual service. Her costar is Benno Furmann, who plays Bodo—a bank robber, among other things.

They meet after Bodo unwittingly causes an accident that leaves Sissi pinned under a truck and choking on her own blood. He crawls under the truck to elude the police, sees that she is dying, and saves her life. I will not tell you how he does this, except to say that the scene, in its horror, its detail, its quiet observation, its reliance on the sound track to tell us what is happening, is overwhelming in its intensity.

It shows greatness—not just because of what I've referred to, but by something more, the detail that Tykwer adds *after* the scene seems to be over. Let us say, without giving too much away, that events have made Sissi acutely aware of the nature of each breath she takes. She has been looking into the eyes of this man who is saving her, and now she becomes aware that his breath is sweet and has sent a "peppermint sting" to her lungs.

Bodo accompanies her into an ambulance (it is his means of escape from the police—every action in this movie seems to have two purposes). She holds desperately to his hand, then passes out, and later finds she has nothing but the button from his coat. He has disappeared. She knows she must find him. It is their destiny. Here is another astonishing scene. She knows a patient at the asylum, a blind man, who like many blind people is acutely aware of his surroundings and may be psychic. She asks him to retrace the route of the man who saved her life.

While all of this is going on, we learn more about an elaborate bank burglary being planned by Bodo and his brother Walter (Joachim Krol), and eventually the lives of Sissi and Bodo cross—not once, not just as a "coincidence," but in a series of interlinking connections that take on a life of their own.

Tykwer uses the elements of genre in his film, but evades generic simplicities. He is using the conventions of a bank heist movie, not to make a bank heist movie, but to lay down a narrative map so that we can clearly see how the characters wander off of it—lose their way in the tangle of their lives and emotions. He looks at his characters a little harder than most directors; he isn't content with one level of writing to describe them, but needs many. Consider an opening sequence in which Bodo is working as a gravedigger and laborer at a funeral home, and is fired for—what would you guess? Do you have an idea? He is fired for crying.

The Princess and the Warrior is not perfect. It is a little too long, and takes us an extra lap around its ironic track. But it's so rich, how can we complain? Tykwer is thirty-six and this is his fourth feature. Like other directors of his generation, he's fascinated by narratives that play with time; like *Memento, Amores Perros,* and *One Night at McCool's,* his film is impatient with straight narratives and linear plots, and wants to filter events through more than one point of view. That's at the structural level. What's special about the film is at a deeper level, down where he engages with the souls of his characters.

The Princess Diaries ★ ½
G, 115 m., 2001

Julie Andrews (Queen Clarisse Renaldi), Anne Hathaway (Mia Thermopolis), Hector Elizondo (Joe), Heather Matarazzo (Lilly Moscovitz), Mandy Moore (Lana Thomas), Caroline Goodall (Mia's Mom, Helen), Robert Schwartzman (Michael Moscovitz), Erik Von Detten (Josh Bryant). Directed by Garry Marshall and produced by Whitney Houston, Debra Martin Chase, and Mario Iscovich. Screenplay by Gina Wendkos, based on the novel by Meg Cabot.

Haven't I seen this movie before? *The Princess Diaries* is a march through the swamp of recycled ugly duckling stories, with occasional pauses in the marsh of sitcom clichés and the bog of Idiot Plots. You recall the Idiot Plot.

That's the plot that would be solved in an instant if anyone on the screen said what was obvious to the audience. A movie like this isn't entertainment. It's more like a party game that you lose if you say the secret word.

The film takes place in the present day, I guess, if through some kind of weird *Pleasantville* time warp the present day had the values and behavior of Andy Hardy movies. It is about a fifteen-year-old girl who doesn't realize she's really the princess of Genovia, which is "between France and Spain" and needs an heir from its royal bloodline if it is not to (a) go out of business, or (b) be taken over by the evil baron and baroness, I'm not sure which. Turns out that Mia Thermopolis (Anne Hathaway) is the daughter of the Prince of Genovia, but has never learned this fact, because her mother, Helen (Caroline Goodall), wanted to lead a normal life and thus left Genovia and her husband, never told Mia about her real father, and raised her normally—that is, in a San Francisco firehouse where she slides down the pole every morning.

The prince has come to an untimely end, and now his mother comes to recruit Mia to take up her royal duties. The mother is Queen Clarisse Renaldi, played by Julie Andrews as a nice woman with very, very, very good manners. The suspense involves: Will Mia accept the throne? And will she choose as her boyfriend the snobbish jerk Josh (Erik Von Detten) or the nice Michael (Robert Schwartzman), older brother of her best friend, Lilly (Heather Matarazzo)? And, for that matter, is there any possibility that Josh will dump a glamorous cheerleader (Mandy Moore) after he sees how Mia looks once she takes off her glasses and does something with her hair? Anyone who doesn't immediately know the answers to these questions either lives in a cave, or wrote this screenplay.

The words "why don't you do something about your hair" have inspired movie transformation scenes since time immemorial, but rarely has the transformation been more of a setup than here. Garry Marshall, the director, hasn't had the nerve to cast a real fifteen-year-old as Mia, but supplies us instead with Anne Hathaway, who is almost twenty-one years old, and is a classic beauty in the Daphne Zuniga tradition. We're expected to believe that this character gets so nervous in class that she throws up while trying to make a speech, and yet the rest of the time is as effortlessly verbal as a stand-up comedian.

One of the creaky problems thrown in the way of the plot is a "scandal" when Mia is photographed in what is not really a very scandalous situation at all, and so perhaps must renounce the throne. Queen Clarisse Renaldi seems reconciled to this. What do you think the chances are that the ruling family of a lucrative tax shelter—Monaco, for example—would abandon their principality because of a newspaper photo of the heir kissing a boy? In the interests of keeping the loot in the family, any heir—even Phoolan Devi, the late Bandit Queen of India—would be considered a viable candidate.

Garry Marshall made the wonderful *Pretty Woman,* but what was his thinking here? Some of the editing is plain sloppy. We are informed, for example, that when a kiss is magical, one of a girl's heels curls up off the floor. Cut to a heel curling up, but stuck to a strand of chewing gum. Whose heel? Whose gum? Nobody's. This is simply an isolated, self-contained shot. Later, at a dinner party, Marshall spends time establishing one of the guests as a drunk, but then the guest disappears without a payoff.

As *The Princess Diaries* creeps from one painfully obvious plot destination to another, we wait impatiently for the characters on-screen to arrive at what has long been clear to the audience. If the movie is determined to be this dim-witted, couldn't it at least move a little more quickly? The metronome is set too slow, as if everyone is acting and thinking in half-time.

Pumpkin ★ ★ ★ ½

R, 113 m., 2002

Christina Ricci (Carolyn McDuffy), Hank Harris (Pumpkin Romanoff), Brenda Blethyn (Judy Romanoff), Dominique Swain (Jeanine Kryszinsky), Marisa Coughlan (Julie Thurber), Sam Ball (Kent Woodlands), Harry J. Lennix (Robert Meary), Michelle Krusiec (Anne Chung). Directed by Anthony Abrams and Adam Larson Broder and produced by Karen Barber, Albert Berger, Christina Ricci, Andrea Sperling, and Ron Yerxa. Screenplay by Broder.

Pumpkin defies description. Maybe it doesn't need a category—it needs a diagnosis. Relentlessly, and sometimes brilliantly, it forces us to decide what we really think, how permissive our taste really is, how far a black comedy can go before it goes too far. It's like a teenage sex comedy crossed with the darkest corners of underground comics. We laugh in three ways: with humor, with recognition, and with disbelief.

The film stars Christina Ricci as Carolyn McDuffy, the peppiest member of a sorority house that dreams of being named Sorority of the Year. To get extra points, the house arranges to coach "special people"—handicapped and retarded athletes—and all of the girls are lined up eagerly when the buses arrive with their tutorial victims. One of them is Pumpkin Romanoff (Hank Harris), who seems to be both mentally and physically challenged, although the movie refuses to permit a verdict about his intelligence level. At first Carolyn is too awkward and embarrassed to deal with Pumpkin—everything she says seems to be offensive—but then she finds she can't get him out of her mind. Pumpkin, of course, has fallen instantly in love with her.

Carolyn has a boyfriend, a BMOC and tennis champion named Kent Woodlands (Sam Ball), who in his own way is also handicapped: He's too handsome, with the improbable good looks of a silent screen idol. But she begins to spend more time with Pumpkin, who at first seems ill-equipped for his chosen sport of discus throwing (he can't stand or throw), but works out tirelessly in his backyard to get in shape.

Pumpkin's mother, Judy (Brenda Blethyn), is an alcoholic who coddles her son and then puts him down. She sees Carolyn as a threat, and when she finds the two in bed together she calls her a slut and a pedophile. This raises an interesting point, since Pumpkin is apparently about fifteen or sixteen, but sex between older women and younger men seems permitted in the movies even though it's taboo the other way around.

Carolyn eventually begins to see the hypocrisy of the Greek system, the shallowness of Kent, and the truly special qualities of Pumpkin. Yes, and there is even a scene where Pumpkin gets an ovation for a discus throw. But this is not one of those heartwarming stories about overcoming obstacles. *Pumpkin* creates inspirational moments only to undermine them, and doubts all good motives. Consider the way the sororities compete for the black and Filipino girls who are going through rush, because they want to add "diversity," and besides, the Filipino "looks almost white." Consider the way Carolyn's Asian sorority sister, Anne Chung (Michelle Krusiec), is never referred to without the word "even" in front of her name: "You can go to the prom with any of the sisters," house president Julie Thurber (Marisa Coughlan) tells Kent. "Even Anne Chung."

The movie takes side shots at other campus targets. Carolyn takes a poetry workshop taught by a black professor (Harry J. Lennix), who announces poetry cannot be taught and that he hates to grade papers, but that, not to worry, "you'll get your stupid credit." Carolyn composes for this class an "Ode to Pasadena" that must be heard to be believed. When she decides to take a stand and leave school, she announces she'll go to "community college," only to discover she has too many credits and has to settle for Long Beach Tech. In her rooming house at Long Beach, the students eat beans, not lamb chops, her favorite at the sorority house.

The climax of the movie involves a fight between Pumpkin and Kent that goes beyond the usual boundaries of commercial comedies, and a car crash that is a deliberate exercise in mocking special effects and stunt explosions. Everything in the movie mocks itself. Even the last shot calls Carolyn's final sincerity into question. But I can say this: *Pumpkin* is alive, and takes chances, and uses the wicked blade of satire in order to show up the complacent political correctness of other movies in its campus genre. It refuses to play it safe. And there is courage in the performances—for example, in the way Sam Ball deals with what happens to his character. Or in the way Christina Ricci sails fearlessly into the risky material. *Pumpkin* may make you mad, but at least you're not angry because it wasn't trying.

Punch-Drunk Love ★ ★ ★ ½
R, 89 m., 2002

Adam Sandler (Barry Egan), Emily Watson (Lena Leonard), Philip Seymour Hoffman (Dean Trumbell), Luis Guzmán (Lance), Mary Lynn Rajskub (Elizabeth), Ashley Clark (Latisha), Julie Hermelin (Kathleen). Directed by Paul Thomas Anderson and produced by Anderson, Daniel Lupi, and Joanne Sellar. Screenplay by Anderson.

There is a new Adam Sandler on view in *Punch-Drunk Love*—angry, sad, desperate. In voice and mannerisms he is the same childlike, love-starved Adam Sandler we've seen in a series of dim comedies, but this movie, by seeing him in a new light, encourages us to look again at those films. Given a director and a screenplay that see through the Sandler persona, that understand it as the disguise of a suffering outsider, Sandler reveals depths and tones we may have suspected but couldn't bring into focus.

The way to criticize a movie, Godard famously said, is to make another movie. In that sense *Punch-Drunk Love* is film criticism. Paul Thomas Anderson says he loves Sandler's comedies—they cheer him up on lonely Saturday nights—but as the director of *Boogie Nights* and *Magnolia*, he must have been able to sense something missing in them, some unexpressed need. The Sandler characters are almost oppressively nice, like needy puppies, and yet they conceal a masked hostility to society, a passive-aggressive need to go against the flow, a gift for offending others while in the very process of being ingratiating.

In *Punch-Drunk Love*, Sandler plays Barry Egan, an executive in a company with a product line of novelty toiletries. Barry has seven sisters, who are all on his case at every moment, and he desperately wishes they would stop invading his privacy, ordering him around and putting him down. He tries at a family gathering to be congenial and friendly, but we can see the tension in his smiling lips and darting eyes, and suddenly he explodes, kicking out the glass patio doors.

This is a pattern. He presents to the world a face of cheerful blandness, and then erupts in terrifying displays of frustrated violence. He does not even begin to understand himself. He seems always on guard, unsure, obscurely threatened. His outbursts here help to explain the curiously violent passages in his previous film, *Mr. Deeds*, which was a remake of a benign Frank Capra comedy. It's as if Sandler is Hannibal Lecter in a Jerry Lewis body.

Most of Sandler's plots are based on predictable, production-line formulas, and after *Punch-Drunk Love* I may begin seeing them as traps containing a resentful captive. The quirky behavior may be a way of calling out for help. In *Big Daddy*, for example, the broad outlines are familiar, but not the creepy way his character trains his adopted five-year-old to be hostile. At one point, ho, ho, they toss tree branches into the path of middle-aged in-line skaters, causing some nasty falls. The hostility veiled as humor in the typical Sandler comedy is revealed in *Punch-Drunk Love* as—hostility.

The film is exhilarating to watch because Sandler, liberated from the constraints of formula, reveals unexpected depths as an actor. Watching this film, you can imagine him in Dennis Hopper roles. He has darkness, obsession, and power. His world is hedged around with mystery and challenge. Consider an opening scene, when he is at work hours before the others have arrived and sees a harmonium dumped in the street in front of his office. It is at once the most innocent and ominous of objects; he runs from it and then peeks around a corner to see if it is still there.

In the Paul Thomas Anderson universe, people meet through serendipity and need, not because they are fulfilling their plot assignments. Barry meets Lena Leonard (Emily Watson), a sweet executive with intently focused eyes, who asks him to look after her broken-down car and later goes out on a dinner date with him. They like each other right away. During the dinner he gets up from his table, goes to the men's room, and in a blind rage breaks everything he can. "Your hand is bleeding," she gently observes, and after they are thrown out of the restaurant she carries on as if the evening is still normal.

Barry is meanwhile enraged by an ongoing battle he is having with a Utah phone sex company. He called the number and was billed for the call, but he was unable to talk easily with the woman at the other end, or even quite conceive of what she wanted him to do. Then she pulled a scam using his credit card number, and this leads to mutual threats and obsceni-

ties over the phone, and to a visit from the porn company's "four blond brothers," who want to intimidate him and extract cash.

Barry is frightened. He knows Lena is going on a business trip to Hawaii. They definitely have chemistry. This would be an ideal time to get off the mainland. He has discovered a loophole in a Healthy Choice promotion that will allow him to earn countless American Airlines frequent-flier miles at very little cost. (This part of the story is based on fact.) It is typical of an Anderson film that Barry, having hit on his mileage scheme, cannot use his miles so quickly, and so simply buys a ticket to Honolulu and meets Lena for a picture-postcard rendezvous on Waikiki Beach. Here and elsewhere, Anderson bathes the screen in romantic colors and fills the sound track with lush orchestrations.

I feel liberated in films where I have absolutely no idea what will happen next. Lena and Barry are odd enough that anything could happen in their relationship. A face-to-face meeting with the Utah porn king (Anderson regular Philip Seymour Hoffman) and another meeting with the four blond brothers are equally unpredictable. And always there is Barry's quick, terrifying anger, a time bomb ticking away beneath every scene.

Punch-Drunk Love is above all a portrait of a personality type. Barry Egan has been damaged, perhaps beyond repair, by what he sees as the depredations of his domineering sisters. It drives him crazy when people nose into his business. He cannot stand to be trifled with. His world is entered by alarming omens and situations that baffle him. The character is vividly seen and the film sympathizes with him in his extremity. Paul Thomas Anderson has referred to *Punch-Drunk Love* as "an art house Adam Sandler film." It may be the key to all of the Adam Sandler films, and may liberate Sandler for a new direction in his work. He can't go on making those moronic comedies forever, can he? Who would have guessed he had such uncharted depths? ☞

Q

Queen of the Damned ★ ★
R, 101 m., 2002

Stuart Townsend (Lestat de Lioncourt), Aaliyah (Akasha), Marguerite Moreau (Jesse Reeves), Vincent Perez (Marius), Paul McGann (David Talbot), Lena Olin (Maharet), Christian Manon (Mael), Claudia Black (Pandora). Directed by Michael Rymer and produced by Jorge Saralegui. Screenplay by Scott Abbott and Michael Petroni, based on the novels *The Vampire Chronicles* by Anne Rice.

Vampires are always in pose mode, which tends to make vampire movies into comedies. The stark horror of *Nosferatu* has long since dribbled down into overwrought melodrama. The buried message of many scenes is: "Regard me well, for here I am, and I am thus." A lot of the dialogue is declamatory, and many sentences are versions of, "Together, we (will, can, must) (rule, change, destroy) the (world, our victims, the people in this bar)."

Queen of the Damned, based on Anne Rice's endless Vampire Chronicles, happily occupies this mode. It is happy to be goofy. *Interview With the Vampire,* Neil Jordan's glossy 1994 version of the earlier Rice novel, was more ambitious and anchored—even sad. This sequel, also about the vampire Lestat, is filled with characters who seem to have taken Gene Simmons as their role model.

The movie stars Stuart Townsend as Lestat, in the role played last time by Tom Cruise. The world got to be too much for him, Lestat explains, and so he withdrew from it and went to sleep 200 years ago. But then "the world didn't sound like the place I had left—but something different, better." Cut to a montage of musical groups, and Lestat pushes back the stone lid of his crypt and materializes during a rehearsal of a rock band. When they ask who he is, he smiles and casts centuries of tradition to the winds: "I am . . . the Vampire Lestat!"

Soon he's a rock god, the lead singer of a Goth band. Other characters emerge. We meet Jesse (Marguerite Moreau), researcher for a London vampire study institute. She likes to play with danger, and even cruises a vampire bar Lestat told her about. We meet the fey Marius (Vincent Perez), the older vampire who turned Lestat on, or out. And Maharet (Lena Olin), who I think is supposed to be a good vampire, or at least one who wishes the others would follow the rules. Along the way we are given vampire feeding lessons: "You must never take the last drop or it will draw you in and you die."

Most noticeably we meet Queen Akasha, the title character, played by Aaliyah, the singer who was killed in a 2001 air crash. She appears first as a statue in a phantasmagorical Egyptian cryptlike shrine, where Lestat plays his violin so fiercely that parts of her stone body seem to glow back into life. She "drank the world dry when she ruled Egypt," Marius tells Lestat. (Historical footnote: The first movie to make the queen of the Egyptians black also makes her a vampire. Is this progress?) Soon Akasha is alive all over, and has the hots for Lestat, making plans about how, together, they will rule the world.

Since this will be her only starring movie role, it's sad that her character has such a narrow emotional range. The Lestat-Akasha romance suffers by being conducted in declarative mode, with Akasha addressing her lover with the intimacy Queen Victoria would have lavished on her footman. Lestat digs her, though, because when he drinks her blood it makes him wild. Nothing good can come of this.

A more intriguing relationship is between Lestat and Marius, who seems to have a thing for him. Marius reappears in Lestat's life after so many centuries that Lestat comments on his outdated apparel. "How did you manage to slip through the fifties in red velvet?" he asks, forgetting that he slept through the 1950s himself and has probably not made much of a study of the decade's clothing styles. He welcomes Marius to Los Angeles and shows him the world from a perch on a painter's scaffold that hangs directly in front of Lestat's leather-clad crotch on a giant Sunset Boulevard outdoor advertisement. We get the feeling Marius would enjoy the view more if he turned around.

There is a showdown. Queen Akasha's subjects, fellow vampires, revolt against her tyrannical rule when she reveals her plans to rule, etc., the world, etc., together, etc., with Lestat.

The others hope to drink all of her blood, so that even if they die, she dies too. But Akasha is not without her defenses. All she has to do is point at enemies and they burst into flame, curl up into charred shadows of themselves, and float upward just like the wrapper from an Amaretti di Saronno cookie.

The movie doesn't reach the level of camp goofiness attained by films like *The Mummy Returns* and *Lara Croft: Tomb Raider*, perhaps because the filmmakers labor under the impression that Anne Rice's works must be treated respectfully. The key to a movie like this is to ask yourself, if these characters were not vampires, what would be interesting about them? The answer is, together they couldn't even rule the people in this bar.

The Quiet American ★ ★ ★ ★
R, 118 m., 2003

Michael Caine (Thomas Fowler), Brendan Fraser (Alden Pyle), Do Thi Hai Yen (Phuong), Rade Serbedzija (Inspector Vigot), Tzi Ma (Hinh), Robert Stanton (Joe Tunney), Holmes Osborne (Bill Granger), Quang Hai (The General), Ferdinand Hoang (Mr. Muoi). Directed by Phillip Noyce and produced by Staffan Ahrenberg and William Horberg. Screenplay by Christopher Hampton and Robert Schenkkan, based on the novel by Graham Greene.

The Englishman is sad and lonely. He suffers from the indignity of growing too old for romance while not yet free of yearning. He is in love for one last time. He doesn't even fully understand it is love until he is about to lose it. He is a newspaper correspondent in Saigon, and she is a dance-hall girl thirty or forty years younger. She loves him because he pays her to. This arrangement suits them both. He tells himself he is "helping" her. Well, he is, and she is helping him.

His name is Fowler, and he is played by Michael Caine in a performance that seems to descend perfectly formed. There is no artifice in it, no unneeded energy, no tricks, no effort. It is there. Her name is Phuong (Do Thi Hai Yen), and like all beautiful women who reveal little of their true feelings, she makes it possible for him to project his own upon her. He loves her for what he can tell himself about her.

Between them steps Alden Pyle (Brendan Fraser), the quiet young American who has come to Vietnam, he believes, to save it. Eventually he also believes he will save Phuong. Young men, like old ones, find it easy to believe hired love is real, and so believe a girl like Phuong would prefer a young man to an old one, when all youth represents is more work.

Graham Greene's novel *The Quiet American* (1955) told the story of this triangle against the background of America's adventure in Vietnam in the early 1950s—when, he shows us, the CIA used pleasant, presentable agents like Pyle to pose as "aid workers" while arranging terrorist acts that would justify our intervention there.

The novel inspired a 1958 Hollywood version in which the director Joseph Mankiewicz turned the story on its head, making Fowler the bad guy and Pyle the hero. Did the CIA have a hand in funding this film? Stranger things have happened: The animated version of *Animal Farm* (1954) was paid for by a CIA front, and twisted Orwell's fable about totalitarianism both East and West into a simplistic anti-Communist cartoon.

Now comes another version of *The Quiet American*, this one directed by the Australian Phillip Noyce and truer to the Greene novel. It is a film with a political point of view, but often its characters lose sight of that in their fascination with each other and with the girl. A question every viewer will have to answer at the end is whether a final death is the result of moral conviction or romantic compulsion.

The film is narrated by Caine's character in that conversational voice weary with wisdom; we are reminded of the tired cynicism of the opening narration in the great film of Greene's *The Third Man*. Pyle has "a face with no history, no problems," Fowler tells us; his own face is a map of both. "I'm just a reporter," he says. "I offer no point of view, I take no action, I don't get involved." Indeed, he has scarcely filed a story in the past year for his paper, the *Times* of London; he is too absorbed in Phuong and opium.

The irony is that Pyle, whom he actually likes at first, jars him into action and involvement. What he finally cannot abide is the younger man's cheerful certainty that he is absolutely right: "Saving the country and saving a woman would be the same thing to a man like that."

As luck would have it, *The Quiet American* was planned for release in the autumn of 2001. It was shelved after 9/11, when Miramax president Harvey Weinstein decided, no doubt correctly, that the national mood was not ripe for a film pointing out that the United States is guilty of terrorist acts of its own. Caine appealed to Weinstein, who a year later allowed the film to be shown at the Toronto Film Festival, where it was well received by the public and critics.

It would be unfortunate if people went to the movie, or stayed away, because of its political beliefs. There is no longer much controversy about the CIA's hand in stirring the Vietnam pot, and the movie is not an exposé but another of Greene's stories about a worn-down, morally exhausted man clinging to shreds of hope in a world whose cynicism has long since rendered him obsolete. Both men "love" Phuong, but for Pyle she is less crucial. Fowler, on the other hand, admits: "I know I'm not essential to Phuong, but if I were to lose her, for me that would be the beginning of death." What Phuong herself thinks is not the point with either man, since they are both convinced she wants them.

Fraser, who often stars as a walking cartoon (*Dudley Do-Right, George of the Jungle*), has shown in other pictures, like *Gods and Monsters,* that he is a gifted actor, and here he finds just the right balance between confidence and blindness: What he does is evil, but he is convinced it is good, and has a simple, sunny view that maddens an old hand like Fowler. The two characters work well together because there is an undercurrent of commonalty: They are both floating in the last currents of colonialism, in which life in Saigon can be very good, unless you get killed.

Phillip Noyce made two great pictures close together, this one and *Rabbit-Proof Fence.* He feels anger as he tells this story, but he conceals it, because the story as it stands is enough. Some viewers will not even intercept the political message. It was that way with Greene: The politics were in the very weave of the cloth, not worth talking about. Here, in a rare Western feature shot in Vietnam, with real locations and sets that look well-worn enough

to be real, with wonderful performances, he suggests a worldview more mature and knowing than the simplistic pieties that provide the public face of foreign policy.

Quitting ★ ★ ½
R, 112 m., 2002

Jia Hongsheng (Hongsheng), Jia Fengsen (Hongsheng's Father), Chai Ziurong (Hongsheng's Mother), Wang Tong (Hongsheng's Sister), Shun Xing (Jia's Roommate), Li Jie (Hongsheng's Musician Friend), Zhang Yang (Director). Directed by Zhang and produced by Peter Loehr. Screenplay by Zhang and Huo Xin.

Quitting is not so much a movie about drug addiction as a movie about sentimentalized Chinese ideas of drug addiction. It is a brave experiment, based on life and using actors who play themselves, but it buys into the whole false notion that artists are somehow too brilliant to be sober—that drugs and booze are almost necessary to tame their creativity, dull their pain, and allow them to tolerate life with the clods around them. Thus the "cure" is not so much to stop using as to stop dreaming; one must become boring to become clean and sober.

Astonishing, how persistent this idea is, since there is nothing more boring than a drunk or an addict, repeating the same failed pattern every day. But China does not embrace the useful disease model of addiction, and in a hospital where the hero is sent, a fellow patient explains, "The Soviets called it hysteria, but the Chinese called it dementia." Addiction is neither. In most cases, it is simply a habitual inability to avoid getting wasted.

If *Quitting* embraced Western ideas, its hero would no doubt quickly find himself attending AA meetings, and while that might be better for his health it might not be better for this movie. *Quitting* stars Jia Hongsheng, who starred in Chinese movies and on television circa 1990, and then, while appearing in the title role of *Kiss of the Spider Woman* on stage in 1992, quickly progressed from pot through heroin into professional and personal dysfunction.

Eventually he had to move in with his sister.

He became a recluse and rejected all work offers. His parents, who were provincial actors, moved to Beijing to take care of him, and the four family members found themselves trapped in an apartment with his disease. Although this is a showbiz family, the parents come from a backwater; Hongsheng believes he receives secret messages from John Lennon, while his father has not even heard of the "Bittles."

Jia Hongsheng plays himself in this story. The parents and other characters play themselves, and the director of the film, Zhang Yang, was the real-life stage director of *Kiss of the Spider Woman*. This gives the film an eerie intrinsic interest: They act in scenes based on remembered pain. This is, however, not a documentary, and a startling shot late in the film underlines the fact that it is artistry, not fact.

The movie's pumped-up scenes of domestic anguish are the least convincing, and when Hongsheng hangs up on TV producers or hides in his room, he is less a suffering person than an addict acting out a tiresome script. When, however, he sits on the grass under a highway overpass with his father and they both drink beer, there is a kind of unforced communion; the father, who has a drinking problem, has promised his wife not to drink, and so as they play hooky together they have a moment of peace.

Zhang Yang's previous film was the popular *Shower* (1999), about a successful son who returns from the provinces to Beijing, where his elderly father and retarded brother run a bathhouse. That film was a warm human comedy, but has connections with *Quitting;* the director cares about how fathers and sons can seem so different and be so much the same.

R

Rabbit-Proof Fence ★ ★ ★ ½
PG, 94 m., 2002

Everlyn Sampi (Molly), Tianna Sansbury (Daisy), Laura Monaghan (Gracie), David Gulpilil (Moodoo), Ningali Lawford (Molly's Mother), Myarn Lawford (Molly's Grandmother), Deborah Mailman (Mavis), Jason Clarke (Constable Riggs), Kenneth Branagh (A. O. Neville). Directed by Phillip Noyce and produced by Noyce, Christine Olsen, and John Winter. Screenplay by Olsen, based on the book by Doris Pilkington Garimara.

The most astonishing words in *Rabbit-Proof Fence* come right at the end, printed on the screen as a historical footnote. The policies depicted in the movie were enforced by the Australian government, we are told, until 1970. Aboriginal children of mixed race were taken by force from their mothers and raised in training schools that would prepare them for lives as factory workers or domestic servants. More than a century after slavery was abolished in the Western world, a Western democracy was still practicing racism of the most cruel description.

The children's fathers were long gone—white construction workers or government employees who enjoyed sex with local Aborigine women and then moved on. But why could the mixed-race children not stay where they were? The offered explanations are equally vile. One is that a half-white child must be rescued from a black society. Another was that too many "white genes" would, by their presumed superiority, increase the power and ability of the Aborigines to cause trouble by insisting on their rights. A third is that, by requiring the lighter-skinned children to marry each other, blackness could eventually be bred out of them. Of course it went without saying that the "schools" they were held in prepared them only for menial labor.

The children affected are known today in Australia as the Stolen Generations. The current Australian government of Prime Minister John Howard still actually refuses to apologize for these policies. Trent Lott by comparison is enlightened.

Phillip Noyce's film is fiction based on fact. The screenplay by Christine Olsen is based on a book by Doris Pilkington Garimara, telling the story of the experiences of her mother, Molly, her aunt Daisy, and their cousin Gracie. Torn from their families by government officials, they were transported some 1,500 miles to a training school, where they huddled together in fear and grief, separated from everyone and everything they had ever known. When they tried to use their own language, they were told to stop "jabbering."

At the time of the adventures in the movie, Molly (Everlyn Sampi) is fourteen, Daisy (Tianna Sansbury) is eight, and Gracie (Laura Monaghan) is ten. The school where they are held is not a Dickensian workhouse; by the standards of the time it is not unkind (that it inflicts the unimaginable pain of separation from family and home does not figure into the thinking of the white educators, who consider they are doing a favor). The girls cannot abide this strange and lonely place. They run away and start walking toward their homes. It will be a journey of 1,500 miles. They have within their heads an instinctive map of the way, and are aided by a fence that stretches for hundreds of miles across the outback, to protect farmlands from a pestilence of rabbits.

The principal white character in the movie is A. O. Neville (Kenneth Branagh), who in 1931 was the administrator of the relocation policies and something of an amateur eugenicist with theories of race and breeding that would have won him a ready audience in Nazi Germany. That Australians could have accepted thinking such as his, and indeed based government policy on it, indicates the sorry fact that many of them thought Aborigines were a step or two down the evolutionary ladder from modern Europeans. That the Aboriginal societies of Australia and New Zealand were remarkably sophisticated was hard for the whites to admit—especially because, the more one credited these native races, the more obvious it was that the land had been stolen from their possession.

As the three girls flee across the vast landscape, they are pursued by white authorities and an Aboriginal tracker named Moodoo

(David Gulpilil), who seems not especially eager to find them. Along the way they are helped by the kindness of strangers, even a white woman. This journey, which evokes some of the same mystery of the Outback as many other Australian films (notably *Walkabout*), is beautiful, harrowing, and sometimes heartbreaking.

The three young stars are all Aboriginals, untrained actors, and Noyce is skilled at the way he evokes their thoughts and feelings. Narration helps fill gaps and supplies details that cannot be explained on-screen. The end of the journey is not the same for all three girls, and there is more heartbreak ahead, which it would be wrong for me to reveal. But I must say this. The final scene of the film contains an appearance and a revelation of astonishing emotional power; not since the last shots of *Schindler's List* have I been so overcome with the realization that real people, in recent historical times, had to undergo such inhumanity.

Raising Victor Vargas ★ ★ ★ ½
R, 88 m., 2003

Victor Rasuk (Victor Vargas), Judy Marte (Judy Ramirez), Melonie Diaz (Melonie), Altagracia Guzman (Grandma), Silvestre Rasuk (Nino Vargas), Krystal Rodriguez (Vicki Vargas), Kevin Rivera (Harold), Wilfree Vasquez (Carlos). Directed by Peter Sollett and produced by Sollett, Scott Macaulay, Robin O'Hara, and Alain de la Mata. Screenplay by Sollett.

Raising Victor Vargas tells the heartwarming story of first love that finds a balance between lust and idealism. Acted by fresh-faced newcomers who never step wrong, it sidesteps the clichés of teenage coming-of-age movies and expands into truth and human comedy. It's the kind of movie you know you can trust, and you give yourself over to affection for these characters who are so lovingly observed.

We meet the Vargas family, who live on the Lower East Side of New York. Grandma (Altagracia Guzman) came from the Dominican Republic. She is raising her three grandchildren: Victor (Victor Rasuk), Nino (Silvestre Rasuk), and Vicki (Krystal Rodriguez). Victor, who is about sixteen, fancies himself a ladies' man but is not as experienced as he seems. Nino looks

up to him. Vicki, who is plump and seems to live on the sofa, is fed up with both boys—and Grandma lives in fear of the hazards that surround them.

In another movie those hazards might involve gangs, drugs, and guns. Not in *Raising Victor Vargas*, which eliminates the usual urban dangers and shows us a home where the values may be old-fashioned but have produced three basically good kids. It's refreshing to find a movie where a Latino family in a poor neighborhood is not portrayed with the usual tired conventions about poverty and crime, but is based on love and strong values. It's only natural that Nino reveals himself as a moderately talented pianist.

If Victor thinks constantly about dating and sex, what boy his age doesn't? As the film opens, he is interrupted during the conquest of Fat Donna, who lives upstairs. It would appear, however, that the interruption came just in time to qualify him still as a virgin. Fat Donna is apparently a neighborhood legend, and although he swears her to secrecy the gossip quickly spreads and his sister cheerfully informs him, "You'll always be known as Fat Donna's boy."

This causes him no small agony, because at the swimming pool he sees the girl of his dreams: Judy Ramirez (Judy Marte), who seems beautiful and elegant and forever inaccessible. The movie's romantic plot involves a complicated scheme in which he convinces Judy's younger brother to arrange an introduction in return for Victor's influence in helping the younger brother meet his sister, Vicki. Meanwhile, Victor's friend Harold falls for Judy's friend Melonie (Melonie Diaz), who seems to be a classic type—the plain girl who is the popular girl's best friend. But then, in a movie tradition that I continue to love, Melonie takes off her glasses and lets down her hair.

The movie is not simply about these three inexperienced and uncertain pairs of lovers. If it were, it would be a typical teenage comedy. It is much deeper and more knowing than that, especially in the way it shows Grandma waging a losing battle to maintain her idea of the family's innocence. Although Victor is a good boy, Grandma imagines his life as a hotbed of sin, and the city as the devil's workshop. When Victor invites Judy to dinner it is a disaster because Grandma has not even suspected their friendship.

There is a delicate progress in the relationship of the two young lovers. Judy for a long time plays hard to get; she's determined to resist the relentless male lust all around her, and demands respect and attention from the boy who will win her heart. Victor is not strong in these qualities, but in a subtle and moving way he begins to learn about them, and the tentative progress of their love is a tender delight.

It is also touching that while Victor, Nino, and Vicki are exasperated by their grandmother's old world ways, they love her and need her. And the film is careful not to make Grandma into a caricature: What she does, she does from love, and when there is a crisis involving a social worker, which threatens the family, Victor finds a silent and tactful way to end it. The screenplay finds reconciliation in a touching story Grandma tells about her childhood.

I was in a discussion the other day about whether a movie can be erotic. Sexual, yes, and explicit, yes—but truly erotic? To achieve that, a film must abandon the details of sexual congress and focus instead on the personalities of its characters. When Victor and Judy finally kiss in this movie, it is a moment more real and joyous than miles of "sex scenes," because by then we know who they are, how they have traveled together to this moment, and what it means to them.

Raising Victor Vargas was written and directed by Peter Sollett. It grew from an award-winning short subject he made with the same actors, who are not experienced professionals but are fresh and true in a way that suggests they're the real thing, and will have fruitful careers.

Note: Like so many movies dealing intelligently with teenage sexuality, Raising Victor Vargas *has been rated R by the MPAA, which awards the PG-13 to comedies celebrating cheap vulgarity, but penalizes sincere expressions of true experience and real-life values.* ☞

Read My Lips ★ ★ ★ ½
NO MPAA RATING, 115 m., 2002

Vincent Cassel (Paul Angeli), Emmanuelle Devos (Carla Bhem), Olivier Gourmet (Marchand), Olivier Perrier (Masson), Olivia Bonamy (Annie), Bernard Alane (Morel). Directed by Jacques Audiard and produced by Jean-Louis Livi and Philippe Carcassonne. Screenplay by Audiard and Tonino Benacquista.

Carla is an office worker whose hearing is impaired, and who can read lips. This skill is crucial in a late scene in *Read My Lips*, a thriller crossed with a psychosexual study. Without giving away surprises, I can say that by reading the lips of Paul, her partner in crime, she is able to reverse a tricky situation. But *Read My Lips* is not a simpleminded movie in which merely being *able* to read lips saves the day. In this brilliant sequence she reads his lips and that *allows* them to set into motion a risky chain of events based on the odds that the bad guys will respond predictably.

By this point in the movie, we are deep into crime, double crosses, beatings, and murder, but *Read My Lips* begins as the story of an office worker—one of those hapless souls who is hardly noticed by the coworkers who leave their half-empty coffee cups on her desk. Carla (Emmanuelle Devos) is in her thirties, with ordinary looks; she seems to exist as an invisible service to others. She has no social life, has neighbors who dump their kids for baby-sitting, and lives in a world of shouts and whispers, depending on the function of her hearing aids. Apparently (it is a little unclear) she was once more deaf than she is now, and is improving.

Carla would like a guy. Her boss suggests she hire an assistant, and immediately we sense her mind at work. What kind of an assistant would she like? A man. What attributes should he have? Nice hands. She eventually hires the spectacularly shaky job candidate Paul (Vincent Cassel), who is fresh out of jail, sleeps rough, has one set of clothes, and, I guess, nice hands. He owes his job to her, and so she treats him a little like the others in the office treat her. There is a sexual undercurrent, complicated because they are both unwilling to seem needy.

Paul has not completely cut his connections to the criminal element in the French city where they live. He moonlights as a bartender, has snaky deals on the side, and finds out almost by accident about a bag of loot that's ripe for the stealing. He can't pull off the job by himself, and enlists Carla, who turns out to have that combination of cunning and hostility

523

that makes successful criminals. Spying on the men with the money, who belong to a dangerous local gang, she perches on a rooftop and uses binoculars to read their lips and discover their plans.

The details of the heist are nicely worked out, and original, as these things go. But the heist is not the point of *Read My Lips*. It is more of a maguffin. The bag and the bad guys are simply the props to justify the way Paul and Carla take their relationship to a new level—how they find, in this dangerous enterprise, a way to use unsuspected skills and discover deep compatibility. Neither Carla, in her office, nor Paul, in his desultory lawlessness, would have ever broken loose and discovered their true potential without the other.

That discovery provides another example of the depth of the screenplay, by director Jacques Audiard and Tonino Benacquista. Just as the lip-reading is not a payoff but a setup, so the relationship of Carla and Paul is not about obvious sex but about a communion of two souls—and sex. A lesser movie would have had them in bed by the halfway mark, in an obligatory sex scene of little motivation, interest, or purpose. Instead, *Read My Lips* is really interested in these two characters. At first they have a simultaneous attraction and repulsion; each finds it sexy that the other one behaves with a certain competitive hostility. Then they share the goal of the crime, which has its own fascination and fulfills both of their natures. And only then, through that experience, do they make a delightful discovery that at deeply buried levels they are connected, in a world where they have never met anyone who feels as they feel.

It is nothing to discover that another person turns you on; that's commonplace. But to discover that you and another person are mutually turned on by deep instincts you bring out in each other—instincts involving the very way you live your lives—is rare, and makes you tremble with joy and risk the unthinkable. The movie is not about deafness, lip-reading, crime, or sex, but about that discovery; the plot simply provides the rails on which it rides.

Real Women Have Curves ★ ★ ★ ½
PG-13, 90 m., 2002

America Ferrera (Ana), Lupe Ontiveros (Carmen), Ingrid Oliu (Estela), George Lopez (Mr. Guzman), Brian Sites (Jimmy). Directed by Patricia Cardosa and produced by Effie Brown and George LaVoo. Screenplay by Josefina Lopez and LaVoo, based on a play by Lopez.

Ana's boyfriend Jimmy tells her, "You're not fat. You're beautiful." She is both. *Real Women Have Curves* doesn't argue that Ana is beautiful on the "inside," like the Gwyneth Paltrow character in *Shallow Hal,* but that she is beautiful inside and out—love handles, big boobs, round cheeks, and all. "Turn the lights on," she shyly tells Jimmy. "I want you to see me. See, this is what I look like."

Ana has learned to accept herself. It is more than her mother can do. Carmen (Lupe Ontiveros) is fat, too, and hates herself for it, and wants her daughter to share her feelings. Ana is smart and could get a college scholarship, but Carmen insists she go to work in a dress factory run by a family member: It's her duty to the family, apparently, to sacrifice her future. The fact that the dress factory is pleasant and friendly doesn't change the reality that it's a dead end; you are at the wrong end of the economy when you make dresses for $18 so that they can be sold for $600.

Ana is a Mexican-American, played by America Ferrera, an eighteen-year-old in her first movie role. Ferrera is a wonder: natural, unforced, sweet, passionate, and always real. Her battle with her mother is convincing in the movie because the director, Patricia Cardosa, doesn't force it into shrill melodrama, but keeps it within the boundaries of a plausible family fight. It is a tribute to the great Lupe Ontiveros that Carmen is able to suggest her love for her daughter, even when it is very hard to see.

There have been several movies recently about the second generation of children of emigrants—Indian, Filipino, Chinese, Korean, Vietnamese—and they follow broad outlines borrowed from life. The parents try to enforce conditions of their homeland on the kids, who are becoming Americanized at blinding speed. While Carmen is insisting on her daughter's virginity, Ana is buying condoms. She insists on a view of her life that is not her parents'. That includes college.

If this movie had been made ten years ago, it might have been shrill, insistent, and dramatic—overplaying its hand. Cardosa and her writers, Josefina Lopez and George LaVoo, are more relaxed, more able to feel affection for all of the characters. Yes, her parents want Ana to work in the dress shop of their older daughter, and yes, they fear losing her—because they sense if she goes away to college she will return as a different person. But the parents are not monsters, and we sense that their love will prevail over their fears.

The film focuses on Ana at a crucial moment, right after high school, when she has decided with a level head and clear eyes to come of age on her own terms. Her parents would not approve of Jimmy, an Anglo, but Ana knows he is a good boy and she feels tender toward him. She also knows he will not be the last boy she dates; she is mature enough to understand herself and the stormy weathers of teenage love. When they have sex, there is a sense in which they are giving each other the gift of a sweet initiation, with respect and tenderness, instead of losing their innocence roughly to strangers in a way without love.

The film's portrait of the dressmaking factory is done with great good humor. Yes, it is very hot there. Yes, the hours are long and the pay is poor. But the women are happy to have jobs and paychecks, and because they like one another there is a lot of laughter. That leads to one of the sunniest, funniest, happiest scenes in a long time. On a hot day, Ana takes off her blouse, and then so do the other women, giggling at their daring, and the music swells up as their exuberance flows over. They are all plump, but Ana, who has a healthy self-image, leads them in celebrating their bodies.

I am so relieved that the MPAA rated this movie PG-13. So often they bar those under seventeen from the very movies they could benefit from the most. *Real Women Have Curves* is enormously entertaining for moviegoers of any age (it won the Audience Award at Sundance 2002). But for young women depressed because they don't look like skinny models, this film is a breath of common sense and fresh air. *Real Women Have Curves* is a re-

minder of how rarely the women in the movies are real. After the almost excruciating attention paid to the world-class beauties in a movie like *White Oleander* (a film in which the more the women suffered the better they looked), how refreshing to see America Ferrera light up the room with a smile from the heart.

Recess: School's Out ★ ★ ½
G, 84 m., 2001

With the voices of: James Woods (Dr. Benedict), Andy Lawrence (T. J. Detweiler), Rickey D'Shon Collins (Vince), Jason Davis (Mikey), Ashley Johnson (Gretchen), Courtland Mead (Gus), Pam Segall (Ashley), Dabney Coleman (Principal Prickly), April Winchell (Miss Finster), Robert Goulet (Mikey's Singing Voice). Directed by Chuck Sheetz and produced by Stephen Swofford. Created by Paul Germain and Joe Ansolabehere. Screenplay by Jonathan Greenberg.

The highest school test scores in the world are recorded in Canada, Iceland, and Norway, according to the brilliant but twisted Dr. Benedict, villain of *Recess: School's Out*. And what else do those countries have in common? "It's snowing all the time." Benedict wants to be president, and part of his strategy is to raise U.S. test scores by using a secret green ray to nudge the moon into a different orbit, ending summer—and therefore summer vacation.

It's up to T. J. Detweiler, plucky grammar school kid, to save Earth, and summer vacation, in *Recess: School's Out*, a spin-off of the animated kids' TV program. He gets the responsibility because he's the only kid left behind when all the others board buses and roar off to summer camp. Meanwhile, Benedict moves his minions and their moon-moving equipment into the Third Street School, "back where it all began."

How so? In the 1960s, we learn, both Benedict and Principal Prickly were idealistic flower children. But then it rained on Benedict's dream, and he turned into the monster he is today. Prickly, on the other hand, simply grew old and lost his youthful enthusiasm in the day-to-day grind. As for Miss Finster, the draconian teacher, it's doubtful she was a child of the 1960s, although she retains some of the

525

lingo (when she gets stuck trying to crawl through a basement window of the school, she cries out, "I'm stuck! Curse these bodacious hips of mine!").

Dr. Benedict, we learn, started out at Third Street School; his career prospered, and he was secretary of education before getting the boot because of his attempts to ban recess. In exile and isolation, his scheme escalated into an attack on the whole summer vacation, and there is a computer simulation of his dream, in which Earth enters a new ice age and the kids presumably all stay inside and study.

Recess is a Disney attempt to reach the same market that Nickelodeon taps with *Rug Rats*, and although it lacks the zany exuberance of *Rugrats in Paris* (2000), it's fast-footed and fun. *Rugrats in Paris* had charms for grown-ups, however, while *Recess: School's Out* seems aimed more directly at grade-schoolers. That makes the 1960s material problematical; do nine-year-olds really care about ancient history? Even if Myra, the fourteen-year-old "singing sensation," performs "Dancin' in the Streets" over the end titles?

The boom in animation has created a lot of voice-over work in Hollywood, and among the voices heard on *Recess* are Dabney Coleman as Principal Prickly, Andy Lawrence as T. J., and Robert Goulet as the singing voice of a character named Mikey (the song is "Green Tambourine," performed in a sequence made by animators who have obviously studied *Yellow Submarine* and the works of Peter Max).

The movie was directed by Chuck Sheetz, who has worked on shows like *King of the Hill* and *The Simpsons*. One of its charms is its defense of recess, which is, we learn, when all the real benefits of primary education take place. I recommend it for kids up to ten or eleven. Parents may find it amusing, but it doesn't have the two-track versatility of *Rugrats in Paris*, which worked for kids on one level and adults on another.

The Recruit ★ ★ ½
PG-13, 105 m., 2003

Al Pacino (Walter Burke), Colin Farrell (James Clayton), Bridget Moynahan (Layla Moore), Gabriel Macht (Zack). Directed by Roger Donaldson and produced by Roger Birnbaum, Jeff Apple, and Gary Barber. Screenplay by Roger Towne, Kurt Wimmer, and Mitch Glazer.

The Recruit reveals that the training process of the Central Intelligence Agency is like a fraternity initiation, but more dangerous. At one point would-be agents are given a time limit to walk into a singles bar and report back to the parking lot with a partner willing to have sex with them. Uh-huh. As for the Company's years of embarrassments and enemy spies within the ranks? "We reveal our failures but not our successes," the senior instructor tells the new recruits. Quick, can you think of any event in recent world history that bears the stamp of a CIA success?

The senior instructor is Walter Burke, played by Al Pacino in a performance that is just plain fun to watch, gruff, blunt, with a weathered charm. He recruits an MIT whiz kid named James Clayton (Colin Farrell), who turns down a big offer from Dell Computers because he wants to know more about the fate of his late father, a CIA agent. Or maybe because he uses a Macintosh.

Clayton is taken to The Farm, a rustic hideaway somewhere in Ontario, doubling for Virginia, where during the entrance exam he locks eyes with the lovely and fragrant Layla (Bridget Moynahan). He also meets Zack (Gabriel Macht), a former Miami cop who speaks English, Spanish, and Farsi.

The training process involves a series of Bondian sequences in which the agents learn such skills as blowing up cars: (a) Throw bomb under car; (b) detonate. They are also taught about biodegradable listening devices, weapons usage, and how to shadow someone. And they are told of an agency superweapon that (I think I heard this right) can plug into an electric socket and disable every digital device connected to the grid. Agents: Be sure Mr. Coffee has completed his brewing cycle before employing weapon.

The early scenes in the film are entertaining, yes, because Pacino works his character for all its grizzled charm, and Colin Farrell is not only enormously likable but fascinates us with his permanent four-day beard. His chemistry with Layla is real enough, but come on: When he walks into that bar to pick up someone, doesn't it occur to him that it is hardly a coincidence that Layla is already there? Mata Hari would make mincemeat of this guy, but the girl shows promise; as Marlene Dietrich usefully observed, "It took more than one man to change my name to Shanghai Lily."

Still, it's intriguing to see these young trainees learning their job, and to hear Pacino's observations, which are epigrammatic ("I don't have answers. Only secrets"), hard-boiled ("They show you your medal. You don't even get to take it home"), complacent ("Our cause is just"), and helpful ("Nothing is what it seems. Trust no one"). Pacino's character wisely sticks to political generalities so that the film can play in foreign markets; the closest it comes to current events is in the mention of Farsi, which is the language of Iran, although, as Michael Caine likes to say, not many people know that.

The first two acts of the film are fun because they're all setup and buildup, and because the romance between James and Layla is no more cornball and contrived than it absolutely has to be. The third act is a mess. It saddles Pacino with the thankless role of the Talking Killer (not that he necessarily kills). That's the guy who has to stand there and explain the complexities of the plot when any real CIA veteran would just blow the other guy away. By the time Pacino wraps things up, we're realizing that the mantras "Nothing is what it seems" and "Trust no one," if taken seriously, reveal the entire plot. There is, however, a neat little misunderstanding at the end that earns a chuckle.

The movie was directed by Roger Donaldson, who does political thrillers about as well as anyone; his *Thirteen Days* (2001), about the Cuban missile crisis, and *No Way Out* (1987), about a scandal in the Department of Defense, were gripping and intelligent, and *The Recruit* is so well directed and acted that only a churl such as myself would question its sanity. It's the kind of movie you can sit back and enjoy, as long as you don't make the mistake of thinking too much.

Red Dragon ★ ★ ★ ½
R, 124 m., 2002

Anthony Hopkins (Hannibal Lecter), Edward Norton (Will Graham), Ralph Fiennes (Francis Dolarhyde), Harvey Keitel (Jack Crawford), Emily Watson (Reba McClane), Mary-Louise Parker (Molly Graham), Philip Seymour Hoffman (Freddy Lounds). Directed by Brett Ratner and produced by Dino De Laurentiis and Martha Schumacher. Screenplay by Ted Tally, based on the book by Thomas Harris.

Red Dragon opens with the pleasure of seeing Hannibal Lecter as he was before leaving civilian life. The camera floats above a symphony orchestra and down into the audience, and we spot Lecter almost at once, regarding with displeasure an inferior musician. Interesting, how the director forces our attention just as a magician forces a card: We notice Lecter because he is located in a strong place on the screen, because his face is lighted to make him pop out from the drabness on either side, and because he is looking directly at the camera.

I felt, I confess, a certain pleasure to find him in the audience. Hannibal Lecter is one of the most wicked villains in movie history, and one of the most beloved. We forgive him his trespasses because (1) they are forced upon him by his nature; (2) most of the time he is helplessly imprisoned, and providing aid to the FBI, or seeming to, after his peculiar fashion; and (3) he is droll and literate, dryly humorous, elegantly mannered. In these days of movie characters who obediently recite the words the plot requires of them, it's a pleasure to meet a man who can hold up his end of the conversation.

The opening, with Hannibal still in civilian life, allows a tense early scene in which the doctor (Anthony Hopkins) receives a late-night visitor, FBI agent Will Graham (Edward Norton). Graham has been assisted by Lecter in examining a series of crimes which, he has just realized, involved cannibalism—and now, as he regards the doctor in the gloom of the shadowed study, it occurs to him, just as it simultaneously occurs to Lecter, that it is clear to both of them who this cannibal might be.

Flash-forward several years. Lecter is in prison, Graham has taken early retirement, but now his old FBI boss (Harvey Keitel) wants to recruit him to solve a pair of serial killings, this time by a man dubbed the Tooth Fairy because he leaves an unmistakable dental imprint at the scenes of his crimes. Graham resists, but photos of the dead families and a poignant look at his own living family do the trick, and he joins the case as a freelance adviser. This requires him to examine crime scenes by creeping through them in pitch darkness in the middle of the night, although there is no reason he could not visit at noon (except, of course, that he wants to share the killer's point of view, and also because the film seeds the darkness with potential danger).

The director is Brett Ratner, who has not achieved the distinction of the three previous directors of Hannibal Lecter movies (Jonathan Demme on *The Silence of the Lambs,* Ridley Scott on *Hannibal,* and Michael Mann on *Manhunter,* the first version of *Red Dragon,* made in 1986). Ratner's credits have included the *Rush Hour* pictures, *The Family Man,* and *Money Talks,* some with their merits, none suggesting he was qualified to be Lecter's next director.

To my surprise, he does a sure, stylish job, appreciating the droll humor of Lecter's predicament, creating a depraved new villain in the Tooth Fairy (Ralph Fiennes), and using the quiet, intense skills of Edward Norton to create a character whose old fears feed into his new ones. There is also humor, of the uneasy he-can't-get-away-with-this variety, in the character of a nosy scandal-sheet reporter (Philip Seymour Hoffman). The screenplay by Ted Tally, who wrote *Lambs,* also supplies a blind girl in peril (Emily Watson), and blind girls have worked dependably since the days of silent pictures.

A movie like *Red Dragon* is all atmosphere and apprehension. Ratner doesn't give us as much violence or as many sensational shocks as Scott did in *Hannibal,* but that's a plus: Lecter is a character who commands contemplation and unease, and too much action just releases the tension. To be sure, Scott was working with a Thomas Harris novel that itself went so high over the top (remember the quadriplegic murdered with an electric eel?) that much of it could not be filmed. But this movie, based on Harris's first novel, has studied *The Silence of the Lambs* and knows that the action comes second to general creepiness. There are stabbings, shootings, fires, explosions, tortures, mutilations, and a flaming corpse in a wheelchair, but within reason.

As the Tooth Fairy figure, named Francis Dolarhyde, Ralph Fiennes comes as close as possible to creating a sympathetic monster.

What he does is unspeakable. What has been done to him is unspeakable. Dolarhyde himself is horrified by his potential, and the character of the blind girl is not merely a cheap gimmick (although it is that, too), but a device that allows him to ask just how far he is prepared to go. We are reminded of another monster and another blind person, in *Bride of Frankenstein* (1932), and in both cases the monster feels relief because the blind cannot see that he is a monster. (In photos of a crime scene, ex-agent Graham notices that mirrors have been broken and shards of the glass put in the eye sockets of victims—perhaps because the Tooth Fairy cannot stand to look at himself, but is driven to a frenzy when others can look at him.)

The movie has been photographed by Dante Spinotti, who also filmed Michael Mann's more cool, stylized version, and here he provides darkness and saturated colors. The Lecter world is one of dampness, lowering clouds, early sunsets, chill in the bones. Lecter himself, when he appears, is like a little fire we can warm ourselves before; he smiles benevolently, knows all, accepts his nature, offers to help, and more often than not has another macabre scheme under way. The early passages of this movie benefit from our knowledge that Lecter will sooner or later appear; it's as if the plot is tiptoeing toward a ledge.

The Lecter character, and the agents who deal with him and the monsters who take him as a role model, create an atmosphere that encourages style in the filmmaking. It is much the same with the best upper-class crime novels. There is violence, yes, but also a lot of carefully described atmosphere, as we enter the attractive lives of the rich and vicious: Consider Nero Wolfe, who, like Hannibal Lecter, hates to interrupt dinner with a murder.

Reign of Fire ★
PG-13, 100 m., 2002

Matthew McConaughey (Denton Van Zan), Christian Bale (Quinn Abercromby), Izabella Scorupco (Alex), Gerard Butler (Creedy), Randall Carlton (Tito), Doug Cockle (Goosh), Duncan Keegan (Michael), Rory Keenan (Devon), Alice Krige (Dragon Slayer's Mother). Directed by Rob Bowman and produced by

Gary Barber, Roger Birnbaum, Lili Fini Zanuck, and Richard D. Zanuck. Screenplay by Gregg Chabot, Kevin Peterka, and Matt Greenberg.

One regards *Reign of Fire* with awe. What a vast enterprise has been marshaled in the service of such a minute idea. Incredulity is our companion, and it is twofold: We cannot believe what happens in the movie, and we cannot believe that the movie was made.

Of course, in a story involving mankind's battle with fire-breathing dragons in the year 2020, there are a few factual matters you let slide. But the movie makes no sense on its own terms, let alone ours. And it is such a grim and dreary enterprise. One prays for a flower or a ray of sunshine as those grotty warriors clamber into their cellars and over their slag heaps. Not since *Battlefield Earth* has there been worse grooming.

The story: A tunnel beneath London breaks open an underground cavern filled with long-dormant fire-breathing dragons. They fly to the surface and attack mankind. When one is destroyed, countless more take its place. Man's weapons only increase the damage. Soon civilization has been all but wiped out; the heroes of the film cower in their underground hiding places and dream of defeating the dragons.

Along comes Van Zan (Matthew McConaughey), the Dragon Slayer. He is bald and bearded, and his zealot's eyes focus in the middle distance as he speaks. He's the kind of tough guy who smokes cigar butts. Not cigars. Butts. He has a disagreement with Quinn Abercromby (Christian Bale), the leader of the group. I am not sure why they so ferociously oppose each other, but I believe their quarrel comes down to: Van Zan thinks they have to fight the dragons, and Quinn thinks they have to fight the dragons but they have to look out real good, because those are dangerous dragons and might follow them home.

There's not much in the way of a plot. Alex (Izabella Scorupco) gets grubby and distraught while standing between the two men and trying to get them to stop shouting so much and listen to her scientific theories. Meanwhile, dragons attack, their animated wings beating as they fry their enemies. Their animation is fairly good, although at one point a dragon in the background flies past the ruined dome of St. Paul's, and you can see one through the other, or vice versa.

I'm wondering why, if civilization has been destroyed, do they have electricity and fuel? Not supposed to ask such questions. They're like, how come everybody has cigarettes in *Water World*? Van Zan figures out that the dragon's fire comes from the way they secrete the ingredients for "natural napalm" in their mouths. His plan: Get real close and fire an explosive arrow into their open mouth at the crucial moment, causing the napalm to blow up the dragon.

He has another bright idea. (Spoiler warning.) All of the dragons they see are females. Many of them carry eggs. Why no males? Because, Van Zan hypothesizes, the dragons are like fish and it only takes a single male to fertilize umpteen eggs. "We kill the male, we kill the species," he says.

Yeah, but . . . there are dragons everywhere. Do they only have one male, total, singular? How about those eggs? Any of them male? And also, after the male is dead, presumably all of the females are still alive, and they must be mad as hell now that they're not getting any action. How come they stop attacking?

I know I have probably been inattentive, and that some of these points are solved with elegant precision in the screenplay. But please do not write to explain, unless you can answer me this: Why are the last words in the movie "Thank God for evolution"? Could it be a ray of hope that the offspring of this movie may someday crawl up onto the land and develop a two-celled brain?

Resident Evil ★

R, 100 m., 2002

Milla Jovovich (Alice/Janus Prospero/Marsha Thompson), Michelle Rodriguez (Rain Ocampo), Eric Mabius (Matt), James Purefoy (Spence Parks), Colin Salmon (James P. Shade), Marisol Nichols (Dana), Joseph May (Blue). Directed by Paul Anderson and produced by Anderson, Jeremy Bolt, Bernd Eichinger, and Samuel Hadida. Screenplay by Anderson.

Resident Evil is a zombie movie set in the twenty-first century and therefore reflects several advances over twentieth-century films. For example, in twentieth-century slasher movies, knife blades make a sharpening noise when being whisked through thin air. In the twenty-first century, large metallic objects make crashing noises just by being looked at.

The vast Umbrella Corporation, whose secret laboratory is the scene of the action, specializes in high-tech weapons and genetic cloning. It can turn a little DNA into a monster with a nine-foot tongue. Reminds me of the young man from Kent. You would think Umbrella could make a door that doesn't make a slamming noise when it closes, but its doors make slamming noises even when they're open. The narration tells us that Umbrella products are in "90 percent of American homes," so it finishes behind Morton salt.

The movie is *Dawn of the Dead* crossed with *John Carpenter's Ghosts of Mars*, with zombies not as ghoulish as the first and trains not as big as the second. The movie does however have Milla Jovovich and Michelle Rodriguez. According to the Internet Movie Database, Jovovich plays "Alice/Janus Prospero/Marsha Thompson," although I don't believe anybody ever calls her anything. I think some of those names come from the original video game. Rodriguez plays "Rain Ocampo," no relation to the Phoenix family. In pairing classical and literary references, the match of Alice and Janus Prospero is certainly the best name combo since Huckleberry P. Jones/Pa Hercules was portrayed by Ugh-Fudge Bwana in *Forbidden Zone* (1980).

The plot: Vials of something that looks like toy coils of plastic DNA models are being delicately manipulated behind thick shields in an airtight chamber by remote-controlled robot hands; when one of the coils is dropped, the factory automatically seals its exits and gasses and drowns everyone inside. Umbrella practices zero tolerance. We learn that the factory, code named The Hive, is buried half a mile below the surface. Seven investigators go down to see what happened. Three are killed, but Alice/Janus Prospero/Marsha, Rain Ocampo, Matt, and Spence survive in order to be attacked for sixty minutes by the dead Hive employees, who have turned into zombies. Meanwhile, the monster with the nine-foot tongue is mutating. (Eventually, its tongue is nailed to the floor of a train car and it is dragged behind

it on the third rail. I hate it when that happens.)

These zombies, like the *Dawn of the Dead* zombies, can be killed by shooting them, so there is a lot of zombie shooting, although not with the squishy green-goo effect of George Romero's 1978 film. The zombies are like vampires, since when one bites you it makes you a zombie. What I don't understand is why zombies are so graceless. They walk with the lurching shuffle of a drunk trying to skate through urped Slurpees to the men's room.

There is one neat effect when characters unwisely venture into a corridor and the door slams shut on them. Then a laser beam passes at head level, decapitating one. Another beam whizzes past at waist level, cutting the second in two while the others duck. A third laser pretends to be high but then switches to low, but the third character outsmarts it by jumping at the last minute. Then the fourth laser turns into a grid that dices its victim into pieces the size of a Big Mac. Since the grid is inescapable, what were the earlier lasers about? Does the corridor have a sense of humor?

Alice/Janus Prospero/Marsha Thompson and her colleagues are highly trained scientists, which leads to the following exchange when they stare at a pool of zombie blood on the floor.

Alice/J.P./M.T./Rain (I forget which): "It's coagulating!"
Matt/Spence (I forget which): "That's not possible!"
"Why not?!?"
"Because blood doesn't do that until you're dead!"

How does the blood on the floor know if you're dead? The answer to this question is so obvious I am surprised you would ask. Because it is zombie blood.

The characters have no small talk. Their dialogue consists of commands, explanations, exclamations, and ejaculations. Yes, an ejaculation can be dialogue. If you live long enough you may find that happening frequently.

Oh, and the film has a Digital Readout. The Hive is set to lock itself forever after sixty minutes have passed, so the characters are racing against time. In other words, after it shuts all of its doors and gasses and drowns everybody, it waits sixty minutes and *really* shuts its doors—big time. No wonder the steel doors make those slamming noises. In their imagination, they're practicing. Creative visualization, it's called. I became inspired, and visualized the theater doors slamming behind me.

Respiro ★ ★ ★
PG-13, 90 m., 2003

Valeria Golino (Grazia), Vincenzo Amato (Pietro), Francesco Casisa (Pasquale), Veronica D'Agostino (Marinella), Filippo Pucillo (Filippo). Directed by Emanuele Crialese and produced by Dominic Process. Screenplay by Crialese.

That there is something not right about Grazia, all the village agrees. "Bring her shot!" her husband calls out at fraught moments, and the children and neighbors hold her down while he jabs her with a needle filled with—what? It calms her down, anyway. There is said to be a doctor in Milan who could help her, but when the entire village unites in favor of the Milan trip, Grazia runs away and is thought to be dead in the sea.

The village is angry at her because Grazia opened the doors of an old stone building and released dozens of stray dogs to run about the streets. Whether they were rabid or just homeless is not clear, and why they were being held instead of put down is not explained, but the men of the village are resourceful, and take to their rooftops with rifles to shoot all the dogs. Then it becomes clear that Grazia must go to Milan: "This can't go on."

The village is on the Italian island of Lampedusa, not far from Tunisia. Whether *Respiro* paints an accurate portrait of its society, I cannot say. Fishing and canning are the local industries, everybody lives in everybody else's pockets, and the harsh sun beats down on a landscape of rock and beach, sea and sky, and sand-colored homes surrounded by children and Vespas.

In this world Grazia (Valeria Golino) is a legend. Young-looking to be the mother of three children, one a teenager, she is married to Pietro (Vincenzo Amato), a handsome fisherman who loves her, but is understandably disturbed when his boat passes a beach where Grazia is swimming nude with their children.

More accurately, she is nude, and her son Pasquale (Francesco Casisa) wants her to put her clothes back on and come home with him.

Pasquale tries to protect his mother. She has what we in the audience diagnose as manic depression, although the movie never declares itself. Mostly she's in the manic phase, too happy, too uncontrolled, burning with a fierce delight that wears out everyone else. Rather than go to Milan, she runs away, and Pasquale helps her hide in a cave he knows, and brings her food while the village searches for her and Pietro grows bereft.

But the story of Grazia is only one of the pleasures of *Respiro*, which won the grand prize in the Critics' Week program at Cannes 2002. The movie, written and directed by the New York University graduate Emanuele Crialese, has a feeling for the rhythms of life on the island, and especially for the way the boys—Grazia's two sons and others—run wild as boys will. We see them trapping birds and cooking them for a treat, depantsing each other, forming tribes constantly at war, and swimming out to returning fishing boats hoping to be thrown a few fish they can trade in the marketplace for chances at winning a train set in the lottery.

When the boys actually win the train set, their bearded and sun-bronzed fishermen fathers behave as all fathers do everywhere, and set up the train "for the kids" because they want to play with it themselves. In the middle of this enterprise, Grazia lures Pietro away for a "nap." It's clear they are still passionately in love. Sex indeed is not far from the surface in this family, and the teenage daughter, Marinella (Veronica D'Agostino), flirts with the new policeman in town, who seems a good deal less sure of his moves than she is.

That's why it's all the more sad when Grazia disappears and Pasquale helps in her deception. Pietro mourns on the beach while Grazia is not far away, living in the cave. How could she do such a heartless thing? Well, because she really does need the man in Milan, although the movie sidesteps that inescapable reality with an ending both poetic and unlikely.

Respiro is a cheerful, life-affirming film, strong in its energy, about vivid characters. It uses mental illness as an entertainment, not a disease. As I watched it, I wondered—do such people really live on Lampedusa, and is this film an accurate reflection of their lives? I have no idea. I tend to doubt it. But perhaps it doesn't matter, since they exist for the ninety minutes of this film, and engage us with their theatricality. Grazia needs help, but her island will not be such a lively place to live if she gets it.

Return to Never Land ★ ★ ★
G, 76 m., 2002

With the voices of: Blayne Weaver (Peter Pan), Harriet Owen (Jane), Corey Burton (Captain Hook), Jeff Bennett (Smee/Starkey and Wibbles), Kath Soucie (Wendy/Narrator), Andrew McDonough (Danny). An animated film directed by Robin Budd and Donovan Cook and produced by Christopher Chase and Dan Rounds. Screenplay by Carter Crocker and Temple Matthews.

The opening titles tell us this is "Peter Pan in Return to Never Land," and indeed, why can't an animated character be a movie star? Years have passed since the end of the first story—London is reeling under the Blitz—and Wendy has grown up, married, and produced a daughter, Jane. But Peter Pan, Tinker Bell, the Lost Boys, and Captain Hook all remain unchanged in Never Land.

During all of those years Hook has continued to search for his lost treasure, which was, he believes, stolen by Peter and hidden somewhere on the island. As the film opens, Jane indulges her mother's stories about fairies that can fly. She doesn't believe them, but is persuaded when kidnapped by Hook and his men—who fly in their pirate ship over London, luckily without engaging any antiaircraft batteries.

Hook believes Jane may be the key to finding the treasure—or at the least a way to pry the secret out of Peter. We can almost sympathize with his impatience. The original *Peter Pan* hurtled through its narrative, and then left him on hold for twenty-five years, gnashing his teeth and spinning his wheels. All the same, Never Land rules apply, and at one point Tinker Bell is grounded because, yes, Jane doesn't believe in fairies.

Of the voice-over talent, Corey Burton is almost inevitably the star, because he's assigned Captain Hook, one of those roles that

sort of directs itself. Blayne Weaver is fine as Peter Pan, but it's interesting that none of the voice talents sing any of the movie's songs; they appear on the sound track as commentaries or parallels to the action.

Return to Never Land is a bright and energetic animated comedy, with all the slick polish we expect from Disney, but it's not much more. This one feels like it had a narrow escape from the direct-to-video market. It's not a major item like *Monsters, Inc.* and lacks the in-jokes and sly references that allow a movie like that to function on two levels. It's more of a Saturday afternoon stop for the kiddies—harmless, skillful, and aimed at grade-schoolers.

Riding in Cars with Boys ★ ★ ★
PG-13, 132 m., 2001

Drew Barrymore (Beverly Donofrio), Sara Gilbert (Tina), Steve Zahn (Raymond), Mika Boorem (Young Beverly), Brittany Murphy (Fay), Adam Garcia (Jason), Lorraine Bracco (Beverly's Mother), James Woods (Beverly's Father), Rosie Perez (Shirley). Directed by Penny Marshall and produced by James L. Brooks, Laurence Mark, Sara Colleton, Richard Sakai, and Julie Ansell. Screenplay by Morgan Upton Ward, based on the memoir by Beverly Donofrio.

"I'm twenty-two, and I still haven't accepted that this is my life," says Beverly Donofrio (Drew Barrymore), the heroine of *Riding in Cars with Boys*. She has a drunken and shiftless husband, a son from a teenage pregnancy, and a run-down house on a dead-end street in a section of town well known to the police. It doesn't help that her father is the chief of police.

Her problems all started not from riding in cars with boys, but from parking in cars with boys, and getting pregnant. Her wisdom in choosing the father didn't help. Ray (Steve Zahn) is an aimless slacker with a basically good heart, not too many smarts, and a life that's moving way too fast for him to keep up while he's using drugs and booze. His wife is manifestly smarter than he is, although not smart enough to avoid blaming her life on everyone but herself.

Riding in Cars with Boys is directed by Penny Marshall and based on a memoir by the real

Beverly Donofrio (reportedly much revised by the screenwriters). It's a brave movie, in the way it centers on a mother who gets trapped in the wrong life, doesn't get out for a long time, takes her misery out on her son, and blames everything on her fate and bad luck. The movie traces a series of developments that dig her deeper into unhappiness. If only she hadn't gotten pregnant. If only the father hadn't been Ray. If only her parents had been easier to talk to. If only . . . well, if only she hadn't gone riding in cars with boys. The best way to avoid the problems of teenage pregnancy, as Beverly would be the first to tell you, is by not getting pregnant.

The movie is a showcase performance for Barrymore, who ages from fifteen to thirty-six, who doggedly plugs away trying to take classes and win college scholarships, who is heroic in her efforts to give her son, Jason, a right start in life, but whose fatal character flaw is that every time she looks at Jason she sees him as the reason for her misery. There's a key scene where Ray is supposed to baby-sit Jason while Beverly goes for a scholarship interview. Ray forgets. She has to take the kid along, and his presence possibly costs her the scholarship. "For me," Jason remembers later, "it's not how Ray let her down, it's about how my mere presence at the age of three crushed all of her dreams."

Steve Zahn's performance is crucial to the film. He has played dim bulbs before *(Joy Ride, Happy, Texas)*, but usually for comic effect. Here he creates a character from the ground up, a dead-on accurate study of a man whose addiction to alcohol and drugs is simply too much for him to negotiate, so that he wakes up already defeated by the struggle ahead. How can you ask a man to do anything constructive when he's already exhausted by the task of feeding his system its daily fix? That he wants to do better, that he loves his son, that he knows his wife's resentment is justified, arouses our pity: He pays the price every second of his trembling existence for his shortcomings.

The movie opens with Jason as a young man, driving with his mother for a meeting with the father he barely remembers. She has written a book about her life, and needs his signature on a release form to protect the publishers against a lawsuit. This meeting will be one

of the most painful scenes in the movie (underlined by the presence of Ray's second wife, played by Rosie Perez as the crown of thorns to top his other sufferings). What Jason sees clearly is that his mother is more concerned about her book than about how Jason will react to this sight of the broken, smelly, pathetic wreck that is his father.

Beverly has been a dutiful mother but not a wise one. No child can carry the burden of a parent's unhappiness, and a parent who demands that is practicing a form of abuse. Because the movie is honest enough to see that, *Riding in Cars with Boys* is brave—not the story of plucky Drew Barrymore struggling through poverty and divorce to become a best-selling author, but the story of a woman whose book, when it is published, will be small consolation.

Perhaps her unhappiness begins with *her* parents—the police chief (James Woods) and his wife (Lorraine Bracco). They are not bad people but, like their daughter, they are more concerned with what is "right" than with how to parent with love. And the failing goes down to the third generation, in a remarkable scene where little Jason rats on his own mother. Desperate for money, she has allowed a neighbor to dry some weed in her oven, and (1) the kid actually tells his grandfather the cop, and (2) the cop actually arrests his own daughter. It's curious how by the end of the movie the mother is not only blaming the son, but the son the mother, and it's the stumblebum father who emerges with some credit for at least blaming himself.

A film like this is refreshing and startling in the way it cuts loose from formula and shows us confused lives we recognize. Hollywood tends to reduce stories like this to simplified redemption parables in which the noble woman emerges triumphant after a lifetime of surviving loser men. This movie is closer to the truth: A lot depends on what happens to you, and then a lot depends on how you let it affect you. Life has not been kind to Beverly, and Beverly has not been kind to life. Maybe there'll be another book in a few years where she sees how, in some ways, she can blame herself.

The Ring ★ ★
PG-13, 115 m., 2002

Naomi Watts (Rachel Keller), Martin Henderson (Noah), Brian Cox (Richard Morgan), David Dorfman (Aidan Keller), Lindsay Frost (Ruth), Amber Tamblyn (Katie), Rachael Bella (Becca), Daveigh Chase (Samara Morgan), Richard Lineback (Innkeeper). Directed by Gore Verbinski and produced by Laurie MacDonald and Walter F. Parkes. Screenplay by Hiroshi Takahashi and Ehren Kruger, based on the novel by Kôji Suzuki.

Rarely has a more serious effort produced a less serious result than in *The Ring,* the kind of dread dark horror film where you better hope nobody in the audience snickers, because the film teeters right on the edge of the ridiculous.

Enormous craft has been put into the movie, which looks just great, but the story goes beyond contrivance into the dizzy realms of the absurd. And although there is no way for everything to be explained (and many events lack any possible explanation), the movie's ending explains and explains and *explains,* until finally you'd rather just give it a pass than sit through one more tedious flashback.

The story involves a video that brings certain death. You look at it, the phone rings, and you find out you have seven days to live. A prologue shows some teenage victims of the dread curse, and then newspaper reporter Rachel Keller (Naomi Watts) gets on the case, helped by eerie drawings by her young son, Aidan (David Dorfman).

The story has been recycled from a popular Japanese thriller by Kôji Suzuki, which was held off the market in this country to clear the field for this remake. Alas, the same idea was ripped off in August 2002 by *FearDotCom,* also a bad movie, but more plain fun than *The Ring,* and with a climax that used brilliant visual effects while this one drags on endlessly.

I dare not reveal too much of the story, but will say that the video does indeed bring death in a week, something we are reminded of as Rachel tries to solve the case while titles tick off the days. A single mom, she enlists Aidan's father, a video geek named Noah (Martin Henderson), to analyze the deadly tape. He tags along for the adventure, which inevitably leads

to their learning to care for each other, I guess, although the movie is not big on relationships. Her investigation leads her to a remote cottage on an island, and to the weird, hostile man (Brian Cox) who lives there. And then the explanations start to pile up.

This is Naomi Watts's first move since *Mulholland Drive,* and I was going to complain that we essentially learn nothing about her character, except that she's a newspaper reporter—but then I remembered that in *Mulholland Drive* we essentially learned nothing except that she was a small-town girl in Hollywood, and by the end of the movie we weren't even sure we had learned that. *Mulholland Drive* however, evoked juicy emotions and dimensions that *The Ring* is lacking, and involved us in a puzzle that was intriguing instead of simply tedious.

There are a couple of moments when we think *The Ring* is going to end, and it doesn't. One is that old reliable where the heroine, soaking wet and saved from death, says, "I want to go home," and the hero cushions her head on his shoulder. But no, there's more. Another is when Aidan says, "You didn't let her out, did you?" That would have been a nice ironic closer, but the movie spells out the entire backstory in merciless detail, until when we're finally walking out of the theater, we're almost ashamed to find ourselves wondering, hey, who was that on the phone? ☞

Rivers and Tides: Andy Goldsworthy Working with Time ★ ★ ★ ½
NO MPAA RATING, 90 m., 2003

A documentary about Scottish environmental artist Andy Goldsworthy. Directed by Thomas Riedelsheimer and produced by Annedore von Donop. Screenplay by Riedelsheimer.

Have you ever watched—no, better, have you ever *been* a young child intent on building something out of the materials at hand in the woods, or by a stream, or at the beach? Have you seen the happiness of an adult joining kids and slowly slipping out of adulthood and into the absorbing process of this . . . and now . . . and over here . . . and build this up . . . and it should go like this?

The artist Andy Goldsworthy lives in that

world of making things. They have no names; they are Things. He brings order to leaves or twigs or icicles and then surrenders them to the process of nature. He will kneel for hours by the oceanside, creating a cairn of stones that balances precariously, the weight on the top holding the sides in place, and then the tide will come in and wash away the sand beneath, and the cairn will collapse, as it must, as it should.

"The very thing that brought the thing to be is the thing that will cause its death," Goldsworthy explains, as his elegant, spiraled constructions once again become random piles of stones on the beach. As with Andy's stones, so with our lives.

Rivers and Tides: Andy Goldsworthy Working with Time is a documentary that opened in San Francisco in mid-2002 and just kept running, moving from one theater to another, finding its audience not so much through word of mouth as through hand-on-elbow, as friends steered friends into the theater, telling them that this was a movie they had to see. I started getting E-mail about it months ago. Had I seen it? I hadn't even heard of it.

It is a film about a man wholly absorbed in the moment. He wanders woods and riverbanks, finding materials and playing with them, fitting them together, piling them up, weaving them, creating beautiful arrangements that he photographs before they return to chaos. He knows that you can warm the end of an icicle just enough to make it start to melt, and then hold it against another icicle, and it will stick. With that knowledge, he makes an ice sculpture, and then it melts in the sun and is over.

Some of his constructions are of magical beauty, as if left behind by beings who disappeared before the dawn. He finds a way to arrange twigs in a kind of web. He makes a spiral of rocks that fans out from a small base and then closes in again, a weight on top holding it together. This is not easy, and he gives us pointers: "Top control can be the death of a work."

Often Andy will be . . . almost there . . . right on the edge . . . holding his breath as one last piece goes into place . . . and then the whole construction will collapse, and he will look deflated, defeated for a moment ("Damn!"), and then start again: "When I build

something I often take it to the very edge of its collapse, and that's a very beautiful balance."

His art needs no explanation. We go into modern art galleries and find work we cannot comprehend as art. We see Damien Hirst's sheep, cut down the middle and embedded in plastic, and we cannot understand how it won the Turner Prize (forgetting that no one thought Turner was making art, either). We suppose that concepts and statements are involved.

But with Andy Goldsworthy, not one word of explanation is necessary because every single one of us has made something like his art. We have piled stones or made architectural constructions out of sand, or played Pick-Up Stix, and we know *exactly* what he is trying to do—and why. Yes, why, because his art takes him into that zone where time drops away and we forget our left-brain concerns and are utterly absorbed by whether this . . . could go like this . . . without the whole thing falling apart.

The documentary, directed, photographed, and edited by Thomas Riedelsheimer, a German filmmaker, goes home with Goldsworthy to Penpont, Scotland, where we see him spending some time with his wife and kids. It follows him to a museum in the south of France, and to an old stone wall in Canada that he wants to rebuild in his own way. It visits with him old stone markers high in mountains, built by early travelers to mark the path.

And it offers extraordinary beauty. We watch as he smashes stones to release their content, and uses that bright red dye to make spectacular patterns in the currents and whirlpools of streams. We see a long rope of linked leaves, bright green, uncoil as it floats downstream. Before, we saw only the surface of the water, but now the movement of the leaves reveals its current and structure. What a happy man. Watching this movie is like daydreaming.

Road to Perdition ★ ★ ★
R, 119 m., 2002

Tom Hanks (Michael Sullivan), Paul Newman (John Rooney), Tyler Hoechlin (Michael Sullivan Jr.), Jude Law (Maguire, aka The Reporter), Anthony LaPaglia (Al Capone), Daniel Craig (Connor Rooney), Stanley Tucci (Frank Nitti), Jennifer Jason Leigh (Annie Sullivan). Directed by Sam Mendes and produced by Mendes,

Dean Zanuck, and Richard D. Zanuck. Screenplay by David Self, based on the graphic novel by Max Allan Collins and Richard Piers Rayner.

Road to Perdition is like a Greek tragedy, dealing out remorseless fates for all the characters. Some tragedies, like "Hamlet," are exhilarating, because we have little idea how quirks of character will bring about the final doom. But the impact of Greek tragedy seems muted to me, because it's preordained. Since *Road to Perdition* is in that tradition, it loses something. It has been compared to *The Godfather,* but *The Godfather* was about characters with free will, and here the characters seem to be performing actions already long since inscribed in the books of their lives.

Yet the movie has other strengths to compensate for the implacable progress of its plot. It is wonderfully acted. And no movie this year will be more praised for its cinematography; Conrad L. Hall's work seems certain to win the Academy Award. He creates a limbo of darkness, shadow, night, fearful faces half-seen, cold, and snow. His characters stand in downpours, the rain running off the brims of their fedoras and soaking the shoulders of their thick wool overcoats. Their feet must always be cold. The photography creates a visceral chill.

The story involves three sets of fathers and sons—two biological, the third emotional—and shows how the lives they lead make ordinary love between them impossible. Tom Hanks plays Michael Sullivan, an enforcer for a suburban branch of the Chicago mob, circa 1931. Tyler Hoechlin plays his son Michael Jr., a solemn-eyed twelve-year-old. After his brother, Peter, asks, "What does Dad do for a job?" Michael Jr. decides to find out for himself. One night he hides in a car, goes along for the ride, and sees a man killed. Not by his father, but what difference does it make?

Sullivan works for John Rooney (Paul Newman), the mob boss, who is trim and focused and uses few words. John's son Connor (Daniel Craig) is a member of the mob. Sullivan finds out that Connor has been stealing from his father, and that sets up the movie's emotional showdown, because Sullivan thinks of John like his own father, and John speaks of Sullivan as a

son. "Your mother knows I love Mr. Rooney," Michael Sr. tells his son. "When we had nothing, he gave us a home."

Men who name their sons after themselves presumably hope the child will turn out a little like them. This is not the case with Michael Sr., who has made a pact with evil in order to support his wife (Jennifer Jason Leigh) and two boys in comfort. Unlike Rooney, he doesn't want his son in the business. The movie's plot asks whether it is possible for fathers to spare their sons from the costs of their sins. It also involves sons who feel they are not the favorite. "Did you like Peter better than me?" Michael Jr. asks his father, after his little brother has been killed. And later Sullivan goes to see Mr. Rooney, and cannot understand why Rooney would prefer his son Connor, who betrayed and stole from him, to his loyal employee who is "like a son."

The movie is directed by Sam Mendes, from a graphic novel by Max Allan Collins and Richard Piers Rayner, much revised by screenwriter David Self. This is only Mendes's second film, but recall that his first, *American Beauty,* won Oscars in 1999 for best picture, director, actor, screenplay—and cinematography, by Conrad Hall. Both films involve men in family situations of unbearable pain, although the first is a comedy (of sorts) and this one certainly is not. Both involve a father who, by leading the life he chooses, betrays his family and even endangers them. Both involve men who hate their work.

The key relationships are between Hanks and Newman, and Hanks and Tyler Hoechlin, the newcomer who plays his son. Newman plays Mr. Rooney as a man who would prefer that as few people be harmed as necessary, but he has an implacable definition of "necessary." He is capable of colorful Corleone-style sayings, as when he declares that his mob will not get involved in labor unions: "What men do after work is what made us rich. No need to screw them at work." Against this benevolence we must set his trade in booze, gambling, and women, and his surgical willingness to amputate any associate who is causing difficulty.

The Hanks character sees the good side of Mr. Rooney so willfully that he almost cannot see the bad. Even after he discovers the worst, he feels wounded more than betrayed. He's a little naive, and it takes Rooney, in a speech Newman delivers with harsh clarity, to disabuse him. Called a murderer, Rooney says: "There are *only* murderers in this room, Michael. Open your eyes. This is the life we chose. The life we lead. And there is only one guarantee—none of us will see heaven."

Sullivan wants his son to see heaven, and that sets up their flight from Rooney justice. Father and son flee, pursued by a hit man (Jude Law) who supplements his income by selling photographs of the people he has killed. The plot all works out in an ending that may seem too neat, unless you reflect that in tragedy there is a place of honor for the *deus ex machina*—the god being lowered by the machinery of the plot into a scene that requires solution.

I mentioned the rain. This is a water-soaked picture, with melting snow on the streets and dampness in every room. That gives Conrad Hall the opportunity to develop and extend one of his most famous shots. In *In Cold Blood* (1967), he has a close-up of Robert Blake, as a convicted killer on the night of his death. He puts Blake near a window, and lights his face through the windowpane, as raindrops slide down the glass. The effect is of tears on his face. In *Road to Perdition,* the light shines through a rain-swept window onto a whole room that seems to weep.

After I saw *Road to Perdition,* I knew I admired it, but I didn't know if I liked it. I am still not sure. It is cold and holds us outside. Yes, there is the love of Hanks for his son, but how sadly he is forced to express it. The troubles of the mob seem caused because Rooney prefers family to good management, but Michael Sullivan's tragedy surely comes because he has put it the other way around—placing Rooney above his family. The movie shares with *The Godfather* the useful tactic of keeping the actual victims out of view. There are no civilians here, destroyed by mob activities. All of the characters, good and bad, are supplied from within the mob. But there is never the sense that any of these characters will tear loose, think laterally, break the chains of their fate. Choice, a luxury of the Corleones, is denied to the Sullivans and Rooneys, and choice or its absence is the difference between Sophocles and Shakespeare. I prefer Shakespeare. ☞

Rock Star ★ ★ ½
R, 110 m., 2001

Mark Wahlberg (Chris "Izzy" Coles), Jennifer Aniston (Emily Poule), Timothy Spall (Manager), Jamie Williams (Mason), Deborah Leydig (Marjorie), William Martin Brennan (Office Drone), Jason Flemyng (Bobby Beers). Directed by Stephen Herek and produced by Toby Jaffe and Robert Lawrence. Screenplay by John Stockwell.

Rock is a business like any other, and musicians are businessmen, and what goes on behind the scenes isn't always pretty. We know this, and we don't want to know this. *Rock Star* is a movie about a copy machine repairman who becomes the lead singer in a famous heavy metal band, and somehow with that premise it should be more fun than it is. (It doesn't even have a crucial moment where the new star saves the day with an emergency copier repair.) Instead, it's a morality play with morose undertones, and for the second movie in a row (after *Planet of the Apes*) here is Mark Wahlberg looking like he doesn't enjoy being out front.

Wahlberg plays Chris "Izzy" Coles, a Pennsylvania copier repairman who sings in the church choir, loves and is loved by his parents and a loyal girlfriend, and leads a local tribute band named Blood Pollution. He idolizes the band Steel Dragon, and insists that his band do only their songs, and only in the exact way they perform them ("You're not nailing the squeal," he tells a guitarist during rehearsal). Eventually his fanaticism makes him such a nuisance that his own band fires him. Miraculously, the lead singer of Steel Dragon is in the process of being kicked out, and the band sees one of Izzy's tapes and hires him as a replacement singer.

This is all loosely inspired by fact. An Ohio office supply salesman named Tim "Ripper" Owens actually did replace Rob Halford, the lead singer in Judas Priest, after warming up as lead singer in a tribute band. Most of the film's other details are, I imagine, fiction—but they portray a world that must be more or less the same for many bands, involving the ordeal of touring, personality clashes, the danger of violence, unhappy relationships, omnipresent groupies, and managers who must be liars, thieves, drug counselors, and psychoanalysts to keep the show on the road.

The best parts of the movie are the early ones, as Izzy fights with his band, stands by his dream, and is supported by his girlfriend Emily (Jennifer Aniston), who at one point goes beyond the call of duty by piercing his nipple so he can wear a ring just like his idol Bobby Beers, the lead singer in Steel Dragon. One of the funniest scenes in the movie involves what appears to be a fight with a cop who breaks into Izzy's bedroom; I won't spoil the punch line.

The members of Steel Dragon are revealed, behind the scenes, to be cynical professionals who casually boot out Bobby Beers, see a tape of Izzy performing, fly him to L.A. for an audition, and hire him. Izzy brings Emily along ("We traded in the first-class ticket for two tourist tickets"), and indeed plans on keeping her by his side during the whole adventure. This is not the way the tour works, and Emily is banned from the band bus; she and the other wives and girlfriends trail behind in a stretch limousine, although an astrologer and a drag queen are allowed on the bus.

We follow Izzy's adventures as a lead singer; he falls down a flight of stairs on his first entrance, and makes a good impression by singing while blood runs down his forehead. Eventually we, and he, understand that he who can be hired can be fired. Timothy Spall anchors this section of the film with his observant, solid performance as the manager, who sees all, knows all, tolerates all until it affects the box office. Aware that Emily feels shut out while groupies cluster around the band, he counsels her to "build up a little tolerance to it, you know?"

Watching *Rock Star* was an instructive experience. Until the halfway mark I approved of it, and then slowly my enthusiasm faded. It stopped being an adventure and started being a parable. Instead of the life and energy in a movie like *Almost Famous,* set in roughly the same period, there was a glum disconsolance. I began to feel that Izzy lacked the imagination to turn the situation into fun, that his rigidity in insisting that Blood Pollution copy Steel Dragon note for note translated to a kind of paralyzing inflexibility.

Where was the juice and joy? By the end of the film I conceded, yes, there are good performances and the period is well captured, but the movie didn't convince me of the feel and the flavor of its experiences.

Note: Rock Star *began production with the title* Metal God, *which is incomparably better; at one point, it was called* So You Wanna Be a Rock Star?—*the inspiration, no doubt, of a ratings-crazed executive who thought it could attract all the Regis Philbin fans.*

Roger Dodger ★ ★ ★
R, 104 m., 2002

Campbell Scott (Roger), Jesse Eisenberg (Nick), Isabella Rossellini (Joyce), Elizabeth Berkley (Andrea), Jennifer Beals (Sophie), Ben Shenkman (Donovan), Mina Badie (Donna). Directed by Dylan Kidd and produced by Anne Chaisson, Kidd, and George VanBuskirk. Screenplay by Kidd.

Roger is an advertising executive who explains that his technique is to make consumers feel miserable so they can restore their happiness by buying the sponsor's product. In his private life, Roger is the product, trying to make women feel miserable about themselves and then offering himself as the cure. Roger is an optimist who keeps on talking, just as if his approach works.

As *Roger Dodger* opens, Roger (Campbell Scott) has just been dumped by his lover, Joyce (Isabella Rossellini), who is also his boss and makes him feel miserable with admirable economy of speech: "I am your boss. You work for me. I have explained to you that I do not wish to see you socially any longer. Find a way to deal with it." Roger can't quite believe her. Indeed, he attends a party at her house that he has specifically not been invited to. He's an optimist in the face of setbacks, a con man who has conned himself.

Into his office and life one day walks his nephew Nick (Jesse Eisenberg), who is sixteen. Roger isn't on speaking terms with Nick's mother, but Nick is another matter, a young man who asks for guidance that Roger feels himself uniquely equipped to provide. Nick knows little of women and wants advice, and Roger starts with theory and then takes Nick nightclub-hopping so they can work on the practice. During one incredibly lucky evening, they meet Andrea and Sophie (Elizabeth Berkley and Jennifer Beals), who are intrigued by Nick's innocence, charmed by his honesty, and delighted by his wit. The kid's naïveté acts like a mirror in which they can study their own attitudes. Roger the coach finds himself on the sidelines.

The movie, written and directed by Dylan Kidd, depends on its dialogue and, like a film by David Mamet or Neil LaBute, has characters who use speech like an instrument. The screenplay would be entertaining just to read, as so very few are. Scott, who usually plays more conventional roles, emerges here as acid and sardonic, with a Shavian turn to his observations, and although his advice is not very useful it is entertaining.

The problem of Nick's young age is one that several other movies, notably *Tadpole*, have negotiated lately. Apparently when it comes to the age of consent for sex, in the movies young males don't count. If an innocent sixteen-year-old girl were taken to a nightclub by her aunt and set up with a couple of thirty-something guys, the MPAA would be outraged and Hollywood terrified. But turn the tables and somehow the glint in Nick's eye takes care of everything.

Roger Dodger effectively deflects criticism in this area by making Roger the victim and the subject. While Nick is funny and earnest and generates many laughs, the movie is really about Roger—about his attempts to tutor his nephew in a lifestyle that has left the older man lonely and single. The film is not just a lot of one-liners, but has a buried agenda, as the funny early dialogue slides down into confusion and sadness. There is a lesson here for Nick, but not the one Roger is teaching.

Rollerball ½★

PG-13, 98 m., 2002

Chris Klein (Jonathan Cross), Jean Reno (Alexi Petrovich), LL Cool J (Marcus Ridley), Rebecca Romijn-Stamos (Aurora), Naveen Andrews (Sanjay), Paul Heyman (Announcer). Directed by John McTiernan and produced by McTiernan, Charles Roven, and Beau St. Clair. Screenplay by William Harrison, Larry Ferguson,

and John Pogue, based on the short story by Harrison.

Rollerball is an incoherent mess, a jumble of footage in search of plot, meaning, rhythm, and sense. There are bright colors and quick movement on the screen, which we can watch as a visual pattern that, in entertainment value, falls somewhere between a kaleidoscope and a lava lamp.

The movie stars Chris Klein, who shot to stardom, so to speak, in the *American Pie* movies and inhabits his violent action role as if struggling against the impulse to blurt out, "People, why can't we all just get along?" Klein is a nice kid. For this role, you need someone who has to shave three times a day.

The movie is set in 2005 in a Central Asian republic apparently somewhere between Uzbekistan and Mudville. Jean Reno plays Petrovich, owner of "the hottest sports start-up in the world," a Rollerball league that crowds both motorcycles and roller skaters on a figure-eight track that at times looks like Roller Derby crossed with demo derby, at other times like a cruddy video game. The sport involves catching a silver ball and throwing it at a big gong so that showers of sparks fly. One of the star players confesses she doesn't understand it, but so what: In the final game Petrovich suspends all rules, fouls, and penalties. This makes no difference that I could see.

Klein plays Jonathan Cross, an NHL draft pick who has to flee America in a hurry for the crime of racing suicidally down the hills of San Francisco flat on his back on what I think is a skateboard. His best friend is Marcus Ridley (LL Cool J), who convinces him to come to Podunkistan and sign for the big bucks. Jonathan is soon attracted to Aurora (Rebecca Romijn-Stamos, from *X-Men*).

"Your face isn't nearly as bad as you think," he compliments her. She has a scar over one eye, but is otherwise in great shape, as we can see because the locker rooms of the future are co-ed. Alas, the women athletes of the future still turn their backs to the camera at crucial moments, carry strategically placed towels, stand behind furniture, and in general follow the rules first established in 1950s nudist volleyball pictures.

I counted three games in the Rollerball sea-

539

son. The third is the championship. There is one road trip, to a rival team's Rollerball arena, which seems to have been prefabricated in the city dump. The games are announced by Paul Heyman, who keeps screaming, "What the hell is going on?" There is no one else in the booth with him. Yet when Aurora wants to show Jonathan that an injury was deliberate, she can call up instant replays from all the cameras on equipment thoughtfully provided in the locker room.

The funniest line in the movie belongs to Jean Reno, who bellows, "I'm this close to a North American cable deal!" North American cable carries Battling Bots, Iron Chefs, Howard Stern, and monster truck rallies. There isn't a person in the audience who couldn't get him that deal. Reno also has the second funniest line. After Jonathan engages in an all-night 120-mph motorcycle chase across the frozen steppes of Bankruptistan, while military planes drop armed Jeeps to chase him, and after he sees his best pal blown to bits *after* leaping across a suspension bridge that has been raised in the middle of the night for no apparent reason, Reno tells him, "Play well tonight."

Oh, and I almost forgot Aurora's breathless discovery after the suspicious death of one of the other players. "His chin strap was cut!" she whispers fiercely to Jonathan. Neither she nor he notices that Jonathan makes it a point never to fasten his own chin strap at any time during a game.

Someday this film may inspire a long, thoughtful book by John Wright, its editor. My guess is that something went dreadfully wrong early in the production. Maybe dysentery or mass hypnosis. And the director, John McTiernan *(Die Hard)*, was unable to supply Wright with the shots he needed to make sense of the story. I saw a Russian documentary once where half the shots were blurred and overexposed because the KGB attacked the negative with X rays. Maybe this movie was put through an MRI scan. Curiously, the signifiers have survived, but not the signified. Characters set up big revelations and then forget to make them. And the long, murky night sequence looks like it was shot, pointlessly, with the green-light NightShot feature on a consumer video camera.

One of the peculiarities of television of the future is a device titled "Instant Global Rating." This supplies a digital readout of how many viewers there are (except on North American cable systems, of course). Whenever something tremendously exciting happens during a game, the rating immediately goes up. This means that people who were not watching somehow sensed they had just missed something amazing, and responded by tuning in. When *Rollerball* finally does get a North American cable deal, I predict the ratings will work in reverse.

The Rookie ★ ★
G, 129 m., 2002

Dennis Quaid (Jimmy), Rachel Griffiths (Lorri), Jay Hernandez ("Wack" Campos), Beth Grant (Olline), Brian Cox (Jim Sr.). Directed by John Lee Hancock and produced by Gordon Gray, Mark Ciardi, and Mark Johnson. Screenplay by Mike Rich.

The Rookie combines two reliable formulas: the Little Team That Goes to State and the Old-Timer Who Realizes His Youthful Dream. When two genres approach exhaustion, sometimes it works if they prop each other up. Not this time, not when we also get the Dad Who Can't Be Pleased However Hard His Son Tries, and the Wife Who Wants Her Husband to Have His Dream but Has a Family to Raise. The movie is so resolutely cobbled together out of older movies that it even uses a totally unnecessary prologue, just because it seems obligatory.

We begin in the wide open spaces of west Texas, where wildcat oil prospectors have a strike in the 1920s. The little town of Big Lake springs up, and in the shadow of one of the rickety old derricks a baseball diamond is scratched out of the dust. Supporting this enterprise, we're told, is St. Rita, "patron saint of hopeless causes." I thought that was St. Jude, but no, the two saints share the same billing. Certainly St. Rita is powerful enough to deal with baseball, but it would take both saints in harness to save this movie.

The story leaps forward in time to the recent past, as we follow a career navy officer (Brian Cox) who moves with his family from town to town while his son, little Jimmy, pounds his baseball mitt and is always getting yanked off his latest team just when it starts to win.

Now it's the present and the Little Leaguer has grown up into big Jimmy (Dennis Quaid), coach of the Big Lake High School baseball team. He's married to Lorri (Rachel Griffiths), they have an eight-year-old, and he has all but forgotten his teenage dream of pitching in the majors. By my calculations thirty years have passed, but his dad, Jim Sr., looks exactly the same age as he did when Jimmy was eight, except for some gray hair, of course. Brian Cox is one of those actors like Walter Matthau who has always been about the same age. I was so misled by the prologue I thought maybe Jim and Jim Sr. were connected in some way with the wildcatters and St. Rita, but apparently the entire laborious prologue is meant simply to establish that baseball was played in Big Lake before Jimmy and Lorri moved there.

All movies of this sort are huggable. They're about nice people, played by actors we like, striving for goals we can identify with. Dennis Quaid is just plain one of the nicest men in the movies, with that big goofy smile, but boy, can he look mean when he narrows his eyes and squints down over his shoulder from the pitching mound.

Faithful readers will know that I have a special regard for Rachel Griffiths, that most intelligent and sexy actress, but what a price she has had to pay for her stardom on HBO's *Six Feet Under.* Instead of starring roles in small, good movies *(My Son the Fanatic, Hilary and Jackie, Me Myself I),* she now gets the big bucks on TV, but her work schedule requires her to take supporting roles in movies that can be slotted into her free time. So here she plays the hero's faithful wife, stirring a pot and buttoning the little boy's shirt, her scenes basically limited to pillow talk, telephone conversations, sitting in the stands and, of course, presenting the hero with the choice of his dream or his family.

The high school team comes from such a small school that, as nearly as I can see, they have only nine members and no subs (Jimmy's eight-year-old is the batboy). It's captained by "Wack" Campos (Jay Hernandez), who is good in the standard role of coach's alter ego. Every single game in the movie, without exception, goes according to the obvious demands of the screenplay, but there is a surprise development when Jimmy pitches batting practice and they're amazed by the speed he still has on his fastball. They make him a deal: If they get to district finals or even state, Jimmy has to try out for the majors again. Is there anyone alive who can hear these lines and not predict what will happen between then and the end of the movie?

The Rookie is comforting, even soothing, to those who like the old songs best. It may confuse those who, because they like the characters, think it is good. It is not good. It is skillful. Learning the difference between good movies and skillful ones is an early step in becoming a moviegoer. *The Rookie* demonstrates that a skillful movie need not be good. It is also true that a good movie need not be skillful, but it takes a heap of moviegoing to figure that one out. And pray to St. Rita.

The Royal Tenenbaums ★ ★ ★ ½
R, 103 m., 2001

Gene Hackman (Royal Tenenbaum), Anjelica Huston (Etheline Tenenbaum), Ben Stiller (Chas Tenenbaum), Gwyneth Paltrow (Margot Helen Tenenbaum), Luke Wilson (Richie Tenenbaum), Owen Wilson (Eli Cash), Danny Glover (Henry Sherman), Bill Murray (Raleigh St. Clair), Seymour Cassel (Dusty), Kumar Pallana (Pagoda), Alec Baldwin (Narrator). Directed by Wes Anderson and produced by Anderson, Barry Mendel, and Scott Rudin. Screenplay by Anderson and Owen Wilson.

Wes Anderson's *The Royal Tenenbaums* exists on a knife edge between comedy and sadness. There are big laughs, and then quiet moments when we're touched. Sometimes we grin at the movie's deadpan audacity. The film doesn't want us to feel just one set of emotions. It's the story of a family that at times could have been created by P. G. Wodehouse, and at other times by John Irving. And it's proof that Wes Anderson and his writing partner, the actor Owen Wilson, have a gift of cockeyed genius.

The Tenenbaums occupy a big house in a kind of dreamy New York. It has enough rooms for each to hide and nurture a personality incompatible with the others. Royal Tenenbaum (Gene Hackman), the patriarch, left home

541

abruptly some years before and has been living in a hotel, on credit, ever since. There was never actually a divorce. His wife, Etheline (Anjelica Huston), remains at home with their three children, who were all child prodigies and have grown into adult neurotics. There's Chas (Ben Stiller), who was a financial whiz as a kid; Margot (Gwyneth Paltrow), who was adopted and won a big prize for writing a school play; and Richie (Luke Wilson), once a tennis champion.

All three come with various partners, children, and friends. The most memorable are Raleigh St. Clair (Bill Murray), a bearded intellectual who has been married to Margot for years but does not begin to know her; Eli Cash (Owen Wilson), who lived across the street, became like a member of the family, and writes best-selling Westerns that get terrible reviews; Henry Sherman (Danny Glover), who was Etheline's accountant for ten years until they suddenly realized they were in love; and such satellites as Pagoda (Kumar Pallana), Royal's faithful servant (who once in India tried to murder Royal and then rescued him from . . . himself), and the bellboy Dusty (Seymour Cassel), who impersonates a doctor when Royal fakes a fatal illness.

Trying to understand the way this flywheel comedy tugs at the heartstrings, I reflected that eccentricity often masks deep loneliness. All the Tenenbaums are islands entire of themselves. Consider that Margot has been a secret smoker since she was thirteen. Why bother? Nobody else in the family cares, and when they discover her deception they hardly notice. Her secrecy was part of her own strategy to stand outside the family, to have something that was her own.

One of the pleasures of the movie is the way it keeps us a little uncertain about how we should be reacting. It's like a guy who seems to be putting you on, and then suddenly reveals himself as sincere, so you're stranded out there with an inappropriate smirk. You can see this quality on-screen in a lot of Owen Wilson's roles—in the half-kidding, half-serious way he finds out just how far he can push people.

The movie's strategy of doubling back on its own emotions works mostly through the dialogue. Consider a sort of brilliant dinner-table conversation where Royal tells the family

he has cancer, they clearly don't believe him (or care), he says he wants to get to know them before he dies, the bitter Chas says he's not interested in that, and Royal pulls out all the stops by suggesting they visit their grandmother. Now watch how it works. Chas and Richie haven't seen her since they were six. Margot says piteously that she has never met her. Royal responds not with sympathy but with a slap at her adopted status: "She wasn't your real grandmother." See how his appeal turns on a dime into a cruel put-down?

Anderson's previous movies were *Bottle Rocket* (1996) and *Rushmore* (1998), both offbeat comedies, both about young people trying to outwit institutions. Anderson and the Wilson brothers met at the University of Texas, made their first film on a shoestring, have quickly developed careers, share a special talent. (That Owen Wilson could cowrite and star in this, and also star in the lugubrious *Behind Enemy Lines,* is one of the year's curiosities.) Like the Farrelly brothers, but kinder and gentler, they follow a logical action to its outrageous conclusion.

Consider, for example, what happens after Royal gets bounced out of his latest hotel and moves back home. His wife doesn't want him and Chas despises him (for stealing from his safety deposit box), so Royal stealthily moves in with a hospital bed, intravenous tubes, private medical care, and Seymour Cassel shaking his head over the prognosis. When this strategy is unmasked, he announces he wants to get to know his grandkids better—wants to teach them to take chances. So he instructs Richie's kids in shoplifting, playing in traffic, and throwing things at taxicabs.

The Royal Tenenbaums is at heart profoundly silly and loving. That's why it made me think of Wodehouse. It stands in amazement as the Tenenbaums and their extended family unveil one strategy after another to get attention, carve out space, and find love. It doesn't mock their efforts, dysfunctional as they are, because it understands them—and sympathizes.

Rugrats Go Wild! ★ ★

PG, 81 m., 2003

With the voices of: Michael Bell (Drew Pickles/Chaz Finster), Jodi Carlisle (Marianne Thornberry), Nancy Cartwright (Chuckie

Finster), Lacey Chabert (Eliza Thornberry), Melanie Chartoff (Didi Pickles), Cheryl Chase (Angelica C. Pickles), Tim Curry (Sir Nigel Thornberry), Elizabeth Daily (Tommy Pickles), Danielle Harris (Debbie Thornberry), Bruce Willis (Spike). Directed by John Eng and Norton Virgien and produced by Gabor Csupo and Arlene Klasky. Screenplay by Kate Boutilier.

The Rugrats meet the Thornberrys in *Rugrats Go Wild!* a merger of the two popular Nickelodeon franchises that confirms our suspicion that Angelica Pickles can shout down anybody, even Debbie Thornberry. The movie has so much shouting, indeed so much noise in general, that I pity parents who will have to listen to it again and again and again after the DVD comes home and goes into an endless loop. The most persuasive argument for the animation of Hayao Miyazaki is that it's sometimes quiet and peaceful.

In the movie, the Pickles family goes on a cruise—not on the magnificent ocean liner that's pulling out just as they arrive at the dock, but on a leaky gutbucket that soon runs into big trouble, as the movie sails into *Perfect Storm* territory with a wall of water that towers above them.

Marooned by the storm on a deserted island, they discover it isn't deserted when they stumble upon Debbie Thornberry sunning herself beside the family's luxury camper. Yes, the Wild Thornberrys are on the island to film a documentary, and Sir Nigel and family more or less rescue the Pickles family, not without many adventures. One intriguing development: Spike, the Pickles's dog, talks for the first time, thanks to the ability of little Eliza Thornberry to speak with animals. (Spike's voice is by Bruce Willis.)

I sat watching the movie and was at a loss for an entry point. Certainly this is not a film an adult would want to attend without a child; unlike *Finding Nemo*, for example, it doesn't play on two levels, but just on one: shrill, nonstop action. That doesn't mean it lacks humor and charm, just that it pitches itself on the level of the Nickelodeon show instead of trying to move it beyond the target audience.

That's what I think, anyway, but as an adult, am I qualified to judge this film? Not long ago I (and 80 percent of the other critics in America) disliked Eddie Murphy's *Daddy Day Care,*

only to be reprimanded by Al Neuharth, founder of *USA Today,* who wrote a column saying we critics were out of touch because he went with his children, aged five to twelve, and they liked it.

I offered Mr. Neuharth a list of a dozen other films his kids would probably like infinitely more, and which would also perhaps challenge and enlighten them, instead of simply bludgeoning them with sitcom slapstick. But on the off chance he was right, I took my grandsons, Emil, aged nine, and Taylor, age five, along with me to *Rugrats Go Wild!* and afterward asked them to rate it on a scale of one to ten.

They both put it at five. "Not as much fun as the TV show," said Emil. "Angelica didn't get to do as much funny stuff." What did they think about the Pickles family meeting the Thornberrys? They were unmoved, not to say indifferent.

My own feeling is that the film is one more assault on the notion that young American audiences might be expected to enjoy films with at least some subtlety and depth and pacing and occasional quietness. The filmmakers apparently believe their audience suffers from ADD, and so they supply breakneck action and screaming sound volumes at all times. That younger viewers may have developed ADD from a diet of this manic behavior on television is probably a fruitful field for study.

Note: The movie is presented in "Odorama." At most screenings, including the one I attended, audience members are given scratch-and-sniff cards with six scents, keyed to numbers that flash on the screen. We can smell strawberries, peanuts, tuna fish, etc. Scratching and sniffing, I determined that the root beer smells terrific, but the peanut butter has no discernible smell at all. The kids around me seemed pretty underwhelmed by this relic from the golden age of exploitation, which was last used by John Waters with his Polyester (1981).

The Rules of Attraction ★ ★
R, 110 m., 2002

James Van Der Beek (Sean Bateman), Shannyn Sossamon (Lauren Hynde), Ian Somerhalder (Paul Denton), Jessica Biel (Lara Holleran), Kip Pardue (Victor Johnson), Kate Bosworth (Kelly), Thomas Ian Nicholas (Mitchell Allen), Joel

Michaely (Raymond). Directed by Roger Avary and produced by Greg Shapiro. Screenplay by Avary, based on the novel by Bret Easton Ellis.

I did not like any of the characters in *The Rules of Attraction*. I cringe to write those words, because they imply a superficial approach to the film. Surely there are films where I hated the characters and admired the work? *In the Company of Men?* No, that gave me a victim to sympathize with. There is no entry portal in *The Rules of Attraction,* and I spent most of the movie feeling depressed by the shallow, selfish, greedy characters. I wanted to be at another party.

Leaving the movie, I reflected that my reaction was probably unfair. *The Rules of Attraction* was based on a novel by Bret Easton Ellis, and while life is too short to read one of his books while a single work of Conrad, Faulkner, or Bellow eludes me, I am familiar enough with his world (through the movies) to know that he agrees his characters are shallow, selfish, and greedy, although perhaps he bears them a certain affection, not least because they populate his books. So I went to see the movie a second time, and emerged with a more evolved opinion: *The Rules of Attraction* is a skillfully made movie about reprehensible people.

The writer-director is Roger Avary, who directed *Killing Zoe* and coauthored Quentin Tarantino's *Pulp Fiction.* (Whether he cast James Van Der Beek as his lead because he looks more like Tarantino than any other working actor, I cannot guess.) In all of his work Avary is fond of free movement up and down the time line, and here he uses an ingenious approach to tell the stories of three main characters who are involved in, I dunno, five or six pairings. He begins with an "End of the World" party at Camden College, the ultimate party school, follows a story thread, then rewinds and follows another. He also uses fast-forward brilliantly to summarize a European vacation in a few hilarious minutes.

The yo-yo time line works because we know, or quickly learn, who the characters are, but sometimes it's annoying, as when we follow one sex romp up to a certain point and then return to it later for the denouement. This style may at times reflect the confused state of mind of the characters, who attend a college where no studying of any kind is ever glimpsed, where the only faculty member in the movie is having an affair with an undergraduate, and where the improbable weekend parties would put the orgies at Hef's pad to shame.

The parties are a lapse of credibility. I cannot believe, for example, that large numbers of coeds would engage in topless lesbian breast play at a campus event, except in the inflamed imaginations of horny undergraduates. But assuming that they would: Is it plausible that the horny undergraduates wouldn't even *look* at them? Are today's undergraduate men so (choose one) blasé, politically correct, or emasculated that, surrounded by the enthusiastic foreplay of countless half-naked women, they would blandly carry on their conversations?

This is not to imply that *The Rules of Attraction* is in any sense a campus sex-romp comedy. There is comedy in it, but so burdened are the students by their heavy loads of alcoholism, depression, drug addiction, and bisexual promiscuity that one yearns for them to be given respite by that cliché of the 1960s, the gratuitous run through meadows and woods. These kids need fresh air.

In the movie, James Van Der Beek plays drug dealer Sean Bateman, who desperately wants to sleep with chic, elusive Lauren (Shannyn Sossamon). She once dated Paul (Ian Somerhalder), who is bisexual and who wants to sleep with Sean, who is straight, but right now if Lauren had her druthers she would bed Victor (Kip Pardue), who stars in the sped-up European trip and slept with half of Europe. (The sexual orientations of most of the major characters come down to: When they're not with the sex they love, they love the sex they're with.) Many but not all of these desired couplings take place, there are distractions from still other willing characters, and a sad suicide involving a character I will not divulge, except to say that when we see how miserable she was in flashbacks to various earlier events, we wonder why, on a campus where promiscuity is epidemic, she had the misfortune to be a one-guy woman.

Avary weaves his stories with zest and wicked energy, and finds a visual style that matches the emotional fragmentation. I have no complaints about the acting, and especially liked the way Shannyn Sossamon kept a kind of impertinent distance from some of the excesses. But by the end, I felt a sad indifference. These characters are not from life, and do not form into a useful fiction. Their excesses of sex and substance abuses are physically unwise, financially unlikely, and emotionally impossible. I do not censor their behavior, but lament the movie's fascination with it. They do not say and perhaps do not think anything interesting. The two other Bret Easton Ellis movies (*Less Than Zero* and *American Psycho*) offered characters who were considerably more intriguing. We had questions about them; they aroused our curiosity. The inhabitants of *The Rules of Attraction* are superficial and transparent. We know people like that, and hope they will get better. ☞

Rush Hour 2 ★ ½
PG-13, 120 m., 2001

Jackie Chan (Detective Inspector Lee), Chris Tucker (Detective James Carter), Chris Penn (Clive), Roselyn Sanchez (Isabella Molina), John Lone (Ricky Tan), Zhang Ziyi (Hu Li), Alan King (Steven Reign). Directed by Brett Ratner and produced by Roger Birnbaum, Jonathan Glickman, Arthur M. Sarkissian, and Jay Stern. Screenplay by Ross LaManna and Jeff Nathanson.

Rush Hour (1998) earned untold millions of dollars, inspiring this sequel. The first film was built on a comic relationship between Jackie Chan and Chris Tucker, as odd-couple cops from Hong Kong and Los Angeles. It was funny because hard work went into the screenplay and the stunts. It was not funny because Chris Tucker is funny whenever he opens his mouth—something he proves abundantly in *Rush Hour 2*, where his endless rants are like an anchor around the ankles of the humor.

Jackie Chan complained, I hear, that the Hollywood filmmakers didn't give him time to compose his usual elaborately choreographed stunts in *Rush Hour 2*, preferring shorter bursts of action. Too bad Brett Ratner, the director, didn't focus instead on shortening Tucker's dialogue scenes. Tucker plays an L.A. cop who, on the evidence of this movie, is a race-fixated

motormouth who makes it a point of being as loud, offensive, and ignorant as he possibly can be.

There is a belief among some black comics that audiences find it funny when they launch extended insults against white people (see also Chris Rock's embarrassing outburst in *Jay and Silent Bob*). My feeling is that audiences of any race find such scenes awkward and unwelcome; I've never heard laughter during them, but have sensed an uncomfortable alertness in the theater. Accusing complete strangers of being racist is aggressive, hostile, and not funny, something Tucker demonstrates to a painful degree in this movie—where the filmmakers apparently lacked the nerve to request him to dial down.

There's one scene that really grated: The Tucker character finds himself in a Vegas casino. He throws a wad of money on a craps table and is given a stack of $500 chips. He is offended: It is racist for the casino to give him $500 chips instead of $1,000 chips, the dealer doesn't think a black man can afford $1,000 a throw, etc. He goes on and on in a shrill tirade against the dealer (an uncredited Saul Rubinek, I think). The dealer answers every verbal assault calmly and firmly. What's extraordinary about this scene is how we identify with the dealer, and how manifestly the Tucker character is acting like the seven-letter word for "jerk." Rubinek wins the exchange.

The movie begins with Tucker and Jackie Chan going to Hong Kong on vacation after their adventures in the previous movie. Soon they're involved in a new case: A bomb has gone off in the American embassy, killing two people. Their investigation leads first to the leader of a local crime triad (John Lone) and then to an American Mr. Big (Alan King). Sex appeal is supplied by Roselyn Sanchez, as an undercover agent, and Zhang Ziyi, from *Crouching Tiger, Hidden Dragon*, as a martial arts fighter.

Jackie Chan is amazing as usual in the action sequences, and Zhang Ziyi has hand-to-hand combat with Chris Tucker in a scene of great energy. There are the usual Chan-style stunts, including one where the heroes dangle above city streets on a flexible bamboo pole. And a couple of those moments, over in a flash, where Chan combines grace, ability, and timing (in one, he slips through a teller's cage, and in another he seems to walk up a scaffolding). Given Chan's so-so command of English, it's ingenious to construct a sequence that silences him with a grenade taped inside his mouth.

But Tucker's scenes finally wear us down. How can a movie allow him to be so obnoxious and make no acknowledgment that his behavior is aberrant? In a nightclub run by Hong Kong gangsters, he jumps on a table and shouts, "Okay, all the triads and ugly women on one side, and all the fine women on the other." He is the quintessential Ugly American, and that's not funny. One rule all comedians should know, and some have to learn the hard way, is that *they* aren't funny—it's the material that gets the laughs. Another rule is that if you're the top dog on a movie set, everybody is going to pretend to laugh at everything you do, so anyone who tells you it's not that funny is trying to do you a favor.

Russian Ark ★ ★ ★ ★
NO MPAA RATING, 96 m., 2002

Sergey Dontsov (The Marquis), Mariya Kuznetsova (Catherine the Great), Leonid Mozgovoy (The Spy), Mikhail Piotrovsky (Himself), David Giorgobiani (Orbeli), Aleksandr Chaban (Boris Piotrovsky), Lev Yeliseyev (Himself), Oleg Khmelnitsky (Himself), Maksim Sergeyev (Peter the Great). Directed by Aleksandr Sokurov and produced by Andrey Deryabin, Jens Meuer, and Karsten Stöter. Screenplay by Anatoly Nikiforov, Boris Khaimsky, Svetlana Proskurina, and Sokurov.

Every review of *Russian Ark* begins by discussing its method. The movie consists of one unbroken shot lasting the entire length of the film, as a camera glides through the Hermitage, the repository of Russian art and history in St. Petersburg. The cinematographer, Tilman Buttner, using a Steadicam and high-definition digital technology, joined with some 2,000 actors in a high-wire act in which every mark and cue had to be hit without fail; there were two broken takes before the third time was the charm.

The subject of the film, which is written, directed, and (in a sense) hosted by Aleksandr Sokurov, is no less than three centuries of

Russian history. The camera doesn't merely take us on a guided tour of the art on the walls and in the corridors, but witnesses many visitors who came to the Hermitage over the years. Apart from anything else, this is one of the best-sustained *ideas* I have ever seen on the screen. Sokurov reportedly rehearsed his all-important camera move again and again with the cinematographer, the actors, and the invisible sound and lighting technicians, knowing that the Hermitage would be given to him for only one precious day.

After a dark screen and the words "I open my eyes and I see nothing," the camera's eye opens upon the Hermitage and we meet the Marquis (Sergey Dontsov), a French nobleman who will wander through the art and the history as we follow him. The voice we heard, which belongs to the never-seen Sokurov, becomes a foil for the Marquis, who keeps up a running commentary. What we see is the grand sweep of Russian history in the years before the Revolution, and a glimpse of the grim times afterward.

It matters little, I think, if we recognize all of the people we meet on this journey; such figures as Catherine II and Peter the Great are identified (Catherine, like many another museum visitor, is searching for the loo), but some of the real people who play themselves, like Mikhail Piotrovsky, the current director of the Hermitage, work primarily as types. We overhear whispered conversations, see state functions, listen as representatives of the Shah apologize to Nicholas I for the killing of Russian diplomats, even see little flirtations.

And then, in a breathtaking opening-up, the camera enters a grand hall and witnesses a formal state ball. Hundreds of dancers, elaborately costumed and bejeweled, dance to the music of a symphony orchestra, and then the camera somehow seems to float through the air to the orchestra's stage and moves among the musicians. An invisible ramp must have been put into place below the camera frame for Buttner and his Steadicam to smoothly climb.

The film is a glorious experience to witness, not least because, knowing the technique and understanding how much depends on every moment, we almost hold our breath. How tragic if an actor had blown a cue or Buttner had stumbled five minutes from the end! The long, long single shot reminds me of a scene in *Nostalgia,* the 1982 film by Russia's Andrei Tarkovsky, in which a man obsessively tries to cross and recross a littered and empty pool while holding a candle that he does not want to go out: The point is not the action itself, but its duration and continuity.

It will be enough for most viewers, as it was for me, to simply view *Russian Ark* as an original and beautiful idea. But Stanley Kauffmann raises an inarguable objection in his *New Republic* review, when he asks, "What is there intrinsically in the film that would grip us if it had been made—even excellently made—in the usual edited manner?" If it were not one unbroken take, if we were not continuously mindful of its 96 minutes—what then? "We sample a lot of scenes," he writes, "that in themselves have no cumulation, no self-contained point.... Everything we see or hear engages us only as part of a directorial tour de force."

This observation is true, and deserves an answer, and I think my reply would be that *Russian Ark,* as it stands, is enough. I found myself in a reverie of thoughts and images, and sometimes, as my mind drifted to the barbarity of Stalin and the tragic destiny of Russia, the scenes of dancing became poignant and ironic. It is not simply what Sokurov shows about Russian history, but what he does not show—doesn't need to show, because it shadows all our thoughts of that country. Kauffmann is right that if the film had been composed in the ordinary way out of separate shots, we would question its purpose. But it is not, and the effect of the unbroken flow of images (experimented with in the past by directors like Hitchcock and Max Ophuls) is uncanny. If cinema is sometimes dreamlike, then every edit is an awakening. *Russian Ark* spins a daydream made of centuries. ☞

S

Safe Conduct ★ ★ ★ ★

NO MPAA RATING, 170 m., 2003

Jacques Gamblin (Jean Devaivre), Denis Podalydès (Jean Aurenche), Charlotte Kady (Suzanne Raymond), Marie Desgranges (Simone Devaivre), Ged Marlon (Jean-Paul Le Chanois), Philippe Morier-Genoud (Maurice Tourneur), Laurent Schilling (Charles Spaak), Maria Pitarresi (Reine Sorignal). Directed by Bertrand Tavernier and produced by Frédéric Bourboulon and Alain Sarde. Screenplay by Jean Cosmos and Tavernier, based on the book by Jean Devaivre.

More than 200 films were made in France during the Nazi Occupation, most of them routine, a few of them good, but none of them, Bertrand Tavernier observes, anti-Semitic. This despite the fact that anti-Semitism was not unknown in the French films of the 1930s. Tavernier's Safe Conduct tells the story of that curious period in French film history through two central characters, a director and a writer, who made their own accommodations while working under the enemy.

The leading German-controlled production company, Continental, often censored scenes it objected to, but its mission was to foster the illusion of life as usual during the Occupation; it would help French morale, according to this theory, if French audiences could see new French films, and such stars as Michel Simon and Danielle Darrieux continued to work.

Tavernier considers the period through the lives of two participants, the assistant director Jean Devaivre (Jacques Gamblin) and the writer Jean Aurenche (Denis Podalydès). The film opens with a flurry of activity at the hotel where Aurenche is expecting a visit from an actress; the proprietor sends champagne to the room, although it is cold and the actress would rather have tea. Aurenche is a compulsive womanizer who does what he can in a passive-aggressive way to avoid working for the Germans while not actually landing in jail. Devaivre works enthusiastically for Continental as a cover for his activities in the French Resistance.

Other figures, some well known to lovers of French cinema, wander through: We see Simon so angry at the visit of a Nazi "snoop" that he cannot remember his lines, and Charles Spaak (who wrote The Grand Illusion in 1937) thrown into a jail cell, but then, when his screenwriting skills are needed, negotiating for better food, wine, and cigarettes in order to keep working while behind bars.

Like Francois Truffaut's The Last Metro (1980), the movie questions the purpose of artistic activity during wartime. But Truffaut's film was more melodramatic, confined to a single theater company and its strategies and deceptions, while Tavernier is more concerned with the entire period of history.

The facts of the time seem constantly available just beneath the veneer of fiction, and sometimes burst through, as in a remarkable aside about Jacques Dubuis, Devaivre's brother-in-law; after he was arrested as a Resistance member, the film tells us, Devaivre's wife never saw her brother again—except once, decades later, as an extra in a French film of the period. We see the moment in a film clip, as the long-dead man collects tickets at a theater. There was debate within the film community about collaborating with the Nazis, and some, like Devaivre, risked contempt for their cooperative attitude because they could not reveal their secret work for the Resistance. Tavernier shows him involved in a remarkable adventure, one of those wartime stories so unlikely they can only be true. Sent home from the set with a bad cold, he stops by the office and happens upon the key to the office of a German intelligence official who works in the same building. He steals some papers, and soon, to his amazement, finds himself flying to England on a clandestine flight to give the papers and his explanation to British officials. They fly him back; a train schedule will not get him to Paris in time, and so he rides his bicycle all the way, still coughing and sneezing, to get back to work. Everyone thinks he has spent the weekend in bed.

You would imagine a film like this would be greeted with rapture in France, but no. The leading French film magazine, Cahiers du Cinema, has long scorned the filmmakers of this older generation as makers of mere "quality," and interprets Tavernier's work as an attack on the New Wave generation that replaced them.

This is astonishingly wrongheaded, since Tavernier (who worked as a publicist for such New Wavers as Godard and Chabrol) is interested in his characters not in terms of the cinema they produced but because of the conditions they survived, and the decisions they made.

Writing in the *New Republic,* Stanley Kauffmann observes: "Those who now think that these film people should have stopped work in order to impede the German state must also consider whether doctors and plumbers and teachers should also have stopped work for the same reason." Well, some would say yes. But that could lead to death, a choice it is easier to urge upon others than to make ourselves.

What Tavernier does here is celebrate filmmakers who did the best they could under the circumstances. Tavernier knew many of these characters; Aurenche and Pierre Bost, a famous screenwriting team, wrote his first film, *The Clockmaker of St. Paul,* and Aurenche worked on several others. In the film's closing moments, we hear Tavernier's own voice in narration, saying that at the end of his life, Aurenche told him he would not have done anything differently.

The Safety of Objects ★ ★

R, 121 m., 2003

Glenn Close (Esther Gold), Dermot Mulroney (Jim Train), Jessica Campbell (Julie Gold), Patricia Clarkson (Annette Jennings), Joshua Jackson (Paul Gold), Moira Kelly (Susan Train), Robert Klein (Howard Gold), Timothy Olyphant (Randy), Alex House (Jake Train), Mary Kay Place (Helen). Directed by Rose Troche and produced by Dorothy Berwin and Christine Vachon. Screenplay by Troche, based on stories by A. M. Homes.

Side by side on a shady suburban street, in houses like temples to domestic gods, three families marinate in misery. They know one another, but what they don't realize is how their lives are secretly entangled. We're intended to pity them, although their troubles are so densely plotted they skirt the edge of irony; this is a literate soap opera in which beautiful people have expensive problems and we wouldn't mind letting them inherit some undistinguished problems of our own.

To be sure, one of the characters has a problem we don't envy. That would be Paul Gold (Joshua Jackson), a bright and handsome teenager who has been in a coma since an accident. Before that he'd been having an affair with the woman next door, Annette Jennings (Patricia Clarkson), so there were consolations in his brief conscious existence.

Now his mother, Esther (Glenn Close), watches over him, reads to him, talks to him, trusts he will return to consciousness. His father, Howard (Robert Klein), doesn't participate in this process, having written off his heir as a bad investment, but listen to how Esther talks to Howard: "You never even put your eyes on him. How do you think that makes him feel?" The dialogue gets a laugh from the heartless audience, but is it intended as funny, thoughtless, ironic, tender, or what? The movie doesn't give us much help in answering that question.

In a different kind of movie, we would be deeply touched by the mother's bedside vigil. In a *very* different kind of movie, like Pedro Almodóvar's *Talk to Her,* which is about two men at the bedsides of the two comatose women they love, we would key in to the weird-sad tone that somehow rises above irony into a kind of sincere, melodramatic excess. But here—well, we know the Glenn Close character is sincere, but we can't tell what the film thinks about her, and we suspect it may be feeling a little more superior to her than it has a right to.

Written and directed by Rose Troche, based on stories by A. M. Homes, *The Safety of Objects* hammers more nails into the undead corpse of the suburban dream. Movies about the Dread Suburbs are so frightening that we wonder why everyone doesn't flee them, like the crowds in the foreground of Japanese monster movies.

The Safety of Objects travels its emotional wastelands in a bittersweet, elegiac mood. We meet a lawyer named Jim Train (Dermot Mulroney), who is passed over for partnership at his law firm, walks out in a rage, and lacks the nerve to tell his wife, Susan (Moira Kelly). Neither one of them knows their young child, Jake (Alex House), is conducting an affair—yes, an actual courtship—with a Barbie doll.

Next door is Helen (Mary Kay Place), who, if she is really going to spend the rest of her life picking up stray men for quick sex, should develop more of a flair. She comes across as desperate, although there's a nice scene where she

549

calls the bluff of a jerk who succeeds in picking her up—and is left with the task of explaining why, if he really expected to bring someone home, his house is such a pigpen.

Let's see who else lives on the street. Annette, the Clarkson character, makes an unmistakable pitch to a handyman, who gets the message, rejects it, but politely thanks her for the offer. Annette is pathetic about men: She forgives her ex-husband anything, even when he skips his alimony payments, and lets a child get away with calling her a loser because she can't afford summer camp.

What comes across is that all of these people are desperately unhappy, are finding no human consolation or contact at home, are fleeing to the arms of strangers, dolls, or the comatose, and place their trust, if the title is to be believed, in the safety of objects. I don't think that means objects will protect them. I think it means they can't hurt them.

Strewn here somewhere are the elements of an effective version of this story—an *Ice Storm* or *American Beauty,* even a *My New Gun.* But Troche's tone is so relentlessly, depressingly monotonous that the characters seem trapped in a narrow emotional range. They live out their miserable lives in one lachrymose sequence after another, and for us there is no relief. *The Safety of Objects* is like a hike through the swamp of despond, with ennui sticking to our shoes.

The Salton Sea ★ ★ ★

R, 103 m., 2002

Val Kilmer (Danny/Tom), Vincent D'Onofrio (Pooh-Bear), Adam Goldberg (Kujo), Luis Guzman (Quincy), Doug Hutchison (Morgan), Anthony LaPaglia (Garcetti), Glenn Plummer (Bobby), Peter Sarsgaard (Jimmy the Finn), Deborah Kara Unger (Colette). Directed by D. J. Caruso and produced by Ken Aguado, Frank Darabont, Eriq LaSalle, and Butch Robinson. Screenplay by Tony Gayton.

The Salton Sea is a low-life black comedy drawing inspiration from *Memento, Pulp Fiction,* and those trendy British thrillers about drug lads. It contains one element of startling originality: its bad guy, nicknamed Pooh-Bear and played by Vincent D'Onofrio in a great, weird,

demented giggle of a performance; imagine a Batman villain cycled through the hallucinations of *Requiem for a Dream.*

The movie opens with what looks like a crash at the intersection of film and *noir:* Val Kilmer sits on the floor and plays a trumpet, surrounded by cash, photos, and flames. He narrates the film and makes a laundry list of biblical figures (Judas, the prodigal son) he can be compared with. As we learn about the murder of his wife and the destruction of his life, I was also reminded of Job.

Kilmer plays Danny Parker, also known as Tom Van Allen; his double identity spans a life in which he is both a jazz musician and a meth middleman, doing speed himself, inhabiting the dangerous world of speed freaks ("tweakers") and acting as an undercover agent for the cops. His life is so arduous we wonder, not for the first time, why people go to such extraordinary efforts to get and use the drugs that make them so unhappy. He doesn't use to get high, but to get from low back to bearable.

The plot involves the usual assortment of lowlifes, scum, killers, bodyguards, dealers, pathetic women, two-timing cops, and strung-out addicts, all employing Tarantinian dialogue about the flotsam of consumer society (you'd be surprised to learn what you might find under Bob Hope on eBay). Towering over them, like a bloated float in a nightmarish Thanksgiving parade, is Pooh-Bear, a drug dealer who lives in a fortified retreat in the desert and brags about the guy who shorted him $11 and got his head clamped in a vise while his brains were removed with a handsaw.

D'Onofrio is a gifted actor and his character performances have ranged from Orson Welles to Abbie Hoffman to the twisted killer with the bizarre murder devices in *The Cell.* Nothing he has done quite approaches Pooh-Bear, an overweight good ol' boy who uses his folksy accent to explain novel ways of punishing the disloyal, such as having their genitals eaten off by a rabid badger. He comes by his nickname because cocaine abuse has destroyed his nose, and he wears a little plastic job that makes him look like Pooh.

The Salton Sea is two movies fighting inside one screenplay. Val Kilmer's movie is about memory and revenge, and tenderness for the abused woman (Deborah Kara Unger) who lives across the hall in his fleabag hotel. Kilmer plays a fairly standard middleman between dealers who might kill him and cops who might betray him. But he sometimes visits a world that is essentially the second movie, a nightmarish comedy. Director D. J. Caruso and writer Tony Gayton *(Murder by Numbers)* introduce scenes with images so weird they're funny to begin with, and then funnier when they're explained. Consider Pooh-Bear's hobby of restaging the Kennedy assassination with pet pigeons in model cars. Note the little details like the pink pillbox hat. Then listen to his driver/bodyguard ask what "JFK" stands for.

On the basis of this film, meth addiction is such a debilitating illness that it's a wonder its victims have the energy for the strange things the screenplay puts them up to. We meet, for example, a dealer named Bobby (Glenn Plummer), whose girlfriend's writhing legs extend frantically from beneath the mattress he sits on, while he toys with a compressed-air spear gun. Bobby looks like a man who has earned that good night's sleep.

The Salton Sea is all pieces and no coherent whole. Maybe life on meth is like that. The plot does finally explain itself, like a dislocated shoulder popping back into place, but then the plot is off the shelf; only the characters and details set the movie aside from its stablemates. I liked it because it was so endlessly, grotesquely, inventive: Watching it, I pictured Tarantino throwing a stick into a swamp, and the movie swimming out through the muck, retrieving it, and bringing it back with its tail wagging.

The Santa Clause 2 ★ ★ ★

G, 95 m., 2002

Tim Allen (Scott/Santa), Judge Reinhold (Neil), Wendy Crewson (Laura Miller), Elizabeth Mitchell (Carol Newman), David Krumholtz (Bernard), Eric Lloyd (Charlie Calvin), Spencer Breslin (Curtis), Liliana Mumy (Lucy). Directed by Michael Lembeck and produced by Robert F. Newmyer, Brian Reilly, and Jeffrey Silver. Screenplay by Don Rhymer, Cinco Paul, Ken Daurio, Ed Decter, and John J. Strauss.

There ain't no sanity clause!
—Chico Marx

True, but there is a *Santa Clause 2*, which requires that Santa get married or else. This information is revealed at the North Pole at the worst possible time, during the pre-Christmas manufacturing rush, when air force listening planes hear what sounds like "tiny hammers" from beneath the snow. The current occupant of the Santa suit is happy supervising his elves and perfecting his chimney-craft, when he's informed of a loophole in his contract: If he doesn't produce a Mrs. Claus in twenty-eight days, he'll stop being Santa and (I'm not real sure about this) the office may even entirely disappear, casting the world's children into gloom.

Already, Santa is thinner, the red suit looks baggy, and the white beard seems to be shedding. The outlook is grim. We recognize Santa from *The Santa Clause*, the 1994 movie that explained how he got the job in the first place. As you may (or very likely may not) recall, Scott Calvin (Tim Allen) was a divorced man who, in attempting to join in the holiday spirit, accidentally . . . well, killed Santa Claus. And then found a card informing him that now *he* was Santa Claus.

In the years that have passed, Scott's ex-wife, Laura (Wendy Crewson), and her nice new husband, Neil (Judge Reinhold), have continued to raise Scott's son, Charlie, but now the kid is involved in a high school graffiti prank and the elves have to break the news to Santa: Charlie has switched lists, from "nice" to "naughty." In a panic, Scott/Santa flies back home to counsel his son and perhaps find a wife, while the North Pole is put under the command of a cloned Santa who soon uses toy soldiers to stage a military coup and establish a dictatorship.

Santa Clause 2 is more of the same tinsel-draped malarkey that made the original film into a big hit, but it's more engaging, assured, and funny, and I like it more. The first movie seemed too desperately cheery; this one has a nice acerbic undertone, even though there is indeed a romance in the works for Santa and Principal Newman (Elizabeth Mitchell), whose experience with corridor passes may come in handy if she has to supervise millions of elves.

The movie is not a special-effects extravaganza like *The Grinch*, but in a way that's a relief. It's more about charm and silliness than about great, hulking, multimillion-dollar high-tech effects. The North Pole looks only a little more elaborate than a department store window, the Clone Santa's troops look like refugees from the March of the Wooden Soldiers, and Santa's mode of transportation is a reindeer named Comet who is not the epitome of grace.

One new touch this time is the Board Meeting of Legendary Characters, which Santa chairs, with members including the Sandman, the Tooth Fairy, Mother Nature, the Easter Bunny, etc., many of them played by well-known actors I will leave you to discover for yourself. I suppose it makes sense that all of these characters would exist in the same universe, and when the Tooth Fairy saves the day, it is through the film's profound understanding of the rules of tooth fairydom.

I almost liked the original *Santa Clause,* but wrote that "despite its charms, the movie didn't push over the top into true inspiration." Now here is *The Santa Clause 2,* which kind of does push over the top, especially with the Clone Santa subplot, and is all-around a better film, although I believe that any universe that includes the Tooth Fairy and the Sandman could easily accommodate, and benefit from, the Marx brothers.   ☞

Save the Last Dance ★ ★ ★
PG-13, 112 m., 2001

Julia Stiles (Sara Johnson), Sean Patrick Thomas (Derek Reynolds), Terry Kinney (Roy), Kerry Washington (Chenille Reynolds), Fredro Starr (Malakai), Vince Green (Snookie), Bianca Lawson (Nikki), Marcello Robinson (Wonk). Directed by Thomas Carter and produced by Robert W. Cort and David Madden. Screenplay by Duane Adler and Cheryl Edwards.

Save the Last Dance begins with standard material but doesn't settle for it. The setup promises clichés, but the development is intelligent, the characters are more complicated than we expect, and the ending doesn't tie everything up in a predictable way. Above all, this is a movie where the characters ask the same questions we do: They're as smart about themselves as we are.

As the film opens, we meet Sara (Julia Stiles),

a morose high school girl on a train. Flashbacks fill us in. She was a promising dancer with an audition at Julliard, but her mother was killed in an accident while driving to see her daughter dance. Now there's no money for school; Sara has lost her comfortable suburban existence and is coming to live with her father, Roy (Terry Kinney), a musician who lives in a walk-up flat in a gritty Chicago neighborhood. Roy is not unfriendly, but isn't the parent type.

The students at Sara's high school are mostly African-American, but as we notice this, we notice something else: The movie doesn't fall into ancient clichés about racial tension, the school is not painted as some kind of blackboard jungle, and the students are not electrified by the arrival of—gasp!—a white girl. They have more important things to think about.

Sara is befriended by a girl named Chenille (Kerry Washington), who shows her how easy it is to get your bag stolen if you leave it untended. In class, she notices Derek (Sean Patrick Thomas), whose comments show he's smart. She's taken to a club on Friday night, dances with Derek (who turns out to be Chenille's brother), and starts to like him. Eventually it becomes a romance, but this is not your basic high school love story, and includes dialogue like, "We spend more time defending our relationship than actually having one."

Derek's best friend is Malakai (Fredro Starr). They've been in trouble together, and Malakai once pulled him out of a situation that could have destroyed his life. Malakai is a petty thief and a gang member; Derek is on a different track (he's just won a scholarship to Georgetown), but loyalty tugs at him when Malakai wants him to come along as backup at a potentially fatal encounter. Derek's choice, and the way the episode ends, may surprise you.

Meanwhile, Derek and Sara dance together—not just at the club, but in a deserted building where he shows her an urban style of dance, and learns of her passion for ballet. All of this is interesting because it is not simply presented as courtship, but as two young people seriously curious about dance. Their romance, when it develops, doesn't show that love is blind, but suggests that it sees very well indeed; the movie doesn't simple-mindedly applaud interracial relationships, and Sara gets bitterly criticized by Derek's sister Chenille: "You come and take one of the few decent men left after drugs, jail, and drive-bys." That overstates the case; there are lots of decent men left, but we understand how she feels.

Do you know who Julia Stiles is? She's one of the most talented of the emerging generation of actresses, although not yet a major star. Born in 1981, acting since she was eleven, she was Ethan Hawke's Ophelia in the modern-dress 2000 version of *Hamlet,* and plays the local teenager who inflames Alec Baldwin in David Mamet's *State and Main* (she was also Freddie Prinze Jr.'s squeeze in the less-than-brilliant *Down to You*). Here she is good in ways that may not be immediately apparent, as when she jockeys for personal space with her bohemian bachelor father, and likes the way she can talk with Derek (ever notice how many teenage lovers in the movies have nothing to say to each other except comments driven directly by the mechanics of the plot?).

Sean Patrick Thomas is good, too, especially in Derek's scenes with Malakai. We see the pull of loyalty struggling with the wisdom of common sense, as Malakai tries to convince him to head into trouble, and Derek fights between his instincts and his intelligence. The movie was directed by Thomas Carter *(Swing Kids, Metro),* who seems determined to let this be the story of these specific characters and not just an exercise in genre. The movie's awake. It surprises you. You can see Derek and Sara thinking. For them, romance is not the end of the story. Their lives are ahead of them. They're going to college. They have plans. Maybe they'll figure in each other's plans. They'll see. You need a lot of luck if you plan to spend your life with the first person you fall in love with in high school.

Saving Silverman ½★
PG-13, 90 m., 2001

Jason Biggs (Darren Silverman), Steve Zahn (Wayne Le Fessier), Jack Black (J. D. McNugent), Amanda Peet (Judith Snodgrass-Fessbeggler), Amanda Detmer (Sandy Perkus), R. Lee Ermey (Coach), Neil Diamond (Himself). Directed by Dennis Dugan and produced by Neal H. Moritz. Screenplay by Greg DePaul and Hank Nelken.

Saving Silverman is so bad in so many different ways that perhaps you should see it, as an example of the lowest slopes of the bell-shaped curve. This is the kind of movie that gives even its defenders fits of desperation.

Consider my friend James Berardinelli, the best of the Web-based critics. No doubt ten days of oxygen deprivation at the Sundance Film Festival helped inspire his three-star review, in which he reports optimistically, "*Saving Silverman* has its share of pratfalls and slapstick moments, but there's almost no flatulence." Here's a critical rule of thumb: You know you're in trouble when you're reduced to praising a movie for its absence of fart jokes, and have to add "almost."

The movie is a male-bonding comedy in which three friends since grade school, now allegedly in their early twenties but looking in two cases suspiciously weathered for anyone under a hard-living thirty-two, are threatened by a romance. Darren Silverman (Jason Biggs), Wayne Le Fessier (Steve Zahn), and J. D. McNugent (Jack Black) grew up together sharing a common passion for the works of Neil Diamond; their sidewalk band, the Diamonds, performs his songs and then passes the hat.

The band is broken up, alas, when Darren is captured by Judith Snodgrass-Fessbeggler (Amanda Peet), a blonde man-eater who immediately bans his friends and starts transforming him into a broken and tamed possession. "He's my puppet and I'm his puppet master!" she declares, proving that she is unfamiliar with the word *mistress,* which does not come as a surprise. In a movie so desperately in need of laughs, it's a mystery why the filmmakers didn't drag Ms. Snodgrass-Fessbeggler's parents onstage long enough to explain their decision to go with the hyphenated last name.

Wayne and J.D. concoct a desperate scheme to save Darren from marriage. They kidnap Judith, convince Darren she is dead, and arrange for him to meet the original love of his life, Sandy Perkus (Amanda Detmer), who is now studying to be a nun. She hasn't yet taken her vows, especially the one of chastity, and is a major babe in her form-fitting novice's habit.

I was going to write that the funniest character in the movie is the boys' former high school coach (R. Lee Ermey, a former marine drill sergeant). It would be more accurate to say the same character would be funny in another movie, but is stopped cold by this one, even though the screenplay tries (when the boys ask Coach what to do with the kidnapped Judith, he replies, "kill her").

The lads don't idolize Neil Diamond merely in theory, but in the flesh, as well. Yes, Diamond himself appears in the film, kids himself, and sings a couple of songs. As a career decision, this ranks somewhere between being a good sport and professional suicide. Perhaps he should have reflected that the director, Dennis Dugan, has directed two Adam Sandler movies (both, it must be said, better than this).

Saving Silverman is Jason Biggs's fourth appearance in a row in a dumb sex comedy (in descending order of quality, they are *American Pie, Boys and Girls,* and *Loser*). It is time for him to strike out in a new direction; the announcement that he will appear in *American Pie II* does not seem to promise that.

Steve Zahn and Jack Black are, in the right movies, splendid comedy actors; Zahn was wonderful in *Happy, Texas,* and Jack Black stole his scenes in *High Fidelity* and *Jesus' Son.* Here they have approximately the charm of Wilson, the soccer ball. Amanda Peet and Amanda Detmer do no harm, although Peet is too nice to play a woman this mean. Lee Ermey is on a planet of his own. As for Neil Diamond, *Saving Silverman* is his first appearance in a fiction film since *The Jazz Singer* (1980), and one can only marvel that he waited twenty years to appear in a second film, and found one even worse than his first one.

Say It Isn't So ★
R, 93 m., 2001

Chris Klein (Gilly Noble), Heather Graham (Jo Wingfield), Orlando Jones (Dig McCaffey), Sally Field (Valdine Wingfield), Richard Jenkins (Walter Wingfield), John Rothman (Larry), Jack Plotnick (Leon), Eddie Cibrian (Jack Mitchelson). Directed by James B. Rogers and produced by Bobby Farrelly, Peter Farrelly, and Bradley Thomas. Screenplay by Peter Gaulke and Gerry Swallow.

Comedy characters can't be successfully em-barrassed for more than a few seconds at a time. Even then, it's best if they don't know what they've done wrong—if the joke's on them, and they don't get it. The "hair gel" scenes in *There's Something About Mary* are a classic example of embarrassment done right. *Say It Isn't So,* on the other hand, keeps a character embarrassed in scene after scene, until he becomes an . . . embarrassment. The movie doesn't understand that embarrassment comes in a sudden painful flush of realization; drag it out, and it's not embarrassment anymore, but public humiliation, which is a different condition, and not funny.

The movie stars Heather Graham and Chris Klein as Jo and Gilly, a hairdresser and a dog-catcher who fall deeply in love and then discover they are brother and sister. Jo flees town to marry a millionaire jerk. Gilly lingers behind in public disgrace until he discovers they are not related after all. But since Jo's family wants her to marry the rich guy, everybody conspires to keep Gilly away. The movie tries for a long-running gag based on the fact that everybody in town mocks Gilly because he slept with his alleged sister. They even write rude remarks in the dust on his truck. This is not funny but merely repetitive.

The movie was produced by the Farrelly brothers, who in *There's Something About Mary* and *Kingpin* showed a finer understanding of the mechanics of comedy than they do here. *Say It Isn't So* was directed by James B. Rogers from a screenplay by Peter Gaulke and Gerry Swallow, who show they are students of Farrel-lyism but not yet graduates. They include obligatory elements like physical handicaps, sexual miscalculations, intestinal difficulties, and weird things done to animals, but few of the gags really work. They know the words but not the music.

Consider a scene in which Chris Klein, as Gilly, punches a cow and his arm becomes lodged in just that portion of the cow's anatomy where both Gilly and the cow would least hope to find it. I can understand intellectually that this could be funny. But to be funny, the character would have to have a great deal invested in *not* appearing like the kind of doofus who would pull such a stunt. Gilly has been established as such a simpleton he has nothing to lose. The cow scene is simply one more cross for him to bear. There is in the movie a legless pilot (Orlando Jones) who prides himself on his heroic aerial abilities. If he had gotten stuck in the cow and been pulled legless down the street—now that would have been funny. Tasteless, yes, and cruel. But not tiresome.

That leads us to another of the movie's miscalculations. Its characters are not smart enough to be properly embarrassed. To be Jo or Gilly is already to be beyond embarrassment, since they wake up already clueless. The genius of *There's Something About Mary* and *Kingpin* was that the characters played by Ben Stiller and Woody Harrelson were smart, clever, played the angles—and still got disgraced. To pick on Gilly and Jo is like shooting fish in a barrel.

Chris Klein's character seems like someone who never gets the joke, who keeps smiling bravely as if everyone can't be laughing at him. We feel sorry for him, which is fatal for a comedy. Better a sharp, edgy character who deserves his comeuppance. Heather Graham's Jo, whose principal character trait is a push-up bra, isn't really engaged by the plot at all, but is blown hither and yon by the winds of fate.

That leaves three characters who are funny a lot of the time: Jo's parents, Valdine and Walter Wingfield (Sally Field and Richard Jenkins), and Dig McCaffey (Orlando Jones), the legless pilot. Valdine is a scheming, money-grubbing con woman who conceals from Gilly the fact that she is not his mother, so that Jo can marry the millionaire. And Walter is her terminally ill husband, communicating through an electronic voice amplifier, who bears a grudge against almost everyone he can see. These characters have the necessary meanness of spirit, and Dig McCaffey is so improbable, as a Jimi Hendrix look-alike, that he gets laughs by sheer incongruity.

On the TV clips, they show the scene where Jo gets so excited while cutting Gilly's hair that she takes a slice out of his ear. Since you have seen this scene, I will use it as an example of comic miscalculation. We see her scissors cutting through the flesh as they amputate an upper slope of his earlobe. This is not funny. It is cringe-inducing. Better to choose an angle where you can't see the actual cut at all, and

then have his entire ear spring loose. Go for the laugh with the idea, not the sight, of grievous injury. And instead of giving Gilly an operation to reattach the missing flesh, have him go through the entire movie without an ear (make a subtle joke by having him always present his good ear to the camera). There are sound comic principles at work here, which *Say It Isn't So* doesn't seem to understand.

Note: The end credits include the usual obligatory outtakes from the movie. These are unique in that they are clearly real and authentic, not scripted. They demonstrate what we have suspected: that real outtakes are rarely funny.

Scooby-Doo ★
PG, 87 m., 2002

Matthew Lillard (Norville "Shaggy" Rogers), Freddie Prinze Jr. (Fred Jones), Sarah Michelle Gellar (Daphne Blake), Linda Cardellini (Velma Dinkley), Rowan Atkinson (Mondavarious), Isla Fisher (Mary Jane), Andrew Bryniarski (Henchman). Directed by Raja Gosnell and produced by Charles Roven. Screenplay by James Gunn, based on characters created by Willam Hanna and Joseph Barbera.

I am not the person to review this movie. I have never seen the *Scooby-Doo* television program, and on the basis of the film I have no desire to start now. I feel no sympathy with any of the characters, I am unable to judge whether the live-action movie is a better idea than the all-cartoon TV approach, I am unable to generate the slightest interest in the plot, and I laughed not a single time, although I smiled more than once at the animated Scooby-Doo himself, an island of amusement in a wasteland of fecklessness.

What I can say, I think, is that a movie like this should in some sense be accessible to a nonfan like myself. I realize that every TV cartoon show has a cadre of fans that grew up with it, have seen every episode many times, and are alert to the nuances of the movie adaptation. But those people, however numerous they are, might perhaps find themselves going to a movie with people like myself—people who found, even at a very young age, that the world was filled with entertainment choices more stimulating than *Scooby-Doo.* If these people can't walk into the movie cold and understand it and get something out of it, then the movie has failed except as an in-joke.

As for myself, scrutinizing the screen helplessly for an angle of approach, one thing above all caught my attention: the director, Raja Gosnell, has a thing about big boobs. I say this not only because of the revealing low-cut costumes of such principals as Sarah Michelle Gellar, but also because of the number of busty extras and background players, who drift by in crowd scenes with what Russ Meyer used to call "cleavage cantilevered on the same principle that made the Sydney Opera House possible." Just as Woody Allen's *Hollywood Ending* is a comedy about a movie director who forges ahead even though he is blind, *Scooby-Doo* could have been a comedy about how a Russ Meyer clone copes with being assigned a live-action adaptation of a kiddie cartoon show.

I did like the dog. Scooby-Doo so thoroughly upstages the live actors that I cannot understand why Warner Bros. didn't just go ahead and make the whole movie animated. While Matthew Lillard, Sarah Michelle Gellar, and Linda Cardellini show pluck in trying to outlast the material, Freddie Prinze Jr. seems completely at a loss to account for his presence in the movie, and the squinchy-faced Rowan *(Mr. Bean)* Atkinson plays the villain as a private joke.

I pray, dear readers, that you not send me mail explaining the genius of *Scooby-Doo* and attacking me for being ill prepared to write this review. I have already turned myself in. Not only am I ill prepared to review the movie, but I venture to guess that anyone who is not literally a member of a *Scooby-Doo* fan club would be equally incapable. This movie exists in a closed universe, and the rest of us are aliens. The Internet was invented so that you can find someone else's review of *Scooby-Doo.* Start surfing.

The Score ★ ★ ★

R, 124 m., 2001

Robert De Niro (Nick Wells), Marlon Brando (Max Baron), Edward Norton (Jackie Teller/ Brian), Angela Bassett (Diane), Jamie Harrold (Stephen), Gary Farmer (Burt). Directed by Frank Oz and produced by Gary Foster, Lee Rich, and Peter Guber. Screenplay by Kario Salem, Lem Dobbs, and Scott Marshall Smith, based on a story by Daniel E. Taylor and Salem.

The Score is the best pure heist movie in recent years. It assembles three generations of great American actors and puts them to work on a break-in of awesome complexity, and has the patience to build real suspense instead of trying to substitute cheap thrills. Its climax is a sustained sequence involving three parallel lines of action, and we're reminded of the best heist movies of the past, like *Grand Slam* (1968), where everything depends on a meticulous and dangerous scenario.

The movie is above all an exercise of traditional craftsmanship. It is very hard to write and direct a screenplay like this, where there can't be loopholes, where the key scenes involve little dialogue and a lot of painstaking physical action, and where the plot surprises, when they come, have been prepared for and earned. Who would have guessed that Frank Oz, a onetime Muppeteer whose work has been mostly in comedy, could direct a *noir* caper that's so lean and involving?

The Score tells the kind of story that explains itself as it goes along, so that by the end we more or less understand how the heist is supposed to work. For that reason, I won't describe specific details of the plot. The setup is another matter, developing characters who are convincing and colorful, as this genre goes, and putting them in relationships that flash with humor and a little mystery.

Robert De Niro stars as Nick Wells, who runs a jazz club in the old town of Montreal but is not, judging by his French, a native. His other job is as a specialist in break-ins, and the title sequence shows him trying to crack a safe in Boston. His rule: Never rob where you live. But now his old friend Max (Marlon Brando), a Montreal crime lord, comes to him with an offer. He knows of an invaluable antique in the Montreal Customs House, and of a way to steal it. The key to his plan: a contact named Jackie (Edward Norton), who is a janitor at the building. Jackie has become a coddled favorite there by pretending to be "Brian," whose speech and movement seem affected by some kind of brain damage.

These three performances are what they need to be and no more. It is a sign of professionalism when an actor can inhabit a genre instead of trying to transcend it. De Niro's Nick is taciturn, weary, ready to retire after the proverbial one last score. Norton is younger and hungrier, and a show-off who angers Nick by fooling him with the Brian performance. Brando's Max is a dialed-down Sidney Green-street character, large, wealthy, a little effeminate; his days of action are behind him, and now he moves other men on the chessboard of his schemes.

To these three characters the screenplay adds a fourth, but does not use her well. This is Diane (Angela Bassett), Nick's girlfriend, who flies into town for brief romantic meetings and is assigned the thankless task of saying yes, she'll marry him—but only if he promises he has retired from his life of crime. Diane is so sadly underwritten that Bassett, a good actress, seems walled in by her dialogue. The filmmakers should have eliminated the role, or found a real purpose for her; as a perfunctory love interest, Diane is a cliché.

There are, however, a couple of flashy supporting roles. When it's necessary to crack the security code used by the agency that guards the Customs House, Nick calls on a friend named Stephen (Jamie Harrold), who lives in a kind of cybernetic war room in his basement, and boasts he's the best: "Give me a KayPro 64 and a dial tone and I can do anything." (There's a running gag about Stephen's mother shouting downstairs to him—a nod to De Niro's character in *The King of Comedy*.) Another supporting role, quieter but necessary, is played by Gary Farmer, the big Canadian Indian actor, who is Nick's strong-arm man.

The dialogue has a nice hard humor to it. When Nick meets a man in the park who is going to sell him a secret, the man comes with another man. "Who's that?" asks Nick. "My cousin," the man says. "See that man reading the newspaper on the bench over there?" says Nick, nodding to the gigantic Farmer. "He's my cousin. So we both have family here."

Brick by brick, the screenplay assembles the pieces of the heist plan. Obligatory elements are respected. We learn that the Montreal Customs House is the most impenetrable building in Quebec, and maybe Canada. We go on a scouting expedition in a labyrinth of tunnels under the building. We're introduced

to high-tech equipment, like miniature cameras and infrared detectors. We study the floor plan. We are alarmed by last-minute changes in plans, when the customs officials finally find out how valuable the treasure is and install motion sensors and three cameras. And then the caper itself unfolds, and of it I will say nothing, except that De Niro's character does incredibly difficult and ingenious things, and we are absorbed.

That's the point. That we sit in the theater in silent concentration, not restless, not stirring, involved in the suspense. Of course there are unanticipated developments. The risk of premature discovery. Twists and turns. But there is not a lot of violence, and the movie honorably avoids a cop-out ending of gunfights and chases. It is true to its story, and the story involves characters, not stunts and special effects. At the end, we feel *satisfied*. We aren't jazzed up by phony fireworks, but satiated by the fulfillment of this clockwork plot that has never cheated. *The Score* is not a great movie, but as a classic heist movie, it's solid professionalism.

The Scorpion King ★ ★ ½

PG-13, 94 m., 2002

The Rock (Mathayus), Steven Brand (Memnon), Michael Clarke Duncan (Balthazar), Kelly Hu (The Sorceress), Bernard Hill (Philos), Grant Heslov (Arpid), Peter Facinelli (Takmet), Ralf Moeller (Thorak). Directed by Chuck Russell and produced by Stephen Sommers, Sean Daniel, James Jacks, and Kevin Misher. Screenplay by Sommers, William Osborne, and David Hayter, based on a story by Sommers and Jonathan Hales.

"Where do you think you are going with my horse?"

"To Gomorrah. Nothing we can say will stop him."

—Dialogue in *The Scorpion King*

And a wise move, too, because *The Scorpion King* is set "thousands of years before the Pyramids," so property values in Gomorrah were a good value for anyone willing to buy and hold. Here is a movie that embraces its goofiness like a Get Out of Jail Free card. The plot is recycled out of previous recycling jobs, the special effects are bad enough that you can grin at them, and the dialogue sounds like the pre-Pyramidal desert warriors are channeling a Fox sitcom (the hero refers to his camel as "my ride").

The film stars The Rock, famous as a WWF wrestling star (Vince McMahon takes a producer's credit), and on the basis of this movie, he can definitely star in movies like this. This story takes place so long ago in prehistory that The Rock was a hero and had not yet turned into the villain of *The Mummy Returns* (2001), and we can clearly see his face and muscular physique—an improvement over the earlier film, in which his scenes mostly consisted of his face being attached to a scorpion so large it looked like a giant lobster. How gigantic was the lobster? It would take a buffalo to play the Turf.

The story: An evil Scorpion King named Memnon (Steven Brand) uses the talents of a sorceress (Kelly Hu) to map his battle plans, and has conquered most of his enemies. Then we meet three Arkadians, professional assassins who have been "trained for generations in the deadly art," which indicates their training began even before they were born. The Arkadian leader Mathayus, played by The Rock, is such a powerful man that early in the film he shoots a guy with an arrow and the force of the arrow sends the guy crashing through a wall and flying through the air. (No wonder he warns, "Don't touch the bow.")

How The Rock morphs from this character into the *Mummy Returns* character is a mystery to me, and, I am sure, to him. Along the trail Mathayus loses some allies and gains others, including a Nubian giant (Michael Clarke Duncan), a scientist who has invented gunpowder, a clever kid, and a wisecracking horse thief. The scene where they vow to kill the Scorpion King is especially impressive, as Mathayus intones, "As long as one of us still breathes, the sorcerer will die!" See if you can spot the logical loophole.*

Mathayus and his team invade the desert stronghold of Memnon, where the sorceress, who comes from or perhaps is the first in a long line of James Bond heroines, sets eyes on him and wonders why she's bothering with the scrawny king. Special effects send Mathayus and others catapulting into harems, falling from castle walls, and narrowly missing death by fire, scorpion, poisonous cobra, swordplay, arrows, explosion, and being buried up to the neck in the sand near colonies of fire ants. And that's not even counting the Valley of the Death, which inspires the neo-Mametian dialogue: "No one goes to the Valley of the Death. That's why it's called the Valley of the Death."

Of all the special effects in the movie, the most impressive are the ones that keep the breasts of the many nubile maidens covered to within one centimeter of the PG-13 guidelines. Kelly Hu, a beautiful woman who looks as if she is trying to remember the good things her agent told her would happen if she took this role, has especially clever long flowing hair, which cascades down over her breasts instead of up over her head even when she is descending a waterfall.

Did I enjoy this movie? Yeah, I did, although not quite enough to recommend it, because it tries too hard to be hyper and not hard enough to be clever. It is what it is, though, and is pretty good at it. Those who would dislike the movie are unlikely to attend it (does anybody go to see The Rock in *The Scorpion King* by accident?). For its target audience, looking for a few laughs, martial arts and stuff that blows up real good, it will be exactly what they expected. It has high energy, the action never stops, the dialogue knows it's funny, and The Rock has the authority to play the role and the fortitude to keep a straight face. I expect him to become a durable action star. There's something about the way he eats those fire ants that lets you know he's thinking, "If I ever escape from this predicament, I'm gonna come back here and fix me up a real mess of fire ants, instead of just chewing on a few at a time."

Now see if you can spot the logical error in my question.

Scotland, PA ★ ★ ½
R, 102 m., 2002

James LeGros (Joe "Mac" McBeth), Maura Tierney (Pat McBeth), Christopher Walken (Lieutenant Ernie McDuff), Kevin Corrigan (Anthony "Banco" Banconi), James Rebhorn (Norm Duncan), Tom Guiry (Malcolm Duncan), Andy Dick (Hippie Jesse), Amy Smart (Hippie Stacy), Timothy "Speed" Levitch (Hippie Hector), Josh Pais (Doug McKenna), Geoff

Dunsworth (Donald Duncan). Directed by Billy Morrissette and produced by Richard Shepard and Jonathan Stern. Screenplay by Morrissette, based on *Macbeth* by Shakespeare.

Scotland, PA translates Shakespeare's *Macbeth* into a comedy set in a Pennsylvania fast-food burger stand, circa 1975. Lady Macbeth rubs unhappily at a grease burn on her hand, the three witches become three local hippies, and poor Duncan, the manager, isn't attacked with a knife but is pounded on the head with a skillet. If you know *Macbeth*, it's funny. Anyone who doesn't is going to think these people are acting mighty peculiar.

Like all good satire, this one is based on venom and loathing. I learn that Billy Morrissette, the writer-director, first began to think of burger stands in Macbethian terms while working in one some twenty years ago. He shared his thoughts with his girlfriend, Maura Tierney, who became his wife, and appropriately plays Lady Macbeth, a.k.a. Mrs. McBeth, in this movie.

The story: "Mac" McBeth (James LeGros) and his wife, Pat, slave unhappily in Duncan's, a fast-food outlet run by Norm Duncan (James Rebhorn). Mac lives with the dream that he will someday be manager. His current boss is Doug McKenna (Josh Pais), who is ripping off Duncan and pocketing receipts. The McBeths tell Duncan about the theft, expecting Mac will be named the new manager. But, no, Duncan picks his two sons, Malcolm (Tom Guiry) and Donald (Geoff Dunsworth) as his heirs.

This is not right, Pat McBeth hisses fiercely to her husband. Especially not after Mac has increased sales by introducing the concept of a drive-through line to Scotland, Pa. Pat badgers her husband to kill Duncan and buy the eatery from his indifferent sons. "We're not bad people, Mac," she argues. "We're just underachievers who have to make up for lost time."

Macbeth is Shakespeare's most violent play, and *Scotland, PA* follows cheerfully in that tradition; after Duncan is pounded on the head, what finishes him off is a headfirst dive into the french-fry grease. The case is so suspicious that the local cops call in Lieutenant Ernie McDuff (Christopher Walken), who affects a kind of genial absentmindedness as a cover for his investigation. "This place really looks great," he tells the proud couple at the grand opening of their McBeth's. "Of course, the last time there was a dead body in the fryer."

Morrissette uses the Shakespeare parallels whenever he can (there is, of course, a ghost at McBeth's opening), and Tierney, in the juiciest role, actually evokes some of the power of the original Lady Macbeth, especially in the way she deals with the torment of her blistered hands. And James LeGros is as feckless and clueless as Shakespeare's Macbeth—easily led, easily deceived, easily disheartened.

The buried joke in many parodies is that events must happen because they did in the original. That works here to explain the remorseless procession of bloody and creepy events. We're expected to engage with the movie on two levels—as itself, and as a parallel to Shakespeare. While modern retellings of Shakespeare often work (as in the Michael Almereyda–Ethan Hawke *Hamlet* or Tim Blake Nelson's *O*), a parody is another matter; like an update, it deprives itself of the purpose of the original. It's even more complicated when the maker of the parody doesn't despise the original, but clearly likes it. Morrissette hates fast food, not *Macbeth*.

I enjoyed the movie in a superficial way, while never sure what its purpose was. I have the curious suspicion that it will be enjoyed most by someone who knows absolutely nothing about Shakespeare, and can see it simply as the story of some very strange people who seem to be reading from the same secret script.

The Scoundrel's Wife ★ ★ ½
R, 99 m., 2003

Tatum O'Neal (Camille Picou), Julian Sands (Dr. Lenz), Tim Curry (Father Antoine), Lacey Chabert (Florida Picou), Eion Bailey (Ensign Jack Burwell), Patrick McCollough (Blue Picou). Directed by Glen Pitre and produced by Peggy Rajski and Jerry Daigle. Screenplay by Michelle Benoit and Pitre.

The Scoundrel's Wife takes place in the small but real bayou fishing village of Cut Off, Louisiana, during World War II. German submarines have been sighted offshore, and the Coast Guard suspects local shrimp boat operators of trading with the enemy. If the premise

559

seems far-fetched, the movie's closing titles remind us that some 600 vessels were attacked by U-boats in American coastal waters, and the movie's plot is inspired by stories heard in childhood by the director, Glen Pitre, who lives in Cut Off to this day.

Pitre is a legendary American regional director, a shrimper's son who graduated from Harvard and went back home to Louisiana to make movies. His early films were shot in the Cajun dialect, starred local people, and played in local movie houses where they quickly made back their investment. I met him at Cannes and again at the Montreal festival—French enclaves where he was being saluted as arguably the world's only Cajun-language filmmaker.

He broke into the mainstream with *Belizaire the Cajun* (1986), starring Armand Assante as a Cajun who defends his people's homes against marauding bands of Anglo rabble-rousers. Found guilty of murder, he stands on a scaffold between two (symbolic?) thieves and tries to talk his way free. He's sort of a bayou version of Gandhi, restraining his anger, able to see the comic side of his predicament, possessed of physical strength and quiet charm.

Now Pitre is back with *The Scoundrel's Wife*, again filmed near home, with local extras joining such stars as Tatum O'Neal, Julian Sands, Tim Curry, Lacey Chabert, and Eion Bailey (of *Band of Brothers*). The film is frankly melodramatic and the climax is hard to believe, but the movie has such a fresh sense of place and such a keen love for its people that it has genuine qualities despite its narrative shortcomings.

O'Neal stars, in her first role since *Basquiat* (1996), as Camille Picou, the widow of a shrimp boat captain who was making ends meet by smuggling in Chinese aliens. He may have been guilty of the murder of some of them, and Camille may have been an accomplice—at least that's what the local people think. She's raising her two teenagers, her son, Blue (Patrick McCollough), and daughter, Florida (Chabert), when World War II begins, and the Coast Guard entrusts a local boy, the untested young ensign Jack Burwell (Bailey), to monitor fishing activities and keep an eye out for spies.

Are there spies in Cut Off? There are certainly suspicious characters. One of them is the German refugee Dr. Lenz (Julian Sands), said to be Jewish, who has settled in as the only local doctor. Another, oddly enough, is the local priest, Father Antoine (Tim Curry), who is charmingly drunk much of the time but also spends ominous evenings in the cemetery, using an iron cross as an antenna for his shortwave radio.

Whether the priest is a spy (and whether the doctor is all he says he is) will not be discussed here. There are two possible romances in the film, one between the widow Picou and the German, the other between the ensign and young Florida. There is also much malicious gossip, all adding up to a scene in the doctor's front yard when a lynch crowd turns up and seems remarkably easy to convince of first one story and then another.

Objectively, *The Scoundrel's Wife* has problems, and there will not be a person in the audience convinced of what happens in the last scene. But I just fired off a note to a campus film critic who was being urged to write more objectively, and asked him, what is a review if not subjective? So let me confess my subjectivity.

I like the bayou flavor of this film, and the fact that it grows from a local story that has been retailed, no doubt, over hundreds of bowls of gumbo. I like the quiet dignity O'Neal brings to her guilt-ridden widow, and I like Curry's willingness to make his priest a true eccentric, instead of trying to hunker down into some bayou method performance. I like the soft, humid beauty of Uta Briesewitz's photography. And if the ending does not convince, well, a lot of family legends do not bear close scrutiny. The movie is finally just a little too ungainly, too jumbled at the end, for me to recommend, but it has heart, and I feel a lot of affection for it.

The Sea ★ ★

NO MPAA RATING, 109 m., 2003

Gunnar Eyjolfsson (Thordur), Hilmir Snaer Gudnason (Agust), Helene De Fougerolles (Francoise), Kristbjorg Kjeld (Kristin), Sven Nordin (Morten), Gudrun S. Gisladottir (Ragnheidur), Sigurdur Skulason (Haraldur), Elva Osk Olafsdottir (Aslaug), Nina Dogg Filippusdottir (Maria), Herdis Thorvaldsdottir (Kata). Directed by Baltasar Kormakur and produced by Kormakur and Jean-Francois

Fonlupt. Screenplay by Kormakur and Olafur Haukur Simonarson, based on a play by Simonarson.

How to spot a film inspired by *King Lear*: An old fart summons home three children amid hints of dividing the kingdom. Once we've spotted this early telltale clue, there can't be many surprises. Each child will fail to do or say what is expected, and the odds are good the O.F. will eventually be wandering in some kind of a wilderness. I've seen the story set in Japan and a farm in Iowa, and now here is *The Sea*, which begins with the Lear figure thundering against changes in the Icelandic fishing industry.

The patriarch is Thordur (Gunnar Eyjolfsson), who owns a fish processing factory in a fading Icelandic fishing village, and refuses to change his ways. His fish are still cleaned by hand, by local women in spotless uniforms, and he rails against the mechanized factory ships that process and ice the fish at sea. He is also loyal to the aging operators of the port's small fishing boats, which are no longer economic.

Still, there is money to be made, or salvaged, from the family business, especially if Thordur sells out to his hated rival and there is a redistribution of local fishing quotas. That is what, in various ways, his desperately neurotic and unhappy family hopes will happen.

We meet the three children, Agust (Hilmir Snaer Gudnason), Haralder (Sigurdur Skulason), and the daughter, Ragnheidur (Gudrun S. Gisladottir). Each is unhappy in a different way. Agust has been living in Paris with his pregnant girlfriend, Maria (Nina Dogg Filippusdottir), squandering his business-school tuition on *la vie bohème*. Haraldur has to endure his harpy of a wife, Aslaug (Elva Osk Olafsdottir), a drunk who runs a sexy lingerie shop. And Ragnheidur, who as the youngest daughter might be suspected of Cordelia tendencies, is a would-be filmmaker in an unhappy marriage.

Ah, but there are more characters. Thordur's wife, Kristin (Kristbjorg Kjeld), is the sister of his first wife, who died in a way that still inspires festering bitterness. And we meet Thordur's old mother, who specializes in spitting out the painful truth at the wrong moment; and various former mistresses, colorful cops, crotchety fishermen, and disloyal business associates.

The characters in Baltasar Kormakur's film are thoroughly wretched, but lack the stature of tragic heroes and are mainly sniveling little rats. They hate their father and each other. The father is clearly wrong about the fishing business, and probably knows it, but hangs onto his old ways out of sheer bloody-mindedness, or to make his family miserable. Since there seems to be no joy in the little village except the kinds that can be purchased with money, it seems ill-mannered of old Thordur to refuse to cash in, and merely sensible of Agust to relocate to Paris.

The Sea is overcrowded and overwritten, with too many shrill denunciations and dramatic surprises; we don't like the characters and, worse, they don't interest us. Surprisingly, the film was nominated by Iceland for this year's Best Foreign Film Oscar. I am surprised because in July 2002 at the Karlovy Vary film festival, I saw a much better film about Icelandic families named *The Seagull's Laughter*, a human comedy about a teenage girl whose life is changed by the return home of a sexy local woman, a bit of a legend who has lived abroad for years. It has the grace and humanity that the lumbering *The Sea* is lacking.

Secretary ★ ★ ★
R, 104 m., 2002

James Spader (E. Edward Grey), Maggie Gyllenhaal (Lee Holloway), Jeremy Davies (Peter), Lesley Ann Warren (Joan Holloway), Stephen McHattie (Burt Holloway), Amy Locane (Theresa). Directed by Steven Shainberg and produced by Shainberg, Andrew Fierberg, and Amy Hobby. Screenplay by Erin Cressida Wilson, based on the story by Mary Gaitskill.

Secretary approaches the tricky subject of sadomasochism with a stealthy tread, avoiding the dangers of making it either too offensive or too funny. Because S&M involves postures that are absorbing for the participants but absurd to the onlooker, we tend to giggle at the wrong times. Here is a film where we giggle at the right times. The director, Steven Shainberg, has succeeded by focusing intently on his characters, making them quirky individuals rather than figures of fun.

The movie, to begin with, is well cast. There

may be better actors than James Spader and Maggie Gyllenhaal, but for this material, I cannot think who they are. About Spader there always seems to be some inarticulated secret hovering, and Gyllenhaal avoids numerous opportunities to make her character seem pathetic, and makes her seem plucky instead—intent on establishing herself and making herself necessary.

Spader plays Mr. Grey, a lawyer whose office looks like the result of intense conversations with an interior designer who has seen too many Michael Douglas movies. Mr. Grey has such bad luck with secretaries that he has an illuminated help-wanted sign out front he can light up, like the VACANCY sign at a motel. Gyllenhaal plays Lee Holloway, who has the illness of self-mutilation and comes from a neurotic family. Released from treatment, Lee takes typing classes, goes looking for work, and has an interview with Mr. Grey. Something unspoken passes between them, and they know they are thinking about the same thing.

Lee is submissive. Spader is dominant and obsessive (he has a fetish for lining up red markers in his desk drawer). He demands perfection, she falls short of the mark, he punishes her, and this becomes a workable relationship. When he loses interest for a time and stops correcting her mistakes, she grows disconsolate; when he sharply calls her back into his office, she is delighted.

The movie does not argue that S&M is good for you, but has a more complex dynamic. By absorbing so much of Mr. Grey's time and attention, Lee, who has abysmal self-esteem, feels that attention is being paid to her. Mr. Grey notices her. He thinks about her. He devises new games for them. He never threatens serious hurt or harm, but instead tends toward role-playing and ritual. What they discover is that, in the long run, S&M is more fun (and less trouble) for the M than for the S. "We can't go on like this twenty-four hours a day," Mr. Grey complains at one point. Lee doesn't see why not.

Jeremy Davies plays Peter, the other key role, sincere to the point of being inarticulate, who for a time dates Lee. Mr. Grey looks on jealously as they do their laundry together, and is faced with the possibility that he might lose his agreeable secretary. That would be the final

straw, since we sense that Mr. Grey is in much worse shape than Lee was ever in. His obsessive-compulsive behavior is driving him nuts, not to mention his clients. Stories about S&M often have an ironic happy ending, but this one, based on a short story by Mary Gaitskill, seems sincere enough: They've found a relationship that works. For them.

The movie's humor comes through the close observation of behavior. It allows us to understand what has happened without specifying it. The lawyer and secretary have subtle little signals by which they step out of their roles and sort of wink, so they both know that they both know what they're doing. Their behavior, which is intended to signify hostility, eventually grows into a deeper recognition of each other's natures and needs. That, of course, leads to affection, which can be tricky, but not for them, because both suspect there is no one else they're ever likely to meet who will understand them quite so completely.

Secret Ballot ★ ★ ★
G, 105 m., 2002

Nassim Abdi (Woman), Cyrus Abidi (Soldier). Directed by Babak Payami and produced by Marco Muller and Payami. Screenplay by Payami.

Secret Ballot is a quixotic new Iranian comedy about a female election agent who is sent to a remote island to collect ballots in a national election. Because we never find out who or what is being elected, there has been much puzzlement among critics about what the election symbolizes. I believe the message is in the messenger: The agent is a *woman.*

"It's election day, don't you know?" the woman tells a bored soldier assigned to drive her around. "There's a letter. You have to guard the ballots."

The soldier studies the letter. "It says an agent will come, not a woman."

"I'm in charge here, mister. I have orders. You must obey or I'll see to it you remain a soldier forever."

Strong words in a culture where the rights of women are limited. I was reminded of *In the Heat of the Night,* in which the whole point is that the Sidney Poitier character insists on being treated with respect. This movie could be titled "They Call Me MISS Election Agent." The plot is secondary to the fact of the character's gender, and in Iran this movie must play with a subtext we can only guess.

But what else is going on? Is the movie intended to show us (a) that democracy exists in Iran, (b) that it is struggling to be born, or (c) that most people find it irrelevant to their daily lives? There's a little of all three during the long day the solider and the woman (both unnamed) spend together. Some citizens, asked to choose two of ten names on the ballot, complain they've never heard of any of them. A fierce old lady shuts her door to the team, but later sends them food, and her courier observes, "Granny Baghoo has her own government here." A man in charge of a solar energy station expresses his opinion with admirable clarity: "I know no one but God almighty, who makes the sun come up. If I vote for anyone, it must be God."

If the woman is the Poitier character, the soldier is like the sheriff played by Rod Steiger. He starts out strongly disapproving of a female agent, but during the course of the day begins to find her persuasive, intriguing, and sympathetic. By the end of the day, when he casts his ballot, it is for her, and we're reminded of the sheriff's little smile as Mister Tibbs gets back on the train.

The director, Babak Payami, has a visual style that is sometimes astonishing, sometimes frustrating, sometimes both. The first shot is of a plane dropping a box by parachute over a dry, empty plain. The camera pans with exquisite subtlety to reveal . . . a bed? Can it be a bed, in the middle of this wilderness? We see that it is. In this hot climate, they sleep outdoors.

As the soldier drives the agent around the island, events do not build so much as accumulate. Mourners in a cemetery tell her women are not allowed inside. Symbol quandary: (a) The fading patriarchy is buried there, or (b) women cannot even die as equals? In the middle of a deserted, unpopulated plain, the soldier brings the jeep to a halt before a red traffic light. Symbol quandary: (a) Outmoded laws must be ignored, or (b) in a democracy the law must be respected everywhere?

As the woman continues her discouraging attempt to involve indifferent islanders in the vote, we are reminded of Dr. Johnson's famous observation in the eighteenth century, when women were as much without rights in England as they are today in the Middle East. After hearing a woman deliver a sermon, he told Mr. Boswell: "It is not done well, but one is surprised to find it done at all."

Watching the movie, I reflected on a persistent subgenre of Iranian cinema, in which characters drive or walk endlessly through enigmatic landscapes, holding conversations of debatable meaning. Kiarostami's *Taste of Cherry* (1997), a Cannes winner much prized by many critics, not by me, follows that pattern. *Secret Ballot* brings to it much more interest and life. Perhaps the lack of cities, names, relationships, and plots provides a certain immunity: A film cannot be criticized for being about what it does not contain.

See Spot Run ★ ½
PG, 94 m., 2001

David Arquette (Gordon Smith), Michael Clarke Duncan (Agent Murdoch), Leslie Bibb (Stephanie), Joe Viterelli (Gino Valente), Angus T. Jones (James), Steven R. Schirripa (Arliss Santino), Anthony Anderson (Benny), Paul Sorvino (Sonny Talia). Directed by John Whitesell and produced by Robert Simonds, Tracey Trench, and Andrew Deane. Screenplay by George Gallo, Dan Baron, and Christian Faber, based on a story by Stuart Gibbs, Craig Titley, and Gallo.

See Spot Run is pitched at the same intellectual level as the earlier stories involving Spot, which I found so immensely involving in the first grade. There are a few refinements. The characters this time are named Gordon, Stephanie, and James, instead of Dick and Jane. And I don't recall the *Spot* books describing the hero rolling around in doggy poo, or a gangster getting his testicles bitten off, but times change. The gangster is named Sonny Talia, in a heroic act of restraint by the filmmakers, who could have named him Gino with no trouble at all.

The movie is a fairly desperate PG-rated comedy about a dog that has been highly trained for the FBI's canine corps. After it bites off one of Talia's indispensables, the mob boss

(Paul Sorvino) orders a hit on the dog, which is hustled into a version of the witness protection program, only to accidentally end up in the possession of young James (Angus T. Jones) and his baby-sitting neighbor, Gordon (David Arquette), who has a crush on James's mother, Stephanie (Leslie Bibb).

This is all setup for a series of slapstick comedy ventures, in which Gordon is humiliated and besmeared while the dog races about proving it is the most intelligent mammal in the picture. The most excruciating sequence has Gordon shinnying up a gutter pipe, which collapses (as all movie gutter pipes always do), tearing off his underpants and depositing him in one of Spot's large, damp, and voluminous gifts to the ecology. When Gordon is thoroughly smeared with caca, what do you think the odds are that (1) the lawn sprinkler system comes on, and (2) the police arrive and demand an explanation?

Another long sequence involves the destruction of a pet store, as mobsters chase the dog and Gordon gets encased in a large ball of bubble wrap, which is inflated by helium, causing him to . . . oh, never mind. And don't get me started on the scene where he lights the zebra fart.

Movies like this demonstrate that when it comes to stupidity and vulgarity, only the best will do for our children. There seems to be some kind of desperate downward trend in American taste, so that when we see a dog movie like this we think back nostalgically to the *Beethoven* dog pictures, which now represent a cultural high-water mark. Consider that there was a time in our society when children were entertained by the *Lassie* pictures, and you can see that the national taste is rapidly spiraling down to the level of a whoopee cushion.

And yes, of course, there are many jokes in *See Spot Run* involving the passing of gas and the placing of blame. Also a fight with two deaf women. Also an electrified dog collar that is activated by a TV channel changer, causing David Arquette to levitate while sparks fly out of his orifices. And a bus that slides over a cliff. And an FBI agent named "Cassavetes," which must be a masochistic in-joke by the filmmakers to remind themselves of how far they have fallen from their early ideals.

The one actor who emerges more or less unharmed is Michael Clarke Duncan, the gentle giant from *The Green Mile*, who is the dog's FBI handler and plays his scenes with the joy of a man whose stream of consciousness must run like this: *No matter how bad this movie is, at least it's better than working for the City of Chicago Department of Streets and Sanitation. I'm still wading through doggy do, but at least now I'm getting paid a movie star salary for doing it.*

Serendipity ★ ½
PG-13, 95 m., 2001

John Cusack (Jon Trager), Kate Beckinsale (Sara Thomas), Molly Shannon (Eve), Jeremy Piven (Dean Kansky), John Corbett (Lars Hammond), Bridget Moynahan (Halley Buchanan), Eugene Levy (Bloomingdale's Salesman). Directed by Peter Chelsom and produced by Simon Fields, Peter Abrams, and Robert L. Levy. Screenplay by Marc Klein.

"If we're meant to meet again, we will."

So says Sara Thomas to Jon Trager. This much has already happened: They have a Meet Cute while fighting over the same pair of cashmere gloves in Bloomingdale's. They feel, if not love, strong attraction at first sight. They go out for hot chocolate. They find out each is dating somebody else. They separate. They return—he for a scarf, she for a parcel. They meet again. He wants her phone number. But no. They must leave themselves in the hands of Fate.

Fate I have no problem with. Leaving themselves in the hands of this screenplay is another matter. It bounces them through so many amazing coincidences and serendipitous parallels and cosmic concordances that Fate is not merely knocking on the door, it has entered with a SWAT team and is banging their heads together and administering poppers.

Jon is played by John Cusack in what is either a bad career move or temporary insanity. Sara is played by Kate Beckinsale, who is a good actress, but not good enough to play this dumb. Jon and Sara have much in common; both are missing an "h." The movie puts them through dramatic and romantic situations so close to parody as to make no difference; one more turn of the screw and this could be a satire of *Sleepless in Seattle.*

Consider. They want to be together. They like each other better than the people they are dating. But they toy with their happiness by setting a series of tests. For example: She says they'll get on separate elevators in a hotel and see if they both push the same button. Odds are against it. They do, however, both push the same button—but do not meet because of a little boy who pushes all the other buttons on Cusack's elevator. I consider this God's way of telling them, "Don't tempt me."

Another test. Jon will write his telephone number on a $5 bill and it will go out in the world, and she will see if it comes back to her. A third test. Sara will write her number in a copy of a novel by Gabriel García Márquez, and if Jon finds it in a used bookstore, well, there you are. (Márquez is fond of coincidences, but *Serendipity* elevates magic realism into the realm of three-card monte.) Jon searches in countless bookstores, having never heard of Bibliofind or Alibris, where for enough money every used bookseller in the world would be happy to have a peek inside his copies of the volume.

Years pass—two or three in the movie, more in the theater. Both are engaged to others. Some smiles are generated by her fiancé, a New Age musician (John Corbett) who illustrates the principle that men who chose to wear their hair very long after about 1980 are afflicted by delusional convictions that they are cooler than anyone else. The plot risks bursting under the strain of its coincidences, as Sara and Jon fly to opposite coasts at the same time and engage in a series of Idiot Plot moves so extreme and wrongheaded that even other characters in the same scene should start shouting helpful suggestions.

By the time these two people finally get together (if they do—I don't want to give anything away) I was thinking of new tests. What if she puts a personal ad in a paper and he has to guess which paper? How about dedicating a song to her, and trusting her to be listening to the radio at that moment, in that city? What about throwing a dart at a spinning world globe? I hope this movie never has a sequel, because Jon and Sara are destined to become the most boring married couple in history. For years to come, people at parties will be whispering, "See that couple over there? The Tragers? Jon and Sara? Whatever you do, don't ask them how they met."

Series 7: The Contenders ★ ★ ½
R, 86 m., 2001

Brooke Smith (Dawn), Glenn Fitzgerald (Jeff), Marylouise Burke (Connie), Richard Venture (Franklin), Michael Kaycheck (Tony), Merritt Wever (Lindsay), Angelina Phillips (Doria), Nada Despotovich (Michelle). Directed by Daniel Minahan and produced by Jason Kliot, Katie Roumel, Christine Vachon, and Joana Vicente. Screenplay by Minahan.

Sometimes the most astonishing thing about a movie is hidden right in plain sight. *Series 7: The Contenders* is a satire on reality TV, taking the world of *Survivor* and *Temptation Island* to its logical extension with a TV show where the contestants kill one another. This is not a new idea; the movie is similar to *The Tenth Victim* (1965) and has also been compared to *Death Race 2000, Running Man, EDtv,* and *The Truman Show* in the way it uses actual lives as TV fodder. The classic short story *The Most Dangerous Game* is also lurking somewhere in its history.

No, it's not the idea that people will kill each other for entertainment that makes *Series 7* jolting. What the movie correctly perceives is that somewhere along the line we've lost all sense of shame in our society. It's not what people will do, but what they'll say—what they eagerly reveal about themselves—that *Series 7* assimilates without even being aware of it. The killing part is the satire, and we expect that to be exaggerated. The dialogue, I suspect, is not intended as satirical at all, but simply reflects the way people think these days. There are still many Americans who choose not to reveal every detail of their private lives the moment a camera is pointed at them, but they don't get on TV much.

Allow me a digression. I was watching *Jerry Springer* the other day, as I often do when I want to investigate the limits of the permissible, and there was a "guest" who was complaining that his girlfriend would not respect his fetish. He likes to vomit during sex. He even had the word for his specialty, but I've forgotten it; "nauseaphilia," no doubt. It was amazing that this guy would reveal his secret on television, but even more astonishing that the girlfriend would also appear, in order to testify how disgusting it was. Anyone so desperate for fame that they will put themselves in a position like that should think, deeply and urgently, about the positive aspects of anonymity.

But what do people say when they meet Springer guests? (1) "Ugh! That was disgusting! You are depraved!" or (2) "I saw you on *Springer*. How do you get on that show?" I suspect the answer is (2).

I make these observations because the characters in *Series 7* have no pride and no shame, and that's more interesting than their willingness to kill one another. The killing is just the gimmick—the satirical hook of the movie—but their willingness to appear on TV and explain the details of their fatal diseases, or allow the cameras to see their filthy hovels, is illuminating. It suggests that fame is the antidote for almost any misfortune.

The movie stars Brooke Smith, that wonderful actress from *Uncle Vanya on 42nd Street,* as Dawn, eight months pregnant, who explains that she must kill people and win the game for the sake of her unborn child. This is a twisted logic with a kind of beauty to it: She kills to defend life. Other contestants include a teenager (Merritt Wever) whose parents drive her to shoot-outs; an ER nurse (Marylouise Burke) whose bloody job and bloody TV role overlap; a father (Michael Kaycheck) with a wife and three kids (he wants to provide for his family); a guy who lurks in a trailer park (Richard Venture); and a testicular cancer victim (Glenn Fitzgerald), who may be in the game because he wants to die.

The Brooke Smith character is the best drawn and most clearly seen, and as she walks into a convenience store and starts blasting away, we notice the reactions of the bystanders. They understand. They know this is only TV. They are not horrified but intrigued, and they're no doubt wondering, "Am I on now?" The overlap between this behavior and some of the actions during the San Diego school shooting recently are uncanny, and disturbing. The kid who went back into the school with the video camera was interviewed *about how much he had been interviewed.*

Real life has caught up with *Series 7* and overlapped it. The movie was filmed before the first airing of a *Survivor* episode, and must have seemed more radical in the screenplay stage than it does now. We observe that the writer-director, Daniel Minahan, has a good feel for the slick graphics and theme songs of this brand of TV, and knows how the bumpers and the teasers work. But the movie has one joke and tells it too often, for too long. It leaves you with time to think about television, celebrity, and shame. Remind me to tell you sometime about the *other* guests on that *Springer* episode.

Sex and Lucía ★ ★ ★
NO MPAA RATING, 128 m., 2002

Paz Vega (Lucía), Tristán Ulloa (Lorenzo), Najwa Nimri (Elena), Daniel Freire (Carlos/Antonio), Javier Cámara (Pepe), Elena Anaya (Belén), Silvia Llanos (Luna), Juan Fernández (Chief). Directed by Julio Medem and produced by Fernando Bovaira and Enrique López Lavigne. Screenplay by Medem.

One of the characters in *Sex and Lucía* is writing a novel. Many of the things that happen in the novel have happened to him. Or he imagines they have, or will. Or they are all only in the novel. It is being read by one of the women who is a character in it. Meanwhile, the audience knows of connections between the characters that they themselves do not suspect. And then there are additional connections because the same actor plays two roles—one real, I guess, and the other . . . well, real too, I guess.

To describe the plot is not possible in a limited space, and besides, I'm not sure I'm up to it. I doubt that anyone seeing this film will completely understand it after one viewing, but that doesn't mean you have to see it twice—it simply means that confusion is part of the effect. The Spanish director, Julio Medem, made a lovely film named *The Lovers of the Arctic Circle* (1998), which was a palindrome—a story that began at both ends and met at the middle (his characters were named, inevitably, Ana and Otto). He likes to toy with the mind of the audience, and he's good at it.

Let's try for a bare outline. We meet Lucía (Paz Vega), a waitress who gets a telephone call leading her to believe her lover has been killed in an accident. He is Lorenzo (Tristán Ulloa). Distraught, she goes to an island he often talked about, and there she meets Carlos (Daniel Freire), a scuba diver who steers her toward a guest house occupied by Elena (Najwa Nimri).

We know, because of a prologue, that Elena is the mother of a daughter by Lorenzo. They met for one magic night on the island and did not exchange names. Hold that for a second, while we flash back six years to the first meeting between Lorenzo and Lucía, who tells him she admires his novel and is in love with him. They become passionate lovers, but eventually he turns sour as he gets bogged down in his second novel. This novel is about how his friend's sister has met Elena, put together the relevant dates and clues, and concluded that Elena's child is Lorenzo's. Lorenzo then goes to see the child, who is being looked after by the sexy Belén (Elena Anaya), who is, I think, Elena's roommate. But there is some confusion here; the scenes where he meets her may exist only in the novel, and Elena may be on the island. On the other hand . . .

But you see how it is. We bookmark the characters, they turn up in various combinations, and Medem describes them as unattached triangles that do not know about one another.

So much for Lucía. What about sex? The movie is an adult film in the 1970s meaning of that term, and has a good deal of sex and nudity, some of it gratuitous, although sometimes, as in this story, gratuitous sex is the most fun. To give you an idea of the film's complications, Carlos the scuba diver is played by the same actor as Antonio, who is the boyfriend of Belén's mother, a former porn actress.

What is the point of all of this? To absorb us, I think. To engage us. The characters are freed by the very absurdity of the plot. They are not required to march lockstep toward a conclusion based on the diminishing number of alternatives left to them. Even at the end of the film, they are drowning in alternatives. And the film itself tells us it has a hole in the middle and then starts over again—as indeed it does, since Lucía falls into a hole and nothing is ever heard again about it.

In notes about the movie, Julio Medem says he wrote a screenplay and then a novel, and then wrote the novel into the screenplay, and so forth. Despite his love of the labyrinthine, he can build a scene, and even if the story parts do not fit, every scene plays strongly in and of itself. The parts work even if the whole leaves me uncertain. Many movies are certain about their whole, but are made of careless parts. Forced to choose, I would take the parts.

Note: The film's digital photography is inadequate to the task of filming under the bright sun of the island. A portentous zoom to the sun is almost ruined because the image is so overexposed you hardly notice the sun. Since voluptuous visuals were obviously part of Medem's plan, he should have used film. Digital is still too anorexic for his purposes.

Sex with Strangers ★ ★
NO MPAA RATING, 105 m., 2002

A documentary directed and produced by Joe and Harry Gantz.

The most intriguing element of *Sex with Strangers* involves not the sex, but the strangers. Here are people who do not allow the use of their last names, yet they cheerfully have sex in front of the camera—and even willingly participate in scenes that make them look cruel, twisted, reckless, and perhaps deranged. We know from the Springer show that shame is no barrier when it comes to collecting your fifteen minutes of fame. But these people act like this, we realize, even when the cameras aren't on. They live this way.

The movie has been produced and directed by Joe and Harry Gantz, who do the *Taxicab Confessions* program for HBO. They follow two couples and a sad threesome through their adventures in the swinging lifestyle, in a documentary that strongly suggests the screwing they're getting isn't worth the screwing they're getting. Even assuming they have an insatiable appetite for sex with strangers, how do they develop an appetite for trolling through the roadside bars of the nation, picking up the kinds of people who can be picked up there? Groucho Marx wouldn't belong to any club that would have him as a member. The stars of this film might be wise not to sleep with anyone who would sleep with them.

We meet James and Theresa, Shannon and Gerard, and Calvin and Sarah and Julie. James and Theresa have it all figured out. They even have their own business cards. They cruise the back roads of the nation, pulling up to bars in their motor home, meeting new friends inside, and inviting them out to the Winnebago for a swap meet. Shannon and Gerard are more complicated: She seems deeply neurotic about the lifestyle, he wants to swing without her, they have a child whom they try to insulate from Mommy and Daddy's ever-changing new friends, and there's even a scene where they chat about their lifestyle with her mother, getting points for "openness" when they should be penalized for inflicting their secrets upon the poor woman.

Now, as for Calvin. He uses the rhetoric of the lifestyle primarily, we suspect, as a way to justify sleeping with both Sarah and Julie, neither one of whom is particularly enthusiastic about his hobby. He wants it all, but isn't a good sport when Sarah and Julie slip off without the middleman.

Although mate-swappers would have you believe that they are open and willing participants in their lifestyle, the evidence on screen suggests that men are a good deal more keen about the practice than women, perhaps because there is an intrinsic imbalance in the pleasures to be had from quickie anonymous sex.

When I first saw the movie, I had fundamental questions about how much of it could be trusted. On *Ebert & Roeper*, I said: "There's a scene where James and Theresa are in a club and they meet another couple and they ask the other couple, 'Do you want to swing?' And the other couple says, 'Sure.' And they say, 'Oh, we have our motor home right outside.' And so they go outside, the two couples, *and the camera*. And I'm wondering: Let's say I wanted to be a swinger, and I've just met two people who are going to take me into their motor home. Am I going to wonder about the fact that this happens to be *videotaped* while it's happening?

When I saw scenes like that, I thought, this has all been rehearsed. It's a setup."

After the show played, I got an e-mail from Joe Gantz, who assured me that all of the scenes in the movie do indeed reflect reality. One key to their footage is that they always have two cameras running all the time, to supply cutaways and reaction shots. Another is that, by definition, they show only couples who agreed to be photographed. If a hypothetical couple got to the motor home and balked at the cameras, they wouldn't be in the movie.

That leads me back to where I began, to curiosity about the mind-set of the people in the film. By openly swapping mates, they have already abandoned conventional notions of privacy and modesty. Perhaps it is only a small additional step to do it on camera. But I didn't find much fascination in the swinging. What they're doing is a matter of plumbing arrangements and mind games, of no erotic or sensuous charge. But *that* they are doing it is thought-provoking. What damage had to be done to their self-esteem, and how, to lead them to this point?

Sexy Beast ★ ★ ★ ½
R, 88 m., 2001

Ray Winstone (Gary "Gal" Dove), Ben Kingsley (Don "Malky" Logan), Ian McShane (Teddy Bass), Amanda Redman (Deedee Dove), Cavan Kendall (Aitch), Julianne White (Jackie), Alvaro Monje (Enrique), James Fox (Harry). Directed by Jonathan Glazer and produced by Jeremy Thomas. Screenplay by Louis Mellis and David Scinto.

Who would have guessed that the most savage mad-dog frothing gangster in recent movies would be played by—Ben Kingsley? Ben Kingsley, who was Gandhi, and the accountant in *Schindler's List*, and the publisher in *Betrayal*, and Dr. Watson in *Without a Clue*? Ben Kingsley, whose previous criminal was the financial wizard Meyer Lansky in *Bugsy*? Yes, Ben Kingsley. Or, as his character, Don Logan, says in *Sexy Beast*, "Yes! Yes! Yes! Yes! Yes."

Logan spits the words into the face of a retired London gangster named Dove. He's an inch away, spitting like a drill sergeant, his face red with anger, the veins throbbing on his forehead, his body coiled in rage. Dove (Ray Winstone), whose nickname is "Gal," lives in a villa on the Costa del Sol in Spain with his wife, Deedee (Amanda Redman), also retired, she from the porn business. He has no desire to return to London to assist in "one last job," a bank heist being masterminded by Logan's boss, Teddy (Ian McShane).

But you can't say no to Don Logan. This is what Dove says about him before he arrives in Spain, and when we meet him, we agree. Logan is dangerous not because he is tough, but because he is fearless and mad. You cannot intimidate a man who has no ordinary feelings. Logan is like a pit bull, hard-wired and untrainable. It's in his nature to please his master, and frighten people. He has a disconcerting habit of suddenly barking out absurdities; he has a lopsided flywheel.

Sexy Beast is in a tradition of movies about Cockney villains. It goes on the list with *The Long Good Friday* and *The Limey*. It loves its characters: Dove, the gangster gone soft; Logan, who is driven to impose his will on others; Teddy, who has a cockeyed plan to drill into a safe-deposit vault from the pool of the Turkish bath next to the bank; and Harry (James Fox), who owns the bank and thinks he is Teddy's lover when in fact he is simply the man who owns the bank.

The heist is absurd in its own way, once Dove gets to London and helps mastermind it. The burglars have total access to the Turkish bath, but it never occurs to them to drain the pool, and so they wear breathing gear while drilling through the walls of the vault next door. The vault predictably fills with water, leading to a wonderful moment when a crook opens a deposit box, finds a container inside, opens it expecting diamonds, and gets a surprise.

The movie opens on an ominous note. While Dove works on his suntan, a boulder bounces down the slope behind his villa, barely misses him, and lands in the pool. In the movie's second act, Don Logan is the boulder. Kingsley's performance has to be seen to be believed. He is angry, seductive, annoyed, wheedling, fed up, ominous, and out of his mind with frustration. I didn't know Kingsley had such notes inside him. Obviously, he can play anyone.

His best scene may be the one when Logan gets on the airplane to fly out of Spain, and the attendant asks him to put out his cigarette. Anyone who lights a cigarette on an airplane these days is asking for it, but Logan is begging for a fight. Notice the improvised lies with which he talks his way out of jail and possibly into a nice check from the airline.

Ray Winstone's work is as strong, but not as flashy. He can play monsters too: He was an abusive father in Gary Oldman's *Nil by Mouth* and Tim Roth's *The War Zone*, and it says something when those two actors cast him as their villain. His Dove is a gangster gone soft, fond of the good life, doting on his wife, able to intimidate civilians but frankly frightened of Logan.

The movie's humor is inseparable from its brutality. The crime boss Teddy (suave and vicious) offers to drive Dove to the airport after the bank job, and that leads to a series of unexpected developments—some jolting, others with deep irony. These are hard men. They could have the Sopranos for dinner, throw up, and have them again.

Shadow Magic ★ ★
PG, 115 m., 2001

Jared Harris (Raymond Wallace), Xia Yu (Liu Jinglun), Xing Yufei (Ling), Liu Peiqi (Master Ren), Lu Liping (Madame Ren), Wang Jingming (Old Liu), Li Yusheng (Lord Tan), Zhang Yukui (Lao Chang). Directed and produced by Ann Hu. Screenplay by Huang Dan, Tang Louyi, Kate Raisz, Bob McAndrew, and Ann Hu.

In Peking in 1902, an Englishman arrives with a hand-cranked projector and a box of the earliest silent movies. Ann Hu's *Shadow Magic* tells the story of how he overcomes tradition to build an audience for the new art form, makes a local disciple, films the people of China, and eventually shows his magic to the empress. It also tells the story of his disciple, a photographer's assistant who is engaged to marry a woman for money but is in love with the daughter of an opera star.

The Englishman, we learn, is based on a real person, although no one seems to have remembered his name (the film calls him Raymond

Wallace). The China in the movie may be based on a real China, but it falls too easily into the forms of movie formulas. Watching the movie, I was reminded of a 1922 novel named *Kimono*, by John Paris, that did an extraordinary job of suggesting how *different* Japan seemed to a British visitor in the early years of the century. Surely China was as intimidating, yet the values and customs in this movie seem familiar to a modern Western viewer. The Englishman should be more of a stranger, and China should be more of a strange land.

Consider a scene late in the movie where Wallace (Jared Harris) and his friend Liu Jinglun (Xia Yu), a young photographer, show the new invention to the Dowager Empress. The screening goes well until there is a fire (film combusts easily in *Shadow Magic*, almost on cue), and the foreigner is condemned to death before the empress pardons him, smiling benevolently as she praises the new art form. Is this what would have happened? Surely to be admitted to the presence of the empress a century ago was fraught with more mystery and drama than the movie suggests, and perhaps the empress herself would have been less like good Queen Victoria, cheerfully hailing progress. The movie is more concerned with the story line (premiere-fire-threat-rescue) than with painting the time and place.

The character Liu Jinglun is painted as an ambitious young man who instantly perceives the wonder of the new invention, while almost everyone else (except, of course, the audiences) seems hostile or indifferent. History suggests it was not this way. Movies were eagerly embraced by the curious in all countries, and the opposition by Liu's possessive father seems contrived (he fears a threat to his photography studio). The romantic subplots involving Liu seem composed on autopilot: There is an arranged marriage with a tubby older widow, which must be avoided if he's to fulfill his secret love for the beautiful young Ling (Xing Yufei).

What the movie does achieve is a lively sense of color and energy. As Wallace and Liu photograph local citizens, we're reminded of *The Star Maker*, a 1995 film by Guiseppe Tornatore *(Cinema Paradiso)* about an itinerant photographer who travels the back roads of Sicily, filming people. He pretends to be making Hollywood screen tests, but actually he is recording something much more precious— the faces of those people at that time.

Shadow Magic ends with some of the footage Raymond and Liu have shot, and that suggests a different kind of film that might have been made. Why not, instead of romantic intrigue and family quarrels in a mildly melodramatic plot, make more of an effort to reconstruct what it must have really been like for that nameless Englishman with his equipment? Why not emphasize the barriers of language, race, and custom, and tell us a little more about the intricacies of the earliest cameras and projectors? Why not trust the subject matter instead of shaping it all to fit a formula? I got the feeling all through *Shadow Magic* that the real story was offscreen.

Shadow of the Vampire ★ ★ ★ ½
R, 93 m., 2001

John Malkovich (F. W. Murnau), Willem Dafoe (Max Schreck), Cary Elwes (Fritz Wagner), Eddie Izzard (Gustav von Wangenheim), Udo Kier (Albin Grau), Catherine McCormack (Greta Schroeder), Ronan Vibert (Wolfgang Muller), Ingeborga Dapkunaite (Micheline). Directed by E. Elias Merhige and produced by Nicolas Cage and Jeff Levine. Screenplay by Steven Katz.

The best of all vampire movies is *Nosferatu*, made by F. W. Murnau in Germany in 1922. Its eerie power only increases with age. Watching it, we don't think about screenplays or special effects. We think: This movie believes in vampires. Max Schreck, the mysterious actor who played Court Orlock the vampire, is so persuasive we never think of the actor, only of the creature.

Shadow of the Vampire, a wicked new movie about the making of *Nosferatu*, has an explanation for Schreck's performance: He really was a vampire. This is not a stretch. It is easier for me to believe Schreck was a vampire than that he was an actor. Examine any photograph of him in the role and decide for yourself. Consider the ratlike face, the feral teeth, the bat ears, the sunken eyes, the fingernail claws that seem to have grown in the tomb. Makeup? He makes the word irrelevant.

In *Shadow of the Vampire*, director E. Elias Merhige and his writer, Steven Katz, do two things at the same time. They make a vampire movie of their own, and they tell a backstage story about the measures that a director will take to realize his vision. Murnau is a man obsessed with his legacy; he lectures his crew on the struggle to create art, promising them, "Our poetry, our music, will have a context as certain as the grave." What they have no way of knowing is that some of them will go to the grave themselves in the service of his poetry. He's made a deal with Schreck: Perform in my movie, and you can dine on the blood of the leading lady.

John Malkovich plays Murnau as a theoretician who is utterly uninterested in human lives other than his own. His work justifies everything. Like other silent directors he has a flamboyant presence, stalking his sets with glasses pushed up on his forehead, making pronouncements, issuing orders, self-pitying about the fools he has to work with and the price he has to pay for his art. After we meet key members of the cast and crew in Berlin, the production moves to Czechoslovakia, where Schreck awaits. Murnau explains that the great actor is so dedicated to his craft that he lives in character the clock around, and must never be spoken to except as Count Orlock.

"Willem Dafoe is Max Schreck." I put quotes around that because it's not just a line for a movie ad but the truth: He embodies the Schreck of *Nosferatu* so uncannily that when real scenes from the silent classic are slipped into the frame, we don't notice much difference. But he is not simply Schreck—or not simply Schreck as the vampire. He is also a venomous and long-suffering creature with unruly appetites, and he angers Murnau by prematurely dining on the cinematographer. Murnau shouts in rage that he *needs* the cinematographer, and now will have to go to Berlin and hire another one. He begs Schreck to keep his appetites in check until the final scene. Schreck muses aloud, "I do not think we need . . . the writer . . ." Scenes like this work as inside comedy, but they also have a practical side: The star is hungry, and because he is the star, he can make demands. This would not be the first time a star has eaten a writer alive.

The fragrant Catherine McCormack plays Greta, the actress whose throat Schreck's fangs will plunge into, for real, in the final scene. She, of course, does not understand this, and is a trouper, putting up with Schreck for the sake of art even though he reeks of decay. Concerned about her close-ups, intoxicated by the joy of stardom, she has no suspicions until, during her crucial scene, her eyes stray to the mirror—and Schreck, of course, is not reflected.

The movie does an uncanny job of recreating the visual feel of Murnau's film. There are shots that look the way moldy basements smell. This material doesn't lend itself to subtlety, and Malkovich and Dafoe chew their lines like characters who know they are always being observed (some directors do more acting on their sets than the actors do). The supporting cast is a curiously, intriguingly, mixed bag: Cary Elwes as Murnau's cinematographer Fritz Wagner (not the one who is eaten), Eddie Izzard as one of the actors, the legendary Udo Kier as the producer.

Vampires for some reason are funny as well as frightening. Maybe that's because the conditions of their lives are so absurd. Some of Anne Rice's vampires have a fairly entertaining time of it, but someone like Schreck, here, seems doomed to spend eternity in psychic and physical horror. There is a nice passage where he submits to a sort of interview from his colleagues, remaining "in character" while answering questions about vampirism. He doesn't make it sound like fun.

"Every horror film seems to become absurd after the passage of years," Pauline Kael wrote in her review of *Nosferatu*, "yet the horror remains." Here Merhige gives us scenes absurd and frightening at the same time, as when Schreck catches a bat that flies into a room, and eats it. Or when Murnau, knowing all that he knows about Schreck, reassures his leading lady: "All you have to do is relax and, as they say, the vampire will do all the work."

Note: Ebert's review of Nosferatu *is at www. suntimes.com/ebert/greatmovies.*

Shallow Hal ★ ★ ★
PG-13, 113 m., 2001

Gwyneth Paltrow (Rosemary Shanahan), Jack Black (Hal Larsen), Jason Alexander (Mauricio), Rene Kirby (Walt), Tony Robbins (Himself),

Susan Ward (Jill), Joe Viterelli (Steve Shanahan), Jill Fitzgerald (Mrs. Shanahan). Directed by Bobby Farrelly and Peter Farrelly, produced by the Farrellys, Bradley Thomas, and Charles B. Wessler. Screenplay by Sean Moynihan and the Farrellys.

Shallow Hal is given words of wisdom at the deathbed of his father, who, under the influence of painkillers, is speaking from the deepest recesses of his being. "Hot young tail," his father says. "That's what it's all about." He makes Hal promise to date only beautiful woman, and to beware of falling in love—"that was the tragic mistake I made with your mother."

Hal (Jack Black) grows up to follow this counsel. He has no meaningful relationships with women because meaningful is not what he's looking for. With his running mate Mauricio (Jason Alexander from *Seinfeld*), whose spray-on hair looks like a felt hat, he prowls the bars. His life is a series of brief encounters, until one day he is trapped on an elevator with Tony Robbins, the self-help guru, who hypnotizes him and tells him to look inside the women he meets, for their inner beauty.

Soon after, Shallow Hal begins to have extraordinary success with women—not least with a nurse and ex–Peace Corps volunteer named Rosemary, who looks exactly like Gwyneth Paltrow, because that's the way Hal's mind is working these days. The movie plays with point-of-view shots to show us that Rosemary actually weighs about 300 pounds, but to Hal she's slender and—well, Gwyneth Paltrow.

At first Rosemary thinks his compliments are ironic insults, and is wounded. Then she realizes he's sincere, and really does think she's beautiful. This has never happened to her before. They begin an enchanted romance, to the consternation of Hal's friends, who can't understand why he's dating this fatso. Of course, if the Tony Robbins hypnosis ever wears off . . .

Shallow Hal, written with Sean Moynihan, is the new movie by the Farrelly brothers, Bobby and Peter. They specialize in skirmishes on the thin line between comedy and cruelty. *There's Something About Mary* had its paraplegic suitor, *Dumb and Dumber* had the little blind boy, *Me, Myself and Irene* was about a

man with a Jekyll-and-Hyde personality, and so on. Whether we laugh or are offended depends on whether our lower or higher sensibilities are in command at the time. The Farrellys have a way of tickling the lower regions while sending the higher centers off on errands. Reader, I confess I have laughed.

Shallow Hal is often very funny, but it is also surprisingly moving at times. It contains characters to test us, especially Walt (Rene Kirby), who has spina bifida and an essentially immobile lower body. Kirby doesn't use a chair or braces, but lopes around on all fours, and is an expert skier, horseman, bicyclist, and acrobat. Because he is clearly handicapped, we think at first his scenes are in "bad taste"—but he doesn't think so; his zest for life allows us to see his inner beauty, and his sense of humor, too, as in a scene where he explains why he's putting on rubber gloves.

There's something about the Farrellys that isn't widely publicized—they're both sincerely involved in work with the mentally retarded. There is a sense that they're not simply laughing at their targets, but sometimes with them, or in sympathy with them. *Shallow Hal* has what look like fat jokes, as when a chair collapses under Rosemary, but the punch line is tilted toward empathy.

Now here's a heartfelt message from Valerie Hawkins of Homewood, Illinois, who writes: "Um, what am I missing, regarding *Shallow Hal*? The trailer prattles on about how Hal now sees only the inner beauty of a woman. No, he doesn't. When he looks at an overweight woman and instead sees her as a thin woman, that's not inner beauty. What he's seeing is a typical tall, thin professional model type— which in some ways is more insulting than if he saw her as she really is and instantly rejected her."

This is persuasive. Hal sees Gwyneth Paltrow, who doesn't spend a lot of time wearing the "fat suit" you've read about in the celeb columns. What if she wore the fat suit in every scene, and he thought she was beautiful because of the Robbins training? This would also be funny; *we* could see her as fat but *he* couldn't. At the same time, screams of rage would come from the producers, who didn't pay Paltrow untold millions to wear a fat suit.

Hawkins has a good argument from our

point of view and hers, but not from Hal's, because he *does* literally see an idealized beauty. To be sure, it is exterior beauty, not interior, but how else to express his experience visually? I think we know to accept the Farrellys' premise as filtered through the realities of the marketplace, in which you do not put Gwyneth Paltrow into a movie where she doesn't look like Gwyneth Paltrow. (John Travolta played an abominable snowman from space in *Battleship Earth*, and look how that went over.) By showing the idealized Gwyneth, the Farrellys set up the third act, in which Shallow Hal does indeed see Paltrow as fat, and has to deal with how he feels about that. If she had been fat all along in the movie's eye, how could his test be made clear visually? Early and late, we see Paltrow as Hal sees her, which is not an evasion but maybe the point.

Whether or not you accept the fat-thin argument, the movie offers a good time. It's very funny across the usual range of Farrelly gags, from the spray-on toupee to a woman with a long second toe to a man with a tail. Gwyneth Paltrow is truly touching. And Jack Black, in his first big-time starring role, struts through with the blissful confidence of a man who knows he was born for stardom, even though he doesn't look like your typical Gwyneth Paltrow boyfriend. He's not so thin, either.

Note: Only the most attentive audience members will catch the Farrellys' subtle reference to a famous poem by Emily Dickinson.

Shanghai Knights ★ ★ ★
PG-13, 107 m., 2003

Jackie Chan (Chon Wang), Owen Wilson (Roy O'Bannon), Aaron Johnson (Charlie), Thomas Fisher (Artie Doyle), Aidan Gillen (Rathbone), Fann Wong (Chon Lin), Donnie Yen (Wu Chow), Oliver Cotton (Jack the Ripper). Directed by David Dobkin and produced by Roger Birnbaum, Gary Barber, and Jonathan Glickman. Screenplay by Alfred Gough and Miles Millar.

Shanghai Knights has a nice mix of calculation and relaxed goofiness, and in Jackie Chan and Owen Wilson it once again teams up two playful actors who manifestly enjoy playing their ridiculous roles. The world of the action comedy is fraught with failure, still more so the period-Western-kung-fu comedy, but here is a movie, like its predecessor *Shanghai Noon* (2000), that bounds from one gag to another like an eager puppy.

The movie opens with the obligatory action prologue required in the Screenwriter's Code: The Great Seal of China is stolen by sinister intruders, and its guardian killed. The guardian, of course, is the father of Chon Wang (Jackie Chan), who, as we join him after the titles, is sheriff of Carson City, Nevada, and busy ticking off the names of the bad guys he has apprehended. Hearing of the tragedy from his beautiful sister, Chon Lin (Fann Wong), Wang hurries to New York to join up with his old comrade in arms Roy O'Bannon (Owen Wilson).

The movie's plot is entirely arbitrary. Nothing has to happen in Nevada, New York, or its ultimate location, London, although I suppose the setup does need to be in China. Every new scene simply establishes the setting for comedy, martial arts, or both. Because the comedy is fun in a broad, genial way, and because Jackie Chan and his costars (including Fann Wong) are martial arts adepts, and because the director, David Dobkin, keeps the picture filled with energy and goodwill, the movie is just the sort of mindless entertainment we're ready for after all of December's distinguished and significant Oscar finalists.

The plot moves to London because, I think, that's where the Great Seal and the evil plotters are, and even more because it needs fresh locations to distinguish the movie from its predecessor. The filmmakers click off locations like Sheriff Chan checking off the bad guys: the House of Lords, Buckingham Palace (fun with the poker-faced guards), Whitechapel and an encounter with Jack the Ripper, Big Ben (homage to Harold Lloyd), Madame Tussaud's. Charlie Chaplin and Arthur Conan Doyle make surprise appearances, surprises I will not spoil.

For Jackie Chan, *Shanghai Knights* is a comeback after the dismal *The Tuxedo* (2002), a movie that made the incalculable error of depriving him of his martial arts skills and making him the captive of a cybernetic suit. Chan's character flip-flopped across the screen in computer-generated action, which is exactly what we don't want in a Jackie Chan movie.

573

The whole point is that he does his own stunts and the audience knows it.

They know it, among other reasons, because over the closing credits there are always outtakes in which Jackie and his costars miss cues, fall wrong, get banged and bounced on assorted body parts, and break up laughing. The outtakes are particularly good this time, even though I cannot help suspecting (unfairly, maybe) that some of them are just as staged as the rest of the movie.   ☞

The Shape of Things ★ ★ ★ ½
R, 96 m., 2003

Paul Rudd (Adam), Rachel Weisz (Evelyn), Gretchen Mol (Jenny), Fred Weller (Phillip). Directed by Neil LaBute and produced by LaBute, Gail Mutrux, Philip Steuer, and Rachel Weisz. Screenplay by LaBute.

The world of Neil LaBute is a battleground of carnage between the sexes. Men and women distrust one another, scheme to humiliate one another, are inspired to fearsome depths of cruelty. Their warfare takes place in the affluent habitats of the white upper-middle class—restaurants, bookstores, coffee shops, corporate offices, campuses, museums, and apartments of tasteful sterility. Although one of his gender wars films was shot in Fort Wayne, Indiana, and the other two in southern California, there is no way to tell that from the information on the screen. All of his characters seem to live in clean, well-lighted, interchangeable places.

The Shape of Things is the third of these films. First came *In the Company of Men* (1997) and *Your Friends and Neighbors* (1998). Then there were two mainstream films, *Nurse Betty* (2000) and *Possession* (2002). Now we are back in the world of chamber dramas involving a handful of intimately linked characters. The first film was driven by a man of ferocious misanthropy. The second involved characters whose everyday selfishness and dishonesty were upstaged by a character of astonishing cruelty. In *The Shape of Things*, while the two couples have their share of character defects, they seem generally within the norm, until we fully understand what has happened.

In a museum, we see Evelyn (Rachel Weisz) step over a velvet rope to take Polaroids of a male nude statue—or, more specifically, of a fig leaf added at a later date. The museum guard, named Adam (Paul Rudd), asks her to step outside the rope, but eventually steps inside it himself, to plead with her not to cause trouble just before his shift ends. He's a student, working part-time.

They begin to see each other. She's a graduate student, working on a project that she describes, as she describes a great many things, as a "thingy." Eventually we meet an engaged couple, Jenny (Gretchen Mol) and Phillip (Fred Weller), who are friends of Adam's. Over a period of months, they notice changes in him. He loses weight. Gets a haircut. Rids himself of a nerdy corduroy jacket that, we learn, Phillip has been urging him to throw away since freshman year. He even has a nose job, which he tries to explain as an accidental injury.

What, or who, is responsible for these changes? Can it be Evelyn, who is now Adam's girlfriend? Adam denies it, although it is not unknown for a woman to make over the new man in her life, and even Jenny observes that most men have traits that stand between them and perfection—traits women are quick to observe and quite willing to change.

The movie unfolds as a series of literate conversations between various combinations of these four articulate people. Their basic subject is one another. They are observant about mannerisms, habits, values, and changes, and feel licensed to make suggestions. There is even a little low-key sexual cheating, involving kissing, and low-key emotional assaults, involving telling about the kissing.

And then . . . but I will not say one more word because the rest of the movie is for you to discover. Let it simply be said that there are no free passes in LaBute's class in gender studies.

The Shape of Things builds a sense of quiet dread under what seems to be an ordinary surface. Characters talk in a normal way, and we suspect that their blandness disguises buried motives. Often they are quite happy to criticize each other, and none of them takes criticism well. These characters are perhaps in training to become the narcissistic, self-absorbed monsters in *Your Friends and Neighbors*.

LaBute has that rarest of attributes, a distinctive voice. You know one of his scenes at once. His dialogue is the dialogue overheard in trendy midscale restaurants, with the words peeled back to suggest the venom beneath. He also has a distinctive view of life, in which men and women are natural enemies—and beyond that, every person is an island surrounded by enemies. This seems like a bleak and extreme view, and yet what happens in his films often feels like the logical extension of what happens to us or around us every day. It is the surface normality of the characters and their world that is scary.

LaBute has been compared to David Mamet, and no doubt there was an influence, seen in the devious plots and the precisely heard, evocative language. But Mamet is much more interested in plotting itself, in con games and deceptions, while in LaBute there is the feeling that some kind of deeper human tragedy is being enacted; his characters deceive and wound one another not for gain or pleasure, but because that is their nature.

Actors have a thankless task in a film like this. All four players are well cast in roles that ask them to avoid "acting" and simply exist on a realistic, everyday level. Like the actors in a Bresson film, they're used for what they intrinsically represent, rather than for what they can achieve through their art. They are like those all around us, and like us, except that LaBute is suspicious of their hidden motives. One person plays a cruel trick in *The Shape of Things*, but we get the uneasy sense that, in LaBute's world, any one of the four could have been that person.

The Shipping News ★ ★

R, 120 m., 2001

Kevin Spacey (Quoyle), Julianne Moore (Wavey), Judi Dench (Agnis), Cate Blanchett (Petal Bear), Rhys Ifans (Nutbeem), Peter Postlethwaite (Tert X. Card), Scott Glenn (Jack Buggit), Allysa Gainer (Bunny), Kaitlin Gainer (Bunny), Lauren Gainer (Bunny). Directed by Lasse Hallstrom and produced by Rob Cowan, Linda Goldstein, Knowlton, Leslie Holleran, and Irwin Winkler. Screenplay by Robert Nelson Jacobs, based on the novel by E. Annie Proulx.

If one person has told me to read *The Shipping News*, half a dozen have. One friend actually pressed a copy of E. Annie Proulx's novel into my hands. They cannot all be wrong. It won the Pulitzer Prize. It must be a wonderful book.

But the movie made from it is relentlessly colorful and cute, until you wonder if the characters stayed up late inventing quirky dialogue and thinking of peculiar behavior they can cultivate.

The movie follows the experiences of Quoyle (Kevin Spacey), a meek ink-man for the *Poughkeepsie News*, as he marries Petal, the local tramp (Cate Blanchett), has a daughter named Bunny, cares for Bunny while Petal sluts around, and then raises her alone after Petal dies, not so really very tragically if you think about it. At about this time he finds a message on his answering machine from his father, informing him, "It's time for your mother and I to put an end to it." That these tragedies range in emotional value from ironic to funny gives you the temperature of the film.

Quoyle and Bunny might have lived on forever in Poughkeepsie, she washing the ink from his coveralls, if Aunt Agnis (Judi Dench) had not happened along with enough gumption to put them all in motion toward Quoyle Point, Newfoundland, where they move back into the family homestead, a frame house on a point so exposed on the rocky coast that cables anchor it against the wind. This house is so decrepit and open to the weather that only in the movies could it be rehabbed into a comfy home after, oh, about three scenes.

The movie's drift is clear: Sad sack and daughter move to eccentric, isolated town where local free spirits will introduce them to the joys of living. Quoyle gets a job on the local paper, the *Gammy Bird*, where arguments rage about sailing vessels versus oil tankers (the tankers have their defender), and the journalists, like all small-town journalists I have ever known, know way more about everything than they can use in the kinds of stories they have to write.

Quoyle meets Wavey (Julianne Moore), who runs the local day-care center, and soon—but you can fill in the blanks. What you may not anticipate are several macabre turns including close calls with death, a severed head, spontaneous resurrection, twelve-year-old grandfathers, and ancient secrets just waiting to be unearthed.

The movie makes good use of the magnificent locations, and abundant use of water; Quoyle is afraid of swimming after traumatic

575

experiences with his father, and has to endure several wet ordeals, one of which I seriously doubt was survivable, and meanwhile even the movie itself seems damp a lot of the time. I liked the feeling of community in the town, the palpable sense of place. But, lord, the characters are tireless in their peculiarities; it's as if the movie took the most colorful folks in Lake Wobegone, dehydrated them, concentrated the granules, shipped them to Newfoundland, reconstituted them with Molson's, and issued them Canadian passports.

Kevin Spacey can effortlessly play the smartest man in every movie. He is not as interesting playing hapless. Julianne Moore is the earth mother, warm, funny, and troubled. Judi Dench is rock-solid dependable as Aunt Agnis. Cate Blanchett is amazingly unrecognizable as Petal, who reminds us of the disused word "hellion." The guys on the newspaper are terrific, especially dreamer Rhys Ifans and dour Peter Postlethwaite, and I liked Scott Glenn as the publisher who would rather go fishing.

All of that said, the film suffers from a severe case of obviously being a film. There is never the sense that Quoyle Point, or any place remotely like it, could exist outside this movie. Maybe this is Canadian magic realism. At the Toronto Film Festival I saw *Rare Birds*, also shot in Newfoundland, starring William Hurt as a restaurant owner and Molly Parker in the Julianne Moore role. It is invaluable as a comparison, because it demonstrates that you can make quite a good human comedy about oddball characters in Newfoundland without going off the deep end. ☞

Showtime ★ ★
PG-13, 95 m., 2002

Robert De Niro (Mitch), Eddie Murphy (Trey), Rene Russo (Chase Renzi), William Shatner (Himself), Frankie Faison (Captain Winship). Directed by Tom Dey and produced by Jane Rosenthal and Jorge Saralegui. Screenplay by Keith Sharon, Alfred Gough, and Miles Millar, based on a story by Saralegui.

The cop buddy comedy is such a familiar genre that a movie can parody it and occupy it at the same time. The characters in *Showtime* do it as a kind of straddle, starting out making fun of

cop buddy clichés and ending up trapped in them. The movie's funny in the opening scenes and then forgets why it came to play.

We meet two cops: Mitch (Robert De Niro), who never had to choose between a red wire and a green wire, and Trey (Eddie Murphy), who is a cop but would rather play one on TV. You can guess from the casting that the movie will have energy and chemistry, and indeed while I watched it my strongest feeling was affection for the actors. They've been around so long, given so much, are so good at what they do. And Rene Russo, as the TV producer who teams them on a reality show, is great at stalking in high heels as if this is the first time she's ever done it without grinding a body part beneath them.

Mitch wants only to do his job. Trey is a hot dog who has learned more from TV than at the police academy. Making a drug bust, he knowledgeably tastes the white powder and finds it's cocaine. "What if it's cyanide?" Mitch asks (or anthrax, we're thinking). "There's a reason real cops don't taste drugs."

We meet Chase Renzi (Russo), TV producer with a problem: Her report on exploding flammable baby pajamas didn't pan out. She's electrified when she sees TV footage of Mitch getting angry with a TV cameraman and shooting his camera. The network sues. Mitch is threatened with suspension, just like in all the *Dirty Harry* movies, but offered an ultimatum: Star in a new reality show with Trey ("You do the show; they drop the suit").

Mitch grudgingly agrees, and some of the best scenes involve the callow Trey instructing the hard-edged Mitch in the art of acting (this is a flip of John Wayne tutoring James Caan in *El Dorado*). During these scenes we're seeing pure De Niro and Murphy, freed from effects and action, simply acting. They're good at it.

Enter a bad guy with a big gun. A gun so big we are surprised not by its power but by the fact that anyone can lift it. An expert testifies: "This gun is like the fifty-foot shark. We know it's there, but nobody has ever seen it." Most of the second half of the movie involves Mitch and Trey chasing down the gun and its owners, who use it in a series of daring robberies. This we have seen before. Oh yes.

The movie was directed by Tom Dey, whose only previous film was *Shanghai Noon* (2000), a buddy movie pairing a Chinese martial arts fighter and a train robber. I learn from the Internet Movie Database that he studied film at Brown University, the Centre des Etudes Critiques in Paris, and the American Film Institute. He probably knows what's wrong with this movie more than I do.

But making movies is an exercise in compromise no less appalling than the making of the "reality" TV show in *Showtime*. My guess: The screenplay ("by Keith Sharon, Alfred Gough, and Miles Millar, based on a story by Jorge Saralegui") was funnier and more satirical until the studio began to doubt the intelligence of the potential audience, and decided to shovel in more action as insurance. As we all know, the first rule of action drama is that when a gun as legendary as a fifty-foot shark comes on-screen in the first act, somebody eventually finds a spent shell casing the size of a shot glass.

Note: Most of the computers in movies for several years have been Macintoshes, maybe because the Mac is the only computer that doesn't look like every other computer and therefore benefits from product placement. But this is the first movie in which an entire iMac commercial runs on TV in the background of a shot.

Shrek ★ ★ ★ ★
PG, 90 m., 2001

With the voices of: Mike Myers (Shrek), Eddie Murphy (The Donkey), Cameron Diaz (Princess Fiona), John Lithgow (Lord Farquaad). Directed by Andrew Adamson and Vicky Jenson and produced by Aron Warner and John H. Williams. Screenplay by Ted Elliott, Terry Rossio, Joe Stillman, and Roger S. H. Schulman, based on the book by William Steig.

There is a moment in *Shrek* when the despicable Lord Farquaad has the Gingerbread Man tortured by dipping him into milk. This prepares us for another moment when Princess Fiona's singing voice is so piercing it causes jolly little bluebirds to explode; making the best of a bad situation, she fries their eggs. This is not your average family cartoon. *Shrek* is jolly and wicked, filled with sly in-jokes and yet somehow possessing a heart.

The movie has been so long in the making at DreamWorks that the late Chris Farley was originally intended to voice the jolly green ogre in the title role. All that work has paid off: The movie is an astonishing visual delight, with animation techniques that seem lifelike and fantastical, both at once. No animated being has ever moved, breathed, or had its skin crawl quite as convincingly as Shrek, and yet the movie doesn't look like a reprocessed version of the real world; it's all made up, right down to, or up to, Shrek's trumpet-shaped ears.

Shrek's voice is now performed by Mike Myers, with a voice that's an echo of his Fat Bastard (the Scotsman with a molasses brogue in *Austin Powers: The Spy Who Shagged Me*). Shrek is an ogre who lives in a swamp surrounded by "Keep Out" and "Beware the Ogre!" signs. He wants only to be left alone, perhaps because he is not such an ogre after all but merely a lonely creature with an inferiority complex because of his ugliness. He is horrified when the solitude of his swamp is disturbed by a sudden invasion of cartoon creatures, who have been banished from Lord Farquaad's kingdom.

Many of these creatures bear a curious correspondence to Disney characters who are in the public domain: The Three Little Pigs turn up, along with the Three Bears, the Three Blind Mice, Tinkerbell, the Big Bad Wolf, and Pinocchio. Later, when Farquaad seeks a bride, the Magic Mirror gives him three choices: Cinderella, Snow White ("She lives with seven men, but she's not easy"), and Princess Fiona. He chooses the beauty who has not had the title role in a Disney animated feature. No doubt all of this, and a little dig at DisneyWorld, were inspired by feelings DreamWorks partner Jeffrey Katzenberg has nourished since his painful departure from Disney—but the elbow in the ribs is more playful than serious. (Farquaad is said to be inspired by Disney chief Michael Eisner, but I don't see a resemblance, and his short stature corresponds not to the tall Eisner but, well, to the diminutive Katzenberg.)

The plot involves Lord Farquaad's desire to wed the Princess Fiona, and his reluctance to slay the dragon that stands between her and would-be suitors. He hires Shrek to attempt the mission, which Shrek is happy to do, providing the loathsome fairy-tale creatures are banished and his swamp returned to its dismal solitude. On his mission, Shrek is joined by a donkey named The Donkey, whose running commentary, voiced by Eddie Murphy, provides some of the movie's best laughs. (The trick isn't that he talks, Shrek observes; "the trick is to get him to shut up.")

The expedition to the castle of the princess involves a suspension bridge above a flaming abyss, and the castle's interior is piled high with the bones of the dragon's previous contenders. When Shrek and The Donkey get inside, there are exuberant action scenes that whirl madly through interior spaces, and revelations about the dragon no one could have guessed. And all along the way, asides and puns, in-jokes and contemporary references, and countless references to other movies.

Voice-overs for animated movies were once, except for the annual Disney classic, quickie jobs that actors took if they were out of work. Now they are starring roles with fat paychecks, and the ads for *Shrek* use big letters to trumpet the names of Myers, Murphy, Cameron Diaz (Fiona), and John Lithgow (Farquaad). Their vocal performances are nicely suited to the characters, although Myers's infatuation with his Scottish brogue reportedly had to be toned down. Murphy in particular has emerged as a star of the voice-over genre.

Much will be written about the movie's technical expertise, and indeed every summer seems to bring another breakthrough on the animation front. After the three-dimensional modeling and shading of *Toy Story*, the even more evolved *Toy Story 2*, *A Bug's Life*, and *Antz*, and the amazing effects in *Dinosaur*, *Shrek* unveils creatures who have been designed from the inside out, so that their skin, muscles, and fat move upon their bones instead of seeming like a single unit. They aren't "realistic," but they're curiously real. The artistry of the locations and setting is equally skilled—not lifelike, but beyond lifelike, in a merry, stylized way.

Still, all the craft in the world would not have made *Shrek* work if the story hadn't been fun and the ogre so lovable. Shrek is not handsome but he isn't as ugly as he thinks; he's a guy we want as our friend, and he doesn't frighten us but stirs our sympathy. He's so immensely likable that I suspect he may emerge as an enduring character, populating sequels and spin-offs. One movie cannot contain him.

Sidewalks of New York ★ ★ ★
R, 100 m., 2001

Edward Burns (Tommy Reilly), Heather Graham (Annie), Rosario Dawson (Maria Tedesco), Brittany Murphy (Ashley), David Krumholtz (Ben), Dennis Farina (Carpo), Stanley Tucci (Griffin), Aida Turturro (Shari). Directed by Edward Burns and produced by Margot Bridger, Burns, Cathy Schulman, and Rick Yorn. Screenplay by Burns.

I saw Edward Burns's *Sidewalks of New York* in September 2001 at the Toronto Film Festival, and enjoyed its lighthearted story of seven lovers who readjust their romantic priorities. It was scheduled to open in a week or two, and I was baffled by Paramount's decision to put it back on the shelf for a couple of months, as if after September 11 no one could possibly contemplate attending a movie named *Sidewalks of New York*.

Now the movie has arrived, the story of lovers, would-be lovers, former lover, and adulterers from each of the city's boroughs, who seem totally preoccupied with themselves. This is as it should be. When you're in love, you think of no one but yourself. Even your thoughts of your loved one are about *your* love, because the idealized other person exists in your imagination. John Donne got this right.

The movie lives at the intersection between Woody Allen and *Sex and the City*. Like *The Brothers McMullen*, Burns's first film, it is about people who spend a lot of time analyzing their motives and measuring their happiness. The film is framed by interviews in which the lovers address the camera directly, talking about themselves and about love, and from their comments we learn one thing for sure: Lovers recycle ancient truisms that have little to do with how they will behave tomorrow, or later tonight.

Like Jacques Rivette's *Va Savoir*, another 2001 movie, the film begins with three couples, and then readjusts the pairings. It actually begins with three and a half couples, because Griffin (Stanley Tucci) is married to Annie

(Heather Graham) and is having an affair with Ashley (Brittany Murphy). He is a dentist, Annie is a real-estate agent, and Ashley is a student at NYU. Judging by recent Manhattan comedies, these are the three most popular occupations in town, after police work and prostitution. Griffin fancies himself a seducer. "I think you have the look of the new millennium," he tells Ashley the first time he sees her. Anyone who considers this a compliment deserves Griffin.

Burns himself plays Tommy, who works for a show not unlike *Entertainment Tonight* (where Burns himself once worked). A love affair has ended, and he has moved out of his apartment and is living temporarily with his boss, Carpo (Dennis Farina), who plays the field and advises Tommy to do likewise. Carpo is the kind of man who believes seduction is all in the cologne. His advice: "A wife and children will drive you to an early grave."

Tommy meets Maria (Rosario Dawson), who teaches rich kids in a private school. She is divorced from Benjamin (David Krumholtz), who supports himself as a doorman while dreaming of a career in music. He cannot believe she left him. We cannot believe she married him. He is a needy whiner who spends way too much energy believing it is only a matter of time until they get back together again. First he seems obnoxious, then you feel a little sorry for him, then he wears down your pity and you figure he got what was coming to him.

Let's see. Griffin, the Tucci character, is having trouble deceiving two women at the same time, which is what he's doing. (A more honest man would merely cheat on his wife with his mistress, but Griffin's nature is such that he also cheats on his mistress with his wife.) His wife, Annie (Graham), shows an apartment to Tommy, and begins to think of her romantic life as still holding promise. His mistress, Ashley, attracts the attention of Benjamin, who continues to annoy his ex-wife, but begins to suspect there may be alternatives to spending his nights ringing her doorbell.

In the Jacques Rivette film, the characters are all French, and so conduct their intrigues while drawing on centuries of experience. Ed Burns's New Yorkers have grown up in a society of psychobabble, and carry around half-digested concepts of guilt, redemption, and finding your karma. The teacher Maria (Dawson) is more centered, because she is the only one who has a job that does not depend on being nice to rich people. (As a waitress, Ashley would also seem to qualify, but in New York waiters are always "really" something else.)

The movie is funny without being hilarious, touching but not tearful, and articulate in the way that Burns is articulate, by nibbling earnestly around an idea as if afraid that the core has seeds. Not a lot is at stake. We would not be surprised if in three years an emotional reassignment has taken place, and all of the new couples, like all of the old ones, have been thrown on the ash-heap of romantic history. Yet *Sidewalks of New York* finds the right note of seeking and optimism among the shoals of hope. It's spiced by a rotter (Tucci) whose self-justifications are ingenious. And by a cynic (Farina) whose advice is sometimes pretty good.

Signs ★ ★ ★ ★
PG-13, 120 m., 2002

Mel Gibson (Graham Hess), Joaquin Phoenix (Merrill Hess), Rory Culkin (Morgan Hess), Abigail Breslin (Bo Hess), Cherry Jones (Officer Caroline Paski), Patricia Kalember (Colleen Hess). Directed by M. Night Shyamalan and produced by Frank Marshall, Sam Mercer, and Shyamalan. Screenplay by Shyamalan.

M. Night Shyamalan's *Signs* is the work of a born filmmaker, able to summon apprehension out of thin air. When it is over, we think not how little has been decided, but how much has been experienced. Here is a movie in which the plot is the rhythm section, not the melody. A movie that stays free of labored explanations and a forced climax, and is about fear in the wind, in the trees, in a dog's bark, in a little girl's reluctance to drink the water. In signs.

The posters show crop circles, those huge geometric shapes in fields of corn and wheat, which were seen all over the world in the 1970s. Their origin was explained in 1991 when several hoaxers came forward and demonstrated how they made them; it was not difficult, they said. Like many supernatural events, however, crop circles live on after their unmasking, and most people today have forgotten, or never knew, that they were explained. *Signs* uses them to evoke the possibility that . . . well, the possibility of anything.

The genius of the film, you see, is that it isn't really about crop circles, or the possibility that aliens created them as navigational aids. I will not even say whether aliens appear in the movie, because whether they do or not is beside the point. The purpose of the film is to evoke pure emotion through the use of skilled acting and direction, and particularly through the sound track. It is not just what we hear that is frightening. It is the way Shyamalan has us listening intensely when there is nothing to be heard. I cannot think of a movie where silence is scarier, and inaction is more disturbing.

Mel Gibson stars, as Father Graham Hess, who lives on a farm in Bucks County, Pennsylvania. We discover he is a priest only belatedly, when someone calls him "father." "It's not 'father' anymore," he says. Since he has two children, it takes us a beat to compute that he must be Episcopalian. Not that it matters, because he has lost his faith. The reason for that is revealed midway in the film, a personal tragedy I will not reveal.

Hess lives on the farm with his brother Merrill (Joaquin Phoenix) and his children, Morgan and Bo (Rory Culkin and Abigail Breslin). There is an old-fashioned farmhouse and barn, and wide cornfields, and from the very first shot there seems to be something . . . out there, or up there, or in there. Hess lives with anxiety gnawing at him. The wind sounds strange. Dogs bark at nothing. There is something *wrong*. The crop circles do not explain the feelings so much as add to them. He catches a glimpse of something in a corn field. Something wrong.

The movie uses TV news broadcasts to report on events around the world, but they're not the handy CNN capsules that supply just what the plot requires. The voices of the anchors reveal confusion and fear. A video taken at a birthday party shows a glimpse of the most alarming thing. "The history of the world's future is on TV right now," Morgan says.

In a time when Hollywood mistakes volume for action, Shyamalan makes quiet films. In a time when incessant action is the style, he persuades us to pay close attention to the smallest nuances. In *The Sixth Sense* (1999) he made a ghost story that until the very end seemed only to be a personal drama—although there was something there, some buried hint, that made us feel all was not as it seemed. In *Unbreakable* (2000) he created a psychological duel between two men, and it was convincing even though we later discovered its surprising underlying nature, and all was redefined.

In *Signs,* he does what Hitchcock said he liked to do, and plays the audience like a piano. There is as little plot as possible, and as much time and depth for the characters as he can create, all surrounded by ominous dread. The possibility of aliens is the catalyst for fear, but this family needs none, because it has already suffered a great blow.

Instead of flashy special effects, Shyamalan creates his world out of everyday objects. A baby monitor that picks up inexplicable sounds. Bo's habit of leaving unfinished glasses of water everywhere. Morgan's bright idea that caps made out of aluminum foil will protect their brains from alien waves. Hess's use of a shiny kitchen knife, not as a weapon, but as a mirror. The worst attack in the film is Morgan's asthma attack, and his father tries to talk him through it, in a scene that sets the entire movie aside and is only about itself.

At the end of the film, I had to smile, recognizing how Shyamalan has essentially ditched a payoff. He knows, as we all sense, that payoffs have grown boring. The mechanical resolution of a movie's problems is something we sit through at the end, but it's the setup and the buildup that keep our attention. *Signs* is all buildup. It's still building when it's over. ☞

Signs and Wonders ★ ★ ★
NO MPAA RATING, 104 m., 2001

Stellan Skarsgard (Alec Fenton), Charlotte Rampling (Marjorie), Deborah Kara Unger (Katherine), Dimitris Katalifos (Andreas), Ashley Remy (Siri), Michael Cook (Marcus), Dave Simonds (Kent). Directed by Jonathan Nossiter and produced by Marin Karmitz. Screenplay by James Lasdun and Nossiter.

Signs and Wonders looks through the eyes of a manic-depressive as the world sends him messages and he hurries to answer them. It shows how exhausting it is to be constantly in the grip of exhilaration, insight, conviction, idealism, and excitement—while bombarded all the time with cosmic coincidences. Nobody in the movie calls this man a manic-depressive, but it's as clear as day—or as the bright yellow suit he turns up wearing one morning, convinced it symbolizes his new and improved psyche. As a drama about the ravages of mental illness, the movie works; too bad most of the critics read it only as a romantic soap opera in which the hero is an obsessive sap. They read the signs but miss the diagnosis.

The movie stars Stellan Skarsgard and Charlotte Rampling as Alec and Marjorie, a married American couple living in Athens. ("It doesn't bother to explain away their foreign accents," complains one critic, although 10 percent of all Americans are first-generation and millions have accents.) She works for the embassy; he has a murky job in finance, and is having an office affair with Katherine (Deborah Kara Unger). The affair has been proceeding satisfactorily for months or maybe years, we gather, until one day Alec, beset with guilt, walks out of his house and uses the phone booth across the street to call back home and confess everything to his wife.

This sudden, dramatic confession marks the start of his bipolar illness. He has become seized with the conviction that vast forces are sweeping through him. He can no longer live a lie. Walking his daughter to school, he joins in her game of counting manholes and clocking various signs and portents in the city streets. For her it's a child's game; for him it becomes an obsession.

Marjorie forgives Alec his affair. Some time later, on the ski slopes in another country, he meets Katherine again—coincidentally, he believes. This random, accidental meeting is for Alec a sign that they were meant to be together, and he leaves Marjorie a second time. Then there is a tense, painful conversation with Katherine, after he explains the significance of their meeting, and why it proved they were predestined to be together. "What if I set it up?" she asks, as a woman who would prefer to be loved for herself rather than as the outward sign of cosmic forces.

I don't think we can be sure if Katherine arranged the meeting or not, but Alec decides she did, and that sends him racing back to Marjorie. Having smashed his family once, and then, as she puts it, returned to smash it again, he has run out of goodwill on the home front—and besides, she's in love with another man. Now come the most fascinating passages in Skarsgard's performance, as his mania becomes more evident. He will baby-sit while she goes out with the other man. He deserves to suffer. He will do penance. Yes! Yes! At one point as she shouts at him, he replies: "I want you to be this angry with me! We need this!" About this time the yellow suit turns up.

The movie is maddeningly obscure about details that do not directly involve Alec. We meet Andreas (Dimitris Katalifos), the man Marjorie plans to marry. He is a left-wing journalist, was tortured by the colonels, has an archive of secrets in his flat about right-wing Greek conspiracies, is perhaps a little paranoid. The twice-jilted Katherine, who comes hunting Alec and assumes a false identity, is also deranged; Marjorie is the sane center of the film. By the end, we are not sure exactly how to explain what happens to Andreas, and the movie leaves a lot of other unanswered questions. Perhaps the answer is, the story spins away from Alec, who as his illness progresses can no longer keep all the connections and meanings in order.

Jonathan Nossiter, the director and cowriter, made the 1997 Sundance prize-winner *Sunday*, about a British actress, down on her luck, who meets a man who may be a famous director or may be a homeless derelict. It's a movie about how people can be who we want them to be. *Signs and Wonders* is about a man who knows what he wants from Marjorie and Katherine, but can't get them to play the roles. They can't keep up with his fevered brain, as he connects, disconnects, reconnects. "I am not a frivolous man!" he cries at one point, aware that unless his signs and wonders are real, he is frivolous indeed. I had a friend once who suffered from manic behavior, and he said, "You know what I used to pray for? Boredom."

Simøne ★ ★
PG-13, 117 m., 2002

Al Pacino (Viktor Taransky), Catherine Keener (Elaine), Evan Rachel Wood (Lainey Taransky),

Rachel Roberts (Simøne), Jay Mohr (Hal Sinclair), Pruitt Taylor Vince (Max Sayer), Winona Ryder (Nicola Anders), Elias Koteas (Hank Aleno). Directed and produced by Andrew Niccol. Screenplay by Niccol.

Simøne tells the story of a director at the end of his rope who inherits a mad inventor's computer program that allows him to create an actress out of thin air. She becomes a big star and the center of a media firestorm, and he's trapped: The more audiences admire her, the less he can reveal she is entirely his work. The movie sets this dilemma within a cynical comedy about modern Hollywood; it's fitfully funny but never really takes off. Out of the corners of our eyes we glimpse the missed opportunities for some real satirical digging.

Al Pacino plays the director, Viktor Taransky, once brilliant, recently the author of a string of flops. Only his young daughter, Lainey (Evan Rachel Wood), still believes in him—a little. His ex-wife, Elaine (Catherine Keener), the head of the studio, has lost all hope for his career and pulls the plug on his latest project when the temperamental star (Winona Ryder) blows up.

Into the life of this desperate man comes another one (Elias Koteas), who has devised a computer program that creates "synthespians." Viktor isn't interested—but then, when the wizard leaves him the program in his will, he starts noodling around with the software and the beautiful, talented, and (above all) cooperative Simøne is the result. She needs, Viktor exults, no hairdresser, makeup, driver, car, trailer, stand-in or stuntwoman—no, not even for the fall from the plane. She is always on time, never complains, says the words just as they're written, and has no problem with nudity.

Viktor creates Simøne's performance on a computer that stands all alone in the middle of an otherwise empty sound stage. The other actors in the movie are told Simøne will be added to their scenes electronically. The premiere of the first movie is a huge success, and of course paparazzi from the supermarket tabloids stalk Viktor in hopes of photographing Simøne. No luck.

The movie was written, produced, and directed by Andrew Niccol, who wrote *The Truman Show* and wrote and directed *Gattaca*, both films about the interface between science and personality. *Simøne* is not in that league. He wants to edge it in the direction of a Hollywood comedy, but the satire is not sharp enough and the characters, including the ex-wife, are too routine.

And there's a bigger problem: Simøne always remains . . . just Simøne. The computer image always looks as if it's about to come to life and never does. One can imagine software bugs that recklessly import other on-line personalities into Simøne: Matt Drudge, for example, or Harry Knowles, or Danni Ashe. One can imagine Simøne suddenly being possessed by Lara Croft, tomb raider, and breaking up a serious dramatic scene with video-game violence. One can imagine . . . well, almost anything except that she remains a well-behaved program. When Simøne "appears" on a chat show, for example, it's kind of funny that she sticks to well-worn subjects like dolphins and smoking, but why not go the extra mile and put her on the Howard Stern show?

Pacino, that splendid actor, does what he can to bring Viktor to life. But the screenplay's too narrow, and prevents him from taking the character beyond a certain point. Most of the big events are handled with sitcom simplicity, and the hungry gossip reporters are presented as they always are, a howling pack with no wit or originality. Even Catherine Keener, as the studio head, simply plays an ex-wife who is a studio head: There's no twist, nothing unexpected.

The problem, I think, is that in aiming for too wide an audience, Niccol has made too shallow a picture. *The Truman Show* and *Gattaca* pushed their premises; *Simøne* settles for the predictable. The story elements echo the sad experience of the team assembled to make *Final Fantasy*, the summer of 2001 sci-fi movie that failed at the box office. That movie was made up entirely of "real" characters generated by computers, including Aki Ross, the heroine, who, all things considered, is a more intriguing woman than Simøne (whose appearance is provided by the actress Rachel Roberts). The *Final Fantasy* team labored four years and achieved everything they dreamed of, and were rejected by the public. Much more interesting than a director who has unimaginable success fall into his lap.

Simon Magus ★ ★

NO MPAA RATING, 106 m., 2001

Noah Taylor (Simon), Stuart Townsend (Dovid), Sean McGinley (Hase), Embeth Davidtz (Leah), Amanda Ryan (Sarah), Rutger Hauer (Squire), Ian Holm (Sirius/Boris), Terence Rigby (Bratislav). Directed by Ben Hopkins and produced by Robert Jones. Screenplay by Hopkins.

If there's anything worse than a laborious fable with a moral, it's the laborious fable without the moral. The more I think about *Simon Magus*, the less I'm sure what it's trying to say. It leads us through a mystical tale about Jews, Poles, and an outcast who takes orders from Satan. Both groups would like to build the local railroad station, but the outcast, a mystic, has visions of these very tracks being used to take Jews to the death camps. Does that mean it doesn't matter who builds the station because the trains will still perform their tragic task? In that case, what's the story about except bleak irony?

The movie takes place in nineteenth-century Silesia, bordering Hungary and Austria. Some twenty Orthodox Jews have a small community near a larger gentile town. The new railroad, bypassing the town, has created hard times for everyone. A Jew named Dovid (Stuart Townsend) wants to build a station and some shops, which will help out the woman he loves, a widowed shopkeeper named Leah (Embeth Davidtz). A gentile named Hase (Sean McGinley) also wants to build the station. The land is controlled by the Squire (Rutger Hauer), a dreamy intellectual.

This would be a story about anti-Semitism and real estate were it not for two other characters. Simon (Noah Taylor) is a Jew who is scorned by his own community because of his crazy ways. From time to time, as he makes his way through the gloomy mists of the town and forest, he is approached by Sirius (Ian Holm), who seems to be the devil. When Satan appears in a movie, I always look around for God, but rarely find him; it's usually up to the human characters to defeat the devil. In this case, Simon's visions of the death trains perhaps suggest that God is taking a century off.

The nonsupernatural side of the story involves the good Dovid and the bad Hase (a villain so obvious he lacks only a mustache to twirl). Both want the Squire to make his land available. The Squire, a lonely and bookish man, wants intellectual companionship—someone to read his poems and keep him company around the fire on long winter evenings. Dovid, a Talmudic scholar but not otherwise widely read, takes lessons from Sarah (Amanda Ryan), who is up on poetry. At one point, she and the Squire get into a literature-quoting contest.

Simon Magus creates a sinister subplot in which the evil Hase tries to trick Simon into taking a box with a Christian baby inside and hiding it in the rabbi's house so that a mob can discover it as proof that the Jews plan to eat it. Simon responds with intelligence that surprises us, but what good purpose does it do to resurrect this slander? Most people now alive would never hear of such ancient anti-Semitic calumnies were it not for movies opposing them. Does Ben Hopkins, the writer-director, imagine audiences nodding sagely as they learn that baby-eating was a myth spread by anti-Semites? Isn't it better to allow such lies to disappear into the mists of the past?

In any event, the story is resolved along standard melodramatic lines, and good (you will not be surprised to learn) triumphs. Yet still those death trains approach inexorably through Simon's visions. The papers are filled these days with stories of Polish villagers who rounded up their local Jews and burned them alive. What difference does it make who builds the train station?

Sinbad: Legend of the Seven Seas ★ ★ ★ ½

PG, 85 m., 2003

With the voices of: Brad Pitt (Sinbad), Catherine Zeta-Jones (Marina), Joseph Fiennes (Proteus), Michelle Pfeiffer (Eris), Dennis Haysbert (Kale). Directed by Patrick Gilmore and Tim Johnson and produced by Jeffrey Katzenberg and Mireille Soria. Screenplay by John Logan.

Sinbad: Legend of the Seven Seas plays like a fire sale in three departments of the genre store: Vaguely Ancient Greek, Hollywood Swashbuckler, and Modern Romance. That it works is because of the high-energy animation, some genuinely beautiful visual concepts, and a story that's a little more sensuous than we expect in animation.

Sinbad, whose voice is by Brad Pitt, is a sailor and pirate whose name and legend have been stretched to accommodate an astonishing range of movie adventures. This time we learn he was a resident of Syracuse, a commoner friend of Prince Proteus (Joseph Fiennes), and left town after his first look at Proteus's intended, Marina (Catherine Zeta-Jones). "I was jealous for the first time," he remembers.

Sinbad runs away and finds a career commanding a pirate vessel with his first mate, a stalwart giant named Kale (Dennis Haysbert). They have indeed sailed the seven seas, all right, if we're to believe his talk of retirement in Fiji. Considering how far Fiji was from Greece in the centuries before the Suez Canal, we rather doubt he has really been there, but no matter: Maybe he's been talking to Realtors.

As the film opens, Sinbad's pirate ship attacks a ship commanded by Proteus, who is in possession of the *Book of Peace*, a sacred volume of incalculable value to the future of Syracuse. This attempted theft goes ahead despite the fact that the two men are old friends and happy to see each other; a pirate is never off duty. Sinbad's scheme is interrupted by Eris (Michelle Pfeiffer), the goddess of chaos, who likes to mix things up and creates a gigantic sea monster to threaten both ships. The battle with the seemingly indestructible monster is one of several astonishing sequences in the film; the others involve sailing off the edge of the world; Tartarus, the realm of the dead, which awaits them over the edge; and a winter vastness presided over by an awesome snowbird. These scenes are animated so fluidly and envision strange sights so colorfully that there is real exhilaration.

The story, directed by Patrick Gilmore and Tim Johnson and written by John Logan, involves the shape shifting, deceptions, switches, and parental ultimatums much beloved by legend. It also exploits the tendency throughout Greek legend for the gods to interfere in the affairs of man. As flies to wanton boys are, Sinbad is to Eris. Although Sinbad did not actually steal the *Book of Peace,* the meddlesome Eris impersonates him and he seems to steal it, and Sinbad is taken prisoner and condemned to die

by King Dymas, father of Proteus. Sinbad protests his innocence; Proteus believes him and offers himself as hostage to free Sinbad to sail off in search of the book. There's a ten-day deadline.

Here's where the sensuous stuff ramps up. Marina, who says she has always wanted to go away to sea, stows away on Sinbad's ship, and that comes in handy when all of the sailors on board are bewitched by seductive Sirens. A female immune to their charms, Marina takes the helm, saves the ship, and furthers the inevitable process by which she falls in love with Sinbad, who, as the character with his name in the title, of course must get the girl.

The scene where the ship sails off the edge of the world to the land of Tartarus involves physics of a nature that Archimedes, a famous native son of Syracuse, would probably not have approved, but what wondrous visuals, and what a haunting realm they discover, filled with the hulls of wrecked ships and the bones of doomed sailors. *Sinbad* is rich with ideas and images, and it exploits the resources of mythology to create such creatures as the snowbird, who at one point locks Syracuse in a grip of ice.

Syracuse itself, for that matter, is a magically seen place, a city of towering turrets atop a mountain range. When Sinbad returns, it is to deal with the crucial question of whether Marina will return to her betrothed or stay with him. This is handled with great tact in a conversation in which both men agree that her basic motivation is to sail away and see the world, although she also, I suspect, has a burning desire to see the bunk in Sinbad's cabin.

Sinbad: Legend of the Seven Seas is another worthy entry in the recent renaissance of animation, and in the summer that also gave us *Finding Nemo,* it's a reminder that animation is the most liberating of movie genres, freed of gravity, plausibility, and even the matters of lighting and focus. There is no way that Syracuse could exist outside animation, and as we watch it, we are sailing over the edge of the human imagination. ☞

Skins ★ ★ ★
R, 87 m., 2002

Graham Greene (Mogie Yellow Lodge), Eric Schweig (Rudy Yellow Lodge), Gary Farmer

(Verdell Weasel Tail), Noah Watts (Herbie), Michelle Thrush (Stella), Lois Red Elk (Aunt Helen), Elaine Miles (Rondella), Nathaniel Arcand (Teen Mogie), Chaske Spencer (Teen Rudy). Directed by Chris Eyre and produced by Jon Kilik and David Pomier. Screenplay by Jennifer D. Lyne, based on the novel *Skins* by Adrian C. Louis.

Skins tells the story of two brothers, both Sioux, one a cop, one an alcoholic "whose mind got short-circuited in Vietnam." They live on the Pine Ridge Reservation, in the shadow of Mount Rushmore and not far from the site of the massacre at Wounded Knee. America's founding fathers were carved, the film informs us, into a mountain that was sacred to the Sioux, and that knowledge sets up a final scene of uncommon power.

The movie is almost brutal in its depiction of life at Pine Ridge, where alcoholism is nine times the national average and life expectancy 50 percent. Director Chris Eyre, whose previous film was the much-loved *Smoke Signals* (1998), has turned from comedy to tragedy and is unblinking in his portrait of a community where poverty and despair are daily realities.

Rudy Yellow Lodge (Eric Schweig), the policeman, is well liked in a job that combines law enforcement with social work. His brother, Mogie (Graham Greene), is the town drunk, but his tirades against society reveal the eloquence of a mind that still knows how to see injustice. Mogie and his buddy Verdell Weasel Tail (Gary Farmer) sit in the sun on the town's main street, drinking and providing a running commentary that sometimes cuts too close to the truth.

Flashbacks show that both brothers were abused as children by an alcoholic father. Mogie probably began life with more going for him, but Vietnam and drinking have flattened him, and it's his kid brother who wears the uniform and draws the paycheck. Those facts are established fairly early, and we think we can foresee the movie's general direction, when Eyre surprises us with a revelation about Rudy: He is a vigilante.

A man is beaten to death in an abandoned house. Rudy discovers the two shiftless kids who did it, disguises himself, and breaks their legs with a baseball bat. Angered by white-owned businesses across the reservation border that make big profits selling booze to the Indians on the day the welfare checks arrive, he torches one of the businesses—only to find he has endangered his brother's life in the process. His protest, direct and angry, is as impotent as every other form of expression seems to be.

When *Skins* premiered at Sundance last January, Eyre was criticized by some for painting a negative portrait of his community. Justin Lin, whose *Better Luck Tomorrow* showed affluent Asian-American teenagers succeeding at a life of crime, was also attacked for not taking a more positive point of view. Recently the wonderful comedy *Barbershop* has been criticized because one character does a comic riff aimed at African-American icons.

In all three cases, the critics are dead wrong because they would limit the artists in their community to impotent feel-good messages instead of applauding their freedom of expression. In all three cases, the critics are also tone-deaf because they cannot distinguish *what* the movies depict from *how* they depict it. That is particularly true with some of the critics of *Barbershop*, who say they have not seen the film. If they did, the audience's joyous laughter might help them understand the context of the controversial dialogue, and the way in which it is answered.

Skins is a portrait of a community almost without resources to save itself. We know from *Smoke Signals* that Eyre also sees another side to his people, but the anger and stark reality he uses here are potent weapons. The movie is not about a crime plot, not about whether Rudy gets caught, not about how things work out. It is about regret. Graham Greene achieves the difficult task of giving a touching performance even though his character is usually drunk, and it is the regret he expresses, to his son and to his brother, that carries the movie's burden of sadness. To see this movie is to understand why the faces on Mount Rushmore are so painful and galling to the first Americans. The movie's final image is haunting.

Slackers no stars
R, 87 m., 2002

Devon Sawa (Dave), Jason Schwartzman (Ethan), James King (Angela), Jason Segel

(Sam), Michael C. Maronna (Jeff), Laura Prepon (Reanna), Mamie Van Doren (Mrs. Van Graaf). Directed by Dewey Nicks and produced by Neal H. Moritz and Erik Feig. Screenplay by David H. Steinberg.

Slackers is a dirty movie. Not a sexy, erotic, steamy, or even smutty movie, but a just plain dirty movie. It made me feel unclean, and I'm the guy who liked *There's Something About Mary* and both *American Pie* movies. Oh, and *Booty Call*. This film knows no shame.

Consider a scene where the heroine's roommate, interrupted while masturbating, continues even while a man she has never met is in the room. Consider a scene where the hero's roommate sings a duet with a sock puppet on his penis. Consider a scene where we cut away from the hero and the heroine to join two roommates just long enough for a loud fart, and then cut back to the main story again.

And consider a scene where Mamie Van Doren, who is seventy-one years old, plays a hooker in a hospital bed who bares her breasts so that the movie's horny creep can give them a sponge bath. On the day when I saw *Slackers*, there were many things I expected and even wanted to see in a movie, but I confess Mamie Van Doren's breasts were not among them.

The movie is an exhausted retread of the old campus romance gag where the pretty girl almost believes the lies of the reprehensible schemer, instead of trusting the nice guy who loves her. The only originality the movie brings to this formula is to make it incomprehensible, through the lurching incompetence of its story structure. Details are labored while the big picture remains unpainted.

Slackers should not be confused with Richard Linklater's *Slacker* (1991), a film that will be treasured long after this one has been turned into landfill. *Slackers* stars the previously blameless Devon Sawa *(SLC Punk! Final Destination)* and Jason Schwartzman *(Rushmore)* as rivals for the attention of the beautiful Angela (James King, who despite her name is definitely a girl). Schwartzman plays Ethan, campus geek; Sawa is Dave, a professional cheater and con man. Ethan obsesses over Angela and blackmails Sawa by threatening to expose his exam-cheating scheme. He demands that Dave "deliver" the girl to him.

This demand cannot be met for a number of reasons. One of them is that Ethan is comprehensively creepy (he not only has an Angela doll made from strands of her hair, but does things with it I will not tire you by describing). Another reason is that Angela falls for Dave. The plot requires Angela to temporarily be blinded to Ethan's repulsiveness and to believe his lies about Dave. These goals are met by making Angela remarkably dense, and even then we don't believe her.

Watching *Slackers*, I was appalled by the poverty of its imagination. There is even a scene where Ethan approaches a girl from behind, thinking she is Angela, and of course she turns around and it is not Angela, but a girl who wears braces and smiles at him so widely and for so long we can almost hear the assistant director instructing her to be sure the camera can see those braces.

But back to the dirt. There is a kind of one-upmanship now at work in Hollywood, inspired by the success of several gross-out comedies, to elevate smut into an art form. This is not an entirely futile endeavor; it can be done, and when it is done well, it can be funny. But most of the wanna-bes fail to understand one thing: It is funny when a character is offensive *despite* himself, but not funny when he is *deliberately* offensive. The classic "hair gel" scene involving Ben Stiller and Cameron Diaz in *There's Something About Mary* was funny because neither one had the slightest idea what was going on.

Knowing that this movie will be block-booked into countless multiplexes, pitying the audiences that stumble into it, I want to stand in line with those kids and whisper the names of other movies now in release: *Monster's Ball, Black Hawk Down, Gosford Park, The Royal Tenenbaums, A Beautiful Mind, The Count of Monte Cristo*. Or even *Orange County*, also about screwed-up college students, but in an intelligent and amusing way. There are a lot of good movies in theaters right now. Why waste two hours (which you can never get back) seeing a rotten one?

The Sleepy Time Gal ★ ★ ★ ½
R, 94 m., 2002

Jacqueline Bisset (Frances), Martha Plimpton

(Rebecca), Nick Stahl (Morgan), Amy Madigan (Maggie), Seymour Cassel (Bob), Peggy Gormley (Betty), Frankie Faison (Jimmy Dupree), Carmen Zapata (Anna). Directed by Christopher Münch and produced by Ruth Charny and Münch. Screenplay by Münch.

Oh, what a sad story this is, about a woman who never accepted anything good in her life because she was hoping for something better. Now she is dying, and in her quiet and civilized way is trying to double back and see what can be retrieved. We think we'll have enough time to tidy up the loose ends, and then death slams down.

The Sleepy Time Gal stars Jacqueline Bisset as Frances, a woman who in some ways has led an admirable life. She made her own way. Very early, she was the late-night disc jockey on a Florida radio station, and her later jobs reflected various causes or passing fancies. She was married twice, had a son by each marriage—and she also, we learn, had a daughter by a third man, and gave her up for adoption. She has not been an attentive mother. One of the sons faithfully attends her bedside, but he observes, "She doesn't really know very much about me"—perhaps not even that he is gay. The other son phones in from London, but will not supply a return number. She wishes she could contact the daughter.

We meet that daughter early in the film. She is Rebecca (Martha Plimpton), raised by foster parents in Boston, now a corporate lawyer. She travels to Daytona Beach to buy a radio station for her employer and has the taxi stop outside a hospital there—the hospital, she knows, where she was born. She looks at it, but what can it tell her? Drive on.

The radio station for many years played rhythm and blues; it was a "race station" when such stations were unknown, says its proud owner Jimmy (Frankie Faison). He wants to give its record collection to the local community college. "I'll be damned if I know what it is that makes this deal so sad," Rebecca says, but Jimmy is not sad; he plans to travel with his wife, maybe to Malaysia. She asks him why he never moved to a bigger market. There were a lot of reasons, he says, and one of them was love. He loved the announcer who was known as the Sleepy Time Gal. Rebecca, looking at her photograph, has no way of knowing it is her mother. That night Rebecca sleeps with Jimmy, who has no way of knowing she is the daughter of the Sleepy Time Gal.

The film is written and directed by Christopher Münch, who made *The Hours and Times* (1991), about a trip to Spain during which John Lennon experiments with homosexuality. In *The Sleepy Time Gal*, he does an unexpected thing. He shows us a story that is not completed and, because of death, will never be completed. Movies are fond of deathbed scenes in which all matters are sealed and wounds cured, but sometimes, with plain bad timing, people just die and leave matters undetermined. Frances has led an interrupted life and her death will not be tidy either.

Consider one of the most beautiful and mysterious scenes in the movie, where she visits the Pennsylvania farm of a former lover and his wife. She is in remission at the time. Bob and Betty (Seymour Cassel and Peggy Gormley) have been happily married for thirty years. But always Betty has known that Frances occupies emotional ground in her husband's mind. She doesn't know they had a daughter, but she senses their feeling for each other and feels no jealousy. That Bob still loves Frances is clear from the first time we see him, in an extraordinary close-up. I have seen Seymour Cassel in countless roles over the years, but did not guess he had a smile like the one he uses to greet Frances at the airport—the smile of a man who is happy as a puppy dog to see her. This smile replaces twenty minutes of exposition.

But see how the visit goes. Listen to the conversation between Frances and Betty, and listen later to how it is recycled in the book Betty writes, which glimpses the love of Bob and Frances from outside. The book is only guessing, but becomes all that remains of that love. Frances flees from Pennsylvania as she has fled, we suspect, from everything: She is not a bad woman, but she mistrusts happiness and is frightened of belonging to anyone.

After the grace of remission, she begins to fail, and the watch at the deathbed is by her son Morgan (Nick Stahl) and nurse Maggie (Amy Madigan). They deal with her and comfort her. They care for her. But this is a difficult woman to deal with. Meanwhile, on the East Coast, Re-

587

becca continues her search for her birth parents. *The Sleepy Time Gal* is not, however, about a deathbed reunion; having given away this child, Frances finds she cannot get her back again at her own convenience.

Münch's screenplay is tenderly observant of his characters. Münch watches them as they float within the seas of their personalities. His scenes are short and often unexpected. The story unfolds in sidelong glances. His people are all stuck with who they are, and speak in thoughtful, well-considered words, as if afraid of being misquoted by destiny.

Life's missed opportunities, at the end, may seem more poignant to us than those we embraced—because in our imagination they have a perfection that reality can never rival. Bob and Frances might never have built a happy marriage ("We felt the pull of our own futures away from each other," she remembers), but their thirty years of unrealized romance has a kind of perfection. Bob's wife understands that, and remembers them both with love. She writes a book. Rebecca, who by now knows who she is and who Bob was, attends a book signing and meets her, but does not introduce herself. So one life slips past another, all of us focused on our plans for eventual perfection.

Snatch ★ ★
R, 103 m., 2001

Brad Pitt (One Punch Mickey), Andy Beckwith (Errol), Ewen Bremner (Mullet), Nikki and Teena Collins (Alex and Susi), Sorcha Cusack (Mum O'Neil), Benicio Del Toro (Franky Four Fingers), Sam Douglas (Rosebud), Mike Reid (Doug the Head), Austin Drage (Gypsy Kid), Dennis Farina (Avi). Directed by Guy Ritchie and produced by Matthew Vaughn. Screenplay by Ritchie.

In my review of *Lock, Stock and Two Smoking Barrels*, Guy Ritchie's 1999 film, I wrote: "In a time when movies follow formulas like zombies, it's alive." So what am I to say of *Snatch*, Ritchie's new film, which follows the *Lock, Stock* formula so slavishly it could be like a new arrangement of the same song?

Once again we descend into a London un-

derworld that has less to do with English criminals than with Dick Tracy. Once again the characters have Runyonesque names (Franky Four Fingers, Bullet Tooth Tony, Boris the Blade, Jack the All-Seeing Eye). Once again the plot is complicated to a degree that seems perverse. Once again titles and narration are used to identify characters and underline developments.

There is one addition of considerable wit: In the previous film, some of the accents were impenetrable to non-British audiences, so this time, in the spirit of fair play, Ritchie has added a character played by Brad Pitt, who speaks a Gypsy dialect even the other characters in the movie can't understand. Pitt paradoxically has more success communicating in this mode than some of the others do with languages we allegedly understand. He sounds like a combination of Adam Sandler and Professor Backwards.

Ritchie is a zany, high-energy director. He isn't interested in crime; he's interested in voltage. As an unfolding event, *Snatch* is fun to watch, even if no reasonable person could hope to understand the plot in one viewing. Ritchie is almost winking at us that the plot doesn't matter, that it's a clothesline for his pyrotechnics (if indeed pyrotechnics can employ clotheslines, but don't get me started).

The plot assembles its lowlifes in interlocking stories involving crooked boxing, stolen diamonds, and pigs. After Franky Four Fingers (Benicio Del Toro) steals a diamond in Antwerp and returns to London, a Russian named Boris the Blade (Rade Sherbedgia) and an American gangster named Avi (Dennis Farina) try to separate him from it—not easy, since it is in a case handcuffed to his wrist.

Meanwhile (somehow I don't think "meanwhile" quite says it), a boxer named Gorgeous George is knocked flat, and two shady promoters find themselves in hock to a crime czar. Desperate to find a winner, they recruit the Gypsy played by Pitt, who is a formidable bare-knuckle fighter that London gamblers won't recognize. Also, bodies are fed to pigs. Pitt's character and the Gypsy community where he lives are the most intriguing parts of the movie.

If this summary seems truncated, it's because an accurate description of this movie dialogue might read like the missing chapters from *Finnegans Wake*. Because the actors have cartoon faces, the action is often outrageous, and Ritchie has an aggressive camera style, the movie is not boring, but it doesn't build, and it doesn't arrive anywhere. It's hard to care much about any of the characters, because from moment to moment what happens to them seems controlled by chance. I mentioned the Marx Brothers in my review of *Lock, Stock,* and I thought of them again here, as strangely dressed weirdos occupy an anarchic nightmare.

I don't want Ritchie to "grow." I don't care if he returns to the kind of material that worked for him the first time around. I just want him to get organized, to find the through-line, to figure out why we would want to see the movie for more than its technique. I can't recommend *Snatch,* but I must report that no movie can be all bad that contains the following dialogue:

U.S. Customs Official: "Anything to declare?"

Avi (Dennis Farina): "Yeah. Don't go to England."

Note: I am not so crass as to mention in my review that Guy Ritchie and Madonna recently became man and wife. I save such biographical details for my footnotes, and would overlook them altogether except that it is blindingly clear to me that he should direct, and she should star in, a British remake of Guys and Dolls.

Solaris ★ ★ ★ ½
PG-13, 98 m., 2002

George Clooney (Chris Kelvin), Natascha McElhone (Rheya Kelvin), Jeremy Davies (Snow), Viola Davis (Helen Gordon), Ulrich Tukur (Gibarian). Directed by Steven Soderbergh and produced by James Cameron, Jon Landau, and Rae Sanchini. Screenplay by Soderbergh, based on the novel by Stanislaw Lem.

Solaris tells the story of a planet that reads minds and obliges its visitors by devising and providing people they have lost, and miss. The catch-22 is that the planet knows no more than its visitors know about these absent people. As the film opens, two astronauts have died in a space station circling the planet, and the two survivors have sent back alarming messages. A psychiatrist named Chris Kelvin (George Clooney) is sent to the station, and when he awakens after his first night on board, his wife, Rheya (Natascha McElhone), is in bed with him. Some time earlier, on Earth, she had committed suicide.

"She's not human," Kelvin is warned by Dr. Helen Gordon (Viola Davis), one of the surviving crew members. Kelvin knows this materialization cannot be his wife, yet is confronted with a person who seems palpably real, shares memories with him, and is flesh and blood. The other survivor, the goofy Snow (Jeremy Davies), asks, "I wonder if they can get pregnant?"

This story originated with a Polish novel by Stanislaw Lem, which is considered one of the major adornments of science fiction. It was made into a 1972 movie of the same name by the Russian master Andrei Tarkovsky. Now Steven Soderbergh has retold it in the kind of smart film that has people arguing about it on their way out of the theater.

The movie needs science fiction to supply the planet and the space station, which furnish the premise and concentrate the action, but it is essentially a psychological drama. When Kelvin arrives on the space station, he finds the survivors seriously spooked. Soderbergh directs Jeremy Davies to escalate his usual style of tics and stutters to the point where a word can hardly be uttered without his hands waving to evoke it from midair.

Even scarier is Gordon, the scientist played by Viola Davis, who has seen whatever catastrophe overtook the station and does not consider Kelvin part of the solution. In his gullibility, will he believe his wife has somehow really been resurrected? And . . . what does the planet *want*? Why does it do this? As a favor, or as a way of luring us into accepting manifestations of its own ego and need? Will the human race eventually be replaced by the Solaris version?

Clooney has successfully survived being named *People* magazine's sexiest man alive by deliberately choosing projects that ignore that image. His alliance with Soderbergh, both as an actor and coproducer, shows a taste for challenge. Here he is intelligent, withdrawn, sad, puzzled. Certain this seems to be his wife, and

589

although he knows intellectually that she is not, still—to destroy her would be ... inhuman. The screenplay develops a painful paradox out of that reality.

The genius of Lem's underlying idea is that the duplicates, or replicants, or whatever we choose to call them, are self-conscious and seem to carry on with free will from the moment they are evoked by the planet. Rheya, for example, says, "I'm not the person I remember. I don't remember experiencing these things." And later, "I'm suicidal because that's how you remember me."

In other words, Kelvin gets back not his dead wife, but a being who incorporates all he knows about his dead wife, and nothing else, and starts over from there. She has no secrets because he did not know her secrets. If she is suicidal, it is because he thought she was. The deep irony here is that all of our relationships in the real world are exactly like that, even without the benefit of Solaris. We do not know the actual other person. What we know is the sum of everything we think we know about them. Even empathy is perhaps of no use; we think it helps us understand how other people feel, but maybe it only tells us how we would feel, if we were them.

At a time when many American movies pump up every fugitive emotion into a clanging assault on the audience, Soderbergh's *Solaris* is quiet and introspective. There are some shocks and surprises, but this is not *Alien*. It is a workshop for a discussion of human identity. It considers not only how we relate to others, but how we relate to our ideas of others—so that a completely phony, nonhuman replica of a dead wife can inspire the same feelings that the wife herself once did. That is a peculiarity of humans: We feel the same emotions for our ideas as we do for the real world, which is why we can cry while reading a book, or fall in love with movie stars. Our idea of humanity bewitches us, while humanity itself stays safely sealed away into its billions of separate containers, or "people."

When I saw Tarkovsky's original film, I felt absorbed in it, as if it were a sponge. It was slow, mysterious, confusing, and I have never forgotten it. Soderbergh's version is more clean and spare, more easily readable, but it pays full attention to the ideas and doesn't compromise. Tarkovsky was a genius, but one who demanded great patience from his audience as he ponderously marched toward his goals. The Soderbergh version is like the same story freed from the weight of Tarkovsky's solemnity. And it evokes one of the rarest of movie emotions, ironic regret. ☞

Someone Like You ★ ★
PG-13, 97 m., 2001

Ashley Judd (Jane Goodale), Greg Kinnear (Ray), Hugh Jackman (Eddie), Ellen Barkin (Diane), Matthew Coyle (Kooky Staff Member), LeAnna Croom (Rebecca), Hugh Downs (Himself), Marisa Tomei (Liz). Directed by Tony Goldwyn and produced by Lynda Obst. Screenplay by Elizabeth Chandler, based on the novel *Animal Husbandry* by Laura Zigman.

Ashley Judd plays Jane, a woman with a theory, in *Someone Like You*. It is the Old Cow, New Cow theory, and she developed it after reading an article in the science section of the newspaper. According to the article, there is no way to get a bull to service the same cow twice. You can paint the old cow blue or spray it with perfume, but the bull's not fooled: Been there, done that. The theory says that men are like bulls, and that's why they are tirelessly motivated to move on from old conquests to new challenges.

This is not precisely a novel theory, although it has been stated in more appealing forms ("If you can't be with the one you love, love the one you're with"). If the theory is correct, it gets men off the hook for their swinish behavior, since we are hard-wired that way and cannot be blamed for millions of years of tunnel-vision evolution. But is it correct? Even about bulls? On the answer to this question depends Jane's future happiness, as well as ours while we are watching the movie.

In *Someone Like You*, Judd plays Jane Goodale, not the chimp lady but a staffer on a daytime talk show hosted by Ellen Barkin. Also on the staff are Ray (Greg Kinnear) and Eddie (Hugh Jackman). Ray is in a relationship. Eddie is a walking, talking example of the Old Cow, New Cow theory, introducing a new cow to his bedroom every night. Jane likes Ray, and Ray, despite his old cow at home, likes Jane, who is a new cow, and so they have an affair, but then she becomes an old cow and the previous old cow begins to look like a new cow again, and so they break up. Jane has meanwhile given up her apartment because she thought she was going to move in with Ray, and so she becomes Eddie's platonic roommate, clocking the cow traffic.

This is, you will have gathered, a pretty lame premise. The screenplay is based on *Animal Husbandry*, a novel by Laura Zigman, unread by me. As a movie, it knows little about men, women, or television shows, but has studied movie formulas so carefully that we can see each new twist and turn as it creeps ever so slowly into view. Will Ray return to Jane? Will she begin to like Eddie? Can Eddie settle for one cow? What about the identity of Ray's mysterious girlfriend? Students of my Law of Economy of Characters will know that movies are thrifty and have a use for all the characters they introduce, and so the solution to that mystery arrives long, long after we have figured it out.

For a movie about a TV show, this one doesn't know much about television. The whole denouement depends on us believing that this high-rated show would do a telephone interview with an anonymous magazine columnist who has become famous for the Old Cow, New Cow theory, and that Jane (who writes the column anonymously) would then decide to blow her cover, burst onto the set, and deliver an endless monologue about how much wiser she is now than she used to be. The chances of a production assistant standing in front of the star of a TV show and talking for several minutes are approximately zero, especially since, let's face it, she's babbling: Her speech reminded me of something in a barnyard. It's not a cow, although it's often found close to one.

The Son ★ ★ ★ ★

NO MPAA RATING, 103 m., 2003

Olivier Gourmet (Olivier), Morgan Marinne (Francis), Isabella Soupart (Magali), Remy Renaud (Philippo), Nassim Hassaini (Omar), Kevin Leroy (Raoul), Felicien Pitsaer (Steve). Directed by Jean-Pierre Dardenne and Luc Dardenne and produced by the Dardennes and Denis Freyd. Screenplay by the Dardennes.

The Son is complete, self-contained, and final. All the critic can bring to it is his admiration. It needs no insight or explanation. It sees everything and explains all. It is as assured and flawless a telling of sadness and joy as I have ever seen.

I agree with Stanley Kauffmann, in the *New Republic*, that a second viewing only underlines the film's greatness, but I would not want to have missed my first viewing, so I will write carefully. The directors, Jean-Pierre Dardenne and Luc Dardenne, do not make the slightest effort to mislead or deceive us. Nor do they make any effort to explain. They simply (not so simply) show, and we lean forward, hushed, reading the faces, watching the actions, intent on sharing the feelings of the characters.

Let me describe a very early sequence in enough detail for you to appreciate how the Dardenne brothers work. Olivier (Olivier Gourmet), a Belgian carpenter, supervises a shop where teenage boys work. He corrects a boy using a power saw. We wonder, because we have been beaten down by formula films, if someone is going to lose a finger or a hand. No. The plank is going to be cut correctly.

A woman comes into the shop and asks Olivier if he can take another apprentice. No, he has too many already. He suggests the welding shop. The moment the woman and the young applicant leave, Olivier slips from the shop and, astonishingly, scurries after them like a feral animal and spies on them through a door opening and the angle of a corridor. A little later, strong and agile, he leaps up onto a metal cabinet to steal a look through a high window.

Then he tells the woman he will take the boy after all. She says the boy is in the shower room. The handheld camera, which follows Olivier everywhere, usually in close medium shot, follows him as he looks around a corner (we intuit it is a corner; two walls form an apparent join). Is he watching the boy take a shower? Is Olivier gay? No. We have seen too many movies. He is simply looking at the boy asleep, fully clothed, on the floor of the shower room. After a long, absorbed look he wakes up the boy and tells him he has a job.

Now you must absolutely stop reading and go see the film. Walk out of the house today, tonight, and see it, if you are open to simplicity, depth, maturity, silence, in a film that sounds in the echo chambers of the heart. *The Son* is a great film. If you find you cannot respond to it, that is the degree to which you have room to grow. I am not being arrogant; I grew during this film. It taught me things about the cinema I did not know.

What did I learn? How this movie is only possible because of the way it was made, and would have been impossible with traditional narrative styles. Like rigorous documentarians, the Dardenne brothers follow Olivier, learning everything they know about him by watching him. They do not point, underline, or send signals by music. There are no reaction shots because the entire movie is their reaction shot. The brothers make the consciousness of the Olivier character into the auteur of the film.

. . . So now you have seen the film. If you were spellbound, moved by its terror and love, struck that the visual style is the only possible one for this story, then let us agree that rarely has a film told us less and told us all, both at the once.

Olivier trains wards of the Belgian state—gives them a craft after they are released from a juvenile home. Francis (Morgan Marinne) was in such a home from his eleventh to sixteenth years. Olivier asks him what his crime was. He stole a car radio.

"And got five years?"

"There was a death."

"What kind of a death?"

There was a child in the car, whom Francis did not see. The child began to cry and would not let go of Francis, who was frightened and "grabbed him by the throat."

"Strangled him," Olivier corrects.

"I didn't mean to," Francis says.

"Do you regret what you did?"

"Obviously."

"Why obviously?"

"Five years locked up. That's worth regretting."

You have seen the film and know what Olivier knows about this death. You have seen it and know the man and boy are at a remote lumberyard on a Sunday. You have seen it and know how *hard* the noises are in the movie,

the heavy planks banging down one upon another. How it hurts even to hear them. The film does not use these sounds or the towers of lumber to create suspense or anything else. It simply respects the nature of lumber, as Olivier does and is teaching Francis to do. You expect, because you have been trained by formula films, an accident or an act of violence. What you could not expect is the breathtaking spiritual beauty of the ending of the film, which is nevertheless no less banal than everything that has gone before.

Olivier Gourmet won the award for best actor at Cannes 2002. He plays an ordinary man behaving at all times in an ordinary way. Here is the key: *Ordinary for him*. The word for his behavior—not his performance, his behavior—is "exemplary." We use the word to mean "praiseworthy." Its first meaning is "fit for imitation."

Everything that Olivier does is exemplary. Walk like this. Hold yourself just so. Measure exactly. Do not use the steel hammer when the wooden mallet is required. Center the nail. Smooth first with the file, then with the sandpaper. Balance the plank and lean into the ladder. Pay for your own apple turnover. Hold a woman who needs to be calmed. Praise a woman who has found she is pregnant. Find out the truth before you tell the truth. Do not use words to discuss what cannot be explained. Be willing to say, "I don't know." Be willing to have a son and teach him a trade. Be willing to be a father.

A recent movie got a laugh by saying there is a rule in *The Godfather* to cover every situation. There can never be that many rules. *The Son* is about a man who needs no rules because he respects his trade and knows his tools. His trade is life. His tools are his loss and his hope.

Songcatcher ★ ★ ★
PG-13, 112 m., 2001

Janet McTeer (Dr. Lily Penleric), Emmy Rossum (Deladis Slocumb), Aidan Quinn (Tom Bledsoe), Pat Carroll (Viney Butler), Jane Adams (Elna Penleric), E. Katherine Kerr (Harriet Tolliver), David Patrick Kelly (Earl Gibbons), Greg Cook (Fate Honeycutt), Iris DeMent (Rose Gentry), Stephanie Roth (Alice Kincaid), Mike Harding (Reese Kincaid). Directed by Maggie Greenwald and produced by Richard Miller and Ellen Rigas-Venetis. Screenplay by Greenwald.

Songcatcher tells the story of a woman who goes into the mountains of Appalachia in 1907, and finds the people singing British ballads that are almost unchanged since they arrived two hundred years earlier. It is also a feminist parable transplanted to earlier times, revealing too much consciousness of modern values. I'm more comfortable with the women I find in Willa Cather's novels, who live at about the same time, who strive to be independent and to be taken seriously, and yet are entirely in and of their worlds. The characters in a serious historical story should not know what happens later.

If we accept *Songcatcher* as a contemporary parable in period costumes, however, there is much to enjoy—not least the sound of the songs themselves. "I have never been anywhere where the music is so much a part of life as it is here," says Dr. Lily Penleric (Janet McTeer), the musicologist, who has fled to the mountains in anger after being passed over for an academic appointment she clearly deserves. The people of these North Carolina hills would as soon sing as talk, and indeed there's a scene where Tom Bledsoe (Aidan Quinn) knocks a man down, and the man stands up and starts to sing.

Tom is a suspicious leader of these people, and doubts Dr. Penleric's motives. He thinks she wants to steal his people's songs. He is right, although she calls it collecting, and hauls heavy Edison equipment up the hillside so she can record the songs on wax cylinders and maybe sell them in stores. She considers this preserving their culture. "The only way to preserve our way of life up here," Tom tells her, "is to preserve your way of life—down there."

We meet the people of the settlement: Viney Butler (Pat Carroll), a Ma Joad type; Deladis Slocumb (Emmy Rossum), a young woman with a voice pure and true; Elna Penleric (Jane Adams), the professor's sister, who has come here to start a one-room school; and her fellow teacher and lover Harriet Tolliver (E. Katherine Kerr), who says she will flee if anyone ever discovers she is a lesbian. Then there's David Patrick Kelly as a coal company representative, who wants to strip mine the land. There are so many issues simmering here in the hollow that

it's a wonder Jeff Greenfield doesn't materialize and hold a town meeting.

The movie has a good amount of sex for a drama about folk music collecting. The lesbians find a secluded glade in the woods, Dr. Penleric and Tom Bledsoe feel powerful urges, and there's a local philanderer named Reese Kincaid (Mike Harding) who cheats on his wife, Alice (Stephanie Roth). The most startling sex scene involves the musicologist and the mountain man; a piercing scream rents the air, and we see Dr. Penleric running through the woods tearing off her clothes before discovering Tom in a clearing and covering him passionately with kisses. The scream comes from a panther (at first I thought it was the noon whistle), and Lilly has been advised by Viney to flee from such an attack by throwing off her clothes to distract it; as a depiction of Victorian morality making the leap into modern lust, this scene will serve.

I liked the tone of the movie, and its spirit. I liked the lashings of melodrama in the midst of the music collecting. Most of all, I liked the songs, especially one sung by Iris DeMent as a woman who loses her home, and by young Emmy Rossum when she is urged to give the newcomer a sample of her singing voice. *Songcatcher* is perhaps too laden with messages for its own good, but it has many moments of musical beauty, and it's interesting to watch Janet McTeer as she starts with Lily Penleric as a cold, abstract academic, and allows her, little by little, to warm in the sun of these songs.

A Song for Martin ★ ★ ★ ½
PG-13, 118 m., 2002

Sven Wollter (Martin), Viveka Seldahl (Barbara), Reine Brynolfsson (Biederman), Lisa Werlinder (Elisabeth), Linda Källgren (Karin), Peter Engman (Philip), Klas Dahlstedt (Erik), Kristina Törnqvist (Dr. Gierlich). Directed by Bille August and produced by August, Lars Kolvig, Michael Lundberg, and Michael Obel. Screenplay by August, based on the novel by Ulla Isaksson.

A Song for Martin tells the story of two people who find sudden, delirious love, and then lose it in one of the most painful ways possible, because of Alzheimer's disease. Their love and loss is all the more poignant because they are such warm, creative people—and perhaps because we sense an ease and acceptance between the two actors, Sven Wollter and Viveka Seldahl, who were married in real life. That she died not long after the movie was made adds another dimension of poignance.

The film, directed by Bille August *(Pelle the Conqueror)*, takes place in cultural circles in Gothenburg, Sweden. Martin, played by Wollter, is a famous conductor and composer, and Barbara (Seldahl) is his first violinist. One day she points out an error to him, he is grateful, they walk back to a hotel together, there is eye contact, and before long they are involved in a romance that must have been smoldering for years. Martin's manager Biederman (Reine Brynolfsson) is quick to spot the situation, and dubious ("Do you think it's wise to fiddle with the fiddler?"), but soon Martin and Barbara have divorced their current spouses and are married and on a passionate honeymoon in Morocco.

The movie probably makes a mistake in giving them both earlier marriages, since leaving those partners raises questions the movie never really deals with. Better to have them meet with their hands free, especially since the movie is not about former marriages but about a good one that turns sad.

The signs of Alzheimer's are at first isolated. Martin forgets Biederman's name. He is sometimes confused. Progress on composing an opera becomes uncertain. "It's as if something fell inside my head," he tells Barbara. The disease progresses, probably more quickly than it would in real life, and there are fairly melodramatic episodes, as when he forgets his purpose on the podium or uses a potted tree for a urinal in a restaurant.

The movie is not about Alzheimer's so much as about loss. Barbara takes them back to the same Moroccan hotel where they had their honeymoon, hoping to reawaken his memories, but it's a disaster, and leads to a scene where he tries to drown them both, in a combination of fear, confusion, and anger. Sometimes she gets angry at him. "All I ask," she tells him, "is a little of the charm you turn on for everyone else." But the man who was Martin is disappearing before her very eyes.

For me the center of the film is the perfor-

mance by Viveka Seldahl. She is a pretty woman with a warm smile, and she embodies the feelings of Barbara so completely that the pain of her loss becomes palpable. The movie is more honest about Alzheimer's, I think, than *Iris*, the film about the novelist Iris Murdoch, who also had the disease. *A Song for Martin* starts at the beginning and goes straight through to the inevitable end, unblinkingly. It doesn't relieve the pressure, as *Iris* does, with flashbacks to happier days. What it knows is that the happier days are behind, and the person who lived them is disappearing. That the body of that person remains present and alive is a particular grief for the survivors.

Songs from the Second Floor ★ ★ ★ ★
NO MPAA RATING, 98 m., 2000

Lars Nordh (Kalle), Stefan Larsson (Stefan), Torbjörn Fahlstrom (Pelle), Sten Andersson (Lasse), Lucio Vucina (Magician), Hanna Eriksson (Mia), Peter Roth (Tomas), Tommy Johansson (Uffe). Directed by Roy Andersson and produced by Lisa Alwert and Andersson. Screenplay by Andersson.

In a sour gray city, filled with pale drunken salarymen and parading flagellants, everything goes wrong, pain is laughed at, businesses fail, traffic seizes up, and a girl is made into a human sacrifice to save a corporation. Roy Andersson's *Songs from the Second Floor* is a collision at the intersection of farce and tragedy—the apocalypse, as a joke on us.

You have never seen a film like this before. You may not enjoy it, but you will not forget it. Andersson is a deadpan Swedish surrealist who has spent the last twenty-five years making "the best TV commercials in the world" (Ingmar Bergman), and now bites off the hand that fed him, chews it thoughtfully, spits it out, and tramples on it. His movie regards modern capitalist society with the detached hilarity of a fanatic saint squatting on his pillar in the desert.

I saw it at the 2000 Cannes Film Festival. Understandably, it did not immediately find a distributor. Predictably, audiences did not flock to it. When I screened it at my 2001 Overlooked Film Festival, there were times when the audience laughed out loud, times when it squinted in dismay, times when it watched in disbelief.

When two of the actors came out onstage afterward, it was somehow completely appropriate that one of them never said a word.

I love this film because it is completely new, starting from a place no other film has started from, proceeding implacably to demonstrate the logic of its despair, arriving at a place of no hope. One rummages for the names of artists to evoke: Bosch, Tati, Kafka, Beckett, Dali. It is "slapstick Ingmar Bergman," says J. Hoberman in the *Village Voice*. Yes, and tragic Groucho Marx.

The film opens ironically with a man in a tanning machine—ironic, because all of the other characters will look like they've spent years in sunless caves. It proceeds with a series of set pieces in which the camera, rarely moving, gazes impassively at scenes of absurdity and despair. A man is fired and clings to the leg of his boss, who marches down a corridor dragging him behind. A magician saws a volunteer in two. Yes. A man with the wrong accent is attacked by a gang. A man burns down his own store and then assures insurance inspectors it was arson, but as they talk we lose interest, because outside on the street a parade of flagellants marches past, whipping themselves in time to their march.

There is the most slender of threads connecting the scenes—the arsonist is a continuing character—but Andersson is not telling a conventional story. He is planting his camera here and there in a city that has simply stopped working, has broken down and is cannibalizing itself. It is a twentieth-century city, but Andersson sees it as an appropriate backdrop for the plague or any other medieval visitation. And its citizens have fallen back on ancient fearful superstition to protect themselves.

Consider the scene where clerics and businessmen, all robed for their offices, gather in a desolate landscape as a young woman walks the plank to her death below. Perhaps the sacrifice of her life will placate the gods who are angry with the corporation. We watch this scene and we are forced to admit that corporations are capable of such behavior: that a tobacco company, for example, expects its customers to walk the plank every day.

Is there no hope in this devastation? A man who corners the market in crucifixes now bitterly tosses out his excess inventory. "I staked everything on a loser," he complains. Does that make the movie anti-Christian? No. It is not anti-anything. It is about the loss of hope, about the breakdown of all systems of hope. Its characters are piggish, ignorant, clueless salarymen who, without salaries, have no way to be men. The movie argues that in an economic collapse our modern civilization would fall from us, and we would be left wandering our cities like the plague victims of old, seeking relief in drunkenness, superstition, sacrifice, sex, and self-mockery.

Oh, but yes, the film is often very funny about this bleak view. I have probably not convinced you of that. It's funny because it stands back and films its scenes in long shot, the camera not moving, so that we can distance ourselves from the action—and we remember the old rule from the silent days: Comedy in long shot, tragedy in close-up. Close shots cause us to identify with the characters, to weep and fear along with them. Long shots allow us to view them objectively, within their environment. *Songs from the Second Floor* is a parade of fools marching blindly to their ruin, and for the moment, we are still spectators and have not been required to join the march. The laughter inspired by the movie is sometimes at the absurd, sometimes simply from relief.

The Son's Room ★ ★ ★ ½
R, 99 m., 2002

Nanni Moretti (Giovanni), Laura Morante (Paola), Jasmine Trinca (Irene), Giuseppe Sanfelice (Andrea), Sofia Vigliar (Arianna), Silvio Orlando (Oscar), Claudia Della Seta (Raffaella), Stefano Accorsi (Tommaso). Directed by Nanni Moretti and produced by Angelo Barbagallo and Moretti. Screenplay by Moretti, Linda Ferri, and Heidrun Schleef.

The Son's Room follows an affluent Italian family through all the stages of grieving. When the teenage son dies in a diving accident, his parents and sister react with instinctive denial, followed by sorrow, anger, the disintegration of their own lives, the picking up of the pieces, and finally a form of acceptance. Because all of these stages are reflected in the clearly seen details of everyday life, the effect is very touching.

The film has been written and directed by

Nanni Moretti, whose 1994 film *Caro Diario (Dear Diary)* was about his own death sentence: Based on fact, it related his feelings when he was diagnosed with cancer and told (mistakenly) that he had a year to live. That film was not quite successful, an uneasy truce between Woody Allen and Elisabeth Kübler-Ross, but *The Son's Room* has a relaxed tenderness and empathy. He got the idea for the story, he has said, when he learned that he and his wife were expecting a son.

Moretti stars as Giovanni, a psychiatrist whose patients rehearse the same problems hour after hour in his office. Can he help them? That's a question he eventually has to ask himself. At home, there is a problem when his son Andrea (Giuseppe Sanfelice) is accused of having stolen a fossil from the school science lab. He denies the charge. Giovanni and his wife, Paola (Laura Morante), get involved, visit the parents of his son's accuser. We see that this is a happy family; the sister Irene (Jasmine Trinca) is on a basketball team, the son studies Latin, and when the parents overhear a conversation indicating that Andrea smokes pot, they are not too concerned. There is a lovely scene where all four sing together during a car trip.

Then the accident takes place, and has the effect of sending mother, father, and daughter spinning into their own private corners. For the father, this means impatience with his clients, and resentment against one whose call on a Sunday derailed Giovanni's plans to go jogging with his son—thus freeing the boy to go diving, and indirectly leading to his death. Grieving mixes with pain as Giovanni imagines the way the day *should* have unfolded, with the two of them on a run, and the son still alive at the end.

We know from the fable of the appointment in Samarra that it is no use trying to outsmart fate, but it is human nature to try—and to torture ourselves when we fail. For Irene, the sister, grief and anger cause her to fight during a basketball game. For Giovanni, they lead to questions about his practice. And then . . . a letter arrives, from Arianna (Sofia Vigliar). It is addressed to the dead Andrea, whom she met for only one day. But somehow there was a connection between them, and she hopes to see him again.

The Son's Room uses this letter, and Ari-

anna's eventual appearance, as its means of resolving the story. To explain how this is done would be unsatisfactory, because Moretti is more concerned with tones and nuances than plot points, and the gradual way Arianna becomes the instrument of acceptance is quietly touching. She represents life that must go on—just as Auden in his poem observes that although Icarus falls into the sea, farmers still plow their fields and dogs go on their doggy errands. Curious, how a late shot of people at dawn says so much by saying nothing at all.

The Son's Room won the Palme d'Or, or top prize, at Cannes. It was a popular choice—too popular, sniffed some, who objected to its mainstream style and frank sentimentality. Yes, but not all movies can be stark, difficult, and obscure. Sometimes in a quite ordinary way a director can reach out and touch us.

Sorority Boys ½★

R, 96 m., 2002

Barry Watson (Dave/Daisy), Harland Williams (Doofer/Roberta), Michael Rosenbaum (Adam/Adina), Melissa Sagemiller (Leah), Heather Matarazzo (Katie). Directed by Wallace Wolodarsky and produced by Larry Brezner and Walter Hamada. Screenplay by Joe Jarvis and Greg Coolidge.

One element of *Sorority Boys* is undeniably good, and that is the title. Pause by the poster on the way into the theater. That will be your high point. It has all you need for a brainless, autopilot, sitcom ripoff: a high concept that is right there in the title, easily grasped at the pitch meeting. The title suggests the poster art, the poster art gives you the movie, and story details can be sketched in by study of *Bosom Buddies, National Lampoon's Animal House,* and the shower scenes in any movie involving girls' dorms or sports teams.

What is unusual about *Sorority Boys* is how it caves in to the homophobia of the audience by not even *trying* to make its cross-dressing heroes look like halfway, even tenth-of-the-way, plausible girls. They look like college boys wearing cheap wigs and dresses they bought at Goodwill. They usually need a shave. One keeps his retro forward-thrusting sideburns and just combs a couple of locks of his wig forward to "cover" them. They look as feminine as the sailors wearing coconut brassieres in *South Pacific.*

Their absolute inability to pass as women leads to another curiosity about the movie, which is that all of the other characters are obviously mentally impaired. How else to explain fraternity brothers who don't recognize their own friends in drag? Sorority sisters who think these are real women and want to pledge them on first sight? A father who doesn't realize that's his *own son* he's trying to pick up?

I know. I'm being too literal. I should be a good sport and go along with the joke. But the joke is not funny. The movie is not funny. If it's this easy to get a screenplay filmed in Hollywood, why did they bother with that Project Greenlight contest? Why not ship all the entries directly to Larry Brezner and Walter Hamada, the producers of *Sorority Boys*, who must wear Santa suits to work?

The plot begins with three members of Kappa Omicron Kappa fraternity, who are thrown out of the KOK house for allegedly stealing party funds. Homeless and forlorn, they decide to pledge the Delta Omicron Gamma house after learning that the DOGs need new members. Dave (Barry Watson) becomes Daisy and is soon feeling chemistry with the DOG president, Leah (Melisa Sagemiller), who is supposed to be an intellectual feminist but can shower nude with him and not catch on he's a man.

Harland Williams and Michael Rosenbaum play the other two fugitive KOKs—roles that, should they become stars, will be invaluable as a source of clips at roasts in their honor. Among the DOGs is the invaluable Heather Matarazzo, who now has a lock on the geeky plain girl roles, even though she is in actual fact sweet and pretty. Just as Latina actresses have risen up in arms against Jennifer Connelly for taking the role of John Forbes Nash's El Salvadoran wife in *A Beautiful Mind,* so ugly girls should picket Heather Matarazzo.

Because the intelligence level of the characters must be low, very low, very very low, for the masquerade to work, the movie contains no wit, only labored gags involving falsies, lipstick, unruly erections, and straight guys who don't realize they're trying to pick up a man. (I imagine yokels in the audience responding with the Gradually Gathering Guffaw as they

catch on. "Hey, Jethro! He don't know she's a guy! Haw! Haw! Haw!") The entire movie, times ten, lacks the humor of a single line in the Bob Gibson/Shel Silverstein song "Mendocino Desperados" ("She was a he, but what the hell, honey / Since you've already got my money...").

I'm curious about who would go to see this movie. Obviously moviegoers with a low opinion of their own taste. It's so obviously what it is that you would require a positive desire to throw away money in order to lose two hours of your life. *Sorority Boys* will be the worst movie playing in any multiplex in America this weekend, and, yes, I realize *Crossroads* is still out there.

Spellbound ★ ★ ★
G, 95 m., 2003

The Spellers: Harry Altman, Angela Arenivar, Ted Brigham, April DeGideo, Neil Kadakia, Nupur Lala, Emily Stagg, Ashley White. A documentary directed by Jeffrey Blitz and produced by Blitz and Sean Welch.

It is useful to be a good speller, up to a point. After that point, you're just showing off. The eight contestants in *Spellbound,* who have come from all over the country to compete in the 1999 National Spelling Bee, are never likely to need words such as "opsimath" in their daily rounds, although "logorrhea" might come in handy. As we watch them drilling with flash cards and work sheets, we hope they will win, but we're not sure what good it will do them.

And yet for some of them, winning the bee will make a substantial difference in their lives— not because they can spell so well, but because the prizes include college scholarships. Take Angela Arenivar, for example. She makes it all the way to the finals in Washington, D.C., from the Texas farm where her father works as a laborer. He originally entered the country illegally, still speaks no English, and is proud beyond all words of his smart daughter.

We cheer for her in the finals, but then we cheer for all of these kids, because it is so easy to remember the pain of getting something wrong in front of the whole class. None of these teenagers is good only at spelling. Jeffrey Blitz takes his documentary into their homes and schools, looks at their families and ambitions, and shows us that they're all smart in a lot of other ways—including the way that makes them a little lonely at times.

Consider Harry Altman. He is a real kid, but has so many eccentricities that he'd be comic relief in a teenage comedy. His laugh would make you turn around in a crowded room. He screws his face up into so many shapes while trying to spell a word that it's a wonder the letters can find their way to the surface. High school cannot be easy for Harry, but he will have his revenge at the twentieth class reunion, by which time he will no doubt be a millionaire or a Nobel winner, and still with that unlikely laugh.

To be smart is to be an outsider in high school. To be seen as smart is even worse (many kids learn to conceal their intelligence). There is a kind of rough populism among adolescents that penalizes those who try harder or are more gifted. In talking with high school kids, I find that many of them go to good or serious movies by themselves, and choose vulgarity and violence when going with their friends. To be a kid and read good books and attend good movies sets you aside. Thank God you have the books and the movies for company—and now the Internet, where bright teenagers find each other.

In *Spellbound*, which was one of this year's Oscar nominees, Blitz begins with portraits of his eight finalists and then follows them to Washington, where they compete on ESPN in the bee, which was founded years ago by Scripps-Howard newspapers. The ritual is time-honored. The word is pronounced and repeated. It may be used in a sentence. Then the contestant has to repeat it, spell it, and say it again.

We've never heard most of the words (cabotinage?). General spelling rules are useful only up to a point, and then memory is the only resource. Some of these kids study up to eight hours a day, memorizing words they may never hear, write, or use. Even when they think they know a word, it's useful to pause and be sure, because once you get to the end of a word you can't go back and start again. You don't win because of your overall score, but because you have been perfect longer than anyone else; the entire bee is a sudden-death overtime.

Oddly enough, it's not tragic when a kid loses. Some of them shrug or grin, and a couple seem happy to be delivered from the pressure

and the burden. One girl is devastated when she misspells a word, but we know it's because she knew it, and knew she knew it, and still got it wrong. They're all winners, in a way, and had to place first in their state or regional contests to get to Washington. When the finalist Nupur Lala, whose parents came from India, returns home to Florida, she's a local hero, and a restaurant hails her on the sign out in front: "Congradulations, Nupur!"

Spider ★ ★ ★
R, 98 m., 2003

Ralph Fiennes (Dennis "Spider" Cleg), Miranda Richardson (Yvonne/Mrs. Cleg), Gabriel Byrne (Bill Cleg), Lynn Redgrave (Mrs. Wilkinson), John Neville (Terrence), Bradley Hall (Young Spider), Gary Reineke (Freddy), Philip Craig (John). Directed by David Cronenberg and produced by Catherine Bailey, Cronenberg, and Samuel Hadida. Screenplay by Patrick McGrath, based on his novel.

He looked like a man cut away from the stake, when the fire has overrunningly wasted all the limbs without consuming them. . . .

So Ahab is described in *Moby-Dick*. The description matches Dennis Cleg, the subject (I hesitate to say "hero") of David Cronenberg's *Spider*. Played by Ralph Fiennes, he is a man eaten away by a lifetime of inner torment; there is not one ounce on his frame that is not needed to support his suffering. Fiennes, so jolly as J. Lo's boyfriend in *Maid in Manhattan*, looks here like a refugee from the slums of hell.

We see him as the last man off a train to London, muttering to himself, picking up stray bits from the sidewalk, staring out through blank, uncomprehending eyes. He finds a boarding-house in a cheerless district, and is shown to a barren room by the gruff landlady (Lynn Redgrave). In the lounge he meets an old man who explains kindly that the house has a "curious character, but one grows used to it after a few years."

This is a halfway house, we learn, and Spider has just been released from a mental institution. In the morning the landlady bursts into his room without knocking—just like a mother, we think, and indeed later he will confuse her with his stepmother. For that matter, his mother, his stepmother, and an alternate version of the landlady are all played by the same actress (Miranda Richardson); we are meant to understand that her looming presence fills every part of his mind that is reserved for women.

The movie is based on an early novel by Patrick McGrath. It enters into the subjective mind of Spider Cleg so completely that it's impossible to be sure what is real and what is not. We see everything through Spider's eyes, and he is not a reliable witness. He hardly seems aware of the present, so traumatized is he by the past. Whether they are trustworthy or not, his childhood memories are the landscape in which he wanders.

In flashbacks, we meet his father, Bill Cleg (Gabriel Byrne) and mother (Richardson). Then we see his father making a rendezvous in a garden shed with Yvonne (also Richardson), a tramp from the pub. The mother discovers them there, is murdered with a spade, and buried right then and there in the garden, with the little boy witnessing everything. Yvonne moves in, and at one point tells young Dennis, "Yes, it's true he murdered your mother. Try and think of me as your mother now."

Why are the two characters played by the same actress? Is this an artistic decision, or a clue to Spider's mental state? We cannot tell for sure, because there is almost nothing in his life that Spider knows for sure. He is adrift in fear. Fiennes plays the character as a man who wants to take back every step, reconsider every word, question every decision. There is a younger version of the character, Spider as a boy, played by Bradley Hall. He is solemn and wide-eyed, is beaten with a belt at one point, has a childhood that functions as an open wound. We understand that this boy is the most important inhabitant of the older Spider's gaunt and wasted body.

The movie is well-made and -acted, but it lacks dimension because it essentially has only one character, and he lacks dimension. We watch him and perhaps care for him, but we cannot identify with him, because he is no longer capable of change and decision. He has long since stopped trying to tell apart his layers of memory, nightmare, experience, and fantasy. He is alone and adrift. He wanders through

memories, lost and sad, and we wander after him, knowing, somehow, that Spider is not going to get better—and that if he does, that would simply mean the loss of his paranoid fantasies, which would leave him with nothing. Sometimes people hold onto illnesses because they are defined by them, given distinction, made real. There seems to be no sense in which Spider could engage the world on terms that would make him any happier.

There are three considerable artists at work here: Cronenberg, Fiennes, and Richardson. They are at the service of a novelist who often writes of grotesque and melancholy characters; he is Britain's modern master of the gothic. His Spider Cleg lives in a closed system, like one of those sealed glass globes where little plants and tiny marine organisms trade their energy back and forth indefinitely. In Spider's globe he feeds on his pain and it feeds on him. We feel that this exchange will go on and on, whether we watch or not. The details of the film and of the performances are meticulously realized; there is a reward in seeing artists working so well. But the story has no entry or exit, and is cold, sad, and hopeless. Afterward, I felt more admiration than gratitude.

Spider-Man ★ ★ ½
PG-13, 121 m., 2002

Tobey Maguire (Spider-Man/Peter Parker), Willem Dafoe (Green Goblin/Norman Osborn), Kirsten Dunst (Mary Jane Watson), James Franco (Harry Osborn), Cliff Robertson (Ben Parker), Rosemary Harris (May Parker), J. K. Simmons (J. Jonah Jameson), Joe Manganiello (Flash Thompson). Directed by Sam Raimi and produced by Laura Ziskin, Ian Brice, and Avi Arad. Screenplay by David Koepp, based on the Marvel comic by Stan Lee and Steve Ditko.

Imagine *Superman* with a Clark Kent more charismatic than the Man of Steel, and you'll understand how *Spider-Man* goes wrong. Tobey Maguire is pitch-perfect as the socially retarded Peter Parker, but when he becomes Spider-Man, the film turns to action sequences that zip along like perfunctory cartoons. Not even during Spidey's first experimental outings do we feel that flesh and blood are contending with gravity. Spidey soars too quickly through the skies of Manhattan; he's as convincing as Mighty Mouse.

The appeal of the best sequences in the Superman and Batman movies is that they lend weight and importance to comic-book images. Within the ground rules set by each movie, they even have plausibility. As a reader of the Spider-Man comics, I admired the vertiginous frames showing Spidey dangling from terrifying heights. He had the powers of a spider and the instincts of a human being, but the movie is split between a plausible Peter Parker and an inconsequential superhero.

Consider a sequence early in the film, after Peter Parker is bitten by a mutant spider and discovers his new powers. His hand is sticky. He doesn't need glasses anymore. He was scrawny yesterday, but today he's got muscles. The movie shows him becoming aware of these facts, but insufficiently amazed (or frightened) by them. He learns how to spin and toss webbing, and finds that he can make enormous leaps. And then there's a scene where he's like a kid with a new toy, jumping from one rooftop to another, making giant leaps, whooping with joy.

Remember the first time you saw the characters defy gravity in *Crouching Tiger, Hidden Dragon*. They transcended gravity, but they didn't dismiss it: They seemed to possess weight, dimension, and presence. Spider-Man, as he leaps across the rooftops, is landing too lightly, rebounding too much like a bouncing ball. He looks like a video-game figure, not like a person having an amazing experience.

The other superbeing in the movie is the Green Goblin, who surfs the skies. He, too, looks like a drawing being moved quickly around a frame, instead of like a character who has mastered a daring form of locomotion. He's handicapped, also, by his face, which looks like a high-tech action figure with a mouth that doesn't move. I understand why it's immobile (we're looking at a mask), but I'm not persuaded; the movie could simply ordain that the Green Goblin's exterior shell has a face that's mobile, and the character would become more interesting. (True, Spider-Man has *no* mouth, and Peter Parker barely opens his—the words slip out through a reluctant slit.)

The film tells Spidey's origin story—who

Peter Parker is, who Aunt May (Rosemary Harris) and Uncle Ben (Cliff Robertson) are, how Peter's an outcast at school, how he burns with unrequited love for Mary Jane Watson (Kirsten Dunst), how he peddles photos of Spider-Man to cigar-chomping editor J. Jonah Jameson (J. K. Simmons).

Peter Parker was crucial in the evolution of Marvel comics because he was fallible and had recognizable human traits. He was a nerd, a loner, socially inept, insecure, a poor kid being raised by relatives. Tobey Maguire gets all of that just right, and I enjoyed the way Dunst is able to modulate her gradually increasing interest in this loser who begins to seem attractive to her. I also liked the complexity of the villain, who in his Dr. Jekyll manifestation is brilliant tycoon Norman Osborn (Willem Dafoe) and in his Mr. Hyde persona is a cackling psychopath. Osborn's son, Harry (James Franco), is a rich kid, embarrassed by his dad's wealth, who is Peter's best and only friend, and Norman is affectionate toward Peter even while their alter egos are deadly enemies. That works, and there's an effective scene where Osborn has a conversation with his invisible dark side.

The origin story is well told, and the characters will not disappoint anyone who values the original comic books. It's in the action scenes that things fall apart. Consider the scene where Spider-Man is given a cruel choice between saving Mary Jane or a cable car full of schoolkids. He tries to save both, so that everyone dangles from webbing that seems about to pull loose. The visuals here could have given an impression of the enormous weights and tensions involved, but instead the scene seems more like a bloodless storyboard of the idea. In other CGI scenes, Spidey swoops from great heights to street level and soars back up among the skyscrapers again with such dizzying speed that it seems less like a stunt than like a fast-forward version of a stunt.

I have one question about the Peter Parker character: Does the movie go too far with his extreme social paralysis? Peter tells Mary Jane he just wants to be friends. "Only a friend?" she repeats. "That's all I have to give," he says. How so? Impotent? Spidey-sense has skewed his sexual instincts? Afraid his hands will get stuck?

Spirited Away ★ ★ ★ ★
PG, 124 m., 2002

With the voices of: Daveigh Chase (Chihiro), Suzanne Pleshette (Yubaba), Jason Marsden (Haku), Susan Egan (Lin), David Ogden Stiers (Kamaji), Michael Chiklis (Chihiro's Father), Lauren Holly (Chihiro's Mother), John Ratzenberger (Assistant Manager). Directed by Hayao Miyazaki (U.S. production directed by Kirk Wise) and produced by Toshio Suzuki and Donald W. Ernst. Screenplay by Miyazaki, Cindy Davis Hewitt, and Donald H. Hewitt.

Spirited Away has been compared to *Alice in Wonderland,* and indeed it tells of a ten-year-old girl who wanders into a world of strange creatures and illogical rules. But it's enchanting and delightful in its own way, and has a good heart. It is the best animated film of recent years, the latest work by Hayao Miyazaki, the Japanese master who is a god to the Disney animators.

Because many adults have an irrational reluctance to see an animated film from Japan (or anywhere else), I begin with reassurances: It has been flawlessly dubbed into English by John Lasseter *(Toy Story),* it was cowinner of this year's Berlin Film Festival against "regular" movies, it passed *Titanic* to become the top-grossing film in Japanese history, and it is the first film ever to make more than $200 million before opening in America.

I feel like I'm giving a pitch on an infomercial, but I make these points because I come bearing news: This is a wonderful film. Don't avoid it because of what you think you know about animation from Japan. And if you only go to Disney animation—well, this is being released by Disney.

Miyazaki's works *(My Neighbor Totoro, Kiki's Delivery Service, Princess Mononoke)* have a depth and complexity often missing in American animation. Not fond of computers, he draws thousand of frames himself, and there is a painterly richness in his work. He's famous for throwaway details at the edges of the screen (animation is so painstaking that few animators draw more than is necessary). And he permits himself silences and contemplation, providing punctuation for the exuberant action and the lovable or sometimes grotesque characters.

Spirited Away is told through the eyes of Chihiro (voice by Daveigh Chase), a ten-year-old girl, and is more personal, less epic, than *Princess Mononoke.* As the story opens, she's on a trip with her parents, and her father unwisely takes the family to explore a mysterious tunnel in the woods. On the other side is what he speculates is an old theme park; but the food stalls still seem to be functioning, and as Chihiro's parents settle down for a free meal, she wanders away and comes upon the film's version of Wonderland, which is a towering bathhouse.

A boy named Haku appears as her guide, and warns her that the sorceress who runs the bathhouse, named Yubaba, will try to steal her name and thus her identity. Yubaba (Suzanne Pleshette) is an old crone with a huge face; she looks a little like a Toby mug, and dotes on a grotesquely huge baby named Bou. Ominously, she renames Chihiro, who wanders through the structure, which is populated, like *Totoro,* with little balls of dust that scurry and scamper underfoot.

In the innards of the structure, Chihiro comes upon the boiler room, operated by a man named Kamaji (David Ogden Stiers), who is dressed in a formal coat and has eight limbs, which he employs in a bewildering variety of ways. At first he seems as fearsome as the world he occupies, but he has a good side, is no friend of Yubaba, and perceives Chihiro's goodness.

If Yubaba is the scariest of the characters and Kamaji the most intriguing, Okutaresama is the one with the most urgent message. He is the spirit of the river, and his body has absorbed the junk, waste, and sludge that has been thrown into it over the years. At one point he actually yields up a discarded bicycle. I was reminded of a throwaway detail in *My Neighbor Totoro,* where a child looks into a bubbling brook, and there is a discarded bottle at the bottom. No point is made; none needs to be made.

Japanese myths often use shape-shifting, in which bodies reveal themselves as facades concealing a deeper reality. It's as if animation was invented for shape-shifting, and Miyazaki does wondrous things with the characters here. Most alarming for Chihiro, she finds that her parents have turned into pigs after gobbling up the free lunch. Okutaresama reveals its true nature after being freed of decades of sludge and discarded household items. Haku is much more than he seems. Indeed, the entire bath-house seems to be under spells affecting the appearance and nature of its inhabitants.

Miyazaki's drawing style, which descends from the classical Japanese graphic artists, is a pleasure to regard, with its subtle use of colors, clear lines, rich detail, and its realistic depiction of fantastical elements. He suggests not just the appearances of his characters, but their natures. Apart from the stories and dialogue, *Spirited Away* is a pleasure to regard just for itself. This is one of the year's best films.

Spirit: Stallion of the Cimarron
★ ★ ★
G, 82 m., 2002

With the voices of: Matt Damon (Narrator), James Cromwell (Cavalry Colonel), Daniel Studi (Little Creek). Directed by Kelly Asbury and Lorna Cook and produced by Mireille Soria and Jeffrey Katzenberg. Screenplay by John Fusco.

The animals do not speak in *Spirit: Stallion of the Cimarron,* and I think that's important to the film's success. It elevates the story from a children's fantasy to one wider audiences can enjoy, because although the stallion's adventures are admittedly pumped-up melodrama, the hero is nevertheless a horse and not a human with four legs. There is a whole level of cuteness that the movie avoids, and a kind of narrative strength it gains in the process.

The latest release from DreamWorks tells the story of Spirit, a wild mustang stallion, who runs free on the great western plains before he ventures into the domain of man and is captured by U.S. Cavalry troops. They think they can tame him. They are wrong, although the gruff-voiced colonel (voice by James Cromwell) makes the stallion into a personal obsession.

Spirit does not want to be broken, shoed, or inducted into the army, and his salvation comes through Little Creek (voice by Daniel Studi), an Indian brave who helps him escape and rides him to freedom. The pursuit by the cavalry is one of several sequences in the film where animation frees chase scenes to run wild, as Spirit and his would-be captors careen down canyons and through towering rock walls, duck under obstacles and end up in a river.

Watching the film, I was reminded of Jack London's classic novel *White Fang,* so unfairly categorized as a children's story even though the book (and the excellent 1991 film) used the dog as a character in a parable for adults. White Fang and Spirit represent holdouts against the taming of the frontier; invaders want to possess them, but they do not see themselves as property.

All of which philosophy will no doubt come as news to the cheering kids I saw the movie with, who enjoyed it, I'm sure, on its most basic level, as a big, bold, colorful adventure about a wide-eyed horse with a stubborn streak. That Spirit does not talk (except for some minimal thoughts that we overhear on voice-over) doesn't mean he doesn't communicate, and the animators pay great attention to body language and facial expressions in scenes where Spirit is frightened of a black-smith, in love with a mare, and the partner of the Indian brave (whom he accepts after a lengthy battle of wills).

There is also a scene of perfect wordless communication between Spirit and a small Indian child who fearlessly approaches the stallion at a time when he feels little but alarm about humans. The two creatures, one giant, one tiny, tentatively reach out to each other, and the child's absolute trust is somehow communicated to the horse. I remembered the great scene in *The Black Stallion* (1979) where the boy and the horse edge together from the far sides of the wide screen.

In the absence of much dialogue, the songs by Bryan Adams fill in some of the narrative gaps, and although some of them simply comment on the action (a practice I find annoying), they are in the spirit of the story. The film is short at eighty-two minutes, but surprisingly moving, and has a couple of really thrilling sequences, one involving a train wreck and the other a daring leap across a chasm. Uncluttered by comic supporting characters and cute sidekicks, *Spirit* is more pure and direct than most of the stories we see in animation—a fable I suspect younger viewers will strongly identify with.

Spun ★ ★ ★
R, 101 m., 2003

Jason Schwartzman (Ross), Mickey Rourke (Cook), Brittany Murphy (Nikki), John Leguizamo (Spider Mike), Mena Suvari (Cookie), Patrick Fugit (Frisbee), Peter Stormare (Cop No. 1), Alexis Arquette (Cop No. 2), Chloe Hunter (April). Directed by Jonas Akerlund and produced by Chris Hanley, Fernando Sulichin, Timothy Wayne Peternel, and Danny Vinik. Screenplay by Will De Los Santos and Creighton Vero.

Spun is a movie about going around and around and around on speed. Sometimes it can be exhausting to have a good time. The characters live within the orbit of Cook, who converts enormous quantities of nonprescription pills into drugs, and Spider Mike, who sells these and other drugs to people who usually can't pay him, leading to a lot of scenarios in which bodily harm is threatened in language learned from TV.

Because Cook is played with the studied weirdness of Mickey Rourke and Spider Mike with the tireless extroversion of John Leguizamo, *Spun* has an effortless wickedness. Rourke in particular has arrived at that point where he doesn't have to play heavy because he is heavy. Leguizamo has the effect of trying to talk himself into and out of trouble simultaneously.

Their world includes characters played by Jason Schwartzman (from *Rushmore*), Mena Suvari (from *American Beauty*), Patrick Fugit (from *Almost Famous*), and Brittany Murphy (from *8 Mile* and *Just Married*). Uncanny, in a way, how they all bring along some of the aura of their famous earlier characters, as if this were a doc about Hollywood youth gone wrong.

Brittany Murphy made quite an impact at the Independent Spirit Awards by being unable to master the concept of reading the five nominees *before* opening the envelope, despite two helpful visits from the stage manager and lots of suggestions from the audience, but with Murphy, you always kind of wonder if she doesn't know exactly what she's doing.

Here she plays Nikki, Cook's girlfriend, which is the kind of situation you end up in when you need a lot of drugs for not a lot of money. She depends on Ross (Schwartzman) to chauffeur her everywhere in his desperately ill Volvo, sometimes taking him off on long missions through the city. These journeys have a queasy undertone since we know (although Ross sometimes forgets) that he has left his own current stripper girlfriend handcuffed to a bed. April (Chloe Hunter), the handcuffed girlfriend, is all the more furious because she realizes Ross is not sadistic but merely confused and absent-minded.

The movie plays like a dark screwball comedy in which people run in and out of doors, get involved with mistaken identities, and desperately try to keep all their plates in the air. The film's charm, which is admittedly an acquired and elusive taste, comes from the fact that *Spun* does not romanticize its characters, does not enlarge or dramatize them, but seems to shake its head incredulously as these screwups persist in ruinous and insane behavior.

Leguizamo is fearless when it comes to depictions of sexual conduct. You may recall him as the transvestite Miss Chi-Chi Rodriguez in *To Wong Foo, Thanks for Everything! Julie Newmar* (1995), or more probably as the energetic Toulouse-Lautrec in *Moulin Rouge,* and he toured in his stage show *John Leguizamo's Sexaholixs.* In *Spun* he demonstrates that although black socks have often played important roles in erotic films, there are still frontiers to be explored. What I have always enjoyed about him is the joy and abandon with which he approaches the right kind of role, as if it is play, not work. Here his energy inspires the others, causing even Patrick Fugit's slothful Frisbee to stir.

The movie is like the low-rent, road show version of those serious drug movies where everybody is macho and deadly. The characters in *Narc* would crush these characters under their thumbs. *Spun* does have two drug cops, played by Peter Stormare and Alexis Arquette, but they work for some kind of TV reality show, are followed by cameras, and are also strung out on speed.

The director, Jonas Akerlund, comes from Sweden via commercials and music videos, and has obviously studied *Requiem for a Dream* carefully, since he uses the same kind of speeded-up visual disconnections to suggest life on meth. His feel for his characters survives his technique, however, and it's interesting how this story and these people seem to have been living before the movie began and will continue after it is over; instead of a plot, we drop in on their lives. When Cook starts the mother of all kitchen fires, for example, he walks toward the camera (obligatory fireball behind him), already looking for a new motel room.

Spy Game ★ ★ ½
R, 115 m., 2001

Robert Redford (Nathan Muir), Brad Pitt (Tom Bishop), Catherine McCormack (Elizabeth), Stephen Dillane (Charles). Directed by Tony Scott and produced by Marc Abraham and Douglas Wick. Screenplay by Michael Frost Beckner and David Arata.

Consider now two spy thrillers: *Spy Game*, with Robert Redford and Brad Pitt, which opened over Thanksgiving, and *The Tailor of Panama*, with Pierce Brosnan and Geoffrey Rush, which opened in March 2001. Both, curiously, star Catherine McCormack as the girl for whom a spy risks all, or seems to, or means to.

Spy Game, directed by Tony Scott, is all style and surface, a slick artifact made of quick cutting and the kind of rough glamour you find in fashion ads; rat-a-tat datelines identify the times and places. *The Tailor of Panama*, directed by John Boormann and based on the John Le Carre novel, moves more deliberately to set up its characters and explore their personalities. *Spy Game* substitutes mannerisms for human nature; there's no time, in a film where individual shots rarely last more than twenty seconds, for deeper attention. The cinematography in *The Tailor of Panama* goes not for surface flash but for tone and mood, for the feel of its locations.

Oddly, although both movies have about the same running times, the slower pace of *The Tailor of Panama* makes it seem shorter than the fast-paced *Spy Game*. Scott's restless camera, with flashbacks and whooshes, resists our attention; it moves so fast that things don't seem to *matter* so much, and because it discourages contemplation, we don't develop a stake in the material. We see it less as a story than as an exercise.

That's not to say the film is without interest. It stars Robert Redford as a veteran CIA spymaster on his last day at work, and Brad Pitt as

the young idealist he recruited after Vietnam. Now Pitt is in a Chinese prison, captured in the act of helping Catherine McCormack escape, and it's Redford who was responsible for her being there. The framework is twenty-four hours during which Redford must scheme, lie, and deceive in order to save Pitt, whom the agency plans to sacrifice; nothing must upset top-level trade talks between the United States and China.

As Redford is quizzed by his masters, flashbacks show him meeting Pitt in Vietnam and later using him in operations in Berlin, Beirut, and Hong Kong. Pitt meets McCormack in Beirut, where she is a nurse and something shadowy besides, and that's where they fall in love, although a movie this fast moving has no time for conversations and tenderness, and so we have to accept their relationship on faith. (These scenes span the years from about 1965 to about 1991, during which the characters look about the same.)

What saves *Spy Game* from death by style is the Redford performance, which uses every resource of his star persona to create a character from thin air. At the end of the movie we still know next to nothing about him (and so, his bosses realize, do they), but he embodies the values the movie is too impatient to establish, and so we sympathize with him, and there's a trickle-down effect: We sympathize with Pitt because Redford does, and we sympathize with McCormack because Pitt does. We have no feelings at all about any of the CIA bosses, and indeed by the end of the film do not even know if they are supposed to be right or wrong (they seem to be doing exactly what Redford taught Pitt to do).

In *The Tailor of Panama*, where Pierce Brosnan plays a veteran British spy, also nearing the end of his career, there is a completely different approach: The visual style serves the story instead of replacing it. We appreciate Brosnan's droll cynicism, his weakness for pleasure, and his appreciation of the way the local British source, a tailor played by Geoffrey Rush, has milked a lot of money out of very little information. There is time for an appreciation of the political realities involved, seen through the eyes of a local radical (Brendan Gleeson), and we reflect that *Spy Game* is so devoid of politics that it could play, just as it stands, in

China—or Afghanistan, now that the theaters are open again. The Catherine McCormack character in *Tailor* is allowed to be sexy, devious, and complicated, qualities that women are not allowed in a Boy's Own story like *Spy Game.*

I sat attentively through *Spy Game,* admired Redford for the way he created a performance that sometimes consisted only of quick shots of his facial expressions, and understood that Pitt's character was conflicted and would have explained why if the screenplay allowed dialogue as long as a paragraph. I was reminded that Redford's earlier spy thriller, Sydney Pollack's *Three Days of the Condor* (1975), had at its heart his brief, sad relationship with Faye Dunaway; it was interested in *how* they cared for each other, while *Spy Game's* Pitt/McCormack pairing is simply declared to exist.

The Tailor of Panama didn't do well at the box office. Maybe people thought it was about a tailor. *Spy Game* at least has a title that gets the idea across. It is not a bad movie, mind you; it's clever and shows great control of craft, but it doesn't care, and so it's hard for us to care about. To see it once is to plumb to the bottom of its mysteries and beyond.

Spy Kids ★ ★ ★ ½
PG, 90 m., 2001

Antonio Banderas (Gregorio Cortez), Alan Cumming (Fegan Floop), Carla Gugino (Ingrid Cortez), Teri Hatcher (Ms. Gradenko), Angela Lanza (Reporter), Daryl Sabara (Juni Cortez), Tony Shalhoub (Minion), Alexa Vega (Carmen Cortez), Cheech Marin (Uncle Felix). Directed by Robert Rodriguez and produced by Elizabeth Avellan and Rodriguez. Screenplay by Rodriguez.

Spy Kids is giddy with the joy of its invention. It's an exuberant, colorful extravaganza, wall-to-wall with wildly original sets and visual gimmicks, and smart enough to escape the kid's film category and play in the mainstream. You can imagine Robert Rodriguez, the writer and director, grinning as he dreamed up this stuff. And being amazed that his visual-effects team could get it all on film so brilliantly.

The movie begins with Antonio Banderas and Carla Gugino as Gregorio and Ingrid Cortez, spies who were once enemies but then fall in love and get married and have two great kids, Carmen (Alexa Vega) and Juni (Daryl Sabara). They retire from the spy business, but then an evil minion named Minion (Tony Shalhoub) kidnaps the parents, and it's up to the spy kids to rescue them and save the world from the threat of robo-kids and Thumb Monsters.

Minion works for the diabolical Fegan Floop (Alan Cumming), whose job as a kiddie-show host masks his scheme to rule the world. His operation, centered in a fantastical seaside castle, includes workers who are all thumbs, literally: thumbs for heads, arms, and legs. Floop runs a cloning operation to turn out exact robotic copies of the children of powerful people. They look like the originals except for eyes with an eerie glow. Their problem: The brains aren't up to speed. Floop's answer: the Third Brain, which Gregorio Cortez secretly took along with him when he left the spy service.

This sounds, I know, like a plot for eight-year-olds, but Rodriguez charges at the material as if he wants to blow Indiana Jones out of the water, and the movie is just one outrageous invention after another. My feeling is that a "family movie" fails if it doesn't entertain the parents, since they're the ones who have to buy the tickets. *Spy Kids* is so endlessly imaginative, so high-spirited, so extravagant with its inspirations, so filled with witty dialogue, that the more you like movies, the more you may like this one.

The plot. After the kidnapping, it's up to the kids to rescue their parents, with a little help from their Uncle Felix (Cheech Marin) and guidance from Ms. Gradenko (Teri Hatcher), who claims to be a friend of their mother's from the old spy days. The kids have repaired to a secret "safe house," which is a lot different inside than outside, and they utilize all sorts of spy gimmicks; some they understand, some they don't. What's neat is the way the kids don't act like kids: They go about their business seriously, and along the way little Juni gains the self-confidence he needs (at school, he was the target of bullies).

Rodriguez has always been in love with special effects (as in his vampire movie *From Dusk Till Dawn*), and here he combines computer-generated images with brightly colored sets that look like a riot in a paint box. The movie's props range from bubble gum that can be used as a tracking device to the parents' car, which doubles as a submarine. And there's great imagination in a scene where the kids commandeer a combination aircraft-speedboat-submarine with a plump fish design that looks like something Captain Nemo might have dreamed up.

With a movie so enchanting and cheerful, I want to resist sociological observations, but it should be noted that Rodriguez has made a mainstream family film in which most of the heroic roles are assigned to Hispanic characters (at one point, the Banderas character even jokes about all the Latinos on Floop's TV show). It should also be observed that he avoids disturbing violence, that the entire movie is in a cheerful kidding spirit, and that the stunts and skills exhibited by the kids look fun, not scary. The props, even the boat-plane-sub, look like extensions of their toys, not like adult inventions that have been scaled down.

Movies like *Spy Kids* are so rare. Families are often reduced to attending scatological dumber-and-dumbest movies like *See Spot Run*—movies that teach vulgarity as a value. *Spy Kids* is an intelligent, upbeat, happy movie that is not about the comedy of embarrassment, that does not have anybody rolling around in dog poop, that would rather find out what it can accomplish than what it can get away with. It's a treasure.

Spy Kids 2: The Island of Lost Dreams
★ ★ ★

PG, 86 m., 2002

Antonio Banderas (Gregorio Cortez), Carla Gugino (Ingrid Cortez), Alexa Vega (Carmen Cortez), Daryl Sabara (Juni Cortez), Steve Buscemi (Romero), Matthew O'Leary (Gary Giggles), Emily Osment (Gerti Giggles), Bill Paxton (Dinky Winks), Ricardo Montalban (Grandpa), Holland Taylor (Grandma). Directed by Robert Rodriguez and produced by Elizabeth Avellan and Rodriguez. Screenplay by Rodriguez.

Spy Kids 2: The Island of Lost Dreams uses the same formula as the wonderful 2001 picture: bright colors, weird gimmicks, fanciful special

effects, goofy villains, sassy dialogue, and lots of moxie. The second installment is a galloping adventure pitting Carmen and Juni Cortez (Alexa Vega and Daryl Sabara), the two original spy kids, against the snot-nosed Gary and Gerti Giggles (Matthew O'Leary and Emily Osment), whose dad has staged a sneaky takeover of the federal spy agency. Soon they're on an invisible island ruled by Romero (Steve Buscemi), a not-quite-mad scientist with a gizmo that could control, or destroy, the world.

Director Robert Rodriguez wrote, directed, edited, and even did some of the digital photography. He seems to have chosen his color palette from those brightly painted little Mexican sculptures you see in gift shops, the ones that have so much energy they make you smile. The whole film has a lively Mexican-American tilt, from the Hispanic backgrounds of the young actors to the surprise appearance of none other than Ricardo Montalban, as Grandpa, in a wheelchair with helicopter capabilities.

The opening sequence is inspired; Carmen and Juni visit a theme park, where the owner (Bill Paxton) proudly explains his great new rides. These rides are so extravagantly, recklessly over the top that I was laughing; we see the Whipper Snapper (customers ride in cars at the end of long ropes that are snapped like whips), the Vomiter (Paxton gets out his umbrella to shield himself from the inevitable customer reaction), and the Juggler, a ride that literally juggles cars containing the patrons.

The daughter of the president of the United States is among the park's guests, and she's a little brat who soon finds herself teetering dangerously on a ledge of the Juggler, while the Spy Kids and the Giggles team compete to rescue her. The Spy Kids save the day, but the Giggleses get the credit, setting off a rivalry that leads to the Island of Lost Dreams.

Just like in the Bond pictures, nothing less than the survival of the world is at stake, but Buscemi plays Romero the scientist as a conflicted character, basically a nice guy who wants to be left alone to tinker with his planet-destroying inventions. The chase to the island involves an undersea journey by the Spy Kids, and, just like in the first movie, pursuit by their worried parents. (The exasperation the kids feel because of their parents' overprotectiveness is mirrored when the grandparents [Montalban and Holland Taylor] come onboard the pursuit sub to give unwanted advice to mom and dad Cortez.)

I liked the special effects, especially a green-and-gold sea monster that was kind of beautiful in its own way, and a many-legged spider man who turns out to have a good heart. The movie is filled with lots of other gimmicks, including Juni's favorite device, a Palm Pilot that has morphed into a personal valet, and creeps across his coat on spider legs to knot his tie.

The dialogue has a certain self-kidding element, as in an exchange where the Kids are searching for the Transmooger, the device that can destroy the world. "There it is!" Carmen shouts. "How do you know?" asks Juni. "Because it's big and round and in the middle of the room."

With *Spy Kids 2: The Island of Lost Dreams,* the Spy Kids franchise establishes itself as a durable part of the movie landscape: a James Bond series for kids. One imagines *Spy Kids 9,* with Alexa Vega and Daryl Sabara promoted to the roles of the parents, Antonio Banderas and Carla Gugino as the grandparents, and kids yet unborn in the title roles.

Standing in the Shadows of Motown
★ ★ ★
PG, 116 m., 2002

A documentary featuring Richard "Pistol" Allen, Jack "Black Jack" Ashford, Bob Babbitt, Johnny Griffith, Joe Hunter, Uriel Jones, Joe Messina, Eddie "Chank" Willis, Benny "Papa Zita" Benjamin, James "Igor" Jamerson, Eddie "Bongo" Brown, Earl "Chunk of Funk" Van Dyke, Robert White, Joan Osborne, Gerald Levert, Me'Shell NdegéOcello, Bootsy Collins, Ben Harper, Chaka Khan, Montell Jordan, and Tom Scott. Directed by Paul Justman and produced by Justman, Sandford Passman, and Allan Slutsky. Screenplay by Walter Dallas and Ntozake Shange, based on the book *Standing in the Shadows of Motown* by Slutsky.

Think of the Supremes, Gladys Knight, Smokey Robinson, Marvin Gaye, Martha Reeves, Stevie Wonder, and the Temptations. You hold decades of pop music history in your mind: the Motown Sound. Now ask who the instrumentalists were on their records. Or don't even

bother, because the question is asked and answered in the affectionate new documentary *Standing in the Shadows of Motown.* In the movie, fans are asked: Who played on the recordings with those artists? Who, for example, was behind Gladys Knight? "The Pips?" asks one Motown fan.

No, it wasn't the Pips, the Miracles, or the Vandellas. The musicians who played behind all of the Motown stars on their studio recordings were the Funk Brothers. The *Funk* Brothers? Paul Justman's documentary, based on a book by Allan Slutsky, gives belated praise for Motown's house musicians, the men who played under all the Motown hits recorded in Detroit.

The hero of the Funk Brothers themselves seems to have been the late James Jamerson, the bass player who used only one finger but seemed able to keep two times at once. Their stories about him are legion. The other original Funks were drummer Benny Benjamin, pianist Joe Hunter, and guitarists Eddie Willis and Joe Messina. The movie talks with or about perhaps a dozen other musicians who played on many or most of the Motown records, but it's difficult to keep them straight—because, of course, they were not famous.

And yet the Motown Sound was, quite simply, their sound. No disrespect to the singers, but, as drummer Steve Gordon observes, "You could have had Deputy Dawg singin' on some of this stuff." The documentary argues that they played on hits that sold more records than the Beatles, Elvis, the Beach Boys, and the Rolling Stones combined—but were almost anonymous.

The first Motown sides were cut in Studio A, which was simply the garage of Berry Gordy, the label's founder. It was down four steps from his kitchen and originally had a dirt floor. Along with the Sun studios in Memphis, it was one of the birthplaces of the last half-century of American hit music. The movie returns to that location ("Hitsville, USA") for sessions in which the surviving Funk Brothers remember the good times and bad, and the very sound of the studio itself.

Sessions would last all day and into the night. A producer would come in with a song and a few chords, and they'd play with it, adapting it to the house style, adding a touch here, a riff there, until it emerged as the big, bold, and sometimes almost unreasonably happy Motown Sound. In one of the movie's best sequences, we see them cobbling a song together almost from scratch. Sometimes, they remember, they were so overworked they'd hide out in a nearby funeral parlor, where Gordy wouldn't think to look for them.

The sound was born in and nurtured by a series of Detroit clubs, places like the Chit Chat and 20 Grand, now closed, where the Funks and other musicians got their start and returned to their roots. Separately they were great and together they were beyond great; it's clear that working steadily behind literally hundreds of hits fused them into a group that all but thought with one mind. As they remember those days, they're like military veterans or the members of a World Series team, and we realize nothing that came after ever held the same joy for them.

The Motown Sound came to an end in 1972, when Gordy moved the label from Detroit to Los Angeles with "no warning and no acknowledgement." The Funks found out from a notice tacked to the door. Some of them followed Motown to the coast, but the magic was gone, and the movie doesn't ask the obvious question: Why didn't some of the singers they worked with know how important they were and demand them, or return to Detroit to record with them?

Standing in the Shadows of Motown interlaces interviews with the surviving Funk Brothers with new performances of many of the hit songs, and some sequences in which events of the past are re-created. The flashback sequences are not especially effective, but are probably better than more talking heads. Or maybe not. The contemporary performers who sing in front of the Funks include Joan Osborne, Ben Harper, Me'Shell NdegéOcello, Montell Jordan, Gerald Levert, Chaka Khan, and the flamboyant Bootsy Collins, who upstages the Funks, not to his own advantage.

What's interesting about these performances is that the singers make no attempt to imitate the original artists, and yet the Funks turn the songs into soundalikes anyway. Is it possible those great Motown stars were more or less created by these unsung musicians? The Funks think that is a distinct possibility. Of course,

the backup singers had a lot to do with it, too, and this movie never gets around to them. They're in the shadows of the shadows.

Star Trek: Nemesis ★ ★
PG-13, 116 m., 2002

Patrick Stewart (Captain Picard), Jonathan Frakes (Commander Riker), Brent Spiner (Data), LeVar Burton (Geordi La Forge), Michael Dorn (Worf), Gates McFadden (Dr. Crusher), Marina Sirtis (Deanna Troi), Tom Hardy (Praetor Shinzon), Ron Perlman (Reman Viceroy). Directed by Stuart Baird and produced by Rick Berman. Screenplay by John Logan.

I'm sitting there during *Star Trek: Nemesis*, the tenth *Star Trek* movie, and I'm smiling like a good sport and trying to get with the dialogue about the isotronic Ruritronic signature from planet Kolarus III, or whatever the hell they were saying, maybe it was "positronic," and gradually it occurs to me that Star Trek is over for me. I've been looking at these stories for half a lifetime, and, let's face it, they're out of gas.

There might have been a time when the command deck of *Starship Enterprise* looked exciting and futuristic, but these days it looks like a communications center for security guards. Starships rocket at light speed halfway across the universe, but when they get into battles the effect is roughly the same as onboard a World War II bomber. Fearsome death rays strike the *Enterprise*, and what happens? Sparks fly out from the ceiling and the crew gets bounced around in their seats like passengers on the No. 36 bus. This far in the future they wouldn't have sparks because they wouldn't have electricity, because in a world where you can beam matter—*beam* it, mind you—from here to there, power obviously no longer lives in the wall and travels through wires.

I've also had it with the force shield that protects the *Enterprise*. The power on this thing is always going down. In movie after movie after movie I have to sit through sequences during which the captain is tersely informed that the front shield is down to 60 percent, or the back shield is down to 10 percent, or the side shield is leaking energy, and the captain tersely orders that power be shifted from the back to the sides or all put in the front, or whatever, and I'm thinking, life is too short to sit through ten movies in which the power is shifted around on these shields. The shields have been losing power for decades now, and here it is the Second Generation of *Star Trek,* and they still haven't fixed them. Maybe they should get new batteries.

I tried to focus on the actors. Patrick Stewart, as Captain Picard, is a wonderful actor. I know because I have seen him elsewhere. It is always said of Stewart that his strength as an actor is his ability to deliver bad dialogue with utter conviction. I say it is time to stop encouraging him. Here's an idea: Instead of giving him bad dialogue, why not give him good dialogue and see what he can do with that? Here is a man who has played Shakespeare.

The plot of *Star Trek: Nemesis* involves a couple of strands, one involving a clone of Data, which somehow seems redundant, and another involving what seems to be a peace feeler from the Romulan empire. In the course of the movie the Romulan Senate is wiped out by a deadly blue powder and the sister planet, Remus, stages an uprising, or something, against being made to work as slaves in the mines. Surely slavery is not an efficient economic system in a world of hyperdrives, but never mind: Turns out that Picard shares something unexpected with his rival commander, although you can no doubt guess what it is, since the movie doesn't work you very hard.

There is a scene in the movie in which one starship rams another one. You would think this would destroy them both, and there are a lot of sparks and everybody has to hold onto their seats, but the *Star Trek* world involves physical laws that reflect only the needs of the plot. If one ship rammed another and they were both destroyed and everyone died, and the movie ended with a lot of junk floating around in space, imagine the faces of the people in the audience.

I think it is time for *Star Trek* to make a mighty leap forward another 1,000 years into the future, to a time when starships do not look like rides in a 1970s amusement arcade, when aliens do not look like humans with funny foreheads, and when wonder, astonishment, and literacy are permitted back into the series. *Star Trek* was kind of terrific once, but now it is a copy of a copy of a copy.

Startup.com ★ ★ ★
R, 103 m., 2001

A documentary directed by Chris Hegedus and Jehane Noujaim and produced by D. A. Pennebaker.

It seemed like a great idea at the time. They'd build a place on-line where people could go to pay their parking tickets. *Startup.com* tells the story of two longtime friends who go into business together, create a Website, raise millions, and at one point are worth $12 million—apiece, I think, but it makes no difference, because by the end of their adventure they have lost everything. The movie's story arc is like *Charly* or *Awakenings,* in which the heroes start low, fly high, and crash.

The friends are named Kaleil Isaza Tuzman and Tom Herman. Their idea is so compelling that Tuzman quits a job at Goodman, Sachs to move to the Internet. The story starts in May 1999, when instant Web millionaires were a dime a dozen, and ends in January 2001. The documentary's last shots were filmed only three weeks before it premiered at Sundance, still wet from the lab. As an inside view of the bursting of the Internet bubble, *Startup.com* is definitive. We sense there were lots of stories more or less like this one.

To film this sort of doc, you need access. The movie has it. One codirector, Jehane Noujaim, was Tuzman's Harvard roommate. She's also the cinematographer, and her digital camera has access to startlingly private moments. The other director, Chris Hegedus, has worked on such insider docs as *The War Room,* the story of the Clinton campaign. She coproduced that one with D. A. Pennebaker, the legendary documentarian, who is also the producer this time.

When the film begins, the new company doesn't even have a name. They settle on govWorks.com. Tuzman and Herman make the rounds of venture capitalists, and it's obvious that Tuzman is the expert pitcher, while Herman, more technically oriented, drives his partner crazy by bringing up bright ideas in meetings on the spur of the moment. Tuzman lectures him to stay on message. Dollar signs dance before their eyes. At one point in Boston they're offered $17 million but lose the deal when they can't get their lawyers on the phone.

Meanwhile, of course, there's the problem of actually writing the software. It would seem to me that paying parking tickets over the Internet would involve basic programming skills plus cosmetic packaging, but no, apparently it's rocket science: Eventually govWorks.com has 200 employees working on the site, and still Tuzman despairs that it's not good enough to be released to the public.

Famous figures float in and out of view. The partners smile from the covers of business magazines. Former Atlanta mayor Maynard Jackson turns up as a consultant. Tuzman appears on TV sitting next to President Clinton, who chairs a summit meeting on the Internet. Meanwhile, Tuzman and Herman, under enormous pressure, go through girlfriends and beards. Herman grows his beard and shaves it off so many times that the filmmakers finally photograph him in front of the mirror with a razor, just to explain the continuity errors. And Tuzman's girlfriends complain that he pays them no attention: "Just a call is all I ask," one says. "A simple call saying you're thinking of me, you're busy, but you miss me. That would keep me going for two weeks." She disappears from the film; her replacement also finds Tuzman a moving target.

There are setbacks. The govWorks office is broken into. Files are stolen. But that's not as big a problem as the disappointing software, and then comes the dot.com meltdown that dries up funds just when the site is turning the corner. On the day govWorks was sold to a competitor, we learn, it landed the big New York City contract.

Noujaim's camera catches painfully intimate moments, as the two old friends argue, split, and Herman leaves the company; in an age-old security ritual, he is "escorted from the building" and guards are told not to readmit him. Today, I learn, Tuzman and Herman are back in business together. My guess is, they could make it this time. The Internet is fundamentally sound. The bubble had to burst to correct its crazy overvaluation. Now that sanity has returned, bright guys like Tuzman

and Herman can find more opportunities. All they need is another great idea. And better software.

Star Wars: Episode II— Attack of the Clones ★ ★
PG, 124 m., 2002

Ewan McGregor (Obi-Wan Kenobi), Natalie Portman (Senator Padme Amidala), Hayden Christensen (Anakin Skywalker), Christopher Lee (Count Dooku), Ian McDiarmid (Palpatine), (voice of) Frank Oz (Yoda), Samuel L. Jackson (Mace Windu), Pernilla August (Shmi Skywalker), Jack Thompson (Cliegg Lars), Temuera Morrison (Jango Fett), Jimmy Smits (Senator Bail Organa). Directed by George Lucas and produced by Rick McCallum. Screenplay by Lucas and Jonathan Hales.

It is not what's there on the screen that disappoints me, but what's not there. It is easy to hail the imaginative computer images that George Lucas brings to *Star Wars: Episode II—Attack of the Clones.* To marvel at his strange new aliens and towering cities and sights such as thousands of clones all marching in perfect ranks into a huge spaceship. To see the beginnings of the dark side in young Anakin Skywalker. All of those experiences are there to be cheered by fans of the *Star Wars* series, and for them this movie will affirm their faith.

But what about the agnostic viewer? The hopeful ticket-buyer walking in not as a cultist but as a moviegoer hoping for a great experience? Is this *Star Wars* critic-proof and scoff-resistant? Yes, probably, at the box office. But as someone who admired the freshness and energy of the earlier films, I was amazed, at the end of *Episode II,* to realize that I had not heard one line of quotable, memorable dialogue. And the images, however magnificently conceived, did not have the impact they deserved. I'll get to them in a moment.

The first hour of *Episode II* contains a sensational chase through the skyscraper canyons of a city, and assorted briefer shots of spaceships and planets. But most of that first hour consists of dialogue, as the characters establish plot points, update viewers on what has happened since *Episode I,* and debate the political crisis facing the Republic. They talk and talk and talk.

And their talk is in a flat utilitarian style: They seem more like lawyers than the heroes of a romantic fantasy.

In the classic movie adventures that inspired *Star Wars,* dialogue was often colorful, energetic, witty, and memorable. The dialogue in *Episode II* exists primarily to advance the plot, provide necessary information, and give a little screen time to continuing characters who are back for a new episode. The only characters in this stretch of the film who have inimitable personal styles are the beloved Yoda and the hated Jar Jar Binks, whose idiosyncrasies turned off audiences for *Phantom Menace.* Yes, Jar Jar's accent may be odd and his mannerisms irritating, but at least he's a unique individual and not a bland cipher. The other characters—Obi-Wan Kenobi, Padme Amidala, Anakin Skywalker—seem so strangely stiff and formal in their speech that an unwary viewer might be excused for thinking they were the clones, soon to be exposed.

Too much of the rest of the film is given over to a romance between Padme and Anakin in which they're incapable of uttering anything other than the most basic and weary romantic clichés, while regarding each other as if love was something to be endured rather than cherished. There is not a romantic word they exchange that has not long since been reduced to cliché. No, wait: Anakin tells Padme at one point: "I don't like the sand. It's coarse and rough and irritating—not like you. You're soft and smooth." I hadn't heard that before.

When it comes to the computer-generated images, I feel that I cannot entirely trust the screening experience I had. I could see that in conception many of these sequences were thrilling and inventive. I liked the planet of rain, and the vast coliseum in which the heroes battle strange alien beasts, and the towering Senate chamber, and the secret factory where clones were being manufactured.

But I felt like I had to lean with my eyes toward the screen in order to see what I was being shown. The images didn't pop out and smack me with delight, the way they did in earlier films. There was a certain fuzziness, an indistinctness that seemed to undermine their potential power.

Later I went on the Web to look at the trailers for the movie, and was startled to see how much brighter, crisper, and more colorful they seemed on my computer screen than in the theater. Although I know that video images are routinely timed to be brighter than movie images, I suspect another reason for this. *Episode II* was shot entirely on digital video. It is being projected in digital video on nineteen screens, but on some 3,000 others, audiences will see it as I did, transferred to film.

How it looks in digital projection I cannot say, although I hope to get a chance to see it that way. I know Lucas believes it looks better than film, but then he has cast his lot with digital. My guess is that the film version of *Episode II* might jump more sharply from the screen in a small multiplex theater. But I saw it on the largest screen in Chicago, and my suspicion is, the density and saturation of the image was not adequate to imprint the image there in a forceful way.

Digital images contain less information than 35mm film images, and the more you test their limits, the more you see that. Not long ago I saw *Patton* shown in 70mm Dimension 150, and it was the most astonishing projection I had ever seen—absolute detail on a giant screen, which was 6,000 times larger than a frame of the 70mm film. That's what large-format film can do, but it's a standard Hollywood has abandoned (except for IMAX), and we are being asked to forget how good screen images can look—to accept the compromises. I am sure I will hear from countless fans who assure me that *Episode II* looks terrific, but it does not. At least, what I saw did not. It may look great in digital projection on multiplex-size screens, and I'm sure it will look great on DVD, but on a big screen it lacks the authority it needs.

I have to see the film again to do it justice. I'm sure I will greatly enjoy its visionary sequences on DVD; I like stuff like that. The dialogue is another matter. Perhaps because a movie like this opens everywhere in the world on the same day, the dialogue has to be dumbed down for easier dubbing or subtitling. Wit, poetry, and imagination are specific to the languages where they originate, and although translators can work wonders, sometimes you get the words but not the music. So it's safer to avoid the music.

But in a film with a built-in audience, why not go for the high notes? Why not allow the dialogue to be inventive, stylish, and expressive? There is a certain lifelessness in some of the acting, perhaps because the actors were often filmed in front of blue screens so their environments could be added later by computer. Actors speak more slowly than they might—flatly, factually, formally, as if reciting. Sometimes that reflects the ponderous load of the mythology they represent. At other times it simply shows that what they have to say is banal. *Episode II—Attack of the Clones* is a technological exercise that lacks juice and delight. The title is more appropriate than it should be.

* * *

I did go back a few days later to see the movie digitally projected.

After seeing the new *Star Wars* movie projected on film, I wrote that the images had "a certain fuzziness, an indistinctness that seemed to undermine their potential power." But I knew the film had been shot on digital video, and that George Lucas believed it should preferably be seen, not on film, but projected digitally. Now I've been able to see the digital version, and Lucas is right: *Star Wars: Episode II—Attack of the Clones* is sharper, crisper, brighter, and punchier on digital than on film.

This will come as melancholy news, I suppose, to the vast majority of fans destined to see the movie through a standard film projector. Although an accurate count is hard to come by, there are apparently about 20 screens in America showing *Episode II* with a digital projector, and about 3,000 showing it on film. Lucas is so eager to promote his vision of the digital future that he is willing to penalize his audience, just to prove a point.

But he *does* prove the point. On Sunday I returned to Chicago's McClurg Court theater, where I had seen *Episode II* on film the previous Tuesday. On Wednesday, technicians from Boeing Digital Cinema swooped down on the theater to install a new Texas Instruments digital projector, and that's how I saw the film a second time—sitting in almost exactly the same seat.

Watching it on film, I wrote: "I felt like I had to lean with my eyes toward the screen in order to see what I was being shown." On digital, the images were bright and clear. Since the movie was being projected on film on another McClurg screen (both screenings were part of a charity benefit) I slipped upstairs, watched a

scene on film, and then hurried downstairs to compare the same scene on video. The difference was dramatic: more detail, more depth, more clarity.

Readers familiar with my preference for film over video projection systems will wonder if I have switched parties. Not at all. It's to be expected that *Episode II* would look better on digital, because it was entirely filmed on digital. Therefore, the digitally projected version is generation one, and the film version is one generation further from the source. Lucas is right as far as a computer-aided special-effects movie like *Episode II* goes, but may be wrong for the vast majority of movies that depict the real world on celluloid.

It is important to understand that *Episode II* is essentially an animated film with humans added to it. This is the flip side of *Who Framed Roger Rabbit*, which was a live-action film with cartoon characters laid on top. Most of the non-human screen images in *Episode II*, and some of the characters (Yoda, Jar Jar Binks) are created entirely in computers. Even in scenes dominated by humans, the backgrounds and locations are often entirely computer-generated.

Whether this is an advance is debatable. I am receiving mail from readers who prefer the earlier *Star Wars* effects, using models, back projection, puppets, and the like. They also question *Spider-Man*, where Spidey's action sequences are animated using CGI, or Computer-Generated Imagery. David Soto of Santa Ana, California, writes: "I liked it, although I wanted to love it. One thing I noticed—for a second I had the impression I was watching a Power Rangers episode." He said CGI made everything "look so fast, so weightless, so unreal."

I agree. In *Episode II*, this is true of the most popular scene in the movie, where Yoda abandons his contemplative and sedentary lifestyle and springs into action. Yes, it's fun to see the surprise Yoda has up his sleeve, but in the scene itself he turns from a substantial, detailed, "realistic" character into a bouncing blob of Yodaness, moving too quickly to be perceived in any detail.

The debate about CGI versus traditional effects will be fueled by *Episode II* and *Spider-Man*. The debate about digital projection is just beginning. My feeling is that movies shot on digital look better projected on video, and that movies shot on film look better projected on film. Of course, every theater, every print, and every projector is different, so results may vary.

What I dislike about Lucas's approach is that he wants to change the entire world of film to suit his convenience. Because his movies are created largely on computers, it suits him to project them digitally. Because the *Star Wars* franchise is so hugely profitable, he hopes he has the clout to swing the movie world behind him—especially since well-funded Boeing and Texas Instruments stand to make millions by grabbing the projection franchise away from film. A century of cinematic tradition may be shown to the exit by Head Usher Jar Jar, while Yoda consoles us with the Force.

Stealing Harvard ★
PG-13, 82 m., 2002

Jason Lee (John Plummer), Tom Green (Duff), Leslie Mann (Elaine), Dennis Farina (Mr. Warner), Megan Mullally (Patty), John C. McGinley (Detective Charles), Chris Penn (David), Tammy Blanchard (Noreen). Directed by Bruce McCulloch and produced by Susan Cavan. Screenplay by Peter Tolan.

The laugh in *Stealing Harvard* comes early, when we see the name of the company where the hero works. It's a home health-care corporation named Homespital. That made me laugh. It made me smile again when the name turned up later. And on the laugh meter, that's about it. This is as lax and limp a comedy as I've seen in a while, a meander through worn-out material.

Jason Lee, who can be engaging in the right material (like *Chasing Amy* and *Almost Famous*), is bland and disposable here, as John Plummer, a young Homespital executive. The firm is owned by his fiancée's father (Dennis Farina), who subjects John to savage cross-examinations on whether he has slept with his daughter. He lies and says he hasn't. He might be telling the truth if he said he wishes he hadn't, since the fiancée, Elaine (Leslie Mann), inexplicably weeps during sex.

Despite his foray into the middle classes, John has not forgotten his superslut sister Patty (Megan Mullally), who despite a life of untiring promiscuity, has a daughter, Noreen (Tammy Blanchard), who has been accepted by Harvard. Carefully preserved home videos show John promising to help with her tuition, and as it happens Noreen needs $29,000—almost exactly the amount Elaine has insisted John have in the bank before she will marry him.

Crime is obviously the way to raise the money, according to John's best pal, Duff (Tom Green), who suggests a break-in at a house where the safe seems to stand open. The owner is, alas, at home, and there is a painfully unfunny sequence in which he forces John to dress in drag and "spoon" to remind him of his late wife. There's another botched robbery in which John and Duff, wearing ski masks, argue over which one gets to call himself Kyle, and so on.

Seeing Tom Green reminded me, how could it not, of his movie *Freddy Got Fingered* (2001), which was so poorly received by film critics that it received only one lonely, apologetic positive review on the Tomatometer. I gave it—let's see—no stars. Bad movie, especially the scene where Green was whirling the newborn infant around his head by its umbilical cord.

But the thing is, I remember *Freddy Got Fingered* more than a year later. I refer to it sometimes. It is a milestone. And for all its sins it was at least an ambitious movie, a go-for-broke attempt to accomplish something. It failed, but it has not left me convinced that Tom Green doesn't have good work in him. Anyone with his nerve and total lack of taste is sooner or later going to make a movie worth seeing.

Stealing Harvard, on the other hand, is a singularly unambitious product, content to paddle lazily in the shallows of sitcom formula. It has no edge, no hunger to be better than it is. It ambles pleasantly through its inanity, like a guest happy to be at a boring party. When you think of some of the weird stuff Jason Lee and Tom Green have been in over the years, you wonder what they did to amuse themselves during the filming.

Stevie ★ ★ ★ ½
NO MPAA RATING, 140 m., 2003

A documentary directed by Steve James and produced by James, Adam Singer, and Gordon Quinn.

Stevie is a brave and painful film, the story of a

man who goes looking for the youngster he met ten years earlier through the Big Brother program. He finds that the news about him is not good, and will get worse. This is a story involving a family so dysfunctional it seems almost to exist for the purpose of wounding and warping this child, Stephen Fielding. As he was wounded, so he has wounded others. That's often the way it goes. They say that child abusers were almost always abused as children. Stevie could be Exhibit A.

The movie is by Steve James, who directed the great documentary *Hoop Dreams* (1994). For years people asked him, "Whatever happened to those kids?"—to the two young basketball players he followed from eighth grade to adulthood. James must often have wondered about the kid nobody ever asked about, Stevie. While he was a student at Southern Illinois University, Steve was a Big Brother to Stevie, but he lost touch in 1985 after graduating. Ten years later, he went back downstate to the little town of Pomona, ten or fifteen miles down the road from Carbondale, to seek out Stevie.

That must have taken some courage, and even on his first return James must have suspected that this story would not have a happy ending. But it has so much truth, as it shows an unhappy childhood reaching out through the years and smacking down its adult survivor.

Here are a few facts, for orientation. Stevie Fielding was not wanted. He was born out of wedlock, does not know who his father is, was raised by a mother who didn't want him, was beaten by her. When she did marry, she turned him over to her new husband's mother to raise. He also made a circuit of foster homes and juvenile centers, where he was raped and beaten regularly.

When we meet Stevie again he is twenty-three and not doing well. His tattoos and Harley T-shirt express a bravado he does not possess, and he makes a poor impression with haystack hair, oversized thick glasses, and bad teeth. The most important person in his life is his girlfriend, Tonya Gregory, who on first impression seems slow, but who on longer acquaintance reveals herself to be smart about Stevie, and loyal to him. His stepsister Brenda is also a support, a surrogate mother who seems the best-adjusted member of his family, per-

haps because, as her husband tells us, "They didn't beat her."

Stevie freely expresses hatred for his mother, Bernice ("Someday I am going to kill her"), and she is one of the villains of the piece, but having stopped drinking, she feels remorse and even blames herself, to a degree, for Stevie's problems—especially the latest one. Between 1995, when Steve James first revisits Stevie, and 1997, when production proper started on this documentary, Stevie was charged with molesting an eight-year-old girl.

Stevie says he is innocent. Even Tonya thinks he is guilty. We do not forgive him this crime because of his tragic childhood, but it helps us understand it—even predict it, or something like it. And as he goes through the court system, Tonya stands by him, Brenda helps him as much as she can, and Bernice, his mother, seems slowly to change for the better—to move in the direction she might have taken if it had not been for her own troubles.

There is no sentimentality in *Stevie*, no escape, no release. "The film does not come to a satisfying ending," writes the critic David Poland. He wanted more of a "lift," and so, I suppose, did I—and Steve James. But although *Hoop Dreams* ended in a way that a novelist could not have improved upon, *Stevie* seems destined to end the way it does, and is the more courageous and powerful for it. A satisfying ending would have been a lie. Most of us are blessed with happy families. Around us are others, nursing deep hurts and guilts and secrets—punished as children for the crime of being unable to fight back.

To watch *Stevie* is to wonder if anything could have been done to change the course of this history. Steve James's Big-Brothering was well intentioned, and his wife, a social worker, believes in help from outside. But this extended family seems to form a matrix of pain and abuse that goes around and around in each generation, and mercilessly down through time to the next. To be born into the family is to have a good chance of being doomed, and Brenda's survival is partly because she got out fast, married young, and kept her distance.

Philip Larkin could have been thinking of this family in his most famous poem, whose opening line cannot be quoted here, but which ends:

Man hands on misery to man.
It deepens like a coastal shelf.
Get out as early as you can,
And don't have any kids yourself.

Search the Web using the first two lines, and you will find a poem that Stevie Fielding might agree with.

Stolen Summer ★ ★ ★
PG, 91 m., 2002

Aidan Quinn (Joe O'Malley), Bonnie Hunt (Margaret O'Malley), Adi Stein (Pete O'Malley), Kevin Pollak (Rabbi Jacobsen), Mike Weinberg (Danny Jacobsen), Lisa Dodson (Mrs. Jacobsen), Brian Dennehy (Father Kelly), Eddie Kaye Thomas (Patrick O'Malley), Ryan Kelley (Seamus O'Malley). Directed by Pete Jones and produced by Ben Affleck, Matt Damon, and Chris Moore. Screenplay by Jones.

Gene Siskel proposed an acid test for a movie: Is this film as good as a documentary of the same people having lunch? At last, with *Stolen Summer*, we get a chance to decide for ourselves. The making of the film has been documented in the HBO series *Project Greenlight*, where we saw the actors and filmmakers having lunch, contract disputes, story conferences, personal vendettas, location emergencies, and even glimpses of hope.

Movies are collisions between egos and compromises. With some there are no survivors. *Stolen Summer* is a delightful surprise because despite all the backstage drama, this is a movie that tells stories that work—is charming, is moving, is funny, and looks professional. That last point is crucial, because as everyone knows, director Pete Jones and his screenplay were chosen in a contest sponsored by Miramax and actors Ben Affleck and Matt Damon. Miramax gave them a break with their screenplay *Good Will Hunting*, and they wanted to return the favor.

Stolen Summer takes place on the South Side of Chicago in the summer of 1976, when an earnest second-grader named Pete O'Malley (Adi Stein) listens in Catholic school and believes every word about working his way into heaven. Seeking advice from a slightly older brother about how to guarantee his passage to

paradise, Pete is startled to learn that the Jews are not seeking to be saved through Jesus. So Pete sets up a free lemonade stand in front of the local synagogue, hoping to convert some Jews and pay for his passage.

There is already a link between Pete's family and that of Rabbi Jacobsen (Kevin Pollak). Pete's dad, Joe (Aidan Quinn), is a fireman who dashed into a burning home and rescued the Jacobsens' young son Danny (Mike Weinberg), who is about Pete's age. Pete has already met the rabbi and now becomes best friends with his son. Although Danny is not much interested in the theology involved, he joins Pete's "quest" to get them both into the Roman Catholic version of heaven. Is Pete's obsession with church rules and heaven plausible for a second-grader? Having been there, done that, I can state that this was not an unknown stage for Catholic school kids to go through, and that I personally knelt in prayer on behalf of my Protestant playmates, which they found enormously entertaining.

The touchier question of "converting the Jews" is handled by the movie so tactfully that it is impossible not to be charmed. The key performance here is by Kevin Pollak, as a rabbi whose counterpoint to Pete's quest involves understated reaction shots and instinctive sympathy and humor. When the Jacobsens invite Pete over for lunch, he makes the sign of the cross, and when the rabbi asks why he's doing it (the unstated words are "at our table"), Pete explains solemnly, "It's like picking up the phone and being sure God is there." Earlier, during his first visit inside the synagogue, Pete is surprised to find no crucifix hanging from the ceiling, and confides to the rabbi: "Sometimes I think of climbing up and loosening the screws and letting him go."

The movie cuts between Pete's quest, which is admittedly a little cutesy, and the completely convincing marriage of his parents, Joe and Margaret (Bonnie Hunt). These are (I know) actors who grew up in Chicago neighborhoods and were raised (I believe) as Catholics, and they are pitch-perfect. Note the scene where Hunt is driving most of her eight kids to Mass and the troublesome Seamus is making too much noise in the backseat. Still driving, she reaches out to him and beckons him closer, saying, "Come closer . . . come on, come on,

I'm not going to hit you," and then smacks him up alongside the head. Every once in a while a movie gives you a moment of absolute truth.

Danny has leukemia, which he explains solemnly to Pete, who is fascinated. Danny's mother is worried about her young son spending so much time with Pete, but the rabbi observes it may be Danny's last chance to act like a normal kid. The "quest" involves such tests as swimming out to a buoy in Lake Michigan, and while we doubt that, even in innocent 1976, second-graders were going to the beach by themselves, we understand the dramatic purpose.

The most fraught scenes in the movie involve the synagogue's decision to thank the O'Malley family after Joe risked his life to save Danny. They settle on a scholarship for Patrick, the oldest O'Malley boy, and the rabbi is startled when Joe turns it down in anger. Joe tells his wife: "It's about the Jews helping out some poor Roman Catholic family so they can go on TV and get free publicity." Is this anti-Semitism? No, I think it's tribalism, and Joe O'Malley would say the same thing about the Episcopalians, the Buddhists, or the Rotary Club. Bonnie Hunt's response is magnificent: If Joe doesn't let his son accept the scholarship, "So help me God, when you come home at night, the only thing colder than your dinner will be your bed."

Stolen Summer is a film combining broad sentiment with sharp observation, although usually not in the same scenes. I don't know if writer-director Jones came from a large Irish-American family on the South Side, but do I even need to ask? The movie even has Brian Dennehy, patron saint of the Chicago stage, as the parish priest. In a time when so many big-budget mainstream movies are witless and heartless, *Stolen Summer* proves that studios might do just about as well by holding a screenplay contest and filming the winner.

The Stoneraft ★ ★ ★
NO MPAA RATING, 117 m., 2003

Ana Padrão (Joana), Gabino Diego (Jose), Icíar Bollain (Maria), Diogo Infante (Joaquim), Federico Luppi (Pedro). Directed and produced by George Sluizer. Screenplay by Yvette Biro and Sluizer, based on the novel by José Saramago.

Certain unexpected shots send an uneasy shudder through the audience. In *Close Encounters* there was the pickup truck waiting at the train crossing when two headlights appeared in the rear window and then, inexplicably, began to rise vertically. In George Sluizer's new film *The Stoneraft*, a dog trots doggily through a country field, and then for no reason leaps across a patch of ground, and continues on his doggy way. A second later, a crack opens up in the ground right where he jumped. How did the dog know?

The film is a low-key disaster picture, made about characters who are inward, thoughtful, talkative. It's about the Iberian Peninsula breaking loose from Europe and sending Spain and Portugal very quickly out into the Atlantic toward a collision with the Azores.

Like all disaster movies, it follows the larger story through several smaller ones. There are five of them, drawn together finally by the dog. Jose (Gabino Diego) discovers that he is being followed everywhere by a flock of birds. Joana (Ana Padrão) uses a stick to idly trace a line in the earth, and finds she cannot erase the line. Joaquim (Diogo Infante) picks up a heavy stone and heaves it into the sea, only to watch amazed as it skips over the waves like a pebble. Maria (Icíar Bollain) starts to unravel a knitted blue sock that has gone wrong, and discovers that her task is never done: "No matter how long I work, there is still more wool." An older man named Pedro (Federico Luppi) can feel the earth trembling even if no one else can.

These people end up in an increasingly crowded Citroën 2CV, driving toward the collision coast as crowds flee in the opposite direction. Eventually the car breaks down and they switch to a horse cart. Some villages are being looted by mobs; in others, people dance in the streets, for tomorrow they may die.

Television covers the fallout. Britain reasserts its claim to Gibraltar. Americans arrive to try to close the widening rift with cables and earth-moving machinery. Governments resign. No one has an explanation, although many believe the film's five heroes may have had something to do with it.

Sluizer is the same director who made *The*

Vanishing (1993), one of the best thrillers ever made, about a man whose wife disappears at a highway rest stop. He later remade it in a Hollywood version that vulgarized his own material. This time, he has reversed the process, taking the tacky American disaster movie and translating it into a quieter and more elegant European version.

It's amusing how few special effects he gets away with. Two entire nations break off from Europe and set sail, and he covers it with a trench in the ground, a flock of birds, a ball of blue wool, and a trained dog. The effect is uncanny and haunting, and I was reminded a little of *On the Beach* (1959), in which the nuclear destruction of the Northern Hemisphere is observed from Australia via low-tech shortwave broadcasts and hearsay reports.

The movie is meant partly as satire; after years of reports about nations breaking away from the EUC, here are two that literally do. There's some social observation: Why does the public assume the man followed by birds represents the cause, not the solution? Much of the story is told at the pace of a leisurely day in the country, as the five characters and the dog muse about the curious turn of events. Is it possible that the small actions of these people could have set into motion the partitioning of subcontinents? After all, doesn't chaos theory teach us that the beating of a butterfly's wings in Asia could theoretically begin a chain of events leading to a hurricane in . . . the Azores, wasn't it?

Stone Reader ★ ★ ★ ½
PG-13, 128 m., 2003

With Carl Brandt, Frank Conroy, Bruce Dobler, Robert C. S. Downs, Robert Ellis, Leslie Fiedler, Ed Gorman, Robert Gottlieb, Dan Guenther, John Kashiwabara, Mark Moskowitz, Dow Mossman, William Cotter Murray, John Seelye. Directed by Mark Moskowitz and produced by Moskowitz and Robert M. Goodman. Screenplay by Moskowitz.

In 1972, a man reads a review of a new novel named *The Stones of Summer* in the *New York Times*. The reviewer believes it is one of the most extraordinary novels of its generation—a masterpiece. The man buys the novel, can't get into it, puts it on the shelf, moves it around with his books for years, and finally reads it. He thinks it's a masterpiece, too. He goes on the Internet to find out what else the author, Dow Mossman, has written. Mossman has written nothing—has disappeared, it would appear, from the face of the Earth.

Stone Reader is the story of the reader's quest for that missing writer. Mark Moskowitz, whose day job is directing political commercials, embarks on a quixotic quest for Dow Mossman, finds him after much difficulty, and discovers why he has been silent for thirty years, and what he has been up to. It will occur to any attentive viewer of the film that Moskowitz could have found Mossman more quickly and easily than he does—that at times he is stretching out the search for its own sake—but then the movie is not really about Mossman anyway. It is about a reader who goes in search of other readers, and it is a love poem to reading.

It is the kind of movie that makes you want to leave the theater and go directly to a bookstore. Maybe to buy *The Stones of Summer*, which got a new edition in autumn 2003, but also to buy—well, it reawakened my interest in Joseph Heller's *Something Happened*, which has been lost in the shadow of his *Catch-22*, and it observes correctly that Kerouac's *On the Road* is a better novel than a lot of people think it is, and it reminded me of Frederick Exley's *A Fan's Notes*, which has been described as the kind of book that, when you meet someone at a party who has also read it, forces you to seek out a quiet corner to talk urgently about it, with much laughter and shaking of heads.

Moskowitz, who narrates the movie and appears in much more of it than Dow Mossman, is a Woody Allenish character who makes the filming into the subject of the film. At one point, he phones his mother for advice on what he should ask Mossman. (At another, he asks her what sort of kid he was at eighteen, when he first bought the novel, and she remembers: "You had a beard, and you used to like to wear only the linings of coats.") When he encounters a fresh interview subject, he is likely to produce a box jammed with books and stack them up between them, reciting the titles like a litany of touchstones. I do not travel around with boxes of books, but get me in conversation with another reader, and I'll recite titles, too. Have you ever read *Quincunx*? *The Raj Quartet*? *A Fine Balance*? Ever heard of that most despairing of all travel books, *The Saddest Pleasure*, by Moritz Thomsen? Does anybody hold up better than Joseph Conrad and Willa Cather? Know any Yeats by heart? Surely P. G. Wodehouse is as great at what he does as Shakespeare was at what he did.

Shakespeare, as it turns out, has been one of Dow Mossman's companions during his missing years. Without telling you very much about where he is now or why he didn't write another novel or what his work has been since 1972, I can nevertheless evoke his presence as a person you would very much like to talk books with. He turns out not to be a tragic recluse, a sad alcoholic, or a depressive, but a man filled with words and good cheer. When he came to my Overlooked Film Festival, where the film played in April, he and the French director Bertrand Tavernier seemed always to be in a corner together, trading enthusiasm about books.

Mark Twain is one of his heroes, and he can cite the chapter of Twain's autobiography that you must read. He is awestruck by Casanova's memoirs. He hated *Shakespeare in Love* because of those scenes where Shakespeare crumpled up a page of foolscap in frustration and threw it away: Paper was too expensive to throw away in those days, Mossman observes, and he is convinced Shakespeare created his plays in his mind while walking around London, and then taught them to his players. Since many of the plays show evidence of being based on actors' prompt copies and scholars can sometimes identify the actor-source who may have been more familiar with some scenes than others, he may be right.

Doesn't matter. What matters is listening to him talk about books with Moskowitz. In the scene where Moskowitz first encounters him, they are soon talking about Shakespeare, not Mossman. Here, we feel, is a man who should appear regularly on National Public Radio, just talking about books he loves.

Before he finds Mossman, Moskowitz interviews several men of letters (no women). Some of them, he hopes, might remember *The Stones of Summer*—such as Robert Gottlieb, the famous editor, or John Kashiwabara, who designed the book cover, or Frank Conroy, who was Mossman's adviser at the University of Iowa. John Seelye, who wrote the original review for the *New York Times*, remembers the book. The late Leslie Fiedler, a towering literary critic, has never heard of it — but Moskowitz interviews him anyway, about the phenomenon of one-book novelists. (Some writers who write many books, like Kerouac, Salinger, Malcolm Lowry, and James T. Farrell, are nevertheless really one-book novelists, they decide.)

Stone Reader is a meandering documentary, frustrating when Moskowitz has Mossman in his sights and *still* delays bagging him while talking to other sources. But at the end, we forgive his procrastination (and remember, with Laurence Sterne and *Tristam Shandy*, that procrastination can be an art if it is done delightfully). Moskowitz has made a wonderful film about readers and reading, writers and writing. Now somebody needs to go to Cedar Rapids and make a whole documentary about Dow Mossman. Call it *The Stone Writer*.

Storytelling ★ ★ ★ ½
R, 87 m., 2002

Fiction
Selma Blair (Vi), Leo Fitzpatrick (Marcus), Robert Wisdom (Mr. Scott).
Nonfiction
Mark Webber (Scooby), John Goodman (Marty), Julie Hagerty (Fern), Jonathan Osser (Mikey), Noah Fleiss (Brady), Lupe Ontiveros (Consuelo), Paul Giamatti (Toby). Directed by Todd Solondz and produced by Ted Hope and Christine Vachon. Screenpaly by Solondz.

For some artists, especially younger ones, the creative impulse is linked directly to the genitals: They create because they hope it makes them sexually attractive. This is a truth so obvious it is rarely mentioned in creative writing circles, although writers as various as Philip Roth, Thomas Wolfe, and Martin Amis have built their careers on it. *Storytelling*, the in-your-face new film by Todd Solondz, is a confessional in which Solondz explores his own methods and motives, and tries to come clean.

The movie contains two stories. The first, *Fiction*, is about a college creative writing student (Selma Blair) whose boyfriend (Leo Fitzpatrick) has cerebral palsy. "You wanna hear my short story now?" he asks her immediately after sex, and it is clear he is trading on sex as a way to win an audience. Although he is the "cripple," that gives him an advantage in her politically correct cosmos, and he milks it. Later, when they've broken up, he observes sadly, "The kinkiness has gone. You've become kind."

She moves on to a one-night stand with her writing professor (Robert Wisdom), a forbidding black man whose tastes run toward rough rape fantasies. She goes looking for trouble, but finds she doesn't like it, and writes a tearful, defiant story about their encounter. When the other students tear it to shreds, she weeps, "But it's the truth!"

All three of these characters are using the pose of "writer" as a way to get sex, get their work read, or both, sometimes at the same time. *Nonfiction,* the longer second section of the film, opens with a would-be documentary filmmaker named Toby (Paul Giamatti) looking at the high school yearbook photo of a girl he now remembers yearningly. Calling her, he finds she is married and has a family, and immediately decides he is making a documentary about an American family and needs hers.

This family, the Livingstons, is Jewish, lives in the suburbs, and is a seething zone of resentment and rage. The father (John Goodman) presides over the dinner table like an enforcer; the mother (Julie Hagerty) is a twittering mass of reconciliation. Scooby (Mark Webber), the oldest son, smokes pot, is sullen, hides in his room. Brady (Noah Fleiss), the middle son, plays football and speculates that Scooby is a "homo." Mikey (Jonathan Osser), the youngest son, has earnest conversations with the El Salvadoran maid, Consuelo (Lupe Ontiveros). She hates the family and her job. Mikey wants to be nice to her but is clueless ("But Consuelo, even though you're poor, don't you have any hobbies or interests or anything?"). When he finds her weeping because her son has been executed for murder, he expresses polite regret before asking her to clean up some grape juice he has spilled. Later, he hypnotizes his father and instructs him to fire her.

Dinner conversation at the Livingstons' is fraught with hazards. When the Holocaust comes up, it is Scooby who observes that since it forced an ancestor to escape to America, "If it wasn't for Hitler, none of us would ever have been born." This gets him immediately banished from the table, a fate that hangs over every meal as the father angrily monitors the conversation.

Alert readers will have noticed that *Storytelling* seems to be working from a list of sensitive or taboo subjects: physical disability, race, rape, facile charges of racism, exploitation of the poor, the Holocaust, homosexuality. I will not reveal the identity of the character who goes into a coma and is apparently braindead; I will observe that this development cheers the editor of Toby's documentary, who tells him it's just what his film needs.

One character does attack Toby's documentary, telling him it's "glib and facile to make fun of these people." "I'm not making fun of them," Toby says. "I love them." Toby, of course, represents Solondz, whose two previous films (*Welcome to the Dollhouse* and *Happiness*) were attacked for making glib and facile fun of the characters. So has this one; Ed Gonzalez of *Slant* refers to Solondz's "cowardly apologias." In a Solondz film there's always a delicate line to be walked between social satire on the one hand and a geek show on the other.

I think Solondz is not cowardly but brave, and does his bourgeois-mugging in full view, instead of concealing it. We live in a time when many comedies mock middle-class American suburban life, but Solondz is one director who does it out in the open, to extremes, pushing the envelope, challenging us to decide what we think. And because his timing is so precise and his ear for dialogue so good, he sometimes tricks us into laughing before we have time to think, gee, we shouldn't be laughing at that.

I saw *Storytelling* at Cannes 2001 and wrote that I wanted to see it again before deciding what I thought about it. I saw it again, and still felt I had to see it again. I saw it a third time. By then I had moved beyond the immediate shock of the material and was able to focus on what a well-made film it was; how concisely Solondz gets the effects he's after.

I was also forced to conclude that I might *never* know for sure what I thought about it— that it was a puzzle without an answer, a demonstration that there are some areas so fraught and sensitive that most people just hurry past them with their eyes averted. By not averting his eyes, Solondz forces us to consider the unthinkable, the unacceptable, the unmentionable. He should not be penalized for going further than the filmmakers who attack the same targets but have better manners—or less nerve.

Note: During the sex scene between the professor and his student, a bright red quadrangle obscures part of the screen. When I saw the movie at Cannes, the audience could see the two characters—graphically, but not in explicit pornographic detail. The MPAA refused to give the film an R rating because of that scene. Solondz refused to cut it, and used the red blocking as a way of underlining the MPAA's censorship. Good for him. And one more reminder that the MPAA and Jack Valenti oppose a workable adult rating for America.

Stuart Little 2 ★ ★ ★
PG, 78 m., 2002

Geena Davis (Eleanor Little), Hugh Laurie (Fredrick Little), Jonathan Lipnicki (George Little). And the voices of: Michael J. Fox (Stuart Little), Nathan Lane (Snowbell), Melanie Griffith (Margalo), James Woods (Falcon). Directed by Rob Minkoff and produced by Lucy Fisher and Douglas Wick. Screenplay by Bruce Joel Rubin and Wick, based on characters from the book *Stuart Little* by E. B. White.

Faithful readers will know that I question the logic of a human-size family with a son who is two inches tall, particularly when the son is a mouse. In watching the first *Stuart Little* (1999), I cringed every time the heavy footfall of one of his parents landed near little Stuart. The mouse is cute, but he was born to be squished.

I vowed to approach *Stuart Little 2* afresh. I would go into full-blown suspension-of-disbelief mode. If there must be a movie about a mouse-child in the real world, then I must accept it—even if the film toys with my fears by putting Stuart into a soccer game with full-size kids. Even Stuart's mom (Geena Davis) gets the shivers at "the thought of all those boys running around with those cleats in their shoes." Stuart's dad (Hugh Laurie) is more optimistic, believing that a Little can do anything

he sets his mind to, and sending the little tyke on dangerous missions, as when he is lowered down the kitchen drain to look for his mother's diamond ring. For that matter, Stuart's daily commute to school in his tiny little red sports car must not be without its hazards.

Stuart Little 2 is not indifferent to the problems involved, not least the compositional problems faced by Steve Poster, its cinematographer, in framing both the six-foot Davis and the two-inch Stuart in the same shot. It provides Stuart (voice by Michael J. Fox) with a friend about his own size, a yellow bird named Margalo (voice by Melanie Griffith). She falls from the sky with a wounded wing, lands in Stuart's sports car, is taken home for first aid, and soon becomes his chum.

There is even a hint of cross-species romance, as Stuart and Margalo go on a date to the drive-in movies (by parking his red sportster in front of the TV). The movie they're watching is Hitchcock's *Vertigo*, about a man who falls in love with a woman who is deceiving him, but Stuart doesn't take the hint, and is blindsided when it turns out (spoiler warning) that Margalo is a con artist, teamed up with a snarky falcon (voice by James Woods). The falcon's advice: "Don't ever make a friend I can eat."

By this point the movie has located itself pretty much two inches above ground level, although there are important roles for the family cat, Snowbell (voice by Nathan Lane), and the family son, George (Jonathan Lipnicki). There's an exciting sequence involving entrapment in a skyscraper, entombment in a garbage barge, and an aerial dogfight between the falcon and Stuart, piloting a model airplane.

Yes, reader, I enjoyed the movie, in its innocent way. It has some of the same charm, if not the same genius, as the movies about Babe the pig. The film imagines Manhattan as a sunny, peaceful place where no one is surprised to see a mouse driving a car, and where the parents are so optimistic that when Stuart goes missing they drive around looking for him—as if you could see a two-inch mouse from the middle of New York traffic.

Of the voices, Melanie Griffith makes Margalo lovable and as sexy as a little yellow bird can be, and Nathan Lane does a virtuoso job with Snowbell, the only cat with dialogue by Damon Runyon. Michael J. Fox's Stuart is stalwart and heroic—the *Braveheart* of mice. As for the parents, Geena Davis and Hugh Laurie deserve some kind of award for keeping straight faces. My only question involves the sweet scene at the end, when Margalo bids them farewell to join the southward migration of geese in the autumn. I think there is a good chance she is a canary, and they don't migrate.

Sugar & Spice ★ ★ ★
PG-13, 93 m., 2001

Marley Shelton (Diane Weston), James Marsden (Jack Bartlett), Mena Suvari (Kansas Hill), Marla Sokoloff (Lisa Janusch), Alexandra Holden (Fern Rogers), Rachel Blanchard (Hannah Wold), Sara Marsh (Lucy Whitman), Melissa George (Cleo Miller), Sean Young (Kansas's Mom). Directed by Francine McDougall and produced by Wendy Finerman. Screenplay by Mandy Nelson.

Sugar & Spice puts your average cheerleader movie to shame. It's sassy and satirical, closer in spirit to *But I'm a Cheerleader* than to *Bring It On*. With its shameless pop culture references, wicked satire, and a cheerleader with the hots for Conan O'Brien, it's more proof that not all movie teenagers have to be dumb. (All right, these cheerleaders *are* dumb—but in a smart movie.) I was surprised by the PG-13 rating; the movie is so in tune with its under-seventeen target audience that it's amazing the MPAA didn't slap it with an R.

The movie takes place at Lincoln High School, with a crepe-headed Honest Abe prancing on the sidelines. We meet the A-team of the cheerleader squad, who seem like a cross between Olympic gymnasts and the pom-pom girl who inflamed Kevin Spacey in *American Beauty*. No wonder: Mena Suvari, who played the pom-pom girl, turns up here as Kansas, a girl whose mom is in prison.

The team leader is Diane (Marley Shelton), a beauty who is stunned when Jack (James Marsden), the captain of the football team, announces at a school assembly that his platform for prom king includes taking her to the prom. They share a wet kiss on stage, and soon Diane is pregnant, which doesn't curtail her cheerleading.

Jack and Diane receive a frosty reception from their parents, but after the movie quotes what for it is scripture ("Papa Don't Preach") they move into a cheap apartment and Jack gets a job at Señor Guacamole. He's fired, there's a financial crisis, and then Diane comes up with an inspiration while watching a heist movie on TV: They can rob a bank!

They do research by watching other crime movies, including *Heat, Point Blank,* and *Reservoir Dogs*. Cleo (Melissa George), the team member with the crush on Conan, makes it more fun by fantasizing Conan's head on the bodies of actors. Hannah (Rachel Blanchard), who has strict churchgoing parents, is allowed to watch only G-rated movies, so she researches *The Apple Dumpling Gang*. Lucy (Sara Marsh), the brains of the outfit, fits it all together. And they rationalize the robbery by saying they can give some of the money to charity: We can buy "one of those starving little kids that Sally Struthers auctions."

The robbery plans include a visit to a local exterminator, who supplies them with guns and insists that his daughter Fern (Alexandra Holden) be allowed to join the cheerleader squad. Fern looks at first like a candidate for one of her dad's poisonous sprays, but cleans up real good. The robbery itself involves disguises: five pregnant Betty dolls and one Richard Nixon. I liked the way a witness, also a cheerleader, sees through the disguises when she observes an "illegal dismount."

The film's narrator is the outsider Lisa (Marla Sokoloff), who has a Bette Midler quality. One of the weirder scenes involves a trip by Kansas to visit her mother (Sean Young) in prison; she needs advice on robbing banks. And the running gag about Conan O'Brien is funny because the passion seems so out of scale with its inspiration. *Sugar & Spice* seems instinctively in sync with its cheerleaders, maybe because it was made by women: director Francine McDougall, writer Mandy Nelson, producer Wendy Finerman. It is not a great high school movie, like *Election,* but it's alive and risky and saucy.

The Sum of All Fears ★ ★ ★ ½
PG-13, 127 m., 2002

Ben Affleck (Jack Ryan), Morgan Freeman (Bill Cabot), James Cromwell (President Fowler),

Liev Schreiber (John Clark), Alan Bates (Richard Dressler), Philip Baker Hall (Defense Secretary Becker), Bruce McGill (Security Adviser Revel), Jamie Harrold (Dillon), Ciaran Hinds (President Nemerov), Bridget Moynahan (Cathy Muller). Directed by Phil Alden Robinson and produced by Mace Neufeld. Screenplay by Paul Attanasio and Daniel Pyne, based on the novel by Tom Clancy.

Oh, for the innocent days when a movie like *The Sum of All Fears* could be enjoyed as a "thriller." In these dark times it is not a thriller but a confirmer, confirming our fears that the world is headed for disaster. The film is about the detonation of a nuclear device in an American city. No less an authority than Warren Buffett recently gave a speech in which he flatly stated that such an event was "inevitable." Movies like *Black Sunday* could exorcise our fears, but this one works instead to give them form.

To be sure, Tom Clancy's horrifying vision has been footnoted with the obligatory Hollywood happy ending, in which world war is averted and an attractive young couple pledge love while sitting on a blanket in the sunshine on the White House lawn. We can walk out smiling, unless we remember that much of Baltimore is radioactive rubble. Human nature is a wonderful thing. The reason the ending is happy is because we in the audience assume we'll be the two on the blanket, not the countless who've been vaporized.

The movie is based on another of Tom Clancy's fearfully factual stories about Jack Ryan, the CIA agent, this time a good deal younger than Harrison Ford's Ryan in *A Clear and Present Danger*, and played by Ben Affleck. It follows the ancient convention in which the hero goes everywhere important and personally performs most of the crucial actions, but it feels less contrived because Clancy has expertise about warfare and national security issues; the plot is a device to get us from one packet of information to another.

The story: In 1973, an Israeli airplane carrying a nuclear bomb crashes in Syria. Many years later, the unexploded bomb is dug up, goes on the black market, and is sold to a right-wing fanatic who has a theory: "Hitler was stupid. He fought America and Russia, instead

of letting them fight one another." The fanatic's plan is to start a nuclear exchange between the superpowers, after which Aryan fascists would pick up the pieces.

The use of the neo-Nazis is politically correct: Best to invent villains who won't offend any audiences. This movie can play in Syria, Saudi Arabia, and Iraq without getting walkouts. It's more likely that if a bomb ever does go off in a big city, the perpetrators will be True Believers whose certainty about the next world gives them, they think, the right to kill us in this one.

In the film, Ryan becomes a sort of unofficial protégé of Bill Cabot (Morgan Freeman), a high-level CIA official and good guy who maintains a "back channel" into the Kremlin to avoid just such misunderstandings as occur. Ryan and Cabot fly to Moscow when a new president assumes power, and the new Soviet leader (Ciaran Hinds) is shown as a reasonable man who must take unreasonable actions (like invading Chechnya) to placate the militarists in his government.

America is being run by President Fowler (tall, Lincolnesque James Cromwell), who is surrounded by advisers cast with some of the most convincing character actors in the movies: Philip Baker Hall, Alan Bates, Bruce McGill, etc. Crucial scenes take place aboard *Air Force One* after Baltimore has been bombed, and we see the president and his cabinet not in cool analytical discussions but all shouting at once. Somehow I am reassured by the notion that our leaders might be really upset at such a time; anyone who can be dispassionate about nuclear war is probably able to countenance one.

There are some frightening special effects in the movie, which I will not describe, because their unexpected appearance has such an effect. There are also several parallel story lines, including one involving a particularly skilled dirty-tricks specialist named John Clark (Liev Schreiber) who I am glad to have on our side. There are also the usual frustrations in which the man with the truth can't get through because of bureaucracy.

Against these strengths are some weaknesses. I think Jack Ryan's one-man actions in postbomb Baltimore are unlikely and way too well-timed. I doubt he would find evildoers still hanging around the scene of their crime. I am not sure all of the threads—identifying the plutonium, finding the shipping manifest and invoice, tracking down the guy who dug up the bomb—could take place with such gratifying precision. And I smile wearily at the necessity of supplying Jack with a girlfriend (Bridget Moynahan), who exists only so that she can (1) be impatient when he is called away from dates on official business; (2) disbelieve his alibis; (3) be heroic; (4) be worried about him; (5) be smudged with blood and dirt; and (6) populate the happy ending. We are so aware of the character's function that we can hardly believe her as a person.

These details are not fatal to the film. Director Phil Alden Robinson and his writers, Paul Attanasio and Daniel Pyne, do a spellbinding job of cranking up the tension; they create a portrait of convincing realism, and then they add the other stuff because, well, if anybody ever makes a movie like this without the obligatory Hollywood softeners, audiences might flee the theater in despair. My own fear is that in the postapocalyptic future, *The Sum of All Fears* will be seen as touchingly optimistic.

Sunshine State ★ ★ ★ ½
PG-13, 141 m., 2002

Edie Falco (Marly Temple), Angela Bassett (Desiree Perry), Jane Alexander (Delia Temple), Ralph Waite (Furman Temple), James McDaniel (Reggie Perry), Timothy Hutton (Jack Meadows), Mary Alice (Eunice Stokes), Bill Cobbs (Dr. Lloyd), Mary Steenburgen (Francine Pickney), Tom Wright (Flash Phillips), Alan King (Murray Silver). Directed by John Sayles and produced by Maggie Renzi. Screenplay by Sayles.

John Sayles's *Sunshine State* looks at first like the story of clashes between social and economic groups: between developers and small landowners, between black and white, between the powerful and their workers, between the Chamber of Commerce and local reality. It's set on a Florida resort island, long stuck in its ways, that has been targeted by a big development company. But this is not quite the story the setup seems to predict.

If the movie had been made twenty or thirty years ago, the whites would have been racists, the blacks victims, and the little businessmen would have struggled courageously to hold out against the developers. But things do change in our country, sometimes slowly for the better, and *Sunshine State* is set at a point in time when all of the players are a little more reconciled, a little less predictable, than they would have been. You can only defend a position so long before the needs of your own life begin to assert themselves.

The island, named Plantation Island, consists of Delrona Beach, a small community of retirees and retail stores, and Lincoln Beach, an enclave of prosperous African-Americans. Both groups have been targeted by a big land development company probably owned by a white-haired golfer named Murray Silver (Alan King), although he exists so far above the world of the little people that it's hard to be sure. The company wants to buy up everything and turn it into a high-rise "beach resort community."

That would doom the Sea-Vue Motel and restaurant, which is run by Marly Temple (Edie Falco, of *The Sopranos*). The motel was built by her parents, Furman and Delia (Ralph Waite and Jane Alexander), and is Furman's life work. But it is not Edie's dream. In a movie made twenty years ago, she would be fighting against the capitalist invaders, but, frankly, she *wants* to sell—and she even begins a little romance with Jack (Timothy Hutton), the architect sent in to size things up.

Over on the Lincoln Beach side, Eunice Stokes (Mary Alice) lives in her tidy white house with a sea view. When she bought this house, it represented a substantial dream for an ambitious black couple; today, it looks a little forlorn. For the first time in years, her daughter Desiree (Angela Bassett) has come to visit. Desiree got pregnant at fifteen with the Florida Flash (Tom Wright), a football hero, and was sent away because Eunice was too proud of her middle-class respectability to risk scandal. Desiree has prospered on TV in Boston and returns with an anesthetist husband.

The Florida Flash, meanwhile, has not prospered. He had an injury on his way to the Heisman Trophy and now sells used cars. Success seems to go wrong on this island; while Francine (Mary Steenburgen), the bubbly Chamber of Commerce pageant chairman, narrates a story of pirates and treasure, her husband tries to kill himself, although neither hanging nor a nail gun does the trick. He's got business difficulties.

Because we are so familiar with the conventional approach to a story like this, it takes time to catch on that Sayles is not repeating the old progressive line about the little guy against big capital. He has made a more observant, elegiac, sad movie, about how the dreams of the parents are not the dreams of the children.

Because Furman wanted a motel, Marly has to work long hours to run it. Because Eunice wanted respectability, Desiree had to run away from home. Because the Chamber of Commerce wants a pageant about "local history," Francine has to concoct one. (The island's real history mostly involves "mass murder, rape, and slavery," she observes, so they'll "Disney-fy it a little bit.") Even the outside predators are not so bad. Timothy Hutton, as the architect, is not typecast as an uncaring pencil pusher who wants to bulldoze the beach, but as a wage earner who moves from one job to another, living in motels, without a family, always on assignment.

Sayles pulls another surprise. His characters are not unyielding. Consider the scene where Marly tells her father she's had it with the motel. Consider the scene where her mother, an Audubon Society stalwart, observes that there might be an angle in selling birdlands and giving the money to the society. Consider Eunice's need to reconsider her daughter's needs and behavior. Look at the daughter's difficulty in reconciling memories of the Florida Flash with the car salesman she sees before her. And consider how at the end of the film, fate and history turn out to play a greater role than any of the great plans.

Sayles's film moves among a large population of characters with grace, humor, and a forgiving irony. The performances by Angela Bassett, Edie Falco, and Mary Alice are at the heart of the story, and there are moments when other characters can illuminate themselves with one flash of dialogue, as Ralph Waite does one day in considering the future of the motel. Some of the characters seem to have drifted in from Altman Land, especially Mary Steenburgen's, whose narration of the pageant is a wildly irrelevant counterpoint to the island's reality. Others, like Tim Hutton's sad architect, seem to

have much more power than they do. And what about Alan King and his golfing buddies? They show that if you have enough money and power, you don't need to get your hands dirty making more (others will do that for you), and you can be genial and philosophical—a sweet, colorful character, subsidized by the unhappiness of others.

Sunshine State is not a radical attack on racism and big business, not a defense of the environment, not a hymn in favor of small communities over conglomerates. It is about the next generation of those issues and the people they involve. Racism has faded to the point where Eunice's proud home on Lincoln Beach no longer makes the same statement. Big business is not monolithic but bumbling. The little motel is an eyesore. The young people who got out, like Desiree, have prospered. Those who stayed, like Marly, have been trapped. And the last scene of the film tells us, I think, that we should hesitate to embrace the future in this nation until we have sufficiently considered the past.

Super Troopers ★ ★ ½
R, 103 m., 2002

Jay Chandrasekhar (Thorny), Kevin Heffernan (Farva), Steve Lemme (Mac), Paul Soter (Foster), Erik Stolhanske (Rabbit), Brian Cox (Captain John O'Hagan), Daniel von Bargen (Chief Grady), Marisa Coughlan (Ursula), Lynda Carter (Governor Jessman). Directed by Jay Chandrasekhar and produced by Richard Perello. Screenplay by Broken Lizard (Jay Chandrasekhar, Kevin Heffernan, Steve Lemme, Paul Soter, and Erik Stolhanske).

Super Troopers plays like it was directed as a do-it-yourself project, following instructions that omitted a few steps, and yet the movie has an undeniable charm. Imagine a group of Vermont state troopers treating their job like an opportunity to stage real-life *Candid Camera* situations. Now imagine that all of the troopers have ambitions to be stand-up comics. And that they were inspired to get into the force by watching *Police Academy* movies. But that they are basically good guys. That kind of describes it.

The movie is set in Spurbury, Vermont, where

there isn't enough crime to go around. That causes a bitter rivalry between the state troopers, led by Captain O'Hagan (Brian Cox), and the city police, led by Chief Grady (Daniel von Bargen). When a dead body turns up in a Winebago and drug smuggling seems to be involved, the two forces compete for clues, arrests, and especially for funds. The state police post, indeed, has been threatened with a complete shutdown by the budget-minded governor (Lynda Carter).

Perhaps because these may be the last weeks they can spend working together, or perhaps simply because they're fundamentally goofy, the troopers pass their days blowing the minds of people they stop on the highway.

Trooper: Do you know how fast you were going?
Terrified kid whose friends are stoned: Sixty-five?
Trooper: Sixty-three.

Other nice touches include (a) using the loudspeaker to instruct a driver to pull over after he has already pulled over, and (b) casually saying "meow" in the middle of a conversation with a curbed driver.

Captain O'Hagan is understandably distressed at the bizarre behavior of his men, and worried about the possible closing of the post. A drug bust would save the day, but his men seem fairly unfocused as they look into a promising case. "Are you suggesting," the local chief asks the troopers, "that a cartoon monkey is bringing drugs into our town?" Well, no, but it's a long story.

There's romantic intrigue when a sweet and sexy local cop named Ursula (Marisa Coughlan) starts to date a trooper named Foster (Paul Soter). This goes against the rules and undermines the rivalry, but may provide a solution to the drug mystery. Foster, however, is not too bright, as when he suggests that he and Ursula get into the backseat of the cruiser. He has forgotten that once you are in the backseat of a cruiser, someone else has to let you out.

During their sessions in local diners, which are long and frequent, the cops trade dialogue like members of a comedy troupe, which indeed they are. The name of their troupe is Broken Lizard, it shares credit for the screenplay,

and the director is Jay Chandrasekhar. He also plays the trooper named Thorny. Vermonters find it obvious that he is of ethnic origin, but are baffled by the challenge of identifying his ethnic group, and there's a running gag as he remains poker-faced while people assume he's Mexican, Arabic, Indian or . . . something.

Broken Lizard, I learn, began as an undergraduate troupe at Colgate in 1989, raised $200,000 to make a movie named *Puddle Cruiser* and, instead of making a distribution deal, did a campus tour to show it. *Super Troopers* aims higher, and may spin off a Fox TV sitcom which, on the basis of this film, might work.

Super Troopers has kind of a revue feel. There is a plot, which somehow arrives at a conclusion, but the movie doesn't tell a story so much as move from one skit to another, with a laidback charm that is more relaxed and selfconfident than the manic laffaminit style of the *Police Academy* pictures. No movie is altogether uninspired that includes lines like, "Desperation is a stinky cologne." I can't quite recommend it—it's too patched together—but I almost can; it's the kind of movie that makes you want to like it.

The Sweetest Thing ★ ½
R, 84 m., 2002

Cameron Diaz (Christina), Christina Applegate (Courtney), Thomas Jane (Peter), Selma Blair (Jane), Jason Bateman (Roger), Parker Posey (Judy). Directed by Roger Kumble and produced by Cathy Konrad. Screenplay by Nancy M. Pimental.

I like Cameron Diaz. I just plain like her. She's able to convey bubble-brained zaniness about as well as anyone in the movies right now, and then she can switch gears and give you a scary dramatic performance in something like *Vanilla Sky*. She's a beauty, but apparently without vanity; how else to account for her appearance in *Being John Malkovich*, or her adventures in *There's Something About Mary*? I don't think she gets halfway enough praise for her talent.

Consider her in *The Sweetest Thing*. This is not a good movie. It's deep-sixed by a compulsion to catalog every bodily fluids gag in *There's Something About Mary* and devise a parallel clone-gag. It knows the words but not the music;

while the Farrelly brothers got away with murder, *The Sweetest Thing* commits suicide.

And yet there were whole long stretches of it when I didn't much care how bad it was—at least, I wasn't brooding in anger about the film—because Cameron Diaz and her costars had thrown themselves into it with such heedless abandon. They don't walk the plank, they tap-dance.

The movie is about three girls who just wanna have fun. They hang out in clubs, they troll for cute guys, they dress like *Maxim* cover girls, they study paperback best-sellers on the rules of relationships, and frequently (this comes as no surprise), they end up weeping in each other's arms. Diaz's running mates, played by Christina Applegate and Selma Blair, are pals and confidantes, and a crisis for one is a crisis for all.

The movie's romance involves Diaz meeting Thomas Jane in a dance club; the chemistry is right but he doesn't quite accurately convey that the wedding he is attending on the weekend is his own. This leads to Diaz's ill-fated expedition into the wedding chapel, many misunderstandings, and the kind of Idiot Plot dialogue in which all problems could be instantly solved if the characters were not studiously avoiding stating the obvious.

The plot is merely the excuse, however, for an astonishing array of sex and body plumbing jokes, nearly all of which dream of hitting a home run like *There's Something About Mary*, but do not. Consider *Mary*'s scene where Diaz has what she thinks is gel in her hair. Funny—because she doesn't know what it really is, and we do. Now consider the scene in this movie where the girls go into a men's room and do not understand that in a men's room a hole in the wall is almost never merely an architectural detail. The payoff is sad, sticky, and depressing.

Or consider a scene where one of the roommates gets "stuck" while performing oral sex. This is intended as a rip-off of the "franks and beans" scene in *Mary*, but gets it all wrong. You simply cannot (I am pretty sure about this) get stuck in the way the movie suggests—no, not even if you've got piercings. More to the point, in *Mary* the victim is unseen, and we picture his dilemma. In *Sweetest Thing*, the victim is seen, sort of (careful framing preserves the R rating), and the image isn't funny. Then we get

several dozen neighbors, all singing to inspire the girl to extricate herself; this might have looked good on the page, but it just plain doesn't work, especially not when embellished with the sobbing cop on the doorstep, the gay cop, and other flat notes.

More details. Sometimes it is funny when people do not know they may be consuming semen (as in *American Pie*) and sometimes it is not, as in the scene at the dry cleaners in this movie. How can you laugh when what you really want to do is hurl? And what about the scene in the ladies' room, where the other girls are curious about Applegate's boobs and she tells them she paid for them and invites them to have a feel, and they do, like shoppers at K-mart? Again, a funny concept. Again, destroyed by bad timing, bad framing, and overkill. Because the director, Roger Kumble, doesn't know how to set it up and pay it off with surgical precision, he simply has women pawing Applegate while the scene dies. An unfunny scene only grows worse by pounding in the concept as if we didn't get it.

So, as I say, I like Cameron Diaz. I like everyone in this movie (I must not neglect the invaluable Parker Posey, as a terrified bride). I like their energy. I like their willingness. I like the opening shot when Diaz comes sashaying up a San Francisco hill like a dancer from *In Living Color* who thinks she's still on the air. I like her mobile, comic face—she's smart in the way she plays dumb. But the movie I cannot like, because the movie doesn't know how to be liked. It doesn't even know how to be a movie.

Sweet Home Alabama ★ ★ ★
PG-13, 102 m., 2002

Reese Witherspoon (Melanie Carmichael), Josh Lucas (Jake Perry), Patrick Dempsey (Andrew Hennings), Fred Ward (Earl Smooter), Mary Kay Place (Pearl Smooter), Jean Smart (Stella Perry), Candice Bergen (Kate Hennings). Directed by Andy Tennant and produced by Stokely Chaffin and Neal H. Moritz. Screenplay by C. Jay Cox.

Among the pieties that Hollywood preaches but does not believe is the notion that small towns are preferable to big cities. Film after film rehearses this belief: Big cities are repositories of greed, alienation, and hypocrisy, while in a small town you will find the front doors left unlocked, peach pies cooling on the kitchen windowsill, and folks down at the diner who all know your name. *Sweet Home Alabama* is the latest, admittedly charming, recycling of this ancient myth.

The fact is that few people in Hollywood have voluntarily gone home again since William Faulkner fled back to Mississippi. The screenwriters who retail the mirage of small towns are relieved to have escaped them. I await a movie where a New Yorker tries moving to a small town and finds that it just doesn't reflect his warmhearted big-city values.

Reese Witherspoon, who is the best reason to see *Sweet Home Alabama*, stars as Melanie Carmichael, a small-town girl who moves to the Big Apple and while still in her twenties becomes a famous fashion designer. She's in love with Andrew (Patrick Dempsey), a JFK Jr. look-alike whose mother (Candice Bergen) is mayor of New York. After he proposes to her in Tiffany's, which he has rented for the occasion, she flies back home to Alabama to take care of unfinished business.

She especially doesn't want Andrew to discover that she is already married to a local boy, and that her family doesn't own a moss-dripped plantation. Her folks live in a luxury mobile home with lots of La-Z-Boys and knitted afghans (La-Z-Boy: the sign of a home where the man makes the decisions). Her husband, Jake (Josh Lucas), was her high school sweetheart, but, looking ahead at a lifetime of dirty diapers and dishes with a loser, she fled north. His plan: Prove himself to earn her respect and get her back again. That's why he's never given her the divorce.

When Melanie returns home, she's greeted by the locals, who remember her high school hijinks (like tying dynamite to a stray cat, ho, ho). Her parents (Fred Ward and Mary Kay Place), who spin away their days lounging around the double-wide practicing sitcom dialogue, look on with love and sympathy, because they know that sooner or later she'll realize that home is right here. A clue comes when the Candice Bergen character advises her prospective in-laws to "go back to your double-wide and fry something."

The Lucas character is more complex, as he needs to be, because the screenplay requires him to keep a secret that common sense insists he divulge immediately. He must meanwhile undergo a subtle transformation so that when we first meet him we think he's a redneck hayseed, and then later he has transmogrified into a sensitive, intelligent, caring male. Oh, and his coon dog still likes her.

The JFK Jr. guy, in the meantime, cannot be permitted to become a total jerk, because the movie's poignancy factor demands that he be understanding, as indeed he would be, with a Jackie look-alike mom who is mayor of New York, a city where, in this movie, nothing bad has happened in recent memory.

So okay, we understand how the formula works, even without learning that C. Jay Cox, the screenwriter, is a student of writing coach Syd Field's theories (i.e., analyze successful movies and copy their structures). We know that the movie absolutely requires that Melanie reject bright lights, big city, and return to the embrace of her hometown. And we know the odds are low that Melanie will get the divorce, return to New York, and marry the mayor's son. (Anyone who thinks I have just committed a spoiler will be unaware of all movies in this genre since *Ma and Pa Kettle*.)

But answer me this. What about Melanie as a person, with her own success and her own ambition? Would a woman with the talent and ambition necessary to become world-famous in the fashion industry before the age of thirty be able, I ask you, be willing, be prepared, to renounce it all to become the spouse of a man who has built a successful business as a (let's say) glassblower?

The chances of that happening are, I submit, extremely thin, and that is why *Sweet Home Alabama* works. It is a fantasy, a sweet, light-hearted fairy tale with Reese Witherspoon at its center. She is as lovable as Doris Day would have been in this role (in fact, Doris Day *was* in this role, in *Please Don't Eat the Daisies*). So I enjoyed Witherspoon and the local color, but I am so very tired of the underlying premise. Isn't it time for the movies to reflect reality, and show the Melanies of the world fleeing to New York as fast as they can? Even if Syd Field flunks you?

Sweet November ★
PG-13, 114 m., 2001

Keanu Reeves (Nelson Moss), Charlize Theron (Sara Deever), Jason Isaacs (Chaz), Greg Germann (Vince), Liam Aiken (Abner). Directed by Pat O'Connor and produced by Deborah Aal, Erwin Stoff, Steven Reuther, and Elliott Kastner. Screenplay by Kurt Voelker.

Sweet November passes off pathological behavior as romantic bliss. It's about two sick and twisted people playing mind games and calling it love. I don't know who I disliked more intensely—Nelson, the abrupt, insulting ad man played by Keanu Reeves, or Sara, Charlize Theron's narcissistic martyr. Reeves at least has the grace to look intensely uncomfortable during several scenes, including one involving a bag full of goodies, which we will get to later.

The movie is a remake of a 1968 film starring Sandy Dennis and Anthony Newley and, if memory serves, the same bed in a San Francisco bay window. Both films have the same conceit, which only a movie producer could believe: A beautiful girl takes men to her bed for one month at a time, to try to help and improve them. "You live in a box, and I can lift the lid," she explains. Why a month? "It's long enough to be meaningful and short enough to stay out of trouble," Sara says—wrong on both counts.

Read no further if you do not already know that she has another reason for term limits. She's dying. In the original movie the disease was described as "quite rare, but incurable." Here we get another clue, when Nelson opens Sara's medicine cabinet and finds, oh, I dunno, at a rough guess, 598 bottles of pills. The girl is obviously overmedicating. Give her a high colonic, send her to detox, and the movie is over.

Nelson is one of those insulting, conceited, impatient, coffee-drinking, cell phone–using, Jaguar-driving advertising executives that you find in only two places: the movies, and real life. His motto is, speed up and smell the coffee. Sara, on the other hand, acts like she has all the time in the world, even though (sob!) she does not. She sits on the hood of Nelson's car and commits other crimes against the male libido that a woman absolutely cannot get away with unless she looks exactly like Charlize

Theron and insists on sleeping with you, and even then she's pushing it.

Nelson gradually learns to accept the gift of herself that she is offering. Actually, he accepts it quickly, the pig, but only gradually appreciates it. So warm, cheerful, perky, plucky, and seductive is Sara that Nelson, and the movie, completely forget for well over an hour that he has an apartment of his own and another girlfriend. By then the inexorable march of the rare but incurable disease is taking its toll, Sara has to go into the hospital, and Nelson finds out the Truth.

Will there be a scene where Sara, with a drip line plugged into every orifice, begs Nelson, "Get me out of here! Take me home!" Do bears eat gooseberries? Will there be a scene where Sara says, "Go away! I don't want you to see me like this!" Do iguanas like papayas? Will there be a scene where Sara's faithful gay friend (Jason Isaacs) bathes and comforts her? Yes, because it is a convention of movies like this that all sexy women have gay friends who materialize on demand to perform nursing and hygiene chores. (Advice to gay friend in next remake: Insist, "Unless I get two good scenes of my own, I've emptied my last bedpan.")

I almost forgot the scene involving the bag full of goodies. Keanu Reeves must have been phoning his agent between every take. The script requires him to climb in through Sara's window with a large bag that contains all of the presents he would ever want to give her, based on all the needs and desires she has ever expressed. I could get cheap laughs by listing the entire inventory of the bag, but that would be unfair. I will mention only one, the dishwashing machine. Logic may lead you to ask, "How can an automatic dishwasher fit inside a bag that Keanu Reeves can sling over his shoulder as he climbs through the window?" I would explain, but I hate it when movie reviews give everything away.

Sweet Sixteen ★ ★ ★ ½
R, 106 m., 2003

Martin Compston (Liam), Annmarie Fulton (Chantelle), William Ruane (Pinball), Michelle Abercromby (Suzanne), Michelle Coulter (Jean), Gary McCormack (Stan), Tommy McKee (Rab), Calum McAllees (Calum). Directed by Ken

Loach and produced by Rebecca O'Brien.
Screenplay by Paul Laverty.

Sweet Sixteen is set in Scotland and acted in a local accent so tricky it needs to be subtitled. Yet it could take place in any American city, in this time of heartless cuts in social services and the abandonment of the poor. I saw the movie at about the same time our lawmakers attacked the pitiful $400 child tax credit, while transferring billions from the working class to the richest 1 percent. Such shameless greed makes me angry, and a movie like *Sweet Sixteen* provides a social context for my feelings, showing a decent kid with no job prospects and no opportunities, in a world where only crime offers a paying occupation.

Yes, you say, but this movie is set in Scotland, not America. True, and the only lesson I can learn from that is that in both countries too many young people correctly understand that society has essentially written them off.

The director of *Sweet Sixteen,* Ken Loach, is political to the soles of his shoes, and his films are often about the difficulties of finding dignity as a working person. His *Bread and Roses* (2000) starred the future Oscar winner Adrien Brody as a union activist in Los Angeles, working to organize a group of nonunion office cleaners and service employees. In *Sweet Sixteen,* there are no jobs, thus no wages.

The movie's hero is a fifteen-year-old named Liam (Martin Compston) who has already been enlisted into crime by his grandfather and his mother's boyfriend. We see the three men during a visit to his mother in prison, where Liam is to smuggle drugs to her with a kiss. He refuses: "You took the rap once for that bastard." But the mother is the emotional and physical captive of her boyfriend, and goes along with his rules and brutality.

The boy is beaten by the two older men, as punishment, and his precious telescope is smashed. He runs away, finds refuge with his seventeen-year-old sister, Chantelle (Annmarie Fulton), and begins to dream of supporting his mother when she is released from prison. He finds a house trailer on sale for 6,000 pounds, and begins raising money to buy it.

Liam and his best friend, Pinball (William Ruane), have up until now raised money by selling stolen cigarettes, but now he moves up a step,

stealing a drug stash from the grandfather and the boyfriend and selling it himself. Eventually he comes to the attention of a local crime lord, who offers him employment—but with conditions, he finds out too late, that are merciless.

Some will recall Loach's great film *Kes* (1969), about a poor English boy who finds joy in training a pet kestrel—a season of self-realization, before a lifetime as a miner down in the pits. *Sweet Sixteen* has a similar character; Liam is sweet, means well, does the best he can given the values he has been raised with. He never quite understands how completely he is a captive of a system that has no role for him.

Yes, he could break out somehow—but we can see that so much more easily than he can. His ambition is more narrow. He dreams of establishing a home where he can live with his mother, his sister, and his sister's child. But the boyfriend can't permit that; it would underline his own powerlessness. And the mother can't make the break with the man she has learned to be submissive to.

The movie's performances have a simplicity and accuracy that are always convincing. Martin Compston, who plays Liam, is a local seventeen-year-old discovered in auditions at his school. He has never acted before, but is effortlessly natural. Michelle Coulter, who plays his mother, is a drug rehab counselor who has also never acted before, and Annmarie Fulton, who plays the sister Chantelle, has studied acting but never appeared in a film.

By using these inexperienced actors (as he often does in his films), Loach gets a spontaneous freshness; scenes feel new because the actors have never done anything like them before, and there are no barriers of style and technique between us and the characters. At the end of *Sweet Sixteen,* we see no hope in the story, but there is hope in the film itself, because to look at the conditions of Liam's life is to ask why, in a rich country, his choices must be so limited. The first crime in his criminal career was the one committed against him by his society. He just followed the example.

Note: The flywheels at the MPAA still follow their unvarying policy of awarding the PG-13 rating to vulgarity and empty-headed violence (2 Fast 2 Furious), while punishing with the R any film like this, which might actually have a useful message for younger viewers.

Swept Away ★
R, 82 m., 2002

Madonna (Amber Leighton), Adriano Giannini (Giuseppe), Bruce Greenwood (Anthony Leighton), Elizabeth Banks (Debi), David Thornton (Mike), Jeanne Tripplehorn (Marina), Michael Beattie (Todd). Directed by Guy Ritchie and produced by Matthew Vaughn. Screenplay by Ritchie.

Swept Away is a deserted island movie during which I desperately wished the characters had chosen one movie to take along if they were stranded on a deserted island, and were showing it to us instead of this one.

The movie is a relatively faithful remake of an incomparably superior 1976 movie with the lovely title, *Swept Away by an Unusual Destiny in the Blue Sea of August.* It knows the words but not the music. It strands two unattractive characters, one bitchy, one moronic, on an island where neither they, nor we, have anyone else to look at or listen to. It's harder for them than it is for us, because they have to go through the motions of an erotic attraction that seems to have become an impossibility the moment the roles were cast.

Madonna stars as Amber, the spoiled rich wife of a patient and long-suffering millionaire. They join two other couples in a cruise on a private yacht from Greece to Italy. The other five passengers recede into unwritten, even unthought-about roles, while Amber picks on Giuseppe (Adriano Giannini), the bearded deckhand. She has decided he is stupid and rude, and insults him mercilessly. So it was in the earlier film, but in this version Amber carries her behavior beyond all reason, until even the rudest and bitchiest rich woman imaginable would have called it a day.

Amber orders Giuseppe to take her out in the dinghy. He demurs: It looks like a storm. She insists. They run out of gas and begin to drift. She insults him some more, and when he succeeds after great effort in catching a fish for them to eat, she throws it overboard. Later she succeeds in putting a hole in the dinghy during a struggle for the flare gun. They drift at sea until they wash up on a deserted island, where the tables are turned and now it is Giuseppe who has the upper hand. Her husband's wealth

is now no longer a factor, but his survival skills are priceless.

All of this is similar to the 1976 movie, even the business of the fish thrown overboard. What is utterly missing is any juice or life in the characters. Giancarlo Giannini and Mariangela Melato became stars on the basis of the original *Swept Away,* which was written and directed by Lina Wertmüller, one of the most successful Italian directors of the 1970s. She was a leftist but not a feminist, and aroused some controversy with a story where it turned out the rich woman liked being ordered around and slapped a little—liked it so much she encouraged the sailor to experiment with practices he could not even pronounce.

This new *Swept Away* is more sentimental, I'm afraid, and the two castaways fall into a more conventional form of love. I didn't believe it for a moment. They have nothing in common, but worse still, neither one has any conversation. They don't say a single interesting thing. That they have sex because they are stranded on the island I can believe. That they are not sleeping in separate caves by the time they are rescued I do not.

The problem with the Madonna character is that she starts out so hateful that she can never really turn it around. We dislike her intensely and thoroughly, and when she gets to the island we don't believe she has learned a lesson or turned nice—we believe she is behaving with this man as she does with all men, in the way best designed to get her what she wants. As for the sailor, does he *really* love her, as he says in that demeaning and pitiful speech toward the end of the film? What is there to love? They shared some interesting times together, but their minds never met.

The ending is particularly unsatisfactory, depending as it does on contrived irony that avoids all of the emotional issues on the table. If I have come this far with these two drips, and sailed with them, and been shipwrecked with them, and listened to their tiresome conversations, I demand that they arrive at some conclusion more rewarding than a misunderstanding based upon a misdelivered letter. This story was about something when Lina Wertmüller directed it, but now it's not about anything at all. It's lost the politics and the social observation and become just another situation romance about a couple of saps stuck in an inarticulate screenplay.

Swimming ★ ★ ★
NO MPAA RATING, 98 m., 2002

Lauren Ambrose (Frankie Wheeler), Joelle Carter (Josee), Jennifer Dundas (Nicola Jenrette), Jamie Harrold (Heath), Josh Pais (Neil Wheeler), Anthony Ruivivar (Kalani). Directed by Robert J. Siegel and produced by Linda Moran and Siegel. Screenplay by Liza Bazadona, Siegel, and Grace Woodard.

Swimming is above all about a young woman's face, and by casting an actress whose face projects that woman's doubts and yearnings, it succeeds. The face belongs to Lauren Ambrose, who you may know as the young redhead on *Six Feet Under.* She plays Frankie, a teenage girl whose parents took early retirement, leaving the family burger stand on the boardwalk in Myrtle Beach, South Carolina, to Frankie and her older married brother, Neil (Josh Pais).

The movie's plot, I fear, is an old reliable: After this summer, nothing will ever be the same again. What saves it is that this summer is unlike other summers we've seen in coming-of-age movies. It's different because Frankie holds her own counsel, doesn't easily reveal her feelings, and is faced with choices that she's not even sure she has to make.

Frankie is a tomboy, invariably dressed in bib overalls and T-shirts, her hair tousled, her face freckled, with apple cheeks. Sexuality for her is an unexplored country. Her best friend is Nicola (Jennifer Dundas), who runs a piercing stand next to the burger joint. (So sincere is Nicola's dedication to piercing that when she gets a cut on her forehead she decides a scar would be cool.) Nicola dresses in an attempt to come across as a sexy blonde, but is loyal: When two cute guys in a car want her to come along but tell her, "lose your friend," she won't play.

One day Josee (Joelle Carter) appears in town. Ostensibly the girlfriend of the hunky lifeguard, she gets a job at the burger joint even though Neil decides she is "the worst waitress I have ever seen." Josee is a sexual creature, who one day out of the blue tells Frankie: "Frankie? I think I want you. I want your body." Frankie's reaction to this news is not to react at all. Life

continues as before, but with confusing desire simmering beneath the surface. It is possible that Josee is the first person to ever express a desire for Frankie, and by doing so she has activated Frankie's ability to feel desirable.

The summer brings other possibilities. Nicola meets Kalani (Anthony Ruivivar), a Marine from Hawaii with an imaginary friend, Ted. Frankie meets Heath (Jamie Harrold), a gawky loner who lives in a van with his dogs and sells tie-dyed T-shirts, which he dyes himself at a local Laundromat. Nicola begins to resent all the time Frankie spends with Josee, and tells her something she doesn't want to know: Josee is cheating with Neil, who has a young family.

Swimming could unfold as a sitcom, or as a desperately sincere drama, but director Robert J. Siegel and his cowriters, Liza Bazadona and Grace Woodard, go for something more delicate and subtle. They use Ambrose's ability to watch and think and not commit, and they allow the summer's choices and possibilities to unfold within her as if her sexuality is awakening and stretching for the first time. What happens, and why, is sweet and innocent, and not pumped up for effect.

Lauren Ambrose's effect in the film reminded me of another early performance many years ago: the work by Cathy Burns in Frank Perry's *Last Summer* (1969). She, too, played a tomboy whose sexuality was unawakened, a member of a group with another young woman (Barbara Hershey) who was sexier and bolder, whose first romance was based more on admiration than lust ("You're so masterful," she tells the boy she admires). Often the movies are no more than opportunities for us to empathize with people we find ourselves in sympathy with. Ambrose has an extraordinary ability to make us like her and care for her, and that is the real subject of the movie—in which, by the way, she never does go swimming.

Swimming Pool ★ ★ ★
R, 102 m., 2003

Charlotte Rampling (Sarah Morton), Ludivine Sagnier (Julie), Charles Dance (John Bosload), Marc Fayolle (Marcel, the Keeper), Jean-Marie Lamour (Franck, the Bartender), Mireille Mossé (Marcel's Daughter). Directed by François Ozon and produced by Olivier Delbosc and Marc Missonnier. Screenplay by Emmanuéle Bernheim and Ozon.

"She threw me a look I caught in my hip pocket," Robert Mitchum's private eye says of Charlotte Rampling's femme fatale in *Farewell, My Lovely* (1975). You don't know what that means, but you know exactly what it means. Rampling has always had the aura of a woman who knows things you would like to do that you haven't even thought of. She played boldly sexual roles early in her career, as in *The Night Porter* (1974), and now, in *Swimming Pool*, a sensuous and deceptive new thriller, she becomes fascinated by a young female predator.

Rampling plays Sarah Morton, a British crime writer whose novels seem to exist somewhere between those of P. D. James and Ruth Rendell. Now she is tired and uncertain, and her publisher offers her a holiday at his French villa. She goes gratefully to the house, shops in the nearby village, and finds she can write again. She is alone except for a taciturn caretaker, who goes into the village at night to live with his daughter, a dwarf who seems older than he is.

Then an unexpected visitor turns up: Julie (Ludivine Sagnier), the daughter her publisher didn't think to tell her about. Sarah is annoyed. Her privacy has been violated. Her privacy and her sense of decorum. Julie is gravid with self-confidence in her emerging sexuality, appears topless at the villa's swimming pool, brings home men to sleep with—men who have nothing in common except Julie's willingness to accommodate them. Sarah is surprised, intrigued, disapproving, curious. She looks down from high windows, spying on the girl who seems so indifferent to her opinion. Eventually she even steals glimpses of the girl's diary.

There is a waiter in the town named Franck (Jean-Marie Lamour), whom Sarah has chatted with and who is perhaps not unaware of her enduring sexuality. But he becomes one of Julie's conquests, too—maybe because Julie senses the older woman's interest in him.

At this point the film takes a turn toward violence, guilt, panic, deception, and concealment, and I will not take the turn with it, because a film like this must be allowed to have its way with you. Let us say that François Ozon,

the director and cowriter (with Emmanuéle Bernheim), understands as Hitchcock did the small steps by which a wrong decision grows in its wrongness into a terrifying paranoid nightmare. And how there is nothing more disturbing than trying to conceal a crime that cries out to be revealed.

There is one moment late in the film that displays Rampling's cool audacity more than any other. The caretaker is about to investigate something that is best not investigated. What she does to startle and distract him I will not hint at, but what a startling moment, and what boldness from Rampling!

Ozon is a director who specializes in films where the absent is more disturbing than the present. Rampling starred in his *Under the Sand* (2000), a film about a husband who apparently drowns and a wife who simply refuses to accept that possibility. He also made the terrifying fifty-seven-minute film *See the Sea* (1997), in which the mother of an infant befriends a young woman hitchhiker and begins to feel that it was a dangerous mistake.

Swimming Pool is more of a conventional thriller than those two—or if it is unconventional, that is a development that doesn't affect the telling of most of the story. After it is over you will want to go back and think things through again, and I can help you by suggesting there is one, and only one, interpretation that resolves all of the difficulties, but if I told you, you would have to kill me. ☞

Swordfish ★ ★ ½
R, 97 m., 2001

John Travolta (Gabriel Shear), Hugh Jackman (Stanley Jobson), Halle Berry (Ginger), Don Cheadle (Agent A. D. Roberts), Vinnie Jones (Marco), Camryn Grimes (Holly Jobson), Sam Shepard (Senator Reisman), Zach Grenier (A. D. Joy). Directed by Dominic Sena and produced by Jonathan D. Krane and Joel Silver. Screenplay by Skip Woods.

Swordfish looks like the result of a nasty explosion down at the Plot Works. It's skillfully mounted and fitfully intriguing, but weaves such a tangled web that at the end I defy anyone in the audience to explain the exact loyalties and motives of the leading characters.

There is one person in the movie who is definitely intended to be a hero, but are the villains really villains? Are they even themselves?

The movie stars Hugh Jackman as a brilliant computer hacker named Stanley, who just spent two years in the pen for the crime of hacking a program used by the FBI to snoop on everybody's e-mail. Now he lives in squalor in a house trailer and yearns for the company of his daughter, whose mother inhabits a drunken stupor.

Enter Ginger (Halle Berry), wearing a sexy little red dress, to recruit Stanley as a hacker for a secret project being masterminded by Gabriel Shear (John Travolta). Stanley demurs: He's been forbidden by the courts to touch a computer. She persists, cornering him in a lap-dancery and giving him one minute (at gunpoint) to hack into a government computer. He succeeds, of course, and is offered $10 million to work for Gabriel, who is (a) a patriot protecting us from bad guys, (b) a bad guy, (c) a double agent pretending to be either a patriot or a bad guy, (d) a freelance, (e) Ginger's lover, or (f) Ginger's target. His true identity is even cloudier than that, but I have said enough.

I will, however, discuss the puzzling role of Ginger, the Halle Berry character. She goes through the motions of being the pretty girl who seduces the hero into working for the secret organization. But this is strange, since Stanley shows little interest in her, and Ginger ostensibly belongs to Gabriel. This does not prevent a scene in which Halle Berry bares her breasts to tempt the untemptable Stanley. This scene came as a huge relief because I thought the movies, in their rush to the PG-13 rating, had forgotten about breasts. In the age of computerized sci-fi special effects, beautiful skin finishes a distant second at the box office. Once teenage boys wanted to see Emmanuelle undulating; now they want to see Keanu Reeves levitating.

Swordfish, to be sure, does have great effects.

One involves a horrific explosion that seems frozen in time while the camera circles it. It's a great visual moment. Another involves a sequence in which a bus is lifted above the city by a helicopter. There's the obligatory scene in which passengers fall to their deaths out the back of the bus—not exploited as well as in Spielberg's *Jurassic Park 2,* but good enough.

For originality, the best scene is a quieter one. Stanley sits at his computer keyboard and looks at six or eight monitors, hacking away in syncopated rhythm to a song about "50,000 volts of (bleeping)." As he works he talks, his words fitting neatly into the music. The song and the action work nicely together, even if we doubt hackers use their keyboards for percussion.

Dominic Sena directed *Gone in 60 Seconds* last year and is getting better. He can't stop himself from including one absolutely gratuitous car chase, but he takes more time with the plot here, and makes good use of Halle Berry to atone for ignoring Angelina Jolie last summer. He also gets a juicy performance out of Travolta, who opens with a monologue that would have been at home in *Get Shorty,* and plays a character whose dialogue is weirdly persuasive. (He defends his violent actions in hard-boiled realpolitik terms.) I also liked Don Cheadle as an FBI agent who supplies one of the few characters in the movie you can count on to be more or less who he says he is.

I see that I have forgotten to even mention that the movie involves a bank robbery and a hostage crisis. Well, it's that kind of film. The robbery and the crisis weave in and out of the plot like motifs in a symphony; we remember them when they're on-screen, but the movie isn't really about them. It's more about pulling the rug out from under the audience every five minutes or so. There comes a time when you seriously think the characters should wear red or blue shirts to keep from passing to the other team.

T

Taboo ★ ★ ★
NO MPAA RATING, 101 m., 2001

Beat Takeshi (Captain Toshizo Hijikata),
Ryuhei Matsuda (Samurai Sozaburo Kano),
Shinji Takeda (Lieutenant Soji Okita), Tadanobu
Asano (Samurai Hyozo Tashiro), Koji Matoba
(Samurai Heibei Sugano), Masa Tommies
(Inspecteur Jo Yamazaki), Masato Ibu (Officer
Koshitaro Ito), Uno Kanda (Geisha Nishikigi-
Dayu). Directed by Nagisa Oshima and
produced by Eiko Oshima, Shigehiro Nakagawa,
and Kazuo Shimizu. Screenplay by Nagisa
Oshima, based on novellas by Ryotaro Shiba.

Nagisa Oshima's *Taboo* tells a story set in the
late samurai period, when a youth of unusual
beauty is admitted into a training program for
warriors, stirring lust among his comrades
and even a superior officer. When the film
premiered at Cannes in May 2000, the joke
was that it would be retitled, "Not to ask, not
to tell."

Homosexuality in the military is as old as
armies, and was sometimes encouraged as a
way of inspiring soldiers to bond; we gather
that within the closed world of the Japanese
samurai, it was acknowledged as a fact of life.
The problem with Sozaburo Kano (Ryuhei
Matsuda) is not that he is gay, but that he is so
beautiful, so feminine, that he is a distraction
and inspires jealousy. He seems fully aware of
his appeal, and enhances it with a kind of
smoldering passivity that dares the other men
to start something.

The movie takes place in Kyoto around
1865, in the last days of traditional samurai.
Threatened by new kinds of fighting, new
channels of power, and the opening of the
country to the West, the men of the Shinsen-
gumi troop adhere all the more rigidly to the
samurai code, even enforcing death as a punishment for severe violations. It is strange that
a candidate as effeminate as Sozaburo would
be one of two finalists chosen after sword-
fighting auditions, but then again there is a
look in the eye of Captain Hijikata (Beat
Takeshi) that hints of hidden agendas.

When Beat Takeshi directs, it is under his
real name of Takeshi Kitano. As director and
star, he is known for violent macho thrillers,
and so his casting here is provocative; imagine
John Wayne in *Red River*, with a stirring beneath his chaps every time he looks at Montgomery Clift. Hijikata is not gay, but Sozaburo
is beautiful enough to inspire a lonely man to
relax his usual standards. A samurai clearly in
love with Sozaburo is Tashiro (Tadanobu
Asano), a brawny type who feels competitive
because both men were recruited at the same
time.

Is Sozaburo capable of fighting well enough
to carry his weight in the samurai army? He
turns out be the best of the young swordsmen,
and when a superior orders him to carry out
the execution of a disobedient samurai, he be-
heads the offender without a blink. The thing
about Sozaburo, indeed, is that he hardly
blinks at anything: Even while another samurai is having sex with him, he hardly seems to
notice.

Is this a weakness of the film? Maybe so.
Oshima, directing his first film in fourteen
years, has found an actor with the physical attributes to play the character, and seems content to leave it at that; his camera regards
Sozaburo as an object of beauty but hardly
seems to engage him. It's as if the young samurai is a platonic ideal of androgynous perfection, and the movie is not about him but
about his effect on the others.

Nagisa Oshima, born in 1932, was a rebel of
the Japanese cinema in the 1960s and 1970s,
and is most famous for *In the Realm of the
Senses* (1976), the story of a love affair that
turned into a sadomasochistic obsession, resulting during one sex scene in the hero's loss
of that implement he might most require if he
hoped to have another one. So great was the
crush to attend that film's Cannes premiere
that one critic was shoved through a plate-
glass window, luckily escaping the hero's fate.
Oshima in recent years has become a Japanese
TV star, and this film was a surprise to those
who assumed he had more or less retired from
filmmaking.

Taboo is not an entirely successful film, but
it isn't boring. There is a kind of understated
humor in the way the senior samurai officers
discuss their troublesome young recruit, and a

melancholy in the way the samurais follow their code as they are ceasing to be relevant or useful. I am not even sure it was a mistake to have Sozaburo be so passive. If he were a more active, complex character, that would generate a wider range of issues, and he works better within the plot as a catalyst.

I am reminded of a story told by Donald Richie, the great writer on Japanese themes. *In the Realm of the Senses* was based on a true story of a woman who castrated her lover at his request. After serving a prison sentence, she was hired by a Tokyo tavern to appear nightly. At the given hour, she would descend a flight of stairs, walk across the room, and exit. The room would always be jammed, Richie reports. "There she goes!" the customers would say. The character of Sozaburo seems to serve something of the same function in this movie.

Tadpole ★ ★

PG-13, 78 m., 2002

Sigourney Weaver (Eve), Aaron Stanford (Oscar Grubman), John Ritter (Stanley Grubman), Bebe Neuwirth (Diane), Robert Iler (Charlie), Adam LeFevre (Phil), Peter Appel (Jimmy), Alicia Van Couvering (Daphne Tisch), Kate Mara (Miranda Spear). Directed by Gary Winick and produced by Alexis Alexanian, Dolly Hall, and Winick. Screenplay by Heather McGowan and Niels Mueller.

Tadpole tells the story of a bright fifteen-year-old who has a crush on his stepmother and actually sleeps with her best friend, in part because the friend is wearing the stepmother's scarf and the lad is powerless over the evocative lure of her perfume. The sexual excursion is not the point of the movie, really, but the setup for its central scene, in which young Oscar has dinner with his father, his stepmother, and the friend, who wickedly threatens to reveal their secret.

Watching the movie at Sundance in January, I tried to accept this premise on its own terms, but could not. Too much has happened in the arena of sexual politics since *The Graduate,* and I kept thinking that since Oscar was fifteen and his stepmother and her friend were about forty, this plot would have been unthinkable if the genders had been reversed. The best friend, far from teasing the new sexual initiate with exposure, would have been terrified of arrest, conviction, and a jail sentence for statutory rape.

I am, I realize, hauling political correctness into a movie where it is not wanted. I know there is even a lighthearted mention of the laws involved. I know I praised *Lovely and Amazing,* which also features a romance between an adult woman and a teenage boy. But *Lovely and Amazing* is about events that happen in a plausible world (the adult is actually arrested). *Tadpole* wants only to be a low-rent *Graduate* clone.

Does it succeed on that level? Not really. True, the dinner scene has its moments, as Oscar (Aaron Stanford) squirms, his lover, Diane (Bebe Neuwirth), grins wickedly, his stepmother, Eve (Sigourney Weaver), keeps up the conversation, and his father, Stanley (John Ritter), practices a suave cluelessness that is his strategy for dealing with life. Neuwirth is really very good here, and the scene supplies the one moment when the movie seems sure of what it wants to do, and how to do it.

The rest of the movie seems perfunctory and derivative, and although I could believe that Oscar would find Eve attractive, I could not quite believe the labored conversations they have, in which he is talking on one level and she on another. It was even less credible that Eve, for a split-second, actually seems to be considering Oscar's desire seriously.

The movie, directed by Gary Winick and written by Heather McGowan and Niels Mueller, gives us Woody Allen's *Manhattan* crossed with Whit Stillman's affluent preppies. Like Stillman's *Metropolitan, Barcelona,* and *The Last Days of Disco,* it gives us a hero who is articulate, multilingual, sophisticated beyond his years, and awesomely self-confident. The difference is that Stillman was seriously intrigued by his young characters, and *Tadpole* uses Oscar primarily as an excuse for transgressive lust.

If Oscar were not forever speaking French and quoting Voltaire, we might see his passion for what it is, the invention of the filmmakers. I never really believed Oscar lusted after Eve the woman, but only after Eve the plot point—the archetypal older woman descended in an unbroken line from Mrs. Robinson.

The film has problems other than credibility. It ends with unseemly haste, it underlines its points too obviously, and its camera moves when it should be still. Some of the flaws may be excused by the filming method; *Tadpole* was filmed in two weeks for about $150,000, and the cast and crew took the minimum wage. When the film played at Sundance, there was a lot of buzz and Winick won the prize as best director. But there was also talk that the digital photography was noticeably washed-out. When Miramax bought the film (for a rumored but no doubt inflated $6 million), word was that the studio would give the visuals an overhaul. They still look unconvincing.

I am reminded of what Gene Siskel used to say whenever a hopeful director told him how little a movie cost. Gene would nod and reply, "I wish you had made it for more." I am in favor of low-budget filmmaking, but I do not consider it a virtue in itself, only a means to an end. In the case of *Tadpole*, the hurried schedule, the shaky digital video, and the lack of character development may all be connected to the fast, cheap shoot. A longer movie (this one is barely feature length at seventy-eight minutes) might have made the relationships more nuanced and convincing. In this version, we can sense the machinery beneath the skin. ☞

The Tailor of Panama ★ ★ ★ ½
R, 109 m., 2001

Pierce Brosnan (Andy Osnard), Geoffrey Rush (Harry Pendel), Jamie Lee Curtis (Louisa Pendel), Brendan Gleeson (Mickie Abraxas), Catherine McCormack (Francesca), Leonor Varela (Marta), Harold Pinter (Uncle Benny), Daniel Radcliffe (Mark Pendel), David Hayman (Luxmore). Directed and produced by John Boorman. Screenplay by Boorman, Andrew Davies, and John Le Carre, based on the novel by Le Carre.

"Welcome to Panama—Casablanca without heroes."

Not that Casablanca had many heroes. The statement is made by Harry Pendel, a tailor in Panama City, to Andy Osnard, a British spy who for his sins has been posted to this diplomatic dead end. The beauty of John Boorman's *The Tailor of Panama* is that the movie has no heroes, either. It's a cynical, droll story about two con men taking advantage of each other and getting away with it because the British and American governments are begging to be lied to. The casting of Pierce Brosnan as Osnard is the perfect touch: Here's a nasty real-world James Bond with no gadgets and no scruples.

The movie is based on the John Le Carre best-seller, showing that when the Cold War ended, its diplomatic gamesmanship continued as farce. In London, we meet Osnard as an amoral cutup in MI6, a gambler and ladies' man with a gift for embarrassing the agency. He's given a chance to redeem himself with the assignment to Panama, where nothing much is happening, although local mischief picks up considerably under his influence.

His strategy: Pick a member of Panama City's British community and use him as a source and conduit for information. He chooses Harry Pendel (Geoffrey Rush), whose firm, Braithwaite and Pendel, claims to be late of London's Saville Row. Actually, as Osnard finds out, there never was a Braithwaite, and Pendel learned to be a tailor while serving a prison term for arson. By threatening to blow Pendel's cover, Osnard gets him to cooperate in a scheme neither one of them quite admits to the other, in which Pendel will supply information which may be dubious, and Osnard will not scrutinize it too suspiciously.

Both men are pragmatists without ideals, although Pendel at least has an inspiration: the safety and security of his American wife (Jamie Lee Curtis) and their two children. That, and his firm, and his farm that is deeply in debt, are all that matter to him. "Where's your patriotism?" Osnard asks him at one point, and he replies: "I had it out in prison—without an anesthetic."

The movie plays as a joy for lovers of well-written, carefully crafted character thrillers. It has a lot of wry, twisted humor. It depends not on chases and killings, but on devious, greedy connivance in a world where everyone is looking out for himself. Its Panama City is still in shock after the Noriega years, and Pendel (who was the dictator's tailor—but then he's the tailor for everyone who can afford him) is well placed to know what's going on. His wife works for the director of the Panama Canal company, and in his tailor shop, which doubles as a club where gentlemen can drop in for a drink or a cigar, he overhears a great deal, although not as much as he tells Osnard he overhears.

He also has genuine contacts with the hidden side of Panama. His shop assistant, the scarred and fierce Marta (Leonor Varela), was a former member of the anti-Noriega underground. And so was his best friend, the shabby, hard-drinking Mickie Abraxas (Brendan Gleeson, from Boorman's *The General*). Both still hold their political ideals, Mickie loudly and defiantly, which inspires Pendel to invent a fictitious radical political movement, which Osnard believes in for reasons of his own.

Osnard, meanwhile, has his eye, and hands, on Francesca (Catherine McCormack), a sexy official in the British embassy, while feeding her boss (David Hayman) his colorful information. Secrets create a vacuum that only more secrets can fill, and soon Osnard is making demands on Pendel, whose wife presumably knows the secrets of the canal company—although not the secrets Pendel invents and passes along.

This round-robin of cynicism and deception takes place against a city of nightclubs and B-girl bars, residential areas and city streets lined with "laundromats" (banks), embassies and the cozy confines of Pendel's shop. Boorman and Le Carre (his executive producer) were wise to shoot the exteriors on location in Panama, where the tropical look makes the overheated schemes seem right at home.

Many thrillers are essentially machines to inject a shock into the audience every few minutes. *The Tailor of Panama* is a real movie, rich and atmospheric, savoring its disreputable characters and their human weaknesses. And there's room for genuine emotion, too, in the way Harry Pendel desperately holds onto the respectability he has conjured out of thin air. And in the way the stubborn, heedless Mickie Abraxas says what he thinks no matter what the risk. The movie is abundant in its gifts, a pleasure for those who like a story to unfold lovingly over a full arc, instead of coming in short, mindless bursts.

Talk to Her ★ ★ ★ ★
R, 112 m., 2002

Javier Cámara (Benigno Martin), Dario Grandinetti (Marco Zuloaga), Leonor Watling (Alicia Roncero), Rosario Flores (Lydia Gonzalez), Geraldine Chaplin (Katerina Bilova), Mariola Fuentes (Rosa). Directed by Pedro Almodóvar and produced by Agustín Almodóvar. Screenplay by Almodóvar.

A man cries in the opening scene of Pedro Almodóvar's *Talk to Her,* but although unspeakably sad things are to happen later in the movie, these tears are shed during a theater performance. Onstage, a woman wanders as if blind or dazed, and a man scurries to move obstacles out of her way—chairs, tables. Sometimes she blunders into the wall.

In the audience, we see two men who are still, at this point, strangers to each other. Marco (Dario Grandinetti) is a travel writer. Benigno (Javier Cámara) is a male nurse. The tears are of empathy, and it hardly matters which man cries, because in the film both will devote themselves to caring for helpless women. What's important are the tears. If he had been the director of *The Searchers* instead of John Ford, Almodóvar told the writer Lorenza Munoz, John Wayne would have cried.

Talk to Her is a film with many themes; it ranges in tone from a soap opera to a tragedy. One theme is that men can possess attributes usually described as feminine. They can devote their lives to a patient in a coma, they can live their emotional lives through someone else, they can gain deep satisfaction from bathing, tending, cleaning up, taking care. The bond that eventually unites the two men in *Talk to Her* is that they share these abilities. For much of the movie, what they have in common is that they wait by the bedsides of women who have suffered brain damage and are never expected to recover.

Marco meets Lydia (Rosario Flores) when she is at the height of her fame, the most famous female matador in Spain. Driving her home one night, he learns her secret: She is fearless about bulls, but paralyzingly frightened of snakes. After Marco catches the snake in her kitchen (we are reminded of Annie Hall's spider), she announces she will never be able to go back into that house again. Soon after, she is gored by a bull and lingers in the twilight of a coma. Marco, who did not know her very well, paradoxically comes to know her better as he attends at her bedside.

Benigno has long been a nurse, and for years tended his dying mother. He first saw the ballerina Alicia (Leonor Watling) as she rehearsed in a studio across from his apartment. She is comatose after a traffic accident. He volunteers to take extra shifts, seems willing to spend twenty-four hours a day at her bedside. He is in love with her.

As the two men meet at the hospital and share their experiences, I was reminded of Julien and Cecilia, the characters in François Truffaut's film *The Green Room* (1978), based on the Henry James story "The Altar of the Dead." Julien builds a shrine to all of his loved ones who have died, fills it with photographs and possessions, and spends all of his time there with "my dead." When he falls in love with Cecilia, he offers her his most precious gift: He shares his dead with her. She gradually comes to understand that for him they are more alive than she is.

That seems to be the case with Benigno, whose woman becomes most real to him now that she is helpless and his life is devoted to caring for her. Marco's motivation is more complex, but both men seem happy to devote their lives to women who do not, and may never, know of their devotion. There is something selfless in their dedication, but something selfish, too, because what they are doing is for their own benefit; the patients would be equally unaware of treatment whether it was kind or careless.

Almodóvar treads a very delicate path here. He accepts the obsessions of the two men, and respects them, but as a director whose films have always revealed a familiarity with the stranger possibilities of human sexual expression, he hints, too, that there is something a little creepy about their devotion. The startling outcome of one of the cases, which I will not reveal, sets an almost insoluble moral dilemma for us. Conventional morality requires us to disapprove of actions that in fact may have been inspired by love and hope.

By Almodóvar's standards this is an almost conventional film; certainly it doesn't involve

itself in the sexual revolving doors of many of his films. But there is a special-effects sequence of outrageous audacity, a short silent film fantasy in which a little man attempts to please a woman with what can only be described as total commitment.

Almodóvar has a way of evoking sincere responses from material which, if it were revolved only slightly, would present a face of sheer irony. *Talk to Her* combines improbable melodrama (gored bullfighters, comatose ballerinas) with subtly kinky bedside vigils and sensational denouements, and yet at the end we are undeniably touched. No director since Fassbinder has been able to evoke such complex emotions with such problematic material.

Tape ★ ★ ★ ½
R, 86 m., 2001

Ethan Hawke (Vince), Robert Sean Leonard (Johnny), Uma Thurman (Amy). Directed by Richard Linklater and produced by Gary Winick, Alexis Alexanian, and Anne Walker-McBay. Screenplay by Stephen Belber, based on his stage play.

Tape made me believe that its events could happen to real people more or less as they appear on the screen, and that is its most difficult accomplishment. To describe the movie makes it sound like an exercise in artifice: Three characters, one motel room, all talk, based on a stage play. But the writing, acting, and direction are so convincing that at some point I stopped thinking about the constraints and started thinking about the movie's freedoms: freedom from idiocy, first of all, since the characters are all smart and articulate, and testing one another's nerves and values. Freedom from big, gassy, meaningless events. Freedom from the tyranny of an overbearing sound track that wants to feel everything for us. Freedom from the expected.

For Ethan Hawke, Robert Sean Leonard, and Uma Thurman, making this movie must have been scary. They have nowhere to run. The motel room is small, and they can't hide from the camera. Small moments must be real because there's nothing to cover them up. Against that is the flexibility of shooting in high-def video, which allows Maryse Alberti's camera to turn and stare and advance and re-coil, commanding the space. This is not one of those films on video where the handheld camera gawks like a nervous home movie. The movements of the actors and camera are thoughtfully blocked, and the result is the *feeling* of spontaneous shooting, rather than its jumpy, handheld reality.

The movie opens with Vince (Hawke) alone in the room, obviously preparing for something. He chugs beers, arranges the furniture, takes off his pants and shirt, and somehow lets us know with body language this is part of a strategy. There's a knock on the door and Johnny (Leonard) enters. They went to high school together a decade ago. Now Johnny is in town (Lansing, Michigan) to show his film in a film festival, and Vince is—what? Attending the festival? In town by a coincidence and heard Johnny was around? It's clear that Johnny, who tries to seem very happy to see his old friend, is not sure.

Conversation. Johnny is confident, balanced, sound. Vince, who snorts some cocaine, is spacy, but not as spacy as he seems. He guides the conversation around to memories of Amy (Uma Thurman), who was Vince's first love. Vince and Amy never made love, however, and that still hurts Vince, although not as much as the fact that Johnny and Amy did make love, during a brief, meaningless fling at the end of senior year. Or—was it love?

Vince batters at Johnny like a prosecutor. Hawke is brilliant in these scenes, which seem loose but, in retrospect, are as controlled as a chess game. Watching his control of body and voice as he flings himself around the room, intimidating Johnny with his command of the space, we see both physical and verbal acting mastery. Johnny's self-possession fades, and he finally makes an admission. But is his admission to be believed? Is he a reliable witness to his own misconduct?

Amy knocks. A surprise to Johnny. And Johnny is a surprise to her. And now Vince's plan becomes clear, with the introduction of a tape that (a) belongs to Vince, (b) contains Johnny's memories, and (c) involves Amy's past. So who should the tape belong to? Who does the past belong to? Who gets to say what it means? Is what happened then as important as what happens now?

In a lesser film, the conflict would be between Vince and Johnny—two boys fighting over the same girl, as she looks dutifully back and forth like a spectator at a tennis match. But she is more than a match for them, and besides, this is a struggle of ethics, not gender. No one is clearly right or wrong. The same information, viewed through different prisms, shifts righteousness from one character to another.

The screenplay by Stephen Belber is based on his own play, which in superficial ways resembles the battle in Mamet's *Oleanna*. Both films are about how the same events can be interpreted differently through male and female eyes. But Mamet is angry and has a point of view—two points of view, really—while Belber's *subject* is points of view. And sneaking along underneath the argument about what happened on that long-ago night is the question of who has the right to make use of it now.

Richard Linklater, the director, has had quite a year. This film follows quickly on the heels of his *Waking Life*, and both films show a director using video instead of being used by it. In *Waking Life* he used video footage as a starting point for an animated film of startling innovation. In *Tape*, he uses video as a way to move intimately and freely through a three-way conversation. Neither film is dominated by its style; both are about their ideas, and the style is at the service of the ideas. For audiences they are stimulating; for other filmmakers, instruction manuals about how to use the tricky new tools.

The Taste of Others ★ ★ ★
NO MPAA RATING, 112 m., 2001

Jean-Pierre Bacri (Castella), Anne Alvaro (Clara), Christiane Millet (Angelique), Brigitte Catillon (Beatrice), Alain Chabat (Deschamps), Agnes Jaoui (Manie), Gérard Lanvin (Moreno), Anne Le Ny (Valerie). Directed by Agnes Jaoui and produced by Christian Berard and Charles Gassot. Screenplay by Jaoui and Jean-Pierre Bacri.

Finding out somebody has bad taste is like discovering he needs dental work. Things were fine until he opened his mouth. Of course, your good taste might be my bad taste, and vice versa. For example, I know there are people who don't go to foreign films, and I am patient with them, as I would be with a child: With luck, they may evolve into more interesting beings. And then they could think about the lessons of *The Taste of Others*.

This is a film about a busy industrialist named Castella (Jean-Pierre Bacri) who is blindsided by love and idealism. As the movie opens his life is affluent but uninspiring. He is surrounded by material comforts, all of them dictated by his wife, an interior decorator. She is the kind of woman who, when she says something loving and affectionate, he has to look up to see if she's talking to him or the dog.

Castella signs up for English lessons, but is impatient at the work required; he gets stuck on the pronunciation of "the." He asks the teacher if she doesn't have a "fun" way to learn English. She doesn't, so he fires her. That night, his wife drags him kicking and screaming to a local dramatic production, and he falls in love with the leading actress. This is, of course, the very same woman who was the English teacher, but at first he doesn't realize that, because now she is surrounded by the aura of Art.

He pursues the actress, named Clara (Anne Alvaro). She is fortyish, attractive but not beautiful, a member of the artsy-fartsy set in their provincial town. She, of course, is not attracted to Castella, who has crass tastes and materialistic values and has led the life of money rather than the life of the mind. But he persists. He sends her flowers. He turns up everywhere. When she doesn't like his dorky mustache, he shaves it off. The movie doesn't present this simply as a romantic infatuation, but goes the additional step: It sees that Castella is in love not only with Clara, but with what she represents: the life of the arts, of the theater, of ideas, of questioning things, of developing your own taste. We are reminded of Jack Nicholson in *As Good as It Gets*, when he tells Helen Hunt, "I love you because you make me want to be a better man."

Meanwhile, things are shaky on the home front. Castella sees a painting he likes, brings it home, and hangs it on the wall. Whether it's a good painting is beside the point: It is *his* painting. When his wife rejects it in horror, he says very quietly, "Angelique . . . I like this picture," and those are words she should listen to very carefully if she values their marriage.

There's a parallel relationship in the movie

between Castella's bodyguard, Moreno (Gerard Lanvin), and the barmaid Manie (played by Agnes Jaoui, the film's director). Manie sells hashish as a sideline, and Moreno disapproves. This, too, is a matter of taste: Anyone who sells drugs is telling you something about themselves that you don't want to know more about. The difference is, you can stop selling drugs, but you may never be able to tell a good painting from a bad one, or know why the decor of a living room should not hurt the eyes. Castella continues his lonely quest, uneasily joining Clara and her bohemian friends in the café they frequent after performances of the play, and eventually—well, people evolve, and taste involves not only judging superficial things, but being able to see beneath them.

One of the delights of *The Taste of Others* is that it is so smart and wears its intelligence lightly. Films about taste are not often made by Hollywood, perhaps because it would so severely limit the box office to require the audience to have any. *The Taste of Others* will be all but impenetrable to anyone unable to appreciate what's going on under the dialogue, under the action, down there at the level where we instinctively make judgments based on taste, style, and judgment. It's not, of course, that there's a right or wrong about taste. It's more that your taste defines the kinds of people who want to share it with you. Here's a test: If, as your taste evolves over a lifetime, you find that it attracts more interesting friends, you're on the right track.

Tears of the Sun ★ ★ ★
R, 121 m., 2003

Bruce Willis (A. K. Waters), Monica Bellucci (Dr. Lena Hendricks), Cole Hauser (Red Atkins), Tom Skerritt (Bill Rhodes), Eamonn Walker (Zee Pettigrew), Nick Chinlund (Slo Slowenski), Fionnula Flanagan (Nurse Grace), Johnny Messner (Kelly Lake). Directed by Antoine Fuqua and produced by Ian Bryce, Mike Lobell, Arnold Rifkin, and Bruce Willis. Screenplay by Patrick Cirillo and Alex Lasker.

Tears of the Sun is a film constructed out of rain, cinematography, and the face of Bruce Willis. These materials are sufficient to build a film almost as good as if there had been a better screenplay. In a case like this, the editor often deserves the credit for concealing what is not there with the power of what remains.

The movie tells the story of a Navy Seals unit that is dropped into a Nigerian civil war zone to airlift four U.S. nationals to safety. They all work at the same mission hospital. The priest and two nuns refuse to leave. The doctor, widow of an American, is also hostile at first ("Get those guns out of my operating room!"), but then she agrees to be saved if she can also bring her patients. She cannot. There is no room on the helicopters for them, and finally Waters (Bruce Willis) wrestles her aboard.

But then he surprises himself. As the chopper circles back over the scene, they see areas already set afire by arriving rebel troops. He cannot quite meet the eyes of the woman, Dr. Lena Hendricks (Monica Bellucci). "Let's turn it around," Willis says. They land, gather about twenty patients who are well enough to walk, and call for the helicopters to return.

But he has disobeyed direct orders, his superior will not risk the choppers, and they will all have to walk through the jungle to Cameroon to be rescued. Later, when it is clear Willis's decision has placed his men and mission in jeopardy, one of his men asks, "Why'd you turn it around?" He replies: "When I figure that out, I'll let you know." And later: "It's been so long since I've done a good thing—the right thing."

There are some actors who couldn't say that dialogue without risking laughter from the audience. Willis is not one of them. His face smeared with camouflage and glistening with rain, his features as shadowed as Marlon Brando's in *Apocalypse Now,* he seems like a dark, violent spirit sent to rescue them from one hell only to lead them into another. If we could fully understand how he does what he does, we would know a great deal about why some actors can carry a role that would destroy others. Casting directors must spend a lot of time thinking about this.

The story is very simple, really. Willis and his men must lead the doctor and her patients through the jungle to safety. Rebel troops pursue them. It's a question of who can walk faster or hide better; that's why it's annoying that Dr. Hendricks is constantly telling Waters, "My people have to rest!" Presumably (a) her African patients from this district have some

experience at walking long distances through the jungle, and (b) she knows they are being chased by certain death, and can do the math.

Until it descends into mindless routine action in the climactic scenes, *Tears of the Sun* is essentially an impressionistic nightmare, directed by Antoine Fuqua, the director who emerged with the Denzel Washington cop picture *Training Day.* His cinematographers, Mauro Fiore and Keith Solomon, create a visual world of black-green saturated wetness, often at night, in which characters swim in and out of view as the face of Willis remains their implacable focal point. There are few words; Willis scarcely has 100 in the first hour. It's all about the conflict between a trained professional soldier and his feelings. There is a subtext of attraction between the soldier and the woman doctor (who goes through the entire film without thinking to button the top of her blouse), but it is wisely left as a subtext.

This film, in this way, from beginning to end, might have really amounted to something. I intuit "input" from producers, studio executives, story consultants, and the like, who found it their duty to dumb it down by cobbling together a conventional action climax. The last half-hour of *Tears of the Sun,* with its routine gun battles, explosions, and machine-gun bursts, is made from off-the-shelf elements. If we can see this sort of close combat done well in a film that is really about it, like Mel Gibson's *We Were Soldiers,* why do we have to see it done merely competently, in a movie that is not really about it?

Where the screenplay originally intended to go, I cannot say, but it's my guess that at an earlier stage it was more thoughtful and sad, more accepting of the hopelessness of the situation in Africa, where "civil war" has become the polite term for genocide. The movie knows a lot about Africa, lets us see that, then has to pretend it doesn't.

Willis, for example, has a scene in the movie where, as a woman approaches a river, he emerges suddenly from beneath the water to grab her, silence her, and tell her he will not hurt her. This scene is laughable, but effective. Laughable, because (a) hiding under the water and breathing through a reed, how can the character know the woman will approach the river at precisely that point? and (b) since he will have to spend the entire mission in the same clothes, is it wise to soak all of his gear when staying dry is an alternative?

Yet his face, so fearsome in camouflage, provides him with a sensational entrance and the movie with a sharp shudder of surprise. There is a way in which movies like *Tears of the Sun* can be enjoyed for their very texture. For the few words Willis uses, and the way he uses them. For the intelligence of the woman doctor, whose agenda is not the same as his. For the camaraderie of the Navy Seals unit, which follows its leader even when he follows his conscience instead of orders. For the way the editor, Conrad Buff, creates a minimalist mood in setup scenes of terse understatement; he doesn't hurry, he doesn't linger. If only the filmmakers had been allowed to follow the movie where it wanted to go—into some existential heart of darkness, I suspect—instead of detouring into the suburbs of safe Hollywood convention.

Ten ★ ★
NO MPAA RATING, 94 m., 2003

Mania Akbari (The Woman), Amin Maher (Her Son), Roya Arabshahi (Passenger), Katayoun Taleidzadeh (Passenger), Mandana Sharbaf (Passenger), Amene Moradi (Passenger). Directed by Abbas Kiarostami and produced by Kiarostami and Marin Karmitz. Screenplay by Kiarostami.

I am unable to grasp the greatness of Abbas Kiarostami. His critical reputation is unmatched: His *Taste of Cherry* (1997) won the Palme d'Or at Cannes, and *The Wind Will Carry Us* (1999) won the Golden Lion at Venice. And yet his films, for example his latest work *Ten*, are meant not so much to be watched as to be written about; his reviews make his points better than he does.

Any review must begin with simple description. *Ten* consists of ten scenes set in the front seat of a car. The driver is always the same. Her passengers include her son, her sister, a friend, an old woman, and a prostitute. The film is shot in digital video, using two cameras, one focused on the driver, the other on the passenger. The cameras are fixed. The film has been described as both fiction and documentary, and is

both: What we see is really happening, but some of it has been planned, and Amin, for example, does not seem to be the driver's son.

Kiarostami's method, I learn from Geoff Andrew's review in *Sight & Sound,* was to audition real people, choose his actors, talk at length with them about their characters and dialogue, and then send them out in the car without him, to play their characters (or perhaps themselves) as they drove the streets and the cameras watched. Beginning with twenty-three hours of footage, he ended with this ninety-four-minute film.

Now you might agree that is a provocative and original way to make a movie. Then I might tell you that *Taste of Cherry* was also set entirely in the front seat of a car—only in that film Kiarostami held the camera and sat alternatively in the seat of the driver and the passenger. And that *The Wind Will Carry Us* was about a man driving around trying to find a place where his cell phone would work. You might observe that his method has become more daring, but you would still be left with movies about people driving and talking.

Ah, but what do we learn about them, and about modern Iran? Andrew, who thinks this is Kiarostami's best film, observes the woman complaining about Iran's "stupid laws" that forbid divorce unless she charges her husband with abuse or drug addiction. He observes that the movie shows prostitution exists in Iran, even though it is illegal. The old woman argues that the driver should try prayer, and she does, showing the nation's religious undercurrent. The friend removes her scarf to show that she has shaved her head, and this is transgressive because women are not allowed to bare their heads in public. And little Amin, the son, seems like a repressive Iranian male in training, having internalized the license of a male-dominant society to criticize and mock his mother.

All very well. But to praise the film for this is like praising a child for coloring between the lines. Where is the reach, the desire to communicate, the passion? If you want to see the themes in *Ten* explored with power and frankness in films of real power, you would turn away from Kiarostami's arid formalism and look instead at a film like Tahmineh Milani's *Two Women* (1998) or Jafar Panahi's *The Circle* (2001), which have the power to deeply move audiences, instead of a willingness to alienate or bore them.

Anyone could make a movie like *Ten*. Two digital cameras, a car, and your actors, and off you go. Of course, much would depend on the actors, what they said, and who they were playing (the little actor playing Amin is awesomely self-confident and articulate on the screen, and effortlessly obnoxious). But if this approach were used for a film shot in Europe or America, would it be accepted as an entry at Cannes?

I argue that it would not. Part of Kiarostami's appeal is that he is Iranian, a country whose films it is somewhat daring to praise. Partly, too, he has a lot of critics invested in his cause, and they do the heavy lifting. The fatal flaw in his approach is that no ordinary moviegoer, whether Iranian or American, can be expected to relate to his films. They exist for film festivals, film critics, and film classes.

The shame is that more accessible Iranian directors are being neglected in the overpraise of Kiarostami. Brian Bennett, who runs the Bangkok Film Festival, told me of attending a Tehran Film Festival with a fair number of Western critics and festival directors. "The moment a film seemed to be about characters or plot," he said, "they all got up and raced out of the room. They had it fixed in their minds that the Iranian cinema consisted of minimalist exercises in style, and didn't want to see narrative films." Since storytelling is how most films work and always have, it is a shame that Iranian stories are being shut out of Western screenings because of a cabal of dilettantes.

Terminator 3: Rise of the Machines
★ ★ ½
R, 109 m., 2003

Arnold Schwarzenegger (Terminator), Kristanna Loken (T-X), Nick Stahl (John Connor), Claire Danes (Kate Brewster), David Andrews (Robert Brewster), Mark Famiglietti (Scott Petersen). Directed by Jonathan Mostow and produced by Mario F. Kassar and Andrew G. Vajna. Screenplay by John Brancato and Michael Ferris.

In the dawning days of science fiction, there was a chasm between the concept-oriented authors and those who churned out space opera.

John W. Campbell Jr.'s *Astounding Science Fiction*, later renamed *Analog* to make the point clear, was the home of the brainy stuff. Bug-eyed monsters chased heroines in aluminum brassieres on the covers of *Amazing, Imagination*, and *Thrilling Wonder Stories*.

The first two Terminator movies, especially the second, belonged to Campbell's tradition of sci-fi ideas. They played elegantly with the paradoxes of time travel, in films where the action scenes were necessary to the convoluted plot. There was actual poignancy in the dilemma of John Connor, responsible for a world that did not even yet exist. The robot Terminator, reprogrammed by Connor, provided an opportunity to exploit Isaac Asimov's Three Laws of Robotics.

But that was an age ago, in 1991. *T2* was there at the birth of computer-generated special effects, and achieved remarkable visuals, especially in the plastic nature of the Terminator played by Robert Patrick, who was made of an infinitely changeable substance that could reconstitute itself from droplets. Now we are in the latter days of CGI, when the process is used not to augment action scenes but essentially to create them. And every week brings a new blockbuster and its $50 million–plus gross, so that audiences don't so much eagerly anticipate the latest extravaganza as walk in with a show-me attitude.

Terminator 3: Rise of the Machines is made in the spirit of these slick new action thrillers and abandons its own tradition to provide wall-to-wall action in what is essentially one long chase and fight punctuated by comic, campy, or simplistic dialogue. This is not your older brother's *Terminator*. It's in the tradition of *Thrilling Wonder Stories; T2* descended from Campbell's *Analog*. The time-based paradoxes are used arbitrarily and sometimes confusingly and lead to an enormous question at the end: How, if that is what happens, are the computer-based machines of the near future created?

Perhaps because the plot is thinner and more superficial, the characters don't have the same impact, either. Nick Stahl plays John Connor, savior of mankind, in the role created by the edgier, more troubled Edward Furlong. Stahl seems more like a hero than a victim of fate, and although he tells us at the outset he lives "off the grid" and feels "the weight of the future bearing down on me," he seems more like an all-purpose action figure than a man who really (like Furlong) feels trapped by an impenetrable destiny.

Early in the film he meets a veterinarian named Kate Brewster (Claire Danes), and after they find they're on the same hit list from the killers of the future, they team up to fight back and save the planet. They are pursued by a new-model Terminator named T-X, sometimes called the Terminatrix, and played by the icy-eyed Kristanna Loken. I know these characters are supposed to be blank-faced and impassive, but somehow Robert Patrick's evil Terminator was ominous and threatening, and Loken's model is more like the mannequin who keeps on coming; significantly, she first appears in the present after materializing in a Beverly Hills shop window. The movie doesn't lavish on her the astonishing shape-shifting qualities of her predecessor.

To protect John and Kate, Terminator T-101 arrives from the future, played by Arnold Schwarzenegger, who has embodied this series from the very first. The strange thing is, this is not the same Terminator he played in T2. "Don't you remember me?" asks Connor. But "hasta la vista, baby" doesn't ring a bell. T-101 does, however, inexplicably remember some old Schwarzenegger movies and at one point intones, "She'll be back."

The movie has several highly evolved action set pieces, as we expect, and there's a running gag involving the cumbersome vehicles that are used. The Terminatrix commandeers a huge self-powered construction crane to mow down rows of cars and buildings, a fire truck is used at another point, and after Kate, John, and the Terminator find a caché of weapons in the coffin of John's mother, a hearse is put into play—at one point, in a development that is becoming a cliché, getting its top sheared off as it races under a truck trailer, so that it becomes a convertible hearse. (Why do movies love convertibles? Because you can see the characters.)

Kate's father is a high-up muckety-muck whose job is a cover for top-secret security work, and that becomes important when the three heroes discover that a nuclear holocaust will begin at 6:18 P.M. Can they get to the nation's underground weapons control facility in time to disarm the war? The chase leads to a

genuinely creative development when a particle accelerator is used to create a magnetic field so powerful it immobilizes the Terminatrix.

The ending of the film must remain for you to discover, but I will say it seems perfunctory—more like a plot development than a denouement in the history of humanity. The movie cares so exclusively about its handful of characters that what happens to them is of supreme importance, and the planet is merely a backdrop.

Is *Terminator 3* a skillful piece of work? Indeed. Will it entertain the Friday-night action crowd? You bet. Does it tease and intrigue us like the earlier films did? Not really. Among recent sci-fi pictures, *Hulk* is in the tradition of science fiction that concerns ideas and personalities, and *Terminator 3* is dumbed down for the multiplex hordes. ☞

Thirteen Conversations About One Thing ★ ★ ★ ★
R, 102 m., 2002

Matthew McConaughey (Troy), John Turturro (Walker), Alan Arkin (Gene), Clea DuVall (Beatrice), Amy Irving (Patricia), Barbara Sukowa (Helen), William Wise (Wade). Directed by Jill Sprecher and produced by Beni Atoori and Gina Resnick. Screenplay by Jill and Karen Sprecher.

Happiness is the subject of *Thirteen Conversations About One Thing*. For that matter, happiness is the subject of every conversation we ever have: the search for happiness, the envy of happiness, the loss of happiness, the guilt about undeserved happiness. The engine that drives the human personality is our desire to be happy instead of sad, entertained instead of bored, inspired instead of disillusioned, informed rather than ignorant. It is not an easy business.

Consider Troy (Matthew McConaughey), the prosecutor who has just won a big conviction. In the movie's opening scene, he's loud and obnoxious in a saloon, celebrating his victory. He spots a sad sack at the bar: Gene (Alan Arkin), who seems to be pessimistic about the possibility of happiness. Gene is a midlevel manager at an insurance company, has to fire someone, and decides to fire Wade, the happiest man in the department, since he can see the sunny side of anything.

Troy buys drinks for Gene. He wants everybody to be happy. Then he drives drunk, hits a pedestrian with his car, and believes he has killed her. As an assistant district attorney he knows how much trouble he's in, and instinctively leaves the scene. His problem becomes an all-consuming guilt, which spoils his ability to enjoy anything in life; he was cut in the accident, and keeps the wound open with a razor blade to punish himself.

The movie finds connections between people who think they are strangers, finding the answer to one person's problem in the question raised by another. We meet Walker (John Turturro), a sardonic college professor, who walks out on his wife (Amy Irving) and begins an affair with a woman (Barbara Sukowa). She realizes that the affair is hardly the point: Walker is going through the motions because he has been told, and believes, that this is how you find happiness. We also meet a house cleaner (Clea DuVall), who is good at her job but works for a client who can only criticize. She is injured for no reason at all, suffers great pain, does not deserve to.

The truth hidden below the surface of the story is a hard one: Nothing makes any sense. We do not get what we deserve. If we are lucky, we get more. If we are unlucky, we get less. Bad things happen to good people, and good things happen to bad people. That's the system. All of our philosophies are a futile attempt to explain it. Let me tell you a story. Not long ago I was in the middle of a cheerful conversation when I slipped on wet wax, landed hard and broke bones in my left shoulder. I was in a fool's paradise of happiness, you see, not realizing that I was working without a net—that in a second my happiness would be rudely interrupted.

I could have hit my head and been killed. Or landed better and not been injured. At best what we can hope for is a daily reprieve from all of the things that can go wrong. *Thirteen Conversations About One Thing* is relentless in the way it demonstrates how little we control our lives. We can choose actions, but we cannot plan outcomes. Follow, for example, the consequences of Alan Arkin's decision to fire the happy man, and then see what happens to Arkin, and then see what happens to the happy man. Or watch as the Matthew McConaughey character grants

reality to something he only thinks he knows. Or see how the Turturro character, so obsessed with his personal timetable, so devoted to his daily and weekly routines, is able to arrange everything to his satisfaction—and then is not satisfied.

The movie is brilliant, really. It is philosophy illustrated through everyday events. Most movies operate as if their events are necessary—that B must follow A. *Thirteen Conversations* betrays B, A, and all the other letters as random possibilities.

The film was directed by Jill Sprecher, and written with her sister, Karen. It's their second, after *Clockwatchers* (1997), the lacerating, funny story about temporary workers in an office and their strategies to prove they exist in a world that is utterly indifferent to them. After these two movies, there aren't many filmmakers whose next film I anticipate more eagerly. They're onto something. They're using films to demonstrate something to us. Movies tell narratives, and the purpose of narrative is to arrange events in an order that seems to make sense and end correctly. The Sprechers are telling us if we believe in these narratives we're only fooling ourselves.

And yet, even so, there is a way to find happiness. That is to be curious about all of the interlocking events that add up to our lives. To notice connections. To be amused or perhaps frightened by the ways things work out. If the universe is indifferent, what a consolation that we are not.

Thirteen Days ★ ★ ★
PG-13, 135 m., 2001

Kevin Costner (Kenny O'Donnell), Bruce Greenwood (John F. Kennedy), Steven Culp (Robert Kennedy), Dylan Baker (Robert McNamara), Henry Strozier (Dean Rusk), Kevin Conway (General Curtis LeMay), Len Cariou (Dean Acheson). Directed by Roger Donaldson and produced by Marc Abraham, Peter O. Almond, Armyan Bernstein, Kevin Costner, and Kevin O'Donnell. Screenplay by David Self, based on a book by Ernest R. May and Philip D. Zelikow.

The 1962 Cuban missile crisis was the closest we've come to a world nuclear war. Khrushchev installed Russian missiles in Cuba, ninety miles from Florida and within striking distance of 80 million Americans. Kennedy told him to remove them, or else. As Russian ships with more missiles moved toward Cuba, a U.S. Navy blockade was set up to stop them. The world waited.

At the University of Illinois, I remember classes being suspended or ignored as we crowded around TV sets and the ships drew closer in the Atlantic. There was a real possibility that nuclear bombs might fall in the next hour. And then Walter Cronkite had the good news: The Russians had turned back. Secretary of State Dean Rusk famously said, "We went eyeball to eyeball, and I think the other fellow just blinked."

The most controversial assertion of Roger Donaldson's *Thirteen Days,* an intelligent new political thriller, is that the guys who blinked were not only the Russians, but also America's own military commanders—who backed down not from Soviet ships but from the White House. The Joint Chiefs of Staff and Air Force general Curtis LeMay are portrayed as rabid hawks itching for a fight. It's up to presidential adviser Kenny O'Donnell (Kevin Costner) and Secretary of Defense Robert McNamara (Dylan Baker) to face down the top brass, who are portrayed as boys eager to play with nuclear toys. "This is a setup," O'Donnell warns President Kennedy (Bruce Greenwood). If fighting breaks out at a low level, say with Castro shooting at an American spy plane, "the chiefs will force us to start shooting."

This version of events, the viewer should be aware, may owe more to the mechanics of screenwriting than to the annals of history. In a movie where the enemy (Khrushchev) is never seen, living and breathing antagonists are a convenience on the screen, and when McNamara and a trigger-happy admiral get into a shouting match it's possible to forget they're both supposed to be good guys. Yet the cold war mentality did engender military paranoia, generals like LeMay were eager to blast the commies, and Kennedy was seen by his detractors as a little soft. "Kennedy's father was one of the architects of Munich," grumbles Dean Acheson, Truman's secretary of state and an architect of the cold war. "Let's hope appeasement doesn't run in the family."

My own feeling is that serious students of the missile crisis will not go to this movie for additional scholarship, and that for the general public it will play, like Oliver Stone's *JFK,* as a parable: Things might not have happened exactly like this, but it sure did feel like they did. I am not even much bothered by the decision to tell the story through the eyes of Kenneth O'Donnell, who according to Kennedy scholars can barely be heard on White House tapes made during the crisis, and doesn't figure significantly in most histories of the event. He functions in the movie as a useful fly on the wall, a man free to be where the president isn't and think thoughts the president can't. (Full disclosure: O'Donnell's son Kevin, the Earthlink millionaire, is an investor in the company of *Thirteen Days* producer Armyan Bernstein.)

Costner plays O'Donnell as a White House jack of all trades, a close adviser whose office adjoins the Oval Office. He has deep roots with the Kennedys. He was Bobby's roommate at Harvard and Jack's campaign manager, he is an utterly loyal confidant, and in the movie he helps save civilization by sometimes taking matters into his own hands. When the Joint Chiefs are itching for an excuse to fight, he urges one pilot to "look through this thing to the other side"—code for asking him to lie to his superiors rather than trigger a war.

The movie's taut, flat style is appropriate for a story that is more about facts and speculation than about action. Kennedy and his advisers study high-altitude photos and intelligence reports, and wonder if Khrushchev's word can be trusted. Everything depends on what they decide. The movie shows men in unknotted ties and shirtsleeves, grasping coffee cups or whiskey glasses and trying to sound rational while they are at some level terrified. What the Kennedy team realizes, and hopes the other side realizes, is that the real danger is that someone will strike first out of fear of striking second.

The movie cuts to military scenes—air bases, ships at sea—but only for information, not for scenes that will settle the plot. In the White House, operatives like O'Donnell make quiet calls to their families, aware they may be saying good-bye forever, that the "evacuation plans" are meaningless except as morale boosters. As Kennedy, Bruce Greenwood is vaguely a look-alike and sound-alike, but like Anthony Hopkins in *Nixon,* he gradually takes on the persona of the character, and we believe him. Steven Culp makes a good Bobby Kennedy, sharp-edged and protective of his brother, and Dylan Baker's resemblance to McNamara is uncanny.

I call the movie a thriller, even though the outcome is known, because it plays like one. We may know that the world doesn't end, but the players in this drama don't, and it is easy to identify with them. They have so much more power than knowledge, and their hunches and guesses may be more useful than war game theories. Certainly past experience is not a guide, because no war will have started or ended like this one.

Donaldson and Costner have worked together before, on *No Way Out* (1987), about a staff member of the secretary of defense. That one was a more traditional thriller, with sex and murders; this time they find almost equal suspense in what's essentially a deadly chess game. In the long run, national defense consists of not blowing everything up in the name of national defense. Suppose nobody had blinked in 1962 and missiles had been fired. Today we would be missing most of the people of Cuba, Russia, and the U.S. Eastern Seaboard, and there'd be a lot of poison in the air. That would be our victory. Yes, Khrushchev was reckless to put the missiles in Cuba, and Kennedy was right to want them out. But it's a good thing somebody blinked.

13 Ghosts ★
R, 90 m., 2001

Tony Shalhoub (Arthur), Embeth Davidtz (Kalina), Matthew Lillard (Rafkin), Shannon Elizabeth (Kathy), Rah Digga (Maggie), J. R. Bourne (Ben Moss), F. Murray Abraham (Cyrus), Alec Roberts (Bobby). Directed by Steve Beck and produced by Gilbert Adler and Dan Cracchiolo. Screenplay by Neal Stevens and Richard D'Ovidio.

13 Ghosts is the loudest movie since *Armageddon.* Flash frames attack the eyeballs while the theater trembles with crashes, bangs, shatters, screams, rumbles, and roars. Forget about fighting the ghosts; they ought to attack the sub-woofer.

The experience of watching the film is literally painful. It hurts the eyes and ears. Aware that their story was thin, that their characters were constantly retracing the same ground and repeating the same words, that the choppy editing is visually incoherent, maybe the filmmakers thought if they turned up the volume the audience might be deceived into thinking something was happening.

When the action pauses long enough for us to see what's on the screen, we have to admire the art direction, special effects, costumes, and makeup. This is a movie that is all craft and little art. It mostly takes place inside a house that is one of the best-looking horror sets I've seen, and the twelve ghosts look like pages from *Heavy Metal,* brought to grotesque life. (The thirteenth ghost is, of course, the key to the mystery.)

The screenplay, inspired by the 1960 William Castle film of the same name but written in a zone all its own, involves dead Uncle Cyrus (F. Murray Abraham), whose research into the occult included a medieval manuscript allegedly dictated by the devil. He leaves his house to his nephew Arthur (Tony Shalhoub), whose wife has tragically died; Arthur moves in with his son, Bobby (Alec Roberts), his daughter, Kathy (Shannon Elizabeth), and Maggie the Nanny (Rah Digga). They're joined by a wisecracking ghostbuster named Rafkin (Matthew Lillard) and Kalina (Embeth Davidtz), a paranormal who knows a lot about Uncle Cyrus, his research, and how the house works.

And does it ever work. Exterior steel panels slide up and down, revealing glass container-cages inside that hold the twelve invisible ghosts, which Cyrus needed in order to ... oh, never mind. What intrigues me is that this house, its shrieks of terror, and its moving walls attract no attention at all from the neighbors, even late in the film when truly alarming things are happening. Maybe the neighbors read the screenplay.

The shatterproof glass cages, we learn, are engraved with "containment spells" that keep the ghosts inside. You can see the ghosts with special glasses, which the cast is issued; when they see them, we see them, usually in shots so maddeningly brief we don't get a good look.

Our consolation, I guess, is that the cast has the glasses but we will have the Pause button when *13 Ghosts* comes out on DVD. The only button this movie needs more than Pause is Delete.

The house, Kalina explains, is really an infernal device: "We are in the middle of a machine designed by the devil and powered by the dead." Gears grind and levers smash up and down, looking really neat, and wheels turn within wheels as it's revealed that the purpose of this machine is to open the "Oculorus Infernum." When a character asks, "What's that?" the answer is not helpful: "It's Latin." Later we learn it is the Eye of Hell, and . . . oh, never mind.

If there are twelve ghosts there must, I suppose, be twelve containment cages, and yet when little Bobby wanders off to the subterranean area with the cages, he gets lost, and his father, sister, the nanny, the psychic, and the ghostbuster wander endlessly up and down what must be the same few corridors, shouting "Bobby! Bobby?" so very, very, very many times that I wanted to cheer when Rafkin finally said what we had all been thinking: "Screw the kid! We gotta get out of this basement!"

The production is first-rate; the executives included Joel Silver and Robert Zemeckis. The physical look of the picture is splendid. The screenplay is dead on arrival. The noise level is torture. I hope *13 Ghosts* plays mostly at multiplexes, because it's the kind of movie you want to watch from the next theater.

Thomas in Love ★ ★

NO MPAA RATING, 97 m., 2001

Benoit Verhaert (Thomas), Aylin Yay (Eva), Magali Pinglaut (Melodie), Micheline Hardy (Nathalie), Alexandre von Sivers (Insurance Agent), Frederic Topart (Psychologist), Serge Lariviere (Receptionist). Directed by Pierre-Paul Renders and produced by Diana Elbaum. Screenplay by Philippe Blasband.

Is this all the better it's going to get? *Thomas in Love* images a cyberfuture in which the hero lives sealed in his apartment, and his entire social life takes place through his computer screen. But the computer technology isn't wildly futuristic; it's a modest extension of today's

on-line chat rooms, pay sex sites, and streaming video. The only big breakthrough is a virtual sex suit, kind of a cross between an EKG hookup and a vibrator, that allows two people to access each other's bodies via the Internet. They have about as much fun as a man operating a robot arm to tighten a radioactive screw.

More advanced virtual sex fantasies have been postulated by William Gibson and others (Arthur C. Clarke imagined a world in which reality was represented to dreamers by direct computer input to their brains). But Pierre-Paul Renders and Philippe Blasband, who directed and wrote *Thomas in Love,* aren't trying to envision a brave new cyberworld; their film is about today's on-line "communities," taken another few steps.

We read about couples who meet on the Internet, meet, sometimes marry, sometimes end up killing each other. The Japanese film *Haru* (1996) was about an e-mail relationship. My notion is, anyone who takes this kind of communication much more seriously than a pen-pal exchange should get a life. I think that's what this film thinks about Thomas.

To be fair, Thomas has special problems. He's agoraphobic, and hasn't stepped foot outside his apartment in eight years. All of his needs are serviced via the Net. Some are mundane (he can't get a vacuum cleaner repairman) and others advanced. His insurance company pays for a therapist who suggests on-line dating services; later, the insurance adjuster himself recommends more direct measures—an on-line prostitute.

We never see Thomas (his voice is by Benoit Verhaert). We only see what he sees—his computer screen. Into view swims his mother, who interrupts his sex with an animated cyberdoll. He begs his mother to call only once a week, but she calls constantly (don't they have a "block address" function in this future?). Through the dating service, he meets Melodie (Magali Pinglaut), a poet with a special interest in her own feet, who is a good sport and buys the cybersex suit. They try it out, but she decides it's "creepy" and she can't do it anymore; she wants to see him in the flesh.

His other on-line connection is with Eva (Aylin Yay), a convict whose sentence consists of providing on-line prostitution to the handicapped. She's crying the first time he visits her, and thinks that's what he wants—to have sex while she cries. Not at all. She makes an interesting slip at one point, talking about how "she" could get in trouble—indicating that the Eva that Thomas sees may be an avatar and not the real Eva.

We sense a growing desperation in Thomas. None of this is working out. He is afraid to leave his apartment, but too miserable to stay there. And the vacuum cleaner still doesn't work. *Thomas in Love* has ominous ideas about the claustrophobic world of on-line living, and although I am always ready to have a faster Internet connection and more bells and whistles on my browser, I don't think I'd much enjoy having Thomas's system.

The movie itself isn't as interesting as the conversations you can have about it. It duplicates Thomas's miserable world so well we want to escape it as urgently as Thomas does. In *Lady in the Lake* (1946), Robert Montgomery experimented with a film in which the camera represents the hero; you never see him, you only see what he sees. It didn't really work, and neither does the virtual version. Our only consolation is that it's better to see what Thomas sees for ninety-seven minutes than to see Thomas. As the complaint rep for the vacuum cleaner company observes, "You don't look too well."

3,000 Miles to Graceland ★ ½
R, 125 m., 2001

Kurt Russell (Michael), Kevin Costner (Murphy), Courteney Cox (Cybil Waingrow), David Kaye (Jesse [Her Son]), Christian Slater (Hanson), Bokeem Woodbine (Franklin), Kevin Pollak (Marshall Damitry), David Arquette (Gus), Jon Lovitz (Jay Peterson), Ice-T (Hamilton). Directed by Demian Lichtenstein and produced by Elie Samaha, Lichtenstein, Richard Spero, Eric Manes, and Andrew Stevens. Screenplay by Richard Recco and Lichtenstein.

Here's a movie without an ounce of human kindness, a sour and mean-spirited enterprise so desperate to please it tries to be a yukky comedy and a hard-boiled action picture at the same time. It's about a gang that robs a casino while masquerading as Elvis impersonators. I was nostalgic for the recent *Sugar and Spice*, in which cheerleaders rob a bank while masquerading as five pregnant Betty dolls (plus one Richard Nixon).

The movie has a heavy-duty cast, with top billing shared by Kurt Russell and Kevin Costner. Russell once played Elvis, very well, on TV, and hits some of the right verbal notes here. Costner, the leader of the gang, chain-smokes and looks mean. His fellow criminals include Christian Slater, David Arquette, and Bokeem Woodbine, who is the black guy and therefore the first to die, following an ancient cliché this movie lacks the wit to rewrite.

The casino robbery involves a gory bloodbath, all gratuitous, all intercut with an Elvis revue on one of the show stages. Not intercut a little, but a lot, complete with dancing girls, until we see so much of the revue we prefer it to the shooting. (Looks like dozens of patrons are killed, but the movie of course forgets this carnage the minute it's over.) The gang makes off with the loot, there is the inevitable squabble over how to divvy it up, and then the movie's most intriguing and inexplicable relationship develops.

This is between Kurt Russell and Courteney Cox, who plays the mom of a bright young kid (David Kaye), and is stranded in the Last Chance Motel, one of those movie sets from a *Road Runner* cartoon. Cox's character is intriguing because we never understand her motivation, and inexplicable because she doesn't, either. She really does like Russell, I guess, and that explains why they're in the sack so quickly, but then the kid, who is about eight, creeps into the bedroom and steals Russell's wallet. The movie never questions the wisdom of showing the kid in the room while his mother is in bed with a stranger. One imagines that the filmmakers were so tickled by the plot point that the moral questions just didn't occur to them.

At a point later in the movie, the Cox character drives off in a car containing most of Russell's loot, while leaving her son behind with him. Would a mother do this? Some would, but most movies wouldn't consider them heroines. There is an "explanation" for her behavior, based on the fact that Russell, a bank robber she has known for about ten minutes, is obviously a good guy and likes the boy—but, come on.

The plot is standard double-reverse, post–*Reservoir Dogs* irony, done with a lot of style and a minimum of thought. It's about behavior patterns, not personalities. Everybody is defined by what they do. Or what they drive: As the film opens, Russell is in a 1957 red Cadillac, and Costner drives a Continental convertible of similar vintage, perhaps because they want to look like Elvis impersonators, more likely because all characters in movies like this drive 1950s cars because modern ones are too small and wimpy.

The cast stays top-drawer right down to the supporting roles. Kevin Pollak turns up as a federal marshal, Jon Lovitz is a money launderer, Ice-T is hired muscle. You guess they all liked the script. But the Russell and Costner characters are so burdened by the baggage of their roles that sometimes they just seem weary, and the energy mostly comes from Courteney Cox—and from the kid, who seems to be smarter than anyone else in the film, and about as experienced.

I will give *3,000 Miles to Graceland* credit for one thing, a terrific trailer. When a bad movie produces a great trailer, it's usually evidence that the raw materials were there for a good movie. I can imagine a blood-soaked caper movie involving Elvis disguises, a lonely tramp, and her bright-eyed son, but it isn't this one.

Till Human Voices Wake Us ★ ½

R, 101 m., 2003

Guy Pearce (Sam Franks), Helena Bonham Carter (Ruby), Lindley Joyner (Young Sam Franks), Brooke Harman (Silvy Lewis). Directed by Michael Petroni and produced by Thomas Augsberger, Matthias Emcke, Shana Levine, Dean Murphy, Nigel Odell, and David Redman. Screenplay by Petroni.

Till Human Voices Wake Us could have been a poem by Edgar Allen Poe, a short story by Stephen King, or a *Twilight Zone* episode by Rod Serling. Poe would have liked the part where the heroine drifts on her back down the river under the starry skies. King would have the hero gasping when he finds only his coat in the boat. And Serling would have informed us, "A man named T. S. Eliot once hinted that you can drown in your sleep and not have the nightmare until you wake up in the morning."

None of these artists would have, however, made this movie. That is because film makes it literal, and the story is too slight to bear up under the weight. *The Twilight Zone* could have done it as video, because it would have represented 20 minutes of running time (instead of 101), and been photographed in that stylized 1950s black-and-white television purity where the exterior shot of every residential street seemed to leave room for a mushroom cloud.

The movie tells a story that kept its key hidden for a long time in the Australian version, which began with two young people in a rural district and only switched over, much later, to a story about two adults (Guy Pearce and Helena Bonham Carter). At least in Australia you thought for half an hour or so that the whole story was about the teenagers (Lindley Joyner and Brooke Harman). In the version shown in the rest of the world, the two stories are intercut, which of course gives away the game, since Young Sam Franks grows up to be Sam Franks, and therefore, according to the Principle of the Unassigned Character, the mysterious girl he meets on the train must therefore be . . .

I am not giving anything away. This is the first movie I have seen where the plot device is revealed by the *fact* of the first flashback. Young Sam has journeyed on into adulthood with a heavy burden of guilt, which he hints at in a lecture he gives on psychology. Freud will be of no help to him, however. Maybe Jung would have some ideas, or Dionne Warwick.

The title comes from *The Love Song of J. Alfred Prufrock*, by T. S. Eliot, which is the favorite poem of—well, I was about to say both women. It looks to me like Silvy, the young woman, is reading from the first edition, which would have been possible in Australia in those days. So is the older woman, named Ruby, at a time when the book was worth about $35,000. A book like that, you take the paperback when you go swimming.

But I am being way too cynical about a film that after all only wants to be sad and bittersweet, redemptive and healing. It doesn't really matter what your literal interpretation is for what happens in that adult summer, since there is a sense in which it doesn't really happen anyway, and the result would be the same no matter what the explanation.

There must still be a kind of moony young adolescent girl for which this film would be enormously appealing, if television has not already exterminated the domestic example of that species. The last surviving example in the wild was run over last week by a snowmobile in Yellowstone.

Time and Tide ★ ★ ★
R, 113 m., 2001

Nicholas Tse (Tyler), Wu Bai (Jack), Anthony Wong (Uncle Ji), Couto Remotigue (Miguel), Candy Lo (Ah Hui), Cathy Chui (Ah Jo). Directed and produced by Tsui Hark. Screenplay by Koan Hui and Hark.

I denounced *The Mummy Returns* for abandoning its characters and using its plot "only as a clothesline for special effects and action sequences." Now I recommend *Time and Tide*, which does exactly the same thing. But there is a difference. While both films rely on nonstop, wall-to-wall action, *Time and Tide* does a better job, and plugs its action and stunt sequences into the real world with everyday props, instead of relying on computers to generate vast and meaningless armies of special-effects creatures.

It's one thing to create an Egyptian-canine-sand warrior on your computer, multiply it by 1,000, and send the results into battle. It's another thing to show a man rappelling down the sides of the interior courtyard of a high-rise apartment building, with the camera following him in a vertiginous descent. In *The Mummy Returns,* you're thinking of the effects. In *Time and Tide,* you're thinking you've never seen anything like *that* before.

Time and Tide is by Tsui Hark, a master of the martial arts action genre, returning to his Hong Kong roots after a series of Hollywood-financed coproductions starring Jean-Claude Van Damme. To describe its plot would be futile. No sane moviegoer should expect to understand most of what happens from a narrative point of view, beyond the broadest outlines of who is more or less good, and who is more or less bad. In general terms, the hero,

Tyler (Nicholas Tse), is trapped in a war between two drug cartels, while simultaneously tracking a lesbian policewoman named Ah Jo (Cathy Chui), who was made pregnant by Tyler during an evening neither one can quite remember. The situation is further complicated by Tyler's friendship with the older mercenary Jack (Wu Bai), who has returned from adventures in South America and has also impregnated a young woman.

That gives us two roughly parallel action strands, populated by characters who look confusingly similar at many moments because we get only glimpses of them surrounded by frenetic action. Does Tsui Hark know this? Yes, and I don't think it bothers him. This is the man whose command of his genre helped make Jet Li into a star, and whose range also encompassed the legendary fantasy *A Chinese Ghost Story.*

Time and Tide is essentially a hyperactive showcase for Tsui Hark's ability to pile one unbelievably complex action sequence on top of another. Characters slip down the sides of parking garages on fire hoses, they crash through plate-glass windows, they roll out of range of sprays of machine-gun fire, they are pulled down staircases by ankle chains, they engage in chases involving every conceivable mode of transportation, and there is a sequence near the end where Tyler assists Ah Jo in giving birth while she uses his gun to fire over his head at their attacking enemies.

Who is Tsui Hark (pronounced "Choy Huck")? After more than sixty features he is the Asian equivalent of Roger Corman, I learn from a *New York Times* profile by Dave Kehr. He was born in Vietnam in 1951 when it was under French rule, immigrated to Hong Kong at fifteen, later studied at Southern Methodist University in Dallas, and edited a newspaper in New York's Chinatown. "From the beginning," Kehr observed, "Mr. Tsui was always willing to go a little bit further than his colleagues." He was "an instinctive postmodernist for whom style was its own justification. [He] created a cinema meant to appeal to the eye, ear, and skin far more than to the brain."

Certainly my eyes, ears, and skin were more involved than my brain as I watched *Time and Tide,* and that explains why I liked it more than *The Mummy Returns,* even though both films could be described as mindless action adventures. With *The Mummy Returns* I was repeatedly reminded that one extravagant visual sequence after another was being tied together with the merest of plot threads, which even the actors treated in a semi-ironic fashion. With *Time and Tide,* the plot might be as tenuous, but the actors treated it with ferocious seriousness (whatever it was), and the presence of flesh-and-blood actors and stunt people created an urgency lacking in the obviously fabricated *Mummy* effects.

After that childbirth-and-gunfire sequence near the end, there's one in which the newborn infant, in a small wooden box, is thrown through the air to save its life. As matters of taste go, is that more defensible than the scene in *Freddy Got Fingered* where Tom Green whirls the newborn infant around his head by its umbilical cord, saving its life? Yes, I would say, it is (the modern film critic is forced into these philosophical choices). It is defensible because there is a difference between thinking, "This is the grossest moment I have ever seen in a movie," and, "Gee, I hope the kid survives!"

The Time Machine ★ ½
PG-13, 96 m., 2002

Guy Pearce (Alexander Hartdegen), Jeremy Irons (Uber Morlock), Sienna Guillory (Emma), Samantha Mumba (Mara), Orlando Jones (Vox), Mark Addy (Dr. Philby). Directed by Simon Wells and produced by Walter F. Parkes and David Valdes. Screenplay by John Logan, based on the novel by H. G. Wells.

The Time Machine is a witless recycling of the H. G. Wells story from 1895, with the absurdity intact but the wonderment missing. It makes use of computer-aided graphics to create a future race of grubby underground beasties who, like the characters in *Battleship Earth,* have evolved beyond the need for bathing and fingernail clippers. Because this race, the Morlocks, is allegedly a Darwinian offshoot of humans, and because they are remarkably unattractive, they call into question the theory that over a long period of time a race grows more attractive through natural selection. They are obviously the result of 800,000 years of ugly brides.

The film stars Guy Pearce as Alexander Hartdegen, a brilliant mathematician who hopes to use Einstein's earliest theories to build a machine to travel through time. He is in love with the beautiful Emma (Sienna Guillory), but on the very night when he proposes marriage a tragedy happens, and he vows to travel back in time in his new machine and change the course of history.

The machine, which lacks so much as a seat belt, consists of whirling spheres encompassing a Victorian club chair. Convenient brass gauges spin to record the current date. Speed and direction are controlled by a joystick. The time machine has an uncanny ability to move in perfect synchronization with Earth, so that it always lands in the same geographical spot, despite the fact that in the future large chunks of the Moon (or all of it, according to the future race of Eloi) have fallen to Earth, which should have had some effect on the orbit. Since it would be inconvenient if a time machine materialized miles in the air or deep underground, this is just as well.

We will not discuss paradoxes of time travel here, since such discussion makes any time travel movie impossible. Let us discuss instead an unintended journey that Hartdegen makes to 8,000 centuries in the future, when Homo sapiens have split in two, into the Eloi and Morlocks. The Morlocks evolved underground in the dark ages after the Moon's fall, and attack on the surface by popping up through dusty sinkholes. They hunt the Eloi for food. The Eloi are an attractive race of brown-skinned people whose civilization seems modeled on paintings by Rousseau; their life is an idyll of leafy bowers, waterfalls, and elegant forest structures, but they are such fatalists about the Morlocks that instead of fighting them off they all but salt and pepper themselves.

Alexander meets a beautiful Eloi woman (Samantha Mumba) and her sturdy young brother, befriends them, and eventually journeys to the underworld to try to rescue her. This brings him into contact with the Uber Morlock, a chalk-faced Jeremy Irons, who did not learn his lesson after playing an evil Mage named Profion in *Dungeons & Dragons.*

In broad outline, this future world matches the one depicted in George Pal's 1960 film *The Time Machine,* although its blond, blue-eyed race of Eloi have been transformed into dusky sun people. One nevertheless tends to question romances between people who were born 800,000 years apart and have few conversations on subjects other than not being eaten. Convenient that when humankind was splitting into two different races, both its branches continued to speak English.

The Morlocks and much of their world have been created by undistinguished animation. The Morlock hunters are supposed to be able to leap great distances with fearsome speed, but the animation turns them into cartoonish characters whose movements defy even the laws of gravity governing bodies in motion. Their movements are not remotely plausible, and it's disconcerting to see that while the Eloi are utterly unable to evade them, Hartdegen, a professor who has scarcely left his laboratory for four years, is able to duck out of the way, bean them with big tree branches, etc.

Guy Pearce, as the hero, makes the mistake of trying to give a good and realistic performance. Irons at least knows what kind of movie he's in, and hams it up accordingly. Pearce seems thoughtful, introspective, quiet, morose. Surely the inventor of a time machine should have a few screws loose, and the glint in his eye should not be from tears. By the end of the movie, as he stands beside the beautiful Eloi woman and takes her hand, we are thinking not of their future together, but about how he got from the Morlock caverns to the top of that mountain ridge in time to watch an explosion that takes only a few seconds. A Morlock could cover that distance, but not a mathematician, unless he has discovered wormholes as well.

Time Out ★ ★ ★
PG-13, 132 m., 2002

Aurelien Recoing (Vincent), Karin Viard (Muriel), Serge Livrozet (Jean-Michel), Jean-Pierre Mangeot (Father), Monique Mangeot (Mother). Directed by Laurent Cantet and produced by Caroline Benjo. Screenplay by Robin Campillo and Cantet.

Vincent loses his job. He cannot bear to confess this to his wife and children, so he invents another one, and the fictional job takes up more of his time than his family does. It is hard work to spend all day producing the illusion of accomplishment out of thin air. Ask anyone from Enron. The film *Time Out* is about modern forms of work that exist only because we say they do. Those best-sellers about modern management techniques are hilarious because the only things that many managers actually manage are their techniques.

Free from his job, Vincent is seduced by the pleasure of getting in his car and just driving around. He lives in France, near the Swiss border, and one day he wanders into an office building in Switzerland, eavesdrops on some of the employees, picks up a brochure, and tells his relatives he works in a place like this. It's an agency associated with the United Nations, and as nearly as I can tell, its purpose is to train managers who can go to Africa and train managers. This is about right. The best way to get a job through a program designed to find you a job is to get a job with the program.

Vincent, played by the sad-eyed, sincere Aurelien Recoing, is not a con man so much as a pragmatist who realizes that since his job exists mostly in his mind anyway, he might as well eliminate the middleman, his employer. He begins taking long overnight trips, sleeping in his car, finding his breakfast at cold, lonely roadside diners at daybreak. He calls his wife frequently with progress reports: The meeting went well, the client needs more time, the project team is assembling tomorrow, he has a new assignment. Since he has not figured out how to live without money, he convinces friends and relatives to invest in his fictional company, and uses that money to live on.

You would think the movie would be about how this life of deception, these lonely weeks on the road, wear him down. Actually, he seems more worn out by the experience of interacting with his family during his visits at home. His wife, Muriel (Karin Viard), a schoolteacher, suspects that something is not quite convincing about this new job. What throws her off is that there was something not quite convincing about his old job too. Vincent's father is the kind of man who, because he can never be pleased, does not distinguish between one form of displeasure and another. Vincent's children are not much interested in their dad's work.

In his travels Vincent encounters Jean-Michel

(Serge Livrozet), who spots him for a phony and might have a place in his organization for the right kind of phony. Jean-Michel imports fake brand-name items. What he does is not legal, but it does involve the sale and delivery of actual physical goods. He is more honest than those who simply exchange theoretical goods; Jean-Michel sells fake Guccis, Enron sells fake dollars.

Time Out is the second film by Laurent Cantet, whose first was *Human Resources* (2000), about a young man from a working-class family who goes off to college and returns as the human resources manager at the factory where his father has worked all of his life as a punch-press operator. One of the son's tasks is to lay off many employees, including his father. The father heartbreakingly returns to his machine even after being fired, because he cannot imagine his life without a job. Vincent in a way is worse off. His job is irrelevant to his life. I admire the closing scenes of the film, which seem to ask whether our civilization offers a cure for Vincent's complaint.

Together ★ ★ ★
R, 106 m., 2001

Lisa Lindgren (Elisabeth), Michael Nyqvist (Rolf), Gustav Hammarsten (Goran), Anja Lundkvist (Lena), Jessica Liedberg (Anna), Ola Norell (Lasse), Shanti Roney (Klas), Sam Kessel (Stefan), Emma Samuelsson (Eva), Henrik Lundstrom (Fredrik), Olle Sarri (Erik). Directed by Lukas Moodysson and produced by Lars Jonsson. Screenplay by Moodysson.

With the recent announcement by its exiled founder that The Body Shop is an empty shell of commercialism, the 1970s I suppose are now officially over. *Together,* a sly, satirical Swedish film, shows the decade coming apart as early as 1975. In a commune in Stockholm, a mixed bag of adults, some with children, try to live according to their ideals, while human nature does its best to force them toward compromise, corruption, and—worst of all—realism.

Watching the film awakened memories of the time: a mother protesting against the gender-coding of pink and blue children's blankets. Arguments about men doing the dishes. Denouncements of Pippi Longstocking as a ma-

terialist and capitalist. A child named Tet, after the North Vietnamese offensive. "Open relationships," which have a way of ending in no relationships at all. By the time the kids start picketing for the right to eat meat, we see their point.

Together is the latest film by Lukas Moodysson, a distinctive new Swedish director whose previous film, *Show Me Love* (1998), told the tender story of two misfit teenage girls who fall in love even though one is probably straight. He has an ability to hold opposing ideas of the same character at the same time, which makes his people more intriguing and convincing than movie characters who are assigned rigid descriptions.

In *Together,* for example, an abused wife comes to the commune with her two children, fleeing her alcoholic husband. When we see the husband, he creates a drunken scene after taking his kids to a Chinese restaurant, and gets arrested. But Moodysson doesn't leave it at that. He shows the husband at work as a plumber, and introduces a minor character—an older man who calls the plumber just because he is lonely. And eventually the plumber turns out to be more redeemable than some of the more righteous members of the commune.

That would include Lena (Anja Lundkvist), married to the commune's leader Goran (Gustaf Hammarsten). They practice an open marriage, which means she makes love to the doctrinaire Marxist Erik (Olle Sarri), and Goran sits uneasily in the kitchen trying to pretend he doesn't mind. One of the movie's great moments is when Goran finally, suddenly, unexpectedly shows he does mind after all.

The movie's best relationship is between two kids: Eva (Emma Samuelsson), the daughter of the alcoholic, and plump, fourteen-year-old Fredrik (Henrik Lundstrom), who lives across the street with uptight parents who hate the commune. The two nearsighted kids discover they have exactly the same eyeglass prescription, and that is an omen, binding them together in an alliance that rejects both the crazy socialism at her house and the rigid conservatism at his. Meeting in the commune's van or in each other's rooms, they form an innocent friendship of mutual support that perhaps shows man's natural state is in the middle and not at the extremes. (There is also the ability of children to turn anything to their own ends. Eva's brother Stephan and his playmate Tet have a game inspired by the Chilean dictator Pinochet, in which they pretend to torture each other with electrodes.)

Sex causes more trouble than it is worth in the commune. One of the marriages has broken up because the wife has decided, for philosophical reasons, to become a lesbian. A gay man attempts unsuccessfully to use pure logic to persuade a straight man to sleep with him. (True, the genitals know no gender, but their owner-operators are rarely as open-minded.) There is a scene where a woman washes the dishes while naked from the waist down, justifying her decision with a medical complaint that might lead even the most open-minded commune member to prefer that she not wash the dishes at all. And all the time there seems to be a powerful subterranean force operating to sort these radical experimenters back into conventional, stable twosomes.

It may be that *Together* only wants to remember a time. That it does with gentle, observant humor. If it has a message, it is that ideas imposed on human nature may be able to shape lives for a while, but in the long run we drift back toward more conventional choices. In the 1970s, hippies defiantly sprawled on the floor—in airports, movie theaters, classrooms, malls. Now they and their children (and grandchildren) have gone back to chairs again, which were invented, as it turns out, for excellent reasons.

Together ★ ★ ★ ½
PG, 116 m., 2003

Tang Yun (Liu Xiaochun), Liu Peiqi (Liu Cheng), Chen Hong (Lili), Wang Zhiwen (Professor Jiang), Chen Kaige (Professor Yu Shifeng), Zhang Qing (Yu Lin). Directed by Chen Kaige and produced by Chen Hong, Kaige, Li Bolun, Yan Xiaoming, and Yang Buting. Screenplay by Kaige and Xue Xiao Lu.

Here is a movie not embarrassed by strong, basic emotions like love and ambition. It has the courage to face them head-on, instead of edging up to them through irony, or disarming them with sitcom comedy. Chen Kaige's *Together* is a movie with the nerve to end with melodramatic sentiment—and get away with it, because it means it. Lots of damp eyes in the audience.

The movie tells the story of Liu Xiaochun (Tang Yun), a thirteen-year-old violin prodigy who lives in a provincial town with his father, Liu Cheng (Liu Peiqi). His father is a cook who decides Xiaochun must advance his studies in Beijing—and so he takes them both there, with his meager savings hidden in his red peasant's hat. Because he is so naive, so direct, so obviously exactly who he is, and because his son really is talented, the uncultured father is able to convince a violin teacher named Jiang (Wang Zhiwen) to take the boy as a student.

Jiang is almost a recluse, a once-talented pianist whose heart was broken by a girl, and who has retreated to a shabby apartment with his cats and his dirty laundry. As he tutors the boy, the boy tutors him, lecturing him on his hygiene and self-pity. The two become close friends, but one day Xiaochun's father decides it is time for him to move up to a better teacher—the famous Yu Shifeng, played by director Chen Kaige himself. Jiang is a realist and agrees with this change, and the leave-taking between the two friends is handled in a touching, unexpected way.

The big city is exciting for young Xiaochun, who meets a woman in her twenties named Lili, played by Chen Hong, who in real life is the director's wife. She tips him for carrying her bag, hires him to play at a party, takes him shopping, and befriends him. She is also involved in a complex and traumatic episode when the boy sells his precious violin (all that is left from his mother, he is told) to buy her a coat.

The young violinist's goal is to be chosen by Professor Yu for an important international contest. A girl named Yu Lin (Zhang Qing), another of Yu's students, is his rival, and both the professor and the girl tell him secrets that force him to reevaluate his world and values. Torn between recognition and his love for his father, he finds a solution in the last scene that is physically impossible (unless the symphony orchestra is playing very, very loudly) but is the perfect outcome for the story—an emotional high point that's dramatic and heartwarming.

The movie is also a story about the old and new China, set in old and new Beijing. Professor Jiang lives in a crowded quarter of dwellings that lean cozily on each other, its streets filled with bicycles and gossip. People know each other. Professor Yu lives in a sterile modern building with Western furnishings. When he suggests that Xiaochun leave his father and live with him, he is essentially asking him to leave an older, more human China, and enter a modern world of ambition, success, and media marketing.

Lili, the pretty neighbor, is caught between those two worlds. She is clearly a good person, yet not above using her beauty to support herself. In this PG-rated movie, however, it's a little hard to figure out exactly what her profession is. I did some Web research and discovered she is "a goodhearted neighbor [who] offers some of the film's most tender moments" (U.S. Conference of Catholic Bishops), "a gold-digging glamour-puss" *(Village Voice)*, or "the proverbial hooker with the heart of gold" *(New York Post)*. Morality is in the eye of the beholder.

For Chen Kaige, *Together* is a comeback after the extravagant *Temptress Moon* (1996) and *The Emperor and the Assassin* (1999). His earlier credits include *Yellow Earth*, a touching story of a soldier collecting rural folk songs, and the masterful *Farewell My Concubine*, about two members of the Peking Opera who survive through a time of political tumult.

Together is powerful in an old-fashioned, big-studio kind of way; Hollywood once had the knack of making audience-pleasers like this, before it got too clever for its own good. Strange, but moviegoers who avoid "art films" and are simply in the mood for a good, entertaining movie would be better off with this Chinese film than with most of the multiplex specials. ☞

Tomcats no stars
R, 92 m., 2001

Jerry O'Connell (Michael Delaney), Shannon Elizabeth (Natalie), Jake Busey (Kyle Brenner), Jaime Pressly (Tricia), Horatio Sanz (Steve), Shelby Stockton (Mistaken Bride), Heather Ankeny (New Girl), Joseph D. Reitman (Dave), David Ogden Stiers (Surgeon), Bill Maher (Carlos). Directed by Gregory Poirier and produced by Alan Riche, Tony Ludwig, and Paul Kurta. Screenplay by Poirier.

The men in *Tomcats* are surrounded by beautiful women, but they hate and fear them. That alone is enough to sink the film, since no reasonable person in the audience can understand why these guys are so weirdly twisted. But then the film humiliates the women, and we wince when it wants us to laugh. Here is a comedy positioned outside the normal range of human response.

The movie belongs to an old and tired movie tradition, in which guys are terrified that wedding bells may be breaking up that old gang of theirs (like *The Brothers,* an African-American version of the theme, but gentler and nicer). There is always one guy who is already (unhappily) married, one who is threatened with marriage, one who claims he will never marry, and then the hero, who wants to marry off the unmarriageable one to win a bet. This plot is engraved on a plaque in the men's room of the Old Writer's Retirement Home.

The twist this time: The guys all agree to pay into a mutual fund. The last one still single collects all the money. The fund quickly grows to nearly $500,000, so their fund must have bought hot tech stocks. (In the sequel, those same stocks—oh, never mind.)

The guy who vows never to marry is Kyle (Jake Busey). He likes to take his dates golfing and run over them with the cart. They bounce right up and keep smiling. The guy who wants to collect the money is Michael (Jerry O'Connell). He comes into a valuable piece of information: Kyle met one perfect woman, cruelly dumped her, and has always wondered if he made a mistake. Michael tracks down the woman, who is Natalie (Shannon Elizabeth), and enlists her in his scheme. She'll seduce and marry Kyle and get her revenge—oh, and she wants half the money too.

The complication, which is so obvious it nearly precedes the setup, is that Michael and Natalie fall for each other. This despite the fact that by going along with his plan she reveals herself as a shameless vixen. The movie then runs through an assembly line of routine situations, including bad jokes about S & M and a proctologist who suspects his wife is a lesbian, before arriving at a sequence of astonishing bad taste.

Read no further if through reckless wrongheadedness you plan to see this movie. What happens is that Kyle develops testicular cancer and has to have surgery to remove one of his testicle teammates. During recovery he develops a nostalgia for the missing sphere, and sends Michael on a mission to the hospital's Medical Waste Storage room to steal back the treasure.

Alas, through a series of mishaps, it bounces around the hospital like the quarry in a handball game before ending up on the cafeteria plate of the surgeon who has just removed it, and now eats it, with relish. The surgeon is played by that accomplished actor David Ogden Stiers, my high school classmate, who also does Shakespeare and probably finds it easier.

The movie has other distasteful scenes, including a bachelor party where the star performer starts with Ping-Pong balls and works up to footballs. If the details are gross, the movie's overall tone is even more offensive. All sex comedies have scenes in which characters are embarrassed, but I can't remember one in which women are so consistently and venomously humiliated, as if they were some kind of hateful plague. The guys in the movie don't even seem to enjoy sex, except as a way of keeping score.

Tomcats was written and directed by Gregory Poirier, who also wrote *See Spot Run* and thus pulls off the neat trick, within one month, of placing two titles on my list of the worst movies of the year. There is a bright spot. He used up all his doggy-do-do ideas in the first picture.

Too Much Sleep ★ ★ ★
NO MPAA RATING, 86 m., 2001

Marc Palmieri (Jack), Pasquale Gaeta (Eddie), Philip Galinsky (Andrew), Nicol Zanzarella (Kate), Judy Sabo Podinker (Judy), Peggy Lord Chilton (Mrs. Bruner). Directed by David Maquiling and produced by Jason Kliot and Joana Vicente. Screenplay by Maquiling.

David Maquiling's *Too Much Sleep* is rich and droll, and yet slight—a film of modest virtues, content to be small, achieving what it intends. It tells the story of a twenty-four-year-old security guard who is separated from his gun through a scam while riding the bus. He can't go to the cops because the gun wasn't registered. So he spends the next few days trying to track down the gun himself.

This summary, however, completely fails to reflect the tone of the movie, which is a coming-of-age comedy about how there are a lot of seriously weird people in the world. Jack (Mark Palmieri) enlists the help of a deli owner named Eddie (Pasquale Gaeta), a know-it-all who has a theory about everything and is an endless source of advice fascinating primarily to himself. Eddie has connections with the cops, and comes up with a list of locals whose M.O. fits the scam on the bus, and Jack wanders from one suspect to another in a kind of disbelieving daze. During this process he comes of age to the extent possible in a few days—at the end of the movie, he is a little older and a little wiser, but not much.

Jack sleeps too much and rarely seems quite awake. He sleeps too much because he has nothing interesting to do. He still lives at home, in a bedroom filled with his possessions from high school, and during the long nights on the job he listens to self-help tapes about starting his own business (he should begin, he learns, "by choosing a name"). He lives in a bland, boring suburb, or so he thinks, but during his odyssey in search of the gun he discovers that it is populated by strange and wonderful people, easily as eccentric as anyone in a De Niro crime movie or an Australian comedy.

These people talk a lot. I especially enjoyed Mrs. Bruner (Peggy Lord Chilton), the mother of a guy Jack urgently wants to question. She chatters away about her son and her late husband, in a conversation where sunny memories suddenly turn cloudy, and her timing and daffy energy is so infectious the whole audience is chuckling, partly in disbelief. (This is her first movie credit; where did she come from? She's like the sister of the Swoozie Kurtz character in *True Stories*.)

I also liked Pasquale Gaeta as Eddie. Guys like this are fun because they are obviously con men, but verbal, entertaining, and ingratiating. Watch the way Eddie shamelessly flatters Mrs. Bruner and makes up facts about her son (whom he has never seen) while Jack is upstairs plundering the kid's room. Eddie is a natural, but why did he take on this job of being Jack's adviser and sidekick in the search for the gun? He hardly knows Jack, has to have their mutual connection described in detail, calls him by the wrong name, and yet is like a father to him.

I think Eddie gets involved in Jack's search because it's in his nature to stick his nose in. To make other people's business his own. To play the role of wise guy. To show how he has the inside info. This is, amazingly, only his second movie; where does David Maquiling, the writer-director, find these engaging naturals?

And who, for that matter, is Maquiling? I learn that he's a Filipino-American who based this seemingly all-American story on a legend from his native land, and that the Eddie character represents a shaman in the original version. Yes, but every culture has shamans, and *Too Much Sleep* has been so Americanized it seems like a road movie (all on city streets) that makes itself up as it goes along. Maquiling loves the specifics of dialogue. He has an ear for word choices, for how people pause for a second after uttering outrageous lies, and for the way the suburbs (his suburbs, at least) are not homogenized flatlands but breed people who go slightly mad in intriguing ways.

When I recommend a movie like this, there are always people who go to see it and challenge me: "What was *that* about?" Sometimes they send me their ticket stubs and demand a refund. They're not used to films this specific and unsprung. Others will cherish it as a treasure. Depends on what you're looking for. *Too Much Sleep* doesn't shake you by the throat with its desire to entertain. It doesn't *want* you to roll in the aisles. It would rather you smiled than laughed out loud. It is enormously amused by the way people invent themselves as characters, and allows itself to be entertained by their preposterous sublimity.

Tortilla Soup ★ ★ ★
PG-13, 100 m., 2001

Hector Elizondo (Martin Naranjo), Jacqueline Obradors (Carmen Naranjo), Tamara Mello (Maribel Naranjo), Elizabeth Pena (Leticia Naranjo), Paul Rodriguez (Orlando), Constance Marie (Yolanda), Nikolai Kinski (Andy), Raquel Welch (Hortensia), Jade Herrera (Eden). Directed by Maria Ripoll and produced by John Bard Manulis. Screenplay by Hui-Ling Wang, Ang Lee, James Schamus, Ramon Menendez, Tom Musca, and Vera Blasi.

There is a quality about Hector Elizondo that is immediately likable, but too often we have to glimpse it in supporting roles; we smile with recognition, and he's gone from the screen. Now comes a starring role that could have been written for him—but wasn't, oddly enough. His Mexican-American patriarch in the wonderful *Tortilla Soup* was originally a Chinese patriarch in the differently wonderful *Eat Drink Man Woman* (1994). That movie, about a Chinese chef and his three daughters, was directed by Ang Lee, and when Samuel Goldwyn Jr. bought the U.S. distribution rights, he wisely bought the remake rights too.

Can a Chinese family be made into a Mexican-American family? Of course, and although six writers worked on the adaptation, for once too many cooks didn't spoil the broth. (One of the writers is Vera Blasi, who directed *Woman on Top*, the 2000 movie with Penelope Cruz as a Brazilian chef.) The underlying idea is universal: We meet a widower who is a great chef, but has entered into the autumn of his life depressed because he has lost his senses of taste and smell. He has to depend on his best friend, a Cuban chef named Thomas, to sample his dishes. Martin Naranjo (Elizondo) now cooks mostly for his family; he presides over a dinner table with his three grown daughters, who all still live at home: Leticia (Elizabeth Pena), a spinster schoolteacher who has abandoned Catholicism to become a born-again Jesus fan; Carmen (Jacqueline Obradors), who is successful in business but feels something is lacking; and Maribel (Tamara Mello), the youngest, with her streaked hair and hip look, who is going through the kind of mild rebellion that leads to boyfriends you can still bring home to dinner.

This father, his daughters, the men in their lives, and the widow (Raquel Welch) who wants to be in his are the ingredients for a warm human comedy that has no great, deep message but simply makes us feel good—especially since Hector Elizondo is so effortlessly able to make us worry and speculate about him, just as his daughters do. Mexican Americans are not often seen in middle-class domestic settings; Hollywood small-mindedly tends to relegate them, like African-Americans, to thrillers and crime movies. Here at last is a Mexican-American home with the kind of kitchen you'd see in *Gourmet* magazine. (The food on the screen was prepared by Mary Sue Milliken and Susan Feniger, the Too Hot Tamales from the Food Network.)

Martin Naranjo is a proud father, old-fashioned but not weird. He and his daughters have arrived at that subtle balancing point in life where he still considers himself taking care of them, but they are starting to think of themselves as taking care of him. He despairs that Leticia, his oldest, will ever get married, or even have sex. He fears that Carmen, the middle girl, has too much sex ("Don't treat me like a slut just because I've had sex in this decade," she tells him). And as for the youngest, the rebellious Maribel, who is this "Brazilian" boy she brings home to dinner? "The only white Brazilians I know," Martin tells him, "are Nazi war criminals." The Brazilian is played by Nikolai Kinski, son of Klaus (who qualifies at least as an honorary South American after *Aguirre* and *Fitzcarraldo*).

Leticia puts her faith in Jesus, and it is rewarded: One day she looks at the high school coach (Paul Rodriguez) in a certain way, and falls in love, and he is already halfway there. When she brings him home for dinner, that is the beginning of the seismic shift in the family's long routine—a shift that the sexy widow Hortensia (Raquel Welch) hopes will move in her favor, while Hortensia's daughter Yolanda (Constance Marie) smiles and keeps her thoughts to herself.

Tortilla Soup, directed by Maria Ripoll, is not a shot-by-shot remake of *Eat Drink Man Woman* by any means, although some plot points (like those involving the best friend Thomas) correspond. What the two films have most in common is their voluptuous food photography. What is it about great food in the movies that seems to stir audiences? Movies as different as *Babette's Feast*, *Like Water for Chocolate*, *Big Night*, *Soul Food*, and *What's Cooking?* (which featured four cuisines) elicit audible sighs from the audience, and Mexico of course has one of the world's great cuisines.

Tortilla Soup follows a familiar formula, in which the movie opens with everyone unmarried, and we suspect it will have to end with everyone happily paired off. But the movie is cast so well that the actors bring life to their predictable destinies, and Elizondo casts a kind of magical warm spell over them all. Watch his

face during the scene where Leticia brings the coach home for dinner. How hard he tries to look stern, and how obviously he wants to fail.

Traffic ★ ★ ★ ★
R, 147 m., 2001

Michael Douglas (Robert Wakefield), Don Cheadle (Montel Gordon), Benicio Del Toro (Javier Rodriguez), Luis Guzman (Ray Castro), Erika Christensen (Caroline Wakefield), Dennis Quaid (Arnie Metzger), Catherine Zeta-Jones (Helena Ayala), Steven Bauer (Carlos Ayala), Albert Finney (Chief of Staff), James Brolin (General Ralph Landry), Jacob Vargas (Manolo Sanchez), Tomas Milian (General Arturo Salazar), Miguel Ferrer (Eduardo Ruiz). Directed by Steven Soderbergh and produced by Edward Zwick, Marshall Herskovitz, and Laura Bickford. Screenplay by Stephen Gaghan.

Our laws against illegal drugs function as a price support system for the criminal drug industry. They do not stop drugs. Despite billions of dollars spent and a toll of death, addiction, crime, corruption, and lives wasted in prison, it is possible today for anyone who wants drugs to get them. "For someone my age," says a high school student in the new film *Traffic*, "it's a lot easier to get drugs than it is to get alcohol."

Who supports the drug law enforcement industry? A good many honest and sincere people, to be sure. Also politicians who may know drug laws are futile, but don't have the nerve to appear soft on the issue. And corrupt lawmen, who find drugs a lucrative source of bribes, kickbacks, and payoffs. And the drug cartels themselves, since the laws make their business so profitable. If the decriminalization of drugs were ever seriously considered in this country, the opponents would include not only high-minded public servants, but the kingpins of the illegal drug industry.

These are the conclusions I draw from *Traffic*, Steven Soderbergh's new film, which traces the drug traffic in North America from the bottom to the top of the supply chain. They may not be your conclusions. Draw your own. Soderbergh himself does not favor legalizing drugs, but believes addiction is a public health problem, not a crime. Certainly drugs breed crime—addicts steal because they must—and a more rational policy would result in a lower crime rate and a safer society.

The movie tells several parallel stories, which sometimes link but usually do not. We meet two Mexican drug enforcement cops. Two San Diego DEA agents. A midlevel wholesaler who imports drugs from Mexico. A high-level drug millionaire who seems to be a respectable businessman. A federal judge who is appointed the U.S. drug czar. And his teenage daughter, who becomes addicted to cocaine and nearly destroys her life. We also meet a Mexican general who has made it his goal to destroy a drug cartel—but not for the reasons he claims. And we see how cooperation between Mexican and American authorities is compromised because key people on both sides may be corrupt, and betray secrets.

The movie is inspired by a five-part *Masterpiece Theater* series named *Traffik,* which ran ten years ago and traced the movement of heroin from the poppy fields of Turkey to the streets of Europe. The story in North America is much the same, which is why adapting this material was so depressingly easy. At every level, the illegal drug business is about making money. If there is anything more lucrative than an addictive substance that is legal, like alcohol or tobacco, it is one that is illegal, like drugs—because the suppliers aren't taxed or regulated and have no overhead for advertising, packaging, insurance, employee benefits, or quality control. Drugs are produced by subsistence-level peasants and move through a distribution chain of street sellers; costs to the end user are kept low to encourage addiction.

Soderbergh's film uses a levelheaded approach. It watches, it observes, it does not do much editorializing. The hopelessness of anti-drug measures is brought home through practical scenarios, not speeches and messages—except for a few. One of the most heartfelt comes from a black man who observes that at any given moment in America, 100,000 white people are driving through black neighborhoods looking for drugs, and a dealer who can make $200 in two hours is hardly motivated to seek other employment.

The key performance in the movie is by Michael Douglas, as Robert Wakefield, an Ohio judge tapped by the White House as the nation's new drug czar. He holds all the usual opinions, mouths all the standard platitudes, shares all the naive assumptions—including his belief that he can destroy one of the Mexican cartels by cooperating with the Mexican authorities. This is true in theory, but in practice his information simply provides an advantage for one cartel over the other.

Wakefield is a good man. His daughter, Caroline (Erika Christensen), is an honor student. One night at a party with other teenagers, she tries cocaine and likes it, very much. We see how easily the drug is available to her, how quickly she gets hooked, how swiftly she falls through the safety nets of family and society. This is the social cost of addiction, and the rationale for passing laws against drugs—but we see that it happens *despite* the laws, and that without a profit motive drugs might not be so easily available in her circle.

In Mexico, we meet two hardworking cops in the drug wars, played by Benicio Del Toro and Jacob Vargas, who intercept a big drug shipment but then are themselves intercepted by troops commanded by an army general (Tomas Milian), who is sort of the J. Edgar Hoover of Mexican drug enforcement. In California, we meet a middleman (Miguel Ferrer) who imports and distributes drugs, and two federal agents (Don Cheadle and Luis Guzman) who are on his trail. And we meet the top executive for this operation, a respectable millionaire (Steven Bauer) and his socialite wife (Catherine Zeta-Jones), who has no idea where her money comes from.

Soderbergh's story, from a screenplay by Stephen Gaghan, cuts between these characters so smoothly that even a fairly complex scenario remains clear and charged with tension. Like Martin Scorsese's *GoodFellas, Traffic* is fascinating at one level simply because it shows how things work—how the drugs are marketed, how the laws are sidestepped. The problem is like a punching bag. You can hammer it all day and still it hangs there, impassive, unchanged.

The movie is powerful precisely because it doesn't preach. It is so restrained that at one moment—the judge's final speech—I wanted one more sentence, making a point, but the movie lets us supply that thought for ourselves. And the facts make their own argument: This war is not winnable on the present terms, and takes a greater toll in human lives than the drugs themselves. The drug war costs $19 billion a year, but scenes near the end of the film suggest that more addicts are helped by two free programs, Alcoholics Anonymous and Narcotics Anonymous, than by all the drug troops put together.

Training Day ★ ★ ★
R, 122 m., 2001

Denzel Washington (Alonzo Harris), Ethan Hawke (Jake Hoyt), Scott Glenn (Roger), Tom Berenger (Stan), Cliff Curtis (Smiley), Snoop Dogg (Sammy), Macy Gray (Sandman's Wife). Directed by Antoine Fuqua and produced by Jeffrey Silver and Bobby Newmeyer. Screenplay by David Ayer.

Training Day is an equal-opportunity police brutality picture, depicting a modern Los Angeles in which the black cop is slimier and more corrupt than anybody ever thought the white cops were. Alonzo Harris, played by Denzel Washington, makes Popeye Doyle look like Officer Friendly. So extreme is his mad dog behavior, indeed, that it shades over into humor: Washington seems to enjoy a performance that's over the top and down the other side.

He plays Alonzo as the meanest, baddest narcotics cop in the city—a dude who cruises the mean streets in his confiscated customized Monte Carlo, extracting tribute and accumulating graft like a medieval warlord shaking down his serfs. His pose is that the job must be done this way: If you don't intimidate the street, it will kill you. This is the lesson he's teaching Jake Hoyt (Ethan Hawke), a young cop who dreams of being promoted to the elite narc squad.

This is Jake's first day of training, and he's been placed in the hands of Alonzo for a taste of street reality. Jake's dream: Get a promotion so he can move his wife and child to a nicer house. This may not turn out to be a wise career move. Just as a warm-up, Alonzo forces him to smoke pot (it turns out to be laced with PCP): If you turn down gifts on the street, he's

told, "You'll be dead." He watches as Alonzo stops two punks who are raping a girl, and then instead of arresting the rapists he thoroughly and competently beats them almost dead.

Dispensing street justice is what it's all about, Alonzo believes; the enemy lives outside the law, and you have to pursue him there. Jake hallucinates for a while because of the PCP, but surfaces to accompany Alonzo on a visit to an old and slimy colleague (Scott Glenn), on a raid on a drug dealer's house, on a visit to what seems to be Alonzo's secret second family, and to a restaurant rendezvous with what appears to be a circle of top cops who mastermind graft and payoffs. Along the way there's a sensational gun battle, although it doesn't draw enough attention to interrupt Alonzo's routine. I'm not saying all of these events in one day are impossible; in the real world, however, by the end of it both cops would be exhausted, and Alonzo would be shaking down a druggist for Ben-Gay.

Is Alonzo for real? Are the city and its cops really this evil? (I am asking about the movie, not life.) At first we wonder if Alonzo isn't putting on a show to test the rookie. The rookie thinks that, too—that if he yields to temptation, he'll be busted. That theory comes to an end when Jake is ordered to kill someone, or be framed for the murder anyway. And Alonzo isn't the exception to the rule: We can tell by the lunchtime summit that he's part of the ruling circle.

For Denzel Washington, *Training Day* is a rare villainous role; he doesn't look, sound, or move like his usual likable characters, and certainly there's no trace of the football coach from *Remember the Titans*. The movie, directed by Antoine Fuqua (*Bait*) and written by David Ayer (*The Fast and the Furious*), keeps pushing him, and by the end it has pushed him right into pure fantasy. Alonzo, in the earlier scenes, seems extreme but perhaps believable; by the end, he's like a monster from a horror film, unkillable and implacable.

A lot of people are going to be leaving the theater as I did, wondering about the logic and plausibility of the last fifteen minutes. There are times when you're distracted from the action on the screen by the need to trace back through the plot and try to piece together how events could possibly have turned out this way. But Ayer's screenplay is ingenious in the way it plants clues and pays them off in unexpected ways; *Training Day* makes as much sense as movies like this usually can. It might have been better if it had stayed closer to life, but it doesn't want to be.

For its kinetic energy and acting zeal, I enjoyed the movie. I like it when actors go for broke. Ethan Hawke is well cast as the cop who believes "we serve and protect" but has trouble accepting the logic of Alonzo's style of serving and protecting. And the supporting roles are well crafted, especially the retired cop played by Scott Glenn, who seems to be sitting on a whole other buried story. Aware as I was of its loopholes and excesses, the movie persuaded me to go along for the ride.

Of course, you can't watch the movie without thinking of the Rodney King and O.J. Simpson sagas, two sides of the same coin, both suggesting the Los Angeles police are not perfect. I found myself wondering what would have happened if the movie had flipped the races, with a rotten white cop showing a black rookie the ropes. Given the way the movie pays off, that might have been doable. But it would have involved flipping the itinerary of the street tours, too; instead of the black cop planting the white boy in the middle of hostile nonwhite environments, you'd have the white cop taking the black rookie to the white drug lords; gated mansions in *Traffic* come to mind. Not as much fun.

The Transporter ★ ★ ½
PG-13, 92 m., 2002

Jason Statham (Frank Martin), Qi Shu (Lai), François Berléand (Tarconi), Matt Schulze (Wall Street). Directed by Corey Yuen and produced by Luc Besson and Steven Chasman. Screenplay by Besson and Robert Mark Kamen.

The marriage of James Bond and Hong Kong continues in *The Transporter*, a movie that combines Bond's luxurious European locations and love of deadly toys with all the tricks of martial arts movies. The movie stars Jason Statham (who has pumped a lot of iron since *Lock, Stock and Two Smoking Barrels*) as Frank Martin, a.k.a. the Transporter, who will transport anything at a price. His three unbreakable rules: Never change the deal, no names, and never look in the package.

Unlike Bond, Martin is amoral and works only for the money. We gather he lost any shreds of patriotism while serving in the British Special Forces, and now hires out his skills to support a lifestyle that includes an oceanside villa on the French Riviera that would retail at $30 million, minimum.

In an opening sequence that promises more than the movie is able to deliver, Martin pilots his BMW for the getaway of a gang of bank robbers. Four of them pile into the car. The deal said there would be three. "The deal never changes," Martin says, as alarms ring and police sirens grow nearer. The robbers scream for him to drive away. He shoots the fourth man. Now the deal can proceed.

And it does, in a chase sequence that is sensationally good, but then aren't all movie chase scenes sensationally good these days? There have been so many virtuoso chase sequences lately that we grow jaded, but this one, with the car bouncing down steps, squeezing through narrow lanes, and speeding backward on expressways, is up there with recent French chases like *Ronin* and *The Bourne Identity*.

The movie combines the skills and trademarks of its director, Corey Yuen, and its writer-producer, Luc Besson. The Hong Kong–based specialist in martial arts movies has forty-three titles to his credit, many of them starring Jet Li and Qi Shu. This is his English-language debut. Besson, now one of the world's top action producers (he has announced nine films for 2003 and also has *Wasabi* in current release), likes partnerships between action heroes and younger, apparently more vulnerable women. Those elements were central in his direction of *La Femme Nikita*, *The Professional*, and *The Fifth Element*. Now he provides Frank Martin with a young woman through the violation of Rule No. 3: Martin looks in the bag.

He has been given a large duffel bag to transport. It squirms. It contains a beautiful young Chinese woman named Lai (Qi Shu, who at age twenty-six has appeared in forty-one movies, mostly erotic or martial arts). He cuts a little hole in the bag so she can sip an orange juice, and before he remembers to consult his rules again he has brought her home to his villa and is embroiled in a plot involving gangsters from Nice and human slave cargoes from China.

The movie is by this point, alas, on autopilot. Statham's character, who had a grim fascination when he was enforcing the rules, turns into just another action hero when he starts breaking them. I actually thought, during the opening scenes, that *The Transporter* was going to rise above the genre, was going to be a study of violent psychology, like *La Femme Nikita*. No luck.

Too much action brings the movie to a dead standstill. Why don't directors understand that? Why don't they know that wall-to-wall action makes a movie *less* interesting—less like drama, more like a repetitive video game? Stunt action sequences are difficult, but apparently not as difficult as good dialogue. Unless you're an early-teens, special-effects zombie, movies get more interesting when the characters are given humanity and dimension.

Frank Martin is an intriguing man in the opening scenes, and we think maybe we'll learn something about his harsh code and lonely profession. But no: We get car leaps from bridges onto auto transporters. Parachute drops onto the tops of moving trucks. Grenades, rocket launchers, machine guns (at one point a friendly inspector asks Martin to explain 50,000 spent rounds of ammo). There is, of course, an underwater adventure, tribute to Besson's early life as the child of scuba diving instructors. At one point Martin tells Lai, "It's quiet. Too quiet." It wasn't nearly quiet enough.

Treasure Planet ★ ★ ½

PG, 95 m., 2002

With the voices of: Joseph Gordon-Levitt (Jim Hawkins [speaking]), John Rzeznik (Jim Hawkins [singing]), Brian Murray (John Silver), David Hyde Pierce (Dr. Doppler), Martin Short (B.E.N.), Emma Thompson (Captain Amelia), Roscoe Lee Browne (Arrow), Michael Wincott (Scroop). Directed by Ron Clements and John Musker and produced by Roy Conli, Clements, and Musker. Screenplay by Clements, Musker, and Rob Edwards, based on the novel *Treasure Island* by Robert Louis Stevenson.

Walt Disney's *Treasure Planet* has zest and humor and some lovable supporting characters, but do we really need this zapped-up version of the Robert Louis Stevenson classic? Eighteenth-century galleons and pirate ships go sailing through the stars, and it somehow just doesn't look right. The film wants to be a pirate movie dressed in *Star Wars* garb, but the pants are too short and the elbows stick out. For anyone who grew up on Disney's 1950 *Treasure Island*, or remembers the 1934 Victor Fleming classic, this one feels like an impostor.

I am not concerned about technical matters. I do not question why spaceships of the future would look like sailing ships of the past. I can believe they could be powered by both rockets and solar winds. It does not bother me that deep space turns out to be breathable. I do not wonder why swashbuckling is still in style in an era of ray guns and laser beams. I accept all of that. It's just that I wonder why I have to. Why not make an animated version of the classic *Treasure Island*? Why not challenge the kids with a version of an actual book written by a great writer, instead of catering to them with what looks like the prototype for a video game?

These are, I suppose, the objections of a hidebound reactionary. I believe that one should review the movie that has been made, not the movie one wishes had been made, and here I violate my own rule. But there was something in me that . . . resisted . . . this movie. I hope it did not blind me to its undeniable charms.

There is, to begin with, a likable hero named Jim Hawkins, whose speaking voice is by Joseph Gordon-Levitt and singing voice by John Rzeznik. Jim is a nice enough kid when we first see him being read to by his mother in his standard-issue Disney fatherless home. But he grows up into a troublemaker, and it is only the possession of a holographic treasure map, and the journey in this movie, that seasons him into a fine young man.

Hoping to sail away to a planet where "the treasures of a thousand worlds" have been deposited, Jim signs on as a cabin boy under the cat-eyed Captain Amelia (voice by Emma Thompson), and is soon befriended by the cook, John Silver (Brian Murray), a cyborg whose right arm contains an amazing collection of attachments and gadgets. Also onboard is the wealthy Dr. Doppler (David Hyde Pierce), who is financing the voyage. (His doglike appearance and Amelia's feline nature make us wonder, when romance blooms, whether theirs is a relationship likely to last.)

I will not be spoiling much, I assume, to suggest that John Silver is more than a cook, and less than a friend. He has mutiny in mind. And the troubles onboard the ship are back-dropped by troubles in space, where a black hole threatens and there is a "space storm" as dangerous as any in the Caribbean.

It is obligatory in all Disney animated features that there be some sort of cute miniature sidekick, and the peppy little creature this time is Morph, a blue blob that can assume almost any shape, is cuddly and frisky, and takes sides. Another supporting character is B.E.N. (Martin Short), a cybernetic navigator who apparently has some fried memory boards and lots of one-liners. He would be obnoxious unless you liked creatures like him, which I do.

Disney experiments with its animation methods in the movie (which is being released simultaneously in regular theaters and on the big IMAX screens, which have recently brought such an awesome presence to *Fantasia* and *Beauty and the Beast*). The foreground characters are two-dimensional in the classical animated style, but the backgrounds are 3-D and computer-generated ("painted," the Web site assures us, but with a computer stylus rather than a brush). Some may find a clash between the two styles, but the backgrounds function as, well, backgrounds, and I accepted them without question.

I'm aware that many, maybe most, of the audience members for this film will never have heard of Robert Louis Stevenson. They may learn in the opening sequence that he once wrote a book named *Treasure Island,* but when this book is opened by Jim's mother it contains no old-fashioned words, only pop-up moving images. For these people, the loss of the story's literary roots may be meaningless. They may wonder what old sailing ships are doing in a futuristic universe, but then there's a lot to wonder about in all animated adventures, isn't there, since none of them are plausible. My guess is that most audiences will enjoy this film more than I did. I remain stubbornly convinced that pirate ships and ocean storms and real whales (as opposed to space whales) are

exciting enough. Even more exciting, because less gimmicky. But there I go again.

The Trials of Henry Kissinger ★ ★ ★
NO MPAA RATING, 80 m., 2002

A documentary directed by Eugene Jarecki and produced by Alex Gibney and Jarecki. Screenplay by Gibney, based on the book by Christopher Hitchens.

The odds are excellent that President Bush did not see this film before appointing Henry Kissinger as the head of a special commission to examine shortcomings of U.S. intelligence in the period before 9/11. *The Trials of Henry Kissinger* charges Kissinger himself with authorizing illegal terrorist acts on behalf of the United States. Did Bush put the fox in charge of the henhouse?

Yes, the film is told from a hostile point of view: It's based on a book by the New Left author Christopher Hitchens, who has made Kissinger-bashing a second career. But many of the facts in it are matters of public record. And it is widely believed, and not just on the left, that Kissinger directly or indirectly brought about the death of the democratically elected Chilean president Salvador Allende. And he is currently the defendant, as Hitchens pointed out recently on www.Slate.com, in a civil suit filed in Washington, D.C., charging that Kissinger gave the order for the assassination of the Chilean general Rene Schneider, who would not support the U.S. call for a military coup. "Every single document in the prosecution case," Hitchens notes, "is a U.S.-government declassified paper."

I am your humble scribe and have no personal knowledge of the truth or falsity of these charges. I note, however, that it may be unwise to assign a man with such a complex image to investigate terrorism. By appointing him to head the investigation into possible failures of U.S. intelligence in the months before 9/11, the president, having resisted such an investigation for more than a year, shows he doesn't really care what anyone thinks.

The Trials of Henry Kissinger, directed by Eugene Jarecki and based on Hitchens's 2001 book *The Trials of Henry Kissinger,* plays like a brief for a war crimes trial against the former secretary of state. It also plays like a roast, with easy jibes about his appetite for dating starlets and his avid careerism (at one point, we learn, he assured friends he would be the White House foreign policy adviser no matter whether Nixon or Humphrey was elected). The movie is not above cheap shots, as when it sets sequences to music.

The film's technique is partisan. It provides Kissinger's critics, including Hitchens, William Shawcross, and Seymour Hersh, with ample time to spell out their charges against Kissinger (samples: He lied to Congress about the bombing of Cambodia, and lengthened the war in Vietnam by sending a secret message to the North Vietnamese that they'd get a better deal if they waited until Nixon was in office). Then Kissinger's defenders are seen and heard, but hardly given equal time. It feels somehow as if the filmmakers have chosen just the words they want, and the context be damned; sophisticated media-watchers will note the editing tricks and suspect the film's motives.

That was also a charge against Hitchens's book: that he was such a rabid hater of Kissinger that he overstated his case, convicting Kissinger of what he suspected as well as what he could prove. More balanced criticisms of Kissinger were drowned out in the resulting controversy, and Hitchens, an easy target, drew attention away from harder targets that might have been less easily answered.

The film is nevertheless fascinating to watch as a portrait of political celebrity and ego. "Power is the greatest aphrodisiac," Kissinger famously said, and he famously proved the truth of that epigram. In the years before his marriage he was seen with a parade of babes on his arm, including Jill St. John, Candice Bergen, Samantha Eggar, Shirley MacLaine, Marlo Thomas, and, yes, Zsa Zsa Gabor. He dined out often and well in New York, Washington, D.C., and world capitals, and his outgoing social life was in distinct contrast with the buttoned-down style of his boss, Nixon.

The movie shows him as a man lustful not so much for sex as for the appearance of conquest (many of his dates were at pains to report they were deposited chastely back home at the end of the evening). He liked the limelight, the power, the access, and he successfully tended the legend that he was indispensable to American foreign policy—so much so that he got credit for some of Nixon's initiatives, such as the opening to China.

He meanwhile exercised great power, not always with discretion if the film is to be believed. There is an agonizing sound bite in which he regretfully observes that there is not always a clear choice between good and evil. Sometimes indeed evil must be done to bring about the greater good. All very well, but if the people of Chile elect a government we don't like, does that give us the right to overthrow it? And even if it does, does that make the man who thought so a wise choice to investigate our current intelligence about terrorism?

The Triumph of Love ★ ★ ★
PG-13, 107 m., 2002

Mira Sorvino (Princess/Phocion/Aspasie), Ben Kingsley (Hermocrates), Jay Rodan (Agis), Fiona Shaw (Leontine), Ignazio Oliva (Harlequin), Rachael Stirling (Hermidas/Corine), Luis Molteni (Dimas). Directed by Clare Peploe and produced by Bernardo Bertolucci. Screenplay by Peploe, Bertolucci, and Marilyn Goldin.

Mira Sorvino has a little teasing smile that is invaluable in *The Triumph of Love*, a movie where she plays a boy who does not look the slightest thing like a boy, but looks exactly like Mira Sorvino playing a boy with a teasing smile. The story, based on an eighteenth-century French play by Pierre Marivaux, is the sort of thing that inspired operas and Shakespeare comedies: It's all premise, no plausibility, and so what?

Sorvino plays a princess who goes for a stroll in the woods one day and happens upon the inspiring sight of a handsome young man named Agis (Jay Rodan) emerging naked from a swim. She knows she must have him. She also knows that he is the true possessor of her throne, that she is an usurper, and that her chances of meeting him are slim. That's because he lives as the virtual prisoner of a brother and sister, a philosopher named Hermocrates (Ben Kingsley) and a scientist named Leontine (Fiona Shaw.)

Hermocrates is a scholar of the sort who, in tales of this sort, spends much time in his study pondering over quaint and curious volumes of forgotten lore. He wears one of those skullcaps with stars and moons on it, and a long robe, and is obsessed, although not without method. His sister, past the second bloom of her youth, is ferociously dedicated to him, and together they raise the young Agis to think rationally of all things, and to avoid the distractions of women, sex, romance, and worldly things.

The scheme of the princess: She and her maid Hermidas (Rachael Stirling) will disguise themselves as young men, penetrate Hermocrates' enclave, and insinuate themselves into the good graces of the brother and sister. Then nature will take its course. This is the sort of plot, like *The Scorpion King*'s, that you either accept or do not accept; if it contained martial arts, skewerings, and explosions, no one would raise an eyebrow. Because it is elegant, mannered, and teasing, some audiences will not want to go along with the joke. Your choice.

The Triumph of Love, as a title, is literally true. Love does conquer Hermocrates, Leontine, and finally Agis. Of course it is not true love in the tiresome modern sense, but romantic love as a plot device. To win Agis, the cross-dressing princess must inveigle herself into the good graces of his guardians by seducing Leontine and Hermocrates. The scene between Sorvino and Shaw is one of the most delightful in the movie, as the prim spinster allows herself reluctantly to believe that she might be irresistible—that this handsome youth might indeed have penetrated the compound hoping to seduce her. The director, Clare Peploe, stages this scene among trees and shrubbery, as the "boy" pursues the bashful sister from sun to shade to sun again.

Now comes the challenge of Hermocrates. Although there are possibilities in the notion that the philosopher might be attracted to a comely young lad, the movie departs from tradition and allows Hermocrates to see through the deception at once: He knows this visitor is a girl, accuses her of it, and is told she disguised herself as a boy only to gain access to his overwhelmingly attractive presence. Hermocrates insists she only wants access to Agis. "He is not the one my heart beats for," she says shyly, and watch Ben Kingsley's face as he understands the implications. Strange, how universal is the human notion that others should find us attractive.

Kingsley is the most versatile of actors, able to suggest, with a slant of the gaze, a cast of the mouth, emotional states that other actors could not achieve with cartwheels. There is a twinkle in his eye. He is as easily persuaded as his sister that this visitor loves him. But is it not cruel that the ripe young imposter deceives both the brother and sister, stealing their hearts as stepping-stones for her own? Not at all, because the ending, in admirable eighteenth-century style, tidies all loose ends, restores order to the kingdom, and allows everyone to live happily ever after, although it is in the nature of things that some will live happier than others.

Clare Peploe, the wife of the great Italian director Bernardo Bertolucci, was born in Tanzania, raised in Britain, educated at the Sorbonne and in Italy, began with her brother Mark as a writer on Antonioni's *Zabriskie Point,* and in addition to cowriting many of Bertolucci's films, has directed three of her own. The sleeper is *High Season* (1988), a comedy set on a Greek island and involving romance, art, spies, and a statue to the Unknown Tourist. If you know the John Huston movie *Beat the Devil* you will have seen its first cousin. With this film, once again she shows a light-hearted playfulness.

The Trumpet of the Swan ★ ½
G, 75 m., 2001

With the voices of: Dee Baker (Louie), Jason Alexander (Father), Mary Steenburgen (Mother), Reese Witherspoon (Serena), Seth Green (Boyd), Carol Burnett (Mrs. Hammerbotham), Joe Mantegna (Monty), Sam Gifaldi (Sam). An animated film directed by Richard Rich and produced by Lin Oliver. Screenplay by Judy Rothman Rofé, based on the novel by E. B. White.

The Trumpet of the Swan is an innocuous family feature that's too little, too late in the fast-moving world of feature animation. I would have found it slow going anyway, but seeing it not long after the triumph of *Shrek* made it seem even tamer and more flat. Maybe younger children will enjoy it at home on video, but older family members will find it thin.

The story is adapted from a 1970 E. B. White fable about a swan named Louie who is born without a voice. While his sisters, Ella and Billie, are trumpeter swans with magnificent calls, Louie paddles around in disconsolate silence. His father, desperate, raids a music store in Billings, Montana, and steals a trumpet, which Louie learns to play.

The young cygnet is a quick study. Encouraged by a local boy named Sam (voice by Sam Gifaldi), Louie enrolls in the local (human) school and learns to communicate by using a blackboard he straps around his neck. But his father's theft of the trumpet weighs upon him, and eventually he flies to Boston and appears in jazz clubs to raise cash to pay for the instrument.

There's more, involving his romance with the feathery Serena (voice by Reese Witherspoon), who in despair over Louie's absence waddles to the altar with the dastardly Boyd (Seth Green). Much is made of the buildup to the Serena-Boyd vows, but once they are interrupted by Louie's last-minute arrival, there are no further wedding scenes, leading thoughtful viewers to wonder whether Serena's nestful of eggs represents a little premarital featherdusting. It wouldn't be the first time a bird fell for a trumpet player.

The Truth About Charlie ★ ★ ★
PG-13, 104 m., 2002

Mark Wahlberg (Joshua Peters), Thandie Newton (Regina Lampert), Tim Robbins (Mr. Bartholomew), Joong-Hoon Park (Il-sang Lee), Lisa Gay Hamilton (Lola), Christine Boisson (Commandant Dominique), Stephen Dillane (Charlie). Directed by Jonathan Demme and produced by Demme, Peter Saraf, and Edward Saxon. Screenplay by Demme, Steve Schmidt, Jessica Bendinger, and Peter Stone.

Regina Lampert has been married for three months. She returns to Paris to find her apartment vandalized and her husband missing. A police official produces her husband's passport—and another, and another. He had many looks and many identities, and is missing in all of them. And now she seems surrounded by unsavory people with a dangerous interest in finding his $6 million. They say she knows where it is. Thank goodness for good, kind Joshua Peters, who turns up protectively whenever he's needed.

This story, right down to the names, will be familiar to lovers of *Charade*, Stanley Donen's 1963 film starring Audrey Hepburn and Cary Grant. Now Jonathan Demme recycles it in *The Truth About Charlie*, with Thandie Newton and Mark Wahlberg in the starring roles. Wahlberg will never be confused with Cary Grant but Newton, now . . . Newton, with her fragile beauty, her flawless complexion, her beautiful head perched atop that extraordinary neck . . . well, you can see how Demme thought of Hepburn when he cast her.

Charade is considered in many quarters to be a masterpiece (no less than the 168th best film of all time, according to the Internet Movie Database). I saw it recently on the sparkling Criterion DVD, enjoyed it, remember it fondly, but do not find it a desecration that Demme wanted to remake it. There are some films that are ineffably themselves, like *The Third Man*, and cannot possibly be remade. Others depend on plots so silly and effervescent that they can be used over and over as vehicles for new generations of actors. *Charade* is in the latter category. If it is true that there will never be another Audrey Hepburn, then it is, I submit, also true that there will never be another Thandie Newton.

I saw her first in *Flirting* (1991), made when she was eighteen. It was a glowing masterpiece about adolescent love. She has been in fifteen films since then, but you may not remember her. She was the lost child in Demme's *Beloved* (1998), looking like a ghost and not herself, and she played Sally Hemings, Thomas Jefferson's slave and lover, in the unsuccessful *Jefferson in Paris* (1995). I liked her in Bernardo Bertolucci's *Besieged* (1998), although the film didn't work and he photographed her with almost unseemly interest. She was in the overlooked but very good *Gridlock'd* (1997), Tupak Shakur's film. If you have seen her at all, it may have been in *Mission: Impossible II*, opposite Tom Cruise.

She carries *The Truth About Charlie*, as she

must, because all of the other characters revolve around her, sometimes literally. Wahlberg has top billing, but that must be a contractual thing; she is the center of the picture, and the news is, she is a star. She has that presence and glow. The plot is essentially a backdrop, as it was in *Charade*, for Paris, suspense, romance, and star power.

I am not sure the plot matters enough to be kept a secret, but I will try not to give away too much. Essentially, Charlie was a deceptive, two-timing louse who made some unfortunate friends. Now that he has gone, several strange people emerge from the woodwork, some to threaten Regina, some, like Mr. Bartholomew (Tim Robbins), to help and advise her. There is an Asian named Il-sang Lee (Joong-Hoon Park) and a femme fatale named Lola (Lisa Gay Hamilton), and a police commandant (Christine Boisson) who appears to seek only the truth. And there is the omnipresent, always helpful Joshua Peters (Wahlberg), who was named Peter Joshua in *Charade*, but there you go.

These people all serve one function: to propel Regina past locations in Paris, from the Champs Elysees to the flea market at Clignancourt, and to accompany her through several costume changes and assorted dangers and escapes. "The history of the cinema," said Jean-Luc Godard, "is of boys photographing girls." There is more to it than that, but both *The Truth About Charlie* and *Charade* prove that is enough.

Tuck Everlasting ★ ★
PG, 90 m., 2002

Alexis Bledel (Winnie Foster), Jonathan Jackson (Jesse Tuck), William Hurt (Angus Tuck), Sissy Spacek (Mae Tuck), Scott Bairstow (Miles Tuck), Amy Irving (Augusta Foster), Victor Garber (Robert Foster), Ben Kingsley (Man in the Yellow Suit). Directed by Jay Russell and produced by Jane Startz and Marc Abraham. Screenplay by Jeffrey Lieber and James V. Hart, based on the book by Natalie Babbitt.

Tuck Everlasting is based on a novel well-known to middle school students but not to me, about a romance between two teenagers, one of whom is 104. It contains a lesson: "Do

not fear death—but rather the unlived life." Wise indeed. But wiser still was Socrates, who said, "The unexamined life is not worth living." The immortals in *Tuck Everlasting* have not examined their endless lives, and the teenage mortal scarcely has a thought in her pretty little head.

The movie, shot in rural Maryland (Blair Witch country), tells of a young woman named Winnie Foster (Alexis Bledel) who feels stifled by strict family rules. Her mother (Amy Irving) frowns disapprovingly on just about anything, but is especially certain that Winnie should never talk to strangers or walk alone in the woods. One day Winnie up and *walks* in the woods, and meets a young man named Jesse (Jonathan Jackson). He warns her against drinking from a spring at the foot of a big old tree, and then his older brother Miles (Scott Bairstow) grabs her and brings her back to their forest cottage on horseback.

These are the Tucks. Mae and Angus, Mom and Dad, are played by Sissy Spacek and William Hurt. Years ago they drank from the spring, and have become immortal. "The spring stops you right where you are," Winnie is told, and that's why Jesse has been 17 for all these years. Although this is not explained, it must stop your mental as well as your physical aging, because at 104 Jesse is not yet desperately bored by being 17.

Earlier, Angus Tuck has spied a stranger in a yellow coat skulking about, and warned the family: "Any strangers in the woods—getting too close—you know what to do. No exceptions." So it appears Winnie must die to protect the secret of the Tucks and their spring. But first Mae Tuck wants to give the poor girl a square meal, and as it becomes clear that Winnie and Jesse are soft on each other, the mean Miles teases: "Don't you wish he'd told you before he kissed you?" (His own mother says Miles is "warm as barbed wire.")

The movie has been handsomely mounted by Jay Russell, whose previous film was *My Dog Skip* (2000), a classic about childhood that was entirely lacking the feather-brained sentimentality of *Tuck Everlasting*. The new movie is slow, quiet, sweet, and maddening in the way it avoids obvious questions: Such as, if one sip from the spring grants immortality, why do the Tucks live for a century in their cottage in the woods? I know what I'd do: Spend ten years apiece in the world's most interesting places. And don't tell me they're afraid city folk will notice how old they are, since the boys live in town and Mae visits them every ten years.

The movie oozes with that kind of self-conscious piety that sometimes comes with the territory when award-winning young people's books are filmed (*Harry Potter* is an exception). The characters seem to lack ordinary human instincts, and behave according to their archetypal requirements. How else to consider the Man in the Yellow Suit (Ben Kingsley), who, if he had given the matter a moment's thought, would know he could stalk the Tucks more successfully with a brown suit? Winnie's father (Victor Garber) is a rather distant man, as befits the form for this genre, in which the women are plucky and the men are either sinister or inessential, unless they are cute teenage boys, of course.

The movie is too impressed with its own solemn insights to work up much entertainment value; is too much fable to be convincing as life; is awkward in the way it tries to convince us Winnie's in danger when we're pretty sure she's not. Even its lesson is questionable. Is it better to live fully for a finite time than to be stuck in eternity? The injunction to live life fully need not come with a time limit. That's why the outcome of the romance is so unsatisfactory. I dare not reveal what happens, except to say that it need not happen, that the explanation for it is logically porous, and that many a young girl has sacrificed more for her love. Besides, just because you're seventeen forever doesn't mean life loses all delight. You can get rid of that horse and carriage and buy a motorcycle.

Tully ★ ★ ★ ½
NO MPAA RATING, 102 m., 2000

Anson Mount (Tully Coates Jr.), Julianne Nicholson (Ella Smalley), Glenn Fitzgerald (Earl Coates), Catherine Kellner (April Reece), Bob Burrus (Tully Coates Sr.). Directed by Hilary Birmingham and produced by Birmingham and Anne Sundberg. Screenplay by Birmingham and Matt Drake, based on the short story "What Happened to Tully" by Tom McNeal.

Tully is set on a Nebraska dairy farm, one without a woman but where thoughts about women are often in the minds of the men. Tully Coates Sr. (Bob Burrus) still loves the wife who walked away from the family years ago. Tully Jr. (Anson Mount) is a ladies' man, dating a local stripper named April (Catherine Kellner). His younger brother Earl (Glenn Fitzgerald) is quieter and more open, with a soft spot for Ella Smalley (Julianne Nicholson), who is home for the summer from studying to be a veterinarian.

In this rural community everyone knows one another. They even think they know each other's secrets, but there are dark secrets at the heart of the Tully family that only the father knows. One, revealed fairly early, is that his wife was not killed in a crash, as he told the boys, but simply abandoned them. The other I will leave for you to discover. The mother is not only alive but dying of cancer in a hospital, where $300,000 in medical bills have caused a lien to be brought against the farm: The Tullys might lose it, after their decades of hard work.

Here in Nebraska the exotic dancers are not very exotic. April is a neighbor girl, who strips in a nearby town because the money is good, but still has small-town notions about going steady. After she and Tully Jr. spend an enjoyable afternoon on the hood of his Cadillac, she claims territorial privilege: From now on, that hood is hers, and she doesn't want to hear about Tully inviting any other girl up there.

Earl has a sort of crush on Ella, who is red-haired and freckled, open-faced and clear about her own feelings. She would like to be dating Tully, but only if he can outgrow his tomcatting and see her as worthy of his loyalty. In her own way, during this summer, she will hook Tully and reel him in, and it may be years before he figures out what really happened. Julianne Nicholson is wonderful in the role, wise about men, aware of her own power.

The anchoring performance in the movie is by Bob Burrus, as the father. Long days alone in the fields have made him taciturn. The boys notice that the lights burn late in the farm office, that he is worried about something, and then they discover their line of credit is cut off at the bank.

During the course of the movie old hurts will be remembered, old secrets revealed, and new loves will form. *Tully,* directed by Hilary Birmingham, cowritten by Birmingham and Matt Drake, and based on a short story by Tom McNeal, doesn't turn those developments into a rural soap opera, but pays close and respectful attention to its characters, allowing them time to develop and deepen—so that, for example, we understand exactly what's happening when Earl warns his brother to be careful with Ella. In other words, don't treat her like another one of his conquests.

Even Ella is bemused by Tully's reputation: "What's it like to drive women crazy?" What Tully is far from understanding is that Ella knows how to drive him crazy, and there is a lovely scene when she takes him to her favorite swimming hole, and allows him to feel desire for her, and pretends that wasn't on her mind. Women know how to win the Tullys, and it's clear that the old man forgives his faithless wife and still loves her.

The movie is a matter-of-fact journal of daily farm life during its opening scenes, and its dramatic secrets are revealed only slowly. At the end, when there is a tragedy, it has been hanging there, waiting to happen, for four or five scenes. Birmingham has a writer's patience and attention to detail, and doesn't hurry things along. She knows that audiences may think they like speed, but they're more deeply moved by depth.

By the end of the film, both times I saw it, there were some tears in the audience. They confirm something I've suspected: Audiences are more touched by goodness than by sadness. Tears come not because something terrible has happened, but because something good has happened that reveals the willingness of people to be brave and kind. We might quarrel with the crucial decision at the end of *Tully,* but we have to honor it, because we know it comes from a good place. So does the whole movie.

The Tuxedo ★ ½
PG-13, 99 m., 2002

Jackie Chan (Jimmy Tong), Jennifer Love Hewitt (Del Blaine), Jason Isaacs (Clark Devlin), Ritchie Coster (Banning), Debi Mazar (Steena), Peter Stormare (Dr. Simms), Mia Cottet (Cheryl). Directed by Kevin Donovan and produced by John H. Williams and Adam Schroeder. Screenplay by Michael Wilson and Michael Leeson.

There is an ancient tradition in action movies that the first scene is a self-contained shocker with no relevance to the rest of the plot. James Bond parachutes from a mountainside, Clint Eastwood disarms a robber, etc. Jackie Chan's *The Tuxedo* opens with a deer urinating in a mountain stream. The deer, the urine, and the stream have nothing to do with the rest of the film.

The movie's plot does involve water. The bad guy wants to add an ingredient to the world's water supply that will cause victims to dehydrate and die. To save themselves, they will have to buy the villain's pure water. Since his opening gambit is to sabotage, I repeat, the *world's* water supply, he will dehydrate everyone except those already drinking only bottled water, and so will inherit a planet of health nuts, which is just as well, since all the fish and animals and birds will dehydrate too, and everyone will have to live on PowerBars.

I have been waiting for a dehydrating villain for some time. My wife is of the opinion that I do not drink enough water. She believes the proper amount is a minimum of eight glasses a day. She often regards me balefully and says, "You're not getting enough water." In hot climates her concern escalates. In Hawaii last summer she had the grandchildren so worked up they ran into the bedroom every morning to see if Grandpa Roger had turned to dust.

The movie's villain, whose name is Banning (Ritchie Coster), has a novel scheme for distributing the formula, or virus, or secret ingredient, or whatever it is, that will make water into a dehydrating agent. He plans to use water striders, those insects that can skate across the surface of a pond. In his secret laboratory he keeps his ultimate weapon, a powerful water strider queen.

Do water striders *have* queens, like bees and ants do? For an authoritative answer I turned to Dr. May Berenbaum, head of the Department of Entomology at the University of Illinois at Urbana-Champaign, and founder of the Insect Fear Film Festival, held every year at the great university.

She says: "Water striders are true bugs (i.e.,

insects with piercing/sucking mouthparts) that run or skate on the surface of bodies of water, feeding on the insects that fall onto the water surface. There are about 500 species of gerrids in the world and, as far as I know, not a single one of those 500 species is eusocial (i.e., has a complex social structure with reproductive division of labor and cooperative brood care). I don't even know of an example of maternal care in the whole group. In short, the answer to your question is an emphatic 'No!' I can't wait to see this film. It definitely sounds like a candidate for a future Insect Fear Film Festival!"

More crushing evidence. Dr. Bruce P. Smith, expert entomologist at Ithaca College, tells me, "There is no known species of water striders that has queens. The most closely related insects that do are some colonial aphid species, and the most familiar (and much more distant relatives) are the ants, bees, wasps, and termites." He adds helpfully, "One mammal does have queens: the naked mole rats of Africa." Revealing himself as a student of insect films, he continues, "If my memory is correct, *Arachnophobia* has a king spider, but no queen—totally absurd!"

So there you have it. Professors Smith and Berenbaum have spoken. The evil Banning has spent untold millions on his secret plans for world domination, and thinks he possesses a water strider queen when he only has a lucky regular water strider living the life of Riley.

But back to *The Tuxedo*. Jackie Chan plays a taxi driver named Jimmy Tong, who is hired by Debi Mazar to be the chauffeur for Clark Devlin (Jason Isaacs), a multimillionaire secret agent whose $2 million tuxedo turns him into a fighting machine (also a dancer, kung-fu expert, etc.). After Devlin is injured by a skateboard bomb, Jackie puts on the suit and soon partners with agent Del Blaine (Jennifer Love Hewitt), who realizes he has a strange accent for a man named Clark Devlin, but nevertheless joins him in battle against Banning.

The movie is silly beyond comprehension, and even if it weren't silly, it would still be beyond comprehension. It does have its moments, as when the tuxedo inadvertently coldcocks James Brown, the Godfather of Soul, and Jackie Chan has to go onstage in place of the hardest-working man in show business. He's very funny as James Brown, although not as funny as James Brown is.

There's something engaging about Jackie Chan. Even in a bad movie, I like him, because what you see is so obviously what you get. This time he goes light on the stunts, at least the stunts he obviously does himself, so that during the closing credits there are lots of flubbed lines and times when the actors break out laughing, but none of those spellbinding shots in which he misses the bridge, falls off the scaffold, etc. And some of the shots are computer-generated, which is kind of cheating, isn't it, with Jackie Chan? Luckily, special effects are not frowned upon at the Insect Fear Film Festival.

28 Days Later ★ ★ ★
R, 108 m., 2003

Cillian Murphy (Jim), Naomie Harris (Selena), Christopher Eccleston (Major Henry West), Megan Burns (Hannah), Brendan Gleeson (Frank), Noah Huntley (Mark). Directed by Danny Boyle and produced by Andrew MacDonald. Screenplay by Alex Garland.

Activists set lab animals free from their cages—only to learn, too late, that they're infected with a "rage" virus that turns them into frothing, savage killers. The virus quickly spreads to human beings, and when a man named Jim (Cillian Murphy) awakens in an empty hospital and walks outside, he finds a deserted London. In a series of astonishing shots, he wanders Piccadilly Circus and crosses Westminster Bridge with not another person in sight, learning from old wind-blown newspapers of a virus that turned humanity against itself.

So opens *28 Days Later*, which begins as a great science fiction film and continues as an intriguing study of human nature. The ending is disappointing—an action shoot-out, with characters chasing each other through the headquarters of a rogue army unit—but for most of the way, it's a great ride. I suppose movies like this have to end with the good and evil characters in a final struggle. The audience wouldn't stand for everybody being dead at the end, even though that's the story's logical outcome.

Director Danny Boyle (*Trainspotting*) shoots on video to give his film an immediate, documentary feel, and also no doubt to make it affordable; a more expensive film would have had more standard action heroes and less time to develop the quirky characters. Spend enough money on this story, and it would have the depth of *Armageddon*. Alex Garland's screenplay develops characters who seem to have a reality apart from their role in the plot—whose personalities help decide what they do and why.

Jim is the everyman, a bicycle messenger whose nearly fatal traffic accident probably saves his life. Wandering London, shouting (unwisely) for anyone else, he eventually encounters Selena (Naomie Harris) and Mark (Noah Huntley), who have avoided infection and explain the situation. (Mark: "Okay, Jim, I've got some bad news.") Selena, a tough-minded black woman who is a realist, says the virus had spread to France and America before the news broadcasts ended; if someone is infected, she explains, you have twenty seconds to kill them before they turn into a berserk, devouring zombie.

That twenty-second limit serves three valuable story purposes: (a) It has us counting "twelve . . . eleven . . . ten" in our minds at one crucial moment; (b) it eliminates the standard story device where a character can keep his infection secret; and (c) it requires the quick elimination of characters we like, dramatizing the merciless nature of the plague.

Darwinians will observe that a virus that acts within twenty seconds will not be an efficient survivor; the host population will soon be dead—and along with it, the virus. I think the movie's answer to this objection is that the "rage" virus did not evolve in the usual way, but was created through genetic manipulation in the Cambridge laboratory where the story begins.

Not that we are thinking much about evolution during the movie's engrossing central passages. Selena becomes the dominant member of the group, the toughest and least sentimental, enforcing a hard-boiled survivalist line. Good-hearted Jim would probably have died if he hadn't met her. Eventually they encounter two other survivors: a big, genial man named Frank (Brendan Gleeson) and his teenage daughter, Hannah (Megan Burns). They're barricaded in a high-rise apartment, and use their hand-cranked radio to pick up a radio broadcast from an army unit near Manchester. Should they trust the broadcast and travel to what is described as a safe zone?

The broadcast reminded me of that forlorn radio signal from the Northern Hemisphere that was picked up in post-bomb Australia in *On the Beach*. After some discussion the group decides to take the risk, and they use Frank's taxi to drive to Manchester. This involves an extremely improbable sequence in which the taxi seems able to climb over gridlocked cars in a tunnel, and another scene in which a wave of countless rats flees from zombies.

Those surviving zombies raise the question: How long can you live once you have the virus? Since London seems empty at the beginning, presumably the zombies we see were survivors until fairly recently. Another question: Since they run in packs, why don't they attack each other? That one, the movie doesn't have an answer for.

The Manchester roadblock, which is indeed maintained by an uninfected army unit, sets up the third act, which doesn't live up to the promise of the first two. The officer in charge, Major Henry West (Christopher Eccleston), invites them to join his men at one of those creepy movie dinners where the hosts are so genial that the guests get suspicious. And then . . . see for yourself.

Naomie Harris, a newcomer, is convincing as Selena, the rock at the center of the storm. We come to realize she was not born tough, but has made the necessary adjustments to the situation. In a lesser movie there would be a love scene between Selena and Jim, but here the movie finds the right tone in a moment where she pecks him on the cheek and he blushes. There is also a touching scene where she offers Valium to young Hannah. They are facing a cruel situation. "To kill myself?" Hannah asks. "No. So you won't care as much."

The conclusion is pretty standard. I can understand why Boyle avoided having everyone dead at the end, but I wish he'd had the nerve that John Sayles showed in *Limbo* with his open ending. My imagination is just diabolical enough that when that jet fighter appears toward the end, I wish it had appeared, circled back—and opened fire. But then I'm never satisfied. *28 Days Later* is a tough, smart, ingenious movie that leads its characters into situations where everything depends on their (and our) understanding of human nature. ☞

25th Hour ★ ★ ★ ½
R, 134 m., 2002

Edward Norton (Monty Brogan), Philip Seymour Hoffman (Jakob Elinsky), Barry Pepper (Frank Slaughtery), Rosario Dawson (Naturelle Rivera), Anna Paquin (Mary D'Annunzio), Brian Cox (James Brogan). Directed by Spike Lee and produced by Julia Chasman, Jon Kilik, Lee, and Tobey Maguire. Screenplay by David Benioff, based on his novel.

Spike Lee's *25th Hour* tells the story of a businessman's last day of freedom before the start of his seven-year prison sentence. During this day he will need to say good-bye to his girlfriend, his father, and his two best friends. And he will need to find someone to take care of his dog. The man's business was selling drugs, but his story could be a microcosm for the Enron thieves. What it has in common is a lack of remorse; the man is sorry he is going to prison, but not particularly sorry for his business practices, which he would still be engaged in if he hadn't been caught.

The man's name is Monty Brogan. He is thoughtful, well spoken, a nice guy. The first time we see him, he's rescuing a dog that has been beaten half to death. He associates with bad guys—the Russian Mafia of New York— but it's hard to picture him at work. He doesn't seem like the type, especially not on the morning of his last day, when an old customer approaches him and he wearily advises him, "Take your jones somewhere else."

Monty is played by Edward Norton as a man who bitterly regrets his greed. He should have gotten out sooner—taken the money and run. He stayed in too long, someone ratted on him, and the feds knew exactly where to look for the cocaine. He dreads prison not so much because of seven lost years, but because he fears he will be raped. His friends see his future more clearly. They are Jakob Elinsky (Philip Seymour Hoffman), a high school English teacher, and Frank Slaughtery (Barry Pepper), a Wall Street trader. Talking sadly with Jakob, Frank spells out Monty's options. He can kill himself. He can become a fugitive. Or he can do the

time, but when he comes out his life will never be the same and he will not be able to put it together in any meaningful way. Frank's verdict: "It's over."

The film reflects this elegiac tone as it follows Monty's last hours of freedom. He has been lucky in his girlfriend, Naturelle (Rosario Dawson), and in his father, James (Brian Cox). Although he suspects that Naturelle could have been his betrayer, we see her as a good-hearted young woman who knows how to read him, who observes at a certain point in the evening that Monty doesn't want company. The father, a retired fireman, runs a bar on Staten Island. Most of his customers are firemen too, and the shadow of 9/11 hangs over them.

Monty has given his father money to pay off the bar's debts. He has moved with Rosario into a nice apartment. Both the father and the girl know where the money comes from. His dad disapproves of drugs, but has a curious way of forgiving his son: He blames himself. Because he was a drunk, because his wife died, it's not all Monty's fault.

The screenplay is by David Benioff, based on his own novel. It contains a brilliant sequence where Monty looks in the mirror of a rest room and spits out a litany of hate for every group he can think of in New York— every economic, ethnic, sexual, and age group gets the f-word, until finally he sees himself in the mirror, and includes himself. This scene seems so typical of Spike Lee (it's like an extension of a sequence in *Do the Right Thing*) that it's a surprise to find it's in the original novel—but then Benioff's novel may have been inspired by Lee's earlier film.

There are two other sequences where we see Lee's unique energy at work. In one of them, also from the book, the father drives Monty to prison and, in a long voice-over monologue, describes an alternative to jail. He tells his son that he could take an exit on the turnpike, head west, start over. In an extraordinary visual illustration of the monologue, we see Monty getting a job in a small town, finding a wife, starting a family, and finally, old and gray, revealing the secret of his life. Wouldn't it be nice to think so. Brian Cox's reading of this passage is another reminder that he is not only the busiest, but also the best of character actors.

The other sequence involves Jakob, the Philip

Seymour Hoffman character. He is a nebbishy English teacher, single, lacking social skills, embracing his thankless job as a form of penance for having been born rich. He is attracted to one of his students, Mary D'Annunzio (Anna Paquin), but does nothing about it, constantly reminding himself that to act would be a sin and a crime. On Monty's last night he takes Naturelle, Jakob, and Frank to a nightclub, and Mary is in the crowd of girls hoping to get past the doorman. From across the street she shouts at Jakob: "Elinsky! Get me in." And we think, yes, she *would* call him by his unadorned last name—the same way she refers to him among her friends.

She does get in, and this continues a parallel story. She is precocious with sexuality yet naive with youth, and the poor schmuck Jakob is finally driven to trying to kiss her, with results that will burn forever in both of their memories. How does this story fit with Monty's? Maybe it shows that we want what we want, no matter the social price. And maybe that's the connection, too, with Frank, who invites Monty over to his big apartment in a building literally overlooking the devastation of the World Trade Center. He has never thought of moving, because the price is right. All three men are willing to see others suffer, in one way or another, or even die, so that they can have what they want. The movie suggests a thought that may not occur to a lot of its viewers: To what degree do we all live that way?

The film is unusual for not having a plot or a payoff. It is about the end of this stage of Monty's life, and so there is no goal he is striving for—unless it is closure with Naturelle and his father. He may not see them again; certainly not like this. The movie criticizes the harsh Rockefeller drug laws, which make drugs more profitable and therefore increase crime. We reflect that when Monty sold drugs, at least his customers knew exactly what they were buying and why. That makes him a little more honest than the corporate executives who relied on trust to con their innocent victims out of billions of dollars.

24 Hour Party People ★ ★ ★ ★
R, 117 m., 2002

Steve Coogan (Tony Wilson), Keith Allen (Roger Ames), Rob Brydon (Ryan Letts), Enzo Cilenti (Pete Saville), Ron Cook (Derek Ryder), Chris Coghill (Bez), Paddy Considine (Rob Gretton), Danny Cunningham (Shaun Ryder), Dave Gorman (John the Postman). Directed by Michael Winterbottom and produced by Andrew Eaton. Screenplay by Frank Cottrell Boyce.

24 *Hour Party People,* which tells the story of the Manchester music scene from the first Sex Pistols concert until the last bankruptcy, shines with a kind of inspired madness. It is based on fact, but Americans who don't know the facts will have no trouble identifying with the sublime posturing of its hero, a television personality named Tony Wilson, who takes himself seriously in a way that is utterly impossible to take seriously.

Wilson, a real man, is played by Steve Coogan, who plays a Wilsonoid TV personality on British TV. That sort of through-the-looking-glass mixing of reality and fancy makes the movie somehow *more* true than a factual documentary would have been. Wilson is a lanky man with the face of a sincere beagle, a flop of hair over his right eyebrow, and an ability to read banal TV copy as if it has earth-shaking profundity. He's usually the only man in the room wearing a suit and tie, but he looks like he put them on without reading the instructions. He is so heartfelt about his lunacies that we understand, somehow, that his mind deals with contradictions by embracing them.

As the film opens, Wilson is attending the first, legendary, Sex Pistols concert in Manchester, England. Here and elsewhere, director Michael Winterbottom subtly blends real newsreel footage with fictional characters so they all fit convincingly into the same shot. Wilson is transfixed by the Pistols as they sing "Anarchy in the UK" and sneer at British tradition. He tells the camera that everyone in the audience will leave the room transformed and inspired, and then the camera pans to show a total of forty-two people, two or three of them half-heartedly dancing in the aisles.

Wilson features the Pistols and other bands on his Manchester TV show. Because of a ban by London TV, his show becomes the only venue for punk rock. Turns out he was right about the Pistols. They let loose something that changed rock music. And they did it in the only way that Wilson could respect, by thoroughly screwing up everything they did, and ending in bankruptcy and failure, followed by Sid Vicious's spectacular murder-suicide flameout. The Sex Pistols became successful because they failed; if they had succeeded, they would have sold out, or become diluted or commercial. I saw Johnny Rotten a few years ago at Sundance, still failing, and it made me feel proud of him.

Tony Wilson, who preaches "anarchism" not as a political position but as an emotional state, knows he has seen the future. He joins with two partners to form Factory Records, which would become one of the most important and least financially successful recording companies in history, and joyously signs the contract in his blood (while declaring "we will have no contracts"). His bands include Joy Division (renamed New Order after the suicide of its lead singer) and Happy Mondays. His company opens a rave club, the Hacienda, which goes broke because the customers ignore the cash bars and spend all their money on Ecstasy.

Wilson hardly cares. When the club closes, he addresses the final night's crowd: "Before you leave, I ask you to invade the offices and loot them." When he meets with investors who want to buy Factory Records, they are startled to learn he has nothing to sell—no contracts, no back catalog, nothing. "We are not really a company," he explains helpfully. "We are an experiment in human nature. I protected myself from the dilemma of selling out by having nothing to sell."

This is a lovable character, all the more so because his conversation uses the offhand goofy non sequiturs of real speech instead of being channeled into a narrow lane of movie dialogue. The writer, Frank Cottrell Boyce, gives Wilson a distinctive voice we come to love. "I went to Cambridge University!" he tells one of his broadcast bosses. "I'm a serious journalist, living in one of the most important times in human history." Yes, but the next day he's interviewing a midget elephant-trainer. He explains how the invention of broccoli funded the James Bond movies (there is a shred of truth there, actually). He quotes Plutarch and William Blake, he says one of his singers is a poet equal to Yeats, he looks at

empty concert halls and observes hopefully that there were only twelve people at the Last Supper (thirteen, actually, counting the talent). And he is courageous in the face of daunting setbacks, pushing on optimistically into higher realms of failure.

The movie works so well because it evokes genuine, not manufactured, nostalgia. It records a time when the inmates ran the asylum, when music lovers got away with murder. It loves its characters. It understands what the Sex Pistols started, and what the 1990s destroyed. And it gets a certain tone right. It kids itself. At one point, Wilson looks straight at the camera and tells us that a scene is missing, "but it will probably be on the DVD."

As the screenwriter of an ill-fated Sex Pistols movie, I met Rotten, Vicious, Cook, Jones, and their infamous manager, Malcolm McLaren, and brushed the fringe of their world. I could see there was no plan, no strategy, no philosophy, just an attitude. If a book on the Sex Pistols had an upraised middle finger on the cover, it wouldn't need any words inside. And yet Tony Wilson goes to see the Pistols and sees before him a delirious opportunity to—to what? Well, obviously, to live in one of the most important times in human history, and to make your mark on it by going down in glorious flames.

Two Can Play That Game ★ ★ ½
R, 90 m., 2001

Vivica A. Fox (Shante Smith), Morris Chestnut (Keith), Anthony Anderson (Tony), Wendy Raquel Robinson (Karen), Gabrielle Union (Conny), Edwards Tamala Jones (Tracye), Mo'Nique (Diedre), Ray Wise (Bill Parker), Bobby Brown (Michael). Directed by Mark Brown and produced by Doug McHenry, Brown, and Paddy Cullen. Screenplay by Brown.

Two Can Play That Game reduces love to rules. At one point it even applies one of Newton's laws of motion to a cheating boyfriend: When one partner has negative energy, we learn, the other person has positive energy, or in any event no energy is lost in the transfer. That the film generates charm from this system is a tribute to the actors.

Vivica A. Fox stars in the film as Shante Smith, its heroine and narrator, who speaks directly to the audience as she talks us through the book of love. She's an ad executive, going with Keith (Morris Chestnut), a professional man with a roving eye. But then, of course, his eye is roving because it's spring, "breakup season," Shante explains. In the winter a man wants to cozy up at home, but the minute those spring outfits hit the streets, his imagination starts to roam.

Shante has three girlfriends, all with men and/or problems of their own: Diedre (Mo'Nique), Karen (Wendy Raquel Robinson), and Tracye (Tamala Jones). At their get-togethers, Shante is the theorist and lecturer, explaining the ways and weaknesses of men—but always confident of her own man, until one day she's shocked when he turns up at her favorite club with a hated rival, Conny (Gabrielle Union) on his arm. Since Keith knew she'd probably be there, this is war.

She fantasizes about flattening Conny with a right to the jaw, but decides on strategy instead, and initiates a ten-day plan designed to inspire any man to mend his ways and come crawling back for forgiveness. This plan includes letting herself be seen with an attractive man, not returning Keith's phone calls, and, on Day Seven, turning up unannounced at his house in full seduction mode, arousing him to the point of frenzy, and then walking out. (The girlfriends engage in some surprisingly crude talk about the results of this practice, with Diedre in particular doubting she could let a situation like that go to waste.) Keith is meanwhile advised by his worldly friend Tony (Anthony Anderson), who anticipates some of Shante's strategies and has some of his own.

The movie intercuts her battle plan with the adventures of her girlfriends, including Karen's inexplicable attraction for Big Mike (Bobby Brown), who when she meets him has a jheri curl and teeth that make Mortimer Snerd look reasonable. She pays for a complete makeover and extensive dental work, and they are blissful together until he catches sight of himself in a mirror and realizes he looks—well, like Bobby Brown.

Among the movie's pleasures is the fact that everybody on the screen is very good-looking, except for Big Mike before his dentistry. Vivica A. Fox, who has made her name in action movies, is so glamorous and bewitching here she may never again need to battle aliens or answer a booty call. Those who know about such things will probably be impressed by the clothes. Those who work for a living will be amused by how, in this movie as in most movies, the characters are given high-powered jobs and then never seem to work at them.

The movie does have charm and moments of humor, but what it doesn't have is romance. The Shante character is so analytical and calculating that life with her might be hell on Earth for poor Keith, even with all of Tony's advice. By Day Seven I was wondering if any man is worthy of (or deserves) such treatment. And Shante doesn't just narrate a little from time to time; she must have half the dialogue in the movie, even interrupting love scenes to explain to the audience in great detail what is happening and why. What we basically have here is *Waiting to Inhale*.

2 Fast 2 Furious ★ ★ ★
PG-13, 100 m., 2003

Paul Walker (Brian O'Connor), Tyrese (Roman Pearce), Eva Mendes (Monica Fuentes), Cole Hauser (Carter Verone), Chris "Ludacris" Bridges (Tej), James Remar (Agent Markham), Devon Aoki (Suki). Directed by John Singleton and produced by Neal H. Moritz. Screenplay by Michael Brandt and Derek Haas.

John Singleton's *2 Fast 2 Furious* tells a story so shamelessly preposterous all we can do is shake our heads in disbelief. Consider that the big climax involves a Miami drug lord who hires two street racers to pick up bags full of money in Miami and deliver them in the Keys, and adds, "You make it, I'll personally hand you one hundred G's at the finish line." Hell, for ten G's I'd rent a van at the Aventura Mall and deliver the goods myself.

But this is not an ordinary delivery. The drivers are expected to drive at speeds ranging from one hundred mph to jet-assisted takeoff velocities, which of course might attract the attention of the police, so the drug lord has to arrange a fifteen-minute "window" with a corrupt cop, whom he persuades by encouraging a rat to eat its way into his intestines.

Does it strike you that this man is going to a lot of extra trouble?

Despite the persuasive rat, the cops do chase the speed racers, but the racers have anticipated this, and drive their cars into a vast garage, after which dozens or hundreds of other supercharged vehicles emerge from the garage, confusing the cops with a high-speed traffic jam. Oh, and some guys in monster trucks crush a lot of squad cars first. It is my instinct that the owners of monster trucks and street machines treat them with tender loving care, and don't casually volunteer to help out a couple of guys (one they've never seen before) by crashing their vehicles into police cars. You can get arrested for that.

Does it sound like I'm complaining? I'm not complaining. I'm grinning. 2 Fast 2 Furious is a video game crossed with a buddy movie, a bad cop–good cop movie, a Miami drug lord movie, a chase movie, and a comedy. It doesn't have a brain in its head, but it's made with skill and style and, boy, is it fast and furious.

How much like a video game is it? The two drivers are named Brian O'Connor (Paul Walker) and Roman Pearce (Tyrese). As they race down city streets at one-fifth the speed of sound, they talk to each other. They can't hear each other, but that doesn't matter, because what they say is exactly the kind of stuff that avatars say in video games. I took some notes:

"Let's see what this thing can do!"

"Watch this, bro!"

"Let's see if you still got it, Brian!"

"How you like them apples!?"

Walker returns from the original The Fast and the Furious (2001), which established Vin Diesel as a star. Rather than appear in this movie, about cops infiltrating his car gang to bust the drug cartel, Diesel decided instead to make A Man Apart, playing a cop fighting the drug cartel. Oddly enough, F&F2 is the better movie.

Walker's costar is Tyrese, a.k.a. Tyrese Gibson, who was so good in Singleton's Baby Boy (2001) and is the engine that drives 2 Fast 2 Furious with energy and charisma. He's like an angrier Vin Diesel. Walker, who gets top billing in both movies, is pleasant but not compelling, sort of a Don Johnson lite.

Other key roles are by Cole Hauser as Carter Verone, the drug lord, whose Colombian parents didn't name him after Jimmy because he's too old for that, but possibly after Mother Maybelle; and Eva Mendes, as Monica Fuentes, the sexy undercover cop who has been on Verone's payroll for nine months and is either sleeping with him or is a sensational conversationalist.

O'Connor and Pearce are teamed up to work undercover as drivers for Verone, and promised that their records will be cleaned up if the mission succeeds. First they have to win their jobs. Verone assembles several teams of drivers and tells them he left a package in his red Ferrari at an auto pound twenty miles away. First team back with the package "gets the opportunity to work with me."

That sets off a high-speed race down Route 95 during which one car is crushed under the wheels of a truck, several more crash, and various racers and, presumably, civilians are killed. O'Connor and Pearce return with the package. As they're driving back, they don't even seem to pass the scene of the incredible carnage they caused in the opposite lanes; just as well, because at 120 mph you don't want to hit a gapers' block.

All of the chases involve the apparently inexhaustible supply of squad cars in South Florida. There's also a traffic jam in the sky, involving police and news helicopters. At one point a copter broadcaster hears a loud noise, looks up, and says, "What was that?" but we never find out what it was, perhaps because the movie is just too fast and too furious to slow down for a helicopter crash.

Two Weeks Notice ★ ★ ★
PG-13, 100 m., 2002

Sandra Bullock (Lucy Kelson), Hugh Grant (George Wade), Alicia Witt (June Carter), Dana Ivey (Ruth Kelson), Robert Klein (Larry Kelson), Heather Burns (Meryl), David Haig (Howard Wade), Dorian Missick (Tony). Directed by Marc Lawrence and produced by Sandra Bullock. Screenplay by Lawrence.

If I tell you Two Weeks Notice is a romantic comedy and it stars Sandra Bullock and Hugh Grant, what do you already know, and what do you need to know?

You already know: That when they meet the first time, they don't like each other. That circumstances bring them together. That they get along fine, but are sometimes scared by that, and back off a little. That they are falling in love without knowing it. That just when they're about to know it, circumstances force them apart. That they seem doomed to live separately, their love never realized. That circumstances bring them back together again. That they finally cave in and admit they're in love.

You need to know: What her job is. What his job is. What they disagree about. What their personality flaws are. And whether, just when their eyes are about to meet, it is a woman who seems to lure him away, or a man who seems to lure her away. You also need to know certain plug-in details of the movie, such as which ethnic groups and ethnic foods it will assign, and what fantasy dreams it will realize.

I have not, by making these observations, spoiled the plot of the movie. I have spoiled the plot of *every* romantic comedy. Just last week I saw *Maid in Manhattan,* and with that one you also know the same things and don't know the same things. The thing is, it doesn't matter that you know. If the actors are charming and the dialogue makes an effort to be witty and smart, the movie will work even though it faithfully follows the ancient formulas.

Romantic comedies are the comfort food of the movies. There are nights when you don't feel like a chef who thinks he's more important than the food. When you feel like sliding into a booth at some Formica joint where the waitress calls you "hon" and writes your order on a green-and-white guest check. Walking into *Two Weeks Notice* at the end of a hectic day, week, month, and year, I *wanted* it to be a typical romantic comedy starring those two lovable people, Sandra Bullock and Hugh Grant. And it was. And some of the dialogue has a real zing to it. There were wicked little one-liners that slipped in under the radar and nudged the audience in the ribs.

She plays a Harvard Law graduate who devotes her life to liberal causes, such as saving the environment and preserving landmarks. He plays a billionaire land developer who devotes his life to despoiling the environment and tearing down landmarks. They disagree about politics and everything else. He is an insufferable egotist, superficial and supercilious, amazed by his own charm and good looks. She is phobic about germs, has a boyfriend she never sees, and thinks anybody who wants to hire her wants to sleep with her.

He is also impulsive, and after she assaults him with a demand to save her favorite landmark, he hires her on the spot, promises he will not offend her sensibilities, and gives her a big salary. He does this, of course, because he plans to violate all of his promises, and because he wants to sleep with her. He may not know that, but we do.

The first half of the movie is just about perfect, of its kind, and I found myself laughing more than I expected to, and even grinning at a colleague who was one seat over, because we were both appreciating how much better the movie was than it had to be. Then a funny thing happens. The movie sort of loses its way.

This happens at about the time the billionaire, whose name is George Wade, agrees to let the lawyer, whose name is Lucy Kelson, quit and go back to her pro bono work. Her replacement is June Carter (Alicia Witt), a dazzling redhead with great legs and flattery skills. We think we know that she is going to be a rat and seduce George, and all the usual stuff. But no. She does make moves in that direction, but from instinct, not design. The fact is, she's essentially a sweet and decent person. At one point I thought I even heard her say she was married, but I must have misheard, as no romantic comedy would ever make the Other Woman technically unavailable.

Anyway, what goes wrong is not Alicia Witt's fault. She plays the role as written. It's just that, by not making her a villain, writer-director Marc Lawrence loses the momentum the formula could have supplied him. The last half of the movie basically involves the key characters being nicer than we expect them to be, more decent than we thought, and less cranked up into emotional overdrive. The result is a certain loss of energy.

I liked the movie anyway. I like the way the characters talk. I like the way they slip in political punchlines, and how some of the dialogue actually makes points about rich and poor, left and right, male and female, Democrat and Republican. The thoughts of these characters are not entirely governed by their genitals.

Sandra Bullock, who produced the film, knew just what she was doing and how to do it. Hugh Grant knew just what he was getting into. Some critics will claim they play their "usual roles," but Grant in particular finds a new note, a little more abrupt, a little more daffy than usual. And they bring to the movie what it must have: two people who we want to see kissing each other, and amusing ways to frustrate us until, of course, they finally do.

U

Under the Sand ★ ★ ★ ½
NO MPAA RATING, 95 m., 2001

Charlotte Rampling (Marie Drillon), Bruno Cremer (Jean Drillon), Jacques Nolot (Vincent), Alexandra Stewart (Amanda), Pierre Vernier (Gerard), Andree Tainsy (Suzanne). Directed by François Ozon and produced by Olivier Delbosc and Marc Missonnier. Screenplay by Ozon.

Her husband disappears and her mind refuses to process that fact. She dozed on the beach, she awoke, and he was gone. Did he drown? Was it an accident or suicide? Or did he simply decide to disappear? Her friends ask these questions, but Marie simply behaves as if he is still there.

She is not delusional. In some sense, in some part of her mind, she knows she will never see him alive again, and perhaps she even agrees with the police that he must have drowned. But that part of her mind is partitioned. Even when she dates other men, even when she sleeps with one, in a real sense her husband is still there, still with her. When she is in bed with another man, he looks on from the doorway, and they exchange a look, and they seem to be agreeing, silently, well, life goes on.

The thing is—it doesn't go on without him. It goes on with him, and she sees him and talks to him. This is not so strange. I know many people who talk about the departed in the present tense. I like it when they do that. When somebody dies, I cannot bring myself to take their telephone number out of my address book, because . . . you never know. Many people believe that their loved ones are with them in spirit. It is only when Marie refers to her husband, Jean, as if he is actually still present as a force in her life that her friends exchange glances.

Under the Sand is a movie of introspection and defiance. It stars Charlotte Rampling, the British actress, as the wife of a Frenchman (Bruno Cremer). We get some ideas about their marriage. Perhaps a reason why some men might commit suicide (a subtle hint about health), but not this man, we think. We do not learn everything there is to know about the

marriage, but it could not have been very unhappy if Marie's mind refuses to allow it to end.

The movie has been written and directed by Francois Ozon. He is thirty-four, has made more than a dozen shorts and a few features. I saw his fifty-two-minute film *See the Sea* in 1997 and have not forgotten it. It is about a woman and her baby living in a seaside cottage; the husband is away. A woman drifter comes by and is befriended by the woman, and a sense of dread grows in us even though we can't put our finger on anything specific in the movie to explain it. There is separate tension growing in the woman, who is in some kind of crisis with the husband that the movie suggests without explaining.

Both of these Ozon films can do what few directors have mastered. They can make us feel exactly what the director intends, without overt or obvious cues. Our emotions are not caused by objective plot events, but well up from the very soul of the film. One of the hardest things for a director to do is to communicate the subjective feelings of a character who refuses to talk about those feelings—who, in Marie's case, does nothing out of the ordinary except to refuse "closure" on her husband's death.

That we are with Marie every step of her emotional journey is a tribute to Ozon, and to Rampling, who in some mysterious way has developed from a journeyman actress of the 1960s into this person capable of communicating the most subtle states with no apparent effort—she just gets on with it, and we are surprised how much we are touched.

Under the Sun ★ ★ ★ ½
NO MPAA RATING, 118 m., 2001

Rolf Lassgard (Olof), Helena Bergstrom (Ellen), Johan Widerberg (Erik), Gunilla Roor (Receptionist), Jonas Falk (Preacher), Linda Ulvaeus (Lena). Directed and produced by Colin Nutley. Screenplay by Nutley, based on the short story "The Little Farm" by H. E. Bates.

It takes more nerve to make a sincere film than an ironic one. Tell the story of a simple and good Swedish farmer, a hayseed who takes out a personals ad to find a wife, and you might be laughed out of town. Who in these days works a farm, has never slept with a woman, and has a heart of gold? *Under the Sun* is a "runny melodrama" with "melancholy mildew," according to Elvis Mitchell, who adds, "If you sit very still, you can probably hear the projectionist sobbing softly." Mitchell, from the *New York Times,* is a splendid critic, but the wrong one for *Under the Sun,* which transmits on a frequency inaudible to the hip. He's too cool for this job. Better to send someone like Andrew Sarris of the *New York Observer,* who finds it gentle, simple, sweet, and lyrical.

Movies like this are not for everyone, but arrive like private messages for their own particular audiences. Accustomed to fast-food films that appeal to the widest conceivable demographics, we're a little stunned by a film making the imaginative leap to the 1950s in rural Sweden—a land more alien to today's moviegoers than anything in *The Mummy Returns.*

I believe farmers like good, kind Olof (Rolf Lassgard) really existed there—a haystack of a man with an unruly shock of straw hair, who inherited the place from his parents, loves his livestock, and lacks any clue about how to meet a woman. I also believe in his younger friend Erik (Johan Widerberg), a country kid with a wild hunger fed by American movies, who drives a Ford convertible, has a ducktail, idolizes Elvis, talks like James Dean with a cigarette bobbing from his lips, and shamelessly uses Olof as a source for "loans" to feed his bets at the racetrack.

I do not believe, however, that very many classified ads for a "housekeeper" would produce in this rural backwoods a candidate like Ellen (Helena Bergstrom), who appears in Olof's life like a wet dream. Blond, voluptuous, red lips, high heels—what business does she have on a farm? The plot eventually supplies an answer, but by the time the answer comes it is unnecessary, because Helena Bergstrom has already answered it in her own way. Hers is a sly and masterful performance, creating a character we are commanded to mistrust, and then turning her into a figure of such fascination and intrigue that by the halfway point we're burning with curiosity about her. What's her angle? Is she too good to be true?

Those are precisely the questions burning in the squirmy mind of Erik. He cannot believe that big, slow, illiterate Olof qualifies for this babe. Erik himself is a pig with women, mistreating his girlfriend of the moment (Linda Ulvaeus) with calculated cruelty. Erik is a player. He makes a move for Ellen, but we never feel it's fueled by lust. It's an autopilot response— he wants to see what happens. At a subterranean level, there is the possibility that Erik doesn't like women at all. (Erik's eventual fate is suggested in two words of dialogue that will sound loudly for students of nautical history.)

Under the Sun is based on a British short story, "The Little Farm" by H. E. Bates, whose work also inspired *Summertime* and *A Month by the Lake.* It has been transplanted to Sweden with no particular strain, since life on this farm is so simple it could be anywhere. What is not simple is the performance by Bergstrom, so carefully modulated that by the end we are hanging on every word and gesture, trying to solve the mystery of her motivation: Can she be as good—or as bad—as she seems? Undulating beneath both possibilities is the daydream shared by many men—that a dreamboat will come along and discover in them qualities concealed from the world at large and certainly invisible to other women. (The inaudible cry of many men is: Let me believe you find me more attractive and fascinating than I have any reason to believe that I am.)

There are two strands of suspense in *Under the Sun*—intrigues about Ellen's intentions regarding Olof and Erik. There is also the enormous question of the sexual future, if any, of this city woman and her farmer friend. He is a virgin, we learn, and so tremulous in the face of sex that he becomes motionless as a terrified rabbit. The writer-director, Colin Nutley, who is married to Bergstrom, photographs her character with an unforced eroticism, having to do with bathing and changing and lingerie and getting sweaty, that makes it clear to us and to Olof that there is a sexual presence on the farm and something will have to be done about it. Eventually something is, in a scene that observes both how complicated sex can be, and how simple.

Two things surprised me about *Under the Sun.* I was surprised how involving this little story became—how much I cared for Olof, wondered about Ellen, despised Erik. And I was also surprised by how comforting and brave it made the life on the farm. There is something real about livestock and fields and big skies, and satisfying about doing a job of real work, and I could almost understand how this sexy, plump-lipped stranger could fall for it. Almost. Sometimes. And then, along with Erik and with Freud, I was maddened by the question: What does she want?

Undisputed ★ ★ ★

R, 96 m., 2002

Wesley Snipes (Monroe Hutchens), Ving Rhames (James "Iceman" Chambers), Peter Falk (Emmanuel "Mendy" Ripstein), Fisher Stevens (James Kroycek), Michael Rooker (Prison Guard), Wes Studi (Mingo Sixkiller). Directed by Walter Hill and produced by David Giler, Hill, Brad Krevoy, and Andrew Sugerman. Screenplay by Hill and Giler.

Walter Hill's *Undisputed* is like a 1940s Warner Bros. B picture, and I mean that as a compliment. With efficiency and laconic skill it sets up the situation, peoples it with clearly drawn characters, and heads for a showdown. There is a kind of pleasure to be had from its directness, from its lack of gimmicks, from its classical form. And just like in the Warner pictures, there is also the pleasure of supporting performances from character actors who come onstage, sing an aria, and leave.

The movie stars Ving Rhames as "Iceman" Chambers, heavyweight champion of the world, recently convicted of rape in a plot obviously inspired by Mike Tyson's misadventures. He's sentenced to the maximum-security Sweetwater Prison in the Mojave Desert, which has an active boxing program. The Sweetwater champion is Monroe Hutchens (Wesley Snipes), and a showdown between the two men is inevitable.

First, though, Iceman has to challenge the leader of the most powerful gang behind bars, and spend some time in solitary as punishment. If he hadn't done that, he explains, he'd be dead. And Monroe has to hear stories about how he's not the undisputed champion any longer.

Also resident in this prison is Emmanuel

"Mendy" Ripstein (Peter Falk), an aging Mafioso who still wields enormous clout inside and beyond the prison walls. He even has his own personal assistant. Ripstein is a fight fan. He agrees with the prevailing opinion that there must be a bout to settle the prison championship, and arranges odds with his Vegas contacts. There will even be a payoff for the two fighters, and Snipes is adamant in negotiating a bigger percentage for himself. The Iceman seems more concerned with survival, and Rhames has a direct, unaffected way with his dialogue that is quietly convincing.

The Falk character is a piece of work. He's like a distillation of Falkness. He squints, he talks out of the side of his mouth, he has a tough-guy accent, he has a way of implying authority. And then he has his aria. This is an unbroken monologue that goes for a minute or two (maybe longer—I was laughing too hard to count), and it is variations on the two themes of the f-word and his wife's bad advice. It touches on the competing charms of California and Florida, comments on state and federal legal details, and rises to a kind of musical grandeur. The screenplay is by Walter Hill and David Giler, who worked together on the *Alien* pictures, but whether they or Falk wrote this monologue is hard to say; it seems to rise from another dimension.

Michael Rooker *(Henry: Portrait of a Serial Killer)* has an important role as the prison guard who coordinates the boxing matches, protected by the benign detachment of the warden. He sets a date for the match, and then the two boxers go into more or less routine training sessions, leading up to the big fight, which is held inside a steel cage. The fight scenes are well choreographed and convincing, and Snipes and Rhames are completely plausible as boxers.

Walter Hill has devoted his career to men's action pictures. He pitted Charles Bronson and James Coburn against each other in his first picture, *Hard Times* (1975), and reinvented the cop buddy movie with Nick Nolte and Eddie Murphy in *48 HRS.* (1982). One day I met the sound men on *Hard Times* and watched them pounding a leather sofa with Ping-Pong paddles to create the sounds of blows landing; *Undisputed* evokes the same cheerful spirit.

Some critics of the movie complain that

there is no hero, since the Iceman has been convicted of rape and Monroe of murder. That is more of a strength than a weakness, depriving us of an obvious favorite and creating a fight in which it is plausible to expect either boxer could win. Of course, Monroe is the underdog, which counts for something, but when you think how obviously the deck is stacked in most boxing movies, this one has a right to call itself suspenseful. On the other hand, with mob involvement, the fight could be fixed. Falk, as Ripstein, has a lovely scene where he expresses himself on that possibility.

Unfaithful ★ ★ ★
R, 123 m., 2002

Diane Lane (Connie Sumner), Richard Gere (Edward Sumner), Olivier Martinez (Paul Martel), Erik Per Sullivan (Charlie Sumner), Myra Lucretia Taylor (Gloria), Michelle Monaghan (Lindsay), Chad Lowe (Bill Stone). Directed by Adrian Lyne and produced by Lyne and G. Mac Brown. Screenplay by Alvin Sargent and William Broyles Jr., based on the film by Claude Chabrol.

"The heart has its reasons," said the French philosopher Pascal, quoted by the American philosopher Woody Allen. It is a useful insight when no other reasons seem apparent. Connie Sumner's heart and other organs have their reasons for straying outside a happy marriage in *Unfaithful,* but the movie doesn't say what they are. This is not necessarily a bad thing, sparing us tortured Freudian explanations and labored plot points. It is almost always more interesting to observe behavior than to listen to reasons.

Connie (Diane Lane) and her husband, Edward (Richard Gere), live with their nine-year-old son, Charlie (Erik Per Sullivan), in one of those Westchester County houses that have a room for every mood. They are happy together, or at least the movie supplies us with no reasons why they are unhappy. One windy day she drives into New York, is literally blown down on top of a rare book dealer named Paul Martel (Olivier Martinez), and is invited upstairs for Band-Aids and a cup of tea. He occupies a large flat filled with shelves of books and art objects.

Martel is your average Calvin Klein model as a bibliophile. He has the Spanish looks, the French accent, the permanent three-day beard, and the strength to suspend a woman indefinitely in any position while making love. He is also cool in his seduction methods. Instead of making a crude pass, he asks her to accept a book as a gift from him, and directs her down an aisle to the last book on the end of the second shelf from the top, where he tells her what page to turn to, and then joins her in reciting the words there: "Be happy for this moment, for this moment is your life."

Does it occur to Connie that Martel planted that book for just such an occasion as this? No, because she likes to be treated in such a way, and soon she's on the phone with a transparent ruse to get up to his apartment again, where Martel overcomes her temporary stall in bed by commanding her: "Hit me!" That breaks the logjam, and soon they're involved in a passionate affair that involves arduous sex in his apartment and quick sex in rest rooms, movie theaters, and corridors. (The movie they go see is Tati's *Monsieur Hulot's Holiday,* which, despite its stature on my list of The Great Movies, fails to compete with furtive experiments that would no doubt have Hulot puffing furiously at his pipe.)

Edward senses that something is wrong. There are clues, but mostly he picks up on her mood, and eventually hires a man to shadow her. Discovering where Martel lives, he visits there one day, and what happens then I will not reveal. What does *not* happen then, I am happy to reveal, is that the movie doesn't turn into a standard thriller in which death stalks Westchester County and the wife and husband fear murder by each other, or by Martel.

That's what's intriguing about the film: Instead of pumping up the plot with recycled manufactured thrills, it's content to contemplate two reasonably sane adults who get themselves into an almost insoluble dilemma. *Unfaithful* contains, as all movies involving suburban families are required to contain, a scene where the parents sit proudly in the audience while their child performs bravely in a school play. But there are no detectives lurking in the shadows to arrest them, and no killers skulking in the parking lot with knives or tire irons. No, the meaning of the scene is simply, movingly, that these two people in desperate trouble are nevertheless able to smile at their son on the stage.

The movie was directed by Adrian Lyne, best known for higher-voltage films like *Fatal Attraction* and *Indecent Proposal*. This film is based on *La Femme Infidele* (1969) by Claude Chabrol, which itself is an update of *Madame Bovary*. Lyne's film is juicier and more passionate than Chabrol's, but both share the fairly daring idea of showing a plot that is entirely about illicit passion and its consequences in a happy marriage. Although cops turn up from time to time in *Unfaithful,* this is not a crime story, but a marital tragedy.

Richard Gere and Diane Lane are well suited to the roles, exuding a kind of serene materialism that seems happily settled in suburbia. It is all the more shocking when Lane revisits Martel's apartment because there is no suggestion that she is unhappy with Gere, starved for sex, or especially impulsive. She goes back up there because—well, because she wants to. He's quite a guy. On one visit he shows her *The Joy of Cooking* in Braille. And then his fingers brush hers as if he's reading *The Joy of Sex* on her skin.

V

Vanilla Sky ★ ★ ★
R, 135 m., 2001

Tom Cruise (David Aames), Penelope Cruz (Sofia Serrano), Kurt Russell (Dr. Curtis McCabe), Cameron Diaz (Julie), Johnny Galecki (Peter), Jean Carol (Woman in New York), Jennifer Aspen (Nina), Zachary Lee (Joshua), Jason Lee (Brian). Directed by Cameron Crowe and produced by Tom Cruise and Paula Wagner. Screenplay by Crowe, based on a film by Alejandro Amenabar and Mateo Gil.

Think it all the way through, and Cameron Crowe's *Vanilla Sky* is a scrupulously moral picture. It tells the story of a man who has just about everything, thinks he can have it all, is given a means to have whatever he wants, and loses it because—well, maybe because he has a conscience. Or maybe not. Maybe just because life sucks. Or maybe he only thinks it does. This is the kind of movie you don't want to analyze until you've seen it two times.

I've seen it two times. I went to a second screening because after the first screening I thought I knew what had happened, but was nagged by the idea that certain things might not have happened the way I thought they had. Now that I've seen it twice, I think I understand it, or maybe not. Certainly it's entertaining as it rolls along, and there is wonderful chemistry of two quite different kinds between Tom Cruise and Cameron Diaz, on the one hand, and Tom Cruise and Penelope Cruz, on the other.

Vanilla Sky, like the 2001 pictures *Memento* and *Mulholland Dr.,* requires the audience to do some heavy lifting. It's got one of those plots that doubles back on itself like an Escher staircase. You get along splendidly one step at a time, but when you get to the top floor you find yourself on the bottom landing. If it's any consolation, its hero is as baffled as we are; it's not that he has memory loss, like the hero of *Memento,* but that in a certain sense he may have no real memory at all.

Cruise stars as David Aames, a thirty-three-year-old tycoon who inherited a publishing empire when his parents were killed in a car crash. His condo is like the Sharper Image catalog died and went to heaven. He has a sex buddy named Julie (Cameron Diaz) and he thinks they can sleep together and remain just friends, but as she eventually has to explain, "When you sleep with someone, your body makes a promise whether you do or not." At a party, he locks eyes with Sofia Serrano (Penelope Cruz), who arrives as the date of his friend Brian (Jason Lee) but ends up spending the night with him. Even though they don't have sex, it looks to me like their bodies are making promises to each other.

At this point the movie starts unveiling surprises that I should not reveal. A lot of surprises. Surprises on top of surprises. The movie is about these surprises, however, and so I must either end this review right now, or reveal some of them.

The End.

Okay, for those of us still in the room, and without revealing *too* much: Julie drives up just as David is leaving after his night with Sofia, offers him a lift, drives off a bridge in Central Park, kills herself, and lands him in front of "the best plastic surgeon in New York" with a horribly scarred face. This time thread is intercut with another one in which a psychiatrist (Kurt Russell) is interrogating David about a murder. He insists there was no murder. Maybe there was and maybe there wasn't, and maybe the victim was who we think it is, and maybe not.

Vanilla Sky has started as if it is about David's life and loves. It reveals an entirely different orientation (which I will not reveal even here in the room), and, to be fair, there is a full explanation. The only problem with the explanation is that it explains the *mechanism* of our confusion, rather than telling us for sure what actually happened.

That's why I went to see it a second time. In general, my second viewing was greatly helped by my first, and I was able to understand events more clearly. But there was one puzzling detail. At the second viewing, I noticed that the first words in the movie ("open your eyes") are unmistakably said in the voice of Sofia, the Penelope Cruz character. If the movie's explanation of this voice is correct, at that point in the movie David has not met Sofia, or heard her voice.

How can we account for her voice appearing before she does? There is a character in the movie who refers to a "splice." We are told where the splice takes place. But consider the source of this information—not the person supplying it, but the underlying source. Is the information reliable? Or does the splice take place, so to speak, before the movie begins? And in that case . . . but see the movie and ask the question for yourself.

Note: Early in the film, there's an astonishing shot of Tom Cruise absolutely alone in Times Square. You might assume, as I did, that computers were involved. Cameron Crowe told me the scene is not faked; the film got city permission to block off Times Square for three hours early on a Sunday morning. Just outside of camera range there are cops and barricades to hold back the traffic.

Va Savoir ★ ★ ★
PG-13, 150 m., 2001

Jeanne Balibar (Camille), Sergio Castillitto (Ugo), Marianne Basler (Sonia), Jacques Bonnaffe (Pierre), Helene de Fougerolles (Do), Bruno Todeschini (Arthur), Catherine Rouvel (Madame Desprez), Claude Berri (Autograph Librarian). Directed by Jacques Rivette and produced by Martine Marignac. Screenplay by Pascal Bonitzer, Christine Laurent, and Rivette.

One reason to see *Va Savoir* is to want to know these people. Art films can encourage escapism too. Some moviegoers like Julia Roberts and others like Jeanne Balibar, but we all have the same pipes and valves pumping away inside. Jeanne Balibar. A little like Audrey Hepburn, the way she wears those little sweaters tightly buttoned over her tummy. Skinny, lithe, confident. Jacques Rivette loves women helplessly. You can say all you want about what a great director he is, but you must remember that he founded the French New Wave along with Jean-Luc Godard, who said, "The history of cinema is boys photographing girls."

Rivette is seventy-three now, and *Va Savoir,* which translates as *Who Knows?* is the kind of film a young man might make if he were seventy-three. It's a farce involving six characters who fall in love with one another in inconvenient and unforeseen combinations. Some of them are involved in the production of a play by Pirandello, who wrote farces about six people—a convenient number for onstage chaos. The action is a farce, with people being locked into rooms, stealing jewelry, cheating on their wives, and challenging each other to ridiculous duels. But the pacing is more leisurely—a farce in waltz time.

Clip and save: Camille (Jeanne Balibar), an actress, has been away from Paris for three years. She returns in a production being directed by Ugo (Sergio Castillitto), her new husband. Pierre (Jacques Bonnaffe) is her old boyfriend, now married to Sonia (Marianne Basler). Dominique (Helene de Fourgerolles), known as Do, is the daughter in a rich family with a famous library. Her half-brother Arthur (Bruno Todeschini) is a rotter who is having an affair with Sonia.

Now rotate everyone one position. Camille finds Pierre just where she knew she would find him, on a bench reading his morning paper. He is a creature of habit. Pierre finds he still loves Camille. Ugo is obsessed with finding a missing play by Goldoni, calls on the rich family and falls in love with Do. This happens while she is on a ladder in the library. No woman ever stands on a ladder in a library in the movies without getting kissed. Arthur goes through the motions of seducing Sonia because he wants to steal her jewels.

Now rotate everyone again. Camille eludes the trap Pierre has set for her. Sonia discovers Arthur's treachery and enlists Camille to steal back the jewelry. Ugo and Camille fight over the play, and Camille walks offstage before her bow on opening night. Ugo discovers Pierre is in love with Camille, and challenges him to a duel. Arthur . . . but you see how it goes.

All of these people are so sleek. In the manner of a certain class of French person, they know exactly who they are, what they stand for, how to behave, and what rules must not be violated even though all the others can be. Around and around they go, bemused, intrigued, as if they are adding elements to an emotional test tube, curious to see whether they will get a love potion or an explosion.

Jacques Rivette loves characters. His best-known films include *Celine and Julie Go Boat-*

ing (1974) and *La Belle Noiseuse* (1991). Both are twice as long as most movies, and consist of the minute and loving appreciation of beautiful young women—not their bodies, but their spirits, their amusement, their style. (Rivette also once made a version of *Joan of Arc*, a reminder that Godard finished his quote by adding, "The history of history is boys burning girls at the stake.")

Va Savoir is the kind of movie you settle into. It's supple and sophisticated, and it's not about much. It has no message and some will say it has no point. But it is a demonstration of grace and wit, it is photographed as a lesson in how to carry yourself, and it has such good manners as it leads us into such absurd situations. The duel has a kind of calm, insane genius to it.

The Vertical Ray of the Sun ★ ★ ★
NO MPAA RATING, 112 m., 2001

Tran Nu Yen-Khe (Lien), Nguyen Nhu Quynh (Suong), Le Khanh (Khanh), Ngo Quang Hai (Brother Hai), Tran Manh Cuong (Khanh's Husband Kien), Chu Ngoc Hung (Suong's Husband Quoc), Le Tuan Anh (Suong's Lover Tuan), Le Van Loc (Hai's Friend Loc). Directed by Tran Anh Hung, and produced by Christophe Rossignon. Screenplay by Tran.

The Vertical Ray of the Sun is beautiful, languorous, passive—it plays like background music for itself. Filmed in a Hanoi that looks more like an Asian love hotel than a city, it's a lush, sensuous work—the film equivalent of those old Mantovani albums with names like *Music for Lovers Only*. It tells the stories of three sisters, two married, one single, and although it contains adulteries in the present, rumors of adultery in the past, one or perhaps two pregnancies, and a hint of incestuous feelings, it would be fair to say that hardly anything happens.

Let me describe one shot. In the left foreground, a woman reclines on a bed. In the right background, a man looks out the window. It is raining. He is smoking. She lights a cigarette. For a time nothing happens except for the pleasure they take in silent companionship and smoking together. This time, passing

in this intimacy without words, is a moment that says so much about their comfort in each other's company that we realize most movies are about people who are *doing* instead of *being*.

Little surprise that the director, Tran Anh Hung, grew up in Paris to love the work of Robert Bresson, that French master of films that were about the essence, not the adventures, of his characters. Tran was born in Vietnam, moved to France with his family at the age of six, and made the remarkable debut film *Scent of Green Papaya* in 1993 when he was still in his twenties. It was the love story of a simple servant girl and a sophisticated rich boy, and it was set in French-ruled Saigon—a Saigon created for the film, astonishingly, entirely on a Parisian sound stage. Then came a trip to Vietnam to film *Cyclo*, a rougher, more realistic story about street life in what had become Ho Chi Minh City. Now here is *Vertical Ray of the Sun*, filmed in Hanoi, but a Hanoi no more realistic than the Paris in MGM musicals like *An American in Paris*.

"I wanted my film to feel like a caress," Tran told Trevor Johnston of the *London Independent*. "It had to have a gentle smile floating through it, a sort of floating feeling." He wanted to find a style, he said, "which didn't present the drama as a series of emotional problems for the various couples." He has been so successful that his film may be maddening for those who expect conflict in their movies. The various couples do in fact have emotional problems, but they live in a sea of such emotional contentment that unhappiness is a wave that crests briefly and falls back, forgotten.

We meet three sisters. Lien, the youngest, is played by Tran Nu Yen-Khe, who is Tran's wife and was the star of *Green Papaya*. She still lives at home with her twin brother, Hai (Ngo Quang Hai). At times they chase each other around the house like children. At other times he awakens to find her in his bed because she "got lonely" in the night. "People think we are courting," she says with delight as they walk in the street. They talk about what he would do if she ever got married. This is emotional, not physical incest.

Their older sister Khanh (Le Khanh) is married to a novelist who says he is stuck on the ending of a novel that may not even have a be-ginning. She has, for me, the most luminous moment in the movie, in a close two-shot where she is filled with something she wants to say and then says it: She is pregnant. Do you know how a woman's lips look when she de-lays with delight, holding back happy news? The pause before she speaks is a moment of such beauty. The third sister is Suong (Nguyen Nhu Quynh), whose husband is obsessed with his photographs of rare plant species. Some-times, she says, she thinks he cares more about his plants than about her. Actually, he also cares about another woman he lives with secretly on the island where he collects his specimens; they have a child. The nature of his life explains his long absences to both women, but Suong has a breathtaking scene where she tells him what she knows, how she knows it, and what she expects him to do about it.

The title, which can also be translated as *At the Height of Summer,* captures a season of heat and humidity when motion is to be avoided and the most luxurious time of the day is wak-ing while it is still cool. The sisters meet to prepare meals, gossip, confess, and speculate. The men are more vaguely drawn. The film finds it so unnecessary to conclude and solve the characters' problems that after it's over you may not be able to remember if it did. It is not about incident, but about nostalgia for the slowness and peace of days past.

Here is Tran again, in the London interview: "My thoughts turned back to my childhood in Danang, remembering the time when I'd be waiting to fall asleep at night, my mind racing from one thing to another, nothing precise. The smell of fruit coming in through the win-dow, a woman's voice singing on the radio. Everything was so vague. It was like a feeling of suspension. If I've ever experienced har-mony in my life it was then. It was just a matter of translating that rhythm and that musicality into the new film."

Reading those words, I was reminded of a little-known but evocative film by Robert Alt-man named *Thieves Like Us* (1974) in which, in a small frame house in the summertime, on Sunday afternoon perhaps, the characters sit dozing in easy chairs, and from a distant room comes the sound of a song on the radio. On such warm and idle afternoons there is the possibility that lovemaking lies ahead, or per-haps it lies behind; it is too much to think about just now.

View from the Top ★ ★ ★
PG-13, 87 m., 2003

Gwyneth Paltrow (Donna), Mark Ruffalo (Ted), Christina Applegate (Christine), Mike Myers (John Whitney), Candice Bergen (Sally), Kelly Preston (Sherry), Rob Lowe (Copilot Steve). Directed by Bruno Barreto and produced by Matthew Baer, Bobby Cohen, and Brad Grey. Screenplay by Eric Wald.

View from the Top stars Gwyneth Paltrow in a sweet and sort of innocent story about a small-town girl who knows life holds more for her, and how a job as a flight attendant becomes her escape route. Along the way she meets friends who help her and friends who double-cross her, a guy who dumps her, and a guy she dumps. And she finds love. What more do you want from a movie?

I confess I expected something else. Flight at-tendants have been asking me for weeks about this movie, which they are in a lather to see. It may be closer to their real lives than they expect. I anticipated an updated version of *Coffee, Tea or Me?* but what I got instead was *Donna the Flight Attendant.* The movie reminded me of career books I read in the seventh grade with ti-tles like *Bob Durham, Boy Radio Announcer.* It's a little more sophisticated, of course, but it has the same good heart, and a teenager thinking of a career in the air might really enjoy it.

So did I, in an uncomplicated way. Paltrow is lovable in the right roles, and here she's joined by two others who are sunny on the screen: Candice Bergen, as the best-selling au-thor/flight attendant who becomes her men-tor, and Mark Ruffalo (from *You Can Count on Me*) as the law student who wants to marry her. The movie knows a secret; most careers do not involve clawing your way to the top, but depend on the kindness of the strangers you meet along the way, who help you just because they feel like it.

We meet Donna (Paltrow) as the daughter of a much-married former exotic dancer from Silver Springs, Nevada. She seems doomed to a life working at the mall until she sees a TV interview with the best-selling Bergen, whose book inspires Donna to train as a flight attendant. Her first stop is a puddle jumper named Sierra Airlines, which flies mostly to and from Fresno, but then she enrolls in training at Royalty Airlines, where the instructor (Mike Myers) is bitter because his crossed eye kept him from flying. Myers finds a delicate balance between lampoon and poignancy—and that's some balance.

Ruffalo plays the sometime law student who comes into her life in Nevada and then again in Cleveland, where she's assigned not to Royalty's transatlantic routes but to the discount Royalty Express. Her first flight is comic (she runs down the aisle screaming, "We're gonna crash!") and then we follow her through intrigues and romantic episodes that lead to a lonely Christmas in Paris when she decides life *still* has to offer more than this.

The movie, directed by Bruno Barreto and written by Eric Wald, is surprising for what it doesn't contain: no scenes involving mile-high clubs, lecherous businessmen, or randy pilots, but the sincere story of a woman who finds her career is almost but not quite enough. Adult audiences may be underwhelmed. Not younger teenage girls, who will be completely fascinated.

The Visit ★ ★ ★
R, 107 m., 2001

Hill Harper (Alex Waters), Obba Babatunde (Tony Waters), Rae Dawn Chong (Felicia McDonald), Billy Dee Williams (Henry Waters), Marla Gibbs (Lois Waters), Phylicia Rashad (Dr. Coles), Talia Shire (Marilyn Coffey), David Clennon (Bill Brenner). Directed and produced by Jordan Walker-Pearlman. Screenplay by Walker-Pearlman, based on the play by Kosmond Russell.

The Visit tells the story of a thirty-two-year-old prison inmate, up for parole, dying of AIDS, trying to come to terms with his past. In a series of prison visits with his parents, his brother, a prison psychiatrist, and a woman who was his childhood friend, he moves slowly from anger to acceptance—he becomes a better person.

This outline sounds perhaps too pious to be absorbing, and the final scenes lay on the message a little thick. But *The Visit* contains some effective performances, not least from Hill Harper as Alex, the hero. I remembered him from *Loving Jezebel* and from a supporting role in *He Got Game*, but wasn't prepared for the depth here; this performance announcing Harper is to be taken seriously. Another surprise comes from Billy Dee Williams; we think of him as a traditional leading man, but here he is as a proud, angry, unyielding father—an authority figure who takes it as a personal affront that his son has gone wrong.

But has he gone wrong? Alex is doing twenty-five years for a rape he says he didn't commit. His mother (Marla Gibbs) believes him. His father remembers that Alex stole from them, lied to them, was a junkie and a thief, and thinks him capable of anything. Alex's brother Tony (Obba Babatunde), well dressed, successful, mirrors the father's attitudes; it diminishes them to have a prisoner in the family.

The movie doesn't crank up the volume with violence and jailhouse clichés, but focuses on this person and his possibilities for change. The key law enforcement officials are not sadistic guards or authoritarian wardens, but people who listen. Phylicia Rashad plays the psychiatrist, trying to lead him past denial into acceptance, and there are several scenes involving a parole board that are driven by insight, not the requirements of the drama. The board members, led by Talia Shire, discuss his case, express their doubts, get mad at one another, seem real.

Rae Dawn Chong plays Felicia, the old friend, who has her own demons; a former addict and a prostitute, she killed an abusive father, but now has her life together and visits Alex at the urging of Tony (it's perceptive of the movie to notice how reluctant family members often recruit volunteers to do their emotional heavy-lifting). Her story and other conversations trigger flashbacks and fantasies, in a story that has enormous empathy for this man at the end of a lost life. (The screenplay by director Jordan Walker-Pearlman is from a play by Kosmond Russell, based on his relationship with a brother in prison.)

Watching the movie, I was reminded of a powerful moment in *The Shawshank Redemption*, when the Morgan Freeman character, paroled as an old man, is asked if he has reformed. He says such words have no meaning. He is no longer the same person who committed the crime. He would give anything, he says, to grab that young punk he once was and shake some sense into him. *The Visit* is about the same process—the fact that the prisoner we see is not the same person who was convicted. If, that is, he is lucky enough to grow and change. The last act of *The Visit* hurries that process too much, but the journey is worth taking.

W

Waking Life ★ ★ ★ ★
R, 99 m., 2001

Featuring the voices and animated likenesses of Wiley Wiggins, Trevor Jack Brooks, Robert C. Solomon, Ethan Hawke, Julie Delpy, Charles Gunning, David Sosa, Alex Jones, Aklilu Gebrewald, Carol Dawson, Lisa Moore, Steve Fitch, Steven Prince, Adam Goldberg, Nicky Katt, David Martinez, Tiana Hux, Speed Levitch, Steven Soderbergh, and Richard Linklater. Directed by Richard Linklater and produced by Anne Walker-McBay, Tommy Pallotta, Palmer West, and Jonah Smith. Screenplay by Linklater and the cast members. Animation directed by Bob Sabiston.

Waking Life could not come at a better time. Opening in the sad and fearful days soon after September 11, it celebrates a series of articulate, intelligent characters who seek out the meaning of their existence and do not have the answers. At a time when madmen think they have the right to kill us because of what they think they know about an afterlife, which is by definition unknowable, those who don't know the answers are the only ones asking sane questions. True believers owe it to the rest of us to seek solutions that are reasonable in the visible world.

The movie is like a cold shower of bracing, clarifying ideas. We feel cleansed of boredom, indifference, futility, and the deadening tyranny of the mundane. The characters walk around passionately discussing ideas, theories, ultimate purposes—just as we've started doing again since the complacent routine of our society was shaken. When we were students we often spoke like this, but in adult life it is hard to find intelligent conversation. "What is my purpose?" is replaced by "What did the market do today?"

The movie is as exhilarating in its style and visuals as in its ideas—indeed, the two are interlocked. Richard Linklater and his collaborators have filmed a series of conversations, debates, rants, monologues, and speculations, and then animated their film using a new process that creates a shimmering, pulsating life on the screen: This movie seems alive, seems vibrating with urgency and excitement.

The animation is curiously realistic. A still from the film would look to you like a drawing. But go to www.wakinglifemovie.com and click on the clips to see how the sound and movement have an effect that is eerily lifelike. The most difficult thing for an animator may be to capture an unplanned, spontaneous movement that expresses personality. By filming real people and then animating them, *Waking Life* captures little moments of real life: a musician putting down her cigarette, a double-take, someone listening while eager to start talking again, a guy smiling as if to say, "I'm not really smiling." And the dialogue has the true ring of everyday life, perhaps because most of the actors helped create their own words: The movie doesn't sound like a script but like eavesdropping.

The film's hero, not given a name, is played by Wiley Wiggins as a young man who has returned to the town where once, years ago, a playmate's folding paper toy (we used to call them "cootie catchers") unfolded to show him the words, "dream is destiny." He seems to be in a dream, and complains that although he knows it's a dream, he can't awaken. He wanders from one person and place to another (something like the camera did in Linklater's first film, *Slackers*). He encounters theories, beliefs, sanity, nuttiness. People try to explain what they believe, but he is overwhelmed until finally he is able to see that the answer is—curiosity itself. To not have the answers is expected. To not ask questions is a crime against your own mind.

If I have made the movie sound somber and contemplative, I have been unfair to it. Few movies are more cheerful and alive. The people encountered by the dreamer in his journey are intoxicated by their ideas—deliriously verbal. We recognize some of them: Ethan Hawke and Julie Delpy, from Linklater's *Before Sunrise,* continue their conversation. Speed Levitch, the manic tour guide from the documentary *The Cruise,* is still on his guided tour of life. Other characters are long known to Linklater, including Robert C. Solomon, a philosopher at the University of Texas, who comes on-screen to say something Linklater remembers him saying in a lecture years ago, that existentialism offers more hope than predestination, because it gives us a reason to try to change things.

I have seen *Waking Life* three times now. I want to see it again—not to master it, or even to remember it better (I would not want to read the screenplay), but simply to experience all of these ideas, all of this passion, the very act of trying to figure things out. It must be depressing to believe that you have been supplied with all the answers, that you must believe them and that to question them is disloyal or a sin. Were we given minds in order to fear the questions?

Waking Up in Reno ★ ½

R, 100 m., 2002

Billy Bob Thornton (Lonnie Earl), Charlize Theron (Candy), Patrick Swayze (Roy), Natasha Richardson (Darlene), Brent Briscoe (Russell Whitehead), Mark Fauser (Boyd). Directed by Jordan Brady and produced by Ben Myron, Robert Salerno, and Dwight Yoakam. Screenplay by Brent Briscoe and Mark Fauser.

Waking Up in Reno is another one of those road comedies where southern roots are supposed to make boring people seem colorful. If these characters were from Minneapolis or Denver, no way anyone would make a film about them. But because they're from Little Rock, Arkansas, and wear stuff made out of snakeskin and carry their own cases of Pabst into the hotel room, they're movie-worthy.

Well, they could be, if they had anything really at risk. But the movie is way too gentle to back them into a corner. They're nice people whose problems are all solved with sitcom dialogue, and the profoundly traditional screenplay makes sure that love and family triumph in the end. Surprising that Billy Bob Thornton, Charlize Theron, Natasha Richardson, and Patrick Swayze would fall for this, but Swayze *did* make *Road House,* so maybe it's not so surprising in his case.

Thornton stars as Lonnie Earl, a Little Rock car dealer who appears in his own commercials and cheats on his wife, Darlene (Richardson). He cheats with Candy (Theron), the wife of his best friend, Roy (Swayze). Actually, they only cheat twice, but if that's like only being a little bit pregnant, maybe she is.

The two couples decide to pull a brand-new SUV off of Lonnie Earl's lot and take a trip to Reno, with stops along the way in Texas (where Lonnie Earl wants to win a seventy-two-ounce steak-eating contest) and maybe at the Grand Canyon. Others have their dreams, too; Darlene has always had a special place in her heart for Tony Orlando, ever since she saw him on the Jerry Lewis telethon. And that's the sort of dialogue detail that's supposed to tip us off how down-home and lovable these people are: They like Tony Orlando, they watch Jerry Lewis. We sense that director Jordan Brady and writers Brent Briscoe and Mark Fauser don't like Tony Orlando and Jerry Lewis as much as the characters do, but the movie's not mean enough to say so, and so any comic point is lost.

That kind of disconnect happens all through the movie: The filmmakers create satirical characters and then play them straight. We're actually expected to sympathize with these caricatures, as Lonnie Earl barely survives the seventy-two-ounce steak and they arrive in Reno for run-ins with the hotel bellboys and the hooker in the bar.

Consider the scene where the helpful bellboy hauls their luggage into their suite and then loiters suggestively for a tip. "Oh, I get it," says Lonnie Earl. "You want your dollar." And he gives him one. The problem here is that no real-life Little Rock car dealer would conceivably believe that the correct tip for luggage for four people would be one dollar. Lonnie Earl must be moderately wealthy, has traveled, has tipped before, is not entirely clueless. But the movie shortchanges his character to get an easy (and very cheap) laugh.

The action in Reno mostly centers around Candy's attempts to get pregnant, her monitoring of her ovular temperature, Roy's obligation to leap into action at every prompt, and the revelation that . . . well, without going into details, let's say secrets are revealed that would more wisely have been left concealed, and that Lonnie Earl, Roy, Candy, and Darlene find themselves in a situation that in the real world could lead to violence but here is settled in about the same way that the Mertzes worked things out with Lucy and Desi.

Yes, the characters are pleasant. Yes, in some grudging way we are happy that they're happy. No, we do not get teary-eyed with sentiment when the movie evokes the Grand Canyon in an attempt to demonstrate that the problems of four little people don't amount to a hill of beans. At the end of the movie titled *Grand Canyon* (1992), I actually was emotionally touched as the characters looked out over the awesome immensity. But then they were real characters, and nothing in *Waking Up in Reno* ever inspired me to think of its inhabitants as anything more than markers in a screenplay.

A Walk to Remember ★ ★ ★

PG, 100 m., 2002

Mandy Moore (Jamie Sullivan), Shane West (Landon Carter), Daryl Hannah (Cynthia Carter), Peter Coyote (Reverend Sullivan), Lauren German (Belinda), Clayne Crawford (Dean). Directed by Adam Shankman and produced by Denise Di Novi and Hunt Lowry. Screenplay by Karen Janszen, based on the novel by Nicholas Sparks.

A Walk to Remember is a love story so sweet, sincere, and positive that it sneaks past the defenses built up in this age of irony. It tells the story of a romance between two eighteen-year-olds that is summarized when the boy tells the girl's doubtful father: "Jamie has faith in me. She makes me want to be different. Better." After all of the vulgar crudities of the typical modern teenage movie, here is one that looks closely, pays attention, sees that not all teenagers are as cretinous as Hollywood portrays them.

Mandy Moore, a natural beauty in both face and manner, stars as Jamie Sullivan, an outsider at school who is laughed at because she stands apart, has values, and always wears the same ratty blue sweater. Her father (Peter Coyote) is a local minister. Shane West plays Landon Carter, a senior boy who hangs with the popular crowd but is shaken when a stupid dare goes wrong and one of his friends is paralyzed in a diving accident. He dates a popular girl and joins in the laughter against Jamie. Then, as punishment for the prank, he is ordered by the principal to join the drama club: "You need to meet some new people."

Jamie's in the club. He begins to notice her in a new way. He asks her to help him rehearse for a role in a play. She treats him with level honesty. She isn't one of those losers who skulks around feeling put-upon; her self-esteem stands apart from the opinion of her peers. She's a smart, nice girl, a reminder that one of the pleasures of the movies is to meet good people.

The plot has revelations that I will not betray. Enough to focus on the way Jamie's serene example makes Landon into a nicer person—encourages him to become more sincere and serious to win her respect. There are setbacks along the way, as in a painful scene at school where she approaches him while he's with his old friends and says, "See you tonight," and he says, "In your dreams." When he turns up at her house, she is hurt and angry, and his excuses sound lame even to him.

The movie walks a fine line with the Peter Coyote character, whose church Landon attends. Movies have a way of stereotyping reactionary Bible-thumpers who are hostile to teen romance. There is a little of that here; Jamie is forbidden to date, for example, although there's more behind her father's decision than knee-jerk strictness. But when Landon goes to the Reverend Sullivan and asks him to have faith in him, the minister listens with an open mind.

Yes, the movie is corny at times. But corniness is all right at times. I forgave the movie its broad emotion because it earned it. It lays things on a little thick at the end, but by then it has paid its way. Director Adam Shankman and his writer, Karen Janszen, working from the novel by Nicholas Sparks, have an unforced trust in the material that redeems, even justifies, the broad strokes. They go wrong only three times: (1) The subplot involving the paralyzed boy should either have been dealt with or dropped. (2) It's tiresome to make the black teenager use "brother" in every sentence, as if he is not their peer but was ported in from another world. (3) As Kuleshov proved more than eighty years ago in a famous experiment, when an audience sees an impassive close-up it supplies the necessary emotion from the context. It can be fatal for an actor to try to "act" in a close-up, and Landon's little smile at the end is a distraction at a crucial moment.

Those are small flaws in a touching movie. The performances by Mandy Moore and Shane

West are so quietly convincing we're reminded that many teenagers in movies seem to think like thirty-year-old stand-up comics. That Jamie and Landon base their romance on values and respect will blindside some viewers of the film, especially since the first five or ten minutes seem to be headed down a familiar teenage movie trail. *A Walk to Remember* is a small treasure.

Warm Water Under a Red Bridge
★ ★ ★

NO MPAA RATING, 119 m., 2002

Koji Yakusho (Yosuke Sasano), Misa Shimizu (Saeko Aizawa), Mitsuko Baisho (Mitsu), Mansaku Fuwa (Gen), Kazuo Kitamura (Taro), Isao Natsuyagi (Masayuki Uomi), Yukiya Kitamura (Shintaro Uomi), Hijiri Kojima (Miki Tagami). Directed by Shohei Imamura and produced by Hisa Iino. Screenplay by Motofumi Tomikawa, Daisuke Tengan, and Imamura, based on a book by Yo Henmi.

Warm Water Under a Red Bridge has modern automobiles and supermarkets, telephones and pepper cheese imported from Europe, but it resonates like an ancient Japanese myth. Imagine a traveler in search of treasure who finds a woman with special needs that only he can fulfill, and who repays him by ending his misery.

Shohei Imamura, one of the greatest Japanese directors, tells this story with the energy and delight of a fairy tale, but we in the West are not likely to see it so naively, because unlike the Japanese we are touchy on the subject of bodily fluids. In Japan, natural functions are accepted calmly as a part of life, and there is a celebrated children's book about farts. No doubt a Japanese audience would view *Warm Water* entirely differently than a North American one—because, you see, the heroine has a condition that causes water to build up in her body, and it can only be released by sexual intercourse.

Water arrives in puddles and rivulets, in sprays and splashes. "Don't worry," Saeko (Misa Shimizu) cheerfully tells Yosuke, the hero. "It's not urine." It is instead—well, what? The water of life? Of growth and renewal? Is she a water goddess? When it runs down the steps of her house and into the river, fish grow large and numerous. And it seems to have a similar effect on Yosuke (Koji Yakusho, from *Shall We Dance?* and *The Eel*). From a pallid, hopeless wanderer in the early scenes, he grows into a bold lover and a brave ocean fisherman.

As the film opens, Yosuke is broke and jobless, fielding incessant cell phone calls from his nagging wife, who wants an update on his job searches. In despair, he hunkers down next to the river with an old philosopher named Taro (Kazuo Kitamura), who tells him a story. Long ago, he says, right after the war, he was stealing to get the money to eat, and he took a gold Buddha from a temple. He left it in an upstairs room of a house next to a red bridge, where he assumes it remains to this day.

Yosuke takes a train to the town named by the old man, finds the bridge, finds the house, and follows Saeko from it into a supermarket where he sees her shoplift some cheese while standing in a puddle. From the puddle he retrieves her earring (a dolphin, of course) and returns it to her, and she asks if he'd like some cheese and then forthrightly tells him, "You saw me steal the cheese. Then you saw the puddle of water."

All true. She explains her problem. The water builds up and must be "vented," often by doing "something wicked" like shoplifting. It is, she adds, building up right now—and soon they are having intercourse to the delight of the fish in the river below.

This story is unthinkable in a Hollywood movie, but there is something about the matter-of-fact way Saeko explains her problem, and the surprised but not stunned way that Yosuke hears her, that takes the edge off. If women are a source of life, and if water is where life began, then—well, whatever. It is important to note that the sex in the movie is not erotic or titillating in any way—it's more like a therapeutic process—and that the movie is not sex-minded, but more delighted with the novelty of Saeko's problem. Only in a nation where bodily functions are discussed in a matter-of-fact way, where nude public bathing is no big deal, where shame about human plumbing has not been ritualized, could this movie play in the way Imamura intended. But seeing it as a Westerner is an enlightening, even liberating, experience.

Imamura, now seventy-six, is also the director of the masterpieces *The Insect Woman* (1963), about a woman whose only priority is her own comfort and survival; *Ballad of Narayama* (1982), the heartbreaking story of a village where the old are left on the side of a mountain to die; and *Black Rain* (1989), not the Michael Douglas thriller, but a harrowing human story about the days and months after the bomb was dropped on Hiroshima.

At his age he seems freed from convention, and in *Warm Water,* for example, he cuts loose from this world to include a dream in which Saeko floats like a embryo in a cosmic cloud. There is also an effortless fusion of old and new. The notion of a man leaving his nagging wife and home and finding succor from a goddess is from ancient myth, and the fact that he would then turn to wrest his living from the sea is not unheard of. But throwing his cell phone overboard, now that's a modern touch.

Wasabi ★ ½
R, 94 m., 2001

Jean Reno (Hubert Fiorentini), Ryoko Hirosue (Yumi Yoshimido), Michel Muller (Momo), Carole Bouquet (Sofia), Ludovic Berthillot (Jean-Baptiste 1), Yan Epstein (Jean-Baptiste 2), Michel Scourneau (Van Eyck), Christian Sinniger (The Squale), Jean-Marc Montalto (Olivier). Directed by Gérard Krawczyk and produced by Luc Besson. Screenplay by Besson.

Jean Reno has the weary eyes and unshaven mug of a French Peter Falk, and some of the same sardonic humor too. He sighs and smokes and slouches his way through thrillers where he sadly kills those who would kill him, and balefully regards women who want to make intimate demands on his time. In good movies *(The Crimson Rivers)* and bad *(Rollerball),* in the ambitious (Michelangelo Antonioni's *Beyond the Clouds*) and the avaricious *(Godzilla),* in comedies *(Just Visiting)* and thrillers *(Ronin),* he shares with Robert Mitchum the unmistakable quality of having seen it all.

Wasabi is not his worst movie, and is far from his best. It is a thriller trapped inside a pop comedy set in Japan, and gives Reno a chirpy young costar who bounces around him like a puppy on visiting day at the drunk tank. She plays his daughter, and he's supposed to like her, but sometimes he looks like he hopes she will turn into an aspirin.

The movie begins in Paris, where Reno plays Hubert Fiorentini, a Dirty Harry type who doesn't merely beat up suspects, but beats up people on the chance that he may suspect them later. During a raid on a nightclub, he makes the mistake of socking the police chief's son so hard the lad flies down a flight of stairs and ends up in a full-body cast. Hubert is ordered to take a vacation.

He shrugs, and thinks to look up an old girlfriend (Carole Bouquet), but then his life takes a dramatic turn. He learns of the death in Japan of a woman he loved years earlier. Arriving for her funeral, he finds she has left him a mysterious key, a daughter he knew nothing about, and $200 million in the bank.

The daughter is named Yumi (Ryoko Hirosue). She is nineteen, has red hair, chooses her wardrobe colors from the Pokemon palette, and bounces crazily through scenes as if life is a music video and they're filming her right now.

The plot involves Yumi's plan to hire the Yakuza (Japanese mafia) to get revenge for her mother's death. If there is a piece of fatherly advice that Hubert the veteran cop could have shared with her, it is that no one related to $200 million should do the least thing to attract the attention of the Yakuza. The plot then unfolds in bewildering alternation between pop comedy and action violence, with Hubert dancing in a video arcade one moment and blasting the bad guys the next.

There is no artistic purpose for this movie. It is product. Luc Besson, who wrote and produced it, has another movie out right now *(The Transporter),* and indeed has written, produced, or announced sixteen other movies since this one was made in far-ago 2001. Jean Reno does what he can in a thankless dilemma, the film ricochets from humor to violence and back again, and Ryoko Hirosue makes us wonder if she is always like that. If she is, I owe an apology to the Powerpuff Girls. I didn't know they were based on real life.

The Wedding Planner ★ ★
PG-13, 100 m., 2001

Jennifer Lopez (Mary Fiore), Matthew McConaughey (Steve Edison), Bridgette

Wilson-Sampras (Fran Donelly), Justin Chambers (Massimo), Alex Rocco (Mary's Father), Erik Hyler (Dancer), Huntley Ritter (Tom). Directed by Adam Shankman and produced by Peter Abrams, Deborah Del Prete, Jennifer Gibgot, Robert L. Levy, and Gigi Pritzker. Screenplay by Pamela Falk and Michael Ellis.

Jennifer Lopez looks soulfully into the eyes of Matthew McConaughey, but is he looking back? One of the many problems of *The Wedding Planner* is that we can't tell and don't much care. When a plot depends on two people falling in love when they absolutely should not, we have to be able to believe at some level that they have been swept up by a destiny beyond their control. McConaughey seems less inflamed by his sudden new romance than resigned to it.

Lopez stars in the title role as Mary Fiore—yes, a wedding planner. With her walkie-talkie headset, cell phone, clipboard, spotters, and video crews, she's mission control as her clients walk down the aisle. Racing to an appointment, she meets Dr. Steve Edison (McConaughey) in one of the most absurd Meet Cutes in many a moon. Her Gucci heel gets stuck in a manhole cover, a garbage Dumpster rolls down a hill toward her, and Steve hurls her out of the way and, of course, lands on top of her; it's love at first full-body contact.

That night they have a perfect date, watching movies in the park. Mary has always been the wedding planner, never the bride (uh-huh—this is as convincing as Julia Roberts's old flame choosing another bride in *My Best Friend's Wedding*). Now she walks on air, until her current client, the millionairess Fran Donelly (Bridgette Wilson-Sampras), introduces Mary to the man Fran will marry, who is, of course, Dr. Steve Edison.

If Steve is engaged, why did he mislead Mary with that night of movies and soul talk? Because he is a dishonest louse, or, as the movie explains it, because he had no idea he would be thunderstruck by love. Since he is in love with Mary, the only sensible thing to do is call off his wedding to Fran and buy a season ticket to movies in the park. But the movie cannot abide common sense, and recycles decades of clichés about the wrong people

getting married and the right ones making stupid decisions.

There are times when the movie's contrivance is agonizing. Consider all the plot mechanics involving Mary's Italian-American father (Alex Rocco) and his schemes to marry her off to Massimo, her childhood playmate from the old country (Calvin Klein model Justin Chambers, sounding as Italian as most people named Chambers). Consider how Mary spends her free time (on a Scrabble team) and how she accepts a proposal of marriage by spelling "OK" with Scrabble tiles when "Yes" would be more appropriate plus get her more points.

And consider a "comic" sequence so awkward and absurd it not only brings the movie to a halt but threatens to reverse its flow. While Mary and Steve wander in a sculpture garden, they accidentally knock over a statue, and the statue's male hardware gets broken off. Mary has some superglue in her purse, and they try to glue the frank and beans back in place, but alas, the broken part becomes stuck to Dr. Steve's palm. If he had gone through the rest of the movie like that it might have added some interest, but no: Mary also has some solvent in her purse. When you have seen Jennifer Lopez ungluing marble genitals from the hand of the man she loves, you have more or less seen everything.

A plot like this is so hopeless that only acting can redeem it. Lopez pulls her share of the load, looking genuinely smitten by this guy, and convincingly crushed when his secret is revealed. But McConaughey is not the right actor for this material. He seems stolid and workmanlike, when what you need is a guy with naughtier eyes: Ben Affleck, Steve Martin, William H. Macy, Alec Baldwin, Matt Dillon.

Bridgette Wilson-Sampras is, however, correctly cast as Fran, the rich bride-to-be. She's an Anna Nicole Smith type who gets the joke and avoids all the usual clichés involving the woman who gets left at the altar, perhaps because she realizes, as we do, that getting dumped by Dr. Steve is far from the worst thing that could happen to her. We sense midway in the movie that Mary and Fran could have more interesting conversations with each other than either one will have with Dr. Steve, and no matter which one marries him, we sense a future, five to eight years from now, after the divorce, when the two girls meet by chance at a spa (I see them at the Golden Door, perhaps, or Rancho La Puerta) and share a good laugh about the doc.

The Weight of Water ★ ★
R, 113 m., 2002

Catherine McCormack (Jean Janes), Sarah Polley (Maren Hontvedt), Sean Penn (Thomas Janes), Josh Lucas (Rich Janes), Elizabeth Hurley (Adaline Gunne), Ciarán Hinds (Louis Wagner), Ulrich Thomsen (John Hontvedt), Anders W. Berthelsen (Evan Christenson), Katrin Cartlidge (Karen Christenson), Vinessa Shaw (Anethe Christenson). Directed by Kathryn Bigelow and produced by A. Kitman Ho, Sigurjon Sighvatsson, and Janet Yang. Screenplay by Alice Arlen and Christopher Kyle, based on the novel by Anita Shreve.

The Weight of Water tells two stories of family jealousy, separated by more than a century and heightened by lurid melodrama, bloody murder, incest, and storms at sea. While either one of the stories could make a plausible thriller, the movie's structure undercuts them both. Unlike *Possession* or *The French Lieutenant's Woman*, in which modern and historical stories are linked in an intriguing way, *The Weight of Water* seems more like an exercise. We don't feel the connection, and every jump in time is a distraction.

The older story is the more absorbing. In 1873, on an island off the coast of New Hampshire, two Norwegian immigrant women are found murdered with an ax. A hapless man named Wagner (Ciarán Hinds) is convicted of the crime after a surviving eyewitness named Maren (Sarah Polley) testifies against him.

By the end of the movie we will have a deeper understanding of the emotional undertow on the island, and we will know that Maren's love for her brother Evan (Anders W. Berthelsen) is at the center of the intrigue. Maren is married to John Hontvedt (Ulrich Thomsen) but does not love him; her brother arrives on the island with his new bride Anethe (Vinessa Shaw), and there is also Maren's sister Karen (Katrin Cartlidge, whose performance is a reminder of

how much we lost when she died at such an early age).

The modern story takes place mostly on a luxury yacht chartered by two brothers, Thomas and Rich Janes (Sean Penn and Josh Lucas). Thomas's wife, Jean (Catherine McCormack), is a famous photographer who is working on a book about the famous crime, which still inspires controversy and revisionist theories. The others are along for the ride, including Rich's girlfriend Adaline (Elizabeth Hurley). We learn, by indirection, tones of voice, and body language, that the Penn character is jealous of his brother, indifferent to his wife, interested in the girlfriend.

The screenplay, by Alice Arlen and Christopher Kyle, doesn't try to force awkward parallels between the two stories, but they are there to be found: hidden and forbidden passion, sibling jealousy, the possibility of violence. The movie tells the two stories so separately, indeed, that each one acts as a distraction from the other. The fact that there are nine major characters and many lines of intrigue doesn't help; *Possession* and *The French Lieutenant's Woman* only had to deal with parallels between a nineteenth-century couple and a twentieth-century couple.

Another problem is that psychological conflicts get upstaged by old-fashioned melodrama. The storm at the end, which I will not describe in detail, involves violence and action that would be right at home in a seafaring thriller, but seems hauled into this material only to provide an exciting action climax. It is not necessary to the material. And the revelations in the historical story would have more depth and resonance if we'd spent more time with the characters—if all of their scenes were not essentially part of the setup.

The movie was directed by Kathryn Bigelow, whose *Strange Days* (1995) was a smart futuristic thriller, inexplicably overlooked by audiences. Her credits also include the effective *K-19: The Widowmaker*, the submarine thriller from earlier this year. I like her work, but with *The Weight of Water* I think her problems began with the very decision to tell these two stories alternately. The actors are splendid, especially Sarah Polley and Sean Penn, but we never feel confident that these two plots fit together, belong together, or work together.

Welcome to Collinwood ★ ★ ½
R, 86 m., 2002

William H. Macy (Riley), Isaiah Washington (Leon), Sam Rockwell (Pero), Michael Jeter (Toto), Luis Guzmán (Cosimo), Patricia Clarkson (Rosalind), Andrew Davoli (Basil), Jennifer Esposito (Carmela), Gabrielle Union (Michelle), George Clooney (Jerzy). Directed by Anthony Russo and Joe Russo and produced by George Clooney and Steven Soderbergh. Screenplay by Russo and Russo.

I wonder if the real problem is that I've seen the original. *Welcome to Collinwood* is a wacky and eccentric heist comedy with many virtues, but it is also a remake of *Big Deal on Madonna Street* (1958), a movie much beloved by me. Some scenes are so close to the original it's kind of uncanny.

Consider the comic climax of the movie, which comes as the gang is trying to break through the wall and get the safe. If you've seen *Big Deal,* you'll remember that great scene. If you haven't, I won't spoil it for you. The surprise element, on top of the humor, makes it something like genius. But when the scene came along in *Welcome to Collinwood,* I knew exactly what would happen, and so the new movie didn't have a chance. All I could do was compare and contrast.

Would the scene work for a fresh audience? I don't see why not. I heard good buzz about *Welcome to Collinwood* at the Toronto Film Festival, and assume that for those who had not seen *Big Deal on Madonna Street,* the scene worked and the movie was a pleasure. The problem is, so many people *have* seen it, one way or another. Made as a satire of *Rififi* (1955), which is the mother of all heist movies, it is itself the mother of all heist comedies. *Big Deal* is a regular on cable, is in the Criterion Collection on DVD, and has been remade many times before, notably by Louis Malle *(Crackers),* Alan Taylor *(Palookaville),* and Woody Allen (the middle section of *Small Time Crooks*).

Directed and written by brothers Anthony and Joe Russo, the movie is set in the seedy Cleveland suburb of Collinwood, which looks unchanged since the depression. We meet members of the hamlet's criminal fraternity, who are incredibly colorful, as if they read Damon Runyon and stay up late taking notes on old crime movies. They have their own lingo. A "malinski" is a guy who will take the rap for you. A "bellini" is a lucrative job. As the film opens, a crook named Cosimo (Luis Guzmán) hears about a bellini and needs a malinski.

He shares his knowledge with his girlfriend (Patricia Clarkson) and unwisely confides in his partner Toto (Michael Jeter, whose character is named after the Italian comedian who played this role in the original). Word spreads through the underworld, and while Cosimo fails to find his malinski, the others sign up for the bellini, which involves a foolproof method to break into a pawnshop where the safe is said to contain $300,000.

The heist spoof genre is durable. Steven Soderbergh, who produced this film, directed *Ocean's Eleven* (2001), which was a remake of *Ocean's Eleven* (1960), which was a remake of the French film *Bob le Flambeur* (1955). In the Russo version, I like the sequence where the gang attempts to film the pawnbroker opening his safe. An arm keeps getting in the way at the crucial moment. After the screening, one crook observes, "As a film, it's a disaster," and another replies, "It's a documentary. It's supposed to look that way."

The break-in gang consists of Toto (Jeter), single dad Riley (William H. Macy), Pero (Sam Rockwell), Leon (Isaiah Washington), and Basil (Andrew Davoli). Romantic distraction comes from Carmela (Jennifer Esposito) and Leon's sister Michelle (Gabrielle Union), who pair with Pero and Basil. Their trainer is the retired safecracker Jerzy (George Clooney), who is in a wheelchair and explains, "I don't go out in the field no more." He charges them $500 to learn the "circular saw method."

The movie is in love with its dialogue, which is in a more mannered and colorful style than real crooks probably have the time to master, and spends too much time lining them all up for conversations. The actual heist is the high point, just as in the Italian film, and so raffish and disorganized was the gang that I can see how someone might enjoy this movie, coming to it for the first time.

Wendigo ★ ★ ½
R, 91 m., 2002

Patricia Clarkson (Kim), Jake Weber (George), Erik Per Sullivan (Miles), John Speredakos (Otis), Christopher Wynkoop (Sheriff), Lloyd Oxendine (Elder), Brian Delate (Everett), Daniel Sherman (Billy). Directed by Larry Fessenden and produced by Jeffrey Levy-Hinte. Screenplay by Fessenden.

Wendigo is a good movie with an ending that doesn't work. While it was not working I felt a keen disappointment, because the rest of the movie works so well. The writer, director, and editor is Larry Fessenden, whose *Habit* (1997) was about a New York college student who found solace, and too much more, in the arms of a vampire. Now Fessenden goes into the Catskills to tell a story that will be compared to *The Blair Witch Project* when it should be compared to *The Innocents*.

The film builds considerable scariness, and does it in the details. Ordinary things happen in ominous ways. Kim and George (Patricia Clarkson and Jake Weber), a couple from New York, drive to the Catskills to spend a weekend in a friend's cottage, bringing along their young son, Miles (Erik Per Sullivan). Even before they arrive, there's trouble. They run into a deer on the road, and three hunters emerge from the woods and complain that the city people killed "their" deer—and worse, broke its antlers.

Two of the hunters seem like all-right guys. The third, named Otis (John Speredakos), is not. Holding a rifle that seems like a threat, he engages in macho name-calling with George, and the scene is seen mostly through the big-eyed point of view of little Miles, in the backseat. He says little, he does little, and the less he says and does, the more his fear becomes real to us. Fessenden is using an effective technique: Instead of scaring us, he scares the kid, and we get scared through empathy and osmosis.

Kim and George are not getting along too well, and that works to increase the tension. They're not fighting out loud, but you can feel the buried unhappiness, and Kim tells him: "You've got all this anger you carry around with you from work and I don't know where,

and he feels it's directed at him." George tries to be nice to Miles, tries to take an interest, but he's not really listening, and kids notice that.

There are bullet holes in the cabin when they get to it. It's cold inside. Miles hears noises and sees things—or thinks he does. The next day at the general store, he is given a wooden figure by a man behind the counter who says it represents a Wendigo, an Indian spirit. His mother asks where he got the figure. "From the man," Miles says. "Nobody works here but me," says a woman behind another counter.

It doesn't sound as effective as it is. The effect is all in the direction, in Fessenden's control of mood. I watched in admiration as he created tension and fear out of thin air. When the boy and his father go sledding, an event takes place so abruptly that it almost happens to us. The way Fessenden handles the aftermath is just right, building suspense without forgetting logic.

The actors have an unforced, natural quality that looks easy but is hard to do. Look and listen at the conversation between Otis and the local sheriff (Christopher Wynkoop). Notice the way they both know what is being said and what is meant, and how they both know the other knows. And look at the way the scene involves us in what will happen next.

The buildup, which continues for most of the film, is very well done. Unfortunately, Fessenden felt compelled, I guess, to tilt over into the supernatural (or the hallucinatory) in a climax that feels false and rushed. Maybe he would have been better off dropping the Wendigo altogether, and basing the story simply on the scariness of a cottage in the woods in winter, and the ominous ways of Otis.

The ending doesn't work, as I've said, but most of the movie works so well I'm almost recommending it anyway—maybe not to everybody, but certainly to people with a curiosity about how a movie can go very right, and then step wrong. Fessenden has not made a perfect film, but he's a real filmmaker.

Wet Hot American Summer ★
R, 97 m., 2001

Janeane Garofalo (Beth), David Hyde Pierce (Henry), Michael Showalter (Coop/Alan

Shemper), Marguerite Moreau (Katie), Paul Rudd (Andy), Christopher Meloni (Gene), Bradley Cooper (Ben), Michael Ian Black (McKinley), Ken Marino (Victor), Marisa Ryan (Abby). Directed by David Wain and produced by Howard Bernstein. Screenplay by Michael Showalter and David Wain.

Hello muddah,
Hello fadduh—
Here I am at *Wet Hot American Summah.*

Wow I hate it
Something fierce—
Except the astrophysicist David Hyde Pierce.

He lives in a
Cottage nearby
And boy can he make Janeane Garofolo sigh.

She's the director
Of Camp Firewood,
Which turns before our eyes into Camp Feel-good.

She is funny
As she's hurrying
Through the camper's names, including David Ben Gurion.

She dreams of bunking
David Hyde Pierce,
Who fears a falling Skylab will crush them first.

(Chorus)
Let me leave,
Oh muddah fadduh—
From this comic romp in Mother Nature . . .
Don't make me stay,
Oh muddah fadduh—
In this idiotic motion picture.

Every camper
And each counselor
Is horny, especially Michael Showalter.

He lusts after
Marguerite Moreau's bod,
But she prefers the lifeguard played by Paul Rudd.

The camp cook,
Chris Meloni,
Goes berserk because he feels attacked by phonies.

He talks to bean cans
And screams and moans
Periodically because of Post-Traumatic Anxiety Syndrome.

(Chorus)
I want to escape,
Oh muddah fadduh—
Life's too short for cinematic torture.
Comedies like this,
Oh muddah fadduh—
Inspire in me the critic as a vulture.

Ben and McKinley
Achieve their fame
As campers whose love dare not speak its name.

Ken Marino
Doesn't go rafting
Prefering Marisa Ryan, who is zaftig.

Watch David Wain's
Direction falter,
Despite the help of cowriter Showalter.

They did The State,
On MTV,
And of the two that is the one you should see

Thoughts of *Meatballs*
Cruelly hamper
Attempts by us to watch as happy campers.

Allan Sherman
Sang on the telly.
I stole from him, and he from Ponchielli.

We Were Soldiers ★ ★ ★ ½

R, 138 m., 2002

Mel Gibson (Hal Moore), Madeleine Stowe (Julie Moore), Sam Elliott (Sergeant Major Plumley), Greg Kinnear (Major Crandall), Chris Klein (Lieutenant Geoghegan), Don Duong (Ahn), Josh Daugherty (Ouelette), Barry Pepper (Joe Galloway), Keri Russell (Barbara Geoghegan). Directed by Randall Wallace and produced by Bruce Davey, Stephen McEveety, and Wallace. Screenplay by Wallace, based on the book by Joe Galloway and Hal Moore.

"I wonder what Custer was thinking," Lieutenant Colonel Hal Moore says, "when he realized he'd moved his men into slaughter." Sergeant Major Plumley, his right-hand man, replies, "Sir, Custer was a pussy." There you have the two emotional poles of *We Were Soldiers*, the story of the first major land battle in the Vietnam War, late in 1964. Moore (Mel Gibson) is a family man and a Harvard graduate who studied international relations. Plumley (Sam Elliott) is an army lifer, hard, brave, unsentimental. They are both about as good as battle leaders get. But by the end of that first battle, they realize they may be in the wrong war.

The reference to Custer is not coincidence. Moore leads the First Battalion of the Seventh Cavalry, Custer's regiment. "We will ride into battle and this will be our horse," Moore says, standing in front of a helicopter. Some 400 of his men ride into battle in the Ia Drang Valley, known as the Valley of Death, and are surrounded by some 2,000 North Vietnamese troops. Moore realizes it's an ambush, and indeed in the film's opening scenes he reads about just such a tactic used by the Vietnamese against the French a few years earlier.

We Were Soldiers, like *Black Hawk Down*, is a film in which the Americans do not automatically prevail in the style of traditional Hollywood war movies. Ia Drang cannot be called a defeat, since Moore's men fought bravely and well, suffering heavy casualties but killing even more Viet Cong. But it is not a victory; it's more the curtain-raiser of a war in which American troops were better trained and better equipped, but outnumbered, outmaneuvered, and finally outlasted.

For much of its length, the movie consists of battle scenes. They are not as lucid and easy to follow as the events in *Black Hawk Down*, but then the terrain is different, the canvas is larger, and there are no eyes in the sky to track troop movements. Director Randall Wallace (who wrote *Braveheart* and *Pearl Harbor*) does make the situation clear from moment to moment, as Moore and his North Vietnamese counterpart try to outsmart each other with theory and instinct.

Wallace cuts between the American troops, their wives back home on an army base, and a tunnel bunker where Ahn (Don Duong), the Viet Cong commander, plans strategy on a map. Both men are smart and intuitive. The enemy knows the terrain and has the advantage of surprise, but is surprised itself at the way the Americans improvise and rise to the occasion.

Black Hawk Down was criticized because the characters seemed hard to tell apart. *We Were Soldiers* doesn't have that problem; in the Hollywood tradition it identifies a few key players, casts them with stars, and follows their stories. In addition to the Gibson and Elliott characters, there are Major Crandall (Greg Kinnear), a helicopter pilot who flies into danger; the gung ho Lieutenant Geoghegan (Chris Klein); and Joe Galloway (Barry Pepper), a photojournalist who was a soldier's son, hitches a ride into battle, and finds himself fighting at the side of the others to save his life.

The key relationship is between Moore and Plumley, and Gibson and Elliott depict it with quiet authority. They're portrayed as professional soldiers with experience from Korea. As they're preparing to ride into battle, Moore tells Plumley, "Better get yourself that M-16." The veteran replies: "By the time I need one, there'll be plenty of them lying on the ground." There are.

Events on the army base center around the lives of the soldiers' wives, including Julie Moore (Madeleine Stowe), who looks after their five children and is the de facto leader of the other spouses. We also meet Barbara Geoghegan (Keri Russell), who, because she is singled out, gives the audience a strong hint that the prognosis for her husband is not good.

Telegrams announcing deaths in battle are delivered by a Yellow Cab driver. Was the army so insensitive that even on a base they couldn't find an officer to deliver the news? That sets up a shameless scene later, when a Yellow Cab pulls up in front of a house and of course the wife inside assumes her husband is dead, only to find him in the cab. This scene is a reminder of Wallace's *Pearl Harbor*, in which the Ben Affleck character is reported shot down over the English Channel and makes a surprise return to Hawaii without calling ahead. Call me a romantic, but when your loved one thinks you're dead, give her a ring.

We Were Soldiers and *Black Hawk Down* both seem to replace patriotism with professionalism. This movie waves the flag more than the other (even the Viet Cong's Ahn looks at the Stars and Stripes with enigmatic thoughtfulness), but the narration tells us, "In the end, they fought for each other." This is an echo of *Black Hawk Down*'s line, "It's about the men next to you. That's all it is."

Some will object, as they did with the earlier film, that the battle scenes consist of Americans killing waves of faceless nonwhite enemies. There is an attempt to give a face and a mind to the Viet Cong in the character of Ahn, but, significantly, he is not listed in the major credits and I had to call the studio to find out his name and the name of the actor who played him. Yet almost all war movies identify with one side or the other, and it's remarkable that *We Were Soldiers* includes a dedication not only to the Americans who fell at Ia Drang, but also to "the members of the People's Army of North Vietnam who died in that place."

I was reminded of an experience fifteen years ago at the Hawaii Film Festival, when a delegation of North Vietnamese directors arrived with a group of their films about the war. An audience member noticed that the enemy was not only faceless, but was not even named: At no point did the movies refer to Americans. "That is true," said one of the directors. "We have been at war so long, first with the Chinese, then the French, then the Americans, that we just think in terms of the enemy."

Whale Rider ★ ★ ★ ★
PG-13, 105 m., 2003

Keisha Castle-Hughes (Pai), Rawiri Paratene (Koro), Vicky Haughton (Flowers), Cliff Curtis (Porourangi), Grant Roa (Rawiri), Mana Taumaunu (Hemi), Rachel House (Shilo), Taungaroa Emile (Dog). Directed by Niki Caro and produced by John Barnett, Frank Hubner, and Tim Sanders. Screenplay by Caro, based on the novel by Witi Ihimaera.

Whale Rider arrives in theaters already proven as one of the great audience-grabbers of recent years. It won the audience awards as the most popular film at both the Toronto and Sundance film festivals, played to standing ovations, left audiences in tears. I recite these facts right at the top of this review because I fear you might make a hasty judgment that you don't want to see a movie about a twelve-year-old Maori girl who dreams of becoming the chief of her peo-ple. Sounds too ethnic, uplifting, and feminist, right?

The genius of the movie is the way it side-steps all of the obvious clichés of the underlying story and makes itself fresh, observant, tough, and genuinely moving. There is a vast difference between movies for twelve-year-old girls, and movies about twelve-year-old girls, and *Whale Rider* proves it.

The movie, which takes place in the present day in New Zealand, begins with the birth of twins. The boy and the mother die. The girl, Pai (Keisha Castle-Hughes), survives. Her father, Porourangi (Cliff Curtis), an artist, leaves New Zealand, and the little girl is raised and much loved by her grandparents, Koro and Nanny Flowers.

Koro is the chief of these people. Porourangi would be next in line, but has no interest in returning home. Pai believes that she could serve as the chief, but her grandfather, despite his love, fiercely opposes this idea. He causes Pai much hurt by doubting her, questioning her achievements, insisting in the face of everything she achieves that she is only a girl.

The movie, written and directed by Niki Caro, inspired by a novel by Witi Ihimaera, describes these events within the rhythms of daily life. This is not a simplistic fable, but the story of real people living in modern times. There are moments when Pai is lost in discouragement and despair, and when her father comes for a visit she almost leaves with him. But, no, her people need her—whether or not her grandfather realizes it.

Pai is played by Keisha Castle-Hughes, a newcomer of whom it can only be said: This is a movie star. She glows. She stands up to her grandfather in painful scenes, she finds dignity, and yet the next second she's running around the village like the kid she is. The other roles are also strongly cast, especially Rawiri Paratene and Vicky Haughton as the grandparents.

One day Koro summons all of the young teenage boys of the village to a series of compulsory lessons on how to be a Maori, and the leader of Maoris. There's an amusing sequence where they practice looking ferocious to scare their enemies. Pai, of course, is banned from these classes, but eavesdrops, and enlists a wayward uncle to reveal some of the secrets of the males.

And then—well, the movie doesn't end as we expect. It doesn't march obediently to standard plot requirements, but develops an unexpected crisis, and an unexpected solution. There is a scene set at a school ceremony, where Pai has composed a work in honor of her people, and asked her grandfather to attend. Despite his anger, he will come, won't he? The movie seems headed for the ancient cliché of the auditorium door that opens at the last moment to reveal the person whom the child onstage desperately hopes to see—but no, that's not what happens.

It isn't that Koro comes or that he doesn't come, but that something else altogether happens. Something on a larger and more significant scale, that brings together all of the themes of the film into a magnificent final sequence. It's not just an uplifting ending, but a transcendent one, inspired and inspiring, and we realize how special this movie really is. So many films by and about teenagers are mired in vulgarity and stupidity; this one, like its heroine, dares to dream.   ☞

What a Girl Wants ★ ★
PG, 104 m., 2003

Amanda Bynes (Daphne Reynolds), Colin Firth (Henry Dashwood), Kelly Preston (Libby Reynolds), Eileen Atkins (Lady Jocelyn), Anna Chancellor (Glynnis), Jonathan Pryce (Alastair Payne), Oliver James (Ian Wallace), Christina Cole (Clarissa). Directed by Dennie Gordon and produced by Denise Di Novi, Bill Gerber, and Hunt Lowry. Screenplay by Jenny Bicks and Elizabeth Chandler, based on the screenplay by William Douglas Home.

Amanda Bynes, the star of *The Amanda Show,* is well known to fans of the Nickelodeon channel, who are so numerous that she is to 'tweeners as Jack Nicholson is to the Academy. She was sort of wonderful in *Big Fat Liar,* a comedy about kids whose screenplay is stolen by a Hollywood professional, and now here she is in *What a Girl Wants,* a comedy whose screenplay was stolen from *The Princess Diaries.*

But I am unfair. What goes around comes around, and to assume this is a retread of *The Princess Diaries* is to overlook its own pedigree. It's based on the 1956 play and 1958 screenplay, *The Reluctant Debutante,* by William Douglas

Home—who, by the way, was the brother of Sir Alec Douglas Home, briefly the British prime minister in the 1960s.

The point, I suppose, is that few movies are truly original, and certainly not *What a Girl Wants* or *The Princess Diaries.* Both are recycled from ancient fairy tales in which a humble child discovers a royal parent and is elevated from pauperdom to princehood, to coin a phrase.

I would not be surprised to learn that Jenny Bicks and Elizabeth Chandler, who adapted Home's screenplay, did homework of their own—because a key plot point in the movie mirrors Sir Alec's own decision, in 1963, to renounce his seat in the House of Lords in order to run for a seat in the Commons. He won, became prime minister after Macmillan, and quickly lost the next election to Harold Wilson.

Do you need to know this? Perhaps not, but then do you need to know the plot of *What a Girl Wants?* The movie is clearly intended for girls between the ages of nine and fifteen, and for the more civilized of their brothers, and isn't of much use to anyone else.

Bynes stars as Daphne Reynolds, who has been raised by her mother, Libby (Kelly Preston), in an apartment above a restaurant in Chinatown, for the excellent reason that we can therefore see shots of Daphne in Chinatown. As nearly as I can recall, no Chinese characters have speaking lines, although one helps to blow out the candles on her birthday cake.

Daphne is the love child of Sir Henry Dashwood (Colin Firth), a handsome British politician who has decided to renounce his seat in the House of Lords in order to run for the Commons (the movie dismisses such minutiae as that Tony Blair has already booted most of the lords out onto the street). Sir Henry had a Meet Cute with Libby in Morocco fifteeen years ago, and they were married by a Bedouin prince, but never had a "real marriage" (a Bedouin prince not ranking as high in this system as a justice of the peace). Then Sir Henry's evil adviser (Jonathan Pryce) plotted to drive them apart, and she fled to Chinatown, believing Sir Henry did not love her and nobly saving him the embarrassment of a pregnant American commoner.

So great is the wealth of the Dashwoods that their country estate, surrounded by a vast expanse of green lawns and many a tree, is smack dab in the middle of London, so central that Daphne can hop off a bus bound for Trafalgar Square and press her pert little nose against its cold iron gates. The Dashwoods, in short, live on real estate worth more than Rhode Island.

Daphne jumps the wall at Dashwood House in order to meet her father, her lovable but eccentric grandmother (Eileen Atkins), her father's competitive fiancée (Anna Chancellor), her father's future stepdaughter (Christina Cole), and her father's adviser (Pryce), who frowns on the notion of introducing a love child on the eve of the election. Now that you know all that, you can easily jot down the rest of the plot for yourself.

There are moments of wit, as when the eccentric grandmother recoils from the American teenager ("No hugs, dear. I'm British. We only show affection to dogs and horses"). And an odd scene where Daphne is locked in a bedroom, released just as Queen Elizabeth II is arriving at a party, and flees in tears—causing her father to choose between chasing her and greeting the queen. My analysis of this scene: (1) He should choose to greet the queen, or nineteen generations of breeding have been for nothing, and (2) Daphne won't get far before being returned, dead or alive, by the Scotland Yard security detail that accompanies the queen when she visits private homes.

I found it a little unlikely, by the way, that the guests at the party were all looking at Daphne and not the queen. Paul Theroux wrote of being at a dinner party for the queen and agonizing over what he should say when she entered the room. Suddenly seeing her famous profile, all he could think of was: "That reminds me! I need to buy postage stamps."

So is this movie worth seeing? Well, everybody in it is either sweet or cute, or eccentric and hateful, and the movie asks the timeless question: Can a little girl from America find love and happiness as the daughter of a wealthy and titled English lord? If you are a fan of Amanda Bynes, you will probably enjoy finding out the answer for yourself. If not, not.

What's the Worst That Can Happen? ★
PG-13, 95 m., 2001

Martin Lawrence (Kevin Caffery), Danny DeVito (Max Fairbanks), John Leguizamo (Berger), Glenne Headly (Gloria), Carmen Ejogo (Amber Belhaven), Bernie Mac (Uncle Jack), Larry Miller (Earl Radburn), Nora Dunn (Lutetia Fairbanks). Directed by Sam Weisman and produced by Lawrence Turman, David Hoberman, Ashok Amritraj, and Wendy Dytman. Screenplay by Matthew Chapman, based on the novel by Donald E. Westlake.

What's the Worst That Can Happen? has too many characters, not enough plot, and a disconnect between the two stars' acting styles. Danny DeVito plays a crooked millionaire, Martin Lawrence plays a smart thief, and they seem to be in different pictures. DeVito as always is taut, sharp, perfectly timed. Lawrence could play in the same key (and does, in an early scene during an art auction), but at other times he bursts into body language that's intended as funny but plays more like the early symptoms of St. Vitus's dance.

There is an old comedy tradition in which the onlookers freeze while the star does his zany stuff. From Groucho Marx to Eddie Murphy to Robin Williams to Jim Carrey, there are scenes where the star does his shtick and the others wait for it to end, like extras in an opera. That only works in a movie that is about the star's shtick. *What's the Worst That Can Happen?* creates a world that plays by one set of comic rules (in which people pretend they're serious) and then Lawrence goes into mime and jive and odd wavings of his arms and verbal riffs, and maybe the people on the set were laughing but the audience doesn't, much.

The plot involves Lawrence as a clever thief named Kevin Caffery, who frequents auctions to find out what's worth stealing. At an art auction, he meets Amber Belhaven (Carmen Ejogo), who is in tears because she has to sell the painting her father left her; she needs money for the hotel bill. She has good reason to be in tears. The painting, described as a fine example of the Hudson River School, goes for

$3,000; some members of the audience will be thinking that's at least $30,000 less than it's probably worth.

If Kevin is supplied with one love interest, Max Fairbanks (DeVito) has several, including his society wife (Nora Dunn), his adoring secretary (Glenne Headly), and Miss September. (When she disappears, Max's assistant, Earl (Larry Miller), observes there are "eleven more months where she came from.") Kevin also has a criminal sidekick named Berger (John Leguizamo), and then there is his getaway driver Uncle Jack (Bernie Mac), and a Boston cop (William Fichtner) who is played for some reason as a flamboyant dandy. If I tell you there are several other characters with significant roles, you will guess that much of the movie is taken up with entrances and exits.

The plot involves Kevin's attempt to burgle Max's luxurious shore estate, which is supposed to be empty but in fact contains Max and Miss September. After the cops are called, Max steals from Kevin a ring given him by Amber Belhaven, and most of the rest of the movie involves Kevin's determination to get it back, intercut with Max's troubles with judges, lawyers, and accountants.

The jokes and the plots are freely and all too sloppily adapted from a Dortmunder novel by Donald E. Westlake, who once told me he only really liked one of the movies made from his books (The Grifters), and probably won't raise the count to two after this one. A comedy needs a strong narrative engine to pull the plot through to the end, and firm directorial discipline to keep the actors from trying to act funny instead of simply being funny. At some point, when a movie like this doesn't work, it stops being a comedy and becomes a documentary about actors trying to make the material work. When you have so many characters played by so many recognizable actors in a movie that runs only ninety-five minutes, you guess that at some point they just cut their losses and gave up.

Note: Again this summer, movies are jumping through hoops to get the PG-13 rating and the under-17 demographic. That's why the battle scenes were toned down and blurred in Pearl Harbor, *and no doubt it's why this movie steals one of the most famous closing lines in comedy*

history, and emasculates it. The Front Page ended with "The son of a bitch stole my watch!" This one ends with "Stop my lawyer! He stole my watch!" Not quite the same, you will agree.

What Time Is It There? ★ ★ ★ ½
NO MPAA RATING, 116 m., 2002

Lee Kang-Sheng (Hsiao Kang), Chen Shiang-Chyi (Shiang-Chyi), Lu Yi-Ching (Mother), Miao Tien (Father), Cecilia Yip (Woman in Paris), Chen Chao-Jung (Man in Subway), Tsai Guei (Prostitute), Arthur Nauczyciel (Man in Phone Booth), David Ganansia (Man in Restaurant), Jean-Pierre Leaud (Man at Cemetery). Directed by Tsai Ming-Lian and produced by Bruno Pesery. Screenplay by Tsai and Yang Pi-Ying.

The reviewers of Tsai Ming-Lian's *What Time Is It There?* have compared it to the work of Yasujiro Ozu, Robert Bresson, Michelangelo Antonioni, Jacques Tati, and Buster Keaton. If none of these names stir admiration and longing in your soul, start with them, not with Tsai. Begin with Keaton and work your way backward on the list, opening yourself to the possibilities of silence, introspection, isolation, and loneliness in the movies. You will notice that the films grow less funny after Keaton and Tati; one of the enigmas about Tsai's work is that it is always funny and always sad, never just one or the other.

Tsai's hero, who indeed shares some of the single-minded self-absorption of the Keaton and Tati characters, is Hsiao Kang (Lee Kang-Sheng), a man who sells wristwatches from a display case on the sidewalks of Taipei. One day he sells a watch to Shiang-Chyi (Chen Shiang-Chyi—remember, family names come first in Chinese societies). He wants to sell her a watch from his case, but she insists on the watch from his wrist, which gives the time in two time zones, because she is flying to Paris.

Hsiao's home life is sad without redemption. In an early scene, we have seen his father, almost too exhausted to exhale the smoke from his cigarettes, die in a dark, lonely room. Hsiao's mother (Lu Yi-Ching) becomes convinced that her dead husband's soul has somehow been channeled into Fatty, the large white fish in a tank in the living room. Since Fatty is

Hsiao's pet and only friend (he confides details of his life to the fish), this is doubly sad: Not only has the father died after bringing no joy to his son's life, but now he has appropriated the fish. You see what I mean about humor and sadness coexisting, neither one conceding to the other.

The movie then develops into a story that seems to involve synchronicity, but actually involves our need for synchronicity. We need to believe that our little lives are in step with distant music, when synchronicity is simply the way coincidence indulges itself in wish fulfillment. The girl goes off to Paris. Hsiao, who has barely spoken to her, and then only about watches, is so struck by longing for her that he begins to reset watches to Paris time. First all of the watches in his display case. Then all of the watches and clocks available to him. Then even a gigantic clock on a building (the parallel to Harold Lloyd's most famous scene is inescapable).

Meanwhile, in Paris, Shiang-Chyi is also lonely. Does she even have a reason for being here? She wanders the streets and travels nowhere in particular on the Metro. Eventually all three lonely people—Hsiao, his mother, and Shiang-Chyi—look for release in sex. Sex is many things, and one of them is a way of reassuring yourself you are alive, that you retain the power to feel and cause feeling. Hsiao seeks out a prostitute, Shiang-Chyi experiments with another woman (who for her purposes could have been a man), and the mother masturbates while thinking of her dead husband.

These three acts take place at about the same time. Synchronicity? Or simply an indication that the loneliness clocks of the three characters started ticking at the same time, and so chime the hour simultaneously? There is another coincidence in the movie: Hsiao watches Truffaut's *The 400 Blows* on video—the scene where Jean-Pierre Leaud wanders the Paris streets because he is afraid to return home. And Shiang-Chyi visits a Paris cemetery where she talks to a strange man sitting on a gravestone. This man is Jean-Pierre Leaud forty-one years later. (It isn't mentioned in the movie, but I think this is the cemetery where Truffaut is buried. Is Leaud visiting the grave of the man who created his life-defining roles?)

What Time Is It There? is not easy. It haunts you, you can't forget it, you admire its conception, and are able to resolve some of the confusions you had while watching it. You realize it is very simple, really, even though at first you thought it was impenetrable. But can you recommend it to others? Does it depend on how advanced they are in their filmgoing? The critics don't seem to agree. Is it true that the movie "proceeds with all the speed of paint drying" *(Film Journal International)* or does Tsai create "shock waves of comedy, which both unleash a wave of euphoria in the audience and communicate the pleasure he gets from filmmaking" *(New York Times)*? Does "a sense of perseverance and comic acceptance trump any self-indulgent ennui" *(Salon)*, or do "emotionally disconnected characters . . . wade through their sterile Taipei surroundings hopelessly grasping for a piece of human comfort" *(Slant)*?

What happens, I think, is that the funny and sad poles of the story checkmate each other. Everything is funny. Everything is sad. There is nothing funnier than an unrequited love. Nothing sadder than an unrequited lover. Nothing tragic, really, about two people who have not connected when they only had two meaningless conversations. But nothing hopeful about two people so unconnected it doesn't matter what city they are in. When Hsiao resets all of the clocks, is that a grand gesture of romance or a pathetic fixation? Which is more depressing—that the mother thinks her husband's soul occupies the fish, or that the fish is her son's only confidant?

A movie that causes us to ask these kinds of questions deserves to be seen. A movie that thinks it knows the answer to them deserves to be pitied. Most movies do not know these questions exist.

When Brendan Met Trudy ★ ★ ★
NO MPAA RATING, 95 m., 2001

Peter McDonald (Brendan), Flora Montgomery (Trudy), Marie Mullen (Mother), Pauline McLynn (Nuala), Don Wycherley (Niall), Maynard Eziashi (Edgar), Eileen Walsh (Siobhan), Barry Cassin (Headmaster). Directed by Kieron J. Walsh and produced by Lynda Myles. Screenplay by Roddy Doyle.

Roddy Doyle has written an original screenplay, and now we know his secret. He wrote the novels that became the rollicking Irish comedies *The Commitments, The Snapper,* and *The Van,* and now here's *When Brendan Met Trudy.* If the title reminds you of *When Harry Met Sally,* that's because half the scenes in the movie are likely to remind you of other movies. Roddy Doyle's secret is, he's a movie fan. The kind of movie fan so fanatic that he creates a hero named Brendan who not only has a poster of Godard's *Breathless* in his office, but another one in his flat.

Brendan, played by Peter McDonald, is a sissy. He runs like a girl, with his arms held out rigidly at his sides, and he sings in the church choir, and he's so shy that when the choir members go into the pub for a pint after practice, he stands by himself at the bar. And there he's standing one night, a sitting duck, when Trudy accosts him. She's the kind of girl who can insult you, pick you up, get you to buy her a drink, keep you at arm's length, and tell you to sod off, simultaneously and charmingly.

Flora Montgomery is the actress. She's got one of those round, regular faces, pretty but frank, like your best friend's sister—the kind of girl you agree would make a great catch for some lucky bloke, but not, you add in an unspoken footnote, for yourself. Trudy doesn't leave Brendan with the free time for such sophistry, however, and soon he is in love with her and proving that he may run like a sissy but he makes love like that Jack Nicholson character with the "Triumph!" T-shirt.

All the same, Brendan has his misgivings. Trudy sneaks out at night, wearing a ski mask. And the TV news reports that young men have been castrated in Dublin by a mysterious masked predator. Could it be Trudy? One night she attempts to add a little spice to their sex by wearing her mask, and he is so terrified that she has to talk him down by confessing she is not a phantom castrator, but merely a thief.

This news comes as a shock to honest Brendan, a schoolteacher whose students openly mock him and whose only escape is going to the movies. Soon Trudy is going to the movies with him, and soon he is going on midnight raids with her, and the Doyle screenplay, directed by Kieron J. Walsh, casts many of their adventures in the form of classic movie scenes, sometimes even with the same dialogue. This is possible because when Brendan finds himself facedown in the gutter, his first thought is not to climb to his feet, but to imagine himself as William Holden in *Sunset Boulevard.*

The more movie references you recognize (from *Once Upon a Time in the West* to *The Producers*), the more you're likely to enjoy *When Brendan Met Trudy,* but the movie works whether you identify the scenes or not. It has that unwound Roddy Doyle humor; the laughs don't hit you over the head, but tickle you behind the knee. And there is, as usual, Doyle's great pleasure in kidding the Irish. At one point Brendan and Trudy visit a miniature Irish landscape, which includes an "Irish Famine Village," and it is so real, they agree "you can almost see them starving." The effect these miniature famine victims have upon Brendan's sex life, and how he deals with it, is making me smile again right now.

White Oleander ★ ★ ½
PG-13, 110 m., 2002

Alison Lohman (Astrid Magnussen), Robin Wright Penn (Starr), Michelle Pfeiffer (Ingrid Magnussen), Renée Zellweger (Claire Richards), Billy Connolly (Barry Kolker), Svetlana Efremova (Rena Grushenka), Patrick Fugit (Paul Trout), Cole Hauser (Ray), Noah Wyle (Mark Richards), Amy Aquino (Miss Martinez). Directed by Peter Kosminsky and produced by John Wells and Hunt Lowry. Screenplay by Mary Agnes Donoghue, based on the novel by Janet Fitch.

White Oleander tells a sad story of crime and foster homes, and makes it look like the movie version. The film takes the materials of human tragedy and dresses them in lovely costumes, southern California locations, and star power. Almost makes it look like fun. The movie's poster shows four women's faces side by side, all blindingly blond: Alison Lohman, Michelle Pfeiffer, Robin Wright Penn, and Renée Zellweger. We suspect there could be another, parallel story of the same events, in which the characters look unhinged and desperate and brunette.

The story is determined to be colorful and melodramatic, like a soap opera where the characters suffer in ways that look intriguing.

When you are a teenage girl and your mother is jailed for murder and you are shipped to a series of foster homes, isn't it a little unlikely that each home would play like an entertaining episode of a miniseries? First you get a sexy foster mom who was "an alcoholic, a cokehead, and dancing topless—and then I was saved by Jesus," although she still dresses like an off-duty stripper. Then you get an actress who lives in a sun-drenched beach house in Malibu, and you become her best friend. Then you get a Russian capitalist who dresses like a gypsy, uses her foster kids as Dumpster-divers, and runs a stall at the Venice Beach flea market. Aren't there any foster mothers who are old, tired, a little mean, and doing it for the money?

The performances are often touching and deserve a better screenplay. I don't hold the beauty of the actresses against them, but I wish the movie had not been so pleased with the way the sunlight comes streaming through their long blond hair and falls on their flawless skin and little white summer dresses.

The movie is narrated by Astrid Magnussen, played by Alison Lohman in several different years and weathers of her life. It's an awesome performance, but it would benefit from the depth and darkness that the movie shies away from. (The movie is all too appropriately rated PG-13; I suspect full justice cannot be done to this material short of an R.) Astrid is the daughter of Ingrid (Michelle Pfeiffer), an artist and free spirit who sits on the roof so the desert winds can find her. "No one had ever seen anyone more beautiful than my mother," Astrid tells us, but there are ominous hints that Ingrid is not an ideal mother, as when she skips Parents Night because "what can they tell me about you that I don't already know?"

Ingrid doesn't date. Doesn't need men. Then makes the mistake of letting Barry (Billy Connolly) into her life (although so fleeting is his role he is barely allowed into the movie). She kills him, observing to her daughter, "He made love to me and then said I had to leave because he had a date." When you hardly know someone and that's how he treats you, he's not worth serving thirty-five years to life.

Astrid then moves on to the series of foster homes, each one so colorful it could be like the adventure of a Dickens character; the Russian is unmistakably a descendent of Fagin, and surely only in a Hollywood fantasy could any of these women qualify as foster mothers. Starr, the former stripper, seems less like a person than a caricature, although the director, Peter Kosminsky, has a good eye for detail and shows how her family takes a jaundiced view of her born-again grandstanding. What happens to bring this foster experience to an end, I will not reveal, except to say that I didn't for a moment believe it; it involves behavior of a sort the movie seems obligated to supply, but never refers to again.

Astrid's best foster experience is with Claire (Renée Zellweger), whose performance is the most convincing in the movie. She plays a one-time horror star, married to a director who is usually absent, and we believe the scenes she has with Astrid because they come from need and honesty.

They also inspire the best scenes between Astrid and her mother; Pfeiffer finds just the right note between jealousy and perception when, on visiting day at the prison, she observes, "You dress like her now." Later she tells her daughter, "I'd like to meet her." "Why?" "Because you don't want me to." And later: "How can you stand to live with poor Claire? I would rather see you in the worst kind of foster home than to live with that woman." The scenes involving Claire most clearly inspire Astrid's developing ideas about her mother.

The third foster experience, with Svetlana Efremova playing the Russian jumble-sale woman, offers a glimpse of the economy's underbelly, but is too choppy and perfunctory to engage us: It feels like it was filmed to add color, and then chopped to reduce the running time. Its only influence on Astrid is to change her wardrobe and hair color, in what feels more like a stunt than a character development.

Pfeiffer's role is the most difficult in the movie, because she has to compress her revelations and emotions into the brief visits of her increasingly dubious daughter. Astrid, who once idealized her mother, now blames her for the loss of happiness with Claire. But even the movie's big emotional payoff loses something because, after all, Ingrid *did* murder Barry, and so what is presented as a sacrifice on behalf of her daughter could also be described as simply doing the right thing.

White Oleander is based on a novel by Janet

Fitch, recommended by Oprah's Book Club, unread by me. I gather it includes still more colorful foster home episodes. Amy Aquino plays Miss Martinez, the social worker who drives Astrid from one foster adventure to the next. She feels like this movie's version of Michael Anthony, the man who introduced each episode of *The Millionaire.* You can imagine her on the TV series, shipping the heroine to a different foster home every week.

Who Is Cletis Tout? ★ ★ ½
R, 95 m., 2002

Christian Slater (Trevor Finch/Cletis Tout), Tim Allen (Critical Jim), Portia de Rossi (Tess), Richard Dreyfuss (Micah). Directed by Chris Ver Wiel and produced by Matthew Grimaldi, Daniel Grodnik, and Robert Snukal. Screenplay by Ver Wiel.

Who Is Cletis Tout? is one of those movies with a plot so labyrinthine you think you should be taking notes and then you realize you are. Like *The Usual Suspects,* it circles around the verbal description of events that are seen in flashback and may or may not be trustworthy. The difference is that *Cletis Tout* is a lot more light-hearted than the usual puzzle movie, and takes its tone from the performance of Tim Allen, as Critical Jim, a hit man who loves the movies.

As the film opens, he sticks a gun in the face of Christian Slater and tells him that in ninety minutes, if money is delivered as planned, he will kill him. In the meantime, he loves a good story. And Slater has one to tell him. Their meeting, Slater explains, is based on a misconception. Critical Jim thinks Slater is Cletis Tout, a man the mob wants dead. But Slater is in fact Trevor Finch, who borrowed Cletis's identity after escaping from prison.

"Flashbacks!" Critical Jim cries. "Yes, I like flashbacks!" So Finch, if that is his name, tells a story about meeting a jewel thief named Micah (Richard Dreyfuss) in prison, and learning from him about a stash of diamonds. Micah we have already seen; he is a gifted magician who stages his robberies while always seeming to be on the sidewalk outside the building. Later, in a prison break, he projects footage of himself against a background of smoke, which seems like a lot of trouble and leaves you wondering

how a guy on a chain gang can smuggle a projector out to the work area.

Anyway. Micah and Finch escape together (jumping onto a train that seems to be speeding way too fast), and then there is the business of the buried diamonds and Micah's daughter, Tess (Portia de Rossi), who either hates Finch or loves him, depending on various stages of the story. "Pitch me!" Critical Jim says, and Finch makes the story good while we try to decide what to believe.

It's endearing, the way Critical Jim has memorized lines of movie dialogue to cover every occasion, but about midway through the movie I began to lose patience with the method, however clever. The underlying story—about the original robbery, the jail break, and the case of mistaken identity involving the mob—is intriguing in itself. Add the beautiful Tess and her carrier pigeons (yes, carrier pigeons) and you have something. Is it entirely necessary to add the layer of the story being told to Critical Jim? Is this not one more unnecessary turn of the screw to make a sound story into a gimmick?

Could be. Or maybe not. By the end of the film I was a little restless, a little impatient at being jerked this way and that by the story devices. There was a lot I liked in *Cletis Tout,* including the performances and the very audacity of details like the magic tricks and the carrier pigeons. But it seemed a shame that the writer and director, Chris Ver Wiel, took a perfectly sound story idea and complicated it into an exercise in style. Less is more.

The Widow of St. Pierre ★ ★ ★ ★
R, 112 m., 2001

Juliette Binoche (Madame La), Daniel Auteuil (Le Capitaine), Emir Kusturica (Neel Auguste), Michel Duchaussoy (Le Gouverneur), Philippe Magnan (President Venot), Christian Charmetant (Commissaire de la Marine), Philippe Du Janerand (Chef Douanier), Reynald Bouchard (Louis Olliver). Directed by Patrice Leconte and produced by Frederic Brillion and Gilles Legrand. Screenplay by Claude Faraldo.

A man gets drunk and commits a senseless murder. He is condemned to death by guillotine. But in the 1850s on a small French fishing island off the coast of Newfoundland, there is no guillotine, and no executioner. The guillotine can be shipped from France. But the island will have to find its own executioner, because superstitious ship's captains refuse to allow one on board.

Time passes, and a strange and touching thing happens. The murderer repents of his crime, and becomes a useful member of the community. He saves a woman's life. He works in a garden started by the wife of the captain of the local military. The judge who condemned him frets, "His popularity is a nuisance." An islander observes, "We committed a murderous brute and we're going to top a benefactor."

The Widow of St. Pierre is a beautiful and haunting film that tells this story, and then tells another subterranean story, about the seasons of a marriage. Le Capitaine (Daniel Auteuil) and his wife, referred to by everyone as Madame La (Juliette Binoche), are not only in love but in deep sympathy with each other. He understands her slightest emotional clues. "Madame La only likes desperate cases," someone says, and indeed she seems stirred by the plight of the prisoner. Stirred and . . . something else. The film is too intelligent and subtle to make obvious what the woman herself hardly suspects, but if we watch and listen closely we realize she is stirred in a sensual way by the prospect of a prisoner who has been condemned to die. Le Capitaine understands this and, because his wife is admirable and he loves her, he sympathizes with it.

The movie becomes not simply a drama about capital punishment, but a story about human psychology. Some audience members may not connect directly with the buried levels of obsession and attraction, but they'll sense them—sense something that makes the movie deeper and sadder than the plot alone can account for. Juliette Binoche, that wonderful actress, is the carrier of this subtlety, and the whole film resides in her face. Sad that most of those who saw her in *Chocolat* will never see, in this film, how much more she is capable of.

The Widow of St. Pierre is a title that carries extra weight. The French called a guillotine a "widow," and by the end of the film it has created two widows. And it has made a sympathetic character of the murderer, named Neel and played by the dark, burly Yugoslavian

director Emir Kusturica. It accomplishes this not by soppy liberal piety, but by leading us to the same sort of empathy the islanders feel. Neel and a friend got drunk and murdered a man for no reason, and can hardly remember it. The friend is dead. Neel is prepared to die, but it becomes clear that death would redress nothing and solve nothing—and that Neel has changed so fundamentally that a different man would be going to the guillotine.

The director is Patrice Leconte, whose films unfailingly move me, and often (but not this time) make me smile. He is obsessed with obsession. He first fascinated me with *Monsieur Hire* (1989), based on a Simenon story about a little man who begins to spy on a beautiful woman whose window faces his. She knows he is looking, and plays her own game, until everything goes wrong. Then there was *The Hairdresser's Husband* (1990), about a man obsessed with hair and the women who cut it. Then *Ridicule* (1996), about a provincial landowner in the reign of Louis XVI, who wants to promote a drainage scheme at court and finds the king will favor only those who make him laugh. Then *The Girl on the Bridge* (1999), about a knife-thrower who recruits suicidal girls as targets for his act—because what do they have to lose?

The Widow of St. Pierre is unlike these others in tone. It is darker, angrier. And yet Leconte loves the humor of paradox, and some of it slips through, as in a scene where Madame La supplies Neel with a boat and advises him to escape to Newfoundland. He escapes, but returns, because he doesn't want to get anyone into trouble. When the guillotine finally arrives, he helps bring it ashore, because he doesn't want to cause work for others on his account. He impregnates a local girl and is allowed to marry, and the islanders develop an affection for him and begin to see the judge as an alien troublemaker from a France they believe "doesn't care about our cod island."

Now watch closely during the scene where Neel marries his pregnant bride. Madame La hides it well during the ceremony, but is distraught. "It's all right; I'm here," Le Capitaine tells her. What's all right? I think she loves Neel. It's not that she wants to be his lover; in the 1850s such a thought would probably not occur. It's that she is happy for him, and is marrying him and having his child vicariously. And Le Capitaine knows that, and loves her the more for it.

The movie is not even primarily about Neel, his crime, his sentence, and the difficulty of bringing about his death. That is the subplot. It is really about the captain and his wife. About two people with good hearts who live in an innocent, less self-aware time, and how the morality of the case and their deeper feelings about Neel all get mixed up together. Eventually Le Capitaine takes a stand, and everyone thinks it is based on politics and ethics, but if we have been paying attention we know better. It is based on his love for his wife, and the ethics are an afterthought.

The Wild Thornberrys Movie ★ ★ ★
PG, 80 m., 2002

With the voices of: Lacey Chabert (Eliza Thornberry), Tom Kane (Darwin the Monkey), Flea (Donnie Thornberry), Tim Curry (Nigel Thornberry), Jodi Carlisle (Marianne Thornberry), Danielle Harris (Debbie Thornberry), Alfre Woodard (Akela the Panther), Marisa Tomei (Bree Blackburn), Rupert Everett (Sloan Blackburn), Brenda Blethyn (Mrs. Fairgood), Melissa Greenspan (Sarah Wellington). Directed by Cathy Malkasian and Jeff McGrath and produced by Gabor Csupo and Arlene Klasky. Screenplay by Kate Boutilier.

The Wild Thornberrys Movie is a jolly surprise, an energetic and eccentric animated cartoon about a decidedly peculiar family making a documentary in Africa. They prowl the plains in their Winnebago, while Mom operates the camera, Dad lectures on nature, and young Eliza Thornberry talks to the animals.

Yes, by saving a tribal priest from a warthog, she has been given this gift on one condition— that she not tell anyone (human) about it. Surprisingly, or perhaps not, the animals are as intelligent and well-spoken as the humans.

The family is drawn in the cheerful, colorful style of *Rugrats,* and indeed codirector Jeff McGrath even worked on the *Rugrats* TV series. Cathy Malkasian, the top-billed codirector, has worked on everything from the *Jumanji* TV series to the Nickelodeon version of the *Thornberrys* itself.

Many kids will already know Eliza (voice by Lacey Chabert) and her family. Her parents, Nigel and Marianne (Tim Curry and Jodi Carlisle), are British, but Eliza is all-American, and her older sister Debbie (Danielle Harris) sounds like a Valley Girl ("That's *so* wrong," she says, confronted with the bright red hindquarters of an ape). Her younger stepbrother Donnie Thornberry (Flea, of the Red Hot Chili Peppers) speaks an unknown language incessantly. Eliza's best friend is Darwin the Monkey (Tom Kane), who sounds upper-class British and is an analyst of the passing scene.

Eliza and Darwin move fearlessly across the plain, protected by her ability to speak to the animals, and one day she convinces Akela the panther (Alfre Woodard) to let her take her three cubs to play. Alas, one of the cubs is snatched by poachers in a helicopter, setting up a thrilling adventure in which Eliza eventually saves an entire herd of elephants from extinction.

But, of course, the story I've described could be told in a dreary, plodding style. The charm of *The Wild Thornberrys Movie* comes from its zany visual style, the energy of the voice-over actors, and the fine balance of action that is thrilling but not too scary. Eliza is a plucky heroine, determined and brave, and the poachers never really have a chance.

There are other elements in the movie, including a trip to boarding school in England, not enjoyed by either Eliza or Darwin, and various innocent bathroom jokes, mostly involving animals; kids have a special fascination for such material, I guess, and here it's handled as tastefully as such tasteless material can be.

The movie reaches just a little further than we expect with the addition of characters such as Nigel Thornberry's parents (his mother is not amused to find worms in her tea) and the poachers Bree and Sloan Blackburn (Marisa Tomei and Rupert Everett), who are not simply villains willing to exterminate hundreds of elephants, but so unashamed about it that their attitude is scarier than their actions. Will such people stop at nothing? Next thing you know, they'll be permitting snowmobiles in our national parks.

Willard ★ ★ ½
PG-13, 100 m., 2003

Crispin Glover (Willard Stiles), R. Lee Ermey (Mr. Martin), Laura Elena Harring (Cathryn), Jackie Burroughs (Henrietta Stiles). Directed by Glen Morgan and produced by Morgan and James Wong. Screenplay by Morgan, based on a book by Gilbert Ralston.

You never know what a rat is going to do next, which is one of the big problems with rats. In *Willard*, you mostly do know what the rats are going to do next, which is a big problem with the film. That's because Willard is able to marshal his rats into disciplined groups that scurry off on missions on his behalf; he is the Dr. Dolittle of pest control.

Willard is a remake of the 1971 film, which was a surprise hit at the box office. My explanation at the time: People had been waiting a long time to see Ernest Borgnine eaten by rats and weren't about to miss the opportunity. This version looks better, moves faster, and is more artistic than the original film, but it doesn't work as a horror film—and since it is a horror film, that's fatal. It has attitude and a look, but the rats aren't scary.

Consider an early scene where Willard (Crispin Glover) goes down in the cellar after his mother complains of rat infestation. The fuse box blows and he's down to a flashlight, and this should be a formula for a scary scene (remember Ellen Burstyn in the attic with a candle in *The Exorcist*). But the scene isn't frightening—ever. The blowing of the fuse is scarier than anything else that happens in the basement.

The plot is essentially a remake of the earlier *Willard*, but with elements suggesting it is a sequel. A portrait that hangs in the family home, for example, shows Bruce Davison as Willard's father—and Davison, of course, was the original Willard. So hold on. If that Willard was this Willard's father, then that means that this Willard's mother (Jackie Burroughs) was that Willard's wife, and has become a shrew just like her mother-in-law, and young Willard still works for an evil man named Mr. Martin (R. Lee Ermey), which was the Borgnine character's name, so he must be Martin Jr. In the new movie, Willard's mom complains about rats in the cellar and Mr. Martin insults Willard and threatens his job, and the sins of the parents are visited on the sequel.

The best thing in the movie is Crispin Glover's performance. He affects dark, sunken eyes and a slight stoop, is very pale, and has one of those haircuts that shouts out: Look how gothic and miserable I am. There is real wit in the performance. And wit, too, in R. Lee Ermey's performance as the boss, which draws heavily on Ermey's real-life experience as a drill sergeant.

The human actors are okay, but the rodent actors (some real, some special effects) are like a prop that turns up on demand and behaves (or misbehaves) flawlessly. A few of the rats pop out: Socrates, Willard's choice for leader, and Ben, who is Ben's choice for leader. Ben is a very big rat (played, according to ominous information I found on the Web, "by an animal that is not a rat").

Laura Elena Harring, the brunette sex bomb from *Mulholland Dr.*, turns up as a worker in Willard's office who worries about him and even comes to his home to see if he's all right. My theory about why she likes him: He is the only man in a 100-mile radius who has never tried to pick her up. Willard is too morose and inward and Anthony Perkinsy. If they'd reinvented the movie as a character study, not so much about the rats as about Willard, they might have come up with something. Here the rats simply sweep across the screen in an animated tide, and instead of thinking, "Eek! Rats!" we're thinking about how it was done. That's not what you're supposed to be thinking about during a horror movie. ☞

Windtalkers ★ ★
R, 133 m., 2002

Nicolas Cage (Sergeant Joe Enders), Adam Beach (Private Ben Yahzee), Roger Willie (Private Charles Whitehorse), Christian Slater (Sergeant Peter "Ox" Henderson), Peter Stormare (Sergeant Eric "Gunny" Hjelmstad), Noah Emmerich (Corporal Charles "Chick" Rogers), Mark Ruffalo (Pappas), Brian Van Holt (Harrigan), Martin Henderson (Nellie). Directed by John Woo and produced by Terence Chang, Tracie Graham, Alison Rosenzweig, and Woo. Screenplay by John Rice and Joe Batteer.

Windtalkers comes advertised as the saga of how Navajo Indians used their language to create an unbreakable code that helped win World War II in the Pacific. That's a fascinating, little-known story and might have made a good movie. Alas, the filmmakers have buried it beneath battlefield clichés, while centering the story on a white character played by Nicolas Cage. I was reminded of *Glory*, the story of heroic African-American troops in the Civil War, which was seen through the eyes of their white commanding officer. Why does Hollywood find it impossible to trust minority groups with their own stories?

The film stars Nicolas Cage as an Italian-American sergeant who is so gung ho his men look at him as if he's crazy. Maybe he is. After defending a position past the point of all reason, he survives bloody carnage, is patched up in Hawaii, and returns to action in a battle to take Saipan, a key stepping-stone in the Pacific war. In this battle he is assigned as the personal watchdog of Private Ben Yahzee (Adam Beach), an almost saintly Navajo. Sergeant Ox Henderson (Christian Slater) is paired with Private Charles Whitehorse (Roger Willie), another Indian. What the Navajos don't know is that the bodyguards have been ordered to kill them, if necessary, to keep them from falling into enemy hands. The code must be protected at all costs.

This is a chapter of history not widely known, and for that reason alone the film is useful. But the director, Hong Kong action expert John Woo, has less interest in the story than in the pyrotechnics, and we get way, way, way too much footage of bloody battle scenes, intercut with thin dialogue scenes that rely on exhausted formulas. We know almost without asking, for example, that one of the white soldiers will be a racist, that another will be a by-the-books commanding officer, that there will be a plucky nurse who believes in the Cage character, and a scene in which a Navajo saves the life of the man who hates him. Henderson and Whitehorse perform duets for the harmonica and Navajo flute, a nice idea, but their characters are so sketchy it doesn't mean much.

The battle sequences are where Woo's heart lies, and he is apparently trying to one-up *Saving Private Ryan, We Were Soldiers,* and the other new entries in the ultraviolent, unapologetically realistic battle film sweepstakes. Alas, the battles in *Windtalkers* play more like a video game. Although Woo is Asian, he treats the enemy Japanese troops as pop-up targets, a faceless horde of screaming maniacs who run headlong into withering fire. Although Americans take heavy casualties (there is a point at which we assume everyone in the movie will be killed), the death ratio is about thirty to one against the Japanese. Since they are defending dug-in positions and the Americans are often exposed, this seems unlikely.

The point of the movie is that the Navajos are able to use their code in order to radio information, call in strikes, and allow secret communication. In the real war, I imagine, this skill was most useful in long-range strategic radio communication. *Windtalkers* devotes minimal time to the code talkers, however, and when they do talk, it's to phone in coordinates for an air strike against big Japanese guns. Since these guns cannot be moved before airplanes arrive, a call in English would have had about the same effect. That Woo shows the Windtalkers in the heat of battle is explained, I think, because he wants to show everything in the heat of battle. The wisdom of assigning two precious code talkers to a small group of frontline soldiers in a deadly hand-to-hand fight situation seems questionable, considering there are only 400 Navajos in the Pacific theater.

The Indians are seen one-dimensionally as really nice guys. The only character of any depth is Cage's Sergeant Enders, who seems to hover between shell shock and hallucinatory flashbacks. There is a final scene between Enders and Yahzee, the Navajo, that reminded me of the male bonding in other Woo movies, in which you may have to shoot the other guy to prove how much you love him. But since the movie has labored to kill off all the supporting characters and spare only the stars, we are in the wrong kind of suspense: Instead of wondering which of these people will survive, we wonder which way the picture will jump in retailing war-movie formulas.

There is a way to make a good movie like *Windtalkers*, and that's to go the indie route. A low-budget Sundance-style picture would focus on the Navajo characters, their personalities and issues. The moment you decide to make *Windtalkers*, a big-budget action movie with a major star and lots of explosions, flying bodies and stuntmen, you give up any possibility that it can succeed on a human scale. The Navajo code talkers have waited a long time to have their story told. Too bad it appears here merely as a gimmick in an action picture.

Winged Migration ★ ★ ★
G, 89 m., 2003

A documentary directed by Jacques Perrin and produced by Christophe Barratier and Perrin. Screenplay by Stéphane Durand and Perrin.

Jacques Perrin's Oscar-nominated *Winged Migration* does for birds what the 1996 documentary *Microcosmos* did for insects: It looks at them intimately, very close up, in shots that seem impossible to explain. That the two plots intersect (birds eat insects) is just one of those things.

The movie, which is awesome to regard, is not particularly informative; it tells us that birds fly south in the winter (unless they live in the Southern Hemisphere, in which case they fly north), that they fly many hundreds or thousands of miles, and that they navigate by the stars, the sun, Earth's gravitational field, and familiar landmarks. These facts are widely known, and the movie's sparse narration tells us little else.

But facts are not the purpose of *Winged Migration*. It wants to allow us to look, simply look, at birds—and that goal it achieves magnificently. There are sights here I will not easily forget. The film opens and closes with long aerial tracking shots showing birds in long-distance flight into the wind, and we realize how very hard it is to fly a thousand miles or more. We see birds stopping to eat (one slides a whole fish down its long neck). We see them feeding their young. We see them courting and mating, and going through chest-thumping rituals that are serious business, if you are a bird. We see cranes locking bills in what looks like play. We see birds trapped in industrial waste. And in a horrifying scene, a bird with a broken wing tries to escape on a sandy beach, but cannot elude the crabs that catch it and pile onto the still-living body, all eager for a bite. In nature, as the film reminds us, life is all about getting enough to eat.

How in the world did they get this footage?

Lisa Nesselson, *Variety*'s correspondent in Paris, supplies helpful information. To begin with, 225 feet of film were exposed for every foot that got into the movie. And some of the birds were raised to be the stars of the film; they were exposed to the sounds of airplanes and movie cameras while still in the shell, and greeted upon their arrival in the world by crew members. (We remember from *Fly Away Home* that newborn birds assume that whoever they see upon emerging must be a parent.)

Some footage was made with cameras in ultralight aircraft. Other shots were taken from hot air balloons. There are shots in which the birds seem to have been scripted—they move toward the camera as it pulls back. And some scenes, I'm afraid, that were manufactured entirely in the editing room, as when we see snowbirds growing alarmed, we hear an avalanche, and then cut to long shots of the avalanche and matching shots of the birds in flight. Somehow we know the camera was not in the path of the avalanche.

I am pleased, actually, that the film has such a tilt toward the visual and away from information. I wouldn't have wanted the narrator to drone away in my ear, reading me encyclopedia articles and making sentimental comments about the beauty of it all. Life is a hard business, and birds work full-time at it. I was shocked by a sequence showing ducks in magnificent flight against the sky, and then dropping one by one as hunters kill them. The birds have flown exhaustingly for days to arrive at this end. It's not so much that I blame the hunters as that I wish the ducks could shoot back.

With a Friend Like Harry ★ ★ ★
R, 117 m., 2001

Laurent Lucas (Michel), Sergi Lopez (Harry), Mathilde Seigner (Claire), Sophie Guillemin (Plum), Laurie Caminata (Sarah), Lorena Caminata (Iris), Victoire de Koster (Jeane). Directed by Dominik Moll and produced by Michel Saint-Jean. Screenplay by Gilles Marchand and Moll.

Michel uses the rest room of a highway oasis to splash some water on his face. He is addressed by a man who smiles too long and stands too close, and pauses as if expecting

Michel to say something. Michel doesn't know what to say. The stranger introduces himself as Harry—an old school friend. Michel doesn't remember him, but Harry's memory is perfect. He remembers the girl they both dated, and quotes a poem Michel wrote for the school magazine.

When people make a closer study of us than we make of ourselves, we grow uneasy. They seem too needy. We want them to get a life. But Harry (Sergi Lopez) has an ingratiating way, and soon has inspired a dinner invitation. Michel (Laurent Lucas) and his wife, Claire (Mathilde Seigner), are on their way to their summer cottage with their noisy daughters. Harry and his girlfriend, Plum (Sophie Guillemin), come along.

We don't like this Harry. He sticks like glue. He insinuates. He makes offers and insists on them. He doesn't respect the distance strangers should keep from one another. He doesn't think of himself as a stranger. It's not wholesome. You can't put your finger on specific transgressions, but his whole style is a violation. He starts conversations Michel has no wish to join. "How do you like Plum?" Harry asks. "She's not brainy like Claire, but she has an animal intelligence that I like. Know what I mean?" Michel doesn't want to know what he means.

With a Friend Like Harry, directed by Dominik Moll, works like a thriller, but we can't put our finger on exactly why we think so. Maybe it's only about an obnoxious pest. Yet Harry is admittedly helpful: Michel and Claire's old car has no air conditioning, and Harry presents them with a brand-new, bright red SUV. No obligation. He wants to. What are friends for?

Harry is a nickname for Satan. Is this Harry the devil? By using the name, the movie nudges us toward the possibility. On the other hand, maybe he's simply a pushy guy named Harry. Maybe the locus of evil is located elsewhere in the movie. Maybe Harry brings out the worst in people.

Movies like this are more intriguing than thrillers where the heroes and villains wear name tags. We know there's danger and possibly violence coming at some point, but we don't know why, or how, or even who will initiate it. Meanwhile, everyday horrors build up the tension. Michel and Claire's family cabin is rude and unfinished, almost a shack. "It needs a lot of work." Yes—but upstairs there is a brand-new bathroom with shocking pink tile. This is the gift of Michel's parents, who wanted to "surprise" them.

What do you do when someone surprises you with a gift that you consider a vulgar eyesore, and you're stuck with it? Are the people who give such gifts really so insensitive? Are their gifts acts of veiled hostility? A new SUV is at least something you want. A shocking pink bathroom is the wrong idea in a rustic country cabin. It might . . . well, it might almost be a gift to be rid of people who insist on such annoyances.

Sergi Lopez, who plays Harry, last appeared in *An Affair of Love,* the insidious French film about the couple who meet through the classifieds and spend one afternoon a week in a hotel room doing something that apparently no one else in the world wants to do, except for them. We never find out what it is. In that movie, before the situation grew complicated, his face bore the contentment of a man whose imaginary pockets are full.

Here he turns up the dial. He's bursting with confidences, reassurances, compliments, generosity. We realize with a shock that the most frightening outcome of the movie would be if it contained no surprises, no revelations, no quirky twist at the end. What would really be terrifying is if Harry is exactly as he seems, and the plot provides no escape for Michel and Claire, and they're stuck with their new friend. *With a Friend Like Harry,* you don't need enemies.

World Traveler ★ ★

R, 104 m., 2002

Billy Crudup (Cal), Julianne Moore (Dulcie), Cleavant Derricks (Carl), David Keith (Richard), Mary McCormack (Margaret), James LeGros (Jack), Liane Balaban (Meg), Karen Allen (Delores). Directed by Bart Freundlich and produced by Tim Perell and Freundlich. Screenplay by Freundlich.

Cal drags a woman out of a bar to look at the stars and listen to his rants about the universe. She pulls loose and asks, "Do you get away with this crap because you look like that?"

Later in the film two kids will ask him if he's a movie star. He's good-looking, in a morose, tormented way, but it's more than that; Cal is charismatic, and strangers are fascinated by his aura of doom and emptiness.

There is another new movie, *About a Boy*, with a hero who complains that he's a "blank." The dialogue is needed in *World Traveler*. Although others are fascinated by Cal's loneliness, his drinking, his lack of a plan, his superficial charm, he is a blank. Early in the film he walks out on his marriage, on the third birthday of his son. Taking the family station wagon, he drives west across the United States and into the emptiness of his soul.

Cal is played by Billy Crudup, one of the best actors in the movies, but there needs to be something *there* for an actor to play, and Cal is like a moony poet who embraces angst as its own reward. Throwing back Jack Daniels in the saloons of the night, he doesn't have a complaint so much as he celebrates one. When we discover that his own father walked out on Cal and his mother, that reads like an motivation but doesn't play like one. It seems too neat— the Creative Writing explanation for his misery.

The film, written and directed by Bart Freundlich, is a road picture, with Cal meeting and leaving a series of other lonely souls without ever achieving closure. It's as if he glimpses them through the windows of his passing car. There's a young hitchhiker who implies an offer of sex, which he doesn't accept. A construction worker named Carl (Cleavant Derricks), who wants friendship and thinks Cal offers it, but is mistaken. A high school classmate (James LeGros, bitingly effective), who provides us with evidence that Cal has been an emotional hit-and-run artist for a long time. Finally there is Dulcie (Julianne Moore), who is drunk and passed out in a bar.

Cal throws her over his shoulder and hauls her back to his motel room to save her from arrest. She involves him in her own madness. Both sense they're acting out interior dramas from obscure emotional needs, and there is a slo-mo scene on a carnival ride that plays like a parody of a good time. Nelson Algren advised, "Never sleep with a woman whose troubles are greater than your own," and Cal would be wise to heed him.

There are moments of sudden truth in the film; Freundlich, who also made *The Myth of Fingerprints* (1998), about an almost heroically depressed family at Thanksgiving, can create and write characters, even if he doesn't always know where to take them.

The construction buddy Carl and his wife (Mary McCormack) spring into focus with a few lines of dialogue. Cal persuades Carl, a recovering alcoholic, to get drunk with him and help him pick up two women in a bar. The next day Carl says his wife is angry at him, and brings her to life with one line of dialogue: "She's mad about the drinking—and the objectification of women." Later, drunk again, Cal meets Carl's wife, who says, "In all the years I've been married to Carl, I've never heard him talk about anyone the way he talks about you." She loves Carl, we see, so much she is moved that he has found a friend. But then Cal tries to make a pass, and the wife looks cold and level at him: "You're not his friend."

Cal isn't anybody's friend. Near the end of his journey, in the western mountains, he meets his father (David Keith). The role is thankless, but Keith does everything possible, and more, to keep the father from being as much a cipher as the son. One senses in *World Traveler* and in his earlier film that Freundlich bears a grievous but obscure complaint against fathers, and circles it obsessively, without making contact.

X

X2: X-Men United ★ ★ ★
PG-13, 124 m., 2003

Patrick Stewart (Charles Xavier), Hugh
Jackman (Wolverine), Ian McKellen
(Magneto), Halle Berry (Storm), Famke Janssen
(Dr. Jean Grey), James Marsden (Cyclops),
Rebecca Romijn-Stamos (Mystique), Brian Cox
(General William Stryker), Alan Cumming
(Nightcrawler), Shawn Ashmore (Iceman),
Aaron Stanford (Pyro), Kelly Hu (Yuriko
Oyama), Anna Paquin (Rogue). Directed by
Bryan Singer and produced by Lauren Shuler
Donner and Ralph Winter. Screenplay by
Michael Dougherty and Daniel P. Harris, based
on the story by David Hayter, Zak Penn, and
Singer and the comic books and characters by
Stan Lee.

X2: X-Men United is the kind of movie you
enjoy for its moments, even though they never
add up. Made for (and possibly by) those with
short attention spans, it lives in the present,
providing one amazing spectacle after another,
and not even trying to develop a story arc. Having trained on the original *X-Men* (2000),
I tried to experience the film entirely in the present, and the fact is, I had a good time. Dumb,
but good.

Like the comic books that inspired it, *X2* begins with the premise that mutant heroes with
specialized superpowers exist among us. Name
the heroes, assign the powers, and you're ready
for perfunctory dialogue leading up to a big
two-page spread in which sleek and muscular
beings hurtle through dramatic showdowns.

Like all the characters in the Marvel Comics
stable, the X-Men have psychological or political problems; in the first movie, they were faced
with genocide, and in this one their right to privacy is violated with the Mutant Registration
Act. Of course, there will be audience members
who believe mutants should have no rights,
and so *X2* provides a valuable civics lesson.
(How you register a mutant who can teleport
or shape-shift is not explained.)

Perhaps not coincidentally, the movie has a
president who looks remarkably like George W.
Bush. The film opens with one of its best scenes,
as a creature with a forked tail attacks the White

House and whooshes down corridors and careens off walls while the Secret Service fires
blindly. The creature's purpose is apparently to
give mutants a bad name, inspiring still more
laws undermining their rights.

Despite all of the havoc and carnage of the
first film, just about everybody is back for the
sequel. Amazing that they weren't all killed.
Charles Xavier (Patrick Stewart) still runs his
private school for young mutants, Magneto (Ian
McKellen) still plots against him, and there is a
new villain named General William Stryker
(Brian Cox), who is assigned by the government
to deal with the mutant threat and uses the
turncoat mutant Yuriko (Kelly Hu) on his team.

The principal mutants are, in credits order,
Wolverine (Hugh Jackman), who has blades
that extend from his knuckles; Storm (Halle
Berry), who can control the weather; Dr. Jean
Grey (Famke Janssen), whose power of telekine-
sis is growing stronger; Cyclops (James Marsden), whose eyes shoot laser beams; Mystique
(Rebecca Romijn-Stamos), a shape shifter
whose shapes are mostly delightful; Nightcrawler (Alan Cumming), the teleporter who
attacked the White House; Iceman (Shawn Ashmore), who can cool your drink and lots of
other things; Pyro (Aaron Stanford), who can
hurl flames but needs a pilot light; and Rogue
(Anna Paquin), who can take on aspects of the
personalities around her.

These superpowers are so oddly assorted
that an X-Man adventure is like a game of chess
where every piece has a different move. Some of
the powers are awesome; Storm stops an aerial
pursuit by generating tornadoes with her mental powers, and Dr. Jean Grey is able to restart
an airplane in midair.

Odd, then, that Wolverine is one of the dominant characters even though his X-Acto
knuckles seem pretty insignificant compared to
the powers of Pyro or Cyclops. In a convention
borrowed from martial arts movies, *X2* pairs
up characters with matching powers, so that
when Wolverine has his titanic battle, it's with
an enemy also equipped with blades. What
would happen if Pyro and Iceman went head to
head? I visualize the two of them in a pool of
hot water.

One might reasonably ask what threat could

possibly be meaningful to mutants with such remarkable powers, but Magneto, who has serious personal issues with mutants, has devised an invention that I will not describe, except to say that it provides some of the movie's best visuals. I also admired the scene where Dr. Jean Grey saves the X-Men's airplane, and the way Famke Janssen brings drama to the exercise of Grey's power instead of just switching it on and off.

Since the earliest days of *Spider-Man,* Marvel heroes have had personal problems to deal with, and there's a classic Stan Lee moment here in the scene where Iceman breaks the news to his parents that he is a mutant. The movie treats the dialogue as a coming-out scene, half-seriously, as if providing inspiration for real-life parents and their children with secrets.

Other possibilities are left for future installments. There's a romance in the movie between Rogue and Iceman, but it doesn't exploit the possibilities of love between mutants with incompatible powers. How inconvenient if during sex your partner was accidentally teleported, frozen, slashed, etc. Does Cyclops wear his dark glasses to bed?

X2: X-Men United lacks a beginning, a middle, and an end, and exists more as a self-renewing loop. In that, it is faithful to comic books themselves, which month after month and year after year seem frozen in the same fictional universe. Yes, there are comics in which the characters age and their worlds change, but the X-Men seem likely to continue forever, demonstrating their superpowers in one showcase scene after another. Perhaps in the next generation a mutant will appear named Scribbler, who can write a better screenplay for them.   ☞

XXX ★ ★ ★ ½
PG-13, 124 m., 2002

Vin Diesel (Xander Cage), Samuel L. Jackson (NSA Agent Gibbons), Asia Argento (Yelena), Marton Csokas (Yorgi), Joe Bucaro III (Virg), TeeJay Boyce (Janelle). Directed by Rob Cohen and produced by Neal H. Moritz. Screenplay by Rich Wilkes.

XXX stars Vin Diesel as a smart-ass Bond with a bad attitude. The filmmakers have broken down the James Bond series into its inevitable components, constructed a screenplay that rips off 007 even in the small details, and then placed Diesel at the center of it—as Xander Cage, extreme sports hero and outlaw. In its own punk way, *XXX* is as good as a good Bond movie, and that's saying something.

Diesel is a tough guy with the shaved head, the tattoos, and the throwaway one-liners (after he's busted for stealing a car and driving it off a bridge, he says, "It was only a Corvette"). In last summer's *The Fast and the Furious,* he hurtled cars down city streets in death-defying races. As we meet him in *XXX,* he's a famous sports daredevil who steals computer chips and cars and is finally hunted down by Gibbons (Samuel L. Jackson), a National Security Agency spymaster with a scarred face and a role inspired by M in the Bond series.

If Bond is a patriot, Xander is a man who looks out only for No. 1, until Gibbons threatens him with prison unless he agrees to go to the Czech Republic and stop a madman with, yes, a plan to destroy and/or conquer the world. This villain, named Yorgi (Marton Csokas), apparently lives in the Prague Castle, which will come as a surprise to President Vaclav Havel. He's a renegade officer of the evil Czech Secret Service; the movie doesn't seem to know that the Cold War is over and Czechs are good guys these days, but never mind: The movie was shot on location in Prague, part of the current filmmaking boom in the republic, and the scenery is terrific.

Director Rob Cohen and producer Neal H. Moritz, who also made *The Fast and the Furious,* follow the Bond formula so carefully this would be a satire if it weren't intended as homage. We click off the 007 checkpoints: (1) villain in lair hidden within mountain, with faceless minions busily going about tasks; (2) a beautiful girl, former KGB, named Yelena (Asia Argento), who seems to be Yorgi's girlfriend but falls for Xander; (3) a techno-geek who supplies Xander with a trick gun and a customized GTO that has an arsenal onboard; (4) stunts involving parachuting, mountains, avalanches, and explosions; (5) a chase at the end to save the world; and (6), my favorite, the obligatory final scene where the hero basks in

Bora Bora with the beautiful girl in a bikini, while his boss tries to convince him to take another job.

Will he take another job? Of course he will. Xander Cage is a new franchise, and Vin Diesel, who was walking around Sundance a few years ago telling everyone he would someday be a big star, was right.

I love the lengths that villains go to in these movies. Consider Yorgi. He has devised an incredibly expensive steel speedboat armed with three rockets containing canisters of poison gas. This speedboat is inside a mountain cavern far below his lair. It is his superweapon for world domination. Fine, except where can a boat go in the landlocked Czech Republic? Down the Danube through Budapest and Vienna? In the event, he decides to attack Prague itself, and we're wondering: Considering how much it cost him to hollow out the mountain and build the boat, why not just put the gas canisters in a car and drive into town? Yorgi is the kind of bad guy who is beloved by the architects of the *Star Wars* defense, staging an attack that is cumbersome, costly, and visible, instead of just delivering the goods by FedEx.

As the boat speeds down the river into town, Xander does a stunt that is not only exciting but, even better, impossible. As the Russian babe pilots the GTO on a road parallel to the river, Xander fires a steel cable that attaches to the boat, and then he transfers from the car to the boat using the cable and a parasail. Wonderful, except . . . do you suppose there are any lampposts, traffic lights, or telephone poles along the road that the cable might get hung up on?

Never mind. Now Xander's onboard, trying to disarm the canisters by using a slicked-up cyber-version of the old standby where he has to decide between the green wire and the red wire. Meanwhile, Gibbons has a vantage point on one of the bridges, and is commanding fighter planes that are prepared to blast the boat out of the water, no doubt thereby dispersing the poison gas, but *c'est la vie.*

See, I like all this stuff, at least when it's done well. Vin Diesel's gruff, monosyllabic style is refreshing as a counterpoint to the gung-ho action, and the romantic scenes with the beautiful Yelena consist of two (2) kisses,

because Xander has a world to save. The music is aggressive heavy metal by the German band Rammstein, and Marton Csokas, as the villain, has one of those fleshy, sneering faces, surrounded by too much greasy hair, that goes with his central European accent. Oddly, he isn't from Transylvania at all, but from New Zealand, and you may have seen him on *Xena.* He likes to play opposite characters with X-names.

Is *XXX* a threat to the Bond franchise? Not a threat so much as a salute. I don't want James Bond to turn crude and muscular on me; I like the suave style. But I like Xander, too, especially since he seems to have studied Bond so very carefully. Consider the movie's big set-piece, totally in the 007 tradition, when Xander parachutes to a mountain top, surveys the bad guys on skimobiles below, throws a grenade to start an avalanche, and then outraces the avalanche on a snowboard while the bad guys are wiped out. Not bad. Now all he has to work on is the kissing.

XX/XY ★ ★ ★ ½
R, 91 m., 2003

Mark Ruffalo (Coles Burroughs), Kathleen Robertson (Thea), Maya Stange (Sam), Petra Wright (Claire), David Thornton (Miles). Directed by Austin Chick and produced by Isen Robbins and Aimee Schoof. Screenplay by Chick.

XX/XY portrays a man that many women will recognize on sight. Coles is like a social climber at a party, always looking past the woman he's with to see if a more perfect woman has just appeared. Women know his type, and sometimes, because he is smart and charming, they go along with the routine. But they're not fooled. Late in the film, when Coles finally tries to commit himself, a woman tells him, "You still haven't chosen me. You're settling for me."

As the film opens in the autumn of 1993, Coles (Mark Ruffalo) is studying film at Sarah Lawrence College. One night at a party he meets Sam (Maya Stange), and asks her, "Would you think I was being too forward if I said, 'Let's go back to your room?'" Her reply: "What would you say if I said, 'Let's go back to my room, but let's bring Thea?'" This was not what he had in mind, but openness to experimentation is obligatory for all Sarah Lawrence students, and besides, Thea (Kathleen Robertson) is intriguing in her outsider rebel way.

What follows is a kinduva sortuva ménage à trois; the possibility hovers that the real reason for including Thea is that she is Sam's roommate and so it seemed like good manners. The next day, as Sam and Coles discuss it on the phone, they both try to backtrack and Coles concludes, "So we're all sorry—but we all had fun." This is, if only Sam could intuit it, an analysis that Coles will be making frequently in the years to come.

Sam likes him. Coles likes her, but he cheats on her anyway, "meaninglessly," with a one-night stand. When he confesses, something breaks between them. When a man tells a woman he loves that he has cheated but "it didn't mean anything," this translates to the woman as, "It is meaningless to me that I cheated on you." Coles doesn't quite grasp this.

As undergraduates the three form the kinds of bonds that do not find closure with graduation. Ten years pass. Coles is now working in the advertising business in Manhattan, and has been living for five years with Claire (Petra Wright). He runs into Sam one day, and finds that she has returned to America after breaking off an engagement in London. She tells him that Thea, who was once so wild, is the first of the three to be married; she runs a restaurant with Miles (David Thornton).

Coles, of course, is attracted to Sam, who looks all the more desirable because she is now the woman he would be cheating with, instead of cheating on. She's on the rebound, and they share a heedless passionate heat. The victim now is Claire, who of all the characters is the wisest about human nature. She is trim, elegant, a little older than Coles, and knows exactly who he is and what he is. When she walks in on Coles and Sam, she walks out again, and conceals what she has seen because she is prepared to accept Coles, up to a point.

All of these lines of sexual intrigue come to a head in a weekend at the Hamptons house of Thea and Miles. To describe what happens would be wrong, but let's suggest it would be a comedy if written by Noel Coward but is not a comedy here. Much depends upon poor Coles, who is addicted to infatuation, and finds fidelity a painful deprivation in a world filled, he thinks, with perfect love that is almost within his grasp.

Mark Ruffalo plays the character with that elusive charm he also revealed in *You Can Count on Me*. In that film he was the unreliable brother of Laura Linney, who loved him but despaired of his irresponsibility. He has a way of smiling at a joke only he can understand. He isn't really a villain (there are no bad people in the movie), but more of a victim of his own inability to commit; he ends up unhappier than any of the people he disappoints.

Maya Stange and Kathleen Robertson find the right notes for their undergraduates who seem to trade places as adults—the reliable one becoming rootless while the daring one settles down. But it is Petra Wright who does the best and most difficult job among the women, finding a painful balance between Claire's self-respect and her desire to hang on to Coles. She is hurt not so much by his sexual infidelity as by his failure to value her seriously enough. "I feel a little like a consolation prize," she says at one point.

One review of this film complains that all of the characters are jerks, and asks why we should care about them. Well, jerks are often the most interesting characters in the movies, and sometimes the ones most like ourselves. *XX/XY* would be dismal if the characters all behaved admirably, but the writer and director, Austin Chick, knows too much about human nature to permit that. The film has a rare insight into the mechanism by which some men would rather pursue happiness than obtain it.

Y

Yi Yi ★ ★ ★ ½
NO MPAA RATING, 173 m., 2001

Nien-Jen Wu (N.J.), Issey Ogata (Mr. Ota), Elaine Jin (Min-Min), Kelly Lee (Ting-Ting), Jonathan Chang (Yang-Yang), Yupang Chang (Fatty), Chen Xisheng (A-Di), Ke Suyun (Sherry Chang-Breitner), Adrian Lin (Lili), Tang Ruyun (Grandma), Michael Tao (Da-Da), Xiao Shushen (Xiao Yan), Xu Shuyuan (Lili's Mother), Zeng Xinyi (Yun-Yun). Directed by Edward Yang and produced by Kawai Shinya and Tsukeda Naoko. Screenplay by Yang.

"Daddy, I can't see what you see and you can't see what I see. How can we know more than half the truth?"

So asks little Yang-Yang, the eight-year-old boy in *Yi Yi*, a movie in which nobody knows more than half the truth, or is happy more than half the time. The movie is a portrait of three generations of a Taiwanese family, affluent and successful, but haunted by lost opportunities and doubts about the purpose of life. Only rarely is a film this observant and tender about the ups and downs of daily existence; I am reminded of *Terms of Endearment*.

The hero of the film is N.J., an electronics executive with a wife, a mother-in-law, an adolescent daughter, an eight-year-old son, and a life so busy that he is rushing through middle age without paying much attention to his happiness. He's stunned one day when he sees a woman in an elevator: "Is it really you?" It is. It is Sherry, his first love, the girl he might have married thirty years ago. Now she lives in Chicago with her husband, Rodney, an insurance executive, but she follows him fiercely to demand, "Why didn't you come that day? I waited and waited. I never got over it."

Why didn't he come? Why did he marry this woman instead of that one? It is a question raised in the first scene of the movie, at another wedding, where a hysterical woman apologizes to the mother of the groom: "It should have been me marrying your son today!" Perhaps, but as a character observes near the end of the film, if he had done things differently, everything might have turned out about the same.

The family lives in a luxury high-rise. We gradually get to know its members and even the neighbors (one couple fights all the time). The mother-in-law has a stroke, goes into a coma, and the family takes turns reading and talking to her. One day N.J. (Wu Nienjen) comes home to find his wife, Min-Min (Elaine Jin), weeping: "I have nothing to say to Mother. I tell her the same things every day. I have so little. How can it be so little? I live a blank. If I ended up like her one day . . ." Yes, but one day, if we live long enough, we all do. Talking to someone in a coma, N.J. observes, is like praying: You're not sure the other party can hear, and not sure you're sincere.

Little Yang-Yang (Jonathan Chang) is too young for such thoughts, and adopts a more positive approach. He takes a photo of the back of his father's head, since the father can't see it and therefore has no way of being sure it is there. And he takes photos of the mosquitoes on the landing outside the apartment, sneaking out of school to collect the prints at the photo shop (his teacher ridicules his "avant-garde art").

Meanwhile, N.J. is visited by memories of Sherry. Should he have married her? One of his few confidants and friends is a Japanese businessman, Mr. Ota (Issey Ogata); it is a measure of the worlds they live in that their conversations must be conducted in English, the only language they have in common. They sing in a karaoke bar, and then Mr. Ota quiets the room by playing sad classical music on the piano. Late one night, returning to a darkened office, N.J. telephones Sherry (Ke Suyun). She wonders if they should start all over with each other.

N.J.'s teenage daughter, Ting-Ting (Kelly Lee), is also considering cheating, with Fatty (Yupang Chang), her best friend's boyfriend. They actually check into a love hotel, but "it's not right," he says. That's the thing about life: You think about transgressions, but a tidal pull pushes you back toward what you know is right.

The point of *Yi Yi* is not to force people into romantic decisions. Many mainstream American films are impatient; in them, people meet, they feel desire, they act on it. If you step back a little from a movie like *3,000 Miles to*

Graceland, you realize it is about stupid, selfish, violent monsters; the movie likes them and thinks it is a comedy. Our films have little time for thought, and our characters are often too superficial for their decisions to have any meaning—they're just plot points.

But the people in *Yi Yi* live considered lives. They feel committed to their families. Their vague romantic yearnings are more like background noise than calls to action. There are some scenes of adultery in the movie, involving characters I have not yet mentioned, but they come across as shabby and sad.

The movie is about the currents of life. But it's not solemn in a Bergmanesque way. N.J. and his family live in a riot of everyday activity; the grandmother in a coma is balanced by Yang-Yang dropping a water balloon on precisely the wrong person. Some scenes edge toward slapstick. Others show characters through the cold, hard windows of modern skyscrapers, bathed in icy fluorescence, their business devoid of any juice or heart.

There was a time when a film from Taiwan would have seemed foreign and unfamiliar—when Taiwan had a completely different culture from ours. The characters in *Yi Yi* live in a world that would be much the same in Toronto, London, Bombay, Sydney; in their economic class, in their jobs, culture is established by corporations, real estate, fast food, and the media, not by tradition. N.J. and Yang-Yang eat at McDonald's, and other characters meet in a Taipei restaurant named New York Bagels. Maybe the movie is not simply about knowing half of the truth, but about knowing the wrong half of the truth.

Note: Yi Yi is unrated; it is appropriate for mature audiences. It was named best film of the year by the National Society of Film Critics.

Y Tu Mama Tambien ★ ★ ★ ★
NO MPAA RATING, 105 m., 2002

Maribel Verdu (Luisa Cortes), Gael Garcia Bernal (Julio Zapata), Diego Luna (Tenoch Iturbide). Directed by Alfonso Cuaron and produced by Alfonso Cuaron and Jorge Vergara. Screenplay by Alfonso Cuaron and Carlos Cuaron.

Y Tu Mama Tambien is described on its Website as a "teen drama," which is like describing *Moulin Rouge* as a musical. The description is technically true but sidesteps all of the reasons to see the movie. Yes, it's about two teenage boys and an impulsive journey with an older woman that involves sexual discoveries. But it is also about the two Mexicos. And it is about the fragility of life and the finality of death. Beneath the carefree road movie that the movie is happy to advertise is a more serious level—and below that, a dead serious level.

The movie, whose title translates as *"And Your Mama, Too,"* is another trumpet blast that there may be a New Mexican Cinema a-bornin'. Like *Amores Perros,* which also stars Gael Garcia Bernal, it is an exuberant exercise in interlocking stories. But these interlock not in space and time, but in what is revealed, what is concealed, and in the parallel world of poverty through which the rich characters move.

The surface is described in a flash: Two Mexican teenagers named Tenoch and Julio, one from a rich family, one middle class, are free for the summer when their girlfriends go to Europe. At a wedding they meet a cousin named Luisa, ten years older, who is sexy and playful. They suggest a weekend trip to the legendary beach named Heaven's Mouth. When her fiancé cheats on her, she unexpectedly agrees, and they set out together on a lark.

This level could have been conventional but is anything but, as directed by Alfonso Cuaron, who cowrote the screenplay with his brother Carlos. Luisa kids them about their sex lives in a lighthearted but tenacious way, until they have few secrets left, and at the same time she teases them with erotic possibilities. The movie is realistic about sex, which is to say, franker and healthier than the smutty evasions forced on American movies by the R rating. We feel a shock of recognition: This is what real people do and how they do it, sexually, and the MPAA has perverted a generation of American movies into puerile, masturbatory snickering.

Whether Luisa will have sex with one or both of her new friends is not for me to reveal. More to the point is what she wants to teach them, which is that men and women learn to share sex as a treasure they must carry together without something spilling—that women are not prizes, conquests, or targets, but the other half of a precarious unity. This is news to the boys, who are obsessed with orgasms (needless to say, their own).

The progress of that story provides the surface arc of the movie. Next to it, in a kind of parallel world, is the Mexico they are driving through. They pass police checkpoints, see drug busts and traffic accidents, drive past shantytowns, and are stopped at a roadblock of flowers by villagers who demand a donation for their queen—a girl in bridal white, representing the Virgin. "You have a beautiful queen," Luisa tells them. Yes, but the roadblock is genteel extortion. The queen has a sizable court that quietly hints a donation is in order.

At times during this journey the sound track goes silent and we hear a narrator who comments from outside the action, pointing out the village where Tenoch's nanny was born, and left at thirteen to seek work. Or a stretch of road where, two years earlier, there was a deadly accident. The narration and the roadside images are a reminder that in Mexico and many other countries a prosperous economy has left an uneducated and penniless peasantry behind.

They arrive at the beach. They are greeted by a fisherman and his family, who have lived here for four generations, sell them fried fish, rent them a place to stay. This is an unspoiled paradise. (The narrator informs us the beach will be purchased for a tourist hotel, and the fisherman will abandon his way of life, go to the city in search of a job, and finally come back here to work as a janitor.) Here the sexual intrigues that have been developing all along will find their conclusion.

Beneath these two levels (the coming-of-age journey, the two Mexicos) is hidden a third.

I will say nothing about it, except to observe there are only two shots in the entire movie that reflect the inner reality of one of the characters. At the end, finally knowing everything, you think back through the film—or, as I was able to do, see it again.

Alfonso Cuaron is Mexican but his first two features were big-budget American films. I thought *Great Expectations* (1998), with Ethan Hawke, Gwyneth Paltrow, and Anne Bancroft, brought a freshness and visual excitement to the updated story. I liked *A Little Princess* (1995) even more. It is clear Cuaron is a gifted director, and here he does his best work to date. Why did he return to Mexico to make it? Because he has something to say about Mexico, obviously, and also because Jack Valenti and the MPAA have made it impossible for a movie like this to be produced in America. It is a perfect illustration of the need for a workable adult rating: too mature, thoughtful, and frank for the R, but not in any sense pornographic. Why do serious film people not rise up in rage and tear down the rating system that infantilizes their work?

The key performance is by Maribel Verdu, as Luisa. She is the engine that drives every scene she's in, as she teases, quizzes, analyzes, and lectures the boys, as if impatient with the task of turning them into beings fit to associate with an adult woman. In a sense she fills the standard role of the sexy older woman, so familiar from countless Hollywood comedies, but her character is so much more than that—wiser, sexier, more complex, happier, sadder. It is true, as some critics have observed, that *Y Tu Mama* is one of those movies where "after that summer, nothing would ever be the same again." Yes, but it redefines "nothing."

Z

Zoolander ★
PG-13, 90 m., 2001

Ben Stiller (Derek Zoolander), Owen Wilson (Hansel), Christine Taylor (Matilda Jeffries), Will Ferrell (Jacobim Mugatu), Jerry Stiller (Maury Ballstein), Milla Jovovich (Katinka), David Pressman (Phil), Matt Levin (Archie). Directed by Ben Stiller and produced by Stuart Cornfeld, Scott Rudin, and Stiller. Screenplay by Drake Sather, Stiller, and John Hamburg, based on a story by Sather and Stiller.

There have been articles lately asking why the United States is so hated in some parts of the world. As this week's Exhibit A from Hollywood, I offer *Zoolander,* a comedy about a plot to assassinate the prime minister of Malaysia because of his opposition to child labor. You might want to read that sentence twice. The logic: Child labor is necessary to the economic health of the fashion industry, and so its opponents must be eliminated. Ben Stiller stars as Derek Zoolander, a moronic male model who is brainwashed to perform the murder.

Malaysia is a mostly Muslim country with a flag that looks a lot like ours: It has the red and white stripes of the American flag, and a blue field in the upper left corner, which instead of stars displays Islamic symbols, the star and crescent. Malaysia is home to the Petronas Towers of Kuala Lumpur, the world's tallest buildings. But you get the point. If the Malaysians made a comedy about the assassination of the president of the United States because of his opposition to slavery, it would seem approximately as funny to us as *Zoolander* would seem to them.

I realize I am getting all serious on you. Obviously, in times like these, we need a little escapism. "Hagrid," a critic at Ain't It Cool News, went to see *Zoolander* feeling "a comedy is just what I needed, and what I feel everybody needs at this time." His verdict? "It's a perfect film to help people forget everything for a few hours, and it's gonna be huge."

Well, you know, I wanted to forget, but the movie kept making me remember. I felt particularly uncomfortable during the scenes involving the prime minister, shown as an elderly

Asian man who is brought to New York to attend a fashion show where he is targeted for assassination. I would give you his name, since he has a lot of screen time, but the movie's Website ignores him and the entry on the Internet Movie Database, which has room to list twenty-six actors, neglects to provide it. Those old Asian actors are just placeholders, I guess, and anyone could play the prime minister.

For that matter, any country could play Malaysia. In years past, movies invented fictional countries to make fun of. Groucho Marx once played Rufus T. Firefly, the dictator of Fredonia, and *The Mouse That Roared* was about the Duchy of Grand Fenwick. Didn't it strike *anybody* connected with this movie that it was in bad taste to name a real country with a real prime minister? A serious political drama would be one thing, but why take such an offensive shot in a silly comedy?

To some degree, *Zoolander* is a victim of bad timing, although I suspect I would have found the assassination angle equally tasteless before September 11. The movie is a satirical jab at the fashion industry, and there are points scored, and some good stuff involving Stiller and Owen Wilson, who play the world's two top male models—funny in itself. The best moments involve the extreme stupidity of the Stiller character. Shown a model of a literary center to be built in his honor, he sweeps it to the floor, exclaiming: "This is a center for ants! How can we teach children to read if they can't even fit inside the building?" Funny, yes, and I like the hand model whose hand is sealed inside a hyperbaric chamber to protect it.

I also admire the ruthlessness with which *Zoolander* points out that the fashion industry does indeed depend on child labor. The back-to-school clothes of American kids are largely made by Third World kids who don't go to school. In fact, the more you put yourself into the shoes (if he had any) of a Muslim twelve-year-old in a sport-shirt factory, the more you might understand why he resents rich Americans, and might be offended by a movie about the assassination of his prime minister (if he had the money to go to a movie). Kids like that don't grow up to think of America as fondly as the people who designed his flag.

Responding quickly to the tragedy of September 11, the makers of *Zoolander* did some last-minute editing. No, they didn't dub over the word "Malaysia" or edit around the assassination of the prime minister. What they did was digitally erase the World Trade Center from the New York skyline, so that audiences would not be reminded of the tragedy, as if we have forgotten. It's a good thing no scenes were shot in Kuala Lumpur, or they probably would have erased the Petronas Towers, to keep us from getting depressed or jealous or anything.

Note: This review, written soon after September 11, is more harsh than it would have been if that tragedy had not taken place.

The Best Films of 2002

It was a year when more movies opened than during any other year in memory. A year when the big Hollywood studios cast their lot with franchises, formulas, sequels, and movies marketed for narrow demographic groups—focusing so much on "product" instead of original work that they seemed likely to be shut out of the Oscars, as they were essentially shut out of the Golden Globes. A year when independent and foreign films showed extraordinary vitality. A wonderful year, that is, for moviegoers who chose carefully, and a mediocre year for those took their chances at the multiplex.

And yet the best movie of the year defied these trends. It was an expensive big-studio production by the most successful director of all time—top-lining a big star, and occupying the popular science fiction genre. But it was brilliant, a film of ideas as well as action, of seamless integration of a strong story with virtuoso special effects.

1. *Minority Report*

Steven Spielberg's movie starred Tom Cruise as a policeman of the future, a man in charge of a program that uses three "precogs," who can foresee the future, allowing them to predict crimes so they can be prevented before they happen. Based on a 1956 story by Philip K. Dick, the movie combined a classic murder plot with sensational futuristic effects and a strong human story.

The Cruise character, still devastated over the disappearance of his young son years earlier, is endangered by an apparent loophole in the precog system. In one of the most extraordinary chase sequences ever filmed, he flees from police while guided by one of the precognatives (Samantha Morton), who gives him instructions based on what is about to happen. The movie is visually dazzling. A sequence involving computer-generated "spiders" who search for Cruise within the elaborate set of a boardinghouse is one of the most impressive displays of technical mastery I have ever seen. It also works

as pure moviemaking. The whole movie does. *Minority Report* is mainstream moviemaking at its most sublime.

2. *City of God*

This Brazilian film will reach a fraction of Spielberg's audience, yet is no less accomplished. A bare plot description makes it sound familiar, and yet in its energy, its dramatic impact, and its exuberant visual style, it is astonishing—the Rio de Janeiro version of *GoodFellas*. Director Fernando Meirelles sets his story in the crime-based culture of the slums of Rio, where opportunities are scarce and drugs and guns are the facts of daily life. He follows a group of kids as they grow up into the city's most famous gangs, and then, after a gang war, shows the whole process starting again.

But that description is pathetically inadequate to describe the film's power and craft. The camera is everywhere, looking, reacting, probing; a fast-forward sequence traces the drug history of one apartment over the years; a subplot shows a character named Rocket who stumbles into a career as a newspaper photographer because he lives in a world of photo opportunities. Meirelles's camera work is flashy, but not tricky; his style is appropriate to the intensity of his story, as the movie races headlong through these Brazilian mean streets.

3. *Adaptation*

What a delightfully dizzying film about itself! Screenwriter Charlie Kaufman is assigned to adapt the book *The Orchid Thief* for the movies. It's an investigation by *New Yorker* writer Susan Orlean into the obsessions of a Florida swamp rat named John Laroche, who steals protected orchids. But the assignment jumps the rails and the movie is about both the book and the struggle to adapt it.

Kaufman and his (fictional) twin brother, Donald, both played by Nicolas Cage, wage a war over movie styles. Charlie is intense and serious, while Donald cheerfully uses commercial formulas to churn out a successful potboiler.

Charlie meanwhile develops a crush on Orlean (Meryl Streep), who in turn is attracted to the intensity she feels from Laroche (Chris Cooper). The movie's director, Spike Jonze, earlier teamed up with Kaufman on *Being John Malkovich*, the best movie of 1999. Once again they've made a film that is, in a way, about the experience of watching it.

4. *Far from Heaven*

In a sense, this is the best film of 1957 that was never made. Todd Haynes deliberately uses the styles, looks, themes, and feel of a 1950s melodrama to investigate two subjects—homosexuality and interracial romance—that were only hinted at in that decade. His model is Douglas Sirk, who in films like *All That Heaven Allows* and *Written on the Wind* used mannered melodrama as a way of dealing with themes that were only subtly hinted at.

Because the movie uses this style sincerely, not ironically, watching it is like watching a well-crafted period film. Julianne Moore stars as a model housewife whose life goes into turmoil when her husband (Dennis Quaid) is revealed as gay, while she begins to feel strong affection for her black gardener (Dennis Haysbert). Like *Adaptation*, this is the kind of movie that makes us more aware of how we experience movies, and why.

5. 13 *Conversations About One Thing*

Directed by Jill Sprecher, cowritten with her sister Karen, this is a movie that circles through a group of characters in search of happiness. Matthew McConaughey plays a prosecutor who finds happiness is not the same thing as success; John Turturro is a professor who thinks he can find it by leaving his wife; Clea DuVall deserves it but is denied it; Alan Arkin is an insurance executive who does not want to cause unhappiness by firing someone.

There have been many movies that circle like a Mobius strip back to where they began. Among recent films, *Pulp Fiction* is the obvious model. Sometimes it's only a device. Here the story circles through its characters to explore the way one life rubs against another, usually by chance, in a way that undoes plans and allows fate to make our decisions. It is also crucial that this film really cares about its characters—does

not see them as markers in a story line, but as people who do, or do not, deserve what they get.

6. *Y Tu Mama Tambien*

Alfonso Cuaron has made three films in one. On the top level, he tells the story of two teenage boys who drive to a legendary beach with a woman some ten years older, who initiates them, not into the world of sex (which they are somewhat familiar with) but into the world of adult feelings. On another level, he uses a narrator to make sad or angry comments about developments in modern Mexico—comments suggested by the places they go and the people they meet. On the deepest level, the movie is about living and dying, and about a character who carries on in the face of despair.

7. *Invincible*

Harmed by thin distribution and wrongheaded reviews, this film by the great Werner Herzog did not find the audience it deserved. It is a fable based on fact, set in 1930s Nazi Germany, about a Polish Jewish strongman, a blacksmith who wins a contest at a circus and is recruited to work for a Berlin charlatan (Tim Roth) who presides over a museum of mesmerism. The showman transforms the simple Jewish man into a fictional Nordic character named Siegfried, but as the strongman realizes what is being done, he rebels. There are countless movies about preludes to the Holocaust, but I can't think of one this innocent, direct, and unblinking in the face of the gathering evil.

8. *Spirited Away*

Hayao Miyazaki of Japan is the greatest living master of animation, and this is a wonderful work about a ten-year-old girl who wanders away from her parents in a ghostly amusement park, and finds herself in a world of fantastical characters. Miyazaki's films aren't ceaselessly eager to make us smile; they use mood, tone, and timing to deeply engage with their characters, which is why adults as well as children find his work so enchanting.

9. *All or Nothing*

The new film by Mike Leigh tells the story of a London minicab driver and his family—a worn down common-law wife, a lonely daughter, a son who is a rude and uncouth couch potato. Hope and cheer have gone out of this family, until a sudden event shocks them back into optimism. With Timothy Spall as the cabbie and Lesley Manville as his kind but despairing wife.

10. *The Quiet American*

A masterful performance by Michael Caine and another, no less assured, by Brendan Fraser, bring touching humanity to this story by Graham Greene, set in the early 1950s. Caine plays a British correspondent in Vietnam, and Fraser is the young American who arrives for apparently innocent reasons. Both fall in love with the same dance hall girl, and are as deceived in romance as in politics. The movie observes that the CIA used terrorist techniques to create a pretense for U.S. military involvement in Vietnam, but in a curious way that is only a backdrop to the deeper story of lost love and wounded idealism.

Overlooked Jury Prize

At film festivals, juries often award a special jury prize to a film that did not win first place and yet is strongly advocated by some of the jury members. It's kind of a minority report. This year my own Overlooked Jury Prize is shared by ten more or less overlooked films that did not reach the audiences they deserved. Some had moderate success, some were almost entirely neglected, some were praised by critics, while others, such as *Femme Fatale* and *The Man from Elysian Fields*, got bitterly divided reviews. Alphabetically:

Diamond Men, written and directed by Daniel M. Cohen, starred Robert Forster in a career performance as a traveling diamond salesman who is required to train his successor (Donnie Wahlberg). They learn from each other, in a plot that coils from business through crime to romance. *Fast Runner*, directed by Zacharias Kunuk, written by Paul Apak Angilirq, is an incredible saga filmed north of the Arctic Circle, and telling a legend of the Inuit peoples, about a feud between brothers that threatens the community.

Femme Fatale was Brian De Palma's elegant, sexy, and masterful thriller, starring Rebecca Romijn-Stamos as a woman who steals a dress made of diamonds—during the Cannes Film Festival. *Frailty*, directed by Bill Paxton, stars him as a father who becomes convinced he is receiving murder directives from an angel. The father enlists his young sons in the killings, in a fearsome reign of terror he says is sanctioned by heaven. *The Grey Zone*, directed by Tim Blake Nelson, tells the story of a revolt by Jewish prisoners in a Nazi death camp, and of an impossible choice presented when a young girl survives the gas chambers. Can one make moral decisions within a closed system that is totally evil?

Ivans xtc., directed by Bernard Rose, written by Rose and Lisa Enos, stars Danny Huston in a performance of startling power, as a Hollywood agent whose cocaine addiction is interrupted by a diagnosis of cancer. As he painfully approaches death, the film watches the sad forms of his courage. *Lovely and Amazing*, written and directed by Nicole Holofcener, is about a mother (Brenda Blethyn) and her three daughters, two adults (Emily Mortimer and Catherine Keener), one a young adopted girl (Raven Goodwin). All these women have body-image problems, explored with sympathy and sharp humor.

The Man from Elysian Fields, directed by George Hickenlooper, written by Phillip Jayson Lasker, stars Andy Garcia as a debt-ridden writer who signs up with an escort agency run by Mick Jagger, and meets a famous old writer (James Coburn) and his wife (Olivia Williams). It is a film about sex, privilege, service—and writing. *Songs from the Second Floor*, written and directed by Roy Andersson, is one of the strangest and most haunting films I've ever seen, as a gray and dismal city approaches the apocalypse with parades of flagellants, bizarre sacrifices, and darkly comic satire. Deadpan surrealism, Tati crossed with Dali.

And *24 Hour Party People*, directed by Michael Winterbottom, written by Frank Cottrell Boyce, tells the story of the Manchester, England, music scene from the first Sex Pistols concert until the last bankruptcy. It shines with the inspired madness of its hero, a TV personality named Tony Wilson, who takes himself seriously in a way that is utterly impossible to take seriously.

Eleventh Place

Top ten lists by their nature are frustrating. After the critic names the best film of the year, does it really matter that one title is seventh and another ninth? One year when I alphabetized my list, however, readers were furious, as if I'd shirked my duty.

There were many films this year I admired or loved or was delighted by. If the jury prize is sort of an alternative top ten, then here are the films tied for eleventh place:

About a Boy, About Schmidt, Antwone Fisher, Auto Focus, Baran, Blade, Blood Work, Bloody Sunday, Bowling for Columbine, Changing Lanes, Chicago, Diaries of Vaslav Nijinsky, Frida, Gangs of New York, Good Girl, Harry Potter and the Chamber of Secrets, How I Killed My Father, Igby Goes Down, Insomnia, Kandahar, The Kid Stays in the Picture, Kwik Stop, Lagaan, Last Orders, Les Destinées, Lilo & Stitch, Lord of the Rings: The Two Towers, Maryam, Metropolis, Me Without You, Moonlight Mile, Nicholas Nickleby, One Hour Photo, Personal Velocity, The Pianist, Piano Teacher, Possession, Pumpkin, Punch-Drunk Love, Rabbit-Proof Fence, Read My Lips, Real Women Have Curves, Red Dragon, Signs, Sleepy Time Gal, Solaris, A Song for Martin, Son's Room, Standing in the Shadows of Motown, Storytelling, Sum of All Fears, Sunshine State, Talk to Her, Tully, 25th Hour, What Time Is It There? and *XXX.*

Interviews

Paul Thomas Anderson and Adam Sandler

October 8, 2002—So there I am at the Toronto Film Festival, eyeing Adam Sandler across the room. He knows and I know that I have never given him a good review. That time we met backstage at *Letterman,* he was very decent, considering. He said he hoped that someday he would make something I liked. Now he has.

The movie is *Punch-Drunk Love,* by Paul Thomas Anderson. The moment it was announced, I got a lot of e-mails from people asking what in the *hell* Anderson was thinking of, making an Adam Sandler movie. Such is the power of Sandler's presence that it didn't occur to them it might be a Paul Thomas Anderson movie. Now I have seen it, and can report that it is both: an Adam Sandler movie by Paul Thomas Anderson. Imagine a Tom Green movie by Martin Scorsese. No, that's easier.

Punch-Drunk Love, which opened October 18, stars Sandler as the peculiar, mannered operator of a small business, who meets a strange woman (Emily Watson) and follows her to Hawaii after discovering that buying $3,000 in pudding will win him enough frequent flier miles. Sandler plays a character not unlike the person he usually portrays—*Variety* didn't call him "the king of moronic farce" for nothing—but the movie looks deeper and finds a pool of anger just below the passive-aggressive surface.

Having admired the movie, I went to the party afterward on the reasonable grounds that I might never again be able to do what I was doing right now. I walked over to Adam Sandler and told him I liked his movie.

"I will have to tell my parents, so they can watch your show again," he said. He talked just the way he talks in the movies: flat and a little childlike, with an edge. "They had to stop watching your show because it made them say bad words."

I said I could understand how that might be. A human tide separated us, and washed me up the next afternoon for an interview with Paul Thomas Anderson, who after *Boogie Nights* (1997) and *Magnolia* (1999) has emerged as one

of the most gifted filmmakers of his generation (he is thirty-two).

The last time I met Anderson, he sat on my back porch in Chicago and promised me that the reproductive equipment of Mark Wahlberg, so memorably on view in *Boogie Nights,* was absolutely and in every respect Wahlberg's own. There had been reports it was a special effect, or a stand-in, whatever. Later I learned that the treasures were not, in fact, authentic. Did I now accuse Anderson of lying? I didn't even bring it up, mostly because I had forgotten it. So quickly do big issues shrink with the passage of time.

I was in a lather to quiz him on Adam Sandler. Why would a brilliant young auteur throw himself on the altar of the king of moronic farce?

"I wanted to work with Sandler so much," he said, "because if I've ever been kinda sad or down or whatever, I just wanna pop in an Adam Sandler movie."

That wouldn't cheer me up, I said.

"I love him," Anderson said, "and he's always made me laugh. I like just about all of his movies and have always felt comfort in watching them. It's Saturday night and if I wanna watch something fun, I'm gonna watch an Adam Sandler movie. Or if I'm sad, I'm popping in an Adam Sandler movie. The last thing I would wanna do is watch *Magnolia,* you know, or *Breaking the Waves.* So I'm looking at Sandler and thinking, God, I wanna get a piece of that. I wanna learn from that dude. What is it that's so appealing about him to so many people? I think he's this great communicator, you know."

He doesn't seem to communicate very well with the critics.

"This sort of bashing from critics that he's taken is just defeatist, really. His films are obviously good because they're obviously communicating something to a lot of people, and they're making them laugh, and that's it, at the end of the day."

I kept an open mind. I hoped to like one of them.

"You should revisit some of them. *The Wedding Singer,* and *Big Daddy,* and especially *Happy Gilmore.* Those three, in particular, I could watch them over and over and over again just from the pure joy that you can feel them putting into making the movie, which is just as much joy as you can feel Robert Altman putting into making *Nashville.*"

I said there was something about Sandler that intrigued me, because he is obviously someone with a real talent, and it made me mad when he hid inside that goofy persona.

"He is a pretty nice dude," Anderson said, "and maybe you pick up on that. The second night that I met him, we went to have dinner and we're walking down the street, and I've never seen anything like it. I've walked down the street with some big movie stars, but walking down the street with him made my heart as warm as you can imagine—because of people's response to him and his sort of openness and response to them. This kid just kinda out of the blue came up and said, 'I'm Jewish, I'm Jewish,' with a real sense of pride in being Jewish, and Adam said, 'Great.' And it was just because of the *Hanukkah Song,* you know. And it was like, I wanna steal some of that. I wanna be around that kind of life force."

We are sprawled in overstuffed leather chairs in a back room of the Windsor Arms in Toronto. We are back here so he can smoke. Anderson wears a wrinkled white dress shirt, blue shorts, and the regulation four-day growth of beard. When he and Sandler decided that Sandler's character would wear a suit and tie throughout *Punch-Drunk Love,* you can see how they thought that would be funny.

Have you made an Adam Sandler movie, or a Paul Thomas Anderson movie? I asked.

"It's like an art house Adam Sandler movie," he said.

It's like you deconstructed the Adam Sandler movies and put them back together again in a new way at a different level.

"That's nice," said Anderson.

Adam Sandler, who generally generates his own films, could never have made this film. Yet his fans will still be seeing Adam Sandler.

Anderson lit a cigarette. "He just appealed to me, point-blank," he said. "He's someone who's taken such a bashing, but still, he was high on my list. In meeting him it all came clear to me.

We have a really similar work ethic. Kind of obsessive and consumed by it. And also, I wanted to learn from him about his attack on stuff. How does he make his movies, what are his concerns? His concerns a lot of times are, what is funny? What will make them laugh? And coming out of making *Magnolia* and living with that for a while, I went, God, I would really like to take a left turn and make myself happy, get rid of all this cancer and crying."

I said that when I look at Sandler's movies I think I see an anger just below the surface.

"Absolutely. I saw this *Best of Adam Sandler* DVD from *Saturday Night Live,* and an amazing thing happened. There's this moment when he's doing this talk show called *The Denise Show,* about his ex-girlfriend who's left him, and his father calls up and says, 'What are you doing? You're embarrassing the family.' And Adam goes into this fit of rage, screaming at his father, and honest to God I saw this moment where it appears as if the whites of his eyes turn black and they roll back in his head. It was like, he just lost his mind. I would play it back, over and over again, and you can see him kinda snap back to reality. The audience is laughing and it's almost like he finally started to hear them laughing a few seconds later."

All comedians are said to be tragic at heart.

"I think it's true. It's probably something to do with feeling like an impostor. You beat yourself up and you make yourself feel like you're kinda worthless. It can turn into a rage."

Have you previewed this film like in a multiplex on Saturday night, in the Valley or somewhere?

"No."

Let's hypothesize two audiences. One audience would be the festivals at Cannes and Toronto and your local art theater. The other audience would be Adam Sandler fans who heard he has a new movie out. Do you think they will see two different films?

"If I've screwed up, they might."

Nicolas Cage, Spike Jonze, and Charlie Kaufman

December 2, 2002—I am engaged in a fierce inner struggle as I begin this article about the brilliant new movie *Adaptation.* Part of me wants to write showbiz gossip. The other part wants to get serious and deal with the cinema of Spike Jonze, the inside-out screenplays of Charlie Kaufman, and the way Nicolas Cage plays twins you can tell apart even though they look the same.

High road or low road? That's the same struggle the movie itself gets involved in. Should it be a movie about an orchid thief? Or a comedy *about* a movie about an orchid thief?

The thief is named John Laroche. He prowls the Everglades, searching for rare orchids that the government says he can't have. A writer for the *New Yorker* named Susan Orlean wrote a book about him named, of course, *The Orchid Thief*, and then Spike Jonze and Charlie Kaufman were brought in to make a movie about it. Jonze directed and Kaufman wrote *Being John Malkovich*, which was the best film of 1999. Now they've teamed up again, with a cast including Meryl Streep as Orlean and Chris Cooper as Laroche.

But it isn't quite that simple. (Hollow laugh.) No, it isn't that simple because *The Orchid Thief* is a book with a great deal of information about orchids. Perhaps too much information. I know, because I started listening to the audio-book and bogged down somewhere in the fourth cassette during long lists of exotic orchids and Victorian orchid hunters who prowled the jungles of the world murdering one another.

Charlie Kaufman came to the same conclusion about the difficulty of writing a screenplay based on *The Orchid Thief*. We know this because *Adaptation*, which is one of the most devious and entertaining screenplays ever written, is *about* how he got bogged down. At the same time he was sweating blood over his keyboard, wouldn't you know that his twin brother, Donald, was hammering out a trashy potboiler while using the screenwriting theories of Robert McKee, the screenplay guru who advises his students to study and emulate (i.e., copy) the most popular screenplays of the past.

There is a crisis in the movie when Donald sells his screenplay for big bucks and Charlie, in desperation, takes a McKee workshop and is given frank, brutal, and profane advice by the great man himself, who pointedly observes that *Casablanca* is the greatest screenplay ever written. The inescapable conclusion is that Charlie's screenplay isn't.

I hope you are not confused yet, because the confusing part only starts now. It starts when I enter a room at the Peninsula Hotel in Chicago to interview Nicolas Cage, Spike Jonze, and Charlie Kaufman. There they are, positioned around the coffee table like my parole board. I have been warned they will not pose for photographs and will not do TV interviews. The publicity for this movie is being handled with all the candor of Putin explaining what was in the gas.

I open with a casual question for Kaufman: "Do you really have a twin brother named Donald?"

The three men jerk visibly. This is obviously the wrong question.

Kaufman looks at Cage and Cage looks at Jonze and Jonze answers. I did not understand what he said, but luckily I had a tape recorder, and so here are his exact words:

"Well, I just wanna . . . that's the first question, that Donald question, which is something we get a lot and we don't wanna—we're not trying to be deceptive about it or trying to be, you know, like, make a trick out of it, but I guess in all earnestness we want to try and leave it part of the experience of the movie is what, you know. These characters, you know, certain aspects of the movie exist in the real world and part of it's fiction and to try and leave that open so people can have that experience going and seeing the movie without necessarily having it all defined and so I guess that's sort of our concern, in part, about sort of opening that can of worms."

In other words, no, Charlie does not have a twin brother named Donald, even though he shares credit on the screenplay. *Adaptation* weaves back and forth between reality and fiction so skillfully, however, that if Charlie doesn't have a twin he might as well.

Real people appear as themselves in the movie, including John Malkovich, Catherine Keener, and John Cusack. There really are a Susan Orlean and a John Laroche, but they are played by Streep and Cooper, wading through the Everglades looking for the Deaths' Head orchid. These scenes are in the book, which is nonfiction. Other scenes, where Nicolas Cage, as Kaufman, stalks Orlean and develops a crush on her, are not in the book, because when the book was written Kaufman and his screenplay were not in the picture.

I hope I am not making this sound like work. *Adaptation* is one of the funniest, smartest, most diabolically twisty movies I have ever seen. And it presents a particularly tricky challenge for the Academy of Motion Picture Arts and Sciences. Kaufman's screenplay will obviously be nominated for the Oscar, but does it belong in the best screenplay adaptation category (as an adaptation of *The Orchid Thief*), or in the best original screenplay category as an original screenplay *about* a screenplay adaptation? And when the presenter opens the envelope and reads out, "Charles and Donald Kaufman," does Charlie accept on behalf of his brother?

But back to the hotel suite. It is clear that Cage, Jonze, and Kaufman know they have made a great movie, and are paralyzingly conflicted about how to go about promoting it. If they don't even want to say whether Charlie has a twin, where do they go from there?

"Nick Cage must not like the movie," Jay Leno told me a few weeks ago, "because he wouldn't come on the show to talk about it."

Maybe it's because he likes it too much. There's no way he can talk about his performance without getting into the matter of the mysterious twin. In the hotel, however, Cage does break down a little. To play the twins, he had to do a lot of scenes in which he was acting opposite himself:

"I'd be literally acting with a tennis ball or an X on a wall, to tell me where to look, and an earpiece in my ear listening to whatever I had already recorded so that I wouldn't overlap dialogue. And then I'd try to move so it worked with my memory of what I'd done as the other character."

"I could always tell whether I was looking at Charlie or Donald," I said.

"Donald has better posture than Charlie, for example," Cage said.

Jonze said, "The only difference physically was that Charlie would be unshaven and Donald would be clean-shaven."

Charlie looks back and forth, fascinated, as we discuss this.

"I think Donald had a little more hair," I said.

"No, he didn't," Cage said. "But it's interesting you would say that, because maybe his greater confidence made him *seem* like he had more hair."

"Or maybe with his better posture he stood up straighter, so I couldn't see the top," I speculated.

"Same amount of hair," Cage repeated.

"Even when they're not talking," Jonze said, "even when they're driving in the car, you know which one is driving."

"I was a fan of Jeremy Irons's performance as twins in *Dead Ringers*," Cage said. "But I'd get frustrated when we would switch the characters three or four times a day. At one point I literally screamed out of frustration and Spike would talk me down."

Some of the funniest and most pointed scenes in the movie involve Robert McKee, who is idolized in some circles and loathed in others because of his writing workshops. In the movie, McKee is called by his real name but played by the actor Brian Cox, who incidentally is a close friend of McKee's.

"You have a lot of people playing themselves in this movie," I said, "but you don't have Robert McKee playing himself."

"It seems consistent," Jonze said, "that since we were gonna have an actor play Susan Orlean, John Laroche, Charlie Kaufman, and Donald Kaufman, that we would have an actor play Robert McKee. And Brian Cox was actually Robert McKee's suggestion. McKee saw it about a month or two ago and he said that it was funny, but it was fair . . ."

There is a point in the movie where it seems to jump the rails and *become* a Robert McKee formula, and I asked if that was a buried ironic commentary on the whole struggle between earnest Charlie and commercial Donald. That question inspired two answers that once again required decryption:

Kaufman: "I mean, we hold all the cards here and so again we don't really wanna say anything about—our opinions about—I mean, in the movie, we don't wanna say anything—it's like, we wanna open up a dialogue with the audience and to do that fairly I think we wanted to present McKee fairly and so . . ."

Jonze: "Leave it open to people's intuition of what they're going into it with, because what they're going into it with is gonna decide what they take out of it."

Which is, in fact, the simple truth. How you react to the ending of *Adaptation* will depend entirely on how you react to other movies.

Some audience members will get all involved and excited and really care. Others will nod with an ironic smile. I will end this article with a piece of advice: If you attend the movie on a date, and one of you is all worked up at the end and the other has an ironic smile, your relationship is going nowhere.

Clint Eastwood

July 31, 2002—Clint Eastwood looks more like Clint Eastwood than ever. The furnace of time has burned away everything that is not essential. He comes to Chicago for a lifetime achievement award and jokes about being seventy-two, but he does not look young or old, only perfected.

He plays an action hero in his new movie, *Blood Work*, which opened August 9, but he does not test credulity by doing impossible things, although what is possible for Eastwood is of course open to negotiation. He plays an FBI agent nearing retirement age. When he chases a killer in the opening scenes, he falls with a heart attack, and when we meet him again two years later, he has had a heart transplant. He goes through the rest of the movie sometimes touching his chest thoughtfully, as if reminding himself of his mortality.

"I'm playing a part where everyone is telling me how bad I look, how I look like crap, how I oughta go home and get some rest," he said, smiling. Eastwood, who has directed himself in twenty of his own films, works with his screen image like an artist long familiar with his medium. In *Space Cowboys* (2000) and this film he makes his age a plot point, and in *Absolute Power* (1997), accused of committing a burglary and climbing down a rope, he replies, "If I could do that, I'd be the star of my AARP meeting."

"You've got to be what you are," he was telling me, two days after he was honored by the Chicago Film Festival. He was going to another event that night, one benefiting a charity important to his wife, Dina. He'd spent the weekend with Dina and some of his kids seeing Chicago, her favorite city.

"There's nothing more silly than someone trying to play what he's not," he said. "I remember a picture a long time ago with Clark Gable and Cameron Mitchell. They were older guys trying to play young, and they kept calling Cameron Mitchell a kid, and the kid was not a day under forty-five or fifty. When you get to a certain age you play what you are and take advantage of that to play roles you weren't capable of when you were younger."

That was his thinking in 1992, he said, when he made *Unforgiven*, which won him Oscars for best picture and best director.

"I bought the screenplay in 1981 and sort of hung onto it for a while because I thought it was something I could mature into. I thought that story would be the perfect way to end the Western for me. It took place on the cusp between two eras, between the Old West and the New West, and it had issues like retribution, gun control, the media making these guys into stars, stuff you didn't find in Westerns very often."

If *Unforgiven* was the end of the Western for Eastwood, his beginning as a star was also in a Western. He had great success on television in the *Rawhide* series from 1959 to 1966, but in the 1950s and 1960s it was conventional wisdom that TV stars could never become movie stars, because people wouldn't pay to see actors they got at home for free.

He'd made eleven movies before the TV series without becoming a star, and in what was perhaps a form of desperation, he accepted an offer to go to Spain and film a Western with an unknown Italian named Sergio Leone. The result, *A Fistful of Dollars*, and its sequel, *For a Few Dollars More*, made Eastwood into a box-office draw, and after his third film with Leone, *The Good, the Bad and the Ugly*, he had all the clout and acceptance he needed to come back to Hollywood and make movies.

"I didn't know if you could make the jump to the big screen," he said. "A few people had. Steve McQueen did small roles and built himself up as a name in pictures. But when I came out of the foreign thing, it was strictly a lucky deal, a rolling of the dice.

"*Fistful* cost about $200,000 to make. It was a Western shot in Spain as an Italian-German-Spanish coproduction, with a screenplay based on a Japanese samurai movie (Kurosawa's *Yojimbo*, 1961). All the producers were arguing among themselves about who was going to pay the bills. It could have been an absolute disaster. But we got lucky with it. And it turned out Sergio Leone was for real. We both came out of the box together."

As a director, Eastwood learned from Leone and from Don Siegel, the American master. They were his mentors (he dedicated *Unforgiven* to them), and they worked fast and lean. Eastwood's own productions are famous for coming in on time and under budget.

"I don't even know if that's a good reputation to have," he said. "You hang around the movies long enough, you realize nobody cares about the economics. But my father, when I was young, used to preach conservationism. Now that means saving the environment, but we grew up in an era when you tried to conserve water and electricity because you were poor and you wanted to save money. Maybe that stuck in my head."

I read a story, I said, that when you and Jeff Daniels were shooting a scene for *Blood Work*, you prevented a crash by grabbing the wheel at the last moment.

He grinned. "It was one of those shots where we're both in the front seat and we're talking, and out of the corner of my eye I saw a situation developing that he didn't see, and just nudged the wheel a little. No big deal.

"Any time you're doing a driving scene and you've got cameras hanging off the car, it's kind of a heady deal. I remember in San Francisco I was driving along—this was on *Dirty Harry*—with boards hanging off the car to mount camera and lights. And I impaled someone in a crosswalk. I wasn't going fast, fortunately. All of a sudden I heard this guy yelling and he was kind of hanging off this board in front of the car. He didn't say much. These days he'd be calling sixteen attorneys. But he just griped and groaned and exchanged a few expletives, and that was about it."

Dustin Hoffman

September 27, 2002—Dustin Hoffman's character in *Moonlight Mile* is named Ben. People immediately think of Benjamin, Hoffman's famous role in *The Graduate*. In the new film they see Ben trying to convince a young man, the fiancé of Ben's murdered daughter, to join him in real estate. They think they have the key: Benjamin has grown up and, like the adults he scorned in *The Graduate*, is offering a young man the key to success.

This is a neat formulation, but I think it starts with the wrong Dustin Hoffman role. In 1984 he starred in Chicago and on Broadway as Willy Loman, the hero of Arthur Miller's *Death of a Salesman*. Willy had lived all of his life on dreams, and all of the dreams had been dashed, and now his hopes for his son, Biff, were being disappointed, too.

In *Moonlight Mile*, written and directed by Brad Silberling, Ben's daughter has been killed. Now he and his wife (Susan Sarandon) rattle around in a lonely marriage. He has dreams of putting together a big parcel of real estate, but she knows that most of his plans come to little. Having lost a daughter, Ben now turns to Joe (Jake Gyllenhaal), who would have been his son-in-law, and treats him as his son—even changing the name of the realty firm to "Floss & Son."

Hoffman, whose work in *Moonlight Mile* has been much praised, accepts the parallels between the two roles.

"I don't think, for myself, that you can do a lot of different things," he told me after the movie's premiere at the Toronto Film Festival. "You try to pretend that you can, but you can't. I worked with Olivier once and he said, 'Dear boy, we've only got about four or five characters. The rest are a variation on a theme.'"

Hoffman at sixty-five still looks intense, focused, vaguely worried. In the movie his voice cracks sometimes, and he will slow down when he wants to be sure he is saying a painful thing in the correct words.

"Some people say you're always doing an autobiography when you act," he said. "I think in life, too, we are constantly doing an autobiography. I cannot stop putting my family into my work. I can't help it. My father is in *Death of a Salesman*. My father is in this. My father was an unsuccessful salesman, and a man who had great difficulty living in the moment. And it was a tragedy of his life and of my life that he . . ."

Instead of finishing that thought, Hoffman related a memory.

"We had the same birthday. He was eighty the same day that I was fifty. A momentous occasion. We took a walk on the beach. I said, 'What do you think, Dad?' He said, 'What do I think? It's all bullshit.' And I think that's the underpinning of this character, Ben. He's doing what my dad did. My father would never admit his despair to anyone. It was always, 'Hey! How are ya?' But you caught it.

"You're not going to get any answers. You want your dad to say he's eighty and he can give you the answers. And he's saying, 'I didn't have them when I was your age, and you're not gonna have them when you're mine.'"

Thinking about *Moonlight Mile*, I can see how Hoffman brought that realization into the movie. The movie gives full attention and sympathy to all of its characters, and doesn't take cheap shots or make anyone into a caricature. Ben's real estate dreams are foolish, but he is not foolish, and he has a scene where he confesses to young Joe that he never really thought he could pull off the deal. It was more that, by *trying* to make the deal work, he was refusing to give in to despair.

Hoffman and Sarandon star with Gyllenhaal and a newcomer named Ellen Pompeo, whose character works at the post office and tends bar and is a local woman whom the grieving Joe begins to take notice of. The movie starts at the time of the funeral of Diane, the murdered daughter, Joe's fiancée, and the world is assaulting them with its sympathy, and they are all maintaining a kind of insouciance, or brave distance, from breaking down. There is a tone of bleak, inconsolable . . . comedy.

"The director lived through this," Hoffman said. "He had a girlfriend who was murdered. He didn't work for four years. I met him in that period. I wasn't interested in the movie because I didn't think I was right for the part, but that's my problem. When he picked the cast, he had us all at a table and he said how happy he was that he got the cast he wanted. And he said, 'We're going to have our first reading.' And then he broke down, and we sat there and he was sobbing, and before we knew it we were crying with him. We didn't know his girlfriend, but there was some mysterious connection that took place."

Nicole Kidman

New York, December 23, 2002—She was dressed to go out for the evening—dress, hair, diamonds, a reminder that the words "movie star" sometimes have to be italicized. Nicole Kidman, who looks plain and dour as Virginia Woolf in *The Hours,* was looking anything but tonight. Maybe that's why she catches people's fancy: She's so glamorous, and then she can turn around and take a role like Woolf and in-

habit it with somber care. After *Eyes Wide Shut* and *The Others* and *Moulin Rouge* and now *The Hours,* it is clear that Kidman is taking deliberate chances to work seriously as an actor.

Consider not only *The Hours,* the most literary and highbrow of the year-end releases, but also the films she will release in 2003. Tonight she was attending the New York premiere of the musical *Chicago,* starring her friend Renée Zellweger. They will star together later in the year in *Cold Mountain,* directed by Anthony Minghella (*The English Patient*). For *Dogville,* she volunteered that she wanted to work with Lars von Trier, the cofounder of the Dogma movement, and will costar with Stellan Skarsgard. In *The Human Stain,* directed by Robert Benton, she stars as an illiterate janitor who begins an affair with a disgraced professor (Anthony Hopkins) twice her age. *Birth* has her opposite the tall, grave Danny Huston in a film by Jonathan Glazer (*Sexy Beast*). And in Franz Oz's *The Stepford Wives,* she stars with Joan and John Cusack.

Is there another big star with such an intriguing series of works in progress? Some of these titles may have considerable box office success, but none of them seem to have been chosen with only that in mind. Kidman, who as the wife of Tom Cruise was sometimes in his shadow, seems determined to establish herself as a freestanding force of her own—tall, yes, and beautiful, yes, but still with something of the studious Australian schoolgirl about her, applying herself to win good marks.

The Hours, based on the Pulitzer Prize–winning novel by Michael Cunningham, stars Kidman as Virginia Woolf, the British novelist who committed suicide in 1941 rather than subject her husband to another season of her mental anguish. Julianne Moore and Meryl Streep also star; the film considers three women whose lives in a way comment on one another.

"That was the only thing I did last year, making this movie," Kidman told me. She was in a period of depression following her divorce. "I just didn't want to work. I was like, 'I'm going to pull out. I can't . . . I just don't . . . I can't cope with anything and I don't want to do it.' And I'm so glad I stuck with it, because I sat down in the cinema and just watched it by myself and I thought, I made a movie with Meryl Streep and

Julianne Moore and three female characters that is so rich and complex."

It seemed so risky when she was making it, she said, that "I really thought, oh, gosh . . . at least it's a small movie and if it doesn't work, nobody will see it. And then it has escalated to this. I just didn't think this sort of movie would garner that kind of attention."

Attention, and Golden Globe nominations for Kidman and Streep, with Moore nominated for *Far from Heaven*. All three are said to be Oscar front-runners.

In the film, Woolf writes a final letter to her husband, Leonard, saying she senses another dark depression coming on and wants to spare him. Then she fills her pockets with stones, walks into the river, and drowns.

"I actually fell in love with Woolf because of her suicide note," Kidman said. "Suicide can be seen as such a selfish act, but you see how she desperately didn't want Leonard to take on any of the blame for it, or the responsibility, and how she says, 'No two people could have been happier.' And that is such a gift to somebody who's devoted their life to you and tried to protect you. I've read all the stuff on her. When she would go crazy and the voices would start, she could just attack him, but yet they really loved each other."

It's heartbreaking, I said, because she was so smart and so good and so ahead of her time.

"And so fragile. She was so brilliant and so profound in her thinking and yet her spirit was so fragile and her physical being was so fragile. When we shot her walking into the river, I remember thinking there's something very strange, eerie, about picking up the stones and putting them in the pocket and just sort of walking into the water and knowing that this is exactly how she did it. I wonder if her presence was somewhere orbiting around watching this as somebody else played her. At school I kind of dabbled in her, but she'd never spoken on a deep level to me because I wasn't open enough or I wasn't experienced enough to receive her— and then to discover her through a movie at a time when I needed to discover her, I think, was a profound experience."

One of the things she admired, she said, was the literacy of the screenplay, based on the novel and written by the playwright David Hare.

"She wants to move back to London, and

Leonard tells her she must stay in Richmond, that London would kill her. She won't give up on it: 'If I have to choose between Richmond and death, then I choose death.' It was just lovely as an actor because film, a lot of the time, is not about the words, it's about the images. But to actually have the chance to say such great words on screen."

The great learning experience of Kidman's acting life, it's clear, was the nearly two years she and Cruise spent working with Stanley Kubrick on his last film, *Eyes Wide Shut* (1999). I speculated that it must have taken them a certain amount of courage to commit to Kubrick, knowing they were in for a demanding ordeal from the famed perfectionist.

"You see," she said, "my madness is, I would have worked with him again. The other night I was at dinner and there was someone who was asking me about Kubrick: 'Wasn't it tortured? It must have been awful.' I said it wasn't. He said, 'But you used to have on so many other things and you were stuck over there.' I said, but I didn't see it as stuck. What was I missing out on? I was working with possibly the greatest director in the world and being stimulated intellectually and emotionally, and I was making a movie. I may not have been making four different movies; I was making one movie that took two years. But I couldn't have been more satiated. They didn't understand that concept. Then I thought, gee, maybe I'm just a little bit loopy. But I loved it. Stanley could really get at you, you know, but he also changed my life. He was a professor of film, he was a professor of philosophy, he was a professor of life, and I was in his vicinity for a few years and I got to learn and grow from that."

It was almost time for Kidman to go downstairs at her hotel and be whisked away to the premiere, but we spent a few minutes talking about movies we'd seen or wanted to see, and then she said:

"Some actors won't go to the movies when they're making one. I like to see movies when I'm working. Because what happens is you sit in the dark and your mind, for whatever reason, gets triggered and you're able to sometimes . . . drift . . . you may not even be present for the whole movie, because you drift off into your own imagination. But you come out with something and suddenly the next day it creates something for you. It's just lovely. The wonder of it is, anything that takes you on a journey, whether it's a novel, whether it's standing in front of a painting, whether it's a movie . . .

"Well, there's a beautiful moment in *Cold Mountain*, actually, where Renée's character and I are lying on the bed and we're reading *Wuthering Heights*. Her character is illiterate, and I'm reading to her, and she asks me, 'She's not gonna marry Linton, is she? She *couldn't* marry Linton. I mean, not if she feels that way about Heathcliffe!'

"And I told Anthony, the director, this is one of my favorite scenes in the movie because you see somebody who can't read still having that moment of the lightbulb going on, and suddenly a story is as important as life."

Patrice Leconte

May 14, 2003—I would like to urge you gently toward those shelves in your friendly video store that hold the titles of Patrice Leconte. If your store does not carry his titles, then it is not your friend.

Patrice Leconte, from France, at fifty-five has made twenty-three films, of which I have been able to see *Monsieur Hire, The Hairdresser's Husband, Ridicule, The Girl on the Bridge, The Widow of St. Pierre,* and now *The Man on the Train.* Two of those films have been on my list of a year's ten best, three more could have been, and the sixth will be.

He is the kind of man who always seems about to tell you a joke, but he is not a comedian. His films often make you laugh, but they are not comedies. They cannot be classified according to any known system of categories, which is why they keep you delighted and curious. If they have a common element, it is serendipity.

Consider *Man on the Train.* It involves a serendipitous meeting between a retired school teacher (Jean Rochefort) and a bank robber with three guns in his luggage (Johnny Hallyday). These men are no longer young. The bank robber gets off the train in a French village on a chilly November day, finds himself talking to the teacher, and is soon the teacher's guest. They talk and drink and smoke and play backgammon and are tactful about respecting each other's privacy. At 10 A.M. on Saturday, the teacher is scheduled for a triple bypass, and the robber is scheduled to hold up a bank.

There is genius in the film's casting. Rochefort, tall and slender, looks aristocratic. Hallyday in his black leather jacket looks like an outlaw rocker, as indeed he is—"the French Elvis," he's always called. To put these two men in the same film would seem unlikely, but Leconte did, again because of serendipity.

"I don't think that a filmmaker is manipulating puppets," Leconte told me last September at the Toronto Film Festival. "On the contrary, I believe a filmmaker is more like a chemist. You mix elements that have nothing to do with each other, and you see what will happen. The starting point for *Man on the Train* was the meeting of these two actors. Put in a few drops of Johnny Hallyday, a few drops of Jean Rochefort, and look what happens. Sometimes it blows up in your face."

What is so special in France about Johnny Hallyday? I asked. "You could also ask, 'Why do Americans like so much Elvis?' What I think is that he has such generosity and such strength that he is the number one and has been number one for forty years. When you have been number one for so long, there's something very magical."

Was it easy to persuade him to make this film? "It was so easy that it was he who came to get me. One day four or five years ago, when I had never met him, he was at the Césars, which are the same thing as the Oscars in France. He said very nice things about my work. He finished by putting his hand on my shoulder and said, 'One day I would like to be filmed by you.'

"I thought it was very touching, even somewhat feminine, because usually a guy like Johnny Hallyday would say, 'It would be nice to do a film together,' but he said, 'I would like to be filmed by you.' And that's how it happened. It was easy to convince him since it was his idea."

We were sitting in a restaurant, crowded at lunchtime, and had already talked about five of Leconte's other films, and I was enormously pleased because I had long been intrigued by this man. He fits into no category, and yet his films are always so elegant, with such a strange mixture of sadness and high spirits. I love the ending of *Man on the Train,* I told him (although I will not spoil it for you). What Leconte says below may seem to be revealing something, but if you see the movie, you will find that it doesn't even touch what happens.

"In the first version of the script," he said, "they died at the same second and that was it. But it was horrifying, much too sad. I wanted the movie to end on a positive note, in a poetic way, fantastic way, to have an ending which was imagined by no one."

In the film, each man is attracted to the life of the other. One day when a pupil of Rochefort's comes to be tutored and the old teacher is not there, the bank robber puts on a straight face and tells the kid, "Your lesson is with me today." And he tutors him on a novel by Balzac, which he has not read. "I especially like that scene," Leconte said, "because Hallyday plays it without looking for any ironic commentary on the situation." Actually Johnny Hallyday might have made a good teacher. "He makes it seem that way."

In *Man on the Train,* Rochefort goes into a barbershop and asks for a short haircut ("halfway between just out of prison and world-class soccer star," he tells the barber). Leconte's *The Hairdresser's Husband* starred Rochefort as a man with a fetish for women cutting hair; he marries a hairdresser, buys a shop for her, and sits in it happily all day.

In *Man on the Train,* I said, I was happy to see Jean Rochefort get a haircut. "The scene is a direct reference to *The Hairdresser's Husband.* And the actor who is playing the hairdresser was the man who gave his hair salon to the hairdresser in that movie. I thought since I'm making a reference anyway, I might as well do it all the way."

Was *The Hairdresser's Husband* a bit autobiographical? "A little bit, yes. I've never wanted to marry a hairdresser, but it was autobiographical on an emotional level. It's an autobiography on the level of confusion and emotion."

Strange, that two of the French directors I value the most, Bertrand Tavernier and Patrice Leconte, are not often highly praised by the French critics. Leconte is a member of the generation after the New Wave (the Next Wave?). I asked him how those great figures affected him. "Well, Godard has become somebody who's very strange today. But he brought so much to

film in the beginning. Godard was the most important element in our desire to do cinema. Because before the New Wave, when you thought of cinema, you were under the impression that films were three hundred kilometers away, that you could never do it. But when I saw his *Breathless,* all of a sudden cinema came closer to me and I told myself I could do this."

These days, I said, the digital revolution has given young directors access to filmmaking at a much smaller expense. "Yes, but not always with the best results. For me the worst example is *Dancer in the Dark.*" That would be the digital video quasi-musical by Lars von Trier, founder of the Dogma movement. "For me, when he's filming with fifty or one hundred cameras, that is the negation of cinema. The point of directing is to have only one camera, but at the right place. And the jury from the Cannes Festival that year, probably because they don't know what cinema is, gave him the Palme d'Or. It made me crazy."

"You don't have to write this down," he said. "But you can, because I really think it." He sighed. "But the New Wave. Well, I didn't know Truffaut at all. I never met him, because he died too early, probably. One of the things that I loved most about Truffaut was that he loved movies. And I would like that on my tomb: This man loved to make movies."

He smiled. "Hopefully, the later the better."

Hayao Miyazaki

September 17, 2002—"I love his films. I study his films. I watch his films when I'm looking for inspiration."

So says John Lasseter, director of *Toy Story* and *A Bug's Life,* about Hayao Miyazaki. Other animators agree that the quiet man from Japan with the mop of gray hair may be the best animation filmmaker in history. His films are so good they force you to rethink how you approach animation.

Lasseter is one of the most successful animators in Hollywood. That he would take time to personally shepherd Miyazaki's *Spirited Away* into a release by Walt Disney is a tribute to the older craftsman. Lasseter, who directed the English-language sound track for the film, joined Miyazaki at the recent Toronto Film Festival.

"The very first screening of *Spirited Away* outside of Japan was at the Pixar animation studios," he said, "and I was stunned at how amazing this film was. North America hasn't had a chance to discover Miyazaki's films. In the animated community he's a hero, like he is to me."

Miyazaki and his partner at Studio Ghibli, Isao Takahata *(Grave of the Fireflies)*, have created works of astonishing depth and artistry; his *Princess Mononoke* was one of the best films of 1999. *Spirited Away*, which won the Berlin Film Festival, has passed *Titanic* at the Japanese box office and is the first film in history to gross $200 million before even opening in North America.

The new film, which may be his best, tells the story of a ten-year-old girl and her parents, who wander into a tunnel in the woods and find what looks like an amusement park. It turns, for the girl, into an *Alice in Wonderland*–type adventure, populated by a sorceress, ghosts, spirits, two-eyed dust balls, a helpful young boy, a boiler-room man with eight limbs, and a fearsome river creature whose body has sopped up decades of pollution.

When I went to talk with Miyazaki, who is sixty-one, I reminded him that in 1999 he said he was going to retire. Now here was another film.

"I wanted to retire," he said, "but life isn't that easy. I wanted to make a movie especially for the daughters of my friends. I opened all the drawers in my head, they were all empty. So I realized I had to make a movie just for ten-year-olds, and *Spirited Away* is my answer."

Revealing. Many directors pitch their movies at ten-year-olds and then claim they are for the "whole family." Miyazaki makes a film that adults found fascinating at the Berlin, Telluride, and Toronto festivals, and claims it is for ten-year-olds.

Speaking through a translator, he said Lasseter "turned into a human bulldozer" to assure the American release: "Without him I don't think we'd be sitting here."

Miyazaki, who is suspicious of computers, personally draws thousands of frames by hand. "We take (handmade) cell animation and digitize it in order to enrich the visual look, but everything starts with the human hand drawing. And the color standard is dictated by the background. We don't make up a color on the computer. Without creating those rigid standards we'll just be caught up in the whirlpool of computerization."

He grinned. "It was an absolute order from the commander." He is the commander.

He defines hand drawing as "2-D" and computer animation as "3-D."

"What we call 2-D is what we draw on paper to create movement and space on a piece of paper. The 3-D is when you create that space inside a computer. I don't think the Japanese creative mind is very suited for 3-D."

I told Miyazaki I love the "gratuitous motion" in his films; instead of every movement being dictated by the story, sometimes people will just sit for a moment, or they will sigh, or look in a running stream, or do something extra, not to advance the story but only to give the sense of time and place and who they are.

"We have a word for that in Japanese," he said. "It's called 'ma.' Emptiness. It's there intentionally."

Is that like the "pillow words" that separate phrases in Japanese poetry?

"I don't think it's like the pillow word." He clapped his hands three or four times. "The time in between my clapping is 'ma.' If you just have nonstop action with no breathing space at all, it's just busyness. But if you take a moment, then the tension building in the film can grow into a wider dimension. If you just have constant tension at eighty degrees all the time you just get numb."

Which helps explain why Miyazaki's films are more absorbing and involving than the frantic cheerful action in a lot of American animation. I asked him to explain that a little more.

"The people who make the movies are scared of silence, so they want to paper and plaster it over," he said. "They're worried that the audience will get bored. They might go up and get some popcorn. But just because it's 80 percent intense all the time doesn't mean the kids are going to bless you with their concentration. What really matters is the underlying emotions—that you never let go of those. What my friends and I have been trying to do since the 1970s is to try and quiet things down a little bit; don't just bombard them with noise and distraction. And to follow the path of children's emotions and feelings as we make a film. If you stay true to joy and astonishment and empathy you don't have to have violence and you don't have to have action. They'll follow you. This is our principle."

He has been amused, he said, to see a lot of animation in live-action movies like *Spider-Man.*

"In a way now, live action is becoming part of that whole soup called animation. Animation has become a word that encompasses so much, and my animation is just a little tiny dot over in the corner. It's plenty for me."

It's plenty for me, too.

Peter O'Toole

Telluride, Colorado, September 15, 2002—Peter O'Toole regarded the Telluride Medal hanging around his neck and intoned: "When fifty years ago this year, I took my first uncertain steps on the stage as an actor, had anyone suggested to me that half a century later I would be up a Rocky in a grand old opry house, being festooned with medals, wandering and relaxing with old and new friends and colleagues, watching the better part of five decades of my life tumble on the screen in the company of the new generation O'Toole, my son Lorcan, I might have said that would be unlikely."

But here he was, at 10,000 feet in the Rocky Mountains, in the Sheridan Opera House, built for miners, restored by the Telluride Film Festival, reporting that he understood Sarah Bernhardt had trod upon these very boards. My job was to interview him. I approached it with hesitation; some actors are eager to please, but O'Toole seems eager not to be annoyed. I was apprehensive until a moment before we went onstage, when I saw him doing an actor's deep-breathing exercises and realized: He isn't here to make my job hard, he's here to win the audience.

And he did, in an hour-long conversation that was arguably the most entertaining in the festival's twenty-nine years. O'Toole is a funny man with impeccable comic timing, elegantly dressed, and he uses a cigarette holder and a pack of Gitanes to punctuate his remarks, sometimes making an audience wait for a cigarette to be extracted, lighted, and inhaled before supplying a punch line.

He is in America this autumn in connection with the launch of the latest restoration of *Lawrence of Arabia,* David Lean's great 1962

film, recently voted the fourth best film ever made in the *Sight & Sound* poll of the world's film directors.

Ebert: This film reminds me of the time when directors and actors and writers thought differently than they do today. The length of it, the ambition of it, the breadth of it, the depth of it. The fact that it had the patience to tell its story without having to blow something up every five seconds.

O'Toole: The script demanded those things. The circumstances demanded all those things. David had the courage to do all those things. We were the right people to do all those things. And we took two years, and I don't think there's one boring second of it. Some say disagreeable seconds, but not boring.

Q: Albert Finney was originally considered for the role?

A: That's right. So was Marlon Brando. I think probably Groucho Marx and Greta Garbo . . .

Q: David Lean found you when you were essentially unknown, and then trusted you for two years with this great undertaking. It must have been a leap of faith on both of your parts.

A: I had a phone call at Stratford-upon-Avon, where I was playing Shylock, and it was David Lean. Would I be able to come to London and have a chat with him? I'd grown my own beard and long hair, which I'd dyed black . . . and David said, "Peter, what do you look like underneath all that stuff?" I said, "Well, I'm quite fair-haired, really, and . . ." He said, "Well, we'd need that. I've seen a film called *The Day They Robbed the Bank of England,* in which you play a young English army officer and you didn't put a foot wrong, and I really want you to do it." And I said, "Who's the producer?" He said, "Sam Spiegel." I said, "Not a chance." Because Sam Spiegel and I didn't get on at all, and we didn't get on for years before *Lawrence of Arabia.* And David said, "Well, look, you're going to hear everybody in the world is about to play this, but please have faith, please trust me, and you'll do it." And Spiegel, of course, was having a baby. He said, "You can't have him. For God's sake, David, you can't have that awful man, that dreadful life." But David stuck to his guns and indeed that's what happened, and then two years later we finished it.

Q: Some actors have trouble staying in character for two hours; you did it for two years. Do you have rushes in the desert? How did you keep on top of a project that lasted that long?

A: I've never looked at a rush in my life. For me, the beginning and the end of everything is the script. It's the words; it's the situations; it's the people. The short answer is, if you watch that film very, very carefully, you can see the decomposition of the flesh. I began when I was, what . . . twenty-eight? And finished when I was thirty, and I can see it, but very few other people can, so I'm told. Nothing really, just concentration, I suppose. I've no idea.

Q: Did your relationship with Sam Spiegel get any better?

A: Not at all. He turned up at one point, on his yacht, when we moved to Spain, and he summoned me on board the yacht. He'd seen the rushes for the nine months we'd done in the desert, and I left the yacht feeling dreadful. Destruction was his game. I couldn't bear the man. When I came off the yacht, there was a little bar and there was the artistic director, John Box, who's alive and well, and I was about to tell him what had happened. He said, "Don't. Don't, don't. I was there for an hour before you." So we helped ourselves to the wine and we finished up—this is so pathetically boyish—climbing up the anchor chain onto his yacht and we stole all his cigars.

Q: As I was looking at these scenes from your career, I must tell you that you made the right decision in not remaining as a film critic. It's true that when you were sixteen, you did film notices?

A: I did, yes.

Q: And then went into the navy and then joined that amazing group of actors that simply transformed the British cinema.

A: In 1953, at the Royal Academy of Dramatic Arts in London, there was Albert Finney, Alan Bates, me and—I always leave people out so they get very upset, but it doesn't matter—Frank Finlay, and on and on and on and on. We were a remarkable little group, and we all moved into the theater, as well as the cinema, and all of us are still alive, which is even more amazing.

Q: Was there a sense of competition in those days?

A: No working actor worth his salt doesn't know what competition means. Yes. In the older days, in the 1800s, theater was on a par with boxing. Yeah, there's always been a very healthy sense of competition between us.

Q: I had a chance to see your 1976 movie *Rogue Male* on cassette. You asked that it be shown here. I'd never heard of it, and I'm at a loss to understand how it fell through the cracks.

A: The crack is called the BBC. *Rogue Male* is deep in my heart. Robert Hunter, the guy I play, he wants to kill Hitler not because of any other reason than the fact that Hitler murdered his fiancée. This is in 1938. When he joins the war effort his purpose is exactly the same. He wants to destroy this man.

Q: You seem to have a particular fascination with the evil of Hitler. You talk about him in your autobiography; even from earliest childhood you were fixated.

A: My dad, who was a bookie, would take me to the news cinema, which was over the railway station. They had an hour program with the Three Stooges, Donald Duck, who I adored, and the Ritz Brothers. I was watching with my father and along came Mussolini, and great hilarious ripe raspberries were thrown at him. Then along came Hitler and there were no raspberries, and I was physically ill at the age of six, seeing this man.

Q: To move on to *Jeffrey Bernard Is Unwell,* the other film that you're showing here, about the lifelong alcoholic who wrote a famous weekly column in the *Spectator* about his adventures . . .

A: Ah, 1955. I was at the Old Vic, and there was a very pretty girl wobbling around. I thought, this is charming; I shall look at her. And I went into the pub next door, waiting for her to come in, and she came in on the arm of the leading man, John Neville. And there was a young chap with sort of Elvis Presley hair and he said, "Yeah, I fancied her, too. Hello, my name is Jeff." And it was Jeff Bernard, a stagehand. He was an extraordinary man, a brilliant man. A cricketer, a film editor, many things, a writer, humorist. [Playwright] Keith Waterhouse took Jeffrey's words and fashioned them into this play, *Jeffrey Bernard Is Unwell.* Keith had been in the pub with Jeff and they'd been laughing and joking and playing cards and losing money, whatever, and Keith went back home, put on his dinner jacket, went to the opera, and sat there nodding off quietly. He thought, "I had so much more fun in the pub. What in the name of Jesus am I doing here?" And, click! His play came to mind because another chum of ours was locked in a pub one night and he spent the entire night in the pub. So that was the premise of the piece.

Q: When you were appearing in the first run of the play in London, Bernard wrote in the *Spectator* about going to the bar in the theater every night in order to accept free drinks from the audience during the intermission. He felt this was really almost as much a benefit as the royalties.

A: Yes, Jeff would turn up every night and he'd nod off during the first half. He'd come into my dressing room, drink all my vodka. I said to him before we began rehearsing, "Jeff, I'm simply not even going to try to impersonate you." He said, "That's very handy, Pete. I've been impersonating you for thirty-five years."

Q: I loved the clip we saw from *The Lion in Winter*. Your confrontation with Katharine Hepburn is astonishing. You were particularly good friends with her?

Q: You said it. I was in a play in London called *The Long and the Short and the Tall*, and there was no lavatory in my dressing room. And after the show I was peeing in the sink, which one does, and a voice said, "Hello, my name is Kate Hepburn and I have come—oh dear, oh dear!" We met, and it was a joy and it was indeed a challenge. Many of us were, a little bit... tired... in the morning. She'd give you about sixty seconds in which to recover and if you weren't there—zip! She'd cut your head off. I adore the girl.

Q: I understand you do the world's greatest impression of John Huston. I wouldn't dream of asking you do to it for us . . . .

A (as Huston): "Don't worry, kid, everything will be fine." There's a marvelous moment when once I was staying with John in Ireland, and came the morning and there was John in a green kimono with a bottle of tequila and two shot glasses, and he said, "Pete, this is the day we're gettin' drunk." We finished up on horses, the pair of us, he in a green kimono, me in my nightie, in the rain, carrying .303 rifles, rough-shooting as in *Rogue Male* but with a shih tzu dog and an Irish wolfhound. Of course, we were incapable of doing anything, and John eventually fell off the horse and broke his leg. And I was accused by his wife of corrupting him.

Q: In addition to being a great actor, you're also an accomplished writer and speaker, and it seems that those sorts of things go with the territory.

A: Well, there's the Gaelic language, the Irish language, which wasn't killed stone dead, but was slowly strangled from about the sixteenth century until this present day. However, the tunes and the rhythms of the Irish language are in the consciousness. And in Ireland the metaphor is as natural as breathing.

Q: Would you ever play W. B. Yeats? You look a little like him.

A: He really was the complete actor-poet. He wandered around with bow ties and bored everyone to tears, and had someone with a harp . . . I imagine that had you met W. B. Yeats in the streets, you'd think, this is the most gruesome man. But he turned out to be the most beautiful lyric poet of the twentieth century and, yeah, I wouldn't mind playing Yeats.

Q: Who of current screenwriters would write your Yeats role? Who would do you justice?

A: Oh, who would do the Yeats justice? I've noticed that recently there are more and more excellent young writers. It goes on and on. I can't think immediately. Maybe it's the boy .. McDonough . . . I can't remember proper nouns at this certain point . . .

Q: Martin McDonough.

A: Perhaps him.

Q (quoting a line of Yeats): "MacDonagh and MacBride . . ."

A: Yeats!

Q: "We know their dreams enough to know they dreamed and are dead."

A: "A terrible beauty is born . . ."

Q: "Far beneath Ben Bulben's head . . ."

A: "Cast a cold eye on life, on death. Horseman, pass by!"

Q: "Too long a sacrifice can make a stone of the heart."

A: "Why shouldn't that old man be mad?"

Al Pacino

Park City, Utah, January 20, 2003—"Somebody asked me today, do I like acting?" Al Pacino was saying. "That stopped me. I had never been asked that."

What did you say?

"Sometimes."

When don't you like it?

"When I'm not working. Bogart was like that. After every picture, he thought he would never work in the movies again. Well, right now, I don't have a single movie on the books. Does that mean I will never work again?"

Unlikely. Pacino at sixty-two works in what he wants, when he wants, moving back and forth between movies and the stage. "The only problem is, I don't have the appetite to make my own pictures. I don't want to direct. So I'm always in a kind of passive position, waiting for someone to come to me with a project. That I sort of don't like."

We sit in a meeting room of the Yarrow Inn, sipping our coffees. He is dressed in a black suit and black sweater, his hair an electric riot, his eyes framed by lines of worry and humor. Unlike many actors who have been so famous for so long, he is unwound and approachable; in conversations he likes to listen, is content to be there, is not looking for openings or recycling sound bites.

It is the day after the Sundance premiere of *People I Know*, in which he plays an exhausted, strung out New York press agent, a man torn between compromise and idealism, using drugs like M&M's. It is a carefully tuned and perceptive performance, in which the character descends into a long night of drugs and is finally so tired and confused he doesn't know if he has witnessed a murder or not. Later, when he's stabbed, he misses that, too.

The performance walks a tightrope between the character's willingness to cover up a scandal involving his last remaining client, and his determination to lure celebrities to a benefit for one of his own liberal causes. The character is said to be inspired by Bobby Zarem, an omnipresent and much beloved New York publicist, although the drugs and the plot are fiction. "I've known Bobby a long time," Pacino says. "I don't know if he even drinks." He has listened to him so closely that if you know Zarem and you close your eyes, it sounds like Bobby's voice from the screen.

The movie, written by Jon Robin Baitz and directed by Dan Algrant, is about the passing of a way of life for the freelance press agent, plant-

ing his clients' names in gossip columns one day and trying to keep them out the next. "I don't think," observed Pacino's own famous publicist, Pat Kingsley, "that I would like to have this movie be made about me." But Kingsley is at the top of her field and heads a big agency, and Eli Wurman, the Pacino character, works out of his rumpled suit and cluttered office, badgering a hapless young man who works for him: "Do you have Regis for the benefit? Call Regis!" ("But, Eli, it's past midnight . . .")

Eli's client (Ryan O'Neal) assigns him to bail out a famous model (Tea Leoni)—on a private jet to whisk her out of town and trouble—but the two end up at a millionaire's sex-and-drugs orgy, after which the evening descends into confusion. What is fascinating about the structure of the story is that the death of the model and the danger to Eli are all held beneath the surface; Eli is so intent on his benefit and so spaced out that he never quite focuses on the immediate situation.

"I like that about the movie," Pacino said. "There was an earlier draft in which the crime stuff was more in the foreground, but no, this isn't a crime movie. It's about Eli's personality. He has a key line: 'I just can't stop.' This is what he does. He knows people. He fixes things. He's got his causes. Maybe he's gay, but he's never explored that possibility. He just keeps moving."

Kim Basinger plays the widow of Eli's brother, who is worried about his health (so is his Dr. Feelgood physician, played by Robert Klein). She offers him a refuge on her Virginia farm, no strings attached, but can Eli stop running?

"When we were getting ready to make the movie," Pacino said, "I said it had to be made cheaply. It's that kind of film. Close to the bone. I was even thinking it might be good to shoot it on digital and blow it up, to give it a kind of immediate feel. There's an edge that you get."

Pacino works both sides of the fence, big and little budgets. His next release will be Roger Donaldson's *The Recruit*, where he plays the CIA boss of young operative Colin Farrell. Then comes a project done for love, not money: the HBO miniseries *Angels in America*, with Pacino as the powerful lawyer Roy Cohn, a gaybashing closeted homosexual.

Pacino is "one of the greatest of all movie stars" (it says so on the Internet Movie Database), but these days he uses his stardom to open doors to nonstar kinds of acting.

"After I won the Tony Award for *The Basic Training of Pavlo Hummel,* I got up there without any kind of a speech prepared, and I found myself saying: 'I am grateful to the theater, which made the movies possible for me, and now I am grateful to the movies, which make theater possible for me.'"

The Polish Twins and Daryl Hannah

July 1, 2003—*Northfork* is about a Montana town that is buried forever beneath a lake, and about the agents who clear out the residents, and the angels who come to console those who linger behind. But that doesn't evoke it; it only describes it.

I am sitting in a coffee shop at the 2003 Sundance Film Festival with the Polish twins, Mark and Michael, who made the film, and Daryl Hannah, who stars in it. She has known them so long they wrote the screenplay on the porch of her house in Telluride when being filmmakers was only their dream. I ask her how she would describe the film.

"You know like when you hear Pink Floyd's 'Dark Side of the Moon' for the first time, and you have to just sit there and let it sink in?" she said.

"There really is a town in Montana that is now underwater," Michael said. "Our dad took us out to dams our grandfather built, and told us about the beautiful houses that were underwater. And there was a lake in Texas where the church steeple came up out of the water."

"The bodies in the cemeteries have to be exhumed," Mark said, "because otherwise the coffins will rise up out of the ground and float to the surface."

The first image of the film shows that happening. The drowned dead returning to the surface. The film stars Daryl Hannah as an angel of indeterminate gender, Nick Nolte as the parish priest, James Woods as one of the government agents who are ordering people out of their homes, and Claire Forlani, Peter Coyote, Anthony Edwards, Jon Gries, and Kyle McLachlan.

"The first day," Michael said, "Jimmy wanted to know, what the —— is this movie about? Then it got to him. He came to the set every day he wasn't shooting. He said it was the best movie he'd ever been in."

"Nick Nolte has seen the film twenty-five times," Mark said. "He's the only one with a copy of the tape."

The movie, which looks as visually elegant and expensive as a big-budget epic, was made for next to nothing. "Nobody really wanted to make this film," the twins said. Their first film (Sundance, class of 1999) was the haunting *Twin Falls Idaho,* in which they played Siamese twins who try to deal with the fact that one is dying. Then they made *Jackpot* (2001), about an itinerent karaoke contestant. Now comes *Northfork,* their first screenplay, financed with maxed-out credit cards, loans from friends, actors who deferred their paychecks, and . . .

"Our dad, Del, built all of the things you see," Mark said. "He's not a true production designer, and there were no sets and no blueprints, just those buildings."

Del isn't a production designer, but you wouldn't guess it from the buildings he created, so lonely and odd in the empty prairie. Nolte preaches a sermon from a church without a back wall, because half the church has already been carted away. A local resident refuses to move, and turns his house into a replica of Noah's Ark.

Daryl Hannah, who hangs out with Sundance types and supports indie films with her acting and encouragement, remembers the summer the brothers sat on her Colorado porch writing the screenplay.

"They were always so quiet," she said. "I said, 'They're really going to be filmmakers!'"

They were. The twins, who are thirty-one, divide the labors: Michael directs, Mark acts (sometimes with Michael), they write and produce together. "Our strength is the way we bounce stuff off each other," Mark said. "We never fight," said Michael.

Their father's side is Austrian; their mother's side is Mexican. Born in El Centro, Texas, where their dad worked for the DEA, they were taken to Montana at every opportunity because that was Del's country, where he was born and raised. There's a lot of their family in the movie: The six federal agents, dressed in dark suits and fedoras, driving fat, dark 1940s sedans, are named after their six uncles: Walter, Willis, Marvin, Matt, Eddie, and Arnold. "Eddie Arnold is a pun," Mark observes.

A kid named Duel Farnes plays Irwin, a dying orphan whose adoptive parents (Claire Forlani and Clark Gregg) return him to the priest, presumably because he is defective: "You gave us a sick child, Father!" The brothers wanted to cast Duel, who was completely inexperienced, but no one else did.

"He had zero support," Michael said. "Even the cinematographer didn't want him. I knew he was perfect for the role. I knew I had really good actors, and they would surround him and not let him fail."

"When Nolte arrived in Montana," Mark said, "he had just gotten off *Hulk*. He has a lot of important scenes with Duel. He said, 'I don't want to meet, see, or play with the kid.' That's because the kid has to feel friendless at the end. The kid has to be able to look in his eyes and know that."

"There is a scene," Hannah said, "where he's lying on the bed and he said, 'Where did my parents go?' He kept his head on the pillow and only moves his eyes. It was . . . amazing."

Robert Rodriguez

August 6, 2002—This is a man with a message, with a gleam in his eye. He has seen the future. He has changed his life. He has found the answers. He is telling me this at 211 words a minute. That's faster than Paul Harvey. I taped our conversation and divided the words by forty-five minutes, which is how I know. He's actually talking faster than that, because some of those words are mine.

His name is Robert Rodriguez, and to know him is to like him. He's thirty-four now. When I met him he was twenty-four, and had just made a film named *El Mariachi* for around $9,000, and it was a big hit. He shot it on a home camera and shoved it through the mail slot of an agent, and the rest is history. He had an enormous hit with *Spy Kids* (2001), a colorful and delightful family entertainment that cost $35 million and grossed many, many times that. Now he's back with *Spy Kids 2*. He's currently editing *Once Upon a Time in Mexico*, starring Antonio Banderas, Johnny Depp, Salma Hayek, Willem Dafoe, and Mickey

Rourke. He is a man who loves his work, his life, the world, and especially the Sony 24fps HD digital video camera.

This is the same camera George Lucas used to shoot *Attack of the Clones*. It was developed by Sony to imitate the look of twenty-four-frame-per-second film, and it costs around $100,000. It is not to be confused with the little cameras most people think of when they think of digital video. Rodriguez believes the HD camera gives him a better picture than film. I disagree. But I've written so much on this issue that it's only fair to let him have his say. Besides, I agree with his other point: that it's faster and cheaper than film, more like play and less like work.

I was not his interviewer but his audience. Rodriguez is so exuberant, so talkative, that at one point I asked him about his good friend Quentin Tarantino, also known to wave his hands a lot and talk nonstop.

When you're in a room together, who stops?

"I stop and I listen," he said, "because I'm from ten kids. He's an only child and he'll talk and he'll talk and he'll talk."

And Rodriguez quietly listens. Uh-huh.

It was Tarantino who told him he should make a third film to follow *El Mariachi* (1992) and *Desperado* (1995), so he would have a Mexican trilogy. Sergio Leone made *A Fistful of Dollars* and *For a Few Dollars More*, both at bargain-basement prices, and then he made the epics *The Good, the Bad and the Ugly* and *Once Upon a Time in the West*. Rodriguez should follow in his footsteps.

"Quentin challenged me." he said. "He told me, 'If you do a third one it has to be *The Good, the Bad and the Ugly*, of this series. It has to be the epic. And you have to call it *Once Upon a Time in Mexico*.'

"I'm thinking, yeah, like when hell freezes over. I ain't gonna go to Mexico again and shoot on film; it's so cumbersome. It's like an anvil around your ankle creatively. I thought, I'm never gonna make that movie, but as soon as I saw the HD cameras, projects I thought were impossible, like that one—hey, I could shoot that in seven weeks and it would look like an epic, like an old Technicolor movie, sharp as a tack. You'll see every pore in every actor's face like an old Sergio Leone movie. I prepared it in two and a half weeks, told the studio we've only got seven weeks to shoot because of the actors' strike coming up. Went out. Shot it. They couldn't believe we brought this huge movie back on time."

The advantages of the HD camera, he said, are that you don't need to spend so much time lighting everything. You can shoot on a moment's notice, and you can see exactly what you've just shot. So you don't have to do another take for insurance.

"It's weird," Rodriguez said. "Usually on a movie you don't see a finished print until the premiere. Now we see on the set better than what we even see at the premiere—digitally. So when an actor comes up to you and says, 'You sure that was good?' You say, yeah, have a look. You show him the digital monitor. You tell him, 'This is the historical record. This is what it's gonna look like on the premiere. You can see the sweat in your eyes.'

"So much of the film-based process of Hollywood is such a hassle. That's why most directors only make one movie every three or four years. Coppola told me he loves directing movies but hates making them. And when something creative is a hassle, something's seriously wrong with the process. You look at a movie and you go, it cost that much? It had all this talent involved—and that's it? That's all you got? Well, I reverse the process."

The Rodriguez Theory is that the less a movie costs, the more freedom he has. He demonstrated that definitively in *Spy Kids 2,* he said. The movie, now playing around the country, is another special-effects extravaganza with the two title characters (Alexa Vega and Daryl Sabara) competing with two snot-nosed rival spy kids to find the secret island of a mad scientist (Steve Buscemi). As before, the spy kids' parents (Antonio Banderas and Carla Gugino) follow along to help, and *this* time, *they're* followed by the spy kids' grandparents (Ricardo Montalban and Holland Taylor).

"The studio said, because the first movie was a $36 million movie, next time spend $60 million. I said, 'I know, you want it bigger and better. But give me the same budget, because the money's not gonna do it. Being *creative* is gonna make it a bigger, better movie.'

"For example, there's a scene where the two kids walk into a room and they can't hear each other talk, but suddenly they can hear each other think. That's a great scene, and it cost five bucks, because it's all in the idea. Better to think up stuff like that than worry, how am I gonna spend $120 million today?"

Rodriguez by now was so warmed up, I felt like I was a studio executive, and this was his pitch.

"I production-design 'em so that I won't overbill 'em," he said. "You have Steve Buscemi standing around this little volcano. There's only three rocks there. I put wheels on them so that when I shot at cross angles, I would roll the rocks over there and line them up and shoot them. The same rocks. And that kind of savings goes throughout. No production designer would ever allow the director to show up and see three rocks and tell him, 'Oh, you can just move 'em, can't you?' But I know what I can get away with, so I save the money, which means I can have creative freedom and be imaginative like a child."

Spy Kids 2 went through most of its postproduction process, Rodriguez said, in his garage, in Austin, Texas. Some towns have garage bands. Austin has garage movies. I remembered Rick Linklater telling me his *Waking Life* was postproduced in *his* garage.

"Once you've abandoned film," Rodriguez said, "you question everything. You ask, why are we doing that like that? That's why I mixed the sound track for this movie in the garage. I edited in my garage, I mixed the sound there. It's 5.1 Dolby. It's a very small garage and I worked hard to emulate a big-room sound."

Austin is really the center of things these days, isn't it?

"It's only because we made it happen. It wasn't like there was something that made filmmaking there easy. People don't live there to work. They work to live there. Because everything's accepted. You do mudslinging artwork? Cool! Rick can go do his crazy animation thing. I'm making giant home movies. Mike Judge is doing *King of the Hill* for TV. It's got a lot of high tech now. And it's a hippie hangout and an artist hangout and musician's hangout.

"When the airport moved, I took over an old hangar, and Rick Linklater, too—we just took hangars and we made film studios out of them so we could shoot in there, so we could work at home. I don't ever wanna feel like I'm working. I just wanna feel like I'm playing all day long.

Playing with my kids, cooking food from scratch, making movies. It all goes together."

Martin Scorsese

New York, December 15, 2002—In 1977, right after he made *Taxi Driver*, Martin Scorsese took out a two-page ad in *Variety* to announce his next production: *The Gangs of New York*.

"It's been on my mind for many, many years," Scorsese was saying the other day. We were having lunch in his hotel suite, and he was eating a bowl full of something that looked like puppy chow, but which he said was on the Zone Diet.

He asked his longtime collaborator Jay Cocks to do a screenplay about the incredibly violent years between 1830 and the Civil War, when gangs ruled New York's streets and engaged in warfare. But then he made *Raging Bull*, and then *The King of Comedy* and then *The Last Temptation of Christ*, and by then, he said, the moment had passed and Hollywood wasn't making pictures like *Gangs* anymore. By which he meant, although he didn't say it, that Hollywood had turned to formulas and was afraid of such an ambitious project.

So twenty years passed and he never stopped thinking about the film, and now here it is, a year after it was first scheduled to be released, surrounded by rumors of power struggles, *Gangs of New York*.

Scorsese's film, which opens Friday, stars Leonardo DiCaprio as Amsterdam Vallon, a tough Irish kid whose father was martyred while leading the Dead Rabbits, a gang of recently arrived immigrants. Daniel Day-Lewis plays William Cutting, also known as Bill the Butcher, leader of a gang called the Nativists, who hate immigrants. Cameron Diaz is Jenny Everdeane, pickpocket and con woman, who was once Bill's woman but now loves Amsterdam.

The film was made at a cost of untold millions (the figure changes from story to story) on enormous sets built at Rome's Cinecitta to duplicate the notorious Five Points area of New York in the decades before the war. No movie has ever depicted American poverty and squalor in this way: Immigrants huddle on shelves in a rooming house, starving children die in the streets, there is no law except the rule of the mighty, and each immigrant or racial tribe battles the others.

"It's not about guys with wigs writing with feathers," Scorsese said, chuckling over his gruel. He is quick to explain, however, that his movie should be seen as an "opera, not a documentary"—that he played with the facts to tell a better story.

He has a scene, for example, when navy ships fire their cannons on rioting draft resisters. "Actually, they unloaded some howitzers and fired from land," he said. "They were joined by army troops fresh from fighting at Gettysburg—I had to cut out the part explaining that—and these troops were impatient at draft resisters and also feared they might be facing a British-led rebellion."

Scorsese tells me these things and many more during our lunch. He is not one of those film promoters who stick to sound bites and are focused on selling their pictures. He talks about whatever comes into his mind, and I learn that he thinks *The River* is Jean Renoir's best movie, that he would love to make a film from a book by Joseph Conrad, that he has finally gotten through James Joyce's *Ulysses*, that he needs to work because he plowed half of his salary back into *Gangs of New York*, and that there will not be a "director's cut" of the film on DVD.

That last he makes particularly clear, because of all the controversy over reported arguments he had with Miramax chief Harvey Weinstein about the length of the film.

"The debate was about how you get a picture to play, not about how long it was," he said. He talked about a long process with his editor, Thelma Schoonmaker, who has worked on all of his pictures, as they made versions that ran from three hours and forty minutes to as little as two hours and thirty-six minutes. They screened before test audiences: "This is a film that needed to be screened that way because it contains a lot of information. How much was getting across? How much wasn't getting across? How much was getting across that you didn't *need* to get across, because you could just drop or forget it?"

At one point, he said, it was too short. Scenes played too fast. "I added three or four minutes, clarified certain other things. The rhythm was still off, I felt. This went on and on over a period of about a year. At one point I put too much back in."

His discussions with Weinstein, he said, were always about finding the length where the picture worked. When that got to the press, it was translated into fights. The movie is currently 168 minutes long, he said, and that is the right length, and that's why there won't be any director's cut—because this is the director's cut.

Scorsese explains these things in a torrent of enthusiasm. I have known him thirty-five years, and this has never changed: He loves movies to an unreasonable, delirious degree, and he has unalloyed zeal for making them and talking about them. Words pour from him. Let me provide statistics. I tape-recorded exactly forty-five minutes of our conversation. It contained 8,731 words, which means he was speaking at 194 words a minute—but even faster, actually, because some of the tape is me, speaking more slowly. I say that just to illustrate that in a time when many people in the film business speak guardedly or even with paranoia, Scorsese wears it all on his sleeve.

The film's art director, Dante Ferretti, created catacombs carved from the rock of Manhattan for the opening scenes. Scorsese said they are based on fact. "Right now in Chinatown they have sweatshops beneath the basements," he said. "A friend of mine did some research a few years ago, going through underground areas in Chinatown. He actually saw sweatshops below."

Are any of the catacombs like those shown in the movie still down there?

"Oh, I think they're there. Just covered over. And I know for a fact that the basements of the Lower East Side where I grew up, you could go in a basement on Elizabeth Street and come out somewhere on Mott Street. That was mainly to get away from the police. And also the Italians used it a lot for making wine down there, which was against the law. The city has a whole ... underneath. I was trying to employ that with these caves."

Now, Scorsese said, he needs to go to work again. "I have a three-year-old to feed," he smiles. What will he make? Two projects are in his mind. One is a biopic based on Dean Martin, which he has been talking about for years. Another is *The Aviator,* based on the early life of Howard Hughes, who has an earth-shaking love affair with Katharine Hepburn.

"You know who looks uncannily like young Howard Hughes?" Scorsese mused. "Leonardo DiCaprio."

Kevin Spacey

Park City, Utah, January 22, 2003—The art of making a deal, Kevin Spacey explains, is not unlike the shell game.

"Under one shell is the actor. He wants to make the movie, but under another shell is his agent, who doesn't want him to commit until the deal is assembled. But the deal can't be assembled without the actor onboard, because he's essential to getting the financing. So the question is: Which shell is the deal under?"

Spacey considered his oatmeal as if the raisins on top would spell out the answer. We were in the coffee shop of the Yarrow Inn, next to a table of Sony digital executives who had just brought us up-to-date on their new cameras. But even a camera is of no use without a deal.

"You take this movie *Pieces of April,*" Spacey said. "It's got some of the best buzz at Sundance. I followed its history. They had a package all together for $8 million. The deal fell apart. They still had their actors—a great cast. So other people stepped up, but for a much more minimal amount. Still, they got it made. The hardest thing in the movie business is getting people to lock and load."

Spacey's own company was instrumental in the production of another much buzzed and well reviewed Sundance entry, *The United States of Leland.* It stars Ryan Gosling as a sensitive, lonely teenager who one day stabs a retarded kid twenty times. Charged with murder, he knows everybody wants to know "why?" but all he can reply is "the sadness." He liked the retarded kid, and used to walk him home from school. Spacey plays the killer's remote and distant father.

Spacey has a movie opening in February, Alan Parker's *The Life of David Gale,* which is about capital punishment and is, he says, incredibly timely because of Governor George Ryan's pardon of Illinois death row inmates. Spacey stars as an activist opposed to executions, who is himself convicted of murder and sent to death row.

"You have to look at both sides," he said. "I think the death penalty is wrong. But what if my sister were murdered? The families of the victims are legitimate in their desire to see the killers die. But how can you be absolutely sure you have the right killer?"

At Sundance, Spacey is seeing movies but not making deals. "I'm taking a year off," he said. "Then, I know what I'll do next. It's based on a book about blackjack called *Bringing Down the House*. It's about these incredibly brilliant MIT students who took the Vegas casinos for a fortune by counting cards at blackjack. They trained rigorously, they were not cheating, they slipped in under the radar because they were mostly minority group members who didn't fit the casino profile for card-counters. It's a great story."

His Sundance entry, *The United States of Leland*, is the kind of smart, sad movie, like *American Beauty*, that could win serious award consideration. It takes place within a suburban lifescape where everything is sunny and well tended on the surface, but loneliness and alienation well up underneath.

The screenplay and direction are by Matthew Ryan Hoge, who had only one minibudget indie film under his belt when Spacey read it. "When I met Matt, I never before in my life have been more convinced that the writer was the right person to direct his own material," Spacey said.

Of course, Spacey's presence in the project is what made it bankable; he was the deal under the third shell. The film stars Don Cheadle as the prison teacher who tries to understand the young killer. "Matthew himself taught classes in prison," Spacey said. Jena Malone is the kid's sort-of girlfriend.

"There was this photo," he said, "of a teenager in San Diego who killed his parents and then shot up a school, and he was in handcuffs and this big orange prison uniform, a tiny kid between two big guards, and he didn't have the slightest idea why he did what he did. This is a movie that explores that ground."

Ryan Gosling's performance is astonishing, coming from the same actor who electrified Sundance two years ago with Henry Bean's *The Believer*, where he played a cocky, smart, angry young Jew who posed as an anti-Semite. As Leland, he is inward, quiet, sensitive, deeply wounded by his childhood.

"His agent told us, 'I've got your Leland,'" Spacey said, "and sent us *The Believer*. Hoge told him, 'No, you haven't,' because there was no connection between that role and Leland. But Ryan came to L.A. to read, and we did a screen test with him and Jena Malone, and we were convinced. He immerses himself in a part. You would never recognize the same actor."

We were talking a day or two after the Golden Globes, and Spacey, the student of the industry, said the big win for *Chicago* was an omen. Like almost everyone else, he expects it to win the Oscar as best picture.

"It's an interesting thing, how films driven by music have been shunned by the Academy, even though they're very good—like *All That Jazz, Fame, Victor/Victoria*, or just now *8 Mile*. For some reason the industry is resistant to the genre, but now, through the direct influence of *Moulin Rouge*, musicals are back on the table, and *Chicago* may break the jinx. Somebody once said that every genre is a bad genre until somebody makes a good movie in it."

Steven Spielberg

New York, December 22, 2002—While many directors spend years in gestation before making a film, Steven Spielberg seems cheerfully productive. In June he released *Minority Report*, an awesomely virtuoso futurist thriller starring Tom Cruise, and now here it is December, and he's back with *Catch Me If You Can*, a more lighthearted film, starring Leonardo DiCaprio as a teenage impostor and Tom Hanks as the FBI man on his trail. The movie is based on the true story of Frank Abagnale Jr., who now advises corporations against the same kinds of cons he once perfected.

We talked last summer; we talk again now. Spielberg seems more relaxed about the new film, which was shot on a much lower budget in a relatively short time, and which must have felt like unwinding after the complexities of *Minority Report*.

I told him I'd just seen *Minority Report* again on the big screen, going down to Times Square to catch it, just to confirm my feeling about how good it was.

Spielberg: I haven't seen it again since it was released. I rarely look back at the movies I've made except when my kids see them for the first time. So I get a chance to see all my own movies again through my kids' eyes, which is always fun, you know, because they tell me whether they like 'em or not right away. Or they walk out. I've had my kids walk out of my pictures.

RE: Which one didn't they like?

Spielberg: They walked out of *Amistad.* I lost my whole family. All my young kids, you know. I wouldn't ever show them the middle passage and I didn't let them see the very beginning, and they were bored by the legal stuff. They left.

RE: With *Catch Me If You Can,* the story of a kid who passes for a doctor and an airline pilot—you personally lived this story, didn't you, because you were putting on a suit and tie and walking onto the studio lot at Universal when you were sixteen years old?

Spielberg: Yeah, just about. I think a little bit less than sixteen. And I did that for a whole summer during my high school vacation.

RE: And every single day you were in violation of the law?

Spielberg: Pretty much so. I was trespassing. There were a number of books they could have thrown at me if they had caught me, but they never caught me.

RE: I was asked the other day about these kids who sneaked into a Hollywood studio to try to replace bad screenplays with good ones, as a kind of public service prank. Of course, that's against the law. And I said, yeah, but you know Spielberg did something like that too. I wonder if you have to bend the laws to get into the industry, one way or another.

Spielberg: I don't know if you have to bend the laws, but I think mine was a unique case. I mean, I just had such a desire to make movies. I had been making movies as a high school student, you know, and so I thought the best thing to do was watch how the professionals did it, so when I went on the Universal lot I was chasing my dreams. Whereas all the things that Frank Abagnale does in *Catch Me If You Can*—his chutzpah is based on getting away with something as he's being chased. So he's being pursued. And I was the pursuer—of a career. That's why I did what I did.

RE: So actually you saw Abagnale's book more as a good idea for a movie than as your life story.

Spielberg: Oh yeah. I thought it was a very original story that only happened once in history and only could have been perpetrated by this guy. Once you meet him you see that he

was so charismatic and so trustworthy. I could see why he could pull the wool over everybody's eyes.

RE: Leonardo DiCaprio is twenty-eight in life, and can look twenty-eight or even older, actually, but he can also look like a high school kid. Is that one of the reasons you cast him? Because he could make that jump in age?

Spielberg: I didn't know how much we could stretch the age, but when he'd comb the bangs over his forehead and he wore the collegiate kind of sweater and he effected a whole different posture of bending over, being very humble, and his voice rose, he was able to step into that character and be totally convincing.

RE: I guess De Niro worked with him early, in *This Boy's Life* (1993), and told Martin Scorsese, "You gotta look out for this kid; he's gonna be good." And then in a sense everybody seems to feel his career was sidetracked by *Titanic* because it was too successful.

Spielberg: That's true.

RE: And so he's making his "comeback" now after having all of that success. You've had a lot of success too. How does that work?

Spielberg: Well, I've had a lot of success, but I've never been traumatized by the cultural phenomenon that came down upon Leo that basically meant that all the credit and all the blame went right to Leonardo DiCaprio. I don't mean blame for the movie, which was perceived as being a really good movie, but the blame for creating such a media circus. Leo was just a cast member. He was an actor playing a role for many, many months and then he suddenly couldn't go anywhere. He was a prisoner. A prisoner of hotel rooms, a prisoner in his own home. He couldn't go anywhere. Everybody's out there with cameras—and then his life became mythological. The rumors were much greater and much more exaggerated than the facts of his personal life. I think it did stall his career by about four or five years.

RE: But by the time you came to cast him, you felt that he was back in the ranks of just being a good actor. Obviously, he's a star but ...

Spielberg: Yeah, but, you know, I've always thought he was a good actor. When I saw *What's Eating Gilbert Grape* (1993), I thought he was a phenomenon. I always wanted to work with him, and he actually predates me on *Catch Me If You Can.* He came first before I decided to direct the movie, so he was already attached to play Frank, and my job was to go over to meet him for the first time, thank him for giving my little daughter Sacha an autograph when *Titanic* came out. I wound up just going crazy for him.

RE: And Tom Hanks was involved at that time or you brought him in?

Spielberg: No, Tom had read the script as a writing sample and called Walter Parkes, the coproducer, and said, "Can I be in this movie? Do you think Steven would let me play the FBI agent? I really know who this guy is." And then Tom called me and he said, "Can I kinda horn in here?" And I said, my God, what do you mean horn in? Then he called Leo and said, "Is it an imposition for me to be in this movie, which is clearly your film? You're carrying it. Would it be an imposition upon you if I played the FBI agent?" Leo thought that heaven had just come down to earth for him. So in a sense, Tom invited himself into the project in such a humble, beautiful way.

RE: You and Tom have a really good relationship, don't you?

Spielberg: Yeah, we do.

RE: As an actor/director, as coproducers and friends.

Spielberg: Friend first.

RE: He's very convincing as just a guy in a suit and a tie and those horn-rimmed glasses, in the hat as the FBI agent. And then at the same time, he can do *Saving Private Ryan*. He has an enormous range.

Spielberg: He's a chameleon. He has amazing range. This is the first movie I think he's ever been in where he has made a meal of anonymity, because he's so anonymous for so long in the picture. He doesn't steal any scenes; he's not trying to out-act anybody. He's just trying to play this pencil pusher whose own FBI agents don't believe all this effort is worth the trouble he's going through.

RE: This movie was a much shorter shoot than *Minority Report* and a lot of your recent films.

Spielberg: It needed pacing; it needed speed, energy on the set, energy with the cast. It needed the cast knowing I was gonna walk away after four or five takes. We had to use our mojos and our intuition to get us there.

RE: You've worked with Tom Cruise as well as with Leonardo DiCaprio, two people who've had to deal with the spotlight of fame. Do you get involved in that or do you just kind of . . .

Spielberg: I'm like a witness to it. I love watching. I went to Japan to open *Minority Report* about a month ago and we walked into 4,000 screaming fans all screaming at the top of their lungs with Japanese accents, "Tom, Tom, Tom." And Tom throws himself into the crowd. He signs autographs, he gets his picture taken with people. He came an hour and a half early to every premiere we did on *Minority Report* in Europe so he could be with the people, let them take his picture, sign their autographs. He is the most generous actor with his own time I have ever experienced when it comes to his fans.

RE: My opinion of *Minority Report* is exactly the same as it was last summer when I had to use a seven-letter word in order to tell you how much I liked it.

Spielberg: It was a beautiful word, though. I'll never forget it.

RE: Is it going to be overlooked at Oscar time just because of that attention-gap problem that the Academy has?

Spielberg: Well, you know, I'm not the one to say whether something deserves attention or not. We directors are in control of everything we do except in the Oscar award season. I'm philosophical about that.

RE: But the problem is that the Academy doesn't look over the whole twelve months of movies.

Spielberg: That's true. They look mainly toward the end of the year, but at the same time, you know, *The Silence of the Lambs* came out in February and won the Oscar over a year later. *Gladiator* came out I believe in May, and won the Oscar almost a year later, and *Private Ryan*, you know, won a lot of Oscars and it came out in July. As far as *Minority Report* is concerned, I'm so philosophical about whether we get recognized. I'd like people in the film to get recognized, but as far as I'm concerned it has very low impact with me right now because the film itself was such a gratifying experience. I had a lot of anxiety about the Oscars until I won with *Schindler's List*, and that was so personally meaningful to me that now, well, I'm kind of sanguine.

Bertrand Tavernier

May 6, 2003—During the Nazi occupation of France, when the country was governed by the German-controlled Vichy administration, 220 films were made by French filmmakers. Bertrand Tavernier is fascinated by this fact: "None of them was anti-Semitic, pro-German, pro-collaboration, or even pro-Vichy. Except for one film, which has two dubious lines, you never had an anti-Semitic remark in the films of that time—even though you had plenty in the 1930s. I wanted to try to understand why."

Tavernier's new film, *Safe Conduct*, is an attempt to reconstruct that wartime period when the Germans ordered the French to keep on making films, because they were good for civilian morale. Hundreds of film workers, including famous directors and actors, continued to work—some for the employment, some as a cover for Resistance activities, some no doubt to save their skins or feed their families. But they did not make pro-Nazi propaganda.

The film combines politics with film history, two areas Tavernier relishes. The French director at sixty-one is a tall, bulky man with a thatch of white hair and a ready smile; after a start as a film critic and publicist, he has directed twenty-nine films and yet found time to write a history of American cinema and to become a familiar face at festivals such as Telluride, where he programs films he loves.

Safe Conduct includes characters based on the assistant director Jean Devaivre (Jacques Gamblin), who performed daring missions for the Resistance, and the writer Jean Aurenche (Denis Podalydes), a womanizer who became expert at seeming to cooperate with the Germans while not doing so. Many years after the war, Aurenche became a friend of Tavernier's, wrote the screenplay for his first film, *The Clockmaker of St. Paul's*, and three others, and told him some of the stories that appear in the film. He died in 1992 at eighty-eight; Devaivre is still alive at ninety-one, and Tavernier helped revive some of his work.

Tavernier says *Safe Conduct* is an examination of why some of those who made films during the period were heroes and many others, not heroes, resisted the Nazis in a passive-aggressive way. The period could have produced shameful films, but did not.

"I think some people had a sense of respon-sibility," Tavernier told me, during a talk after the April 25 screening of his film *L.627* (1991) at my Overlooked Film Festival at the University of Illinois at Urbana. At the festival, he was in nonstop conversation with everyone from fellow director Neil LaBute to undergraduate film fans; few people have such a boundless love of the movies.

He told a story about a meeting between Jean Aurenche and Alfred Greven, the head of Continental, the German-controlled production company, who asked Aurenche for the names of Jewish screenwriters, allegedly because he wanted to use them.

"Aurenche told me this was the worst moment of his life, because he was talking to somebody who was appointed by Joseph Goebbels. He told Greven: 'If I knew some Jewish people I don't think I would mention the names to you.' And Greven said, 'You know that I can send you to Germany just like that.' And Aurenche transformed that into a joke. He said, 'You will not do that, Mr. Greven, because we are alike. If I had been working class, a worker, or the waiter there, I would never have spoken to you like that. But we are both bourgeois and the bourgeois do not eat each other.' He made Greven laugh and he got away with it. That's the kind of scene I like to deal with in a film, and the kind of scene *Safe Conduct* is about."

Aurenche's dodge isn't the stuff of classic movie heroism, but it meets Tavernier's definition: "The French novelist Rolland said that a hero is a man who does what he can."

The director Maurice Tourneur is shown as a character in the film, which also notes the stars Michel Simon and Danielle Darrieux, but Tavernier said he wasn't interested in the story of great actors.

"I was interested in the story of the screenwriters, the technicians, the workers, people who are suffering. The story of the foot soldier. Those are the people in *Safe Conduct*, the people who were trying not to help the Germans, or were working for the Germans because that was a way to hide the fact that you were in the Resistance."

Oddly enough, this French film about French filmmakers was not well received in France, especially by the critics of the legendary magazine *Cahiers du Cinéma*, which launched the early writing careers of François Truffaut and

Claude Chabrol (and Tavernier). *Cahiers* showcased the auteur theory, hailed the French New Wave, and attacked the earlier generation for what were contemptuously described as merely well-made films. That generation, of course, includes the characters in *Safe Conduct*.

"They thought that by telling the story of the people who tried to be brave in 1942, I was attacking the New Wave," Tavernier said. "That is totally mad. I've been a great defender of the New Wave. I was the press agent of Jean-Luc Godard; I worked on films of Claude Chabrol, of Agnès Varda, of Jacques Demy, of Jacques Rivette. But I did a film which is about work, about the people who tried to do films during the Occupation. And working there meant that you could become a collaborator, or you could avoid collaborating. And it was harder for the bottom people."

The character of Greven, who ruled the French film industry during the Occupation, is played by Christian Berkel in the film and fascinates Tavernier.

"Greven was a mysterious character because he was appointed by Goebbels, but he disobeyed every order of Goebbels. Goebbels wanted him to produce empty films, films which had no content, which would simply amuse and entertain. But Greven produced a lot of ambitious films and some of them made Goebbels furious."

The Nazi propaganda czar told Greven that *La Symphonie Fantastique*, the life story of Berlioz, "is superbly directed, it's a masterpiece, but it's a film which is totally nationalistic. It is awakening the French nationalist. I did not put you in charge to wake French nationalism and have people applaud at each screening!"

"But two months after that," Tavernier said, "Greven produced *Le Corbeau* by Clouzot, which is one of the strongest films made during that period. It is about anonymous letters, about people informing. So why did Greven behave like that? And why did he produce an adaptation of Emile Zola, who was first on the Nazi blacklist because of the Dreyfuss case? Those are the sorts of questions I'm dealing with in *Safe Conduct*."

Essays

Unhappy *Happy Times*

August 23, 2002—Movies can bridge cultural boundaries, but sometimes they also confuse them. Consider the tricky case of *Happy Times*, a new film by the distinguished Chinese director Zhang Yimou. As I wrote in my review:

"It is about a group of unemployed men who build a fake room in an abandoned factory, move a blind girl into it, tell her it is in a hotel, and become her client for daily massages, paying her with blank pieces of paper they hope she will mistake for money.

"On the basis of that description, you will assume that this movie is cruel and depraved.... [but] *Happy Times* is a comedy, and has been compared to Chaplin's *City Lights,* which was also about a jobless man trying to help a blind girl."

In my review, I speculated on the chances of the story being used in a Hollywood movie (none), and wondered if there was a culture gap at work. I wrote: "When American critics praise the movie (and most of them have), they are making some kind of concession to its Chinese origins. A story that would be unfilmable by Hollywood becomes, in Chinese hands, 'often uproariously funny' *(New York Magazine),* 'subtle and even humorous' *(Film Journal International),* and 'wise, gentle and sad' *(New York Times)."*

Toward the end of my review, I confessed: "... if I found it creepy beyond all reason, that is no doubt because I have been hopelessly corrupted by the decadent society I inhabit. Or ... are there moviegoers in China who also find *Happy Times* odd in the extreme? ... The Web is worldwide and perhaps I will hear from a Chinese reader or two."

I have. I have heard from readers in China, and from Chinese Americans from Maine to California. And I am no closer to an answer to my question.

Brian Hu of Berkeley, California, wrote me: "I watched the film with another Chinese American and we both found it uproariously funny. In fact, I can't think of another film this year that has made me laugh as much. At first I thought, finally, a major director has made a universally simple, humorous, and meaningful film that all Americans can easily enjoy and learn from. But reading your review, I'd reconsider it.

"Americans simply are not aware of Chinese comedic traditions. We may know Hong Kong cinema for its wild action movies, but we don't realize that a good fraction of Cantonese-language films are comedies, just as a good part of Hollywood films are comedies. Sadly, the truth is, violence translates well; comedy does not. Chinese comedy is often quite sadistic. Think of those Asian game shows that are parodied on American TV, where contestants do crazy things like endure freezing weather in their underwear while a laugh track of Japanese junior high students giggling plays in the background. Americans may find it cruel, but many Chinese find it hilarious.

"That's not to say Chinese people are sadistic. They just find some things that we find 'cruel and depraved' to be funny. On the other hand, I have not yet met one Taiwanese or mainland Chinese who enjoyed *Pulp Fiction* or *Fargo* like we do here in America. Chinese audiences find films like *Happy Times* charming and affectionate, because although it's cruel, it's cruel on a simple, harmless level, something you certainly can't say about Tarantino's comedies. It's like Harpo Marx vs. Neil LaBute."

And now here is Ye Meng of Beijing, China, who writes for MonkeyPeaches.com, a site devoted to Chinese film news:

"When the film was released in China one and a half years ago, reviews from most audiences and critics were generally very negative. They found the film dull, shallow, and illusory. Most of them thought the plot was ridiculously illogical and the setup of the story was too far away from real life. They said Zhang Yimou's handprint was nowhere to be found and the entire film was carried away by Zhao Benshan (who played Zhao), a very well-known comedian in China. Not surprisingly, the film did really poorly in China.

"However, a small number of moviegoers and critics did find the film touching, humorous, and bittersweet. They said the film was reflecting the life of the little people, their struggle for better life, and their simple and maybe even naive love to total strangers. Many social phenomena shown in the film, like laid-off workers, shut-down state-owned factories, and disparity between the rich and poor, are all very real. What is not so real is the story. In fact, director Zhang Yimou intended to put the characters in a strange position and let them play ridiculous. 'My goal is very simple—showing the audiences some humor and letting them laugh with a bitter taste,' he said. '*Happy Times* won't be my greatest work and it won't have very rich social content.'

"I think you will only buy the film if you can forgive the story setting and try to find out what the director really wanted to tell. The film somehow went wrong probably because Zhang Yimou was incapable of handling comedy, and his own touch was outshined by so many stars, especially Zhao Benshan, who he brought onboard to remedy such incapability.

"The ending being shown to international audiences is not the original ending being shown in China. The original ending is: Zhao forges a letter from the father of Wu Ying, the blind girl. When he starts reading the letter, which is filled with beautiful lies, for her, the camera is gradually pulled away and credits start to show up.

"Zhang Yimou and his writing team struggled on the script for almost a year and he said what made him finally decide to shoot the film was simply because he loved the ending. When asked about the ending, he said: 'We can live with nothing but we must have dreams. This is a film about the dreams of the poor people.' However, many Chinese audiences hated it and to make sure the film sold well internationally, a second ending was shot.

"The new ending is favored by Sony, the film's North American distributor. However, according to an on-line survey conducted by a movie theater in Beijing, only 9.24 percent of the audiences preferred the new ending."

And now here is Jue Wang of Bangor, Maine:

"Hey, I read your review for the Chinese film *Happy Times* and you asked for the opinion of a Chinese person. Well, I'm Chinese. Sort of. I moved to North America when I was seven, and I saw the movie in its Chinese version a year ago, in eighth grade.

"I didn't find the movie creepy like you did, but I don't think it should be viewed as a comedy. Certainly, no one I know thought the picture was funny, as a whole. I'm not sure there's a genre for this movie (even in China). Maybe 'overly depressing attempt at poignancy.'

"I think the problem was that the director tried too hard to carry a message. It wasn't wholeheartedly funny, but it also wasn't convincingly sad.

"Anyway, my point is, most Chinese people agree with you: This isn't the director's best pic. Well, I agree with you, anyway. I don't think it's possible to market this movie to an American audience, anyway. The 'creepy' part is hard to ignore. Even for China. Well, some in China."

Beyond the Valley of My Memories

February 7, 2003—It may be one of the ten best movies of the 1970s, as the critic Richard Corliss once said, or it may be saddled with a script by a neophyte screenwriter, as Gene Siskel once said, but *Beyond the Valley of the Dolls* was one of the great experiences of my life. When Russ Meyer, the king of the Bs, called up in 1969 to ask me to write a screenplay at Twentieth Century Fox, he began an adventure later described as the maniacs taking over the studio. In six reckless weeks, starting with only a title, we created the movie from scratch. "This is not a sequel!" the ads said. "There has never been anything like it!"

BVD was made during that brief period when major studios produced X-rated films, although today it looks more like an R. It cost $900,000, including the development costs for two discarded screenplays by Jacqueline Susann, and became one of the most profitable movies on the studio's books. But the official Fox history doesn't even mention it, and although *Beyond* has briefly been available on VHS and laser disc, both formats are long out of print, maybe because studio management preferred to forget its dalliance with the X.

Only recently, with a younger generation of executives who grew up with the film as a cult favorite, has it come back into favor; a DVD is planned for later this year, and I have been approached about a Broadway version. Last year the studio struck a new 35-mm print, which played to sold-out houses at the Film Forum in New York.

My friendship with Russ Meyer began in a sense in 1960, when his first film, *The Immoral Mr. Teas,* opened at the Illini Theater in my hometown of Champaign-Urbana, Illinois. It played on and off for two years, and was a staple during exam weeks. Meyer, who had photographed many of the first year's playmates for Hugh Hefner, adopted the *Playboy* standard of "the girl next door" and invented the "nudie" genre. His films didn't feature tacky strippers, but wholesome young women in a format that looked but didn't touch. (Mr. Teas, played by Meyer's old army buddy Bill Teas, was a dentures deliveryman who suffered from a strange condition that allowed him to see women unclothed.)

By the mid-1960s, Meyer had moved on to his "drive-in period," producing movies with little nudity but lots of cleavage and violence. Two of them inspired the names of rock bands: *Mud Honey* and the immortal *Faster, Pussycat! Kill! Kill!* Then in 1968 came *Vixen!* which cost $72,000, grossed $6 million, and inspired a front-page article in the *Wall Street Journal* by the aptly named Steven Lovelady, crowning Meyer the "King of the Nudies." Lovelady mentioned Meyer's auteur status and cult following (*Teas,* according to the distinguished critic Leslie Fiedler, was "the best comedy of 1960").

I wrote a letter to the *Journal* applauding its recognition of a director whose dynamic editing style and distinctive energy were exciting whether or not he made skin flicks. Meyer wrote back with thanks, called me the next time he was in Chicago, and we became friends. When Richard Zanuck and David Brown, then running Fox, offered him a contract and the title *Beyond the Valley of the Dolls,* he hired me to write the screenplay, and I took a six-week leave from the *Chicago Sun-Times.* We moved into a three-room office on the Fox lot and concocted the screenplay in sessions involving yellow legal pads and much laughter.

The lot was not a happy place in those days. "Jeez, you guys gotta save the studio," moaned the legendary publicist Jet Fore. "Every pro-

ducer in town has his nephew up in the hills trying to remake *Easy Rider,* and whadda we got in the can? Nothing but a Western and two war movies." (The Western was *Butch Cassidy and the Sundance Kid,* and the war movies were *Patton* and *M*A*S*H.*)

Working with Meyer was exhilarating but demanding. He equated writing with typing. He kept his office door open, and whenever he couldn't hear my typewriter keys, he'd shout, "What's the matter?" We screened the original *Valley of the Dolls* (neither one of us ever read the book), thought it was pretty bad, and agreed to do a satire on the same formula: Three sexy young women come to Hollywood seeking fame and fortune, but fall afoul of sex, drugs, and vanity. Our heroines would not be movie stars, however, but members of an all-girl rock trio, the Carrie Nations. The movie, we reassured Jet Fore, would be "the first rock camp horror exploitation musical."

The story came from my own inflamed imagination, stoked by Meyer's love of absurd melodrama. I remember one day when I started laughing uproariously at about page 104.

"What's the matter?" Meyer shouted.

I hurried into his office. "Z-Man is a girl!" I said.

"He's what?" he asked.

"Z-Man has been a woman all along!" I explained. "He reveals his secret to Wonder Boy during the orgy scene!"

Meyer nodded judiciously. "You can never have too many women in the picture."

The film was cast with veterans of other Meyer pictures, like Erica *(Vixen)* Gavin, Chuck *(Cherry, Harry and Raquel!)* Napier, Haji *(Pussycat),* and Henry Rowland as a mysterious bartender named Martin Bormann. Blink and you'll miss Pam Grier's first screen appearance. Veteran Meyer composer Stu Phillips signed on, penning such songs as "Look Up at the Bottom" and "Come with the Gentle People." I introduced Russ to his future wife, Fox contract starlet Edy Williams, at the studio commissary, and she was cast as Ashley St. Ives. (The character was originally named Ashley Famous, after the agency headed by Ted Ashley, but Zanuck and Brown vetoed that.) Two Playboy playmates, Cynthia Myers and Dolly Read, were cast, along with the beautiful African-American model Marcia McBroom, as the Carrie Nations. John Lazar played the crucial role of Ronnie "Z-Man" Barzell. The Strawberry Alarm Clock was signed to appear in a party scene.

As the film went into production, the skin flick era was ending and hard-core pornography was appearing on American screens. Russ and I went to see *I Am Curious (Yellow)* on Hollywood Boulevard, and he emerged shaking his head.

"I'll never do hard-core," he said. "First, I don't want to share my grosses with the mob. Second, I've never been that interested in what goes on below the waist."

Russ was, as everyone knew or could have guessed from his films, a breast man.

"Where do you find those women?" I asked him.

"After they surpass a certain bra size," he said, "they find me."

The movie went into production with the distinguished cinematographer Fred Koenekamp behind the camera. Russ, a Signal Corps cameraman in World War II and a perfectionist who had always shot his own films, drove Fred nuts with demands for tighter focus.

The actors were briefed by Meyer before every scene, in solemn tones. Chuck Napier told me one day: "You wrote this, Roger. It reads like a comedy to me. But, hell, Russ treats it like Eugene O'Neill. He's lecturing us on character motivation and symbolism and deep meanings."

Russ knew it was a comedy, but never admitted that to the actors: "No actor can be funny by trying to be funny," he told me.

Beyond the Valley of the Dolls was released on June 17, 1970, a day shy of my twenty-eighth birthday. The critic John Simon found it was "rather like a Grandma Moses illustration for a work by the Marquis de Sade." Vincent Canby wrote in the *New York Times:* "Any movie that Jacqueline Susann thinks would damage her reputation as a writer cannot be all bad."

Thirty-three years after the film's first release, it remains an indestructible cult classic, long ignored by the studio, unavailable on video, sometimes seen on cable, still finding new fans. Students at the University of Colorado performed their own stage version for me at Boulder five years ago. When the film had

its twentieth anniversary screening in 1990 at the University of Southern California, the students recited the dialogue in unison with the screen. When it played at the University of Texas, an academic declared, "On a structural level, Meyer is, absurd as it may seem, the logical successor to Sergei Eisenstein." At the just-concluded Sundance Film Festival, directors Larry Charles of *Seinfeld* and Dan Algrant of *People I Know* told me they'd seen it many times. Mike Myers pays homage in his Austin Powers movies ("This is my happening—and it freaks me out!").

The 1970s are now enshrined as the golden age of American movies, when directors did their thing and the studios let them get away with it. No one got away with more than Russ Meyer did on *BVD*, making a subversive indie satire within the very system itself and getting the decade off on the right foot.

What do I think about the film today? Russ, who often cited *Li'l Abner* as his greatest artistic influence, was the auteur and I was merely the acolyte, but quite frankly and in all due modesty, I think it is the best rock camp horror exploitation musical ever made. Is it actually one of the ten best movies of the decade? Richard Corliss is one of two critics who think so, according to Leonard Maltin's *Film Guide*, although I have never been able to find out who the other one is. Maybe it is me.

Ten Oscar Memories

March 16, 2003—Oscar turns seventy-five this year, old enough to write a second volume of its memoirs. The Academy Awards are always called Hollywood's Prom Night, and like all prom nights they inspire a lot of memories and photographs and scrapbooks, and sometimes you go rummaging through them.

Everyone remembers Rob Lowe dancing with Snow White (except for me—I was stuck on an elevator to the press room and didn't see it). No one will ever forget Roberto Begnini climbing over the seats to claim his Oscar, or the unflappable David Niven confronted with a streaker, or Jack Palance pumping off those one-armed push-ups, or Sally Field crying, "You really love me." So those are everybody's memories. Here are ten of my own, alphabetically:

—Halle Berry's acceptance speech last year after winning best actress for *Monster's Ball*. There were those who said she went on too long, or was too emotional, but for me it was the perfect speech, combining the emotion of the moment with the context of history.

She was the first black woman to win as best actress, and as she named those who prepared the way for her, from Dorothy Dandridge, Lena Horne, and Diahann Carroll to "the women that stand beside me, Jada Pinkett, Angela Bassett, Vivica Fox" and then to "every nameless, faceless woman of color that now has a chance because this door tonight has been opened," well, there were tears in my eyes.

—Charlie Chaplin's honorary Oscar, in 1972, for his lifetime of work. They held his award right to the end of the show, where they thought it would be most dramatic. After a filmed tribute, Chaplin appeared on stage and walked to the front, and there should have been a magical moment, but some director or network executive or busybody got worried that the show was running too long, and superimposed a sponsor's trademark over Chaplin before fading to the credits. Wrong, cruel, stupid.

—How in the world did *Chariots of Fire* win in 1982? I remember a conversation I had at Cannes in May 1981 with David Puttnam and Jake Eberts, who produced it, and Hugh Hudson, who directed it. This was not an interview but just a discussion about whether the film would "play" in America. British Olympic runners in the 1924 Olympics? One a Jew, one a Christian, both running out of faith?

The movie opened in late 1981 in four theaters and slowly built an audience through word of mouth. It was still playing in some theaters a year later. With today's mass release patterns, it would have been dead in a weekend. It's worth remembering the other four best film nominees that year: *Atlantic City, On Golden Pond, Raiders of the Lost Ark,* and *Reds.* Four films that have stood the test of time—but, yes, *Chariots of Fire* would play in America.

—Bette Davis is one of three people often credited with naming the Oscar (she said its backside reminded her of a former husband). The legendary star was a presenter in 1986, after suffering a stroke in 1983, and it appeared to many viewers that she was completely confused at the podium. Not entirely true, or at least not her fault.

What happened was that she departed for a moment from the TelePrompTer. The prompter operator begin to scroll to catch up with what he thought was being left out, then scrolled back when he realized she wanted to return to the copy, and all she could see were lines of type scrolling up and down unhelpfully. To set the record straight, she appeared with Johnny Carson the next night, just to show everyone she hadn't lost it. That was the night she got an ovation simply for lighting a cigarette.

—Isaac Hayes, performing the theme song from *Shaft* in 1972. He materialized out of a cloud of smoke, decked in chains, like a Hell's Angel riding a piano rather than a motorcycle. It may not have been a great song, but did Oscar ever have a greater entrance?

—There was a time when many Americans thought Bob Hope was the permanent Oscar emcee. He hosted the show eight times by himself, and seven times with cohosts, between 1953 and 1978, and that included the first telecast of the Oscars in 1953. That year I listened on the radio, in the hospital, after having my appendix removed, and it seemed to me that the Academy Awards were unimaginably distant and grand. The fact that Hope could joke about them made him grander still. Listening on the radio made them seem so glamorous in my mind's eye that the real thing has never quite equaled the images in my imagination that night.

—In the spring of 1993, the Italian master Federico Fellini was given an honorary Academy Award, and in October of that year he was dead of a heart attack. But it is not Fellini I remember. What I remember is his wife, Giulietta Masina, sitting in the front row and weeping as he accepted the Oscar. She was weeping with both sorrow and joy, because she knew he was a dying man.

—The best Oscar day I ever spent was in the company of Dr. Haing S. Ngor, who was nominated for best supporting actor for *The Killing Fields.* The Cambodian doctor had never acted a day in his life before being cast in the film as a journalist who barely escapes with his life from the tyranny of the Khmer Rouge.

I asked if I could follow him around. First he

did the morning TV shows. Then he went to Tuxedo Center on Sunset and rented formal wear. Then he went to a Thai restaurant not far away, which was in fact run by Cambodians, where he caused a sensation when he walked in; by the time lunch was over, every Cambodian within five miles had gathered at the restaurant.

Ngor did not have the slightest expectation that he would win, but he'd had an incredible journey from the killing fields to the Oscars, and he was determined to enjoy every moment. He had a camera and photographed everything. As it happened, he *did* win the Oscar that night, and went on to act in sixteen more movies and TV shows before being shot dead in 1996 in a robbery-homicide.

—Sir Laurence Olivier won an honorary Oscar in 1979, and gave a speech so dramatic you could hear a pin drop. The camera cut to Jon Voight, in the audience, and you could read his lips, "Wow."

The next day, as it happened, I went to interview Michael Caine, who told me he had received a call that morning from Olivier: "He wanted to know what I thought of his speech. I said, 'Magnificent—but what did it mean?' Larry said: 'Exactly, dear boy! Utterly meaningless. I'm afraid I went up at the crucial moment and forgot everything I intended to say, so I just fell back on the old Shakespearean actors' tactic, where you mumble something about life and death and being off to Salisbury, and hope to get close enough to the wings to hear the prompter."

So great an actor was Olivier, however, that he sold the speech convincingly, and his listeners, convinced they had heard something profound, demanded the transcript. Then they puzzled over it.

—"The thing I regret most about the times I produced the Oscar show," the director Norman Jewison told me, "was the time John Wayne called up and said he wanted to be a presenter. Just hearing his voice on the phone was awesome. But he called a little late and we had already sent out invitations to all the presenters, so we didn't have an opening, and that's what I had to tell him."

That would have been in the late 1970s, maybe 1978, Jewison said. In 1979, Wayne was a presenter at the Oscars—giving the best pic-

ture award to *The Deer Hunter.* By then everybody knew he was dying. In 1963, after a lung cancer operation, he said he'd "beaten the big C," and for a long time, that was true. But he had open-heart surgery in 1978, and was operated on early in 1979 for stomach cancer.

When he walked onstage, his face was thin, his step was slow, he was apparently in pain, but he walked up to the podium unaided, and did the job to great applause. A few months later, in June 1979, he died.

"Watching that was an inspiration," Jewison said. "What courage the man had. Why did I turn him down the year before? John Wayne! Why didn't I shuffle some people around? What was I thinking?"

2003 Oscars

May 24, 2003—Oscar's kind of movie, *Chicago* is.

But it was a squeaker. *The Pianist,* a film about a Holocaust survivor by the exiled Roman Polanski, stole some of its thunder at the seventy-fifth anniversary Academy Awards by winning for best director, actor, and screenplay.

The other headline from the evening: Michael Moore's kind of president, George Bush isn't.

Chicago won for best picture and five other categories. Its star, Catherine Zeta-Jones, won for best supporting actress, and it also won Oscars for art direction, costumes, sound, and editing.

But *The Pianist* staged a late rally, and Adrien Brody did some scene-stealing with his win for best actor. After a back-bending kiss for presenter Halle Berry, he delivered heartfelt thanks, and then, as the orchestra was signaling him to wrap it up, he said, "Cut it out—I got one shot at this," and brought the audience to its feet: "Whoever you pray to, whether it's God or Allah, may He watch over you. Let's pray for a peaceful and swift resolution."

Nicole Kidman was tearful as she accepted for best actress for *The Hours,* saying, "Russell Crowe told me not to cry, and I'm crying." She added, "Why do you come to the Academy Awards when the world is in such turmoil? Because art is important." She sent blessings to families touched by the war, then looked down at her mother and said, "All my life I've wanted to make my mother proud." Then she looked down at her mother and daughter, whom she had made proud.

Clouds of war shadowed the Oscar ceremony, as ABC cut away to grim war updates from Peter Jennings, but in the first 100 minutes there were surprisingly few politically oriented comments. "No red carpet—that'll show 'em!" Steve Martin quipped in his opening line.

Then all bets were off when the Left's designated hitter, documentary winner Michael Moore *(Bowling for Columbine)*, let loose: Inviting his fellow nominees onstage, he said: "They're here in solidarity with me. We like nonfiction and we live in fictitious times, with fictitious election results, a fictitious president, sending us to war for fictitious reasons . . . shame on you, Mr. Bush!"

Moore's remarks were greeted by both cheers and boos, some stood and others remained seated, and Oscarcast director Gil Cates signaled the orchestra to play after Moore's allotted forty-five seconds.

Steve Martin's comment about the scene backstage: "The teamsters are helping Michael Moore into the trunk of his limo."

But Moore arrived intact in the backstage press room. "Don't report there was a split decision in the house just because five loud people booed," Moore lectured the press, saying the house was completely behind him. It sounded more divided than that to me, however, and as a reporter I must say what I heard and not what Moore tells me. To be sure, he had a better view.

There were other political comments, but not at Moore's volume, and presenters Susan Sarandon and Dustin Hoffman, whose political views are well known, stuck mostly to their scripts.

A very pregnant Catherine Zeta-Jones, winning for best supporting actress, said, "My hormones are way too out of control to be dealing with this." She acknowledged husband Michael Douglas for her award—"and this one, too," she said, glancing down toward her unborn child.

Chris Cooper won, as widely expected, in the best supporting actor category for his randy swamp rat in *Adaptation*. His speech included the first reference to world events, in a low-key way: "In light of all the troubles in this world, I wish us all peace."

Eminem's "Lose Yourself," from *8 Mile*, was a somewhat unexpected winner for best original song, inspiring an acceptance speech from cowriter Luis Resto, who kept referring to Eminem as "Marshall," following the time-honored Hollywood custom of using an actor's real name to show how well you know someone, but no doubt confusing some of Eminem's fans.

In the screenplay categories, Ronald Harwood's adapted screenplay for *The Pianist* won along with Pedro Almodóvar's original screenplay, *Talk to Her*. Almodóvar dedicated his prize to those "who raise their voices against the war."

The best foreign film winner, Caroline Link's *Nowhere in Africa*, has a chance to become one of those subtitled films that break through to a wider English-speaking audience. From the moment I first saw it, at the July 2003 Karlovy Vary Film Festival, I was brashly predicting it would win the Oscar, so I'm not very surprised. It tells the story of a German Jewish family that flees Hitler to work on a rural farm in Kenya, where the African landscape enraptures the young daughter while her parents struggle with a failing marriage.

Peter O'Toole's honorary Oscar won a standing ovation as the orchestra played the theme from *Lawrence of Arabia*. The seventy-year-old legend, composed and stylish, said, "As I totter into antiquity, movie magic enchants me still."

As expected, the legendary and beloved Conrad L. Hall, who died earlier this year, won the Oscar for best cinematography. His son, Conrad W. Hall, also a cinematographer, accepted for him. Hall used minimal light levels to create dark moods, notably in his last film, *Road to Perdition*.

The evening's first real upset came in the best musical score category, where Elliot Goldenthal won for *Frida*, upsetting veterans Elmer Bernstein, John Williams, and Philip Glass.

The *Chicago* mini-bandwagon got rolling early with the awards for art direction and costume design. When John Myhre and Gordon Sim, *Chicago* winners for art direction, came backstage, they were asked by a reporter for the *Toronto Sun* why the film was shot in Toronto and not Chicago. They praised Toronto crews and technicians, etc., and then a member of the press not a million miles from my seat riposted, "That's true in Chicago, too. Great crews!" The thought that *Chicago* was not filmed in Chicago continues to seem inexplicable.

The first award of the evening was one of the biggest upsets. In the new animation category, the Oscar went to *Spirited Away,* by the great Japanese master Hayao Miyazaki. Although Miyazaki is considered the greatest animator of all time and is a god to Hollywood animators, it was widely expected that the voters would go for one of the leading domestic entries, like Disney's *Lilo & Stitch* or DreamWorks' *Spirit: Stallion of the Cimarron.* To be sure, Disney got a piece of the Oscar, by distributing the Miyazaki film.

Steve Martin got big laughs with digs at Kathy Bates and Jack Nicholson, and with smart one-liners ("I loved *Lord of the Rings*— that was a great download"). And with a zinger: "As a special gesture, the proceeds from tonight's Oscarcast will be divvied up among huge corporations."

Later in the show, a scene that belongs on all future videos of Oscar highlights: the seventy-fifth anniversary parade of past Oscar winners, gathered onstage, from the earlier winners to this year's victors.

Vincent Gallo, *The Brown Bunny,* and Me

June 3, 2003—Vincent Gallo has put a curse on my colon and a hex on my prostate. He called me a "fat pig" in the *New York Post* and told the *New York Observer* I have "the physique of a slave trader." He is angry at me because I said his *The Brown Bunny* was the worst movie in the history of the Cannes Film Festival.

I was not alone in my judgment. *Screen International,* the British trade paper, convenes a panel of critics to score the official entries. *The Brown Bunny* scored 0.6 out of a possible 5— the lowest score in its history, the paper said.

This came as a blow to the French. Their national pride could not abide the notion that an American film was worse than any of their own, and so a few days later they countered with Bertrand Blier's *Les Cotelettes.*

"It actually scored even worse with our forlorn international critics," Colin Brown, editor of *Screen International,* told me: "seven zeroes, versus Gallo's five zeroes."

Bunny's press screening "was remarkable for the unrestrained hostility of the audience,"

wrote A. O. Scott in the *New York Times.* At the end, the audience "gave voice to that French form of abuse that sounds like a cross between the lowing of a cow and the hooting of an owl."

During a scene where Gallo shares a bicycle with a young woman, I became so nostalgic for *Butch Cassidy* that I softly sang "Raindrops Keep Fallin' on My Head." I stopped after six words when my wife jabbed me in the ribs. I was overheard by a writer for the *Hollywood Reporter,* who included it in his coverage about how badly the film was received, and that is another reason Gallo has put the heebie-jeebies on my colon and prostate. I am not too worried. I had a colonoscopy once, and they let me watch it on TV. It was more entertaining than *The Brown Bunny.*

A day after the fiasco of the movie's premiere, *Screen International* ran a remarkable interview in which Gallo apologized for his film, calling it "a disaster and a waste of time," and adding, "I apologize to the financiers of the film, but I must assure you it was never my intention to make a pretentious film, a self-indulgent film, a useless film, an unengaging film." He added that the official screening "was the worst feeling I ever had in my life," and said he would never watch the film again.

On Monday Gallo told the *New York Post*'s page six that *Screen International* "made up" his quotes. He added: "I'm sorry I'm not gay or Jewish, so I don't have a special interest group of journalists who support me." Such comments might seem politically incorrect, but not to Gallo, who says he is a conservative Republican, although since his film ends with a hardcore oral sex scene, he is not likely to be fielding many group bookings from the Moral Majority.

But was Gallo actually misquoted?

"Absolutely insane stuff from Gallo," editor Colin Brown assured me. "Not only is everything we wrote in Cannes exactly as he spewed it out, word for word, it was all recorded on audiotape." He adds: "It makes me wonder whether this is not all some great marketing ploy on his part. I have actually come across people who say *Brown Bunny* is top of their list of films they most want to see out of Cannes this year."

Fionnuala Halligan, who wrote the *Screen International* piece, says she quoted Gallo accurately and sent me a copy of his transcript. "By the end he is shouting and spitting and his invective is so unpleasant, I feel quite shaken listening to it again," she told me. "I don't think it was a good day for him to meet the press as he was obviously extremely upset. He was very late and all the interviews that had previously been arranged got lumped into one group, which is fortunate for me, as he probably would have thumped me otherwise."

Gallo all but wept in a Cannes interview as he described the pain of "growing up ugly," but empathy has its limits, and he had no tears for a fat pig and slave trader such as myself. It is true that I am fat, but one day I will be thin, and he will still be the director of *The Brown Bunny*.

In Memoriam

James Coburn

He was sometimes accused of taking it easy during the early years of his career, but James Coburn, who died Monday, November 18, 2002, at seventy-four, had a strong finish.

The man who joked and grinned his way through *Our Man Flint* and its sequels won an Academy Award in 1997 for his performance as a brutal patriarch in *Affliction*. And he is superb as a dying writer in *The Man from Elysian Fields*, which is currently in theaters.

In that film, Coburn has a conversation with Andy Garcia, as a younger writer who asks him what he'd like to come back as in another lifetime. "I could never have it better than I have in my own lifetime," he replies, and there is the temptation to hear Coburn speaking through the character.

Coburn's credits included some of the best-known movies of his time, from *The Great Escape* to *The Magnificent Seven* (where he had few lines but stole the show with a knife scene). Like many actors, he enjoyed doing voice-over work for feature-length animation, and scored a success last year as Henry J. Waternoose, the CEO of *Monsters, Inc.*

He talked to me about his work, his personal style, and his health during a rambling interview at the 1980 Toronto Film Festival. Here is the text of that interview:

Toronto—James Coburn is one of those movie stars who inspire an instinctive reaction in a lot of people. They seem to believe he's getting away with something. Maybe it's that grin, the one that somehow suggests that fate has given Coburn a free lifetime pass. In the 1960s, that decade when the generation under thirty seemed drenched in euphoria, Coburn's grin hinted that he was . . . well, always stoned.

Now it is 1980, and the grin still hints at the same thing. James Coburn is not, however, always stoned. He just looks that way; it's part of his image. At this moment, in fact, Coburn may be the cleanest-living star in Hollywood. He sits in a duplex hotel suite in Toronto and holds out his hand and flexes it.

"See that? A few months ago, I could not make a fist. I had arthritis so bad I couldn't walk up a flight of stairs. I was down in Mexico doing a cameo role in a Western, and they had to hoist me onto the horse, and riding on the horse was excruciatingly painful. Me! I was always so healthy."

Being an archetypal southern Californian, Coburn refused to accept his fate. In southern California there is a folk belief that the human body will wear indefinitely if you tune it as carefully as your Mercedes. Coburn therefore placed his body at the disposal of the state's healing industries: "The first thing I did was to get completely detoxified. No drugs, no booze, no caffeine, no nicotine, nothing. Then I went on a water fast, which tapered into an organic fruit juice fast. I underwent acupuncture. I had deep muscle massage. I did meditation. I used megavitamin therapy. I underwent a program of high colonic irrigation. Essentially what I was doing was completely cleaning out my body, getting rid of the garbage."

Did it work?

"For me, it worked. The arthritis is gone. I can move again. For anybody else, who knows?"

In the 1960s, I told him, when the James Coburn image first became famous through movies like *Our Man Flint,* there was the sense that you were always into things like meditation, Eastern philosophical systems, deep meanings, all the flower child things. What's interesting is that you've never really changed that image . . .

"I meditate, I take good care of myself, sure. I try not to get too involved in the details."

There were always reports that you'd used LSD.

"That's right. I took LSD several years before it became popular and well known. There was a doctor who was experimenting with its effects, and I got involved as one of the subjects—this was before my acting career had even started to take off. I had a lot of trips. It was all very . . . interesting."

When Coburn's acting in a movie, there's a strange feeling sometimes that he's kidding the movie, as if there's some level of subtle self-parody going on. In his *Biographical Dictionary of Film*, David Thomson observes: "Increasingly, he was the best thing in his movies, smiling privately, seeming to suggest that he was in contact with some profound source of amusement."

"Really?" said Coburn. "Part of that may just be that I'm feeling well. You can sense that in a movie, if the actor is feeling well and not pushing himself. Apart from that, I just try to do the job. I try not to get too involved.

"You have to find a way to concentrate. You're on the set, there's often a long wait between the times you're actually shooting, they're taking pains to get everything else perfect, and then suddenly it's your turn and you're expected to create this whole moment out of the air.

"I try to focus my mind, put myself wholly into it, do it, and then forget it. Walk away from it. You never really know when you're on a set how things are going to work out, anyway. There are so many other people involved in the end product, that any attempt to sit there in front of the camera and figure it all out and second-guess is just futile."

Coburn was in Toronto for the world premiere, at the Festival of Festivals, of his new movie, *Loving Couples*. It's a changing-partners sex farce, with Coburn and Shirley MacLaine playing a married couple who are both doctors. MacLaine treats a young man (Stephen Collins) who has hurt himself in a fall. She falls in love with him and begins to have an affair. Meanwhile, the young man's girlfriend (Susan Sarandon) finds out about the affair, spills the beans to Coburn, and, as they share their mutual misery, they fall in love too. Disaster strikes when both illicit couples meet during an out-of-town weekend at a resort hotel.

"What do I know about all of this?" Coburn asked. "Not much. I recently got divorced, after seventeen years. Marriage is something everyone should make one real try at, I think. Seventeen years is a real try. Now there's a woman I'm seeing, but she's in London and I'm in Los Angeles and we both have careers, which is just fine, because it means we can meet for two or three intense weeks and then split for three or four months, and we enjoy the intimacy without the involvement. I like being free."

Coburn's most famous role was, of course, our man Flint, and he said he's getting a little tired of people still coming to him after all these years with jokes involving trick cigarette lighters. The *Flint* films came after some early-1960s supporting roles in movies like *The Magnificent Seven,* where he had no dialogue but an unforgettable bit with a knife, and *The Great Escape.* Flint made Coburn into a world star: "In Marrakech, little kids were coming up to me in the casbah, asking me where my harem was."

But Coburn's own favorite movies, he said, were made by his favorite director, Sam Peckinpah, who used him for the first time in *Major Dundee*—a 1965 Western that was not widely seen at the time, but has become, in retrospect, one of Peckinpah's masterpieces. He used him again in *Pat Garrett and Billy the Kid* (1973), a revisionist version of Western history, and in *Cross of Iron* (1977), a war movie made under great difficulty in Yugoslavia, and released to a puzzled critical reception.

From the Yugoslavian experience, however, comes Coburn's favorite story about Peckinpah: "Sam would simply hole up on the weekends with a whiskey bottle. So we went to him and said, 'Come, on, Sam! We're only a few hours' drive from Venice. Let's go look at the gondolas.' Sam came along. But when he got to his hotel in Venice, he went straight upstairs and stayed there. The next day, in the lobby of the hotel, I ran into Federico Fellini. I told him Sam was upstairs. Fellini insisted on being taken to meet him. He said Peckinpah was one of his favorite directors.

"So, we went upstairs. I knocked on Sam's door. Sam growled, 'Who is it?' I said it was me. He said to come in. We walked in. He was lying stark naked on top of his bed with a bottle in his hand. 'Sam,' I said, 'I'd like you to meet Federico Fellini.' Sam opened his eyes, sat straight up in bed, said, 'Thank you so very much for giving us all those wonderful films,' and fell back on the bed again. And that was the historic meeting of two great directors."

Buddy Hackett

"There was a Vegas casino that offered me twice what I was making," Buddy Hackett was explaining to me one day. "I went to look at their showroom, and I said I could never work there. The money didn't matter, because in that room I would never get a laugh."

Why was that? I asked.

"Because the stage was above the eye line of the audience. You had to look up to see the act. It was great for sight lines but lousy for comedy, because you can never laugh at anybody you're looking up at. A comic, you have to be looking down at him. My favorite rooms, the audience is above the stage, stadium-style."

What's the logic behind that?

"You look up at drama, down at comedy. A singer, looking up is okay. A comic, it's death."

So when you go to the movies, I said, should you sit in the balcony for a comedy and on the main floor for a drama?

"Seems to me," he said.

This was one of many conversations we had in the mid-1990s, when we both found ourselves installed simultaneously at the Pritikin Longevity Center, which at that time was on the beach at Santa Monica. Hackett, a great comedian who died June 30, 2003, at seventy-eight, was engaged in a lifelong struggle with weight and cholesterol, although once he had me feel his calf muscles: "Hard as steel! I'm a great skier."

Hackett lived nearby, but checked into Pritikin to isolate himself from life's temptations. Other regulars were Rodney Dangerfield and Mel Brooks, who ate at Pritikin twice a week with his wife, Anne Bancroft. At lunch, Hackett would preside over a table of his guests, other comics, including George Gobel, Jan Murray, and Soupy Sales.

Once a woman approached the table and said she had a joke she wanted to tell.

"Lady," said Hackett, "go tell your joke at a table where amateurs are sitting. We're professionals here. We got all the jokes we can handle."

One night Buddy brought over a tape of *Bud and Lou* (1978), a movie where he played comedian Lou Costello. He felt he'd done good work in a less-than-great film, and wanted his Pritikin friends to see it. Hackett's Costello comes across, as many comics do in private life, as a lonely and sad man, and I felt Hackett did a good job of portraying that—even though I never sensed gloom in his own makeup.

Hackett said he once thought he was on the edge of a great movie role. Martin Scorsese called him up and said he wanted to come over and talk to him about working in *GoodFellas*.

"He comes over to the house," Buddy says, "and he tells me the scene. Ray Liotta is walking into the nightclub and the waiters seat him, and I'm on stage doing my act. So I ask, what do you want me to say? Where's the script? And Scorsese says there isn't any script. I'll just be in the background telling part of a joke. *Part* of a joke?"

Hackett's face grew dark.

"I stood up and walked over to the window. I invited Scorsese to stand next to me. 'Isn't that a beautiful lawn?' I said. He agreed that it was one of the most beautiful lawns he had ever seen.

"Take a real good look," I told him, "because you will never be back in this house again. Part of a joke! Get the —— outta here!"

One day I told Buddy a true story. It took place in 1979, I said. Jack Lemmon came to Chicago to promote *The China Syndrome*. He told Gene Siskel and myself he wanted to relax and suggested we go to the Gaslight Club, where he heard there was good jazz.

Four women at another table were celebrating a birthday. They looked at our table and giggled and finally one of them approached our table with a menu.

"Here comes the autograph request," Lemmon said.

"Mr. Siskel," the woman said, "I enjoy your reviews so much! Would you autograph my menu?"

Gene agreed with a smile.

"You've made my day," the woman said.

"In that case," Gene said, "your day isn't over. Did you notice who I am sitting with?"

The woman looked over.

"Ohmigod! Jack Lemmon! Oh, Mr. Lemmon, you are my favorite actor. I didn't expect to see you here! Would you sign my menu?"

Lemmon agreed. Then Gene said, "And your day still isn't over. Look who's sitting right here!"

The woman looked at me, and her face broke into a delighted smile.

"Buddy Hackett!!!" she said.

After I told this story to Buddy, he nodded thoughtfully.

"The question is," he said, "didn't she know how I look or didn't she know how you look?"

Richard Harris

Richard Harris, the boisterous, brawling, sometimes brilliant Irish actor, is dead at seventy-two. A charter member of the acting generation known as the Angry Young Men, he capped his career playing a very old and wise man—Albus Dumbledore, the headmaster of Hogwart's School in *Harry Potter and the Sorcerer's Stone* (2001).

He had almost finished filming his role in the forthcoming sequel, *Harry Potter and the Chamber of Secrets,* when he was struck ill earlier this year with Hodgkin's disease. A few of his scenes had to be shot with a double.

Harris was a mercurial stage actor who was often linked with Richard Burton, Peter O'Toole, and Oliver Reed as a legendary drinker and bar fighter. "Let's face it," Reed told me in 1969, "they like somebody like Richard Harris or myself, somebody who's a boozer and gets in fights and is colorful as hell."

But Harris stopped drinking, on medical advice, in the early 1980s, and told me at the time: "I locked myself in my house with a bottle in every room and told my brother, 'If I don't come out in a week, come in for me because I'll be dead.' I went cold turkey. Haven't had a drink since. The difference between me and Richard Burton is, I stopped drinking and am still appearing in *Camelot.* He did not, and is not."

After a sensational debut as a rugby player in *This Sporting Life* (1963), Harris played a series of tough-guy roles and then surprised everyone with his performance as the gentle King Arthur in *Camelot* (1968). His most famous role was probably *A Man Called Horse* (1970), in which he played a British traveler in the American West who is captured by Indians, survives a grueling test of his manhood, and is welcomed into the tribe. The movie inspired two lesser sequels.

Sixty of his seventy movies were "crap," he said, and he was equally free in criticizing his fellow actors. Unhappy with the scripts he was being offered, Harris largely withdrew from films in the 1980s, continuing to tour in *Camelot,* with which he drew full houses all over the world. In 1990 he made a comeback with *The Field,* a grim, dour Irish story about a man who determines to transform a wasteland into farmland by hauling buckets of seaweed to it on his back. The role won him an Academy Award nomination, and a few years later he won more praise for his work in Clint East-

wood's *Unforgiven,* as English Bob, a gunslinger who travels with his own biographer.

The Harry Potter movies, near the end of his life, made him a legion of new fans, as the *Star Wars* pictures had earlier done for Sir Alec Guinness. But he advised his fellow actors not to take it too seriously: "There is real life out there. This is all make-believe crap."

When I talked with Harris for the last time, in September 2001, it was late at night at the Toronto Film Festival, and he was sitting at an outdoor café with a pint of forbidden lager. It struck me at the time that he seemed subdued and even sad. He was diagnosed earlier this year with Hodgkin's, a cancer affecting the lymph nodes, and it claimed him in a London hospital on October 22, 2002.

Katharine Hepburn

The first lady of the movies is dead. Katharine Hepburn, who ruled the screen in a career spanning seven decades, won four Academy Awards and was nominated for eight others, died Sunday, June 29, 2003, at her home in Old Saybrook, Connecticut. She was ninety-six.

She made her first film in 1932, her final film in 1994, and embodied during all that time one of the most distinctive of screen presences. She almost always played a lady—sometimes with grease on her face, as in *The African Queen*—and her characters were resolute, forthright, self-assured, and unbending (but able to bend in moments of tenderness or hilarity). She played opposite the top leading men of her time, including Spencer Tracy, Cary Grant, James Stewart, and John Wayne, effortlessly upstaging all of them when required.

No one else looked like her or sounded like her. She was tall, not curvaceous, with a beauty too sharply defined to be called pretty, and a voice that betrayed her background as a New England blue blood. "I strike people as peculiar in some way," she said in an interview with the *New York Times,* "although I don't quite understand why. Of course, I have an angular face, an angular body and, I suppose, an angular personality, which jabs into people."

Married once while young, to a man she confessed she treated terribly and dumped after winning her first Oscar, she had one great love affair in her life, with Spencer Tracy. They lived together from 1940 until 1967, when he died seventeen days after they finished their final movie together, *Guess Who's Coming to Dinner*. They never married, because Tracy, a Catholic, would not divorce his wife. But I remember Glenna Syse, the late *Sun-Times* drama critic, returning from a Chicago press conference when Hepburn was appearing on stage here. "Someone asked her if she had been in love," Glenna smiled, "and she said, 'You should not ask such a question! And you should not have to ask such a question!'"

Another interviewer who got as good as he gave was my late colleague Gene Siskel, who once dared to ask about her decision to continue acting despite a tremor that affected her face and voice. Her reply: "What choice do I have?"

Hepburn's career began in the early years of the talkies, which cherished her distinctive voice, even though studios despaired of casting her as conventional characters. She won her first Oscar, in the somewhat autobiographical role of a hopeful actress, for *Morning Glory* (1933), was a distinctive Jo in *Little Women* (1933), and in following years had a remarkable string of successes in *Alice Adams* (1935), *Sylvia Scarlett* (1936), *Mary of Scotland* (1936), *Stage Door* (1937), *Bringing Up Baby* (1938), *Holiday* (1938), *The Philadelphia Story* (1940), and *Woman of the Year* (1942). Has any other actress ever had a run like that?

Bringing Up Baby was the classic Howard Hawks comedy where she and Cary Grant try to raise a baby leopard. George Stevens's *Woman of the Year* (1942) was her first film with Tracy. They worked together nine times, including George Cukor's *Keeper of the Flame* (1942), Frank Capra's *State of the Union* (1948), and Cukor's *Adam's Rib* (1949) and *Pat and Mike* (1952), as couples who made verbal sparring into an art form. In 1951, she went with Humphrey Bogart and director John Huston to Africa for the legendary location shoot of *The African Queen*, where at times she was den mother, wardrobe seamstress, cook, and peacemaker. "Nature, Mr. Allnut," her missionary character famously told the scruffy Bogart character, "is what we are put in this world to rise above."

Although she famously waded through African rivers and emerged unharmed, it was while making *Summertime* (1955) in Venice that she contracted a chronic eye infection while insisting on doing her own stunt by falling into the Grand Canal.

George Cukor, her favorite director and life-long friend, told me Hepburn always stayed in one of his guest cottages while in Hollywood. After the eye problem, he said, she insisted that there be no chlorine in his pool: "You can always tell when Miss Hepburn is in attendance, because the pool is filled with green slime."

Cukor, who directed her first film, *A Bill of Divorcement* (1932), visited the Chicago Film Festival not long after Stanley Kramer's *Guess Who's Coming to Dinner* was finished. He told me, "There are many, many talented young performers in movies these days. But the other day I saw a preview of Tracy and Hepburn in *Guess Who's Coming to Dinner,* and all I could think was, well, now, there are two people who know how to act."

He noted that Kramer went ahead with shooting even though Tracy was not insurable because of ill health. During the shooting, Hepburn acted as Tracy's nurse as well as costar, cherishing their scenes together and keeping watch on his stamina. Hepburn won an Oscar for her role, as the wife of the curmudgeon Tracy, who opposed the desire of his daughter (Katharine Houghton) to marry an African-American physician (Sidney Poitier). The film was considered a daring breakthrough at the time.

Miss Hepburn's sense of quality control rarely failed her. When RKO tried to shoehorn her into a series of inane comedies, she broke free from her contract and became one of the first Hollywood stars to work as an independent. *The Philadelphia Story,* which had a heroine some thought was modeled on Miss Hepburn's personality, was her breakthrough, and she never looked back.

Her taste was often daring. In 1959 she made *Suddenly Last Summer,* and in 1962 she took on one of her most challenging roles, as the matriarch in Eugene O'Neill's *Long Day's Journey into Night.* It was an early film by the gifted director Sidney Lumet.

She was the only actress to win back-to-back Oscars, for *Guess Who's Coming to Dinner* (1967) and as Eleanor of Aquitaine, opposite Peter O'Toole, in *The Lion in Winter* (1968), the latter shared with Barbra Streisand (*Funny Girl*) in an unprecedented tie. She won again for *On Golden Pond* (1981), where she played the loving wife of a stubborn man (Henry Fonda) who has not reconciled with their daughter (Jane Fonda). The sincerity of the Academy was made manifest by Miss Hepburn's refusal to attend Oscar ceremonies to accept her awards, although she appeared at the Oscars for other purposes.

Another of Hepburn's adventurous projects was a film of Edward Albee's play *A Delicate Balance* (1972). She made it for the American Film Theater project, a series of films of plays that was long unavailable but has just been released on DVD. Against all of Hollywood's expectations, she enjoyed working with John Wayne in *Rooster Cogburn* (1975), and wrote in her autobiography that he was always on time, always knew the scene, was "very impatient with anyone who was inefficient. And did not bother to cover it up." She could have been describing herself.

Katharine Hepburn was born May 12, 1907, to a successful physician in Hartford, Connecticut; years later she confessed to taking two years off her age. She was active in undergraduate dramatic productions at Bryn Mawr, and after early success in summer stock and on Broadway, she moved to Hollywood in 1932 and won an Oscar the next year. She was the first to point out that her family's wealth and her own upbringing helped her get started in show business, but it was talent that gave her stardom and longevity, despite her unconventional looks and voice. As the Tracy character observed in *Pat and Mike,* "There ain't much meat on her, but what there is, is choice."

Bob Hope

Bob Hope, who died July 27, 2003, at one hundred, became such an American icon that his mere presence made people smile. That was the lesson I learned one day in 1980, when I joined him aboard a private jet after he'd made a personal appearance.

The *World Book Encyclopedia* had chosen Hope as its Man of the Year. My assignment: interview him. *Chicago Sun-Times* columnist Irv Kupcinet talked to him constantly, and gave me the number of his assistant, Ken Kantor. Hope was quickly on the line: "I have to fly up to San Francisco to appear at the Anheuser-Busch stockholder's meeting. Meet me there and we can fly back to Burbank on the Budweiser jet."

Our talk touched on the quality of his fame. He had long since surpassed the categories of movie star, radio-TV star, stand-up comic, and recording artist, and he had become a spokesman for—well, Hope. Not just Hope the man, but hope the quality, since his never-failing ebullience was a tonic for his audiences, especially the countless servicemen he entertained on battlefronts and at far-flung outposts.

When I asked him what he had done at the stockholder's meeting, he said he had walked onstage and surprised company head August Busch. Just that, essentially. His presence was a recognition of Busch and the company and the audience, and he got a standing ovation—and at his age, he observed, standing ovations were a good reason to get up in the morning.

Hope's best films included *The Cat and the Canary* (1939); *My Favorite Blonde* (1942); *Road to Morocco* (1942) and *Road to Utopia* (1946), which were the best of the *Road* movies; *The Paleface* (1948) and *Son of Paleface* (1952); and *Monsieur Beaucaire* (1946). The *Paleface* movies costarred Jane Russell, and a Hope trademark was the proximity of a sexy girl who seemed forever out of his reach. He specialized in asides to fellow cast members and the audience, and he created a character who was often a dauntless coward. In *Road to Utopia,* he walks into a rough-and-tough Alaska saloon and orders a lemonade. When the grizzled miners look offended, he snarls, "In a dirty glass!"

The quality of Hope's films had flagged by the time I came on the movie-reviewing scene. His last starring role in a theatrical film was in 1972, with *Cancel My Reservation.* I wrote that it wasn't remotely funny, "unless you are a '50s freak and do not find it amazing that a 1972 movie should have references to Bing Crosby's golf game and *The $64,000 Question.*"

But he had once been a cutting-edge movie comedian, valued by Woody Allen as the best of his time. His one-liners invented the stand-up routines later perfected by Johnny Carson, Jay Leno, and Dave Letterman. He paired with Crosby in the *Road* pictures, which pointed the way for Dean Martin and Jerry Lewis, who were essentially playing the same two characters. And he didn't tell the same old jokes over and over but had a legendary stable of writers who supplied new topical humor from the day's headlines—a technique later adapted by Mort Sahl, Dick Gregory and a whole school of young stand-ups who followed them, including Jay Leno.

Hope created the modern definition of the Academy Awards host; before Hope, the Oscar emcee was just that, a master of ceremonies. After Hope the job became a role, filled by Carson, Billy Crystal, Steve Martin, and all the others. He emceed the Oscars for the first time in 1939, and did it eighteen times between then and 1977, when, in the aftermath of Vietnam and Watergate, his upbeat wisecracks seemed dated. He never won an Oscar, except for an honorary one, inspiring his famous line "At my house, the Oscars are known as Passover."

Before the 1967 show he told me the most dramatic Oscar moment was in 1961, when Elizabeth Taylor won for *Butterfield 8,* after having narrowly escaped death with an emergency tracheotomy.

"That was the year she had been critically ill, and it wasn't known until the last minute whether she'd even attend the ceremony. When her name was called and she stood up and walked toward the stage, everyone held his breath, waiting for her to collapse, but she made it. What a woman!" he said. Being Bob Hope, he couldn't help adding, "In fact, she even made it to the party afterward."

He lived so long that younger generations barely know who he was. One of the richest men in Hollywood, he lived for years in the same comfortable but scarcely palatial house in the Toluca Lake neighborhood of the San Fernando Valley. When we landed at the Burbank airport, he got into his own car and drove himself home. For anyone old enough to have known him in his prime, he was a legend, an institution—and a very funny man.

All the obituaries will end the same way, and so will mine.

Thanks for the memories.

Gregory Peck

Gregory Peck died peacefully in his sleep on June 12, 2003, the week after his famous character Atticus Finch from *To Kill a Mockingbird* was named by the American Film Institute as the greatest movie hero of all time.

The veteran star, who won an Oscar for that performance and was nominated for four others, was eighty-seven. Peck's wife, Veronique, was holding his hand when he died, family spokesman Monroe Friedman told the Associated Press: "He just went to sleep. He had just been getting older and more fragile. He wasn't really ill. He just sort of ran his course and died of old age."

He seemed somewhat frail when I saw him last, at the Cannes Film Festival in 2000, when he attended the glittering annual benefit for AMFAR, the AIDS charity. He and Veronique, a French journalist who became his second wife in 1954, sat near Elizabeth Taylor and greeted friends and admirers with the same quiet courtesy he brought to the role of Atticus.

A star during five decades, the tall, ruggedly handsome Peck was also a Hollywood leader offscreen, as president of the Motion Picture Academy and the first chairman of the AFI. He was a liberal activist who produced a film opposing the Vietnam War in 1972, four years after President Lyndon Johnson awarded him the Medal of Freedom.

It was as the courtly, righteous small-town lawyer in *To Kill a Mockingbird* that Peck found the role of a lifetime. Released in 1962, set in Alabama in 1932, it is currently ranked thirty-fifth on the Internet Movie Database's vote for the best films of all time. Atticus Finch is a lawyer picked to defend a black man accused of raping a poor white girl, and he stands up against the racist fury of the town in crafting his defense—while at the same time leaving indelible memories for his daughter, Scout, and her brother, Jem.

Oddly enough, his very first role as an actor was one he would return to in one of his most famous movies. While he was an English major at Berkeley, he was recruited by a campus theater to play Captain Ahab in *Moby-Dick.* "I wasn't any good," he told critic Bob Thomas some fifty years later, "but I ended up doing five plays my last year in college." After graduating, he headed for Broadway to try his luck as an actor, broke into Hollywood in 1944, and was a great star almost from the first, winning four Oscar nominations for best actor in five years, for *The Keys of the Kingdom* (1944), *The Yearling* (1946), *Gentleman's Agreement* (1947), and *Twelve O'Clock High* (1949). In 1956 the director John Huston cast him once again as Ahab in

Moby-Dick. The movie was not entirely successful—maybe the novel resisted adaptation—but it become a hit, and one of Peck's most famous roles, not least because he insisted on doing some of his stunts himself and was nearly drowned while strapped to a prop whale that held him too long underwater.

Fittingly, he rounded out his career in the Melville classic; his final role was in a 1998 TV version of *Moby-Dick,* where he played Father Mapple, the preacher who paints a fearsome portrait of the deep in a sermon. Peck's last leading role in a movie was in *Old Gringo* (1989), where Yankee spinster Jane Fonda travels to Mexico and meets a mysterious stranger (Peck) she doesn't realize is Ambrose Bierce, an author thought to have died years earlier.

One of the films Peck was proudest of was *Gentleman's Agreement,* a pioneering attack on anti-Semitism. Hollywood had traditionally been reluctant to tackle the issue, and Peck was warned that his stature as a movie hero could be endangered by playing the role of a investigative reporter who poses as a Jew, but he went ahead anyway, and the film won an Oscar nomination for Peck as well as capturing best picture.

For viewers of the movie channels and home video, the four films for which Peck is probably most familiar are *Mockingbird;* Alfred Hitchcock's *Spellbound* (1945), with Peck as the possibly sinister new head of a mental asylum with Ingrid Bergman on the staff; *Roman Holiday* (1953), opposite Audrey Hepburn; and *The Guns of Navarone* (1961). In *Roman Holiday* he and Hepburn toured the Eternal City on a Vespa, inspiring countless tourists (myself included) to do the same thing on their first visits there. In *The Guns of Navarone,* he helped to establish the modern action "event" picture. Movie fans also know him from the horror hit *The Omen* (1976), from the title role of *MacArthur* (1977), and from *The Boys from Brazil* (1978), where he played one of his rare villains, the Nazi butcher Dr. Josef Mengele; the reviews advised Peck to stick to heroes, and indeed there was something innately courteous and upright about him that fit more easily into heroic roles than evil ones.

Gregory Peck was almost the last survivor among the great Hollywood leading men who came up in the 1940s—the era of Cary Grant, James Stewart, Robert Mitchum, and Joseph Cotten, among many others. He looked like a movie star, at a time when stars were expected to; the modern trend toward quirky character-type stars like Jack Nicholson was still in the future.

If Atticus Finch was his most famous and successful role, perhaps that is because Peck and Finch were very much alike in their dignity, their deep convictions, their instinctive humanity. When he won the Academy's Jean Hersholt Humanitarian Award in 1968, he said he was embarrassed to be called a humanitarian simply for doing what he believed in. But his stature was such that, like Hersholt, he is one of those few Hollywood citizens who might appropriately have an award named after him.

Film Festivals

Telluride Film Festival
Telluride Report No. 1:
High Expectations

Telluride, Colorado, August 30, 2002—The schedule of each year's Telluride Film Festival is as closely guarded as the Oscar winners. Until they arrive, gasping for air, in this pretty little mountain town at the 10,000-foot level, festival ticket holders have no idea what they'll be seeing.

Rumors start early. At the Denver airport, waiting for the shuttle to Montrose, I was informed that Martin Scorsese's *Gangs of New York* will be sneaked here this year. That is almost certainly not true (never say never). Then again, if somebody had told me that Telluride was going to resurrect the three-screen, three-camera Cinerama process, I would have doubted it. And they are.

The festival presents the Telluride Medal to three distinguished guests every year. This year the honorees will be Peter O'Toole, at seventy still one of a kind; Paul Schrader, the outsider writer-director who wrote *Raging Bull* (1980), the most recent film in the recent *Sight & Sound* list of the greatest movies; and D. A. Pennebaker, seventy-seven, the great documentarian.

Schrader's forthcoming *Auto Focus,* starring Greg Kinnear as the sex-addicted TV star Bob Crane, will be premiered at the festival, as will Pennebaker's *Only the Strong Survive,* codirected with Chris Hegedus, which is about such surviving Motown stars as Sam Moore, Wilson Pickett, Mary Wilson, Isaac Hayes, and Jerry Butler and the Chi-Lites. Pennebaker's Bob Dylan doc *Don't Look Back* (1967) and his *Monterey Pop* (1969) were two of the groundbreakers of music documentaries.

The hottest ticket at Telluride this year may be *Bowling for Columbine,* the new Michael Moore documentary about America's fascination with guns. It was here in the Rocky Mountains in 1989 that Moore's *Roger & Me,* an attack on the corporate culture of General Motors, first put the jolly populist on the map.

Terry Gilliam, whose visionary and fanciful epics like *Brazil* are often misunderstood by their distributors, is here with *Lost in La Mancha,* a doc about his failed efforts to make a movie of Don Quixote. Appropriately enough, O'Toole includes a Quixote among his credits, as the star of the 1972 musical *Man of La Mancha.*

Schrader's film about Bob Crane, which shows the fading star having sex every night almost out of a sense of duty to his fans, will be joined by two controversial films containing high-voltage sex: *Irreversible,* by Gaspar Noé, which inspired an uproar at Cannes with an extended rape scene; and *Ken Park,* by Larry Clark and the cinematographer Ed Lachman, about the unhappy, aggressive lives of California teens. Clark is known for two other controversial films about teenagers, *Kids* and *Bully.*

Also back at Telluride this year is French director Bertrand Tavernier, a former guest programmer here, who will premiere his *Safe Passage,* about directors like Jean Aurenche and Henri-George Clouzot, who successfully made films during the Nazi occupation of France. Another Telluride favorite, Canada's David Cronenberg, is here with *Spider,* starring Ralph Fiennes as a Londoner who has lost his hold on reality.

Arriving with strong buzz from European festivals, Phillip Noyce's *Rabbit-Proof Fence* tells the story, based on truth, of three Aboriginal children stolen from their families in the 1930s to be turned into Australian domestic servants.

Godfrey Reggio, whose speeded-up documentaries *Koyaanisqatsi* and *Powaqqatsi* were sensations here, is back with *Naqoyqatsi,* using high-def digital photography in a concert that questions its own technology. The Philip Glass score is performed by Yo-Yo Ma.

And there will be an exhibit of the art of Chuck Jones, the great animator who died earlier this year, and was a faithful Telluride visitor. The animator of Bugs Bunny, Elmer Fudd, and the gang already has a cinema named after him here, and his widow, Marian, will be honored at the opening of the exhibit.

And Cinerama? The festival has constructed a giant screen with three projectors to recapture the glory days of the 1950s obsession with bigger and bigger pictures. For Telluride, this effort is not even a first: In the early 1980s it linked together three projectors for the three-screen revival of Abel Gance's long-lost silent masterpiece *Napoleon* (1927). The director himself, then in his nineties, sat in the window of his room at the Sheridan Opera House and saw his work projected under the stars in Elks Park, across the street.

Telluride Report No. 2: *Auto Focus* is Strong Opener

September 3, 2002—Bob Crane seems to have been an awfully nice guy. Not a faithful husband, not a great father, but a helluva nice guy to run into late at night in a bar or a strip club, especially if you were young, female, and a fan of *Hogan's Heroes*. Chances are he would even oblige you by having sex.

Auto Focus, the brilliant new film by Paul Schrader, documents Crane's rise and, mostly, his fall in a haunting showbiz biopic. Starring Greg Kinnear as Crane and Willem Dafoe as John Carpenter, Crane's running mate in the swinging underworld, the movie follows a family man who stumbled into TV success, discovers the world of groupies, and seems to sleep with them because it seems like the polite thing to do.

Auto Focus is premiered here this weekend at the twenty-ninth Telluride Film Festival, which includes a tribute to Schrader, whose directing credits include *American Gigolo* and *Light Sleeper,* and whose screenplays include *Taxi Driver* and *Raging Bull.*

Schrader joins two other veteran directors whose new films have been embraced by the sophisticated Telluride audience: Spain's Pedro Almodóvar, whose *Talk to Her* has been called his best work, and Finland's Aki Kaurismäki's *The Man Without a Past,* which combines his deadpan humor with something deeper.

Schrader's *Auto Focus* is set in the years before and after *Hogan's Heroes,* a TV sitcom that depended on the charm of the Crane character, who got away with murder in a German POW camp. Happily married, a family man, a practicing Catholic, Crane meets Carpenter on the set one day and his life makes a U-turn.

The other man is involved in the electronics industry, shows Crane the first portable video cameras and cassette recorders, and invites him to a strip club. Soon Crane is sitting in on the drums at strip clubs every night after work, and staying out even later as he and Carpenter seduce legions of women and record most of their conquests on film. Crane seems oblivious to the danger to his career; he stars in Disney's *Superdad* while Polaroids of his orgies circulate through Hollywood.

The brilliance of the film comes in the way it sees how essentially unsatisfying, even deadening, Crane's life becomes—a treadmill to promiscuity. Schrader somehow succeeds in making a film with wall-to-wall sex in which sadness and loneliness, not passion, are the subject. And then there is the creepy subtext of Crane's relationship with Carpenter, who wants to think of himself as more than the TV star's procurer.

Kinnear is uncanny as Crane, looking a lot like him and effortlessly suggesting the autopilot charm that is all the scarier because, we suspect, it is sincere. Dafoe's character has a murkier role, involved in what may be unexpressed homosexual jealousy between two men whose actions are always hetero. Schrader places them in a world that looks like a *Playboy* bachelor pad, circa 1964, with all the right drinks, clothes, toys—and then he shades that world into the emerging hippie and psychedelic era.

Talk to Her, the Almodóvar film, sounds in summary like another one of the lurid soap operas he specializes in. As the film opens, a hospital intern spends even his off-hours at the bedside of a beautiful young woman in a coma. Soon the victim is joined by another—a beautiful female bullfighter, gored and comatose, who also has a tireless admirer. The two men, logging countless hours at their bedsides, become friends, and it's intriguing how their relationships with the sleeping beauties are so fulfilling for them. Then something sensational takes place, and causes upheaval in what seemed like a static situation. There is melodramatic sensationalism at the end, as always with Almodóvar, but this time it's curiously moving.

The Man Without a Past is another of those Kaurismäki films in which passive people glide thoughtfully through extraordinary situations.

Its hero awakens with no memory, tries to reenter society, is honest when he says he has no idea who he is, and seems to become a blank slate on which many others try to write their ideas about him. But this is not a drama about amnesia; it's more of a wry examination of how we all unconsciously believe we "are" the people whose names we bear, when in fact our names and histories may simply be randomly accumulated and have little to do with who we really are.

These three films had Telluride off to a strong start. All weekend, movies unreeled from dawn to past midnight, and then of course there's the Labor Day ice cream social in the town park, with great directors sitting on bales of hay and discussing their work. Not like your average festival.

Telluride Report No. 3:
Columbine Documentary Premieres

September 3, 2002—At some point early in his life, Michael Moore must have found himself wearing a baseball cap, a windbreaker, and a shirt hanging outside his jeans, and decided he liked the look. That's what he was wearing when I met him at the Telluride Film Festival in 1989, and that's what he was wearing this year. It is also what he wears in *Bowling for Columbine,* his new documentary film, when he goes calling on K-Mart executives and Charlton Heston, the spokesman for the National Rifle Association.

He is not necessarily wearing the same shirt and jeans, you understand. His closet must look a lot like Archie's and Jughead's, with rows of identical uniforms. The clothes send a message: Here is a man of the people, working-class. He may be on television but he is not of television. In his films, he is a huge hulking presence at the edge of the screen, doggedly firing questions at people who desperately wish they were elsewhere. His face is usually in shadow because of the baseball cap.

Bowling for Columbine, which had its U.S. premiere here over the weekend, as funny and abrasive as his hit *Roger & Me,* and much more sorrowful, is about the American love affair with guns. And not just with guns, but with shooting: A higher percentage of Canadians than Americans own guns, we learn, but they hardly ever shoot anyone with them. Gunshot

deaths in the United States are ten to twenty times higher than in other developed nations.

For once Moore does not seem to have the answers to all the questions he asks, and there is a certain humility at moments in this film. He talks to gun owners who say they feel safer with guns in the house, and then he meditates on whether media coverage of violence may be making them feel threatened. One of his many eye-opening statistics is that in recent years violent death has been down 20 percent, but coverage of it on TV has been up 600 percent.

In the most astonishing sequence in the film, he takes two survivors of the Columbine massacre on a trip to K-Mart corporate headquarters. Both teens still have bullets in their bodies that were purchased at K-Mart, and in a Moore brainstorm they want to see if they can return them for a refund. One of the boys actually shows a K-Mart spokesperson the bullet scars on his back. K-Mart sends the usual series of P.R. types to deal with Moore's delegation, and we're reminded of the General Motors spokesmen in *Roger & Me.*

But then a totally unexpected thing happens. K-Mart tells Moore and the boys it will stop selling ammunition in its stores. Moore is stunned: No one has ever agreed with one of his demands before. He has the K-Mart spokesperson repeat her promise. It's true. K-Mart won't sell bullets.

That may help a little, but comedian Chris Rock may be on to something in the film when he observes how cheap bullets are (the Columbine bullets were seventeen cents apiece). Why not price them at $5,000, he suggests: "And then you wouldn't have any innocent bystanders."

I'll review the movie at length when it opens, including Moore's interview with Charlton Heston and the way he links Michigan's "work for welfare" laws to the death of a six-year-old. After the Telluride screening, Ian Waldron-Mantgani, a teenage film critic from Liverpool, was shaking, literally shaking, as he left the theater. He was not alone.

* * *

At most film festivals, movie professionals attend only to do business. At Telluride, they come for pleasure even when they don't have a film to flog. Two of the recent guest programmers at Telluride have been novelist Salman

Rushdie and British stage director Peter Sellars. Both were back this year, on their own, for fun. "Last year I spent all my time watching the films I programmed," Rushdie told me. "This year I can go to films I haven't seen." Also here on a busman's holiday: the great Werner Herzog, the French master Bertrand Tavernier (who has a film, but comes even when he doesn't), the documentarian Ken Burns, and the Czech-American filmmaker Ivan Passer. All hanging around, catching screenings, debating movies on street corners.

* * *

The most astonishing technical feat at this year's festival is without doubt the cinematography in *Russian Ark,* the new film by Aleksandr Sokurov of Russia. The movie is ninety-six minutes long, and was filmed in one single take by German cameraman Tilman Buettner, using a Steadicam mounting and a new Sony HD digital camera.

To describe the film as a journey through the Hermitage Museum in St. Petersburg would be missing the point. Using the great museum as his location, Sokurov follows a "time traveler" as he wanders through 300 years of Russian history. The camera movements are meticulous as the traveler encounters one group of actors after another, eavesdrops on conversations, examines paintings, witnesses a period of Soviet history when the museum was shuttered, and then waltzes into an astonishing gala ball with 2,000 costumed extras dancing in a vast ballroom.

* * *

Spider, the new film by David Cronenberg, is a bleak, moving meditation on the adult life of a man who was destroyed by his childhood and is still haunted by it. Ralph Fiennes stars in the story, based on a novel by Patrick McGrath. The time line moves between his present existence in a halfway house for mental patients, and his childhood, when his brutal father (Gabriel Byrne) murdered his mother and moved in a floozy from the pub (both women are played by Miranda Richardson). The subject of the film is really the sadness and confusion in the mind of Clegg, the hero, whose tragic childhood seems destined to rerun in his mind until he dies.

Telluride Report No. 4: Sneak Preview of *Frida*

September 3, 2002—After a screening at Telluride the audience spills outside and starts arguing about the film they've just seen. There is no escaping this process: It is a small town and everyone is on foot. To get instant feedback on a new film, all the curious director has to do is mingle.

On the last day of the festival, two directors would have discovered that Telluride loved their films. The codirectors of another film would have found that Telluride was variously horrified, intrigued, offended, and moved by a film some called courageous and many called depraved.

The two home runs were Julie Taymor's *Frida,* the new biopic starring Salma Hayek as the passionate Mexican artist Frida Kahlo, and *Safe Passage,* Bertrand Tavernier's ambitious drama about how French filmmakers worked during the Nazi occupation.

The courageous and/or depraved film was *Ken Park,* by Larry Clark and Ed Lachman, which is about teenage sexuality in a small California town. With graphic scenes of nudity and sexual conduct, it is an adult movie destined to stir enormous controversy.

* * *

Frida was an unannounced sneak preview here, in advance of the movie's official North American premiere in the Toronto Film Festival. It's a personal triumph for Salma Hayek, who seems certain to win an Oscar nomination, and a triumph, too, for Julie Taymor. She had sensational success as the director of *The Lion King* on Broadway and made the visionary Shakespeare adaptation *Titus* (2000), which some critics failed to understand was a masterpiece.

Now she is back with a film about Frida Kahlo, a Mexican painter who was horribly injured in a bus accident, who walked with a limp and was in constant pain, and yet found the energy to produce a flood of paintings and to marry Diego Rivera, the most famous and flamboyant Mexican artist of the twentieth century.

The film is visualized in a tumble of bright colors, sometimes bursting free into fanciful imaginary scenes; it's magic realism crossed with the left-wing politics of Kahlo and Rivera. Alfred Molina, a British actor of Spanish-Italian heritage, plays Rivera as a man who frankly admits he is a womanizer, and has been so diagnosed by a doctor. Frida, his third wife, does not ask him to be faithful but expects him to be loyal. And so he is, during adventures including a trip to New York, when he creates a famous mural for Rockefeller Center. It imprudently depicted Lenin, and he clashed with Nelson Rockefeller, who famously had the mural pounded to bits.

If Frida had not been crippled (she was often in a cast or brace), it is difficult to imagine how she could have celebrated her life any more. The movie suggests that among her own affairs there was one with Leon Trotsky and another, in Paris, with the black American singer Josephine Baker. Not a shabby dance card.

* * *

Safe Passage is a salute by Tavernier to French filmmakers who somehow continued to work under the Germans without working for them. In introducing the film, Tavernier quoted François Truffaut, who said that during that period Italian filmmakers for the most part caved in to fascism, but the French were "98 percent" resistant to the Nazis.

Not everyone would agree that those who worked for the German-controlled Continental studio were patriots, but in Tavernier's retelling, most did what they could to slip anti-Nazi messages into seemingly innocent entertainments. And one, assistant director Jean Devaivre (Jacques Gamblin), seized an opportunity to steal classified Nazi documents and delivered them to the British during a secret night flight that ended in a parachuting.

One of the subtexts of the film is how everyone, even Nazis, are a little in awe of the movies, and prepared to bend the rules. At one point a Jewish screenwriter, Charles Spaak, is given day passes from prison to work on a movie the Germans are interested in. Tavernier creates a palpable sense of wartime conditions; everyone is cold all the time, and there is so little to eat that the main courses for a dinner scene are constructed out of sculpted rutabagas (extras nevertheless gobble them down).

* * *

Now as to *Ken Park*. The title refers to a teenager whose name, spelled backward, is Krap Nek; one of the narrators of the film is not sure whether being teased about his name led Ken to the movie's opening scene, in which he skateboards to a playground, sets a video camera to film himself, and shoots himself through the head. This shocking opening sets the tone for the film, which shows suburban teenage boys and a girl living in an emotionally starved universe with parents who are indifferent at best, drunken and abusive at worst.

The kids' weapon, as they fight back against their cruel home lives, is sex, and the movie uses graphic detail in a series of scenes where a boy dangerously practices autoerotic asphyxiation, a girl ties her boyfriend to the bed (he is savagely beaten when her father discovers them), an alcoholic father assaults his own son, and one boy has simultaneous affairs with his teenage girlfriend and her mother. The film ends in a three-way orgy. Yes. To say some members of the audience were stunned would be putting it mildly. One woman began to laugh hysterically until she was quieted by those around her.

Ed Lachman, one of the codirectors, is a distinguished cinematographer, working with Werner Herzog on a series of risky documentaries and more recently on such titles as *The Limey* and *Erin Brockovich*. Larry Clark, the other codirector, has specialized in films about alienated and transgressive teenagers. His *Kids* (1995) and *Bully* (2001) were both films I admired for the forthright way they dealt with their alienated characters.

This time, I have serious doubts. This is not the place for a formal review, and I want to see the film again before writing more about it, but I wonder if the filmmakers have not strayed beyond the task of depicting these lives, and lingered on lurid details with a kind of unsavory curiosity.

Toronto Film Festival
Toronto Film Festival Advance

Toronto, Canada, September 4, 2002—After Cannes, the Toronto Film Festival is the most important in the world. Last year's festival was ripped in two on September 11. I walked out of a screening, heard the news, and the world had changed. Now comes the twenty-seventh annual festival. Are movies important in the new world we occupy? Yes, I think they are, because they are the most powerful artistic device for creating empathy—for helping us understand the lives of others.

We turn to Toronto every September in a spirit of hope. After a year during which slavish attention has been showered on the latest installments of the big studio franchises, when movies have opened to $60 million weekends and been forgotten by the end of the month, Toronto declares the opening of Good Movie Season, which runs from the festival's opening night until the deadline for Oscar nominations.

Yet even though the next Oscar winner will quite possibly premiere during the week, Toronto is not about Oscar handicapping, but about the little film you find in a half-empty screening on Tuesday morning, or in one of the twenty-seat "VIP" screening rooms, which seem devoted to Not Very Important pictures. I have here a list of all of the films in this year's festival, and it is probable that the best one is hiding somewhere in the fine print.

There are 343 films this year, too many for any one person to see, but at Toronto we can be reasonably sure they are well chosen, because the festival employs expert programmers in each area. One of the pleasures of a screening is to hear it introduced by the programmer who found it and has become its advocate.

Critics are asked how we decide which films to see. Some are obvious picks: premieres of big films that will soon be opening (*Phone Booth* by Joel Schumacher and *Spirited Away* by Hayao Miyazaki). Also obvious are the new films by famous directors (Atom Egoyan), or by filmmakers we have a special affection for (Paul Schrader). But the discoveries come simply through buzz. You stand in line, you talk to the people next to you before the movie starts, and you begin to realize you have heard the same title mentioned three or four times.

I run my finger down the names of the directors in this year's festival. For the experienced moviegoer the names are trademarks, suggesting a certain kind of quality or experience. Among the Galas, we find Denzel Washington making his directorial debut with *Antwone Fisher,* and the veteran Brian De Palma back with *Femme Fatale.* Veteran filmgoers know, even if the world does not, that directors like Patrice Leconte (*L'Homme du*

Train) and Julie Taymor *(Frida)* can probably be counted on.

We will not conceivably miss the new films by David Cronenberg *(Spider)*, Atom Egoyan *(Ararat)*, Neil Jordan *(The Good Thief)*, Todd Haynes *(Far from Heaven)*, and Jim Sheridan *(In America)*, and because we know that there is a renaissance in the South Korean cinema right now, we will go to *Chihwaseon,* by Im Kwon-taek, because logic suggests that in a year when new Korean films are the subject of the National Harvest section, a film that spun out from that section into the Galas must be special. And we will go to Shekhar Kapur's *The Four Feathers* because we're intrigued by the notion that a story of British colonialism has now been retold by an Indian director. We await the revisionist *Gunga Din.*

Every year at Toronto I meet members of the trail mix brigade. These are festival-goers who take vacations from their jobs, cross-index the program with a fury, and squeeze in five or six screenings a day by devising ingenious itineraries and living on bottled water and trail mix. They carry knapsacks filled with the necessities of serial moviegoing, from aspirin to ponchos to house slippers. They explain their strategies to me. One instant friend last year said she had given up on trying to predict which films to see, and had decided to simply attend as many screenings in the Master's section as possible, on the logical grounds that a great director might make a great movie.

If you were to adopt that course this year, look at some of the directors you would encounter: Abbas Kiarostami, the fierce minimalist from Iran; Mike Leigh, the British outsider who ironically has become one of the UK's few bankable filmmakers; Frederick Wiseman, the great documentarian; Aki Kaurismäki, the Finnish master of human tragicomedy; Marco Bellocchio, Italy's enfant terrible grown wise; Catherine Breillat, the French specialist in erotic brinksmanship; Ken Loach, the British poet of the laboring classes; Chen Kaige, the Chinese master; and a selection of gifted Indian directors.

Other directors spring out from other sections. Takeshi Kitano, the hard-boiled pokerface from Japan. Gus Van Sant, whose *Gerry* was the most perplexing, discussed, hated, and defended film at Sundance. Michael Almereyda, who made the risky Ethan Hawke *Hamlet.* Larry Clark, of *Kids* and *Bully,* teamed with the maverick cinematographer Ed Lachman for *Ken Park.* Rebecca Miller, whose *Personal Velocity* was a Sundance treasure. Claire Denis, the French poet of personal experience. Curtis Hanson of *L.A. Confidential.* Robert Duvall, with that tango film he's been talking about making for years. Michael Moore's *Bowling for Columbine,* the Cannes success about America's gun culture. Matt Dillon's first directorial effort. Steve James's first feature doc since *Hoop Dreams.* Bruce Beresford, Patricia Rozema, Tom Tykwer, Paul Thomas Anderson, Phillip Noyce (twice), Alan Rudolph, Pedro Almodóvar, Deepa Mehta, Amos Gitai, Agnieszka Holland, Nancy Savoca, Rod Lurie . . . and, good God, Kenneth Anger. . . .

And, of course, the shadow of 9/11 will fall over all of this work, most particularly during the premiere of *11'09"01,* a collection of eleven-minute films by eleven directors about 9/11. Already there is controversy over what has been called "anti-American content" in some of the films, although it is hard to quarrel with Mira Nair's segment, about a Pakistani-American who, the IMDb reports, died while helping firefighters and then was described as a possible terrorist.

I put down the list of this year's films and I am eager to begin. Against the juggernaut of $30 million publicity campaigns, festivals like Toronto make their passionate stand. It is a little like throwing stones at a tank, but at least for ten days we're not in the tank.

Toronto Report No. 2

September 5, 2002—If the twenty-seventh Toronto Film Festival closes after two days, it will have shown six wonderful films and one magnificently bloody-minded one—and I do not exclude the possible greatness of entries I have not yet seen.

The wonderful films are *Nowhere in Africa, Personal Velocity, Respiro, Russian Ark, Secretary,* and *Talk to Her.* The defiantly screwy one is *Gerry,* which after it played at Sundance had people standing face-to-face in the snow trading praise and denunciation.

Nowhere in Africa is the sleeper, a German film about a Jewish family that flees Hitler and escapes to Kenya, where the father supervises a farm far from anything they know. Although Africa was his idea, he grows disenchanted with the farm at the same time that his wife, reluctant at first, begins to care for it. Their daughter, on the edge of adolescence, absorbs Africa through every pore, and becomes the friend and confidante of Owuor, the family's cook.

There is irony in the film, as when Jews are briefly interned by the British as enemy nationals. And beauty, and moments of surprising emotional intensity. Director Caroline Link paints Africa with calm realism; there are hazards of man and nature, but the movie doesn't descend to adventure melodrama, focusing instead on the human experiences of these refugees so far from home. The tensions of the marriage and the growth of the daughter are evoked with insight and tenderness. My hunch is that *Nowhere in Africa* could become a North American box office success.

Personal Velocity, directed by Rebecca Miller, won the Grand Jury prize at Sundance, where I was deeply touched by its insights into the lives of three women. Kyra Sedgwick is Delia, who marries a wife-beater, escapes the marriage with her children, and tries to survive as a waitress. Parker Posey is Greta, a cookbook editor whose safe but boring marriage is threatened by an unexpected newcomer. And Fairuza Balk is Paula, whose life is saved by fate, who finds herself pregnant, who befriends a battered hitchhiker. The depth of the film is hardly hinted at by such descriptions; Miller sees into these women and understands them with a deep sympathy. It is a wonderful film.

Respiro, directed by Emanuele Crialese, won the Critics' Week at Cannes. It is a film with its feet in the sand and its fancies flying free; the story sounds like neorealism, but the treatment is more like magic realism. Valeria Golino stars, as a woman whose passions and sadnesses have led others in a small fishing village to believe she should be sent to Milan for treatment. The popular diagnosis is manic depression, but then everybody in the village seems a little manic-depressive, including her son, who stage-manages her escape and brings her food, while her husband has himself lowered dangerously over cliffs in a search for her. The movie played last weekend at Telluride, where it scored a triumph.

Aleksandr Sokurov's *Russian Ark,* also at Telluride, is one of the most astonishing films ever made. Shot with a Sony HD digital camera, it consists of *one* unbroken ninety-five-minute shot as the camera and an invisible narrator follow a "time traveler" through the Hermitage in St. Petersburg. The film is not in any sense merely a guided tour of the museum, but a journey through 300 years of Russian history, sometimes illuminated by the museum's treasures, sometimes enacted by actors (including Soviet bureaucrats during a period when the museum was closed). The final breathtaking scene has the Steadicam gliding through 2,000 costumed extras at a ball.

After the screening I spoke with cinematographer John Bailey, who was awestruck by the control and stamina of the cameraman, Tilman Buttner. Bailey photographed *The Anniversary Party,* a feature shot on digital (but not HD), and admired the look of *Russian Ark* immensely, although as an old celluloid hand he felt a ninety-five-minute shot would have been possible on Super 16, and might have looked even better.

Steven Shainberg's *Secretary* is another one of those pictures where the casting is crucial, and it is difficult to imagine without James Spader and Maggie Gyllenhaal. She plays a painfully shy young woman who practices self-mutilation. He is a perfectionist martinet, a desperately miserable lawyer who loses all of his secretaries because he berates them mercilessly. She likes being berated, and before long they are locked in a sadomasochistic relationship. It's fun at first, then less fun for the lawyer, who has to do all the work. The movie is essentially a human comedy, although it takes some time to realize that.

Most of the critics in London, where I recently saw it, believe Pedro Almodóvar's *Talk to Her* is his best film. They may be right, although it's more serious and sorrowful than his usual work. It tells the story of two men who, through quite different circumstances, find themselves keeping vigil at the bedsides of two women in comas. Onto these sleeping beauties they project needs and desires, and curiously grow to enjoy their silent companionship. They also get to know each other.

The movie is in one sense another of Almodóvar's lurid soap operas, and in another sense a meditation on relationships, fantasy, and loyalty. It is compelling to the viewer, who gets so hooked on the situation that the day-to-day conditions of the patients become curiously important. More I will not say, because the movie has surprises and an ironic ending. But I will mention a little silent film that appears halfway through the longer one, in which a little man pleasures his woman in what one can only describe as the best means at his disposal.

And now to *Gerry.* You may hate it, but you may want to see it, because your fellow moviegoers will be talking of nothing else. Directed by Gus Van Sant, it was written by and stars Casey Affleck and Matt Damon as two young men who go on a hike in the desert and get lost. And there you have it. They remain lost for a very long time (I would not dream of telling you if they ever get found), and they talk about a good many things, at first in good cheer, later in desperation.

There are moments of humor worthy of silent comedy, as when one gets atop a big rock and is not sure how to get down, and monologues of droll wit. But to describe the film in those terms is to miss its heart, which is silent and empty and lost and thirsty and despairing. Gus Van Sant is one of the few directors with the nerve to point his camera into the desert and just keep walking, and Affleck and Damon achieve something in their performances that is existential grandeur, if you like the film, and transcendent stupidity, if you don't.

Toronto Report No. 3

September 6, 2002—There is a moment in *Bowling for Columbine* when Michael Moore is at a loss for words for perhaps for the first time in his life. The moment comes at the conclusion of one of the public psychodramas he has become expert in staging, in which he dramatizes evildoing (as defined by Moore) in the way calculated to maximize the embarrassment of the evildoer.

His staging is brilliant. He recruits two of the young Columbine shooting victims to accompany him on a visit to K-Mart corporate headquarters—where, he muses, they might ask to return merchandise, specifically the K-Mart bullets still in their bodies. The purpose of the visit is to request K-Mart to stop selling ammunition. After an initial contact with a P. R. person proves unsatisfactory, Moore and the students go to a K-Mart and the teenagers easily purchase hundreds of rounds of ammunition.

Then Moore and his camera and the kids return to K-Mart, where a spokesperson tells them, yes, that K-Mart will phase out the sale of ammunition over the next ninety days. Moore can't believe his ears. He asks the K-Mart rep to repeat what she just said. She does. Moore has won. "This has never happened before," he tells the Columbine survivors.

Bowling for Columbine, which plays in the Toronto Film Festival, is a departure for Moore in other ways. He is a little kinder and gentler, and less certain than usual. His subject is guns in America. He wants to know why so many Americans die of gunshot wounds every year. Why, for example, does Canada, with gun ownership comparable to the United States, have only a fraction of the shootings?

This is a question Moore does not and probably cannot answer, and so his movie lacks the moral clarity of *Roger & Me*, his attack on General Motors, in which he was convinced he was absolutely right. His tone in *Bowling for Columbine* is often funny or sarcastic, as before, but it is joined now by a new sorrowful note. Audiences watching the film are sometimes blindsided by emotion, and I have seen people crying during the K-Mart episode and earlier surveillance camera footage of the Columbine massacre itself.

If Moore has an answer, it is that America may have talked itself into feeling endangered. He notes that while gunshot deaths and violent crime in general have gone down 20 percent, coverage of violence on the TV news has increased by 600 percent. "If it bleeds, it leads," TV news directors chant. Moore corners poor Charlton Heston, who says he has a loaded gun in the house for protection. "Do you feel threatened?" he asks. "No," says Heston, who lives behind a gated wall. Maybe it's just the principle of the thing.

* * *

The festival's opening weekend has turned into a logistical nightmare for journalists trying to cover it in some sort of organized way. The big movies seem to be front-loaded, so that three or even four press screenings of important titles compete at the same time.

"It's because of 9/11," a festival insider told me. "The studios wanted to play all their stuff before Wednesday, because they're convinced everyone will go home early."

If I were a wise producer's rep—like my friend Jeff (The Dude) Dowd, for example—I would advise my clients to schedule their movies for late in the week, when visiting critics will be looking for screenings and copy. As things now stand, the schedule is so crowded that some pictures have press screenings that overlap with interview times. Maybe you see the first thirty minutes, run out to interview the director about the story so far, and then hurry back to see how it ends.

* * *

If I could see only one film on Saturday, I would make it Hayao Miyazaki's *Spirited Away*. This is a great film. Like all of Miyazaki's work, it appeals as much to adults as children—perhaps more so, because the subtlety of his visual universe may be lost on the kids as they focus on the story.

This is a film about a little girl, standoffish with her parents, who is separated from them during a vacation trip and wanders into what seems to be a theme park and then into a mysterious bathhouse run by a grotesque sorceress. (There is an eight-limbed man pumping the levers in the boiler room, a creature Miyazaki's animation was born to render.) The last time Miyazaki came to Toronto, with *Princess Mononoke*, he told me it would be his last film. Not quite. *Spirited Away* is perhaps his best.

The Portuguese master Manoel de Oliveira, now ninety-three, has made fourteen of his thirty-five films since 1990. I'm going to interview Miyazaki (who is only sixty-two) during the festival, and will tactfully point this out.

Toronto Report No. 4: Veteran Actors at Home in Their Roles

September 9, 2002—It can be exciting to watch young actors trying as hard as they can to be good. But there's something sort of inspiring about an older actor who has made so many movies over so many years that he knows how to do it without thinking. Within the first few minutes of *The Quiet American, Frida,* and *The Good Thief,* I could tell that Michael Caine, Alfred Molina, and Nick Nolte were completely at ease within their roles. They knew themselves, their bodies, their faces, their voices, and they could play them like Willie Nelson plays that old guitar with the hole in it. It's better to have a guitar without a hole, but after you've played on it long enough, an instrument is you.

Michael Caine in the right role is a superb actor, something we need reminding after watching him squirm in *Austin Powers in Goldmember*. Why bother to give Austin a father if you don't write a role for him? Caine is a hard-working actor who cheerfully takes all sorts of roles (when he won his first Oscar in 1987 he missed the ceremony because he was making *Jaws: The Revenge*). In *The Quiet American*, where he plays a *London Times* reporter in Vietnam, circa 1952, we know within a few minutes that he is not only right but inevitable for the role.

In Phillip Noyce's movie, he is in love with a taxi dancer (Hai Yen Do), and in competition with a young, confident American (Brendan Fraser) who is in love with her, too—but more earnestly and urgently and "sincerely," which is the way with young Americans. What neither man can entirely admit is that their money has a great deal to do with their appeal.

Caine finds a certain measured pace for the film; he has the leisurely movements of a man long in the tropics and no stranger to opium. The camera does not make the slightest concession to vanity, and we can see all of his years in his face, but because Caine's face has become beloved to us in so many other movies, there is a positive comfort in regarding it. Caine plays villains, comic characters, caricatures, but when he plays a man with a good heart and painful knowledge, there is no improving on him. He plays his character, Fowler, as if it is the most natural thing in the world. Just as Caine at thirty-three was naturally and inevitably Alfie, at fifty-three had "found his answer" in *Hannah and Her Sisters*, and only last year was magnificently human as a dying man in *Last Orders*, so at sixty-nine he has found another role completely within his gift and instincts.

Alfred Molina is only forty-nine. I first really noticed him in *Prick Up Your Ears* (1987), playing Kenneth Halliwell, jealous lover of the playwright Joe Orton. There and elsewhere he played an insecure man, unhappy within his skin, but in his new film, *Frida*, we sense that Molina is comfortable and confident, expansive and roguish. Is this simply the character? Is

it because he plays the legendary Mexican painter Diego Rivera? Not really. There is a kind of unstudied confidence in his performance, which seems to feed on his personal style. My guess is that Molina in person would be more like Rivera than most of his other characters. Of course it doesn't matter if I'm right; what matters is that he makes me feel that way.

Frida, directed by Julie Taymor, whose *Titus* is an unacknowledged masterpiece, played over the weekend in the Toronto festival. Most of the attention went to Salma Hayek, as of course it should, since she is electric and fascinating as the artist Frida Kahlo, who was (to Diego's astonishment) his match. But her performance certainly benefits from Molina's absolute assurance as Rivera. She calls him "fatso" the first time she sees him, when he is already a great man and she only a schoolgirl, but his size is not a flaw but a badge of honor: He is big in every way, and must present to the world a body that argues that fact. In movies like *Chocolat* (2000), where Molina played a supercilious count, we feel he's acting. In *Frida* we feel he's expanding with relief into a role that fits.

Now consider Nick Nolte, who is sixty-one and looks, not older, exactly, but more used and worn than his age suggests. In Neil Jordan's *The Good Thief*, he plays a shambling wreck on the French Riviera, a gambler named Bob who drives himself to smoke, to drink, to shoot heroin. Sometimes he dresses well, but at other times, at night in the rain after bad times, he looks like the Swamp Thing. Nolte came to attention as the improbably handsome star of the miniseries *Rich Man, Poor Man* (1976), and has been fighting ever since against the pretty boy image—a battle he has decisively won.

There is a moment in the film where the police inspector, who likes Bob, looks at his old mug shots, and one of them is Nolte in the 1970s. Many men would be grateful to be so good-looking, but that was obviously not an image Nolte was comfortable with, and for fifteen years at least (since *Extreme Prejudice*, 1987, where he was a lean Texas Ranger) he has been perfecting the hero as slob. I swear that one year at the Independent Spirit Awards he was wearing the bathrobe he put on when he got out of bed that morning.

The Good Thief is still another movie inspired by Jean-Pierre Melville's *Bob le Flam-*

beur (1955), which was also remade as both versions of *Ocean's 11*. Bob the High Roller is an aging, much imprisoned character whom even the cops like. He masterminds a complicated heist, and survives its risks because he is true to his essential self—he's a gambler, not a criminal.

Nolte inhabits the role like a bed he wants to sleep late in. We feel we are touching his real nature. He plays a man of huge appetites (look how tiny a cigarette seems in his hand), but the drugs and booze do not fill the empty places. Only romance can do that.

Nolte, Molina, and Caine are victors. They have survived the countless ways the movies have of wearing actors down and chewing them up. They have survived by gravitating toward roles they have trained for a lifetime to play. Watching the opening of *The Quiet American*, I wondered why I seemed to be smiling a little, and then I realized that I felt positive affection for Michael Caine, and I sensed that his character would engage me all the way through. As it did. The movie magazines have the twenty-three-year-old stars du jour on their covers, but let them put in the time and see if they turn out this well.

Toronto Report No. 5: *Heaven* Is Controversial Hit

September 9, 2002—We have a saying in Chicago: Don't drive the Dan Ryan Expressway until you've driven it three times. Nobody should see Todd Haynes's *Far from Heaven* unless they've seen a lot of movies, especially from the 1950s. Unless you know what he's doing, you're likely to hate it. This is among the most daring films in the Toronto Film Festival, and is likely to be the most misunderstood.

The movie has been made in the style and tone of those Universal-International social melodramas of the 1950s, especially such Douglas Sirk titles as *All That Heaven Allows*, *There's Always Tomorrow*, *Written on the Wind*, and *Imitation of Life*. It copies the look down to the leisurely treetop pans past autumn leaves. It is a period movie in the most difficult way possible—a movie not simply set in a period, but filmed as if it were made at the time, and with the values of the time. Most period films are set in the past but embody the values of the present.

Like the Sirk films, *Far from Heaven* deals with characters who risk society's disapproval in order to follow their hearts. In Sirk's *All That Heaven Allows*, the movie that most resembles this one, middle-aged widow Jane Wyman falls in love with her young gardener, Rock Hudson. In the Haynes version, the housewife (Julianne Moore) finds herself drawn to her black gardener (Dennis Haysbert), while her husband (Dennis Quaid) struggles with his homosexuality.

Homosexual romances were usually dealt with by implication in the 1950s. It takes an act of deconstruction like Mark Rappaport's *Rock Hudson's Home Movies* to understand, for example, what was going on between Hudson and Robert Stack as they go through the motions of competing for Lauren Bacall in *Written on the Wind*. If homosexuality dared not speak its name in the 1950s, interracial romance was as deeply buried, in convoluted plotlines like *Imitation of Life*, where the daughter of the movie star's maid passes for white.

Haynes's *Far from Heaven* is frankly about the homosexuality of the husband and the attraction between the wife and the gardener. Here is the daring thing: Haynes treats these two elements as they would have been treated in 1957. Homosexuality is a "problem" that Quaid tells a shrink makes him feel "despicable." And Moore and Haysbert, who never so much as kiss, have their lives so destroyed by gossip that he has to sell his business and leave town.

The movie shows that both forms of love were forbidden by society, but finds there is something poignant about the interracial couple and something shameful about the gay man. There is sadness as the woman smiles to the man as he leaves town on the train (in a quote of the last shot from *In the Heat of the Night*), but no joy when we see her husband in a hotel room with his lover. This, too, is true to the period: Gay rights lagged at least a decade behind civil rights in terms of public enlightenment.

"Who's gonna go see this movie?" I was asked after the screening, by a friend who is one of the most knowledgeable movie people in Canada. He said he admired it, "but I'm old enough to remember the 1950s, and the movies of the 1950s. Show this to a young audience today, and the gays will hate it and the blacks will laugh at it."

Perhaps they will, because they will bring

today's values to a film that deliberately does not embody them. The movie is valuable precisely as a time capsule. It reconstructs how ordinary suburbanites in middle America (Hartford, Connecticut) dealt with race and sex by not dealing with them at all. It depicts "liberals" who "support the NAACP" but know no blacks except their domestic servants.

One scene is a mirror of *All That Heaven Allows*, where Rock Hudson was the gardener and, like Haysbert here, wore plaid shirts, drove a pickup, and always seemed to be pruning something in the garden just when the lady of the house needed a heart-to-heart. Haysbert tells Moore he needs to pick up some plants and asks her to "come along for the ride," just as Hudson does with Wyman, and in both movies nosy neighbors see them together and start whispering. The thing many people suspected about Sirk's films at the time—the thing that attracted gay directors like Fassbinder and Haynes to his style and material—is that he always seemed to be hinting that his story lines were really about something else that Hollywood wouldn't let him represent.

Everyone is polite and chirpy and maddeningly conventional in *Far from Heaven*, and the conversational tone is set early, when Moore's son tells her: "Aw, shucks." He is of an age when today's suburban white boys enrich their vocabularies with hop-hop. There is a jolt when Haynes breaks the form brilliantly: Quaid, drunk, angry, and in anguish, shouts at his wife and uses an f-word that would never have been heard in a 1950s movie. They are both shocked, he apologizes, and they hug each other; the moment shows a ruder but more truthful age preparing to break through.

Will blacks laugh at the movie? Will gays be angry? Well, blacks have had decades of experience at not laughing out loud at white Hollywood product. Both black and gay critics have written about watching mainstream films for the oblique hints of stories beneath the surface. My feeling is that perceptive viewers will be able to see what Haynes is attempting. And *Far from Heaven* does work as drama. I sensed that the audience was as involved, and in much the same way, as they would have been while seeing a good 1957 movie.

Certainly *Far from Heaven* has been the hottest ticket so far at the Toronto Film Festival;

there was a mob scene at the press and industry screening, as two theaters filled up early and hundreds of angry people were shut outside. A volunteer muttered into her walkie-talkie, "Things are getting ugly." When hundreds of people spontaneously turn up an hour early for a screening, that indicates a particular desire to see the movie. Most audiences at Toronto form fifteen minutes before showtime.

I was among those shut out. When I was finally able to see the film, later that evening, I noticed that every single member of the audience remained seated until the last credit had rolled and the last note of Elmer Bernstein's period score had played. Usually, festival-goers bolt for the doors. Were they deeply moved, or just contemplative? Hard to say. Haynes has made the film in utter sincerity. There is not a shred of irony in it. No satire, no condescension to the characters or the story. He has made it as seriously as Sirk would have. "It made me feel," said my friend the veteran filmgoer. "I felt something. I really did." Haynes cares for his characters.

You have to experience *Far from Heaven* in the terms of the time. You can't approach it as if it were made this year, even though it was. If Hollywood had been able to make movies that dealt openly with homosexuality and race in 1957, it might have made this one. And we would have been the better for it.

Toronto Report No. 6: Eminem's Film Debut

September 9, 2002—A midterm report on the twenty-seventh Toronto Film Festival:

Whether Eminem can play anyone else is still to be discovered. That he can play himself was convincingly demonstrated Sunday night at a sneak screening of *8 Mile*, the quasi-autobiographical film based on his early days as a white hip-hop artist in Detroit, circa 1995.

The movie, directed by Curtis Hanson (*Wonder Boys, L.A. Confidential*), sidesteps the ancient puzzle of how to showcase a rock star in his first film role, by taking a semi-documentary approach. That also worked years ago for the Beatles in *A Hard Day's Night*.

"When I joined the Directors Guild," Hanson told me after the screening, "my signatory was Don Siegel. He directed Elvis in *Flaming Star*. I took that as an omen."

8 Mile, with a title that refers to the dividing line between mostly black Detroit and its mostly white suburbs, shows Eminem as a poor, earnest, worried, inward kid whose best friends are members of the local black rap scene. As the film opens, his character has been dropped by his pregnant girlfriend and moves back into the trailer home of his mother (Kim Basinger, very good), who is, as he notes in a lyric, sleeping with a guy he went to school with.

The movie is unflinching in its view of a violent home life, which is hard on the hero's little sister. He rides with his black friends, engages in the risky practice of tagging police cars with paint fired from a gun, works long shifts as a punch-press operator, gets in fights with rival singers, and engages in the weekly competitions between hip-hop artists at a local club. Eminem emerges from the film as a grungy, sympathetic proletarian, although in his next film he could stand to lighten up a little. The rough cut shown at Toronto was an audience-pleaser, and the prospects for continuing film success seem much more likely than, for example, Britney Spears after her ill-advised debut, *Crossroads.*

* * *

Best male performance in the festival so far: Michael Caine in Phillip Noyce's *The Quiet American.* This may in fact be the best performance of Caine's career, and seems certain to win him another Oscar nomination. He is immediately affecting as a weary, cynical *London Times* correspondent in Vietnam, circa 1952, who meets an earnest young American (Brendan Fraser) who has been sent by the CIA to finance and fake an insurrection that will serve as an excuse for American troop involvement. Caine and Fraser compete for the love of the same local girl, a taxi dancer (Hai Yen Do) who, neither man quite seems to understand, sincerely loves them both, but would love neither without his money.

Best female performance so far: Julianne Moore in Todd Haynes's *Far from Heaven,* where she is pitch-perfect in the kind of role Jane Wyman, Lana Turner, and Dorothy Malone played in Douglas Sirk's weepy Universal melodramas in the 1950s. It is a performance on two levels. She is convincing as a suburban housewife who begins a risky friendship with the black gardener, and discovers her husband

is a homosexual. She is also convincing as an actress playing that role in a 1957 movie, which is crucial, since Haynes has essentially made a movie Sirk should have made in the 1950s, but couldn't because of Hollywood restrictions.

Moore starred earlier in Haynes's *Safe* (1995), as a housewife who becomes allergic to her entire world, and retreats to a sheltered existence. The distance between these two roles is a measure of her reach; the conviction in each role is a measure of her depth.

Most emotional ending: the final shots of Phillip Noyce's powerful *Rabbit-Proof Fence,* which I will not breathe a word about, because they blindside the audience and leave many in tears.

* * *

Sooner or later the festival will have to deal with the crisis affecting the Press and Industry screenings. Some 2,000 tickets have been sold at $850 each to "industry members," who are entitled to attend all the press screenings and also get early dibs on public tickets. This is the best deal at the festival, which is why so many "industry members" have signed on.

Add the 750 accredited press at the festival, and you have 2,750 pass holders who all think they are entitled to a seat at screenings with 200 to 700 available seats. The screenings for *Talk to Her, Auto Focus, Jet Lag, Far from Heaven,* and *Eight Women* were all filled up by pass holders who got in line up to an hour in advance; those arriving any later were turned away. The distributors of *Far from Heaven* looked on impotently as the critics of *Variety,* the *New York Times,* the *National Post, New York,* and *USA Today,* plus festival godfather Norman Jewison, were turned away.

"First come, first served," said the hard-working volunteers. Yes, but distributors don't spend money to bring their films here for those who are first in line—they want them to be seen by working critics and buyers, not just movie fans with $850. That's what the public screenings are for. At Cannes and elsewhere, the press is guaranteed admission by arriving fifteen minutes before the start time; after that, the queue is admitted.

And speaking of director Norman Jewison and his wife, Dixie, does the festival have two better friends? The Jewisons, backers of the fest from its earliest days, turn up faithfully at several screenings a day. Norman, in his inevitable baseball cap, is irrepressibly enthusiastic, seeks out young directors, is always discovering something wonderful. And on the fest's first Sunday they host a barbecue for festival guests in the big backyard of the Canadian Center for Advanced Film Study—which, by the way, is also Norman's baby.

And by the way: Does Eminem or anyone else know who started the ubiquitous modern custom of wearing baseball caps while not playing baseball? It was Norman Jewison, who discovered in the late 1950s that the cap kept the sun out of his eyes while he was lining up outdoor shots. Other directors and cinematographers followed, actors copied them, and a fashion fad was born. Fact.

Toronto Report No. 7: *The Guys* Premieres on Anniversary

September 10, 2002—The enormity of the attack on the World Trade Center struck many artists dumb; what can be said, and how? Anne Nelson's play *The Guys*, which was quickly produced in New York and has starred many different actors, reduces the story to two people: one who remembers his fallen comrades, and one who wants to help him word his memories. Now it has been made into a film, which premieres on September 11, 2002, at the Toronto festival.

The Guys stars Anthony LaPaglia as a fire captain who will need to eulogize his friends at memorial services and worries about what to say. Sigourney Weaver is the professional writer who volunteers to help him. As a long day darkens into evening, Jim Simpson's film shows these two people in conversation about the captain's friends—their quirks, their strengths, their humanity.

At breakfast in Toronto on Tuesday, Simpson said he studied Louis Malle's *My Dinner with Andre* for ideas about how to keep the conversation alive. His camera is subtle and his framing exact as the two people speak, and the film wisely avoids news footage, depending on words to make us see these men who went into the towers and never returned.

Weaver spoke about the slow process by which the writer sets the captain at ease, so that his first stilted words loosen into a flow of memories. And Nelson said the play was an idea that fell into her life: "I had done something like the writer in the story, and it occurred to me that this was a way to approach the loss we all felt."

* * *

There was sadness Monday night at the dinner before Mike Leigh's *All or Nothing*, because Leigh and his actors Timothy Spall and Lesley Manville had worked with and loved the great actress Katrin Cartlidge. She died Saturday, at forty-one, suddenly, of septicemia resulting from pneumonia; she had been in the hospital only two days. Cartlidge, an actress of power and grace, starred for Leigh in *Naked, Career Girls,* and *Topsy-Turvy,* and took courageous chances in Lars von Trier's *Breaking the Waves* and Lodge Kerrigan's *Claire Dolan.*

Leigh and his friends learned the news after arriving in Toronto; he quietly passed around a respectful obituary from the *Guardian.* What he said I will not quote, because it was personal and heartfelt.

Leigh's *All or Nothing* is a tender, wonderful film starring Spall as a minicab driver, married to a Safeway cashier; they have two pudgy children, one a lonely caretaker at an old folks' home, the other a profane and rude couch potato. We also meet friends and neighbors, in a story that deals with the small dramas, hopes, and fears of life in poverty. Then a family crisis breaks the dreary pattern, and leads to a great scene between Spall and Manville, as his wife, which in terms of heartbreaking simplicity says as much as can be said about why it is worthwhile, or not, to slog on through a difficult life.

* * *

You may vaguely remember the controversy over *Fortunate Son,* J. H. Hatfield's 1999 biography of George W. Bush, which alleged that the future president had been arrested for cocaine possession, and that charges were dropped after the intervention of his father. The book was a cause célèbre and a best-seller for about a week; then it was revealed that Hatfield had served time for attempted murder, the book was pulped by its publisher, St. Martin's Press, and the charges were forgotten.

Horns and Halos, a documentary at the Toronto Film Festival, continues the story as a portrait of Hatfield, a loose cannon. Directed by Suki Hawley and Michael Galinsky, the film follows Hatfield as he finds another publisher—the Soft Skull Press, run by Sander Hicks, a twenty-nine-year-old guerrilla who operates out of basement offices in the New York building where he is also the janitor.

Hicks republishes the book, gets Hatfield on *60 Minutes,* and takes him to Book Expo in Chicago, but once again the author becomes his own worst enemy. A new introduction written for the Soft Skull edition inspires a lawsuit by a former associate who, Hatfield alleges, was involved with him in the murder scheme.

Hatfield's own story is tragic, as you will find if you see the movie. He was much criticized after the first edition for using anonymous sources for his story of George W. Bush's alleged cocaine use. So, at a Book Expo press conference he names as a source none other than Karl Rove, then and now political adviser to the president. Can this be true? The movie raises substantial doubts about Hatfield's reliability. But he sure came up with a humdinger.

* * *

Justin Lin's *Better Luck Tomorrow,* one of the best films in this year's festival, arrives in Toronto for a fall launch after its controversial Sundance premiere. It's a knowing, deeply cynical view of the success ethic among adolescent Asian-Americans in an affluent California community, who begin by selling exam answers and gradually escalate into drugs and murder. The hero considers turning himself in, but "I couldn't let one mistake get in the way of everything I'd worked for."

After the Sundance screening, a member of the audience angrily asked Lin, "How could you make such a bleak, negative, amoral film? Don't you have a responsibility to paint a more positive and helpful portrait of your community?"

Lin replied that he had made the film he wanted to make, the way he had wanted to make it. He felt it depicted a reality among teenagers of any race. I usually don't speak during the Q&A sessions after screenings, but I couldn't restrain myself. I told the man I thought he was being condescending: "You would never make a comment like that to a white filmmaker." Lin's responsibility, I felt, was to make the best film he could. To limit minority filmmakers to "positive" stories is a form of racism.

* * *

No better documentary has been made in re-

cent years than Steve James's *Hoop Dreams* (1994), about two inner-city Chicago kids who dream of the NBA and are recruited by a rich suburban Catholic high school. Filmed over the course of five years, it had the drama of fiction.

Now comes James's new documentary, *Stevie,* playing at Toronto. This one doesn't have the neat, almost poetic ending of *Hoop Dreams,* because sometimes life doesn't turn out that way. James tells the story about how when he was in college he was a Big Brother to an eleven-year-old named Stevie Fielding.

When he graduated and left Stevie behind, James says, he felt there was unfinished business. More than a decade later, he went back to find him. One would like to hope, as James originally does, that a well-intentioned outsider can make a difference. But what he finds is a family so profoundly dysfunctional that it's likely Stevie never really had a chance. The movie is deeply sorrowful and impossible to forget.

Toronto Report No. 8: September 11 Story Told in Eleven Short Films

September 12, 2002—The eleven films by eleven filmmakers in the film *11'09"01,* all trying to address 9/11 in eleven minutes, are uneven and not entirely satisfying. One wonders if the producers should have recruited directors of shorts rather than features, but four of them have undeniable impact, and one is devastating.

The film, which caused much discussion at the Venice Film Festival, had its North American premiere here at the Toronto festival and will go into limited release. With its eleven viewpoints from all over the world, not all of them pro-American, it celebrates, the opening titles say, "subjective conscience" and "free expression."

Yes, but would it have killed at least one of these eleven directors to make a clear-cut attack on the terrorists? The banner headline in the *Toronto Star* the day after the movie's screening reported that Prime Minister Jean Chrétien "ties 9/11 terror to Western 'greed.'" We in the West have much to be ashamed of, but oddly enough, I don't think al-Qaida's hatred of us is based on our greed; we are infidels who deserve to die because we pray to the wrong God.

The overpowering episode is by Alejandro

González Iñárritu of Mexico, best known for *Amores Perros*. He keeps his screen entirely black for most of the eleven minutes, occasionally interrupting it with flashes of bodies falling from the burning World Trade Center. We realize after a while that the muffled thuds on the sound track are the bodies landing.

The sound track begins and ends with a collage of excited voices, and during the eleven minutes we also hear snatches of newscasts and part of a cell phone call from a passenger on one of the hijacked airplanes ("We have a little problem on the plane, and I wanted to say I love you . . .").

Toward the end, there is the sound of fearsome hammering, and we realize with a chill that this is the sound of the floors collapsing, one on top of another, growing louder. It must have been recorded from a radio inside the building; it is the last thing the terrified people inside the towers heard. This film is so strong because it allows us to use our imaginations. It generates almost unbearable empathy.

Another of the best films is by Ken Loach of Great Britain, who films a Chilean writing a letter to Americans in which he offers his sympathy. Then he recalls that on another Tuesday, September 11, in 1973, the democratically elected government of Chile was overthrown by a CIA-funded military coup, President Salvador Allende was murdered, and the right-wing dictator Pinochet was installed as the U.S. puppet to rule over a reign of torture and terror. I wrote in my notes: "Do unto others as you would have them do unto you."

The third powerful film is by Mira Nair of India, who tells the true story of a Pakistani mother in New York whose son got on the subway to go to medical school and never returned. She was questioned by the FBI, her son was named as a suspected terrorist, and only six months later was his body found in the rubble, where, as a trained medic, he had gone to help. His hero's coffin was draped in the American flag.

One of the most sympathetic films comes from Iran. Samira Makhmalbaf's film shows a teacher trying to explain to her students—Afghan refugees in Iran—what has happened in New York. The kids get into a discussion about God, and whether he would kill some people to make others; "God isn't crazy," one child finally decides. None of the children can imagine a tall building, so the teacher takes them to stand beneath a smokestack, and the smoke from the top makes an eerie mirror of the catastrophe.

Other films miss the mark. Amos Gitai of Israel shows a TV news reporter broadcasting live from the scene of a suicide bombing when she is taken off the air because of the news from New York. This situation could have generated an interesting film, but the reporter is depicted as so self-centered and goofy that the piece derails. A film by Egypt's Youssef Chahine also has an interesting premise—a director is visited by the ghost of a U.S. Marine who was killed in the Beirut bombing—but the piece is unfocused, half-realized.

The only note of humor comes in a charming film from Burkina Faso, in Africa, where five poor boys believe they have spotted Osama bin Laden in their town, and plot to capture him and win the $25 million reward. They are not entirely off the track; the actor hired to play bin Laden could be his double.

Other films are from Bosnia's Danis Tanovic, who shows women continuing to march with the names of their dead despite the deaths in New York; Japan's Shohei Imamura, who shows a man who survived the atomic bombing but has become convinced he is a snake; Sean Penn of the United States, who stars Ernest Borgnine as an old man who rejoices when his dead wife's flowers bloom, not realizing they get sunlight because the towers have fallen; and France's Claude Lelouch, with a sentimental piece about a deaf woman who does not realize what has happened until her boyfriend returns alive, covered with dust.

Hawaii Film Festival
Hawaii Report No. 1

Honolulu, November 5, 2002—I'm often asked what purpose film festivals serve. My answer this morning is: The Hawaii Film Festival allowed me to see *Charlotte Sometimes* last night. This is an Asian-American "art film" that is about two relationships, but doesn't fit into any conventional category involving love or romance. It's more about secrets, power, and buried issues between Asian-American men and women. It is written, directed, and acted with the penetrating shorthand of a short story; we experience the plot at firsthand, without tiresome dialogue in which people explain things they already know, so that the audience can be briefed.

Going into the film, I expected some kind of a conventional boy-girl story, in which the problem is that the boy and girl are not in love, and that's fixed by the happy ending. This movie is not about those moronic movie romances. It is about very particular people with needs and fears, and the way they dance around the lies that separate them.

Michael Idemoto stars as Michael, an auto mechanic. He reads all the time, is intellectual, moody, lonely, inherited the garage from his family. He lives in his childhood home, which he has divided. His tenant is Lori (Eugenia Yuan). She has a boyfriend named Justin (Matt Westmore), but after their loud and energetic lovemaking she often knocks on Michael's door for companionship.

One day in a bar Michael meets Darcy (Jacqueline Kim). She is intimidating: formidably smart, mysteriously perverse. They spend a long night of drinking and talking. There is something there, between them, but when Darcy suggests sex, Michael dances away because that is too easy, and he wants to get to know her first. She says sex is a shortcut to knowing. She only has a few days—she doesn't say why—and then she has to leave. (No, it isn't because she's dying. This is a smart movie.)

I began to realize this would not be the story of how they ended up in each other's arms, but how they got past each other's defenses—or under each other's skins. Darcy appears and disappears. She is inquisitive about the nature of his relationship with Lori: Are they really only friends? Jacqueline Kim suggests a need and pain in her character that is never forced, but always there, just out of sight, and scary.

The writer-director, Eric Byler, who says he dislikes expository dialogue, presents Darcy and Michael in an uncannily realistic way: This relationship, with all of its trying and testing, its game playing and sudden darts toward feeling, is more real than most movies allow. There are scenes in which we sense more is going on than

anyone admits, but the movie lets us speculate without spoiling everything with dramatic revelations. We *participate* in this film. The actors reject layers of actorly mannerisms to come out clean and clear as plausible, quirky individuals. Byler avoids underlining everything with big close-ups and reaction shots, but traps the characters in space together as they try to figure out what they mean to one another. This is a relationship picture that plays like an emotional thriller.

Charlotte Sometimes is the best of the films I've seen so far at the Hawaii festival, which has emerged as a premiere showcase for films of the Pacific Rim. Now underwritten by Louis Vuitton Hawaii, the festival has 200 films and some forty premieres this year, in commercial theaters on Waikiki Beach, at a multiplex at the old Dole cannery, and at the Hawaii Academy of Arts. Enormous crowds turn out, many of them movie fanatics; at *Charlotte Sometimes* I met Bob Chin, of the famous crab house in Wheeling, Illinois, who spends part of his year in Hawaii and was positioned in the front row of the balcony with several family members for their fifth movie of the day.

There are seminars as well as screenings. Donald Richie, the famed Japanese film expert, did a seminar on *Men Who Tread on the Tiger's Tail,* a 1945 Kurosawa film I had never heard of. Peter Pau, the cinematographer of *Crouching Tiger, Hidden Dragon,* is here to talk about his techniques and take home the Eastman Kodak Cinematography Award. The actress Elizabeth Lindsay appeared with the Honolulu Symphony and narrated her sad and powerful film *And Then There Were None,* about the extinction of the Hawaiian people. In the afternoons, I am doing a shot-by-shot seminar on *Citizen Kane.*

Many of the films at Hawaii never penetrate to the mainstream. Eric Byler told me he still doesn't have a distributor for *Charlotte Sometimes,* perhaps because it is both Asian-American and, well, seriously good. Its buried theme, he said, is the way American society tends to "exoticize" Asian females while marginalizing Asian males. In a movie where all the actors are Asian, this theme is internalized; there is no white character to provide a villain, and that's another example of its subtlety.

What films like this represent is a breakthrough for Asian-American filmmakers. For the first generation, it was enough that their films existed: Wow! Asians in an American movie! Now the filmmakers have lost their self-consciousness, have freed themselves from the need to fit into conventional patterns. Films like *Charlotte Sometimes* and Justin Lin's Sundance hit *Better Luck Tomorrow*, also showing here, show Asian-American characters who do not "represent their community" or project a "positive image" or do anything else except what characters in all good movies do: be themselves, in a way that is fascinating and illuminating.

Hawaii Report No. 2: The Winners

November 11, 2002—*The Maori Merchant of Venice*, a film of Shakespeare's play translated into the Maori language, won the coveted Audience Award here as the most popular film at the Louis Vuitton Hawaii Film Festival. The translation was done to illustrate the capability of the Maori language, spoken by the native peoples of New Zealand; the film was made by Maori theater veterans who love Shakespeare.

The Golden Maile Award, given by a jury and named for the most noble of Hawaii's plants, went to Aparna Sen's *Mr. and Mrs. Iyer*, from India, the story of a Hindu woman and her child, who meet a Muslim man on a journey. When their bus is attacked by a mob of Hindus, she saves the man's life by claiming him as her husband.

The Golden Maile Award for best documentary went to *Spellbound*, Jeff Blitz's film about the National Spelling Bee. This film, a big audience favorite at several festivals, follows eight good spellers on their way to the national finals, and seems destined for theatrical release.

The Maori Merchant of Venice, directed by Don C. Selwyn, transposes Venice to New Zealand through the use of local waterways, the harbor district, and Italian-inspired buildings. The story, translated from Shakespeare in 1945 by the scholar Pei Te Hurinui Jones, is translated back into modern English in the subtitles.

The role of Shylock is played by Waihoroi Shortland, a burly bullet-headed man who looks like a James Bond villain, but talks like a scholar and is a noted author. He told me that Maori and Shakespeare's language are a good fit because both are classical and easily permit allusions and poetry. Jones first began translating Shakespeare because so many translations from English into Maori consisted of matter-of-fact prose that did not exploit the language's more poetic and fanciful properties.

Selwyn, a longtime New Zealand actor, producer, and director, told me he "doubted" the film would find theatrical release in North America, and indeed the blinkered major distributors would scarcely see this as a follow-up to *Shakespeare in Love*. But it is in love with Shakespeare, which is another matter altogether.

Among other films I saw here at the twenty-second Hawaii festival, one I especially admired was Hao Jiangi's *Life Show*, from China, starring Si Wu as a pretty, thirty-fiveish single woman who sits for long nights in her food stall at the "night market," selling duck's necks to hungry night workers. Her family surrounds her with problems: One brother is in jail with drug troubles, another has an acquisitive wife who hardly wants to raise their son. Night after night, a middle-aged man comes to sit across from her stall and regard her, and eventually they become friends.

There is much more than that, all to be discovered when you see the film. This is not a love story but more of a sad, poetic evocation of the woman's life choices. Is the food stand her lifelong destiny? Why must she always be the responsible family member? The film is in the emerging elliptical style from China, in which plot points are not hammered home but made by implication, or contained in the elegant, darkly shadowed compositions.

I also admired *Way Past Cool*, by Adam Davidson, which is sort of a blood-soaked *George Washington* about young African-American boys introduced too early and too sadly to guns. Davidson said one of his inspirations was the Little Rascals, and indeed his twelve-year-olds have the same impish spirit, but are entering a deadly world of tragic consequences. He makes his point well and not without humor, although many audience members are going to turn away at the sight of characters too young to survive in their urban environment.

YMCA Baseball Team, the opening-night film, was from Korea, and began the festival's salute to Korean cinema. It takes place circa

1902, when the Japanese have made a historically damaging treaty with Korea, and, in a story based on fact, tells of the first Korean baseball team and a crucial game with a more experienced Japanese team. The film combines more or less predictable sports footage with director Kim Hyun-seok's deadpan comic timing, and is vastly more amusing than the premise suggests. In theme, it's a reminder of *Lagaan,* the recent Bollywood film about a cricket match between Indians and British.

Sundance Film Festival
Sundance Report No. 1 (Advance)

Park City, Utah, January 16, 2003—I have just spent an hour with the 2003 program for the Sundance Film Festival, and I am churning with eagerness to get at these films. On the basis of track records, this could be the strongest Sundance in some time—and remember, last year's festival kicked off an extraordinary year for indie films.

Sundance is the only American film festival that's a must (if you include Canada, there's also Toronto). For ten days in the snows of Park City, the movie crowd breaks in its new goose-down parkas and trudges through the drifts to screenings all over town. The excitement of seeing a great new film is equaled only by the thrill of having your car towed by the town's fanatic traffic gestapo.

More than 1,000 films are submitted to Sundance every year, and about 10 percent get chosen by a staff that starts viewing submissions in the autumn. This year's reality was summarized with admirable frankness by Geoff Gilmore, the festival director, who told the *Hollywood Reporter:* "A couple of years ago, we saw an enormous amount of crap get produced and there was a lot of money out there to produce it. A lot of the films we have at the festival this year are the result of the creative passion and tenacity and perseverance that you have to have to get a film made these days, and the films reflect that."

Yes. There are no longer dot.coms webcasting from Main Street, but the indie filmmakers will still be working the sidewalks with the Sundance trademark, a postcard begging you to attend their screenings. I hurl myself into this maelstrom with a certain glee, clicking off three, four, or even five or (once) six films a day. I get dinner invitations, which inspire a hollow laugh. To have dinner at Sundance is to miss one or even two movies, and the true festival goer exists on sandwiches and brownies sold by the Friends of the Library.

The festival opens Thursday night in Salt Lake City with the world premiere of Ed Solomon's *Levity,* a film with an intriguing cast: Billy Bob Thornton, Morgan Freeman, Holly Hunter, and Kirsten Dunst. The film involves a prisoner released after twenty-two years, who returns to a community center in his old neighborhood and to the same issues that put him behind bars. For Holly Hunter, the opening night will be followed on Tuesday by the Tribute to Independent Vision Award, an honor given every year to a heroic indie spirit.

After Thursday night, everybody moves up the hill to the ski town of Park City. It is an irony that Sundance first became popular because Hollywood types could use it as an excuse to write off their ski vacations; these days they are way too busy to ski.

The Park City opening night films include Keith Gordon's *The Singing Detective,* with Robert Downey Jr. in the title role, and Dan Algrant's *People I Know,* starring Al Pacino as a New York press agent. The Downey film is based on the legendary BBC television series by Dennis Potter, who reinvented it in this screenplay written as he was dying. The Pacino movie is said to be inspired by the legendary and beloved Bobby Zarem, a New York publicist who sends out a blizzard of handwritten notes, breathlessly FedExed. I am one of the people Zarem knows, but then of course he knows everyone. When I ran into him in Elaine's in December he cautioned me that the film contains "a lot of fiction." That could also be said (although I did not say it) about his notes.

To summarize the week ahead would involve us here in a long list of titles, stars, and directors, and as I have seen none of these films, I'd be shooting in the dark. But of course that's what you do at Sundance. You circle the films by interesting directors, because they act as brand names. Then, while you're standing in line, you begin to absorb the buzz. You hear about a little film you must not miss, and before long you find yourself at *Memento* or *Better Luck Tomorrow* or *The Blair Witch Project* (yes, there was a time at Sundance when even that was a little film no one had heard of).

The indie distributors troll the screenings, looking for films to purchase. So heated is the competition that one year Miramax's Harvey Weinstein was actually in a shoving match over a film. The film-spotters are paranoid because of the big ones that got away. After all, Miramax and everyone else except for tiny Artisan passed on *Blair Witch,* and everyone except for Lions Gate passed on *My Big Fat Greek Wedding.* Both films grossed north of $200 million.

Now let me suggest some of the potential treasures this year. Neil LaBute, whose career began with *In the Company of Men* at Sundance, is back with *The Shape of Things,* starring Paul Rudd and Rachel Weisz in a story of college kids searching for meaning. Gael Garcia Bernal, the hot Mexican star of *Amores Perros* and *Y Tu Mama Tambien,* is in Matthew Parkhill's *dot the i,* a love triangle. Claire Danes and Joaquin Phoenix are in *It's All About Love,* a futuristic fantasy by Dogma pioneer Thomas Vinterberg.

Sundance discovery Edward Burns *(The Brothers McMullen)* and Dustin Hoffman are in James Foley's con-man story *Confidence.* Troy Garity, son of Jane Fonda and Tom Hayden, stars in Frank Pierson's *Soldier's Girl,* about a young army trainee who falls in love with a transgendered dancer. The Polish twins, Mark and Michael *(Twin Falls, Idaho),* are here with *Northfork,* starring James Woods, Nick Nolte, and Daryl Hannah in the story of holdouts against government relocation. Seinfeld's Larry Charles and Bob Dylan are collaborators on *Masked and Anonymous,* a futuristic satire starring Jeff Bridges and Penelope Cruz.

Danny Glover and Whoopi Goldberg star in Ernest Dickerson's *Good Fences,* about a pioneering middle-class black couple in 1970s suburbia. The inimitable Philip Seymour Hoffman and Minnie Driver are in Richard Kwietnioski's *Owning Mahowny,* the story of a bank manager who is a compulsive gambler. Campbell Scott is all over the map, starring in three films,

including Alan Rudolph's *The Secret Lives of Dentists,* based on the Jane Smiley novel about jealous rage.

That's only a sample of the major premieres. There are equally intriguing titles in the sidebar sections, including the dramatic and documentary competitions and the World Cinema showcase. And on the closing weekend, Oliver Stone's *Commandante,* based on thirty hours of the director's conversations with Fidel Castro. I'll be filing more or less daily reports from the festival, which annually reminds us that the movies can be original and challenging, once you break free of the mainstream lockstep.

Sundance Report No. 2

January 17, 2003—Robert Redford remembers the first year of the Sundance Film Festival: "We had thirty or forty films in two theaters. I was standing in the street outside the Egyptian Theater, handing out brochures like a street hawker, trying to talk people into coming inside. I saw David Puttnam, who was running Columbia at that time, and gave him the pitch. He went in, saw Jim McBride's *The Big Easy,* and bought it. That was the first film bought at Sundance."

But not the last. On the opening day in Park City, Redford sat in Wahso, an upscale Asian grill on Main Street, and considered what he had wrought. This year 3,600 films were submitted to the festival, and 140 were selected. The town is jammed. Sidewalks are shoulder-to-shoulder with filmmakers, buyers, sellers, publicists, and fans. "It can't get any bigger," Redford said. His little festival has become the most important in America.

Redford himself is an uneasy figurehead. Although he welcomed the opening night crowd at Thursday's gala down the hill in Salt Lake City, "I don't want to be out front," he said. "In the early years, I was right in the middle—tossed around like a cork in a rapids. Now I step aside and enjoy the festival."

He protests too much. Redford's shadow looms large in this corner of Utah, where his Sundance resort also screens festival entries; afterward moviegoers can have a drink at an antique bar built in Ireland for the Hole-in-the-Wall Gang, bought by Redford in Thermopolis, Wyoming, and lovingly restored, bullet holes and all. In the summer, his Sundance Institute is a workshop where veterans work with young directors, writers, and actors, improving films that often get made and praised. No single person has done more for the independent film movement than the one-time matinee idol who now, at sixty-five frets: "Celebrity is distracting us from important issues. We're going to war and all you hear about are the ten top celebrity this and that."

This year's festival benefits in a curious way from the economic downturn, Redford said. In the go-go years of the 1990s, when dot.com money poured into film, there was an "over-population of filmmakers with digital formats, making it almost too easy to make a movie without a whole lot of credentials. There was a danger of losing audiences who couldn't take all the junk." Good independent films always find a way, he said, and he thinks this year's selection is better than average—"and also funnier. I think you'll find more lightness this year."

Redford has always been a political liberal, and "in the current political climate," he said, "with the administration leaning further and further toward secrecy and stonewalling, independent films are a way to get out information."

He remembered the shell shock of last year's festival, under the cloud of 9/11. This year "the anxiety is still there, and the government has responded with an attack on freedom of speech and expression. The Constitution is under attack under the disguise of patriotism. The administration forgets that dissent is the American way. A lot of this year's movies will reflect that."

As a writer and director, Redford is personally voting for indie films. He's making *Clearing*, a low-budget film with a Dutch director named Peter Jan Brugge, costarring Helen Mirren and Willem Dafoe. He's talking with Danish filmmaker Lasse Hallstrom about a film costarring Morgan Freeman. And he will direct a sequel to *The Candidate*, the 1972 film he still remembers as one of the best times he ever had: "We shot it in forty days on $1.6 million."

Down the street from where we're talking, the separate Slamdance Festival also opens today, providing a home for the best of the Sundance refuseniks. "The more the merrier," Redford said. "I'm glad some films can be

shown that we had to turn down. The selection process is so brutal. We can't show them all.

"But sometimes a film slips through. I remember one year I was in an elevator in New York and this kid accosted me. He looked like a panhandler. It was Edward Burns. He hands me a tape and begs me to watch it. I get that all the time, but I thought, what the hell, that's what it's all about. So I watched it. And I liked it. It was forty minutes too long, but it was good, and he trimmed it. That was *The Brothers McMullen* (1995), which went on to win the festival."

Sundance Report No. 3

January 20, 2003—The question from the audience was pretty direct: "Did you draw on experiences in your own life in this performance?" Robert Downey Jr. who among his other gifts is a physical comedian, seemed to implode, crouching over, his arms shielding him. Charlie Chaplin—whom he once played—might have approved of the pantomime. The body language said: You had to ask that, didn't you?

Downey, whose career appears to be back on track after a seemingly endless series of drug troubles, stars in Keith Gordon's *The Singing Detective* as a writer whose entire body is covered with painful eczema. The film played on the Park City opening night of the Sundance Film Festival. His character's face has so many pits, boils, and eruptions that he calls himself the Pizza Man. Even the slightest movement is agony, and he mentally escapes to a parallel universe of *film noir* in which he imagines gangsters and private eyes and gun molls—who occasionally burst into song-and-dance numbers based on 1950s rock 'n' roll.

The film is a much shorter version of the famous 1986 BBC series written by Dennis Potter, who himself suffered from an excruciating skin ailment. The screenplay was the last work he finished before his death. Gordon directs unblinkingly, with close-ups of the suffering hero, but the film is curiously resilient and not as depressing as it sounds—a brave spirit's defiant thumb in the eye of disease.

Downey's performance is remarkable in the way it works with the physical condition. At times his voice is choked and harsh, because it hurts to move his lips, and yet at other times he gets laughs with perfectly timed looks and grins and grimaces. Then there are scenes where in his imagination he is magically restored. Onstage, he kidded with the audience and with his costars Robin Wright Penn, Katie Holmes, and Carla Gugino, but after the question referring to his troubled past, he joked, "An hour from now I'm gonna be drunk." That didn't get much of a laugh.

* * *

The Dude is writing his autobiography. Jeff Dowd, the movie publicist and producers' rep who inspired *The Big Lebowski* by the Coen brothers, says it will be titled *Classic Tales and Rebel Rants from the Dude.*

I ran into the Dude at the Sundance screening of *People I Know,* the new movie starring Al Pacino and very loosely based on the life of another famous publicist, Bobby Zarem of New York and Savannah. All you can say is, when it comes to the drug use of their two fictional alter egos, Robert Downey finishes a distant third.

"It's great writing this book," the Dude enthused. "All I gotta do is look up stuff on Google and I find all my facts. Like I'll type in a place I was, and the stories will remind me of stuff that happened there." He says his book is inspired by a statement of the novelist Gabriel García Márquez: "People want to hear about events as they wish they had happened, and not as they did happen."

* * *

The festival opened on a disappointing note Thursday night with a gala screening in Salt Lake City of *Levity,* Ed Solomon's lugubrious parable about a killer who wants to redeem himself. You'd think a movie starring Billy Bob Thornton, Morgan Freeman, Holly Hunter, and Kirsten Dunst would have moments of impact just by default, but the actors were boxed in by a maudlin screenplay, slowed down to a crawl.

Thornton plays a man who as a teenager killed a supermarket clerk, served seventeen years in prison, and emerges looking curiously like a sixty-year-old. He has long, straggly gray hair that's a constant distraction, because it looks so spectacularly wrong. He returns to his old neighborhood, meets Freeman, who runs a storefront mission for troubled kids, and then encounters Hunter, the sister of his victim. Also hanging around is Dunst, as a troubled girl who attends nearby raves, gets drunk, passes out, and attracts Thornton's sympathy.

The movie takes place in one of those universes inhabited only by its key characters—plus, of course, the chorus of troubled kids, who are strewn "casually" about the set like the cowboys in Oklahoma. So small is this world that at midnight, in a darkened alley, Hunter's son encounters his enemy, and then Thornton stumbles across the violent situation, and then Hunter herself turns up. Thornton, usually such a watchable and surprising actor, adopts the wrong emotional choice for this role: He's a low-energy sad sack, his conversation a mournful dirge. Flashes of wit by the others disappear into the black hole of his depression.

Before Sundance screenings, the directors often come out and say something like, "I hope you enjoy the movie." Solomon (who wrote *Men in Black,* but cannot be blamed for *Men in Black II*) gave the longest speech I have ever heard before a movie, twenty minutes or so, thanking even his lawyers and accountants and telling us he tried to write the story at twenty-one and again in his thirties before finally arriving at this version. He settled too soon.

Sundance Report No. 4

January 20, 2003—Is *Commandante* a bad film because it shows Fidel Castro, the old baseball star, effortlessly fielding Oliver Stone's softball questions? Or is it a good film for the very same reason?

A debate raged in the lobby of the 1,300-seat Eccles Center after the Sundance premiere of Stone's new film. Harlan Jacobson, covering for *USA Today,* was outraged. He recently returned from the Havana Film Festival filled with questions he would have liked to ask Castro, and Stone avoided all of them. Why, for example, didn't Stone ask the Cuban dictator if his interview represented an opening to the Cuban exiles in Florida?

My own tendency was to approach the film as a phenomenon. Most of us have never seen Castro except in film clips from one of his endless speeches. Here he is unplugged, over a period of three days, talking with Stone in his office, touring a medical school, making a neighborhood visit, eating meals, introducing his children, talking about politics, theology, philosophy, and Ernest Hemingway.

Like all documentaries, *Commandante* documents what is in front of the camera, and smart viewers don't take it at face value. If Stone asks the wrong questions, well, then this could be a documentary showing how Fidel's charm seduced the famous American director. I think Jacobson is in danger of reviewing the film he would have made, instead of the film that Stone, for better or worse, has made.

Stone does, for the record, ask some hard questions—about Cuban torturers in Hanoi, about prejudice against blacks and homosexuals in Cuba, about political prisoners. Castro's answers are masterful in the way they rephrase and deflect. Most fascinating is their conversation about the Cuban missile crisis, which in Castro's eyes was a Big Powers chess game with unsophisticated Cuba caught in the middle.

Commandante is one of ten films I've seen so far at Sundance 2003, although as usual the buzz suggests I've missed some key titles. I'm playing catch-up today, abandoning my plans in order to attend screenings of movies that everybody's talking about. You plan your screenings and then buzz sweeps them away.

Here are some of the highlights, and otherwise, of the first four days:

Aidan Quinn, the Chicagoan who now works frequently in Ireland, is here with the angry, moving *Song for a Raggy Boy*, directed by Aisling Walsh. His performance is direct and strong, a rebuke to the usual wimpy teachers in school stories. Set in 1939 at a church-run Irish reformatory school for young boys, it stars Quinn as a lay teacher, an idealistic veteran of the Spanish civil war, where he lost the woman he loved. Now he faces a horrifying situation of brutality and sexual abuse; the genial, compromising priest in charge is intimidated by another priest, a sadistic disciplinarian. Arriving hard on the heels of *The Magdalene Sisters*, another attack on Irish church institutions, it continues the rewriting of Irish history. If Bill Donohue of the Catholic League hated the earlier film, he will implode after this one.

David Gordon Green's *George Washington* was one of the best films of 2000. Now, at only twenty-seven, he's back with the stylistically similar *All the Real Girls*, set in the industrial landscapes of a North Carolina mill town and watching and listening with a special lyrical intensity to the love affair between Paul (Paul Schneider) and Noel (Zooey Deschanel), who feel their love is special and yet are doomed to test it. Green has a gift for moments of acute observation, for dialogue both naturalistic and uninflected, for mood over plot, for poetry over prose. It's a lovely film.

After the screening of Thomas Vinterberg's *It's All About Love*, a woman in the audience stood up and asked him to forgive her, but "I don't have a clue what the movie is about. Can you explain it, so I know what to say to my friends?" Vinterberg, one of the founders of the Dogma movement and the director of the powerful *Celebration*, was not pleased. "The film speaks for itself," he said.

Alas, it does not. It is a murky, slow, boring, and pointless parable set in the near future, when there is a global ice age and other strange phenomena, like hearts that stop because of love, and Ugandans who suddenly begin to fly. The lead character, played by Claire Danes, is an ice-skater who is about to be replaced by doubles. Not since Robert Altman's *Quintet*, also set in snow and ice and in the future, has there been such an inexplicable film by an important director.

Dopamine, directed by Mark Decena, is set amid the ashes of the dot.com boom in San Francisco, where a computer programmer (John Livingston) attempts to create an animated bird that will become a child's loyal friend. He meets a young woman (Sabrina Lloyd) at a bar one night, and again when she's the teacher in a classroom where he tests his little bird. They fall in love, but does he want a love that is unquestioning and loyal and programmed by him? The movie has a sweet offhand romantic tone, in which old-fashioned notions of love encounter the alienation of demanding occupations.

Of *dot the i*, the film by Matthew Parkhill, I can only say that it has several twists too many. It begins as a perfectly good, indeed engrossing, love story involving a Brazilian (Gael Garcia Bernal of *Y Tu Mama Tambien*) and a Spaniard (Natalia Verbeke), who Meet Cute in a London restaurant and fall in love during the last week before her planned marriage to the rich Brit James d'Arcy. This story, followed through to the end, would have been enough, especially with its witty parallels to *The Graduate.* But then Parkhill makes a U-turn into one of those plots where everything has to be reevaluated and nothing is as it seems. A summation during which d'Arcy explains, or doesn't explain, is relentless in its endless detail.

Confidence is the new film by James Foley (*At Close Range, Glengarry Glen Ross*). It's about a con game, masterminded by Edward Burns and enlisting Rachel Weisz, Paul Giamatti, Andy Garcia, Luis Guzman, and, in a supercharged cameo, Dustin Hoffman as a porn king and bookie with ADD.

It's a well-made commercial film, but the question I had as I watched the movie was— why is it at Sundance? It's a big-budget caper picture with well-known stars, and will be released to thousands of theaters. Isn't Sundance supposed to be a showcase for the independent cinema? Are the evening premieres in the big Eccles Center being skewed toward higher-profile movies? I depart now for the auditorium of the Park City Library, a less glamorous venue, to see two of those films I've heard so much about.

Sundance Report No. 5

January 21, 2003—"I've worked hard to stay in shape," William H. Macy was saying, "but who would have guessed my first love scene would come when I was fifty?"

He grinned that William H. Macy grin, rueful, surprised, like a kid who got away with something. He was answering questions after the Sundance screening of *The Cooler,* a film in which he plays Bernie Lootz, a man with such bad luck that casino boss Alec Baldwin hires him to simply stand next to gamblers on a winning streak. That's all it takes.

The movie combines elements of *Casino* with the flip side of *Leaving Las Vegas.* We get a lot of backstage casino lore, but this time when the loser meets the hooker, it's true love. Maria Bello costars as Natalie, a casino waitress who starts dating him for her own reasons, but stays because, to her amazement, she's head over heels. That's when Bernie's luck changes.

The movie, directed by Wayne Kramer, combines fantasy elements involving luck with a hard-edged portrait of a vicious casino boss, played by Alec Baldwin in a performance that makes the guy oily, hateful, and somehow plucky—he's holding out for old-style Vegas in the face of modern times. The new money guys don't even believe in coolers.

The Cooler was the first film I saw Monday during a day of catch-up, going to movies with big buzz. Since most Sundance movies arrive unseen by anyone except the selection committee, you get accurate tips just by listening to people. I walked into the Eccles Center, for example, just as *Pieces of April* was getting out, and twenty people told me they loved it. So there I was at the second screening, in the auditorium of the Park City Library.

This one is a honey. One distributor told me with lust in her voice, "I could make this into the next *Greek Wedding.*" Well, maybe. The film takes place on Thanksgiving, as April (Katie Holmes) and her boyfriend Bobby (Derek Luke) prepare Thanksgiving dinner for her family, who are driving into the city. As she desperately tries to borrow a stove for her turkey, we follow the progress of the family: father Oliver Platt, mother Patricia Clarkson, younger brother, and grandma with Alzheimer's.

The key to the film is that everyone in it is basically nice, and a little crazy, especially the Clarkson character, who is fighting breast cancer and uses that as an opportunity to get laughs. At one point she urgently tells her husband to pull over, and says she has to make a big announcement. "We all have to give a lot of thought," she says, and they think she'll talk about her possible death, but she finishes, "to how we are going to hide the food we don't eat."

Nobody has any confidence in April's cooking, and the scene where she and Bobby stuff the turkey is some kind of a classic. Derek Luke plays Bobby as a nice guy, saner than April, and this film, coming after his work as *Antwone Fisher,* shows his range: He'll be a star. "I'm still living the dream," he told me in the library corridor. "Don't wake up," I advised him.

Neil LaBute came to fame with the Sundance premiere of his great first film *In the Company of Men* (1997), and is back this year with *The Shape of Things.* The earlier film was about a man playing a cruel joke on a woman. This one, which is otherwise totally different, is about a woman playing a cruel joke on a man. Based on a play LaBute wrote and directed in

London, the movie is about two couples: Adam and Evelyn (Paul Rudd and Rachel Weisz) and Phil and Jenny (Fred Weller and Gretchen Mol). They attend college together, where Adam and Phil were former but polar opposite roommates. Adam, overweight and unkempt, starts dating the daring Evelyn; their Meet Cute takes place in a museum where Adam is a guard and Evelyn wants to spray paint a penis on the fig leaf of a statue.

Soon they're in love, and she is transforming him. She makes him lose weight, get a nose job, and throw away the cord jacket he's been wearing since he was a freshman. But she clashes with Phil, a loose screw who hates her on sight (he wants to marry Jenny underwater, in scuba gear). All of this seems like the setup for a campus comedy, but not in the world of Neil LaBute, where the sexes have arrived at Armageddon, and the last act involves pain and humiliation. Once again LaBute proves himself one of the most literate, penetrating, and darkly humorous of directors.

Sundance Report No. 6

January 21, 2003—A story of two encounters, one with a man whose work I love, another with a man whose work I am in violent disagreement with.

Encounter One. I ran into Steve James, whose *Hoop Dreams* is one of the best documentaries ever made, in the back row at the Park City Library. He's here with his new doc, *Stevie*, which I saw and admired at Toronto, and which is a big success here—the story of his return to visit a troubled downstate Illinois kid whom he was Big Brother to years earlier. How has Stevie turned out? Not well, it seems.

James was brimming with good cheer. His film has been picked up by Lions Gate for distribution, and short-listed in the doc category for the Academy Awards. Considering that *Hoop Dreams,* the greatest doc of recent years, was turned off after fifteen minutes by the obtuse Academy selection committee, this is sweet revenge.

Steve was back a minute later with an update that explains how buzz works at Sundance. "I just ran into one of the van drivers," he said. "The guy told me he has driven two vanloads of people who had just seen *Stevie,* and they liked it so much he just bought a ticket for himself."

Encounter Two. Bill Aho lives in Salt Lake City, but he is a candidate for the most hated man in Hollywood. He's the CEO of ClearPlay, a software company that offers a product that sits between you and a DVD, skipping some scenes and muting certain words. In theory, this software is simply navigational, but in practice it enables censorship: An editor goes through an R-rated movie, say, and skips all the sex and violence and bleeps all the four-letter words.

Aho is being sued by major studios and the Directors Guild, who claim his software is a violation of artists' rights and copyright law. He asked what I thought of it. I said I was against it: Movie viewers should either see a movie or not see it, but the filmmakers have a right for it to be presented as they made it.

"But what if a critic says the first half of a movie is good, but skip the second half?" he asked.

"Fine," I said. "Then it's a matter of opinion. You can always switch off a DVD."

"But we are just doing it for you," he said.

"If I do it myself, it's a matter of choice," I said, "but if you do it, you're a censor and a parasite, living off someone else's work."

He flinched. "I don't like that characterization," he said. I kind of regretted it myself, since he seemed like a nice guy. But I love movies too much to ever accept ClearPlay. Let younger viewers see movies intended for them. When they are adults, let them decide. Of what purpose is a version of *Gangs of New York* consisting of people getting ready to do things, and standing around after they have done them, with their lips moving but no sounds coming out?

Sundance Report No. 7: Bob Dylan

January 23, 2003—"Do you consider yourself a photographer?" asked Tom Bernard. He is the cohoncho of Sony Classics.

I held up my camera and shrugged.

"Good," he said, "Dylan wants a photographer backstage right now. Come with me."

This is like hearing that George Bush wants to meet a liberal. While photographers for *People, Entertainment Weekly,* and *Premiere* were surging against the barricades, Bernard led me backstage to the Green Room at the big Eccles Center.

There are two premieres every night at Eccles. Big stars come and go. Only Bob Dylan inspired a media riot. His new movie, *Masked and Anonymous*, was premiering, and two days earlier the volunteer ushers were warning me, "It's gonna be crazy."

Consider. Dylan has never made a hit feature. He is indeed the fountainhead of half the popular music of the last four decades, but the flow has long since reached the sea. Yet it's clear he's the biggest star at Sundance.

Bernard and I made our way through the backstage gloom to the Green Room. The door opened. I looked inside and it was like a Jack Davis drawing for *Mad* magazine—one of those drawings where dozens of stars elbow each other for floor space.

I saw (in alphabetical order) Penelope Cruz, Bob Dylan, John Goodman, Daryl Hannah, Laura Elena Harring, Val Kilmer, Jessica Lange, Mickey Rourke, Christian Slater, and Luke Wilson. All but Hannah appear in the movie. A star-studded cast, you say? Ah, but the movie *also* stars (in alphabetical order) Jeff Bridges, Angela Bassett, Steven Bauer, Bruce Dern, Ed Harris, Shawn Michael Howard, Reggie Lee, Cheech Marin, and Chris Penn.

Alas, Bob Dylan's need for a photographer was no longer operational. Geoffrey Gilmore, director of the festival, asked the group to leave for the auditorium, and as they filed past me I looked through my viewfinder for Dylan, but could not find him. I did, however, get photos of Daryl Hannah, Penelope Cruz, and Laura Elena Harring, which was considerable consolation.

In the wings of the stage, I finally found Dylan, his hair falling down from within a Billabong knit hat. He wore a leather jacket and a winter scarf, and looked as happy as a man unexpectedly delayed on his way to his execution.

As director Larry Charles of *Seinfeld* fame introduced his cast, there was applause for everyone—the atmosphere was electric—but a roar and then a *standing ovation* for Dylan, before the movie had even started. Then we all settled in to watch what Charles described as "a work in progress."

It's a work, all right, but progress eludes it. Dylan stars as Jack Fate, a singer once famous, now on the skids, who is recruited by promoter John Goodman to do a benefit concert in a war zone of a Third World nation (downtown Los Angeles supplied the locations).

Dylan travels to the concert by bus, wearing a quasi-military uniform that looks like a khaki version of a Michael Jackson castoff. Once there, he is plunged into a plot involving Angela Bassett as his father's former lover, Jeff Bridges as an insulting journalist, Penelope Cruz as Bridges's wife, and Jessica Lange as Goodman's assistant or wife, I'm not sure which, who is another example of the movie character who is required to smoke all the time in every single scene, as a trait. No one else in the movie smokes at all.

Masked and Anonymous can be described as homage, if you are a Dylan fan, or idolatry, if you are not. His character is treated by all the others as an awesome legend. He occupies his scenes like a judge, gazing at the others as if measuring their worthiness to share the frame with him.

How is Dylan as an actor? It is impossible to tell, because he never has dialogue that is more than one sentence in length, never engages in actual conversation with any of the others, and looks enigmatic and/or ridiculous in a second braided and buttoned Michael Jackson castoff and an oversize cowboy hat. A similar costume might be appropriate for the band members at an impoverished southwestern high school.

Charles uses an unvarying strategy to shoot Dylan: Let Goodman, for example, fulminate and expostulate; cut to Dylan; Dylan utters enigmatic one-liner; cut away. Occasionally this format is interrupted by Dylan deadpanning a song, and the songs are indeed good to hear, although it is a little puzzling why he thinks a revolutionary war zone in the Third World needs to hear "Dixie."

Masked and Anonymous is one of the oddest movies I have ever seen. Obviously everyone involved in it was besotted, if not mesmerized, by Dylan. All of those big stars must have agreed to their cameos because this was Dylan's first dramatic role since—I dunno, Sam Peckinpah's *Pat Garrett and Billy the Kid* (1973). It's a little sad to see them acting their hearts away in scenes where Dylan sits there like a toad, impassive, unmoving, oracular, waiting for the close-up in which he utters yet another oblique epigram.

The thing that comes across is his lack of

generosity. If the party is in your honor, you should make an effort to have a good time. Dylan seems to be appearing as a favor. Whether he wrote his dialogue or someone else did, he might have suggested that Jack Fate be given more dimension, more depth, more humanity, more . . . words.

As the Goodman character prepares for the big benefit concert, he introduces Jack Fate's warm-up acts, which include a magician, a "rubber woman," a ventriloquist, and celebrity look-alikes of the pope, Abraham Lincoln, and Gandhi. These last three stand around pointlessly. How much wiser if a celebrity look-alike of Dylan had also been used, and Jack Fate had been portrayed by somebody who came to play.

Sundance Report No. 8

January 24, 2003—Now the buzz has taken over and I am seeing mostly good, sometimes great, films. You open the Sundance catalog on the first day of the festival and choose your films for the first weekend, and after that you go where the buzz sends you, because audiences are always honest. The best rule of Sundance: Ignore the hype, believe the buzz.

With *American Splendor*, the buzz started even before Sundance, and with reason. This one is plain brilliant. It tells the story of Harvey Pekar, who you may vaguely remember as David Letterman's most obstreperous guest in the 1980s. He works as a file clerk and writes comic books based on his own boring life and suspicious personality, which are illustrated by the great R. Crumb and have become classics. He even finds a bride, as dubious about life as he is.

The film does something I have never seen before, and does it with perfect effect. It combines fictional scenes starring Paul Giamatti as Pekar, with documentary scenes starring Pekar himself. His wife, Joyce, is portrayed both by Hope Davis and by herself, and the story unfolds not only as fiction and fact, but also as animation and voice-over narration. We even see the actual Letterman segments. Sounds like a gimmick, but the result, in this film by Shari Springer Berman and Robert Pulcini, is a funny, quirky biopic of astonishing originality.

Another masterpiece: *Northfork*, by the Pol-

ish brothers. Michael directed, Mark acted, they coproduced and cowrote, and the result is a visionary epic set in Montana in the 1950s, where a town is about to be buried forever beneath the waters of a dam. The movie is a haunting parable, in which angels visit the town, one of its little boys becomes an angel, and six men with black overcoats, black fedoras, and black autos go on their grim rounds, evicting the residents who refuse to leave. (One local has built an ark around his house.)

This is a ghostly, evocative movie that works with visuals, oblique dialogue, and sad symbolism to evoke a mood—in this case, a great sadness about the town that will soon haunt the bottom of a lake. Nick Nolte stars as a preacher who stays behind with the dying boy, Daryl Hannah is an androgynous angel, James Woods is one of the eviction agents going implacably on his rounds. After *Twin Falls, Idaho*, more evidence that the Polish twins are the real thing.

There was no movie at Sundance I enjoyed more, in a pure movie way, than Gurinder Chadha's *Bend It Like Beckham*. It stars the lithe, athletic, joyous Parminder Nagra as Jess, the daughter of a traditional Indian family living in London. Her parents want her to go to college and marry a nice boy, preferably Sikh. She wants to play professional women's soccer, and has troubling romantic feelings about the young Irish man who coaches the team. Indian family life is seen in exuberant richness (yes, there is a wedding and lots of dancing), in a movie that shamelessly combines melodrama, romance, comedy, and sports. Pure exuberant fun.

One of the great performances this year is by Philip Seymour Hoffman in *Owning Mahowny*. He plays a Toronto bank clerk, engaged to a teller played by Minnie Driver; in his secret life he is a compulsive gambler. We watch in horrified fascination as a $1,300 debt grows to $10.2 million, as he steals money from the bank to try to gamble his way out of debt. John Hurt plays the professional but quirky Atlantic City casino manager who watches, fascinated, as this strange nebbishy man arrives with larger and larger piles of cash; there is a sequence involving a winning streak that's among the most gripping gambling scenes ever filmed.

"That does it," said the woman in front of me after *Thirteen* was over. "I'm not having kids." This is one of the buzz champs of Sundance, the story of a thirteen-year-old teenager (Evan Rachel Wood) who is hurtled into a life of shoplifting, smoking, drinking, piercing, drugs, and older boys, under the influence of her new friend (Nikki Reed). Her mother (Holly Hunter), a recovering alcoholic and addict, is sincere and loving, but doesn't understand how quickly her daughter's life is changing.

The most astonishing thing about the movie: It was cowritten by the director, Catherine Hardwicke, with Nikki Reed herself. They met when Hardwicke started dating the girl's father. Nikki was troubled, and the older woman suggested she write something about her life, little suspecting that this harrowing story would emerge. Nikki Reed, who proves herself not only a writer but an actor of remarkable power and energy, is now fourteen.

Capturing the Friedmans is a documentary about a Great Neck, Long Island, family that is devastated in the 1980s when both the father and one of his three sons are charged with sexually molesting minors. What is remarkable is that another son obsessively videotaped the whole experience at the time. His camera is so omnipresent his family forgets it, as we watch family fights, strategy sessions with lawyers, everyday life, and the last nights of freedom for the two men. The trials were among the first to be televised, so the film uses that footage, too—and yet, knowing so much, even being inside the family, we can't decide if the teenage son is guilty.

Rhythm of the Saints is about another troubled family, and this time the occult arts come into play. The rising star Daniella Alonso stars as a lively teenage beauty from Washington Heights, whose mother (Sarita Choudhury) works nights—giving her boyfriend opportunity to molest the daughter. The girl and her friends consult practitioners of the voodoo arts of Haiti to cast a spell on the molester, in a plot that turns out to be a lot more complicated than that. Touching performances from Choudhury and Alonso, who look remarkably like mother and daughter.

Another movie Sundance audiences love is *The Station Agent,* starring Peter Dinklage as a dwarf railroad buff who inherits an old train station in the wilds of New Jersey. Moving in, he meets a nearby divorcée (Patricia Clarkson) and a goofy, lonely guy who runs a hot dog wagon (Bobby Cannavale). Dinklage plays a silent loner, the hot dog man is compulsively nosy, and the divorcée is a sweetheart who carries a deep sadness. Dinklage provides a rare movie portrait of a little person seen seriously and with perception.

Sundance Report No. 9

January 27, 2003—Wrapping up the final films I saw at Sundance this year:

The technical writer lives in the basement of the apartment building like a reclusive subterranean species, chain-smoking and typing arcane instructions for the operation of unnamed devices. He never leaves the building. He is friendly with a dying woman and on speaking terms with the desk clerk, and that is all, and it is enough. Then the swingers move in upstairs.

Scott Saunders's *The Technical Writer,* a strange and haunting Sundance entry, is more character study than story. Michael Harris stars as the writer, unkempt, bearded, hostile. Pamela Gordon is the dying woman, and Tatum O'Neal and William Forsythe are the swingers. Oh, and another apartment contains two Russian prostitutes. Eventually, not without difficulty, O'Neal lures him out of the building and then into her bed, but this isn't one of those simplistic movies in which sex is the answer, or even the question. The movie has more to do with loneliness, tenderness, and finding something to be true to.

Alan Rudolph's *The Secret Lives of Dentists* has some of the same themes. Campbell Scott and Hope Davis star as dentists, married to each other and with three children, the youngest one going through a stage where she hates her mother. By accident Scott discovers that his wife is apparently having an affair, and this begins a long, uneasy period in which this fact hovers over their marriage. He refuses to confront her, because that would open the whole can of worms: separation, divorce, custody, alimony. So they communicate by silences and absences, and meanwhile a laconic fantasy figure (Denis Leary) gives Scott harsh advice from the underside of his id. Based on Jane Smiley's novel *The Age of Grief,* the movie is acute in the way it shows two long-married people communicating by the very fact of non-communication.

Camp is one of the audience favorites this year; the musical numbers are applauded by the audience. It takes place at an upstate New York camp for gifted young performers, some of them gay, who put on shows and a benefit, and jockey for plum roles and compliments. A straight boy gets a gay boy as his roommate, and asks him if he has ever experimented with heterosexual sex. The gay kid asks, "You mean have sex with a straight guy?" The plot is intercut with musical numbers, remarkably well performed, and if the love stories are predictable, the energy level is high and there is little question some of these performers will actually make it to Broadway.

Perhaps representing a return of the musical, in a year when *Chicago* seems destined for the top Oscar, Alex Proyas's *Garage Days* is a visually exuberant, high-spirited story from Australia about Sydney wannabes who form a rock band. Their sex lives are infinitely more tangled than the kids' in *Camp,* but then they're a little older and more worn and, as one admits, not very good. But they love their music, and Proyas *(Dark City)* uses dazzling graphics and special effects to underline, subvert, and kid their stories.

Ernest Dickerson, whose *Our America* was one of the best of last year's films, is back with *Good Fences,* where Danny Glover and Whoopi Goldberg star in what begins as a suburban comedy and then takes a U-turn to the dark side. Glover is a successful lawyer, later a judge, who with his wife integrates an all-white neighborhood in Greenwich, Connecticut All goes well until a black welfare queen from Florida buys the house next door, testing their values and, in Glover's case, his sanity. The light tone of the early scenes makes the movie's turn to tragedy rather startling; Goldberg makes the transition successfully, but Glover's character is so oddly written that all he can do is struggle. The movie plays next month on Showtime.

Buffalo Soldiers was set for release in the autumn of 2001, but was yanked by Miramax after 9/11. Set in West Germany right before the fall of the Berlin Wall, it stars Joaquin Phoenix as an ambitious young GI who heads a ring of black marketeers and drug dealers on a U.S. Army base. Scott Glenn is the hard-bitten top sergeant who makes life impossible for him after the kid starts dating the sergeant's daughter (Anna Paquin). Of course, he's also having an affair with the wife (Elizabeth McGovern) of his commanding officer (Ed Harris). True, the movie is not patriotic in its view of greedy slackers in the peacetime army, but it is hardly political enough to deserve the water bottle that was hurled at the cast by an angry audience member after the screening. Those who do not want to hear bad news are often the angriest when it comes.

And now the 2003 Sundance festival is over and it is time for melancholy list-making. I've seen more than thirty films, but I did not see *In America, Soldier's Girl, Whale Rider, Bukowski: Born Into This, The Weather Underground, Off the Map, Laurel Canyon, The Murder of Emmett Till, Normal, Raising Victor Vargas,* or *A Decade Under the Influence,* all films I have been reliably assured I absolutely should have seen. Four movies a day is more or less my capacity, and there must also be time for interviewing, writing, eating, and not getting enough sleep.

Sundance Report No. 10: The Winners

January 27, 2003—*American Splendor,* a brilliant hybrid of fiction and documentary, won the Grand Prize here Saturday as the best feature in the 2003 Sundance Film Festival. The movie, directed by Shari Springer Berman and Robert Pulcini, tells the story of a Cleveland file clerk named Harvey Pekar, who wrote a famous series of comic books documenting his boring life and discontented psyche. His books eventually made him a favorite guest on the David Letterman program in the 1980s, until he wore out his welcome with unscripted criticisms of the show.

The movie stars Paul Giamatti and Hope Davis as Pekar and his wife, Joyce, who eventually wrote comics of her own. It also features the real Mr. and Mrs. Pekar, playing themselves. The story moves seamlessly between fact and fiction, allowing us for the first time to judge biopic performances by a side-by-side comparison with the people who inspired them.

The grand prize in the documentary category went to another hybrid, Andrew Jarecki's *Capturing the Friedmans,* which tells the story of a Great Neck, Long Island, family devastated when the father and a teenage son were both convicted of child sexual abuse. Another son consistently videotaped his family, even during fights and strategy sessions, and this footage from the 1980s is combined with recent documentary footage to explore the guilt or innocence of its subjects.

The Sundance Audience Awards are based on votes by filmgoers. *The Station Agent,* by Tom McCarthy, won as favorite fiction film with its story of a dwarf (Peter Dinklage) who inherits an abandoned train station and meets a nearby divorcée (Patricia Clarkson) and a talkative hot dog vendor (Bobby Cannavale). Among the docs, the audience voted for *My Flesh and Blood,* by Jonathan Karsh, which tells the story of an adoptive mother named Susan Tom and her eleven children with special needs.

The new World Cinema Audience Award for a foreign film went to Niki Caro's *Whale Rider,* from New Zealand, about a hereditary chief who dies, leaving not a son but a daughter to lead the tribe.

Awards for best direction went to Catherine Hardwicke for *Thirteen,* which starred Holly Hunter as a mother faced with a daughter who is growing up with alarming recklessness, and to Jonathan Karsh, for *My Flesh and Blood.*

Patricia Clarkson won a special jury prize for her outstanding performances in *The Station Agent, Pieces of April,* and *All the Real Girls.* Charles Busch was honored for his drag performance in *Die Mommie Die.*

Chicagoans Dana Kupper, Gordon Quinn, and Peter Gilbert of Kartemquin Films won the cinematography award for their work in Steve James's *Stevie,* the story of James's search for a troubled boy he once mentored. Many of the same filmmakers were involved in the great documentary *Hoop Dreams.* Kupper's advice to new doc photographers: "When in doubt, zoom out." In the dramatic category, best cinematography went to Derek Cianfrance for his work on the street-racing picture *Quattro Noza.*

A prison writing workshop inspired *What I Want My Words to Do for You,* which won the Freedom of Expression Award. The Waldo Salt Screenwriting Award went to Tom McCarthy, for *The Station Agent.*

The jury honored *All the Real Girls,* by David Gordon Green *(George Washington),* and *What Alice Found,* by A. Dean Bell, "for their emotional truth."

Special jury prizes went to two other docs, Stanley Nelson's *The Murder of Emmett Till,* about the Chicago boy killed by Southern racists, and Blue Hedaegh and Grover Babcock's *A Certain Kind of Death,* about unclaimed bodies. Nelson paid tribute to Emmett's mother, Mamie, who worked with the filmmakers but did not live to see the film.

The prize for best short film went to *Terminal Bar,* by Stefen Nadelman, who pressed a tape of the film into my hands after the ceremony. I viewed it half an hour later, and was fascinated by its portrait of "the toughest bar in New York," which used to be across from the Port Authority bus terminal at 8th Avenue and 42d Street. Nadelman's father tended bar there for ten years, making a photographic record of hundreds of regulars. The father's flat, amused, but detached descriptions of the scene and his photographs are like a textbook on applied alcoholism.

Overlooked Film Festival

Champaign, Illinois, April 23, 2003—Five years ago we unveiled a new film festival that was still in the process of inventing itself. What did "overlooked" mean, anyway? It was clear that it honored films that had not received the attention they deserved. But it could also include formats (70-mm, Todd AO Vision), periods (the silent era), and genres (documentaries, animé, musicals) that had been overlooked. It was best to allow the word "overlooked" to remain flexible.

Now we are back in the Virginia Theater for our fifth anniversary. Joining us are friends from that first festival—Scott and Heavenly Wilson, who were here for the screening of *Shiloh* and are back for the screening of *The Right Stuff.* Also back again are the brilliant and tireless Nancy Casey, festival executive producer; Professor Nate Kohn, festival director; Nickie Dalton, festival manager; and assistant director Mary Susan Britt. In the booth again are our world-class projection experts, James Bond and Steve Kraus. And the festival would be impossible without the skilled staff of the Virginia Theater and our valued volunteers. My gratitude also to Dean Kim Rotzoll of the College of Communications, who with Dean Casey first approached me with the idea of the festival.

We also welcome back our audiences, who think nothing of four films a day. Some have even asked me if a midnight screening is possible. Actually, this year we tried—we really tried—to scale back to three screenings on Thursday and Friday, but as Nate Kohn and I debated various rundowns we found we simply could not bear to trim even one film from our lineup.

This year's films come from a variety of inspirations. We will be showing the trailers from the 2002 Karlovy Vary Film Festival, in the Czech Republic. I served on their jury last summer, and my wife, Chaz, and I joined the hilarity as they played. So infectious were the trailers that on closing night the jury actually danced onstage while singing the trailer song. (By the way, the three performers are not professional actors but were technicians attached to the festival.)

In a festival celebrating the "overlooked," we have found a form of film preservation most audiences will not even have heard of: the Japanese tradition of the "benshi," or simultaneous commentator. I learned about benshis from a book by Professor David Bordwell, the famed film scholar from the University of Wisconsin, who is an Overlooked guest this year. In the Japanese silent era, the benshi stood next to the screen and interpreted the dialogue and action in a parallel performance that was as popular as the film itself; benshis headlined their own theaters. If benshis are overlooked, what could be more overlooked than a Mexican benshi performance? Festival director Nate Kohn discovered Claudio Valdes Kurl, a Mexican theater director who has adapted *The Grey Automobile,* a Mexican silent film about a real-life gang, into a benshi performance including live actors who work in Japanese, Spanish, and English, with startling sound effects. Bordwell

will join the artists and me in the onstage discussion of this transfer of the benshi tradition from one culture to another.

Speaking of silent films, when I am in Los Angeles I like to go to the Silent Film Theater on Fairfax Avenue, where Charlie Lustman introduces the films and during the intermission serves his mother's cookies. Lustman will host our Saturday morning matinee of sparkling 35-mm prints of silent comedy classics by Lloyd, Keaton, Chaplin, Laurel and Hardy, and the Little Rascals. Performing on the Virginia's organ will be the renowned silent accompanist Dean Mora.

Another silent program will welcome back the Alloy Orchestra of Cambridge, Massachusetts, specialists in performing the scores of silent films. This year they're bringing us Douglas Fairbanks in *The Black Pirate* (1926), an early experiment in two-strip Technicolor (an overlooked format!).

With three silent programs this year, it is only appropriate that our traditional Sunday afternoon musical be *Singin' in the Rain,* the greatest of all Hollywood musicals, which is about the transition from silents to talkies. How is it "overlooked"? Simply that in its fiftieth anniversary year, with a brilliant new 35-mm restored print, it would be a crime to overlook it. We will have its great star Donald O'Connor (of Danville, Illinois) onstage for a tribute afterward.

Other films were found in various ways. I discovered Bertrand Tavernier's *L.627* at the 1992 Telluride festival, where he has been a regular guest and programmer for many years. I met Tavernier in 1976 at the Chicago festival, where his first film, *The Clockmaker,* made a deep impression, and have watched him become the leading filmmaker from France while always maintaining a direct and personal enthusiasm for movies. Few people are more knowledgeable about film.

His *L.627,* made with deep personal motives, examines the dilemma of unenforceable drug laws in a time of unacceptable and rising drug abuse. It is as relevant in America as in France, and offers not easy answers but a penetrating examination of the human issues involved. The "drug movie" has become a Hollywood genre, all about guns and chases and ironic dialogue, all completely missing the point. *L.627* looks at drugs with accuracy, sadness, and anger. A great film.

Haskell Wexler I have known even longer than Tavernier; I met him in Chicago in 1968 when he was filming *Medium Cool.* Its message of protest in a time of political turmoil is as relevant today as it was then. He is, of course, one of the world's greatest cinematographers, winner of two Oscars, nominated for five, but more important, he is a man of conscience and commitment. We are also graced by his wife, the gifted actress Rita Taggart, whose sense of humor makes her a living national treasure.

I found *Charlotte Sometimes* at the 2002 Hawaii Film Festival, and was amazed by its artistry. Its story of gender and racial issues is all the more challenging because handled in such a subtle way. Although it still seeks distribution, its power was acknowledged by the Independent Spirit Awards (the "indie Oscars"), where it was nominated for the John Cassavetes Award, and Jacqueline Kim was nominated as best supporting actress. Director Eric Byler, Miss Kim, Michael Idemoto, and John Manulis will join us after the screening.

Also at this year's Indie Spirits, I met director Jill Sprecher and cowriter Karen Sprecher, whose *13 Conversations About One Thing* was on my list of the best films of 2002. They were nominated for best screenplay, and Alan Arkin for best supporting actor. I love the way their story loops through its characters, not as a Tarantinesque stunt, but as a demonstration of how ethical decisions have a ripple effect on the lives we touch. The Sprecher sisters will join us onstage.

And standing next to me as I chatted with the Sprechers was Robert Goodman, producer of another Overlooked entry, *The Stone Reader.* This is a documentary that graduate students were born to see. The story of director Mark Moskowitz's years-long search for the author of a great 1972 novel, it leads down a long trail of literary critics, agents, and publishers to finally end at a family home in Cedar Rapids, Iowa. The author of *The Stones of Summer,* Dow Mossman, will join us onstage with Moskowitz, as will Jeff Lipsky.

From the moment I saw Neil LaBute's *In the Company of Men* at the 1997 Sundance Film Festival, I knew that a great new American writer-director had emerged. His *Your Friends and Neighbors* (1998) is the flowering of the pitiless critique he makes of modern manners and mores. His characters are materialistic, selfish, and narcissistic, and yet feel good about themselves, because they live up to the shabby values of their environment. The *New Statesman* recently wrote that no playwright in the world today is doing better work than Neil LaBute; he will join us after his film.

I was in the audience at the New York Film Festival for the world premiere of Bob Rafelson's *Five Easy Pieces,* and more than thirty years later I wrote of that experience: "This was the direction American movies should take: into idiosyncratic characters, into dialogue with an ear for the vulgar and the literate, into a plot free to surprise us about the characters, into an existential ending not required to be happy. *Five Easy Pieces* was a fusion of the personal cinema of John Cassavetes and the new indie movement that was tentatively emerging. It was, you could say, the first Sundance film." Since then, Rafelson has remained on the cutting edge, and his *Blood and Wine* (1997) struck me as a reinvention and reinvigoration of the crime genre. Jack Nicholson, working for the fourth time with Rafelson, and Michael Caine, with his unforgettable steadfastness in the face of death, and Jennifer Lopez, in her second major role, work without a net and handle hard scenes like easy pieces. Rafelson will join us after the screening.

And, we learn, he spent time as a young man working in the Japanese film industry, and will be a resource for our Japanese programs. They include *Shall We Dance?,* Masayuki Suo's 1997 film that begins in existential loneliness, edges into comedy, and ends by celebrating universal human nature. This is the kind of foreign film that makes me want to grab people and shake them, and say, "You don't know what you're missing!"

I decided to invite Gurinder Chadha's *What's Cooking?* at a specific time and place—during the closing credits of her new film *Bend It Like Beckham,* at the 2003 Sundance Film Festival. She led her cast and crew in a jolly singalong during the credits, and I realized that although I may have seen deeper and more profound films at Sundance, I had not seen one that was more purely enjoyable.

What's Cooking? is no less fun but emotionally deeper; an affirmation of the American melting pot in the story of Thanksgiving feasts prepared by four families: African-American, Jewish, Latino, and Vietnamese. What is remarkable is how much drama and truth she finds in each of her four stories, how her film is not just a comic round-robin but a thoughtful story about who we are and why we give thanks. In this time of national emergency, we need films like this more than ever.

That brings us to our curtain-raiser, the opening-night film, Phil Kaufman's *The Right Stuff* (1983). This is one of the great modern American films; I put it first on my list of the year's top ten. When it opened, everyone expected it to become a box office sensation, but,

inexplicably, it did not find a large audience. Why not? Some said a newsweekly cover, linking it to the presidential campaign of John Glenn, confused people, who thought it was about politics. But how many people make their moviegoing decisions based on *Newsweek* covers?

The Right Stuff, the story of America's first steps into space, has since found wide audiences on home video, but this is a movie that shouts out to be seen on a big screen—and the Virginia's vast expanse will show us the epic as it was intended to be seen, thanks to a pristine new print from Warner Bros. Scott Wilson, who plays test pilot Scott Crossfield, the archrival of Chuck Yeager, will join us onstage, once again helping us launch a festival that gets less overlooked every year.

Cannes Film Festival
Cannes Report No. 1

Cannes, France, May 14, 2003—Music from the films of Fellini floats over the Cannes Film Festival from speakers along the beachfront. It is bittersweet and a little nostalgic, and that reflects the mood as this fifty-sixth festival opens. There are no doubt masterpieces concealed among the official entries, but excitement is muted as the festival opens, and the high point looks to be the world premiere of Clint Eastwood's *Mystic River.* It's rumored the Sean Penn performance is Oscar material.

Eastwood, of course, is a Cannes favorite; the crowds screaming "Cleent! Cleent!" during his appearance here with *White Hunter, Black Heart* in 1990 were matched in enthusiasm only by the mobs when Jimmy Stewart visited for the revival of *The Glenn Miller Story.* Whether Eastwood will be as rapturously received in these days of French anti-Americanism is a good question, but probably so: At Cannes, Hollywood is considered an independent nation properly appreciated only by the French.

This is the year when many of the films Cannes hoped for were not ready on time, and the Official Selection bears certain signs of being the Official Compromise. Nevertheless, there are some films I eagerly anticipate, not least: *The Fog of War,* the new documentary by

Errol Morris about, and with the participation of, former secretary of defense Robert McNamara; *Dogville,* Lars von Trier's three-hour drama with Nicole Kidman as a fugitive on the run; Gus van Sant's *Elephant,* which begins on an ordinary day in an American high school; Francois Ozon's *Swimming Pool,* with Charlotte Rampling as a mystery writer; *The Barbarian Invasion,* by Denys Arcand of Quebec, which opens "after the collapse of the American empire"; and Vincent Gallo's *The Brown Bunny,* about a trip across America in search of love.

The festival usually opens with a French blockbuster, followed by a Hollywood blockbuster, both playing out of competition, and this year's American b-b is the French premiere of *The Matrix Reloaded.*

A vast, metallic tent, looking vaguely like the hangar for a pregnant spaceship, has been erected on the jetty beyond the harbor for the *Matrix* party; if the film's secretive, Chicago-born directors, the Wachowski brothers, attend it, it will be their first public appearance in four years. These kickoff parties cost untold millions (of dollars, francs, euros, whatever), but the *Matrix* shindig is unlikely to top the all-time champion, the *Moulin Rouge* party two years ago, at which excitement reached such a fever pitch that Rupert Murdoch, master of media and owner of the studio, climbed up on a chair the better to see the hootchie-kootchie girls his minions had imported from Paris.

Many journalists arrived here a day late this year, after the national strike called in France on Tuesday by workers concerned about their pensions. And there is a certain apprehension about SARS in the air here; a passenger on the London–Nice flight, who was sneezing loudly, found himself surrounded by empty seats on the crowded airport bus.

My own festival begins Thursday, with the first three of thirty or forty screenings. I approach the fifty-sixth event knowing that, although I may never write a film that plays at Cannes, I have at least written a title that played here. In 1979 I wrote *Who Killed Bambi*, an original screenplay for the Sex Pistols. It was never made, but imagine my gratification to see that *Qui a Tué Bambi?*, by Gilles Marchand, will play out of competition this year. Marchand, I discover, shares my birthday. There may be something occult involved here.

Cannes Report No. 2

May 15, 2003—For all of the countless words and hours of news I've absorbed about Afghanistan, nothing has provided such an evocative portrait of that troubled land as a film by a twenty-three-year-old Iranian woman that plays here this weekend.

Panj E Asr, which translates as *At Five in the Afternoon*, looks through the eyes of some women who uncertainly test their new freedoms after the fall of the Taliban. One, who attends school, is asked by the teacher why she doesn't wear the uniform. It is because, she explains, if her father knew she was a student, he would punish her and forbid her to attend classes. It is clear that it is one thing in Afghanistan for women to have more rights, and another for them to feel free to exercise them.

The film is an official selection at the fifty-sixth Cannes Film Festival. Its director, Samira Makhmalbaf, is already a veteran; her *The Apple* (1998) played here when she was only eighteen, and her *Blackboards* won the Grand Jury Prize here in 2000. Her father is the veteran Iranian director Mohsen Makhmalbaf *(Kandahar, The Silence)*, and after dropping

out of school at fifteen (she found the teachers incompetent, she says in her Web biography), she worked as an assistant for her father before striking out on her own.

Blackboards, the story of itinerant teachers traveling remote mountain areas of Iran with their blackboards strapped to their backs, is a spare and forbidding film—too much style, not enough feeling, I thought. But with *At Five in the Afternoon*, which she wrote with her father, Makhmalbaf seems so caught up in the emotions of her characters that she's made a universal and touchable film.

It's impossible not to be moved by a scene where three Afghan women, who have heard that Pakistan has, or had, or might have had, a woman president, answer questions about what they would do if they were president. One woman, who recalls that the Taliban killed her father and whipped her, says she would outlaw the Taliban, but she would not take vengeance. Her generosity is all the more touching because she has so little chance of ever being the president.

The inescapable feeling in the film is that women constitute a separate nation in their land, where many men believe they should be illiterate and without the vote or property. They meet secretly for classes and discussions, in a true definition of sisterhood, and then once again cover their faces and return to the world of men. In an image that occurs twice in the film, the heroine rides with her father on a cart that slowly sinks below the horizon on a desolate road, disappearing into the vast land.

Makhmalbaf's film has the kind of urgency in which the message defines the style, and it is what festivals like Cannes are for. Cannes is also, of course, for extravaganzas like the multimillion-dollar European premiere and party for *The Matrix Reloaded*, which played here as news arrived of its record-breaking U.S. opening. Italian star Monica Bellucci, who plays the sultry Persephone in the movie, was here to officially open the festival, and was joined by costars Keanu Reeves, Carrie-Anne Moss, and Hugo Weaving (whose character is multiplied by 100 in one scene).

The Boulevard Croisette was filled with the usual throngs for the black-tie evening ceremony; families bring folding chairs and picnic hampers, and jostle for a sight of the rich and famous, who promenade up the red-carpeted grand staircase in a blizzard of flash pictures. It is a little like, in another day, the poor people of Paree craning their necks for a glimpse of Marie Antoinette. Compared to Cannes, the red carpet arrivals at the Oscars are like opening day at a car dealership.

Among the other early successes this year is an American film, Campbell Scott's *Off the Map*, based on a play by Joan Ackermann about a family living on its own in a desolate area of New Mexico. It is narrated by the adult voice of their eleven-year-old daughter (Valentina de Angelis), who begins by telling us it was the summer of her father's depression.

Her father is played by Sam Elliott, a magnificent, grizzled presence—inward, quiet, often weeping—and her mother is Joan Allen, who suggests her husband take pills for his chemical imbalance but is speechless when he says simply, "I would prefer not to." A stranger (Jim True-Frost) arrives; he is an inspector for the IRS, intending to audit their returns, but he cares not for auditing and stays as an outrider of the family. Allen, usually an upright WASP (she played Pat Nixon) is here a bronzed, part-Indian prairie woman, who gardens naked and imparts some of her mysticism to her daughter.

Another strong film: *The Strays*, by French veteran André Téchiné, which stars Emmanuelle Béart as a mother fleeing from Paris with her thirteen-year-old son and six-year-old daughter at the time of the German invasion. Their car is destroyed during a Nazi attack on a road filled with helpless refugees, and they escape into a woods with a young man (Gaspard Ulliel), who helps them survive and find a house where they live for a time. What is his mystery? And how will this bourgeois Parisian woman adapt to the wartime urgency of survival?

As I write, the weekend is upon us. Cannes is usually thronged with tourists on its first weekend, the roads out of town lined with campers, the cafés jammed, sightseers everywhere. It is said the crowds may be smaller this year, because a series of national transportation strikes will make it harder to get here. But with stars like Béart scheduled for the red carpet treatment, it will take more than a strike to keep the idolaters away.

Cannes Report No. 3

May 17, 2003—I have seen seven movies here since my last report, and together they will not gross as much as the popcorn sales for *The Matrix Reloaded* in one good-sized state—California, say. I moderated a panel of independent American directors Saturday, put together by the Independent Film Channel at the Variety Pavilion, and *The Matrix* loomed like a thundercloud over the table. As box office records were falling like so many clones of Agent Smith, here we were talking about retarded ice fishermen in Wisconsin and a Cleveland file clerk who inspired an underground comic book.

Is there no point to our enterprise? Should we simply go home and buy Warner Bros. stock? Complicating the matter: *The Matrix Reloaded* is not at all a bad movie, and indeed one of the directors on the panel observed that the Wachowski brothers had made it with real passion. This in the week when Al Neuharth, founder of *USA Today*, attacked American movie critics because they disliked Eddie Murphy's *Daddy Day Care* while his children, ages five to twelve, loved it. Obviously, critics whose taste is more demanding than that of the Neuharth children are indulging in snotty negativism.

The late C. P. Snow, a British scientist who wrote novels, defined two worlds of the twentieth century—one humanist, the other rational. His task, as he saw it, was to bridge the gap between people who wrote novels and people who split atoms. Today the movie industry is split by the same divide. On the one hand, the "novelists," who make one-of-a-kind movies about people they find interesting. On the other hand, the "scientists," who combine box office formulas with high-tech special effects to create movies that function effortlessly to gross billions of dollars.

Allan Mindel comes down on the side of the handmade films. The director of *Milwaukee, Minnesota* said he hates digital, he hates video, he hates special effects, he hates computerized editing. He wants to dig in up to his elbows in old-fashioned moviemaking techniques. He doesn't even own a CD player, he said, "except for the one that came in the car."

He was the traditionalist on the panel, the director of a film starring Troy Garity as the retarded ice fisherman who gets involved in a plot far, far too complicated to describe here—especially since Mindel also came out against critics who synopsize the plots.

Somewhere in the middle was Gus Van Sant, who made *Good Will Hunting,* which won nine nominations and two Oscars, and who also made *Gerry,* that film where Matt Damon and Casey Affleck got lost in the desert and wandered and wandered and wandered—and that *is* the synopsis. Van Sant is here with an official selection, *Elephant,* an HBO film that paints a stark and unforgiving portrait of two students who carry out a massacre at their high school. Van Sant could see the point in studio pictures and antistudio pictures, all depending on the needs of the director for each individual film.

The conversation tilted back and forth between mediums and messages: celluloid versus video, indie films versus blockbusters. Ross McElwee, whose *Sherman's March* (1986) is one of the most praised of American documentaries, is at Cannes with *Bright Leaves,* his new film about tobacco. Like all his films, it is autobiographical; an ancestor developed Bull Durham leaves. Despite his low budgets, he said, he shoots on film—and then curses his decision during the laborious steps in editing and lab work, until finally, when he sees the completed print, "I say, oh, yeah, now I remember why I work in film."

Shari Springer Berman and Robert Pulcini, who are at Cannes with their Sundance winner *American Splendor,* used both film and video in their biopic about Harvey Pekar, the file clerk and comic-book hero who was a regular on the Letterman show in the 1980s, until he pushed Dave a little too far.

The film combines fictional footage shot on film, in which Paul Giamatti and Hope Davis play Pekar and his wife, Joyce Brabner, with video doc footage in which Pekar and Brabner play themselves. The contrast between the two looks was useful, Berman said, in making the fictional and doc parts look apart from each other.

Jean-François Pouliot, the Montreal-born director of *La Grande Seduction,* said there was a reason for that: Video and film send different kinds of messages to our minds, and film seems to be a record of the past while video feels as if it is happening right now.

Kenneth Bowser was on the panel representing his doc *Easy Riders, Raging Bulls,* about the period in the late 1960s and early 1970s when directors were given a free rein at the studios, and a golden age of American cinema was the result. Could such a day come back again?

The directors doubted it, but pointed out that festivals like Sundance testify to the strength of indie films, which are easier to make in the age of video, although Allan Mindel doesn't like the way they look. Even Mindel, however, conceded that there was sometimes a place for video, mentioning Richard Linklater's *Tape* and Ethan Hawke's *Chelsea Walls* as works that would have been impossible on film.

As the panel broke up, hopeful would-be filmmakers surged toward the table to press their screenplays into the hands of these directors who might want to film them. Gus Van Sant had a couple under his arm as he left.

There is always room for hope. Just the day before, I interviewed Campbell Scott in a Q&A session at the American Pavilion, and he recalled how the script for Dylan Kidd's *Roger Dodger* (2002) came into his hands. This was a film that Scott starred in and coproduced, and Kidd directed. And how did they meet? Kidd was a waiter at the time, Scott was dining at his table, and Kidd asked him to read the screenplay. Actors are routinely advised never to read scripts that do not arrive via agencies, because of the danger of plagiarism suits. But there was something about the way Kidd presented himself and described the story, Scott said, that convinced him to ignore the conventional advice and read the thing. Now that could make a movie.

Cannes Report No. 4

May 18, 2003—Derek Malcolm will take your bet. The distinguished film critic of the *Guardian,* Britain's venerable left-wing daily, sets the odds on the winner of the Cannes top prize, the Palme d'Or. He takes actual money. He pays off at the end of the festival. This is not a joke.

"I've been doing this for years," Malcolm told me. We were standing in the crowd outside the morning press screening, and he seemed relaxed; his eyes were not scanning the crowd for gendarmes.

Is it legal? I asked.

"I don't know. It is in England."

Do you make a profit?

"Almost every year. One year there was a tie for the Palme d'Or. That wasn't a good year for me."

So you give me the odds, I hand you money, you put the money in your pocket, and you take my bet? Then if I win you pay me?

"That's how it works. Every year there are a few silly buggers who don't leave me their addresses, and of course I can't call them because the festival is over and they've moved out of their hotels."

So what are the odds this year?

"Well, of course they change daily. Right now I can give you 5-to-2 on *Dogville*, 7-to-2 on the Babenco film, and 5-to-1 on Samira Makhmalbaf."

Dogville is the three-hour film by Lars von Trier, founder of the Dogma movement, and it stars Nicole Kidman. Babenco is Hector Babenco (*Pixote, Kiss of the Spider Woman*), the Brazilian director who is here with *Carandiru*, about a doctor who provides an eyewitness account of a prison hellhole in São Paolo. Samira Makhmalbaf is the twenty-three-year-old Iranian director of *At Five in the Afternoon*, the well-received film about women in post-Taliban Afghanistan.

What about Peter Greenaway? I asked. Greenaway is the British director whose films are sometimes brilliant and always impenetrable. He is here with *The Tulse Luper Suitcases, Part One: The Moab Story*, described as encompassing twentieth-century history from the discovery of uranium in Colorado to the fall of the Berlin Wall.

"Greenaway is 50-to-1," he said.

I told Malcolm I heard that before joining the ranks of film critics, he was a jockey.

"Quite right. But a National Hunt jockey—over the sticks, not around the track. In fact, I first joined the *Guardian* as their turf correspondent."

And is it true, I asked, that you are such a keen sportsman that you once flew back to London from the Venice Film Festival for one day to captain the *Guardian*'s cricket team?

"It was a very important match."

Now what if I bet on a film and it loses the Palme d'Or but wins the Grand Jury Prize?

"No payouts for place or show. I only handle the Palme d'Or. I have my hands full as it is, going to see all of these movies."

Cannes Report No. 5

May 19, 2003—The so-far disappointing 2003 Cannes Film Festival stirred from its torpor over the weekend with sex, violence, and Dogma. This being Cannes, Dogma got the most attention, as Lars von Trier, founder of the minimalist Dogma movement, unveiled his three-hour *Dogville*. This is one of the most confounding and exasperating films of the festival, and maybe it is brilliant, but I will not be able to determine that until I have recovered from the ordeal of sitting through it.

If it is brilliant, it is the kind of brilliance only the most evolved of filmgoers will want to experience. Imagine *Our Town* as a gangster-Western-feminist avant-garde experiment in which (I think but am not sure) the message is that fascists will win out every time over do-gooder liberals.

At the midpoint of the festival, *Dogville* is probably the front-runner for the Palme d'Or, which says something about the weak level of entries this year. My personal favorite, the Iranian film *At Five in the Afternoon*, will probably pick up a prize, and it's possible that Gus Van Sant's *Elephant*, inspired by the Columbine massacre, will win something.

Elephant received a standing ovation after its official black-tie screening, but also received a scathing review from *Variety*'s important Todd McCarthy ("pointless at best and irresponsible at worst"). It is a low-key, uninflected record of two high school students who methodically kill classmates and teachers, in scenes that seem modeled on Columbine news footage. No motives are offered or messages arrived at—and in a way that is appropriate, because to try to "explain" Columbine in the usual screenwriting terms would be pointless at best, if not irresponsible at worst. I think Van Sant simply intends to watch, and invite us to watch with him, this chilling and inexplicable tragedy.

Bertrand Bonello's *Tiresia*, an official selection from France, may win no prizes and indeed may be denounced as lurid and melodramatic, but it held my attention from beginning to end, as did *Elephant*, but as did not *Dogville*. It is based on the Greek myth of

Tiresias, who (Bonello's notes inform us) was both a man and a woman, blinded but then made clairvoyant.

That is also what happens to the title character, a Brazilian transvestite prostitute picked up in Paris by a man who keeps her locked up for weeks—and then, when the lack of hormones causes her femininity to fade, blinds her and dumps her by a road. Ah, but there is much more, as Tiresia is found by a young girl and nursed back to health, only to inspire another tragedy and what might best be explained as a virgin birth. Bonello makes Tiresia look completely convincing as both a man and a woman, by the admirable logic of casting both a woman and a man in the role.

But back to *Dogville*. Imagine an opening shot of a tiny mining town in the Rockies, seen from above as chalk outlines on the floor of a soundstage. The white marks create the "houses" of the characters, who are permitted a few props in their rooms. Sound effects contribute opening doors, ringing bells, barking dogs, etc.

To this town comes a fugitive named Grace (Nicole Kidman), pursued by gangsters (led by James Caan) who drive 1930s cars, wear fedoras, and pack machine guns. Tom (Paul Bettany), who is the town everyman, hides Grace in the abandoned mine shaft (five wooden arches on the stage floor), and later introduces Grace to the town, which is at first suspicious, then accepting, and then, when the gangsters seem about ready to return, disloyal.

A narrator functions uncannily like the stage manager in *Our Town*, introducing everyone, telling us where they live, and commenting on their activities. The large cast is distinguished (Ben Gazzara, Blair Brown, Philip Baker Hall, Stellan Skarsgard, Harriet Andersson, Patricia Clarkson, Jeremy Davies, Jean-Marc Barr, Lauren Bacall), but they speak as if afraid of being overheard, and live in a dim light that makes the whole movie hushed and murky and very, very long. Tom represents the face of ineffectual liberalism, and if the gangsters represent fascism, then the ending suggests that force and violence will win out over humane ideas every time.

The ending is brutal, abrupt, and cruel. The same unblinking cruelty is seen in *Tiresia* and

Elephant. All three films inspired walkouts right after particularly cruel moments, and while I have seen a lot of violence over the years at Cannes, I cannot remember many films that seemed so pitiless and unredeeming. Is the message that there is no hope?

I've seen ten other films so far at the festival, but perhaps, after this report of films of woe, I should close with François Ozon's *Swimming Pool*, another official entry, from France but mostly in English. It returns us to the more genteel tradition of the British country house murder, in this case starring Charlotte Rampling as a mystery writer who vacations in her publisher's home in France, there encounters the publisher's oversexed daughter (Ludivine Sagnier), and finds herself in a web of sex and, yes, murder—followed, in the British tradition, with much about gardening tools and the disposal of the body.

There are surprises in *Swimming Pool*, enormous ones, with a real doozy at the end. The film sets up apparent paradoxes that had the critics debating it all day; what's refreshing is that it deals with murder in the ancient tradition of Agatha Christie, in which there are plots and clues and stuff like that, while the other three films stare unblinkingly into the face of evil.

Cannes Report No. 6

May 19, 2003—Where is the Cannes of the past? The Cannes of great, joyous movies and silly starlets and larger-than-life characters and long, lazy lunches on the beach? How did it get replaced by this melancholy impostor, this festival of murder and nihilism and hopelessness?

As I write, the daily demonstration is unwinding beneath my window—teachers, this time, banging garbage can lids against park benches and shouting slogans, while the police eye them balefully. A dusty wind comes down from the hills, scattering café napkins and menus into the street. The first movie I saw today, Michael Haneke's *Le Temps du Loup*, was about the dog-eat-dog world of survivors in a postapocalyptic universe. The second, Kurosawa Kiyoshi's *Bright Future*, ended with the hero's father committing suicide by grabbing a jellyfish. In three recent movies, everyone was shot dead at the end.

I do not ask for jolly, simple, and cheerful movies. You know me better than that. But a morose funk has settled on this year's festival, in which each film is more despairing than the last, and the overall message is: Life is hell, and then you die. Even the stars aren't fun anymore. Arnold Schwarzenegger came all the way here to stand before a *Terminator 3* display in front of the Carlton Hotel and say "I'm back!" Unquote.

Nicole Kidman has been a good sport in support of Lars von Trier's *Dogville,* but now there is a controversy about whether it is anti-American. In the good old days, when a film was anti-American, you knew it. My own feeling: Von Trier shows that liberalism is weak-kneed and doomed to lose to fascism. Lots of machine guns at the end, trained on the weaklings of Dogville. Maybe Dogville is America and the gangsters are the Bush administration. Maybe that's it. Search me.

There was a little Italian comedy, *Il Cuore Altrove* by Pupi Avati, on the weekend, and it wasn't very good, but at least it made me smile and had some charm in its story of a clueless thirty-five-year-old bachelor who is seduced and abandoned by a heartless blind beauty. It was a human comedy with people who had simple, elemental motives like lust, greed, and vanity. How brave was this cheer, in the face of the festival's doomsday obsession.

On the big screen on the beach every night they are showing the films of Fellini, and there is also a retrospective of works by Chaplin. These are reminders that the movies can rescue us from our misery, as well as rubbing our noses in it.

My motto: No good movie is depressing; all bad movies are depressing. *Do the Right Thing* was depressing, but exhilarating in its greatness. I am depressed this year because one film after another has been unspeakably awful. There are good ones, of course; I exempt *At Five in the Afternoon,* from Iran; and the Turkish film *Uzak,* about a country cousin who comes to visit and disrupts the life of his city relative; and *Elephant,* Gus Van Sant's stark meditation on Columbine; and a few others.

But even the Turkish film has been seized by the fierce, paralyzing minimalism that now passes for style. In the glory days of Cannes, style was Fellini's gracefully moving camera

and shots that seemed to sing. Or audacious experiments by Tarantino, Spike Lee, and the Coen brothers. Or the freshness of the New Wave. Or the audacity of Fassbinder and the vision of Kurosawa.

Then along came Angelopoulos from Greece and Kiarostami from Iran, with their fashionably dead films in which shots last forever, and grim, middle-aged men with mustaches sit and look and think and smoke and think and look and sit and smoke and shout and drive around and smoke until finally there is a closing shot that lasts forever and has no point.

The Turkish director of *Uzak,* Nuri Bilge Ceylan, seems to have been infected by his Greek and Iranian neighbors, and takes a perfectly sound story and slows it down into a mannered exercise. I sort of liked it anyway, this tale of a neat and solitary intellectual whose life is disrupted by his ill-mannered visitor. The last shot, as he is seen alone and isolated in a wintry, desolate cityscape, shows that now he can sink again into his solitary misery. But consider this: The only time the audience chuckled, and applauded lightly, was more than an hour into the film—when a reverse shot revealed that two rooms we thought were separate were, in fact, *just opposite ends of the same room!* Such a meager pleasure, in the festival where Francis Ford Coppola revealed the boundless creative energy of *Apocalypse Now.*

There are films here I've loved. The Sundance winner *American Splendor,* about the blue-collar comic-book author Harvey Pekar, is one of them, but it's out of competition. Maybe that's my problem: I've been faithfully attending every single Competition film, when maybe I should be plundering the sidebar programs. I know that many major directors (Altman, the Coens, and Bertolucci among them) were not able to finish their new films in time for Cannes. But even so, this year's official entries are the weakest in memory, almost a salon of refuseniks. When your film is rejected by Sundance, you can always try Slamdance. What is this? Slamcannes?

Cannes Report No. 7

May 21, 2003—Coming up for air like an exhausted swimmer, the Cannes Film Festival produced two splendid films on Wednesday morning, after a week of the most dismal entries in memory. Denys Arcand's *The Barbarian Invasion,* from Quebec, and Errol Morris's documentary *The Fog of War,* about Robert McNamara, are in their different ways both masterpieces about old men who find a kind of wisdom.

But that is not the headline. The news is that on Tuesday night, Cannes showed a film so shockingly bad that it created a scandal here on the Riviera not because of sex, violence, or politics, but simply because of its awfulness.

Those who saw Vincent Gallo's *The Brown Bunny* have been gathering ever since, with hushed voices and sad smiles, to discuss how wretched it was. Those who missed it hope to get tickets, for no other film has inspired such discussion. "The worst film in the history of the festival," I told a TV crew posted outside the theater. I have not seen every film in the history of the festival, yet I feel my judgment will stand.

Imagine ninety tedious minutes of a man driving across America in a van. Imagine long shots through a windshield as it collects bug splats. Imagine not one but two scenes in which he stops for gas. Imagine a long shot on the Bonneville Salt Flats where he races his motorcycle until it disappears as a speck in the distance, followed by another shot in which a speck in the distance becomes his motorcycle. Imagine a film so unendurably boring that at one point, when he gets out of his van to change his shirt, there is applause.

And then, after half the audience has walked out and those who remain stay because they will never again see a film so amateurish, narcissistic, self-indulgent, and bloody-minded, imagine a scene where the hero's lost girl reappears, performs fellatio in a hard-core scene, and then reveals the sad truth of their relationship.

Of Vincent Gallo, the film's star, writer, producer, director, editor, and only begetter, it can be said that this talented actor must have been out of his mind to make this film and allow it to be seen. Of Chloe Sevigny, who plays the girlfriend, Daisy, it must be said that she brings a truth and vulnerability to her scene that exists on a level far above the movie it is in.

If Gallo had thrown away all of the rest of the movie and made the Sevigny scene into a short film, he would have had something. That this film was admitted into Cannes as an Official Selection is inexplicable. By no standard,

through no lens, in any interpretation, does it qualify for Cannes. The quip is: This is the most anti-American film at Cannes, because it is so anti-American to show it as an example of American filmmaking.

But enough of horror. Now to grace, truth, and humanity. Denys Arcand's *The Barbarian Invasion,* which could be a hit on the art film circuit, concerns the dying days of a professor named Rémy, played by Rémy Girard in a performance brimming with life, energy, defiance, humor, and regret. He has been a wicked womanizer all his life, is alienated from his children, is informed he has a short time to live.

His son Sébastien (Stéphane Rousseau) flies in from London to be at the old man's bedside, and tries to make his dying more comfortable; in one astonishing scene, told that heroin is a better painkiller than morphine, he simply goes to the Montreal narcotics squad to ask where he can buy it. Old friends and lovers gather at the bedside, as the measure is taken of Rémy's life and times. There is Rabelaisian humor in the film, and real sadness; there were so many tears and sniffles at the press screening that it appeared even journalists have feelings.

Errol Morris's *The Fog of War* is based on twenty hours of interviews with Robert McNamara, who tries to explain the mistakes that led to Vietnam. As the secretary of defense under Kennedy and Johnson, he was seen as the architect of the war, and here he unflinchingly accepts responsibility, while at the same time regretting the wrongheadedness that continued the war long after it was obviously misguided. One timely observation: If we can't persuade nations with comparable values of the worth of our actions, then we should reconsider them.

McNamara at eighty-five is forceful, plainspoken, merciless on himself and others. This is not a sad old man but a man who is still healthy, powerful, and thoughtful, who analyzes his actions with no apologies and no evasions. I doubt that Donald Rumsfeld will want to see this film, but it could prove enormously valuable to him.

As we head into the weekend, Clint Eastwood's *Mystic River* looks like an oasis in the desert. There have been a few fine films here, noted in earlier dispatches, but nobody can remember a year when the overall quality of the official selections was so low. At least with Eastwood, we are likely to get a real movie, with characters and a story and all that good stuff. By contrast, although I have met some admirers of Lars von Trier's portentous three-hour parable *Dogville,* I have not met any who are eager to sit through it again.

See also "Vincent Gallo, *The Brown Bunny,* and Me" on page 762.

Cannes Report No. 8

May 22, 2003—Three conversations at Cannes:

When Errol Morris first showed Robert McNamara the Interrotron, the former secretary of defense balked. "What's *that?*" he asked the famed documentarian. Morris explained that his device linked two video cameras and two video screens so that he and his subjects can look each other in the eye while talking. In most video interviews, the subject is looking to the side of the camera. With the Interrotron, he is looking straight down the barrel—making eye contact with the viewer.

McNamara had agreed to a one-hour interview with Morris, whose subjects over the years have included the metaphysician Stephen Hawking, as well as lion tamers, pet cemetery operators, electric chair inventors, death row inmates, wild turkey hunters in Florida, a student of the naked mole rat, and an autistic woman who designed most of the cattle chutes in America.

Morris knew within the first five minutes, he says, that he wanted to do a feature film about McNamara. Eventually McNamara grew to accept the Interrotron, and in Morris's startling and persuasive new film, *The Fog of War,* he looks us straight in the eye as he reevaluates his role in the Vietnam War.

It is an extraordinary performance, from a man who at eighty-five still skis and climbs mountains, and takes no guff from Morris. He talks about his realization that the war was unwinnable, about a private memo to Lyndon Johnson, about whether he resigned or LBJ fired him. "When I raised that question with Kay Graham, publisher of the *Washington Post,*" he recalls, "she told me, 'Of *course* you were fired.'"

Morris is one of the most distinctive filmmakers in America, a man who combines documentary subjects with haunting, rhythmic graphics and, in his later films, other-worldly scores by Philip Glass. *The Fog of War* is a presentation of a man's thoughts, memories, and conscience, all woven together into a tapestry of realism and regret.

After the Cannes premiere of the movie, I joined Morris at dinner with James Blight, a professor in international relations at Brown, and his wife, Janet Lang. They are close friends of McNamara, who lives in Aspen.

"Bob had a lot of doubts about making this film," Blight said. "He wondered if he would be left to hang out to dry by Morris. He'd never seen one of Errol's films before. It took a lot of nerve."

Yes, but the gamble was worth it, because instead of a dry, talking-head documentary, Morris has captured the man himself, a man who held enormous power and responsibility, tried to exercise it well, and was clear-eyed enough to see that Vietnam was not winnable.

Morris is an intellectual with a touch of mysticism, a man whose approach to facts sometimes seems musical, as if he wants them to bow and sway to inner rhythms. His motto, he told me, is from the novelist Harry Crews, who wrote, "I want more *this,* not more *of* this."

* * *

Gus Van Sant's official entry, *Elephant,* has drawn praise from European critics but scathing reviews from *Variety* and the *Hollywood Reporter.* It has been called anti-American and irresponsible, but also fearless and strong. It is clearly inspired by the Columbine murders, and follows two teenage shooters through their last day on Earth, but it identifies no causes and delivers no messages.

"I want the audience to make its own observations and draw its own conclusions," Van Sant told me one morning over Perrier at the beach. "Who knows why those boys acted as they did? The police have dozens of hours of tapes they made, but have never released them. Maybe then we will find some answers. I think Todd McCarthy (the *Variety* critic) was bothered by the style, but shifted that to questions about how such a thing could happen. That's like saying he has no thoughts of his own on the matter. Since he obviously does, he is really commenting on my approach and not the events."

Van Sant also drew criticisms, many of them

passionate, after his previous film, *Gerry*, which starred Matt Damon and Casey Affleck in the story of two men who get lost in the desert, and walk, and walk, and walk, without benefit of a bottled Hollywood plot to rescue them and lend meaning to their wandering.

That kind of experiment is more interesting, Van Sant said, than conventional studio pictures. His early films, like *Drugstore Cowboy*, lived in the indie world, and then he had a great success with *Good Will Hunting*, which made him a lot of money and defined him for the first time as bankable in studio terms.

"I came to realize since I had no need to make a lot of money, I should make films I find interesting, regardless of their outcome and audience. Cheap films, unencumbered by enormous salaries."

Elephant uses high school students from Van Sant's home town of Portland, Oregon, and looks professional in a cold, sharp-edged, glossy way, but it's "interesting," in his terms, because it simply regards events based on that tragic day, without trying to explain them.

* * *

Most people at Cannes have never heard of Harvey Pekar, his wife, Joyce Brabner, and their adopted daughter, Danielle Batone. But to comic-book fans, Pekar is famous for chronicling the story of his life, bringing unexpected drama and poignancy to the existence of a man who worked all his life as a government file clerk. And now Cannes knows him too, because of *American Splendor*, a film by Shari Springer Berman and Robert Pulcini that combines a fictional story starring Paul Giamatti and Hope Davis with real-life footage of Pekar, Brabner, and Batone.

The film is not in competition, because it won at Sundance in January, but many feel it's the best film they've seen here, and a much better standard-bearer for American cinema than Vincent Gallo's booed and derided official entry *The Brown Bunny*.

Within ten seconds of sitting down to talk to the three "real" characters, you realize that what you see is what you get. Pekar is *exactly* as he appears in the comics and movie—sardonic, doubtful, wary, protective, insecure. He confides that he was once offered a talk show by Fox, but didn't want to risk his government pension after thirty years.

Joyce and Danielle do a lot of the talking. When Harvey observes that money from the movie will pay for the fifteen-year-old's education, Danielle confides that she wants to study movies, but doesn't want to be an actress, because then she might be unemployable over forty. Instead, she says, she wants to work behind the scenes. More longevity that way. Harvey nods approvingly.

Harvey was a famous guest on the Letterman show in the 1980s, until he was bounced for insisting on ranting about GE's ownership of NBC. He only did the show, he says, to help sales of his comic books. "And it didn't sell any books, so why was I bothering?"

The stupidest question she's been asked, Joyce said, is whether when she married Harvey twenty years ago this week she knew she would be sharing a stage with him at the Cannes Film Festival. "I just tell them, of course I did."

Some readers of the American Splendor comic books over the years have doubted that Pekar was *really* a government file clerk in Cleveland. The movie shows him at work, and at his retirement party. "He's grade G-4," Joyce said. "G-2 is minimum wage. Isn't that something, after thirty years as a file clerk?" Yes, but it got them to Cannes.

Cannes Report No. 9: The Winners

May 27, 2003—In a stunning surprise, Gus Van Sant's *Elephant*, a low-budget independent film inspired by the Columbine shootings, won both the Palme d'Or and the Best Director Award here Sunday at the fifty-sixth Cannes Film Festival.

The early favorite, *Dogville*, directed by Lars von Trier and starring Nicole Kidman, was completely shut out, as was Clint Eastwood's praised and popular *Mystic River*.

The Cannes rules specify that only one prize can be given to a film. But the jury asked festival president Gilles Jacob for an "exception," said its president, the director Patrice Chereau. That exception permitted not only the double award for *Elephant* but also two prizes apiece for *The Barbarian Invasions,* from Quebec, and *Uzak,* from Turkey.

The fact that three films shared six of the festival's seven major awards may have been a way for the jury to reflect the general opinion that this year the official competition was unusually weak. It included two films, Vincent Gallo's *The Brown Bunny* and Bertrand Blier's *Les Cotelettes*, that were booed with true enthusiasm.

A special jury prize was voted to Samira Makhmalbaf, the twenty-three-year-old Iranian director whose *At Five in the Afternoon* was about Afghan women who are free of the Taliban but not yet free of a restrictive patriarchal society. In the film, Afghan women talk about what they would do if they were president. In her speech, Makhmalbaf said she would not personally want to be president "in a world where the most powerful president is George W. Bush." Her logic was shaky but her meaning clear.

Denys Arcand, the sixty-one-year-old director of *The Barbarian Invasions,* speculated that he would retire after the unfriendly Cannes reception of *Stardom,* his unsuccessful 2000 film. Good thing he reconsidered. His film, about a dying teacher who is joined by his friends and family during his last few days, was an enormous audience hit here—and also with the jury, which gave Arcand's film the Screenplay Award, and also named Marie-Josée Croze best actress, for her performance as a heroin addict who helps the dying man's son get drugs for him.

Uzak, by Nuri Bilge Ceylan of Turkey, won the Grand Jury Prize, generally considered to be second place, and the Best Actor Award was shared by its two actors, Muzaffer Ozdemir and Mehmet Emin Toprak. Tragically, Toprak was killed in an auto accident a day after learning the film had been accepted by Cannes. In the movie, he plays a country cousin who comes to visit his reclusive city relative, and overstays his welcome as issues from their past bubble beneath the surface.

The Critics' Prize, voted on by journalists at the festival and given independently of the jury, went to the Sundance winner *American Splendor,* inspired by the autobiographical comic books of the redoubtable Cleveland file clerk Harvey Pekar. The Camera d'Or Award, for the best first film, was given by a jury headed by director Wim Wenders to *Osama,* by Sedigh Barmak of Iran. *Milwaukee, Minnesota,* by the American indie director Allan Mindel, won as the best feature in the Critics' Week.

The jury, which included two Americans, director Steven Soderbergh and actress Meg Ryan, is traditionally secluded for its secret deliberations, while rumors, most of them inaccurate, race down the Boulevard Croisette. Their prizes are the most important in the world, after the Oscars, and a good deal more inventive.

Their work was cut out for them this year, by an Official Selection containing a few fine films, many bad films, and a few terrible films. "It was not the best of years," Jacob observed diplomatically. Von Trier's *Dogville,* a three-hour dirge set in Colorado but filmed entirely on an artificial soundstage set, was thought to be the winner by default, but found no favor with the jury.

Van Sant's film is sure to ride its Cannes victory to a high-profile opening in North America. It stars unknown high school students from Portland, Oregon, in the Columbine-inspired story of two teenagers who stage a massacre. Some admired it, some hated it; many speculated that its portrait of a violence-prone America helped it win.

The Barbarian Invasions and Eastwood's *Mystic River* were probably the two films audiences enjoyed the most, and both seem destined for box office success. The Arcand film was snatched up by Miramax, whose president, Harvey Weinstein, complained there wasn't much else worth buying here this year.

Questions for the Movie Answer Man

Academy Awards

Q. We know that Oscar has a short memory and rarely honors films released in the first half of the year. Why doesn't the Academy have *two* ceremonies—one for films released between January and August and another for the "prestige" items of the fall and winter?

—Joe Sadowski, Minneapolis, Minnesota

A. Two Oscarcasts? Twice as many envelopes? A Billy Crystal and Steve Martin tag team? And of course in the weeks before them, two Golden Globes, two People's Choice Awards, and two special issues of *Entertainment Weekly*? The real reason the Academy nominates mostly recent films is not because it can't remember the earlier films, but because an Oscar can't help a film that has already played out in theaters and on video. The studios put their promotional clout behind films that are still in theaters or newly on video. It takes an extraordinary film from early in the year to swim against this tide.

Q. I think Meryl Streep is great, but the articles that came out after the Oscar nominations are technically wrong. They claim Streep has passed Katharine Hepburn in total number of nominations. In general, yes. But two of Streep's nominations are for supporting actress, leaving her with eleven for lead actress. All of Hepburn's are for lead actress; none for supporting. That leaves Hepburn with twelve and Streep with eleven in the lead category. I know it is a small point.

—Myron Heaton, Las Vegas, Nevada

A. But not an invisible one.

Q. You mentioned in your Oscar nominations write-up that the nomination for Donald Kaufman for coauthoring *Adaptation*'s screenplay was the first time the Academy knowingly nominated a fictitious personality. This is actually the second time this has happened, the first being Roderick Jaynes's nomination as editor for *Fargo*. Jaynes is of course a pseudonym used by both Joel and Ethan Coen.

—Rhett Miller, Calgary, Alberta

A. A key distinction is that Joel and Ethan Coen both actually exist.

Q. Liz Smith quoted you as saying, "At least Scorsese lost to a real director and not to Rob Marshall." What makes you think he isn't a real director?

—Charles Smith, Chicago, Illinois

A. He is a real director and a gifted one. I wrote him to apologize. I spoke carelessly. I meant to say something like "a veteran director," meaning someone who, like Polanski, has a body of work and is not a first-timer. Scorsese has lost twice in the past to first-timers (Robert Redford and Kevin Costner).

Actors of Color

Q. Vin Diesel recently said he considers himself "multicultural," rather than belonging to any particular ethnicity. He has a production company called "One Race." I find both these items to be incredibly refreshing. I couldn't understand why, during last spring's Academy Awards, everyone kept referring to Halle Berry as an African-American, even though such ethnicity makes up only half her identity. In other words, she's just as multicultural as Diesel is. Agree?

—Nick Curtis, Macomb, Illinois

A. One of the most heartening trends in movies is away from color coding and toward diversity in casting. Vin Diesel is a good example. On the basis of *The Fast and the Furious* and his new *XXX*, in which he plays a badass James Bond–style character, he's poised to become the major action star of his generation. On a Website devoted to his work, he says his ethnicity is a mystery, because his mother has never revealed the identity or race of his father: "I am truly multiracial. I never knew my

815

biological father. All I know from my mother is that I have connections to many different cultures." He adds, "I am definitely a person of color."

Adaptation

Q. Just out of curiosity, do you happen to know how much of *Adaptation* is true?
—Daniel Lee, Los Angeles, California

A. Susan Orlean really did write a book about an orchid fanatic named John Laroche. There really is a screenplay guru named Robert McKee. That's about it, although Charlie Kaufman's struggles with the screenplay are no doubt inspired by fact.

Alex & Emma

Q. In your review of *Alex & Emma,* you state that the couple falls in love because Hollywood's romantic storytelling rules dictate that they must. It is implied that this is bad. On the other hand, in your review of *Bringin' Down the House,* you lamented the fact that the two leads did not get together. Aren't you contradicting yourself in saying that one movie is bad for following a stock convention while another is also flawed for not following the same stock convention?
—J. C. Genter, Atlanta, Georgia

A. Not at all. The rule applies in both cases. *Bringin' Down the House* violated it despite the manifest chemistry between Steve Martin and Queen Latifah and the audience's desire to see them together—instead of paired off with subsidiary drips. *Alex & Emma* is not bad because the two characters fall in love, but bad because we don't care, the flashback strategy is clunky, the movie isn't funny, the multiple roles are a yawn, and because Luke Wilson and Kate Hudson never convince us their characters care deeply about one another—while Martin and Latifah do.

Q. I've been surprised that in the many reviews of the new film *Alex & Emma* (including your own), there has been no mention of the 1964 William Holden–Audrey Hepburn film *Paris When It Sizzles*—which has almost the exact same plot: Holden is a screenwriter who has to finish a script for Noel Coward before the weekend is over. . . . He and stenog-

rapher Hepburn act out the plot in their fantasies and fall in love in the process.
—Al Featherston, Durham, North Carolina

A. I've not seen *Paris When It Sizzles,* but many other Answer Man readers made the same observation. Both films seem to have been inspired by the experience of Dostoyevsky, who, to pay urgent gambling debts, dictated his novel *The Gambler* in thirty days to a stenographer and fell in love with her. The resemblance seems uncanny.

Antwone Fisher

Q. Am I the only one knocked out by the work of Viola Davis this season? I just saw *Antwone Fisher,* and her one-scene, near-wordless bit as Antwone's mother was absolutely jaw dropping. That on top of her role as Julianne Moore's maid in *Far from Heaven* and the straight-talking scientist in *Solaris,* convinces me she should be given the best-supporting actress Oscar right now for her body of work.
—Joe Baltake, film critic, *Sacramento Bee*

A. Davis won a 2001 Tony Award for August Wilson's *King Hedley II* and was also in the Steven Soderberg films *Out of Sight* and *Traffic,* in addition to *Solaris.* The three roles you mention, all within a few months, have made a strong impression.

Q. Having read the book that *Antwone Fisher* is based on, I was quite surprised to find that the Japanese woman who was the first girlfriend of the real Antwone Fisher was omitted and replaced by an African-American woman in the film. Why is this so?
—James Edwards, Chicago, Illinois

A. A Fox Searchlight rep says that while *Antwone Fisher* is inspired by a true story, "not everything in the film is fact. Antwone had several women in his life and the character of Cheryl is a composite of those women."

Audiences

Q. What can be done to make people (especially teenagers) act properly in movie theaters, and increase the level of cinematic literacy? I ask this because of my appalling experience last night watching *The Lord of the Rings: The Two Towers.* Back when I was in high school, we would socialize at pizza joints. We would talk nonstop, laugh uproariously, make calls from a pay phone, switch seats and tables. Now, here in Jupiter, Florida, teenagers do these things inside movie theaters, except they use cell phones instead of pay phones. While *The Two Towers* was on-screen, teenagers in the audience chatted away, swapped seats, laughed at their jokes, and made and received cell phone calls. I'm pretty sure that a girl in my row called a friend sitting about ten rows back. I was floored. Do parents teach their kids even rudimentary manners?

Equally disturbing is what happened in two key scenes in the movie. Moviegoers laughed when Gollum suffers from his split-personality episodes. I wish *The Two Towers* could have been released as an NC-17 movie to keep the morons out. From now on I'll watch big movies late on school nights.

—Holden Lewis, Jupiter, Florida

A. Cell phones have no place in a movie theater, and anyone who uses one there should be required to wear a badge saying, "I am an inconsiderate moron." The time is coming when theater chains will be forced to take action against audience misbehavior, because it is alienating so much of its customer base. With big pictures, perhaps some multiplex screens could be set aside for the civilized.

Q. I wanted to share with the Answer Man two wonderful visits to the cinema I had recently, both of which were improved by audience "participation." The first was to a sneak preview to *The Ring*, a most frightening film I attended with about one hundred teenage girls in the theater, shrieking and squealing and squirming in their seats as the psychological terror unfolded on the screen. The second was to *Spirited Away*, which many forward-thinking parents had taken their small children to see; each of them was rapt with attention and the wonderful adventure "spirited" them away both with terror and delight. In both cases the audience added to the whole experience because they reacted in a myriad of ways, bringing me along with them. Let it not be said that the home theater can ever replace seeing a movie with a live audience.

—Miles Blanton, Carrboro, North Carolina

A. Let it not, indeed. Although I would suggest that the audience for *The Ring* took almost nothing of value away from the theater, while the audience for *Spirited Away* took great artistry and a sense of wonder. Both films deal with young girls. The heroine of *Spirited Away* has enchanting adventures and learns lessons in life; the heroine of *The Ring* is horribly mistreated and gets revenge as a serial killer, murdering people seven days after they get her phone call.

Q. My husband and I have always been avid moviegoers, but since we have two young children and baby-sitters are not in the budget, opportunities to go to films together are rare. While I absolutely love going to movies alone, my husband refuses to do so. He seems to be phobic about going alone, and at age thirty-four, has never done so, not once! I have tried to describe the enjoyment to be had (I have just sneaked away to see *Nicholas Nickleby* and *Gangs of New York* all by myself) but have been unable to assuage his fears that he won't be able to enjoy the experience without someone he knows sitting right next to him.

—Barbara Diamond, New York, New York

A. When a movie is really working, we are always alone, because we are within the reverie it creates. Tell him that one of the reasons we go to the movies is to leave ourselves behind for two hours and identify with the characters—so if it's a good movie he won't be alone for long.

Austin Powers in Goldmember

Q. In your review of *Austin Powers in Goldmember,* you wrote, "Meanwhile, we learn that Dr. Evil plans to flood the earth with a beam projected from an orbiting satellite that looks like a gigantic brassiere." You are one great gallopin' git, aren't you? If you are not intelligent enough to follow a plot as simplistic as *Goldmember,* then why would you expect people to give one whit of attention to your reviews? For the record his plan was to use a giant tractor beam that extended out of his giant submarine to pull an asteroid made of pure gold down from outer space, crashing into the North Pole, causing the ice caps to melt and destroy the world. To demonstrate his power he used the beam to pull the giant brassiere

817

out of orbit. Which is the part that you remember.

—Mike Frei, Syracuse, New York

A. Yeah, I always remember the part about the giant brassiere.

Auto Focus

Q. Your review of *Auto Focus* from Telluride was the final straw for me. How you can rave about a film that contains "wall-to-wall sex" escapes me. I guess I'm just a fogy about such matters. Films aren't often being made for people like me, and the critics have forgotten that people like me exist.

—Paul Montgomery, Chicago, Illinois

A. I have not forgotten that people like you exist, but I am not you, just as you are not me, and unless I honestly report my own opinion, I am of no use to you or anyone else. I admire Paul Schrader's new film very much; Greg Kinnear is surprisingly effective in charting Bob Crane's self-destruction. Certainly sexual addiction is a valid subject for a movie, but I didn't "rave" about the sex. I wrote, "Schrader somehow succeeds in making a film with wall-to-wall sex in which sadness and loneliness, not passion, is the subject." There is a difference between a movie that *is* wall-to-wall sex, and a movie that is *about* it. Here is a crucial rule for anyone seriously interested in movies: It's not *what* the movie is about that makes it good or bad, but *how* it is about it.

Back Roads

Q. I live in Phoenix but lived in L.A. for years, and drove to and from Phoenix and Las Vegas many times. Thus, I fail to see why such road trips in movies (*Banger Sisters* and others) are usually on nonexistent, desolate, two-lane roads. Is it to emphasize the bleakness and emptiness of the desert? Is it a semi-accurate homage to *Psycho*? Is it Western *film* noir? Certainly most of the characters in such movies would appreciate the existence of Interstates 10 and 15.

—Mike Galloway, Phoenix, Arizona

A. Top ten reasons they use back roads: (1) more colorful; (2) meet weirdos and coots along the way; (3) can be shot anywhere; (4) remote roads can be closed off for stunt driving, but freeways can't be; (5) gas stations have one attendant, no customers, saving on extras; (6) two-lane roads go better with the vintage convertibles that many movie heroes drive; (7) if you get in trouble, you're on your own; (8) long shot from high angle shows one car on lonely road, while on a freeway you couldn't single it out; (9) wild animals are plausible if required; (10) nudity not a problem.

Barbershop

Q. My husband and I saw *Barbershop* and I've been reading about the controversy stirred by Jesse Jackson. He believes that comments made by one character are disrespectful to Martin Luther King Jr. and Rosa Parks and should be deleted from video and DVD releases of the film. Then I read Mary Mitchell's column in the *Sun-Times*. My mother agrees with Rev. Jackson. I agree with Mary Mitchell. Jackson hasn't made this much noise about a movie in a long time. How many movies have black people as pimps, whores, drug dealers, addicts, murderers, and illiterate children? What did Jackson say about *In Too Deep*, the film that depicted black people engaged in gang activity, men beating women down in the street, and the head of the gang named God? A Web search listed zero hits of Jackson protesting such films. The scene in *Barbershop* should not be cut from the tapes and DVDs. How should the director and producers of *Barbershop* handle this situation?

—Troylene Ladner, Jersey City, New Jersey

A. The movie's producers included George Tillman Jr. and Robert Teitel, who also made *Soul Food*. They have handled the controversy correctly, by joining MGM in saying the film will not be censored in its home video release. Many critics of *Barbershop* made the crucial error of not seeing the film before attacking it. It has not generated any significant protest from its audiences—because, in context, the scene is not offensive. Most audiences enjoy it and understand where it's coming from.

Rev. Jackson and other attackers overlook a crucial rule in film criticism: "It's not *what* it's about, but *how* it's about it." Yes, the character played by Cedric the Entertainer disses several African-American heroes. But it's clear he's playing the part of an instigator, clowning for shock value. He is immediately shouted down by another character: "What you're saying is not true! It's wrong and disrespectful!" Rosa Parks is an American heroine, but I imagine anyone with the gumption to do what she did isn't going to be fazed by a loudmouth barber. In context, the movie doesn't disrespect her but shows affection for the conversational back and forth and ups and downs of these black working men.

It is sad that Jackson singled out for blame an independent African-American production of good-heartedness and humor. His decision could have a negative effect on other independent producers hoping to find financing for family movies about the daily lives of ordinary black people. And the controversy may have cost Cedric the Entertainer an Oscar nomination. Kweisi Mfume, president of the NAACP, who has seen the film, is correct when he says, "I thought it was a funny film, that it honestly replicates life and situational comedy that takes place in a barbershop. Given the context in which the remarks were made—here is one person being shouted down by everyone else—it's clear this is an older person with views not commonly held by those who regularly participate, and he has no credibility."

Bend It Like Beckham

Q. I've seen Bend It Like Beckham but still don't understand what "bend it" means. Is it a British phrase or a soccer phrase?
—Kenny Hom, Campbell, California

A. It is a British soccer phrase. David Beckham, "the Michael Jordan of British soccer," is said to be able to bend the flight of the ball to his will, much as Jordan seemed able to fly.

Q. About the Answer Man discussion of Bend It Like Beckham and its title: The distributors of the movie apparently considered the expression "bend it" to be too subtle for the non-English speaking European audience. In Germany, an English language title was used for all the publicity material. However, that title was Kick It Like Beckham. In France they used a French language title Joue la comme Beckham, which translates as Play It Like Beckham. French and German cinemagoers were expected to know who Beckham is. In America, the whole title was presumably expected

to be incomprehensible, so they didn't attempt to change it.
—Michael Jennings, London, England

A. Yet the movie is a box office hit; after seven weeks on the charts, it was averaging $3,600 per screen and has grossed some $10 million, which is sensational for an import. Except for the big movies that buy their grosses, word of mouth is more important than titles and advertising put together.

Q. Please advise parents to take their children to Bend It Like Beckham despite the PG-13 rating. The ratings system is unforgivably arbitrary. Here is a movie that is a wonderful self-esteem builder for girls and quite inspirational. Some parents bring their younger children to see it (the kids love it of course), but others are hesitant due to the rating. How can the Austin Powers films, which I laughed at but are full of adolescent sexual humor, have the same rating as this gem?
—Alexandra Schultz, Sound Beach, New York

A. The ratings system makes no distinction between the sublime and the ridiculous. For parents who want to know in great detail exactly what is in a movie, there is no better authority than ScreenIt.com, which charts an amazing number of categories, from sex to smoking to "bad attitude," and simply provides the facts, without any political or religious spin.

Better Luck Tomorrow

Q. I just saw Better Luck Tomorrow and enjoyed it tremendously. However, most of my friends were disappointed by the ending. I myself would have liked to see more of the characters' reactions to the killing (especially Ben's after Stephanie chooses him). Then I read in a review that Ben's concluding voice-over narrative was modified from the version shown at Sundance in 2002, ostensibly to soften the ending and make the film more palatable for a wider audience. What was different in the original version?
—Brian Wong, New York, New York

A. When I saw the film at Sundance, Ben considers turning himself in to the police, but says, "I couldn't let one mistake get in the way of everything I'd worked for. I know the difference between right and wrong, but I guess in the end I really wanted to go to a good college." I thought this ending struck the right note of irony and cynicism. When I talked to director Justin Lin at the Wisconsin Film Festival last month, he said that Paramount and MTV had given him money to complete the film the way, he implied, he originally wanted to. I like the current ending but miss the impact of the original ending. I think the DVD should include both.

Beyond the Valley of the Dolls

Q. It is generally acknowledged that the character of "Z-Man" in your script of *Beyond the Valley of the Dolls* is based (loosely, I presume) on Phil Spector. Have you given any thought concerning the violent conclusion of the film given the recent events in Spector's life? I know it is a morbid question but hey, I'm a morbid chap.

—James Boswell, Wollongong, Australia

A. "Inspired by uninformed and feverish fantasies about Phil Spector" would be more accurate, since neither Russ Meyer nor myself ever met Spector or knew any more about him than your average music fan. Speculation on the morbid parallels I will leave to morbid chaps like you.

The Birth of a Nation

Q. Many critics don't give *The Birth of a Nation* the credit that it deserves. It revolutionized cinema; it was like the *Citizen Kane* of the silent era. It may show racism, but so do many other films. Take *The Searchers* for instance; that movie is hailed by most critics to be one of the best movies ever made, and it is racist toward Indians. Do critics refuse to talk about or give credit to *The Birth of a Nation* because they're afraid they'll be called racist, or do they just think it's not a good movie?

—Jay Liverman, Virginia Beach, Virginia

A. In writing my series of Great Movies reviews, I postponed my inevitable confrontation with D. W. Griffith's *Birth of a Nation.* The movie was enormously important and influential, but the second half, in particular, is racist to a degree far beyond anything contained in *The Searchers.* The Griffith film I

have included in my Great Movies series is *Broken Blossoms* (1919), which was Hollywood's first depiction, however timid, of an interracial romance.

Griffith defended himself against charges of racism, writing to *Sight & Sound* magazine in 1947 to protest: "I am not now and never have been 'anti-Negro' or 'anti' any other race. . . . In filming *The Birth of a Nation,* I gave my best knowledge to the proven facts, and presented the known truth, about the Reconstruction period in the American South."

Nevertheless, the film's racist caricatures of African-Americans and its glorification of the Ku Klux Klan is there to be seen on the screen, and did much to revive the moribund Klan. The film was picketed on its release by the NAACP. Griffith himself made *Intolerance* (1916) the year after *The Birth of a Nation* as a form of amends. My guess is he was not willfully racist so much as ignorant and naive, as many Americans were at the time; the film was even praised by President Woodrow Wilson—who was himself at one point in his life a member of the Klan.

Note: I have since reviewed Birth of a Nation *for the Great Movies series.*

Blockbuster Stores

Q. Being a fan of DVD, I've been growing more and more uneasy with the saturation of full-frame DVD titles into stores. Blockbuster and Wal-Mart are the worst offenders, rarely even offering the original theatrical wide-screen version at all. Does it cause you any worry that just when millions of DVD players will be under Christmas trees, people will still go on watching chopped up versions of movies?

—Blake A. Smith, Kitchener, Ontario

A. It does. The chains give their customers little credit for intelligence and, incredibly, still believe many of them do not understand letterboxing. The obvious solution is to offer wide screen on one side of a disk, and "full frame" (sliced-and-diced) on the other side.

It's my belief that no true movie lover has any business going into Blockbuster in the first place, since its policies have done so much harm to modern American cinema. By refusing to handle NC-17 movies, Blockbuster has all but destroyed the freedom of American directors to make studio pictures intended for adults. At the same time, by killing the safety valve of the "adult" rating, Blockbuster has contributed to the downward leakage of unsuitable material into the R and PG-13 categories. Thus it corrupts youth while appearing sanctimonious.

A recent *Boston Globe* article by Geoff Edgers documents another Blockbuster transgression. Two of the most acclaimed recent foreign films, *Y Tu Mama Tambien* and *The Piano Teacher,* have been "sanitized" for Blockbuster. Edgers notes many cuts in *Y Tu Mama* and adds that at the end: "The dramatic seduction scene is neutered in a way that completely alters the film." There is no point in seeing these films unless you see them in the theatrical version, so DVD renters should patronize stores that offer movies in their original forms.

Q. I have a question about your discussion of Blockbuster and the content-sanitizing of the DVD of *Y Tu Mama Tambien.* Have all DVD versions of *Y Tu Mama Tambien* been edited in content or only the ones sold and rented at Blockbuster?

—Ken Gelwasser, Hollywood, Florida

A. Blockbuster is offering only the sanitized version. Some stores are offering both. What you want to look for is the unedited theatrical version, which is being sold on-line at Amazon.com and sold and rented at facets.org and netflix.com.

Q. I work part-time at a Blockbuster Video store. I tried to get this job because I love movies and while the job doesn't pay as well as some others it offers five free rentals per week. I completely agree with nearly everything you said about Blockbuster. If they didn't give me the movies for free I wouldn't go there. Because of all this, when I saw the Answer Man question about the spread of full-frame (pan-and-scan) DVD titles, I was thrilled. This is something that has always bothered me. I cannot stand to watch pan-and-scan movies and had always loved the fact that most DVDs came as letterbox by default. But you write, "The chains give their customers little credit for intelligence, and, incredibly, still believe many of them do not understand letterboxing." While I would love to believe this, I can tell you, the chains are correct in their assumptions.

I can't count how many times per day people come up to me and ask if we "have the DVDs without those black bars on the top and bottom." The vast majority of these same customers have no idea and actually believe letterbox cuts off the top and bottom, not understanding that pan-and-scan cuts off the sides. I try to explain the truth to them but they usually don't care. The assumption that the general public deserves more credit is sadly untrue.

—Mike Fortier Jr., Worcester, Massachusetts

A. I can understand why people with small screens might resist letterboxing, which is why I see nothing wrong with offering the choice of letterbox on one side of a disc and pan and scan on the other. It would not be that hard to offer an in-store demo of the difference. Here, recommended by reader Joao Solimeo of Valinhos, Brazil, is a Website with an excellent explanation of letterboxing: www.ryanwright.com/ht/oar.shtml.

Q. More about Blockbuster's refusal to stock wide-screen formats: Earlier this week, I considered renting *Unfaithful* at a Blockbuster and decided against it because, out of the forty DVDs available, all copies were full-screen. When I complained to the high school kid checking me out, he actually said that Blockbuster had no control over that because "they buy what the director wants the audience to see." I looked at him dumbfounded. Later, after I was able to rent the wide-screen version from a local video store, I realized that I should have said, "If the director wants the audience to see a movie that is the shape of my TV screen, why on earth would he make it in the wide-screen aspect ratio?"

—Katie Dahlquist, Austin, Texas

A. Blockbuster's policy is okay for people with small-screen TVs, but as screens grow larger and home theater systems more popular, it is lingering in the dark ages.

Q. I don't know if you've heard yet, but Blockbuster has changed its policy and is now opting for wide-screen DVDs when available.

So congratulations. Scratch one more personal cause off your list.

—Alan Podmore, Canoga Park, California

A. After years of claiming that consumers preferred sliced-and-diced movies that were either (a) missing the sides, or (b) panning back and forth like crazy to see everything, Blockbuster has joined the twenty-first century. Blake Lugash, Blockbuster spokesman, said in a news story, "We try to follow our customer preferences. As DVD becomes increasingly popular, they become more familiar with the features and with the benefits of letterboxing. They've learned it's a superior format to full-frame." This implies of course, that Blockbuster knew that all along. I agree with Lugash that the best policy is a two-sided disc offering both formats.

Bowling for Columbine

Q. I am sorry you had to reprint Internet crap in your column today. It is a lie to say anything but the following:

1. I was handed that gun in that bank and walked out with it and have it in my possession to this day. I *never* had to go to any gun shop. The scene happened just the way you saw it. I'd be happy to send you all the raw footage.

2. The Columbine shooters *did* go to the bowling alley that morning. I can supply you with the five witnesses, including their teacher. It's all there in the investigation conducted by the state of Colorado.

I don't understand why, after all these years, you would run stuff that wasn't true. It was hugely disappointing to read it.

—Michael Moore, Flint, Michigan

A. Moore is referring to my Oscar predictions piece, in which I wrote that his *Bowling for Columbine* was probably going to win the Oscar, and added: "Recent charges that he made up stuff probably won't hurt it, because somehow you know, watching it, that Moore has granted himself poetic license. So, okay, the Columbine killers *didn't* go bowling earlier that morning, as a news report falsely claimed. So, okay, that bank didn't hand you the rifle as a premium right there in the bank, but made you go to a gun shop to pick it up."

His message does not precisely address the second item. I believe Moore was handed the gun right there in the bank, but I am not sure an average customer would have been. As for the first item, Moore has a disagreement with the Jefferson County sheriff's office. According to Andy Ihnatko of Boston, who has been researching the film and talked to the Jefferson County sheriff's office, teachers and students at the class did not see the killers there, and they were marked absent. Moore, on the other hand, says he has five eyewitnesses. Currently I am being copied on a voluminous correspondence between Moore and Ihnatko, with both sides citing persuasive information, and I confess that I cannot determine objective fact. All I know is that *Bowling for Columbine* is a brilliant polemic.

Q. On your weekly show you stated that you hoped Michael Moore would make a politically charged speech if he won the Oscar this year, and that it should be audacious and controversial, in the spirit of his documentaries (I'd call them pseudo-docs). Then on *Jay Leno* you exclaimed that Moore's actual speech was the worst moment of the night, and Moore disappointed you because he had the audience in the palm of his hand and then deliberately polarized it. Isn't this speech and all his antics afterward the entire point to Michael Moore? How can you say he disappointed you when he did exactly what you wanted him to do?

—Chiranjit Goswami, Winnipeg, Manitoba

A. On *Ebert & Roeper*, I said I hoped Moore would win the Oscar and deliver one of those "offensive political speeches they hate to sit through." Be careful what you ask for; you may get it.

On a day of bad war news, Moore cued the Academy negatively with his hurried delivery and defensive body language. He came on fast and strong; they instinctively recoiled from being identified with him. In a similar speech the day before at the Indie Spirits, he took his time, made eye contact, and used the much better line, "The message for the children of Columbine is that violence is an acceptable way to resolve disputes."

At the Oscars, when the boos grew louder,

he got rattled, I think, and shouted "Shame on you, Mr. Bush!"—which was guaranteed to turn a large part of the audience against him. Moore turned a standing ovation into a mixed reception by replaying his old tapes when a new speech for that day, occasion, and mood was called for.

Interestingly enough, Moore agrees. He told me, "I completely blew it by not saying what I wanted to say, or using my sense of humor. I have played this over in my head so many times. I don't disagree with what I said in terms of content. It's about the delivery. I didn't expect to win, and I started to panic. It was a classic example of poor delivery, improper reading of the room, and not feeling comfortable in the moment."

Q. As someone who was at the Kodak Theater on Sunday, believe me there were more than five loud people who booed Michael Moore that night (as he claims).

—Ziggy Kozlowski, Los Angeles, California

A. As a reporter, I was offended when Moore walked into the backstage pressroom and immediately started spin control. Instead of acknowledging he had been booed and dealing with that, he lectured the press to "tell the truth—don't say it was a divided house because five loud people were booing." Everyone in that room had heard a lot of booing ("at least half the house," the *New York Times* reported). To paraphrase a famous Richard Pryor line, Moore was asking us, "Who you gonna believe? Me, or your lyin' ears?"

By the next day, he was quoted that the boos of his enemies were somehow amplified, that the boos came from a claque in the balcony, that stagehands were behind it. Everything but boos from the grassy knoll. He even said some of the booers were booing the other booers. If anyone knows that you cheer in order to drown out boos, it's the Academy.

But Moore told me that press reports of his comments about booing were not accurate. "I didn't say anything about stagehands. That was written in the *Los Angeles Times*. My ears heard the booing but my eyes didn't see anybody booing. My relatives in the balcony said some people were booing the booers. I agree that's the wrong approach: You should try to

cheer over them. By the time I got backstage, I was in a fog. When I study the ABC tapes, I still don't see anyone on the main floor booing."

Q. I was the *Bowling for Columbine* producer who scouted the bank that gives you a gun. I was there for Michael Moore's only and entire visit to the bank and was dismayed to see you repeating an outright lie about this scene. Mike walked into North County Bank and walked out with a gun in less than an hour. He opened a CD account, they faxed in his check, it came back all clear, and a bank official handed him his rifle. The crew, Mike, and I then drove directly to the barbershop where Mike bought the bullets for his new rifle just as you see in the film. All this occurred before lunch that day, the final day of filming. Then everyone flew home. Maybe you ought to expose the origin of this lie rather than repeat this easily refuted fabrication.

—Jeff Gibbs, Traverse City, Michigan

A. I am happy to oblige. It originated at http://www.opinionjournal.com/forms/print-This.htmlid=110003233.

Of the bank incident Gibbs mentions, author John Fund writes, "Jan Jacobson, the bank employee who worked with Mr. Moore on his account, says that only happened because Mr. Moore's film company had worked for a month to stage the scene. 'What happened at the bank was a prearranged thing,' she says. The gun was brought from a gun dealer in another city, where it would normally have to be picked up. 'Typically, you're looking at a week to ten days waiting period,' she says."

I asked Michael Moore about this report. His response: "I walked in cold. It happened exactly as you see in the film. A producer did call ahead and said I wanted to come in. It is not true that an ordinary person could not have walked in and gotten a gun. No need to go to a gun shop; they had five hundred guns in their vault. There's a 2001 story in the *St. Petersburg Times* about how the bank is proud as a peacock about its gun offer."

Another critical analysis of the film is at www.hardylaw.net/Truth_About_Bowling.html. On this site, David T. Hardy, a lawyer associated with the National Rifle Association, raises questions about the accuracy and fairness of many sequences in the movie. One point he makes is that *Bowling for Columbine* misquotes a plaque on a B-52 bomber at the Air Force Academy. Hardy writes, "Moore solemnly pronounces that the plaque under it 'proudly proclaims that the plane killed Vietnamese people on Christmas Eve of 1972.' ... The plaque actually reads, 'Flying out of Utapao Royal Thai Naval Airfield in southeast Thailand, the crew of *Diamond Lil* shot down a MIG northeast of Hanoi during 'Linebacker II' action on Christmas Eve 1972.'"

Moore's response: "I was making a point about the carpet bombing of Vietnam during the 1972 Christmas offensive. I did not say exactly what the plaque said but was paraphrasing."

I think here he is fudging. Few audience members would have considered it a paraphrase. It would also appear that his depiction of a Charlton Heston speech is less than accurate. You can compare the *Bowling for Columbine* version at http://ufies.org/archives/000586.html with this transcript of Heston's original speech: www.nrawinningteam.com/meeting99/hestsp1.html.

I sometimes suspect that Moore takes as his motto these words by Huck Finn about an earlier book in which Huck figured: "That book was made by Mr. Mark Twain, and he told the truth, mainly. There was things which he stretched. But mainly he told the truth."

Moore told me, "I don't know what category to put my films in. They're like a film version of the op-ed page, and not a traditional documentary. They are cinematic essays presenting my point of view. I may be right or wrong, but if I state something as a fact, I need the viewers to trust that those facts are correct."

The debate about specific facts in *Bowling for Columbine* has grown in such intensity and attention to detail that it requires the dedication of a Kennedy-assassination buff. The Answer Man recommends you read both of the sites above, as well as www.michaelmoore.com, where he says he is posting a point-by-point reply to his critics, complete with documents, affidavits, etc. I also recommend that Moore preface his next film with the quote from Mark Twain.

Bringing Down the House

Q. Your review of *Bringing Down the House* confused me somewhat. You were troubled that the movie didn't pair off the characters in the end as any other movie would have. Usually, you complain about the formulaic endings of movies.

—Christopher Dodd, Champaign, Illinois

A. Lots of people pointed out that contradiction. My dislike of formulas is trumped by the mutual attraction between Steve Martin and Queen Latifah, which seemed like a force of nature in *Bringing Down the House,* so that the film's unconvincing U-turn at the end felt wrong.

Broccoli and Broccoli

Q. In your review for *24 Hour Party People,* you write that the Wilson character "explains how the invention of broccoli funded the James Bond movies," and then comment, "There is a shred of truth there, actually." Please, don't leave us hanging! What's the connection between broccoli and Her Majesty's Secret Service?

—Phil Edwards, Dayton, Ohio

A. Albert R. "Cubby" Broccoli (1909–96) produced most of the James Bond pictures. According to *New York Times* articles at the time of his death, "He was descended from the Broccoli family of Calabria in Italy, which crossed cauliflower and rabe and named the new vegetable after themselves," and "Mr. Broccoli said one of his uncles brought the first broccoli seeds into the United States in the 1870s."

Q. Cubby Broccoli produced James Bond movies, as you noted recently, but broccoli isn't named for him, according to the *Oxford English Dictionary,* which says the word is an Italian diminutive for "shoot" or "stalk." Broccoli turned up in English about 1700. One wonders where the *New York Times* obituary, which you quoted, got the idea the veggie was named for Cubby's ancestors. A P.R. firm working overtime?

—Jim Breig, East Greenbush, New York

A. Jack Noland of Lisbon, Portugal, cites the *Random House Dictionary* and *World Book* in likewise questioning this factoid, and wonders, "Could ol' Cubby be yanking our stalk?"

Q. The Answer Man recently revived the story that an ancestor of James Bond producer Cubby Broccoli invented the vegetable of the same name, and indeed named it after himself. This account seemed unlikely to me. A quick check in a dictionary reveals that "broccoli" derives from the Italian word *broccolo,* meaning "the flowering top of a cabbage."

Also, an Internet site provides a brief précis on the origins of the broccoli plant with no mention of Cubby or his grandfather. It seems safe to say that although Cubby's family might or might not have had something to do with cultivating or popularizing the vegetable, it is presumptuous to credit them with its invention.

—Charles Nielson, Arlington, Virginia

A. Unless they invented it and then named themselves after it? All I know is that the story was recounted in Broccoli's *New York Times* obituary. In double-checking it, I was disappointed to find it was not written by Johnny Apple.

Buster

Q. About your item that the name Buster did not exist before it was used by Buster Keaton: The comic strip character Buster Brown debuted in May 1902, when Buster Keaton was six years old, and quickly became the most spectacularly successful comic strip of its time. So the name "Buster" was certainly in circulation before Keaton became famous.

—Andy Ihnatko, Boston, Massachusetts

A. Not quite. Believe it or not, biographies record that Buster Keaton was nicknamed when he was two, and already a famous member of the family vaudeville act, and both the comic strip and Buster Brown shoes were named after him.

The Cat's Meow

Q. Kenneth Anger's appearance at the Siskel Film Center prompted me to browse through my copy of his book, *Hollywood Babylon.* I was surprised to see that Anger's chapter on the mysterious death of Thomas Ince is virtually identical to the version related in Peter Bogdanovich's film *The Cat's Meow*—including the suggestion that Louella Parsons was given a lifetime contract in return for her silence. I was under the impression that the film's depiction of Parsons as an eyewitness was an original idea, but obviously that is not the case.

—Rich Gallagher, Fishkill, New York

A. The Anger version is the one most commonly told, but in making the film, Bogdanovich told me, he also relied on another source: "Orson Welles had a fascinating version of that story. According to him, Willie (Hearst) was convinced Marion (Davies, his mistress) was having an affair with Charlie Chaplin. During a cruise on Hearst's yacht, Hearst was overcome with jealousy and took a shot at a man he thought was Chaplin. It was a case of mistaken identity, and Thomas Ince was killed. The true story of the death never came out. In fact, despite his fame at the time, the cause of Ince's death was never established, there was never an investigation, and no one on the yacht was ever questioned."

Charles Napier

Q. I was disappointed that Charles Napier did not appear in Jonathan Demme's *The Truth About Charlie.* Napier's appearance in Demme's films was a fun cinematic footnote. Do you know if Napier is still alive or still working?

—Michael Green, Phoenix, Arizona

A. Napier, still alive and working, has the distinction of being a favorite actor of both Jonathan Demme and Russ Meyer. He was the guard whose face was stolen by Hannibal Lecter in *The Silence of the Lambs* and played the sheriff in *Cherry, Harry & Raquel.* Demme tells me he tried to find a role for Napier in *The Truth About Charlie* but just wasn't able to.

Q. In your most recent Answer Man column, you cite Charles Napier as playing the guard in *The Silence of the Lambs* who gets his face stolen by Hannibal Lector. This is incorrect. Alex Coleman played the unfortunate victim, Pembrey, while Napier ended up being strung crucifix-style from the rafters.

—Adam Lindsley, Santa Monica, California

A. You are correct. That was a query about why Jonathan Demme, who almost always uses Napier in his films, did not have him in *The Truth About Charlie*. Napier must have lots of fans; eleven readers, one from Argentina, pointed out the error.

Citizen Kane

Q. I recently took my ten-year-old son and fourteen-year-old daughter to see *Citizen Kane,* which they loved. They were unnaturally alert during the scene in which Kane throws a party celebrating the hiring of talented reporters from his rival newspaper, and trots out a line of chorus girls. Whereupon everyone bursts into a song, "There is a man, a certain man . . ." After a few lines, my kids were mouthing the words. I was incredulous until they told me these were the lyrics to a song by the White Stripes, "The Union Forever," on the hit album *White Blood Cells.*

While the tune is utterly different, the lyrics are exactly those in the film and they are bracketed by other significant lines from the *Kane* script. Yet the CD liner copy reads, "All songs written and performed by the White Stripes." *Citizen Kane* is neither mentioned nor credited. Is this flagrant, unpunished plagiarism, or did Jack and Meg White receive special dispensation from the Orson Welles estate?

—Phil Freshman, St. Louis Park, Minnesota

A. Early in the White Stripes song, the lyrics say "sure I'm C. F. K.," which would be Charles Foster Kane. Later this dialogue is quoted from the screenplay: "I'm not interested in gold mines, oil wells, shipping, or real estate." (In the movie Kane adds, "I think I might like to run a newspaper.") The song then quotes more dialogue by Kane: "What would I liked to have been? Everything you hate." Here are some of the purloined lyrics:

there is a man
a certain man
and for the poor
you may be sure
that he'll do all he can.
who is this one?
[whose favorite son?]
just by his action

has the traction
magnates
on the run?
who likes to smoke?
enjoys a joke?

A contact tells me Warner Bros., which now owns the DVD rights, believes the lyrics were lifted from *Citizen Kane* without permission, and the studio's legal department is investigating.

Q. About your item on how a White Stripes song quotes lyrics from a song in *Citizen Kane,* and that the Warner Bros. legal department is looking into it: Clearly the Stripes are fans of the film, and their song is part tribute. Jack White is an old soul with interest in roots, musical and otherwise. That the young hipsters might be turned onto *Citizen Kane* via White Stripes is a good thing.

—Mike Spearns, St. John's, Newfoundland

A. The usage is homage, not plagiarism. There is no reason to lift those particular lyrics other than to evoke Citizen Kane. The only astonishment for me is how long it took for the tribute to be noticed. There may be unacknowledged homages and quotations still lurking here and there, in some of the most unlikely songs and films, as prizes for alert audiences. I personally once hid some poetry by H. D., but I won't say where.

City of God

Q. I wholeheartedly agree that the bone-shattering *City of God* belongs near the top of a Top Ten list. But are you sure you've got the right year? As far as I can tell, this movie had no theatrical release in 2002—even in L.A., it's not slated to open until January 17. Indeed, in the few dozen Top Ten lists I scanned, only you and *Screen Daily* (a European publication) cited it, which I consider rock-solid proof that your peers must have considered it off-limits.

—Kevin Bourrillion, San Francisco, California

A. I mentioned in my article that I knew I was jumping the gun. But *City of God* is so extraordinary that I wanted to include it on this year's list, which might do it some good, rather than wait a year. Foreign films have a hard enough time at the box office. Since several thousand North Americans have seen *City of God* at film festivals and it is eligible for the 2002 foreign-language Oscar, I feel my timing is justified.

Q. Of course I am biased, being a Brazilian, but don't you think that *City of God* deserved an Oscar nomination? Here in Brazil it's one of the biggest box office hits ever. The film received critical acclaim everywhere. We were all hoping for it to win the award. So, what happened? Is the theme too strong for Oscar? Is it just bad luck? Don't you think it's one of the best films of the year?
—João Solimeo, Vinhedo, Brazil

A. So good, I put it second on my list of the ten best films of 2002. *City of God* has already been voted among the top two hundred films of all time on the Internet Movie Database, and scores over 90 percent on the Tomatometer. It's a black eye for the Academy that it was not even nominated, calling the whole foreign film nomination process into question yet once again. This is one of those monstrous fiascoes like the Academy members who turned off *Hoop Dreams* after fifteen minutes.

How did this miscarriage of taste take place? Miramax, the film's U.S. distributor, has no official statement. However, an insider tells me privately, "When we had about sixty walkouts at our official Academy screening we knew things weren't looking good. Unfortunately, the Academy randomly assigns screening dates and ours was in early December, way before the good reviews and press came out. I guess the bottom line is that this film didn't appeal to the people on this committee, who are older and have a history of not going for edgier fare. There were some real champions but the nominations are based on an average and those walkouts killed the average."

The Academy members capable of walking out on *City of God* should disqualify themselves from future voting, as a final service to the Academy.

Commercials and Movies

Q. When we went to see *The Two Towers* at our local theater (owned by Regal) we were forced to sit through thirty minutes of commercials and advertisements. This was prior to the usual amount of trailers. The audience that night was close to rioting after the first fifteen minutes of ads and I understood their frustration. The trailers I don't mind but if I wanted to see commercials I would stay home and watch TV. Any thoughts on how we can stop this before it gets any worse?
—Joanna Land, Irvine, California

A. I agree with you: I've paid to get in and don't deserve to have commercials inflicted on me. There is another insidious possibility: Movies are currently held to about two hours because theaters want to "turn over" the audience three times a night. If twenty or thirty minutes of commercials are added, will directors be pressured to hold their movies to ninety minutes? There are trade reports that theater ad packages are being promoted as a new advertising medium. What may sink this trend is the intense resentment audiences feel against the commercials. If I were a sponsor, I would think twice before buying ads so that an audience could boo my trademark.

Q. I got a good laugh out of that Answer Man question about ads in theaters. I happen to work for Regal as a manager. Regal is evil and greedy, but maybe not in that order. Each week we receive a list of commercials that must be on-screen. And every week, each movie has a minimum of eight to ten commercials. The corporate office is very focused on how much revenue advertisements provide. Everything else is secondary to making sure all commercials are running—including customer complaints.

Now, in coordination with RegalCinemedia, Regal Entertainment will begin implementing a prefeature program: twenty minutes of commercials preceding the start time of the feature—projected digitally. I wonder how well this will work. Considering that shows will have to end at least twenty minutes before the prefeature program, this will largely limit the number of shows per day.
—Name withheld

A. If I were faced with twenty minutes of paid advertising before a movie, I would simply walk out and demand my money back. Commercials are fine when they underwrite TV or subsidize newspapers, which could not exist without them. But when I pay for a ticket, I am personally subsidizing the screening, and resent being made into a captive victim. I received an avalanche of mail on this subject and cannot understand why advertisers would want to attract hostility toward their products by deliberately offending potential customers.

Q. I enjoyed your Answer Man response to the question about ads before movies. I always wonder how much the theater gets paid. I mean, I pay $9.50 to get in. I can't imagine that all of the ads bring in more than a quarter per person. Is it really worth alienating your customer for a quarter? I don't think marketing people realize a lot of folks hate ads. The McDonald's across the street from Wrigley field has flat-screen LCD monitors, flashing ads at you while you wait in line. How much could they possibly earn from those monitors? Does it offset the negative reaction it creates in some people?

I enjoy the Century theaters in Evanston. But I went in to buy a Coke, paid them something like four dollars, and they handed me a cup for self-serve. The soda dispenser was filthy, and I couldn't tell which kind of lid was the right size. Buying a movie Coke, it always grates me that the price is out of line. But there was something about having to fill it up myself, the dirty station, and having to hassle with the lid that did me in. I haven't bought a Coke since. I go to the convenience store and buy a twenty-ounce bottle, and sneak it in. They've pushed me over to the wrong side of the law.

What do they pay the people behind the counter? Six dollars an hour, with no benefits? How many Cokes per hour can one person serve? What's the difference in profits between a self-serve Coke and one that their person makes? It doesn't make business sense. These guys are trying to squeeze more money out of people in lots of little ways, making the experience of going to the movies that much more unpleasant. At some point they will cross over a line, and people will stop going. I don't know where that point is, but I know it exists.
—Alex Strasheim, Chicago, Illinois

A. Theater chains obsessed with the bottom line should realize that the real bottom line is their customers.

Q. When I saw *Anger Management* this week, I discovered a ridiculous new advertising medium being shoved down the audience's throat. Several scenes at the main character's apartment began with an outside view of his building. On top of the building was a clearly computer-generated billboard advertising the "U.S. Army: An Army of One." The camera focused on the billboard for several seconds, and I felt increasingly disgusted. What have we come to? Are producers of these mainstream movies being paid to literally rent out space during their running time?
—Daniel Lennard, Chicago, Illinois

A. A rep for Columbia Pictures tells me: "The army billboard is not product placement. It was computer-generated. A Happy Madison Production, the production company on *Anger Management,* is a big supporter of the military and that is why they made it an army billboard."

Q. I read the letter in your Answer Man column about TV commercials playing in movie theaters. I, too, am pissed off about this. If advertisers don't want their commercials to be scorned by moviegoers, perhaps they could sponsor a short film. That would add to the entertainment value of my movie ticket and maybe even encourage me to buy from that advertiser.
—Herb Kane, criticdoctor.com

A. Having heard moviegoers boo and ridicule the paid commercials, I am puzzled why advertisers would want to offend audiences in this way. Since theaters place great emphasis on how many times they can show a movie in a day, the addition of twenty minutes of paid commercials will sooner or later result in pressure for shorter movies—a penalty for filmmakers and audience.

John Fithian, president of the National Association of Theater Owners, has been quoted as saying: "You can either have movies with ads and pay $7 a ticket, or you can pay $12 a ticket and not have commercials." If anyone has found a first-run theater that has lowered its prices because of commercials, please let me know. In the meantime, Chicago attorney Douglas Litowitz has filed a class action lawsuit against commercials in movie theaters, and has a Website about his campaign at www.nomovieads.com.

Complaint Department

Q. Who can I sue?? The movie *Saving Private Ryan* had to be, by far, the world's worst movie of all time. Thank God it was on TV & I did not spend $ to see it, how could you give it a 4-star rating? Any *Combat* episode is 10k times better. You have to be getting a kick-back, or be on dope, to not recognize a stink-bomb.
—Ross Lyngstad, Warrenton, Oregon

A. I suggest you sue your local educators.

Q. I was astonished by how many movies you gave four-star reviews to in 2002. Assuming that all these movies are of masterpiece caliber, what's the point of making a year-end Top Ten list if you can't give each film rightful acknowledgment?
—Jon Crylen, Schaumburg, Illinois

A. What's the point of not giving them four stars if they deserve them? Last year was a very good year at the movies, and I don't grade on the curve. When it comes time to make the Top Ten list, which is somewhat arbitrary anyway, I try to choose the best of the best.

Confessions of a Dangerous Mind

Q. *Confessions of a Dangerous Mind,* the fantasy-biography of TV producer Chuck Barris, revives an old debate surrounding *The Newlywed Game.* In the film, we see a clip from the game show in which host Bob Eubanks asks a young wife named Olga, "Where is the oddest place you have ever had the urge to make whoopee?" After some bashful hemming and hawing, the woman answers, "In the butt." Her husband laughs heartily while Eubanks, stunned, tries to rephrase the question.

Now, it was my understanding that this *Newlywed Game* moment was an urban legend, and that Eubanks had denied that such an exchange ever took place. Did the creators of *Confessions of a Dangerous Mind* unearth the original risqué footage, or did they simply fabricate the clip in imitation of the legend?
—Maureen Stabile, Streamwood, Illinois

A. Director George Clooney tells me he thought it was an urban legend, too, until Barris produced the actual footage.

The Core

Q. In your review for *The Core,* you mentioned that the film is not very scientifically accurate. The screenwriter would beg to differ. John Rogers went to quite a bit of trouble to make his film as accurate as possible. He has his panties in a bunch over the dismissal of the film as scientific fantasy and has been responding, as in a letter to Ain't It Cool News.
—Bruce Labbate, Atlanta, Georgia

A. I read his letter, and man! This guy is angry enough to personally drill to the earth's core in his birthday suit. I concede that his portrait of the earth's interior draws on facts (up to a point), but then it shades off into total fantasy, and besides, are we going to this movie for accuracy, anyway? Most of the criticism of the science was affectionate. Mine was.

Credit Cookies

Q. Is there a term for the inconsiderate filmgoers who rush to leave as soon as the credits roll, but then *stop and block your view* so they can stand and gawk at the surprise outtakes? This situation almost caused a fight at a recent showing of *Bruce Almighty.* As soon as the credits started, 60 to 70 percent of the crowd immediately jumped out of their seats to leave. But the outtakes started playing, and these same people, who were in such a hurry, suddenly stopped in their tracks, gawked up at the screen, and completely blocked the view of those of us who had decided to stay. Seated patrons asked the gawkers to please sit back down, only to be met by hostile shouts of, "Oh, be quiet. The movie's over. Why don't *you* stand up?" Were we seated moviegoers within in our rights to ask them to sit down or walk out?
—Bill Dal Cerro, Chicago, Illinois

A. Absolutely. By now even the slowest-witted moviegoers must know that deleted scenes and outtakes, known as credit cookies, are a part of any comedy. Barbarians who stand up and block the view should obviously be called Cookie Monsters, and I advise you to throw popcorn at them. Best credit cookies of the year: director Gurinder Chadha, at the end of *Bend It Like Beckham,* leading her cast and crew in singing the chutney soca song "Hot, Hot, Hot."

Crying at the Movies

Q. I recently saw *About Schmidt,* starring Jack Nicholson, at the fortieth New York Film Festival. I'm a twenty-year-old male film studies major, but couldn't help myself from shamelessly bursting into tears at the end of this film, the first time I have ever cried at the movies. When was the last time you cried at a movie?

—Brian Betancourt, Columbia University, New York, New York

A. At the end of Philip Noyce's *Rabbit-Proof Fence,* at the Toronto Film Festival.

Daddy Day Care

Q. In your review of *Daddy Day Care* you write about the rival school run by Anjelica Huston: "It looks to me like a pretty good school, with the kids speaking foreign languages and discussing advanced science projects. Obviously, in the terms of this movie, any school where the kids have to study is bad, just as a school where the kids can run around and raise hell is good." I agree with you that *Daddy Day Care* does not look like the best environment for children, but you cannot possibly believe the other school looks good, making four-year-olds study SAT words, learn Portuguese, and being deprived of anything resembling fun!

—Andrew Shusterm Merrick, New York

A. Which school would you send your kids to?

Digital Projection

Q. What are your thoughts on the recent announcement that all Landmark Theaters are converting to digital screening systems? I am convinced that this is bad news; current top-of-the-line systems are putting out a 1.5k image and experts say that only a 4k image will truly approximate 35-mm film. Yet as near as I can tell the Landmark screens are going to use DVD quality or less (inferior even to the 1.5k resolution that *Attack of the*

Clones was shown at last summer). I guess there are two good things about it: that it could allow some really low-budget independent films easier distribution, and that the quality will so rankle filmgoers that it will push back total digital adoption even further (Landmark screens usually show films for the art house crowds, who can be the most finicky customers).

—Richard Huffman, Seattle, Washington

A. As I understand it, Landmark does not plan to replace traditional celluloid projection, but to augment it with video projectors that will allow the booking of low-budget indie films without the expense of making and shipping prints. This is an inventive step toward getting such films seen. A year or two ago it appeared that film would be replaced by digital projection, but that bubble has burst. Digital projection is not ready for prime time in terms of its quality, and no workable system for distributing and encrypting it has been devised.

DVDs

Q. As a movie lover I was delighted with the success of the DVD format for home viewing. Unfortunately, now I often have to choose between the letterboxing and better picture quality of a DVD and the more clearly audible dialogue of a VHS tape. Why is the dialogue on so many DVDs overshadowed by the music and background sounds? Most recently I purchased *The Lord of the Rings: Fellowship of the Ring* on DVD and had to turn on the English captioning because of the poor sound mixing. Are the new DVDs designed for the newer digital TVs and no longer compatible with conventional TV systems? Even my friends with quality surround sound are having this problem on certain DVD releases.

—Karen Eubanks, Calgary, Alberta

A. In the theater, movie dialogue is carried on the center channel, and music and sound effects are on the surround channels. DVDs do the same thing. A good home entertainment system will have a receiver capable of decoding them, and a center speaker in addition to the "stereo" speakers on the side. New TVs can handle DVDs.

Q. I've just experienced *Waking Life* on video and I am disappointed with Fox's blanket disclaimer at the opening of the DVD. If "the opinions expressed in this movie do not necessarily reflect those of 20th Century–Fox," then I can't help but ask, what *does?* This movie, unlike any other, respects and represents the myriad of human states in which we find ourselves today. Was this blanket disclaimer in response to feeling of unease among the media "in the wake of 911?"
—George Partida, Carson, California

A. Good lord! A movie with an opinion! In fact, countless opinions, as the movie's hero wanders around Austin and listens to dozens of talkative folks. My guess is that 20th Century–Fox, being a studio and not a person, has no opinions on anything, so it doesn't necessarily disagree with them, either.

Q. When I watched *Moulin Rouge* in the theater, I found it to be an incoherent, in-your-face, style-without-substance kind of movie. I would never have recommended it to anyone, not even lovers of the musical. I just bought the DVD for my girlfriend, and while rewatching it with her, I found it to be extremely entertaining. I could not believe how much dislike I had on the first viewing, and yet so much joy on the second. Should we always trust our initial instincts with a movie when judging it?
—Vincent Santino, Phoenix, Arizona

A. Yes. If you saw it in a theater again, you would probably feel the same way. The phenomenon of *Moulin Rouge* is that for many people it seems to play better on DVD than on the big screen, maybe because they can get more distance from its passionate stylistic aggression. I liked it on the screen, loved it on DVD.

Q. What do you think of self-destructing DVDs? With disposable movies, the late fees that video chains rely on will dry up. Imagine a world littered with disposable copies of *The Mummy Returns*. On the other hand, think of all the time I'll save not returning DVDs. They'll make fine coasters or you can throw them away like a Frisbee.
—Mike Breiburg, Studio City, California

A. Technology described at www.flexplay.com provides a "limited-time viewing window beginning after it is removed from the packaging." Once you open the DVD and watch it you throw it away, eliminating the return to the store. This may be a mixed blessing for video stores, because returning the old movies is often when you get inspired to rent new ones. It could, however, provide a competitive edge if a single video chain licenses it and advertises no-return DVDs.

Q. Of late I've had the notion that DVDs have been coming down in price. To see whether this is correct, I crunched a lot of numbers, and found that between 1998 and this year my average DVD purchase went down from $22.85 to $14.25. Up to now I have crossed my fingers. The DVD seemed too good to be true. I was expecting the industry to realize their mistake and triple or quadruple the price, explaining it was too good for the likes of me! But to my joy, the DVD format has increased in strength, and competition has driven down the prices instead.
—Chuck Kuenneth, Chicago, Illinois

A. Prices of VHS tapes were often in the $89 range, because studios made most of their money selling them to video stores for subsequent rental. The business strategy for DVDs was to make them a "sell-through" medium, like CDs and paperback books. The format has been successful beyond the industry's wildest dreams. Recently some big consumer electronics chains have stopped selling VHS tapes altogether to make more room for the discs.

Q. I would like to commend Wal-Mart on their new DVD releases. There is a shiny, silver sticker that reads, "Special Limited Release! Formatted to fit your TV! No black bars on top and bottom!" It's bad enough that these morons disfigure artwork, but now they're using their ignorance as a marketing pitch!
—Lee Stringer, Brampton, Ontario

A. In a few years Wal-Mart will be selling wide-screen TVs, and their customers will be bringing in those DVDs and demanding a refund because there are black bars on the left and right.

Q. About the topic of "missing DVDs." I'd like to add *Wings of Desire* and *A Matter of Life and Death* to the list. What causes the holdup in getting some of these to DVD?

—Scott Held, Detroit, Michigan

A. Usually it's a problem of copyright; sometimes adequate film materials are not available. Also missing: *La Dolce Vita, The High and the Mighty, El Topo.* The long-awaited Visconti film *The Leopard,* with its famous Burt Lancaster performance, is now reportedly in the pipeline.

Editing for Content

Q. You have mentioned before your view on the Clean Flick movie chain and chains like it. What is your opinion of editing a film for television or for an airline flight?

—Peter Felt, Provo, Utah

A. It happens. I never watch airline movies and avoid channels that censor their films. I believe the director has a better idea of what should be in the film than some bluenose video jockey. Companies like Clean Flick "edit" movies to remove offending words and images. They produce such annoying results that some of their frustrated customers are inspired to seek out the actual film. The Directors Guild of America is currently suing to stop the practice—but is on shaky ground, since it agrees (over the dead bodies of some of its members) with airline and broadcast censorship.

My notion is that religions should be robust enough to trust their members. A religion should arm you to go into the world, not wall you off from it. One thing censorship achieves is to create an aura of forbidden glamour. How well I remember, as a callow adolescent, studying the Legion of Decency's "condemned" film list in *Our Sunday Visitor. Summer with Monica* especially inflamed my imagination. Years later I discovered it was an early Ingmar Bergman drama of alienation, condemned for nihilism, not sex.

Q. I was surprised by your comments about ClearPlay in your article from Sundance. Your main argument is, "Filmmakers have a right for their films to be presented as they made them." This is an example of your personal bias in favor of filmmakers over viewers. I'm a father with small children, and I hope you would not oppose my "right" to manually use the remote control to skip over one or more parts of a film that have content that I feel is inappropriate.

As a practical matter, in a busy family a parent does not have the time to preview every film they might want to share with their children, so it's quite possible to bring home a film with one or more scenes that are inappropriate. ClearPlay may or may not help with this problem, but certainly you shouldn't discount its fundamental function, which is to filter out content that might be too difficult for a younger viewer to absorb.

—Allen Broadman, Montvale, New Jersey

A. The responsibility of parents does not stop at, or even include, editing out parts of movies that were not meant for children in the first place. It begins with the positive decision to offer the children appropriate entertainment. Sites such as ScreenIt.com provide in-depth, objective information about the suitability of films for various age groups. What purpose does it serve for a child to see *8 Mile* after the ClearPlay software has cleaned it up? What are they left with? What do they get from it? As for adults, they must be big boys and girls and decide for themselves. The idea that software would stand between me and a movie is sad and insulting.

Q. In *Back to the Future* on TNT they showed a scene of Marty writing a letter to Doc Brown, warning him about being shot by terrorists in the future. As Marty reads the letter aloud, I noticed that him saying "by terrorists" had been muted. And when they showed a close-up of the letter, the words "by terrorists" had been digitally erased!

—Steven Knauts, Atlanta, Georgia

A. Bob Gale, the producer of the movie, says he is amazed that TNT would take out "terrorist." He doesn't think director Bob Zemeckis knows about it, and it couldn't have come from the studio, so it must have come from TNT. All of my queries to TNT have gone unanswered. A splendid new DVD edition of the *Future* trilogy provides access to the unedited films.

Eight Legged Freaks

Q. Shouldn't the movie *Eight Legged Freaks*, without a hyphen, be about eight freaks who have legs?

—John Vieira, Calgary, Alberta

A. For years we have had to struggle with the Grocer's Apostrophe, the extra apostrophe after the name of a fruit or vegetable ("banana's," "onion's"). Now we are faced with the Eight Legged Hyphen.

8 Mile

Q. Because of the release of *8 Mile*, more and more discussions have been surfacing about the validity of rap music as an art form. A disturbing trend that I've been seeing recently is to label rappers/rap music as "talentless" by those that are not fans of the genre. Now while you can expect comments such as that from kids and teenagers full of antimainstream angst, it becomes downright sad to see it from mainstream movie reviewers (á la Rex Reed).

While the movie contains quite a few clichés, much of it rings completely true; this is coming from someone who was surrounded with that environment growing up. As a movie critic who was once an aspiring rapper from the Detroit inner city, I can say that the process of writing and performing a rap drew on much more "ability" than something like writing a movie review, because of all of the different kinds of skills and talents that it draws upon at once. How is it that so many who make a living critiquing talents have such a problem recognizing it when it is something that they don't necessarily like?

—Aaron "Ator" McCray, Detroit, Michigan

A. The ability required to perform an art form is not related to the ability of others to enjoy it. If I told you that grand opera requires much more ability than rap music, would you abandon Eminem for Verdi? What we are talking about here is that great imponderable, personal taste. I happen to admire *8 Mile* and think Eminem is talented, but my taste in music does not run toward the angry and cheerless.

11'09"01

Q. Where can one rent or buy the film *11'09"01*, which premiered at the Toronto Film Festival?

—Jay Mitchell, Olympia Fields, Illinois

A. This is a film in which eleven directors from eleven countries were given eleven minutes each to make a film about September 11th. It has not yet been picked up for theatrical distribution in the United States, perhaps because some of the films express a viewpoint critical of the United States. The best of the eleven, overwhelmingly powerful, is by Mexico's Alejandro Gonzáles Iñárritu (*Amores Perros*), whose screen is darkened for most of the running time, then interrupted with brief flashes of falling bodies. The sound track includes a fearsome hammering of the floors in one of the towers as they collapsed, and were recorded on a radio inside the tower. *Note: The film was released in September 2003.*

End Credits

Q. Why don't studios repeat the title of the film in the end credits? I often turn on a movie after it has started on TV and never find out what movie I am watching so that I can rent the DVD and see the first part that I missed.

—Paul Cady, Oak Park, Illinois

A. This is pure common sense and I expect your suggestion to be adopted immediately.

Far from Heaven

Q. In the end credits for *Far from Heaven*, I noticed that one of the assistants to director Todd Haynes was listed as Slats Grobnik. Is this a real person or an in-joke by someone paying tribute to Mike Royko's famous fictional character?

—Greg Nelson, Chicago, Illinois

A. I asked Todd Haynes, who replies, "I love that you noticed the ghostly presence of Slats on the credits of *Far from Heaven*. I have to claim utter Chi-town ignorance of the legend and defer entirely to my talented friend Jon Raymond, who agreed to be my assistant on the film, and knew of the history of Mike Royko's sidekick and decided to cloak himself accordingly. Jon, who's actually visiting his hometown of Portland this week where I now live, was very chuffed to hear you'd picked up on this."

Q. Why did Douglas Sirk, who's back on the pop culture radar thanks to *Far from Heaven,* quit making movies from 1960 to the mid '70s? Was he ill? Fed up with moviemaking? Retired and living somewhere in Tahiti, with Marlon Brando's ex-girlfriends?

—Laura Emerick, Chicago, Illinois

A. Todd Haynes's *Far from Heaven* is set in 1957 and is a deliberate reconstruction of the look, feel, and style of the melodramas Sirk made during that decade, such as *All That Heaven Allows, Written on the Wind,* and *Magnificent Obsession.* Born in 1900, Sirk was a German (real name Claus Detlev Sierck) who left Germany in 1937. Ill health forced his retirement after *Imitation of Life* in 1959 and he returned to Germany, where he was embraced by members of the German New Wave like Rainer Werner Fassbinder, himself heavily influenced by Sirk. Helped by this new generation, he made three short films between 1975 and 1978.

Fargo Urban Legend

Q. A long-standing urban legend has come to an end. An article in the *London Guardian* by Paul Berczeller followed up on the story about the woman from Japan who allegedly went to North Dakota and supposedly froze while looking for the buried roadside treasure left at the end of *Fargo.* While it turns out to be a sad story about a young woman's suicide, it ultimately had nothing to do with the movie.

—Jason Bergman, Brooklyn, New York

A. You betcha.

Femme Fatale

Q. Your four-star rating of *Femme Fatale* flies in the face of every other review I have read. (I must admit that not only have I not seen this movie, and it's entirely likely, unfortunately, that I will never see it in its original theatrical form here in Singapore.) I conclude that (a) you must have a crush on Rebecca Romijn-Stamos (but who among us doesn't)

and (b) others are blind to the charms of this movie.

—Tony McFadden, Singapore

A. *Femme Fatale* is one of the great recent triumphs of pure movie style, and my praise is far from alone. Critics I admire, such as Jonathan Rosenbaum of the *Chicago Reader,* A. O. Scott of the *New York Times,* David Edelstein of Slate.com, Charles Taylor of Salon.com, and Ed Gonzalez of Slant.com also loved it. Perhaps audiences and critics have been so bludgeoned by in-your-face sensationalism that they have lost the taste for elegance, eroticism, and wit.

Finding Nemo

Q: I just watched *Finding Nemo* and thoroughly enjoyed the film; however, did I catch an anti-American comment at one point? Marlin is telling the fish back home that his son has been kidnapped by humans. One of the other fish says humans are terrible because they believe they own everything and can do as they please. Another fish says something like, "Yeah, they were probably Americans." No matter what one's political leanings may be, this is a rather curious addition to a major studio film.

—Carl Little, Halifax, Nova Scotia

A. The comment is incredibly unfair, since Nemo was kidnapped by Australian humans. You should reflect, however, that in saying Americans think they can do as they please, the poor little fish is only reflecting current administration policy.

555-XXXX

Q. In a recent Answer Man, you refer to "the nonexistent 555 prefix." The 555 prefix does exist now, though, so I expect moviemakers will resort to using more normal-sounding numbers from now on. One example: call 800-555-TELL and you can order movie tickets.

—Binky Melnik, New York City

A. For years "555" was reserved for movie numbers. Another citadel of movie trivia falls. But at least the California 2GAT123 license plate still turns up all the time.

From Justin to Kelly

Q. The studio releasing *From Justin to Kelly* did not screen the movie for critics. Isn't this pretty much the kiss of death for a new release? When was the last time a movie that wasn't screened for critics wound up being a megahit at the box office?

—Andrew Milner, Bryn Mawr, Pennsylvania

A. The strategy almost always backfires, generating more negative publicity than it prevents. A wise old publicist told me that while negative reviews can hurt ambitious pictures, they can't hurt junk, because the public knows it's junk and doesn't mind; therefore, the reviews simply provide more publicity. "Has anyone," he asked me, "ever stayed away from a *Friday the 13th* movie because it got bad reviews?" *From Justin to Kelly* tanked badly at the box office, and might have benefited by the buzz of opening-day reviews, however negative. Among deserving pictures that the studio didn't screen, I recall Disney's *Tombstone,* a superior Western; the lack of critics' screenings during the crucial Christmas season may have cost Val Kilmer an Oscar nomination for his brilliant Doc Holliday.

Funniest Title

Q. Following the Answer Man shebang about the funniest movie title of all time, I would like to pose the following question. Is the quote "Those aren't pillows" the funniest line of movie dialogue ever?

—Ali Arikan, London, England

A. The problem with funny dialogue is that it usually needs a context to work. If we remember the scene from *Planes, Trains, and Automobiles,* yes, that is great dialogue. But what about dialogue that doesn't depend on context and is funny all by itself? Something like, for example, "Everybody needs money! That's why they call it money!"

Heather Rose

Q. I read on an Australian Website that Heather Rose has passed away. As one who admired and loved her film *Dance Me to My Song,* I wonder if you can give more details.

—Susan Lake, Urbana, Illinois

A. Heather Rose, who brought sunshine to my first Overlooked Film Festival in 1999, died suddenly on October 5, 2002, a day after her thirty-sixth birthday. She wrote and starred in *Dance Me to My Song,* which was directed by Rolf de Heer and won a standing ovation at Cannes in 1998. A victim of severe cerebral palsy, she communicated by typing voice messages on a computer with the one finger she could control. In the movie, she plays a character who has two goals: (1) to meet a man and make love, and (2) to have revenge on the corrupt caregiver who insults her, ignores her, and steals from her. Despite her handicaps, she is triumphant. The movie is powerful and deeply affecting, a masterpiece that never blinks in regarding the nature of her disabilities, but it has not found distribution in the United States—perhaps because of competition at the time with *The Theory of Flight,* a sentimental and manipulative movie about a woman with ALS, starring Helena Bonham Carter and Kenneth Branagh. In that one, the heroine was taken flying in her new lover's handmade plane. The Heather Rose character's journey to the sidewalk in front of her house is much more difficult and inspiring.

The Hours

Q. The *Hollywood Reporter* said on January 29, 2003, that *The Hours* was disqualified in the best makeup category because of a technicality—some digital work had been done on Kidman's prosthetic nose. What the heck does that actually mean? What did they *do* to the schnoz? And why would they *need* to do it? You hear about an actor's hairline being filled in digitally, but what could it mean for a nose? Why didn't they simply make the prosthetic the way they wanted it to look in the first place?

—Mary Jo Kaplan, New York, New York

A. I'm told it's not so much a question of creating Virginia Woolf's distinctive nose as of making it look absolutely realistic in big-screen color close-ups. If it didn't look right in postproduction scrutiny, it was too late to reshoot the scenes, but not too late to make subtle digital improvements.

Hulk

Q. The Hulk never knows when he'll be angry enough to metamorphose into a giant of extra proportions; yet whenever he does metamorphose, he always has his shorts on. I'm a science fiction fanatic but I've never come across the explanation as to how Hulk is not running around totally naked.

—Her Lao, Saint Paul, Minnesota

A. "I'm as fascinated as you about that," Hulk actor Eric Bana told the *London Observer.* "Obviously it's got to do with the fact that otherwise we'd have a large green penis flopping around, and that would diminish the chances of us opening in four thousand cinemas across the country."

In a World . . .

Q. Studios still produce trailers that start with "In a world . . ." and then gather momentum with quick cuts and explosions, followed by a supposedly cool line by the star. Having just seen the clever trailer for Jerry Seinfeld's new movie *The Comedian,* I wonder if you think the days of the mind-numbingly predictable voice-over are numbered?

—G. Doig, Glasgow, Scotland

A. The new Seinfeld trailer may nor may not sell tickets, but it's one of the funniest I've seen. It stars the "In a world . . ." guy himself, Hal Douglas, described by Miramax publicist Tracy Ury as "perhaps the most recognizable trailer voice in the business." The trailer is a merciless dig at all the weary catchphrases that trailers recycle over and over again. It's at www.apple.com/trailers/miramax/comedian.html.

Irreversible

Q. In your review of the brilliant (though shocking and disturbing) French film *Irreversible,* you wrote that La Tenia is "discovered and beaten brutally." That's actually not the case. The man savagely beaten to death, although believed to be La Tenia, is someone else. He seemed to be either La Tenia's friend or his bodyguard. In essence, the wrong man was punished. Marcus and Pierre never actually get their revenge. I actually had to see the movie twice before I realized it, but it's true.

This actually makes the movie even *more* depressing and disturbing.

—Joey Di Girolamo, Miami, Florida

A. I wrongly identified the beating victim, as several readers wrote me. My excuse: At the time La Tenia is being sought, we have not seen the rape and do not know what the rapist looks like. Nor do we get a clear view of the man actually being beaten. As Darren Fernandi of Brampton, Ontario, observed, "Half the people I saw it with made this same mistake." When I did see La Tenia (in the backward chronology of the film) I did not realize he was not the man beaten in the earlier scene. That they beat the wrong man is indeed even more depressing, although one could argue that all of the movie's violence is equally wrong—the revenge turning "ordinary" men into creatures as violent as the rapist. I will correct the review on-line. But please, no messages about whether I ever change a review on-line. Of course I do, to correct mistakes above all. It is intended as a current resource, not a historical record.

Q. In an interview with Salon.com, *Irreversible* director Gaspar Noé mentioned that the scene in the gay nightclub included a sound track that consisted of "27 Hz of infrasound—a low frequency sound which the police use to quell riots." Did you notice such an effect when you watched that segment? What are your thoughts on the practicality of putting such a difficult sound in the movie?

—Gautham Thomas, Berkeley, California

A. Noé told Salon's Jean Tang: "We added 27 Hz of infrasound. . . . You can't hear it, but it makes you shake. In a good theater with a subwoofer, you may be more scared by the sound than by what's happening on the screen. A lot of people can take the images but not the sound. Those reactions are physical."

I asked an expert about this. David Bondelevich is lecturer on cinema sound at the University of Southern California. He tells me, "I haven't seen the film, but it doesn't make a lot of sense. Infrasonic sound is below the normally audible frequency range, which would be below 20 Hz. There has been research showing that 12 Hz can make you nauseated if played at very high levels. Based on this theory, police are investigating the possibility of creating weapons similar to the ones used in *Minority Report.* (Fringe elements insist they are already in use.) However, theatrical sound systems are not capable of accurately reproducing sound at infrasonic frequencies, so it sounds like propaganda to me. Remember 'Sensurround'? It had a similar theory. Their press releases claimed 'People were sent screaming from the theater' and made sick in their seats, even though all it produced was make a normal rumbling sound. It was just a well-designed marketing ploy."

Jackass

Q. During your recent appearance on *Charlie Rose,* you made the following statement: "If I laugh, I have to tell you it's funny. I went to see *Jackass,* a shameful movie. I laughed all the way through it. I mean, I have to tell you that." This was a shocking thing to hear. I anticipated your review of *Jackass: The Movie,* and none was given. Why did you not write a review and then specifically cite this movie in your interview?
—Jeff Griffith-Perham, Norwood, Massachusetts

A. In October more than forty major movies opened, and I reviewed all of them. On two weekends in a row, I published twelve reviews. On October 25, one of those weekends, I took a pass on *Jackass,* but reviewed these films: *All the Queen's Men, Auto Focus, Bloody Sunday, The Comedian, Das Experiment, Ghost Ship, The Grey Zone, Naqoyqatsi, Paid in Full, Real Women Have Curves, The Truth About Charlie,* and *Waking Up in Reno.* Have I received one single e-mail thanking me for these reviews? Nope. Only complaints that I did not review *Jackass.*

Q. Why is it that such drivel like *Jackass: The Movie* can get more than 2,400 screens for its opening, and incredible films like *Spirited Away* are sidelined into 150 theaters? Is there no justice in the film industry?
—Michael Wayne Howe, Chicago, Illinois

A. There is justice but not taste. Many moviegoers are afraid to attend a film they

hear might be good, but eager to see a film they hear is incredibly bad. On the weekend when *Jackass* opened, I reviewed twelve movies, some of them worthy of four stars, but received countless queries from readers disappointed that I had overlooked *Jackass.* I did go to see *Jackass,* and felt it was about as reviewable as the geek show at a carnival. But I've received this provocative dissent by Christopher Claxton of Honolulu:

"The film *Jackass: The Movie does* have a certain social value. It is a time capsule for suburban youth boredom. When I was a teen, my friends and I would do Jackassian stunts such as jumping off of the garage roof or riding in shopping carts. Suburbia has become a prisonlike environment, where every house looks the same and the only oasis is the shopping center, which is the legal drug of the masses. *Jackass,* like early punk rock, is born out of frustrated youth trying to break the walls of a sterilized suburban society. Johnny Knoxville and his band of desperadoes, like the Ramones or the Sex Pistols, are just taking a preexisting art form to the next level. This is why I believe this film is worthy of a review, be it negative or otherwise."

James Bond

Q. I like the idea that James Bond, like the characters in *The Simpsons* and *The Family Circle,* exists in an eternal present. The world around him is subject to time, but he and his supporting cast never age or change. In the newest movie, Q's warehouse includes the stiletto shoe and rocket backpack from previous Bond adventures. It made me wonder if Bond is supposed to be able to "remember" that he tangled with Dr. No back in the '60s. Or does time somehow contract around Bond—so that the adventures in his movies happened, not over the past forty years, but only over a decade or two? Does Bond's universe know he doesn't age? Does Bond know?
—Nick Califano, Deer Park, New York

A. Yeah, and Tarzan is getting way up there.

Q. In a recent Answer Man you were asked why James Bond never seems to remember that he has a past. My hypothesis: When a Bond is retired or killed, a new Bond is groomed to replace him. We have seen five different faces for Bond so far (not counting *Casino Royale*) and it would be fair to assume that the legend of Bond is nurtured and exploited by MI6. After all, why else would five different secret agents introduce themselves as such? It even explains Lazenby's quip at the beginning of *On Her Majesty's Secret Service,* "This never happened to the other fella."

—Ramsey Brown, Denver, Colorado

A. You realize this means Monypenny is a promiscuous slut?

Q. In a scene from the new James Bond movie, *Die Another Day,* I believe I saw Bond pick up *A Field Guide to Birds of the West Indies.* It is a well-known fact that Ian Fleming took the name of one of the authors of this book, James Bond, and used it to name his secret agent that would later acquire worldwide fame as a film franchise. Is this an unbelievable coincidence, an intended homage, or am I incorrect in my information or just seeing things?

—Daniel Robinson, Scarsdale, New York

A. No, yes, and you are not.

Q. One plot point from the otherwise fine new Bond movie *Die Another Day* was not resolved: Just what exactly *are* "African conflict diamonds"? I was unable to find out *any* information about them on an Internet search after watching the movie. Do they exist or is this a maguffin invented by the screenwriters? If they do exist, how are they different from ordinary diamonds, since, as I recall, the characters in the movie mentioned that these particular diamonds are highly illegal.

—Ed Vaira, San Diego, California

A. They are diamonds illegal to buy and sell because they come from (i.e., are stolen in or from) conflict areas. A March 2001 UN report says, "The General Assembly recognized that conflict diamonds are a crucial factor in prolonging brutal wars in parts of Africa, and underscored that legitimate diamonds contribute to prosperity and development elsewhere on the continent. In Angola and Sierra Leone, conflict diamonds continue to fund the rebel groups."

Q. In your review of *Die Another Day* you

said Bond says, "My friends call me James Bond" and Jinx replies, "Well that's a mouthful." That is incorrect; the lovely Halle Berry actually replies, "Well that's a mouthful" when James Bond tells her he is an ornithologist.

—Yusuf Artam, Wayne, New Jersey

A. You are completely correct. I scribbled a note in the dark and double-checked the quote at IMDb.com without noticing that it appears the way I quote it only in the *trailer* where nothing is ever the same as it is in the movie.

John Wayne and Marijuana

Q. Recently I came across an Italian poster for the 1952 John Wayne movie *Big Jim McLain.* In Italy, it seems, the movie was called *Marijuana.* Fascinated, I rented the movie, and found out it was an anticommunist film that starred the Duke and James Arness as HUAC investigators out to break up a ring of communists in Hawaii. There was no mention whatsoever of marijuana in the movie. My guess is that, as communism was not considered inherently evil in Europe in the 1950s, they changed the plot of the film to have Wayne and Arness chasing a drug gang. But to do so, they would have had to reshoot a considerable amount of the movie. Is this what happened, or is there some other explanation for the Italian title?

—Jeff Schwager, Seattle, Washington

A. I turned for an answer to Randy Roberts, professor of history at Purdue University and coauthor with James S. Olson of *John Wayne: American* (1995), a biographical study. He replies, "I really wish I could help you but the Italian version of the film is something I know nothing about. The conclusions of the questioner seem sound, but I don't believe anything was reshot. I know from living for a while in Europe that European titles often are quite different than American ones, but *Marijuana* seems just way out there."

Kings of New York

Q. What's your reaction to screenwriter William Goldman's article in *Variety* trashing Martin Scorsese? In the article he calls Scorsese an ape and a lousy storyteller.

—Joshua Thompson, Revere, Massachusetts

A. Goldman embarrassed himself with the article, which was mean-spirited, green-eyed, and wrong.

Larry Clark and Ken Park

Q. Larry Clark, the director of the controversial teenage sex movie *Ken Park,* recently got into a fight with his British distributor and the film was pulled from the London Film Festival. What's the story?

—Greg Nelson, Chicago, Illinois

A. Clark wrote an e-mail about the incident that was forwarded to me by his publicist, Reid Rosefelt. Greatly condensed, it says that Clark grew angry at his British distributor, Hamish McAlpine, during a dinner at which McAlpine said September 11th was the best thing that ever happened to America, and continued by praising Yassar Arafat and making disparaging comments about Israel and Jews. When he praised Hamas, Clark wrote, "I said what about the innocent little children and babies who get blown up? He said, 'They ———— deserve to die' and I lost it and punched him in the nose. I hit him a few more times. He went to the hospital with a broken nose and I went to jail for four hours before they let me go. He now says he will not release *Ken Park* and pulled the film from the London Film Festival. . . . But, if I had awoken this morning after listening to him last night and hadn't hit him, I don't think I could have looked at myself in the mirror."

McAlpine later told the *London Guardian,* "I was not prepared to put up with the presence of a racist man." McAlpine thought Clark was racist because he was anti-Palestine, and Clark thought McAlpine was racist because he was anti-Israel. Clark is taking anger-management classes. The film is without a British distributor.

La-Z-Boys

Q. In your review of *Sweet Home Alabama,* you note the La-Z-Boy reclining rockers in the home of Reese Witherspoon's parents, and then write: "La-Z-Boy: the sign of a home where the man makes the decisions." If the La-Z-Boy company doesn't license this slogan from you, then they are not the shrewd organization I've grown to know and love. Here is

a corollary to your observation: A La-Z-Boy in anything referred to as "the rumpus room" doesn't count. And how do you know for sure that the woman makes all the decisions in a relationship? You walk into the house and it's not immediately obvious where the TV is.

—Andy Ihnatko, Norwood, Massachusetts

A. Thank you for the photo of your tastefully appointed living room, with the old NeXTCube UNIX workstation serving as an end table. I also enjoyed the colorful aquarium made from a recycled Macintosh. Is there a Mrs. Ihnatko?

The League of Extraordinary Gentlemen

Q. In your review of *The League of Extraordinary Gentlemen,* you write, "Venice of all cities doesn't have graves because the occupants would be underwater," and "Venetians find it prudent to bury their dead in aboveground crypts." But Venice has, to my knowledge, at least two graveyards, both famous. Of main interest is La Isola di San Michele, an entire island dedicated to the cemetery hosting the bodies of such famous persons as Ezra Pound, Joseph Brodsky, and Igor Stravinsky. The other burial site is La Basilica di Santa Maria Gloriosa dei Frari, a cathedral that hosts the bodies of Monteverdi and Titian, and the heart (but not body) of sculptor Canova. While Titian and Canova's remains are in similar large, embellished crypts, Monteverdi's are almost certainly buried below ground level—there is a marble slab marking his grave.

—Alexander Staubo, Oslo, Norway

A. You are correct. I got caught by an urban legend. There are burial places in Venice. However, Venice does not have a *graveyard* of the Hammer horror film variety, as seen in the film. I was interested to learn on the Internet Movie Database that although a long segment of the story is set in Venice, no scenes were shot there. Of course the real city could not accommodate the car chase.

Left to Right

Q. In reading some articles on *Star Wars,* I read that the left-to-right direction is considered positive in film, and good guys move in this direction. I have not been observant enough to notice this, so is this a common practice for directors? And what are some reasons to identify the left-to-right direction as positive?

—Victor Chen, Houston, Texas

A. Yes, movement to the right is considered positive, to the left negative. Louis D. Giannetti writes in *Understanding Movies,* his invaluable book about cinematic language, "Since the eye tends to read a picture from left to right, physical movement in this direction seems psychologically natural, whereas movement from right to left often seems inexplicably tense and uncomfortable."

Q. In your response to Victor Chen of Houston, you said that movement from left to right on the screen was more psychologically natural for viewers. I'm wondering if this is instinctual throughout all cultures? In Arab and Asian countries for instance, where they learn to read right to left, do they perceive right to left movement as being more natural? Do their movies reflect this?

—Tim Cummins, Fort Worth, Texas

A. Some two dozen Answer Man readers asked the same question. I was quoting from Louis D. Giannetti's invaluable *Understanding Movies,* now in its ninth edition. He writes, "Since the eye tends to read a picture from left to right, physical movement in this direction seems psychologically natural, whereas movement from right to left often seems inexplicably tense and uncomfortable." Directors often use that insight to subtly underline the emotional effect of scenes; Hitchcock, for example, rarely violates it. Essentially, the right is more intrinsically weighted than the left, the top than the bottom, the foreground than the background. The balance point, where an object seems ideally placed, is not true center, but a little higher and to the right.

But is that only true in Western countries, where we read from left to right? I telephoned Professor Giannetti at Case Western Reserve University in Cleveland. He said he picked up the insight from the work of art historian E. H. Gombrich. "When I started asking around," he said, "cinematographers told me they don't look at it that way. Especially when

they're working out of doors, the direction and quality of the light determines everything. But they said directors do often use the left-to-right rule, composing their shots as a theater director would; the practice derives from stagecraft, and the importance of stage right.

"In the case of Asian directors, someone like Kurosawa does seem to use left to right. Ozu of course is the exception to every rule, and composes every shot independently. I'm not that familiar with Middle Eastern directors, so can't say. But I doubt the rule comes from the fact we read from left to right. It seems to reflect something innate in our minds. Classical theories of painting also reflect the left-right rule, and if you flip left and right by looking at a painting in a mirror, something looks wrong about it."

The Answer Man now expects to hear from Asian and Middle Eastern readers, and will share their insights.

The Life of David Gale

Q. Your zero-star rating for *The Life of David Gale* was partly based on the ending. Without you explaining that ending, I cannot really appreciate the review without seeing the film. I think with zero-star reviews like this you might want to consider spoilers. As a reader of your *Hated, Hated, Hated* book, I'm tempted to take a sedative and go see *David Gale* merely to understand your review.

—Mark Kornweibel, Playa del Rey, California

A. Fair enough. Spoiler warning! After the hero (Kevin Spacey) is executed for the alleged murder of his fellow death-penalty opponent (Laura Linney), the reporter (Kate Winslet) is devastated at having failed to save his life. Then she receives a video from him. On it, she discovers that Linney, who was dying, committed suicide, aided by Spacey and another activist, who together framed Spacey for the murder to discredit the death penalty. This tape represents the biggest story of her career, of course she will report on it. The result: Spacey has died in vain and discredited his own cause by making death-penalty opponents look like unprincipled frauds. The movie's ending exists only to supply a balm and cheap thrill to the audience, and trashes the logic of all that has gone before.

The Master of Disguise

Q. In his film *Master of Disguise* Dana Carvey is seen portraying an Indian man, replete with turban and snake-charming regalia. While these stereotypes are appalling, what drove me over the edge was to see him with his skin painted brown. As a South Asian, I see this as no different from the blackface used by white actors in Hollywood so long ago.

—Sridhar Reddy, Chicago, Illinois

A. When used for comic purposes, black, brown, yellow, red, and whiteface are not generally appropriate, although exceptions are possible, justified by the material. If it's any consolation, the movie may not be seen by many people. Rottentomatoes.com offers a Tomatometer, which summarizes the reviews and declares every movie "fresh" or "rotten." Sehn Duong, an editor there, writes me: "*Master of Disguise* received not a single recommendation from forty-eight print and on-line critics. This will rank it as the worst-reviewed film of all time on our site." Since he wrote, the score has changed to 61-1. The movie's only supporter is David Cornelius of the Amazing Colossal Website, who writes, "I know I shouldn't have laughed, but hey, those farts got to my inner nine-year-old."

The Matrix Reloaded

Q. I finally figured out why everyone in *The Matrix Reloaded* wears cool sunglasses: So that when the special effects guys replace the actors with phony computer-generated stunt doubles, only the grown-ups will notice. The eyes never lie. I mean, do they really think we didn't notice that Neo was a graphic toward the end of the "Battle of 100 Agent Smiths"? Or that a number of the Agent Smiths didn't even look like Hugo Weaving? This is sloppy stuff.

—Jeff Young, Las Vegas, Nevada

A. For kids raised on video games, it may have been the human actors who looked fishy.

Q. I know you have tremendous respect for Stanley Kauffmann of the *New Republic* (as do I), but what do you think of his comments that the *Matrix* films do not deserve to be reviewed, because they are essentially childish fluff? In my opinion, he should review them,

because no matter your opinion of the film, they are important from a cultural standpoint and if he thinks they're garbage, he should write a review explaining why. Mostly, I'm just upset because he's a great writer and I want to hear his take. Kauffmann wrote, "Several readers have asked why I have not reviewed either the first *Matrix* film or its sequel, especially since the theme has evoked so much serious comment. But serious themes are hardly new in science fiction. In the 1950s, when I was a book editor, I dealt with, among other sorts of books, some science fiction, including novels by Ray Bradbury, Arthur C. Clarke, Frederik Pohl, and C. M. Kornbluth, most of which were built on serious ideas and were really readable, not mere aggrandized juvenilia à la *The Matrix*. Intellectuals comparable to those who are now discussing the *Matrix* films might just as easily have examined back then the core themes of *Fahrenheit 451* by Bradbury and *The Space Merchants* by Pohl and Kornbluth. In any case this quite familiar utilization of serious thought does not in itself make the *Matrix* films more than the adolescent fodder that they are."

—Steven Bevier, East Lansing, Michigan

A. I don't know about you, but I think this *does* "explain why."

Q. I agree with the reader who was disappointed in Stanley Kauffmann for not reviewing the *Matrix* films. Kauffmann is a lucid and insightful critic, and if he feels *The Matrix* is "adolescent" and "trite," then I'd like to read exactly why. But I also regard critics as having an obligation to review major releases, especially those with a popular cultural impact. Why else become a critic? I wonder about those who try to build a career championing "small" films and obscure directors. It's like becoming a sports writer and refusing to cover the Super Bowl. When Kauffmann doesn't write even a few paragraphs on the films, it seems like a dereliction of duty.

—D. Newbert, University of New Mexico

A. Kauffmann, a critic I have admired since I was in college, reviews one or two films a week. Believe it or not, most weeks there are films more deserving of his lucid insights than *The Matrix Reloaded*. On the *New Republic*

Website, note particularly his review of *The Son*, a film of astonishing brilliance. I can think of many reasons to become a critic other than the "obligation to review major releases," and one of them is the obligation to review major films.

Q. Last night, we went to go see *The Matrix Reloaded—The IMAX Experience*. We felt ripped off. The image projected filled two-thirds of the screen and appeared no bigger than the giant screens at modern multiplexes. But at $11.50, three dollars more than the regular ticket price, we anticipated a true IMAX experience. What kind of print are they projecting? How can they get away with calling this an IMAX experience without filling the whole screen?

—John Aden, Denver Colorado

A. The IMAX screen has a ratio of 1.33:1, or four feet wide for every three feet tall. *The Matrix Reloaded* was filmed in the ratio of 2.35:1. Therefore, to show you the entire width of the picture, IMAX has to "letterbox" it. If the whole IMAX screen were filled, they'd have to cut off the sides of the image, and that would make you even unhappier. It was the preference of the Wachowski brothers that it be shown by IMAX in this way. There are definite advantages to seeing it in IMAX. Erica Chesney, an IMAX spokesman, tells me: "*The IMAX Experience* delivers a more immersive experience in terms of size, sound, and clarity. IMAX screens are four times larger than conventional 35mm screens, so the IMAX presentation of *The Matrix Reloaded* is proportionally bigger. *Matrix Reloaded: The IMAX Experience* is ten times clearer and provides a more detailed, brighter presentation. The IMAX sound system also delivers twelve thousand watts of digital surround sound."

MaxiVision vs. Digital

Q. I was amused by the e-mailer who said he was "convinced of the greatness" of MaxiVision, though he had never seen it in use. Cost issues aside, why should MaxiVision be considered superior to digital? And why don't we hear more about it in the general press?

—David Newbert, Albuquerque, New Mexico

A. Apart from the fact that it would cost only 8 percent as much to install, would play any film ever made, and would not have to be replaced every three to five years, MaxiVision is superior to digital projection because—well, because it is. The picture quality is four times as good. A few weeks ago, George Lucas invited a lot of directors up to Skywalker Ranch to lecture them that film was dead and digital was the future. He is a zealot for digital, but I was encouraged that a director like Oliver Stone actually told Lucas, "Film is what we do. It's what we use. You'll be known as the man who killed cinema." In his demo, Lucas showed them a new digital version of *Monsters, Inc.* and an old, beaten-up film print. (This was cheating, because *Monsters, Inc.* was digital to begin with, so film was one generation down.) His point was that digital remains fresh while prints get beaten up over time. True, but MaxiVision uses a vibration-free motor and ionized air so that the film is never touched by the projector housing. A valid demonstration would have been side-by-side comparisons of two films shot on celluloid, one projected digitally, the other conventionally. Even more interesting: MaxiVision against anything Lucas could throw at it.

Why don't we hear more about MaxiVision in the general press? Because the easy solution is simply to repeat the digital mantra. The *Los Angeles Times* story about the séance at Skywalker Ranch raised serious questions about digital, but seemed unaware that there were alternatives. A heavyweight investment firm, Suisse Bank/First Boston, has issued a research report arguing against digital and in favor of MaxiVision, but the press is still mesmerized by the mirage of digital.

Minority Report

Q. In *Minority Report* there is a scene where Tom Cruise is on a train and a stranger, who is reading the newspaper, looks up at him in suspicion. This man seemed to resemble Cruise's directorial buddy Cameron Crowe, who on his last project, *Vanilla Sky,* had Spielberg make a cameo.

—Ryan Kirkby, Waterloo, Ontario

A. Cameron Crowe replies, "Okay, I admit it. It's me. Steven Spielberg came to the *Vanilla Sky* set one day to visit Tom Cruise, and I urged him to walk into the birthday sequence we were filming. He was a big hit, improvised dialogue, stayed a couple hours, and left threatening to put me into *Minority Report*. Months later, his costumer came to our office with an armful of bizarre ill-fitting clothes, and told me I'd been cast as a futuristic bum. Mercifully, Spielberg later recast me as a businessman on the subway holding an interactive *USA Today*. Excitedly chomping on an unlit cigar, he explained the *USA Today* would be alive with moving images, a newspaper from the future. He's a truly joyful director. Cameron Diaz, who was also visiting his set that day, plays a businesswoman talking on a cell phone right behind me. Diaz and Cruise gave me acting tips, which I promptly forgot. It's a great movie, one of Spielberg's very best. Not even my poor acting could hold him back."

Q. On the DVD of *Minority Report* there is a line of dialogue that sounds blatantly changed through ADR post-recording. It goes something like this: "... taking a shower while this large fellow with an attitude you can't even knock down with a hammer whispers in your ear 'Oh Nancy, oh Nancy.'" Now, the word "attitude" in that sentence doesn't make a whole lot of sense. Several people have reported that they remember different wording in the theatrical release, which would make the line a lot more coherent (if obscene).
—Joshua Zyber, Jamaica Plain, Massachusetts

A. Dreamworks Home Video, which released the DVD, says, "Absolutely no audio was changed for the home video release of *Minority Report*." This does not exclude the possibility that an offending expression was cleaned up in the original release, to qualify for the PG-13 rating.

Q. I couldn't agree with you more on your choice of *Minority Report* as the best film of the year. I think Spielberg's film is one of the greatest sci-fi films every made. Much like *Blade Runner*, it will be recognized for its greatness in time. Yet upon its release and even now it hasn't received the accolades it so richly deserves. Why do you think that is? Do you feel it was too intelligent for some viewers?
—Tony Hough, Oak Park, Illinois

A. Some people never saw it because it was science fiction. Others discounted it because Spielberg's popularity distracts from his talent. It is ambitious and visionary in the way of silent films like *Metropolis,* and his technical skills are at the service of the story, instead of in place of it.

Movie Critics

Q. I was just wondering if you caught last week's episode of *Curb Your Enthusiasm,* which featured a food critic who was obscene, crude, and had a trademark "thumbs-up, thumbs-down" method for his show. As I recall, you gave Larry David's *Sour Grapes* a zero-star review. Is there any satisfaction or pride in knowing that some writer-directors take your reviews so personally?
—Scott Mertz, Omaha, Nebraska

A. Larry David may have been aiming at critics in general, not at me, since *Sour Grapes* scored a perfect zero among major critics on the Tomatometer. There is a reason for that. *Sour Grapes* was a terrible movie. *Curb Your Enthusiasm,* on the other hand, is a wonderful TV show and I like it a lot. I did wince when the critic's thumbs got broken.

Q. Peter Bart, the editor of *Variety,* recently wrote a column attacking film critics and their Top Ten lists, calling them elitist, obscurantist, and brain-damaged. Then Michael Medved echoed Bart's complaint in *USA Today,* adding that endorsing obscure nonhits "not only enhances a critic's conviction that he serves some important purpose, but also strengthens his sense of superiority, suggesting that the reviewer possesses knowledge, refinement, and sophistication that set him apart from ordinary moviegoers." Your opinion?
—Susan Lake, Urbana, Illinois

A. Peter Bart usually writes a well-informed column, but every six months or so he is overtaken by an embarrassing fit of lunacy and writes a silly know-nothing column that his editor should spike. Whoops, he's the editor. His column complains that critics do not reflect mass-market tastes and list too many small films. But surely that is the function of the critic? Top Ten lists are not a science, anyway. Their greatest usefulness is for readers looking for rental ideas. On my own list, I included both the "obscurantist" film *Invincible,* by Werner Herzog, and Steven Spielberg's box office hit *Minority Report.* I hope Bart's head doesn't explode as he ponders this.

As for the quote from Medved: I couldn't have said it better. Yes, like any self-respecting critic, I believe I "serve an important purpose, and that I possess knowledge, refinement, and sophistication that set me apart from ordinary moviegoers." It is interesting that Medved doesn't believe this statement describes himself.

Q. I am a student at Queen's University in Canada and have recently begun reviewing theater productions for the campus newspaper. I feel I have a good sense as a reviewer. I am critical but fair. I am certainly not afraid (as I find some are) to give praise when praise is due. I have been criticized for my subjectivity. I'll be the first to admit that I do discuss my personal reaction to a piece. What are your thoughts on the subjective/objective responsibilities of a reviewer?

—Graham Kosakoski, Kamloops, British Columbia

A. Subjectivity is the only possible approach to reviewing. What is a review but an opinion? Those who call for you to be objective are revealing that they have not given the matter a moment's serious thought. Most times, those calling for objectivity are essentially saying they wish you had written a review that reflected their subjective opinion.

Q. The Answer Man wrote: "One of the great mysteries is why people will cheerfully attend movies they expect to be bad, but approach good movies with great caution." Here is my theory: People are aware that film is a powerful medium and fear being challenged by it. They have plunked down nine dollars for an entertaining two hours, and do not want the movie to interrupt their good time by calling into question their values and beliefs (and, in some cases, prejudices). When a review says, "This movie will leave you with nothing to think about," that's precisely what they're looking for. If it's a bad movie, all the better; they can deride it with a sense of superiority.

—James R. Temple, Seattle Washington

A. As I never tire of repeating, "No good movie is depressing. All bad movies are depressing." I am exhilarated after a great tragedy, dejected after a bad comedy.

Movie Dogs

Q. I recently wrote a review on IMDb.com for *Accidental Tourist* and I found myself mentioning Edward, the charming dog in the film. Does the Answer Man have any favorite movie dogs?

—Jeff Leach, Keene, New Hampshire

A. I'm torn between Verdell, played by Jill in *As Good as It Gets,* and Docky, who played the unfortunate dog in *There's Something About Mary.* There is also the telepathic dog named Blood in *A Boy and His Dog.*

Movie Ratings

Q. In your review of *Martin Lawrence Live: Runteldat,* you noted "If it proves nothing else, this movie establishes that it is impossible for a film to get the NC-17 rating from the MPAA for language alone." Except for Lawrence's first concert picture, *You So Crazy,* which received an NC-17 in 1994. And so did *Dice Rules* (1991), with Andrew Dice Clay.

—Jeremy Gruenwald, Hoffman Estates, Illinois

A. The R rating suggested to me that the MPAA had relaxed its standards. MPAA spokesman Richard Taylor tells me, "The ratings board must have determined that the language contained in the more recent film by Mr. Lawrence was of a less explicit, less crude nature than that found in *You So Crazy.* This is not to say that the language in *Runteldat* is family fare, which is why it still received a rating requiring a parent or adult guardian to accompany anyone under the age of seventeen." I may have to rent *You So Crazy* to remind myself of the amazing language it must have contained, since the new Lawrence film leaves few words unsaid and it is impossible to imagine language more "explicit and crude."

Q. The MPAA rating for *Jackass* gives the film an R for "dangerous, sometimes extremely crude stunts, language and nudity." Ignoring the "extremely crude" remark (which seems to be more of an aesthetic judgment), aren't all stunts "dangerous"? Regardless of the danger or crudity how in the hell can a movie (stop reading if you are eating) show a guy make his own yellow snow-cone (you know what I mean), consume said snow-cone and then regurgitate said snow-cone and only get an R—while Paul Schrader has to pixelize grainy video footage before he can get an R for *Auto Focus*?

—Peter Sobczynski, Chicago, Illinois

A. If there is a pattern to the MPAA's reasoning, it's that you can do things in a vulgar comedy that are off-limits in a serious drama.

Q. I've noticed that films are often changed for their release in England. When there are scenes of people using nunchakus, or head-butting other people, those scenes are deleted in the U.K. release. Why? I know they have more strict laws governing guns, but nunchakus and head butts?

—Randall Poblete, Hercules, California

A. The British film critic Ian Waldron-Mantgani replies, "The British Board of Film Classification had a long-standing policy of removing shots of swinging nunchakus and connecting head butts, possibly because of legal restrictions. (Weapons such as nunchakus and star knives are banned in the U.K., after they became popular hoodlum weapons when the kung-fu craze hit Britain hard in the '70s and early '80s.) *Teenage Mutant Ninja Turtles* was a famous example of both head butts and nunchakus being cut from a U.K. release. The BBFC may have relaxed its guidelines after longtime chairman James Ferman retired and Robin Duval took over. I know that the recent cinema and video releases of *A Clockwork Orange* were passed uncut, and if I'm not mistaken that movie features shots of both nunchakus and head butts. Undoubtedly the gateway is now open for *Droogs vs. Donatello,* the movie we've all been waiting for."

Q. Maybe the MPAA is finally getting things right. In today's *Boston Globe* they gave *How to Lose a Guy in 10 Days* a PG-13 rating for "profanity, sexual situations, karaoke." I don't mind my kids hearing a little tasteful cussing, but karaoke? Never.

—Jose Dundee, Boston, Massachusetts

A. The official MPAA site mentions only "some sex-related material." Doesn't even discuss the type of microphone used.

Q. One of the things I love most about DVD is that the studios will sometimes release two versions of a film at once—the regular theatrical release and the definitive director's cut. This means I get to see the film as it was originally intended by the authors of the film before it was watered down by the ratings boards and the studio executive brass with their marketing department. But why do the studios have to wait until the DVD to do this? Why can't the studios release more than one version of a film into theaters at the same time—a version for teens or people that are faint of heart, and a version for those of us who can stomach a bit more "realism" or want to see the director's original vision? Curtis Hanson's *8 Mile,* with Eminem, reported the biggest opening ever for an R-rated movie. It seems to me the studio could have made a bundle more money and kept everyone happy by distributing two versions of his film.

—Euan B. Sharp, St. Catharines, Ontario

A. Since then, of course, *The Matrix Reloaded* has shattered all records for an R-rated film.

I was told by an exhibitor at Cannes, "Once you buy a ticket, we basically don't know which multiplex screen you go to." So those under seventeen buy a ticket to another movie, then slip into the *Matrix Reloaded* theater. Of course, Warner Bros., distributor of *Reloaded,* doesn't collect the money on that ticket, which may go to a family film. The ratings system today has little meaning except as a guide to parents, who should not deceive themselves that theaters will, or can, enforce it. When the DVDs come out, Blockbuster refuses to carry unrated or NC-17-rated film, so directors of unrated films (like *Requiem for a Dream*) are forced to create an R-rated version for the Blockbuster stores. It's not so much that the movie can't play in theaters unrated as that it can't get into Blockbuster that way.

Movie Scores

Q. While watching the most recent trailer for *Lord of the Rings: The Two Towers,* I immediately recognized the music as the excellent score from *Requiem for a Dream*. I am familiar with the practice of recycling music for trailers—I can't count the number of times I have heard the score from *Aliens*—but why bother, with a sequel to a hugely successful movie with a ready-made score? If it was slapped on for time's sake, I might understand, but the version I heard on the trailer sounds reorchestrated and tweaked, as if specifically for *LOTR*. Granted, the urgency and sadness of the music fit the tone of the trailer perfectly, but did the studio think the existing score from the first *Rings* film not moving enough?

—Kermit Holden, Atlanta, Georgia

A. You have good ears. Yes, the *Requiem* score was used, and yes, it was reorchestrated. I contacted the Answer Man's expert source David Bondelevich, award-winning music editor and lecturer at the University of Southern California. He at first assumed that "rescoring it would be prohibitively expensive," but his contact at the Ant Farm, which created the trailer, said otherwise.

Nathan D. Duvall, music producer at the Ant Farm, explained: "In many cases a trailer is created in two days and there isn't enough time to create original music. With *Two Towers* the editor who cut the trailer fell in love with the *Requiem* score but found that it didn't quite adhere to the typical trailer music formula. To solve this we created a larger orchestration that arched to a big resolution. *Requiem* is a more intimate feature yet it has a haunting melody that easily translates to a more broad feature in *Two Towers*.

"The *Rings* score is well placed in the first minute of the *Two Towers* trailer but the editor found that she needed something different since *Towers* is a different act in the trilogy. Once you have introduced the known characters and reminded the audience of their separate journeys we needed to depart from the old score. Howard Shore had not yet completed his score for *Two Towers* by the time we finished our trailer so we couldn't use any of the new music. As far as creative decisions go, our partner here at the Ant Farm who holds the *Rings* account, Barbara Glazer, supported our attempt with the revised *Requiem* theme. And all creative decisions are finally approved by [*LOTR* director] Peter Jackson."

My Big Fat Greek Wedding

Q. *My Big Fat Greek Wedding*, cost only $5 million to make and is on its way to grossing $150 million. Is this *the* most successful film ever made or have there been any films topping it in terms of "total gross/production cost?"

—Eric Schmidt, New Berlin, Wisconsin

A. *The Blair Witch Project* had a budget of $35,000 and grossed well over $150 million.

Q. *My Big Fat Greek Wedding* is dedicated to Jon Anderson. What can you tell me about him?

—Susan Lake, Urbana, Illinois

A. Jon Anderson, a gifted and much loved stage manager at Second City in Chicago, was married to actress Christina Dunne, a former roommate of the film's writer and star, Nia Vardalos. He died tragically of symptoms associated with the flu about three years ago. His father, Jon Anderson, is a legendary Chicago journalist.

Q. I read in *USA Today* that *My Big Fat Greek Wedding* is going to inspire a TV sitcom, but that CBS wants to change the name to *My Big Loud Greek Family*. What do you think of this change?

—Susan Lake, Urbana Illinois

A. Substituting "family" for "wedding" is fair enough. But "loud" is all wrong; it clangs. I'm told, however, that CBS cannot use "fat" because of small print in the film's original contract. It would probably be better for everyone, including the owners of the film, if the language was waived and "fat" went into the sitcom title.

My Wife Is an Actress

Q. I just saw *My Wife Is an Actress* and I have a question. Why is that movies about the making of other movies can never manage to come up with a decent plot for the film-within-the-film? The movie that Charlotte Gainsbourg's making with Terence Stamp looks every bit as ludicrous and uninteresting as *Rendezvous,* the film that the Julia Roberts and Blair Underwood characters are working on Steven Soderbergh's *Full Frontal.* Who'd pay to see these films anyway? This flaw seems unavoidable. It's plagued everything from François Truffaut's otherwise fine *Day for Night* to Julia Roberts's *America's Sweethearts*.

—Joe Baltake, *Sacramento Bee*

A. I think the inner movies are considered throwaway exercises; if they were too good, they'd be distractions. While agreeing that the movie within *Full Frontal* is bad I would, however, argue that it is better than the film containing it—a first.

Never Again

Q. I haven't seen *Never Again* and I probably won't, but I have one comment about your review, where you said that a woman wouldn't tell her stylist about her sexual exploits in a voice loud enough to be heard by all. You are definitely wrong about that. I have been a monthly visitor to hair salons for many years, and you wouldn't believe the things some women (and men, I might add) say in front of everyone. I have never understood it, but some women seem to use the salon like a confessional.

—Kay Robart, Austin, Texas

A. I continue to doubt that the woman in *Never Again* would have said those things in that way in real life. Then again, no one goes to a beauty salon looking for real life.

Q. About the Answer Man discussion of *Never Again*, in which you doubted that the character would talk so loudly about her sex life in a beauty salon: Kay Robart of Austin, Texas, wrote you saying you wouldn't believe the things some women say in front of everyone. I have been going to salons for a very long time and women *do not* talk about sex, let alone loud enough for everyone to hear. Then again she is from Texas.

—Joanne Plummer, Chicago, Illinois

A. She's the sweetest little rosebud that Texas ever knew.

Q. About the Answer Man discussion of *Never Again*, in which you doubted that the character would talk so loudly about her sex life in a beauty salon: Kay Robart of Austin, Texas, wrote you saying you wouldn't believe the things some women say in front of others. Then Joanne Plummer of Chicago,

Illinois, disputed that claim and used Kay's Texas residency as an explanation for such vulgar behavior. Being a Texan myself, I want it to be known that I have had countless sexual encounters in which I performed remarkably well. I suppose it's my own fault for taking offense to the pompous chuckle you fueled by an inaccurate generalization of Southern etiquette. After all, you *are* from Chicago.

—Dana Byron, Houston, Texas

A. The question isn't whether you performed well, but *whether you talked about it in a beauty parlor.* Countless people perform well. The well-bred do not discuss it loudly before strangers and do not categorize such behavior as "etiquette." Of course, I *am* from Chicago.

Q. About the Answer Man discussion of the sexual gossip in the beauty parlor in *Never Again*: Any woman who grew up in a small town probably knows the toe-curling full-voice chat in the local "beauty parlor" (think of *Steel Magnolias*). By definition, it's not a public place, even if it's a place of business. The customers are "regulars," they all know each other, and there are no men present. And yes, what's discussed can be a little startling. Most "stylists" or the Flip 'n' Clip franchise in any larger city would not qualify—I haven't heard any real beauty parlor gossip in twenty years. Don't know if there are any neighborhoods in Chicago where you can find the real everyone-knows-your-name places.

—Cathy Pittard, Arlington, Texas

A. Oddly enough, I have just seen a preview of the new comedy *Barbershop*, which takes place in the mostly but not exclusively male domain of a barbershop on Chicago's South Side. Sexual discussions are not unknown there, with the emphasis on booty—who's got it, who needs it, who wants it.

Now Read the Book

Q. In three of your recent reviews—*The Rules of Attraction, Tuck Everlasting,* and *White Oleander*—you mention that you have not read the novels the films are based upon. Do you think that reading them may enhance your viewing? Do you ever seek out books to read before/after seeing the movie? And, if you have read the novel, do you try and forget about it whilst watching the film, or do you make a comparison? (In your review of *The Fellowship of the Ring* you constantly refer to the book.)

—Adam Whyte, Scotland

A. I use different approaches for different films. There is not time to read every book that every movie is based on, and so my usual approach is to judge the movie as a movie. If I have read the book, and useful insights occur, I will use them. I am currently reading *The Shipping News*, by E. Annie Proulx, which many people assured me was better than the movie. They are correct.

Nuisances in Theaters

Q. Last night, my husband and I went to see *K-19: The Widowmaker*. Midway through the film, I was distracted by a bright light, and saw a man using some kind of LCD device. The man was answering e-mail messages on his PDA! When the movie ended, I told him he was rude and inconsiderate. He told me he'd had an emergency. I told him that if there was an emergency, it was his responsibility to handle it without impacting others. He told me that if I continued to harass him, he would have me arrested for assault. I quickly dashed ahead. When he came down the escalator, I had the manager and the security guard waiting for him. The security guard approached him, but he insisted that I was the harasser and the security guard let him go. (For the record, I used to be a hospital IS director; when I went to the movies, I always put my pager on vibrate and sat as close as possible to the end of a row, so I could exit quickly.) What do you think audience members and theater managers should do in such situations?

—Jan Lisa Huttner, Chicago, Illinois

A. Illuminated PDAs, cell phones, and pens that light up in the dark have absolutely no place in a movie theater. I applaud the policy of the Telluride Film Festival regarding cell phones that ring: One offense, and you are ejected from the theater. A second offense, and your device is confiscated until the end of the festival. For practical reasons, in a theater, the offender should be offered the choice of leaving or checking his device with the manager.

Owning Mahoney

Q. About the gambling movie *Owning Mahoney*, you said, "At least Seymour Hoffman was playing interesting games—unlike video poker and slots, like Bill Bennett." Although Bill Bennett lost over $8 million and no doubt was a fool who I have lost a great deal of respect for, your statement could not be more incorrect. Although 99.9 percent or more gamblers will lose money over the long term, I and many others like me have been playing video poker for many years, and some games (that pay over 100 percent return) can be played for profit *if* one is willing to memorize and learn the proper cards to hold based on the overall payout that the machine offers for various hands. I personally have played almost ten million hands at video poker and have never had a losing year gambling. Video poker, as far as I am concerned, is by far the most "interesting" game and can be the most profitable. You need only ask other professional gamblers about this to verify it.

—Larry M., Las Vegas, Nevada

A. I consider gambling to be entertainment, not a reasonable way to support yourself. In my experience with casinos, it is a lot more fun to play poker, blackjack, roulette, etc., than to sit for hours in solitude and isolation in front of a machine. The thought of playing ten million hands of video poker, while there are so many friends to make, movies to see, and places to visit, strikes me as depressing. The real sin of William Bennett was to condemn himself to all of those hours shut off from human life—from his friends, his family, his ideas.

Phone Booth

Q. I haven't heard anyone mention that *Phone Booth* is very much like *Liberty Stands Still* with Linda Fiorentino and Wesley Snipes. Snipes is the sniper, and Linda Fiorentino is the person stuck on the phone (cell phone in this case). The sniper forces her to cuff herself to the hot-dog cart she is standing next to.

—George C. Glanzmann, Buena Park, California

A. It's often the case that similar films come out at about the same time. *Liberty Stands Still* (which I have not seen) came out first, playing on cable in August 2002 and then going to video in October. *Phone Booth* premiered at the September 2002 Toronto Film Festival but a theatrical release was delayed because of the uncomfortable similarity to the case of the Beltway Sniper (this did not seem to deter Lions Gate, producer of *Liberty*). *Phone Booth* went into production first, in November 2000; *Liberty Stands Still* started shooting in February 2001.

The Pianist

Q. Roman Polanski's *The Pianist* inspired me to recall Ernst Lubitsch's *To Be or Not to Be* (1942), a film of a very different tone that also takes place in Nazi-occupied Warsaw. Then I remembered that a character in the troupe recites the "If we are pricked, do we not bleed?" passage to a colleague at least twice to establish his Shakespearean bona fides. Hearing a character recite that speech in the middle of *The Pianist,* I knew that Polanski has not lost his sense of humor. Yes, the speech is dramatically appropriate on its own merits, but knowledge of the Lubitsch reference changes it from appropriate to brilliant.

—Art Rothstein, San Francisco, California

A. This kind of movie cross-reference is like a hidden treasure.

Piracy

Q. As you know, I take notes via audiotape recorder at screenings. As you probably also know, Fox, Warner, and now Sony are putting in a "no electronic devices" policy at their screenings. Although I've informed them that I'm only recording my verbal notes and not the movie, they won't let me bring in my recorder. They state piracy concerns, although I doubt anyone would want to hear me mumbling into the microphone.

—Jim Judy, ScreenIt.com, Washington, D.C.

A. Why is it that otherwise intelligent people roll over and play dead when the magic word "security" is invoked? At a recent screening of *Finding Nemo,* a security guard searched my sandwich bag from the deli. I could have had an entire arsenal of recording devices in my pockets, for all he knew. Odd, too, that these policies are enforced for advance press screenings, where all guests are presumably professionals who would lose their jobs if caught at digital piracy. Will the studios also screen Friday-night multiplex crowds? Instead of spending untold fortunes on security personnel for every screening (for that is what it will take), they should simply offer a $1,000 cash reward for anyone turning in a pirate. I have a feeling that would work.

In your case, this idiotic policy is doubly depressing, because it handicaps one of the single most useful movie sites on the Web. ScreenIt.com is always listed in the top three or four review sites on Google. Anyone visiting the site will know you provide detailed and exhausting information for parents on the content of movies. The tape recorder is obviously necessary for you to do your job. Since there is, so far as I know, no market for audio recordings of new movies, the studios are penalizing you out of their own ignorance and laziness—or, more likely, are in thrall to their security experts, whose own jobs depend on dreaming up this sort of busywork.

Q. I don't know how it is in Chicago, but the critics' screenings in Philadelphia have been heavy with ridiculous security. Critics are scanned, frisked, probed, and body-checked. Bags are searched and cell phones are confiscated. At the local screening of Fox's *Down with Love,* the *Philadelphia Inquirer's* Carrie Rickey refused to relinquish her cell phone and was refused admittance to the screening. She demanded an apology from Fox (for being treated "like a criminal") and a refund of the $12 she spent on cab fares to and from the screening. Similar treatment occurred at *X-Men 2* and, to a lesser degree, at *The Matrix Reloaded.*

Do studio officials actually think that full-time, paid professional critics would download one of their films at a screening or be stupid enough to even try? Do you think they take the same precautions at regular paid performances for the public, where such an event is more likely to occur? The thievery of copyrighted works is more likely to occur at those awful evening, radio-sponsored screenings or at public performances. I can't figure out if this is yet another anticritic ploy by the studios or if it's just another example of the rampant sense of self-importance in the movie industry.

—Joe Baltake, film critic, *Sacramento Bee*

A. Carrie Rickey was correct to protest. Subjecting film critics to the equivalent of strip searches is meaningless while audiences at public screenings are not screened at all. It strikes me that many "security measures" exist primarily to provide income for the security industry, and to give inattentive studio executives the impression that something is being done, when nothing really is.

Pirates of the Caribbean

Q. I saw *Pirates* over the weekend and loved it. I read your review and noted that you said it seemed as though Johnny Depp was "channeling a drunken drag queen." It seemed to me he was channeling the Rolling Stones' Keith Richard, from the accent and eyeliner, right down to the trinkets hanging from his hair. Is it possible Depp used Richards as the model for Jack Sparrow? Has he given any interviews saying such?

—J. M. DePaul, Lewiston, Idaho

A. It happens that he has. David Geyer of Wheeling, West Virginia, supplies me with this Depp quote from the *Boston Globe:* "Keith Richards has been a hero forever and ever. It wasn't an imitation. It was more kind of a salute to him." Apologies to Keith Richards for confusing him with a drunken drag queen and vice versa.

Politics and Movies

Q. I was offended by your remarks about Trent Lott, which were totally unnecessary and irrelevant to a review of *Gods and Generals*. Please stick to reviewing movies, not giving political statements.

—Susan Bean, Lee's Summit, Missouri

A. I wrote that *Gods and Generals* was a Civil War movie that Trent Lott might enjoy. So it actually is, in my opinion. The movie embodies a nostalgic view of the war in which whites on both sides are noble, heroic, and pious, and African-Americans are all but invisible. That was the vision Lott seemed to be evoking when he said that if the segregationist Strom Thurmond had been elected in 1948, "We wouldn't have all these troubles today."

But you raise a larger question: Do political opinions belong in movie reviews? When they are relevant to the movie, of course they do. Where did so many Americans get the notion that there is something offensive about expressing political opinions? Movies are often about politics, sometimes when they least seem to be, and the critic must be honest enough to reveal his own beliefs in reviewing them, instead of hiding behind a mask of false objectivity.

When I read other critics on tricky movies, I seek those who disagree with me. For example, Mark Steyn, the conservative political columnist, doubles as the film critic for the *Spectator,* a conservative British weekly that has been my favorite magazine for more than twenty-five years. I read his reviews faithfully. Presumably they are informed by his conservatism, but since he is such an intelligent and engaging writer, I had rather be informed I am wrong by Steyn, than correct by a liberal drone. If you disagree with something I write, tell me so, argue with me, correct me—but don't tell me to shut up. That's not the American way.

Q. I recently saw *The O'Reilly Factor* where he was challenging Hollywood politics. He listed a few conservatives among the majority of liberals in Hollywood. Being a liberal, I feel this is a good thing, since most films I find thoughtful and intelligent involve liberals (*T-2* and *The Sixth Sense* starring Arnie and Bruce are a few exceptions). The only questionable actor in Hollywood is Mel Gibson. What are his political views?

—Samuel Mills, Salt Lake City, Utah

A. Mel Gibson is a conservative. As for O'Reilly's views, he is correct. Liberals tend to be drawn toward the arts more than conservatives, just as conservatives tend to appear more often on Fox News than liberals.

Q. In your recent Answer Man column, you note that liberals rather than conservatives tend to be drawn to the arts and to Hollywood. Since the vast majority of films being released year in and year out are garbage, could it be said that liberals are, in fact, drawn to garbage?

—Barry O'Connell, Kenosha, Wisconsin

A. Logical error. People less drawn to the arts are more inclined to pay to see garbage.

Q. The fifteenth anniversary celebration of the film *Bull Durham* was canceled by the Baseball Hall of Fame because actors in that film have recently exercised some freedom of speech. Haven't actors learned from the McCarthy era that actors and writers (i.e., people who have the public's attention) don't have the same rights as citizens and are still subject to blacklisting, or don't they care?

—Manuel Sutton, Chula Vista, California

A. Celebrities who speak out politically are made into targets as a way of discouraging dissent. I have not heard a single thing Susan Sarandon and Tim Robbins (the stars of *Bull Durham*) have said about the war, but I have heard countless attacks on them for saying it. When you attack the messenger instead of the message, you are essentially saying, "Since you disagree with me, shut up." This is profoundly anti-American.

Q. Some groups have launched a protest against Disney for using Ellen DeGeneres as the voice-over talent for Dory, the blue fish in *Finding Nemo*. Since she is a lesbian, they feel she is not a "suitable role model" for families attending the film. What do you think?

—Susan Lake, Urbana, Illinois

A. I think their protest is silly, immoral, and dangerous. Silly, because the voice of an animated fish is not a role model for sexuality. Immoral, because they wish to deny employment to DeGeneres because of her God-given sexual identity. Dangerous, because this is another example of a slash-and-burn mentality that works through hate and intimidation. My feeling is that moderate Americans are getting weary of these tactics.

Q. Something smells, uh, fishy. In your latest Answer Man column, you printed a letter saying there were "some groups" protesting *Finding Nemo* because of Ellen DeGeneres's

involvement in the film. I've looked and looked, but the only references I can find to anybody protesting *Finding Nemo* both come from the *Chicago Sun-Times*, one of those being your column, the other being a similarly unsourced quote from the "Quick Takes" column. By contrast, the Christian/family sites making comments about *Finding Nemo* have nothing but positive things to say.

Now, I too think that anyone who protests a movie in this manner is an idiot; however, I'm also not particularly fond of beating up straw men to prove that I'm not one of these idiots. Who are these anti-Nemo groups?

—Brian Lundmark, Norman, Oklahoma

A. It was wrong to refer to "some groups." The protest came from only one source that I'm aware of: Tom Perrault, editor of Crosswalk.com, a Christian family group. He writes, "Ellen DeGeneres is, apparently, the only female they could find to voice one of the main characters. Clearly, the Pixar/Disney folks just assume that Ellen is a perfect casting choice, and only those in the hate-mongering religious right would have any issues with the selection. . . . Although Ellen might be a sweet person (I have no idea) and a good choice for the role (whatever), we're once again reminded just how far removed most of us are from the cultural epicenter of America.

With literally hundreds and hundreds of perfectly viable options, Disney goes with someone whose personal lifestyle is antithetical to the throngs of families who are supposed to eagerly flock to the theaters."

Q. I must say I take exception to your use of Vincent Gallo's assertion that he is a "conservative Republican" as ammo in your response to his "curse" on you. You tack on his political affiliations like they are part of the evidence against him. I can think of plenty of loony, self-pontificating liberals in show business, but I've never heard you use it against them. While you are certainly justified in defending yourself against Gallo's ridiculous personal attacks, the inclusion of his political views seems like your way of trying to scapegoat a viewpoint from the unrelated ravings of an obviously troubled individual.

—Gabriel Frost, Boston, Massachusetts

A. When man bites dog, that's news. When Tim Robbins directs *Dead Man Walking*, that's not news. When Vincent Gallo is a conservative Republican, that's big news.

Punch-Drunk Love

Q. I saw a preview last night for *Punch-Drunk Love*, the newest offering from the Adam Sandler hit factory. Today, I looked for it on IMDb.com, and it already has fifty-eight votes from people who "saw" this movie. Is this movie really showing somewhere, or is somebody cooking the star ratings on IMDb.com?

—Ben Brown, Wilmette, Illinois

A. The movie played at Cannes in May, so it has been publicly seen; 78 percent of those voting gave it a "10," the highest rating. This movie is obviously a contender for the 2012 *Sight & Sound* poll of the greatest films of all time.

Q. Sadly, all my suspicions came true when I went to see *Punch-Drunk Love* this past weekend. Oh, not about the movie, which was beautifully done and surprisingly touching. No, as I feared, I found myself in a theater full of *Billy Madison* and *Happy Gilmore* worshippers who were programmed to laugh when Sandler cried, and look confused in between bodily harm jokes. In your experience, can we expect Sandler to make more movies like *PDL,* or is the following of his first audience going to force him to continue *SNL* vehicles forever?

—Ryan Cooke, Denton, Texas

A. Sandler has been bitten by the hands that feed him. *Punch-Drunk Love* has not appealed to his traditional audiences, and there is a big disconnect between critics and fans. According to the Tomatometer, 85 percent of major critics praised the film, and yet Cinemascore.com shows that exiting moviegoers rated it between C+ and F.

Matt Fields, who operates the Athena Theater in Athens, Ohio (home of Ohio University's twenty thousand students), writes me, "There are actually people out there who think that *Punch-Drunk* is Sandler's worst movie. Sony has just expanded *Punch-Drunk* to 1,200 theaters (still not very wide) and as they have expanded it, the per-screen average has tumbled. It just isn't playing to crowds outside of large metro areas. I just think that the moviegoing public isn't very sophisticated. I am always surprised how many college students don't know anything about art films at all. It seems that an earlier generation grew up on Godard while today's is growing up on *Jackass*."

Q. I've been waiting all year for *Punch-Drunk Love* to open. Now it has, and I'm frustrated by the fact that The Powers That Be have not deemed me worthy of viewing it. It is not playing in any of the over a dozen theaters within reasonable driving distance of my home (in southern New Hampshire). I'm not so naive as to think that a letter of complaint will have any constructive effect, but I want to do it anyway. My question is, who is responsible for the decision not to let me see this film and others like it? If I'm going to write a pointless letter, at least I want it to be thrown away by the right person's secretary.

—Ron Spiegelhalter, Merrimack, New Hampshire

A. I would contact the home office of the chains operating theaters in your area. They obviously believe that while southern New Hampshire is ripe for moronic Adam Sandler movies, it is not ready for a good Adam Sandler movie. A kind of redlining goes on, in which "art films" are booked in the cities but denied to less populated areas. Woody Allen once claimed that none of his films has ever played south of the Mason-Dixon line. An exaggeration, but with a grain of truth.

Q. In the film *Punch-Drunk Love,* I noticed several moments when bands of color appeared during scenes. Do you feel that these bands of color are supposed to signify something, that they are unintentional, or that they were created by the cinematographer for artistic purposes? I have my own theory that the glares, which appear in a variety of colors, actually symbolize the emotions being experienced by Barry, the main character. Any thoughts?

—Ryan Lisee, Voluntown, Connecticut

A. If that is your theory, then that is what they symbolize for you. There is never a right answer to the question of what something symbolizes, because symbolizing, of necessity, takes place in the mind of the beholder, not the creator. Remember Ebert's First Law of Symbolism: If you have to ask what it symbolized, it didn't.

Raising Victor Vargas

Q. When have you become so jaded that you sidestep the unnecessary vulgarities in *Raising Victor Vargas,* which caused about a dozen viewers (including myself) to walk out after twenty minutes? The positive review may have been deserved otherwise, but the language did not allow a lot of people to hang around long enough to find out. How sad that we think foul mouths are inspiring.

—Paul Victor, Pasadena, California

A. The MPAA rated the film R "for strong language." I am sad that you and others left this wonderful, life-affirming film which has no gangs, no guns, no drugs, and shows a Latino family that stays together during the crisis of the hero's coming-of-age. The language is exactly as real people do often speak in today's world. I am not jaded in "sidestepping" it but simply realistic about current norms.

It is a shame that the MPAA, in its (unsuccessful) attempt to warn you, put the movie off-limits to teenagers who could have learned and benefited from it. As I wrote in my review, "Like so many movies dealing intelligently with teenage sexuality, *Raising Victor Vargas* has been rated R by the MPAA, which awards the PG-13 to comedies celebrating cheap vulgarity but penalizes sincere expressions of true experience and real-life values." If you are looking for a new film with no strong language, the MPAA awards the PG-13 to *2 Fast 2 Furious.* But which has the more moral values?

Realtors®

Q. In your Recent Review of *Hollywood Homicide,* you Referenced a Capitalization Rule of which I was previously Unaware. I am an English major, so I'd like to think I'm on top of things when it comes to grammar. When did it become a Rule to capitalize the word "Realtor"? How can someone put a trademark on an occupation? Suppose I wanted to impose an arbitrary Rule about capitalization, even within this e-mail, just to make Myself seem more important? Why should a Realtor be allowed more latitude than a Customer Care Representative when it comes to grammar?

—Miguel E. Rodriguez, Tampa, Florida

A. Sean Hanson, a reader in North Bend, Oregon, tells me, "The answer is that, according to the Associated Press style book, Realtor is trademarked. So, you were better off just calling him a real estate agent." Indeed, "Realtor" is a "federally registered collective membership mark owned exclusively by the National Association of Realtors," and only members can use it. I have decided I am in sympathy with them, since "Two Thumbs Up" is a trademark registered by Gene Siskel and me, and people rip it off all the time. Just the other day some Realtor used it in an ad. Now I am thinking of trademarking Reviewor, and can think of other possibilities, such as Lawyor, Singor, and Proctologor.

The Ring

Q. With movie competition so intense but dull these days, I am pining for the days when studios promoted their movies with flair, like William Castle did. Case in point: With *The Ring,* wouldn't it be neat if the theater required all viewers to complete a form before the show, so that each can be tracked in case they died in seven days? Also, how about having a phone ring inside the theater right after the first showing of *The*

—Hilton Mock, Stanford, California

A. Your message ended prematurely in the middle of the title. I hope this was simply an e-mail glitch.

Road to Perdition

Q. In *The Road to Perdition,* those wool coats in the rain kept taking me out of the movie. Ever get a wool coat wet? It's *stinky!* And heavy! Well-dressed gangsters with any brains in their heads woulda been wearing raincoats. All I could think was, "My God! How can they stand upright with twenty pounds of stinky wet sheep hanging from their shoulders?"

—Binky Melnick, New York

A. The road to perdition is long, hard, and wet.

The Rules of Attraction

Q. As a current student at a major university, I have to say that you are out of touch in your review of *The Rules of Attraction* when you doubt that "large numbers of coeds would engage in topless lesbian breast play at a campus event," and that undergraduate men wouldn't even look at them. I have seen everything in the film, except the suicide, on my campus. And yes, when there are fifteen topless girls, you stop paying much attention. You can say that it is awful, and perhaps it is, but don't say that it isn't reality.
—Joseph Gallo, Auburn, Alabama

Josh Fiero of Lafayette, Louisiana, also writes me: "There is a party at Rice called Night of Decadence, which undergraduates attend in their underwear—and sometimes significantly less if they're feeling adventurous. Whatever the film's faults may be, it's a more accurate portrayal of college life today than most folks out in the real world would want to admit."

A. I am counting the seconds until Howard Stern does a live broadcast from one of these campus events.

Russian Ark

Q. In your review of *Russian Ark,* you mentioned that it is one continuous shot throughout the entire film. Apart from this film and Alfred Hitchcock's *Rope,* I can't think of any other time this has been done. Has this technique been used before?
—Wes R. Benash, Marlton, New Jersey

A. Hitchcock's shot was only apparently unbroken; each magazine held only ten minutes of film, so the camera had to move behind something to mask the reloading. *Ark* really was one take. So was *Time Code,* a 2000 film directed by Mike Figgis. In fact, it was four takes, using four simultaneous continuous shots, ninety-three minutes apiece.

The Santa Clause 2

Q. I await your review of *The Santa Clause 2* with great interest. I liked the first *Santa Clause* with Tim Allen, though I didn't find it quite as enjoyable as you did. But at a preview of *Clause 2,* I couldn't reconcile Christmas with a "dictator Santa" and "children elves" working in a sweatshop. Where were all their parents? Santa employs a legion of orphaned elves? I found it all a bit disturbing and I don't think I'd take very young kids to see it. An evil Santa is too much for parents to explain after the credits roll.
—Maria Toscana, Chicago, Illinois

A. My review has now appeared; I liked *Clause 2* better than the original, but I confess I didn't think of the impact on younger kids. Yeah, it's a little weird with Clone Santa staging a military coup with all those toy soldiers. I guess maybe the cutoff is: Kids who believe in Santa are too young for this movie.

The Searchers

Q. I recently heard an interesting theory about John Ford's 1956 classic, *The Searchers.* It was suggested to me that Ethan Edwards, John Wayne's racist ex-Confederate soldier in search of his Comanche-captured nieces, killed his oldest niece, Lucy. The evidence that was given is that when he tells his searching partners, Martin and Brad, that he found Lucy's body, he is furiously digging his knife into the sand. This and the fact that we know for a fact he originally planned to kill the other niece, Debbie, make it seem very possible that Ethan slit Lucy's throat. I was wondering what your thoughts were on this and if John Ford himself had ever addressed the theory in an interview.
—Pete Dragovich, Bemidji State University, Minnesota

A. Ethan originally said he would kill Debbie because she had become "the leavin's of a Comanche buck." I referred your question to David Bordwell, the famed critic and professor at the University of Wisconsin, and he replies:
"Interesting, but I think it's implausible. I think that Ethan's obsession grows in the course of the hunt, and he doesn't 'originally' plan to kill Debbie—at least the film doesn't present any clear-cut moment of decision. I think that finding Lucy presumably ravaged by her captors ("Do I have to draw ya a picture?") may be part of the cause of his decision to kill Debbie. It's fairly late in the film

that Marty gives voice to the prediction that Ethan will kill Debbie, and until then I don't think we can be sure.

"I don't find the digging with the knife particularly revealing because Ethan is often expressing himself in florid physical gestures (e.g., the way he gesticulates airily about Comanches leading you off the scent) and because (I think) he says he buried Lucy, so his digging with the knife may be an angry reenactment of that too. In all, if Ethan kills Lucy I think our uncertainty about what he will do when he finds Debbie suffers, and I don't think Hollywood movies (except sometimes for Hitchcock or Sternberg) are this elliptical about key events."

Sex in the Cinema

Q. I have a theory as to why many people, parents in particular (including my own father), object more to the depiction of sexual content in movies than the depiction of violent content. Sex makes humans (and any animal for that matter) more vulnerable to an attack. Violence is supposed to repel attackers. My thinking is that if parents have to deal with anyone being attacked, they would prefer that their own offspring be the attacker rather than the attackee. It's all on a subconscious level, I guess.

—Jan Lookabaugh, Gurnee, Illinois

A. You may be correct, although it is a sad commentary that sex is so often seen in terms of aggression instead of in terms of tenderness and love, and violence is so often seen as a solution instead of a problem.

Shanghai Knights

Q. In your review of *Shanghai Knights,* you say, "The whole point is that [Jackie Chan] does his own stunts, and the audience knows it." I'm curious what you think of Chan's recent admission that this is no longer true—he does use a stuntman for stunts that he does not feel safe doing.

—Geoffrey Romer, Claremont, California

A. We may be up against an urban legend. The authoritative Website www.jackiechan-kids.com says that Chan has *never* done all of his own stunts and never claimed that he did, although he sometimes just smiled when oth-

ers made that statement. Why doesn't he do his own stunts? The reply: "He'd be stupid to do *all* the stunts in *all* his movies. And as Jackie has said many times, 'I may be crazy but I'm not stupid.'

"Jackie began his career in the movies as a stuntman and did many dangerous things that no one else would do because he was trying to make a name for himself. After he established himself as a well-regarded stuntman, he no longer had to do it all to prove anything to anyone. So he began to do as much as he wanted to do. In the old days, that meant nearly all the stunts. . . . As he got older, he began to use stunt doubles for several reasons. The studios . . . sometimes insisted that he use stunt doubles so that their star wouldn't be put in any danger. He also began to be more careful about his own body. Doctors warned him about doing things that might cause permanent damage."

The Shipping News

Q. You couldn't mention in the Answer Man that you were reading *The Shipping News* without expecting to hear from your most persistent Newfoundlander reader. Here's an exercise in reverse engineering for you. Having read the book, do you have an actor in mind who you would have cast as Quoyle, instead of Kevin Spacey? Two names I heard bandied around years ago were Randy Quaid and John Lithgow, for physical reasons, I assume. A wife of a friend once told me she imagined me as Quoyle as she read it. He has wisely divorced her since.

—Mike Spearns, St. John's, Newfoundland

A. Timothy Spall, of course.

The Shortest Review

Q. What is the shortest review you've ever written?

—Chris Phillips, Los Angeles, California

A. I don't know. But I know the shortest movie review of all time. *I Am a Camera* on both stage and screen inspired the review "Me no Leica," which has been attributed to John Collier, Kenneth Tynan, and others.

Q. I am crushed to read that the shortest movie review ever written was "Me no Leica." For years, I've told everyone that the shortest

855

and funniest movie review was the great James Agee's summing-up of *You Were Meant for Me.* He wrote: "That's what you think."
—Steve Bailey, Jacksonville Beach, Florida

A. There are many contenders for the crown. Kathleen Davis of Grand Blanc, Michigan, remembers a review of *Ernest Scared Stupid* that said, "Ernest doesn't need to be scared to be stupid." Michael LeWitt remembers a review of the play *How Now, Dow Jones?* which read: "Standard and poor." Andrew Feldstein of Brighton, Michigan, thinks one of the Detroit papers reviewed *Casual Sex?* with "No thanks." Matthew Bricker of Iowa City, Iowa, and a dozen other readers cited Leonard Maltin's review of *Isn't It Romantic* ("No"), and Steve Lipson of Washington, D.C., says Maltin made the *Guinness Book* with that review.

But there've been other one-word reviews. Bob Cousins of Lethbridge, Alberta, says the Canadian weekly *Maclean's* reviewed *Orca* with "Ugh." John Hobson of Bolingbrook, Illinois, says Alexander Woolcott's review of the Broadway play *Wham!* was "Ouch!" Alan McDermott of Kansas City, Missouri, says Pauline Kael reviewed *Lipstick* with "Smeared." The most minimalist review of all may have been by Gene Siskel; Mitch Derry of Austin, Texas, recalls that his review of *Rabbit, Run* consisted only of blank space.

Q. I was wondering if you've seen the interview with director Spike Jonze on the *Being John Malkovich* DVD. It's very short and consists mostly of him driving a car, answering a few questions incoherently, and looking as if he is going to be sick. Suddenly he gets out of the car and vomits. End of interview.
—Connie Boyd, Denver, Colorado

A. Getting back to the previous question, about the shortest movie reviews, Rich Adis of Highland Park, Illinois, remembers a review of mine: "Five minutes into *Succubus,* the man in front of me stepped into the aisle and threw up. I knew how he felt." Spike Jonze is first choice for the *Succubus* commentary track.

The *Sight & Sound* Polls

Q. About the lack of post-1980 films in the *Sight & Sound* polls: One of the problems

with putting recent films on an all-time list is that you have to live with a film for a considerable time before it can achieve such status. If you see a film when you're twenty-five and you think it's great, you need to see it again when you're thirty-five and forty-five to see if this was true greatness or just a transient reaction.
—Tim Gregorek, Chicago, Illinois

A. It takes time for a great film to emerge from the pack, and I generally avoid films less than ten years old in my Great Movies series. Strange, though, that in the 1992 *S&S* poll *Raging Bull* was the most recent film, and in 2002 it still is—not a single all-time great in the last twenty years. (For more information see my 2003 *Yearbook.*)

Q. I am disappointed with the latest *Sight & Sound* poll. The omission of both Keaton (the greatest filmmaker who ever lived) and Chaplin from both the critics' and directors' lists is disheartening. I feel sorry for all the people who will never be exposed to the beauty of Keaton and Murnau, the pathos of Chaplin, the revolutionary techniques of Griffith and Eisenstein, and the fierceness of Lang. I'm involved in my high school film club. Some members wanted to show *Fight Club, Requiem for a Dream,* and any Wes Anderson or Kevin Smith film. I'm not saying those films are bad, it just illustrates ignorance concerning our film heritage. I convinced them to let me show Keaton's *The General, Steamboat Bill, Jr.,* and *The Navigator.* Everyone was laughing their heads off.
—Matt Stieg, Carmel, Indiana

A. The critics included two silent films on their list *(Sunrise* and *Potemkin),* the directors none. I don't know if Keaton is the greatest filmmaker in the history of the cinema, but he is certainly the greatest actor-director.

Q. I was fascinated by the wide range of films that received at least one vote in the recent *Sight & Sound* poll, but I was shocked that not a single Disney animated movie received even one vote! I expected to see at least *Beauty and the Beast* or *Snow White* and was stunned they weren't there. Why do you think this is? Do people in the business believe animated movies are on a different level than the standard fare?

—David Becker, North Wales, Pennsylvania

A. The *Sight & Sound* votes are influenced by the auteur theory and the notion of the Great Director; animation by its nature is teamwork. Although Disney was shut out, the Japanese master Hayao Miyazaki got two votes for *My Neighbor Totoro,* and three for *Spirited Away.*

Q. Were documentary films excluded from the *Sight & Sound* poll? I was surprised you didn't include *Gates of Heaven, Hoop Dreams,* or the *Up* documentaries on your own list. Perhaps there is an unspoken mind-set that comparing documentaries to fiction films is like comparing apples and oranges.

—Mike Spearns, St. John's, Newfoundland

A. I voted for *Gates of Heaven* in a previous poll, and my votes this time reflect "No diminution of my esteem for titles on my earlier lists." But it seemed like a vote for a doc was wasted on the *S&S* crowd.

Q. You noted that you didn't vote for documentaries in the *Sight & Sound* poll as you felt it would be wasted on them. Did you change your list in any other ways to tailor for the *S&S* crowd? What documentaries would you have considered for the list?

—Rick Pittman, Toronto, Ontario

A. The *Up* documentaries are a noble use of film, Errol Morris's *Gates of Heaven* continues to amaze me, and there are many others just from recent years, like *Hoop Dreams, Crumb,* and *Paradise Lost.* In voting, I specified that I had undiminished affection for the films on my previous list, but did some judicious switching, for example, replacing Ozu's *Floating Weeds* with his *Tokyo Story,* which I felt had a better chance of getting votes. I was right, and it made the Top Ten. But making such a list is agonizing. Countless readers have asked me why I left off this or that film, and there is no answer. I wisely refuse to vote in all polls except this one, every ten years.

Q. About the *S&S* poll: I wonder what justification there could be for considering *The Godfather* and *The Godfather Part II* as a

single entry, while excluding *The Godfather Part III*? Seems to me they should be judged individually or as a trilogy. Do you agree?

—Jeff Schwager, Seattle, Washington

A. Combining the votes of the two films (which therefore placed second with the directors and fourth with the critics) seems sneaky enough to deserve an asterisk. The poll says Parts I and II got twenty-seven votes from the directors and twenty-three from the critics. If you look at the breakdown, Part II actually outpolled Part I among those voting individually (critics 13 to 8, directors 15 to 12). Eight critics and six directors voted for the two together; one critic and one director voted for the trilogy. A lack of ground rules conspired to favor the *Godfather* team.

Q. *Sight & Sound* has recently released the results of a poll asking what the best films of the last twenty-five years are. What do you think of the results of this poll?

—M. Lingo, Bodega Bay, California

A. *Sight & Sound* is the magazine of the British Film Institute. Because so few recent films made their September 2002 list of the Top Ten films of all time, they asked for votes on films of the past quarter-century. The results: 1. *Apocalypse Now* (Francis Ford Coppola); 2. *Raging Bull* (Martin Scorsese); 3. *Fanny and Alexander* (Ingmar Bergman); 4. *GoodFellas* (Martin Scorsese); 5. *Blue Velvet* (David Lynch); 6. *Do the Right Thing* (Spike Lee); 7. *Blade Runner* (Ridley Scott); 8. *Chungking Express* (Wong Kar-Wai); 9. *Distant Voices, Still Lives* (Terence Davies); 10. (tie) *Once Upon a Time in America* (Sergio Leone) and *A One and a Two* (Edward Yang).

The Top Ten directors were Martin Scorsese, Krzysztof Kieslowski, Wong Kar-Wai, Abbas Kiarostami, Michael Mann, David Lynch, Pedro Almodóvar, Francis Ford Coppola, and a tie between Spike Lee and Ingmar Bergman.

All polls are a matter of apples and oranges. I miss such titles as *Pulp Fiction* and Kieslowski's trilogy *(Blue, White,* and *Red);* and on the director's list, where is Robert Altman? But it's a good list, especially compared to the idiocy of the recent Zagat survey of one thousand films, which is based on the premise that the people at Blockbuster have better taste than you do.

Signs

Q. Although I enjoyed M. Night Shyamalan's film *Signs,* I wondered how closely Night paid attention in science class when giving the aliens such a ridiculous weakness involving water. You'd think for such an advanced species, they could tell that our planet is 70 percent covered by the stuff.
—S. Legge, Ottawa, Ontario

A. The aliens are not the most impressive aspect of the movie, which I liked because of its creepy atmosphere, not its credibility. I did, however, think it was interesting to make them truly odd instead of dressing them in alien suits or *Star Trek* makeup. Although *Signs* did an astonishing $60 million in its first weekend, unprecedented for such a low-key picture, most of the Answer Man's mail about it was negative: "about as scary as a first grader in a mummy suit" (J. Romanchuk, Haiku, Hawaii); "The first view of the aliens looks like 8-mm film of *Big Foot!*" (Ron Goldstein, Porter Ranch, California). R. Luckey of Scottsdale, Arizona, liked the movie, especially the kids, but wonders why no one asked where the other end of the baby monitor unit was.

Sinbad: Legend of the Seven Seas

Q. Watching *Sinbad: Legend of the Seven Seas,* I couldn't help noticing that the setting is in mythological Greece. As I recall, the original Sinbad story takes place in the Arabian world. Is Sinbad an Arabian, or Greek? I really don't see a reason for the filmmaker to consciously alter the story to avoid the Arab culture.
—Eiyo Baba, Honolulu, Hawaii

A. According to my *Brewer's Dictionary of Phrase and Fable,* Sinbad is a character in *The Arabian Nights,* where he is described as a wealthy citizen of Baghdad. Why did they make him Greek? Do the math. What puzzles me more are his plans to retire to Fiji.

Solaris

Q. I heard a teaser on the radio that promised to reveal the most disliked film in the past twenty years. Before the revelation,

I wondered what high-profile recent film it would be. Perhaps the irresponsible *Jackass.* But no, exit polling condemned *Solaris* with an F for all ages and genders. Doesn't the exit polling just indicate the studio has lured in the wrong audience with two trailers, one a promise of a love story and the other of ominous adventure?
—Walter Scott, Schaumburg, Illinois

A. It was a very good movie, but the ads pitched it to the wrong audience. *Solaris* is a love story, but on a more thoughtful and subtle level than some audiences can appreciate. Matt Singer of Morganville, New Jersey, writes, "I saw *Solaris* this weekend, and while I was interested and involved throughout, most of the audience I saw it with was not. About a third of the way through, people started to leave." If they walked out, that means they didn't understand the premise well enough to care how it turned out. Yet the premise is clear to any attentive viewer. Many audience members have no interest in narrative development, and attend only for shocks, thrills, and laughs.

Spellbinding

Q. Have you ever called a movie "spellbinding" in your career as a critic? It seems to me that when movie trailers use that as a quote, it's a red flag, as if to say, "No real critics cared enough to formulate sincere praises of this movie."
—Paul Zaic, Dumfries, Virginia

A. A computer text search of some five thousand reviews from 1967 to 2001 shows that I have used the word twenty-one times, although not always positively. Sample titles: *Amarcord, Carrie, My Dinner with Andre, Lone Star, Titanic.* I am pleased to discover I have not used it at all since December 1997. By way of comparison, in the same time period I used the word *labyrinthine* eighty-two times.

Subtitles

Q. I have noticed lately that you are writing an awful lot of reviews for foreign movies that aren't even in English. They are in another language with English subtitles. Now I am as cultured as the next person, but do you honestly think many U.S. theaters are showing movies like *Jian Gui,* which is in Cantonese, Mandarin, and Thai? And even if they were, who do you think would watch these movies? Are there just not enough movies coming out lately that are in English?

—Kreg Cremer, Boyertown, Pennsylvania

A. Somebody must have seen *Jian Gui,* released in North America as *The Eye,* because Tom Cruise has purchased the remake rights. Same thing happened with the Japanese film *Ringu* (1998), remade as *The Ring,* which was a big hit. Fans of the Asian horror genre eagerly seek out movies like this. More to the point: If you don't go to subtitled films, you are *not* "as cultured as the next person," and will miss some of the best movies every year. Start with Chen Keige's new film *Together.* I'll bet you like it.

Swimming Pool

Q. Okay, my friend and I saw *Swimming Pool* over the weekend. We really enjoyed it, and Charlotte Rampling was wonderful, but—we can't seem to find the one thing you mention in your review that would explain the ending. We promise to keep it to ourselves.

—Thomas V. Hogan, Chicago, Illinois

A. In my review, I wrote, "After it is over you will want to go back and think things through again, and I can help you by suggesting there is one, and only one, interpretation that resolves all of the difficulties, but if I told you, you would have to kill me." Nevertheless, more than a dozen readers have requested the interpretation. I am therefore issuing the sternest possible *Spoiler Warning!* If you have not seen the movie you do *not* want to read further. The key that closes all loopholes is this: There was never a French daughter at the villa at any time. She was entirely the creation of the novelist's imagination, along with her diary, her sex life, the death, et cetera. At the very end of the film, we get a glimpse of the publisher's real daughter.

Tadpole

Q. I saw the preview for *Tadpole,* and I have three questions. (1) Why is it when a teenage boy has sex with older women (as in *Tadpole, American Pie,* and episodes of *Dawson's Creek* and *Frasier*) it's portrayed as a funny or touch-ing coming-of-age situation, but when a teenage boy has sex with an older man ("*L.I.E.,*" "*Our Lady of the Assassins*") it's portrayed as exploitation? (2) In your review of *L.I.E.,* you described the character of Big John, an older man who has sex with fourteen- and fifteen-year-old boys, as "an admitted pedophile." Is the older woman who has sex with the fifteen-year-old boy in *Tadpole* an "admitted pedophile"? (3) Why does *L.I.E.* merit an NC-17 rating, but *Tadpole* gets a PG-13?

—Richard Lindsay, New Haven, Connecticut

A. (1) There is a double standard at work. Society views men as sexual predators, and when the tables are turned on them, that is seen as comic. (2) Not admittedly, but, yes, legally a pedophile. (3) *L.I.E.* was a more serious and specific film, deserving an R rating. If it had been about heterosexual sex, it probably would have received one, instead of the NC-17.

Technical Matters

Q. Every once in a while during a movie I notice a little black oval in the upper right-hand corner of the picture. It seems to only be there for one or two frames, and then it's gone. I originally thought that it was just an imperfection that can develop when films start to wear, but then I noticed it on movies even during the first show of the day. What is this oval?

—Jon Paine, Provo, Utah

A. That's the signal that a reel is ending and the projectionist needs to switch to the other projector. However, many booths these days put the whole movie on one big reel, making reel changes unnecessary.

Terminator 3

Q. I represent the Greenbrier Golf Resort in White Sulpher Springs, West Virginia. In your review of *Terminator 3,* you mentioned that a part of *T3* was filmed at a decommissioned underground bunker in White Sulpher Springs. There is one such underground bunker at the Greenbrier but the movie was not filmed there.

—Kelly A. Cahill, the Greenbrier

A. How did I get that wrong information? After the *T3* screening, a fellow movie critic told me he had attended a movie junket that was held in that very same decommissioned bunker at White Sulphur Springs, a hideout originally designed to shelter key government figures in the event of nuclear war. He said he recognized it in the movie. It was a set, however, and so credit goes to production designer Jeff Mann for fooling a onetime visitor with his verisimilitude.

Test Screenings

Q. Yesterday, as I was entering a movie theater, I was invited to a test screening of the upcoming film *Adaptation*. As a movie geek, I accepted excitedly. However, I began to wonder: How can the creators of ostensibly artistic and creative films (as this one seems to be) justify the asking of Joe Six-Pack's opinions? I don't mean to sound insulting, but what the hell does the public know?

I'll bet that if *Waking Life* had test screenings most people would have labeled it a trifle of a film and terribly boring. I say this because when I left the theater after seeing that strangely moving picture most people were saying terrible things about the film. We already have the MPAA, special interest groups, and a myriad of other sources hindering the artistic vision of a filmmaker. It's really disheartening that the creators of *Being John Malkovich* could stoop so low as to ask me my opinions of their movie. I'm seventeen, what do I know?

—Dan Schwartz, Paradise Valley, Arizona

A. Many directors find test screenings invaluable; Billy Wilder, for example, killed the first reel of *Sunset Boulevard* after a screening. If the screenings are used by the filmmakers themselves to get feedback on a rough cut, that's valid. Too often, however, studio executives use preview screenings as a weapon to enforce their views on directors, and countless movies have had stupid happy endings tacked on after such screenings. (Classic case, probably apocryphal: the test audiences for *Messenger: The Story of Joan of Arc*, who were unhappy that she had to burn at the stake.) An exposé in the *Wall Street Journal* a few years ago revealed that one marketing company fabricated test results to meet the requirements of the executives.

3-D

Q. As the leading IMAX 3-D filmmaker (meaning I have made more of them than anyone else: five out of twenty-four), I have followed your comments on this new form with much interest. I totally disagree with your point of view, yet I find myself in agreement with your review of *Ghosts of the Abyss*. Mr. Cameron shot *Ghosts* like a 35-mm 3-D film, not like a large-format 3-D experience. Contrary to the 3-D of old, IMAX 3-D is a totally new language of cinema.

In the past, 3-D filmmakers created a window enabling them to use the space behind that window and in front of that window. In IMAX 3-D, the screen is so big, the audience is barely aware of the frame around the picture and there is no need for a "window." The filmmaker tries to create a filmic space and then transport the audience into that filmic space and let it decide where to look. The challenge with IMAX 3-D is that it is such a new language; the grammar still needs to be developed.

With *Ghosts of the Abyss*, Cameron uses the feature film language and transposes it to the giant screen. It does not work and it stands in the way of the full enjoyment of the audience. Why, for example, converge the camera on Bill Paxton, making it very uncomfortable to even try to look at the other characters around the table? Had the filmmaker shot with parallel cameras (one of the few basic rules already established for large-format 3-D), the 3-D space would have been even more impressive and the audience would have been transported into the room and be able to decide who to look at.

—Ben Stassen, Brussels, Belgium

A. The true IMAX 3-D movies, involving those $200 glasses with the built-in stereo headphones, are indeed much more impressive than the plain vanilla approach of Cameron. Another factor: There was obviously no room for the big IMAX cameras in his miniature sub, not to mention in his little robots Jake and Elwood, and he shot in high-def video, which gives him a good picture, but not one comparable to the native IMAX process, which uses a much larger negative. I concede that true IMAX 3-D looks much better than any previous 3-D process, but remain unconvinced that 3-D is necessary in cinematic storytelling. It is a mistake when the medium distracts from the message.

Together

Q. In your review of *Together,* you said, "It's a little hard to figure out exactly what her (Lili's) profession is." Then you did some Web research and quoted several comments. I think maybe you would like to know what director Chen Kaige himself said about the character, who is played by his real-life wife Chen Hong. He told the Chinese paper *Nanfang Daily* in December 2001 (I translated it into English myself): "The role Chen Hong played is just the same as every one of us; a person earns money to live. Except, her profession is a little bit vague, because even by the end of the film, people still don't know what she does. I don't think the relationship between [the character of] Chen Hong and the boy (Xiao Chun, played by Tang Yun) is an 'unethical affair.'

"What is really attracting the boy is her beauty and he lost his mother since he was very young. Therefore, the support she offers to the boy is no doubt a kind of mother's love. Their relationship is very complicated but is also very pure." I think the director has made it very clear, or intentionally unclear, on Lili's profession. Anything else would be speculation.

—Ye Meng, Beijing, China

A. Which didn't stop critics from speculating. In my review, I quoted a range of opinions, from the *New York Post* ("the proverbial hooker with the heart of gold") to the U.S. Conference of Catholic Bishops ("a good-hearted neighbor [who] offers some of the film's most tender moments"). It seems clear that Lili is supported by men who do not seem motivated primarily by charity. By making her profession vague, however, Chen Keige protects his wonderful movie's suitability for families.

Tomatometer

Q. Last week the Tomatometer at rottentomatoes.com read 98 percent favorable for Miyazaki's *Spirited Away,* because of a single

negative review by someone whose name I can't recall now. Today I see that the green splatter is gone, and the meter is pegged out at a solid 100 percent "fresh." If there's one film that I've seen recently that deserves a 100 percent tomato rating, it's this one, so I have no objection to the removal of that negative link. But I am wondering how often RT adjusts its ratings in this way. Do they do it according to some standard, or in response to user complaints?

—Joe Lippl, Minneapolis, Minnesota

A. Stephen Wang, chief technical officer of Rotten tomatoes, first replied: "Mr. Lippl makes reference to the once 'rotten' and now 'fresh' review for *Spirited Away* by esteemed film critic Rob Blackwelder of SPLICEDwire. I believe this is a rare case where a reader's enlightened response to his review shed light on the film that changed Rob's own critical view of the movie. This demonstrates that on-line criticism enjoys the benefit of a healthy back and forth with its readers."

Now it gets stranger: In an addendum to his negative but three-star review at SPLICEDwire.com, Blackwelder says he upped his star rating after reader Jon Cook wrote him explaining that the movie is a metaphor about prostitution in modern Japan. Huh? My reactions: (1) Jon Cook is committing the classical critical error of bringing something to a film that is not in it and claiming he found it there; and (2) assuming for the sake of argument that it *is* about prostitution, it does such a poor job of communicating this that Blackwelder should have given it fewer, not more, stars.

Toronto Locations

Q. I was saddened by your need to lash out against the filming of *Chicago* in Toronto. It is easier to take shots at films made in Canada than to understand that some of the finest crews in the world are based in the great country to the north. I worked on *Chicago* for five months. One simple point to be aware of: Your crews get more money to do less than we do.

—Adam Nahanni, Toronto, Ontario

A. I doubt if they do less, but they are paid

more, given the value of the Canadian dollar and the difference in the labor union situation. When Gord Sim, the Oscar winner for set decoration on *Chicago,* was backstage in the press room, he was asked by a Toronto friend of mine about the oddity that *Chicago* was filmed in Toronto. He replied somewhat evasively by praising the great crews in Toronto. I remarked that Chicago has great crews, too.

Let's face it: If it cost 25 percent more to film in Toronto than Chicago, he would have been praising the Chicago crews. I have nothing against films shot in Toronto, a city I love. But if a musical named *O Canada* were currently being filmed in Chicago, how would that make you feel?

Troma Films

Q. In his new book *Make Your Own Damn Movie* Troma Films president Lloyd Kaufman accuses you of purposely ignoring his company's movies. He complains that when they distributed acclaimed director Dario Argento's *The Stendhal Syndrome* in New York and Los Angeles, you didn't review it on your TV show. He also mentions that while *Tromeo & Juliet* and *Terror Firmer* played theaters in Chicago, you didn't review them in your newspaper. Knowing your policy is to review as many movies as possible, I would be interested in knowing your answer to Kaufman's complaint.

—Keith Bailey, Victoria, British Columbia

A. So many critics failed to cover *Tromeo & Juliet* that there are not enough reviews to quality for a Tomatometer rating at rottentomatoes.com, although the *New York Times* kinda liked it and *New Times* said, "It stands head and shoulders above almost every other Troma movie." I have no bias against the delightful Mr. Kaufman, who makes me smile every time I see him at Cannes, especially when he is dressed as the Toxic Avenger. I am looking forward to his next production, *Tales from the Crapper.*

28 Days Later

Q. Several critics have accused *28 Days Later* of having amateurish camerawork. I found the film to be quite beautiful (as in the painted flowers scene). *28 Days Later* may not adhere to the ideal compositions of Hollywood films, but (especially in the beginning) the nontraditional placement of the main character puts more emphasis on his surroundings, making the viewer aware of the entire frame; the emptiness becomes intoxicating. The shot choices themselves enhance the reality of this devastated world. I would argue that this is one of the best-shot films of the year. A search at IMDb.com would reveal that cinematographer Anthony Dod Mantle is more than a competent visual artist, having been responsible for some of the most renowned Dogma films, including the much anticipated "Dogville."

—Christopher Claxton, Honolulu, Hawaii

A. The film's style is precisely suited to its subject. Critics who disliked the cinematography perhaps have a narrow taste for elegant, polished, and "beautiful" photography, but you are correct that Mantle's opening scenes are even more effective because he has the hero wandering in the frame, instead of the frame following the hero.

Two Taps

Q. In response to your recent Answer Man glossary entry—the "Two Taps" Rule—you asked if there was anyone who actually taps the car twice as their friend in the car is leaving following a conversation. Sadly, I've been doing it for the past ten years. I will be talking to a friend who pulled up to say hello. As they leave, I say my good-bye and enunciate it with two taps to roof, hood, top of car, any part that's near. Why do I do this? To be honest, I think I saw it in a movie once, began imitating it, and I've been caught ever since.

—Erik Grebner, Decatur, Illinois

A. That glossary entry, contributed by Mike Mascarin of Windsor, Ontario, asking, "Has anyone ever done this?" inspired more responses than any other glossary entry in the column's history. Sample comments:

"I do it because I'll be getting home late at night and just want my friend to know so they won't hit me. Either that or it's something I picked up from my dad."

—Zachary Freiesleben, Grandville, Michigan

"I cannot recall if I started doing this after seeing someone perform the action in a film, but it's something I've done for decades."

—Terry Davidson, Lakewood, California

"Could this have its roots in horseriding or Westerns? I dimly recall at least one instance where a character places another atop a horse, and slaps the horse twice to get it moving."

—Geoffrey Booth, Ithaca, New York

"Isn't this derived from the racing world? I can recall Formula One pit crews tapping drivers on the helmet when their cars were ready to go."

—Bill Burns, Boca Raton, Florida

2001: A Space Odyssey

Q. Since I saw it in 1968 I've wondered about a blooper in *2001: A Space Odyssey.* There is a scene aboard the PanAm shuttle where a stewardess picks a floating pen out of the air. Just as she grasps it you hear a clicking sound. I discovered the floating effect was created by attaching the pen to a round sheet of glass, lit not to show reflections, and rotated to suggest zero gravity. There is no reason at all to hear the sound of her fingernails making contact with the glass, but in all the versions I have seen, the click remains.

—Jeff Young, Las Vegas, Nevada

A. Sir Arthur C. Clarke, who wrote the screenplay, e-mails me from Sri Lanka: "I am afraid Mr. Jeff Young is suffering from terminal tinnitus. I and my staff have all played the DVD of 2001 and it has also been listened to by my blind masseur, whose hearing, as you can imagine, is very good. There isn't a trace of a click at the point indicated. There are a couple of errors in the film: When Dave Bowman opens the hatch he holds his breath, which is the worst possible thing to have done. (I wasn't there when that was filmed!) And some of the walking on the moon, particularly in the interior scenes, is wrong—they would be bouncing around because of the low gravity. Incidentally did you ever see the TV from SkyLab, when the astronauts ran around its circumference, and deliberately reproduced the same scene in 2001!"

Q. I was wondering if the "Star Child" scene

at the end of *2001: A Space Odyssey* is based on a passage from James Joyce's *Ulysses.* Here is the passage:

"Would the departed never nowhere nohow reappear? Ever would he wander, self compelled, to the extreme limit of his cometary orbit, beyond the fixed stars and variable suns and telescopic planets . . . to the extreme boundary of space . . . he would somehow appear reborn above delta in the constellation of Cassiopeia and . . . return an estranged avenger, a wreaker of justice on malefactors."

The idea of a child ("reborn") in space wreaking havoc on malefactors sounds a lot like the "Star Child," especially if you read Clarke's book, where he destroys a nuclear weapon.

—Alberto Diamante, Toronto, Ontario

A. Sir Arthur C. Clarke e-mails me from Sri Lanka: "Ashamed (?) to admit I've never read a word of Joyce—though I believe he invented the useful name 'quark.' Now involved with a much better Irish writer—Lord Dunsany has asked me to write intros to two of his g'father's books."

Q. Some Answer Man readers must have been surprised to learn, in Sir Arthur C. Clarke's message to you about James Joyce, that he prefers the Irish writer Lord Dunsany to Joyce. This might be interesting: Clarke and Dunsany maintained a correspondence and both are writers of fantasy. Ergo, Clarke's judgment is no surprise. Lord Dunsany was a familiar name in my childhood in the '30s and '40s, but no more than a name. The Q&A drove me to the Internet and library, and by now I have read and enjoyed Dunsany. There is a great tradition of fantasy in Irish literature.

—Harry Ward, Glen Ellyn, Illinois

A. For me, the big difference between Dunsany and Joyce is that I have finished every Dunsany work that I started. In the movie *Finding Forrester,* there was one absolutely accurate bit of set decoration: The tattered stack of well-read paperbacks next to the young hero's bed included one book that looked brand-new: Joyce's *Finnegans Wake,* which many purchase but few read.

Was That . . . ?

Q. In *Red Dragon,* I could swear that Emily Watson's ex-boyfriend was played by Frank Whaley and that the museum curator who showed Francis Dollarhyde the painting of the dragon was Mary Beth Hurt but I couldn't find their names in the credits or on the IMDb.com page for this new movie. Could you confirm?

—Jeff Young, Las Vegas, Nevada

A. A rep for Universal Publicity says yes, Frank Whaley and Mary Beth Hurt did make uncredited appearances in the movie.

Whale Rider

Q. I applaud your cogent argument against the MPAA on this week's *Ebert & Roeper* show. My question is this: How can you be prevented from endorsing *Whale Rider* because of its PG-13 rating, yet one can go to any toy store and find *Lord of the Rings* toys and even *Matrix* toys that are tied into films with PG-13 or even R ratings? Is it because *Whale Rider* is an independent film?

—Paul Hardister, Arlington, Virginia

A. The controversy arose over my quote in the *Whale Rider* ads: "Take the kids and they'll see a movie that will touch their hearts and minds." The MPAA informed the distributor that it had to remove the line, because a film with a PG-13 rating can't be marketed to children. This raises several problems. (1) I said "Take the kids," not "Send them in alone." (2) Kids can in any event attend PG-13 movies by themselves. They only need the parent or adult for an R movie. (3) It is my right and duty as a critic to make such judgments, and surely the distributor has a right to quote them. (4) This is a sad example of a system that has lost all reason and now categorizes an inspiring family film (yes, family!) like *Whale Rider* with *Charlie's Angel's Full Throttle* and *2 Fast 2 Furious.*

Q. The MPAA has deemed *Whale Rider* as a PG-13 film, suggesting to parents that children under thirteen may not be able to handle the material. It is rated PG-13 because of "brief language and a momentary drug reference." I walked out of this film thinking that the rating was no less than G, and yet one "momen-tary drug reference" has made it of danger to a child. I could not even find a drug reference in the film, and yet the MPAA would not suggest bringing a child to see this wonderful movie. They are telling the parents that they should sooner take a kid to *Daddy Day Care* (PG) than *Whale Rider.*

—Nick Teddy, Santa Rosa, California

A. Josh Dorst of Ft. Lauderdale writes that he, too, "seemed to miss the drug references." If you look quickly, you may be able to spot what looks like a marijuana pipe, perhaps recently used, in the uncle's room. The "language" involves one "s" word, one "damn," and three nonsexual references to "dicks." The MPAA has lost all reason if it thinks it reflects how the majority of parents would evaluate this film.

Q. Your bio states that you're into Darwinian thought, so let me pose this: Why is it that wonderful movies like *Whale Rider* and *Raising Victor Vargas* aren't giving rise to more great films and making the expensive, overblown Hollywood clunkers extinct?

—Ed Weiss, Toronto, Ontario

A. I think the problem begins, not with evolving better movies, but in evolving better audiences. Have you noticed that television for the most part only feeds off new movies, never expressing an opinion about them? Many moviegoers would like to see better films, but are overwhelmed by hype and marketing. Movie critics are busy little bees, pollinating as fast as we can, but the hydroponic movies look juicier than our organic crops, even if they taste like crap.

Willard

Q. I just got back from seeing *Willard* and also came to the conclusion, before reading your review, that the creature who played Ben was not a rat. But what was he?

—David Mitchell, Franklin, Massachusetts

A. Peter Debruge, the well-informed assistant editor of AOL Movies, writes me: "Ben is played in the new version of *Willard* by an African Gambian rat, the world's largest type of rat. That said, I haven't seen *Ben,* the sequel to the original *Willard,* where he may have been played by another type of animal (or by poodles in rat costumes, as *Willard* rat wrangler Boone Narr used in the movie *Rats*)."

X2: X-Men United

Q. In your review for the first *X-Men* film, you stated that you were wondering how Wolverine, whose knuckles turn into switchblades, gets to be the top-ranking superhero—as opposed to Storm who should be more powerful because she can control a tropical storm. Would it not be correct to say that Storm can be killed by the switchblades that emerge from Wolverine's knuckles, whereas Wolverine's wounds would heal almost immediately?

Also, I think the top-ranking superhero would be Professor Charles Xavier, since not only is he the leader of the X-Men, but he can control the mind of every single human being and mutant on the planet Earth simultaneously. Total mind control must be the most powerful of all the mutant powers.

—Mike Furlong, Roy, Utah

A. I persist in my notion that being able to create tornadoes and control the weather is a greater superpower than being able to heal quickly. Once Wolverine heals, he's still just a guy with blades on his knuckles. As for Professor Xavier, since he has total mind control over every human and mutant on the planet—why are there *X-Men* movies at all, since he could have controlled and solved everything before the movies began? No doubt I will receive the answer in communications from countless X-heads, but it does seem like a paradox, no?

Ebert's Little Movie Glossary

These are contributions to my glossary project. Hundreds of entries were collected in *Ebert's Bigger Little Movie Glossary,* published in 1999. Contributions are always welcome.

* * *

Awake and Ready to Scare. When a character touches another to check whether they're sleeping or dead, the immobile person inevitably wakes up and grabs him in tune with a strong musical note.

—Gerardo Valero, Mexico City, Mexico

Big Head Poster. The prevailing ad style for modern movies, featuring an extralarge picture of one highly paid star. See the ad for *Notting Hill,* which features a normal-size Hugh Grant casually walking past a Big Head of Julia Roberts.

—Merwyn Grote, St. Louis, Missouri

"Brains in Vats" Movie. Named for Wilder Penfield's brain experiments in the mid–twentieth century, these are movies in which the reality of events is caused by some sort of device that makes the brain "think" it is experiencing those events. See the *Matrix* movies, *Existenz, Total Recall, Open Your Eyes, Vanilla Sky,* and others. Currently in vogue as a replacement for the dreaded "It Was All a Dream" movie.

—Mike Spearns, St. Johns, Newfoundland

California Sunrise. As viewed from North America, the sun rises from the Atlantic at an angle up and to the right, and sets into the Pacific at a corresponding angle down and to the right. Lazy California directors fake an East Coast sunrise by filming a California sunset and running it backward, though this causes the sun to rise up and to the left.

—Tom DeLorey, Blue Island, Illinois

Cast-Thinning Device. Any event or coincidence utilized to eliminate the majority of a cast for the purpose of focusing on a smaller core group. Examples: Nearly the entire staff of the shark research facility leaving for the weekend in *Deep Blue Sea,* the stubborn passengers who just wouldn't listen to Gene Hackman in *The Poseidon Adventure,* and most Dead Teenager Movies.

—Jason Willis, Eugene, Oregon

Ebert's First Law of Symbolism. If you have to ask what it symbolized, it didn't.

—R. E.

Eyewitness as Prime Suspect. When an innocent person discovers a dead body they invariably pick up the murder weapon in order to leave their fingerprints.

—Roger Plummer, Chicago, Illinois

The Fat Lady Will Sing. An amazing percentage of Hollywood movies taking place in modern Australia show the Sydney Opera House as an establishing shot.

—Joseph Goodfriend, Chicago, Illinois

Gauntlet Chalk Talk. The protagonists need to break into an Impregnable Fortress, for a heist or a rescue. Before embarking on their quest, one of the characters will describe all of the hazards on the way to their goal in a voice-over while the camera swoops through the gauntlet of sensors, traps, and guards they must somehow bypass.

—John Franklin, Norman, Oklahoma

Homeroom Syndrome. In a movie set at a school, all the important characters take all the same classes with the same teacher at the same time, regardless of major or class year.

—Eric Lanyard, Los Angeles, California

Hoo-ha Rule, or Eleven on Pacino's Dial. The *Spinal Tap*-esque volume level to which Al Pacino's voice often and inexplicably raises. Examples: *Scent of a Woman* ("If I were the man I was five years ago, I'd take a *flame thrower* to this place!"); *Heat* ("You can get killed walking your *doggie!*"); *The Devil's Advocate* ("God likes to watch. He's a prankster. Think about it. He gives man *instincts!*")

—Christopher M. Terry, Atlanta, Georgia

Human "Off" Switch. This is a spot on the back of the human head or neck, which when struck renders the victim immediately unconscious. Mr. Spock just had to touch it, but even weak humans can make the mightiest warriors go "lights-out." To take just one film as an example: In *The Princess Bride*, Westley switches off Inigo after their swordfight, Rugen switches off Westley after the Fire Swamp, and Fezzik switches off the Albino outside the Pit of Despair.

—Paul Wieder, Chicago, Illinois

Industrial Strength Bubble Bath. The preferred soap of movie characters because it creates mountains of superlong-lasting suds that hide "naughty bits" for an indefinite period of time. Should the character stand up, ISBB clings provocatively to the R- or X-rated parts of the body.

—Merwyn Grote, St. Louis, Missouri

Licking the Llama. When a comic actor makes out with an extremely beautiful person, the kiss is often revealed to be nothing more than a dream sequence, and in fact the actor is being licked by a slobbering animal.

—Brad Sorensen, Ottawa, Ontario

Load-Bearing Artifact. Every ancient temple has one central treasure that is also its keystone. When it is removed, the temple promptly collapses.

—Petrea Mitchell and Chris French, Beaverton, Oregon

Ma Bell, Phone Home. Even in new movies, no one has voice mail. Everyone uses full-size, old-fashioned answering machines, so that if anyone calls and the recipient is not home, the audience gets to hear the message out loud. — See *Cast Away* and *Ghost World.*

—Joseph Goodfriend, Chicago, Illinois

Monty Python Holy Grail Moment. In every bombastic, overhyped film epic, there is inevitably a moment that outsmarts itself by reminding us of *Monty Python and the Holy Grail.* See the Elf Alliance proclamation during

The Lord of the Rings: The Two Towers battle sequence, or the fanciful riot-wear before the opening fight in *Gangs of New York.*

—Pat McDonald, Chicago, Illinois

Nontransferable Like Rule. You will never actually love a film that claims you will love it because you liked another film. Examples: "If you liked *A Fish Called Wanda,* you'll love *Nuns on the Run.*" Or "If you liked *Who Framed Roger Rabbit,* you'll love *Cool World.*"

—Joseph Goodfriend, Chicago, Illinois

Number 42 Crosstown Expedience Route. The bus that runs directly between where the characters are and where the scriptwriter needs them to be, every day of the week, at any time of day or night.

—Petrea Mitchell, Beaverton, Oregon

Overhead Hitchcock Rule. All films showing a car passing a vacant country intersection will shoot the intersection from an above angle. This angle is a direct homage to Hitchcock's influential establishing shot for the crop duster sequence in *North by Northwest.* See *Road to Perdition; One False Move; O, Brother, Where Art Thou?; Cast Away,* etc.

—Steven Dalli, Los Angeles, California

Rearview Rejections. The tendency for rearview mirrors in cars to disappear and reappear from scene to scene, depending on whether the cinematographer thinks they're casting unflattering shadows or obscuring actors' faces.

—Merwyn Grote, St. Louis, Missouri

Rule of Loose 6's and 9's. Every time a room door features the numbers 6 or 9, the screw will be loose on the number and it will eventually reveal itself to be 9 or 6. Recent example: *Minority Report.*

—Mitchell Schnurbach, Hollywood, Florida

Rule of the White Suit. In any thriller, the man dressed all in white is a villain. If his ensemble includes a matching hat, he is the chief villain.

—Petrea Mitchell, Beaverton, Oregon

Two Taps Means Go Rule. When a character sees another off in a car, he will always tap the roof of the car. Do drivers need this signal? Has anyone ever done this?

—Mike Mascarin, Windsor, Ontario

Very Tough Love Syndrome. Bad guy issues dire threat, follows it with an affectionate slap on the cheek that is a little too hard.

—R. E.

"We've Been Expecting You." Whenever a hero fights his way into the villain's fortress, escaping multiple assassination attempts, he will be caught and taken to the villain, who will invariably greet him, "We've been expecting you."

—Gerardo Valero, Mexico City, Mexico

Reviews Appearing in All Editions of the *Movie Home Companion, Video Companion,* or *Movie Yearbook*

A

Abandon, 2002, PG-13, ★★½	2004
About a Boy, 2002, PG-13, ★★★½	2004
About Last Night . . . , 1986, R, ★★★★	1998
About Schmidt, 2002, R, ★★★½	2004
Above the Law, 1988, R, ★★★	1995
Above the Rim, 1994, R, ★★★	1995
Absence of Malice, 1981, PG, ★★★	1998
Absolute Power, 1997, R, ★★★½	1998
Accidental Tourist, The, 1988, PG, ★★★★	1998
Accompanist, The, 1994, PG, ★★★½	1998
Accused, The, 1988, R, ★★★	1998
Ace Ventura: Pet Detective, 1994, PG-13, ★	1998
Ace Ventura: When Nature Calls, 1995, PG-13, ★½	1998
Adam Sandler's Eight Crazy Nights, 2002, PG-13, ★★	2004
Adaptation, 2002, R, ★★★★	2004
Addams Family, The, 1991, PG-13, ★★	1997
Addams Family Values, 1993, PG-13, ★★★	1998
Addicted to Love, 1997, R, ★★	1998
Addiction, The, 1995, NO MPAA RATING, ★★½	1997
Adjuster, The, 1992, R, ★★★	1998
Adventures of Baron Munchausen, The, 1989, PG, ★★★	1998
Adventures of Ford Fairlane, The, 1990, R, ★	1992
Adventures of Huck Finn, The, 1993, PG, ★★★	1998
Adventures of Priscilla, Queen of the Desert, The, 1994, R, ★★½	1998
Adventures of Rocky & Bullwinkle, The, 2000, PG, ★★★	2003
Adventures of Sebastian Cole, The, 1999, R, ★★★	2002
Affair of Love, An, 2000, R, ★★★½	2003
Affair of the Necklace, The, 2001, R, ★★	2004
Affliction, 1999, R, ★★★★	2002
Afterglow, 1998, R, ★★★	2001
After Hours, 1985, R, ★★★★	1998
After Life, 1999, NO MPAA RATING, ★★★★	2002
After the Rehearsal, 1984, R, ★★★★	1998
Against All Odds, 1984, R, ★★★	1998
Agent Cody Banks, 2003, R, ★★½	2004
Age of Innocence, The, 1993, PG, ★★★★	1998
Agnes Browne, 2000, R, ★★½	2003
Agnes of God, 1985, PG-13, ★	1989
A.I. Artificial Intelligence, 2001, PG-13, ★★★	2004
Aimee & Jaguar, 2000, NO MPAA RATING, ★★★	2003
Air Bud, 1997, PG, ★★★	2000
Air Bud 2: Golden Receiver, 1998, G, ★½	2001
Air Force One, 1997, R, ★★½	2000
Airplane!, 1980, PG, ★★★	1998
Airport, 1970, G, ★★	1996
Airport 1975, 1974, PG, ★★½	1996
Aladdin, 1992, G, ★★★	1998
Alan Smithee Film Burn Hollywood Burn, An, 1998, R, no stars	2001
Alaska, 1996, PG, ★★★	1999
Albino Alligator, 1997, R, ★★	2000
Alex & Emma, 2003, PG-13, ★½	2004
Alex in Wonderland, 1971, R, ★★★★	1998
Ali, 2001, R, ★★	2004
Alice, 1990, PG-13, ★★★	1998
Alice Doesn't Live Here Anymore, 1974, PG, ★★★★	1998
Alien³, 1992, R, ★½	1997
Alien Nation, 1988, R, ★★	1994
Alien Resurrection, 1997, R, ★½	2000
Aliens, 1986, R, ★★★½	1998
Alive, 1993, R, ★★½	1997
All About Lily Chou-Chou, 2002, NO MPAA RATING, ★★	2004
All About My Mother, 1999, R, ★★★½	2002
All Dogs Go to Heaven, 1989, G, ★★★	1998
Allegro Non Tropo, 1977, NO MPAA RATING, ★★★½	1995
Alligator, 1980, R, ★	1990
All Night Long, 1981, R, ★★	1986
All of Me, 1984, PG, ★★★½	1998
All or Nothing, 2002, R, ★★★★	2004
All the Little Animals, 1999, R, ★★★	2002
. . . All the Marbles, 1981, R, ★★	1986

Note: The right-hand column is the year in which the review last appeared in *Roger Ebert's Movie Home Companion, Roger Ebert's Video Companion,* or *Roger Ebert's Movie Yearbook.*

All the President's Men, 1976, PG, ★★★½ 1998
All the Pretty Horses, 2000, PG-13, ★★★½ 2003
All the Queen's Men, 2002, NO MPAA
   RATING, ★ 2004
All the Real Girls, 2003, R, ★★★★ 2004
All the Right Moves, 1983, R, ★★★ 1998
All the Vermeers in New York, 1992,
   NO MPAA RATING, ★★★ 1998
Almost an Angel, 1990, PG, ★★½ 1995
Almost Famous, 2000, R, ★★★★ 2003
Almost Salinas, 2003, PG, ★½ 2004
Along Came a Spider, 2001, R, ★★ 2004
Altered States, 1980, R, ★★★½ 1998
Always, 1989, PG, ★★ 1997
Amadeus, 1984, PG, ★★★★ 1998
Amandla!, 2003, PG-13, ★★★ 2004
Amarcord, 1974, R, ★★★★ 1998
Amateur, 1995, R, ★★½ 1996
Amati Girls, The, 2001, PG, ★ 2004
Amelie, 2001, R, ★★★½ 2004
American Beauty, 1999, R, ★★★★ 2002
American Buffalo, 1996, R, ★★½ 1999
American Dream, 1992, NO MPAA
   RATING, ★★★★ 1998
American Flyers, 1985, PG-13, ★★½ 1995
American Gigolo, 1980, R, ★★★½ 1998
American Graffiti, 1973, PG, ★★★★ 1998
American History X, 1998, R, ★★★ 2001
American in Paris, An, 1952, G, ★★★½ 1997
American Me, 1992, R, ★★★½ 1998
American Movie, 2000, R, ★★★★ 2004
American Outlaws, 2001, PG-13, ★ 2004
American Pie, 1999, R, ★★★ 2002
American Pie 2, 2001, R, ★★★ 2004
American President, The, 1995,
   PG-13, ★★★★ 1998
American Psycho, 2000, R, ★★★ 2004
American Rhapsody, 2001, PG-13, ★★★ 2004
American Tail: Fievel Goes West, An,
   1991, G, ★★½ 1998
American Werewolf in London, An, 1981,
   R, ★★ 1998
American Werewolf in Paris, An, 1997,
   R, ★ 2000
America's Sweethearts, 2001, PG-13, ★★ 2004
Amistad, 1997, R, ★★★ 2000
Amityville II: The Possession, 1982,
   R, ★★ 1988
Among Giants, 1999, R, ★★★ 2002
Amores Perros, 2001, R, ★★★½ 2004
Amos & Andrew, 1993, PG-13, ★★½ 1995
Anaconda, 1997, PG-13, ★★★½ 1998

Analyze That, 2002, R, ★★ 2004
Analyze This, 1999, R, ★★★ 2002
Anastasia, 1997, G, ★★★½ 2000
Angela's Ashes, 2000, R, ★★½ 2004
Angel at My Table, An, 1991, R, ★★★★ 1998
Angel Baby, 1997, NO MPAA
   RATING, ★★★ 2000
Angel Eyes, 2001, R, ★★★ 2004
Angel Heart, 1987, R, ★★★½ 1998
Angelo My Love, 1983, R, ★★★½ 1995
Angels and Insects, 1996, NO MPAA
   RATING, ★★★½ 1999
Angels in the Outfield, 1994, PG, ★★ 1996
Anger Management, 2003, PG-13, ★★ 2004
Angie, 1994, R, ★★½ 1997
Angus, 1995, PG-13, ★★★ 1998
Anna and the King, 1999, PG-13, ★★ 2002
Anna Karenina, 1997, PG-13, ★½ 2000
Anne Frank Remembered, 1996,
   PG, ★★★½ 1999
Annie, 1982, PG, ★★★ 1998
Annie Hall, 1977, PG, ★★★½ 1998
Anniversary Party, The, 2001, R, ★★★ 2004
Another Day in Paradise, 1999, R, ★★★ 2002
Another 48 HRS, 1990, R, ★★ 1996
Another Woman, 1988, PG, ★★★★ 1998
AntiTrust, 2001, PG-13, ★★ 2004
Antonia and Jane, 1991, NO MPAA
   RATING, ★★★ 1998
Antonia's Line, 1996, NO MPAA
   RATING, ★★★★ 1999
Antwone Fisher, 2002, PG-13, ★★★½ 2004
Antz, 1998, PG, ★★★½ 2001
Any Given Sunday, 1999, R, ★★★ 2002
Anywhere But Here, 1999, PG-13, ★★★ 2002
Any Which Way You Can, 1980, PG, ★★ 1988
Apocalypse Now, 1979, R, ★★★★ 1998
Apocalypse Now Redux, 2001,
   R, ★★★★ 2004
Apollo 13, 1995, PG, ★★★★ 1998
Apostle, The, 1998, PG-13, ★★★★ 2001
Applegates, The, 1991, R, ★★ 1994
Apprenticeship of Duddy Kravitz,
   The, 1974, PG, ★★★ 1998
Apt Pupil, 1998, R, ★★ 2001
Arachnophobia, 1990, PG-13, ★★★ 1998
Ararat, 2002, R, ★★½ 2004
Aria, 1988, R, ★★★ 1998
Ariel, 1990, NO MPAA RATING, ★★★ 1998
Arizona Dream, 1995, R, ★★★ 1998
Arlington Road, 1999, R, ★★ 2002
Armageddon, 1998, PG-13, ★ 2001

Arrival, The, 1996, PG-13, ★★★½ — 1999
Artemisia, 1998, R, ★★★ — 2001
Arthur, 1981, PG, ★★★½ — 1998
Article 99, 1992, R, ★½ — 1993
As Good As It Gets, 1997, PG-13, ★★★ — 2000
Assassination Tango, 2003, R, ★★★ — 2004
Assassins, 1995, R, ★½ — 1997
Assault, The, 1987, NO MPAA
   RATING, ★★★ — 1995
Assignment, The, 1997, R, ★★★½ — 2000
Associate, The, 1996, PG-13, ★★ — 1999
Astronaut's Wife, The, 1999, R, ★★½ — 2002
Asylum, 1972, PG, ★★ — 1991
At Close Range, 1986, R, ★★★½ — 1998
At First Sight, 1999, PG-13, ★★ — 2002
Atlantis: The Lost Empire, 2001,
   PG, ★★★½ — 2004
At Play in the Fields of the Lord, 1991,
   R, ★★★½ — 1998
At the Max, 1992, R, ★★★★ — 1998
August, 1996, PG, ★½ — 1999
Au Revoir les Enfants, 1988, PG, ★★★★ — 1998
Austin Powers: International Man of
   Mystery, 1997, PG-13, ★★★ — 1998
Austin Powers: The Spy Who Shagged
   Me, 1999, PG-13, ★★½ — 2002
Austin Powers in Goldmember, 2002,
   PG-13, ★★ — 2004
Auto Focus, 2002, R, ★★★★ — 2004
Autumn Sonata, 1978, PG, ★★★★ — 1998
Autumn Tale, 1999, PG, ★★★★ — 2002
Avalon, 1990, PG, ★★★½ — 1998
Awakening, The, 1980, R, ★ — 1986
Awakenings, 1990, PG-13, ★★★★ — 1998

B

Babe, 1995, G, ★★★ — 1998
Babe, The, 1992, PG, ★ — 1993
Babe: Pig in the City, 1998, G, ★★★★ — 2001
Baby, It's You, 1983, R, ★★★ — 1998
Baby Boom, 1987, PG, ★★★ — 1995
Baby Boy, 2001, R, ★★★½ — 2004
Babyfever, 1994, R, ★★★ — 1998
Baby Geniuses, 1999, PG, ½★ — 2002
Baby's Day Out, 1994, PG, ★½ — 1996
Baby . . . The Secret of the Lost Legend,
   1985, PG, ★ — 1987
Bachelor Party, 1984, R, ★★★ — 1995
Backbeat, 1994, R, ★★ — 1997
Backdraft, 1991, R, ★★★ — 1996
Back Roads, 1981, R, ★★ — 1987
Back to School, 1986, PG-13, ★★★ — 1998

Back to the Beach, 1987, PG, ★★★½ — 1998
Back to the Future, 1985, PG, ★★★½ — 1998
Back to the Future Part II, 1989,
   PG, ★★★ — 1998
Back to the Future Part III, 1990,
   PG, ★★½ — 1998
Bad Boys, 1983, R, ★★★½ — 1998
Bad Boys, 1995, R, ★★ — 1996
Bad Company, 1995, R, ★★★½ — 1998
Bad Company, 2002, PG-13, ★★ — 2004
Bad Dreams, 1988, R, ½★ — 1990
Bad Girls, 1994, R, ★½ — 1996
Bad Influence, 1990, R, ★★★ — 1998
Badlands, 1974, PG, ★★★★ — 1998
Bad Lieutenant, 1993, NC-17, ★★★★ — 1998
Bad Manners, 1998, R, ★★★ — 2001
Bagdad Cafe, 1988, PG, ★★★½ — 1998
Baise-Moi, 2001, NO MPAA RATING, ★ — 2004
Bait, 2000, R, ★★★ — 2003
Ballad of Little Jo, The, 1993, R, ★★★ — 1998
Ballad of Ramblin' Jack, 2000, NO MPAA
   RATING, ★★★ — 2003
Ballad of the Sad Café, The, 1991, NO
   MPAA RATING, ★★★ — 1998
Ballistic: Ecks vs. Sever, 2002, R, ½★ — 2004
Bambi, 1942, G, ★★★½ — 1997
Bamboozled, 2000, R, ★★ — 2003
Bandit Queen, 1995, NO MPAA
   RATING, ★★★ — 1998
Bandits, 2001, PG-13, ★★ — 2004
Bang, 1997, NO MPAA RATING, ★★★½ — 2000
Banger Sisters, The, 2002, R, ★★★ — 2004
Bang the Drum Slowly, 1973, PG, ★★★★ — 1998
B.A.P.S., 1997, PG-13, no stars — 2000
Baran, 2002, PG, ★★★½ — 2004
Barbershop, 2002, PG-13, ★★★ — 2004
Barb Wire, 1996, R, ★★½ — 1999
Barcelona, 1994, PG-13, ★★★ — 1998
Barenaked in America, 2000, NO MPAA
   RATING, ★★★ — 2003
Barfly, 1987, R, ★★★★ — 1998
Bar Girls, 1995, R, ★½ — 1997
Barney's Great Adventure, 1998, G, ★★★ — 2001
Bartleby, 2002, PG-13, ★★½ — 2004
Barton Fink, 1991, R, ★★★½ — 1998
BASEketball, 1998, R, ★½ — 2001
Basic, 2003, R, ★ — 2004
Basic Instinct, 1992, R, ★★ — 1998
Basketball Diaries, The, 1995, R, ★★ — 1996
Basquiat, 1996, R, ★★★½ — 1999
Batman, 1989, PG-13, ★★ — 1998
Batman & Robin, 1997, PG-13, ★★ — 1998

Black Marble, The, 1980, PG, ★★★½   1998

Black Rain (Japan), 1990, NO MPAA RATING, ★★★½   1998

Black Rain (Michael Douglas), 1989, R, ★★   1993

Black Robe, 1991, R, ★★½   1994

Black Stallion, The, 1980, G, ★★★★   1998

Black Stallion Returns, The, 1983, PG, ★★½   1986

Black Widow, 1987, R, ★★½   1991

Blade, 1998, R, ★★★   2001

Blade Runner, 1982, R, ★★★   1998

Blade Runner: The Director's Cut, 1992, R, ★★★   1997

Blade II, 2002, R, ★★★½   2004

Blair Witch Project, The, 1999, R, ★★★★   2002

Blame It on Rio, 1984, R, ★   1987

Blast from the Past, 1999, PG-13, ★★★   2002

Blaze, 1989, R, ★★★½   1998

Blind Date, 1987, PG-13, ★★½   1988

Blink, 1994, R, ★★★½   1998

Bliss, 1997, R, ★★★½   1998

Blood and Wine, 1997, R, ★★★½   1998

Blood, Guts, Bullets and Octane, 1999, NO MPAA RATING, ★★½   2002

Blood Simple, 1985, R, ★★★★   1998

Blood Simple: 2000 Director's Cut, 2000, R, ★★★★   2003

Blood Work, 2002, R, ★★★½   2004

Bloody Sunday, 2002, R, ★★★½   2004

Blow, 2001, R, ★★½   2004

Blown Away, 1994, R, ★★   1996

Blow Out, 1981, R, ★★★★   1998

Blue, 1994, R, ★★★½   1998

Blue Angel, The, 2001, NO MPAA RATING, ★★★½   2004

Blue Car, 2003, R, ★★★½   2004

Blue Chips, 1994, PG-13, ★★★   1998

Blue Collar, 1978, R, ★★★★   1998

Blue Collar Comedy Tour: The Movie, 2003, PG-13, ★★★   2004

Blue Crush, 2002, PG-13, ★★★   2004

Blue Kite, The, 1994, NO MPAA RATING, ★★★★   1998

Blue Lagoon, The, 1980, R, ½★   1991

Blues Brothers, The, 1980, R, ★★★   1998

Blues Brothers 2000, 1998, PG-13, ★★   2001

Blue Sky, 1994, PG-13, ★★★   1998

Blue Steel, 1990, R, ★★★   1998

Blue Streak, 1999, PG-13, ★★★   2002

Blue Velvet, 1986, R, ★   1998

Blume in Love, 1973, R, ★★★★   1998

Blush, 1996, NO MPAA RATING, ★★½   1999

Boat Trip, 2003, R, ½★   2004

Bob Roberts, 1992, R, ★★★   1998

Bodies, Rest and Motion, 1993, R, ★★   1994

Body Double, 1984, R, ★★★½   1998

Bodyguard, The, 1992, R, ★★★   1998

Body of Evidence, 1993, R, ½★   1994

Body Shots, 1999, R, ★★   2002

Body Snatchers, 1994, R, ★★★★   1998

Bogus, 1996, PG, ★★★   1999

Boiler Room, 2000, R, ★★★½   2003

Bolero, 1984, NO MPAA RATING, ½★   1993

Bone Collector, The, 1999, R, ★★   2002

Bonfire of the Vanities, The, 1990, R, ★★½   1998

Boogie Nights, 1997, R, ★★★★   2000

Book of Shadows: Blair Witch 2, 2000, R, ★★   2003

Boomerang, 1992, R, ★★★   1998

Boost, The, 1988, R, ★★★½   1998

Bootmen, 2000, R, ★½   2003

Booty Call, 1997, R, ★★★   1998

Bopha!, 1993, PG-13, ★★★½   1998

Born on the Fourth of July, 1989, R, ★★★★   1998

Born Yesterday, 1993, PG, ★   1994

Borrowers, The, 1998, PG, ★★★   2001

Borstal Boy, 2002, NO MPAA RATING, ★★   2004

Bostonians, The, 1984, PG, ★★★   1998

Bounce, 2000, PG-13, ★★★   2003

Bound, 1996, R, ★★★★   1999

Bound by Honor, 1993, R, ★★   1994

Bounty, The, 1984, PG, ★★★★   1998

Bourne Identity, 2002, PG-13, ★★★   2004

Bowfinger, 1999, PG-13, ★★★½   2002

Bowling for Columbine, 2002, R, ★★★½   2004

Boxer, The, 1998, R, ★★★   2001

Box of Moonlight, 1997, R, ★★★   2000

Boyfriends and Girlfriends, 1988, PG, ★★★   1998

Boys, 1996, PG-13, ★★   1999

Boys and Girls, 2000, PG-13, ★★   2003

Boys Don't Cry, 1999, R, ★★★★   2002

Boys on the Side, 1995, R, ★★★½   1998

Boy Who Could Fly, The, 1986, PG, ★★★   1996

Boyz N the Hood, 1991, R, ★★★★   1998

Brady Bunch Movie, The, 1995, PG-13, ★★   1997

Brainscan, 1994, R, ★★   1995

Brainstorm, 1983, PG, ★★   1986

Chuck Berry Hail! Hail! Rock 'n' Roll, 1987, PG, ★★★★ 1998

Chungking Express, 1996, PG-13, ★★★ 1999

Cider House Rules, The, 1999, PG-13, ★★ 2002

Cinderella, 1950, G, ★★★ 1997

Cinema Paradiso, 1989, NO MPAA RATING, ★★★½ 1998

Cinema Paradiso: The New Version, 2002, R, ★★★½ 2004

Circle, The, 2001, NO MPAA RATING, ★★★½ 2004

Circle of Friends, 1995, PG-13, ★★★½ 1998

Citizen Kane, 1941, NO MPAA RATING, ★★★★ 1998

Citizen Ruth, 1997, R, ★★★ 2000

City by the Sea, 2002, R, ★★★ 2004

City Hall, 1996, R, ★★½ 1999

City Heat, 1984, PG, ½★ 1991

City of Angels, 1998, PG-13, ★★★ 2001

City of Ghosts, 2003, R, ★★★ 2004

City of God, 2003, R, ★★★★ 2004

City of Hope, 1991, R, ★★★★ 1998

City of Industry, 1997, R, ★½ 2000

City of Joy, 1992, PG-13, ★★★ 1995

City of Lost Children, 1995, R, ★★★ 1998

City of Women, 1981, R, ★★½ 1991

City Slickers, 1991, PG-13, ★★★½ 1998

City Slickers II: The Legend of Curly's Gold, 1994, PG-13, ★★ 1995

Civil Action, A, 1999, PG-13, ★★★½ 2002

Claim, The, 2001, R, ★★★½ 2004

Claire Dolan, 2000, NO MPAA RATING, ★★★½ 2003

Claire's Knee, 1971, PG, ★★★★ 1998

Clan of the Cave Bear, 1985, R, ★½ 1989

Clash of the Titans, 1981, PG, ★★★½ 1998

Class Action, 1991, R, ★★★ 1995

Class of 1984, The, 1982, R, ★★★½ 1995

Class of 1999, 1990, R, ★★ 1992

Clay Pigeons, 1998, R, ★★½ 2001

Clean and Sober, 1988, R, ★★★½ 1998

Clean, Shaven, 1995, NO MPAA RATING, ★★★½ 1998

Clerks, 1994, R, ★★★ 1998

Client, The, 1994, PG-13, ★★½ 1998

Cliffhanger, 1993, R, ★★★ 1998

Clifford, 1994, PG, ½★ 1995

Clockers, 1995, R, ★★★½ 1998

Clockstoppers, 2002, PG, ★★½ 2004

Clockwatchers, 1998, PG-13, ★★★½ 2001

Close Encounters of the Third Kind: The Special Edition, 1980, PG, ★★★★ 1998

Closer You Get, The, 2000, PG-13, ★★ 2003

Closet, The, 2001, R, ★★½ 2004

Close to Eden, 1992, NO MPAA RATING, ★★★ 1998

Clueless, 1995, PG-13, ★★★½ 1998

Coal Miner's Daughter, 1980, PG, ★★★ 1998

Cobb, 1994, R, ★★ 1996

Coca-Cola Kid, The, 1985, NO MPAA RATING, ★★★ 1987

Cocktail, 1988, R, ★★ 1993

Cocoon, 1985, PG-13, ★★★ 1998

Cocoon: The Return, 1988, PG, ★★½ 1997

Code of Silence, 1985, R, ★★★½ 1998

Cold Comfort Farm, 1995, PG, ★★★ 1999

Cold Fever, 1996, NO MPAA RATING, ★★★ 1999

Collateral Damage, 2002, R, ★★★ 2004

Color of Money, The, 1986, R, ★★½ 1998

Color of Night, 1994, R, ★½ 1996

Color of Paradise, The, 2000, PG, ★★★½ 2003

Color Purple, The, 1985, PG-13, ★★★★ 1998

Colors, 1988, R, ★★★ 1998

Coma, 1978, PG, ★★★ 1995

Come Back to the 5 & Dime, Jimmy Dean, Jimmy Dean, 1982, PG, ★★★ 1998

Comedian, 2002, R, ★★ 2004

Come See the Paradise, 1991, R, ★★★ 1998

Comfort of Strangers, The, 1991, R, ★★½ 1994

Coming Home, 1978, R, ★★★★ 1998

Commandments, 1997, R, ★★ 2000

Commitments, The, 1991, R, ★★★ 1998

Company Man, 2001, PG-13, ½★ 2004

Company of Wolves, The, 1985, R, ★★★ 1987

Competition, The, 1981, PG, ★★★ 1995

Compromising Positions, 1985, R, ★★ 1987

Con Air, 1997, R, ★★★ 1998

Conan the Barbarian, 1982, R, ★★★ 1998

Conan the Destroyer, 1984, PG, ★★★ 1998

Coneheads, 1993, PG, ★½ 1995

Confessions of a Dangerous Mind, 2002, R, ★★★½ 2004

Confidence, 2003, R, ★★ 2004

Congo, 1995, PG-13, ★★★ 1998

Conspiracy Theory, 1997, R, ★★½ 2000

Conspirators of Pleasure, 1998, NO MPAA RATING, ★★★ 2001

Contact, 1997, PG, ★★★½ 1998

Contempt, 1997, NO MPAA RATING, ★★★ 2000

Contender, The, 2000, R, ★★★★ 2003

Continental Divide, 1981, PG, ★★★ 1998

Conversation, The, 1974, PG, ★★★★ 1998
Cookie, 1989, R, ★★ 1992
Cookie's Fortune, 1999, PG-13, ★★★★ 2002
Cook, the Thief, His Wife and Her
  Lover, The, 1990, NO MPAA
  RATING, ★★★★ 1998
Cool Runnings, 1993, PG, ★★½ 1995
Cop, 1988, R, ★★★ 1998
Cop and a Half, 1993, PG, ★★★ 1995
Cop Land, 1997, R, ★★ 2000
Cops and Robbersons, 1994, PG, ★★ 1995
Copycat, 1995, R, ★★★½ 1998
Core, The, 2003, PG-13, ★★½ 2004
Corky Romano, 2001, PG-13, ½★ 2004
Corrina, Corrina, 1994, PG, ★★½ 1997
Corruptor, The, 1999, R, ★½ 2002
Cotton Club, The, 1984, R, ★★★★ 1998
Cotton Mary, 2000, R, ★★ 2003
Count of Monte Cristo, 2002,
  PG-13, ★★★ 2004
Country, 1984, PG, ★★★½ 1998
Country Bears, The, 2002, G, ★★ 2004
Country Life, 1995, PG-13, ★★★½ 1998
Coupe de Ville, 1990, PG-13, ★½ 1992
Cousin Bette, 1998, R, ★★★ 2001
Cousins, 1989, PG-13, ★★★½ 1998
Cowboys, The, 1972, PG, ★★½ 1991
Coyote Ugly, 2000, PG-13, ★★ 2003
Cradle 2 the Grave, 2003, R, ★★ 2004
Cradle Will Rock, 1999, R, ★★★ 2002
Craft, The, 1996, R, ★★ 1999
Crash, 1997, NC-17, ★★★½ 1998
Crazy/Beautiful, 2001, PG-13, ★★★ 2004
Crazy in Alabama, 1999, PG-13, ★★ 2002
Crazy People, 1990, R, ★★ 1992
Creator, 1985, R, ★★½ 1987
Creepshow, 1982, R, ★★★ 1995
Crew, The, 2000, PG-13, ★½ 2003
Cries and Whispers, 1973, R, ★★★★ 1998
Crime and Punishment in Suburbia,
  2000, R, ★★★ 2003
Crime of Father Amaro, 2002, R, ★★★ 2004
Crimes and Misdemeanors, 1989,
  PG-13, ★★★★ 1998
Crimes of Passion, 1984, R, ★½ 1994
Crimson Rivers, The, 2001, R, ★★★½ 2004
Crimson Tide, 1995, R, ★★★½ 1998
Critical Care, 1997, R, ★★★ 2000
Critters, 1986, PG-13, ★★★ 1998
Crocodile Dundee, 1986, PG-13, ★★ 1998
Crocodile Dundee in Los Angeles, 2001,
  PG, ★★ 2004

Crocodile Hunter: Collision Course,
  The, PG, ★★★ 2004
Cronos, 1994, NO MPAA RATING, ★★★ 1998
Crooklyn, 1994, PG-13, ★★★½ 1998
Crossing Delancey, 1988, PG, ★★½ 1995
Crossing Guard, The, 1995, R, ★★½ 1997
Cross My Heart, 1987, R, ★★½ 1989
Crossover Dreams, 1985, PG-13, ★★★ 1995
Crossroads, 1985, R, ★★★½ 1998
Crossroads, 2002, PG-13, ★½ 2004
Crouching Tiger, Hidden Dragon,
  2000, PG-13, ★★★★ 2003
Croupier, 2000, NO MPAA RATING, ★★★ 2003
Crow, The, 1994, R, ★★★½ 1998
Crucible, The, 1996, PG-13, ★★ 1999
Cruel Intentions, 1999, R, ★★★ 2002
Cruise, The, 1998, NO MPAA
  RATING, ★★★ 2001
Crumb, 1995, R, ★★★★ 1997
Crush, 2002, R, ★★★ 2004
Crusoe, 1989, PG-13, ★★★½ 1995
Cry-Baby, 1990, PG-13, ★★★ 1998
Cry Freedom, 1987, PG, ★★½ 1997
Crying Game, The, 1992, R, ★★★★ 1998
Cry in the Dark, A, 1988, PG-13, ★★★ 1998
Cup, The, 2000, G, ★★★ 2003
Curdled, 1996, R, ★★ 1999
Cure, The, 1995, PG-13, ★★½ 1996
Curly Sue, 1991, PG, ★★★ 1998
Curse of the Jade Scorpion, 2001,
  PG-13, ★★½ 2004
Curse of the Pink Panther, 1983, PG, ★½ 1986
Cutthroat Island, 1995, PG-13, ★★★ 1998
Cutting Edge, The, 1992, PG, ★★½ 1994
CyberWorld 3D, 2000, NO MPAA
  RATING, ★★★ 2003
Cyborg, 1989, R, ★ 1992
Cyrano de Bergerac, 1990, PG, ★★★½ 1998

D

Dad, 1989, PG, ★★ 1993
Daddy Nostalgia, 1991, PG, ★★★½ 1998
Dadetown, 1996, NO MPAA RATING, ★★ 1998
Dalmatians, 1996, G, ★★½ 1999
Damage, 1993, R, ★★★★ 1998
Dancer in the Dark, 2000, R, ★★★½ 2003
Dancer Upstairs, The, 2003, R, ★★★ 2004
Dances with Wolves, 1990,
  PG-13, ★★★★ 1998
Dance with a Stranger, 1985, R, ★★★★ 1998
Dance with Me, 1998, PG, ★★★ 2001
Dancing at Lughnasa, 1998, PG, ★★½ 2001

Dangerous Beauty, 1998, R, ★★★½ — 2001
Dangerous Ground, 1997, R, ★★ — 1998
Dangerous Liaisons, 1988, R, ★★★ — 1998
Dangerous Lives of Altar Boys, The, 2002, R, ★★½ — 2004
Dangerous Minds, 1995, R, ★½ — 1997
Daniel, 1983, R, ★★½ — 1987
Dante's Peak, 1997, PG-13, ★★½ — 1998
Daredevil, 2003, PG-13, ★★★ — 2004
Dark Blue, 2003, R, ★★★ — 2004
Dark Blue World, 2002, R, ★★ — 2004
Dark City, 1998, R, ★★★★ — 2001
Dark Crystal, The, 1982, PG, ★★½ — 1991
Dark Days, 2000, NO MPAA RATING, ★★★½ — 2003
Dark Eyes, 1987, NO MPAA RATING, ★★★½ — 1998
Dark Half, The, 1993, R, ★★ — 1994
Dark Obsession, 1991, NC-17, ★★★ — 1998
D.A.R.Y.L., 1985, PG, ★★★ — 1998
Das Experiment, 2002, NO MPAA RATING, ★★★ — 2004
Date with an Angel, 1987, PG, ★ — 1989
Daughters of the Dust, 1992, NO MPAA RATING, ★★★ — 1998
Dave, 1993, PG-13, ★★★½ — 1998
Dawn of the Dead, 1979, R, ★★★★ — 1998
Day After Trinity, The, 1980, NO MPAA RATING, ★★★★ — 1998
Day for Night, 1974, PG, ★★★★ — 1998
Day I Became a Woman, The, 2001, NO MPAA RATING, ★★★½ — 2004
Daylight, 1996, PG-13, ★★ — 1999
Day of the Dead, 1985, R, ★½ — 1992
Day of the Jackal, The, 1973, PG, ★★★★ — 1998
Days of Heaven, 1978, PG, ★★★★ — 1998
Days of Thunder, 1990, PG-13, ★★★ — 1998
Daytrippers, The, 1997, NO MPAA RATING, ★★ — 2000
Dazed and Confused, 1993, R, ★★★ — 1998
D.C. Cab, 1983, R, ★★ — 1986
Dead, The, 1987, PG, ★★★ — 1998
Dead Again, 1991, R, ★★★★ — 1998
Dead Calm, 1989, R, ★★★ — 1998
Dead Man Walking, 1995, R, ★★★★ — 1999
Dead of Winter, 1987, PG-13, ★★½ — 1993
Dead Poets Society, 1989, PG, ★★ — 1998
Dead Pool, The, 1988, R, ★★★½ — 1998
Dead Presidents, 1995, R, ★★½ — 1998
Dead Ringers, 1988, R, ★★½ — 1993
Dead Zone, The, 1983, R, ★★★½ — 1998

Dear America: Letters Home from Vietnam, 1988, PG-13, ★★★★ — 1998
Dear God, 1996, PG, ★ — 1999
Death and the Maiden, 1995, R, ★★★ — 1998
Death in Venice, 1971, PG, ★★½ — 1994
Death to Smoochy, 2002, R, ½★ — 2004
Deathtrap, 1982, R, ★★★ — 1998
Death Wish, 1974, R, ★★★ — 1998
Death Wish 3, 1985, R, ★ — 1993
Death Wish II, 1982, R, no stars — 1993
Debut, The, 2002, NO MPAA RATING, ★★★ — 2004
Deceived, 1991, PG-13, ★★ — 1993
Deceiver, 1998, R, ★★ — 2001
Deconstructing Harry, 1997, R, ★★★½ — 2000
Deep Blue Sea, 1999, R, ★★★ — 2002
Deep Cover, 1992, R, ★★★½ — 1998
Deep Crimson, 1998, NO MPAA RATING, ★★★½ — 2001
Deep End, The, 2001, R, ★★★½ — 2004
Deep End of the Ocean, The, 1999, PG-13, ★½ — 2002
Deep Impact, 1998, PG-13, ★★½ — 2001
Deep Rising, 1998, R, ★½ — 2001
Deer Hunter, The, 1978, R, ★★★★ — 1998
Defending Your Life, 1991, PG, ★★★½ — 1998
Defense of the Realm, 1987, PG, ★★★ — 1998
Deja Vu, 1998, PG-13, ★★★½ — 2001
Deliver Us from Eva, 2003, R, ★★ — 2004
Delta Force, The, 1985, R, ★★★ — 1998
Denise Calls Up, 1996, PG-13, ★★ — 1999
Dennis the Menace, 1993, PG, ★★½ — 1995
Desert Blue, 1999, R, ★★★ — 2002
Desert Hearts, 1985, R, ★★½ — 1988
Designated Mourner, The, 1997, R, ★★★ — 2000
Desperado, 1995, R, ★★ — 1997
Desperate Hours, 1990, R, ★★ — 1992
Desperately Seeking Susan, 1985, PG-13, ★★★ — 1998
Desperate Measures, 1998, R, ★★ — 2001
Destiny, 1999, NO MPAA RATING, ★★½ — 2002
Deterrence, 2000, R, ★★★ — 2003
Deuce Bigalow: Male Gigolo, 1999, R, ★½ — 2002
Devil in a Blue Dress, 1995, R, ★★★ — 1998
Devil's Advocate, 1997, R, ★★½ — 2000
Devil's Backbone, The, 2001, R, ★★★ — 2004
Devil's Own, The, 1997, R, ★★½ — 1998
Diabolique, 1955, NO MPAA RATING, ★★★½ — 1999
Diabolique, 1995, R, ★★ — 1997

Driven, 2001, PG-13, ★★¹/₂ — 2004
Driving Miss Daisy, 1989, PG, ★★★★ — 1998
Drop Dead Gorgeous, 1999, PG-13, ★★ — 2002
Drop Zone, 1994, R, ★★¹/₂ — 1997
Drowning by Numbers, 1991, NO MPAA RATING, ★★ — 1995
Drowning Mona, 2000, PG-13, ★★ — 2003
Dr. Seuss' How the Grinch Stole Christmas, 2000, PG, ★★ — 2003
Dr. Strangelove, 1964, PG, ★★★★ — 1997
Dr. T and the Women, 2000, R, ★★★ — 2003
Drugstore Cowboy, 1989, R, ★★★★ — 1998
Drumline, 2002, PG-13, ★★★ — 2004
Dry White Season, A, 1989, R, ★★★★ — 1998
D3: The Mighty Ducks, 1996, PG, ★ — 1999
Dudley Do-Right, 1999, PG, ★★¹/₂ — 2002
Duets, 2000, R, ★★¹/₂ — 2003
Dumb and Dumber, 1994, PG-13, ★★ — 1998
Dune, 1984, PG-13, ★ — 1988
Dungeons & Dragons, 2000, PG-13, ★¹/₂ — 2003
Dutch, 1991, PG-13, ★¹/₂ — 1993
Dying Young, 1991, R, ★★ — 1994
DysFunKtional Family, 2003, R, ★★★ — 2004

E

Earth, 1999, NO MPAA RATING, ★★★ — 2002
Earth Girls Are Easy, 1989, PG, ★★★ — 1998
East Is East, 2000, R, ★★★ — 2003
East/West, 2000, PG-13, ★★¹/₂ — 2003
Easy Money, 1983, R, ★★¹/₂ — 1994
Easy Rider, 1969, R, ★★★★ — 1997
Eating Raoul, 1983, R, ★★ — 1995
Eddie, 1996, PG-13, ★¹/₂ — 1999
Eddie and the Cruisers, 1983, PG, ★★ — 1987
Edge, The, 1997, R, ★★★ — 2000
Edge of 17, 1999, NO MPAA RATING, ★★ — 2002
Edge of the World, The, 2000, NO MPAA RATING, ★★★ — 2003
Ed's Next Move, 1996, R, ★★★ — 1999
EdTV, 1999, PG-13, ★★¹/₂ — 2002
Educating Rita, 1983, PG, ★★ — 1995
Education of Little Tree, The, 1998, PG, ★★★ — 2001
Edward Scissorhands, 1990, PG-13, ★★ — 1997
Ed Wood, 1994, R, ★★★¹/₂ — 1998
Eel, The, 1998, NO MPAA RATING, ★★★ — 2001
Efficiency Expert, The, 1992, PG, ★★★ — 1998
Eighth Day, The, 1997, NO MPAA RATING, ★★★ — 2000
8 Heads in a Duffel Bag, 1997, R, ★★ — 2000
Eight Legged Freaks, 2002, PG-13, ★★★ — 2004
Eight Men Out, 1988, PG, ★★ — 1993

8 Mile, 2002, R, ★★★ — 2004
8MM, 1999, R, ★★★ — 2002
Eight Seconds, 1994, PG-13, ★★ — 1995
8 Women, 2002, R, ★★★ — 2004
8¹/₂ Women, 2000, R, ★★★ — 2003
84 Charing Cross Road, 1987, PG, ★★ — 1993
84 Charlie Mopic, 1989, R, ★★★ — 1998
Election, 1999, R, ★★★¹/₂ — 2002
Electric Dreams, 1984, PG, ★★★¹/₂ — 1989
Electric Horseman, The, 1979, PG, ★★★ — 1998
Eleni, 1985, PG, ★★★ — 1987
Elephant Man, The, 1980, PG, ★★ — 1995
Elizabeth, 1998, R, ★★★¹/₂ — 2001
Elling, 2002, R, ★★★ — 2004
El Mariachi, 1993, R, ★★★ — 1998
El Norte, 1983, R, ★★★★ — 1998
Emerald Forest, The, 1985, R, ★★ — 1988
Emma, 1996, PG, ★★★ — 1999
Emmanuelle, 1975, X, ★★★ — 1998
Emperor's Club, The, 2002, PG-13, ★★★ — 2004
Emperor's New Clothes, 2002, PG, ★★★ — 2004
Emperor's New Groove, The, 2000, G, ★★★ — 2003
Emperor's Shadow, The, 1999, NO MPAA RATING, ★★★ — 2002
Empire, 2002, R, ★★¹/₂ — 2004
Empire of the Sun, 1987, PG, ★★¹/₂ — 1995
Empire Strikes Back, The, 1980, PG, ★★★★ — 1998
Empire Strikes Back, The (reissue), 1997, PG, ★★★★ — 2000
Encounter in the Third Dimension, 1999, NO MPAA RATING, ★★ — 2002
Endless Love, 1981, R, ★★ — 1991
End of Days, 1999, R, ★★ — 2002
End of the Affair, The, 1999, R, ★★¹/₂ — 2002
End of Violence, The, 1997, R, ★★ — 2000
Endurance, 1999, G, ★★★ — 2002
Endurance, The, 2002, G, ★★★¹/₂ — 2004
Enemies, a Love Story, 1989, R, ★★★¹/₂ — 1998
Enemy at the Gates, 2001, R, ★★★ — 2004
Enemy Mine, 1985, PG-13, ★★¹/₂ — 1988
Enemy of the State, 1998, R, ★★★ — 2001
Englishman Who Went Up a Hill But Came Down a Mountain, The, 1995, PG, ★★★ — 1998
English Patient, The, 1996, R, ★★★★ — 1999
Enigma, 2002, R, ★★★ — 2004
Enough, 2002, PG-13, ★¹/₂ — 2004
Entrapment, 1999, PG-13, ★★★ — 2002
Equilibrium, 2002, R, ★★★ — 2004
Eraser, 1995, R, ★★★ — 1999

Four Rooms, 1995, R, ★★ 1998
1492: Conquest of Paradise, 1992,
  PG-13, ★★★ 1996
Fourth Protocol, The, 1987, R, ★★★½ 1998
Fourth War, The, 1990, R, ★★★ 1998
Four Weddings and a Funeral, 1994,
  R, ★★★½ 1998
Fox and the Hound, The, 1981, G, ★★★ 1998
Foxes, 1980, R, ★★★ 1998
Frailty, 2002, R, ★★★★ 2004
Frances, 1983, R, ★★★½ 1998
Frankie and Johnny, 1991, R, ★★½ 1995
Frankie Starlight, 1995, R, ★★★½ 1998
Frantic, 1988, R, ★★★ 1998
Fraternity Vacation, 1985, R, ★ 1990
Freddy Got Fingered, 2001, R, no stars 2004
Freeway, 1997, R, ★★★½ 1998
Free Willy, 1993, PG, ★★★½ 1998
Free Willy 3: The Rescue, 1997, PG, ★★★ 2000
French Kiss, 1995, PG-13, ★★ 1997
French Lieutenant's Woman, The, 1981,
  R, ★★★½ 1998
Frenzy, 1972, R, ★★★★ 1998
Frequency, 2000, PG-13, ★★★½ 2003
Fresh, 1994, R, ★★★★ 1998
Freshman, The, 1990, PG, ★★★½ 1998
Frida, 2002, R, ★★★½ 2004
Friday After Next, 2002, R, ★★ 2004
Friday the 13th, Part II, 1981, R, ½★ 1993
Fried Green Tomatoes, 1992,
  PG-13, ★★★ 1998
Friends & Lovers, 1999, NO MPAA
  RATING, ½★ 2002
Friends of Eddie Coyle, The, 1973,
  R, ★★★★ 1998
Frighteners, The, 1996, R, ★ 1999
Fright Night, 1985, R, ★★★ 1996
Fringe Dwellers, The, 1987,
  PG-13, ★★★½ 1996
Frogs for Snakes, 1999, R, no stars 2002
From Dusk Till Dawn, 1996, R, ★★★ 1999
From Hell, 2001, R, ★★★ 2004
From the Journals of Jean Seberg, 1996,
  NO MPAA RATING, ★★★½ 1999
Frozen Assets, 1992, PG-13, no stars 1994
Fugitive, The, 1993, PG-13, ★★★★ 1998
Full Frontal, 2002, R, ★½ 2004
Full Metal Jacket, 1987, R, ★★½ 1998
Full Monty, The, 1997, R, ★★★ 2000
Full Moon on Blue Water, 1988, R, ★★ 1992
Funeral, The, 1996, R, ★★★ 1999
Funny Farm, 1988, PG, ★★★½ 1998

F/X, 1985, R, ★★★½ 1998
F/X 2: The Deadly Art of Illusion, 1991,
  PG-13, ★★ 1993

G

Gabbeh, 1997, NO MPAA RATING, ★★★ 2000
Galaxy Quest, 1999, PG, ★★★ 2002
Gambler, The, 1974, R, ★★★★ 1998
Game, The, 1997, R, ★★★½ 2000
Gamera: Guardian of the Universe,
  1997, NO MPAA RATING, ★★★ 2000
Gandhi, 1982, PG, ★★★★ 1998
Gang Related, 1997, R, ★★★ 2000
Gangs of New York, 2002, R, ★★★½ 2004
Gangster No. 1, 2002, R, ★★★ 2004
Garden of the Finzi-Continis, The, 1971,
  R, ★★★★ 1998
Gates of Heaven, 1978, NO MPAA
  RATING, ★★★★ 1998
Gattaca, 1997, PG-13, ★★★½ 2000
Gauntlet, The, 1977, R, ★★★ 1998
General, The, 1999, R, ★★★½ 2002
General's Daughter, The, 1999, R, ★★½ 2002
Genghis Blues, 1999, NO MPAA RATING,
  ★★★½ 2002
George of the Jungle, 1997, PG, ★★★ 1998
George Stevens: A Filmmaker's Journey,
  1985, PG, ★★★½ 1996
George Washington, 2001, NO MPAA
  RATING, ★★★★ 2004
Georgia, 1996, R, ★★★½ 1999
Germinal, 1994, R, ★★★ 1998
Geronimo: An American Legend, 1993,
  PG-13, ★★★½ 1998
Gerry, 2003, R, ★★★ 2004
Getaway, The, 1994, R, ★ 1995
Get Bruce, 1999, R, ★★★ 2002
Get on the Bus, 1996, R, ★★★★ 1999
Get Real, 1999, R, ★★★ 2002
Getting Away with Murder, 1995,
  R, ★★ 1999
Getting Even with Dad, 1994, PG, ★★ 1995
Getting It Right, 1989, R, ★★★★ 1998
Getting to Know You, 2000, NO MPAA
  RATING, ★★★ 2003
Gettysburg, 1993, PG, ★★★ 1998
Ghost, 1990, PG-13, ★★½ 1998
Ghost and the Darkness, The, 1996,
  R, ½★ 1999
Ghostbusters, 1984, PG, ★★★½ 1998
Ghost Dog: The Way of the Samurai,
  2000, R, ★★★ 2003

Heathers, 1989, R, ★★¹/₂ — 1994
Heaven, 1987, PG-13, ★★ — 1990
Heaven, 2002, R, ★★★ — 2004
Heaven and Earth, 1993, R, ★★★¹/₂ — 1998
Heaven Help Us, 1985, R, ★★¹/₂ — 1989
Heavenly Creatures, 1994, R, ★★★¹/₂ — 1998
Heavenly Kid, The, 1985, PG-13, ★ — 1987
Heaven's Gate, 1981, R, ¹/₂★ — 1994
Heaven's Prisoners, 1995, R, ★★ — 1999
Heavy, 1996, NO MPAA RATING, ★★★¹/₂ — 1999
Hedwig and the Angry Inch, 2001, R, ★★★ — 2004
He Got Game, 1998, R, ★★★¹/₂ — 2001
Heidi Fleiss, Hollywood Madam, 1995, NO MPAA RATING, ★★★★ — 1999
Heist, 2001, R, ★★★¹/₂ — 2004
Hellbound: Hellraiser II, 1988, R, ¹/₂★ — 1990
Hell Night, 1981, R, ★ — 1986
Henry and June, 1990, NC-17, ★★★ — 1998
Henry V, 1989, NO MPAA RATING, ★★★¹/₂ — 1998
Henry Fool, 1998, R, ★★¹/₂ — 2001
Henry: Portrait of a Serial Killer, 1986, NO MPAA RATING, ★★★¹/₂ — 1998
Her Alibi, 1989, PG, ¹/₂★ — 1993
Hercules, 1997, G, ★★★¹/₂ — 1998
Here on Earth, 2000, PG-13, ★★ — 2003
Hero, 1992, PG-13, ★★ — 1994
Hero and the Terror, 1987, R, ★★ — 1991
Herod's Law, 2003, R, ★★ — 2004
Hidden, The, 1987, R, ★★★ — 1996
Hidden Agenda, 1990, R, ★★★ — 1998
Hidden Fortress, The, 1958, NO MPAA RATING, ★★★★ — 1997
Hideaway, 1995, R, ★★★ — 1998
Hideous Kinky, 1999, R, ★★★ — 2002
High Anxiety, 1978, PG, ★★¹/₂ — 1995
High Art, 1998, R, ★★★¹/₂ — 2001
High Crimes, 2002, PG-13, ★★★ — 2004
Higher Learning, 1995, R, ★★★ — 1998
High Fidelity, 2000, R, ★★★★ — 2003
High Hopes, 1989, NO MPAA RATING, ★★★★ — 1998
Highlander 2: The Quickening, 1991, R, ¹/₂★ — 1993
High Road to China, 1983, PG, ★★ — 1987
High School High, 1996, PG-13, ★¹/₂ — 1999
High Season, 1988, R, ★★★ — 1998
Hilary and Jackie, 1999, R, ★★★¹/₂ — 2002
Hi-Lo Country, The, 1999, R, ★★ — 2002
Himalaya, 2001, NO MPAA RATING, ★★★ — 2004

History of the World—Part I, 1981, R, ★★ — 1995
Hitcher, The, 1985, R, no stars — 1990
Hocus Pocus, 1993, PG, ★ — 1995
Hoffa, 1992, R, ★★★¹/₂ — 1998
Holes, 2003, PG, ★★★¹/₂ — 2004
Hollow Man, 2000, R, ★★ — 2003
Hollywood Ending, 2002, PG-13, ★★¹/₂ — 2004
Hollywood Homicide, 2003, PG-13, ★★★ — 2004
Hollywood Shuffle, 1987, R, ★★★ — 1998
Holy Man, 1998, PG, ★★ — 2001
Holy Smoke!, 2000, R, ★★¹/₂ — 2003
Homage, 1996, R, ★★¹/₂ — 1999
Home Alone, 1990, PG, ★★¹/₂ — 1998
Home Alone 2: Lost in New York, 1992, PG, ★★ — 1995
Home Alone 3, 1997, PG, ★★★ — 2000
Home and the World, The, 1986, NO MPAA RATING, ★★★ — 1987
Home Fries, 1998, PG-13, ★★★ — 2001
Home Movie, 2002, NO MPAA RATING, ★★★ — 2004
Home of Our Own, A, 1993, PG, ★★★ — 1998
Home of the Brave, 1986, NO MPAA RATING, ★★★¹/₂ — 1998
Homeward Bound: The Incredible Journey, 1993, G, ★★★ — 1998
Homeward Bound II: Lost in San Francisco, 1996, G, ★★ — 1999
Homicide, 1991, R, ★★★★ — 1998
Honey, I Blew Up the Kid, 1992, PG, ★¹/₂ — 1994
Honey, I Shrunk the Kids, 1989, PG, ★★ — 1995
Honeymoon in Vegas, 1992, PG-13, ★★★¹/₂ — 1998
Honkytonk Man, 1982, PG, ★★★ — 1998
Hoodlum, 1997, R, ★★★ — 2000
Hook, 1991, PG, ★★ — 1994
Hoop Dreams, 1994, PG-13, ★★★★ — 1998
Hoosiers, 1987, PG, ★★★★ — 1998
Hope and Glory, 1987, PG-13, ★★★ — 1998
Hope Floats, 1998, PG-13, ★★ — 2001
Horseman on the Roof, The, 1995, R, ★★★ — 1999
Horse Whisperer, The, 1998, PG-13, ★★★ — 2001
Hot Chick, The, 2002, PG-13, ¹/₂★ — 2004
Hotel de Love, 1997, R, ★★¹/₂ — 2000
Hotel Terminus, 1988, NO MPAA RATING, ★★★ — 1996
Hot Shots! Part Deux, 1993, PG-13, ★★★ — 1998
Hot Spot, The, 1990, R, ★★★ — 1996

J

King David, 1985, PG-13, ★ — 1987
Kingdom Come, 2001, PG, ★★ — 2004
King Is Alive, The, 2001, R, ★★★ — 2004
King Lear, 1972, PG, ★★★ — 1998
King of Comedy, The, 1983, PG, ★★★ — 1998
King of Marvin Gardens, The, 1972,
 R, ★★★ — 1998
King of Masks, The, 1999, NO MPAA
 RATING, ★★★ — 2002
King of New York, 1990, R, ★★ — 1993
King of the Gypsies, 1978, R, ★★★ — 1998
King of the Hill, 1993, PG-13, ★★★★ — 1998
Kinjite: Forbidden Subjects, 1989, R, ★ — 1993
Kiss Before Dying, A, 1991, R, ★★★ — 1998
Kissed, 1997, NO MPAA RATING, ★★★ — 1998
Kissing a Fool, 1998, R, ★ — 2001
Kissing Jessica Stein, 2002, R, ★★★ — 2004
Kiss Me, Guido, 1997, R, ★★ — 2000
Kiss of Death, 1995, R, ★★ — 1996
Kiss of the Dragon, 2001, R, ★★★ — 2004
Kiss of the Spider Woman, 1985,
 R, ★★★½ — 1998
Kiss or Kill, 1997, R, ★★★ — 2000
Kiss the Girls, 1997, R, ★★★½ — 2000
Klute, 1971, R, ★★★½ — 1998
Knight's Tale, A, 2001, PG-13, ★★★ — 2004
K-9, 1989, PG, ★★ — 1993
K-19: The Widowmaker, 2002,
 PG-13, ★★★ — 2004
Knockaround Guys, 2002, R, ★★★ — 2004
Kolya, 1997, PG-13, ★★★½ — 1998
Koyaanisqatsi, 1983, NO MPAA
 RATING, ★★★ — 1998
K-PAX, 2001, PG-13, ★★★ — 2004
Krays, The, 1990, R, ★★★½ — 1998
Krippendorf's Tribe, 1998, PG-13, ★★ — 2001
K2, 1992, R, ★★ — 1994
Kundun, 1998, PG-13, ★★★ — 2001
Kung Fu Master, 1989, R, ★★★ — 1998
Kurt & Courtney, 1998, NO MPAA
 RATING, ★★★ — 2001
Kwik Stop, 2002, NO MPAA
 RATING, ★★★½ — 2004

L

La Bamba, 1987, PG-13, ★★★ — 1998
La Belle Noiseuse, 1992, NO MPAA
 RATING, ★★★★ — 1998
La Cage aux Folles, 1979, R, ★★★★ — 1998
La Ceremonie, 1997, NO MPAA
 RATING, ★★★ — 2000

La Cienaga, 2001, NO MPAA
 RATING, ★★★ — 2004
La Ciudad (The City), 2000, NO MPAA
 RATING, ★★★ — 2003
L.A. Confidential, 1997, R, ★★★★ — 2000
La Cucaracha, 1999, R, ★★★ — 2002
Ladies Man, The, 2000, R, ★ — 2003
Lady and the Duke, The, 2002,
 PG-13, ★★★ — 2004
Ladybird, Ladybird, 1995, NO MPAA
 RATING, ★★★★ — 1998
Lady in White, 1988, PG-13, ★★★ — 1995
Lady Sings the Blues, 1972, R, ★★★ — 1998
La Femme Nikita, 1991, R, ★★★ — 1998
Lagaan: Once Upon a Time in India,
 2002, PG, ★★★½ — 2004
Lair of the White Worm, The, 1988,
 R, ★★ — 1991
Lakeboat, 2001, R, ★★★ — 2004
Lake Placid, 1999, R, ★ — 2002
La Lectrice, 1989, R, ★★★★ — 1998
Land and Freedom, 1995, NO MPAA
 RATING, ★★★ — 1999
Land Before Time, The, 1988, G, ★★★ — 1996
Land Girls, The, 1998, R, ★★½ — 2001
Lantana, 2002, R, ★★★½ — 2004
Lara Croft Tomb Raider, 2001,
 PG-13, ★★★ — 2004
Larger Than Life, 1996, PG, ★½ — 1999
Lassiter, 1984, R, ★★★ — 1995
Last Action Hero, The, 1993, PG-13, ★★½ — 1995
Last Boy Scout, The, 1991, R, ★★★ — 1996
Last Castle, The, 2001, R, ★★★ — 2004
Last Dance, 1995, R, ★★½ — 1999
Last Days, The, 1999, NO MPAA
 RATING, ★★★½ — 2002
Last Days of Chez Nous, The, 1993,
 R, ★★★½ — 1998
Last Days of Disco, The, 1998,
 R, ★★★½ — 2001
Last Detail, The, 1974, R, ★★★★ — 1998
Last Dragon, The, 1985, PG-13, ★★½ — 1991
Last Emperor, The, 1987, PG-13, ★★★★ — 1998
Last Exit to Brooklyn, 1990, R, ★★★½ — 1998
Last Flight of Noah's Ark, The, 1980,
 G, ½★ — 1986
Last House on the Left, 1972, R, ★★★½ — 1998
Last Kiss, The, 2002, R, ★★ — 2004
Last Man Standing, 1996, R, ★ — 1999
Last Metro, The, 1980, NO MPAA
 RATING, ★★★ — 1998

Last Night, 1999, R, ★★★ — 2002

Last of the Dogmen, 1995, PG, ★★★ — 1998

Last of the Mohicans, The, 1992, R, ★★★ — 1998

Last Orders, The, 2002, R, ★★★¹/₂ — 2004

L.A. Story, 1991, PG-13, ★★★★ — 1998

Last Picture Show, The, 1971, R, ★★★★ — 1998

La Strada, 1954, NO MPAA RATING, ★★★¹/₂ — 1997

Last Resort, 2001, NO MPAA RATING, ★★★ — 2004

Last Seduction, The, 1994, NO MPAA RATING, ★★★★ — 1998

Last September, The, 2000, R, ★★ — 2003

Last Starfighter, The, 1984, PG, ★★¹/₂ — 1991

Last Supper, The, 1995, R, ★★★ — 1999

Last Tango in Paris, 1972, X, ★★★★ — 1998

Last Temptation of Christ, The, 1988, R, ★★★★ — 1998

Last Waltz, The, 2002, PG, ★★★ — 2004

Late for Dinner, 1991, PG, ★★¹/₂ — 1993

Late Marriage, 2002, NO MPAA RATING, ★★★ — 2004

Late Show, The, 1977, PG, ★★★★ — 1998

L'Auberge Espagnole, 2003, R, ★★★ — 2004

Laurel Canyon, 2003, R, ★★ — 2004

Lawless Heart, 2003, R, ★★★ — 2004

Lawn Dogs, 1998, NO MPAA RATING, ★¹/₂ — 2001

Lawrence of Arabia, 1962, PG, ★★★★ — 1997

Laws of Gravity, 1992, R, ★★★ — 1996

Leading Man, The, 1998, R, ★★★ — 2001

League of Extraordinary Gentlemen, 2003, PG-13, ★ — 2004

League of Their Own, A, 1992, PG, ★★★ — 1998

Lean on Me, 1989, PG-13, ★★¹/₂ — 1993

Leap of Faith, 1992, PG-13, ★★★ — 1998

Leave It to Beaver, 1997, PG, ★★★ — 2000

Leaving Las Vegas, 1995, R, ★★★★ — 1998

Leaving Normal, 1992, R, ★★¹/₂ — 1994

Le Cercle Rouge, 2003, NO MPAA RATING, ★★★★ — 2004

Left Luggage, 2001, NO MPAA RATING, ★★ — 2004

Legally Blonde, 2001, PG-13, ★★★ — 2004

Legally Blonde 2: Red, White and Blonde, 2003, PG-13, ★★ — 2004

Legend, 1986, PG, ★★ — 1989

Legend of Bagger Vance, The, 2000, PG-13, ★★★¹/₂ — 2003

Legend of Hell House, The, 1973, PG, ★★★¹/₂ — 1995

Legend of 1900, The, 1999, R, ★★¹/₂ — 2002

Legend of Rita, The, 2001, NO MPAA RATING, ★★★¹/₂ — 2004

Legend of the Drunken Master, The, 2000, R, ★★★¹/₂ — 2003

Legends of the Fall, 1995, R, ★★★ — 1998

Léolo, 1993, NO MPAA RATING, ★★★★ — 1998

Les Destinées, 2002, NO MPAA RATING, ★★★¹/₂ — 2004

Les Miserables, 1998, PG-13, ★★¹/₂ — 2001

Less Than Zero, 1987, R, ★★★★ — 1998

Les Voleurs (The Thieves), 1996, R, ★★★¹/₂ — 1999

Lethal Weapon, 1987, R, ★★★★ — 1998

Lethal Weapon 2, 1989, R, ★★★¹/₂ — 1998

Lethal Weapon 3, 1992, R, ★★★ — 1998

Lethal Weapon 4, 1998, R, ★★ — 2001

Let Him Have It, 1992, R, ★★★¹/₂ — 1998

Let's Spend the Night Together, 1983, PG, ★★¹/₂ — 1994

Let's Talk About Sex, 1998, R, ★ — 2001

Levity, 2003, R, ★¹/₂ — 2004

L'Humanite, 2000, NO MPAA RATING, ★★★¹/₂ — 2003

Liam, 2001, R, ★★★¹/₂ — 2004

Lianna, 1983, R, ★★★¹/₂ — 1998

Liar Liar, 1997, PG-13, ★★★ — 1998

Liberty Heights, 1999, R, ★★★¹/₂ — 2002

Licence to Kill, 1989, PG-13, ★★★¹/₂ — 1998

L.I.E., 2001, NC-17, ★★★ — 2004

Life, 1999, R, ★★★ — 2002

Life and Debt, 2001, NO MPAA RATING, ★★★ — 2004

Life as a House, 2001, R, ★★¹/₂ — 2004

Life Is Beautiful, 1998, PG-13, ★★★¹/₂ — 2001

Life Is Sweet, 1991, NO MPAA RATING, ★★★★ — 1998

Life Less Ordinary, A, 1997, R, ★★ — 2000

Life of David Gale, The, 2003, R, no stars — 2004

Life or Something Like It, 2002, PG-13, ★ — 2004

Life Stinks, 1991, PG-13, ★★★ — 1998

Life with Mikey, 1993, PG, ★★ — 1995

Light It Up, 1999, R, ★★¹/₂ — 2002

Lightning Jack, 1994, PG-13, ★★ — 1995

Light of Day, 1987, PG-13, ★★★¹/₂ — 1998

Light Sleeper, 1992, R, ★★★★ — 1998

Like Father, Like Son, 1987, PG-13, ★ — 1991

Like Mike, 2002, PG, ★★★ — 2004

Like Water for Chocolate, 1993, R, ★★★★ — 1998

Lilo & Stitch, 2002, PG, ★★★¹/₂ — 2004

Love Streams, 1984, PG-13, ★★★★ 1998
Love the Hard Way, 2003, NO MPAA
RATING, ★★★ 2004
Love! Valour! Compassion!, 1997,
R, ★★★ 1998
Love Walked In, 1998, R, ★★ 2001
Loving Jezebel, 2000, R, ★★½ 2003
Low Down, The, 2001, NO MPAA
RATING, ★★★ 2004
Lucas, 1985, PG-13, ★★★★ 1998
Lucie Aubrac, 1999, R, ★★½ 2002
Lucky Break, 2002, PG-13, ★★★ 2004
Lucky Numbers, 2000, R, ★★ 2003
Lumiere & Company, 1996, NO MPAA
RATING, ★★★ 1999
Lumumba, 2001, NO MPAA
RATING, ★★★ 2004
Lust in the Dust, 1985, R, ★★ 1990
Luzhin Defence, The, 2001, PG-13, ★★½ 2004

M

Maborosi, 1997, NO MPAA
RATING, ★★★★ 1998
Mac, 1993, R, ★★★½ 1998
Macbeth, 1972, R, ★★★★ 1998
Madadayo, 2000, NO MPAA
RATING, ★★★ 2003
Madame Bovary, 1991, NO MPAA
RATING, ★★★ 1998
Madame Butterfly, 1996, NO MPAA
RATING, ★★★ 1999
Madame Sousatzka, 1988, PG-13, ★★★★ 1998
Mad City, 1997, PG-13, ★★½ 2000
Mad Dog and Glory, 1993, R, ★★★½ 1998
Mad Dog Time, 1996, R, no stars 1999
Made, 2001, R, ★★★ 2004
Made in America, 1993, PG-13, ★★★ 1998
Madeline, 1998, PG, ★★★ 2001
Mad Love, 1995, PG-13, ★★★ 1998
Mad Max Beyond Thunderdome, 1985,
R, ★★★★ 1998
Madness of King George, The, 1995, NO
MPAA RATING, ★★★★ 1998
Mafia!, 1998, PG-13, ★★ 2001
Magnolia, 2000, R, ★★★★ 2003
Maid in Manhattan, 2002, PG-13, ★★★ 2004
Majestic, The, 2001, PG, ★★★½ 2004
Major Payne, 1995, PG-13, ★★★ 1998
Making Love, 1982, R, ★★ 1988
Making Mr. Right, 1987, PG-13, ★★★½ 1998
Malcolm X, 1992, PG-13, ★★★★ 1998
Malena, 2000, R, ★★ 2003

Malibu's Most Wanted, 2003,
PG-13, ★★½ 2004
Malice, 1993, R, ★★ 1995
Mambo Kings, The, 1992, R, ★★★½ 1998
Man Apart, A, 2003, R, ★★ 2004
Manchurian Candidate, The, 1962,
PG-13, ★★★★ 1997
Mandela, 1997, NO MPAA RATING, ★★★ 2000
Man from Elysian Fields, The, 2002,
R, ★★★★ 2004
Manhattan, 1979, R, ★★★½ 1998
Manhattan Murder Mystery, 1993,
PG, ★★★ 1998
Manhattan Project, The, 1986,
PG-13, ★★★★ 1998
Manic, 2003, R, ★★ 2004
Man in the Iron Mask, The, 1998,
PG-13, ★★½ 2001
Man in the Moon, The, 1991,
PG-13, ★★★★ 1998
Manito, 2003, NO MPAA RATING, ★★★½ 2004
Mannequin, 1987, PG, ½★ 1990
Manny and Lo, 1996, R, ★★★½ 1999
Man of Iron, 1980, NO MPAA
RATING, ★★★★ 1998
Man of the Century, 1999, R, ★★★ 2002
Manon of the Spring, 1987, PG, ★★★★ 1998
Man on the Moon, 1999, R, ★★★½ 2002
Man on the Train, The, 2003, R, ★★★★ 2004
Mansfield Park, 1999, PG-13, ★★★★ 2002
Man Who Cried, The, 2001, R, ★★★ 2004
Man Who Knew Too Little, The, 1997,
PG, ★ 2000
Man Who Loved Women, The, 1983,
R, ★★ 1988
Man Who Wasn't There, The, 2001,
R, ★★★ 2004
Man Who Would Be King, The, 1975,
PG, ★★★★ 1998
Man Without a Face, The, 1993,
PG-13, ★★★ 1998
Man Without a Past, The, 2003,
PG-13, ★★★½ 2004
Man With Two Brains, The, 1983, R, ★★ 1995
Map of the Human Heart, 1993,
R, ★★★★ 1998
Map of the World, A, 2000, R, ★★★½ 2003
Margaret's Museum, 1997, R, ★★★½ 1998
Marie, 1985, PG-13, ★★★ 1987
Marie Baie des Anges, 1998, R, ★ 2001
Marius and Jeannette, 1998, NO MPAA
RATING, ★★ 2001

Mighty Ducks, The, 1992, PG, ★★ — 1994
Mighty Joe Young, 1998, PG, ★★★ — 2001
Mighty Morphin Power Rangers:
The Movie, 1995, PG, ¹/₂★ — 1997
Mighty Peking Man, 1999, NO MPAA
RATING, ★★★ — 2002
Mighty Quinn, The, 1989, R, ★★★★ — 1998
Mighty Wind, A, 2003, PG-13, ★★¹/₂ — 2004
Milagro Beanfield War, The, 1988,
R, ★★¹/₂ — 1993
Miles from Home, 1988, R, ★★★ — 1998
Milk Money, 1994, PG-13, ★ — 1996
Miller's Crossing, 1990, R, ★★★ — 1998
Mimic, 1997, R, ★★★¹/₂ — 2000
Minority Report, 2002, PG-13, ★★★★ — 2004
Minus Man, The, 1999, R, ★★★ — 2002
Miracle Mile, 1989, R, ★★★ — 1998
Miracle on 34th Street, 1994, PG, ★★★ — 1998
Mirror Has Two Faces, The, 1996,
PG-13, ★★★ — 1999
Misery, 1990, R, ★★★ — 1998
Mishima, 1985, R, ★★★★ — 1998
Miss Congeniality, 2000, PG-13, ★★ — 2003
Miss Firecracker, 1989, PG, ★★★¹/₂ — 1998
Missing, 1982, R, ★★★ — 1998
Mission, The, 1986, PG, ★★¹/₂ — 1993
Mission Impossible, 1996, PG-13, ★★★ — 1999
Mission Impossible 2, 2000,
PG-13, ★★★ — 2003
Mission to Mars, 2000, PG-13, ★★¹/₂ — 2003
Mississippi Burning, 1988, R, ★★★★ — 1998
Mississippi Masala, 1992, R, ★★★¹/₂ — 1998
Miss Julie, 2000, R, ★★★ — 2003
Mister Johnson, 1991, PG-13, ★★★ — 1998
Mo' Better Blues, 1990, R, ★★★ — 1998
Moderns, The, 1988, NO MPAA
RATING, ★★★ — 1998
Mod Squad, The, 1999, R, ★★ — 2002
Mommie Dearest, 1981, PG, ★ — 1998
Mona Lisa, 1986, R, ★★★★ — 1998
Money Pit, The, 1986, PG-13, ★ — 1991
Money Talks, 1997, R, ★★★ — 2000
Money Train, 1995, R, ★¹/₂ — 1997
Mon Homme, 1998, NO MPAA
RATING, ★★ — 2001
Monkeybone, 2001, PG-13, ★¹/₂ — 2004
Monkey Trouble, 1994, PG, ★★★ — 1998
Monsieur Hire, 1990, PG-13, ★★★★ — 1998
Monsignor, 1982, R, ★ — 1987
Monsoon Wedding, 2002, R, ★★★¹/₂ — 2004
Monster's Ball, 2002, R, ★★★★ — 2004
Monsters, Inc., 2001, G, ★★★ — 2004

Month by the Lake, A, 1995, PG, ★★★¹/₂ — 1998
Monty Python's Meaning of Life, 1983,
R, ★★¹/₂ — 1995
Monument Ave., 1998, NO MPAA
RATING, ★★★ — 2001
Moonlighting, 1982, PG, ★★★★ — 1998
Moonlight Mile, 2002, PG-13, ★★★★ — 2004
Moon Over Parador, 1988, PG-13, ★★ — 1993
Moonstruck, 1987, PG, ★★★★ — 1998
Morning After, The, 1986, R, ★★★ — 1996
Mortal Thoughts, 1991, R, ★★★ — 1998
Moscow on the Hudson, 1984,
R, ★★★★ — 1998
Mosquito Coast, The, 1986, PG, ★★ — 1993
Motel Hell, 1980, R, ★★★ — 1996
Mother, 1997, PG-13, ★★★¹/₂ — 1998
Mother and the Whore, The, 1999,
NO MPAA RATING, ★★★★ — 2002
Mother Night, 1996, R, ★★¹/₂ — 1999
Mother's Day, 1980, R, no stars — 1991
Mothman Prophecies, The, 2002,
PG-13, ★★ — 2004
Moulin Rouge, 2001, PG-13, ★★★¹/₂ — 2004
Mountains of the Moon, 1990,
R, ★★★¹/₂ — 1998
Mouse Hunt, 1997, PG, ★★ — 2000
Movern Callar, 2002, NO MPAA
RATING, ★★★¹/₂ — 2004
Mr. and Mrs. Bridge, 1991,
PG-13, ★★★★ — 1998
Mr. Baseball, 1992, PG-13, ★★★ — 1998
Mr. Death: The Rise and Fall of
Fred A. Leuchter Jr., 2000,
PG-13, ★★★★ — 2003
Mr. Deeds, 2002, PG-13, ★¹/₂ — 2004
Mr. Destiny, 1990, PG-13, ★★ — 1992
Mr. Holland's Opus, 1996, PG, ★★★¹/₂ — 1999
Mr. Jealousy, 1998, R, ★★¹/₂ — 2001
Mr. Jones, 1993, R, ★★★ — 1998
Mr. Magoo, 1997, PG, ¹/₂★ — 2000
Mr. Mom, 1983, PG, ★★ — 1987
Mr. Nice Guy, 1998, PG-13, ★★★ — 2001
Mr. Saturday Night, 1992, R, ★★★ — 1995
Mrs. Brown, 1997, PG, ★★★¹/₂ — 2000
Mrs. Dalloway, 1998, PG-13, ★★★¹/₂ — 2001
Mrs. Doubtfire, 1993, PG-13, ★★¹/₂ — 1998
Mrs. Parker and the Vicious Circle,
1994, R, ★★★¹/₂ — 1998
Mrs. Winterbourne, 1996, PG-13, ★★¹/₂ — 1999
Mr. Wonderful, 1993, PG-13, ★¹/₂ — 1995
Much Ado About Nothing, 1993,
PG-13, ★★★ — 1998

Mulan, 1998, G, ★★★½	2001
Mulholland Dr. , 2001, R, ★★★★	2004
Mulholland Falls, 1996, R, ★★★½	1999
Multiplicity, 1996, PG-13, ★★½	1999
Mumford, 1999, R, ★★★½	2002
Mummy, The, 1999, PG-13, ★★★	2002
Mummy Returns, The, 2001, PG-13, ★★	2004
Muppet Christmas Carol, The, 1992, G, ★★★	1998
Muppet Movie, The, 1979, G, ★★★½	1998
Muppets from Space, 1999, G, ★★	2002
Muppets Take Manhattan, The, 1984, G, ★★★	1998
Muppet Treasure Island, 1996, G, ★★½	1999
Murder at 1600, 1997, R, ★★½	1998
Murder by Numbers, 2002, R, ★★★	2004
Murder in the First, 1995, R, ★★	1996
Murder on the Orient Express, 1974, PG, ★★★	1998
Muriel's Wedding, 1995, R, ★★★½	1998
Murphy's Romance, 1985, PG-13, ★★★	1998
Muse, The, 1999, PG-13, ★★★	2002
Music Box, 1990, PG-13, ★★	1993
Music Lovers, The, 1971, R, ★★	1993
Music of Chance, The, 1993, NO MPAA RATING, ★★★	1998
Music of the Heart, 1999, PG, ★★★	2002
Musketeer, The, 2001, PG-13, ★★½	2004
My Beautiful Laundrette, 1986, R, ★★★	1998
My Best Friend, 2000, NO MPAA RATING, ★★★	2003
My Best Friend's Wedding, 1997, PG-13, ★★★	1998
My Big Fat Greek Wedding, 2002, PG, ★★★	2004
My Bodyguard, 1980, PG, ★★★½	1998
My Brilliant Career, 1980, NO MPAA RATING, ★★★½	1998
My Cousin Vinny, 1992, R, ★★½	1998
My Dinner with André, 1981, NO MPAA RATING, ★★★★	1998
My Dog Skip, 2000, PG, ★★★	2003
My Fair Lady, 1964, G, ★★★★	1997
My Family, 1995, R, ★★★★	1998
My Father's Glory, 1991, G, ★★★★	1998
My Father the Hero, 1994, PG, ★★	1995
My Favorite Martian, 1999, PG, ★★	2002
My Favorite Season, 1995, NO MPAA RATING, ★★★	1999
My Favorite Year, 1982, PG, ★★★½	1998
My Fellow Americans, 1996, PG-13, ★★½	1999
My First Mister, 2001, R, ★★★	2004

My Giant, 1998, PG, ★★	2001
My Girl, 1991, PG, ★★★½	1998
My Girl 2, 1994, PG, ★★	1995
My Heroes Have Always Been Cowboys, 1991, PG, ★★	1992
My Left Foot, 1989, R, ★★★★	1998
My Life, 1993, PG-13, ★★½	1995
My Life So Far, 1999, PG-13, ★★★	2002
My Mother's Castle, 1991, PG, ★★★★	1998
My Name Is Joe, 1999, R, ★★★½	2002
My Own Private Idaho, 1991, R, ★★★½	1998
My Son the Fanatic, 1999, R, ★★★½	2002
My Stepmother Is an Alien, 1988, PG-13, ★★	1993
Mystery, Alaska, 1999, R, ★★½	2002
Mystery Men, 1999, PG-13, ★★	2002
Mystery Science Theater 3000: The Movie, 1996, PG-13, ★★★	1999
Mystery Train, 1990, R, ★★★½	1998
Mystic Masseur, The, 2002, PG, ★★★	2004
Mystic Pizza, 1988, R, ★★★½	1998
Myth of Fingerprints, The, 1997, R, ★½	2000
My Tutor, 1983, R, ★★★	1986
My Wife Is an Actress, 2002, R, ★★½	2004

N

Nadine, 1987, PG, ★★½	1993
Naked, 1994, NO MPAA RATING, ★★★★	1998
Naked Gun, The, 1988, PG-13, ★★★½	1998
Naked Gun 2½: The Smell of Fear, The, 1991, PG-13, ★★★	1998
Naked Gun 33⅓: The Final Insult, 1994, PG-13, ★★★	1998
Naked in New York, 1994, R, ★★★	1998
Naked Lunch, 1992, R, ★★½	1994
Name of the Rose, The, 1986, R, ★★½	1995
Naqoyqatsi, 2002, PG, ★★★	2004
Narc, 2003, R, ★★★	2004
Narrow Margin, 1990, R, ★½	1992
Nashville, 1975, R, ★★★★	1998
Nasty Girl, The, 1991, PG-13, ★★½	1993
National Lampoon's Animal House, 1978, R, ★★★★	1998
National Lampoon's Christmas Vacation, 1989, PG-13, ★★	1995
National Lampoon's Loaded Weapon I, 1993, PG-13, ★	1994
National Lampoon's Van Wilder, 2002, R, ★	2004
Natural, The, 1984, PG, ★★	1995
Natural Born Killers, 1994, R, ★★★★	1998
Navy Seals, 1990, R, ★½	1992

Necessary Roughness, 1991, PG-13, ★★★ 1996
Needful Things, 1993, R, ★¹/₂ 1995
Negotiator, The, 1998, R, ★★★¹/₂ 2001
Neighbors, 1981, R, ★★★ 1996
Nell, 1994, PG-13, ★★★ 1998
Nelly and Monsieur Arnaud, 1996, NO
  MPAA RATING, ★★★¹/₂ 1999
Nenette et Boni, 1997, NO MPAA
  RATING, ★★★ 2000
Net, The, 1995, PG-13, ★★★ 1998
Network, 1976, R, ★★★★ 1998
Never Again, 2002, R, ★★ 2004
Never Been Kissed, 1999, PG-13, ★★★ 2002
NeverEnding Story, The, 1984, PG, ★★★ 1998
Never Say Never Again, 1983,
  PG, ★★★¹/₂ 1998
New Age, The, 1994, R, ★★★¹/₂ 1998
New Guy, The, 2002, PG-13, ★★ 2004
New Jack City, 1991, R, ★★★¹/₂ 1998
New Jersey Drive, 1995, R, ★★★ 1998
Newsies, 1992, PG, ★¹/₂ 1993
Newton Boys, The, 1998, PG-13, ★★ 2001
New York, New York, 1977, PG, ★★★ 1998
New York Stories, 1989, PG 1998
Next Best Thing, The, 2000, PG-13, ★ 2003
Niagara, Niagara, 1998, R, ★★★ 2001
Nicholas Nickleby, 2003, PG, ★★★¹/₂ 2004
Nick and Jane, 1997, R, ¹/₂★ 2000
Nico and Dani, 2001, NO MPAA
  RATING, ★★★ 2004
Nico Icon, 1996, NO MPAA
  RATING, ★★★ 1999
Night and the City, 1992, R, ★★ 1994
Night at the Roxbury, A, 1998, PG-13, ★ 2001
Night Falls on Manhattan, 1997,
  R, ★★★ 2000
Nightmare on Elm Street 3: Dream
  Warriors, 1987, R, ★¹/₂ 1990
Night of the Living Dead, 1990, R, ★ 1992
Night on Earth, 1992, R, ★★★ 1998
Nightwatch, 1998, R, ★★ 2001
Nil by Mouth, 1998, R, ★★★¹/₂ 2001
Nina Takes a Lover, 1995, R, ★★ 1997
9¹/₂ Weeks, 1985, R, ★★★¹/₂ 1998
Nine Months, 1995, PG-13, ★★ 1998
Nine Queens, 2002, R, ★★★ 2004
1984, 1984, R, ★★★¹/₂ 1998
Nine to Five, 1980, PG, ★★★ 1998
Ninth Gate, The, 2000, R, ★★ 2003
Nixon, 1995, R, ★★★★ 1998
Nobody's Fool, 1986, PG-13, ★★ 1991
Nobody's Fool, 1995, R, ★★★¹/₂ 1998

No Escape, 1994, R, ★★ 1995
No Looking Back, 1998, R, ★★ 2001
Nomads, 1985, R, ★¹/₂ 1987
No Man's Land, 1987, R, ★★★ 1998
No Man's Land, 2001, R, ★★★¹/₂ 2004
No Mercy, 1986, R, ★★★ 1996
Normal Life, 1996, R, ★★★¹/₂ 1999
Norma Rae, 1979, PG, ★★★ 1998
North, 1994, PG, no stars 1997
North Dallas Forty, 1979, R, ★★★¹/₂ 1998
Northfork, 2003, PG-13, ★★★★ 2004
Nosferatu, 1979, R, ★★★★ 1998
No Such Thing, 2002, R, ★ 2004
Not Another Teen Movie, 2001, R, ★★ 2004
Nothing But a Man, 1964, NO MPAA
  RATING, ★★★¹/₂ 1997
Nothing in Common, 1986, PG, ★★¹/₂ 1988
Nothing to Lose, 1997, R, ★★ 2000
Not One Less, 2000, G, ★★★ 2003
Notting Hill, 1999, PG-13, ★★★ 2002
Not Without My Daughter, 1990,
  PG-13, ★★★ 1998
Novocaine, 2001, R, ★★★ 2004
No Way Out, 1987, R, ★★★★ 1998
Nowhere in Africa, 2003, NO MPAA
  RATING, ★★★★ 2004
Nuns on the Run, 1990, PG-13, ★ 1993
Nurse Betty, 2000, R, ★★★ 2003
Nuts, 1987, R, ★★ 1993
Nutty Professor, The, 1996, PG-13, ★★★ 1999
Nutty Professor II: The Klumps, 2000,
  PG-13, ★★★ 2003

O

O, 2001, R, ★★★ 2004
Object of Beauty, The, 1991, R, ★★★¹/₂ 1998
Object of My Affection, The, 1998,
  R, ★★ 2001
O Brother, Where Art Thou?, 2000,
  PG-13, ★★¹/₂ 2003
Ocean's Eleven, 2001, PG-13, ★★★ 2004
October Sky, 1999, PG, ★★★¹/₂ 2002
Odd Couple II, The, 1998, PG-13, ★¹/₂ 2001
Off Beat, 1986, PG, ★★★¹/₂ 1995
Officer and a Gentleman, An, 1982,
  R, ★★★★ 1998
Office Space, 1999, R, ★★★ 2002
Of Mice and Men, 1992, PG-13, ★★★¹/₂ 1998
Oh, God!, 1977, PG, ★★★¹/₂ 1998
Oh, God! Book II, 1980, PG, ★★ 1995
Oh, God! You Devil, 1984, PG, ★★★¹/₂ 1998
Old Gringo, 1989, R, ★★ 1993

Q

Q, 1982, R, ★★½	1993
Q&A, 1990, R, ★★★½	1998
Queen Margot, 1994, R, ★★	1997
Queen of Hearts, 1989, NO MPAA RATING, ★★★½	1998
Queen of the Damned, 2002, R, ★★	2004
Queens Logic, 1991, R, ★★½	1994
Quest for Camelot, 1998, G, ★★	2001
Quest for Fire, 1982, R, ★★★½	1998
Quick and the Dead, The, 1995, R, ★★	1996
Quick Change, 1990, R, ★★★	1995
Quicksilver, 1985, PG, ★★	1987
Quiet American, The, 2003, R, ★★★★	2004
Quigley Down Under, 1990, PG-13, ★★½	1994
Quills, 2000, R, ★★★½	2003
Quitting, 2002, R, ★★½	2004
Quiz Show, 1994, PG-13, ★★★½	1998

R

Rabbit-Proof Fence, 2002, PG, ★★★½	2004
Race the Sun, 1996, PG, ★½	1999
Racing with the Moon, 1984, PG, ★★★½	1998
Radio Days, 1987, PG, ★★★★	1998
Radio Flyer, 1992, PG-13, ★½	1994
Rage: Carrie 2, The, 1999, R, ★★	2002
Rage in Harlem, A, 1991, R, ★★★	1998
Raggedy Man, 1981, PG, ★★★½	1995
Raging Bull, 1980, R, ★★★★	1998
Ragtime, 1981, PG, ★★★½	1998
Raiders of the Lost Ark, 1981, PG, ★★★★	1998
Rainbow, The, 1989, R, ★★★	1998
Raining Stones, 1994, NO MPAA RATING, ★★★½	1998
Rainmaker, The, 1997, PG-13, ★★★	2000
Rain Man, 1988, R, ★★★½	1998
Raise the Red Lantern, 1992, PG, ★★★★	1998
Raise the Titanic, 1980, PG, ★★½	1986
Raising Arizona, 1987, PG-13, ★½	1995
Raising Victor Vargas, 2003, R, ★★★½	2004
Rambling Rose, 1991, R, ★★★	1998
Rambo: First Blood Part II, 1985, R, ★★★	1996
Ran, 1985, R, ★★★★	1998
Random Hearts, 1999, R, ★★½	2002
Ransom, 1996, R, ★★★	1999
Rapa Nui, 1994, R, ★★	1997
Rapture, The, 1991, R, ★★★★	1998
Ravenous, 1999, R, ★★★	2002

Razor's Edge, The, 1984, PG-13, ★★½	1988
Reach the Rock, 1998, R, ★	2001
Read My Lips, 2002, NO MPAA RATING, ★★★½	2004
Ready to Rumble, 2000, PG-13, ★★	2003
Ready to Wear, 1994, R, ★★½	1997
Real Blonde, The, 1998, R, ★★★	2001
Real Genius, 1985, PG-13, ★★★½	1998
Reality Bites, 1994, PG-13, ★★	1995
Real McCoy, The, 1993, PG-13, ★★	1995
Real Women Have Curves, 2002, PG-13, ★★★½	2004
Re-Animator, 1985, NO MPAA RATING, ★★★	1998
Recess: School's Out, 2001, G, ★★½	2004
Recruit, The, 2003, PG-13, ★★½	2004
Red, 1994, R, ★★★★	1998
Red Corner, 1997, R, ★★	2000
Red Dragon, 2002, R, ★★★½	2004
Red Heat, 1988, R, ★★★	1998
Red Planet, 2000, PG-13, ★★★	2003
Red Rock West, 1994, R, ★★★½	1998
Reds, 1981, PG, ★★★½	1998
Red Sonja, 1985, PG-13, ★½	1987
Red Violin, The, 1999, NO MPAA RATING, ★★★½	2002
Ref, The, 1994, R, ★★★	1998
Regarding Henry, 1991, PG-13, ★★	1994
Regret to Inform, 1999, NO MPAA RATING, ★★★	2002
Reign of Fire, 2002, PG-13, ★	2004
Reindeer Games, 2000, R, ★½	2003
Relic, The, 1997, R, ★★★	1998
Remains of the Day, 1993, PG, ★★★½	1998
Remember the Titans, 2000, PG, ★★★	2003
Renaissance Man, 1994, PG-13, ★½	1995
Rendevous in Paris, 1996, NO MPAA RATING, ★★★½	1999
Replacement Killers, The, 1998, R, ★★★	2001
Replacements, The, 2000, PG-13, ★★	2003
Repo Man, 1984, R, ★★★	1998
Requiem for a Dream, 2000, NO MPAA RATING, ★★★½	2003
Rescuers Down Under, The, 1990, G, ★★★	1998
Reservoir Dogs, 1992, R, ★★½	1998
Resident Evil, 2002, R, ★	2004
Respiro, 2003, PG-13, ★★★	2004
Restoration, 1996, R, ★★★½	1999
Return of the Jedi (special edition), 1997, PG, ★★★★	1998

Return of the Living Dead, 1985, R, ★★★	1987
Return of the Secaucus Seven, 1981, NO MPAA RATING, ★★★	1998
Return to Me, 2000, PG, ★★★	2003
Return to Never Land, 2002, G, ★★★	2004
Return to Oz, 1985, PG, ★★	1987
Return to Paradise, 1998, R, ★★★½	2001
Return with Honor, 1999, NO MPAA RATING, ★★★	2002
Revenge, 1990, R, ★★½	1993
Revenge of the Nerds II, 1987, PG-13, ★½	1990
Revenge of the Pink Panther, 1978, PG, ★★★	1995
Reversal of Fortune, 1990, R, ★★★★	1998
Rhapsody in August, 1992, PG, ★★★	1998
Rhinestone, 1984, PG, ★	1987
Rich and Famous, 1981, R, ★★½	1987
Richard Pryor Here and Now, 1983, R, ★★★★	1996
Richard Pryor Live on the Sunset Strip, 1982, R, ★★★★	1996
Richard III, 1996, R, ★★★½	1999
Richie Rich, 1994, PG, ★★★	1998
Rich in Love, 1993, PG-13, ★★★	1998
Rich Man's Wife, The, 1996, R, ★★½	1999
Ride with the Devil, 1999, R, ★★	2002
Ridicule, 1996, R, ★★★½	1999
Riding in Cars with Boys, 2001, PG-13, ★★★	2004
Right Stuff, The, 1983, PG, ★★★★	1998
Ring, The, 2002, PG-13, ★★	2004
Ringmaster, 1998, R, ★★	2001
Rising Sun, 1993, R, ★★	1995
Risky Business, 1983, R, ★★★★	1998
Rita, Sue and Bob Too, 1987, R, ★★★	1996
River, The, 1985, PG-13, ★★	1991
River Runs Through It, A, 1992, PG, ★★★½	1998
Rivers and Tides: Andy Goldsworthy Working with Time, 2003, NO MPAA RATING, ★★★½	2004
River's Edge, 1987, R, ★★★½	1998
River Wild, The, 1994, PG-13, ★★	1997
Road House, 1989, R, ★★½	1993
Road to El Dorado, The, 2000, PG, ★★★	2003
Road to Perdition, 2002, R, ★★★	2004
Road Trip, 2000, R, ★★	2003
Road Warrior, The, 1982, R, ★★★½	1998
Robin Hood: Prince of Thieves, 1991, PG-13, ★★	1997
RoboCop, 1987, R, ★★★	1998
RoboCop II, 1990, R, ★★	1995
RoboCop 3, 1993, PG-13, ★½	1995
Rob Roy, 1995, R, ★★★½	1998
Rock, The, 1996, R, ★★★½	1999
Rocketeer, The, 1991, PG-13, ★★★	1998
Rocket Man, 1997, PG, ★★★	2000
Rock Star, 2001, R, ★★½	2004
Rocky, 1976, PG, ★★★★	1998
Rocky II, 1979, PG, ★★★	1998
Rocky IV, 1986, PG, ★★	1993
Rocky V, 1990, PG-13, ★★	1993
Rocky Horror Picture Show, The, 1975, R, ★★½	1998
Roger & Me, 1989, R, ★★★★	1998
Roger Dodger, 2002, R, ★★★	2004
Rollerball, 2002, PG-13, ½★	2004
Romance, 1999, NO MPAA RATING, ★★★	2002
Romancing the Stone, 1984, PG, ★★★	1998
Romeo Is Bleeding, 1994, R, ★★	1995
Romeo Must Die, 2000, R, ★½	2003
Romy and Michele's High School Reunion, 1997, R, ★★★	1998
Ronin, 1998, R, ★★★	2001
Rookie, The, 2002, G, ★★	2004
Rookie of the Year, 1993, PG, ★★★	1996
Room for Romeo Brass, A, 2000, R, ★★★	2003
Room with a View, A, 1985, PG-13, ★★★★	1998
Rosalie Goes Shopping, 1990, PG, ★★★	1998
Rose, The, 1979, R, ★★★	1998
Rosetta, 2000, R, ★★★½	2003
Rosewood, 1997, R, ★★★½	1998
Rough Magic, 1997, PG-13, ★★	1998
Roujin-Z, 1996, PG-13, ★★★	1999
Rounders, 1998, R, ★★★	2001
'Round Midnight, 1986, R, ★★★★	1998
Roxanne, 1987, PG, ★★★½	1998
Royal Tenenbaums, The, 2001, R, ★★★½	2004
Ruby, 1992, R, ★★	1994
Ruby in Paradise, 1993, NO MPAA RATING, ★★★★	1998
Rudy, 1993, PG, ★★★½	1998
Rudyard Kipling's Second Jungle Book: Mowgli and Baloo, 1997, PG, ★½	2000
Rudyard Kipling's the Jungle Book, 1994, PG, ★★★	1998
Rugrats, 1998, G, ★★	2001
Rugrats Go Wild!, 2003, PG, ★★	2004
Rugrats in Paris, 2000, G, ★★★	2003

Simon Magus, 2001, NO MPAA
RATING, ★★ — 2004

Simpatico, 2000, R, ★¹⁄₂ — 2003

Simple Men, 1992, R, ★★ — 1995

Simple Plan, A, 1998, R, ★★★★ — 2001

Simple Wish, A, 1997, PG, ★¹⁄₂ — 2000

Simply Irresistible, 1999, PG-13, ★★★ — 2002

Sinbad: Legend of the Seven Seas, 2003,
PG, ★★★¹⁄₂ — 2004

Sing, 1989, PG-13, ★★★ — 1996

Singin' in the Rain, 1952, G, ★★★★ — 1997

Singles, 1992, PG-13, ★★★ — 1998

Single White Female, 1992, R, ★★★ — 1996

Sirens, 1994, R, ★★★¹⁄₂ — 1998

Sister Act, 1992, PG, ★★¹⁄₂ — 1996

Sister Act 2: Back in the Habit, 1993,
PG, ★★ — 1995

Sisters, 1973, R, ★★★ — 1998

Six Days, Seven Nights, 1998,
PG-13, ★★¹⁄₂ — 2001

Sixteen Candles, 1984, PG, ★★★ — 1998

6th Day, The, 2000, PG-13, ★★★ — 2003

Sixth Man, The, 1997, PG-13, ★¹⁄₂ — 2000

Sixth Sense, The, 1999, PG-13, ★★★ — 2002

Skin Deep, 1989, R, ★★★ — 1998

Skins, 2002, R, ★★★ — 2004

Skulls, The, 2000, PG-13, ★ — 2003

Slacker, 1991, R, ★★★ — 1998

Slackers, 2002, R, no stars — 2004

Slam, 1998, R, ★★¹⁄₂ — 2001

SlamNation, 1998, NO MPAA
RATING, ★★★ — 2001

Slappy and the Stinkers, 1998, PG, ★★ — 2001

Slaves of New York, 1989, R, ¹⁄₂★ — 1993

SLC Punk!, 1999, R, ★★★ — 2002

Sleeper, 1973, PG, ★★★¹⁄₂ — 1998

Sleeping with the Enemy, 1991, R, ★¹⁄₂ — 1994

Sleepless in Seattle, 1993, PG, ★★★ — 1998

Sleepy Hollow, 1999, R, ★★★¹⁄₂ — 2002

Sleepy Time Gal, The, 2002, R, ★★★¹⁄₂ — 2004

Sleuth, 1972, PG, ★★★★ — 1998

Sliding Doors, 1998, PG-13, ★★ — 2001

Sling Blade, 1996, R, ★★★¹⁄₂ — 1999

Slugger's Wife, The, 1985, PG-13, ★★ — 1986

Slums of Beverly Hills, 1998, R, ★★★ — 2001

Small Change, 1976, PG, ★★★★ — 1998

Small Soldiers, 1998, PG-13, ★★¹⁄₂ — 2001

Small Time Crooks, 2000, PG, ★★★ — 2003

Smash Palace, 1982, R, ★★★★ — 1998

Smiling Fish and Goat on Fire, 2000,
R, ★★★ — 2003

Smilla's Sense of Snow, 1997, R, ★★★ — 1998

Smoke, 1995, R, ★★★ — 1998

Smoke Signals, 1998, PG-13, ★★★ — 2001

Smokey and the Bandit II, 1980, PG, ★ — 1986

Smooth Talk, 1986, PG-13, ★★★¹⁄₂ — 1998

Snake Eyes, 1998, R, ★ — 2001

Snapper, The, 1993, R, ★★★¹⁄₂ — 1998

Snatch, 2001, R, ★★ — 2004

Sneakers, 1992, PG-13, ★★¹⁄₂ — 1994

Sniper, 1993, R, ★★★ — 1996

Snow Day, 2000, PG, ★¹⁄₂ — 2003

Snow Falling on Cedars, 2000,
PG-13, ★★★¹⁄₂ — 2003

Soapdish, 1991, PG-13, ★★★¹⁄₂ — 1998

So I Married an Axe Murderer, 1993,
PG-13, ★★¹⁄₂ — 1995

Solaris, 2002, PG-13, ★★★¹⁄₂ — 2004

Soldier of Orange, 1980, PG, ★★★¹⁄₂ — 1986

Soldier's Daughter Never Cries, A, 1998,
R, ★★★¹⁄₂ — 2001

Soldier's Story, A, 1984, PG, ★★¹⁄₂ — 1993

Solomon and Gaenor, 2000, R, ★★ — 2003

Some Kind of Wonderful, 1987,
PG-13, ★★★ — 1998

Some Mother's Son, 1996, R, ★★★ — 1999

Someone Like You, 2001, PG-13, ★★ — 2004

Someone to Watch Over Me, 1987,
R, ★★ — 1992

Something to Talk About, 1995,
R, ★★★¹⁄₂ — 1998

Something Wild, 1986, R, ★★★¹⁄₂ — 1998

Sometimes a Great Notion, 1971,
PG, ★★★ — 1998

Somewhere in Time, 1980, PG, ★★ — 1988

Sommersby, 1993, PG-13, ★★ — 1994

Son, The, 2003, NO MPAA
RATING, ★★★★ — 2004

Sonatine, 1998, R, ★★★¹⁄₂ — 2001

Songcatcher, 2001, PG-13, ★★★ — 2004

Song for Martin, A, 2002, PG-13, ★★★¹⁄₂ — 2004

Songs from the Second Floor, 2002, NO
MPAA RATING, ★★★★ — 2004

Songwriter, 1985, R, ★★★¹⁄₂ — 1996

Son-in-Law, 1993, PG-13, ★★ — 1995

Son's Room, The, 2002, R, ★★★¹⁄₂ — 2004

Sophie's Choice, 1982, R, ★★★★ — 1998

Sorority Boys, 2002, R, ¹⁄₂★ — 2004

Soul Food, 1997, R, ★★★¹⁄₂ — 2000

Soul Man, 1986, PG-13, ★ — 1989

Sounder, 1972, G, ★★★★ — 1998

Sour Grapes, 1998, R, no stars — 2001

South, 2000, NO MPAA RATING, ★★★ — 2003
South Central, 1992, R, ★★★ — 1996
Southern Comfort, 1981, R, ★★★ — 1996
South Park: Bigger, Longer and Uncut, 1999, R, ★★½ — 2002
Spaceballs, 1987, PG, ★★½ — 1991
Space Cowboys, 2000, PG-13, ★★★ — 2003
Space Jam, 1996, PG, ★★★½ — 1999
Spanish Prisoner, The, 1998, PG, ★★★½ — 2001
Spartacus, 1960, PG-13, ★★★ — 1997
Spawn, 1997, PG-13, ★★★½ — 2000
Special Effects Documentary, 1996, NO MPAA RATING, ★★★ — 1999
Species, 1995, R, ★★ — 1997
Speechless, 1994, PG-13, ★★ — 1996
Speed, 1994, R, ★★★★ — 1997
Speed 2: Cruise Control, 1997, PG-13, ★★★½ — 2000
Spellbound, 2003, G, ★★★ — 2004
Sphere, 1998, PG-13, ★½ — 2001
Spice World, 1998, PG, ½★ — 2001
Spider, 2003, R, ★★★ — 2004
Spider-Man, 2002, PG-13, ★★ — 2004
Spider's Stratagem, The, 1973, PG, ★★★ — 1998
Spike of Bensonhurst, 1988, R, ★★★ — 1998
Spirited Away, 2002, PG, ★★★★ — 2004
Spirit: Stallion of the Cimarron, 2002, G, ★★★ — 2004
Spitfire Grill, The, 1996, PG-13, ★★ — 1999
Splash, 1984, PG, ★½ — 1993
Spring Break, 1983, R, ★ — 1988
Sprung, 1997, R, ★½ — 2000
Spun, 2003, R, ★★★ — 2004
Spy Game, 2001, R, ★★½ — 2004
Spy Kids, 2001, PG, ★★★½ — 2004
Spy Kids 2: The Island of Lost Dreams, 2002, PG, ★★★ — 2004
Spy Who Loved Me, The, 1977, PG, ★★★½ — 1998
Stairway to Heaven, 1946, PG, ★★★★ — 1997
Stakeout, 1987, R, ★★★ — 1996
Stand and Deliver, 1988, PG-13, ★★½ — 1994
Standing in the Shadows of Motown, 2002, PG, ★★★ — 2004
Stanley & Iris, 1990, PG-13, ★★½ — 1993
Stardust Memories, 1980, PG, ★★ — 1997
STAR 80, 1983, R, ★★★★ — 1998
Stargate, 1994, PG-13, ★ — 1997
Star Is Born, A, 1954 (1983), PG, ★★★★ — 1997
Star Kid, 1998, PG, ★★★ — 2001

Starmaker, The, 1996, R, ★★★ — 1999
Starman, 1984, PG, ★★★ — 1998
Star Maps, 1997, R, ★★ — 2000
Stars Fell on Henrietta, The, 1995, PG, ★★ — 1997
Starship Troopers, 1997, R, ★★ — 2000
Star Trek: The Motion Picture, 1979, G, ★★★ — 1998
Star Trek II: The Wrath of Khan, 1982, PG, ★★★ — 1998
Star Trek III: The Search for Spock, 1984, PG, ★★★ — 1998
Star Trek IV: The Voyage Home, 1986, PG, ★★★½ — 1998
Star Trek V: The Final Frontier, 1989, PG, ★★ — 1997
Star Trek VI: The Undiscovered Country, 1991, PG, ★★★ — 1998
Star Trek: Generations, 1994, PG, ★★ — 1997
Star Trek: First Contact, 1996, PG-13, ★★★½ — 1999
Star Trek: Insurrection, 1998, PG, ★★ — 2001
Star Trek: Nemesis, 2002, PG-13, ★★ — 2004
Startup.com, 2001, R, ★★★ — 2004
Star Wars, 1977, PG, ★★★★ — 1997
Star Wars (special edition), PG, 1997, ★★★★ — 1998
Star Wars: Episode I—The Phantom Menace, 1999, PG, ★★★½ — 2002
Star Wars: Episode II—Attack of the Clones, 2002, PG, ★★ — 2004
State and Main, 2000, R, ★★★ — 2003
State of Grace, 1990, R, ★★★½ — 1998
Stay Hungry, 1976, R, ★★★ — 1996
Staying Alive, 1983, PG, ★ — 1994
Staying Together, 1989, R, ★★ — 1993
Stealing Beauty, 1996, R, ★★ — 1999
Stealing Harvard, 2002, PG-13, ★ — 2004
Steal This Movie, 2000, R, ★★★ — 2003
Steam: The Turkish Bath, 1999, NO MPAA RATING, ★★ — 2002
Steel Magnolias, 1989, PG, ★★★ — 1998
Stella, 1990, PG-13, ★★★½ — 1998
St. Elmo's Fire, 1985, R, ★½ — 1987
Stepfather, The, 1987, R, ★★½ — 1994
Stephen King's Silver Bullet, 1985, R, ★★★ — 1988
Stepmom, 1998, PG-13, ★★ — 2001
Stepping Out, 1991, PG, ★★ — 1994
Stevie, 1981, NO MPAA RATING, ★★★★ — 1998
Stevie, 2003, NO MPAA RATING, ★★★½ — 2004
Stigmata, 1999, R, ★★ — 2002

Still Crazy, 1999, R, ★★★	2002
Sting II, The, 1983, PG, ★★	1986
Stir Crazy, 1980, R, ★★	1987
Stir of Echoes, 1999, R, ★★★	2002
Stolen Summer, 2002, PG, ★★★	2004
Stoneraft, The, 2003, NO MPAA RATING, ★★★	2004
Stone Reader, 2003, PG-13, ★★★¹⁄₂	2004
Stonewall, 1996, NO MPAA RATING, ★★¹⁄₂	1999
Stop Making Sense, 1984, NO MPAA RATING, ★★★¹⁄₂	1998
Stop! Or My Mom Will Shoot, 1992, PG-13, ¹⁄₂★	1994
Stormy Monday, 1988, R, ★★★¹⁄₂	1998
Story of Qiu Ju, The, 1993, NO MPAA RATING, ★★★¹⁄₂	1997
Story of Us, The, 1999, R, ★	2002
Story of Women, 1990, R, ★★¹⁄₂	1993
Storytelling, 2002, R, ★★★¹⁄₂	2004
Storyville, 1992, R, ★★★¹⁄₂	1998
Straight Out of Brooklyn, 1991, R, ★★★	1998
Straight Story, The, 1999, G, ★★★★	2002
Straight Talk, 1992, PG, ★★	1994
Straight Time, 1978, R, ★★★¹⁄₂	1998
Strange Days, 1995, R, ★★★★	1998
Stranger Among Us, A, 1992, PG-13, ★¹⁄₂	1994
Stranger than Paradise, 1984, R, ★★★★	1998
Strapless, 1990, R, ★★★	1998
Strawberry and Chocolate, 1995, R, ★★★¹⁄₂	1998
Streamers, 1984, R, ★★★★	1998
Streetcar Named Desire, A, 1951, PG, ★★★★	1997
Street Smart, 1987, R, ★★★	1998
Streets of Fire, 1984, PG, ★★★	1988
Streetwise, 1985, R, ★★★★	1998
Strictly Ballroom, 1993, PG, ★★★	1998
Strictly Business, 1991, PG-13, ★★¹⁄₂	1993
Striking Distance, 1993, R, ★¹⁄₂	1995
Stripes, 1981, R, ★★★¹⁄₂	1998
Stripper, 1986, R, ★★★	1987
Striptease, 1996, R, ★★	1999
Stroker Ace, 1983, PG, ★¹⁄₂	1986
Stroszek, 1978, NO MPAA RATING, ★★★★	1998
Stuart Little, 1999, PG, ★★	2002
Stuart Little 2, 2002, PG, ★★★	2004
Stuart Saves His Family, 1995, PG-13, ★★★	1998
Stuff, The, 1985, R, ★¹⁄₂	1987
Stunt Man, The, 1980, R, ★★	1988
Substance of Fire, The, 1997, R, ★★★	2000
Substitute, The, 1996, R, ★	1999

Suburban Commando, 1991, PG, ★	1993
subUrbia, 1997, R, ★★★¹⁄₂	1998
Such a Long Journey, 2000, NO MPAA RATING, ★★★¹⁄₂	2003
Sudden Death, 1995, R, ★★¹⁄₂	1998
Sudden Impact, 1983, R, ★★★	1998
Sugar & Spice, 2001, PG-13, ★★★	2004
Sugar Hill, 1994, R, ★★★★	1998
Sugar Town, 1999, R, ★★★	2002
Summer House, The, 1993, NO MPAA RATING, ★★★	1998
Summer of ʼ42, 1971, R, ★★¹⁄₂	1987
Summer of Sam, 1999, R, ★★★¹⁄₂	2002
Sum of All Fears, The, 2002, PG-13, ★★★¹⁄₂	2004
Sunday, 1997, NO MPAA RATING, ★★★	2000
Sunday Bloody Sunday, 1971, R, ★★★★	1998
Sunset Park, 1996, R, ★★	1999
Sunshine, 2000, R, ★★★	2003
Sunshine State, 2002, PG-13, ★★★¹⁄₂	2004
Super, The, 1991, R, ★★	1995
Supergirl, 1984, PG, ★★	1988
Superman, 1978, PG, ★★★★	1998
Superman II, 1981, PG, ★★★★	1998
Superman III, 1983, PG, ★★¹⁄₂	1998
Superstar, 1999, PG-13, ★	2002
Superstar: The Life and Times of Andy Warhol, 1991, NO MPAA RATING, ★★★	1997
Super Troopers, 2002, R, ★★¹⁄₂	2004
Sure Thing, The, 1985, PG-13, ★★★¹⁄₂	1998
Surrender, 1987, PG, ★★	1989
Survivors, The, 1983, R, ★¹⁄₂	1991
Suspect, 1987, R, ★★¹⁄₂	1993
Swamp Thing, 1982, R, ★★★	1998
Swann in Love, 1984, R, ★★★	1996
Swan Princess, The, 1994, G, ★★★	1998
Sweet and Lowdown, 1999, PG-13, ★★★¹⁄₂	2002
Sweet Dreams, 1985, PG-13, ★★	1988
Sweetest Thing, The, 2002, R, ★¹⁄₂	2004
Sweet Hereafter, The, 1997, R, ★★★★	2000
Sweet Home Alabama, 2002, PG-13, ★★★	2004
Sweetie, 1990, R, ★★★¹⁄₂	1998
Sweet Liberty, 1986, PG, ★★¹⁄₂	1993
Sweet Nothing, 1996, R, ★★★	1999
Sweet November, 2001, PG-13, ★	2004
Sweet Sixteen, 2003, R, ★★★¹⁄₂	2004
Swept Away, 2002, R, ★	2004
Swept from the Sea, 1998, PG-13, ★★	2001

Swimming, 2002, NO MPAA RATING, ★★★ — 2004

Swimming Pool, 2003, R, ★★★ — 2004

Swimming to Cambodia, 1987, NO MPAA RATING, ★★★ — 1998

Swimming with Sharks, 1995, R, ★★★ — 1998

Swindle, The, 1999, NO MPAA RATING, ★★★ — 2002

Swingers, 1996, R, ★★★ — 1999

Swing Kids, 1993, PG-13, ★ — 1994

Swing Shift, 1984, PG, ★★★ — 1988

Switch, 1991, R, ★★½ — 1994

Switchback, 1997, R, ★★ — 2000

Switchblade Sisters, 1997, R, ★ — 1999

Switching Channels, 1988, PG-13, ★★★ — 1996

Swoon, 1992, NO MPAA RATING, ★★★ — 1996

Swordfish, 2001, R, ★★½ — 2004

Sylvester, 1985, PG, ★★★ — 1988

Synthetic Pleasures, 1996, NO MPAA RATING, ★★½ — 1999

T

Table for Five, 1983, PG, ★½ — 1986

Taboo, 2001, NO MPAA RATING, ★★★ — 2004

Tadpole, 2002, PG-13, ★★ — 2004

Tailor of Panama, The, 2001, R, ★★★½ — 2004

Talented Mr. Ripley, The, 1999, R, ★★★★ — 2002

Tale of Springtime, A, 1992, PG, ★★★½ — 1998

Talk Radio, 1988, R, ★★★★ — 1998

Talk to Her, 2002, R, ★★★★ — 2004

Tall Guy, The, 1990, R, ★★★½ — 1998

Tall Tale: The Unbelievable Adventures of Pecos Bill, 1995, PG, ★★★ — 1998

Tampopo, 1987, NO MPAA RATING, ★★★★ — 1998

Tango, 1999, PG-13, ★★★½ — 2002

Tango and Cash, 1989, R, ★ — 1992

Tango Lesson, The, 1997, PG, ★★★½ — 2000

Tank Girl, 1995, R, ★★ — 1996

Tao of Steve, The, 2000, PG-13, ★★★ — 2003

Tap, 1989, PG-13, ★★★ — 1998

Tape, 2001, R, ★★★½ — 2004

Taps, 1981, PG, ★★★ — 1998

Tarzan, 1999, G, ★★★★ — 2002

Tarzan, the Ape Man, 1981, R, ★★½ — 1993

Taste of Cherry, The, 1998, NO MPAA RATING, ★ — 2001

Taste of Others, The, 2001, NO MPAA RATING, ★★★ — 2004

Tatie Danielle, 1991, NO MPAA RATING, ★★★ — 1996

Taxi Blues, 1991, NO MPAA RATING, ★★★ — 1998

Taxi Driver, 1976, R, ★★★★ — 1997

Taxi Driver: 20th Anniversary Edition, 1995, R, ★★★★ — 1999

Taxing Woman, A, 1988, NO MPAA RATING, ★★ — 1992

Teachers, 1984, R, ★★ — 1986

Teaching Mrs. Tingle, 1999, PG-13, ★½ — 2002

Tears of the Sun, 2003, R, ★★★ — 2004

Tea with Mussolini, 1999, PG, ★★½ — 2002

Teenage Mutant Ninja Turtles, 1990, PG, ★★½ — 1994

Teenage Mutant Ninja Turtles II: The Secret of the Ooze, 1991, PG, ★ — 1994

Teen Wolf Too, 1987, PG, ½★ — 1989

Telling Lies in America, 1997, PG-13, ★★★ — 2000

Tell Them Willie Boy Is Here, 1970, PG, ★★★½ — 1996

Temptress Moon, 1997, R, ★★ — 2000

10, 1979, R, ★★★★ — 1998

Ten, 2003, NO MPAA RATING, ★★ — 2004

Tender Mercies, 1983, PG, ★★★ — 1998

10 Things I Hate About You, 1999, PG-13, ★★½ — 2002

Tequila Sunrise, 1988, R, ★★½ — 1994

Terminal Velocity, 1994, PG-13, ★★ — 1996

Terminator 2: Judgment Day, 1991, R, ★★★½ — 1998

Terminator 3: Rise of the Machines, 2003, R, ★★½ — 2004

Terms of Endearment, 1983, PG, ★★★★ — 1998

Terrorist, The, 2000, NO MPAA RATING, ★★★½ — 2003

Terror Train, 1980, R, ★ — 1986

Tess, 1980, PG, ★★★★ — 1998

Testament, 1983, PG, ★★★★ — 1998

Tetsuo II: Body Hammer, 1997, NO MPAA RATING, ★★★ — 2000

Tex, 1982, PG, ★★★★ — 1998

Texas Chainsaw Massacre, The, 1974, R, ★★ — 1995

Texasville, 1990, R, ★★★½ — 1998

That Obscure Object of Desire, 1977, R, ★★★★ — 1998

That Old Feeling, 1997, PG-13, ★ — 1998

That's Dancing!, 1985, PG, ★★★ — 1998

That's Entertainment!, 1974, G, ★★★★ — 1998

That's Entertainment! III, 1994, G, ★★★½ — 1998

That's the Way I Like It, 1999,
PG-13, ★★★   2002

That Thing You Do!, 1996, PG, ★★★   1999

That Was Then . . . This Is Now, 1985,
R, ★★   1987

Thelma & Louise, 1991, R, ★★★½   1998

Thelonious Monk: Straight, No Chaser,
1989, PG-13, ★★★½   1998

Theory of Flight, The, 1999, R, ★★½   2002

Theremin: An Electronic Odyssey, 1995,
NO MPAA RATING, ★★★½   1998

Therese, 1987, NO MPAA RATING, ★★★½   1996

There's Something About Mary, 1998,
R, ★★★   2001

They Call Me Bruce, 1983, PG, ★★   1986

They Shoot Horses, Don't They?, 1970,
PG, ★★★★   1998

Thief, 1981, R, ★★★½   1996

Thief, The, 1998, R, ★★★   2001

Thieves Like Us, 1974, R, ★★★½   1998

Thin Blue Line, The, 1988, NO MPAA
RATING, ★★★½   1998

Thing, The, 1982, R, ★★½   1995

Things Change, 1988, PG, ★★★   1998

Things to Do in Denver When You're
Dead, 1996, R, ★★½   1999

Thin Line Between Love and Hate, A,
1996, R, ★★½   1999

Thin Red Line, The, 1999, R, ★★★   2002

Third Miracle, The, 2000, R, ★★★   2003

Thirteen, 2000, NO MPAA
RATING, ★★★½   2003

Thirteen Conversations About One
Thing, 2002, R, ★★★★   2004

Thirteen Days, 2001, PG-13, ★★★   2004

13 Ghosts, 2001, R, ★   2004

13th Warrior, The, 1999, R, ★½   2002

35 Up, 1992, NO MPAA RATING, ★★★★   1998

36 Fillette, 1989, NO MPAA
RATING, ★★★½   1996

Thirty-two Short Films About Glenn
Gould, 1994, NO MPAA
RATING, ★★★★   1998

This Boy's Life, 1993, R, ★★★½   1998

This Is Elvis, 1981, PG, ★★★½   1998

This Is My Father, 1999, R, ★★★   2002

This Is My Life, 1992, PG-13, ★★★   1996

This Is Spinal Tap, 1984, R, ★★★★   1998

Thomas and the Magic Railroad, 2000,
G, ★   2003

Thomas Crown Affair, The, 1999,
R, ★★½   2002

Thomas in Love, 2001, NO MPAA
RATING, ★★   2004

Thousand Acres, A, 1997, R, ★★   2000

Three Kings, 1999, R, ★★★★   2002

Three Lives and Only One Death, 1997,
NO MPAA RATING, ★★★   2000

Three Men and a Baby, 1987, PG, ★★★   1998

Three Men and a Little Lady, 1990,
PG, ★★   1994

Three Musketeers, The, 1993, PG, ★★   1995

3 Ninjas Kick Back, 1994, PG, ★★½   1995

Three of Hearts, 1993, R, ★★★   1996

Three Seasons, 1999, PG-13, ★★★   2002

Threesome, 1994, R, ★★★   1996

3,000 Miles to Graceland, 2001, R, ★½   2004

Three to Tango, 1999, PG-13, ★   2002

3 Women, 1977, PG, ★★★★   1998

Throw Momma from the Train, 1987,
PG-13, ★★   1993

Thunderheart, 1992, R, ★★★½   1998

THX 1138, 1971, PG, ★★★   1998

Ticket to Heaven, 1981, R, ★★★½   1998

Tie Me Up! Tie Me Down!, 1990, NO
MPAA RATING, ★★   1993

Tiger's Tale, A, 1988, R, ★★   1989

Tightrope, 1984, R, ★★★½   1998

Till Human Voices Wake Us, 2003, R, ★½   2004

'Til There Was You, 1997, PG-13, ½★   1998

Tim Burton's Nightmare Before
Christmas, 1993, PG, ★★★½   1998

Time and Tide, 2001, R, ★★★   2004

Time Bandits, 1981, PG, ★★★   1998

Time Code, 2000, R, ★★★   2003

Timecop, 1994, R, ★★   1997

Time for Drunken Horses, A, 2000, NO
MPAA RATING, ★★★   2003

Time Machine, 2002, PG-13, ★½   2004

Time of Destiny, A, 1988, PG-13, ★★★½   1998

Time Out, 2002, PG-13, ★★★   2004

Time Regained, 2000, NO MPAA
RATING, ★★★½   2003

Times of Harvey Milk, The, 1985, NO
MPAA RATING, ★★★½   1997

Tin Cup, 1996, R, ★★★   1999

Tin Drum, The, 1980, R, ★★   1988

Tin Men, 1987, R, ★★★   1998

Titan A.E., 2000, PG, ★★★½   2003

Titanic, 1997, PG-13, ★★★★   2000

Titus, 2000, R, ★★★½   2003

To Be or Not To Be, 1983, R, ★★★   1998

To Die For, 1995, R, ★★★½   1998

Together, 2001, R, ★★★   2004

Together, 2003, PG, ★★★½ — 2004

To Gillian on Her 37th Birthday, 1996, PG-13, ★★ — 1999

Tokyo Story, 1953, G, ★★★★ — 1997

To Live, 1994, NO MPAA RATING, ★★★½ — 1998

To Live and Die in L.A., 1985, R, ★★★★ — 1998

Tom and Viv, 1995, PG-13, ★★½ — 1996

Tomcats, 2001, R, no stars — 2004

Tommy, 1975, PG, ★★★ — 1998

Tomorrow Never Dies, 1997, PG-13, ★★★ — 2000

Too Beautiful for You, 1990, R, ★★★½ — 1998

Too Much Sleep, 2001, NO MPAA RATING, ★★★ — 2004

Tootsie, 1982, PG, ★★★★ — 1998

Topaz, 1970, PG, ★★★½ — 1998

Top Gun, 1986, PG, ★★½ — 1998

Top Secret!, 1984, R, ★★★½ — 1998

Topsy-Turvy, 2000, R, ★★★★ — 2003

Torch Song Trilogy, 1988, R, ★★★½ — 1998

Tortilla Soup, 2001, PG-13, ★★★ — 2004

To Sleep with Anger, 1990, PG, ★★½ — 1993

Total Recall, 1990, R, ★★★½ — 1998

Toto le Heros, 1992, NO MPAA RATING, ★★½ — 1994

Touch, 1997, R, ★★½ — 2000

Tough Enough, 1983, PG, ★★★ — 1986

Tough Guys Don't Dance, 1987, R, ★★½ — 1993

To Wong Foo, Thanks for Everything! Julie Newmar, 1995, PG-13, ★★½ — 1997

Toys, 1992, PG-13, ★★½ — 1994

Toy Story, 1995, G, ★★★½ — 1998

Toy Story 2, 1999, G, ★★★½ — 2002

Track 29, 1988, R, ★★★ — 1996

Trading Places, 1983, R, ★★★½ — 1998

Traffic, 2001, R, ★★★★ — 2004

Training Day, 2001, R, ★★★ — 2004

Trainspotting, 1996, R, ★★★ — 1998

Transporter, The, 2002, PG-13, ★★½ — 2004

Traveller, 1997, R, ★★★ — 2000

Treasure Planet, 2002, PG, ★★½ — 2004

Trees Lounge, 1996, R, ★★★½ — 1999

Trekkies, 1999, PG, ★★★ — 2002

Trespass, 1992, R, ★★½ — 1994

Trial, The, 1994, NO MPAA RATING, ★★½ — 1996

Trial, The, 2000, NO MPAA RATING, ★★★★ — 2003

Trial and Error, 1997, PG-13, ★★★ — 1998

Trials of Henry Kissinger, The, 2002, NO MPAA RATING, ★★★ — 2004

Tribute, 1981, PG, ★★★ — 1996

Trick, 1999, R, ★★ — 2002

Trippin', 1999, R, ★★½ — 2002

Trip to Bountiful, The, 1985, PG, ★★★½ — 1998

Triumph of Love, The, 2002, PG-13, ★★★ — 2004

Trixie, 2000, R, ★★ — 2004

Tron, 1982, PG, ★★★★ — 1998

Troop Beverly Hills, 1989, PG, ★★ — 1994

Trouble in Mind, 1985, R, ★★★★ — 1998

Troublesome Creek: A Midwestern, 1997, NO MPAA RATING, ★★★ — 2000

True Believer, 1989, R, ★★★ — 1996

True Colors, 1991, R, ★★ — 1994

True Confessions, 1981, R, ★★★ — 1996

True Crime, 1999, R, ★★★ — 2002

True Lies, 1994, R, ★★★ — 1998

True Love, 1989, R, ★★★ — 1996

True Romance, 1993, R, ★★★ — 1998

True Stories, 1986, PG-13, ★★★½ — 1998

Truly, Madly, Deeply, 1991, NO MPAA RATING, ★★★ — 1998

Truman Show, The, 1998, PG, ★★★★ — 2001

Trumpet of the Swan, The, 2001, G, ★½ — 2004

Trust, 1991, R, ★★ — 1994

Truth About Cats and Dogs, The, 1996, PG-13, ★★★½ — 1999

Truth About Charlie, The, 2002, PG-13, ★★★ — 2004

Truth or Dare, 1991, R, ★★★½ — 1998

Tucker: The Man and His Dream, 1988, PG, ★★½ — 1993

Tuck Everlasting, 2002, PG, ★★ — 2004

Tully, 2002, NO MPAA RATING, ★★★½ — 2004

Tumbleweeds, 1999, PG-13, ★★★ — 2002

Tune in Tomorrow . . . , 1990, PG-13, ★★½ — 1993

Turbulence, 1997, R, ★ — 1998

Turk 182!, 1985, PG-13, ★ — 1987

Turning Point, The, 1977, PG, ★★★½ — 1998

Turn It Up, 2000, R, ★½ — 2003

Turtle Diary, 1985, PG-13, ★★★½ — 1998

Tuxedo, The, 2002, PG-13, ★½ — 2004

Twelfth Night, 1996, PG, ★★★½ — 1999

12 Monkeys, 1996, R, ★★★ — 1999

Twenty Bucks, 1994, R, ★★★ — 1996

20 Dates, 1999, R, ½★ — 2002

28 Days, 2000, PG-13, ★★★ — 2003

28 Days Later, 2003, R, ★★★ — 2004

28 Up, 1985, NO MPAA RATING, ★★★★ — 1998

25th Hour, 2002, R, ★★★½ — 2004

24 Hour Party People, 2002, R, ★★★★ — 2004

24-Hour Woman, The, 1999, R, ★★★ — 2002

X, Y, Z

Index

A

Aaliyah: *Queen of the Damned,* 517

Aaron, Caroline: *Never Again,* 461

Abadal, Ignasi: *Nine Queens,* 466

Abandon, 1

Abdi, Cyrus: *Secret Ballot,* 562

Abdi, Nassim: *Secret Ballot,* 562

Abedini, Hossein: *Baran,* 50

Abercromby, Michelle: *Sweet Sixteen,* 628

Abernathy, Lewis: *Ghosts of the Abyss,* 236

About a Boy, 2

About Schmidt, 3

Abraham, F. Murray: *13 Ghosts,* 647

Abrams, Abiola Wendy: *Jump Tomorrow,* 335

Abrams, Anthony: dir., *Pumpkin,* 514

Accorsi, Stefano: *Last Kiss, The,* 364; *Son's Room, The,* 595

Acevedo, Kirk: *Dinner Rush,* 166

Ackert, David: *Maryam,* 420

Adams, Amy: *Catch Me If You Can,* 105

Adams, Bryan: *House of Fools,* 286

Adams, Jane: *Anniversary Party, The,* 31; *Songcatcher,* 592

Adams, Jay: *Dogtown and Z-Boys,* 170

Adams, Joey Lauren: *Harvard Man,* 268

Adams, Orny: *Comedian,* 131

Adams, Tacey: *Good Housekeeping,* 248

Adam Sandler's Eight Crazy Nights, 4

Adamson, Andrew: dir., *Shrek,* 577

Adaptation, 5

Aday, Meat Loaf: *Focus,* 219

Addy, Mark: *Down to Earth,* 175; *Knight's Tale, A,* 350; *Time Machine, The,* 652

Ade, Melyssa: *Jason X,* 326

Adebimpe, Tunde: *Jump Tomorrow,* 335

Adjemian, Martin: *La Cienaga,* 356

Aernouts, Kenny: *Innocence,* 302

Affair of the Necklace, The, 7

Affleck, Ben: *Changing Lanes,* 111; *Daredevil,* 152; *Jay and Silent Bob Strike Back,* 327; *Pearl Harbor,* 497; *Sum of All Fears, The,* 621

Affleck, Casey: *Gerry,* 233; *Ocean's Eleven,* 475

Agapova, Lyubov: *Lilya 4-Ever,* 389

Agent Cody Banks, 8

Aghdashloo, Shohre: *Maryam,* 420

Agudelo, Wilmar: *Our Lady of the Assassins,* 489

Ahola, Jouko: *Invincible,* 310

A.I. Artificial Intelligence, 8

Aiello, Danny: *Dinner Rush,* 166

Aiken, Liam: *Sweet November,* 628

Aird, Holly: *Possession,* 510

Akbari, Mania: *Ten,* 642

Akerlund, Jonas: dir., *Spun,* 603

Akers, Michelle: *I Remember Me,* 312

Akhtar, Fatemeh Cheragh: *Day I Became a Woman, The,* 156

Akinnuoye-Agbaje, Adewale: *Bourne Identity, The,* 85; *Mummy Returns, The,* 450

Akinshina, Oksana: *Lilya 4-Ever,* 389

Alajar, Gina: *Debut, The,* 158

Alane, Bernard: *Read My Lips,* 523

Albers, Hans: *Blue Angel, The,* 79

Alcázar, Damián: *Crime of Father Amaro, The,* 141; *Herod's Law,* 277

Alex & Emma, 10

Alexander, Erika: *Full Frontal,* 228; *Love Liza,* 398

Alexander, Jane: *Sunshine State,* 623

Alexander, Jason: *Shallow Hal,* 571; *Trumpet of the Swan, The,* 666

Alexander, Kala: *Blue Crush,* 82

Alexi-Malle, Adam: *Man Who Wasn't There, The,* 416

Ali, 11

Alice, Mary: *Sunshine State,* 623

All About Lily Chou-Chou, 13

Allen, Douglas: *Diamond Men,* 162

Allen, Karen: *In the Bedroom,* 306; *World Traveler,* 715

Allen, Keith: *My Wife Is an Actress,* 457; *24 Hour Party People,* 674

Allen, Ray: *Harvard Man,* 268

Allen, Richard "Pistol": *Standing in the Shadows of Motown,* 607

Allen, Tessa: *Enough,* 194

Allen, Tim: *Big Trouble,* 69; *Joe Somebody,* 331; *Santa Clause 2, The,* 551; *Who Is Cletis Tout?,* 709

Allen, Woody: dir., *Company Man,* 132; actor and dir., *Curse of the Jade Scorpion, The,* 147; actor and dir., *Hollywood Ending,* 281

All or Nothing, 13

All the Queen's Men, 15

All the Real Girls, 16

Almani, Mariam Palvin: *Circle, The,* 122

Almela, Laura: *Amores Perros,* 27

Almodóvar, Pedro: dir., *Talk to Her,* 637

Almost Salinas, 17

Along Came a Spider, 18

Alonso, Marie Conchita: *Chasing Papi,* 116

Alpay, David: *Ararat,* 36

Altman, Bruce: *L.I.E.,* 382

Altman, Harry: *Spellbound,* 597

Altman, Robert: dir., *Gosford Park,* 250

Alva, Tony: *Dogtown and Z-Boys,* 170

Alvarez, Juan Carlos: *Our Lady of the Assassins,* 489

Alvaro, Anne: *Taste of Others, The,* 639

Alyx, Karen: *Girls Can't Swim,* 240

Amado, Chisco: *Nico and Dani,* 465

Amandla!, 19

Amati Girls, The, 20

Amato, Bruno: *Just a Kiss,* 337

Amato, Vincenzo: *Respiro,* 531

Ambrose, Lauren: *Swimming,* 631

Amelie, 21

Amenabar, Alejandro: dir., *Others, The,* 487

American Outlaws, 22